IFRS® Standards Part C

**required for accounting periods
beginning on 1 January 2018,
excluding changes not yet required**

This edition is issued in three parts

PART C
Contains the Bases for Conclusions that accompany
the Standards and the IFRS® Practice Statements.

**For the unaccompanied Standards and the Accompanying
Guidance see Parts A and B of this edition:**

*Part A contains the text of IFRS Standards including
IAS® Standards, IFRIC® Interpretations and
SIC® Interpretations, together with The Conceptual Framework
for Financial Reporting*

*Part B (Accompanying Guidance) contains the
documents—Illustrative Examples and Implementation
Guidance—that accompany the Standards, together
with IFRS® Practice Statements.*

IFRS® Standards together with their accompanying documents are issued by the International Accounting Standards Board (the Board).

Disclaimer: To the extent permitted by applicable law, the Board and the IFRS Foundation (Foundation) expressly disclaim all liability howsoever arising from this publication or any translation thereof whether in contract, tort or otherwise to any person in respect of any claims or losses of any nature including direct, indirect, incidental or consequential loss, punitive damages, penalties or costs.

Information contained in this publication does not constitute advice and should not be substituted for the services of an appropriately qualified professional.

ISBN for this part: 978-1-911040-70-5
ISBN for complete publication (three parts): 978-1-911040-67-5

The Foundation has trade marks registered around the world (Marks) including 'IAS®', 'IASB®', 'IFRIC®', 'IFRS®', the IFRS® logo, 'IFRS for SMEs®', IFRS for SMEs® logo, the 'Hexagon Device', 'International Accounting Standards®', 'International Financial Reporting Standards®', 'IFRS Taxonomy®' and 'SIC®'. Further details of the Foundation's Marks are available from the Licensor on request.

The Foundation is a not-for-profit corporation under the General Corporation Law of the State of Delaware, USA and operates in England and Wales as an overseas company (Company number: FC023235) with its principal office at 30 Cannon Street, London, EC4M 6XH.

Contents

continued...

IFRIC Interpretations

continued...

IASB documents published to accompany

The *Conceptual Framework for Financial Reporting*

The *Conceptual Framework for Financial Reporting* (the *Conceptual Framework*) was issued by the International Accounting Standards Board. It superseded the *Framework for the Preparation and Presentation of Financial Statements* in September 2010.

The text of the *Conceptual Framework* is contained in Part A of this edition. This part presents the following accompanying documents:

BASIS FOR CONCLUSIONS ON CHAPTERS 1 AND 3

Contents

Basis for Conclusions on
Chapter 1: *The objective of general purpose financial reporting*

This Basis for Conclusions accompanies, but is not part of, Chapter 1.

Introduction

BC1.1   This Basis for Conclusions summarises considerations of the International Accounting Standards Board in reaching the conclusions in Chapter 1 *The objective of general purpose financial reporting*. It includes reasons for accepting some alternatives and rejecting others. Individual Board members gave greater weight to some factors than to others.

BC1.2   The Board developed this chapter jointly with the US Financial Accounting Standards Board (FASB). Consequently, this Basis for Conclusions also includes some references to the FASB's literature.

Background

BC1.3   The Board began the process of developing the objective of financial reporting by reviewing its own framework and concepts as well as those of other standard-setters. In July 2006 the Board published for public comment a discussion paper on this topic. That same paper was also published by the FASB. The Board and the FASB received 179 responses. In its redeliberations of the issues on this topic, the Board considered all of the comments received and information gained from other outreach initiatives. In May 2008 the Board and the FASB jointly published an exposure draft. The boards received 142 responses. The Board reconsidered all of the issues on this topic. This document is the result of those reconsiderations.

General purpose financial reporting

BC1.4   Consistently with the Board's responsibilities, the *Conceptual Framework* establishes an objective of financial reporting and not just of financial statements. Financial statements are a central part of financial reporting, and most of the issues that the Board addresses involve financial statements. Although the scope of FASB Concepts Statement No. 1 *Objectives of Financial Reporting by Business Enterprises* was financial reporting, the other FASB concepts statements focused on financial statements. The scope of the Board's *Framework for the Preparation and Presentation of Financial Statements*, which was published by the Board's predecessor body in 1989 (hereinafter called *Framework* (1989)), dealt with financial statements only. Therefore, for both boards the scope of the *Conceptual Framework* is broader.

BC1.5   Some constituents suggested that advances in technology may make general purpose financial reporting obsolete. New technologies, for example the use of eXtensible Business Reporting Language (XBRL), may make it practicable in the future for reporting entities either to prepare or to make available the information necessary for different users to assemble different financial reports to meet their individual information needs.

BC1.6   To provide different reports for different users, or to make available all of the information that users would need to assemble their own custom-designed reports, would be expensive. Requiring users of financial information to assemble their own reports might also be unreasonable, because many users would need to have a greater understanding of accounting than they have now. Therefore, the Board concluded that for now a general purpose financial report is still the most efficient and effective way to meet the information needs of a variety of users.

BC1.7 In the discussion paper, the Board used the term *general purpose external financial reporting*. External was intended to convey that internal users such as management were not the intended beneficiaries for general purpose financial reporting as established by the Board. During redeliberations, the Board concluded that this term was redundant. Therefore, Chapter 1 uses *general purpose financial reporting*.

Financial reporting of the reporting entity

BC1.8 Some respondents to the exposure draft said that the reporting entity is not separate from its equity investors or a subset of those equity investors. This view has its roots in the days when most businesses were sole proprietorships and partnerships that were managed by their owners who had unlimited liability for the debts incurred in the course of the business. Over time, the separation between businesses and their owners has grown. The vast majority of today's businesses have legal substance separate from their owners by virtue of their legal form of organisation, numerous investors with limited legal liability and professional managers separate from the owners. Consequently, the Board concluded that financial reports should reflect that separation by accounting for the entity (and its economic resources and claims) rather than its primary users and their interests in the reporting entity.

Primary users

BC1.9 The objective of financial reporting in paragraph OB2 refers to existing and potential investors, lenders and other creditors. The description of the primary users in paragraph OB5 refers to existing and potential investors, lenders and other creditors who cannot require reporting entities to provide information directly to them. Paragraph OB10 states that 'regulators and members of the public other than investors, lenders and other creditors' may find information in general purpose financial reports useful but clearly states that those are not the parties to whom general purpose financial reports are primarily directed.

BC1.10 Paragraph 9 of the *Framework* (1989) stated that users included 'present and potential investors, employees, lenders, suppliers and other trade creditors' (and later added advisers in the discussion of investors' needs), all of which are intended to be encompassed by the phrase in paragraph OB2. Paragraph 9 of the *Framework* (1989) also included a list of other potential users such as customers, governments and their agencies, and the public, which is similar to the list in paragraph OB10 of those who may be interested in financial reports but are not primary users.

BC1.11 Paragraph 10 of the *Framework* (1989) stated that 'as investors are providers of risk capital to the entity, the provision of financial statements that meet their needs will also meet most of the needs of other users that financial statements

can satisfy', which might have been read to narrow the focus to investors only. However, paragraph 12 explicitly stated that the objective of financial statements is to provide information 'that is useful to a wide range of users in making economic decisions.' Thus, the *Framework* (1989) focused on investors' needs as representative of the needs of a wide range of users but did not explicitly identify a group of primary users.

BC1.12 FASB Concepts Statement 1 referred to 'present and potential investors and creditors and other users in making rational investment, credit, and similar decisions' (paragraph 34). It also stated that 'major groups of investors are equity securityholders and debt securityholders' and 'major groups of creditors are suppliers of goods and services who extend credit, customers and employees with claims, lending institutions, individual lenders, and debt securityholders' (paragraph 35). One difference in emphasis from the *Framework* (1989), which emphasised providers of risk capital, is that Concepts Statement 1 referred to 'both those who desire safety of investment and those who are willing to accept risk to obtain high rates of return' (paragraph 35). However, like the *Framework* (1989), Concepts Statement 1 stated that the terms investors and creditors 'also may comprehend security analysts and advisors, brokers, lawyers, regulatory agencies, and others who advise or represent the interests of investors and creditors or who otherwise are interested in how investors and creditors are faring' (paragraph 35).

BC1.13 Paragraphs OB3, OB5 and OB10 differ from the *Framework* (1989) and Concepts Statement 1 for two reasons—to eliminate differences between the *Framework* and Concepts Statement 1 and to be more direct by focusing on users making decisions about providing resources (but not to exclude advisers). The reasons are discussed in paragraphs BC1.15–BC1.24.

Should there be a primary user group?

BC1.14 The discussion paper and the exposure draft proposed identifying a group of primary users of financial reports. Some respondents to the exposure draft said that other users who have not provided, and are not considering providing, resources to the entity, use financial reports for a variety of reasons. The Board sympathised with their information needs but concluded that without a defined group of primary users, the *Conceptual Framework* would risk becoming unduly abstract or vague.

Why are existing and potential investors, lenders and other creditors considered the primary users?

BC1.15 Some respondents to the discussion paper and the exposure draft suggested that the primary user group should be limited to existing shareholders or the controlling entity's majority shareholders. Others said that the primary users should be existing shareholders and creditors, and that financial reports should focus on their needs.

BC1.16 The reasons why the Board concluded that the primary user group should be the existing and potential investors, lenders and other creditors of a reporting entity are:

(a) Existing and potential investors, lenders and other creditors have the most critical and immediate need for the information in financial reports and many cannot require the entity to provide the information to them directly.

(b) The Board's and the FASB's responsibilities require them to focus on the needs of participants in capital markets, which include not only existing investors but also potential investors and existing and potential lenders and other creditors.

(c) Information that meets the needs of the specified primary users is likely to meet the needs of users both in jurisdictions with a corporate governance model defined in the context of shareholders and those with a corporate governance model defined in the context of all types of stakeholders.

BC1.17 Some respondents expressed the view that the specified primary user group was too broad and that it would result in too much information in the financial reports. However, *too much* is a subjective judgement. In developing financial reporting requirements that meet the objective of financial reporting, the boards will rely on the qualitative characteristics of, and the cost constraint on, useful financial information to provide discipline to avoid providing too much information.

Should there be a hierarchy of users?

BC1.18 Some respondents to the exposure draft who supported the composition of the primary user group also recommended that the Board should establish a hierarchy of primary users because investors, lenders and other creditors have different information needs. However, the Board observed that individual users may have information needs and desires that are different from, and possibly conflict with, those of other users with the same type of interest in the reporting entity. General purpose financial reports are intended to provide common information to users and cannot accommodate every request for information. The Board will seek the information set that is intended to meet the needs of the maximum number of users in cost-beneficial ways.

Information needs of other users who are not within the primary user group

Management's information needs

BC1.19 Some constituents questioned the interaction between general purpose financial reporting and management's needs. The Board stated that some of the information directed to the primary users is likely to meet some of management's needs but not all of them. However, management has the ability to access additional financial information, and consequently, general purpose financial reporting need not be explicitly directed to management.

Regulators' information needs

BC1.20 Some constituents said that maintaining financial stability in capital markets (the stability of a country's or region's economy or financial systems) should be

an objective of financial reporting. They stated that financial reporting should focus on the needs of regulators and fiscal policy decision-makers who are responsible for maintaining financial stability.

BC1.21   Other constituents opposed establishing an objective to maintain financial stability. They said that financial statements should present the economic reality of the reporting entity with as little bias as possible, but that such a presentation is not necessarily inconsistent with a financial stability objective. By presenting economic reality, financial statements could lead to more informed decision-making and thereby support financial stability even if that is not the primary aim.[1]

BC1.22   However, advocates of a financial stability objective had a different outcome in mind. They did not encourage the Board to require reporting entities to provide information for use by regulators and fiscal policy decision-makers. Instead, they recommended that the Board consider the consequences of new financial reporting standards for the stability of the world's economies and financial systems and, at least at times, assign greater weight to that objective than to the information needs of investors, lenders and other creditors.

BC1.23   The Board acknowledged that the interests of investors, lenders and other creditors often overlap with those of regulators. However, expanding the objective of financial reporting to include maintaining financial stability could at times create conflicts between the objectives that the Board is not well-equipped to resolve. For example, some may take the view that the best way to maintain financial stability is to require entities not to report, or to delay reporting, some changes in asset or liability values. That requirement would almost certainly result in depriving investors, lenders and other creditors of information that they need. The only way to avoid conflicts would be to eliminate or de-emphasise the existing objective of providing information to investors, lenders and other creditors. The Board concluded that eliminating that objective would be inconsistent with its basic mission, which is to serve the information needs of participants in capital markets. The Board also noted that providing relevant and faithfully represented financial information can improve users' confidence in the information, and thus contribute to promoting financial stability.

Usefulness for making decisions

BC1.24   Both the Board's and the FASB's previous frameworks focused on providing information that is useful in making economic decisions as the fundamental objective of financial reporting. Those frameworks also stated that financial information that is useful in making economic decisions would also be helpful in assessing how management has fulfilled its stewardship responsibility.

---

1   One group expressing that view was the Financial Crisis Advisory Group (FCAG). The FCAG comprised approximately 20 senior leaders with broad experience in international financial markets and an interest in the transparency of financial reporting information. The FCAG was formed in 2009 to advise the Board and the FASB about the standard-setting implications of the financial crisis and of potential changes in the global regulatory environment.

BC1.25 The discussion paper that led to Chapter 1 stated that the objective of financial reporting should focus on resource allocation decisions. Although most respondents to the discussion paper agreed that providing useful information for decision-making was the appropriate objective, they said that investors, lenders and other creditors make other decisions that are aided by financial reporting information in addition to resource allocation decisions. For example, shareholders who vote on whether to retain directors or replace them, and on how members of management should be remunerated for their services, need information on which to base their decisions. Shareholders' decision-making process may include evaluating how management of the entity performed against management in competing entities in similar circumstances.

BC1.26 The Board agreed with these respondents and noted that, in most cases, information designed for resource allocation decisions would also be useful for assessing management's performance. Therefore, in the exposure draft leading to Chapter 1, the Board proposed that the objective of financial reporting is to provide financial information about the reporting entity that is useful to present and potential investors, lenders and other creditors in making decisions in their capacity as capital providers. The exposure draft also described the role financial statements can have in supporting decisions related to the stewardship of an entity's resources.

BC1.27 The exposure draft discussed the *Objective of Financial Reporting* and *Decision-usefulness* in separate sections. The Board combined those two sections in Chapter 1 because usefulness in making decisions is the objective of financial reporting. Consequently, both sections addressed the same points and provided more detail than was necessary. Combining those two sections resulted in eliminating the separate subsections on usefulness in assessing cash flow prospects and usefulness in assessing stewardship. The Board did not intend to imply that assessing prospects for future cash flow or assessing the quality of management's stewardship is more important than the other. Both are important for making decisions about providing resources to an entity, and information about stewardship is also important for resource providers who have the ability to vote on, or otherwise influence, management's actions.

BC1.28 The Board decided not to use the term *stewardship* in the chapter because there would be difficulties in translating it into other languages. Instead, the Board described what stewardship encapsulates. Accordingly, the objective of financial reporting acknowledges that users make resource allocation decisions as well as decisions as to whether management has made efficient and effective use of the resources provided.

The objective of financial reporting for different types of entities

BC1.29 The Board also considered whether the objective of general purpose financial reporting should differ for different types of entities. Possibilities include:

(a) smaller entities versus larger entities;

(b) entities with listed (publicly traded) debt or equity financial instruments versus those without such instruments; and

(c)   closely held entities versus those with widely dispersed ownership.

BC1.30   External users of financial reporting have similar objectives, irrespective of the type of entities in which they invest. Therefore, the Board concluded that the objective of general purpose financial reports is the same for all entities. However, cost constraints and differences in activities among entities may sometimes lead the Board to permit or require differences in reporting for different types of entities.

Information about a reporting entity's resources, claims against the entity and changes in resources and claims

The significance of information about financial performance

BC1.31   A long-standing assertion by many constituents is that a reporting entity's financial performance as represented by comprehensive income and its components is the most important information.[2] Concepts Statement 1 (paragraph 43) stated:

> The primary focus of financial reporting is information about an enterprise's performance provided by measures of comprehensive income and its components. Investors, creditors, and others who are concerned with assessing the prospects for enterprise net cash inflows are especially interested in that information.

In contrast, the *Framework* (1989) considered information on the reporting entity's financial position and financial performance of equal importance.

BC1.32   To be useful for decision-making, financial reports must provide information about a reporting entity's economic resources and claims, and the change during a period in economic resources and claims. A reporting entity cannot provide reasonably complete information about its financial performance (as represented by comprehensive income, profit or loss or other similar terms) without identifying and measuring its economic resources and the claims. Consequently, the Board concluded that to designate one type of information as the primary focus of financial reporting would be inappropriate.

BC1.33   In discussing the financial position of an entity, the exposure draft referred to *economic resources and claims on them*. The chapter uses the phrase *economic resources of the reporting entity and the claims against the reporting entity* (see paragraph OB12). The reason for the change is that in many cases, claims against an entity are not claims on specific resources. In addition, many claims will be satisfied using resources that will result from future net cash inflows. Thus, while all claims are claims against the entity, not all are claims against the entity's existing resources.

Financial position and solvency

BC1.34   Some constituents have suggested that the main purpose of the statement of financial position should be to provide information that helps assess the

---

2   Concepts Statement 1 referred to *earnings and its components*. However, FASB Concepts Statement No. 6 *Elements of Financial Statements* substituted the term *comprehensive income* for the term *earnings*. The latter term is reserved for a component of comprehensive income.

reporting entity's solvency. The question is not whether information provided in the financial reports should be helpful in assessing solvency; clearly, it should. Assessing solvency is of interest to investors, lenders and other creditors, and the objective of general purpose financial reporting is to provide information that is useful to them for making decisions.

BC1.35 However, some have suggested that the statement of financial position should be directed towards the information needs of lenders, other creditors and regulators, possibly to the detriment of investors and other users. To do so would be inconsistent with the objective of serving the common information needs of the primary user group. Therefore, the Board rejected the notion of directing the statement of financial position (or any other particular financial statement) towards the needs of a particular subset of users.

BASIS FOR CONCLUSIONS ON CHAPTER 2:
THE REPORTING ENTITY

[to be added]

CONTENTS

Basis for Conclusions on
Chapter 3: *Qualitative characteristics of useful financial information*

This Basis for Conclusions accompanies, but is not part of, Chapter 3.

Introduction

BC3.1 This Basis for Conclusions summarises considerations of the Board in reaching the conclusions in Chapter 3 *Qualitative characteristics of useful financial information*. It includes reasons for accepting some alternatives and rejecting others. Individual Board members gave greater weight to some factors than to others.

BC3.2 The Board developed the chapter jointly with the US Financial Accounting Standards Board (FASB). Consequently, this Basis for Conclusions also includes some references to the FASB's literature.

Background

BC3.3 The Board began the process of developing the qualitative characteristics of useful financial information by reviewing its own framework and concepts as well as those of other standard-setters. In July 2006 the Board published for public comment a discussion paper on this topic. That same paper was also published by the FASB. The Board and the FASB received 179 responses. In its redeliberations of the issues on this topic, the Board considered all of the comments received and information gained from other outreach initiatives. In May 2008 the Board and the FASB jointly published an exposure draft. The boards received 142 responses. The Board reconsidered all of the issues. This document is the result of those reconsiderations.

The objective of financial reporting and the qualitative characteristics of useful financial information

BC3.4 Alternatives are available for all aspects of financial reporting, including recognition, derecognition, measurement, classification, presentation and disclosure. When developing financial reporting standards, the Board will choose the alternative that goes furthest towards achieving the objective of financial reporting. Providers of financial information will also have to choose among the alternatives if there are no applicable standards available, or if application of a particular standard requires judgements or options, to achieve the objective of financial reporting.

BC3.5 Chapter 1 specifies that the objective of general purpose financial reporting is to provide financial information about the reporting entity that is useful to existing and potential investors, lenders and other creditors in making decisions about providing resources to the entity. The decision-makers on which this *Conceptual Framework* focuses are existing and potential investors, lenders and other creditors.

BC3.6 That objective by itself leaves a great deal to judgement and provides little guidance on how to exercise that judgement. Chapter 3 describes the first step in making the judgements needed to apply that objective. It identifies and describes the qualitative characteristics that financial information should have if it is to meet the objective of financial reporting. It also discusses cost, which is a pervasive constraint on financial reporting.

BC3.7 Subsequent chapters will use the qualitative characteristics to help guide choices about recognition, measurement and the other aspects of financial reporting.

Fundamental and enhancing qualitative characteristics

BC3.8 Chapter 3 distinguishes between the fundamental qualitative characteristics that are the most critical and the enhancing qualitative characteristics that are less critical but still highly desirable. The discussion paper did not explicitly distinguish between those qualitative characteristics. The Board made the distinction later because of confusion among respondents to the discussion paper about how the qualitative characteristics relate to each other.

BC3.9 Some respondents to the exposure draft stated that all of the qualitative characteristics should be considered equal, and that the distinction between fundamental and enhancing qualitative characteristics was arbitrary. Others said that the most important qualitative characteristic differs depending on the circumstances; therefore, differentiating among the qualitative characteristics was not appropriate.

BC3.10 The Board does not agree that the distinction is arbitrary. Financial information without the two fundamental qualitative characteristics of relevance and faithful representation is not useful, and it cannot be made useful by being more comparable, verifiable, timely or understandable. However, financial information that is relevant and faithfully represented may still be useful even if it does not have any of the enhancing qualitative characteristics.

Fundamental qualitative characteristics

Relevance

BC3.11 It is self-evident that financial information is useful for making a decision only if it is capable of making a difference in that decision. *Relevance* is the term used in the *Conceptual Framework* to describe that capability. It is a fundamental qualitative characteristic of useful financial information.

BC3.12 The definition of relevance in the *Conceptual Framework* is consistent with the definition in FASB Concepts Statement No. 2 *Qualitative Characteristics of Accounting Information*. The *Framework* (1989) definition of relevance was that information is relevant only if it actually makes a difference in users' decisions. However, users consider a variety of information from many sources, and the extent to which a decision is affected by information about a particular economic phenomenon is difficult, if not impossible, to determine, even after the fact.

BC3.13 In contrast, whether information is *capable* of making a difference in a decision (relevance as defined in the *Conceptual Framework*) can be determined. One of the primary purposes of publishing exposure drafts and other due process documents is to seek the views of users on whether information that would be required by proposed financial reporting standards is capable of making a difference in their decisions. The Board also assesses relevance by meeting users to discuss proposed standards, potential agenda decisions, effects on reported information of applying recently implemented standards and other matters.

Predictive and confirmatory value

BC3.14 Many decisions by investors, lenders and other creditors are based on implicit or explicit predictions about the amount and timing of the return on an equity investment, loan or other credit instrument. Consequently, information is capable of making a difference in one of those decisions only if it will help users to make new predictions, confirm or correct prior predictions or both (which is the definition of predictive or confirmatory value).

BC3.15 The *Framework* (1989) identified predictive value and confirmatory value as components of relevance, and Concepts Statement 2 referred to predictive value and feedback value. The Board concluded that confirmatory value and feedback value were intended to have the same meaning. The Board and the FASB agreed that both boards would use the same term (confirmatory value) to avoid giving the impression that the two frameworks were intended to be different.

The difference between predictive value and related statistical terms

BC3.16 Predictive value, as used in the *Conceptual Framework*, is not the same as predictability and persistence as used in statistics. Information has predictive value if it can be used in making predictions about the eventual outcomes of past or current events. In contrast, statisticians use predictability to refer to the accuracy with which it is possible to foretell the next number in a series and persistence to refer to the tendency of a series of numbers to continue to change as it has changed in the past.

Materiality

BC3.17 Concepts Statement 2 and the *Framework* (1989) discussed materiality and defined it similarly. Concepts Statement 2 described materiality as a constraint on financial reporting that can be considered only together with the qualitative characteristics, especially relevance and faithful representation. The *Framework* (1989), on the other hand, discussed materiality as an aspect of relevance and did not indicate that materiality has a role in relation to the other qualitative characteristics.

BC3.18 The discussion paper and the exposure draft proposed that materiality is a pervasive constraint in financial reporting because it is pertinent to all of the qualitative characteristics. However, some respondents to the exposure draft agreed that although materiality is pervasive, it is not a constraint on a reporting entity's ability to report information. Rather, materiality is an aspect of relevance, because immaterial information does not affect a user's decision. Furthermore, a standard-setter does not consider materiality when developing standards because it is an entity-specific consideration. The boards agreed with those views and concluded that materiality is an aspect of relevance that applies at the individual entity level.

Faithful representation

BC3.19   The discussion of faithful representation in Chapter 3 differs from that in the previous frameworks in two significant ways. First, it uses the term *faithful representation* instead of the term *reliability*. Second, substance over form, prudence (conservatism) and verifiability, which were aspects of reliability in Concepts Statement 2 or the *Framework* (1989), are not considered aspects of faithful representation. Substance over form and prudence were removed for the reasons described in paragraphs BC3.26–BC3.29. Verifiability is now described as an enhancing qualitative characteristic rather than as part of this fundamental qualitative characteristic (see paragraphs BC3.34–BC3.36).

Replacement of the term reliability

BC3.20   Concepts Statement 2 and the *Framework* (1989) used the term *reliability* to describe what is now called faithful representation.

BC3.21   Concepts Statement 2 listed representational faithfulness, verifiability and neutrality as aspects of reliability and discussed completeness as part of representational faithfulness.

BC3.22   The *Framework* (1989) said:

> Information has the quality of reliability when it is free from material error and bias and can be depended upon by users to represent faithfully that which it either purports to represent or could reasonably be expected to represent.

The *Framework* (1989) also discussed substance over form, neutrality, prudence and completeness as aspects of faithful representation.

BC3.23   Unfortunately, neither framework clearly conveyed the meaning of reliability. The comments of respondents to numerous proposed standards indicated a lack of a common understanding of the term *reliability*. Some focused on *verifiability* or *free from material error* to the virtual exclusion of faithful representation. Others focused more on faithful representation, perhaps combined with neutrality. Some apparently think that reliability refers primarily to precision.

BC3.24   Because attempts to explain what reliability was intended to mean in this context have proved unsuccessful, the Board sought a different term that would more clearly convey the intended meaning. The term *faithful representation*, the faithful depiction in financial reports of economic phenomena, was the result of that search. That term encompasses the main characteristics that the previous frameworks included as aspects of reliability.

BC3.25   Many respondents to the discussion paper and the exposure draft opposed the Board's preliminary decision to replace *reliability* with *faithful representation*. Some said that the Board could have better explained what reliable means rather than replacing the term. However, many respondents who made those comments assigned a different meaning to reliability from what the Board meant. In particular, many respondents' descriptions of reliability more closely resembled the Board's notion of verifiability than its notion of reliability. Those comments led the Board to affirm its decision to replace the term *reliability* with *faithful representation*.

Substance over form

BC3.26   Substance over form is not considered a separate component of faithful representation because it would be redundant. Faithful representation means that financial information represents the substance of an economic phenomenon rather than merely representing its legal form. Representing a legal form that differs from the economic substance of the underlying economic phenomenon could not result in a faithful representation.

Prudence (conservatism) and neutrality

BC3.27   Chapter 3 does not include prudence or conservatism as an aspect of faithful representation because including either would be inconsistent with neutrality. Some respondents to the discussion paper and exposure draft disagreed with that view. They said that the framework should include conservatism, prudence or both. They said that bias should not always be assumed to be undesirable, especially in circumstances when bias, in their view, produces information that is more relevant to some users.

BC3.28   Deliberately reflecting conservative estimates of assets, liabilities, income or equity has sometimes been considered desirable to counteract the effects of some management estimates that have been perceived as excessively optimistic. However, even with the prohibitions against deliberate misstatement that appear in the existing frameworks, an admonition to be prudent is likely to lead to a bias. Understating assets or overstating liabilities in one period frequently leads to overstating financial performance in later periods—a result that cannot be described as prudent or neutral.

BC3.29   Other respondents to the exposure draft said that neutrality is impossible to achieve. In their view, relevant information must have purpose, and information with a purpose is not neutral. In other words, because financial reporting is a tool to influence decision-making, it cannot be neutral. Obviously, reported financial information is expected to influence the actions of users of that information, and the mere fact that many users take similar actions on the basis of reported information does not demonstrate a lack of neutrality. The Board does not attempt to encourage or predict specific actions of users. If financial information is biased in a way that encourages users to take or avoid predetermined actions, that information is not neutral.

Can faithful representation be empirically measured?

BC3.30   Empirical accounting researchers have accumulated considerable evidence supporting relevant and faithfully represented financial information through correlation with changes in the market prices of entities' equity or debt instruments. However, such studies have not provided techniques for empirically measuring faithful representation apart from relevance.

BC3.31   Both previous frameworks discussed the desirability of providing statistical information about how faithfully a financial measure is represented. That would not be unprecedented. Other statistical information is sometimes reflected in financial reports. For example, some entities disclose value at risk from derivative financial instruments and similar positions. The Board expects that the use of statistical concepts for financial reporting in some situations will continue to be important. Unfortunately, the boards have not identified any way to quantify the faithfulness of the representations in a financial report.

Enhancing qualitative characteristics

Comparability

BC3.32   Comparability was an important concept in both the *Framework* (1989) and Concepts Statement 2, but the two previous frameworks disagreed on its importance. The *Framework* (1989) stated that comparability is as important as relevance and faithful representation.[3] Concepts Statement 2 described comparability as a quality of the relationship between two or more pieces of information that, although important, is secondary to relevance and faithful representation.

BC3.33   Relevant and faithfully represented information is most useful if it can be readily compared with similar information reported by other entities and by the same entity in other periods. One of the most important reasons that financial reporting standards are needed is to increase the comparability of reported financial information. However, even if it is not readily comparable, relevant and faithfully represented information is still useful. Comparable information, however, is not useful if it is not relevant and may mislead if it is not faithfully represented. Therefore, *comparability* is considered an enhancing qualitative characteristic instead of a fundamental qualitative characteristic.

Verifiability

BC3.34   Verifiable information can be used with confidence. Lack of verifiability does not necessarily render information useless, but users are likely to be more cautious because there is a greater risk that the information does not faithfully represent what it purports to represent.

BC3.35   The *Framework* (1989) did not explicitly include verifiability as an aspect of reliability, but Concepts Statement 2 did. However, the two frameworks are not as different as it might appear because the definition of reliability in the *Framework* (1989) contained the phrase *and can be depended upon by users*, which implies that users need assurance on the information.

BC3.36   The discussion paper stated that reported financial information should be verifiable to assure users that it is free from material error and bias and can be depended on to represent what it purports to represent. Therefore, verifiability was considered an aspect of faithful representation. Some respondents pointed out that including verifiability as an aspect of faithful representation could result in excluding information that is not readily verifiable. Those respondents recognised that many forward-looking estimates that are very important in providing relevant financial information (for example, expected cash flows, useful lives and salvage values) cannot be directly verified. However, excluding information about those estimates would make the financial reports much less

---

3   The term *reliability* was used instead of *faithful representation*, but the meaning was intended to be similar.

useful. The Board agreed and repositioned verifiability as an enhancing qualitative characteristic, very desirable but not necessarily required.

Timeliness

BC3.37 The *Framework* (1989) discussed timeliness as a constraint that could rob information of relevance. Concepts Statement 2 described timeliness as an aspect of relevance. However, the substance of timeliness as discussed in the two previous frameworks was essentially the same.

BC3.38 The discussion paper described timeliness as an aspect of relevance. However, some respondents pointed out that timeliness is not part of relevance in the same sense that predictive and confirmatory value are. The Board was persuaded that timeliness is different from the other components of relevance.

BC3.39 Timeliness is very desirable, but it is not as critical as relevance and faithful representation. Timely information is useful only if it is relevant and faithfully represented. In contrast, relevant and faithfully represented information may still be useful (especially for confirmatory purposes) even if it is not reported in as timely a manner as would be desirable.

Understandability

BC3.40 Both the *Framework* (1989) and Concepts Statement 2 included understandability, a qualitative characteristic that enables users to comprehend the information and therefore make it useful for making decisions. Both frameworks also similarly described that for financial information to be understandable, users should have a reasonable degree of financial knowledge and a willingness to study the information with reasonable diligence.

BC3.41 Despite those discussions of understandability and users' responsibilities for understanding financial reports, misunderstanding persists. For example, some have expressed the view that a new accounting method should not be implemented because some users might not understand it, even though the new accounting method would result in reporting financial information that is useful for decision-making. They imply that understandability is more important than relevance.

BC3.42 If understandability considerations were fundamental, it might be appropriate to avoid reporting information about very complicated things even if the information is relevant and faithfully represented. Classifying understandability as an enhancing qualitative characteristic is intended to indicate that information that is difficult to understand should be presented and explained as clearly as possible.

BC3.43 To clarify another frequently misunderstood point, the *Conceptual Framework* explains that users are responsible for *actually* studying reported financial information with reasonable diligence rather than only being *willing* to do so (which was the statement in the previous frameworks). In addition, the *Conceptual Framework* states that users may need to seek the aid of advisers to understand economic phenomena that are particularly complex.

Qualitative characteristics not included

BC3.44 *Transparency, high quality, internal consistency, true and fair view or fair presentation* and *credibility* have been suggested as desirable qualitative characteristics of financial information. However, transparency, high quality, internal consistency, true and fair view or fair presentation are different words to describe information that has the qualitative characteristics of relevance and representational faithfulness enhanced by comparability, verifiability, timeliness and understandability. Credibility is similar but also implies trustworthiness of a reporting entity's management.

BC3.45 Interested parties sometimes suggested other criteria for standard-setting decisions, and the Board has at times cited some of those criteria as part of the rationale for some decisions. Those criteria include simplicity, operationality, practicability or practicality, and acceptability.

BC3.46 Those criteria are not qualitative characteristics. Instead, they are part of the overall weighing of benefits and costs of providing useful financial information. For example, a simpler method may be less costly to apply than a more complex method. In some circumstances, a simpler method may result in information that is essentially the same as, but somewhat less precise than, information produced by a more complex method. In that situation, a standard-setter would include the decrease in faithful representation and the decrease in implementation cost in weighing benefits against costs.

The cost constraint on useful financial reporting

BC3.47 Cost is a pervasive constraint that standard-setters, as well as providers and users of financial information, should keep in mind when considering the benefits of a possible new financial reporting requirement. Cost is not a qualitative characteristic of information. It is a characteristic of the process used to provide the information.

BC3.48 The Board has attempted and continues to attempt to develop more structured methods of obtaining information about the cost of gathering and processing the information that proposed standards would require entities to provide. The primary method used is to request interested parties, sometimes formally (such as by field tests and questionnaires), to submit cost and benefit information for a specific proposal that is quantified to the extent feasible. Those requests have resulted in helpful information and have led directly to changes to proposed requirements to reduce the costs without significantly reducing the related benefits.

IASB documents published to accompany

IFRS 1

First-time Adoption of International Financial Reporting Standards

The text of the unaccompanied standard, IFRS 1, is contained in Part A of this edition. Its effective date when issued was 1 July 2009. The text of the Accompanying Guidance on IFRS 1 is contained in Part B of this edition. This part presents the following documents:

BASIS FOR CONCLUSIONS

APPENDIX TO THE BASIS FOR CONCLUSIONS
Amendments to Basis for Conclusions on other IFRSs

Contents

Basis for Conclusions on
IFRS 1 *First-time Adoption of International Financial Reporting Standards*

This Basis for Conclusions accompanies, but is not part of, IFRS 1.

In this Basis for Conclusions the terminology has not been amended to reflect the changes made by IAS 1 Presentation of Financial Statements *(as revised in 2007).*

This Basis for Conclusions has not been revised to reflect the restructuring of IFRS 1 in November 2008, but cross-references have been updated.

Introduction

BC1   This Basis for Conclusions summarises the International Accounting Standards Board's considerations in reaching the conclusions in IFRS 1 *First-time Adoption of International Financial Reporting Standards.* Individual Board members gave greater weight to some factors than to others.

BC2   SIC-8 *First-time Application of IASs as the Primary Basis of Accounting,* issued in 1998, dealt with matters that arose when an entity first adopted IASs. In 2001, the Board began a project to review SIC-8. In July 2002, the Board published ED 1 *First-time Application of International Financial Reporting Standards,* with a comment deadline of 31 October 2002. The Board received 83 comment letters on ED 1. IFRS 1 was issued by the Board in June 2003.

BC2A   IFRS 1 replaced SIC-8. The Board developed the IFRS to address concerns that:

      (a)   some aspects of SIC-8's requirement for full retrospective application caused costs that exceeded the likely benefits for users of financial statements. Moreover, although SIC-8 did not require retrospective application when this would be impracticable, it did not explain whether a first-time adopter should interpret impracticability as a high hurdle or a low hurdle and it did not specify any particular treatment in cases of impracticability.

      (b)   SIC-8 could require a first-time adopter to apply two different versions of a standard if a new version were introduced during the periods covered by its first financial statements prepared under IASs and the new version prohibited retrospective application.

      (c)   SIC-8 did not state clearly whether a first-time adopter should use hindsight in applying recognition and measurement decisions retrospectively.

      (d)   there was some doubt about how SIC-8 interacted with specific transitional provisions in individual standards.

BC2B   Like SIC-8, IFRS 1 requires retrospective application in most areas. Unlike SIC-8, it:

      (a)   includes targeted exemptions to avoid costs that would be likely to exceed the benefits to users of financial statements, and a small number of other exceptions for practical reasons.

(b)   clarifies that an entity applies the latest version of IFRSs.

(c)   clarifies how a first-time adopter's estimates in accordance with IFRSs relate to the estimates it made for the same date in accordance with previous GAAP.

(d)   specifies that the transitional provisions in other IFRSs do not apply to a first-time adopter.

(e)   requires enhanced disclosure about the transition to IFRSs.

BC3   The project took on added significance because of the requirement for listed European Union companies to adopt IFRSs in their consolidated financial statements from 2005. Several other countries announced that they would permit or require entities to adopt IFRSs in the next few years. Nevertheless, the Board's aim in developing the IFRS was to find solutions that would be appropriate for any entity, in any part of the world, regardless of whether adoption occurs in 2005 or at a different time.

Restructuring of the IFRS

BC3A   Since it was issued in 2003, IFRS 1 has been amended many times to accommodate first-time adoption requirements resulting from new or amended IFRSs. Because of the way IFRS 1 was structured, those amendments made the IFRS more complex and less clear. As more amendments become necessary, this problem will become worse.

BC3B   As part of its improvements project in 2007, therefore, the Board proposed to change the structure of IFRS 1 without amending its substance. Respondents to the exposure draft published in October 2007 supported the restructuring. The revised structure of the IFRS issued in November 2008 is easier for the reader to understand and is better designed to accommodate future changes. The focus of the restructuring was to move to appendices all specific exemptions and exceptions from the requirements of IFRSs. Exemptions are categorised into business combinations, exemptions and short-term exemptions. Exemptions are applicable to all first-time adopters regardless of their date of transition to IFRSs. Short-term exemptions are those exemptions applicable to users for a short time. Once those exemptions have become out of date, they will be deleted.

Scope

BC4   The IFRS applies to an entity that presents its first IFRS financial statements (a first-time adopter). Some suggested that an entity should not be regarded as a first-time adopter if its previous financial statements contained an explicit statement of compliance with IFRSs, except for specified (and explicit) departures. They argued that an explicit statement of compliance establishes that an entity regards IFRSs as its basis of accounting, even if the entity does not comply with every requirement of every IFRS. Some regarded this argument as especially strong if an entity previously complied with all recognition and measurement requirements of IFRSs, but did not give some required disclosures—for example, segmental disclosures that IAS 14 *Segment Reporting*[1] requires or the explicit statement of compliance with IFRSs that IAS 1 *Presentation of Financial Statements* requires.

BC5   To implement that approach, it would be necessary to establish how many departures are needed—and how serious they must be—before an entity would conclude that it has not adopted IFRSs. In the Board's view, this would lead to complexity and uncertainty. Also, an entity should not be regarded as having adopted IFRSs if it does not give all disclosures required by IFRSs, because that approach would diminish the importance of disclosures and undermine efforts to promote full compliance with IFRSs. Therefore, the IFRS contains a simple test that gives an unambiguous answer: an entity has adopted IFRSs if, and only if, its financial statements contain an explicit and unreserved statement of compliance with IFRSs (paragraph 3 of the IFRS).

BC6   If an entity's financial statements in previous years contained that statement, any material disclosed or undisclosed departures from IFRSs are errors. The entity applies IAS 8 *Accounting Policies, Changes in Accounting Estimates and Errors* in correcting them.

Repeated application of IFRS 1

BC6A   In *Annual Improvements 2009–2011 Cycle* (issued in May 2012) the Board addressed a request to clarify whether an entity may apply IFRS 1:

(a)   if the entity meets the criteria for applying IFRS 1 and has applied IFRS 1 in a previous reporting period; or

(b)   if the entity meets the criteria for applying IFRS 1 and has applied IFRSs in a previous reporting period when IFRS 1 did not exist.

For example, an entity may have applied IFRS 1 in a previous reporting period to meet listing requirements in a foreign jurisdiction. The entity then delists and no longer presents financial statements in accordance with IFRSs. In a subsequent reporting period, the reporting requirements in the entity's local jurisdiction may change from national GAAP to IFRSs. Consequently, the entity is again required to present its financial statements in accordance with IFRSs.

BC6B   The Board noted that the scope of IFRS 1 focuses on whether an entity's financial statements are its first IFRS financial statements (a term defined in Appendix A). If an entity's financial statements meet the definition of 'first IFRS financial statements', the entity is required to apply IFRS 1 in accordance with paragraph 2(a). However, use of the term 'first' raises the question whether IFRS 1 can be applied more than once.

BC6C   In the June 2011 exposure draft the Board proposed to clarify that an entity is required to apply IFRS 1 when the entity's most recent previous annual financial statements do not contain an explicit and unreserved statement of compliance with IFRSs, even if the entity has applied IFRS 1 in a reporting period before the period reported in the most recent previous annual financial statements. However, in the light of respondents' comments on the June 2011 exposure draft, the Board decided that an entity that meets the criteria for applying IFRS 1

---

1   In 2006 IAS 14 was replaced by IFRS 8 *Operating Segments*.

and that has applied IFRSs in a previous reporting period (regardless of whether it used IFRS 1 or SIC-8 *First-Time Application of IASs*, if either, when previously adopting) may choose to apply IFRS 1 when it re-adopts IFRSs. The Board decided that the entity should be allowed, rather than required, to apply IFRS 1 because, as explained in paragraph IN5 of IFRS 1, IFRS 1 grants limited exemptions from some requirements of IFRSs on the assumption that the cost of complying with some IFRSs would be likely to exceed the benefits to users of financial statements. However, the costs of applying IFRSs in full might not exceed the benefits of doing so for an entity that had previously applied IFRSs. Consequently, the Board concluded that an entity returning to IFRSs might determine that the benefits of applying IFRSs as if it had continued to do so without interruption would exceed the costs of preparing such information, and that an entity should not be prohibited from following that approach. In applying such an approach, an entity should apply IFRSs retrospectively in accordance with IAS 8 *Accounting Policies, Changes in Estimates and Errors* as if the entity had never stopped applying IFRSs. The Board noted that hindsight is not applied by an entity in preparing IFRS financial statements, whether that entity is applying IFRS 1, or whether that entity applies IFRSs retrospectively as if the entity had never stopped applying them in accordance with IAS 8. The Board noted that paragraphs 14–17 of IFRS 1 and paragraph 53 of IAS 8 provide guidance in this regard.

BC6D   The Board also noted that, in accordance with paragraph 2 of IFRS 1, an entity that has never applied IFRSs in the past would continue to be required to apply IFRS 1 in its first IFRS financial statements.

BC6E   The Board also decided that the entity shall disclose the reason why it stopped applying IFRSs and the reason why it is resuming reporting in accordance with IFRSs. The Board thinks that this disclosure requirement provides users with useful information and would discourage the intentional omission of the statement of compliance with IFRSs solely to allow an entity to take advantage of the exemptions in IFRS 1. The Board also decided that an entity that does not elect to apply IFRS 1 shall explain the reasons why it has elected to apply IFRSs as if it had never stopped applying them. The Board believes that this disclosure ensures that useful information will be provided to users.

Basic concepts

Useful information for users

BC7   In developing recognition and measurement requirements for an entity's opening IFRS balance sheet, the Board referred to the objective of financial statements, as set out in the *Framework for the Preparation and Presentation of Financial Statements*. The *Framework*[2] states that the objective of financial statements is to provide information about the financial position, performance and changes in financial position of an entity that is useful to a wide range of users in making economic decisions.

---

2   References to the *Framework* are to IASC's *Framework for the Preparation and Presentation of Financial Statements*, adopted by the IASB in 2001. In September 2010 the IASB replaced the *Framework* with the *Conceptual Framework for Financial Reporting*.

BC8   The *Framework* identifies four qualitative characteristics that make information in financial statements useful to users. In summary, the information should be:

     (a)   readily understandable by users.

     (b)   relevant to the decision-making needs of users.

     (c)   reliable, in other words financial statements should:

         (i)   represent faithfully the transactions and other events they either purport to represent or could reasonably be expected to represent;

         (ii)   represent transactions and other events in accordance with their substance and economic reality and not merely their legal form;

         (iii)   be neutral, that is to say, free from bias;

         (iv)   contend with the uncertainties that inevitably surround many events and circumstances by the exercise of prudence; and

         (v)   be complete within the bounds of materiality and cost.

     (d)   comparable with information provided by the entity in its financial statements through time and with information provided in the financial statements of other entities.

Comparability

BC9   The previous paragraph notes the need for comparability. Ideally, a regime for first-time adoption of IFRSs would achieve comparability:

     (a)   within an entity over time;

     (b)   between different first-time adopters; and

     (c)   between first-time adopters and entities that already apply IFRSs.

BC10   SIC-8 gave priority to ensuring comparability between a first-time adopter and entities that already applied IASs. It was based on the principle that a first-time adopter should comply with the same standards as an entity that already applied IASs. However, the Board decided that it is more important to achieve comparability over time within a first-time adopter's first IFRS financial statements and between different entities adopting IFRSs for the first time at a given date; achieving comparability between first-time adopters and entities that already apply IFRSs is a secondary objective.

Current version of IFRSs

BC11   Paragraphs 7–9 of the IFRS require a first-time adopter to apply the current version of IFRSs, without considering superseded or amended versions.[3] This:

     (a)   enhances comparability, because the information in a first-time adopter's first IFRS financial statements is prepared on a consistent basis over time;

---

3   *Annual Improvements Cycle 2011–2013* clarified that this paragraph does not require an entity to use a more recent version of an IFRS. It only explains the advantages of applying a more recent version of an IFRS. See paragraph BC11A for further details.

(b)   gives users comparative information prepared using later versions of IFRSs that the Board regards as superior to superseded versions; and

(c)   avoids unnecessary costs.

BC11A   Paragraph 7 requires an entity to use the IFRSs that are effective at the end of its first IFRS reporting period. Paragraph 8 allows a first-time adopter to apply a new IFRS that is not yet mandatory if that IFRS permits early application. Notwithstanding the advantages, set out in paragraph BC11, of applying a more recent version of an IFRS, paragraphs 7–8 permit an entity to use either the IFRS that is currently mandatory or the new IFRS that is not yet mandatory, if that new IFRS permits early application. Paragraph 7 requires an entity to apply the same version of the IFRS throughout the periods covered by the entity's first IFRS financial statements. Consequently, if a first-time adopter chooses to early apply a new IFRS, that new IFRS will be applied throughout all the periods presented in its first IFRS financial statements on a retrospective basis, unless IFRS 1 provides an exemption or an exception that permits or requires otherwise.

BC12   In general, the transitional provisions in other IFRSs do not apply to a first-time adopter (paragraph 9 of the IFRS). Some of these transitional provisions require or permit an entity already reporting in accordance with IFRSs to apply a new requirement prospectively. These provisions generally reflect a conclusion that one or both of the following factors are present in a particular case:

(a)   Retrospective application may be difficult or involve costs exceeding the likely benefits. The IFRS permits prospective application in specific cases where this could occur (paragraphs BC30–BC73).

(b)   There is a danger of abuse if retrospective application would require judgements by management about past conditions after the outcome of a particular transaction is already known. The IFRS prohibits retrospective application in some areas where this could occur (paragraphs BC74–BC84).

BC13   Some have suggested three further reasons for permitting or requiring prospective application in some cases:

(a)   to alleviate unforeseen consequences of a new IFRS if another party uses financial statements to monitor compliance with a contract or agreement. However, in the Board's view, it is up to the parties to an agreement to determine whether to insulate the agreement from the effects of a future IFRS and, if not, how they might renegotiate it so that it reflects changes in the underlying financial condition rather than changes in reporting (paragraph 21[4] of the *Preface to International Financial Reporting Standards*).

(b)   to give a first-time adopter the same accounting options as an entity that already applies IFRSs. However, permitting prospective application by a first-time adopter would conflict with the Board's primary objective of comparability within an entity's first IFRS financial statements (paragraph BC10). Therefore, the Board did not adopt a general policy of giving first-time adopters the same accounting options of prospective

---

4   amended to paragraph 20 when the *Preface* was revised in January 2010.

application that existing IFRSs give to entities that already apply IFRSs. Paragraphs BC20–BC23 discuss one specific case, namely derecognition of financial assets and financial liabilities.

(c)   to avoid difficult distinctions between changes in estimates and changes in the basis for making estimates. However, a first-time adopter need not make this distinction in preparing its opening IFRS balance sheet, so the IFRS does not include exemptions on these grounds. If an entity becomes aware of errors made under previous GAAP, the IFRS requires it to disclose the correction of the errors (paragraph 26 of the IFRS).

BC14   The Board will consider case by case when it issues a new IFRS whether a first-time adopter should apply that IFRS retrospectively or prospectively. The Board expects that retrospective application will be appropriate in most cases, given its primary objective of comparability over time within a first-time adopter's first IFRS financial statements. However, if the Board concludes in a particular case that prospective application by a first-time adopter is justified, it will amend the IFRS on first-time adoption of IFRSs. As a result, IFRS 1 will contain all material on first-time adoption of IFRSs and other IFRSs will not refer to first-time adopters (except, when needed, in the Basis for Conclusions and consequential amendments).

BC15   Under the proposals in ED 1, a first-time adopter could have elected to apply IFRSs as if it had always applied IFRSs. This alternative approach was intended mainly to help an entity that did not wish to use any of the exemptions proposed in ED 1 because it had already been accumulating information in accordance with IFRSs without presenting IFRS financial statements. To enable an entity using this approach to use the information it had already accumulated, ED 1 would have required it to consider superseded versions of IFRSs if more recent versions required prospective application. However, as explained in paragraphs BC28 and BC29, the Board abandoned ED 1's all-or-nothing approach to exemptions. Because this eliminated the reason for the alternative approach, the Board deleted it in finalising the IFRS.

Opening IFRS balance sheet

BC16   An entity's opening IFRS balance sheet is the starting point for its accounting in accordance with IFRSs. The following paragraphs explain how the Board used the *Framework* in developing recognition and measurement requirements for the opening IFRS balance sheet.

Recognition

BC17   The Board considered a suggestion that the IFRS should not require a first-time adopter to investigate transactions that occurred before the beginning of a 'look back' period of, say, three to five years before the date of transition to IFRSs. Some argued that this would be a practical way for a first-time adopter to give a high level of transparency and comparability, without incurring the cost of investigating very old transactions. They noted two particular precedents for transitional provisions that have permitted an entity to omit some assets and liabilities from its balance sheet:

(a) A previous version of IAS 39 *Financial Instruments: Recognition and Measurement*[5] prohibited restatement of securitisation, transfer or other derecognition transactions entered into before the beginning of the financial year in which it was initially applied.

(b) Some national accounting standards and IAS 17 *Accounting for Leases* (superseded in 1997 by IAS 17 *Leases*) permitted prospective application of a requirement for lessees to capitalise finance leases. Under this approach, a lessee would not be required to recognise finance lease obligations and the related leased assets for leases that began before a specified date.

BC18 However, limiting the look back period could lead to the omission of material assets or liabilities from an entity's opening IFRS balance sheet. Material omissions would undermine the understandability, relevance, reliability and comparability of an entity's first IFRS financial statements. Therefore, the Board concluded that an entity's opening IFRS balance sheet should:

(a) include all assets and liabilities whose recognition is required by IFRSs, except:

(i) some financial assets or financial liabilities derecognised in accordance with previous GAAP before the date of transition to IFRSs (paragraphs BC20–BC23); and

(ii) goodwill and other assets acquired, and liabilities assumed, in a past business combination that were not recognised in the acquirer's consolidated balance sheet in accordance with previous GAAP and also would not qualify for recognition in accordance with IFRSs in the balance sheet of the acquiree (paragraphs BC31–BC40).

(b) not report items as assets or liabilities if they do not qualify for recognition in accordance with IFRSs.

BC19 Some financial instruments may be classified as equity in accordance with previous GAAP but as financial liabilities in accordance with IAS 32 *Financial Instruments: Presentation*. Some respondents to ED 1 requested an extended transitional period to enable the issuer of such instruments to renegotiate contracts that refer to debt-equity ratios. However, although a new IFRS may have unforeseen consequences if another party uses financial statements to monitor compliance with a contract or agreement, that possibility does not, in the Board's view, justify prospective application (paragraph BC13(a)).

Derecognition in accordance with previous GAAP

BC20 An entity may have derecognised financial assets or financial liabilities in accordance with its previous GAAP that do not qualify for derecognition in accordance with IAS 39.[6] ED 1 proposed that a first-time adopter should recognise those assets and liabilities in its opening IFRS balance sheet. Some

---

5 IFRS 9 *Financial Instruments* replaced IAS 39. IFRS 9 applies to all items that were previously within the scope of IAS 39.

6 IFRS 9 *Financial Instruments* replaced IAS 39. IFRS 9 applies to all items that were previously within the scope of IAS 39.

respondents to ED 1 requested the Board to permit or require a first-time adopter not to restate past derecognition transactions, on the following grounds:

(a)   Restating past derecognition transactions would be costly, especially if restatement involves determining the fair value of retained servicing assets and liabilities and other components retained in a complex securitisation. Furthermore, it may be difficult to obtain information on financial assets held by transferees that are not under the transferor's control.

(b)   Restatement undermines the legal certainty expected by parties who entered into transactions on the basis of the accounting rules in effect at the time.

(c)   IAS 39 did not, before the improvements proposed in June 2002, require (or even permit) entities to restate past derecognition transactions. Without a similar exemption, first-time adopters would be unfairly disadvantaged.

(d)   Retrospective application would not result in consistent measurement, as entities would need to recreate information about past transactions with the benefit of hindsight.

BC21   The Board had considered these arguments in developing ED 1. The Board's reasons for the proposal in ED 1 were as follows:

(a)   The omission of material assets or liabilities would undermine the understandability, relevance, reliability and comparability of an entity's financial statements. Many of the transactions under discussion are large and will have effects for many years.

(b)   Such an exemption would be inconsistent with the June 2002 exposure draft of improvements to IAS 39.

(c)   The Board's primary objective is to achieve comparability over time within an entity's first IFRS financial statements. Prospective application by a first-time adopter would conflict with that primary objective, even if prospective application were available to entities already applying IFRSs.

(d)   Although a new IFRS may have unforeseen consequences if another party uses financial statements to monitor compliance with a contract or agreement, that possibility does not justify prospective application (paragraph BC13(a)).

BC22   Nevertheless, in finalising the IFRS, the Board concluded that it would be premature to require a treatment different from the current version of IAS 39 before completing the proposed improvements to IAS 39. Accordingly, the IFRS originally required the same treatment as the then current version of IAS 39 for derecognition transactions before the effective date of the then current version of IAS 39, namely that any financial assets or financial liabilities derecognised in accordance with previous GAAP before financial years beginning on 1 January 2001 remain derecognised. The Board agreed that when it completed the improvements to IAS 39, it might amend or delete this exemption.

BC22A   The Board reconsidered this issue in completing the revision of IAS 39 in 2003. The Board decided to retain the transition requirements as set out in IFRS 1, for the reasons given in paragraph BC20. However, the Board amended the date from which prospective application was required to transactions that occur on or after 1 January 2004 in order to overcome the practical difficulties of restating transactions that had been derecognised before that date. In 2010 the Board was asked to reconsider whether 1 January 2004 is the appropriate date from which a first-time adopter should be required to restate past derecognition transactions. Constituents were concerned that, as time passes, the fixed transition date of 1 January 2004 becomes more remote and increasingly less relevant to the financial reports as additional jurisdictions adopt IFRSs. The Board accepted that the cost of reconstructing transactions back in time to 1 January 2004 was likely to outweigh the benefit to be achieved in doing so. It therefore amended the fixed date of 1 January 2004 in paragraph B2 to 'the date of transition to IFRSs'. The Board also amended the wording of the illustration in paragraph B2, in order to clarify that it is providing an example.

BC22B   The Board also noted that financial statements that include financial assets and financial liabilities that would otherwise be omitted under the provisions of the IFRS would be more complete and therefore more useful to users of financial statements. The Board therefore decided to permit retrospective application of the derecognition requirements. It also decided that retrospective application should be limited to cases when the information needed to apply the IFRS to past transactions was obtained at the time of initially accounting for those transactions. This limitation prevents the unacceptable use of hindsight.

BC23   The Board removed from IAS 39 the following consequential amendments to IAS 39 made when IFRS 1 was issued, because, for first-time adopters, these clarifications are clear in paragraphs IG26–IG31 and IG53 of the guidance on implementing IFRS 1. These were:

(a)   the clarification that an entity is required to apply IAS 39 to all derivatives or other interests retained after a derecognition transaction, even if the transaction occurred before the effective date of IAS 39; and

(b)   the confirmation that there are no exemptions for special purpose entities[7] that existed before the date of transition to IFRSs.

Measurement

BC24   The Board considered whether it should require a first-time adopter to measure all assets and liabilities at fair value in the opening IFRS balance sheet. Some argued that this would result in more relevant information than an aggregation of costs incurred at different dates, or of costs and fair values. However, the Board concluded that a requirement to measure all assets and liabilities at fair value at the date of transition to IFRSs would be unreasonable, given that an entity may use an IFRS-compliant cost-based measurement before and after that date for some items.

---

7   SIC-12 *Consolidation—Special Purpose Entities* was withdrawn and superseded by IFRS 10 *Consolidated Financial Statements* issued in May 2011. There is no longer specific accounting guidance for special purpose entities because IFRS 10 applies to all types of entities.

       © IFRS Foundation

BC25   The Board decided as a general principle that a first-time adopter should measure all assets and liabilities recognised in its opening IFRS balance sheet on the basis required by the relevant IFRSs. This is needed for an entity's first IFRS financial statements to present understandable, relevant, reliable and comparable information.

Benefits and costs

BC26   The *Framework* acknowledges that the need for a balance between the benefits of information and the cost of providing it may constrain the provision of relevant and reliable information. The Board considered these cost-benefit constraints and developed targeted exemptions from the general principle described in paragraph BC25. SIC-8 did not include specific exemptions of this kind, although it provided general exemptions from:

(a)   retrospective adjustments to the opening balance of retained earnings 'when the amount of the adjustment relating to prior periods cannot be reasonably determined'.

(b)   provision of comparative information when it is 'impracticable' to provide such information.

BC27   The Board expects that most first-time adopters will begin planning on a timely basis for the transition to IFRSs. Accordingly, in balancing benefits and costs, the Board took as its benchmark an entity that plans the transition well in advance and can collect most information needed for its opening IFRS balance sheet at, or very soon after, the date of transition to IFRSs.

BC28   ED 1 proposed that a first-time adopter should use either all the exemptions in ED 1 or none. However, some respondents disagreed with this all-or-nothing approach for the following reasons:

(a)   Many of the exemptions are not interdependent, so there is no conceptual reason to condition use of one exemption on use of other exemptions.

(b)   Although it is necessary to permit some exemptions on pragmatic grounds, entities should be encouraged to use as few exemptions as possible.

(c)   Some of the exemptions proposed in ED 1 were implicit options because they relied on the entity's own judgement of undue cost or effort and some others were explicit options. Only a few exemptions were really mandatory.

(d)   Unlike the other exceptions to retrospective application, the requirement to apply hedge accounting prospectively was not intended as a pragmatic concession on cost-benefit grounds. Retrospective application in an area that relies on designation by management would not be acceptable, even if an entity applied all other aspects of IFRSs retrospectively.

BC29   The Board found these comments persuasive. In finalising the IFRS, the Board grouped the exceptions to retrospective application into two categories:

(a) Some exceptions consist of optional exemptions (paragraphs BC30–BC63E).

(b) The other exceptions prohibit full retrospective application of IFRSs to some aspects of derecognition (paragraphs BC20–BC23), hedge accounting (paragraphs BC75–BC80), and estimates (paragraph BC84).

Exemptions from other IFRSs

BC30 An entity may elect to use one or more of the following exemptions:

(a) business combinations (paragraphs BC31–BC40);

(b) deemed cost (paragraphs BC41–BC47K);

(c) employee benefits (paragraphs BC48–BC52);

(d) cumulative translation differences (paragraphs BC53–BC55);

(e) compound financial instruments (paragraphs BC56–BC58);

(f) investments in subsidiaries, jointly controlled entities[8] and associates (paragraphs BC58A–BC58M);

(g) assets and liabilities of subsidiaries, associates and joint ventures (paragraphs BC59–BC63);

(h) designation of previously recognised financial instruments (paragraph BC63A);

(i) share-based payment transactions (paragraph BC63B);

(j) changes in existing decommissioning, restoration and similar liabilities included in the cost of property, plant and equipment (paragraphs BC63C and BC63CA);

(k) leases (paragraphs BC63D–BC63DB);

(l) borrowing costs (paragraph BC63E);

(m) severe hyperinflation (paragraphs BC63F–BC63J); and

(n) joint arrangements (paragraphs BC63K and BC63L).

Business combinations[9]

BC31 The following paragraphs discuss various aspects of accounting for business combinations that an entity recognised in accordance with previous GAAP before the date of transition to IFRSs:

(a) whether retrospective restatement of past business combinations should be prohibited, permitted or required (paragraphs BC32–BC34).

(b) whether an entity should recognise assets acquired and liabilities assumed in a past business combination if it did not recognise them in accordance with previous GAAP (paragraph BC35).

---

8 'Jointly controlled entities' were defined in IAS 31 *Interests in Joint Ventures*. IFRS 11 *Joint Arrangements*, issued in May 2011, replaced IAS 31 and changed the terminology.

9 In October 2012 the Board issued *Investment Entities* (Amendments to IFRS 10, IFRS 12 and IAS 27), which stated that Appendix C of IFRS 1 should only apply to business combinations within the scope of IFRS 3 *Business Combinations*.

(c)   whether an entity should restate amounts assigned to the assets and liabilities of the combining entities if previous GAAP brought forward unchanged their pre-combination carrying amounts (paragraph BC36).

(d)   whether an entity should restate goodwill for adjustments made in its opening IFRS balance sheet to the carrying amounts of assets acquired and liabilities assumed in past business combinations (paragraphs BC37–BC40).

BC32   Retrospective application of IFRS 3 *Business Combinations* could require an entity to recreate data that it did not capture at the date of a past business combination and make subjective estimates about conditions that existed at that date. These factors could reduce the relevance and reliability of the entity's first IFRS financial statements. Therefore, ED 1 would have prohibited restatement of past business combinations (unless an entity used the proposed alternative approach, discussed in paragraph BC15, of applying IFRSs as if it had always applied IFRSs). Some respondents agreed, arguing that restatement of past business combinations would involve subjective, and potentially selective, use of hindsight that would diminish the relevance and reliability of financial statements.

BC33   Other respondents disagreed. They argued that:

(a)   effects of business combination accounting can last for many years. Previous GAAP may differ significantly from IFRSs, and in some countries there are no accounting requirements at all for business combinations. Previous GAAP balances might not result in decision-useful information in these countries.

(b)   restatement is preferable and may not involve as much cost or effort for more recent business combinations.

BC34   In the light of these comments, the Board concluded that restatement of past business combinations is conceptually preferable, although for cost-benefit reasons this should be permitted but not required. The Board decided to place some limits on this election and noted that information is more likely to be available for more recent business combinations. Therefore, if a first-time adopter restates any business combination, the IFRS requires it to restate all later business combinations (paragraph C1 of the IFRS).

BC35   If an entity did not recognise a particular asset or liability in accordance with previous GAAP at the date of the business combination, ED 1 proposed that its deemed cost in accordance with IFRSs would be zero. As a result, the entity's opening IFRS balance sheet would not have included that asset or liability if IFRSs permit or require a cost-based measurement. Some respondents to ED 1 argued that this would be an unjustifiable departure from the principle that the opening IFRS balance sheet should include all assets and liabilities. The Board agreed with that conclusion. Therefore, paragraph C4(f) of the IFRS requires that the acquirer should recognise those assets and liabilities and measure them on the basis that IFRSs would require in the separate balance sheet of the acquiree.

BC36   In accordance with previous GAAP, an entity might have brought forward unchanged the pre-combination carrying amounts of the combining entities' assets and liabilities. Some argued that it would be inconsistent to use these carrying amounts as deemed cost in accordance with IFRSs, given that the IFRS does not permit the use of similar carrying amounts as deemed cost for assets and liabilities that were not acquired in a business combination. However, the Board identified no specific form of past business combination, and no specific form of accounting for past business combinations, for which it would not be acceptable to bring forward cost-based measurements made in accordance with previous GAAP.

BC37   Although the IFRS treats amounts assigned in accordance with previous GAAP to goodwill and other assets acquired and liabilities assumed in a past business combination as their deemed cost in accordance with IFRSs at the date of the business combination, an entity needs to adjust their carrying amounts in its opening IFRS balance sheet, as follows.

(a)   Assets and liabilities measured in accordance with IFRSs at fair value[10] or other forms of current value: remeasure to fair value or that other current value.

(b)   Assets (other than goodwill) and liabilities for which IFRSs apply a cost-based measurement: adjust the accumulated depreciation or amortisation since the date of the business combination if it does not comply with IFRSs. Depreciation is based on deemed cost, which is the carrying amount in accordance with previous GAAP immediately following the business combination.

(c)   Assets (other than goodwill) and liabilities not recognised in accordance with previous GAAP: measure on the basis that IFRSs would require in the separate balance sheet of the acquiree.

(d)   Items that do not qualify for recognition as assets and liabilities in accordance with IFRSs: eliminate from the opening IFRS balance sheet.

BC38   The Board considered whether a first-time adopter should recognise the resulting adjustments by restating goodwill. Because intangible assets and goodwill are closely related, the Board decided that a first-time adopter should restate goodwill when it:

(a)   eliminates an item that was recognised in accordance with previous GAAP as an intangible asset but does not qualify for separate recognition in accordance with IFRSs; or

(b)   recognises an intangible asset that was subsumed within goodwill in accordance with previous GAAP.

However, to avoid costs that would exceed the likely benefits to users, the IFRS prohibits restatement of goodwill for most other adjustments reflected in the opening IFRS balance sheet, unless a first-time adopter elects to apply IFRS 3 retrospectively (paragraph C4(g) of the IFRS).

BC39   To minimise the possibility of double-counting an item that was included in goodwill in accordance with previous GAAP, and is included in accordance with

---

10   IFRS 13 *Fair Value Measurement*, issued in May 2011, defines fair value and contains the requirements for measuring fair value.

IFRSs either within the measurement of another asset or as a deduction from a liability, the IFRS requires an entity to test goodwill recognised in its opening IFRS balance sheet for impairment (paragraph C4(g)(ii) of the IFRS). This does not prevent the implicit recognition of internally generated goodwill that arose after the date of the business combination. However, the Board concluded that an attempt to exclude such internally generated goodwill would be costly and lead to arbitrary results.

BC40 Some respondents to ED 1 suggested that a formal impairment test should be required only if there is a possibility of double-counting—ie when additional, previously unrecognised, assets relating to a past business combination are recognised in the opening IFRS balance sheet (or an indicator of impairment is present). However, the Board decided that a first-time adopter should carry out a formal impairment test of all goodwill recognised in its opening IFRS balance sheet, as previous GAAP might not have required a test of comparable rigour.

Deemed cost

BC41 Some measurements in accordance with IFRSs are based on an accumulation of past costs or other transaction data. If an entity has not previously collected the necessary information, collecting or estimating it retrospectively may be costly. To avoid excessive cost, ED 1 proposed that an entity could use the fair value of an item of property, plant and equipment at the date of transition to IFRSs as its deemed cost at that date if determining a cost-based measurement in accordance with IFRSs would involve undue cost or effort.

BC42 In finalising the IFRS, the Board noted that reconstructed cost data might be less relevant to users, and less reliable, than current fair value data. Furthermore, the Board concluded that balancing costs and benefits was a task for the Board when it sets accounting requirements rather than for entities when they apply those requirements. Therefore, the IFRS permits an entity to use fair value as deemed cost in some cases without any need to demonstrate undue cost or effort.

BC43 Some expressed concerns that the use of fair value would lead to lack of comparability. However, cost is generally equivalent to fair value at the date of acquisition. Therefore, the use of fair value as the deemed cost of an asset means that an entity will report the same cost data as if it had acquired an asset with the same remaining service potential at the date of transition to IFRSs. If there is any lack of comparability, it arises from the aggregation of costs incurred at different dates, rather than from the targeted use of fair value as deemed cost for some assets. The Board regarded this approach as justified to solve the unique problem of introducing IFRSs in a cost-effective way without damaging transparency.

BC44 The IFRS restricts the use of fair value as deemed cost to those assets for which reconstructing costs is likely to be of limited benefit to users and particularly onerous: property, plant and equipment, investment property (if an entity elects to use the cost method in IAS 40 *Investment Property*) and intangible assets that meet restrictive criteria (paragraphs D5 and D7 of the IFRS).

BC45 Under the revaluation model in IAS 16 *Property, Plant and Equipment*, if an entity revalues an asset, it must revalue all assets in that class. This restriction prevents selective revaluation of only those assets whose revaluation would lead to a particular result. Some suggested a similar restriction on the use of fair value as deemed cost. However, IAS 36 *Impairment of Assets* requires an impairment test if there is any indication that an asset is impaired. Thus, if an entity uses fair value as deemed cost for assets whose fair value is above cost, it cannot ignore indications that the recoverable amount of other assets may have fallen below their carrying amount. Therefore, the IFRS does not restrict the use of fair value as deemed cost to entire classes of asset.

BC46   Some revaluations in accordance with previous GAAP might be more relevant to users than original cost. If so, it would not be reasonable to require time-consuming and expensive reconstruction of a cost that complies with IFRSs. In consequence, the IFRS permits an entity to use amounts determined using previous GAAP as deemed cost for IFRSs in the following cases:

(a)   if an entity revalued one of the assets described in paragraph BC44 using its previous GAAP and the revaluation met specified criteria (paragraphs D6 and D7 of the IFRS).

(b)   if an entity established a deemed cost in accordance with previous GAAP for some or all assets and liabilities by measuring them at their fair value at one particular date because of an event such as a privatisation or initial public offering (paragraph D8 of the IFRS).

BC46A   In *Improvements to IFRSs* issued in May 2010, the Board extended the scope of paragraph D8 for the use of the deemed cost exemption for an event-driven fair value. In some jurisdictions, local law requires an entity to revalue its assets and liabilities to fair value for a privatisation or initial public offering (IPO) and to treat the revalued amounts as deemed cost for the entity's previous GAAP. Before the amendment made in May 2010, if that revaluation occurred after the entity's date of transition to IFRSs, the entity could not have used that revaluation as deemed cost for IFRSs. Therefore, the entity would have had to prepare two sets of measurements for its assets and liabilities—one to comply with IFRSs, and one to comply with local law. The Board considered this unduly onerous. Therefore, the Board amended paragraph D8 to allow an entity to recognise an event-driven fair value measurement as deemed cost when the event occurs, provided that this is during the periods covered by its first IFRS financial statements. In addition, the Board concluded that the same relief should apply to an entity that adopted IFRSs in periods before the effective date of IFRS 1 or applied IFRS 1 in a previous period, provided the measurement date is within the period covered by its first IFRS financial statements.

BC46B   The Board also decided to require the entity to present historical costs or other amounts already permitted by IFRS 1 for the periods before that date. In this regard, the Board considered an approach where an entity could 'work back' to the deemed cost on the date of transition, using the revaluation amounts obtained on the measurement date, adjusted to exclude any depreciation, amortisation or impairment between the two dates. Although some believed that this presentation would have provided greater comparability throughout the first IFRS reporting period, the Board rejected it because making such adjustments would require hindsight and the computed carrying amounts on the date of transition to IFRSs would be neither the historical costs of the revalued assets nor their fair values on that date.

BC47 Paragraph D6 of the IFRS refers to revaluations that are broadly comparable to fair value or reflect an index applied to a cost that is broadly comparable to cost determined in accordance with IFRSs. It may not always be clear whether a previous revaluation was intended as a measure of fair value or differs materially from fair value. The flexibility in this area permits a cost-effective solution for the unique problem of transition to IFRSs. It allows a first-time adopter to establish a deemed cost using a measurement that is already available and is a reasonable starting point for a cost-based measurement.

BC47A Under their previous GAAP many oil and gas entities accounted for exploration and development costs for properties in development or production in cost centres that include all properties in a large geographical area. (In some jurisdictions, this is referred to as full cost accounting.) Those entities will in most cases have to determine the carrying amounts for oil and gas assets at the date of transition to IFRSs. Information about oil and gas assets recorded in an accounting system using this method of accounting will almost always be at a larger unit of account than the unit of account that is acceptable under IFRSs. Amortisation at the IFRS unit of account level would also have to be calculated (on a unit of production basis) for each year, using a reserves base that has changed over time because of changes in factors such as geological understanding and prices for oil and gas. In many cases, particularly for older assets, this information may not be available. The Board was advised that even if such information is available the effort and associated cost to determine the opening balances at the date of transition would usually be very high.

BC47B IFRS 1 permits an entity to measure an item of property, plant and equipment at its fair value at the date of transition to IFRSs and to use that fair value as the item's deemed cost at that date. Determining the fair value of oil and gas assets is a complex process that begins with the difficult task of estimating the volume of reserves and resources. When the fair value amounts must be audited, determining significant inputs to the estimates generally requires the use of qualified external experts. For entities with many oil and gas assets, the use of this fair value as deemed cost alternative would not meet the Board's stated intention of avoiding excessive cost (see paragraph BC41).

BC47C The Board decided that for oil and gas assets in the development or production phases, it would permit entities that used the method of accounting described in paragraph BC47A under their previous GAAP to determine the deemed cost at the date of transition to IFRSs using an allocation of the amount determined for a cost centre under the entity's previous GAAP on the basis of the reserves associated with the oil and gas assets in that cost centre.

BC47D The deemed cost of oil and gas assets determined in this way may include amounts that would not have been capitalised in accordance with IFRSs, such as some overhead costs, costs that were incurred before the entity obtained legal rights to explore a specific area (and cannot be capitalised in accordance with IAS 38 *Intangible Assets*) and, most significantly, unsuccessful exploration costs. This is a consequence of having included these costs in the single carrying amount under the method of accounting described in paragraph BC47A. To avoid the use of deemed costs resulting in an oil and gas asset being measured at more than its recoverable amount, the Board decided that oil and gas assets should be tested for impairment at the date of transition to IFRSs.

BC47E   Not all oil and gas entities used the method of accounting described in paragraph BC47A under their previous GAAP. Some used a method of accounting that requires a unit of account that is generally consistent with IFRSs and does not cause similar transition issues. Therefore, the Board decided that the exemption would apply only to entities that used the method of accounting described in paragraph BC47A under their previous GAAP.

BC47F   In *Improvements to IFRSs* issued in May 2010, the Board extended the use of the deemed cost exemption to entities with operations subject to rate regulation. An entity might have items of property, plant and equipment or intangible assets that it holds for use in operations subject to rate regulation, or that it once used for this purpose and now holds for other purposes. Under previous GAAP, an entity might have capitalised, as part of the carrying amount of items of property, plant and equipment or intangible assets held for use in operations subject to rate regulation, amounts that do not qualify for capitalisation under IFRSs. For example, when setting rates regulators often permit entities to capitalise, as part of the cost of property, plant and equipment or intangible assets acquired, constructed or produced over time, an allowance for the cost of financing the asset's acquisition, construction or production. This allowance typically includes an imputed cost of equity. IFRSs do not permit an entity to capitalise an imputed cost of equity.

BC47G   Before this amendment, an entity with such items whose carrying amounts include amounts that do not qualify for capitalisation under IFRSs would have had either to restate those items retrospectively to remove the non-qualifying amounts, or to use the exemption in paragraph D5 (fair value as deemed cost). Both of those alternatives pose significant practical challenges, the cost of which can often outweigh the benefit.

BC47H   Typically, once amounts are included in the total cost of an item of property, plant and equipment, they are no longer tracked separately. The restatement of property, plant and equipment to remove amounts not in compliance with IFRSs would require historical information that, given the typical age of some of the assets involved, is probably no longer available and would be difficult to estimate. Obtaining the fair value information necessary to use the exemption in paragraph D5 may not be a practical alternative, given the lack of readily available fair value information for those assets.

BC47I   The Board decided it would permit entities with operations subject to rate regulation to use as deemed cost at the date of transition to IFRSs the carrying amount of the items of property, plant and equipment or intangible assets determined under the entity's previous GAAP. The Board views this exemption as consistent with the exemptions already included in IFRS 1 in that it avoids excessive costs while meeting the objectives of the IFRS.

BC47J   The Board understands that most first-time adopters with operations subject to rate regulation have previously accounted for property, plant and equipment largely in accordance with a historical cost model consistent with IAS 16. The

Board concluded that the cost and effort required to achieve total compliance in this area for the purposes of preparing an entity's first IFRS financial statements is not warranted to meet the objective of providing a suitable starting point for accounting under IFRSs. IFRS 1 requires that each item for which the exemption is used is tested for impairment, either individually or at the cash-generating unit to which the item belongs in accordance with IAS 36, at the date of transition. This requirement provides further assurance that this objective is met.

BC47K   Consistent with the Board's rationale for the use of fair value as deemed cost in paragraphs BC43 and BC44, this exemption means that an entity will report the same cost data as if it had acquired an asset with the same remaining service potential for that amount at the date of transition to IFRSs. An entity's use of this exemption results in a new cost basis for the item and previous GAAP depreciation methods and capitalisation policies are not relevant. Thus, if an entity uses this exemption for items of property, plant and equipment or intangible assets, it does not also apply the exemption for borrowing costs provided in paragraph D23.

Employee benefits

BC48   [Deleted]

BC49   The revision of IAS 19 in 1998 increased the reported employee benefit liabilities of some entities. IAS 19 permitted entities to amortise that increase over up to five years. Some suggested a similar transitional treatment for first-time adopters. However, the Board has no general policy of exempting transactions occurring before a specific date from the requirements of new IFRSs (paragraph 21[11] of the *Preface to International Financial Reporting Standards*). Therefore, the Board did not include a similar transitional provision for first-time adopters.

BC50   An entity's first IFRS financial statements may reflect measurements of pension liabilities at three dates: the reporting date, the end of the comparative year and the date of transition to IFRSs. Some suggested that obtaining three separate actuarial valuations for a single set of financial statements would be costly. Therefore, they proposed that the Board should permit an entity to use a single actuarial valuation, based, for example, on assumptions valid at the reporting date, with service costs and interest costs based on those assumptions for each of the periods presented.

BC51   However, the Board concluded that a general exemption from the principle of measurement at each date would conflict with the objective of providing understandable, relevant, reliable and comparable information for users. If an entity obtains a full actuarial valuation at one or two of these dates and rolls that (those) valuation(s) forward or back to the other date(s), any such roll forward or roll back needs to reflect material transactions and other material events (including changes in market prices and interest rates) between those dates (IAS 19 paragraph 57).

BC52   [Deleted]

---

11   amended to paragraph 20 when the *Preface* was revised in January 2010

Cumulative translation differences

BC53 IAS 21 *The Effects of Changes in Foreign Exchange Rates* requires an entity to classify some cumulative translation differences (CTDs) relating to a net investment in a foreign operation as a separate component of equity. The entity transfers the CTDs to the income statement on subsequent disposal of the foreign operation. The proposals in ED 1 would have permitted a first-time adopter to use the CTDs in accordance with previous GAAP as the deemed CTDs in accordance with IFRSs if reconstructing CTDs would have involved undue cost or effort.

BC54 Some respondents to ED 1 argued that it would be more transparent and comparable to exempt an entity from the requirement to identify CTDs at the date of transition to IFRSs, for the following reasons:

(a) An entity might know the aggregate CTDs, but might not know the amount for each subsidiary. If so, it could not transfer that amount to the income statement on disposal of that subsidiary. This would defeat the objective of identifying CTDs as a separate component of equity.

(b) The amount of CTDs in accordance with previous GAAP might be inappropriate as it might be affected by adjustments made on transition to IFRSs to assets and liabilities of foreign entities.

BC55 The Board found these arguments persuasive. Therefore, a first-time adopter need not identify the CTDs at the date of transition to IFRSs (paragraphs D12 and D13 of the IFRS). The first-time adopter need not show that identifying the CTDs would involve undue cost or effort.

Compound financial instruments

BC56 IAS 32 requires an entity to split a compound financial instrument at inception into separate liability and equity components. Even if the liability component is no longer outstanding, retrospective application of IAS 32 would involve separating two portions of equity. The first portion is in retained earnings and represents the cumulative interest accreted on the liability component. The other portion represents the original equity component of the instrument.

BC57 Some respondents to ED 1 argued that separating these two portions would be costly if the liability component of the compound instrument is no longer outstanding at the date of transition to IFRSs. The Board agreed with those comments. Therefore, if the liability component is no longer outstanding at the date of transition to IFRSs, a first-time adopter need not separate the cumulative interest on the liability component from the equity component (paragraph D18 of the IFRS).

BC58 Some respondents requested an exemption for compound instruments even if still outstanding at the date of transition to IFRSs. One possible approach would be to use the fair value of the components at the date of transition to IFRSs as deemed cost. However, as the IFRS does not include any exemptions for financial liabilities, the Board concluded that it would be inconsistent to create such an exemption for the liability component of a compound instrument.

Investments in subsidiaries, jointly controlled entities[12] and associates

BC58A   IAS 27 *Consolidated and Separate Financial Statements* requires an entity, in its separate financial statements, to account for investments in subsidiaries, jointly controlled entities and associates either at cost or in accordance with IAS 39.[13,14] For those investments that are measured at cost, the previous version of IAS 27 (before *Cost of an Investment* in a *Subsidiary, Jointly Controlled Entity or Associate* was issued in May 2008) required an entity to recognise income from the investment only to the extent the entity received distributions from post-acquisition retained earnings (the 'cost method'). Distributions received in excess of such profits were regarded as a recovery of investment and were recognised as a reduction in the cost of the investment.

BC58B   For some jurisdictions, these aspects of IAS 27 led to practical difficulties on transition to IFRSs. In order to apply IAS 27 retrospectively, it would be necessary:

(a)   to measure the fair value of the consideration given at the date of acquisition; and

(b)   to determine whether any dividends received from a subsidiary after its acquisition were paid out of pre-acquisition retained earnings, which would reduce the carrying amount of the investment in the subsidiary in the parent's separate financial statements.

BC58C   If a parent held an investment in a subsidiary for many years, such an exercise might be difficult, or even impossible, and perhaps costly. For example, in some jurisdictions, entities accounted for some previous acquisitions that were share-for-share exchanges using so-called 'merger relief' or 'group reconstruction relief'. In this situation, the carrying amount of the investment in the parent's separate financial statements was based on the nominal value of the shares given rather than the value of the purchase consideration. This might make it difficult or impossible to measure the fair value of the shares given.

BC58D   The Board published *Cost of an Investment in a Subsidiary*, an exposure draft of proposed amendments to IFRS 1, in January 2007. In response to the issues outlined in paragraphs BC58A–BC58C, the Board proposed two exemptions from applying the requirements of IAS 27 retrospectively upon first-time adoption of IFRSs:

(a)   an alternative approach for determining the cost of an investment in a subsidiary in the separate financial statements of a parent; and

(b)   simplification of the process for determining the pre-acquisition retained earnings of that subsidiary.

---

12   'Jointly controlled entities' were defined in IAS 31 *Interests in Joint Ventures*. IFRS 11 *Joint Arrangements*, issued in May 2011, replaced IAS 31 and changed the terminology.

13   The consolidation guidance was removed from IAS 27 and the Standard was renamed *Separate Financial Statements* by IFRS 10 *Consolidated Financial Statements* issued in May 2011. The accounting requirements for separate financial statements were not changed.

14   IFRS 9 *Financial Instruments* replaced IAS 39. IFRS 9 applies to all items that were previously within the scope of IAS 39.

BC58E   In developing that exposure draft, the Board considered three ways of determining a deemed cost of an investment in a subsidiary at the parent's date of transition to IFRSs in its separate financial statements. These were:

(a)   the previous GAAP cost of the investment (previous GAAP deemed cost).

(b)   the parent's interest in the subsidiary's assets less liabilities, using the carrying amounts that IFRSs would require in the subsidiary's statement of financial position (net asset deemed cost).

(c)   the fair value of the investment (fair value deemed cost).

BC58F   The Board decided that the net asset deemed cost option would provide relevant information to users about the subsidiary's financial position at the date of transition to IFRSs and would be relatively easy to determine. The fair value deemed cost option would provide relevant information at the date of transition to IFRSs, but might be more costly and difficult to determine.

BC58G   In some situations, the cost of an investment in a subsidiary determined using the previous GAAP carrying amount might bear little resemblance to cost determined in accordance with IAS 27. Therefore, the Board rejected the use of a deemed cost based on the previous GAAP carrying amount. The Board proposed to allow entities a choice between the net asset deemed cost and the fair value deemed cost.

BC58H   Respondents to the exposure draft stated that the previous GAAP carrying amount is a more appropriate deemed cost. They argued that:

(a)   a net asset deemed cost would not include goodwill or other intangible assets that might be present in a carrying amount determined in accordance with previous GAAP. When this is the case, the net asset deemed cost option would understate the assets of the entities for which it is used. The resulting reduction in the carrying amount of the investment could reduce the distributable profits of the parent.

(b)   it was difficult to see why, in the light of the exemption in IFRS 1 from applying IFRS 3 retrospectively, the Board did not propose to permit the cost of the investment in a subsidiary in accordance with previous GAAP to be used as a deemed cost. When an entity had chosen not to apply IFRS 3 retrospectively to a past business combination, it would be logical not to require it to restate the cost of the related investment in the separate financial statements of the parent.

BC58I   In the light of respondents' comments, the Board observed that, in many instances, neither the previous GAAP carrying amount nor the net asset deemed cost represents 'cost'—both numbers could be viewed as being equally arbitrary.

BC58J   In order to reduce the cost of adopting IFRSs in the parent entity's separate financial statements without significantly reducing the benefits of those statements, the Board decided to allow entities a choice between the previous GAAP carrying amount and the fair value as deemed cost.

BC58K   The Board also agreed with respondents that similar issues arise for investments in associates and jointly controlled entities.[15] As a result, paragraph D15 of the IFRS applies to such investments.

BC58L   The Board published its revised proposals in *Cost of an Investment in a Subsidiary, Jointly Controlled Entity or Associate*, an exposure draft of proposed amendments to IFRS 1 and IAS 27, in December 2007. Respondents generally supported the proposed amendments to IFRS 1. The Board included the amendments in *Cost of an Investment in a Subsidiary, Jointly Controlled Entity or Associate* issued in May 2008.

BC58M   In developing the December 2007 exposure draft, the Board decided to address the simplification of the process for determining the pre-acquisition retained earnings of a subsidiary more generally through an amendment to IAS 27 (see paragraph 38A of IAS 27 and paragraphs BC66D–BC66J[16] of the Basis for Conclusions on IAS 27).

Assets and liabilities of subsidiaries, associates and joint ventures

BC59   A subsidiary may have reported to its parent in the previous period using IFRSs without presenting a full set of financial statements in accordance with IFRSs. If the subsidiary subsequently begins to present financial statements that contain an explicit and unreserved statement of compliance with IFRSs, it becomes a first-time adopter at that time. This might compel the subsidiary to keep two parallel sets of accounting records based on different dates of transition to IFRSs, because some measurements in accordance with the IFRS depend on the date of transition to IFRSs.

BC60   In developing ED 1, the Board concluded that a requirement to keep two parallel sets of records would be burdensome and not be beneficial to users. Therefore, ED 1 proposed that a subsidiary would not be treated as a first-time adopter for recognition and measurement purposes if the subsidiary was consolidated in IFRS financial statements for the previous period and all owners of the minority interests consented.[17]

BC61   Some respondents to ED 1 opposed the exemption, on the following grounds:

    (a)   The exemption would not eliminate all differences between the group reporting package and the subsidiary's own financial statements. The reporting package does not constitute a full set of financial statements, the parent may have made adjustments to the reported numbers (for example, if pension cost adjustments were made centrally), and the group materiality threshold may be higher than for the subsidiary.

---

15 'Jointly controlled entities' were defined in IAS 31 *Interests in Joint Ventures*. IFRS 11 *Joint Arrangements*, issued in May 2011, replaced IAS 31 and changed the terminology.

16 renumbered to paragraphs 12 and BC16–BC22 when IAS 27 was amended in May 2011.

17 In January 2008 the IASB issued an amended IAS 27 *Consolidated and Separate Financial Statements*, which amended 'minority interests' to 'non-controlling interests'. The consolidation requirements in IAS 27 were superseded by IFRS 10 *Consolidated Financial Statements* issued in May 2011. The term 'non-controlling interests' and the requirements for non-controlling interests were not changed.

(b)   The Board's objective of comparability between different entities adopting IFRSs for the first time at the same date (paragraph BC10) should apply equally to any entity, including subsidiaries, particularly if the subsidiary's debt or equity securities are publicly traded.

BC62   However, the Board retained the exemption because it will ease some practical problems. Although the exemption does not eliminate all differences between the subsidiary's financial statements and a group reporting package, it does reduce them. Furthermore, the exemption does not diminish the relevance and reliability of the subsidiary's financial statements because it permits a measurement that is already acceptable in accordance with IFRSs in the consolidated financial statements of the parent. Therefore, the Board also eliminated the proposal in ED 1 that the exemption should be conditional on the consent of minorities.

BC63   In finalising the IFRS, the Board simplified the description of the exemption for a subsidiary that adopts IFRSs after its parent. In accordance with the IFRS, the subsidiary may measure its assets and liabilities at the carrying amounts that would be included in the parent's consolidated financial statements, based on the parent's date of transition to IFRSs, if no adjustments were made for consolidation procedures and for the effects of the business combination in which the parent acquired the subsidiary.[18] Alternatively, it may elect to measure them at the carrying amounts required by the rest of the IFRS, based on the subsidiary's date of transition to IFRSs. The Board also extended the exemption to an associate or joint venture that becomes a first-time adopter later than an entity that has significant influence or joint control over it (paragraph D16 of the IFRS). However, if a parent adopts IFRSs later than a subsidiary, the parent cannot, in its consolidated financial statements, elect to change IFRS measurements that the subsidiary has already used in its financial statements, except to adjust for consolidation procedures and for the effects of the business combination in which the parent acquired the subsidiary[19] (paragraph D17 of the IFRS).

Designation of previously recognised financial instruments

BC63A   IAS 39[20] permits an entity to designate, on initial recognition only, a financial instrument as (a) available for sale[21] (for a financial asset) or (b) a financial asset or financial liability at fair value through profit or loss (provided the asset or liability qualifies for such designation in accordance with paragraph 9(b)(i), 9(b)(ii)). Despite this requirement, an entity that had already applied IFRSs before the effective date of IAS 39 (as revised in March 2004) may (a) designate a previously recognised financial asset as available for sale on initial application of IAS 39 (as revised in March 2004), or (b) designate a previously recognised

---

18 In October 2012 the Board issued *Investment Entities* (Amendments to IFRS 10, IFRS 12 and IAS 27), which removed option D16(a) for investments in subsidiaries of investment entities, as defined in IFRS 10 *Consolidated Financial Statements*, required to be measured at fair value through profit or loss.

19 In October 2012 the Board issued *Investment Entities* (Amendments to IFRS 10, IFRS 12 and IAS 27), which amended paragraph D17 to clarify its application to investment entities, as defined in IFRS 10.

20 IFRS 9 *Financial Instruments* replaced IAS 39. IFRS 9 applies to all items that were previously within the scope of IAS 39.

21 IFRS 9 *Financial Instruments* eliminated the category of available-for-sale financial assets.

financial instrument as at fair value through profit or loss in the circumstances specified in paragraph 105B of IAS 39. The Board decided that the same considerations apply to first-time adopters as to entities that already apply IFRSs. Accordingly, a first-time adopter of IFRSs may similarly designate a previously recognised financial instrument in accordance with paragraph D19 of the IFRS. Such an entity shall disclose the fair value of the financial assets or financial liabilities designated into each category at the date of designation and their classification and carrying amount in the previous financial statements.

Share-based payment transactions

BC63B   IFRS 2 *Share-based Payment* contains various transitional provisions. For example, for equity-settled share-based payment arrangements, IFRS 2 requires an entity to apply IFRS 2 to shares, share options or other equity instruments that were granted after 7 November 2002 and had not vested at the effective date of IFRS 2. IFRS 2 is effective for annual periods beginning on or after 1 January 2005. There are also transitional arrangements for liabilities arising from cash-settled share-based payment transactions, and for modifications of the terms or conditions of a grant of equity instruments to which IFRS 2 has not been applied, if the modification occurs after the effective date of IFRS 2. The Board decided that, in general, first-time adopters should be treated in the same way as entities that already apply IFRSs. For example, a first-time adopter should not be required to apply IFRS 2 to equity instruments that were granted on or before 7 November 2002. Similarly, a first-time adopter should not be required to apply IFRS 2 to equity instruments that were granted after 7 November 2002 if those equity instruments vested before 1 January 2005. In addition, the Board decided that a first-time adopter should not be required to apply IFRS 2 to equity instruments that were granted after 7 November 2002 if those equity instruments vested before the date of transition to IFRSs. Similarly, the Board decided that a first-time adopter should not be required to apply IFRS 2 to liabilities arising from cash-settled share-based payment transactions if those liabilities were settled before the date of transition to IFRSs.

Changes in existing decommissioning, restoration and similar liabilities included in the cost of property, plant and equipment

BC63C   IFRIC 1 *Changes in Existing Decommissioning, Restoration and Similar Liabilities* requires specified changes in decommissioning, restoration and similar liabilities to be added to, or deducted from, the cost of the assets to which they relate, and the adjusted depreciable amount to be depreciated prospectively over the remaining useful life of those assets. Retrospective application of this requirement at the date of transition would require an entity to construct a historical record of all such adjustments that would have been made in the past. In many cases this will not be practicable. The Board agreed that, as an alternative to complying with this requirement, an entity should be permitted to include in the depreciated cost of the asset, at the date of transition to IFRSs, an amount calculated by discounting the liability at that date back to, and depreciating it from, when the liability was first incurred.

BC63CA Paragraph D21 of the IFRS exempts from the requirements of IFRIC 1 *Changes in Existing Decommissioning, Restoration and Similar Liabilities* changes in decommissioning costs incurred before the date of transition to IFRSs. Use of this exemption would require detailed calculations that would not be practicable for entities that used the method of accounting described in paragraph BC47A under their previous GAAP. The Board noted that adjustments to liabilities as a result of initial adoption of IFRSs arise from events and transactions before the date of transition to IFRSs and are generally recognised in retained earnings. Therefore, the Board decided that, for entities that used the method of accounting described in paragraph BC47A, any adjustment for a difference between decommissioning, restoration and similar liabilities measured in accordance with IAS 37 and the liability determined under the entity's previous GAAP should be accounted for in the same manner.

Leases

BC63D   IFRIC 4 *Determining whether an Arrangement contains a Lease* contains transitional provisions because the IFRIC acknowledged the practical difficulties raised by full retrospective application of the Interpretation, in particular the difficulty of going back potentially many years and making a meaningful assessment of whether the arrangement satisfied the criteria at that time. The Board decided to treat first-time adopters in the same way as entities that already apply IFRSs.

BC63DA   IFRIC 4 permits an entity to apply its requirements to arrangements existing at the start of the earliest period for which comparative information is presented on the basis of facts and circumstances existing at the start of that period. Before adopting IFRSs, a jurisdiction might adopt a national standard having the same effect as the requirements of IFRIC 4, including the same transitional provisions. An entity in that jurisdiction might then apply requirements having the same effect as the requirements of IFRIC 4 to some or all arrangements (even if the wording of those requirements is not identical). However, the entity might apply the requirements at a date different from the date in the transitional provisions of IFRIC 4. IFRS 1 would require such an entity to reassess that accounting retrospectively on first-time adoption. This might result in additional costs, with no obvious benefits. Accordingly, the Board decided that if a first-time adopter made the same determination under previous GAAP as that required by IFRIC 4 but at a date other than that required by IFRIC 4, the first-time adopter need not reassess that determination when it adopts IFRSs.

BC63DB   The Board considered a more general modification to IFRS 1. It considered whether to modify IFRS 1 so that entities need not reassess, at the date of transition to IFRSs, prior accounting if that prior accounting permitted the same prospective application as IFRSs with the only difference from IFRSs being the effective date from when that accounting was applied. In this regard, the Board noted that any such proposal must apply to assessments resulting in the *same* determination, rather than *similar* determinations, because it would be too difficult to determine and enforce what constitutes a sufficient degree of similarity. The Board noted that many of the circumstances in which this situation might arise have been dealt with in IFRS 1 or other IFRSs. Accordingly, the Board decided to focus on IFRIC 4 only.

Borrowing costs

BC63E   IAS 23 *Borrowing Costs* (as revised in 2007) contains transitional provisions because the Board acknowledged that if an entity has been following the accounting policy of immediately recognising borrowing costs as an expense and has not previously gathered the necessary information for capitalisation of borrowing costs, getting the information retrospectively may be costly. First-time adopters of IFRSs face problems similar to those facing entities that already apply IFRSs. Moreover, although first-time adopters have the option of using fair value as the deemed cost of an asset at the date of transition to IFRSs, this option is not applicable to all qualifying assets, such as inventories. Furthermore, the Board concluded that the existence of the deemed cost option is not sufficient to justify a more stringent requirement for the application of IAS 23 for first-time adopters than for entities that already apply IFRSs. A more stringent requirement for the adoption of the capitalisation treatment could be justified when IFRS 1 was originally issued because capitalisation was then an option. The requirements for the application of mandatory capitalisation, on the other hand, should be the same for entities that already apply IFRSs and for first-time adopters. Therefore, the Board decided to amend IFRS 1, allowing first-time adopters transitional provisions equivalent to those available to entities that already apply IFRSs in paragraphs 27 and 28 of IAS 23, as revised in 2007.

BC63EA   In *Annual Improvements 2009–2011 Cycle* (issued in May 2012) the Board addressed some concerns that were raised by first-time adopters about the transitional provisions for borrowing costs relating to qualifying assets for which the commencement date for capitalisation was before the date of transition to IFRSs. Interested parties found it unclear whether borrowing costs capitalised in accordance with previous GAAP should be retained, restated or eliminated in the opening statement of financial position. Interested parties also questioned the accounting, after the date of transition, for borrowing costs that relate to such qualifying assets when these qualifying assets are under construction at the date of transition. They wanted clarification as to whether the first-time adopter should apply the requirements of IAS 23 *Borrowing Costs* or whether it should continue applying its previous GAAP even if that previous GAAP is not consistent with IAS 23.

BC63EB   The Board clarified that when the entity chooses to apply the exemption in paragraph D23 of IFRS 1, the borrowing costs that were capitalised in accordance with previous GAAP should be carried forward in the opening statement of financial position. This is because gathering the information for capitalisation of borrowing costs under IAS 23 and identifying and eliminating the amounts (if any) capitalised in past years under previous GAAP may be costly. In addition, the Board clarified that an entity should account for borrowing costs that are incurred after the date of transition and that relate to qualifying assets under construction at the date of transition in accordance with IAS 23, regardless of whether the entity capitalised or recognised in profit and loss borrowing costs under previous GAAP. The Board determined that this requirement would ensure useful information to users of financial statements. A first-time adopter could also choose to apply the requirements of IAS 23 from a date earlier than the date of transition, in which case it should account for borrowing costs in accordance with IAS 23 on or after the earlier date selected.

Severe hyperinflation

BC63F   In 2010 the Board was asked to clarify how an entity should resume presenting financial statements in accordance with IFRSs after a period of severe hyperinflation, during which the entity had been unable to comply with IAS 29 *Financial Reporting in Hyperinflationary Economies*. An entity would be unable to comply with IAS 29 if a reliable general price index is not available to all entities with that same functional currency, and exchangeability between the currency and a relatively stable foreign currency does not exist. However, once the functional currency changes to a non-hyperinflationary currency, or the currency ceases to be severely hyperinflationary, an entity would be able to start applying IFRSs to subsequent transactions.

BC63G   The Board noted that IFRSs did not provide sufficient guidance in these circumstances. The Board therefore decided to amend IFRS 1 to provide guidance on how an entity can present IFRS financial statements after its currency ceases to be severely hyperinflationary, by presenting an opening IFRS statement of financial position on or after the functional currency normalisation date. The Board believed that allowing an entity to apply the exemption when presenting an opening IFRS statement of financial position after, and not just on, the functional currency normalisation date, would address practical concerns that may arise if the functional currency normalisation date and the entity's date of transition to IFRSs are different. The Board decided that this amendment would also be available to entities that were emerging from a period of severe hyperinflation but had not applied IFRSs in the past.

BC63H   The Board decided to permit an entity emerging from a period of severe hyperinflation to elect to measure its assets and liabilities at fair value. That fair value could then be used as the deemed cost in its opening IFRS statement of financial position. The Board believed that this approach would expand the scope of the deemed cost exemptions in IFRS 1 to enable them to be applied in these specific circumstances. However, because severe hyperinflation is a specific set of circumstances, the Board wanted to ensure that the fair value measurement option was applied only to those assets and liabilities that were held before the functional currency normalisation date, and not to other assets and liabilities held by the entity at the time it made the transition to IFRSs. Furthermore, where a parent entity's functional currency has been subject to severe hyperinflation, but its subsidiary company's functional currency has not been subject to severe hyperinflation, the Board decided it was inappropriate for such a subsidiary company to be able to apply this exemption.

BC63I   The Board decided that any adjustments arising on electing to measure assets and liabilities at fair value in the opening IFRS statement of financial position arise from events and transactions before the date of transition to IFRSs. Consequently, those adjustments should be accounted for in accordance with paragraph 11 of IFRS 1, and an entity should recognise those adjustments directly in retained earnings (or, if appropriate, in another category of equity) at the date of transition to IFRSs.

BC63J   The Board observed that entities are required to apply paragraph 21 of IFRS 1 and prepare and present comparative information in accordance with IFRSs. The Board noted that preparation of information in accordance with IFRSs for periods before the functional currency normalisation date may not be possible; hence the exemption refers to a date of transition on or after the functional currency normalisation date. This may lead to a comparative period of less than 12 months. The Board identified that entities should consider whether disclosure of non-IFRS comparative information and historical summaries, in accordance with paragraph 22 of IFRS 1, would provide useful information to users of financial statements. The Board also noted that an entity should clearly explain the transition to IFRSs in accordance with paragraphs 23–28.

Joint arrangements

BC63K   During its redeliberation of the exposure draft ED 9 *Joint Arrangements* the Board decided not to require entities changing from proportionate consolidation to the equity method to adjust any differences between the two accounting methods retrospectively. Instead an entity should determine the opening balance of the investment relating to its interest in a joint venture as the aggregate of the carrying amounts of the assets and liabilities that the entity had been previously proportionately consolidated, including any goodwill arising from acquisition as at the beginning of the earliest period presented. The Board decided to treat first-time adopters in the same way as entities that already apply IFRSs with the following exception.

BC63L   A first-time adopter is required to test for impairment the opening investment in accordance with IAS 36 at the earliest period presented, regardless of whether there is any indication that the investment may be impaired. The Board noted that this is a more stringent requirement for the application of IFRS 11 *Joint Arrangements* by first-time adopters, but is aligned with the requirement for first-time adopters to apply IAS 36 in testing goodwill for impairment at the date of transition to IFRSs regardless of whether there is any indication that the goodwill may be impaired.

BC63M   *Consolidated Financial Statements, Joint Arrangements and Disclosure of Interests in Other Entities: Transition Guidance* (Amendments to IFRS 10, IFRS 11 and IFRS 12), issued in June 2012, amended IFRS 11 to require the transition adjustments of that IFRS to be recognised at the beginning of the annual period immediately preceding the first annual period for which IFRS 11 is applied (the 'immediately preceding period') instead of the beginning of the earliest period presented. The Board agreed that IFRS 1 should not be amended to reflect those amendments because the adjustments required on transition to IFRS should be reflected at the date of transition, which may be earlier than the beginning of the immediately preceding period. Consequently, paragraph D31 was amended to clarify that, when a first-time adopter is applying the transition guidance of IFRS 11, they shall apply the requirements at the date of transition, which is the same as the beginning of the earliest IFRS period presented.

Other possible exemptions rejected

BC64   The Board considered and rejected suggestions for other exemptions. Each such exemption would have moved the IFRS away from a principle-based approach, diminished transparency for users, decreased comparability over time within an entity's first IFRS financial statements and created additional complexity. In the Board's view, any cost savings generated would not have outweighed these disadvantages. Paragraphs BC65–BC73 discuss some of the specific suggestions the Board considered for embedded derivatives, hyperinflation, intangible assets and transaction costs on financial instruments.

Embedded derivatives

BC65   IAS 39[22] requires an entity to account separately for some embedded derivatives at fair value. Some respondents to ED 1 argued that retrospective application of this requirement would be costly. Some suggested either an exemption from retrospective application of this requirement, or a requirement or option to use the fair value of the host instrument at the date of transition to IFRSs as its deemed cost at that date.

BC66   The Board noted that US GAAP provides an option in this area. Under the transitional provisions of SFAS 133 *Accounting for Derivative Instruments and Hedging Activities*, an entity need not account separately for some pre-existing embedded derivatives. Nevertheless, the Board concluded that the failure to measure embedded derivatives at fair value would diminish the relevance and reliability of an entity's first IFRS financial statements. The Board also observed that IAS 39 addresses an inability to measure an embedded derivative and the host contract separately. In such cases, IAS 39 requires an entity to measure the entire combined contract at fair value.

Hyperinflation

BC67   Some argued that the cost of restating financial statements for the effects of hyperinflation in periods before the date of transition to IFRSs would exceed the benefits, particularly if the currency is no longer hyperinflationary. However, the Board concluded that such restatement should be required, because hyperinflation can make unadjusted financial statements meaningless or misleading.

Intangible assets

BC68   For the following reasons, some proposed that a first-time adopter's opening IFRS balance sheet should exclude intangible assets that it did not recognise in accordance with previous GAAP:

(a)   Using hindsight to assess retrospectively when the recognition criteria for intangible assets were met could be subjective, open up possibilities for manipulation and involve costs that might exceed the benefits to users.

---

22   The Board amended the requirements in IAS 39 to identify and separately account for embedded derivatives and relocated them to IFRS 9 *Financial Instruments*. This Basis for Conclusions has not been updated for changes in requirements since IFRIC 9 *Reassessment of Embedded Derivatives* was issued in March 2006.

(b) The benefits expected from intangible assets are often not related directly to the costs incurred. Therefore, capitalising the costs incurred is of limited benefit to users, particularly if the costs were incurred in the distant past.

(c) Such an exclusion would be consistent with the transitional provisions in IAS 38 *Intangible Assets*. These encourage (but do not require) the recognition of intangible assets acquired in a previous business combination that was an acquisition and prohibit the recognition of all other previously unrecognised intangible assets.

BC69 In many cases, internally generated intangible assets do not qualify for recognition in accordance with IAS 38 at the date of transition to IFRSs because an entity did not, in accordance with previous GAAP, accumulate cost information or did not carry out contemporaneous assessments of future economic benefits. In these cases, there is no need for a specific requirement to exclude those assets. Furthermore, when these assets do not qualify for recognition, first-time adopters will not generally, in the Board's view, need to perform extensive work to reach this conclusion.

BC70 In other cases, an entity may have accumulated and retained sufficient information about costs and future economic benefits to determine which intangible assets (whether internally generated or acquired in a business combination or separately) qualify in accordance with IAS 38 for recognition in its opening IFRS balance sheet. If that information is available, no exclusion is justified.

BC71 Some argued that fair value should be used as deemed cost for intangible assets in the opening IFRS balance sheet (by analogy with a business combination). ED 1 would not have permitted this. However, in finalising the IFRS, the Board concluded that this approach should be available for those intangible assets for which IFRSs already permit fair value measurements. Therefore, in accordance with the IFRS, a first-time adopter may elect to use fair value or some previous GAAP revaluations of intangible assets as deemed cost for IFRSs, but only if the intangible assets meet:

(a) the recognition criteria in IAS 38 (including reliable measurement of original cost); and

(b) the criteria in IAS 38 for revaluation (including the existence of an active market) (paragraph D7 of the IFRS).

Transaction costs: financial instruments

BC72 To determine the amortised cost of a financial asset or financial liability using the effective interest method, it is necessary to determine the transaction costs incurred when the asset or liability was originated. Some respondents to ED 1 argued that determining these transaction costs could involve undue cost or effort for financial assets or financial liabilities originated long before the date of transition to IFRSs. They suggested that the Board should permit a first-time adopter:

(a) to use the fair value of the financial asset or financial liability at the date of transition to IFRSs as its deemed cost at that date; or

(b)   to determine amortised cost without considering transaction costs.

BC73   In the Board's view, the unamortised portion of transaction costs at the date of transition to IFRSs is unlikely to be material for most financial assets and financial liabilities. Even when the unamortised portion is material, reasonable estimates should be possible. Therefore, the Board created no exemption in this area.

Retrospective designation

BC74   The Board considered practical implementation difficulties that could arise from the retrospective application of aspects of IAS 39:[23]

    (a)   hedge accounting (paragraphs BC75–BC80);

    (b)   government loans (paragraphs BC80A–BC80E);

    (c)   the treatment of cumulative fair value changes on available-for-sale financial assets[24] at the date of transition to IFRSs (paragraphs BC81–BC83); and

    (d)   'day 1' gain or loss recognition (paragraph BC83A).

Hedge accounting[25]

BC75   Before beginning their preparations for adopting IAS 39 (or a local standard based on IAS 39), it is unlikely that most entities would have adopted IAS 39's criteria for (a) documenting hedges at their inception and (b) testing the hedges for effectiveness, even if they intended to continue the same hedging strategies after adopting IAS 39. Furthermore, retrospective designation of hedges (or retrospective reversal of their designation) could lead to selective designation of some hedges to report a particular result.

BC76   To overcome these problems, the transitional requirements in IAS 39 require an entity already applying IFRSs to apply the hedging requirements prospectively when it adopts IAS 39. As the same problems arise for a first-time adopter, the IFRS requires prospective application by a first-time adopter.

BC77   ED 1 included a redrafted version of the transitional provisions in IAS 39 and related *Questions and Answers* (Q&As) developed by the IAS 39 Implementation Guidance Committee. The Board confirmed in the Basis for Conclusions published with ED 1 that it did not intend the redrafting to create substantive changes. However, in the light of responses to ED 1, the Board decided in finalising IFRS 1 that the redrafting would not make it easier for first-time adopters and others to understand and apply the transitional provisions and Q&As. However, the project to improve IAS 32 and IAS 39 resulted in certain amendments to the transition requirements. In addition, this project incorporated selected other Q&As (ie not on transition) into IAS 39. The Board therefore took this opportunity to consolidate all the guidance for first-time adopters in one place, by incorporating the Q&As on transition into IFRS 1.

---

23 IFRS 9 *Financial Instruments* replaced IAS 39. IFRS 9 applies to all items that were previously within the scope of IAS 39.

24 IFRS 9 *Financial Instruments* eliminated the category of available-for-sale financial assets.

25 IFRS 9 *Financial Instruments* replaced the hedge accounting requirements in IAS 39.

        © IFRS Foundation

BC78   Some respondents to ED 1 asked the Board to clarify what would happen if hedge accounting in accordance with previous GAAP involved hedging relationships of a type that does not qualify for hedge accounting in accordance with IAS 39. The problem can be seen most clearly for a hedge of a net position (macro hedge). If a first-time adopter were to use hedge accounting in its opening IFRS balance sheet for a hedge of a net position, this would involve either:

(a)   recognising deferred debits and credits that are not assets and liabilities (for a fair value hedge); or

(b)   deferring gains or losses in equity when there is, at best, a weak link to an underlying item that defines when they should be transferred to the income statement (for a cash flow hedge).

BC79   As either of these treatments would diminish the relevance and reliability of an entity's first IFRS financial statements, the Board decided that an entity should not apply hedge accounting in its opening IFRS balance sheet to a hedge of a net position that does not qualify as a hedged item in accordance with IAS 39. However, the Board concluded that it would be reasonable (and consistent with IAS 39 paragraph 133[26]) to permit a first-time adopter to designate an individual item as a hedged item within the net position, provided that it does so no later than the date of transition to IFRSs, to prevent selective designation. For similar reasons, the Board prohibited hedge accounting in the opening IFRS balance sheet for any hedging relationship of a type that does not qualify for hedge accounting in accordance with IAS 39 (see paragraph B5 of the IFRS).

BC80   Some respondents to ED 1 suggested that an entity adopting IFRSs for the first time in 2005 could not meet IAS 39's documentation and effectiveness criteria by the date of transition to IFRSs (1 January 2004 for many entities). Some requested an exemption from these criteria until the beginning of the latest period covered by the first IFRS financial statements (1 January 2005 for many entities). However, for the following reasons, the Board did not create an exemption in this area:

(a)   The Board's primary objective is comparability within a first-time adopter's first IFRS financial statements and between different first-time adopters switching to IFRSs at the same time (paragraph BC10).

(b)   The continuation of previous GAAP hedge accounting practices could permit the non-recognition of derivatives or the recognition of deferred debits and credits that are not assets and liabilities.

(c)   The Board's benchmark for cost-benefit assessments was an entity that has planned the transition to IFRSs and is able to collect the necessary information at, or very soon after, the date of transition to IFRSs (paragraph BC27). Entities should not be 'rewarded' by concessions if they failed to plan for transition, nor should that failure be allowed to undermine the integrity of their opening IFRS balance sheet. Entities switching to IFRSs in 2005 need to have their hedge accounting systems in place by the beginning of 2004. In the Board's view, that is a

---

26 In IAS 39, as revised in 2003, paragraph 133 was replaced by paragraphs 84 and AG101.

challenging but achievable timetable. Entities preparing to switch to IFRSs in 2004 should have been aware of the implications of IAS 39 already and the exposure draft of improvements to IAS 39, published in June 2002, proposed very few changes in this area, so delayed transition is not justified for these entities either.

Government loans

BC80A   IAS 20 *Accounting for Government Grants and Disclosure of Government Assistance* (as revised in May 2008) introduced a requirement that government loans with a below-market rate of interest shall be measured at fair value on initial recognition. At the time this requirement was added, the Board recognised that applying it retrospectively may require entities to measure the fair value of loans at an earlier date. Accordingly, the Board decided that entities should apply this requirement in IAS 20 prospectively, with earlier application permitted.

BC80B   In 2011 the application of this requirement by first-time adopters was brought to the Board's attention. The Board noted that the general requirement in IFRS 1 for first-time adopters to apply IFRSs retrospectively at the date of transition to IFRSs could require some entities to measure such government loans at fair value at a date before the date of transition to IFRSs. This may lead to an entity applying hindsight if it must derive a fair value that needs significant unobservable inputs. Accordingly, the Board decided to add an exception to the retrospective application of IFRSs to require that first-time adopters shall apply the requirements of IAS 20 prospectively to government loans existing at the date of transition to IFRSs, unless the necessary information was obtained at the time of initially accounting for that loan. As a result of not applying IAS 20 and IFRS 9 retrospectively to government loans at the date of transition, the corresponding benefit of the government loan at a below-market rate of interest is not recognised as a government grant.

BC80C   The Board proposed the exception in October 2011 in the exposure draft *Government Loans* (proposed amendments to IFRS 1). In recognition of comments on the exposure draft, the Board revised paragraph B10 to specify that an entity applies IAS 32 *Financial Instruments: Presentation* to classify the government loans as a financial liability or an equity instrument, and to limit the scope of the exemption to matters of recognition and measurement. This will give first-time adopters the same relief as existing preparers and will mean that if a first-time adopter had classified government loans in equity under its previous GAAP, it will reclassify those loans as liabilities, if those loans meet the definition of a financial liability in IAS 32. The Board also clarified that an entity should use its previous GAAP carrying amount of such loans at the date of transition to IFRSs as the carrying amount in the opening IFRS statement of financial position. IFRS 9 should be applied to such loans subsequently.

BC80D   Some respondents to the exposure draft asked why the retrospective application of IAS 20 should be optional, rather than mandatory, if the information needed to apply IFRS 9 had been obtained. The Board thought that mandatory restatement could require an onerous search to determine whether this information had been obtained when initially accounting for loans that were received many years ago.

BC80E   The Board noted that prohibiting the application of this option on a loan-by-loan basis might introduce further complexity into IFRS 1. This is because it may raise further questions, such as whether the retrospective application would be permitted for all the loans for which the information needed was obtained at the time, even if there are other similar loans for which the fair value information was not obtained at that time; and whether the retrospective application should be restricted to all loans received after a certain date and for which all necessary information was obtained to enable retrospective application. The Board concluded that the exception proposed in paragraph B11 should be available on a loan-by-loan basis.

BC80F   In November 2013 the Board amended the examples in the guidance on hedge accounting so that they conformed to IFRS 9, which replaced the hedge accounting requirements in IAS 39.

Available-for-sale financial assets[27]

BC81   Retrospective application of IAS 39[28] to available-for-sale financial assets requires a first-time adopter to recognise the cumulative fair value changes in a separate component of equity in the opening IFRS balance sheet, and transfer those fair value changes to the income statement on subsequent disposal or impairment of the asset. This could allow, for example, selective classification of assets with cumulative gains as available for sale (with subsequent transfers to the income statement on disposal) and assets with cumulative losses as held for trading (with no transfers on disposal).

BC82   IAS 39 confirmed the proposal in the exposure draft of June 2002 to give an entity that already applies IFRSs an option to designate any financial asset as at fair value through profit or loss when it first applies the proposed improvements. Although this requirement could increase the risk of selective classification by first-time adopters of the kind discussed in the previous paragraph, the Board noted that an entity could achieve a similar result by selective disposal of some assets before the date of transition to IFRSs. Therefore, the Board concluded that it should treat first-time adopters in the same way as entities that already apply IFRSs by requiring retrospective application.

BC83   Some respondents to ED 1 commented that the cost of determining the amount to be included in a separate component of equity would exceed the benefits. However, the Board noted that these costs would be minimal if a first-time adopter carried the available-for-sale financial assets in accordance with previous GAAP at cost or the lower of cost and market value. These costs might be more significant if it carried them at fair value, but in that case it might well classify the assets as held for trading. Therefore, the Board made no changes to ED 1's proposal that a first-time adopter should apply IAS 39 retrospectively to available-for-sale financial assets.

BC83A   IFRS 1 originally required retrospective application of the 'day 1' gain or loss recognition requirements in IAS 39 paragraph AG76. After the revised IAS 39 was issued, constituents raised concerns that retrospective application

---

27   IFRS 9 *Financial Instruments* eliminated the category of available-for-sale financial assets.
28   IFRS 9 *Financial Instruments* replaced IAS 39. IFRS 9 applies to all items that were previously within the scope of IAS 39.

diverge from the requirements of US GAAP, would be difficult and expensive to implement, and might require subjective assumptions about what was observable and what was not. In response to these concerns, the Board decided to permit entities to apply the requirements in the last sentence of IAS 39 paragraph AG76 and in paragraph AG76A, in any one of the following ways:

(a)   retrospectively;

(b)   prospectively to transactions entered into after 25 October 2002; or

(c)   prospectively to transactions entered into after 1 January 2004.

In 2010 the Board was asked to reconsider whether the fixed dates of 25 October 2002 and 1 January 2004 continued to be appropriate for first-time adopters. Constituents were concerned that, as time passes, these fixed dates become more remote and increasingly less relevant to the financial reports as additional jurisdictions adopt IFRSs. The Board accepted that the cost of reconstructing transactions back in time to 25 October 2002 or 1 January 2004 was likely to outweigh the benefit to be achieved in doing so. It therefore amended the fixed dates included in paragraph D20 of IFRS 1 to permit a first-time adopter to apply the 'day 1' gain or loss recognition requirement in IAS 39 paragraphs AG76 and AG76A prospectively from 'the date of transition to IFRSs'.[29]

Estimates

BC84   An entity will have made estimates in accordance with previous GAAP at the date of transition to IFRSs. Events between that date and the reporting date for the entity's first IFRS financial statements might suggest a need to change those estimates. Some of those events might qualify as adjusting events in accordance with IAS 10 *Events after the Balance Sheet Date*.[30] However, if the entity made those estimates on a basis consistent with IFRSs, the Board concluded that it would be more helpful to users—and more consistent with IAS 8—to recognise the revision of those estimates as income or expense in the period when the entity made the revision, rather than in preparing the opening IFRS balance sheet (paragraphs 14–17 of the IFRS).

Presentation and disclosure

Comparative information

BC85   IAS 1 requires an entity to disclose comparative information (in accordance with IFRSs) for the previous period. Some suggested that a first-time adopter should disclose comparative information for more than one previous period. For entities that already apply IFRSs, users normally have access to financial statements prepared on a comparable basis for several years. However, this is not the case for a first-time adopter.

---

29 IFRS 9 *Financial Instruments* replaced IAS 39. Paragraphs AG76 and AG76A of IAS 39 were relocated to IFRS 9 as paragraphs B5.4.8 and B5.4.9. However, in May 2011, IFRS 13 deleted paragraphs B5.4.8 and B5.4.9 of IFRS 9. In 2014 the requirements for amortised cost measurement and impairment were added to IFRS 9 as Sections 5.4 and 5.5. Paragraphs B5.4.8 and B5.4.9 of IFRS 9 now contains requirements related to amortised cost measurement.
30 In September 2007 the IASB amended the title of IAS 10 *Events after the Balance Sheet Date* to *Events after the Reporting Period* as a consequence of the revision of IAS 1 *Presentation of Financial Statements* in 2007.

BC86   Nevertheless, the Board did not require a first-time adopter to present more comparative information than IAS 1 requires, because such a requirement would impose costs out of proportion to the benefits to users, and increase the risk that preparers might need to make arbitrary assumptions in applying hindsight.

BC87   ED 1 proposed that if the first IFRS financial statements include more than one year of comparative information, the additional comparative information should comply with IFRSs. Some respondents to ED 1 noted that some regulators require entities to prepare more than two years of comparatives. They argued the following:

(a)   A requirement to restate two years of comparatives would impose excessive costs and lead to arbitrary restatements that might be biased by hindsight.

(b)   Consider an entity adopting IFRSs in 2005 and required by its regulator to give two years of comparatives. Its date of transition to IFRSs would be 1 January 2003—several months before the publication of the IFRS and of the standards resulting from the improvements project. This could contradict the Board's assertion in paragraph BC27 above that most preparers could gather most information they need for their opening IFRS balance sheet at, or soon after, the date of transition to IFRSs.

BC88   In response to these comments, the Board deleted this proposal. Instead, if a first-time adopter elects to give more than one year of comparative information, the additional comparative information need not comply with IFRSs, but the IFRS requires the entity:

(a)   to label previous GAAP information prominently as not being prepared in accordance with IFRSs.

(b)   to disclose the nature of the main adjustments that would make it comply with IFRSs (paragraph 22 of the IFRS).

BC89   Some respondents to ED 1 suggested that it would be onerous to prepare comparative information in accordance with IAS 32 and IAS 39[31] about financial instruments. They suggested that an entity should be able to apply IAS 39 prospectively from the beginning of the year of its first IFRS financial statements (eg 1 January 2005 for many first-time adopters). They noted that US companies were not required to restate comparatives on the introduction of SFAS 133 *Accounting for Derivative Instruments and Hedging Activities*. However, given the Board's emphasis on comparability within the first IFRS financial statements (paragraph BC10) and the assumption of timely planning (paragraph BC27), the Board introduced no general exemption in this area.

BC89A   Nevertheless, the Board noted that the revised IAS 32 and IAS 39[32] were not issued until December 2003. Additionally, the Board's decision to re-expose its proposals for portfolio hedges of interest rate risk had the effect that some of the

---

31   IFRS 9 *Financial Instruments* replaced IAS 39. IFRS 9 applies to all items that were previously within the scope of IAS 39.

32   IFRS 9 *Financial Instruments* replaced IAS 39. IFRS 9 applies to all items that were previously within the scope of IAS 39.

requirements will not be finalised until early 2004. The Board was sympathetic to concerns that entities that will be required to comply with IFRSs for the first time in 2005 could not make a timely transition to IFRSs because IAS 39 will not be issued in final form until after the start of 2004. Therefore, the Board decided to exempt entities adopting IFRSs for the first time before 1 January 2006 from producing comparative information that complies with IAS 32 and IAS 39, as revised in 2003, in their first IFRS financial statements.

BC89B   In the light of respondents' comments on the June 2011 exposure draft *Improvements to IFRSs*, the Board amended paragraph 21 as part of *Annual Improvements 2009–2011 Cycle* (issued in May 2012) because it considered that the requirements for comparative information for a first-time adopter should be different from the requirements for comparative information for an existing preparer. The Board noted that a first-time adopter should not be exempted from presenting three statements of financial position and related notes because it might not have presented this information previously on a basis consistent with IFRSs.

BC89C   In addition, the Board considered that a first-time adopter may provide additional comparative information that is presented in accordance with previous GAAP to help the user understand the effects of the transition to IFRSs in accordance with paragraph 22 of IFRS 1. For example, a law or a regulator requires an entity to present the first comparative financial statements in accordance with both IFRSs and previous GAAP and the second comparative in accordance with previous GAAP only. The presentation of this information is an exception from the requirement in paragraph 38C of IAS 1 (to allow an entity to present comparative information in addition to the minimum comparative information required by IFRSs).

Historical summaries

BC90   Some entities choose, or are required, to present in their financial statements historical summaries of selected data covering periods before the first period for which they present full comparative information. Some argued that an entity should present this information in accordance with IFRSs, to ensure comparability over time. However, the Board concluded that such a requirement would cause costs out of proportion to the benefit to users. The IFRS requires disclosure of the nature of the main adjustments needed to make historical summaries included in financial statements or interim financial reports comply with IFRSs (paragraph 22 of the IFRS). Historical summaries published outside financial statements or interim financial reports are beyond the scope of the IFRS.

Explanation of transition to IFRSs

BC91   The IFRS requires disclosures about the effect of the transition from previous GAAP to IFRS. The Board concluded that such disclosures are essential, in the first (annual) IFRS financial statements as well as in interim financial reports (if any), because they help users understand the effect and implications of the transition to IFRSs and how they need to change their analytical models to make the best use of information presented using IFRSs. The required disclosures relate to both:

(a)   the most recent information published in accordance with previous GAAP, so that users have the most up-to-date information; and

(b)   the date of transition to IFRSs. This is an important focus of attention for users, preparers and auditors because the opening IFRS balance sheet is the starting point for accounting in accordance with IFRSs.

BC92   Paragraph 24(a) and (b) of the IFRS requires reconciliations of equity and total comprehensive income. The Board concluded that users would also find it helpful to have information about the other adjustments that affect the opening IFRS balance sheet but do not appear in these reconciliations. Because a reconciliation could be voluminous, the IFRS requires disclosure of narrative information about these adjustments, as well as about adjustments to the cash flow statement (paragraph 25 of the IFRS).

BC92A   The Board decided to require a first-time adopter to include in its first IFRS financial statements a reconciliation of total comprehensive income (or, if an entity did not report such a total, profit or loss) in accordance with previous GAAP to total comprehensive income in accordance with IFRSs for the latest period reported in accordance with previous GAAP.

BC92B   The Board observed that the amendments to IAS 1 in 2007 regarding the presentation of income and expense might result in users having to change their analytical models to include both income and expense that are recognised in profit or loss and those recognised outside profit or loss. Accordingly, the Board concluded that it would be helpful to those users to provide information on the effect and implication of the transition to IFRSs on all items of income and expense, not only those recognised in profit or loss.

BC92C   The Board acknowledged that GAAP in other jurisdictions might not have a notion of total comprehensive income. Accordingly, it decided that an entity should reconcile to total comprehensive income in accordance with IFRSs from the previous GAAP equivalent of total comprehensive income. The previous GAAP equivalent might be profit or loss.

BC93   Paragraph 26 of the IFRS states that the reconciliations should distinguish changes in accounting policies from the correction of errors. Some respondents to ED 1 argued that complying with this requirement could be difficult or costly. However, the Board concluded that both components are important and their disclosure should be required because:

(a)   information about changes in accounting policies helps explain the transition to IFRSs.

(b)   information about errors helps users assess the reliability of financial information. Furthermore, a failure to disclose the effect of material errors would obscure the 'results of the stewardship of management, or the accountability of management for the resources entrusted to it' (*Framework*, paragraph 14[33]).

BC94   For impairment losses (and reversals) recognised in preparing the opening IFRS balance sheet, paragraph 24(c) of the IFRS requires the disclosures that IAS 36

---

33   superseded by Chapter 1 of the *Conceptual Framework*

would require if those impairment losses (and reversals) were recognised during the period beginning with the date of transition to IFRSs. The rationale for this requirement is that there is inevitably subjectivity about impairment losses. This disclosure provides transparency about impairment losses recognised on transition to IFRSs. These losses might otherwise receive less attention than impairment losses recognised in earlier or later periods.

BC95   Paragraph 30 of the IFRS requires disclosures about the use of fair value as deemed cost. Although the adjustment arising from the use of this exemption appears in the reconciliations discussed above, this more specific disclosure highlights it. Furthermore, this exemption differs from the other exemptions that might apply for property, plant and equipment (previous GAAP revaluation or event-driven fair value measurement). The latter two exemptions do not lead to a restatement on transition to IFRSs because they apply only if the measurement was already used in previous GAAP financial statements.

Interim financial reports

BC96   IAS 34 *Interim Financial Reporting* states that the interim financial report is 'intended to provide an update on the latest complete set of annual financial statements' (paragraph 6). Thus, IAS 34 requires less disclosure in interim financial statements than IFRSs require in annual financial statements. However, an entity's interim financial report in accordance with IAS 34 is less helpful to users if the entity's latest annual financial statements were prepared using previous GAAP than if they were prepared in accordance with IFRSs. Therefore, the Board concluded that a first-time adopter's first interim financial report in accordance with IAS 34 should include sufficient information to enable users to understand how the transition to IFRSs affected previously reported annual, as well as interim, figures (paragraphs 32 and 33 of the IFRS).

Accounting policy changes in the year of adoption

BC97   In *Improvements to IFRSs* issued in May 2010, the Board clarified unclear wording concerning how changes in accounting policies should be addressed by a first-time adopter when those changes occur after the publication of the entity's first interim financial report. The Board decided that a first-time adopter is exempt from all the requirements of IAS 8 for the interim financial report it presents in accordance with IAS 34 for part of the period covered by its first IFRS financial statements and for its first IFRS financial statements. The Board concluded that to comply with IFRS 1's requirement to explain its transition to IFRSs, an entity should be required to explain any changes in its accounting policies or the IFRS 1 exemptions it applied between its first IFRS interim financial report and its first IFRS financial statements. The Board decided that the most useful information it could require was updated reconciliations between previous GAAP and IFRSs.

Short-term exemptions from IFRSs

BC98   [Deleted][34]

Deletion of short-term exemptions (amendments issued in December 2016)

BC99   In *Annual Improvements to IFRS Standards 2014–2016 Cycle*, the Board deleted the short-term exemptions in paragraphs E3–E7 and the related effective date paragraphs. The Board noted that the reliefs provided in those paragraphs were no longer applicable. The reliefs provided had been available to entities only for reporting periods that had passed.

---

34 *Annual Improvements to IFRS Standards 2014–2016 Cycle*, issued in December 2016, deleted some short-term exemptions for first-time adopters (see paragraph BC99), and as a consequence deleted paragraph BC98.

Appendix
Amendments to Basis for Conclusions on other IFRSs

This appendix contains amendments to the Basis for Conclusions on other IFRSs that are necessary to ensure consistency with IFRS 1 (as revised in 2008).

* * * * *

The amendments contained in this appendix when the revised IFRS 1 was issued in 2008 have been incorporated into the text of the Basis for Conclusions on IFRS 6 and IASs 27 and 39 as issued at 27 November 2008.

IASB documents published to accompany

IFRS 2

Share-based Payment

The text of the unaccompanied standard, IFRS 2, is contained in Part A of this edition. Its effective date when issued was 1 January 2005. The text of the Accompanying Guidance on IFRS 2 is contained in Part B of this edition. This part presents the following documents:

BASIS FOR CONCLUSIONS

Contents

© IFRS Foundation

Basis for Conclusions on
IFRS 2 *Share-based Payment*

This Basis for Conclusions accompanies, but is not part of, IFRS 2.

Introduction

BC1　This Basis for Conclusions summarises the International Accounting Standards Board's considerations in reaching the conclusions in IFRS 2 *Share-based Payment*. Individual Board members gave greater weight to some factors than to others.

BC2　Entities often issue[1] shares or share options to pay employees or other parties. Share plans and share option plans are a common feature of employee remuneration, not only for directors and senior executives, but also for many other employees. Some entities issue shares or share options to pay suppliers, such as suppliers of professional services.

BC3　Until the issue of IFRS 2, there has been no International Financial Reporting Standard (IFRS) covering the recognition and measurement of these transactions. Concerns have been raised about this gap in international standards. For example, the International Organization of Securities Commissions (IOSCO), in its 2000 report on international standards, stated that IASC (the IASB's predecessor body) should consider the accounting treatment of share-based payment.

BC4　Few countries have standards on the topic. This is a concern in many countries, because the use of share-based payment has increased in recent years and continues to spread. Various standard-setting bodies have been working on this issue. At the time the IASB added a project on share-based payment to its agenda in July 2001, some standard-setters had recently published proposals. For example, the German Accounting Standards Committee published a draft accounting standard *Accounting for Share Option Plans and Similar Compensation Arrangements* in June 2001. The UK Accounting Standards Board led the development of the Discussion Paper *Accounting for Share-based Payment*, published in July 2000 by IASC, the ASB and other bodies represented in the G4+1.[2] The Danish Institute of State Authorised Public Accountants issued a Discussion Paper *The Accounting Treatment of Share-based Payment* in April 2000. More recently, in December 2002, the Accounting Standards Board of Japan published a Summary Issues Paper on share-based payment. In March 2003, the US Financial Accounting Standards Board (FASB) added to its agenda a project to review US accounting requirements on share-based payment. Also, the Canadian Accounting Standards Board (AcSB) recently completed its project on share-based payment. The AcSB standard requires recognition of all share-based payment

---

1　The word 'issue' is used in a broad sense. For example, a transfer of shares held in treasury (own shares held) to another party is regarded as an 'issue' of equity instruments. Some argue that if options or shares are granted with vesting conditions, they are not 'issued' until those vesting conditions have been satisfied. However, even if this argument is accepted, it does not change the Board's conclusions on the requirements of the IFRS, and therefore the word 'issue' is used broadly, to include situations in which equity instruments are conditionally transferred to the counterparty, subject to the satisfaction of specified vesting conditions.

2　The G4+1 comprised members of the national accounting standard-setting bodies of Australia, Canada, New Zealand, the UK and the US, and IASC.

transactions, including transactions in which share options are granted to employees (discussed further in paragraphs BC281 and BC282).

BC5 Users of financial statements and other commentators are calling for improvements in the accounting treatment of share-based payment. For example, the proposal in the IASC/G4+1 Discussion Paper and ED 2 *Share-based Payment*, that share-based payment transactions should be recognised in the financial statements, resulting in an expense when the goods or services are consumed, received strong support from investors and other users of financial statements. Recent economic events have emphasised the importance of high quality financial statements that provide neutral, transparent and comparable information to help users make economic decisions. In particular, the omission of expenses arising from share-based payment transactions with employees has been highlighted by investors, other users of financial statements and other commentators as causing economic distortions and corporate governance concerns.

BC6 As noted above, the Board began a project to develop an IFRS on share-based payment in July 2001. In September 2001, the Board invited additional comment on the IASC/G4+1 Discussion Paper, with a comment deadline of 15 December 2001. The Board received over 270 letters. During the development of ED 2, the Board was also assisted by an Advisory Group, consisting of individuals from various countries and with a range of backgrounds, including persons from the investment, corporate, audit, academic, compensation consultancy, valuation and regulatory communities. The Board received further assistance from other experts at a panel discussion held in New York in July 2002. In November 2002, the Board published an Exposure Draft, ED 2 *Share-based Payment*, with a comment deadline of 7 March 2003. The Board received over 240 letters. The Board also worked with the FASB after that body added to its agenda a project to review US accounting requirements on share-based payment. This included participating in meetings of the FASB's Option Valuation Group and meeting the FASB to discuss convergence issues.

BC6A In 2007 the Board added to its agenda a project to clarify the scope and accounting for group cash-settled share-based payment transactions in the separate or individual financial statements of the entity receiving the goods or services when that entity has no obligation to settle the share-based payment. In December 2007 the Board published *Group Cash-settled Share-based Payment Transactions* (proposed amendments to IFRS 2). The resulting amendments issued in June 2009 also incorporate the requirements of two Interpretations—IFRIC 8 *Scope of IFRS 2* and IFRIC 11 *IFRS 2—Group and Treasury Share Transactions*. As a consequence, the Board withdrew both Interpretations.

Scope

BC7 Much of the controversy and complexity surrounding the accounting for share-based payment relates to employee share options. However, the scope of IFRS 2 is broader than that. It applies to transactions in which shares or other equity instruments are granted to employees. It also applies to transactions with parties other than employees, in which goods or services are received as consideration for the issue of shares, share options or other equity instruments. The term 'goods' includes inventories, consumables, property, plant and equipment, intangible assets and other non-financial assets. Lastly, the IFRS applies to payments in cash (or other assets) that are 'share-based' because the amount of the payment is based on the price of the entity's shares or other equity instruments, eg cash share appreciation rights.

Broad-based employee share plans, including employee share purchase plans

BC8 Some employee share plans are described as 'broad-based' or 'all-employee' plans, in which all (or virtually all) employees have the opportunity to participate, whereas other plans are more selective, covering individual or specific groups of employees (eg senior executives). Employee share purchase plans are often broad-based plans. Typically, employee share purchase plans provide employees with an opportunity to buy a specific number of shares at a discounted price, ie at an amount that is less than the fair value of the shares. The employee's entitlement to discounted shares is usually conditional upon specific conditions being satisfied, such as remaining in the service of the entity for a specified period.

BC9 The issues that arise with respect to employee share purchase plans are:

(a) are these plans somehow so different from other employee share plans that a different accounting treatment is appropriate?

(b) even if the answer to the above question is 'no', are there circumstances, such as when the discount is very small, when it is appropriate to exempt employee share purchase plans from an accounting standard on share-based payment?

BC10 Some respondents to ED 2 argued that broad-based employee share plans should be exempt from an accounting standard on share-based payment. The reason usually given was that these plans are different from other types of employee share plans and, in particular, are not a part of remuneration for employee services. Some argued that requiring the recognition of an expense in respect of these types of plans was perceived to be contrary to government policy to encourage employee share ownership. In contrast, other respondents saw no difference between employee share purchase plans and other employee share plans, and argued that the same accounting requirements should therefore apply. However, some suggested that there should be an exemption if the discount is small.

BC11 The Board concluded that, in principle, there is no reason to treat broad-based employee share plans, including broad-based employee share purchase plans, differently from other employee share plans (the issue of 'small' discounts is considered later). The Board noted that the fact that these schemes are available only to employees is in itself sufficient to conclude that the benefits provided represent employee remuneration. Moreover, the term 'remuneration' is not limited to remuneration provided as part of an individual employee's contract: it encompasses all benefits provided to employees. Similarly, the term services encompasses all benefits provided by the employees in return, including increased productivity, commitment or other enhancements in employee work performance as a result of the incentives provided by the share plan.

BC12 Moreover, distinguishing regular employee services from the additional benefits received from broad-based employee share plans would not change the conclusion that it is necessary to account for such plans. No matter what label is placed on the benefits provided by employees—or the benefits provided by the entity—the transaction should be recognised in the financial statements.

BC13 Furthermore, that governments in some countries have a policy of encouraging employee share ownership is not a valid reason for according these types of plans a different accounting treatment, because it is not the role of financial reporting to give favourable accounting treatment to particular transactions to encourage entities to enter into them. For example, governments might wish to encourage entities to provide pensions to their employees, to lessen the future burden on the state, but that does not mean that pension costs should be excluded from the financial statements. To do so would impair the quality of financial reporting. The purpose of financial reporting is to provide information to users of financial statements, to assist them in making economic decisions. The omission of expenses from the financial statements does not change the fact that those expenses have been incurred. The omission of expenses causes reported profits to be overstated and hence the financial statements are not neutral, are less transparent and comparable, and are potentially misleading to users.

BC14 There remains the question whether there should be an exemption for some plans, when the discount is small. For example, FASB Statement of Financial Accounting Standards No. 123 *Accounting for Stock-Based Compensation* contains an exemption for employee share purchase plans that meet specified criteria, of which one is that the discount is small.

BC15 On the one hand, it seems reasonable to exempt an employee share purchase plan if it has substantially no option features and the discount is small. In such situations, the rights given to the employees under the plan probably do not have a significant value, from the entity's perspective.

BC16 On the other hand, even if one accepts that an exemption is appropriate, specifying its scope is problematic, eg deciding what constitutes a small discount. Some argue that a 5 per cent discount from the market price (as specified in SFAS 123) is too high, noting that a block of shares can be sold on the market at a price close to the current share price. Furthermore, it could be argued that it is unnecessary to exempt these plans from the standard. If the rights given to the employees do not have a significant value, this suggests that the amounts involved are immaterial. Because it is not necessary to include immaterial information in the financial statements, there is no need for a specific exclusion in an accounting standard.

BC17 For the reasons given in the preceding paragraph, the Board concluded that broad-based employee share plans, including broad-based employee share purchase plans, should not be exempted from the IFRS.

BC18 However, the Board noted that there might be instances when an entity engages in a transaction with an employee in his/her capacity as a holder of equity instruments, rather than in his/her capacity as an employee. For example, an entity might grant all holders of a particular class of its equity instruments the right to acquire additional equity instruments of the entity at a price that is less than the fair value of those equity instruments. If an employee receives such a right because he/she is a holder of that particular class of equity instruments, the Board concluded that the granting or exercise of that right should not be subject to the requirements of the IFRS, because the employee has received that right in his/her capacity as a shareholder, rather than as an employee.

Transactions in which an entity cannot identify some or all of the goods or services received (paragraph 2)[3]

BC18A   The Board incorporated into IFRS 2 the consensus of IFRIC 8 in *Group Cash-settled Share-based Payment Transactions* issued in June 2009. This section summarises the IFRIC's considerations in reaching that consensus, as approved by the Board.

BC18B   IFRS 2 applies to share-based payment transactions in which the entity receives or acquires goods or services. However, in some situations it might be difficult to demonstrate that the entity has received goods or services. This raises the question of whether IFRS 2 applies to such transactions. In addition, if the entity has made a share-based payment and the identifiable consideration received (if any) appears to be less than the fair value of the share-based payment, does this situation indicate that goods or services have been received, even though those goods or services are not specifically identified, and therefore that IFRS 2 applies?

BC18C   When the Board developed IFRS 2, it concluded that the directors of an entity would expect to receive some goods or services in return for equity instruments issued (paragraph BC37). This implies that it is not necessary to identify the specific goods or services received in return for the equity instruments granted to conclude that goods or services have been (or will be) received. Furthermore, paragraph 8 of the IFRS establishes that it is not necessary for the goods or services received to qualify for recognition as an asset in order for the share-based payment to be within the scope of IFRS 2. In this case, the IFRS requires the cost of the goods or services received or receivable to be recognised as expenses.

BC18D   Accordingly, the Board concluded that the scope of IFRS 2 includes transactions in which the entity cannot identify some or all of the specific goods or services received. If the value of the identifiable consideration received appears to be less than the fair value of the equity instruments granted or liability incurred, typically,[4] this circumstance indicates that other consideration (ie unidentifiable goods or services) has been (or will be) received.

---

3   Paragraphs BC18A–BC18D are added as a consequence of *Group Cash-settled Share-based Payment Transactions* (Amendments to IFRS 2) issued in June 2009.

4   In some cases, the reason for the transfer would explain why no goods or services have been or will be received. For example, a principal shareholder, as part of estate planning, transfers some of his shares to a family member. In the absence of factors that indicate that the family member has provided, or is expected to provide, any goods or services to the entity in return for the shares, such a transaction would be outside the scope of IFRS 2.

Transfers of equity instruments to employees (paragraphs 3 and 3A)[5]

BC19   In some situations, an entity might not issue shares or share options to employees (or other parties) direct. Instead, a shareholder (or shareholders) might transfer equity instruments to the employees (or other parties).

BC20   Under this arrangement, the entity has received services (or goods) that were paid for by its shareholders. The arrangement could be viewed as being, in substance, two transactions—one transaction in which the entity has reacquired equity instruments for nil consideration, and a second transaction in which the entity has received services (or goods) as consideration for equity instruments issued to the employees (or other parties).

BC21   The second transaction is a share-based payment transaction. Therefore, the Board concluded that the entity should account for transfers of equity instruments by shareholders to employees or other parties in the same way as other share-based payment transactions. The Board reached the same conclusion with respect to transfers of equity instruments of the entity's parent, or of another entity within the same group as the entity, to the entity's employees or other suppliers.

BC22   However, such a transfer is not a share-based payment transaction if the transfer of equity instruments to an employee or other party is clearly for a purpose other than payment for goods or services supplied to the entity. This would be the case, for example, if the transfer is to settle a shareholder's personal obligation to an employee that is unrelated to employment by the entity, or if the shareholder and employee are related and the transfer is a personal gift because of that relationship.

BC22A   In December 2007 the Board published an exposure draft *Group Cash-settled Share-based Payment Transactions* proposing amendments to IFRS 2 and IFRIC 11 to clarify the accounting for such transactions in the separate or individual financial statements of the entity receiving goods or services. The Board proposed to include specified types of such transactions within the scope of IFRS 2 (not IAS 19 *Employee Benefits*), regardless of whether the group share-based payment transaction is cash-settled or equity-settled.

BC22B   Nearly all of the respondents to the exposure draft agreed that the group cash-settled transactions between a parent and a subsidiary described in the exposure draft should be within the scope of IFRS 2. Respondents generally believed that including these transactions is consistent with IFRS 2's main principle that the entity should recognise the goods or services that it receives in a share-based transaction. However, respondents also expressed concerns that the proposed scope:

(a)   adopted a case-by-case approach and was inconsistent with the definitions of share-based payment transactions in IFRS 2.

(b)   was unclear and increased the inconsistency in the scope requirements among the applicable IFRSs, including IFRIC 11.

---

5   Paragraphs BC22A–BC22G are added as a consequence of *Group Cash-settled Share-based Payment Transactions* (Amendments to IFRS 2) issued in June 2009.

BC22C   Many respondents expressed concerns that similar transactions would continue to be treated differently. Because no amendments to the definitions of share-based payment transactions were proposed, some transactions might not be included within the scope of IFRS 2 because they did not meet those definitions. The Board agreed with respondents that the proposals did not achieve the objective of including all share-based payment transactions within the scope of IFRS 2 as intended.

BC22D   When finalising the amendments issued in June 2009, the Board reaffirmed the view it had intended to convey in the proposed amendments, namely that the entity receiving the goods or services should account for group share-based payment transactions in accordance with IFRS 2. Consequently, IFRS 2 applies even when the entity receiving the goods or services has no obligation to settle the transaction and regardless of whether the payments to the suppliers are equity-settled or cash-settled. To avoid the need for further guidance on the scope of IFRS 2 for group transactions, the Board decided to amend some of the defined terms and to supersede paragraph 3 by a new paragraph 3A to state clearly the principles applicable to those transactions.

BC22E   During its redeliberations of the proposed amendments, the Board agreed with respondents' comments that, as proposed, the scope of IFRS 2 remained unclear and inconsistent between the standard and related Interpretations. For example, the terms 'shareholder' and 'parent' have different meanings: a shareholder is not necessarily a parent, and a parent does not have to be a shareholder. The Board noted that share-based payment transactions among group entities are often directed by the parent, indicating a level of control. Therefore, the Board clarified the boundaries of a 'group' by adopting the same definition as in paragraph 4 of IAS 27 *Consolidated and Separate Financial Statements*, which includes only a parent and its subsidiaries.[6]

BC22F   Some respondents to the exposure draft questioned whether the proposals should apply to joint ventures. Before the Board's amendments, the guidance in paragraph 3 (now superseded by paragraph 3A) stated that when a shareholder transferred equity instruments of the entity (or another group entity), the transaction would be within the scope of IFRS 2 for the entity receiving the goods or services. However, that guidance did not specify the accounting by a shareholder transferor. The Board noted that the defined terms in Appendix A, as amended, would clearly state that any entity (including a joint venture) that receives goods or services in a share-based payment transaction should account for the transaction in accordance with the IFRS, regardless of whether that entity also settles the transaction.

BC22G   Furthermore, the Board noted that the exposure draft and related discussions focused on clarifying guidance for transactions involving group entities in the separate or individual financial statements of the entity receiving the goods or services. Addressing transactions involving related parties outside a group structure in their separate or individual financial statements would significantly expand the scope of the project and change the scope of IFRS 2. Therefore, the

---

6   The consolidation requirements in IAS 27 were superseded by IFRS 10 *Consolidated Financial Statements* issued in May 2011. The definition of control changed but the definition of a group was not substantially changed.

Board decided not to address transactions between entities not in the same group that are similar to share-based payment transactions but outside the definitions as amended. This carries forward the existing guidance of IFRS 2 for entities not in the same group and the Board does not intend to change that guidance.

Transactions within the scope of IFRS 3 *Business Combinations*

BC23   An entity might acquire goods (or other non-financial assets) as part of the net assets acquired in a business combination for which the consideration paid included shares or other equity instruments issued by the entity. Because IFRS 3 applies to the acquisition of assets and issue of shares in connection with a business combination, that is the more specific standard that should be applied to that transaction.

BC24   Therefore, equity instruments issued in a business combination in exchange for control of the acquiree are not within the scope of IFRS 2. However, equity instruments granted to employees of the acquiree in their capacity as employees, eg in return for continued service, are within the scope of IFRS 2. Also, the cancellation, replacement, or other modifications to share-based payment arrangements because of a business combination or other equity restructuring should be accounted for in accordance with IFRS 2.

BC24A   IFRS 3 (as revised in 2008) changed the definition of a business combination. The previous definition of a business combination was 'the bringing together of separate entities or businesses into one reporting entity'. The revised definition of a business combination is 'a transaction or other event in which an acquirer obtains control of one or more businesses'.

BC24B   The Board was advised that the changes to that definition caused the accounting for the contribution of a business in exchange for shares issued on formation of a joint venture by the venturers to be within the scope of IFRS 2. The Board noted that common control transactions may also be within the scope of IFRS 2 depending on which level of the group reporting entity is assessing the combination.

BC24C   The Board noted that during the development of revised IFRS 3 it did not discuss whether it intended IFRS 2 to apply to these types of transactions. The Board also noted that the reason for excluding common control transactions and the accounting by a joint venture upon its formation from the scope of revised IFRS 3 was to give the Board more time to consider the relevant accounting issues. When the Board revised IFRS 3, it did not intend to change existing practice by bringing such transactions within the scope of IFRS 2, which does not specifically address them.

BC24D   Accordingly, in *Improvements to IFRSs* issued in April 2009, the Board amended paragraph 5 of IFRS 2 to confirm that the contribution of a business on the formation of a joint venture and common control transactions are not within the scope of IFRS 2.

Transactions within the scope of IAS 32 *Financial Instruments: Presentation* and IAS 39 *Financial Instruments: Recognition and Measurement*[7]

BC25 The IFRS includes consequential amendments to IAS 32 and IAS 39 (both as revised in 2003)[8] to exclude from their scope transactions within the scope of IFRS 2.

BC26 For example, suppose the entity enters into a contract to purchase cloth for use in its clothing manufacturing business, whereby it is required to pay cash to the counterparty in an amount equal to the value of 1,000 of the entity's shares at the date of delivery of the cloth. The entity will acquire goods and pay cash at an amount based on its share price. This meets the definition of a share-based payment transaction. Moreover, because the contract is to purchase cloth, which is a non-financial item, and the contract was entered into for the purpose of taking delivery of the cloth for use in the entity's manufacturing business, the contract is not within the scope of IAS 32 and IAS 39.

BC27 The scope of IAS 32 and IAS 39 includes contracts to buy non-financial items that can be settled net in cash or another financial instrument, or by exchanging financial instruments, with the exception of contracts that were entered into and continue to be held for the purpose of the receipt or delivery of a non-financial item in accordance with the entity's expected purchase, sale or usage requirements. A contract that can be settled net in cash or another financial instrument or by exchanging financial instruments includes (a) when the terms of the contract permit either party to settle it net in cash or another financial instrument or by exchanging financial instruments; (b) when the ability to settle net in cash or another financial instrument, or by exchanging financial instruments, is not explicit in the terms of the contract, but the entity has a practice of settling similar contracts net in cash or another financial instrument, or by exchanging financial instruments (whether with the counterparty, by entering into offsetting contracts, or by selling the contract before its exercise or lapse); (c) when, for similar contracts, the entity has a practice of taking delivery of the underlying and selling it within a short period after delivery for the purpose of generating a profit from short-term fluctuations in price or dealer's margin; and (d) when the non-financial item that is the subject of the contract is readily convertible to cash (IAS 32, paragraphs 8–10 and IAS 39, paragraphs 5–7).

BC28 The Board concluded that the contracts discussed in paragraph BC27 should remain within the scope of IAS 32 and IAS 39 and they are therefore excluded from the scope of IFRS 2.

Recognition of equity-settled share-based payment transactions

BC29 When it developed ED 2, the Board first considered conceptual arguments relating to the recognition of an expense arising from equity-settled share-based payment transactions, including arguments advanced by respondents to the

---

7   IFRS 9 *Financial Instruments* replaced IAS 39. IFRS 9 applies to all items that were previously within the scope of IAS 39. Paragraphs BC25–BC28 refer to matters relevant when IFRS 2 was issued.
8   The title of IAS 32 was amended in 2005.

Discussion Paper and other commentators. Some respondents who disagreed with the recognition of an expense arising from particular share-based payment transactions (ie those involving employee share options) did so for practical, rather than conceptual, reasons. The Board considered those practical issues later (see paragraphs BC294–BC310).

BC30 The Board focused its discussions on employee share options, because that is where most of the complexity and controversy lies, but the question of whether expense recognition is appropriate is broader than that—it covers all transactions involving the issue of shares, share options or other equity instruments to employees or suppliers of goods and services. For example, the Board noted that arguments made by respondents and other commentators against expense recognition are directed solely at employee share options. However, if conceptual arguments made against recognition of an expense in relation to employee share options are valid (eg that there is no cost to the entity), those arguments ought to apply equally to transactions involving other equity instruments (eg shares) and to equity instruments issued to other parties (eg suppliers of professional services).

BC31 The rationale for recognising all types of share-based payment transactions—irrespective of whether the equity instrument is a share or a share option, and irrespective of whether the equity instrument is granted to an employee or to some other party—is that the entity has engaged in a transaction that is in essence the same as any other issue of equity instruments. In other words, the entity has received resources (goods or services) as consideration for the issue of shares, share options or other equity instruments. It should therefore account for the inflow of resources (goods or services) and the increase in equity. Subsequently, either at the time of receipt of the goods or services or at some later date, the entity should also account for the expense arising from the consumption of those resources.

BC32 Many respondents to ED 2 agreed with this conclusion. Of those who disagreed, some disagreed in principle, some disagreed for practical reasons, and some disagreed for both reasons. The arguments against expense recognition in principle were considered by the Board when it developed ED 2, as were the arguments against expense recognition for practical reasons, as explained below and in paragraphs BC294–BC310.

BC33 Arguments commonly made against expense recognition include:

(a) the transaction is between the shareholders and the employees, not the entity and the employees.

(b) the employees do not provide services for the options.

(c) there is no cost to the entity, because no cash or other assets are given up; the shareholders bear the cost, in the form of dilution of their ownership interests, not the entity.

(d)   the recognition of an expense is inconsistent with the definition of an expense in the conceptual frameworks used by accounting standard-setters, including the IASB's *Framework for the Preparation and Presentation of Financial Statements*.[9]

(e)   the cost borne by the shareholders is recognised in the dilution of earnings per share (EPS); if the transaction is recognised in the entity's accounts, the resulting charge to the income statement would mean that EPS is 'hit twice'.

(f)   requiring the recognition of a charge would have adverse economic consequences, because it would discourage entities from introducing or continuing employee share plans.

'The entity is not a party to the transaction'

BC34   Some argue that the effect of employee share plans is that the existing shareholders transfer some of their ownership interests to the employees and that the entity is not a party to this transaction.

BC35   The Board did not accept this argument. Entities, not shareholders, set up employee share plans and entities, not shareholders, issue share options to their employees. Even if that were not the case, eg if shareholders transferred shares or share options direct to the employees, this would not mean that the entity is not a party to the transaction. The equity instruments are issued in return for services rendered by the employees and the entity, not the shareholders, receives those services. Therefore, the Board concluded that the entity should account for the services received in return for the equity instruments issued. The Board noted that this is no different from other situations in which equity instruments are issued. For example, if an entity issues warrants for cash, the entity recognises the cash received in return for the warrants issued. Although the effect of an issue, and subsequent exercise, of warrants might be described as a transfer of ownership interests from the existing shareholders to the warrant holders, the entity nevertheless is a party to the transaction because it receives resources (cash) for the issue of warrants and further resources (cash) for the issue of shares upon exercise of the warrants. Similarly, with employee share options, the entity receives resources (employee services) for the issue of the options and further resources (cash) for the issue of shares on the exercise of options.

'The employees do not provide services'

BC36   Some who argue that the entity is not a party to the transaction counter the points made above with the argument that employees do not provide services for the options, because the employees are paid in cash (or other assets) for their services.

BC37   Again, the Board was not convinced by this argument. If it were true that employees do not provide services for their share options, this would mean that entities are issuing valuable share options and getting nothing in return.

---

9   References to the *Framework* are to IASC's *Framework for the Preparation and Presentation of Financial Statements*, adopted by the IASB in 2001. In September 2010 the IASB replaced the *Framework* with the *Conceptual Framework for Financial Reporting*.

Employees do not pay cash for the share options they receive. Hence, if they do not provide services for the options, the employees are providing nothing in return. If this were true, by issuing such options the entity's directors would be in breach of their fiduciary duties to their shareholders.

BC38 Typically, shares or share options granted to employees form one part of their remuneration package. For example, an employee might have a remuneration package consisting of a basic cash salary, company car, pension, healthcare benefits, and other benefits including shares and share options. It is usually not possible to identify the services received in respect of individual components of that remuneration package, eg the services received in respect of healthcare benefits. But that does not mean that the employee does not provide services for those healthcare benefits. Rather, the employee provides services for the entire remuneration package.

BC39 In summary, shares, share options or other equity instruments are granted to employees because they are employees. The equity instruments granted form a part of their total remuneration package, regardless of whether that represents a large part or a small part.

'There is no cost to the entity, therefore there is no expense'

BC40 Some argue that because share-based payments do not require the entity to sacrifice any cash or other assets, there is no cost to the entity, and therefore no expense should be recognised.

BC41 The Board regards this argument as unsound, because it overlooks that:

(a) every time an entity receives resources as consideration for the issue of equity instruments, there is no outflow of cash or other assets, and on every other occasion the resources received as consideration for the issue of equity instruments are recognised in the financial statements; and

(b) the expense arises from the consumption of those resources, not from an outflow of assets.

BC42 In other words, irrespective of whether one accepts that there is a cost to the entity, an accounting entry is required to recognise the resources received as consideration for the issue of equity instruments, just as it is on other occasions when equity instruments are issued. For example, when shares are issued for cash, an entry is required to recognise the cash received. If a non-monetary asset, such as plant and machinery, is received for those shares instead of cash, an entry is required to recognise the asset received. If the entity acquires another business or entity by issuing shares in a business combination, the entity recognises the net assets acquired.

BC43 The recognition of an expense arising out of such a transaction represents the consumption of resources received, ie the 'using up' of the resources received for the shares or share options. In the case of the plant and machinery mentioned above, the asset would be depreciated over its expected life, resulting in the recognition of an expense each year. Eventually, the entire amount recognised for the resources received when the shares were issued would be recognised as an expense (including any residual value, which would form part of the measurement of the gain or loss on disposal of the asset). Similarly, if another business or entity is acquired by an issue of shares, an expense is recognised when the assets acquired are consumed. For example, inventories acquired will be recognised as an expense when sold, even though no cash or other assets were disbursed to acquire those inventories.

BC44   The only difference in the case of employee services (or other services) received as consideration for the issue of shares or share options is that usually the resources received are consumed immediately upon receipt. This means that an expense for the consumption of resources is recognised immediately, rather than over a period of time. The Board concluded that the timing of consumption does not change the principle; the financial statements should recognise the receipt and consumption of resources, even when consumption occurs at the same time as, or soon after, receipt. This point is discussed further in paragraphs BC45–BC53.

'Expense recognition is inconsistent with the definition of an expense'

BC45   Some have questioned whether recognition of an expense arising from particular share-based payment transactions is consistent with accounting standard-setters' conceptual frameworks, in particular, the *Framework*, which states:

> Expenses are decreases in economic benefits during the accounting period in the form of outflows or *depletions of assets* or incurrences of liabilities that result in decreases in equity, other than those relating to distributions to equity participants. (paragraph 70,[10] emphasis added)

BC46   Some argue that if services are received in a share-based payment transaction, there is no transaction or event that meets the definition of an expense. They contend that there is no outflow of assets and that no liability is incurred. Furthermore, because services usually do not meet the criteria for recognition as an asset, it is argued that the consumption of those services does not represent a depletion of assets.

BC47   The *Framework* defines an asset and explains that the term 'asset' is not limited to resources that can be recognised as assets in the balance sheet (*Framework*, paragraphs 49 and 50).[11] Although services to be received in the future might not meet the definition of an asset,[12] services are assets when received. These assets are usually consumed immediately. This is explained in FASB Statement of Financial Accounting Concepts No. 6 *Elements of Financial Statements*:

> Services provided by other entities, including personal services, cannot be stored and are received and used simultaneously. They can be assets of an entity only momentarily—as the entity receives and uses them—although their use may create or add value to other assets of the entity ... (paragraph 31)

---

10 now paragraph 4.25 of the *Conceptual Framework*
11 now paragraphs 4.4 and 4.5 of the *Conceptual Framework*
12 For example, the entity might not have control over future services.

BC48   This applies to all types of services, eg employee services, legal services and telephone services. It also applies irrespective of the form of payment. For example, if an entity purchases services for cash, the accounting entry is:

Dr   Services received
   Cr Cash paid

BC49   Sometimes, those services are consumed in the creation of a recognisable asset, such as inventories, in which case the debit for services received is capitalised as part of a recognised asset. But often the services do not create or form part of a recognisable asset, in which case the debit for services received is charged immediately to the income statement as an expense. The debit entry above (and the resulting expense) does not represent the cash outflow—that is what the credit entry was for. Nor does it represent some sort of balancing item, to make the accounts balance. The debit entry above represents the resources received, and the resulting expense represents the consumption of those resources.

BC50   The same analysis applies if the services are acquired with payment made in shares or share options. The resulting expense represents the consumption of services, ie a depletion of assets.

BC51   To illustrate this point, suppose that an entity has two buildings, both with gas heating, and the entity issues shares to the gas supplier instead of paying cash. Suppose that, for one building, the gas is supplied through a pipeline, and so is consumed immediately upon receipt. Suppose that, for the other building, the gas is supplied in bottles, and is consumed over a period of time. In both cases, the entity has received assets as consideration for the issue of equity instruments, and should therefore recognise the assets received, and a corresponding contribution to equity. If the assets are consumed immediately (the gas received through the pipeline), an expense is recognised immediately; if the assets are consumed later (the gas received in bottles), an expense is recognised later when the assets are consumed.

BC52   Therefore, the Board concluded that the recognition of an expense arising from share-based payment transactions is consistent with the definition of an expense in the *Framework*.

BC53   The FASB considered the same issue and reached the same conclusion in SFAS 123:

> Some respondents pointed out that the definition of expenses in FASB Concepts Statement No. 6, *Elements of Financial Statements*, says that expenses result from outflows or using up of assets or incurring of liabilities (or both). They asserted that because the issuance of stock options does not result in the incurrence of a liability, no expense should be recognised. The Board agrees that employee stock options are not a liability—like stock purchase warrants, employee stock options are equity instruments of the issuer. However, equity instruments, including employee stock options, are valuable financial instruments and thus are issued for valuable consideration, which...for employee stock options is employee services. Using in the entity's operations the benefits embodied in the asset received results in an expense ... (Concepts Statement 6, paragraph 81, footnote 43, notes that, in

concept most expenses decrease assets. However, if receipt of an asset, such as services, and its use occur virtually simultaneously, the asset often is not recorded.) [paragraph 88]

'Earnings per share is "hit twice"'

BC54   Some argue that any cost arising from share-based payment transactions is already recognised in the dilution of earnings per share (EPS). If an expense were recognised in the income statement, EPS would be 'hit twice'.

BC55   However, the Board noted that this result is appropriate. For example, if the entity paid the employees in cash for their services and the cash was then returned to the entity, as consideration for the issue of share options, the effect on EPS would be the same as issuing those options direct to the employees.

BC56   The dual effect on EPS simply reflects the two economic events that have occurred: the entity has issued shares or share options, thereby increasing the number of shares included in the EPS calculation—although, in the case of options, only to the extent that the options are regarded as dilutive—and it has also consumed the resources it received for those options, thereby decreasing earnings. This is illustrated by the plant and machinery example mentioned in paragraphs BC42 and BC43. Issuing shares affects the number of shares in the EPS calculation, and the consumption (depreciation) of the asset affects earnings.

BC57   In summary, the Board concluded that the dual effect on diluted EPS is not double-counting the effects of a share or share option grant—the same effect is not counted twice. Rather, two different effects are each counted once.

'Adverse economic consequences'

BC58   Some argue that to require recognition (or greater recognition) of employee share-based payment would have adverse economic consequences, in that it might discourage entities from introducing or continuing employee share plans.

BC59   Others argue that if the introduction of accounting changes did lead to a reduction in the use of employee share plans, it might be because the requirement for entities to account properly for employee share plans had revealed the economic consequences of such plans. They argue that this would correct the present economic distortion, whereby entities obtain and consume resources by issuing valuable shares or share options without accounting for those transactions.

BC60   In any event, the Board noted that the role of accounting is to report transactions and events in a neutral manner, not to give 'favourable' treatment to particular transactions to encourage entities to engage in those transactions. To do so would impair the quality of financial reporting. The omission of expenses from the financial statements does not change the fact that those expenses have been incurred. Hence, if expenses are omitted from the income statement, reported profits are overstated. The financial statements are not neutral, are less transparent and are potentially misleading to users. Comparability is impaired, given that expenses arising from employee share-based payment transactions vary from entity to entity, from sector to sector, and from year to year. More fundamentally, accountability is impaired, because the entities are not accounting for transactions they have entered into and the consequences of those transactions.

Measurement of equity-settled share-based payment transactions

BC61   To recognise equity-settled share-based payment transactions, it is necessary to decide how the transactions should be measured. The Board began by considering how to measure share-based payment transactions in principle. Later, it considered practical issues arising from the application of its preferred measurement approach. In terms of accounting principles, there are two basic questions:

(a)   which measurement basis should be applied?

(b)   when should that measurement basis be applied?

BC62   To answer these questions, the Board considered the accounting principles applying to equity transactions. The *Framework* states:

> Equity is the residual interest in the assets of the enterprise after deducting all of its liabilities ... The amount at which equity is shown in the balance sheet is dependent upon the measurement of assets and liabilities. Normally, the aggregate amount of equity only by coincidence corresponds with the aggregate market value of the shares of the enterprise ... (paragraphs 49 and 67)[13]

BC63   The accounting equation that corresponds to this definition of equity is:

assets minus liabilities equals equity

BC64   Equity is a residual interest, dependent on the measurement of assets and liabilities. Therefore, accounting focuses on recording changes in the left side of the equation (assets minus liabilities, or net assets), rather than the right side. Changes in equity arise from changes in net assets. For example, if an entity issues shares for cash, it recognises the cash received and a corresponding increase in equity. Subsequent changes in the market price of the shares do not affect the entity's net assets and therefore those changes in value are not recognised.

BC65   Hence, the Board concluded that, when accounting for an equity-settled share-based payment transaction, the primary accounting objective is to account for the goods or services received as consideration for the issue of equity instruments. Therefore, equity-settled share-based payment transactions should be accounted for in the same way as other issues of equity instruments, by recognising the consideration received (the change in net assets), and a corresponding increase in equity.

BC66   Given this objective, the Board concluded that, in principle, the goods or services received should be measured at their fair value at the date when the entity obtains those goods or as the services are received. In other words, because a change in net assets occurs when the entity obtains the goods or as the services are received, the fair value of those goods or services at that date provides an appropriate measure of the change in net assets.

---

13   now paragraphs 4.4 and 4.22 of the *Conceptual Framework*

BC67   However, for share-based payment transactions with employees, it is usually difficult to measure directly the fair value of the services received. As noted earlier, typically shares or share options are granted to employees as one component of their remuneration package. It is usually not possible to identify the services rendered in respect of individual components of that package. It might also not be possible to measure independently the fair value of the total package, without measuring directly the fair value of the equity instruments granted. Furthermore, options or shares are sometimes granted as part of a bonus arrangement, rather than as a part of basic remuneration, eg as an incentive to the employees to remain in the entity's employ, or to reward them for their efforts in improving the entity's performance. By granting share options, in addition to other remuneration, the entity is paying additional remuneration to obtain additional benefits. Estimating the fair value of those additional benefits is likely to be difficult.

BC68   Given these practical difficulties in measuring directly the fair value of the employee services received, the Board concluded that it is necessary to measure the other side of the transaction, ie the fair value of the equity instruments granted, as a surrogate measure of the fair value of the services received. In this context, the Board considered the same basic questions, as mentioned above:

    (a)   which measurement basis should be applied?

    (b)   when should that measurement basis be applied?

Measurement basis

BC69   The Board discussed the following measurement bases, to decide which should be applied in principle:

    (a)   historical cost

    (b)   intrinsic value

    (c)   minimum value

    (d)   fair value.

Historical cost

BC70   In jurisdictions where legislation permits, entities commonly repurchase their own shares, either directly or through a vehicle such as a trust, which are used to fulfil promised grants of shares to employees or the exercise of employee share options. A possible basis for measuring a grant of options or shares would be the historical cost (purchase price) of its own shares that an entity holds (own shares held), even if they were acquired before the award was made.

BC71   For share options, this would entail comparing the historical cost of own shares held with the exercise price of options granted to employees. Any shortfall would be recognised as an expense. Also, presumably, if the exercise price exceeded the historical cost of own shares held, the excess would be recognised as a gain.

BC72   At first sight, if one simply focuses on the cash flows involved, the historical cost basis appears reasonable: there is a cash outflow to acquire the shares, followed by a cash inflow when those shares are transferred to the employees (the exercise price), with any shortfall representing a cost to the entity. If the cash flows related to anything other than the entity's own shares, this approach would be appropriate. For example, suppose ABC Ltd bought shares in another entity, XYZ Ltd, for a total cost of CU500,000,[14] and later sold the shares to employees for a total of CU400,000. The entity would recognise an expense for the CU100,000 shortfall.

BC73　　But when this analysis is applied to the entity's own shares, the logic breaks down. The entity's own shares are not an asset of the entity.[15] Rather, the shares are an interest in the entity's assets. Hence, the distribution of cash to buy back shares is a return of capital to shareholders, and should therefore be recognised as a decrease in equity. Similarly, when the shares are subsequently reissued or transferred, the inflow of cash is an increase in shareholders' capital, and should therefore be recognised as an increase in equity. It follows that no revenue or expense should be recognised. Just as the issue of shares does not represent revenue to the entity, the repurchase of those shares does not represent an expense.

BC74　　Therefore, the Board concluded that historical cost is not an appropriate basis upon which to measure equity-settled share-based payment transactions.

Intrinsic value

BC75　　An equity instrument could be measured at its intrinsic value. The intrinsic value of a share option at any point in time is the difference between the market price of the underlying shares and the exercise price of the option.

BC76　　Often, employee share options have zero intrinsic value at the date of grant—commonly the exercise price is at the market value of the shares at grant date. Therefore, in many cases, valuing share options at their intrinsic value at grant date is equivalent to attributing no value to the options.

BC77　　However, the intrinsic value of an option does not fully reflect its value. Options sell in the market for more than their intrinsic value. This is because the holder of an option need not exercise it immediately and benefits from any increase in the value of the underlying shares. In other words, although the ultimate benefit realised by the option holder is the option's intrinsic value at the date of exercise, the option holder is able to realise that future intrinsic value because of having held the option. Thus, the option holder benefits from the right to participate in future gains from increases in the share price. In addition, the

---

14　All monetary amounts in this Basis for Conclusions are denominated in 'currency units (CU)'.

15　The Discussion Paper discusses this point: Accounting practice in some jurisdictions may present own shares acquired as an asset, but they lack the essential feature of an asset—the ability to provide future economic benefits. The future economic benefits usually provided by an interest in shares are the right to receive dividends and the right to gain from an increase in value of the shares. When a company has an interest in its own shares, it will receive dividends on those shares only if it elects to pay them, and such dividends do not represent a gain to the company, as there is no change in net assets: the flow of funds is simply circular. Whilst it is true that a company that holds its own shares in treasury may sell them and receive a higher amount if their value has increased, a company is generally able to issue shares to third parties at (or near) the current market price. Although there may be legal, regulatory or administrative reasons why it is easier to sell shares that are held as treasury shares than it would be to issue new shares, such considerations do not seem to amount to a fundamental contrast between the two cases. (Footnote to paragraph 4.7) option holder benefits from the right to defer payment of the exercise price until the end of the option term. These benefits are commonly referred to as the option's 'time value'.

BC78   For many options, time value represents a substantial part of their value. As noted earlier, many employee share options have zero intrinsic value at grant date, and hence the option's value consists entirely of time value. In such cases, ignoring time value by applying the intrinsic value method at grant date understates the value of the option by 100 per cent.

BC79   The Board concluded that, in general, the intrinsic value measurement basis is not appropriate for measuring share-based payment transactions, because omitting the option's time value ignores a potentially substantial part of an option's total value. Measuring share-based payment transactions at such an understated value would fail to represent those transactions faithfully in the financial statements.

Minimum value

BC80   A share option could be measured at its minimum value. Minimum value is based on the premise that someone who wants to buy a call option on a share would be willing to pay at least (and the option writer would demand at least) the value of the right to defer payment of the exercise price until the end of the option's term. Therefore, minimum value can be calculated using a present value technique. For a dividend-paying share, the calculation is:

(a)   the current price of the share, minus

(b)   the present value of expected dividends on that share during the option term (if the option holder does not receive dividends), minus

(c)   the present value of the exercise price.

BC81   Minimum value can also be calculated using an option pricing model with an expected volatility of effectively zero (not exactly zero, because some option pricing models use volatility as a divisor, and zero cannot be a divisor).

BC82   The minimum value measurement basis captures part of the time value of options, being the value of the right to defer payment of the exercise price until the end of the option's term. It does not capture the effects of volatility. Option holders benefit from volatility because they have the right to participate in gains from increases in the share price during the option term without having to bear the full risk of loss from decreases in the share price. By ignoring volatility, the minimum value method produces a value that is lower, and often much lower, than values produced by methods designed to estimate the fair value of an option.

BC83   The Board concluded that minimum value is not an appropriate measurement basis, because ignoring the effects of volatility ignores a potentially large part of an option's value. As with intrinsic value, measuring share-based payment transactions at the option's minimum value would fail to represent those transactions faithfully in the financial statements.

Fair value

BC84 Fair value is already used in other areas of accounting, including other transactions in which non-cash resources are acquired through the issue of equity instruments. For example, consideration transferred in a business combination is measured at fair value, including the fair value of any equity instruments issued by the entity.

BC85 Fair value, which is the amount at which an equity instrument granted could be exchanged between knowledgeable, willing parties in an arm's length transaction, captures both intrinsic value and time value and therefore provides a measure of the share option's total value (unlike intrinsic value or minimum value). It is the value that reflects the bargain between the entity and its employees, whereby the entity has agreed to grant share options to employees for their services to the entity. Hence, measuring share-based payment transactions at fair value ensures that those transactions are represented faithfully in the financial statements, and consistently with other transactions in which the entity receives resources as consideration for the issue of equity instruments.

BC86 Therefore, the Board concluded that shares, share options or other equity instruments granted should be measured at their fair value.

BC87 Of the respondents to ED 2 who addressed this issue, many agreed with the proposal to measure the equity instruments granted at their fair value. Some respondents who disagreed with the proposal, or who agreed with reservations, expressed concerns about measurement reliability, particularly in the case of smaller or unlisted entities. The issues of measurement reliability and unlisted entities are discussed in paragraphs BC294–BC310 and BC137–BC144, respectively.

Measurement date

BC88 The Board first considered at which date the fair value of equity instruments should be determined for the purpose of measuring share-based payment transactions with employees (and others providing similar services).[16] The possible measurement dates discussed were grant date, service date, vesting date and exercise date. Much of this discussion was in the context of share options rather than shares or other equity instruments, because only options have an exercise date.

---

16 When the Board developed the proposals in ED 2, it focused on the measurement of equity-settled transactions with employees and with parties other than employees. ED 2 did not propose a definition of the term 'employees'. When the Board reconsidered the proposals in ED 2 in the light of comments received, it discussed whether the term might be interpreted too narrowly. This could result in a different accounting treatment of services received from individuals who are regarded as employees (eg for legal or tax purposes) and substantially similar services received from other individuals. The Board therefore concluded that the requirements of the IFRS for transactions with employees should also apply to transactions with other parties providing similar services. This includes services received from (1) individuals who work for the entity under its direction in the same way as individuals who are regarded as employees for legal or tax purposes and (2) individuals who are not employees but who render personal services to the entity similar to those rendered by employees. All references to employees therefore include other parties providing similar services.

BC89 In the context of an employee share option, grant date is when the entity and the employee enter into an agreement, whereby the employee is granted rights to the share option, provided that specified conditions are met, such as the employee's remaining in the entity's employ for a specified period. Service date is the date when the employee renders the services necessary to become entitled to the share option.[17] Vesting date is the date when the employee has satisfied all the conditions necessary to become entitled to the share option. For example, if the employee is required to remain in the entity's employ for three years, vesting date is at the end of that three-year period. Exercise date is when the share option is exercised.

BC90 To help determine the appropriate measurement date, the Board applied the accounting concepts in the *Framework* to each side of the transaction. For transactions with employees, the Board concluded that grant date is the appropriate measurement date, as explained in paragraphs BC91–BC105. The Board also considered some other issues, as explained in paragraphs BC106–BC118. For transactions with parties other than employees, the Board concluded that delivery date is the appropriate measurement date (ie the date the goods or services are received, referred to as service date in the context of transactions with employees), as explained in paragraphs BC119–BC128.

The debit side of the transaction

BC91 Focusing on the debit side of the transaction means focusing on measuring the fair value of the resources received. This measurement objective is consistent with the primary objective of accounting for the goods or services received as consideration for the issue of equity instruments (see paragraphs BC64–BC66). The Board therefore concluded that, in principle, the goods or services received should be measured at their fair value at the date when the entity obtains those goods or as the services are received.

BC92 However, if the fair value of the services received is not readily determinable, then a surrogate measure must be used, such as the fair value of the share options or shares granted. This is the case for employee services.

BC93 If the fair value of the equity instruments granted is used as a surrogate measure of the fair value of the services received, both vesting date and exercise date measurement are inappropriate because the fair value of the services received during a particular accounting period is not affected by subsequent changes in the fair value of the equity instrument. For example, suppose that services are received during years 1–3 as the consideration for share options that are exercised at the end of year 5. For services received in year 1, subsequent changes in the value of the share option in years 2–5 are unrelated to, and have no effect on, the fair value of those services when received.

BC94 Service date measurement measures the fair value of the equity instrument at the same time as the services are received. This means that changes in the fair

---

17 Service date measurement theoretically requires the entity to measure the fair value of the share option at each date when services are received. For pragmatic reasons, an approximation would probably be used, such as the fair value of the share option at the end of each accounting period, or the value of the share option measured at regular intervals during each accounting period.

value of the equity instrument during the vesting period affect the amount attributed to the services received. Some argue that this is appropriate, because, in their view, there is a correlation between changes in the fair value of the equity instrument and the fair value of the services received. For example, they argue that if the fair value of a share option falls, so does its incentive effects, which causes employees to reduce the level of services provided for that option, or demand extra remuneration. Some argue that when the fair value of a share option falls because of a general decline in share prices, remuneration levels also fall, and therefore service date measurement reflects this decline in remuneration levels.

BC95 The Board concluded, however, that there is unlikely to be a high correlation between changes in the fair value of an equity instrument and the fair value of the services received. For example, if the fair value of a share option doubles, it is unlikely that the employees work twice as hard, or accept a reduction in the rest of their remuneration package. Similarly, even if a general rise in share prices is accompanied by a rise in remuneration levels, it is unlikely that there is a high correlation between the two. Furthermore, it is likely that any link between share prices and remuneration levels is not universally applicable to all industry sectors.

BC96 The Board concluded that, at grant date, it is reasonable to presume that the fair value of both sides of the contract are substantially the same, ie the fair value of the services expected to be received is substantially the same as the fair value of the equity instruments granted. This conclusion, together with the Board's conclusion that there is unlikely to be a high correlation between the fair value of the services received and the fair value of the equity instruments granted at later measurement dates, led the Board to conclude that grant date is the most appropriate measurement date for the purposes of providing a surrogate measure of the fair value of the services received.

The credit side of the transaction

BC97 Although focusing on the debit side of the transaction is consistent with the primary accounting objective, some approach the measurement date question from the perspective of the credit side of the transaction, ie the issue of an equity instrument. The Board therefore considered the matter from this perspective too.

Exercise date

BC98 Under exercise date measurement, the entity recognises the resources received (eg employee services) for the issue of share options, and also recognises changes in the fair value of the option until it is exercised or lapses. Thus, if the option is exercised, the transaction amount is ultimately 'trued up' to equal the gain made by the option holder on exercise of the option. However, if the option lapses at the end of the exercise period, any amounts previously recognised are effectively reversed, hence the transaction amount is ultimately trued up to equal zero. The Board rejected exercise date measurement because it requires share options to be treated as liabilities, which is inconsistent with the definition of liabilities in the *Framework*. Exercise date measurement requires share options to be treated as liabilities because it requires the remeasurement of share options after initial recognition, which is inappropriate if the share options are equity instruments. A share option does not meet the definition of a liability, because it does not contain an obligation to transfer cash or other assets.

Vesting date, service date and grant date

BC99   The Board noted that the IASC/G4+1 Discussion Paper supported vesting date measurement, and rejected grant date and service date measurement, because it concluded that the share option is not issued until vesting date. It noted that the employees must perform their side of the arrangement by providing the necessary services and meeting any other performance criteria before the entity is obliged to perform its side of the arrangement. The provision of services by the employees is not merely a condition of the arrangement, it is the consideration they use to 'pay' for the share option. Therefore, the Discussion Paper concluded, in economic terms the share option is not issued until vesting date. Because the entity performs its side of the arrangement on vesting date, that is the appropriate measurement date.

BC100   The Discussion Paper also proposed recognising an accrual in equity during the vesting period to ensure that the services are recognised when they are received. It proposed that this accrual should be revised on vesting date to equal the fair value of the share option at that date. This means that amounts credited to equity during the vesting period will be subsequently remeasured to reflect changes in the value of that equity interest before vesting date. That is inconsistent with the *Framework* because equity interests are not subsequently remeasured, ie any changes in their value are not recognised. The Discussion Paper justified this remeasurement by arguing that because the share option is not issued until vesting date, the option is not being remeasured. The credit to equity during the vesting period is merely an interim measure that is used to recognise the partially completed transaction.

BC101   However, the Board noted that even if one accepts that the share option is not issued until vesting date, this does not mean that there is no equity interest until then. If an equity interest exists before vesting date, that interest should not be remeasured. Moreover, the conversion of one type of equity interest into another should not, in itself, cause a change in total equity, because no change in net assets has occurred.

BC102   Some supporters of vesting date suggest that the accrual during the performance period meets the definition of a liability. However, the basis for this conclusion is unclear. The entity is not required to transfer cash or other assets to the employees. Its only commitment is to issue equity instruments.

BC103   The Board concluded that vesting date measurement is inconsistent with the *Framework*, because it requires the remeasurement of equity.

BC104   Service date measurement does not require remeasurement of equity interests after initial recognition. However, as explained earlier, the Board concluded that incorporating changes in the fair value of the share option into the transaction amount is unlikely to produce an amount that fairly reflects the fair value of the services received, which is the primary objective.

BC105   The Board therefore concluded that, no matter which side of the transaction one focuses upon (ie the receipt of resources or the issue of an equity instrument), grant date is the appropriate measurement date under the *Framework*, because it does not require remeasurement of equity interests and it provides a reasonable surrogate measure of the fair value of the services received from employees.

Other issues

IAS 32 Financial Instruments: Disclosure and Presentation[18]

BC106   As discussed above, under the definitions of liabilities and equity in the *Framework*, both shares and share options are equity instruments, because neither instrument requires the entity to transfer cash or other assets. Similarly, all contracts or arrangements that will be settled by the entity issuing shares or share options are classified as equity. However, this differs from the distinction between liabilities and equity applied in IAS 32. Although IAS 32 also considers, in its debt/equity distinction, whether an instrument contains an obligation to transfer cash or other assets, this is supplemented by a second criterion, which considers whether the number of shares to be issued (and cash to be received) on settlement is fixed or variable. IAS 32 classifies a contract that will or may be settled in the entity's own equity instruments as a liability if the contract is a non-derivative for which the entity is or may be obliged to deliver a variable number of the entity's own equity instruments; or a derivative that will or may be settled other than by the exchange of a fixed amount of cash or another financial asset for a fixed number of the entity's own equity instruments.

BC107   In some cases, the number of share options to which employees are entitled varies. For example, the number of share options to which the employees will be entitled on vesting date might vary depending on whether, and to the extent that, a particular performance target is exceeded. Another example is share appreciation rights settled in shares. In this situation, a variable number of shares will be issued, equal in value to the appreciation of the entity's share price over a period of time.

BC108   Therefore, if the requirements of IAS 32 were applied to equity-settled share-based payment transactions, in some situations an obligation to issue equity instruments would be classified as a liability. In such cases, final measurement of the transaction would be at a measurement date later than grant date.

BC109   The Board concluded that different considerations applied in developing IFRS 2. For example, drawing a distinction between fixed and variable option plans and requiring a later measurement date for variable option plans has undesirable consequences, as discussed in paragraphs BC272–BC275.

BC110   The Board concluded that the requirements in IAS 32, whereby some obligations to issue equity instruments are classified as liabilities, should not be applied in the IFRS on share-based payment. The Board recognises that this creates a difference between IFRS 2 and IAS 32. Before deciding whether and how that difference should be eliminated, the Board concluded that it is necessary to

---

18   In August 2005 IAS 32 was amended as IAS 32 *Financial Instruments: Presentation*.

address this issue in a broader context, as part of a fundamental review of the definitions of liabilities and equity in the *Framework*, particularly because this is not the only debt/equity classification issue that has arisen in the share-based payment project, as explained below.

Suggestions to change the definitions of liabilities and equity

BC111   In concluding that, for transactions with employees, grant date is the appropriate measurement date under the *Framework*, the Board noted that some respondents to ED 2 and the Discussion Paper support other measurement dates because they believe that the definitions of liabilities and equity in the *Framework* should be revised.

BC112   For example, some supporters of vesting date argue that receipt of employee services between grant date and vesting date creates an obligation for the entity to pay for those services, and that the method of settlement should not matter. In other words, it should not matter whether that obligation is settled in cash or in equity instruments—both ought to be treated as liabilities. Therefore, the definition of a liability should be modified so that all types of obligations, however settled, are included in liabilities. But it is not clear that this approach would necessarily result in vesting date measurement. A share option contains an obligation to issue shares. Hence, if all types of obligations are classified as liabilities, then a share option would be a liability, which would result in exercise date measurement.

BC113   Some support exercise date measurement on the grounds that it produces the same accounting result as 'economically similar' cash-settled share-based payments. For example, it is argued that share appreciation rights (SARs) settled in cash are substantially similar to SARs settled in shares, because in both cases the employee receives consideration to the same value. Also, if the SARs are settled in shares and the shares are immediately sold, the employee ends up in exactly the same position as under a cash-settled SAR, ie with cash equal to the appreciation in the entity's share price over the specified period. Similarly, some argue that share options and cash-settled SARs are economically similar. This is particularly true when the employee realises the gain on the exercise of share options by selling the shares immediately after exercise, as commonly occurs. Either way, the employee ends up with an amount of cash that is based on the appreciation of the share price over a period of time. If cash-settled transactions and equity-settled transactions are economically similar, the accounting treatment should be the same.

BC114   However, it is not clear that changing the distinction between liabilities and equity to be consistent with exercise date measurement is the only way to achieve the same accounting treatment. For example, the distinction could be changed so that cash-settled employee share plans are measured at grant date, with the subsequent cash payment debited directly to equity, as a distribution to equity participants.

BC115   Others who support exercise date measurement do not regard share option holders as part of the ownership group, and therefore believe that options should not be classified as equity. Option holders, some argue, are only potential owners of the entity. But it is not clear whether this view is held generally, ie applied to all types of options. For example, some who support exercise date measurement for employee share options do not necessarily advocate the same approach for share options or warrants issued for cash in the market. However, any revision to the definitions of liabilities and equity in the *Framework* would affect the classification of all options and warrants issued by the entity.

BC116   Given that there is more than one suggestion to change the definitions of liabilities and equity, and these suggestions have not been fully explored, it is not clear exactly what changes to the definitions are being proposed.

BC117   Moreover, the Board concluded that these suggestions should not be considered in isolation, because changing the distinction between liabilities and equity affects all sorts of financial interests, not just those relating to employee share plans. All of the implications of any suggested changes should be explored in a broader project to review the definitions of liabilities and equity in the *Framework*. If such a review resulted in changes to the definitions, the Board would then consider whether the IFRS on share-based payment should be revised.

BC118   Therefore, after considering the issues discussed above, the Board confirmed its conclusion that grant date is the appropriate date at which to measure the fair value of the equity instruments granted for the purposes of providing a surrogate measure of the fair value of services received from employees.

Share-based payment transactions with parties other than employees

BC119   In many share-based payment transactions with parties other than employees, it should be possible to measure reliably the fair value of the goods or services received. The Board therefore concluded that the IFRS should require an entity to presume that the fair value of the goods or services received can be measured reliably.[19] However, in rare cases in which the presumption is rebutted, it is necessary to measure the transaction at the fair value of the equity instruments granted.

BC120   Some measurement issues that arise in respect of share-based payment transactions with employees also arise in transactions with other parties. For example, there might be performance (ie vesting) conditions that must be met before the other party is entitled to the shares or share options. Therefore, any

---

19   ED 2 proposed that equity-settled share-based payment transactions should be measured at the fair value of the goods or services received, or by reference to the fair value of the equity instruments granted, whichever fair value is more readily determinable. For transactions with parties other than employees, ED 2 proposed that there should be a rebuttable presumption that the fair value of the goods or services received is the more readily determinable fair value. The Board reconsidered these proposed requirements when finalising the IFRS. It concluded that it would be more consistent with the primary accounting objective (explained in paragraphs BC64–BC66) to require equity-settled share-based payment transactions to be measured at the fair value of the goods or services received, unless that fair value cannot be estimated reliably (eg in transactions with employees). For transactions with parties other than employees, the Board concluded that, in many cases, it should be possible to measure reliably the fair value of the goods or services received, as noted above. Hence, the Board concluded that the IFRS should require an entity to presume that the fair value of the goods or services received can be measured reliably.

conclusions reached on how to treat vesting conditions in the context of share-based payment transactions with employees also apply to transactions with other parties.

BC121 Similarly, performance by the other party might take place over a period of time, rather than on one specific date, which again raises the question of the appropriate measurement date.

BC122 SFAS 123 does not specify a measurement date for share-based payment transactions with parties other than employees, on the grounds that this is usually a minor issue in such transactions. However, the date at which to estimate the fair value of equity instruments issued to parties other than employees is specified in the US interpretation EITF 96-18 *Accounting for Equity Instruments That Are Issued to Other Than Employees for Acquiring, or in Conjunction with Selling, Goods or Services*:

> [The measurement date is] the earlier of the following:
>
> (a)   The date at which a commitment for performance by the counterparty to earn the equity instruments is reached (a "performance commitment"), or
>
> (b)   The date at which the counterparty's performance is complete. (extract from Issue 1, footnotes excluded)

BC123 The second of these two dates corresponds to vesting date, because vesting date is when the other party has satisfied all the conditions necessary to become unconditionally entitled to the share options or shares. The first of the two dates does not necessarily correspond to grant date. For example, under an employee share plan, the employees are (usually) not committed to providing the necessary services, because they are usually able to leave at any time. Indeed, EITF 96-18 makes it clear that the fact that the equity instrument will be forfeited if the counterparty fails to perform is not sufficient evidence of a performance commitment (Issue 1, footnote 3). Therefore, in the context of share-based payment transactions with parties other than employees, if the other party is not committed to perform, there would be no performance commitment date, in which case the measurement date would be vesting date.

BC124 Accordingly, under SFAS 123 and EITF 96-18, the measurement date for share-based payment transactions with employees is grant date, but for transactions with other parties the measurement date could be vesting date, or some other date between grant date and vesting date.

BC125 In developing the proposals in ED 2, the Board concluded that for transactions with parties other than employees that are measured by reference to the fair value of the equity instruments granted, the equity instruments should be measured at grant date, the same as for transactions with employees.

BC126 However, the Board reconsidered this conclusion during its redeliberations of the proposals in ED 2. The Board considered whether the delivery (service) date fair value of the equity instruments granted provided a better surrogate measure of the fair value of the goods or services received from parties other than employees than the grant date fair value of those instruments. For example, some argue that if the counterparty is not firmly committed to delivering the goods or services, the counterparty would consider whether the fair value of the equity instruments at the delivery date is sufficient payment for the goods or services when deciding whether to deliver the goods or services. This suggests that there is a high correlation between the fair value of the equity instruments at the date the goods or services are received and the fair value of those goods or services. The Board noted that it had considered and rejected a similar argument in the context of transactions with employees (see paragraphs BC94 and BC95). However, the Board found the argument more compelling in the case of transactions with parties other than employees, particularly for transactions in which the counterparty delivers the goods or services on a single date (or over a short period of time) that is substantially later than grant date, compared with transactions with employees in which the services are received over a continuous period that typically begins on grant date.

BC127 The Board was also concerned that permitting entities to measure transactions with parties other than employees on the basis of the fair value of the equity instruments at grant date would provide opportunities for entities to structure transactions to achieve a particular accounting result, causing the carrying amount of the goods or services received, and the resulting expense for the consumption of those goods or services, to be understated.

BC128 The Board therefore concluded that for transactions with parties other than employees in which the entity cannot measure reliably the fair value of the goods or services received at the date of receipt, the fair value of those goods or services should be measured indirectly, based on the fair value of the equity instruments granted, measured at the date the goods or services are received.

Transactions in which the entity cannot identify specifically some or all of the goods or services received (paragraph 13A)[20]

BC128A The Board incorporated into IFRS 2 the consensus of IFRIC 8 in *Group Cash-settled Share-based Payment Transactions* issued in June 2009. This section summarises the IFRIC's considerations in reaching that consensus, as approved by the Board.

BC128B IFRS 2 presumes that the consideration received for share-based payments is consistent with the fair value of those share-based payments. For example, if the entity cannot estimate reliably the fair value of the goods or services received, paragraph 10 of the IFRS requires the entity to measure the fair value of the goods or services received by reference to the fair value of the share-based payment made to acquire those goods or services.

BC128C The Board noted that it is neither necessary nor appropriate to measure the fair value of goods or services as well as the fair value of the share-based payment for every transaction in which the entity receives goods or non-employee services. However, when the value of the identifiable consideration received appears to be less than the fair value of the share-based payment, measurement of both the goods or the services received and the share-based payment may be necessary in order to measure the value of the unidentifiable goods or services received.

BC128D Paragraph 13 of the IFRS stipulates a rebuttable presumption that the value of identifiable goods or services received can be reliably measured. The Board

---

20 Paragraphs BC128A–BC128H are added as a consequence of amendments to IFRS 2 *Group Cash-settled Share-based Payment Transactions* issued in June 2009.

noted that goods or services that are unidentifiable cannot be reliably measured and that this rebuttable presumption is relevant only for identifiable goods or services.

BC128E The Board noted that when the goods or services received are identifiable, the measurement principles in the IFRS should be applied. When the goods or services received are unidentifiable, the Board concluded that the grant date is the most appropriate date for the purposes of providing a surrogate measure of the value of the unidentifiable goods or services received (or to be received).

BC128F The Board noted that some transactions include identifiable and unidentifiable goods or services. In this case, it would be necessary to measure at the grant date the fair value of the unidentifiable goods or services received and to measure the value of the identifiable goods or services in accordance with the IFRS.

BC128G For cash-settled transactions in which unidentifiable goods or services are received, it is necessary to remeasure the liability at each subsequent reporting date in order to be consistent with the IFRS.

BC128H The Board noted that the IFRS's requirements in respect of the recognition of the expense arising from share-based payments would apply to identifiable and unidentifiable goods or services. Therefore, the Board decided not to issue additional guidance on this point.

Fair value of employee share options

BC129 The Board spent much time discussing how to measure the fair value of employee share options, including how to take into account common features of employee share options, such as vesting conditions and non-transferability. These discussions focused on measuring fair value at grant date, not only because the Board regarded grant date as the appropriate measurement date for transactions with employees, but also because more measurement issues arise at grant date than at later measurement dates. In reaching its conclusions in ED 2, the Board received assistance from the project's Advisory Group and from a panel of experts. During its redeliberations of the proposals in ED 2, the Board considered comments by respondents and advice received from valuation experts on the FASB's Option Valuation Group.

BC130 Market prices provide the best evidence of the fair value of share options. However, share options with terms and conditions similar to employee share options are seldom traded in the markets. The Board therefore concluded that, if market prices are not available, it will be necessary to apply an option pricing model to estimate the fair value of share options.

BC131 The Board decided that it is not necessary or appropriate to prescribe the precise formula or model to be used for option valuation. There is no particular option pricing model that is regarded as theoretically superior to the others, and there is the risk that any model specified might be superseded by improved methodologies in the future. Entities should select whichever model is most appropriate in the circumstances. For example, many employee share options have long lives, are usually exercisable during the period between vesting date and the end of the option's life, and are often exercised early. These factors should be considered when estimating the grant date fair value of share options. For many entities, this might preclude the use of the Black-Scholes-Merton formula, which does not take into account the possibility of exercise before the end of the share option's life and may not adequately reflect the effects of expected early exercise. This is discussed further below (paragraphs BC160–BC162).

BC132   All option pricing models take into account the following option features:

- the exercise price of the option

- the current market price of the share

- the expected volatility of the share price

- the dividends expected to be paid on the shares

- the rate of interest available in the market

- the term of the option.

BC133   The first two items define the intrinsic value of a share option; the remaining four are relevant to the share option's time value. Expected volatility, dividends and interest rate are all based on expectations over the option term. Therefore, the option term is an important part of calculating time value, because it affects the other inputs.

BC134   One aspect of time value is the value of the right to participate in future gains, if any. The valuation does not attempt to predict what the future gain will be, only the amount that a buyer would pay at the valuation date to obtain the right to participate in any future gains. In other words, option pricing models estimate the value of the share option at the measurement date, not the value of the underlying share at some future date.

BC135   The Board noted that some argue that any estimate of the fair value of a share option is inherently uncertain, because it is not known what the ultimate outcome will be, eg whether the share option will expire worthless or whether the employee (or other party) will make a large gain on exercise. However, the valuation objective is to measure the fair value of the rights granted, not to predict the outcome of having granted those rights. Hence, irrespective of whether the option expires worthless or the employee makes a large gain on exercise, that outcome does not mean that the grant date estimate of the fair value of the option was unreliable or wrong.

BC136   A similar analysis applies to the argument that share options do not have any value until they are in the money, ie the share price is greater than the exercise price. This argument refers to the share option's intrinsic value only. Share options also have a time value, which is why they are traded in the markets at prices greater than their intrinsic value. The option holder has a valuable right to participate in any future increases in the share price. So even share options that are at the money have a value when granted. The subsequent outcome of that option grant, even if it expires worthless, does not change the fact that the share option had a value at grant date.

Application of option pricing models to unlisted and newly listed entities

BC137   As explained above, two of the inputs to an option pricing model are the entity's share price and the expected volatility of its share price. For an unlisted entity, there is no published share price information. The entity would therefore need to estimate the fair value of its shares (eg based on the share price of similar entities that are listed, or on a net assets or earnings basis). It would also need to estimate the expected volatility of that value.

BC138   The Board considered whether unlisted entities should be permitted to use the minimum value method instead of a fair value measurement method. The minimum value method is explained earlier, in paragraphs BC80–BC83. Because it excludes the effects of expected volatility, the minimum value method produces a value that is lower, often much lower, than that produced by methods designed to estimate the fair value of an option. Therefore, the Board discussed how an unlisted entity could estimate expected volatility.

BC139   An unlisted entity that regularly issues share options or shares to employees (or other parties) might have an internal market for its shares. The volatility of the internal market share prices provides a basis for estimating expected volatility. Alternatively, an entity could use the historical or implied volatility of similar entities that are listed, and for which share price or option price information is available, as the basis for an estimate of expected volatility. This would be appropriate if the entity has estimated the value of its shares by reference to the share prices of these similar listed entities. If the entity has instead used another methodology to value its shares, the entity could derive an estimate of expected volatility consistent with that methodology. For example, the entity might value its shares on the basis of net asset values or earnings, in which case it could use the expected volatility of those net asset values or earnings as a basis for estimating expected share price volatility.

BC140   The Board acknowledged that these approaches for estimating the expected volatility of an unlisted entity's shares are somewhat subjective. However, the Board thought it likely that, in practice, the application of these approaches would result in underestimates of expected volatility, rather than overestimates, because entities were likely to exercise caution in making such estimates, to ensure that the resulting option values are not overstated. Therefore, estimating expected volatility is likely to produce a more reliable measure of the fair value of share options granted by unlisted entities than an alternative valuation method, such as the minimum value method.

BC141   Newly listed entities would not need to estimate their share price. However, like unlisted entities, newly listed entities could have difficulties in estimating expected volatility when valuing share options, because they might not have sufficient historical share price information upon which to base an estimate of expected volatility.

BC142   SFAS 123 requires such entities to consider the historical volatility of similar entities during a comparable period in their lives:

> For example, an entity that has been publicly traded for only one year that grants options with an average expected life of five years might consider the pattern and level of historical volatility of more mature entities in the same industry for the first six years the stock of those entities were publicly traded. (paragraph 285b)

BC143　The Board concluded that, in general, unlisted and newly listed entities should not be exempt from a requirement to apply fair value measurement and that the IFRS should include implementation guidance on estimating expected volatility for the purposes of applying an option pricing model to share options granted by unlisted and newly listed entities.

BC144　However, the Board acknowledged that there might be some instances in which an entity—such as (but not limited to) an unlisted or newly listed entity—cannot estimate reliably the grant date fair value of share options granted. In this situation, the Board concluded that the entity should measure the share option at its intrinsic value, initially at the date the entity obtains the goods or the counterparty renders service and subsequently at each reporting date until the final settlement of the share-based payment arrangement, with the effects of the remeasurement recognised in profit or loss. For a grant of share options, the share-based payment arrangement is finally settled when the options are exercised, forfeited (eg upon cessation of employment) or lapse (eg at the end of the option's life). For a grant of shares, the share-based payment arrangement is finally settled when the shares vest or are forfeited.

Application of option pricing models to employee share options

BC145　Option pricing models are widely used in, and accepted by, the financial markets. However, there are differences between employee share options and traded share options. The Board considered the valuation implications of these differences, with assistance from its Advisory Group and other experts, including experts in the FASB's Option Valuation Group, and comments made by respondents to ED 2. Employee share options usually differ from traded options in the following ways, which are discussed further below:

(a)　there is a vesting period, during which time the share options are not exercisable;

(b)　the options are non-transferable;

(c)　there are conditions attached to vesting which, if not satisfied, cause the options to be forfeited; and

(d)　the option term is significantly longer.

Inability to exercise during the vesting period

BC146　Typically, employee share options have a vesting period, during which the options cannot be exercised. For example, a share option might be granted with a ten-year life and a vesting period of three years, so the option is not exercisable for the first three years and can then be exercised at any time during the remaining seven years. Employee share options cannot be exercised during the vesting period because the employees must first 'pay' for the options, by providing the necessary services. Furthermore, there might be other specified periods during which an employee share option cannot be exercised (eg during a closed period).

BC147 In the finance literature, employee share options are sometimes called Bermudian options, being partly European and partly American. An American share option can be exercised at any time during the option's life, whereas a European share option can be exercised only at the end of the option's life. An American share option is more valuable than a European share option, although the difference in value is not usually significant.

BC148 Therefore, other things being equal, an employee share option would have a higher value than a European share option and a lower value than an American share option, but the difference between the three values is unlikely to be significant.

BC149 If the entity uses the Black-Scholes-Merton formula, or another option pricing model that values European share options, there is no need to adjust the model for the inability to exercise an option in the vesting period (or any other period), because the model already assumes that the option cannot be exercised during that period.

BC150 If the entity uses an option pricing model that values American share options, such as the binomial model, the inability to exercise an option during the vesting period can be taken into account in applying such a model.

BC151 Although the inability to exercise the share option during the vesting period does not, in itself, have a significant effect on the value of the option, there is still the question whether this restriction has an effect when combined with non-transferability. This is discussed in the following section.

BC152 The Board therefore concluded that:

(a) if the entity uses an option pricing model that values European share options, such as the Black-Scholes-Merton formula, no adjustment is required for the inability to exercise the options during the vesting period, because the model already assumes that they cannot be exercised during that period.

(b) if the entity uses an option pricing model that values American share options, such as a binomial model, the application of the model should take account of the inability to exercise the options during the vesting period.

Non-transferability

BC153 From the option holder's perspective, the inability to transfer a share option limits the opportunities available when the option has some time yet to run and the holder wishes either to terminate the exposure to future price changes or to liquidate the position. For example, the holder might believe that over the remaining term of the share option the share price is more likely to decrease than to increase. Also, employee share option plans typically require employees to exercise vested options within a fixed period of time after the employee leaves the entity, or to forfeit the options.

BC154   In the case of a conventional share option, the holder would sell the option rather than exercise it and then sell the shares. Selling the share option enables the holder to receive the option's fair value, including both its intrinsic value and remaining time value, whereas exercising the option enables the holder to receive intrinsic value only.

BC155   However, the option holder is not able to sell a non-transferable share option. Usually, the only possibility open to the option holder is to exercise it, which entails forgoing the remaining time value. (This is not always true. The use of other derivatives, in effect, to sell or gain protection from future changes in the value of the option is discussed later.)

BC156   At first sight, the inability to transfer a share option could seem irrelevant from the entity's perspective, because the entity must issue shares at the exercise price upon exercise of the option, no matter who holds it. In other words, from the entity's perspective, its commitments under the contract are unaffected by whether the shares are issued to the original option holder or to someone else. Therefore, in valuing the entity's side of the contract, from the entity's perspective, non-transferability seems irrelevant.

BC157   However, the lack of transferability often results in early exercise of the share option, because that is the only way for the employees to liquidate their position. Therefore, by imposing the restriction on transferability, the entity has caused the option holder to exercise the option early, thereby resulting in the loss of time value. For example, one aspect of time value is the value of the right to defer payment of the exercise price until the end of the option term. If the option is exercised early because of non-transferability, the entity receives the exercise price much earlier than it would otherwise have done.

BC158   Non-transferability is not the only reason why employees might exercise share options early. Other reasons include risk aversion, lack of wealth diversification, and termination of employment (typically, employees must exercise vested options soon after termination of employment; otherwise the options are forfeited).

BC159   Recent accounting standards and proposed standards (including ED 2) address the issue of early exercise by requiring the expected life of a non-transferable share option to be used in valuing it, rather than the contractual option term. Expected life can be estimated either for the entire share option plan or for subgroups of employees participating in the plan. The estimate takes into account factors such as the length of the vesting period, the average length of time similar options have remained outstanding in the past and the expected volatility of the underlying shares.

BC160   However, comments from respondents to ED 2 and advice received from valuation experts during the Board's redeliberations led the Board to conclude that using a single expected life as an input into an option pricing model (eg the Black-Scholes-Merton formula) was not the best solution for reflecting in the share option valuation the effects of early exercise. For example, such an approach does not take into account the correlation between the share price and early exercise. It would also mean that the share option valuation does not take into account the possibility that the option might be exercised at a date that is later than the end of its expected life. Therefore, in many instances, a more flexible model, such as a binomial model, that uses the share option's contractual life as an input and takes into account the possibility of early exercise on a range of different dates in the option's life, allowing for factors such as the correlation between the share price and early exercise and expected employee turnover, is likely to produce a more accurate estimate of the option's fair value.

BC161   Binomial lattice and similar option pricing models also have the advantage of permitting the inputs to the model to vary over the share option's life. For example, instead of using a single expected volatility, a binomial lattice or similar option pricing model can allow for the possibility that volatility might change over the share option's life. This would be particularly appropriate when valuing share options granted by entities experiencing higher than usual volatility, because volatility tends to revert to its mean over time.

BC162   For these reasons, the Board considered whether it should require the use of a more flexible model, rather than the more commonly used Black-Scholes-Merton formula. However, the Board concluded that it was not necessary to prohibit the use of the Black-Scholes-Merton formula, because there might be instances in which the formula produces a sufficiently reliable estimate of the fair value of the share options granted. For example, if the entity has not granted many share options, the effects of applying a more flexible model might not have a material impact on the entity's financial statements. Also, for share options with relatively short contractual lives, or share options that must be exercised within a short period of time after vesting date, the issues discussed in paragraph BC160 may not be relevant, and hence the Black-Scholes-Merton formula may produce a value that is substantially the same as that produced by a more flexible option pricing model. Therefore, rather than prohibit the use of the Black-Scholes-Merton formula, the Board concluded that the IFRS should include guidance on selecting the most appropriate model to apply. This includes the requirement that the entity should consider factors that knowledgeable, willing market participants would consider in selecting the option pricing model to apply.

BC163   Although non-transferability often results in the early exercise of employee share options, some employees can mitigate the effects of non-transferability, because they are able, in effect, to sell the options or protect themselves from future changes in the value of the options by selling or buying other derivatives. For example, the employee might be able, in effect, to sell an employee share option by entering into an arrangement with an investment bank whereby the employee sells a similar call option to the bank, ie an option with the same exercise price and term. A zero-cost collar is one means of obtaining protection from changes in the value of an employee share option, by selling a call option and buying a put option.

BC164   However, it appears that such arrangements are not always available. For example, the amounts involved have to be sufficiently large to make it worthwhile for the investment bank, which would probably exclude many employees (unless a collective arrangement was made). Also, it appears that investment banks are unlikely to enter into such an arrangement unless the entity is a top listed company, with shares traded in a deep and active market, to enable the investment bank to hedge its own position.

BC165 It would not be feasible to stipulate in an accounting standard that an adjustment to take account of non-transferability is necessary only if the employees cannot mitigate the effects of non-transferability through the use of other derivatives. However, using expected life as an input into an option pricing model, or modelling early exercise in a binomial or similar model, copes with both situations. If employees were able to mitigate the effects of non-transferability by using derivatives, this would often result in the employee share options being exercised later than they would otherwise have been. By taking this factor into account, the estimated fair value of the share option would be higher, which makes sense, given that non-transferability is not a constraint in this case. If the employees cannot mitigate the effects of non-transferability through the use of derivatives, they are likely to exercise the share options much earlier than is optimal. In this case, allowing for the effects of early exercise would significantly reduce the estimated value of the share option.

BC166 This still leaves the question whether there is a need for further adjustment for the combined effect of being unable to exercise or transfer the share option during the vesting period. In other words, the inability to exercise a share option does not, in itself, appear to have a significant effect on its value. But if the share option cannot be transferred and cannot be exercised, and assuming that other derivatives are not available, the holder is unable to extract value from the share option or protect its value during the vesting period.

BC167 However, it should be noted why these restrictions are in place: the employee has not yet 'paid' for the share option by providing the required services (and fulfilling any other performance conditions). The employee cannot exercise or transfer a share option to which he/she is not yet entitled. The share option will either vest or fail to vest, depending on whether the vesting conditions are satisfied. The possibility of forfeiture resulting from failure to fulfil the vesting conditions is taken into account through the application of the modified grant date method (discussed in paragraphs BC170–BC184).

BC168 Moreover, for accounting purposes, the objective is to estimate the fair value of the share option, not the value from the employee's perspective. The fair value of any item depends on the expected amounts, timing, and uncertainty of the future cash flows relating to the item. The share option grant gives the employee the right to subscribe to the entity's shares at the exercise price, provided that the vesting conditions are satisfied and the exercise price is paid during the specified period. The effect of the vesting conditions is considered below. The effect of the share option being non-exercisable during the vesting period has already been considered above, as has the effect of non-transferability. There does not seem to be any additional effect on the expected amounts, timing or uncertainty of the future cash flows arising from the combination of non-exercisability and non-transferability during the vesting period.

BC169 After considering all of the above points, the Board concluded that the effects of early exercise, because of non-transferability and other factors, should be taken into account when estimating the fair value of the share option, either by modelling early exercise in a binomial or similar model, or using expected life rather than contracted life as an input into an option pricing model, such as the Black-Scholes-Merton formula.

Vesting conditions

BC170   Employee share options usually have vesting conditions. The most common condition is that the employee must remain in the entity's employ for a specified period, say three years. If the employee leaves during that period, the options are forfeited. There might also be other performance conditions, eg that the entity achieves a specified growth in share price or earnings.

BC171   Vesting conditions ensure that the employees provide the services required to 'pay' for their share options. For example, the usual reason for imposing service conditions is to retain staff; the usual reason for imposing other performance conditions is to provide an incentive for the employees to work towards specified performance targets.

BC171A   In 2005 the Board decided to take on a project to clarify the definition of vesting conditions and the accounting treatment of cancellations. In particular, the Board noted that it is important to distinguish between non-vesting conditions, which need to be satisfied for the counterparty to become entitled to the equity instrument, and vesting conditions such as performance conditions. In February 2006 the Board published an exposure draft *Vesting Conditions and Cancellations*, which proposed to restrict vesting conditions to service conditions and performance conditions. Those are the only conditions that determine whether *the entity receives the services* that entitle the counterparty to the share-based payment, and therefore whether the share-based payment vests. In particular, a share-based payment may vest even if some non-vesting conditions have not been met. The feature that distinguishes a performance condition from a non-vesting condition is that the former has an explicit or implicit service requirement and the latter does not.

BC171B   In general, respondents to the exposure draft agreed with the Board's proposals but asked for clarification of whether particular restrictive conditions, such as 'non-compete provisions', are vesting conditions. The Board noted that a share-based payment vests when the counterparty's entitlement to it is no longer conditional on future service or performance conditions. Therefore, conditions such as non-compete provisions and transfer restrictions, which apply after the counterparty has become entitled to the share-based payment, are not vesting conditions. The Board revised the definition of 'vest' accordingly.

BC172   Some argue that the existence of vesting conditions does not necessarily imply that the value of employee share options is significantly less than the value of traded share options. The employees have to satisfy the vesting conditions to fulfil their side of the arrangement. In other words, the employees' performance of their side of the arrangement is what they do to pay for their share options. Employees do not pay for the options with cash, as do the holders of traded share options; they pay with their services. Having to pay for the share options does not make them less valuable. On the contrary, it proves that the share options are valuable.

BC173　Others argue that the possibility of forfeiture without compensation for part-performance suggests that the share options are less valuable. The employees might partly perform their side of the arrangement, eg by working for part of the period, then have to leave for some reason, and forfeit the share options without compensation for that part performance. If there are other performance conditions, such as achieving a specified growth in the share price or earnings, the employees might work for the entire vesting period, but fail to meet the vesting conditions and therefore forfeit the share options.

BC174　Similarly, some argue that the entity would take into account the possibility of forfeiture when entering into the agreement at grant date. In other words, in deciding how many share options to grant in total, the entity would allow for expected forfeitures. Hence, if the objective is to estimate at grant date the fair value of the entity's commitments under the share option agreement, that valuation should take into account that the entity's commitment to fulfil its side of the option agreement is conditional upon the vesting conditions being satisfied.

BC175　In developing the proposals in ED 2, the Board concluded that the valuation of rights to share options or shares granted to employees (or other parties) should take into account all types of vesting conditions, including both service conditions and performance conditions. In other words, the grant date valuation should be reduced to allow for the possibility of forfeiture due to failure to satisfy the vesting conditions.

BC176　Such a reduction might be achieved by adapting an option pricing model to incorporate vesting conditions. Alternatively, a more simplistic approach might be applied. One such approach is to estimate the possibility of forfeiture at grant date, and reduce the value produced by an option pricing model accordingly. For example, if the valuation calculated using an option pricing model was CU15, and the entity estimated that 20 per cent of the share options would be forfeited because of failure to satisfy the vesting conditions, allowing for the possibility of forfeiture would reduce the grant date value of each option granted from CU15 to CU12.

BC177　The Board decided against proposing detailed guidance on how the grant date value should be adjusted to allow for the possibility of forfeiture. This is consistent with the Board's objective of setting principles-based standards. The measurement objective is to estimate fair value. That objective might not be achieved if detailed, prescriptive rules were specified, which would probably become outdated by future developments in valuation methodologies.

BC178　However, respondents to ED 2 raised a variety of concerns about the inclusion of vesting conditions in the grant date valuation. Some respondents were concerned about the practicality and subjectivity of including non-market performance conditions in the share option valuation. Some were also concerned about the practicality of including service conditions in the grant date valuation, particularly in conjunction with the units of service method proposed in ED 2 (discussed further in paragraphs BC203–BC217).

BC179　Some respondents suggested the alternative approach applied in SFAS 123, referred to as the modified grant date method. Under this method, service conditions and non-market performance conditions are excluded from the grant date valuation (ie the possibility of forfeiture is not taken into account when estimating the grant date fair value of the share options or other equity instruments, thereby producing a higher grant date fair value), but are instead taken into account by requiring the transaction amount to be based on the number of equity instruments that eventually vest. Under this method, on a cumulative basis, no amount is recognised for goods or services received if the equity instruments granted do not vest because of failure to satisfy a vesting condition (other than a market condition), eg the counterparty fails to complete a specified service period, or a performance condition (other than a market condition) is not satisfied.

BC180   After considering respondents' comments and obtaining further advice from valuation experts, the Board decided to adopt the modified grant date method applied in SFAS 123. However, the Board decided that it should not permit the choice available in SFAS 123 to account for the effects of expected or actual forfeitures of share options or other equity instruments because of failure to satisfy a service condition. For a grant of equity instruments with a service condition, SFAS 123 permits an entity to choose at grant date to recognise the services received based on an estimate of the number of share options or other equity instruments expected to vest, and to revise that estimate, if necessary, if subsequent information indicates that actual forfeitures are likely to differ from previous estimates. Alternatively, an entity may begin recognising the services received as if all the equity instruments granted that are subject to a service requirement are expected to vest. The effects of forfeitures are then recognised when those forfeitures occur, by reversing any amounts previously recognised for services received as consideration for equity instruments that are forfeited.

BC181   The Board decided that the latter method should not be permitted. Given that the transaction amount is ultimately based on the number of equity instruments that vest, it is appropriate to estimate the number of expected forfeitures when recognising the services received during the vesting period. Furthermore, by ignoring expected forfeitures until those forfeitures occur, the effects of reversing any amounts previously recognised might result in a distortion of remuneration expense recognised during the vesting period. For example, an entity that experiences a high level of forfeitures might recognise a large amount of remuneration expense in one period, which is then reversed in a later period.

BC182   Therefore, the Board decided that the IFRS should require an entity to estimate the number of equity instruments expected to vest and to revise that estimate, if necessary, if subsequent information indicates that actual forfeitures are likely to differ from previous estimates.

BC183   Under SFAS 123, market conditions (eg a condition involving a target share price, or specified amount of intrinsic value on which vesting or exercisability is conditioned) are included in the grant date valuation, without subsequent reversal. That is to say, when estimating the fair value of the equity instruments at grant date, the entity takes into account the possibility that the market condition may not be satisfied. Having allowed for that possibility in the grant date valuation of the equity instruments, no adjustment is made to the number of equity instruments included in the calculation of the transaction amount, irrespective of the outcome of the market condition. In other words, the entity recognises the goods or services received from a counterparty that satisfies all other vesting conditions (eg services received from an employee who remains in service for the specified service period), irrespective of whether that market condition is satisfied. The treatment of market conditions therefore contrasts with the treatment of other types of vesting conditions. As explained in paragraph BC179, under the modified grant date method, vesting conditions are not taken into account when estimating the fair value of the equity instruments at grant date, but are instead taken into account by requiring the transaction amount to be based on the number of equity instruments that eventually vest.

BC184   The Board considered whether it should apply the same approach to market conditions as is applied in SFAS 123. It might be argued that it is not appropriate to distinguish between market conditions and other types of performance conditions, because to do so could create opportunities for arbitrage, or cause an economic distortion by encouraging entities to favour one type of performance condition over another. However, the Board noted that it is not clear what the result would be. On the one hand, some entities might prefer the 'truing up' aspect of the modified grant date method, because it permits a reversal of remuneration expense if the condition is not met. On the other hand, if the performance condition is met, and it has not been incorporated into the grant date valuation (as is the case when the modified grant date method is used), the expense will be higher than it would otherwise have been (ie if the performance condition had been incorporated into the grant date valuation). Furthermore, some entities might prefer to avoid the potential volatility caused by the truing up mechanism. Therefore, it is not clear whether having a different treatment for market and non-market performance conditions will necessarily cause entities to favour market conditions over non-market performance conditions, or vice versa. Furthermore, the practical difficulties that led the Board to conclude that non-market performance conditions should be dealt with via the modified grant date method rather than being included in the grant date valuation do not apply to market conditions, because market conditions can be incorporated into option pricing models. Moreover, it is difficult to distinguish between market conditions, such as a target share price, and the market condition that is inherent in the option itself, ie that the option will be exercised only if the share price on the date of exercise exceeds the exercise price. For these reasons, the Board concluded that the IFRS should apply the same approach as is applied in SFAS 123.

Option term

BC185   Employee share options often have a long contractual life, eg ten years. Traded options typically have short lives, often only a few months. Estimating the inputs required by an option pricing model, such as expected volatility, over long periods can be difficult, giving rise to the possibility of significant estimation error. This is not usually a problem with traded share options, given their much shorter lives.

BC186   However, some share options traded over the counter have long lives, such as ten or fifteen years. Option pricing models are used to value them. Therefore, contrary to the argument sometimes advanced, option pricing models can be (and are being) applied to long-lived share options.

BC187　Moreover, the potential for estimation error is mitigated by using a binomial or similar model that allows for changes in model inputs over the share option's life, such as expected volatility, and interest and dividend rates, that could occur and the probability of those changes occurring during the term of the share option. The potential for estimation error is further mitigated by taking into account the possibility of early exercise, either by using expected life rather than contracted life as an input into an option pricing model or by modelling exercise behaviour in a binomial or similar model, because this reduces the expected term of the share option. Because employees often exercise their share options relatively early in the share option's life, the expected term is usually much shorter than contracted life.

Other features of employee share options

BC188　Whilst the features discussed above are common to most employee share options, some might include other features. For example, some share options have a reload feature. This entitles the employee to automatic grants of additional share options whenever he/she exercises previously granted share options and pays the exercise price in the entity's shares rather than in cash. Typically, the employee is granted a new share option, called a reload option, for each share surrendered when exercising the previous share option. The exercise price of the reload option is usually set at the market price of the shares on the date the reload option is granted.

BC189　When SFAS 123 was developed, the FASB concluded that, ideally, the value of the reload feature should be included in the valuation of the original share option at grant date. However, at that time the FASB believed that it was not possible to do so. Accordingly, SFAS 123 does not require the reload feature to be included in the grant date valuation of the original share option. Instead, reload options granted upon exercise of the original share options are accounted for as a new share option grant.

BC190　However, recent academic research indicates that it is possible to value the reload feature at grant date, eg Saly, Jagannathan and Huddart (1999).[21] However, if significant uncertainties exist, such as the number and timing of expected grants of reload options, it might not be practicable to include the reload feature in the grant date valuation.

BC191　When it developed ED 2, the Board concluded that the reload feature should be taken into account, where practicable, when measuring the fair value of the share options granted. However, if the reload feature was not taken into account, then when the reload option is granted, it should be accounted for as a new share option grant.

BC192　Many respondents to ED 2 agreed with the proposals in ED 2. However, some disagreed. For example, some disagreed with there being a choice of treatments. Some respondents supported always treating reload options granted as new

---

21　P J Saly, R Jagannathan and S J Huddart. 1999. Valuing the Reload Features of Executive Stock Options. *Accounting Horizons* 13 (3): 219–240.

grants whereas others supported always including the reload feature in the grant date valuation. Some expressed concerns about the practicality of including the reload feature in the grant date valuation. After reconsidering this issue, the Board concluded that the reload feature should not be included in the grant date valuation and therefore all reload options granted should be accounted for as new share option grants.

BC193   There may be other features of employee (and other) share options that the Board has not yet considered. But even if the Board were to consider every conceivable feature of employee (and other) share options that exist at present, new features might be developed in the future.

BC194   The Board therefore concluded that the IFRS should focus on setting out clear principles to be applied to share-based payment transactions, and provide guidance on the more common features of employee share options, but should not prescribe extensive application guidance, which would be likely to become outdated.

BC195   Nevertheless, the Board considered whether there are share options with such unusual or complex features that it is too difficult to make a reliable estimate of their fair value and, if so, what the accounting treatment should be.

BC196   SFAS 123 states that 'it should be possible to reasonably estimate the fair value of most stock options and other equity instruments at the date they are granted' (paragraph 21). However, it states that, 'in unusual circumstances, the terms of the stock option or other equity instrument may make it virtually impossible to reasonably estimate the instrument's fair value at the date it is granted'. The standard requires that, in such situations, measurement should be delayed until it is possible to estimate reasonably the instrument's fair value. It notes that this is likely to be the date at which the number of shares to which the employee is entitled and the exercise price are determinable. This could be vesting date. The standard requires that estimates of compensation expense for earlier periods (ie until it is possible to estimate fair value) should be based on current intrinsic value.

BC197   The Board thought it unlikely that entities could not reasonably determine the fair value of share options at grant date, particularly after excluding vesting conditions[22] and reload features from the grant date valuation. The share options form part of the employee's remuneration package, and it seems reasonable to presume that an entity's management would consider the value of the share options to satisfy itself that the employee's remuneration package is fair and reasonable.

BC198   When it developed ED 2, the Board concluded that there should be no exceptions to the requirement to apply a fair value measurement basis, and therefore it was not necessary to include in the proposed IFRS specific accounting requirements for share options that are difficult to value.

BC199   However, after considering respondents' comments, particularly with regard to unlisted entities, the Board reconsidered this issue. The Board concluded that, in rare cases only, in which the entity could not estimate reliably the grant date

---

22   ie vesting conditions other than market conditions.

fair value of the equity instruments granted, the entity should measure the equity instruments at intrinsic value, initially at grant date and subsequently at each reporting date until the final settlement of the share-based payment arrangement, with the effects of the remeasurement recognised in profit or loss. For a grant of share options, the share-based payment arrangement is finally settled when the share options are exercised, are forfeited (eg upon cessation of employment) or lapse (eg at the end of the option's life). For a grant of shares, the share-based payment arrangement is finally settled when the shares vest or are forfeited. This requirement would apply to all entities, including listed and unlisted entities.

Recognition and measurement of services received in an equity-settled share-based payment transaction

During the vesting period

BC200   In an equity-settled share-based payment transaction, the accounting objective is to recognise the goods or services received as consideration for the entity's equity instruments, measured at the fair value of those goods or services when received. For transactions in which the entity receives employee services, it is often difficult to measure directly the fair value of the services received. In this case, the Board concluded that the fair value of the equity instruments granted should be used as a surrogate measure of the fair value of the services received. This raises the question how to use that surrogate measure to derive an amount to attribute to the services received. Another related question is how the entity should determine when the services are received.

BC201   Starting with the latter question, some argue that shares or share options are often granted to employees for past services rather than future services, or mostly for past services, irrespective of whether the employees are required to continue working for the entity for a specified future period before their rights to those shares or share options vest. Conversely, some argue that shares or share options granted provide a future incentive to the employees and those incentive effects continue after vesting date, which implies that the entity receives services from employees during a period that extends beyond vesting date. For share options in particular, some argue that employees render services beyond vesting date, because employees are able to benefit from an option's time value between vesting date and exercise date only if they continue to work for the entity (since usually a departing employee must exercise the share options within a short period, otherwise they are forfeited).

BC202   However, the Board concluded that if the employees are required to complete a specified service period to become entitled to the shares or share options, this requirement provides the best evidence of when the employees render services in return for the shares or share options. Consequently, the Board concluded that the entity should presume that the services are received during the vesting period. If the shares or share options vest immediately, it should be presumed that the entity has already received the services, in the absence of evidence to the contrary. An example of when immediately vested shares or share options are not for past services is when the employee concerned has only recently begun working for the entity, and the shares or share options are granted as a signing bonus. But in this situation, it might nevertheless be necessary to recognise an expense immediately, if the future employee services do not meet the definition of an asset.

BC203 Returning to the first question in paragraph BC200, when the Board developed ED 2 it developed an approach whereby the fair value of the shares or share options granted, measured at grant date and allowing for all vesting conditions, is divided by the number of units of service expected to be received to determine the deemed fair value of each unit of service subsequently received.

BC204 For example, suppose that the fair value of share options granted, before taking into account the possibility of forfeiture, is CU750,000. Suppose that the entity estimates the possibility of forfeiture because of failure of the employees to complete the required three-year period of service is 20 per cent (based on a weighted average probability), and hence it estimates the fair value of the options granted at CU600,000 (CU750,000 × 80%). The entity expects to receive 1,350 units of service over the three-year vesting period.

BC205 Under the units of service method proposed in ED 2, the deemed fair value per unit of service subsequently received is CU444.44 (CU600,000/1,350). If everything turns out as expected, the amount recognised for services received is CU600,000 (CU444.44 × 1,350).

BC206 This approach is based on the presumption that there is a fairly bargained contract at grant date. Thus the entity has granted share options valued at CU600,000 and expects to receive services valued at CU600,000 in return. It does not expect all share options granted to vest because it does not expect all employees to complete three years' service. Expectations of forfeiture because of employee departures are taken into account when estimating the fair value of the share options granted, and when determining the fair value of the services to be received in return.

BC207 Under the units of service method, the amount recognised for services received during the vesting period might exceed CU600,000, if the entity receives more services than expected. This is because the objective is to account for the services subsequently received, not the fair value of the share options granted. In other words, the objective is not to estimate the fair value of the share options granted and then spread that amount over the vesting period. Rather, the objective is to account for the services subsequently received, because it is the receipt of those services that causes a change in net assets and hence a change in equity. Because of the practical difficulty of valuing those services directly, the fair value of the share options granted is used as a surrogate measure to determine the fair value of each unit of service subsequently received, and therefore the transaction amount is dependent upon the number of units of service actually received. If more are received than expected, the transaction amount will be greater than CU600,000. If fewer services are received, the transaction amount will be less than CU600,000.

BC208 Hence, a grant date measurement method is used as a practical expedient to achieve the accounting objective, which is to account for the services actually received in the vesting period. The Board noted that many who support grant date measurement do so for reasons that focus on the entity's commitments under the contract, not the services received. They take the view that the entity has conveyed to its employees valuable equity instruments at grant date and that the accounting objective should be to account for the equity instruments conveyed. Similarly, supporters of vesting date measurement argue that the entity does not convey valuable equity instruments to the employees until vesting date, and that the accounting objective should be to account for the equity instruments conveyed at vesting date. Supporters of exercise date measurement argue that, ultimately, the valuable equity instruments conveyed by the entity to the employees are the shares issued on exercise date and the objective should be to account for the value given up by the entity by issuing equity instruments at less than their fair value.

BC209   Hence all of these arguments for various measurement dates are focused entirely on what the entity (or its shareholders) has given up under the share-based payment arrangement, and accounting for that sacrifice. Therefore, if 'grant date measurement' were applied as a matter of principle, the primary objective would be to account for the value of the rights granted. Depending on whether the services have already been received and whether a prepayment for services to be received in the future meets the definition of an asset, the other side of the transaction would either be recognised as an expense at grant date, or capitalised as a prepayment and amortised over some period of time, such as over the vesting period or over the expected life of the share option. Under this view of grant date measurement, there would be no subsequent adjustment for actual outcomes. No matter how many share options vest or how many share options are exercised, that does not change the value of the rights given to the employees at grant date.

BC210   Therefore, the reason why some support grant date measurement differs from the reason why the Board concluded that the fair value of the equity instruments granted should be measured at grant date. This means that some will have different views about the consequences of applying grant date measurement. Because the units of service method is based on using the fair value of the equity instruments granted, measured at grant date, as a surrogate measure of the fair value of the services received, the total transaction amount is dependent upon the number of units of service received.

BC211   Some respondents to ED 2 disagreed with the units of service method in principle, because they did not accept that the fair value of the services received should be the accounting focus. Rather, the respondents focused on accounting for the 'cost' of the equity instruments issued (ie the credit side of the transaction rather than the debit side), and took the view that if the share options or shares are forfeited, no cost was incurred, and thus any amounts recognised previously should be reversed, as would happen with a cash-settled transaction.

BC212   Some respondents also disagreed with the treatment of performance conditions under the units of service method, because if the employee completes the required service period but the equity instruments do not vest because of the performance condition not being satisfied, there is no reversal of amounts recognised during the vesting period. Some argue that this result is unreasonable because, if the performance condition is not satisfied, then the employee did not perform as required, hence it is inappropriate to recognise an expense for services received or consumed, because the entity did not receive the specified services.

BC213 The Board considered and rejected the above arguments made against the units of service method in principle. For example, the Board noted that the objective of accounting for the services received, rather than the cost of the equity instruments issued, is consistent with the accounting treatment of other issues of equity instruments, and with the IASB *Framework*. With regard to performance conditions, the Board noted that the strength of the argument in paragraph BC212 depends on the extent to which the employee has control or influence over the achievement of the performance target. One cannot necessarily conclude that the non-attainment of the performance target is a good indication that the employee has failed to perform his/her side of the arrangement (ie failed to provide services).

BC214 Therefore, the Board was not persuaded by those respondents who disagreed with the units of service method in principle. However, the Board also noted that some respondents raised practical concerns about the method. Some respondents regarded the units of service method as too complex and burdensome to apply in practice. For example, if an entity granted share options to a group of employees but did not grant the same number of share options to each employee (eg the number might vary according to their salary or position in the entity), it would be necessary to calculate a different deemed fair value per unit of service for each individual employee (or for each subgroup of employees, if there are groups of employees who each received the same number of options). Then the entity would have to track each employee, to calculate the amount to recognise for each employee. Furthermore, in some circumstances, an employee share or share option scheme might not require the employee to forfeit the shares or share options if the employee leaves during the vesting period in specified circumstances. Under the terms of some schemes, employees can retain their share options or shares if they are classified as a 'good leaver', eg a departure resulting from circumstances not within the employee's control, such as compulsory retirement, ill health or redundancy. Therefore, in estimating the possibility of forfeiture, it is not simply a matter of estimating the possibility of employee departure during the vesting period. It is also necessary to estimate whether those departures will be 'good leavers' or 'bad leavers'. And because the share options or shares will vest upon departure of 'good leavers', the expected number of units to be received and the expected length of the vesting period will be shorter for this group of employees. These factors would need to be incorporated into the application of the units of service method.

BC215 Some respondents also raised practical concerns about applying the units of service method to grants with performance conditions. These concerns include the difficulty of incorporating non-market and complex performance conditions into the grant date valuation, the additional subjectivity that this introduces, and that it was unclear how to apply the method when the length of the vesting period is not fixed, because it depends on when a performance condition is satisfied.

BC216   The Board considered the practical concerns raised by respondents, and obtained further advice from valuation experts concerning the difficulties highlighted by respondents of including non-market performance conditions in the grant date valuation. Because of these practical considerations, the Board concluded that the units of service method should not be retained in the IFRS. Instead, the Board decided to adopt the modified grant date method applied in SFAS 123. Under this method, service conditions and non-market performance conditions are excluded from the grant date valuation (ie the possibility of forfeiture is not taken into account when estimating the grant date fair value of the share options or other equity instruments, thereby producing a higher grant date fair value), but are instead taken into account by requiring that the transaction amount be based on the number of equity instruments that eventually vest.[23] Under this method, on a cumulative basis, no amount is recognised for goods or services received if the equity instruments granted do not vest because of failure to satisfy a vesting condition (other than a market condition), eg the counterparty fails to complete a specified service period, or a performance condition (other than a market condition) is not satisfied.

BC217   However, as discussed earlier (paragraphs BC180–BC182), the Board decided that it should not permit the choice available in SFAS 123 to account for the effects of expected or actual forfeitures of share options or other equity instruments because of failure to satisfy a service condition. The Board decided that the IFRS should require an entity to estimate the number of equity instruments expected to vest and to revise that estimate, if necessary, if subsequent information indicates that actual forfeitures are likely to differ from previous estimates.

Share options that are forfeited or lapse after the end of the vesting period

BC218   Some share options might not be exercised. For example, a share option holder is unlikely to exercise a share option if the share price is below the exercise price throughout the exercise period. Once the last date for exercise is passed, the share option will lapse.

BC219   The lapse of a share option at the end of the exercise period does not change the fact that the original transaction occurred, ie goods or services were received as consideration for the issue of an equity instrument (the share option). The lapsing of the share option does not represent a gain to the entity, because there is no change to the entity's net assets. In other words, although some might see such an event as being a benefit to the remaining shareholders, it has no effect on the entity's financial position. In effect, one type of equity interest (the share option holders' interest) becomes part of another type of equity interest (the shareholders' interest). The Board therefore concluded that the only accounting entry that might be required is a movement within equity, to reflect that the share options are no longer outstanding (ie as a transfer from one type of equity interest to another).

---

23   The treatment of market conditions is discussed in paragraphs BC183 and BC184. As noted in paragraph BC184, the practical difficulties that led the Board to conclude that non-market conditions should be dealt with via the modified grant date method rather than being included in the grant date valuation do not apply to market conditions, because market conditions can be incorporated into option pricing models.

BC220 This is consistent with the treatment of other equity instruments, such as warrants issued for cash. When warrants subsequently lapse unexercised, this is not treated as a gain; instead the amount previously recognised when the warrants were issued remains within equity.[24]

BC221 The same analysis applies to equity instruments that are forfeited after the end of the vesting period. For example, an employee with vested share options typically must exercise those options within a short period after cessation of employment, otherwise the options are forfeited. If the share options are not in the money, the employee is unlikely to exercise the options and hence they will be forfeited. For the same reasons as are given in paragraph BC219, no adjustment is made to the amounts previously recognised for services received as consideration for the share options. The only accounting entry that might be required is a movement within equity, to reflect that the share options are no longer outstanding.

Modifications to the terms and conditions of share-based payment arrangements

BC222 An entity might modify the terms of or conditions under which the equity instruments were granted. For example, the entity might reduce the exercise price of share options granted to employees (ie reprice the options), which increases the fair value of those options. During the development of ED 2, the Board focused mainly on the repricing of share options.

BC223 The Board noted that the IASC/G4+1 Discussion Paper argued that if the entity reprices its share options it has, in effect, replaced the original share option with a more valuable share option. The entity presumably believes that it will receive an equivalent amount of benefit from doing so, because otherwise the directors would not be acting in the best interests of the entity or its shareholders. This suggests that the entity expects to receive additional or enhanced employee services equivalent in value to the incremental value of the repriced share options. The Discussion Paper therefore proposed that the incremental value given (ie the difference between the value of the original share option and the value of the repriced share option, as at the date of repricing) should be recognised as additional remuneration expense. Although the Discussion Paper discussed repricing in the context of vesting date measurement, SFAS 123, which applies a grant date measurement basis for employee share-based payment, contains reasoning similar to that in the Discussion Paper.

BC224 This reasoning seems appropriate if grant date measurement is applied on the grounds that the entity made a payment to the employees on grant date by granting them valuable rights to equity instruments of the entity. If the entity is prepared to replace that payment with a more valuable payment, it must believe it will receive an equivalent amount of benefit from doing so.

BC225 The same conclusion is drawn if grant date measurement is applied on the grounds that some type of equity interest is created at grant date, and thereafter

---

24 However, an alternative approach is followed in some jurisdictions (eg Japan and the UK), where the entity recognises a gain when warrants lapse. But under the *Framework*, recognising a gain on the lapse of warrants would be appropriate only if warrants were liabilities, which they are not.

changes in the value of that equity interest accrue to the option holders as equity participants, not as employees. Repricing is inconsistent with the view that share option holders bear changes in value as equity participants. Hence it follows that the incremental value has been granted to the share option holders in their capacity as employees (rather than equity participants), as part of their remuneration for services to the entity. Therefore additional remuneration expense arises in respect of the incremental value given.

BC226   It could be argued that if (a) grant date measurement is used as a surrogate measure of the fair value of the services received and (b) the repricing occurs between grant date and vesting date and (c) the repricing merely restores the share option's original value at grant date, then the entity may not receive additional services. Rather, the repricing might simply be a means of ensuring that the entity receives the services it originally expected to receive when the share options were granted. Under this view, it is not appropriate to recognise additional remuneration expense to the extent that the repricing restores the share option's original value at grant date.

BC227   Some argue that the effect of a repricing is to create a new deal between the entity and its employees, and therefore the entity should estimate the fair value of the repriced share options at the date of repricing to calculate a new measure of the fair value of the services received subsequent to repricing. Under this view, the entity would cease using the grant date fair value of the share options when measuring services received after the repricing date, but without reversal of amounts recognised previously. The entity would then measure the services received between the date of repricing and the end of the vesting period by reference to the fair value of the modified share options, measured at the date of repricing. If the repricing occurs after the end of the vesting period, the same process applies. That is to say, there is no adjustment to previously recognised amounts, and the entity recognises—either immediately or over the vesting period, depending on whether the employees are required to complete an additional period of service to become entitled to the repriced share options—an amount equal to the fair value of the modified share options, measured at the date of repricing.

BC228   In the context of measuring the fair value of the equity instruments as a surrogate measure of the fair value of the services received, after considering the above points, the Board concluded when it developed ED 2 that the incremental value granted on repricing should be taken into account when measuring the services received, because:

(a)   there is an underlying presumption that the fair value of the equity instruments, at grant date, provides a surrogate measure of the fair value of the services received. That fair value is based on the share option's original terms and conditions. Therefore, if those terms or conditions are modified, the modification should be taken into account when measuring the services received.

(b)   a share option that will be repriced if the share price falls is more valuable than one that will not be repriced. Therefore, by presuming at grant date that the share option will not be repriced, the entity underestimated the fair value of that option. The Board concluded that, because it is impractical to include the possibility of repricing in the estimate of fair value at grant date, the incremental value granted on repricing should be taken into account as and when the repricing occurs.

BC229   Many of the respondents to ED 2 who addressed the issue of repricing agreed with the proposed requirements. After considering respondents' comments, the Board decided to retain the approach to repricing as proposed in ED 2, ie recognise the incremental value granted on repricing, in addition to continuing to recognise amounts based on the fair value of the original grant.

BC230   The Board also discussed situations in which repricing might be effected by cancelling share options and issuing replacement share options. For example, suppose an entity grants at-the-money share options with an estimated fair value of CU20 each. Suppose the share price falls, so that the share options become significantly out of the money, and are now worth CU2 each. Suppose the entity is considering repricing, so that the share options are again at the money, which would result in them being worth, say, CU10 each. (Note that the share options are still worth less than at grant date, because the share price is now lower. Other things being equal, an at-the-money option on a low priced share is worth less than an at-the-money option on a high priced share.)

BC231   Under ED 2's proposed treatment of repricing, the incremental value given on repricing (CU10 − CU2 = CU8 increment in fair value per share option) would be accounted for when measuring the services rendered, resulting in the recognition of additional expense, ie additional to any amounts recognised in the future in respect of the original share option grant (valued at CU20). If the entity instead cancelled the existing share options and then issued what were, in effect, replacement share options, but treated the replacement share options as a new share option grant, this could reduce the expense recognised. Although the new grant would be valued at CU10 rather than incremental value of CU8, the entity would not recognise any further expense in respect of the original share option grant, valued at CU20. Although some regard such a result as appropriate (and consistent with their views on repricing, as explained in paragraph BC227), it is inconsistent with the Board's treatment of repricing.

BC232   By this means, the entity could, in effect, reduce its remuneration expense if the share price falls, without having to increase the expense if the share price rises (because no repricing would be necessary in this case). In other words, the entity could structure a repricing so as to achieve a form of service date measurement if the share price falls and grant date measurement if the share price rises, ie an asymmetrical treatment of share price changes.

BC233   When it developed ED 2, the Board concluded that if an entity cancels a share or share option grant during the vesting period (other than cancellations because of employees' failing to satisfy the vesting conditions), it should nevertheless continue to account for services received, as if that share or share option grant had not been cancelled. In the Board's view, it is very unlikely that a share or share option grant would be cancelled without some compensation to the counterparty, either in the form of cash or replacement share options. Moreover, the Board saw no difference between a repricing of share options and a cancellation of share options followed by the granting of replacement share options at a lower exercise price, and therefore concluded that the accounting treatment should be the same. If cash is paid on the cancellation of the share or share option grant, the Board concluded that the payment should be accounted for as the repurchase of an equity interest, ie as a deduction from equity.

BC234 The Board noted that its proposed treatment means that an entity would continue to recognise services received during the remainder of the original vesting period, even though the entity might have paid cash compensation to the counterparty upon cancellation of the share or share option grant. The Board discussed an alternative approach applied in SFAS 123: if an entity settles unvested shares or share options in cash, those shares or share options are treated as having immediately vested. The entity is required to recognise immediately an expense for the amount of compensation expense that would otherwise have been recognised during the remainder of the original vesting period. Although the Board would have preferred to adopt this approach, it would have been difficult to apply in the context of the proposed accounting method in ED 2, given that there is not a specific amount of unrecognised compensation expense—the amount recognised in the future would have depended on the number of units of service received in the future.

BC235 Many respondents who commented on the treatment of cancellations disagreed with the proposals in ED 2. They commented that it was inappropriate to continue recognising an expense after a grant has been cancelled. Some suggested other approaches, including the approach applied in SFAS 123. After considering these comments, and given that the Board had decided to replace the units of service method with the modified grant date method in SFAS 123, the Board concluded that it should adopt the same approach as applied in SFAS 123 to cancellations and settlements. Under SFAS 123, a settlement (including a cancellation) is regarded as resulting in the immediate vesting of the equity instruments. The amount of remuneration expense measured at grant date but not yet recognised is recognised immediately at the date of settlement or cancellation.

BC236 In addition to the above issues, during its redeliberation of the proposals in ED 2 the Board also considered more detailed issues relating to modifications and cancellations. Specifically, the Board considered:

(a) a modification that results in a decrease in fair value (ie the fair value of the modified instrument is less than the fair value of the original instrument, measured at the date of the modification).

(b) a change in the number of equity instruments granted (increase and decrease).

(c) a change in services conditions, thereby changing the length of the vesting period (increase and decrease).

(d) a change in performance conditions, thereby changing the probability of vesting (increase and decrease).

(e) a change in the classification of the grant, from equity to liabilities.

BC237 The Board concluded that having adopted a grant date measurement method, the requirements for modifications and cancellations should ensure that the entity cannot, by modifying or cancelling the grant of shares or share options, avoid recognising remuneration expense based on the grant date fair values. Therefore, the Board concluded that, for arrangements that are classified as equity-settled arrangements (at least initially), the entity must recognise the grant date fair value of the equity instruments over the vesting period, unless the employee fails to vest in those equity instruments under the terms of the original vesting conditions.

BC237A   During the deliberations of its proposals in the exposure draft *Vesting Conditions and Cancellations* published in February 2006, the Board considered how failure to meet a non-vesting condition should be treated. The Board concluded that in order to be consistent with the grant date measurement method, failure to meet a non-vesting condition should have no accounting effect when neither the entity nor the counterparty can choose whether that condition is met. The entity should continue to recognise the expense, based on the grant date fair value, over the vesting period unless the employee fails to meet a vesting condition.

BC237B   However, the Board concluded that the entity's failure to meet a non-vesting condition is a cancellation if the entity can choose whether that non-vesting condition is met. Furthermore, the Board noted that no non-arbitrary or unambiguous criteria exist to distinguish between a decision by the counterparty not to meet a non-vesting condition and a cancellation by the entity. The Board considered establishing a rebuttable presumption that a counterparty's failure to meet a non-vesting condition is (or is not) a cancellation, unless it can be demonstrated that the entity had no (or had some) influence over the counterparty's decision. The Board did not believe that the information about the entity's decision-making processes that is publicly available would be sufficient to determine whether the presumption has been rebutted. Therefore, the Board concluded that a failure to meet a non-vesting condition should be treated as a cancellation when either the entity or the counterparty can choose whether that non-vesting condition is met.

Accounting for a modification of a share-based payment transaction that changes its classification from cash-settled to equity-settled (2016 amendments)[25]

BC237C   This section summarises the Board's considerations when finalising its proposals to address the accounting for a modification to the terms and conditions of a share-based payment that changes the classification of the transaction from cash-settled to equity-settled. These changes were proposed in the Exposure Draft *Classification and Measurement of Share-based Payment Transactions* (Proposed amendments to IFRS 2) published in November 2014 (November 2014 ED).

BC237D   The Board was informed that there are situations in which a cash-settled share-based payment is modified by cancelling it and replacing it with a new equity-settled share-based payment, and, at the replacement date, the fair value of the replacement award is different from the recognised value of the original award. Interested parties told the Board that there is diversity in practice

---

25 Paragraphs BC237C–BC237L are added as a consequence of amendments to IFRS 2 *Classification and Measurement of Share-based Payment Transactions*, issued in June 2016.

because IFRS 2 does not provide specific requirements for these situations and asked the Board to clarify the accounting.

BC237E The Board decided that paragraphs 27 and B42–B44 of IFRS 2, which set out the requirements for modifications to the terms and conditions of equity-settled share-based payments, should not be applied by analogy to account for the fact patterns raised. This is because the requirement in paragraph 27 of IFRS 2 to recognise a minimum amount for the equity-settled share-based payment following a modification is inconsistent with the requirement in paragraph 30 of IFRS 2 to remeasure the liability for a cash-settled share-based payment at fair value at the end of each reporting date until the liability is settled.

BC237F Accordingly, the Board decided to require that the equity-settled share-based payment transaction be recognised in equity to the extent to which goods or services have been received at the modification date. The Board required this measurement to be made by reference to the modification-date fair value of the equity instruments granted. The Board noted that, at the original grant date, there was a shared understanding that the entity would pay cash for services to be rendered by the counterparty. However, at the modification date, the entity and the counterparty have a new shared understanding that the entity will issue equity instruments to the counterparty. Therefore, the Board concluded that the modification-date fair value should be used to measure the modified equity-settled share-based payment.

BC237G Furthermore, the Board noted that the liability for the original cash-settled share-based payment is derecognised on the modification date as it is considered to be settled when the entity grants the replacement equity-settled share-based payment. This is because, at the modification date, the entity is no longer obliged to transfer cash (or other assets) to the counterparty.

BC237H The Board observed that any difference between the carrying amount of the derecognised liability and the amount of recognised equity on the modification date is recognised immediately in profit or loss. The Board observed that this is consistent with how cash-settled share-based payments are measured in accordance with paragraph 30 of IFRS 2. The Board further observed that recognising the difference in value between the original and the replacement award in profit or loss is also consistent with the requirements for the extinguishment of a financial liability (that has been extinguished fully or partially by the issue of equity instruments) in paragraph 3.3.3 of IFRS 9 *Financial Instruments* and with paragraph 9 of IFRIC *Interpretation 19 Extinguishing Financial Liabilities with Equity Instruments*.

BC237I Respondents to the November 2014 ED questioned whether the guidance in paragraph B44A would also apply to a situation in which the modification changes the vesting period of the share-based payment transaction. The Board confirmed in paragraph B44B that the guidance in paragraph B44A is applied when the modification occurs during or after the vesting period, and when the vesting period is extended or shortened.

BC237J The Board provided guidance in paragraph B44C to account for a grant of equity instruments that has been identified as a replacement for a cancelled cash-settled share-based payment. The Board observed that if an entity does not identify a grant of equity instruments as a replacement, the entity would have to reverse the expense recognised for the cash-settled share-based payment and recognise an expense for the new equity-settled share-based payment. The Board noted that this accounting treatment is different from the accounting for modifications of equity-settled awards when the entity does not identify new equity instruments granted as replacement equity instruments for the cancelled equity instrument (as set out in paragraph 28(c) of IFRS 2). In that case, the entity does not reverse the expense recognised for the cancelled original equity-settled award and recognises an expense for the new grant of equity instruments.

BC237K   Some respondents to the November 2014 ED suggested that the Board add examples to the implementation guidance of IFRS 2 to illustrate the accounting for other types of modifications of share-based payments (for example, a modification from equity-settled to cash-settled). The Board decided that it was not necessary to include additional examples (other than adding paragraph IG19B and IG Example 12C which illustrates the application of paragraphs B44A–B44C), because the existing implementation guidance in IFRS 2 could be applied by analogy. For example, Example 9 illustrates a grant of shares to which a cash settlement alternative is subsequently added.

Effective date and transition (2016 amendments)

BC237L   In response to the comments received on the November 2014 ED, the Board decided to provide specific transition requirements in paragraph 59A of IFRS 2 for each of the amendments. The Board also decided to permit an entity to apply all of the amendments retrospectively if, (and only if), the necessary information to do so is available without the use of hindsight.

Share appreciation rights settled in cash

BC238   Some transactions are 'share-based', even though they do not involve the issue of shares, share options or any other form of equity instrument. Share appreciation rights (SARs) settled in cash are transactions in which the amount of cash paid to the employee (or another party) is based upon the increase in the share price over a specified period, usually subject to vesting conditions, such as the employee's remaining with the entity during the specified period. (Note that the following discussion focuses on SARs granted to employees, but also applies to SARs granted to other parties.)

BC239   In terms of accounting concepts, share-based payment transactions involving an outflow of cash (or other assets) are different from transactions in which goods or services are received as consideration for the issue of equity instruments.

BC240   In an equity-settled transaction, only one side of the transaction causes a change in assets, ie an asset (services) is received but no assets are disbursed. The other side of the transaction increases equity; it does not cause a change in assets. Accordingly, not only is it not necessary to remeasure the transaction amount upon settlement, it is not appropriate, because equity interests are not remeasured.

BC241   In contrast, in a cash-settled transaction, both sides of the transaction cause a change in assets, ie an asset (services) is received and an asset (cash) is ultimately disbursed. Therefore, no matter what value is attributed to the first asset (services received), eventually it will be necessary to recognise the change in assets when the second asset (cash) is disbursed. Thus, no matter how the transaction is accounted for between the receipt of services and the settlement in cash, it will be 'trued up' to equal the amount of cash paid out, to account for both changes in assets.

BC242   Because cash-settled SARs involve an outflow of cash (rather than the issue of equity instruments) cash SARs should be accounted for in accordance with the usual accounting for similar liabilities. That sounds straightforward, but there are some questions to consider:

(a)   should a liability be recognised before vesting date, ie before the employees have fulfilled the conditions to become unconditionally entitled to the cash payment?

(b)   if so, how should that liability be measured?

(c)   how should the expense be presented in the income statement?

Is there a liability before vesting date?

BC243   It could be argued that the entity does not have a liability until vesting date, because the entity does not have a present obligation to pay cash to the employees until the employees fulfil the conditions to become unconditionally entitled to the cash; between grant date and vesting date there is only a contingent liability.

BC244   The Board noted that this argument applies to all sorts of employee benefits settled in cash, not just SARs. For example, it could be argued that an entity has no liability for pension payments to employees until the employees have met the specified vesting conditions. This argument was considered by IASC in IAS 19 *Employee Benefits*. The Basis for Conclusions states:

> Paragraph 54 of the new IAS 19 summarises the recognition and measurement of liabilities arising from defined benefit plans ... Paragraph 54 of the new IAS 19 is based on the definition of, and recognition criteria for, a liability in IASC's *Framework* ... The Board believes that an enterprise has an obligation under a defined benefit plan when an employee has rendered service in return for the benefits promised under the plan ... The Board believes that an obligation exists even if a benefit is not vested, in other words if the employee's right to receive the benefit is conditional upon future employment. For example, consider an enterprise that provides a benefit of 100 to employees who remain in service for two years. At the end of the first year, the employee and the enterprise are not in the same position as at the beginning of the first year, because the employee will only need to work for one year, instead of two, before becoming entitled to the benefit. Although there is a possibility that the benefit may not vest, that difference is an obligation and, in the Board's view, should result in the recognition of a liability at the end of the first year. The measurement of that

obligation at its present value reflects the enterprise's best estimate of the probability that the benefit may not vest. (IAS 19, Basis for Conclusions, paragraphs BC11–BC14)[26]

BC245 Therefore, the Board concluded that, to be consistent with IAS 19, which covers other cash-settled employee benefits, a liability should be recognised in respect of cash-settled SARs during the vesting period, as services are rendered by the employees. Thus, no matter how the liability is measured, the Board concluded that it should be accrued over the vesting period, to the extent that the employees have performed their side of the arrangement. For example, if the terms of the arrangement require the employees to perform services over a three-year period, the liability would be accrued over that three-year period, consistently with the treatment of other cash-settled employee benefits.

How should the liability be measured?

BC246 A simple approach would be to base the accrual on the entity's share price at the end of each reporting period. If the entity's share price increased over the vesting period, expenses would be larger in later reporting periods compared with earlier reporting periods. This is because each reporting period will include the effects of (a) an increase in the liability in respect of the employee services received during that reporting period and (b) an increase in the liability attributable to the increase in the entity's share price during the reporting period, which increases the amount payable in respect of past employee services received.

BC247 This approach is consistent with SFAS 123 (paragraph 25) and FASB Interpretation No. 28 *Accounting for Stock Appreciation Rights and Other Variable Stock Option or Award Plans*.

BC248 However, this is not a fair value approach. Like share options, the fair value of SARs includes both their intrinsic value (the increase in the share price to date) and their time value (the value of the right to participate in future increases in the share price, if any, that may occur between the valuation date and the settlement date). An option pricing model can be used to estimate the fair value of SARs.

BC249 Ultimately, however, no matter how the liability is measured during the vesting period, the liability—and therefore the expense—will be remeasured, when the SARs are settled, to equal the amount of the cash paid out. The amount of cash paid will be based on the SARs' intrinsic value at the settlement date. Some support measuring the SAR liability at intrinsic value for this reason, and because intrinsic value is easier to measure.

BC250 The Board concluded that measuring SARs at intrinsic value would be inconsistent with the fair value measurement basis applied, in most cases, in the rest of the IFRS. Furthermore, although a fair value measurement basis is more complex to apply, it was likely that many entities would be measuring the fair value of similar instruments regularly, eg new SAR or share option grants, which would provide much of the information required to remeasure the fair

---

26 IAS 19 *Employee Benefits* (as amended in June 2011) renumbered and amended paragraphs BC11–BC14 as paragraphs BC52–BC55. The amendments changed the terminology for consistency with IAS 19.

value of the SAR at each reporting date. Moreover, because the intrinsic value measurement basis does not include time value, it is not an adequate measure of either the SAR liability or the cost of services consumed.

BC251   The question of how to measure the liability is linked with the question how to present the associated expense in the income statement, as explained below.

How should the associated expense be presented in the income statement?

BC252   SARs are economically similar to share options. Hence some argue that the accounting treatment of SARs should be the same as the treatment of share options, as discussed earlier (paragraph BC113). However, as noted in paragraphs BC240 and BC241, in an equity-settled transaction there is one change in net assets (the goods or services received) whereas in a cash-settled transaction there are two changes in net assets (the goods or services received and the cash or other assets paid out). To differentiate between the effects of each change in net assets in a cash-settled transaction, the expense could be separated into two components:

- an amount based on the fair value of the SARs at grant date, recognised over the vesting period, in a manner similar to accounting for equity-settled share-based payment transactions, and

- changes in estimate between grant date and settlement date, ie all changes required to remeasure the transaction amount to equal the amount paid out on settlement date.

BC253   In developing ED 2, the Board concluded that information about these two components would be helpful to users of financial statements. For example, users of financial statements regard the effects of remeasuring the liability as having little predictive value. Therefore, the Board concluded that there should be separate disclosure, either on the face of the income statement or in the notes, of that portion of the expense recognised during each accounting period that is attributable to changes in the estimated fair value of the liability between grant date and settlement date.

BC254   However, some respondents to ED 2 disagreed with the proposed disclosure, arguing that it was burdensome and inappropriate to require the entity to account for the transaction as a cash-settled transaction and also calculate, for the purposes of the disclosure, what the transaction amount would have been if the arrangement was an equity-settled transaction.

BC255   The Board considered these comments and also noted that its decision to adopt the SFAS 123 modified grant date method will make it more complex for entities to determine the amount to disclose, because it will be necessary to distinguish between the effects of forfeitures and the effects of fair value changes when calculating the amount to disclose. The Board therefore concluded that the disclosure should not be retained as a mandatory requirement, but instead should be given as an example of an additional disclosure that entities should consider providing. For example, entities with a significant amount of cash-settled arrangements that experience significant share price volatility will probably find that the disclosure is helpful to users of their financial statements.

Share-based payment transactions with a net settlement feature for withholding tax obligations (2016 amendments)[27]

BC255A   This section summarises the Board's considerations when it finalised its proposals to address the classification of a share-based payment transaction with a net settlement feature for withholding tax obligations, contained in the November 2014 ED.

BC255B   Some jurisdictions have tax laws or regulations that oblige an entity to withhold an amount for an employee's tax obligation associated with a share-based payment and to transfer that amount, normally in cash, to the tax authority on the employee's behalf. Those tax withholding obligations vary from jurisdiction to jurisdiction. To fulfill this obligation, many plans include a net settlement feature that permits or requires the entity to deduct from the total number of equity instruments that it otherwise would deliver to the employee, the number of equity instruments needed to equal the monetary value of the tax obligation that the employee incurs as a result of the share-based payment transaction. The entity transfers the amount withheld to the tax authority in cash or other assets.

BC255C   The Board received a request to address the classification of such a share-based payment transaction. Specifically, the Board was asked whether the portion of the share-based payment that the entity withholds to satisfy the employee's tax obligation should be classified as cash-settled or equity-settled, if the transaction would otherwise have been classified as an equity-settled share-based payment transaction.

BC255D   There were two views on this issue:

(a)   View 1—The share-based payment has two components and each component is accounted for consistently with its manner of settlement. The portion that the entity withholds, and for which it incurs a liability to transfer cash (or other assets) to the tax authority, should be accounted for as a cash-settled share-based payment transaction. The portion of the share-based payment that the entity settles by issuing equity instruments to the employee is accounted for as an equity-settled share-based payment.

(b)   View 2—The entire share-based payment transaction should be classified as an equity-settled share-based payment transaction, because the net settlement should be viewed as if the entity had repurchased some of the equity instruments issued to the employee (ie the entity would apply the requirements in paragraph 29 of IFRS 2 for a repurchase of vested equity instruments).

BC255E   View 1 is based on the view that the entity is settling part of the share-based payment transaction in cash; ie the entity has an obligation to transfer cash (or other assets) to the tax authority to settle the employee's tax obligation on the employee's behalf. Paragraph 34 of IFRS 2 requires a share-based payment

---

27   Paragraphs BC255A–BC255P are added as a consequence of amendments to IFRS 2 *Classification and Measurement of Share-based Payment Transactions*, issued in June 2016.

transaction, or components of that transaction, to be classified as cash-settled if, and to the extent that, the entity has incurred a liability to settle in cash or other assets.

BC255F   View 2 is based on the view that the entity is acting as an agent when it transfers cash to the tax authority because the employee has the tax obligation. Under this view, it is as if the entity settles the share-based payment transaction in its entirety by issuing equity instruments to the employee. As a separate (yet simultaneous) transaction, the entity repurchases a portion of those equity instruments from the employee. The entity then remits the cash value of the repurchased equity instruments to the tax authority on behalf of the employee to settle the employee's tax obligation in relation to the share-based payment.

BC255G   The Board observed that paragraph 34 of IFRS 2 indicates that a share-based payment transaction, or components of that transaction, should be classified as a cash-settled share-based payment transaction if, and to the extent that, the entity has incurred a liability to settle in cash or other assets. Consequently a transaction with such a net settlement feature would be divided into two components and each component would be accounted for consistently with how it is settled (View 1). Consequently, the component that reflects the entity's obligation to pay cash to the tax authority would be accounted for as a cash-settled share-based payment and the component that reflects the entity's obligation to issue equity instruments to the employee would be accounted for as an equity-settled share-based payment.

BC255H   The Board observed that the entity's payment to the tax authority represents, in substance, a payment to the counterparty (ie the employee) for the services received from the counterparty, despite the fact that the entity transfers the cash to the tax authority. This is because:

(a)   when the entity pays the amount withheld to the tax authority on behalf of the employee, the entity is acting as an agent for the employee; however,

(b)   the entity is also acting as a principal because it is fulfilling its obligation to the employee (ie the counterparty in the share-based payment transaction) to transfer cash (or other assets) for the goods or services received.

BC255I   Nevertheless, despite the requirements in paragraph 34, the Board decided to make an exception with the result that the transaction would be classified as equity-settled in its entirety if it would have been so classified had it not included the net settlement feature. The Board decided that this exception should be limited to the share-based payment transaction described in paragraph 33E.

BC255J   The Board decided to make the exception because it observed that dividing the specific transaction described in paragraph 33E into two components could be a significant operational challenge for preparers and thus impose cost in excess of the benefit of distinguishing the two components. This is because dividing the transaction into two components requires an entity to estimate changes that affect the amount that the entity is required to withhold and remit to the tax authority on the employee's behalf in respect of the share-based payment. As that estimate changes, the entity would need to reclassify a portion of the share-based payment between cash-settled and equity-settled.

BC255K Respondents to the November 2014 ED observed that this ED did not specifically address the accounting for the amount paid by the entity to the tax authority. In response to these concerns the Board decided to explain how the requirements of paragraph 29 of IFRS 2 would be applied. Paragraph 33G explains that the accounting for the amount transferred to the tax authority in respect of the employee's tax obligation associated with the share-based payment is consistent with the accounting described in paragraph 29 of this Standard (ie as if the entity had repurchased the vested equity instruments). This amendment does not address the recognition and measurement of any liability to the tax authority.

BC255L The Board observed that withholding shares to fund the payment (in cash or other assets) to the tax authority could result in a significant difference between the amount paid and the amount at which the share-based payment was measured. This is because the amount payable to the tax authority may reflect settlement-date fair value, whereas the amount recognised for the equity-settled share-based payment during the vesting period would reflect grant-date fair value.

BC255M The Board further observed that it could be necessary to inform users about the future cash flow effects associated with the share-based payment arrangement as the settlement of the tax payment to the tax authority approaches. Therefore, the Board decided to require an entity to disclose the estimated amount that it expects to transfer to the tax authority when this disclosure is needed to inform users about the future cash-flow effects associated with the share-based payment. The Board did not specify the basis for calculating such an estimate.

BC255N The Board also received questions about the accounting when the number of equity instruments withheld exceeds the number of equity instruments needed to equal the monetary value of the employee's tax obligation in respect of the share-based payment. The Board observed that the classification exception (in paragraph 33F) for the classification of a share-based payment award with a net settlement feature would not apply to any equity instruments withheld in excess of the number required to equal the monetary value of the employee's tax obligation. Consequently, when that excess amount is paid to the employee in cash (or other assets), and consistent with existing requirements, the excess number of equity instruments withheld should be separated and accounted for as a cash-settled share-based payment.

BC255O Some respondents to the November 2014 ED asked the Board to clarify whether the exception in paragraph 33F (ie relief from dividing the share-based payment into its different components) applies to arrangements other than those in which an entity is obliged by tax laws or regulations to withhold an employee's tax obligation. For example, an entity may not be obliged by tax laws or regulations to withhold an amount for an employee's tax obligation but it is the entity's normal practice to withhold such an amount. The Board noted that its intent is to limit the exception to circumstances in which the tax laws or regulations impose the obligation on the entity to withhold an amount for the employee's tax obligation associated with a share-based payment for the exception in paragraph 33F to apply.

BC255P   Furthermore, the Board added paragraph IG19A and IG Example 12B to the Guidance on Implementing IFRS 2 to illustrate a share-based payment transaction with a net settlement feature for withholding tax obligations.

Share-based payment transactions with cash alternatives

BC256   Under some employee share-based payment arrangements the employees can choose to receive cash instead of shares or share options, or instead of exercising share options. There are many possible variations of share-based payment arrangements under which a cash alternative may be paid. For example, the employees may have more than one opportunity to elect to receive the cash alternative, eg the employees may be able to elect to receive cash instead of shares or share options on vesting date, or elect to receive cash instead of exercising the share options. The terms of the arrangement may provide the entity with a choice of settlement, ie whether to pay the cash alternative instead of issuing shares or share options on vesting date or instead of issuing shares upon the exercise of the share options. The amount of the cash alternative may be fixed or variable and, if variable, may be determinable in a manner that is related, or unrelated, to the price of the entity's shares.

BC257   The IFRS contains different accounting methods for cash-settled and equity-settled share-based payment transactions. Hence, if the entity or the employee has the choice of settlement, it is necessary to determine which accounting method should be applied. The Board considered situations when the terms of the arrangement provide (a) the employee with a choice of settlement and (b) the entity with a choice of settlement.

The terms of the arrangement provide the employee with a choice of settlement

BC258   Share-based payment transactions without cash alternatives do not give rise to liabilities under the *Framework*, because the entity is not required to transfer cash or other assets to the other party. However, this is not so if the contract between the entity and the employee gives the employee the contractual right to demand the cash alternative. In this situation, the entity has an obligation to transfer cash to the employee and hence a liability exists. Furthermore, because the employee has the right to demand settlement in equity instead of cash, the employee also has a conditional right to equity instruments. Hence, on grant date the employee was granted rights to a compound financial instrument, ie a financial instrument that includes both debt and equity components.

BC259   It is common for the alternatives to be structured so that the fair value of the cash alternative is always the same as the fair value of the equity alternative, eg where the employee has a choice between share options and SARs. However, if this is not so, then the fair value of the compound financial instrument will usually exceed both the individual fair value of the cash alternative (because of the possibility that the shares or share options may be more valuable than the cash alternative) and that of the shares or options (because of the possibility that the cash alternative may be more valuable than the shares or options).

BC260 Under IAS 32, a financial instrument that is accounted for as a compound instrument is separated into its debt and equity components, by allocating the proceeds received for the issue of a compound instrument to its debt and equity components. This entails determining the fair value of the liability component and then assigning the remainder of the proceeds received to the equity component. This is possible if those proceeds are cash or non-cash consideration whose fair value can be reliably measured. If that is not the case, it will be necessary to estimate the fair value of the compound instrument itself.

BC261 The Board concluded that the compound instrument should be measured by first valuing the liability component (the cash alternative) and then valuing the equity component (the equity instrument)—with that valuation taking into account that the employee must forfeit the cash alternative to receive the equity instrument—and adding the two component values together. This is consistent with the approach adopted in IAS 32, whereby the liability component is measured first and the residual is allocated to equity. If the fair value of each settlement alternative is always the same, then the fair value of the equity component of the compound instrument will be zero and hence the fair value of the compound instrument will be the same as the fair value of the liability component.

BC262 The Board concluded that the entity should separately account for the services rendered in respect of each component of the compound financial instrument, to ensure consistency with the IFRS's requirements for equity-settled and cash-settled share-based payment transactions. Hence, for the debt component, the entity should recognise the services received, and a liability to pay for those services, as the employees render services, in the same manner as other cash-settled share-based payment transactions (eg SARs). For the equity component (if any), the entity should recognise the services received, and an increase in equity, as the employees render services, in the same way as other equity-settled share-based payment transactions.

BC263 The Board concluded that the liability should be remeasured to its fair value as at the date of settlement, before accounting for the settlement of the liability. This ensures that, if the entity settles the liability by issuing equity instruments, the resulting increase in equity is measured at the fair value of the consideration received for the equity instruments issued, being the fair value of the liability settled.

BC264 The Board also concluded that, if the entity pays cash rather than issuing equity instruments on settlement, any contributions to equity previously recognised in respect of the equity component should remain in equity. By electing to receive cash rather than equity instruments, the employee has surrendered his/her rights to receive equity instruments. That event does not cause a change in net assets and hence there is no change in total equity. This is consistent with the Board's conclusions on other lapses of equity instruments (see paragraphs BC218–BC221).

The terms of the arrangement provide the entity with a choice of settlement

BC265   For share-based payment transactions in which the terms of the arrangement provide the entity with a choice of whether to settle in cash or by issuing equity instruments, the entity would need first to determine whether it has an obligation to settle in cash and therefore does not, in effect, have a choice of settlement. Although the contract might specify that the entity can choose whether to settle in cash or by issuing equity instruments, the Board concluded that the entity will have an obligation to settle in cash if the choice of settlement in equity has no commercial substance (eg because the entity is legally prohibited from issuing shares), or if the entity has a past practice or a stated policy of settling in cash, or generally settles in cash whenever the counterparty asks for cash settlement. The entity will also have an obligation to settle in cash if the shares issued (including shares issued upon the exercise of share options) are redeemable, either mandatorily (eg upon cessation of employment) or at the counterparty's option.

BC266   During its redeliberations of the proposals in ED 2, the Board noted that the classification as liabilities or equity of arrangements in which the entity appears to have the choice of settlement differs from the classification under IAS 32, which requires such an arrangement to be classified either wholly as a liability (if the contract is a derivative contract) or as a compound instrument (if the contract is a non-derivative contract). However, consistently with its conclusions on the other differences between IFRS 2 and IAS 32 (see paragraphs BC106–BC110), the Board decided to retain this difference, pending the outcome of its longer-term Concepts project, which includes reviewing the definitions of liabilities and equity.

BC267   Even if the entity is not obliged to settle in cash until it chooses to do so, at the time it makes that election a liability will arise for the amount of the cash payment. This raises the question how to account for the debit side of the entry. It could be argued that any difference between (a) the amount of the cash payment and (b) the total expense recognised for services received and consumed up to the date of settlement (which would be based on the grant date value of the equity settlement alternative) should be recognised as an adjustment to the employee remuneration expense. However, given that the cash payment is to settle an equity interest, the Board concluded that it is consistent with the *Framework* to treat the cash payment as the repurchase of an equity interest, ie as a deduction from equity. In this case, no adjustment to remuneration expense is required on settlement.

BC268   However, the Board concluded that an additional expense should be recognised if the entity chooses the settlement alternative with the higher fair value because, given that the entity has voluntarily paid more than it needed to, presumably it expects to receive (or has already received) additional services from the employees in return for the additional value given.

Share-based payment transactions among group entities (2009 amendments)[28]

BC268A   This section summarises the Board's considerations when finalising its proposals contained in the exposure draft *Group Cash-settled Share-based Payment Transactions* published in December 2007. Until the Board amended IFRS 2 in 2009, IFRIC 11 provided guidance on how an entity that received the goods or services from its suppliers should account for some specific group equity-settled share-based payment transactions in its separate or individual financial statements. Therefore, the amendments issued in June 2009 incorporated substantially the same consensus contained in IFRIC 11. The relevant matters the IFRIC considered when reaching the consensus contained in IFRIC 11, as approved by the Board, are also carried forward in this section.

BC268B   The exposure draft published in December 2007 addressed two arrangements in which the parent (not the entity itself) has an obligation to make the required cash payments to the suppliers of the entity:

(a)   Arrangement 1 – the supplier of the entity will receive cash payments that are linked to the price of the equity instruments of the entity.

(b)   Arrangement 2 – the supplier of the entity will receive cash payments that are linked to the price of the equity instruments of the parent of the entity.

BC268C   The Board noted that like those group equity-settled share-based payment transactions originally addressed in IFRIC 11, the two arrangements described in paragraph BC268B did not meet the definition of either an equity-settled or a cash-settled share-based payment transaction. The Board considered whether a different conclusion should be reached for such arrangements merely because they are cash-settled rather than equity-settled. Paragraphs BC22A–BC22F explain the Board's considerations in finalising the amendments to clarify the scope of IFRS 2. The section below summarises the Board's considerations in finalising the amendments relating to the measurement of such transactions.

BC268D   The Board noted that the arrangements described in paragraph BC268B are

(a)   for the purpose of providing benefits to the employees of the subsidiary in return for employee services, and

(b)   share-based and cash-settled.

In addition, the Board noted that the guidance in paragraph 3 (now superseded by paragraph 3A) already stated that when a shareholder transferred equity instruments of the entity (or another group entity), the transaction would be within the scope of IFRS 2 for the entity receiving the goods or services.

BC268E   For these reasons, in the exposure draft published in December 2007 the Board proposed to amend IFRS 2 and IFRIC 11 to require that, in the separate or individual financial statements of the entity receiving the goods or services, the entity should measure the employee services in accordance with the

---

28   Paragraphs BC268A–BC268O are added as a consequence of amendments to IFRS 2 *Group Cash-settled Share-based Payment Transactions* issued in June 2009.

requirements applicable to cash-settled share-based payment transactions on the basis of the fair value of the corresponding liability incurred by the parent. Specifically, until the liability incurred by the parent is settled, the entity should recognise any changes in the fair value of the liability in profit or loss and changes in the entity's equity as adjustments to contributions from the parent.

BC268F   Because group cash-settled share-based payment transactions did not meet the definition of either an equity-settled or a cash-settled share-based payment transaction, some respondents did not object to measuring them as cash-settled on the basis that the accounting reflects the form of the payment received by the entity's suppliers. However, many respondents questioned the basis for the conclusions reached, citing reasons that included:

(a)   the lack of a 'push-down' accounting concept in current IFRSs that would require the parent's costs incurred on behalf of the subsidiary to be attributed to the subsidiary,

(b)   conflicts with the *Framework* and with other IFRSs that prohibit remeasurement of equity, and

(c)   conflicts with the rationale in the Basis for Conclusions on IFRS 2 related to the remeasurement of cash-settled share-based payment transactions when the entity itself has no obligation to its suppliers.

BC268G   The Board agreed with respondents that the entity receiving goods or services has no obligation to distribute assets and that the parent's settlement is an equity contribution to the entity. The Board noted that regardless of how such group transactions are structured or accounted for in the separate or individual financial statements of the group entities, the accounting measurement in the consolidated financial statements of the group will be the same. The Board also noted that the share-based payment expense measured on grant date results in the same fair value for both the entity receiving goods or services and the entity settling the transaction, regardless of whether it is measured as equity-settled or as cash-settled.

BC268H   To address the comments received from respondents, the Board reviewed two issues to determine the appropriate subsequent measurement in the separate or individual financial statements of the entity receiving the goods or services. The first issue was whether the entity should recognise in its separate or individual financial statements:

(a)   Approach 1 – an expense of the same amount as in the consolidated financial statements, or

(b)   Approach 2 – an expense measured by classifying the transaction as equity-settled or cash-settled evaluated from its own perspective, which may not always be the same as the amount recognised by the consolidated group.

BC268I   The Board noted that IFRSs have no broad-based guidance to address push-down accounting or the accounting in separate or individual financial statements for the allocation of costs among group entities. When addressing defined benefit plans that share risks between entities under common control, IAS 19 requires an expense to be recognised by the subsidiary on the basis of the cash amount charged by the group plan. When there are no repayment arrangements, in the separate or individual financial statements, the subsidiary should recognise a cost equal to its contribution payable for the period. This is consistent with Approach 2 described in paragraph BC268H.

BC268J   The Board therefore decided to adopt Approach 2. However, the approach adopted in IFRS 2 is different from that in IAS 19 in that the entity receiving goods or services in a share-based payment transaction recognises an expense even when it has no obligation to pay cash or other assets. The Board concluded that this approach is consistent with the expense attribution principles underlying IFRS 2.

BC268K   The Board noted that Approach 2 is consistent with the rationale that the information provided by general purpose financial reporting should 'reflect the perspective of the entity rather than the perspective of the entity's equity investors ....' because the reporting entity is deemed to have substance of its own, separate from that of its owners. Approach 1 reflects the perspective of the entity's owners (the group) rather than the rights and obligations of the entity itself.

BC268L   The Board also noted that the consensus reached in IFRIC 11 reflected Approach 1 described in paragraph BC268H for some scenarios and Approach 2 for others. The Board concluded that this was undesirable and decided that there should be a single approach to measurement that would apply in all situations.

BC268M   The second issue the Board considered was identifying the criteria for classifying group share-based payment transactions as equity-settled or cash-settled. How a transaction is classified determines the subsequent measurement in the separate or individual financial statements of both the entity receiving the goods or services and the entity settling the transaction, if different. The Board reviewed the two classification criteria set out in the consensus in IFRIC 11 for group equity-settled transactions:

(a)   based on the nature of the award given to the employees—therefore, classified as *equity-settled* if the entity's own equity instruments are given, regardless of which entity grants or settles it; otherwise classified as *cash-settled* even when the entity receiving the goods or services has no obligation.

(b)   based on the entity's own rights and obligations—therefore, classified as *cash-settled* if the entity has an obligation to settle, regardless of the nature of the consideration; otherwise classified as *equity-settled*.

BC268N   The Board noted that, on its own, either of the two criteria described above would not consistently reflect the entity's perspective when assessing the appropriate classification for transactions described in paragraph BC268B. The Board concluded that the entity should consider both criteria in IFRIC 11, ie *equity-settled* when suppliers are given the entity's own equity instruments or when the entity receiving the goods or services has no obligation to settle and *cash-settled* in all other circumstances. The Board also noted that when the entity receiving goods or services has no obligation to deliver cash or other assets to its suppliers, accounting for the transaction as cash-settled in its separate or individual financial statements is not appropriate. The equity-settled basis is more consistent with the principles and rationales in both IFRS 2 and IFRIC 11. Therefore, the Board decided that the entity receiving the goods or services should classify both of the group cash-settled share-based payment transactions described in paragraph BC268B as *equity-settled* in its separate or individual financial statements.

BC268O This conclusion is the main change to the proposals in the exposure draft. The Board concluded that the broader principles it developed during its redeliberations addressed the three main concerns expressed by respondents described in paragraph BC268F. Those principles apply to all group share-based payment transactions, whether they are cash-settled or equity-settled. The Board's conclusions do not result in any changes to the guidance in IFRIC 11 that addressed similar group equity-settled share-based payment transactions. Other than the change described above, the Board reaffirmed the proposals in the exposure draft. Therefore, the Board concluded that it was not necessary to re-expose the amendments before finalising them.

Transfers of employees between group entities (paragraphs B59–B61)

BC268P When it developed the consensus in IFRIC 11, the IFRIC noted that some share-based payment arrangements involve a parent granting rights to the employees of more than one subsidiary with a vesting condition that requires the employees to work for the group for a particular period. Sometimes, an employee of one subsidiary transfers employment to another subsidiary during the vesting period, without the employee's rights under the original share-based payment arrangements being affected.

BC268Q The IFRIC noted that the terms of the original share-based payment arrangement require the employees to work for the group, rather than for a particular group entity. Thus, the IFRIC concluded that the change of employment should not result in a new grant of equity instruments in the financial statements of the subsidiary to which the employees transferred employment. The subsidiary to which the employee transfers employment should measure the fair value of the services received from the employee by reference to the fair value of the equity instruments at the date those equity instruments were originally granted to the employee by the parent. For the same reason, the IFRIC concluded that the transfer itself should not be treated as an employee's failure to satisfy a vesting condition. Thus, the transfer should not trigger any reversal of the charge previously recognised in respect of the services received from the employee in the separate or individual financial statements of the subsidiary from which the employee transfers employment.

BC268R The IFRIC noted that paragraph 19 of the IFRS requires the cumulative amount recognised for goods or services as consideration for the equity instruments granted to be based on the number of equity instruments that eventually vest. Accordingly, on a cumulative basis, no amount is recognised for goods or services if the equity instruments do not vest because of failure to satisfy a vesting condition other than a market condition as defined in Appendix A. Applying the principles in paragraph 19, the IFRIC concluded that when the employee fails to satisfy a vesting condition other than a market condition, the services from that employee recognised in the financial statements of each group entity during the vesting period should be reversed.

BC268S   When finalising the 2009 amendments to IFRS 2 for group share-based payment transactions, the Board concluded that the guidance in IFRIC 11 should apply to all group share-based payment transactions classified as equity-settled in the entity's separate or individual financial statements in accordance with paragraphs 43A–43C.

Overall conclusions on accounting for employee share options

BC269   The Board first considered all major issues relating to the recognition and measurement of share-based payment transactions, and reached conclusions on those issues. It then drew some overall conclusions, particularly on the treatment of employee share options, which is one of the most controversial aspects of the project. In arriving at those conclusions, the Board considered the following issues:

- convergence with US GAAP

- recognition versus disclosure of expenses arising from employee share-based payment transactions

- reliability of measurement of the fair value of employee share options.

Convergence with US GAAP

BC270   Some respondents to the Discussion Paper and ED 2 urged the Board to develop an IFRS that was based on existing requirements under US generally accepted accounting principles (US GAAP).

BC271   More specifically, respondents urged the Board to develop a standard based on SFAS 123. However, given that convergence of accounting standards was commonly given as a reason for this suggestion, the Board considered US GAAP overall, not just one aspect of it. The main pronouncements of US GAAP on share-based payment are Accounting Principles Board Opinion No. 25 *Accounting for Stock Issued to Employees*, and SFAS 123.

APB 25

BC272   APB 25 was issued in 1972. It deals with employee share plans only, and draws a distinction between non-performance-related (fixed) plans and performance-related and other variable plans.

BC273   For fixed plans, an expense is measured at intrinsic value (ie the difference between the share price and the exercise price), if any, at grant date. Typically, this results in no expense being recognised for fixed plans, because most share options granted under fixed plans are granted at the money. For performance-related and other variable plans, an expense is measured at intrinsic value at the measurement date. The measurement date is when both the number of shares or share options that the employee is entitled to receive and the exercise price are fixed. Because this measurement date is likely to be much later than grant date, any expense is subject to uncertainty and, if the share price is increasing, the expense for performance-related plans would be larger than for fixed plans.

BC274   In SFAS 123, the FASB noted that APB 25 is criticised for producing anomalous results and for lacking any underlying conceptual rationale. For example, the requirements of APB 25 typically result in the recognition of an expense for performance-related share options but usually no expense is recognised for fixed share options. This result is anomalous because fixed share options are usually more valuable at grant date than performance-related share options. Moreover, the omission of an expense for fixed share options impairs the quality of financial statements:

> The resulting financial statements are less credible than they could be, and the financial statements of entities that use fixed employee share options extensively are not comparable to those of entities that do not make significant use of fixed options. (SFAS 123, paragraph 56)

BC275   The Discussion Paper, in its discussion of US GAAP, noted that the different accounting treatments for fixed and performance-related plans also had the perverse effect of discouraging entities from setting up performance-related employee share plans.

SFAS 123

BC276   SFAS 123 was issued in 1995. It requires recognition of share-based payment transactions with parties other than employees, based on the fair value of the shares or share options issued or the fair value of the goods or services received, whichever is more reliably measurable. Entities are also encouraged, but not required, to apply the fair value accounting method in SFAS 123 to share-based payment transactions with employees. Generally speaking, SFAS 123 draws no distinction between fixed and performance-related plans.

BC277   If an entity applies the accounting method in APB 25 rather than that in SFAS 123, SFAS 123 requires disclosures of pro forma net income and earnings per share in the annual financial statements, as if the standard had been applied. Recently, a significant number of major US companies have voluntarily adopted the fair value accounting method in SFAS 123 for transactions with employees.

BC278   The FASB regards SFAS 123 as superior to APB 25, and would have preferred recognition based on the fair value of employee options to be mandatory, not optional. SFAS 123 makes it clear that the FASB decided to permit the disclosure-based alternative for political reasons, not because it thought that it was the best accounting solution:

> ... the Board ... continues to believe that disclosure is not an adequate substitute for recognition of assets, liabilities, equity, revenues and expenses in financial statements ... The Board chose a disclosure-based solution for stock-based employee compensation to bring closure to the divisive debate on this issue—not because it believes that solution is the best way to improve financial accounting and reporting.

> (SFAS 123, paragraphs 61 and 62)

BC279   Under US GAAP, the accounting treatment of share-based payment transactions differs, depending on whether the other party to the transaction is an employee or non-employee, and whether the entity chooses to apply SFAS 123 or APB 25 to transactions with employees. Having a choice of accounting methods is generally regarded as undesirable. Indeed, the Board recently devoted much time and effort to developing improvements to existing international standards, one of the objectives of which is to eliminate choices of accounting methods.

BC280   Research in the US demonstrates that choosing one accounting method over the other has a significant impact on the reported earnings of US entities. For example, research by Bear Stearns and Credit Suisse First Boston on the S&P 500 shows that, had the fair value measurement method in SFAS 123 been applied for the purposes of recognising an expense for employee stock-based compensation, the earnings of the S&P 500 companies would have been significantly lower, and that the effect is growing. The effect on reported earnings is substantial in some sectors, where companies make heavy use of share options.

BC281   The Canadian Accounting Standards Board (AcSB) recently completed its project on share-based payment. In accordance with the AcSB's policy of harmonising Canadian standards with those in the US, the AcSB initially proposed a standard that was based on US GAAP, including APB 25. After considering respondents' comments, the AcSB decided to delete the guidance drawn from APB 25. The AcSB reached this decision for various reasons, including that, in its view, the intrinsic value method is flawed. Also, incorporating the requirements of APB 25 into an accounting standard would result in preparers of financial statements incurring substantial costs for which users of financial statements would derive no benefit—entities would spend a great deal of time and effort on understanding the rules and then redesigning option plans, usually by deleting existing performance conditions, to avoid recognising an expense in respect of such plans, thereby producing no improvement in the accounting for share option plans.

BC282   The Canadian standard was initially consistent with SFAS 123. That included permitting a choice between fair value-based accounting for employee stock-based compensation expense in the income statement and disclosure of pro forma amounts in the notes to both interim and annual financial statements. However, the AcSB recently amended its standard to remove the choice between recognition and disclosure, and therefore expense recognition is mandatory for financial periods beginning on or after 1 January 2004.

BC283   Because APB 25 contains serious flaws, the Board concluded that basing an IFRS on it is unlikely to represent much, if any, improvement in financial reporting. Moreover, the perverse effects of APB 25, particularly in discouraging performance-related share option plans, may cause economic distortions. Accounting standards are intended to be neutral, not to give favourable or unfavourable accounting treatments to particular transactions to encourage or discourage entities from entering into those transactions. APB 25 fails to achieve that objective. Performance-related employee share plans are common in Europe (performance conditions are often required by law) and in other parts of the world outside the US, and investors are calling for greater use of performance conditions. Therefore, the Board concluded that introducing an accounting standard based on APB 25 would be inconsistent with its objective of developing high quality accounting standards.

BC284　That leaves SFAS 123. Comments from the FASB, in the SFAS 123 Basis for Conclusions, and from the Canadian AcSB when it developed a standard based on SFAS 123, indicate that both standard-setters regard it as inadequate, because it permits a choice between recognition and disclosure. (This issue is discussed further below.) The FASB added to its agenda in March 2003 a project to review US accounting requirements on share-based payment, including removing the disclosure alternative in SFAS 123, so that expense recognition is mandatory. The Chairman of the FASB commented:

> Recent events have served as a reminder to all of us that clear, credible and comparable financial information is essential to the health and vitality of our capital market system. In the wake of the market meltdown and corporate reporting scandals, the FASB has received numerous requests from individual and institutional investors, financial analysts and many others urging the Board to mandate the expensing of the compensation cost relating to employee stock options ... While a number of major companies have voluntarily opted to reflect these costs as an expense in reporting their earnings, other companies continue to show these costs in the footnotes to their financial statements. In addition, a move to require an expense treatment would be consistent with the FASB's commitment to work toward convergence between U.S. and international accounting standards. In taking all of these factors into consideration, the Board concluded that it was critical that it now revisit this important subject. (FASB News Release, 12 March 2003)

BC285　During the Board's redeliberations of the proposals in ED 2, the Board worked with the FASB to achieve convergence of international and US standards, to the extent possible, bearing in mind that the FASB was at an earlier stage in its project—the FASB was developing an Exposure Draft to revise SFAS 123 whereas the IASB was finalising its IFRS. The Board concluded that, although convergence is an important objective, it would not be appropriate to delay the issue of the IFRS, because of the pressing need for a standard on share-based payment, as explained in paragraphs BC2–BC5. In any event, at the time the IASB concluded its deliberations, a substantial amount of convergence had been achieved. For example, the FASB agreed with the IASB that all share-based payment transactions should be recognised in the financial statements, measured on a fair value measurement basis, including transactions in which share options are granted to employees. Hence, the FASB agreed that the disclosure alternative in SFAS 123 should be eliminated.

BC286　The IASB and FASB also agreed that, once both boards have issued final standards on share-based payment, the two boards will consider undertaking a convergence project, with the objective of eliminating any remaining areas of divergence between international and US standards on this topic.

Recognition versus disclosure

BC287　A basic accounting concept is that disclosure of financial information is not an adequate substitute for recognition in the financial statements. For example, the *Framework* states:

Items that meet the recognition criteria should be recognised in the balance sheet or income statement. The failure to recognise such items is not rectified by disclosure of the accounting policies used nor by notes or explanatory material. (paragraph 82)[29]

BC288 A key aspect of the recognition criteria is that the item can be measured with reliability. This issue is discussed further below. Therefore, this discussion focuses on the 'recognition versus disclosure' issue in principle, not on measurement reliability. Once it has been determined that an item meets the criteria for recognition in the financial statements, failing to recognise it is inconsistent with the basic concept that disclosure is not an adequate substitute for recognition.

BC289 Some disagree with this concept, arguing that it makes no difference whether information is recognised in the financial statements or disclosed in the notes. Either way, users of financial statements have the information they require to make economic decisions. Hence, they believe that note disclosure of expenses arising from particular employee share-based payment transactions (ie those involving awards of share options to employees), rather than recognition in the income statement, is acceptable.

BC290 The Board did not accept this argument. The Board noted that if note disclosure is acceptable, because it makes no difference whether the expense is recognised or disclosed, then recognition in the financial statements must also be acceptable for the same reason. If recognition is acceptable, and recognition rather than mere disclosure accords with the accounting principles applied to all other expense items, it is not acceptable to leave one particular expense item out of the income statement.

BC291 The Board also noted that there is significant evidence that there is a difference between recognition and disclosure. First, academic research indicates that whether information is recognised or merely disclosed affects market prices (eg Barth, Clinch and Shibano, 2003).[30] If information is disclosed only in the notes, users of financial statements have to expend time and effort to become sufficiently expert in accounting to know (a) that there are items that are not recognised in the financial statements, (b) that there is information about those items in the notes, and (c) how to assess the note disclosures. Because gaining that expertise comes at a cost, and not all users of financial statements will become accounting experts, information that is merely disclosed may not be fully reflected in share prices.

BC292 Second, both preparers and users of financial statements appear to agree that there is an important difference between recognition and disclosure. Users of financial statements have strongly expressed the view that all forms of share-based payment, including employee share options, should be recognised in the financial statements, resulting in the recognition of an expense when the goods or services received are consumed, and that note disclosure alone is inadequate. Their views have been expressed by various means, including:

---

29 now paragraph 4.37 of the *Conceptual Framework*

30 M E Barth, G Clinch and T Shibano. 2003. Market Effects of Recognition and Disclosure. *Journal of Accounting Research* 41(4): 581–609.

(a)   users' responses to the Discussion Paper and ED 2.

(b)   the 2001 survey by the Association for Investment Management and Research of analysts and fund managers—83 per cent of survey respondents said the accounting method for all share-based payment transactions should require recognition of an expense in the income statement.

(c)   public comments by users of financial statements, such as those reported in the press or made at recent US Senate hearings.

BC293   Preparers of financial statements also see a major difference between recognition and disclosure. For example, some preparers who responded to the Discussion Paper and ED 2 were concerned that unless expense recognition is required in all countries, entities that are required to recognise an expense would be at a competitive disadvantage compared with entities that are permitted a choice between recognition and disclosure. Comments such as these indicate that preparers of financial statements regard expense recognition as having consequences that are different from those of disclosure.

Reliability of measurement

BC294   One reason commonly given by those who oppose the recognition of an expense arising from transactions involving grants of share options to employees is that it is not possible to measure those transactions reliably.

BC295   The Board discussed these concerns about reliability, after first putting the issue into context. For example, the Board noted that when estimating the fair value of share options, the objective is to measure that fair value at the measurement date, not the value of the underlying share at some future date. Some regard the fair value estimate as inherently uncertain because it is not known, at the measurement date, what the final outcome will be, ie how much the gain on exercise (if any) will be. However, the valuation does not attempt to estimate the future gain, only the amount that the other party would pay to obtain the right to participate in any future gains. Therefore, even if the share option expires worthless or the employee makes a large gain on exercise, this does not mean that the grant date estimate of the fair value of that option was unreliable or wrong.

BC296   The Board also noted that accounting often involves making estimates, and therefore reporting an estimated fair value is not objectionable merely because that amount represents an estimate rather than a precise measure. Examples of other estimates made in accounting, which may have a material effect on the income statement and the balance sheet, include estimates of the collectability of doubtful debts, estimates of the useful life of fixed assets and the pattern of their consumption, and estimates of employee pension liabilities.

BC297   However, some argue that including in the financial statements an estimate of the fair value of employee share options is different from including other estimates, because there is no subsequent correction of the estimate. Other estimates, such as employee pension costs, will ultimately be revised to equal the amount of the cash paid out. In contrast, because equity is not remeasured, if the estimated fair value of employee share options is recognised, there is no remeasurement of the fair value estimate—unless exercise date measurement is used—so any estimation error is permanently embedded in the financial statements.

BC298   The FASB considered and rejected this argument in developing SFAS 123. For example, for employee pension costs, the total cost is never completely trued up unless the scheme is terminated, the amount attributed to any particular year is never trued up, and it can take decades before the amounts relating to particular employees are trued up. In the meantime, users of financial statements have made economic decisions based on the estimated costs.

BC299   Moreover, the Board noted that if no expense (or an expense based on intrinsic value only, which is typically zero) is recognised in respect of employee share options, that also means that there is an error that is permanently embedded in the financial statements. Reporting zero (or an amount based on intrinsic value, if any) is never trued up.

BC300   The Board also considered the meaning of reliability. Arguments about whether estimates of the fair value of employee share options are sufficiently reliable focus on one aspect of reliability only—whether the estimate is free from material error. The *Framework*, in common with the conceptual frameworks of other accounting standard-setters, makes it clear that another important aspect of reliability is whether the information can be depended upon by users of financial statements to represent faithfully what it purports to represent. Therefore, in assessing whether a particular accounting method produces reliable financial information, it is necessary to consider whether that information is representationally faithful. This is one way in which reliability is linked to another important qualitative characteristic of financial information, relevance.

BC301   For example, in the context of share-based payment, some commentators advocate measuring employee share options at intrinsic value rather than fair value, because intrinsic value is regarded as a much more reliable measure. Whether intrinsic value is a more reliable measure is doubtful—it is certainly less subject to estimation error, but is unlikely to be a representationally faithful measure of remuneration. Nor is intrinsic value a relevant measure, especially when measured at grant date. Many employee share options are issued at the money, so have no intrinsic value at grant date. A share option with no intrinsic value consists entirely of time value. If a share option is measured at intrinsic value at grant date, zero value is attributed to the share option. Therefore, by ignoring time value, the amount attributed to the share option is 100 per cent understated.

BC302   Another qualitative characteristic is comparability. Some argue that, given the uncertainties relating to estimating the fair value of employee share options, it is better for all entities to report zero, because this will make financial statements more comparable. They argue that if, for example, for two entities the 'true' amount of expense relating to employee share options is CU500,000, and estimation uncertainties cause one entity to report CU450,000 and the other to report CU550,000, the two entities' financial statements would be more comparable if both reported zero, rather than these divergent figures.

BC303   However, it is unlikely that any two entities will have the same amount of employee share-based remuneration expense. Research (eg by Bear Stearns and Credit Suisse First Boston) indicates that the expense varies widely from industry to industry, from entity to entity, and from year to year. Reporting zero rather than an estimated amount is likely to make the financial statements much less comparable, not more comparable. For example, if the estimated employee share-based remuneration expense of Company A, Company B and Company C is CU10,000, CU100,000 and CU1,000,000 respectively, reporting zero for all three companies will not make their financial statements comparable.

BC304   In the context of the foregoing discussion of reliability, the Board addressed the question whether transactions involving share options granted to employees can be measured with sufficient reliability for the purpose of recognition in the financial statements. The Board noted that many respondents to the Discussion Paper asserted that this is not possible. They argue that option pricing models cannot be applied to employee share options, because of the differences between employee options and traded options.

BC305   The Board considered these differences, with the assistance of the project's Advisory Group and other experts, and has reached conclusions on how to take account of these differences when estimating the fair value of employee share options, as explained in paragraphs BC145–BC199. In doing so, the Board noted that the objective is to measure the fair value of the share options, ie an estimate of what the price of those equity instruments would have been on grant date in an arm's length transaction between knowledgeable, willing parties. The valuation methodology applied should therefore be consistent with valuation methodologies that market participants would use for pricing similar financial instruments, and should incorporate all factors and assumptions that knowledgeable, willing market participants would consider in setting the price.

BC306   Hence, factors that a knowledgeable, willing market participant would not consider in setting the price of an option are not relevant when estimating the fair value of shares, share options or other equity instruments granted. For example, for share options granted to employees, factors that affect the value of the option from the individual employee's perspective only are not relevant to estimating the price that would be set by a knowledgeable, willing market participant. Many respondents' comments about measurement reliability, and the differences between employee share options and traded options, often focused on the value of the option from the employee's perspective. Therefore, the Board concluded that the IFRS should emphasise that the objective is to estimate the fair value of the share option, not an employee-specific value.

BC307   The Board noted that there is evidence to support a conclusion that it is possible to make a reliable estimate of the fair value of employee share options. First, there is academic research to support this conclusion (eg Carpenter 1998, Maller, Tan and Van De Vyver 2002).[31] Second, users of financial statements regard the estimated fair values as sufficiently reliable for recognition in the financial statements. Evidence of this can be found in a variety of sources, such

---

31   J N Carpenter. 1998. The exercise and valuation of executive stock options. *Journal of Financial Economics* 48: 127–158. R A Maller, R Tan and M Van De Vyver. 2002. How Might Companies Value ESOs? *Australian Accounting Review* 12 (1): 11–24.

as the comment letters received from users of financial statements who responded to the Discussion Paper and ED 2. Users' views are important, because the objective of financial statements is to provide high quality, transparent and comparable information to help users make economic decisions. In other words, financial statements are intended to meet the needs of users, rather than preparers or other interest groups. The purpose of setting accounting standards is to ensure that, wherever possible, the information provided in the financial statements meets users' needs. Therefore, if the people who use the financial statements in making economic decisions regard the fair value estimates as sufficiently reliable for recognition in the financial statements, this provides strong evidence of measurement reliability.

BC308   The Board also noted that, although the FASB decided to permit a choice between recognition and disclosure of expenses arising from employee share-based payment transactions, it did so for non-technical reasons, not because it agreed with the view that reliable measurement was not possible:

> The Board continues to believe that use of option-pricing models, as modified in this statement, will produce estimates of the fair value of stock options that are sufficiently reliable to justify recognition in financial statements. Imprecision in those estimates does not justify failure to recognize compensation cost stemming from employee stock options. That belief underlies the Board's encouragement to entities to adopt the fair value based method of recognizing stock-based employee compensation cost in their financial statements. (SFAS 123, Basis for Conclusions, paragraph 117)

BC309   In summary, if expenses arising from grants of share options to employees are omitted from the financial statements, or recognised using the intrinsic value method (which typically results in zero expense) or the minimum value method, there will be a permanent error embedded in the financial statements. So the question is, which accounting method is more likely to produce the smallest amount of error and the most relevant, comparable information—a fair value estimate, which might result in some understatement or overstatement of the associated expense, or another measurement basis, such as intrinsic value (especially if measured at grant date), that will definitely result in substantial understatement of the associated expense?

BC310   Taking all of the above into consideration, the Board concluded that, in virtually all cases, the estimated fair value of employee share options at grant date can be measured with sufficient reliability for the purposes of recognising employee share-based payment transactions in the financial statements. The Board therefore concluded that, in general, the IFRS on share-based payment should require a fair value measurement method to be applied to all types of share-based payment transactions, including all types of employee share-based payment. Hence, the Board concluded that the IFRS should not allow a choice between a fair value measurement method and an intrinsic value measurement method, and should not permit a choice between recognition and disclosure of expenses arising from employee share-based payment transactions.

Transitional provisions

Share-based payment transactions among group entities

BC310A The Board noted a potential difficulty when an entity retrospectively applies the amendments made by *Group Cash-settled Share-based Payment Transactions* issued in June 2009. An entity might not have accounted for some group share-based payment transactions in accordance with IFRS 2 in its separate or individual financial statements. In a few cases, an entity that settles a group share-based payment transaction may have to apply hindsight to measure the fair value of awards now required to be accounted for as cash-settled. However, the Board noted that such transactions would have been accounted for in accordance with IFRS 2 in the group's consolidated financial statements. For these reasons and those outlined in paragraph BC268G, if the information necessary for retrospective application is not available, the Board decided to require an entity to use amounts previously recognised in the group's consolidated financial statements when applying the new requirements retrospectively in the entity's separate or individual financial statements.

Consequential amendments to other Standards

Tax effects of share-based payment transactions

BC311 Whether expenses arising from share-based payment transactions are deductible, and if so, whether the amount of the tax deduction is the same as the reported expense and whether the tax deduction arises in the same accounting period, varies from country to country.

BC312 If the amount of the tax deduction is the same as the reported expense, but the tax deduction arises in a later accounting period, this will result in a deductible temporary difference under IAS 12 *Income Taxes*. Temporary differences usually arise from differences between the carrying amount of assets and liabilities and the amount attributed to those assets and liabilities for tax purposes. However, IAS 12 also deals with items that have a tax base but are not recognised as assets and liabilities in the balance sheet. It gives an example of research costs that are recognised as an expense in the financial statements in the period in which the costs are incurred, but are deductible for tax purposes in a later accounting period. The Standard states that the difference between the tax base of the research costs, being the amount that will be deductible in a future accounting period, and the carrying amount of nil is a deductible temporary difference that results in a deferred tax asset (IAS 12, paragraph 9).

BC313 Applying this guidance indicates that if an expense arising from a share-based payment transaction is recognised in the financial statements in one accounting period and is tax-deductible in a later accounting period, this should be accounted for as a deductible temporary difference under IAS 12. Under that Standard, a deferred tax asset is recognised for all deductible temporary differences to the extent that it is probable that taxable profit will be available against which the deductible temporary difference can be used (IAS 12, paragraph 24).

BC314   Whilst IAS 12 does not discuss reverse situations, the same logic applies. For example, suppose the entity is able to claim a tax deduction for the total transaction amount at the date of grant but the entity recognises an expense arising from that transaction over the vesting period. Applying the guidance in IAS 12 suggests that this should be accounted for as a taxable temporary difference, and hence a deferred tax liability should be recognised.

BC315   However, the amount of the tax deduction might differ from the amount of the expense recognised in the financial statements. For example, the measurement basis applied for accounting purposes might not be the same as that used for tax purposes, eg intrinsic value might be used for tax purposes and fair value for accounting purposes. Similarly, the measurement date might differ. For example, US entities receive a tax deduction based on intrinsic value at the date of exercise in respect of some share options, whereas for accounting purposes an entity applying SFAS 123 would recognise an expense based on the option's fair value, measured at the date of grant. There could also be other differences in the measurement method applied for accounting and tax purposes, eg differences in the treatment of forfeitures or different valuation methodologies applied.

BC316   SFAS 123 requires that, if the amount of the tax deduction exceeds the total expense recognised in the financial statements, the tax benefit for the excess deduction should be recognised as additional paid-in capital, ie as a direct credit to equity. Conversely, if the tax deduction is less than the total expense recognised for accounting purposes, the write-off of the related deferred tax asset in excess of the benefits of the tax deduction is recognised in the income statement, except to the extent that there is remaining additional paid-in capital from excess tax deductions from previous share-based payment transactions (SFAS 123, paragraph 44).

BC317   At first sight, it may seem questionable to credit or debit directly to equity amounts that relate to differences between the amount of the tax deduction and the total recognised expense. The tax effects of any such differences would ordinarily flow through the income statement. However, some argue that the approach in SFAS 123 is appropriate if the reason for the difference between the amount of the tax deduction and the recognised expense is that a different measurement date is applied.

BC318   For example, suppose grant date measurement is used for accounting purposes and exercise date measurement is used for tax purposes. Under grant date measurement, any changes in the value of the equity instrument after grant date accrue to the employee (or other party) in their capacity as equity participants. Therefore, some argue that any tax effects arising from those valuation changes should be credited to equity (or debited to equity, if the value of the equity instrument declines).

BC319   Similarly, some argue that the tax deduction arises from an equity transaction (the exercise of options), and hence the tax effects should be reported in equity. It can also be argued that this treatment is consistent with the requirement in IAS 12 to account for the tax effects of transactions or events in the same way as the entity accounts for those transactions or events themselves. If the tax deduction relates to both an income statement item and an equity item, the associated tax effects should be allocated between the income statement and equity.

BC320   Others disagree, arguing that the tax deduction relates to employee remuneration expense, ie an income statement item only, and therefore all of the tax effects of the deduction should be recognised in the income statement. The fact that the taxing authority applies a different method in measuring the amount of the tax deduction does not change this conclusion. A further argument is that this treatment is consistent with the *Framework*, because reporting amounts directly in equity would be inappropriate, given that the government is not an owner of the entity.

BC321   The Board noted that, if one accepts that it might be appropriate to debit/credit to equity the tax effect of the difference between the amount of the tax deduction and the total recognised expense where that difference relates to changes in the value of equity interests, there could be other reasons why the amount of the tax deduction differs from the total recognised expense. For example, grant date measurement may be used for both tax and accounting purposes, but the valuation methodology used for tax purposes might produce a higher value than the methodology used for accounting purposes (eg the effects of early exercise might be ignored when valuing an option for tax purposes). The Board saw no reason why, in this situation, the excess tax benefits should be credited to equity.

BC322   In developing ED 2, the Board concluded that the tax effects of share-based payment transactions should be recognised in the income statement by being taken into account in the determination of tax expense. It agreed that this should be explained in the form of a worked example in a consequential amendment to IAS 12.

BC323   During the Board's redeliberation of the proposals in ED 2, the Board reconsidered the points above, and concluded that the tax effects of an equity-settled share-based payment transaction should be allocated between the income statement and equity. The Board then considered how this allocation should be made and related issues, such as the measurement of the deferred tax asset.

BC324   Under IAS 12, the deferred tax asset for a deductible temporary difference is based on the amount the taxation authorities will permit as a deduction in future periods. Therefore, the Board concluded that the measurement of the deferred tax asset should be based on an estimate of the future tax deduction. If changes in the share price affect that future tax deduction, the estimate of the expected future tax deduction should be based on the current share price.

BC325   These conclusions are consistent with the proposals in ED 2 concerning the measurement of the deferred tax asset. However, this approach differs from SFAS 123, which measures the deferred tax asset on the basis of the cumulative recognised expense. The Board rejected the SFAS 123 method of measuring the deferred tax asset because it is inconsistent with IAS 12. As noted above, under IAS 12, the deferred tax asset for a deductible temporary difference is based on the amount the taxation authorities will permit as a deduction in future periods. If a later measurement date is applied for tax purposes, it is very unlikely that the tax deduction will ever equal the cumulative expense, except by coincidence. For example, if share options are granted to employees, and the entity receives a tax deduction measured as the difference between the share price and the exercise price at the date of exercise, it is extremely unlikely that the tax deduction will ever equal the cumulative expense. By basing the measurement of the deferred tax asset on the cumulative expense, the SFAS 123 method is likely to result in the understatement or overstatement of the deferred tax asset. In some situations, such as when share options are significantly out of the money, SFAS 123 requires the entity to continue to recognise a deferred tax asset even when the possibility of the entity recovering that asset is remote. Continuing to recognise a deferred tax asset in this situation is not only inconsistent with IAS 12, it is inconsistent with the definition of an asset in the *Framework*, and the requirements of other IFRSs for the recognition and measurement of assets, including requirements to assess impairment.

BC326 The Board also concluded that:

(a) if the tax deduction received (or expected to be received, measured as described in paragraph BC324) is less than or equal to the cumulative expense, the associated tax benefits received (or expected to be received) should be recognised as tax income and included in profit or loss for the period.

(b) if the tax deduction received (or expected to be received, measured as described in paragraph BC324) exceeds the cumulative expense, the excess associated tax benefits received (or expected to be received) should be recognised directly in equity.

BC327 The above allocation method is similar to that applied in SFAS 123, with some exceptions. First, the above allocation method ensures that the total tax benefits recognised in the income statement in respect of a particular share-based payment transaction do not exceed the tax benefits ultimately received. The Board disagreed with the approach in SFAS 123, which sometimes results in the total tax benefits recognised in the income statement exceeding the tax benefits ultimately received because, in some situations, SFAS 123 permits the unrecovered portion of the deferred tax asset to be written off to equity.

BC328 Second, the Board concluded that the above allocation method should be applied irrespective of why the tax deduction received (or expected to be received) differs from the cumulative expense. The SFAS 123 method is based on US tax legislation, under which the excess tax benefits credited to equity (if any) arise from the use of a later measurement date for tax purposes. The Board agreed with respondents who commented that the accounting treatment must be capable of being applied in various tax jurisdictions. The Board was concerned that requiring entities to examine the reasons why there is a difference between the tax deduction and the cumulative expense, and then account for the tax effects accordingly, would be too complex to be applied consistently across a wide range of different tax jurisdictions.

BC329 The Board noted that it might need to reconsider its conclusions on accounting for the tax effects of share-based payment transactions in the future, for example, if the Board reviews IAS 12 more broadly.

Accounting for own shares held

BC330 IAS 32 requires the acquisition of treasury shares to be deducted from equity, and no gain or loss is to be recognised on the sale, issue or cancellation of treasury shares. Consideration received on the subsequent sale or issue of treasury shares is credited to equity.

BC331 This is consistent with the *Framework*. The repurchase of shares and their subsequent reissue or transfer to other parties are transactions with equity participants that should be recognised as changes in equity. In accounting terms, there is no difference between shares that are repurchased and cancelled, and shares that are repurchased and held by the entity. In both cases, the repurchase involves an outflow of resources to shareholders (ie a distribution), thereby reducing shareholders' investment in the entity. Similarly, there is no difference between a new issue of shares and an issue of shares previously repurchased and held in treasury. In both cases, there is an inflow of resources from shareholders, thereby increasing shareholders' investment in the entity. Although accounting practice in some jurisdictions treats own shares held as assets, this is not consistent with the definition of assets in the *Framework* and the conceptual frameworks of other standard-setters, as explained in the Discussion Paper (footnote to paragraph 4.7 of the Discussion Paper, reproduced earlier in the footnote to paragraph BC73).

BC332 Given that treasury shares are treated as an asset in some jurisdictions, it will be necessary to change that accounting treatment when this IFRS is applied, because otherwise an entity would be faced with two expense items—an expense arising from the share-based payment transaction (for the consumption of goods and services received as consideration for the issue of an equity instrument) and another expense arising from the write-down of the 'asset' for treasury shares issued or transferred to employees at an exercise price that is less than their purchase price.

BC333 Hence, the Board concluded that the requirements in the relevant paragraphs of IAS 32 regarding treasury shares should also be applied to treasury shares purchased, sold, issued or cancelled in connection with employee share plans or other share-based payment arrangements.

Definition of vesting condition (2013 amendments)

BC334 The Board decided to clarify the definition of 'vesting conditions' in IFRS 2 to ensure the consistent classification of conditions attached to a share-based payment. Previously, this Standard did not separately define 'performance condition' or 'service condition', but instead described both concepts within the definition of vesting conditions.

BC335 The Board decided to separate the definitions of performance condition and service condition from the definition of vesting condition to make the description of each condition clearer.

BC336   In response to the comments received on the Exposure Draft *Annual Improvements to IFRSs 2010–2012 Cycle* (Proposed amendments to International Financial Reporting Standards) (the 'ED'), published in May 2012, the Board addressed the following concerns that had been raised about the definitions of performance condition, service condition and market condition:

(a)   whether a performance target can be set by reference to the price (or value) of another entity (or entities) that is (are) within the group;

(b)   whether a performance target that refers to a longer period than the required service period may constitute a performance condition;

(c)   whether the specified period of service that the counterparty is required to complete can be either implicit or explicit;

(d)   whether a performance target needs to be influenced by an employee;

(e)   whether a share market index target may constitute a performance condition or a non-vesting condition;

(f)   whether the definition of performance condition should indicate that it includes a market condition;

(g)   whether a definition of non-vesting condition is needed; and

(h)   whether the employee's failure to complete a required service period due to termination of employment is considered to be a failure to satisfy a service condition.

Whether a performance target can be set by reference to the price (or value) of another entity (or entities) that is (are) within the group

BC337   The Board decided to clarify that within the context of a share-based payment transaction that involves entities in the same group, a performance target can be defined by the price (or value) of the equity instruments of another entity in that group. This amendment is consistent with the guidance in paragraphs 3A and 43A–43D of IFRS 2. Paragraph 3A, which provides guidance about the scope of IFRS 2, states that "a share-based payment transaction may be settled by another group entity (or a shareholder of any group entity) on behalf of the entity receiving or acquiring the goods or services".

BC338   The Board decided to make a similar amendment to the definition of market condition to indicate that a market condition can be based on the market price of the entity's equity instruments or the equity instruments of another entity in the same group.

Whether a performance target that refers to a longer period than the required service period may constitute a performance condition

BC339   The Board observed that IFRS 2 was not clear about the duration of a performance target relative to the duration of the related service condition. Some understood IFRS 2 to require that the duration of the performance has to be wholly within the period of the related service requirement; others understood that a performance target could be achieved over a period that extends beyond the period for which the employee is required to provide a service.

BC340   During its deliberations prior to the issue of the ED, the Board decided to clarify that the duration of the performance condition needed to be wholly within the period of the related service requirement. This meant that the period of achieving the performance target could not start before, or end after, the service period. This requirement was reflected in the ED.

BC341   Some respondents to the ED disagreed with the requirement that the duration of the performance condition needed to be wholly within the period of the related service, because they asserted that it was common for a performance target to start before the service period. For example, a performance target could be set as a measure of the growth in earnings per share (the 'EPS target') between the most recently published financial statements on the grant date and the most recently published financial statements before the vesting date.

BC342   Other respondents noted that if the beginning of the period for achieving the performance target was restricted, then a relatively minor difference in the way that the awards are structured could lead to a different classification of the performance target (ie as either a non-vesting condition or a performance (vesting) condition), which could consequently lead to differences in the way in which the award would be accounted for in accordance with the guidance in IFRS 2.

BC343   In response to the comments received on the ED, the Board decided to revise the proposed definition of performance condition. In this revision, the Board decided to ease the restriction on when the period for a performance target could start. It therefore decided to clarify that the start of the period of achieving the performance target could be before the service period, provided that the commencement date of the performance target is not substantially before the commencement of the service period.

BC344   However, the Board decided to retain the proposal in the ED that the period over which the performance target is achieved should not extend beyond the service period. It thought that this decision was consistent with the definition of a performance condition, which was previously included within the definition of a vesting condition. The definition of a performance condition requires the counterparty to complete a specified period of service and to meet the performance target(s) while the counterparty is rendering the service required. The definition of performance condition reflects the principle in paragraph 7 of IFRS 2, which states that "An entity shall recognise the goods or services received or acquired in a share-based payment transaction when it obtains the goods or as the services are received".

BC345   The Board also decided to add the words "ie a **service condition**" to criterion (a) of the definition of performance condition in order to create a cross-reference to the definition of service condition.

Whether the specified period of service that the counterparty is required to complete can be either implicit or explicit

BC346　In the definition of performance condition, the Board decided to highlight a feature that distinguishes a performance condition from a non-vesting condition in accordance with paragraph BC171A of IFRS 2; namely, that a performance condition has an explicit or implicit service requirement and a non-vesting condition does not. This is so that, in order to constitute a performance condition, a performance target needs to be accompanied by a service requirement, which can be implicit or explicit. The Board observed that if the share-based payment arrangement does not contain an explicit requirement to provide services, the arrangement may still contain an implicit service condition.

Whether a performance target needs to be influenced by an employee

BC347　During its deliberations the Board observed that for a target to constitute a performance condition it needs to be both 'within the influence' of the employee and in the interest of the entity. Consequently, the Board proposed that the definition of performance condition should make clear that a performance target is defined by reference to the entity's own operations (or activities) or the price (or value) of its equity instruments (including shares and share options).

BC348　In response to the ED, some respondents indicated that the reason why the performance target needed to be within the influence of the employee was unclear and found it to be contradictory to the proposed definition of performance condition. This is because in the proposed definition, the performance target was defined by reference to the performance of the entity, that is, by reference to the entity's own operations (or activities) or the price (or value) of its equity instruments. Some other respondents also raised some difficulties that they expected to encounter when applying the proposed guidance. In this respect, the respondents stated that determining whether a performance target is within the influence of the employee would be difficult to apply in the case of a group of entities; for example, the profit or share price of a group of companies could be seen to be 'remote from the influence of' an employee of a particular subsidiary of the group.

BC349　The Board observed that requiring a performance target to be within the influence of the employee could be misinterpreted as meaning that the Board's intention was to challenge management to explain how the performance of the employee affects the performance target. The Board confirmed that it was not its intention to do so. It observed that the link between the employee's service/performance against a given performance target is management's responsibility. It noted that each employee has, in varying degrees, an influence over an entity's (or group's) overall performance, that is, over an entity's (or group's) own operations (or activities) or the price (or value) of its equity instruments. Consequently, the Board decided to omit the requirement that the target "needs to be within the influence of the employee" to avoid further confusion.

BC350   In its review of the definition of performance condition the Board also considered what, if any, level of correlation is required between an employee's responsibility and the performance target. Potential diversity in practice had emerged because some were of the view that if share based payment awards are granted to employees conditional on the entity-wide profit, it is not clear that the profit target constitutes a performance condition on the basis that the employee might have so little influence on the entity-wide profit that it is not clear whether the target is able to sufficiently incentivise an individual employee's actions. Others held the view that because the entity is in business in order to make a profit, it is reasonable to assume that all employees contribute directly or indirectly to the entity-wide profit, ie that the whole body of employees contribute towards the entity-wide profit.

BC351   In the ED the Board observed that it is reasonable to assume that the performance target that is set by management for an employee's share-based payment appropriately incentivises the employee to provide an increased quality and/or quantity of service to benefit the entity. Consequently, the Board decided that the definition of performance condition should make clear that a performance target may relate either to the performance of the entity as a whole or to some part of it, such as a division or an individual employee.

BC352   Respondents to the ED questioned whether it was the Board's intention to require an entity to demonstrate, or provide evidence of, the correlation between an employee's responsibility and the performance target in order for that target to be a performance condition. During its deliberations, the Board confirmed that it was not its intention to require an entity to prove this correlation.

Whether a share market index target may constitute a performance condition or a non-vesting condition

BC353   The Board analysed the case in which a share-based payment is conditional on a share market index target and whether it would be considered a performance condition or a non-vesting condition. For example, a grant might be conditional on a stock exchange index (of which the entity's shares are a part) reaching a specified target and the employee remaining in service up to the date that the target is met.

BC354   The Board observed that some might argue that the share market index target with the implicit service requirement constitutes a performance condition, because an employee is required to provide service to the entity, and that the time estimated to affect the share market index target implicitly determines how long the entity receives the required service. Others might argue that the share market index target is a non-vesting condition because it is not related to the performance of the entity (ie instead it is related to, or based on, not only the entity's share price but also the share price of other unrelated entities).

BC355   In the ED the Board observed that the share market index target would be considered a non-vesting condition because it is not related to the performance of the entity or of another entity in the same group, even if the shares of the entity or of another entity in the same group form part of that index. The Board also observed that a share market index target may be predominantly affected by many external variables or factors involved in its determination, including macroeconomic factors such as the risk-free interest rate or foreign exchange rates and, consequently, it is remote from the influence of the employee.

BC356   Respondents to the ED agreed that it would be reasonable to assume that the share market index target is a non-vesting condition but some thought that it should not be based on the level of influence exercised by an employee over the performance target or on whether the target is affected by external variables or factors. This is because, in their view, the level of influence and the effect of external variables are subjective reasons that are difficult to measure.

BC357   The Board decided to reaffirm its position that a share market index is a non-vesting condition but, on the basis of the comments received, it is clarifying that the reason why it is a non-vesting condition is because a share market index not only reflects the performance of an entity but, in addition, also reflects the performance of other entities outside the group.

BC358   The Board also considered a similar case in which the entity's share price makes up a substantial part of the share market index. The Board determined that even in such a case the condition should still be considered a non-vesting condition because it reflects the performance of other entities that are outside the group.

Whether the definition of performance condition should indicate that it includes a market condition

BC359   A respondent to the ED noted that the final sentence of the definition of vesting conditions, which states that "a performance condition might include a market condition", is contradictory. This is because a market condition:

(a)   is a target that is related to the market price of the entity's equity instruments; and

(b)   includes no explicit requirement for the counterparty to complete a specified period of service.

BC360   The Board observed that, on the basis of the definition of performance condition, a performance target that is related to the market price of an entity's equity instruments and to the completion of a specified period of service is considered a market (performance) condition. Consequently, the Board disagreed that an inconsistency existed in the definitions of performance condition and market condition. To avoid confusion in the definitions of performance condition and market condition, the Board decided to:

(a)   delete the last sentence in the definition of vesting condition (ie "a performance condition might include a market condition"); and

(b)   indicate within the definition of performance condition that performance conditions are either market conditions or non-market conditions.

BC361   The Board decided to confirm that a market condition is a type of performance condition. The Board considered that a condition that is not subject to a service requirement is not a performance condition, and instead, is considered a non-vesting condition. In making this clarification, the Board did not change the measurement requirements in IFRS 2 for a market condition.

Whether a definition of 'non-vesting condition' is needed

BC362   Respondents to the ED thought that clarity could be further improved in IFRS 2 by defining a 'non-vesting condition'.

BC363   The Board noted that there is no formal definition of non-vesting condition in IFRS 2, but Implementation Guidance on the split between vesting and non-vesting conditions is provided in a flowchart in paragraph IG24 of IFRS 2.

BC364   The Board determined that the creation of a stand-alone definition of non-vesting condition would not be the best alternative for providing clarity on this issue. This is because the Board observed that the concept of a non-vesting condition can be inferred from paragraphs BC170–BC184 of IFRS 2, which clarify the definition of vesting conditions. In accordance with this guidance it can be inferred that a non-vesting condition is any condition that does not determine whether the entity receives the services that entitle the counterparty to receive cash, other assets or equity instruments of the entity under a share-based payment arrangement. In other words, a non-vesting condition is any condition that is not a vesting condition. On the basis of its analysis the Board decided to not add a definition of non-vesting condition.

Whether the employee's failure to complete a required service period due to termination of employment is considered to be a failure to satisfy a service condition

BC365   When considering a possible revision of the definition of service condition, the Board observed that in IFRS 2 there is no specific guidance on how to account for a share-based payment award when the entity terminates an employee's employment.

BC366   The Board noted, however, that paragraph 19 of this Standard regards the employee's failure to complete a specified service period as a failure to satisfy a service condition. In the ED the Board proposed to clarify within the definition of service condition that if the employee fails to complete a specified service period, the employee thereby fails to satisfy a service condition, regardless of the reason for that failure. The Board also noted that the accounting consequence is that the compensation expense would be reversed if an employee fails to complete a specified service period.

BC367   Some respondents to the ED thought that more clarity could be provided in the proposed guidance. This is because they noted that in some circumstances in which an employee is unable to perform the service condition by completing the stipulated service period (such as when the employee is ill or dies in service), it would normally be expected that part of the award would vest and that the related compensation expense should not be reversed. They noted that, to the extent that a portion of the award vests, that portion should be recognised as an expense.

BC368   In response to the comments received, the Board noted that the objective of the proposed amendment to the definition of service condition is to clarify that the termination of an employee's employment is a situation in which the employee fails to complete a specified service period and, consequently, is considered a situation in which the service condition is not met.

BC369   The Board observed that in circumstances in which equity instruments do not vest because of failure to satisfy a vesting condition, paragraph 19 of IFRS 2 states that "on a cumulative basis, no amount is recognised for goods or services received if the equity instruments granted do not vest because of a failure to satisfy a vesting condition". The Board observed that in circumstances in which the equity instruments either partly or fully vest on cessation of employment, paragraph 23 of IFRS 2 states that "the entity shall make no subsequent adjustment to total equity after vesting date". The Board also noted that, in accordance with paragraph 28, "if a grant of equity instruments is cancelled or settled during the vesting period (other than a grant cancelled by forfeiture when the vesting conditions are not satisfied) the entity shall account for the cancellation or settlement as an acceleration of vesting, and shall therefore recognise immediately the amount that otherwise would have been recognised for services received over the remainder of the vesting period". Noting the guidance already provided in IFRS 2, the Board concluded that further guidance was not necessary.

Transition provisions

BC370   The Board considered the transition provisions and effective date of the amendment to IFRS 2. The Board noted that the changes to the definitions of vesting conditions and market condition and the addition of performance condition and service condition might result in changes to the grant-date fair value of share-based payment transactions for which the grant date was in previous periods. To avoid the use of hindsight, it decided that an entity would apply the amendments to IFRS 2 prospectively to share-based payment transactions for which the grant date is on or after 1 July 2014. Earlier application should be permitted.

Effects of vesting conditions on the measurement of a cash-settled share-based payment (2016 amendments)[32]

BC371   This section summarises the Board's considerations when it finalised its proposals to address the accounting for the effects of vesting conditions on the measurement of a cash-settled share-based payment, contained in the November 2014 ED.

BC372   The Board received a request regarding the measurement requirements in IFRS 2 for cash-settled share-based payment transactions that include a performance condition.

BC373   The Board noted that IFRS 2 requires the use of fair value as a principle in measuring share-based payment transactions. The Board observed that paragraphs 19–21A of IFRS 2 provide the requirements for measuring the fair value of equity-settled share-based payment transactions that include vesting and non-vesting conditions. The Board also observed that, in the case of cash-settled share-based payment transactions, paragraph 33 of IFRS 2 requires an entity to measure the liability, initially and at the end of each reporting

---

32   Paragraphs BC371–BC382 are added as a consequence of amendments to IFRS 2 *Classification and Measurement of Share-based Payment Transactions* issued in June 2016.

period until settled, at fair value. The entity is required to apply an option pricing model, taking into account the terms and conditions on which the cash-settled share-based payments were granted and the extent to which the employees have rendered service to date.

BC374 However, IFRS 2 does not specifically address the impact of vesting and non-vesting conditions on the measurement of the fair value of the liability incurred in a cash-settled share-based payment transaction. Specifically, it was unclear whether an entity should apply, by analogy, the requirements in paragraphs 19–21A of IFRS 2 for measuring equity-settled share-based payment transactions when measuring cash-settled share-based payment transactions that include vesting and non-vesting conditions.

BC375 The Board observed that, in accordance with paragraph 6A, IFRS 2 uses the term 'fair value' in a way that differs in some respects from the definition of fair value in IFRS 13 *Fair Value Measurement*. When applying IFRS 2, an entity is required to measure fair value in accordance with that Standard (and not in accordance with IFRS 13) for cash-settled and equity-settled awards. Consequently, the Board decided to add paragraphs 33A–33D on how market and non-market vesting conditions and non-vesting conditions should be reflected in the measurement of a cash-settled share-based payment transaction. The Board decided that those conditions should be reflected in the measurement of cash-settled share-based payments in a manner consistent with how they are reflected in the measurement of an equity-settled share-based payment transaction.

BC376 The Board further observed that measuring the fair value of the liability incurred in a cash-settled share-based payment transaction by analogy to the requirements for equity-settled share-based payment transactions would avoid the practical difficulties of measuring the effects of vesting conditions (other than market conditions) on the fair value of the awards. Those practical difficulties were identified by the Board when it originally issued IFRS 2, and are explained in paragraph BC184 of IFRS 2.

BC377 Consequently the Board decided to amend paragraphs 30–31, and 33 and added paragraphs 33A–33D to clarify the effect that market and non-market vesting conditions and non-vesting conditions have on the measurement of the liability incurred in a cash-settled share-based payment transaction.

BC378 The Board observed that if an employee does not receive the payment because of a failure to satisfy any condition, this should result in remeasuring the liability to zero. The amendments make clear that the cumulative amount ultimately recognised for goods or services received as consideration for a cash-settled share-based payment will be equal to the amount of cash (or other assets) that is paid.

BC379 Furthermore, the Board amended paragraph IG19 and added IG Example 12A to the Guidance on Implementing IFRS 2 to illustrate the impact of a performance condition on the measurement of a cash-settled share-based payment transaction.

BC380 Respondents to the November 2014 ED questioned the meaning of 'best available estimate', as that notion was used in the proposal, for estimating the fair value of a cash-settled share-based payment. The Board noted that the term 'best available estimate' is already used in IFRS 2 and is not a new notion. This term is also used in paragraph 20 of IFRS 2 for estimating the number of equity instruments expected to vest of an equity-settled share-based payment. The Board further observed that analysing such a notion would potentially involve examining similar notions in other Standards and observed that such notions would be better examined as part of a broader project.

BC381   Respondents to the November 2014 ED suggested that the Board should add an explicit requirement for the disclosure of a contingent liability when vesting is not probable (and thus no liability is recognised, as illustrated in Year 1 of Example 12A). The Board observed that adding such a requirement is not necessary because the general requirement in paragraph 50 of IFRS 2 already requires entities to

> ...disclose information that enables users of the financial statements to understand the effect of share-based payment transactions on the entity's profit or loss for the period and on its financial position.

BC382   Some respondents to the November 2014 ED suggested that the Board should add other examples to the Guidance on Implementing IFRS 2 to illustrate the effects of vesting and non-vesting conditions on the measurement of cash-settled awards. The Board did not think this was necessary because of the existing examples in the implementation guidance that illustrate the effects of market and non-market vesting conditions and of non-vesting conditions on equity-settled awards. These examples also serve to illustrate the effects of such conditions on cash-settled awards because the amendments require consistent treatment for both types of awards.

IASB documents published to accompany

IFRS 3

Business Combinations

The text of the unaccompanied standard, IFRS 3, is contained in Part A of this edition. Its effective date when issued was 1 July 2009. The text of the Accompanying Guidance on IFRS 3 is contained in Part B of this edition. This part presents the following documents:

BASIS FOR CONCLUSIONS

APPENDIX TO THE BASIS FOR CONCLUSIONS
Amendments to the Basis for Conclusions on other IFRSs

DISSENTING OPINIONS

Contents

BENEFITS AND COSTS **BC435**

APPENDIX

Amendments to the Basis for Conclusions on other IFRSs

DISSENTING OPINIONS

Basis for Conclusions on
IFRS 3 *Business Combinations*

This Basis for Conclusions and its appendix accompany, but are not part of, IFRS 3.

Background information

In 2001 the International Accounting Standards Board began a project to review IAS 22 *Business Combinations* (revised in 1998) as part of its initial agenda, with the objective of improving the quality of, and seeking international convergence on, the accounting for business combinations. The Board decided to address the accounting for business combinations in two phases.

As part of the first phase, the Board published in December 2002 ED 3 *Business Combinations*, together with an exposure draft of proposed related amendments to IAS 36 *Impairment of Assets* and IAS 38 *Intangible Assets*, with a comment deadline of 4 April 2003. The Board received 136 comment letters.

The Board concluded the first phase in March 2004 by issuing simultaneously IFRS 3 *Business Combinations* and revised versions of IAS 36 and IAS 38. The Board's primary conclusion in the first phase was that virtually all business combinations are acquisitions. Accordingly, the Board decided to require the use of one method of accounting for business combinations—the acquisition method.

The US Financial Accounting Standards Board (FASB) also conducted a project on business combinations in multiple phases. The FASB concluded its first phase in June 2001 by issuing FASB Statements No. 141 *Business Combinations* (SFAS 141) and No. 142 *Goodwill and Other Intangible Assets*. The scope of that first phase was similar to IFRS 3 and the FASB reached similar conclusions on the major issues.

The two boards began deliberating the second phase of their projects at about the same time. They decided that a significant improvement could be made to financial reporting if they had similar standards for accounting for business combinations. They therefore agreed to conduct the second phase of the project as a joint effort with the objective of reaching the same conclusions.

The second phase of the project addressed the guidance for applying the acquisition method. In June 2005 the boards published an exposure draft of revisions to IFRS 3 and SFAS 141, together with exposure drafts of related amendments to IAS 27 *Consolidated and Separate Financial Statements* and Accounting Research Bulletin No. 51 *Consolidated Financial Statements*, with a comment deadline of 28 October 2005. The boards received more than 280 comment letters.

The boards concluded the second phase of the project by issuing their revised standards, IFRS 3 *Business Combinations* (as revised in 2008) and FASB Statement No. 141 (revised 2007) *Business Combinations* and the related amendments to IAS 27 and FASB Statement No. 160 *Noncontrolling Interests in Consolidated Financial Statements*.

Introduction

BC1   This Basis for Conclusions summarises the considerations of the International Accounting Standards Board (IASB) and the US Financial Accounting Standards Board (FASB) in reaching the conclusions in their revised standards, IFRS 3 *Business Combinations* (as revised in 2008) and FASB Statement No. 141 (revised 2007) *Business Combinations* (SFAS 141(R)). It includes the reasons why each board accepted particular approaches and rejected others. Individual board members gave greater weight to some factors than to others.

BC2   The revised IFRS 3 and SFAS 141(R) carry forward without reconsideration the primary conclusions each board reached in IFRS 3 (issued in 2004) and FASB Statement No. 141 (SFAS 141, issued in 2001), both of which were titled *Business Combinations*. The conclusions carried forward include, among others, the requirement to apply the *purchase method* (which the revised standards refer to as the *acquisition method*) to account for all business combinations and the identifiability criteria for recognising an intangible asset separately from goodwill. This Basis for Conclusions includes the reasons for those conclusions, as well as the reasons for the conclusions the boards reached in their joint deliberations that led to the revised standards. Because the provisions of the revised standards on applying the acquisition method represent a more extensive change to SFAS 141 than to the previous version of IFRS 3, this Basis for Conclusions includes more discussion of the FASB's conclusions than of the IASB's in the second phase of their respective business combinations projects.

BC3   In discussing the boards' consideration of comments on exposure drafts, this Basis for Conclusions refers to the exposure draft that preceded the previous version of IFRS 3 as *ED 3* and to the one that preceded SFAS 141 as the *1999 Exposure Draft*; it refers to the joint exposure draft that preceded the revised standards as the *2005 Exposure Draft*. Other exposure drafts published by each board in developing IFRS 3 or SFAS 141 are explained in the context of the issues they addressed. As used in this Basis for Conclusions, *the revised IFRS 3*, *SFAS 141(R)* and *the revised standards* refer to the revised versions of IFRS 3 and SFAS 141; references to *IFRS 3* and *SFAS 141* are to the original versions of those standards.

BC4   The IASB and the FASB concurrently deliberated the issues in the second phase of the project and reached the same conclusions on most of them. The table of differences between the revised IFRS 3 and SFAS 141(R) (presented after the illustrative examples) describes the substantive differences that remain; the most significant difference is the measurement of a non-controlling interest in an acquiree (see paragraphs BC205–BC221). In addition, the application of some provisions of the revised standards on which the boards reached the same conclusions may differ because of differences in:

(a)   other accounting standards of the boards to which the revised standards refer. For example, recognition and measurement requirements for a few particular assets acquired (eg a deferred tax asset) and liabilities assumed (eg an employee benefit obligation) refer to existing IFRSs or US generally accepted accounting principles (GAAP) rather than fair value measures.

(b)   disclosure practices of the boards. For example, the FASB requires particular supplementary information or particular disclosures by public entities only. The IASB has no similar requirements for supplementary information and does not distinguish between listed and unlisted entities.

(c)   particular transition provisions for changes to past accounting practices of US and non-US companies that previously differed.

Definition of a business combination

BC5   The FASB's 1999 Exposure Draft proposed that a *business combination* should be defined as occurring when one entity acquires net assets that constitute a business or acquires equity interests in one or more other entities and thereby obtains control over that entity or entities. Many respondents who commented on the proposed definition said that it would exclude certain transactions covered by APB Opinion No. 16 *Business Combinations* (APB Opinion 16), in particular, transactions in which none of the former shareholder groups of the combining entities obtained control over the combined entity (such as roll-ups, put-togethers and so-called mergers of equals). During its redeliberations of the 1999 Exposure Draft, the FASB concluded that those transactions should be included in the definition of a business combination and in the scope of SFAS 141. Therefore, paragraph 10 of SFAS 141 indicated that it also applied to business combinations in which none of the owners of the combining entities as a group retain or receive a majority of the voting rights of the combined entity. However, the FASB acknowledged at that time that some of those business combinations might not be acquisitions and said that it intended to consider in another project whether business combinations that are not acquisitions should be accounted for using the fresh start method rather than the purchase method.

BC6   IFRS 3 defined a business combination as 'the bringing together of separate entities or businesses into one reporting entity.' In developing IFRS 3, the IASB considered adopting the definition of a business combination in SFAS 141. It did not do so because that definition excluded some forms of combinations encompassed in IAS 22 *Business Combinations* (which IFRS 3 replaced), such as those described in paragraph BC5 in which none of the former shareholder groups of the combining entities obtained control over the combined entity. Accordingly, IFRS 3 essentially retained the definition of a business combination from IAS 22.

BC7   The definition of a business combination was an item of divergence between IFRS 3 and SFAS 141. In addition, the definition in SFAS 141 excluded combinations in which control is obtained by means other than acquiring net assets or equity interests. An objective of the second phase of the FASB's project leading to SFAS 141(R) was to reconsider whether the accounting for a change in control resulting in the acquisition of a business should differ because of the way in which control is obtained.

BC8   The FASB considered several alternatives for improving the definition of a business combination, including adopting the definition of a business combination in IFRS 3. That definition would encompass all transactions or other events that are within the scope of the revised standards. The FASB concluded, however, that the definition of a business combination in IFRS 3 was too broad for its purposes because it would allow for the inclusion in a business combination of one or more businesses that the acquirer does not control.

BC9   Because the FASB considers all changes of control in which an entity acquires a business to be economically similar transactions or events, it decided to expand the definition of a business combination to include all transactions or other events in which an entity obtains control of a business. Application of the expanded definition will improve the consistency of accounting guidance and the relevance, completeness and comparability of the resulting information about the assets, liabilities and activities of an acquired business.

BC10   The IASB also reconsidered the definition of a business combination. The result was that the IASB and the FASB adopted the same definition. The IASB observed that the IFRS 3 definition could be read to include circumstances in which there may be no triggering economic event or transaction and thus no change in an economic entity, per se. For example, under the IFRS 3 definition, an individual's decision to prepare combined financial statements for all or some of the entities that he or she controls could qualify as a business combination. The IASB concluded that a business combination should be described in terms of an economic event rather than in terms of consolidation accounting and that the definition in the revised standards satisfies that condition.

BC11   The IASB also observed that, although the IFRS 3 definition of a business combination was sufficiently broad to include them, formations of joint ventures were excluded from the scope of IFRS 3. Because joint ventures are also excluded from the scope of the revised standards, the revised definition of a business combination is intended to include all of the types of transactions and other events initially included in the scope of IFRS 3.

BC12   Some respondents to the 2005 Exposure Draft who consider particular combinations of businesses to be 'true mergers' said that the definition of a business combination as a transaction or other event in which an acquirer obtains control of one or more businesses seemed to exclude true mergers. The boards concluded that the most straightforward way of indicating that the scope of the revised standards, and the definition of a business combination, is intended to include true mergers, if any occur, is simply to state that fact.

BC13   Some respondents to the 2005 Exposure Draft also said that it was not clear that the definition of a business combination, and thus the scope of the revised standards, includes reverse acquisitions and perhaps other combinations of businesses. The boards observed that in a reverse acquisition, one entity—the one whose equity interests are acquired—obtains economic (although not legal) control over the other and is therefore the acquirer, as indicated in paragraph B15 of the revised IFRS 3. Therefore, the boards concluded that it is unnecessary to state explicitly that reverse acquisitions are included in the definition of a business combination and thus within the scope of the revised standards.

Change in terminology

BC14   As defined in the revised standards, a business combination could occur in the absence of a purchase transaction. Accordingly, the boards decided to replace the term *purchase method*, which was previously used to describe the method of accounting for business combinations that the revised standards require, with the term *acquisition method*. To avoid confusion, this Basis for Conclusions uses that term throughout, including when it refers to IFRS 3 and SFAS 141 (and earlier exposure drafts or other documents), which used the term *purchase method*.

Definition of a business

BC15   The definition of a business combination in the revised standards provides that a transaction or other event is a business combination only if the assets acquired and liabilities assumed constitute a business (an acquiree), and Appendix A defines a *business*.

BC16   SFAS 141 did not include a definition of a business. Instead, it referred to EITF Issue No. 98-3 *Determining Whether a Nonmonetary Transaction Involves Receipt of Productive Assets or of a Business* for guidance on whether a group of net assets constitutes a business. Some constituents said that particular aspects of the definition and the related guidance in EITF Issue 98-3 were both unnecessarily restrictive and open to misinterpretation. They suggested that the FASB should reconsider that definition and guidance as part of this phase of the project, and it agreed to do so. In addition to considering how its definition and guidance might be improved, the FASB, in conjunction with the IASB, decided that the boards should strive to develop a joint definition of a business.

BC17   Before issuing IFRS 3, the IASB did not have a definition of a business or guidance similar to that in EITF Issue 98-3. Consistently with the suggestions of respondents to ED 3, the IASB decided to provide a definition of a business in IFRS 3. In developing that definition, the IASB also considered the guidance in EITF Issue 98-3. However, the definition in IFRS 3 benefited from deliberations in this project to that date, and it differed from EITF Issue 98-3 in some aspects. For example, the definition in IFRS 3 did not include either of the following factors, both of which were in EITF Issue 98-3:

(a)   a requirement that a business be self-sustaining; or

(b)   a presumption that a transferred set of activities and assets in the development stage that has not commenced planned principal operations cannot be a business.

BC18   In the second phase of their business combinations projects, both boards considered the suitability of their existing definitions of a business in an attempt to develop an improved, common definition. To address the perceived deficiencies and misinterpretations, the boards modified their respective definitions of a business and clarified the related guidance. The more significant modifications, and the reasons for them, are:

(a)   to continue to exclude self-sustaining as the definition in IFRS 3 did, and instead, provide that the integrated set of activities and assets must be **capable** of being conducted and managed for the purpose of providing a return in the form of dividends, lower costs or other economic benefits directly to investors or other owners, members or participants. Focusing on the capability to achieve the purposes of the business helps avoid the unduly restrictive interpretations that existed in accordance with the former guidance.

(b)   to clarify the meanings of the terms *inputs, processes* and *outputs* that were used in both EITF Issue 98-3 and IFRS 3. Clarifying the meanings of those terms, together with other modifications, helps eliminate the need for extensive detailed guidance and the misinterpretations that sometimes stem from such guidance.

(c)   to clarify that inputs and processes applied to those inputs are essential and that although the resulting outputs are normally present, they need not be present. Therefore, an integrated set of assets and activities could qualify as a business if the integrated set is capable of being conducted and managed to produce the resulting outputs. Together with item (a), clarifying that outputs need not be present for an integrated set to be a business helps avoid the unduly restrictive interpretations of the guidance in EITF Issue 98-3.

(d)   to clarify that a business need not include all of the inputs or processes that the seller used in operating that business if a market participant is capable of continuing to produce outputs, for example, by integrating the business with its own inputs and processes. This clarification also helps avoid the need for extensive detailed guidance and assessments about whether a missing input or process is minor.

(e)   to continue to exclude a presumption that an integrated set in the development stage is not a business merely because it has not yet begun its planned principal operations, as IFRS 3 did. Eliminating that presumption is consistent with focusing on assessing the capability to achieve the purposes of the business (item (a)) and helps avoid the unduly restrictive interpretations that existed with the former guidance.

BC19   The boards also considered whether to include in the revised standards a presumption similar to the one in EITF Issue 98-3 that an asset group is a business if goodwill is present. Some members of the FASB's resource group suggested that that presumption results in circular logic that is not especially useful guidance in practice. Although the boards had some sympathy with those views, they noted that such a presumption could be useful in avoiding interpretations of the definition of a business that would hinder the stated intention of applying the revised standards' guidance to economically similar transactions. The presumption might also simplify the assessment of whether a particular set of activities and assets meets the definition of a business. Therefore, the revised standards' application guidance retains that presumption.

BC20   The boards considered whether to expand the scope of the revised standards to all acquisitions of groups of assets. They noted that doing so would avoid the need to distinguish between those groups that are businesses and those that are not. However, both boards noted that broadening the scope of the revised standards beyond acquisitions of businesses would require further research and deliberation of additional issues and delay the implementation of the revised standards' improvements to practice. The boards therefore did not extend the scope of the revised standards to acquisitions of all asset groups. Paragraph 2(b) of the revised IFRS 3 describes the typical accounting for an asset acquisition.

BC21   SFAS 141(R) amends FASB Interpretation No. 46 (revised December 2003) *Consolidation of Variable Interest Entities* (FASB Interpretation 46(R)) to clarify that the initial consolidation of a variable interest entity that is a business is a business combination. Therefore, the assets, liabilities and non-controlling interests of the variable interest entity should be measured in accordance with the requirements of SFAS 141(R). Previously, FASB Interpretation 46(R) required assets, liabilities and non-controlling interests of variable interest entities that are businesses to be measured at fair value. The FASB concluded that variable interest entities that are businesses should be afforded the same exceptions to fair value measurement and recognition that are provided for assets and liabilities of acquired businesses. The FASB also decided that upon the initial consolidation of a variable interest entity that is not a business, the assets (other than goodwill), liabilities and non-controlling interests should be recognised and measured in accordance with the requirements of SFAS 141(R), rather than at fair value as previously required by FASB Interpretation 46(R). The FASB reached that decision for the same reasons described above, ie if SFAS 141(R) allows an exception to fair value measurement for a particular asset or liability, it would be inconsistent to require the same type of asset or liability to be measured at fair value. Except for that provision, the FASB did not reconsider the requirements in FASB Interpretation 46(R) for the initial consolidation of a variable interest entity that is not a business.

Method of accounting for business combinations

BC22   Both IAS 22 and APB Opinion 16 permitted use of either the acquisition method or the pooling of interests (pooling) method of accounting for a business combination, although the two methods were not intended as alternatives for the same set of facts and circumstances. ED 3 and the 1999 Exposure Draft proposed, and IFRS 3 and SFAS 141 required, use of the acquisition method to account for all business combinations. The boards did not redeliberate that conclusion during the project that led to the revised standards.

BC23   In developing IFRS 3 and SFAS 141, the IASB and the FASB considered three possible methods of accounting for business combinations—the pooling method, the acquisition method and the fresh start method. In assessing those methods, both boards were mindful of the disadvantages of having more than one method of accounting for business combinations, as evidenced by the experience with IAS 22 and APB Opinion 16. The boards concluded that having more than one method could be justified only if the alternative method (or methods) could be demonstrated to produce information that is more decision-useful and if unambiguous and non-arbitrary boundaries could be established that unequivocally distinguish when one method is to be applied instead of another. The boards also concluded that most business combinations are acquisitions and, for the reasons discussed in paragraphs BC24–BC28, that the acquisition method is the appropriate method for those business combinations.

Respondents to ED 3 and the 1999 Exposure Draft generally agreed. Therefore, neither the pooling method nor the fresh start method could be appropriately used for all business combinations.

Reasons for adopting the acquisition method

BC24   Both boards concluded that the acquisition method is the appropriate method of accounting for all business combinations in which one entity obtains control of one or more other businesses[1] because that method is consistent with how the accounting model generally accounts for transactions in which assets are acquired and liabilities are assumed or incurred. Therefore, it produces information that is comparable with other accounting information.

BC25   The acquisition method views a combination from the perspective of the acquirer—the entity that obtains control of the other combining businesses. The acquirer purchases or otherwise obtains control over net assets and recognises in its financial statements the assets acquired and liabilities assumed, including those not previously recognised by the acquiree. Consequently, users of financial statements are better able to assess the initial investments made and the subsequent performance of those investments and compare them with the performance of other entities. In addition, by initially recognising almost all of the assets acquired and liabilities assumed at their fair values, the acquisition method includes in the financial statements more information about the market's expectation of the value of the future cash flows associated with those assets and liabilities, which enhances the relevance of that information.

BC26   Most of the respondents to ED 3 supported the proposal to eliminate the pooling method and to require all business combinations to be accounted for by applying the acquisition method, pending the IASB's future consideration of whether the fresh start method might be applied to some combinations. Respondents to the 1999 Exposure Draft generally agreed that most business combinations are acquisitions, and many said that all combinations involving only two entities are acquisitions. Respondents also agreed that the acquisition method is the appropriate method of accounting for business combinations in which one of the combining entities obtains control over the other combining entities. However, some qualified their support for the acquisition method as contingent upon the FASB's decisions about some aspects of applying that method, particularly the accounting for goodwill.

BC27   The boards concluded that most business combinations, both two-party transactions and those involving three or more entities (multi-party combinations), are acquisitions. The boards acknowledged that some multi-party combinations (in particular, those that are commonly referred to as roll-up or put-together transactions) might not be acquisitions; however, they noted that the acquisition method has generally been used to account for them. The boards decided not to change that practice at this time. Consequently, the

---

1   In October 2012 the Board issued *Investment Entities* (Amendments to IFRS 10, IFRS 12 and IAS 27), which removed from the scope of IFRS 3 *Business Combinations* the acquisition by an investment entity, as defined in IFRS 10 *Consolidated Financial Statements*, of an investment in a subsidiary required to be measured at fair value through profit or loss.

revised standards require the acquisition method to be used to account for all business combinations, including those that some might not consider acquisitions.

BC28 Both boards considered assertions that exceptions to the acquisition method should be provided for circumstances in which identifying the acquirer is difficult. Respondents taking that view generally said that the pooling method would provide better information in those circumstances. Although acknowledging that identifying the acquirer sometimes may be difficult, the boards concluded that it would be practicable to identify an acquirer in all business combinations. Moreover, in some jurisdictions an acquirer must be identified for tax purposes, regardless of how difficult it may be to do so. Both boards also concluded that in no circumstances does the pooling method provide better information than the acquisition method.

Reasons for rejecting the pooling method

Mergers and acquisitions are economically similar

BC29 Some observers, including some respondents to the ED 3 and to the 1999 Exposure Draft, argued that business combinations in which the predominant form of consideration is equity interests, generally referred to as *mergers*, are different from acquisitions and should be accounted for differently. They said that the pooling method is appropriate for a merger because ownership interests are continued (either completely or substantially), no new capital is invested and no assets are distributed, post-combination ownership interests are proportional to those before the combination, and the intention is to unite commercial strategies. Those respondents said that a merger should be accounted for in terms of the carrying amounts of the assets and liabilities of the combining entities because, unlike acquisitions in which only the acquirer survives the combination, all of the combining entities effectively survive a merger.

BC30 Most respondents who favoured retaining the pooling method also supported limiting its application. Many of those respondents suggested limiting use of the pooling method to 'true mergers' or 'mergers of equals', which they described as combinations of entities of approximately equal size or those in which it is difficult to identify an acquirer.

BC31 The boards also considered the assertion that the pooling method properly portrays true mergers as a transaction between the owners of the combining entities rather than between the combining entities. The boards rejected that assertion, noting that business combinations are initiated by, and take place because of, a transaction between the combining entities themselves. The entities—not their owners—engage in the negotiations necessary to carry out the combination, although the owners must eventually participate in and approve the transaction.

BC32 Many respondents agreed with the boards that although ownership interests are continued in a combination effected by an exchange of equity instruments, those interests **change** as a result of the combination. The former owners of each entity no longer have an exclusive interest in the net assets of the pre-combination entities. Rather, after the business combination, the owners of the combining entities have a residual interest in the net assets of the combined entity. The information provided by the pooling method fails to reflect that and is therefore not a faithful representation.

BC33   Both boards observed that all business combinations entail some bringing together of commercial strategies. Accordingly, the intention to unite commercial strategies is not unique to mergers and does not support applying a different accounting method to some combinations from that applied to others.

BC34   Some respondents said that, economically, mergers are virtually identical to acquisitions, making them in-substance acquisitions. Some noted that shares could have been issued for cash and that cash then used to effect the combination, with the result being economically the same as if shares had been used to effect the combination.

BC35   Both boards concluded that 'true mergers' or 'mergers of equals' in which none of the combining entities obtains control of the others are so rare as to be virtually non-existent, and many respondents agreed. Other respondents stated that even if a true merger or merger of equals did occur, it would be so rare that a separate accounting treatment is not warranted. The boards also observed that respondents and other constituents were unable to suggest an unambiguous and non-arbitrary boundary for distinguishing true mergers or mergers of equals from other business combinations and concluded that developing such an operational boundary would not be feasible. Moreover, even if those mergers could feasibly be distinguished from other combinations, both boards noted that it does not follow that mergers should be accounted for on a carry-over basis. If they were to be accounted for using a method other than the acquisition method, the fresh start method would be better than the pooling method.

Information provided is not decision-useful

BC36   Some proponents of the pooling method argued that it provides decision-useful information for the business combinations for which they favour its use. They said that the information is a more faithful representation than the information that the acquisition method would provide for those combinations. However, other respondents said that the information provided by the acquisition method is more revealing than that provided by the pooling method. Respondents also noted that the pooling method does not hold management accountable for the investment made and the subsequent performance of that investment. In contrast, the accountability that results from applying the acquisition method forces management to examine business combination deals carefully to see that they make economic sense.

BC37   Both boards observed that an important part of decision-useful information is information about cash-generating abilities and cash flows generated. The IASB's *Framework*[2] *for the Preparation and Presentation of Financial Statements* says that 'The economic decisions that are taken by users of financial statements require an evaluation of the ability of an entity to generate cash and cash equivalents

---

2   In this Basis for Conclusions references to the *Framework* are to IASC's *Framework for the Preparation and Presentation of Financial Statements*, adopted by the IASB in 2001. In September 2010 the IASB replaced the *Framework* with the *Conceptual Framework for Financial Reporting*.

and of the timing and certainty of their generation' (paragraph 15).[3] FASB Concepts Statement No. 1 *Objectives of Financial Reporting by Business Enterprises* indicates that '... financial reporting should provide information to help investors, creditors, and others assess the amounts, timing, and uncertainty of prospective net cash inflows to the related enterprise' (paragraph 37; footnote reference omitted). Neither the cash-generating abilities of the combined entity nor its future cash flows generally are affected by the method used to account for the combination. However, fair values reflect the expected cash flows associated with acquired assets and assumed liabilities. Because the pooling method records the net assets acquired at their carrying amounts rather than at their fair values, the information that the pooling method provides about the cash-generating abilities of those net assets is less useful than that provided by the acquisition method.

BC38   Both boards also concluded that the information provided by the pooling method is less relevant because it has less predictive value and feedback value than the information that is provided by other methods. It is also less complete because it does not reflect assets acquired or liabilities assumed that were not included in the pre-combination financial statements of the combining entities. The pooling method also provides a less faithful representation of the combined entity's performance in periods after the combination. For example, by recording assets and liabilities at the carrying amounts of predecessor entities, post-combination revenues may be overstated (and expenses understated) as the result of embedded gains that were generated by predecessor entities but not recognised by them.

BC39   The *Framework* and FASB Concepts Statement No. 2 *Qualitative Characteristics of Accounting Information* describe comparability as an important characteristic of decision-useful information. Use of different accounting methods for the same set of facts and circumstances makes the resulting information less comparable and thus less useful for making economic decisions. As discussed in paragraphs BC29–BC35, the boards concluded that all business combinations are economically similar. Accordingly, use of the same method to account for all combinations enhances the comparability of the resulting financial reporting information. Both boards observed that the acquisition method, but not the pooling method, could reasonably be applied to all business combinations in which one party to the combination obtains control over the combined entity.

BC40   Opponents of the pooling method generally said that eliminating that method would enhance the comparability of financial statements of entities that grow by means of acquisitions. Both boards agreed.

Inconsistent with historical cost accounting model

BC41   Both boards observed that the pooling method is an exception to the general concept that exchange transactions are accounted for in terms of the fair values of the items exchanged. Because the pooling method records the combination in terms of the pre-combination carrying amounts of the parties to the transaction, it fails to record and thus to hold management accountable for the investment made in the combination.

---

3   superseded by Chapter 1 of the *Conceptual Framework*.

BC42　Some respondents to the FASB's 1999 Exposure Draft who advocated use of the pooling method asserted that it is consistent with the historical cost model and that eliminating the pooling method would be a step towards adopting a fair value model. They argued that before eliminating the pooling method, the FASB should resolve the broad issue of whether to adopt a fair value model in place of the historical cost model. The FASB disagreed, noting that, regardless of the merits of a fair value model, the pooling method is an aberration that is inconsistent with the historical cost model.

BC43　Although the historical cost model is frequently described as being 'transaction based', the fair value model also records all transactions. In both models, transactions are recognised on the basis of the fair values exchanged at the transaction date. In contrast, the pooling method does not result in recognising in the records of the combined entity the values exchanged; instead, only the carrying amounts of the predecessor entities are recognised. Failure to record those values can adversely affect the relevance and reliability of the combined entity's financial statements for years—and even decades—to come. For those reasons, both boards concluded that the pooling method is inconsistent with the historical cost model. Requiring use of the acquisition method is not a step towards adopting a fair value accounting model. Rather, it eliminates an exception to the historical cost model and requires accounting for assets acquired and liabilities assumed in a business combination consistently with other acquisitions of assets and incurrences of liabilities.

Disclosure not an adequate response

BC44　In urging that the pooling method should be retained, a few respondents to the 1999 Exposure Draft said that any perceived problems with having two methods of accounting could be addressed by enhanced disclosures in the notes to the financial statements. However, they generally did not specify what those disclosures should be and how they would help overcome the comparability problems that inevitably result from having two methods.

BC45　The FASB considered whether enhanced disclosures might compensate for the deficiencies of the pooling method but doubted the usefulness of almost any disclosures short of disclosing what the results would have been had the acquisition method been used to account for the business combination. Providing disclosures that would enable users of financial statements to determine what the results would have been had the transaction been accounted for by the acquisition method would be a costly solution that begs the question of why the acquisition method was not used to account for the transaction in the first place. Thus, the FASB rejected enhanced disclosures as a viable alternative.

Not cost-beneficial

BC46　Some of the boards' constituents cited cost-benefit considerations as a reason for retaining the pooling method. They argued that the pooling method is a quicker and less expensive way to account for a business combination because it does not require an entity to hire valuation experts to value assets for accounting purposes.

BC47   Other constituents favoured eliminating the pooling method for cost-benefit reasons. Some argued that the pooling method causes preparers of financial statements, auditors, regulators and others to spend unproductive time dealing with the detailed criteria required by IAS 22 or APB Opinion 16 in attempts to qualify some business combinations for the pooling method. Others noted that using the acquisition method of accounting for all business combinations would eliminate the enormous amount of interpretative guidance necessary to accommodate the pooling method. They also said that the benefits derived from making the acquisition method the only method of accounting for business combinations would significantly outweigh any issues that might arise from accounting for the very rare true merger or merger of equals by the acquisition method.

BC48   Both boards concluded that requiring a single method of accounting is preferable because having more than one method would lead to higher costs associated with applying, auditing, enforcing and analysing the information produced by the different methods. The IASB's conclusions on benefits and costs are more fully discussed in paragraphs BC435–BC439.

Perceived economic consequences not a valid reason for retention

BC49   Some of the respondents to ED 3 and the 1999 Exposure Draft who favoured retaining the pooling method cited public policy considerations or other perceived economic consequences of eliminating it. Some argued that eliminating the pooling method would require some investors to adjust to different measures of performance, potentially affecting market valuations adversely in some industries during the transition period. Others argued that it would impede desirable consolidation in some industries, reduce the amount of capital flowing into those industries, slow the development of new technology and adversely affect entrepreneurial culture. Some argued that eliminating the pooling method would reduce the options available to some regulatory agencies and possibly require regulated entities to maintain a second set of accounting records.

BC50   Other respondents did not share those views. Some said that because business combinations are (or should be) driven by economic rather than accounting considerations, economically sound deals would be completed regardless of the method used to account for them. Others noted that the financial community values business combinations in terms of their fair values rather than book values; therefore, those transactions should initially be recognised in the financial statements at fair value.

BC51   Both boards have long held that accounting standards should be neutral; they should not be slanted to favour one set of economic interests over another. Neutrality is the absence of bias intended to attain a predetermined result or to induce a particular behaviour. Neutrality is an essential aspect of decision-useful financial information because biased financial reporting information cannot faithfully represent economic phenomena. The consequences of a new financial reporting standard may indeed be negative for some interests in either the short term or the long term. But the dissemination of unreliable and potentially misleading information is, in the long run, harmful for all interests.

BC52 Both boards rejected the view that the pooling method should be retained because eliminating it could have adverse consequences for some economic interests. Accounting requirements for business combinations should seek neither to encourage nor to discourage business combinations. Instead, those standards should produce unbiased information about those combinations that is useful to investors, creditors and others in making economic decisions about the combined entity.

Acquisition method flaws remedied

BC53 Some respondents to ED 3 or to the 1999 Exposure Draft supported retaining the pooling method because of perceived problems associated with the acquisition method. Most of those comments focused on the effects of goodwill amortisation.

BC54 Both boards concluded that the pooling method is so fundamentally flawed that it does not warrant retention, regardless of perceived problems with the acquisition method. The boards also observed that the most frequently cited concern is remedied by the requirement of IAS 36 *Impairment of Assets* and FASB Statement No. 142 *Goodwill and Other Intangible Assets* (SFAS 142) to test goodwill for impairment and recognise a loss if it is impaired rather than to amortise goodwill.

The fresh start method

BC55 In the fresh start method, none of the combining entities is viewed as having survived the combination as an independent reporting entity. Rather, the combination is viewed as the transfer of the net assets of the combining entities to a new entity that assumes control over them. The history of that new entity, by definition, begins with the combination.

BC56 In the first part of their respective business combinations projects, both the IASB and the FASB acknowledged that a case could be made for using the fresh start method to account for the relatively rare business combination that does not clearly qualify as an acquisition. Such a combination might be defined either as one in which an acquirer cannot be identified or as one in which the acquirer is substantially modified by the transaction. However, the boards observed that those transactions have been accounted for by the acquisition method and they decided not to change that practice.

BC57 Neither the IASB nor the FASB has on its agenda a project to consider the fresh start method. However, both boards have expressed interest in considering whether joint venture formations and some formations of new entities in multi-party business combinations should be accounted for by the fresh start method. Depending on the relative priorities of that topic and other topics competing for their agendas when time becomes available, the boards might undertake a joint project to consider those issues at some future date.

Scope

BC58   The revised standards exclude from their scope some transactions that were also excluded from the scope of both IFRS 3 and SFAS 141. However, the revised standards include within their scope combinations involving only mutual entities and combinations achieved by contract alone, which were excluded from the scope of IFRS 3 and SFAS 141. Paragraphs BC59–BC79 discuss the boards' reasons for those conclusions.

Joint ventures and combinations of entities under common control

BC59   Formations of joint ventures and combinations of entities under common control are excluded from the scope of the revised standards. Those transactions were also excluded from the scope of both IFRS 3 and SFAS 141, and the boards continue to believe that issues related to such combinations are appropriately excluded from the scope of this project. The boards are aware of nothing that has happened since IFRS 3 and SFAS 141 were issued to suggest that the revised standards should be delayed to address the accounting for those events.

BC60   In developing IFRS 3, the IASB considered whether it should amend the definition of joint control in IAS 31 *Interests in Joint Ventures*[4] because it was concerned that its decision to eliminate the pooling method would create incentives for business combinations to be structured to meet the definition of a joint venture. After considering comments on the definition proposed in ED 3, the IASB revised the definition of joint control in IAS 31 to clarify that:

(a)   unanimous consent on **all** financial and operating decisions is not necessary for an arrangement to satisfy the definition of a joint venture—unanimous consent on only strategic decisions is sufficient.

(b)   in the absence of a contractual agreement requiring unanimous consent to strategic financial and operating decisions, a transaction in which the owners of multiple businesses agree to combine their businesses into a new entity (sometimes referred to as a roll-up transaction) should be accounted for by the acquisition method. Majority consent on such decisions is not sufficient.

BC61   In developing SFAS 141, the FASB noted that constituents consider the guidance in paragraph 3(d) of APB Opinion No. 18 *The Equity Method of Accounting for Investments in Common Stock* in assessing whether an entity is a joint venture, and it decided not to change that practice in its project on business combinations.

Annual Improvements Cycle 2011–2013

BC61A   The IASB observed that there was uncertainty about whether paragraph 2(a) of IFRS 3, which excludes the formation of joint ventures from the scope of IFRS 3, should have been amended to refer to joint arrangements when IFRS 11 was issued. IFRS 11 had changed the use of the term 'joint venture' from having a general meaning that included 'jointly controlled operations', 'jointly controlled assets' and 'jointly controlled entities', to meaning a specific type of

---

4   IFRS 11 *Joint Arrangements*, issued in May 2011, replaced IAS 31.

joint arrangement, which does not include 'joint operations'. The IASB did not change the wording of the scope exclusion in paragraph 2(a) of IFRS 3 for 'the formation of a joint venture' when it replaced IAS 31 with IFRS 11 *Joint Arrangements*, although it had not intended to change the scope of IFRS 3.

BC61B   There was also uncertainty about whether the scope exclusion in paragraph 2(a) of IFRS 3 addresses:

(a)   the accounting by the joint arrangements themselves in their financial statements only; or also

(b)   the accounting by the parties to the joint arrangement for their interests in the joint arrangement.

BC61C   The IASB noted that paragraph 2(a) of IFRS 3 should exclude formations of every type of joint arrangement (ie joint ventures and joint operations) from the scope of IFRS 3. It also noted that paragraph 2(a) of IFRS 3 excludes, from the scope of IFRS 3, only the accounting by the joint arrangements themselves in their financial statements.

BC61D   The IASB concluded that paragraph 2(a) of IFRS 3 should be amended to address all types of joint arrangements and to remove uncertainty about the financial statements to which it applies.

BC61E   Consequently, the IASB amended paragraph 2(a) of IFRS 3 to:

(a)   exclude the formation of all types of joint arrangements from the scope of IFRS 3 by replacing 'joint venture' with 'joint arrangement'; and

(b)   clarify that the only scope exclusion needed from the scope of IFRS 3 is the accounting for the formation of a joint arrangement in the financial statements of the joint arrangement itself.

Not-for-profit organisations

BC62   The FASB also decided to exclude from the scope of SFAS 141(R) business combinations of not-for-profit organisations and acquisitions of for-profit businesses by not-for-profit organisations. Some aspects of combinations of not-for-profit organisations are different from combinations of business entities. For example, it cannot be presumed that combinations of organisations that serve a public interest are necessarily exchange transactions in which willing parties exchange equal values. For that reason, the FASB is addressing the accounting for combinations of not-for-profit organisations in a separate project. It published an exposure draft in October 2006 that addresses accounting for combinations of not-for-profit organisations.

BC63   IFRSs generally do not have scope limitations for not-for-profit activities in the private or public sector. Although IFRSs are developed for profit-oriented entities, a not-for-profit entity might be required, or choose, to apply IFRSs. A scope exclusion for combinations of not-for-profit organisations is not necessary.

Combinations of mutual entities

BC64   During its deliberations leading to SFAS 141, the FASB concluded that combinations involving only mutual entities should also be accounted for using the acquisition method but decided not to mandate its use until the FASB had considered implementation questions raised about the application of that method. Similarly, IFRS 3 did not require use of the acquisition method for combinations of mutual entities, although the IASB had also concluded that the acquisition method was appropriate for those combinations. Instead, as part of the first phase of its business combinations project, the IASB published an exposure draft of proposed amendments to IFRS 3—*Combinations by Contract Alone or Involving Mutual Entities*, which proposed an interim approach for accounting for those combinations until the IASB had considered related implementation issues in the second phase of its project. In the light of respondents' comments, the IASB decided not to proceed with the proposals in the exposure draft, primarily for reasons of timing and impending consideration of those issues in the second phase of this project.

BC65   After SFAS 141 was issued, the FASB began a joint project with the Canadian Accounting Standards Board (AcSB). The objective of that project was to develop guidance for combinations of two or more mutual entities. In October 2001 the FASB and the AcSB held a round-table discussion with representatives of mutual banks, credit unions, co-operatives and other mutual entities. In January 2004 the FASB met representatives of organisations of co-operative and other mutual entities to discuss its tentative conclusions and specific concerns raised by constituents. In addition, the FASB conducted field visits to three mutual entities in 2004.

BC66   A few participants in those meetings indicated a preference for the fresh start method as an alternative to the acquisition method for particular mergers, especially for those in which it is difficult to identify the acquirer. On both occasions, however, those participants acknowledged the costs and practical difficulties that a fresh start alternative would impose, especially on entities with recurring combinations. After considering those views, the FASB concluded that any potential advantages of using the fresh start method for some combinations of mutual entities would be outweighed by the disadvantages of having two methods of accounting.

BC67   During the deliberations leading to the 2005 Exposure Draft, some representatives of mutual entities reiterated concerns expressed during the development of SFAS 141 about requiring all combinations of mutual entities to be accounted for using the acquisition method. Many of those constituents reiterated public policy concerns similar to those discussed in paragraphs BC49–BC52. For example, some said that eliminating the pooling method could impede desirable combinations and reduce the amount of capital flowing into their industries. They suggested, for example, that the requirement to identify an acquirer could impede mergers of neighbouring mutual entities when both the fact and appearance of a merger of equals are of paramount importance to their directors, members and communities. The boards did not find those arguments persuasive for the same reasons discussed in paragraphs BC49–BC52.

BC68   Although mutual entities have particular characteristics that distinguish them from other business entities, the boards noted that the two types of entities also have many common characteristics. The boards also observed that the economic motivations for combinations of mutual entities, such as to provide their constituents with a broader range of, or access to, services and cost savings through economies of scale, are similar to those for combinations of other business entities. For example:

(a) although mutual entities generally do not have shareholders in the traditional sense of investor-owners, they are in effect 'owned' by their members and are in business to serve their members or other stakeholders. Like other businesses, mutual entities strive to provide their members with a financial return or benefits. A mutual entity generally does that by focusing on providing its members with its products and services at lower prices. For example, the benefit provided by a credit union may be a lower interest rate on a borrowing than might be obtainable through an investor-owned financial institution. In a wholesale buying co-operative, the benefit might be lower net costs, after reflecting patronage dividends.

(b) members' interests in a mutual entity are generally not transferable like other ownership interests. However, they usually include a right to share in the net assets of the mutual entity in the event of its liquidation or conversion to another form of entity.

(c) a higher percentage of combinations of mutual entities than of combinations of other business entities occur without an exchange of cash or other readily measurable consideration, but such combinations are not unique to mutual entities. Business combinations of other entities, particularly private entities, also take place without an exchange of cash or other readily measurable consideration.

BC69 Thus, the boards concluded that the attributes of mutual entities are not sufficiently different from those of other entities to justify different accounting for business combinations. The boards also concluded that the benefits of requiring combinations of mutual entities to be accounted for by the acquisition method would justify the related costs. Therefore, combinations of mutual entities were included within the scope of the 2005 Exposure Draft.

BC70 Many of the respondents to the 2005 Exposure Draft who commented on combinations of mutual entities objected to including them in the scope of the revised standards and thus requiring them to be accounted for by the acquisition method. Respondents objected to the use of the acquisition method for conceptual, practical and cost-benefit reasons. For example, some said that a combination involving only mutual entities is a 'true pooling of interests' and that the acquisition method would not reflect the economics of the transactions. Some also said that it would often be difficult to identify an acquirer. Some also noted the absence of readily measurable consideration transferred in many combinations of mutual entities, which would make it necessary to use other valuation techniques to develop the fair values needed to apply the acquisition method. For those reasons, respondents also said that using the acquisition method for combinations of mutual entities would not be cost-beneficial. Respondents proposed other methods of accounting for mutual entities, including the pooling method, the fresh start method and a net asset method that was the same as the modified version of the acquisition method proposed by the IASB in its exposure draft mentioned in paragraph BC64.

BC71   In considering those comments, the boards noted that respondents' reasons for their objections to the acquisition method were generally the same as the factors discussed in paragraphs BC67 and BC68. For the same reasons discussed in those paragraphs, the boards affirmed their conclusion that the attributes of mutual entities are not sufficiently different from those of investor-owned entities to justify a different method of accounting for combinations of mutual entities. The boards also noted that, regardless of the intentions of the combining entities, the general result of a combination involving only mutual entities is that one entity obtains control of the other entity (or entities). Thus, combinations involving only mutual entities are included in the scope of the revised standards.

BC72   Some representatives of mutual entities suggested that the revised standards should permit an acquisition of a mutual entity to be reported as an increase in the retained earnings of the acquirer (combined entity) as had been the practice in accordance with the pooling method of accounting. The boards observed that in a combination of two investor-owned entities in which the acquirer issues its equity shares as consideration for all of the acquiree's equity shares, the fair value of the acquiree's equity is recognised as an addition to the acquirer's equity—generally as an increase to the acquirer's ordinary shares and capital. Thus, the equity (net assets) of the combined entity is increased from the acquisition of the acquiree (and the fair value of its net assets), but retained earnings of the acquirer are unaffected. The boards concluded that business combinations of two investor-owned entities are economically similar to those of two mutual entities in which the acquirer issues member interests for all the member interests of the acquiree. Thus, the boards concluded that those similar transactions should be similarly reported. Therefore, the revised standards clarify that if the only consideration exchanged is the member interests of the acquiree for the member interests of the acquirer (or the member interests of the newly combined entity), the amount of the acquiree's net assets is recognised as a direct addition to capital or equity, not retained earnings (paragraph B47 of the revised IFRS 3).

BC73   During the boards' redeliberations of the 2005 Exposure Draft, some representatives of mutual entities also proposed that the entire amount of the acquiree's net assets recognised in accordance with the revised standards should be considered a gain on a bargain purchase. They contended that the exchange of member interests in at least some forms of mutual entities does not constitute consideration because the interests the acquirer transfers have no economic value. The boards disagreed, noting that one mutual entity—the acquiree—would presumably not be willing to transfer its net assets to the control of another—the acquirer—in exchange for nothing of value.

BC74   The FASB also considered more specific concerns of representatives of credit unions about adverse economic consequences for those entities. Those representatives argued that requiring the application of the acquisition method would impede consolidation within that industry and might misrepresent the financial soundness and regulatory capital of two credit unions that combine their operations. They noted that in the United States, applicable federal law defines net worth for credit unions as the 'retained earnings balance of the credit union, as determined under generally accepted accounting principles.'

Because the regulatory definition of net worth is narrower than equity under US GAAP, they expressed concern that the exclusion of the equity of an acquired credit union from retained earnings of the combined entity could make a financially sound combined entity appear to be financially unsound. Thus, they suggested that credit unions should be permitted to continue to report the equity of an acquired mutual entity as an addition to retained earnings of the combined entity. The FASB was not persuaded by those arguments; it believes that Statement 141(R) will not affect the ability of credit unions to restructure and combine with other credit unions.

BC75   Additionally, constituents told the FASB that the number of combinations of credit unions in which the regulatory net worth calculation could be significantly affected is relatively small in any given year. The FASB also noted that the regulatory filings of credit unions and other entities and the needs of their regulators are separate matters beyond the purpose of financial statements. The FASB's Concepts Statement 2 states that a necessary and important characteristic of accounting information is neutrality. In the context of business combinations, neutrality means that accounting standards should neither encourage nor discourage business combinations but rather provide information about those combinations that is fair and even-handed. The FASB observed that its public policy goal is to issue accounting standards that result in neutral and representationally faithful financial information. Eliminating use of the pooling method for all entities and requiring all entities, including mutual entities, to report the resulting increase directly in equity other than retained earnings is consistent with that public policy goal.

BC76   Some respondents to the 2005 Exposure Draft said that co-operatives do not fit within the definition of a mutual entity and that co-operatives are sufficiently different from other entities to justify a different method of accounting for combinations involving only co-operatives. To support their view, they cited factors such as differences in legal characteristics and different purposes of co-operatives in addition to providing economic benefits to members.

BC77   The boards considered the differences between, for example, a co-operative that provides electricity to its members in a rural area and other types of mutual entities, such as a mutual insurance company. The boards acknowledged particular differences between the two types of entities, for example, the co-operative issues member shares and the mutual insurance company does not. In addition, the objective of the co-operative may include providing more social and cultural benefits to its community in addition to the economic benefits provided to its members than does another type of mutual entity. However, the boards concluded that co-operatives generally provide direct and indirect economic benefits such as dividends and lower costs of services, including credit, or other products directly to its members. The boards concluded that differences in the amount of social and cultural benefits an entity seeks to provide do not justify a conclusion that co-operatives are sufficiently different from other mutual entities that they do not fit within the definition of a mutual entity in the revised standards. Thus, co-operatives are included in the definition of a mutual entity in the revised standards.

Combinations achieved by contract alone

BC78 Both boards also concluded that business combinations achieved by contract alone should be included in the scope of the revised standards. Those combinations were not included in the scope of either IFRS 3 or SFAS 141, although the boards understand that practice in the United States generally was to account for them in accordance with SFAS 141. For example, in EITF Issue No. 97-2 *Application of FASB Statement No. 94 and APB Opinion No. 16 to Physician Practice Management Entities and Certain Other Entities with Contractual Management Arrangements*, the Task Force reached a consensus that a transaction in which a physician practice management entity executes a management agreement with the physician practice should be accounted for as a business combination. Technically, that transaction would not meet the definition of a business combination in APB Opinion 16 or SFAS 141 because the physician practice management entity does not acquire either equity interests in, or the net assets of, the physician practice.

BC79 The boards understand that difficulties may arise in applying the acquisition method to combinations achieved by contract alone. In particular, such business combinations normally do not involve the payment of readily measurable consideration and in rare circumstances it might be difficult to identify the acquirer. However, as for combinations of mutual entities and for the reasons discussed above, the boards concluded that the acquisition method can and should be applied in accounting for such business combinations. In reaching that conclusion, the boards also concluded that in a business combination achieved by contract alone:

(a) difficulties in identifying the acquirer are not a sufficient reason to justify a different accounting treatment, and no further guidance is necessary for identifying the acquirer for combinations by contract alone.

(b) in the United States, these transactions are already being accounted for by the acquisition method and insurmountable issues have not been encountered.

(c) determining the fair value of the identifiable assets acquired and liabilities assumed and calculating the related goodwill should be consistent with decisions reached in the second phase of the project.

Applying the acquisition method

BC80 The 2005 Exposure Draft identified four steps in applying the acquisition method, and it discussed the requirements for applying the acquisition method in terms of those steps:

(a) identifying the acquirer;

(b) determining the acquisition date;

(c) measuring the fair value of the acquiree; and

(d) measuring and recognising the assets acquired and the liabilities assumed.

BC80A   In contrast, the revised standards indicate (paragraph 5 of the revised IFRS 3) that applying the acquisition method requires:

(a)   identifying the acquirer;

(b)   determining the acquisition date;

(c)   recognising and measuring the identifiable assets acquired, liabilities assumed and any non-controlling interest in the acquiree; and

(d)   recognising and measuring goodwill or a gain from a bargain purchase.

BC81   The main changes to the list of steps in applying the acquisition method are to eliminate measuring the fair value of the acquiree as a whole and to add recognising and measuring goodwill as a separate step. The primary reason for those changes is the boards' decision to focus on measuring the components of the business combination, including any non-controlling interest in the acquiree, rather than measuring the fair value of the acquiree as a whole. The boards observed that neither the requirements of the 2005 Exposure Draft nor those of the revised standards for applying the acquisition method result in a fair value measure of either the acquiree as a whole or the acquirer's interest in the acquiree. For example, the revised standards do not provide for recognising a loss if the acquirer overpays for the acquiree, ie if the acquisition-date fair value of the consideration transferred exceeds the acquisition-date fair value of the acquirer's interest in the acquiree. The IASB's decision to allow an acquirer to choose to measure any non-controlling interest in the acquiree at fair value or on the basis of its proportionate interest in the acquiree's identifiable net assets adds another potential difference between the results of applying the requirements of the revised IFRS 3 and measuring the acquisition-date fair value of the acquiree as a whole. (See paragraphs BC209–BC221 for discussion of the reasons why the IASB provided that choice.) Paragraphs BC330 and BC331 discuss the reasons why the revised standards also eliminate the related presumption in the 2005 Exposure Draft that the consideration transferred in exchange for the acquiree measures the fair value of the acquirer's interest in the acquiree.

Identifying the acquirer

BC82   The boards' decision that all business combinations within the scope of the revised standards should be accounted for by the acquisition method means that the acquirer must be identified in every business combination.

BC83   The IASB and the FASB separately developed the guidance on identifying the acquirer that appeared in IFRS 3 and SFAS 141, respectively. Paragraphs BC84–BC92 discuss the FASB's development of the guidance in SFAS 141 and paragraphs BC93–BC101 discuss the IASB's development of the guidance in IFRS 3. Paragraphs BC102–BC105 discuss the boards' joint consideration of how to identify the acquirer in a business combination in the second phase of their projects on business combinations.

Developing the guidance in SFAS 141

BC84   SFAS 141's guidance on identifying the acquirer focused on the types of business combinations included in its scope, which excluded transactions in which one entity obtains control over one or more other entities by means other than transferring assets, incurring liabilities or issuing equity securities. Thus, SFAS 141 did not include the general guidance that the entity that obtains control is the acquirer, although that was the effect of the guidance for the combinations within its scope.

BC85   In developing its 1999 Exposure Draft, the FASB affirmed the guidance in APB Opinion 16 that in a business combination effected primarily through the distribution of cash or other assets or by incurring liabilities, the acquirer is generally the entity that distributes cash or other assets or assumes or incurs liabilities. The FASB considered a variety of suggestions on factors that should be considered in identifying the acquirer in a business combination effected through an exchange of equity interests. The guidance proposed in the 1999 Exposure Draft reflected the FASB's conclusion that all pertinent facts and circumstances should be considered when identifying the acquirer, particularly the relative voting rights in the combined entity after the combination. That proposed guidance said that the existence of unusual or special voting arrangements and options, warrants or convertible securities should be considered in determining which shareholder group retained or received the larger portion of the voting rights in the combined entity. In addition, factors related to the composition of the board of directors and senior management of the combined entity should be considered and should be weighted equally with the factors related to voting rights.

BC86   Respondents to the 1999 Exposure Draft who commented on the proposed criteria for identifying the acquirer generally agreed that they were appropriate. Some respondents said that the proposed guidance was an improvement over APB Opinion 16 because it provided additional factors to consider in determining which shareholder group retained or received the larger share of the voting rights in the combined entity. However, many respondents suggested improvements to the proposed criteria, and some suggested that the FASB should consider other criteria.

BC87   Several respondents suggested that the FASB should retain the presumptive approach in APB Opinion 16 for identifying the acquirer in transactions effected through an exchange of equity interests. That approach presumes that, in the absence of evidence to the contrary, the acquirer is the combining entity whose owners as a group retain or receive the larger share of the voting rights in the combined entity. Other respondents suggested that the factors to be considered in identifying the acquirer should be provided in the form of a hierarchy. Some of those respondents also suggested that the FASB should provide additional guidance explaining how factors relating to voting rights (unusual special voting arrangements and options, warrants or convertible securities) would affect the determination of the acquirer.

BC88   In considering those suggestions, the FASB observed, as it did in developing the 1999 Exposure Draft, that because each business combination is unique, the facts and circumstances relevant to identifying the acquirer in one combination may be less relevant in another. Therefore, SFAS 141 did not retain the presumptive approach in APB Opinion 16 nor did it provide hierarchical guidance because to do so would have implied that some factors are always more important than others in identifying the acquirer. However, as suggested by respondents, the FASB modified the proposed guidance to explain how some of the factors influence the identification of the acquirer.

BC89 The 1999 Exposure Draft did not propose requiring consideration of the payment of a premium over the market value of the equity securities acquired as evidence of the identity of the acquirer. Some respondents to the 1999 Exposure Draft said that the payment of a premium is a strong indicator of the identity of the acquirer. Upon reconsideration, the FASB decided to include in SFAS 141 the payment of a premium as a criterion to be considered in identifying the acquirer.

BC90 In developing SFAS 141, the FASB observed that identifying the acquirer might be difficult in some multi-party business combinations, particularly those that might not be acquisitions but are required to be accounted for as such. The FASB noted that in those circumstances it might be helpful to consider additional factors such as which of the entities initiated the combination and whether the reported amounts of assets, revenues and earnings of one of the combining entities significantly exceed those of the others. Respondents to the 1999 Exposure Draft generally agreed, and SFAS 141 included that guidance.

BC91 In addition, as suggested by respondents, the FASB decided that SFAS 141 should explicitly state that in some business combinations, such as reverse acquisitions, the entity that issues the equity interests may not be the acquirer. In a reverse acquisition, one entity (Entity A) obtains ownership of the equity instruments of another entity (Entity B), but Entity A issues enough of its own voting equity instruments as consideration in the exchange transaction for control of the combined entity to pass to the owners of Entity B.

BC92 If a new entity is formed to issue equity instruments to effect a business combination, SFAS 141 required that one of the combining entities that existed before the combination must be identified as the acquirer for essentially the same reasons as those discussed in paragraphs BC98–BC101 in the context of IFRS 3's similar requirement.

Developing the guidance in IFRS 3

BC93 As proposed in ED 3, IFRS 3 carried forward from IAS 22 the principle that in a business combination accounted for using the acquisition method the acquirer is the combining entity that obtains control of the other combining entities or businesses. The IASB observed that using the control concept as the basis for identifying the acquirer is consistent with using the control concept in IAS 27 *Consolidated and Separate Financial Statements* to define the boundaries of the reporting entity and to provide the basis for establishing the existence of a parent-subsidiary relationship.[5] IFRS 3 also carried forward the guidance in IAS 22 that control is the power to govern the financial and operating policies of the other entity so as to obtain benefits from its activities. IFRS 3 also provided the same guidance as IAS 22 for identifying the acquirer if one of the combining

---

5 The consolidation requirements in IAS 27 were superseded, and the definition of control was revised, by IFRS 10 *Consolidated Financial Statements* issued in May 2011.

entities might have obtained control even if it does not acquire more than one-half of the voting rights of another combining entity.

Identifying an acquirer in a business combination effected through an exchange of equity interests

BC94   In developing ED 3 and IFRS 3, the IASB decided not to carry forward the guidance in IAS 22 on identifying which of the combining entities is the acquirer in a reverse acquisition. IAS 22 required the entity whose owners control the combined entity to be treated as the acquirer. That approach presumed that in a business combination effected through an exchange of equity interests, the entity whose owners control the combined entity is always the entity with the power to govern the financial and operating policies of the other entity so as to obtain benefits from its activities. The IASB observed that because the presumption is not always accurate, carrying it forward would in effect override the control concept for identifying the acquirer.

BC95   The IASB observed that the control concept focuses on the relationship between two entities, in particular, whether one entity has the power to govern the financial and operating policies of another so as to obtain benefits from its activities. Therefore, determining which of the combining entities has, as a consequence of the combination, the power to govern the financial and operating policies of the other so as to obtain benefits from its activities is fundamental to identifying the acquirer, regardless of the form of the consideration.

BC96   The IASB also observed that in some reverse acquisitions, the acquirer may be the entity whose equity interests have been acquired and the acquiree is the issuing entity. For example, a private entity might arrange to have itself 'acquired' by a smaller public entity through an exchange of equity interests as a means of obtaining a stock exchange listing. As part of the agreement, the directors of the public entity resign and are replaced by directors appointed by the private entity and its former owners. The IASB observed that in such circumstances, the private entity, which is the legal subsidiary, has the power to govern the financial and operating policies of the combined entity so as to obtain benefits from its activities. Treating the legal subsidiary as the acquirer in such circumstances is thus consistent with applying the control concept for identifying the acquirer. Treating the legal parent as the acquirer in such circumstances would place the form of the transaction over its substance, thereby providing less useful information than would be provided using the control concept to identify the acquirer.

BC97   Therefore, the IASB proposed in ED 3 that the acquirer in a business combination effected through an issue of equity interests should be identified by considering all pertinent facts and circumstances to determine which of the combining entities has the power to govern the financial and operating policies of the other so as to obtain benefits from its activities. Pertinent facts and circumstances include, but are not limited to, the relative ownership interests of the owners of the combining entities. Respondents to ED 3 generally supported that requirement, which was consistent with the requirement of SFAS 141.

Identifying an acquirer if a new entity is formed to effect a business combination

BC98　If a new entity is formed to issue equity instruments to effect a business combination, ED 3 proposed and IFRS 3 required one of the combining entities that existed before the combination to be identified as the acquirer on the basis of the evidence available. In considering that requirement, the IASB identified two approaches to applying the acquisition method that had been applied in various jurisdictions. The first approach viewed business combinations from the perspective of one of the combining entities that existed before the combination. Under that approach, the acquirer must be one of the combining entities that existed before the combination and therefore cannot be a new entity formed to issue equity instruments to effect a combination. The second approach viewed business combinations from the perspective of the entity providing the consideration, which could be a newly formed entity. Under that approach, the acquirer must be the entity providing the consideration. Some jurisdictions interpreted IAS 22 as requiring the first approach; other jurisdictions interpreted IAS 22 as requiring the second approach.

BC99　If a new entity is formed to issue equity instruments to effect a business combination involving two or more other entities, viewing the combination from the perspective of the entity providing the consideration would result in the newly formed entity applying the acquisition method to each of the other combining entities. The IASB noted that the result would be the same as applying the fresh start method to account for the business combination, which would potentially provide users of the financial statements with more relevant information than requiring one of the pre-existing entities to be treated as the acquirer.

BC100　The IASB also considered whether treating a new entity formed to issue equity instruments to effect a business combination as the acquirer would place the form of the transaction over its substance, because the new entity may have no economic substance. The formation of such entities is often related to legal, tax or other business considerations that do not affect the identification of the acquirer. For example, a combination of two entities that is structured so that one entity directs the formation of a new entity to issue equity instruments to the owners of both of the combining entities is, in substance, no different from a transaction in which one of the combining entities directly acquires the other. Therefore, the transaction should be accounted for in the same way as a transaction in which one of the combining entities directly acquires the other. To do otherwise would impair both the comparability and the reliability of the information.

BC101　The IASB concluded that the users of an entity's financial statements are provided with more useful information about a business combination when that information faithfully represents the transaction it purports to represent. Therefore, IFRS 3 required the acquirer to be one of the combining entities that existed before the combination.

Convergence and clarification of SFAS 141's and IFRS 3's guidance for identifying the acquirer

BC102   The deliberations of the FASB and the IASB described in paragraphs BC84–BC101 resulted in similar but not identical guidance for identifying the acquirer in SFAS 141 and IFRS 3. But the guidance was worded differently, and the boards were concerned that differences in identifying the acquirer could arise. Therefore, as part of the effort to develop a common standard on accounting for business combinations, the boards decided to develop common guidance for identifying the acquirer that could be applied internationally. For example, the FASB adopted the IASB's definition of an acquirer as the entity that obtains control of the other combining entities, and both boards decided to include in the revised standards an explicit reference to their other standards that provide guidance for identifying the acquirer. That guidance, although previously implicit, was not in SFAS 141. The intention of the boards is to conform and clarify their guidance but not to change the substance of the provisions for identifying an acquirer previously provided in SFAS 141 and IFRS 3.

BC103   Some respondents to the 2005 Exposure Draft noted that the existing IASB and FASB definitions of control in their respective consolidations standards are somewhat different and, in rare instances, may lead to identifications of different acquirers. The boards agreed with that observation, but they affirmed their conclusion in developing the 2005 Exposure Draft that developing a common definition of control is outside the scope of the business combinations project.

Identifying the acquirer in business combinations involving only mutual entities

BC104   The boards considered whether differences between mutual entities and investor-owned entities or differences between combinations of mutual entities and combinations of investor-owned entities result in a need for different or additional guidance for identifying the acquirer in combinations of mutual entities. The boards did not note any such differences. As a result, the boards concluded that an acquirer must be identified for all business combinations, including those involving only mutual entities.

BC105   The boards also concluded that the indicators for identifying the acquirer in a business combination are applicable to mutual entities and that no additional indicators are needed to identify the acquirer in those combinations. Both boards acknowledged that difficulties may arise in identifying the acquirer in combinations of two virtually equal mutual entities but observed that those difficulties also arise in combinations of two virtually equal investor-owned entities. The boards concluded that those difficulties, which are not unique to mutual entities, could be resolved in practice.

Determining the acquisition date

BC106   IFRS 3 and SFAS 141 carried forward without reconsideration the provisions of IAS 22 and APB Opinion 16, respectively, on determining the acquisition date.

With one exception that applies only to SFAS 141 (see paragraphs BC108–BC110), that guidance resulted in the same acquisition date as the guidance in the revised standards.

BC107 In both IFRS 3 and SFAS 141, the guidance on the acquisition date, which IFRS 3 also referred to as the *exchange date*, was incorporated within the guidance on determining the cost of the acquisition rather than being stated separately. The revised standards clarify the acquisition-date guidance to make explicit that the acquisition date is the date that the acquirer obtains control of the acquiree. Paragraphs BC338–BC342 discuss the related issue of the measurement date for equity securities transferred as consideration in a business combination and the changes the revised standards make to the previous requirements on that issue.

BC108 The FASB also eliminated the 'convenience' exception that SFAS 141 carried forward from APB Opinion 16 and the reporting alternative permitted by Accounting Research Bulletin No. 51 *Consolidated Financial Statements* (ARB 51). SFAS 141, paragraph 48, permitted an acquirer to designate an effective date other than the date that assets or equity interests are transferred or liabilities are assumed or incurred (the acquisition date) if it also reduced the cost of the acquiree and net income as required by that paragraph to compensate for recognising income before consideration was transferred. Paragraph 11 of ARB 51 permitted an acquirer to include a subsidiary that was purchased during the year in the consolidation as though it had been acquired at the beginning of the year and to deduct the pre-acquisition earnings at the bottom of the consolidated income statement.

BC109 The FASB concluded that to represent faithfully an acquirer's financial position and results of operations, the acquirer should account for all business combinations at the acquisition date. In other words, its financial position should reflect the assets acquired and liabilities assumed at the acquisition date—not before or after they are obtained or assumed. Moreover, the acquirer's financial statements for the period should include only the cash inflows and outflows, revenues and expenses and other effects of the acquiree's operations after the acquisition date.

BC110 Very few respondents to the 2005 Exposure Draft commented on the proposed guidance on determining the acquisition date. Those who did so generally raised practicability issues related to eliminating the ability to designate an effective date other than the acquisition date. The boards concluded that the financial statement effects of eliminating that exception were rarely likely to be material. For example, for convenience an entity might wish to designate an acquisition date of the end (or the beginning) of a month, the date on which it closes its books, rather than the actual acquisition date during the month. Unless events between the 'convenience' date and the actual acquisition date result in material changes in the amounts recognised, that entity's practice would comply with the requirements of the revised standards. Therefore, the boards decided to retain the guidance in the 2005 Exposure Draft about determining the acquisition date.

Recognising and measuring the identifiable assets acquired, the liabilities assumed and any non-controlling interest in the acquiree

Recognition

BC111   The revised standards' recognition principle is stated in paragraph 10 of the revised IFRS 3. Paragraphs BC112–BC130 discuss the recognition conditions the acquirer is to use in applying the recognition principle. The revised standards also provide guidance for recognising particular assets and liabilities, which is discussed in paragraphs BC131–BC184. The revised standards' guidance on classifying and designating assets acquired and liabilities assumed is discussed in paragraphs BC185–BC188, and the limited exceptions to the recognition principle provided in the revised standards are discussed in paragraphs BC263–BC303.

Conditions for recognition

BC112   The boards decided that to achieve a reasonably high degree of consistency in practice and to resolve existing inconsistencies, the revised standards should provide guidance on applying the recognition principle. That guidance emphasises two fundamental conditions. To measure and recognise an item as part of applying the acquisition method, the item acquired or assumed must be:

(a)   an asset or liability at the acquisition date; and

(b)   part of the business acquired (the acquiree) rather than the result of a separate transaction.

An asset or a liability at the acquisition date

BC113   In determining whether an item should be recognised at the acquisition date as part of the business combination, the boards decided that the appropriate first step is to apply the definitions of assets and liabilities in the IASB's *Framework* or FASB Concepts Statement No. 6 *Elements of Financial Statements*, respectively.

BC114   The boards observed that in accordance with both IFRS 3 and SFAS 141, and their predecessors and the related interpretative guidance, particular items were recognised **as if** they were assets acquired or liabilities assumed at the acquisition date even though they did not meet the definition of an asset or a liability. That practice was related to the previous emphasis on measuring the cost of (or investment in) the acquiree rather than the acquisition-date fair values of the assets acquired and liabilities assumed. For example, as discussed in paragraphs BC365–BC370, some expenses for services received in connection with a business combination were capitalised as part of the cost of the acquiree (and recognised as part of goodwill) **as if** they were an asset at the acquisition date. In addition, some future costs that an acquirer expected to incur often were viewed as a cost of the acquiree and recognised **as if** they were a liability at the acquisition date—expected restructuring costs were an example. The boards concluded that the representational faithfulness, consistency and understandability of financial reporting would be improved by eliminating such practices.

Part of the business combination

BC115 The second condition for recognising an asset acquired or a liability assumed or incurred in a business combination is that the asset or liability must be part of the business combination transaction rather than an asset or a liability resulting from a separate transaction. Making that distinction requires an acquirer to identify the components of a transaction in which it obtains control over an acquiree. The objective of the condition and the guidance on identifying the components of a business combination is to ensure that each component is accounted for in accordance with its economic substance.

BC116 The boards decided to provide application guidance to help address concerns about the difficulty of determining whether a part of the consideration transferred is for the acquiree or is for another purpose. The boards observed that parties directly involved in the negotiations of an impending business combination may take on the characteristics of related parties. Therefore, they may be willing to enter into other agreements or include as part of the business combination agreement some arrangements that are designed primarily for the benefit of the acquirer or the combined entity, for example, to achieve more favourable financial reporting outcomes after the business combination. Because of those concerns the boards decided to develop a principle for determining whether a particular transaction or arrangement entered into by the parties to the combination is part of what the acquirer and acquiree exchange in the business combination or is a separate transaction.

BC117 The boards concluded that a transaction that is designed primarily for the economic benefit of the acquirer or the combined entity (rather than the acquiree or its former owners before the business combination) is not part of the exchange for the acquiree. Those transactions should be accounted for separately from the business combination. The boards acknowledge that judgement may be required to determine whether part of the consideration paid or the assets acquired and liabilities assumed stems from a separate transaction. Accordingly, the 2005 Exposure Draft included both a general principle and implementation guidance for applying that principle, including several examples.

BC118 Respondents' comments on the proposed guidance on identifying the components of a business combination transaction were mixed. For example, some respondents said that the general principle was clear and provided adequate guidance; others said that the proposed principle was not clear. Several respondents said that the focus on determining whether a transaction benefits the acquiree or the acquirer was not clear because a transaction or event that benefits the acquiree would also benefit the combined entity because the acquiree is part of the combined entity.

BC119 The boards agreed with respondents that the proposed principle for distinguishing between components of a business combination needed improvement. Accordingly, they revised the principle to focus on whether a transaction is entered into by or on behalf of the acquirer or **primarily** for the benefit of the acquirer or the combined entity, rather than **primarily** for the benefit of the acquiree or its former owners **before the combination** (paragraph 52 of the revised IFRS 3).

BC120   The boards also concluded that the focus of the principle should be on identifying whether a business combination includes separate transactions that should be accounted for separately in accordance with their economic substance rather than solely on assessing whether a transaction is part of the exchange for the acquiree (paragraph 51 of the revised IFRS 3). Focusing solely on whether assets or liabilities are part of the exchange for the acquiree might not result in all transactions being accounted for in accordance with their economic substance. For example, if an acquirer asks the acquiree to pay some or all of the acquisition-related costs on its behalf and the acquiree has paid those costs before the acquisition date, at the acquisition date the acquiree will show no liability for those costs. Therefore, some might think that the principle as stated in the 2005 Exposure Draft does not apply to the transactions giving rise to the acquisition-related costs. The boards concluded that focusing instead on whether a transaction is separate from the business combination will more clearly convey the intention of the principle and thus will provide users with more relevant information about the financial effects of transactions and events entered into by the acquirer. The acquirer's financial statements will reflect the financial effects of all transactions for which the acquirer is responsible in accordance with their economic substance.

BC121   To help in applying the principle, paragraph 52 of the revised IFRS 3 includes three examples of transactions that are separate from the transaction in which an acquirer obtains control over an acquiree, and Appendix B provides additional application guidance.

BC122   The first example in paragraph 52 is directed at ensuring that a transaction that in effect settles a pre-existing relationship between the acquirer and the acquiree is excluded from the accounting for the business combination. Assume, for example, that a potential acquiree has an asset (receivable) for an unresolved claim against the potential acquirer. The acquirer and the acquiree's owners agree to settle that claim as part of an agreement to sell the acquiree to the acquirer. The boards concluded that if the acquirer makes a lump sum payment to the seller-owner, part of that payment is to settle the claim and is not part of the consideration transferred to acquire the business. Thus, the portion of the payment that relates to the claim settlement should be excluded from the accounting for the business combination and accounted for separately. In effect, the acquiree relinquished its claim (receivable) against the acquirer by transferring it (as a dividend) to the acquiree's owner. Thus, at the acquisition date the acquiree has no receivable (asset) to be acquired as part of the combination, and the acquirer would account for its settlement payment separately. The FASB observed that the conclusion that a transaction that settles a pre-existing relationship is not part of applying the acquisition method is consistent with the conclusion in EITF Issue No. 04-1 *Accounting for Preexisting Relationships between the Parties to a Business Combination*, which is incorporated into SFAS 141(R) and therefore superseded.

BC123   The second and third examples are also directed at ensuring that payments that are not part of the consideration transferred for the acquiree are excluded from the business combination accounting. The boards concluded that the payments for such transactions or arrangements should be accounted for separately in accordance with the applicable requirements for those transactions.

Paragraph BC370 also discusses potential abuses related to the third example—payments to reimburse the acquiree or its former owners for paying the acquirer's costs incurred in connection with the business combination.

BC124 To provide additional help in identifying the components of a business combination, paragraph B50 of the revised IFRS 3 includes three factors to be considered in assessing a business combination transaction: (a) the reason for the transaction, (b) who initiated the transaction and (c) the timing of the transaction. Although those factors are neither mutually exclusive nor individually conclusive, the boards decided that the factors could help in considering whether a transaction or event is arranged primarily for the economic benefit of the acquirer or the combined entity or primarily for the benefit of the acquiree and its former owners before the business combination.

IFRS 3's criterion on reliability of measurement

BC125 IFRS 3 included another recognition criterion for assets acquired or liabilities assumed in a business combination. That criterion required an asset or liability to be recognised separately from goodwill only if it could be reliably measured. In its deliberations leading to the revised IFRS 3, the IASB decided to eliminate reliability of measurement as an overall criterion, which it observed is unnecessary because reliability of measurement is a part of the overall recognition criteria in the *Framework*.

IFRS 3's criterion on probability of an inflow or outflow of benefits

BC126 IFRS 3 provided that an acquirer should recognise the acquiree's identifiable assets (other than intangible assets) and liabilities (other than contingent liabilities) only if it is probable that the asset or liability will result in an inflow or outflow of economic benefits. The revised IFRS 3 does not contain that probability recognition criterion and thus it requires the acquirer to recognise identifiable assets acquired and liabilities assumed regardless of the degree of probability of an inflow or outflow of economic benefits.

BC127 The recognition criteria in the *Framework* include the concept of probability to refer to the degree of uncertainty that the future economic benefits associated with an asset or liability will flow to or from the entity.

BC128 During the development of the revised IFRS 3, the IASB reconsidered items described in IAS 37 *Provisions, Contingent Liabilities and Contingent Assets* as contingent assets and contingent liabilities. Analysing the rights or obligations in such items to determine which are conditional and which are unconditional clarifies the question of whether the entity has an asset or a liability at the acquisition date.[6] As a result, the IASB concluded that many items previously described as contingent assets or contingent liabilities meet the definition of an asset or a liability in the *Framework* because they contain unconditional rights or obligations as well as conditional rights or obligations. Once the unconditional right in an asset (the unconditional obligation in a liability) is identified, the question to be addressed becomes what is the inflow (outflow) of economic benefits relating to that unconditional right (unconditional obligation).

---

6 Paragraphs BC11–BC17 and BC22–BC26 of the Basis for Conclusions on the draft amendments to IAS 37, published for comment in June 2005, discuss this issue in more detail.

BC129   The IASB noted that the *Framework* articulates the probability recognition criterion in terms of a flow of economic benefits rather than just direct cash flows. If an entity has an unconditional obligation, it is certain that an outflow of economic benefits from the entity is required, even if there is uncertainty about the timing and the amount of the outflow of benefits associated with a related conditional obligation. Hence, the IASB concluded that the liability (the unconditional obligation) satisfies the *Framework*'s probability recognition criterion. That conclusion applies equally to unconditional rights. Thus, if an entity has an unconditional right, it is certain that it has the right to an inflow of economic benefits, and the probability recognition criterion is satisfied.

BC130   Therefore, the IASB decided that inclusion of the probability criterion in the revised IFRS 3 is unnecessary because an unconditional right or obligation will always satisfy the criterion.   In addition, the IASB made consequential amendments to paragraphs 25 and 33 of IAS 38 *Intangible Assets* to clarify the reason for its conclusion that the probability recognition criterion is always considered to be satisfied for intangible assets that are acquired separately or in a business combination. Specifically, the amendment indicates that an entity expects there to be an inflow of economic benefits embodied in an intangible asset acquired separately or in a business combination, even if there is uncertainty about the timing and the amount of the inflow.

Recognising particular identifiable assets acquired and liabilities assumed

BC131   To help ensure the consistent application of the requirements of the revised standards, the boards decided to provide specific recognition guidance for particular types of identifiable assets acquired and liabilities assumed in a business combination. That guidance and the reasons for it are discussed in the following paragraphs.

Liabilities associated with restructuring or exit activities of the acquiree

BC132   The revised standards explain that an acquirer recognises liabilities for restructuring or exit activities acquired in a business combination only if they meet the definition of a liability at the acquisition date (paragraph 11 of the revised IFRS 3).   Costs associated with restructuring or exiting an acquiree's activities that are not liabilities at that date are recognised as post-combination activities or transactions of the combined entity when the costs are incurred. In considering acquired restructuring or exit activities the FASB and the IASB began at different points because the requirements of SFAS 141 and IFRS 3 on the issue differed.

BC133   In applying SFAS 141, acquirers looked to EITF Issue No. 95-3 *Recognition of Liabilities in Connection with a Purchase Business Combination* for guidance on recognising liabilities associated with restructuring or exit activities of an acquirer. EITF Issue 95-3 provided that the costs of an acquirer's plan (a) to exit an activity of an acquired company, (b) to involuntarily terminate the employment of employees of an acquired company or (c) to relocate employees of an acquired company should be recognised as liabilities assumed in a purchase business combination if specified conditions were met.   Those conditions did not require the existence of a present obligation to another party.

In developing the 2005 Exposure Draft, the FASB concluded, as it did in FASB Statement No. 146 *Accounting for Costs Associated with Exit or Disposal Activities* (SFAS 146), that only present obligations to others are liabilities under the definition in the FASB's Concepts Statement 6. An exit or disposal plan, by itself, does not create a present obligation to others for costs an entity expects to incur under the plan. Thus, an entity's commitment to an exit or disposal plan, by itself, is not a sufficient condition for recognition of a liability. Consistently with that conclusion, SFAS 141(R) nullifies the guidance in EITF Issue 95-3, which was not consistent with SFAS 146.

BC134   Before the IASB issued IFRS 3, IAS 22, like EITF Issue 95-3, required the acquirer to recognise as part of allocating the cost of a combination a provision for terminating or reducing the activities of the acquiree (*a restructuring provision*) that was not a liability of the acquiree at the acquisition date, provided that the acquirer had satisfied specified criteria. The criteria in IAS 22 were similar to those in EITF Issue 95-3. In developing ED 3 and IFRS 3, the IASB considered the view that a restructuring provision that was not a liability of the acquiree at the acquisition date should nonetheless be recognised by the acquirer as part of allocating the cost of the combination if the specified conditions were met. Those supporting this view, including some respondents to ED 3, argued that:

(a)   the estimated cost of terminating or reducing the activities of the acquiree would have influenced the price paid by the acquirer for the acquiree and therefore should be taken into account in measuring goodwill.

(b)   the acquirer is committed to the costs of terminating or reducing the activities of the acquiree because of the business combination. In other words, the combination is the past event that gives rise to a present obligation to terminate or reduce the activities of the acquiree.

BC135   In developing IFRS 3, the IASB rejected those arguments, noting that the price paid by the acquirer would also be influenced by future losses and other 'unavoidable' costs that relate to the future conduct of the business, such as costs of investing in new systems. IFRS 3 did not provide for recognising those costs as liabilities because they do not represent liabilities of the acquiree at the acquisition date, although the expected future outflows may affect the value of existing recognised assets. The IASB concluded that it would be inconsistent to recognise 'unavoidable' restructuring costs that arise in a business combination but to prohibit recognition of a liability for other 'unavoidable' costs to be incurred as a result of the combination.

BC136   The IASB's general criteria for identifying and recognising restructuring provisions are set out in IAS 37. IAS 37 states that a constructive obligation to restructure (and therefore a liability) arises only when the entity has developed a detailed formal plan for the restructuring and either raised a valid expectation in those affected that it will carry out the restructuring by publicly announcing details of the plan or begun implementing the plan. IAS 37 requires such a liability to be recognised when it becomes probable that an outflow of resources embodying economic benefits will be required to settle the obligation and the amount of the obligation can be reliably estimated.

BC137　IFRS 3 reflected the IASB's conclusion that if the criteria in paragraph 31 of IAS 22 for the recognition of a restructuring provision were carried forward, similar items would be accounted for differently. The timing of the recognition of restructuring provisions would differ, depending on whether a plan to restructure arises in connection with, or in the absence of, a business combination. The IASB decided that such a difference would impair the usefulness of the information provided to users about an entity's plans to restructure because both comparability and reliability would be diminished. Accordingly, IFRS 3 contained the same requirements as the revised IFRS 3 for recognising liabilities associated with restructuring or exit activities.

BC138　Few of the comments on the 2005 Exposure Draft from respondents who apply IFRSs in preparing their financial statements addressed its proposal on accounting for costs to restructure or exit activities of an acquiree (restructuring costs). Those who did so generally agreed with its proposal to carry forward the requirement of IFRS 3 for recognising liabilities associated with restructuring or exit activities of an acquiree. But the provisions of the 2005 Exposure Draft on that issue represented a change to GAAP in the United States, and the FASB received several responses objecting to the proposed change. It also received some responses that agreed with them, generally for the same reasons that the boards proposed the provisions in the 2005 Exposure Draft.

BC139　Respondents who disagreed with the proposed accounting for liabilities associated with restructuring or exit activities of an acquiree generally cited one or more of the following reasons in support of their view:

(a)　Acquirers factor restructuring costs into the amount they are willing to pay for the acquiree. Therefore, those costs should be included in accounting for the business combination.

(b)　It is not clear why the boards decided that restructuring costs should not be recognised as liabilities assumed in the business combination when those costs are more likely to be incurred than some of the liabilities related to contingencies that the boards proposed to recognise as liabilities assumed in a combination.

(c)　Capitalising restructuring costs as part of a business combination would be consistent with the accounting for other asset acquisitions in which the amount capitalised is equal to the amount paid to acquire and place the asset in service.

BC140　The boards were not persuaded by those views. They observed that the view described in paragraph BC139(a) is essentially the same as the view of some respondents to ED 3 discussed in paragraph BC134(a). In addition, the boards noted that the acquirer does not pay the acquiree or its owners for the anticipated costs to restructure or exit activities and the acquirer's plans to do so do not give rise to an obligation and associated liability at the acquisition date. The acquirer ordinarily incurs a liability associated with such costs after it gains control of the acquiree's business.

BC141　The boards also disagreed with the view that the accounting for costs to restructure or exit some of an acquiree's activities is inconsistent with the requirements of the revised standards on contingencies. On the contrary, the two requirements are consistent with each other because both require recognition of a liability only if an obligation that meets the definition of a liability exists at the acquisition date.

BC142   The boards also observed that the requirements of the revised standards on restructuring costs are consistent with current practice in accounting for many similar costs expected to be incurred in conjunction with other acquisitions of assets. For example, one airline might acquire an aircraft from another airline. The acquirer was likely to consider the costs of changing the logo on the aircraft and making any other intended changes to its configuration in deciding what it was willing to pay for the aircraft. Other airlines bidding for the aircraft might also have plans to change the aircraft if they were the successful bidders. The nature and extent of the changes each airline expected to make and the costs each would incur were likely to differ.

BC143   In accordance with both US GAAP and IFRSs, the airline would recognise none of those expected, post-acquisition costs at the date the aircraft is acquired. Instead, those costs are accounted for after control of the aircraft is obtained. If the costs add to the value of the aircraft and meet the related requirements of US GAAP or IFRSs, they will be recognised as assets (probably as an addition to the carrying amount of the aircraft). Otherwise, those additional costs are likely to be charged to expense when incurred.

Operating leases

BC144   In accordance with both FASB Statement No. 13 *Accounting for Leases* (SFAS 13) and IAS 17 *Leases*, an acquiree that is the lessee in an operating lease does not recognise separately the rights and obligations embodied in operating leases. The boards considered whether to require, for example, the separate recognition of an asset acquired for an acquiree's rights to use property for the specified period and related renewal options or other rights and a liability assumed for an acquiree's obligations to make required lease payments for an operating lease acquired in a business combination. However, at the time they considered how to account for operating leases in a business combination, they were considering adding to their agendas a joint project on accounting for leases. That project was added in 2006. Accordingly, the boards concluded that the revised standards should be consistent with the existing accounting requirements on accounting for leases. Therefore, the revised standards provide that the acquirer recognises no assets or liabilities related to an operating lease in which the acquiree is the lessee other than those referred to in paragraphs B29 and B30 of the revised IFRS 3, which are discussed in the following paragraphs.

BC145   The 2005 Exposure Draft proposed that the amount by which the terms of an operating lease are favourable or unfavourable in relation to market terms should be recognised as a separate intangible asset, regardless of whether the acquiree is the lessee or the lessor. For the FASB, that proposal would have carried forward the related guidance in SFAS 141 for leases in which the acquiree is the lessee. Some respondents suggested that, instead, the measure of the fair value of an asset subject to an operating lease in which the acquiree is the lessor should take into account the favourable or unfavourable aspect of the lease terms.

BC146   The boards considered this issue in the context of their respective guidance in other standards on how to determine the fair value of an asset. As noted above, the proposal in the 2005 Exposure Draft was generally consistent with US GAAP for business combinations. However, FASB Statement No. 157 *Fair Value Measurements* (SFAS 157) does not provide guidance on the *unit of valuation*—the level at which an asset or liability is aggregated or disaggregated to determine what is being measured. The IASB also does not have general guidance on determining the unit of valuation. However, IAS 40 *Investment Property* provides that the fair value of investment property takes into account rental income from current leases, and the IASB understands that practice in measuring the fair value of investment property is to take into account the contractual terms of the leases and other contracts in place relating to the asset.

BC147   The FASB concluded that SFAS 141 should retain the guidance in the 2005 Exposure Draft that the favourable or unfavourable aspect of an operating lease in which the acquiree is the lessor should be separately recognised as an intangible asset or liability. It concluded that separately reporting that amount rather than embedding an aspect of a lease contract in the fair value of the leased asset would provide more complete information to users of the post-combination financial statements. In addition, the FASB noted that reporting the favourable or unfavourable aspect of the lease contract separately would facilitate appropriate amortisation of that amount over the term of the lease rather than over the remaining life of the leased asset. Unlike IAS 16 *Property, Plant and Equipment*, US GAAP does not require an item of property, plant or equipment to be separated into components, with the components depreciated or amortised over different useful lives.

BC148   The IASB decided to require the acquirer in a business combination to follow the guidance in IAS 40 for assets subject to operating leases in which the acquiree is the lessor. The IASB observed that, for lessors who choose the cost option in IAS 40, both IAS 16 and IAS 38 require use of a depreciation or amortisation method that reflects the pattern in which the entity expects to consume the asset's future economic benefits. In addition, IAS 16 requires each part of an item of property, plant and equipment that has a cost that is significant in relation to the total cost of the item to be depreciated separately. Thus, an entity would be required to adjust the depreciation or amortisation method for the leased asset to reflect the timing of cash flows attributable to the underlying leases. Therefore, although the presentation of operating leases and the underlying leased assets in the statement of financial position will differ depending on whether an entity applies IFRSs or US GAAP, the IASB observed that the identifiable net assets and the depreciation or amortisation recognised in the post-combination financial statements will be the same.

Research and development assets

BC149   The revised standards require an acquirer to recognise all tangible and intangible research and development assets acquired in a business combination, as was proposed in the 2005 Exposure Draft. Previously, FASB Interpretation No. 4 *Applicability of FASB Statement No. 2 to Business Combinations Accounted for by the Purchase Method* (FASB Interpretation 4) required an acquirer to measure and immediately recognise as expense tangible and intangible assets to be used in research and development that had no alternative future use. A research and development asset was recognised as such only if it had an alternative future use. In contrast, IFRS 3 did not require a research and development asset to have an alternative future use for it to be recognised. The revised standards therefore do not change the provisions of IFRS 3 on that issue. Accordingly, most of the discussion in paragraphs BC150–BC156 pertains to the FASB's consideration of this issue.

BC150　The FASB concluded that the requirement to write off assets to be used in research and development activities immediately if they have no alternative future use resulted in information that was not representationally faithful. In addition, eliminating that requirement furthers the goal of international convergence of accounting standards. Therefore, SFAS 141(R) supersedes FASB Interpretation 4 and requires research and development assets acquired in a business combination to be recognised regardless of whether they have an alternative future use.

BC151　Relatively few respondents to the 2005 Exposure Draft commented on the proposed accounting for research and development assets. Those who did so generally disagreed with those proposals (they also generally applied US GAAP rather than IFRSs), citing either or both of the following concerns as support for their view:

(a)　In-process research and development may not meet the definition of an asset in the FASB's Concepts Statement 6 because its low likelihood of success does not represent **probable** future economic benefits.

(b)　The fair value of in-process research and development may not be measurable with sufficient reliability for recognition in financial statements.

The boards rejected both of those views for the reasons explained in the following paragraphs.

BC152　The boards agreed with respondents that the likelihood that an individual research and development project will result in a profitable product is often low. However, the boards also noted that the use of the word *probable* in the FASB's Concepts Statement 6 refers only to something that is not certain. The definition does not use that term as a recognition criterion that specifies the degree of probability of the inflow or outflow of future economic benefits that must be present for an item to qualify for recognition. Therefore, the boards concluded that in-process research and development acquired in a business combination will generally satisfy the definition of an asset because the observable exchange at the acquisition date provides evidence that the parties to the exchange expect future economic benefits to result from that research and development. Uncertainty about the outcome of an individual project is reflected in measuring its fair value.

BC153　The boards also agreed that determining the fair value of in-process research and development requires the use of estimates and judgement, and the resulting amount will generally not be as reliable as the fair values of other assets for which quoted prices in active markets are available. However, the boards observed that use of estimates and judgement, by itself, does not mean that information is unreliable; reliability does not require precision or certainty. For example, paragraph 86 of the IASB's *Framework*[7] says that 'In many cases, cost or value must be estimated; the use of reasonable estimates is an essential part of the preparation of financial statements and does not undermine their reliability.' The boards also noted that the requirement to measure the fair value of in-process research and development assets acquired in a business combination is not new—not even in US GAAP. In accordance with FASB Interpretation 4, that amount was measured but immediately written off. Moreover, respondents to the 2005 Exposure Draft that apply IFRSs generally did not mention any problems with complying with the provisions of IFRS 3 on research and development assets, which are the same as those in the revised standards.

BC154   In developing the 2005 Exposure Draft, the FASB also considered whether it could make further improvements by extending the recognition provisions of SFAS 141(R) for research and development assets to purchases of in-process research and development assets outside a business combination. At that time, the FASB decided not to do so because the additional time needed to deliberate the related issues would have unduly delayed the revised standards.

BC155   Some respondents to the 2005 Exposure Draft objected to the resulting inconsistent US GAAP requirements for research and development assets acquired in a business combination and those acquired in another type of transaction. The FASB agreed with respondents that inconsistent accounting for research and development assets depending on how they are acquired is undesirable. Therefore, the FASB expects to reconsider the accounting for research and development assets acquired by means other than in a business combination separately from its project on business combinations.

BC156   The FASB also decided to provide guidance on the impairment testing of in-process research and development projects that are temporarily idled or abandoned. It did that by means of an amendment to SFAS 142.

Distinguishing identifiable intangible assets from goodwill

BC157   Early in their respective projects on accounting for business combinations, the IASB and the FASB both observed that intangible assets make up an increasing proportion of the assets of many (if not most) entities. The boards also observed that intangible assets acquired in a business combination were often included in the amount recognised as goodwill.

BC158   Both the IASB and the FASB decided that they needed to provide explicit criteria for determining whether an acquired intangible asset should be recognised separately from goodwill. The FASB provided such criteria in SFAS 141 and the IASB provided similar, although not identical, criteria in IAS 38.[8] One reason for providing such criteria was the boards' conclusion that the decision-usefulness of financial statements would be enhanced if intangible assets acquired in a business combination were distinguished from goodwill. For example, the FASB's Concepts Statement No. 5 *Recognition and Measurement in Financial*

---

7   now paragraph 4.41 of the *Conceptual Framework*
8   More detailed information about the IASB's reasoning in developing the criteria in IAS 38 is available in its Basis for Conclusions.

Statements of Business Enterprises says that classification in financial statements facilitates analysis by grouping items with essentially similar characteristics and separating items with essentially different characteristics. Analysis aimed at objectives such as predicting amounts, timing and uncertainty of future cash flows requires financial information segregated into reasonably homogeneous groups.

BC159   In developing its 1999 Exposure Draft, the FASB considered various characteristics that might distinguish other intangible assets from goodwill. Because the FASB concluded that identifiability is the characteristic that conceptually distinguishes other intangible assets from goodwill, the 1999 Exposure Draft proposed that intangible assets that are identifiable and reliably measurable should be recognised as assets separately from goodwill. Most respondents to the 1999 Exposure Draft agreed that many intangible assets are identifiable and that various intangible assets are reliably measurable. However, respondents' views on the proposed recognition criteria varied. Many of those respondents suggested alternative recognition criteria and many urged the FASB to clarify the term *reliably measurable*.

BC160   The FASB considered those suggestions and decided to modify the proposed recognition criteria to provide a clearer distinction between intangible assets that should be recognised separately from goodwill and those that should be subsumed into goodwill. The FASB then published a revised exposure draft *Business Combinations and Intangible Assets—Accounting for Goodwill* (2001 Exposure Draft) which proposed that an intangible asset should be recognised separately from goodwill if either:

(a)   control over the future economic benefits of the asset results from contractual or other legal rights (the contractual-legal criterion); or

(b)   the intangible asset is capable of being separated or divided and sold, transferred, licensed, rented or exchanged (either separately or as part of a group of assets) (the separability criterion).

The FASB concluded that sufficient information should exist to measure reliably the fair value of an asset that satisfies either of those criteria. Thus, the change in the recognition criteria eliminated the need explicitly to include *reliably measurable* as a recognition criterion or to clarify the meaning of that term.

BC161   IAS 38 (as issued by the IASB's predecessor body in 1998) clarified that the definition of an intangible asset required an intangible asset to be identifiable to distinguish it from goodwill. However, it did not define the term *identifiable*. Instead, IAS 38 stated that an intangible asset could be distinguished from goodwill if the asset was separable, though separability was not a necessary condition for identifiability.

BC162   In developing IFRS 3, the IASB affirmed the conclusion in IAS 38 that identifiability is the characteristic that conceptually distinguishes other intangible assets from goodwill. In addition, the IASB concluded that to provide a definitive basis for identifying and recognising intangible assets separately from goodwill, the concept of identifiability needed to be articulated more clearly. As a result of that consideration, which is discussed in paragraphs BC163–BC165, the IASB developed more definitive criteria for distinguishing between identifiable intangible assets and goodwill and included those criteria in both IFRS 3 and IAS 38 (as revised in 2004).

Reasons for the contractual-legal criterion

BC163　In developing IFRS 3 and SFAS 141, the IASB and the FASB observed that many intangible assets arise from rights conveyed legally by contract, statute or similar means. For example, franchises are granted to car dealers, fast food outlets and professional sports teams. Trademarks and service marks may be registered with the government. Contracts are often negotiated with customers or suppliers. Technological innovations are often protected by patents. In contrast, goodwill arises from the collection of assembled assets that make up an acquiree or the value created by assembling a collection of assets through a business combination, such as the synergies that are expected to result from combining two or more businesses. Therefore, both boards concluded that the fact that an intangible asset arises from contractual or other legal rights is an important characteristic that distinguishes many intangible assets from goodwill and an acquired intangible asset with that characteristic should be recognised separately from goodwill.

Reasons for the separability criterion

BC164　As already noted (paragraph BC161), the original version of IAS 38 included separability as a characteristic that helps to distinguish intangible assets from goodwill. In developing IFRS 3, the IASB affirmed that conclusion for the reasons discussed in the following paragraphs.

BC165　In developing IFRS 3 and SFAS 141, the IASB and the FASB observed that some intangible assets that do not arise from rights conveyed by contract or other legal means are nonetheless capable of being separated from the acquiree and exchanged for something else of value. Others, like goodwill, cannot be separated from an entity and sold or otherwise transferred. Both boards thus concluded that separability is another important characteristic that distinguishes many intangible assets from goodwill. An acquired intangible asset with that characteristic should be recognised separately from goodwill.

BC166　The FASB's 2001 Exposure Draft proposed that an intangible asset that was not separable individually would meet the separability criterion if it could be sold, transferred, licensed, rented or exchanged along with a group of related assets or liabilities. Some respondents suggested that the FASB should eliminate that requirement, arguing that unless the asset is separable individually it should be included in the amount recognised as goodwill. Others asked the FASB to clarify the meaning of the term *group of related assets*, noting that even goodwill can be separated from the acquiree if the asset group sold constitutes a business.

BC167　The FASB noted that some intangible assets are so closely related to another asset or liability that they are usually sold as a 'package' (eg deposit liabilities and the related depositor relationship intangible asset). If those intangible assets were subsumed into goodwill, gains might be inappropriately recognised if the intangible asset was later sold along with the related asset or obligation. However, the FASB agreed that the proposed requirement to recognise an intangible asset separately from goodwill if it could be sold or transferred as part of an asset group was a broader criterion than it had intended. For those reasons, SFAS 141 provided, as do the revised standards, that an intangible asset that is not separable individually meets the separability criterion if it can be separated from the entity and sold, transferred, licensed, rented or exchanged in combination with a related contract, other identifiable asset or other liability.

BC168　Some respondents to the 2001 Exposure Draft suggested limiting the separability criterion to intangible assets that are separable **and** are traded in observable exchange transactions. Although the FASB agreed that exchange transactions provide evidence of an asset's separability, it concluded that those transactions were not necessarily the only evidence of separability and it did not adopt that suggestion.

BC169　Other respondents suggested that the separability criterion should be modified to require recognition of an intangible asset separately from goodwill only if management of the entity **intends** to sell, lease or otherwise exchange the asset. The FASB rejected that suggestion because it concluded that the asset's **capability** of being separated from the entity and exchanged for something else of value is the pertinent characteristic of an intangible asset that distinguishes it from goodwill. In contrast, management's intentions are not a characteristic of an asset.

The FASB's reasons for rejecting other recognition criteria suggested for SFAS 141

BC170　Some respondents suggested that the FASB should eliminate the requirement to recognise intangible assets separately from goodwill. Others suggested that all intangible assets with characteristics similar to goodwill should be included in the amount recorded as goodwill. The FASB rejected those suggestions because they would diminish rather than improve the decision-usefulness of reported financial information.

BC171　Some respondents doubted their ability to measure reliably the fair values of many intangible assets. They suggested that the only intangible assets that should be recognised separately from goodwill are those that have direct cash flows and those that are bought and sold in observable exchange transactions. The FASB rejected that suggestion. Although the fair value measures of some identifiable intangible assets might lack the precision of the measures for other assets, the FASB concluded that the information that will be provided by recognising intangible assets at their estimated fair values is a more faithful representation than that which would be provided if those intangible assets were subsumed into goodwill. Moreover, including finite-lived intangible assets in goodwill that is not being amortised would further diminish the representational faithfulness of financial statements.

Convergence of criteria in SFAS 141 and IFRS 3

BC172　The criteria in IFRS 3 for determining if an intangible asset is identifiable and thus should be recognised separately from goodwill included the same contractual or legal and separability conditions as SFAS 141. However, IFRS 3 also included a requirement that the fair value of an identifiable intangible asset should be reliably measurable to be recognised separately. In developing the 2005 Exposure Draft, the boards considered how best to achieve convergence of their respective recognition criteria for intangible assets.

BC173   In developing IFRS 3, the IASB noted that the fair value of identifiable intangible assets acquired in a business combination is normally measurable with sufficient reliability to be recognised separately from goodwill. The effects of uncertainty because of a range of possible outcomes with different probabilities are reflected in measuring the asset's fair value; the existence of such a range does not demonstrate an inability to measure fair value reliably. IAS 38 (before amendment by the revised IFRS 3) included a rebuttable presumption that the fair value of an intangible asset with a finite useful life acquired in a business combination can be measured reliably. The IASB had concluded that it might not always be possible to measure reliably the fair value of an asset that has an underlying contractual or legal basis. However, IAS 38 provided that the only circumstances in which it might not be possible to measure reliably the fair value of an intangible asset that arises from legal or other contractual rights acquired in a business combination were if it either:

(a)   is not separable; or

(b)   is separable, but there is no history or evidence of exchange transactions for the same or similar assets, and otherwise estimating fair value would depend on immeasurable variables.

BC174   In developing the 2005 Exposure Draft, the IASB concluded that separate recognition of intangible assets, on the basis of an estimate of fair value, rather than subsuming them in goodwill, provides better information to the users of financial statements even if a significant degree of judgement is required to estimate fair value. For that reason, the IASB decided to propose consequential amendments to IAS 38 to remove the reliability of measurement criterion for intangible assets acquired in a business combination. In redeliberating the proposals in the 2005 Exposure Draft, the IASB affirmed those amendments to IAS 38.

Illustrative list of intangible assets

BC175   The illustrative examples that accompanied IFRS 3 included a list of examples of identifiable intangible assets that might be acquired in a business combination. A similar list accompanies the revised IFRS 3 (see the illustrative examples). The list reflects various changes to similar lists in the exposure drafts that the boards published earlier in their respective projects on business combinations. The boards observed that the list is not exhaustive, and a particular type of intangible asset that was included on an earlier list might not be mentioned in the illustrative examples. That does not necessarily mean that the intangible asset does not qualify as identifiable in accordance with the criteria in the revised standards. An acquirer must consider the nature of each acquired intangible asset in determining whether those criteria are met.

Assembled workforce

BC176   In developing SFAS 141, the FASB did not consider whether an assembled workforce met either the contractual-legal or the separability criterion for recognition as an identifiable intangible asset. Instead, SFAS 141 precluded separate recognition of an assembled workforce because of the FASB's conclusion that techniques to measure the value of an assembled workforce with sufficient reliability were not currently available. IFRS 3 and IAS 38, on the other hand, did not explicitly preclude separate recognition of an assembled workforce. However, paragraph 15 of IAS 38 noted that an entity would not usually have sufficient control over the expected future economic benefits arising from an assembled workforce for it to meet the definition of a separate intangible asset.

BC177   In developing the 2005 Exposure Draft, the boards concluded that an acquirer should not recognise an assembled workforce as a separate intangible asset because it meets neither the contractual-legal nor the separability criterion. The views of respondents who commented on recognition of an assembled workforce were mixed. Some agreed with its proposed recognition prohibition. Others suggested that the boards should reconsider that prohibition; they generally said that an assembled workforce is already valued in many situations for the purpose of calculating a 'contributory asset charge' in determining the fair value of some intangible assets. (In using an 'excess earnings' income valuation technique, a contributory asset charge is required to isolate the cash flows generated by the intangible asset being valued from the contribution to those cash flows made by other assets, including other intangible assets. Contributory asset charges are hypothetical 'rental' charges for the use of those other contributing assets.) Those respondents opposed a prohibition on recognising an assembled workforce as a separate intangible asset; they favoured permitting acquirers to assess whether an assembled workforce is separable in each situation and to recognise those that are separable.

BC178   In reconsidering the proposal in the 2005 Exposure Draft, the boards concluded that the prohibition of recognising an assembled workforce should be retained. Because an assembled workforce is a collection of employees rather than an individual employee, it does not arise from contractual or legal rights. Although individual employees might have employment contracts with the employer, the collection of employees, as a whole, does not have such a contract. In addition, an assembled workforce is not separable, either as individual employees or together with a related contract, identifiable asset or liability. An assembled workforce cannot be sold, transferred, licensed, rented or otherwise exchanged without causing disruption to the acquirer's business. In contrast, an entity could continue to operate after transferring an identifiable asset. Therefore, an assembled workforce is not an identifiable intangible asset to be recognised separately from goodwill.

BC179   The boards observed that neither IAS 38 nor SFAS 141 defined an assembled workforce, and that inconsistencies have resulted in practice. In addition, some who objected to the recognition prohibition in the 2005 Exposure Draft apparently consider that an assembled workforce represents the intellectual capital of the skilled workforce—the (often specialised) knowledge and experience that employees of an acquiree bring to their jobs. However, the boards view an assembled workforce as an existing collection of employees that permits an acquirer to continue to operate an acquired business from the acquisition date and they decided to include that definition in the revised standards (paragraph B37 of the revised IFRS 3).

BC180   The boards observed that the value of intellectual capital is, in effect, recognised because it is part of the fair value of the entity's other intangible assets, such as proprietary technologies and processes and customer contracts and relationships. In that situation, a process or methodology can be documented and followed to the extent that the business would not be materially affected if a particular employee left the entity. In most jurisdictions, the employer usually 'owns' the intellectual capital of an employee. Most employment contracts stipulate that the employer retains the rights to and ownership of any intellectual property created by the employee. For example, a software program created by a particular employee (or group of employees) would be documented and generally would be the property of the entity. The particular programmer who created the program could be replaced by another software programmer with equivalent expertise without significantly affecting the ability of the entity to continue to operate. But the intellectual property created in the form of a software program is part of the fair value of that program and is an identifiable intangible asset if it is separable from the entity. In other words, the prohibition of recognising an assembled workforce as an intangible asset does not apply to intellectual property; it applies only to the value of having a workforce in place on the acquisition date so that the acquirer can continue the acquiree's operations without having to hire and train a workforce.

Reacquired rights

BC181　As part of a business combination, an acquirer may reacquire a right that it had previously granted to the acquiree to use the acquirer's recognised or unrecognised intangible assets. Examples of such rights include a right to use the acquirer's trade name under a franchise agreement or a right to use the acquirer's technology under a technology licensing agreement. The 2005 Exposure Draft proposed, and the revised standards require, an acquirer to recognise such a reacquired right as an identifiable intangible asset (paragraph B35 of the revised IFRS 3). The fair value of a reacquired right is to be amortised over the remaining term of the contract that gave rise to the right. For entities applying US GAAP, that guidance is not new; it is the same as the related guidance in EITF Issue 04-1. (Paragraphs BC308–BC310 discuss the measurement of reacquired rights.)

BC182　A few respondents to the 2005 Exposure Draft disagreed with recognising a reacquired right as an identifiable intangible asset because they considered that doing so was the same as recognising an internally generated intangible asset. Some suggested recognising a reacquired right as the settlement of a pre-existing relationship; others said that a reacquired right should be recognised as part of goodwill.

BC183　The boards rejected the alternative of treating a reacquired right as the termination of a pre-existing relationship because reacquisition of, for example, a franchise right does not terminate the right. After a business combination, the right to operate a franchised outlet in a particular region continues to exist. The difference is that the acquirer, rather than the acquiree by itself, now controls the franchise right.

BC184　The boards also rejected recognising a reacquired right as part of goodwill. Supporters of that alternative consider that such a right differs from other identifiable intangible assets recognised in a business combination because, from the perspective of the combined entity, a franchising relationship with an outside party no longer exists. As already noted, however, the reacquired right and the related cash flows continue to exist. The boards concluded that recognising that right separately from goodwill provides users of the financial statements of the combined entity with more decision-useful information than subsuming the right into goodwill. The boards also observed that a reacquired right meets the contractual-legal and the separability criteria and therefore qualifies as an identifiable intangible asset.

Classifying and designating assets acquired and liabilities assumed

BC185   In some situations, IFRSs and US GAAP provide for different accounting depending on how a particular asset or liability is classified or designated. For example, in accordance with both IAS 39 *Financial Instruments: Recognition and Measurement*[9] and FASB Statement No. 115 *Accounting for Certain Investments in Debt and Equity Securities*, the accounting for particular financial instruments differs depending on how the instrument is classified, for example, as at fair value through profit or loss, available for sale or held to maturity. Another example is the accounting for a derivative instrument in accordance with either IAS 39[10] or FASB Statement No.133 *Accounting for Derivative Instruments and Hedging Activities* (SFAS 133), which depends on whether the derivative is designated as a hedge, and if so, the type of hedge designated.

BC186   The 2005 Exposure Draft proposed that the classification of an acquired lease would not change from the acquiree's classification at lease inception unless the terms of the lease were modified as a result of the business combination in a way that would require a different classification in accordance with IAS 17 or SFAS 13. But that exposure draft did not address classification or designation issues pertaining to other types of contracts. Some respondents and others asked the boards to provide additional guidance on when the acquirer in a business combination should reconsider and perhaps change the classification or designation of a contract for the purpose of applying other accounting requirements.

BC187   The boards decided that providing a general principle for classifying or designating contracts acquired in a business combination would facilitate consistent implementation of the revised standards. They observed that application of the acquisition method results in the initial recognition in the acquirer's financial statements of the assets acquired and liabilities assumed in a business combination. Therefore, in concept, the acquirer should classify and designate all items acquired in a business combination at the acquisition date in the context of the contractual terms, economic conditions and other pertinent factors at that date. That concept underlies the classification and designation principle (paragraph 15 of the revised IFRS 3).

BC188   In the two situations described in paragraph 17 of the revised IFRS 3, classification of a lease contract as an operating lease or a finance lease and classification of a contract as an insurance or reinsurance contract or a deposit contract, other IFRSs and US GAAP require an entity to classify a contract only at

9   IFRS 9 *Financial Instruments* replaced IAS 39. IFRS 9 applies to all items that were previously within the scope of IAS 39.
10   IFRS 9 *Financial Instruments* replaced the hedge accounting requirements in IAS 39.

its inception, on the basis of contractual terms and other factors at that date. Because those requirements apply to specific types of contracts regardless of the identity of the parties to the contract, the boards concluded that such requirements should also apply in accounting for a business combination. Thus, the revised standards provide an exception to the principle for classifying and designating assets acquired and liabilities assumed in a business combination for the two types of contracts identified in paragraph 17.

Recognition, classification and measurement guidance for insurance and reinsurance contracts

BC189　SFAS 141(R) provides guidance specific to insurance and reinsurance contracts acquired or assumed in a business combination, primarily by means of amendments to other insurance-related standards. Paragraphs BC190–BC195 discuss that guidance. Paragraph BC196 discusses the IASB's guidance on recognition and measurement of insurance contracts in a business combination, which is provided in IFRS 4 *Insurance Contracts*.

BC190　The FASB decided that insurance and reinsurance contracts acquired in a business combination should be accounted for on a fresh start (new contract) basis. Accordingly, all assets and liabilities arising from the rights and obligations of insurance and reinsurance contracts acquired in a business combination are recognised at the acquisition date, measured at their acquisition-date fair values. That recognition and measurement might include a reinsurance recoverable, a liability to pay future contract claims and claims expenses on the unexpired portion of the acquired contracts and a liability to pay incurred contract claims and claims expenses. However, those assets acquired and liabilities assumed would not include the acquiree's insurance and reinsurance contract accounts such as deferred acquisition costs and unearned premiums that do not represent future cash flows. The FASB considers that model the most consistent with the acquisition method and with the accounting for other types of contracts acquired in a business combination.

BC191　The FASB also decided to require the acquirer to carry forward the acquiree's classification of a contract as an insurance or reinsurance contract (rather than a deposit) on the basis of the terms of the acquired contract and any related contracts or agreements at the inception of the contract. If the terms of those contracts or agreements have been modified in a manner that would change the classification, the acquirer determines the classification of the contract on the basis of its terms and other pertinent factors as of the modification date, which may be the acquisition date. Consideration of related contracts and arrangements is important in assessing whether a contract qualifies as insurance or reinsurance because they can significantly affect the amount of risk transferred.

BC192　SFAS 141(R) also requires the fair value of the insurance and reinsurance contracts acquired in a business combination to be separated into (a) insurance and reinsurance US GAAP accounting balances using the acquirer's accounting policies and (b) an intangible asset (or, at times that are expected to be rare, another liability). That guidance permits the acquirer to report the acquired business subsequently on the same basis as its written business (with the exception of the amortisation of the intangible asset). Other contracts providing for third-party contingent commissions would be accounted for in the same way as other contingencies, and contracts that provide guarantees of the adequacy of claims liabilities would be accounted for as indemnifications.

BC193   The FASB concluded that the intangible asset should be amortised on a basis consistent with the measurement of the liability. For example, for most short-duration contracts such as property and liability insurance contracts, US GAAP claims liabilities are not discounted, so amortising the intangible asset like a discount using an interest method could be an appropriate method. For particular long-duration contracts such as most traditional life insurance contracts, using a basis consistent with the measurement of the liability would be similar to the guidance provided in paragraph 31 of FASB Statement No. 60 *Accounting and Reporting by Insurance Enterprises* (SFAS 60).

BC194   The FASB considered several implementation issues identified by respondents to the 2005 Exposure Draft but decided that specifying the fresh start model for acquired insurance and reinsurance contracts and providing limited guidance on subsequent accounting, including requiring the intangible asset to be amortised on a basis consistent with the liability, should be sufficient to resolve most practice issues. That level of guidance is also consistent with the limited guidance provided by IFRS 4.

BC195   The FASB decided to provide the guidance on recognition and measurement, including subsequent measurement, of insurance and reinsurance contracts acquired in a business combination by means of an amendment to SFAS 60. That parallels the location of the IASB's business combination guidance for insurance contracts in IFRS 4 and will make it easier to address any changes in that guidance that might result if the FASB and the IASB eventually undertake a joint project to reconsider comprehensively the accounting for insurance contracts.

BC196   Paragraphs 31–33 of IFRS 4 deal with limited aspects of insurance contracts acquired in a business combination. That guidance was developed in phase I of the IASB's project on insurance contracts. The IASB decided not to amend those paragraphs in phase II of the business combinations project, so as not to pre-empt phase II of the IASB's project on insurance contracts. In May 2007 the IASB published its initial thoughts for phase II of that project in a discussion paper *Preliminary Views on Insurance Contracts*.

Measurement

BC197   Paragraph 18 of the revised IFRS 3 establishes the principle that the identifiable assets acquired and liabilities assumed should be measured at their acquisition-date fair values. The reasons for that principle and its application to contingencies and non-controlling interests are discussed in paragraphs BC198–BC245, and the definition of fair value[11] is discussed in paragraphs BC246–BC251. The revised standards provide guidance on determining the acquisition-date fair value of particular types of assets acquired,

---

11 IFRS 13 *Fair Value Measurement*, issued in May 2011, defines fair value and contains the requirements for measuring fair value.

which is discussed in paragraphs BC252–BC262. The exceptions to the measurement principle are discussed in paragraphs BC279–BC311.

Why establish fair value as the measurement principle?

Identifiable assets acquired and liabilities assumed

BC198   In developing the measurement principle in the revised standards, the boards concluded that fair value is the most relevant attribute for assets acquired and liabilities assumed in a business combination. Measurement at fair value also provides information that is more comparable and understandable than measurement at cost or on the basis of allocating the total cost of an acquisition. Both IFRS 3 and SFAS 141 required allocation of that cost on the basis of the fair value of the assets acquired and the liabilities assumed. However, other guidance in those standards required measurements that were other than fair value. Moreover, SFAS 141's requirements for measuring identifiable assets acquired and liabilities assumed in an acquisition achieved in stages (a step acquisition) and in acquisitions of less than all of the equity interests in the acquiree resulted in another difference between fair value measurement of identifiable assets and liabilities and the process of accumulating and allocating costs. Those requirements were the same as the benchmark treatment in IAS 22, which IFRS 3 replaced. The following paragraphs discuss both the IASB's reasons for that change to IAS 22 and the FASB's reasons for the change to SFAS 141's requirements for step acquisitions, as well as providing additional discussion of the reasons for the fair value measurement principle in the revised standards.

BC199   In developing IFRS 3 and SFAS 141(R), respectively, the boards examined the inconsistencies that resulted from applying the benchmark treatment in IAS 22 and the provisions of SFAS 141, and the related implementation guidance, to acquisitions of businesses. For a step acquisition, that process involved accumulating the costs or carrying amounts of earlier purchases of interests in an entity, which may have occurred years or decades ago. Those amounts were added to the current costs to purchase incremental interests in the acquiree on the acquisition date. The accumulated amounts of those purchases were then allocated to the assets acquired and liabilities assumed. Allocating the accumulated amounts generally resulted in recognising the identifiable assets and liabilities of the acquiree at a mixture of current exchange prices and carry-forward book values for each earlier purchase rather than at their acquisition-date fair values. Users of financial statements have long criticised those practices as resulting in information that lacks consistency, understandability and usefulness. For example, in response to the September 1991 FASB Discussion Memorandum *Consolidation Policy and Procedures*, an organisation representing lending officers said:

> [We believe] that the assets and liabilities of the subsidiary [acquiree] reported in the consolidation should reflect the full values established by the exchange transaction in which they were purchased. … [We believe] the current practice of reporting individual assets and liabilities at a mixture of some current exchange prices and some carry-forward book values is **dangerously misleading**. [emphasis added]

BC200　　The boards concluded that no useful purpose is served by reporting the assets or liabilities of a newly acquired business using a mixture of their fair values at the date acquired and the acquirer's historical costs or carrying amounts. Amounts that relate to transactions and events occurring before the business is included in the acquirer's financial statements are not relevant to users of those financial statements.

BC201　　The boards also observed the criticisms of the information resulting from application of the cost accumulation and allocation process to acquisitions of businesses that resulted in ownership of less than all of the equity interests in the acquiree. In those circumstances, application of the cost accumulation and allocation process also resulted in identifiable assets and liabilities being assigned amounts that were generally not their acquisition-date fair values. For example, in its 1993 Position Paper *Financial Reporting in the 1990s and Beyond* the Association for Investment Management and Research (AIMR)[12] said:

> An even more difficult situation arises when Firm B acquires less than total ownership of Firm A. Under current practice, only the proportionate share of Firm A's assets and liabilities owned by Firm B are re-valued, but all of Firm A's assets and liabilities—partially re-valued, partially not—are consolidated with those of Firm B, none of whose assets and liabilities have been re-valued. What a mélange! **The result is a combination of historic and current values that only a mystic could sort out with precision.** [page 28, emphasis added]

BC202　　In contrast, if all of the interests in the business were acquired in a single purchase, the process of assigning that current purchase price generally resulted in the assets and liabilities being measured and recognised at their acquisition-date fair values. Thus, the reported amounts of assets and liabilities differed depending on whether an acquirer purchased all of the equity interests in an acquiree in one transaction or in multiple transactions.

BC203　　The boards concluded that measuring assets acquired or liabilities assumed at amounts other than their fair values at the acquisition date does not faithfully represent their economic values or the acquirer's economic circumstances resulting from the business combination. As discussed in paragraph BC37, an important purpose of financial statements is to provide users with relevant and reliable information about the performance of the entity and the resources under its control. That applies regardless of the extent of the ownership interest a parent holds in a particular subsidiary. The boards concluded that measurement at fair value enables users to make a better assessment of the cash-generating abilities of the identifiable net assets acquired in the business combination and the accountability of management for the resources entrusted to it. Thus, the fair value measurement principle in the revised standards will improve the completeness, reliability and relevance of the information reported in an acquirer's financial statements. The boards also concluded that application of that measurement principle should not impose undue incremental costs on entities because it was also necessary to measure the fair values of assets acquired and liabilities assumed under the provisions of IFRS 3

12　Subsequently, the AIMR changed its name to the CFA Institute. References to the organisation in this Basis for Conclusions use its name at the date it published a particular paper.

and SFAS 141, even though those fair values were not always the amounts at which assets and liabilities were recognised.

BC204 Thus, the revised standards reflect the decisions of the IASB and the FASB to develop a standard (and related application guidance) for measuring assets acquired and liabilities assumed in a business combination that:

(a) is consistent with the general principle of initially measuring assets acquired and liabilities assumed at their fair values, thereby improving the relevance and comparability of the resulting information about the assets acquired and liabilities assumed;

(b) eliminates inconsistencies and other deficiencies of the purchase price allocation process, including those in acquisitions of businesses that occur in stages and those in which the acquirer obtains a business without purchasing all, or perhaps any, of the acquiree's equity interests on the acquisition date; and

(c) can be applied in practice with a reasonably high degree of consistency and without imposing undue costs.

Non-controlling interests

BC205 The 2005 Exposure Draft proposed that a non-controlling interest in an acquiree should be determined as the sum of the non-controlling interest's proportional interest in the identifiable assets acquired and liabilities assumed plus the non-controlling interest's share of goodwill. Thus, because goodwill is measured as a residual, the amount recognised for a non-controlling interest in an acquiree would also have been a residual. Also, an important issue in deciding how to measure a non-controlling interest was whether its share of goodwill should be recognised (often referred to as the 'full goodwill versus partial goodwill issue'). In developing the 2005 Exposure Draft, the boards concluded that it should be recognised (in other words, they selected the 'full goodwill' alternative).

BC206 In redeliberating the 2005 Exposure Draft, the boards observed that they had specified the mechanics of determining the reported amount of a non-controlling interest but had not identified its measurement attribute. The result of those mechanics would have been that the non-controlling interest was effectively measured as the 'final residual' in a business combination. That is to say, the reported amount of the non-controlling interest depended on the amount of goodwill attributed to it, and goodwill is measured as a residual. Thus, in a sense, a non-controlling interest would have been the residual after allocating the residual, or the residual of a residual.

BC207 The boards concluded that, in principle, it is undesirable to have two residual amounts in accounting for a business combination. They also observed that goodwill cannot be measured as other than as a residual; measuring the fair value of goodwill directly would not be possible. In contrast, an acquirer can measure the fair value of a non-controlling interest, for example, on the basis of market prices for the shares held by non-controlling shareholders or by applying another valuation technique. The non-controlling interest in the acquiree is a component of a business combination in which less than 100 per cent of the equity interests are acquired, and the boards concluded that, in concept, the non-controlling interest, like other components of the combination, should be measured at fair value. The boards concluded that the decision-usefulness of information about a non-controlling interest would be improved if the revised standards specified a measurement attribute for a non-controlling interest rather than merely mechanics for determining that amount. They also concluded that, in principle, the measurement attribute should be fair value. The boards also understand from consultation with some constituents who use financial statements for making (or making recommendations about) investment decisions that information about the acquisition-date fair value of a non-controlling interest would be helpful in estimating the value of shares of the parent company, not only at the acquisition date but also at future dates.

BC208   The boards also observed that a non-controlling interest is a component of equity in the acquirer's consolidated financial statements and that measuring a non-controlling interest at its acquisition-date fair value is consistent with the way in which other components of equity are measured. For example, outstanding shares of the parent company, including shares issued to former owners of an acquiree to effect a business combination, were measured in the financial statements at their fair value (market price) on the date they were issued. Accordingly, the fair value measurement principle in SFAS 141(R) applies to a non-controlling interest in an acquiree, and the revised IFRS 3 permits an acquirer to measure a non-controlling interest in an acquiree at its acquisition-date fair value.

IFRS 3's choice of measurement basis for a non-controlling interest

BC209   The IASB concluded that, in principle, an acquirer should measure all components of a business combination, including any non-controlling interest in an acquiree, at their acquisition-date fair values. However, the revised IFRS 3 permits an acquirer to choose whether to measure any non-controlling interest in an acquiree at its fair value or as the non-controlling interests' proportionate share of the acquiree's identifiable net assets.

BC210   Introducing a choice of measurement basis for non-controlling interests was not the IASB's first preference. In general, the IASB believes that alternative accounting methods reduce the comparability of financial statements. However, the IASB was not able to agree on a single measurement basis for non-controlling interests because neither of the alternatives considered (fair value and proportionate share of the acquiree's identifiable net assets) was supported by enough board members to enable a revised business combinations standard to be issued. The IASB decided to permit a choice of measurement basis for non-controlling interests because it concluded that the benefits of the other improvements to, and the convergence of, the accounting for business combinations developed in this project outweigh the disadvantages of allowing this particular option.

BC211   The following sections (a) provide additional information about the measurement alternatives considered by the IASB, (b) summarise the main effects of permitting a choice in measurement basis and (c) discuss the effect on convergence.

Measurement alternatives

BC212   Although the IASB supports the principle of measuring all components of a business combination at fair value, support for that principle was not unanimous. Some IASB members did not support that principle because it would require measuring non-controlling interests at fair value. For that reason, those IASB members supported making an exception to the measurement principle for the non-controlling interest in an acquiree.

BC213   Some other IASB members supported an exception for the non-controlling interest for different reasons. Some advocated an exception on the basis that they did not have sufficient evidence to assess the marginal benefits of reporting the acquisition-date fair value of non-controlling interests. Those members concluded that, generally, the fair value of the non-controlling interest could be measured reliably, but they noted that it would be more costly to do so than measuring it at its proportionate share of the acquiree's identifiable net assets. Those members observed that many respondents had indicated that they saw little information of value in the reported non-controlling interest, no matter how it is measured.

BC214   Those IASB members who did not support making an exception concluded that the marginal benefits of reporting the acquisition-date fair value of non-controlling interests exceed the marginal costs of measuring it.

BC215   The IASB considered making it a requirement to measure non-controlling interests at fair value unless doing so would impose undue cost or effort on the acquirer. However, feedback from constituents and staff research indicated that it was unlikely that the term *undue cost or effort* would be applied consistently. Therefore, such a requirement would be unlikely to increase appreciably the consistency with which different entities measured non-controlling interests.

BC216   The IASB reluctantly concluded that the only way the revised IFRS 3 would receive sufficient votes to be issued was if it permitted an acquirer to measure a non-controlling interest either at fair value or at its proportionate share of the acquiree's identifiable net assets, on a transaction-by-transaction basis.

Effects of the optional measurement of non-controlling interests

BC217   The IASB noted that there are likely to be three main differences in outcome that occur when the non-controlling interest is measured as its proportionate share of the acquiree's identifiable net assets, rather than at fair value. First, the amounts recognised in a business combination for non-controlling interests and goodwill are likely to be lower (and these should be the only two items affected on initial recognition). Second, if a cash-generating unit is subsequently impaired, any resulting impairment of goodwill recognised through income is likely to be lower than it would have been if the non-controlling interest had been measured at fair value (although it does not affect the impairment loss attributable to the controlling interest).

BC218   The third difference arises if the acquirer subsequently purchases some (or all) of the shares held by the non-controlling shareholders. If the non-controlling interests are acquired, presumably at fair value, the equity of the group is reduced by the non-controlling interests' share of any unrecognised changes in the fair value of the net assets of the business, including goodwill. If the non-controlling interest is measured initially as a proportionate share of the acquiree's identifiable net assets, rather than at fair value, that reduction in the reported equity attributable to the acquirer is likely to be larger. This matter was considered further in the IASB's deliberations on the proposed amendments to IAS 27.[13]

Convergence

BC219   Both boards decided that, although they would have preferred to have a common measurement attribute for non-controlling interests, they had considered and removed as many differences between IFRS 3 and SFAS 141 as was practicable.

BC220   The boards were unable to achieve convergence of their respective requirements in several areas because of existing differences between IFRSs and US GAAP requirements outside a business combination. The boards observed that the accounting for impairments in IFRSs is different from that in US GAAP. This means that even if the boards converged on the initial measurement of non-controlling interests, and therefore goodwill, the subsequent accounting for goodwill would not have converged. Although this is not a good reason for allowing divergence in the initial measurement of non-controlling interests, it was a mitigating factor.

BC221   Because most business combinations do not involve a non-controlling interest, the boards also observed that the revised standards will align most of the accounting for most business combinations regardless of the different accounting for non-controlling interests in the revised standards.

Subsequent improvements to IFRS 3

BC221A   In *Improvements to IFRSs* issued in May 2010, the Board addressed a concern that permitting the measurement choice for certain components of non-controlling interest might result in inappropriate measurement of those components in some circumstances. The Board decided to limit the choice to non-controlling interests that are present ownership instruments and entitle their holders to a proportionate share of the entity's net assets in the event of liquidation. The amendment requires the acquirer to measure all other components of non-controlling interest at the acquisition-date fair value, unless IFRSs require another measurement basis. For example, if a share-based payment transaction is classified as equity, an entity measures it in accordance with IFRS 2 *Share-based Payment*. Without this amendment, if the acquirer chose to measure non-controlling interest at its proportionate share of the acquiree's identifiable net assets, the acquirer might have measured some equity instruments at nil. In the Board's view, this would result in not recognising economic interests that other parties have in the acquiree. Therefore, the Board amended IFRS 3 to limit the scope of the measurement choice.

---

13   The consolidation requirements in IAS 27 were superseded by IFRS 10 *Consolidated Financial Statements* issued in May 2011. The requirements with respect to transactions between owners in their capacity as owners did not change.

Measuring assets and liabilities arising from contingencies, including subsequent measurement

BC222 FASB Statement No. 5 *Accounting for Contingencies* (SFAS 5) defines a *contingency* as an existing condition, situation or set of circumstances involving uncertainty as to possible gain or loss to an entity that will ultimately be resolved when one or more future events occur or fail to occur. SFAS 141(R) refers to the assets and liabilities to which contingencies relate as *assets and liabilities arising from contingencies*. For ease of discussion, this Basis for Conclusions also uses that term to refer broadly to the issues related to contingencies, including the issues that the IASB considered in developing its requirements on recognising and measuring contingent liabilities in a business combination (paragraphs BC242–BC245 and BC272–BC278).

BC223 The revised standards require the assets and liabilities arising from contingencies that are recognised as of the acquisition date to be measured at their acquisition-date fair values. That requirement is generally consistent with the measurement requirements of IFRS 3, but it represents a change in the way entities generally applied SFAS 141. In addition, the IASB's measurement guidance on contingent liabilities carries forward the related guidance in IFRS 3, pending completion of the project to revise IAS 37 (paragraphs BC272–BC276). Accordingly, the FASB's and the IASB's conclusions on measuring assets and liabilities arising from contingencies are discussed separately.

The FASB's conclusions on measuring assets and liabilities arising from contingencies

BC224 The amount of an asset or a liability arising from a contingency recognised in accordance with SFAS 141 was seldom the acquisition-date fair value. Rather, it was often the settlement amount or a best estimate of the expected settlement amount on the basis of circumstances existing at a date after the acquisition date.

BC225 In developing the 2005 Exposure Draft, the FASB considered whether to require a strict SFAS 5 approach for the initial measurement and recognition of all contingencies in a business combination. That would mean that contingencies that did not meet the SFAS 5 'probability' criterion would be measured at zero (or at a minimum amount that qualifies as probable) rather than at fair value. Some constituents said that applying SFAS 5 in accounting for a business combination might be a practical way to reduce the costs and measurement difficulties involved in obtaining the information and legal counsel needed to measure the fair value of numerous contingencies that the acquiree had not recognised in accordance with SFAS 5.

BC226 The FASB observed that paragraph 17(a) of SFAS 5 states that 'Contingencies that might result in gains usually are not reflected in the accounts since to do so might be to recognize revenue prior to its realization.' Thus, to apply SFAS 5 in accounting for a business combination in the same way it is applied in other situations was likely to result in non-recognition of gain contingencies, including those for which all of the needed information is available at the acquisition date. The FASB concluded that that would be a step backwards; SFAS 141 already required the recognition of gain contingencies at the acquisition date and for which fair value is determinable (paragraphs 39 and 40(a) of SFAS 141). Also, in accordance with SFAS 5's requirements, contingent losses that arise outside a business combination are not recognised unless there is a high likelihood of a future outflow of resources. In addition, because goodwill is calculated as a residual, omitting an asset for an identifiable contingent gain would also result in overstating goodwill. Similarly, omitting a liability for a contingent loss would result in understating goodwill. Thus, the FASB rejected the SFAS 5 approach in accounting for a business combination.

BC227 The FASB also considered but rejected retaining existing practice based on FASB Statement No. 38 *Accounting for Preacquisition Contingencies of Purchased Enterprises* (SFAS 38), which SFAS 141 carried forward without reconsideration. For the reasons described in the preceding paragraph, the FASB concluded that continuing to permit the delayed recognition of most assets and liabilities arising from contingencies that occurred in applying SFAS 141 and the related guidance would fail to bring about needed improvements in the accounting for business combinations. The FASB decided that requiring an acquirer to measure at fair value and recognise any assets and liabilities arising from contingencies that meet the conceptual elements definition would help bring about those needed improvements, in particular, improvements in the completeness of reported financial information.

BC228 Some respondents to the 2005 Exposure Draft were concerned about the ability to measure reliably the fair value of assets and liabilities arising from contingencies at the acquisition date. The FASB concluded that measuring the fair value of an asset or a liability arising from a contractual contingency with sufficient reliability as of the acquisition date should not be more difficult than measuring the fair value of many other assets and liabilities that the revised standards require to be measured at fair value as of that date. The terms of the contract, together with information developed during the acquisition process, for example, to determine the price to be paid, should provide the needed information. Sufficient information is also likely to be available to measure the acquisition-date fair value of assets and liabilities arising from non-contractual contingencies that satisfy the more-likely-than-not criterion (see paragraphs BC270 and BC271). The FASB acknowledges that non-contractual assets and liabilities that do not meet that criterion at the acquisition date are most likely to raise difficult measurement issues and concerns about the reliability of those measures. To address those reliability concerns, the FASB decided that an acquirer should not measure and recognise such assets and liabilities. Rather, assets and liabilities arising from non-contractual contingencies that do not satisfy the more-likely-than-not criterion at the acquisition date are accounted for in accordance with other US GAAP, including SFAS 5.

BC229 The FASB also observed that respondents who are concerned about the reliability with which the fair values of assets and liabilities arising from contingencies can be measured may be interpreting *reliable measurement* differently from the FASB. To determine a reliable measure of the fair value of a contingency, the acquirer need not be able to determine, predict or otherwise know the ultimate settlement amount of that contingency at the acquisition date (or within the measurement period) with certainty or precision.

BC230   In 2006 the FASB and the IASB published for comment the first discussion paper in their joint project to improve their respective conceptual frameworks. Paragraph QC21 of that paper—*Preliminary Views on an improved Conceptual Framework for Financial Reporting: The Objective of Financial Reporting and Qualitative Characteristics of Decision-useful Financial Reporting Information*—discusses the relationship between faithful representation, the quality of decision-useful financial reporting information that pertains to the reliability of information, and precision. It says that accuracy of estimates is desirable and some minimum level of accuracy is necessary for an estimate to be a faithful representation of an economic phenomenon. However, faithful representation implies neither absolute precision in the estimate nor certainty about the outcome.

BC231   The FASB concluded that the fair values of assets and liabilities arising from contingencies meeting the recognition criteria of SFAS 141(R) are measurable with sufficient reliability as of the acquisition date for recognition in accounting for a business combination if the estimates are based on the appropriate inputs and each input reflects the best available information about that factor. The FASB acknowledges that the fair value measured at the acquisition date will not be the amount for which the asset or liability is ultimately settled, but it provides information about the current value of an asset or a liability by incorporating uncertainty into the measure.

Subsequent measurement of assets and liabilities arising from contingencies

BC232   The FASB observed that applying SFAS 5 in the post-combination period to a recognised liability or asset arising from a contingency that did not meet the SFAS 5 probability threshold at the acquisition date would result in derecognising that liability or asset and reporting a gain or loss in income of the post-combination period. That result would not faithfully represent the economic events occurring in that period. The FASB noted that similar concerns about the potential for misleading reporting consequences do not exist for many financial instruments arising from contingencies, such as options, forward contracts and other derivatives. Such assets and liabilities generally would continue to be measured at fair value in accordance with other applicable US GAAP, which also provides guidance on how to report subsequent changes in the fair values of financial instruments in earnings or comprehensive income. Thus, the FASB decided that it must address the subsequent measurement of assets and liabilities arising from contingencies recognised in a business combination. However, it limited the scope of that effort to assets and liabilities that would be subsequently subject to SFAS 5.

BC233   The FASB considered five alternatives for subsequent measurement of assets and liabilities arising from contingencies that would be subject to SFAS 5 if not acquired or assumed in a business combination:

> Alternative 1— Subsequently measuring at fair value
>
> Alternative 2—Subsequently reporting amounts initially recognised in a business combination at their acquisition-date fair values until the acquirer obtains new information about the possible outcome of the contingency. When new information is obtained the acquirer evaluates that new information and measures a liability at the **higher** of its

acquisition-date fair value or the amount that would be recognised if applying SFAS 5 and an asset at the **lower** of its acquisition-date fair value or the best estimate of its future settlement amount

Alternative 3—'Freezing' amounts initially recognised in a business combination

Alternative 4—Applying an interest allocation method (similar to the model in FASB Statement No. 143 *Accounting for Asset Retirement Obligations* (SFAS 143))

Alternative 5—Applying a deferred revenue method, but only to those items that relate to revenue-generating activities.

BC234   Paragraphs BC224–BC231 discuss the reasons for the FASB's decision to require fair value measurement for initial recognition of assets and liabilities arising from contingencies. For many of those same reasons, the FASB considered requiring Alternative 1—subsequent measurement at fair value. For a variety of reasons, the FASB ultimately rejected that alternative. Adopting this alternative would mean that for some entities (maybe many entities) assets and liabilities arising from contingencies acquired in a business combination would be reported at fair value, while other similar assets and liabilities would be reported at SFAS 5 amounts—different measurement of similar assets and liabilities would make financial reports more difficult to understand. The FASB noted that a project on business combinations would not be the appropriate place to address broadly perceived deficiencies in SFAS 5. Moreover, at the same time as SFAS 141(R) was finalised, the FASB was considering adding a project to its technical agenda to reconsider comprehensively the accounting for contingencies in SFAS 5. (The FASB added a project to reconsider the accounting for contingencies to its agenda in September 2007.) The FASB concluded that requiring assets and liabilities arising from contingencies to be subsequently measured at fair value was premature and might prejudge the outcome of its deliberations in that project.

BC235   The FASB decided, as a practical alternative, to require Alternative 2. In accordance with that approach, the acquirer continues to report an asset or liability arising from a contingency recognised as of the acquisition date at its acquisition-date fair value in the absence of new information about the possible outcome of the contingency. When such new information is obtained, the acquirer evaluates that information and measures the asset or liability as follows:

(a)   a liability is measured at the **higher** of:

(i)   its acquisition-date fair value; and

(ii)   the amount that would be recognised if applying SFAS 5.

(b)   an asset is measured at the **lower** of:

(i)   its acquisition-date fair value; and

(ii)   the best estimate of its future settlement amount.

BC236   The FASB concluded that this alternative was a practical bridge between improved reporting at the acquisition date and subsequent accounting under the existing requirements of SFAS 5. It would not prejudge the outcome of deliberations that the FASB will have in a project to reconsider SFAS 5. It also addressed the concerns of some constituents that requiring contingencies to be subsequently measured at fair value would result in contingencies acquired or assumed in a business combination being measured differently from contingencies that arise outside of a business combination.

BC237   The FASB observed that this alternative provides slightly different guidance for liabilities from its guidance for assets. Unlike liabilities, it could not require assets to be measured at the lower of their acquisition-date fair values or *the amounts that would be recognised if applying* SFAS 5. Because SFAS 5 does not allow recognition of gain contingencies, the amount that would be recognised by applying SFAS 5 to an asset would be zero. Thus, the FASB decided that an asset arising from a contingency should be measured at the lower of its acquisition-date fair value or *the best estimate of its future settlement amount.* The FASB believes that that measure is similar to the measure required by SFAS 5 for liabilities (loss contingencies). The FASB also observed that the approach for assets allows for the recognition of impairments to the asset; it requires an asset to be decreased to the current estimate of the amount the acquirer expects to collect.

BC238   The FASB rejected Alternative 3—freezing the amounts initially recognised. The FASB observed that this alternative results in less relevant information than Alternative 2. Because the FASB views Alternative 2 as a practical and operational solution, it saw no compelling reason to adopt a less optimal alternative. The FASB also rejected Alternative 4—the interest allocation method. In accordance with that method, the contingency would be remeasured using a convention similar to SFAS 143 whereby interest rates are held constant for initial cash flow assumptions. The FASB noted that the reasons for selecting the interest allocation method in SFAS 143 for long-term asset retirement obligations, including concerns about income statement volatility, are not compelling for contingencies such as warranties and pending litigation that generally have shorter lives.

BC239   In accordance with Alternative 5—the deferred revenue method—the acquisition-date fair value of a deferred revenue liability (performance obligation) would be amortised after the acquisition date, like the approach for separately priced extended warranties and product maintenance contracts acquired outside a business combination. Accruals would be added to the contingency for subsequent direct costs. The FASB acknowledged that the costs to apply that measurement approach would be lower than other measurement approaches. However, the FASB concluded that the potential reduction in costs does not justify (a) creating inconsistencies in the subsequent accounting for particular classes of contingencies acquired or assumed in a business combination and (b) the diminished relevance of the resulting information. Thus, the FASB also rejected Alternative 5. Some respondents to the 2005 Exposure Draft supported recognition of subsequent changes in the amounts recognised for assets and liabilities arising from contingencies either as adjustments to goodwill or in comprehensive income rather than in earnings. Some who favoured reporting such changes as adjustments to goodwill did so at least in part because of the difficulties they see in distinguishing between changes that result from changes in circumstances after the acquisition date and changes that pertain more to obtaining better information about circumstances that existed at that date. They noted that the latter are measurement period adjustments, many of which result in adjustments to goodwill.

BC240   The FASB understands that distinguishing between measurement period adjustments and other changes in the amounts of assets and liabilities arising from contingencies will sometimes be difficult. It observed, however, that similar difficulties exist for other assets acquired and liabilities assumed in a business combination; changes in the amounts of those assets and liabilities after the acquisition date are included in earnings. The FASB saw no compelling reason to treat items arising from contingencies differently.

BC241   Those who favoured reporting subsequent changes in the amounts recognised for assets and liabilities arising from contingencies in other comprehensive income rather than in earnings generally analogised to the present accounting for available-for-sale securities. They said that items arising from contingencies were not 'realised' until the contingency is resolved. The FASB rejected that alternative because it saw no compelling reason to add to the category of items that are initially recognised as other comprehensive income and later 'recycled' to earnings. The FASB considers reporting subsequent changes in the amounts of items arising from contingencies in earnings not only conceptually superior to reporting those changes only in comprehensive income but also consistent with the way in which other changes in amounts of items acquired or assumed in a business combination are recognised.

The IASB's conclusions on initial and subsequent measurement of contingent liabilities

BC242   As noted in paragraph BC223, the IASB's measurement guidance on contingencies carries forward the related guidance in IFRS 3 (except for clarifying that an acquirer cannot recognise a contingency that is not a liability), pending completion of the project to revise IAS 37. Accordingly, contingent liabilities recognised in a business combination are initially measured at their acquisition-date fair values.

BC243   In developing IFRS 3, the IASB observed that not specifying the subsequent accounting for contingent liabilities recognised in a business combination might result in inappropriately derecognising some or all of those contingent liabilities immediately after the combination.

BC244   In ED 3 the IASB proposed that a contingent liability recognised in a business combination should be excluded from the scope of IAS 37 and subsequently measured at fair value with changes in fair value recognised in profit or loss until the liability is settled or the uncertain future event described in the definition of a contingent liability is resolved. In considering respondents' comments on this issue, the IASB noted that subsequently measuring such contingent liabilities at fair value would be inconsistent with the conclusions it reached on the accounting for financial guarantees and commitments to provide loans at below-market interest rates when it revised IAS 39.[14]

BC245 The IASB decided to revise the proposal in ED 3 for consistency with IAS 39. Therefore, the revised IFRS 3 requires contingent liabilities recognised in a business combination to be measured after their initial recognition at the higher of:

(a) the amount that would be recognised in accordance with IAS 37; and

(b) the amount initially recognised less, when appropriate, cumulative amortisation recognised in accordance with IAS 18 *Revenue*.[15]

Definition of fair value[16]

BC246 The revised IFRS 3 and SFAS 141(R) each use the same definition of fair value that the IASB and the FASB respectively use in their other standards. Specifically, IAS 39[17] and other IFRSs define fair value as 'the amount for which an asset could be exchanged, or a liability settled, between knowledgeable, willing parties in an arm's length transaction' and the revised IFRS 3 uses that definition. SFAS 157, on the other hand, defines fair value as 'the price that would be received to sell an asset or paid to transfer a liability in an orderly transaction between market participants at the measurement date' and that definition is used in SFAS 141(R).[18]

BC247 The IASB considered also using the definition of fair value from SFAS 157 but decided that to do so would prejudge the outcome of its project on fair value measurements. Similarly, the FASB considered using the definition of fair value from IFRS 3 but decided that to do so would be inappropriate in the light of SFAS 157, which it intends for use in all situations in which a new standard requires measurement at fair value.

BC248 The boards acknowledge that the differing definitions of fair value might result in measuring the fair values of assets acquired and liabilities assumed in a business combination differently depending on whether the combination is accounted for in accordance with the revised IFRS 3 or SFAS 141(R). However, the boards consulted valuation experts on the likely effects of the differing definitions of fair value. As a result of that consultation, the boards understand that such differences are unlikely to occur often. The boards also observed that the definitions use different words to articulate essentially the same concepts in two general areas—the non-performance risk and credit standing of financial liabilities and the market-based measurement objective.

---

14 IFRS 9 *Financial Instruments* relocated to IFRS 9 the requirements on the accounting for financial guarantees and commitments to provide loans at below-market interest rates.

15 IFRS 15 *Revenue from Contracts with Customers*, issued in May 2014, replaced IAS 18 *Revenue* and amended paragraph 56 of IFRS 3 for consistency with the requirements in IFRS 15.

16 IFRS 13, issued in May 2011, defines fair value.

17 IFRS 9 *Financial Instruments* replaced IAS 39. IFRS 9 applies to all items that were previously within the scope of IAS 39.

18 IFRS 13, issued in May 2011, is the result of the IASB's and the FASB's joint project on fair value measurement. As a result, the definition of fair value in IFRSs is identical to the definition in US GAAP (Topic 820 *Fair Value Measurement* in the *FASB Accounting Standards Codification*® codified SFAS 157).

BC249 SFAS 157 defines non-performance risk as the risk that an obligation will not be fulfilled and indicates that it affects the fair value of a liability. Non-performance risk includes but may not be limited to the reporting entity's own credit risk. In comparison, IFRSs do not use the term *non-performance risk* in discussing the fair value of a liability. However, IAS 39 requires the fair value of a financial liability to reflect its credit risk. Although the words are different, the boards believe that the underlying concepts are essentially the same.

BC250 The definition of fair value from SFAS 157 indicates that it is a price in an orderly transaction between market participants. In comparison, IFRSs indicate that fair value reflects an arm's length transaction between knowledgeable, willing parties. Paragraphs 42–44 of IAS 40 discuss what a *transaction between knowledgeable, willing parties* means:

> ... In this context, 'knowledgeable' means that both the willing buyer and the willing seller are reasonably informed about the nature and characteristics of the investment property, its actual and potential uses, and market conditions at the end of the reporting period ...

> ... The willing seller is motivated to sell the investment property at market terms for the best price obtainable. The factual circumstances of the actual investment property owner are not a part of this consideration because the willing seller is a hypothetical owner (eg a willing seller would not take into account the particular tax circumstances of the investment property owner).

> The definition of fair value refers to an arm's length transaction. An arm's length transaction is one between parties that do not have a particular or special relationship that makes prices of transactions uncharacteristic of market conditions. The transaction is presumed to be between unrelated parties, each acting independently.

Thus, although the two definitions use different words, the concept is the same—fair value is a market-based measure in a transaction between unrelated parties.

BC251 However, differences in the results of applying the different definitions of fair value may occur in particular areas. For example, SFAS 157 defines fair value as an exit price between market participants and IFRSs define fair value as an exchange price in an arm's length transaction. Most valuation experts the boards consulted said that, because transaction costs are not a component of fair value in either definition, an exit price for an asset or liability acquired or assumed in a business combination would differ from an exchange price (entry or exit) only (a) if the asset is acquired for its defensive value or (b) if a liability is measured on the basis of settling it with the creditor rather than transferring it to a third party. However, the boards understand that ways of measuring assets on the basis of their defensive value in accordance with paragraph A12 of SFAS 157 are developing, and it is too early to tell the significance of any differences that might result. It is also not clear that entities will use different methods of measuring the fair value of liabilities assumed in a business combination.

Measuring the acquisition-date fair values of particular assets acquired

Assets with uncertain cash flows (valuation allowances)

BC252   Both IFRS 3 and SFAS 141 required receivables to be measured at the present values of amounts to be received determined at appropriate current interest rates, less allowances for uncollectibility and collection costs, if necessary. The boards considered whether an exception to the fair value measurement principle is necessary for assets such as trade receivables and other short-term and long-term receivables acquired in a business combination. Several of the boards' constituents suggested that an exception should be permitted for practical and other reasons, including concerns about comparing credit losses on loans acquired in a business combination with those on originated loans. In developing the 2005 Exposure Draft, however, the boards saw no compelling reason for such an exception. The boards observed that using an acquiree's carrying basis and including collection costs is inconsistent with the revised standards' fair value measurement requirement and the underlying notion that the acquirer's initial measurement, recognition and classification of the assets acquired and liabilities assumed begins on the acquisition date. Because uncertainty about collections and future cash flows is included in the fair value measure of a receivable, the 2005 Exposure Draft proposed that the acquirer should not recognise a separate valuation allowance for acquired assets measured at fair value.

BC253   In developing the 2005 Exposure Draft, the FASB acknowledged that including uncertainties about future cash flows in a fair value measure, with no separate allowance for uncollectible amounts, differed from the current practice for SEC registrants. That practice was established in SEC Staff Accounting Bulletin Topic 2.A.5 *Adjustments to Allowances for Loan Losses in Connection with Business Combinations* which states that generally the acquirer's estimation of the uncollectible portion of the acquiree's loans should not change from the acquiree's estimation before the acquisition. However, the FASB also observed that fair value measurement is consistent with guidance in AICPA Statement of Position 03-3 *Accounting for Certain Loans or Debt Securities Acquired in a Transfer* (AICPA SOP 03-3), which prohibits 'carrying over' or creating valuation allowances in the initial accounting of all loans acquired in transfers that are within its scope, including business combinations accounted for as an acquisition.

BC254   In developing the 2005 Exposure Draft, the boards also acknowledged that the fair value measurement approach has implications for the capital requirements for financial institutions, particularly banks. The boards noted, however, that regulatory reporting requirements are a separate matter that is beyond the scope of general purpose financial reporting.

BC255   Some respondents to the 2005 Exposure Draft who commented on this issue agreed with the proposal, but many who commented on it disagreed with not recognising a separate valuation allowance for receivables and similar assets. Some of those respondents favoured retaining the guidance in IFRS 3 and SFAS 141. They said that the costs of measuring the fair value of trade receivables, loans, receivables under financing leases and the like would be high; they did not think the related benefits would justify those costs. Some also said that software systems currently available for loans and other receivables do not provide for separate accounting for acquired and originated loans; they have to account manually for loans to which AICPA SOP 03-3 applies, incurring significant costs to do so.

BC256　As they did in developing the 2005 Exposure Draft, the boards acknowledged that the requirement to measure receivables and similar assets at fair value with no separate valuation allowance may lead to additional costs for some entities. However, the boards observed that entities that apply IAS 39[19] are required to measure financial assets acquired outside a business combination, as well as those originated, at fair value on initial recognition. The boards do not think financial or other assets should be measured differently because of the nature of the transaction in which they are acquired. Because the boards saw no compelling reason to provide an exception to the measurement principle for receivables or other assets with credit risk, they affirmed their conclusion that the benefits of measuring receivables and similar assets at fair value justify the related costs.

BC257　Some respondents to the 2005 Exposure Draft said that separate recognition of valuation allowances for loans and similar assets was important to users in evaluating the credit assumptions built into loan valuations. They suggested that the fair value of receivables should be split into three components: (a) the gross contractual amounts, (b) a separate discount or premium for changes in interest rates and (c) a valuation allowance for the credit risk, which would be based on the contractual cash flows expected to be uncollectible. In evaluating that alternative presentation, the boards noted that the valuation allowance presented would differ from the valuation allowance for receivables under IAS 39 and SFAS 5, each of which is determined on the basis of incurred, rather than expected, losses. Thus, how to determine the valuation allowance on an ongoing basis would be problematic. For example, if requirements for other receivables were applied, an immediate gain would be recognised for the difference between incurred losses and expected losses. In contrast, if the valuation allowance for receivables acquired by transfer, including in a business combination, rather than by origination was determined subsequently on an expected loss basis, the result would be a new accounting model for those receivables. The boards concluded that this project is not the place to consider the broader issues of how best to determine the valuation allowances for receivables, regardless of the manner in which the receivables are acquired.

Disclosure of information about receivables acquired

BC258　Some constituents asked the boards to consider requiring additional disclosures about receivables measured at fair value to help in assessing considerations of credit quality included in the fair value measures, including expectations about receivables that will be uncollectible. Those constituents were concerned that without additional disclosure, it would be impossible to determine the contractual cash flows and the amount of the contractual cash flows not expected to be collected if receivables were recognised at fair value. In response

---

19　IFRS 9 *Financial Instruments* replaced IAS 39. IFRS 9 applies to all items that were previously within the scope of IAS 39.

to those comments, the boards decided to require disclosure of the fair value of receivables acquired, the gross contractual amounts receivable and the best estimate at the acquisition date of the contractual cash flows not expected to be collected. The disclosures are required for each major class of receivable.

BC259   In January 2007 the FASB added a project to its technical agenda to improve disclosures relating to the allowance for credit losses associated with financing receivables. As part of that project, the FASB is considering potential new disclosures and enhanced current disclosures about the credit quality of an entity's portfolio, the entity's credit risk exposures, its accounting policies on valuation allowances and possibly other areas.

BC260   The boards observed that the work involved in developing a complete set of credit quality disclosures to be made for receivables acquired in a business combination would be similar to that required in the FASB's disclosure project related to valuation allowances. Combining those efforts would be a more efficient use of resources. Accordingly, the FASB decided to include disclosures that should be made in a business combination in the scope of its project on disclosures related to valuation allowances and credit quality, and the IASB will monitor that project. In the interim, the disclosures required by the revised standards (paragraph B64(h) of the revised IFRS 3) will provide at least some, although perhaps not all, of the information users need to evaluate the credit quality of receivables acquired.

Assets that the acquirer intends not to use or to use in a way that is different from the way other market participants would use them

BC261   While the revised standards were being developed, the FASB received enquiries about inconsistencies in practice in accordance with SFAS 141 related to measuring particular intangible assets that an acquirer intends not to use or intends to use in a way different from the way other market participants would use them. For example, if the acquirer did not intend to use a brand name acquired in a business combination, some entities assigned no value to the asset and other entities measured it at the amount at which market participants could be expected to exchange the asset, ie at its fair value.

BC262   To avoid such inconsistencies in practice, the boards decided to clarify the measurement of assets that an acquirer intends not to use (paragraph B43 of the revised IFRS 3). The intention of both IFRS 3 and SFAS 141 was that assets, both tangible and intangible, should be measured at their fair values regardless of how or whether the acquirer intends to use them. The FASB observed that measuring such assets in accordance with their highest and best use is consistent with SFAS 157. Paragraph A12 of SFAS 157 illustrates determining the fair value of an in-process research and development project acquired in a business combination that the acquirer does not intend to complete. The IASB understands from its consultation with preparers, valuation experts and auditors that IFRS 3 was applied in the way the revised standards require.[20]

---

20 IFRS 13, issued in May 2011, describes the concept of highest and best use and provides examples of its application in a business combination.

Exceptions to the recognition or measurement principle

BC263 As indicated in paragraphs 14 and 20 of the revised IFRS 3, the revised standards include limited exceptions to its recognition and measurement principles. Paragraphs BC265–BC311 discuss the types of identifiable assets and liabilities for which exceptions are provided and the reasons for those exceptions.

BC264 It is important to note that not every item that falls into a particular type of asset or liability is an exception to either the recognition or the measurement principle (or both). For example, contingent liabilities are identified as an exception to the recognition principle because the revised IFRS 3 includes a recognition condition for them in addition to the recognition conditions in paragraphs 11 and 12. Although applying that additional condition will result in not recognising some contingent liabilities, those that meet the additional condition will be recognised in accordance with the recognition principle. Another example is employee benefits, which are identified as a type of asset or liability for which exceptions to both the recognition and the measurement principles are provided. As discussed further in paragraphs BC296–BC300, the acquirer is required to recognise and measure liabilities and any related assets resulting from the acquiree's employee benefit arrangements in accordance with IAS 19 *Employee Benefits* rather than by applying the recognition and measurement principles in the revised IFRS 3. Applying the requirements of IAS 19 will result in recognising many, if not most, types of employee benefit liabilities in the same way as would result from applying the recognition principle (see paragraph BC297). However, others, for example withdrawal liabilities from multi-employer plans for entities applying US GAAP, are not necessarily consistent with the recognition principle. In addition, applying the requirements of IAS 19 generally will result in measuring liabilities for employee benefits (and any related assets) on a basis other than their acquisition-date fair values. However, applying the requirements of SFAS 146 to one-off termination benefits results in measuring liabilities for those benefits at their acquisition-date fair values.

Exception to the recognition principle

Assets and liabilities arising from contingencies

BC265 Both the FASB's conclusions on recognising assets and liabilities arising from contingencies and the IASB's conclusions on recognising contingent liabilities resulted in exceptions to the recognition principle in the revised standards because both will result in some items being unrecognised at the acquisition date. However, the details of the exceptions differ. The reasons for those exceptions and the differences between them are discussed in paragraphs BC266–BC278.

The FASB's conclusions on assets and liabilities arising from contingencies

BC266 SFAS 141 carried forward without reconsideration the requirements of SFAS 38, which required an acquirer to include in the purchase price allocation the fair value of an acquiree's contingencies if their fair value could be determined during the allocation period. For those contingencies whose fair value could not be determined during the allocation period, SFAS 141 required the acquirer to recognise the contingency in earnings when the occurrence of the contingency became probable and its amount could be reasonably estimated.

BC267　Members of its resource group and others told the FASB that in practice acquirers often did not recognise an acquiree's assets and liabilities arising from contingencies at the acquisition date. Instead, contingencies were recognised after the acquisition date at an amount determined at that later date either because their amount could not be 'reasonably estimated' or because the contingency was determined not to meet the SFAS 5 'probability' criterion for recognition.

BC268　The 2005 Exposure Draft proposed that an acquirer should recognise all assets and liabilities arising from an acquiree's contingencies if they meet the definition of an asset or a liability in the FASB's Concepts Statement 6 regardless of whether a contingency meets the recognition criteria in SFAS 5. The FASB, like the IASB, concluded that to represent faithfully the economic circumstances at the acquisition date, in principle, all identifiable assets acquired and liabilities assumed should be recognised separately from goodwill, including assets and liabilities arising from contingencies at the acquisition date.

BC269　Respondents to the 2005 Exposure Draft that apply US GAAP expressed concern about how to deal with uncertainty about whether and when a contingency gives rise to an asset or a liability that meets the definition in the FASB's Concepts Statement 6, referred to as *element uncertainty*. An example cited by some respondents involved an acquiree's negotiations with another party at the acquisition date for reimbursement of costs incurred on the other party's behalf. How should the acquirer determine whether that contingency gave rise to an asset that should be recognised as part of the accounting for the business combination? Respondents suggested several means of dealing with element uncertainty, which generally involved introducing a threshold either for all contingencies or for the non-contractual contingencies an acquirer is required to recognise at the acquisition date. Other respondents suggested requiring recognition of only those assets and liabilities arising from contingencies whose fair values can be reliably determined, which would be similar to the requirements of SFAS 141.

BC270　The FASB understands the potential difficulty of resolving element uncertainty, especially for assets or liabilities arising from non-contractual contingencies. It considered whether to deal with element uncertainty by requiring assets and liabilities arising from contingencies to be recognised only if their fair values are reliably measurable. The FASB concluded that applying the guidance in SFAS 157 on measuring fair value should result in an estimate of the fair value of assets and liabilities arising from contingencies that is sufficiently reliable for recognition. The FASB also observed that adding a measurement condition is an indirect way of dealing with uncertainty involving recognition; it would be better to deal with such uncertainty more directly.

BC271　The FASB concluded that most cases of significant uncertainty about whether a potential asset or liability arising from a contingency meets the pertinent definition (element uncertainty) are likely to involve non-contractual contingencies. To help preparers and their auditors deal with element uncertainty, the FASB decided to add a requirement for the acquirer to assess whether it is **more likely than not** that the contingency gives rise to an asset or a liability as defined in the FASB's Concepts Statement 6. For an asset arising from a contingency, applying that criterion focuses on whether it is more likely than not that the acquirer has obtained control of a future economic benefit as a result of a past transaction or other event. For a liability, the more-likely-than-not criterion focuses on whether the acquirer has a present obligation to sacrifice future economic benefits as a result of a past transaction or other event. If that criterion is met at the acquisition date, the acquirer recognises the asset or liability, measured at its acquisition-date fair value, as part of the accounting for the business combination. If that criterion is not met at the acquisition date, the acquirer accounts for the non-contractual contingency in accordance with other US GAAP, including SFAS 5, as appropriate. The FASB concluded that adding the more-likely-than-not criterion would permit acquirers to focus their efforts on the more readily identifiable contingencies of acquirees, thereby avoiding spending disproportionate amounts of time searching for contingencies that, even if identified, would have less significant effects.

The IASB's conclusions on contingent liabilities

BC272   In developing the 2005 Exposure Draft, the IASB concluded that an asset or a liability should be recognised separately from goodwill if it satisfies the definitions in the *Framework*. In some cases, the amount of the future economic benefits embodied in the asset or required to settle the liability is contingent (or conditional) on the occurrence or non-occurrence of one or more uncertain future events. That uncertainty is reflected in measurement. The FASB reached a consistent conclusion.

BC273   At the same time as it published the 2005 Exposure Draft, the IASB also published for comment a separate exposure draft containing similar proposals on the accounting for contingent assets and contingent liabilities within the scope of IAS 37. At that time, the IASB expected that the effective date of the revised IAS 37 would be the same as the effective date of the revised IFRS 3. However, the IASB now expects to issue a revised IAS 37 at a later date. Accordingly, except for clarifying that an acquirer should not recognise a so-called contingent liability that is not an obligation at the acquisition date, the IASB decided to carry forward the related requirements in the original IFRS 3. The IASB expects to reconsider and, if necessary, amend the requirements in the revised IFRS 3 when it issues the revised IAS 37.

BC274   The IASB concluded that an acquirer should recognise a contingent liability assumed in a business combination only if it satisfies the definition of a liability in the *Framework*. This is consistent with the overall objective of the second phase of the project on business combinations in which an acquirer recognises the assets acquired and liabilities assumed at the date control is obtained.

BC275   However, the IASB observed that the definition of a contingent liability in IAS 37 includes both (a) 'possible obligations' and (b) present obligations for which either it is not probable that an outflow of resources embodying economic benefits will be required to settle the obligation or the amount of the obligation cannot be measured reliably. The IASB concluded that a contingent liability assumed in a business combination should be recognised only if it is a present obligation. Therefore, unlike the previous version of IFRS 3, the revised IFRS 3 does not permit the recognition of 'possible obligations'.

BC276 Like its decision on the recognition of contingent liabilities assumed in a business combination, the IASB concluded that an acquirer should recognise a contingent asset acquired in a business combination only if it satisfies the definition of an asset in the *Framework*. However, the IASB observed that the definition of a contingent asset in IAS 37 includes only 'possible assets'. A contingent asset arises when it is uncertain whether an entity has an asset at the end of the reporting period, but it is expected that some future event will confirm whether the entity has an asset. Accordingly, the IASB concluded that contingent assets should not be recognised, even if it is virtually certain that they will become unconditional or non-contingent. If an entity determines that an asset exists at the acquisition date (ie that it has an unconditional right at the acquisition date), that asset is not a contingent asset and should be accounted for in accordance with the appropriate IFRS.

Convergence

BC277 The result of the FASB's and the IASB's conclusions on recognising assets and liabilities arising from contingencies is that the criteria for determining which items to recognise at the acquisition date differ, at least for the short term. That lack of convergence is inevitable at this time, given the status of the IASB's redeliberations on its revision of IAS 37 and the fact that the FASB had no project on its agenda to reconsider the requirements of SFAS 5 while the boards were developing the revised standards. (The FASB added a project to reconsider the accounting for contingencies to its agenda in September 2007.) To attempt to converge on guidance for recognising assets and liabilities arising from contingencies in a business combination now would run the risk of establishing requirements for a business combination that would be inconsistent with the eventual requirements for assets and liabilities arising from contingencies acquired or incurred by means other than a business combination.

BC278 However, the boards observed that the assets or liabilities arising from contingencies that are recognised in accordance with the FASB's recognition guidance and the contingent liabilities recognised in accordance with the IASB's recognition guidance will be measured consistently. In other words, the initial measurement requirements for assets and liabilities arising from contingencies recognised at the acquisition date have converged. However, the boards acknowledge that the subsequent measurement requirements differ because SFAS 5's measurement guidance differs from that in IAS 37. The reasons for the boards' conclusion on measuring those assets and liabilities are discussed in paragraphs BC224–BC245.

Exceptions to both the recognition and measurement principles

Income taxes

BC279 The 2005 Exposure Draft proposed, and the revised standards require, that a deferred tax asset or liability should be recognised and measured in accordance with either IAS 12 *Income Taxes* or FASB Statement No. 109 *Accounting for Income Taxes* (SFAS 109) respectively. IAS 12 and SFAS 109 establish requirements for recognising and measuring deferred tax assets and liabilities—requirements that are not necessarily consistent with the recognition and measurement principles in the revised standards.

BC280   The boards considered identifying deferred tax assets and liabilities as an exception to only the measurement principle because most, if not all, of the requirements of IAS 12 and SFAS 109 are arguably consistent with the revised standards' recognition principle.   The recognition principle requires the acquirer to recognise at the acquisition date the assets acquired and liabilities assumed that meet the conceptual definition of an asset or a liability at that date. However, the boards concluded that exempting deferred tax assets and liabilities from both the recognition and the measurement principles would more clearly indicate that the acquirer should apply the recognition and measurement provisions of IAS 12 and SFAS 109 and their related interpretations or amendments.

BC281   Deferred tax assets or liabilities generally are measured at undiscounted amounts in accordance with IAS 12 and SFAS 109. The boards decided not to require deferred tax assets or liabilities acquired in a business combination to be measured at fair value because they observed that:

(a)   if those assets and liabilities were measured at their acquisition-date fair values, their subsequent measurement in accordance with IAS 12 or SFAS 109 would result in reported post-combination gains or losses in the period immediately following the acquisition even though the underlying economic circumstances did not change. That would not faithfully represent the results of the post-combination period and would be inconsistent with the notion that a business combination that is a fair value exchange should not give rise to the recognition of immediate post-combination gains or losses.

(b)   to measure those assets and liabilities at their acquisition-date fair values and overcome the reporting problem noted in (a) would require a comprehensive consideration of whether and how to modify the requirements of IAS 12 and SFAS 109 for the subsequent measurement of deferred tax assets or liabilities acquired in a business combination. Because of the complexities of IAS 12 and SFAS 109 and the added complexities that would be involved in tracking deferred tax assets acquired and liabilities assumed in a business combination, the boards concluded that the benefits of applying the revised standards' fair value measurement principle would not warrant the costs or complexities that would cause.

Respondents to the 2005 Exposure Draft generally supported that exception to the fair value measurement requirements.

BC282   To align IAS 12 and SFAS 109 more closely and to make the accounting more consistent with the principles in the revised standards, the boards decided to address four specific issues pertaining to the acquirer's income tax accounting in connection with a business combination:

(a)   accounting for a change in the acquirer's recognised deferred tax asset that results from a business combination;

(b)   accounting for a change after the acquisition date in the deferred tax benefits for the acquiree's deductible temporary differences or operating loss or tax credit carryforwards acquired in a business combination;

(c)   accounting for tax benefits arising from tax-deductible goodwill in excess of goodwill for financial reporting; and

(d)   accounting for changes after the acquisition date in the uncertainties pertaining to acquired tax positions.

BC283   The boards addressed the first issue because the existing requirements of IAS 12 and SFAS 109 differed, with IAS 12 accounting for a change in recognised deferred tax assets separately from the business combination and SFAS 109 including a change in the acquirer's valuation allowance for its deferred tax asset in the business combination accounting. The FASB decided to converge with the IAS 12 requirement on the first issue, which the IASB decided to retain. Thus, the acquirer would recognise the change in its recognised deferred tax assets as income or expense (or a change in equity), as required by IAS 12, in the period of the business combination.

BC284   Because the boards considered the first issue primarily in an attempt to achieve convergence, they limited their consideration to the requirements of IAS 12 and SFAS 109. The FASB acknowledged that both alternatives are defensible on conceptual grounds. However, it concluded that on balance the benefits of converging with the IAS 12 method outweigh the costs related to a change in the accounting in accordance with SFAS 109. SFAS 141(R) therefore amends SFAS 109 accordingly.

BC285   Most of the respondents to the 2005 Exposure Draft supported its proposal on accounting for changes to the acquirer's own deferred taxes in conjunction with a business combination. But some disagreed; they said that an acquirer factors its expected tax synergies into the price it is willing to pay for the acquiree, and therefore those tax synergies constitute goodwill. Those respondents were concerned about the potential for double-counting the synergies once in the consideration and a second time by separately recognising the changes in the acquirer's income taxes.

BC286   The boards acknowledged that in some situations a portion of the tax synergies might be factored into the price paid in the business combination. However, they concluded that it would be difficult, if not impossible, to identify that portion. In addition, an acquirer would not pay more for an acquiree because of tax synergies unless another bidder would also pay more; an acquirer would not knowingly pay more than necessary for the acquiree. Therefore, in some situations none (or only a very small portion) of the tax synergies are likely to be factored into the price paid. The boards also observed that the revised standards (paragraph 51 of the revised IFRS 3) require only the portion of the consideration transferred for the acquiree and the assets acquired and liabilities assumed in the exchange for the acquiree to be included in applying the acquisition method. Excluding effects on the acquirer's ability to utilise its deferred tax asset is consistent with that requirement. Therefore, the boards decided to retain the treatment of changes in an acquirer's tax assets and liabilities proposed in the 2005 Exposure Draft.

BC287   The revised standards also amend IAS 12 and SFAS 109 to require disclosure of the amount of the deferred tax benefit (or expense) recognised in income in the period of the acquisition for the reduction (or increase) of the acquirer's valuation allowance for its deferred tax asset that results from a business combination. The boards decided that disclosure of that amount is necessary to enable users of the acquirer's financial statements to evaluate the nature and financial effect of a business combination.

BC288   The second issue listed in paragraph BC282 relates to changes after the acquisition date in the amounts recognised for deferred tax benefits acquired in a business combination. IAS 12 and SFAS 109 both required subsequent recognition of acquired tax benefits to reduce goodwill. However, IAS 12 and SFAS 109 differed in that:

(a)   IAS 12 did not permit the reduction of other non-current intangible assets, which SFAS 109 required; and

(b)   IAS 12 required the recognition of offsetting income and expense in the acquirer's profit or loss when subsequent changes are recognised.

BC289   In developing the 2005 Exposure Draft, the FASB concluded that the fair value of other long-lived assets acquired in a business combination should no longer be reduced for changes in a valuation allowance after the acquisition date. That decision is consistent with the boards' decision not to adjust other acquired assets or assumed liabilities, with a corresponding adjustment to goodwill, for the effects of other events occurring after the acquisition date.

BC290   Few respondents to the 2005 Exposure Draft addressed this issue, and the views of those who commented differed. Some favoured providing for reduction of goodwill indefinitely because they view the measurement exception for deferred tax assets as resulting in a measure that is drastically different from fair value. Those who supported not permitting the indefinite reduction of goodwill said that, conceptually, changes in estimates pertaining to deferred taxes recognised in a business combination should be treated the same as other revisions to the amounts recorded at acquisition. The boards agreed with those respondents that a measurement exception should not result in potentially indefinite adjustments to goodwill. The revised standards provide other limited exceptions to the recognition and measurement principles, for example, for employee benefits—none of which result in indefinite adjustments to goodwill for subsequent changes.

BC291   The 2005 Exposure Draft proposed a rebuttable presumption that the subsequent recognition of acquired tax benefits within one year of the acquisition date should be accounted for by reducing goodwill. The rebuttable presumption could have been overcome if the subsequent recognition of the tax benefits resulted from a discrete event or circumstance occurring after the acquisition date. Recognition of acquired tax benefits after the one-year period would be accounted for in profit or loss (or, if IAS 12 or SFAS 109 so requires, outside profit or loss). Respondents suggested particular modifications to that proposal, including removing the rebuttable presumption about subsequent recognition of acquired tax benefits within one year of the acquisition date and treating increases and decreases in deferred tax assets consistently. (IAS 12 and

SFAS 109 provided guidance on accounting for decreases.) The boards agreed with those suggestions and revised the requirements of the revised standards accordingly.

BC292 As described in paragraph BC282(c), the boards considered whether a deferred tax asset should be recognised in a business combination for any excess amount of tax-deductible goodwill over the goodwill for financial reporting purposes (excess tax goodwill). From a conceptual standpoint, the excess tax goodwill meets the definition of a temporary difference. Not recognising the tax benefit of that temporary difference at the date of the business combination would be inappropriate and inconsistent with IAS 12 and SFAS 109; it would also be inconsistent with the recognition principle in the revised standards. Thus, the revised IFRS 3 clarifies IAS 12 and SFAS 141(R) amends SFAS 109 accordingly.

BC293 On the issue in paragraph BC282(d), respondents to the 2005 Exposure Draft suggested that the revised standards should address how to account for subsequent adjustments to amounts recognised for acquired income tax uncertainties. Respondents supported accounting for subsequent adjustments to amounts recognised for tax uncertainties using the same approach as the accounting for subsequent adjustments to acquired deferred tax benefits.

BC294 The FASB agreed with respondents' suggestion that an acquirer should recognise changes to acquired income tax uncertainties after the acquisition in the same way as changes in acquired deferred tax benefits. Therefore, SFAS 141(R) amends FASB Interpretation No. 48 *Accounting for Uncertainty in Income Taxes* (FASB Interpretation 48) to require a change to an acquired income tax uncertainty within the measurement period that results from new information about facts and circumstances that existed at the acquisition date to be recognised through a corresponding adjustment to goodwill. If that reduces goodwill to zero, an acquirer would recognise any additional increases of the recognised income tax uncertainty as a reduction of income tax expense. All other changes in the acquired income tax uncertainties would be accounted for in accordance with FASB Interpretation 48.

BC295 The IASB also considered whether to address the accounting for changes in acquired income tax uncertainties in a business combination. IAS 12 is silent on income tax uncertainties. The IASB is considering tax uncertainties as part of the convergence income tax project. Therefore, the IASB decided not to modify IAS 12 as part of this project to address specifically the accounting for changes in acquired income tax uncertainties in a business combination.

Employee benefits

BC296 The revised standards provide exceptions to both the recognition and measurement principles for liabilities and any related assets resulting from the employee benefit arrangements of an acquiree. The acquirer is required to recognise and measure those assets and liabilities in accordance with IAS 19 or applicable US GAAP.

BC297 As with deferred tax assets and liabilities, the boards considered identifying employee benefits as an exception only to the measurement principle. The boards concluded that essentially the same considerations discussed in paragraph BC280 for deferred tax assets and liabilities also apply to employee benefits. In addition, the FASB observed that FASB Statements No. 43 *Accounting for Compensated Absences* and 112 *Employers' Accounting for Postemployment Benefits* require recognition of a liability for compensated absences or post-employment benefits, respectively, only if payment is probable. Arguably, a liability for those benefits exists, at least in some circumstances, regardless of whether payment is probable. Accordingly, to make it clear that the acquirer should apply the recognition and measurement requirements of IAS 19 or applicable US GAAP without separately considering the extent to which those requirements are consistent with the principles in the revised standards, the boards exempted employee benefit obligations from both the recognition and the measurement principles.

BC298 The FASB decided to amend FASB Statements No. 87 *Employers' Accounting for Pensions* (SFAS 87) and 106 *Employers' Accounting for Postretirement Benefits Other Than Pensions* (SFAS 106) to require the acquirer to exclude from the liability it recognises for a single-employer pension or other post-retirement benefit plan the effects of expected plan amendments, terminations or curtailments that it has no obligation to make at the acquisition date. However, those amendments also require the acquirer to include in the liability it recognises at the acquisition date the expected withdrawal liability for a multi-employer plan if it is probable at that date that the acquirer will withdraw from the plan. For a pension or other post-retirement benefit plan, the latter requirement brings into the authoritative literature a provision that previously appeared only in the Basis for Conclusions on SFASs 87 and 106. The FASB acknowledges that the provisions for single-employer and multi-employer plans are not necessarily consistent, and it considered amending SFASs 87 and 106 to require recognition of withdrawal liabilities not yet incurred in post-combination financial statements of the periods in which withdrawals occur. However, it observed that the liability recognised upon withdrawal from a multi-employer plan represents the previously unrecognised portion of the accumulated benefits obligation, which is recognised as it arises for a single-employer plan. In addition, the FASB observed that some might consider the employer's contractual obligation upon withdrawal from a multi-employer plan an unconditional obligation to 'stand ready' to pay if withdrawal occurs and therefore a present obligation. Therefore, the FASB decided not to require the same accounting for expected withdrawals from a multi-employer plan as it requires for expected terminations or curtailments of a single-employer plan.

BC299 The effect of the revised standards' measurement exception for liabilities and any related assets resulting from the acquiree's employee benefit plans is more significant than the related recognition exception. The boards concluded that it was not feasible to require all employee benefit obligations assumed in a business combination to be measured at their acquisition-date fair values. To do so would effectively require the boards to reconsider comprehensively the relevant standards for those employee benefits as a part of their business combinations projects. Given the complexities in accounting for employee benefit obligations in accordance with existing requirements, the boards decided that the only practicable alternative is to require those obligations, and any related assets, to be measured in accordance with their applicable standards.

BC300   The 2005 Exposure Draft proposed exempting only employee benefits subject to SFASs 87 and 106 from its fair value measurement requirement. Some respondents observed that existing measurement requirements for other types of employee benefits are not consistent with fair value and said that those benefits should also be exempted. The FASB agreed and modified the measurement exception for employee benefits accordingly.

Indemnification assets

BC301   A few constituents asked about the potential inconsistency if an asset for an indemnification is measured at fair value at the acquisition date and the related liability is measured using a different measurement attribute. Members of the FASB's resource group raised the issue primarily in the context of FASB Interpretation 48, which requires an entity to measure a tax position that meets the more-likely-than-not recognition threshold at the largest amount of tax benefit that is more than 50 per cent likely to be realised upon ultimate settlement with a taxing authority.

BC302   The boards understand that a business combination sometimes includes an indemnification agreement under which the former owners of the acquiree are required to reimburse the acquirer for any payments the acquirer eventually makes upon settlement of a particular liability. If the indemnification pertains to uncertainty about a position taken in the acquiree's tax returns for prior years or to another item for which the revised standards provide a recognition or measurement exception, not providing a related exception for the indemnification asset would result in recognition or measurement anomalies. For example, for an indemnification pertaining to a deferred tax liability, the acquirer would recognise at the acquisition date a liability to the taxing authority for the deferred taxes and an asset for the indemnification due from the former owners of the acquiree. In the absence of an exception, the asset would be measured at fair value, and the liability would be measured in accordance with the pertinent income tax accounting requirements, such as FASB Interpretation 48 for an entity that applies US GAAP, because income taxes are an exception to the fair value measurement principle. Those two amounts would differ. The boards agreed with constituents that an asset representing an indemnification related to a specific liability should be recognised and measured on the same basis as that liability.

BC303   The boards also provided an exception to the recognition principle for indemnification assets. The reasons for that exception are much the same as the reasons why the boards exempted deferred tax assets and liabilities and employee benefits from that principle. Providing an exception to the recognition principle for indemnification assets clarifies that the acquirer does not apply that principle in determining whether or when to recognise such an asset. Rather, the acquirer recognises the asset when it recognises the related liability. Therefore, the revised standards provide an exception to the recognition and measurement principles for indemnification assets.

Exceptions to the measurement principle

BC304   In addition to the exceptions to both the recognition and measurement principles discussed above, the revised standards provide exceptions to the measurement principle for particular types of assets acquired or liabilities assumed in a business combination. Those exceptions are discussed in paragraphs BC305–BC311.

Temporary exception for assets held for sale

BC305   The 2005 Exposure Draft proposed that non-current assets qualifying as held for sale at the acquisition date under IFRS 5 *Non-current Assets Held for Sale and Discontinued Operations* or FASB Statement No. 144 *Accounting for the Impairment or Disposal of Long-Lived Assets* (SFAS 144) should be measured as those standards require—at fair value less costs to sell. The purpose of that proposed exception was to avoid the need to recognise a loss for the selling costs immediately after a business combination (referred to as a *Day 2 loss* because in theory it would be recognised on the day after the acquisition date). That Day 2 loss would result if the assets were initially measured at fair value but the acquirer then applied either IFRS 5 or SFAS 144, requiring measurement at fair value less costs to sell, for subsequent accounting. Because that loss would stem entirely from different measurement requirements for assets held for sale acquired in a business combination and for assets already held that are classified as held for sale, the reported loss would not faithfully represent the activities of the acquirer.

BC306   After considering responses to the 2005 Exposure Draft, the boards decided that the exception to the measurement principle for assets held for sale should be eliminated. The definitions of fair value[21] in the revised standards, and their application in other areas focuses on market data. Costs that a buyer (acquirer) incurs to purchase or expects to incur to sell an asset are excluded from the amount at which an asset is measured. The boards concluded that disposal costs should also be excluded from the measurement of assets held for sale.

BC307   However, avoiding the Day 2 loss described in paragraph BC305 will require the boards to amend IFRS 5 and SFAS 144 to require assets classified as held for sale to be measured at fair value rather than at fair value less costs to sell. The boards decided to do that, but their respective due process procedures require those amendments to be made in separate projects to give constituents the opportunity to comment on the proposed changes. Although the boards intend the amendments of IFRS 5 and SFAS 144 to be effective at the same time as the revised standards, they decided as an interim step to include a measurement exception until completion of the amendments.

Reacquired rights

BC308   The revised standards (paragraph 29 of the revised IFRS 3) require the fair value of a reacquired right recognised as an intangible asset to be measured on the basis of the remaining contractual term of the contract that gave rise to the right, without taking into account potential renewals of that contract. In developing the 2005 Exposure Draft, the boards observed that a reacquired right is no longer a contract with a third party. An acquirer who controls a reacquired right could assume indefinite renewals of its contractual term, effectively making the reacquired right an intangible asset with an indefinite life. (The

---

21   IFRS 13, issued in May 2011, defines fair value and describes the effect that transaction costs have on a fair value measurement.

boards understood that some entities had been classifying reacquired rights in that way.) The boards concluded that a right reacquired from an acquiree has in substance a finite life; a renewal of the contractual term after the business combination is not part of what was acquired in the business combination. Accordingly, the 2005 Exposure Draft proposed, and the revised standards require, limiting the period over which the intangible asset is amortised (its useful life) to the remaining contractual term of the contract from which the reacquired right stems.

BC309　The 2005 Exposure Draft did not include guidance on determining the fair value of a reacquired right. Some constituents indicated that determining that value is a problem in practice, and the boards agreed that the revised standards should include guidance on that point. To be consistent with the requirement for determining the useful life of a reacquired right, the boards concluded that the fair value of the right should be based on the remaining term of the contract giving rise to the right. The boards acknowledge that market participants would generally reflect expected renewals of the term of a contractual right in the fair value of a right traded in the market. The boards decided, however, that determining the fair value of a reacquired right in that manner would be inconsistent with amortising its value over the remaining contractual term. The boards also observed that a contractual right transferred to a third party (traded in the market) is not a **reacquired** right. Accordingly, the boards decided that departing from the assumptions that market participants would use in measuring the fair value of a reacquired right is appropriate.

BC310　A few constituents asked for guidance on accounting for the sale of a reacquired right after the business combination. The boards concluded that the sale of a reacquired right is in substance the sale of an intangible asset, and the revised standards require the sale of a reacquired right to be accounted for in the same way as sales of other assets (paragraph 55 of the revised IFRS 3). Thus, the carrying amount of the right is to be included in determining the gain or loss on the sale.

Share-based payment awards

BC311　FASB Statement No. 123 (revised 2004) *Share-Based Payment* (SFAS 123(R)) requires measurement of share-based payment awards using what it describes as the *fair-value-based method*. IFRS 2 *Share-based Payment* requires essentially the same measurement method, which the revised IFRS 3 refers to as the *market-based measure*. For reasons identified in those standards, application of the measurement methods they require generally does not result in the amount at which market participants would exchange an award at a particular date—its fair value at that date. Therefore, the revised standards provide an exception to the measurement principle for share-based payment awards. The reasons for that exception are essentially the same as the reasons already discussed for other exceptions to its recognition and measurement principles that the revised standards provide. For example, as with both deferred tax assets and liabilities and assets and liabilities related to employee benefit arrangements, initial measurement of share-based payment awards at their acquisition-date fair values would cause difficulties with the subsequent accounting for those awards in accordance with IFRS 2 or SFAS 123(R).

Un-replaced and voluntarily replaced share-based payment transactions

BC311A   In *Improvements to IFRSs* issued in May 2010, the Board addressed a concern that there was insufficient application guidance for share-based payment transactions that are replaced in the context of a business combination. After the revised IFRS 3 was issued in 2008, some constituents raised concerns about the lack of explicit guidance with respect to share-based payment transactions of the acquiree that the acquirer chooses to replace, even though either they are unaffected by the business combination or vesting is accelerated as a consequence of the business combination. In addition, some were concerned that the measurement guidance for share-based payment transactions applies only to replacement awards but not to acquiree awards that the acquirer chooses not to replace. In response to those concerns, the Board added explicit guidance in paragraphs B56 and B62A to clarify that those awards should be accounted for in the same way as acquiree awards that the acquirer is obliged to replace.

BC311B   Employee share-based payment awards might expire in the event of a business combination. When this occurs, the acquirer may choose to grant a new award to those employees voluntarily. The new award granted in such circumstances can only be for future services, because the acquirer has no obligation to the employees in respect of past services that they provided to the acquiree. Accordingly, paragraph B56 requires the whole of the market-based value of the new award to be accounted for as a post-combination expense, which is recognised in accordance with IFRS 2. This accounting treatment is different from that required in circumstances when the employee share-based payment award does not expire in the event of a business combination. When an unexpired award is replaced by the acquirer, part of the market-based value of the replacement award reflects the acquiree's obligation that remains outstanding at the date of the business combination, and is accounted for as part of the consideration transferred in the business combination. The balance of the market-based value of the replacement award is accounted for as a post-combination expense for the services to be received over the period to when the replacement award vests, in accordance with IFRS 2. The accounting for the replacement of unexpired awards is the same for awards that are replaced voluntarily by the acquirer and those that the acquirer is obliged to replace because the substance is the same in both circumstances.

Recognising and measuring goodwill or a gain from a bargain purchase

BC312   Consistently with IFRS 3 and SFAS 141, the revised standards require the acquirer to recognise goodwill as an asset and to measure it as a residual.

Goodwill qualifies as an asset

BC313   The FASB's 1999 and 2001 Exposure Drafts listed six components of the amount that in practice, under authoritative guidance in effect at that time, had been recognised as goodwill. The IASB's ED 3 included a similar, but not identical, discussion. The components and their descriptions, taken from the FASB's exposure drafts, were:

Component 1—The excess of the fair values over the book values of the acquiree's net assets at the date of acquisition.

Component 2—The fair values of other net assets that the acquiree had not previously recognised. They may not have been recognised because they failed to meet the recognition criteria (perhaps because of measurement difficulties), because of a requirement that prohibited their recognition, or because the acquiree concluded that the costs of recognising them separately were not justified by the benefits.

Component 3—The fair value of the *going concern* element of the acquiree's existing business. The going concern element represents the ability of the established business to earn a higher rate of return on an assembled collection of net assets than would be expected if those net assets had to be acquired separately. That value stems from the synergies of the net assets of the business, as well as from other benefits (such as factors related to market imperfections, including the ability to earn monopoly profits and barriers to market entry—either legal or because of transaction costs—by potential competitors).

Component 4—The fair value of the expected synergies and other benefits from combining the acquirer's and acquiree's net assets and businesses. Those synergies and other benefits are unique to each combination, and different combinations would produce different synergies and, hence, different values.

Component 5—Overvaluation of the consideration paid by the acquirer stemming from errors in valuing the consideration tendered. Although the purchase price in an all-cash transaction would not be subject to measurement error, the same may not necessarily be said of a transaction involving the acquirer's equity interests. For example, the number of ordinary shares being traded daily may be small relative to the number of shares issued in the combination. If so, imputing the current market price to all of the shares issued to effect the combination may produce a higher value than those shares would command if they were sold for cash and the cash then used to effect the combination.

Component 6—Overpayment or underpayment by the acquirer. Overpayment might occur, for example, if the price is driven up in the course of bidding for the acquiree; underpayment may occur in a distress sale (sometimes termed a fire sale).

BC314   The boards observed that the first two components, both of which relate to the acquiree, are conceptually not part of goodwill. The first component is not itself an asset; instead, it reflects gains that the acquiree had not recognised on its net assets. As such, that component is part of those assets rather than part of goodwill. The second component is also not part of goodwill conceptually; it primarily reflects intangible assets that might be recognised as individual assets.

BC315   The fifth and sixth components, both of which relate to the acquirer, are also not conceptually part of goodwill. The fifth component is not an asset in and of itself or even part of an asset but, rather, is a measurement error. The sixth component is also not an asset; conceptually it represents a loss (in the case of overpayment) or a gain (in the case of underpayment) to the acquirer. Thus, neither of those components is conceptually part of goodwill.

BC316 The boards also observed that the third and fourth components are part of goodwill. The third component relates to the acquiree and reflects the excess assembled value of the acquiree's net assets. It represents the pre-existing goodwill that was either internally generated by the acquiree or acquired by it in prior business combinations. The fourth component relates to the acquiree and the acquirer jointly and reflects the excess assembled value that is created by the combination—the synergies that are expected from combining those businesses. The boards described the third and fourth components collectively as 'core goodwill'.

BC317 The revised standards try to avoid subsuming the first, second and fifth components of goodwill into the amount initially recognised as goodwill. Specifically, an acquirer is required to make every effort:

(a) to measure the consideration accurately (eliminating or reducing component 5);

(b) to recognise the identifiable net assets acquired at their fair values rather than their carrying amounts (eliminating or reducing component 1); and

(c) to recognise all acquired intangible assets meeting the criteria in the revised standards (paragraph B31 of the revised IFRS 3) so that they are not subsumed into the amount initially recognised as goodwill (reducing component 2).

BC318 In developing IFRS 3 and SFAS 141, the IASB and the FASB both considered whether 'core goodwill' (the third and fourth components) qualifies as an asset under the definition in their respective conceptual frameworks. (That consideration was based on the existing conceptual frameworks. In 2004, the IASB and the FASB began work on a joint project to develop an improved conceptual framework that, among other things, would eliminate both substantive and wording differences between their existing frameworks. Although the asset definition is likely to change as a result of that project, the boards observed that nothing in their deliberations to date indicates that any such changes are likely to call into question whether goodwill continues to qualify as an asset.)

Asset definition in the FASB's Concepts Statement 6

BC319 Paragraph 172 of the FASB's Concepts Statement 6 says that an item that has future economic benefits has the capacity to serve the entity by being exchanged for something else of value to the entity, by being used to produce something of value to the entity or by being used to settle its liabilities.

BC320 The FASB noted that goodwill cannot be exchanged for something else of value to the entity and it cannot be used to settle the entity's liabilities. Goodwill also lacks the capacity singly to produce future net cash inflows, although it can—in combination with other assets—produce cash flows. Thus, the future benefit associated with goodwill is generally more nebulous and may be less certain than the benefit associated with most other assets. Nevertheless, goodwill generally provides future economic benefit. The FASB's Concepts Statement 6 observes that 'Anything that is commonly bought and sold has future economic benefit, including the individual items that a buyer obtains and is willing to pay for in a "basket purchase" of several items or in a business combination' (paragraph 173).

BC321 For the future economic benefit embodied in goodwill to qualify as an asset, the acquirer must control that benefit. The FASB observed that the acquirer's control is demonstrated by means of its ability to direct the policies and management of the acquiree. The FASB also observed that the past transaction or event necessary for goodwill to qualify as the acquirer's asset is the transaction in which it obtained the controlling interest in the acquiree.

Asset definition in the IASB's Framework

BC322 Paragraph 53 of the IASB's *Framework*[22] explains that 'The future economic benefit embodied in an asset is the potential to contribute, directly or indirectly, to the flow of cash and cash equivalents to the entity.'

BC323 The IASB concluded that core goodwill represents resources from which future economic benefits are expected to flow to the entity. In considering whether core goodwill represents a resource **controlled** by the entity, the IASB considered the assertion that core goodwill arises, at least in part, through factors such as a well-trained workforce, loyal customers and so on, and that these factors cannot be regarded as controlled by the entity because the workforce could leave and the customers could go elsewhere. However, the IASB, like the FASB, concluded that control of core goodwill is provided by means of the acquirer's power to direct the policies and management of the acquiree. Therefore, both the IASB and the FASB concluded that core goodwill meets the conceptual definition of an asset.

Relevance of information about goodwill

BC324 In developing SFAS 141, the FASB also considered the relevance of information about goodwill. Although the IASB's Basis for Conclusions on IFRS 3 did not explicitly discuss the relevance of information about goodwill, the FASB's analysis of that issue was available to the IASB members as they developed IFRS 3, and they saw no reason not to accept that analysis.

BC325 More specifically, in developing SFAS 141, the FASB considered the views of users as reported by the AICPA Special Committee[23] and as expressed by the Financial Accounting Policy Committee (FAPC) of the Association for Investment Management and Research (AIMR) in its 1993 position paper *Financial Reporting in the 1990s and Beyond*. The FASB observed that users have mixed views about whether goodwill should be recognised as an asset. Some are troubled by the lack of comparability between internally generated goodwill and acquired goodwill that results under present standards, but others do not appear to be particularly bothered by it. However, users appear to be reluctant to give up information about goodwill acquired in a business combination. In the view of

---

22 now paragraph 4.8 of the *Conceptual Framework*.
23 AICPA Special Committee on Financial Reporting, *Improving Business Reporting—A Customer Focus* (New York: AICPA, 1994).

the AICPA Special Committee, users want to retain the option of being able to use that information. Similarly, the FAPC said that goodwill should be recognised in financial statements.

BC326   The FASB also considered the growing use of 'economic value added' (EVA)[24] and similar measures, which are increasingly being employed as means of assessing performance. The FASB observed that such measures commonly incorporate goodwill, and in business combinations accounted for by the pooling method, an adjustment was commonly made to incorporate a measure of the goodwill that was not recognised under that method. As a result, the aggregate amount of goodwill is included in the base that is subject to a capital charge that is part of the EVA measure and management is held accountable for the total investment in the acquiree.

BC327   The FASB also considered evidence about the relevance of goodwill provided by a number of research studies that empirically examined the relationship between goodwill and the market value of business entities.[25] Those studies generally found a positive relationship between the reported goodwill of entities and their market values, thereby indicating that investors in the markets behave as if they view goodwill as an asset.

Measuring goodwill as a residual

BC328   The revised standards require the acquirer to measure goodwill as the excess of one amount (described in paragraph 32(a) of the revised IFRS 3) over another (described in paragraph 32(b) of the revised IFRS 3). Therefore, goodwill is measured as a residual, which is consistent with IFRS 3 and SFAS 141, in which the IASB and the FASB, respectively, concluded that direct measurement of goodwill is not possible. The boards did not reconsider measuring goodwill as a residual in the second phase of the business combinations project. However, the boards simplified the measurement of goodwill acquired in a business combination achieved in stages (a step acquisition). In accordance with IFRS 3 and SFAS 141, an entity that acquired another entity in a step acquisition measured goodwill by reference to the cost of each step and the related fair value of the underlying identifiable net assets acquired. This process was costly because it required the acquirer in a step acquisition to determine the amounts allocated to the identifiable net assets acquired at the date of each acquisition, even if those steps occurred years or decades earlier. In contrast, the revised

---

24   EVA was developed by the consulting firm of Stern Stewart & Company (and is a registered trademark of Stern Stewart) as a financial performance measure that improves management's ability to make decisions that enhance shareholder value.

25   Refer to, for example, Eli Amir, Trevor S Harris and Elizabeth K Venuti, 'A Comparison of the Value-Relevance of U.S. versus Non-U.S. GAAP Accounting Measures Using Form 20-F Reconciliations', *Journal of Accounting Research*, Supplement (1993): 230–264; Mary Barth and Greg Clinch, 'International Accounting Differences and Their Relation to Share Prices: Evidence from U.K., Australian and Canadian Firms', *Contemporary Accounting Research* (spring 1996): 135–170; Keith W Chauvin and Mark Hirschey, 'Goodwill, Profitability, and the Market Value of the Firm', *Journal of Accounting and Public Policy* (summer 1994): 159–180; Ross Jennings, John Robinson, Robert B Thompson and Linda Duvall, 'The Relation between Accounting Goodwill Numbers and Equity Values', *Journal of Business Finance and Accounting* (June 1996): 513–533; and Mark G McCarthy and Douglas K Schneider, 'Market Perception of Goodwill: Some Empirical Evidence', *Accounting and Business Research* (winter 1995): 69–81.

standards require goodwill to be measured once—at the acquisition date. Thus, the revised standards reduce the complexity and costs of accounting for step acquisitions.

BC329　Both boards decided that all assets acquired and liabilities assumed, including those of an acquiree (subsidiary) that is not wholly-owned, as well as, in principle, any non-controlling interest in the acquiree, should be measured at their acquisition-date fair values (or in limited situations, their amounts determined in accordance with other US GAAP or IFRSs). Thus, SFAS 141(R) eliminates the past practice of not recognising the portion of goodwill related to the non-controlling interests in subsidiaries that are not wholly-owned. However, as discussed in paragraphs BC209–BC211, the IASB concluded that the revised IFRS 3 should permit entities to measure any non-controlling interest in an acquiree as its proportionate share of the acquiree's identifiable net assets. If an entity chooses that alternative, only the goodwill related to the acquirer is recognised.

Using the acquisition-date fair value of consideration to measure goodwill

BC330　As discussed in paragraph BC81, the revised standards do not focus on measuring the acquisition-date fair value of either the acquiree as a whole or the acquirer's interest in the acquiree as the 2005 Exposure Draft did. Consistently with that change, the boards also eliminated the presumption in the 2005 Exposure Draft that, in the absence of evidence to the contrary, the acquisition-date fair value of the consideration transferred is the best evidence of the fair value of the acquirer's interest in the acquiree at that date. Therefore, the revised standards describe the measurement of goodwill in terms of the recognised amount of the consideration transferred—generally its acquisition-date fair value (paragraph 32 of the revised IFRS 3)—and specify how to measure goodwill if the fair value of the acquiree is more reliably measurable than the fair value of the consideration transferred or if no consideration is transferred (paragraph 33 of the revised IFRS 3).

BC331　Because business combinations are generally exchange transactions in which knowledgeable, unrelated willing parties exchange equal values, the boards continue to believe that the acquisition-date fair value of the consideration transferred provides the best evidence of the acquisition-date fair value of the acquirer's interest in the acquiree in many, if not most, situations. However, that is not the case if the acquirer either makes a bargain purchase or pays more than the acquiree is worth at the acquisition date if the acquirer underpays or overpays. The revised standards provide for recognising a gain in the event of a bargain purchase, but they do not provide for recognising a loss in the event of an overpayment (paragraph BC382). Therefore, the boards concluded that focusing directly on the fair value of the consideration transferred rather than on the fair value of the acquirer's interest in the acquiree, with a presumption that the two amounts are usually equal, would be a more straightforward way of describing how to measure goodwill. (The same conclusion applies to measuring the gain on a bargain purchase, which is discussed in paragraphs BC371–BC381.) That change in focus will also avoid unproductive disputes in practice about whether the consideration transferred or another valuation technique provides the best evidence for measuring the acquirer's interest in the acquiree in a particular situation.

Using the acquirer's interest in the acquiree to measure goodwill

BC332   The boards acknowledge that in the absence of measurable consideration, the acquirer is likely to incur costs to measure the acquisition-date fair value of its interest in the acquiree and incremental costs to have that measure independently verified.   The boards observed that in many of those circumstances companies already incur such costs as part of their due diligence procedures.   For example, an acquisition of a privately held entity by another privately held entity is often accomplished by an exchange of equity shares that do not have observable market prices.   To determine the exchange ratio, those entities generally engage advisers and valuation experts to assist them in valuing the acquiree as well as the equity transferred by the acquirer in exchange for the acquiree.   Similarly, a combination of two mutual entities is often accomplished by an exchange of member interests of the acquirer for all of the member interests of the acquiree.   In many, but not necessarily all, of those cases the directors and managers of the entities also assess the relative fair values of the combining entities to ensure that the exchange of member interests is equitable to the members of both entities.

BC333   The boards concluded that the benefits in terms of improved financial information resulting from the revised standards outweigh the incremental measurement costs that the revised standards may require.   Those improvements include the increased relevance and understandability of information resulting from applying the revised standards' measurement principle and guidance on recognising and measuring goodwill, which are consistent with reflecting the change in economic circumstances that occurs at that date.

BC334   The 2005 Exposure Draft included illustrative guidance for applying the fair value measurement requirement if no consideration is transferred or the consideration transferred is not the best evidence of the acquisition-date fair value of the acquiree. That illustrative guidance drew on related guidance in the FASB's exposure draft that preceded SFAS 157. Because SFAS 157 provides guidance on using valuation techniques such as the market approach and the income approach for measuring fair value, the FASB decided that it is unnecessary for SFAS 141(R) to provide the same guidance.

BC335   The IASB decided not to include in the revised IFRS 3 guidance on using valuation techniques to measure the acquisition-date fair value of the acquirer's interest in the acquiree.   The IASB has on its agenda a project to develop guidance on measuring fair value.   While deliberations on that project are in progress, the IASB considers it inappropriate to include fair value measurement guidance in IFRSs.

BC336   The FASB, on the other hand, completed its project on fair value measurement when it issued SFAS 157. SFAS 141(R), together with SFAS 157, provides broadly applicable measurement guidance that is relevant and useful in measuring the acquirer's interest in the acquiree. However, both boards were concerned that without some discussion of special considerations for measuring the fair value of mutual entities, some acquirers might neglect to consider relevant assumptions that market participants would make about future member benefits when using a valuation technique. For example, the acquirer of a co-operative entity should consider the value of the member discounts in its determination of the fair value of its interest in the acquiree. Therefore, the boards decided to include a discussion of special considerations in measuring the fair value of mutual entities (paragraphs B47–B49 of the revised IFRS 3).[26]

Measuring consideration and determining whether particular items are part of the consideration transferred for the acquiree

BC337   Paragraphs BC338–BC360 discuss the boards' conclusions on measuring specific items of consideration that are often transferred by acquirers. Paragraphs BC361–BC370 then discuss whether particular replacement awards of share-based remuneration and acquisition-related costs incurred by acquirers are part of the consideration transferred for the acquiree.

Measurement date for equity securities transferred

BC338   The guidance in IFRS 3 and SFAS 141 on the measurement date for equity securities transferred as consideration in a business combination differed, and SFAS 141's guidance on that issue was contradictory. Paragraph 22 of SFAS 141, which was carried forward from APB Opinion 16, said that the market price for a reasonable period before and after the date that the terms of the acquisition are agreed to and announced should be considered in determining the fair value of the securities issued. That effectively established the agreement date as the measurement date for equity securities issued as consideration. However, paragraph 49 of SFAS 141, which was also carried forward from APB Opinion 16, said that the cost of an acquiree should be determined as of the acquisition date. IFRS 3, on the other hand, required measuring the consideration transferred in a business combination at its fair value on the exchange date, which was the acquisition date for a combination in which control is achieved in a single transaction. (IFRS 3, like SFAS 141, included special guidance on determining the cost of a business combination in which control is achieved in stages.) In their deliberations leading to the 2005 Exposure Draft, the boards decided that the fair value of equity securities issued as consideration in a business combination should be measured at the acquisition date.

BC339   In reaching their conclusions on this issue, the boards considered the reasons for the consensus reached in EITF Issue No. 99-12 *Determination of the Measurement Date for the Market Price of Acquirer Securities Issued in a Purchase Business Combination*. That consensus states that the value of the acquirer's marketable equity securities issued to effect a business combination should be determined on the basis of the market price of the securities over a reasonable period before and after the terms of the acquisition are agreed to and announced. The arguments for that consensus are based on the view that the announcement of a transaction, and the related agreements, normally bind the parties to the transaction so that the acquirer is obliged at that point to issue the equity securities at the closing date.

---

26 The combination of IFRS 3 and IFRS 13, issued in May 2011, provides guidance for measuring the fair value of an acquirer's interest in the acquiree (including mutual entities).

If the parties are bound to the transaction at the agreement (announcement) date, the value of the underlying securities on that date best reflects the value of the bargained exchange. The boards did not find those arguments compelling. The boards observed that to make the announcement of a recommended transaction binding generally requires shareholders' authorisation or another binding event, which also gives rise to the change in control of the acquiree.

BC340 Additionally, the boards noted that measuring the fair value of equity securities issued on the agreement date (or on the basis of the market price of the securities for a short period before and after that date) did not result in a consistent measure of the consideration transferred. The fair values of all other forms of consideration transferred are measured at the acquisition date. The boards decided that all forms of consideration transferred should be valued on the same date, which should also be the same date as when the assets acquired and liabilities assumed are measured. The boards also observed that negotiations between an acquirer and an acquiree typically provide for share adjustments in the event of material events and circumstances between the agreement date and acquisition date. In addition, ongoing negotiations after announcement of agreements, which are not unusual, provide evidence that agreements are generally not binding at the date they are announced. Lastly, the boards also observed that the parties typically provide for cancellation options if the number of shares to be issued at the acquisition date would not reflect an exchange of approximately equal fair values at that date.

BC341 Respondents to the 2005 Exposure Draft expressed mixed views on the measurement date for equity securities. Some supported the proposal to measure equity securities at their fair value on the acquisition date, generally for the same reasons given in that exposure draft. Others, however, favoured use of the agreement date. They generally cited one or more of the following as support for their view:

(a) An acquirer and a target entity both consider the fair value of a target entity on the agreement date in negotiating the amount of consideration to be paid. Measuring equity securities issued as consideration at fair value on the agreement date reflects the values taken into account in negotiations.

(b) Changes in the fair value of the acquirer's equity securities between the agreement date and the acquisition date may be caused by factors unrelated to the business combination.

(c) Changes in the fair value of the acquirer's equity securities between the agreement date and the acquisition date may result in inappropriate recognition of either a bargain purchase or artificially inflated goodwill if the fair value of those securities is measured at the acquisition date.

BC342 In considering those comments, the boards observed, as they did in the 2005 Exposure Draft, that valid conceptual arguments can be made for both the agreement date and the acquisition date. However, they also observed that the parties to a business combination are likely to take into account expected changes between the agreement date and the acquisition date in the fair value of the acquirer and the market price of the acquirer's securities issued as consideration. The argument against acquisition date measurement of equity securities noted in paragraph BC341(a) is mitigated if acquirers and targets generally consider their best estimates at the agreement date of the fair values of the amounts to be exchanged on the acquisition dates. The boards also noted that measuring the equity securities on the acquisition date avoids the complexities of dealing with situations in which the number of shares or other consideration transferred can change between the agreement date and the acquisition date. The boards therefore concluded that equity instruments issued as consideration in a business combination should be measured at their fair values on the acquisition date.

Contingent consideration, including subsequent measurement

BC343 In accordance with the guidance in SFAS 141, which was carried forward from APB Opinion 16 without reconsideration, an acquirer's obligations to make payments conditional on the outcome of future events (often called *contingent consideration*) were not usually recognised at the acquisition date. Rather, acquirers usually recognised those obligations when the contingency was resolved and consideration was issued or became issuable. In general, issuing additional securities or distributing additional cash or other assets upon resolving contingencies on the basis of reaching particular earnings levels resulted in delayed recognition of an additional element of cost of an acquiree. In contrast, issuing additional securities or distributing additional assets upon resolving contingencies on the basis of security prices did not change the recognised cost of an acquiree.

BC344 The IASB carried forward in IFRS 3 the requirements for contingent consideration from IAS 22 without reconsideration. In accordance with IFRS 3, an acquirer recognised consideration that is contingent on future events at the acquisition date only if it is probable and can be measured reliably. If the required level of probability or reliability for recognition was reached only after the acquisition date, the additional consideration was treated as an adjustment to the accounting for the business combination and to goodwill at that later date.

BC345 Therefore, in accordance with both SFAS 141 and IFRS 3, unlike other forms of consideration, an obligation for contingent consideration was not always measured at its acquisition-date fair value and its remeasurement either sometimes (SFAS 141) or always (IFRS 3) resulted in an adjustment to the business combination accounting.

BC346 In developing the 2005 Exposure Draft, both boards concluded that the delayed recognition of contingent consideration in their previous standards on business combinations was unacceptable because it ignored that the acquirer's agreement to make contingent payments is the obligating event in a business combination transaction. Although the amount of the future payments the acquirer will make is conditional on future events, the obligation to make them if the specified future events occur is unconditional. The same is true for a right to the return of previously transferred consideration if specified conditions are met. Failure to recognise that obligation or right at the acquisition date would not faithfully represent the economic consideration exchanged at that date.

Thus, both boards concluded that obligations and rights associated with contingent consideration arrangements should be measured and recognised at their acquisition-date fair values.

BC347   The boards considered arguments that it might be difficult to measure the fair value of contingent consideration at the acquisition date. The boards acknowledged that measuring the fair value of some contingent payments may be difficult, but they concluded that to delay recognition of, or otherwise ignore, assets or liabilities that are difficult to measure would cause financial reporting to be incomplete and thus diminish its usefulness in making economic decisions.

BC348   Moreover, a contingent consideration arrangement is inherently part of the economic considerations in the negotiations between the buyer and seller. Such arrangements are commonly used by buyers and sellers to reach an agreement by sharing particular specified economic risks related to uncertainties about future outcomes. Differences in the views of the buyer and seller about those uncertainties are often reconciled by their agreeing to share the risks in such ways that favourable future outcomes generally result in additional payments to the seller and unfavourable outcomes result in no or lower payments. The boards observed that information used in those negotiations will often be helpful in estimating the fair value of the contingent obligation assumed by the acquirer.

BC349   The boards noted that most contingent consideration obligations are financial instruments, and many are derivative instruments. Reporting entities that use such instruments extensively, auditors and valuation professionals are familiar with the use of valuation techniques for estimating the fair values of financial instruments. The boards concluded that acquirers should be able to use valuation techniques to develop estimates of the fair values of contingent consideration obligations that are sufficiently reliable for recognition. The boards also observed that an effective estimate of zero for the acquisition-date fair value of contingent consideration, which was often the result under IFRS 3 and SFAS 141, was unreliable.

BC350   Some respondents to the 2005 Exposure Draft were especially concerned about the reliability with which the fair value of performance-based contingent consideration can be measured. The IASB and the FASB considered those concerns in the context of related requirements in their standards on share-based payments (IFRS 2 and SFAS 123(R), respectively), neither of which requires performance conditions that are not market conditions to be included in the market-based measure of an award of share-based payment at the grant date. For example, remuneration cost is recognised for a share option with vesting requirements that depend on achievement of an earnings target based on the number of equity instruments expected to vest and any such cost recognised during the vesting period is reversed if the target is not achieved. Both IFRS 2 and SFAS 123(R) cite constituents' concerns about the measurability at the grant date of the expected outcomes associated with performance conditions as part of the reason for that treatment.

BC351   The boards concluded that the requirements for awards of share-based payment subject to performance conditions should not determine the requirements for contingent (or conditional) consideration in a business combination. In addition, the boards concluded that the negotiations between buyer and seller inherent in a contingent consideration arrangement in a business combination provide better evidence of its fair value than is likely to be available for most share-based payment arrangements with performance conditions.

BC352   The boards also noted that some contingent consideration arrangements oblige the acquirer to deliver its equity securities if specified future events occur. The boards concluded that the classification of such instruments as either equity or a liability should be based on existing IFRSs or US GAAP, as indicated in paragraph 40 of the revised IFRS 3.

Subsequent measurement of contingent consideration

BC353   For reasons similar to those discussed in the context of contingent liabilities (paragraphs BC232 and BC243), the boards concluded that the revised standards must address subsequent accounting for contingent consideration. For consistency with the accounting for other obligations that require an entity to deliver its equity shares, the boards concluded that obligations for contingent payments that are classified as equity should not be remeasured after the acquisition date.

BC354   The boards observed that many obligations for contingent consideration that qualify for classification as liabilities meet the definition of derivative instruments in IAS 39[27] or SFAS 133. To improve transparency in reporting particular instruments, the boards concluded that all contracts that would otherwise be within the scope of those standards (if not issued in a business combination) should be subject to their requirements if issued in a business combination. Therefore, the boards decided to eliminate their respective provisions (paragraph 2(f) of IAS 39 and paragraph 11(c) of SFAS 133) that excluded contingent consideration in a business combination from the scope of those standards. Accordingly, liabilities for payments of contingent consideration that are subject to the requirements of IAS 39 or SFAS 133 would subsequently be measured at fair value at the end of each reporting period, with changes in fair value recognised in accordance with whichever of those standards an entity applies in its financial statements.

BC355   In considering the subsequent accounting for contingent payments that are liabilities but are not derivatives, the boards concluded that, in concept, all liabilities for contingent payments should be accounted for similarly. Therefore, liabilities for contingent payments that are not derivative instruments should also be remeasured at fair value after the acquisition date. The boards concluded that applying those provisions would faithfully represent the fair value of the liability for the contingent payment of consideration that remains a liability until settled.

BC356   The boards also considered whether subsequent changes in the fair values of liabilities for contingent consideration should be reflected as adjustments to the consideration transferred in the business combination (usually in goodwill).

---

27   IFRS 9 *Financial Instruments* replaced IAS 39. IFRS 9 applies to all items that were previously within the scope of IAS 39.

© IFRS Foundation

Some respondents to the 2005 Exposure Draft favoured that alternative because they thought that changes in the fair value of contingent consideration effectively resolve differing views of the acquirer and the former owners of the acquiree about the acquisition-date fair value of the acquiree. The boards acknowledged that a conclusive determination at the acquisition date of the fair value of a liability for contingent consideration might not be practicable in the limited circumstances in which particular information is not available at that date. As discussed in more detail in paragraphs BC390–BC400, the boards decided that the revised standards should provide for provisional measurement of the fair value of assets acquired or liabilities assumed or incurred, including liabilities for contingent payments, in those circumstances.

BC357 Except for adjustments during the measurement period to provisional estimates of fair values at the acquisition date, the boards concluded that subsequent changes in the fair value of a liability for contingent consideration do not affect the acquisition-date fair value of the consideration transferred. Rather, those subsequent changes in value are generally directly related to post-combination events and changes in circumstances related to the combined entity. Thus, subsequent changes in value for post-combination events and circumstances should not affect the measurement of the consideration transferred or goodwill on the acquisition date. (The boards acknowledge that some changes in fair value might result from events and circumstances related in part to a pre-combination period. But that part of the change is usually indistinguishable from the part related to the post-combination period and the boards concluded that the benefits in those limited circumstances that might result from making such fine distinctions would not justify the costs that such a requirement would impose.)

BC358 The boards also considered arguments that the results of the requirements of the revised standards for recognition of changes in the fair value of contingent consideration after the acquisition date are counter-intuitive because they will result in:

(a) recognising gains if the specified milestone or event requiring the contingent payment is not met. For example, the acquirer would recognise a gain on the reversal of the liability if an earnings target in an earn-out arrangement is not achieved.

(b) recognising losses if the combined entity is successful and the amount paid exceeds the estimated fair value of the liability at the acquisition date.

BC359 The boards accept the consequence that recognising the fair value of a liability for payment of contingent consideration is likely to result subsequently in a gain if smaller or no payments are required or result in a loss if greater payments are required. That is a consequence of entering into contingent consideration arrangements related to future changes in the value of a specified asset or liability or earnings of the acquiree after the acquisition date. For example, if a contingent consideration arrangement relates to the level of future earnings of the combined entity, higher earnings in the specified periods may be partially offset by increases in the liability to make contingent payments based on earnings because the acquirer has agreed to share those increases with former owners of the acquiree.

BC360　The boards also observed that liabilities for contingent payments may be related to contingencies surrounding an outcome for a particular asset or another liability. In those cases, the effect on income of the period of a change in the fair value of the liability for the contingent payment may be offset by a change in the value of the asset or other liability. For example, after an acquisition the combined entity might reach a favourable settlement of pending litigation of the acquiree for which it had a contingent consideration arrangement. If the combined entity is thus required to make a contingent payment to the seller of the acquiree that exceeds the initially estimated fair value of the liability for contingent consideration, the effect of the increase in that liability may be offset in part by the reduction in the liability to the litigation claimant. Similarly, if the acquirer is not required to make a contingent payment to the seller because an acquired research and development project failed to result in a viable product, the gain from the elimination of the liability may be offset, in whole or in part, by an impairment charge to the asset acquired.

Clarification on the accounting for contingent consideration in a business combination

BC360A　The IASB clarified the accounting for contingent consideration arising from business combinations.

Classification of contingent consideration in a business combination

BC360B　The IASB noted that the classification requirements in paragraph 40 of IFRS 3 were unclear as to when, if ever, "other applicable IFRSs" would need to be used to determine the classification of contingent consideration as a financial liability or as an equity instrument. Consequently, the IASB deleted the reference to "other applicable IFRSs" in paragraph 40.

Subsequent measurement of contingent consideration in a business combination

BC360C　The IASB also noted that the requirements for subsequent measurement in paragraph 58 require contingent consideration, other than that which meets the definition of equity in accordance with IAS 32 *Financial Instruments: Presentation*, to be subsequently measured at fair value. However, paragraph 58 then refers to IFRS 9 *Financial Instruments* (or IAS 39, if IFRS 9 has not yet been applied), IAS 37 or other IFRSs as appropriate, which may not require subsequent measurement at fair value.

Subsequent measurement of contingent consideration that is a financial instrument

BC360D　The IASB noted that the requirements for subsequent measurement in paragraph 58 for contingent consideration that is a financial instrument within the scope of IFRS 9 (or IAS 39[28]) were inconsistent with the accounting requirements of IFRS 9 (or IAS 39). Because paragraph 58 referred to IFRS 9 (or IAS 39), which allows amortised cost measurement in some circumstances, contingent consideration that is a financial liability might be classified as being measured at amortised cost. This would conflict with the requirement in paragraph 58 that such contingent consideration should be subsequently measured at fair value. Consequently, the IASB amended the classification requirements of IFRS 9 (and IAS 39) to ensure that the subsequent measurement requirement for contingent consideration that is a financial liability is fair value. The IASB thinks that this clarifies the original intention for subsequent measurement of contingent consideration as explained in paragraph BC355.

BC360E In redeliberating this issue, the IASB decided that it would not be possible for contingent consideration that is a financial asset that meets the requirements in IFRS 9 to be subsequently measured at amortised cost (because the contractual terms of contingent consideration that is a financial asset would not give rise on specified dates to cash flows that are solely payments of principal and interest on the principal amount outstanding). Consequently, the IASB decided that the proposed amendments to paragraph 4.1.2 of IFRS 9 in the Exposure Draft *Annual Improvements to IFRSs 2010–2012 Cycle* were not needed.

BC360F The IASB also decided that changes in fair value of any contingent consideration that is a financial asset or a financial liability should be recognised in profit or loss. Consequently, the IASB decided to amend paragraph 5.7.5 of IFRS 9 to ensure that any change in the fair value of investments in equity instruments that are contingent consideration in a business combination should be presented in profit or loss. The IASB noted that it was unlikely that contingent consideration that is an asset would meet the definition of equity. However, it decided to amend the paragraph to ensure that all contingent consideration that is made up of financial instruments is accounted for consistently.

Subsequent measurement of contingent consideration that is a non-financial asset or a non-financial liability

BC360G The IASB also noted that the subsequent measurement requirements in paragraph 58(b) for contingent consideration that is a non-financial asset or a non-financial liability may conflict with the measurement requirements in other applicable Standards. The conflict arises because paragraph 58 refers to changes in the fair value of contingent consideration but paragraph 58(b) refers to Standards that do not require fair value as a measurement basis, for example, IAS 37. Consequently, the IASB deleted the reference to "IAS 37 or other IFRSs as appropriate" from paragraph 58(b). This, therefore, maintains fair value as the subsequent measurement basis for all non equity contingent consideration to which IFRS 3 applies. The IASB thinks that this clarifies the original intention for subsequent measurement of contingent consideration as explained in paragraph BC355.

---

28 IFRS 9 *Financial Instruments* replaced IAS 39. IFRS 9 applies to all items that were previously within the scope of IAS 39.

BC360H   The IASB also decided that the full change in the fair value of any contingent consideration that is a non-financial asset or a non-financial liability should be recognised in profit or loss.

Other considerations given to subsequent measurement of contingent consideration

BC360I   The IASB considered alternatives for the subsequent measurement requirements for contingent consideration. It considered whether all references to other Standards, including references to IFRS 9 (or IAS 39[29]), should be removed and instead all necessary guidance for the subsequent measurement of contingent consideration should be included in IFRS 3. It decided, however, to amend IFRS 9 (and IAS 39) as a consequential amendment derived from the amendment to IFRS 3 and to retain the link to IFRS 9 (or IAS 39) so that the general guidance in IFRS 9 (or IAS 39) applies to contingent consideration that is within the scope of IFRS 9 (or IAS 39). The IASB also considered whether some liability contingent consideration should be measured at fair value with some fair value changes being presented in other comprehensive income. It decided that it was preferable that the guidance was consistent for all liability contingent consideration and, consequently, it decided that all liability contingent consideration should be subsequently measured at fair value with any resulting gain or loss, including gain or loss attributable to changes in own credit risk, being recognised in profit or loss.

Disclosure

BC360J   Some stakeholders had asked whether the IASB had intended the disclosure requirements in IFRS 7 *Financial Instruments: Disclosures* to apply to contingent consideration, noting that there are disclosure requirements for contingent consideration in IFRS 3. The IASB thinks that it is appropriate for the disclosure requirements of IFRS 7 to apply to contingent consideration that is a financial instrument within the scope of IFRS 7. Consequently, the IASB decided not to make any changes to the scope of IFRS 7 to exclude such financial instruments.

Replacement awards

BC361   An acquirer sometimes issues replacement awards to benefit the employees of the acquiree for past services, for future services or for both. Accordingly, the 2005 Exposure Draft included guidance for determining the extent to which replacement awards are for past services (and thus part of the consideration transferred in the business combination) or future services (and thus not part of the consideration transferred). In developing that guidance, the boards' objective was, as far as possible, to be consistent with the guidance in their respective standards on share-based payments.

BC362   Few respondents to the 2005 Exposure Draft commented on this issue, and those who did so generally agreed with the proposals, at least as they related to entities that apply IFRS 2 in accounting for share-based payment awards granted otherwise than in a business combination. However, in redeliberating the 2005

---

29   IFRS 9 *Financial Instruments* replaced IAS 39. IFRS 9 applies to all items that were previously within the scope of IAS 39.

Exposure Draft, the FASB observed that some of its proposals on share-based payment awards were not consistent with SFAS 123(R), which was published after the related deliberations in the second phase of its business combinations project. For example, the 2005 Exposure Draft proposed that the excess, if any, of the fair value of replacement awards over the fair value of the replaced acquiree awards should be immediately recognised as remuneration cost in the post-combination financial statements even if employees were required to render future service to earn the rights to the replacement awards. SFAS 123(R), on the other hand, requires recognition of additional remuneration cost arising in a modification of the terms of an award (which is the same as the replacement of one award with another) over the requisite service period. The FASB concluded that, in general, the requirements of SFAS 141(R) on accounting for replacements of share-based payment awards should be consistent with the requirements for other share-based payment awards in SFAS 123(R). To achieve that goal the FASB modified the guidance in SFAS 141(R) on accounting for any excess of the fair value of replacement awards over the fair value of the replaced awards.

BC363   In addition, the FASB's constituents raised questions about other aspects of the guidance on accounting for the replacement of share-based payment awards. Those questions generally related to interpretative guidance that SFAS 123(R) superseded or nullified without providing comparable guidance—specifically, FASB Interpretation No. 44 *Accounting for Certain Transactions involving Stock Compensation* and EITF Issue No. 00-23 *Issues Related to the Accounting for Stock Compensation under APB Opinion No. 25 and FASB Interpretation No. 44*. Paragraphs B56–B62 of the revised IFRS 3 provide guidance to help in resolving those implementation questions. In developing that guidance, the FASB sought to apply the same principles to the replacement of share-based payment awards in a business combination that are applied to share-based payment awards in other situations. The IASB agreed with that goal, and it decided that the guidance on accounting for replacement awards of share-based payment is consistent with the guidance in IFRS 2 on accounting for modification of share-based payment awards.

BC364   The boards concluded that the guidance in the revised standards is consistent with the objective that the consideration transferred for an acquired business includes those payments that are for the business and excludes those payments that are for other purposes. Remuneration for future services to be rendered to the acquirer by former owners or other employees of the acquiree is not, in substance, consideration for the business acquired.

Acquisition-related costs

BC365   The boards considered whether acquisition-related costs are part of the consideration transferred in exchange for the acquiree. Those costs include an acquirer's costs incurred in connection with a business combination (a) for the services of lawyers, investment bankers, accountants and other third parties and (b) for issuing debt or equity instruments used to effect the business combination (issue costs). Generally, acquisition-related costs are charged to expense as incurred, but the costs to issue debt or equity securities are an exception. Currently, the accounting for issue costs is mixed and conflicting practices have developed in the absence of clear accounting guidance. The FASB is addressing issue costs in its project on liabilities and equity and has tentatively decided that those costs should be recognised as expenses as incurred. Some FASB members would have preferred to require issue costs to effect a business combination to be recognised as expenses, but they did not think that the business combinations project was the place to make that decision. Therefore, the FASB decided to allow mixed practices for accounting for issue costs to continue until the project on liabilities and equity resolves the issue broadly.

BC366 The boards concluded that acquisition-related costs are not part of the fair value exchange between the buyer and seller for the business. Rather, they are separate transactions in which the buyer pays for the fair value of services received. The boards also observed that those costs, whether for services performed by external parties or internal staff of the acquirer, do not generally represent assets of the acquirer at the acquisition date because the benefits obtained are consumed as the services are received.

BC367 Thus, the 2005 Exposure Draft proposed, and the revised standards require, the acquirer to exclude acquisition-related costs from the measurement of the fair value of both the consideration transferred and the assets acquired or liabilities assumed as part of the business combination. Those costs are to be accounted for separately from the business combination, and generally recognised as expenses when incurred. The revised standards therefore resolve inconsistencies in accounting for acquisition-related costs in accordance with the cost-accumulation approach in IFRS 3 and SFAS 141, which provided that the cost of an acquiree included *direct* costs incurred for an acquisition of a business but excluded *indirect* costs. Direct costs included out-of-pocket or incremental costs, for example, finder's fees and fees paid to outside consultants for accounting, legal or valuation services for a successful acquisition, but direct costs incurred in unsuccessful negotiations were recognised as expenses as incurred. Indirect costs included recurring internal costs, such as maintaining an acquisition department. Although those costs also could be directly related to a successful acquisition, they were recognised as expenses as incurred.

BC368 Some respondents to the 2005 Exposure Draft said that acquisition-related costs, including costs of due diligence, are unavoidable costs of the investment in a business. They suggested that, because the acquirer intends to recover its due diligence cost through the post-acquisition operations of the business, that transaction cost should be capitalised as part of the total investment in the business. Some also argued that the buyer specifically considers those costs in determining the amount that it is willing to pay for the acquiree. The boards rejected those arguments. They found no persuasive evidence indicating that the seller of a particular business is willing to accept less than fair value as consideration for its business merely because a particular buyer may incur more (or less) acquisition-related costs than other potential buyers for that business. Furthermore, the boards concluded that the intentions of a particular buyer, including its plans to recover such costs, are a separate matter that is distinct from the fair value measurement objective in the revised standards.

BC369   The boards acknowledge that the cost-accumulation models in IFRS 3 and SFAS 141 included some acquisition-related costs as part of the carrying amount of the assets acquired. The boards also acknowledge that all asset acquisitions are similar transactions that, in concept, should be accounted for similarly, regardless of whether assets are acquired separately or as part of a group of assets that may meet the definition of a business. However, as noted in paragraph BC20, the boards decided not to extend the scope of the revised standards to all acquisitions of groups of assets. Therefore, the boards accept that, at this time, accounting for most acquisition-related costs separately from the business combination, generally as an expense as incurred for services received in connection with a combination, differs from some standards or accepted practices that require or permit particular acquisition-related costs to be included in the cost of an asset acquisition. The boards concluded, however, that the revised standards improve financial reporting by eliminating inconsistencies in accounting for acquisition-related costs in connection with a business combination and by applying the fair value measurement principle to all business combinations. The boards also observed that in practice under IFRS 3 and SFAS 141, most acquisition-related costs were subsumed in goodwill, which was also not consistent with accounting for asset acquisitions.

BC370   The boards also considered concerns about the potential for abuse. Some constituents, including some respondents to the 2005 Exposure Draft, said that if acquirers could no longer capitalise acquisition-related costs as part of the cost of the business acquired, they might modify transactions to avoid recognising those costs as expenses. For example, some said that a buyer might ask a seller to make payments to the buyer's vendors on its behalf. To facilitate the negotiations and sale of the business, the seller might agree to make those payments if the total amount to be paid to it upon closing of the business combination is sufficient to reimburse the seller for payments it made on the buyer's behalf. If the disguised reimbursements were treated as part of the consideration transferred for the business, the acquirer might not recognise those expenses. Rather, the measure of the fair value of the business and the amount of goodwill recognised for that business might be overstated. To mitigate such concerns, the revised standards require any payments to an acquiree (or its former owners) in connection with a business combination that are payments for goods or services that are not part of the acquired business to be assigned to those goods or services and accounted for as a separate transaction. The revised standards specifically require an acquirer to determine whether any portion of the amounts transferred by the acquirer are separate from the consideration exchanged for the acquiree and the assets acquired and liabilities assumed in the business combination. The revised standards (see paragraphs 51–53 and B50 of the revised IFRS 3) provide guidance for making that determination.

Bargain purchases

BC371   Paragraphs 34–36 of the revised IFRS 3 set out the accounting requirements for a bargain purchase. The boards consider bargain purchases anomalous transactions—business entities and their owners generally do not knowingly and willingly sell assets or businesses at prices below their fair values. However, bargain purchases have occurred and are likely to continue to occur.

Circumstances in which they occur include a forced liquidation or distress sale (eg after the death of a founder or key manager) in which owners need to sell a business quickly, which may result in a price that is less than fair value.

BC372 The boards observed that an economic gain is inherent in a bargain purchase. At the acquisition date, the acquirer is better off by the amount by which the fair value of what is acquired exceeds the fair value of the consideration transferred (paid) for it. The boards concluded that, in concept, the acquirer should recognise that gain at the acquisition date. However, the boards acknowledged that although the reasons for a forced liquidation or distress sale are often apparent, sometimes clear evidence might not exist, for example, if a seller uses a closed (private) process for the sale and to maintain its negotiating position is unwilling to reveal the main reason for the sale. The appearance of a bargain purchase without evidence of the underlying reasons would raise concerns in practice about the existence of measurement errors.

BC373 Constituents, including some respondents to the 2005 Exposure Draft, expressed concerns about recognising gains upon the acquisition of a business, particularly if it is difficult to determine whether a particular acquisition is in fact a bargain purchase. They also suggested that an initial determination of an excess of the acquisition-date fair value (or other recognised amounts) of the identifiable net assets acquired over the fair value of the consideration paid by the acquirer plus the recognised amount of any non-controlling interest in the acquiree might arise from other factors, including:

(a) errors in measuring the fair values of (i) the consideration paid for the business, (ii) the assets acquired or (iii) the liabilities assumed; and

(b) using measures in accordance with IFRSs or US GAAP that are not fair values.

Distinguishing a bargain purchase from measurement errors

BC374 The boards acknowledged concerns raised by constituents that a requirement to recognise gains on a bargain purchase might provide an opportunity for inappropriate gain recognition from intentional errors resulting from the acquirer's:

(a) understating or failing to identify the value of items of consideration that it transferred;

(b) overstating values attributed to particular assets acquired; or

(c) understating or failing to identify and recognise particular liabilities assumed.

BC375 The boards think that problems surrounding intentional measurement errors by acquirers are generally best addressed by means other than setting standards specifically intended to avoid abuse. Strong internal control systems and the use of independent valuation experts and external auditors are among the means by which both intentional and unintentional measurement errors are minimised. Standards specifically designed to avoid abuse would inevitably lack neutrality. (See paragraph BC51 for a discussion of the need for neutrality in accounting and accounting standards.) However, the boards share constituents' concerns about the potential for inappropriate gain recognition resulting from measurement bias or undetected measurement errors. Thus, the boards decided (see paragraph 36 of the revised IFRS 3) to require the acquirer to reassess whether it has correctly identified all of the assets acquired and all of the liabilities assumed before recognising a gain on a bargain purchase. The acquirer must then review the procedures used to measure the amounts the revised standards require to be recognised at the acquisition date for all of the following:

(a) the identifiable assets acquired and liabilities assumed;

(b) the non-controlling interest in the acquiree, if any;

(c) for a business combination achieved in stages, the acquirer's previously held equity interest in the acquiree; and

(d) the consideration transferred.

The objective of that review is to ensure that appropriate consideration has been given to all available information in identifying the items to be measured and recognised and in determining their fair values. The boards believe that the required review will mitigate, if not eliminate, undetected errors that might have existed in the initial measurements.

BC376 The boards acknowledged, however, that the required review might be insufficient to eliminate concerns about unintentional measurement bias. They decided to address that concern by limiting the extent of gain that can be recognised. Thus, the revised standards provide that a gain on a bargain purchase is measured as the excess of:

(a) the net of the acquisition-date amounts of the identifiable assets acquired and liabilities assumed; over

(b) the acquisition-date fair value of the consideration transferred plus the recognised amount of any non-controlling interest in the acquiree and, if the transaction is an acquisition achieved in stages, the acquisition-date fair value of the acquirer's previously held equity interest in the acquiree.

That means that a gain on a bargain purchase and goodwill cannot both be recognised for the same business combination. The 2005 Exposure Draft defined a bargain purchase as a transaction in which the fair value of the acquirer's interest in the acquiree exceeds the consideration transferred for it, but it would have required that any resulting goodwill should be written off before a gain was recognised. The result of the revised standards' requirement is the same, but there will be no goodwill to write off if the gain is measured with reference to the identifiable net assets acquired rather than the fair value of the acquirer's interest in the acquiree. In addition, the revised standards require (paragraph B64(n) of the revised IFRS 3) the acquirer to disclose information about a gain recognised on a bargain purchase.

BC377 The main purpose of the limitation on gain recognition is to mitigate the potential for inappropriate gain recognition through measurement errors, particularly those that might result from unintended measurement bias. The main purpose of the disclosure requirement is to provide information that enables users of an acquirer's financial statements to evaluate the nature and financial effect of business combinations that occur during the period. The boards acknowledged, however, that the limitation and disclosure requirements may also help to mitigate constituents' concerns about potential abuse, although that is not their primary objective.

BC378 Moreover, the boards believe that concerns about abuse resulting from the opportunity for gain recognition may be overstated. Financial analysts and other users have often told the boards that they give little weight to one-off or unusual gains, such as those resulting from a bargain purchase transaction. In addition, the boards noted that managers of entities generally have no incentive to overstate assets acquired or understate liabilities assumed in a business combination because that would generally result in higher post-combination expenses—when the assets are used or become impaired or liabilities are remeasured or settled.

Distinguishing a bargain purchase from a 'negative goodwill result'

BC379 The boards acknowledged that a so-called negative goodwill result remains a possibility (although in most situations, a remote possibility) because the revised standards continue to require particular assets acquired and liabilities assumed to be measured at amounts other than their acquisition-date fair values. The boards observed, however, that the revised standards address most deficiencies in past requirements on accounting for business combinations that previously led to negative goodwill results—ie a result that had the appearance but not the economic substance of a bargain purchase. For example, often no liability was recognised for some contingent payment arrangements (eg earn-outs) at the acquisition date, which could result in the appearance of a bargain purchase by understating the consideration paid. The revised standards, in contrast, require the measurement and recognition of substantially all liabilities at their fair values on the acquisition date.

BC380 The boards also considered concerns raised by some constituents that a buyer's expectations of future losses and its need to incur future costs to make a business viable might give rise to a negative goodwill result. In other words, a buyer would be willing to pay a seller only an amount that is, according to that view, less than the fair value of the acquiree (or its identifiable net assets) because to make a fair return on the business the buyer would need to make further investments in that business to bring its condition to fair value. The boards disagreed with that view for the reasons noted in paragraphs BC134–BC143 in the context of liabilities associated with restructuring or exit activities of the acquiree, as well as those that follow.

BC381 Fair values are measured by reference to unrelated buyers and sellers that are knowledgeable and have a common understanding about factors relevant to the business and the transaction and are also willing and able to transact business in the same market(s) and have the legal and financial ability to do so. The boards are aware of no compelling reason to believe that, in the absence of duress, a seller would willingly and knowingly sell a business for an amount less than its fair value. Thus, the boards concluded that careful application of the revised standards' fair value measurement requirements will mitigate concerns that negative goodwill might result and be misinterpreted as a bargain purchase transaction.

Overpayments

BC382　The boards considered whether the revised standards should include special provisions to account for a business combination in which a buyer overpays for its interest in the acquiree. The boards acknowledged that overpayments are possible and, in concept, an overpayment should lead to the acquirer's recognition of an expense (or loss) in the period of the acquisition. However, the boards believe that in practice any overpayment is unlikely to be detectable or known at the acquisition date. In other words, the boards are not aware of instances in which a buyer knowingly overpays or is compelled to overpay a seller to acquire a business. Even if an acquirer thinks it might have overpaid in some sense, the amount of overpayment would be difficult, if not impossible, to quantify. Thus, the boards concluded that in practice it is not possible to identify and reliably measure an overpayment at the acquisition date. Accounting for overpayments is best addressed through subsequent impairment testing when evidence of a potential overpayment first arises.

Additional guidance for particular types of business combinations

BC383　To help entities apply the acquisition method as required by the revised standards, the boards decided to provide additional guidance for business combinations achieved in stages and those achieved without the transfer of consideration. Paragraphs BC384–BC389 discuss the guidance provided on business combinations achieved in stages. The guidance on combinations achieved without the transfer of consideration merely responds to a question about how to report the acquiree's net assets in the equity section of the acquirer's post-combination statement of financial position, and this Basis for Conclusions does not discuss that guidance further.

Business combinations achieved in stages

BC384　In a business combination achieved in stages, the acquirer remeasures its previously held equity interest at its acquisition-date fair value and recognises the related gain or loss in profit or loss (paragraph 42 of the revised IFRS 3). The boards concluded that a change from holding a non-controlling investment in an entity to obtaining control of that entity is a significant change in the nature of and economic circumstances surrounding that investment. That change warrants a change in the classification and measurement of that investment. Once it obtains control, the acquirer is no longer the owner of a non-controlling investment asset in the acquiree. As in present practice, the acquirer ceases its accounting for an investment asset and begins reporting in its financial statements the underlying assets, liabilities and results of operations of the acquiree.[30] In effect, the acquirer exchanges its status as an owner of an investment asset in an entity for a controlling financial interest in all of the underlying assets and liabilities of that entity (acquiree) and the right to direct how the acquiree and its management use those assets in its operations.

BC385 In August 2003 the FASB held a round-table meeting with members of its resource group on business combinations and other constituents to discuss, among other things, the decision to require an acquirer to remeasure any previously held equity investment in an acquiree at its acquisition-date fair value and to recognise in earnings any gain or loss. The users of financial statements indicated they did not have significant concerns with that change to present practice, as long as the amount of the gain or loss is clearly disclosed in the financial statements or in the notes. Paragraph B64(p) of the revised IFRS 3 requires that disclosure.

BC386 The boards rejected the view expressed by some constituents that the carrying amount of any pre-acquisition investment should be retained in the initial accounting for the cost of the business acquired. The boards concluded that cost-accumulation practices led to many of the inconsistencies and deficiencies in financial reporting as required by SFAS 141 and, to a lesser extent, by IFRS 3 (see paragraphs BC198–BC202).

BC387 Some constituents also expressed concern about what they described as allowing an opportunity for gain recognition on a purchase transaction. The boards noted that the required remeasurement could also result in loss recognition. Moreover, the boards rejected the characterisation that the result is to recognise a gain or loss on a purchase. Rather, under today's mixed attribute accounting model, economic gains and losses are recognised as they occur for some, but not all, financial instruments. If an equity interest in an entity is not required to be measured at its fair value, the recognition of a gain or loss at the acquisition date is merely a consequence of the delayed recognition of the economic gain or loss that is present in that financial instrument. If the investment asset had been measured at fair value at the end of each reporting period, the gain or loss would have been recognised as it occurred and measurement of the asset at its acquisition-date fair value would result in no further gain or loss.

BC388 Some respondents who agreed that an acquirer should remeasure its previously held equity interest at fair value would recognise any resulting gain or loss in other comprehensive income rather than in profit or loss. Those respondents said that the accounting for previously held equity interests is similar to the accounting for available-for-sale securities. Changes in the value of available-for-sale securities are recognised in other comprehensive income. They view each step in a step acquisition as a transaction in which the acquirer only obtains more shares in the acquiree. Because the shares that the acquirer previously held have not been exchanged or sold, they think that the recognition of profit or loss is not appropriate.

---

30 In October 2012 the Board issued *Investment Entities* (Amendments to IFRS 10, IFRS 12 and IAS 27), which required investment entities, as defined in IFRS 10, to measure their investments in subsidiaries, other than those providing investment-related services or activities, at fair value through profit or loss.

BC389　The boards understand that the required treatment of a previously held equity investment in a step acquisition is different from the initial recognition of gains or losses on available-for-sale securities.[31] However, the boards noted that changes in the value of available-for-sale securities are recognised in profit or loss when the securities are derecognised. In a business combination achieved in stages, the acquirer derecognises its investment asset in an entity in its consolidated financial statements when it achieves control. Thus, the boards concluded that it is appropriate to recognise any resulting gain or loss in profit or loss at the acquisition date.

Measurement period

BC390　The revised standards provide an acquirer with a reasonable period after the acquisition date, a *measurement period*, during which to obtain the information necessary to identify and measure the items specified in paragraph 46 of the revised IFRS 3 as of the acquisition date in accordance with the requirements of the revised standards. If sufficient information is not available at the acquisition date to measure those amounts, the acquirer determines and recognises provisional amounts until the necessary information becomes available.

BC391　The boards concluded that providing for retrospective adjustments during the measurement period should help to resolve concerns about the quality and availability of information at the acquisition date for measuring the fair values of particular items at that date. Constituents especially indicated such concerns about contingent liabilities and contingent consideration arrangements, which also affect the amount of goodwill or the gain recognised on a bargain purchase.

BC392　The boards decided to place constraints on the period for which it is deemed reasonable to be seeking information necessary to complete the accounting for a business combination. The measurement period ends as soon as the acquirer receives the necessary information about facts and circumstances that existed as of the acquisition date or learns that the information is not obtainable. However, in no circumstances may the measurement period exceed one year from the acquisition date. The boards concluded that allowing a measurement period longer than one year would not be especially helpful; obtaining reliable information about circumstances and conditions that existed more than a year ago is likely to become more difficult as time passes. Of course, the outcome of some contingencies and similar matters may not be known within a year. But the objective of the measurement period is to provide time to obtain the information necessary to measure the fair value of the item as of the acquisition date. Determining the ultimate settlement amount of a contingency or other item is not necessary. Uncertainties about the timing and amount of future cash flows are part of the measure of the fair value of an asset or liability.

BC393　The boards also concluded that acquirers should provide users of their financial statements with relevant information about the status of items that have been measured only provisionally. Thus, paragraph B67(a) of the revised IFRS 3 specifies particular disclosures about those items.

31　IFRS 9 *Financial Instruments* eliminated the category of available-for-sale financial assets.

BC394   Both IFRS 3 and SFAS 141 included a period during which an acquirer might measure particular amounts provisionally if the necessary information was not available at the acquisition date. Neither of those provisions was identical to the measurement period guidance in the revised standards, although IFRS 3's was quite similar. However, the measurement period provisions in the revised standards differ in important ways from the allocation period guidance of SFAS 141 and its cost-allocation method. The revised standards emphasise the principle that assets acquired, liabilities assumed and any non-controlling interest in the acquiree should be measured at their acquisition-date fair values. SFAS 141's allocation period and its post-combination adjustments delayed the recognition of assets and liabilities, and those assets and liabilities were not measured at their acquisition-date fair values when they were recognised. Therefore, the FASB decided to replace the SFAS 141 term *allocation period* and its guidance with the measurement period guidance in the revised standards.

BC395   The FASB also decided that to improve the quality of comparative information reported in financial statements and to converge with the requirements of IFRS 3, SFAS 141(R) should require an acquirer:

(a)   to recognise adjustments made during the measurement period to the provisional values of the assets acquired and liabilities assumed as if the accounting for the business combination had been completed at the acquisition date.

(b)   to adjust comparative information in previously issued financial statements, including any change in depreciation, amortisation or other income effect recognised as a result of completing the initial accounting.

BC396   SFAS 141 was silent about whether adjustments during its allocation period were to be reported retrospectively, but the FASB noted that in practice the effects of those adjustments were typically reported in the post-combination period, not retrospectively. The FASB acknowledged concerns that retrospective adjustments and adjusting previously issued comparative information are more costly. The FASB observed, however, that applying measurement period adjustments retrospectively would result in at least two significant benefits: (a) improvements in comparative period information and (b) avoidance of divergent accounting between US entities and others and the reduction of reconciling items and their attendant costs. The FASB concluded, as had the IASB in developing IFRS 3, that those overall benefits outweigh the potential costs of retrospective application.

BC397   Some respondents to the 2005 Exposure Draft (generally those who apply US GAAP rather than IFRSs) disagreed with retrospective application of measurement period adjustments. They regarded measurement period adjustments as similar to changes in estimates, which are accounted for prospectively. They noted that FASB Statement No. 154 *Accounting Changes and Error Corrections* (SFAS 154) and IAS 8 *Accounting Policies, Changes in Accounting Estimates and Errors* both require retrospective adjustment only for changes in accounting policy or restatement for errors.

BC398   In considering those responses, the boards observed that measurement period adjustments in a business combination differ from the changes in estimates dealt with by SFAS 154 and IAS 8. Measurement period adjustments result from information about assets, liabilities and non-controlling interests **as of** the acquisition date that becomes available only after that date. In contrast, adjustments for changes in estimates generally result from changes in facts and circumstances that affect an estimate, for example, a change in technology that affects the useful life of an asset.

BC399　The boards concluded that adjustments during the measurement period following a business combination are more analogous to adjusting events after the end of the reporting period (IAS 10 *Events after the Reporting Period*) than to changes in estimates. The effects of events that occur after the end of an accounting period but before the financial statements for the period are authorised for issue and provide evidence of a condition that existed at the date of the financial statements are reflected in financial statements as of that date. Similarly, the effects of information that first becomes available during the measurement period and provides evidence of conditions or circumstances that existed at the acquisition date should be reflected in the accounting as of that date.

BC400　To recognise measurement period adjustments only prospectively would be inconsistent with the recognition and measurement principles in the revised standards. Thus, although the boards understand the practical and other difficulties with retrospective adjustments, on balance, they concluded that requiring such adjustments in this situation is appropriate.

Disclosures

BC401　Because a business combination often results in a significant change to an entity's operations, the nature and extent of the information disclosed about the transaction bear on users' abilities to assess the effects of such changes on post-combination profit or loss and cash flows. Accordingly, as part of their respective projects that led to IFRS 3 and SFAS 141, the IASB and the FASB both considered the usefulness of the disclosure requirements required by IAS 22 and APB Opinion 16, respectively, for the acquisition method. IFRS 3 and SFAS 141 carried forward disclosures from the earlier requirements for business combinations that remained relevant, eliminated those that did not and modified those that were affected by changes in the recognition or measurement requirements. In the second phase of their projects on business combinations, the boards undertook essentially the same sort of reconsideration of the disclosure requirements in IFRS 3 and SFAS 141, and they also considered particular disclosures requested by respondents to the 2005 Exposure Draft.

BC402　The remainder of this section first reviews the changes that SFAS 141 and IFRS 3 made to the disclosure requirements of APB Opinion 16 and IAS 22 respectively (paragraphs BC403–BC418). Paragraphs BC419–BC428 then discuss the changes the revised standards make to the disclosure requirements of SFAS 141 and IFRS 3.

Disclosure requirements of SFAS 141

Disclosure of information about the purchase price allocation and pro forma sales and earnings

BC403　The 1999 Exposure Draft would have required tabular disclosure of the fair values allocated to each of the major classes of assets and liabilities presented in the statement of financial position and the acquiree's related carrying amounts immediately before its acquisition. That exposure draft also proposed eliminating the pro forma sales and earnings disclosures required by APB Opinion 16.

BC404　Approximately half of the respondents who commented on the proposed requirement to disclose information about the purchase price allocation agreed that the information would be useful in assessing post-acquisition earnings and cash flows of the acquirer. However, some respondents questioned the usefulness of the proposed disclosure of information about the acquiree's carrying amounts of assets acquired and liabilities assumed, particularly if the financial statements of the acquiree were not audited or were prepared on a basis other than US GAAP. After considering those views, the FASB affirmed its conclusion that information about the allocation of the purchase price to major classes of assets and liabilities in the statement of financial position would be useful in assessing the amount and timing of future cash flows. However, it agreed that information about the related carrying amounts might be of limited usefulness. Thus, SFAS 141 required disclosure of information about the allocation of the purchase price to each major class of asset and liability in the acquiree's statement of financial position but not their previous carrying amounts.

BC405　After considering respondents' views, the FASB included in SFAS 141 the pro forma disclosure requirements from APB Opinion 16. However, the FASB also continued the exemption of non-public entities from the pro forma disclosure requirements. Preparers and auditors of financial statements of non-public entities urged the FASB to continue that exemption, which was initially provided by FASB Statement No. 79 *Elimination of Certain Disclosures for Business Combinations by Nonpublic Enterprises*.

Disclosures related to goodwill

BC406　The FASB's 2001 Exposure Draft (see paragraph BC160 for a discussion of that exposure draft) would have required the acquirer to disclose (a) the reasons for the acquisition, including a description of the factors that led to a purchase price that resulted in goodwill and (b) the amount of goodwill assigned to each reportable segment. The requirement to disclose goodwill by reportable segment was limited to entities that are within the scope of FASB Statement No. 131 *Disclosures about Segments of an Enterprise and Related Information*. That exposure draft also proposed requiring disclosure of the amount of goodwill expected to be deductible for tax purposes if the goodwill initially recognised in a material business combination was significant in relation to the total cost of the acquiree. After considering the comments of respondents, the FASB affirmed its conclusion that the information would be useful in estimating the amount and timing of future impairment losses, and SFAS 141 required that disclosure.

Disclosure of information about intangible assets other than goodwill

BC407　If the amount assigned to intangible assets was significant in relation to the total cost of an acquiree, SFAS 141 required disclosure of the following information to help users of financial statements assess the amount and timing of future cash flows:

(a)　the total amount assigned to intangible assets subject to amortisation and the total amount assigned to those that are not subject to amortisation;

(b)　the amount assigned to each major intangible asset class;

(c)　for intangible assets subject to amortisation, the weighted average amortisation period in total and for each major intangible asset class; and

(d)　the amount of any significant residual value assumed, both in total and for each major class of intangible asset.

Other disclosure requirements

BC408　The 1999 Exposure Draft proposed, and SFAS 141 required, disclosure of specified information for a series of immaterial business combinations that are material in the aggregate completed in a reporting period:

(a)　the number of entities acquired and a brief description of them;

(b)　the aggregate cost of the acquired entities, the number of equity interests issued or issuable and the value assigned to them;

(c)　the aggregate amount of any contingent payments, options or commitments and the accounting treatment that will be followed should any such contingency occur (if potentially significant in relation to the aggregate cost of the acquired entities); and

(d)　the information about goodwill required for a material acquisition if the aggregate amount assigned to goodwill or to other intangible assets acquired was significant in relation to the aggregate cost of the acquired entities.

BC409　In addition, the 1999 Exposure Draft proposed, and SFAS 141 required, that the information required to be disclosed for a completed business combination would also be disclosed for a material business combination completed after the balance sheet date but before the financial statements are authorised for issue (unless disclosure of such information was not practicable). That requirement was consistent with auditing standards on subsequent events.

Disclosures in interim financial information

BC410　Several analysts and other users recommended that the FASB should require disclosure of supplemental pro forma revenues and earnings in interim financial information because that information would be more useful if it was available earlier. SFAS 141 amended APB Opinion No. 28 *Interim Financial Reporting* to require disclosure of that information.

Disclosure requirements of IFRS 3

BC411   IFRS 3 identified three objectives that its disclosure requirements were intended to meet, specifically, to provide the users of an acquirer's financial statements with information that enables them to evaluate:

(a)   the nature and financial effect of business combinations that were effected during the reporting period or after the balance sheet date but before the financial statements were authorised for issue.

(b)   the financial effects of gains, losses, error corrections and other adjustments recognised in the current period that relate to business combinations that were effected in the current period or in previous periods.

(c)   changes in the carrying amount of goodwill during the period.

BC412   The IASB began its discussion of the disclosure requirements necessary to meet the objectives by assessing the disclosure requirements in SIC-28 *Business Combinations—"Date of Exchange" and Fair Value of Equity Instruments* and IAS 22. The IASB concluded that information disclosed in accordance with SIC-28 about equity instruments issued as part of the cost of a business combination helped to meet the first of the three objectives outlined above. Therefore, IFRS 3 carried forward the disclosure requirements in SIC-28.

BC413   The IASB also concluded that information previously disclosed in accordance with IAS 22 about business combinations classified as acquisitions and goodwill helped to meet the objectives in paragraph BC411. Therefore, IFRS 3 carried forward the related disclosure requirements in IAS 22, amended as necessary to reflect changes IFRS 3 made to the provisions of IAS 22. For example, IAS 22 required disclosure of the amount of any adjustment during the period to goodwill or 'negative goodwill' resulting from subsequent identification or changes in value of the acquiree's identifiable assets and liabilities. IFRS 3 required an acquirer, with specified exceptions, to adjust the initial accounting for a combination after that accounting was complete only to correct an error. Thus, IFRS 3 revised the IAS 22 disclosure requirement to require disclosure of information about error corrections required to be disclosed by IAS 8.

BC414   The IASB then assessed whether any additional disclosure requirements should be included in IFRS 3 to ensure that the three disclosure objectives were met and considered the disclosure requirements in the corresponding standards of its partner standard-setters. As a result, and after considering respondents' comments on ED 3, the IASB identified, and IFRS 3 required, the following additional disclosures to help meet the first of the three disclosure objectives in paragraph BC411:

(a)   For each business combination effected during the period:

(i)   the amounts recognised at the acquisition date for each class of the acquiree's assets, liabilities and contingent liabilities and, if practicable, the carrying amounts of each of those classes, determined in accordance with IFRSs, immediately before the combination. If such disclosure was impracticable, an entity disclosed that fact, together with an explanation of why disclosure was impracticable.

(ii) a description of the factors that contributed to the recognition of goodwill—including a description of each intangible asset that was not recognised separately from goodwill and an explanation of why the intangible asset's fair value could not be measured reliably. If the acquirer's interest in the acquiree's identifiable net assets exceeded the cost, the acquirer was required to describe the nature of that excess.

(iii) the amount of the acquiree's profit or loss since the acquisition date included in the acquirer's profit or loss for the period, unless disclosure was impracticable. If such disclosure was impracticable, the acquirer disclosed that fact, together with an explanation of why disclosure was impracticable.

(b) The information required to be disclosed for each business combination that was effected during the period in aggregate for business combinations that are individually immaterial.

(c) The revenue and profit or loss of the combined entity for the period as though the acquisition date for all business combinations that were effected during the period had been the beginning of that period, unless such disclosure was impracticable.

BC415 To aid in meeting the second disclosure objective in paragraph BC411, IFRS 3 also required disclosure of the amount and an explanation of any gain or loss recognised in the current period that both:

(a) related to the identifiable assets acquired or liabilities or contingent liabilities assumed in a business combination that was effected in the current or a previous period; and

(b) was of such size, nature or incidence that disclosure was relevant to an understanding of the combined entity's financial performance.

BC416 To help achieve the third disclosure objective in paragraph BC411, the IASB concluded that the previous requirement to disclose a reconciliation of the carrying amount of goodwill at the beginning and end of the period should be amended to require separate disclosure of net exchange rate differences arising during the period in accordance with IAS 21 *The Effects of Changes in Foreign Exchange Rates*.

BC417 The IASB observed that there might be situations in which the information disclosed under the specific requirements would not completely satisfy IFRS 3's three disclosure objectives. In that situation, IFRS 3 required disclosure of any additional information necessary to meet those objectives.

BC418 IFRS 3 also required the acquirer to disclose the number of equity instruments issued or issuable as part of the cost of a business combination, the fair value of those instruments and the basis for determining that fair value. Although IAS 22 did not explicitly require disclosure of that information, the IASB concluded that the acquirer should have provided it as part of disclosing the cost of acquisition and a description of the purchase consideration paid or contingently payable in accordance with paragraph 87(b) of IAS 22. The IASB decided that to avoid inconsistent application, IFRS 3 should explicitly require disclosure of that information.

Disclosure requirements of the revised standards

BC419   The boards decided that the revised standards should include overall objectives for the disclosure of information that would be useful to investors, creditors and others in evaluating the financial effects of a business combination. The objectives, which are stated in paragraphs 59 and 61 of the revised IFRS 3, are, in substance, the same as those in IFRS 3 and the 2005 Exposure Draft. Respondents to the 2005 Exposure Draft who discussed the proposed disclosures generally agreed with the disclosure objectives. In reconsidering that exposure draft, however, the boards noted that the third objective in IFRS 3, to provide information that enables users of an entity's financial statements to evaluate changes in the carrying amount of goodwill during the period, is effectively included in the objective in paragraph 61. Thus, the boards combined those two objectives.

BC420   In addition, both boards concluded, as the IASB did in developing IFRS 3, that it is not necessary (or possible) to identify all of the specific information that may be necessary to meet those objectives for all business combinations. Rather, the revised standards specify particular disclosures that are generally required to meet those objectives and require acquirers to disclose any additional information about the circumstances surrounding a particular business combination that they consider necessary to meet those objectives (paragraph 63 of the revised IFRS 3).

BC421   Changes to the disclosure requirements of IFRS 3 and SFAS 141 include the elimination of disclosures of amounts or information that was based on applying the cost allocation (purchase price) method for assigning amounts to assets and liabilities that is replaced by the revised standards' fair value measurement principle. Some of those disclosures are modified to retain the information but conform the amounts to be disclosed with the fair value measurement principle.

BC422   The boards added some disclosure requirements to those in IFRS 3, SFAS 141 or both and modified or eliminated others. Those changes are described below, together with an indication of how the changes relate to each board's previous requirements and references to related discussions in other parts of this Basis for Conclusions where pertinent.[32]

(a)   In response to requests from some commentators on the 2005 Exposure Draft, the boards added to both IFRS 3 and SFAS 141 disclosure of information about receivables acquired. (paragraphs BC258–BC260)

---

32 IFRS 13, issued in May 2011, requires disclosures about fair value measurements after initial recognition. Although the disclosures required by IFRS 13 are not required for IFRS 3, the wording has been aligned.

(b) The boards modified both IFRS 3's and SFAS 141's disclosures about contingent consideration in a business combination to make them consistent with the revised standards' requirements for contingent consideration. Paragraph B64(g) of the revised IFRS 3 describes the specific disclosures now required.

(c) The FASB added to SFAS 141 disclosure of the revenue and earnings of the acquiree, if practicable, for a minimum of the period from the acquisition date to the end of the current year. The disclosure is required only from public business entities for the current year, the current interim period and cumulative interim periods from the acquisition date to the end of the current year. IFRS 3 already required disclosure of the amount of the acquiree's profit or loss included in the acquirer's profit or loss for the period, unless that was impracticable; the IASB added revenues to that disclosure. (paragraphs BC423–BC428)

(d) The FASB modified SFAS 141's disclosure of supplemental pro forma information about results of operations for the comparable prior period presented to focus on revenue and earnings of the combined entity for the comparable prior reporting period as though the acquisition date for all business combinations during the current year had been the beginning of the comparable prior annual reporting period. The disclosure is required only from public entities and only if practicable. The IASB decided not to add that disclosure. (paragraph BC428)

(e) The FASB replaced SFAS 141's disclosure of the period for which the results of operations of the acquiree are included in the income statement of the combined entity with disclosure of the acquisition date—a disclosure that IFRS 3 already required. SFAS 141(R) no longer permits the alternative practice of reporting revenues and expenses of the acquiree as if the acquisition occurred as of the beginning of the year (or a designated date) with a reduction to eliminate the acquiree's pre-acquisition period earnings. (paragraphs BC108–BC110)

(f) The boards revised both IFRS 3's and SFAS 141's disclosures about contingencies, at the acquisition date and subsequently, to make them consistent with the requirement of the revised standards on assets and liabilities arising from contingencies. The IASB's and the FASB's disclosures on contingencies differ because the recognition requirements to which they relate differ. (paragraphs BC265–BC278)

(g) The FASB added to SFAS 141 disclosure of the amount of acquisition-related costs, which IFRS 3 already required, and the boards added to both IFRS 3 and SFAS 141 disclosure of the amount of acquisition-related costs recognised as expense and the statement of comprehensive income line item in which that expense is reported.

(h) The FASB eliminated SFAS 141's requirement to disclose the amount of in-process research and development acquired that had been measured and immediately written off to expense in accordance with FASB Interpretation 4. SFAS 141(R) no longer permits that practice. (paragraphs BC149–BC155)

(i)   The boards added to both IFRS 3 and SFAS 141 disclosure of the acquisition-date fair value or other recognised amount of the non-controlling interest in the acquiree and the valuation techniques and key model inputs used for determining that value. An entity that prepares its financial statements in accordance with IFRSs also discloses the measurement basis selected for the non-controlling interest.

(j)   For a business combination achieved in stages, the boards added to both IFRS 3 and SFAS 141 disclosure of the fair value of the acquirer's previously held equity interest in the acquiree, the amount of gain or loss recognised in accordance with paragraph 42 of the revised IFRS 3 and the line item in the statement of comprehensive income in which that gain or loss is recognised.

(k)   The FASB replaced SFAS 141's disclosure of extraordinary gains recognised for 'negative goodwill' with disclosure of the amount of any gain recognised in the period for a bargain purchase, the line item in the statement of comprehensive income in which it is recognised and a description of the reasons why the transaction resulted in a gain (paragraphs BC371–BC381). IFRS 3 already required disclosure of that amount (although it was not called a gain on a bargain purchase).

(l)   The boards added to both IFRS 3 and SFAS 141 the disclosures described in paragraph B64(l) of the revised IFRS 3 about transactions that are separate from the acquisition of assets and assumption of liabilities in the exchange for the acquiree. The 2005 Exposure Draft proposed requiring disclosures about only pre-existing relationships between the acquirer and acquiree. The boards broadened the disclosure to all separate transactions in response to comments on the exposure draft.

(m)   The boards revised the disclosures in IFRS 3 and SFAS 141 about aspects of the purchase price allocation not yet completed to make them consistent with the requirements of the revised standards about the measurement period. The specific disclosures required are in paragraph B67(a) of the revised IFRS 3.

(n)   The IASB eliminated IFRS 3's required disclosure of the acquiree's carrying amounts in accordance with IFRSs for each class of its assets and liabilities immediately before the combination. The IASB concluded that providing that disclosure could often involve significant costs because the acquiree might not be applying IFRSs and that those costs might exceed the benefits of the information to users.

Disclosure of information about post-combination revenue and profit or loss of the acquiree

BC423   Paragraph B64(q) of the revised IFRS 3 requires an entity to disclose, for each business combination (and for individually immaterial business combinations that are material collectively), the amounts of revenue and profit or loss of the acquiree since the acquisition date included in the consolidated statement of comprehensive income for the period. At its August 2003 round-table discussion with users of financial statements, the FASB discussed the potential usefulness of information about increases or decreases in post-combination revenues and earnings from acquired businesses versus revenues and earnings from the operations already owned by the acquirer (organic growth). The FASB also asked whether that information would be preferable to the pro forma supplemental disclosure of revenue and results of operations of the combined entity for the current period as though the acquisition date for all business combinations during the year had been as of the beginning of the annual reporting period. SFAS 141 carried that disclosure forward from APB Opinion 16 and IFRS 3 required a similar disclosure.

BC424　The FASB also questioned whether those disclosures are directed at similar objectives and, if so, whether one may be preferable. The FASB observed that making post-combination distinctions might be too costly or impossible if the operations of the acquiree are integrated with those of the acquirer. Although users acknowledged that point, they indicated that information about actual post-combination revenues and earnings is preferable to the pro forma disclosures and should be required whenever possible. Some also said that distinguishing acquired revenues from organic revenues is most important and suggested that acquirers should be required to provide that information for a twelve-month period following an acquisition rather than only to the end of the annual period.

BC425　The boards agreed with users that the information about post-combination revenues and profit or loss of the acquiree is useful. However, for practical reasons, the boards concluded that the revised standards should provide an exception to that requirement if distinguishing the post-combination earnings of the acquiree from earnings of the combined entity is impracticable. The boards also decided that in those circumstances the acquirer should disclose that fact and the reasons why it is impracticable to provide the post-combination information. The period for that disclosure is limited to the end of the current annual period because the boards concluded that the information needed to provide the disclosure during that period will generally be available. A short period is often required to integrate an acquiree's operations fully with those of the acquirer. The boards also observed that the usefulness of the separate information diminishes as the operations of the acquiree are integrated with the combined entity.

BC426　The FASB proposed in its version of the 2005 Exposure Draft that the post-combination disclosures should focus on *results of operations* rather than on revenues and earnings. *Results of operations* was defined as revenue, income before extraordinary items and the cumulative effect of accounting changes, earnings and earnings per share. In considering the responses to the exposure draft and opportunities for further convergence, the FASB decided to revise its disclosures to focus on revenues and earnings, which is consistent with the related requirements of the IASB. The boards observed that the term *results of operations* is not used or defined in IFRSs; it would thus have been more difficult for the IASB to converge with the disclosures initially proposed by the FASB.

BC427　The FASB considered expanding the disclosure of post-combination revenues and earnings of an acquiree to all entities because the information would be valuable to any investor, not merely investors in public business entities. To do so would also converge with the requirements of the IASB. However, the FASB was concerned about imposing the additional costs on non-public entities because it believes that the benefits to users of those entities would not be sufficient to warrant imposing those costs. The FASB also observed that the IASB has not completed its separate deliberations on its small and medium-sized entities project and thus does not have an established practice of differential disclosure for circumstances in which it is clear that the benefits would be sufficient for some entities but not so clear for all entities. Because of those cost-benefit concerns, the FASB decided not to extend this disclosure requirement to all entities.

BC428   If comparative financial statements are presented, the FASB decided to require disclosure of supplemental pro forma information about the revenue and earnings of the combined entity for the comparable prior reporting period as though the acquisition date for all business combinations during the current year had been the beginning of the comparable prior annual reporting period. The disclosure is required only for public entities and only if practicable. The IASB considered also requiring that disclosure, but it observed that the needed information would be particularly difficult and costly to obtain in the international environment. An entity that prepares its financial statements in accordance with IFRSs might in a given year acquire other entities that had previously applied the domestic reporting requirements of several different countries. Because the IASB did not consider it feasible to require the disclosure in the international environment, the revised IFRS 3 requires only disclosure of revenues and profit or loss for the current reporting period determined as though the acquisition date for all combinations during the period had been as of the beginning of the annual reporting period.

Effective date and transition

BC429   SFAS 141(R) is effective for business combinations for which the acquisition date is on or after the beginning of the first annual reporting period beginning on or after 15 December 2008, ie for 2009 financial statements. The IASB decided to provide a slightly later effective date. The revised IFRS 3 is effective for business combinations for which the acquisition date is on or after the beginning of the first annual reporting period beginning on or after 1 July 2009. The IASB made a commitment to its constituents that there would be a transition period of approximately 18 months between the publication date and the effective date of the revised IFRS 3 as part of its commitment to have a period of stability following the initial transition to IFRSs. The FASB decided to make SFAS 141(R) effective as soon as practicable, ie for 2009 financial statements. The FASB believes that that effective date provides sufficient time for entities and their auditors to analyse, interpret and prepare for implementation of the provisions of SFAS 141(R).

BC430   The boards also concluded that the effective date of the revised standards should be the same as that of the amendments to their respective consolidation standards (FASB Statement No. 160 *Noncontrolling Interests in Consolidated Financial Statements* and the IASB's amendments to IAS 27). Particular provisions in those amendments, which address the subsequent accounting for an acquiree in consolidated financial statements, are related to provisions in the revised standards that address the initial accounting for an acquiree at the acquisition date.[33] The boards concluded that linking the timing of the changes in accounting required by those amendments to those required by the revised standards would minimise disruptions to practice, which benefits both preparers and users of financial statements.

BC431   SFAS 141(R) prohibits early application and the revised IFRS 3 permits early application. The FASB's Investors Technical Advisory Committee and other users of financial statements told the FASB that providing alternatives for when entities adopt a new standard impairs comparability. The IASB observed, however, that the changes to IFRS 3 are less extensive than the changes to SFAS 141. In addition, the IASB observed that IAS 27 is silent on the accounting for changes in controlling ownership interests in a subsidiary and it wanted entities to be able to adopt the guidance in the amended IAS 27 as soon as it is published. Accordingly, the IASB retained the proposal in the 2005 Exposure Draft to permit entities to adopt the revised IFRS 3 early if they so choose.

BC432   The IASB and the FASB also concluded that the revised standards should be applied prospectively. As with most other requirements that relate to particular types of transactions, applying the revised standards retrospectively would not be feasible.

Effective date and transition for combinations of mutual entities or by contract alone

BC433   IFRS 3 excluded from its scope combinations of mutual entities and those achieved by contract alone. In developing IFRS 3, the IASB decided that these combinations should be excluded from its scope until the IASB published interpretative guidance for the application of the acquisition method to those transactions. The revised IFRS 3 provides that guidance. The effective date for combinations of mutual entities and those achieved by contract alone is the same as the effective date for all other entities applying the revised IFRS 3.

BC434   For the reasons outlined in paragraph BC180 of IFRS 3 the IASB concluded that the transitional provisions for combinations involving mutual entities only or those achieved by contract alone should be prospective. Given that these combinations were not within the scope of IFRS 3, they may have been accounted for differently from what IFRS 3 required. The transitional provisions in IFRS 3 took into consideration that entities may have used a range of alternatives in accounting for combinations in the past. The IASB concluded that the transitional provisions for these combinations should incorporate the transitional provisions in IFRS 3 for other business combinations. In addition, the IASB concluded that the transitional provisions should provide that an entity should continue to classify prior combinations in accordance with its previous accounting for such combinations. This is consistent with the prospective approach. Those provisions are contained in paragraphs B68 and B69 of the revised IFRS 3.

---

33   The consolidation requirements in IAS 27 were superseded by IFRS 10 *Consolidated Financial Statements* issued in May 2011. The requirements for the subsequent accounting for an acquiree in consolidated financial statements were not changed.

Transition requirements for contingent consideration from a business combination that occurred before the effective date of IFRS 3 (as revised in 2008)

BC434A   In *Improvements to IFRSs* issued in May 2010, the Board addressed a perceived conflict in the guidance on accounting for contingent consideration in a business combination. The perceived conflict related to the transition guidance for contingent consideration arising from business combinations that had been accounted for in accordance with IFRS 3 (as issued in 2004). Before their deletion in January 2008, paragraph 3(c) of IFRS 7, paragraph 4(c) of IAS 32 and paragraph 2(f) of IAS 39[34] excluded contingent consideration arrangements from the scope of those IFRSs. To allow the acquirer to account for contingent consideration as required by IFRS 3 (revised 2008), the Board deleted those scope exceptions in the second phase of its project on business combinations.

BC434B   Some interpreted the deletion of the scope exception as meaning that IAS 39 would apply to all contingent consideration, including contingent consideration from business combinations with an acquisition date earlier than the application date of IFRS 3 (revised 2008). However, this interpretation is inconsistent with the transition guidance in paragraph 65 of IFRS 3 (revised 2008).

BC434C   Therefore, the Board reproduced paragraphs 32–35 of IFRS 3 (as issued in 2004) as paragraphs 65B–65E in IFRS 3 (revised 2008) and made the conforming changes to IFRS 7, IAS 32 and IAS 39. The Board did this to clarify that the requirements in IAS 39 do not apply to contingent consideration that arose from a business combination whose acquisition date preceded the application of IFRS 3 (revised 2008) and to provide guidance on how to account for such balances. The Board believes that the amendments will not cause IFRS 3 to diverge from FASB ASC Topic 805 *Business Combinations* (SFAS 141(R) *Business Combinations*).

Effective date and transition for clarifications of the accounting for contingent consideration that arises from business combinations

BC434D   *Annual Improvements to IFRSs 2010–2012 Cycle*, issued in December 2013, clarifies the accounting for contingent consideration that arises from business combinations. The IASB considered whether the transition provisions of paragraph 19 in IAS 8 should apply, which require retrospective application. The IASB considered that the amendments required fair value measurement, and that some entities might not have previously applied fair value measurement for the subsequent measurement of contingent consideration. Retrospective application might therefore require the determination of fair value for contingent consideration, which might not have been previously measured at fair value following initial recognition. It may be impracticable for an entity to determine the fair value of such contingent consideration without using hindsight. Consequently, the IASB decided to require prospective application to avoid the risk of hindsight being applied. The IASB also decided

---

34   IFRS 9 *Financial Instruments* replaced IAS 39. IFRS 9 applies to all items that were previously within the scope of IAS 39.

© IFRS Foundation

on a 1 July 2014 mandatory effective date for the amendments to IFRS 3 and the consequential amendments to IAS 37 as well as to IFRS 9 and IAS 39, depending on the financial instruments Standard that is applied by the entity at the time that this amendment becomes effective.

Scope exceptions for joint ventures

BC434E   *Annual Improvements Cycle 2011–2013* issued in December 2013 amended paragraph 2(a) and added paragraph 64J to clarify the scope exception in paragraph 2(a) of IFRS 3. It took into consideration the transition provisions and effective date of the amendment to IFRS 3. In order to be consistent with the prospective initial application of IFRS 3, the IASB decided that an entity shall apply the amendment to IFRS 3 prospectively for annual periods beginning on or after 1 July 2014.

Benefits and costs

BC435   The objective of financial statements is to provide information about the financial position, performance and changes in financial position of an entity that is useful to a wide range of users in making economic decisions. However, the benefits derived from information should exceed the cost of providing it. The evaluation of benefits and costs is substantially a judgemental process. Furthermore, the costs do not necessarily fall on those who enjoy the benefits. For these reasons, it is difficult to apply a cost-benefit test in any particular case. In making its judgement, the IASB considers:

(a)   the costs incurred by preparers of financial statements;

(b)   the costs incurred by users of financial statements when information is not available;

(c)   the comparative advantage that preparers have in developing information, when compared with the costs that users would incur to develop surrogate information; and

(d)   the benefit of better economic decision-making as a result of improved financial reporting.

In the second phase of the business combinations project the IASB also considered the costs and benefits of the revised IFRS 3 relative to IFRS 3.

BC436   The IASB concluded that the revised IFRS 3 benefits both preparers and users of financial statements by converging to common high quality, understandable and enforceable accounting standards for business combinations in IFRSs and US GAAP. This improves the comparability of financial information around the world and it also simplifies and reduces the costs of accounting for entities that issue financial statements in accordance with both IFRSs and US GAAP.

BC437   The revised IFRS 3 builds on the core principles established by IFRS 3. However, the IASB sought to improve the understandability, relevance, reliability and comparability of information provided to users of financial statements as follows:

(a) **Scope**

The revised IFRS 3 has a broader scope than IFRS 3. Those entities that will now be required to apply the acquisition method might incur additional costs to obtain valuations and account for intangible assets and goodwill after the acquisition date. However, the IASB observes that much of the information required to account for a business combination by applying the acquisition method is already prepared by those entities that are currently applying the pooling of interests method. There might be additional costs associated with presenting this information within the financial statements, such as audit costs, but much of the information will already be available to management. The IASB concluded therefore that the benefits of improved comparability and faithful representation outweigh the costs that those entities will incur.

(b) **Non-controlling interest**

Paragraph 19 of the revised IFRS 3 provides preparers of financial statements with a choice for each business combination to measure initially a non-controlling interest either at fair value or as the non-controlling interest's proportionate share of the acquiree's identifiable net assets. Paragraphs BC209–BC221 discuss the benefits and costs associated with granting a choice on how non-controlling interests should be measured.

(c) **Contingent consideration**

Paragraph 58 of the revised IFRS 3 requires contingent consideration that is classified as a liability and is within the scope of IAS 39[35] to be remeasured to fair value (or for those within the scope of IAS 37 or another IFRS, to be accounted for in accordance with that IFRS)[36] and that contingent consideration classified as equity is not remeasured. The IASB understands that remeasuring the fair value of contingent consideration after the acquisition date results in additional costs to preparers. Preparers will need to measure the fair value of these arrangements or will need to obtain external valuations at the end of each reporting period. However, users have stated that the information they receive under IFRS 3 is too late to be useful. The IASB concluded therefore that the benefits of relevance and representational faithfulness and the increased information that would be provided to users outweigh the costs.

(d) **Acquisition-related costs**

Paragraph 53 of the revised IFRS 3 requires the costs the acquirer incurs in connection with a business combination to be accounted for separately from the business combination. The IASB concluded that this treatment would improve the understandability of the information

---

35 IFRS 9 *Financial Instruments* replaced IAS 39. IFRS 9 applies to all items that were previously within the scope of IAS 39.

36 *Annual Improvements to IFRSs 2010–2012 Cycle*, issued in December 2013, amended IFRS 3, IFRS 9, IAS 37 and IAS 39 to clarify that contingent consideration in a business combination that is classified as an asset or a liability shall be subsequently measured at fair value with changes in fair value recognised in profit or loss.

provided to users of financial statements. The IASB observed that the new requirement does not create significant additional costs for preparers of financial statements because paragraph 67(d) of IFRS 3 already required disclosure of acquisition-related costs.

(e) **Business combinations achieved in stages**

The revised IFRS 3 establishes the acquisition date as the single measurement date for all assets acquired, liabilities assumed and any non-controlling interest in the acquiree.

In a business combination achieved in stages, the acquirer also remeasures its previously held equity interest in the acquiree at its acquisition-date fair value and recognises the resulting gain or loss, if any, in profit or loss. In contrast, IFRS 3 required that for a business combination achieved in stages each exchange transaction should be treated separately by the acquirer, using the cost of the transaction and fair value information at the date of each exchange transaction, to determine the amount of any goodwill associated with that transaction. Therefore, the previous treatment required a comparison of the cost of the individual investments with the acquirer's interest in the fair values of the acquiree's identifiable assets and liabilities at each step. The IASB concluded that the revised treatment of business combinations achieved in stages would improve understandability and relevance of the information provided as well as reduce the cost of accounting for such transactions.

BC438   The IASB concluded that the guidance in the revised IFRS 3 is not unduly complex. Indeed, it eliminates guidance that many have found to be complex, costly and arbitrary and that has been the source of considerable uncertainties and costs in the marketplace. Moreover, the revised IFRS 3 does not introduce a new method of accounting but rather expands the use of the acquisition-method of accounting that is familiar, has been widely used and for which there is a substantial base of experience. However, the IASB also sought to reduce the costs of applying the revised IFRS 3 by:

(a) requiring particular assets and liabilities (eg those related to deferred taxes and employee benefits) to continue to be measured in accordance with existing accounting standards rather than at fair value;

(b) carrying over the basic requirements of IFRS 3 on contingent liabilities assumed in a business combination into the revised IFRS 3 until the IASB has comprehensively reconsidered the accounting for contingencies in its liabilities project; and

(c) requiring the revised IFRS 3 to be applied prospectively rather than retrospectively.

BC439   The IASB acknowledges that those steps may result in some sacrifice to the benefits of improved information in financial statements in accordance with the revised IFRS 3. However, the IASB concluded that the complexities and related costs that would result from applying the fair value measurement requirement to all assets and liabilities, at this time, and requiring retrospective application are not justified.

Appendix
Amendments to the Basis for Conclusions on other IFRSs

This appendix contains amendments to the Basis for Conclusions on other IFRSs that are necessary in order to ensure consistency with IFRS 3 (as revised in 2008) and the related amendments to other IFRSs. Amended paragraphs are shown with new text underlined and deleted text struck through.

* * * * *

The amendments contained in this appendix when the revised IFRS 3 was issued in 2008 have been incorporated into the text of the Basis for Conclusions on IFRSs 2, 4 and 5 and on IASs 36 and 38 as issued at 10 January 2008.

Dissenting opinions

Dissent of Mary E Barth, Robert P Garnett and John T Smith

DO1   Professor Barth and Messrs Garnett and Smith dissent from the publication of IFRS 3 *Business Combinations* (as revised in 2008), for the reasons set out below.

Measurement of non-controlling interest

DO2   Professor Barth and Mr Smith disagree with the Board's decision to make an exception to the IFRS's measurement principle and permit acquirers a free choice, acquisition by acquisition, to measure any non-controlling interest in an acquiree as the non-controlling interest's proportionate share of the acquiree's identifiable net assets, rather than at fair value (paragraph 19 of the IFRS).

DO3   Professor Barth and Mr Smith agree with the measurement principle as explained in paragraph BC207 that the acquirer should recognise the identifiable assets acquired, the liabilities assumed and any non-controlling interest in the acquiree at their acquisition-date fair values. Paragraph BC209 indicates that the Board also supports this principle, but decided to make an exception. Professor Barth and Mr Smith support the Board's general view that exceptions should be avoided because they undermine principle-based standards, but understand that they are necessary in well-justified circumstances. Professor Barth and Mr Smith do not believe that an exception to this principle, with a free choice in applying it, is justified in this situation.

DO4   First, Professor Barth and Mr Smith are among those Board members mentioned in paragraph BC213 who believe that non-controlling interests can be measured reliably. Second, Professor Barth and Mr Smith believe that the benefits of consistently measuring all assets acquired and liabilities assumed outweigh the costs involved in conducting the measurement. To address concerns about costs exceeding benefits in particular acquisitions, they would have supported an exception to the principle based on undue cost or effort. Such an exception would not have been a free choice, but would have required assessment of the facts and circumstances associated with the acquisition. Professor Barth and Mr Smith disagree with the Board's decision to permit a free choice, rather than to adopt such an exception. They also disagree with the Board's decision not to require fair value measurement even for acquisitions of listed acquirees, for which the cost would be nil. Third, a consequence of failure to measure non-controlling interests at fair value is that acquired goodwill is not measured at fair value. In addition to being an exception to the IFRS's measurement principle, this has several undesirable effects beyond the initial accounting for goodwill. The Board acknowledges these in paragraphs BC217 and BC218. In particular, if goodwill is impaired the impairment loss is understated, and if the acquirer subsequently purchases more of the non-controlling interests equity is reduced more than it would be had goodwill been measured initially at fair value. Fourth, based on staff research, the choice will benefit only a minority of acquirers because most acquisitions are for 100 per cent of the acquiree. As noted above, any benefit is reduced if such acquirers subsequently impair goodwill or acquire more of the non-controlling interest because of the resulting anomalous accounting results.

DO5 Professor Barth and Mr Smith agree with the Board that permitting entities a choice between alternative accounting methods impairs comparability, as noted in paragraph BC210. They disagree with the Board's decision not to support a single method, particularly a method consistent with the IFRS's measurement principle. However, Professor Barth and Mr Smith disagree with the Board that the benefits of other changes to the IFRS outweigh the disadvantages of permitting entities that acquire less than 100 per cent of an acquiree a free choice as to how to account for the acquisition. Although Professor Barth and Mr Smith agree with the other changes to IFRS 3, they believe that these changes are not as important as having a consistent measurement principle.

DO6 In addition to improving the accounting for business combinations, a primary goal of the business combinations project was to achieve convergence between IFRS 3 and FASB Statement No. 141 (revised 2007) *Business Combinations* (SFAS 141(R)). Professor Barth and Mr Smith strongly support that goal. The Board's decision to make the exception to the measurement principle for non-controlling interests creates a divergence from SFAS 141(R). Both the FASB and the IASB made compromises to achieve a converged result in other aspects of the IFRS, and the FASB made a number of changes to its standard that conform to IFRS 3 (as issued in 2004). Professor Barth and Mr Smith believe that the Board's compromise on this particular issue diminishes the importance of convergence, establishes a precedent for allowing a choice when the two boards cannot reach agreement and may suggest that full convergence in the long term cannot be achieved. This is particularly concerning for this decision given that the Board supports the principle underlying the FASB's answer, there are comparability costs inherent in a free choice of accounting methods and there are likely to be few benefits arising from the exception.

DO7 Mr Garnett dissents from the issue of the IFRS because it both establishes a measurement principle for non-controlling interests with which he disagrees, and permits an exception to that principle. Whilst the exception permits the accounting that he considers appropriate, the use of alternative accounting methods reduces the comparability of financial statements.

DO8 Mr Garnett observes that the application of the measurement principle that an acquirer should measure the components of a business combination, including non-controlling interests, at their acquisition-date fair values results in the recognition of not only the purchased goodwill attributable to the acquirer as a result of the acquisition transaction, but also the goodwill attributable to the non-controlling interest in the acquiree. This is often referred to as the 'full goodwill' method.

DO9 Mr Garnett considers that goodwill is unlike other assets since it cannot be identified separately, or measured directly. Purchased goodwill is a residual resulting from a calculation that absorbs the effects of recognition and measurement exceptions made in the IFRS (such as the accounting for employee benefit plans and deferred taxes) and any differences between an entry price used in valuing the business as a whole and the valuation of the individual assets and liabilities acquired.

DO10　　Mr Garnett notes that the 'parent-only' approach to goodwill in the previous version of IFRS 3 (as issued in 2004) avoids this difficulty by measuring goodwill as the difference between the fair value of the consideration paid by the parent for the acquiree and its share of the fair value of the identifiable net assets of the acquiree. Thus, purchased goodwill is the amount implicit in the acquisition transaction and excludes any goodwill attributable to non-controlling interests. This method gives rise to more reliable measurement because it is based on the purchase consideration, which can usually be reliably measured, and it reflects faithfully the acquisition transaction to which the non-controlling interests were not a party.

A business combination achieved in stages

DO11　　Mr Garnett disagrees with the requirement in a business combination achieved in stages to recognise the effect of remeasuring any previously-held equity interest in the acquiree to fair value through profit or loss (paragraph 42 of the IFRS), because that investment was not part of the exchange. Mr Garnett agrees that gaining control is a significant economic event that warrants a change from investment accounting to consolidation. However, the previous investment has not been sold. Under current IFRSs, gains and losses on cost method, available-for-sale and equity method investments are recognised in profit or loss only when the investment is sold (other than impairment). Mr Garnett would have recognised the effect of those remeasurements as a separate component of other comprehensive income instead of profit or loss.

IASB documents published to accompany

IFRS 4

Insurance Contracts

The text of the unaccompanied standard, IFRS 4, is contained in Part A of this edition. Its effective date when issued was 1 January 2005. The text of the Accompanying Guidance on IFRS 4 is contained in Part B of this edition. This part presents the following documents:

BASIS FOR CONCLUSIONS

DISSENTING OPINIONS

CONTENTS

Basis for Conclusions on
IFRS 4 *Insurance Contracts*

This Basis for Conclusions accompanies, but is not part of, IFRS 4.

Introduction

BC1   This Basis for Conclusions summarises the International Accounting Standards Board's considerations in reaching the conclusions in IFRS 4 *Insurance Contracts*. Individual Board members gave greater weight to some factors than to others.

Background

BC2   The Board decided to develop an International Financial Reporting Standard (IFRS) on insurance contracts because:

    (a)   there was no IFRS on insurance contracts, and insurance contracts were excluded from the scope of existing IFRSs that would otherwise have been relevant (eg IFRSs on provisions, financial instruments and intangible assets).

    (b)   accounting practices for insurance contracts were diverse, and also often differed from practices in other sectors.

BC3   The Board's predecessor organisation, the International Accounting Standards Committee (IASC), set up a Steering Committee in 1997 to carry out the initial work on this project. In December 1999, the Steering Committee published an *Issues Paper*, which attracted 138 comment letters. The Steering Committee reviewed the comment letters and concluded its work by developing a report to the Board in the form of a *Draft Statement of Principles* (DSOP). The Board started discussing the DSOP in November 2001. The Board did not approve the DSOP or invite formal comments on it, but made it available to the public on the IASB's Website.

BC4   Few insurers report using IFRSs at present, although many more are expected to do so from 2005. Because it was not feasible to complete this project for implementation in 2005, the Board split the project into two phases so that insurers could implement some aspects in 2005. The Board published its proposals for phase I in July 2003 as ED 5 *Insurance Contracts*. The deadline for comments was 31 October 2003 and the Board received 135 responses. After reviewing the responses, the Board issued IFRS 4 in March 2004.

BC5   The Board's objectives for phase I were:

    (a)   to make limited improvements to accounting practices for insurance contracts, without requiring major changes that may need to be reversed in phase II.

    (b)   to require disclosure that (i) identifies and explains the amounts in an insurer's financial statements arising from insurance contracts and (ii) helps users of those financial statements understand the amount, timing and uncertainty of future cash flows from insurance contracts.

Tentative conclusions for phase II

BC6　The Board sees phase I as a stepping stone to phase II and is committed to completing phase II without delay once it has investigated all relevant conceptual and practical questions and completed its due process. In January 2003, the Board reached the following tentative conclusions for phase II:

    (a)　The approach should be an asset-and-liability approach that would require an entity to identify and measure directly the contractual rights and obligations arising from insurance contracts, rather than create deferrals of inflows and outflows.

    (b)　Assets and liabilities arising from insurance contracts should be measured at their fair value, with the following two caveats:

        (i)　Recognising the lack of market transactions, an entity may use entity-specific assumptions and information when market-based information is not available without undue cost and effort.

        (ii)　In the absence of market evidence to the contrary, the estimated fair value of an insurance liability shall not be less, but may be more, than the entity would charge to accept new contracts with identical contractual terms and remaining maturity from new policyholders. It follows that an insurer would not recognise a net gain at inception of an insurance contract, unless such market evidence is available.

    (c)　As implied by the definition of fair value:[1]

        (i)　an undiscounted measure is inconsistent with fair value.

        (ii)　expectations about the performance of assets should not be incorporated into the measurement of an insurance contract, directly or indirectly (unless the amounts payable to a policyholder depend on the performance of specific assets).

        (iii)　the measurement of fair value should include an adjustment for the premium that marketplace participants would demand for risks and mark-up in addition to the expected cash flows.

        (iv)　fair value measurement of an insurance contract should reflect the credit characteristics of that contract, including the effect of policyholder protections and insurance provided by governmental bodies or other guarantors.

    (d)　The measurement of contractual rights and obligations associated with the closed book of insurance contracts should include future premiums specified in the contracts (and claims, benefits, expenses, and other additional cash flows resulting from those premiums) if, and only if:

1　IFRS 13 *Fair Value Measurement*, issued in May 2011, defines fair value and contains the requirements for measuring fair value.

       (i)   policyholders hold non-cancellable continuation or renewal rights that significantly constrain the insurer's ability to reprice the contract to rates that would apply for new policyholders whose characteristics are similar to those of the existing policyholders; and

       (ii)   those rights will lapse if the policyholders stop paying premiums.

(e) Acquisition costs should be recognised as an expense when incurred.

(f) The Board will consider two more questions later in phase II:

       (i)   Should the measurement model unbundle the individual elements of an insurance contract and measure them individually?

       (ii)   How should an insurer measure its liability to holders of participating contracts?

BC7 In two areas, those tentative conclusions differ from the IASC Steering Committee's recommendations in the DSOP:

(a) the use of a fair value measurement objective rather than entity-specific value. However, that change is not as significant as it might seem because entity-specific value as described in the DSOP is indistinguishable in most respects from estimates of fair value determined using measurement guidance that the Board has tentatively adopted in phase II of its project on business combinations.[2]

(b) the criteria used to determine whether measurement should reflect future premiums and related cash flows (paragraph BC6(d)).

BC8 Since January 2003, constraints on Board and staff resources have prevented the Board from continuing work to determine whether its tentative conclusions for phase II can be developed into a standard that is consistent with the IASB *Framework*[3] and workable in practice. The Board intends to return to phase II of the project in the second quarter of 2004. It plans to focus at that time on both conceptual and practical issues, as in any project. Only after completing its deliberations will the Board proceed with an Exposure Draft of a proposed IFRS. The Board's deliberations in all projects include a consideration of alternatives and whether those alternatives represent conceptually superior approaches to financial reporting issues. Consequently, the Board will examine existing practices throughout the world to ascertain whether any could be deemed to be a superior answer suitable for international adoption.

---

2   The Board completed the second phase of its project on business combinations in 2008 by issuing a revised IFRS 3 *Business Combinations* and an amended version of IAS 27 *Consolidated and Separate Financial Statements*. The consolidation requirements in IAS 27 were superseded by IFRS 10 *Consolidated Financial Statements* issued in May 2011. IFRS 13, issued in May 2011, defines fair value and contains the requirements for measuring fair value.

3   References to the *Framework* are to IASC's *Framework for the Preparation and Presentation of Financial Statements*, adopted by the IASB in 2001. In September 2010 the IASB replaced the *Framework* with the *Conceptual Framework for Financial Reporting*.

BC9 As discussed in paragraph BC84, ED 5 proposed a 'sunset clause', which the Board deleted in finalising the IFRS. Although respondents generally opposed the sunset clause, many applauded the Board's signal of its commitment to complete phase II without delay.

Scope

BC10 Some argued that the IFRS should deal with all aspects of financial reporting by insurers, to ensure that the financial reporting for insurers is internally consistent. They noted that regulatory requirements, and some national accounting requirements, often cover all aspects of an insurer's business. However, for the following reasons, the IFRS deals with insurance contracts of all entities and does not address other aspects of accounting by insurers:

(a) It would be difficult, and perhaps impossible, to create a robust definition of an insurer that could be applied consistently from country to country. Among other things, an increasing number of entities have major activities in both insurance and other areas.

(b) It would be undesirable for an insurer to account for a transaction in one way and for a non-insurer to account in a different way for the same transaction.

(c) The project should not reopen issues addressed by other IFRSs, unless specific features of insurance contracts justify a different treatment. Paragraphs BC166–BC180 discuss the treatment of assets backing insurance contracts.

Definition of insurance contract

BC11 The definition of an insurance contract determines which contracts are within the scope of IFRS 4 rather than other IFRSs. Some argued that phase I should use existing national definitions of insurance contracts, on the following grounds:

(a) Before phase II gives guidance on applying IAS 39 *Financial Instruments: Recognition and Measurement*[4] to difficult areas such as discretionary participation features and cancellation and renewal rights, it would be premature to require insurers to apply IAS 39 to contracts that contain these features and rights.

(b) The definition adopted for phase I may need to be amended again for phase II. This could compel insurers to make extensive changes twice in a short time.

BC12 However, in the Board's view, it is unsatisfactory to base the definition used in IFRSs on local definitions that may vary from country to country and may not be most relevant for deciding which IFRS ought to apply to a particular type of contract.

BC13 Some expressed concerns that the adoption of a particular definition by the IASB could lead ultimately to inappropriate changes in definitions used for other

---

4 IFRS 9 *Financial Instruments* replaced IAS 39. IFRS 9 applies to all items that were previously within the scope of IAS 39.

purposes, such as insurance law, insurance supervision or tax. The Board emphasises that any definition used in IFRSs is solely for financial reporting and is not intended to change or pre-empt definitions used for other purposes.

BC14　Various Standards issued by IASC used definitions or descriptions of insurance contracts to exclude insurance contracts from their scope. The scope of IAS 37 *Provisions, Contingent Liabilities and Contingent Assets* and of IAS 38 *Intangible Assets* excluded provisions, contingent liabilities, contingent assets and intangible assets that arise in insurance enterprises from contracts with policyholders. IASC used this wording when its insurance project had just started, to avoid prejudging whether the project would address insurance contracts or a broader class of contracts. Similarly, the scope of IAS 18 *Revenue*[5] excluded revenue arising from insurance contracts of insurance enterprises.

BC15　The following definition of insurance contracts was used to exclude insurance contracts from the scope of an earlier version of IAS 32 *Financial Instruments: Disclosure and Presentation* and IAS 39.

> An insurance contract is a contract that exposes the insurer to identified risks of loss from events or circumstances occurring or discovered within a specified period, including death (in the case of an annuity, the survival of the annuitant), sickness, disability, property damage, injury to others and business interruption.

BC16　This definition was supplemented by a statement that IAS 32 and IAS 39 did, nevertheless, apply when a financial instrument 'takes the form of an insurance contract but principally involves the transfer of financial risks.'

BC17　For the following reasons, the Board discarded the previous definition in IAS 32 and IAS 39:

(a)　The definition gave a list of examples, but did not define the characteristics of the risks that it was intended to include.

(b)　A clearer definition reduces the uncertainty about the meaning of the phrase 'principally involves the transfer of financial risks'. This will help insurers adopting IFRSs for the first-time ('first-time adopters') in 2005 and minimises the likelihood of further changes in classification for phase II. Furthermore, the previous test could have led to many contracts being classified as financial instruments even though they transfer significant insurance risk.

BC18　In developing a new definition, the Board also considered US GAAP. The main FASB statements for insurers deal with financial reporting by insurance entities and do not define insurance contracts explicitly. However, paragraph 1 of SFAS 113 *Accounting and Reporting for Reinsurance of Short-Duration and Long-Duration Contracts* states:

> Insurance provides indemnification against loss or liability from specified events and circumstances that may occur or be discovered during a specified period. In exchange for a payment from the policyholder (a premium), an insurance enterprise agrees to pay the policyholder if specified events occur or are discovered.

5　IFRS 15 *Revenue from Contracts with Customers*, issued in May 2014, replaced IAS 18 *Revenue*. IFRS 15 also excludes from its scope revenue arising from insurance contracts.

BC19   Paragraph 6 of SFAS 113 applies to any transaction, regardless of its form, that indemnifies an insurer against loss or liability relating to insurance risk. The glossary appended to SFAS 113 defines insurance risk as:

> The risk arising from uncertainties about both (a) the ultimate amount of net cash flows from premiums, commissions, claims, and claim settlement expenses paid under a contract (often referred to as underwriting risk) and (b) the timing of the receipt and payment of those cash flows (often referred to as timing risk). Actual or imputed investment returns are not an element of insurance risk. Insurance risk is fortuitous—the possibility of adverse events occurring is outside the control of the insured.

BC20   Having reviewed these definitions from US GAAP, the Board developed a new definition of insurance contract for the IFRS and expects to use the same definition for phase II. The following aspects of the definition are discussed below:

(a)   insurance risk (paragraphs BC21–BC24);

(b)   insurable interest (paragraphs BC25–BC29);

(c)   quantity of insurance risk (paragraphs BC30–BC37);

(d)   expiry of insurance-contingent rights and obligations (paragraphs BC38 and BC39);

(e)   unbundling (paragraphs BC40–BC54); and

(f)   weather derivatives (paragraphs BC55–BC60).

Insurance risk

BC21   The definition of an insurance contract in the IFRS focuses on the feature that causes accounting problems unique to insurance contracts, namely insurance risk. The definition of insurance risk excludes financial risk, defined using a list of risks that also appears in IAS 39's[6] definition of a derivative.

BC22   Some contracts have the legal form of insurance contracts but do not transfer significant insurance risk to the issuer. Some argue that all such contracts should be treated as insurance contracts, for the following reasons:

(a)   These contracts are traditionally described as insurance contracts and are generally subject to regulation by insurance supervisors.

(b)   Phase I will not achieve great comparability between insurers because it will permit a diverse range of treatments for insurance contracts. It would be preferable to ensure consistency at least within a single insurer.

---

6   IFRS 9 *Financial Instruments* replaced IAS 39. IFRS 9 applies to all items that were previously within the scope of IAS 39.

(c)   Accounting for some contracts under IAS 39[7] and others under local GAAP is unhelpful to users. Moreover, some argued that IAS 39 contains insufficient, and possibly inappropriate, guidance for investment contracts.[8]

(d)   The guidance proposed in ED 5 on significant insurance risk was too vague, would be applied inconsistently and relied on actuarial resources in short supply in many countries.

BC23   However, as explained in the *Framework*, financial statements should reflect economic substance and not merely legal form. Furthermore, accounting arbitrage could occur if the addition of an insignificant amount of insurance risk made a significant difference to the accounting. Therefore, the Board decided that contracts described in the previous paragraph should not be treated as insurance contracts for financial reporting.

BC24   Some respondents suggested that an insurance contract is any contract under which the policyholder exchanges a fixed amount (ie the premium) for an amount payable if an insured event occurs. However, not all insurance contracts have explicit premiums (eg insurance cover bundled with some credit card contracts). Adding a reference to premiums would have introduced no more clarity and might have required more supporting guidance and explanations.

Insurable interest

BC25   In some countries, the legal definition of insurance requires that the policyholder or other beneficiary should have an insurable interest in the insured event. For the following reasons, the definition proposed in 1999 by the former IASC Steering Committee in the Issues Paper did not refer to insurable interest:

(a)   Insurable interest is defined in different ways in different countries. Also, it is difficult to find a simple definition of insurable interest that is adequate for such different types of insurance as insurance against fire, term life insurance and annuities.

(b)   Contracts that require payment if a specified uncertain future event occurs cause similar types of economic exposure, whether or not the other party has an insurable interest.

BC26   Because the definition proposed in the Issues Paper did not include a notion of insurable interest, it would have encompassed gambling. Several commentators on the Issues Paper stressed the important social, moral, legal and regulatory differences between insurance and gambling. They noted that policyholders buy insurance to reduce risk, whereas gamblers take on risk (unless they use a gambling contract as a hedge). In the light of these comments, the definition of an insurance contract in the IFRS incorporates the notion of insurable interest. Specifically, it refers to the fact that the insurer accepts risk from the policyholder by agreeing to compensate the policyholder if an uncertain event

---

7   IFRS 9 *Financial Instruments* replaced IAS 39. IFRS 9 applies to all items that were previously within the scope of IAS 39.

8   'Investment contract' is an informal term referring to a contract issued by an insurer that does not expose the insurer to significant insurance risk and is therefore within the scope of IAS 39.

adversely affects the policyholder. The notion of insurable interest also appears in the definition of financial risk, which refers to a non-financial variable not specific to a party to the contract.

BC27 This reference to an adverse effect is open to the objections set out in paragraph BC25. However, without this reference, the definition of an insurance contract might have captured any prepaid contract to provide services whose cost is uncertain (see paragraphs BC74–BC76 for further discussion). This would have extended the meaning of the term 'insurance contract' too far beyond its traditional meaning.

BC28 Some respondents to ED 5 were opposed to including the notion of insurable interest, on the following grounds:

(a) In life insurance, there is no direct link between the adverse event and the financial loss to the policyholder. Moreover, it is not clear that survival adversely affects an annuitant. Any contract that is contingent on human life should meet the definition of insurance contract.

(b) This notion excludes some contracts that are, in substance, used as insurance, such as weather derivatives (see paragraphs BC55–BC60 for further discussion). The test should be whether there is a reasonable expectation of some indemnification to policyholders. A tradable contract could be brought within the scope of IAS 39.[9]

(c) It would be preferable to eliminate the notion of insurable interest and replace it with the notion that insurance is a business that involves assembling risks into a pool that is managed together.

BC29 The Board decided to retain the notion of insurable interest because it gives a principle-based distinction, particularly between insurance contracts and other contracts that happen to be used for hedging. Furthermore, it is preferable to base a distinction on the type of contract, rather than the way an entity manages a contract or group of contracts. Moreover, the Board decided that it was unnecessary to refine this notion for a life insurance contract or life-contingent annuity, because such contracts typically provide for a predetermined amount to quantify the adverse effect (see paragraph B13 of the IFRS).

Quantity of insurance risk

BC30 Paragraphs B22–B28 of Appendix B of the IFRS discuss how much insurance risk must be present before a contract qualifies as an insurance contract. In developing this material, the Board noted the conditions in US GAAP for a contract to be treated as an insurance contract. SFAS 113 requires two conditions for a contract to be eligible for reinsurance accounting, rather than deposit accounting:

(a) the contract transfers significant insurance risk from the cedant to the reinsurer (which does not occur if the probability of a significant variation in either the amount or timing of payments by the reinsurer is remote); and

---

9 IFRS 9 *Financial Instruments* replaced IAS 39. IFRS 9 applies to all items that were previously within the scope of IAS 39.

(b)   either:

    (i)   there is a reasonable possibility that the reinsurer will suffer a significant loss (based on the present value of all cash flows between the ceding and assuming enterprises under reasonably possible outcomes); or

    (ii)   the reinsurer has assumed substantially all of the insurance risk relating to the reinsured portions of the underlying insurance contracts (and the cedant has retained only insignificant insurance risk on the reinsured portions).

BC31   Under paragraph 8 of SFAS 97 *Accounting and Reporting by Insurance Enterprises for Certain Long-Duration Contracts and for Realized Gains and Losses from the Sale of Investments*, an annuity contract is considered an insurance contract unless (a) the probability that life contingent payments will be made is remote[10] or (b) the present value of the expected life-contingent payments relative to the present value of all expected payments under the contract is insignificant.

BC32   The Board noted that some practitioners use the following guideline in applying US GAAP: a reasonable possibility of a significant loss is a 10 per cent probability of a 10 per cent loss. In this light, the Board considered whether it should define the amount of insurance risk in quantitative terms in relation to, for example:

    (a)   the probability that payments under the contract will exceed the expected (ie probability-weighted average) level of payments; or

    (b)   a measure of the range of outcomes, such as the range between the highest and lowest level of payments or the standard deviation of payments.

BC33   Quantitative guidance creates an arbitrary dividing line that results in different accounting treatments for similar transactions that fall marginally on different sides of the line. It also creates opportunities for accounting arbitrage by encouraging transactions that fall marginally on one side or the other of the line. For these reasons, the IFRS does not include quantitative guidance.

BC34   The Board also considered whether it should define the significance of insurance risk by referring to materiality, which the *Framework* describes as follows. 'Information is material if its omission or misstatement could influence the economic decisions of users taken on the basis of the financial statements.' However, a single contract, or even a single book of similar contracts, could rarely generate a loss that is material in relation to the financial statements as a whole. Therefore, the IFRS defines the significance of insurance risk in relation to the individual contract (paragraph B25). The Board had two reasons for this:

    (a)   Although insurers manage contracts on a portfolio basis, and often measure them on that basis, the contractual rights and obligations arise from individual contracts.

---

10 Paragraph 8 of SFAS 97 notes that the term remote is defined in paragraph 3 of SFAS 5 *Accounting for Contingencies* as 'the chance of the future event or events occurring is slight.'

(b) An assessment contract by contract is likely to increase the proportion of contracts that qualify as insurance contracts. If a relatively homogeneous book of contracts is known to consist of contracts that all transfer insurance risk, the Board did not intend to require insurers to examine each contract within that book to identify a few non-derivative contracts that transfer insignificant insurance risk (paragraph B25 of the IFRS). The Board intended to make it easier, not harder, for a contract to meet the definition.

BC35 The Board also rejected the notion of defining the significance of insurance risk by expressing the expected (ie probability-weighted) average of the present values of the adverse outcomes as a proportion of the expected present value of all outcomes, or as a proportion of the premium. This notion had some intuitive appeal because it would consider both amount and probability. However, it would have meant that a contract could start as an investment contract (ie a financial liability) and become an insurance contract as time passes or probabilities are reassessed. In the Board's view, requiring continuous monitoring over the life of the contract would be too onerous. Instead, the Board adopted an approach that requires this decision to be made once only, at the inception of a contract. The guidance in paragraphs B22–B28 of the IFRS focuses on whether insured events could cause an insurer to pay additional amounts, judged contract by contract.

BC36 Some respondents objected to ED 5's proposal that insurance risk would be significant if a single plausible event could cause a loss that is more than trivial. They suggested that such a broad notion of significant insurance risk might permit abuse. Instead, they suggested referring to a reasonable possibility of a significant loss. However, the Board rejected this suggestion because it would have required insurers to monitor the level of insurance risk continually, which could have given rise to frequent reclassifications. It might also have been too difficult to apply this notion to remote catastrophic scenarios; indeed, some respondents asked the Board to clarify whether the assessment should include such scenarios. In finalising the IFRS, the Board clarified the terminology by (a) replacing the notion of a plausible scenario with an explanation of the need to ignore scenarios that have no commercial substance and (b) replacing the term 'trivial' with the term 'insignificant'.

BC37 Some respondents asked the Board to clarify the basis of comparison for the significance test, because of uncertainty about the meaning of the phrase 'net cash flows arising from the contract' in ED 5. Some suggested that this would require a comparison with the profit that the issuer expects from the contract. However, the Board had not intended this reading, which would have led to the absurd conclusion that any contract with a profitability of close to zero might qualify as an insurance contract. In finalising the IFRS, the Board confirmed in paragraphs B22–B28 that:

(a) the comparison is between the amounts payable if an insured event occurs and the amounts payable if no insured event occurs. Implementation Guidance in IG Example 1.3 addresses a contract in which the death benefit in a unit-linked contract is 101 per cent of the unit value.

(b)   surrender charges that might be waived on death are not relevant in assessing how much insurance risk a contract transfers because their waiver does not compensate the policyholder for a pre-existing risk. Implementation Guidance in IG Examples 1.23 and 1.24 is relevant.

Expiry of insurance-contingent rights and obligations

BC38   Some respondents suggested that a contract should no longer be treated as an insurance contract after all insurance-contingent rights and obligations have expired. However, this suggestion could have required insurers to set up new systems to identify these contracts. Therefore, paragraph B30 states that an insurance contract remains an insurance contract until all rights and obligations expire. IG Example 2.19 in the Implementation Guidance addresses dual-trigger contracts.

BC39   Some respondents suggested that a contract should not be regarded as an insurance contract if the insurance-contingent rights and obligations expire after a very short time. The IFRS includes material that may be relevant: paragraph B23 explains the need to ignore scenarios that lack commercial substance and paragraph B24(b) notes that there is no significant transfer of pre-existing risk in some contracts that waive surrender penalties on death.

Unbundling

BC40   The definition of an insurance contact distinguishes insurance contracts within the scope of the IFRS from investments and deposits within the scope of IAS 39.[11] However, many insurance contracts contain a significant deposit component (ie a component that would, if it were a separate instrument, be within the scope of IAS 39). Indeed, virtually all insurance contracts have an implicit or explicit deposit component, because the policyholder is generally required to pay premiums before the period of risk; therefore, the time value of money is likely to be one factor that insurers consider in pricing contracts.

BC41   To reduce the need for guidance on the definition of an insurance contract, some argue that an insurer should 'unbundle' the deposit component from the insurance component. Unbundling has the following consequences:

(a)   The insurance component is measured as an insurance contract.

(b)   The deposit component is measured under IAS 39 at either amortised cost or fair value. This might not be consistent with the basis used for insurance contracts.

(c)   Premium receipts for the deposit component are recognised not as revenue, but rather as changes in the deposit liability. Premium receipts for the insurance element are typically recognised as revenue.

(d)   A portion of the transaction costs incurred at inception is allocated to the deposit component if this allocation has a material effect.

BC42   Supporters of unbundling deposit components argue that:

---

11 IFRS 9 *Financial Instruments* replaced IAS 39. IFRS 9 applies to all items that were previously within the scope of IAS 39.

(a)   an entity should account in the same way for the deposit component of an insurance contract as for an otherwise identical financial instrument that does not transfer significant insurance risk.

(b)   the tendency in some countries for banks to own insurers (and vice versa) and the similarity of products offered by the insurance and fund management sectors suggest that insurers, banks and fund managers should account for the deposit component in a similar manner.

(c)   many groups sell products ranging from pure investments to pure insurance, with all variations in between. Unbundling would avoid sharp discontinuities in the accounting between a product that transfers just enough insurance risk to be an insurance contract, and another product that falls marginally on the other side of the line.

(d)   financial statements should make a clear distinction between premium revenue derived from products that transfer significant insurance risk and premium receipts that are, in substance, investment or deposit receipts.

BC43   The Issues Paper published in 1999 proposed that the deposit component should be unbundled if it is either disclosed explicitly to the policyholder or clearly identifiable from the terms of the contract. However, commentators on the Issues Paper generally opposed unbundling, giving the following reasons:

(a)   The components are closely interrelated and the value of the bundled product is not necessarily equal to the sum of the individual values of the components.

(b)   Unbundling would require significant and costly systems changes.

(c)   Contracts of this kind are a single product, regulated as insurance business by insurance supervisors and should be treated in a similar way for financial reporting.

(d)   Some users of financial statements would prefer that either all products are unbundled or no products are unbundled, because they regard information about gross premium inflows as important. A consistent use of a single measurement basis might be more useful as an aid to economic decisions than mixing one measurement basis for the deposit component with another measurement basis for the insurance component.

BC44   In the light of these arguments, the DSOP proposed that an insurer or policyholder should not unbundle these components. However, that was against the background of an assumption that the treatments of the two components would be reasonably similar. This may not be the case in phase I, because phase I permits a wide range of accounting treatments for insurance components. Nevertheless, the Board did not wish to require costly changes in phase I that might be reversed in phase II. Therefore, the Board decided to require unbundling only when it is easiest to perform and the effect is likely to be greatest (paragraphs 10–12 of the IFRS and IG Example 3 in the Implementation Guidance).

BC45   The Board acknowledges that there is no clear conceptual line between the cases when unbundling is required and the cases when unbundling is not required. At one extreme, the Board regards unbundling as appropriate for large customised contracts, such as some financial reinsurance contracts, if a failure to unbundle them could lead to the complete omission from the balance sheet of material contractual rights and obligations. This may be especially important if a contract was deliberately structured to achieve a specific accounting result. Furthermore, the practical problems cited in paragraph BC43 are much less significant for these contracts.

BC46   At the other extreme, unbundling the surrender values in a large portfolio of traditional life insurance contracts would require significant systems changes beyond the intended scope of phase I. Furthermore, failing to unbundle these contracts would affect the measurement of these liabilities, but not lead to their complete omission from the insurer's balance sheet. In addition, a desire to achieve a particular accounting result is much less likely to influence the precise structure of these transactions.

BC47   The option for the policyholder to surrender a traditional life insurance contract at an amount that differs significantly from its carrying amount is an embedded derivative and IAS 39[12] would require the insurer to separate it and measure it at fair value. That treatment would have the same disadvantages, described in the previous paragraph, as unbundling the surrender value. Therefore, paragraph 8 of the IFRS exempts an insurer from applying this requirement to some surrender options embedded in insurance contracts. However, the Board saw no conceptual or practical reason to create such an exemption for surrender options in non-insurance financial instruments issued by insurers or by others.

BC48   Some respondents opposed unbundling in phase I on the following grounds, in addition to the reasons given in paragraph BC43:

      (a)   Insurance contracts are, in general, designed, priced and managed as packages of benefits. Furthermore, the insurer cannot unilaterally terminate the agreement or sell parts of it. In consequence, any unbundling required solely for accounting would be artificial. Insurance contracts should not be unbundled unless the structure of the contract is clearly artificial.

      (b)   Unbundling may require extensive systems changes that would increase the administrative burden for 2005 and not be needed for phase II.

      (c)   There would be no need to require unbundling if the Board strengthened the liability adequacy test, defined significant insurance risk more narrowly and confirmed that contracts combined artificially are separate contracts.

      (d)   The unbundling conditions in ED 5 were vague and did not explain the underlying principle.

---

12   The Board amended the requirements in IAS 39 to identify and separately account for embedded derivatives and relocated them to IFRS 9 *Financial Instruments*. This Basis for Conclusions has not been updated for changes in requirements since IFRIC 9 *Reassessment of Embedded Derivatives* was issued in March 2006.

        © IFRS Foundation

(e) Because ED 5 did not propose recognition criteria, insurers would use local GAAP to judge whether assets and liabilities were omitted. This would defeat the stated reason for unbundling.

(f) If a contract is unbundled, the premium for the deposit component is recognised not as premium revenue but as a balance sheet movement (ie as a deposit receipt). Requiring this would be premature before the Board completes its project on reporting comprehensive income.

BC49 Some suggested other criteria for unbundling:

(a) All contracts should be unbundled, or unbundling should always be permitted at least. Unbundling is required in Australia and New Zealand.

(b) All non-insurance components (for example, service components) should be unbundled, not only deposit components.

(c) Unbundling should be required only when the components are completely separable, or when there is an account in the name of the policyholder.

(d) Unbundling could affect the presentation of revenue more than it affects liability recognition. Therefore, unbundling should also be required if it would have a significant effect on reported revenue and is easy to perform.

BC50 Some respondents argued that the test for unbundling should be two-sided (ie the cash flows of the insurance component and the investment component do not interact) rather than the one-sided test proposed in ED 5 (ie the cash flows from the insurance component do not affect the cash flows from the deposit component). Here is an example where this might make a difference: in some life insurance contracts, the death benefit is the difference between (a) a fixed amount and (b) the value of a deposit component (for example, a unit-linked investment). The deposit component can be measured independently, but the death benefit depends on the unit value so the insurance component cannot be measured independently.

BC51 The Board decided that phase I should not require insurers to set up systems to unbundle the products described in the previous paragraph. However, the Board decided to rely on the condition that provides an exemption from unbundling if all the rights and obligations under the deposit component are recognised. If this condition is not met, unbundling is appropriate.

BC52 Some argued that it is irrelevant whether the insurance component affects the deposit component. They suggested that a deposit component exists if the policyholder will receive a minimum fixed amount of future cash flows in the form of either a return of premium (if no insured event occurs) or an insurance recovery (if an insured event occurs). However, the Board noted that this focus on a single cash flow would not result in unbundling if a financial instrument and an insurance contract are combined artificially into a single contract and the cash flows from one component offset cash flows from the other component. The Board regarded that result as inappropriate and open to abuse.

BC53   In summary, the Board retained the approach broadly as in ED 5. This requires unbundling if that is needed to ensure the recognition of rights and obligations arising from the deposit component and those rights and obligations can be measured separately. If only the second of these conditions is met, the IFRS permits unbundling, but does not require it.

BC54   Some respondents suggested that if a contract has been artificially separated through the use of side letters, the separate components of the contract should be considered together. The Board did not address this because it is a wider issue for the Board's possible future work on linkage (ie accounting for separate transactions that are connected in some way). The footnote to paragraph B25 refers to simultaneous contracts with the same counterparty.

Weather derivatives

BC55   The scope of IAS 39[13] previously excluded contracts that require a payment based on climatic, geological, or other physical variables (if based on climatic variables, sometimes described as weather derivatives). It is convenient to divide these contracts into two categories:

(a)   contracts that require a payment only if a particular level of the underlying climatic, geological, or other physical variables adversely affects the contract holder. These are insurance contracts as defined in the IFRS.

(b)   contracts that require a payment based on a specified level of the underlying variable regardless of whether there is an adverse effect on the contract holder. These are derivatives and the IFRS removes a previous scope exclusion to bring them within the scope of IAS 39.

BC56   The previous scope exclusion was created mainly because the holder might use such a derivative in a way that resembles the use of an insurance contract. However, the definition of an insurance contract in the IFRS now provides a principled basis for deciding which of these contracts are treated as insurance contracts and which are treated as derivatives. Therefore, the Board removed the scope exclusion from IAS 39 (see paragraph C3 of Appendix C of the IFRS). Such contracts are within the scope of the IFRS if payment is contingent on changes in a physical variable that is specific to a party to the contract, and within the scope of IAS 39 in all other cases.

BC57   Some respondents suggested that a weather derivative should be treated as:

(a)   an insurance contract if it is expected to be highly effective in mitigating an existing risk exposure.

(b)   a derivative financial instrument otherwise.

BC58   Some argued that some weather derivatives are, in substance, insurance contracts. For example, under some contracts, the policyholder can claim a fixed sum based on rainfall levels at the nearest weather station. The contract was purchased to provide insurance against low rainfall but was structured like this because of difficulties in measuring actual loss suffered and because of the

---

13 IFRS 9 *Financial Instruments* replaced IAS 39. IFRS 9 applies to all items that were previously within the scope of IAS 39.

moral hazard of having a rainfall gauge on the policyholder's property. It can reasonably be expected that the rainfall at the nearest weather station will affect the holder, but the physical variable specified in the contract (ie rainfall) is not specific to a party to the contract. Similarly, some insurers use weather derivatives as a hedge against insurance contracts they issue and view them as similar to reinsurance.

BC59   Some suggested that weather derivatives should be excluded from the scope of the IFRS because they are tradable instruments that behave like other derivatives and have an observable market value, rather than because there is no contractual link between the holder and the event that triggers payment.

BC60   The IFRS distinguishes an insurance contract (in which an adverse effect on the policyholder is a contractual precondition for payment) from other instruments, such as derivatives and weather derivatives (in which an adverse effect is not a contractual precondition for payment, although the counterparty may, in fact, use the instrument to hedge an existing exposure). In the Board's view, this is an important and useful distinction. It is much easier to base a classification on the terms of the contract than on an assessment of the counterparty's motive (ie hedging or trading). Consequently, the Board made no change to ED 5's proposals for the treatment of weather derivatives.

Scope exclusions

BC61   The scope of the IFRS excludes various items that may meet the definition of insurance contracts, but are, or will be, covered by existing or proposed future IFRSs (paragraph 4). The following paragraphs discuss:

(a)   financial guarantees and insurance against credit risk (paragraphs BC62–BC68);

(b)   product warranties (paragraphs BC69–BC72);

(c)   accounting by policyholders (paragraph BC73); and

(d)   prepaid service contracts (paragraphs BC74–BC76).

Financial guarantees and insurance against credit risk

BC62   The Basis for Conclusions on IAS 39[14] explains the reasons for the Board's conclusions on financial guarantee contracts.

BC63–   [Deleted]
BC68

Product warranties

BC69   A product warranty clearly meets the definition of an insurance contract if an entity issues it on behalf of another party (such as a manufacturer, dealer or retailer). The scope of the IFRS includes such warranties.

BC70   A product warranty issued directly by a manufacturer, dealer or retailer also meets the definition of an insurance contract. Although some might think of this as 'self-insurance', the risk retained arises from existing contractual

---

14   IFRS 9 *Financial Instruments* replaced IAS 39. IFRS 9 applies to all items that were previously within the scope of IAS 39.

obligations towards the customer. Some may reason that the definition of insurance contracts should exclude such direct warranties because they do not involve a transfer of risk from buyer to seller, but rather a crystallisation of an existing responsibility. However, in the Board's view, excluding these warranties from the definition of insurance contracts would complicate the definition for only marginal benefit.

BC71 Although such direct warranties create economic exposures similar to warranties issued on behalf of the manufacturer, dealer or retailer by another party (ie the insurer), the scope of the IFRS excludes them because they are closely related to the underlying sale of goods and because IAS 37 addresses product warranties. IAS 18[15] deals with the revenue received for such warranties.

BC72 In a separate project, the Board is exploring an asset and liability approach to revenue recognition. If this approach is implemented, the accounting model for these direct product warranties may change.[16]

Accounting by policyholders

BC73 The IFRS does not address accounting and disclosure by policyholders for direct insurance contracts because the Board does not regard this as a high priority for phase I. The Board intends to address accounting by policyholders in phase II (see IASB *Update* February 2002 for the Board's discussion of accounting by policyholders). IFRSs address some aspects of accounting by policyholders for insurance contracts:

(a) IAS 37 addresses accounting for reimbursements from insurers for expenditure required to settle a provision.

(b) IAS 16 addresses some aspects of compensation from third parties for property, plant and equipment that was impaired, lost or given up.

(c) Because policyholder accounting is outside the scope of the IFRS, the hierarchy of criteria in paragraphs 10–12 of IAS 8 *Accounting Policies, Changes in Accounting Estimates and Errors* applies to policyholder accounting (see paragraphs BC77–BC86).

(d) A policyholder's rights and obligations under insurance contracts are outside the scope of IAS 32 and IAS 39.[17]

Prepaid service contracts

BC74 Some respondents noted that the definition proposed in ED 5 captured some prepaid contracts to provide services whose cost is uncertain. Because these contracts are not normally regarded as insurance contracts, these respondents suggested that the Board should change the definition or exclude these contracts from the scope of the IFRS. Respondents cited two specific examples.

---

15 IFRS 15 *Revenue from Contracts with Customers*, issued in May 2014, replaced IAS 18 *Revenue*.

16 IFRS 15 *Revenue from Contracts with Customers*, issued in May 2014, replaced IAS 18 *Revenue* and completed the Board's Revenue Recognition project.

17 IFRS 9 *Financial Instruments* replaced IAS 39. IFRS 9 applies to all items that were previously within the scope of IAS 39.

(a)   Fixed fee service contracts if the level of service depends on an uncertain event, for example maintenance contracts if the service provider agrees to repair specified equipment after a malfunction. The fixed service fee is based on the expected number of malfunctions, although it is uncertain that the machines will actually break down. The malfunction of the equipment adversely affects its owner and the contract compensates the owner (in kind, rather than cash).

(b)   Some car breakdown assistance if (i) each breakdown has little incremental cost because employed patrols provide most of the assistance, (ii) the motorist pays for all parts and repairs, (iii) the service provider's only responsibility is to take the car to a specified destination (eg the nearest garage, home or the original destination), (iv) the need to provide assistance (and the related cost) is known within hours and (v) the number of call-outs is limited.

BC75   The Board saw no conceptual reason to change either the definition of insurance contracts or the scope of the IFRS in the light of the two examples cited by respondents. Paragraphs B6 and B7 of the IFRS note that complying with the IFRS in phase I is unlikely to be particularly burdensome in these two examples, for materiality reasons. The Board may need to review this conclusion in phase II.

BC76   Some respondents argued that the proposals in ED 5 were directed primarily at entities that are generally regarded as insurers. They suggested that the Board should not impose these proposals on entities that have a relatively small amount of a given transaction type. The Board concluded that these comments were primarily about materiality. IAS 1 *Presentation of Financial Statements* and IAS 8 address materiality and the Board decided that no further guidance or specific exemption was needed in this case.

Temporary exemption from some other IFRSs

BC77   Paragraphs 10–12 of IAS 8 specify a hierarchy of criteria that an entity should use in developing an accounting policy if no IFRS applies specifically to an item. Without changes made in the IFRS, an insurer adopting IFRSs in 2005 would have needed to assess whether its accounting policies for insurance contracts comply with these requirements. In the absence of guidance, there might have been uncertainty about what would be acceptable. Establishing what would be acceptable could have been costly and some insurers might have made major changes in 2005 followed by further significant changes in phase II.

BC78   To avoid unnecessary disruption for both users and preparers in phase I that would not have eased the transition to phase II, the Board decided to limit the need for insurers to change their existing accounting policies for insurance contracts. The Board did this by the following measures:

(a)   creating a temporary exemption from the hierarchy in IAS 8 that specifies the criteria an entity uses in developing an accounting policy if no IFRS applies specifically to an item. The exemption applies to insurers, but not to policyholders.

(b)   limiting the impact of that exemption from the hierarchy by five specific requirements (relating to catastrophe provisions, liability adequacy, derecognition, offsetting and impairment of reinsurance assets, see paragraphs BC87–BC114).

(c)   permitting some existing practices to continue but prohibiting their introduction (paragraphs BC123–BC146).

BC79   Some respondents opposed the exemption from the hierarchy on the grounds that it would permit too much diversity and allow fundamental departures from the *Framework* that could prevent an insurer's financial statements from presenting information that is understandable, relevant, reliable and comparable. The Board did not grant the exemption from the hierarchy in IAS 8 lightly, but took this unusual step to minimise disruption in 2005 for both users (eg lack of continuity of trend data) and preparers (eg systems changes).

BC80   ED 6 *Exploration for and Evaluation of Mineral Resources* proposes a temporary exemption from paragraphs 11 and 12 of IAS 8 (ie sources of guidance), but not from paragraph 10 (ie relevance and reliability). That proposed exemption is narrower than in IFRS 4 because ED 6 leaves a relatively narrow range of issues unaddressed. In contrast, because IFRS 4 leaves many significant aspects of accounting for insurance contracts until phase II, a requirement to apply paragraph 10 of IAS 8 to insurance contracts would have had much more pervasive effects and insurers would have needed to address matters such as completeness, substance over form and neutrality.

BC81   Some suggested that the Board should specifically require an insurer to follow its national accounting requirements (national GAAP) in accounting for insurance contracts during phase I, to prevent selection of accounting policies that do not form a comprehensive basis of accounting to achieve a predetermined result ('cherry-picking'). However, defining national GAAP would have posed problems. Further definitional problems could have arisen because some insurers do not apply the national GAAP of their own country. For example, some non-US insurers with a US listing apply US GAAP. Moreover, it is unusual and, arguably, beyond the Board's mandate to impose requirements set by another body.

BC82   In addition, an insurer might wish to improve its accounting policies to reflect other accounting developments with no counterpart in national GAAP. For example, an insurer adopting IFRSs for the first time might wish to amend its accounting policies for insurance contracts for greater consistency with accounting policies that it uses for contracts within the scope of IAS 39.[18] Similarly, an insurer might wish to improve its accounting for embedded options and guarantees by addressing both their time value and their intrinsic value, even if no similar improvements are made to its national GAAP.

BC83   Therefore, the Board decided that an insurer could continue to follow the accounting policies that it was using when it first applied the phase I

---

18 IFRS 9 *Financial Instruments* replaced IAS 39. IFRS 9 applies to all items that were previously within the scope of IAS 39.

requirements, with some exceptions noted below. An insurer could also improve those accounting policies if specified criteria are met (see paragraphs 21–30 of the IFRS).

BC84   The criteria in paragraphs 10–12 of IAS 8 include relevance and reliability. Granting an exemption from those criteria, even temporarily, is a highly unusual step. The Board was prepared to contemplate that step only as part of an orderly and relatively fast transition to phase II. Because the exemption is so exceptional, ED 5 proposed that it would apply only for accounting periods beginning before 1 January 2007. Some described this time limit as a 'sunset clause'.

BC85   Many respondents opposed the sunset clause. They argued the following:

(a)   If the exemption expired in 2007 before phase II is in force, there would be considerable confusion, disruption and cost for both users and preparers. It would not be appropriate to penalise users and preparers if the Board does not complete phase II on time.

(b)   The sunset clause might be perceived as putting pressure on the Board to complete phase II without adequate consultation, investigation and testing.

The Board accepted the validity of these objections to the sunset clause and deleted it.

BC86   The Board decided to maintain some requirements that follow from the criteria in IAS 8. The Board acknowledges that it is difficult to make piecemeal changes to recognition and measurement practices in phase I because many aspects of accounting for insurance contracts are interrelated with aspects that will not be completed until phase II. However, abandoning these particular requirements would detract from the relevance and reliability of an insurer's financial statements to an unacceptable degree. Moreover, these requirements are not interrelated to a great extent with other aspects of recognition and measurement and the Board does not expect phase II to reverse these requirements. The following points are discussed below:

(a)   catastrophe and equalisation provisions (paragraphs BC87–BC93)

(b)   liability adequacy (paragraphs BC94–BC104)

(c)   derecognition (paragraph BC105)

(d)   offsetting (paragraph BC106)

(e)   impairment of reinsurance assets (paragraphs BC107–BC114).

Catastrophe and equalisation provisions

BC87   Some insurance contracts expose the insurer to infrequent but severe catastrophic losses caused by events such as damage to nuclear installations or satellites or earthquake damage. Some jurisdictions permit or require catastrophe provisions for contracts of this type. The catastrophe provisions are generally built up gradually over the years out of the premiums received, usually following a prescribed formula, until a specified limit is reached. They are intended to be used on the occurrence of a future catastrophic loss that is covered by current or future contracts of this type. Some countries also permit or require equalisation provisions to cover random fluctuations of claim expenses around the expected value of claims for some types of insurance contract (eg hail, credit, guarantee and fidelity insurance) using a formula based on experience over a number of years.

BC88   Those who favour recognising catastrophe or equalisation provisions as liabilities base their view on one or more of the following arguments:

(a)   Such provisions represent a deferral of unearned premiums that are designed to provide for events that are not expected, on average, to occur in any single contract period but are expected to occur over an entire cycle of several contract periods. Although contracts cover only one period in form, in substance contracts are commonly renewed, leading to pooling of risks over time rather than within a single period. Indeed, some jurisdictions make it difficult for an insurer to stop offering insurance against some forms of risk, such as hurricanes.

(b)   In some jurisdictions, an insurer is required to segregate part of the premium (the catastrophe premium). The catastrophe premium is not available for distribution to shareholders (except on liquidation) and, if the insurer transfers the contract to another insurer, it must also transfer the catastrophe premium.

(c)   In years when no catastrophe occurs (or when claims are abnormally low), such provisions portray an insurer's long-term profitability faithfully because they match the insurer's costs and revenue over the long term. Also, they show a pattern of profit similar to one obtained through reinsurance, but with less cost and administrative burden.

(d)   Such provisions enhance solvency protection by restricting the amounts distributed to shareholders and by restricting a weak company's ability to expand or enter new markets.

(e)   Such provisions encourage insurers to accept risks that they might otherwise decline. Some countries reinforce this encouragement with tax deductions.

BC89   For the following reasons, the IFRS prohibits the recognition as a liability of provisions for possible future claims under contracts that are not in existence at the reporting date (such as catastrophe and equalisation provisions):

(a)   Such provisions are not liabilities as defined in the *Framework*, because the insurer has no present obligation for losses that will occur after the end of the current contract period. As the *Framework* states, the matching concept does not allow the recognition of items in the balance sheet that do not meet the definition of assets or liabilities. Recognising deferred credits as if they were liabilities would diminish the relevance and reliability of an insurer's financial statements.

(b)   Even if the insurance law requires an insurer to segregate catastrophe premiums so that they are not available for distribution to shareholders in any circumstances, earnings on those segregated premiums will ultimately be available to shareholders. Therefore, those segregated amounts are appropriately classified as equity, not as a liability.

(c)   Recognising such provisions obscures users' ability to examine the impact of past catastrophes and does not contribute to their analysis of an insurer's exposure to future catastrophes. Given adequate disclosure, knowledgeable users understand that some types of insurance expose an insurer to infrequent but severe losses. Moreover, the analogy with reinsurance contracts is irrelevant, because reinsurance actually changes the insurer's risk profile.

(d)   The objective of general purpose financial statements is not to enhance solvency but to provide information that is useful to a wide range of users for economic decisions. Moreover, the recognition of provisions does not, by itself, enhance solvency. However, if the objective of financial statements were to enhance solvency and such provisions were an appropriate means of enhancing solvency, it would follow that the insurer should recognise the entire provision immediately, rather than accumulating it over time. Furthermore, if catastrophes (or unusual experience) in one period are independent of those in other periods, the insurer should not reduce the liability when a catastrophe (or unusually bad experience) occurs. Also, if diversification over time were a valid basis for accounting, above-average losses in early years should be recognised as assets, yet proponents of catastrophe and equalisation provisions do not advocate this.

(e)   Recognising catastrophe or equalisation provisions is not the only way to limit distributions to shareholders. Other measures, such as solvency margin requirements and risk-based capital requirements, could play an important role. Another possibility is for an insurer to segregate a portion of its equity for retention to meet possible losses in future years.

(f)   The objective of general purpose financial statements is not to encourage or discourage particular transactions or activities, but to report neutral information about transactions and activities. Therefore, accounting requirements should not try to encourage insurers to accept or decline particular types of risks.

(g)   If an insurer expects to continue writing catastrophe cover, presumably it believes that the future business will be profitable. It would not be representationally faithful to recognise a liability for future contracts that are expected to be profitable.

(h)   There is no objective way to measure catastrophe and equalisation provisions, unless an arbitrary formula is used.

BC90   Some suggested that it is not appropriate to eliminate catastrophe and equalisation provisions in phase I as a piecemeal amendment to existing approaches. However, the Board concluded that it could prohibit these provisions without undermining other components of existing approaches. There is no credible basis for arguing that catastrophe or equalisation 'provisions' are recognisable liabilities under IFRSs and there is no realistic prospect that the Board will permit them in phase II. Indeed, as noted above, paragraphs 10–12 of IAS 8 require an entity to consider various criteria in developing an accounting policy for an item if no IFRS applies specifically to that item. In the Board's view, if the IFRS had not suspended that requirement, it would clearly have prohibited the recognition of such items as a liability. Accordingly, the IFRS preserves this prohibition (see paragraph 14(a) of the IFRS).

BC91 Some respondents presented additional arguments for permitting the recognition of catastrophe and equalisation provisions as a liability:

(a) Some insurers measure insurance contracts without margins for risk, but instead recognise catastrophe or equalisation provisions. If catastrophe provisions are eliminated in phase I, this change might be partly reversed in phase II if insurers are then required to include margins for risk.

(b) Some insurers regard these provisions as relating partly to existing contracts and partly to future contracts. Splitting these components may be difficult and involve systems changes that might not be needed in phase II.

BC92 For the following reasons, these arguments did not persuade the Board:

(a) Present imperfections in the measurement of recognisable liabilities do not justify the recognition of other items that do not meet the definition of a liability.

(b) Additions to these provisions are often based on a percentage of premium revenue. If the risk period has already expired, that premium does not relate to an existing contractual obligation. If the risk period has not yet fully expired, the related portion of the premium relates to an existing contractual obligation, but most existing models defer all the related premium as unearned premium, so recognising an additional provision would be double-counting (unless the contract were known to be underpriced).

BC93 Accordingly, the Board retained the proposal in ED 5 to eliminate these provisions. However, although the IFRS prohibits their recognition as a liability, it does not prohibit the segregation of a component of equity. Changes in a component of equity are not recognised in profit or loss. IAS 1 requires a statement of changes in equity.

Liability adequacy

BC94 Many existing accounting models have tests to confirm that insurance liabilities are not understated, and that related amounts recognised as assets, such as deferred acquisition costs, are not overstated. The precise form of the test depends on the underlying measurement approach. However, there is no guarantee that these tests exist everywhere and the credibility of IFRSs could suffer if an insurer claims to comply with IFRSs but fails to recognise material and reasonably foreseeable losses arising from existing contractual obligations. To avoid this, the IFRS requires a liability adequacy test[19] (see paragraphs 15–19).

---

19 ED 5 described this as a 'loss recognition test'.

BC95   The Board's intention was not to introduce piecemeal elements of a parallel measurement model, but to create a mechanism that reduces the possibility that material losses remain unrecognised during phase I. With this in mind, paragraph 16 of the IFRS defines minimum requirements that an insurer's existing test must meet. If the insurer does not apply a test that meets those requirements, it must apply a test specified by the Board. To specify a test on a basis that already exists in IFRSs and minimise the need for exceptions to existing principles, the Board decided to draw on IAS 37.

BC96   The liability adequacy test also applies to deferred acquisition costs and to intangible assets representing the contractual rights acquired in a business combination or portfolio transfer. As a result, when the Board revised IAS 36 *Impairment of Assets* in 2004, it excluded deferred acquisition costs and those intangible assets from the scope of IAS 36.

BC97   The Board considered whether it should retain the impairment model in IAS 36 for deferred acquisition costs, and perhaps also the related insurance liabilities. However, the IAS 36 model cannot be applied to deferred acquisition costs alone, without also considering the cash flows relating to the recognised liability. Indeed, some insurers capitalise acquisition costs implicitly through deductions in the measurement of the liability. Moreover, it would be confusing and difficult to apply this model to liabilities without some re-engineering. In the Board's view, it is simpler to use a model that is designed for liabilities, namely the IAS 37 model. In practice, a re-engineered IAS 36 model and IAS 37 might not lead to very different results.

BC98   Some respondents suggested that the Board should specify that the cash flows considered in a liability adequacy test should include the effect of embedded options and guarantees, such as guaranteed annuity rates. They expressed concerns that many national practices have not required insurers to recognise these exposures, which can be very large.

BC99   Although the Board's objective was not to develop a detailed liability adequacy test, it observed that the size of exposures to embedded guarantees and options and the failings of many national practices in this area warranted specific requirements, even in phase I. Accordingly, the Board decided that the minimum requirements for an existing liability adequacy test should include considering cash flows resulting from embedded options and guarantees. The Board did not specify how those cash flows should be considered but noted that an insurer would consider this matter in developing disclosures of its accounting policies. If an existing liability adequacy test does not meet the minimum requirements, a comparison is made with the measurement that IAS 37 would require. IAS 37 refers to the amount that an entity would rationally pay to settle the obligation or transfer it to a third party. Implicitly, this amount would consider the possible effect of embedded options and guarantees.

BC100   ED 5 did not specify the level of aggregation for the liability adequacy test and some respondents asked the Board to clarify this. Paragraph 18 of the IFRS confirms that the aggregation requirements of the existing liability adequacy test apply if the test meets the minimum requirements specified in paragraph 16 of the IFRS. If that test does not meet those minimum requirements, there is no conceptual justification for offsetting a loss on one contract against an otherwise unrecognisable gain on another contract. However, the Board concluded that a contract-by-contract assessment would impose costs that exceed the likely benefits to users. Therefore, paragraph 18 states that the comparison is made at the level of a portfolio of contracts that are subject to broadly similar risks and managed together as a portfolio. More precise definition would be difficult and is not needed, given the Board's restricted objective of ensuring at least a minimum level of testing for the limited life of phase I.

BC101   It is beyond the scope of phase I to create a detailed accounting regime for insurance contracts. Therefore, the IFRS does not specify:

(a)   what criteria determine when existing contracts end and future contracts start.

(b)   whether or how the cash flows are discounted to reflect the time value of money or adjusted for risk and uncertainty.

(c)   whether the liability adequacy test considers both the time value and the intrinsic value of embedded options and guarantees.

(d)   whether additional losses recognised because of the liability adequacy test are recognised by reducing the carrying amount of deferred acquisition costs or by increasing the carrying amount of the related insurance liabilities.

BC102   Some respondents asked the Board to clarify that no formal liability adequacy test is needed if an entity can demonstrate that its method of measuring insurance liabilities means that they are not understated. Paragraph 15 of the IFRS requires an insurer to 'assess whether its recognised insurance liabilities are adequate, using current estimates of future cash flows'. The fundamental point is that future cash flows must be considered in some way, and not merely be assumed to support the existing carrying amount. The IFRS does not specify the precise means of ensuring this, as long as the minimum requirements in paragraph 16 are met.

BC103   Some respondents read the liability adequacy test proposed in ED 5 as requiring fair value measurement as a minimum. That was not the Board's intention. An insurer needs to refer to IAS 37 only if the minimum requirements in paragraph 16 are not met.

BC104   Some respondents noted that many existing liability adequacy tests require measurements that do not include a risk margin. However, IAS 37 requires such a margin. To achieve consistency, these respondents suggested that a liability adequacy test under IAS 37 should also exclude these margins. The Board did not adopt this suggestion. The idea behind using IAS 37 for phase I was to take an existing measurement basis 'off the shelf' rather than create a new model.

Derecognition

BC105   The Board identified no reasons why derecognition requirements for insurance liabilities and insurance assets should differ from those for financial liabilities and financial assets. Therefore, the derecognition requirements for insurance liabilities are the same as for financial liabilities (see paragraph 14(c) of the IFRS). However, because derecognition of financial assets is a controversial topic, the IFRS does not address derecognition of insurance assets.

Offsetting

BC106 A cedant (ie the insurer that is the policyholder under a reinsurance contract) does not normally have a right to offset amounts due from a reinsurer against amounts due to the underlying policyholder. Normal offsetting criteria prohibit offsetting when no such right exists. When these criteria are not met, a gross presentation gives a clearer picture of the cedant's rights and obligations, and related income and expense (see paragraph 14(d) of the IFRS).

Reinsurance assets

Impairment of reinsurance assets

BC107 ED 5 proposed that a cedant should apply IAS 36 *Impairment of Assets* to its reinsurance assets. Respondents opposed this proposal for the following reasons:

(a) This would compel many cedants to change their accounting model for reinsurance contracts in a way that is inconsistent with the accounting for the underlying direct insurance liability.

(b) IAS 36 would require the cedant to address matters that are beyond the scope of phase I for the underlying direct insurance liability, such as the cash flows to be discounted, the discount rate and the approach to risk. Some saw IAS 36 as an indirect way of imposing something similar to a fair value model. There would also have been systems implications.

(c) Reinsurance assets are essentially a form of financial asset and should be subject, for impairment testing, to IAS 39[20] rather than IAS 36.

BC108 The Board concluded that an impairment test for phase I (a) should focus on credit risk (arising from the risk of default by the reinsurer and also from disputes over coverage) and (b) should not address matters arising from the measurement of the underlying direct insurance liability. The Board decided that the most appropriate way to achieve this was an incurred loss model based on that in IAS 39 (see paragraph 20 of the IFRS).

Gains and losses on buying reinsurance

BC109 The IFRS defines a reinsurance contract as an insurance contract issued by one insurer (the reinsurer) to compensate another insurer (the cedant) for losses on one or more contracts issued by the cedant. One consequence is that the level of insurance risk required to meet the definition of an insurance contract is the same for a reinsurance contract as for a direct insurance contract.

BC110 National accounting requirements often define reinsurance contracts more strictly than direct insurance contracts to avoid distortion through contracts that have the legal form of reinsurance but do not transfer significant insurance

---

20 IFRS 9 *Financial Instruments* replaced IAS 39. IFRS 9 applies to all items that were previously within the scope of IAS 39.

risk (sometimes known as financial reinsurance). One source of such distortions is the failure to discount many non-life insurance claims liabilities. If the insurer buys reinsurance, the premium paid to the reinsurer reflects the present value of the liability and is, therefore, less than the previous carrying amount of the liability. Reporting a gain on buying the reinsurance is not representationally faithful if no economic gain occurred at that time. The accounting gain arises largely because of the failure to use discounting for the underlying liability. Similar problems arise if the underlying insurance liability is measured with excessive prudence.

BC111 The Board decided that it would not use the definition of a reinsurance contract to address these problems because the Board found no conceptual reason to define a reinsurance contract more or less strictly than a direct insurance contract. Instead, ED 5 addressed these problems through the following proposals:

(a) prohibiting derecognition if the liability is not extinguished (paragraphs 14(c) of the IFRS and BC105) and prohibiting the offsetting of reinsurance assets against the related direct insurance liabilities (paragraphs 14(d) of the IFRS and BC106).

(b) requiring unbundling in some cases (paragraphs 10–12 of the IFRS, IG Example 3 in the Implementation Guidance and paragraphs BC40–BC54).

(c) limiting the recognition of gains when an insurer buys reinsurance.

BC112 Respondents to ED 5 generally opposed the proposal described in paragraph BC111(c), on the following grounds:

(a) These piecemeal amendments to existing accounting models were beyond the scope of phase I and would require new systems that might not be needed in phase II.

(b) The proposals would have been difficult to apply to more complex reinsurance contracts, including excess of loss contracts and contracts that reinsure different layers of a portfolio of underlying direct insurance contracts.

(c) The proposals would have created inconsistencies with the measurement of the underlying direct insurance contracts.

(d) The artificial gain recognised at inception of some reinsurance contracts mitigates an artificial loss that arose earlier from excessive prudence or lack of discounting. If the net exposure has been reduced by reinsurance, there is no reason to continue to overstate the original liability.

(e) Any deferral of profit on buying reinsurance should be recognised as a liability, not as a reduction in the carrying amount of the reinsurance asset. This would permit assets and liabilities relating to the same underlying insurance contracts to be measured on a consistent basis and would also be consistent with other accounting bases such as US GAAP.

(f)   Any restrictions in phase I should be targeted more precisely at financial reinsurance transactions (ie transactions that do not meet the definition of an insurance contract or that have significant financial components) or contracts that provide retroactive cover (ie ones that cover events that have already occurred).

(g)   The liability adequacy test and unbundling proposals would have provided sufficient safeguards against the recognition of excessive profits.

BC113   The Board considered limiting the proposed requirements to cases where significant distortions in reported profit were most likely to occur, for example retroactive contracts. However, developing such a distinction would have been time-consuming and difficult, and there would have been no guarantee of success. The Board also considered drawing on requirements in US GAAP but decided not to include detailed requirements of this kind as a temporary and only partly effective solution. The proposals in ED 5 were an attempt to develop a simpler temporary solution. The responses indicated that the proposed solution contained too many imperfections to achieve its purpose.

BC114   The Board decided to delete the proposal in ED 5 and replace it with a specific disclosure requirement for gains and losses that arose on buying reinsurance (see paragraph 37(b) of the IFRS).

Other existing practices

BC115   The IFRS does not address:

(a)   acquisition costs (paragraphs BC116–BC119);

(b)   salvage and subrogation (paragraphs BC120 and BC121); and

(c)   policy loans (paragraph BC122).

Acquisition costs

BC116   Acquisition costs are the costs that an insurer incurs to sell, underwrite and initiate a new insurance contract. The IFRS neither prohibits nor requires the deferral of acquisition costs, nor does it prescribe what acquisition costs are deferrable, the period and method of their amortisation or whether an insurer should present deferred acquisition costs as an asset or as a reduction in insurance liabilities. The treatment of deferred acquisition costs is an integral part of existing models and cannot be amended easily without a more fundamental review of those models in phase II.

BC117   The treatment of acquisition costs for insurance contracts in phase I may differ from the treatment of transaction costs incurred for investment contracts (ie financial liabilities). IAS 39[21] requires specified transaction costs to be presented as a deduction in determining the initial carrying amount of a financial liability. The Board did not wish to create exceptions to the definition of the transaction costs to which this treatment applies. Those costs may be

---

21   IFRS 9 *Financial Instruments* replaced IAS 39. IFRS 9 applies to all items that were previously within the scope of IAS 39.

defined more broadly or more narrowly than the acquisition costs that an insurer is required or permitted to defer using its existing accounting policies.

BC118   Some entities incur significant costs in originating long-term savings contracts. Some respondents argued that most, if not all, of these costs relate to the right to charge future investment management fees rather than to the financial liability that is created when the first instalment is received. They asked the Board to clarify whether the cost of originating those rights could be recognised as a separate asset rather than as a deduction in determining the initial carrying amount of the financial liability. They noted that this treatment would:

(a)   simplify the application of the effective interest method for a financial liability carried at amortised cost.

(b)   prevent the recognition of a misleading loss at inception for a financial liability that contains a demand feature and is carried at fair value. IAS 39 states that the fair value of such a liability is not less than the amount payable on demand (discounted, if applicable, from the first date when that amount could be required to be paid).

BC119   In response to these comments, the Board decided that incremental costs directly attributable to securing an investment management contract should be recognised as an asset if they meet specified criteria, and that incremental costs should be defined in the same way as in IAS 39. The Board clarified these points by adding guidance to the illustrative examples accompanying IAS 18 *Revenue*.[22]

Salvage and subrogation

BC120   Some insurance contracts permit the insurer to sell (usually damaged) property acquired in settling the claim (ie salvage). The insurer may also have the right to pursue third parties for payment of some or all costs (ie subrogation). The Board will consider salvage and subrogation in phase II.

BC121   In the following two related areas, the IFRS does not amend IAS 37:

(a)   Gains on the expected disposal of assets are not taken into account in measuring a provision, even if the expected disposal is closely linked to the event giving rise to the provision. Instead, an entity recognises gains on expected disposals of assets at the time specified by the IFRS dealing with the assets concerned (paragraphs 51 and 52 of IAS 37).

(b)   Paragraphs 53–58 of IAS 37 address reimbursements for some or all of the expenditure required to settle a provision.

The Board is working on a project to amend various aspects of IAS 37.

Policy loans

BC122   Some insurance contracts permit the policyholder to obtain a loan from the insurer. The DSOP proposed that an insurer should treat these loans as a

---

22 IFRS 15 *Revenue from Contracts with Customers*, issued in May 2014, replaced IAS 18 *Revenue*. The guidance on the accounting for incremental costs directly attributable to securing an investment management contract was replaced by requirements in IFRS 15.

prepayment of the insurance liability, rather than as the creation of a separate financial asset. Because the Board does not regard this issue as a priority, phase I does not address it.

Changes in accounting policies

Relevance and reliability

BC123 IAS 8 prohibits a change in accounting policies that is not required by an IFRS, unless the change will result in the provision of reliable and more relevant information. Although the Board wished to avoid imposing unnecessary changes in phase I, it saw no need to exempt insurers from the requirement to justify changes in accounting policies. Therefore, paragraph 22 of the IFRS permits an insurer to change its accounting policies for insurance contracts if, and only if, the change makes the financial statements more relevant and no less reliable or more reliable and no less relevant, judged by the criteria in IAS 8.[23] As the Board's conclusions for phase II develop (see paragraphs BC6–BC8), they will give insurers further context for judgements about whether a change in accounting policies will make their financial statements more relevant and reliable.

BC124 The IFRS contains further specific requirements supporting paragraph 22:

    (a)   paragraph 24 permits an insurer to change its accounting policies for some insurance liabilities that it designates, without satisfying the normal requirement in IAS 8 that an accounting policy should be applied to all similar items (paragraphs BC174–BC177).

    (b)   paragraph 25 permits the following practices to continue but prohibits their introduction:

        (i)   measuring insurance liabilities on an undiscounted basis (paragraphs BC126 and BC127).

        (ii)   measuring contractual rights to future investment management fees at an amount that exceeds their fair value as implied by a comparison with current fees charged by other market participants for similar services (paragraphs BC128–BC130).

        (iii)   using non-uniform accounting policies for the insurance contracts of subsidiaries (paragraphs BC131 and BC132).

    (c)   paragraph 26 prohibits the introduction of additional prudence if an insurer already measures insurance liabilities with sufficient prudence (paragraph BC133).

    (d)   paragraphs 27–29 create a rebuttable presumption against the introduction of future investment margins in the measurement of insurance contracts (paragraphs BC134–BC144).

---

23 Unlike IAS 8, paragraph 22 of the IFRS permits changes in accounting policies that make the financial statements more reliable and no less relevant. This permits improvements that make financial statements more reliable even if they do not achieve full reliability. In IAS 8 and the *Framework*, reliability is not synonymous with verifiability but includes characteristics such as neutrality and substance over form.

(e)   paragraph 30 addresses 'shadow accounting' (paragraphs BC181–BC184).

(f)   paragraph 45 permits an insurer to redesignate financial assets as 'at fair value through profit or loss' when it changes its accounting policies for insurance liabilities (paragraphs BC145 and BC146).

BC125   Some respondents suggested that phase I should not permit changes in accounting policies, to prevent lack of comparability (especially within a country) and management discretion to make arbitrary changes. However, the Board decided to permit changes in accounting policies for insurance contracts if they make the financial statements more relevant and no less reliable, or more reliable and no less relevant.

Discounting

BC126   In present practice, most general insurance claims liabilities are not discounted. In the Board's view, discounting of insurance liabilities results in financial statements that are more relevant and reliable. However, because the Board will not address discount rates and the basis for risk adjustments until phase II, the Board concluded that it could not require discounting in phase I. Nevertheless, the IFRS prohibits a change from an accounting policy that involves discounting to one that does not involve discounting (paragraph 25(a)).

BC127   Some respondents to ED 5 opposed discounting for contracts in which almost all the cash flows are expected to arise within one year, on materiality and cost-benefit grounds. The Board decided to create no specific exemption for these liabilities, because the normal materiality criteria in IAS 8 apply.

Investment management fees

BC128   Under some insurance contracts, the insurer is entitled to receive a periodic investment management fee. Some suggest that the insurer should, in determining the fair value of its contractual rights and obligations, discount the estimated future cash flows at a discount rate that reflects the risks associated with the cash flows. Some insurers use this approach in determining embedded values.

BC129   However, in the Board's view, this approach can lead to results that are not consistent with a fair value measurement. If the insurer's contractual asset management fee is in line with the fee charged by other insurers and asset managers for comparable asset management services, the fair value of the insurer's contractual right to that fee would be approximately equal to what it would cost insurers and asset managers to acquire similar contractual rights.[24] Therefore, paragraph 25(b) of the IFRS confirms that an insurer cannot introduce an accounting policy that measures those contractual rights at more than their fair value as implied by fees charged by others for comparable services; however, if an insurer's existing accounting policies involve such measurements, it may continue to use them in phase I.

BC130   The Board's agenda includes a project on revenue recognition.

---

24 This approach is consistent with the discussion of servicing rights and obligations in IAS 39.

Uniform accounting policies on consolidation

BC131   IAS 27 *Consolidated and Separate Financial Statements* requires entities to use uniform accounting policies.[25] However, under current national requirements, some insurers consolidate subsidiaries without conforming the measurement of insurance liabilities using the subsidiaries' own local GAAP to the accounting policies used by the rest of the group.

BC132   The use of non-uniform accounting policies reduces the relevance and reliability of financial statements. However, prohibiting this would force some insurers to change their accounting policies for the insurance liabilities of some subsidiaries in phase I. This could have required systems changes that might no longer be needed in phase II. Therefore, the Board decided that an insurer already using non-uniform accounting policies for insurance contracts could continue to do so in phase I. However, if an insurer already uses uniform accounting policies for insurance contracts, it could not switch to a policy of using non-uniform accounting policies (paragraph 25(c) of the IFRS).

Excessive prudence

BC133   Insurers sometimes measure insurance liabilities on what is intended to be a highly prudent basis that lacks the neutrality required by the *Framework*. However, phase I does not define how much prudence is appropriate and cannot, therefore, eliminate excessive prudence. Consequently, the IFRS does not attempt to prohibit existing measurements of insurance liabilities that lack neutrality because of excessive prudence. Nevertheless, it prohibits the introduction of additional prudence if an insurer already measures insurance liabilities with sufficient prudence (see paragraph 26 of the IFRS). The liability adequacy test in paragraphs 15–19 addresses the converse problem of understated insurance liabilities.

Future investment margins

BC134   In the Board's view, the cash flows from an asset are irrelevant for the measurement of a liability (unless those cash flows affect (a) the cash flows arising from the liability or (b) the credit characteristics of the liability). Many existing measurement practices for insurance liabilities conflict with this principle because they use a discount rate based on the estimated return from the assets that are deemed to back the insurance liabilities. However, the Board concluded that it could not eliminate these practices until phase II gives guidance on discount rates and the basis for risk adjustments.

BC135   ED 5 stated that an accounting policy change makes financial statements less relevant and reliable if it introduces a practice of including future investment margins. On the following grounds, some respondents opposed this proposal, which would have prohibited the introduction of any measurements that reflect future investment margins:

---

25 The consolidation requirements in IAS 27 were superseded by IFRS 10 *Consolidated Financial Statements* issued in May 2011, but the accounting policy requirements were not changed.

(a) The proposal prejudges a phase II issue. Most actuaries and insurers believe that a fair value measure (ie one calibrated to transactions involving insurance contracts) must include some consideration of asset performance because product pricing, reinsurance and market transactions are observed to reflect this feature.

(b) A current market rate results in more relevant and reliable information than an out-of-date discount rate prescribed by a regulator, even if the current market rate reflects expected asset returns.

(c) Asset-based discount rates are a feature of most existing national systems, including some modern systems that use current estimates of future cash flows and current (albeit asset-based) discount rates. The prohibition proposed in ED 5 would have prevented an insurer from replacing its existing accounting policies for insurance contracts with another comprehensive basis of accounting for insurance contracts that is, in aggregate, more relevant and reliable despite the disadvantage of using an asset-based discount rate.

(d) Because US GAAP uses an asset-based discount rate for some insurance liabilities, the prohibition would have prevented insurers from adopting US GAAP for their insurance liabilities in phase I. This would have been unfair because some insurers that have already adopted IFRSs apply US GAAP to their insurance contracts and could continue to do so in phase I.

BC136 In the light of these comments, the Board replaced the prohibition proposed in ED 5 with a rebuttable presumption, which could be overcome if the other components of a change in accounting policies increase the relevance and reliability of an insurer's financial statements sufficiently to outweigh the disadvantage of introducing the practice in question (see paragraph 28 of the IFRS for an example).

BC137 The IFRS identifies two practices that include future investment margins in the measurement of insurance liabilities: (a) using a discount rate that reflects the estimated return on the insurer's assets,[26] (b) projecting the returns on those assets at an estimated rate of return, discounting those projected returns at a different rate and including the result in the measurement of the liability. Some suggested that (b) should be eliminated in phase I because they regarded it as less acceptable than (a). However, the Board noted that although (b) appears more obviously incorrect than (a), these two practices have the same effect and are logically equivalent.

---

26 Some approaches attempt to find a portfolio of assets ('replicating portfolio') with characteristics that replicate the characteristics of the liability very closely. If such a portfolio can be found, it may be appropriate to use the expected return on the replicating portfolio as the discount rate for the liability, with suitable adjustments for differences in their characteristics. However, replicating portfolio approaches should not be regarded as using an asset-based discount rate because they attempt to measure the characteristics of the liability. They are not based on the characteristics of the actual assets held, which may or may not match those of the liability.

Future investment margins and embedded value

BC138　In addition to considering asset-based discount rates in general, the Board also considered a specific measurement technique that, at least in present practice, typically reflects future investment margins, namely embedded value. Embedded value is an indirect method of measuring an insurance liability. Indirect methods measure the liability by discounting all cash flows arising from both the book of insurance contracts and the assets supporting the book, to arrive at a net measurement for the contracts and supporting assets. The measurement of the assets is then deducted to arrive at a measurement of the book of contracts.[27] In contrast, direct methods measure the liability by discounting future cash flows arising from the book of insurance contracts only. If the same assumptions are made in both methods, direct and indirect methods can produce the same results.[28]

BC139　Life insurers in an increasing number of countries disclose embedded value information. Most disclose this information outside the financial statements or as supplementary information (usually unaudited), but a few use it as a measurement in their balance sheets.[29]

BC140　Some respondents felt that embedded value methodology is far more relevant and reliable than most local accounting methods, and insurers should be permitted to adopt it. They noted that embedded values are often an important consideration in determining prices for acquisitions of insurers and of blocks of insurance contracts. Furthermore, embedded value and similar indirect methods are often used in accounting for the insurance liabilities assumed in these acquisitions.

BC141　For the following reasons, some suggested that phase I should prohibit embedded value measurements in the balance sheet.

(a)　Embedded value approaches are largely unregulated at present and there is diversity in their application. For example, some view the methods used to reflect risk as fairly crude, diverse and not always fully consistent with capital market prices.

(b)　Embedded value methods today typically involve two practices whose introduction ED 5 regarded as unacceptable:

(i)　reflecting future investment margins in the measurement of the 'embedded value' asset associated with insurance liabilities (see paragraphs BC134–BC144).

(ii)　measuring contractual rights to future investment management fees at an amount that exceeds their fair value as implied by a comparison with current fees charged by other market participants for similar services (see paragraphs BC128–BC130).

27　If embedded values are recognised in the statement of financial position, they are typically presented as two components: an insurance liability and a separate intangible asset. This is similar to the expanded presentation that the IFRS permits in a business combination or portfolio transfer.

28　Luke N Girard, *Market Value of Insurance Liabilities: Reconciling the Actuarial Appraisal and Option Pricing Methods*, North American Actuarial Journal, Volume 4, Number 1.

29　IAS 1 *Presentation of Financial Statements* (as revised in 2007) replaced the term 'balance sheet' with 'statement of financial position'.

(c)   In current practice, embedded values are generally determined on a single best estimate basis that does not reflect the full range of possible outcomes. This does not generally adequately address embedded guarantees and options, such as embedded interest rate guarantees. Until recently, embedded values would have ignored these items if they were out of the money. Indeed, in some cases, they might have been ignored even if they were in the money, because of assumptions about future investment performance. More attention is now being devoted to these options and guarantees and embedded value methods may begin to address them more rigorously, but that development is not yet complete.

BC142   However, for the following reasons, the IFRS permits continued use of embedded value measurements:

(a)   One objective of phase I is to avoid disturbing existing practice for insurance contracts, unless a change creates a significant improvement and leads in a direction consistent with the likely direction of phase II. Prohibiting the continued use of embedded values would not meet that criterion.

(b)   Embedded value methods are based on estimates of future cash flows, not an accumulation of past transactions. The advantages of this may, in some cases, outweigh the disadvantage of including future investment margins. Therefore, eliminating embedded value methods may not result in more relevant and reliable financial statements in every case.

(c)   Given that the Board did not prohibit asset-based discount rates for other measurements of insurance liabilities in phase I, there is no compelling reason in phase I to prohibit embedded value measurements that contain future investment margins.

(d)   Although embedded value measurements today typically include future investment margins, some practitioners have suggested improving embedded value methods by adjusting the asset cash flows fully for risk to make them consistent with market prices.

BC143   It follows from the Board's conclusions on relevance and reliability (paragraphs BC123–BC125), investment management fees (paragraphs BC128–BC130) and future investment margins (paragraphs BC134–BC137) that an insurer can introduce embedded value measurements in its balance sheet only if all the following conditions are met:

(a)   the new accounting policy will result in more relevant and reliable financial statements (paragraph 22 of the IFRS). This is not an automatic decision and will depend on a comparison of the insurer's existing accounting with the way in which it intends to apply embedded value.

(b)   this increase in relevance and reliability is sufficient to overcome the rebuttable presumption against including future investment margins (paragraph 29 of the IFRS).

(c)   the embedded values include contractual rights to future investment management fees at an amount that does not exceed their fair value as implied by a comparison with current fees charged by other market participants for similar services (paragraph 25(b) of the IFRS and paragraphs BC128–BC130).

BC144   In some measurement approaches, the discount rate is used to determine the present value of a future profit margin, which is then attributed to different periods using a formula. However, in other approaches (such as most applications of embedded value), the discount rate determines the measurement of the liability directly. The Board concluded that it is highly unlikely that an insurer could overcome the rebuttable presumption in the latter case (see paragraph 29 of the IFRS).

Redesignation of financial assets

BC145   When an insurer changes its accounting policies for insurance liabilities, it is permitted, but not required, to reclassify some or all financial assets as 'at fair value through profit or loss'. This permits an insurer to avoid artificial mismatches when it improves its accounting policies for insurance liabilities. The Board also decided:

(a)   not to restrict redesignation to assets backing the insurance contracts for which the accounting policies were changed. The Board did not wish to create unnecessary barriers for those insurers that wish to move to a more consistent measurement basis that reflects fair values.

(b)   not to introduce an option to reclassify financial assets as 'available for sale'.[30] Such reclassification would have caused changes in carrying amount to be recognised directly in equity for assets, but in profit or loss for insurance liabilities. An insurer can avoid this inconsistency by classifying the financial assets as 'at fair value through profit or loss'.

BC146   IAS 39[31] permits redesignation of assets in specified circumstances when an entity adopts the revised IAS 39. IFRS 1 *First-time Adoption of International Financial Reporting Standards* contains corresponding provisions for first-time adopters.

Acquisition of insurance contracts in business combinations and portfolio transfers

BC147   When an entity acquires another entity in a business combination, IFRS 3 *Business Combinations* requires the acquirer to measure at fair value the identifiable assets and liabilities acquired. Similar requirements exist under many national accounting frameworks. Nevertheless, in practice, insurers have often used an expanded presentation that splits the fair value of acquired insurance contracts into two components:

(a)   a liability measured in accordance with the insurer's accounting policies for insurance contracts that it issues; and

---

30 IFRS 9 *Financial Instruments* eliminated the category of available-for-sale financial assets.
31 IFRS 9 *Financial Instruments* replaced IAS 39. IFRS 9 applies to all items that were previously within the scope of IAS 39.

(b) an intangible asset, representing the difference between (i) the fair value of the contractual insurance rights acquired and insurance obligations assumed and (ii) the amount described in (a). Life insurers often describe this intangible asset by names such as the present value of in force business (PVIF), present value of future profits (PVFP or PVP) or value of business acquired (VOBA). Similar principles apply in non-life insurance, for example if claims liabilities are not discounted.

BC148 For the following reasons, the Board decided to permit these existing practices during phase I (paragraph 31 of the IFRS):

(a) One objective of phase I is to avoid prejudging most phase II issues and to avoid requiring systems changes for phase I that might need to be reversed for phase II. In the meantime, disclosure about the nature of, and changes in, the related intangible asset provides transparency for users.

(b) The IFRS gives no guidance on how to determine the fair value of the insurance liabilities, because that would be premature in phase I. Thus, fair values identified during phase I might need to be changed in phase II.

(c) It may be difficult to integrate a fair value measurement at the date of a business combination into subsequent insurance contract accounting without requiring systems changes that could become obsolete in phase II.

BC149 The intangible asset described above is generally amortised over the estimated life of the contracts. Some insurers use an interest method of amortisation, which appears appropriate for an asset that essentially comprises the present value of a set of contractual cash flows. However, it is doubtful whether IAS 38 *Intangible Assets* would have permitted its use. Therefore, the Board decided that this asset should remain outside the scope of IAS 38 and its subsequent measurement should be consistent with the measurement of the related insurance liability (paragraph 31(b) of the IFRS). Because this asset would be covered by the liability adequacy test in paragraphs 15–19, the Board also excluded it from the scope of IAS 36 *Impairment of Assets*.

BC150 IAS 36 and IAS 38 still apply to customer lists and customer relationships reflecting the expectation of contracts that are not part of the contractual insurance rights and contractual insurance obligations that existed at the date of a business combination. An illustrative example published with IFRS 3 deals with customer relationships acquired together with a portfolio of one-year motor insurance contracts.

BC151 Measurements of the intangible asset described in paragraph BC147(b) sometimes include future investment margins. Those margins are subject to the same requirements as future investment margins included in the measurement of the related insurance liability (see paragraphs BC134–BC144).

BC152 In some cases, an insurer's accounting policies under previous GAAP (ie those used before it adopted IFRSs) involved measuring the intangible asset described in paragraph BC147(b) on a basis derived from the carrying amounts of other assets and liabilities. In such cases, if an entity changes the measurements of its assets and liabilities on adopting IFRSs for the first time, shadow accounting may become relevant (see paragraphs BC181–BC184 for a discussion of shadow accounting).

BC153　Some respondents requested an exemption from fair value measurement for insurance liabilities assumed in a business combination. They argued that there is still too much uncertainty about how fair value should be defined and determined.[32] However, insurers have apparently been able to cope with the existing requirements in IFRSs and in national standards. The Board saw no compelling reason for a new exemption.

Discretionary participation features

BC154　Some insurance contracts contain a discretionary participation feature as well as a guaranteed element. The insurer has discretion over the amount and/or timing of distributions to policyholders, although that discretion may be subject to some contractual constraints (including related legal and regulatory constraints) and competitive constraints. Distributions are typically made to policyholders whose contracts are still in force when the distribution is made. Thus, in many cases, a change in the timing of a distribution means that a different generation of policyholders will benefit.

BC155　Although the issuer has contractual discretion over distributions, it is usually likely that current or future policyholders will ultimately receive some part of the accumulated surplus available, at the reporting date, for distribution to holders of contracts with discretionary participation features (ie distributable surplus). The main accounting question is whether that part of the distributable surplus is a liability or a component of equity. The Board will explore that question in phase II.

BC156　Features of this kind are found not only in insurance contracts but also in some investment contracts (ie financial liabilities). Requiring a particular accounting treatment in phase I for investment contracts with these features would create the risk that the Board might decide on a different treatment in phase II. Furthermore, in some cases, holders of insurance contracts and investment contracts have a contractual right to share in discretionary payments out of the same pool of assets. If the Board required a particular treatment for the discretionary participation features of the investment contracts in phase I, it might prejudge the treatment of these features in insurance contracts that are linked to the same pool of assets.

BC157　For these reasons, the Board decided not to address most aspects of the accounting treatment of such features in phase I, in either insurance contracts or investment contracts. However, paragraphs 34 and 35 of the IFRS confirm that it is unacceptable to classify a discretionary participation feature as an intermediate category that is neither liability nor equity, because this would be

---

32　IFRS 13, issued in May 2011, defines fair value and contains the requirements for measuring fair value.

inconsistent with the *Framework*. If a balance sheet item does not meet the *Framework*'s definition of, and recognition criteria for, assets or liabilities, that item is included in equity.

BC158 Furthermore, ED 5 proposed a requirement for the issuer of an investment contract containing such a feature to recognise a liability measured at no less than the amount that would result from applying IAS 39[33] to the guaranteed element of the contract. Because issuers need not determine the IAS 39 measurement of the guaranteed element if the total recognised liability is clearly higher, ED 5 noted the Board's expectation that issuers would not need extensive new systems to comply with this requirement.

BC159 Some respondents objected that determining the result of applying IAS 39 to the guaranteed element would either have virtually no effect (in which case the requirement would be unnecessary) or require extensive new systems (causing costs exceeding the likely benefit to users). In finalising the IFRS, the Board adopted a more flexible approach that limits the need for systems to apply IAS 39 to the guaranteed element alone, while still requiring some rigour to avoid the understatement of the financial liability. Specifically, paragraph 35 permits two approaches for a discretionary participation feature in a financial liability:

(a) The issuer may classify the entire discretionary participation feature as a liability, but need not separate it from the guaranteed element (and so need not determine the result of applying IAS 39 to the guaranteed element). An issuer choosing this approach is required to apply the liability adequacy test in paragraphs 15–19 of the IFRS to the contract.

(b) The issuer may classify part or all of the feature as a separate component of equity. If so, the liability recognised cannot be less than the result of applying IAS 39 to the guaranteed element. The issuer need not determine that measurement if the total liability recognised is clearly higher.

BC160 There may be timing differences between retained earnings under IFRSs and distributable surplus (ie the accumulated amount that is contractually eligible for distribution to holders of discretionary participation features). For example, distributable surplus may exclude unrealised investment gains that are recognised under IFRSs. The resulting timing differences are analogous, in some respects, to temporary differences between the carrying amounts of assets and liabilities and their tax bases. The IFRS does not address the classification of these timing differences because the Board will not determine until phase II whether the distributable surplus is all equity, all liability or part equity and part liability.

BC161 The factor that makes it difficult to determine the appropriate accounting for these features is constrained discretion, in other words, the combination of

---

33 IFRS 9 *Financial Instruments* replaced IAS 39. IFRS 9 applies to all items that were previously within the scope of IAS 39.

discretion and constraints on that discretion. If participation features lack discretion, they are embedded derivatives and within the scope of IAS 39.[34]

BC162   The definition of a discretionary participation feature does not capture an unconstrained contractual discretion to set a 'crediting rate' that is used to credit interest or other returns to policyholders (as found in the contracts described in some countries as 'universal life' contracts). Some view these features as similar to discretionary participation features because crediting rates are constrained by market forces and the insurer's resources. The Board will revisit the treatment of these features in phase II.

BC163   Some respondents asked the Board to clarify the treatment of premiums received for financial instruments containing discretionary participation features. Conceptually the premium for the guaranteed element is not revenue, but the treatment of the premium for the discretionary participation feature could depend on matters that will not be resolved until phase II. Furthermore, requiring the premium to be split could involve system changes that might become redundant in phase II. To avoid unnecessary disruption in phase I, the Board decided that entities could continue presenting premiums as revenue, with a corresponding expense representing the change in the liability.

BC164   Conceptually, if part or all of a discretionary participation feature is classified as a component of equity, the related portion of the premium should not be included in profit or loss. However, the Board concluded that requiring each incoming premium to be split would require systems changes beyond the scope of phase I. Therefore, the Board decided that an issuer could recognise the entire premium as revenue without separating the portion that relates to the equity component. However, the Board confirmed that the portion of profit or loss attributable to the equity component is presented as an allocation of profit or loss (in a manner similar to the presentation of minority interests[35]), not as expense or income.

BC165   Some suggested that investment contracts containing a discretionary participation feature should be excluded from the fair value disclosure required by IAS 32.[36] They noted both conceptual and practical problems in determining the fair value of an instrument of this kind. However, instead of creating a new exclusion from the required disclosure of fair value, the Board added new paragraph 91A to IAS 32. This extends existing requirements in IAS 32 governing those unquoted equity instruments whose fair value cannot be determined reliably.

---

34 The Board amended the requirements in IAS 39 to identify and separately account for embedded derivatives and relocated them to IFRS 9 *Financial Instruments*. This Basis for Conclusions has not been updated for changes in requirements since IFRIC 9 *Reassessment of Embedded Derivatives* was issued in March 2006.

35 In January 2008 the IASB issued an amended IAS 27 *Consolidated and Separate Financial Statements*, which amended 'minority interests' to 'non-controlling interests'. The consolidation requirements in IAS 27 were superseded by IFRS 10 *Consolidated Financial Statements* issued in May 2011. The term 'non-controlling interests' and the requirements for non-controlling interests were not changed.

36 In August 2005, the IASB relocated all disclosures relating to financial instruments to IFRS 7 *Financial Instruments: Disclosures*.

Issues related to IAS 39[37],[38]

Assets held to back insurance contracts

BC166   The IFRS does not address financial or non-financial assets held by insurers to back insurance contracts.[39] IAS 39 identifies four categories of financial asset, with three different accounting treatments. In developing IAS 39, the Board's predecessor (IASC) acknowledged that most countries had a mixed measurement model, measuring some financial assets at amortised cost and others at fair value. IASC decided to retain, but regulate and structure, the different approaches as follows:

(a)   financial assets classified as 'at fair value through profit or loss' (including all financial assets held for trading) are measured at fair value, with all changes in their fair value recognised in profit or loss. Furthermore, all derivatives are deemed to be held for trading, and hence measured at fair value, because this is the only method that provides sufficient transparency in the financial statements.

(b)   available-for-sale assets (ie those that do not fall into any of the other categories) are measured at fair value, with changes in their fair value recognised in equity until the asset is derecognised or becomes impaired. Measurement at fair value is appropriate given that available-for-sale assets may be sold in response to, for example, changes in market prices or a liquidity shortage.

(c)   assets with a fixed maturity may be measured at amortised cost if the entity intends to hold them to maturity and shows that it has the ability to do so. This treatment is based on the view of some that changes in market prices are irrelevant if an asset is held to maturity because those changes will reverse before maturity (unless the asset becomes impaired).

(d)   loans and receivables are measured at amortised cost. IASC was persuaded that there are difficulties in estimating the fair value of such loans, and that further progress was needed in valuation techniques before fair value should be required.

BC167   Some expressed concerns that accounting mismatches would arise in phase I if financial assets (particularly interest-bearing investments) held to back insurance contracts are measured at fair value under IAS 39 whilst insurance liabilities are measured on a different basis. If the insurer classifies the assets as 'available for sale', this difference in measurement basis would not affect profit or loss but it could lead to some volatility in equity. Some do not regard that

---

37   IFRS 9 *Financial Instruments* replaced IAS 39. IFRS 9 applies to all items that were previously within the scope of IAS 39, unless an insurer applies the temporary exemption from IFRS 9 in paragraphs 20A–20Q and 39B–39J of IFRS 4. That temporary exemption is discussed in paragraphs BC228–BC299.

38   IFRS 9 *Financial Instruments* eliminated the category of available-for-sale financial assets.

39   IFRS 9 applies to an insurer's financial assets, including financial assets held to back insurance contracts. In September 2016, the Board issued *Applying IFRS 9 Financial Instruments with IFRS 4 Insurance Contracts* (Amendments to IFRS 4) to address concerns arising from the different effective dates of IFRS 9 and the forthcoming insurance contracts Standard. Those amendments include a temporary exemption from IFRS 9 for insurers that meet specified criteria and an option for insurers to apply the overlay approach to designated financial assets.

© IFRS Foundation

volatility as a faithful representation of changes in the insurer's financial position. In developing ED 5, after discussing various suggestions for reducing that volatility,[40] the Board decided:

(a)   not to relax the criteria in IAS 39 for classifying financial assets as 'held to maturity'. Relaxing those criteria would undermine the fundamental assertion that an entity has both the intent and ability to hold the assets until maturity. The Board noted that an insurer may be able to classify some of its fixed maturity financial assets as held to maturity if it intends not to sell them before maturity and, in addition to meeting the other conditions set out in IAS 39, concludes that an unexpected increase in lapses or claims would not compel it to sell those assets (except in the 'disaster scenario' discussed in IAS 39 paragraph AG21).

(b)   not to create a new category of assets carried at amortised cost: assets held to back insurance liabilities. The creation of such a category would lead to a need for arbitrary distinctions and complex attribution procedures that would not make an insurer's financial statements more relevant and reliable, and could require insurers to develop costly systems. The Board reviewed a precedent that exists in Japan for such a category, but was not persuaded that the procedures adopted there can overcome these difficulties. Moreover, if an insurer may sell assets in response to, for example, changes in market prices or a liquidity shortage, the only appropriate measurement is fair value.

(c)   not to create a new category of 'available-for-settlement' liabilities, analogous to available-for-sale assets, measured at fair value, with changes in fair value recognised in equity. The creation of such a category would make it necessary to find some basis for distinguishing between that category and the existing category of non-trading financial liabilities, or to permit a free choice of accounting treatments. The Board has identified no basis for such a distinction, nor for deciding which of these two categories would be the new residual category. Furthermore, creating such a category could require insurers to develop new systems with no certainty that those systems would be needed in phase II.

BC168   In developing ED 5, the Board concluded that the reasons given above outweigh the effects of any accounting mismatch on an insurer's reported equity. Therefore, the Board decided not to exempt insurers from these existing requirements, even temporarily.

BC169   Insurers may be particularly sensitive to equity reported in general purpose financial statements in some countries where this amount is used in assessing compliance with regulatory capital requirements. However, although insurance supervisors are important users of general purpose financial statements, those financial statements are not directed at specific needs of insurance supervisors that other users do not share. Furthermore, supervisors generally have the

---

40   The Board discussed this subject at its meeting in November 2002. It was also one of the major topics raised by insurance participants at two half-day sessions during the financial instruments round tables in March 2003. Before finalising ED 5, the Board discussed the subject again in April 2003.

power to obtain additional information that meets their specific needs. In the Board's view, creating new exemptions from IAS 39 in this area would not have been the best way to meet the common needs of users (including insurance supervisors) of an insurer's general purpose financial statements.

BC170   Some argued that banks enjoy an 'advantage' that is not available to insurers. Under IAS 39, a bank may measure its core banking-book assets and liabilities (loans and receivables and non-trading financial liabilities) at amortised cost, whereas an insurer would have no such option for many of the assets held to back its core insurance activities. However, as noted in paragraph BC166(d), IASC permitted amortised cost measurement for loans and receivables because it had concerns about difficulties in establishing their fair value. This factor does not apply to many assets held by insurers to back insurance liabilities.

BC171   Many of the respondents to ED 5 urged the Board to explore ways of reducing the accounting mismatch described above. The Board discussed this subject at length at all three meetings at which it discussed the responses to ED 5 before finalising the IFRS. In addition, the Board discussed it with the Standards Advisory Council. It was also raised at a meeting of the Board's Insurance Advisory Committee in September 2003, which six Board members attended together with the project staff. Individual Board members and staff also had many discussions with interested parties, including users, insurers, actuaries, auditors and regulators.

BC172   It is important to distinguish two different types of mismatch:

(a)   *accounting mismatch* arises if changes in economic conditions affect assets and liabilities to the same extent, but the carrying amounts of those assets and liabilities do not respond equally to those economic changes. Specifically, accounting mismatch occurs if an entity uses different measurement bases for assets and liabilities.

(b)   *economic mismatch* arises if the values of, or cash flows from, assets and liabilities respond differently to changes in economic conditions. It is worth noting that economic mismatch is not necessarily eliminated by an asset-liability management programme that involves investing in assets to provide the optimal risk-return trade-off for the package of assets and liabilities.

BC173   Ideally, a measurement model would report all the economic mismatch that exists and would not report any accounting mismatch. The Board considered various alternatives, observing that all had advantages and disadvantages. Some alternatives would have amended IAS 39 to extend the use of cost or amortised cost measurements. However, the Board noted the following:

(a)   Fair value is a more relevant measurement than amortised cost for financial assets that an entity might sell in response to changing market and other conditions.

(b)   In its response to ED 5, the Association for Investment Management and Research (AIMR) strongly urged the Board not to extend the use of amortised cost in IAS 39. The AIMR is a non-profit professional association of more than 67,200 financial analysts, portfolio managers, and other investment professionals in 116 countries.

(c) An accounting model that measured both assets and liabilities at amounts based on current interest rates would provide information about the degree of economic mismatch. A model that measured both at historical values, or ignored the time value of money in measuring some insurance liabilities, would not. Financial analysts often observe that information about economic mismatch is very important to them.

(d) Some suggested that insurers wish to follow a strategy that involves holding fixed maturity investments to maturity, with some flexibility to sell investments if insurance claims or lapses are unusually high. They recommended relaxing restrictions in IAS 39 so that insurers using such a strategy could use the held-to-maturity category more easily. However, in discussions with individual Board members and staff, insurers generally indicated that they also wished to keep the flexibility to make sales in the light of changing demographic and economic conditions so that they can seek the best trade-off between risk and return. That is a valid and understandable business objective, but it is difficult to argue that cost could be more relevant than fair value in such cases. Although IAS 32[41] requires disclosure of the fair value of financial assets carried at amortised cost, disclosure does not rectify inappropriate measurement.

(e) Some noted that they wished to keep the flexibility to sell corporate bonds before a major downgrade occurs. They viewed the guidance in IAS 39 as restricting their ability to do this. Moreover, because a 'tainting' requirement in IAS 39 prohibits the use of the held-to-maturity category after most sales from this category, insurers are reluctant to use this classification for corporate bonds. The application guidance in IAS 39 gives examples of cases when sales of held-to-maturity investments do not 'taint' all other such investments. For example, paragraph AG22(a) of IAS 39 refers to a sale following a significant deterioration in the issuer's creditworthiness. The Board noted that some appeared to read that guidance as limited to changes in a credit rating by an external credit rating agency, although the guidance also refers to internal ratings that meet particular criteria.

(f) The Japanese precedent mentioned in paragraph BC167(b) creates some discipline by placing restrictions on the use of amortised cost, but for systems or other reasons not all insurers in Japan adopt this approach. Furthermore, this approach permits a cost approach if the durations (ie average maturities) of insurance liabilities match those of the related assets within a specified band of 80–125 per cent. If any economic mismatch arises within that band, this approach does not recognise it. In addition, gains and losses on selling assets held at amortised cost are generally recognised immediately in profit or loss (except that some gains are deferred and amortised if sales are not compatible with the duration matching strategy).

---

41 In August 2005, the IASB relocated all disclosures relating to financial instruments to IFRS 7 *Financial Instruments: Disclosures*.

(g)   Some Board members and staff met representatives of major European insurers to explore the possibility of (i) extending the use of amortised cost if specified, relatively strict, criteria are met and (ii) combining that with a simplified attempt to identify 'ineffectiveness' resulting from the fact that the assets and liabilities would not respond identically to changes in interest rates. This approach would have avoided some of the practical and conceptual problems inherent in the Japanese approach discussed above. However, this untried approach had been developed at short notice and not all details had been worked through. Moreover, many insurers may not be able or willing to invest in systems that could need amendment in phase II.

(h)   That a mixed measurement model can create an accounting mismatch is undeniable. Furthermore, it costs time and money for insurers to explain the effects even to sophisticated users. Insurers are very concerned that less sophisticated users may misinterpret the resulting information. If a simple, transparent and conceptually acceptable way could have been found to eliminate the accounting mismatch at an acceptable cost without also obscuring the economic mismatch, that change might have been beneficial. However, the Board could find no such way in the short term. The Board also noted that any change could have required major systems changes and that there appeared to be no consensus among insurers on a single method.

(i)   Extending the use of amortised cost would have created an inconsistency with US GAAP. The accounting mismatch described in paragraphs BC167 and BC172 has existed for some years in US GAAP, which requires insurers to account for their financial assets in broadly the same way as under IAS 39. Furthermore, the US Financial Accounting Standards Board decided in January 2004 not to add to its agenda a project to reconsider US GAAP for investments held by life insurance companies.

BC174   In the light of these considerations, the Board concluded that changing the measurement requirements in IAS 39 for financial assets, even temporarily, would diminish the relevance and reliability of an insurer's financial statements. The Board observed that the accounting mismatch arose more from imperfections in existing measurement models for insurance liabilities than from deficiencies in the measurement of the assets. It would have been a retrograde step to try to mitigate the accounting mismatch by adopting a less relevant measurement of the assets—a measurement that would also have obscured some of the economic mismatch.

BC175   The Board considered whether it could mitigate the accounting mismatch by permitting improvements to the measurement of insurance liabilities. The Board noted that introducing a current market-based discount rate for insurance liabilities rather than a historical discount rate would improve the relevance and reliability of an insurer's financial statements. Therefore, such a change would have been permitted by the proposals in ED 5 and is also permitted by the IFRS. However, IAS 8 requires consistent accounting policies for similar transactions. For systems and other reasons, some insurers may not wish, or be able, in phase I to introduce a current market-based discount rate for all insurance liabilities.

BC176　The Board concluded that the increase in relevance and reliability from introducing a current discount rate could outweigh the disadvantages of permitting accounting policies that are not applied consistently to all similar liabilities. Accordingly, the Board decided to permit, but not require, an insurer to change its accounting policies so that it remeasures designated insurance liabilities for changes in interest rates. This election permits a change in accounting policies that is applied to some liabilities, but not to all similar liabilities as IAS 8 would otherwise require. The Board noted that insurers might sometimes be able to develop simplified models that give a reasonable estimate of the effect of interest rate changes.

BC177　The Board also noted the following:

(a)　No single proposal would have eliminated the accounting mismatch for a broad cross-section of insurers without also obscuring the economic mismatch.

(b)　No single proposal would have been acceptable to a broad cross-section of insurers.

(c)　No single proposal could have been implemented by a broad cross-section of insurers without major systems changes. In other words, no solution was available that built on common industry approaches and systems. Furthermore, the systems needed to implement successfully the approach discussed with some European insurers (see paragraph BC173(g)) would also allow the approach permitted by paragraph 24 of the IFRS (adjusting designated liabilities for changes in interest rates). Indeed, paragraph 24 imposes fewer restrictions than the approach discussed with European insurers because it does not require the assets to match the liability cash flows closely, since any mismatch in cash flows is reflected in profit or loss.

(d)　Adjusting the discount rate for designated liabilities will not eliminate all the accounting mismatch described above and some, perhaps many, insurers will choose not to make that adjustment. The reasons for this are as follows:

(i)　As noted above, many insurers may not have systems to adjust liabilities for changes in interest rates and may not wish to develop such systems, even for designated liabilities as opposed to all liabilities.

(ii)　Changes in discount rates would not affect the measurement of insurance liabilities that are carried at an accumulated account value.

(iii)　Changes in discount rates would not affect the measurement of financial liabilities with a demand feature, because IAS 39 states that their fair value is not less than the amount payable on demand (discounted, if applicable, from the first date when that amount could be required to be paid). Although this last point is not strictly relevant for insurance contracts, many life insurers issue investment contracts for which it is relevant.

BC178   In summary, the Board decided not to amend existing measurement requirements in IAS 39 for financial assets because such amendments would have reduced the relevance and reliability of financial statements to an unacceptable extent. Although such amendments could have eliminated some of the accounting mismatch, they would also have obscured any economic mismatch that exists. The following points summarise amendments made to ED 5 that might mitigate the accounting mismatch in some cases, as well as relevant observations made by the Board:

(a)   The Board decided to permit, but not require, an insurer to change its accounting policies so that it remeasures designated insurance liabilities for changes in interest rates (see paragraph BC176).

(b)   The Board clarified the applicability of the practice sometimes known as 'shadow accounting' (paragraphs BC181–BC184).

(c)   The Board amended IAS 40 *Investment Property* to permit two separate elections when an entity selects the fair value model or the cost model for investment property. One election is for investment property backing contracts (which could be either insurance contracts or financial instruments) that pay a return linked directly to the fair value of, or returns from, specified assets including that investment property. The other election is for all other investment property (see paragraph C12 of the IFRS).[42]

(d)   The Board observed that some entities appeared to have misread the application guidance in IAS 39 on sales of held-to-maturity investments following a significant deterioration in the issuer's creditworthiness. Specifically, as noted in paragraph BC173(e), some appeared to have read it as limited to changes in a credit rating by an external credit rating agency, although the guidance also refers to internal ratings that meet particular criteria.

(e)   The Board observed that IAS 1 and IAS 32 do not preclude a presentation identifying a separate component of equity to report a portion of the change (and cumulative change) in the carrying amount of fixed-maturity available-for-sale financial assets. An insurer could use such a presentation to highlight the effect on equity of changes in interest rates that (i) changed the carrying amount of assets but (ii) did not change the carrying amount of liabilities that respond economically to those changing interest rates.

BC179   IAS 40 permits an entity to use a fair value model for investment property, but IAS 16 does not permit this model for owner-occupied property. An entity may measure its owner-occupied property at fair value using the revaluation model in IAS 16, but changes in its fair value must be recognised in revaluation surplus

---

42 The amendments contained in paragraph C12 are now incorporated as paragraphs 32A–32C of IAS 40.

rather than in profit or loss. Some insurers regard their owner-occupied property as an investment and prefer to use a fair value model for it. However, the Board decided not to make piecemeal changes to IAS 16 and IAS 40 at this stage.

BC180 The Board noted that shadow accounting (paragraphs BC181–BC184) may be relevant if there is a contractual link between payments to policyholders and the carrying amount of, or returns from, owner-occupied property. If an insurer elects to use shadow accounting, changes in the measurement of the liability resulting from revaluations of the property are recognised directly in equity, through the statement of changes in equity.

Shadow accounting

BC181 In some accounting models, realised gains or losses on an insurer's assets have a direct effect on the measurement of some or all of its insurance liabilities.[43]

BC182 When many of those models were constructed, unrealised gains and most unrealised losses were not recognised in financial statements. Some of those models were extended later to require some financial assets to be measured at fair value, with changes in fair value recognised directly in equity (ie the same treatment as for available-for-sale financial assets under IAS 39). When this happened, a practice sometimes known as 'shadow accounting' was developed with the following two features:

(a) A recognised but unrealised gain or loss on an asset affects the measurement of the insurance liability in the same way that a realised gain or loss does.

(b) If unrealised gains or losses on an asset are recognised directly in equity, the resulting change in the carrying amount of the insurance liability is also recognised in equity.

BC183 Some respondents asked the Board to clarify whether the proposals in ED 5 permitted shadow accounting. The Board concluded the following:

(a) In principle, gains and losses on an asset should not influence the measurement of an insurance liability (unless the gains or losses on the asset alter the amounts payable to policyholders). Nevertheless, this is a feature of some existing measurement models for insurance liabilities and the Board decided that it was not feasible to eliminate this practice in phase I (see paragraph BC134 for further discussion in the context of future investment margins).

(b) Shadow accounting permits all recognised gains and losses on assets to affect the measurement of insurance liabilities in the same way, regardless of whether (i) the gains and losses are realised or unrealised and (ii) unrealised gains and losses are recognised in profit or loss or directly in equity. This is a logical application of a feature of some existing models.

---

43 Throughout this section, references to insurance liabilities are also relevant for (a) related deferred acquisition costs and (b) intangible assets relating to insurance contracts acquired in a business combination or portfolio transfer.

(c)   Because the Board does not expect that feature of existing models to survive in phase II, insurers should not be required to develop systems to apply shadow accounting.

(d)   If an unrealised gain or loss on an asset triggers a shadow accounting adjustment to a liability, that adjustment should be recognised in the same way as the unrealised gain or loss.

(e)   In some cases and to some extent, shadow accounting might mitigate volatility caused by differences between the measurement basis for assets and the measurement basis for insurance liabilities. However, that is a by-product of shadow accounting and not its primary purpose.

BC184   Paragraph 30 of the IFRS permits, but does not require, shadow accounting. The Implementation Guidance includes an illustrative example to show how shadow accounting might become relevant in an environment where the accounting for assets changes so that unrealised gains are recognised (IG Example 4). Because the Board does not expect the feature underlying the use of shadow accounting to survive in phase II, the Board decided not to give further guidance.

Investment contracts

BC185   Many insurers issue investment contracts (ie financial instruments that do not transfer enough insurance risk to qualify as insurance contracts). Under IAS 39, the issuer measures investment contracts at either amortised cost or, with appropriate designation at inception, at fair value. Some aspects of the measurements under IAS 39 differ from the measurements that are often used at present under national accounting requirements for these contracts:

(a)   The definition and treatment of transaction costs under IAS 39 may differ from the definition and treatment of acquisition costs in some national requirements.

(b)   The condition in IAS 39 for treating a modification of a financial liability (or the exchange of the new liability for an old liability) as an extinguishment of the original liability may differ from equivalent national requirements.

(c)   Future cash flows from assets do not affect the amortised cost or fair value of investment contract liabilities (unless the cash flows from the liabilities are contractually linked to the cash flows from the assets).

(d)   The amortised cost of a financial liability is not adjusted when market interest rates change, even if the return on available assets is below the effective interest rate on the liability (unless the change in rates causes the liability cash flows to change).

(e)   The fair value of a financial liability with a demand feature is not less than the amount payable on demand.

(f)   The fair value of a financial instrument reflects its credit characteristics.[44]

(g)   Premiums received for an investment contract are not recognised as revenue under IAS 39, but as balance sheet movements, in the same way as a deposit received.

BC186   Some argued that the Board should not require insurers to change their accounting for investment contracts in phase I because the scope of phase I is intended to be limited and because the current treatment of such contracts is often very similar to the treatment of insurance contracts. However, the Board saw no reason to delay the application of IAS 39 to contracts that do not transfer significant insurance risk. The Board noted that some of these contracts have features, such as long maturities, recurring premiums and high initial transaction costs, that are less common in other financial instruments. Nevertheless, applying a single set of accounting requirements to all financial instruments will make an insurer's financial statements more relevant and reliable.

BC187   Some contracts within the scope of IAS 39 grant cancellation or renewal rights to the holder. The cancellation or renewal rights are embedded derivatives and IAS 39 requires the issuer to measure them separately at fair value if they are not closely related to their host contract (unless the issuer elects to measure the entire contract at fair value).

Embedded derivatives

BC188   Some suggested that the Board should exempt insurers from the requirement to separate embedded derivatives contained in a host insurance contract and measure them at fair value under IAS 39. They argued that:

(a)   separating these derivatives would require extensive and costly systems changes that might not be needed for phase II.

(b)   some of these derivatives are intertwined with the host insurance contract in a way that would make separate measurement arbitrary and perhaps misleading, because the fair value of the whole contract might differ from the sum of the fair values of its components.

BC189   Some suggested that the inclusion of embedded options and guarantees in the cash flows used for a liability adequacy test could permit the Board to exempt some embedded derivatives from fair value measurement under IAS 39. Most proponents of this exemption implied that including only the intrinsic value of these items (ie without their time value) would suffice. However, because excluding the time value of these items could make an entity's financial statements much less relevant and reliable, the Board did not create such an exemption.

BC190   In the Board's view, fair value is the only relevant measurement basis for derivatives, because it is the only method that provides sufficient transparency in the financial statements. The cost of most derivatives is nil or immaterial.

---

44   IFRS 13, issued in May 2011, states that the fair value of a liability reflects the effect of non-performance risk, which includes, but may not be limited to, an entity's own credit risk.

Hence if derivatives were measured at cost, they would not be included in the balance sheet and their success (or otherwise) in reducing risk, or their role in increasing risk, would not be visible. In addition, the value of derivatives often changes disproportionately in response to market movements (put another way, they are highly leveraged or carry a high level of risk). Fair value is the only measurement basis that can capture this leveraged nature of derivatives—information that is essential to communicate to users the nature of the rights and obligations inherent in derivatives.

BC191 IAS 39 requires entities to account separately for derivatives embedded in non-derivative contracts. This is necessary:

(a) to ensure that contractual rights and obligations that create similar risk exposures are treated in the same way whether or not they are embedded in a non-derivative contract.

(b) to counter the possibility that entities might seek to avoid the requirement to measure derivatives at fair value by embedding a derivative in a non-derivative contract.

BC192 The requirement to separate embedded derivatives already applied to a host contract of any kind before the IFRS was issued. Exempting insurance contracts from that existing requirement would have been a retrograde step. Furthermore, much of the effort needed to measure embedded derivatives at fair value arises from the need to identify the derivatives and from other steps that will still be needed if the Board requires fair value measurement for phase II. In the Board's view, the incremental effort needed to identify the embedded derivatives separately in phase I is relatively small and is justified by the increased transparency that fair value measurement brings. IG Example 2 in the Implementation Guidance gives guidance on the treatment of various forms of embedded derivative.

BC193 Some embedded derivatives meet the definition of an insurance contract. It would be contradictory to require a fair value measurement in phase I of an insurance contract that is embedded in a larger contract when such measurement is not required for a stand-alone insurance contract. Therefore, the IFRS confirms that this is not required (paragraph 8). For the same reason, the Board concluded that an embedded derivative is closely related to the host insurance contract if the embedded derivative and host insurance contract are so interdependent that an entity cannot measure the embedded derivative separately (see new paragraph AG33(h) of IAS 39). Without this conclusion, paragraph 12 of IAS 39 would have required the insurer to measure the entire contract at fair value. An alternative approach would have been to retain that requirement, but require measurement at cost if an insurance contract cannot be measured reliably at fair value in its entirety, building on a similar treatment in IAS 39 for unquoted equity instruments. However, the Board did not intend to require fair value measurement for insurance contracts in phase I. Therefore, the Board decided not to require this even when it is possible to measure reliably the fair value of an insurance contract containing an embedded derivative.

BC194 The Board acknowledges that insurers need not, during phase I, recognise some potentially large exposures to items such as guaranteed annuity options and guaranteed minimum death benefits. These items create risks that many regard as predominantly financial, but if the payout is contingent on an event that creates significant insurance risk, these embedded derivatives meet the definition of an insurance contract. The IFRS requires specific disclosures about these items (paragraph 39(e)). In addition, the liability adequacy test requires an entity to consider them (see paragraphs BC94–BC104).

Elimination of internal items

BC195 Some respondents suggested that financial instruments issued by one entity to a life insurer in the same group should not be eliminated from the group's consolidated financial statements if the life insurer's assets are earmarked as security for policyholders' savings.

BC196 The Board noted that these financial instruments are not assets and liabilities from the group's perspective. The Board saw no justification for departing from the general principle that all intragroup transactions are eliminated, even if they are between components of an entity that have different stakeholders, for example policyholder funds and shareholder funds. However, although the transactions are eliminated, they may affect future cash flows. Hence, they may be relevant in measuring liabilities.

BC197 Some respondents argued that non-elimination would be consistent with the fact that financial instruments issued can (unless they are non-transferable) be plan assets in defined benefit plans under IAS 19 *Employee Benefits*. However, the Board did not view IAS 19 as a precedent in this area. IAS 19 requires a presentation net of plan assets because investment in plan assets reduces the obligation (IAS 19 Basis for Conclusions paragraph BC66). This presentation does not result in the recognition of new assets and liabilities.

Issues related to IFRS 9

BC197A In July 2014, the Board issued the completed version of IFRS 9 *Financial Instruments*. It replaces IAS 39 and has an effective date of 1 January 2018. In September 2016, the Board issued *Applying IFRS 9* Financial Instruments *with IFRS 4* Insurance Contracts (Amendments to IFRS 4) to address concerns arising from the different effective dates of IFRS 9 and the forthcoming insurance contracts Standard. Those amendments are discussed in paragraphs BC228–BC299.

Income taxes

BC198 Some respondents argued that discounting should be required, or at least permitted, for deferred tax relating to insurance contracts. The Board noted that discounting of a temporary difference is not relevant if an item's tax base and carrying amount are both determined on a present value basis.

Disclosure

BC199 The disclosure requirements are designed as a pair of high level principles, supplemented by some specified disclosures to meet those objectives.

Implementation Guidance, published in a separate booklet,[45] discusses how an insurer might satisfy the requirements.

BC200   Although they agreed that insurers should be allowed flexibility in determining the levels of aggregation and amount of disclosure, some respondents suggested that the Board should introduce more specific and standardised disclosure requirements. Others suggested that the draft Implementation Guidance published with ED 5 was at too high a level to ensure consistency and comparability and that its non-mandatory nature might diminish its usefulness. Some were concerned that different levels of aggregation by different insurers could reduce comparability.

BC201   Nevertheless, the Board retained ED 5's approach. The Board viewed this as superior to requiring a long list of detailed and descriptive disclosures, because concentrating on the underlying principles:

(a)   makes it easier for insurers to understand the rationale for the requirements, which promotes compliance.

(b)   avoids 'hard-wiring' into the IFRS disclosures that may become obsolete, and encourages experimentation that will lead to improvements as techniques develop.

(c)   avoids requiring specific disclosures that may not be needed to meet the underlying objectives in the circumstances of every insurer and could lead to information overload that obscures important information in a mass of detail.

(d)   gives insurers flexibility to decide on an appropriate level of aggregation that enables users to see the overall picture but without combining information that has different characteristics.

BC202   Some respondents expressed the following general concerns about the proposed disclosure requirements in ED 5:

(a)   The proposed volume of disclosure was excessive and some of it would duplicate extensive material included in some countries in prudential returns.

(b)   Some of the proposed disclosures would be difficult and costly to prepare and audit, make it difficult to prepare timely financial statements and provide users with little value.

(c)   The proposals in ED 5 would require excessive disclosure of sensitive pricing information and other confidential proprietary information.

(d)   Some of the disclosures exceeded those required in other industries, which singled out insurers unfairly. Some felt that the level of disclosure would be particularly burdensome for small insurers, whereas others referred to the difficulty of aggregating information in a meaningful way for large international groups.

---

45 but included in this volume.

BC203   The two principles and most of the supporting requirements are applications of existing requirements in IFRSs, or relatively straightforward analogies with existing IFRS requirements (particularly IFRS 7 *Financial Instruments: Disclosures*).

BC203A   IFRS 7 was issued in August 2005 and replaced the disclosure requirements in IAS 32, including those on which the disclosures originally in IFRS 4 were based. Accordingly, the Board amended the disclosure requirements in IFRS 4 to be consistent with IFRS 7, when possible. The Board noted that:

(a)   insurers will have both insurance contracts and financial instruments. In particular, some of the investment products issued by insurers are financial instruments, not insurance contracts as defined in IFRS 4. It is more useful for users and easier for preparers if the risk disclosures for insurance contracts and financial instruments are the same.

(b)   making the disclosure requirements of IFRS 4 consistent with IFRS 7 makes the disclosures easier to prepare. In particular, IFRS 7 removes the 'terms and conditions' disclosure previously in paragraph 39(b) of IFRS 4. Some commentators on ED 5 (the Exposure Draft that preceded IFRS 4) objected to this disclosure requirement, believing it to be onerous and not to provide the most useful information.

(c)   the disclosures in IFRS 7 are designed to be implemented as a package, and if implemented piecemeal would result in less useful information for users. For example, the risk disclosures replace the 'terms and conditions' disclosure previously in paragraph 60(a) of IAS 32 and paragraph 39(b) of IFRS 4. Merely updating the reference in paragraph 39(d) from IAS 32 to IFRS 7 would have resulted in some, but not all, of the risk disclosures being applicable to insurance contracts and the 'terms and conditions' disclosure being retained.

(d)   as discussed in paragraph BC207, significant changes to the risk disclosures in paragraphs 38–39A are not expected as a result of phase II of the project on insurance contracts (although consequential changes may be needed to the accounting-related disclosures in paragraphs 36 and 37).

BC203B   Some respondents, particularly preparers, did not agree that IFRS 4 should be amended as part of IFRS 7. In particular, some respondents argued that sensitivity analysis of market risk would be problematic for insurance contracts; they disagreed that such an analysis would be relatively easy to understand or calculate while issues relating to the measurement of fair value for insurance contracts remain unresolved. Those respondents suggested that disclosure requirements on sensitivity analysis should be considered during phase II of the project on insurance contracts, rather than in finalising IFRS 7. The Board noted that this requirement should not be unduly onerous for insurers, nor require them to provide quantitative information, because the sensitivity analysis applies only to changes in market risk variables that have an effect on profit or loss and equity in the period being reported. In addition, the Board noted that a sensitivity analysis is intended to replace the terms and conditions disclosures, which entities found onerous. The Board did not want to *require* insurers to comply with the older terms and conditions disclosures while allowing other entities to use the less onerous sensitivity analysis. However, the Board also noted that providing the sensitivity analysis would mean systems changes for some entities. Because the purpose of IFRS 4 was to minimise such changes pending the outcome of phase II, the Board did not want to require extensive systems changes for insurance contracts as a result of IFRS 7.

BC203C To address the concerns of those who do not want to make systems changes and those who want to substitute the new sensitivity analysis for the terms and conditions disclosures, the Board decided to permit a choice of sensitivity analysis disclosures for insurance risk only. Paragraph 39A of IFRS 4 has been added so that entities will be able to choose between providing:

(a) the terms and conditions disclosures, together with the qualitative sensitivity analysis currently permitted by IFRS 4; or

(b) the quantitative sensitivity analysis required by IFRS 7 (and permitted, but not required, by IFRS 4).

The Board permitted entities to choose to disclose a combination of qualitative and quantitative sensitivity analysis for insurance risk because it believes that entities should not be prevented from providing more useful information for some insurance risks, even if they do not have the ability to provide this information for all insurance risks. The Board noted that this option was a temporary solution to the problems cited in paragraph BC203B and would be eliminated in phase II.

BC204 Many respondents asked the Board to clarify the status of the Implementation Guidance. In particular, some felt that the Implementation Guidance appeared to impose detailed and voluminous requirements that contradicted the Board's stated intention in paragraph BC201. In response to requests from respondents, the Board added paragraph IG12 to clarify the status of the implementation guidance on disclosure.

BC205 Some suggested that some of the disclosures, particularly those that are qualitative rather than quantitative or convey management's assertions about possible future developments, should be located outside the financial statements in a financial review by management. However, in the Board's view, the disclosure requirements are all essential and should be part of the financial statements.

BC206 Some argued that the disclosure requirements could be particularly onerous and less relevant for a subsidiary, especially if the parent guarantees the liabilities or the parent reinsures all the liabilities. However, the Board decided that no exemptions from the disclosure principles were justified. Nevertheless, the high level and flexible approach adopted by the Board enables a subsidiary to disclose the required information in a way that suits its circumstances.

BC207 Some respondents expressed concerns that the disclosure proposals in ED 5 might require extensive systems changes in phase I that might not be needed in phase II. The Board expects that both disclosure principles will remain largely unchanged for phase II, although the guidance to support them may need refinement because different information will be available and because insurers will have experience of developing systems to meet the disclosure principles in phase I.

Materiality

BC208   Some respondents expressed concerns that the IFRS (reinforced by the Implementation Guidance) might require disclosure of excessively detailed information that might not be beneficial to users. In response to these concerns, the Board included in the Implementation Guidance a discussion of materiality taken from IAS 1.

BC209   Some respondents suggested that some of the qualitative disclosures should not be subject to the normal materiality threshold, which might, in their view, lead to excessive disclosure. They proposed using different terminology, such as 'significant', to reinforce that message. However, the Board noted that not requiring disclosure of material information would be inconsistent with the definition of materiality. Thus, the Board concluded that the disclosure should, in general, rely solely on the normal definition of materiality.

BC210   In one place, the IFRS refers to a different notion. Paragraph 37(c) refers to the assumptions that have the greatest effect on the measurement of assets, liabilities, income and expense arising from insurance contracts. Because many assumptions could be relevant, the Board decided to narrow the scope of the disclosure somewhat.

Explanation of recognised amounts

Assumptions

BC211   The first disclosure principle in the IFRS requires disclosure of amounts in an insurer's balance sheet[46] and income statement[47] that arise from insurance contracts (paragraph 36 of the IFRS). In support of this principle, paragraph 37(c) and (d) requires disclosure about assumptions and changes in assumptions. The disclosure of assumptions both assists users in testing reported information for sensitivity to changes in those assumptions and enhances their confidence in the transparency and comparability of the information.

BC212   Some expressed concerns that information about assumptions and changes in assumptions might be costly to prepare and of limited usefulness. There are many possible assumptions that could be disclosed: excessive aggregation would result in meaningless information, whereas excessive disaggregation could be costly, lead to information overload, and reveal commercially sensitive information. In response to these concerns, the disclosure about the assumptions focuses on the process used to derive them.

BC213   Some respondents argued that it is difficult to disclose meaningful information about changes in interdependent assumptions. As a result, an analysis by sources of change often depends on the order in which the analysis is performed. To acknowledge this difficulty, the IFRS does not specify a rigid format or contents for this analysis. This allows insurers to analyse the changes

---

46   IAS 1 *Presentation of Financial Statements* (as revised in 2007) replaced the term 'balance sheet' with 'statement of financial position'.

47   IAS 1 (revised 2007) requires an entity to present all income and expense items in one statement of comprehensive income or in two statements (a separate income statement and a statement of comprehensive income).

in a way that meets the objective of the disclosure and is appropriate for the risks they face and the systems that they have, or can enhance at a reasonable cost.

Changes in insurance liabilities

BC214 Paragraph 37(e) of the IFRS requires a reconciliation of changes in insurance liabilities, reinsurance assets and, if any, deferred acquisition costs. IAS 37 requires broadly comparable disclosure of changes in provisions, but the scope of IAS 37 excludes insurance contracts. Disclosure about changes in deferred acquisition costs is important because some existing methods use adjustments to deferred acquisition costs as a means of recognising some effects of remeasuring the future cash flows from an insurance contract (for example, to reflect the result of a liability adequacy test).

Nature and extent of risks arising from insurance contracts

BC215 The second disclosure principle in the IFRS requires disclosure of information that enables users to understand the nature and extent of risks arising from insurance contracts (paragraph 38 of the IFRS). The Implementation Guidance supporting this principle builds largely on existing requirements in IFRSs, particularly the disclosures for financial instruments in IFRS 7.

BC216 Some respondents read the draft Implementation Guidance accompanying ED 5 as implying that the IFRS would require disclosures of estimated cash flows. That was not the Board's intention because insurers cannot be expected to have systems to prepare detailed estimates of cash flows in phase I (beyond what is needed for the liability adequacy test). The Board revised the Implementation Guidance to emphasise that the second disclosure principle requires disclosure **about** cash flows (ie disclosure that helps users understand their amount, timing and uncertainty), not disclosure **of** cash flows.[48]

Insurance risk

BC217 For insurance risk (paragraph 39(c)), the disclosures are intended to be consistent with the spirit of the disclosures required by IAS 32.[49] The usefulness of particular disclosures about insurance risk depends on the circumstances of a particular insurer. Therefore, the requirements are written in general terms to allow practice in this area to evolve.

Sensitivity analysis

BC218 Paragraph 39(c)(i) requires disclosure of a sensitivity analysis. The Board decided not to include specific requirements that may not be appropriate in every case and could impede the development of more useful forms of disclosure or become obsolete.

---

48 IFRS 7 replaced the required disclosures about cash flows with required disclosures about the nature and extent of risks.

49 In August 2005, the IASB relocated all disclosures relating to financial instruments to IFRS 7 *Financial Instruments: Disclosures*.

BC219   IAS 32 requires disclosure of a sensitivity analysis only for assumptions that are not supported by observable market prices or rates. However, because the IFRS does not require a specific method of accounting for embedded options and guarantees, including some that are partly dependent on observable market prices or rates, paragraph 39(c)(i) requires a sensitivity analysis for all variables that have a material effect, including variables that are observable market prices or rates.

Claims development

BC220   Paragraph 39(c)(iii) requires disclosure about claims development. The US Securities and Exchange Commission requires property and casualty insurers to provide a table showing the development of provisions for unpaid claims and claim adjustment expenses for the previous ten years, if the provisions exceed 50 per cent of equity. The Board noted that the period of ten years is arbitrary and decided instead to set the period covered by this disclosure by reference to the length of the claims settlement cycle. Therefore, the IFRS requires that the disclosure should go back to the period when the earliest material claim arose for which there is still uncertainty about the amount and timing of the claims payments, but need not go back more than ten years (subject to transitional exemptions in paragraph 44 of the IFRS). Furthermore, the proposal applies to all insurers, not only to property and casualty insurers. However, because an insurer need not disclose this information for claims for which uncertainty about the amount and timing of claims payments is typically resolved within one year, it is unlikely that many life insurers would need to give this disclosure.

BC221   In the US, disclosure of claims development is generally presented in management's discussion and analysis, rather than in the financial statements. However, this disclosure is important because it gives users insights into the uncertainty surrounding estimates about future claims, and also indicates whether a particular insurer has tended to overestimate or underestimate ultimate payments. Therefore, the IFRS requires it in the financial statements.

Probable maximum loss

BC222   Some suggested that an insurer—particularly a general insurer—should disclose the probable maximum loss (PML) that it would expect if a reasonably extreme event occurred. For example, an insurer might disclose the loss that it would suffer from a severe earthquake of the kind that would be expected to recur every one hundred years, on average. However, given the lack of a widely agreed definition of PML, the Board concluded that it is not feasible to require disclosure of PML or similar measures.

Exposures to interest rate risk or market risk

BC223   As discussed in paragraphs BC193 and BC194, the Board confirmed that an insurer need not account at fair value for embedded derivatives that meet the definition of an insurance contract, but also create material exposures to interest rate risk or market risk. For many insurers, these exposures can be large. Therefore, paragraph 39(e) of the IFRS specifically requires disclosures about these exposures.

Fair value of insurance liabilities and insurance assets

BC224   ED 5 proposed that an insurer should disclose the fair value of its insurance liabilities and insurance assets. This proposal was intended (a) to give useful information to users of an insurer's financial statements and (b) to encourage insurers to begin work on systems that use updated information, to minimise the transition period for phase II.

BC225   Some respondents supported the proposed disclosure of fair value, arguing that it is important information for users. Some felt that this would be particularly important given the range of measurement practices in phase I. However, many respondents (including some who supported a fair value disclosure requirement in principle) suggested that the Board should delete this requirement or suspend it until phase II is completed. They offered the following arguments:

(a)   Requiring such disclosure would be premature before the Board resolves significant issues about fair value measurement and gives adequate guidance on how to determine fair value.[50] The lack of guidance would lead to lack of comparability for users, place unreasonable demands on preparers and pose problems of auditability. Furthermore, disclosure cannot rectify that lack of comparability because it is difficult to describe the features of different models clearly and concisely.

(b)   Disclosure by 2006 (as proposed in ED 5) would be impracticable because insurers would not have time to create and test the necessary systems.

(c)   Expecting insurers to begin work on an unknown objective would be costly and waste time. Furthermore, in the absence of agreed methods for developing fair value, the systems developed for phase I disclosures of fair value might need changes for phase II.

(d)   The proposal asked for a mandate for the IASB to interpret its own requirement before explaining what it means.

BC226   The Board did not view the proposed requirement to disclose fair value as conditional on the measurement model for phase II. In the Board's view, disclosure of the fair value of insurance liabilities and insurance assets would provide relevant and reliable information for users even if phase II does not result in a fair value model. However, the Board agreed with respondents that requiring disclosure of fair value would not be appropriate at this stage.

Disclosures about the temporary exemption from IFRS 9 and the overlay approach

BC226A   In September 2016, the Board issued Applying IFRS 9 Financial Instruments with IFRS 4 Insurance Contracts (Amendments to IFRS 4) to address concerns arising from the different effective dates of IFRS 9 and the forthcoming insurance contracts Standard. Paragraphs BC239 and BC269–BC273 discuss the additional disclosures that an insurer is required to provide if it applies those amendments.

---

50   IFRS 13, issued in May 2011, defines fair value and contains the requirements for measuring fair value.

Summary of changes from ED 5

BC227 The following is a summary of the main changes from ED 5 to the IFRS. The Board:

(a) clarified aspects of the definition of an insurance contract (paragraphs BC36 and BC37).

(b) clarified the requirement to unbundle deposit components in some (limited) circumstances (paragraphs BC40–BC54).

(c) deleted the 'sunset clause' proposed in ED 5 (paragraphs BC84 and BC85).

(d) clarified the need to consider embedded options and guarantees in a liability adequacy test (paragraph BC99) and clarified the level of aggregation for the liability adequacy test (paragraph BC100).

(e) replaced the impairment test for reinsurance assets. Instead of referring to IAS 36 (which contained no scope exclusion for reinsurance assets before the Board issued IFRS 4), the test will refer to IAS 39 (paragraphs BC107 and BC108).

(f) deleted the proposed ban on recognising a gain at inception of a reinsurance contract, and replaced this with a disclosure requirement (paragraphs BC109–BC114).

(g) clarified the treatment of acquisition costs for contracts that involve the provision of investment management services (paragraphs BC118 and BC119).

(h) changed the prohibition on introducing asset-based discount rates into a rebuttable presumption (paragraphs BC134–BC144).

(i) clarified aspects of the treatment of discretionary participation features (paragraphs BC154–BC165) and created an explicit new exemption from the requirement to separate, and measure at fair value, some options to surrender a contract with a discretionary participation feature (paragraph 9 of the IFRS).

(j) introduced an option for an insurer to change its accounting policies so that it remeasures designated insurance liabilities in each period for changes in interest rates. This election permits a change in accounting policies that is applied to some liabilities, but not to all similar liabilities as IAS 8 would otherwise require (paragraphs BC174–BC177).

(k) amended IAS 40 to permit two separate elections for investment property when an entity selects the fair value model or the cost model. One election is for investment property backing contracts that pay a return linked directly to the fair value of, or returns from, that investment property. The other election is for all other investment property (paragraph BC178).

(l) clarified the applicability of shadow accounting (paragraphs BC181–BC184).

(m) clarified that an embedded derivative is closely related to the host insurance contract if they are so interdependent that an entity cannot measure the embedded derivative separately (ie without considering the host contract) (paragraph BC193).

(n) clarified that the Implementation Guidance does not impose new disclosure requirements (paragraph BC204).

(o) deleted the proposed requirement to disclose the fair value of insurance contracts from 2006 (paragraphs BC224–BC226).

(p) provided an exemption from applying most disclosure requirements for insurance contracts to comparatives that relate to 2004 (paragraphs 42–44 of the IFRS).

(q) confirmed that unit-denominated payments can be measured at current unit values, for both insurance contracts and investment contracts, avoiding the apparent need to separate an 'embedded derivative' (paragraph AG33(g) of IAS 39, inserted by the IFRS).

Applying IFRS 9 with IFRS 4

Background

BC228 In July 2014, the Board issued the completed version of IFRS 9. IFRS 9 sets out the requirements for recognising and measuring financial instruments. It replaces IAS 39 and is effective for annual periods beginning on or after 1 January 2018 with early application permitted.

BC229 In late 2015, the Board was at an advanced stage in its project to replace IFRS 4 with a new Standard for insurance contracts but noted that the effective date of that replacement will be after the effective date of IFRS 9. Both IFRS 9 and the forthcoming insurance contracts Standard are expected to result in major accounting changes for most insurers.[51] Some interested parties expressed concern that there could be undesirable consequences, such as additional accounting mismatches and volatility in profit or loss, when IFRS 9 is applied before the forthcoming insurance contracts Standard. The Board agreed that these concerns should be addressed.

BC230 Accordingly, in September 2016 the Board amended IFRS 4 by issuing *Applying IFRS 9 Financial Instruments with IFRS 4 Insurance Contracts* (Amendments to IFRS 4), which confirmed with modifications the proposals in the Exposure Draft published in December 2015 (the 2015 ED). The Amendments to IFRS 4 introduce:

(a) an optional overlay approach that permits insurers to reclassify between profit or loss and other comprehensive income (OCI) an amount equal to the difference between the amount reported in profit or loss for designated financial assets applying IFRS 9 and the amount that would have been reported in profit or loss for those assets if the insurer had applied IAS 39 (paragraphs BC237–BC247); and

---

51 All references in paragraphs BC228–BC299 to an insurer shall be read as also referring to an issuer of a financial instrument that contains a discretionary participation feature.

(b)   an optional temporary exemption from IFRS 9 for insurers whose activities are predominantly connected with insurance (paragraphs BC248–BC277).[52]

BC231   Although creating options within IFRSs can reduce comparability, the Board made both the overlay approach and the temporary exemption from IFRS 9 optional. This permits insurers that are eligible for the temporary exemption from IFRS 9 or the overlay approach to choose not to apply them and instead apply the improved accounting requirements in IFRS 9 without adjustment. Comparability is discussed further in paragraphs BC288–BC289.

BC232   Some interested parties suggested that the Board should permit all insurers to defer the application of IFRS 9. They expressed concern that two sets of major accounting changes in a short period of time could result in significant cost and effort for preparers and users of financial statements and also expressed the view that applying IFRS 9 before the effects of the forthcoming insurance contracts Standard can be fully evaluated would require insurers to 'apply IFRS 9 twice'.

BC233   However, the Board decided that the temporary exemption from IFRS 9 should not be available for all insurers but rather should be limited to insurers that are significantly affected by the different effective dates of IFRS 9 and the forthcoming insurance contracts Standard. The Board concluded that for other insurers the disadvantages of the temporary exemption would outweigh the advantages. In particular, the Board noted that IFRS 9 introduces significant improvements in accounting for financial instruments that should be implemented promptly. These improvements are particularly important for insurers because they hold significant investments in financial instruments. In fact, most users of financial statements with whom the Board and staff held discussions supported the application of IFRS 9 on its effective date because it would result in significantly improved information about insurers' financial instruments. As a result, most users of financial statements preferred the overlay approach over the temporary exemption.

BC234   The Board also observed that there are differing views on whether applying these two sets of major accounting changes consecutively in a short period of time, rather than simultaneously, would result in significant incremental costs for preparers. The Board concluded that the incremental costs for preparers of applying IFRS 9 before applying the forthcoming insurance contracts Standard when compared to applying both Standards at the same time would be limited. This is because all insurers will ultimately have to apply both Standards and incur the costs necessary to do so.

BC235   The Board noted that the concerns about having to 'apply IFRS 9 twice' seem to arise from the Board's decision to provide transition reliefs on initial application of the forthcoming insurance contracts Standard for those insurers that have previously applied IFRS 9. Those transition reliefs would permit, but not require, an insurer to reassess the business model for financial assets and

---

52 For the avoidance of doubt, any reference to IFRS 9 includes all of its appendices. For example, Appendix C of IFRS 9 specifies amendments to other IFRSs that apply when an entity applies IFRS 9. Those amendments do not apply when an entity applies the temporary exemption from IFRS 9, except as necessary to provide the disclosures required by the Amendments to IFRS 4.

designate or de-designate financial assets under the fair value option and the OCI presentation election for investments in equity instruments based on the facts and circumstances that exist on the date of transition to the forthcoming insurance contracts Standard. The Board observed that the incremental costs of applying those reliefs would be limited because they are optional rather than mandatory and, if applied, would affect only particular financial assets.

BC236 In addition, the Board noted that insurers applying IFRS 9 with IFRS 4 would be able to address concerns about additional accounting mismatches and volatility in profit or loss by using the existing accounting options in IFRS 4 until the forthcoming insurance contracts Standard is applied. In particular, in such circumstances, IFRS 4 permits shadow accounting (see paragraph 30 of IFRS 4), the use of current market interest rates in the measurement of insurance contracts (see paragraph 24 of IFRS 4) and changes in an insurer's accounting policies for insurance contracts (see paragraph 22 of IFRS 4).

Overlay approach

BC237 An insurer applying the overlay approach applies IFRS 9, and consequently provides:

(a) the significantly improved information about financial instruments that results from applying IFRS 9, in particular information on credit risk, that will enable improved analysis by users of financial statements; and

(b) information about financial instruments that is comparable to the information provided by entities that apply IFRS 9 without the overlay approach.

BC238 Furthermore, the overlay approach provides additional information to users of financial statements that will enable them to understand the effects of applying IFRS 9 to the designated financial assets. Applying the overlay approach, an insurer adjusts profit or loss for the designated financial assets so that it reports the same overall amount that it would have reported in profit or loss if IAS 39 had been applied to those financial assets. However, because the insurer makes an offsetting adjustment to OCI, total comprehensive income is not affected (ie total comprehensive income is the same as applying IFRS 9 without the overlay approach). The carrying amounts of all financial assets are determined applying IFRS 9.

BC239 The adjustment to profit or loss for the designated financial assets addresses the additional accounting mismatches and volatility in profit or loss that may arise from applying IFRS 9 before applying the forthcoming insurance contracts Standard. The accompanying presentation and disclosure requirements make the effect of the overlay adjustment transparent.

Eligibility for the overlay approach

BC240 The overlay approach is intended to address the additional accounting mismatches and volatility in profit or loss that may arise if an insurer applies IFRS 9 before applying the forthcoming insurance contracts Standard. To meet that objective:

(a)   an insurer may elect to apply the overlay approach only when it first applies IFRS 9;[53] and

(b)   a financial asset is eligible for designation if, and only if, it meets both of the following criteria:

(i)   it is measured at fair value through profit or loss (FVPL) applying IFRS 9 but would not have been measured at FVPL in its entirety applying IAS 39. This criterion limits application of the overlay approach to those financial assets for which the application of IFRS 9 may result in additional volatility in profit or loss. An example is a financial asset that is measured at FVPL applying IFRS 9 but that would have been bifurcated into a derivative and a host applying IAS 39.

(ii)   it is not held in respect of an activity that is unconnected with contracts within the scope of IFRS 4. The forthcoming insurance contracts Standard will not affect assets held in respect of an activity that is unconnected with contracts within the scope of IFRS 4. For example, financial assets held in respect of banking activities or financial assets held in funds relating to investment contracts that are outside the scope of IFRS 4 would not be eligible for designation. On the other hand, financial assets held for insurance regulatory requirements (or for internal capital objectives for the insurance business) are eligible because the forthcoming insurance contracts Standard may affect them.

BC241   Insurers may choose whether to apply the overlay approach, and to what extent. The availability of such a choice reduces comparability among insurers. However, the Board decided not to require insurers to apply the overlay approach to all eligible financial assets. That is because there is no loss of information when an insurer applies the overlay approach to only some financial assets. As described in paragraphs BC238 and BC243, when an insurer applies the overlay approach, it applies IFRS 9 to all its financial assets and provides additional information about the designated financial assets. Moreover, not requiring an insurer to designate all eligible financial assets minimises the cost of applying the overlay approach and permits insurers to decide how broadly to apply it. Insurers may have different approaches to designating eligible financial assets depending on the extent of, and the insurers' desire to address, the additional accounting mismatches and volatility in profit or loss that may arise from the financial assets they hold.

BC242   Finally, the Board considered the risk that an insurer could apply the overlay approach selectively with the intention of managing reported profit or loss. However, the following features of the overlay approach mitigate this risk:

---

53 This includes applying the overlay approach after previously applying either the temporary exemption from IFRS 9 or only the requirements in IFRS 9 for the presentation of gains and losses on financial liabilities designated as at fair value through profit or loss (the 'own credit' requirements).

(a)   IFRS 9 is applied to designated financial assets, consistently with financial assets that are not designated, and the accompanying presentation and disclosure requirements make the effect of applying the overlay approach transparent.

(b)   an insurer may elect to apply the overlay approach only when it first applies IFRS 9.

(c)   an insurer must continue to apply the overlay approach to a designated financial asset until the asset is derecognised, unless the financial asset no longer meets the eligibility criterion described in paragraph BC240(b)(ii) or the insurer stops applying the overlay approach to all designated financial assets. Disclosures are required when an insurer changes its designation of financial assets to make such changes transparent.

(d)   when an entity no longer has contracts within the scope of IFRS 4, it must stop applying the overlay approach and cannot recommence applying it.

Presentation

BC243   IFRS 9 must be applied to measure designated financial assets and the income and expense presented in profit or loss for those assets must reflect the application of that Standard. The amount reclassified between profit or loss and OCI (the overlay adjustment) is presented as a separate line item in profit or loss and in OCI, separately from other components in OCI. These presentation requirements are intended to make the overlay adjustment transparent, improve comparability with entities applying IFRS 9 without the overlay approach, and provide users of financial statements with information about the effect on an insurer's financial results of applying IFRS 9 to designated financial assets before the forthcoming insurance contracts Standard.

BC244   The Board decided not to provide additional presentation guidance for the overlay adjustment and instead decided to rely on the requirements in IAS 1 for the presentation of line items in the statement of comprehensive income. Applying IAS 1, the overlay adjustment will be grouped in OCI with other items that will be reclassified subsequently to profit or loss. Additionally, applying IAS 1, line items in profit or loss are presented pre-tax unless otherwise specified. Therefore, the overlay adjustment is presented in profit or loss on a pre-tax basis.

Interaction with other requirements

BC245   The Board observed that reclassifying an amount between profit or loss and OCI applying the overlay approach may have consequential effects for including other items in OCI, such as income taxes. The Board decided that it was unnecessary to develop specific requirements for those consequential effects because other IFRSs, such as IAS 12 *Income Taxes*, contain the relevant requirements.

BC246   When an insurer applies the overlay approach, shadow accounting may be applicable if, and only if, the designated financial assets have a direct effect on the measurement of some or all of its insurance liabilities, related deferred acquisition costs and related intangible assets (see paragraph 30 of IFRS 4). The

Board observed that applying both the overlay approach and shadow accounting enables an insurer to report the same profit or loss as if it had applied IAS 39 to the designated financial assets. At the same time, the overall effect on total comprehensive income reflects the result of applying IFRS 9 to those assets.

Transition

BC247 An insurer can apply the overlay approach only when it applies IFRS 9. As a result, the approach to transition and comparative information for the overlay approach is consistent with the approach in IFRS 9. IFRS 9 requires an entity to apply IFRS 9 retrospectively, subject to specified transition reliefs. Accordingly, the insurer must also apply the overlay approach retrospectively. IFRS 9 permits an entity to restate comparative information on transition to IFRS 9, except in specified circumstances in which restatement is prohibited. Accordingly, the insurer is required to restate comparative information to reflect the overlay approach when that comparative information is restated applying IFRS 9, but otherwise is prohibited from doing so.

Temporary exemption from IFRS 9

BC248 The Board observed that although the overlay approach addressed concerns about the additional accounting mismatches and volatility in profit or loss that may arise when IFRS 9 is applied in conjunction with IFRS 4, it would result in additional costs compared to applying IFRS 9 without the overlay approach (see paragraph BC294) or allowing insurers to continue to apply IAS 39.

BC249 Accordingly, the Board introduced a temporary exemption from IFRS 9 for a limited period for insurers whose activities are predominantly connected with insurance. An insurer applying the temporary exemption continues to apply IAS 39 rather than applying IFRS 9. The Board concluded that, for such insurers in that limited period, the temporary exemption reduces costs in a way that would outweigh the following disadvantages:

(a) users of financial statements would not have the significantly improved information about financial instruments provided by applying IFRS 9; and

(b) cross-sector comparability would be reduced.

BC250 The Board decided that the temporary exemption from IFRS 9 should not be available to insurers whose activities are not predominantly connected with insurance because the disadvantages for users of financial statements would outweigh the benefits for those insurers of applying the temporary exemption.

Eligibility for the temporary exemption

BC251 An insurer may apply the temporary exemption from IFRS 9 if, and only if:

(a) it has not previously applied IFRS 9[54] (see paragraph BC253); and

---

54 However, an entity that has applied only the requirements in IFRS 9 for the presentation of gains and losses on financial liabilities designated as at FVPL (the 'own credit' requirements) is not precluded from applying the temporary exemption from IFRS 9. If an entity applies those own credit requirements, it must apply the relevant requirements in IFRS 7 (as amended by IFRS 9 (2010)).

(b)   its activities are predominantly connected with insurance, which is assessed on the basis of the following two criteria:

    (i)   the insurer has a significant amount of liabilities arising from contracts within the scope of IFRS 4 (see paragraph BC258); and

    (ii)   the percentage of the insurer's liabilities connected with insurance relative to all its liabilities meets a specified threshold (see paragraphs BC254–BC257).

BC252   Insurers must assess their eligibility for the temporary exemption from IFRS 9 at the reporting entity level. That is, an entity as a whole is assessed by considering all its activities. As a result, an insurer applies either IAS 39 or IFRS 9 to all its financial assets and financial liabilities (see paragraphs BC260–BC263).

Qualifying criteria

BC253   The Board decided that an insurer that has previously applied IFRS 9 is not permitted to apply the temporary exemption from IFRS 9. This is because:

(a)   applying the temporary exemption after applying IFRS 9 would disrupt trend information several times (ie on transition to IFRS 9, followed by transition back into IAS 39, followed by another transition to IFRS 9 when the insurer applies the forthcoming insurance contracts Standard); and

(b)   if the insurer has already applied IFRS 9, it will have explained the effects of that application to the users of its financial statements, and the temporary exemption would not reduce the costs of applying IFRS 9 before applying the forthcoming insurance contracts Standard.

BC254   In the 2015 ED, the Board proposed that an insurer that has not yet applied IFRS 9 would be eligible for the temporary exemption from IFRS 9 only if its predominant activity is issuing contracts within the scope of IFRS 4. Under those proposals, an insurer would have made that determination by comparing the carrying amount of its liabilities arising from contracts within the scope of IFRS 4 to the total carrying amount of all its liabilities.

BC255   However, in the light of the feedback received on the 2015 ED, particularly from some users of financial statements, the Board broadened the qualifying criteria for the temporary exemption from IFRS 9 in order to improve comparability among peers in the insurance sector. Specifically, in addition to the liabilities arising from contracts within the scope of IFRS 4, the Board decided to treat the following liabilities as being connected with insurance for the purposes of assessing whether an insurer's activities are predominantly connected with insurance:

(a)   non-derivative investment contract liabilities measured at FVPL applying IAS 39 (including those designated as at FVPL to which the insurer has applied the requirements in IFRS 9 for the presentation of gains and losses). Even though they do not meet the definition of an insurance contract applying IFRS 4, the Board noted that those investment contracts are sold alongside similar products with significant insurance risk and are regulated as insurance contracts in many jurisdictions.

Also, such investment contracts are generally measured at FVPL. Accordingly, the Board concluded that insurers with significant investment contracts measured at FVPL should not be precluded from qualifying for the temporary exemption. However, the Board noted that insurers generally measure at amortised cost most non-derivative financial liabilities that are associated with non-insurance activities and therefore decided that such financial liabilities cannot be treated as connected with insurance.

(b) liabilities that arise because the insurer issues, or fulfils its obligations arising from: (i) contracts within the scope of IFRS 4 and (ii) non-derivative investment contracts measured at FVPL. The Board noted that even if an insurer undertakes only insurance activities, other connected liabilities may arise, such as liabilities for salaries and other employment benefits for the employees of the insurance activities. Accordingly, the Board decided that these other liabilities should be treated as being connected with insurance for the purposes of assessing an insurer's predominant activities.

BC256 To avoid ambiguity and undue effort in determining eligibility for the temporary exemption from IFRS 9, particularly because it is available only for a limited period and is an exemption from the requirements that otherwise must be applied to financial instruments, the Board concluded that it was important to clearly identify the targeted population. Accordingly, the Board decided that there should be a threshold that determines when an insurer's activities are considered to be predominantly connected with insurance. That determinative threshold is met when the percentage of the total carrying amount of an insurer's liabilities connected with insurance relative to the total carrying amount of all its liabilities is greater than 90 per cent. Nevertheless, the Board acknowledged that an assessment based solely on this threshold has shortcomings. Accordingly, the Board decided that when an insurer narrowly fails to meet the threshold, the insurer is still able to qualify for the temporary exemption as long as more than 80 per cent of its liabilities are connected with insurance, and it does not engage in a significant activity unconnected with insurance.

BC257 The Board considered that an insurer with one or more significant activities unconnected with insurance is comparable to other conglomerates, and is less likely to be comparable to entities that are regarded purely as 'insurers'. For insurers engaged in significant activities unconnected with insurance, the Board decided that the benefits for users of financial statements of comparability with non-insurance entities outweigh the benefits of the temporary exemption from IFRS 9. To achieve an appropriate balance between clearly identifying those insurers that qualify for the temporary exemption and creating 'bright lines', the Board concluded that the insurer should consider both quantitative and qualitative factors to determine whether it has a significant activity unconnected with insurance.

BC258 The Board emphasised that its objective is to provide the temporary exemption from IFRS 9 only to insurers significantly affected by the different effective dates of IFRS 9 and the forthcoming insurance contracts Standard. That objective is met only if the insurer has a significant amount of liabilities arising from contracts within the scope of IFRS 4. Accordingly, the Board decided that, to qualify for the temporary exemption, the carrying amount of an insurer's liabilities arising from contracts within the scope of IFRS 4 must be significant compared to the total carrying amount of all its liabilities. Otherwise, applying only the criterion discussed in paragraphs BC251(b)(ii) and BC255, an insurer could qualify for the temporary exemption even if, for example, it had very few contracts within the scope of IFRS 4. The Board acknowledged that determining 'significance' will require judgement but decided not to provide additional guidance on its meaning because this term is used in other IFRSs and is already applied in practice.

BC259   The Board also clarified that deposit components and embedded derivatives that an insurer unbundles from insurance contracts applying paragraphs 7–12 of IFRS 4, and accounts for using IAS 39, are considered liabilities arising from contracts within the scope of IFRS 4 for the purposes of assessing eligibility for the temporary exemption from IFRS 9.

Assessment at the reporting entity level

BC260   The Board concluded that a reporting entity would provide more understandable and useful information by accounting for its financial assets and financial liabilities applying either IFRS 9 or IAS 39 (ie if the temporary exemption from IFRS 9 applies at the reporting entity level). This is the primary reason why the Board decided that the temporary exemption from IFRS 9 should be available only if the entity as a whole qualifies by considering all of its activities. In considering the feedback on the 2015 ED, the Board discussed suggestions from some respondents that the eligibility for the temporary exemption should be assessed both at and below the reporting entity level. The following views were expressed in support of that approach:

(a)   some respondents stated that users of financial statements do not rely on the information in a group's consolidated primary financial statements for sector comparisons of conglomerates and instead focus on other types of information (eg segmental information). Therefore, in those respondents' view, consolidated financial statements that include both IFRS 9 and IAS 39 information would not cause difficulties for many users of financial statements.

(b)   some respondents argued that avoiding the additional costs of applying IFRS 9 before applying the forthcoming insurance contracts Standard is as important for the insurance activities within a diversified group as it is for a group in its entirety.

BC261   However, the Board rejected the suggestion to permit insurers to apply the temporary exemption from IFRS 9 below the reporting entity level. The Board noted that:

(a)   IFRSs require a reporting entity to use consistent accounting policies because this enables users of financial statements to compare the reporting entity with other reporting entities, and provides more understandable and useful information about the reporting entity's assets and liabilities. Consistent accounting policies also reduce accounting complexities arising from intra-group transactions. Conglomerates that engage in both insurance and non-insurance activities frequently have complex corporate and financial structures, and engage in complex transactions. Any requirement or option to split these entities into constituent parts would necessarily be complex in order to encompass all possible structures and activities—both complex to articulate and complex for users of financial statements to understand.

(b) most users of financial statements and regulators supported assessing eligibility for the temporary exemption from IFRS 9 at the reporting entity level. This is because they were concerned about the implications of applying the temporary exemption below the reporting entity level—specifically, applying both IFRS 9 and IAS 39 in one set of consolidated financial statements. They stated that such an approach would make financial statements more complex to understand and compare. Users of financial statements told the Board that understanding how IAS 39 and IFRS 9 are applied to different parts of an entity and analysing two significant changes in the accounting for financial instruments in a short period of time (ie the changes arising from initially applying IFRS 9 to only some parts of a reporting entity and then the changes arising from subsequently applying IFRS 9 to the rest of its activities) would be more confusing compared to an entity continuing to apply IAS 39 or applying IFRS 9.

BC262 Nonetheless, the Board observed that if a group fails to qualify for the temporary exemption from IFRS 9 because its activities are not predominately connected with insurance, then the group could provide additional information to explain more clearly the effects of applying IFRS 9 with IFRS 4. In particular, although the group would apply IFRS 9 to all financial assets and financial liabilities reported in its consolidated financial statements:

(a) the overlay approach would be available to address additional accounting mismatches and volatility in profit or loss associated with the group's insurance activities arising from the different effective dates of IFRS 9 and the forthcoming insurance contracts Standard.

(b) the group would have had to disclose segmental information in accordance with IFRS 8 *Operating Segments* for its insurance activities using IAS 39, if such information is used in internal management reports and if insurance activities are an operating segment. Even if the group did not produce such segmental information, the group could still choose to disclose additional information for its insurance activities using IAS 39. This would facilitate comparisons with other insurers applying IAS 39.

BC263 In addition, if an individual reporting entity, such as a subsidiary, undertakes activities predominantly connected with insurance, and prepares separate or individual financial statements, it could apply the temporary exemption from IFRS 9 in those separate or individual financial statements, even though it is required to produce information using IFRS 9 for inclusion in the consolidated financial statements. That subsidiary may decide that the cost of applying the temporary exemption (ie IAS 39) in its separate or individual financial statements is justified despite also needing to prepare IFRS 9 information for consolidation.

Initial assessment and reassessment of predominant activities

BC264 The 2015 ED proposed that an entity would assess whether it qualifies for the temporary exemption from IFRS 9 on the date that it would otherwise be required to initially apply IFRS 9; ie the first day of the annual period beginning on or after 1 January 2018. However, respondents told the Board that entities would need to perform the assessment earlier than that proposed date because they would need adequate time to implement IFRS 9 if they did not qualify for the temporary exemption. Therefore, the Board decided that an entity assesses whether its activities are predominantly connected with insurance at its annual reporting date (ie the end of its annual period) that immediately precedes 1 April 2016. This assessment date is intended to reduce uncertainty and provide adequate time for entities to implement IFRS 9 if they do not qualify for the temporary exemption.

BC265 An entity that previously qualified for the temporary exemption from IFRS 9 is required to reassess whether its activities are predominantly connected with insurance at a subsequent annual reporting date if, and only if, there was a change in its activities as described in paragraphs 20H–20I of IFRS 4 during the annual period that ended on that date (for example, the acquisition or disposal of a business line). The Board observed that a change in an entity's activities is expected to be very infrequent and provided further guidance on the nature of such changes. The Board considered that a change merely in the level of an entity's insurance liabilities relative to its total liabilities over time would not trigger a reassessment because such a change, in the absence of other events, would be unlikely to indicate a change in the entity's activities.

BC266 The entity's financial statements would reflect the effects of a change in its activities only after the change has been completed. Therefore, an entity performs the reassessment using the carrying amounts of its liabilities at the annual reporting date immediately following the completion of the change in its activities. For example, an entity would reassess whether its activities are predominantly connected with insurance at the annual reporting date immediately following the completion of an acquisition.

BC267 When an entity concludes, as a result of a reassessment, that its activities are no longer predominantly connected with insurance, the entity is permitted to continue to apply the temporary exemption from IFRS 9 only until the end of the annual period that began immediately after that reassessment. Nevertheless, the entity must apply IFRS 9 in annual periods beginning on or after 1 January 2021, which is the fixed expiry date of the temporary exemption. The Board concluded that this provides entities with time to implement IFRS 9 after a change in their activities. But all entities must apply IFRS 9 by the fixed expiry date of the temporary exemption, and a change in their activities would not affect the preparations needed to implement IFRS 9 by that date.

BC268 Similarly, an entity that previously did not qualify for the temporary exemption from IFRS 9 and has not applied IFRS 9 is permitted to reassess its eligibility at a subsequent reporting date before 31 December 2018 (the effective date of IFRS 9) if, and only if, there was a change in the entity's activities as described in paragraphs 20H–20I of IFRS 4. The Board concluded that this provision, which was not included in the 2015 ED, was appropriate as a result of its decision to set an earlier initial assessment date than was proposed in that ED (see paragraph BC264).

Disclosure

BC269   The temporary exemption from IFRS 9 will delay the provision of better information by some insurers and reduce comparability among insurers and between insurers and other entities. To mitigate these disadvantages, the Board decided that an insurer applying the temporary exemption must disclose information to enable users of financial statements to make some comparisons between insurers applying the temporary exemption and entities applying IFRS 9.

BC270   In requiring these disclosures, the Board was conscious of the need to minimise the extent to which an insurer would need to prejudge considerations that it will make when it later applies IFRS 9. The Board also noted that disclosures based on the assessment of the business model applying IFRS 9 or disclosures that would effectively require an insurer to apply the IFRS 9 impairment requirements would be unduly burdensome for preparers, though some users of financial statements had suggested that such disclosures would be useful.

BC271   In response to the 2015 ED, most regulators and users of financial statements supported the disclosure objectives proposed by the Board. They also suggested that the Board require additional disclosures to assist in cross-sector comparisons and in better understanding the credit risk of financial assets held by insurers applying the temporary exemption from IFRS 9. In contrast, some preparers expressed the view that the Board should not require disclosures that would require insurers applying the temporary exemption to apply any aspect of IFRS 9.

BC272   The Board concluded that it could balance the potential cost for preparers with improved comparability for users of financial statements and regulators by requiring:

(a)   fair value information for all financial assets, separated into groups that would identify a population that is similar to the population that would be separately disclosed as mandatorily measured at FVPL applying IFRS 9; and

(b)   credit risk information for a specific population of financial assets that is similar to the population to which the IFRS 9 expected credit loss requirements would apply.

Insurers applying the temporary exemption from IFRS 9 must use the requirements in IFRS 9, including any consequential amendments that IFRS 9 made to other IFRSs (such as IFRS 7), that are necessary to provide those disclosures.

BC273   Paragraph 30 of IAS 8 requires an entity to disclose information when it has not applied a new IFRS that has been issued but is not yet effective. Accordingly, the

Board observed that insurers are required to provide information about the expected effect of the Amendments to IFRS 4 before they are effective, including whether the insurer expects to apply the temporary exemption from IFRS 9.

Transition

BC274 The Board noted that no special transition provisions are needed for the temporary exemption from IFRS 9. This is because, when an insurer first applies:

(a) the temporary exemption, it would continue applying IAS 39 and start providing the disclosures required by the Amendments to IFRS 4, using the relevant provisions in IFRS 9 that are necessary to provide those disclosures; and

(b) IFRS 9 after previously applying the temporary exemption, it would apply the transition requirements in IFRS 9 and stop providing the required disclosures relating to the temporary exemption.

Fixed expiry date for the temporary exemption

BC275 The forthcoming insurance contract Standard will replace IFRS 4 and therefore, the temporary exemption from IFRS 9 will no longer exist when the insurer first applies that forthcoming Standard. However, the Board decided that, even if the forthcoming insurance contract Standard is not effective by 1 January 2021, all insurers must apply IFRS 9 for annual periods beginning on or after 1 January 2021.

BC276 The Board considered the view that an insurer should be required to apply IFRS 9 only when it applies the forthcoming insurance contracts Standard. However, the Board disagreed with that view because IFRS 9 provides significant improvements to the accounting requirements for financial instruments. Hence, the Board decided that a temporary exemption from IFRS 9 would be acceptable only if it is in place for a short period of time. Therefore, insurers are required to apply IFRS 9 no later than 2021.

BC277 In contrast, the Board rejected a fixed expiry date for the overlay approach. Unlike insurers applying the temporary exemption from IFRS 9, insurers applying the overlay approach will provide the improved financial instrument information required by IFRS 9 and information about the effects on designated assets of moving from IAS 39 to IFRS 9. Accordingly, the rationale set out in paragraph BC276 for setting a fixed expiry date for the temporary exemption does not apply to the overlay approach. However, the forthcoming insurance contract Standard will replace IFRS 4 and therefore, the overlay approach in IFRS 4 will no longer exist when the insurer first applies that forthcoming Standard.

Temporary exemption from specific requirements in IAS 28

BC278 When an entity applies the equity method, paragraphs 35–36 of IAS 28 *Investments in Associates and Joint Ventures* require the entity to adjust its associate's or joint venture's accounting policies to conform them to the entity's accounting policies. The 2015 ED did not propose any relief from this requirement. However, in the light of the feedback received, the Board decided that:

(a) an entity that applies IFRS 9 would be permitted, but not required, to retain the IAS 39 accounting used by any associate or joint venture that applies the temporary exemption from IFRS 9 in its financial statements;

(b) an entity that applies the temporary exemption from IFRS 9 would be permitted, but not required, to retain the IFRS 9 accounting used by any associate or joint venture in its financial statements; and

(c) these reliefs would be available separately for each associate or joint venture.

BC279 These reliefs are intended to reduce the costs of applying the equity method when an entity does not qualify for the temporary exemption from IFRS 9, and thus applies IFRS 9, but one or more of the entity's associates or joint ventures is eligible and chooses to continue to apply IAS 39 (or vice versa).

BC280 The Board observed that when providing these reliefs, cost and benefit considerations for accounting for associates and joint ventures using the equity method are different to those for subsidiaries that are consolidated, for the following reasons:

(a) users of financial statements lose less information when entities apply equity accounting using different accounting policies for similar transactions than when entities prepare consolidated financial statements using different accounting policies for similar transactions. Under the equity method, the assets and liabilities of the associate and joint venture are not controlled by the entity and therefore are not considered as part of the group. Accordingly, the reliefs affect only the net amounts recognised through the equity method instead of all the items related to financial instruments presented in the group's financial statements.

(b) significant additional practical difficulties or costs may arise for an entity to apply uniform accounting policies when equity accounting is applied compared to when preparing consolidated financial statements because the entity does not control an associate or joint venture.

BC281 The Board concluded that similar reliefs are not needed for the overlay approach because that approach is applied on an instrument-by-instrument basis—that is, an entity need not apply the overlay approach to all eligible financial assets. Accordingly, when applying the equity method, the entity could retain (or modify) the overlay approach applied by an associate or joint venture or retain the associate's or joint venture's full IFRS 9 accounting.

First-time adopter

BC282 The Board decided that the concerns raised by some interested parties about the different effective dates of IFRS 9 and the forthcoming insurance contracts Standard could be equally applicable to some first-time adopters. This might be the case, for example, when a first-time adopter previously applied accounting policies for financial instruments under a national GAAP that was not significantly different from IFRSs. Consequently, the Board decided to permit first-time adopters to apply the overlay approach, described in paragraph 35B of IFRS 4, or the temporary exemption from IFRS 9, described in paragraph 20A of IFRS 4, consistently with existing IFRS preparers if, and only if, those first-time adopters meet the same criteria. For example, a first-time adopter would assess whether its activities are predominately connected with insurance in the same way, and on the same date, as an existing IFRS preparer.

Effects analysis of Applying IFRS 9 with IFRS 4

BC283　The Board is committed to assessing and sharing knowledge about the likely costs of implementing proposed new requirements and the likely ongoing costs and benefits of each new IFRS—the costs and benefits are collectively referred to as 'effects'. The Board gains insight on the likely effects of the proposals for new or revised IFRSs through its formal exposure of proposals, analysis and consultations with relevant parties.

BC284　In evaluating the likely effects of the Amendments to IFRS 4, the Board has considered the following:

> (a)　how the overlay approach and the temporary exemption from IFRS 9 affect the financial statements of those applying IFRS;
>
> (b)　whether the changes improve the comparability of financial information between different reporting periods for an individual entity and among different entities in a particular reporting period;
>
> (c)　whether the changes will improve the ability of users of financial statements to assess the future cash flows of an entity;
>
> (d)　whether the improvements to financial reporting will result in better economic decision-making;
>
> (e)　the likely effect on compliance costs for preparers; and
>
> (f)　whether the likely costs of analysis for users of financial statements are affected.

Financial statements of those applying IFRS

BC285　The Amendments to IFRS 4 would affect only those insurers that have not applied IFRS 9 (other than the requirements for the presentation of gains and losses on financial liabilities designated as at FVPL). Accordingly, non-insurers, or insurers that have already applied IFRS 9, will not be affected by the changes.

BC286　The Amendments to IFRS 4 introduce the overlay approach—the option to reclassify between profit or loss an amount equal to the incremental effect on profit or loss of applying IFRS 9 to designated financial assets until the insurer applies the forthcoming insurance contracts Standard. That approach will affect the financial statements as follows:

(a) the overlay approach will change the reported profit or loss and total OCI. However, the overlay approach will not change the carrying amounts reported on the statement of financial position, nor will it change total comprehensive income.

(b) insurers will present a line item for the amount reclassified in the statement of profit or loss, and in OCI separately from other components of OCI.

(c) insurers will provide disclosures to explain how the overlay adjustment is calculated and the effect of that adjustment on the financial statements.

BC287 The Amendments to IFRS 4 also, as an alternative, permit an insurer meeting specified criteria to apply a temporary exemption from IFRS 9—the option to defer the application of IFRS 9 until the earlier of the date when the insurer applies the forthcoming insurance contracts Standard or the fixed expiry date of the temporary exemption. The temporary exemption from IFRS 9 will affect the financial statements as follows:

(a) the carrying amounts reported in the statement of financial position and the profit or loss and total comprehensive income reported in the statement of profit or loss and OCI will be different compared to if the insurer had applied IFRS 9. However, there will be no effect on comparability with the insurer's prior period financial statements because the insurer will continue to apply IAS 39.

(b) insurers applying the temporary exemption will provide disclosures that will enable users of financial statements to make comparisons between entities applying the temporary exemption and entities applying IFRS 9.

Comparability

BC288 The financial statements of insurers that apply the overlay approach or the temporary exemption from IFRS 9 will not be directly comparable with entities that apply IFRS 9. Furthermore, making those two approaches optional also reduces comparability among entities. However, the Board has sought to mitigate the concerns about comparability by deciding the following:

(a) the effect of the overlay approach must be presented as a separate line item in profit or loss and in OCI, separately from other components of OCI. This will help users of financial statements to compare entities that apply the overlay approach and those that apply IFRS 9 without the overlay approach.

(b) the scope of the temporary exemption is restricted with the intention that any reduction in comparability affects only peers within the insurance sector. In addition, based on the feedback received, the Board expects that in a particular jurisdiction, insurers that qualify for the temporary exemption would select the same options relating to the overlay approach or the temporary exemption, which would improve comparability in practice within a jurisdiction.

(c) the disclosure requirements provide some information that will enable users of financial statements to compare entities that apply the temporary exemption with those that apply IFRS 9.

(d) there is a fixed expiry date for the temporary exemption from IFRS 9. That fixed expiry date, and the Board's commitment to completing the forthcoming insurance contracts Standard expeditiously, mean that any reduction in comparability will last only for a short period of time (ie until the temporary exemption expires or the forthcoming insurance contracts Standard is applied).

(e) eligibility for the temporary exemption is assessed at the reporting entity level and an entity applies either IAS 39 or IFRS 9 to all its financial assets and financial liabilities. Accordingly, an entity may apply either the temporary exemption or the overlay approach in its financial statements, but not both (except in the limited case of equity accounting as discussed in paragraphs BC278–BC281).

BC289 Nevertheless, the Board acknowledged that full comparability cannot be achieved by these decisions because such comparability would be achieved only if all insurers applied IFRS 9 when it becomes effective or if all entities, including insurers, deferred IFRS 9. The Board concluded that deferring the effective date of IFRS 9 for all entities would be a disproportionate response to the issues raised because it would mean that preparers and users of financial statements would not benefit from the better reporting that results from applying IFRS 9.

Usefulness in assessing the future cash flows of an entity and better economic decision-making

BC290 The Board received mixed feedback as to whether the Amendments to IFRS 4 would result in financial statements that are more useful in assessing the cash flows of an insurer:

(a) many users of financial statements did not support the temporary exemption from IFRS 9 because:

(i) they expected no additional difficulty in their analysis as a result of the additional accounting mismatches and volatility in profit or loss that might arise if IFRS 9 was applied before the forthcoming insurance contracts Standard; and

(ii) they already saw volatility when analysing insurers and were able to make adjustments necessary to understand the financial performance of such insurers.

(b) however, some users expressed concerns about potential additional volatility in profit or loss and supported the overlay approach, the temporary exemption, or both, because reporting such volatility could:

(i) make the financial statements of insurers less understandable and less attractive for investment; and

        (ii)   make it more difficult to predict long-term economic performance and to forecast earnings based on profit or loss information.

BC291   The Board expects that the temporary exemption from IFRS 9 would not impair a user's existing ability to assess an insurer's future cash flows because the insurer would continue to apply the existing requirements in IAS 39. However, insurers applying the temporary exemption would not provide users of financial statements with the better information that would be available from entities applying IFRS 9. In addition, the application of the temporary exemption may impair the usefulness of information for economic decision-making because of the reduced comparability among entities. The Board has sought to mitigate the concern about comparability as described in paragraph BC288.

BC292   The Board expects that the overlay approach would provide users of financial statements with better information to assess future cash flows and make economic decisions than would be the case if an insurer applies the temporary exemption from IFRS 9. This is because insurers applying the overlay approach would provide the improved financial instrument information resulting from applying IFRS 9. In addition, insurers applying the overlay approach would provide additional information that would help users of financial statements to understand the effects, on designated financial assets, of applying IFRS 9.

Effect on compliance costs for preparers

BC293   The temporary exemption from IFRS 9 will be more costly for preparers than just applying IAS 39 because of the additional disclosures required. However, the Board does not consider those costs to be unduly onerous because those disclosures do not require the insurer to apply IFRS 9 in its entirety, and in particular, do not require the application of the expected credit loss model in IFRS 9.

BC294   IAS 39 already requires insurers to disclose fair value information for financial assets eligible for designation under the overlay approach and that is the only additional information needed to apply that approach. However, the overlay approach will be more costly than applying:

    (a)   only IFRS 9, because an insurer will need to decide which financial assets to designate and will then need to continue to track and measure those designated assets in accordance with IAS 39.

    (b)   the temporary exemption from IFRS 9, because an insurer applying the overlay approach will incur costs to apply IFRS 9 earlier than if it applied the temporary exemption. However, all insurers applying the temporary exemption will apply IFRS 9 in the future and thus will incur the necessary costs to do so at that point.

BC295   Nevertheless, the Board noted that the insurers would already have systems in place to measure the designated financial assets in accordance with IAS 39 because the information required to apply the overlay approach is the same as the information previously prepared when the insurer applied IAS 39. Moreover, the Board noted that if an insurer determines that the costs of the overlay approach are excessive, that insurer could choose not to apply the overlay approach or to apply it to only some of its eligible assets.

BC296 Finally, instead of applying the temporary exemption from IFRS 9 or the overlay approach, the Board noted that an insurer could choose to address the additional accounting mismatches and volatility in profit or loss by providing additional disclosures that explain those effects to the users of its financial statements or by using existing accounting options in IFRS 4 (see paragraph BC236).

The costs of analysis for users of financial statements

BC297 The overlay approach and the temporary exemption from IFRS 9 may increase the costs of analysis for users of financial statements, particularly if a user of financial statements invests across insurance and other sectors. This is because the Amendments to IFRS 4 reduce comparability, especially as the temporary exemption and the overlay approach are optional. The Board has sought to mitigate this concern as described in paragraph BC288.

BC298 Furthermore, the Board observed that the overlay approach would provide mitigating benefits for users of financial statements because it allows an insurer to address concerns about the different effective dates of IFRS 9 and the forthcoming insurance contracts Standard in a transparent manner, while applying the improved financial reporting requirements in IFRS 9.

BC299 The temporary exemption from IFRS 9 would reduce the accounting mismatches and volatility in profit or loss that may arise from applying IFRS 9 before the forthcoming insurance contracts Standard. However, the Board noted that, if an insurer applies the temporary exemption, it would not provide users of financial statements with the improved information about financial instruments that is required by IFRS 9. The Board has mitigated that loss of information by:

(a) limiting the temporary exemption to insurers whose activities are predominantly connected with insurance;

(b) requiring eligibility for the temporary exemption to be assessed at the reporting entity level so that an entity applies either IAS 39 or IFRS 9 to all its financial assets and financial liabilities;

(c) requiring insurers applying the temporary exemption to provide additional disclosures; and

(d) setting a fixed expiry date for the temporary exemption.

Dissenting opinions on IFRS 4

DO1   Professor Barth and Messrs Garnett, Gélard, Leisenring, Smith and Yamada dissent from the issue of IFRS 4.

Dissent of Mary E Barth, Robert P Garnett, Gilbert Gélard, James J Leisenring and John T Smith

DO2   Messrs Garnett and Gélard dissent for the reasons given in paragraphs DO3 and DO4 and Mr Garnett also dissents for the reasons given in paragraphs DO5 and DO6. Professor Barth and Messrs Leisenring and Smith dissent for the reasons given in paragraphs DO3–DO8 and Mr Smith also dissents for the reasons given in paragraphs DO9–DO13.

Temporary exemption from paragraphs 10–12 of IAS 8

DO3   Professor Barth and Messrs Garnett, Gélard, Leisenring and Smith dissent because IFRS 4 exempts an entity from applying paragraphs 10–12 of IAS 8 *Accounting Policies, Changes in Accounting Estimates and Errors* when accounting for insurance and reinsurance contracts. They believe that all entities should be required to apply these paragraphs. These Board members believe that the requirements in IAS 8 have particular relevance and applicability when an IFRS lacks specificities, as does IFRS 4, which allows the continuation of a variety of measurement bases for insurance and reinsurance contracts. Because of the failure to consider the IASB *Framework*,[55] continuation of such practices may result in the inappropriate recognition of, or inappropriate failure to recognise, assets, liabilities, equity, income and expense. In these Board members' view, if an entity cannot meet the basic requirements of paragraphs 10–12 of IAS 8, it should not be allowed to describe its financial statements as being in accordance with International Financial Reporting Standards.

DO4   These Board members' concerns are heightened by the delay in completing phase II of the Board's project on accounting for insurance contracts. Although phase II is on the Board's active agenda, it is unlikely that the Board will be able to develop an IFRS on insurance contracts in the near term. Accordingly, it is likely that the exemption from IAS 8 will be in place for some time.

Future investment margins and shadow accounting

DO5   Professor Barth and Messrs Garnett, Leisenring and Smith dissent for the further reason that they would not permit entities to change their accounting policies for insurance and reinsurance contracts to policies that include using future investment margins in the measurement of insurance liabilities. They agree with the view expressed in paragraph BC134 that cash flows from an asset are irrelevant for the measurement of a liability (unless those cash flows affect the cash flows arising from the liability or the credit characteristics of the liability). Therefore, they believe that changing to an accounting policy for insurance contracts that uses future investment margins to measure liabilities arising

---

55   References to the *Framework* are to IASC's *Framework for the Preparation and Presentation of Financial Statements*, adopted by the IASB in 2001. In September 2010 the IASB replaced the *Framework* with the *Conceptual Framework for Financial Reporting*.

from insurance contracts reduces the relevance and reliability of an insurer's financial statements. They do not believe that other aspects of an accounting model for insurance contracts can outweigh this reduction.

DO6   These four Board members also would not permit entities to change their accounting policies for insurance and reinsurance contracts to policies that include using what is called shadow accounting. They do not believe that the changes in the carrying amount of insurance liabilities (including related deferred acquisition costs and intangible assets) under shadow accounting should be recognised directly in equity. That these changes in the measurement of the liability are calculated on the basis of changes in the measurement of assets is irrelevant. These Board members believe that these changes in insurance liabilities result in expenses that under the IASB *Framework* should be recognised in profit or loss.

Financial instruments with a discretionary participation feature[56]

DO7   Professor Barth and Messrs Leisenring and Smith would not permit entities to account for a financial instrument with a discretionary participation feature on a basis that differs from that required by IAS 32 *Financial Instruments: Disclosure and Presentation* and IAS 39 *Financial Instruments: Recognition and Measurement*. Those Standards require entities to separate the components of a compound financial instrument, recognise the liability component initially at fair value, and attribute any residual to the equity component. These three Board members believe that the difficulty in determining whether a discretionary participation feature is a liability or equity does not preclude applying the measurement requirements in IAS 39 to the liability and equity components once the entity makes that determination. These three Board members believe that an entity would misstate interest expense if the financial liability component is not initially measured at its fair value.

DO8   These three Board members would require entities to ensure in all cases that the liability recognised for financial instruments with a discretionary participation feature is no less than the amount that would result from applying IAS 39 to the guaranteed element. Paragraph 35 of IFRS 4 requires this if an entity classifies none or some of the feature as a liability, but not if it classifies all of the feature as a liability.

Financial instruments[57]

DO9   Mr Smith also dissents from IFRS 4 because he believes it defines insurance contracts too broadly and makes unnecessary exceptions to the scope of IAS 32 and IAS 39. In his view, this permits the structuring of contractual provisions to avoid the requirements of those Standards, diminishing their effectiveness and adding considerable complexity in interpreting and applying them and IFRS 4. He believes that many of the exceptions, based on the desire to avoid systems changes, are unnecessary because they generally are unrelated to the second phase of the project on insurance contracts, and they create a disincentive to

---

56   IFRS 9 *Financial Instruments* replaced IAS 39. IFRS 9 applies to all items that were previously within the scope of IAS 39.

57   IFRS 9 *Financial Instruments* replaced IAS 39. IFRS 9 applies to all items that were previously within the scope of IAS 39.

enhance systems before the second phase of that project is completed. Mr Smith believes that IAS 32 and IAS 39 already contain the appropriate solutions when measurements cannot be made reliably and those solutions make systems limitations transparent.

DO10   Paragraph 10 of IFRS 4 requires an insurer to unbundle a deposit component of an insurance contract if the insurer can measure the deposit component separately and the insurer's accounting policies do not otherwise require it to recognise all rights and obligations arising from the deposit component. Mr Smith notes that the deposit component consists entirely of financial liabilities or financial assets. Therefore, he believes that the deposit component of all insurance contracts should be unbundled. Mr Smith notes that IAS 32 already requires the liability component of a compound financial instrument to be separated at its fair value with any residual accounted for as equity. He believes this approach could be applied by analogy when an insurance contract contains a financial liability and would represent a superior solution.

DO11   IFRS 4 amends IAS 39 by stating that an embedded derivative and the host insurance contract are closely related if they are so interdependent that the entity cannot measure the embedded derivative separately. This creates an exemption from the requirement in IAS 39 to account for such embedded derivatives at fair value. Mr Smith disagrees with that change. In particular, if a contract permits a policyholder to obtain a derivative-based cash settlement in lieu of maintaining insurance, Mr Smith believes that the derivative-based cash settlement alternative is a financial liability and should be measured at fair value.

DO12   For the contracts discussed in the previous paragraph, Mr Smith believes that IAS 39 already provides a superior solution that will not promote structuring to take advantage of an exception to IAS 39. It requires the entire contract to be measured at fair value when an embedded derivative cannot be reliably separated from the host contract. However, Mr Smith would amend IAS 39 to require measurement at cost if a contract cannot be measured reliably at fair value in its entirety and contains a significant insurance component as well as an embedded derivative. This amendment would be consistent with similar requirements in IAS 39 for unquoted equity instruments. To make systems limitations more transparent, Mr Smith would add the disclosure required by IAS 32, including the fact that fair value cannot be measured reliably, a description of the insurance contracts in question, their carrying amounts, an explanation of why fair value cannot be measured reliably and, if possible, the range of estimates within which fair value is likely to fall.

DO13   Mr Smith would exclude from the definition of an insurance contract those contracts that are regarded as transferring significant insurance risk at inception only because they include a pricing option permitting the holder to purchase insurance at a specified price at a later date. He would also exclude from the definition those contracts in which the insurance component has expired. He believes that any remaining obligation is a financial instrument that should be accounted for under IAS 39.

Dissent of Tatsumi Yamada

DO14   Mr Yamada dissents from the issue of IFRS 4 because he believes that it does not resolve appropriately the mismatch in measurement base between financial assets of insurers and their insurance liabilities. Specifically:

(a)   he disagrees with the inclusion of an option to introduce a current discount rate for designated insurance liabilities.

(b)   he believes that the Board should have provided a practicable means to reduce the effect of the accounting mismatch using methods based partly on some existing practices that involve broader, but constrained, use of amortised cost.

Option to introduce a current discount rate

DO15   Mr Yamada disagrees with paragraph 24 of the IFRS, which creates an option to introduce a current market-based discount rate for designated insurance liabilities. He has sympathy for the view expressed in paragraph BC175 that introducing a current market-based discount rate for insurance liabilities rather than a historical discount rate would improve the relevance and reliability of an insurer's financial statements. However, as explained in paragraph BC126, 'the Board will not address discount rates and the basis for risk adjustments until phase II.' Therefore, Mr Yamada believes that it is not appropriate to deal with measurement of insurance liabilities in phase I of this project.

DO16   In addition, Mr Yamada believes that there should be a stringent test to assess whether changes in the carrying amount of the designated insurance liabilities mitigate the changes in carrying amount of financial assets. Without such a test, management will have a free choice to decide the extent to which it introduces remeasurement of insurance liabilities. Therefore, he does not agree with the Board's conclusion in paragraph BC176 that 'the increase in relevance and reliability from introducing a current discount rate could outweigh the disadvantages of permitting accounting policies that are not applied consistently to all similar liabilities'.

DO17   Furthermore, the option introduced by paragraph 24 is not an effective way to reduce the accounting mismatch, in Mr Yamada's view. He agrees with the Board's analysis that 'many insurers may not have systems to adjust liabilities for changes in interest rates and may not wish to develop such systems, even for designated liabilities as opposed to all liabilities', as explained in paragraph BC177(d)(i).

Assets held to back insurance liabilities[58]

DO18   As stated in paragraph BC171, many of the respondents to ED 5 urged the Board to explore ways of reducing the accounting mismatch. Mr Yamada notes that IFRS 4 provides some limited solutions for the accounting mismatch by clarifying that shadow accounting can be used and amending IAS 40 to permit two separate elections when an entity selects the fair value model or the cost model for investment property. IFRS 4 also provides an option to introduce a

---

58 IFRS 9 *Financial Instruments* replaced IAS 39. IFRS 9 applies to all items that were previously within the scope of IAS 39.

current market-based discount rate for designated insurance liabilities but, for reasons given in paragraphs DO15–DO17, Mr Yamada does not support that option.

DO19 Mr Yamada believes that it would have been appropriate to provide a more broadly applicable way of mitigating the effect of the accounting mismatch. Because phase I is only a stepping stone to phase II, Mr Yamada is of the view that the only practicable solution in the short term is one based on the existing practices of insurers. He believes that if remeasurement of insurance liabilities by a current market-based discount rate is allowed as means of resolving the mismatch, a new category of assets carried at amortised cost such as the Japanese 'debt securities earmarked for policy reserve' (DSR) should also have been allowed in phase I.

DO20 Although Mr Yamada acknowledges that the DSR approach would not lead to more relevant and reliable measurements, he notes that insurers have several years' experience of using this approach, which was created in 2000 when Japan introduced an accounting standard for financial instruments that is similar to IASs 32 and 39. He believes that no perfect solution is available in phase I and together with the disclosure of fair value information required by IAS 32, the DSR approach would provide a reasonable solution for phase I. Therefore he does not agree with the Board's conclusion in paragraph BC178 that amending the existing measurement requirements in IAS 39 for financial assets 'would have reduced the relevance and reliability of financial statements to an unacceptable extent'. Indeed, Mr Yamada believes the exemption in IFRS 4 from paragraphs 10–12 of IAS 8 could impair the relevance and reliability of financial statements more than introducing the DSR approach would have done.

Dissent of Mary Tokar from *Applying IFRS 9* Financial Instruments *with IFRS 4* Insurance Contracts (Amendments to IFRS 4) as issued in September 2016

DO1 Ms Tokar dissents from the issue of the Amendments to IFRS 4 because she disagrees with providing a temporary exemption from IFRS 9 for insurers whose activities are predominantly connected with insurance. She believes that it is important for IFRS 9 to be applied without delay because of the significant improvements that IFRS 9 requires in accounting for financial assets, including a new impairment model that is based on expected credit losses and the related enhanced disclosures about credit risk. She notes that these improvements were made in response to calls from regulators and users of financial statements after the global financial crisis and many of those parties have called for these improvements to be introduced without delay. She also notes that the temporary exemption from IFRS 9 will reduce comparability among reporting entities, including among insurers.

DO2 Ms Tokar agrees that there are valid concerns about the different effective dates of IFRS 9 and the forthcoming insurance contracts Standard. She agrees that the classification and measurement requirements in IFRS 9 may lead to new accounting mismatches and, hence, an increase in reported volatility within profit or loss for those insurers that measure insurance contracts on a cost basis under IFRS 4. She also notes that some of that volatility is expected to be offset in profit or loss when the forthcoming insurance contracts Standard is applied because that forthcoming Standard is expected to require insurers to measure insurance contracts using current estimates of future cash flows discounted at a current rate.

DO3 Ms Tokar believes that the amendment to permit insurers to use the overlay approach makes a temporary exemption from IFRS 9 unnecessary. She notes that the overlay approach deals more appropriately with the concerns expressed about additional accounting mismatches and volatility because the overlay approach:

(a) provides users of financial statements with the benefits of the improved accounting required by IFRS 9 but also removes the effect of potential additional volatility from profit or loss for designated financial assets until the forthcoming insurance contracts Standard is applied.

(b) makes it easier for users of financial statements to compare the financial statements of insurers that apply the overlay approach with those that do not, as well as with other entities that hold similar financial assets. This comparability will be reduced if some insurers apply a temporary exemption from IFRS 9.

DO4 Ms Tokar observed that the Board and staff undertook extensive outreach with users of financial statements while developing, and following the publication of, the Exposure Draft in December 2015. This outreach was global and involved both users specialising in insurance activities and non-specialist users. Many users expressed the view that entities should apply IFRS 9 in 2018 (ie when that Standard is mandatory), even if this is before the application of the forthcoming insurance contracts Standard, because IFRS 9 provides improved information about financial instruments. Those users of financial statements expressed the view that if the Board decided to address preparers' concerns regarding increases in accounting mismatches and volatility then only the overlay approach should be used. They expressed this preference because the overlay approach maintains the comparability of financial statements by requiring all entities to apply IFRS 9 while addressing volatility in a transparent way.

DO5 Ms Tokar also notes that, as a result of the Amendments to IFRS 4, three different reporting outcomes will exist for insurers: (a) application of IFRS 9 without the overlay approach; (b) application of IFRS 9 with the overlay approach; and (c) use of the temporary exemption from IFRS 9. She believes that this variety in approaches to accounting for financial instruments may significantly reduce comparability among insurers, and between insurers and other entities. She observes that reduced comparability is one of the concerns expressed by users of financial statements about the temporary exemption.

IASB documents published to accompany

IFRS 5

Non-current Assets Held for Sale and Discontinued Operations

The text of the unaccompanied standard, IFRS 5, is contained in Part A of this edition. Its effective date when issued was 1 January 2005. The text of the Accompanying Guidance on IFRS 5 is contained in Part B of this edition. This part presents the following documents:

BASIS FOR CONCLUSIONS

DISSENTING OPINIONS

CONTENTS

Basis for Conclusions on
IFRS 5 *Non-current Assets Held for Sale and Discontinued Operations*

This Basis for Conclusions accompanies, but is not part of, IFRS 5.

Introduction

BC1   This Basis for Conclusions summarises the International Accounting Standards Board's considerations in reaching the conclusions in IFRS 5 *Non-current Assets Held for Sale and Discontinued Operations*. Individual Board members gave greater weight to some factors than to others.

BC2   In September 2002 the Board agreed to add a short-term convergence project to its active agenda. The objective of the project is to reduce differences between IFRSs and US GAAP that are capable of resolution in a relatively short time and can be addressed outside major projects. The project is a joint project with the US Financial Accounting Standards Board (FASB).

BC3   As part of the project, the two boards agreed to review each other's deliberations on each of the selected possible convergence topics, and choose the highest quality solution as the basis for convergence. For topics recently considered by either board, there is an expectation that whichever board has more recently deliberated that topic will have the higher quality solution.

BC4   As part of the review of topics recently considered by the FASB, the Board discussed the requirements of SFAS 144 *Accounting for the Impairment or Disposal of Long-Lived Assets*, as they relate to assets held for sale and discontinued operations. The Board did not consider the requirements of SFAS 144 relating to the impairment of assets held for use. Impairment of such assets is an issue that is being addressed in the IASB research project on measurement being led by the Canadian Accounting Standards Board.

BC5   Until the issue of IFRS 5, the requirements of SFAS 144 on assets held for sale and discontinued operations differed from IFRSs in the following ways:

(a)   if specified criteria are met, SFAS 144 requires non-current assets that are to be disposed of to be classified as held for sale. Such assets are remeasured at the lower of carrying amount and fair value less costs to sell and are not depreciated or amortised. IFRSs did not require non-current assets that are to be disposed of to be classified separately or measured differently from other non-current assets.

(b)   the definition of discontinued operations in SFAS 144 was different from the definition of discontinuing operations in IAS 35 *Discontinuing Operations* and the presentation of such operations required by the two standards was also different.

BC6   As discussed in more detail below, the Board concluded that introducing a classification of assets that are held for sale would substantially improve the information available to users of financial statements about assets to be sold.

BC7   The Board published its proposals in an Exposure Draft, ED 4 *Disposal of Non-current Assets and Presentation of Discontinued Operations*, in July 2003 with a comment deadline of 24 October 2003. The Board received over 80 comment letters on the Exposure Draft.

Scope of the IFRS

BC8   In ED 4, the Board proposed that the IFRS should apply to all non-current assets except:

  (a)   goodwill,

  (b)   financial instruments within the scope of IAS 39 *Financial Instruments: Recognition and Measurement*,[1]

  (c)   financial assets under leases, and

  (d)   deferred tax assets and assets arising from employee benefits.

BC9   In reconsidering the scope, the Board noted that the use of the term 'non-current' caused the following problems:

  (a)   assets that are acquired with the intention of resale were clearly intended to be within the scope of ED 4, but would also be within the definition of current assets and so might be thought to be excluded. The same was true for assets that had been classified as non-current but were now expected to be realised within twelve months.

  (b)   it was not clear how the scope would apply to assets presented in accordance with a liquidity presentation.

BC10   The Board noted that it had not intended that assets classified as non-current in accordance with IAS 1 *Presentation of Financial Statements* would be reclassified as current assets simply because of management's intention to sell or because they reached their final twelve months of expected use by the entity. The Board decided to clarify in IFRS 5 that assets classified as non-current are not reclassified as current assets until they meet the criteria to be classified as held for sale in accordance with the IFRS. Further, assets of a class that an entity would normally regard as non-current and are acquired exclusively with a view to resale are not classified as current unless they meet the criteria to be classified as held for sale in accordance with the IFRS.

BC11   In relation to assets presented in accordance with a liquidity presentation, the Board decided that non-current should be taken to mean assets that include amounts expected to be recovered more than twelve months after the balance sheet date.

BC12   These clarifications ensure that all assets of the type normally regarded by the entity as non-current will be within the scope of the IFRS.

BC13   The Board also reconsidered the exclusions from the scope proposed in ED 4. The Board noted that the classification and presentation requirements of the

---

1   IFRS 9 *Financial Instruments* replaced IAS 39. IFRS 9 applies to all items that were previously within the scope of IAS 39. This paragraph refers to matters relevant when IFRS 5 was issued.

IFRS are applicable to all non-current assets and concluded that any exclusions should relate only to the measurement requirements. In relation to the measurement requirements, the Board decided that non-current assets should be excluded only if (i) they are already carried at fair value with changes in fair value recognised in profit or loss or (ii) there would be difficulties in determining their fair value less costs to sell. The Board therefore concluded that only the following non-current assets should be excluded from the measurement requirements of the IFRS:

Assets already carried at fair value with changes in fair value recognised in profit or loss:

(a)   financial assets within the scope of IAS 39.[2]

(b)   non-current assets that have been accounted for using the fair value model in IAS 40 *Investment Property*.

(c)   non-current assets that have been measured at fair value less estimated point-of-sale costs in accordance with IAS 41 *Agriculture*.[3]

Assets for which there might be difficulties in determining their fair value:

(a)   deferred tax assets.

(b)   assets arising from employee benefits.

(c)   assets arising from insurance contracts.

BC14   The Board acknowledged that the scope of the IFRS would differ from that of SFAS 144 but noted that SFAS 144 covers the impairment of non-current assets held for use as well as those held for sale. Furthermore, other requirements in US GAAP affect the scope of SFAS 144. The Board therefore concluded that convergence with the scope of SFAS 144 would not be possible.

BC14A   The Board identified a need to clarify the disclosure requirements for non-current assets (or disposal groups) classified as held for sale or discontinued operations in accordance with IFRS 5. Some believed that IFRS 5 and other IFRSs that specifically refer to non-current assets (or disposal groups) classified as held for sale or discontinued operations set out all the disclosures required in respect of those assets or operations. Others believed that all disclosures required by IFRSs whose scope does not specifically exclude non-current assets (or disposal groups) classified as held for sale or discontinued operations apply to such assets (or disposal groups).[4]

BC14B   The Board noted that paragraph 30 of IFRS 5 requires an entity to 'present and disclose information that enables users of the financial statements to evaluate the financial effects of discontinued operations and disposals of non-current assets (or disposal groups).' Paragraph BC17 below states that 'the Board concluded that providing information about assets and groups of assets and

---

2   IFRS 9 *Financial Instruments* replaced IAS 39. IFRS 9 applies to all items that were previously within the scope of IAS 39. This paragraph refers to matters relevant when IFRS 5 was issued.

3   In *Improvements to IFRSs* issued in May 2008 the Board amended IAS 41: the term 'estimated point-of-sale costs' was replaced by 'costs to sell'. IFRS 13 *Fair Value Measurement*, issued in May 2011, defines fair value and contains the requirements for measuring fair value.

4   Paragraphs BC14A–BC14E were added as a consequence of amendments to IFRS 5 by *Improvements to IFRSs* issued in April 2009.

liabilities to be disposed of is of benefit to users of financial statements. Such information should assist users in assessing the timing, amount and uncertainty of future cash flows.'

BC14C   The Board noted that some IFRSs other than IFRS 5 require specific disclosures for non-current assets (or disposal groups) classified as held for sale or discontinued operations. For instance, paragraph 68 of IAS 33 *Earnings per Share* requires an entity to disclose the amount per share for discontinued operations. The Board also noted that the requirements of IAS 1 on fair presentation and materiality also apply to such assets (or disposal groups).

BC14D   The Board also noted that when a disposal group includes assets and liabilities that are not within the scope of the measurement requirements of IFRS 5, disclosures about measurement of those assets and liabilities are normally provided in the other notes to the financial statements and do not need to be repeated, unless they better enable users of the financial statements to evaluate the financial effects of discontinued operations and disposals of non-current assets (or disposal groups).

BC14E   Consequently, in *Improvements to IFRSs* issued in April 2009, the Board clarified that IFRS 5 and other IFRSs that specifically refer to non-current assets (or disposal groups) classified as held for sale or discontinued operations set out all the disclosures required in respect of those assets or operations. Additional disclosures about non-current assets (or disposal groups) classified as held for sale may be necessary to comply with the general requirements of IAS 1, in particular paragraphs 15 and 125 of that Standard.

Classification of non-current assets to be disposed of as held for sale

BC15   Under SFAS 144, long-lived assets are classified as either (i) held and used or (ii) held for sale. Before the issue of this IFRS, no distinction was made in IFRSs between non-current assets held and used and non-current assets held for sale, except in relation to financial instruments.

BC16   The Board considered whether a separate classification for non-current assets held for sale would create unnecessary complexity in IFRSs and introduce an element of management intent into the accounting. Some commentators suggested that the categorisation 'assets held for sale' is unnecessary, and that if the focus were changed to 'assets *retired* from active use' much of the complexity could be eliminated, because the latter classification would be based on actuality rather than what they perceive as management intent. They assert that it is the potential abuse of the classification that necessitates many of the detailed requirements in SFAS 144. Others suggested that, if existing IFRSs were amended to specify that assets retired from active use are measured at fair value less costs to sell and to require additional disclosure, some convergence with SFAS 144 could be achieved without creating a new IFRS.

BC17   However, the Board concluded that providing information about assets and groups of assets and liabilities to be disposed of is of benefit to users of financial statements. Such information should assist users in assessing the timing, amount and uncertainty of future cash flows. The Board understands that this was also the assessment underpinning SFAS 144. Therefore the Board concluded that introducing the notion of assets and disposal groups held for sale makes IFRSs more complete.

BC18   Furthermore, although the held for sale classification begins from an intention to sell the asset, the other criteria for this classification are tightly drawn and are significantly more objective than simply specifying an intention or commitment to sell. Some might argue that the criteria are too specific. However, the Board believes that the criteria should be specific to achieve comparability of classification between entities. The Board does not believe that a classification 'retired from active use' would necessarily require fewer criteria to support it. For example, it would be necessary to establish a distinction between assets retired from active use and those that are held as back-up spares or are temporarily idle.

BC19   Lastly, if the classification and measurement of assets held for sale in IFRSs are the same as in US GAAP, convergence will have been achieved in an area of importance to users of financial statements.

BC20   Most respondents to ED 4 agreed that a separate classification for non-current assets that are no longer held to be used is desirable. However, the proposals in ED 4 were criticised for the following reasons:

(a)   the criteria were too restrictive and rules-based.

(b)   a commitment to sell needs to be demonstrated, consistently with the requirements of IAS 37 *Provisions, Contingent Liabilities and Contingent Assets* relating to restructuring provisions.

(c)   the classification should be for assets retired from active use.

(d)   assets to be abandoned should be treated in the same way as assets to be sold.

BC21   The Board noted that a more flexible definition would be open to abuse. Further, changing the criteria for classification could cause divergence from US GAAP. The Board has, however, reordered the criteria to highlight the principles.

BC22   The Board also noted that the requirements of IAS 37 establish when a liability is incurred, whereas the requirements of the IFRS relate to the measurement and presentation of assets that are already recognised.

BC23   Finally, the Board reconfirmed the principle behind the classification proposals in ED 4, which is that the carrying amount of the assets will be recovered principally through sale. Applying this principle to assets retired from active use, the Board decided that assets retired from active use that do not meet the criteria for classification as assets held for sale should not be presented separately because the carrying amount of the asset may not be recovered principally through sale. Conversely, the Board decided that assets that meet the criteria to be classified as held for sale and are being used should not be precluded from being separately classified. This is because, if a non-current asset is available for immediate sale, the remaining use of the asset is incidental to its recovery through sale and the carrying amount of the asset will be recovered principally through sale.

BC24   Applying the same principle to assets to be abandoned, the Board noted that their carrying value will never be recovered principally through sale.

Plan to sell the controlling interest in a subsidiary[5]

BC24A   In 2007 the Board considered situations in which an entity is committed to a plan to sell the controlling interest in a subsidiary and, after the sale, retains a non-controlling interest in its former subsidiary, taking the form of an investment in an associate, an investment in a joint venture or a financial asset. The Board considered how the classification as held for sale applies to the subsidiary in the consolidated financial statements of the entity.

BC24B   The Board noted that paragraph 6 states that 'An entity shall classify a non-current asset (or disposal group) as held for sale if its carrying amount will be recovered principally through a sale transaction rather than through continuing use.' The Board also noted that IAS 27 *Consolidated and Separate Financial Statements* (as amended in January 2008) defines control and requires a parent to consolidate a subsidiary until control is lost.[6] At the date control is lost, all the subsidiary's assets and liabilities are derecognised and any investment retained in the former subsidiary is recognised. Loss of control is a significant economic event that changes the nature of an investment. The parent-subsidiary relationship ceases to exist and an investor-investee relationship begins that differs significantly from the former parent-subsidiary relationship. Therefore, the new investor-investee relationship is recognised and measured initially at the date when control is lost.

BC24C   The Board concluded that, under the sale plan described above, the controlling interest in the subsidiary is, in substance, exchanged for a non-controlling interest. Therefore, in the Board's view, being committed to a plan involving loss of control of a subsidiary should trigger classification as held for sale. The Board also noted that this conclusion is consistent with IAS 27.

BC24D   The Board noted that the subsidiary's assets and liabilities meet the definition of a disposal group in accordance with paragraph 4. Therefore, the Board concluded that all the subsidiary's assets and liabilities should be classified as held for sale, not only the portion of the interest to be disposed of, regardless of whether the entity will retain a non-controlling interest.

BC24E   The Board considered the comments received on the proposal set out in its exposure draft of October 2007. In response to comments from some respondents, the Board clarified in the amendment that the criteria for classification as held for sale need to be met.

---

5   This section and paragraphs BC77A and BC79A were added as a consequence of amendments to IFRS 5 by *Improvements to IFRSs* issued in May 2008.

6   The consolidation requirements in IAS 27 were superseded, and the definition of control was consequently revised, by IFRS 10 *Consolidated Financial Statements* issued in May 2011. The requirement to consolidate a subsidiary until control is lost did not change. In October 2012 the Board issued *Investment Entities* (Amendments to IFRS 10, IFRS 12 and IAS 27), which required investment entities, as defined in IFRS 10 *Consolidated Financial Statements*, to measure their investments in subsidiaries, other than those providing investment-related services or activities, at fair value through profit or loss.

Assets to be exchanged for other non-current assets

BC25   Under SFAS 144, long-lived assets that are to be exchanged for similar productive assets cannot be classified as held for sale. They are regarded as disposed of only when exchanged. The Basis for Conclusions on SFAS 144 explains that this is because the exchange of such assets is accounted for at amounts based on the carrying amount of the assets, not at fair value, and that using the carrying amount is more consistent with the accounting for a long-lived asset to be held and used than for a long-lived asset to be sold.

BC26   Under IAS 16 *Property, Plant and Equipment*, as revised in 2003, an exchange of assets is normally measured at fair value. The SFAS 144 reasoning for the classification of such assets as held for sale does not, therefore, apply. Consistently with IAS 16, the IFRS treats an exchange of assets as a disposal and acquisition of assets unless the exchange has no commercial substance.

BC27   The FASB has published an exposure draft proposing to converge with the requirements in IAS 16 for an exchange of assets to be measured at fair value. The exposure draft also proposes a consequential amendment to SFAS 144 that would make exchanges of assets that have commercial substance eligible for classification as held for sale.

Measurement of non-current assets held for sale

BC28   SFAS 144 requires a long-lived asset or a disposal group classified as held for sale to be measured at the lower of its carrying amount and fair value less costs to sell. A long-lived asset classified as held for sale (or included within a disposal group) is not depreciated, but interest and other expenses attributable to the liabilities of a disposal group are recognised.

BC29   As explained in the Basis for Conclusions on SFAS 144, the remaining use in operations of an asset that is to be sold is incidental to the recovery of the carrying amount through sale. The accounting for such an asset should therefore be a process of valuation rather than allocation.

BC30   The FASB further observed that once the asset is remeasured, to depreciate the asset would reduce its carrying amount below its fair value less costs to sell. It also noted that should there be a decline in the value of the asset after initial classification as held for sale and before eventual sale, the loss would be recognised in the period of decline because the fair value less costs to sell is evaluated each period.

BC31   The counter-argument is that, although classified as held for sale, the asset is still being used in operations, and hence cessation of depreciation is inconsistent with the basic principle that the cost of an asset should be allocated over the period during which benefits are obtained from its use. Furthermore, although the decline in the value of the asset through its use would be reflected in the recognised change in fair value, it might also be masked by an increase arising from changes in the market prices of the asset.

BC32   However, the Board noted that IAS 16 requires an entity to keep the expected useful life and residual values of property, plant and equipment up to date, and IAS 36 *Impairment of Assets* requires an immediate write-down to the higher of value in use and fair value less costs to sell. An entity should, therefore, often achieve a measurement effect for individual assets that are about to be sold under other IFRSs similar to that required by this IFRS as follows. Under other IFRSs, if the fair value less costs to sell is higher than carrying amount there will be no impairment and no depreciation (because the residual value will have been updated). If fair value less costs to sell is lower than carrying amount, there will be an impairment loss that reduces the carrying amount to fair value less costs to sell and then no depreciation (because the residual value will have been updated), unless value in use is higher than fair value less costs to sell. If value in use is higher than fair value less costs to sell, there would be small differences between the treatment that would arise under other IFRSs and the treatment under IFRS 5. Under other IFRSs there would be an impairment loss to the extent that the carrying amount exceeds value in use rather than to the extent that the carrying amount exceeds fair value less costs to sell. Under other IFRSs, there would also then be depreciation of the excess of value in use (the new carrying amount of the asset) over fair value less costs to sell (its residual value). However, for assets classified as held for sale, value in use will differ from fair value less costs to sell only to the extent of the net cash flows expected to arise before the sale. If the period to sale is short, this amount will usually be relatively small. The difference in impairment loss recognised and subsequent depreciation under other IFRSs compared with the impairment loss and no subsequent depreciation under IFRS 5 would, therefore, also be small.

BC33   The Board concluded that the measurement requirements of IFRS 5 for individual assets would often not involve a significant change from the requirements of other IFRSs. Furthermore, the Board agreed with the FASB that the cash flows arising from the asset's remaining use were incidental to the recovery of the asset through sale and, hence, concluded that individual assets classified as held for sale should be measured at the lower of carrying amount and fair value less costs to sell and should not be depreciated.

BC34   For disposal groups, there could be greater differences between the requirements in other IFRSs and the requirements of IFRS 5. For example, the fair value less costs to sell of a disposal group may reflect internally generated goodwill to the extent that it is higher than the carrying value of the net assets in the disposal group. The residual value of the non-current assets in the disposal group may, nonetheless, be such that, if they were accounted for in accordance with IAS 16, those assets would be depreciated.

BC35   In such a situation, some might view the requirements in IFRS 5 as allowing internally generated goodwill to stop the depreciation of non-current assets. However, the Board does not agree with that view. Rather, the Board believes that the internally generated goodwill provides a buffer against the recognition of an impairment loss on the disposal group. The same effect arises from the impairment requirements in IAS 36. The non-depreciation of the non-current assets in the disposal group is, as with individual assets, a consequence of the basic principle underlying the separate classification, that the carrying amount of the asset will be recovered principally through sale, not continuing use, and that amounts recovered through continuing use will be incidental.

BC36   In addition, it is important to emphasise that IFRS 5 permits only an asset (or disposal group) that is to be *sold* to be classified as held for sale. Assets to be abandoned are classified as held and used until disposed of, and thus are depreciated. The Board agrees with the FASB's observation that a distinction can be drawn between an asset that is to be sold and an asset that is to be abandoned, because the former will be recovered principally through sale and the latter through its continuing use. Therefore, it is logical that depreciation should cease in the former but not the latter case.

BC37   When an asset or a disposal group held for sale is part of a foreign operation with a functional currency that is different from the presentation currency of the group, an exchange difference will have been recognised in equity[7] arising from the translation of the asset or disposal group into the presentation currency of the group. IAS 21 *The Effects of Changes in Foreign Exchange Rates* requires the exchange difference to be 'recycled' from equity to profit or loss on disposal of the operation. The question arises whether classification as held for sale should trigger the recycling of any exchange differences. Under US GAAP (EITF 01-5 *Application of FASB Statement No. 52 to an Investment Being Evaluated for Impairment That Will Be Disposed Of*) the accumulated foreign currency translation adjustments previously recognised in other comprehensive income that are expected to be recycled in income at the time of sale are included in the carrying amount of the asset (or disposal group) being tested for impairment.

BC38   In its project on reporting comprehensive income, the Board may reconsider the issue of recycling. Therefore, it did not wish to make any interim changes to the requirements in IAS 21. Hence, the IFRS does not permit any exchange differences to be recycled on the classification of an asset or a disposal group as held for sale. The recycling will take place when the asset or disposal group is sold.

The allocation of an impairment loss to a disposal group

BC39   Under SFAS 144 and the proposals in ED 4, assets within the disposal group that are not within the scope of the IFRS are adjusted in accordance with other standards before measuring the fair value less costs to sell of the disposal group. Any loss or gain recognised on adjusting the carrying amount of the disposal group is allocated to the carrying amount of the long-lived assets of the group.

BC40   This is different from the requirements of IAS 36 for the allocation of an impairment loss arising on a cash-generating unit. IAS 36 requires an impairment loss on a cash-generating unit to be allocated first to reduce the carrying amount of goodwill and then to reduce pro rata the carrying amounts of the other assets in the unit.

BC41   The Board considered whether the allocation of an impairment loss for a disposal group should be consistent with the requirements of IAS 36 or with the requirements of SFAS 144. The Board concluded that it would be simplest to

---

7   As a consequence of the revision of IAS 1 *Presentation of Financial Statements* (as revised in 2007) such a difference is recognised in other comprehensive income.

require the same allocation as is required by IAS 36 for cash-generating units. Although this is different from SFAS 144, the disposal group as a whole will be measured at the same amount.

Newly acquired assets

BC42   SFAS 144 requires, and ED 4 proposed, newly acquired assets that meet the criteria to be classified as held for sale to be measured at fair value less costs to sell on initial recognition. So, in those instances, other than in a business combination, in which an entity acquires a non-current asset that meets the criteria to be classified as held for sale, a loss is recognised in profit or loss if the cost of the asset exceeds its fair value less costs to sell. In the more common cases in which an entity acquires, as part of a business combination, a non-current asset (or disposal group) that meets the criteria to be classified as held for sale, the difference between fair value and fair value less costs to sell is recognised in goodwill.

BC43   Some respondents to ED 4 noted that measuring newly acquired assets not part of a business combination at fair value less costs to sell was inconsistent with the general proposal that assets classified as held for sale should be measured at the *lower of carrying amount* and fair value less costs to sell. The Board agreed and amended the requirement so that it is clear that the newly acquired assets (or disposal groups) are measured on initial recognition at the lower of what their carrying amount would be were they not classified as held for sale (ie cost) and fair value less costs to sell.

BC44   In relation to business combinations, the Board noted that conceptually the assets should be recognised initially at fair value and then immediately classified as held for sale, with the result that the costs to sell are recognised in profit or loss, not goodwill. In theory, if the entity had factored the costs to sell into the purchase price, the reduced price would lead to the creation of negative goodwill, the immediate recognition of which in profit or loss would offset the loss arising from the costs to sell. Of course, in practice, the reduced price will usually result in lower net positive goodwill rather than negative goodwill to be recognised in profit or loss. For that reason, and for the sake of convergence, the Board concluded that in a business combination non-current assets that meet the criteria to be classified as held for sale on acquisition should be measured at fair value less costs to sell on initial recognition.

BC45   The Board and the FASB are considering which items should form part of the business combination transaction more generally in their joint project on the application of the purchase method. This consideration includes whether the assets and liabilities recognised in the transaction should be based on the acquirer's or the acquiree's perspective. The outcome of those deliberations may affect the decision discussed in paragraph BC44.[8]

---

8   In their joint project on the application of the acquisition method, the Board and the FASB clarified that the classification of assets acquired in a business combination as held for sale should be based on the acquirer's perspective. Therefore, the acquirer would have to satisfy the criteria in paragraphs 6–11 of IFRS 5 at the acquisition date in order to classify assets acquired as held for sale on initial recognition.

Recognition of subsequent increases in fair value less costs to sell

BC46 The Board considered whether a subsequent increase in fair value less costs to sell should be recognised to the extent that it reversed previous impairments. SFAS 144 requires the recognition of a subsequent increase in fair value less costs to sell, but not in excess of the cumulative loss previously recognised for a write-down to fair value less costs to sell. The Board decided that, under IFRSs, a gain should be recognised to the extent that it reverses any impairment of the asset, either in accordance with the IFRS or previously in accordance with IAS 36. Recognising a gain for the reversal of an impairment that occurred before the classification of the asset as held for sale is consistent with the requirement in IAS 36 to recognise reversals of impairment.

Recognition of impairment losses and subsequent gains for assets that, before classification as held for sale, were measured at revalued amounts in accordance with another IFRS

BC47 ED 4 proposed that impairment losses and subsequent gains for assets that, before classification as held for sale, were measured at revalued amounts in accordance with another IFRS should be treated as revaluation decreases and increases according to the standard under which the assets had previously been revalued, consistently with the requirements of IAS 36, except to the extent that the losses and gains are caused by the initial recognition of, or changes in, costs to sell. ED 4 also proposed that costs to sell should always be recognised in profit or loss.

BC48 Many respondents disagreed with these proposals, because of their complexity and because of the resulting inconsistent treatment of assets classified as held for sale. The Board considered the issues raised and decided that assets that were already carried at fair value with changes in fair value recognised in profit or loss should not be subject to the measurement requirements of the IFRS. The Board believes that, for such assets, continued measurement at fair value gives better information than measurement at the lower of carrying amount and fair value less costs to sell. The Board did not, however, believe that such treatment was appropriate for assets that had been revalued in accordance with IAS 16 and IAS 38, because those standards require depreciation to continue and the revaluation change would not necessarily be recognised in profit or loss. The Board concluded that assets that had been revalued in accordance with IAS 16 and IAS 38 should be treated in the same way as any assets that, before classification as held for sale, had not been revalued. Such an approach results in a consistent treatment for assets that are within the scope of the measurement requirements of the IFRS and, hence, a simpler standard.

Measurement of assets reclassified as held for use

BC49 Under SFAS 144, when an entity changes its plan to sell the asset and reclassifies a long-lived asset from held for sale to held and used, the asset is measured at the lower of (a) the carrying amount before the asset (or disposal group) was classified as held for sale, adjusted for any depreciation (or amortisation) that would have been recognised had the asset (or disposal group) been continuously classified as held and used and (b) its fair value at the date of the decision not to sell.

BC50   The underlying principle is to restore the carrying value of the asset to what it would have been had it never been classified as held for sale, taking into account any impairments that may have occurred. In fact, SFAS 144 requires that, for held and used assets, an impairment is recognised only if the carrying amount of the asset exceeds the sum of the undiscounted cash flows expected to result from its use and eventual disposal. Thus, the carrying amount of the asset if it had never been classified as held for sale might exceed its fair value. As a result, SFAS 144 does not necessarily lead to the asset reverting to its original carrying amount. However, the Basis for Conclusions on SFAS 144 notes that the FASB concluded it would be inappropriate to write up the carrying amount of the asset to an amount greater than its fair value solely on the basis of an undiscounted cash flow test. Hence, it arrived at the requirement for measurement at the lower of (a) the asset's carrying amount had it not been classified as held for sale and (b) fair value at the date of the decision not to sell the asset.

BC51   IAS 36 has a different measurement basis for impaired assets, ie recoverable amount. The Board concluded that to be consistent with the principle of SFAS 144 and also to be consistent with the requirements of IAS 36, an asset that ceases to be classified as held for sale should be measured at the lower of (a) the carrying amount that would have been recognised had the asset not been classified as held for sale and (b) its recoverable amount at the date of reclassification. Whilst this is not full convergence, the difference arises from differences in the US GAAP and IFRS impairment models.

Removal of exemption from consolidation for subsidiaries acquired and held exclusively with a view to resale

BC52   SFAS 144 removed the exemption from consolidation in US GAAP for subsidiaries held on a temporary basis on the grounds that all assets held for sale should be treated in the same way, ie as required by SFAS 144 rather than having some assets consolidated and some not.

BC53   The Board agreed that all subsidiaries should be consolidated and that all assets (and disposal groups) that meet the criteria to be classified as held for sale should be treated in the same way. The exemption from consolidation in IAS 27 *Consolidated and Separate Financial Statements* for subsidiaries acquired and held exclusively with a view to resale prevents those assets and disposal groups within such subsidiaries that meet the criteria to be classified as held for sale from being treated consistently with other assets and disposal groups. ED 4 therefore proposed that the exemption in IAS 27 should be removed.[9]

BC54   Some respondents disagreed with this proposal, on the grounds that the information provided by consolidation of such subsidiaries would be less useful

---

9   The consolidation requirements in IAS 27 were superseded by IFRS 10 *Consolidated Financial Statements* issued in May 2011. IFRS 10 does not contain an exception from consolidation for subsidiaries acquired and held exclusively with a view to resale.

than that provided by the current requirement to measure the investment in such subsidiaries at fair value. The Board noted that the impact of the proposals in ED 4 would be limited to the following:

(a) the measurement of a subsidiary that currently is within the scope of the exemptions would change from fair value as required by IAS 39[10] to the lower of cost and fair value less costs to sell.

(b) any change in fair value of the investment in the subsidiary would, in accordance with the current requirements in IAS 27, be presented as a single amount in profit or loss as a held-for-trading financial asset[11] in accordance with IAS 39. As discussed in paragraph BC72, the subsidiary would be a discontinued operation and, in accordance with the IFRS's requirements (see paragraphs BC73–BC76), any recognised change in the value of the disposal group that comprises the subsidiary would be presented as a single amount in profit or loss.

(c) the presentation in the balance sheet would change from a single amount for the investment in the subsidiary to two amounts—one for the assets and one for the liabilities of the disposal group that is the subsidiary.[12]

BC55　The Board reaffirmed its conclusion set out in paragraph BC53. However, it noted that the limited impact of the proposals apply only to the amounts required to be presented on the face of the balance sheet and the income statement. Providing the required analyses of those amounts in the notes could potentially involve the entity having to obtain significantly more information. The Board therefore decided not to require the disclosure of the analyses of the amounts presented on the face of the balance sheet and income statement for newly acquired subsidiaries and to clarify in an example the computational short cuts that could be used to arrive at the amounts to be presented on the face of the balance sheet and income statement.

Presentation of non-current assets held for sale

BC56　SFAS 144 requires an entity to present:

(a) a long-lived asset classified as held for sale separately in the balance sheet; and

(b) the assets and liabilities of a disposal group classified as held for sale separately in the asset and liability sections of the balance sheet. The major classes of those assets and liabilities are separately disclosed either on the face of the balance sheet or in the notes.

BC57　In the Basis for Conclusions on SFAS 144 the FASB noted that information about the nature of both assets and liabilities of a disposal group is useful to users.

10　IFRS 9 *Financial Instruments* replaced IAS 39. IFRS 9 applies to all items that were previously within the scope of IAS 39. This paragraph refers to matters relevant when IFRS 5 was issued.

11　IFRS 9 *Financial Instruments* eliminated the category of held-for-trading financial assets. This paragraph refers to matters relevant when IFRS 5 was issued.

12　Greater disaggregation of the disposal group in the statement of financial position is permitted but not required.

Separately presenting those items in the balance sheet provides information that is relevant. Separate presentation also distinguishes those assets that are not being depreciated from those that are being depreciated. The Board agreed with the FASB's views.

BC58   Respondents to ED 4 noted that the separate presentation within equity of amounts relating to assets and disposal groups classified as held for sale (such as, for example, unrealised gains and losses on available-for-sale assets[13] and foreign currency translation adjustments) would also provide useful information. The Board agreed and has added such a requirement to the IFRS.

Timing of classification as, and definition of, discontinued operations

BC59   With the introduction of SFAS 144, the FASB broadened the scope of a discontinued operation from a 'segment of a business' to a 'component of an entity'. A component is widely drawn, the criterion being that it comprises 'operations and cash flows that can be clearly distinguished, operationally and for financial reporting purposes, from the rest of the entity'. SFAS 144 states that a component may be a segment, a reporting unit, a subsidiary or an asset group.

BC60   However, at the same time, the FASB specified more restrictive criteria for determining *when* the component is classified as discontinued and hence when its results are presented as discontinued. SFAS 144 requires a component to be classified as discontinued only if it has been disposed of or if it meets the criteria for classification as an asset 'held for sale'.

BC61   The definition of a discontinuing operation in IAS 35 as a 'major line of business' or 'geographical area of operations' is closer to the former, and narrower, US GAAP definition. The trigger in IAS 35 for classifying the operation as discontinuing is the earlier of (a) the entity entering into a binding sale agreement and (b) the board of directors approving and announcing a formal disposal plan. Although IAS 35 refers to IAS 37 for further guidance on what constitutes a plan, the criteria are less restrictive than those in SFAS 144.

BC62   Paragraph 12 of the *Framework*[14] states that the objective of financial statements is to provide information about the financial position, performance and changes in financial position of an entity that is useful to a wide range of users in making economic decisions. Paragraph 15 of the *Framework* goes on to state that the economic decisions that are taken by users of financial statements require an evaluation of the ability of an entity to generate cash and cash equivalents. Separately highlighting the results of discontinued operations provides users with information that is relevant in assessing the ongoing ability of the entity to generate cash flows.

---

13 IFRS 9 *Financial Instruments* eliminated the category of available-for-sale financial assets. This paragraph refers to matters relevant when IFRS 5 was issued.

14 References to the *Framework* are to IASC's *Framework for the Preparation and Presentation of Financial Statements*, adopted by the IASB in 2001. In September 2010 the IASB replaced the *Framework* with the *Conceptual Framework for Financial Reporting*. Paragraphs 12 and 15 were superseded by Chapter 1 of the *Conceptual Framework*.

BC63   In terms of the timing of classifying an operation as discontinued, the Board considered whether more useful information is provided by making the classification conditional upon a firm decision to discontinue an operation (the current IAS 35 approach) or conditional upon the classification of an operation as held for sale.

BC64   The Board decided that, to be consistent with the presentation of assets held for disposal and in the interests of convergence, an operation should be classified as discontinued when it is disposed of or classified as held for sale.

BC65   IAS 35 also adopts a different approach from US GAAP when criteria for classification as discontinued are met after the period-end but before the financial statements are issued. SFAS 144 requires some disclosure; however, the component is *not* presented as a discontinued operation. IAS 35 requires the component to be classified as discontinuing.

BC66   The Board believes that, consistently with IAS 10 *Events after the Balance Sheet Date*,[15] a component should not be classified as discontinued in the financial statements unless it meets the criteria to be so classified at the balance sheet date.

BC67   In terms of the definition of a discontinued operation, ED 4 proposed adopting the SFAS 144 definition of a discontinued operation. The Board argued that under existing IAS 35 there may be disposal transactions that, although likely to have an impact on the ongoing operations of the entity, do not meet the criteria for classification as a discontinuing activity. For example, an entity might dispose of a significant portion, but not all, of its cash-generating units operating in a particular geographical area. Under IAS 35, that might not meet the definition of a discontinuing operation. Under SFAS 144, if the relevant criteria were met, it would.

BC68   However, a substantial majority of respondents to ED 4 disagreed with this proposal. They preferred instead to retain the IAS 35 criterion that a discontinued operation should be a major line of business or geographical area of operations.

BC69   The Board reconsidered the issue in the light of the comments received and concluded that the size of unit that could be classified as discontinued in accordance with SFAS 144 was too small, with the result that the information provided by separately presenting discontinued operations may not be as useful as it could be.

BC70   The Board also noted that the FASB Emerging Issues Task Force (EITF) is considering practical problems that have arisen in implementing the criteria for discontinued operations in SFAS 144. Specifically, the EITF is considering (a) the cash flows of the component that should be considered in the determination of whether cash flows have been or will be eliminated from the ongoing operations of the entity and (b) the types of continuing involvement that constitute significant continuing involvement in the operations of the disposal

---

15 In September 2007 the title of IAS 10 was amended from *Events after the Balance Sheet Date* to *Events after the Reporting Period* as a consequence of the revision of IAS 1 *Presentation of Financial Statements* in 2007.

component. As a result of these practical problems, the Board further concluded that it was not appropriate to change the definition of a discontinued operation in a way that was likely to cause the same problems in practice as have arisen under SFAS 144.

BC71   The Board therefore decided that it would retain the requirement in IAS 35 that a discontinued operation should be a major line of business or geographical area of operations, noting that this will include operations that would have been excluded from the US definition before SFAS 144, which was based on a reporting segment. However, the Board regards this as an interim measure and intends to work with the FASB to arrive at a converged definition within a relatively short time.

BC72   Lastly, the Board considered whether newly acquired subsidiaries that meet the criteria to be classified as held for sale should always be classified as discontinued. The Board concluded that they should be so classified because they are being disposed of for one of the following reasons:

(a)   the subsidiary is in a different line of business from the entity, so disposing of it is similar to disposing of a major line of business.

(b)   the subsidiary is required to be disposed of by regulators because the entity would otherwise have too much of a particular type of operation in a particular geographical area. In such a case the subsidiary must be a significant operation.

Changes to a plan of sale (amendment 2011)

BC72A   During its redeliberation of the exposure draft ED 9 *Joint Arrangements* the Board decided that if a disposal group or non-current asset that ceases to be classified as held for sale is a subsidiary, a joint operation, a joint venture, an associate, or a portion of an interest in a joint venture or associate, an entity should amend its financial statements for the periods since the classification as held for sale was made.

Changes to a plan of sale or to a plan of distribution to owners

BC72B   The Board received a request to clarify the accounting for a change in a disposal plan from a plan to sell to a plan to distribute a dividend in kind to its shareholders. Paragraph 26 of IFRS 5 was interpreted by some, but not all, as requiring this change to be considered as a change to a plan of sale that would be accounted for in accordance with paragraphs 27–29 of IFRS 5

BC72C   In analysing this issue the Board observed that there was no specific guidance in IFRS 5 for the discontinuation of held-for-distribution accounting, when an entity determines that the asset (or disposal group) is no longer available for immediate distribution to owners or that the distribution to owners is no longer 'highly probable', in accordance with paragraph 12A of IFRS 5.

BC72D   The Board observed that IFRIC 17 *Distribution of Non-cash Assets to Owners* amended IFRS 5 by adding paragraphs 5A, 12A and 15A to provide guidance for the held-for-distribution classification. However, this amendment did not provide guidance for when an entity reclassifies an asset (or disposal group) from held for sale to held for distribution to owners (or vice versa), or when held-for-distribution accounting is discontinued. The Board noted that paragraphs 27–29 of IFRS 5 should have been considered for amendment by IFRIC 17 and the fact that they were not amended at the time was an oversight.

BC72E   The Board observed that the current guidance in IFRS 5 could be read in a way that a change from a plan to sell a non-current asset (or disposal group) to a plan to distribute a non-current asset (or disposal group) automatically results in a change to a plan of sale and that the guidance in paragraphs 27–29 of IFRS 5 should be applied.

BC72F   The Board observed that, consistently with paragraphs 5A of IFRS 5 and BC60 of IFRIC 17, it was the intention of the Board to have consistent criteria and accounting requirements for an asset (or disposal group) classified as held for sale and for an asset (or disposal group) classified as held for distribution to owners. In addition:

(a)   the conditions required by paragraph 8 of IFRS 5 for a sale to be considered highly probable are similar to the conditions required by paragraph 12A of IFRS 5 for a distribution to owners to be considered highly probable, so they should be accounted for in the same way; and

(b)   paragraph 5A of IFRS 5 confirms that the classification, presentation and measurement requirements in IFRS 5 that are applicable for an asset (or disposal group) that is classified as held for sale also apply to an asset (or disposal group) that is classified as held for distribution to owners.

BC72G   The Board noted that, on the basis of the current guidance in paragraphs 5A, 8 and 12A of IFRS 5 and the explanations in the Basis for Conclusions on IFRIC 17, the change from being held for sale to held for distribution to owners (or vice versa) when an entity reclassifies an asset (or disposal group) directly from one method of disposal to the other should not be considered a new plan (to sell or distribute). Instead, it should be treated as a continuation of the original plan. This means that an entity moves from one method of disposal to the other without any time lag, so that there is no interruption of the application of the requirements in IFRS 5. This would involve applying the classification, presentation and measurement requirements required for each type of disposal in IFRS 5.

BC72H   Consequently, when an entity reclassifies an asset (or disposal group) directly from held for sale to held for distribution to owners (or vice versa), the Board decided to clarify that such a reclassification shall not be treated as a change to a plan of sale (or distribution to owners) and an entity shall not follow the guidance in paragraphs 27–29 of IFRS 5 to account for this change.

BC72I   In response to the comments received on the Exposure Draft *Annual Improvements to IFRSs 2012–2014 Cycle* (the '2013 Annual Improvements Exposure Draft'), published in December 2013, the Board clarified that at the time of the change in the disposal plan, an entity would need to measure the non-current asset (or disposal group) in accordance with paragraph 15 or 15A of IFRS 5, and recognise any write-down in value (impairment loss) or gain for the subsequent increase in the fair value less costs to sell/costs to distribute a non-current asset (or disposal group) in accordance with paragraphs 20–25 of IFRS 5.

BC72J   In response to the comments received on the 2013 Annual Improvements Exposure Draft, the Board further clarified that a change from being held for sale to held for distribution to owners (or vice versa) via a direct reclassification is not a new plan of disposal and does not change the requirements in IFRS 5 to determine whether a sale (or a distribution to owners) is highly probable, in accordance with paragraph 8 (or 12A) of IFRS 5. Consequently, the determination of the 12-month period should not restart when such a change in the method of disposal occurs, but should instead continue to be the same as initially determined by management in its assessment of whether the sale and/or distribution to owners is highly probable. The Board also noted that the period required to complete a sale or distribution to owners can be extended if the conditions in paragraph 9 of IFRS 5 are met. The Board noted that when an entity changes its planned method of disposal via a direct reclassification, it does not restate prior periods to reflect the new method of disposal.

BC72K   To address the lack of guidance in circumstances when an asset no longer meets the criteria for held for distribution to owners (without meeting the held-for-sale criteria), the Board decided to clarify that an entity should cease to apply held-for-distribution accounting in the same way as it ceases to apply the held-for-sale accounting when it no longer meets the held-for-sale criteria.

BC72L   In response to the comments received on the 2013 Annual Improvements Exposure Draft, the Board concluded that the amendments to IFRS 5 are required to be applied, on a prospective basis, to changes in the method of disposal that occur after the first application of the amendments. This is because this requirement is consistent with the transition requirements provided by IFRIC 17 when it amended IFRS 5 (see paragraph 44D of IFRS 5). The Board considered that prospective application is also required to avoid the potential use of hindsight, because an entity might not have collected all the relevant information at the time of the change in the plan to allow the entity to account for this change.

Presentation of discontinued operations

BC73   SFAS 144 requires the results of a discontinued operation to be presented as a separate component in the income statement (net of income tax) for all periods presented.

BC74   IAS 35 did not require the results of a discontinuing operation to be presented as a net amount on the face of the income statement. Instead, specified items are disclosed either in the notes or on the face of the income statement.

BC75   In ED 4, the Board noted that it was considering the presentation of discontinued operations in the income statement in its project on reporting comprehensive income and that it did not wish to prejudge the outcome of that project by changing the requirements of IAS 35 in respect of the components to be disclosed. Given that the project on reporting comprehensive income will not be completed as soon as previously expected, the Board decided to proceed with its decisions on the presentation of discontinued operations in this IFRS.

BC76   The Board believes that discontinued operations should be shown in a section of the income statement separately from continuing operations because of the different cash flows expected to arise from the two types of operations. The Board concluded that it is sufficient to show a single net figure for discontinued operations on the face of the income statement because of the limited future cash flows expected to arise from the operations. The IFRS therefore permits an analysis of the single net amount to be presented either in the notes or in the income statement.[16]

BC77   A substantial majority of the respondents to ED 4 supported such a presentation.

BC77A   The Board considered the comments received on the draft amendments in the 2007 exposure draft of proposed *Improvements to International Financial Reporting Standards*. Some respondents asked the Board to clarify the effects of the proposed amendment on the income statement when the disposal group meets the definition of a discontinued operation. The Board concluded that when a subsidiary is a disposal group that meets the definition of a discontinued operation in accordance with paragraph 32, an entity that is committed to a sale plan involving loss of control of the subsidiary should disclose the information required by paragraphs 33–36. The Board agreed with respondents that presentation should not differ simply because of the form of the disposal group.

Transitional arrangements

BC78   Some respondents to ED 4 noted that there could be difficulties in obtaining the information necessary to apply the IFRS retrospectively. The Board agreed that hindsight might be involved in determining at what date assets or disposal groups met the criteria to be classified as held for sale and their fair value at that date. Problems might also arise in separating the results of operations that would have been classified as discontinued operations in prior periods and that had been derecognised in full before the effective date of the IFRS.

BC79   The Board therefore decided to require application of the IFRS prospectively and allow retrospective application only when the necessary information had been obtained in the prior periods in question.

BC79A   The Board concluded that the effective date of the amendments in paragraphs 8A and 36A for presentation purposes should be 1 July 2009 to be consistent with the effective date of the amendments to IAS 27 (as amended in January 2008) for measurement purposes. Because paragraph 45(c) of IAS 27 provides an exception to retrospective application of the amendments relating to the loss of control of a subsidiary for measurement purposes, the Board required an entity to consider the applicable transitional provisions in IAS 27 when implementing the amendments in paragraphs 8A and 36A.[17]

---

16 IAS 1 *Presentation of Financial Statements* (as revised in 2007) requires an entity to present all income and expense items in one statement of comprehensive income or in two statements (a separate income statement and a statement of comprehensive income).

17 The consolidation requirements in IAS 27 were superseded by IFRS 10 *Consolidated Financial Statements* issued in May 2011. Paragraph 45(c) in IAS 27 was moved to paragraph C6(c) of IFRS 10; however, the transition provisions were not changed.

Terminology

BC80   Two issues of terminology arose in developing the IFRS:

    (a)   the use of the term 'probable' and

    (b)   the use of the term 'fair value less costs to sell'.[18]

BC81   In SFAS 144, the term *probable* is described as referring to a future sale that is 'likely to occur'. For the purposes of IFRSs, probable is defined as 'more likely than not'. To converge on the same meaning as SFAS 144 and to avoid using the term 'probable' with different meanings in IFRSs, this IFRS uses the phrase 'highly probable'. The Board regards 'highly probable' as implying a significantly higher probability than 'more likely than not' and as implying the same probability as the FASB's phrase 'likely to occur'. This is consistent with the Board's use of 'highly probable' in IAS 39.[19]

BC82   The measurement basis 'fair value less costs to sell' used in SFAS 144 is the same as the measurement 'net selling price' used in IAS 36 (as issued in 1998). SFAS 144 defines fair value of an asset as 'the amount at which that asset could be bought or sold in a current transaction between willing parties, that is, other than in a forced or liquidation sale', and costs to sell as 'the incremental direct costs to transact a sale, that is, the costs that result directly from and are essential to a sale transaction and that would not have been incurred by the entity had the decision to sell not been made.' IAS 36 defines net selling price as the amount obtainable from the sale of an asset in an arm's length transaction between knowledgeable, willing parties, less the costs of disposal. Costs of disposal are incremental costs directly attributable to the disposal of an asset, excluding finance costs and income tax expenses.

BC83   The Board considered using the phrase 'net selling price' to be consistent with IAS 36. However, it noted that 'fair value' is used in many IFRSs. The Board concluded that it would be preferable to use the same phrase as SFAS 144 so that it is clear that convergence on this point had been achieved and to amend IAS 36 so that the terminology in IAS 36 is consistent with other IFRSs. Therefore, a consequential amendment made by IFRS 5 replaces 'net selling price' with 'fair value less costs to sell' throughout IAS 36.

Summary of changes from ED 4

BC84   The major changes from the proposals in ED 4 are:

    (a)   clarification that assets classified as non-current are not reclassified as current until they meet the criteria to be classified as held for sale (paragraph BC10).

    (b)   goodwill and financial assets under leases are included in the scope of the measurement provisions of the IFRS (paragraphs BC8–BC14).

---

18 IFRS 13, issued in May 2011, defines fair value and contains the requirements for measuring fair value.

19 IFRS 9 *Financial Instruments* replaced IAS 39. IFRS 9 applies to all items that were previously within the scope of IAS 39. This paragraph refers to matters relevant when IFRS 5 was issued.

(c)   non-current assets carried at fair value with changes recognised in profit or loss are excluded from the measurement provisions of the IFRS (paragraphs BC8–BC14).

(d)   assets that are revalued in accordance with IAS 16 or IAS 38 are, when classified as held for sale, treated consistently with assets that had not previously been revalued (paragraphs BC47 and BC48).

(e)   the allocation of an impairment loss on a disposal group is consistent with the order of allocation of impairment losses in IAS 36 (paragraphs BC39–BC41).

(f)   the criterion in IAS 35 that a discontinued operation should be a major line of business or area of geographical operations has been added (paragraphs BC67–BC71).

(g)   discontinued operations can be presented on the face of the income statement as a single amount (paragraphs BC73–BC77).

Comparison with relevant aspects of SFAS 144

BC85   The following table sets out the extent of convergence with SFAS 144:

Requirement	Extent of convergence with SFAS 144
Scope	Some differences in scope arising from other differences between IFRSs and US GAAP.
Criteria for classification as held for sale	Fully converged.
Treatment of assets to be exchanged	Fully converged if FASB proposals on exchanges of non-monetary assets are finalised.
Treatment of assets to be abandoned	Fully converged.
Measurement on initial classification	Converged, other than cumulative exchange differences recognised directly in equity[a] that are included in the carrying amount of the asset (or disposal group) under US GAAP but are not under IFRS 5.
Subsequent measurement	Converged on the principles, but some differences arising from different requirements on reversals of previous impairments.

continued...

...continued

Requirement	Extent of convergence with SFAS 144
Changes to a plan to sell	Converged on reclassification and on measurement, except for differences arising from different requirements on reversals of previous impairments.
Presentation of assets classified as held for sale	Fully converged.
Definition of a discontinued operation	Not converged but the Board intends to work with the FASB to arrive at a converged definition within a relatively short time.
Timing of classification of an operation as discontinued	Fully converged.
Presentation of a discontinued operation	Converged except that SFAS 144 requires the presentation of pre- and post-tax profits on the face of the income statement and IFRS 5 requires the presentation of post-tax profit only (although disaggregation is permitted).

(a) As a consequence of the revision of IAS 1 *Presentation of Financial Statements* (as revised in 2007) such differences are recognised in other comprehensive income.

Dissenting opinions

Dissent of Anthony T Cope and Harry K Schmid

DO1   Messrs Cope and Schmid dissent from the issue of IFRS 5.

Dissent of Anthony T Cope

DO2   Mr Cope dissents because, in his view, the IFRS fails to meet fully the needs of users in this important area.

DO3   In deciding to undertake this project, the Board had two objectives—to improve users' ability to assess the amount, timing and uncertainty of future cash flows, and to converge with US GAAP. The ability to identify assets (or asset groups) whose value will be recovered principally through sale rather than through operations has significant implications for future cash flows. Similarly, separate presentation of discontinued operations enables users to distinguish those parts of a business that will not contribute to future cash flows.

DO4   The importance of identifying and disaggregating these components was emphasised in the 1994 report of the Special Committee on Financial Reporting of the American Institute of Certified Public Accountants (the AICPA Jenkins Committee). The Jenkins Committee report, arguably the most extensive and authoritative survey of user needs ever undertaken, recommended that:

> [The definition of discontinued operations] should be broadened to include all significant discontinued operations whose assets and results of operations and activities can be distinguished physically and operationally and for business reporting purposes.

The sections of SFAS 144 dealing with discontinued operations were the direct response of the FASB to this recommendation.

DO5   Indeed, the Board appeared to agree in its initial deliberations. In ED 4, the Board stated:

> [The Board] further concluded that the definition of discontinued operations in SFAS 144 leads to more useful information being presented and disclosed for a wider range of operations than did the existing definition in IAS 35. That information is important to users in their assessment of the amount, timing and uncertainty of future cash flows.

Mr Cope continues to agree with that statement.

DO6   However, the Board ultimately has decided to retain the definition in IAS 35, thus failing to gain convergence on an important point in a project designed to achieve such convergence, and failing to respond to the stated needs of users.

DO7   The reason given for the Board's action is that implementation problems with SFAS 144 have emerged in the US. (Most of these problems seem to be with the guidance concerning the definition in SFAS 144, rather than the definition itself.) In paragraph BC71, the Board describes its action as an interim measure, and plans to work with the FASB to arrive promptly at a converged solution. In Mr Cope's view, it would have been much preferable to have converged first, and then dealt with any implementation problems jointly with the FASB.

Dissent of Harry K Schmid

DO8 The main reasons for Mr Schmid's dissent are:

(a) depreciation/amortisation of non-current assets that are still in active use should not cease only because of a management decision to sell the assets that has not yet been fully carried out; and

(b) measurement of assets should not be based on a management decision that has not yet been fully carried out, requiring a very rule-based Standard.

DO9 Mr Schmid believes that not depreciating/amortising assets classified as held for sale but still in active use is conceptually wrong and is especially problematic for discontinued operations because such operations represent a separate major line of business or geographical area of operations. Mr Schmid does not accept that measurement at the lower of carrying amount and fair value less costs to sell acts as a proxy for depreciation because, in most such cases, the fair value less costs to sell will be higher than the carrying amount as the fair value of such disposal groups will often reflect internally generated goodwill. Therefore, non-current assets in such disposal groups will simply remain at their carrying amounts even though they are still actively used, up to one year or even longer. In addition, the net profit shown separately in the income statement for discontinued operations will not be meaningful because depreciation/amortisation charges are not deducted for the continued use of the assets and this profit cannot be compared with the information restated in comparative periods where depreciation had been charged.

DO10 The proposed classification 'held for sale' and resulting measurement of non-current assets (or disposal groups) so classified is based on a management decision that has not yet been fully carried out and demands detailed (anti-abuse) rules to define the classification and to fix the time boundaries during which these assets can remain within the classification. The final result is, in Mr Schmid's view, an excessively detailed and rule-based Standard.

DO11 Mr Schmid believes that a more simple and straightforward solution would have been possible by creating a special category of non-current assets retired from active use. The concept 'retired from active use' would have been simple to apply and management intentions would be removed from the Standard. The classification would equally apply to any form of disposal (sale, abandonment, exchange, spin-off etc); no detailed (anti-abuse) rules and no illustrations would be necessary and the Standard would be simple and based on a clear and unambiguous principle. Mr Schmid, on this point, does not agree with the conclusions in paragraph BC18 that a classification 'retired from active use' would not require fewer criteria to support it than the category 'assets held for sale'.

DO12 Mr Schmid agrees with paragraph BC17 of the Basis for Conclusions, but in order to provide information of intended sales of non-current assets, especially discontinued operations, disclosure could have been required to take effect as soon as such assets are likely to be sold, even if they are still in active use.

DO13   Mr Schmid is fully in favour of seeking, whenever possible, convergence with US GAAP, but only if the converged solution is of high quality. He is of the opinion that this is not the case for this Standard for the reasons given.

IASB documents published to accompany

IFRS 6

Exploration for and Evaluation of Mineral Resources

The text of the unaccompanied standard, IFRS 6, is contained in Part A of this edition. Its effective date when issued was 1 January 2013. This part presents the following documents:

BASIS FOR CONCLUSIONS

DISSENTING OPINIONS

Contents

Basis for Conclusions on
IFRS 6 *Exploration for and Evaluation of Mineral Resources*

This Basis for Conclusions accompanies, but is not part of, IFRS 6.

Introduction

BC1   This Basis for Conclusions summarises the International Accounting Standards Board's considerations in reaching the conclusions in IFRS 6 *Exploration for and Evaluation of Mineral Resources*. Individual Board members gave greater weight to some factors than to others.

Reasons for issuing the IFRS

BC2   Paragraphs 10–12 of IAS 8 *Accounting Policies, Changes in Accounting Estimates and Errors* specify a hierarchy of criteria that an entity should use in developing an accounting policy if no IFRS applies specifically to an item. Without the exemption in IFRS 6, an entity adopting IFRSs in 2005 would have needed to assess whether its accounting policies for the exploration for and evaluation of mineral resources complied with those requirements. In the absence of guidance, there might have been uncertainty about what would be acceptable. Establishing what would be acceptable could have been costly and some entities might have made major changes in 2005 followed by further significant changes once the Board completes its comprehensive review of accounting for extractive activities.

BC3   To avoid unnecessary disruption for both users and preparers at this time, the Board proposed to limit the need for entities to change their existing accounting policies for exploration and evaluation assets. The Board did this by:

(a)   creating a temporary exemption from parts of the hierarchy in IAS 8 that specify the criteria an entity uses in developing an accounting policy if no IFRS applies specifically.

(b)   limiting the impact of that exemption from the hierarchy by identifying expenditures to be included in and excluded from exploration and evaluation assets and requiring all exploration and evaluation assets to be assessed for impairment.

BC4   The Board published its proposals in January 2004. ED 6 *Exploration for and Evaluation of Mineral Resources* had a comment deadline of 16 April 2004. The Board received 55 comment letters.

BC5   In April 2004 the Board approved a research project to be undertaken by staff from the national standard-setters in Australia, Canada, Norway and South Africa that will address accounting for extractive activities generally. The research project team is assisted by an advisory panel, which includes members from industry (oil and gas and mining sectors), accounting firms, users and securities regulators from around the world.

Scope

BC6   In the Board's view, even though no IFRS has addressed extractive activities directly, all IFRSs (including International Accounting Standards and Interpretations) are applicable to entities engaged in the exploration for and evaluation of mineral resources that make an unreserved statement of compliance with IFRSs in accordance with IAS 1 *Presentation of Financial Statements*. Consequently, each IFRS must be applied by all such entities.

BC7   Some respondents to ED 6 encouraged the Board to develop standards for other stages in the process of exploring for and evaluating mineral resources, including pre-exploration activities (ie activities preceding the exploration for and evaluation of mineral resources) and development activities (ie activities after the technical feasibility and commercial viability of extracting a mineral resource are demonstrable). The Board decided not to do this for two reasons. First, it did not want to prejudge the comprehensive review of the accounting for such activities. Second, the Board concluded that an appropriate accounting policy for pre-exploration activities could be developed from an application of existing IFRSs, from the *Framework's*[1] definitions of assets and expenses, and by applying the general principles of asset recognition in IAS 16 *Property, Plant and Equipment* and IAS 38 *Intangible Assets*.

BC8   The Board also decided not to expand the scope of IFRS 6 beyond that proposed in ED 6 because to do so would require additional due process, possibly including another exposure draft. In view of the many entities engaged in extractive activities that would be required to apply IFRSs from 1 January 2005, the Board decided that it should not delay issuing guidance by expanding the scope of the IFRS beyond the exploration for and evaluation of mineral resources.

Definition of exploration and evaluation assets

BC9   Most respondents to ED 6 agreed with the Board's proposed definition of exploration and evaluation assets, but asked for changes or clarifications to make the Board's intentions clearer:

(a)   some respondents asked the Board to distinguish between exploration and pre-exploration expenditures.

(b)   others asked the Board to define exploration and evaluation activities separately, reflecting the different risk profiles of such activities or the requirements of other jurisdictions.

(c)   other respondents asked for further guidance on what constitute mineral resources, principally examples of what constitutes a mineral reserve.

---

1   References to the *Framework* are to IASC's *Framework for the Preparation and Presentation of Financial Statements*, adopted by the IASB in 2001. In September 2010 the IASB replaced the *Framework* with the *Conceptual Framework for Financial Reporting*.

Expenditures incurred before the exploration for and evaluation of mineral resources

BC10   Respondents seemed to be concerned that the Board was extending the scope of the proposals to include expenditures incurred before the acquisition of legal rights to explore in a specific area in the definition of exploration and evaluation expenditure. Some were concerned that such an extension would open the way for the recognition of such expenditures as assets; others preferred this result. In drafting IFRS 6, the Board could not identify any reason why the *Framework* was not applicable to such expenditures.

BC11   The Board decided not to define pre-acquisition or pre-exploration expenditures. However, the IFRS clarifies that expenditures before the entity has obtained legal rights to explore in a specific area are not exploration and evaluation expenditures and are therefore outside the scope of the IFRS.

BC12   The Board noted that an appropriate application of IFRSs might require pre-acquisition expenditures related to the acquisition of an intangible asset (eg expenditures directly attributable to the acquisition of an exploration licence) to be recognised as part of the intangible asset in accordance with IAS 38. Paragraph 27(a) of IAS 38 states that the cost of a separately acquired intangible asset comprises its purchase price, including import duties and non-refundable purchase taxes, and some directly attributable costs.

BC13   Similarly, the Board understands that expenditures incurred before the exploration for and evaluation of mineral resources cannot usually be associated with any specific mineral property and thus are likely to be recognised as an expense as incurred. However, such expenditures need to be distinguished from expenditures on infrastructure—for example access roads—necessary for the exploration work to proceed. Such expenditures should be recognised as property, plant and equipment in accordance with paragraph 3 of IAS 16.

Separate definitions of 'exploration' and 'evaluation'

BC14   Some respondents asked the Board to provide separate definitions of exploration and evaluation. The Board considered using the definitions provided in the Issues Paper *Extractive Industries* published by its predecessor, the Board of the International Accounting Standards Committee, in November 2000, because those definitions would be acceptable to many respondents, particularly because they are based on definitions that have been used for a number of years in both the mining and the oil and gas sectors.

BC15   The Board concluded that distinguishing between evaluation and exploration would not improve the IFRS. Exploration and evaluation are accounted for in the same way.

Mineral resources

BC16   Some respondents asked the Board to define mineral resources more precisely. The Board concluded that, for the purposes of the IFRS, elaboration was unnecessary. The items listed in the definition of exploration for and evaluation of mineral resources were sufficient to convey the Board's intentions.

Recognition of exploration and evaluation assets

Temporary exemption from IAS 8 paragraphs 11 and 12

BC17 A variety of accounting practices are followed by entities engaged in the exploration for and evaluation of mineral resources. These practices range from deferring on the balance sheet nearly all exploration and evaluation expenditure to recognising all such expenditure in profit or loss as incurred. The IFRS permits these various accounting practices to continue. Given this diversity, some respondents to ED 6 opposed any exemption from paragraphs 11 and 12 of IAS 8. These respondents were concerned that entities could give the appearance of compliance with IFRSs while being inconsistent with the stated objectives of the IASB, ie to provide users of financial statements with financial information that was of high quality, transparent and comparable. The Board did not grant the exemption from parts of IAS 8 lightly, but took this step to minimise disruption, especially in 2006 (or 2005, for those entities that adopt the IFRS early), both for users (eg lack of continuity of trend data) and for preparers (eg systems changes).

BC18 IFRS 4 *Insurance Contracts* provides a temporary exemption from paragraphs 10–12 of IAS 8. That exemption is broader than in IFRS 6 because IFRS 4 leaves many significant aspects of accounting for insurance contracts until phase II of the Board's project on that topic. A requirement to apply paragraph 10 of IAS 8 to insurance contracts would have had much more pervasive effects and insurers would have needed to address matters such as completeness, substance over form and neutrality. In contrast, IFRS 6 leaves a relatively narrow range of issues unaddressed and the Board did not think that an exemption from paragraph 10 of IAS 8 was necessary.

BC19 ED 6 made it clear that the Board intended to suspend only paragraphs 11 and 12 of IAS 8, implying that paragraph 10 should be followed when an entity was determining its accounting policies for exploration and evaluation assets. However, it was apparent from some comments received that the Board's intention had not been understood clearly. Consequently, the IFRS contains a specific statement that complying with paragraph 10 of IAS 8 is mandatory.

BC20 Respondents who objected to the Board's proposal in ED 6 to permit some accounting practices to continue found it difficult to draw a meaningful distinction between the exploration for and evaluation of mineral resources and scientific research. Both activities can be costly and have significant risks of failure. These respondents would support bringing the exploration for and evaluation of mineral resources within the scope of IAS 16 and IAS 38. The Board is similarly concerned that existing accounting practices might result in the inappropriate recognition of exploration and evaluation assets. However, it is also concerned that accounting for exploration and evaluation expenditures in accordance with IAS 38 might result in the overstatement of expenses. In the absence of internationally accepted standards for such expenditures, the Board concluded that it could not make an informed judgement in advance of the comprehensive review of accounting for extractive activities.

BC21 Some suggested that the Board should require an entity to follow its national accounting requirements (ie national GAAP) in accounting for the exploration for and evaluation of mineral resources until the Board completes its comprehensive review of accounting for extractive activities, to prevent the selection of accounting policies that do not form a comprehensive basis of accounting. Consistently with its conclusions in IFRS 4, the Board concluded that defining national GAAP would have posed problems. Further definitional problems could have arisen because some entities do not apply the national GAAP of their own country. For example, some non-US entities with extractive activities in the oil and gas sector apply US GAAP. Moreover, it is unusual and, arguably, beyond the Board's mandate to impose requirements set by another body.

BC22   Therefore, the Board decided that an entity could continue to follow the accounting policies that it was using when it first applied the IFRS's requirements, provided they satisfy the requirements of paragraph 10 of IAS 8 and with some exceptions noted below. An entity could also improve those accounting policies if specified criteria are met (see paragraphs 13 and 14 of the IFRS).

BC23   The Board acknowledges that it is difficult to make piecemeal changes to recognition and measurement practices at this time because many aspects of accounting for extractive activities are interrelated with aspects that will not be considered until the Board completes its comprehensive review of accounting for extractive activities. However, not imposing the requirements in the IFRS would detract from the relevance and reliability of an entity's financial statements to an unacceptable degree.

BC23A   In 2008, as part of its annual improvements project, the Board considered the guidance on the treatment in IAS 7 *Statement of Cash Flows* of some types of expenditures incurred with the objective of generating future cash flows when those expenditures are not recognised as assets in accordance with IFRSs. Some entities classify such expenditures as cash flows from operating activities and others classify them as investing activities. Examples of such expenditures are those for exploration and evaluation activities, which can be recognised according to IFRS 6 as either an asset or an expense.[2]

BC23B   The Board noted that the exemption in IFRS 6 applies only to recognition and measurement of exploration and evaluation assets, not to the classification of related expenditures in the statement of cash flows. Consequently, the Board amended paragraph 16 of IAS 7 to state that only an expenditure that results in a recognised asset can be classified as a cash flow from investing activities.

Elements of cost of exploration and evaluation assets

BC24   ED 6 paragraph 7 listed examples of expenditures related to the exploration for and evaluation of mineral resources that might be included in the cost of an exploration and evaluation asset. ED 6 paragraph 8 listed expenditures that could not be recognised as an exploration and evaluation asset. Respondents expressed a desire for greater clarity with respect to these paragraphs and more examples of types of expenditures that would be included or excluded.

---

2   Paragraphs BC23A and BC23B were added as a consequence of an amendment to IAS 7 included in *Improvements to IFRSs* issued in April 2009.

BC25   In the light of the responses, the Board decided to redraft the guidance to state that the list is not exhaustive and that the items noted are examples of expenditures that might, but need not always, satisfy the definition of exploration and evaluation expenditure. In addition, the Board noted that IFRSs require that expenditures should be treated consistently for comparable activities and between reporting periods. Any change in what is deemed to be an expenditure qualifying for recognition as an exploration and evaluation asset should be treated as a change in an accounting policy accounted for in accordance with IAS 8. Pending the comprehensive review of accounting for extractive activities, the Board does not think that it is feasible to define what expenditures should be included or excluded.

BC26   ED 6 paragraph 8 proposed to prohibit expenditure related to the development of a mineral resource from being recognised as an exploration and evaluation asset. Respondents expressed difficulty identifying expenditures on 'development'. The Board did not define 'development of a mineral resource' because this is beyond the scope of the IFRS.

BC27   However, the Board noted that development of a mineral resource once the technical feasibility and commercial viability of extracting the mineral resource had been determined was an example of the development phase of an internal project. Paragraph 57 of IAS 38 provides guidance that should be followed in developing an accounting policy for this activity.

BC28   ED 6 proposed that administration and other general overhead costs should be excluded from the initial measurement of exploration and evaluation assets. Several respondents suggested that general and administrative and overhead costs *directly attributable* to the exploration and evaluation activities should qualify for inclusion in the carrying amount of the asset. These respondents saw this treatment as consistent with the treatment of such costs with respect to inventory (paragraph 11 of IAS 2 *Inventories*) and intangible assets (paragraph 67(a) of IAS 38). However, the Board noted that such a treatment would seem to be inconsistent with paragraph 19(d) of IAS 16. The IFRS was not regarded as the appropriate Standard in which to resolve this inconsistency, and the Board decided to delete the reference in the IFRS to administrative and other general overheads. The treatment of such expenditures would be an accounting policy choice; the chosen policy should be consistent with one of the treatments available under IFRSs.

Measurement after recognition

BC29   The IFRS permits an entity recognising exploration and evaluation assets to measure such assets, after recognition, using either the cost model or the revaluation model in IAS 16 and IAS 38. The model chosen should be consistent with how the entity classifies the exploration and evaluation assets. Those revaluation models permit the revaluation of assets when specified requirements are met (see paragraphs 31–42 of IAS 16 and paragraphs 72–84 of IAS 38). The revaluation model in IAS 38 can be used only if the asset's fair value can be determined by reference to an active market; the revaluation model in IAS 16 refers only to 'market-based evidence'. The Board was troubled by this inconsistency and was concerned that entities might choose accounting policies to achieve a more advantageous measurement of exploration and evaluation assets.

BC30   A few respondents were also concerned with the option proposed in ED 6. Some did not agree that exploration and evaluation assets should be revalued, preferring an arbitrary prohibition of remeasurement. Others were concerned about the reliability of the measure. The Board concluded that no substantive reasons had been presented for reaching a conclusion different from that in ED 6. Although the revaluation of an exploration asset in accordance with IAS 16 or IAS 38 might not be widespread, it was not appropriate to prohibit remeasurement of specific types of IAS 16 or IAS 38 assets on a selective basis.

BC31   Exploration and evaluation assets may arise as a result of a business combination. The Board noted that IFRS 3 *Business Combinations* applies to all entities asserting compliance with IFRSs and that any exploration and evaluation assets acquired in a business combination should be accounted for in accordance with IFRS 3.

Presentation of exploration and evaluation assets

BC32   ED 6 noted that the Board had not yet considered whether exploration and evaluation assets are tangible or intangible. Several respondents suggested that the Board should give some direction on this issue.

BC33   Some exploration and evaluation assets are treated as intangible assets (eg drilling rights), whereas others are clearly tangible (eg vehicles and drilling rigs). A tangible asset may be used in the development of an intangible one. For example, a portable drilling rig may be used to drill test wells or take core samples, clearly part of the exploration activity. To the extent that the tangible asset is consumed in developing an intangible asset, the amount reflecting that consumption is part of the cost of the intangible asset. However, using the drilling rig to develop an intangible asset does not change a tangible asset into an intangible asset.

BC34   Pending completion of the comprehensive review of accounting practices for extractive activities, the Board did not wish to decide whether and which exploration and evaluation assets should be classified as tangible or intangible. However, the Board concluded that an entity should classify the elements of exploration and evaluation assets as tangible or intangible according to their nature and apply this classification consistently. This classification is the foundation for other accounting policy choices as described in paragraphs BC29–BC31 and for the disclosures required by the IFRS.

Impairment of exploration and evaluation assets

BC35   When it developed ED 6, the Board decided that an entity recognising exploration and evaluation assets should test those assets for impairment, and that the impairment test to be applied should be that in IAS 36 *Impairment of Assets*. Respondents accepted the general proposition that exploration and evaluation assets should be tested for impairment. However, the Board's proposals for a special 'cash-generating unit for exploration and evaluation assets' (the special CGU) were not thought appropriate or useful.

Assessment of impairment

BC36 In some cases, and particularly in exploration-only entities, exploration and evaluation assets do not generate cash flows and there is insufficient information about the mineral resources in a specific area for an entity to make reasonable estimates of exploration and evaluation assets' recoverable amount. This is because the exploration for and evaluation of the mineral resources has not reached a stage at which information sufficient to estimate future cash flows is available to the entity. Without such information, it is not possible to estimate either fair value less costs to sell or value in use, the two measures of recoverable amount in IAS 36. Respondents noted that this would lead to an immediate write-off of exploration assets in many cases.

BC37 The Board was persuaded by respondents' arguments that recognising impairment losses on this basis was potentially inconsistent with permitting existing methods of accounting for exploration and evaluation assets to continue. Therefore, pending completion of the comprehensive review of accounting for extractive activities, the Board decided to change the approach to recognition of impairment; the assessment of impairment should be triggered by changes in facts and circumstances. However, it also confirmed that, once an entity had determined that an exploration and evaluation asset was impaired, IAS 36 should be used to measure, present and disclose that impairment in the financial statements, subject to special requirements with respect to the level at which impairment is assessed.

BC38 Paragraph 12 of ED 6 proposed that an entity that had recognised exploration and evaluation assets should assess those assets for impairment annually and recognise any resulting impairment loss in accordance with IAS 36. Paragraph 13 proposed a set of indicators of impairment that an entity would consider in addition to those in IAS 36. Respondents stated that these indicators would not achieve the Board's intended result, especially in circumstances in which the information necessary for an assessment of mineral reserves was not available.

BC39 The Board replaced the proposals in paragraphs 12 and 13 of ED 6 with an exception to the recognition requirements in IAS 36. The Board decided that, until the entity had sufficient data to determine technical feasibility and commercial viability, exploration and evaluation assets need not be assessed for impairment. However, when such information becomes available, or other facts and circumstances suggest that the asset might be impaired, the exploration and evaluation assets must be assessed for impairment. The IFRS suggests possible indicators of impairment.

The level at which impairment is assessed

BC40 When it developed ED 6, the Board decided that there was a need for consistency between the level at which costs were accumulated and the level at which impairment was assessed. Without this consistency, there was a danger that expenditures that would form part of the cost of an exploration and evaluation asset under one of the common methods of accounting for the exploration for and evaluation of mineral resources would need to be recognised in profit or loss in accordance with IAS 36. Consequently, ED 6 proposed that an entity recognising exploration and evaluation assets should make a one-time election to test those assets either at the level of the IAS 36 cash-generating unit (CGU) or at the level of a special CGU. ED 6 explained that any assets other than exploration and evaluation assets included within the special CGU should continue to be subject to separate impairment testing in accordance with IAS 36, and that impairment test should be performed before the special CGU was tested for impairment.

BC41   Respondents disagreed with the Board's proposal. In particular, and for various reasons, they did not accept that the special CGU would provide the relief it was intended to provide, because:

(a)   small, start-up or exploration-only entities might not have adequate cash flows to support exploration and evaluation assets that were not cash-generating.

(b)   entities applying the successful efforts method of accounting typically conduct impairment tests property by property. However, because of the way in which the special CGU was defined in ED 6 such entities would be forced to carry out impairment tests at the CGU level.

(c)   the special CGU permitted management extensive discretion.

In addition, there was concern that, because the exploration and evaluation assets could be aggregated with other assets in the special CGU, there would be confusion about the appropriate measurement model to apply (fair value less costs to sell or value in use). As a result, many respondents to ED 6 did not think that the Board had achieved its intention in this respect, and said that they preferred to apply IAS 36 without the special CGU.

BC42   Although the Board disagreed with some of the arguments put forward by respondents, it acknowledged that the special CGU seemed to be more confusing than helpful. This suggested that it was not needed. Paragraph BC20 of the Basis for Conclusions on ED 6 noted the Board's reluctance to introduce a special CGU. Removing the special CGU would eliminate much of the complexity in the proposed IFRS and the confusion among constituents. It would also mean that entities with extractive activities would assess their assets for impairment at the same level as other entities—providing a higher level of comparability than might otherwise be the case.

BC43   Board members noted that paragraph 22 of IAS 36 requires impairment to be assessed at the individual asset level 'unless the asset does not generate cash inflows that are largely independent of those from other assets or groups of assets'. In addition, paragraph 70 of IAS 36 requires that 'if an active market exists for the output produced by an asset or group of assets, that asset or group of assets shall be identified as a cash-generating unit'. In some cases in which exploration and evaluation assets are recognised, eg in the petroleum sector, each well is potentially capable of producing cash inflows that are observable and capable of reliable measurement because there is an active market for crude oil. The Board was concerned that removing the special CGU would cause entities recognising exploration and evaluation assets to test for impairment at a very low level.

BC44 The issue was highlighted in the July 2004 issue of *IASB Update*, in the project summary and in the *Effect of Redeliberations* documents available on the IASB's Website. These documents were also sent to the Board's research project team and others with a request to encourage their constituents to respond to the issues raised. The Board received 16 comment letters.

BC45 The majority of respondents continued to support the elimination of the special CGU. They also supported the notion that entities should test impairment at the level of the cost centre and suggested that the Board should consider defining an 'asset' as it applied to exploration and evaluation assets. The respondents argued that such an approach would reflect more accurately the way in which the industry manages its operations. The Board was persuaded by these arguments and decided that it should permit entities some flexibility in allocating exploration and evaluation assets to cash-generating units or groups of units, subject to an upper limit on the size of the units or groups of units.

BC46 The Board decided that its approach to the impairment of goodwill in the 2004 revisions to IAS 36 paragraphs 80–82 offered the best model available within IFRSs to accomplish its objective. It noted that entities might be able to monitor exploration and evaluation assets for internal management purposes at the level of an oilfield or a contiguous ore body. The Board did not intend to require impairment to be assessed at such a low level. Consequently, the IFRS permits CGUs to be aggregated. However, the Board decided to require the level at which impairment was assessed to be no larger than a segment, based on either the entity's primary or the entity's secondary segment reporting format in accordance with IAS 14 *Segment Reporting*. The Board concluded, consistently with the approach to goodwill in IAS 36, that this approach was necessary to ensure that entities managed on a matrix basis could test exploration and evaluation assets for impairment at the level of reporting that reflects the way they manage their operations. This requirement is no less rigorous than ED 6's requirement that the special CGU should 'be no larger than a segment'.[3]

BC47 Consequently, the Board decided to remove the proposed special CGU. In doing so, it noted that eliminating this requirement would have the following benefits:

(a) once an impairment was identified, the measurement, presentation and disclosure of impairment would be more consistent across entities recognising exploration and evaluation assets.

(b) it would remove the confusion about what practices entities recognising exploration and evaluation assets for the first time should follow.

---

3 In 2006 IAS 14 was replaced by IFRS 8 *Operating Segments*, which does not require the identification of primary and secondary segments. See paragraph BC150A of the Basis for Conclusions on IAS 36 *Impairment of Assets*.

(c)   it would remove the risk noted in some comment letters that the special CGU could become the 'industry norm', limiting the Board's options when the comprehensive review of accounting for extractive activities is completed.

Reversal of impairment losses

BC48   The reversal of impairment losses when specified requirements (ie those set out in paragraphs 109–123 of IAS 36) are met is required of all entities for all assets (excluding goodwill and equity investments classified as available for sale). Respondents to ED 6 who commented on this issue and who disagreed with the ability to reverse impairment losses advanced no new arguments why the Board should prohibit reversal of impairment losses in the case of exploration and evaluation assets. Consequently, the Board reaffirmed its conclusion that it would not be appropriate to propose an exemption from the requirement to reverse impairment losses for exploration and evaluation assets.

Changes in accounting policies

BC49   IAS 8 prohibits a change in accounting policies that is not required by an IFRS, unless the change will result in the provision of reliable and more relevant information. Although the Board wished to avoid imposing unnecessary changes in this IFRS, it did not believe it should exempt entities from the requirement to justify changes in accounting policies. Consistently with its conclusions in IFRS 4, the Board decided to permit changes in accounting policies for exploration and evaluation assets if they make the financial statements more relevant and no less reliable, or more reliable and no less relevant judged by the criteria in IAS 8.

Disclosures

BC50   The disclosure requirements in the IFRS are based on a principle that an entity should disclose information that identifies and explains the amounts recognised in its financial statements that arise from the exploration for and evaluation of mineral resources, supplemented by specified disclosures to meet that objective.

BC51   Although respondents agreed that entities should be allowed flexibility in determining the levels of aggregation and amount of disclosure, they suggested that the Board should introduce more specific and standardised disclosure requirements. Some respondents were concerned that the variety of accounting for the exploration for and evaluation of mineral resources could reduce comparability.

BC52   The Board concluded that the ED 6 approach was superior to requiring a long list of detailed and prescriptive disclosures because concentrating on the underlying principle:

(a)   makes it easier for entities to understand the rationale for the requirements, which promotes compliance.

    (b)   avoids requiring specific disclosures that may not be needed to meet the underlying objectives in the circumstances of every entity and could lead to information overload that obscures important information in a mass of detail.

    (c)   gives entities flexibility to decide on an appropriate level of aggregation that enables users to see the overall picture, but without combining information that has different characteristics.

    (d)   permits reporting exploration and evaluation expenditure by segment on either an annual basis or an accumulated basis.

BC53   Some respondents suggested that the Board should require disclosures similar to those in paragraphs 73 and 74 of IAS 16 or in paragraphs 118–125 of IAS 38. Both IAS 16 and IAS 38 contain scope exclusions for exploration and evaluation assets. Therefore, entities recognising these assets could claim that the requirements were not applicable. The Board decided that, although the scope of those standards excludes exploration and evaluation assets, their required disclosures would provide information relevant to an understanding of the financial statements and useful to users. Consequently, the Board concluded that the IFRS should confirm that the disclosures of IASs 16 and 38 are required consistently with how the entity classifies its exploration and evaluation assets (ie tangible (IAS 16) or intangible (IAS 38)).

BC54   In addition, some respondents suggested that the Board should require disclosure of non-financial information, including:

    (a)   commercial reserve quantities;

    (b)   rights to explore for, develop and produce wasting resources;

    (c)   disclosures about stages after exploration and evaluation; and

    (d)   the number of years since exploration started, and an estimation of the time remaining until a decision could be made about the technical feasibility and commercial viability of extracting the mineral resource.

Commercial reserves

BC55   The Board acknowledged that information about commercial reserve quantities is, perhaps, the most important disclosure for an entity with extractive activities. However, it noted that commercial reserves are usually determined after the exploration and evaluation stage has ended and it concluded that such disclosure was beyond the stated scope of the IFRS.

Stages after exploration and evaluation

BC56   As with commercial reserves, the Board concluded that, although information about stages after exploration and evaluation would be useful to users of financial statements, such disclosure is beyond the scope of the IFRS.

Project timing

BC57   The Board also concluded that disclosure of the number of years since exploration started and the estimated time remaining until a decision could be made about development would apply only to large scale exploration activities.

It noted that if the project is significant, paragraph 112(c) of IAS 1 already requires its disclosure, ie as additional information that is necessary for an understanding of the financial statements.

Effective date

BC58 ED 6 proposed that the IFRS should be effective for annual periods beginning on or after 1 January 2005. The Board decided to change the effective date to 1 January 2006 to allow entities more time to make the transition to the IFRS. It also decided to permit an entity that wishes or is required to adopt IFRSs before 1 January 2006 to adopt IFRS 6 early.

Transition

BC59 The Board did not propose any special transition in ED 6. Consequently, paragraphs 14–27 of IAS 8 would apply to any changes in accounting that are necessary as a result of the IFRS.

BC60 Some respondents expressed concern about the application of the proposals to prior periods—especially those related to impairment and the inclusion or exclusion of some expenditures from exploration and evaluation assets. In particular, respondents requested that if the Board were to require restatement, it should give transitional guidance on how to identify elements previously recognised as exploration and evaluation assets now outside the definition.

BC61 IAS 8 would require entities recognising exploration and evaluation assets to determine whether there were any facts and circumstances indicating impairment in prior periods. The Board concluded that retrospective application was not likely to involve the use of hindsight because the facts and circumstances identified in the IFRS are generally objective indicators and whether they existed at a particular date should be a question of fact. However, the Board noted that it provided transitional relief in IFRS 4 for applying the liability adequacy test to comparative periods on the basis of impracticability, principally because the liability adequacy test involves the use of current estimates of future cash flows from an entity's insurance contracts. The Board does not expect that IFRS 6's approach to impairment will involve current estimates of future cash flows and other variables to the same extent. However, it is aware that the variety of approaches to assessing recoverability means that current estimates of future cash flows and other variables are likely to be in use by some entities.

BC62 Therefore, consistently with IFRS 4, the Board concluded that if it is impracticable to apply the impairment test to comparative information that relates to annual periods beginning before 1 January 2006, an entity should disclose that fact.

BC63 Some respondents were concerned that entities would have difficulty in compiling the information necessary for 2004 comparative figures, and suggested that entities should be exempted from restating comparatives on transition, given that the IFRS would be introduced close to 1 January 2005, and could result in substantial changes.

BC64   The Board considered a similar issue when it developed ED 7 *Financial Instruments: Disclosures*, in which it concluded that entities that apply the requirements proposed in ED 7 only when they become mandatory should be required to provide comparative disclosures because such entities will have enough time to prepare the information.

BC65   In ED 7, the Board decided to propose that an entity that both (a) adopts IFRSs for the first time before 1 January 2006 and (b) applies the IFRS before that date should be exempt from the requirement to produce comparative information in the first year of application. The Board compared the concerns raised by constituents in response to ED 6 and the issues it considered in developing ED 7 and decided that its conclusions in ED 7 were also appropriate for the IFRS.

BC65A   [Deleted][4]

Summary of changes from ED 6

BC66   The following is a summary of the main changes from ED 6 to the IFRS. The Board:

(a)   deleted the specific prohibition against including administration and other general overhead costs in the initial measurement of an exploration and evaluation asset (paragraph BC28).

(b)   introduced a requirement for the entity to classify exploration and evaluation assets as either tangible or intangible according to the nature of the asset acquired and to apply this classification consistently (paragraphs BC32–BC34).

(c)   amended the impairment principle so that an impairment is recognised on the basis of an assessment of facts and circumstances and measured, presented and disclosed in accordance with IAS 36, subject to the modification of the level at which the impairment is assessed (paragraphs BC36–BC39).

(d)   deleted the indicators of impairment proposed in ED 6 and replaced them with examples of facts and circumstances that would suggest that an exploration and evaluation asset was impaired (paragraphs BC36–BC39).

(e)   deleted the special cash-generating unit for exploration and evaluation assets and instead required that the entity determine an accounting policy for allocating exploration and evaluation assets to a cash-generating unit or units for the purpose of the impairment test (paragraphs BC40–BC47).

---

4   Paragraph BC65A was deleted as a result of revisions to IFRS 1 *First-time Adoption of International Financial Reporting Standards* in November 2008 as it was no longer applicable.

(f)   amended the effective date of the IFRS so that the IFRS is effective for annual periods beginning on or after 1 January 2006 (paragraph BC58).

(g)   provided transitional relief for entities adopting IFRSs for the first time and adopting the IFRS before 1 January 2006 (paragraphs BC59–BC65).

Dissenting opinions

Dissent of Robert P Garnett, James J Leisenring, Warren J McGregor and John T Smith

DO1   Messrs Garnett, Leisenring, McGregor and Smith dissent from the issue of IFRS 6.

DO2   These four Board members dissent because they would not permit entities the alternative of continuing their existing accounting treatment for exploration and evaluation assets. In particular, they believe that all entities should be required to apply paragraphs 11 and 12 of IAS 8 *Accounting Policies, Changes in Accounting Estimates and Errors* when developing an accounting policy for exploration and evaluation assets. These Board members believe that the requirements in IAS 8 have particular relevance and applicability when an IFRS lacks specificities, as is the case for entities recognising exploration and evaluation assets. This is especially true because the IFRS allows the continuation of a variety of measurement bases for these items and, because of the failure to consider the *Framework*,[5] may result in the inappropriate recognition of assets. In the view of these Board members, if an entity cannot meet those requirements, it should not be allowed to describe its financial statements as being in accordance with International Financial Reporting Standards.

DO3   Messrs Garnett and McGregor also disagree with the modifications to the requirements of IAS 36 for the purpose of assessing exploration and evaluation assets for impairment contained in paragraphs 18–22 of the IFRS. They think that the requirements of IAS 36 should be applied in their entirety to exploration and evaluation assets. Failure to do so could result in exploration and evaluation assets continuing to be carried forward when such assets are not known to be recoverable. This could result in the exclusion of relevant information from the financial statements because of the failure to recognise impairment losses on a timely basis and the inclusion of unreliable information because of the inclusion of assets that do not faithfully represent the transactions and other events that they purport to represent.

DO4   The four Board members' concerns are heightened by the absence as yet from the Board's main agenda of a project on accounting for exploration for and evaluation of mineral resources generally. Although a research project has begun, it is unlikely that the Board will be able to develop financial reporting standards in the medium term. Accordingly, it is likely that the concession referred to in paragraph DO2 and, in Messrs Garnett and McGregor's cases, in paragraph DO3, will remain in place for some time.

---

5   The reference to the *Framework* is to IASC's *Framework for the Preparation and Presentation of Financial Statements*, adopted by the IASB in 2001. In September 2010 the IASB replaced the *Framework* with the *Conceptual Framework for Financial Reporting*.

IASB documents published to accompany

IFRS 7

Financial Instruments: Disclosures

The text of the unaccompanied standard, IFRS 7, is contained in Part A of this edition. Its effective date when issued was 1 January 2007. The text of the Accompanying Guidance on IFRS 7 is contained in Part B of this edition. This part presents the following documents:

BASIS FOR CONCLUSIONS

APPENDIX TO THE BASIS FOR CONCLUSIONS
Amendments to Basis for Conclusions on other IFRSs

Contents

Basis for Conclusions on
IFRS 7 *Financial Instruments: Disclosures*

This Basis for Conclusions accompanies, but is not part of, IFRS 7.

In this Basis for Conclusions the terminology has not been amended to reflect the changes made by IAS 1 Presentation of Financial Statements *(as revised in 2007).*

The requirements of IAS 39 relating to classification and measurement of items within the scope of IAS 39 were relocated to IFRS 9 Financial Instruments, *and IFRS 7 was amended accordingly. The text of this Basis for Conclusions has been amended for consistency with those changes.*

Introduction

BC1　This Basis for Conclusions summarises the International Accounting Standards Board's considerations in reaching the conclusions in IFRS 7 *Financial Instruments: Disclosures*. Individual Board members gave greater weight to some factors than to others.

BC2　During the late 1990s, the need for a comprehensive review of IAS 30 *Disclosures in the Financial Statements of Banks and Similar Financial Institutions* became apparent. The Board's predecessor, the International Accounting Standards Committee (IASC), issued a number of Standards that addressed, more comprehensively, some of the topics previously addressed only for banks in IAS 30. Also, fundamental changes were taking place in the financial services industry and in the way in which financial institutions manage their activities and risk exposures. This made it increasingly difficult for users of banks' financial statements to assess and compare their financial position and performance, their associated risk exposures, and their processes for measuring and managing those risks.

BC3　In 1999 IASC added a project to its agenda to revise IAS 30 and in 2000 it appointed a steering committee.

BC4　In 2001 the Board added this project to its agenda. To assist and advise it, the Board retained the IAS 30 steering committee, renamed the Financial Activities Advisory Committee (FAAC), as an expert advisory group. FAAC members had experience and expertise in banks, finance companies and insurance companies and included auditors, financial analysts, preparers and regulators. The FAAC's role was:

(a)　to provide input from the perspective of preparers and auditors of financial statements of entities that have significant exposures to financial instruments; and

(b)　to assist the Board in developing a standard and implementation guidance for risk disclosures arising from financial instruments and for other related disclosures.

BC5　The Board published its proposals in July 2004 as ED 7 *Financial Instruments: Disclosures*. The deadline for comments was 27 October 2004. The Board received 105 comment letters. After reviewing the responses, the Board issued IFRS 7 in August 2005.

BC5A   In October 2008 the Board published an exposure draft *Improving Disclosures about Financial Instruments* (proposed amendments to IFRS 7). The aim of the proposed amendments was to enhance disclosures about fair value and liquidity risk. The Board received 89 comment letters. After reviewing the responses, the Board issued amendments to IFRS 7 in March 2009. The Board decided to require application of the amendments for periods beginning on or after 1 January 2009. The Board noted that, although the effective date of IFRSs and amendments to IFRSs is usually 6–18 months after issue, the urgent need for enhanced disclosures about financial instruments demanded earlier application.

BC5B   In January 2011 the IASB and the US national standard-setter, the Financial Accounting Standards Board (FASB), published the exposure draft *Offsetting Financial Assets and Financial Liabilities*. This was in response to requests from users of financial statements and recommendations from the Financial Stability Board to achieve convergence of the boards' requirements for offsetting financial assets and financial liabilities. The different requirements result in a significant difference between amounts presented in statements of financial position prepared in accordance with IFRSs and amounts presented in statements of financial position prepared in accordance with US GAAP, particularly for entities that have large amounts of derivative activities. The proposals in the exposure draft would have replaced the requirements for offsetting financial assets and financial liabilities and would have established a common approach with the FASB. After considering the responses to the exposure draft, the boards decided to maintain their respective offsetting models. However, to meet the needs of users of financial statements, the boards agreed jointly on additional disclosures to enable users of financial statements to evaluate the effect or potential effect of netting arrangements, including rights of set-off associated with an entity's recognised financial assets and recognised financial liabilities, on the entity's financial position. *Disclosures—Offsetting Financial Assets and Financial Liabilities* (Amendments to IFRS 7) was issued in December 2011 and is effective for annual periods beginning on or after 1 January 2013 and interim periods within those annual periods.

Scope (paragraphs 3–5)

The entities to which the IFRS applies

BC6   Although IFRS 7 arose from a project to revise IAS 30 (a Standard that applied only to banks and similar financial institutions), it applies to all entities that have financial instruments. The Board observed that the reduction in regulatory barriers in many countries and increasing competition between banks, non-bank financial services firms, and financial conglomerates have resulted in many entities providing financial services that were traditionally provided only by entities regulated and supervised as banks. The Board concluded that this development would make it inappropriate to limit this project to banks and similar financial institutions.

BC7   The Board considered whether entities that undertake specified activities commonly undertaken by banks and other financial institutions, namely deposit-taking, lending and securities activities, face unique risks that would require a standard specific to them. However, the Board decided that the scope of this project should include disclosures about risks arising from financial instruments in all entities for the following reasons:

(a) disclosures about risks associated with financial instruments are useful to users of the financial statements of all entities.

(b) the Board found it could not satisfactorily define deposit-taking, lending, and securities activities. In particular, it could not satisfactorily differentiate an entity with securities activities from an entity holding a portfolio of financial assets for investment and liquidity management purposes.

(c) responses to the Exposure Draft of Improvements to IAS 32 *Financial Instruments: Disclosure and Presentation*, published in June 2002, indicated that IAS 32's risk disclosure requirements, applicable to all entities, could be improved.

(d) the exclusion of some financial instruments would increase the danger that risk disclosures could be incomplete and possibly misleading. For example, a debt instrument issued by an entity could significantly affect its exposures to liquidity risk, interest rate risk and currency risk even if that instrument is not held as part of deposit-taking, lending and securities activities.

(e) users of financial statements need to be able to compare similar activities, transactions and events of different entities on a consistent basis. Hence, the disclosure principles that apply to regulated entities should not differ from those that apply to non-regulated, but otherwise similar, entities.

BC8 The Board decided that the scope of the IFRS should be the same as that of IAS 32 with one exception. The Board concluded that the IFRS should not apply to derivatives based on interests in subsidiaries, associates or joint ventures if the derivatives meet the definition of an equity instrument in IAS 32. This is because equity instruments are not remeasured and hence:

(a) they do not expose the issuer to balance sheet and income statement risk; and

(b) the disclosures about the significance of financial instruments for financial position and performance are not relevant to equity instruments.

Although these instruments are excluded from the scope of IFRS 7, they are within the scope of IAS 32 for the purpose of determining whether they meet the definition of equity instruments.

Exemptions considered by the Board

Insurers

BC9 The Board considered whether the IFRS should apply to entities that both have financial instruments and issue insurance contracts. The Board did not exempt these entities because financial instruments expose all entities to risks regardless of what other assets and liabilities they have. Accordingly, an entity that both issues insurance contracts and has financial instruments applies IFRS 4 *Insurance Contracts* to its insurance contracts and IFRS 7 to its financial assets and financial liabilities. However, many of the disclosure requirements in IFRS 4 were applications of, or relatively straightforward analogies with, existing requirements in IAS 32. Therefore, the Board also updated the disclosures required by IFRS 4 to make them consistent with IFRS 7, with modifications that reflect the interim nature of IFRS 4.

Small and medium-sized entities

BC10   The Board considered whether it should exempt small and medium-sized entities from the scope of the IFRS. The Board noted that the extent of disclosures required by the IFRS will depend on the extent to which the entity uses financial instruments and the extent to which it has assumed associated risks. The IFRS requires entities with few financial instruments and few risks to give few disclosures. Also, many of the requirements in the IFRS are based on information provided internally to the entity's key management personnel. This helps to avoid unduly onerous requirements that would not be appropriate for smaller entities. Accordingly, the Board decided not to exempt such entities from the scope of IFRS 7. However, it will keep this decision under review in its project on financial reporting for small and medium-sized entities.

Subsidiaries

BC11   Some respondents to ED 7 stated that there is little public interest in the financial statements of some entities, such as a wholly-owned subsidiary whose parent issues publicly available financial statements. These respondents stated that such subsidiaries should be exempt from some of the requirements of IFRS 7 in their individual financial statements. However, deciding whether such an entity should prepare general purpose financial statements is a matter for the entity and local legislators and regulators. If such an entity prepares financial statements in accordance with IFRSs, users of those statements should receive information of the same quality as users of any general purpose financial statements prepared in accordance with IFRSs. The Board confirmed its view that no exemptions from the general requirements of any Standard should be given for the financial statements of subsidiaries.

Disclosures about the significance of financial instruments for financial position and performance (paragraphs 7–30, B4 and B5)[1]

BC12   The Board relocated disclosures from IAS 32 to IFRS 7, so that all disclosure requirements for financial instruments are in one Standard. Many of the disclosure requirements about the significance of financial instruments for an entity's financial position and performance were previously in IAS 32. For these disclosures, the relevant paragraphs from the Basis for Conclusions on IAS 32 have been incorporated into this Basis for Conclusions. This Basis for Conclusions does not discuss requirements that the Board did not reconsider either in revising IAS 32 in 2003 or in developing IFRS 7.

---

1   IFRS 9 *Financial Instruments* deleted paragraph B4 of IFRS 7.

The principle (paragraph 7)

BC13   The Board decided that the disclosure requirements of IFRS 7 should result from the explicit disclosure principle in paragraph 7. The Board also decided to specify disclosures to satisfy this principle. In the Board's view, entities could not satisfy the principle in paragraph 7 unless they disclose the information required by paragraphs 8–30.

Balance sheet disclosures (paragraphs 8–19 and B4)[2]

Categories of financial assets and financial liabilities (paragraph 8)

BC14   Paragraph 8 requires entities to disclose financial assets and financial liabilities by the measurement categories in IFRS 9 *Financial Instruments*. The Board concluded that disclosures for each measurement category would assist users in understanding the extent to which accounting policies affect the amounts at which financial assets and financial liabilities are recognised.

BC15   The Board also concluded that separate disclosure of the carrying amounts of financial assets and financial liabilities that are designated upon initial recognition as financial assets and financial liabilities at fair value through profit or loss and those mandatorily measured at fair value is useful because such designation is at the discretion of the entity.

Financial assets or financial liabilities at fair value through profit or loss (paragraphs 9–11, B4 and B5)[3]

BC16   IFRS 9 permits entities to designate a non-derivative financial liability as at fair value through profit or loss, if specified conditions are met. If entities do so, they are required to provide the disclosures in paragraphs 10–11. The Board's reasons for these disclosures are set out in the Basis for Conclusions on IFRS 9, paragraphs BCZ5.29–BCZ5.34.

BC17   The requirements in paragraphs 9, 11 and B5(a) are related to the Amendments to IAS 39 Financial Instruments: Recognition and Measurement—*The Fair Value Option*, issued in June 2005.[4] The reasons for those requirements are discussed in the Basis for Conclusions on those Amendments.

BC18   Paragraph 10(a) requires disclosure of the change in fair value of a financial liability designated as at fair value through profit or loss that is attributable to changes in the liability's credit risk. The Board previously considered this disclosure in its deliberations on the fair value measurement of financial liabilities in IAS 39.

BC19   Although quantifying such changes might be difficult in practice, the Board concluded that disclosure of such information would be useful to users of financial statements and would help alleviate concerns that users may misinterpret the profit or loss effects of changes in credit risk, especially in the

---

2   IFRS 9 *Financial Instruments* deleted paragraph B4 of IFRS 7.
3   IFRS 9 *Financial Instruments* deleted paragraph B4 of IFRS 7.
4   IFRS 9 *Financial Instruments* replaced IAS 39. IFRS 9 applies to all items that were previously within the scope of IAS 39. This paragraph refers to matters relevant when IFRS 7 was issued.

absence of disclosures. Therefore, in finalising the revisions to IAS 32 in 2003, it decided to require disclosure of the change in fair value of the financial liability that is not attributable to changes in a benchmark interest rate. The Board believed that this is often a reasonable proxy for the change in fair value that is attributable to changes in the liability's credit risk, in particular when such changes are large, and would provide users with information with which to understand the profit or loss effect of such a change in credit risk.

BC20   However, some respondents to ED 7 stated that they did not agree that the IAS 32 disclosure provided a reasonable proxy, except for straightforward debt instruments. In particular, there could be other factors involved in the change in an instrument's fair value unrelated to the benchmark interest rate, such as the effect of an embedded derivative. Respondents also cited difficulties for unit-linked insurance contracts, for which the amount of the liability reflects the performance of a defined pool of assets. The Board noted that the proxy that was developed in IAS 32 assumed that it is not practicable for entities to determine directly the change in fair value arising from changes in credit risk. However, the Board acknowledged and shared these concerns.

BC21   As a result, the Board amended this requirement to focus directly on the objective of providing information about the effects of changes in credit risk:

(a)   by permitting entities to provide a more faithful representation of the amount of change in fair value that is attributable to changes in credit risk if they could do so. However, such entities are also required to disclose the methods used and provide their justification for concluding that those methods give a more faithful representation than the proxy in paragraph 10(a)(i).

(b)   by amending the proxy disclosure to be the amount of change in fair value that is not attributable to changes in market conditions that give rise to market risk. For example, some entities may be able to identify part of the change in the fair value of the liability as attributable to a change in an index. In these cases, the proxy disclosure would exclude the amount of change attributable to a change in an index. Similarly, excluding the amount attributable to a change in an internal or external investment fund makes the proxy more suitable for unit-linked insurance contracts.

BC22   The Board decided that when an entity has designated a financial liability as at fair value through profit or loss, it should disclose the difference between the carrying amount and the amount the entity would contractually be required to pay at maturity to the holders of the liability (see paragraph 10(b)). The fair value may differ significantly from the settlement amount, in particular for financial liabilities with a long duration when an entity has experienced a significant deterioration in creditworthiness since their issue. The Board concluded that knowledge of this difference would be useful to users of financial statements. Also, the settlement amount is important to some financial statement users, particularly creditors.

Reclassification (paragraphs 12B–12D)

BC23   IAS 32 required disclosure of the reason for reclassification of financial assets at cost or amortised cost rather than at fair value. The Board extended this requirement to include disclosure of the reason for reclassifications and of the amount reclassified into and out of each category. As noted in paragraph BC14, the Board regards such information as useful because the categorisation of financial instruments has a significant effect on their measurement.

BC23A   In October and November 2008 the Board amended IAS 39[5] to permit reclassification of particular financial assets in some circumstances. The Board decided to require additional disclosures about the situations in which any such reclassification is made, and the effects on the financial statements. The Board regards such information as useful because the reclassification of a financial asset can have a significant effect on the financial statements.

BC23B   The Board issued the requirements relating to the reclassification of financial assets in IFRS 9 *Financial Instruments* and revised accordingly the disclosure requirements relating to the reclassification of financial assets.

BC24   [Deleted]

Offsetting financial assets and financial liabilities

Background

BC24A   Following requests from users of financial statements and recommendations from the Financial Stability Board, in June 2010 the IASB and the FASB added a project to their respective agendas to improve and potentially achieve convergence of the requirements for offsetting financial assets and financial liabilities. The different requirements result in a significant difference between amounts presented in statements of financial position prepared in accordance with IFRSs and amounts presented in statements of financial position prepared in accordance with US GAAP, particularly for entities that have large amounts of derivative activities.

BC24B   Consequently, in January 2011 the IASB and the FASB published the exposure draft *Offsetting Financial Assets and Financial Liabilities*. The exposure draft proposed common offsetting requirements for IFRSs and US GAAP and proposed disclosures about financial assets and financial liabilities that are subject to rights of set-off and related arrangements.

BC24C   Most respondents to the exposure draft supported the boards' efforts towards achieving convergence, but their responses to the proposals varied. Many IFRS preparers agreed with the proposals, stating that the underlying principle and proposed criteria were similar to those in IAS 32 and reflect an entity's credit and liquidity exposure to such instruments. Some US GAAP preparers indicated that offsetting in the statement of financial position in accordance with the proposed criteria provided more relevant information than the current model, except for derivatives and repurchase or reverse repurchase agreements.

---

5   IFRS 9 *Financial Instruments* replaced IAS 39. IFRS 9 applies to all items that were previously within the scope of IAS 39. This paragraph refers to matters relevant when IFRS 7 was issued.

BC24D   There was no consensus among users of financial statements regarding if, or when, to present gross or net information in the statement of financial position. However, there was consensus that both gross and net information are useful and necessary for analysing financial statements. Users of financial statements supported achieving convergence of the IFRS and US GAAP requirements, and also supported improving disclosures so that financial statements prepared in accordance with IFRSs and US GAAP would be more comparable. Comparable information is important to investors for calculating their ratios and performing their analyses.

BC24E   As a result of the feedback received on the exposure draft, the IASB and the FASB decided to maintain their respective offsetting models. However, the boards noted that requiring common disclosures of gross and net amounts of recognised financial instruments that are (a) set off in the statement of financial position and (b) subject to enforceable master netting arrangements and similar agreements, even if not set off in the statement of financial position, would be helpful for users of financial statements. Accordingly, the boards agreed on common disclosure requirements by amending and finalising the disclosures initially proposed in the exposure draft.

Scope (paragraph 13A)

BC24F   The disclosures in the exposure draft would have applied to all recognised financial assets and recognised financial liabilities subject to a right of set-off, and/or for which an entity had either received or pledged cash or other financial instruments as collateral.

BC24G   Respondents to the exposure draft noted that paragraphs 14, 15 and 36(b) of IFRS 7 already require disclosures of financial instrument collateral received and pledged and other credit enhancements. US GAAP has similar disclosure requirements. Consequently, if an entity has no financial assets or financial liabilities subject to a right of set-off (other than collateral agreements or credit enhancements), the boards concluded that there would be no incremental value in providing additional disclosure information for such instruments.

BC24H   For example, some respondents were concerned that providing disclosure of conditional rights to set off loans and customer deposits at the same financial institution would be a significant operational burden. Such rights are often a result of statute, and entities do not typically manage their credit risk related to such amounts based on these rights of set-off. In addition, entities that have contractual rights to set off customer deposits with loans only in situations such as events of default see these rights as a credit enhancement and not as the primary source of credit mitigation. Respondents argued that the cost of including these amounts in the amended disclosures would outweigh the benefit because users of financial statements did not request information related to these instruments when discussing the offsetting disclosure requirements.

BC24I   The boards agreed and decided to limit the scope of the disclosures to all financial instruments that meet the boards' respective offsetting models and recognised financial assets and recognised financial liabilities that are subject to an enforceable master netting arrangement or a similar agreement. The boards specifically excluded loans and customer deposits with the same financial institution from the scope of these requirements (except in the limited cases when the respective offsetting model is satisfied). This reduced scope still responds to the needs of users of financial statements for information about amounts that have been set off in accordance with IFRSs and amounts that have been set off in accordance with US GAAP. The types of instruments that fall within the scope of these disclosures include the instruments that cause significant differences between amounts presented in statements of financial position prepared in accordance with IFRSs and amounts presented in statements of financial position prepared in accordance with US GAAP.

BC24J   If there is an associated collateral agreement for such instruments, an entity would disclose amounts subject to such agreements in order to provide full information about its exposure in the normal course of business, as well as in the events of default and insolvency or bankruptcy.

BC24K   Other respondents requested that the scope of the proposed disclosures be further amended to exclude financial instruments for which the lender has the right to set off the related non-financial collateral in the event of default. Although non-financial collateral agreements may exist for some financial instruments, those preparers do not necessarily manage the credit risk related to such financial instruments on the basis of the non-financial collateral held.

BC24L   The disclosures focus on the effects of recognised financial instruments and financial instrument set-off agreements on an entity's financial position. The boards also noted that a comprehensive reconsideration of credit risk disclosures was not within the scope of this project. They therefore restricted the scope of the disclosures to exclude financial instruments with rights of set-off only for non-financial collateral.

BC24M   A few respondents were concerned that the proposals seem to be designed for financial institutions and would impose requirements on non-financial institutions. They questioned the benefit that such disclosures would provide to investors in non-financial entities.

BC24N   Although the boards acknowledged that financial institutions would be among those most affected, they did not agree that the disclosures are only relevant for financial institutions. Other industries have similar financial instrument activities and use enforceable master netting arrangements and similar agreements to mitigate exposure to credit risks. Consequently, the boards concluded that the required disclosures provide useful information about an entity's arrangements, irrespective of the nature of the entity's business.

Disclosure of quantitative information for recognised financial assets and recognised financial liabilities within the scope of paragraph 13A (paragraph 13C)

BC24O   The boards understood that recognised financial instruments included in the disclosure requirements in paragraph 13C of IFRS 7 may be subject to different measurement requirements. For example, a payable related to a repurchase agreement may be measured at amortised cost, while a derivative asset or derivative liability subject to the same disclosure requirements (for example, in paragraph 13C(a) of IFRS 7) will be measured at fair value. In addition, the fair value amount of any financial instrument collateral received or pledged and subject to paragraph 13C(d)(ii) of IFRS 7 should be included in the disclosures to provide users of financial statements with the best information about an entity's exposure. Consequently, a financial asset or financial liability disclosure table may include financial instruments measured at different amounts. To provide users of financial statements with the information they need to evaluate the amounts disclosed in accordance with paragraph 13C of IFRS 7, the boards decided that an entity should describe any resulting measurement differences in the related disclosures.

Disclosure of the net amounts presented in the statement of financial position (paragraph 13C(c))

BC24P   When providing feedback on the proposals in the exposure draft, users of financial statements emphasised that information in the notes should be clearly reconciled back to the amounts in the statement of financial position. The boards therefore decided that if an entity determines that the aggregation or disaggregation of individual financial statement line item amounts provides more relevant information when disclosing amounts in accordance with paragraph 13C of IFRS 7, the entity must still reconcile the amounts disclosed in paragraph 13C(c) of IFRS 7 back to the individual line item amounts in the statement of financial position.

Disclosure of the amounts subject to an enforceable master netting arrangement or similar agreement that are not otherwise included in paragraph 13C(b) (paragraph 13C(d))

BC24Q   Paragraph 13C(d)(i) of IFRS 7 requires disclosure of amounts related to recognised financial instruments that do not meet some or all of the offsetting criteria in paragraph 42 of IAS 32. This may include current rights of set-off that do not meet the criterion in paragraph 42(b) of IAS 32, or conditional rights of set-off that are enforceable and exercisable only in the event of default, or only in the event of insolvency or bankruptcy of any of the counterparties. Although such rights do not qualify for set-off in accordance with IAS 32, users of financial statements are interested in arrangements that an entity has entered into that mitigate the entity's exposure to such financial instruments in the normal course of business and/or in the events of default and insolvency or bankruptcy.

BC24R   Paragraph 13C(d)(ii) of IFRS 7 requires disclosure of amounts of cash and financial instrument collateral (whether recognised or unrecognised) that do not meet the criteria for offsetting in the statement of financial position but that relate to financial instruments within the scope of these disclosure requirements. Depending on the terms of the collateral arrangement, collateral will often reduce an entity's exposure in the events of default and insolvency or bankruptcy of a counterparty to the contract. Collateral received or pledged against financial assets and financial liabilities may often be liquidated immediately upon an event of default. Consequently, the boards concluded that the amounts of collateral that are not set off in the statement of financial position but that are associated with other netting arrangements should be included in the amounts disclosed as required by paragraph 13C(d)(ii) of IFRS 7.

Limits on the amounts disclosed in paragraph 13C(d) (paragraph 13D)

BC24S The boards concluded that an aggregate disclosure of the amount of cash collateral and/or the fair value of collateral in the form of other financial instruments would be misleading when some financial assets and financial liabilities are over-collateralised and others have insufficient collateral. To prevent an entity from inappropriately obscuring under-collateralised financial instruments with others that are over-collateralised, paragraph 13D of IFRS 7 restricts the amounts of cash and/or financial instrument collateral to be disclosed in respect of a recognised financial instrument to more accurately reflect an entity's exposure. However, if rights to collateral can be enforced across financial instruments, such rights can be included in the disclosure provided in accordance with paragraph 13D of IFRS 7. At no point in time should under-collateralisation be obscured.

Disclosure by type of financial instrument or by counterparty

BC24T The exposure draft proposed disclosures by class of financial instrument. An entity would have been required to group financial assets and financial liabilities separately into classes that were appropriate to the nature of the information disclosed, taking into account the characteristics of those financial instruments and the applicable rights of set-off. Many preparers were concerned that the cost of disclosing amounts related to rights of set-off in the events of default and insolvency or bankruptcy by class of financial instrument would outweigh the benefit. They also indicated that they often manage credit exposure by counterparty and not necessarily by class of financial instrument.

BC24U Many users of financial statements indicated that disclosure of recognised amounts subject to enforceable master netting arrangements and similar agreements (including financial collateral) that were not set off in the statement of financial position would be useful irrespective of whether the amounts are disclosed by counterparty or by type or by class of financial instrument, as long as they can reconcile these amounts back to the statement of financial position. In evaluating whether the disclosures should be provided by type or by class of financial instrument or by counterparty, the boards noted that the objective of these disclosures (paragraph 13B of IFRS 7) is that an entity should disclose information to enable users of its financial statements to evaluate the effect or potential effect of netting arrangements on the entity's financial position.

BC24V The boards decided to reduce the burden on preparers by requiring disclosure by type of financial instrument rather than by class. Disclosure by type of financial instrument may (or may not) differ from the class of financial instrument used for other disclosures in IFRS 7, but is appropriate in circumstances where a difference would better achieve the objective of the disclosures required by these amendments. The boards also decided to provide flexibility as to whether the information required by paragraph 13C(c)–(e) of IFRS 7 is presented by type of financial instrument or by counterparty. This would allow preparers to present the disclosures in the same way that they manage their credit exposure.

BC24W The Board also noted that paragraph 31 of IFRS 7 requires an entity to disclose information that enables users of its financial statements to evaluate the nature and extent of risks arising from financial instruments to which the entity is exposed at the end of the reporting period. In addition, paragraph 34 of IFRS 7 requires the disclosure of concentrations of risk for each type of risk. Consequently, the Board noted that, irrespective of whether the disclosures were required to be provided by type or by class of financial instrument or by counterparty, entities are already required to disclose information about risks and how they are managed, including information about concentrations of credit risk.

Other considerations

Reconciliation between IFRSs and US GAAP

BC24X   Some users of financial statements asked for information to help them reconcile between the amounts set off in accordance with IFRSs and the amounts set off in accordance with US GAAP. The boards recognised that the amounts disclosed in accordance with paragraph 13C(b), (c) and (d) of IFRS 7 will probably be different for financial statements prepared in accordance with IFRSs and those prepared in accordance with US GAAP. However, the amounts disclosed in accordance with paragraph 13C(a) and (e) of IFRS 7 are generally not affected by the offsetting criteria applied in the statement of financial position. These amounts are important for users of financial statements to understand the effects of netting arrangements on an entity's financial position in the normal course of business and in the events of default and insolvency or bankruptcy.

BC24Y   Consequently, while the amended disclosure requirements do not directly reconcile the IFRS and US GAAP amounts, they provide both gross and net information on a comparable basis. The boards considered that requiring a full reconciliation between IFRSs and US GAAP was unnecessary, particularly given the relative costs and benefits. Such reconciliation would have required preparers to apply two sets of accounting requirements and to track any changes to the related accounting standards and to contracts in the related jurisdictions.

Tabular information

BC24Z   The disclosures require amounts to be presented in a tabular format (ie a table) unless another format is more appropriate. The boards believe that a tabular format best conveys an overall understanding of the effect of any rights of set-off and other related arrangements on an entity's financial position and improves the transparency of such information.

Transition and effective date

BC24AA   The boards identified two transition approaches in the exposure draft—prospective and retrospective.

BC24AB   Prospective transition is generally appropriate only in situations where it is not practicable to apply a standard to all prior periods. The boards did not believe that this was the case with the proposed disclosure requirements. Retrospective transition would require an entity to apply the new requirements to all periods presented. This would maximise consistency of financial information between periods. Retrospective transition would enable analysis and understanding of comparative accounting information among entities. In addition, the scope of the disclosures was reduced and the disclosures amended to require less detailed information than originally proposed, which would make them less burdensome for preparers to apply retrospectively.

BC24AC   The exposure draft did not propose an effective date, but instead asked respondents for information about the time and effort that would be involved in implementing the proposed requirements. The boards indicated that they would use such feedback, as well as the responses in their *Request for Views on Effective Dates and Transition Methods*, and the timing of other planned accounting and reporting standards, to determine an appropriate effective date for the proposals in the exposure draft.

BC24AD   Some respondents suggested that the offsetting proposals should have the same effective date as the other components of the IASB's project to replace IAS 39 with IFRS 9 *Financial Instruments*. If an earlier date was required, it was suggested that application should be restricted only to the accounting period being presented, rather than providing comparative information, because of the potential burden of applying the proposed disclosure requirements.

BC24AE   At the time the amended disclosure requirements were issued (December 2011), IFRS 9 was not yet mandatorily effective. However, the Board did not believe that the IFRS 9 project would change the offsetting disclosures. Aligning the effective date of these amendments with the effective date of the financial instruments project could result in postponing the effective date of the common disclosure requirements, which would mean a delay in providing users of financial statements the information that they need. For users of financial statements to benefit from the increased comparability, and because the offsetting and IFRS 9 projects are independent of one another, the boards decided that common disclosures should be effective as early as possible.

BC24AF   In addition, the boards did not think that a long transition period was needed, because the amended disclosures had a reduced scope and less detailed information than originally proposed in the exposure draft and were related to the presentation of instruments that entities have already recognised and measured. The boards therefore decided that the effective date for the amended disclosures should be for annual periods beginning on or after 1 January 2013, and interim periods within those annual periods.

BC24AG   As described in greater detail in other sections of this Basis for Conclusions, the disclosures required by paragraphs 13B–13E of IFRS 7 are a result of requests from users of financial statements for information to enable them to compare statements of financial position prepared in accordance with IFRSs with statements of financial position prepared in accordance with US GAAP, particularly for entities that have large amounts of derivative activities.

BC24AH   The information required in paragraphs 13B–13E of IFRS 7 will enable users of financial statements to evaluate the effect or potential effect of netting arrangements, including rights of set-off associated with an entity's recognised financial assets and recognised financial liabilities, on the entity's financial position for financial statements presented in accordance with IFRSs and those presented in accordance with US GAAP.

BC24AI The Board noted that paragraph 10(f) of IAS 1 *Presentation of Financial Statements* requires an entity to provide a statement of financial position as at the beginning of the earliest comparative period when an entity applies an accounting policy retrospectively or makes a retrospective restatement of items in its financial statements, or when it reclassifies items in its financial statements. In the case of *Disclosures—Offsetting Financial Assets and Financial Liabilities* (Amendments to IFRS 7), because the change relates only to disclosures and there is no associated change in accounting policy, or a resulting restatement or reclassification, it was noted that paragraph 10(f) of IAS 1 does not apply for these amendments to IFRS 7.

Cost-benefit considerations

BC24AJ Before issuing an IFRS or an amendment to an IFRS, the Board seeks to ensure that it will meet a significant need and that the overall benefits of the resulting information justify the costs of providing it. As described in greater detail in other sections of this Basis for Conclusions on *Disclosures—Offsetting Financial Assets and Financial Liabilities* (Amendments to IFRS 7), the Board considered that there is significant benefit to market participants in providing these disclosures. The disclosures address a significant difference between the amounts presented in statements of financial position prepared in accordance with IFRSs and amounts presented in statements of financial position prepared in accordance with US GAAP, particularly for entities that have large amounts of derivative activities. The disclosures therefore make the amounts presented in accordance with both sets of standards more comparable.

BC24AK During redeliberations, the Board considered feedback related to the costs of providing the disclosures proposed in the exposure draft. As described in greater detail in other sections of this Basis for Conclusions, the Board decided to limit the scope of the disclosures because these changes would reduce the cost to preparers while still providing the information that users of financial statements had requested.

BC24AL On the basis of the considerations described in the Basis for Conclusions on these amendments, and summarised in paragraphs BC24AJ and BC24AK, the Board concluded that the benefits of *Disclosures—Offsetting Financial Assets and Financial Liabilities* (Amendments to IFRS 7) outweigh the costs to preparers of applying these amendments.

Collateral (paragraphs 14 and 15)

BC25 Paragraph 15 requires disclosures about collateral that the entity holds if it is permitted to sell or repledge the collateral in the absence of default by the owner. Some respondents to ED 7 argued for an exemption from this disclosure if it is impracticable to obtain the fair value of the collateral held. However, the Board concluded that it is reasonable to expect an entity to know the fair value of collateral that it holds and can sell even if there is no default.

Allowance account for credit losses (paragraph 16)[6]

BC26 When a separate account is used to record impairment losses (such as an allowance account or similar account used to record a collective impairment of assets), paragraph 16 requires a reconciliation of that account to be disclosed. The Board was informed that analysts and other users find this information useful in assessing the adequacy of the allowance for impairment losses for such entities and when comparing one entity with another. However, the Board decided not to specify the components of the reconciliation. This allows entities flexibility in determining the most appropriate format for their needs.

BC27 Respondents to ED 7 asked the Board to require entities to provide equivalent information if they do not use an allowance account. The Board decided not to add this disclosure in finalising the IFRS. It concluded that, for virtually all entities, IAS 39's requirement to consider impairment on a group basis would necessitate the use of an allowance or similar account. The accounting policy disclosures required by paragraph B5(d) also include information about the use of direct adjustments to carrying amounts of financial assets.

Compound financial instruments with multiple embedded derivatives (paragraph 17)

BC28 IAS 32 requires the separation of the liability and equity components of a compound financial instrument. The Board notes that this is more complicated for compound financial instruments with multiple embedded derivative features whose values are interdependent (for example, a convertible debt instrument that gives the issuer a right to call the instrument back from the holder, or the holder a right to put the instrument back to the issuer) than for those without such features. If the embedded equity and non-equity derivative features are interdependent, the sum of the separately determined values of the liability and equity components will not equal the value of the compound financial instrument as a whole.

BC29 For example, the values of an embedded call option feature and an equity conversion option feature in a callable convertible debt instrument depend in part on each other if the holder's equity conversion option is extinguished when the entity exercises the call option or vice versa. The following diagram illustrates the joint value arising from the interaction between a call option and an equity conversion option in a callable convertible bond. Circle L represents the value of the liability component, ie the value of the straight debt and the embedded call option on the straight debt, and Circle E represents the value of the equity component, ie the equity conversion option on the straight debt.

---

6 IFRS 9 *Financial Instruments* replaced IAS 39. IFRS 9 applies to all items that were previously within the scope of IAS 9. This paragraph refers to matters relevant when IFRS 7 was issued.

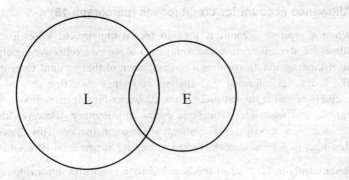

The total area of the two circles represents the value of the callable convertible bond. The difference between the value of the callable convertible bond as a whole and the sum of the separately determined values for the liability and equity components is the joint value attributable to the interdependence between the call option feature and the equity conversion feature. It is represented by the intersection between the two circles.

BC30   Under the approach in IAS 32, the joint value attributable to the interdependence between multiple embedded derivative features is included in the liability component. A numerical example is set out as Illustrative Example 10 accompanying IAS 32.

BC31   Even though this approach is consistent with the definition of equity as a residual interest, the Board recognises that the allocation of the joint value to either the liability component or the equity component is arbitrary because it is, by its nature, joint. Therefore, the Board concluded that it is important to disclose the existence of issued compound financial instruments with multiple embedded derivative features that have interdependent values. Such disclosure highlights the effect of multiple embedded derivative features on the amounts recognised as liabilities and equity.

Defaults and breaches (paragraphs 18 and 19)

BC32   Paragraphs 18 and 19 require disclosures about defaults and breaches of loans payable and other loan agreements. The Board concluded that such disclosures provide relevant information about the entity's creditworthiness and its prospects of obtaining future loans.

Income statement and equity (paragraph 20)

Items of income, expenses, gains or losses (paragraph 20(a))

BC33   Paragraph 20(a) requires disclosure of income statement gains and losses by the measurement classifications in IFRS 9 (which complement the balance sheet disclosure requirement described in paragraph BC14). The Board concluded that the disclosure is needed for users to understand the financial performance of an entity's financial instruments, given the different measurement bases in IFRS 9.

BC34   Some entities include interest and dividend income in gains and losses on financial assets and financial liabilities measured at fair value through profit or loss and others do not. To assist users in comparing income arising from financial instruments across different entities, the Board decided that an entity should disclose how the income statement amounts are determined. For example, an entity should disclose whether net gains and losses on financial assets or financial liabilities measured at fair value through profit or loss include interest and dividend income (see Appendix B, paragraph B5(e)).

Fee income and expense (paragraph 20(c))

BC35   Paragraph 20(c) requires disclosure of fee income and expense (other than amounts included in determining the effective interest rate) arising from financial assets or financial liabilities and from trust and other fiduciary activities that result in the entity holding or placing assets on behalf of individuals, trusts, retirement benefit plans, and other institutions. This information indicates the level of such activities and helps users to estimate possible future income of the entity.

Other Disclosures—Hedge Accounting

BC35A   The Board divided its project to replace IAS 39 into three phases. As the Board completed each phase, it deleted the relevant portions in IAS 39 and replaced it with chapters in IFRS 9. The third phase of the project to replace IAS 39 related to hedge accounting. As a consequence of the decisions the Board made when it replaced the hedge accounting guidance in IAS 39, the Board also considered changes to the disclosure requirements related to hedge accounting contained in IFRS 7.

BC35B   During its deliberations, the Board engaged in outreach activities with users of financial statements. This outreach included soliciting views on presentation and disclosures. The Board used the responses received from those outreach activities to develop the proposed hedge accounting disclosures.

BC35C   The Board was told that many users did not find the hedge accounting disclosures in financial statements helpful. Many also think that the hedge accounting disclosures that were originally in IFRS 7 did not provide transparency on an entity's hedging activities.

BC35D   To provide relevant information that enhances the transparency on an entity's hedging activities, the Board proposes hedge accounting disclosures that meet particular objectives. Clear disclosure objectives allow an entity to apply its judgement when it provides information that is useful and relevant to users of financial statements.

BC35E   The following sub-sections set out the Board's considerations regarding the proposed hedge accounting disclosures.

General considerations

Scope of the hedge accounting disclosures

BC35F   An entity might enter into a transaction to manage an exposure to a particular risk that might not qualify for hedge accounting (for various reasons), for example, an item that is not eligible to be designated as a hedged item or hedging instrument. Information on such transactions might enable users to understand why an entity has entered into a transaction and how it manages the particular risk, even though those transactions do not qualify for hedge accounting.

BC35G However, the Board thought that mandating such disclosures would require it to determine the part of an entity's risk management that was relevant for the purpose of this disclosure and then define that part to make the disclosure requirement operational. The Board did not believe that this would be feasible as part of its hedge accounting project as it requires a much wider scope because the disclosures would not depend on the accounting treatment.

BC35H Furthermore, users of financial statements can often obtain information on an entity's hedging activities from information in management reports and sources outside the financial reporting context. That often gives a reasonable overview of why hedge accounting might be difficult to achieve. Consequently, the Board decided not to propose in its 2010 Exposure Draft *Hedge Accounting* (the '2010 Hedge Accounting Exposure Draft') disclosures about hedging when hedge accounting does not apply.

BC35I Most respondents to the 2010 Hedge Accounting Exposure Draft agreed with the Board's proposed scope for hedge accounting disclosures (ie to provide information about risk exposures that an entity hedges and for which hedge accounting is applied). However, some did raise concerns about the potential lack of information that will be available to users of financial statements about those risk exposures an entity hedges but for which hedge accounting is not applied.

BC35J The Board noted that IFRS 7 requires entities to provide qualitative and quantitative disclosure about the nature and extent of risks arising from financial instruments to which the entity is exposed at the end of the reporting period and how those risks are being managed. The Board believes that, as part of these disclosures, entities would provide information for users of financial statements to understand how it manages risk exposures for which hedge accounting is not applied.

BC35K Consequently, the Board decided to retain the scope of the hedge accounting disclosures as proposed in the 2010 Hedge Accounting Exposure Draft, that is, to provide information to users of financial statements on exposures that an entity hedges and for which hedge accounting is applied.

Location of disclosures

BC35L The Board decided that all hedge accounting disclosures should be presented in one location within an entity's financial statements. However, if such information is already presented elsewhere the Board decided that, in order to avoid duplication, an entity should be allowed to incorporate that information by cross-reference, which is similar to the approach used by IFRS 7 for some disclosures that can be incorporated by reference. The Board thinks that the information will be more transparent and easier to understand if it is presented in one location within the entity's financial statements.

Disclosures by risk category

BC35M   The Board noted that recognition and measurement requirements allow for only a partial reflection of the economic hedging activities in the financial statements, which results in a limitation of an entity's reporting of its hedging activities. Hence, the Board considered that the transparency of an entity's hedging activities could be enhanced by an approach that considers:

     (a)   information that provides a clear picture of those risk management activities of an entity that are captured by hedge accounting (this information is not necessarily provided in the primary financial statements); and

     (b)   information that is included in the primary financial statements.

BC35N   To provide information that is useful to users of financial statements, there should be a clear link between the hedge accounting information that is outside the primary financial statements and the hedge accounting within those. To provide such a link, the Board decided that an entity should provide hedge accounting disclosures by risk category. Consequently, an entity should disclose by risk category:

     (a)   information that is not included in the primary financial statements (see paragraphs BC35P–BC35BB); and

     (b)   information that is included in the primary financial statements (see paragraphs BC35CC–BC35SS).

BC35O   The Board decided not to prescribe the risk categories by which the disclosures need to be disaggregated. In the Board's view an entity should apply judgement and categorise risks on the basis of how it manages its risks through hedging. For example, an entity manages its floating interest rate risk using interest rate swaps (to change it to a fixed interest rate) for some hedging relationships (cash flow hedges), while it also uses cross-currency interest rate swaps to manage both the floating interest rate and foreign exchange risk of other hedging relationships (cash flow hedges). Consequently, the entity would have one risk category for floating interest rate risk and another risk category for foreign exchange risk combined with floating interest rate risk. However, an entity should apply its risk categories consistently throughout all the proposed hedge accounting disclosures.

The risk management strategy

BC35P   Users of financial statements need to understand how an entity's risk management strategy is applied. Understanding an entity's risk management strategy for each risk helps users to understand the accounting information disclosed.

BC35Q   Consequently, in its 2010 Hedge Accounting Exposure Draft, the Board proposed that an entity should provide an explanation of its risk management strategy for each category of risk.

BC35R   Most respondents to the 2010 Hedge Accounting Exposure Draft agreed with this proposal. However, some raised concerns that the 2010 Hedge Accounting

Exposure Draft was not clear enough on how much detail should be provided by entities to comply with the disclosure requirement.

BC35S The Board noted that an entity will identify and ultimately describe their risk management strategies based on how it manages risk. Because entities manage risk in different ways, the Board did not think that users of financial statements would necessarily understand an entity's risk management strategy if it required a specific list of information to be disclosed. Instead, the Board decided to add additional guidance on the type of information that should be included in a risk management description.

The amount, timing and uncertainty of future cash flows

BC35T The Board decided that, in order to meet the objectives of hedge accounting disclosures, an entity would have to provide sufficient quantitative information to help users of financial statements understand how its risk management strategy for each particular risk affects the amount, timing and uncertainty of future cash flows. In this context, risk exposure refers only to risks that the entity has decided to hedge and for which hedge accounting is applied.

BC35U Consequently, in its 2010 Hedge Accounting Exposure Draft, the Board proposed that an entity should provide:

(a) quantitative information on the risk exposure that the entity manages and the extent to which the entity hedges that exposure; and

(b) a breakdown of that information for each future period that a hedging relationship (which exists at the reporting date) covers.

BC35V The Board also proposed that an entity should disclose information about the sources of hedge ineffectiveness of hedging relationships for each particular risk category. In the Board's view this would assist users in identifying the reasons for hedge ineffectiveness that is recognised in profit or loss. It would also help users to determine how hedging relationships will affect profit or loss.

BC35W Most respondents disagreed with the Board's proposal to require entities to disclose information on the risk exposure and the hedged rate. They commented that this would result in the disclosure of commercially sensitive information (ie the risk exposure and the hedged rate). They believed that those who do not elect to apply hedge accounting would potentially have an unfair advantage because although they do not have to disclose anything, they could nonetheless gain insight into their competitor's hedge positions. Commercial sensitivity was also of concern to those entities whose competitors are not listed companies or who do not report under IFRSs.

BC35X The Board noted that the proposal in the 2010 Hedge Accounting Exposure Draft focused on the hedged risk (ie the hedged item). Consequently, it would result in disclosures about forward looking information and the rates at which future transactions are hedged. The Board acknowledged that this would potentially provide competitors with insight into an entity's costing structure. Consequently, the Board decided not to require information to be disclosed about the total risk exposure because of the potential forward looking nature of this information. The Board also decided to change the focus of the proposed disclosure from the hedged item to the hedging instrument. In other words, the disclosure would require information on some of the terms and conditions of the hedging instrument to be provided. The Board believes that this information will still be relevant and useful for users of financial statements in inferring the exposure that an entity is exposed to and what the effects will be on future cash flows as a result of how the entity manages the particular risk.

BC35Y   The Board also discussed situations in which an entity uses a 'dynamic' hedging process, ie a situation in which entities assess their overall exposure to a particular risk and then designate hedging relationships for constantly evolving exposures that require frequent discontinuations and restarts of hedging relationships. This is particularly the case for hedges of open portfolios. The Board noted that, because the general hedge accounting model allows hedge accounting for hedges of groups and net positions in relation to closed portfolios, entities need to use a 'dynamic' hedging process for an open portfolio. This means that entities designate hedging relationships for an open portfolio as if it were a closed portfolio for a short period and at the end of that period look at the open portfolio as the next closed portfolio for another short period. The dynamic nature of this process involves frequent discontinuations and restarts of hedging relationships.

BC35Z   The Board considered that, in those circumstances, providing information about the terms and conditions of the hedging instruments would not be useful given that the hedging instruments are part of a particular hedging relationship for only a short period at a time and are then designated into a new hedging relationship or left undesignated. In contrast, the disclosure requirement related to the terms and conditions of the hedging instrument was designed to provide information for situations in which an entity hedges a risk that remains broadly the same over the entire hedged period. Consequently, the Board decided to exempt entities from the requirement to disclose the terms and conditions of the hedging instruments in situations in which they use a 'dynamic' hedging process that involves frequent discontinuations and restarts of hedging relationships.

BC35AA   The Board was of the view that it was more important for users to understand why entities use hedge accounting in the context of 'dynamic' hedging processes than to provide users with information about the terms and conditions of a hedging instrument that is part of a hedging relationship for only a short period at a time (and the designation of which changes frequently). Consequently, the Board decided that, in such circumstances, an entity should expand its discussion of the risk management strategy by providing the following information about how the entity uses hedge accounting to reflect its risk management strategy:

(a)   information about what the ultimate risk management strategy is (for the dynamic hedging process);

(b)   a description of how it reflects its risk management strategy by using hedge accounting and designating the particular hedging relationships; and

(c)   an indication of how frequently the hedging relationships are discontinued and restarted as part of the dynamic hedging process.

BC35BB   The Board also noted that, because the designated hedging relationships change frequently, the specific relationships at the reporting date might not be representative of the normal volumes during the period. The Board therefore decided to require entities to disclose when the volumes at the reporting date are unrepresentative of normal volumes during the period (similar to the disclosure requirement on sensitivity analyses for market risk in paragraph 42).

BC35CC   One function of hedge accounting is to mitigate the recognition and measurement anomalies between the accounting for hedging instruments and the accounting for hedged items. Hedge accounting disclosures should therefore increase the transparency of how an entity has mitigated these recognition and measurement anomalies. Doing so will help users identify how hedge accounting has affected the entity's statement of profit or loss and other comprehensive income and statement of financial position.

The effects of hedge accounting on financial position and performance

BC35DD   To provide information on the effects of hedge accounting on the statement of profit or loss and other comprehensive income and the statement of financial position, the Board proposed disclosures that should be presented in a tabular format that separates the information by risk category and by type of hedge. Providing disclosures in a tabular format allows users to identify clearly the relevant numbers and their effects on the entity's statement of profit or loss and other comprehensive income and statement of financial position.

BC35EE   During the Board's initial outreach, users said that they do not analyse an entity's hedging activities by type of hedging relationship (for example, a cash flow hedge or a fair value hedge). They said that it is more important to understand the risks that the entity manages and the results after hedging. However, to provide information effectively on the effects of hedge accounting on the statement of profit or loss and other comprehensive income and the statement of financial position, the information should reflect the accounting that was applied (for example, cash flow hedge accounting or fair value hedge accounting). The Board believed that if the proposed table is prepared by risk category and by type of hedge, the table would provide sufficient links between the accounting information and the risk management information.

BC35FF   The Board did not propose prescribing levels of aggregation or disaggregation for the information that should be disclosed in a tabular format. An entity should apply judgement when it determines the appropriate level of aggregation or disaggregation. However, the Board proposed that an entity should consider other disclosure requirements in IFRS 7 when it considers the appropriate level of aggregation or disaggregation. For example, users should be able to take amounts that are disclosed and measured at fair value and make comparisons between the fair value disclosures and the proposed hedge accounting disclosures.

BC35GG   Cash flow hedge accounting requires an entity to defer gains or losses on the hedging instrument in other comprehensive income. The deferred amounts are reflected in the statement of changes in equity in the cash flow hedge reserve. IAS 1 requires an entity to prepare a reconciliation for each component of equity between the carrying amount at the beginning and at the end of the period. In conformity with its objectives for hedge accounting disclosures, the Board proposed that the reconciliation required by IAS 1 should have the same level of detail as the information that identifies the effects of hedge accounting on the statement of profit or loss and other comprehensive income. The Board also proposed that the reconciliation should be by type of risk. The Board considered that such a disclosure would allow users of financial statements to evaluate the effects of hedge accounting on equity and the statement of profit or loss and other comprehensive income.

BC35HH   Many respondents to the 2010 Hedge Accounting Exposure Draft agreed with the Board's proposal to explain the effects of hedge accounting disclosures using a tabular disclosure format. However, some respondents raised concerns that the proposal seems too prescriptive. Some also commented that they did not think that the tabular disclosure, as proposed, provided a clear enough link between hedged items and hedging instruments for the purpose of explaining hedge ineffectiveness. A few respondents also commented that the disclosures did not allow them to differentiate between financial instruments that have been designated as hedging instruments and those that have not. These respondents believe that it is helpful to understand the purpose and effect of financial instruments if their designation is made clear through disclosures.

BC35II   The Board thinks that providing a tabular disclosure format separated by type of hedge (ie fair value hedges or cash flow hedge), risk category and by risk management strategy provides a sufficient link between the accounting information and the risk management information.

BC35JJ   The Board did not propose any more specific format other than requiring information to be disclosed in a tabular format. The Board thought that entities should have the freedom to present the disclosures that require a tabular format however they feel is best in order to provide users with the most useful information.

BC35KK   While the 2010 Hedge Accounting Exposure Draft was open for public comment, the Board issued IFRS 13 *Fair Value Measurement*. As a consequence of issuing that IFRS, the Board moved the fair value disclosures in IFRS 7 to IFRS 13. To improve the usefulness of the hedge accounting disclosures, the Board decided to require entities to use the same level of aggregation or disaggregation it used for other IFRS 7 or IFRS 13 disclosures related to the same underlying information.

BC35LL   In its redeliberations of the 2010 Hedge Accounting Exposure Draft, the Board also considered a disclosure that would allow understanding how the hedge ineffectiveness that is recognised in the statement of comprehensive income relates to the changes in the values of the hedging instruments and the hedged items. The Board decided to require disclosure of the change in fair value of the hedging instruments and the change in the value of the hedged items on the basis that is used to calculate the hedge ineffectiveness that is recognised in the statement of comprehensive income. Those are the changes in value during the period (after taking into account the effect of the 'lower of' test for cash flow hedges and hedges of a net investment in a foreign operation). This means that the difference between the amount included in the table for hedged items and the amount included in the table for hedging instruments equals the hedge ineffectiveness recognised in the statement of comprehensive income.

BC35MM The Board also did not think that it was necessary to provide a specific disclosure that indicates which financial instruments have been designated as hedging instruments and which have not. The Board thought that such a disclosure would provide potentially misleading information to users of financial statements. This is because users of financial statements might think that all financial instruments not designated as hedging instruments might be held for speculative purposes. This is not necessarily the case. Entities might hold financial instruments for hedging purposes but may decide not to elect hedge accounting. In addition to this, the Board thought that, because entities need to provide the information that requires a tabular format based on the same level of aggregation or disaggregation as in IFRS 13, users of financial statements should be able to identify the financial instruments not designated as hedging instruments by simply comparing the disclosures with each other. In addition, users should be able to understand how an entity manages the risks it is exposed to as a result of financial instruments using the disclosure requirements in IFRS 7 that are not related to the hedge accounting disclosures.

Time value of options accumulated through other comprehensive income

BC35NN The Board proposed accounting requirements that involve other comprehensive income for the time value of an option when an entity elects to separate the time value of the option and designate (as the hedging instrument) only its intrinsic value. Consequently, the Board also considered disclosures regarding the amounts that would be recognised in other comprehensive income under these proposals.

BC35OO The Board noted that IAS 1 requires an entity to prepare a reconciliation for each component of equity between the carrying amount at the beginning and at the end of the period. Consequently, as a result of IAS 1, an entity would disclose the amounts in relation to the time value of options that would be accumulated in other comprehensive income and the movements in that balance.

BC35PP However, in its 2010 Hedge Accounting Exposure Draft, the Board proposed that an entity should differentiate between transaction related hedged items and time-period related hedged items when providing the reconciliation of the accumulated other comprehensive income. This disaggregation would provide additional information about what cumulative amount in other comprehensive income would become an expense item over time and what amount would be transferred when a particular transaction occurs.

BC35QQ Most respondents agreed with the Board's proposal and consequently, the Board decided to retain the proposal from its 2010 Hedge Accounting Exposure Draft. However, as a consequence of the Board's decision to also allow an alternative accounting treatment for forward elements and foreign currency basis spreads, the Board also required that for the purpose of the IAS 1, amounts recognised in accumulated other comprehensive income that relate to forward elements and foreign currency basis spreads should be reconciled separately from amounts in relation to time value of options.

Hedging credit risk using credit derivatives

BC35RR   For situations in which entities hedge credit risk using credit derivatives the Board decided to mitigate accounting mismatches in relation to credit derivatives accounted for at fair value through profit or loss by also using fair value through profit or loss accounting for the hedged credit exposure. Consequently, the Board also considered disclosures to provide transparency when entities apply that accounting.

BC35SS   The Board considered that the following information would be useful for understanding the accounting in such situations:

(a)   a reconciliation of amounts at the beginning and end of the period for the nominal amount and for the fair value of the credit derivatives;

(b)   the gain or loss recognised in profit or loss as a result of changing the accounting for a credit exposure to fair value through profit or loss; and

(c)   when an entity discontinues fair value through profit or loss accounting for credit exposures, the fair value that becomes the new deemed cost or amortisable amount (for loan commitments) and the related nominal or principal amount.

Other disclosures—fair value (paragraphs 25–30)[7]

BC36   Many entities use fair value information internally in determining their overall financial position and in making decisions about individual financial instruments. It is also relevant to many decisions made by users of financial statements because, in many circumstances, it reflects the judgement of the financial markets about the present value of expected future cash flows relating to an instrument. Fair value information permits comparisons of financial instruments having substantially the same economic characteristics, regardless of why they are held and when and by whom they were issued or acquired. Fair values provide a neutral basis for assessing management's stewardship by indicating the effects of its decisions to buy, sell or hold financial assets and to incur, maintain or discharge financial liabilities. The Board decided that when an entity does not measure a financial asset or financial liability in its balance sheet at fair value, it should provide fair value information through supplementary disclosures to assist users to compare entities on a consistent basis.

BC37   Disclosure of fair value is not required for investments in unquoted equity instruments[8] and derivatives linked to such equity instruments if their fair value cannot be measured reliably.[9] Similarly, IFRS 4 does not specify the accounting required for contracts containing a discretionary participation

---

7   IFRS 13 *Fair Value Measurement*, issued in May 2011, defines fair value and contains requirements for measuring fair value and for disclosing information about fair value measurements. As a consequence paragraphs 27–27B of IFRS 7 have been deleted.

8   IFRS 13, issued in May 2011, defines a Level 1 input as a quoted price in an active market for an identical asset or liability. Level 2 inputs include quoted prices for identical assets or liabilities in markets that are not active. As a result IAS 39 and IFRS 9 refer to such equity instruments as 'an equity instrument that does not have a quoted price in an active market for an identical instrument (ie a Level 1 input)'.

9   IFRS 9 changed the measurement requirements for investments in equity instruments.

feature pending phase II of the Board's project on insurance contracts. Accordingly, disclosure of fair value is not required for contracts containing a discretionary participation feature, if the fair value of that feature cannot be measured reliably. For all other financial assets and financial liabilities, it is reasonable to expect that fair value can be determined with sufficient reliability within constraints of timeliness and cost. Therefore, the Board concluded that there should be no other exception from the requirement to disclose fair value information for financial assets or financial liabilities.

BC38   To provide users of financial statements with a sense of the potential variability of fair value estimates, the Board decided that information about the use of valuation techniques should be disclosed, in particular the sensitivities of fair value estimates to the main valuation assumptions.[10] In forming this conclusion, the Board considered the view that disclosure of sensitivities could be difficult, particularly when there are many assumptions to which the disclosure would apply and these assumptions are interdependent. However, the Board noted that a detailed quantitative disclosure of sensitivity to all assumptions is not required (only those that could result in a significantly different estimate of fair value are required) and that the disclosure does not require the entity to reflect interdependencies between assumptions when making the disclosure. Additionally, the Board considered whether this disclosure might imply that a fair value established by a valuation technique is less reliable than one established by other means. However, the Board noted that fair values estimated by valuation techniques are more subjective than those established from an observable market price, and concluded that users need information to help them assess the extent of this subjectivity.

BC39   Paragraph 28 requires disclosure about the difference that arises if the transaction price differs from the fair value of a financial instrument that is determined in accordance with paragraph B5.4.8 of IFRS 9.[11] Those disclosures relate to matters addressed in the December 2004 amendment to IAS 39 *Transition and Initial Recognition of Financial Assets and Financial Liabilities*. That amendment does not specify how entities should account for those initial differences in subsequent periods. The disclosures required by paragraph 28 inform users about the amount of gain or loss that will be recognised in profit or loss in future periods. The Board noted that the information required to provide these disclosures would be readily available to the entities affected.

BC39A   Statement of Financial Accounting Standards No. 157 *Fair Value Measurements* (SFAS 157) issued by the US Financial Accounting Standards Board requires disclosures that are based on a three-level fair value hierarchy for the inputs used in valuation techniques to measure fair value. The Board was asked by some users of financial statements to include similar disclosure requirements in IFRS 7 to provide more information about the relative reliability of the inputs to fair value measurements. The Board concluded that such a hierarchy would improve comparability between entities about the effects of fair value

---

10   IFRS 13, issued in May 2011, resulted in paragraph 27B(e) of IFRS 7 being deleted.

11   IFRS 13, issued in May 2011, contains the requirements for measuring fair value. As a consequence of issuing that IFRS, paragraph B5.4.8 of IFRS 9 was deleted. However, in 2014 the requirements for amortised cost measurement and impairment were added to IFRS 9 as Sections 5.4 and 5.5. Paragraph B5.4.8 of IFRS 9 now contains requirements related to amortised cost measurement.

measurements as well as increase the convergence of IFRSs and US generally accepted accounting principles (GAAP). Therefore, the Board decided to require disclosures for financial instruments on the basis of a fair value hierarchy.[12]

BC39B   Because its own fair value measurement project was not yet completed, the Board decided not to propose a fair value hierarchy for measurement but only for disclosures. The fair value hierarchy for disclosures is the same as that in SFAS 157 but uses IFRS language pending completion of the fair value measurement project. Although the implicit fair value hierarchy for measurement in IFRS 9 is different from the fair value hierarchy in SFAS 157, the Board recognised the importance of using a three-level hierarchy for disclosures that is the same as that in SFAS 157.

BC39C   The Board noted the following three-level measurement hierarchy implicit in IFRS 9:

(a)   financial instruments quoted in an active market;

(b)   financial instruments whose fair value is evidenced by comparison with other observable current market transactions in the same instrument (ie without modification or repackaging) or based on a valuation technique whose variables include only data from observable markets; and

(c)   financial instruments whose fair value is determined in whole or in part using a valuation technique based on assumptions that are not supported by prices from observable current market transactions in the same instrument (ie without modification or repackaging) and not based on available observable market data.

BC39D   For example, the Board acknowledged that some financial instruments that, for measurement purposes, are considered to have an active market in accordance with paragraphs B5.4.3–B5.4.5 of IFRS 9 might be in Level 2 for disclosure purposes. Also, the application of paragraph B5.4.9 of IFRS 9 might result in no gain or loss being recognised on the initial recognition of a financial instrument that is in Level 2 for disclosure purposes.[13]

BC39E   The introduction of the fair value disclosure hierarchy does not affect any measurement or recognition requirements of other IFRSs. In particular, the Board noted that the recognition of gains or losses at inception of a financial instrument (as required by paragraph B5.4.8 of IFRS 9[14]) would not change as a result of the fair value disclosure hierarchy.

---

12 IFRS 13, issued in May 2011, contains a three-level fair value hierarchy for the inputs used in the valuation techniques used to measure fair value and for the related disclosures.

13 IFRS 13, issued in May 2011, contains the requirements for measuring fair value. As a consequence of issuing that IFRS, paragraphs B5.4.3–B5.4.5 of IFRS 9 were deleted and paragraph B5.4.9 of IFRS 9 was relocated to paragraphs B5.1.2A and B5.2.2A. However, in 2014 the requirements for amortised cost measurement and impairment were added to IFRS 9 as Sections 5.4 and 5.5. Paragraphs B5.4.3–B5.4.5 and paragraph B5.4.9 of IFRS 9 now contain requirements related to amortised cost measurement.

14 IFRS 13, issued in May 2011, contains the requirements for measuring fair value. As a consequence of issuing that IFRS, paragraph B5.4.8 of IFRS 9 was deleted. However, in 2014 the requirements for amortised cost measurement and impairment were added to IFRS 9 as Sections 5.4 and 5.5. Paragraph B5.4.8 of IFRS 9 now contains requirements related to amortised cost measurement.

BC39F   The Board decided to require additional disclosures for instruments with fair value measurements that are in Level 3 of the fair value hierarchy.[15] These disclosures inform users of financial statements about the effects of those fair value measurements that use the most subjective inputs.

BC39G   After reviewing comments received on the exposure draft, the Board decided not to require disclosure by level of the fair value hierarchy for financial instruments that are not measured at fair value in the statement of financial position. The Board noted that paragraphs 25 and 27 of IFRS 7, which require the disclosure of the fair value of each class of assets and liabilities in a way that permits it to be compared with its carrying amount, and the methods and assumptions applied in determining fair values, were retained.[16]

Disclosures about the nature and extent of risks arising from financial instruments (paragraphs 31–42 and B6–B28)

BC40   The Board was informed that users of financial statements value information about the risks arising from financial instruments, such as credit risk, liquidity risk and market risk, to which entities are exposed, and the techniques used to identify, measure, monitor and control those risks. Therefore, the Board decided to require disclosure of this information. The Board also decided to balance two objectives:

(a)   consistent requirements should apply to all entities so that users receive comparable information about the risks to which entities are exposed.

(b)   the disclosures provided should depend on the extent of an entity's use of financial instruments and the extent to which it assumes associated risks. Entities with many financial instruments and related risks should provide more disclosure to communicate those risks to users of financial statements. Conversely, entities with few financial instruments and related risks may provide less extensive disclosure.

BC41   The Board decided to balance these two objectives by developing an IFRS that sets out principles and minimum requirements applicable to all entities, supported by guidance on implementing the IFRS. The requirements in paragraphs 33–42 combine qualitative disclosures of the entity's exposure to risks arising from financial instruments, and the way in which management views and manages these risks, with quantitative disclosures about material risks arising from financial instruments. The extent of disclosure depends on the extent of the entity's exposure to risks arising from financial instruments. The guidance on implementing the IFRS illustrates how an entity might apply the IFRS. This guidance is consistent with the disclosure requirements for banks developed by the Basel Committee (known as Pillar 3), so that banks can prepare, and users receive, a single co-ordinated set of disclosures about financial risk.

BC42   The Board noted that because entities view and manage risk in different ways, disclosures based on how an entity manages risk are unlikely to be comparable

---

15   IFRS 13, issued in May 2011, requires disclosures about fair value measurements. As a consequence paragraphs 27–27B of IFRS 7 have been deleted.

16   IFRS 13, issued in May 2011, resulted in paragraph 27 of IFRS 7 being deleted.

between entities. In addition, for an entity that undertakes limited management of risks arising from financial instruments, such disclosures would convey little or no information about the risks the entity has assumed. To overcome these limitations, the Board decided to specify disclosures about risk exposures applicable to all entities. These disclosures provide a common benchmark for financial statement users when comparing risk exposures across different entities and are expected to be relatively easy for entities to prepare. Entities with more developed risk management systems would provide more detailed information.

Interaction between qualitative and quantitative disclosures (paragraph 32A)

BC42A   In *Improvements to IFRSs* issued in May 2010, the Board addressed a perceived lack of clarity in the intended interaction between the qualitative and quantitative disclosures of the nature and extent of risks arising from financial instruments. The Board emphasised the interaction between qualitative and quantitative disclosures about the nature and extent of risks arising from financial instruments. This enables users to link related disclosures and hence form an overall picture of the nature and extent of risks arising from financial instruments. The Board concluded that an explicit emphasis on the interaction between qualitative and quantitative disclosures will contribute to disclosure of information in a way that better enables users to evaluate an entity's exposure.

Location of disclosures of risks arising from financial instruments (paragraph B6)

BC43   Many respondents to ED 7 argued that disclosures about risks in paragraphs 31–42 should not be part of the financial statements for the following reasons:

(a)   the information would be difficult and costly to audit.

(b)   the information is different from information generally included in financial statements because it is subjective, forward-looking and based on management's judgement. Thus, the information does not meet the criteria of comparability, faithful representation and completeness.

(c)   inclusion of such information in a management commentary section outside the financial statements would be consistent with practice in other jurisdictions, including the US. Having this information in the financial statements would put IFRS preparers at a disadvantage relative to their US peers.

BC44   Respondents raised concerns that the disclosure of sensitivity analysis in particular should not be part of the financial statements. Respondents stated that sensitivity analysis cannot be prepared with the degree of reliability expected of information in the financial statements, and that the subjectivity in the sensitivity analysis and the hypothetical alternative values could undermine the credibility of the fair values recognised in the financial statements.

BC45   The Board considered whether the disclosures should be part of the information provided by management outside the financial statements. The Board noted that respondents generally regarded the disclosures proposed in ED 7 as useful, even if they did not agree that they should be located in the financial statements. The Board's view is that financial statements would be incomplete and potentially misleading without disclosures about risks arising from financial instruments. Hence, it concluded that such disclosures should be part of the financial statements. The Board rejected the argument that increased transparency puts an entity at a disadvantage; greater certainty on the part of investors can provide a significant advantage by lowering the entity's cost of capital.

BC46   The Board also noted that some entities might prefer to present the information required by the IFRS together with material such as a management commentary or risk report that is not part of the financial statements. Some entities might be required by regulatory authorities to provide in a separate report information similar to that required by the IFRS. Accordingly, the Board decided these disclosures should be given in the financial statements or incorporated by cross-reference from the financial statements to some other statement that is available to users of the financial statements on the same terms as the financial statements and at the same time.

Quantitative disclosures (paragraphs 34–42 and B7–B28)

Information based on how the entity manages risk (paragraphs 34 and B7)

BC47   The Board concluded that disclosures about an entity's exposure to risks arising from financial instruments should be required, and should be based on how the entity views and manages its risks, ie using the information provided to key management personnel (for example, its board of directors or chief executive officer). This approach:

(a)   provides a useful insight into how the entity views and manages risk;

(b)   results in information that has more predictive value than information based on assumptions and methods that management does not use, for instance, in considering the entity's ability to react to adverse situations;

(c)   is more effective in adapting to changes in risk measurement and management techniques and developments in the external environment;

(d)   has practical advantages for preparers of financial statements, because it allows them to use the data they use in managing risk; and

(e)   is consistent with the approach used in IAS 14 *Segment Reporting*.[17]

BC47A   In *Improvements to IFRSs* issued in May 2010, the Board removed the reference to materiality from paragraph 34(b) of IFRS 7. The Board noted that the reference could imply that disclosures in IFRS 7 are required even if those disclosures are not material, which was not the Board's intention.

---

17 In 2006 IAS 14 was replaced by IFRS 8 *Operating Segments*.

© IFRS Foundation

Information on averages

BC48   The Board considered whether it should require quantitative information about average risk exposures during the period. It noted that information about averages is more informative if the risk exposure at the reporting date is not typical of the exposure during the period. However, information about averages is also more onerous to prepare. On balance, the Board decided to require disclosure of the exposures at the reporting date in all cases and to require additional information only if the information provided at the reporting date is unrepresentative of the entity's exposure to risk during the period.

Credit risk (paragraphs 36–38, B9 and B10)

Disclosure objectives

BC48A   In developing the impairment disclosure requirements in this IFRS, the Board sought to supplement the existing disclosures to meet the additional information needs of users of financial statements that will arise specifically from an impairment model based on expected credit losses. When relevant, the Board has considered the comments received on the disclosure requirements proposed in the original Exposure Draft *Financial Instruments: Amortised Cost and Impairment* (the '2009 Impairment Exposure Draft') and the Board-only appendix to the Supplementary Document *Financial Instruments: Impairment*.

BC48B   During the development of the expected credit loss requirements, the Board acknowledged that any approach that attempts to reflect expected credit losses will be subject to measurement uncertainty and will place greater emphasis on management's judgement and the quality of the information used.

BC48C   However, the Board believes that this level of judgement is necessary given the differences in how entities approach credit risk management. The Board considered that information is useful and relevant when it enables users of financial statements to predict the likely amounts, timing and uncertainty of future cash flows. Accordingly, the Board identified three objectives for the disclosure requirements and this IFRS requires both qualitative and quantitative disclosures to assist users of financial statements to understand and identify:

    (a)   an entity's credit risk management practices and how they relate to the recognition and measurement of expected credit losses;

    (b)   the amounts in the financial statements that arise from expected credit losses that are measured in accordance with IFRS 9, including the changes in the estimate of expected credit losses and the reasons for the changes; and

    (c)   an entity's credit risk profile (ie the credit risk inherent in an entity's financial instruments), including significant credit concentrations at the reporting date.

Credit risk management practices

BC48D   Requiring entities to estimate expected credit losses will increase the significance of forecasts and the use of an entity's judgement. In addition, IFRS 9 requires entities to incorporate new types of information into the measurement of expected credit losses as compared to IAS 39. In the Board's view it is helpful for users of financial statements to understand the information entities use to estimate expected credit losses.

BC48E   When developing the proposals in the 2013 Exposure Draft *Financial Instruments: Expected Credit Losses* (the '2013 Impairment Exposure Draft') the Board noted that disclosures about the methods, assumptions and information used to estimate expected credit losses have been a core part of the disclosure package since the 2009 Impairment Exposure Draft, and are important for understanding how an entity applies the expected credit loss requirements. However, the Board acknowledges that different entities will use different information and techniques for assessing whether they should recognise lifetime expected credit losses. The information and techniques that an entity uses will depend on the nature of its financial instruments and other factors.

BC48F   The 2013 Impairment Exposure Draft acknowledged and permitted this. The Board considered that to understand how an entity has applied the proposed expected credit loss requirements, the following information would be relevant and useful:

(a)   how significant increases in credit risk are assessed and identified;

(b)   how default is defined and the reasons for selecting that definition;

(c)   how an entity assesses that financial assets are credit-impaired; and

(d)   the write-off policy applied.

BC48G   Respondents to the 2013 Impairment Exposure Draft supported the disclosure of that qualitative information, with a few respondents requesting the disclosure of more qualitative information about the modification of financial instruments and how an entity has incorporated macroeconomic information in its estimates of expected credit losses.

BC48H   As noted in paragraph BC5.252 of IFRS 9, the notion of default is fundamental to the application of the impairment model, particularly because it affects the population that is subject to the 12-month expected credit loss measure. The Board noted during redeliberations on the 2013 Impairment Exposure Draft that default can be interpreted in various ways, ranging from broad judgemental definitions based on qualitative factors to narrower non-judgemental definitions focusing only on non-payment. The appropriate definition also depends on the nature of the financial instrument in question. Given the various interpretations of default, the Board decided to require the disclosure of an entity's definition of default and the reasons for its selection.

BC48I   The Board considered that an explanation of how forward-looking information, including macroeconomic information, has been incorporated in the measurement of expected credit losses would provide relevant and useful information, given the requirement in IFRS 9 to consider all reasonable and supportable information that is available without undue cost and effort when determining whether there has been a significant increase in credit risk since initial recognition. The Board also considered that an explanation of how an entity has applied the requirements in paragraph 5.5.12 of IFRS 9 for the modification of contractual cash flows of financial assets, including how an entity determines whether the credit risk of modified financial assets has improved so that is not considered to be significantly increased compared to initial recognition, would enhance the understanding of how an entity manages credit risk through modifications and restructurings.

BC48J   The 2013 Impairment Exposure Draft proposed that an entity should disclose the nominal amount of financial assets that have been written off but that are still subject to enforcement activity. This was included because feedback from users of financial statements indicated users would like to understand the extent to which recoveries of written off assets are still possible. The Board acknowledged this desire, however it determined that the disclosure of the aggregate amount of financial assets that have been written off but that remain subject to enforcement activity would not provide the most relevant information for this purpose. For example, the nominal amount could be very high (particularly as time passes, if the asset legally continues to accrue interest) even though the prospect of recovering any amounts outstanding might be extremely low. In addition, the Board received feedback from preparers that tracking these amounts for an extended period would be operationally burdensome. As a result, the Board decided to modify the disclosure and require that entities disclose the amount of financial assets that have been written off during the period, while narrative information is provided about financial assets that have previously been written off but that are still subject to enforcement activity.

BC48K   The Board also proposed narrative disclosures to complement the quantitative disclosures. In the Board's view, users of financial statements would further benefit from a qualitative explanation of changes in estimates of expected credit losses. Estimates of expected credit losses may change, for example, because of changes in the volume of financial instruments, changes in overall market conditions or as a result of a significant event (for example, a sovereign debt crisis, weather-related events or other disasters). The disclosures should therefore include a qualitative narrative describing how significant events have affected the entity's estimate of expected credit losses.

Financial instruments evaluated on an individual basis

BC48L   Previously paragraph 37(b) of IFRS 7 required an analysis of financial instruments that are individually determined to be credit-impaired as at the end of the reporting period, including an analysis of the factors that the entity considered when determining that those financial instruments are credit-impaired. Many entities already disclose the loan balance and loss allowance amount for both collectively and individually assessed credit-impaired loans. Consequently, the 2013 Impairment Exposure Draft proposed amendments to those requirements to limit them to financial instruments that an entity assesses individually for recognition of lifetime expected credit losses.

BC48M   During outreach activities, users of financial statements noted that it is important for them to understand which financial instruments an entity assesses on an individual basis, especially when that individual assessment is because of an increase in credit risk and closer management of the instrument. While these financial instruments may not have experienced an increase in credit risk greater than those evaluated on a group basis, the Board concluded that this distinction helps users of financial statements to understand how an entity is monitoring and managing credit risk, so it is useful even when the difference is not attributable to differences in credit risk.

BC48N   However, several respondents to the 2013 Impairment Exposure Draft argued that a disclosure of the gross carrying amount of financial assets (and the amount recognised as a loss allowance for loan commitments and financial guarantee contracts) that are assessed on an individual basis is not relevant in an impairment model based on expected credit losses. These respondents argued that unlike in IAS 39, the loss allowance does not result from objective evidence of impairment on an individual asset.

BC48O   The Board noted that conceptually, an assessment on an individual or collective basis should render the same result. However, as noted in paragraph B5.5.2 of IFRS 9, an entity may not have access to reasonable and supportable information that enables it to identify significant increases in credit on an individual basis prior to financial assets becoming past due. Furthermore, an entity may only be able to incorporate forward-looking information in its estimates of expected credit losses on a collective basis. The Board therefore decided instead to require the disclosure of information about how an entity has grouped financial instruments if they are assessed or measured on a collective basis.

Amounts arising from expected credit losses

Reconciliation of the gross carrying amount and loss allowance

BC48P   The Supplementary Document proposed the mandatory use of a loss allowance account for credit losses, with separate disclosure of reconciliations for the two groups of financial assets that an entity would distinguish for the purpose of determining the loss allowance (ie assets in the 'good book' and assets in the 'bad book'). Almost all respondents supported the mandatory use of a loss allowance account. Consequently, the 2013 Impairment Exposure Draft retained that proposal.

BC48Q   The 2013 Impairment Exposure Draft also retained the proposal in the Supplementary Document to show a reconciliation of the gross carrying amount of financial assets separately for each of the groups of financial assets that an entity would distinguish between for the purpose of determining the loss allowance (ie 12-month expected credit losses and lifetime expected credit losses) and each of the related loss allowances. Respondents (including preparers) generally supported disclosing a reconciliation (ie flow information) of changes in the loss allowance and stated that it was operational and useful. However, similar to the feedback received on the Supplementary Document, respondents to the 2013 Impairment Exposure Draft commented that showing separate reconciliations of the gross carrying amount of financial assets was onerous, especially when they were required to disclose the effect of the change of financial assets between those with loss allowances measured at amounts equal to 12-month and lifetime expected credit losses. They noted that when loss allowances are determined on a collective (ie portfolio) basis, an entity does not allocate loss allowances to individual financial assets. Preparers also stated that the costs associated with the disclosure, and any disclosure about flow information, would be substantial. In order to provide this information for open portfolios, an entity would be required to track changes in the credit risk of individual financial instruments and calculate the change in the loss allowance that results from new loans, derecognised assets, changes between 12-month and lifetime loss allowances and changes in estimates of credit losses. They noted that this would be contrary to the requirement in IFRS 9 which requires lifetime expected credit losses to be recognised even if a significant increase in credit risk cannot be identified on an individual financial instrument basis.

BC48R   During outreach, users of financial statements have consistently and strongly expressed the view that the change in the gross carrying amount of financial assets and the effect on the loss allowance are critical elements in understanding the credit quality of an entity's financial instruments and its credit risk management practices. They held the view that the reconciliation of the gross carrying amount of financial instruments would greatly enhance transparency of an entity's financial asset portfolio. While these disclosures would require systems changes and the cost of providing the information would be high, the Board noted that such reconciliations provide key information about movements between 12-month and lifetime loss allowances and about the causes of changes in expected credit losses and about the effect of changes in volume and credit quality.

BC48S   The Board therefore decided to retain the requirement to provide a reconciliation of the changes in the loss allowance. However, in the light of the feedback about the operational burden of reconciling the changes in the gross carrying amount of financial assets, the Board clarified that the objective of that reconciliation is to provide information about the key drivers for changes in the gross carrying amount to the extent that it contributes to changes in the loss allowance during the period. Examples of such key drivers for change could include new originations and purchases, deterioration of existing financial instruments resulting in the loss allowance changing to lifetime expected credit losses and financial assets being written off during the period. The Board also acknowledged that although the most relevant and useful information will be provided by disclosing the gross movements between loss allowance measurement categories, in some circumstances, or for some types of financial assets, information will be more useful if the movements are disclosed on a net basis (for example trade receivables accounted for in accordance with the general approach in IFRS 9).

Loan commitments and financial guarantee contracts

BC48T   The 2013 Impairment Exposure Draft proposed that expected credit losses on loan commitments and financial guarantee contracts should be recognised as a provision in the statement of financial position. The Board noted that it would be inappropriate to recognise a loss allowance for such financial instruments because there is no corresponding asset with which to present that loss allowance.

BC48U   The Board noted feedback on the 2013 Impairment Exposure Draft that indicated that for most loan commitments and financial guarantee contracts, entities estimate expected credit losses on an instrument (facility) level and are therefore not able to distinguish the expected credit losses related to the drawn component (the financial asset) and the undrawn component (the loan commitment). Consequently, it would not seem appropriate to attempt to allocate expected credit losses to each of these components for the purposes of presenting the loss allowance on each component separately and any allocation would probably be arbitrary.

BC48V   The Board therefore decided that the loss allowance on a loan commitment or a financial guarantee contract should be presented together with the loss allowance for expected credit losses on the associated financial asset, if an entity cannot separately identify the expected credit losses related to the separate components. To the extent that the amount of expected credit losses on a loan commitment or a financial guarantee contract exceeds the carrying amount of the associated financial asset recognised in the statement of financial position, the remaining balance should be presented as a provision.

Purchased or originated credit-impaired assets

BC48W   The Board sought to enhance the comparability of financial assets that are credit-impaired on initial recognition with those that are not. Consequently, the Board decided that an entity should disclose the undiscounted expected credit losses that are implicit in the pricing at initial recognition for purchased or originated credit-impaired financial assets. Users of financial statements have indicated that such a disclosure would be helpful in alleviating some of the complexity in this area of accounting and would allow them to see the possible contractual cash flows that an entity could collect if there was a favourable change in expectations of credit losses for such assets.

Modifications

BC48X   Throughout the Impairment project, users of financial statements have noted that an area in which current disclosures and information is insufficient is that of restructurings and modifications. Particularly during the global financial crisis, users have expressed frustration at the difficulty of understanding the extent of restructuring activity that entities are undertaking in respect of their financial assets.

BC48Y   The 2013 Impairment Exposure Draft proposed to require the disclosure of the gross carrying amount of financial assets that have been modified during their life at a time when the loss allowance was measured at lifetime expected credit losses and for which the measurement of the loss allowance had subsequently changed back to 12-month expected credit losses. This proposed requirement resulted from users of financial statements requesting information to enable them to understand the amount of financial assets that have been modified and that have subsequently improved in credit quality. During redeliberations the Board noted operational concerns raised in feedback from preparers about the need to meet such a requirement by tracking individual financial assets, particularly even long after such assets have returned to a performing status and are no longer closely monitored for credit risk management purposes. The Board noted that the usefulness of the information would decrease over time as an increasing number of assets are required to be included in the disclosure. The Board therefore decided to limit the requirement to financial assets that have previously been modified at a time when the loss allowance was measured at lifetime expected credit losses and for which the loss allowance has changed back to 12-month expected credit losses during the reporting period.

BC48Z   During redeliberations of the 2013 Impairment Exposure Draft the Board received feedback that the modification guidance in IFRS 9 should be limited to modifications of credit-impaired assets or modifications undertaken for credit risk management purposes. The Board rejected these views and confirmed that the scope of this guidance applies to all modifications of contractual cash flows, regardless of the reason for the modification. In making this decision, the Board noted that an amortised cost carrying amount equates to the present value of the expected contractual cash flows, discounted at the effective interest rate. Consequently, the carrying amount should reflect changes in those contractual cash flows, irrespective of the reason for the modification occurring. In addition, it was noted that any change in contractual terms will have an impact on credit risk, even if small. Furthermore, the Board noted that it has been told previously that identifying those modifications that have been performed for credit risk management (ie non-commercial) purposes is operationally challenging. Consequently, the disclosures in paragraph 35J of IFRS 7 apply to all modifications of contractual cash flows.

Collateral and credit risk mitigation disclosures

BC48AA   Collateral and other credit risk mitigants are important factors in an entity's estimate of expected credit losses. For instance, an entity with more heavily collateralised loans will, all other things being equal, record a smaller loss allowance for credit losses than an entity with unsecured loans. The previous requirements of paragraph 36(b) of IFRS 7 required the disclosure of information similar to that proposed in the 2013 Impairment Exposure Draft. However, the Board received feedback that these collateral disclosures were too onerous and costly to prepare, and therefore proposed to limit the quantitative collateral disclosure requirements to those financial instruments that become credit-impaired subsequent to initial recognition.

BC48BB   Feedback on the 2013 Impairment Exposure Draft indicated that respondents remained concerned about the disclosure of quantitative information about collateral for financial instruments that become credit-impaired subsequent to initial recognition. The Board maintained the view that information about the financial effect of collateral is useful. However, the Board noted that it did not intend to require providing information about the fair value of collateral. In addition, the Board decided that qualitative information should be disclosed about how collateral and other credit enhancements have been incorporated into the measurement of expected credit losses on all financial instruments.

Credit risk exposure

BC48CC   Because the recognition of lifetime expected credit losses is based on a significant increase in credit risk since initial recognition, there could be a wide range of initial credit risk for which 12-month expected credit losses is recognised (for example, loans that are originated with a high credit risk but have not increased in credit risk subsequently would have a loss allowance based on 12-month expected credit losses as would high quality loans that have not significantly increased in credit risk since initial recognition). To provide users of financial statements with information about the changes in the loss allowance and the entity's exposure to credit risk on financial instruments, the 2013 Impairment Exposure Draft proposed a disaggregation of the carrying amounts of financial instruments into credit risk categories, for both 12-month and lifetime expected credit losses.

BC48DD   Disaggregating by credit risk shows the entity's exposure to credit risk and its credit risk profile at a given point in time (ie the reporting date). Users of financial statements indicated that they were concerned about the relative nature of the disclosure that is based on the range of credit risk relevant to the entity's portfolio and that it would lack comparability as a result (ie a high risk for one entity may only be a medium risk for another). Furthermore, without vintage information, a user would not be able to determine whether changes in the risk profile are a result of changes in the credit risk of existing financial instruments or a result of the credit risk of new instruments recognised during the period. However, they believed that risk disaggregation would still provide insight into an entity's exposure to credit risk and were therefore in favour of including it in the notes to the financial statements. The Board required the disclosure because changes in risk will affect the measurement of expected credit losses and it would therefore provide users of financial statements with information about the drivers of the change in the measurement. The Board also noted that this disclosure, particularly when considered together with the reconciliation of the gross carrying amount and loss allowance, provides relevant and useful information about credit risk migration and changes in overall credit risk over time.

BC48EE   The Board considered adding language to the proposed disclosure that would have required an entity to reconcile this disclosure to internal credit rating grades. However, responses to the Supplementary Document considered this internal risk-rating information to be proprietary and therefore objected to this level of specificity. Consequently, the Board decided not to propose this reconciliation.

BC48FF   Some respondents to the 2013 Impairment Exposure Draft also commented that the disclosure was incompatible with the credit risk management practices for some asset classes and for non-financial entities, and noted that the disclosure should be aligned with an entity's internal credit risk approach. In the light of this feedback the Board decided to remove the requirement to provide a disaggregation across a minimum of three credit risk rating grades, and instead require that the disaggregation to be aligned with how credit risk is managed internally. The Board additionally decided to permit the use of an ageing analysis for financial assets for which delinquency information is the only borrower-specific information available to assess significant increases in credit risk.

Simplified approach for trade receivables, contract assets and lease receivables

BC48GG   This IFRS includes exceptions to the general disclosures for trade receivables, contract assets and lease receivables when an entity applies the simplified approach. The Board noted that these exemptions provide relief that is consistent with the intention to simplify the application of the impairment model for these categories of financial assets to alleviate some of the practical concerns of tracking changes in credit risk.

Maximum exposure to credit risk (paragraphs 36(a), B9 and B10)

BC49 Paragraph 36(a) requires disclosure of an entity's maximum exposure to credit risk at the reporting date. Some respondents to ED 7 stated that these disclosures would not provide useful information when there are no identified problems in a loan portfolio, and it is not likely that collateral would be called on. However, the Board disagreed because it believes that such information:

(a) provides users of financial statements with a consistent measure of an entity's exposure to credit risk; and

(b) takes into account the possibility that the maximum exposure to loss may differ from the amount recognised in the balance sheet.

BC49A In *Improvements to IFRSs* issued in May 2010, the Board enhanced consistency within IFRS 7 by clarifying that the disclosure requirement in paragraph 36(a) applies only to financial assets whose carrying amounts do not show the reporting entity's maximum exposure to credit risk. Such an approach is consistent with the approach taken in paragraph 29(a), which states that disclosure of fair value is not required when the carrying amount is a reasonable approximation of fair value. Moreover, the Board concluded that the requirement might be duplicative for assets that are presented in the statement of financial position because the carrying amount of these assets often represents the maximum exposure to credit risk. In the Board's view, the disclosure requirement should focus on the entity's exposure to credit risk that is not already reflected in the statement of financial position.

BC50 Some respondents to ED 7 questioned whether the maximum exposure to credit risk for a derivative contract is its carrying amount because fair value does not always reflect potential future exposure to credit risk (see paragraph B10(b)). However, the Board noted that paragraph 36(a) requires disclosure of the amount that best represents the maximum exposure to credit risk *at the reporting date*, which is the carrying amount.

Collateral held as security and other credit enhancements (paragraphs 36(b) and 37(c))

BC51 ED 7 proposed that, unless impracticable, the entity should disclose the fair value of collateral held as security and other credit enhancements, to provide information about the loss the entity might incur in the event of default. However, many respondents to ED 7 disagreed with this proposal on cost/benefit grounds. Respondents indicated that fair value information might not be available for:

(a) small entities and entities other than banks, which may find it onerous to acquire information about collateral;

(b) banks that collect precise information on the value of collateral only on origination, for loans whose payments are made on time and in full (for example a mortgage portfolio secured by properties, for which valuations are not kept up to date on an asset-by-asset basis);

(c) particular types of collateral, such as a floating charge on all the assets of an entity; and

(d) insurers that hold collateral for which fair value information is not readily available.

BC52 The Board also noted respondents' concerns that an aggregate disclosure of the fair value of collateral held would be misleading when some loans in a portfolio are over-collateralised, and other loans have insufficient collateral. In these circumstances, netting the fair value of the two types of collateral would under-report the amount of credit risk. The Board agreed with respondents that the information useful to users is not the total amount of credit exposure less the total amount of collateral, but rather is the amount of credit exposure that is left after available collateral is taken into account.

BC53 Therefore, the Board decided not to require disclosure of the fair value of collateral held, but to require disclosure of only a description of collateral held as security and other credit enhancements. The Board noted that such disclosure does not require an entity to establish fair values for all its collateral (in particular when the entity has determined that the fair value of some collateral exceeds the carrying amount of the loan) and, thus, would be less onerous for entities to provide than fair values.

Credit quality of financial assets that are neither past due nor impaired (paragraph 36(c))[18]

BC54 The Board noted that information about credit quality gives a greater insight into the credit risk of assets and helps users assess whether such assets are more or less likely to become impaired in the future. Because this information will vary between entities, the Board decided not to specify a particular method for giving this information, but rather to allow each entity to devise a method that is appropriate to its circumstances.

Financial assets with renegotiated terms (paragraph 36(d))

BC54A In *Improvements to IFRSs* issued in May 2010, the Board addressed a practical concern relating to the disclosure requirements for renegotiated financial assets. The Board deleted the requirement in paragraph 36(d) to disclose the carrying amount of financial assets that would otherwise be past due or impaired whose terms have been renegotiated. The Board considered the difficulty in identifying financial assets whose terms have been renegotiated to avoid becoming past due or impaired (rather than for other commercial reasons). The Board noted that the original requirement was unclear about whether the requirement applies only to financial assets that were renegotiated in the current reporting period or whether past negotiations of those assets should be considered. Moreover, the Board was informed that commercial terms of loans are often renegotiated regularly for reasons that are not related to impairment. In practice it is difficult, especially for a large portfolio of loans, to ascertain which loans were renegotiated to avoid becoming past due or impaired.

---

18 IFRS 9 *Financial Instruments* deleted paragraph 36(c) of IFRS 7.

Financial assets that are either past due or impaired (paragraph 37)[19]

BC55   The Board decided to require separate disclosure of financial assets that are past due or impaired to provide users with information about financial assets with the greatest credit risk (paragraph 37). This includes:

(a)   an analysis of the age of financial assets, including trade receivables, that are past due at the reporting date, but not impaired (paragraph 37(a)). This information provides users with information about those financial assets that are more likely to become impaired and helps users to estimate the level of future impairment losses.

(b)   an analysis of financial assets that are individually determined to be impaired at the reporting date, including the factors the entity considered in determining that the financial assets are impaired (paragraph 37(b)). The Board concluded that an analysis of impaired financial assets by factors other than age (eg nature of the counterparty, or geographical analysis of impaired assets) would be useful because it helps users to understand why the impairment occurred.

BC55A   In *Improvements to IFRSs* issued in May 2010, the Board addressed a concern that the disclosure of the fair value of collateral was potentially misleading. Within a class of assets some might be over-collateralised while others might be under-collateralised. Hence, aggregate disclosure of the fair value might be misleading. Therefore, the Board removed from paragraph 37(c) the requirement to disclose the fair value of collateral and other credit enhancements. However, the Board believes that information on the financial effect of such assets is useful to users. Hence, the Board included in paragraph 36(b) a requirement to disclose a description of collateral held as security and of other credit enhancements and to disclose their financial effect.

Collateral and other credit enhancements obtained (paragraph 38)

BC56   Paragraph 38 requires the entity to disclose the nature and carrying amount of assets obtained by taking possession of collateral held as security or calling on other credit enhancements and its policy for disposing of such assets. The Board concluded that this information is useful because it provides information about the frequency of such activities and the entity's ability to obtain and realise the value of the collateral. ED 7 had proposed that the entity should disclose the fair value of the assets obtained less the cost of selling them, rather than the carrying amount. The Board noted that this amount might be more relevant in the case of collateral obtained that is expected to be sold. However, it also noted that such an amount would be included in the impairment calculation that is reflected in the amount recognised in the balance sheet and the purpose of the disclosure is to indicate the amount recognised in the balance sheet for such assets.

BC56A   In *Improvements to IFRSs* issued in May 2010, the Board enhanced consistency within IFRS 7 by clarifying that paragraph 38 requires entities to disclose the amount of foreclosed collateral held at the reporting date. This is consistent

---

19   IFRS 9 *Financial Instruments* deleted paragraph 37 of IFRS 7.

with the objective in IFRS 7 to disclose information that enables users to evaluate the nature and extent of risks arising from financial instruments to which the entity is exposed at the end of the reporting period.

Liquidity risk (paragraphs 34(a), 39, B10A and B11A–B11F)

BC57   The Board decided to require disclosure of a maturity analysis for financial liabilities showing the remaining earliest contractual maturities (paragraph 39(a) and paragraphs B11–B16 of Appendix B).[20] Liquidity risk, ie the risk that the entity will encounter difficulty in meeting commitments associated with financial liabilities, arises because of the possibility (which may often be remote) that the entity could be required to pay its liabilities earlier than expected. The Board decided to require disclosure based on the earliest contractual maturity date because this disclosure shows a worst case scenario.

BC58   Some respondents expressed concerns that such a contractual maturity analysis does not reveal the expected maturity of liabilities, which, for some entities—eg banks with many demand deposits—may be very different. They suggested that a contractual maturity analysis alone does not provide information about the conditions expected in normal circumstances or how the entity manages deviations from expected maturity. Therefore, the Board decided to require a description of how the entity manages the liquidity risk portrayed by the contractual maturity analysis.

BC58A   In March 2009 the Board amended the disclosure requirements on the nature and extent of liquidity risk by:

(a)   amending the definition of liquidity risk to clarify that paragraph 39 applies only to financial liabilities that will result in the outflow of cash or another financial asset. This clarifies that the disclosure requirements would not apply to financial liabilities that will be settled in the entity's own equity instruments and to liabilities within the scope of IFRS 7 that are settled with non-financial assets.

(b)   emphasising that an entity must provide summary quantitative data about its exposure to liquidity risk based on information provided internally to key management personnel of the entity as required by paragraph 34(a). This reinforces the principles of IFRS 7.

(c)   amending the requirement in paragraph 39 to disclose a contractual maturity analysis.

BC58B   The requirements in paragraph 39(a) and (b) relate to minimum benchmark disclosures as set out in paragraph 34(b) and are expected to be relatively easy to apply. However, the Board noted that the requirement to provide disclosures based on the remaining contractual maturities was difficult to apply for some derivative financial liabilities and did not always result in information that reflects how many entities manage liquidity risk for such instruments. Hence, for some circumstances the Board eliminated the previous requirement to disclose contractual maturity information for derivative financial liabilities.

---

20 Amendments to IFRS 7 issued in March 2009 amended paragraph 39 and paragraphs B11–B16. The paragraph references in paragraph BC57 have not been amended as a result of these amendments.

However, the Board retained minimum contractual maturity disclosures for non-derivative financial liabilities (including issued financial guarantee contracts within the scope of the IFRS) and for some derivative financial liabilities.

BC58C   The Board noted that for non-derivative financial liabilities (including issued financial guarantee contracts within the scope of the IFRS) and some derivative financial liabilities, contractual maturities are essential for an understanding of the timing of cash flows associated with the liabilities. Therefore, this information is useful to users of financial statements. The Board concluded that disclosures based on the remaining contractual maturities of these financial liabilities should continue to be required.

BC58D   The Board also emphasised the existing requirement to disclose a maturity analysis for financial assets held for managing liquidity risk, if that information is required to enable users of its financial statements to evaluate the nature and extent of liquidity risk. The Board also emphasised that an entity must explain the relationship between qualitative and quantitative disclosures about liquidity risk so that users of financial statements can evaluate the nature and extent of liquidity risk.

Market risk (paragraphs 40–42 and B17–B28)

BC59   The Board decided to require disclosure of a sensitivity analysis for each type of market risk (paragraph 40) because:

(a)   users have consistently emphasised the fundamental importance of sensitivity analysis;

(b)   a sensitivity analysis can be disclosed for all types of market risk and by all entities, and is relatively easy to understand and calculate; and

(c)   it is suitable for all entities—including non-financial entities—that have financial instruments. It is supported by disclosures of how the entity manages the risk. Thus, it is a simpler and more suitable disclosure than other approaches, including the disclosures of terms and conditions and the gap analysis of interest rate risk previously required by IAS 32.

The Board noted that information provided by a simple sensitivity analysis would not be comparable across entities. This is because the methodologies used to prepare the sensitivity analysis and the resulting disclosures would vary according to the nature of the entity and the complexity of its risk management systems.

BC60   The Board acknowledged that a simple sensitivity analysis that shows a change in only one variable has limitations. For example, the analysis may not reveal non-linearities in sensitivities or the effects of interdependencies between variables. The Board decided to meet the first concern by requiring additional disclosure when the sensitivity analysis is unrepresentative of a risk inherent in a financial instrument (paragraph 42). The Board noted that it could meet the second concern by requiring a more complex sensitivity analysis that takes into account the interdependencies between risks. Although more informative, such an analysis is also more complex and costly to prepare. Accordingly, the Board decided not to require such an analysis, but to permit its disclosure as an alternative to the minimum requirement when it is used by management to manage risk.

BC61   Respondents to ED 7 noted that a value-at-risk amount would not show the effect on profit or loss or equity. However, entities that manage on the basis of value at risk would not want to prepare a separate sensitivity analysis solely for the purpose of this disclosure. The Board's objective was to require disclosures about sensitivity, not to mandate a particular form of sensitivity disclosure. Therefore, the Board decided not to require disclosure of the effects on profit or loss and equity if an alternative disclosure of sensitivity is made.

BC62   Respondents to ED 7 requested the Board to provide more guidance and clarification about the sensitivity analysis, in particular:

(a)   what is a reasonably possible change in the relevant risk variable?

(b)   what is the appropriate level of aggregation in the disclosures?

(c)   what methodology should be used in preparing the sensitivity analysis?

BC63   The Board concluded that it would not be possible to provide comprehensive guidance on the methodology to be used in preparing the sensitivity analysis. The Board noted that more comparable information would be obtained if it imposed specific requirements about the inputs, process and methodology of the analysis, for example disclosure of the effects of a parallel shift of the yield curve by 100 basis points. However, the Board decided against such a specific requirement because a reasonably possible change in a relevant risk variable (such as interest rates) in one economic environment may not be reasonably possible in another (such as an economy with higher inflation). Moreover, the effect of a reasonably possible change will vary depending on the entity's risk exposures. As a result, entities are required to judge what those reasonably possible changes are.

BC64   However, the Board decided that it would provide high level application guidance about how the entity should assess what is a reasonably possible change and on the appropriate level of aggregation in the disclosures. In response to comments received on ED 7, the Board also decided to clarify that:

(a)   an entity should not aggregate information about material exposures to risk from significantly different economic environments. However, if it has exposure to only one type of market risk in only one economic environment, it might not show disaggregated information.

(b)   the sensitivity analysis does not require entities to determine what the profit or loss for the period would have been had the relevant risk variable been different. The sensitivity analysis shows the effect on current period profit or loss and equity if a reasonably possible change in the relevant risk variable had been applied to the risk exposures in existence at the balance sheet date.

(c)   a reasonably possible change is judged relative to the economic environments in which the entity operates, and does not include remote or 'worst case' scenarios or 'stress tests'.

(d) entities are required to disclose only the effects of the changes at the limits of the reasonably possible range of the relevant risk variable, rather than all reasonably possible changes.

(e) the time frame for which entities should make an assessment about what is reasonably possible is the period until the entity next presents these disclosures, usually its next annual reporting period.

The Board also decided to add a simple example of what a sensitivity analysis might look like.

Operational risk

BC65 The Board discussed whether it should require disclosure of information about operational risk. However, the Board noted that the definition and measurement of operational risk are in their infancy and are not necessarily related to financial instruments. It also decided that such disclosures would be more appropriately located outside the financial statements. Therefore, the Board decided to defer this issue to its research project on management commentary.

Disclosures relating to transfers of financial assets

Background

BC65A In March 2009, in conjunction with the Memorandum of Understanding between the IASB and the US Financial Accounting Standards Board (FASB) to improve and achieve convergence of IFRS and US standards for derecognition, the IASB published an exposure draft to replace the derecognition requirements of IAS 39[21] and to improve the disclosure requirements in IFRS 7 relating to the transfer of financial assets and liabilities. In response to feedback received on the exposure draft the IASB developed more fully the alternative model described in the exposure draft and the boards discussed the alternative model.

BC65B In May 2010 the boards reconsidered their strategies and plans for the derecognition project in the light of:

(a) their joint discussions of the alternative derecognition model described in the exposure draft;

(b) the June 2009 amendments to the US GAAP derecognition guidance by the FASB, which reduced the differences between IFRSs and US GAAP by improving requirements relating to derecognition of financial assets and liabilities; and

(c) the feedback the IASB received from national standard-setters on the largely favourable effects of the IFRS derecognition requirements during the financial crisis.

BC65C As a result, in June 2010 the IASB and the FASB agreed that their near-term priority was on increasing the transparency and comparability of their standards by improving and aligning the disclosure requirements in IFRSs and

---

21 IFRS 9 *Financial Instruments* replaced IAS 39. IFRS 9 applies to all items that were previously within the scope of IAS 39.

US GAAP for financial assets transferred to another entity. The boards also decided to conduct additional research and analysis, including a post-implementation review of some of the FASB's recently amended requirements, as a basis for assessing the nature and direction of any further efforts to improve or align IFRSs and US GAAP.

BC65D   As a result, the Board decided to finalise the derecognition disclosures and related objectives, proposed in the exposure draft. Accordingly, in October 2010 the Board issued *Disclosures—Transfers of Financial Assets* (Amendments to IFRS 7), requiring disclosures to help users of financial statements:

(a)   to understand the relationship between transferred financial assets that are not derecognised in their entirety and the associated liabilities; and

(b)   to evaluate the nature of and risks associated with the entity's continuing involvement in derecognised financial assets.

Transferred financial assets that are not derecognised in their entirety

BC65E   When financial assets are transferred but not derecognised, there has been an exchange transaction that is not reflected as such in the financial statements as a result of the accounting requirements. The Board concluded that in those situations, users of financial statements need to understand the relationship between those transferred financial assets and the associated liabilities that an entity recognises. Understanding that relationship helps users of financial statements in assessing an entity's cash flow needs and the cash flows available to the entity from its assets.

BC65F   The Board observed that IFRS 7 required disclosures about transferred financial assets that are not derecognised in their entirety. The Board decided to continue requiring those disclosures because they provide information that is useful in understanding the relationship between transferred financial assets that are not derecognised and associated liabilities.

BC65G   However, the Board also decided that the following additional disclosures were necessary:

(a)   a qualitative description of the nature of the relationship between transferred assets and associated liabilities, including restrictions arising from the transfer on the reporting entity's use of the transferred assets; and

(b)   a schedule that sets out the fair value of the transferred financial assets, the associated liabilities and the net position when the counterparty to the associated liabilities has recourse only to the transferred assets.

BC65H   The Board concluded that these disclosures would provide information that is useful in assessing the extent to which the economic benefits generated by assets of an entity cannot be used in an unrestricted manner, as is implied when assets are recognised in an entity's statement of financial position. In addition, the disclosures would provide information about liabilities that will be settled entirely from the proceeds received from the transferred assets, and thus identify liabilities for which the counterparties do not have claims on the assets of the entity in general. For those assets for which the underlying cash flows are committed to be used to satisfy related liabilities, the Board noted that a schedule that sets out the fair value of the transferred financial assets, the associated liabilities and the net position (in addition to showing the cash flow relationship between those assets and liabilities) also provides a means of understanding the net exposure of an entity following a transfer transaction that fails derecognition.

Transferred financial assets that are derecognised in their entirety

BC65I   The Board was asked by users of financial statements, regulators and others to review the disclosure requirements for what are often described as 'off balance sheet' activities. Transfers of financial assets, particularly securitisation of financial assets, were identified as forming part of such activities.

BC65J   The Board concluded that when an entity retains continuing involvement in financial assets that it has derecognised, users of financial statements would benefit from information about the risks to which the entity remains exposed. Such information is relevant in assessing the amount, timing and uncertainty of the entity's future cash flows.

BC65K   The Board observed that IFRS 7 already requires certain disclosures by class of financial instrument or by type of risk. However, the IFRS requires the information at an aggregated level, so information specific to derecognition transactions is often not available. In response to requests from users and others the Board concluded that disclosures specific to derecognition transactions were necessary.

BC65L   The Board concluded that the disclosures should focus on the risk exposure of an entity, and should provide information about the timing of the return and the cash outflow that would or may be required to repurchase the derecognised financial assets in the future. The Board reasoned that a combination of disclosures about the strike price or repurchase price to repurchase assets, the fair value of its continuing involvement, the maximum exposure to loss and qualitative information about an entity's obligations to provide financial support are relevant in understanding an entity's exposure to risks.

BC65M   In addition, the Board concluded that information about an entity's gain or loss on derecognition and the timing of recognition of that gain or loss provides information about the proportion of an entity's profit or loss that arises from transferring financial assets in which the entity also retains continuing involvement. Such information is useful in assessing the extent to which an entity generates profits from transferring financial assets while retaining some form of continuing involvement and thus exposure to risk.

BC65N   The Board observed that the total amount of proceeds from transfer activity (that qualifies for derecognition) in a reporting period may not be evenly distributed throughout the reporting period (eg if a substantial proportion of the total amount of transfer activity takes place in the closing days of a reporting period). The Board decided that if transfer activity is concentrated around the end of reporting periods, disclosure of this fact provides an indication of whether transfer transactions are undertaken for the purpose of altering the appearance of the statement of financial position rather than for an ongoing commercial or financing purpose. In such cases, the amendments require disclosure of when the greatest transfer activity took place within that reporting period, the amount recognised from the transfer activity in that part of the reporting period, and the total amount of proceeds from transfer activity in that part of the reporting period.

Application of the disclosure requirements to a servicing contract

BC65O   Paragraphs 42A–42H of IFRS 7 require an entity to provide disclosures for all transferred financial assets that are not derecognised in their entirety and for any continuing involvement in a transferred asset that is derecognised in its entirety, existing at the reporting date, irrespective of when the related transfer transaction occurred.

BC65P   The Board received a request to clarify whether servicing contracts constitute continuing involvement for the purposes of applying the disclosure requirements in paragraphs 42E–42H of IFRS 7. The question raised was whether paragraph 42C(c) of IFRS 7 excludes servicing contracts from the scope of those disclosure requirements.

BC65Q   The Board observed that paragraph 42C(c) of IFRS 7 discusses arrangements whereby an entity retains the contractual rights to receive the cash flows of a financial asset but assumes a contractual obligation to pay the cash flows to one or more entities and the conditions in paragraph 3.2.5(a)–(c) of IFRS 9 are met; ie it is a 'pass-through arrangement'.[22] Paragraph 42C(c) of IFRS 7 confirms that the cash flows collected to be passed through are not themselves continuing involvement for the purposes of the transfer disclosure requirements. Consequently, the Board observed that the servicer's obligation to pass through to one or more entities the cash flows that it collects from a transferred financial asset is not in itself continuing involvement for the purposes of the disclosure requirements, because the activity of passing through cash flows does not in itself constitute an interest in the future performance of the transferred financial asset. The Board observed, however, that a servicing contract is generally continuing involvement for the purposes of the transfer disclosure requirements because, in most cases, the servicer has an interest in the future performance of the transferred financial assets as a result of that contract. That would be the case if the amount and/or timing of the servicing fee depended on the amount and/or timing of the cash flows collected from the transferred financial asset. This would be true irrespective of how the servicer receives its servicing fee; ie whether the servicer retains a portion of the cash flows collected from the transferred financial asset as its fee or it passes through all of the cash flows collected and receives its fee separately from the transferee or another entity.

BC65R   On the basis of these observations, the Board noted that paragraphs 42C and B30 of IFRS 7 are considered to determine whether a servicing contract gives rise to continuing involvement for the purposes of the transfer disclosure

---

22   If IFRS 9 has not been applied early, the equivalent reference is paragraph 19(a)–(c) of IAS 39.

requirements. The Board decided to add guidance to the Application Guidance of IFRS 7 to clarify how the guidance in paragraph 42C of IFRS 7 is applied to servicing contracts.

BC65S   During its discussions on this issue, the Board noted that for the purpose of applying the disclosure requirements in paragraphs 42E–42H of IFRS 7, continuing involvement as described in paragraph 42C of IFRS 7 has a different meaning from that used in paragraphs 3.2.6(c)(ii) and 3.2.16 of IFRS 9.[23] The Board considered, but decided against, making a clarification in respect of this point because it thought that this difference was already clear from the description of continuing involvement in the two IFRSs.

Effective date and transition (paragraphs 43–44A)

BC66   The Board is committed to maintaining a 'stable platform' of substantially unchanged Standards for annual periods beginning on or before 1 January 2005, when many entities will adopt IFRSs for the first time. In addition, some preparers will need time to make the system changes necessary to comply with the IFRS. Therefore, the Board decided that the effective date of IFRS 7 should be annual periods beginning on or after 1 January 2007, with earlier application encouraged.

BC67   The Board noted that entities that apply IFRS 7 only when it becomes mandatory will have sufficient time to prepare comparative information. This conclusion does not apply to entities that apply IFRS 7 early. In particular, the time would be extremely short for those entities that would like to apply IFRS 7 when they first adopt IFRSs in 2005, to avoid changing from local GAAP to IAS 32 and IAS 30 when they adopt IFRSs and then changing again to IFRS 7 only one or two years later. Therefore, the Board gave an exemption from providing comparative disclosure in the first year of application of IFRS 7 to any entity that both (a) is a first-time adopter of IFRSs and (b) applies IFRS 7 before 1 January 2006. The Board noted that such an exemption for first-time adopters exists in IAS 32 and IFRS 4 and that the reasons for providing the exemption apply equally to IFRS 7.

BC68   The Board also considered whether it should provide an exemption from presenting all or some of the comparative information to encourage early adoption of IFRS 7 by entities that already apply IFRSs.

BC69   The Board noted that IFRS 7 contains two types of disclosures: accounting disclosures (in paragraphs 7–30) that are based on requirements previously in IAS 32 and new risk disclosures (in paragraphs 31–42). The Board concluded that existing users of IFRSs already will have complied with the requirements of IAS 32 and will not encounter difficulty in providing comparative information for the accounting disclosures.

BC70   The Board noted that most of the risk disclosures, in particular those about market risk, are based on information collected at the end of the reporting period. The Board concluded that although IFRS 7 was published in August 2005, it will still be possible for entities to collect the information that they

---

23   If IFRS 9 has not been applied early, the equivalent references are paragraphs 20(c)(ii) and 30 of IAS 39.

require to comply with IFRS 7 for accounting periods beginning in 2005. However, it would not always be possible to collect the information needed to provide comparative information about accounting periods that began in 2004. As a result, the Board decided that entities that apply IFRS 7 for accounting periods beginning in 2005 (ie before 1 January 2006) need not present comparative information about the risk disclosures.

BC71   The Board also noted that comparative disclosures about risk are less relevant because these disclosures are intended to have predictive value. As a result information about risk loses relevance more quickly than other types of disclosure, and any disclosures required by previous GAAP are unlikely to be comparable with those required by IFRS 7. Accordingly, the Board decided that an entity that is not a first-time adopter and applies IFRS 7 for annual periods beginning before 1 January 2006 need not present comparative disclosures about the nature and extent of risks arising from financial instruments. In reaching this conclusion, the Board noted that the advantages of encouraging more entities to apply IFRS 7 early outweighed the disadvantage of the reduced information provided.

BC72   The Board considered and rejected arguments that it should extend the exemption:

(a)   from providing comparative information to first-time adopters that applied IFRS 7 before 1 January 2007 (rather than only those that applied IFRS 7 before 1 January 2006). The Board concluded that an entity that intends to adopt IFRSs for the first time on or after 1 January 2006 will have sufficient time to collect information for its accounting period beginning on or after 1 January 2005 and, thus, should not have difficulty in providing the comparative disclosures for accounting periods beginning on or after 1 January 2006.

(b)   from providing comparative disclosures about the significance of financial instruments to all entities adopting the IFRS for annual periods beginning before 1 January 2006 (rather than only to first-time adopters). The Board concluded that only first-time adopters warranted special relief so that they would be able to adopt IFRS 7 early without first having to adopt IAS 32 and IAS 30 for only one period. Entities that are not first-time adopters already apply IAS 32 and IAS 30 and have no particular need to adopt IFRS 7 before 1 January 2007.

(c)   from providing comparative disclosures about risk to periods beginning before 1 January 2007 (rather than 2006). The Board noted that entities adopting IFRS 7 after 1 January 2006 would have a full calendar year to prepare after the publication of the IFRS.

BC72A   *Annual Improvements to IFRSs 2012–2014 Cycle*, issued in September 2014, amended paragraph B30 and added paragraph B30A of IFRS 7. The Board considered whether the amendment should apply to any period presented that begins before the annual period for which the entity first applies the amendment. The Board noted that paragraph 42E(b) of IFRS 7 requires disclosure of the fair value of the assets and liabilities that represent the entity's continuing involvement in the derecognised financial assets. Application of the amendment to such a period might therefore require an entity to determine the fair value as at the end of the period for a servicing asset or servicing liability, which the entity might not have previously determined. It might be impracticable for an entity to determine the fair value of such a servicing asset or servicing liability without using hindsight. The Board also noted that paragraph 44M of IFRS 7 provides transition relief by which the entity need not apply the transfer disclosure requirements to comparative periods. Consequently, to avoid the risk of hindsight being applied, the Board decided to require the application of the amendment only to annual periods beginning on or after the beginning of the annual period for which the amendment is applied for the first time. Furthermore, for the same reason, the Board observed that those transition provisions should be available to first-time adopters. The Board has characterised the transition provisions in paragraph 44AA of IFRS 7 as retrospective despite this relief, because entities are required to look back to past derecognition events to determine whether a servicing asset or servicing liability needs to be disclosed.[24]

Applicability of the offsetting amendments to IFRS 7 to condensed interim financial statements (paragraph 44R)

BC72B   The Board was asked to clarify the applicability of the amendments to IFRS 7 *Disclosure–Offsetting Financial Assets and Financial Liabilities* (the 'amendments to IFRS 7 concerning offsetting'), issued in December 2011, to condensed interim financial statements. It was asked to clarify the meaning of the reference to 'interim periods within those annual periods', used in paragraph 44R of IFRS 7. There was uncertainty about whether the disclosures required by paragraphs 13A–13F and B40–B53 of IFRS 7 were required to be included in condensed interim financial statements prepared in accordance with IFRS and, if so, whether those disclosures should be presented in every set of condensed interim financial statements, or only in those interim financial statements presented in the first year in which the disclosure requirements are effective or for which disclosure would be required under the principles in IAS 34 *Interim Financial Reporting*.

BC72C   The Board noted that IAS 34 was not consequentially amended upon issue of the amendments to IFRS 7 concerning offsetting and that when the Board intends to require an entity to provide a disclosure in condensed interim financial statements in all circumstances it amends IAS 34. Consequently, the Board decided to amend paragraph 44R of IFRS 7 within the *Annual Improvements to IFRSs 2012–2014 Cycle* in order to clarify that the additional disclosure required by the amendments to IFRS 7 concerning offsetting is not specifically required for all interim periods. However, when considering this amendment, the Board noted that the additional disclosure is required to be given in condensed interim financial statements prepared in accordance with IAS 34 when its inclusion would be required in accordance with the general requirements of that IFRS. IAS 34 requires the disclosure of information in condensed interim financial

---

24   *Annual Improvements to IFRS Standards 2014–2016 Cycle*, issued in December 2016, amended IFRS 1 *First-time Adoption of International Financial Reporting Standards* by deleting the short-term exemption for first-time adopters (see paragraph BC99 of IFRS 1), because it was no longer applicable.

statements when its omission would make the condensed interim financial statements misleading. The Board noted that in accordance with paragraph 15 of IAS 34 "an entity shall include in its interim financial report an explanation of events and transactions that are significant to an understanding of the changes in financial position and performance of the entity since the end of the last annual reporting period". The Board further noted that in accordance with paragraph 25 of IAS 34: "The overriding goal is to ensure that an interim financial report includes all information that is relevant to understanding an entity's financial position and performance during the interim period".

Summary of main changes from the Exposure Draft

BC73   The main changes to the proposals in ED 7 are:

(a)   ED 7 proposed disclosure of the amount of change in the fair value of a financial liability designated as at fair value through profit or loss that is not attributable to changes in a benchmark interest rate as a proxy for the amount of change in fair value attributable to changes in the instrument's credit risk. The IFRS permits entities to determine the amount of change in fair value attributable to changes in the instrument's credit risk using an alternative method if the entity believes that its alternative method gives more faithful representation. The proxy disclosure has been amended to be the amount of change in fair value that is not attributable to changes in market conditions that give rise to market risk. As a result, entities may exclude factors other than a change in a benchmark interest rate when calculating the proxy.

(b)   a requirement has been added for disclosures about the difference between the transaction price at initial recognition (used as fair value in accordance with paragraph B5.4.8[25] of IFRS 9) and the results of a valuation technique that will be used for subsequent measurement.

(c)   no disclosure is required of the fair value of collateral pledged as security and other credit enhancements as was proposed in ED 7.

(d)   the sensitivity analysis requirements have been clarified.

(e)   the exemption from presenting comparatives has been widened.

(f)   the capital disclosures are a stand-alone amendment to IAS 1, rather than part of the IFRS. No disclosure is required of whether the entity has complied with capital targets set by management and of the consequences of any non-compliance with those targets.

(g)   the amendments to IFRS 4 related to IFRS 7 have been modified to reduce systems changes for insurers.

---

25   IFRS 13, issued in May 2011, contains the requirements for measuring fair value. As a consequence of issuing that IFRS, paragraph B5.4.8 of IFRS 9 was deleted. However, in 2014 the requirements for amortised cost measurement and impairment were added to IFRS 9 as Sections 5.4 and 5.5. Paragraph B5.4.8 of IFRS 9 now contains requirements related to amortised cost measurement.

Appendix
Amendments to Basis for Conclusions on other IFRSs

This appendix contains amendments to the Basis for Conclusions on other IFRSs that are necessary in order to ensure consistency with IFRS 7. In the amended paragraphs, new text is underlined and deleted text is struck through.

* * * * *

The amendments contained in this appendix when IFRS 7 was issued in 2005 have been incorporated into the text of the Basis of Conclusions on IFRS 4 and on IASs 32, 39 and 41 as issued at 18 August 2005.

IASB documents published to accompany

IFRS 8

Operating Segments

The text of the unaccompanied standard, IFRS 8, is contained in Part A of this edition. Its effective date when issued was 1 January 2009. The text of the Accompanying Guidance on IFRS 8 is contained in Part B of this edition. This part presents the following documents:

BASIS FOR CONCLUSIONS

APPENDICES TO THE BASIS FOR CONCLUSIONS

A Background information and basis for conclusions of the US Financial Accounting Standards Board on SFAS 131

B Amendments to the Basis for Conclusions on other IFRSs

DISSENTING OPINIONS

CONTENTS

Basis for Conclusions on
IFRS 8 *Operating Segments*

This Basis for Conclusions and its appendices accompany, but are not part of, IFRS 8.

Introduction

BC1   This Basis for Conclusions summarises the International Accounting Standards Board's considerations in reaching the conclusions in IFRS 8 *Operating Segments*. Individual Board members gave greater weight to some factors than to others.

BC2   In September 2002 the Board decided to add a short-term convergence project to its active agenda. The project is being conducted jointly with the United States standard-setter, the Financial Accounting Standards Board (FASB). The objective of the project is to reduce differences between IFRSs and US generally accepted accounting principles (US GAAP) that are capable of resolution in a relatively short time and can be addressed outside major projects.

BC3   As part of the project, the Board identified differences between IAS 14 *Segment Reporting* and the US standard SFAS 131 *Disclosures about Segments of an Enterprise and Related Information*, reviewed academic research findings on segment reporting, in particular relating to the implementation of SFAS 131, and had meetings with users of financial statements.

Differences between IAS 14 and SFAS 131

BC4   The requirements of SFAS 131 are based on the way that management regards an entity, focusing on information about the components of the business that management uses to make decisions about operating matters. In contrast, IAS 14 requires the disaggregation of the entity's financial statements into segments based on related products and services, and on geographical areas.

BC5   The requirements of SFAS 14 *Financial Reporting for Segments of a Business Enterprise*, the predecessor to SFAS 131, were similar to those of IAS 14. In particular, both standards required the accounting policies underlying the disaggregated information to be the same as those underlying the entity information, since segment information was regarded as a disaggregation of the entity information. The approach to segment disclosures in SFAS 14 was criticised for not providing information about segments based on the structure of an entity's internal organisation that could enhance a user's ability to predict actions or reactions of management that could significantly affect the entity's future cash flow prospects.

Academic research findings

BC6   Most of the academic research findings on segment reporting indicated that application of SFAS 131 resulted in more useful information than its predecessor, SFAS 14. According to the research, the management approach of SFAS 131:

(a)   increased the number of reported segments and provided more information;

(b) enabled users to see an entity through the eyes of management;

(c) enabled an entity to provide timely segment information for external interim reporting with relatively low incremental cost;

(d) enhanced consistency with the management discussion and analysis or other annual report disclosures; and

(e) provided various measures of segment performance.

Meetings with users

BC7 The Board discussed segment reporting at several meetings with users of financial statements. Most of the users supported the management approach of SFAS 131 for the reasons mentioned in the previous paragraph. In particular, they supported an approach that would enable more segment information to be provided in interim financial reports.

BC8 Consequently the Board decided to adopt the US approach and published its proposals as an exposure draft in ED 8 *Operating Segments* in January 2006. The deadline for comments was 19 May 2006. The Board received 182 comment letters. After reviewing the responses, the Board issued IFRS 8 in November 2006.

Adoption of management approach

BC9 In the Basis for Conclusions on ED 8, the Board noted that the primary benefits of adopting the management approach in SFAS 131 are that:

(a) entities will report segments that correspond to internal management reports;

(b) entities will report segment information that will be more consistent with other parts of their annual reports;

(c) some entities will report more segments; and

(d) entities will report more segment information in interim financial reports.

In addition, the Board noted that the proposed IFRS would reduce the cost of providing disaggregated information for many entities because it uses segment information that is generated for management's use.

BC10 Most respondents to the Exposure Draft supported the adoption of the management approach. They considered the management approach appropriate, and superior to the approach of IAS 14. These respondents observed that the management approach for segment reporting allows users to review an entity's operations from the same perspective as management. They noted that although the IAS 14 approach would enhance comparability by requiring entities to report segment information that is consistent with IFRSs, the disclosures will not necessarily correspond to segment information that is reported to management and is used for making decisions.

BC11 Other respondents disagreed with the management approach. They argued that convergence should instead be achieved by changing SFAS 131 to IAS 14. In their view the latter approach is superior because it provides comparability of information across entities by defining measures of segment revenue, segment expense, segment result, segment assets and segment liabilities.

BC12   Yet other respondents agreed with the management approach for the identification of segment assets, but disagreed with the management approach for the measurement of the various segment disclosures. In particular, they doubted whether the publication of internally reported amounts would generate significant benefit for investors if those amounts differ from IFRS amounts.

BC13   The Board noted that if IFRS amounts could be prepared reliably and on a timely basis for segments identified using the management approach, that approach would provide the most useful information. However, the Board observed that IFRS amounts for segments cannot always be prepared on a sufficiently timely basis for interim reporting.

BC14   The Board also noted the requirements in the IFRS for an explanation of the measurements of segment profit or loss and segment assets and for reconciliations of the segment amounts to the amounts recognised in the entity's financial statements. The Board was satisfied that users would be able to understand and judge appropriately the basis on which the segment amounts were determined.

BC15   The Board concluded that the advantages of the management approach, in particular the ability of entities to prepare segment information on a sufficiently timely basis for inclusion in interim financial reports, outweighed any disadvantages arising from the potential for segments to be reported in accordance with non-IFRS accounting policies.

BC16   Given the Board's support for the principles of the management approach required by SFAS 131 and the objectives of the short-term convergence project, the Board decided that the simplest and most complete way to achieve convergence would be to use the text of SFAS 131 for the IFRS.

BC17   The FASB's thinking behind the management approach of SFAS 131 is presented in its Background Information and Basis for Conclusions. Because the Board has adopted that approach, the FASB's Background Information and Basis for Conclusions are reproduced in Appendix A to this Basis for Conclusions. The few differences from SFAS 131 that the Board has included in the IFRS are noted in paragraph BC60 below.

Scope of the standard

BC18   In ED 8, the Board proposed extending the scope of the IFRS to all entities that have public accountability rather than just entities whose securities are publicly traded. The Board noted that it was premature to adopt the proposed definition of public accountability that is being considered in a separate Board project on small and medium-sized entities (SMEs). However, the Board decided that the scope of the standard should be extended to include entities that hold assets in a fiduciary capacity for a broad group of outsiders. The Board concluded that the

SMEs project is the most appropriate context in which to decide whether to extend the scope of the requirements on segment reporting to other entities.

BC19   Some respondents to ED 8 commented that the scope of the IFRS should not be extended until the Board has reached a conclusion on the definitions of 'fiduciary capacity' and 'public accountability' in the SMEs project. They argued that the terms needed clarification and definition.

BC20   The Board accepted these concerns and decided that the IFRS should not apply to entities that hold assets in a fiduciary capacity. However, the Board decided that publicly accountable entities should be within the scope of the IFRS, and that a future amendment of the scope of the IFRS should be proposed to include publicly accountable entities once the definition has been properly developed in the SMEs project. The proposed amendment will therefore be exposed at the same time as the exposure draft of the proposed IFRS for SMEs.

BC21   A number of respondents to ED 8 suggested that the scope exemption of paragraph 6 of IAS 14 should be included in the IFRS. This paragraph provided an exemption from segment reporting in the separate financial statements of the parent when a financial report contains both consolidated financial statements and the parent's separate financial statements. The Board agreed that on practical grounds such an exemption was appropriate.

BC22   In ED 8 the Board proposed that if an entity not required to apply the IFRS chooses to disclose segment information in financial statements that comply with IFRSs, that entity would be required to comply with the requirements of the IFRS. Respondents commented that this was unnecessarily restrictive. For example, they observed that requiring full compliance with the IFRS would prevent an entity outside its scope from voluntarily disclosing sales information for segments without also disclosing segment profit or loss. The Board concluded that an entity should be able to provide segment information on a voluntary basis without triggering the need to comply fully with the IFRS, so long as the disclosure is not referred to as segment information.

BC23   A respondent to ED 8 asked for clarification on whether the scope of the proposed IFRS included the consolidated financial statements of a group whose parent has no listed financial instruments, but includes a listed minority interest[1] or a subsidiary with listed debt. The Board decided that such consolidated financial statements should not be included in the scope and that the scope should be clarified accordingly. The Board also noted that the same clarification should be made to the scope of IAS 33 *Earnings per Share*.

Aspects of the management approach

Specific measurement requirements for some items

BC24   In ED 8, the Board invited comments on whether the proposed IFRS should depart from the management approach in SFAS 131 by setting measurement

---

1   In January 2008 the IASB issued an amended IAS 27 *Consolidated and Separate Financial Statements*, which amended 'minority interest' to 'non-controlling interests'. The consolidation requirements in IAS 27 were superseded by IFRS 10 *Consolidated Financial Statements* issued in May 2011. The term 'non-controlling interests' and the requirements for non-controlling interests were not changed.

requirements for specified items. Some respondents to ED 8 supported an approach that would define the measurement of the key terms such as segment revenues, segment expenses, segment results, segment assets and segment liabilities in order to enhance comparability between reporting entities. Other respondents disagreed with any departure from SFAS 131 on the grounds that defined measurements for specified items would eliminate the major benefits of the management approach.

BC25 The IFRS requires the entity to explain the measurements of segment profit or loss and segment assets and liabilities and to provide reconciliations of the total segment amounts to the amounts recognised in the entity's financial statements. The Board believes that such reconciliations will enable users to understand and judge the basis on which the segment amounts were determined. The Board also noted that to define the measurement of such amounts would be a departure from the requirements of SFAS 131 that would involve additional time and cost for entities and would be inconsistent with the management perspective on segment information.

BC26 Therefore, the Board decided not to require defined measures of segment revenues, segment expenses, segment result, segment assets and segment liabilities.

Matrix form of organisations

BC27 In ED 8 the Board proposed that when more than one set of segments could be identified, for example when entities use a matrix form of organisation, the components based on products and services should be the basis for the operating segments. Some respondents noted that matrix organisational structures are commonly used for large complex organisations and that mandating the use of components based on products and services was inconsistent with the management approach. The Board agreed with this view. Accordingly, the IFRS requires the identification of operating segments to be made by reference to the core principle of the IFRS.

Quantitative thresholds

BC28 In ED 8 the Board proposed quantitative thresholds for identifying reportable segments. Some respondents argued that such requirements represent adoption of a rule-based, rather than a principle-based, approach. In addition, some respondents commented that the inclusion of a 10 per cent threshold could create a precedent for determining materiality in other areas.

BC29 The Board considered an approach whereby any material operating segment would be required to be disclosed separately. However, the Board was concerned that there might be uncertainty about the meaning of materiality in relation to disclosure. Furthermore, such a requirement would be a significant change from the wording of SFAS 131. Thus, the Board was concerned that the change would be from an easily understandable and familiar set of words that converges with SFAS 131 to a potentially confusing principle. Accordingly, the Board decided to retain the quantitative thresholds.

Interaction of aggregation criteria and quantitative thresholds

BC30   One respondent commented that the ranking of the aggregation criteria for operating segments and the quantitative thresholds for determining reportable segments was unclear in ED 8. However, the flow chart in paragraph IG7 of the implementation guidance indicates that the aggregation criteria take precedence over the quantitative thresholds. The Board also noted that the wording in SFAS 131 was clear because the paragraph on aggregation refers to aggregation into a 'single operating segment'. The quantitative thresholds then determine which operating segments are reportable segments. The term 'operating' has been inserted in paragraph 12 of the IFRS.

Aggregation of operating segments

BC30A   The Board received a request to consider including a disclosure in paragraph 22 that would require a description of the operating segments that have been aggregated and the economic indicators that have been assessed to decide whether operating segments have 'similar economic characteristics' in accordance with paragraph 12. The Board observed that:

(a)   paragraph 12 does not elaborate upon the meaning of "similar economic characteristics" except to say that operating segments that share similar economic characteristics would be expected to exhibit a similar long term financial performance. In addition, determining whether operating segments have similar economic characteristics requires the use of judgement.

(b)   paragraph 22(a) currently contains a requirement to disclose the factors used to identify the entity's reportable segments, including the basis of organisation, and suggests, as an example, disclosing whether operating segments have been aggregated. However, there is no explicit, or indeed apparent, requirement in paragraph 22(a) to disclose the aggregation of operating segments.

BC30B   The Board noted that the disclosure is complementary to the information required by paragraph 22(a). The Board thinks that including a disclosure requirement in paragraph 22 would provide users of financial statements with an understanding of the judgements made by management on how (and the reasons why) operating segments have been aggregated. The judgements made by management may relate to the application of any of the criteria in paragraph 12, which states that two or more operating segments may be aggregated into a single operating segment if aggregation is consistent with the core principle of IFRS 8, the segments have similar economic characteristics and the segments are similarly based on the factors listed in paragraph 12(a)–(e). Consequently, the Board added paragraph 22(aa) to complement the disclosure required in paragraph 22(a). The requirements in paragraph 22(b) remain the same and its wording has not been modified.

Inclusion of US guidance

BC31   The Board discussed the extent to which the IFRS should address the practical problems that have arisen from applying SFAS 131 in the US. The Board considered the FASB *Q&A 131 Segment Information: Guidance on Applying Statement 131* and Emerging Issues Task Force (EITF) 04-10 *Determining Whether to Aggregate Operating Segments that do not Meet the Quantitative Threshold.*

BC32 EITF 04-10 addresses the issue of whether to aggregate operating segments that do not meet the quantitative thresholds. It requires quantitative thresholds to be aggregated only if aggregation is consistent with the objective and core principles of SFAS 131, the segments have similar economic characteristics, and the segments share a majority of the aggregation criteria listed in paragraph 17(a)–(e) of SFAS 131. The Board agreed with the approach adopted in EITF 04-10 and concluded that the same requirement should be included in the IFRS.

BC33 FASB *Q&A 131—Segment Information: Guidance on Applying Statement 131* is an implementation guide that provides the views of the FASB staff on certain questions on SFAS 131. Because it was not issued by the FASB itself, the Board decided not to include this material in the IFRS.

Information about segment assets

BC34 Several respondents noted that, whilst a measure of segment profit or loss can be expected in every entity's internal reporting, a measure of segment assets is not always available, particularly in service industries or other industries with low utilisation of physical assets. Respondents suggested that in such circumstances a measure of segment assets should be disclosed only if those amounts were regularly provided to the chief operating decision maker.

BC35 ~~The Board noted that requiring disclosure of a measure of segment assets only when such a measure is reviewed by the chief operating decision maker would create divergence from SFAS 131. The Board also supported a minimum disclosure of segment profit or loss and segment assets. The Board therefore concluded that measures of segment profit or loss and total segment assets should be disclosed for all segments regardless of whether those measures are reviewed by the chief operating decision maker.[2]~~

BC35A After IFRS 8 was issued, the Board was informed that the reasons originally set out in paragraph BC35 contradict long-standing interpretations published in the US for the application of SFAS 131 and create an unintended difference from practice in the US under SFAS 131. After reconsideration and discussion of the interaction between the disclosure and measurement requirements in the IFRS (paragraphs 23 and 25), the Board concluded that those reasons no longer reflected its thinking. Therefore, the Board amended paragraph 23 by *Improvements to IFRSs* issued in April 2009 to clarify that a measure of segment assets should be disclosed only if that amount is regularly provided to the chief operating decision maker.

Reconciliation of segment assets

BC35B The Board received a request to clarify in paragraph 28(c) that a reconciliation of the total of the reportable segments' assets to the entity's assets should only be

---

2 Paragraph BC35 was deleted and paragraph BC35A added as a consequence of *Improvements to IFRSs* issued in April 2009.

disclosed if that amount is regularly provided to the chief operating decision maker. This clarification would make this paragraph consistent with paragraphs 23 and 28(d). The Board agreed with the request and decided to modify paragraph 28(c) to achieve this.

Information about segment liabilities

BC36　ED 8 did not propose disclosure of segment liabilities because there is no such requirement in SFAS 131. The reasons for this are set out in paragraph 96 of the Basis for Conclusions on SFAS 131, included as Appendix A to this Basis for Conclusions.

BC37　Some respondents proposed adding a requirement for each entity to disclose information about segment liabilities, if such information is regularly provided to the chief operating decision maker. They argued that information about segment liabilities would be helpful to users. Other respondents favoured information about net segment assets rather than gross segment assets.

BC38　The Board noted that if segment liabilities are considered in assessing the performance of, and allocating resources to, the segments of an entity, such disclosure would be consistent with the management approach. The Board also noted support for this disclosure from some commentators, particularly users of financial statements. Accordingly the Board decided to require disclosure of a measure of segment liabilities if those amounts are regularly provided to the chief operating decision maker notwithstanding that such a requirement would create divergence from SFAS 131.

Level of reconciliations

BC39　ED 8 proposed that an entity should provide reconciliations of total reportable segment amounts for specified items to amounts the entity recognised in accordance with IFRSs. It did not propose such reconciliations for individual reportable segments.

BC40　Several respondents expressed concern about the level of detail provided by the proposed reconciliations. They argued that if the IFRS allows segment information to be measured on the basis of management information, it should require reconciliations for individual reportable segments between the segment amounts and the equivalent amounts measured in accordance with an entity's IFRS accounting policies. They added that reconciling only total reportable segment amounts to amounts presented in the financial statements does not provide useful information.

BC41　Other respondents supported the proposed reconciliations on the grounds that more detailed reconciliations would not be more understandable to users and might be confusing. They believed that the additional costs to reporting entities were not justified.

BC42　The Board noted that a requirement to provide reconciliations at the individual reportable segment level would effectively lead to two complete segment reports—one according to internal measures and the other according to IFRSs. The Board concluded that the cost of providing two sets of segment information would outweigh the benefits.

Lack of a competitive harm exemption

BC43　The Board discussed whether entities should be exempt from aspects of the IFRS if disclosure could cause competitive damage or erosion of shareholder value. The Board considered an alternative approach whereby entities could be required to provide reasons for non-disclosure on a 'comply or explain' basis.

BC44　The Board concluded that a 'competitive harm' exemption would be inappropriate because it would provide a means for broad non-compliance with the IFRS. The Board noted that entities would be unlikely to suffer competitive harm from the required disclosures since most competitors have sources of detailed information about an entity other than its financial statements.

BC45　Respondents also commented that the requirements of the IFRS would place small listed companies at a disadvantage to non-listed companies, which are outside the scope of the IFRS. The Board noted that the relative advantage/disadvantage of an entity being publicly listed is not a matter for the Board to consider.

Adoption of the term 'impracticable'

BC46　Some respondents to ED 8 expressed concern that entities were to be allowed not to give entity-wide disclosures about products and services and geographical areas if '... the necessary information is not available and the cost to develop it would be excessive.' They argued that the test to be applied for non-disclosure should be that of impracticability as defined in IAS 1 *Presentation of Financial Statements*.

BC47　The Board noted that the wording in ED 8 ensures convergence with SFAS 131. Using the term 'impracticable' as defined in IAS 1 would change the requirement and create divergence from SFAS 131. Therefore, the Board decided to retain the wording of ED 8.

Entity-wide disclosures

Geographical information

BC48　The IFRS requires an entity to disclose geographical information about non-current assets, excluding specified items. The Board considered comments made by some respondents who advocated country-by-country disclosure, others who requested specific items of geographical information to be disclosed, and some who expressed reservations with the proposed requirement relating to disclosure of country of domicile.

BC49　A coalition of over 300 organisations from more than 50 countries known as the Publish What You Pay campaign requested that the scope of the IFRS should be extended to require additional disclosure on a country-by-country basis. The objective of such additional disclosure would be to promote greater transparency in the management of amounts paid by the oil, gas and mining industries to governments in developing or transitional countries that are resource-rich. The view of these campaigners was that publication of specific payments made by those companies to governments is in the interest of all users of financial statements.

BC50 Because the IFRS is being developed in a short-term convergence project to converge with SFAS 131, the Board decided that issues raised by the Publish What You Pay campaign relating to country-by-country disclosures should not be addressed in the IFRS. The Board was of the view that such issues merit further discussion with bodies that are currently engaged in similar issues, for example the United Nations, International Public Sector Accounting Standards Board, International Monetary Fund, World Bank, regional development banks and Financial Stability Forum.

Exemption from entity-wide disclosures

BC51 Several respondents suggested different geographical disclosures from those proposed in ED 8. For example, some preferred disclosures by geographical areas rather than by individual country. Others favoured geographical disclosure of profit or loss as well as non-current assets. Several respondents expressed the view that disclosure of total assets would be more relevant than non-current assets. Some took the view that disclosures should be made of both current and non-current assets. Other respondents recommended that financial assets should be disclosed as well as non-current assets. Some respondents expressed the view that disclosure of non-current assets should not be required if those amounts are not reviewed by the chief operating decision maker.

BC52 In developing ED 8, the Board decided to adopt the requirements in SFAS 131. Paragraphs 104–107 of the Basis for Conclusions on SFAS 131 provide the rationale for the geographical disclosures required.

BC53 None of the suggested alternative disclosures was broadly supported by the user responses. The Board noted that entities that wish to give additional information are free to do so. The Board therefore concluded that the disclosure requirement taken from SFAS 131 should not be changed.

Country of domicile

BC54 Some respondents asserted that disclosures relating to the country of domicile were inappropriate for many entities. They expressed the view that such information would be relevant when a large proportion of an entity's business is carried out in its country of domicile. They noted, however, that in many circumstances the country of domicile represents a small proportion of the entity's business and in these cases the information required would not be relevant. In addition, they argued that SFAS 131 had been designed for entities in the US, for whom the 'country of domicile' is in itself a significant geographical area. These respondents suggested that disclosures should instead be required about the country of principal activities.

BC55 The IFRS requires disclosures for any country that is individually material. The Board noted that identifying the country of principal activities may be difficult and subjective. Accordingly, the Board decided not to require entities to identify the country of principal activities.

Subtotal for tangible non-current assets

BC56 Paragraphs 14 and 15 of the Basis for Conclusions on ED 8 highlighted a potential difference from SFAS 131. SFAS 131 requires disclosure of 'long-lived assets' excluding intangible assets, whereas ED 8 proposed disclosure of 'non-current assets' including intangible assets. The Board reconsidered whether, in the interest of convergence, the IFRS should require disclosure of the subtotal of tangible non-current assets.

BC57　　The Board concluded that a separate disclosure of a subtotal of tangible non-current assets was unnecessary on the grounds that the incremental benefit does not justify such disclosure. However, the Board noted that entities that wish to provide that information are free to do so.

Information about major customers

BC58　　ED 8 proposed that, in respect of the disclosures about major customers, a group of entities known to be under common control should be treated as a single customer. Some respondents noted that this could be difficult when entities are state-controlled. The Board noted that it was considering proposals to amend IAS 24 *Related Party Disclosures* with regard to state-controlled entities, and a consequential amendment to the IFRS on reporting segments might result from those proposals. In the meantime, the Board decided to require in the IFRS that a government (whether national, state, provincial, territorial, local or foreign) and entities known to the reporting entity to be controlled by that government should be treated as a single customer. This makes the requirements relating to government-controlled entities the same as those relating to privately controlled entities.

Interim financial information

BC59　　The Board decided that the changes to IAS 34 *Interim Financial Reporting* proposed in ED 8 should be amended to clarify that interim disclosure of information on segment profit or loss items is required only if the specified amounts are included in the measure of segment profit or loss reviewed by the chief operating decision maker. The Board reached this conclusion because it noted that such disclosure is consistent with the management approach.

Differences from SFAS 131

BC60　　In developing the IFRS, the Board included the following differences from SFAS 131:

(a)　　The FASB *Guidance on Applying Statement 131* indicates that the FASB staff believe that 'long-lived assets', as that phrase is used in paragraph 38 of SFAS 131, implies hard assets that cannot be readily removed, which would appear to exclude intangibles. Non-current assets in the IFRS include intangibles (see paragraphs BC56 and BC57).

(b)　　SFAS 131 does not require disclosure of a measure of segment liabilities. The IFRS requires disclosure of segment liabilities if such a measure is regularly provided to the chief operating decision maker (see paragraphs BC36–BC38).

(c)   SFAS 131 requires an entity with a matrix form of organisation to determine operating segments based on products and services. The IFRS requires such an entity to determine operating segments by reference to the core principle of the IFRS (see paragraph BC27).

Transitional provisions

BC61   Under its transitional provisions, SFAS 131 was not required to be applied to interim financial statements in the initial year of its application. However, in the second year of application, comparative information relating to interim periods in the initial year of application was required. The Basis for Conclusions on SFAS 131 explained that the reason for these transitional requirements was that some of the information that is required to be reported for interim periods is based on information reported in the most recent annual financial statements. Interim segment information would not be as meaningful without a full set of annual segment information to use as a comparison and to provide an understanding of the basis on which it is provided.

BC62   The Board did not agree with the transitional provision for interim financial statements in SFAS 131. The Board noted that the IFRS is not effective until 2009, giving entities adequate time to prepare. Furthermore, the Board was aware that some entities adopting IFRSs for the first time may wish to present comparative information in accordance with the IFRS rather than IAS 14.

CONTENTS

Background information and basis for conclusions of the US Financial Accounting Standards Board on SFAS 131

Introduction

41.   This appendix summarizes considerations that were deemed significant by Board members in reaching the conclusions in this Statement. It includes reasons for accepting certain approaches and rejecting others. Individual Board members gave greater weight to some factors than to others.

Background Information

42.   FASB Statement No. 14, *Financial Reporting for Segments of a Business Enterprise*, was issued in 1976. That Statement required that business enterprises report segment information on two bases: by industry and by geographic area. It also required disclosure of information about export sales and major customers.

43.   The Board concluded at the time it issued Statement 14 that information about components of an enterprise, the products and services that it offers, its foreign operations, and its major customers is useful for understanding and making decisions about the enterprise as a whole. Financial statement users observe that the evaluation of the prospects for future cash flows is the central element of investment and lending decisions. The evaluation of prospects requires assessment of the uncertainty that surrounds both the timing and the amount of the expected cash flows to the enterprise, which in turn affect potential cash flows to the investor or creditor. Users also observe that uncertainty results in part from factors related to the products and services an enterprise offers and the geographic areas in which it operates.

44.   In its 1993 position paper, *Financial Reporting in the 1990s and Beyond*, the Association for Investment Management and Research (AIMR) said:

> [Segment data] is vital, essential, fundamental, indispensable, and integral to the investment analysis process. Analysts need to know and understand how the various components of a multifaceted enterprise behave economically. One weak member of the group is analogous to a section of blight on a piece of fruit; it has the potential to spread rot over the entirety. Even in the absence of weakness, different segments will generate dissimilar streams of cash flows to which are attached disparate risks and which bring about unique values. Thus, without disaggregation, there is no sensible way to predict the overall amounts, timing, or risks of a complete enterprise's future cash flows. There is little dispute over the analytic usefulness of disaggregated financial data. [pages 59 and 60]

45.   Over the years, financial analysts consistently requested that financial statement data be disaggregated to a much greater degree than it is in current practice. Many analysts said that they found Statement 14 helpful but inadequate. In its 1993 position paper, the AIMR emphasized that:

> There is no disagreement among AIMR members that segment information is totally vital to their work. There also is general agreement among them that the current segment reporting standard, Financial Accounting Standard No. 14, is inadequate. Recent work by a subcommittee of the [Financial Accounting Policy Committee] has confirmed that a substantial majority of analysts seek and, when it is available, use quarterly segment data. [page 5]

46.   The Canadian Institute of Chartered Accountants (CICA) published a Research Study, *Financial Reporting for Segments*, in August 1992. An FASB Research Report, *Reporting Disaggregated Information*, was published in February 1993. In March 1993, the FASB and the Accounting Standards Board (AcSB) of the CICA agreed to pursue their projects jointly.

47.   In May 1993, the FASB and the AcSB jointly issued an Invitation to Comment, *Reporting Disaggregated Information by Business Enterprises*. That Invitation to Comment identified certain issues related to disclosure of information about segments, solicited comments on those issues, and asked readers to identify additional issues. The boards received 129 comment letters from U.S. and Canadian respondents.

48.   In late 1993, the FASB and the AcSB formed the Disaggregated Disclosures Advisory Group to advise and otherwise support the two boards in their efforts to improve disaggregated disclosures. The members of the group included financial statement issuers, auditors, financial analysts, and academics from both the United States and Canada. In January 1994, the FASB and the AcSB began discussing changes to Statement 14 and *CICA Handbook* Section 1700, "Segmented Information." The two boards met with and otherwise actively solicited the views of analysts and preparers of financial statements about possible improvements to the current segment reporting requirements. FASB and AcSB members and staff also discussed disaggregated disclosures at meetings of several groups of analysts, including the AIMR's Financial Accounting Policy Committee.

49.   In 1991, the AICPA formed the Special Committee on Financial Reporting (the Special Committee) to make recommendations to improve the relevance and usefulness of business reporting. The Special Committee, which comprised financial statement auditors and preparers, established focus groups of credit analysts and equity analysts to assist in formulating its recommendations. The Special Committee issued its report, *Improving Business Reporting—A Customer Focus*, in 1994. That report listed improvements in disclosures of business segment information as its first recommendation and included the following commentary:

> ... for users analyzing a company involved in diverse businesses, financial information about business segments often is as important as information about the company as a whole. Users suggest that standard setters assign the highest priority to improving segment reporting because of its importance to their work and the perceived problems with current reporting of segment information. [page 68]

50.   The report of the Special Committee listed the following as among the most important improvements needed:

(a)   Disclosure of segment information in interim financial reports

(b)   Greater number of segments for some enterprises

(c)   More information about segments

(d)   Segmentation that corresponds to internal management reports (e)　　Consistency of segment information with other parts of an annual report.

Similar recommendations had been made in each of the last 20 years in evaluations of corporate reporting conducted by the AIMR.

51.　The two boards reached tentative conclusions about an approach to segment reporting that was substantially different from the approach in Statement 14 and Section 1700. Key characteristics of the new approach were that (a) information would be provided about segments of the enterprise that corresponded to the structure of the enterprise's internal organization, that is, about the divisions, departments, subsidiaries, or other internal units that the chief operating decision maker uses to make operating decisions and to assess an enterprise's performance, (b) specific amounts would be allocated to segments only if they were allocated in reports used by the chief operating decision maker for evaluation of segment performance, and (c) accounting policies used to produce the disaggregated information would be the same as those used in the reports used by the chief operating decision maker in allocating resources and assessing segment performance.

52.　In February 1995, the staffs of the FASB and the CICA distributed a paper, "Tentative Conclusions on Financial Reporting for Segments" (Tentative Conclusions), to selected securities analysts, the FASB Task Force on Consolidations and Related Matters, the Disaggregated Disclosures Advisory Group, the FASB's Emerging Issues Task Force, the Financial Accounting Standards Advisory Council, the AcSB's list of Associates,[3] and members of representative organizations that regularly work with the boards. The paper also was announced in FASB and CICA publications and was sent to anyone who requested a copy. Board and staff members discussed the Tentative Conclusions with various analyst and preparer groups. Approximately 80 comment letters were received from U.S. and Canadian respondents.

53.　In January 1996, the FASB and the AcSB issued virtually identical Exposure Drafts, *Reporting Disaggregated Information about a Business Enterprise.* The FASB received 221 comment letters and the AcSB received 73 comment letters in response to the Exposure Drafts. A field test of the proposals was conducted in March 1996. A public meeting was held in Toronto in October 1996 to discuss results and concerns with field test participants. Other interested parties attended a public meeting in Norwalk in October 1996 to discuss their concerns about the proposals in the Exposure Drafts. The FASB decided that it could reach an informed decision on the project without holding a public hearing.

54.　The FASB and the AcSB exchanged information during the course of redeliberating the proposals in their respective Exposure Drafts. AcSB members and CICA staff attended FASB meetings, and FASB members and staff attended AcSB meetings in late 1996 and in 1997 to discuss the issues raised by respondents. Both boards reached agreement on all of the substantive issues to achieve virtually identical standards for segment reporting in the United States

---

3　Associates are individuals and organizations with a particular interest in financial reporting issues that have volunteered to provide an outside reaction to AcSB positions at an early stage in the AcSB's deliberations.

and Canada. Members of the Segment Disclosures Advisory Group (formerly the Disaggregated Disclosures Advisory Group) discussed a draft of the standards section in March 1997.

55. The International Accounting Standards Committee (IASC) issued an Exposure Draft of a proposed International Accounting Standard that would replace International Accounting Standard IAS 14, *Reporting Financial Information by Segment*, in December 1995. Although many of its provisions are similar to those of the FASB and AcSB Exposure Drafts, the IASC's proposal is based on different objectives and is different from those Exposure Drafts. A member of the IASC Segments Steering Committee participated in FASB meetings during the redeliberations of the Exposure Draft, and members of the FASB participated in meetings of the IASC Segments Steering Committee. Many of the respondents to the Exposure Drafts encouraged the FASB and the AcSB to work closely with the IASC to achieve similar standards for segment reporting. The IASC expects to issue a standard on segment reporting later in 1997. Although there likely will be differences between the IASC's requirements for segment reporting and those of this Statement, the boards expect that it will be possible to prepare one set of segment information that complies with both the IASC requirements and those of this Statement.

56. This Statement addresses the following key issues:

(a) What is the appropriate basis for defining segments?

(b) What accounting principles and allocations should be used?

(c) What specific items of information should be reported?

(d) Should segment information be reported in condensed financial statements for interim periods?

Defining Operating Segments of an Enterprise

57. The Board concluded that the *industry approach* to segment disclosures in Statement 14 was not providing the information required by financial statement users and that disclosure of disaggregated information should be based on operating segments. This Statement defines an operating segment as a component of an enterprise (a) that engages in business activities from which it may earn revenues and incur expenses, (b) whose operating results are regularly reviewed by the enterprise's chief operating decision maker to make decisions about resources to be allocated to the segment and to assess its performance, and (c) for which discrete financial information is available.

58. The AIMR's 1993 position paper and the report of the AICPA Special Committee criticized Statement 14's industry segment approach to reporting segment information. The AIMR's position paper included the following:

> FAS 14 requires disclosure of line-of-business information classified by "industry segment." Its definition of segment is necessarily imprecise, recognizing that there are numerous practical problems in applying that definition to different business entities operating under disparate circumstances. That weakness in FAS 14 has been exploited by many enterprises to suit their own financial reporting purposes. As a result, we have seen one of the ten largest firms in the country report all of its operations as being in a single, very broadly defined industry segment. [page 60]

The report of the Special Committee said that "[financial statement users] believe that many companies define industry segments too broadly for business reporting and thus report on too few industry segments" (page 69).

59. The report of the AICPA Special Committee also said that " ... the primary means to improving industry segment reporting should be to align business reporting with internal reporting" (page 69), and the AIMR's 1993 position paper recommended that:

> ... priority should be given to the production and dissemination of financial data that reflects and reports sensibly the operations of specific enterprises. If we could obtain reports showing the details of how an individual business firm is organized and managed, we would assume more responsibility for making meaningful comparisons of those data to the unlike data of other firms that conduct their business differently. [pages 60 and 61]

Almost all of the users and many other constituents who responded to the Exposure Draft or who met with Board and staff members agreed that defining segments based on the structure of an enterprise's internal organization would result in improved information. They said that not only would enterprises be likely to report more detailed information but knowledge of the structure of an enterprise's internal organization is valuable in itself because it highlights the risks and opportunities that management believes are important.

60. Segments based on the structure of an enterprise's internal organization have at least three other significant advantages. First, an ability to see an enterprise "through the eyes of management" enhances a user's ability to predict actions or reactions of management that can significantly affect the enterprise's prospects for future cash flows. Second, because information about those segments is generated for management's use, the incremental cost of providing information for external reporting should be relatively low. Third, practice has demonstrated that the term *industry* is subjective. Segments based on an existing internal structure should be less subjective.

61. The AIMR and other users have commented that segment information is more useful if it is consistent with explanatory information provided elsewhere in the annual report. They note that the business review section and the chairman's letter in an annual report frequently discuss the enterprise's operations on a basis different from that of the segment information in the notes to the financial statements and the management's discussion and analysis section, which is required by SEC rules to correspond to the segment information provided to comply with Statement 14. That appears to occur if the enterprise is not managed in a way that corresponds to the way it defines segments under the requirements of Statement 14. Segmentation based on the structure of an enterprise's internal organization should facilitate consistent discussion of segment financial results throughout an enterprise's annual report.

62. Some respondents to the Exposure Draft opposed the Board's approach for several reasons. Segments based on the structure of an enterprise's internal organization may not be comparable between enterprises that engage in similar activities and may not be comparable from year to year for an individual enterprise. In addition, an enterprise may not be organized based on products and services or geographic areas, and thus the enterprise's segments may not be

susceptible to analysis using macroeconomic models. Finally, some asserted that because enterprises are organized strategically, the information that would be reported may be competitively harmful to the reporting enterprise.

63. The Board acknowledges that comparability of accounting information is important. The summary of principal conclusions in FASB Concepts Statement No. 2, *Qualitative Characteristics of Accounting Information*, says: "Comparability between enterprises and consistency in the application of methods over time increases the informational value of comparisons of relative economic opportunities or performance. The significance of information, especially quantitative information, depends to a great extent on the user's ability to relate it to some benchmark." However, Concepts Statement 2 also notes a danger:

> Improving comparability may destroy or weaken relevance or reliability if, to secure comparability between two measures, one of them has to be obtained by a method yielding less relevant or less reliable information. Historically, extreme examples of this have been provided in some European countries in which the use of standardized charts of accounts has been made mandatory in the interest of interfirm comparability but at the expense of relevance and often reliability as well. That kind of uniformity may even adversely affect comparability of information if it conceals real differences between enterprises. [paragraph 116]

64. The Board was concerned that segments defined using the approach in Statement 14 may appear to be more comparable between enterprises than they actually are. Statement 14 included the following:

> Information prepared in conformity with [Statement 14] may be of limited usefulness for comparing an industry segment of one enterprise with a similar industry segment of another enterprise (i.e., for interenterprise comparison). Interenterprise comparison of industry segments would require a fairly detailed prescription of the basis or bases of disaggregation to be followed by all enterprises, as well as specification of the basis of accounting for intersegment transfers and methods of allocating costs common to two or more segments. [paragraph 76]

65. Statement 14 explained why the Board chose not to develop a detailed prescription of the bases of disaggregation:

> ... differences among enterprises in the nature of their operations and in the extent to which components of the enterprise share common facilities, equipment, materials and supplies, or labor force make unworkable the prescription of highly detailed rules and procedures that must be followed by all enterprises. Moreover, ... differences in the accounting systems of business enterprises are a practical constraint on the degree of specificity with which standards of financial accounting and reporting for disaggregated information can be established. [paragraph 74]

Those same considerations persuaded the Board not to adopt more specific requirements in this Statement. Both relevance and comparability will not be achievable in all cases, and relevance should be the overriding concern.

66. The AICPA Special Committee, some respondents to the Exposure Draft, and other constituents recommended that the Board require that an enterprise use an alternative method of segmentation for external reporting if its internal organization is not based on differences in products and services or geography.

Some specifically recommended adoption of the proposal in the IASC Exposure Draft that was commonly referred to as a "safety net." The IASC Exposure Draft approach to identifying primary and secondary operating segments calls for review of management's organization of segments, but both primary and secondary segments are required to be defined either on the basis of related products and services or on the basis of geography. That is, regardless of management's organization, segments must be grouped either by related products and services or by geographic areas, and one set must be presented as primary segments and the other as secondary segments.

67. The Board recognizes that an enterprise may not be divided into components with similar products and services or geographic areas for internal purposes and that some users of financial statements have expressed a desire for information organized on those bases. However, instead of an alternative method of segmentation, which would call for multiple sets of segment information in many circumstances, the Board chose to require disclosure of additional information about products and services and about geographic areas of operations for the enterprise as a whole if the basic segment disclosures do not provide it.

68. One reason for not prescribing segmentation along bases of only related products and services or geography is that it is difficult to define clearly the circumstances in which an alternative method that differs from the management approach would be applied consistently. An enterprise with a relatively narrow product line may not consider two products to be similar, while an enterprise with a broad product line may consider those same two products to be similar. For example, a highly diversified enterprise may consider all consumer products to be similar if it has other businesses such as financial services and road construction. However, an enterprise that sells only consumer products might consider razor blades to be different from toasters.

69. A second reason for rejecting that approach is that an alternative method of segmentation would increase the cost to some enterprises to prepare the information. A management approach to defining segments allows enterprises to present the information that they use internally and facilitates consistent descriptions of the components of an enterprise from one part of the annual report to another. An enterprise could be organized by its products and services, geography, a mixture of both products and services and geography, or other bases, such as customer type, and the segment information required by this Statement would be consistent with that method of organization. Furthermore, the enterprise-wide disclosures about products and services will provide information about the total revenues from related products and services, and the enterprise-wide disclosures about geography will provide information about the revenues and assets of an enterprise both inside and outside its home country. If material, individual foreign country information also is required.

70. The Board recognizes that some enterprises organize their segments on more than one basis. Other enterprises may produce reports in which their activities are presented in a variety of ways. In those situations, reportable segments are to be determined based on a review of other factors to identify the enterprise's operating segments, including the nature of the activities of each component,

the existence of managers responsible for them, and the information provided to the board of directors. In many enterprises, only one set of data is provided to the board of directors. That set of data generally is indicative of how management views the enterprise's activities.

Reportable Segments

71. The Board included a notion of reportable segments, a subset of operating segments, in this Statement by defining aggregation criteria and quantitative thresholds for determining which operating segments should be reported separately in the financial statements.

72. A so-called pure management approach to segment reporting might require that an enterprise report all of the information that is reviewed by the chief operating decision maker to make decisions about resource allocations and to assess the performance of the enterprise. However, that level of detail may not be useful to readers of external financial statements, and it also may be cumbersome for an enterprise to present. Therefore, this Statement uses a modified management approach that includes both aggregation criteria and quantitative thresholds for determining reportable operating segments. However, an enterprise need not aggregate similar segments, and it may present segments that fall below the quantitative thresholds.

Aggregation of Similar Operating Segments

73. The Board believes that separate reporting of segment information will not add significantly to an investor's understanding of an enterprise if its operating segments have characteristics so similar that they can be expected to have essentially the same future prospects. The Board concluded that although information about each segment may be available, in those circumstances the benefit would be insufficient to justify its disclosure. For example, a retail chain may have 10 stores that individually meet the definition of an operating segment, but each store may be essentially the same as the others.

74. Most respondents commented on the aggregation criteria in the Exposure Draft. Many said that the criteria were unreasonably strict, to the extent that nearly identical segments might not qualify for aggregation. Some respondents linked their concerns about competitive harm and too many segments directly to the aggregation criteria, indicating that a relaxation of the criteria would significantly reduce those concerns. To better convey its intent, the Board revised the wording of the aggregation criteria and the introduction to them. However, the Board rejected recommendations that the criteria be indicators rather than tests and that the guidance require only the expectation of similar long-term performance of segments to justify aggregation because those changes might result in a level of aggregation that would cause a loss of potentially valuable information. For the same reason, the Board also rejected suggestions that segments need be similar in only a majority of the characteristics in paragraph 17 to justify aggregation. The Board recognizes that determining when two segments are sufficiently similar to justify aggregating them is difficult and subjective. However, the Board notes that one of the reasons that

the information provided under Statement 14 did not satisfy financial statement users' needs is that segments with different characteristics in important areas were at times aggregated.

Quantitative Thresholds

75. In developing the Exposure Draft, the Board had concluded that quantitative criteria might interfere with the determination of operating segments and, if anything, might unnecessarily reduce the number of segments disclosed. Respondents to the Exposure Draft and others urged the Board to include quantitative criteria for determining which segments to report because they said that some enterprises would be required to report too many segments unless specific quantitative guidelines allowed them to omit small segments. Some respondents said that the Exposure Draft would have required disclosure of as many as 25 operating segments, which was not a result anticipated by the Board in its deliberations preceding the Exposure Draft. Others said that enterprises would report information that was too highly aggregated unless quantitative guidelines prevented it. The Board decided that the addition of quantitative thresholds would be a practical way to address respondents' concerns about competitive harm and proliferation of segments without fundamentally changing the management approach to segment definition.

76. Similar to the requirements in Statement 14, the Board decided to require that any operating segment that constitutes 10 percent or more of reported revenues, assets, or profit or loss be reported separately and that reportable segments account for at least 75 percent of an enterprise's external revenues. The Board decided to retain that guidance for the quantitative thresholds because it can be objectively applied and because preparers and users of financial statements already understand it.

77. Inclusion of quantitative thresholds similar to those in Statement 14 necessitates guidance on how to report operating segments that do not meet the thresholds. The Board concluded that enterprises should be permitted to aggregate information about operating segments that do not meet the thresholds with information about other operating segments that do not meet the thresholds if a majority of the aggregation criteria in paragraph 17 are met. That is a more liberal aggregation provision than that for individually material operating segments, but it prohibits aggregation of segments that are dissimilar.

78. Paragraph 125 of Concepts Statement 2 states that "... magnitude by itself, without regard to the nature of the item and the circumstances in which the judgment has to be made, will not generally be a sufficient basis for a materiality judgment." That guidance applies to segment information. An understanding of the material segments of an enterprise is important for understanding the enterprise as a whole, and individual items of segment information are important for understanding the segments. Thus, an item of segment information that, if omitted, would change a user's decision about that segment so significantly that it would change the user's decision about the enterprise as a whole is material even though an item of a similar magnitude might not be considered material if it were omitted from the consolidated financial statements. Therefore, enterprises are encouraged to report information about segments that do not meet the quantitative thresholds if

management believes that it is material. Those who are familiar with the particular circumstances of each enterprise must decide what constitutes *material*.

Vertically Integrated Enterprises

79.   The Board concluded that the definition of an operating segment should include components of an enterprise that sell primarily or exclusively to other operating segments of the enterprise if the enterprise is managed that way. Information about the components engaged in each stage of production is particularly important for understanding vertically integrated enterprises in certain businesses, for example, oil and gas enterprises. Different activities within the enterprise may have significantly different prospects for future cash flows, and users of financial statements have asserted that they need to know results of each operation.

80.   Some respondents to the Exposure Draft opposed the requirement to report vertically integrated segments separately. They said that the segment results may not be comparable between enterprises and that transfer prices are not sufficiently reliable for external reporting purposes. The Board considered an approach that would have required separate reporting of vertically integrated segments only if transfer prices were based on quoted market prices and if there was no basis for combining the selling segment and the buying segment. However, that would have been a significant departure from the management approach to defining segments. The Board also was concerned that the criteria would be unworkable. Therefore, the Board decided to retain the Exposure Draft's provisions for vertically integrated segments.

Accounting Principles and Allocations

81.   The Board decided that the information to be reported about each segment should be measured on the same basis as the information used by the chief operating decision maker for purposes of allocating resources to segments and assessing segments' performance. That is a management approach to measuring segment information as proposed in the Exposure Draft. The Board does not think that a separate measure of segment profit or loss or assets should have to be developed solely for the purpose of disclosing segment information. For example, an enterprise that accounts for inventory using a specialized valuation method for internal purposes should not be required to restate inventory amounts for each segment, and an enterprise that accounts for pension expense only on a consolidated basis should not be required to allocate pension expense to each operating segment.

82.   The report of the AICPA Special Committee said that the Board "should allow companies to report a statistic on the same basis it is reported for internal purposes, if the statistic is reported internally. The usefulness of information prepared only for [external] reporting is questionable. Users want to understand management's perspective on the company and the implications of key statistics." It also said that "key statistics to be reported [should] be limited to statistics a company has available ..." (page 72).

83. Respondents to the Exposure Draft had mixed reactions to its measurement guidance. Very few suggested that the Board require allocations solely for external reporting purposes. Most agreed that allocations are inherently arbitrary and may not be meaningful if they are not used for management purposes. No respondents suggested that intersegment transfers should be reported on any basis other than that used internally. However, some respondents recommended that information about each segment be provided based on the accounting principles used in the enterprise's general-purpose financial statements. Some observed that unadjusted information from internal sources would not necessarily comply with generally accepted accounting principles and, for that reason, might be difficult for users to understand. Other respondents argued that comparability between enterprises would be improved if the segment information were provided on the basis of generally accepted accounting principles. Finally, a few questioned the verifiability of the information.

84. The Board decided not to require that segment information be provided in accordance with the same generally accepted accounting principles used to prepare the consolidated financial statements for several reasons. Preparing segment information in accordance with the generally accepted accounting principles used at the consolidated level would be difficult because some generally accepted accounting principles are not intended to apply at a segment level. Examples include allocation of the cost of an acquisition to individual assets and liabilities of a subsidiary using the purchase method of accounting, accounting for the cost of enterprise-wide employee benefit plans, accounting for income taxes in an enterprise that files a consolidated income tax return, and accounting for inventory on a last-in, first-out basis if the pools include items in more than one segment. In addition, there are no generally accepted accounting principles for allocating joint costs, jointly used assets, or jointly incurred liabilities to segments or for pricing intersegment transfers. As a consequence, it generally is not feasible to present segment profitability in accordance with generally accepted accounting principles.

85. The Board recognizes that segment information is subject to certain limitations and that some of that information may not be susceptible to the same degree of verifiability as some other financial information. However, verifiability is not the only important qualitative characteristic of accounting information. Verifiability is a component of reliability, which is one of two characteristics that contribute to the usefulness of accounting information. The other is relevance, which is equally important. Concepts Statement 2 states:

> Although financial information must be both relevant and reliable to be useful, information may possess both characteristics to varying degrees. It may be possible to trade relevance for reliability or vice versa, though not to the point of dispensing with one of them altogether. ... trade-offs between characteristics may be necessary or beneficial.
>
> In a particular situation, the importance attached to relevance in relation to the importance of other decision specific qualities of accounting information (for example, reliability) will be different for different information users, and their willingness to trade one quality for another will also differ. [paragraphs 42 and 45]

86.   It is apparent that users are willing to trade a degree of reliability in segment information for more relevant information. The AIMR's 1993 position paper states:

> Analysts need financial statements structured so as to be consistent with how the business is organized and managed. That means that two different companies in the same industry may have to report segment data differently because they are structured differently themselves. [page 20]

But, as previously noted, the position paper says that, under those circumstances, analysts "would assume more responsibility for making meaningful comparisons of those data to the unlike data of other firms that conduct their business differently" (page 61).

87.   The Board believes that the information required by this Statement meets the objective of reliability of which both representational faithfulness and verifiability are components. An auditor can determine whether the information reported in the notes to the financial statements came from the required source by reviewing management reports or minutes from meetings of the board of directors. The information is not required to be provided on a specified basis, but the enterprise is required to explain the basis on which it is provided and to reconcile the segment information to consolidated enterprise totals. Adequate explanation and an appropriate reconciliation will enable a user to understand the information and its limitations in the context of the enterprise's financial statements. The auditor can test both the explanation of segment amounts and the reconciliations to consolidated totals. Furthermore, because management uses that information in its decision-making processes, that information is likely to be highly reliable. The information provided to comply with Statement 14 was more difficult to verify in many situations and was less reliable. Because it was prepared solely for external reporting purposes, it required allocations that may have been arbitrary, and it was based on accounting principles that may have been difficult to apply at the segment level.

88.   Paragraph 29 requires amounts allocated to a segment to be allocated on a reasonable basis. However, the Board believes that the potential increased reliability that might have been achieved by requiring allocation of consolidated amounts is illusory because expenses incurred at the consolidated level could be allocated to segments in a variety of ways that could be considered "reasonable." For example, an enterprise could use either the number of employees in each segment or the segment's total salary expense in relation to the consolidated amounts as a basis for allocating pension expense to segments. Those two approaches to allocation could result in significantly different measures of segment profit or loss. However, both the number of employees and the total salary expense might be reasonable bases on which to allocate total pension expense. In contrast, it would not seem reasonable for an enterprise to allocate pension expense to a segment that had no employees eligible for the pension plan. Because of the potential for misleading information that may result from such allocations, the Board decided that it is appropriate for this Statement to require that amounts allocated to a segment be allocated on a reasonable basis.

89.   The Board also considered explicitly requiring that revenues and expenses directly incurred by or directly attributable to an operating segment be reported

by that segment. However, it decided that, in some cases, whether an item of revenue or expense is attributable to an operating segment is a matter of judgment. Further, such an explicit requirement would be an additional modification of the management approach to measurement. While the Board decided not to include an explicit requirement, it believes that many items of revenue or expense clearly relate to a particular segment and that it would be unlikely that the information used by management would omit those items.

90. To assist users of financial statements in understanding segment disclosures, this Statement requires that enterprises provide sufficient explanation of the basis on which the information was prepared. That disclosure must include any differences in the basis of measurement between the consolidated amounts and the segment amounts. It also must indicate whether allocations of items were made symmetrically. An enterprise may allocate an expense to a segment without allocating the related asset; however, disclosure of that fact is required. Enterprises also are required to reconcile to the consolidated totals in the enterprise's financial statements the totals of reportable segment assets, segment revenues, segment profit or loss, and any other significant segment information that is disclosed.

91. In addition, the advantages of reporting unadjusted management information are significant. That practice is consistent with defining segments based on the structure of the enterprise's internal organization. It imposes little incremental cost on the enterprise and requires little incremental time to prepare. Thus, the enterprise can more easily report segment information in condensed financial statements for interim periods and can report more information about each segment in annual financial statements. Information used by management also highlights for a user of financial statements the risks and opportunities that management considers important.

Information to Be Disclosed about Segments

92. The items of information about each reportable operating segment that must be disclosed as described in paragraphs 25–31 represent a balance between the needs of users of financial statements who may want a complete set of financial statements for each segment and the costs to preparers who may prefer not to disclose any segment information. Statement 14 required disclosure of internal and external revenues; profit or loss; depreciation, depletion, and amortization expense; and unusual items as defined in APB Opinion No. 30, *Reporting the Results of Operations—Reporting the Effects of Disposal of a Segment of a Business, and Extraordinary, Unusual and Infrequently Occurring Events and Transactions*, for each segment. Statement 14 also required disclosure of total assets, equity in the net income of investees accounted for by the equity method, the amount of investment in equity method investees, and total expenditures for additions to long-lived assets. Some respondents to the Exposure Draft objected to disclosing any information that was not required by Statement 14, while others recommended disclosure of additional items that are not required by this Statement. This Statement calls for the following additional disclosures only if the items are included in the measure of segment profit or loss that is reviewed by the chief operating decision maker: significant noncash items, interest revenue, interest expense, and income tax expense.

93.   Some respondents to the Exposure Draft expressed concern that the proposals would increase the sheer volume of information compared to what was required to be reported under Statement 14. The Board considers that concern to be overstated for several reasons. Although this Statement requires disclosure of more information about an individual operating segment than Statement 14 required for an industry segment, this Statement requires disclosure of information about only one type of segment—reportable operating segments—while Statement 14 required information about two types of segments—industry segments and geographic segments. Moreover, Statement 14 required that many enterprises create information solely for external reporting, while almost all of the segment information that this Statement requires is already available in management reports. The Board recognizes, however, that some enterprises may find it necessary to create the enterprise-wide information about products and services, geographic areas, and major customers required by paragraphs 36–39.

94.   The Board decided to require disclosure of significant noncash items included in the measure of segment profit or loss and information about total expenditures for additions to long-lived segment assets (other than financial instruments, long-term customer relationships of a financial institution, mortgage and other servicing rights, deferred policy acquisition costs, and deferred tax assets) if that information is reported internally because it improves financial statement users' abilities to estimate cash-generating potential and cash requirements of operating segments. As an alternative, the Board considered requiring disclosure of operating cash flow for each operating segment. However, many respondents said that disclosing operating cash flow in accordance with FASB Statement No. 95, *Statement of Cash Flows*, would require that they gather and process information solely for external reporting purposes. They said that management often evaluates cash generated or required by segments in ways other than by calculating operating cash flow in accordance with Statement 95. For that reason, the Board decided not to require disclosure of cash flow by segment.

95.   Disclosure of interest revenue and interest expense included in reported segment profit or loss is intended to provide information about the financing activities of a segment. The Exposure Draft proposed that an enterprise disclose gross interest revenue and gross interest expense for all segments in which reported profit or loss includes those items. Some respondents said that financial services segments generally are managed based on net interest revenue, or the "spread," and that management looks only to that data in its decision-making process. Therefore those segments should be required to disclose only the net amount and not both gross interest revenue and expense. Those respondents noted that requiring disclosure of both gross amounts would be analogous to requiring nonfinancial services segments to disclose both sales and cost of sales. The Board decided that segments that derive a majority of revenue from interest should be permitted to disclose net interest revenue instead of gross interest revenue and gross interest expense if management finds that amount to be more relevant in managing the segment. Information about interest is most important if a single segment comprises a mix of financial and nonfinancial operations. If a segment is primarily a financial operation, interest

revenue probably constitutes most of segment revenues and interest expense will constitute most of the difference between reported segment revenues and reported segment profit or loss. If the segment has no financial operations or only immaterial financial operations, no information about interest is required.

96.   The Board decided not to require the disclosure of segment liabilities. The Exposure Draft proposed that an enterprise disclose segment liabilities because the Board believed that liabilities are an important disclosure for understanding the financing activities of a segment. The Board also noted that the requirement in FASB Statement No. 94, *Consolidation of All Majority-Owned Subsidiaries*, to disclose assets, liabilities, and profit or loss about previously unconsolidated subsidiaries was continued from APB Opinion No. 18, *The Equity Method of Accounting for Investments in Common Stock*, pending completion of the project on disaggregated disclosures. However, in commenting on the disclosures that should be required by this Statement, many respondents said that liabilities are incurred centrally and that enterprises often do not allocate those amounts to segments. The Board concluded that the value of information about segment liabilities in assessing the performance of the segments of an enterprise was limited.

97.   The Board decided not to require disclosure of research and development expense included in the measure of segment profit or loss. The Exposure Draft would have required that disclosure to provide financial statement users with information about the operating segments in which an enterprise is focusing its product development efforts. Disclosure of research and development expense was requested by a number of financial statement users and was specifically requested in both the report of the AICPA's Special Committee and the AIMR's 1993 position paper. However, respondents said that disclosing research and development expense by segment may result in competitive harm by providing competitors with early insight into the strategic plans of an enterprise. Other respondents observed that research and development is only one of a number of items that indicate where an enterprise is focusing its efforts and that it is much more significant in some enterprises than in others. For example, costs of employee training and advertising were cited as items that often are more important to some enterprises than research and development, calling into question the relevance of disclosing only research and development expense. Additionally, many respondents said that research and development expense often is incurred centrally and not allocated to segments. The Board therefore decided not to require the disclosure of research and development expense by segment.

Interim Period Information

98.   This Statement requires disclosure of limited segment information in condensed financial statements that are included in quarterly reports to shareholders, as was proposed in the Exposure Draft. Statement 14 did not apply to those condensed financial statements because of the expense and the time required for producing segment information under Statement 14. A few respondents to the Exposure Draft said that reporting segment information in interim financial statements would be unnecessarily burdensome. However, users contended that, to be timely, segment information is needed more often than annually and

that the difficulties of preparing it on an interim basis could be overcome by an approach like the one in this Statement. Managers of many enterprises agree and have voluntarily provided segment information for interim periods.

99. The Board decided that the condensed financial statements in interim reports issued to shareholders should include disclosure of segment revenues from external customers, intersegment revenues, a measure of segment profit or loss, material changes in segment assets, differences in the basis of segmentation or the way segment profit or loss was measured in the previous annual period, and a reconciliation to the enterprise's total profit or loss. That decision is a compromise between the needs of users who want the same segment information for interim periods as that required in annual financial statements and the costs to preparers who must report the information. Users will have some key information on a timely basis. Enterprises should not incur significant incremental costs to provide the information because it is based on information that is used internally and therefore already available.

Restatement of Previously Reported Information

100. The Board decided to require restatement of previously reported segment information following a change in the composition of an enterprise's segments unless it is impracticable to do so. Changes in the composition of segments interrupt trends, and trend analysis is important to users of financial statements. Some financial statement issuers have said that their policy is to restate one or more prior years for internal trend analysis. Many reorganizations result in discrete profit centers' being reassigned from one segment to another and lead to relatively simple restatements. However, if an enterprise undergoes a fundamental reorganization, restatement may be very difficult and expensive. The Board concluded that in those situations restatement may be impracticable and, therefore, should not be required. However, if an enterprise does not restate its segment information, the enterprise is required to provide current-period segment information on both the old and new bases of segmentation in the year in which the change occurs unless it is impracticable to do so.

Enterprise-Wide Disclosures

101. Paragraphs 36–39 require disclosure of information about an enterprise's products and services, geographic areas, and major customers, regardless of the enterprise's organization. The required disclosures need be provided only if they are not included as part of the disclosures about segments. The Exposure Draft proposed requiring additional disclosures about products and services and geographic areas *by segment*. Many respondents said that that proposal would have resulted in disclosure of excessive amounts of information. Some enterprises providing a variety of products and services throughout many countries, for example, would have been required to present a large quantity of information that would have been time-consuming to prepare and of questionable benefit to most financial statement users. The Board decided that additional disclosures provided on an enterprise-wide basis rather than on a segment basis would be appropriate and not unduly burdensome. The Board also agreed that those enterprise-wide disclosures are appropriate for all

enterprises including those that have a single operating segment if the enterprise offers a range of products and services, derives revenues from customers in more than one country, or both.

102.   Based on reviews of published information about public enterprises, discussions with constituents, and a field test of the Exposure Draft, the Board believes that most enterprises are organized by products and services or by geography and will report one or both of those types of information in their reportable operating segment disclosures. However, some enterprises will be required by paragraphs 36–39 to report additional information because the enterprise-wide disclosures are required for all enterprises, even those that have a single reportable segment.

Information about Products and Services

103.   This Statement requires that enterprises report revenues from external customers for each product and service or each group of similar products and services for the enterprise as a whole. Analysts said that an analysis of trends in revenues from products and services is important in assessing both past performance and prospects for future growth. Those trends can be compared to benchmarks such as industry statistics or information reported by competitors. Information about the assets that are used to produce specific products and deliver specific services also might be useful. However, in many enterprises, assets are not dedicated to specific products and services and reporting assets by products and services would require arbitrary allocations.

Information about Geographic Areas

104.   This Statement requires disclosure of information about both revenues and assets by geographic area. Analysts said that information about revenues from customers in different geographic areas assists them in understanding concentrations of risks due to negative changes in economic conditions and prospects for growth due to positive economic changes. They said that information about assets located in different areas assists them in understanding concentrations of risks (for example, political risks such as expropriation).

105.   Statement 14 requires disclosure of geographic information by geographic region, whereas this Statement requires disclosure of individually material countries as well as information for the enterprise's country of domicile and all foreign countries in the aggregate. This Statement's approach has two significant benefits. First, it will reduce the burden on preparers of financial statements because most enterprises are likely to have material operations in only a few countries or perhaps only in their country of domicile. Second, and more important, it will provide information that is more useful in assessing the impact of concentrations of risk. Information disclosed by country is more useful because it is easier to interpret. Countries in contiguous areas often experience different rates of growth and other differences in economic conditions. Under the requirements of Statement 14, enterprises often reported information about broad geographic areas that included groupings such as Europe, Africa, and the Middle East. Analysts and others have questioned the usefulness of that type of broad disclosure.

106. Respondents to the Exposure Draft questioned how revenues should be allocated to individual countries. For example, guidance was requested for situations in which products are shipped to one location but the customer resides in another location. The Board decided to provide flexibility concerning the basis on which enterprises attribute revenues to individual countries rather than requiring that revenues be attributed to countries according to the location of customers. The Board also decided to require that enterprises disclose the basis they have adopted for attributing revenues to countries to permit financial statement users to understand the geographic information provided.

107. As a result of its decision to require geographic information on an enterprise-wide basis, the Board decided not to require disclosure of capital expenditures on certain long-lived assets by geographic area. Such information on an enterprise-wide basis is not necessarily helpful in forecasting future cash flows of operating segments.

Information about Major Customers

108. The Board decided to retain the requirement in Statement 14, as amended by FASB Statement No. 30, *Disclosure of Information about Major Customers*, to report information about major customers because major customers of an enterprise represent a significant concentration of risk. The 10 percent threshold is arbitrary; however, it has been accepted practice since Statement 14 was issued, and few have suggested changing it.

Competitive Harm

109. A number of respondents to the Exposure Draft noted the potential for competitive harm as a result of disclosing segment information in accordance with this Statement. The Board considered adopting special provisions to reduce the potential for competitive harm from certain segment information but decided against it. In the Invitation to Comment, the Tentative Conclusions, and the Exposure Draft, the Board asked constituents for specific illustrations of competitive harm that has resulted from disclosing segment information. Some respondents said that public enterprises may be at a disadvantage to nonpublic enterprises or foreign competitors that do not have to disclose segment information. Other respondents suggested that information about narrowly defined segments may put an enterprise at a disadvantage in price negotiations with customers or in competitive bid situations.

110. Some respondents said that if a competitive disadvantage exists, it is a consequence of an obligation that enterprises have accepted to gain greater access to capital markets, which gives them certain advantages over nonpublic enterprises and many foreign enterprises. Other respondents said that enterprises are not likely to suffer competitive harm because most competitors have other sources of more detailed information about an enterprise than that disclosed in the financial statements. In addition, the information that is required to be disclosed about an operating segment is no more detailed or specific than the information typically provided by a smaller enterprise with a single operation.

111. The Board was sympathetic to specific concerns raised by certain constituents; however, it decided that a competitive-harm exemption was inappropriate because it would provide a means for broad noncompliance with this Statement. Some form of relief for single-product or single-service segments was explored; however, there are many enterprises that produce a single product or a single service that are required to issue general-purpose financial statements. Those statements would include the same information that would be reported by single-product or single-service segments of an enterprise. The Board concluded that it was not necessary to provide an exemption for single-product or single-service segments because enterprises that produce a single product or service that are required to issue general-purpose financial statements have that same exposure to competitive harm. The Board noted that concerns about competitive harm were addressed to the extent feasible by four changes made during redeliberations: (a) modifying the aggregation criteria, (b) adding quantitative materiality thresholds for identifying reportable segments, (c) eliminating the requirements to disclose research and development expense and liabilities by segment, and (d) changing the second-level disclosure requirements about products and services and geography from a segment basis to an enterprise-wide basis.

Cost-Benefit Considerations

112. One of the precepts of the Board's mission is to promulgate standards only if the expected benefits of the resulting information exceed the perceived costs. The Board strives to determine that a proposed standard will fill a significant need and that the costs incurred to satisfy that need, as compared with other alternatives, are justified in relation to the overall benefits of the resulting information. The Board concluded that the benefits that will result from this Statement will exceed the related costs.

113. The Board believes that the primary benefits of this Statement are that enterprises will report segment information in interim financial reports, some enterprises will report a greater number of segments, most enterprises will report more items of information about each segment, enterprises will report segments that correspond to internal management reports, and enterprises will report segment information that will be more consistent with other parts of their annual reports.

114. This Statement will reduce the cost of providing disaggregated information for many enterprises. Statement 14 required that enterprises define segments by both industry and by geographical area, ways that often did not match the way that information was used internally. Even if the reported segments aligned with the internal organization, the information required was often created solely for external reporting because Statement 14 required certain allocations of costs, prohibited other cost allocations, and required allocations of assets to segments. This Statement requires that information about operating segments be provided on the same basis that it is used internally. The Board believes that most of the enterprise-wide disclosures in this Statement about products and services, geography, and major customers typically are provided in current financial statements or can be prepared with minimal incremental cost.

Applicability to Nonpublic Enterprises and Not-for-Profit Organizations

115.   The Board decided to continue to exempt nonpublic enterprises from the requirement to report segment information. Few users of nonpublic enterprises' financial statements have requested that the Board require that those enterprises provide segment information.

116.   At the time the Board began considering improvements to disclosures about segment information, FASB Statement No. 117, *Financial Statements of Not-for-Profit Organizations*, had not been issued and there were no effective standards for consolidated financial statements of not-for-profit organizations. Most not-for-profit organizations provided financial information for each of their funds, which is a form of disaggregated information. The situation in Canada was similar. Thus, when the two boards agreed to pursue a joint project, they decided to limit the scope to public business enterprises.

117.   The Board provided a limited form of disaggregated information in paragraph 26 of Statement 117, which requires disclosure of expense by functional classification. However, the Board acknowledges that the application of that Statement may increase the need for disaggregated information about not-for-profit organizations. A final Statement expected to result from the FASB Exposure Draft, *Consolidated Financial Statements: Policy and Procedures*, also may increase that need by requiring aggregation of information about more entities in the financial statements of not-for-profit organizations.

118.   The general approach of providing information based on the structure of an enterprise's internal organization may be appropriate for not-for-profit organizations. However, the Board decided not to add not-for-profit organizations to the scope of this Statement. Users of financial statements of not-for-profit organizations have not urged the Board to include those organizations, perhaps because they have not yet seen the effects of Statement 117 and the Exposure Draft on consolidations. Furthermore, the term *not-for-profit organizations* applies to a wide variety of entities, some of which are similar to business enterprises and some of which are very different. There are likely to be unique characteristics of some of those entities or special user needs that require special provisions, which the Board has not studied. In addition, the AcSB has recently adopted standards for reporting by not-for-profit organizations that are different from Statement 117. In the interest of completing this joint project in a timely manner, the Board decided not to undertake the research and deliberations that would be necessary to adapt the requirements of this Statement to not-for-profit organizations at this time. Few respondents to the Exposure Draft disagreed with the Board's position.

Effective Date and Transition

119.   The Board concluded that this Statement should be effective for financial statements issued for fiscal years beginning after December 15, 1997. In developing the Exposure Draft, the Board had decided on an effective date of December 15, 1996. The Board believed that that time frame was reasonable because almost all of the information that this Statement requires is generated by systems already in place within an enterprise and a final Statement was

expected to be issued before the end of 1996. However, respondents said that some enterprises may need more time to comply with the requirements of this Statement than would have been provided under the Exposure Draft.

120.   The Board also decided not to require that segment information be reported in financial statements for interim periods in the initial year of application. Some of the information that is required to be reported for interim periods is based on information that would have been reported in the most recent annual financial statements. Without a full set of segment information to use as a comparison and to provide an understanding of the basis on which it is provided, interim information would not be as meaningful.

© IFRS Foundation

Appendix B
Amendments to Basis for Conclusions on other IFRSs

This appendix contains amendments to the Basis for Conclusions on other IFRSs that are necessary in order to note the replacement of IAS 14 by IFRS 8.

* * * * *

The amendments contained in this appendix when IFRS 8 was issued in 2006 have been incorporated into the text of the Basis for Conclusions on IFRSs 1, 6 and 7 and IASs 27 and 36 as issued at 30 November 2006.

Dissenting opinions

Dissent of Gilbert Gélard and James J Leisenring

DO1   Messrs Gélard and Leisenring dissent from the issue of the IFRS because it does not require a defined measure of segment profit or loss to be disclosed and does not require the measure of profit or loss reported to be consistent with the attribution of assets to reportable segments.

DO2   By not defining segment profit or loss, the IFRS allows the reporting of any measure of segment profit or loss as long as that measure is reviewed by the chief operating decision maker. Items of revenue and expense directly attributable to a segment need not be included in the reported profit or loss of that segment, and allocation of items not directly attributable to any given segment is not required. Messrs Gélard and Leisenring believe that the IFRS should require amounts directly incurred by or directly attributable to a segment to be included in that segment's profit or loss, and measurement of a segment's profit or loss to be consistent with the attribution of assets to the segment.

DO3   Messrs Gélard and Leisenring support the disclosure of information to enable users of financial statements to evaluate the activities of an entity and the economic environment in which it operates. However, they believe that the IFRS will not meet this objective, even with the required disclosures and reconciliation to the entity's annual financial statements, because it does not define segment profit or loss and does not require consistent attribution of assets and profit or loss to segments.

DO4   Messrs Gélard and Leisenring support the management approach for defining reportable segments and support requiring disclosure of selected segment information in interim financial reports. They believe, however, that the definitions of segment revenue, expense, result, assets and liabilities in paragraph 16 of IAS 14 *Segment Reporting* should be retained in the IFRS and applied to segments identified by the management approach. They believe that proper external reporting of segment information should not permit the use of non-GAAP measures because they might mislead users.

DO5   Messrs Gélard and Leisenring also believe that the changes from IAS 14 are not justified by the need for convergence with US GAAP. IAS 14 is a disclosure standard and therefore does not affect the reconciliation of IFRS amounts to US GAAP, though additional disclosure from what is required now by IAS 14 might be needed to comply with US GAAP.

Dissent of Stephen Cooper from the amendment issued in April 2009

DO1   Mr Cooper dissents from the amendment to IFRS 8 *Operating Segments* made by *Improvements to IFRSs* issued in April 2009.

DO2   In his view the changes are unnecessary considering that the provisions in the *Framework*[4] regarding materiality already enable a reporting entity not to disclose segment assets when those assets are small relative to segment profit and not relevant to the understanding of the business. Mr Cooper believes that allowing a reporting entity not to disclose segment assets merely because this is not reported to the chief operating decision maker weakens IFRS 8, and may result in segment assets not being disclosed even when they are important to understanding the performance and financial position of that business.

---

4   The reference to the *Framework* is to IASC's *Framework for the Preparation and Presentation of Financial Statements*, adopted by the IASB in 2001. In September 2010 the IASB replaced the *Framework* with the *Conceptual Framework for Financial Reporting*.

IASB documents published to accompany

IFRS 9

Financial Instruments

The text of the unaccompanied standard, IFRS 9, is contained in Part A of this edition. Its effective date when issued was 1 January 2018. The text of the Accompanying Guidance on IFRS 9 is contained in Part B of this edition. This part presents the following documents:

CONTENTS

Basis for Conclusions on
IFRS 9 *Financial Instruments*

This Basis for Conclusions accompanies, but is not part of, IFRS 9.

IFRS 9 replaced IAS 39 Financial Instruments: Recognition and Measurement. *When revised in 2003 IAS 39 was accompanied by a Basis for Conclusions summarising the considerations of the IASB as constituted at the time, in reaching some of its conclusions in that Standard. That Basis for Conclusions was subsequently updated to reflect amendments to the Standard. For convenience the IASB has incorporated into its Basis for Conclusions on IFRS 9 material from the Basis for Conclusions on IAS 39 that discusses matters that the IASB has not reconsidered. That material is contained in paragraphs denoted by numbers with the prefix BCZ. In those paragraphs cross-references to the Standard have been updated accordingly and minor necessary editorial changes have been made. In 2003 and later some IASB members dissented from the issue of IAS 39 and subsequent amendments, and portions of their dissenting opinions relate to requirements that have been carried forward to IFRS 9. Those dissenting opinions are set out in an appendix after this Basis for Conclusions.*

Paragraphs describing the IASB's considerations in reaching its own conclusions on IFRS 9 are numbered with the prefix BC.

Introduction

BCIN.1   This Basis for Conclusions summarises the considerations of the International Accounting Standards Board (IASB) when developing IFRS 9 *Financial Instruments*. Individual IASB members gave greater weight to some factors than to others.

BCIN.2   The IASB has long acknowledged the need to improve the requirements for financial reporting of financial instruments to enhance the relevance and understandability of information about financial instruments for users of financial statements. That need became more urgent in the light of the global financial crisis that started in 2007 ('the global financial crisis'), so the IASB decided to replace IAS 39 *Financial Instruments: Recognition and Measurement* in its entirety as expeditiously as possible. To do this the IASB divided the project into several phases. In adopting this approach, the IASB acknowledged the difficulties that might be created by differences in timing between this project and others, in particular the project on insurance contracts.

Classification and measurement

BCIN.3   IFRS 9 is a new Standard that deals with the accounting for financial instruments. When developing IFRS 9, the IASB considered the responses to its 2009 Exposure Draft *Financial Instruments: Classification and Measurement* (the '2009 Classification and Measurement Exposure Draft').

BCIN.4   That 2009 Classification and Measurement Exposure Draft contained proposals for all items within the scope of IAS 39. However, some respondents said that the IASB should finalise its proposals on the classification and measurement of financial assets while retaining the existing requirements for financial liabilities (including the requirements for embedded derivatives and the fair value option) until the IASB had more fully considered the issues relating to financial liabilities. Those respondents pointed out that the IASB had accelerated its project on financial instruments because of the global financial crisis, which had placed more emphasis on issues in the accounting for financial assets than for financial liabilities. They suggested that the IASB should consider issues related to financial liabilities more closely before finalising the requirements for classification and measurement of financial liabilities.

BCIN.5   The IASB noted those concerns and, as a result, in November 2009 it finalised the first chapters of IFRS 9, dealing with the classification and measurement of financial assets. In the IASB's view, requirements for classification and measurement are the foundation for a financial reporting standard on accounting for financial instruments, and the requirements on associated matters (for example, on impairment and hedge accounting) have to reflect those requirements. In addition, the IASB noted that many of the application issues that arose in the global financial crisis were related to the classification and measurement of financial assets in accordance with IAS 39.

BCIN.6   Thus, financial liabilities, including derivative liabilities, initially remained within the scope of IAS 39. Taking that course enabled the IASB to obtain further feedback on the accounting for financial liabilities, including how best to address accounting for changes in own credit risk.

BCIN.7   Immediately after issuing IFRS 9, the IASB began an extensive outreach programme to gather feedback on the classification and measurement of financial liabilities. The IASB obtained information and views from its Financial Instruments Working Group (FIWG) and from users of financial statements, regulators, preparers, auditors and others from a range of industries across different geographical regions. The primary messages that the IASB received were that the requirements in IAS 39 for classifying and measuring financial liabilities were generally working well but that the effects of the changes in a liability's credit risk ought not to affect profit or loss unless the liability is held for trading. As a result of the feedback received, the IASB decided to retain almost all of the requirements in IAS 39 for the classification and measurement of financial liabilities and carry them forward to IFRS 9 (see paragraphs BC4.46–BC4.53).

BCIN.8   By taking that course, the issue of accounting for the effects of changes in credit risk does not arise for most liabilities and would remain only in the context of financial liabilities designated as measured at fair value under the fair value option. Thus, in May 2010, the IASB published the Exposure Draft *Fair Value Option for Financial Liabilities* (the '2010 Own Credit Risk Exposure Draft'), which proposed that the effects of changes in the credit risk of liabilities designated under the fair value option would be presented in other comprehensive income. The IASB considered the responses to the 2010 Own Credit Risk Exposure Draft and finalised the requirements, which were then added to IFRS 9 in October 2010.

BCIN.9   In November 2012 the IASB published the Exposure Draft *Classification and Measurement: Limited Amendments to IFRS 9* (Proposed amendments to IFRS 9 (2010)) (the '2012 Limited Amendments Exposure Draft'). In that Exposure Draft, the IASB proposed limited amendments to the classification and measurement requirements in IFRS 9 for financial assets with the aims of:

(a) considering the interaction between the classification and measurement of financial assets and the accounting for insurance contract liabilities;

(b) addressing specific application questions that had been raised by some interested parties since IFRS 9 was issued; and

(c) seeking to reduce key differences with the US national standard-setter, the Financial Accounting Standards Board's (FASB) tentative classification and measurement model for financial instruments.

BCIN.10 Accordingly, the 2012 Limited Amendments Exposure Draft proposed limited amendments to clarify the application of the existing classification and measurement requirements for financial assets and to introduce a fair value through other comprehensive income measurement category for particular debt investments. Most respondents to the 2012 Limited Amendments Exposure Draft—as well as participants in the IASB's outreach programme—generally supported the proposed limited amendments. However, many asked the IASB for clarifications or additional guidance on particular aspects of the proposals. The IASB considered the responses in the comment letters and the information received during its outreach activities when it finalised the limited amendments in July 2014.

Amortised cost and impairment methodology

BCIN.11 In October 2008, as part of a joint approach to dealing with the financial reporting issues arising from the global financial crisis, the IASB and the FASB set up the Financial Crisis Advisory Group (FCAG). The FCAG considered how improvements in financial reporting could help to enhance investor confidence in financial markets. In its report, published in July 2009, the FCAG identified weaknesses in the current accounting standards for financial instruments and their application. Those weaknesses included the delayed recognition of credit losses on loans (and other financial instruments) and the complexity of multiple impairment approaches. One of the FCAG's recommendations was to explore alternatives to the incurred credit loss model that would use more forward looking information.

BCIN.12 Following a Request for Information that the IASB posted on its website in June 2009, the IASB published, in November 2009, the Exposure Draft *Financial Instruments: Amortised Cost and Impairment* (the '2009 Impairment Exposure Draft'). Comments received on the 2009 Impairment Exposure Draft and during outreach indicated support for the concept of such an impairment model, but highlighted the operational difficulties of applying it.

BCIN.13 In response, the IASB decided to modify the impairment model proposed in the 2009 Impairment Exposure Draft to address those operational difficulties while replicating the outcomes of that model that it proposed in that Exposure Draft as closely as possible. These simplifications were published in the Supplementary Document *Financial Instruments: Impairment* in January 2011, however the IASB did not receive strong support on these proposals.

BCIN.14 The IASB started developing an impairment model that would reflect the general pattern of deterioration in the credit quality of financial instruments and in which the amount of the expected credit losses recognised as a loss allowance or provision would depend on the level of deterioration in the credit quality of financial instruments since initial recognition.

BCIN.15 In 2013 the IASB published the Exposure Draft *Financial Instruments: Expected Credit Losses* (the '2013 Impairment Exposure Draft'), which proposed to recognise a loss allowance or provision at an amount equal to lifetime expected credit losses if there was a significant increase in credit risk after initial recognition of a financial instrument and at 12-month expected credit losses for all other instruments.

BCIN.16 Most respondents to the 2013 Impairment Exposure Draft—as well as participants in the IASB's outreach and field work programme—generally supported the proposed impairment model. However, many asked the IASB for clarifications or additional guidance on particular aspects of the proposals. The IASB considered the responses in the comment letters and the information received during its outreach activities when it finalised the impairment requirements in July 2014.

Hedge accounting

BCIN.17 In December 2010 the IASB published the Exposure Draft *Hedge Accounting* (the '2010 Hedge Accounting Exposure Draft'). That Exposure Draft contained an objective for hedge accounting that aimed to align accounting more closely with risk management and to provide useful information about the purpose and effect of hedging instruments. It also proposed requirements for:

(a) what financial instruments qualify for designation as hedging instruments;

(b) what items (existing or expected) qualify for designation as hedged items;

(c) an objective-based hedge effectiveness assessment;

(d) how an entity should account for a hedging relationship (fair value hedge, cash flow hedge or a hedge of a net investment in a foreign operation as defined in IAS 21 *The Effects of Changes in Foreign Exchange Rates*); and

(e) hedge accounting presentation and disclosures.

BCIN.18 After the publication of the 2010 Hedge Accounting Exposure Draft, the IASB began an extensive outreach programme to gather feedback on the hedge accounting proposals. The IASB obtained information and views from users of financial statements, preparers, treasurers, risk management experts, auditors, standard-setters and regulators from a range of industries across different geographical regions.

BCIN.19 The views from participants in the IASB's outreach activities were largely consistent with the views in the comment letters to the 2010 Hedge Accounting Exposure Draft. The IASB received strong support for the objective of aligning accounting more closely with risk management. However, many asked the IASB for added clarification on some of the fundamental changes proposed in the 2010 Hedge Accounting Exposure Draft.

BCIN.20   The IASB considered the responses in the comment letters to the 2010 Hedge Accounting Exposure Draft and the information received during its outreach activities when it finalised the requirements for hedge accounting that were then added to IFRS 9 in November 2013.

Scope (Chapter 2)

BC2.1   The scope of IAS 39 was not raised as a matter of concern during the global financial crisis and, hence, the IASB decided that the scope of IFRS 9 should be based on that of IAS 39. Consequently, the scope of IAS 39 was carried forward to IFRS 9. It has been changed only as a consequence of other new requirements, such as to reflect the changes to the accounting for expected credit losses on loan commitments that an entity issues (see paragraph BC2.8). As a result, most of paragraphs in this section of the Basis for Conclusions were carried forward from the Basis for Conclusion on IAS 39 and describe the IASB's rationale when it set the scope of that Standard.

Loan commitments

BCZ2.2   Loan commitments are firm commitments to provide credit under pre-specified terms and conditions. In the IAS 39 implementation guidance process, the question was raised whether a bank's loan commitments are derivatives accounted for at fair value under IAS 39. This question arises because a commitment to make a loan at a specified rate of interest during a fixed period of time meets the definition of a derivative. In effect, it is a written option for the potential borrower to obtain a loan at a specified rate.

BCZ2.3   To simplify the accounting for holders and issuers of loan commitments, the IASB decided to exclude particular loan commitments from the scope of IAS 39. The effect of the exclusion is that an entity will not recognise and measure changes in fair value of these loan commitments that result from changes in market interest rates or credit spreads. This is consistent with the measurement of the loan that results if the holder of the loan commitment exercises its right to obtain financing, because changes in market interest rates do not affect the measurement of an asset measured at amortised cost (assuming it is not designated in a category other than loans and receivables).[1]

BCZ2.4   However, the IASB decided that an entity should be permitted to measure a loan commitment at fair value with changes in fair value recognised in profit or loss on the basis of designation at inception of the loan commitment as a financial liability through profit or loss. This may be appropriate, for example, if the entity manages risk exposures related to loan commitments on a fair value basis.

BCZ2.5   The IASB further decided that a loan commitment should be excluded from the scope of IAS 39 only if it cannot be settled net. If the value of a loan commitment can be settled net in cash or another financial instrument, including when the entity has a past practice of selling the resulting loan assets shortly after origination, it is difficult to justify its exclusion from the requirement in IAS 39 to measure at fair value similar instruments that meet the definition of a derivative.

---

1   IFRS 9 eliminated the category of loans and receivables.

BCZ2.6   Some comments received on the Exposure Draft that preceded the issuance of these requirements in IAS 39 disagreed with the IASB's proposal that an entity that has a past practice of selling the assets resulting from its loan commitments shortly after origination should apply IAS 39 to all of its loan commitments. The IASB considered this concern and agreed that the words in that Exposure Draft did not reflect the IASB's intention. Thus, the IASB clarified that if an entity has a past practice of selling the assets resulting from its loan commitments shortly after origination, it applies IAS 39 only to its loan commitments in the same class.

BCZ2.7   Finally, in developing the requirements in IAS 39, the IASB decided that commitments to provide a loan at a below-market interest rate should be initially measured at fair value, and subsequently measured at the higher of (a) the amount that would be recognised under IAS 37 and (b) the amount initially recognised less, where appropriate, cumulative amortisation recognised in accordance with IAS 18 *Revenue*.[2] It noted that without such a requirement, liabilities that result from such commitments might not be recognised in the balance sheet, because in many cases no cash consideration is received.

BC2.8   In developing IFRS 9, the IASB decided to retain the accounting in IAS 39 for loan commitments, except to reflect the new impairment requirements. Consequently, in accordance with Section 5.5 of IFRS 9, an entity must apply the impairment requirements of IFRS 9 to loan commitments that are not otherwise within the scope of that Standard. Additionally, IFRS 9 requires that an issuer of a loan commitment to provide a loan at a below-market interest rate must measure it at the higher of (a) the amount of the loss allowance determined in accordance with Section 5.5 of that Standard and (b) the amount initially recognised less, when appropriate, the cumulative amount of income recognised in accordance with the principles of IFRS 15. The IASB did not change the accounting for loan commitments held by potential borrowers.

Financial guarantee contracts

BCZ2.9   In finalising IFRS 4 *Insurance Contracts* in early 2004, the IASB reached the following conclusions:

(a)   Financial guarantee contracts can have various legal forms, such as that of a guarantee, some types of letter of credit, a credit default contract or an insurance contract. However, although this difference in legal form may in some cases reflect differences in substance, the accounting for these instruments should not depend on their legal form.

(b)   If a financial guarantee contract is not an insurance contract, as defined in IFRS 4, it should be within the scope of IAS 39. This was the case before the IASB finalised IFRS 4.

(c)   As required before the IASB finalised IFRS 4, if a financial guarantee contract was entered into or retained on transferring to another party financial assets or financial liabilities within the scope of IAS 39, the issuer should apply IAS 39 to that contract even if it is an insurance contract, as defined in IFRS 4.

---

2   IFRS 15 *Revenue from Contracts with Customers*, issued in May 2014, replaced IAS 18.

(d) Unless (c) applies, the following treatment is appropriate for a financial guarantee contract that meets the definition of an insurance contract:

    (i) At inception, the issuer of a financial guarantee contract has a recognisable liability and should measure it at fair value. If a financial guarantee contract was issued in a stand-alone arm's length transaction to an unrelated party, its fair value at inception is likely to equal the premium received, unless there is evidence to the contrary.

    (ii) Subsequently, the issuer should measure the contract at the higher of the amount determined in accordance with IAS 37 *Provisions, Contingent Liabilities and Contingent Assets* and the amount initially recognised less, when appropriate, cumulative amortisation recognised in accordance with IAS 18.[3]

BCZ2.10 Mindful of the need to develop a 'stable platform' of Standards for 2005, the IASB finalised IFRS 4 in early 2004 without specifying the accounting for these contracts and then published an Exposure Draft *Financial Guarantee Contracts and Credit Insurance* in July 2004 to expose for public comment the conclusion set out in paragraph BCZ2.9(d). The IASB set a comment deadline of 8 October 2004 and received more than 60 comment letters. Before reviewing the comment letters, the IASB held a public education session at which it received briefings from representatives of the International Credit Insurance & Surety Association and of the Association of Financial Guaranty Insurers.

BCZ2.11 Some respondents to the Exposure Draft of July 2004 argued that there were important economic differences between credit insurance contracts and other forms of contract that met the proposed definition of a financial guarantee contract. However, both in developing the Exposure Draft of July 2004 and in subsequently discussing the comments received, the IASB was unable to identify differences that would justify differences in accounting treatment.

BCZ2.12 Some respondents to the Exposure Draft of July 2004 noted that some credit insurance contracts contain features, such as cancellation and renewal rights and profit-sharing features, that the IASB will not address until Phase II of its project on insurance contracts. They argued that the Exposure Draft did not give enough guidance to enable them to account for these features. The IASB concluded it could not address such features in the short term. The IASB noted that when credit insurers issue credit insurance contracts, they typically recognise a liability measured as either the premium received or an estimate of the expected losses. However, the IASB was concerned that some other issuers of financial guarantee contracts might argue that no recognisable liability existed at inception. To provide a temporary solution that balances these competing concerns, the IASB decided the following:

(a) If the issuer of financial guarantee contracts has previously asserted explicitly that it regards such contracts as insurance contracts and has used accounting applicable to insurance contracts, the issuer may elect to apply either IAS 39 or IFRS 4 to such financial guarantee contracts.

---

3   IFRS 15, issued in May 2014, replaced IAS 18.

(b)   In all other cases, the issuer of a financial guarantee contract should apply IAS 39.

BCZ2.13   The IASB does not regard criteria such as those described in paragraph BCZ2.12(a) as suitable for the long term, because they can lead to different accounting for contracts that have similar economic effects. However, the IASB could not find a more compelling approach to resolve its concerns for the short term. Moreover, although the criteria described in paragraph BCZ2.12(a) may appear imprecise, the IASB believes that the criteria would provide a clear answer in the vast majority of cases. Paragraph B2.6 in IFRS 9 gives guidance on the application of those criteria.

BCZ2.14   The IASB considered convergence with US generally accepted accounting principles (GAAP). In US GAAP, the requirements for financial guarantee contracts (other than those covered by US Standards specific to the insurance sector) are in FASB Interpretation 45 *Guarantor's Accounting and Disclosure Requirements for Guarantees, Including Indirect Guarantees of Indebtedness of Others* (FIN 45). The recognition and measurement requirements of FIN 45 do not apply to guarantees issued between parents and their subsidiaries, between entities under common control, or by a parent or subsidiary on behalf of a subsidiary or the parent. Some respondents to the Exposure Draft of July 2004 asked the IASB to provide a similar exemption. They argued that the requirement to recognise these financial guarantee contracts in separate or individual financial statements would cause costs disproportionate to the likely benefits, given that intragroup transactions are eliminated on consolidation. However, to avoid the omission of material liabilities from separate or individual financial statements, the IASB did not create such an exemption.

BCZ2.15   The IASB issued the amendments for financial guarantee contracts in August 2005. After those amendments, the recognition and measurement requirements for financial guarantee contracts within the scope of IAS 39 were consistent with FIN 45 in some areas, but differed in others:

(a)   Like FIN 45, IAS 39 requires initial recognition at fair value.

(b)   IAS 39 requires systematic amortisation, in accordance with IAS 18[4], of the liability recognised initially. This is compatible with FIN 45, though FIN 45 contains less prescriptive requirements on subsequent measurement. Both IAS 39 and FIN 45 include a liability adequacy (or loss recognition) test, although the tests differ because of underlying differences in the Standards to which those tests refer (IAS 37 and Statement of Financial Accounting Standards No. 5 *Accounting for Contingencies*).

(c)   Like FIN 45, IAS 39 permits a different treatment for financial guarantee contracts issued by insurers.

(d)   Unlike FIN 45, IAS 39 does not contain exemptions for parents, subsidiaries or other entities under common control. However, any differences are reflected only in the separate or individual financial statements of the parent, subsidiaries or common control entities.

---

4   IFRS 15, issued in May 2014, replaced IAS 18.

BCZ2.16   Some respondents to the Exposure Draft of July 2004 asked for guidance on the treatment of financial guarantee contracts by the holder. However, this was beyond the limited scope of the project.

BC2.17   In developing IFRS 9, the IASB decided to retain the accounting in IAS 39 for financial guarantee contracts, except to reflect the new impairment requirements. Consequently, financial guarantee contracts that are within the scope of IFRS 9 and that are not measured at fair value through profit or loss, are measured at the higher of (a) the amount of the loss allowance determined in accordance with Section 5.5 of that Standard and (b) the amount initially recognised less, when appropriate, the cumulative amount of income recognised in accordance with the principles of IFRS 15.

Contracts to buy or sell a non-financial item

BCZ2.18   Before the amendments in 2003, IAS 39 and IAS 32 were not consistent with respect to the circumstances in which a commodity-based contract meets the definition of a financial instrument and is accounted for as a derivative. The IASB concluded that the amendments should make them consistent on the basis of the notion that a contract to buy or sell a non-financial item should be accounted for as a derivative when it (i) can be settled net or by exchanging financial instruments and (ii) is not held for the purpose of receipt or delivery of the non-financial item in accordance with the entity's expected purchase, sale or usage requirements (a 'normal' purchase or sale). In addition, the IASB concluded that the notion of when a contract can be settled net should include contracts:

(a)   where the entity has a practice of settling similar contracts net in cash or another financial instrument or by exchanging financial instruments;

(b)   for which the entity has a practice of taking delivery of the underlying and selling it within a short period after delivery for the purpose of generating a profit from short-term fluctuations in price or dealer's margin; and

(c)   in which the non-financial item that is the subject of the contract is readily convertible to cash.

Because practices of settling net or taking delivery of the underlying and selling it within a short period after delivery also indicate that the contracts are not 'normal' purchases or sales, such contracts are within the scope of IAS 39 and are accounted for as derivatives. The IASB also decided to clarify that a written option that can be settled net in cash or another financial instrument, or by exchanging financial instruments, is within the scope of the Standard and cannot qualify as a 'normal' purchase or sale.

Accounting for a contract to buy or sell a non-financial item as a derivative

BCZ2.19   In the third phase of its project to replace IAS 39 with IFRS 9, the IASB considered replacing the hedge accounting requirements in IAS 39. As part of those deliberations, the IASB considered the accounting for executory contracts that gives rise to accounting mismatches in some situations. The IASB's decision is discussed in more detail below.

BCZ2.20   Contracts accounted for in accordance with IAS 39 include those contracts to buy or sell a non-financial item that can be settled net in cash (including net settlement in another financial instrument or by exchanging financial instruments), as if the contracts were financial instruments. In addition, IAS 39 specifies that there are various ways in which a contract to buy or sell a non-financial item can be settled net in cash. For example, a contract is considered to be settleable net in cash even if it is not explicit in the terms of the contract, but the entity has a practice of settling similar contracts net in cash.

BCZ2.21   However, such contracts are excluded from the scope of IAS 39 if they were entered into and continue to be held for the purpose of the receipt or delivery of a non-financial item in accordance with the entity's expected purchase, sale or usage requirements. This is commonly referred to as the 'own use' scope exception of IAS 39. The own use scope exception in IAS 39 mostly applies to contracts for commodity purchases or sales.

BCZ2.22   It is not uncommon for a commodity contract to be within the scope of IAS 39 and meet the definition of a derivative. Many commodity contracts meet the criteria for net settlement in cash because in many instances commodities are readily convertible to cash. When such a contract is accounted for as a derivative, it is measured at fair value with changes in the fair value recognised in profit or loss. If an entity enters into a derivative to hedge the change in the fair value of the commodity contract, that derivative is also measured at fair value with changes in fair value recognised in profit or loss. Because the changes in the fair value of the commodity contract and the derivative are recognised in profit or loss, an entity does not need hedge accounting.

BCZ2.23   However, in situations in which a commodity contract is not within the scope of IAS 39, it is accounted for as a normal sale or purchase contract ('executory contract'). Consequently, if an entity enters into a derivative contract to hedge changes in the fair value arising from a commodity supply contract that is not within the scope of IAS 39, an accounting mismatch is created. This is because the change in the fair value of the derivative is recognised in profit or loss while the change in the fair value of the commodity supply contract is not recognised (unless the contract is onerous).

BCZ2.24   To eliminate this accounting mismatch, an entity could apply hedge accounting. It could designate the commodity supply contracts (which meet the definition of a firm commitment) as a hedged item in a fair value hedge relationship. Consequently, the commodity supply contracts would be measured at fair value and the fair value changes would offset the changes in the fair value of the derivative instruments (to the extent that those are effective hedges). However, hedge accounting in these circumstances is administratively burdensome and often produces a less meaningful result than fair value accounting. Furthermore, entities enter into large volumes of commodity contracts and some positions may offset each other. An entity would therefore typically hedge on a net basis. Moreover, in many business models, this net position also includes physical long positions such as commodity inventory. That net position as a whole is then managed using derivatives to achieve a net position (after hedging) of nil (or close to nil). The net position is typically monitored, managed and adjusted daily. Because of the frequent movement of the net position and therefore the frequent adjustment of the net position to nil or close to nil by using derivatives, an entity would have to adjust the fair value hedge relationships frequently if the entity were to apply hedge accounting.

BCZ2.25 The IASB noted that in such situations hedge accounting would not be an efficient solution because entities manage a net position of derivatives, executory contracts and physical long positions in a dynamic way. Consequently, the IASB considered amending the scope of IAS 39 so that it would allow a commodity contract to be accounted for as a derivative in such situations. The IASB considered two alternatives for amending the scope of IAS 39:

(a) allowing an entity to elect to account for commodity contracts as derivatives (ie a free choice); or

(b) accounting for a commodity contract as a derivative if that is in accordance with the entity's fair value-based risk management strategy.

BCZ2.26 The IASB noted that giving an entity the choice to account for commodity contracts as derivatives would be tantamount to an elective 'own use' scope exception, which would have outcomes that would be similar to the accounting treatment in US GAAP. This approach would, in effect, allow an entity to elect the own use scope exception instead of derivative accounting at inception or a later date. Once the entity had elected to apply the scope exception it would not be able to change its election and switch to derivative accounting.

BCZ2.27 However, the IASB noted that such an approach would not be consistent with the approach in IAS 39 because:

(a) the accounting treatment in accordance with IAS 39 is dependent on, and reflects, the purpose (ie whether it is for 'own use') for which the contracts to buy or sell non-financial items are entered into and continue to be held for. This is different from a free choice, which would allow, but not require, the accounting treatment to reflect the purpose of the contract.

(b) in accordance with IAS 39, if similar contracts have been settled net, a contract to buy or sell non-financial items that can be settled net in cash must be accounted for as a derivative. Hence, a free choice would allow an entity to account for a commodity contract as a derivative regardless of whether similar contracts have been settled net in cash.

Consequently, in the Exposure Draft *Hedge Accounting* (the '2010 Hedge Accounting Exposure Draft'), the IASB decided not to propose that entities can elect to account for commodity contracts as derivatives.

BCZ2.28 Alternatively, the IASB considered applying derivative accounting to commodity contracts if that is in accordance with the entity's underlying business model and how the contracts are managed. Consequently, the actual type of settlement (ie whether settled net in cash) would not be conclusive for the evaluation of the appropriate accounting treatment. Instead, an entity would consider not only the purpose (based solely on the actual type of settlement) but also how the contracts are managed. As a result, if an entity's underlying business model changes and the entity no longer manages its commodity contracts on a fair value basis, the contracts would revert to the own use scope exception. This would be consistent with the criteria for using the fair value option for financial instruments (ie eliminating an accounting mismatch or if the financial instruments are managed on a fair value basis).

BCZ2.29　Consequently, the IASB proposed that derivative accounting would apply to contracts that would otherwise meet the own use scope exception if that is in accordance with the entity's fair value-based risk management strategy. The IASB believed that this approach would faithfully represent the financial position and the performance of entities that manage their entire business on a fair value basis, provide more useful information to users of financial statements, and be less onerous for entities than applying hedge accounting.

BCZ2.30　Most respondents to the 2010 Hedge Accounting Exposure Draft supported the IASB's approach of using fair value accounting for resolving the accounting mismatch that arises when a commodity contract that is outside the scope of IAS 39 is hedged with a derivative. Those who supported the proposal thought that it would facilitate a better presentation of the overall economic effects of entering into such hedging transactions.

BCZ2.31　However, some respondents were concerned that the proposal would have unintended consequences by creating an accounting mismatch for some entities. They argued that in scenarios in which there are other items that are managed within a fair value-based risk management strategy and those other items are not measured at fair value under IFRS, applying derivative accounting to 'own use contracts' would introduce (instead of eliminate) an accounting mismatch. For example, in the electricity industry the risk management for some power plants and the related electricity sales is on a fair value basis. If these entities had to apply derivative accounting for customer sales contracts it would create an accounting mismatch. This accounting mismatch would result in artificial profit or loss volatility if the power plant is measured at cost under IAS 16 *Property, Plant and Equipment*. Another example raised by respondents was that of entities risk-managing the own use contracts, inventory and derivatives on a fair value basis. An accounting mismatch would arise if the inventory is measured in accordance with IAS 2 *Inventories* at the lower of cost and net realisable value while the own use contracts are measured at fair value.

BCZ2.32　Some respondents also requested that the IASB remove the precondition that an entity achieves a nil or close to nil net risk position in order to qualify for accounting for executory contracts as derivatives. They argued that if the condition was not removed it would limit the benefits of the proposal. This is because some entities, while generally seeking to maintain a net risk position close to nil, may sometimes take an open position depending on market conditions. These respondents noted that, from an entity's perspective, whether it takes a position or manages its exposure close to nil, it is still employing a fair value-based risk management strategy and that the financial statements should reflect the nature of its risk management activities.

BCZ2.33　Some also requested that the IASB clarify whether the proposal required that a fair value-based risk management strategy is adopted at an entity level or whether the business model can be assessed at a level lower than the entity level.

These respondents commented that within an entity, a part of the business may be risk-managed on a fair value basis while other businesses within the entity may be managed differently.

BCZ2.34 In the light of the arguments raised by respondents to the 2010 Hedge Accounting Exposure Draft, the IASB discussed whether an alternative would be extending the fair value option in IFRS 9 (for situations in which it eliminates or significantly reduces an accounting mismatch) to contracts that meet the own use scope exception. The IASB noted that because the fair value option would be an election by the entity, it would address the concerns raised about creating unintended accounting mismatches (see paragraph BCZ2.31) while still providing an efficient solution to the problem that the IASB wanted to address through its 2010 Hedge Accounting Exposure Draft.

BCZ2.35 The IASB considered that the disadvantage of providing an election (ie different accounting outcomes as the result of the entity's choice) by extending the fair value option in IFRS 9 was outweighed by the benefits of this alternative because:

(a) it is consistent with the IASB's objective to represent more faithfully the financial position and performance of entities that risk-manage an entire business on a fair value basis;

(b) it provides operational relief for entities that risk-manage an entire business on a dynamic fair value basis (ie it is less onerous than applying hedge accounting); and

(c) it does not have the unintended consequences of creating an accounting mismatch in some situations.

BCZ2.36 The IASB also considered whether specific transition requirements were needed for this amendment to IAS 39. Without those, the amendment would, by default, apply retrospectively. However, the IASB noted that because the decision is to be made at inception of a contract, the transition to the amended scope of IAS 39 would in effect be prospective in that the election would not be available for contracts that already exist on the date on which an entity applies the amendment for the first time.

BCZ2.37 The IASB considered that this transition would detrimentally affect financial statements because of the co-existence of two different accounting treatments (derivative and executory contract accounting) for similar contracts until all own use contracts that existed on transition would have matured. The IASB also noted that this effect may create a practical disincentive that would dissuade entities from making the election for new contracts. This could result in a failure to achieve the benefit of reducing accounting mismatches that the changes were designed to address.

BCZ2.38 Consequently, the IASB decided to provide entities with an option to elect accounting as at fair value through profit or loss for own use contracts that already exist on the date on which an entity applies the amendment for the first time. The IASB decided that that option would apply on an 'all-or-none basis' for all similar contracts in order to prevent selective use of this option for similar contracts. The IASB also noted that because these contracts would previously have been outside the scope of IFRS 7 *Financial Instruments: Disclosures*, entities would not have measured the fair value of these contracts for measurement or disclosure purposes. Consequently, restating comparatives would be impracticable because it would involve hindsight.

Business combination forward contracts

BCZ2.39 The IASB was advised that there was diversity in practice regarding the application of the exemption in paragraph 2(g) of IAS 39 (now paragraph 2.1(f) of IFRS 9).[5] That paragraph applies to particular contracts associated with a business combination and results in those contracts not being accounted for as derivatives while, for example, necessary regulatory and legal processes are being completed.

BCZ2.40 As part of the *Improvements to IFRSs* issued in April 2009, the IASB concluded that that paragraph should be restricted to forward contracts between an acquirer and a selling shareholder to buy or sell an acquiree in a business combination at a future acquisition date and should not apply to option contracts, whether or not currently exercisable, that on exercise will result in control of an entity.

BCZ2.41 The IASB concluded that the purpose of paragraph 2(g) is to exempt from the provisions of IAS 39 contracts for business combinations that are firmly committed to be completed. Once the business combination is consummated, the entity follows the requirements of IFRS 3. Paragraph 2(g) applies only when completion of the business combination is not dependent on further actions of either party (and only the passage of a normal period of time is required). Option contracts allow one party to control the occurrence or non-occurrence of future events depending on whether the option is exercised.

BCZ2.42 Several respondents to the Exposure Draft that proposed the amendment expressed the view that it should also apply to contracts to acquire investments in associates, referring to paragraph 20 of IAS 28. However, the acquisition of an interest in an associate represents the acquisition of a financial instrument. The acquisition of an interest in an associate does not represent an acquisition of a business with subsequent consolidation of the constituent net assets. The IASB noted that paragraph 20 of IAS 28 explains only the methodology used to account for investments in associates. This should not be taken to imply that the principles for business combinations and consolidations can be applied by analogy to accounting for investments in associates and joint ventures. The IASB concluded that paragraph 2(g) should not be applied by analogy to contracts to acquire investments in associates and similar transactions. This conclusion is consistent with the conclusion the IASB reached regarding impairment losses on investments in associates as noted in the *Improvements to IFRSs* issued in May 2008 and stated in paragraph BC27 of the Basis for Conclusions on IAS 28.

BCZ2.43 Some respondents to the Exposure Draft that proposed the amendment raised concerns about the proposed transition requirement. The IASB noted that determining the fair value of a currently outstanding contract when its

---

5 In October 2012 the IASB issued *Investment Entities* (Amendments to IFRS 10, IFRS 12 and IAS 27), which amended paragraph 2(g) of IAS 39 (now paragraph 2.1(f) of IFRS 9) to clarify that the exception should only apply to forward contracts that result in a business combination within the scope of IFRS 3 *Business Combinations*.

inception was before the effective date of this amendment would require the use of hindsight and might not achieve comparability. Accordingly, the IASB decided not to require retrospective application. The IASB also rejected applying the amendment prospectively only to new contracts entered into after the effective date because that would create a lack of comparability between contracts outstanding as of the effective date and contracts entered into after the effective date. Consequently, the IASB concluded that the amendment to paragraph 2(g) should be applied prospectively to all unexpired contracts for annual periods beginning on or after 1 January 2010.

Recognition and derecognition (Chapter 3)

Derecognition of a financial asset

The original IAS 39[6]

BCZ3.1 Under the original IAS 39, several concepts governed when a financial asset should be derecognised. It was not always clear when and in what order to apply those concepts. As a result, the derecognition requirements in the original IAS 39 were not applied consistently in practice.

BCZ3.2 As an example, the original IAS 39 was unclear about the extent to which risks and rewards of a transferred asset should be considered for the purpose of determining whether derecognition is appropriate and how risks and rewards should be assessed. In some cases (eg transfers with total returns swaps or unconditional written put options), the Standard specifically indicated whether derecognition was appropriate, whereas in others (eg credit guarantees) it was unclear. Also, some questioned whether the assessment should focus on risks and rewards or only risks and how different risks and rewards should be aggregated and weighed.

BCZ3.3 To illustrate, assume an entity sells a portfolio of short-term receivables of CU100[7] and provides a guarantee to the buyer for credit losses up to a specified amount (say CU20) that is less than the total amount of the receivables, but higher than the amount of expected losses (say CU5). In this case, should (a) the entire portfolio continue to be recognised, (b) the portion that is guaranteed continue to be recognised or (c) the portfolio be derecognised in full and a guarantee be recognised as a financial liability? The original IAS 39 did not give a clear answer and the IAS 39 Implementation Guidance Committee—a group set up by the IASB's predecessor body to resolve interpretative issues raised in practice—was unable to reach an agreement on how IAS 39 should be applied in this case. In developing proposals for improvements to IAS 39, the IASB concluded that it was important that IAS 39 should provide clear and consistent guidance on how to account for such a transaction.

---

6   In this Basis for Conclusions, the phrase 'the original IAS 39' refers to the Standard issued by the IASB's predecessor body, the International Accounting Standards Committee (IASC) in 1999 and revised in 2000.

7   In this Basis for Conclusions, monetary amounts are denominated in 'currency units (CU)'.

Exposure draft of proposed amendments to IAS 39 published in 2002

BCZ3.4   To resolve the problems, the exposure draft published in 2002 proposed an approach to derecognition under which a transferor of a financial asset continues to recognise that asset to the extent the transferor has a continuing involvement in it. Continuing involvement could be established in two ways: (a) a reacquisition provision (such as a call option, put option or repurchase agreement) and (b) a provision to pay or receive compensation based on changes in value of the transferred asset (such as a credit guarantee or net cash-settled option).

BCZ3.5   The purpose of the approach proposed in the exposure draft was to facilitate consistent implementation and application of IAS 39 by eliminating conflicting concepts and establishing an unambiguous, more internally consistent and workable approach to derecognition. The main benefits of the proposed approach were that it would greatly clarify IAS 39 and provide transparency on the balance sheet about any continuing involvement in a transferred asset.

Comments received

BCZ3.6   Many respondents to the exposure draft agreed that there were inconsistencies in the existing derecognition requirements in IAS 39. However, there was limited support for the proposed continuing involvement approach. Respondents expressed conceptual and practical concerns, including:

(a)   any benefits of the proposed changes did not outweigh the burden of adopting a different approach that had its own set of (as yet unidentified and unsolved) problems;

(b)   the proposed approach was a fundamental change from that in the original IAS 39;

(c)   the proposal did not achieve convergence with US GAAP;

(d)   the proposal was untested; and

(e)   the proposal was not consistent with the *Framework for the Preparation and Presentation of Financial Statements*.

BCZ3.7   Many respondents expressed the view that the basic approach in the original IAS 39 should be retained and the inconsistencies removed. The reasons included: (a) the existing IAS 39 had proven to be reasonable in concept and operational in practice and (b) the approach should not be changed until the IASB developed an alternative comprehensive approach.

Revisions to IAS 39

BCZ3.8   In response to the comments received, the IASB decided to revert to the derecognition concepts in the original IAS 39 and to clarify how and in what order the concepts should be applied. In particular, the IASB decided that an evaluation of the transfer of risks and rewards should precede an evaluation of the transfer of control for all types of transactions.

BCZ3.9   Although the structure and wording of the derecognition requirements were substantially amended, the IASB concluded that the requirements in the revised

IAS 39 should not be substantially different from those in the original IAS 39. In support of this conclusion, it noted that the application of the requirements in the revised IAS 39 generally resulted in answers that could have been obtained under the original IAS 39. In addition, although there would be a need to apply judgement to evaluate whether substantially all risks and rewards had been retained, this type of judgement was not new compared with the original IAS 39. However, the revised requirements clarified the application of the concepts in circumstances in which it was previously unclear how IAS 39 should be applied (this guidance is now in IFRS 9). The IASB concluded that it would be inappropriate to revert to the original IAS 39 without such clarifications.

BCZ3.10 The IASB also decided to include guidance in the Standard that clarified how to evaluate the concepts of risks and rewards and of control. The IASB regarded such guidance as important to provide a framework for applying the concepts in IAS 39 (this guidance is now in IFRS 9). Although judgement was still necessary to apply the concepts in practice, the guidance was expected to increase consistency in how the concepts were applied.

BCZ3.11 More specifically, the IASB decided that the transfer of risks and rewards should be evaluated by comparing the entity's exposure before and after the transfer to the variability in the amounts and timing of the net cash flows of the transferred asset. If the entity's exposure, on a present value basis, had not changed significantly, the entity would conclude that it had retained substantially all risks and rewards. In this case, the IASB concluded that the asset should continue to be recognised. This accounting treatment was consistent with the treatment of repurchase transactions and some assets subject to deep in-the-money options under the original IAS 39. It was also consistent with how some interpreted the original IAS 39 when an entity sells a portfolio of short-term receivables but retains all substantive risks through the issue of a guarantee to compensate for all expected credit losses (see the example in paragraph BCZ3.3).

BCZ3.12 The IASB decided that control should be evaluated by looking to whether the transferee has the practical ability to sell the asset. If the transferee could sell the asset (eg because the asset was readily obtainable in the market and the transferee could obtain a replacement asset if it needed to return the asset to the transferor), the transferor had not retained control because the transferor did not control the transferee's use of the asset. If the transferee could not sell the asset (eg because the transferor had a call option and the asset was not readily obtainable in the market, so that the transferee could not obtain a replacement asset), the transferor had retained control because the transferee was not free to use the asset as its own.

BCZ3.13 The original IAS 39 also did not contain guidance on when a part of a financial asset could be considered for derecognition. The IASB decided to include such guidance in the Standard to clarify the issue (this guidance is now in IFRS 9). It decided that an entity should apply the derecognition principles to a part of a financial asset only if that part contained no risks and rewards relating to the part not being considered for derecognition. Accordingly, a part of a financial asset would be considered for derecognition only if it comprised:

(a)   only specifically identified cash flows from a financial asset (or a group of similar financial assets);

(b)   only a fully proportionate (pro rata) share of the cash flows from a financial asset (or a group of similar financial assets); or

(c)   only a fully proportionate (pro rata) share of specifically identified cash flows from a financial asset (or a group of similar financial assets).

In all other cases the derecognition principles would be applied to the financial asset in its entirety.

Arrangements under which an entity retains the contractual rights to receive the cash flows of a financial asset but assumes a contractual obligation to pay the cash flows to one or more recipients

BCZ3.14   The original IAS 39 did not provide explicit guidance about the extent to which derecognition is appropriate for contractual arrangements in which an entity retains its contractual right to receive the cash flows from an asset, but assumes a contractual obligation to pay those cash flows to another entity (a 'pass-through arrangement'). Questions were raised in practice about the appropriate accounting treatment and divergent interpretations evolved for more complex structures.

BCZ3.15   To illustrate the issue using a simple example, assume the following. Entity A makes a five-year interest-bearing loan (the 'original asset') of CU100 to Entity B. Entity A then enters into an agreement with Entity C in which, in exchange for a cash payment of CU90, Entity A agrees to pass to Entity C 90 per cent of all principal and interest payments collected from Entity B (as, when and if collected). Entity A accepts no obligation to make any payments to Entity C other than 90 per cent of exactly what has been received from Entity B. Entity A provides no guarantee to Entity C about the performance of the loan and has no rights to retain 90 per cent of the cash collected from Entity B nor any obligation to pay cash to Entity C if cash has not been received from Entity B. In the example above, does Entity A have a loan asset of CU100 and a liability of CU90 or does it have an asset of CU10? To make the example more complex, what if Entity A first transfers the loan to a consolidated special purpose entity (SPE), which in turn passes through to investors the cash flows from the asset? Does the accounting treatment change because Entity A first sold the asset to an SPE?[8]

BCZ3.16   To address these issues, the exposure draft of proposed amendments to IAS 39 in 2002 included guidance to clarify under which conditions pass-through arrangements could be treated as a transfer of the underlying financial asset. The IASB concluded that an entity does not have an asset and a liability, as defined in the Framework,[9] when it enters into an arrangement to pass through cash flows from an asset and that arrangement meets specified conditions. In

---

8   SIC-12 Consolidation—Special Purpose Entities was withdrawn and superseded by IFRS 10 Consolidated Financial Statements issued in May 2011. There is no longer specific accounting guidance for special purpose entities because IFRS 10 applies to all types of entities.

9   References to the Framework are to IASC's Framework for the Preparation and Presentation of Financial Statements, adopted by the IASB in 2001. In September 2010 the IASB replaced the Framework with the Conceptual Framework for Financial Reporting.

these cases, the entity acts more as an agent of the eventual recipients of the cash flows than as an owner of the asset. Accordingly, to the extent that those conditions are met the arrangement is treated as a transfer and considered for derecognition even though the entity may continue to collect cash flows from the asset. Conversely, to the extent the conditions are not met, the entity acts more as an owner of the asset with the result that the asset should continue to be recognised.

BCZ3.17   Respondents to the exposure draft (2002) were generally supportive of the proposed changes. Some respondents asked for further clarification of the requirements and the interaction with the requirements for consolidation of special purpose entities (in SIC-12 *Consolidation—Special Purpose Entities*). Respondents in the securitisation industry noted that under the proposed guidance many securitisation structures would not qualify for derecognition.

BCZ3.18   Considering these and other comments, the IASB decided to proceed with its proposals to issue guidance on pass-through arrangements and to clarify that guidance in finalising the revised IAS 39 (this guidance is now in IFRS 9).

BCZ3.19   The IASB concluded that the following three conditions must be met for treating a contractual arrangement to pass through cash flows from a financial asset as a transfer of that asset:

(a)   The entity has no obligation to pay amounts to the eventual recipients unless it collects equivalent amounts from the original asset. However, the entity is allowed to make short-term advances to the eventual recipient so long as it has the right of full recovery of the amount lent plus accrued interest.

(b)   The entity is prohibited by the terms of the transfer contract from selling or pledging the original asset other than as security to the eventual recipients for the obligation to pay them cash flows.

(c)   The entity has an obligation to remit any cash flows it collects on behalf of the eventual recipients without material delay. In addition, during the short settlement period, the entity is not entitled to reinvest such cash flows except for investments in cash or cash equivalents and where any interest earned from such investments is remitted to the eventual recipients.

BCZ3.20   These conditions followed from the definitions of assets and liabilities in the *Framework*. Condition (a) indicates that the transferor has no liability (because there is no present obligation to pay cash), and conditions (b) and (c) indicate that the transferor has no asset (because the transferor does not control the future economic benefits associated with the transferred asset).

BCZ3.21   The IASB decided that the derecognition tests that apply to other transfers of financial assets (ie the tests of transferring substantially all the risks and rewards and control) should also apply to arrangements to pass through cash flows that meet the three conditions but do not involve a fully proportional share of all or specifically identified cash flows. Thus, if the three conditions are met and the entity passes on a fully proportional share, either of all cash flows (as in the example in paragraph BCZ3.15) or of specifically identified cash flows (eg 10 per cent of all interest cash flows), the proportion sold is derecognised, provided the entity has transferred substantially all the risks and rewards of ownership. Thus, in the example in paragraph BCZ3.15, Entity A would report a loan asset of CU10 and derecognise CU90. Similarly, if an entity enters into an arrangement that meets the three conditions above, but the arrangement is not on a fully proportionate basis, the contractual arrangement would have to meet the general derecognition conditions to qualify for derecognition. This ensures consistency in the application of the derecognition model, whether a transaction is structured as a transfer of the contractual right to receive the cash flows of a financial asset or as an arrangement to pass through cash flows.

BCZ3.22   To illustrate a disproportionate arrangement using a simple example, assume the following. Entity A originates a portfolio of five-year interest-bearing loans of CU10,000. Entity A then enters into an agreement with Entity C in which, in exchange for a cash payment of CU9,000, Entity A agrees to pay to Entity C the first CU9,000 (plus interest) of cash collected from the loan portfolio. Entity A retains rights to the last CU1,000 (plus interest), ie it retains a subordinated residual interest. If Entity A collects, say, only CU8,000 of its loans of CU10,000 because some debtors default, Entity A would pass on to Entity C all of the CU8,000 collected and Entity A keeps nothing of the CU8,000 collected. If Entity A collects CU9,500, it passes CU9,000 to Entity C and retains CU500. In this case, if Entity A retains substantially all the risks and rewards of ownership because the subordinated retained interest absorbs all of the likely variability in net cash flows, the loans continue to be recognised in their entirety even if the three pass-through conditions are met.

BCZ3.23   The IASB recognised that many securitisations might fail to qualify for derecognition either because one or more of the three conditions (now in paragraph 3.2.5 of IFRS 9) were not met or because the entity has retained substantially all the risks and rewards of ownership.

BCZ3.24   Whether a transfer of a financial asset qualifies for derecognition does not differ depending on whether the transfer is direct to investors or through a consolidated SPE or trust that obtains the financial assets and, in turn, transfers a portion of those financial assets to third-party investors.

Transfers that do not qualify for derecognition

BCZ3.25   The original IAS 39 did not provide guidance about how to account for a transfer of a financial asset that does not qualify for derecognition. The amendments included such guidance (that guidance is now in IFRS 9). To ensure that the accounting reflects the rights and obligations that the transferor has in relation to the transferred asset, there is a need to consider the accounting for the asset as well as the accounting for the associated liability.

BCZ3.26   When an entity retains substantially all the risks and rewards of the asset (eg in a repurchase transaction), there are generally no special accounting considerations because the entity retains upside and downside exposure to gains and losses resulting from the transferred asset. Consequently, the asset continues to be recognised in its entirety and the proceeds received are recognised as a liability. Similarly, the entity continues to recognise any income from the asset along with any expense incurred on the associated liability.

Continuing involvement in a transferred asset

BCZ3.27 The IASB decided that if the entity determines that it has neither retained nor transferred substantially all of the risks and rewards of an asset and that it has retained control, the entity should continue to recognise the asset to the extent of its continuing involvement. This is to reflect the transferor's continuing exposure to the risks and rewards of the asset and that this exposure is not related to the entire asset, but is limited in amount. The IASB noted that precluding derecognition to the extent of the continuing involvement is useful to users of financial statements in such cases, because it reflects the entity's retained exposure to the risks and rewards of the financial asset better than full derecognition.

BCZ3.28 When the entity transfers some significant risks and rewards and retains others and derecognition is precluded because the entity retains control of the transferred asset, the entity no longer retains all the upside and downside exposure to gains and losses resulting from the transferred asset. Consequently, the revised IAS 39 required (and IFRS 9 now requires) the asset and the associated liability to be measured in a way that ensures that any changes in value of the transferred asset that are not attributed to the entity are not recognised by the entity.

BCZ3.29 For example, special measurement and income recognition issues arise if derecognition is precluded because the transferor has retained a call option or written a put option and the asset is measured at fair value. In those situations, in the absence of additional guidance, application of the general measurement and income recognition requirements for financial assets and financial liabilities may result in accounting that does not represent the transferor's rights and obligations related to the transfer.

Improved disclosure requirements issued in October 2010

BC3.30 In March 2009 the IASB published an Exposure Draft *Derecognition* (Proposed amendments to IAS 39 and IFRS 7) (the '2009 Derecognition Exposure Draft'). In June 2009 the IASB held public round tables in North America, Asia and Europe to discuss the proposals in the 2009 Derecognition Exposure Draft. In addition to the round tables, the IASB undertook an extensive outreach programme with users, preparers, regulators, auditors, trade associations and others.

BC3.31 However, in June 2010 the IASB revised its strategy and work plan. The IASB and the US Financial Accounting Standards Board (FASB) decided that their near-term priority should be to increase the transparency and comparability of their standards by improving and aligning US GAAP and IFRS disclosure requirements for financial assets transferred to another entity. The boards also decided to conduct additional research and analysis, including a post-implementation review of the FASB's recently amended requirements, as a basis for assessing the nature and direction of any further efforts to improve or align IFRS and US GAAP. As a result, the IASB finalised the disclosure requirements that were included in the 2009 Derecognition Exposure Draft with a view to aligning the disclosure requirements in IFRS with US GAAP requirements for transfers of financial assets. Those disclosure requirements were issued in October 2010 as an amendment to IFRS 7. In October 2010 the requirements in IAS 39 for derecognition of financial assets and financial liabilities were carried forward unchanged to IFRS 9.

BC3.32 *[This paragraph refers to amendments that are not yet effective, and is therefore not included in this edition.]*

Classification (Chapter 4)

Classification of financial assets

BC4.1 In IFRS 9 as issued in 2009 the IASB aimed to help users to understand the financial reporting of financial assets by:

(a) reducing the number of classification categories and providing a clearer rationale for measuring financial assets in a particular way that replaces the numerous categories in IAS 39, each of which has specific rules dictating how an asset can or must be classified;

(b) applying a single impairment method to all financial assets not measured at fair value, which replaces the many different impairment methods that are associated with the numerous classification categories in IAS 39; and

(c) aligning the measurement attribute of financial assets with the way the entity manages its financial assets ('business model') and their contractual cash flow characteristics, thus providing relevant and useful information to users for their assessment of the amounts, timing and uncertainty of the entity's future cash flows.

BC4.2 The IASB believes that IFRS 9 both helps users to understand and use the financial reporting of financial assets and eliminates much of the complexity in IAS 39. The IASB disagrees with the assertion made by a dissenting IASB member that IFRS 9 does not meet the objective of reducing the number of classification categories for financial assets and eliminating the specific rules associated with those categories. Unlike IAS 39, IFRS 9 provides a clear rationale for measuring a financial asset at either amortised cost or fair value, and hence helps users to understand the financial reporting of financial assets. IFRS 9 aligns the measurement attribute of financial assets with the way the entity manages its financial assets ('business model') and their contractual cash flow characteristics. In so doing, IFRS 9 significantly reduces complexity by eliminating the numerous rules associated with each classification category in IAS 39. Consistently with all other financial assets, hybrid contracts with financial asset hosts are classified and measured in their entirety, thereby eliminating the complex and rule-based requirements in IAS 39 for embedded derivatives. Furthermore, IFRS 9 requires a single impairment method, which replaces the different impairment methods associated with the many classification categories in IAS 39. The IASB believes that these changes will help users to understand the financial reporting of financial assets and to better assess the amounts, timing and uncertainty of future cash flows.

Measurement categories for financial assets

BC4.3   Some users of financial statements support a single measurement method—fair value—for all financial assets. They view fair value as more relevant than other measurements in helping them to assess the effect of current economic events on an entity. They assert that having one measurement attribute for all financial assets promotes consistency in valuation, presentation and disclosure and improves the usefulness of financial statements.

BC4.4   However, many users and others, including many preparers and auditors of financial statements and regulators, do not support the recognition in the statement of comprehensive income of changes in fair value for financial assets that are not held for trading or are not managed on a fair value basis. Some users say that they often value an entity on the basis of its business model and that in some circumstances cost-based information provides relevant information that can be used to predict likely actual cash flows.

BC4.5   Some, including some of those who generally support the broad application of fair value for financial assets, raise concerns about the use of fair value when fair value cannot be determined within a narrow range. Those views were consistent with the general concerns raised during the financial crisis. Many also believe that other issues, including financial statement presentation, need to be addressed before a comprehensive fair value measurement requirement would be feasible.

BC4.6   In response to those views, the IASB decided that measuring all financial assets at fair value is not the most appropriate approach to improving the financial reporting for financial instruments. Accordingly, the 2009 Exposure Draft *Financial Instruments: Classification and Measurement* (the '2009 Classification and Measurement Exposure Draft') proposed that entities should classify financial assets into two primary measurement categories: amortised cost and fair value (the 'mixed attribute approach'). The IASB noted that both of those measurement methods can provide useful information to users of financial statements for particular types of financial assets in particular circumstances.

BC4.7   Almost all respondents to the 2009 Classification and Measurement Exposure Draft supported the mixed attribute approach, stating that amortised cost provides relevant and useful information about particular financial assets in particular circumstances because it provides information about the entity's likely actual cash flows. Some respondents said that fair value does not provide such information because it assumes that the financial asset is sold or transferred on the measurement date.

BC4.8   Accordingly, IFRS 9 requires some financial assets to be measured at amortised cost if particular conditions are met.

Fair value information in the statements of financial position and financial performance

BC4.9   Some respondents to the 2009 Classification and Measurement Exposure Draft proposed that fair value information should be presented in the statement of financial position for financial assets measured at amortised cost. Some of those supporting such presentation said that the information provided would be more reliable and timely if it were required to be presented in the statement of financial position instead of in the notes.

BC4.10 The IASB also considered whether the total gains and losses for the period related to fair value measurements in Level 3 of the fair value measurement hierarchy (paragraph 27A of IFRS 7 describes the levels in the fair value hierarchy[10]) should be presented separately in the statement of comprehensive income. Those supporting such presentation said that its prominence would draw attention to how much of the total fair value gain or loss for the period was attributable to fair value measurements that are subject to more measurement uncertainty.

BC4.11 The IASB decided that it would reconsider both issues at a future date. The IASB noted that the Level 3 gains or losses for the period are required to be disclosed in the notes to the financial statements in accordance with IFRS 7.[11] The IASB also noted that neither proposal had been exposed for public comment and further consultation was required. The IASB decided that these two issues should form part of convergence discussions with the FASB.

Approach to classifying financial assets

BC4.12 The 2009 Classification and Measurement Exposure Draft proposed that an entity should classify its financial assets into two primary measurement categories on the basis of the financial assets' characteristics and the entity's business model for managing them. Thus, a financial asset would be measured at amortised cost if two conditions were met:

(a) the financial asset has only basic loan features; and

(b) the financial asset is managed on a contractual yield basis.

A financial asset that did not meet both conditions would be measured at fair value.

BC4.13 Most respondents supported classification on the basis of the contractual terms of the financial asset and how an entity manages groups of financial assets. Although they agreed with the principles proposed in the 2009 Classification and Measurement Exposure Draft, some did not agree with the way the approach was described and said that more application guidance was needed, in particular to address the following issues:

(a) the order in which the two conditions are considered;

(b) how the 'managed on a contractual yield basis' condition should be applied; and

(c) how the 'basic loan features' condition should be applied.

---

10 IFRS 13 *Fair Value Measurement*, issued in May 2011, defines fair value and contains requirements for measuring fair value and for disclosing information about fair value measurements. IFRS 13 contains a three-level fair value hierarchy for the inputs used in valuation techniques to measure fair value and for the related disclosures. As a consequence paragraph 27A of IFRS 7 has been deleted.

11 IFRS 13, issued in May 2011, requires disclosures about fair value measurements. As a consequence paragraph 27B(c) and (d) of IFRS 7 has been deleted.

BC4.14　Most respondents agreed that the two conditions for determining how financial assets are measured were necessary. However, many questioned the order in which the two conditions should be considered. The IASB agreed with those who commented that it would be more efficient for an entity to consider the business model condition first. Consequently, the IASB clarified that entities would consider the business model first. However, the IASB noted that the contractual cash flow characteristics of any financial asset within a business model that has the objective of collecting contractual cash flows must also be assessed to ensure that amortised cost provides relevant information to users.

The entity's business model

BC4.15　The IASB concluded that an entity's business model affects the predictive quality of contractual cash flows—ie whether the likely actual cash flows will result primarily from the collection of contractual cash flows. Accordingly, the 2009 Classification and Measurement Exposure Draft proposed that a financial asset should be measured at amortised cost only if it is 'managed on a contractual yield basis'. This condition was intended to ensure that the measurement of a financial asset provides information that is useful to users of financial statements in predicting likely actual cash flows.

BC4.16　Almost all respondents to the exposure draft agreed that classification and measurement should reflect how an entity manages its financial assets. However, most expressed concern that the term 'managed on a contractual yield basis' would not adequately describe that principle and that more guidance was needed.

BC4.17　In August 2009 the FASB posted on its website a description of its tentative approach to classification and measurement of financial instruments. That approach also considers the entity's business model. Under that approach, financial instruments would be measured at fair value through profit or loss unless:

> ... an entity's business strategy is to hold debt instruments with principal amounts for collection or payment(s) of contractual cash flows rather than to sell or settle the financial instruments with a third party ...

The FASB also provided explanatory text:

> ... an entity's business strategy for a financial instrument would be evaluated based on how the entity manages its financial instruments rather than based on the entity's intent for an individual financial instrument. The entity also would demonstrate that it holds a high proportion of similar instruments for long periods of time relative to their contractual terms.

BC4.18　The IASB had intended 'managed on a contractual yield basis' to describe a similar condition. However, it decided not to use the FASB's proposed guidance because the additional guidance included would still necessitate significant judgement. In addition, the IASB noted that the FASB's proposed approach might be viewed as very similar to the notion of 'held to maturity' in IAS 39, which could result in 'bright line' guidance on how to apply it. Most respondents believed the IASB should avoid such bright lines and that an entity should be required to exercise judgement.

BC4.19 Therefore, in response to the concerns noted in paragraph BC4.16, the IASB clarified the condition by requiring an entity to measure a financial asset at amortised cost only if the objective of the entity's business model is to hold the financial asset to collect the contractual cash flows. The IASB also clarified in the application guidance that:

(a) it is expected that an entity may sell some financial assets that it holds with an objective of collecting the contractual cash flows. Very few business models entail holding all instruments until maturity. However, frequent buying and selling of financial assets is not consistent with a business model of holding financial assets to collect contractual cash flows.

(b) an entity needs to use judgement to determine at what level this condition should be applied. That determination is made on the basis of how an entity manages its business. It is not made at the level of an individual financial asset.

BC4.20 The IASB noted that an entity's business model does not relate to a choice (ie it is not a voluntary designation) but instead it is a matter of fact that can be observed by the way an entity is managed and information is provided to its management.

BC4.21 For example, if an investment bank uses a trading business model, it could not easily become a savings bank that uses an 'originate and hold' business model. Consequently, a business model is very different from 'management intentions', which can relate to a single instrument. The IASB concluded that sales or transfers of financial instruments before maturity would not be inconsistent with a business model with an objective of collecting contractual cash flows, as long as such transactions were consistent with that business model; instead of with a business model that has the objective of realising changes in fair values.

Contractual cash flow characteristics

BC4.22 The 2009 Classification and Measurement Exposure Draft proposed that only financial instruments with basic loan features could be measured at amortised cost. It specified that a financial instrument has basic loan features if its contractual terms give rise on specified dates to cash flows that are solely payments of principal and interest on the principal amount outstanding. For the purposes of this condition, interest is consideration for the time value of money and the credit risk associated with the principal amount outstanding during a particular period of time, which may include a premium for liquidity risk.

BC4.23 The objective of the effective interest method for financial instruments measured at amortised cost is to allocate interest revenue or expense to the relevant period. Cash flows that are interest always have a close relation to the amount advanced to the debtor (the 'funded' amount) because interest is consideration for the time value of money and the credit risk associated with the issuer of the instrument and with the instrument itself. The IASB noted that the effective interest method is not an appropriate method to allocate cash flows that are not principal or interest on the principal amount outstanding. The IASB concluded that if a financial asset contains contractual cash flows that are not principal or interest on the principal amount outstanding then a valuation overlay to contractual cash flows (fair value) is required to ensure that the reported financial information provides useful information.

BC4.24 Most respondents to the 2009 Classification and Measurement Exposure Draft agreed with the principle that classification should reflect the contractual terms of the financial asset. However, many objected to the label 'basic loan features' and requested more guidance to apply the principle to particular financial assets. Respondents were also concerned that the 2009 Classification and Measurement Exposure Draft did not discuss 'immaterial' or 'insignificant' features that they believed ought not to affect classification.

BC4.25 The IASB decided to clarify how contractual cash flow characteristics should affect classification and improve the examples that illustrate how the condition should be applied. It decided not to add application guidance clarifying that the notion of materiality applies to this condition, because that notion applies to every item in the financial statements. However, it did add application guidance that a contractual cash flow characteristic does not affect the classification of a financial asset if it is 'not genuine'.

Application of the two classification conditions to particular financial assets

Investments in contractually linked instruments (tranches)

BC4.26 A structured investment vehicle may issue different tranches to create a 'waterfall' structure that prioritises the payments by the issuer to the holders of the different tranches. In typical waterfall structures, multiple contractually linked instruments effect concentrations of credit risk in which payments to holders are prioritised. Such structures specify the order in which any losses that the issuer incurs are allocated to the tranches. The 2009 Classification and Measurement Exposure Draft concluded that tranches providing credit protection (albeit on a contingent basis) to other tranches are leveraged because they expose themselves to higher credit risk by writing credit protection to other tranches. Hence their cash flows do not represent solely payments of principal and interest on the principal amount outstanding. Thus, only the most senior tranche could have basic loan features and might qualify for measurement at amortised cost, because only the most senior tranche would receive credit protection in all situations.

BC4.27 The 2009 Classification and Measurement Exposure Draft proposed that the classification principle should be based on whether a tranche could provide credit protection to any other tranches in any possible scenario. In the IASB's view, a contract that contains credit concentration features that create ongoing subordination (not only in a liquidation scenario) would include contractual cash flows that represent a premium for providing credit protection to other tranches. Only the most senior tranche does not receive such a premium.

BC4.28 In proposing this approach, the IASB concluded that subordination in itself should not preclude amortised cost measurement. The ranking of an entity's instruments is a common form of subordination that affects almost all lending transactions. Commercial law (including bankruptcy law) typically sets out a basic ranking for creditors. This is required because not all creditors' claims are contractual (eg claims regarding damages for unlawful behaviour and for tax liabilities or social insurance contributions). Although it is often difficult to determine exactly the degree of leverage resulting from this subordination, the IASB believes that it is reasonable to assume that commercial law does not intend to create leveraged credit exposure for general creditors such as trade creditors. Thus, the IASB believes that the credit risk associated with general creditors does not preclude the contractual cash flows representing the payments of principal and interest on the principal amount outstanding. Consequently, the credit risk associated with any secured or senior liabilities ranking above general creditors should also not preclude the contractual cash flows from representing payments of principal and interest on the principal amount outstanding.

BC4.29 Almost all respondents disagreed with the approach in the 2009 Classification and Measurement Exposure Draft for investments in contractually linked instruments for the following reasons:

(a) It focused on form and legal structure instead of the economic characteristics of the financial instruments.

(b) It would create structuring opportunities because of the focus on the existence of a waterfall structure, without consideration of the characteristics of the underlying instruments.

(c) It would be an exception to the overall classification model, driven by anti-abuse considerations.

BC4.30 In particular, respondents argued that the proposals in the 2009 Classification and Measurement Exposure Draft would conclude that some tranches provide credit protection and therefore were ineligible for measurement at amortised cost, even though that tranche might have a lower credit risk than the underlying pool of instruments that would themselves be eligible for measurement at amortised cost.

BC4.31 The IASB did not agree that the proposals in the 2009 Classification and Measurement Exposure Draft were an exception to the overall classification model. In the IASB's view, those proposals were consistent with many respondents' view that any financial instrument that creates contractual subordination should be subject to the proposed classification criteria and no specific guidance should be required to apply the classification approach to these instruments. However, it noted that, for contractually linked instruments that effect concentrations of credit risk, many respondents did not agree that the contractual cash flow characteristics determined by the terms and conditions of the financial asset in isolation best reflected the economic characteristics of that financial asset.

BC4.32 Respondents proposed other approaches in which an investor 'looks through' to the underlying pool of instruments of a waterfall structure and measures the instruments at fair value if looking through is not possible. They made the following points:

(a) *Practicability*: The securitisation transactions intended to be addressed were generally over-the-counter transactions in which the parties involved had sufficient information about the assets to perform an analysis of the underlying pool of instruments.

(b) *Complexity*: Complex accounting judgement was appropriate to reflect the complex economic characteristics of the instrument. In particular, in order to obtain an understanding of the effects of the contractual terms and conditions, an investor would have to understand the underlying pool of instruments. Also, requiring fair value measurement if it were not practicable to look through to the underlying pool of instruments would allow an entity to avoid such complexity.

(c) *Mechanics*: Amortised cost measurement should be available only if all of the instruments in the underlying pool of instruments had contractual cash flows that represented payments of principal and interest on the principal amount outstanding. Some also suggested that instruments that change the cash flow variability of the underlying pool of instruments in a way that is consistent with representing solely payments of principal and interest on the principal amount outstanding, or aligned currency/interest rates with the issued notes, should not preclude amortised cost measurement.

(d) *Relative exposure to credit risk*: Many favoured use of a probability-weighted approach to assess whether an instrument has a lower or higher exposure to credit risk than the average credit risk of the underlying pool of instruments.

BC4.33 The IASB was persuaded that classification solely on the basis of the contractual features of the financial asset being assessed for classification would not capture the economic characteristics of the instruments when a concentrated credit risk arises through contractual linkage. Consequently, the IASB decided that, unless it is impracticable, an entity should 'look through' to assess the underlying cash flow characteristics of the financial assets and to assess the exposure to credit risk of those financial assets relative to the underlying pool of instruments.

BC4.34 The IASB concluded that the nature of contractually linked instruments that effect concentrations of credit risk justifies this approach because the variability of cash flows from the underlying pool of instruments is a reference point, and tranching only reallocates credit risk. Thus, if the contractual cash flows of the assets in the underlying pool represent payments of principal and interest on the principal amount outstanding, any tranche that is exposed to the same or lower credit risk (as evidenced by the cash flow variability of the tranche relative to the overall cash flow variability of the underlying instrument pool) would also be deemed to represent payments of principal and interest on the principal amount outstanding. The IASB also took the view that such an approach would address many of the concerns raised in the comment letters with regard to structuring opportunities and the focus on the contractual form of the financial asset, instead of its underlying economic characteristics. The IASB also noted that in order to understand and make the judgement about whether particular types of financial assets have the required cash flow characteristics, an entity would have to understand the characteristics of the underlying issuer to ensure that the instrument's cash flows are solely payments of principal and interest on the principal amount outstanding.

BC4.35 To apply this approach, the IASB decided that an entity should:

(a) determine whether the contractual terms of the issued instrument (the financial asset being classified) give rise to cash flows that are solely payments of principal and interest on the principal amount outstanding. The IASB concluded that the issued instrument must have contractual cash flows that are solely payments of principal and interest on the principal amount outstanding.

(b) look through to the underlying pool of instruments until it can identify the instruments that are creating (instead of simply passing through) the cash flows.

(c) determine whether one or more of the instruments in the underlying pool has contractual cash flows that are solely payments of principal and interest on the principal amount outstanding. The IASB concluded that the underlying pool must contain one or more instruments that have contractual cash flows that are solely payments of principal and interest on the principal amount outstanding.

(d) assess whether any other instruments in the underlying pool only:

(i) reduce the cash flow variability of the underlying pool of instruments in a way that is consistent with representing solely payments of principal and interest on the principal amount outstanding, or

(ii) align the cash flows of the issued financial assets with the underlying pool of financial instruments.

The IASB concluded that the existence of such instruments does not preclude the cash flows from representing solely payments of principal and interest on the principal amount outstanding. The IASB determined that the existence of other instruments in the pool would, however, preclude the cash flows representing solely payments of principal and interest on the principal amount outstanding. For example, an underlying pool that contains government bonds and an instrument that swaps government credit risk for (riskier) corporate credit risk would not have cash flows that represent solely principal and interest on the principal amount outstanding.

(e) measure at fair value any issued instrument in which any of the financial instruments in the underlying pool:

(i) have cash flows that do not represent solely payments of principal and interest on the principal amount outstanding; or

(ii) could change so that cash flows may not represent solely payments of principal and interest on the principal amount outstanding at any point in the future.

(f)   measure at fair value any issued instrument whose exposure to credit risk in the underlying pool of financial instruments is greater than the exposure to credit risk of the underlying pool of financial instruments. The IASB decided that if the range of expected losses on the issued instrument is greater than the weighted average range of expected losses on the underlying pool of financial instruments, then the issued instrument should be measured at fair value.

BC4.36   The IASB also decided that if it were not practicable to look through to the underlying pool of financial instruments, entities should measure the issued instrument at fair value.

Financial assets acquired at a discount that reflects incurred credit losses

BC4.37   The 2009 Classification and Measurement Exposure Draft proposed that if a financial asset is acquired at a discount that reflects incurred credit losses, it cannot be measured at amortised cost because:

(a)   the entity does not hold such financial assets to collect the cash flows arising from those assets' contractual terms; and

(b)   an investor acquiring a financial asset at such a discount believes that the actual losses will be less than the losses that are reflected in the purchase price. Thus, that asset creates exposure to significant variability in actual cash flows and such variability is not interest.

BC4.38   Almost all respondents disagreed with the IASB's conclusion that these assets cannot be held to collect the contractual cash flows. They regarded that conclusion as an exception to a classification approach based on the entity's business model for managing the financial assets. In particular, they noted that entities could acquire and subsequently manage such assets as part of an otherwise performing asset portfolio for which the objective of the entity's business model is to hold the assets to collect contractual cash flows.

BC4.39   Respondents also noted that an entity's expectations about actual future cash flows are not the same as the contractual cash flows of the financial asset. Those expectations are irrelevant to an assessment of the financial asset's contractual cash flow characteristics.

BC4.40   The IASB agreed that the general classification approach in IFRS 9 should apply to financial assets acquired at a discount that reflects incurred credit losses. Thus, when such assets meet the conditions in paragraph 4.1.2, they are measured at amortised cost.

Alternative approaches to classifying assets

BC4.41   In its deliberations leading to the 2009 Classification and Measurement Exposure Draft, the IASB discussed alternative approaches to classification and measurement. In particular, it considered an approach in which financial assets that have basic loan features, are managed on a contractual yield basis and meet the definition of loans and receivables in IAS 39 would be measured at amortised cost. All other financial assets would be measured at fair value. The fair value changes for each period for those financial assets with basic loan features that are managed on a contractual yield basis would be disaggregated and presented as follows:

(a) changes in recognised value determined on an amortised cost basis (including impairments determined using the incurred loss impairment requirements in IAS 39) would be presented in profit or loss; and

(b) any difference between the amortised cost measure in (a) and the fair value change for the period would be presented in other comprehensive income.

BC4.42 The IASB also considered variants in which all financial assets and financial liabilities would be measured at fair value. One variant would be to present both the amounts in paragraph BC4.41(a) and (b) in profit or loss, but separately. Another variant would be to measure all financial instruments (including financial assets that meet the two conditions specified in the 2009 Classification and Measurement Exposure Draft and meet the definition of loans and receivables in IAS 39) at fair value in the statement of financial position. All financial instruments (including financial liabilities) with basic loan features that are managed on a contractual yield basis would be disaggregated and presented as described in paragraph BC4.41(a) and (b).

BC4.43 Respondents noted that the alternative approach described in paragraph BC4.41 and both variants described in paragraph BC4.42 would result in more financial assets and financial liabilities being measured at fair value. Respondents also noted that the alternative approach would apply only to financial assets. Lastly, almost all respondents noted that splitting gains and losses between profit or loss and other comprehensive income would increase complexity and reduce understandability. The IASB concluded that those approaches would not result in more useful information than the approach in IFRS 9 and did not consider them further.

BC4.44 The IASB also considered and rejected the following approaches to classification:

(a) *Classification based on the definition of held for trading:* A few respondents suggested that all financial assets and financial liabilities that are not 'held for trading' should be eligible for measurement at amortised cost. However, in the IASB's view, the notion of 'held for trading' is too narrow and cannot appropriately reflect all situations in which amortised cost does not provide useful information.

(b) *Three-category approach:* Some respondents suggested retaining a three-category approach, ie including a third category similar to the available-for-sale category in IAS 39. However, in the IASB's view, such an approach would neither significantly improve nor reduce the complexity of the reporting for financial instruments.

(c) *Classification based only on the business model:* A small number of respondents thought the contractual terms of the instrument condition was unnecessary and that classification should depend solely on the entity's business model for managing financial instruments. However, in the IASB's view, determining classification solely on the basis of how an entity manages its financial instruments would result in misleading information that is not useful to a user in understanding the risks associated with complex or risky instruments. The IASB concluded, as had almost all respondents, that the contractual cash flow characteristics condition is required to ensure that amortised cost is used only when it provides information that is useful in predicting the entity's future cash flows.

(d)   *Amortised cost as the default option:* The IASB considered developing conditions that specified when a financial asset must be measured at fair value, with the requirement that all other financial instruments would be measured at amortised cost. The IASB rejected that approach because it believes that new conditions would have to be developed in the future to address innovative financial products. In addition, the IASB noted that such an approach would not be practical because an entity can apply amortised cost only to some types of financial instruments.

(e)   *Originated loan approach:* In developing an approach to distinguish between financial assets measured at fair value and amortised cost the IASB considered a model in which only loans originated by the entity would qualify for amortised cost measurement. The IASB acknowledged that for originated instruments the entity potentially has better information about the future contractual cash flows and credit risk than for purchased loans. However, the IASB decided not to pursue that approach, mainly because some entities manage originated and purchased loans in the same portfolio. Distinguishing between originated and purchased loans, which would be done mainly for accounting purposes, would involve systems changes. In addition, the IASB noted that 'originated loans' might easily be created by placing purchased loans into an investment vehicle. The IASB also noted that the definition of loans and receivables in IAS 39 had created application problems in practice.

Tainting

BC4.45   The IASB considered whether it should prohibit an entity from classifying a financial asset as measured at amortised cost if the entity had previously sold or reclassified financial assets instead of holding them to collect the contractual cash flows. A restriction of this kind is often called 'tainting'. However, the IASB believes that classification based on the entity's business model for managing financial assets and the contractual cash flow characteristics of those financial assets provides a clear rationale for measurement. A tainting provision would increase the complexity of application, be unduly prohibitive in the context of that approach and could give rise to classification that is inconsistent with the classification approach in IFRS 9. However, in 2009 the IASB amended IAS 1 *Presentation of Financial Statements* to require an entity to present separately in the statement of comprehensive income all gains and losses arising from the derecognition of financial assets measured at amortised cost. The IASB also amended IFRS 7 in 2009 to require an entity to disclose an analysis of those gains and losses, including the reasons for derecognising those financial assets. Those requirements enable users of financial statements to understand the effects of derecognising before maturity instruments measured at amortised cost and also provides transparency in situations where an entity has measured financial assets at amortised cost on the basis of having an objective of managing those assets in order to collect the contractual cash flows but regularly sells them.

Classification of financial liabilities

BC4.46 Immediately after issuing the first chapters of IFRS 9 in November 2009, the IASB began an extensive outreach programme to gather feedback on the classification and measurement of financial liabilities, in particular how best to address the effects of changes in the fair value of a financial liability caused by changes in the risk that the issuer will fail to perform on that liability. The IASB obtained information and views from its FIWG and from users, regulators, preparers, auditors and others from a range of industries across different geographical regions. The IASB also developed a questionnaire to ask users of financial statements how they use information about the effects of changes in liabilities' credit risk (if at all) and what their preferred method of accounting is for selected financial liabilities. The IASB received over 90 responses to that questionnaire.

BC4.47 During the outreach programme, the IASB explored several approaches for classification and subsequent measurement of financial liabilities that would exclude the effects of changes in a liability's credit risk from profit or loss, including:

(a) measuring liabilities at fair value and presenting in other comprehensive income the portion of the change in fair value that is attributable to changes in the liability's credit risk. A variant of this alternative would be to present in other comprehensive income the entire change in fair value.

(b) measuring liabilities at an 'adjusted' fair value whereby the liability would be remeasured for all changes in fair value except for the effects of changes in its credit risk (ie 'the frozen credit spread method'). In other words, the effects of changes in its credit risk would be ignored in the primary financial statements.

(c) measuring liabilities at amortised cost. This would require estimating the cash flows over the life of the instrument, including those cash flows associated with any embedded derivative features.

(d) bifurcating liabilities into hosts and embedded features. The host contract would be measured at amortised cost and the embedded features (eg embedded derivatives) would be measured at fair value through profit or loss. The IASB discussed either carrying forward the bifurcation requirements in IAS 39 for financial liabilities or developing new requirements.

BC4.48 The primary message that the IASB received from users of financial statements and others during its outreach programme was that the effects of changes in a liability's credit risk ought not to affect profit or loss unless the liability is held for trading. That is because an entity generally will not realise the effects of changes in the liability's credit risk unless the liability is held for trading.

BC4.49　In addition to that view, there were several other themes in the feedback that the IASB received:

(a)　Symmetry between how an entity classifies and measures its financial assets and its financial liabilities is not necessary and often does not result in useful information. Most constituents said that in its deliberations on financial liabilities the IASB should not be constrained or biased by the requirements in IFRS 9 for financial assets.

(b)　Amortised cost is the most appropriate measurement attribute for many financial liabilities because it reflects the issuer's legal obligation to pay the contractual amounts in the normal course of business (ie on a going concern basis) and in many cases, the issuer will hold liabilities to maturity and pay the contractual amounts. However, if a liability has structured features (eg embedded derivatives), amortised cost is difficult to apply and understand because the cash flows can be highly variable.

(c)　The bifurcation methodology in IAS 39 is generally working well and practice has developed since those requirements were issued. For many entities, bifurcation avoids the issue of own credit risk because the host is measured at amortised cost and only the derivative is measured at fair value through profit or loss. Many constituents, including users of financial statements, favoured retaining bifurcation for financial liabilities even though they supported eliminating it for financial assets. That was because bifurcation addresses the issue of own credit risk, which is only relevant for financial liabilities. Users preferred structured assets to be measured at fair value in their entirety. Many constituents were sceptical that a new bifurcation methodology could be developed that was less complex and provided more useful information than using the bifurcation methodology in IAS 39. Moreover, a new bifurcation methodology would be likely to have the same classification and measurement outcomes as the existing methodology in most cases.

(d)　The IASB should not develop a new measurement attribute. The almost unanimous view was that a 'full' fair value amount is more understandable and useful than an 'adjusted' fair value amount that ignores the effects of changes in the liability's credit risk.

(e)　Even for preparers with sophisticated valuation expertise, it is difficult to determine the amount of change in the fair value of a liability that is attributable to changes in its credit risk. Under existing Standards only entities that elect to designate liabilities under the fair value option are required to determine that amount. If the IASB were to extend that requirement to more entities and to more financial liabilities, many entities would have significant difficulty determining that amount and could incur significant costs in doing so.

BC4.50　Although there were common themes in the feedback received, there was no consensus on which of the alternative approaches being explored by the IASB was the best way to address the effects of changes in liabilities' credit risk. Many constituents said that none of the alternatives being discussed was less complex or would result in more useful information than the existing bifurcation requirements.

BC4.51   As a result of the feedback received, the IASB decided to retain almost all of the existing requirements for the classification and measurement of financial liabilities. The IASB decided that the benefits of changing practice at this point do not outweigh the costs of the disruption that such a change would cause. Accordingly, in October 2010 the IASB carried forward almost all of the requirements unchanged from IAS 39 to IFRS 9.

BC4.52   By retaining almost all of the existing requirements, the issue of credit risk is addressed for most liabilities because they would continue to be subsequently measured at amortised cost or would be bifurcated into a host, which would be measured at amortised cost, and an embedded derivative, which would be measured at fair value. Liabilities that are held for trading (including all derivative liabilities) would continue to be subsequently measured at fair value through profit or loss, which is consistent with the widespread view that all fair value changes for those liabilities should affect profit or loss.

BC4.53   The issue of credit risk would remain only in the context of financial liabilities designated under the fair value option. Thus, in May 2010 the IASB published an Exposure Draft *Fair Value Option for Financial Liabilities* (the '2010 Own Credit Risk Exposure Draft'), which proposed that the effects of changes in the credit risk of liabilities designated under the fair value option would be presented in other comprehensive income. The IASB considered the responses to 2010 Own Credit Risk Exposure Draft and finalised amendments to IFRS 9 in October 2010 (see paragraphs BC5.35–BC5.64). Those amendments also eliminated the cost exception for particular derivative liabilities that will be settled by delivering unquoted equity instruments[12] whose fair values cannot be reliably determined (see paragraph BC5.20).

Option to designate a financial asset or financial liability at fair value through profit or loss

Background to the fair value option in IAS 39

BCZ4.54   In 2003 the IASB concluded that it could simplify the application of IAS 39 (as revised in 2000) for some entities by permitting the use of fair value measurement for any financial instrument. With one exception, this greater use of fair value is optional. The fair value measurement option does not require entities to measure more financial instruments at fair value.

BCZ4.55   IAS 39 (as revised in 2000)[13] did not permit an entity to measure particular categories of financial instruments at fair value with changes in fair value recognised in profit or loss. Examples included:

(a)   originated loans and receivables, including a debt instrument acquired directly from the issuer, unless they met the conditions for classification as held for trading (now in Appendix A of IFRS 9).

---

12   IFRS 13, issued in May 2011, defines a Level 1 input as a quoted price in an active market for an identical asset or liability. Level 2 inputs include quoted prices for identical assets or liabilities in markets that are not active. As a result IFRS 9 refers to such equity instruments as 'an equity instrument that does not have a quoted price in an active market for an identical instrument (ie a Level 1 input)'.

13   IFRS 9 eliminated the loans and receivables and available-for-sale categories.

(b)   financial assets classified as available for sale, unless as an accounting policy choice gains and losses on all available-for-sale financial assets were recognised in profit or loss or they met the conditions for classification as held for trading (now in Appendix A of IFRS 9).

(c)   non-derivative financial liabilities, even if the entity had a policy and practice of actively repurchasing such liabilities or they formed part of an arbitrage/customer facilitation strategy or fund trading activities.

BCZ4.56   The IASB decided in IAS 39 (as revised in 2003) to permit entities to designate irrevocably on initial recognition any financial instruments as ones to be measured at fair value with gains and losses recognised in profit or loss ('fair value through profit or loss'). To impose discipline on this approach, the IASB decided that financial instruments should not be reclassified into or out of the category of fair value through profit or loss. In particular, some comments received on the exposure draft of proposed amendments to IAS 39 published in June 2002 suggested that entities could use the fair value option to recognise selectively changes in fair value in profit or loss. The IASB noted that the requirement (now in IFRS 9) to designate irrevocably on initial recognition the financial instruments for which the fair value option is to be applied results in an entity being unable to 'cherry pick' in this way. This is because it will not be known at initial recognition whether the fair value of the instrument will increase or decrease.

BCZ4.57   Following the issue of IAS 39 (as revised in 2003), as a result of continuing discussions with constituents on the fair value option, the IASB became aware that some, including prudential supervisors of banks, securities companies and insurers, were concerned that the fair value option might be used inappropriately. These constituents were concerned that:

(a)   entities might apply the fair value option to financial assets or financial liabilities whose fair value is not verifiable. If so, because the valuation of these financial assets and financial liabilities is subjective, entities might determine their fair value in a way that inappropriately affects profit or loss.

(b)   the use of the option might increase, instead of decreasing, volatility in profit or loss, for example if an entity applied the option to only one part of a matched position.

(c)   if an entity applied the fair value option to financial liabilities, it might result in an entity recognising gains or losses in profit or loss associated with changes in its own creditworthiness.

BCZ4.58   In response to those concerns, the IASB published in April 2004 an exposure draft of proposed restrictions to the fair value option contained in IAS 39 (as revised in 2003). After discussing comments received from constituents and a series of public round-table meetings, the IASB issued an amendment to IAS 39 in June 2005 permitting entities to designate irrevocably on initial recognition financial instruments that meet one of three conditions as ones to be measured at fair value through profit or loss.

BCZ4.59   In those amendment to the fair value option, the IASB identified three situations in which permitting designation at fair value through profit or loss either results in more relevant information ((a) and (b) below) or is justified on the grounds of reducing complexity or increasing measurement reliability ((c) below). These are:

(a)   when such designation eliminates or significantly reduces a measurement or recognition inconsistency (sometimes referred to as an 'accounting mismatch') that would otherwise arise (paragraphs BCZ4.61–BCZ4.63);

(b)   when a group of financial assets, financial liabilities or both is managed and its performance is evaluated on a fair value basis, in accordance with a documented risk management or investment strategy (paragraphs BCZ4.64–BCZ4.66); and

(c)   when an instrument contains an embedded derivative that meets particular conditions (paragraphs BCZ4.67–BCZ4.70).

BCZ4.60   The ability for entities to use the fair value option simplifies the application of IAS 39 by mitigating some anomalies that result from the different measurement attributes. In particular, for financial instruments designated in this way:

(a)   it eliminates the need for hedge accounting for hedges of fair value exposures when there are natural offsets, and thereby eliminates the related burden of designating, tracking and analysing hedge effectiveness.

(b)   it eliminates the burden of separating embedded derivatives.

(c)   it eliminates problems arising from a mixed measurement model when financial assets are measured at fair value and related financial liabilities are measured at amortised cost. In particular, it eliminates volatility in profit or loss and equity that results when matched positions of financial assets and financial liabilities are not measured consistently.

(d)   the option to recognise unrealised gains and losses on available-for-sale financial assets in profit or loss is no longer necessary.

(e)   it de-emphasises interpretative issues around what constitutes trading.

Designation eliminates or significantly reduces an accounting mismatch

BCZ4.61   IAS 39, like comparable standards in some national jurisdictions, imposed (and IFRS 9 now imposes) a mixed attribute measurement model. It required some financial assets and liabilities to be measured at fair value, and others to be measured at amortised cost. It required some gains and losses to be recognised in profit or loss, and others to be recognised initially as a component of equity.[14] This combination of measurement and recognition requirements could result in inconsistencies, which some refer to as 'accounting mismatches', between the accounting for an asset (or group of assets) and a liability (or group of liabilities). The notion of an accounting mismatch necessarily involves two propositions. First, an entity has particular assets and liabilities that are measured, or on

---

14 As a consequence of the revision of IAS 1 *Presentation of Financial Statements* in 2007 these other gains and losses are recognised in other comprehensive income.

which gains and losses are recognised, inconsistently; second, there is a perceived economic relationship between those assets and liabilities. For example, a liability may be considered to be related to an asset when they share a risk that gives rise to opposite changes in fair value that tend to offset, or when the entity considers that the liability funds the asset.

BCZ4.62 Some entities could overcome measurement or recognition inconsistencies by using hedge accounting or, in the case of insurers, shadow accounting. However, the IASB recognised that those techniques are complex and do not address all situations. In developing the amendment to the fair value option in 2004, the IASB considered whether it should impose conditions to limit the situations in which an entity could use the option to eliminate an accounting mismatch. For example, it considered whether entities should be required to demonstrate that particular assets and liabilities are managed together, or that a management strategy is effective in reducing risk (as is required for hedge accounting to be used), or that hedge accounting or other ways of overcoming the inconsistency are not available.

BCZ4.63 The IASB concluded that accounting mismatches arise in a wide variety of circumstances. In the IASB's view, financial reporting is best served by providing entities with the opportunity to eliminate perceived accounting mismatches whenever that results in more relevant information. Furthermore, the IASB concluded that the fair value option may validly be used in place of hedge accounting for hedges of fair value exposures, thereby eliminating the related burden of designating, tracking and analysing hedge effectiveness. Hence, the IASB decided not to develop detailed prescriptive guidance about when the fair value option could be applied (such as requiring effectiveness tests similar to those required for hedge accounting) in the amendment on the fair value option. Instead, the IASB decided to require disclosures (now in IFRS 7) about:

- the criteria an entity uses for designating financial assets and financial liabilities as at fair value through profit or loss

- how the entity satisfies the conditions for such designation

- the nature of the assets and liabilities so designated

- the effect on the financial statement of using this designation, namely the carrying amounts and net gains and losses on assets and liabilities so designated, information about the effect of changes in a financial liability's credit quality on changes in its fair value, and information about the credit risk of loans or receivables and any related credit derivatives or similar instruments.

A group of financial assets, financial liabilities or both is managed and its performance is evaluated on a fair value basis

BCZ4.64 IAS 39 required financial instruments to be measured at fair value through profit or loss in only two situations, namely when an instrument is held for trading or when it contains an embedded derivative that the entity is unable to measure separately. However, the IASB recognised that some entities manage and evaluate the performance of financial instruments on a fair value basis in other situations. Furthermore, for instruments managed and evaluated in this way, users of financial statements may regard fair value measurement as providing more relevant information. Finally, it is established practice in some industries in some jurisdictions to recognise all financial assets at fair value through profit or loss. (This practice was permitted for many assets in IAS 39 (as revised in 2000) as an accounting policy choice in accordance with which gains and losses on all available-for-sale financial assets were reported in profit or loss.)

BCZ4.65 In the amendment to IAS 39 relating to the fair value option issued in June 2005, the IASB permitted financial instruments managed and evaluated on a fair value basis to be measured at fair value through profit or loss. The IASB also introduced two requirements to make this category operational. These requirements are that the financial instruments are managed and evaluated on a fair value basis in accordance with a documented risk management or investment strategy, and that information about the financial instruments is provided internally on that basis to the entity's key management personnel.

BCZ4.66 In looking to an entity's documented risk management or investment strategy, the IASB made no judgement on what an entity's strategy should be. However, the IASB noted that users, in making economic decisions, would find useful both a description of the chosen strategy and how designation at fair value through profit or loss is consistent with it. Such disclosures are required (now in IFRS 7). The IASB also noted that the required documentation of the entity's strategy need not be item by item, nor need it be in the level of detail required for hedge accounting. However, it should be sufficient to demonstrate that using the fair value option is consistent with the entity's risk management or investment strategy. In many cases, the entity's existing documentation, as approved by its key management personnel, should be sufficient for this purpose.

The instrument contains an embedded derivative that meets particular conditions

BCZ4.67 IAS 39 required virtually all derivative financial instruments to be measured at fair value. This requirement extended to derivatives that are embedded in an instrument that also includes a non-derivative host if the embedded derivative met particular conditions. Conversely, if the embedded derivative did not meet those conditions, separate accounting with measurement of the embedded derivative at fair value is prohibited. Consequently, to satisfy these requirements, the entity must:

(a) identify whether the instrument contains one or more embedded derivatives,

(b) determine whether each embedded derivative is one that must be separated from the host instrument or one for which separation is prohibited, and

(c) if the embedded derivative is one that must be separated, determine its fair value at initial recognition and subsequently.

BCZ4.68 For some embedded derivatives, like the prepayment option in an ordinary residential mortgage, this process is fairly simple. However, entities with more complex instruments have reported that the search for and analysis of embedded derivatives (steps (a) and (b) in paragraph BCZ4.67) significantly increase the cost of complying with the Standard. They report that this cost could be eliminated if they had the option to fair value the combined contract.

BCZ4.69 Other entities report that one of the most common uses of the fair value option is likely to be for structured products that contain several embedded derivatives. Those structured products will typically be hedged with derivatives that offset all (or nearly all) of the risks they contain, whether or not the embedded derivatives that give rise to those risks are separated for accounting purposes. Hence, the simplest way to account for such products is to apply the fair value option so that the combined contract (as well as the derivatives that hedge it) is measured at fair value through profit or loss. Furthermore, for these more complex instruments, the fair value of the combined contract may be significantly easier to measure and hence be more reliable than the fair value of only those embedded derivatives that are required to be separated.

BCZ4.70 The IASB sought to strike a balance between reducing the costs of complying with the embedded derivatives provisions and the need to respond to the concerns expressed regarding possible inappropriate use of the fair value option. The IASB determined that allowing the fair value option to be used for any instrument with an embedded derivative would make other restrictions on the use of the option ineffective, because many financial instruments include an embedded derivative. In contrast, limiting the use of the fair value option to situations in which the embedded derivative must otherwise be separated would not significantly reduce the costs of compliance and could result in less reliable measures being included in the financial statements. Consequently, the IASB decided to specify situations in which an entity cannot justify using the fair value option in place of assessing embedded derivatives—when the embedded derivative does not significantly modify the cash flows that would otherwise be required by the contract or is one for which it is clear with little or no analysis when a similar hybrid instrument is first considered that separation is prohibited.

The role of prudential supervisors

BCZ4.71 The IASB considered the circumstances of regulated financial institutions such as banks and insurers in determining the extent to which conditions should be placed on the use of the fair value option. The IASB recognised that regulated financial institutions are extensive holders and issuers of financial instruments and so are likely to be among the largest potential users of the fair value option. However, the IASB noted that some of the prudential supervisors that oversee these entities expressed concern that the fair value option might be used inappropriately.

BCZ4.72 The IASB noted that the primary objective of prudential supervisors is to maintain the financial soundness of individual financial institutions and the stability of the financial system as a whole. Prudential supervisors achieve this objective partly by assessing the risk profile of each regulated institution and imposing a risk-based capital requirement.

BCZ4.73 The IASB noted that these objectives of prudential supervision differ from the objectives of general purpose financial reporting. The latter is intended to provide information about the financial position, performance and changes in financial position of an entity that is useful to a wide range of users in making economic decisions. However, the IASB acknowledged that for the purposes of determining what level of capital an institution should maintain, prudential supervisors may wish to understand the circumstances in which a regulated financial institution has chosen to apply the fair value option and evaluate the rigour of the institution's fair value measurement practices and the robustness of its underlying risk management strategies, policies and practices. Furthermore, the IASB agreed that certain disclosures would assist both prudential supervisors in their evaluation of capital requirements and investors in making economic decisions. In particular, the IASB decided to require an entity to disclose how it has satisfied the conditions for using the fair value option, including, for instruments that are now within paragraph 4.2.2(b) of IFRS 9, a narrative description of how designation at fair value through profit or loss is consistent with the entity's documented risk management or investment strategy.

Application of the fair value option to a component or a proportion (instead of the entirety) of a financial asset or a financial liability

BCZ4.74 Some comments received on the exposure draft of proposed amendments to IAS 39 published in June 2002 argued that the fair value option should be extended so that it could also be applied to a component of a financial asset or a financial liability (eg changes in fair value attributable to one risk such as changes in a benchmark interest rate). The arguments included (a) concerns regarding inclusion of own credit risk in the measurement of financial liabilities and (b) the prohibition on using non-derivatives as hedging instruments (cash instrument hedging).

BCZ4.75 The IASB concluded that IAS 39 should not extend the fair value option to components of financial assets or financial liabilities. It was concerned (a) about difficulties in measuring the change in value of the component because of ordering issues and joint effects (ie if the component is affected by more than one risk, it may be difficult to isolate accurately and measure the component); (b) that the amounts recognised in the balance sheet would be neither fair value nor cost; and (c) that a fair value adjustment for a component might move the carrying amount of an instrument away from its fair value. In finalising the 2003 amendments to IAS 39, the IASB separately considered the issue of cash instrument hedging (see paragraphs BC144 and BC145 of the Basis for Conclusions on IAS 39).

BCZ4.76 Other comments received on the April 2004 exposure draft of proposed restrictions on the fair value option contained in IAS 39 (as revised in 2003) suggested that the fair value option should be extended so that it could be applied to a proportion (ie a percentage) of a financial asset or financial liability. The IASB was concerned that such an extension would require prescriptive guidance on how to determine a proportion. For example, if an entity were to issue a bond totalling CU100 million in the form of 100 certificates each of CU1 million, would a proportion of 10 per cent be identified as 10 per cent of each certificate, CU10 million specified certificates, the first (or last) CU10 million certificates to be redeemed, or on some other basis? The IASB was also concerned that the remaining proportion, not being subject to the fair value option, could give rise to incentives for an entity to 'cherry pick' (ie to realise financial assets or financial liabilities selectively so as to achieve a desired accounting result). For these reasons, the IASB decided not to allow the fair value option to be applied to a proportion of a single financial asset or financial liability (that restriction is now in IFRS 9). However, if an entity simultaneously issues two or more identical financial instruments, it is not precluded from designating only some of those instruments as being subject to the fair value option (for example, if doing so achieves a significant reduction in a recognition or measurement inconsistency). Thus, in the above example, the entity could designate CU10 million specified certificates if to do so would meet one of the three criteria in paragraph BCZ4.59.

Option to designate a financial asset at fair value

BC4.77 As noted above, IAS 39 allowed entities an option to designate on initial recognition any financial asset or financial liability as measured at fair value through profit or loss if one (or more) of the following three conditions is met:

(a) Doing so eliminates or significantly reduces a measurement or recognition inconsistency (sometimes referred to as an 'accounting mismatch') that would otherwise arise from measuring assets or liabilities on different bases or recognising the gains and losses on them on different bases.

(b) A group of financial assets, financial liabilities or both is managed and its performance is evaluated on a fair value basis, in accordance with a documented risk management or investment strategy, and information about the group is provided internally on that basis to the entity's key management personnel.

(c) The financial asset or financial liability contains one or more embedded derivatives (and particular other conditions now described in paragraph 4.3.5 of IFRS 9 are met) and the entity elects to account for the hybrid contract in its entirety.

BC4.78 However, in contrast to IAS 39, IFRS 9 requires:

(a) any financial asset that is not managed within a business model that has the objective of collecting contractual cash flows to be measured at fair value; and

(b) hybrid contracts with financial asset hosts to be classified in their entirety, hence eliminating the requirement to identify and account for embedded derivatives separately.

Accordingly, the IASB concluded that the conditions described in paragraph BC4.77(b) and (c) are unnecessary for financial assets.

BC4.79 The IASB retained the eligibility condition described in paragraph BC4.77(a) because it mitigates some anomalies that result from the different measurement attributes used for financial instruments. In particular, it eliminates the need for fair value hedge accounting of fair value exposures when there are natural offsets. It also avoids problems arising from a mixed measurement model when some financial assets are measured at amortised cost and related financial liabilities are measured at fair value. A separate phase of the project is considering hedge accounting, and the fair value option will be better considered in that context. The IASB also noted that particular industry sectors believe it is important to be able to mitigate such anomalies until other IASB projects are completed (eg insurance contracts). The IASB decided to defer consideration of changes to the eligibility condition set out in paragraph BC4.77(a) as part of the future exposure draft on hedge accounting.

BC4.80　Almost all the respondents to the 2009 Classification and Measurement Exposure Draft supported the proposal to retain the fair value option if such designation eliminates or significantly reduces an accounting mismatch. Although some respondents would prefer an unrestricted fair value option, they acknowledged that an unrestricted fair value option has been opposed by many in the past and it is not appropriate to pursue it now.

Option to designate a financial liability at fair value

Eligibility conditions

BC4.81　During its discussions about subsequent classification and measurement of financial liabilities in 2010 (see paragraphs BC4.46–BC4.53), the IASB considered whether it was necessary to propose any changes to the eligibility conditions for designating financial liabilities under the fair value option. However, the IASB decided that such changes were not necessary because the IASB was not changing the underlying classification and measurement approach for financial liabilities. Consequently, the 2010 Own Credit Risk Exposure Draft proposed to carry forward the three eligibility conditions.

BC4.82　Most respondents agreed with that proposal in the 2010 Own Credit Risk Exposure Draft. The IASB confirmed the proposal and decided to carry forward to IFRS 9 the three eligibility conditions in October 2010. Some would have preferred an unrestricted fair value option. However, they acknowledged that an unrestricted fair value option had been opposed by many in the past and it was not appropriate to pursue it now.

Embedded derivatives

Hybrid contracts with a host that is an asset within the scope of IFRS 9

BC4.83　An embedded derivative is a derivative component of a hybrid contract that also includes a non-derivative host, with the effect that some of the cash flows of the combined contract vary like the cash flows of a stand-alone derivative contract. IAS 39 required an entity to assess all contracts to determine whether they contain one or more embedded derivatives that are required to be separated from the host and accounted for as stand-alone derivatives.

BC4.84　Many respondents to the Discussion Paper *Reducing Complexity in Reporting Financial Instruments* commented that the requirements and guidance in IAS 39 were complex, rule-based and internally inconsistent. Respondents, and others, also noted the many application problems that arose from requirements to assess all non-derivative contracts for embedded derivatives and, if required, to account for and measure those embedded derivatives separately as stand-alone derivatives.

BC4.85   In 2009 the IASB discussed three approaches for accounting for embedded derivatives:

    (a)   to maintain the requirements in IAS 39;

    (b)   to use 'closely related' (used in IAS 39 to determine whether an embedded derivative is required to be separated from the host) to determine the classification for the contract in its entirety; and

    (c)   to use the same classification approach for all financial assets (including hybrid contracts).

BC4.86   The IASB rejected the first two approaches. The IASB noted that both would rely on the assessment of whether an embedded derivative is 'closely related' to the host. The 'closely related' assessment is based on a list of examples that are inconsistent and unclear. That assessment is also a significant source of complexity. Both approaches would result in hybrid contracts being classified using conditions different from those that would be applied to all non-hybrid financial instruments. Consequently, some hybrid contracts whose contractual cash flows do not solely represent payments of principal and interest on the principal amount outstanding might be measured at amortised cost. Similarly, some hybrid contracts whose contractual cash flows do meet the conditions for measurement at amortised cost might be measured at fair value. The IASB also believes that neither approach would make it easier for users of financial statements to understand the information that financial statements present about financial instruments.

BC4.87   Therefore, the 2009 Classification and Measurement Exposure Draft proposed that entities should use the same classification approach for all financial instruments, including hybrid contracts with hosts within the scope of the proposed IFRS ('financial hosts'). The IASB concluded that a single classification approach for all financial instruments and hybrid contracts with financial hosts was the only approach that responded adequately to the criticisms described above. The IASB noted that using a single classification approach improves comparability by ensuring consistency in classification, and hence makes it easier for users to understand the information that financial statements present about financial instruments.

BC4.88   In the responses to the 2009 Classification and Measurement Exposure Draft, some respondents, mainly preparers, stated their preference for keeping or modifying the bifurcation model that was in IAS 39. They noted that:

    (a)   eliminating the requirement to account for embedded derivatives as stand-alone derivatives would lead to increased volatility in profit or loss and result in accounting that did not reflect the underlying economics and risk management or business model considerations in a transaction. For example, the components of some hybrid financial instruments may be managed separately.

    (b)   structuring opportunities would be created, for example if an entity entered into two transactions that have the same economic effect as entering into a single hybrid contract.

BC4.89 However, the IASB confirmed the proposals in the 2009 Classification and Measurement Exposure Draft for the following reasons:

(a) The elimination of the embedded derivatives guidance for hybrid contracts with financial hosts reduces the complexity in financial reporting of financial assets by eliminating another classification approach and improves the reporting for financial instruments. Many constituents agreed with this conclusion.

(b) In the IASB view, the underlying rationale for separate accounting for embedded derivatives is not to reflect risk management activities, but to avoid entities circumventing the recognition and measurement requirements for derivatives. Accordingly it is an exception to the definition of the unit of account (the contract) motivated by a wish to avoid abuse. It would reduce complexity to eliminate an anti-abuse exception.

(c) The IASB noted the concerns about structuring opportunities referred to in paragraph BC4.88(b). However, two contracts represent two units of account. Reconsideration of the unit of account forms part of a far broader issue for financial reporting that is outside the scope of the IASB's considerations in IFRS 9. In addition, embedded derivative features often do not have contractual cash flows that represent payments of principal and interest on the principal amount outstanding and thus the entire hybrid contract would not be eligible to be measured at amortised cost. However, the IASB noted that this would provide more relevant information because the embedded derivative feature affects the cash flows ultimately arising from the hybrid contract. Thus, applying the classification approach to the hybrid contract in its entirety would depict more faithfully the amount, timing and uncertainty of future cash flows.

(d) In the IASB's view, accounting for the hybrid contract as one unit of account is consistent with the project's objective—to improve the usefulness for users in their assessment of the timing, amount and uncertainty of future cash flows of financial instruments and to reduce the complexity in reporting financial instruments.

This decision applies only to hybrid contracts with a host that is an asset within the scope of IFRS 9.

BC4.90 The IASB decided not to consider at this time changes to the requirements in IAS 39 for embedded derivatives in hybrid contracts with non-financial hosts. The IASB acknowledged that those requirements are also complex and have resulted in some application problems, including the question of whether particular types of non-financial contracts are within the scope of IAS 39. The IASB accepted the importance of ensuring that any proposals for hybrid contracts with non-financial hosts should also address which non-financial contracts should be within the scope of IFRS 9. The IASB also noted the importance for many non-financial entities of hedge accounting for non-financial items, and the relationship to both scope and embedded derivative requirements. Consequently, the IASB concluded that the requirements for hybrid contracts with non-financial hosts should be addressed in a later phase of the project to replace IAS 39.

Hybrid contracts with a host that is not an asset within the scope of IFRS 9

BC4.91   As discussed in paragraphs BC4.46–BC4.53, in 2010 the IASB decided to retain almost all of the requirements in IAS 39 for the classification and measurement of financial liabilities. Consequently, those requirements (including the requirements related to embedded derivatives) were carried forward unchanged to IFRS 9. Constituents told the IASB that the bifurcation methodology in IAS 39 for financial liabilities is generally working well in practice and practice has developed since those requirements were issued. Many constituents, including users of financial statements, favoured retaining bifurcation for financial liabilities even though they supported eliminating it for financial assets. That was because bifurcation addresses the issue of own credit risk, which is only relevant for financial liabilities.

Embedded foreign currency derivatives

BCZ4.92   A rationale for the embedded derivatives requirements is that an entity should not be able to circumvent the recognition and measurement requirements for derivatives merely by embedding a derivative in a non-derivative financial instrument or other contract, for example, a commodity forward in a debt instrument. To achieve consistency in accounting for such embedded derivatives, all derivatives embedded in financial instruments that are not measured at fair value with gains and losses recognised in profit or loss ought to be accounted for separately as derivatives. However, as a practical expedient, an embedded derivative need not be separated if it is regarded as closely related to its host contract. When the embedded derivative bears a close economic relationship to the host contract, such as a cap or a floor on the interest rate on a loan, it is less likely that the derivative was embedded to achieve a desired accounting result.

BCZ4.93   The original IAS 39 specified that a foreign currency derivative embedded in a non-financial host contract (such as a supply contract denominated in a foreign currency) was not separated if it required payments denominated in the currency of the primary economic environment in which any substantial party to the contract operates (their functional currencies) or the currency in which the price of the related good or service that is acquired or delivered is routinely denominated in international commerce (such as the US dollar for crude oil transactions). Such foreign currency derivatives are regarded as bearing such a close economic relationship to their host contracts that they do not have to be separated.

BCZ4.94   The requirement to separate embedded foreign currency derivatives may be burdensome for entities that operate in economies in which business contracts denominated in a foreign currency are common. For example, entities domiciled in small countries may find it convenient to denominate business contracts with entities from other small countries in an internationally liquid currency (such as the US dollar, euro or yen) instead of the local currency of any of the parties to the transaction. In addition, an entity operating in a hyperinflationary economy may use a price list in a hard currency to protect against inflation, for example, an entity that has a foreign operation in a hyperinflationary economy that denominates local contracts in the functional currency of the parent.

BCZ4.95 In revising IAS 39, the IASB concluded that an embedded foreign currency derivative may be integral to the contractual arrangements in the cases mentioned in the previous paragraph. It decided that a foreign currency derivative in a contract should not be required to be separated if it is denominated in a currency that is commonly used in business transactions (that are not financial instruments) in the environment in which the transaction takes place (that guidance is now in IFRS 9). A foreign currency derivative would be viewed as closely related to the host contract if the currency is commonly used in local business transactions, for example, when monetary amounts are viewed by the general population not in terms of the local currency but in terms of a relatively stable foreign currency, and prices may be quoted in that foreign currency (see IAS 29 *Financial Reporting in Hyperinflationary Economies*).

Embedded prepayment penalties

BCZ4.96 The IASB identified an apparent inconsistency in the guidance in IAS 39 (as issued in 2003). The inconsistency related to embedded prepayment options in which the exercise price represented a penalty for early repayment (ie prepayment) of the loan. The inconsistency related to whether these are considered closely related to the loan.

BCZ4.97 The IASB decided to remove this inconsistency by amending paragraph AG30(g) in April 2009 (now paragraph B4.3.5(e) of IFRS 9). The amendment makes an exception to the examples in paragraph AG30(g) of embedded derivatives that are not closely related to the underlying. This exception is in respect of prepayment options, the exercise prices of which compensate the lender for the loss of interest income because the loan was prepaid. This exception is conditional on the exercise price compensating the lender for loss of interest by reducing the economic loss from reinvestment risk.

Reassessment of embedded derivatives

BC4.98 In October 2010 the IASB incorporated into IFRS 9 the consensus in IFRIC 9 *Reassessment of Embedded Derivatives*. This section summarises the considerations of the International Financial Reporting Interpretations Committee (IFRIC) in reaching that consensus, as approved by the IASB, and the IASB's consideration for amending IFRIC 9 in April 2009.

BCZ4.99 When an entity first becomes a party to particular hybrid contracts it is required to assess whether any embedded derivative contained in the contract needs to be separated from the host contract and accounted for as a derivative. However, the issue arises whether an entity is required to continue to carry out this assessment after it first becomes a party to a contract, and if so, with what frequency.

BCZ4.100 The question is relevant, for example, when the terms of the embedded derivative do not change but market conditions change and the market was the principal factor in determining whether the host contract and embedded derivative are closely related. Instances when this might arise are given in paragraph B4.3.8(d) of IFRS 9. Paragraph 4.3.8(d) states that an embedded foreign currency derivative is closely related to the host contract provided it is not leveraged, does not contain an option feature, and requires payments denominated in one of the following currencies:

(a)   the functional currency of any substantial party to that contract;

(b)   the currency in which the price of the related good or service that is acquired or delivered is routinely denominated in commercial transactions around the world (such as the US dollar for crude oil transactions); or

(c)   a currency that is commonly used in contracts to purchase or sell non-financial items in the economic environment in which the transaction takes place (eg a relatively stable and liquid currency that is commonly used in local business transactions or external trade).

BCZ4.101   Any of the currencies specified in (a)–(c) above may change. Assume that when an entity first became a party to a contract, it assessed the contract as containing an embedded derivative that was closely related and hence not accounted for separately. Assume that subsequently market conditions change and that if the entity were to reassess the contract under the changed circumstances it would conclude that the embedded derivative is not closely related and therefore requires separate accounting. (The converse could also arise.) The issue was whether the entity should make such a reassessment.

BCZ4.102   When the IFRIC considered this issue in 2006, it noted that the rationale for the requirement to separate particular embedded derivatives is that an entity should not be able to circumvent the recognition and measurement requirements for derivatives merely by embedding a derivative in a non-derivative financial instrument or other contract (for example, by embedding a commodity forward in a debt instrument). Changes in external circumstances are not ways to circumvent the requirements. The IFRIC therefore concluded that reassessment was not appropriate for such changes.

BCZ4.103   The IFRIC noted that as a practical expedient IAS 39 did not require the separation of embedded derivatives that are closely related (that guidance is now in IFRS 9 for hybrid contracts with a host that is not an asset within the scope of that IFRS). Many financial instruments contain embedded derivatives. Separating all of these embedded derivatives would be burdensome for entities. The IFRIC noted that requiring entities to reassess embedded derivatives in all hybrid instruments could be onerous because frequent monitoring would be required. Market conditions and other factors affecting embedded derivatives would have to be monitored continuously to ensure timely identification of a change in circumstances and amendment of the accounting treatment accordingly. For example, if the functional currency of the counterparty changes during the reporting period so that the contract is no longer denominated in a currency of one of the parties to the contract, then a reassessment of the hybrid instrument would be required at the date of change to ensure the correct accounting treatment in future.

BCZ4.104 The IFRIC also recognised that although IAS 39 was silent on the issue of reassessment it gave relevant guidance when it stated that for the types of contracts now covered by paragraph B4.3.8(b) of IFRS 9 the assessment of whether an embedded derivative is closely related was required only at inception. Paragraph B4.3.8(b) of IFRS 9 states:

> An embedded floor or cap on the interest rate on a debt contract or insurance contract is closely related to the host contract, provided the cap is at or above the market rate of interest and the floor is at or below the market rate of interest *when the contract is issued*, and the cap or floor is not leveraged in relation to the host contract. Similarly, provisions included in a contract to purchase or sell an asset (eg a commodity) that establish a cap and a floor on the price to be paid or received for the asset are closely related to the host contract if both the cap and floor were out of the *money at inception* and are not leveraged. [Emphasis added]

BCZ4.105 The IFRIC also considered the implications of requiring subsequent reassessment. For example, assume that an entity, when it first becomes a party to a contract, separately recognises a host asset[15] and an embedded derivative liability. If the entity were required to reassess whether the embedded derivative was to be accounted for separately and if the entity concluded some time after becoming a party to the contract that the derivative was no longer required to be separated, then questions of recognition and measurement would arise. In the above circumstances, the IFRIC identified the following possibilities:

(a) The entity could remove the derivative from its balance sheet and recognise in profit or loss a corresponding gain or loss. This would lead to recognition of a gain or loss even though there had been no transaction and no change in the value of the total contract or its components.

(b) The entity could leave the derivative as a separate item in the balance sheet. The issue would then arise as to when the item was to be removed from the balance sheet. Should it be amortised (and, if so, how would the amortisation affect the effective interest rate of the asset), or should it be derecognised only when the asset is derecognised?

(c) The entity could combine the derivative (which is recognised at fair value) with the asset (which is recognised at amortised cost). This would alter both the carrying amount of the asset and its effective interest rate even though there had been no change in the economics of the whole contract. In some cases, it could also result in a negative effective interest rate.

The IFRIC noted that, under its view that subsequent reassessment is appropriate only when there has been a change in the terms of the contract that significantly modifies the cash flows that otherwise would be required by the contract, the above issues do not arise.

BCZ4.106 The IFRIC noted that IAS 39 required (and now IFRS 9 requires) an entity to assess whether particular embedded derivatives need to be separated from particular host contracts and accounted for as a derivative when it first becomes a party to

---

15 Hybrid contracts with a host that is an asset within the scope of IFRS 9 are now classified and measured in their entirety in accordance with section 4.1 of that IFRS.

a contract. Consequently, if an entity purchases a contract that contains an embedded derivative it assesses whether the embedded derivative needs to be separated and accounted for as a derivative on the basis of conditions at that date.

Improvements to IFRSs issued in April 2009

BCZ4.107 In 2009 the IASB observed that the changes to the definition of a business combination in the revisions to IFRS 3 *Business Combinations* (as revised in 2008) caused the accounting for the formation of a joint venture by the venturer to be within the scope of IFRIC 9. Similarly, the Board noted that common control transactions might raise the same issue depending on which level of the group reporting entity is assessing the combination.

BCZ4.108 The IASB observed that during the development of the revised IFRS 3, it did not discuss whether it intended IFRIC 9 to apply to those types of transactions. The IASB did not intend to change existing practice by including such transactions within the scope of IFRIC 9. Accordingly, in *Improvements to IFRSs* issued in April 2009, the IASB amended paragraph 5 of IFRIC 9 (now paragraph B4.3.12 of IFRS 9) to clarify that IFRIC 9 did not apply to embedded derivatives in contracts acquired in a combination between entities or businesses under common control or the formation of a joint venture.

BCZ4.109 Some respondents to the Exposure Draft *Post-implementation Revisions to IFRIC Interpretations* published in January 2009 expressed the view that investments in associates should also be excluded from the scope of IFRIC 9. Respondents noted that paragraphs 20–23 of IAS 28 *Investments in Associates*[16] state that the concepts underlying the procedures used in accounting for the acquisition of a subsidiary are also adopted in accounting for the acquisition of an investment in an associate.

BCZ4.110 In its redeliberations, the IASB confirmed its previous decision that no scope exemption in IFRIC 9 was needed for investments in associates. However, in response to the comments received, the IASB noted that reassessment of embedded derivatives in contracts held by an associate is not required by IFRIC 9 in any event. The investment in the associate is the asset the investor controls and recognises, not the underlying assets and liabilities of the associate.

Reclassification

Reclassification of financial assets

BC4.111 The 2009 Classification and Measurement Exposure Draft proposed to prohibit reclassification of financial assets between the amortised cost and fair value categories. The IASB's rationale for that proposal was as follows:

(a) Requiring (or permitting) reclassifications would not make it easier for users of financial statements to understand the information that financial statements provide about financial instruments.

---

16 In May 2011, the IASB amended IAS 28 and changed its title to *Investments in Associates and Joint Ventures*.

(b)   Requiring (or permitting) reclassifications would increase complexity because detailed guidance would be required to specify when reclassifications would be required (or permitted) and the subsequent accounting for reclassified financial instruments.

(c)   Reclassification should not be necessary because classification is based on the entity's business model and that business model is not expected to change.

BC4.112   In their responses, some users questioned the usefulness of reclassified information, noting concerns about the consistency and rigour with which any requirements would be applied. Some were also concerned that opportunistic reclassifications would be possible.

BC4.113   However, almost all respondents (including most users) argued that prohibiting reclassification is inconsistent with a classification approach based on how an entity manages its financial assets. They noted that in an approach based on an entity's business model for managing financial assets, reclassifications would provide useful, relevant and comparable information to users because it would ensure that financial statements faithfully represent how those financial assets are managed at the reporting date. In particular, most users stated that, conceptually, reclassifications should not be prohibited when the classification no longer reflects how the instruments would be classified if the items were newly acquired. If reclassification were prohibited, the reported information would not reflect the amounts, timing and uncertainty of future cash flows.

BC4.114   The IASB was persuaded by these arguments and decided that reclassification should not be prohibited. The IASB noted that prohibiting reclassification decreases comparability for like instruments managed in the same way.

BC4.115   Some respondents contended that reclassifications should be permitted, instead of required, but did not explain their justification. However, the IASB noted that permitting reclassification would decrease comparability, both between different entities and for instruments held by a single entity, and would enable an entity to manage its profit or loss by selecting the timing of when future gains or losses are recognised. Consequently, the IASB decided that reclassification should be required when the entity's business model for managing those financial assets changes.

BC4.116   The IASB noted that, as highlighted by many respondents, such changes in business model would be very infrequent, significant and demonstrable and determined by the entity's senior management as a result of external or internal change.

BC4.117   The IASB considered arguments that reclassification should also be permitted or required when contractual cash flow characteristics of a financial asset vary (or may vary) over that asset's life based on its original contractual terms. However, the IASB noted that, unlike a change in business model, the contractual terms of a financial asset are known at initial recognition. An entity classifies the financial asset at initial recognition on the basis of the contractual terms over the life of the instrument. Consequently, the IASB decided that reclassification on the basis of a financial asset's contractual cash flows should not be permitted.

BC4.118   The IASB considered how reclassifications should be accounted for. Almost all respondents said that reclassifications should be accounted for prospectively and should be accompanied by robust disclosures. The IASB reasoned that if classification and reclassification are based on the business model within which they are managed, classification should always reflect the business model within which the financial asset was managed at the reporting date. To apply the reclassification retrospectively would not reflect how the financial assets were managed at the prior reporting dates.

BC4.119   The IASB also considered the date at which reclassifications could take effect. Some respondents stated that reclassifications should be reflected in the entity's financial statements as soon as the entity's business model for the relevant instruments changes. To do otherwise would be contradictory to the objective of reclassification—ie to reflect how the instruments are managed. However, the IASB decided that reclassifications should take effect from the beginning of the following reporting period. In the IASB's view, entities should be prevented from choosing a reclassification date to achieve an accounting result. The IASB also noted that a change in an entity's business model is a significant and demonstrable event; therefore, an entity will most likely disclose such an event in its financial statements in the reporting period in which the change in business model takes place.

BC4.120   The IASB also considered and rejected the following approaches:

(a)   *Disclosure approach:* Quantitative and qualitative disclosure (instead of reclassification) could be used to address when the classification no longer reflects how the financial assets would be classified if they were newly acquired. However, in the IASB's view, disclosure is not an adequate substitute for recognition.

(b)   *One-way reclassification:* Reclassification would be required only to fair value measurement, ie reclassification to amortised cost measurement would be prohibited. Proponents of this approach indicated that such an approach might minimise abuse of the reclassification requirements and result in more instruments being measured at fair value. However, in the IASB's view, there is no conceptual reason to require reclassification in one direction but not the other.

Reclassification of financial liabilities

BC4.121   Consistently with its decision in 2010 to retain most of the existing requirements for classifying and measuring financial liabilities (and relocate them to IFRS 9), the IASB decided to retain the requirements that prohibit reclassifying financial liabilities between amortised cost and fair value. The IASB noted that IFRS 9 requires reclassification of assets in particular circumstances. However, in line with the feedback received during the IASB's outreach programme, the classification and measurement approaches for financial assets and financial liabilities are different; therefore the IASB decided that it is unnecessary and inappropriate to have symmetrical requirements for reclassification. Moreover, although the reclassification of financial assets has been a controversial topic in recent years, the IASB is not aware of any requests or views that support reclassifying financial liabilities.

Changes in circumstances that are not reclassifications

BCZ4.122 The definition of a financial asset or financial liability at fair value through profit or loss excludes derivatives that are designated and effective hedging instruments. Paragraph 50 of IAS 39 prohibited (and unless particular conditions are met, paragraphs 4.4.1 and 4.4.2 of IFRS 9 prohibit) the reclassification of financial instruments into or out of the fair value through profit or loss category after initial recognition. The IASB noted that the prohibition on reclassification might be read as preventing a derivative financial instrument that becomes a designated and effective hedging instrument from being excluded from the fair value through profit or loss category in accordance with the definition. Similarly, it might be read as preventing a derivative that ceases to be a designated and effective hedging instrument from being accounted for at fair value through profit or loss.

BCZ4.123 The IASB decided that the prohibition on reclassification should not prevent a derivative from being accounted for at fair value through profit or loss when it does not qualify for hedge accounting and vice versa. Consequently, in *Improvements to IFRSs* issued in May 2008, the IASB addressed this point (now in paragraph 4.4.3 of IFRS 9).

Limited amendments for financial assets (July 2014)

BC4.124 When the IASB issued IFRS 9 in 2009, it acknowledged the difficulties that might be created by differences in timing between the classification and measurement phase of the project to replace IAS 39 and the Insurance Contracts project. The IASB consistently stated that the interaction between IFRS 9 and the Insurance Contracts project would be considered once the IASB's insurance contracts model had been developed sufficiently.

BC4.125 In addition, after IFRS 9 was issued in 2009, the IASB received feedback from interested parties in various jurisdictions that had chosen to apply IFRS 9 early or who had reviewed IFRS 9 in detail in preparation for application. Some asked questions or raised application issues related to the requirements for classifying and measuring financial assets.

BC4.126 Finally, when the IASB was developing the first requirements of IFRS 9, its priority was to make improvements to the accounting for financial instruments available quickly. Consequently, the IASB issued the classification and measurement requirements for financial assets in IFRS 9 in 2009 while the FASB was still developing its classification and measurement model. However, the boards remained committed to trying to achieve increased comparability internationally in the accounting for financial instruments.

BC4.127 Accordingly, in November 2011 the IASB decided to consider making limited amendments to IFRS 9 with the following objectives:

(a) consider the interaction between the classification and measurement of financial assets and the accounting for insurance contract liabilities;

(b) address specific application questions raised by interested parties since IFRS 9 was issued; and

(c)   seek to reduce key differences with the FASB's tentative classification and measurement model for financial instruments.

BC4.128   In making this decision, the IASB noted that IFRS 9 was fundamentally sound and would result in useful information being provided to users of financial statements. Feedback from interested parties since IFRS 9 was issued had confirmed that it was operational. Accordingly, although some interested parties might have preferred the IASB to discuss additional issues, it decided to consider only limited amendments to IFRS 9 in line with the objectives set out in paragraph BC4.127.

BC4.129   In limiting the scope of the deliberations, the IASB was also mindful of the need to complete the entire project on financial instruments on a timely basis and minimise the cost and disruption to entities that have already applied, or have begun preparations to apply, IFRS 9. Thus, the IASB decided to focus only on the following issues:

(a)   the basis for, and the scope of, a possible third measurement category for financial assets (ie fair value through other comprehensive income);

(b)   the assessment of a financial asset's contractual cash flow characteristics—specifically, whether, and if so what, additional guidance is required to clarify how the assessment is to be applied and whether bifurcation of financial assets should be reintroduced; and

(c)   interrelated issues arising from these topics (for example, disclosure requirements and the model for financial liabilities).

BC4.130   At the same time, the FASB had been discussing its tentative model for classifying and measuring financial instruments. Consequently, consistently with their long-standing objective to increase international comparability in the accounting for financial instruments, in January 2012, the IASB and the FASB decided to jointly deliberate these issues. However, the boards were mindful of their different starting points. Specifically, the IASB was considering limited amendments to the existing requirements in IFRS 9 whereas the FASB was considering a comprehensive new model.

BC4.131   The boards' joint deliberations led to the publication of the Exposure Draft *Classification and Measurement: Limited Amendments to IFRS 9* (Proposed amendments to IFRS 9 (2010)) (the '2012 Limited Amendments Exposure Draft') and the FASB's proposed Accounting Standards Update *Financial Instruments—Overall (Subtopic 825-10): Recognition and Measurement of Financial Assets and Financial Liabilities* in November 2012 and February 2013 respectively. While the publications had different scopes (ie to reflect the fact that the IASB was proposing limited amendments to IFRS 9 whereas the FASB was proposing a comprehensive new model) the key aspects of the boards' respective classification and measurement models were largely aligned.

BC4.132   The comment periods on the IASB's and the FASB's proposals ended on 28 March 2013 and 15 May 2013 respectively. The boards developed a plan for joint redeliberations on the basis of the feedback received. That plan reflected the fact that the feedback differed in a number of ways. Specifically, many of the FASB's respondents questioned whether a new comprehensive classification and measurement model was needed and raised concerns about the complexity of the proposals. Many of those respondents advocated that the FASB should consider making targeted improvements to current US GAAP (particularly to the current requirements for bifurcating financial instruments). Consequently, while agreeing to joint redeliberations, the FASB indicated that after those redeliberations were complete, it would consider whether it would confirm the model that the boards had been jointly discussing or pursue another approach (for example, targeted improvements to US GAAP). In contrast, overall, the IASB's respondents continued to support the classification and measurement model in IFRS 9 and supported the proposed limited amendments to that model. The boards' plan for redeliberations also reflected the fact that the boards had different scopes for their redeliberations, which reflected their different starting points. Accordingly the boards' project plan envisaged both joint and separate redeliberations.

BC4.133   At joint public meetings in September through November 2013, the boards discussed the key aspects of their respective models—specifically, the assessment of an asset's contractual cash flow characteristics and the assessment of an entity's business model for managing financial assets (including the basis for, and the scope of, the fair value through other comprehensive income measurement category). Most of the decisions were made jointly and there was general agreement on the key aspects. However, there were differences in the boards' decisions on specific details, such as the assessment of some contingent and prepayment features as well as the articulation of particular aspects of the business model assessment.

BC4.134   Subsequent to the joint discussions, the FASB continued to discuss at FASB-only public meetings the assessment of an asset's contractual cash flow characteristics and the assessment of an entity's business model for managing financial assets. The FASB tentatively decided in December 2013 and January 2014 that it would not continue to pursue the model that the boards had been jointly discussing. Instead, the FASB tentatively decided to consider targeted improvements to current US GAAP guidance for classifying and measuring financial assets.

BC4.135   At its February 2014 meeting, the IASB received and discussed an update on the FASB's tentative decisions. Although the IASB expressed disappointment that the boards had failed to achieve a more converged outcome, it decided to proceed with finalising the limited amendments to IFRS 9. The IASB noted that its stakeholders continue to support the classification and measurement model in IFRS 9 and also supported the proposed limited amendments to that model. The IASB also noted that the minor revisions to the proposed limited amendments that were made during the redeliberations of those proposals were largely to confirm and clarify the proposals in response to the feedback received on the 2012 Limited Amendments Exposure Draft.

The entity's business model

BC4.136   The requirements issued in IFRS 9 (2009) required an entity to assess its business model for managing financial assets. A financial asset was measured at amortised cost only if it was held within a business model whose objective was to hold financial assets in order to collect contractual cash flows (a 'hold to collect' business model), subject also to an assessment of the asset's contractual cash flow characteristics. All other financial assets were measured at fair value through profit or loss. Paragraph BC4.15–BC4.21 describe the IASB's rationale for that assessment.

BC4.137 Most interested parties have consistently agreed that financial assets should be classified and measured on the basis of the objective of the business model in which the assets are held, and also have consistently agreed that assets held within a hold to collect business model ought to be measured at amortised cost. However, after IFRS 9 was issued in 2009, some interested parties asked the IASB to clarify particular aspects of the hold to collect business model, including:

(a) the level of sales activity that is consistent with a hold to collect business model;

(b) the effect on the classification of an entity's financial assets if the entity's sales activity in a particular period appears to contradict the hold to collect business model objective—specifically, the consequences both on the classification of assets that the entity currently holds (ie those assets that the entity has already recognised) and on the classification of assets that it may hold in the future; and

(c) how to classify some portfolios of assets—in particular, so-called 'liquidity portfolios' that banks hold to satisfy their actual or potential liquidity needs, often in response to regulatory requirements.

More generally, some interested parties said that significant judgement was needed to classify some financial assets and, as a result, there was some inconsistency in views in practice about whether the objective of particular business models was to hold to collect contractual cash flows.

BC4.138 In addition, some interested parties expressed the view that IFRS 9 should contain a third measurement category: fair value through other comprehensive income. These views mainly related to:

(a) whether measurement at fair value through profit or loss appropriately reflects the performance of financial assets that are managed both in order to collect contractual cash flows and for sale. Some believed that the requirements for the business model assessment issued in IFRS 9 (2009) resulted in classification outcomes that were too stark, ie an entity either holds financial assets to collect contractual cash flows or it is required to measure the assets at fair value through profit or loss.

(b) the potential accounting mismatch that may arise as a result of the interaction between the classification and measurement of financial assets in accordance with IFRS 9 and the accounting for insurance contract liabilities under the IASB's tentative decisions in its Insurance Contracts project. That was because the 2013 Exposure Draft *Insurance Contracts* (the '2013 Insurance Contracts Exposure Draft') proposed that insurance contract liabilities would be measured on the statement of financial position using a current value approach, but the effects of changes in the discount rate used to measure that current value would be required to be disaggregated and presented in other comprehensive income.

(c)   the tentative classification and measurement model that the FASB was considering immediately prior to the start of the boards' joint deliberations, which contemplated three measurement categories: amortised cost, fair value through other comprehensive income and fair value through profit or loss.

BC4.139   Accordingly, in the 2012 Limited Amendments Exposure Draft, the IASB proposed to clarify the objective of the hold to collect business model by providing additional application guidance. The IASB also proposed to introduce a third measurement category; that is, a measurement category for particular financial assets with simple contractual cash flows that are managed both in order to collect contractual cash flows and for sale.

The hold to collect business model

BC4.140   As a result of the application questions raised by interested parties and the diversity in views expressed since IFRS 9 was issued in 2009, the IASB decided to propose clarifications to the hold to collect business model. The IASB noted that these clarifications are relevant irrespective of whether a third measurement category is ultimately introduced to IFRS 9. That is, in the IASB's view, the proposed clarifications would not change (narrow the scope of) the population of financial assets that are eligible to be measured at amortised cost on the basis of the business model in which they are held in order to accommodate an additional measurement category. Instead, the proposals reaffirmed the existing principle in IFRS 9 that financial assets are measured at amortised cost only if they are held within a hold to collect business model (subject also to the assessment of the asset's contractual cash flow characteristics). The proposals also clarified and supplemented that principle with additional application guidance on the types of business activities and the frequency and nature of sales that are consistent, and inconsistent, with a hold to collect business model.

BC4.141   The 2012 Limited Amendments Exposure Draft stated that in order to assess whether the objective of the business model is to hold financial assets to collect contractual cash flows, an entity needs to consider the frequency and significance of past sales activity and the reason for those sales, as well as expectations about future sales activity. The IASB noted that that assessment is consistent with determining whether the cash flows from the financial assets will arise from the collection of their contractual cash flows. The IASB also noted that it expects that sales out of the amortised cost measurement category will be less frequent than sales out of the other measurement categories, because holding assets to collect contractual cash flows is integral to achieving the objective of a hold to collect business model, while selling financial assets to realise cash flows (including fair value changes) is only incidental to that objective. However, the 2012 Limited Amendments Exposure Draft clarified that the credit quality of financial assets is relevant to the entity's ability to collect the assets' contractual cash flows. Consequently, selling a financial asset when its credit quality has deteriorated is consistent with an objective to collect contractual cash flows.

BC4.142   Respondents to the 2012 Limited Amendments Exposure Draft generally agreed that financial assets should be classified and measured on the basis of the objective of the business model within which the assets are held, and specifically agreed with the hold to collect business model for classifying financial assets at amortised cost. However, some respondents expressed concern about what they perceived to be an unduly narrow amortised cost measurement category and expressed the view that the application guidance seemed similar to the guidance for held-to-maturity assets in IAS 39. Specifically, the respondents said that the proposals placed too much emphasis on the frequency and volume of sales instead of focusing on the reasons for those sales and whether those sales are consistent with a hold to collect business model. In addition, while respondents agreed that selling a financial asset when its credit quality has deteriorated is consistent with an objective of collecting contractual cash flows, some asked whether such sales would be acceptable only if they occur once the entity has actually incurred a loss (or there has been significant credit deterioration and therefore lifetime expected credit losses are recognised on the financial asset in accordance with the proposals published in the Exposure Draft *Financial Instruments: Expected Credit Losses* (the '2013 Impairment Exposure Draft'). Some respondents also expressed the view that selling financial assets to manage concentrations of credit risk (for example, selling financial assets in order to limit the amount of instruments held that are issued in a particular jurisdiction) should not be inconsistent with a hold to collect business model.

BC4.143   In response to the feedback received, the IASB decided to emphasise that the business model assessment in IFRS 9 focuses on how the entity actually manages financial assets in order to generate cash flows. The IASB noted that amortised cost is a simple measurement technique that allocates interest over time using the effective interest rate, which is based on contractual cash flows. Accordingly, amortised cost provides relevant and useful information about the amounts, timing and uncertainty of cash flows only if the contractual cash flows will be collected. In order to supplement that principle and improve the clarity of the application guidance related to the hold to collect business model, the IASB also decided to expand the discussion in IFRS 9 on the activities that are commonly associated with the hold to collect business model.

BC4.144   The IASB confirmed that although the objective of an entity's business model may be to hold financial assets in order to collect contractual cash flows, the entity need not hold all of those assets until maturity. Some sales out of the hold to collect business model are expected to occur (ie some financial assets will be derecognised for accounting purposes before maturity). The IASB noted that the level of sales activity (ie the frequency and value of sales), and the reasons for those sales, play a role in assessing the objective of the business model because that assessment focuses on determining how the entity actually manages assets to generate cash flows from the financial assets.

BC4.145   The IASB decided to clarify that the value and frequency of sales do not determine the objective of the business model and therefore should not be considered in isolation. Instead, information about past sales and expectations about future sales (including the frequency, value and nature of such sales) provide evidence about the objective of the business model. Information about sales and sales patterns are useful in determining how an entity manages its financial assets and how cash flows will be realised. Information about historical sales helps an entity to support and verify its business model assessment; that is, such information provides evidence about whether cash flows have been realised in a manner that is consistent with the entity's stated objective for managing those assets. The IASB noted that while an entity should consider historical sales information, that information does not imply that newly originated or newly purchased assets should be classified differently from period to period solely on the basis of sales activity in prior periods. In other words, fluctuations in sales activity in particular periods do not necessarily mean that the entity's business model has changed. The entity will need to consider the reasons for those sales and whether they are consistent with a hold to collect business model. For example, a change in the regulatory treatment of a particular type of financial asset may cause an entity to undertake a significant rebalancing of its portfolio in a particular period. Given its nature, the selling activity in that example would likely not in itself change the entity's overall assessment of its business model if the selling activity is an isolated (ie one-time) event. The entity also needs to consider information about past sales within the context of the conditions that existed at that time as compared to existing conditions and expectations about future conditions.

BC4.146 The IASB decided to emphasise that sales due to an increase in the asset's credit risk enhance the entity's ability to collect contractual cash flows. Accordingly, the IASB noted that selling a financial asset when concerns arise about the collectability of the contractual cash flows is consistent with the objective of a hold to collect business model. The IASB noted that this guidance does not require that the entity wait to sell the financial asset until it has incurred a credit loss or until there has been a significant increase in credit risk (and lifetime expected credit losses are recognised on the asset). Instead, a sale would be consistent with the objective of a hold to collect business model if the asset's credit risk has increased based on reasonable and supportable information, including forward looking information.

BC4.147 The IASB also discussed whether sales due to managing concentrations of credit risk are consistent with a hold to collect business model. The IASB decided that such sales should be assessed in the same manner as other sales. Specifically, an entity must assess whether the assets' credit risk has increased (based on reasonable and supportable, including forward looking, information) and, if so, such sales would be consistent with a hold to collect business model. If not, the entity would need to consider the frequency, value and timing of such sales, as well as the reasons for those sales, to determine whether they are consistent with a hold to collect business model. The IASB noted that the notion of credit concentration risk is applied fairly broadly in practice and may include changes in the entity's investment policy or strategy that are not related to credit deterioration. The IASB noted that frequent sales that are significant in value and labelled as 'due to credit concentration risk' (but that are not related to an increase in the assets' credit risk) are likely to be inconsistent with the objective of collecting contractual cash flows.

Fair value through other comprehensive income

BC4.148　The requirements issued in IFRS 9 (2009) stated that financial assets were measured at either amortised cost or fair value through profit or loss.[17] However, as discussed in paragraph BC4.138, the IASB received feedback from some interested parties subsequent to IFRS 9 being issued in 2009 that the Standard should contain a third measurement category: fair value through other comprehensive income. In that feedback, some questioned whether measuring financial assets at fair value through profit or loss if those assets are not held within a hold to collect business model always results in useful information. In addition, some were concerned about the potential accounting mismatch that may arise because of the interaction between the classification and measurement of financial assets under IFRS 9 and the proposed accounting for insurance contract liabilities under the IASB's Insurance Contracts project. Others pointed out that, at the time, the FASB was considering a tentative model that included a fair value through other comprehensive income measurement category.

BC4.149　In response to that feedback, the IASB proposed in the 2012 Limited Amendments Exposure Draft to introduce into IFRS 9 a fair value through other comprehensive income measurement category for particular financial assets. Specifically, the 2012 Limited Amendments Exposure Draft proposed that an entity would be required to measure a financial asset at fair value through other comprehensive income (unless the asset qualifies for, and the entity elects to apply, the fair value option) if the asset:

(a)　has contractual cash flow characteristics that give rise on specified dates to cash flows that are solely payments of principal and interest on the principal amount outstanding; and

(b)　is held within a business model in which assets are managed both in order to collect contractual cash flows and for sale (a 'hold to collect and sell' business model).

BC4.150　The IASB noted that the performance of a hold to collect and sell business model will be affected by both the collection of contractual cash flows and the realisation of fair values. Accordingly, the IASB decided that both amortised cost and fair value information are relevant and useful and therefore decided to propose that both sets of information are presented in the financial statements. Specifically, the 2012 Limited Amendments Exposure Draft proposed that the assets would be measured at fair value in the statement of financial position and the following amortised cost information would be presented in profit or loss:

(a)　interest revenue using the effective interest method that is applied to financial assets measured at amortised cost; and

(b)　impairment gains and losses using the same methodology that is applied to financial assets measured at amortised cost.

17　The requirements issued in IFRS 9 (2009) permitted an entity to make an irrevocable election at initial recognition to present fair value gains and losses on particular investments in equity instruments in other comprehensive income. That election is discussed in paragraph 5.7.5 of IFRS 9 and was outside of the scope of the 2012 Limited Amendments Exposure Draft.

The difference between the total change in fair value and the amounts recognised in profit or loss would be presented in other comprehensive income.

BC4.151 The IASB noted in the 2012 Limited Amendments Exposure Draft that amortised cost information in profit or loss reflects the entity's decision to hold the assets to collect contractual cash flows unless, and until, the entity sells the assets in order to achieve the objective of the business model. Fair value information reflects the cash flows that would be realised if, and when, the assets are sold. In addition, the 2012 Limited Amendments Exposure Draft proposed that when an asset measured at fair value through other comprehensive income is derecognised, the cumulative fair value gain or loss that was recognised in other comprehensive income is reclassified ('recycled') from equity to profit or loss as a reclassification adjustment (in accordance with IAS 1). The IASB noted that amortised cost information would not be provided in profit or loss unless the gains or losses previously accumulated in other comprehensive income are recycled to profit or loss when the financial asset is derecognised—and, therefore, recycling was a key feature of the proposed fair value through other comprehensive income measurement category.

BC4.152 However, the IASB acknowledged that requiring recycling for these financial assets is different from other requirements in IFRS 9 that prohibit recycling. Specifically, in accordance with IFRS 9, an entity is prohibited from recycling the gains and losses accumulated in other comprehensive income related to the following financial instruments:

(a) investments in equity instruments for which an entity has made an irrevocable election at initial recognition to present fair value changes in other comprehensive income (see paragraphs 5.7.5 and B5.7.1 of IFRS 9); or

(b) financial liabilities designated under the fair value option for which the effects of changes in the liability's credit risk are presented in other comprehensive income (see paragraphs 5.7.7 and B5.7.9 of IFRS 9).

BC4.153 However, the IASB noted in the 2012 Limited Amendments Exposure Draft that some of the reasons for prohibiting recycling of those gains or losses do not apply to financial assets measured at fair value through other comprehensive income. Specifically:

(a) *investments in equity instruments:* paragraph BC5.25(b) discusses the reasons why these gains and losses accumulated in other comprehensive income are not recycled. One of the primary reasons is that recycling would create the need to assess these equity investments for impairment. The impairment requirements in IAS 39 for investments in equity instruments were very subjective and indeed were among the most criticised accounting requirements during the global financial crisis. In contrast, IFRS 9 does not contain impairment requirements for investments in equity instruments. For financial assets mandatorily measured in accordance with the new fair value through other comprehensive income category, the IASB proposed that the same impairment approach would apply to those financial assets as is applied to financial assets measured at amortised cost. While recycling is prohibited, the IASB observed that an entity is not prohibited from presenting information in the financial statements about realised gains or losses on investments in equity instruments; for example, as a separate line item in other comprehensive income.

(b) *financial liabilities designated under the fair value option*: paragraphs BC5.52–BC5.57 discuss the reasons why these own credit gains and losses accumulated in other comprehensive income are not recycled. One of the primary reasons is that if the entity repays the contractual amount, which will often be the case for these financial liabilities, the cumulative effect of changes in the liability's credit risk over its life will net to zero because the liability's fair value will ultimately equal the contractual amount due. In contrast, for financial assets measured at fair value through other comprehensive income, selling financial assets is integral to achieving the objective of the business model and therefore the gains and losses accumulated in other comprehensive income will not net to zero.

BC4.154 Consistently with providing amortised cost information in profit or loss, the IASB proposed that for the purposes of recognising foreign exchange gains and losses under IAS 21 *The Effects of Changes in Foreign Exchange Rates*, a financial asset measured at fair value through other comprehensive income should be treated as if it was measured at amortised cost in the foreign currency. Consequently, exchange differences on the amortised cost (ie interest revenue calculated using the effective interest method and impairment gains and losses) would be recognised in profit or loss, with all other exchange differences recognised in other comprehensive income.

BC4.155 In addition to providing relevant and useful information for financial assets that are held within a hold to collect and sell business model, the IASB noted in the 2012 Limited Amendments Exposure Draft that the introduction of the fair value through other comprehensive income measurement category may improve consistency between the classification and measurement of financial assets under IFRS 9 and the accounting for insurance contract liabilities under the IASB's tentative decisions at that time in its Insurance Contracts project. That is because the 2013 Insurance Contracts Exposure Draft proposed that insurance contract liabilities would be measured on the statement of financial position using a current value approach but the effects of changes in the discount rate used to measure that current value would be presented in other comprehensive income. Consequently, when the entity holds both insurance contract liabilities and financial assets that qualify to be measured at fair value through other comprehensive income, particular changes in both the fair value of the financial assets (ie those changes other than interest revenue and impairment gains and losses) and the current value of the insurance contract liabilities (ie those changes arising from the effects of changes in the discount rate) would be presented in other comprehensive income.

BC4.156 The majority of respondents to the 2012 Limited Amendments Exposure Draft agreed with the introduction of the fair value through other comprehensive income measurement category. Some of those respondents agreed with the measurement category as proposed by the IASB, while others agreed in principle with the proposals but made suggestions related to the conditions for that new measurement category. For example, some respondents expressed the view that a financial asset should be measured at fair value through other comprehensive income as long as it is held in a hold to collect and sell business model (ie irrespective of the asset's contractual cash flow characteristics) and others suggested that the fair value through other comprehensive income measurement category should be an option (either in addition to, or instead of, a mandatory measurement category). The suggestion that the fair value through other comprehensive income measurement category should be an option was most often made within the context of further reducing accounting mismatches between the classification and measurement of financial assets under IFRS 9 and accounting for insurance contract liabilities under the IASB's tentative decisions in its Insurance Contracts project. In addition, some respondents raised questions about the distinction between the fair value through other comprehensive income measurement category and the fair value through profit or loss measurement category. Some of these respondents asked the IASB to more clearly articulate the principle underpinning the fair value through other comprehensive income measurement category. A few respondents asked whether it would be more straightforward to define the conditions to measure a financial asset at fair value through profit or loss and therefore suggested that fair value through other comprehensive income should be the residual measurement category. They noted that this would be more aligned with the available-for-sale category in IAS 39.

BC4.157 Consistently with the proposal in the 2012 Limited Amendments Exposure Draft and the feedback received on that proposal, the IASB confirmed the introduction of a third measurement category—fair value through other comprehensive income—into IFRS 9. The IASB believes that this measurement category is appropriate for financial assets that have contractual cash flows that are solely payments of principal and interest and that are held in a hold to collect and sell business model. For those financial assets, the IASB believes that both amortised cost and fair value information are relevant and useful because such information reflects how cash flows are realised. That is, holding financial assets to collect contractual cash flows is integral to achieving the objective of the hold to collect and sell business model and therefore the amounts presented in profit or loss provide amortised cost information while the entity holds the assets. Other fair value changes are not presented in profit or loss until (and unless) they are realised through selling, which acknowledges that such changes may reverse while the entity holds the asset. However, because selling assets is also integral to achieving the objective of the hold to collect and sell business model, those other fair value changes are presented in other comprehensive income and the financial asset is presented at fair value in the statement of financial position.

BC4.158 Also, in order to be measured at fair value through other comprehensive income, a financial asset must have contractual cash flows that are solely payments of principal and interest on the principal amount outstanding. This is because amortised cost information is presented in profit or loss for assets measured at fair value through other comprehensive income and, as the IASB has consistently stated, the amortised cost measurement attribute provides relevant and useful information only for financial assets with 'simple' contractual cash flows (ie contractual cash flows that are solely principal and interest). Amortised cost is a relatively simple measurement technique that allocates interest over the relevant time period using the effective interest rate. As discussed in paragraph BC4.23, the IASB's long-held view is that the effective interest method, which underpins amortised cost measurement, is not an appropriate method for allocating 'complex' contractual cash flows (ie contractual cash flows that are not solely principal and interest).

BC4.159 The IASB also discussed during its redeliberations whether the fair value through other comprehensive income measurement category should be optional—either in addition to, or instead of, a mandatory measurement category. However, the IASB believes that such an option would be inconsistent with, and indeed would undermine, its decision to classify financial assets as measured at fair value through other comprehensive income on the basis of their contractual cash flows and the business model within which they are held. Indeed, the overall structure of IFRS 9 is based on classifying financial assets on the basis of those two conditions. Moreover, the IASB noted that users of financial statements have both consistently opposed permitting too much optionality in accounting requirements and have also advocated accounting requirements that provide comparability. However, the IASB acknowledged that accounting mismatches could arise as a result of the classification and measurement of financial assets under IFRS 9. In particular, such mismatches could arise because of the accounting for insurance contract liabilities under the IASB's tentative decisions in its Insurance Contracts project. In response to those potential mismatches, the IASB noted that the introduction of the fair value through other comprehensive income measurement category, which reflects a hold to collect and sell business model, and the extension of the existing fair value option in IFRS 9 to financial assets that would otherwise be measured at fair value through other comprehensive income (see paragraphs BC4.210–BC4.211), are both relevant to many entities that have insurance contract liabilities. Consequently, the IASB believes that those requirements will assist in improving the interaction between the accounting for financial assets and the proposed accounting for insurance contract liabilities as compared to the requirements issued in IFRS 9 (2009). The IASB noted that, in a sense, these amendments to the requirements in IFRS 9 for the classification and measurement of financial assets provide a number of 'tools' that the IASB can consider when it finalises the accounting for insurance contract liabilities. Moreover, the IASB noted that it will consider the feedback related to the accounting model for insurance contract liabilities and whether that model should be modified to reflect the interaction with the classification and measurement model for financial assets in IFRS 9 as it continues to discuss its Insurance Contracts project.

BC4.160 In order to improve the clarity of the application guidance related to the hold to collect and sell business model, the IASB decided to emphasise that holding and selling are not the *objectives* of the business model, but instead are the *outcomes* of the business model. That is, collecting contractual cash flows and selling financial assets are the outcomes of the way in which an entity manages its financial assets to achieve the objective of a particular business model. For example, an entity with a long-term investment strategy that has an objective of matching the cash flows on long-term liabilities or matching the duration of liabilities with the cash flows on financial assets may have a hold to collect and sell business model. The IASB decided to clarify that measuring financial assets at fair value through other comprehensive income provides relevant and useful information to users of financial statements only when realising cash flows by collecting contractual cash flows and selling financial assets are both integral to achieving the objective of the business model.

BC4.161   The IASB acknowledges that a third measurement category adds complexity to IFRS 9 and may seem similar to the available-for-sale category in IAS 39. However, the IASB believes that measuring particular financial assets at fair value through other comprehensive income reflects the assets' performance better than measuring those assets at either amortised cost or fair value through profit or loss. The IASB also believes that the fair value through other comprehensive income measurement category in IFRS 9 is fundamentally different to the available-for-sale category in IAS 39. That is because there is a clear and logical rationale for measuring particular financial assets at fair value through other comprehensive income, which is based on the existing structure in IFRS 9 (ie financial assets are classified on the basis of their contractual cash flow characteristics and the business model in which they are held). In contrast, the available-for-sale category in IAS 39 was essentially a residual classification and, in many cases, was a free choice. Moreover, IFRS 9 requires the same interest revenue recognition and impairment approach for assets measured at amortised cost and fair value through other comprehensive income, whereas IAS 39 applied different impairment approaches to different measurement categories. Consequently, the IASB believes that the added complexity of a third measurement category (compared to the requirements issued in IFRS 9 (2009)) is justified by the usefulness of the information provided to users of financial statements.

BC4.162   The IASB noted during its redeliberations that some interested parties have expressed concerns that the introduction of the fair value through other comprehensive income measurement category would increase the use of fair value compared to the requirements issued in IFRS 9 (2009). However, as discussed in paragraph BC4.140, the introduction of the third measurement category and the clarifications to the hold to collect business model clarify, instead of change (narrow the scope of), the population of financial assets that were intended to be eligible to be measured at amortised cost. The clarifications to the guidance for the hold to collect business model address particular application questions raised by interested parties by reaffirming the existing principle in IFRS 9. The introduction of the fair value through other comprehensive income measurement category affects only assets that are not held in a hold to collect business model and thus would otherwise be measured at fair value through profit or loss under the requirements issued in IFRS 9 (2009).

Fair value through profit or loss

BC4.163   IFRS 9 (as issued in 2009) had only two measurement categories: amortised cost and fair value through profit or loss. A financial asset was measured at amortised cost only if it met particular conditions. All other financial assets were measured at fair value through profit or loss; ie fair value through profit or loss was the residual measurement category.[18]

BC4.164   The 2012 Limited Amendments Exposure Draft proposed to introduce a third measurement category—fair value through other comprehensive income—and, during the deliberations leading to that Exposure Draft, the IASB considered whether fair value through profit or loss should remain the residual measurement category. The IASB acknowledged that there might be some benefits in making fair value through other comprehensive income the residual measurement category, because, arguably, a clearer distinction could be made between the conditions for the amortised cost measurement category and the conditions for the fair value through profit or loss measurement category. That is, it would be easier to define the two 'ends' of the classification spectrum (ie amortised cost and fair value through profit or loss) with the 'middle' (ie fair value through other comprehensive income) as the residual. As noted in paragraph BC4.156, a few respondents to the 2012 Limited Amendments Exposure Draft expressed this view.

BC4.165   However, the IASB has consistently noted that the residual measurement category must provide useful information for all of the instruments classified in that category. Amortised cost information is provided in profit or loss for both the amortised cost measurement category and the fair value through other comprehensive income measurement category, and this information is relevant only for financial assets with particular contractual cash flow characteristics that are held within particular business models. That is, amortised cost information is relevant only if the financial asset has contractual cash flows that are solely payments of principal and interest and the asset is held in a business model in which collecting contractual cash flows is integral to achieving its objective. As a result, the IASB believes that it would be inappropriate if either amortised cost or fair value through other comprehensive income was the residual measurement category. Furthermore, the IASB believes that defining the conditions for the fair value through other comprehensive income measurement category strengthens and clarifies the conditions for the amortised cost measurement category.

BC4.166   Consequently, the IASB reaffirmed the existing requirement in IFRS 9—and the proposal in the 2012 Limited Amendments Exposure Draft—that the fair value through profit or loss measurement category is the residual measurement category. In addition, to respond to feedback received, the IASB confirmed that financial assets that are held for trading purposes and financial assets that are managed and whose performance is evaluated on a fair value basis must be measured at fair value through profit or loss, because they are held neither in a hold to collect business model nor in a hold to collect and sell business model. Instead, the entity makes decisions on the basis of changes in, and with the objective of realising, the assets' fair value. Thus, the IASB believes that relevant

---

18   As noted previously, IFRS 9 (as issued in 2009) permitted an entity to make an irrevocable election at initial recognition to present fair value gains and losses on particular investments in equity instruments in other comprehensive income. That election is discussed in paragraph 5.7.5 of IFRS 9 and was outside of the scope of the 2012 Limited Amendments Exposure Draft.

and useful information about the amounts, timing and uncertainty of future cash flows is provided to users of financial statements only if these financial assets are measured at fair value through profit or loss.

Other considerations

BC4.167 In the deliberations leading to the publication of the 2012 Limited Amendments Exposure Draft, the IASB considered an alternative approach to assessing the business model in which financial assets are held. The approach was a 'business-activity approach' and was similar to the tentative approach that the FASB had been considering immediately prior to the start of the boards' joint deliberations. In summary, the business-activity approach would have classified financial assets on the basis of the business activity that the entity uses in acquiring and managing those financial assets, subject to an assessment of the asset's contractual cash flow characteristics. The business-activity approach focused on the strategy that resulted in an entity's initial recognition of the financial asset. Under this approach, the relevant business activities were 'customer financing' or 'lending', which would result in measurement at amortised cost; 'investing', which would result in measurement at fair value through other comprehensive income; and 'holding for sale' or 'actively managing (or monitoring) the assets at fair value', which would result in measurement at fair value through profit or loss. In order to be considered a lending (or customer financing) business activity, in addition to holding the financial assets to collect substantially all of the contractual cash flows, the entity must also have had the ability to negotiate adjustments to the contractual cash flows with the counterparty in the event of a potential credit loss.

BC4.168 The IASB noted that the business-activity approach would be different from the approach to classifying financial assets in IFRS 9 (as issued in 2009). In addition, the IASB noted that measuring financial assets at amortised cost only if the entity has the ability to negotiate the asset's terms with the counterparty might be unduly costly to implement and complex to apply and also might result in different classification of lending activities solely as a result of the different legal frameworks in different jurisdictions. The IASB also noted that, under the business-activity approach, the form of the financial asset would affect its classification; for example, widely-held bonds would typically fail to meet the criteria to be measured at amortised cost, because the holder is generally unable to renegotiate the terms with the counterparty on a bilateral basis. Accordingly, the IASB decided not to pursue the business-activity approach and instead confirmed the approach in IFRS 9, in which financial assets are measured at amortised cost if they are held with an objective to collect contractual cash flows (subject to the assessment of the asset's contractual cash flow characteristics) and reaffirmed the rationale for the business model assessment set out in paragraphs BC4.15–BC4.21.

BC4.169 In addition, during its deliberations leading to the publication of the 2012 Limited Amendments Exposure Draft, the IASB noted that the 2009 Classification and Measurement Exposure Draft had solicited views on alternative approaches in which fair value changes for particular financial assets would be disaggregated, with the result that a portion of the fair value change would be presented in profit or loss and a portion of the fair value change would be presented in other comprehensive income. Those alternative approaches, as well as the feedback received and the IASB's rationale for ultimately rejecting the approaches, are described in more detail in paragraphs BC4.41–BC4.43. The IASB believes that the fair value through other comprehensive income measurement category that was proposed in the 2012 Limited Amendments Exposure Draft, and subsequently added to IFRS 9, is different from, and significantly less complex than, those alternative approaches. For example, the alternative approaches continued to rely on the definition of 'loans and receivables' in IAS 39 (in addition to the assessments of the entity's business model and the asset's contractual cash flows). Moreover, the alternative approaches prohibited recycling and therefore did not present both fair value and amortised cost information in the financial statements. As discussed in paragraph BC4.157, presenting both sets of information was an important factor in the IASB's decision to add the fair value through other comprehensive income measurement category to IFRS 9.

Contractual cash flow characteristics[19]

Solely payments of principal and interest

BC4.170   IFRS 9 (as issued in 2009) required an entity to assess the contractual cash flow characteristics of financial assets. A financial asset was measured at amortised cost only if its contractual terms gave rise on specified dates to cash flows that are solely payments of principal and interest on the principal amount outstanding, subject to the assessment of the business model within which the asset is held. For the purposes of assessing the contractual cash flow characteristics of a financial asset, interest was consideration for the time value of money and for the credit risk associated with the principal amount outstanding during a particular period of time. Paragraph BC4.22 noted that a premium for liquidity risk may be included.

BC4.171   The IASB's long-standing view has been that amortised cost provides relevant and useful information about particular financial assets in particular circumstances because, for those assets, it provides information about the amount, timing and uncertainty of future cash flows. Amortised cost is calculated using the effective interest method, which is a relatively simple measurement technique that allocates interest over the relevant time period using the effective interest rate.

BC4.172   The objective of the requirement in IFRS 9 to assess an asset's contractual cash flows is to identify instruments for which the effective interest method results in relevant and useful information. The IASB believes that the effective interest method is suitable only for instruments with 'simple' cash flows that represent solely principal and interest. In contrast, as set out in paragraph BC4.23, the effective interest method is not an appropriate method for allocating contractual cash flows that are not principal and interest on the principal

---

19   In this section, the discussion about amortised cost information is relevant to both financial assets in the amortised cost measurement category and financial assets in the fair value through other comprehensive income measurement category. That is because, for the latter, the assets are measured at fair value in the statement of financial position and amortised cost information is provided in profit or loss.

© IFRS Foundation

amount outstanding. Instead those more complex cash flows require a valuation overlay to contractual cash flows (ie fair value) to ensure that the reported financial information provides useful information.

BC4.173 Most interested parties have consistently agreed that a financial asset should be classified and measured on the basis of its contractual cash flow characteristics and have found this requirement to be operational. However, subsequent to the issue of IFRS 9 in 2009, the IASB received some questions about how this assessment should be applied to particular financial assets. Specifically, the requirements in paragraph B4.1.13 of IFRS 9 (2009) set out an example of a financial asset with an interest rate tenor mismatch (that is, the variable interest rate on the financial asset is reset every month to a three-month interest rate or the variable interest rate is reset to always reflect the original maturity of the asset). The discussion of the example (Instrument B) concluded that such contractual cash flows are not payments of principal and interest, because the interest rate does not represent consideration for the time value of money for the tenor of the instrument (or the reset period). Subsequent to the issuance of IFRS 9 in 2009, many interested parties raised concerns related to that example. Specifically, those interested parties asked about the assessment of a financial asset's contractual cash flows when the consideration for the time value of money element of the interest rate is not perfect (ie it is 'modified') because of a contractual term such as an interest rate tenor mismatch feature. Generally, stakeholders expressed concerns that the application guidance issued in IFRS 9 (2009) could lead to an unduly narrow interpretation of the meaning of interest.

BC4.174 The IASB acknowledged these concerns. In the 2012 Limited Amendments Exposure Draft, it proposed a notion of a modified economic relationship between principal and the consideration for time value of money and credit risk—and also proposed corresponding clarifications to Instrument B in paragraph B4.1.13 of IFRS 9. Specifically, the IASB proposed that a financial asset does not necessarily need to be measured at fair value through profit or loss if the economic relationship between principal and the consideration for time value of money and credit risk is modified by an interest rate tenor mismatch feature. Instead, an entity would be required to assess the effect of the modified relationship on the financial asset's contractual cash flows relative to a 'perfect' benchmark instrument (ie a financial instrument with the same credit quality and with the same contractual terms except for the contractual term under evaluation). If the modification could result in contractual cash flows that are more than insignificantly different from the benchmark cash flows, the contractual terms of the financial asset would not give rise to cash flows that are solely payments of principal and interest on the principal amount outstanding. In other words, in the 2012 Limited Amendments Exposure Draft, the IASB clarified that the relationship between principal and the consideration for time value of money and credit risk does not need to be perfect, but only relatively minor modifications of that relationship are consistent with payments that are solely principal and interest.

BC4.175 While developing the 2012 Limited Amendments Exposure Draft, the IASB received feedback about interest rates in regulated environments that modify the economic relationship between principal and the consideration for the time value of money and the credit risk. Interested parties noted that in such environments the base interest rates are set by a central authority and may not be reset in a manner that reflects the reset period. In these circumstances, the effect of the interest rate tenor mismatch feature could be significant. Furthermore, in such environments, there may not be any financial instruments available that are priced on a different basis. Thus, some raised concerns about how to determine whether the cash flows on such instruments are solely payments of principal and interest and whether the proposed notion of a modified economic relationship was operational and appropriate in such environments. The IASB noted that it would gather further feedback during the comment period on whether the clarifications proposed in the 2012 Limited Amendments Exposure Draft appropriately addressed the concerns related to interest rates in regulated environments.

BC4.176 Nearly all respondents to the 2012 Limited Amendments Exposure Draft agreed that a financial asset with a modified economic relationship between principal and the consideration for the time value of money and the credit risk should be considered to have contractual cash flows that are solely payments of principal and interest. However, many respondents believed that the clarification did not go far enough in addressing common application questions and expressed concern that some financial assets that they view as 'plain vanilla' or 'normal lending' would still not have contractual cash flows that are solely payments of principal and interest. Specifically, these respondents expressed the view that the assessment of a modified economic relationship still implied an unduly narrow and strict interpretation of the time value of money element of an interest rate. They stated that amortised cost could provide useful information for a broader range of financial instruments. They asked the IASB to clarify the scope of the assessment of a modified economic relationship (for example, whether it should apply only to interest rate tenor mismatch features or more broadly to all circumstances in which the time value of money element is modified (ie imperfect)) and to reconsider the threshold used in that assessment (ie the threshold of 'not more than insignificantly different' from benchmark cash flows). Respondents also requested broader clarifications about the meaning of the time value of money as that notion is used in the description of interest in IFRS 9.

BC4.177 In its redeliberations, the IASB acknowledged respondents' questions and concerns and, as a result, decided to clarify the following items:

(a) The objective of the time value of money element is to provide consideration for *only* the passage of time, in the absence of a return for other risks (such as credit risk or liquidity risk) or costs associated with holding the financial asset. In assessing the time value of money element, the entity must consider the currency in which the financial asset is denominated, because interest rates vary by currency. In addition, as a general proposition, there must be a link between the interest rate and the period for which the interest rate is set, because the appropriate rate for an instrument varies depending on the term for which the rate is set.

(b)   However, in some circumstances, the time value of money element could provide consideration for only the passage of time even if that element is modified by, for example, an interest rate tenor mismatch feature or a feature that sets the interest rate by reference to an average of particular short and long-term interest rates. In these cases, an entity must assess whether the time value of money element provides consideration for only the passage of time by performing either a quantitative or qualitative assessment. The objective of that assessment is to establish (on an undiscounted basis) how different the financial asset's contractual cash flows (ie taking into account all of the contractual cash flows) could be from the cash flows that would arise if the time value of money element were perfect (ie if there were a perfect link between the interest rate and the period for which that rate is set). The IASB decided not to prescribe when an entity must perform a quantitative versus a qualitative assessment.

(c)   If the modified time value of money element could result in cash flows that are significantly different on an undiscounted basis from the 'perfect' cash flows (described as benchmark cash flows), either in a single reporting period or cumulatively over the life of the financial instrument, the financial asset does not have contractual cash flows that are solely payments of principal and interest. The IASB was persuaded by respondents' feedback that the 'not more than insignificantly different' threshold in the 2012 Limited Amendments Exposure Draft was unduly restrictive and, as a result, particular financial assets would be measured at fair value through profit or loss even though the objective of the modified time value of money element was in fact to provide consideration for only the passage of time. However, the IASB noted that the objective of a modified time value of money element is not to provide consideration for just the passage of time, and thus the contractual cash flows are not solely payments of principal and interest, if the contractual cash flows could be significantly different from the benchmark cash flows.

BC4.178   The IASB also noted that, as a general proposition, the market in which the transaction occurs is relevant to the assessment of the time value of money element. For example, in Europe it is common to reference interest rates to LIBOR and in the United States it is common to reference interest rates to the prime rate. However the IASB noted that a particular interest rate does not necessarily reflect consideration for only the time value of money merely because that rate is considered 'normal' in a particular market. For example, if an interest rate is reset every year but the reference rate is always a 15-year rate, it would be difficult for an entity to conclude that such a rate provides consideration for only the passage of time, even if such pricing is commonly used in that particular market. Accordingly the IASB believes that an entity must apply judgement to conclude whether the stated time value of money element meets the objective of providing consideration for only the passage of time.

Regulated interest rates

BC4.179 The IASB noted that in some jurisdictions the government or regulatory authority establishes interest rates and, in some cases, the objective of the time value of money element may not be to provide consideration for only the passage of time. However, the IASB decided that such a regulated interest rate is a proxy for the time value of money element if that interest rate provides consideration that is broadly consistent with the passage of time and does not provide exposure to risks or volatility in the contractual cash flows that are inconsistent with a basic lending arrangement.

BC4.180 The IASB acknowledged that this approach for regulated interest rates is broader than the approach for interest rates that are established freely by market participants. However, the IASB noted that these regulated rates are set for public policy reasons and thus are not subject to structuring to achieve a particular accounting result. For example, the IASB noted that French retail banks collect deposits on special 'Livret A' savings accounts. The interest rate is determined by the central bank and the government according to a formula that reflects protection against inflation and an adequate remuneration that incentivises entities to use these particular savings accounts. This is because legislation requires a particular portion of the amounts collected by the retail banks to be lent to a governmental agency that uses the proceeds for social programmes. The IASB noted that the time value element of interest on these accounts may not provide consideration for only the passage of time; however the IASB believes that amortised cost would provide relevant and useful information as long as the contractual cash flows do not introduce risks or volatility that are inconsistent with a basic lending arrangement.

Other clarifications

BC4.181 Respondents to the 2012 Limited Amendments Exposure Draft also asked the IASB to clarify the overall objective of the assessment of a financial asset's contractual cash flow characteristics and also raised the following specific questions and concerns related to that assessment:

(a) the meaning of 'principal'—respondents asked the IASB to clarify the meaning of principal, in particular within the context of financial assets that are originated or purchased at a premium or discount to par;

(b) the meaning of 'interest'—respondents asked whether elements other than the time value of money and credit risk (for example, consideration for liquidity risk, funding costs and a profit margin) could be consistent with contractual cash flows that are solely payments of principal and interest; and

(c) de minimis features—respondents asked whether a contractual feature would affect the classification and measurement of a financial asset if, in all scenarios, that feature could impact the contractual cash flows only by a de minimis amount.

BC4.182 In response to the feedback received, the IASB decided to clarify the application guidance in IFRS 9 as follows:

(a) for the purposes of applying the condition in paragraphs 4.1.2(b) and 4.1.2A(b) of IFRS 9, principal is the fair value of the financial asset at initial recognition. The IASB believes that this meaning reflects the economics of the financial asset from the perspective of the current holder; in other words, the entity would assess the contractual cash flow characteristics by comparing the contractual cash flows to the amount that it actually invested. However, the IASB acknowledged that the principal amount may change over the life of the financial asset (for example, if there are repayments of principal).

(b) for the purposes of applying the condition in paragraphs 4.1.2(b) and 4.1.2A(b) of IFRS 9, the consideration for the time value of money and the credit risk are typically the most significant elements of interest; however, they may not be the only elements. In discussing the elements of interest (and indeed the overall objective of the assessment of an asset's contractual cash flows), the IASB considered the concept of a 'basic lending arrangement' (the form of which need not be that of a loan). In such an arrangement, the IASB noted that interest may include consideration for elements other than the time value of money and credit risk. Specifically, interest may include consideration for risks such as liquidity risk and costs associated with holding the asset (such as administrative costs) as well as a profit margin. But elements that introduce exposure to risks or variability in the contractual cash flows that are unrelated to lending (such as exposure to equity or commodity price risk) are not consistent with a basic lending arrangement. The IASB also noted that the assessment of interest focuses on *what* the entity is being compensated for (ie whether the entity is receiving consideration for basic lending risks, costs and a profit margin or is being compensated for something else), instead of *how much* the entity receives for a particular element. For example, the IASB acknowledged that different entities may price the credit risk element differently.

(c) a contractual feature does not affect the classification and measurement of a financial asset if the impact of that feature on the asset's contractual cash flows could only ever be de minimis. The IASB noted that to make this determination an entity must consider the potential effect of the feature in each reporting period and cumulatively over the life of the instrument. For example, a feature would not have a de minimis effect if it could give rise to a significant increase in contractual cash flows in one reporting period and a significant decrease in contractual cash flows in another reporting period, even if these amounts offset each other on a cumulative basis.

Contractual terms that change the timing or amount of contractual cash flows, including prepayment and extension features

BC4.183 The requirements issued in IFRS 9 (2009) provided guidance for contractual terms that permit the issuer (ie the debtor) to prepay a financial instrument or that permit the holder (ie the creditor) to put the financial instrument back to the issuer before maturity (ie 'prepayment features') and contractual terms that permit the issuer or holder to extend the contractual term of the financial instrument (ie 'extension features'). In summary, that guidance stated that prepayment and extension features result in contractual cash flows that are solely payments of principal and interest only if:

(a)   the prepayment or extension feature is not contingent on future events, other than to protect the holder or issuer against particular events or circumstances; and

(b)   the terms of the prepayment or extension feature result in contractual cash flows that are solely payments of principal and interest.

The guidance for prepayment features stated that the prepayment amount may include reasonable additional compensation for the early termination of the contract.

BC4.184   The requirements issued in IFRS 9 (2009) also stated that a contractual term that changes the timing or amount of payments of principal or interest does not result in contractual cash flows that are solely payments of principal and interest unless the term is a variable interest rate that is consideration for the time value of money and credit risk or the term is a prepayment or extension feature (as in paragraph BC4.183). However if a contractual term is not genuine, it does not affect the classification of a financial asset. (Consistently with IAS 32, a contractual feature is not genuine if it affects the asset's contractual cash flows only on the occurrence of an event that is extremely rare, highly abnormal and very unlikely to occur.)

BC4.185   Although the 2012 Limited Amendments Exposure Draft did not propose any amendments to these requirements, some respondents asked the IASB to reconsider or clarify particular aspects of the guidance. In particular, some respondents asked why the requirements issued in IFRS 9 (2009) provided specific guidance for prepayment and extension features that are contingent on future events ('contingent prepayment and extension features'), but did not provide guidance for other types of features that are contingent on future events ('other contingent features'). Respondents also asked whether (and if so, why) the nature of the future event in itself affects whether the financial asset's contractual cash flows are solely payments of principal and interest. These respondents generally expressed the view that an entity should focus on the contractual cash flows that could arise over the life of the financial instrument (ie both before and after the future event), instead of on the nature of the future event itself.

BC4.186   In addition, some respondents expressed the view that a contingent feature should not affect the classification and measurement of a financial asset if the likelihood is remote that the future event will occur. Some of these respondents were specifically concerned about contingently convertible instruments or so-called 'bail-in' instruments. While the contractual terms of these instruments vary, generally, interested parties raised concerns about contingently convertible instruments that convert into equity instruments of the issuer on the basis of a predetermined ratio if a specified event occurs (for example, if the issuer's regulatory capital ratios decline below a specific threshold). In the case of a bail-in instrument, interested parties generally raised concerns about instruments with a contractual feature that requires (or permits) a portion or all of the unpaid amounts of principal and interest to be written off if a specified event occurs (for example, if the issuer has insufficient regulatory capital or is at a point of non-viability). These respondents expressed the view that these instruments should not be measured at fair value through profit or loss merely as a result of the contingent cash flow characteristics (ie the conversion into a predetermined number of the issuer's equity instruments or the write-off of particular unpaid amounts upon the occurrence of a particular future event) if it is unlikely that the future event will occur.

BC4.187 Other respondents asked whether a financial asset could have contractual cash flows that are solely payments of principal and interest if the asset is purchased or originated at a significant premium or discount to the contractual par amount but is prepayable at that par amount. These respondents noted that if principal is described as the fair value of the financial asset at initial recognition, then the prepayment amount (ie par) will not represent unpaid amounts of principal and interest. That is because the prepayment amount will either be *more than* unpaid amounts of principal and interest (if the asset is purchased or originated at a significant discount) or *less than* unpaid amounts of principal and interest (if the asset is purchased or originated at a significant premium). Respondents stated that discounts and premiums are generally expected to arise when the entity does not expect that the asset will be prepaid (even though prepayment is contractually possible). Many raised this issue specifically within the context of purchased credit-impaired financial assets. Many of these assets will be purchased at a significant discount to par, which reflects the credit impairment, but the contractual terms may include a prepayment feature. Respondents expressed the view that an entity should not be required to measure purchased credit-impaired financial assets at fair value through profit or loss merely as a result of the prepayment feature, particularly because it is highly unlikely that such an asset will be prepaid at its contractual par amount since it is credit impaired.

BC4.188 In its redeliberations of the 2012 Limited Amendments Exposure Draft, the IASB decided to clarify the application guidance in IFRS 9 as follows:

(a) all contingent features must be assessed in the same way. That is, there is no distinction between contingent prepayment and extension features and other types of contingent features.

(b) for all contingent features, the nature of the future event in itself does not determine whether a financial asset's contractual cash flows are solely payments of principal and interest. However, the IASB noted that there often is an important interaction between the nature of the future event and the resulting contractual cash flows. Consequently, it is often helpful (or perhaps even necessary) for the entity to consider the nature of the future event to determine whether the resulting contractual cash flows are solely payments of principal and interest. For example, if the nature of the future event is unrelated to a basic lending arrangement (for example, a particular equity or commodity index reaches or exceeds a particular level), it is unlikely that the resulting contractual cash flows are solely payments of principal and interest, because those cash flows are likely to reflect a return for equity or commodity price risk.

BC4.189 In addition, the IASB confirmed the guidance in IFRS 9 that an entity is not permitted to take into account the probability that the future event will occur, unless the contingent feature is not genuine. In other words, a financial asset must be measured at fair value through profit or loss if a remote (but genuine) contingency would result in contractual cash flows that are not solely payments of principal and interest (and those contractual cash flows are not de minimis). In reaching that conclusion, the IASB considered an alternative approach in which a contingent feature would not affect the classification and measurement of a financial asset if the likelihood is remote that the future event will occur. The IASB rejected this approach because it is inconsistent with its long-standing view that amortised cost provides relevant and useful information only for financial assets with simple contractual cash flows. As noted in paragraph BC4.23, the effective interest method is not appropriate for measuring contractual cash flows that are not solely payments of principal and interest, but instead those cash flows require a valuation overlay to contractual cash flows (ie fair value) to ensure that the reported financial information is relevant and useful.

BC4.190 In particular, the IASB noted that contingently convertible instruments and bail-in instruments could give rise to contractual cash flows that are not solely payments of principal and interest and indeed are structured for regulatory purposes such that they have contractual characteristics similar to equity instruments in particular circumstances. Consequently, the IASB believes that amortised cost does not provide relevant or useful information to users of financial statements about those financial instruments, in particular if the likelihood of that future event occurring increases. At a minimum, the IASB observed that it would be necessary to reclassify the financial asset so that it is measured at fair value through profit or loss if the future event becomes more likely than remote. Thus, the IASB observed that an approach that is based on whether the likelihood of a future event is remote would create additional complexity, because the entity would need to continuously reassess whether the likelihood of the future event has increased such that it is no longer remote, and if so, the entity would need to reclassify the financial asset so that it is measured at fair value through profit or loss at that point.

BC4.191 However, the IASB acknowledged that, as the result of legislation, some governments or other authorities have the power in particular circumstances to impose losses on the holders of some financial instruments. The IASB noted that IFRS 9 requires the holder to analyse the *contractual terms* of a financial asset to determine whether the asset gives rise to cash flows that are solely payments of principal and interest on the principal amount outstanding. In other words, the holder would not consider the payments that arise only as a result of the government's or other authority's legislative power as cash flows in its analysis. That is because that power and the related payments are not *contractual terms* of the financial instrument.

BC4.192 Moreover, the IASB decided to provide a narrow exception for particular prepayable financial assets. The exception would apply to financial assets that would otherwise have contractual cash flows that are solely payments of principal and interest but do not meet that condition only as a result of the prepayment feature. Such financial assets would be eligible to be measured at amortised cost or fair value through other comprehensive income (subject to the assessment of the business model in which they are held) if the following three conditions are met:

(a)   the financial asset is purchased or originated at a premium or discount to the contractual par amount;

(b)   the prepayment amount substantially represents the contractual par amount and accrued (but unpaid) contractual interest, which may include reasonable additional compensation for the early termination of the contract; and

(c)   the fair value of the prepayment feature on initial recognition of the financial asset is insignificant.

BC4.193   This exception would require some financial assets that otherwise do not have contractual cash flows that are solely payments of principal and interest to be measured at amortised cost or fair value through other comprehensive income (subject to the assessment of the business model in which they are held). In particular, the IASB observed that this exception will apply to many purchased credit-impaired financial assets with contractual prepayment features. If such an asset was purchased at a deep discount, apart from the exception described in paragraph BC4.192, the contractual cash flows would not be solely payments of principal and interest if, contractually, the asset could be repaid immediately at the par amount. However that contractual prepayment feature would have an insignificant fair value if it is very unlikely that prepayment will occur. The IASB was persuaded by the feedback that stated that amortised cost would provide useful and relevant information to users of financial statements about such financial assets, because the exception applies only to those financial assets that are prepayable at the contractual par amount. Consequently, the prepayment amount does not introduce variability that is inconsistent with a basic lending arrangement because that variability would result only from the time value of money and credit risk elements; ie the entity would receive more of the contractual cash flows than it previously expected, and it would receive those contractual cash flows immediately. The IASB believes that information about that variability would be appropriately captured by amortised cost via the catch-up adjustment mechanism.

BC4.194   Similarly, the IASB observed that this exception will apply to some financial assets that are originated at below-market interest rates. For example, this scenario may arise when an entity sells an item (for example, an automobile) and, as a marketing incentive, provides financing to the customer at an interest rate that is below the prevailing market rate. At initial recognition the entity would measure the financial asset at fair value[20] and, as a result of the below-market interest rate, the fair value would be at a discount to the par amount. If the customer has a contractual right to repay the par amount at any point before maturity, then without an exception, the contractual cash flows may not be solely payments of principal and interest. The IASB observed that

---

20   Unless the financial asset is a trade receivable that does not have a significant financing component (determined in accordance with IFRS 15). Such a trade receivable is measured at initial recognition in accordance with paragraph 5.1.3 in IFRS 9.

such a contractual prepayment feature likely would have an insignificant fair value because it is unlikely that the customer will choose to prepay; in particular, because the interest rate is below-market and thus the financing is advantageous. Consistently with the discussion in paragraph BC4.193, the IASB believes that amortised cost would provide relevant and useful information to users of financial statements about this financial asset, because the prepayment amount does not introduce variability that is inconsistent with a basic lending arrangement.

BC4.195 Paragraphs BC4.193–BC4.194 discuss circumstances in which a financial asset is originated or purchased at a *discount* to the par amount. However, the IASB noted that its rationale for the exception described in paragraph BC4.192 is equally relevant for assets that are originated or purchased at a *premium* and therefore decided that the exception should apply symmetrically to both circumstances.

Bifurcation

BC4.196 The requirements issued in IFRS 9 (2009) did not bifurcate hybrid contracts with financial asset hosts. Instead, all financial assets were classified in their entirety. Since 2009, many interested parties have expressed support for that approach. However, others have expressed the view that hybrid financial assets should be bifurcated into a derivative component and a non-derivative host. Much of the feedback that was received after IFRS 9 was issued in 2009 was similar to the feedback that was received during the deliberations that led to that Standard being issued. That feedback is summarised in paragraph BC4.88. In addition, some have noted that:

(a) components of some hybrid financial assets are managed separately and therefore bifurcation may provide more relevant information to users of financial statements about how the entity manages those instruments;

(b) an embedded feature that has an insignificant fair value at initial recognition (for example, because it is contingent on a future event that the entity believes is unlikely to occur) could cause a hybrid financial asset to be measured at fair value through profit or loss in its entirety; and

(c) it is important to have symmetry in the bifurcation of financial assets and financial liabilities and, consequently, hybrid financial assets should be bifurcated because the IASB retained bifurcation for hybrid financial liabilities.

BC4.197 During the deliberations that led to the publication of the 2012 Limited Amendments Exposure Draft, the IASB reconsidered whether bifurcation should be pursued for financial assets or financial liabilities (or both) and, if so, what the basis for that bifurcation should be. The IASB considered three approaches:

(a) 'closely-related' bifurcation (ie bifurcation using the 'closely-related' bifurcation criteria in IAS 39, which have been carried forward to IFRS 9 for financial liabilities);

(b) 'principal-and-interest' bifurcation; or

(c)   no bifurcation (ie the financial instrument would be classified in its entirety).

BC4.198   In the 2012 Limited Amendments Exposure Draft, the IASB did not propose any changes to the requirements in IFRS 9 related to the bifurcation of financial instruments. As a result, hybrid financial assets are not bifurcated but are instead classified and measured in their entirety. Hybrid financial liabilities are bifurcated (unless the entity elects to apply the fair value option) on the basis of the closely-related criteria that were carried forward to IFRS 9 from IAS 39.

BC4.199   In reaching that conclusion, the IASB noted that, consistently with paragraphs BC4.46–BC4.53 and BC4.91, interested parties have consistently told the IASB that the bifurcation methodology in IAS 39 for financial liabilities is generally working well in practice and practice has developed since those requirements were issued. Specifically, many constituents, including users of financial statements, strongly supported retaining bifurcation for financial liabilities even though they supported eliminating it for financial assets. That was primarily because bifurcation addresses the issue of own credit risk, which is relevant only for financial liabilities.

BC4.200   In contrast, while the closely-related bifurcation methodology in IAS 39 works well for financial liabilities, it does not complement the guidance in IFRS 9 that requires an entity to assess the asset's contractual cash flow characteristics. For example, if IFRS 9 were to require both an assessment of the asset's contractual cash flow characteristics *and* a closely-related bifurcation assessment, the IASB would need to determine which of those assessments should have primacy. For example, the IASB discussed a scenario in which a financial asset had contractual cash flows that were not solely payments of principal and interest but did not contain an embedded derivative that required bifurcation. Specifically, the IASB considered how such a financial asset should be subsequently measured; ie either in its entirety at fair value through profit or loss because its contractual cash flows were not solely payments of principal and interest or, alternatively, in its entirety at amortised cost (or fair value through other comprehensive income, depending on the business model in which is it held) because it did not contain an embedded derivative that required bifurcation. Similar challenges would arise for a financial asset that had contractual cash flows that were solely payments of principal and interest but contained an embedded derivative that required bifurcation. As a result, the IASB concluded that combining the assessment in IFRS 9 of the asset's contractual cash flow characteristics with a closely-related bifurcation assessment would be complex and likely would give rise to contradictory outcomes—and indeed, in some cases, seemed unworkable. Consequently, the IASB decided not to pursue this approach for financial assets.

BC4.201   Under a principal-and-interest bifurcation approach, if a financial asset had cash flows that were not solely payments of principal and interest, that asset would be assessed to determine whether it should be bifurcated into a host (with cash flows that are solely payments of principal and interest) and an embedded residual feature. The host could qualify for a measurement category other than fair value through profit or loss, depending on the business model within which it was held. The embedded feature would be measured at fair value through profit or loss. The IASB also considered variations of this approach whereby bifurcation would be required only if the embedded feature met the definition of a derivative or if the components were separately managed. If these conditions were not met, the financial asset would be measured in its entirety at fair value through profit or loss.

BC4.202 The IASB noted that if principal-and-interest bifurcation is based on the separate management of the components of the instrument, such an approach would be an instrument-by-instrument assessment of the management of a financial asset. That would be inconsistent with the existing assessment in IFRS 9 of the business model, which requires the management of financial assets to be assessed at a higher level of aggregation. The IASB also noted that a principal-and-interest bifurcation approach might seem generally compatible with the existing requirements in IFRS 9, but, in fact, it would introduce new concepts into the classification and measurement of financial assets and would undoubtedly raise questions about how the host and embedded feature should be defined and measured. The IASB observed that introducing a principal-and-interest bifurcation approach into IFRS 9 would significantly increase complexity, especially because it would then contain two bifurcation approaches (ie one for hybrid financial assets and another for hybrid financial liabilities). The IASB also observed that there was significant risk of unintended consequences related to introducing a new bifurcation approach. Consequently, the IASB decided not to pursue this approach for financial assets.

BC4.203 Accordingly, during the deliberations that led to the 2012 Limited Amendments Exposure Draft, the IASB confirmed its decision that hybrid contracts with financial asset hosts should be classified and measured in their entirety. In reaching that conclusion, the IASB cited its original rationale for prohibiting bifurcation, which is set out in paragraphs BC4.83–BC4.90.

BC4.204 Some respondents to the 2012 Limited Amendments Exposure Draft from particular jurisdictions continued to express a preference for bifurcating hybrid financial assets. However, most respondents did not suggest that bifurcation should be reintroduced and some respondents specifically stated that they disagreed with reintroducing it. As a result, the IASB reconfirmed the requirements in IFRS 9 that hybrid contracts with financial asset hosts should not be bifurcated but should instead be classified and measured in their entirety.

Investments in contractually linked instruments (tranches)

BC4.205 In accordance with the requirements in paragraphs B4.1.21–B4.1.26 of IFRS 9 (issued in 2009), investments in contractually linked instruments (tranches) may have contractual cash flows that are solely payments of principal and interest if (in summary):

(a) the contractual terms of the tranche being assessed for classification give rise to cash flows that are solely payments of principal and interest on the principal amount outstanding;

(b) the underlying pool of instruments contains only instruments that have contractual cash flows that are solely principal and interest on the principal amount outstanding, that reduce cash flow variability on the instruments in the pool or that align the cash flows of the tranches with the cash flows of the instruments in the pool to address particular differences; and

(c)   the exposure to credit risk inherent in the tranche being assessed is equal to, or lower than, the overall exposure to credit risk of the underlying pool of financial instruments.

BC4.206   After IFRS 9 was issued in 2009, the IASB received questions about whether a tranche could have contractual cash flows that are solely payments of principal and interest if the tranche is prepayable in the event that the underlying pool of financial instruments is prepaid or if the underlying pool includes instruments that are collateralised by assets that do not meet the conditions set out in paragraphs B4.1.23–B4.1.24 of IFRS 9 (as issued in 2009). The IASB noted that a key principle underpinning the assessment of contractually linked instruments is that an entity should not be disadvantaged simply as a result of holding an investment indirectly (ie via an investment in a tranche) if the underlying pool of instruments have contractual cash flows that are solely payments of principal and interest and the tranche is not exposed to leverage or more credit risk than the credit risk of the underlying pool of financial instruments. Accordingly, in the 2012 Limited Amendments Exposure Draft, the IASB proposed to clarify that a tranche may have contractual cash flows that are solely payments of principal and interest even if:

(a)   the tranche is prepayable in the event that the underlying pool of financial instruments is prepaid. The IASB noted that because the underlying pool of assets must have contractual cash flows that are solely payments of principal and interest then, by extension, any prepayment features in those underlying financial assets must also be solely payments of principal and interest.

(b)   financial assets in the underlying pool are collateralised by assets that do not meet the conditions set out in paragraphs B4.1.23 and B4.1.24 of IFRS 9. In such cases, the entity would disregard the possibility that the pool may contain the collateral in the future unless the entity acquired the instrument with the intention of controlling the collateral. The IASB noted that this is consistent with IFRS 9; ie financial assets can themselves still have contractual cash flows that are solely payments of principal and interest if they are collateralised by assets that do not have contractual cash flows that are solely payments of principal and interest.

BC4.207   Respondents supported these proposals but asked the IASB to consider additional clarifications to the requirements for contractually linked instruments:

(a)   in assessing whether the instruments in the underlying pool meet the requirements in paragraphs B4.1.23 or B4.1.24 of IFRS 9, a detailed instrument-by-instrument analysis of the pool may not be necessary; however, the entity is required to use judgement and perform sufficient analysis to determine whether those requirements are met; and

(b) an entity may assess the requirement in paragraph B4.1.21(c) of IFRS 9 by comparing the credit rating of a tranche to the weighted average credit rating of the financial assets in the underlying pool (ie comparing the credit rating of the tranche being assessed for classification to what the credit rating would be on a *single* tranche that funded the entire underlying pool of financial instruments).

BC4.208 The IASB agreed with the points in paragraph BC4.207 and indeed noted that those clarifications are consistent with the original intention of the requirements for contractually linked instruments. The IASB therefore decided to clarify the relevant paragraphs in the application guidance to IFRS 9. However, it noted that the clarification described in paragraph BC4.206(a) would be addressed as a result of the general clarifications made to the requirements for contingent prepayment features.

Other limited amendments

BC4.209 As a result of introducing the fair value through other comprehensive income measurement category into IFRS 9, the IASB considered particular interrelated issues—specifically, whether the existing requirements issued in IFRS 9 (2009) for the fair value option and for reclassifications should be extended to financial assets measured at fair value through other comprehensive income.

Fair value option for financial assets otherwise measured at fair value through other comprehensive income

BC4.210 In accordance with the requirements issued in IFRS 9 (2009), entities are permitted to designate financial assets that would otherwise be measured at amortised cost as measured at fair value through profit or loss if, and only if, such designation eliminates or significantly reduces a measurement or recognition inconsistency (sometimes referred to as an 'accounting mismatch'). Such designation is available at initial recognition and is irrevocable.

BC4.211 The IASB decided that the same fair value option that is available to financial assets that would otherwise be measured at amortised cost should be available for financial assets that would otherwise be measured at fair value through other comprehensive income. The IASB noted that the rationale set out in paragraph BC4.79 for permitting the fair value option for assets measured at amortised cost is equally applicable for financial assets measured at fair value through other comprehensive income.

Reclassifications into and out of the fair value through other comprehensive income measurement category

BC4.212 Paragraph 4.1.1 of IFRS 9 (as issued in 2009) required that an entity reclassify all affected financial assets when it changes its business model for managing financial assets. Paragraphs BC4.111–BC4.120 set out the IASB's rationale for the reclassification requirements.

BC4.213 The IASB noted that the number of measurement categories does not affect that rationale and therefore decided that the reclassification requirements issued in IFRS 9 (2009) should also apply to financial assets measured at fair value through other comprehensive income. Consequently, when an entity changes its business model for managing financial assets, it must reclassify all affected financial assets, including those in the fair value through other comprehensive income measurement category. Consistently with the requirements issued in IFRS 9 (2009), all reclassifications into and out of the fair value through other comprehensive income measurement category are applied prospectively from the reclassification date and previously recognised gains or losses (including impairment gains or losses) or interest revenue are not restated.

BC4.214   The IASB noted that because amortised cost information is provided in profit or loss for financial assets that are measured at fair value through other comprehensive income, reclassifications between the amortised cost measurement category and the fair value through other comprehensive income measurement category do not change the recognition of interest revenue or the measurement of expected credit losses. Specifically, the entity would have established the effective interest rate when the financial asset was originally recognised and would continue to use that rate if the financial asset is reclassified between the amortised cost measurement category and the fair value through other comprehensive income measurement category. Similarly, the measurement of expected credit losses does not change because both measurement categories apply the same impairment approach.

BC4.215   The IASB also decided to extend the relevant disclosure requirements in IFRS 7 and the relevant presentation requirements in IAS 1 to reclassifications into and out of the fair value through other comprehensive income measurement category.

Measurement (Chapter 5)

Fair value measurement considerations[21]

BCZ5.1   The IASB decided to include in the revised IAS 39 (published in 2002) expanded guidance about how to determine fair values (the guidance is now in IFRS 9), in particular for financial instruments for which no quoted market price is available (now paragraphs B5.4.6–B5.4.13 of IFRS 9). The IASB decided that it is desirable to provide clear and reasonably detailed guidance about the objective and use of valuation techniques to achieve reliable and comparable fair value estimates when financial instruments are measured at fair value.

Use of quoted prices in active markets

BCZ5.2   The IASB considered comments received that disagreed with the proposal in the exposure draft published in 2002 that a quoted price is the appropriate measure of fair value for an instrument quoted in an active market. Some respondents argued that (a) valuation techniques are more appropriate for measuring fair value than a quoted price in an active market (eg for derivatives) and (b) valuation models are consistent with industry best practice, and are justified because of their acceptance for regulatory capital purposes.

---

21   IFRS 13, issued in May 2011, contains the requirements for measuring fair value. As a consequence paragraphs 5.4.1–5.4.3 and B5.4.1–B5.4.13 of IFRS 9 have been deleted. *Annual Improvements to IFRSs 2010–2012 Cycle*, issued in December 2013, added paragraph BC138A to the Basis for Conclusions on IFRS 13 to clarify the IASB's reason for deleting paragraph B5.4.12.

BCZ5.3   However, the IASB confirmed that a quoted price is the appropriate measure of
fair value for an instrument quoted in an active market, notably because (a) in
an active market, the quoted price is the best evidence of fair value, given that
fair value is defined in terms of a price agreed by a knowledgeable, willing buyer
and a knowledgeable, willing seller; (b) it results in consistent measurement
across entities; and (c) fair value (now defined in IFRS 9) does not depend on
entity-specific factors. The IASB further clarified that a quoted price includes
market-quoted rates as well as prices.

Entities that have access to more than one active market

BCZ5.4   The IASB considered situations in which entities operate in different markets.
An example is a trader that originates a derivative with a corporate in an active
corporate retail market and offsets the derivative by taking out a derivative with
a dealer in an active dealers' wholesale market. The IASB decided to clarify that
the objective of fair value measurement is to arrive at the price at which a
transaction would occur at the balance sheet date in the same instrument
(ie without modification or repackaging) in the most advantageous active
market[22] to which an entity has immediate access. Thus, if a dealer enters into a
derivative instrument with the corporate, but has immediate access to a more
advantageously priced dealers' market, the entity recognises a profit on initial
recognition of the derivative instrument. However, the entity adjusts the price
observed in the dealer market for any differences in counterparty credit risk
between the derivative instrument with the corporate and that with the dealers'
market.

Bid-ask spreads in active markets

BCZ5.5   The IASB confirmed the proposal in the exposure draft published in 2002 that
the appropriate quoted market price for an asset held or liability to be issued is
usually the current bid price and, for an asset to be acquired or liability held, the
asking price.[23] It concluded that applying mid-market prices to an individual
instrument is not appropriate because it would result in entities recognising
upfront gains or losses for the difference between the bid-ask price and the
mid-market price.

BCZ5.6   The IASB discussed whether the bid-ask spread should be applied to the net open
position of a portfolio containing offsetting market risk positions, or to each
instrument in the portfolio. It noted the concerns raised by constituents that
applying the bid-ask spread to the net open position better reflects the fair value
of the risk retained in the portfolio. The IASB concluded that for offsetting risk
positions, entities could use mid-market prices to determine fair value, and
hence may apply the bid or asking price to the net open position as appropriate.
The IASB believes that when an entity has offsetting risk positions, using the
mid-market price is appropriate because the entity (a) has locked in its cash

---

22   IFRS 13, issued in May 2011, states that a fair value measurement assumes that the transaction to
sell an asset or to transfer a liability takes place in the principal market, or in the absence of a
principal market, the most advantageous market for the asset or liability.

23   IFRS 13, issued in May 2011, states that fair value is measured using the price within the bid-ask
spread that is most representative of fair value in the circumstances.

flows from the asset and liability and (b) potentially could sell the matched position without incurring the bid-ask spread.[24]

BCZ5.7 Comments received on the exposure draft published in 2002 revealed that some interpret the term 'bid-ask spread' differently from others and from the IASB. Thus, the IASB clarified that the spread represents only transaction costs.

No active market

BCZ5.8 The exposure draft published in 2002 proposed a three-tier fair value measurement hierarchy as follows:

(a) For instruments traded in active markets, use a quoted price.

(b) For instruments for which there is not an active market, use a recent market transaction.

(c) For instruments for which there is neither an active market nor a recent market transaction, use a valuation technique.

BCZ5.9 The IASB decided to simplify the proposed fair value measurement hierarchy[25] by requiring the fair value of financial instruments for which there is not an active market to be determined by using valuation techniques, including recent market transactions between knowledgeable, willing parties in an arm's length transaction.

BCZ5.10 The IASB also considered constituents' comments regarding whether an instrument should always be recognised on initial recognition at the transaction price or whether gains or losses may be recognised on initial recognition when an entity uses a valuation technique to estimate fair value. The IASB concluded that an entity may recognise a gain or loss at inception only if fair value is evidenced by comparison with other observable current market transactions in the same instrument (ie without modification or repackaging) or is based on a valuation technique incorporating only observable market data. The IASB concluded that those conditions were necessary and sufficient to provide reasonable assurance that fair value was other than the transaction price for the purpose of recognising upfront gains or losses. The IASB decided that in other cases, the transaction price gave the best evidence of fair value.[26] The IASB also noted that its decision achieved convergence with US GAAP.[27]

---

24 IFRS 13, issued in May 2011, permits an exception to the fair value measurement requirements when an entity manages its financial assets and financial liabilities on the basis of the entity's net exposure to market risks or the credit risk of a particular counterparty, allowing the entity to measure the fair value of its financial instruments on the basis of the entity's net exposure to either of those risks.

25 IFRS 13, issued in May 2011, contains a three-level fair value hierarchy for the inputs used in the valuation techniques used to measure fair value.

26 IFRS 13, issued in May 2011, describes when a transaction price might not represent the fair value of an asset or a liability at initial recognition.

27 FASB Statement of Financial Accounting Standards No. 157 *Fair Value Measurements* (SFAS 157) superseded EITF Issue No. 02-3 *Issues Involved in Accounting for Derivative Contracts Held for Trading Purposes and Involved in Energy Trading and Risk Management Activities* (Topic 820 *Fair Value Measurement* in the *FASB Accounting Standards Codification*® codified SFAS 157). As a result, IFRS and US GAAP have different requirements for when an entity may recognise a gain or loss when there is a difference between fair value and the transaction price at initial recognition.

Measurement of financial liabilities with a demand feature[28]

BCZ5.11–
BCZ5.12   [Deleted]

Exception in IAS 39 from fair value measurement for some unquoted equity instruments[29] (and some derivative assets linked to those instruments)

BC5.13   The IASB believes that measurement at amortised cost is not applicable to equity investments because such financial assets have no contractual cash flows and hence there are no contractual cash flows to amortise. IAS 39 contained an exception from fair value measurement for investments in equity instruments (and some derivatives linked to those investments) that do not have a quoted price in an active market and whose fair value cannot be reliably measured. Those equity investments were required to be measured at cost less impairment, if any. Impairment losses are measured as the difference between the carrying amount of the financial asset and the present value of estimated future cash flows discounted at the current market rate of return for a similar financial asset.

BC5.14   The 2009 Classification and Measurement Exposure Draft proposed that all investments in equity instruments (and derivatives linked to those investments) should be measured at fair value for the following reasons:

(a)   For investments in equity instruments and derivatives, fair value provides the most relevant information. Cost provides little, if any, information with predictive value about the timing, amount and uncertainty of the future cash flows arising from the instrument. In many cases, fair value will differ significantly from historical cost (this is particularly true for derivatives measured at cost under the exception).

(b)   To ensure that a financial asset accounted for under the cost exception is not carried above its recoverable amount, IAS 39 required an entity to monitor instruments measured at cost for any impairment. Calculating any impairment loss is similar to determining fair value (ie the estimated future cash flows are discounted using the current market rate of return for a similar financial asset and compared with the carrying amount).

(c)   Removing the exception would reduce complexity because the classification model for financial assets would not have a third measurement attribute and would not require an additional impairment methodology. Although there might be an increase in the complexity of determining fair values on a recurring basis that complexity would be offset (at least partially) by the fact that all equity instruments and derivatives have one common measurement attribute; thus the impairment requirements would be eliminated.

---

28 IFRS 13, issued in May 2011, resulted in the relocation of paragraphs BCZ5.11 and BCZ5.12 of IFRS 9 to paragraphs BCZ102 and BCZ103 of IFRS 13. As a consequence minor necessary edits have been made to that material.
29 IFRS 13, issued in May 2011, defines a Level 1 input as a quoted price in an active market for an identical asset or liability. Level 2 inputs include quoted prices for identical assets or liabilities in markets that are not active. As a result IFRS 9 refers to such equity instruments as 'an equity instrument that does not have a quoted price in an active market for an identical instrument (ie a Level 1 input)'.

BC5.15   Many respondents agreed that cost does not provide useful information about future cash flows arising from equity instruments and that conceptually such equity instruments should be measured using a current measurement attribute such as fair value. Some of those respondents generally agreed with the removal of the exception, but suggested that disclosures would have to include information about the uncertainties surrounding measurement.

BC5.16   However, many respondents (mainly preparers from non-financial entities and some auditors) disagreed with the proposal to eliminate the current cost exception on the grounds of the reliability and usefulness of fair value measurement and the cost and difficulty involved in determining fair value on a recurring basis. They generally preferred to keep a cost exception, similar to that in IAS 39. Some noted that the proposals would not reduce complexity, because they would increase complexity in measurement. Furthermore, a few believed that cost could provide useful information if the financial asset is held for the long term.

BC5.17   The IASB considered those arguments as follows:

   (a)   *Reliability and usefulness of fair value measurement*
          Respondents noted that IAS 39 included a cost exception because of the lack of reliability of fair value measurement for particular equity instruments and contended that this rationale is still valid. They believed that, given the lack of available reliable information, any fair value measurement would require significant management judgement or might be impossible. They also believed that comparability would be impaired by the requirement to measure such equity instruments at fair value. However, those respondents had considered the question of reliability of fair value for the instruments concerned in isolation. In the IASB's view, the usefulness of information must be assessed against all four of the qualitative characteristics in the *Framework*: reliability, understandability, relevance and comparability. Thus, cost is a reliable (and objective) amount, but has little, if any, relevance. In the IASB's view measuring all equity instruments at fair value, including those that are currently measured using the cost exception in IAS 39, meets the criteria in the *Framework* for information to be reliable if appropriate measurement techniques and inputs are employed. The IASB noted that its project on fair value measurement will provide guidance on how to meet that objective.[30]

   (b)   *Cost and difficulty involved in determining fair value on a recurring basis*
          Many respondents, particularly in emerging economies, said that they faced difficulty in obtaining information that might be relied on to use in valuation. Others said that they would inevitably rely heavily on external experts at significant cost. Many questioned whether the requirement to determine fair value on a recurring basis would involve significant costs and efforts that are not offset by the incremental benefit to usefulness from fair value. The IASB considered the costs of requiring such equity investments to be measured at fair value from the

---

30 IFRS 13, issued in May 2011, contains the requirements for measuring fair value.

perspectives of valuation methodology and expertise, as well as the ability to obtain the information required for a fair value measurement. The IASB noted that valuation methods for equity investments are well-developed and are often far less complex than those required for other financial instruments that are required to be measured at fair value, including many complex derivative products. Although some expressed concern that smaller entities applying IFRS might not have internal systems or expertise to determine easily the fair value of equity investments held, the IASB noted that basic shareholder rights generally enable an entity to obtain the necessary information to perform a valuation. The IASB acknowledged that there are circumstances in which the cost of determining fair value could outweigh the benefits from fair value measurement. In particular, the IASB noted that, in some jurisdictions, entities hold high numbers of unquoted equity instruments that are currently accounted for under the cost exception and the value of a single investment is considered low. However, the IASB concluded that if the volume of the investments individually or aggregated is material the incremental benefit of fair value generally outweighs the additional cost because of the impact of the investments on the financial performance and position of the entity.[31]

BC5.18　The IASB noted that there are some circumstances in which cost might be representative of fair value and decided to provide additional application guidance on those circumstances to alleviate some of the concerns expressed. However, the IASB also noted that those circumstances would never apply to equity investments held by particular entities such as financial institutions and investment funds.

BC5.19　The IASB considered whether a simplified approach to measurement should be provided for equity instruments when fair value measurement was impracticable. The IASB also discussed possible simplified measurement approaches, including management's best estimate of the price it would accept to sell or buy the instrument, or changes in the share of net assets. However, the IASB concluded that a simplified measurement approach would add complexity to the classification approach and reduce the usefulness of information to users of financial statements. Those disadvantages would not be offset by the benefit of reduced cost to preparers of financial statements.

Elimination of the cost exception for particular derivative liabilities

BC5.20　Consistently with the requirements in IFRS 9 for some investments in equity instruments and some derivative assets linked to those instruments (see paragraphs BC5.13–BC5.19), the IASB decided in 2010 that the cost exception should be eliminated for derivative liabilities that will be physically settled by

---

31　IFRS 13, issued in May 2011, defines a Level 1 input as a quoted price in an active market for an identical asset or liability. Level 2 inputs include quoted prices for identical assets or liabilities in markets that are not active. As a result IFRS 9 refers to such equity instruments as 'an equity instrument that does not have a quoted price in an active market for an identical instrument (ie a Level 1 input)'.

delivering unquoted equity instruments whose fair values cannot be reliably determined. That proposal was included in the 2009 Classification and Measurement Exposure Draft.

Gains and losses

Investments in equity instruments

BC5.21 IFRS 9 permits an entity to make an irrevocable election to present in other comprehensive income changes in the value of any investment in equity instruments that is not held for trading. The term 'equity instrument' is defined in IAS 32 *Financial Instruments: Presentation*. The IASB noted that in particular circumstances a puttable instrument (or an instrument that imposes on the entity an obligation to deliver to another party a pro rata share of the net assets of the entity only on liquidation) is classified as equity. However, the IASB noted that such instruments do not meet the definition of an equity instrument.

BC5.22 In the IASB's view, fair value provides the most useful information about investments in equity instruments to users of financial statements. However, the IASB noted arguments that presenting fair value gains and losses in profit or loss for some equity investments may not be indicative of the performance of the entity, particularly if the entity holds those equity instruments for non-contractual benefits, rather than primarily for increases in the value of the investment. An example could be a requirement to hold such an investment if an entity sells its products in a particular country.

BC5.23 The IASB also noted that, in their valuation of an entity, users of financial statements often differentiate between fair value changes arising from equity investments held for purposes other than generating investment returns and equity investments held for trading. Thus, the IASB believes that separate presentation in other comprehensive income of gains and losses for some investments could provide useful information to users of financial statements because it would allow them to identify easily, and value accordingly, the associated fair value changes.

BC5.24 Almost all respondents to the 2009 Classification and Measurement Exposure Draft supported recognition of fair value gains and losses in other comprehensive income for particular equity investments. They agreed that an entity should make an irrevocable election to identify those equity instruments. However, some users did not support these proposals in the 2009 Classification and Measurement Exposure Draft.

BC5.25 The concerns expressed in the comment letters were as follows:

(a) *Dividends*: The 2009 Classification and Measurement Exposure Draft proposed that dividends on equity instruments measured at fair value with changes recognised in other comprehensive income would also be recognised in other comprehensive income. Nearly all respondents objected to that proposal. They argued that dividends are a form of income that should be presented in profit or loss in accordance with IAS 18 *Revenue* and noted that those equity investments are sometimes funded with debt instruments whose interest expense is recognised in profit or loss. As a result, presenting dividends in other comprehensive income would create a 'mismatch'. Some listed investment funds stated that without recognising dividend income in profit or loss their financial statements would become meaningless to their investors. The IASB agreed with those arguments. The IASB noted that structuring opportunities might remain because dividends could represent a return of investment, instead of a return on investment. Consequently, the IASB decided that dividends that clearly represent a recovery of part of the cost of the investment are not recognised in profit or loss. However, in the IASB's view, those structuring opportunities would be limited because an entity with the ability to control or significantly influence the dividend policy of the investment would not account for those investments in accordance with IFRS 9.[32] Furthermore, the IASB decided to require disclosures that would allow a user to compare easily the dividends recognised in profit or loss and the other fair value changes.

(b) *Recycling:* Many respondents, including many users, did not support the proposal to prohibit subsequent transfer ('recycling') of fair value changes to profit or loss (on derecognition of the investments in an equity instrument). Those respondents supported an approach that maintains a distinction between realised and unrealised gains and losses and said that an entity's performance should include all realised gains and losses. However, the IASB concluded that a gain or loss on those investments should be recognised once only; therefore, recognising a gain or loss in other comprehensive income and subsequently transferring it to profit or loss is inappropriate. In addition, the IASB noted that recycling of gains and losses to profit or loss would create something similar to the available-for-sale category in IAS 39 and would create the requirement to assess the equity instrument for impairment, which had created application problems. That would not significantly improve or reduce the complexity of the financial reporting for financial assets. Accordingly, the IASB decided to prohibit recycling of gains and losses into profit or loss when an equity instrument is derecognised.

(c) *Scope of exception:* Some respondents asked the IASB to identify a principle that defined the equity instruments to which the exception should apply. However, they did not specify what that principle should be. The IASB previously considered developing a principle to identify other equity investments whose fair value changes should be presented in profit or loss (or other comprehensive income), including a distinction based on whether the equity instruments represented a 'strategic investment'. However, the IASB decided that it would be difficult, and perhaps impossible, to develop a clear and robust principle that would identify investments that are different enough to justify a different presentation requirement. The IASB considered whether a list of indicators could be used to support the principle, but decided that such a list would inevitably be rule-based and could not be comprehensive

---

32 In October 2012 the IASB issued *Investment Entities* (Amendments to IFRS 10, IFRS 12 and IAS 27), which required investment entities, as defined in IFRS 10 *Consolidated Financial Statements*, to measure their investments in subsidiaries, other than those providing investment-related services or activities, at fair value through profit or loss.

enough to address all possible situations and factors. Moreover, the IASB noted that such an approach would create complexity in application without necessarily increasing the usefulness of information to users of financial statements.

(d) *Irrevocability of the exception:* A small number of respondents believed that an entity should be able to reclassify equity instruments into and out of the fair value through other comprehensive income category if an entity starts or ceases to hold the investments for trading purposes. However, the IASB decided that the option must be irrevocable to provide discipline to its application. The IASB also noted that the option to designate a financial asset as measured at fair value is also irrevocable.

BC5.26 An entity may transfer the cumulative gain or loss within equity. In the light of jurisdiction-specific restrictions on components of equity, the IASB decided not to provide specific requirements related to that transfer.

BC5.27 IFRS 9 amended IFRS 7 in 2009 to require additional disclosures about investments in equity instruments that are measured at fair value through other comprehensive income. The IASB believes those disclosures will provide useful information to users of financial statements about instruments presented in that manner and the effect of that presentation.

BC5.28 The IASB noted that permitting an option for entities to present some gains and losses in other comprehensive income is an exception to the overall classification and measurement approach and adds complexity. However, the IASB believes that the requirement that the election is irrevocable, together with the additional disclosures required, addresses many of those concerns.

Liabilities designated as at fair value through profit or loss

Previous discussions related to the effects of changes in a liability's credit risk

BCZ5.29 In 2003 the IASB discussed the issue of including changes in the credit risk of a financial liability in its fair value measurement. It considered responses to the exposure draft of proposed amendments to IAS 39 published in June 2002 that expressed concern about the effect of including this component in the fair value measurement and that suggested the fair value option should be restricted to exclude all or some financial liabilities. However, the IASB concluded that the fair value option could be applied to any financial liability, and decided not to restrict the option in IAS 39 (as revised in 2003) because to do so would negate some of the benefits of the fair value option set out in paragraph BCZ4.60.

BCZ5.30 The IASB considered comments on the exposure draft published in 2002 that disagreed with the view that, in applying the fair value option to financial liabilities, an entity should recognise income as a result of deteriorating credit quality (and expense as a result of improving credit quality). Commentators noted that it is not useful to report lower liabilities when an entity is in financial difficulty precisely because its debt levels are too high, and that it would be difficult to explain to users of financial statements the reasons why income would be recognised when a liability's creditworthiness deteriorates. These comments suggested that fair value should exclude the effects of changes in the instrument's credit risk.

BCZ5.31 However, the IASB noted that because financial statements are prepared on a going concern basis, credit risk affects the value at which liabilities could be repurchased or settled. Accordingly, the fair value of a financial liability reflects the credit risk relating to that liability. Consequently, it decided to include credit risk relating to a financial liability in the fair value measurement of that liability for the following reasons:

(a) Entities realise changes in fair value, including fair value attributable to the liability's credit risk, for example, by renegotiating or repurchasing liabilities or by using derivatives.

(b) Changes in credit risk affect the observed market price of a financial liability and hence its fair value.

(c) It is difficult from a practical standpoint to exclude changes in credit risk from an observed market price.

(d) The fair value of a financial liability (ie the price of that liability in an exchange between a knowledgeable, willing buyer and a knowledgeable, willing seller) on initial recognition reflects its credit risk. The IASB believes that it is inappropriate to include credit risk in the initial fair value measurement of financial liabilities, but not subsequently.

BCZ5.32 In 2003 the IASB also considered whether the component of the fair value of a financial liability attributable to changes in credit quality should be specifically disclosed, separately presented in the income statement, or separately presented in equity. The IASB decided that whilst separately presenting or disclosing such changes might be difficult in practice, disclosure of such information would be useful to users of financial statements and would help alleviate the concerns expressed. Consequently, it decided to require a disclosure to help identify the changes in the fair value of a financial liability that arise from changes in the liability's credit risk. The IASB believes this is a reasonable proxy for the change in fair value that is attributable to changes in the liability's credit risk, in particular when such changes are large, and will provide users with information with which to understand the profit or loss effect of such a change in credit risk.

BCZ5.33 The IASB decided to clarify that this issue relates to the credit risk of the financial liability, instead of the creditworthiness of the entity. The IASB noted that this more appropriately describes the objective of what is included in the fair value measurement of financial liabilities.

BCZ5.34 The IASB also noted that the fair value of liabilities secured by valuable collateral, guaranteed by third parties or ranking ahead of virtually all other liabilities is generally unaffected by changes in the entity's creditworthiness.

BC5.34A IFRS 13, issued in May 2011, includes requirements for measuring the fair value of a liability issued with an inseparable third-party credit enhancement from the issuer's perspective.

Requirements added to IFRS 9 in October 2010 to address the effects of changes in credit risk for liabilities designated as at fair value through profit or loss

BC5.35   As noted above, if an entity designates a financial liability under the fair value option, IAS 39 required the entire fair value change to be presented in profit or loss. However, many users and others told the IASB over a long period of time that changes in a liability's credit risk ought not to affect profit or loss unless the liability is held for trading. That is because an entity generally will not realise the effects of changes in the liability's credit risk unless the liability is held for trading.

BC5.36   To respond to that long-standing and widespread concern, in May 2010 the IASB proposed that the effects of changes in a liability's credit risk should be presented in other comprehensive income. The proposals in the 2010 Own Credit Risk Exposure Draft would have applied to all liabilities designated under the fair value option.

BC5.37   However, in its deliberations leading to the 2010 Own Credit Risk Exposure Draft, the IASB discussed whether such treatment would create or enlarge an accounting mismatch in profit or loss in some limited cases. The IASB acknowledged that this might be the case if an entity holds large portfolios of financial assets that are measured at fair value through profit or loss and there is an economic relationship between changes in the fair value of those assets and the effects of changes in the credit risk of the financial liabilities designated under the fair value option. A mismatch would arise because the entire change in the fair value of the assets would be presented in profit or loss but only a portion of the change in the fair value of the liabilities would be presented in profit or loss. The portion of the liabilities' fair value change attributable to changes in their credit risk would be presented in other comprehensive income. To address potential mismatches, the IASB set out an alternative approach in the 2010 Own Credit Risk Exposure Draft whereby the effects of changes in the liabilities' credit risk would be presented in other comprehensive income unless such treatment would create or enlarge an accounting mismatch in profit or loss (in which case, the entire fair value change would be presented in profit or loss). The 2010 Own Credit Risk Exposure Draft stated that the determination about potential mismatches would be made when the liability is initially recognised and would not be reassessed. The IASB asked respondents for feedback on the alternative approach.

BC5.38   Many respondents preferred the alternative approach. They agreed that in almost all cases the effects of changes in credit risk ought not to be presented in profit or loss. However, those respondents said that if such treatment would create or enlarge an accounting mismatch in profit or loss, the entire fair value change should be presented in profit or loss. Respondents thought such cases would be rare and asked the IASB to provide guidance on how to determine whether presenting the effects of changes in credit risk in other comprehensive income would create or enlarge an accounting mismatch in profit or loss.

BC5.39   The IASB agreed with the responses and finalised the alternative approach. Consequently, entities are required to present the effects of changes in the liabilities' credit risk in other comprehensive income unless such treatment would create or enlarge an accounting mismatch in profit or loss (in which case, the entire fair value change is required to be presented in profit or loss). The IASB acknowledged that that approach will introduce some additional complexity to financial reporting because not all liabilities designated under the fair value option will be treated the same. However, the IASB decided that it was necessary to address circumstances in which the proposals would create or enlarge a mismatch in profit or loss. Although the IASB expects those circumstances to be rare, they could be significant in some industries in some jurisdictions.

BC5.40 The IASB discussed how an entity should determine whether a mismatch would be created or enlarged. It decided that an entity has to assess whether it expects that changes in the credit risk of a liability will be offset by changes in the fair value of another financial instrument. The IASB decided that such an assessment must be based on an economic relationship between the characteristics of the liability and the characteristics of the other financial instrument. Such a relationship does not arise by coincidence.

BC5.41 The IASB believes that in many cases the relationship will be contractual (as described in paragraph B5.7.10 of IFRS 9) but decided that a contractual relationship is not required. Requiring a contractual relationship would have created a very high threshold for presenting the effects of changes in a liability's credit risk in profit or loss and the IASB decided that such a high threshold was too strict to accommodate all of the possible scenarios in which a mismatch would be created or enlarged by presenting those amounts in other comprehensive income.

BC5.42 However, to increase transparency about an entity's determination about potential mismatches, the IASB decided to require disclosures about an entity's methodology for making that determination. Also, an entity is required to apply its methodology consistently. The determination must be made at initial recognition of the liability and is not reassessed, which is consistent with the entity's overall election to use the fair value option.

BC5.43 Some respondents to the 2010 Own Credit Risk Exposure Draft asked whether the IASB intended that the proposals should apply to loan commitments and financial guarantee contracts that are designated under the fair value option. Those respondents suggested that the proposals should not apply to those items because the IASB's intention seemingly had always been to address the issue of own credit risk for non-derivative liabilities. The respondents noted that loan commitments and financial guarantee contracts either meet the definition of a derivative or are very similar to a derivative from an economic perspective and therefore changes in their fair value should always be presented in profit or loss. The IASB agreed with those respondents and decided that all changes in the fair value of loan commitments and financial guarantee contracts designated under the fair value option should be presented in profit or loss. In addition to the comments put forward by respondents, the IASB also noted that phase II of the insurance project was discussing whether all financial guarantee contracts should be within the scope of that proposed Standard.

Alternative approaches to address the issue of own credit risk

BC5.44   In 2010 the IASB discussed and rejected the following approaches for addressing the issue of credit risk:

(a)   *Present the effects of changes in credit risk directly in equity:* Some believe that the effects of changes in credit risk should not affect the entity's performance; therefore they believe that those amounts should be presented directly in equity. The IASB rejected this approach in the 2010 Own Credit Risk Exposure Draft because it believes that changes in the liability's credit risk ought to affect the entity's performance if the liability is measured at fair value. If those amounts were presented directly in equity, they would never be presented in the entity's statement of comprehensive income. The IASB acknowledged that IFRS does not provide a clear objective for when an item should be presented in other comprehensive income instead of in profit or loss or whether the amounts in other comprehensive income should be reclassified to profit or loss. However, the IASB believes that presenting the effects of changes in credit risk in other comprehensive income is preferable to presenting them directly in equity because the latter would create a new problem by causing confusion or creating inconsistencies in what items are presented directly in equity. The IASB noted that remeasurements of assets and liabilities should not be presented directly in equity because remeasurements are not transactions with equity holders. The IASB asked respondents for feedback on presenting directly in equity the effects of changes in a liability's credit risk and almost all respondents, including users, did not support it. Accordingly the IASB did not pursue this alternative.

(b)   *Present the entire change in the fair value of liabilities in other comprehensive income:* Some believe that the entire change in fair value (not just the portion attributable to changes in credit risk) should be presented in other comprehensive income. They argue that this approach would avoid the difficult question of how to measure the effects of changes in credit risk. The IASB rejected this approach because it believes that at least some of the change in fair value should be presented in profit or loss. The IASB's objective was to address issues related to the effects of changes in liabilities' credit risk; therefore, presenting the entire change in fair value in other comprehensive income is not appropriate. Also, this approach would result in mismatches in profit or loss because changes in the fair value of an entity's assets would be presented in profit or loss and changes in the fair value of its liabilities would be presented in other comprehensive income (see similar discussion in paragraph BC5.37). Moreover, this alternative would raise difficult questions about what (if any) amounts should be presented in profit or loss during the life of the liability (eg interest or other financing costs). The IASB has discussed the topic of disaggregating finance costs from other fair value changes on numerous occasions without reaching any conclusions.

Presenting the effects of changes in credit risk in other comprehensive income via a one-step or two-step approach

BC5.45 The 2010 Own Credit Risk Exposure Draft proposed a 'two-step approach' for presenting a liability's credit risk in the statement of comprehensive income, with the result that those changes would not affect profit or loss. In the first step, the entity would present the entire fair value change in profit or loss. In the second step, the entity would 'back out' from profit or loss the portion of the fair value change that is attributable to changes in the liability's credit risk and present that amount in other comprehensive income.

BC5.46 The 2010 Own Credit Risk Exposure Draft also set out a 'one-step approach', which would present the portion of the fair value change that is attributable to changes in the liability's credit risk directly in other comprehensive income. All other portions of the fair value change would be presented in profit or loss.

BC5.47 The IASB acknowledged that the only difference between those two approaches is how the effects of changes in the liability's credit risk are presented. The two-step approach would present those amounts first in profit or loss and then transfer them to other comprehensive income, whereas the one-step approach would present them directly in other comprehensive income.

BC5.48 The IASB proposed the two-step approach in the 2010 Own Credit Risk Exposure Draft because it thought that it would present more clearly all of the relevant information in the primary financial statements, but it decided to ask respondents which approach they supported.

BC5.49 Almost all respondents, including users, supported the one-step approach. They said that the one-step approach is more efficient and less complicated than the two-step approach. They pointed out that both approaches have the same net result in profit or loss and other comprehensive income. Respondents said that there is little (if any) added benefit of the 'gross' presentation in the two-step approach and the extra line items on the face of the performance statement result in unnecessary clutter. Furthermore, respondents noted the IASB's exposure draft published in May 2010 on the presentation of items in other comprehensive income. That exposure draft proposes that the profit or loss section and other comprehensive income should be displayed as separate components within an overall statement of profit or loss and other comprehensive income. Respondents questioned whether the two-step approach would have any added benefit if the Board finalised the proposals in that exposure draft.

BC5.50 Users told the IASB that the two-step approach would not be more helpful to their analysis than the one-step approach. Some users noted that the effects of changes in a liability's credit risk should not be presented in profit or loss, even if those effects were subsequently backed out.

BC5.51 The IASB was persuaded by respondents' arguments and decided to require the one-step approach. The IASB noted that no information is lost by using the one-step approach because IFRS 7 and IAS 1 *Presentation of Financial Statements* require entities to disclose (either on the financial statements or in the notes) all of the information required by the two-step approach.

Reclassifying amounts to profit or loss

BC5.52   The 2010 Own Credit Risk Exposure Draft proposed to prohibit reclassification of gains or losses to profit or loss (on derecognition of the liability or otherwise)—sometimes called 'recycling'. In the Basis for Conclusions on that Exposure Draft, the IASB noted that the proposal was consistent with the requirements in IFRS 9 that prohibit recycling for investments in equity instruments that are measured at fair value with changes presented in other comprehensive income.

BC5.53   Moreover, the IASB noted that if the entity repays the contractual amount, the cumulative effect over the life of the instrument of any changes in the liability's credit risk will net to zero because its fair value will equal the contractual amount. Consequently, for many liabilities, the issue of reclassification is irrelevant.

BC5.54   Most respondents to the 2010 Own Credit Risk Exposure Draft disagreed with that proposal and urged the IASB to require reclassification if the liability was derecognised and the effects of changes in its credit risk were realised. They acknowledged that there would not be any amount to reclassify if the entity repays the contractual amount. But they believe that if the entity repays an amount other than the contractual amount, the realised amounts in other comprehensive income should be reclassified. Those respondents view other comprehensive income as a 'temporary holding place' for unrealised gains and losses. They believe that unrealised and realised amounts are fundamentally different and thus should not be treated the same. The former are still uncertain and may never be crystallised. In contrast, the latter have crystallised and are backed by cash flows.

BC5.55   However, the IASB was not persuaded and confirmed the proposal to prohibit reclassification. The IASB acknowledged that it needs to address the overall objective of other comprehensive income, including when an item should be presented in other comprehensive income instead of in profit or loss and whether amounts in other comprehensive income should be reclassified to profit or loss (and if so, when). However, in the absence of such an objective, the IASB noted that its decision is consistent with the requirements in IFRS 9 that prohibit recycling for investments in equity instruments that are measured at fair value with changes presented in other comprehensive income.

BC5.56   However, to provide users with information about how much of the accumulated other comprehensive income balance has been realised during the current reporting period (ie how much would have been reclassified if the IASB had required reclassification upon derecognition), the IASB decided to require entities to disclose that amount.

BC5.57   Also, consistently with the requirements for equity investments measured at fair value with changes presented in other comprehensive income, the IASB decided that an entity may transfer the cumulative gain or loss within equity.

Determining the effects of changes in the liability's credit risk

BC5.58   IFRS 7 required an entity, when designating a financial liability under the fair value option, to disclose the amount of the change in fair value that is attributable to changes in the liability's credit risk. The application guidance in IFRS 7 provided a default method for determining that amount. If the only relevant changes in market conditions for the liability are changes in an observed (benchmark) interest rate, that method attributes all changes in fair value, other than changes in the benchmark interest rate, to changes in the credit risk of the liability. In the Basis for Conclusions on IFRS 7, the IASB acknowledged that quantifying the change in a liability's credit risk might be difficult in practice. It noted that it believes that the default method provides a reasonable proxy for changes in the liability's credit risk, in particular when such changes are large, and would provide users with information with which to understand the effect on profit or loss of such a change in credit risk. However, IFRS 7 permitted entities to use a different method if it provides a more faithful representation of the changes in the liability's credit risk.

BC5.59   During the IASB's outreach programme preceding the publication of the 2010 Own Credit Risk Exposure Draft, preparers told the IASB that the default method in IFRS 7 is appropriate in many circumstances but a more sophisticated method is sometimes needed to reflect faithfully the effects of changes in the liabilities' credit risk (eg when the volume of liabilities outstanding significantly changed during the reporting period).

BC5.60   In the user questionnaire conducted during that outreach programme, the IASB asked users whether the default method in IFRS 7 was appropriate for determining the change in a liability's credit risk. Most users said that it was an appropriate method. Many users noted the difficulty in determining that amount more precisely.

BC5.61   Therefore, for the purposes of measuring the effects of changes in the credit risk of a liability, the 2010 Own Credit Risk Exposure Draft proposed to use the guidance in IFRS 7. Under the proposals, the default method would be carried forward but entities would continue to be permitted to use a different method if it provides a more faithful representation of the amount of the change in fair value that is attributable to changes in the liability's credit risk.

BC5.62   Most respondents agreed with the proposals in the 2010 Own Credit Risk Exposure Draft. Those respondents agreed that the guidance in IFRS 7 for measuring the effects of changes in a liability's credit risk is appropriate and operational. They noted that determining the effects of changes in a liability's credit risk can be complex, and therefore it was necessary to allow some flexibility in how it is measured. They acknowledged that the default method described in IFRS 7 is imprecise but said that it is a reasonable proxy in many cases. Moreover, although some respondents acknowledged that the default method does not isolate changes in a liability's credit risk from some other changes in fair value (eg general changes in the price of credit or changes in liquidity risk), those respondents said that it is often very difficult or impossible to separate those items. However, some respondents (including those who supported the IASB's proposals in the 2010 Own Credit Risk Exposure Draft) asked for some clarification on particular aspects of the guidance in IFRS 7.

BC5.63   Consistently with the majority of responses, the IASB decided to confirm the proposals in the 2010 Own Credit Risk Exposure Draft to use the guidance in IFRS 7 related to determining the effects of changes in a liability's credit risk.

Thus, that guidance was carried forward from IFRS 7 to IFRS 9. However, to respond to some of the questions raised in the comment letters, the IASB decided to clarify the difference between the creditworthiness of the entity and the credit risk of a liability. Moreover, the IASB addressed the difference between a liability's credit risk and asset-specific performance risk—and confirmed that a change in a liability's credit risk does not include changes in asset-specific performance risk. Furthermore, the IASB noted that in some cases a liability might not have credit risk. Consequently, the IASB included additional examples in the application guidance to clarify those points.

BC5.64 Also, the IASB clarified that the default method illustrated in IFRS 7 (and relocated to IFRS 9) is appropriate only if the only relevant changes in market conditions for a liability are changes in an observed (benchmark) interest rate. If that is not the case, an entity is required to use a more precise method. Moreover, an entity is always permitted to use a different method if that method more faithfully represents the effects of changes in a liability's credit risk.

Amortised cost measurement

Effective interest rate

BCZ5.65 In developing the revised IAS 39, the IASB considered whether the effective interest rate for all financial instruments should be calculated on the basis of estimated cash flows (consistently with the original IAS 39) or whether the use of estimated cash flows should be restricted to groups of financial instruments with contractual cash flows being used for individual financial instruments. The IASB agreed to reconfirm the position in the original IAS 39 because it achieves consistent application of the effective interest method throughout the Standard.

BCZ5.66 The IASB noted that future cash flows and the expected life can be reliably estimated for most financial assets and financial liabilities, in particular for a group of similar financial assets or similar financial liabilities. However, the IASB acknowledged that in some rare cases it might not be possible to estimate the timing or amount of future cash flows reliably. It therefore decided to require that if it is not possible to estimate reliably the future cash flows or the expected life of a financial instrument, the entity should use contractual cash flows over the full contractual term of the financial instrument.

BCZ5.67 The IASB also decided to clarify that expected future defaults should not be included in estimates of cash flows because this would be a departure from the incurred loss model for impairment recognition.[33] At the same time, the IASB noted that in some cases, for example, when a financial asset is acquired at a deep discount, credit losses have occurred and are reflected in the price. If an entity does not take into account such credit losses in the calculation of the effective interest rate, the entity would recognise a higher interest income than

---

33 The IASB did not change this approach to determining the effective interest rate for financial instruments (other than those that are purchased or originated credit impaired) when changing from an incurred loss in IAS 39 to an expected credit loss impairment model. This was because the decoupled approach in IFRS 9 considers the recognition of interest revenue and the recognition of expected credit losses separately.

that inherent in the price paid. The IASB therefore decided to clarify that such credit losses are included in the estimated cash flows when computing the effective interest rate.

BCZ5.68 The revised IAS 39 refers to all fees 'that are an integral part of the effective interest rate'. The IASB included this reference to clarify that IAS 39 relates only to those fees that are determined to be an integral part of the effective interest rate in accordance with IAS 18.[34]

BCZ5.69 Some commentators noted that it was not always clear how to interpret the requirement in the original IAS 39 that the effective interest rate must be based on discounting cash flows through maturity or the next market-based repricing date. In particular, it was not always clear whether fees, transaction costs and other premiums or discounts included in the calculation of the effective interest rate should be amortised over the period until maturity or the period to the next market-based repricing date.

BCZ5.70 For consistency with the estimated cash flows approach, the IASB decided to clarify that the effective interest rate is calculated over the expected life of the instrument or, when applicable, a shorter period. A shorter period is used when the variable (eg interest rates) to which the fee, transaction costs, discount or premium relates is repriced to market rates before the expected maturity of the instrument. In such a case, the appropriate amortisation period is the period to the next such repricing date.

BCZ5.71 The IASB identified an apparent inconsistency in the guidance in the revised IAS 39. It related to whether the revised or the original effective interest rate of a debt instrument should be applied when remeasuring the instrument's carrying amount on the cessation of fair value hedge accounting. A revised effective interest rate is calculated when fair value hedge accounting ceases. The IASB removed this inconsistency as part of *Improvements to IFRSs* issued in May 2008 by clarifying that the remeasurement of an instrument in accordance with paragraph AG8 (now paragraph B5.4.6 of IFRS 9) is based on the revised effective interest rate calculated in accordance with paragraph 92 (now paragraph 6.5.10 of IFRS 9), when applicable, instead of the original effective interest rate.

Presentation of interest revenue

BC5.72 As part of its work on the Impairment project (Section 5.5 of IFRS 9), the IASB published the 2009 Exposure Draft *Financial Instruments: Amortised Cost and Impairment* (the '2009 Impairment Exposure Draft'). The 2009 Impairment Exposure Draft proposed a model in which an entity would have considered initial expectations of credit losses when determining the effective interest rate on financial assets. Consequently, interest revenue would have represented the economic yield, or the effective return, on those financial assets. In contrast, the decoupled approach in IFRS 9 considers the recognition of interest revenue and the recognition of expected credit losses separately. Under this approach, an entity recognises interest on the gross carrying amount of a financial asset without taking expected credit losses into consideration (except when financial

---

34 IFRS 15, issued in May 2014, replaced IAS 18. See paragraphs B5.4.1–B5.4.3 of IFRS 9 for the requirements for fees that are an integral part of the effective interest rate.

assets become credit-impaired or are credit-impaired on initial recognition). Paragraphs BC5.88–BC5.91 discusses further the reasons why the IASB did not proceed with the proposals in the 2009 Impairment Exposure Draft in finalising IFRS 9.

BC5.73 Respondents told the IASB that calculating an effective interest rate that considers initial expected credit losses is operationally burdensome, particularly for open portfolios of financial assets. In addition, users of financial statements stressed the need for an interest revenue recognition model that allows them to continue to analyse net interest margin and credit losses separately.

BC5.74 Consequently, the IASB proposed in the 2013 Impairment Exposure Draft, consistently with the proposals in the Supplementary Document *Financial Instruments: Impairment* (the 'Supplementary Document'), that, an entity would calculate interest revenue on the gross carrying amount of a financial asset using an effective interest rate that is not adjusted for expected credit losses. However, the IASB noted that there are some financial assets for which credit risk has increased to such an extent that presenting interest revenue on the basis of the gross carrying amount of the financial asset, that reflects the contractual return, would no longer faithfully represent the economic return. The 2013 Impairment Exposure Draft therefore proposed that if a financial asset is credit-impaired at the reporting date, an entity should change the interest revenue calculation from being based on the gross carrying amount to the amortised cost of a financial asset (ie the amount net of the loss allowance) at the beginning of the following reporting period.

BC5.75 The IASB received feedback on the 2013 Impairment Exposure Draft that showed the majority of respondents agreed that the interest revenue calculation should change to a calculation on a net basis for some financial assets, because it best supported faithful representation. These requirements only affect the calculation and presentation of interest revenue and not the measurement of the loss allowance.

BC5.76 The IASB acknowledged the concerns of using 'incurred loss' criteria in a model based on expected credit losses. However, in the IASB's view, it was necessary to retain the faithful representation of interest revenue, while minimising the operational challenges of requiring entities to calculate interest revenue on the amortised cost amount for all financial assets.

BC5.77 Financial assets that are credit-impaired at the reporting date and on which interest revenue is calculated on the amortised cost of a financial asset are a subset of financial assets with a loss allowance measured at lifetime expected credit losses. IFRS preparers are already required to determine interest on the amortised cost amount of these financial assets in accordance with IAS 39 and therefore the IASB noted that this requirement would result in a minimal change in practice. Accordingly, the IASB decided to retain the scope of assets on which interest is calculated on the amortised cost amount of a financial asset that is credit-impaired as identified in by IAS 39 (but excluding the concept of 'incurred but not reported').

BC5.78 The IASB is of the view that, conceptually, an entity should assess whether financial assets have become credit-impaired on an ongoing basis, thus altering the presentation of interest revenue as the underlying economics change. However, the IASB noted that such an approach would be unduly onerous for preparers to apply. Thus, the IASB decided that an entity should be required to make the assessment of whether a financial asset is credit-impaired at the reporting date and then change the interest calculation from the beginning of the following reporting period.

BC5.79 However, a few respondents to the 2013 Impairment Exposure Draft supported presenting nil interest revenue on credit-impaired financial assets for operational reasons. In accordance with such an approach an entity would be required to offset interest revenue on a subset of financial assets with an equal amount of expected credit losses. The IASB noted that an advantage of presenting nil interest revenue is the operational simplicity. The only information that an entity would need to know to apply this approach would be the interest revenue on the subset of financial assets. That is, an entity would not be required to identify the loss allowance related to that subset of financial assets. However, the IASB noted that such an approach would blend together the effect of the unwinding of the present value of expected cash flows with other expected credit losses. In the IASB's view, a nil interest approach would not improve the calculation of interest revenue, because it would not faithfully represent the economic return in a manner that is consistent with the measurement of the gross carrying amount and expected credit losses at a present value.

BC5.80 Consequently, the IASB decided to confirm the requirement to present interest revenue on a net basis and to do so from the beginning of the reporting period following the reporting period when the financial instrument became credit-impaired.

Write-off

BC5.81 In the IASB's view, a definition of 'write-off' is necessary to faithfully represent the gross carrying amount of the financial assets within the scope of IFRS 9. The definition is also necessary for the newly introduced disclosure requirements about expected credit losses. The 2009 Impairment Exposure Draft proposed definitions and requirements related to the term 'write off'. Following positive comments about those definitions, the IASB decided to retain the definitions and requirements related to the term 'write-off' in IFRS 9 with minimal changes to the definition proposed in the 2009 Impairment Exposure Draft.

Impairment

Background

Objectives for depicting expected credit losses

BC5.82 For financial assets measured at amortised cost and debt instruments measured at fair value through other comprehensive income the effect of changes in credit risk are more relevant to an investor's understanding of the likelihood of the collection of future contractual cash flows than the effects of other changes, such as changes in market interest rates. This is because an integral aspect of both business models is to collect contractual cash flows.

BC5.83   The IASB noted that a model that faithfully represents the economic phenomenon of expected credit losses should provide users of financial statements with relevant information about the amount, timing and uncertainty of an entity's future cash flows. It should also ensure that the amounts that an entity reports are comparable, timely and understandable. Furthermore, the IASB also sought to ensure that the model address the criticisms of the incurred loss model in IAS 39. These criticisms included the concerns that the model in IAS 39 overstated interest revenue in periods before a credit loss event occurs, delayed the recognition of credit losses and was complex due to its multiple impairment approaches.

BC5.84   In developing a model that depicts expected credit losses, the IASB observed that:

(a)   when an entity prices a financial instrument, part of the yield, the credit risk premium, compensates the entity for the credit losses initially expected (for example, an entity will typically demand a higher yield for those instruments with higher expected credit losses at the date the instrument is issued). Consequently, no economic loss is suffered at initial recognition simply because the credit risk on a financial instrument is high at that time, because those expected credit losses are implicit in the initial pricing of the instrument.

(b)   for most financial instruments, the pricing is not adjusted for changes in expected credit losses in subsequent periods. Consequently, subsequent changes in expected credit losses are economic losses (or gains) of the entity in the period in which they occur.

BC5.85   Expected credit losses, in isolation, are not directly observable. However, because the credit risk premium is a component of the market yield for financial instruments, the indirect measurement of expected credit losses is a daily occurrence in the pricing of such instruments in the market. A number of models exist to assist market participants and regulators in the measurement of expected credit losses. But, because expected credit losses are not directly observable, their measurement is inherently based on judgement and any model that attempts to depict expected credit losses will be subject to measurement uncertainty.

BC5.86   Some interested parties would prefer an impairment model that results in a more conservative, or prudential, depiction of expected credit losses. Those interested parties argue that such a depiction would better meet the needs of both the regulators who are responsible for maintaining financial stability and investors and other users of financial statements. However, to be consistent with the *Conceptual Framework*, faithful representation of expected credit losses implies that the depiction of those credit losses is neutral and free from bias. The depiction of expected credit losses in an unbiased way informs the decisions of a broad range of users of financial statements, including regulators and investors and creditors. In the IASB's view, incorporating a degree of conservatism would be arbitrary and would result in a lack of comparability. The risk of an outcome other than the probability-weighted expected outcome is only relevant for particular purposes, such as determining the extent of economic or regulatory capital requirements.

Alternative models considered to depict expected credit losses

The model proposed in the 2009 Impairment Exposure Draft

BC5.87 In November 2009 the IASB published the 2009 Impairment Exposure Draft, which proposed that an entity should measure amortised cost at the expected (credit-adjusted) cash flows discounted at the original credit-adjusted effective interest rate, ie the effective interest rate adjusted for the initial expected credit losses. The IASB was aware that these proposals were a fundamentally new approach to impairment accounting for financial reporting purposes that was much more closely linked to credit risk management concepts. In order to fully understand the consequences of this, the IASB established a panel of credit risk experts (the Expert Advisory Panel (EAP)) to provide input during the comment period.

BC5.88 In the IASB's view, the model in the 2009 Impairment Exposure Draft most faithfully represents expected credit losses and would determine the carrying amount, interest revenue and impairment gains or losses to be recognised through a single, integrated calculation. Thus, an entity would recognise:

(a) the initial expected credit losses over the life of the asset through the credit-adjusted effective interest rate; and

(b) any changes in expected credit losses when those changes occurred.

BC5.89 Users of financial statements have told the IASB that they support a model that distinguishes between the effect of initial estimates of expected credit losses and subsequent changes in those estimates. They noted that such a distinction would provide useful information about changes in credit risk and the resulting economic losses. Many other respondents also supported the concepts in the 2009 Impairment Exposure Draft, but said that the proposals would present significant operational challenges. In particular, they highlighted the following:

(a) estimating the full expected cash flows for all financial instruments;

(b) applying a credit-adjusted effective interest rate to those cash flow estimates; and

(c) maintaining information about the initial estimate of expected credit losses.

BC5.90 These operational challenges arose because entities typically operate separate accounting and credit risk management systems. To have applied the 2009 Impairment Exposure Draft, entities would have had to have integrated those separate systems. The IASB was told that this would have required substantial costs and lead time. Respondents noted that these operational challenges would be especially acute for open portfolios (ie portfolios to which new financial instruments are added over time).

BC5.91 The IASB initially considered different approaches to address the specific operational challenges that respondents raised while at the same time replicating the outcomes of the 2009 Impairment Exposure Draft to the maximum extent possible.

Simplifications to address operational challenges of the 2009 Impairment Exposure Draft

BC5.92 To address the operational challenges outlined in paragraph BC5.89 and as suggested by the EAP, the IASB decided to decouple the measurement and allocation of initial expected credit losses from the determination of the effective interest rate (except for purchased or originated credit-impaired financial assets). Thus, an entity would measure the financial asset and the loss allowance separately using the original effective interest rate (ie not adjusted for initial expected credit losses). The IASB considered that such an approach would address some of the operational challenges of the 2009 Impairment Exposure Draft by allowing an entity to leverage its existing accounting and credit risk management systems and reduce the extent of integration between these systems.

BC5.93 As a result of the decoupling simplification, an entity would measure the present value of expected credit losses using the original effective interest rate. This presents a dilemma, because measuring expected credit losses using such a rate double-counts the expected credit losses that were priced into the financial asset at initial recognition. The IASB therefore concluded that recognising the lifetime expected credit losses from initial recognition would be inappropriate under a model that discounts expected credit losses using the original effective interest rate. The IASB further concluded that a recognition mechanism was required that preserves, to as great an extent as possible, the objective of the 2009 Impairment Exposure Draft and reduces the effect of this double-counting. Thus, the IASB proposed to pursue a model that recognises two different amounts based on the extent of increases in credit risk since initial recognition. Such a dual-measurement model would require an entity to recognise:

(a) a portion of the lifetime expected credit losses from initial recognition as a proxy for recognising the initial expected credit losses over the life of the financial asset; and

(b) the lifetime expected credit losses when credit risk has increased since initial recognition (ie when the recognition of only a portion of the lifetime expected credit losses is no longer appropriate because the entity has suffered a significant economic loss).

BC5.94 The IASB considered the interaction between the timing of the recognition of the full lifetime expected credit losses, and the size of the portion of the lifetime expected credit losses that are recognised before that, to be a determinant of what would provide a more faithful representation of the economic loss. Thus, if an entity recognises a smaller portion of the lifetime expected credit losses initially, it should recognise the full lifetime expected credit losses earlier than if it had been required to recognise a larger portion of the lifetime expected credit losses initially.

BC5.95 As a result of the decoupling simplification as discussed in paragraphs BC5.92–BC5.93, the IASB acknowledges that any model that recognises different amounts of expected credit losses based on the extent of increases in credit risk since initial recognition cannot perfectly replicate the outcome of the model in the 2009 Impairment Exposure Draft. Furthermore, while there is always recognition of some expected credit losses, such a model retains a criterion for when lifetime expected credit losses are recognised. Once that criterion is met, the recognition of lifetime expected credit losses results in a loss representing the difference between the portion that was recognised previously and the lifetime expected credit losses (a 'cliff effect'). In the IASB's view, any approach that seeks to approximate the outcomes of the model in the 2009 Impairment Exposure Draft without the associated operational challenges will include a recognition threshold for lifetime expected credit losses and a resulting cliff effect.

The model proposed in the Supplementary Document

BC5.96　Based on the feedback from the 2009 Impairment Exposure Draft and the simplifications considered to address the challenges of that model, the IASB published the Supplementary Document in January 2011. The Supplementary Document proposed a two-tier loss allowance, which would be recognised as follows:

(a)　the higher of, a time-proportionate allowance (TPA) or expected credit losses for the foreseeable future, for the good book. If applying a TPA, an entity would recognise the lifetime expected credit losses over the weighted average life of the portfolio of assets.

(b)　the lifetime expected credit losses for the bad book. Financial assets would be moved to the bad book if the collectability of contractual cash flows on a financial asset became so uncertain that the entity's credit risk management objective changes from receiving the regular payments to recovery of all, or a portion of, the asset.

BC5.97　The Supplementary Document proposed to reflect the relationship between expected credit losses and interest revenue using the TPA. The TPA would achieve this through the allocation of expected credit losses over time, indirectly 'adjusting' the contractual interest. However, the TPA does this through a short cut and therefore it would not represent the economics as faithfully as the 2009 Impairment Exposure Draft did. Because the TPA allocates both the initial expected credit losses and the subsequent changes in lifetime expected credit losses over time, the measurement results in an understatement of changes in expected credit losses until the entity recognises lifetime expected credit losses. This effect is particularly problematic for financial assets that increase in credit risk and thus whose expected credit losses increase early in the asset's life.

BC5.98　Allocating the change in estimated expected credit losses in this way results in the deferred recognition of the full amount of the change in expected credit losses and, consequently, the TPA closely replicated the outcome of the model in the 2009 Impairment Exposure Draft only in situations in which expectations of credit losses do not change or the credit losses emerge at, or close to, maturity (extremely back-ended losses). This shortcoming was addressed by including a foreseeable future floor in the SD. However, because the calculation of the TPA relied on the weighted average age over the weighted average life of the portfolio, the outcome may not have reflected the economics of a growing or declining portfolio.

BC5.99　The TPA calculation proposed by the Supplementary Document (whereby the loss allowance was, at a minimum, equal to the expected credit losses in the foreseeable future) was unique and would not be a calculation required to be used by entities for other purposes. Some of the identified operational challenges of the proposals in the 2009 Impairment Exposure Draft would still exist, including the need to change systems to calculate the weighted average age and the weighted average life of open portfolios, as would the need to estimate the full expected cash flows for all financial assets.

BC5.100 The IASB did not receive strong support for the proposals in the Supplementary Document. Many respondents were concerned that the Supplementary Document required an entity to make two calculations to measure the loss allowance balance for the good book. They viewed the dual calculation as operationally difficult, lacking conceptual merit and providing confusing information to users of financial statements, because the basis for these loss calculations could change over time for the same financial assets and be different for different financial assets. Respondents also expressed concerns about the calculation of expected credit losses for the foreseeable future, with many expressing confusion about the conceptual basis for the time period. Many also noted that the term 'foreseeable future' had not been sufficiently defined to ensure consistent application. Furthermore, feedback on the Supplementary Document proposals were geographically split, with respondents in the US generally preferring the foreseeable future floor while respondents outside the US generally preferred the TPA approach.

BC5.101 Although the IASB did not receive strong support for the proposals in the Supplementary Document, some respondents, particularly users of financial statements and prudential regulators, supported the distinction between 'good book' and 'bad book' assets even if they were concerned that the criteria for transferring from the 'good book' to the 'bad book' were not sufficiently clear. On balance, the IASB decided not to further pursue this two-tier approach.

The model proposed in the 2013 Impairment Exposure Draft

BC5.102 The model proposed in the 2013 Impairment Exposure Draft continued to build on a tiered approach by requiring an entity to measure:

(a) the expected credit losses for a financial instrument at an amount equal to the lifetime expected credit losses, if the credit quality on that financial instrument has decreased significantly (or the credit risk increases significantly) since initial recognition; and

(b) the expected credit losses for a financial instrument at an amount equal to the 12-month expected credit losses for all other financial instruments.

BC5.103 The model proposed in the 2013 Impairment Exposure Draft eliminated the operational challenge of estimating the full expected cash flows for all financial instruments by limiting the recognition of lifetime expected credit losses to financial instruments for which credit risk has increased significantly since initial recognition.

BC5.104 To assist entities that have less sophisticated credit risk management systems, the 2013 Impairment Exposure Draft included simplifications to account for trade receivables and lease receivables. The proposed simplifications would reduce the need to track increases in credit risk by requiring (or allowing) an entity to recognise lifetime expected credit losses from the date of initial recognition.

BC5.105 The 2013 Impairment Exposure Draft proposed that interest revenue would be calculated using the effective interest method using the effective interest rate unadjusted for expected credit losses, except for purchased or originated credit-impaired financial assets, in which case the entity would use a credit-adjusted effective interest rate.

BC5.106 Overall, the majority of participants in the outreach conducted by the IASB while developing this model, including users of financial statements, supported a model that distinguishes between instruments for which credit risk has increased significantly since initial recognition and those that have not. In the IASB's view, this requirement for recognising lifetime expected credit losses strikes the best balance between the benefits of making distinctions on the basis of an increase in credit risk and the costs and complexity of making that assessment. Furthermore, the proposals aimed to limit the new information that an entity would be required to capture and maintain about the initial credit risk of financial assets by using information that preparers have said is consistent with current credit risk management systems.

BC5.107 To further reduce the cost of assessing the increases in credit risk, the proposed model included practical expedients and rebuttable presumptions (see paragraphs BC5.180–BC5.194) to assess if there have been significant increases in credit risk.

BC5.108 On the basis of the comments received about the proposals in the 2013 Impairment Exposure Draft, the IASB proceeded to refine the proposals while developing IFRS 9 and its requirements to account for impairment based on expected credit losses.

Joint deliberations with the FASB

BC5.109 In May 2010, the FASB published a proposed Accounting Standards Update *Accounting for Financial Instruments and Revisions to the Accounting for Derivative Instruments and Hedging Activities* (the '2010 proposed Update') that included proposals for impairment as part of its comprehensive approach to replacing the accounting requirements for financial instruments in US Generally Accepted Accounting Principles (US GAAP). The FASB's objective for credit impairment was to develop a single model for all financial instruments that provides more timely credit loss information for users of financial statements.

BC5.110 Many respondents to both the IASB's 2009 Impairment Exposure Draft and the FASB's 2010 proposed Update commented that achieving a common outcome for impairment accounting would be highly desirable. The boards agreed and, in January 2011, jointly published the Supplementary Document, which built on their individual original Exposure Drafts and sought to incorporate the objectives of both boards' original impairment proposals (see paragraphs BC5.96–BC5.101 for further discussions on the Supplementary Document's proposals and feedback).

BC5.111 The feedback received on the Supplementary Document, combined with the importance of achieving convergence, encouraged the IASB and the FASB to jointly develop an alternative expected credit loss model. In May 2011, the boards decided to jointly develop a model that would reflect the general pattern of increases in the credit risk of financial instruments, the so-called 'three-bucket model'. In the three-bucket model, the amount of the expected credit losses recognised as a loss allowance would depend on the extent of increases in the credit risk on financial instruments since initial recognition.

BC5.112 However, in response to feedback received from respondents in the US about that model, in July 2012 the FASB decided to develop an alternative expected credit loss model.

BC5.113 In December 2012, the FASB published the proposed Accounting Standards Update *Financial Instruments—Credit Losses* (the '2012 proposed Update'). The proposed Update would require an entity to measure the net amortised cost at the present value of cash flows that it expects to collect, discounted at the original effective interest rate. To achieve this, an entity would recognise a loss allowance for expected credit losses from initial recognition at an amount equal to the lifetime expected credit losses. The comment period on this document overlapped with the IASB's comment period on the 2013 Impairment Exposure Draft.

BC5.114 Feedback received by the IASB on the 2013 Impairment Exposure Draft and by the FASB on the 2012 proposed Update was shared at joint board meetings to enable the boards to consider the comments received and differences in the opinions of their respective stakeholders. For many respondents to the 2013 Impairment Exposure Draft convergence was still preferable; however, many noted that their preference was subject to the impairment model being similar to that proposed in the IASB's 2013 Impairment Exposure Draft. Only a limited number of the IASB's respondents preferred convergence to the 2012 proposed Update model exposed by the FASB. Furthermore, very few respondents demanded convergence at the cost of finalising the requirements in a timely manner. Many respondents urged the IASB to finalise the proposed model as soon as possible, with or without convergence, stressing the importance of improving the accounting for the impairment of financial assets in IFRS as soon as possible.

BC5.115 The FASB and the IASB reported differences in views from the users of the financial statements. The FASB reported that users of financial statements overwhelmingly supported its 2012 proposed Update model. The IASB however reported on its outreach activities that a majority of non-US users preferred an impairment model similar to what was proposed in the 2013 Impairment Exposure Draft, while the majority of US users preferred a model similar to that proposed by the FASB.

BC5.116 Because of the importance of the user perspective and the apparent inconsistency in feedback subsequent to the comment letter analysis discussed in July 2013, the IASB conducted further outreach activities to understand the reasons for the difference in the feedback received by the IASB and the FASB on their respective proposals. The IASB identified the following:

(a)   the starting point of how preparers apply US GAAP for loss allowances is different from the starting point of IFRS preparers. The IASB believe that this difference in starting point has influenced users' perceptions of the two proposed models.

(b)   the interaction between the role of prudential regulators and loss allowances is historically stronger in the US.

(c)   many users of financial statements in the US place greater weight on the adequacy of loss allowances in the balance sheet.

BC5.117   Before and during the redeliberations the IASB was made aware of the feedback received from all respondents, including the users of financial statements. The issue of convergence was discussed at length throughout the course of the project. Having considered all the feedback and the points discussed in paragraphs BC5.114–BC5.116, the IASB decided to proceed with the model proposed in the 2013 Impairment Exposure Draft.

Scope

BC5.118   In addition to financial assets that are measured at amortised cost (including trade receivables) and at fair value through other comprehensive income, the IASB decided to include the following within the scope of the impairment requirements of IFRS 9:

(a)   loan commitments and financial guarantee contracts for the issuer, that are not measured at fair value through profit or loss;

(b)   lease receivables that are accounted for in accordance with IAS 17 *Leases*; and

(c)   contract assets that are recognised and measured in accordance with IFRS 15.

Financial assets measured at fair value through other comprehensive income

BC5.119   The objective of the fair value through other comprehensive income measurement category is to provide users of financial statements with information on both a fair value and an amortised cost basis. To achieve that objective, paragraph 5.7.10 of IFRS 9 requires an entity to calculate interest revenue and impairment gains or losses in a manner that is consistent with the requirements that are applicable to financial assets measured at amortised cost. Thus, the IASB decided that the requirements for the recognition and measurement of expected credit losses shall apply to the fair value through other comprehensive income measurement category, in the same way as for assets measured at amortised cost. However, the loss allowance is recognised in other comprehensive income instead of reducing the carrying amount of the financial asset in the statement of financial position.

BC5.120   The IASB has noted feedback that recommended including a practical expedient that will provide relief from recognising 12-month expected credit losses on financial assets measured at fair value through other comprehensive income, when the fair value of the financial asset exceeds its amortised cost or when the loss allowance is insignificant. Interested parties noted that such a practical expedient would reduce the operational burden of assessing whether increases in credit risk since initial recognition are significant on financial assets that are already measured at fair value. They also noted that it would not be appropriate to recognise impairment gains or losses in profit or loss on financial assets that were purchased in an active market that prices the initial expectations of credit losses into the financial asset.

BC5.121 The IASB rejected these views. The IASB noted that not all debt instruments acquired in an active market are measured at fair value through other comprehensive income. In accordance with paragraph 4.1.2 of IFRS 9, such instruments can also be measured at amortised cost if the business model criteria are met (subject to the cash flow characteristics criteria). Having separate impairment models for similar financial assets that are measured differently would be inconsistent with the IASB's objective of having a single impairment model.

BC5.122 Furthermore, the IASB observed that a fair value-based practical expedient is inconsistent with the general impairment approach, which is based on an entity's assessment of the changes in the risk of a default occurring since initial recognition. Introducing a fair value-based practical expedient would represent a different impairment approach and would not result in the amounts recognised in profit or loss being the same as if the financial assets were measured at amortised cost.

BC5.123 The IASB noted that the assessment of credit risk is based on management's view of collecting contractual cash flows instead of on the perspective of a market participant as is the case with fair value measurement. It was noted that market prices are not in themselves intended to be a determinant of whether credit risk has increased significantly because, for example, market prices can be affected by factors that are not relevant to credit risk (such as changes in the level of general interest rates and the price of liquidity). However, the IASB noted that market prices are an important source of information that should be considered in assessing whether credit risk has changed. It was also noted that market information is relevant for financial instruments within the scope of the impairment model irrespective of the classification in accordance with IFRS 9. This is because the form of a financial asset (as a bond or a loan) does not determine its classification in accordance with IFRS 9 and because the accounting for expected credit losses is the same for financial assets measured at amortised cost and those measured at fair value through other comprehensive income.

BC5.124 In the IASB's view, applying a single impairment model to both financial assets at amortised cost and financial assets at fair value through other comprehensive income will facilitate comparability of amounts that are recognised in profit or loss for assets with similar economic characteristics. In addition, the IASB noted that having a single impairment model reduces a significant source of complexity for both users of financial statements and preparers compared with applying IAS 39. The IASB's view was strongly supported by respondents to the 2013 Impairment Exposure Draft. During its redeliberations on the 2013

Impairment Exposure Draft, the IASB, having noted the support from respondents, confirmed the inclusion of these financial assets within the scope of the impairment requirements.

Loan commitments and financial guarantee contracts

BC5.125 Loan commitments and financial guarantee contracts outside the scope of IAS 39 were previously accounted for in accordance with IAS 37 *Provisions, Contingent Liabilities and Contingent Assets*. The Supplementary Document asked respondents whether an entity should apply the same impairment model to loan commitments and financial guarantee contracts as for financial assets measured at amortised cost. On the basis of the support from respondents to the Supplementary Document, the 2013 Impairment Exposure Draft retained the proposal that an entity should recognise expected credit losses that result from loan commitments and financial guarantee contracts when there is a present contractual obligation to extend credit.

BC5.126 The vast majority of respondents to the 2013 Impairment Exposure Draft agreed that loan commitments and financial guarantee contracts should be within the scope of the impairment model because:

(a) expected credit losses on loan commitments and financial guarantee contracts (off balance sheet exposures) are similar to those on loans and other on balance sheet exposures. The only difference is that in the latter case, the borrower has already drawn down the loan whereas in the former case it has not.

(b) in practice, loan commitments and financial guarantee contracts are often managed using the same credit risk management approach and information systems as loans and other on balance sheet items.

(c) a single impairment model for all credit exposures, irrespective of their type, removes the complexity previously caused by different impairment models in IFRS.

BC5.127 However, many of the respondents that supported including loan commitments and financial guarantee contracts within the scope of the impairment requirements proposed that the expected credit losses should be measured over the behavioural life of the product, instead of over the contractual life as was proposed (see paragraphs BC5.254–BC5.261).

BC5.128 The IASB therefore confirmed the inclusion within the scope of the impairment requirements of loan commitments that are not measured at fair value through profit or loss in accordance with IFRS 9 and financial guarantee contracts to which IFRS 9 is applied and that are not measured at fair value through profit or loss.

Trade receivables, contract assets and lease receivables

BC5.129 The 2009 Impairment Exposure Draft proposed that entities should apply an expected credit loss model to trade receivables. It also proposed a practical expedient by which they could use a provision matrix as the basis for measurement. Many respondents told the IASB that applying an expected credit loss model to non-interest-bearing trade receivables would not provide useful information because of their short maturity. They also noted that there would be operational challenges for non-financial institutions and less sophisticated financial institutions in applying an expected credit loss model. Consequently, the IASB conducted further outreach to gather information about current practice and the operational challenges of applying an expected credit loss model to trade receivables. That outreach indicated that the practical application of the impairment requirements in IAS 39 often results in credit losses not being recognised until trade receivables become past due.

BC5.130   In finalising IFRS 9, the IASB concluded that requiring entities to recognise a loss allowance on a more forward-looking basis before trade receivables become past due would improve financial reporting.

BC5.131   The IASB also noted in both the 2009 and 2013 Impairment Exposure Drafts, that, although the requirements in IAS 17 result in the measurement of a lease receivable in a manner that is similar to financial assets that are measured at amortised cost in accordance with IFRS 9, there are differences in the application of the effective interest method. In addition, the cash flows included in lease contracts could include features such as contingent payments that would not be present in other financial instruments. The existence of contingent and variable lease payments results in:

(a)   specific requirements for identifying the cash flows that are included in the measurement of the lease receivable (such as the criteria for including contingent lease payments, the treatment of renewal options and the bifurcation of any embedded derivatives); and

(b)   a consequential effect on determining the discount rate (ie given (a), the discount rate cannot always be determined in the same way as the effective interest rate for a financial asset measured at amortised cost).

BC5.132   The IASB decided that these differences do not justify applying a different impairment model and therefore included lease receivables within the scope of the impairment requirements in IFRS 9. In reaching this decision, the IASB concluded that the impairment model could be applied to lease receivables as long as:

(a)   the cash flows assessed for expected credit losses are consistent with those included in the measurement of the lease receivable; and

(b)   the rate used to discount the expected credit losses is consistent with the rate that is determined in accordance with IAS 17.

BC5.133   Some respondents to the 2013 Impairment Exposure Draft noted that the IASB has an active project affecting the accounting treatment of lease receivables that is yet to be finalised. They requested further clarification of the interaction between the expected credit loss requirements and the proposed accounting for lease receivables in accordance with that project. The IASB acknowledged these concerns and noted that it will further consider this interaction if needed when deliberating the accounting treatment for lease receivables as part of the leases project.

BC5.134   When finalising IFRS 15, the IASB noted that although contract assets are specifically excluded from the scope of IFRS 9 and accounted for in accordance with IFRS 15, the exposure to credit risk on contract assets is similar to that of trade receivables. The IASB therefore decided to include contract assets in the scope of the impairment requirements. The IASB also decided that if an entity applies IFRS 9 before it applies IFRS 15, an entity should apply the impairment requirements in IFRS 9 to those receivables that arise from transactions that are accounted for in accordance with IAS 18 *Revenue* and IAS 11 *Construction Contracts*.

Recognition of expected credit losses

General approach

BC5.135   On the basis of the feedback received from respondents on the proposals in the 2013 Impairment Exposure Draft about the usefulness of the information and the responsiveness of the impairment model to changes in credit risk, the IASB decided to finalise the proposed approach. In doing so, the IASB considered that this expected credit loss approach will improve financial reporting because:

(a)   financial statements will clearly distinguish between financial instruments for which credit risk has increased significantly since initial recognition and those for which it has not;

(b)   a loss allowance at an amount equal to at least 12-month expected credit losses will be recognised throughout the life of financial assets, thereby reducing the systematic overstatement of interest revenue in accordance with the requirements in IAS 39, and acting as a proxy for the recognition of initial expected credit losses over time as proposed in the 2009 Impairment Exposure Draft;

(c)   a loss allowance at an amount equal to lifetime expected credit losses will be recognised when credit risk has significantly increased since initial recognition, resulting in the timely recognition of expected credit losses; and

(d)   amounts reported about expected credit losses will better reflect the effective return and the changes in the credit risk on financial instruments compared to the requirements in IAS 39.

Collective and individual assessment of changes in credit risk

BC5.136   It was apparent in responses and comments received on the 2013 Impairment Exposure Draft that some respondents were of the view that the proposals would not require (or even allow) lifetime expected credit losses to be recognised on financial instruments unless there was evidence of significant increases in credit risk at an individual instrument level. The IASB also became aware that some understood the 2013 Impairment Exposure Draft as only requiring lifetime expected credit losses to be recognised when a financial asset became past due.

BC5.137   In considering the feedback received, the IASB confirmed that the objective of the impairment requirements is to capture lifetime expected credit losses on all financial instruments that have significant increases in credit risk, regardless of whether it is on an individual or a collective basis.

BC5.138   Consequently, the IASB considered whether the impairment requirements in Section 5.5 of IFRS 9 should specify whether an entity should evaluate financial instruments individually or collectively when deciding whether it should recognise lifetime expected credit losses. In accordance with IFRS 9, the unit of account is the individual financial instrument. The timeliness of capturing significant increases in credit risk primarily depends on whether the entity has reasonable and supportable information that is available without undue cost or effort to identify significant increases in credit risk in a timely manner before financial assets become past due. However, when credit risk management systems are heavily dependent on past due information, there may be a delay between identifying significant increases in credit risk and when the increase in credit risk has actually occurred.

BC5.139   The IASB observed that any delay is minimised when credit risk management systems capture a comprehensive range of credit risk information that is forward-looking and is updated on a timely basis at the individual instrument level. The delay is more apparent for portfolios of financial instruments that are managed on the basis of past due information.

BC5.140   The IASB noted that in some circumstances the segmentation of portfolios based on shared credit risk characteristics may assist in determining significant increases in credit risk for groups of financial instruments. The IASB considered that individual financial assets could be grouped into segments on the basis of common borrower-specific information and the effect of forward-looking information (ie changes in macroeconomic indicators) that affect the risk of a default occurring could be considered for each segment. As a result, an entity could use the change in that macroeconomic indicator to determine that the credit risk of one or more segments of financial instruments in the portfolio has increased significantly, although it is not yet possible to identify the individual financial instruments for which credit risk has increased significantly. The IASB also noted that in other cases an entity may use reasonable and supportable information to determine that the credit risk of a homogeneous portion of a portfolio should be considered to have increased significantly in order to meet the objective of recognising all significant increases in credit risk.

BC5.141   The IASB noted that measuring expected credit losses on a collective basis approximates the result of using comprehensive credit risk information that incorporates forward-looking information at an individual instrument level. However, financial instruments should not be grouped in order to measure expected credit losses on a collective basis in a way that obscures significant increases in credit risk on individual financial instruments within the group.

BC5.142   The IASB observed that, although an entity may group financial instruments in a portfolio with similar characteristics to identify significant increases in credit risk, ultimately, information will emerge that may enable an entity to distinguish between instruments that are more likely to default from instruments that are not. As the passage of time reduces the uncertainty about the eventual outcome, the risk of a default occurring on the financial instruments in the portfolio should diverge until the financial instruments either default or are collected in full. Consequently, the appropriate level of grouping is expected to change over time in order to capture all significant increases in credit risk. The IASB concluded that an entity should not group financial instruments at a higher level of aggregation if a subgroup exists for which the recognition of lifetime expected credit losses is more appropriate.

Timing of the recognition of lifetime expected credit losses

BC5.143 Some respondents to the 2009 Impairment Exposure Draft and the Supplementary Document believed that the value of a financial asset measured at amortised cost is most faithfully represented by discounting the expected cash flows (ie contractual cash flows reduced for expected credit losses) at the original effective interest rate (ie the effective interest rate that is not reduced for initial expected credit losses). In other words, an entity would be required to recognise a loss allowance for lifetime expected credit losses, discounted using the original effective interest rate, from initial recognition. Those respondents believe that because credit losses do not occur rateably throughout the life of a loan, or throughout the life of a portfolio of loans, there is a fundamental disconnect between the 'lumpy' pattern of actual credit losses and a time-based accounting approach that attempts to link the recognition of credit losses that are anticipated at initial recognition of the financial asset with the recognition of interest revenue.

BC5.144 The IASB considered and rejected this view. At initial recognition, the timing of initial expected credit losses affects the amount of the adjustment to the effective interest rate. Thus, an earlier expected credit loss would give rise to a larger credit adjustment to the effective interest rate than a later expected credit loss of an equal nominal value. Because the pattern of initially expected credit losses is priced into the asset as represented by its present value, compensation is received for the amount and timing of those initially expected credit losses. Thus, in the IASB's view, if initial credit loss expectations do not subsequently change:

(a) interest revenue should reflect the credit-adjusted effective return over time; and

(b) there is no credit loss (or gain), because no economic loss (or gain) has occurred.

BC5.145 Respondents also believe that the evaluation of the creditworthiness that influences pricing is based on historical experience for groups of similar assets. This means that, while the credit spread that is charged on the lender's overall portfolio of individual loans may be expected to compensate the entity for credit losses for a large portfolio of assets over time, the credit spread on any individual asset is not necessarily established in a way that compensates the lender for expected credit losses on that particular asset.

BC5.146 The IASB considered and rejected these views. First, expected credit losses are a probability-weighted estimate of expected cash shortfalls. Thus, the pricing of individual instruments would reflect the probability of credit losses and would be no different to the pricing of an instrument that is part of a portfolio. Market participants price individual instruments consistently, irrespective of whether they will hold that instrument in isolation or as part of a portfolio. Second, it is not necessary to measure separately the initial expected credit losses and the compensation for those credit losses, and then precisely match the amount and timing of those credit losses and the related compensation. An estimate of expected credit losses at initial recognition (which an entity could estimate in a number of different ways) would be sufficient for the purposes of determining the credit adjustment to the effective interest rate. Indeed, any models requiring the recognition of the lifetime expected credit losses at initial recognition would require an entity to make the same estimate.

BC5.147   A few respondents also argued that the amortised cost amount of a financial asset should reflect the present value of the cash flows that are expected to be collected, discounted at the original effective interest rate (ie a rate that is not adjusted for initial expected credit losses). They believe that it is misleading to investors to allow the balance sheet to reflect a greater amount.

BC5.148   The IASB considered and rejected that view. The original effective interest rate is the rate that exactly discounts the expected cash flows (before deducting expected credit losses) of the asset to the transaction price (ie the fair value or principal) at initial recognition. Thus, the original effective interest rate already takes into consideration an entity's initial estimate of expected credit losses (ie it reflects the riskiness of the contractual cash flows). One of the general principles of any present value technique is that the discount rate should reflect assumptions that are consistent with those inherent in the cash flows that are being discounted. Requiring the entity to further deduct an amount from the transaction price that represents the same amount that it has already discounted from the contractual cash flows results in the entity double-counting its initial estimate of expected credit losses. The effect of this would be most apparent at initial recognition, because the carrying amount of the asset would be below the transaction price.

BC5.149   As noted in paragraph BC5.103, the impairment model proposed in the 2013 Impairment Exposure Draft eliminated the operational challenge of having to estimate the full expected (credit-loss adjusted) cash flows for all financial instruments. It did this by limiting the measurement of lifetime expected credit losses to financial instruments for which credit risk has significantly increased since initial recognition. The majority of participants in the outreach conducted by the IASB while developing the proposals in the 2013 Impairment Exposure Draft noted that if financial instruments were to move too quickly to a lifetime expected credit loss measurement (for example, on the basis of minor increases in credit risk) the costs of implementing the model (ie one that would require lifetime expected credit losses to be measured on many financial assets in addition to requiring a distinction to be made on the basis of the extent of the change in the credit risk) might not be justified.

BC5.150   Respondents to the 2013 Impairment Exposure Draft strongly supported the proposal to recognise lifetime expected credit losses only when the credit risk of a financial instrument has increased significantly since initial recognition, because it captures the underlying economics of a transaction while easing operational complexities. They also noted that:

(a)   it reflects and provides a clear indication that an economic loss occurred as a result of changes in credit risk from initial expectations.

(b)   it avoids excessive front-loading of expected credit losses.

(c)   measuring lifetime expected credit losses for financial instruments that have signs of significant increases in credit risk would be operationally simpler because more data is available for these financial instruments.

(d)   the proposal would result in recognising lifetime expected credit losses in a timelier and more forward-looking manner compared to IAS 39. Respondents therefore believed that the proposal addresses the concerns of the G20 and others about the delayed recognition of credit losses under an incurred loss approach.

BC5.151   Consequently, in the light of the support and arguments presented, the IASB decided to require an entity to recognise lifetime expected credit losses when the credit risk of a financial instrument has increased significantly since initial recognition.

BC5.152   The IASB received requests to clarify whether a financial instrument for which the interest rate on the instrument has been repriced to reflect an increase in credit risk should continue to have a loss allowance measured at an amount equal to 12-month expected credit losses, even if the increase in credit risk since initial recognition is assessed to be significant. The IASB considered that, conceptually, the loss allowance on such an instrument should continue to be measured at 12-month expected credit losses. This is because the contractual interest rate has been repriced to reflect the entity's expectations about credit losses and is similar to the economic position on initial recognition of a similar financial instrument with a similar credit risk at origination. However, the IASB noted that requiring an entity to assess whether the increase in the interest rate appropriately compensates it for the increase in credit risk would give rise to operational complexity similar to that arising from the 2009 Impairment Exposure Draft. The IASB further noted that the objective of the impairment requirements is to recognise lifetime expected credit losses for financial instruments if there have been significant increases in credit risk since initial recognition.

BC5.153   The IASB also considered that when a financial instrument is repriced to take into account an increase in credit risk, the risk of a default occurring on the financial instrument has increased, implying that the customer is more likely to default than was expected at initial recognition. The fact that the entity is entitled to a higher yield because of the increase in credit risk does not mean that the risk of a default occurring on the financial instrument has not increased. The IASB therefore decided that, on balance, the assessment of whether lifetime expected credit losses should be recognised should be based solely on the increase in the risk of a default occurring since initial recognition.

Determining significant increases in credit risk

Use of changes in the risk of a default occurring

BC5.154   In the 2013 Impairment Exposure Draft, the IASB proposed using the risk of a default occurring on a financial instrument to determine whether there has been an increase in credit risk since initial recognition. The IASB noted that the risk of a default occurring is a measurement of the financial instrument's credit risk that does not require the full estimation of expected credit losses. The

2009 Impairment Exposure Draft required the tracking of the initial expected credit losses and the measurement of all subsequent changes in those expected credit losses. In contrast, the model proposed in the 2013 Impairment Exposure Draft required:

(a)   the tracking of the initial risk of a default occurring (a component of the expected credit losses); and

(b)   an assessment of the significance of subsequent changes in the risk of a default occurring to decide whether the recognition of lifetime expected credit losses is required.

BC5.155   Many respondents to the proposals in the 2013 Impairment Exposure Draft agreed that an assessment of when to recognise lifetime expected credit losses should take into consideration only the changes in credit risk (ie the risk of a default occurring) instead of changes in the amount of expected credit losses. These respondents noted that the risk of a default occurring was considered the most relevant factor in assessing credit risk, and that tracking only the risk of a default occurring makes the model more operational, because that generally aligns with their credit risk management practices.

BC5.156   Respondents to the 2013 Impairment Exposure Draft supported the proposed principle-based approach of assessing significant increases in credit risk instead of prescriptive rules and 'bright lines'. However, some requested clarification about the information that needs to be considered in that assessment. In particular, some thought that the 2013 Impairment Exposure Draft could be interpreted to explicitly require the use of a mechanistic approach to determine the 'probability of default' when assessing significant increases in credit risk. Respondents were concerned that this would require the explicit calculation and storage of the lifetime probability of default curve for a financial instrument to compare the expected remaining lifetime probability of default at inception with the remaining lifetime probability of default at the reporting date.

BC5.157   The IASB noted that it did not intend to prescribe a specific or mechanistic approach to assess changes in credit risk and that the appropriate approach will vary for different levels of sophistication of entities, the financial instrument and the availability of data. The IASB confirmed that the use of the term 'probability of a default' occurring was intended to capture the concept of the risk of a default occurring. A specific probability of default measure is one way in which that could be assessed, but the IASB decided that it would not be appropriate to require particular sources of information to be used to make the assessment. This is because credit analysis is a multifactor and holistic analysis, and when making that analysis entities have differences in the availability of data. Such differences include whether a specific factor is relevant, and its weight compared to other factors which will depend on the type of product, characteristics of the financial instrument and the customer as well as the geographical region. However, to reduce the risk of misinterpretation, the IASB decided to change the terminology from 'probability of a default occurring' to 'risk of a default occurring'.

BC5.158 In the IASB's view, the recognition requirements for lifetime expected credit losses in IFRS 9 strike the best balance between the benefits of making distinctions on the basis of increases in credit risk and the costs and complexity of making that assessment.

Approaches for determining significant increases in credit risk considered and rejected

BC5.159 The IASB considered a number of alternative approaches for determining when to recognise lifetime expected credit losses to make the impairment model in IFRS 9 more operational.

Absolute level of credit risk

BC5.160 The IASB considered whether lifetime expected credit losses should be recognised on the basis of an assessment of the absolute credit risk of a financial instrument at each reporting date. Under this approach, an entity would recognise lifetime expected credit losses on all financial instruments at, or above, a particular credit risk at the reporting date. An approach based on the absolute credit risk at each reporting date would be much simpler to apply, because it does not require tracking of credit risk at initial recognition. However, such an approach would provide very different information. It would not approximate the economic effect of initial credit loss expectations and subsequent changes in expectations. In addition, if the absolute credit risk threshold for recognising lifetime expected credit losses was too high, too many financial instruments would be below the threshold and expected credit losses would be understated. If the absolute threshold was too low, too many financial instruments would be above the threshold, overstating the expected credit losses (for example, financial instruments with a high credit risk that an entity prices appropriately to compensate for the higher credit risk would always have lifetime expected credit losses recognised). Furthermore, depending on which absolute credit risk threshold is selected, such an approach might be similar to the incurred loss model in IAS 39 (in which the absolute threshold is objective evidence of impairment). Consequently, the IASB rejected this approach.

BC5.161 Although the IASB rejected using an absolute level of credit risk for the recognition of lifetime expected credit losses, it noted that the assessment of significant increases in credit risk could be implemented more simply by determining the maximum initial credit risk accepted by the reporting entity for a particular portfolio of financial instruments and then comparing the credit risk of financial instruments in that portfolio at the reporting date to that maximum initial credit risk. However, the IASB noted that this would only be possible for portfolios of financial instruments with similar credit risk at initial recognition. Such an approach would enable a change in credit risk to be the basis for the recognition of lifetime expected credit losses, but does not require specific tracking of the credit risk on an individual financial instrument since initial recognition.

Change in the credit risk management objective

BC5.162 Some interested parties suggested that lifetime expected credit losses should be recognised when an entity's credit risk management objective changes; for example, when contractual cash flows are no longer received consistently with the terms of the contract, the entity changes its credit risk management objective from collecting past due amounts to recovery of the total (or part of the) contractual amount outstanding and the financial assets are being monitored on an individual basis. While recognising lifetime expected credit losses when the credit risk management objective changes would be operationally simpler (ie financial instruments that are being managed differently would be identified immediately, with no need to assess a change in credit risk since initial recognition), the approach would be likely to have a similar effect to the incurred loss model in IAS 39. Because the management of a financial instrument may change only relatively late compared with when significant increases in credit risk occur, the IASB considered this to be a less timely approach to recognising lifetime expected credit losses.

Credit underwriting policies

BC5.163   Some interested parties suggested that lifetime expected credit losses should be recognised when a financial instrument's credit risk at the reporting date is higher than the credit risk at which the entity would originate new loans for that particular class of financial instruments (ie if the level of credit risk exceeded the credit underwriting limit for that class of financial instruments at the reporting date).

BC5.164   The IASB noted a number of disadvantages to this approach. In a similar way to an approach based on the absolute level of credit risk or a change in the credit risk management objective, this approach would not require the change in credit risk since initial recognition to be assessed. It would thus be inconsistent with the IASB's objective of reflecting increases in credit risk and linking that to pricing. The objective of setting credit underwriting limits also follows a different objective compared to that of financial reporting, which could result in a misstatement of expected credit losses. For example, changes in underwriting policies may occur for business reasons, such as wishing to increase lending, resulting in changes to the recognition of expected credit losses on existing financial instruments irrespective of changes in credit risk.

BC5.165   The IASB further noted that the underwriting standards at the time that a financial instrument is initially recognised do not in themselves provide evidence of a significant increase in credit risk. This is because the new financial instruments cannot, by definition, have experienced significant increases in credit risk at initial recognition. Furthermore, the underwriting standards of new financial instruments are not relevant to the credit risk of existing financial instruments. However, the IASB notes that particular vintages may be more prone to increases in credit risk, and thus financial instruments of particular vintages may need to be monitored and assessed with increased vigilance.

Counterparty assessment

BC5.166   Some interested parties suggested that an entity should recognise lifetime expected credit losses on all financial instruments it holds with the same borrower (ie counterparty), if the credit risk of the borrower has reached a specified level at the reporting date (including on newly originated or purchased financial instruments for which the yield appropriately reflects the credit risk at the reporting date). Respondents supporting this approach noted that they manage credit risk on a counterparty level instead of an individual instrument level and that assessing significant increases in credit risk on an instrument level was in their view counterintuitive. This was because different loss allowance measurements could be recognised for similar instruments held with the same counterparty, depending on when the instruments were initially recognised.

BC5.167 The IASB noted that the objective of the impairment requirements is to reflect the economics of lending to provide users of financial statements with relevant information about the performance of financial instruments instead of the performance of a counterparty. A counterparty assessment could misstate expected credit losses if its credit risk had changed; for example, because it would not reflect that a recently recognised financial instrument of a counterparty was priced taking into consideration the current credit risk. Furthermore, like the absolute approach, this approach might be similar to the incurred loss model in IAS 39 in effect, depending on which level of credit risk is selected as the threshold for recognising lifetime expected credit losses. The IASB also noted that not all entities manage credit risk on a counterparty level and that a counterparty assessment of credit risk could produce very different information compared to the information resulting from the impairment model in IFRS 9.

BC5.168 However, the IASB acknowledged that assessing credit risk on a basis that considers a customer's credit risk (ie the risk that a customer will default on its obligations) more holistically may nevertheless be consistent with the impairment requirements. An overall assessment of a counterparty's credit risk could be undertaken, for example, to make an initial assessment of whether credit risk has increased significantly, as long as such an assessment satisfies the requirements for recognising lifetime expected credit losses and the outcome would not be different to the outcome if the financial instruments had been individually assessed.

Extent of increase in credit risk required

BC5.169 The model proposed in the 2013 Impairment Exposure Draft requires an entity to initially account for a portion of expected credit losses. However, the IASB decided that, if an entity suffers a significant economic loss, recognition of only a portion of the lifetime expected credit losses is no longer appropriate and it should recognise the full lifetime expected credit losses. The IASB considered how significant the extent of the increase in credit risk should be, from both an economic and a practical perspective, to justify the recognition of lifetime expected credit losses.

BC5.170 In the IASB's joint deliberations with the FASB, the boards had tentatively agreed that the deterioration criteria for the recognition of lifetime expected credit losses should be that the credit quality had deteriorated more than insignificantly subsequent to the initial recognition of the financial instrument. However, in the IASB's outreach undertaken while developing the model proposed in the 2013 Impairment Exposure Draft, participants expressed concern that this criterion would have the result that even a minor change in the credit quality would satisfy the test. In response to that concern, the 2013

Impairment Exposure Draft proposed that the criterion for the recognition of lifetime expected credit losses is significant increases in credit risk, expressed as an increase in the risk of a default occurring since initial recognition.

BC5.171 During outreach and as part of their responses to the 2013 Impairment Exposure Draft, some interested parties and respondents asked the IASB to specify the amount of change in the risk of a default occurring that would require the recognition of lifetime expected credit losses. Those making this request argued that this would provide clarity and improve comparability. The IASB did not pursue this approach for the following reasons:

(a) not all entities use an explicit probability of default to measure or assess credit risk—in particular, entities other than regulated financial institutions. The IASB observed that entities manage financial instruments and credit risk in different ways, with different levels of sophistication and by using different information. If the IASB were to propose a precise definition of significant increases in credit risk, for example, a change of 5 per cent in the probability of default, then an entity would need to calculate a probability of default measure to make the assessment. Thus, the costs of assessing changes in credit risk would increase.

(b) the measure for the risk of a default occurring (ie probability of default) selected would be arbitrary and it would be difficult to properly reflect the structure and pricing of credit that an entity should consider for different types of financial instruments, maturities and initial credit risk. Selecting a single measure could not properly reflect the assessment of credit across entities, products and geographical regions. Because of the arbitrariness of defining the extent of increases in credit risk, the IASB questioned the perceived comparability that would result.

BC5.172 Consequently, the IASB confirmed its view that the requirements for when to recognise lifetime expected credit losses should be clear but also be broadly defined and objective based.

BC5.173 The IASB noted that the assessment of the significance of the change in the risk of a default occurring for different financial instruments would depend on the credit risk at initial recognition and the time to maturity. This is because it would be consistent with the structure of credit risk and therefore with the pricing of financial instruments. In the IASB's view, an entity should consider the term structure and the initial credit risk in assessing whether it should recognise lifetime expected credit losses. Doing so will improve the comparability of the requirements for financial instruments with different maturities and different initial credit risks. For example, all other things being equal, a given increase (in absolute terms) in the risk of a default occurring reflects a greater increase in credit risk the shorter the term of the financial instrument and the lower its initial credit risk. This would also be consistent with the IASB's understanding of existing models for measuring credit risk, such as those underlying external credit ratings, option pricing models and their variants, including the models for measuring the risk of a default occurring for the purposes of prudential regulatory requirements.

BC5.174   If an entity were not required to consider both the initial credit risk and the time until maturity, the assessment would benefit shorter-term financial instruments with low credit risk and would disadvantage longer-term instruments with high credit risk. In addition, not reflecting the term structure might also result in the assessment that the risk of a default occurring has changed merely because of the passage of time. This could happen even if an entity had expected such a change at initial recognition. In the IASB's view, the assessment of the criteria should not change solely because the maturity date is closer.

BC5.175   To assist in the application of the impairment requirements, the IASB decided to provide application guidance, including guidance about the types of information that an entity should consider. The IASB reaffirmed its view that an entity should use the best information that is available without undue cost and effort when measuring expected credit losses.

Use of changes in the risk of a default occurring within the next 12 months

BC5.176   The 2013 Impairment Exposure Draft required the determination of an increase in credit risk to be based on changes in the risk of a default occurring over the life of a financial instrument but noted that a 12-month measure could be used "if the information considered did not suggest that the outcome would differ".

BC5.177   Many respondents to the 2013 Impairment Exposure Draft noted that the assessment of significant increases in credit risk could be made more operational by aligning it with credit risk management practices, including enabling the use of a 12-month instead of lifetime risk of a default occurring when assessing changes in credit risk. Many of these respondents were however concerned that the 2013 Impairment Exposure Draft would require entities to compare the outcome from a 12-month assessment and prove that it would not differ from the outcome of a lifetime assessment.

BC5.178   In response to the feedback, the IASB noted that, ideally, an entity should use changes in the lifetime risk of a default occurring to assess changes in credit risk since initial recognition. However, the IASB observed that changes in the risk of a default occurring within the next 12 months generally should be a reasonable approximation of changes in the risk of a default occurring over the remaining life of a financial instrument and thus would not be inconsistent with the requirements. The IASB also noted that some entities use a 12-month probability of default measure for prudential regulatory requirements. These entities could therefore use their existing systems and methodologies as a starting point for determining significant increases in credit risk, thus reducing the costs of implementation.

BC5.179   However, the IASB noted that there may be circumstances in which the use of the risk of a default occurring within the next 12 months will not be appropriate. For example, this may be the case for financial instruments with a payment profile in which significant payment obligations occur beyond the next 12 months or when there are changes in macroeconomic or other credit-related factors that are not adequately reflected in the risk of a default occurring in the next 12 months. Consequently, an entity may use changes in the risk of a default occurring within the next 12 months unless circumstances indicate that a lifetime assessment is necessary to meet the objective of identifying significant increases in credit risk since initial recognition.

Financial instruments that have low credit risk at the reporting date

BC5.180 The IASB proposed in the 2013 Impairment Exposure Draft that irrespective of the change in credit risk from initial recognition, an entity should not recognise lifetime expected credit losses on financial instruments with low credit risk at the reporting date. The IASB proposed this to reduce the operational costs and to make the model more cost-effective. The IASB observed that for financial instruments with low credit risk, the effect of this simplification on the timing of recognition, and the amount of expected credit losses would be minimal. This would be the case even if the recognition of lifetime expected credit losses occurred later than it otherwise would have if there had been no simplification. In the IASB's view, this would help to achieve an appropriate balance between the benefits of distinguishing between financial instruments on the basis of changes in credit risk and the costs of making that distinction. The IASB also noted that financial instruments of such a quality were not the primary focus for the recognition of lifetime expected credit losses.

BC5.181 The 2013 Impairment Exposure Draft proposed that the credit risk on a financial instrument should be considered low if the financial instrument has a low risk of default, and the borrower has a strong capacity to meet its contractual cash flow obligations in the near term. The 2013 Impairment Exposure Draft noted that this is the case even if adverse changes in economic and business conditions in the longer term may, but will not necessarily, reduce the ability to fully recover cash flows in the long term. It was noted that such credit risk is typically equivalent to the investment grade market convention, ie an entity need not assess the extent of the increase in credit risk since initial recognition for financial instruments with credit risk that is equivalent to investment grade.

BC5.182 Respondents to the 2013 Impairment Exposure Draft had mixed views on the inclusion of the low credit risk simplification. Most respondents supported a simplification based on low credit risk and noted that it reduces the costs of implementation and avoids recognising lifetime expected credit losses inappropriately. However, a number of clarifications were suggested regarding the meaning of low credit risk and its application. Some noted that the low credit risk simplification could paradoxically increase operational complexity because, in addition to assessing the change in credit risk, the absolute credit risk at the reporting date would need to be assessed.

BC5.183 In response, the IASB noted that the intention was to reduce operational complexity and therefore decided to retain the low credit risk simplification but to *allow* instead of *require* this to be used. This would allow entities to better align the assessment of increases in credit risk for the purpose of IFRS 9 with their internal credit risk systems.

BC5.184 The IASB considered whether to allow reporting entities to have an accounting policy choice on whether to apply the requirement to assess whether a financial instrument is considered to have low credit risk at the reporting date. It noted that the intention of the low credit risk concept was to provide relief from tracking changes in the credit risk of high quality financial instruments and that requiring an entity to apply it as an accounting policy choice for a class of financial instrument would be inconsistent with this intention. The assessment of low credit risk can therefore be made on an instrument-by-instrument basis.

BC5.185 Some respondents were confused about the role of the low credit risk simplification. For example, some were concerned that as soon as a financial instrument was no longer low credit risk, lifetime expected credit losses would be required to be recognised irrespective of the initial credit risk on the financial instrument.

BC5.186 The IASB therefore clarified that:

(a) the objective of the low credit risk simplification is to provide operational relief for high quality financial instruments, in other words, those with a low risk of default.

(b) an increase in credit risk that results in a financial instrument no longer being considered to have low credit risk at the reporting date is not an automatic trigger for the recognition of lifetime expected credit losses. Instead, if a financial instrument is not low credit risk at the reporting date, an entity should assess the extent of the increase in credit risk and recognise lifetime expected credit losses only when the increase since initial recognition is significant in accordance with the usual requirements.

BC5.187 Respondents also raised questions about the ambiguity of using 'investment grade' as an example of low credit risk. Respondents were concerned that only financial instruments that are externally rated by a credit rating agency as investment grade would be considered to have low credit risk. They also questioned whether the reference to investment grade referred to global or national rating scales.

BC5.188 The IASB noted that:

(a) financial instruments are not required to be externally rated to meet the low credit risk requirements. Instead, the reference to investment grade serves only as an example of a financial instrument that may be considered to have low credit risk. The credit risk can be determined using alternative measures, such as internal rating grades based on commonly understood notions of credit risk.

(b) its intention was to use a globally comparable notion of low credit risk instead of a level of risk determined, for example, by an entity or jurisdiction's view of risk based on entity-specific or jurisdictional factors.

(c) ratings should consider or be adjusted to take into consideration the specific risks of the financial instruments being assessed.

BC5.189 Consequently, the IASB confirmed that low credit risk refers to a level of credit risk that is akin to a globally accepted definition of low credit risk. Credit risk ratings and methodologies that are consistent with these requirements and that consider the risks and the type of financial instruments that are being assessed may be used to apply the requirements in paragraph 5.5.10 of IFRS 9.

More than 30 days past due rebuttable presumption

BC5.190 In the 2013 Impairment Exposure Draft, the IASB proposed that an entity may consider information about delinquency or past due status, together with other, more forward-looking information, in its assessment of the increases in credit risk since initial recognition, if appropriate. To supplement the requirement to determine the extent of increases in credit risk since initial recognition, and to ensure that its application does not revert to an incurred loss notion, the IASB proposed a rebuttable presumption that the credit risk on a financial instrument has increased significantly, and that lifetime expected credit losses shall be recognised, when a financial asset is more than 30 days past due.

BC5.191 The majority of respondents to the 2013 Impairment Exposure Draft considered that the rebuttable presumption results in an appropriate balance between identifying significant increases in credit risk and the cost of tracking and assessing those increases in credit risk. Respondents noted that the outcome is broadly in line with existing credit risk management practices (ie looking at past due information). Field test participants observed that there was generally a correlation between financial instruments that are more than 30 days past due and significant increases in the 12-month probability of default. However, some respondents did not support having a past due measure as an indication of when there has been a significant increase in credit risk. They believe that a past due measure creates a bright line for the recognition of lifetime expected credit losses and, because past due status is a lagging indicator of increases in credit risk, it will fail to identify significant increases in credit risk on a timely basis.

BC5.192 In response, the IASB confirmed that, consistent with the forward-looking nature of expected credit losses, an entity should use forward-looking information, such as the price for credit risk, probabilities of default and internal or external credit ratings, to update the measurement of expected credit losses and when assessing whether to recognise lifetime expected credit losses. However, the IASB acknowledged the feedback that supported the view that many entities manage credit risk on the basis of information about past due status and have a limited ability to assess credit risk on an instrument-by-instrument basis in more detail on a timely basis.

BC5.193 The IASB therefore decided to retain the rebuttable presumption, but also wanted to ensure that this did not contribute to the delayed recognition of lifetime expected credit losses. The IASB clarified that the objective of the rebuttable presumption in paragraph 5.5.11 of IFRS 9 is not to be an absolute indicator of when lifetime expected credit losses should be recognised, but serves as a backstop for when there has been a significant increase in credit risk. The IASB noted that the application of the rebuttable presumption should identify significant increases in credit risk before financial assets become credit-impaired or an actual default occurs. The IASB also noted that, ideally, significant increases in credit risk should be identified before financial assets become past due.

BC5.194 The IASB decided to confirm the ability of an entity to rebut the presumption if the entity has reasonable and supportable information to support a more lagging past due measure. The IASB acknowledged that 30 days past due might not be an appropriate indicator for all types of products or jurisdictions.

However, it noted that to be able to rebut the presumption, an entity would need reasonable and supportable information that indicates that the credit risk has not increased significantly. Furthermore, an entity is not required to rebut the presumption on an instrument-by-instrument basis but can rebut it if the entity has information that indicates that, for a particular product, region or customer type, more than 30 days past due is not representative of the point at which credit risk increases significantly. The IASB noted that if significant increases in credit risk were identified before a financial asset(s) was 30 days past due, the presumption does not need to be rebutted.

Recognition of 12-month expected credit losses

BC5.195   During the development of the 2013 Impairment Exposure Draft, the IASB considered what measure of expected credit losses would be both appropriate and cost-effective for financial instruments before significant increases in credit risk have occurred. The IASB accepted the concerns of interested parties about the operational complexity of the methods proposed in the 2009 Impairment Exposure Draft and the Supplementary Document. The IASB also accepted that significant judgement would be required for any estimation technique that an entity might use. Consequently, the IASB decided that an entity should measure the loss allowance at an amount equal to 12-month expected credit losses. In the IASB's view, the overall result of such a measurement, combined with the earlier recognition of the full lifetime expected credit losses compared to IAS 39, achieves an appropriate balance between the benefits of a faithful representation of expected credit losses and the operational costs and complexity. The IASB acknowledged that this is an operational simplification, and that cost-benefit is the only conceptual justification for the 12-month time horizon.

BC5.196   The majority of respondents to the 2013 Impairment Exposure Draft supported the IASB's reasoning, noting that the recognition of 12-month expected credit losses is a pragmatic solution to achieve an appropriate balance between faithfully representing the underlying economics of a transaction and the cost of implementation. Furthermore, it would allow preparers to make use of existing reporting systems that some regulated financial institutions already apply and would therefore be less costly to implement for those entities. In addition, users of financial statements considered 12 months a reliable period to estimate expected credit losses for financial instruments that have not significantly increased in credit risk.

BC5.197   However, some respondents proposed alternative measures for the loss allowance on financial instruments for which there were no significant increases in credit risk since initial recognition. These alternatives and the IASB's reasons for rejecting them are discussed in paragraphs BC5.200–BC5.209.

BC5.198   In finalising the Standard, the IASB acknowledged that the recognition of 12-month expected credit losses would result in an overstatement of expected credit losses for financial instruments, and a resulting understatement of the value of any related financial asset, immediately after initial recognition of those financial instruments. In particular, the initial carrying amount of financial assets would be below their fair value. However, isolating initial credit loss expectations for recognition over the life of financial instruments is operationally complex. Furthermore, this measurement of expected credit losses serves as a practical approximation of the adjustment of the effective interest rate for credit risk as required by the 2009 Impairment Exposure Draft. The recognition of a portion of expected credit losses for financial instruments for which there have not been significant increases in credit risk also limits the requirement to perform the more costly and complex calculation of the lifetime expected credit losses. In addition, in the IASB's view, measuring 12-month expected credit losses for some financial instruments would be less costly than always calculating the lifetime expected credit losses as proposed in the Supplementary Document.

BC5.199 The IASB decided to retain the recognition of 12-month expected credit losses for the measurement and allocation of initial expected credit losses, which was necessary as a result of the decision to decouple the measurement and allocation of initial expected credit losses from the determination of the effective interest rate as proposed in the 2009 Impairment Exposure Draft. The IASB considered such a measure of expected credit losses to be superior to the alternatives discussed below.

Approaches to recognition of 12-month expected credit losses considered and rejected

No allowance for instruments without a significant increase in credit risk

BC5.200 Some respondents did not agree with recognising any expected credit loss allowance for financial instruments that have not experienced significant increases in credit risk since initial recognition. These respondents considered initial expectations of credit losses to be included in the pricing of a financial instrument and they were conceptually opposed to the recognition of a loss allowance on initial recognition.

BC5.201 The IASB acknowledged that not recognising an allowance balance for financial instruments for which credit risk has not increased significantly would be consistent with the requirement in paragraph 5.1.1 of IFRS 9 that a financial asset should be recognised at fair value on initial recognition. However, only recognising lifetime expected credit losses when there have been significant increases in credit risk, without recognising any expected credit losses before that to reflect the changes in initial expectations of credit risk since initial recognition, would fail to appropriately reflect the economic losses experienced as a result of those (non-significant) changes. Expected credit losses are implicit in the initial pricing for the instrument, but subsequent changes in those expectations represent economic losses (or gains) in the period in which they occur. Not reflecting changes in credit risk before the change is considered significant would therefore fail to recognise those economic losses (or gains).

BC5.202 The IASB noted that not recognising any expected credit losses before there have been significant increases in credit risk would not be consistent with preserving, to as great an extent as possible, the objective of the 2009 Impairment Exposure Draft (see paragraphs BC5.87–B5.88). In the view of the IASB, this approach would fail to appropriately reflect the economic effects of over-recognition of interest revenue prior to losses being recognised and would also fail to recognise economic losses experienced as a result of non-significant changes in credit risk or significant increases not yet identified.

Recognise a portion of lifetime expected credit losses larger than 12-month expected credit losses

BC5.203   The IASB considered whether an entity should recognise a portion of lifetime expected credit losses that is greater than 12-month expected credit losses before there are significant increases in credit risk. However, it rejected requiring a larger portion of expected credit losses to be recognised because:

(a)   as noted in paragraph BC5.198, the IASB acknowledges that the 12-month measure is a practical concession that initially overstates expected credit losses before there are significant increases in credit risk. Recognising a greater portion would further increase the overstatement of expected credit losses and, thus, when considered with the much earlier timing of the recognition of lifetime expected credit losses, would be a less faithful representation of the underlying economics.

(b)   12-month expected credit losses would allow preparers to make use of existing reporting systems that some regulated financial institutions already apply and would therefore be less costly to implement for those entities.

Recognise expected credit losses for the loss emergence period

BC5.204   This alternative would require entities to consider all reasonable and supportable information available, including historical information, in order to determine the average period of time over which meaningful increases in credit risk are expected to occur.

BC5.205   The IASB acknowledged that different asset classes have different loss patterns and different loss emergence periods. Consequently, estimating expected credit losses over the relevant period of time it takes for an event to happen and for the effects to be known, may have conceptual merit. However, the IASB noted that 'emergence' notions fit more naturally in an incurred loss model in which it is difficult to identify when a loss has been incurred on individual instruments.

BC5.206   The IASB also noted that emergence periods may change over the life of financial instruments and depend on the economic cycle. As a result, the IASB considered that this approach would be more operationally difficult than one that has a defined period, because an entity would have to continually assess that it was using the appropriate emergence period.

Recognise expected credit losses for the foreseeable future

BC5.207   The Supplementary Document proposed that the loss allowance for financial assets in the good book should be calculated as the greater of the time-proportionate amount and expected credit losses for the foreseeable future (see paragraphs BC5.96–BC5.101).

BC5.208   The feedback received about the foreseeable future floor for the good book was geographically split, with respondents outside the US generally opposing it. Furthermore, respondents expressed concerns about the calculation of expected credit losses for the foreseeable future, with many expressing confusion about the underlying conceptual basis for such a limitation to the time period. Many also noted that, despite the conceptual concerns, the term 'foreseeable future' was not sufficiently defined to ensure consistent application.

BC5.209　In response to the concerns raised about the foreseeable future, the IASB rejected the approach. To address these concerns about the ambiguity of the foreseeable future definition in the Supplementary Document, the IASB decided to define the measurement objective for financial instruments for which credit risk has not increased significantly as 12-month expected credit losses. The IASB did not receive any new information that caused it to change its view.

Symmetry

BC5.210　The IASB's view is that an entity should recognise favourable changes in credit risk consistently with unfavourable changes in credit risk (ie the model should be 'symmetrical'), but only to the extent that those favourable changes represent a reversal of risk that was previously recognised as unfavourable changes. In accordance with the general model, if the credit risk on financial instruments, for which lifetime expected credit losses have been recognised, subsequently improves so that the requirement for recognising lifetime expected credit losses is no longer met, the loss allowance should be measured at an amount equal to 12-month expected credit losses with a resulting gain recognised in profit or loss. Doing so would reflect the fact that the expectations of credit losses have moved back towards the initial expectations. For purchased or originated credit-impaired financial assets (to which the general model does not apply (see paragraph BC5.214–BC5.220), an entity would recognise a gain if credit risk improves after initial recognition, reflecting an increase in the expected cash flows.

BC5.211　To address concerns about potential earnings management, the IASB considered requiring a change back to a loss allowance measured at an amount equal to 12-month expected credit losses to be based on stricter criteria than is required for the recognition of lifetime expected credit losses. The IASB rejected such a requirement because it reduces the usefulness, neutrality and faithful representation of expected credit losses, and anti-abuse considerations should not override that. The IASB also noted that such arbitrary distinctions can have unintended consequences, such as creating a disincentive to recognise lifetime expected credit losses, because of the higher hurdle to change back to the recognition of 12-month expected credit losses.

BC5.212　As a result of this, the 2013 Impairment Exposure Draft proposed that the model should be symmetrical with lifetime expected credit losses being recognised, and ceasing to be recognised, depending on whether the credit risk at the reporting date has increased significantly since initial recognition. Nearly all respondents to the 2013 Impairment Exposure Draft agreed that the approach should be symmetrical. In doing so, they noted that this would be consistent with the objective of a model based on changes in credit risk and would faithfully represent the underlying economics.

BC5.213　Consequently, the IASB confirmed its reasoning in the 2013 Impairment Exposure Draft and confirmed that a loss allowance measured at an amount equal to 12-month expected credit losses shall be re-established for financial instruments for which the criteria for the recognition of lifetime expected credit losses are no longer met.

Purchased or originated credit-impaired financial assets

BC5.214　The 2013 Impairment Exposure Draft proposed to carry forward the scope and requirements in paragraph AG5 of IAS 39. That paragraph required an entity to include the initial expected credit losses in the estimated cash flows when calculating the effective interest rate for financial assets that are credit-impaired on initial recognition. In addition, it was proposed that an entity calculate interest revenue from financial assets subject to this measurement requirement by applying the credit-adjusted effective interest rate to the amortised cost of the financial asset (adjusted for any loss allowance).

BC5.215　Some users of financial statements expressed a preference for a single impairment model for all financial assets to ensure comparability. However, in the IASB's view, applying the general approach to purchased or originated credit-impaired financial assets would not achieve the desired comparability. This is because, in the IASB's view, the model proposed in the 2009 Impairment Exposure Draft more faithfully represents the underlying economics for these financial assets than the general approach proposed in the 2013 Impairment Exposure Draft, and the benefits of this better representation outweigh the costs for these financial assets.

BC5.216　The IASB noted that, while the scope of the requirements for financial assets that are credit-impaired at initial recognition usually relates to purchased financial assets, in unusual circumstances financial assets could be originated that would be within this scope. However, this does not mean that all financial assets originated at a high credit risk are within the scope—the financial assets have to be credit-impaired on initial recognition. In confirming that a financial asset could be credit-impaired on origination the IASB focussed on the potential for the modification of contractual cash flows to result in derecognition. The IASB considered an example in which a substantial modification of a distressed asset resulted in derecognition of the original financial asset. Such a case is an example of the rare situation in which a newly originated financial asset may be credit-impaired—it would be possible for the modification to constitute objective evidence that the new asset is credit-impaired at initial recognition.

BC5.217　Consistent with the 2009 Impairment Exposure Draft, for these financial assets, the 2013 Impairment Exposure Draft considered the initial credit loss expectations to be part of the effective interest rate and thus interest revenue will represent the effective yield on the asset. An entity will recognise changes in the initial expected credit losses as gains or losses. Paragraph BC5.89 sets out the operational challenges that would have arisen if the 2009 Impairment Exposure Draft had applied to all financial assets. However, in developing the proposals in the 2013 Impairment Exposure Draft, the IASB observed that this requirement in IAS 39 has not presented issues in practice and proposed to retain it, and to use a scope that is based on IAS 39 to minimise the operational challenges for preparers.

BC5.218 Respondents to the 2013 Impairment Exposure Draft almost unanimously supported the proposals for purchased or originated credit-impaired financial assets. These respondents noted that the proposals were the conceptually correct outcome, similar to the 2009 Impairment Exposure Draft, and appropriately reflect the economics of the transaction and management's objective when acquiring or originating such assets. Respondents additionally noted that the proposals were operable because they are consistent with the existing accounting treatment in accordance with IAS 39.

BC5.219 However, some respondents preferred a gross-up approach, whereby an allowance is recognised for initial expected credit losses and is used to gross-up the carrying amount of the purchased or originated credit-impaired financial asset. These respondents considered that it would be operationally simpler to have a gross presentation of expected credit losses for all financial assets, and comparability would be improved if there was an allowance balance for purchased or originated credit-impaired financial assets like there is for other financial assets.

BC5.220 The IASB noted in response that even if the loss allowance balance was calculated for purchased or originated credit-impaired financial assets at initial recognition, the carrying amounts would not be comparable. Purchased or originated credit-impaired assets are initially recognised at fair value and would be grossed-up for the loss allowance balance, resulting in a carrying amount above fair value. In contrast, other assets within the scope of IFRS 9 are carried net of the loss allowance, and so would be grossed-up to fair value. The IASB therefore rejected these arguments. Consequently, the IASB decided to confirm the proposals in the 2013 Impairment Exposure Draft.

Simplified approach for trade receivables, contract assets and lease receivables

BC5.221 The 2013 Impairment Exposure Draft proposed that trade receivables that do not have a significant financing component in accordance with IFRS 15 should be accounted for as follows:

(a) an entity would be required to measure the trade receivable at initial recognition at the transaction price as defined in IFRS 15 (ie the invoiced amount in many cases); and

(b) an entity would be required to recognise a loss allowance for lifetime expected credit losses on those trade receivables throughout their life.

BC5.222 Most respondents to the 2013 Impairment Exposure Draft supported the approach proposed for trade receivables without a significant financing component. Respondents noted that most trade receivables without a significant financing component would have a maturity that is less than one year, so the lifetime expected credit losses and the 12-month expected credit losses would be the same, or very similar. In addition, respondents supported the recognition of these trade receivables at transaction price, because it aligns the requirements in IFRS 9 with revenue recognition requirements and results in the amortised cost of these receivables at initial recognition being closer to fair value.

BC5.223 Respondents indicated that they would not have significant operational difficulty in applying an impairment model based on expected credit losses to their trade receivables without a significant financing component. While these participants acknowledge that such an impairment model would require a change in practice, they believe that they can incorporate forward-looking information within their current methodologies. In addition, the outreach participants noted that the IASB had made the application of the impairment model to current trade receivables (ie those that are not past due) more operational without the loss of useful information.

BC5.224 The IASB therefore decided to retain the proposed approach for trade receivables without a significant financing component.

BC5.225 In the 2013 Impairment Exposure Draft, the IASB noted that, in its view, a provision matrix can be an acceptable method to measure expected credit losses for trade receivables in accordance with the objectives for the measurement of expected credit losses in IFRS 9. An entity would adjust historical provision rates, which are an average of historical outcomes, to reflect relevant information about current conditions as well as reasonable and supportable forecasts and their implications for expected credit losses, including the time value of money. Such a technique would be consistent with the measurement objective of expected credit losses as set out in IFRS 9. The 2013 Impairment Exposure Draft therefore proposed that entities would have a choice of an accounting policy both for trade receivables that have a significant financing component in accordance with IFRS 15 and separately for lease receivables in accordance with IAS 17. Those accounting policy choices would allow entities to decide between fully applying the proposed model or recognising a loss allowance for lifetime expected credit losses from initial recognition until derecognition (the simplified approach). The IASB noted that allowing this option for trade receivables and lease receivables would reduce comparability. However, the IASB believed it would alleviate some of the practical concerns of tracking changes in credit risk for entities that do not have sophisticated credit risk management systems.

BC5.226 The IASB noted that feedback on the 2013 Impairment Exposure Draft indicated that many respondents agreed that the operational relief was of greater weight than concerns about comparability, and supported the simplified approach as an accounting policy choice. In addition, the IASB noted that removing the accounting policy choice would require either removing the simplified approach or making it mandatory, neither of which the IASB considered appropriate. In the IASB's view, the benefits of achieving comparability do not outweigh the costs to implement the full model in this case. The IASB therefore decided to confirm these proposals in IFRS 9. As noted in paragraph BC5.134, the IASB decided that the impairment requirements in IFRS 9 should also apply to contract assets that are recognised and measured in accordance with IFRS 15. Because the nature of contract assets and the exposure to credit risk is similar to trade receivables, the IASB decided that an entity should have the same accounting policy choice as for trade receivables with a significant financing component and for lease receivables.

Modifications of contractual cash flows

BC5.227   Some modifications of contractual cash flows result in the derecognition of a financial instrument and the recognition of a new financial instrument in accordance with IFRS 9. However, modifications frequently do not result in the derecognition of a financial instrument. The IASB considered how the proposed model will apply to these financial instruments with modified contractual cash flows.

BC5.228   In the 2013 Impairment Exposure Draft the IASB proposed that, when an entity is assessing whether it should recognise a loss allowance at an amount equal to 12-month expected credit losses or lifetime expected credit losses, it should compare the credit risk of the modified financial instrument at the reporting date to the credit risk of the (unmodified) financial instrument at initial recognition when the modification has not resulted in derecognition. The simplification for financial instruments with low credit risk would also apply to modified financial instruments.

BC5.229   This decision reflected the fact that financial instruments that are modified but not derecognised are not new financial instruments from an accounting perspective and, as a result, the amortised cost measurement would keep the same original effective interest rate. Consequently, the impairment model should apply as it does for other financial instruments, reflecting the changes in credit risk since initial recognition.

BC5.230   The IASB further noted that when the modification of a financial asset results in the derecognition of the asset and the subsequent recognition of the modified financial asset, the modified asset is considered a 'new' asset from an accounting perspective. The IASB observed that entities should consider whether a modified financial asset is originated credit-impaired at initial recognition (see paragraphs BC5.214–BC5.220). If not, subsequent recognition of a loss allowance would be determined in accordance with the requirements in Section 5.5 of IFRS 9.

BC5.231   The IASB also proposed in the 2013 Impairment Exposure Draft that the modification requirements should apply to all modifications or renegotiations of the contractual cash flows of financial instruments. Although most respondents supported the proposals, some noted that they would have preferred that the requirements be limited to modifications of credit-impaired assets or modifications undertaken for credit risk management purposes. These respondents believed that the proposed requirements do not represent the economics of modifications performed for commercial or other reasons that are unrelated to credit risk management.

BC5.232   However, the IASB has previously considered the difficulty of identifying the reason for modifications and renegotiations. Before May 2010, IFRS 7 required the disclosure of the carrying amount of financial assets that would otherwise be past due or credit-impaired but whose terms have been renegotiated. The IASB received feedback from constituents that it is operationally difficult to determine the purpose of modifications (ie whether they are performed for commercial or credit risk management reasons). The IASB noted in paragraph BC54A of IFRS 7 the difficulty in identifying financial assets whose terms have been renegotiated for reasons other than credit reasons, especially when commercial terms of loans are often renegotiated regularly for reasons that are not related to impairment. This led the IASB to remove this requirement from IFRS 7.

BC5.233 The IASB further noted that these requirements were consistent with the previous requirements in paragraph AG8 of IAS 39, which did not differentiate between modifications based on the reason for the modification. Paragraph AG8 applied to all revisions of estimates of payments or receipts. This is because amortised cost is a measurement method whereby the carrying amount equates to the present value of the estimated future cash payments or receipts discounted at the effective interest rate. Consequently, the amortised cost amount should be updated in all cases in which those cash flows are modified (or expectations change other than in respect of impairment changes).

BC5.234 The IASB also noted that even if the intention of a modification could be clearly identified to be for commercial purposes, any change in the contractual terms of a financial instrument will have a consequential effect on the credit risk of the financial instrument since initial recognition and will affect the measurement of the loss allowance. Furthermore, the difficulty involved in discerning the purpose of modifications, and to what extent a modification is related to credit risk reasons, could create opportunities for manipulation. This could happen if entities were able to select a 'preferred' treatment for modifications simply because of the purpose of the modification. Limiting the scope of the modification requirements in Section 5.5 of IFRS 9 to those undertaken for credit reasons could therefore result in different accounting treatments for the same economic event.

BC5.235 Consequently, the IASB decided to confirm the proposals in the 2013 Impairment Exposure Draft that the modification requirements should apply to all modifications or renegotiations of the contractual terms of financial instruments.

Assessment of significant increases in credit risk

BC5.236 The IASB considered whether an entity should assess the increase in credit risk by comparing it to the credit risk at the point of modification. However, the IASB noted that if the original financial instrument has not been derecognised, the modified financial instrument is not a new financial instrument. The IASB also noted that by using such an approach the financial instrument would, by definition, not have experienced an increase in credit risk that is more than insignificant since modification. As a result, if the IASB took this approach, an entity would recognise 12-month expected credit losses for every modified financial instrument at the point of modification.

BC5.237 Thus, the IASB decided that an entity should compare the credit risk at the reporting date with the credit risk as at initial recognition of the unmodified financial instrument in a manner that is consistent with that applied to all other financial instruments. An entity should base the risk of default occurring after a modification on the ability to meet the modified contractual cash flows. This should include an assessment of historical and forward-looking information and an assessment of the credit risk over the remaining life of the instrument, which should include the circumstances that led to the modification. Consequently, the credit risk on a financial asset will not necessarily decrease merely because of a modification.

Symmetry

BC5.238 The IASB observed that it is not unusual for distressed financial instruments to be modified more than once and, therefore, the assessment of whether lifetime expected credit losses should continue to be recognised after modification may be perceived to be based on projections that are optimistic. The IASB considered prohibiting modified financial instruments that continue to be recognised reverting to a loss allowance at an amount equal to 12-month expected credit losses or alternatively proposing more restrictive criteria than usual before allowing 12-month expected credit losses to be re-established.

BC5.239 The IASB concluded that the expected credit loss requirements should allow the loss allowance on such modified financial instruments to revert to being measured at an amount equal to 12-month expected credit losses when they no longer meet the requirements for the recognition of lifetime expected credit losses, consistent with the treatment of unmodified financial instruments. In the IASB's view, this faithfully represents the economics of the transaction and it should not override that faithful representation for anti-abuse purposes. In addition, the IASB observed that entities also modify financial instruments for reasons other than increases in credit risk and, therefore, it would be difficult from an operational standpoint to prescribe asymmetrical guidance only for financial assets that have been modified because of credit risk factors (see paragraphs BC5.227–BC5.235).

Adjustment of gross carrying amount

BC5.240 As explained in more detail in paragraphs BC5.102–BC5.108, IFRS 9 requires a decoupled approach to interest revenue and recognition of expected credit losses for financial assets. In accordance with a decoupled approach, an entity would calculate the interest revenue by multiplying the effective interest rate by the gross carrying amount (ie the amount that does not include an adjustment for the loss allowance). As a result, not adjusting the carrying amount upon a modification would result in inflating interest revenue and the loss allowance.

BC5.241 Consequently, the IASB decided that an entity should adjust the gross carrying amount of a financial asset if it modifies the contractual cash flows and recognise modification gains or losses in profit or loss. For example, if credit losses are crystallised by a modification, an entity should recognise a reduction in the gross carrying amount. There may be situations in which adjusting the gross carrying amount result in the recognition of a gain. Except for purchased or originated credit-impaired financial assets, the new gross carrying amount will represent the future contractual cash flows discounted at the original effective interest rate.

Measurement of expected credit losses

BC5.242 The 2013 Impairment Exposure Draft and 2009 Impairment Exposure Draft proposed to define expected credit losses as the expected present value of all cash shortfalls over the remaining life of the financial instrument. The IASB decided to retain the emphasis on the objective of the measurement of expected credit losses, and to keep the requirements principle-based instead of specifying techniques to measure expected credit losses. Respondents have commented that adopting such a principle-based approach would help reduce complexity and mitigate operational challenges by allowing an entity to use techniques that work best in its specific circumstances.

Loan commitments and financial guarantee contracts

BC5.243 The 2013 Impairment Exposure Draft proposed that an entity should recognise expected credit losses that result from loan commitments and financial guarantee contracts when there is a present contractual obligation to extend credit. The IASB believe that expected credit losses of obligations to extend credit (off balance sheet exposures) are similar to those of loans and other on balance sheet exposures. The only difference is that, in the latter case, the borrower has already drawn down the loan whereas in the former case it has not. The recognition of a liability for expected credit losses was limited to loan commitments and financial guarantee contracts with a present contractual obligation to extend credit. Without a present contractual obligation to extend credit, an entity may withdraw its loan commitment before it extends credit. Consequently, the IASB concluded that a liability does not exist for loan commitments or financial guarantee contracts when there is no present contractual obligation to extend credit.

BC5.244 The 2013 Impairment Exposure Draft proposed that the impairment requirements should apply to these financial instruments in the same way as for other financial instruments, including the assessment of the increase in credit risk to decide whether it should recognise 12-month or lifetime expected credit losses. When measuring expected credit losses of loan commitments and financial guarantee contracts, additional uncertainty arises in respect of one of the input factors: the exposure at default. To measure the exposure at default of the loan commitments, the issuer needs to estimate the amount that a borrower will have drawn down at the time of default. That is, the issuer needs to estimate the part of the undrawn facility that the borrower will convert into a funded amount, typically referred to as a credit conversion factor or a utilisation rate. Some financial institutions are required to make similar assessments for regulatory capital purposes.

BC5.245 Respondents to the Supplementary Document, and participants in the IASB's outreach that preceded the publication of the 2013 Impairment Exposure Draft, noted that estimating future drawdowns over the lifetime of the financial instrument will introduce additional complexities. These additional complexities arise because of the uncertainty involved in estimating the behaviour of customers over a longer period. Interested parties were concerned that the requirements would hold entities to a standard of accuracy that they would not be able to meet.

BC5.246 The IASB considered and rejected the following alternatives that were suggested for measuring future drawdowns:

(a) limiting the estimate of future drawdowns to the next 12 months. While it would be less complex to use an estimate over a 12-month time period, such a limit would be arbitrary and inconsistent with estimating lifetime expected credit losses.

(b) estimating future drawdowns based only on historical information. While it would be less complex to limit the estimate to historical information, it would be inconsistent with the objective of an impairment model based on expected credit losses. Historical utilisation rates might be a good indicator for future drawdowns, but an entity would also need to consider the need to make adjustments for current and future expectations when estimating expected credit losses.

(c) using the credit conversion factor provided by prudential regulators. Regulators typically provide credit conversion factors over a 12-month period. Generally, they are not forward-looking, and are specific to product types or particular to the entity. Similarly as for the issues mentioned in (a)–(b), applying such a standardised parameter when estimating expected credit losses is inconsistent with the general approach. It also would also not address the issue for entities that are not subject to such regulations.

BC5.247 The IASB acknowledged the complexity involved in estimating future drawdowns over the life of financial instruments. Nevertheless, this estimate is necessary to have a consistent application of the impairment model. The IASB considered that not having it would defeat the purpose of removing the inconsistency between on balance sheet and off balance sheet exposures. Consequently, the IASB decided that for financial instruments that include both a loan and an undrawn commitment component and the entity's contractual ability to demand repayment and cancel the undrawn commitment does not limit the entity's exposure to credit losses to the contractual notice period, an entity shall estimate the usage behaviour over the period that the entity is exposed to credit risk and expected credit losses would not be mitigated by credit risk management actions, even if that period extends beyond the maximum contractual period (see paragraphs BC5.254–BC5.261).

Definition of default

BC5.248 The 2013 Impairment Exposure Draft did not define default. Instead, it proposed allowing entities to use different definitions of default including, when applicable, regulatory definitions of default. In making this decision, the IASB observed that expected credit losses are not expected to change as a result of differences in the definition of default that was applied, because of the counterbalancing interaction between the way an entity defines default and the credit losses that arise as a result of that definition of default.

BC5.249 Although the 2013 Impairment Exposure Draft did not ask a specific question on the definition of default, some respondents commented on the topic and most of those respondents recommended that default should be clearly described or defined. Those respondents noted that the notion of default is fundamental to the application of the model, particularly because it affects the population that is subject to the 12-month expected credit loss measure. Some of those respondents considered the term 'default event' to be ambiguous, and were unclear whether the notion of default should align more closely with indicators about significant increases in credit risk or with the indicators for credit-impaired financial assets. Those respondents also expressed concern that the absence of prescriptive guidance could result in inconsistent application. Regulators, in particular, were concerned about the delayed recognition of expected credit losses if default were interpreted solely as non-payment.

BC5.250 Other respondents supported the proposal not to define default, and noted that the point of default would be different for different instruments and across jurisdictions and legal systems. These respondents noted that any attempt to be more prescriptive or provide guidance would add confusion and could result in differing default definitions for credit risk management, regulatory and accounting purposes.

BC5.251 The IASB noted during its redeliberations on the 2013 Impairment Exposure Draft that default can be interpreted in various ways, ranging from broad judgemental definitions based on qualitative factors to narrower, non-judgemental definitions focusing only on non-payment. The appropriate definition also depends on the nature of the financial instrument in question. One of the objectives of the 2013 Impairment Exposure Draft was to allow entities to leverage existing credit risk management systems. Because of the various interpretations of default, the IASB was concerned that defining it could result in a definition for financial reporting that is inconsistent with that applied internally for credit risk management. That could result in the impairment model being applied in a way that does not provide useful information about actual credit risk management.

BC5.252 Consequently, the IASB decided not to specifically define default in IFRS 9. However, to address the feedback received and noting in particular the effect on the financial instruments captured within the scope of the 12-month expected credit losses, the IASB decided to include a rebuttable presumption that default does not occur later than 90 days past due unless an entity has reasonable and supportable information to support a more lagging default criterion. The IASB also decided to emphasise that an entity should consider qualitative indicators of default when appropriate (for example, for financial instruments that include covenants that can lead to events of default) and clarify that an entity should apply a default definition that is consistent with its credit risk management practices for the relevant financial instruments, consistently from one period to another. The IASB noted that an entity may have multiple definitions of default, for example, for different types of products.

BC5.253 The IASB noted that this rebuttable presumption serves as a 'backstop' to ensure a more consistent population of financial instruments for which significant increases in credit risk is determined when applying the model. It was also noted that the purpose of the rebuttable presumption is not to delay the default event until a financial asset becomes 90 days past due, but to ensure that entities will not define default later than that point without reasonable and supportable information to substantiate the assertion (for example, financial instruments that include covenants that can lead to events of default). The IASB acknowledges that defining the backstop as 90 days past due is arbitrary, but it considered that any number of days would be arbitrary and that 90 days past due best aligned with current practice and regulatory requirements in many jurisdictions.

Period over which to estimate expected credit losses

BC5.254 Respondents to the 2013 Impairment Exposure Draft widely supported the proposed requirements for loan commitments and financial guarantee contracts in general, and no new arguments were raised that the IASB considered would call into question its prior analysis. However, the majority of respondents that supported including loan commitments within the scope of the proposed model noted that expected credit losses on some loan commitments should be estimated over the behavioural life of the financial instrument, instead of over the contractual commitment period. Although they noted that the use of the contractual period would be conceptually appropriate, there was concern that using the contractual period:

(a) would be contrary to how the exposures are handled for credit risk management and regulatory purposes;

(b) could result in insufficient allowances for the exposures arising from these contracts; and

(c) would result in outcomes for which no actual loss experience exists on which to base the estimates.

BC5.255 Respondents noted that the use of the contractual period was of particular concern for some types of loan commitments that are managed on a collective basis, and for which an entity usually has no practical ability to withdraw the commitment before a loss event occurs and to limit the exposure to credit losses to the contractual period over which it is committed to extend the credit. Respondents noted that this applies particularly to revolving credit facilities such as credit cards and overdraft facilities. For these types of facilities, estimating the expected credit losses over the behavioural life of the instruments was viewed as more faithfully representing their exposure to credit risk.

BC5.256 Respondents also noted that those revolving credit facilities lack a fixed term or repayment structure and allow borrowers flexibility in how frequently they make drawdowns on the facility. Such facilities can be viewed as a combination of an undrawn loan commitment and a drawn-down loan asset. Typically, these facilities can be contractually cancelled by a lender with little or no notice, requiring repayment of any drawn balance and cancellation of any undrawn commitment under the facility. There would be no need on a conceptual basis to recognise expected credit losses on the undrawn portion of these facilities, because the exposure period could be as little as one day under the proposals in the 2013 Impairment Exposure Draft.

BC5.257 Outreach performed during the comment period on the 2013 Impairment Exposure Draft indicated that, in practice, lenders generally continue to extend credit under these types of financial instruments for a duration longer than the contractual minimum and only withdraw the facility if observable credit risk on the facility has increased significantly. The IASB noted that, for such facilities, the contractual maturities are often set for protective reasons and are not actively enforced as part of the normal credit risk management processes. Participants also noted that it may be difficult to withdraw undrawn commitments on these facilities for commercial reasons unless there has been an increase in credit risk. Consequently, economically, the contractual ability to demand repayment and cancel the undrawn commitment does not necessarily prevent an entity from being exposed to credit losses beyond the contractual notice period.

BC5.258   The IASB noted that the expected credit losses on these type of facilities can be significant and that restricting the recognition of a loss allowance to expected credit losses in the contractual notice period would arguably be inconsistent with the notion of expected credit losses (ie it would not reflect actual expectations of loss) and would not reflect the underlying economics or the way in which those facilities are managed for credit risk purposes. The IASB also noted that the amount of expected credit losses for these facilities could be significantly lower if the exposure is restricted to the contractual period, which may be inconsistent with an economic assessment of that exposure.

BC5.259   The IASB further noted that from a credit risk management perspective, the concept of expected credit losses is as relevant to off balance sheet exposures as it is to on balance sheet exposures. These types of financial instruments include both a loan (ie financial asset) and an undrawn commitment (ie loan commitment) component and are managed, and expected credit losses are estimated, on a facility level. In other words there is only one set of cash flows from the borrower that relates to both components. Expected credit losses on the on balance sheet exposure (the financial asset) are not estimated separately from the expected credit losses on the off balance sheet exposure (the loan commitment). Consequently, the period over which the expected credit losses are estimated should reflect the period over which the entity is expected to be exposed to the credit risk on the instrument as a whole.

BC5.260   The IASB remains of the view that the contractual period over which an entity is committed to provide credit (or a shorter period considering prepayments) is the correct conceptual outcome. The IASB noted that most loan commitments will expire at a specified date, and if an entity decides to renew or extend its commitment to extend credit, it will be a new instrument for which the entity has the opportunity to revise the terms and conditions. Consequently, the IASB decided to confirm that the maximum period over which expected credit losses for loan commitments and financial guarantee contracts are estimated is the contractual period over which the entity is committed to provide credit.

BC5.261   However, to address the concerns raised about the financial instruments noted in paragraphs BC5.254–BC5.257, the IASB decided that for financial instruments that include both a loan and an undrawn commitment component and the entity's contractual ability to demand repayment and cancel the undrawn commitment does not limit the entity's exposure to credit losses to the contractual notice period, an entity shall estimate expected credit losses over the period that the entity is expected to be exposed to credit risk and expected credit losses would not be mitigated by credit risk management actions, even if that period extends beyond the maximum contractual period. When determining the period over which the entity is exposed to credit risk on the financial instrument, the entity should consider factors such as relevant historical information and experience on similar financial instruments. The measurement of expected credit losses should take into account credit risk management actions that are taken once an exposure has increased in credit risk, such as the reduction or withdrawal of undrawn limits.

Probability-weighted outcome

BC5.262 The requirement in paragraph 5.5.17 of IFRS 9 states that the estimates of cash flows are expected values. Hence, estimates of the amounts and timing of cash flows are based on probability-weighted possible outcomes.

BC5.263 The term 'expected' as used in the terms 'expected credit losses', 'expected value' and 'expected cash flow' is a technical term that refers to the probability-weighted mean of a distribution and should not be confused with a most likely outcome or an entity's best estimate of the ultimate outcome.

BC5.264 In the IASB's view, an expected value measurement is the most relevant measurement basis because it provides information about the timing, amounts and uncertainty of an entity's future cash flows. This is because an expected value measurement would:

(a) include consideration of expected credit losses using all the available evidence, including forward-looking information. Thus, an entity will be required to consider multiple scenarios and possible outcomes and their probability of occurrence.

(b) reflect that the pricing of financial instruments includes the consideration of expected credit losses. Although entities might not attribute specific credit loss estimates to individual financial instruments, and although competitive pressures might influence pricing, entities still consider credit loss expectations for the credit risk of similar obligors when pricing loans on origination and purchase.

(c) not revert (at any time) to an incurred credit loss model—all financial instruments have risk of a default occurring and the measurement will therefore reflect that risk of default and not the most likely outcome.

(d) have the same objective regardless of whether an entity performs the measurement at an individual or a portfolio level. Consequently, there is no need to specify specific conditions or criteria for grouping financial instruments for the purposes of measurement.

(e) provide useful information to users of financial statements (ie information about the risk that the investment might not perform).

BC5.265 The IASB observed that an entity can use a variety of techniques to meet the objective of an expected value without requiring detailed statistical models. The calculation of an expected value need not be a rigorous mathematical exercise whereby an entity identifies every single possible outcome and its probability. Instead, when there are many possible outcomes, an entity can use a representative sample of the complete distribution for determining the expected value. The main objective is that at least two outcomes are considered: the risk of a default and the risk of no default. Based on the feedback received and fieldwork performed, the IASB believes that many preparers are already performing calculations for internal purposes that would provide an appropriate measure of expected values.

BC5.266　The IASB also acknowledged that an entity may use various techniques to measure expected credit losses, including, for the 12-month expected credit losses measurement, techniques that do not include an explicit 12-month probability of default as an input, such as a loss rate methodology. The requirements in Section 5.5 of IFRS 9 do not list acceptable techniques or methods for measuring the loss allowance. The IASB was concerned that listing acceptable methods might rule out other appropriate methods for measuring expected credit losses, or be interpreted as providing unconditional acceptance of a particular method even when such a measurement would result in an amount that is not consistent with the required attributes of an expected credit loss measurement. Instead, Section 5.5 of IFRS 9 sets out the objectives for the measurement of expected credit losses, allowing entities to decide the most appropriate techniques to satisfy those objectives.

Time value of money

BC5.267　Consistent with the proposals in the Supplementary Document, the 2013 Impairment Exposure Draft proposed to allow an entity to discount expected credit losses using the risk-free rate, the effective interest rate on the related financial asset or any rate in between these two rates.

BC5.268　In developing the proposals in the Supplementary Document, the IASB noted that, conceptually, the discount rate for cash flows of an asset cannot be below the risk-free rate. The IASB further noted that the discount rate used in the 2009 Impairment Exposure Draft is conceptually appropriate for calculations of amortised cost. However, if the IASB were to propose that the upper limit should be the credit-adjusted effective interest rate from the 2009 Impairment Exposure Draft, entities would need to calculate that rate to decide whether they could use a rate that is more readily determinable. Therefore, such a proposal would not avoid the operational complexity of determining that credit-adjusted effective interest rate, which would be counter-productive. Thus, the IASB proposed that an entity should use any rate between the risk-free rate and the effective interest rate, not adjusted for credit risk, as the discount rate.

BC5.269　The IASB observed that some credit risk management systems discount expected cash flows to the date of default. The proposals would require an entity to discount expected credit losses to the reporting date.

BC5.270　Most respondents to the Supplementary Document supported flexibility in an entity choosing which discount rate it should apply. These respondents agreed that this flexibility was helpful for easing the operational challenges of determining and maintaining the discount rate. They also felt that it was appropriate to allow preparers to choose a rate that is suitable for the level of sophistication of their systems and their operational capability. Those who did not support permitting flexibility in determining the appropriate rate wanted to maintain comparability between entities.

BC5.271 The IASB confirmed these proposals in the 2013 Impairment Exposure Draft, but additionally proposed that an entity should disclose the discount rate it used and any significant assumptions that it made in determining that rate. This choice of discount rates did not apply to purchased or originated credit-impaired financial assets, on which the amortised cost measurement always uses the credit-adjusted effective interest rate.

BC5.272 Given the support previously expressed for the proposals in the Supplementary Document, the 2013 Impairment Exposure Draft did not specifically ask respondents to comment on the proposals relating to the discount rate when calculating expected credit losses. However, a number of respondents commented on the proposals, the majority of which disagreed with them. The reasons for their disagreement included that:

(a) using the effective interest rate would be consistent with the proposals for originated or purchased credit-impaired financial assets and financial assets that are credit-impaired at the reporting date (ie the rate used to recognise interest revenue should be the same as the rate used to discount expected credit losses);

(b) discounting cash flows using a risk-free rate disregards any compensation that the entity receives to compensate it for credit risk; and

(c) the permitted range of discount rates is too flexible and differences in the amount of the loss allowance due to different discount rates could be material.

BC5.273 Considering these views, the IASB noted that the advantages of using the effective interest rate to discount expected credit losses included:

(a) that the effective interest rate is the conceptually correct rate and is consistent with amortised cost measurement;

(b) it limits the range of rates that an entity can use when discounting cash shortfalls, thereby limiting the potential for manipulation;

(c) it enhances comparability between entities; and

(d) it avoids the adjustment that arises when financial assets become credit-impaired (interest revenue is required to be calculated on the carrying amount net of expected credit losses) if a rate other than the effective interest rate has been used up to that point.

BC5.274 The IASB acknowledged that, unlike the requirements of IAS 39, in which shortfalls on cash flows were only measured on a subset of financial instruments, the impairment requirements will result in expected credit losses being measured on all financial instruments in the scope of the requirements. Respondents have previously noted that they would have to integrate their credit risk management and accounting systems to improve the interaction between them if they have to discount cash shortfalls using the effective interest rate. However, the IASB noted that even in accordance with the requirements of IAS 39 to use the effective interest rate to discount expected cash flows, there are operational challenges with using the effective interest rate for open portfolios and that entities use approximations of the effective interest rate.

BC5.275   Consequently, on the basis of the feedback received and the advantages noted in paragraph BC5.273, the IASB decided to require the use of the effective interest rate (or an approximation of it) when discounting expected credit losses.

Loan commitments and financial guarantee contracts

BC5.276   The 2013 Impairment Exposure Draft proposed that because loan commitments and financial guarantee contracts are unfunded, the effective interest method and, hence, an effective interest rate, would not be applicable. This is because the IASB considered that those financial instruments by themselves, before they are drawn down, do not give rise to the notion of interest and that, instead, their cash flow profiles are akin to that of derivatives. The fact that interest revenue does not apply is reflected in the accounting for loan commitments and financial guarantee contracts within the scope of IFRS 9. For those loan commitments and financial guarantee contracts, revenue recognition of the related fee income does not use the effective interest method. Consequently, the IASB did not consider it appropriate to simply extend the requirements for the discount rate for measuring expected credit losses that arise from financial assets to the requirements for the discount rate for measuring expected credit losses that arise from loan commitments and financial guarantee contracts.

BC5.277   As a result, the IASB proposed in the 2013 Impairment Exposure Draft that the discount rate to be applied when discounting the expected credit losses that arise from a loan commitment or a financial guarantee contract would be the rate that reflects:

(a)   current market assessments of the time value of money (ie a rate that does not provide consideration for credit risk such as a risk-free rate); and

(b)   the risks that are specific to the cash flows, to the extent that the risks are taken into account by adjusting the discount rate instead of adjusting the cash flows that are being discounted.

BC5.278   Consistent with their feedback in paragraph BC5.272, respondents commented on the disconnect between the discount rate used for the financial asset component (the drawn balance) and the loan commitment component (the undrawn commitment). They noted that this was an unnecessary complication, because, in accordance with the proposals, the measurement of expected credit losses associated with the loan commitment would change when the facility is drawn, merely as a result of the difference in discount rate. Furthermore, respondents noted that for credit risk management purposes, a single discount rate is usually applied to these facilities as a whole. The loan commitment relates directly to the recognised financial asset for which the effective interest rate has already been determined. The effective interest rate applied to the financial asset therefore already reflects an assessment of the time value of money and the risks that are specific to the cash flows on the loan commitment. This rate could be considered to represent a reasonable approximation of the discount rate for loan commitments.

BC5.279   Consequently, the IASB agreed that the expected credit losses on loan commitments should be discounted using the same effective interest rate (or an approximation of it) that is used to discount the expected credit losses on the financial asset. However, for financial guarantee contracts and loan commitments for which the effective interest rate cannot be determined, the discount rate should be determined as proposed in the 2013 Impairment Exposure Draft.

Reasonable and supportable information

BC5.280 Consistent with the proposals in the 2013 Impairment Exposure Draft, the Supplementary Document and the 2009 Impairment Exposure Draft, the IASB specified that the information set required for measuring expected credit losses in accordance with Section 5.5 of IFRS 9 is the best information that is available without undue cost or effort, and that this includes reasonable and supportable forward-looking information.

BC5.281 In the IASB's view, historical information is an important foundation on which to measure expected credit losses. However, an entity should adjust the historical information using reasonable and supportable information that is available without undue cost or effort to reflect current observable data and forecasts of future conditions if such forecasts are different from past information. The IASB noted that an entity is not required to incorporate forecasts of future conditions over the entire remaining life of a financial instrument. Instead, paragraph B5.5.50 of IFRS 9 acknowledges the difficulty arising from estimating expected credit losses as the forecast horizon increases. In some cases, the best reasonable and supportable information could be the unadjusted historical information, depending on the nature of that information and when it was calculated compared to the reporting date, but it should not be assumed to be appropriate in all circumstances. The IASB notes that even if an unadjusted historical measure was not appropriate, it could still be used as a starting point from which adjustments are made to estimate expected credit losses on the basis of reasonable and supportable information that incorporates both current and forward-looking information.

Prudential information

BC5.282 Some respondents to the 2013 Impairment Exposure Draft asked the IASB to ensure that the requirements for measuring expected credit losses in accordance with Section 5.5 of IFRS 9 are aligned to the prudential capital frameworks. Certain prudential regulation and capital adequacy systems, such as the framework developed by the Basel Committee on Banking Supervision, already require financial institutions to calculate 12-month expected credit losses as part of their regulatory capital requirements. However, some of those systems only use credit loss experience based on historical events to set out 'provisioning' levels over the entire economic cycle ('through-the-cycle'). Furthermore, through-the-cycle approaches consider a range of possible economic outcomes instead of those that are actually expected at the reporting date. This would result in a loss allowance that does not reflect the economic characteristics of the financial instruments at the reporting date.

BC5.283 The IASB notes that financial reporting, including estimates of expected credit losses, are based on information, circumstances and events at the reporting date. The IASB expects entities to be able to use some regulatory measures as a basis for the calculation of expected credit losses in accordance with the requirements in IFRS 9. However, these calculations may have to be adjusted to meet the measurement requirements in Section 5.5 of IFRS 9. Only information that is available without undue cost or effort and supportable at the reporting date should be considered. This may include information about current economic conditions as well as reasonable and supportable forecasts of future economic conditions, as long as the information is supportable and available without undue cost or effort when the estimates are made.

BC5.284   Some interested parties are also of the view that loss allowance balances should be used to provide a counter-cyclical effect by building up loss allowances in good times to be used in bad times. This would, however, mask the effect of changes in credit loss expectations.

BC5.285   Some users of financial statements would prefer a representation of credit losses with a conservative or prudential bias, arguing that such a representation would better meet the needs of regulators, who are responsible for maintaining financial stability, and investors. The IASB notes that the objective of the impairment requirements is to faithfully represent the economic reality of expected credit losses in relation to the carrying amount of a financial asset. The IASB does not include in this objective the recognition of a loss allowance that will sufficiently cover unexpected credit losses, because that is not the primary objective of general purpose financial reporting.

BC5.286   The impairment requirements in IFRS 9 are based on the information available at the reporting date and are designed to reflect economic reality, instead of adjusting the assumptions and inputs applied to achieve a counter-cyclical effect. For example, when credit risk improves, the measurement of the loss allowance will faithfully represent that change. This is consistent with the objective of general purpose financial statements.

Hedge accounting (Chapter 6)

BC6.1–   [Relocated to paragraphs BCE.174–BCE.238]
BC6.75

The objective of hedge accounting

BC6.76   Hedge accounting is an exception to the normal recognition and measurement requirements in IFRS. For example, the hedge accounting guidance in IAS 39 permitted:

(a)   the recognition of items that would otherwise have not been recognised (for example, a firm commitment);

(b)   the measurement of an item on a basis that is different from the measurement basis that is normally required (for example, adjusting the measurement of a hedged item in a fair value hedge); and

(c)   the deferral of the changes in the fair value of a hedging instrument for a cash flow hedge in other comprehensive income. Such changes in fair value would otherwise have been recognised in profit or loss (for example, the hedging of a highly probable forecast transaction).

BC6.77   The IASB noted that, although hedge accounting was an exception from normal accounting requirements, in many situations the information that resulted from applying those normal requirements without using hedge accounting either did not provide useful information or omitted important information. Hence, the IASB concluded that hedge accounting should be retained.

BC6.78 In the IASB's view, a consistent hedge accounting model requires an objective that describes when and how an entity should:

(a) override the general recognition and measurement requirements in IFRS (ie when and how an entity should apply hedge accounting); and

(b) recognise effectiveness and/or ineffectiveness of a hedging relationship (ie when and how gains and losses should be recognised).

BC6.79 The IASB considered two possible objectives of hedge accounting—that hedge accounting should:

(a) provide a link between an entity's risk management and its financial reporting. Hedge accounting would convey the context of hedging instruments, which would allow insights into their purpose and effect.

(b) mitigate the recognition and measurement anomalies between the accounting for derivatives (or other hedging instruments) and the accounting for hedged items and manage the timing of the recognition of gains or losses on derivative hedging instruments used to mitigate cash flow risk.

BC6.80 However, the IASB rejected both objectives for hedge accounting. The IASB thought that an objective that linked an entity's risk management and financial reporting was too broad: it was not clear enough what risk management activity was being referred to. Conversely, the IASB thought that an objective that focused on the accounting anomalies was too narrow: it focused on the mechanics of hedge accounting instead of on why hedge accounting was being done.

BC6.81 Consequently, the IASB decided to propose in the 2010 Hedge Accounting Exposure Draft an objective that combined elements of both objectives. The IASB considered that the proposed objective of hedge accounting reflected a broad articulation of a principle-based approach with a focus on the purpose of the entity's risk management activities. In addition, the objective also provided for a focus on the statement of financial position and the statement of comprehensive income, thereby reflecting the effects of the individual assets and liabilities associated with the risk management activities on those statements. This reflected the IASB's intention: that entities should provide useful information about the purpose and effect of hedging instruments for which hedge accounting is applied.

BC6.82 The IASB also noted that, despite that an entity's risk management activities were central to the objective of hedge accounting, an entity would only achieve hedge accounting if it met all the qualifying criteria.

BC6.83 Almost all respondents to the 2010 Hedge Accounting Exposure Draft as well as participants in the IASB's outreach activities supported the objective of hedge accounting proposed in the 2010 Hedge Accounting Exposure Draft.

Open portfolios

BC6.84 Closed hedged portfolios are hedged portfolios in which items cannot be added, removed or replaced without treating each change as the transition to a new portfolio (or a new layer). The hedging relationship specifies at inception the hedged items that form that particular hedging relationship.

BC6.85 In practice, risk management often assesses risk exposures on a continuous basis and at a portfolio level. Risk management strategies tend to have a time horizon (for example, two years) over which an exposure is hedged. Consequently, as time passes new exposures are continuously added to such hedged portfolios and other exposures are removed from them. These are referred to as open portfolios.

BC6.86 Hedges of open portfolios introduce complexity to the accounting for such hedges. Changes could be addressed by treating them like a series of closed portfolios with a short life (ie by periodic discontinuations of the hedging relationships for the previous closed portfolios of items and designations of new hedging relationships for the revised closed portfolios of items). However, this gives rise to complexities related to tracking, amortisation of hedge adjustments and the reclassification of gains or losses deferred in accumulated other comprehensive income. Furthermore, it may be impractical to align such an accounting treatment with the way in which the exposures are viewed from a risk management perspective, which may update hedge portfolios more frequently (for example, daily).

BC6.87 The IASB decided not to specifically address open portfolios or 'macro' hedging (ie hedging at the level that aggregates portfolios) as part of the 2010 Hedge Accounting Exposure Draft. The IASB considered hedge accounting only in the context of groups of items that constitute a gross or net position for which the items that make up that position are included in a specified overall group of items (see paragraphs BC6.427–BC6.467).

BC6.88 Consequently, for fair value hedge accounting for a portfolio hedge of interest rate risk the 2010 Hedge Accounting Exposure Draft did not propose replacing the requirements in IAS 39.

BC6.89 The IASB received feedback from financial institutions as well as from entities outside the financial sector that addressing situations in which entities use a dynamic risk management strategy was important. Financial institutions also noted that this was important because some of their risk exposures might only qualify for hedge accounting in an open portfolio context (for example, non-interest bearing demand deposits).

BC6.90 The IASB noted that this is a complex topic that warrants thorough research and feedback from interested parties. Accordingly, the IASB decided to separately deliberate on the accounting for macro hedging as part of its active agenda with the objective of issuing a Discussion Paper. The IASB noted that this would enable IFRS 9 to be completed more quickly and would enable the new 'general' hedge accounting requirements to be available as part of IFRS 9. The IASB also noted that during the project on accounting for macro hedging the status quo of 'macro hedge accounting' under previous Standards would broadly be maintained so that entities would not be worse off in the meantime.

BC6.91   The IASB noted that broadly maintaining the status quo of 'macro hedge accounting' meant that:

(a)   an entity could continue to apply IAS 39 for fair value hedge accounting for a portfolio hedge of interest rate risk (see paragraph BC6.88), which includes the application of the specific 'macro hedge accounting' requirements in IAS 39; but

(b)   all cash flow hedges would be within the scope of the hedge accounting model of IFRS 9—including those that are colloquially referred to as 'macro cash flow hedges' under IAS 39 today.

BC6.92   The IASB noted that this approach appropriately reflected the interaction between the IAS 39 hedge accounting requirements and the new hedge accounting model it had developed for IFRS 9 for the following reasons:

(a)   the new hedge accounting model does apply to situations in which entities manage risk in a 'macro' context, for example, for risk exposures that result from large groups of items that are managed on an aggregated level, including open portfolios. It also applies to all types of hedges and risks. But entities must use the designations that are available under the new hedge accounting model (and can only apply hedge accounting if they meet the qualifying criteria).

(b)   the new hedge accounting model does not however provide specific 'customised' solutions that would be an exception to (instead of an application of) the model designed to make the implementation of hedge accounting in those situations easier. For example, it does not provide an exception to allow a net position cash flow hedge for interest rate risk or to allow non-interest bearing demand deposits to be designated as hedged items.

(c)   the specific fair value hedge accounting for a portfolio hedge of interest rate risk is an exception to the hedge accounting model in IAS 39 and is strictly limited to that particular type of hedge. This exception does not fit into the new hedge accounting model. The IASB decided that in order to retain this exception pending the completion of the project on accounting for macro hedging, a scope exception that allows the continued application of IAS 39 for this particular type of hedge is appropriate.

(d)   in contrast, cash flow hedge accounting in a 'macro' context was an application of the (general) hedge accounting model under IAS 39. Consequently, it is consistent with that approach to include 'macro cash flow hedge accounting' as an application of the new hedge accounting model.

BC6.93   However, the IASB received feedback that some entities were unsure whether and how 'macro cash flow hedge accounting' could also be applied under the hedge accounting requirements of IFRS 9. In response, the IASB considered whether it could address those concerns by carrying forward the Implementation Guidance that accompanied IAS 39 and that illustrated 'macro cash flow hedge accounting'. The IASB noted that to do so would be inconsistent with its decision not to carry forward any of the hedge accounting

Implementation Guidance that accompanied IAS 39. The IASB also noted that making an exception by carrying forward some parts of the Implementation Guidance but not others could have unintended consequences because it would inevitably create the perception that the IASB had endorsed some parts while it had rejected others.

BC6.94 The IASB also noted that carrying forward Implementation Guidance could not be justified as a means to address any concerns about whether a particular accounting practice complies with the hedge accounting requirements. Implementation Guidance only accompanies, but is not part of, a Standard, which means that it does not override the requirements of a Standard.

BC6.95 Consequently, the IASB decided to retain its original approach of not carrying forward any of the hedge accounting related Implementation Guidance that accompanied IAS 39. However, the IASB emphasised that not carrying forward the Implementation Guidance did not mean that it had rejected that guidance.

BC6.96 The IASB also received feedback that some entities were concerned that 'proxy hedging' would not be possible under the hedge accounting model in IFRS 9—a concern that was highlighted by the 'macro cash flow hedge accounting' related Implementation Guidance that accompanied IAS 39 not being carried forward. 'Proxy hedging' is a colloquial reference to the use of designations of hedging relationships that do not exactly represent an entity's actual risk management. Examples include using a designation of a gross amount of an exposure (gross designation) when risks are actually managed on a net position basis, and using designations of variable-rate debt instruments in cash flow hedges when risk management is based on managing the interest rate risk of prepayable fixed-rate debt instruments or deposits (such as core deposits). Similarly, 'proxy hedging' can involve designating fixed-rate debt instruments in fair value hedges when risk management is based on managing the interest rate risk of variable-rate debt instruments.

BC6.97 The IASB noted that its rationale for not including a scope exception from the IFRS 9 hedge accounting requirements for 'macro cash flow hedge accounting' reflected that designations of hedging relationships that represent 'proxy hedging' are possible. The IASB was aware that many financial institutions use 'proxy hedging' as described in paragraph BC6.96.

BC6.98 The IASB considered that in those situations the designation for hedge accounting purposes was inevitably not the same as the entity's risk management view of its hedging, but that the designation reflects risk management in that it relates to the same type of risk that was being managed and the instruments used for that purpose. For example, like IAS 39, IFRS 9 also does not allow cash flow hedges of interest rate risk to be designated on a net position basis but entities must instead designate gross positions. This requires so called 'proxy hedging' because the designation for hedge accounting purposes is on a gross position basis even though risk management typically manages on a net position basis. This 'proxy hedging' also includes approaches that for risk management purposes determine the net interest rate risk position on the basis of fixed-rate items. A cash flow hedge designation can still reflect those approaches in that the net interest rate risk position can be viewed as having a dual character: the hedges bridge, for example, the economic mismatch between fixed-rate assets and variable-rate funding (existing variable-rate funding as well as funding to be obtained in the future to continue to fund the assets as existing funding matures). Such an economic mismatch can be regarded as fair value interest rate risk when looking at the assets and as cash flow interest rate risk when looking at the funding. The net position hedging combines the two aspects because both affect the net interest margin. Hence, both fair value and cash flow interest rate risk are inherent aspects of the hedged exposure. However, hedge accounting requires the designation of the hedging relationship as either a fair value hedge or as a cash flow hedge. The IASB noted that in that sense, even if a fair value hedge designation better represented a risk management perspective that considers the fixed-rate assets as the primary or leading aspect, a cash flow hedge designation would still reflect the risk management because of the dual character of the risk position. Consequently, the IASB regarded 'proxy hedging' as an eligible way of designating the hedged item under IFRS 9 as long as that still reflected risk management, which was the case in this situation.

BC6.99 The IASB noted that in such situations entities have to select some items that give rise to interest rate risk and that qualify for designation as a hedged item and designate them as a gross exposure in order to achieve hedge accounting. The IASB acknowledged that in those circumstances there is typically no obvious link between any particular designated hedged item and the designated hedging instrument, and that entities select items for designation that are most suitable for hedge accounting purposes. This means that different entities can have different ways of selecting those items depending on their situation (for example, whether designating an interest rate risk exposure related to a financial asset or a financial liability).

BC6.100 The IASB also noted that designations of hedging relationships that reflect 'proxy hedging' were not unique to hedging of interest rate risk by banks in, for example, a 'macro' context. Despite the objective of the project to represent, in the financial statements, the effect of an entity's risk management activities, the IASB considered that this would in many situations not be possible as a simple, exact '1:1 copy' of the actual risk management perspective. In the IASB's view this was already apparent from other aspects of the hedge accounting model of IFRS 9, for example:

(a) the mere fact that the IASB had limited net position cash flow hedges to foreign currency risk meant that for all other types of hedged risks an entity would have to designate gross amounts (gross designation). But this did not mean that cash flow hedge accounting was prohibited for all other risks that are managed on a net position basis.

(b) an entity that actually hedges on a risk component basis in accordance with its risk management view might not meet the criteria for designating the hedged item as a risk component. But this did not mean that the entity was prohibited from applying hedge accounting altogether. Instead, it was only prohibited from using that particular designation of a risk component. Consequently, the entity could designate the item in its entirety as the hedged item and apply hedge accounting (if it met the qualifying criteria on the basis of that designation).

(c) for many entities the actual risk management is based on a 'flow perspective' for cash flow hedges, which only considers mismatches in the variable cash flows of the hedging instrument and the hedged item as a source of hedge ineffectiveness. However, the measurement of hedge effectiveness for hedge accounting purposes does not allow an entity to assume perfect hedge effectiveness in those circumstances (or limiting the analysis to only the variable cash flows of the hedging instrument). However, this did not mean that hedge accounting was prohibited. Instead, it meant that the entity had to measure hedge ineffectiveness as required for accounting purposes.

(d) the presentation of hedges of net positions requires the use of a separate line item in the income statement instead of directly adjusting the line items affected by the hedged items (for example, grossing up revenue and cost of sales). In contrast, entities' actual risk management often considers the respective line items as hedged at the respective rates that were locked in by the hedges. This difference between the risk management and accounting views did not mean that an entity was prohibited from using hedge accounting. Instead, it meant that the entity had to follow the presentation requirements for accounting purposes if it wanted to apply hedge accounting.

BC6.101 Consequently, the IASB did not agree that designations of hedging relationships under IFRS 9 could not represent 'proxy hedging'. The IASB also decided to provide further guidance on how 'proxy hedging' is related to the discontinuation of hedge accounting (see paragraph BC6.331).

BC6.102 However, the IASB also received feedback from some entities that they did not want to have to apply the hedge accounting requirements of IFRS 9 before the IASB's project on accounting for macro hedging was completed. Those entities cited concerns about remaining uncertainty as to whether IAS 39—compliant practices of designating hedging relationships for portfolio hedging or macro hedging activities would still be available, the costs of assessing whether those practices are IFRS 9—compliant and the risk of having to change those practices twice. Some entities questioned whether it was appropriate to require entities to re-examine and potentially make changes to their hedge accounting while the project on accounting for macro hedging was ongoing.

BC6.103 The IASB considered whether it should provide a scope exception to the hedge accounting requirements of IFRS 9 to address those concerns over the interaction with macro hedging activities. This scope exception would be separate from that for fair value hedge accounting for a portfolio hedge of interest rate risk, which complements the hedge accounting requirements of IFRS 9 and which the IASB had already proposed in the 2010 Hedge Accounting Exposure Draft (see paragraph BC6.88). In this case the IASB considered whether there was a need to allow entities to continue to apply IAS 39 to cash flow hedges in the context of macro hedging activities. In the IASB's view it was not necessary from a technical perspective to make any changes in addition to the clarifications that it had already provided (see paragraphs BC6.93–BC6.101). However, the IASB acknowledged that it had not yet completed its project on accounting for macro hedging and that providing a choice to continue to apply the hedge accounting requirements in IAS 39 would allow entities to wait for the complete picture related to the accounting for hedging activities before applying a new hedge accounting model.

BC6.104 Consequently, the IASB considered whether it could provide a specific scope exception that would confine the continued application of IAS 39 to situations in which entities seek to apply 'macro cash flow hedge accounting'. However, the IASB determined that such a specific scope would be difficult to describe, resulting in added complexity and the risk that interpretation questions would arise. The IASB therefore decided to provide entities with an accounting policy choice between applying the hedge accounting requirements of IFRS 9 (including the scope exception for fair value hedge accounting for a portfolio hedge of interest rate risk) and continuing to apply the existing hedge accounting requirements in IAS 39 for all hedge accounting until its project on the accounting for macro hedging is completed. The IASB noted that an entity could subsequently decide to change its accounting policy and commence applying the hedge accounting requirements of IFRS 9 at the beginning of any reporting period (subject to the other transition requirements of IFRS 9). The IASB also emphasised that, once IFRS 9 as amended in November 2013 is applied, the new disclosure requirements related to hedge accounting are part of IFRS 7 and would consequently apply to all entities using hedge accounting under IFRS (even if electing to continue to apply IAS 39 for hedge accounting).

Hedge accounting for equity investments designated as at fair value through other comprehensive income

BC6.105 In accordance with IFRS 9 an entity may, at initial recognition, make an irrevocable election to present subsequent changes in the fair value of some investments in equity instruments in other comprehensive income. Amounts recognised in other comprehensive income for such equity instruments are not reclassified to profit or loss. However, IAS 39 defined a hedging relationship as a relationship in which the exposure to be hedged could affect profit or loss. Consequently, an entity could not apply hedge accounting if the hedged exposure affected other comprehensive income without reclassification out of other comprehensive income to profit or loss because only such a reclassification would mean that the hedged exposure could ultimately affect profit or loss.

BC6.106 For its 2010 Hedge Accounting Exposure Draft, the IASB considered whether it should amend the definition of a fair value hedge to state that the hedged exposure could affect either profit or loss or other comprehensive income, instead of only profit or loss. However, the IASB had concerns about the mechanics of matching the changes in the fair value of the hedging instrument with the changes in the value of the hedged item attributable to the hedged risk. Furthermore, the IASB was concerned about how to account for any related hedge ineffectiveness. To address these concerns, the IASB considered alternative approaches.

BC6.107 The IASB considered whether the hedge ineffectiveness should remain in other comprehensive income when the changes in the value of the hedged item attributable to the hedged risk are bigger than the changes in the fair value of the hedging instrument. This approach would:

(a) be consistent with the IASB's decision on classification and measurement (the first phase of the IFRS 9 project), whereby changes in the fair value of the equity investment designated as at fair value through other comprehensive income should not be reclassified to profit or loss; but

(b) contradict the hedge accounting principle that hedge ineffectiveness should be recognised in profit or loss.

BC6.108 Conversely, if the hedge ineffectiveness were recognised in profit or loss it would:

(a) be consistent with the hedge accounting principle that hedge ineffectiveness should be recognised in profit or loss; but

(b) contradict the prohibition of reclassifying from other comprehensive income to profit or loss gains or losses on investments in equity instruments accounted for as at fair value through other comprehensive income.

BC6.109 Consequently, in its 2010 Hedge Accounting Exposure Draft the IASB proposed prohibiting hedge accounting for investments in equity instruments designated as at fair value through other comprehensive income, because it could not be achieved within the existing framework of hedge accounting. Introducing another framework would add complexity. Furthermore, the IASB did not want to add another exception (ie contradicting the principle in IFRS 9 of not reclassifying between other comprehensive income and profit or loss, or contradicting the principle of recognising hedge ineffectiveness in profit or loss) to the existing exception of accounting for investments in equity instruments (ie the option to account for those investments at fair value through other comprehensive income).

BC6.110 However, the IASB noted that dividends from such investments in equity instruments are recognised in profit or loss. Consequently, a forecast dividend from such investments could be an eligible hedged item (if all qualifying criteria for hedge accounting are met).

BC6.111 Almost all respondents to the 2010 Hedge Accounting Exposure Draft disagreed with the IASB's proposal to prohibit hedge accounting for investments in equity instruments designated as at fair value through other comprehensive income. Those respondents argued that hedge accounting should be available for equity investments at fair value through other comprehensive income so that hedge accounting can be more closely aligned with risk management activities. In particular, respondents commented that it was a common risk management strategy for an entity to hedge the foreign exchange risk exposure of equity investments (irrespective of the accounting designation at fair value through profit or loss or other comprehensive income). In addition, an entity might also hedge the equity price risk even though it does not intend to sell the equity investment because it might still want to protect itself against equity volatility.

BC6.112   In the light of those concerns, the IASB reconsidered whether it should allow investments in equity instruments designated as at fair value through other comprehensive income to be designated as a hedged item in a fair value hedge. Some respondents argued that the inconsistencies that the IASB had discussed in its original deliberations (see paragraphs BC6.107–BC6.108) could be overcome by using a differentiating approach, whereby if fair value changes of the hedging instrument exceeded those of the hedged item hedge ineffectiveness would be presented in profit or loss and otherwise in other comprehensive income. However, the IASB noted that the cumulative ineffectiveness presented in profit or loss or other comprehensive income over the total period of the hedging relationship might still contradict the principle of not recycling to profit or loss changes in the fair value of equity investments at fair value through other comprehensive income. Hence, the IASB rejected that approach.

BC6.113   The IASB noted that recognising hedge ineffectiveness always in profit or loss would be inconsistent with the irrevocable election of presenting in other comprehensive income fair value changes of investments in equity instruments (see paragraph BC6.108). The IASB considered that that outcome would defeat its aim to reduce complexity in accounting for financial instruments.

BC6.114   The IASB considered that an approach that would recognise hedge ineffectiveness always in other comprehensive income (without recycling) could facilitate hedge accounting in situations in which an entity's risk management involves hedging risks of equity investments designated as at fair value through other comprehensive income without contradicting the classification and measurement requirements of IFRS 9. The IASB noted that, as a consequence, hedge ineffectiveness would not always be presented in profit or loss but would always follow the presentation of the value changes of the hedged item.

BC6.115   The IASB considered that, on balance, the advantages of the approach that always recognises hedge ineffectiveness in other comprehensive income (without recycling) for those investments in equity instruments would outweigh any disadvantages and, overall, that this alternative was superior to the other alternatives that the IASB had contemplated. Hence, the IASB decided to include this approach in the final requirements.

BC6.116   The IASB also considered whether hedge accounting should be more generally available for exposures that only affect other comprehensive income (but not profit or loss). However, the IASB was concerned that such a broad scope might result in items qualifying for hedge accounting that might not be suitable hedged items and hence have unintended consequences. Consequently, the IASB decided against making hedge accounting more generally available to such exposures.

Hedging instruments

Qualifying instruments

Derivatives embedded in financial assets

BC6.117   IAS 39 required the separation of derivatives embedded in hybrid financial assets and liabilities that are not closely related to the host contract (bifurcation). In accordance with IAS 39, the separated derivative was eligible for designation as a hedging instrument. In accordance with IFRS 9, hybrid financial assets are measured in their entirety (ie including any embedded derivative) at either amortised cost or fair value through profit or loss. No separation of any embedded derivative is permitted.

BC6.118 In the light of the decision that it made on IFRS 9, the IASB considered whether derivatives embedded in financial assets should be eligible for designation as hedging instruments. The IASB considered two alternatives:

(a) an entity could choose to separate embedded derivatives solely for the purpose of designating the derivative component as a hedging instrument; or

(b) an entity could designate a risk component of the hybrid financial asset, equivalent to the embedded derivative, as the hedging instrument.

BC6.119 The IASB rejected both alternatives. Consequently, the IASB proposed not to allow derivative features embedded in financial assets to be eligible hedging instruments (even though they can be an integral part of a hybrid financial asset that is measured at fair value through profit or loss and designated as the hedging instrument in its entirety—see paragraph BC6.129). The reasons for the IASB's decision are summarised in paragraphs BC6.120–BC6.121.

BC6.120 Permitting an entity to separate embedded derivatives for the purpose of hedge accounting would retain the IAS 39 requirements in terms of their eligibility as hedging instruments. However, the IASB noted that the underlying rationale for separating embedded derivatives in IAS 39 was not to reflect risk management activities, but instead to prevent an entity from circumventing the requirements for the recognition and measurement of derivatives. The IASB also noted that the designation of a separated embedded derivative as a hedging instrument in accordance with IAS 39 was not very common in practice. Hence, the IASB considered that reintroducing the separation of embedded derivatives for hybrid financial assets does not target hedge accounting considerations, would consequently not be an appropriate means to address any hedge accounting concerns and in addition would reintroduce complexity for situations that are not common in practice.

BC6.121 Alternatively, permitting an entity to designate, as the hedging instrument, a risk component of a hybrid financial asset would allow that entity to show more accurately the results of its risk management activities. However, such an approach would be a significant expansion of the scope of the Hedge Accounting project because the IASB would need to address the question of how to disaggregate a hedging instrument into components. In order to be consistent, a similar question would need to be addressed for non-financial items (for example, non-financial liabilities in IAS 37 Provisions, Contingent Liabilities and Contingent Assets with currency or commodity risk elements). The IASB did not want to expand the scope of the hedge accounting project beyond financial instruments because the outcome of exploring this alternative would be highly uncertain, could possibly necessitate a review of other Standards and could significantly delay the project.

BC6.122   The IASB therefore retained its original decision when deliberating its 2010 Hedge Accounting Exposure Draft.

Non-derivative financial instruments

BC6.123   Hedge accounting shows how the changes in the fair value or cash flows of a hedging instrument offset the changes in the fair value or cash flows of a designated hedged item attributable to the hedged risk if it reflects an entity's risk management strategy.

BC6.124   IAS 39 permitted non-derivative financial assets and non-derivative financial liabilities (for example, monetary items denominated in a foreign currency) to be designated as hedging instruments only for a hedge of foreign currency risk. Designating a non-derivative financial asset or liability denominated in a foreign currency as a hedge of foreign currency risk in accordance with IAS 39 was equivalent to designating a risk component of a hedging instrument in a hedging relationship. This foreign currency risk component is determined in accordance with IAS 21 *The Effects of Changes in Foreign Exchange Rates*. Because the foreign currency risk component is determined in accordance with foreign currency translation requirements in IAS 21, it is already available for incorporation by reference in the financial instruments Standard. Consequently, permitting the use of a foreign currency risk component for hedge accounting purposes did not require separate, additional requirements for risk components within the hedge accounting model.

BC6.125   Not allowing the disaggregation of a non-derivative financial instrument used as a hedge into risk components, other than foreign currency risk, has implications for the likelihood of achieving hedge accounting for those instruments. This is because the effects of components of the cash instrument that are not related to the risk being hedged cannot be excluded from the hedging relationship and consequently from the effectiveness assessment. Consequently, depending on the size of the components that are not related to the risk being hedged, in most scenarios it will be difficult to demonstrate that there is an economic relationship between the hedged item and the hedging instrument that gives rise to an expectation that their values will systematically change in response to movements in either the same underlying or underlyings that are economically related in such a way that they respond in a similar way to the risk that is being hedged.

BC6.126   In the light of this consequence, the IASB considered whether it should permit non-derivative financial instruments to be eligible for designation as hedging instruments for risk components other than foreign currency risk. The IASB noted that permitting this would require developing an approach for disaggregating non-derivative hedging instruments into components. For reasons similar to those set out in paragraph BC6.121 the IASB decided not to explore such an approach.

BC6.127   The IASB also considered two alternatives to the requirements of IAS 39 (those requirements that limit the eligibility of non-derivative financial instruments as hedging instruments to hedges of foreign currency risk). The IASB considered whether for hedges of all types of risk (ie not limited to hedges of foreign currency risk) it should extend the eligibility as hedging instruments to non-derivative financial instruments:

(a) that are classified as at fair value through profit or loss; or (alternatively to those); and

(b) that are part of other categories of IFRS 9.

BC6.128 The IASB noted that extending the eligibility to non-derivative financial instruments in categories other than fair value through profit or loss would give rise to operational problems because to apply hedge accounting would require changing the measurement of non-derivative financial instruments measured at amortised cost when they are designated as hedging instruments. The IASB considered that the only way to mitigate this issue was to allow for the designation of components of the non-derivative financial instrument. This would limit the change in measurement to a component of the instrument attributable to the hedged risk. However, the IASB had already rejected that idea in its deliberations (see paragraph BC6.126).

BC6.129 However, the IASB noted that extending the eligibility to non-derivative financial instruments that are measured at fair value through profit or loss, if designated in their entirety (instead of only some risk components of them), would not give rise to the need to change the measurement or the recognition of gains and losses of the financial instrument. The IASB also noted that extending the eligibility to these financial instruments would align the new hedge accounting model more closely with the classification model of IFRS 9 and make it better able to address hedging strategies that could evolve in the future. Consequently, the IASB proposed in its 2010 Hedge Accounting Exposure Draft that non-derivative financial instruments that are measured at fair value through profit or loss should also be eligible hedging instruments if they are designated in their entirety (in addition to hedges of foreign currency risk for which the hedging instrument can be designated on a risk component basis—see paragraph BC6.124).

BC6.130 Generally, respondents to the 2010 Hedge Accounting Exposure Draft agreed that distinguishing between derivative and non-derivative financial instruments was not appropriate for the purpose of determining their eligibility as hedging instruments. Many respondents believed that extending the eligibility criteria to non-derivative financial instruments at fair value through profit or loss would allow better representation of an entity's risk management activities in the financial statements. The feedback highlighted that this was particularly relevant in countries that have legal and regulatory restrictions on the use and availability of derivative financial instruments.

BC6.131 Some respondents argued that there was no conceptual basis to restrict the eligibility of non-derivative financial instruments to those that are measured at fair value through profit or loss. In their view all non-derivative financial instruments should be eligible as hedging instruments.

BC6.132 Other respondents thought that that the proposals were not restrictive enough, particularly in relation to non-derivative financial instruments that are measured at fair value through profit or loss as a result of applying the fair value option. Those respondents thought that the IASB should specifically restrict the use of non-derivative financial instruments designated under the fair value option because these have usually been elected to be measured at fair value to eliminate an accounting mismatch and hence should not qualify for hedge accounting. Some respondents also questioned whether a financial liability that is measured at fair value, with changes in the fair value attributable to changes in the liability's credit risk presented in other comprehensive income, would be an eligible hedging instrument under the proposals in the 2010 Hedge Accounting Exposure Draft.

BC6.133 The IASB noted that in its deliberations leading to the 2010 Hedge Accounting Exposure Draft it had already considered whether non-derivative financial instruments measured at amortised cost should also be eligible for designation as hedging instruments. The IASB remained concerned that designating as hedging instruments those non-derivative financial instruments that were not already accounted for at fair value through profit or loss would result in hedge accounting that would change the measurement or recognition of gains and losses of items that would otherwise result from applying IFRS 9. For example, the IASB noted that it would have to determine how to account for the difference between the fair value and the amortised cost of the non-derivative financial instrument upon designation as a hedging instrument. Furthermore, upon discontinuation of the hedging relationship, the measurement of the non-derivative financial instrument would revert to amortised cost resulting in a difference between its carrying amount as of the date of discontinuation (the fair value as at the discontinuation date which becomes the new deemed cost) and its maturity amount. The IASB considered that addressing those aspects would inappropriately increase complexity.

BC6.134 The IASB was also concerned that allowing non-derivative financial instruments that are not already accounted for at fair value through profit or loss to be designated as hedging instruments would mean that the hedge accounting model would not only change the measurement basis of the hedged item, as the existing hedge accounting model already does, but also the measurement basis of hedging instruments. Hence, it could, for example, result in situations in which a natural hedge (ie an accounting match) is already achieved on an amortised cost basis between two non-derivative financial instruments, but hedge accounting could still be used to change the measurement basis of both those instruments to fair value (one as a hedged item and the other as the hedging instrument).

BC6.135 Consequently, the IASB decided that non-derivative financial instruments should be eligible hedging instruments only if they are already accounted for at fair value through profit or loss.

BC6.136 The IASB also discussed whether or not those non-derivative financial instruments that are accounted for at fair value through profit or loss as a result of applying the fair value option should be eligible for designation as a hedging instrument. The IASB considered that any designation as a hedging instrument should not contradict the entity's election of the fair value option (ie recreate the accounting mismatch that the election of the fair value option addressed). For example, if a non-derivative financial instrument that has previously been designated under the fair value option is included in a cash flow hedge relationship, the accounting for the non-derivative financial instrument under the fair value option would have to be overridden. This is because all (or part) of the changes in the fair value of that hedging instrument are recognised in other comprehensive income. However, recognising the changes in fair value in other comprehensive income re-introduces the accounting mismatch that the application of the fair value option eliminated in the first instance. The IASB noted that similar considerations apply to fair value hedges and hedges of net investments in foreign operations.

BC6.137 Consequently, the IASB considered whether it should introduce a general prohibition against designating, as hedging instruments, non-derivative financial instruments that are accounted for at fair value through profit or loss as a result of electing the fair value option. However, such a prohibition would not necessarily be appropriate. The IASB noted that one of the items underlying the fair value option might be sold or terminated at a later stage (ie the circumstances that made the fair value option available might be subject to change or later disappear). However, because the fair value option is irrevocable it would mean a non-derivative financial instrument for which the fair value option was initially elected could never qualify as a hedging instrument even if there was no longer a conflict between the purpose of the fair value option and the purpose of hedge accounting. A general prohibition would not allow the use of hedge accounting at a later stage even when hedge accounting might then mitigate an accounting mismatch (without recreating another one).

BC6.138 The IASB noted that when a non-derivative financial instrument is accounted for at fair value through profit or loss as a result of electing the fair value option, the appropriateness of its use as a hedging instrument depends on the relevant facts and circumstances underlying the fair value option designation. The IASB considered that if an entity designates as a hedging instrument a financial instrument for which it originally elected the fair value option, and this results in the mitigation of an accounting mismatch (without recreating another one), using hedge accounting was appropriate. However, the IASB emphasised that if applying hedge accounting recreates, in the financial statements, the accounting mismatches that electing the fair value option sought to eliminate, then designating the financial instrument for which the fair value option was elected as a hedging instrument would contradict the basis (qualifying criterion) on which the fair value option was elected. Hence, in those situations there would be a conflict between the purpose of the fair value option and the purpose of hedge accounting as they could not be achieved at the same time but instead would, overall, result in another accounting mismatch. Consequently, the IASB emphasised that designating the non-derivative financial instrument as a hedging instrument in those situations would call into question the legitimacy of electing the fair value option and would be inappropriate. The IASB considered that, to this effect, the requirements of the fair value option were sufficient and hence no additional guidance was necessary.

BC6.139 As a result, the IASB decided not to introduce a general prohibition against the eligibility of designating as hedging instruments non-derivative financial instruments accounted for at fair value through profit or loss as a result of electing the fair value option.

BC6.140   The IASB also considered whether it needed to provide more guidance on when a non-derivative financial liability designated as at fair value through profit or loss under the fair value option would qualify as a hedging instrument. The IASB noted that IFRS 9 refers to liabilities for which the fair value option is elected as "liabilities designated at fair value through profit or loss", irrespective of whether the effects of changes in the liability's credit risk are presented in other comprehensive income or (if that presentation would enlarge an accounting mismatch) in profit or loss. However, for the eligibility as a hedging instrument, the IASB considered that it would make a difference whether the effects of changes in the liability's credit risk are presented in other comprehensive income or profit or loss. The IASB noted that if a financial liability whose credit risk related fair value changes are presented in other comprehensive income was an eligible hedging instrument there would be two alternatives for what could be designated as part of the hedging relationship:

(a)   only the part of the liability that is measured at fair value through profit or loss, in which case the hedging relationship would exclude credit risk and hence any related hedge ineffectiveness would not be recognised; or

(b)   the entire fair value change of the liability, in which case the presentation in other comprehensive income of the changes in fair value related to changes in the credit risk of the liability would have to be overridden (ie using reclassification to profit or loss) to comply with the hedge accounting requirements.

BC6.141   Consequently, the IASB decided to clarify its proposal by adding an explicit statement that a financial liability is not eligible for designation as a hedging instrument if under the fair value option the amount of change in the fair value attributable to changes in the liability's own credit risk is presented in other comprehensive income.

Internal derivatives as hedging instruments

BC6.142   An entity may follow different risk management models depending on the structure of its operations and the nature of the hedges. Some use a centralised treasury or similar function that is responsible for identifying the exposures and managing the risks borne by various entities within the group. Others use a decentralised risk management approach and manage risks individually for entities in the group. Some also use a combination of those two approaches.

BC6.143   Internal derivatives are typically used to aggregate risk exposures of a group (often on a net basis) to allow the entity to manage the resulting consolidated exposure. However, IAS 39 was primarily designed to address one-to-one hedging relationships. Consequently, in order to explore how to align accounting with risk management, the IASB considered whether internal derivatives should be eligible for designation as hedging instruments. However, the IASB noted that the ineligibility of internal derivatives as hedging instruments was not the root cause of misalignment between risk management and hedge accounting. Instead, the challenge was how to make hedge accounting operational for groups of items and net positions.

BC6.144   The IASB noted that, for financial reporting purposes, the mitigation or transformation of risk is generally only relevant if it results in a transfer of risk to a party outside the reporting entity. Any transfer of risk within the reporting entity does not change the risk exposure from the perspective of that reporting entity as a whole. This is consistent with the principles of consolidated financial statements.

BC6.145 For example, a subsidiary might transfer cash flow interest rate risk from variable-rate funding to the group's central treasury using an interest rate swap. The central treasury might decide to retain that exposure (instead of hedging it out to a party external to the group). In that case, the cash flow interest rate risk of the stand-alone subsidiary has been transferred (the swap is an external derivative from the subsidiary's perspective). However, from the group's consolidated perspective, the cash flow interest rate risk has not changed but merely been reallocated between different parts of the group (the swap is an internal derivative from the group's perspective).

BC6.146 Consequently, in the deliberations leading to the 2010 Hedge Accounting Exposure Draft, the IASB decided that internal derivatives should not be eligible hedging instruments in the financial statements of the reporting entity (for example, intragroup derivatives in the consolidated financial statements) because they do not represent an instrument that the reporting entity uses to transfer the risk to an external party (ie outside the reporting entity). This meant that the related requirements in IAS 39 would be retained.

BC6.147 The IASB retained its original decision when redeliberating its 2010 Hedge Accounting Exposure Draft.

Intragroup monetary items as hedging instruments

BC6.148 In accordance with IAS 39, the difference arising from the translation of intragroup monetary items in the consolidated financial statements in accordance with IAS 21 was eligible as a hedged item but not as a hedging instrument. This may appear inconsistent.

BC6.149 The IASB noted that, when translating an intragroup monetary item, IAS 21 requires the recognition of a gain or loss in the consolidated statement of profit or loss and other comprehensive income. Consequently, in the IASB's view, considering intragroup monetary items for eligibility as hedging instruments would require a review of the requirements in IAS 21 at the same time as considering any hedge accounting requirements. The IASB noted that at that time there was no active project on foreign currency translation. Hence, it decided that it should not address this issue as part of its project on hedge accounting. Consequently, in the deliberations leading to the 2010 Hedge Accounting Exposure Draft, the IASB decided not to allow intragroup monetary items to be eligible hedging instruments (ie to retain the restriction in IAS 39).

BC6.150 The IASB retained its original decision when redeliberating its 2010 Hedge Accounting Exposure Draft.

Written options

BC6.151 In its 2010 Hedge Accounting Exposure Draft, the IASB retained the restriction in IAS 39 that a written option does not qualify as a hedging instrument except when it is used to hedge a purchased option or unless it is combined with a purchased option as one derivative instrument (for example, a collar) and that derivative instrument is not a net written option.

BC6.152 However, respondents to the 2010 Hedge Accounting Exposure Draft commented that a stand-alone written option should not be excluded from being eligible for designation as a hedging instrument if it is jointly designated with other instruments such that in combination they do not result in a net written option. Those respondents highlighted that entities sometimes enter into two separate option contracts because of, for example, legal or regulatory considerations, and that the two separate option contracts achieve, in effect, the same economic outcome as one contract (for example, a collar contract).

BC6.153 The IASB considered that the eligibility of an option contract to be designated as a hedging instrument should depend on its economic substance instead of its legal form. Consequently, the IASB decided to amend the requirements such that a written option and a purchased option (regardless of whether the hedging instrument arises from one or several different contracts) can be jointly designated as the hedging instrument, provided that the combination is not a net written option. The IASB also noted that by aligning the accounting for combinations of written and purchased options with that for derivative instruments that combine written and purchased options (for example, a collar contract), the assessment of what is, in effect, a net written option would be the same, ie it would follow the established practice under IAS 39. That practice considers the following cumulative factors to ascertain that an interest rate collar or other derivative instrument that includes a written option is not a net written option:

(a) no net premium is received either at inception or over the life of the combination of options. The distinguishing feature of a written option is the receipt of a premium to compensate the writer for the risk incurred.

(b) except for the strike prices, the critical terms and conditions of the written option component and the purchased option component are the same (including underlying variable or variables, currency denomination and maturity date). Also, the notional amount of the written option component is not greater than the notional amount of the purchased option component.

Hedged items

Qualifying items

Financial instruments held within a business model whose objective is to collect or pay contractual cash flows

BC6.154 Against the background of potential interaction with the classification of financial instruments in accordance with IFRS 9, the IASB, in its deliberations leading to the 2010 Hedge Accounting Exposure Draft, considered the eligibility for hedge accounting of financial instruments held within a business model whose objective is to collect or pay contractual cash flows. The IASB focused on fair value hedges of interest rate risk because other risks (for example, foreign currency risk) affect cash flows that are collected or paid and the application of hedge accounting seemed clearly appropriate. More specifically, the IASB was concerned about whether a desire to enter into a fair value hedge can be seen as calling into question whether the entity's business model is to hold the financial instrument to collect (or pay) contractual cash flows, instead of selling (or settle/transfer) the instrument before contractual maturity in order to realise the fair value changes. Consequently, some argue that, on the basis of the assertion underlying the business model assessment, the entity should be interested only in the contractual cash flows arising from those investments and not in the changes in fair value.

BC6.155 The IASB discussed several situations in which a fair value hedge of interest rate risk does not contradict the fact that a financial instrument is held with the objective to collect or pay contractual cash flows. One example is an entity that seeks to invest in a variable-rate asset of a particular credit quality, but could only obtain a fixed-rate asset of the desired credit quality. That entity could create the cash flow profile of a variable-rate asset indirectly by buying both the available fixed-rate investment and entering into an interest rate swap that transforms the fixed-interest cash flows from that asset into variable-interest cash flows. The IASB noted that this and other examples demonstrated that what is a fair value hedge for accounting purposes is, from a risk management perspective, often a choice between receiving (or paying) fixed versus variable interest cash flows, instead of a strategy to protect against fair value changes. Hence, the IASB considered that a fair value hedge of interest rate risk would not in itself contradict the assertion that a financial instrument is held with the objective to collect or pay contractual cash flows.

BC6.156 The IASB also noted that, under the classification model for financial instruments in IFRS 9, an entity may sell or transfer some financial instruments that qualify for amortised cost, even if they are held with the objective to collect or pay contractual cash flows. Consequently, the IASB decided that fair value hedge accounting should be available for financial instruments that are held with the objective to collect or pay contractual cash flows.

BC6.157 The IASB retained its original decisions when redeliberating its 2010 Hedge Accounting Exposure Draft.

Designation of derivatives

BC6.158 The guidance on implementing IAS 39 stated that derivatives could be designated as hedging instruments only, not as hedged items (either individually or as part of a group of hedged items). As the sole exception, paragraph AG94 in the application guidance in IAS 39 allowed a purchased option to be designated as a hedged item. In practice, this has generally prevented derivatives from qualifying as hedged items. Similarly, positions that are a combination of an exposure and a derivative ('aggregated exposures') failed to qualify as hedged items. The implementation guidance accompanying IAS 39 provided the rationale for not permitting derivatives (or aggregated exposures that include a derivative) to be designated as hedged items. It stated that derivative instruments were always deemed to be held for trading and measured at fair value with gains or losses recognised in profit or loss unless they are designated as hedging instruments.

BC6.159　However, this rationale is difficult to justify in the light of the exception to permit some purchased options to qualify as hedged items irrespective of whether the option is a stand-alone derivative or an embedded derivative. If a stand-alone purchased option can be a hedged item then prohibiting derivatives that are part of an aggregated exposure to be part of a hedged item is arbitrary. Many raised similar concerns in response to the Discussion Paper *Reducing Complexity in Reporting Financial Instruments* about the prohibition of designating derivatives as hedged items.

BC6.160　The IASB noted that an entity was sometimes economically required to enter into transactions that result in, for example, both interest rate risk and foreign currency risk. While those two exposures can be managed together at the same time and for the entire term, the IASB noted that entities often use different risk management strategies for the interest rate risk and foreign currency risk. For example, for 10-year fixed-rate debt denominated in a foreign currency an entity may hedge the foreign currency risk for the entire term of the debt instrument but require fixed-rate exposure in its functional currency only for the short to medium term (say, two years) and floating-rate exposure in its functional currency for the remaining term to maturity. At the end of each of the two-year intervals (ie on a two-year rolling basis) the entity fixes the next two years (if the interest level is such that the entity wants to fix interest rates). In such a situation an entity may enter into a 10-year fixed-to-floating cross-currency interest rate swap that swaps the fixed-rate foreign currency debt into a variable-rate functional currency exposure. This is then overlaid with a two-year interest rate swap that—on the basis of the functional currency—swaps variable-rate debt into fixed-rate debt. In effect, the fixed-rate foreign currency debt and the 10-year fixed-to-floating cross-currency interest rate swap in combination are viewed as a 10-year variable-rate debt functional currency exposure for risk management purposes.

BC6.161　Consequently, for the purpose of its 2010 Hedge Accounting Exposure Draft, the IASB concluded that the fact that an aggregated exposure is created by including an instrument that has the characteristics of a derivative should not, in itself, preclude the designation of that aggregated exposure as a hedged item.

BC6.162　Most respondents to the 2010 Hedge Accounting Exposure Draft supported the proposal to allow aggregated exposures to be designated as hedged items. Those respondents noted that the proposal better aligns hedge accounting with an entity's risk management by allowing hedge accounting to be used for common ways in which entities manage risks. In addition, those respondents noted that the proposal removes the arbitrary restrictions that were in IAS 39 and moves closer towards a principle-based requirement. The IASB therefore decided to retain the notion of an aggregated exposure as proposed in the 2010 Hedge Accounting Exposure Draft.

BC6.163　The main requests that respondents made to the IASB were:

　　(a)　to provide examples that would illustrate the accounting mechanics for aggregated exposures;

　　(b)　to clarify that accounting for aggregated exposures is not tantamount to 'synthetic accounting'; and

(c)   to clarify whether an entity would, in a first step (and as a precondition), have to achieve hedge accounting for the combination of the exposure and the derivative that together constitute the aggregated exposure so that, in a second step, the aggregated exposure itself can then be eligible as the hedged item in the other hedging relationship.

BC6.164   In response to the request for examples of the accounting mechanics for aggregated exposures, the IASB decided to provide illustrative examples to accompany IFRS 9. The IASB considered that numerical examples illustrating the mechanics of the accounting for aggregated exposures would, at the same time, address other questions raised in the feedback on the proposals, such as how hedge ineffectiveness is recognised and the type of the hedging relationships involved. Moreover, the IASB noted that those examples would also demonstrate that the proposed accounting for aggregated exposures is very different from 'synthetic accounting', which would reinforce the second clarification that respondents had requested.

BC6.165   The IASB thought that the confusion about 'synthetic accounting' arose from accounting debates in the past about whether two items should be treated for accounting purposes as if they were one single item. This would have had the consequence that a derivative could have assumed the accounting treatment for a non-derivative item (for example, accounting at amortised cost). The IASB noted that, in contrast, under the 2010 Hedge Accounting Exposure Draft's proposal for aggregated exposures the accounting for derivatives would always be at fair value and hedge accounting would be applied to them. Hence, the IASB emphasised that accounting for aggregated exposures does not allow 'synthetic accounting'.

BC6.166   The IASB noted that most respondents had correctly understood the 2010 Hedge Accounting Exposure Draft (ie that it does not allow 'synthetic accounting') but the IASB was still concerned because any misconception that aggregated exposures are tantamount to 'synthetic accounting' would result in a fundamental accounting error. Hence, the IASB decided to provide, in addition to illustrative examples, an explicit statement confirming that derivatives that form part of an aggregated exposure are always recognised as separate assets or liabilities and measured at fair value.

BC6.167   The IASB also discussed the request to clarify whether an entity would have to first (as a precondition) achieve hedge accounting for the combination of the underlying exposure and the derivative that constitute the aggregated exposure (the first level relationship) so that the aggregated exposure itself can be eligible as the hedged item in the other hedging relationship (the second level relationship). The IASB noted that the effect of not achieving hedge accounting for the first level relationship depended on the circumstances (in particular, the types of hedge used). In many circumstances, it would make the accounting for the aggregated exposure more complicated and the outcome inferior compared to achieving hedge accounting for the first level relationship. However, the IASB considered that achieving hedge accounting for the first level relationship was not required to comply with the general hedge accounting requirements for the second level relationship (ie the hedging relationship in which the aggregated exposure is the hedged item). Consequently, the IASB decided not to make achieving hedge accounting for the first level relationship a prerequisite for qualifying for hedge accounting for the second level relationship.

BC6.168   The IASB also clarified two other aspects that had been raised by some respondents:

(a)   that the notion of an aggregated exposure includes a highly probable forecast transaction of an aggregated exposure if that aggregated exposure, once it has occurred, is eligible as a hedged item; and

(b)   how to apply the general requirements of designating a derivative as the hedging instrument in the context of aggregated exposures. The IASB noted that the way in which a derivative is included in the hedged item that is an aggregated exposure must be consistent with the designation of that derivative as the hedging instrument at the level of the aggregated exposure (ie at the level of the first level relationship—if applicable, ie if hedge accounting is applied at that level). If the derivative is not designated as the hedging instrument at the level of the aggregated exposure, it must be designated in its entirety or as a proportion of it. The IASB noted that, consistent with the general requirements of the hedge accounting model, this also ensures that including a derivative in an aggregated exposure does not allow splitting a derivative by risk, by parts of its term or by cash flows.

Designation of hedged items

Designation of a risk component

BC6.169   IAS 39 distinguished the eligibility of risk components for designation as the hedged item by the type of item that includes the component:

(a)   for financial items, an entity could designate a risk component if that risk component was separately identifiable and reliably measurable; however,

(b)   for non-financial items, an entity could only designate foreign currency risk as a risk component.

BC6.170   Risk components of non-financial items, even when they are contractually specified, were not eligible risk components in accordance with IAS 39. Consequently, other than for foreign currency risk, a non-financial item was required to be designated as the hedged item for all risks. The rationale for including this restriction in IAS 39 was that permitting risk components (portions) of non-financial assets and non-financial liabilities to be designated as the hedged item for a risk other than foreign currency risk would compromise the principles of identification of the hedged item and effectiveness testing because the portion could be designated so that no ineffectiveness would ever arise.

BC6.171   The hedge accounting model in IAS 39 used the entire item as the default unit of account and then provided rules to govern what risk components of that entire item were available for separate designation in hedging relationships. This has resulted in the hedge accounting requirements being misaligned with many risk management strategies. The outcome was that the normal approach for risk management purposes was treated as the exception by the hedge accounting requirements.

BC6.172　Many of the comment letters received on the Discussion Paper *Reducing Complexity in Reporting Financial Instruments* criticised the prohibition on designating risk components for non-financial items. This was also the most common issue raised during the IASB's outreach activities.

BC6.173　The IASB noted that the conclusion in IAS 39, that permitting, as hedged items, risk components of non-financial assets and non-financial liabilities would compromise the principles of identification of the hedged item and effectiveness testing, was not appropriate in all circumstances. As part of its deliberations, the IASB considered whether risk components should be eligible for designation as hedged items when they are:

(a)　contractually specified; and

(b)　not contractually specified.

BC6.174　Contractually specified risk components determine a currency amount for a pricing element of a contract independently of the other pricing elements and, therefore, independently of the non-financial item as a whole. Consequently, these components are separately identifiable. The IASB also noted that many pricing formulas that use a reference to, for example, benchmark commodity prices are designed in that way to ensure that there is no gap or misalignment for that risk component compared with the benchmark price. Consequently, by reference to that risk component, the exposure can be economically fully hedged using a derivative with the benchmark as the underlying. This means that the hedge effectiveness assessment on a risk components basis accurately reflects the underlying economics of the transaction (ie that there is no or very little ineffectiveness).

BC6.175　However, in many situations risk components are not an explicit part of a fair value or a cash flow. Nonetheless, many hedging strategies involve the hedging of components even if they are not contractually specified. There are different reasons for using a component approach to hedging, including:

(a)　the entire item cannot be hedged because there is a lack of appropriate hedging instruments;

(b)　it is cheaper to hedge the single components individually than the entire item (for example, because an active market exists for the risk components, but not for the entire item); and

(c)　the entity makes a conscious decision to hedge only particular parts of the fair value or cash flow risk (for example, because one of the risk components is particularly volatile and it therefore justifies the costs of hedging it).

BC6.176　The IASB learned from its outreach activities that there are circumstances in which entities are able to identify and measure many risk components (not only foreign currency risk) of non-financial items with sufficient reliability. Appropriate risk components (if they are not contractually specified) can be determined only in the context of the particular market structure related to that risk. Consequently, the determination of appropriate risk components requires an evaluation of the relevant facts and circumstances (ie careful analysis and knowledge of the relevant markets). The IASB noted that as a result there is no 'bright line' to determine eligible risk components of non-financial items.

BC6.177 Consequently, in its 2010 Hedge Accounting Exposure Draft, the IASB proposed that risk components (both those that are and those that are not contractually specified) should be eligible for designation as hedged items as long as they are separately identifiable and reliably measurable. This proposal would align the eligibility of risk components of non-financial items with that of financial items in IAS 39.

BC6.178 Most respondents to the 2010 Hedge Accounting Exposure Draft supported the IASB's proposal and its rationale for allowing risk components (both those that are and those that are not contractually specified) to be eligible for designation as hedged items. Those respondents noted that the proposal on risk components was a key aspect of the new hedge accounting model because it would allow hedge accounting to reflect that, in commercial reality, hedging risk components was the norm and hedging items in their entirety was the exception.

BC6.179 Many respondents noted that IAS 39 was biased against hedges of non-financial items such as commodity hedges. They considered the distinction between financial and non-financial items for determining which risk components would be eligible hedged items as arbitrary and without conceptual justification. The main request by respondents was for additional guidance or clarifications.

BC6.180 Only a few respondents disagreed with the IASB's proposal on risk components. Those respondents believed that, in situations in which non-contractually specified risk components of non-financial items would be designated as hedged items, no hedge ineffectiveness would be recognised.

BC6.181 The IASB noted that the debate about risk components suffered from some common misunderstandings. In the IASB's opinion, the root cause of those misunderstandings is the large number of markets and circumstances in which hedging takes place. This results in an inevitable lack of familiarity with many markets. In the light of the arguments raised and to address some of the misunderstandings, the IASB focused its discussions on non-contractually specified risk components of non-financial items and, in particular, on:

(a) the effect of risk components; and

(b) hedge ineffectiveness when designating a risk component.

BC6.182 The IASB noted that some believe that designating a risk component as a hedged item should not be allowed if it could result in the value of that risk component moving in an opposite direction to the value of the entire item (ie its overall price). For example, if the hedged risk component increases in value this would offset the loss on the hedging instrument, while decreases in the value of other unhedged risk components remain unrecognised.

BC6.183 The IASB noted that this was not specific to non-contractually specified risk components of non-financial items, but that it applied to risk components in general. For example, consider an entity that holds a fixed-rate bond and the benchmark interest rate decreases but the bond's spread over the benchmark increases. If the entity hedges only the benchmark interest rate using a benchmark interest rate swap, the loss on the swap is offset by a fair value hedge adjustment for the benchmark interest rate component of the bond (even though the bond's fair value is lower than its carrying amount after the fair value hedge adjustment because of the increase in the spread).

BC6.184　The IASB also noted that designating a risk component was not tantamount to 'hiding losses' or avoiding their recognition by applying hedge accounting. Instead, it would help to mitigate accounting mismatches that would otherwise result from how an entity manages its risks. If hedge accounting is not applied, only the gain or loss from the change in the fair value of the financial instrument that hedges the risk is recognised in profit or loss, whereas the gain or loss on the entire item that gives rise to the risk remains fully unrecognised (until it is realised in a later period) so that any offset is obscured. If designation on a risk component basis is not available, that initially creates an issue of whether the hedge qualifies at all for hedge accounting and is inconsistent with the economic decision of hedging done on a components basis. Consequently, the accounting assessment would be completely disconnected from the decision making of an entity, which is driven by risk management purposes. The IASB also noted that this consequence would be amplified by the fact that the hedged component is not necessarily the main or largest component (for example, in the case of a power purchase agreement with a contractual pricing formula that includes indexations to fuel oil and inflation, only the inflation risk but not the fuel oil price risk is hedged).

BC6.185　The IASB noted that even if hedge accounting can be achieved between the hedging instrument and the item (which includes the hedged risk component) in its entirety, the accounting outcome would be more akin to a fair value option for the entire item than reflecting the effect of the economic hedge. However, because hedge accounting would be disconnected from what is economically hedged, there would also be ramifications for the hedge ratio that would have to be used for designating the hedging relationship. The hedge ratio that an entity actually uses (ie for decision making purposes driven by risk management) would be based on the economic relationship between the underlyings of the hedged risk component and the hedging instrument. This is the sensible basis for hedging decisions. However, for accounting purposes, an entity would be forced to compare changes in the value of the hedging instrument to those of the entire item. This means that, in order to improve the offset for the hedging relationship that is designated for accounting purposes, an entity would have to create a deliberate mismatch compared to the economic hedging relationship, which is tantamount to distorting the economic hedge ratio for accounting purposes. The IASB noted that distorting the hedge ratio also meant that prohibiting the designation of hedged items on a risk components basis would, ultimately, not necessarily result in the financial statements reflecting the change in the value of the unhedged risk component as a gain or loss for which there is no offset. Hence, prohibiting that kind of designation would not achieve transparency about the changes in the value of unhedged components by showing a gain or loss for which there is no offset.

BC6.186 The IASB also noted that designating risk components as hedged items would reflect the fact that risk management typically operates on a 'by risk' basis instead of on a 'by item' basis (which is the unit of account for financial reporting purposes). Hence, the use of risk components as hedged items would reflect what in commercial reality is the norm instead of requiring that all hedged items are 'deemed' to be hedged in their entirety (ie for all risks).

BC6.187 The IASB also considered the effect that risk components have on the recognition of hedge ineffectiveness. A few respondents believed that if a risk component was designated as the hedged item, it would result in no hedge ineffectiveness being recognised.

BC6.188 The IASB noted that the effect of designating a risk component as the hedged item was that it became the point of reference for determining offset (ie the fair value change on the hedging instrument would be compared to the change in value of the designated risk component instead of the entire item). This would make the comparison more focused because it would exclude the effect of changes in the value of risks that are not hedged, which would also make hedge ineffectiveness a better indicator of the success of the hedge. The IASB noted that the hedge accounting requirements would apply to the risk component in the same way as they apply to other hedged items that are not risk components. Consequently, even when a risk component was designated as the hedged item, hedge ineffectiveness could still arise and would have to be measured and recognised. For example:

(a) a floating-rate debt instrument is hedged against the variability of cash flows using an interest rate swap. The two instruments are indexed to the same benchmark interest rate but have different reset dates for the variable payments. Even though the hedged item is designated as the benchmark interest rate related variability in cash flows (ie as a risk component), the difference in reset dates causes hedge ineffectiveness. There is no market structure that would support identifying a 'reset date' risk component in the variable payments on the floating rate debt that would mirror the reset dates of the interest rate swap. In particular, the terms and conditions of the interest rate swap cannot be simply imputed by projecting terms and conditions of the interest rate swap onto floating-rate debt.

(b) a fixed-rate debt instrument is hedged against fair value interest rate risk using an interest rate swap. The two instruments have different day count methods for the fixed-rate payments. Even though the hedged item is designated as the benchmark interest rate related change in fair value (ie as a risk component), the difference in the day count methods causes hedge ineffectiveness. There is no market structure that would support identifying a 'day count' risk component in the payments on the debt that would mirror the day count method of the interest rate swap. In particular, the terms and conditions of the interest rate swap cannot be simply imputed by projecting terms and conditions of the interest rate swap onto the fixed-rate debt.

(c)   an entity purchases crude oil under a variable-price oil supply contract that is indexed to a light sweet crude oil benchmark. Because of the natural decline of the benchmark oil field the derivatives market for that benchmark has suffered a significant decline in liquidity. In response, the entity decides to use derivatives for a different benchmark for light sweet crude oil in a different geographical area because the derivatives market is much more liquid. The changes in the crude oil price for the more liquid benchmark and the less liquid benchmark are closely correlated but vary slightly. The variation between the two oil benchmark prices causes hedge ineffectiveness. There is no market structure that would support identifying the more liquid benchmark as a component in the variable payments under the oil supply contract. In particular, the terms and conditions of the derivatives indexed to the more liquid benchmark cannot simply be imputed by projecting terms and conditions of those derivatives onto the oil supply contract.

(d)   an entity is exposed to price risk from forecast purchases of jet fuel. The entity's jet fuel purchases are in North America and Europe. The entity determines that the relevant crude oil benchmark for jet fuel purchases at its North American locations is West Texas Intermediate (WTI) whereas it is Brent for jet fuel purchases at its European locations. Hence, the entity designates as the hedged item a WTI crude oil component for its jet fuel purchases in North America and a Brent crude oil component for its jet fuel purchases in Europe. Historically, WTI and Brent have been closely correlated and the entity's purchase volume in North America significantly exceeds its European purchase volume. Hence, the entity uses one type of hedge contract—indexed to WTI—for all its crude oil components. Changes in the price differential between WTI and Brent cause hedge ineffectiveness related to the forecast purchases of jet fuel in Europe. There is no market structure that would support identifying WTI as a component of Brent. In particular, the terms and conditions of the WTI futures cannot simply be imputed by projecting terms and conditions of those derivatives onto the forecast jet fuel purchases in Europe.

BC6.189   Consequently, the IASB noted that the designation of a risk component as a hedged item did not mean that no hedge ineffectiveness arises or that it would not be recognised.

BC6.190   The IASB noted that the concerns about hedge ineffectiveness not being recognised related particularly to non-contractually specified risk components of non-financial items. However, the IASB considered that this was not a financial versus non-financial item problem. Determining the hedge ineffectiveness, for example, for a fixed-rate debt instrument when designating the benchmark interest rate component as the hedged item is no more or less troublesome than doing so for commodity price risk. In both cases the appropriate designation of a risk component depends on an appropriate analysis of the market structure. The IASB noted that the derivative markets for commodity risk had evolved and had resulted in customs that helped improve the effectiveness of hedging. For example, very liquid commodity benchmarks have evolved, allowing for a market volume for derivatives that is far larger than the physical volume of the underlying commodity, thus facilitating benchmarks that can be widely used.

BC6.191 In the light of those considerations and the responses received on the 2010 Hedge Accounting Exposure Draft, the IASB decided to retain the notion of risk components as eligible hedged items. Because of the large variety of markets and circumstances in which hedging takes place, the IASB considered that, in order to avoid arbitrary discrimination against some markets, risks or geographies, there was no alternative to using a criteria-based approach to identifying eligible risk components. Consequently, the IASB decided that for risk components (of both financial and non-financial items) to qualify as eligible hedged items, they must be separately identifiable and reliably measureable. In response to requests from respondents, the IASB also decided to expand the examples of how to determine eligible risk components, including illustrations of the role of the market structure.

BC6.192 The IASB also discussed the proposal in the 2010 Hedge Accounting Exposure Draft to prohibit the designation of non-contractually specified inflation risk components of financial instruments. That prohibition was carried over from IAS 39. The IASB noted that an outright ban meant that the general criteria for the eligibility of risk components could not be applied and, as a result, would leave no room for the possibility that in some situations there might be circumstances that could support identifying a risk component for inflation risk. On the other hand, the IASB was concerned that the removal of the restriction would encourage the use of inflation risk components for hedge accounting when it was not necessarily appropriate to do so. This would be the case when a risk component, instead of being supported by the market structure and independently determined for the hedged item, would, for example, be determined by simply projecting the terms and conditions of the inflation derivative that was actually used as the hedge onto the hedged item. In the light of this trade-off, the IASB also considered that financial markets continuously evolve and that the requirements should be capable of addressing changes in the market over time.

BC6.193 On balance, the IASB decided to remove the prohibition. However, it was concerned that its decision could be misunderstood as simply 'rubber stamping' the use of inflation risk components for hedge accounting without proper application of the criteria for designating risk components. The IASB therefore agreed to include a caution in the final requirements that, in order to determine whether inflation risk is an eligible risk component, a careful analysis of the facts and circumstances is required so that the criteria for designating risk components are properly applied. Consequently, the IASB decided to add a rebuttable presumption related to non-contractually specified inflation risk components of financial instruments.

Designation of 'one-sided' risk components

BC6.194 IAS 39 permitted an entity to designate changes in the cash flows or fair value of a hedged item above or below a specified price or other variable (a 'one-sided' risk). So, an entity might hedge an exposure to a specific type of risk of a financial instrument (for example, interest rates) above a pre-determined level (for example, above 5 per cent) using a purchased option (for example, an interest rate cap). In this situation an entity hedged some parts of a specific type of risk (ie interest exposure above 5 per cent).

BC6.195 Furthermore, the IASB noted that hedging one-sided risk exposures is a common risk management activity. The IASB also noted that the main issue that relates to the hedging of one-sided risk is the use of options as hedging instruments. Consequently, the IASB decided to permit the designation of one-sided risk components as hedged items, as was the case in IAS 39 for some risk components. However, the IASB decided to change the accounting for the time value of options (see paragraphs BC6.386–BC6.413).

BC6.196 The IASB retained its original decisions about the eligibility of one-sided risk components as hedged items when redeliberating its 2010 Hedge Accounting Exposure Draft.

Components of a nominal amount—designation of a component that is a proportion

BC6.197 The IASB noted that components that form some quantifiable nominal part of the total cash flows of the instrument are typically separately identifiable. For example, a proportion, such as 50 per cent, of the contractual cash flows of a loan includes all the characteristics of that loan. In other words, changes in the value and cash flows for the 50 per cent component are half of those for the entire instrument.

BC6.198 The IASB noted that a proportion of an item forms the basis of many different risk management strategies and are commonly hedged in practice (often in combination with risk components). The IASB concluded that if the effectiveness of the hedging relationship can be measured, an entity should be permitted to designate a proportion of an item as a hedged item (as previously permitted by IAS 39).

BC6.199 The IASB retained its original decisions when redeliberating its 2010 Hedge Accounting Exposure Draft.

Components of a nominal amount—designation of a layer component

BC6.200 IAS 39 required an entity to identify and document anticipated (ie forecast) transactions that are designated as hedged items with sufficient specificity so that when the transaction occurs, it is clear whether the transaction is or is not the hedged transaction. As a result, IAS 39 permitted forecast transactions to be identified as a 'layer' component of a nominal amount, for example, the first 100 barrels of the total oil purchases for a specific month (ie a layer of the total oil purchase volume). Such a designation accommodates the fact that there is some uncertainty surrounding the hedged item related to the amount or timing. This uncertainty does not affect the hedging relationship to the extent that the hedged volume occurs (irrespective of which particular individual items make up that volume).

BC6.201 The IASB considered whether similar considerations should also apply to a hedge of an existing transaction or item in some situations. For example, a firm commitment or a loan might also involve some uncertainty because:

(a) a contract might be cancelled for breach of contract (ie non-performance); or

(b) a contract with an early termination option (for repayment at fair value) might be terminated before maturity.

BC6.202 Because there is uncertainty for both anticipated transactions and existing transactions and items, the IASB decided not to distinguish between such transactions and items for the purposes of designating a layer component.

BC6.203 The IASB noted that designating as the hedged item a component that is a proportion of an item can give rise to a different accounting outcome when compared with designating a layer component. If the designation of those components is not aligned with the risk management strategy of the entity, it might result in profit or loss providing confusing or less useful information to users of financial statements.

BC6.204 In the IASB's view there might be circumstances when it is appropriate to designate a layer component as a hedged item. Consequently, in its 2010 Hedge Accounting Exposure Draft the IASB proposed to permit the designation of a layer component as the hedged item (for anticipated and existing transactions). The IASB also proposed that a layer component of a contract that includes a prepayment option should not be eligible as a hedged item in a fair value hedge if the option's fair value is affected by changes in the hedged risk. The IASB noted that if the prepayment option's fair value changed in response to the hedged risk a layer approach would be tantamount to identifying a risk component that was not separately identifiable (because the change in the value of the prepayment option owing to the hedged risk would not be part of how the hedge effectiveness would be measured).

BC6.205 Most respondents to the 2010 Hedge Accounting Exposure Draft agreed with the proposed change for fair value hedges, which would allow an entity to designate a layer component from a defined nominal amount. They agreed that such layers would allow entities to better reflect what risk they actually hedge.

BC6.206 However, many respondents disagreed with the IASB's proposal to prohibit, in any circumstances, the designation of a layer component in a fair value hedge for all contracts that include any prepayment option whose fair value is affected by changes in the hedged risk. Those respondents' main objection was that the proposal was inconsistent with common risk management strategies and that the fair value changes of a prepayment option were irrelevant in the context of a bottom layer.

BC6.207   In the light of the comments received, the IASB discussed:

(a)   whether the prohibition to designate a layer component as the hedged item in a fair value hedge should relate to an entire item or contract containing a prepayment option or whether it should relate only to those situations in which the designated layer contains a prepayment option;

(b)   whether a layer component can be designated as the hedged item in a fair value hedge if it includes the effect of a related prepayment option; and

(c)   whether the requirement should differentiate between written and purchased prepayment options, thereby allowing a layer component to be designated for items with a purchased option, ie if the entity is the option holder (for example, a debtor's call option included in prepayable debt).

BC6.208   The IASB discussed situations in which a contract is prepayable for only a part of its entire amount, which means that the remainder is not prepayable and hence does not include a prepayment option. For example, a loan with a principal amount of CU100 and a maturity of five years that allows the debtor to repay (at par) up to CU10 at the end of each year would mean that only CU40 is prepayable (at different points in time), whereas CU60 is non-prepayable but has a five-year fixed term. Because the CU60 is fixed-term debt that is not affected by prepayments, its fair value does not include the effect of a prepayment option. Consequently, the changes in the fair value related to the CU60 are unrelated to the fair value changes of the prepayment option for other amounts. This means that if the CU60 were designated as a layer component, the hedge ineffectiveness would appropriately exclude the change in the fair value of the prepayment option. The IASB considered that this would be consistent with its rationale for proposing to prohibit a layer component of an (entire) item or contract that contains a prepayment option (see paragraph BC6.204) to be designated. However, the IASB noted that the changes in fair value of the amounts that are prepayable (ie the CU40 at inception, CU30 after one year, CU20 after two years and CU10 after three years) include a prepayment option and the designation of a layer for these amounts would therefore contradict the IASB's rationale (see paragraph BC6.204). The IASB noted that the layer of CU60 in this example should not be confused with a bottom layer of CU60 that is expected to remain at maturity from a total amount of CU100 that is prepayable in its entirety. The difference is that the expected remaining amount of a larger prepayable amount is the expected eventual outcome of a variable contractual maturity, whereas the CU60 in this example is the definite outcome of a fixed contractual maturity.

BC6.209   Consequently, the IASB decided to:

(a)   confirm the proposals in the 2010 Hedge Accounting Exposure Draft to allow a layer-based designation of a hedged item (when the item does not include a prepayment option whose fair value is affected by changes in the hedged risk); and

(b)   to allow a layer-based designation for those amounts that are not prepayable at the time of designation of a partially prepayable item.

BC6.210   The IASB also discussed whether a layer component should be available for designation as the hedged item in a fair value hedge if it includes the effect of a related prepayment option when determining the change in fair value of the hedged item.

BC6.211   Including the change in fair value of the prepayment option that affects a layer when determining hedge ineffectiveness has the following consequences:

(a)   the designated hedged item would include the entire effect of changes in the hedged risk on the fair value of the layer, ie including those resulting from the prepayment option; and

(b)   if the layer was hedged with a hedging instrument (or a combination of instruments that are designated jointly) that does not have option features that mirror the layer's prepayment option, hedge ineffectiveness would arise.

BC6.212   The IASB noted that a designation of a layer as the hedged item, if it included the effects of a related prepayment option when determining the change in fair value of the hedged item, would not conflict with its rationale for proposing the requirements related to the implication of prepayment options for layer designations (see paragraph BC6.204).

BC6.213   Consequently, the IASB decided that designating a layer as the hedged item should be allowed if it includes the effect of a related prepayment option when determining the change in fair value of the hedged item.

BC6.214   The IASB also considered whether it should differentiate between written and purchased prepayment options for the purpose of determining the eligibility of a layer-based designation of a hedged item in a fair value hedge. Some respondents had argued that if the entity was the option holder, it would control the exercise of the option and could therefore demonstrate that the option was not affected by the hedged risk.

BC6.215   However, the IASB noted that the hedged risk affects the fair value of a prepayment option irrespective of whether the particular option holder actually exercises it at that time or intends to actually exercise it in the future. The fair value of the option captures the possible outcomes and hence the risk that an amount that would be in the money might be repaid at a different amount than at fair value before taking the prepayment option into account (for example, at par). Consequently, the IASB noted that whether a prepayment option is a purchased or a written option does not affect the change in the option's absolute fair value but instead determines whether it is either a gain or a loss from the entity's perspective. In other words, the IASB considered that the aspect of who controls the exercise of the option relates to whether any intrinsic value would be realised (but not whether it exists).

BC6.216   Consequently, the IASB decided not to differentiate between written and purchased prepayment options for the purpose of the eligibility of a layer-based designation of hedged items.

Relationship between components and the total cash flows of an item

BC6.217   IAS 39 allowed an entity to designate the LIBOR component of an interest-bearing asset or liability provided that the instrument has a zero or positive spread over LIBOR. When an entity has an interest-bearing debt instrument with an interest rate that is below LIBOR (or linked to a reference rate that is demonstrably below LIBOR), it would not be able to designate a hedging relationship based on a LIBOR risk component that assumes LIBOR cash flows that would exceed the actual cash flows on that debt instrument. However, for an asset or liability with a negative spread to LIBOR, an entity could still achieve hedge accounting by designating all of the cash flows of the hedged item for LIBOR interest rate risk (which is different from designating a LIBOR component that assumes cash flows exceeding those of the hedged item).

BC6.218   When an entity (particularly a bank) has access to sub-LIBOR funding (bearing a variable-interest coupon at LIBOR minus a spread or an equivalent fixed-rate coupon), the negative spread represents a positive margin for the borrower. This is because banks on average pay LIBOR for their funding in the interbank market. Another example of when this occurs is when the reference rate is highly correlated with LIBOR and the negative spreads arise because of the better credit risk of the contributors to the reference index compared with LIBOR. When entering into hedging relationships, an entity cannot obtain (at a reasonable cost) a standardised hedging instrument for all transactions that are priced sub-LIBOR. Consequently, such an entity uses hedging instruments that have LIBOR as their underlying.

BC6.219   In the deliberations leading to the 2010 Hedge Accounting Exposure Draft, the IASB noted that it had received feedback on the sub-LIBOR issue from its outreach activities that accompanied those deliberations. That feedback showed that some participants believed that designating a risk component that assumes cash flows that would exceed the actual cash flows of the financial instrument reflected risk management in situations in which the hedged item has a negative spread to the benchmark rate. They believed that it should be possible to hedge the LIBOR risk as a benchmark component and treat the spread as a negative residual component. They argued that they were hedging their exposure to the variability of cash flows attributable to LIBOR (or a correlated index) using LIBOR swaps.

BC6.220   In the deliberations leading to the 2010 Hedge Accounting Exposure Draft, the IASB noted that, for risk management purposes, an entity normally does not try to hedge the effective interest rate of the financial instrument but instead the change in the variability of the cash flows attributable to LIBOR. By doing this, such an entity ensures that exposure to benchmark interest rate risk is managed and that the profit margin of the hedged items (ie the spread relative to the benchmark) is protected against LIBOR changes, provided that LIBOR is not below the absolute value of the negative spread. This risk management strategy provides offsetting changes related to the LIBOR-related interest rate risk in a similar way to situations in which the spread above LIBOR is zero or positive. However, if LIBOR falls below the absolute value of that negative spread it would result in 'negative' interest, or interest that is inconsistent with the movement of market interest rates (similar to a 'reverse floater'). The IASB noted that these outcomes are inconsistent with the economic phenomenon to which they relate.

BC6.221　To avoid those outcomes, the IASB proposed retaining the restriction in IAS 39 for the designation of risk components when the designated component would exceed the total cash flows of the hedged item. However, the IASB emphasised that hedge accounting would still be available on the basis of designating all the cash flows of an item for a particular risk, ie a risk component for the actual cash flows of the item (see paragraph BC6.217).

BC6.222　The IASB received mixed views on its proposal to retain this restriction. Some agreed with the restriction and the IASB's rationale for retaining it. Others were concerned that the restriction was inconsistent with common risk management practices. Those who disagreed believed that it should be possible to designate as the hedged item a benchmark risk component that is equivalent to the entire LIBOR and to treat the spread between the entire LIBOR and the contractual rate as a negative residual component. Their view reflects the fact that they are hedging their exposure to the variability of cash flows attributable to LIBOR (or a correlated index) using LIBOR swaps (see paragraph BC6.226 for an example). In their view, the IASB's proposal would not allow them to properly reflect the hedging relationship, and would force them to recognise hedge ineffectiveness that, in their view, would not reflect their risk management strategy.

BC6.223　In response to the concerns raised, the IASB considered whether it should allow the designation of risk components on a benchmark risk basis that assumes cash flows exceeding the total actual cash flows of the hedged item.

BC6.224　As part of its redeliberations, the IASB discussed how contractual terms and conditions that determine whether an instrument has a zero interest rate floor or 'negative' interest (ie no floor) might affect the designation of a full LIBOR component of a sub-LIBOR instrument.

BC6.225　The IASB discussed an example of an entity that has a liability that pays a fixed rate and grants a loan at a floating rate with both instruments being priced at sub-LIBOR interest rates. The entity enters into a LIBOR-based interest rate swap with the aim of locking in the margin that it will earn on the combined position. If the entity wants to designate the hedged item on the basis of the interest rate risk that results from its financial asset, this would be an example of a cash flow hedge of variable-rate interest cash flows from a sub-LIBOR asset.

BC6.226　The IASB noted that if the floating-rate asset had a zero interest rate floor and LIBOR decreased below the absolute value of the negative spread on the asset, the return on the asset (after taking into account the effect of the swap) would increase as a result of the interest rate swap not having a floor. This means that if designated on a full LIBOR risk component basis, the hedging relationship would have outcomes that would be inconsistent with the notion of a locked margin. In this example, the margin could become variable instead of being locked. The IASB was of the view that, in the context of hedge accounting, this would give rise to hedge ineffectiveness that must be recognised in profit or loss. The IASB noted that this hedge ineffectiveness resulted from the absence of offsetting cash flows and hence represented a genuine economic mismatch between changes in cash flows on the floating-rate asset and the swap. Hence, if a full LIBOR component was imputed for interest bearing instruments that are priced sub-LIBOR, it would inappropriately defer hedge ineffectiveness in other comprehensive income. In the IASB's view this would be tantamount to accrual accounting for the interest rate swap.

BC6.227 In contrast, the IASB noted that if the floating-rate asset had no floor, the sub-LIBOR instrument included in the hedging relationship would still have changes in their cash flows that would move with LIBOR even if LIBOR was below the absolute value of the spread. Consequently, the variability in cash flows of the hedging instrument that locks the margin would be offset by the variability of the cash flows of the sub-LIBOR instrument irrespective of the LIBOR level. In other words, the LIBOR-related cash flow variability when the asset had no floor would be equivalent to that of a full LIBOR component and therefore the proposed requirement would not prohibit designating the hedged item accordingly (ie as changes in cash flows of a full LIBOR risk component).

BC6.228 As a result, the IASB decided to confirm the proposal in the 2010 Hedge Accounting Exposure Draft that if a component of the cash flows of a financial or non-financial item is designated as the hedged item, that component must be less than or equal to the total cash flows of the entire item.

BC6.229 Furthermore, the IASB noted that the examples carried over from IAS 39 to the 2010 Hedge Accounting Exposure Draft only included financial items because under IAS 39 the issue could only apply to that type of item. But, given that under the new hedge accounting model this issue also applies to non-financial items that are traded below their respective benchmark price, the IASB decided to add an example of a hedge of commodity price risk in a situation in which the commodity is priced at a discount to the benchmark commodity price.

Qualifying criteria for hedge accounting

Effectiveness assessment

BC6.230 To qualify for hedge accounting in accordance with IAS 39, a hedge had to be highly effective, both prospectively and retrospectively. Consequently, an entity had to perform two effectiveness assessments for each hedging relationship. The prospective assessment supported the expectation that the hedging relationship would be effective in the future. The retrospective assessment determined that the hedging relationship had been effective in the reporting period. All retrospective assessments were required to be performed using quantitative methods. However, IAS 39 did not specify a particular method for testing hedge effectiveness.

BC6.231 The term 'highly effective' referred to the degree to which the hedging relationship achieved offsetting between changes in the fair value or cash flows of the hedging instrument and changes in the fair value or cash flows of the hedged item attributable to the hedged risk during the hedge period. In accordance with IAS 39, a hedge was regarded as highly effective if the offset was within the range of 80–125 per cent (often colloquially referred to as a 'bright line test').

BC6.232   In the deliberations leading to the 2010 Hedge Accounting Exposure Draft, the IASB noted that it had received feedback on the hedge effectiveness assessment under IAS 39 from its outreach activities that accompanied those deliberations. The feedback showed that:

(a)   many participants found that the hedge effectiveness assessment in IAS 39 was arbitrary, onerous and difficult to apply;

(b)   as a result, there was often little or no link between hedge accounting and the risk management strategy; and

(c)   because hedge accounting was not achieved if the hedge effectiveness was outside the 80–125 per cent range, it made hedge accounting difficult to understand in the context of the risk management strategy of the entity.

BC6.233   Consequently, in its 2010 Hedge Accounting Exposure Draft the IASB proposed a more principle-based hedge effectiveness assessment. The IASB proposed that a hedging relationship meets the hedge effectiveness requirements if it:

(a)   meets the objective of the hedge effectiveness assessment (ie that the hedging relationship will produce an unbiased result and minimise expected hedge ineffectiveness); and

(b)   is expected to achieve other than accidental offsetting.

BC6.234   Most respondents to the 2010 Hedge Accounting Exposure Draft supported the removal of the 80–125 per cent quantitative test. Those respondents also supported the IASB in avoiding the use of bright lines in hedge accounting generally and the move towards a more principle-based effectiveness assessment.

BC6.235   Only a few respondents disagreed with the proposal, largely because they believed that the quantitative threshold in IAS 39 was appropriate. They also believed that an approach that was completely principle-based would generate operational difficulties and would have the potential to inappropriately extend the application of hedge accounting.

BC6.236   The sections below elaborate on the IASB's considerations.

The objective of the hedge effectiveness assessment

BC6.237   Traditionally, accounting standard-setters have set high thresholds for hedging relationships to qualify for hedge accounting. The IASB noted that this resulted in hedge accounting that was considered by some as arbitrary and onerous. Furthermore, the arbitrary 'bright line' of 80–125 per cent resulted in a disconnect between hedge accounting and risk management. Consequently, it made it difficult to explain the results of hedge accounting to users of financial statements. To address those concerns, the IASB decided that it would propose an objective-based model for testing hedge effectiveness instead of the 80–125 per cent 'bright line test' in IAS 39.

BC6.238   During its deliberations, the IASB initially considered an objective-based assessment to determine which hedging relationships would qualify for hedge accounting. The IASB's intention was that the assessment should not be based on a particular level of hedge effectiveness. The IASB decided that, in order to avoid the arbitrary outcomes of the assessment under IAS 39, it had to remove, instead of just move, the bright line. The IASB held the view that the objective of the hedge effectiveness assessment should reflect the fact that hedge accounting was based on the notion of offset.

BC6.239 In accordance with the approach that the IASB initially considered, the effectiveness assessment would have aimed only to identify accidental offsetting and prevent hedge accounting in those situations. This assessment would have been based on an analysis of the possible behaviour of the hedging relationship during its term to ascertain whether it could be expected to meet the risk management objective. The IASB believed that the proposed approach would therefore have strengthened the relationship between hedge accounting and risk management practice.

BC6.240 However, the IASB was concerned that this approach might not be rigorous enough. This was because, without clear guidance, an entity might designate hedging relationships that would not be appropriate because they would give rise to systematic hedge ineffectiveness that could be avoided by a more appropriate designation of the hedging relationship and hence be biased. The IASB noted that the bright line of 80–125 per cent in IAS 39 created a trade-off when an entity chose a hedge ratio that would have a biased result, because that result came at the expense of higher ineffectiveness and hence increased the risk of falling outside that range. However, the IASB noted that the 80–125 per cent range would be eliminated by its proposals and therefore decided to extend its initial objective of the effectiveness assessment so that it also included the hedge ratio. Consequently, in its 2010 Hedge Accounting Exposure Draft, the IASB proposed that the objective of assessing the effectiveness of a hedging relationship was that the entity designated the hedging relationship so that it gave an unbiased result and minimised expected ineffectiveness.

BC6.241 The IASB noted that many types of hedging relationships inevitably involve some ineffectiveness that cannot be eliminated. For example, ineffectiveness could arise because of differences in the underlyings or other differences between the hedging instrument and the hedged item that the entity accepts in order to achieve a cost-effective hedging relationship. The IASB considered that when an entity establishes a hedging relationship there should be no expectation that changes in the value of the hedging instrument will systematically either exceed or be less than the change in value of the hedged item. As a result, the IASB proposed in its 2010 Hedge Accounting Exposure Draft that hedging relationships should not be established (for accounting purposes) in such a way that they include a deliberate mismatch in the weightings of the hedged item and of the hedging instrument.

BC6.242 However, many respondents to the 2010 Hedge Accounting Exposure Draft asked the IASB to provide further guidance on the objective-based effectiveness assessment, particularly on the notions of 'unbiased result' and 'minimise expected hedge ineffectiveness'. Those respondents were concerned that the requirements, as drafted in the 2010 Hedge Accounting Exposure Draft, could be interpreted to be more restrictive and onerous than the bright line effectiveness test in IAS 39 and would be inconsistent with risk management practice. More specifically, those respondents were concerned that the objective of the hedge effectiveness assessment as drafted in the 2010 Hedge Accounting Exposure Draft could be interpreted as requiring entities to set up a hedging relationship that was 'perfectly effective'. They were concerned that this would result in an effectiveness assessment that would be based on a bright line of 100 per cent effectiveness, and that such an approach:

(a) would not take into account that, in many situations, entities do not use a hedging instrument that would make the hedging relationship 'perfectly effective'. They noted that entities use hedging instruments that do not achieve perfect hedge effectiveness because the 'perfect' hedging instrument is:

(i) not available; or

(ii) not cost-effective as a hedge (compared to a standardised instrument that is cheaper and/or more liquid, but does not provide the perfect fit).

(b) could be interpreted as a mathematical optimisation exercise. In other words, they were concerned that it would require entities to search for the perfect hedging relationship at inception (and on a continuous basis), because if they did not, the results could be considered to be biased and hedge ineffectiveness would probably not be 'minimised'.

BC6.243 In the light of the concerns about the use of hedging instruments that are not 'perfectly effective', the IASB noted that the appropriate hedge ratio was primarily a risk management decision instead of an accounting decision. When determining the appropriate hedge ratio, risk management would take into consideration, among other things, the following factors:

(a) the availability of hedging instruments and the underlyings of those hedging instruments (and, as a consequence, the level of the risk of differences in value changes involved between the hedged item and the hedging instrument);

(b) the tolerance levels in relation to expected sources of hedge ineffectiveness (which determine when the hedging relationship is adjusted for risk management purposes); and

(c) the costs of hedging (including the costs of adjusting an existing hedging relationship).

BC6.244 The IASB's intention behind its proposal in the 2010 Hedge Accounting Exposure Draft was that an entity would choose the actual hedge basing its decision on commercial considerations, designate it as the hedging instrument and use it as a starting point to determine the hedge ratio that would comply with the proposed requirements. In other words, the IASB did not intend that an entity would have to consider the hedge effectiveness and related hedge ratio that could have been achieved with a different hedging instrument that might have been a better fit for the hedged risk if it did not enter into that hedging instrument.

BC6.245 The IASB also reconsidered the proposed objective of the hedge effectiveness assessment in the light of the concerns that it might result in a mathematical optimisation exercise. In particular, the IASB considered the effect of its proposal in situations in which a derivative is designated as a hedging instrument only after its inception so that it is already in or out of the money at the time of its designation (often colloquially referred to as a 'late hedge'). The IASB considered whether the hedge ratio would have to be adjusted to take into account the (non-zero) fair value of the derivative at the time of its designation. This is because the fair value of the hedging instrument at the time of its designation is a present value. Over the remaining life of the hedging instrument this present value will accrete to the undiscounted amount (the 'unwinding of the discount'). The IASB noted that there is no offsetting fair value change in the hedged item for this effect (unless the hedged item was also in or out of the money in an equal but opposite way). Consequently, in situations in which the derivative is designated as the hedging instrument after its inception, an entity would expect that the changes in the value of the hedging instrument will systematically either exceed or be less than the changes in the value of the hedged item (ie the hedge ratio would not be 'unbiased'). To meet the proposed objective of the hedge effectiveness assessment an entity would need to explore whether it could adjust the hedge ratio to avoid the systematic difference between the value changes of the hedging instrument and the hedged item over the hedging period. However, to determine the ratio that would avoid that systematic difference, an entity would need to know what the actual price or rate of the underlying will be at the end of the hedging relationship. Hence, the IASB noted that the proposed objective of the hedge effectiveness assessment could be interpreted to the effect that, in the (quite common) situations in which an entity has a 'late hedge', the proposed hedge effectiveness requirements would not be met. This is because the entity would not be able to identify a hedge ratio for the designation of the hedging relationship that would not involve an expectation that the changes in value of the hedging instrument will systematically either exceed or be less than the changes in the value of the hedged item. The IASB did not intend this outcome when it developed its proposals in its 2010 Hedge Accounting Exposure Draft.

BC6.246 The IASB noted that the feedback about the requirement that the hedging relationship should minimise hedge ineffectiveness suggested that identifying a 'minimum' would involve considerable effort in all situations in which the terms of the hedging instrument and the hedged item are not fully matched. Hence, the requirement to minimise hedge ineffectiveness would bring back many of the operational problems of the hedge effectiveness assessment in IAS 39. Furthermore, regardless of the effort involved, it would be difficult to demonstrate that the 'minimum' had been identified.

BC6.247 The IASB noted that when it developed its 2010 Hedge Accounting Exposure Draft, it included the notions of 'unbiased' and 'minimise expected hedge ineffectiveness' to ensure that:

(a)   entities would not deliberately create a difference between the quantity actually hedged and the quantity designated as the hedged item in order to achieve a particular accounting outcome; and

(b)   an entity would not inappropriately designate a hedging relationship such that it would give rise to systematic hedge ineffectiveness, which could be avoided by a more appropriate designation.

The IASB noted that both aspects could result in undermining the 'lower of' test for cash flow hedges or achieving fair value hedge adjustments on a greater quantity of the hedged item than an entity actually hedged (ie fair value accounting would be disproportionately expanded compared to the quantity actually hedged).

BC6.248   Taking into account the responses to the 2010 Hedge Accounting Exposure Draft, the IASB decided to remove the terms 'unbiased' (ie no expectation that changes in the value of the hedging instrument will systematically either exceed or be less than the changes in the value of the hedged item such that they would produce a biased result) and 'minimising expected hedge ineffectiveness'. Instead, the IASB decided to state, more directly, that the entity's designation of the hedging relationship shall use a hedge ratio based on:

(a)   the quantity of the hedged item that it actually hedges; and

(b)   the quantity of the hedging instrument that it actually uses to hedge that quantity of hedged item.

BC6.249   The IASB noted that this approach has the following advantages:

(a)   the use of the hedge ratio resulting from the requirement in this Standard provides information about the hedge ineffectiveness in situations in which an entity uses a hedging instrument that does not provide the best fit (for example, because of cost-efficiency considerations). The IASB noted that the hedge ratio determined for risk management purposes has the effect of showing the characteristics of the hedging relationship and the entity's expectations about hedge ineffectiveness. This includes hedge ineffectiveness that results from using a hedging instrument that does not provide the best fit.

(b)   it also aligns hedge accounting with risk management and hence is consistent with the overall objective of the new hedge accounting model.

(c)   it addresses the requests from respondents to the 2010 Hedge Accounting Exposure Draft for clarification that the relevant hedging instrument to be considered in the hedge effectiveness assessment is the actual hedging instrument the entity decided to use.

(d)   it retains the notion proposed in the 2010 Hedge Accounting Exposure Draft that the hedge ratio is not a free choice for accounting purposes as it was in IAS 39 (subject to passing the 80–125 per cent bright line test).

BC6.250   The IASB noted that the only situation open to abuse is if the entity purposefully (for risk management purposes) used a hedge ratio that would be considered 'inappropriately loose' from an accounting perspective, for example:

(a)   if an entity uses an excess quantity of the hedging instrument it would have more costs and risks because of having more hedging instruments than needed to mitigate the risks resulting from the hedged items. However, from an accounting perspective, this would not lead to any advantage because it would create fair value changes for the hedging instrument that affect profit or loss for both fair value hedges and cash flow hedges. The result of an entity using an excess quantity of the hedging instrument would therefore solely be the presentation of fair value changes within profit or loss as hedge ineffectiveness instead of other or trading gains or losses. This would increase the hedge ineffectiveness in an entity's financial statements while having no impact on overall profit or loss.

(b)   if an entity uses a quantity of the hedging instrument that is too small it would leave, economically, a gap in its hedging. From an accounting perspective, this might create an advantage for fair value hedges if an entity wanted to achieve fair value hedge adjustments on a greater quantity of 'hedged items' than it would achieve when using an appropriate hedge ratio. In addition, for cash flow hedges, an entity could abuse the lower of test because the hedge ineffectiveness arising from the larger change in fair value on the hedged item compared to that on the hedging instrument would not be recognised. Consequently, even though using a 'deficit' quantity of the hedging instrument would not be economically advantageous, from an accounting perspective it might have the desired outcome for an entity.

BC6.251   The IASB noted that the potential for abuse, as illustrated above, was implicitly addressed in IAS 39 by the 80–125 per cent bright line of the retrospective hedge effectiveness assessment. Given its decision to remove that bright line (see paragraph BC6.237), the IASB decided to explicitly address this potential for abuse. As a consequence, this Standard requires that, for the purpose of hedge accounting, an entity shall not designate a hedging relationship in a manner that reflects an imbalance between the weightings of the hedged item and the hedging instrument that would create hedge ineffectiveness (irrespective of whether recognised or not) that could result in an accounting outcome that would be inconsistent with the purpose of hedge accounting.

Other than accidental offsetting

BC6.252   IAS 39 was based on a purely accounting-driven percentage-based bright line test (the 80–125 per cent range). This disconnected accounting from risk management (see paragraph BC6.237). Consequently, the IASB proposed replacing the bright line test with a notion that aims to reflect the way entities look at the design and monitoring of hedging relationships from a risk management perspective. Inherent in this was the notion of 'other than accidental offsetting'. This linked the risk management perspective with the hedge accounting model's general notion of offset between gains and losses on hedging instruments and hedged items. The IASB also considered that this link reflected the intention that the effectiveness assessment should not be based on a particular level of effectiveness (hence avoiding a new bright line).

BC6.253   Many respondents to the 2010 Hedge Accounting Exposure Draft asked the IASB to provide further guidance on the notion of 'other than accidental offsetting'. Many also suggested that the IASB revise the proposed guidance by introducing a direct reference to the aspect of an economic relationship between the hedged item and the hedging instrument that was included in the application guidance proposed in the 2010 Hedge Accounting Exposure Draft.

BC6.254   The IASB noted that qualifying criteria that use terminology such as 'other than accidental offsetting' can be abstract. The feedback suggested that this makes the relevant aspects or elements of the hedge effectiveness assessment more difficult to understand. The IASB considered that it could address the respondents' request and reduce the abstractness of this proposal by avoiding the use of an 'umbrella term' and instead making explicit all aspects that the requirement comprises. This would provide greater clarity and facilitate a better understanding of what aspects are relevant when assessing hedge effectiveness.

BC6.255   Consequently, the IASB decided to replace the term 'other than accidental offsetting' with requirements that better conveyed its original notion:

(a)   an economic relationship between the hedged item and the hedging instrument, which gives rise to offset, must exist at inception and during the life of the hedging relationship; and

(b)   the effect of credit risk does not dominate the value changes that result from that economic relationship.

A 'reasonably effective' threshold

BC6.256   A few respondents suggested that the IASB could consider using a 'qualitative threshold' instead of a principle-based hedge effectiveness assessment. Those respondents believed that, in order to meet the hedge effectiveness criteria, a hedging relationship should be required to be 'reasonably effective' in achieving offsetting changes in the fair value of the hedged item and in the fair value of the hedging instrument.

BC6.257   The IASB noted that a 'reasonably effective' criterion would retain the threshold design of the effectiveness assessment that was used in IAS 39. The IASB considered that moving, instead of removing, the threshold would not address the root cause of the problem (see paragraph BC6.237). The suggested approach would instead only change the level of the threshold. The IASB considered that, even though the threshold would be of a qualitative nature, it would still create a danger of reverting back to a quantitative measure (such as the percentage range of IAS 39) in order for it to be operational. The IASB noted that similar concerns had been raised as part of the feedback to the 2010 Hedge Accounting Exposure Draft.

BC6.258   The IASB also noted that one of the major concerns that respondents had raised about the reference in the 2010 Hedge Accounting Exposure Draft to 'unbiased result' was that it could be perceived as requiring entities to identify the 'perfect' hedging instrument or that the entity's commercial decision of which hedging instrument to actually use could be restricted or second guessed (see paragraph BC6.242).

BC6.259   The IASB considered that using a reference to 'reasonably effective' would give rise to similar concerns because it would raise the question of how much ineffectiveness that results from the choice of the actual hedging instrument is 'reasonable' (similar to the notion of 'unbiased' proposed in the 2010 Hedge Accounting Exposure Draft). The IASB was also concerned that this might have a particular impact on emerging economies because entities in those economies often have to transact hedging instruments in more liquid markets abroad, which means that it is more difficult for them to find a hedging instrument that fits their actual exposure than it is for entities in economies with those liquid markets.

BC6.260 Furthermore, the IASB was concerned that using the single term 'reasonably effective' would mingle different aspects, which would be tantamount to aggregating the different aspects of the effectiveness assessment that the IASB had considered (ie the economic relationship, the effect of credit risk and the hedge ratio). The IASB noted that it was clear from feedback received on its proposed objective of the hedge effectiveness assessment that a single term was too abstract if the notion described by that term included a number of different aspects (see also paragraph BC6.254).

BC6.261 Consequently, the IASB decided not to use a qualitative 'reasonably effective' threshold for assessing hedge effectiveness.

Frequency of assessing whether the hedge effectiveness requirements are met

BC6.262 In the deliberations leading to the 2010 Hedge Accounting Exposure Draft, as a consequence of its proposed hedge effectiveness requirements, the IASB considered how frequently an entity should assess whether the hedge effectiveness requirements were met. The IASB decided that an entity should perform this assessment at the inception of the hedging relationship.

BC6.263 Furthermore, the IASB considered that an entity should assess, on an ongoing basis, whether the hedge effectiveness requirements are still met, including any adjustment (rebalancing) that might be required in order to continue to meet those requirements (see paragraphs BC6.300–BC6.313). This was because the proposed hedge effectiveness requirements should be met throughout the term of the hedging relationship. The IASB also decided that the assessment of those requirements should be only forward-looking (ie prospective) because it related to expectations about hedge effectiveness.

BC6.264 Hence, in the deliberations leading to the 2010 Hedge Accounting Exposure Draft, the IASB concluded that the reassessment of the hedge ratio should be performed at the beginning of each reporting period or upon a significant change in the circumstances underlying the effectiveness assessment, whichever comes first.

BC6.265 Given that the changes made to the proposed hedge effectiveness requirements when redeliberating the 2010 Hedge Accounting Exposure Draft did not affect the IASB's rationale for its proposals for the frequency of the assessment, the IASB retained its original decision.

Method of assessing hedge effectiveness

BC6.266 The method used to assess the effectiveness of the hedging relationship needs to be suitable to demonstrate that the objective of the hedge effectiveness assessment has been achieved. The IASB considered whether the effectiveness of a hedging relationship should be assessed on either a qualitative or a quantitative basis.

BC6.267 Hedging relationships have one of two characteristics that affect the complexity of the hedge effectiveness assessment:

(a) the critical terms of the hedged item and hedging instrument match or are closely aligned. If there are no substantial changes in the critical terms or in the credit risk of the hedging instrument or hedged item, the hedge effectiveness can typically be determined using a qualitative assessment.

(b) the critical terms of the hedged item and hedging instrument do not match and are not closely aligned. These hedging relationships involve an increased level of uncertainty about the degree of offset and so the effectiveness of the hedge during its term is more difficult to evaluate.

BC6.268 Qualitative hedge effectiveness assessments use a comparison of the terms of the hedged item and the hedging instrument (for example, the commonly termed 'critical-terms-match' approach). The IASB considered that, in the context of an effectiveness assessment that does not use a threshold, it can be appropriate to assess the effectiveness qualitatively for a hedging relationship for which the terms of the hedging instrument and the hedged item match or are closely aligned.

BC6.269 However, assessing the hedging relationship qualitatively is less effective than a quantitative assessment in other situations. For example, when analysing the possible behaviour of hedging relationships that involve a significant degree of potential ineffectiveness resulting from terms of the hedged item that are less closely aligned with the hedging instrument, the extent of future offset has a high level of uncertainty and is difficult to determine using a qualitative approach. The IASB considered that a quantitative assessment would be more suitable in such situations.

BC6.270 Quantitative assessments or tests encompass a wide spectrum of tools and techniques. The IASB noted that selecting the appropriate tool or technique depends on the complexity of the hedge, the availability of data and the level of uncertainty of offset in the hedging relationship. The type of assessment and the method used to assess hedge effectiveness therefore depends on the relevant characteristics of the hedging relationship. Consequently, in the deliberations leading to the 2010 Hedge Accounting Exposure Draft, the IASB decided that an entity should assess the effectiveness of a hedging relationship either qualitatively or quantitatively depending on the relevant characteristics of the hedging relationship and the potential sources of ineffectiveness. However, the IASB decided not to prescribe any specific method of assessing hedge effectiveness.

BC6.271 The IASB retained its original decisions when redeliberating its 2010 Hedge Accounting Exposure Draft.

Accounting for qualifying hedging relationships

Hedge of a foreign currency risk of a firm commitment

BC6.272 IAS 39 allowed an entity to choose fair value hedge accounting or cash flow hedge accounting for hedges of the foreign currency risk of a firm commitment.

When developing the 2010 Hedge Accounting Exposure Draft, the IASB considered whether it should continue to allow this choice.

BC6.273　The IASB noted that requiring an entity to apply cash flow hedge accounting for all hedges of foreign currency risk of a firm commitment could result in what some regard as 'artificial' other comprehensive income and equity volatility (see paragraphs BC6.353–BC6.354). The IASB also noted that, by requiring an entity to apply cash flow hedge accounting, the lower of test would apply to transactions that already exist (ie firm commitments).

BC6.274　However, the IASB also noted that requiring an entity to apply fair value hedge accounting for all hedges of foreign currency risk of a firm commitment would require a change in the type of hedging relationship to a fair value hedge when the foreign currency cash flow hedge of a forecast transaction becomes a hedge of a firm commitment. This results in operational complexity. For example, this would require changing the measurement of ineffectiveness from a 'lower of' test to a symmetrical test.

BC6.275　The IASB also noted that for existing hedged items (such as firm commitments) foreign currency risk affects both the cash flows and the fair value of the hedged item and hence has a dual character.

BC6.276　Consequently, the IASB proposed in its 2010 Hedge Accounting Exposure Draft to continue to permit an entity the choice of accounting for a hedge of foreign currency risk of a firm commitment as either a cash flow hedge or a fair value hedge.

BC6.277　The IASB retained its original decision when redeliberating its 2010 Hedge Accounting Exposure Draft.

Measuring the ineffectiveness of a hedging relationship

BC6.278　Because the measurement of hedge ineffectiveness is based on the actual performance of the hedging instrument and the hedged item, the IASB in its deliberations leading to the 2010 Hedge Accounting Exposure Draft decided that hedge ineffectiveness should be measured by comparing the changes in their values (on the basis of currency unit amounts).

BC6.279　The IASB retained its original decision when redeliberating its 2010 Hedge Accounting Exposure Draft.

Time value of money

BC6.280　The objective of measuring hedge ineffectiveness is to recognise, in profit or loss, the extent to which the hedging relationship did not achieve offset (subject to the restrictions that apply to the recognition of hedge ineffectiveness for cash flow hedges—often referred to as the lower of test).

BC6.281　The IASB noted that hedging instruments are subject to measurement either at fair value or amortised cost, both of which are present value measurements. Consequently, in order to be consistent, the amounts that are compared with the changes in the value of the hedging instrument must also be determined on a present value basis. The IASB noted that hedge accounting does not change the measurement of the hedging instrument, but that it might change only the location of where the change in its carrying amount is presented. As a result, the same basis (ie present value) for the hedged item must be used in order to avoid a mismatch when determining the amount to be recognised as hedge ineffectiveness.

BC6.282　Consequently, in the deliberations leading to the 2010 Hedge Accounting Exposure Draft, the IASB decided that the time value of money must be considered when measuring the ineffectiveness of a hedging relationship.

BC6.283　The IASB retained its original decision when redeliberating its 2010 Hedge Accounting Exposure Draft.

Hypothetical derivatives

BC6.284　In its deliberations leading to the 2010 Hedge Accounting Exposure Draft, the IASB considered the use of a 'hypothetical derivative', which is a derivative that would have critical terms that exactly match those of a hedged item. The IASB considered the use of a hypothetical derivative in the context of the hedge effectiveness assessment as well as for the purpose of measuring hedge ineffectiveness.

BC6.285　The IASB noted that the purpose of a hypothetical derivative is to measure the change in the value of the hedged item. Consequently, a hypothetical derivative is not a method in its own right for assessing hedge effectiveness or measuring hedge ineffectiveness. Instead, a hypothetical derivative is one possible way of determining an input for other methods (for example, statistical methods or dollar-offset) to assess the effectiveness of the hedging relationship or to measure ineffectiveness.

BC6.286　Consequently, in the deliberations leading to the 2010 Hedge Accounting Exposure Draft, the IASB decided that an entity can use the fair value of a hypothetical derivative to calculate the fair value of the hedged item. This allows determining changes in the value of the hedged item against which the changes in the fair value of the hedging instrument are compared to assess hedge effectiveness and measure ineffectiveness. The IASB noted that this notion of a hypothetical derivative means that using a hypothetical derivative is only one possible way to determine the change in the value of the hedged item and would result in the same outcome as if that change in the value was determined by a different approach (ie it is a mathematical expedient).

BC6.287　When redeliberating its 2010 Hedge Accounting Exposure Draft the IASB considered feedback that disagreed with this proposal. The main reasons cited for disagreement were:

(a)　cash flow hedges and fair value hedges are different concepts. Unlike fair value hedges, cash flow hedges are not based on a valuation concept and therefore do not give rise to hedge ineffectiveness from differences in value changes between the hedging instrument and the hedged item as long as their variable cash flows match. However, some conceded that credit risk was a source of hedge ineffectiveness even if all variable cash flows were perfectly matched.

(b)   the new hedge accounting model has the objective of aligning hedge accounting more closely with risk management. Risk management has a 'flow perspective' that considers cash flow hedges as (fully) effective if the variable cash flows of the actual derivative match those of the hedged item (ie if the entity uses a 'perfect derivative' to hedge the risk exposure).

(c)   the accounting treatment for the effect of a foreign currency basis spread is inconsistent with that for the time value of options and the forward element of forward contracts, ie the notion of 'costs of hedging' that the new hedge accounting model introduces. The foreign currency basis spread is also a cost of hedging and should be treated consistently with the other types of costs of hedging.

BC6.288   The IASB considered whether a cash flow hedge is a different concept from a fair value hedge. The IASB noted that IFRS uses a hedge accounting model that is based on a valuation at the reporting date of both the hedging instrument and the hedged item (valuation model); hedge (in)effectiveness is then measured by comparing the changes in the value of the hedging instrument and the hedged item. Consequently, for determining the effective part of a cash flow hedge, an entity also needs to look at the change in cash flows on a present value basis, ie based on a valuation. Consequently, simply comparing the cash flow variability of the hedging instrument and the hedged item (ie a pure 'flow perspective' without involving a valuation) was not appropriate.

BC6.289   The IASB also noted that IFRS uses a hedge accounting model that does not allow perfect hedge effectiveness to be assumed, and that this applies even if for a cash flow hedge the critical terms of the hedging instrument and the hedged item perfectly match. Doing so could conceal differences in credit risk or liquidity of the hedging instrument and the hedged item, which are potential sources of hedge ineffectiveness for fair value hedges and cash flow hedges alike.

BC6.290   The IASB therefore rejected the view that cash flow hedges and fair value hedges were different concepts in that the former represented a mere comparison of cash flows whereas only the latter represented a comparison of valuations. Consequently, the IASB also rejected the view that a hypothetical derivative is meant to represent the 'perfect hedge' instead of the hedged item. Instead, the IASB confirmed its view that for fair value hedges and cash flow hedges the hedge accounting model:

(a)   is a valuation model; and

(b)   requires that the value of the hedged item is measured independently of the value of the hedging instrument.

BC6.291   The IASB noted that the objective of aligning hedge accounting with risk management meant that the IASB developed a new hedge accounting model that would facilitate hedge accounting in more circumstances than the previous one and would provide more useful information about the risk management associated with hedging. But this objective did not mean that an entity could override accounting requirements with its particular risk management view.

BC6.292   Consequently, the IASB rejected the view that if risk management considered cash flow hedges as fully effective when the variable cash flows of the actual derivative match those of the hedged item (ie if the entity uses a 'perfect derivative') that hedge should also be considered as fully effective for accounting purposes.

BC6.293   The IASB then considered the concern that the accounting treatment for the effect of a foreign currency basis spread was inconsistent with that for the time value of options and the forward element of forward contracts, ie the notion of 'costs of hedging' that the new hedge accounting model introduces.

BC6.294   The IASB noted that its proposals would result in hedge ineffectiveness arising from the fair value changes of the hedging instrument that are attributable to the effect of a foreign currency basis spread. Taking the example of a cross-currency interest rate swap that is a hedge of the foreign currency risk (and the interest rate risk) of a debt instrument that is denominated in a foreign currency, the IASB noted that the cross-currency interest rate swap included a pricing element that reflected that the derivative instrument resulted in the exchange of two currencies. This led to the IASB questioning whether there was a similar feature or characteristic in the hedged item that would offset the effect of the foreign currency basis spread on the fair value of the cross-currency interest rate swap. The IASB noted that the hedged debt instrument was a single-currency instrument, ie unlike the cross-currency interest rate swap, the hedged item itself did not involve the exchange of two currencies. Instead, any exchange of the debt instrument's currency of denomination for another currency was a circumstance of the holder or issuer of that debt instrument instead of a characteristic or feature of the debt instrument itself.

BC6.295   The IASB noted that whether reflecting the effect of the foreign currency basis spread within hedge ineffectiveness, as proposed in the 2010 Hedge Accounting Exposure Draft, was inconsistent with the new hedge accounting model depended on whether that spread could be regarded as a cost of hedging. Foreign currency basis spreads are an economic phenomenon that would not exist in a perfect market because the existence of such a spread creates economic arbitrage opportunities that would result in its reduction to zero. However, in the actual markets for cross-currency swaps the foreign currency basis spread is not zero because of factors that prevent perfect arbitrage. Those factors include, for example, the credit risk embedded in the underlying reference rates of the currencies as well as the demand and supply for the particular financial product (for example, cross-currency interest rate swaps), which relates to specific situations in foreign currency (product) markets. Also, the interaction between the spot and the forward foreign currency markets can sometimes have an effect.

BC6.296   The IASB considered that, overall, a foreign currency basis spread could be considered as a charge to convert one currency into another. Consequently, the IASB agreed that the foreign currency basis spread could be subsumed under the notion of 'costs of hedging' that it had developed for the accounting for the time value of options and the forward element of forward contracts. The IASB therefore decided to expand the notion of 'costs of hedging' so as to include foreign currency basis spreads. In the IASB's view, this would provide the most transparent accounting, reflect best the economics of the transaction and fit into the new hedge accounting model.

BC6.297 The IASB also considered whether it should expand the notion of 'costs of hedging' by broadening the exception it had proposed for the time value of options and the forward element of forward contracts or by replacing that exception with a broader principle. The IASB acknowledged that, conceptually, a principle would be preferable but it was concerned that using a broader principle for the costs of hedging could result in some types of hedge ineffectiveness being inappropriately deferred in accumulated other comprehensive income as costs of hedging.

BC6.298 Consequently, the IASB decided to expand the notion of 'costs of hedging' but only for foreign currency basis spreads by broadening the exception for the forward elements of forward contracts so that it also covers those spreads.

BC6.299 The IASB also decided to more closely align the structure of this exception with that used for the accounting for the time value of options. The IASB noted that for hedges of transaction related hedged items, using the forward rate method to measure the hedged item would allow entities to achieve an equivalent accounting outcome for the forward element of forward contracts (see paragraphs BC6.418–BC6.420). However, the IASB acknowledged that in order to allow a similar accounting outcome not only for the forward element of forward contracts but also for foreign currency basis spreads, entities would need to be able to apply the notion of 'costs of hedging', including for hedges of transaction related hedged items. Consequently, the IASB introduced the notion of 'costs of hedging' also for those types of cost of hedging for both hedges of time-period related hedged items and for hedges of transaction related hedged items.

Rebalancing the hedging relationship

BC6.300 IAS 39 did not allow adjustments that were not envisaged and documented at the inception of the hedge to be treated as adjustments to a continuing hedging relationship. IAS 39 treated adjustments to an existing hedging relationship that were not envisaged at the inception of the hedging relationship as a discontinuation of the original hedging relationship and the start of a new one. The IASB noted that this resulted from a hedge accounting model that did not include the notion of accounting for changes to an existing hedging relationship as a continuation of that relationship.

BC6.301 The IASB noted that this is inconsistent with risk management practices. There are instances where, although the risk management objective remains the same, adjustments to an existing hedging relationship are made because of changes in circumstances related to the hedging relationship's underlyings or risk variables. For example, such adjustments are often required to re-align the hedging relationship with risk management policies in view of changed circumstances. Hence, those adjustments to the hedged item or hedging instrument do not change the original risk management objective but instead reflect a change in how it is executed owing to the changes in circumstances. The IASB considered that in those situations the revised hedging relationship should be accounted for as a continuation of the existing hedging relationship. The IASB referred to such adjustments of hedging relationships as 'rebalancing'.

BC6.302 In its deliberations leading to the 2010 Hedge Accounting Exposure Draft, the IASB also considered the ramifications of the proposed hedge effectiveness requirements, which, for some changes in circumstances, would create the need for an adjustment to the hedging relationship to ensure that those requirements would continue to be met. An example is a change in the relationship between two variables in such a way that the hedge ratio would need to be adjusted in order to avoid a level of ineffectiveness that would fail the effectiveness requirements (which would not be met when using the original hedge ratio in the new circumstances).

BC6.303 The IASB concluded that, in such situations, if the original risk management objective remained unaltered, the adjustment to the hedging relationship should be treated as the continuation of the hedging relationship. Consequently, the IASB proposed that an adjustment to a hedging relationship is treated as a rebalancing when that adjustment changes the hedge ratio in response to changes in the economic relationship between the hedged item and the hedging instrument but risk management otherwise continues the originally designated hedging relationship.

BC6.304 However, if the adjustment represents an overhaul of the existing hedging relationship, the IASB considered that treating the adjustment as a rebalancing would not be appropriate. Instead, the IASB considered that such an adjustment should result in the discontinuation of that hedging relationship. An example is a hedging relationship with a hedging instrument that experiences a severe deterioration of its credit quality and hence is no longer used for risk management purposes.

BC6.305 Most respondents to the 2010 Hedge Accounting Exposure Draft agreed that the hedge accounting model should include a notion whereby a hedging relationship can be adjusted and accounted for as the continuation of an existing hedging relationship. Respondents thought that the inclusion of the concept of rebalancing would enhance the application of hedge accounting and would be a better representation of what entities do as part of their risk management activities. However, some respondents requested that the IASB clarify the circumstances in which rebalancing is required or permitted. They were unsure as to whether rebalancing has been designed in the narrower sense to only deal with adjustments to the hedge ratio in the context of the hedge effectiveness requirements, or whether in a wider sense it also relates to the adjustment of hedged volumes when the hedge ratio is still appropriate (ie when the entity simply wants to hedge more or less than originally).

BC6.306 Even though respondents generally supported the concept of rebalancing, some were concerned that, on the basis of how the hedge effectiveness requirement was proposed in the 2010 Hedge Accounting Exposure Draft, it would be unclear when to rebalance and that the IASB should provide more guidance to ensure consistent application. Some respondents also thought that rebalancing should be permitted but not mandatory. They argued that risk management often chose not to adjust its (economic) hedging relationships based on a mathematical optimisation exercise that was implied in the 2010 Hedge

Accounting Exposure Draft (see paragraph BC6.242). This was because of cost-effectiveness considerations or simply because the hedge was still within the tolerance limits that an entity might use for adjusting the hedging relationship. There was concern that the wording, as proposed in the 2010 Hedge Accounting Exposure Draft, implied a continuous optimisation exercise (ie to always have the perfect hedge ratio) and would therefore require constant rebalancing. Consequently, almost all respondents (directly or indirectly) requested that the IASB clarify that rebalancing should only be required when done for risk management purposes. They believed that hedge accounting should follow and represent rebalancing based on what an entity actually did for risk management purposes but that rebalancing should not be triggered merely by accounting requirements.

BC6.307 In the light of the feedback, the IASB decided to retain the notion of rebalancing but to add some clarification on:

(a) whether rebalancing should be mandatory or voluntary; and

(b) the notion of rebalancing.

Mandatory or voluntary rebalancing

BC6.308 The IASB noted that its decision on the hedge effectiveness assessment when deliberating the 2010 Hedge Accounting Exposure Draft had ramifications for rebalancing. This decision resulted in designating hedging relationships using a hedge ratio based on the quantity of the hedged item that the entity actually hedges and the quantity of the hedging instrument that it actually uses to hedge that quantity of hedged item. However, this is provided that the hedge ratio would not reflect an imbalance that would create hedge ineffectiveness that could result in an accounting outcome that would be inconsistent with the purpose of hedge accounting (see paragraphs BC6.248–BC6.251). The IASB considered that this decision addressed the main concerns respondents had about rebalancing (ie how rebalancing for hedge accounting purposes related to rebalancing for risk management purposes).

BC6.309 The IASB's proposal in the 2010 Hedge Accounting Exposure Draft included the notion of proactive rebalancing as a complement to the proposed hedge effectiveness assessment in order to allow an entity to adjust hedging relationships on a timely basis and at the same time strengthen the link between hedge accounting and risk management. However, the IASB considered that its decision on the hedge effectiveness assessment when deliberating the 2010 Hedge Accounting Exposure Draft (see paragraph BC6.248) had an effect on rebalancing that would facilitate the adjustments to a hedging relationship that the 2010 Hedge Accounting Exposure Draft had addressed by the proposed notion of proactive rebalancing. In other words, if an entity adjusted the hedge ratio in response to changes in the economic relationship between the hedged item and the hedging instrument for risk management purposes (including adjustments that the 2010 Hedge Accounting Exposure Draft would have considered 'proactive'), the hedging relationship for hedge accounting purposes would usually be adjusted in the same way. Consequently, the IASB considered that the notion of proactive rebalancing had become obsolete.

BC6.310 The IASB also noted that the decisions that it made on the hedge effectiveness assessment when deliberating the 2010 Hedge Accounting Exposure Draft addressed respondents' concerns about the frequency of rebalancing because those decisions also clarified that rebalancing was not a mathematical optimisation exercise (see paragraphs BC6.248–BC6.249).

Clarification of the term 'rebalancing'

BC6.311 The IASB noted that it had already clarified the notion of 'rebalancing' as a result of its decision on the hedge effectiveness assessment when deliberating the 2010 Hedge Accounting Exposure Draft (see paragraphs BC6.308–BC6.310). However, the IASB considered whether it also needed to provide clarification on the scope of rebalancing—in other words, what adjustments to a hedging relationship constitute rebalancing.

BC6.312 The IASB noted that the notion of rebalancing, as proposed in its 2010 Hedge Accounting Exposure Draft, was used in the context of adjusting the designated quantities of the hedging instrument or hedged item in order to maintain a hedge ratio that complies with the hedge effectiveness requirements. Changes to designated quantities of a hedging instrument or of a hedged item for different purposes did not constitute the notion of 'rebalancing' that was proposed in the 2010 Hedge Accounting Exposure Draft.

BC6.313 Consequently, the IASB decided to clarify that rebalancing only covers adjustments to the designated quantities of the hedged item or of the hedging instrument for the purpose of maintaining a hedge ratio that complies with the requirements of the hedge effectiveness assessment (ie not when the entity simply wants to hedge more or less than it did originally).

Discontinuation of hedge accounting

Mandatory or voluntary discontinuation of hedge accounting

BC6.314 In accordance with IAS 39, an entity had to discontinue hedge accounting when the hedging relationship ceased to meet the qualifying criteria (including when the hedging instrument no longer existed or was sold). However, in accordance with IAS 39, an entity also had a free choice to voluntarily discontinue hedge accounting by simply revoking the designation of the hedging relationship (ie irrespective of any reason).

BC6.315 The IASB noted that entities voluntarily discontinued hedge accounting often because of how the effectiveness assessment in IAS 39 worked. For example, entities revoked the designation of a hedging relationship and re-designated it as a new hedging relationship in order to apply a different method of assessing hedge ineffectiveness from the method originally documented (expecting that the new method would be a better fit). Another example was entities that revoked the designation of a hedging relationship because they wanted to adjust the hedge ratio following a change in the relationship between the hedged item and the hedging instrument (typically in response to a change in the relationship between different underlyings). The hedging relationship was then re-designated, including the adjustment to the volume of the hedging instrument or the hedged item, in order to achieve the new hedge ratio. The IASB noted that in those situations the hedging relationship was discontinued and then restarted even though the risk management objective of the entity had not changed. In the IASB's view, those outcomes created a disconnect between the hedge accounting model in IAS 39 and hedging from a risk management perspective and also undermined the usefulness of the information provided.

BC6.316 In its deliberations leading to the 2010 Hedge Accounting Exposure Draft, the IASB concluded that the proposed hedge accounting model would improve the link between hedge accounting and risk management because:

(a) the new hedge effectiveness assessment requirements would not involve a percentage band or any other bright line criterion and would result in changing the method for assessing hedge effectiveness in response to changes in circumstances as part of a continuing hedging relationship; and

(b) the notion of rebalancing would allow the hedge ratio to be adjusted as part of a continuing hedging relationship.

BC6.317 The IASB also noted that sometimes a hedging relationship was discontinued because of a decrease in the hedged quantities of forecast transactions (ie the volume that remains highly probable of occurring falls or is expected to fall below the volume designated as the hedged item). Under IAS 39 this had resulted in discontinuing hedge accounting for the hedging relationship as designated, ie the volume designated as the hedged item in its entirety. The IASB considered that the quantity of forecast transactions that were still highly probable of occurring was in fact a continuation of the original hedging relationship (albeit with a lower volume). Hence, the IASB decided to propose in its 2010 Hedge Accounting Exposure Draft that hedge accounting should be discontinued only for the volume that was no longer highly probable of occurring and that the remaining volume that was still highly probable of occurring should be accounted for as a continuation of the original hedging relationship. In the IASB's view, this would more closely align hedge accounting with risk management and provide more useful information.

BC6.318 However, the IASB was concerned that this accounting might possibly undermine the requirement that forecast transactions must be highly probable in order to qualify as a hedged item. Hence, the IASB decided to also propose to clarify that a history of having designated hedges of forecast transactions and having subsequently determined that the forecast transactions are no longer expected to occur would call into question the entity's ability to predict similar forecast transactions accurately. This would affect the assessment of whether similar forecast transactions are highly probable and hence their eligibility as hedged items.

BC6.319 In view of its aim to better link hedge accounting to risk management and provide more useful hedge accounting information, the IASB also discussed whether it should retain an entity's choice to revoke the designation of a hedging relationship, taking into consideration that the designation of a hedging relationship (and hence the discontinuation of hedge accounting) at will does not result in useful information. The IASB noted that this would allow hedge accounting to be discontinued even if the entity for risk management purposes continued to hedge the exposure in accordance with its risk management objective that was part of the qualifying criteria that initially allowed the entity to achieve hedge accounting. The IASB considered that, in such situations, voluntary discontinuation of hedge accounting would be arbitrary and unjustifiable. Hence, the IASB decided to propose not to allow entities a free choice to revoke the designation of a hedging relationship in this situation. The IASB also noted that if the hedging relationship no longer reflected the risk management objective for that particular hedging relationship, discontinuation of hedge accounting was not a choice but was required because the qualifying criteria would no longer be met. The IASB considered that applying hedge accounting without a risk management objective would not provide useful information.

BC6.320   In its deliberations leading to the 2010 Hedge Accounting Exposure Draft, the IASB did not consider new designations of any hedging relationships of the acquiree in the consolidated financial statements of the acquirer following a business combination. The IASB noted that this was a requirement of IFRS 3 *Business Combinations* and hence not within the scope of its project on hedge accounting.

BC6.321   The responses to the proposals on the discontinuation of hedge accounting in the 2010 Hedge Accounting Exposure Draft provided mixed views. Those who agreed thought that the proposals would strengthen the reliability of financial reporting because the ability to change accounting for no valid reason would be reduced.

BC6.322   More specifically, those who agreed also thought that the model in IAS 39 provided an opportunity for structuring. They noted that allowing a hedging relationship to be arbitrarily discontinued at any point in time is not conceptually sound and does not result in useful information.

BC6.323   Even though many respondents agreed with the proposals, there were also requests that the IASB provide additional guidance on the meaning of 'risk management' and at what level it should be considered for the purpose of hedge accounting.

BC6.324   Generally, those who disagreed with the proposals argued that if starting hedge accounting was voluntary, ceasing it should also be voluntary. Some respondents who disagreed did so because they believed that voluntary discontinuation was necessary in scenarios in which an entity decided to terminate a hedging relationship on the basis that the hedge was no longer cost efficient (for example, a high administrative burden makes it is too onerous and costly to apply hedge accounting). Some of these respondents raised the concern that voluntary discontinuation was an important tool in the current hedge accounting model for financial institutions that normally run hedging programmes based on portfolios of items on a macro basis. Those portfolios were subject to constant changes and entities removed the hedge designation with the aim of adjusting the hedging relationship for new hedged items and hedging instruments.

BC6.325   Others who disagreed argued that not allowing voluntary discontinuation was inconsistent with the mechanics of cash flow hedge accounting. For example, when an entity entered into a cash flow hedge for forecast sales in a foreign currency, the risk management strategy aimed to protect the cash flows until settlement of the invoice. However, hedge accounting was only applied until the moment when the sales invoice became an on-balance-sheet item, after which the entity obtained a natural offset in the statement of profit or loss and other comprehensive income because of the translation of the hedged item in accordance with IAS 21 and the accounting for the hedging instrument at fair value through profit or loss. Those respondents thought that voluntary discontinuation of the hedging relationship was necessary at the time that the forecast transaction became an on-balance-sheet item (for example, a trade receivable).

BC6.326 Based on this feedback, the IASB, in its redeliberations, considered:

(a) whether voluntary discontinuation should be allowed, given that hedge accounting remained optional; and

(b) how the link of the proposed discontinuation requirements to the risk management objective and strategy would work.

BC6.327 The IASB noted that even though the application of hedge accounting remained optional, it facilitated the provision of useful information for financial reporting purposes (ie how hedging instruments are used to manage risk). The IASB considered that this purpose could not be ignored when considering the voluntary discontinuation of hedge accounting. If an entity chose to apply hedge accounting, it did so with the aim of using that particular accounting to represent in the financial statements the effect of pursuing a particular risk management objective. If the risk management objective had not changed and the other qualifying criteria for hedge accounting were still met, the ability to discontinue hedge accounting would undermine the aspect of consistency over time in accounting for, and providing information about, that hedging relationship. The IASB noted that a free choice to discontinue hedge accounting reflected a view that hedge accounting is a mere accounting exercise that does not have a particular meaning. Consequently, the IASB considered that it was not valid to argue that because hedge accounting was voluntary, the discontinuation of hedge accounting should also be voluntary.

BC6.328 In addition, the IASB noted that other optional accounting treatments of IFRS does not allow the entity to overturn its initial election:

(a) the fair value option in IAS 39 and IFRS 9; and

(b) the lessee's option to account for a property interest held under an operating lease as an investment property, which is available (irrevocably) on a property-by-property basis.

BC6.329 The IASB also did not think that the ability to voluntarily discontinue hedge accounting was necessary for hedge accounting to work as intended in particular situations mentioned in the feedback (see paragraphs BC6.324–BC6.325). The IASB considered that the impression of some respondents that voluntary discontinuation was necessary in those situations resulted from a lack of clarity about the distinction between the notions of risk management strategy and risk management objective. The IASB noted that that distinction was important for determining when the discontinuation of a hedging relationship was required (or not allowed). The IASB also noted that the term 'risk management strategy' was used in the 2010 Hedge Accounting Exposure Draft as a reference to the highest level at which an entity determines how it manages risk. In other words, the risk management strategy typically identified the risks to which the entity was exposed and set out how the entity responded to them. Conversely, the 2010 Hedge Accounting Exposure Draft used the term 'risk management objective' (for a hedging relationship) to refer to the objective that applies at the level of that particular hedging relationship (instead of what the entity aims to achieve with the overall strategy). In other words, it related to how the particular designated hedging instrument is used to hedge the particular exposure designated as the hedged item.

BC6.330 The IASB noted that a risk management strategy could (and often would) involve many different hedging relationships whose risk management objectives relate to executing that risk management strategy. Hence, the risk management objective for a particular hedging relationship could change even though an entity's risk management strategy remained unchanged. The IASB's intention was to prohibit voluntary discontinuation of hedge accounting when the risk management objective at the level of a particular hedging relationship (ie not only the risk management strategy) remained the same and all other qualifying criteria were still met.

BC6.331 Consequently, the IASB decided to prohibit the voluntary discontinuation of hedge accounting when the risk management objective for a particular hedging relationship remains the same and all the other qualifying criteria are still met. However, the IASB also decided to add additional guidance on how the risk management objective and the risk management strategy relate to each other using examples that contrast these two notions, including for situations in which 'proxy hedging' designations are used.

Novation of derivatives

BC6.332 When deliberating its 2010 Hedge Accounting Exposure Draft, the IASB received an urgent request to clarify whether an entity is required to discontinue hedge accounting for hedging relationships in which a derivative has been designated as a hedging instrument when that derivative is novated to a central counterparty (CCP) due to the introduction of a new law or regulation.[35] This question applied equally to the designation of hedging instruments in accordance with IAS 39 and under the new hedge accounting model for IFRS 9 that the IASB was redeliberating. Consequently, the IASB considered this question and possible solutions, both in the context of hedge accounting under IAS 39 and IFRS 9.[36]

BC6.333 The IASB considered the derecognition requirements of IFRS 9 to determine whether the novation in such a circumstance would lead to the derecognition of

---

35 In this context, the term 'novation' indicates that the parties to a derivative agree that one or more clearly counterparties replace their original counterparty to each of the parties. For this purpose, a clearing counterparty is a central counterparty or an entity or entities, for example, a clearing member of a clearing organisation or a client of a clearing member of a clearing organisation, that are acting as counterparty in order to effect clearing by a central counterparty.

36 The references in the Basis for Conclusions of this Standard are to the relevant requirements of IFRS 9. The Basis for Conclusions of the equivalent amendments to IAS 39 referred to the relevant requirements in that Standard (which were equivalent).

an existing derivative that had been designated as a hedging instrument. The IASB noted that a derivative should be derecognised only when it meets both the derecognition criteria for a financial asset and the derecognition criteria for a financial liability in circumstances in which the derivative involves two-way payments between parties (ie the payments are or could be from and to each of the parties).

BC6.334 The IASB observed that paragraph 3.2.3(a) of IFRS 9 requires that a financial asset is derecognised when the contractual rights to the cash flows from the financial asset expire. The IASB noted that through novation to a CCP, a party (Party A) to the original derivative has new contractual rights to cash flows from a (new) derivative with the CCP, and this new contract replaces the original contract with a counterparty (Party B). Thus, the original derivative with Party B has expired and, as a consequence, the original derivative through which Party A has engaged with Party B meets the derecognition criteria for a financial asset.

BC6.335 The IASB also observed that paragraph B3.3.1(b) of IFRS 9 states that a financial liability is extinguished when the debtor is legally released from primary responsibility for the liability. The IASB noted that the novation to the CCP would release Party A from the responsibility to make payments to Party B and would also oblige Party A to make payments to the CCP. Consequently, the original derivative through which Party A has transacted with Party B also meets the derecognition criteria for a financial liability.

BC6.336 Consequently, the IASB concluded that the novation of a derivative to a CCP would be accounted for as the derecognition of the original derivative and the recognition of the (new) novated derivative.

BC6.337 Taking into account the conclusion of the assessment on the derecognition requirements, the IASB considered the guidance it had proposed on the discontinuation of hedge accounting, which would require an entity to discontinue hedge accounting prospectively if the hedging instrument expires or is sold, terminated or exercised. The IASB noted that novation to a CCP would require the entity to discontinue hedge accounting because the derivative that was designated as a hedging instrument has been derecognised and consequently the hedging instrument in the existing hedging relationship no longer exists.

BC6.338 The IASB was, however, concerned about the financial reporting effects that would arise from novations that result from new laws or regulations. The IASB noted that the requirement to discontinue hedge accounting meant that although an entity could designate the new derivative as the hedging instrument in a new hedging relationship, this could result in more hedge ineffectiveness, especially for cash flow hedges, compared to a continuing hedging relationship. This is because the derivative that would be newly designated as the hedging instrument would be on terms that would be different from a new derivative, ie it was unlikely to be 'at-market' (for example, a non-option derivative such as a swap or forward might have a significant fair value) at the time of the novation.

BC6.339 The IASB, taking note of this financial reporting effect, was convinced that accounting for the hedging relationship that existed before the novation as a continuing hedging relationship, in this specific situation, would provide more useful information to users of financial statements. The IASB also considered the feedback from outreach that involved the members of the International Forum of Accounting Standard Setters (IFASS) and securities regulators and noted that this issue is not limited to a specific jurisdiction because many jurisdictions have introduced, or are expected to mandate, laws or regulations that encourage or require the novation of derivatives to a CCP.

BC6.340   The IASB noted that the widespread legislative changes across jurisdictions were prompted by a G20 commitment to improve transparency and regulatory oversight of over-the-counter (OTC) derivatives in an internationally consistent and non-discriminatory way. Specifically, the G20 agreed to improve OTC derivatives markets so that all standardised OTC derivatives contracts are cleared through a CCP.

BC6.341   Consequently, the IASB decided to publish, in January 2013, the Exposure Draft *Novation of Derivatives and Continuation of Hedge Accounting* (the '2013 Novation of Derivatives and Continuation of Hedge Accounting Exposure Draft'), which proposed amendments to IAS 39 and revisions to the IASB's hedge accounting proposals to IFRS 9. In the 2013 Novation of Derivatives and Continuation of Hedge Accounting Exposure Draft, the IASB proposed revised requirements for the discontinuation of hedge accounting to provide relief from discontinuing hedge accounting when the novation to a CCP is required by new laws or regulations and meets particular criteria.

BC6.342   When developing the 2013 Novation of Derivatives and Continuation of Hedge Accounting Exposure Draft, the IASB tentatively decided that the terms of the novated derivative should be unchanged other than the change in counterparty. However, the IASB noted that, in practice, other changes may arise as a direct consequence of the novation. For example, in order to enter into a derivative with a CCP it may be necessary to make adjustments to the collateral arrangements. Such narrow changes that are a direct consequence of, or are incidental to, the novation were acknowledged in the proposals. However, this would not include changes to, for example, the maturity of the derivatives, the payment dates or the contractual cash flows or the basis of their calculation, except for changes that may arise as a consequence of transacting with a CCP.

BC6.343   When developing the 2013 Novation of Derivatives and Continuation of Hedge Accounting Exposure Draft, the IASB also discussed whether to require an entity to disclose that it has been able to continue hedge accounting by applying the relief provided by these proposals. The IASB considered that it was not appropriate to mandate a specific disclosure in this situation because, from the perspective of a user of financial statements, hedge accounting would continue.

BC6.344   The vast majority of respondents agreed that the proposed revisions are necessary. However, a few respondents expressed disagreement with the proposal on the basis that they disagreed with the IASB's conclusion that hedge accounting would be required to be discontinued as a result of such novations. In expressing such disagreement some noted that the guidance on the discontinuation of hedge accounting expressly acknowledges that certain replacements or rollovers of hedging instruments are not expirations or terminations for the purposes of discontinuing hedge accounting. The IASB noted that this exception applies if "[a] replacement or rollover is part of, and consistent with, the entity's documented risk management objective". The IASB questioned whether replacement of a contract as a result of unforeseen legislative changes (even if documented) fits the definition of a replacement that is part of a 'documented risk management objective'.

BC6.345 Even though the vast majority of respondents agreed with the proposal, a considerable majority of respondents disagreed with the scope of the proposals. They believed that the proposed scope of 'novation required by laws or regulations' is too restrictive and that the scope should therefore be expanded by removing this criterion. In particular, they argued that voluntary novation to a CCP should be provided with the same relief as novation required by laws or regulations. A few respondents further requested that the scope should not be limited to novation to a central counterparty and that novation in other circumstances should also be considered.

BC6.346 When considering respondents' comments, the IASB noted that voluntary novation to a CCP could be prevalent in some circumstances such as novation in anticipation of regulatory changes, novation owing to operational ease, and novation induced but not actually mandated by laws or regulations as a result of the imposition of charges or penalties. The IASB also noted that many jurisdictions would not require the existing stock of outstanding historical derivatives to be moved to CCPs, although this was encouraged by the G20 commitment.

BC6.347 The IASB observed, however, that for hedge accounting to continue, voluntary novation to a CCP should be associated with laws or regulations that are relevant to central clearing of derivatives. The IASB noted that while a novation need not be required by laws or regulations for hedge accounting to be allowed to continue, allowing all novations to CCPs to be accommodated was broader than the IASB had intended. In addition, the IASB agreed that hedge accounting should continue when novations are performed as a consequence of laws or regulations or the introduction of laws or regulations but noted that the mere possibility of laws or regulations being introduced was not a sufficient basis for the continuation of hedge accounting.

BC6.348 Some respondents were concerned that restricting the relief to novation directly to a CCP was too narrow. In considering respondents' comments, the IASB noted that in some cases a CCP has a contractual relationship only with its 'clearing members', and therefore an entity must have a contractual relationship with a clearing member in order to transact with a CCP; a clearing member of a CCP provides a clearing service to its client who cannot access a CCP directly. The IASB also noted that some jurisdictions are introducing a so-called 'indirect clearing' arrangement in their laws or regulations to effect clearing with a CCP, by which a client of a clearing member of a CCP provides a (indirect) clearing service to its client in the same way as a clearing member of a CCP provides a clearing service to its client. In addition, the IASB observed that an intragroup novation can also occur in order to access a CCP; for example, if only particular group entities can transact directly with a CCP.

BC6.349 On the basis of respondents' comments, the IASB decided to expand the scope of the amendments by providing relief for novations to entities other than a CCP if such novation is undertaken with the objective of effecting the clearing with a CCP instead of limiting relief to situations in which novation is direct to a CCP. The IASB decided that in those circumstances the novation had occurred in order to effect clearing through a CCP, albeit indirectly. The IASB thus decided to also include such novations in the scope of the amendments because they are consistent with the objective of the proposed amendments—they enable hedge accounting to continue when novations occur as a consequence of laws or regulations or the introduction of laws or regulations that increase the use of CCPs. However, the IASB noted that when parties to a hedging instrument enter into novations with different counterparties (for example, with different clearing members), these amendments only apply if each of those parties ultimately effects clearing with the same central counterparty.

BC6.350 Respondents raised a concern about the phrase 'if and only if' that was used in the 2013 Novation of Derivatives and Continuation of Hedge Accounting Exposure Draft when describing that the relief is provided 'if and only if' the criteria are met. In considering respondents' comments, the IASB noted that the 2013 Novation of Derivatives and Continuation of Hedge Accounting Exposure Draft was intended to address a narrow issue—novation to CCPs—and therefore changing the phrase 'if and only if' to 'if' would target the amendment on the fact patterns that the IASB sought to address. The IASB noted that this would have the effect of requiring an analysis of whether the general conditions for the continuation of hedge accounting are satisfied in other cases (for example, as was raised by some respondents, in determining the effect of intragroup novations in consolidated financial statements).

BC6.351 The 2013 Novation of Derivatives and Continuation of Hedge Accounting Exposure Draft did not propose any additional disclosures. The vast majority of respondents agreed with this. The IASB confirmed that additional disclosures are not required. However, the IASB noted that an entity may consider disclosures in accordance with IFRS 7, which requires qualitative and quantitative disclosures about credit risk.

BC6.352 The IASB also decided to retain the transition requirements proposed in the 2013 Novation of Derivatives and Continuation of Hedge Accounting Exposure Draft so that the revised guidance should apply retrospectively and early application should be permitted. The IASB noted that even with retrospective application, if an entity had previously discontinued hedge accounting as a result of a novation, that (pre-novation) hedge accounting relationship could not be reinstated because doing so would be inconsistent with the requirements for hedge accounting (ie hedge accounting cannot be applied retrospectively).

Fair value hedges

Accounting for fair value hedges

BC6.353 In its deliberations leading to the 2010 Hedge Accounting Exposure Draft, the IASB considered reducing the complexity of hedge accounting by replacing the fair value hedge accounting mechanics with the cash flow hedge accounting mechanics. Such an approach would recognise gains or losses on the hedging instruments outside profit or loss in other comprehensive income instead of requiring the hedged item to be remeasured. The IASB considered such an approach because it would:

(a) improve the usefulness of the reported information for users of financial statements. In accordance with such an approach, all hedging activities to which hedge accounting is applied (including hedges of fair value risk) would be reflected in other comprehensive income, resulting in greater transparency and comparability. In addition, the measurement of the hedged item would not be affected.

(b) simplify existing requirements. Although fair value and cash flow hedge accounting are designed to address different exposures, the same mechanisms can be used to reflect how an entity manages these exposures in the financial statements. Eliminating one of two different methods (fair value hedge accounting or cash flow hedge accounting) would reduce complexity. Such an approach would align fair value hedge accounting and cash flow hedge accounting, resulting in a single method for hedge accounting.

(c) be an expeditious approach to finalise this phase of the project to replace IAS 39. Such an approach would draw on the existing mechanics of cash flow hedge accounting in IAS 39 and, consequently, such an approach would not require much further development.

BC6.354 However, during its outreach activities conducted before publishing the 2010 Hedge Accounting Exposure Draft, the IASB received mixed views on this approach. Some supported the approach for the reasons that the IASB had considered, which was consistent with the feedback received on the Discussion Paper *Reducing Complexity in Reporting Financial Instruments*. However, others raised concerns that such an approach:

(a) would not reflect the underlying economics. They argued that if an entity applies a fair value hedge, the hedged item exists and hence there is an actual gain or loss on the hedged item (not just an anticipated gain or loss on a forecast transaction that does not yet exist). Consequently, hedge accounting should not cause 'artificial' volatility in other comprehensive income and equity.

(b) would make the movements in other comprehensive income less understandable.

(c) would make it difficult to identify the type of risk management strategy that the entity employs.

(d) could result in scenarios in which equity would be significantly reduced or even negative because of losses on the hedging instrument deferred in other comprehensive income. This could have serious implications in terms of solvency and regulatory requirements.

BC6.355 In the light of the views received, the IASB decided to propose a different approach in the 2010 Hedge Accounting Exposure Draft. The IASB proposed to continue to account for fair value hedges differently from cash flow hedges. However, the IASB proposed some changes to the presentation and mechanics of fair value hedge accounting:

(a)   in relation to the gain or loss on remeasuring the hedging instrument—IAS 39 required the gain or loss to be recognised in profit or loss. The IASB proposed to require the recognition of the gain or loss in other comprehensive income.

(b)   in relation to the gain or loss on the hedged item—IAS 39 required such a gain or loss to result in an adjustment to the carrying amount of the hedged item and to be recognised in profit or loss. The IASB proposed to require the gain or loss to be recognised as an asset or a liability that is presented in a separate line item in the statement of financial position and in other comprehensive income. That separate line item would have been presented within assets (or liabilities) for those reporting periods for which the hedged item is an asset (or a liability).

BC6.356   The IASB noted that the separate line item represented measurement adjustments to the hedged items instead of separate assets or liabilities in their own right. The IASB thought that the additional line item might be perceived to add complexity and would increase the number of line items in the statement of financial position. In addition, the IASB noted that this approach is more complex than the approach initially considered, which would have eliminated fair value hedge accounting mechanics.

BC6.357   However, the IASB decided to propose these changes because they would:

(a)   eliminate the mixed measurement for the hedged item (for example, an amount that is amortised cost with a partial fair value adjustment).

(b)   avoid volatility in other comprehensive income and equity that some consider artificial.

(c)   present in one place (ie other comprehensive income) the effects of risk management activities (for both cash flow and fair value hedges).

(d)   provide information in the statement of comprehensive income about the extent of the offsetting achieved for fair value hedges.

BC6.358   Most respondents supported providing the information proposed in the 2010 Hedge Accounting Exposure Draft, but many disagreed with providing this information on the face of the financial statements.

BC6.359   With respect to recognising gains or losses on the hedging instrument and the hedged item in other comprehensive income, many respondents thought that the use of other comprehensive income should be limited until the IASB completed a project on what 'other comprehensive income' represents. Many respondents expressed a preference for the approach in IAS 39 (ie presenting the gain or loss on the hedging instrument and the hedged item in profit or loss). As an alternative, those respondents suggested that the gain or loss on the hedging instrument and the hedged item should be disclosed in the notes to the financial statements.

BC6.360   With respect to presenting separate line items in the statement of financial position, many respondents expressed concern about the excessive number of additional line items in the statement of financial position that could result from the proposals in the 2010 Hedge Accounting Exposure Draft. Those respondents thought that the statement of financial position would appear too cluttered. As an alternative, those respondents suggested that entities disclose the accumulated adjustment made to the carrying amount of the hedged item in the notes to the financial statements.

BC6.361   In the light of this feedback, the IASB, in its redeliberations, decided to retain the fair value hedge accounting mechanics that were in IAS 39. However, the IASB also decided that it would require information to be disclosed so that users of financial statements could understand the effects of hedge accounting on the financial statements and that all hedge accounting disclosures are presented in a single note or separate section in the financial statements (those disclosure requirements were included in IFRS 7).

Linked presentation for fair value hedges

BC6.362   During its outreach activities conducted before the publication of the 2010 Hedge Accounting Exposure Draft, the IASB was alerted to the effect on financial reporting that fair value hedge accounting has on hedges of the foreign currency risk of firm commitments in a specific industry. This issue is a particular concern to that industry because of the magnitude of firm commitments that are denominated in a foreign currency because of the industry's business model. In response to that concern, the IASB considered whether applying linked presentation for fair value hedges of firm commitments might be appropriate. Linked presentation is a way of presenting information so that it shows how particular assets and liabilities are related. Linked presentation is not the same as offsetting, which presents a net asset or liability. Linked presentation displays the 'gross' amount of related items in the statement of financial position (while the net amount is included in the total for assets or liabilities).

BC6.363   The industry was concerned that the presentation resulting from fair value hedge accounting would not reflect the economic effects of hedges of foreign currency risk. For example, an entity that has a large firm commitment for a sale denominated in a foreign currency enters into currency forward contracts to hedge the foreign currency risk of that firm commitment (the forward contract and the firm commitment could be considered 'linked transactions'). The fair value of the derivative liability (asset) and the firm commitment asset (liability) could be significant depending on the volatility of the currency being hedged. That industry was concerned that, as a result, on the basis of the statement of financial position, the entity would appear to be exposed to a higher risk than it actually was. In that industry's view, confusion might arise because the statement of financial position would show large amounts for total assets and total liabilities and hence a high leverage (which typically suggests higher risk) even though the entity hedged the foreign currency risk of the firm commitment and thus sought to reduce risk.

BC6.364   That industry argued that linked presentation of the firm commitment (recognised as a result of fair value hedge accounting) and the hedging instrument could present the effect of an entity's hedging activity and the relationship of the hedged item and the hedging instrument. Linked presentation would not require changing the requirements of offsetting in IAS 32 or other requirements in IAS 39 and IFRS 9.

BC6.365 Moreover, that industry argued that a firm commitment is recognised in the statement of financial position only when fair value hedge accounting is applied. Consequently, that industry advocated that a firm commitment and the related hedging instrument should be accounted for as two parts of a single transaction. That industry also argued that totals for assets and liabilities that include only the 'net' amount (of the linked transactions) would be most appropriate for financial analysis purposes. That industry believed that the ratios, such as leverage, should be calculated on the basis of the difference between the hedged item and the hedging instrument, ie the net amount instead of the gross amount of those items.

BC6.366 The IASB noted that while linked presentation could provide some useful information about a particular relationship between an asset and a liability, it does not differentiate between the types of risk that are covered by that relationship and those that are not. Consequently, linked presentation could result in one net amount for an asset and liability that are 'linked' even though that link (ie the relationship) affects only one of several risks underlying the asset or liability (for example, only the currency risk but not the credit risk or interest rate risk). Furthermore, the IASB did not consider that linked presentation would result in more appropriate totals of assets and liabilities for the purpose of ratio analysis because the hedging affected only one risk but not all risks. Instead, the IASB believed that disclosures about hedging would be a better alternative for providing information that allows users of financial statements to assess the relevance of the information for their own analysis.

BC6.367 Consequently, the IASB decided not to propose the use of linked presentation for the purposes of hedge accounting.

BC6.368 Most respondents to the 2010 Hedge Accounting Exposure Draft agreed with the IASB's conclusion not to allow linked presentation. Some respondents also thought that linked presentation is not an appropriate topic for a project on hedge accounting, but instead that it should be considered as a separate project or as part of a project on either financial statement presentation or the *Conceptual Framework*.

BC6.369 However, those respondents that supported linked presentation argued that, without it, entities that use hedge accounting would be perceived to be riskier than those that do not, and that the true economic effects of hedges of foreign currency risk of firm commitments would not be reflected.

BC6.370 The IASB noted that in the absence of a clear principle for linked presentation, it should be considered in a broader context than just hedge accounting. Consequently, the IASB decided not to require or allow the use of linked presentation for the purpose of hedge accounting.

Cash flow hedges

The 'lower of' test

BC6.371 When a hedge accounting relationship is fully effective, the fair value changes of the hedging instrument perfectly offset the value changes of the hedged item. Hedge ineffectiveness arises when the value changes of the hedging instrument exceed those of the hedged item, or when the value changes of the hedging instrument are less than those of the hedged item.

BC6.372 For cash flow hedges, recognising in profit or loss gains and losses arising on the hedged item in excess of the gains and losses on the hedging instrument is problematic because many hedged items of cash flow hedges are highly probable forecast transactions. Those hedged items do not yet exist although they are expected to occur in the future. Hence, recognising gains and losses on those items in excess of the gains and losses on the hedging instrument is tantamount to recognising gains and losses on items that do not yet exist (instead of a deferral of the gain or loss on the hedging instrument). The IASB noted that this would be conceptually questionable as well as a counter-intuitive outcome.

BC6.373 IAS 39 required a 'lower of' test for determining the amounts that were recognised for cash flow hedges in other comprehensive income (the effective part) and profit or loss (the ineffective part). The 'lower of' test ensured that cumulative changes in the value of the hedged items that exceed cumulative fair value changes of the hedging instrument are not recognised. In contrast, the lower of test did not apply to fair value hedges because, for that type of hedge, the hedged item exists. For example, while a firm commitment might not be recognised in accordance with IFRS, the transaction already exists. Conversely, a forecast transaction does not yet exist but will occur only in the future.

BC6.374 In its deliberations leading to the 2010 Hedge Accounting Exposure Draft, the IASB discussed whether the requirements for measuring the hedge ineffectiveness that is recognised in profit or loss should be aligned for fair value hedges and cash flow hedges. The IASB noted that the requirements could be aligned by also applying the lower of test to fair value hedges or by eliminating it for cash flow hedges. In the IASB's view, aligning the requirements would reduce complexity. However, the IASB considered that, for conceptual reasons, recognising gains and losses on items that do not yet exist instead of only deferring the gain or loss on the hedging instrument was not appropriate. On the other hand, the IASB considered that the nature of fair value hedges is different from that of cash flow hedges. Also applying the lower of test to fair value hedges, even though that test was designed to address only the specific characteristics of cash flow hedges, was not justified. Consequently, the IASB decided to retain the lower of test for cash flow hedges and not to introduce it for fair value hedges.

Basis adjustments for hedges of forecast transactions that will result in the recognition of a non-financial asset or a non-financial liability

BC6.375 A forecast transaction could subsequently result in the recognition of a non-financial asset or a non-financial liability. Similarly, a forecast transaction for a non-financial asset or non-financial liability could subsequently result in the recognition of a firm commitment for which fair value hedge accounting is applied. In these cases IAS 39 permitted an entity an accounting policy choice:

(a) to reclassify the associated gains or losses that were recognised in other comprehensive income to profit or loss in the same period or periods during which the asset acquired or liability assumed affects profit or loss; or

(b) to remove the associated gains or losses that were recognised in other comprehensive income and include them in the initial cost or other carrying amount of the asset or liability. This approach was commonly referred to as a 'basis adjustment'.

BC6.376 In its deliberations leading to the 2010 Hedge Accounting Exposure Draft, the IASB considered whether to continue allowing this accounting policy choice. The IASB noted that if an entity was precluded from applying a basis adjustment, this would require the entity to track the hedging gains and losses separately (after the hedging relationship had ended) and to match them to the period or periods in which the non-financial item that had resulted from the hedged transaction affected profit or loss. The entity would also need to consider whether or not the remaining amount in other comprehensive income was recoverable in one or more future periods. In contrast, if an entity applied a basis adjustment, the hedging gain or loss was included in the carrying amount of the non-financial item and automatically recognised in profit or loss in the period in which the related non-financial item affected profit or loss (for example, through depreciation expense for items of property, plant and equipment or cost of sales for inventories). It would also be automatically considered when an entity tested a non-financial asset for impairment. The IASB noted that for a non-financial asset that is tested for impairment as part of a cash-generating unit, tracking amounts in other comprehensive income and including them in the impairment test is difficult (even more so if the composition of cash-generating units changes over time).

BC6.377 The IASB acknowledged that there were different views on whether a basis adjustment would achieve or reduce comparability. One view was that two identical assets purchased at the same time and in the same way (except for the fact that one was hedged) should have the same initial carrying amount. From this viewpoint, basis adjustments would impair comparability.

BC6.378 The other view was that basis adjustments allowed identical assets for which the acquisitions are subject to the same risk to be measured so that they had the same initial carrying amount. For example, Entity A and Entity B want to purchase the same asset from a supplier that has a different functional currency. Entity A is able to secure the purchase contract denominated in its functional currency. Conversely, while Entity B also wants to fix the purchase price in its functional currency, it has to accept a purchase contract denominated in the functional currency of the supplier (ie a foreign currency) and is therefore exposed to the variability in cash flows arising from movements in the exchange rate. Hence, Entity B hedges its exposure to foreign currency risk using a currency forward contract which, in effect, fixes the price of the purchase in its functional currency. When taking into account the currency forward contract,

Entity B has, in effect, the same foreign currency risk exposure as Entity A. From this viewpoint, basis adjustments would enhance comparability.

BC6.379 The IASB also considered the interaction between basis adjustments and the choice of accounting for a hedge of foreign currency risk of a firm commitment as either a cash flow hedge or a fair value hedge (see paragraphs BC6.272–BC6.277). The IASB noted that for hedges of the foreign currency risk of a firm commitment the basis adjustment at the end of the cash flow hedge has the same effect on the presentation of the hedged item as accounting for the hedge as a fair value hedge. Thus, using fair value hedge accounting for those firm commitments was tantamount to a basis adjustment. The IASB thought that, in this context, basis adjustments would also enhance comparability.

BC6.380 Consequently, the IASB decided to eliminate the accounting policy choice in IAS 39 and require basis adjustments. The IASB decided that when the entity removes the associated gain or loss that was recognised in other comprehensive income in order to include it in the initial cost or other carrying amount of the asset or liability, that gain or loss should be directly applied against the carrying amount of the asset or liability.   This means that it would not be a reclassification adjustment (see IAS 1 *Presentation of Financial Statements*) and hence would not affect other comprehensive income when removing it from equity and adding it to, or deducting it from, the asset or liability. The IASB noted that accounting for the basis adjustment as a reclassification adjustment would distort comprehensive income because the amount would affect comprehensive income twice but in different periods:

(a)   first (in other comprehensive income) in the period in which the non-financial item is recognised; and

(b)   again in the later periods when the non-financial item affects profit or loss (for example, through depreciation expense or cost of sales).

The IASB also noted that presenting a basis adjustment as a reclassification adjustment would create the misleading impression that the basis adjustment was a performance event.

BC6.381 The IASB acknowledged that the total comprehensive income across periods will be distorted because the gain or loss on the hedging instrument during the period of the cash flow hedge is recognised in other comprehensive income, whereas the cumulative hedging gain or loss that is removed from the cash flow hedge reserve (ie from equity) and directly applied to the subsequently recognised non-financial item does not affect other comprehensive income. The IASB considered that one type of distortion of other comprehensive income was inevitable (ie either in the period of the basis adjustment or over the total period) and hence there was a trade-off. The IASB concluded that, on balance, the effect of a reclassification adjustment in the period of the basis adjustment would be more misleading than the effect over the total period of not using a reclassification adjustment.

BC6.382 The IASB retained its original decision when deliberating its 2010 Hedge Accounting Exposure Draft.

Hedges of a net investment in a foreign operation

BC6.383 In its deliberations leading to the 2010 Hedge Accounting Exposure Draft, the IASB decided not to address a hedge of a net investment in a foreign operation as part of its hedge accounting project. The IASB noted that a net investment in a foreign operation was determined and accounted for in accordance with IAS 21. The IASB also noted that the hedge of a net investment in a foreign operation also related to IAS 21. Hence, similar to the issue of considering intragroup monetary items for eligibility as hedging instruments for hedges of foreign exchange risk (see paragraph BC6.149), the IASB considered that comprehensively addressing this type of hedge would require a review of the requirements in IAS 21 at the same time as considering the hedge accounting requirements.

BC6.384 Consequently, the IASB proposed retaining the requirements of IAS 39 for a hedge of a net investment in a foreign operation.

BC6.385 The IASB retained its original decision when redeliberating its 2010 Hedge Accounting Exposure Draft.

Accounting for the time value of options

BC6.386 IAS 39 allowed an entity a choice:

(a) to designate an option-type derivative as a hedging instrument in its entirety; or

(b) to separate the time value of the option and designate as the hedging instrument only the intrinsic value element.

BC6.387 The IASB noted that under the IAS 39 hedge accounting model entities typically designated option-type derivatives as hedging instruments on the basis of their intrinsic value. Consequently, the undesignated time value of the option was treated as held for trading and was accounted for as at fair value through profit or loss, which gave rise to significant volatility in profit or loss. This particular accounting treatment is disconnected from the risk management view, whereby entities typically consider the time value of an option (at inception, ie included in the premium paid) as a cost of hedging. It is a cost of obtaining protection against unfavourable changes of prices, while retaining participation in any favourable changes.

BC6.388 Against this background, the IASB, in its deliberations leading to the 2010 Hedge Accounting Exposure Draft, considered how best to portray the time value of options (in the context of hedging exposures only against changes to one side of a specified level—a 'one-sided risk'). The IASB noted that the standard-setting debate about accounting for the time value of options had historically been focused on hedge ineffectiveness. Many typical hedged transactions (such as firm commitments, forecast transactions or existing items) do not involve a time value notion because they are not options. Hence, such hedged items do not have a change in their value that offsets the fair value change related to the time value of the option that is used as a hedging instrument. The IASB concluded that, unless the time value of the option was excluded from being designated as the hedging instrument, hedge ineffectiveness would arise.

BC6.389   However, the IASB noted that the time value of an option could also be considered from a different perspective—that of a premium for protection against risk (an 'insurance premium' view).

BC6.390   The IASB noted that entities that use purchased options to hedge one-sided risks typically consider the time value that they pay as a premium to the option writer or seller as similar to an insurance premium. In order to protect themselves against the downside of an exposure (an adverse outcome) while retaining the upside, they have to compensate someone else for assuming the inverse asymmetrical position, which has only the downside but not the upside. The time value of an option is subject to 'time decay'. This means that it loses its value over time as the option approaches expiry, which occurs at an increasingly rapid rate. At expiry the option's time value reaches zero. Hence, entities that use purchased options to hedge one-sided risks know that over the life of the option they will lose the time value that they paid. This explains why entities typically view the premium paid as being similar to an insurance premium and hence as a cost of using this hedging strategy.

BC6.391   The IASB considered that by taking an insurance premium view, the accounting for the time value of options could be aligned with the risk management perspective as well as with other areas of accounting. The IASB noted that under IFRS some costs of insuring risks were treated as transaction costs that were capitalised into the costs of the insured asset (for example, freight insurance paid by the buyer in accordance with IAS 2 Inventories or IAS 16 *Property, Plant and Equipment*), whereas costs of insuring some other risks were recognised as expenses over the period for which the entity was insured (for example, fire insurance for a building). Hence, the IASB considered that aligning the accounting for the time value of options with such other areas would provide more comparable results that would also be more aligned with how preparers and users of financial statements think about the issue.

BC6.392   The IASB took the view that, like the distinction between the different types of costs of insuring risk, the time value of options should be distinguished by the type of hedged item that the option hedges, into time value that is:

(a)   transaction related (for example, the forecast purchase of a commodity); or

(b)   time-period related (for example, hedging an existing commodity inventory for commodity price changes).

BC6.393   The IASB considered that for transaction related hedged items the cumulative change in fair value of the option's time value should be accumulated in other comprehensive income and be reclassified in a way similar to that for cash flow hedges. In the IASB's view, this would best reflect the character of transaction costs (like those capitalised for inventory or property, plant and equipment).

BC6.394   In contrast, the IASB considered that for time-period related hedged items the nature of the time value of the option used as the hedging instrument is that of a cost for obtaining protection against a risk over a particular period of time. Hence, the IASB considered that the cost of obtaining the protection should be allocated as an expense over the relevant period on a systematic and rational basis. The IASB noted that this would require accumulating the cumulative change in fair value of the option's time value in other comprehensive income and amortising the original time value by transferring in each period an amount to profit or loss. The IASB considered that the amortisation pattern should be determined on a systematic and rational basis, which would best reflect principle-based standard-setting.

BC6.395 The IASB also considered situations in which the option used has critical terms (such as the nominal amount, the life and the underlying) that do not match the hedged item. This raises the following questions:

(a) which part of the time value included in the premium relates to the hedged item (and therefore should be treated as costs of hedging) and which part does not?

(b) how should any part of the time value that does not relate to the hedged item be accounted for?

BC6.396 The IASB proposed in the 2010 Hedge Accounting Exposure Draft that the part of the time value of the option that relates to the hedged item should be determined as the time value that would have been paid for an option that perfectly matches the hedged item (for example, with the same underlying, maturity and notional amount). The IASB noted that this would require an option pricing exercise using the terms of the hedged item as well as other relevant information about the hedged item (in particular, the volatility of its price or cash flow, which is a driver of an option's time value).

BC6.397 The IASB noted that the accounting for the time value of the option would need to distinguish whether the initial time value of the purchased option (actual time value) is higher or lower than the time value that would have been paid for an option that perfectly matches the hedged item (aligned time value). The IASB noted that if, at inception of the hedging relationship, the actual time value is higher than the aligned time value, the entity pays a higher premium than that which reflects the costs of hedging. Hence, the IASB considered that the amount that is recognised in accumulated other comprehensive income should be determined only on the basis of the aligned time value, whereas the remainder of the actual time value should be accounted for as a derivative.

BC6.398 Conversely, the IASB noted that if, at inception of the hedging relationship, the actual time value is lower than the aligned time value, the entity actually pays a lower premium than it would have to pay to cover the risk fully. The IASB considered that in this situation, in order to avoid accounting for a higher time value of an option than was actually paid, the amount that is recognised in accumulated other comprehensive income would have to be determined by reference to the lower of the cumulative fair value change of:

(a) the actual time value; and

(b) the aligned time value.

BC6.399 The IASB also considered whether the balances accumulated in other comprehensive income would require an impairment test. The IASB decided that because the accounting for the time value of the option was closely linked to hedge accounting, an impairment test that uses features of the hedge accounting model would be appropriate. Hence, for transaction related hedged items the impairment test would be similar to that for the cash flow hedge reserve. For time-period related hedged items the IASB considered that the part of the option's time value that remains in accumulated other comprehensive income should be immediately recognised in profit or loss when the hedging relationship is discontinued. That would reflect that the reason for amortising the amount would no longer apply after the insured risk (ie the hedged item) no longer qualifies for hedge accounting. The IASB noted that impairment of the hedged item affects the criteria for qualifying hedges and if those are no longer met it would result in an impairment loss for the remaining unamortised balance of the time value of the option.

BC6.400　Most of the respondents to the 2010 Hedge Accounting Exposure Draft agreed with the 'insurance premium' view. They thought that the proposal provided a better representation of the performance and effect of the entity's risk management strategy than under IAS 39. In their view, the proposals alleviated undue profit or loss volatility and reflected the economic substance of the transaction. They also thought that the costs of hedging should be associated with the hedged item instead of being mischaracterised as hedge ineffectiveness.

BC6.401　However, there were mixed views about the complexity of the proposals, in particular in relation to:

(a)　the requirement to differentiate between transaction related and time-period related hedged items; and

(b)　the requirement to measure the fair value of the aligned time value. Those concerns included the concern that the costs of implementing the proposals could outweigh the benefits, for instance, for less sophisticated (for example, smaller) entities.

BC6.402　Some respondents did not agree with the proposed accounting for transaction related hedged items. Some argued that time value should always be expensed over the option period.

BC6.403　In the light of this feedback the IASB considered in its redeliberations:

(a)　whether the time value of an option should always be expensed over the life of the option instead of applying the accounting as proposed in the 2010 Hedge Accounting Exposure Draft;

(b)　whether it should remove the differentiation between transaction related and time-period related hedged items and replace it with a single accounting treatment; and

(c)　whether it should simplify the requirement to account for the fair value of the aligned time value.

BC6.404　The IASB discussed whether the time value of an option should always be expensed over the life of the option instead of applying the accounting as proposed in the 2010 Hedge Accounting Exposure Draft. The IASB noted that such an accounting treatment would have outcomes that would be inconsistent with the notion of the time value being regarded as costs of hedging. This is because it could result in recognising an expense in periods that are unrelated to how the hedged exposure affects profit or loss.

BC6.405 The IASB also reconsidered whether it was appropriate to defer in accumulated other comprehensive income the time value of options for transaction related hedged items. The IASB noted that the deferred time value does not represent an asset in itself, but that it is an ancillary cost that is capitalised as part of the measurement of the asset acquired or liability assumed. This is consistent with how other Standards treat ancillary costs. The IASB also noted that the 2010 Hedge Accounting Exposure Draft included an impairment test to ensure that amounts that are not expected to be recoverable are not deferred.

BC6.406 The IASB also discussed whether the proposals in the 2010 Hedge Accounting Exposure Draft could be simplified by removing the differentiation between transaction related and time-period related hedged items. However, the IASB noted that a single accounting treatment would be inconsistent with other Standards because it would not distinguish situations in a similar way (see paragraphs BC6.391–BC6.392). Hence, the IASB considered that the suggested single accounting treatment would essentially treat unlike situations as alike. The IASB noted that this would actually diminish comparability and hence not be an improvement to financial reporting.

BC6.407 The IASB also considered whether it should paraphrase the requirements as a single general principle to clarify the accounting for transaction related and time-period related hedged items, instead of having requirements that distinguish between those two types of hedged items. However, on balance the IASB decided that this approach risked creating confusion, particularly because it would still involve the two different types of accounting treatments.

BC6.408 The IASB also discussed possible ways to simplify the requirements to account for the fair value of the aligned time value. As part of those discussions the IASB considered:

(a) applying the proposed accounting treatment for the time value of options to the entire amount of the time value paid even if it differs from the aligned time value. This means that entities would not need to perform a separate valuation for the fair value of the aligned time value. However, the IASB considered that only the time value that relates to the hedged item should be treated as a cost of hedging. Hence, any additional time value paid should be accounted for as a derivative at fair value through profit or loss.

(b) providing entities with a choice (for each hedging relationship or alternatively as an accounting policy choice) to account for the time value of options either as proposed in the 2010 Hedge Accounting Exposure Draft or in accordance with the treatment in IAS 39. In the latter case, the amount recognised in profit or loss as a 'trading instrument' is the difference between the change in the fair value of the option in its entirety and the change in fair value of the intrinsic value. In contrast, the proposals in the 2010 Hedge Accounting Exposure Draft would require two option valuations (ie the change in fair value of the actual time value of the option and the aligned time value of the option). However, the IASB noted that the accounting treatment in accordance with IAS 39 would, in effect, present the change in fair value of the time value as a trading profit or loss. This accounting treatment would not be consistent with the character of the changes in the time value that the IASB is seeking to portray, ie that of costs of hedging. In addition, the IASB noted that providing a choice would reduce comparability between entities and it would make financial statements more difficult to understand.

BC6.409 Consequently, the IASB decided to retain the accounting requirements related to the time value of options proposed in the 2010 Hedge Accounting Exposure Draft (ie that the accounting would depend on the nature of the hedged item and that the new accounting treatment only applied to the aligned time value).

Zero-cost collars

BC6.410 The proposed accounting treatment for the time value of options in the 2010 Hedge Accounting Exposure Draft only addressed situations in which the option had a time value (other than nil) at inception. That proposed accounting would not have applied to situations in which there was a combination of a purchased and a written option (one being a put option and one being a call option) that at inception of the hedging relationship had a net time value of nil (often referred to as 'zero-cost collars' or 'zero premium collars').

BC6.411 Many respondents to the 2010 Hedge Accounting Exposure Draft commented that the proposed accounting for purchased options should also apply to all zero-cost collars. They thought that without generally aligning the accounting treatment for the time value of zero-cost collars and options, it would encourage entities to undertake particular types of transactions and replace zero-cost collars with collars with a nominal cost only to achieve a desired accounting outcome.

BC6.412 Furthermore, those respondents noted that even though the zero-cost collar had no net time value at inception, the time value of the collar would fluctuate during the life of the hedge. They noted that time value was subject to 'time decay' and that both the purchased and the written option would lose their time value over time as the collar approaches expiry. They argued that the time value of zero-cost collars should also be recognised in other comprehensive income during the life of the hedging relationship. They considered it unjustified to limit the proposed accounting to options that have an initial time value of greater than nil, given that one of the main concerns being addressed by the proposal was the volatility resulting from changes in the time value over the life of the hedge.

BC6.413 In the light of those arguments, the IASB decided to align the accounting treatment for changes in the time value of options and zero-cost collars.

Accounting for the forward element of forward contracts

BC6.414 IAS 39 allowed an entity a choice between:

(a) designating a forward contract as a hedging instrument in its entirety; or

(b) separating the forward element and designating as the hedging instrument only the spot element.

BC6.415   If not designated, the forward element was treated as held for trading and was accounted for as at fair value through profit or loss, which gave rise to significant volatility in profit or loss.

BC6.416   The IASB noted that the characteristics of forward elements depended on the underlying item, for example:

     (a)   for foreign exchange rate risk, the forward element represents the interest differential between the two currencies;

     (b)   for interest rate risk, the forward element reflects the term structure of interest rates; and

     (c)   for commodity risk, the forward element represents what is called the 'cost of carry' (for example, it includes costs such as storage costs).

BC6.417   Respondents to the 2010 Hedge Accounting Exposure Draft as well as participants in the IASB's outreach activities requested that the IASB consider extending the proposal on the accounting for the time value of options (see paragraphs BC6.386–BC6.413) to forward elements.

BC6.418   The IASB noted that even though under IAS 39 the hedge accounting requirements were identical for forward elements and options, the actual accounting implications were different. In contrast to many typical situations in which options were used to hedge transactions that did not involve a time value notion because they were not options (see paragraph BC6.388), in situations in which forward contracts were used the value of hedged items typically did have a forward element that corresponded to that of the hedge. The IASB noted that this meant that an entity could choose to designate the forward contract in its entirety and use the 'forward rate method' to measure the hedged item.

BC6.419   Using the forward rate method, the forward element is essentially included in the hedging relationship by measuring the change in the value of the hedged item on the basis of forward prices or rates. An entity can then recognise the forward element as costs of hedging by using the forward rate method, resulting in, for example:

     (a)   capitalising the forward element into the cost of the acquired asset or liability assumed; or

     (b)   reclassifying the forward element into profit or loss when the hedged item (for example, hedged sales denominated in a foreign currency) affects profit or loss.

BC6.420   Consequently, changes in forward elements are not recognised in profit or loss until the hedged item affects profit or loss. The IASB noted that this outcome was equivalent to what it had proposed in its 2010 Hedge Accounting Exposure Draft for accounting for the time value of options that hedge transaction related hedged items. Hence, the IASB considered that, for situations similar to hedges of transaction related hedged items using options, applying the forward rate method would, in effect, achieve an accounting outcome that treated the forward element like costs of hedging. This would be consistent with the IASB's overall approach to accounting for the costs of hedging and would therefore not require any amendments to the proposals in the 2010 Hedge Accounting Exposure Draft.

BC6.421 However, the IASB acknowledged that in situations that were equivalent to those addressed by its decision on the accounting for time-period related hedged items that were hedged using options, its proposals in the 2010 Hedge Accounting Exposure Draft (like IAS 39) would prevent an entity from achieving an equivalent accounting outcome for the forward element of a forward contract. The reason was that, like IAS 39, the proposals in the 2010 Hedge Accounting Exposure Draft did not allow the forward element to be amortised. For example, if an entity hedged the fair value changes resulting from the price changes of its existing commodity inventory (ie a time-period related hedged item) it could, under the proposals in the 2010 Hedge Accounting Exposure Draft (like IAS 39), either:

(a) use the forward rate method (ie forward elements are capitalised into the cost of inventory, instead of being accounted for as at fair value through profit or loss over the time of the hedge); or

(b) designate as the hedging instrument only changes in the spot element (ie fair value changes in the forward element of the forward contract are recognised in profit or loss).

Neither of the above accounting outcomes are aligned with the treatment for the time value of options for time-period related hedged items that requires that the time value is amortised on a systematic and rational basis.

BC6.422 The IASB also noted that the accounting for monetary financial assets and liabilities denominated in a foreign currency had an important consequence. Like IAS 39, IFRS 9 (see paragraph B5.7.2) requires an entity to apply IAS 21 to those assets and liabilities, which means that they are translated into the entity's functional currency by using the spot exchange rate. Hence, the forward rate method does not provide a solution when entities hedge monetary financial assets and liabilities denominated in a foreign currency.

BC6.423 Consequently, the IASB acknowledged that aligning the accounting for forward elements with the accounting for the time value of options was a particular concern to entities that, for example, had more funding in their functional currency than they could invest in financial assets in their functional currency. To generate an economic return on their surplus funds, such entities exchange those funds into a foreign currency and invest in assets denominated in that foreign currency. To manage their exposure to foreign exchange risk (and to stabilise their net interest margin), such entities commonly enter into foreign exchange derivatives. Such transactions usually involve the following simultaneously:

(a) swapping the functional currency surplus funds into a foreign currency;

(b) investing the funds in a foreign currency financial asset for a period of time; and

(c) entering into a foreign exchange derivative to convert the foreign currency funds back into the functional currency at the end of the investment period. This amount typically covers the principal plus the interest at maturity.

BC6.424 The difference between the forward rate and the spot rate (ie the forward element) represents the interest differential between the two currencies at inception. The net economic return (ie the interest margin) over the investment period is determined by adjusting the yield of the investment in the foreign currency by the forward points (ie the forward element of the foreign exchange derivative) and then deducting the interest expense. The combination of the three transactions described in paragraph BC6.423 allows the entity to, in effect, 'lock in' a net interest margin and generate a fixed economic return over the investment period.

BC6.425 Respondents argued that risk management viewed the forward elements as an adjustment of the investment yield on foreign currency denominated assets. They believed that, as in the case of the accounting for the time value of options, it gave rise to a similar need for adjusting profit or loss against other comprehensive income to represent the cost of achieving a fixed economic return in a way that is consistent with the accounting for that return.

BC6.426 In the light of the arguments raised by respondents, the IASB decided to permit forward points that exist at inception of the hedging relationship to be recognised in profit or loss over time on a systematic and rational basis and to accumulate subsequent fair value changes through other comprehensive income. The IASB considered that this accounting treatment would provide a better representation of the economic substance of the transaction and the performance of the net interest margin.

Hedges of a group of items

BC6.427 IAS 39 restricted the application of hedge accounting for groups of items. For example, hedged items that together constitute an overall net position of assets and liabilities could not be designated into a hedging relationship with that net position as the hedged item. Other groups were eligible if the individual items within that group had similar risk characteristics and shared the risk exposure that was designated as being hedged. Furthermore, the change in the fair value attributable to the hedged risk for each individual item in the group had to be approximately proportional to the overall change in the fair value of the group for the hedged risk. The effect of those restrictions was that a group would generally qualify as a hedged item only if all the items in that group would qualify for hedge accounting for the same hedged risk on an individual basis (ie each as an individual hedged item).

BC6.428 In response to the Discussion Paper *Reducing Complexity in Reporting Financial Instruments*, many commented that restricting the ability to achieve hedge accounting for groups of items, including net positions, had resulted in a hedge accounting model that was inconsistent with the way in which an entity actually hedges (ie for risk management purposes). Similar concerns about the restrictions of IAS 39 for applying hedge accounting to groups of items were raised as part of the IASB's outreach activities for its Hedge Accounting project.

BC6.429   In practice, most entities hedge their risk exposures using different approaches, resulting in hedges of:

(a)   individual items;

(b)   groups of items that form a gross position; or

(c)   groups of (partially) offsetting items or risks that result in a net position.

BC6.430   The group hedging approach involves identifying the risk from particular groups of items (including a net position), and then hedging some or all of that risk with one or more hedging instruments. The group hedging approach views the risk at a higher aggregated level. The reasons for taking this approach include:

(a)   items in the group have some offsetting risk positions that provide a natural hedge for some of those risks and therefore those offsetting risks do not need to be separately hedged;

(b)   hedging derivatives that hedge different risks together can be more readily available than individual derivatives that each hedge a different risk;

(c)   it is more expedient (cost, practicality, etc) to enter into fewer derivatives to hedge a group instead of hedging individual exposures;

(d)   the minimisation of counterparty credit risk exposure, because offsetting risk positions are hedged on a net basis (this aspect is particularly important for an entity that has regulatory capital requirements); and

(e)   the reduction of gross assets/liabilities in the statement of financial position, because offset accounting may not be achieved if multiple derivatives (with offsetting risk exposures) are entered into.

BC6.431   The restrictions in IAS 39 prevented an entity that hedges on a group or net basis from presenting its activities in a manner that is consistent with its risk management practice. For example, an entity may hedge the net (ie residual) foreign currency risk from a sequence of sales and expenses that arise over several reporting periods (say, two years) using a single foreign currency derivative. Such an entity could not designate the net position of sales and expenses as the hedged item. Instead, if it wanted to apply hedge accounting it had to designate a gross position that best matched its hedging instrument. However, the IASB noted there were a number of reasons why this could render information less useful, for example:

(a)   a matching hedged item might not exist, in which case hedge accounting cannot be applied.

(b)   if the entity did identify and designate a matching gross exposure from the sequence of sales and expenses, that item would be portrayed as the only hedged item and would be presented at the hedged rate. All other transactions (for instance, in earlier reporting periods) would appear unhedged and would be recognised at the prevailing spot rates, which would give rise to volatility in some reporting periods.

(c)   if the designated hedged transaction did not arise, but the net position remained the same, hedge ineffectiveness would be recognised for accounting purposes even though it does not exist from an economic perspective.

BC6.432   Consequently, in its 2010 Hedge Accounting Exposure Draft, the IASB proposed that groups of items (including net positions) should be eligible for hedge accounting. However, the IASB also proposed limiting the application of cash flow hedge accounting for some types of groups of items that constitute a net position (see paragraphs BC6.442–BC6.447).

BC6.433   Respondents to the 2010 Hedge Accounting Exposure Draft supported the proposal to allow hedge accounting for groups and net positions and most supported the IASB's rationale for doing so. However, some disagreed with specific aspects of the IASB's proposals in the 2010 Hedge Accounting Exposure Draft. Their concerns focused on the proposals related to cash flow hedges of net positions.

BC6.434   The following subsections set out the IASB's considerations about the application of hedge accounting in the context of groups of items.

Criteria for the eligibility of a group of items as a hedged item

BC6.435   An individual hedge approach involves an entity entering into one or more hedging instruments to manage a risk exposure from an individual hedged item to achieve a desired outcome. This is similar for a group hedge approach. However, for a group hedge approach an entity seeks to manage the risk exposure from a group of items. Some of the risks in the group may offset (for their full term or for a partial term) and provide a hedge against each other, leaving the group residual risk to be hedged by the hedging instrument.

BC6.436   An individual hedge approach and a group hedge approach are similar in concept. Hence, the IASB decided that the requirements for qualifying for hedge accounting should also be similar. Consequently, the IASB proposed that the eligibility criteria that apply to individual hedged items should also apply to hedges of groups of items. However, some restrictions were retained for cash flow hedges of net positions.

BC6.437   The IASB retained its original decision when redeliberating its 2010 Hedge Accounting Exposure Draft.

Designation of a layer component of a nominal amount for hedges of a group of items

BC6.438   The IASB proposed in its 2010 Hedge Accounting Exposure Draft that an entity could designate a layer component of a nominal amount (a 'layer') of a single item in a hedging relationship. The IASB also considered whether it would be appropriate to extend that decision on single items to groups of items and hence allow the designation of a layer of a group in a hedging relationship.

BC6.439   The IASB noted that the benefits of identifying a layer component of a nominal amount of a group of items are similar to the benefits it had considered for layer components of single items (see paragraphs BC6.200–BC6.204). In addition, the IASB also noted other reasons that support the use of components for groups of items:

(a) uncertainties such as a breach (or cancellation) of contracts, or prepayment, can be better modelled when considering a group of items;

(b) in practice, hedging layers of groups of items (for example, a bottom layer) is a common risk management strategy; and

(c) arbitrarily identifying and designating (as hedged items) specific items from a group of items that are exposed to the same hedged risk can:

    (i) give rise to arbitrary accounting results if the designated items do not behave as originally expected (while other items, sufficient to cover the hedged amount, do behave as originally expected); and

    (ii) can provide opportunities for earnings management (for example, by choosing to transfer and derecognise particular items from a group of homogeneous items when only some were specifically designated into a fair value hedge and therefore have fair value hedge adjustments attached to them).

BC6.440 The IASB noted that, in practice, groups of items hedged together are not likely to be groups of identical items. Given the different types of groups that could exist in practice, in some cases it could be easy to satisfy the proposed conditions and in some cases it could be more challenging or even impossible. The IASB considered that it is not appropriate to define the cases in which the proposed conditions were satisfied because it would depend on the specific facts and circumstances. The IASB therefore considered a criteria-based approach would be more operational and appropriate. Such an approach would allow hedge accounting to be applied in situations in which the criteria are easy to meet as well as in cases in which, although the criteria are more challenging to meet, an entity is prepared to undertake the necessary efforts (for example, to invest in systems in order to achieve compliance with the hedge accounting requirements).

BC6.441 The IASB retained its original decision when redeliberating its 2010 Hedge Accounting Exposure Draft.

Cash flow hedges of a group of items that constitutes a net position that qualifies for hedge accounting

BC6.442 In a cash flow hedge, changes in the fair value of the hedging instrument are deferred in other comprehensive income to be reclassified later from accumulated other comprehensive income to profit or loss when the hedged item affects profit or loss. For hedges of net positions, items in the group have some offsetting risk positions that provide a natural hedge for some of the risks in the group (ie the gains on some items offset the losses on others). Hence, for a cash flow hedge of a net position that is a group of forecast transactions, the cumulative change in value (from the inception of the hedge) that arises on some forecast transactions (to the extent that it is effective in achieving offset) must be deferred in other comprehensive income. This is necessary because the gain or loss that arises on the forecast transactions that occur in the early phase of the hedging relationship must be reclassified to profit or loss in the later phase until the last hedged item in the net position affects profit or loss.

BC6.443 The forecast transactions that constitute a hedged net position might differ in their timing such that they affect profit or loss in different reporting periods. For example, sales and unrelated expenditure hedged for foreign currency risk might affect profit or loss in different reporting periods. When this happens, the cumulative change in value of the designated sales (to be reclassified later when the expenditure is recognised as an expense) needs to be excluded from profit or loss and instead be deferred in other comprehensive income. This is required in order to ensure that the effect of the sales on profit or loss is based on the hedged exchange rate.

BC6.444 Hence, in its deliberations leading to the 2010 Hedge Accounting Exposure Draft, the IASB noted that cash flow hedge accounting for net positions of forecast transactions would involve a deferral in accumulated other comprehensive income of cumulative gains and losses on some forecast transactions, from the time they occurred until some other forecast transactions would affect profit or loss in later reporting periods. The IASB considered that this would be tantamount to measuring the transactions that occurred first at a different amount from the transaction amount (or other amount that would be required under general IFRS requirements) in contemplation of other forecast transactions that were expected to occur in the future and that would have an offsetting gain or loss. When those other transactions occurred, their measurement would be adjusted for the amounts deferred in accumulated other comprehensive income on forecast transactions that had occurred earlier.

BC6.445 The IASB acknowledged that this approach would not result in the recognition of gains and losses on items that do not yet exist but would instead defer gains and losses on some forecast transactions as those transactions occurred. However, the IASB considered that this approach would be a significant departure from general IFRS regarding the items that resulted from the forecast transactions. The IASB noted that this departure would affect the forecast transactions:

(a) that occurred in the early phases of the hedging relationship, ie those for which gains and losses were deferred when the transaction occurred; and

(b) those that occurred in the later phases of the hedging relationship and were adjusted for the gains or losses that had been deferred on the forecast transactions as those transactions had occurred in the early phases of the hedging relationship.

BC6.446 The IASB noted that the accounting for the forecast transactions that occurred in the later phases of the hedging relationship was comparable to that of forecast transactions that were hedged items in a cash flow hedge. However, the treatment of the forecast transactions that occurred in the early phases of the hedging relationship would be more similar to that of a hedging instrument than to that of a hedged item. The IASB concluded that this would be a significant departure from general IFRS requirements and the requirements of the hedge accounting model for hedging instruments.

BC6.447　Consequently, in its 2010 Hedge Accounting Exposure Draft, the IASB proposed that a cash flow hedge of a net position should not qualify for hedge accounting when the offsetting risk positions would affect profit or loss in different periods. The IASB noted that when the offsetting risk positions affected profit or loss in the same period those concerns would not apply in the same way as no deferral in accumulated other comprehensive income of cumulative gains and losses on forecast transactions would be required. Hence, the IASB proposed that such net positions should be eligible as hedged items.

BC6.448　Some respondents to the 2010 Hedge Accounting Exposure Draft agreed with the IASB's rationale for not allowing the application of cash flow hedge accounting to net positions that consist of forecast transactions that would affect profit or loss in different reporting periods. They believed that without this restriction the potential for earnings management would arise. Despite agreeing with the proposals, some respondents asked the IASB to provide additional guidance on the treatment of the amounts deferred in accumulated other comprehensive income if, in a cash flow hedge of a net position, the offsetting risk positions that were initially expected to affect profit or loss in the same reporting period subsequently changed and, as a result, were expected to affect profit or loss in different periods.

BC6.449　Others requested the IASB to reconsider the restriction on the application of hedge accounting to cash flow hedges of a net position with offsetting risk positions that affect profit or loss in different reporting periods. Those respondents believed that this restriction would not allow entities to properly reflect their risk management activities. In addition, some respondents requested that the IASB consider the annual reporting period as the basis for this restriction (if retained) instead of any reporting period (ie including an interim reporting period), noting that the frequency of reporting would otherwise affect the eligibility for this form of hedge accounting.

BC6.450　The IASB noted that the feedback on its proposals in the 2010 Hedge Accounting Exposure Draft reflected two different perspectives:

(a)　a treasury perspective—this is a cash flow perspective. The respondents who provided comments from this perspective typically look at cash inflows and cash outflows arising from both sides of the net position. The treasury view stops at the level of the cash flows and does not take into account the time lag that might exist between the cash flow and the recognition of related income or expense in profit or loss. From this perspective, once the first forecast transaction is recognised, the natural hedge lapses and the remainder of the net position will be hedged by entering into an additional derivative (or alternatively by using, for example, the foreign currency denominated cash instrument that arises as a result of the occurrence of the first forecast transaction). Subsequently (ie at the time of settlement of the second forecast transaction), the cash flows from the financial instrument being used as a hedging instrument will be used to settle the payments resulting from the forecast transaction.

(b)   an accounting perspective—this perspective focuses on how to present the effect of the two forecast transactions in profit or loss and in which accounting period. This goes beyond the cash flow view of the treasury perspective. This is because the way in which the item affects profit or loss can be different, while the cash flow is a point-in-time event. For example, while the purchase of services and the sales of goods can be designated as part of a net position in a way that they will affect profit or loss in one reporting period, purchases of property, plant and equipment affect profit or loss over several different reporting periods through the depreciation pattern. Similarly, if inventory is sold in the period after it was purchased, the cash flow and the related effect on profit or loss occur in different periods.

BC6.451   In the light of the comments received, the IASB reconsidered the restriction on cash flow hedges of net positions with offsetting risk positions that affect profit or loss in different reporting periods, as proposed in the 2010 Hedge Accounting Exposure Draft. The IASB did not think that it was appropriate to completely remove the restriction. However, the IASB considered whether there was an alternative approach that could better reflect an entity's risk management activities but that would also address the earnings management concerns that had been raised.

BC6.452   The IASB noted that entities would only be able to reflect their risk management activities if it removed the restriction on the application of hedge accounting to cash flow hedges of a net position with offsetting risk positions that affect profit or loss in different reporting periods. However, the IASB noted that it could address the concerns about earnings management by introducing some requirements for documenting the hedging relationship instead of prohibiting the designation altogether.

BC6.453   The IASB noted that the potential for earnings management could be addressed if the recognition pattern for profit or loss arising from the hedged net position for all reporting periods affected was set at the inception of the hedge, in such a way that it was clear what amounts would affect profit or loss, when they would affect profit or loss and to which hedged volumes and types of items they related.

BC6.454   However, the IASB had concerns about applying cash flow hedges for net positions to many different types of risks because it might have unintended consequences for some risks. The IASB noted that foreign currency risk was the risk most commented on by respondents and the risk that the IASB intended to address by this type of hedge.

BC6.455   Consequently, the IASB decided that cash flow hedges of net positions would only be available for hedges of foreign currency risk (but no other risks). In addition, the IASB decided to remove the restriction that the offsetting risk positions in a net position must affect profit or loss in the same reporting period. However, the IASB was concerned that without sufficiently specific documentation of the items within the designated net position, an entity could use hindsight to allocate the hedging gains or losses to those items so as to achieve a particular result in profit or loss (selection effect). Consequently, the IASB decided that for all items within the designated net position for which there could be a selection effect, an entity must specify each period in which the transactions are expected to affect profit or loss as well as the nature and volume of each type of forecast transaction in such a way that it eliminates the selection effect. For example, depending on the circumstances, eliminating a selection effect could require that specifying the nature of a forecast purchase of items of property, plant and equipment includes aspects such as the depreciation pattern for items of the same kind, if the nature of those items is such that the depreciation pattern could vary depending on how the entity uses those items (such as different useful lives because of being used in different production processes). The IASB noted that this would also address the issue that some respondents had raised about changes in the original expectations of when the risk positions would affect profit or loss resulting in items affecting profit or loss in different reporting periods (see paragraph BC6.449).

Presentation for groups of items that are a net position

BC6.456 For cash flow hedges of groups of items with offsetting risk positions (ie net positions), the hedged items might affect different line items in the statement of profit or loss and other comprehensive income. Consequently, this raises the question of how hedging gains or losses should be presented for a cash flow hedge of such a group. In its deliberations leading to the 2010 Hedge Accounting Exposure Draft, the IASB noted that hedging gains or losses would need to be grossed up to offset each of the hedged items individually.

BC6.457 The IASB noted that if it proposed to adjust (gross up) all the affected line items in the statement of profit or loss and other comprehensive income it would result in the recognition of gross (partially offsetting) gains or losses that did not exist, and that this would not be consistent with general accounting principles. Consequently, in its 2010 Hedge Accounting Exposure Draft, the IASB decided not to propose adjusting (grossing up) all affected line items in the statement of profit or loss and other comprehensive income.

BC6.458 Instead, the IASB proposed that in the statement of profit or loss or other comprehensive income hedging gains or losses for cash flow hedges of a net position should be presented in a separate line item. This would avoid the problem of distorting gains or losses with amounts that did not exist. However, the IASB acknowledged that this results in additional disaggregation of information in the statement of profit or loss and other comprehensive income. This would also result in hedges of net positions being presented differently from hedges of gross positions.

BC6.459 In a fair value hedge, changes in the fair value of both the hedged item and the hedging instrument, for changes in the hedged risk, are recognised in the statement of profit or loss and other comprehensive income. Because the treatment of gains or losses for both the hedged item and the hedging instrument is the same, the IASB did not believe any changes to the fair value hedge accounting mechanics were necessary to accommodate net positions. However, in situations in which some hedging gains or losses are considered a modification of revenue or an expense (for example, when the net interest accrual on an interest rate swap is considered a modification of the interest revenue or expense on the hedged item), those gains or losses should be presented in a separate line when the hedged item is a net position. In the

IASB's view, in those situations the same reasons applied that it had considered for cash flow hedges in relation to their presentation in the statement of profit or loss and other comprehensive income.

BC6.460 Most of the respondents to the 2010 Hedge Accounting Exposure Draft supported the IASB's proposal to require the hedging gains or losses to be presented in a separate line item for a hedging relationship that includes a group of items with offsetting risks that affect different line items in the statement of profit or loss and other comprehensive income.

BC6.461 The IASB decided to retain the proposal in the 2010 Hedge Accounting Exposure Draft, as it would make transparent that an entity is hedging on a net basis and would clearly present the effect of those hedges of net positions on the face of the statement of profit or loss and other comprehensive income.

Identifying the hedged item for hedges of a group of items that constitutes a net position

BC6.462 The IASB considered in its deliberations leading to the 2010 Hedge Accounting Exposure Draft how an entity that applies hedge accounting to net positions should identify the hedged item. The IASB concluded that an entity would need to designate a combination of gross positions if it were to apply the hedge accounting mechanics to the hedged position. Consequently, the IASB proposed that an entity could not designate a merely abstract net position (ie without specifying the items that form the gross positions from which the net position arises) as the hedged item.

BC6.463 The IASB retained its original decision when redeliberating its 2010 Hedge Accounting Exposure Draft.

Hedges of a group of items that results in a net position of nil

BC6.464 In its deliberations leading to the 2010 Hedge Accounting Exposure Draft, the IASB noted that when an entity managed and hedged risks on a net basis, the proposals would allow the entity to designate the net risk from hedged items into a hedging relationship with a hedging instrument. For an entity that hedges on such a basis, the IASB acknowledged that there might be circumstances in which, by coincidence, the net position of hedged items for a particular period was nil.

BC6.465 The IASB considered whether, when an entity hedges risk on a net basis, a nil net position should be eligible for hedge accounting. Such a hedging relationship could be, in its entirety, outside the scope of hedge accounting if it did not include any financial instruments. Furthermore, eligibility for hedge accounting would be inconsistent with the general requirement that a hedging relationship must contain both an eligible hedged item and an eligible hedging instrument.

BC6.466 However, the IASB noted that the accounting result of prohibiting the application of hedge accounting to nil net positions could distort the financial reporting of an entity that otherwise hedged (with eligible hedging instruments) and applied hedge accounting on a net basis, for example:

(a) in periods in which hedge accounting is permitted (because a net position exists and is hedged with a hedging instrument), the transactions would affect profit or loss at an overall hedged rate or price; whereas

(b) in periods in which hedge accounting would not be permitted (because the net position is nil), transactions would affect profit or loss at prevailing spot rates or prices.

BC6.467 Consequently, the IASB proposed that nil net positions should qualify for hedge accounting. However, the IASB noted that such situations would be coincidental and hence it expected that nil net positions would be rare in practice.

BC6.468 The IASB retained its original decision when redeliberating its 2010 Hedge Accounting Exposure Draft.

Hedging credit risk using credit derivatives

The IASB's deliberations leading to the 2010 Hedge Accounting Exposure Draft

The issue

BC6.469 Many financial institutions use credit derivatives to manage their credit risk exposures arising from their lending activities. For example, hedges of credit risk exposure allow financial institutions to transfer the risk of credit loss on a loan or a loan commitment to a third party. This might also reduce the regulatory capital requirement for the loan or loan commitment while at the same time allowing the financial institution to retain nominal ownership of the loan and to preserve the relationship with the client. Credit portfolio managers frequently use credit derivatives to hedge the credit risk of a proportion of a particular exposure (for example, a facility for a particular client) or the bank's overall lending portfolio.

BC6.470 However, the credit risk of a financial item is not a risk component that meets the eligibility criteria for hedged items. The spread between the risk-free rate and the market interest rate incorporates credit risk, liquidity risk, funding risk and any other unidentified risk component and margin elements. Although it is possible to determine that the spread includes credit risk, the credit risk cannot be isolated in a way that would allow the change in fair value that is attributable solely to credit risk to be separately identifiable (see also paragraph BC6.503).

BC6.471 As an alternative to hedge accounting, IFRS 9 permits an entity to designate, as at fair value through profit or loss, at initial recognition, financial instruments that are within the scope of that Standard if doing so eliminates or significantly reduces an accounting mismatch. However, the fair value option is only available at initial recognition, is irrevocable and an entity must designate the financial item in its entirety (ie for its full nominal amount). Because of the various optional features and the drawdown behavioural pattern of the loans and loan commitments, credit portfolio managers often engage in a flexible and active risk management strategy. Credit portfolio managers most often hedge less than 100 per cent of a loan or loan commitment. They might also hedge longer periods than the contractual maturity of the loan or the loan commitment. Furthermore, the fair value option is available only for instruments that are within the scope of IFRS 9. Most of the loan commitments for which credit risk is managed fall within the scope of IAS 37, not IFRS 9. Consequently, most financial institutions do not (and often cannot) elect to apply the fair value option because of the associated restrictions and scope.

BC6.472 As a result, financial institutions that use credit default swaps to hedge the credit risk of their loan portfolios measure their loan portfolios at amortised cost and do not recognise most loan commitments (ie those that meet the scope exception of IFRS 9). The changes in fair value of the credit default swaps are recognised in profit or loss in every reporting period (as for a trading book). The accounting outcome is an accounting mismatch of gains and losses of the loans and loan commitments versus those of the credit default swaps, which creates volatility in profit or loss. During the IASB's outreach programme, many users of financial statements pointed out that that outcome does not reflect the economic substance of the credit risk management strategy of financial institutions.

BC6.473 In its 2010 Hedge Accounting Exposure Draft, the IASB proposed that a risk component should be separately identifiable and reliably measurable in order to qualify as a hedged item. As mentioned before, measuring the credit risk component of a loan or a loan commitment is complex. Consequently, to accommodate an equivalent to hedge accounting when entities hedge credit risk, a different accounting requirement would have to be developed specifically for this type of risk, or the proposed hedge accounting requirements would have to be significantly modified (for example, in relation to eligible hedged items and effectiveness testing).

Alternatives considered by the IASB

BC6.474 In its deliberations leading to the 2010 Hedge Accounting Exposure Draft, the IASB considered three alternative approaches to hedge accounting in order to address situations in which credit risk is hedged by credit derivatives. Those alternatives would, subject to qualification criteria, permit an entity with regard to the hedged credit exposure (for example, a bond, loan or loan commitment):

(a) Alternative 1:

    (i) to elect fair value through profit or loss only at initial recognition;

    (ii) to designate a component of nominal amounts; and

    (iii) to discontinue fair value through profit or loss accounting.

(b) Alternative 2:

    (i) to elect fair value through profit or loss at initial recognition or subsequently (if subsequently, the difference between the then carrying amount and the then fair value is recognised immediately in profit or loss);

    (ii) to designate a component of nominal amounts; and

    (iii) to discontinue fair value through profit or loss accounting.

(c)   Alternative 3:

    (i)   to elect fair value through profit or loss at initial recognition or subsequently (if subsequently, the difference between the then carrying amount and the then fair value is amortised or deferred);

    (ii)   to designate a component of nominal amounts; and

    (iii)   to discontinue fair value through profit or loss accounting.

BC6.475   The election of fair value through profit or loss would be available for a financial instrument (or a proportion of it) that is managed in such a way that an economic relationship on the basis of the same credit risk exists with credit derivatives (measured at fair value through profit or loss) that causes offset between changes in fair value of the financial instrument and the credit derivatives. This would also apply to financial instruments that fall outside the scope of IFRS 9, for example, loan commitments. Instead of the qualifying criteria for hedge accounting (see paragraphs BC6.230–BC6.271), the IASB considered the following qualifying criteria for electing fair value through profit or loss:

    (a)   the name of the credit exposure matches the reference entity of the credit derivative (name matching); and

    (b)   the seniority of the financial instrument matches that of the instruments that can be delivered in accordance with the credit derivative.

BC6.476   The qualification criteria in BC6.475 are set with a view to accommodating economic hedges of credit risk that would otherwise qualify for hedge accounting, but for the fact that the credit risk component within the hedged exposure cannot be separately identified and hence is not a risk component that meets the eligibility criteria for hedged items. Those qualification criteria are also consistent with regulatory requirements and the risk management strategy underlying the current business practice of financial institutions. However, using name matching as a qualifying criterion means that index-based credit default swaps would not meet that criterion.

BC6.477   For discontinuation, the IASB considered the following criteria:

    (a)   the qualifying criteria are no longer met; and

    (b)   retaining the measurement at fair value through profit or loss is not needed because of any other requirements.

BC6.478   Given the rationale for electing fair value through profit or loss, an entity would typically discontinue accounting at fair value through profit or loss if the discontinuation criteria in BC6.477 are met, because that would ensure that the accounting is aligned with how the exposure is managed (ie the credit risk is no longer managed using credit derivatives). The IASB noted that in circumstances when the discontinuation criteria apply, the financial instrument, if fair value through profit or loss accounting had not already been elected, would not qualify (any more) for that election. Hence, the IASB considered that it would be logical to make the discontinuation of fair value through profit or loss accounting mandatory (instead of optional) if the discontinuation criteria are fulfilled.

BC6.479 Alternative 1 permits electing fair value through profit or loss for a component of the nominal amount of the financial instrument if qualifying criteria are met. This is available only at initial recognition. Fair value through profit or loss can be discontinued if the qualification criteria are met. Loan commitments that fall outside the scope of IFRS 9 could also be eligible in accordance with this alternative if the qualification criteria are met. In accordance with Alternative 1, at the date of discontinuation of accounting for the financial instrument at fair value through profit or loss, the fair value of the financial instrument will be its deemed cost. For loan commitments outside the scope of IFRS 9 the recognition and measurement criteria of IAS 37 would apply.

BC6.480 The IASB noted that a significant disadvantage of Alternative 1 is that in many situations in practice (when a financial institution obtains credit protection for an exposure after the initial recognition of that exposure) this alternative is not aligned with the credit risk management strategy and would therefore not reflect its effect. An advantage of Alternative 1 is that it is less complex than the other alternatives that the IASB considered. By not permitting the election of fair value through profit or loss after initial recognition (or inception of a loan commitment), the difference at later points in time between the carrying amount and the fair value of the financial instrument will not arise.

BC6.481 In addition to the election of fair value through profit or loss at initial recognition in accordance with Alternative 1, Alternative 2 also permits that election after initial recognition. This means that the election is available again for an exposure for which fair value through profit or loss was elected previously (which logically cannot apply if the election is restricted to initial recognition). An example is a volatile longer-term exposure that was previously deteriorating and was then protected by credit default derivatives, then significantly improved so that the credit derivatives were sold, but then again deteriorated and was protected again. This ensures that an entity that uses a credit risk management strategy that protects exposures that drop below a certain quality or risk level could align the accounting with their risk management.

BC6.482 The IASB noted that when the financial instrument is elected for measurement as at fair value through profit or loss after initial recognition, a difference could arise between its carrying amount and its fair value. This difference is a result of the change in the measurement basis (for example, from amortised cost to fair value for a loan). The IASB considers this type of difference a measurement change adjustment. Alternative 2 proposes to recognise the measurement change adjustment in profit or loss immediately. At the date of discontinuation of fair value through profit or loss accounting, the fair value will be the deemed cost (as in Alternative 1). If the financial instrument is elected again after a previous discontinuation, the measurement change adjustment at that date is also recognised immediately in profit or loss.

BC6.483 A significant advantage of Alternative 2 is that it would eliminate the accounting mismatch and produce more consistent and relevant information. It is reflective of how credit exposures are managed. Credit exposures are actively managed by credit risk portfolio managers. Alternative 2 allows the effects of such an active and flexible risk management approach to be reflected appropriately and significantly reduces the measurement inconsistency between the credit exposures and the credit derivatives.

BC6.484 A disadvantage of Alternative 2 is that it is more complex than Alternative 1. Furthermore, it might appear susceptible to earnings management. An entity can decide at what time to elect fair value through profit or loss accounting for the financial instrument and thus when the difference between the carrying amount and the fair value at that date would be recognised in profit or loss. The accounting impact of immediately recognising the measurement change adjustment in profit or loss may also deter an entity from electing fair value through profit or loss accounting. For example, when an entity decides to take out credit protection at a time when the fair value has already moved below the carrying amount of the loan because of credit concerns in the market, it will immediately recognise a loss if it elects fair value through profit or loss accounting.

BC6.485 On the other hand, the advantage of recognising the measurement change adjustment immediately in profit or loss is that it is operationally simpler than Alternative 3. Alternative 3 provides the same eligibility of fair value through profit or loss accounting and its discontinuation as Alternative 2. Consequently, it also allows financial institutions to achieve an accounting outcome that reflects their credit risk management strategy.

BC6.486 An important difference between Alternatives 2 and 3 is the treatment of the measurement change adjustment (ie the difference that could arise between the carrying amount and the fair value of the financial instrument when fair value through profit or loss accounting is elected after initial recognition of the credit exposure). Alternative 3 proposes that the measurement change adjustment should be amortised for loans and deferred for loan commitments that fall within the scope of IAS 37.

BC6.487 As in Alternative 2, a significant advantage of Alternative 3 is that it would eliminate the accounting mismatch and produce more consistent and relevant information. It allows the effects of an active and flexible risk management approach to be reflected appropriately and significantly reduces the measurement inconsistency between the credit exposures and the credit derivatives. An advantage of Alternative 3 over Alternative 2 is that it would be less susceptible to earnings management and would not deter the election of fair value through profit or loss in scenarios after initial recognition of the exposure when the fair value of the exposure has already declined.

BC6.488 However, a disadvantage of Alternative 3 is that it is the most complex of the alternatives. The IASB noted that the measurement change adjustment in accordance with Alternative 3 would have presentation implications. The measurement change adjustment could be presented in the statement of financial position in the following ways:

(a) as an integral part of the carrying amount of the exposure (ie it could be added to the fair value of the loan): this results in a mixed amount that is neither fair value nor amortised cost;

(b)   presentation as a separate line item next to the line item that includes the credit exposure: this results in additional line items in the statement of financial position and may easily be confused as a hedging adjustment; or

(c)   in other comprehensive income.

BC6.489   The IASB noted that disclosures could make the measurement change adjustment transparent.

BC6.490   However, in the light of the complexities that these three alternatives would introduce, the IASB decided not to propose allowing elective fair value accounting for hedged credit exposures (such as loans and loan commitments).

The feedback received on the 2010 Hedge Accounting Exposure Draft

BC6.491   Many respondents to the 2010 Hedge Accounting Exposure Draft were of the view that the IASB should consider how to accommodate hedges of credit risk using credit derivatives under IFRS. Respondents commented that hedges of credit risk using credit derivatives are becoming an increasingly significant practice issue in the application of IFRS. They noted that this issue is just as significant as other issues that had been addressed in the 2010 Hedge Accounting Exposure Draft (for example, the time value of options, hedges of aggregated exposures and risk components of non-financial items). They also noted that financial reporting under IFRS should allow entities to reflect the effects of such activities in the financial statements consistently with the overall hedge accounting objective to better reflect risk management activities.

BC6.492   Respondents also commented that IFRS today fails to represent the effect of credit risk management activities and distort the financial performance of financial institutions. They noted that, because of the accounting mismatch between loans and loan commitments on the one hand and the related credit derivatives on the other hand, the profit or loss under IFRS is significantly more volatile for financial institutions that hedge their credit risk exposures than for financial institutions that do not hedge.

BC6.493   Many respondents noted that the objective of hedge accounting would not be met if IFRS would not provide a way to account for hedges of credit risk so that financial statements can reflect the credit risk management activities of financial institutions.

BC6.494   Most users of financial statements commented that the IASB should address this issue. Many also noted that the financial statements currently reflect accounting-driven volatility when credit risk is hedged and that those financial statements do not align with those risk management activities.

BC6.495   Participants in the outreach provided the same feedback. Most of them were also of the view that this is an important practice issue that the IASB should address.

BC6.496   However, the feedback was mixed on how the IASB should address or resolve this issue. Many respondents were of the view that it was difficult to reliably measure credit risk as a risk component for the purposes of hedge accounting.

However, some respondents suggested that for some types of instruments the credit risk component of financial instruments could be reliably measured on the basis of credit default swap (CDS) prices, subject to some adjustments.

BC6.497 Many agreed that the alternatives set out in the Basis for Conclusions of the 2010 Hedge Accounting Exposure Draft (see paragraph BC6.474) were too complex, although some respondents supported elective fair value through profit or loss accounting as an alternative to hedge accounting. Of the three fair value through profit or loss alternatives, most respondents supported Alternative 3.

BC6.498 Respondents who supported elective fair value through profit or loss accounting thought that it would be operational and believed that it would be no more complex than the other possible approaches, for example, identifying risk components. Most preferred Alternative 3 as it would align most closely with the dynamic credit risk management approach of many financial institutions. Some users of financial statements supported elective fair value through profit or loss accounting because they thought that the benefits of providing a better depiction of the economics of the risk management activities would outweigh the complexity.

The IASB's redeliberations of the 2010 Hedge Accounting Exposure Draft

BC6.499 In the light of the feedback received on its 2010 Hedge Accounting Exposure Draft, the IASB decided to specifically address the accounting for hedges of credit risk using credit derivatives. In its redeliberations the IASB explored various accounting alternatives.

Treating credit risk as a risk component

BC6.500 The IASB noted that for credit risk there are unique differences between how the relevant risk might affect the hedging instrument and the hedged risk exposure when compared to other risk components.

BC6.501 The IASB also noted that there is sometimes uncertainty about whether voluntary debt restructurings constitute a credit event under a standard credit default swap contract. Whether an event constitutes a credit event is determined by a committee consisting of representatives of banks and fund entities. This can (and in practice did) result in situations in which the fair value of a debt instrument has decreased, reflecting the market view of credit losses on those debt instruments while any payout on credit default swaps for those debt instruments depends on how the difficulties of the debtor will be resolved and what related measures might be considered a credit event. This is a factor that affects credit default swaps in a different way than the actual underlying debt. It is an additional factor inherent in credit default swaps that is not inherent in the debt as such. Hence, there could be scenarios in which, for example, an impairment loss on a loan might not be compensated by a payout from a credit default swap that is linked to the obligor of that debt. Also, market liquidity and the behaviour of speculators trying to close positions and taking gains affect the credit default swap and the debt market in different ways.

BC6.502 The IASB also noted that when a financial institution enters into a credit default swap to hedge the credit exposure from a loan commitment it might result in a situation in which the reference entity defaults while the loan commitment remains undrawn or partly undrawn. In such situations the financial institution receives compensation from the payout on the credit default swaps without actually incurring a credit loss.

BC6.503 Furthermore, the IASB considered the implications of the fact that, upon a credit event, the protection buyer receives the notional principal less the fair value of the reference entity's obligation. Hence, the compensation received for credit risk depends on the fair value of the reference instrument. The IASB noted that, for a fixed-rate loan, the fair value of the reference instrument is also affected by changes in market interest rates. In other words, on settlement of the credit default swap, the entity also settles the fair value changes attributable to interest rate risk—and not solely fair value changes attributable to the credit risk of the reference entity. Hence, the way credit default swaps are settled reflects that credit risk inextricably depends on interest rate risk. This in turn reflects that credit risk is an 'overlay' risk that is affected by all other value changes of the hedged exposure because those value changes determine the value of what is lost in case of a default.

BC6.504 Hence, the IASB considered that credit risk is not a separately identifiable risk component and thus does not qualify for designation as a hedged item on a risk component basis.

Exception to the general risk component criteria

BC6.505 The IASB then considered whether it should provide an exception to the general risk component criteria specifically for credit risk.

BC6.506 Some respondents suggested that, as an exception to the general risk component criteria, the IASB should consider an approach that would provide a reasonable approximation of the credit risk. This approach could be based on the guidance in IFRS 7 and IFRS 9 for the measurement of an entity's own credit risk on financial liabilities designated as at fair value through profit or loss. Those respondents noted that if this method of determining own credit risk for such liabilities is acceptable in IFRS 7 and IFRS 9, the IASB should provide the same 'relief' for measuring the credit risk component for the purposes of hedge accounting.

BC6.507 The IASB noted that, in finalising the requirement for the fair value option for financial liabilities in IFRS 9, it retained the default method in the application guidance in IFRS 7 to determine the effects of changes in the liability's credit risk. The IASB received comments on its 2010 Own Credit Risk Exposure Draft that determining the effects of changes in a liability's credit risk can be complex, and that it was therefore necessary to allow some flexibility in how a liability's credit risk could be measured. Respondents to that Exposure Draft, like the IASB, acknowledged that the default method was imprecise but considered the result a reasonable proxy in many cases. Moreover, the IASB noted that respondents to the 2010 Own Credit Risk Exposure Draft did acknowledge that the 'IFRS 7 method' did not isolate changes in a liability's credit risk from other changes in fair value (for example, general changes in the price of credit or changes in liquidity risk). Those respondents said that it was often very difficult or impossible to separate those items.

BC6.508 The IASB noted that the IFRS 7 method (which was incorporated into IFRS 9) involves the use of an observed market price at the beginning and end of the period to determine the change in the effects of credit. That method requires entities to deduct any changes in market conditions from changes in the fair value of the instrument. Any residual amount is deemed to be attributable to changes in credit. The IASB noted that the loans and loan commitments for which the credit risk is hedged very often have no observable market price and that, in order to achieve a close approximation of the credit risk, complex modelling would be involved to arrive at a 'market price'. Applying the IFRS 7 method would then require the deduction of valuations for parts of the instrument and analysing them for changes in market conditions to arrive at a credit risk component. This would also be complex when trying to achieve a close approximation of the credit risk.

BC6.509 Furthermore, the IASB noted that the loans and loan commitments for which the credit exposure is hedged often have embedded options whose fair value depends on both market and non-market conditions. For example, the exercise of prepayment options could be because of changes in general interest rates (a market condition) while loans are typically refinanced (exercise of the prepayment option) well in advance of the scheduled maturity, irrespective of movements in general interest rates. Hence, in order to achieve a close approximation of the credit risk, isolating the changes for market conditions on those embedded options could involve significant judgement and could become extremely complex.

BC6.510 The IASB also considered that applying the IFRS 7 method in a way that was operational (ie so that the approximation would provide relief) would mean using many of the same simplifications that some had suggested for applying the general risk component criteria to credit risk (for example, using a standardised haircut for prepayment and term-out options, and ignoring immaterial options).

BC6.511 The IASB considered that for exchange-traded bonds for which market prices are readily observable and that do not have embedded options, the IFRS 7 method might result in an approximation or proxy for the credit risk component in some circumstances. However, the IASB was concerned that for loans and loan commitments that are not actively traded, the IFRS 7 method could become a complicated 'circular' pricing exercise and in any case it would very likely result in only a rough approximation or imprecise measurement of the credit risk component.

BC6.512 The IASB further noted that it had acknowledged the shortcomings of the approach used for IFRS 7 and IFRS 9 and that the approach was only a proxy for measuring credit risk. Hence, the IASB had actively sought to limit the application of this approach by retaining the bifurcation requirement for hybrid financial liabilities, even though bifurcation of financial assets was eliminated. Hence, the approach was only applied to financial liabilities designated as at fair value through profit or loss.

BC6.513 The IASB acknowledged that in order to ensure that hedge ineffectiveness is recognised the qualifying criteria for risk components use a higher degree of precision than a mere proxy. Also, for the classification and measurement of financial liabilities the IASB sought to minimise the application of this proxy by retaining the separation of embedded derivatives. Consequently, the IASB decided that also using the guidance in IFRS 7 and IFRS 9 for the measurement of an entity's own credit risk on financial liabilities designated as at fair value through profit or loss for the purpose of measuring credit risk as a hedged item would be inappropriate.

BC6.514   The IASB also considered whether it should permit 'residual risks' as an eligible hedged item. Such an approach would allow an entity to designate as the hedged item those changes in cash flows or fair value of an item that are not attributable to a specific risk or risks that meet the separately identifiable and reliably measurable criteria for risk components. For example, an entity could designate as the hedged item the fair value changes of a loan that are attributable to all risks other than interest rate risk.

BC6.515   The IASB noted that that approach would have the advantage of not requiring an entity to directly measure credit risk. However, the IASB noted that this approach would entail similar complexity as the IFRS 7 method for financial instruments with multiple embedded options. Hence, determining the part of the fair value changes that is attributable to a specific risk (for example, interest rate risk) could be complex.

BC6.516   The IASB also noted that that approach would have other disadvantages:

(a)   the problem that credit risk inextricably depends on interest rate risk because of the nature of credit risk as an overlay risk (see paragraphs BC6.503–BC6.504) would remain; and

(b)   entities would struggle with the hedge effectiveness assessment of the new hedge accounting model as it would be difficult to establish and demonstrate a direct economic relationship between the 'residual risk' and the hedging instrument (ie the credit default swap), which gives rise to offset—a requirement to qualify for hedge accounting.

BC6.517   Consequently, the IASB decided against permitting 'residual risks' as an eligible hedged item.

Applying financial guarantee contract accounting

BC6.518   The IASB considered whether the accounting for financial guarantee contracts in IFRS 9 could be applied to credit derivatives.

BC6.519   The IASB noted that credit derivatives, such as credit default swaps, do not typically meet the definition of a financial guarantee contract in IFRS 9 because:

(a)   the credit events that trigger payment on a standardised credit default swap (for example, bankruptcy, repudiation, moratorium or restructuring) might not directly relate to the failure to pay on the particular debt instrument held by an entity; and

(b)   in order to meet the definition of a financial guarantee contract, it must be a precondition for payment that the holder is exposed to, and has incurred a loss on, the failure of the debtor to make payments on the guaranteed asset when due. However, it is not a precondition for entering into a credit default swap that the holder is exposed to the underlying reference financial instrument (ie an entity can hold a 'naked' position).

BC6.520 The IASB noted that it would have to broaden the definition of 'financial guarantee contract' in order to include such credit derivatives. The IASB also noted that accounting for credit default swaps as financial guarantee contracts would mean that credit default swaps would not be measured at fair value but at 'cost', ie it would result in applying accrual accounting to a derivative financial instrument.

BC6.521 The IASB therefore rejected this alternative.

Applying the accounting for the time value of options

BC6.522 Some respondents to the 2010 Hedge Accounting Exposure Draft suggested that the premium paid on credit default swaps is similar to buying protection under an insurance contract and, accordingly, the premium should be amortised to profit or loss. Those respondents supported applying to credit default swaps the accounting treatment for the time value of options that was proposed in the 2010 Hedge Accounting Exposure Draft. They argued that, from a risk management perspective, changes in the fair value of the derivative during the reporting period were irrelevant, as long as the issuer of the debt was solvent because if there was no credit event the fair value of the credit default swap on maturity would be zero. Hence, those respondents believed that 'interim' fair value changes could be recognised in other comprehensive income similarly to the accounting treatment proposed in the 2010 Hedge Accounting Exposure Draft for the time value of options.

BC6.523 The IASB noted that in contrast to 'normal' options for which the time value paid is known from the beginning (hence the amount to be amortised or deferred is known), for a credit default swap the premium is contingent on the occurrence of a credit event and hence the total premium that is ultimately paid is not known at the outset. This is because the premium for a credit default swap, or at least a large part of the premium, is paid over time—but only until a credit event occurs. The IASB noted that in order to apply the same accounting as for the time value of options, the contingent nature of the credit default swap premium would have to be ignored so that the amortisation of the premium to profit or loss could be based on the assumption that no credit event occurs—even though that risk is reflected in the fair value of the credit default swap. The IASB also noted that in substance this would be 'as-you-go' accounting for the credit default swap premium (ie recognising it in profit or loss on an accrual basis).

BC6.524 The IASB also noted that applying to credit default swaps the same accounting treatment as for the time value of options would require splitting the fair value of the credit default swap into an intrinsic value and a time value. This raises the question of whether the credit default swap would only have time value (and hence no intrinsic value) until a credit event occurs, ie whether before a credit event occurs the entire fair value of the credit default swap should be deemed to be its time value.

BC6.525 The IASB considered that it would be inappropriate to simply attribute the entire fair value of the credit default swap before a credit event to time value.

The IASB noted that hedged items such as bonds or loans have 'intrinsic' value but not an equivalent to time value. In an effective economic hedge, the changes in the intrinsic value in the hedged item would offset the changes in the intrinsic value of the hedging instrument. During times of financial difficulty, but before a credit event (for example, before an actual default), the fair value of the loan would have decreased because of credit deterioration. Also, the fair value of the related credit default swap would increase because of the higher risk of default. Hence, the IASB considered that the increase in fair value of the credit default swap includes some intrinsic value element even though it would be difficult to isolate and separately quantify it.

BC6.526 The IASB also noted that if the entire fair value on a credit default swap was treated as time value before default, there could be an accounting mismatch when an entity recognised an impairment loss on the loan or loan commitment before default. This is because all fair value changes from the credit default swap would still be recognised in other comprehensive income. One solution might be to recycle the amount recognised as an impairment loss on the loan or loan commitment from other comprehensive income to profit or loss and hence to simply deem the amount of the impairment loss to be the intrinsic value of the credit default swap. The IASB considered that this would give rise to the same problems as other approximations it had discussed when it rejected an exception to the general risk component criteria, namely that any mismatch of economic gains or losses from the hedge would not be recognised as hedge ineffectiveness. Instead, under this approach profit or loss recognition for the credit default swap would be the same as accrual accounting while assuming perfect hedge effectiveness.

BC6.527 The IASB therefore rejected this alternative.

Applying an 'insurance approach'

BC6.528 Some respondents to the 2010 Hedge Accounting Exposure Draft supported an 'insurance approach' or accrual accounting for credit derivatives. They argued that such an approach would best address the accounting mismatch between loans or loan commitments and credit derivatives and would reflect the risk management of financial institutions.

BC6.529 The IASB considered that under an insurance approach the following accounting could be applied to a credit default swap that is used to manage credit exposures:

(a) any premium paid at the inception of the credit default swap (or its fair value if an existing contract is used) would be amortised over the life of that contract;

(b) the periodic premium would be expensed as paid each period (including adjustments for premium accruals);

(c) the fair value of the credit default swap would be disclosed in the notes; and

(d) in the assessment of impairment, the cash flow that might result from the credit default swap in case of a credit event is treated in the same way as cash flows that might result from the collateral or guarantee of a collateralised or guaranteed financial asset. In other words, the loan or loan commitment for which credit risk is managed using the credit default swap is treated like a collateralised or guaranteed financial asset with the credit default swap accounted for like collateral or a guarantee.

BC6.530 The IASB noted that the insurance approach is a simple and straightforward solution if a credit default swap is used as credit protection for one particular credit exposure with a matching (remaining) maturity. Also, situations in which the maturity of the credit default swap exceeds that of the credit exposure could be addressed by using an 'aligned' credit default swap (similar to the notion of 'aligned' time value that is used for the new accounting treatment for the time value of options; see paragraphs BC6.386–BC6.409). However, the aligned credit default swap would only address maturity mismatches. It would not capture other differences between the actual credit default swap and the hedged credit exposure (for example, that a loan might be prepayable) because the insurance approach only intends to change the accounting for the credit default swap instead of adjusting the credit exposure for value changes that reflect all of its characteristics.

BC6.531 The IASB considered that the insurance approach would have a simple interaction with an impairment model as a result of treating the credit default swap like collateral or a guarantee, which means it would affect the estimate of the recoverable cash flows. Hence, this interaction would be at the most basic level of the information that any impairment model uses so that the effect would not differ by type of impairment model (assuming only credit derivatives with a remaining life equal to, or longer than, the remaining exposure period would qualify for the insurance approach).

BC6.532 However, the IASB noted that difficulties would arise when the insurance approach was discontinued before the credit exposure matures. In such a situation the consequences of using accrual (or 'as-you-go') accounting for the credit default swap would become obvious, ie it would be necessary to revert from off-balance-sheet accounting to measurement at fair value.

BC6.533 The IASB also noted that under the insurance approach neither the credit derivative nor the loan or loan commitment would be recognised in the statement of financial position at fair value. Hence, any mismatch of economic gains or losses (ie economic hedge ineffectiveness) between loans or loan commitments and the credit derivatives would not be recognised in profit or loss. In addition, it would result in omitting the fair value of the credit default swap from the statement of financial position even though fair value provides important and relevant information about derivative financial instruments.

BC6.534 The IASB therefore rejected this alternative.

Applying a 'deemed credit adjustment approach'

BC6.535 The IASB also considered an approach that would adjust the carrying amount of the hedged credit exposure against profit or loss. The adjustment would be the change in the fair value of a credit default swap that matches the maturity of the hedged credit exposure ('aligned' credit default swap value). The mechanics of this would be similar to how, in a fair value hedge, the gain or loss on the hedged item that is attributable to a risk component adjusts the carrying amount of the hedged item and is recognised in profit or loss. Essentially, the cumulative change in the fair value of the aligned credit default swap would be deemed to be the credit risk component of the exposure in a fair value hedge of credit risk (ie act as a proxy for credit risk—'deemed credit adjustment'). When the deemed credit adjustment approach is discontinued before the credit exposure matures an accounting treatment that is similar to that used for discontinued fair value hedges could be used.

BC6.536   The IASB noted that the deemed credit adjustment approach would retain the measurement of credit default swaps at fair value through profit or loss. Hence, in contrast to the insurance approach (see paragraphs BC6.528–BC6.534), an advantage of this approach would be that the accounting for the credit default swap would not be affected by any switches between periods for which the credit derivative is used and those for which it is not used to manage a particular credit exposure.

BC6.537   However, the IASB was concerned that the interaction between the deemed credit adjustment approach and impairment accounting would be significantly more complex than under the insurance approach because the deemed credit adjustment and the impairment allowance would be 'competing mechanisms' in the accounting for impairment losses. This would also involve the danger of double counting for credit losses. The interaction would depend on the type of impairment model and would be more difficult in conjunction with an expected loss model.

BC6.538   The IASB therefore rejected this alternative.

Allowing entities to elect fair value accounting for the hedged credit exposure

BC6.539   Because the discussions of those various alternatives did not identify an appropriate solution, the IASB reconsidered the alternatives it had contemplated in its original deliberations leading to the 2010 Hedge Accounting Exposure Draft (see paragraph BC6.474).

BC6.540   The IASB considered that only Alternatives 2 and 3 of allowing an entity to elect fair value through profit or loss accounting for the hedged credit exposure would be viable. Given that Alternative 1 would be limited to an election only on initial recognition of the credit exposure (or when entering into a loan commitment), the IASB was concerned that, in many situations in practice (when an entity obtains credit protection for an exposure after the initial recognition of that exposure or entering into the loan commitment), this alternative would not be aligned with the credit risk management strategy and would therefore fail to resolve the problem (ie that no useful information is provided).

BC6.541   The IASB noted that Alternative 3 would involve amortising the measurement change adjustment (ie the difference between the carrying amount, or nil for an unrecognised loan commitment, and the fair value of the financial instrument when it is elected for measurement at fair value through profit or loss after initial recognition or after entering into a loan commitment) over the life of the financial instrument hedged for credit risk. As a consequence, to ensure that the measurement change adjustment is not inappropriately deferred but recognised immediately in profit or loss when impaired, the measurement change adjustment would require an impairment test. This would result in interaction with the impairment model.

BC6.542 The IASB was concerned that the interaction of Alternative 3 with the impairment model could create a compatibility problem and might be a potential restriction of the impairment phase of its project to replace IAS 39.

BC6.543 Hence, the IASB reconsidered Alternative 2, noting that:

(a) the status quo under IAS 39, in which credit default swaps are accounted for at fair value through profit or loss while credit exposures are accounted for at amortised cost or are unrecognised (for example, many loan commitments), does not convey the full picture. It results in the recognition of gains on credit default swaps while the impairment is recognised on a different measurement basis and with a time lag because of the impairment models. Hence, in a situation in which the situation of a lender deteriorates but it has protected itself, gains are shown even though the protection keeps the situation neutral at best.

(b) Alternative 2 would use fair value accounting for both the credit default swap and the credit exposure. This would best capture all economic mismatches but would come at the expense of inevitably including in the remeasurement interest rate risk in addition to credit risk. Alternative 2 would have the clearest objective of all the approaches considered (fair value measurement) and, as a result, it would require the least guidance. The IASB noted that under Alternative 2 there could be concerns about earnings management because on electing fair value accounting the difference to the previous carrying amount of the credit exposure would be immediately recognised in profit or loss. However, the IASB also noted that some would consider that outcome as relevant because it would signal a different approach to managing credit risk and this difference would often be a loss that is a reflection of any lag in the impairment model behind the 'market view'. To be consistent, this should be removed by changing the measurement basis when switching to a fair value-based credit risk management.

(c) the accounting under Alternative 2 is completely de-linked from the impairment model and consequently has the least interaction with impairment of all approaches considered.

(d) Alternative 2 is operationally the least complex of the approaches considered.

BC6.544 The IASB considered that, on balance, the advantages of Alternative 2 outweighed its disadvantages and, overall, that it was superior to all other approaches. Hence, the IASB decided to include Alternative 2 in the final requirements.

BC6.545 In response to feedback received on the 2010 Hedge Accounting Exposure Draft, the IASB also decided to align the accounting for the discontinuation of fair value through profit or loss accounting for loan commitments with that for loans (ie use amortisation unless a higher liability is required by IAS 37, instead of simply reverting to that Standard as contemplated during the IASB's initial deliberations—see paragraphs BC6.479 and BC6.482). The IASB's reasons for also using an amortisation approach for loan commitments were that:

(a) it would prevent an immediate gain from the derecognition of the loan commitment under IAS 37 if the probable threshold is not met when discontinuing fair value through profit or loss accounting. This would reduce concerns about earnings management.

(b) the amortisation of the carrying amount when discontinuing fair value through profit or loss accounting would use the effective interest method. This would require the entity to assume that a loan had been drawn under the loan commitment in order to determine an amortisation profile. The rationale for this alternative is that a credit loss only results from a loan commitment if that loan commitment gets drawn and the resulting loan is not repaid. Hence, an amortisation on an 'as if drawn' basis would be appropriate for the amortisation of the carrying amount.

(c) this accounting also provides operational relief for loan commitments that allow repayments and redraws (for example, a revolving facility). It would avoid the need to capitalise any remaining carrying amount into individual drawings to ensure its amortisation, which would be operationally complex.

Effective date and transition (Chapter 7)

Effective date

Requirements issued in IFRS 9 (2009)

BC7.1 The IASB recognises that many countries require time for translation and for introducing the mandatory requirements into law. In addition, entities require time to implement new standards. The IASB usually sets an effective date of between six and eighteen months after issuing a Standard. However, the IASB has adopted a phased approach to publishing IFRS 9, so this is not possible.

BC7.2 In the response to the 2009 Classification and Measurement Exposure Draft, respondents urged that:

(a) it would be helpful to preparers if the IASB were to permit all phases of the project to replace IAS 39 to be adopted at the same time.

(b) it would be helpful to entities that issue insurance contracts if the effective date of IFRS 9 were aligned with the forthcoming Standard on accounting for insurance contracts. Most of an insurer's assets are financial assets and most of its liabilities are insurance liabilities or financial liabilities. Thus, if an insurer applies IFRS 9 before it applies any new Standard on insurance contracts, it might face two rounds of major changes in a short period. This would be disruptive for both users and preparers.

(c) because a number of countries will adopt IFRS in the next few years, it would be helpful to entities in those countries if the IASB did not require them to make two changes in a short period of time.

BC7.3   With these factors in mind, the IASB decided it should require entities to apply the requirements of IFRS 9 for annual periods beginning on or after 1 January 2013. The IASB intends that this date will allow entities to adopt at the same time the guidance from all phases of the project to replace IAS 39. (Paragraphs BC7.9A–BC7.9E, BC7.9F–BC7.9H and BC7.9J–BC7.9N describe the IASB's subsequent decisions on the effective date of IFRS 9.)

BC7.4   The IASB will consider delaying the effective date of IFRS 9 if the impairment phase of the project to replace IAS 39 makes such a delay necessary, or if the new Standard on insurance contracts has a mandatory effective date later than 2013, to avoid an insurer having to face two rounds of changes in a short period.

BC7.5   The IASB decided to permit earlier application of IFRS 9 to allow an entity to apply the new requirements on classification and measurement of financial assets. This enables entities to use IFRS 9 (as issued in November 2009) in their 2009 annual financial statements and meets one of the objectives of the phased approach, ie to have improved classification and measurement requirements for financial assets in place for 2009 year-ends. (Paragraphs BC7.7–BC7.9, BC7.9H and BC7.9O–BC7.9T describe the IASB's subsequent decisions on the early application of IFRS 9.)

BC7.6   The effect of transition will be significant for some entities. As a result, there will be less comparability between entities that apply IFRS 9 and those that do not. Accordingly, IFRS 9 includes additional disclosures about the transition to IFRS 9.

Requirements added to IFRS 9 in October 2010

BC7.7   The IASB chose to complete the project to replace IAS 39 in phases to respond to requests that the accounting for financial instruments should be improved quickly. However, the IASB is concerned that if an entity is permitted to adopt one phase early without also adopting early all of the preceding phases, there would be a period of significant incomparability among entities until all of the phases of the project are mandatorily effective. That is because there will be many possible combinations of which requirements are adopted early and which are not. Moreover, the period of incomparability would be significant because the phases will not be mandatorily effective before 1 January 2013. (Paragraphs BC7.9A–BC7.9E, BC7.9F–BC7.9H and BC7.9J–BC7.9N describe the IASB's subsequent decisions on the effective date of IFRS 9.)

BC7.8   Consequently, in the 2010 Own Credit Risk Exposure Draft the IASB proposed that if an entity elects to apply any finalised requirements early, the entity must also apply any preceding requirements in IFRS 9 that it does not already apply. Some respondents did not agree with this proposal and urged the IASB to permit an entity to adopt the proposals in the 2010 Own Credit Risk Exposure Draft early without also adopting early the requirements in IFRS 9 for financial assets. As an alternative, some respondents asked the IASB to finalise the proposals as an amendment to IAS 39, which could be applied immediately, instead of adding the proposals to IFRS 9. Those respondents thought that the proposals in the 2010 Own Credit Risk Exposure Draft are unrelated to the requirements for financial assets and would be less complex to implement. However, the IASB was not persuaded that the benefits of permitting an entity to adopt early only the proposals in the 2010 Own Credit Risk Exposure Draft exceeded the significant incomparability that would result. Moreover, the IASB noted that the transition requirements in IFRS 9 for financial assets require an entity to reassess some financial liabilities designated under the fair value option. Consequently, there is a linkage between the two phases and to permit entities to adopt early only the proposals in the 2010 Own Credit Risk Exposure Draft would be inappropriate and confusing. Moreover, the IASB decided that it would be inappropriate to amend IAS 39 while it was in the process of replacing it. For those reasons, the IASB decided to confirm the proposals in the 2010 Own Credit Risk Exposure Draft. (Paragraphs BC7.35–BC7.40 describe the IASB's subsequent decisions on the early application of the own credit risk requirements.)

BC7.9 However, if an entity chooses to adopt a phase early, the IASB does not require the entity to adopt subsequent phases early. The IASB decided that it would be unfair to require an entity to anticipate the outcomes of unfinished phases in order to make a decision about adopting a phase early. Moreover, the IASB decided that an entity is permitted to adopt early the requirements in IFRS 9 issued in 2009 without adopting early the requirements that were added to IFRS 9 in 2010. (Paragraphs BC7.9O–BC7.9T describe the IASB's subsequent decisions on the early application of IFRS 9.)

Mandatory effective date of IFRS 9—November 2011

BC7.9A IFRS 9 (2009) and IFRS 9 (2010) were issued with a mandatory effective date of 1 January 2013. At the time, the IASB noted that it would consider delaying the effective date of IFRS 9, if:

(a) the impairment phase of the project to replace IAS 39 made such a delay necessary; or

(b) the new Standard on insurance contracts had a mandatory effective date later than 2013, to avoid an insurer having to face two rounds of changes in a short period.

BC7.9B In July 2011 the IASB noted that in order to enable an appropriate period for implementation before the mandatory effective date of the new requirements, the impairment and hedge accounting phases of the project to replace IAS 39 would not be mandatory for periods beginning before 1 January 2013. In addition, any new requirements for the accounting for insurance contracts would not have a mandatory effective date as early as 1 January 2013.

BC7.9C As a result of these considerations, in August 2011 the IASB published the Exposure Draft *Mandatory Effective Date of IFRS 9* (the '2011 Mandatory Effective Date Exposure Draft'). In the 2011 Mandatory Effective Date Exposure Draft, the IASB proposed that the mandatory effective date of IFRS 9 should be deferred to annual periods beginning on or after 1 January 2015. The IASB noted that it did not want to discourage entities from applying IFRS 9 and stressed that early application would still be permitted.

BC7.9D In its redeliberations on the 2011 Mandatory Effective Date Exposure Draft, the IASB decided to confirm its proposal that IFRS 9 would be required to be applied for annual periods beginning on or after 1 January 2015. In doing so, the IASB noted that there are compelling reasons for all project phases to be implemented at the same time and that, based on current circumstances, it is still appropriate to pursue an approach of requiring the same effective date for all phases of this project. (Paragraphs BC7.9F–BC7.9H and BC7.9J–BC7.9N describe the IASB's subsequent decisions on the effective date of IFRS 9.)

BC7.9E However, the IASB noted that it is difficult to assess the amount of lead time that will be necessary to implement all phases of the project because the entire project to replace IAS 39 is not yet complete. Ultimately this may affect the IASB's conclusion on the appropriateness of requiring the same mandatory effective date for all phases of this project.

Requirements added to, and amendments of, IFRS 9 in November 2013

Mandatory effective date of IFRS 9—November 2013

BC7.9F The 2012 Limited Amendments Exposure Draft did not propose to change the mandatory effective date of IFRS 9 and the IASB did not ask a question on that topic. However, as part of the 2013 Impairment Exposure Draft, the IASB noted that all phases of IFRS 9 would have the same effective date and asked respondents for feedback on the lead time that would be needed to implement the proposals on expected credit losses and what the resulting mandatory effective date for IFRS 9 should be.

BC7.9G Many respondents to the 2012 Limited Amendments Exposure Draft urged the IASB to confirm as soon as possible that the mandatory effective date of IFRS 9 of 1 January 2015 would be deferred. Respondents noted that the IASB has a practice of allowing a minimum of 18 months between the finalisation of a Standard and the mandatory effective date. They noted that even if the remaining phases of IFRS 9 were completed by the end of 2013, there would not be 18 months remaining until 1 January 2015. The feedback received in response to the 2013 Impairment Exposure Draft indicated that entities believed that they would need around three years to implement the proposed impairment model.

BC7.9H In the light of the feedback received, the IASB decided to defer the mandatory effective date of IFRS 9. The IASB decided that it will be able to determine the appropriate mandatory effective date only after it finalises the requirements for impairment and classification and measurement and has considered the lead time that is necessary to implement those new requirements. Consequently, the IASB decided that the mandatory effective date should not be specified in IFRS 9 but will be determined when the outstanding phases are finalised. However, the IASB confirmed that in the meantime application of IFRS 9 is still permitted. (Paragraphs BC7.9J–BC7.9N describe the IASB's subsequent decisions on the effective date of IFRS 9. Paragraphs BC7.35–BC7.40 describe the IASB's decisions in November 2013 on the early application of the own credit risk requirements.)

Hedge accounting

BC7.9I The IASB decided that the effective date of the hedge accounting requirements should be aligned with the effective date for the other requirements of IFRS 9 (see paragraph BC7.9H) and confirmed that the hedge accounting requirements cannot be applied prior to the application of the classification and measurement requirements in IFRS 9.

Requirements added to IFRS 9 in July 2014

Mandatory effective date of IFRS 9

BC7.9J   The IASB concluded that the mandatory effective date for IFRS 9 would largely depend on the time and effort required to implement the impairment requirements. Accordingly, the 2013 Impairment Exposure Draft requested feedback on how much time entities would require to implement those requirements.

BC7.9K   Some respondents noted that the impairment model that would be incorporated into IFRS 9 is arguably the most important part of the IASB's response to the global financial crisis. Consequently, although they believe that sufficient time should be allowed for the implementation of IFRS 9, they expressed concern about any delay that is not strictly necessary. These respondents recommended that the IASB should allow no more than two years for the implementation of IFRS 9.

BC7.9L   However, most respondents noted that they would require approximately three years, noting the following reasons:

(a)   entities would need to make system and model changes, in particular credit risk management systems, to monitor significant increases in credit risk and to modify credit risk models to incorporate appropriate forward-looking data;

(b)   entities may have limited availability of historical and trend information. Such information is needed to build relevant models and incorporate forward-looking data in measuring expected credit losses;

(c)   entities would need to undertake parallel testing and running of new systems before final implementation; and

(d)   entities would need to consider the interaction of the expected credit loss requirements with various other regulatory reforms and regulatory capital requirements. Respondents noted that resource constraints would hamper their efforts for a quicker implementation.

BC7.9M   In addition, the IASB noted that most respondents to the IASB's 2013 Insurance Contracts Exposure Draft commented that it would be ideal if the requirements of the new Standard on insurance contracts could have the same mandatory effective date as IFRS 9. Those respondents were concerned that the designations and assessments that an entity would make on initial application of IFRS 9 might not be the same as those that the entity would have made if it had been applying the new Standard on insurance contracts at the same time. Although the IASB had not concluded deliberations on the Standard on insurance contracts, it had tentatively decided that it would allow approximately three years between finalising that Standard and its mandatory effective date.

BC7.9N   The IASB noted that IFRS 9 is relevant to a broad range of entities. Accordingly, it concluded that it may not be appropriate to delay the application of IFRS 9 solely to mitigate the concerns of insurers since it would delay the benefits of improved financial reporting for a broad range of entities. However, in balancing the competing objectives of timely implementation of IFRS 9 and allowing entities sufficient time to implement IFRS 9 and, at the same time, considering the concerns raised in response to the 2013 Insurance Contracts Exposure Draft, the IASB concluded that a mandatory effective date of 1 January 2018 would be appropriate. In the IASB's view, that date would allow sufficient time for entities to implement IFRS 9 and give it the opportunity to progress its project on insurance contracts so that affected entities would be able to understand the direction of the insurance contracts requirements prior to implementing IFRS 9.

Early application of IFRS 9

BC7.9O   Prior to IFRS 9 being issued in July 2014, three versions of IFRS 9 existed—IFRS 9 (2009), IFRS 9 (2010) and IFRS 9 (2013)—and each of these previous versions of IFRS 9 permitted early application. The relevant rationale is set out in paragraphs BC7.5, BC7.7–BC7.9 and BC7.9H–BC7.9I. In addition, an entity is permitted to early apply only the requirements in IFRS 9 related to the presentation of 'own credit' gains and losses on financial liabilities designated under the fair value option; ie without applying the other requirements in IFRS 9. The relevant rationale is set out in paragraphs BC7.35–BC7.40.

BC7.9P   In the 2012 Limited Amendments Exposure Draft, the IASB proposed to limit the versions of IFRS 9 available for early application. Specifically, entities:

(a)   would be permitted to early apply the completed version of IFRS 9; but

(b)   entities would not be permitted to newly early apply a previous version of IFRS 9 if the entity's relevant date of initial application is six months or more after the completed version of IFRS 9 is issued. However, if the entity's relevant date of initial application is less than six months after the completed version of IFRS 9 is issued, an entity would be permitted to continue to apply that version until the completed version of IFRS 9 becomes mandatorily effective.

These proposals did not affect the provision in IFRS 9 that permits an entity to early apply only the requirements related to the presentation of 'own credit' gains and losses on financial liabilities designated under the fair value option. Moreover, the proposals did not affect those entities that chose to early apply a previous version of IFRS 9 before the completed version of IFRS 9 was issued. Those entities would be permitted to continue to apply that previous version of IFRS 9 until the completed version of IFRS 9 is mandatorily effective.

BC7.9Q   In considering those proposals, the IASB noted that having multiple versions of IFRS 9 available for early application (in addition to IAS 39) is complex and significantly reduces the comparability of information that is provided to users of financial statements.

BC7.9R   The IASB acknowledged in the 2012 Limited Amendments Exposure Draft that the phased approach to replacing IAS 39 (including the phased approach to the application of, and transition to, IFRS 9) was originally developed in response to requests from the G20, the Financial Stability Board and others that improvements to the accounting for financial instruments should be available quickly. For this reason, the classification and measurement requirements in IFRS 9 were issued before the phases for impairment and hedge accounting were completed. However, the IASB noted that when the completed version of IFRS 9 is issued (ie when all of the phases of the project to replace IAS 39 are completed), the lack of comparability, as well as the complexity, that results from permitting entities to early apply more than one version of IFRS 9 is no longer justified.

BC7.9S   Despite the conclusion in paragraph BC7.9R, the IASB decided to propose that an entity would be permitted to early apply a previous version of IFRS 9 for six months after the completed version of IFRS 9 is issued. This was a practical accommodation to minimise the cost and disruption to entities that are preparing to apply a previous version of IFRS 9 at the time that the completed version is issued.

BC7.9T   Of those respondents who commented on these proposals in the 2012 Limited Amendments Exposure Draft, nearly all agreed. Many agreed with the IASB's rationale that this would increase comparability compared to the phased early application that is currently permitted. Consequently, the IASB confirmed the proposals set out in paragraph BC7.9P.

Transition related to IFRS 9 as issued in November 2009

BC7.10   IAS 8 *Accounting Policies, Changes in Accounting Estimates and Errors* states that retrospective application results in the most useful information to users because the information presented for all periods is comparable. Consequently, the 2009 Classification and Measurement Exposure Draft proposed retrospective application subject to some transition relief in particular circumstances. The IASB considered the difficulties and associated costs of full retrospective application of the proposals in the 2009 Classification and Measurement Exposure Draft.

BC7.11   Most respondents agreed, in principle, with requiring retrospective application, but many questioned the practicability of the approach. In particular, many noted that the extensive exceptions to retrospective application that would be required to make such transition practicable significantly reduced (and possibly eliminated) any benefit that users might obtain from requiring comparative information to be restated.

BC7.12   The IASB considered whether to require prospective application, but noted that such an approach does not provide comparable information for users of financial statements. In addition, the IASB noted that any transition approach (such as prospective application) that requires resetting the effective interest rate for financial assets measured at amortised cost reduces the usefulness of information about interest income.

BC7.13   The IASB decided to require retrospective application but provide transition relief to address particular difficulties that might arise from retrospective application. The IASB also noted that IAS 8 sets out transition requirements that apply if retrospective application is impracticable and prohibits the use of hindsight when applying a new accounting policy to a prior period.

Transition relief

Impracticability exceptions

BC7.14 The IASB acknowledged that it may be impracticable for an entity to apply the effective interest method or impairment requirements in IAS 39 retrospectively in some situations. The process would be cumbersome, in particular for an entity with a large number of financial assets that were previously measured at fair value but are measured at amortised cost in accordance with the approach in IFRS 9. Several loss events and reversals might have occurred between the date when the asset was initially recognised and the date of initial application of the Standard. IFRS 9 requires that if applying the impairment requirements is impracticable or requires the use of hindsight, an entity should use previously determined fair value information to determine whether a financial asset was impaired in comparative periods. IFRS 9 also requires that the fair value at the date of initial application of the new requirements should be treated as the new amortised cost carrying amount of that financial asset in that case. The IASB rejected proposals that entities should be permitted, but not required, to treat the fair value at the date of initial application as amortised cost because it would impair comparability and require significant guidance about when such an option should be permitted. (Paragraphs BC7.72–BC7.81 describe the IASB's subsequent decisions on transition to the new impairment requirements.)

BC7.15 The IASB noted that an entity would not have determined the fair value of an investment in an unquoted equity instrument[37] (or a derivative on such an investment) that was previously accounted for in accordance with paragraphs 46(c) and 66 of IAS 39. Moreover, an entity will not have the necessary information to determine fair value retrospectively without using hindsight. Accordingly, IFRS 9 requires such instruments to be measured at fair value at the date of initial application.

Hybrid contracts

BC7.16 An entity may not have previously determined the fair value of a hybrid contract in its entirety. Moreover, an entity will not have the necessary information to determine fair value retrospectively without using hindsight. However, an entity would have been required to measure both the embedded derivative and host separately at fair value to apply the disclosure requirements in IFRS 7. Consequently, in comparative periods, IFRS 9 requires the sum of the fair value of the embedded derivative and the host to be used as an approximation of the fair value of the entire hybrid contract.

BC7.17 The proposals in the 2009 Classification and Measurement Exposure Draft would have resulted in fair value measurement for many hybrid contracts for which the embedded derivative was accounted for separately in accordance with IAS 39. Some respondents asked for such treatment under IAS 39 to be 'grandfathered'. The IASB noted that many such requests had been related to

---

37 IFRS 13, issued in May 2011, defines a Level 1 input as a quoted price in an active market for an identical asset or liability. Level 2 inputs include quoted prices for identical assets or liabilities in markets that are not active. As a result, IFRS 9 refers to such equity instruments as 'an equity instrument that does not have a quoted price in an active market for an identical instrument (ie a Level 1 input)'.

the proposed treatment of hybrid contracts with financial liability hosts, which were not included in IFRS 9 (2009). Consequently, the IASB decided not to permit an option to grandfather hybrid contracts with financial asset hosts that were bifurcated in accordance with IAS 39 as an accounting policy choice because it would impair comparability, and because some such contracts may still have a significant remaining maturity.

Assessment of the objective of the entity's business model for managing financial assets

BC7.18   IFRS 9 requires an entity to assess whether the objective of an entity's business model is to manage financial assets to collect the contractual cash flows on the basis of circumstances at the date of initial application. The IASB believes it would be difficult, and perhaps impossible, to assess that condition on the basis of circumstances when the instrument first satisfied the recognition criterion in IAS 39.

Assessment of qualifying criteria for the fair value option

BC7.19   The IASB decided that the assessment of whether a financial asset or financial liability meets the eligibility criterion for designation under the fair value option should be based on the circumstances at the date of initial application. IFRS 9 changes the classification of some financial assets, including eliminating two of the three eligibility criteria in IAS 39 for the fair value option for financial assets. Consequently, the IASB believes that an entity should reconsider at transition its original assessment of whether to designate a financial asset or financial liability as at fair value through profit or loss.

Comparative information

BC7.20   As noted above, many respondents were concerned that the inevitable exceptions to full retrospective application would result in restated information that is incomplete. They proposed an approach similar to that used on first-time adoption of IFRS and when entities adopted IAS 39 in 2005, in which the requirement to provide comparative information was waived. Some respondents believe that such an approach would address the concerns that, although IAS 1 requires only one year of comparative information, the legal and regulatory frameworks in many jurisdictions require further comparative periods to be presented. In those situations, the restatement of comparatives would be virtually impossible for an entity wishing to adopt IFRS 9 early.

BC7.21   In the IASB's view, waiving the requirement to restate comparatives strikes a balance between the conceptually preferable method of full retrospective application (as stated in IAS 8) and the practicability of adopting the new classification model within a short time frame. Accordingly, the IASB decided that it would permit, but not require, restatement of comparative periods by entities that implement IFRS 9 for reporting periods beginning before 1 January 2012. However, those considerations would be less applicable for entities that adopted outside a short time frame. Consequently, restated comparative information is required if an entity adopts IFRS 9 for reporting periods beginning after 1 January 2012. (Paragraphs BC7.34A–BC7.34M and BC7.82–BC7.84 describe the IASB's subsequent decisions on restating comparative information.)

Date of initial application

BC7.22　The 2009 Classification and Measurement Exposure Draft stated that the date of initial application would be the date when an entity first applies the requirements in the Standard. Many respondents questioned whether the date of initial application could be an arbitrary date between the date of issue of the Standard (or even earlier) and the mandatory effective date, resulting in a loss of comparability over a long period of time. The IASB agreed that a free choice would impair comparability, but noted it intended that entities should be able to apply the Standard in 2009 or 2010 financial statements. Accordingly, the Standard requires the date of initial application to be the beginning of a reporting period, but provides relief from this requirement for entities applying the Standard for reporting periods beginning on or before 1 January 2011.

Hedge accounting

BC7.23　The IASB decided not to carry forward the specific transition provisions on hedge accounting proposed in the 2009 Classification and Measurement Exposure Draft because they are not necessary.

Transitional disclosures

BC7.24　The 2009 Classification and Measurement Exposure Draft proposed disclosures for entities that apply the new IFRS 9 early. However, many noted that such disclosures would be useful for all entities applying IFRS 9 for the first time, and not only early adopters. The IASB noted that the information necessary to make those disclosures would be readily available to the entity to make the necessary journal entries on transition and to account for the financial assets in the future. Accordingly, IFRS 9 requires all entities to supply additional disclosures on transition. (Paragraphs BC7.34A–BC7.34M and BC7.63–BC7.68 describe the IASB's subsequent decisions on disclosures at transition to IFRS 9.)

BC7.25　The IASB rejected a proposal in the comment letters that entities should apply disclosures similar to those based on IFRS 1 *First-time Adoption of International Financial Reporting Standards* explaining the transition to the new Standard. The IASB noted that the disclosures in IFRS 1 relate to first-time adoption and not to changes in accounting policies. Disclosures about changes in an accounting policy are required by IAS 8.

Transition related to the requirements added to IFRS 9 in October 2010

BC7.26　As noted above, IAS 8 states that retrospective application results in the most useful information to users because the information presented for all periods is comparable. The IASB noted that IFRS 7 already requires disclosure of the amount of the change in fair value that is attributable to changes in the credit risk of the liability. Consequently, entities are already calculating the information necessary to present the effects of changes in liabilities' credit risk in other comprehensive income. Thus, the 2010 Own Credit Risk Exposure Draft proposed retrospective application and almost all respondents agreed. The IASB confirmed that proposal.

BC7.27 The IASB did not change the classification and measurement approach for financial liabilities, including the eligibility conditions for the fair value option for financial liabilities. Consequently, the proposals in the 2010 Own Credit Risk Exposure Draft did not permit entities to make new designations or revoke its previous designations as a result of the proposals. Some respondents believed that the IASB should permit entities to reassess their designations in the light of the new requirements related to own credit risk.

BC7.28 However, the IASB was not persuaded that there is a compelling reason to permit entities to reassess their elections, especially because the underlying classification and measurement approach has not changed. As noted in paragraph BC7.19, when an entity initially applies IFRS 9 to assets, it is required to reassess particular liabilities designated under the fair value option. That was necessary because the requirements issued in IFRS 9 (2009) introduced a new classification and measurement approach for financial assets, which would change the classification of some (and perhaps many) financial assets. Those changes require an entity to reassess liabilities designated under the fair value option to the extent that designation was originally elected to address an accounting mismatch. However, the IASB believed that a similar case could not be made for the requirements added to IFRS 9 in 2010. And because the requirements issued in IFRS 9 (2009) already require reassessment of particular liabilities, the IASB believes that a second reassessment would make transition unnecessarily complex. Consequently, the IASB decided to confirm the proposal in the 2010 Own Credit Risk Exposure Draft.

Transition relief

BC7.29 When the IASB issued the new requirements for financial assets in November 2009, it granted some transition relief from full retrospective transition. To be consistent with the transition requirements for assets, the IASB decided to grant similar transition relief for the requirements added to IFRS 9 in October 2010:

(a) The requirements are not applied to liabilities that have been derecognised at the date of initial application. The IASB concluded that applying the requirements in IFRS 9 to some derecognised items but not others would be confusing and unnecessarily complex.

(b) An entity is required to assess whether presenting the effects of changes in a liability's credit risk in other comprehensive income would create or enlarge an accounting mismatch in profit or loss on the basis of facts and circumstances that exist at the date of initial application. This is consistent with the other transition requirements in IFRS 9 related to the fair value option. Moreover, the IASB noted that the conclusion will most likely be the same regardless of whether it is made on the basis of facts and circumstances that existed at initial recognition of the liability or at the date of initial application.

(c) Derivative liabilities that were previously accounted for at cost are measured at fair value at the date of initial application. Consistently with the requirements for financial assets, an entity will not have the necessary information to determine fair value retrospectively without using hindsight.

(d) An entity is not required to restate prior periods if the requirements are adopted for reporting periods beginning before 1 January 2012. The IASB decided that it would be inappropriate and confusing to require an entity to restate prior periods for some of the requirements in IFRS 9 but not others. However, the IASB decided that if the entity elects to restate prior periods to reflect the requirements added to IFRS 9 in October 2010, it must also restate prior periods to reflect the other requirements in IFRS 9. That conclusion is consistent with the IASB's decision that if an entity elects to adopt the requirements early, it must at the same time adopt early all of the requirements in IFRS 9 that it does not already apply. (Paragraphs BC7.34A–BC7.34M and BC7.82–BC7.84 describe the IASB's subsequent decision on restating comparative information.)

Transitional insurance issues

BC7.30 The IASB noted that insurers may face particular problems if they apply IFRS 9 before they apply the new Standard on insurance contracts (the new IFRS 4). To avoid accounting mismatches in profit or loss, many insurers classify many of their financial assets as available-for-sale. If those insurers apply IFRS 9 before the new IFRS 4, they might decide to classify many of their financial assets at amortised cost (assuming they meet the relevant conditions in IFRS 9). When those insurers later apply the new IFRS 4, they may wish to reclassify those assets from amortised cost to fair value through profit or loss, but that may not generally be possible in accordance with IFRS 9. Thus, those insurers might have either to classify those assets at fair value through profit or loss during the intervening period or to continue to classify them at amortised cost when they apply the new IFRS 4. Either choice might lead to an accounting mismatch.

BC7.31 The IASB considered whether it could reduce such mismatches by maintaining the available-for-sale category for insurers until they can apply the new IFRS 4. However, if the IASB did so, it would have to create detailed and arbitrary descriptions of the entities and instruments to which that approach would apply. The IASB concluded that permitting the continuation of that category would not provide more useful information for users.

BC7.32 The IASB will consider in developing the new IFRS 4 whether to provide an option for insurers to reclassify some or all financial assets when they first apply the new IFRS 4. This would be similar to the option in paragraph 45 of IFRS 4 and paragraph D4 of IFRS 1. The IASB included such an option in IFRS 4 for reasons that may be equally valid for phase II.

Shadow accounting for participating contracts

BC7.33 Some insurers expressed concerns that an accounting mismatch will arise if the assets backing participating insurance liabilities include equity investments and the insurer elects to present gains and losses on those investments in other comprehensive income. That accounting mismatch would arise because paragraph 30 of IFRS 4 does not give explicit authority to apply 'shadow accounting' in such cases.

BC7.34 The IASB acknowledges that this accounting mismatch is undesirable. However, for the following reasons, the IASB did not amend paragraph 30 of IFRS 4:

(a) This accounting mismatch will arise only if an insurer elects to present gains and losses on equity investments in other comprehensive income.

(b) As described in paragraph BC5.23, in creating the option to present gains and losses on equity investments in other comprehensive income, the IASB's intention was to provide a presentation alternative for some equity investments in which presenting fair value gains and losses in profit or loss may not be indicative of the performance of the entity, particularly if the entity holds those equity instruments for non-contractual benefits, rather than primarily to generate increases in the value of the investment. The IASB did not intend to provide an alternative for investments in any other circumstances, including if an entity intends to hold an equity investment over a long time frame. In the IASB's view, if an insurer holds investments with the primary objective of realising a profit from increases in their value, for the benefit of either the insurer itself or its policyholders, the most transparent place to present those value changes is in profit or loss.

Disclosures on transition from IAS 39 to IFRS 9—November 2011

BC7.34A When IFRS 9 (2009) and IFRS 9 (2010) were issued, they provided limited relief from restating comparative financial statements. Entities that adopted the Standard for reporting periods beginning before 1 January 2012 were not required to restate prior periods. At the time, the IASB's view was that waiving the requirement to restate comparative financial statements struck a balance between the conceptually preferable method of full retrospective application (as stated in IAS 8) and the practicability of adopting the new classification model within a short time frame.

BC7.34B In August 2011 the IASB published the 2011 Mandatory Effective Date Exposure Draft. At the time, the IASB noted that these practicability considerations would be less relevant for entities that adopted outside a short time frame, and therefore proposed that restated comparative financial statements would continue to be required if an entity adopts IFRS 9 for reporting periods beginning on or after 1 January 2012.

BC7.34C Some respondents to the 2011 Mandatory Effective Date Exposure Draft believed that comparative financial statements should be required to be restated for the following reasons:

(a) The presentation of restated comparative financial statements is consistent with IAS 8.

(b) A delay in the mandatory effective date of IFRS 9 would allow a sufficient time frame for entities to prepare restated comparative financial statements.

(c)   IAS 39 and IFRS 9 are sufficiently different from each other, so restatement will be necessary to provide meaningful information to users of financial statements.

BC7.34D   In contrast, those who did not believe that comparative financial statements should be required to be restated argued that:

(a)   Comparative relief was granted for IAS 32 and IAS 39 upon first-time adoption of IFRS for European reporting entities.

(b)   Comparability is impaired by the transition requirements, which are complex and inconsistent across various phases of the project, reducing the usefulness of the comparative information (for example, the classification and measurement phase requires retrospective application with some transition reliefs, whereas the hedge accounting phase requires prospective application).

(c)   Time pressures similar to those existing when IFRS 9 (2009) and IFRS 9 (2010) were initially issued will nonetheless exist when the last phase of the project to replace IAS 39 is issued.

BC7.34E   Respondents to the 2011 Mandatory Effective Date Exposure Draft also raised specific implementation issues that increased the cost of applying the classification and measurement requirements of IFRS 9 in periods prior to their date of initial application. These reasons were the interaction between the date of initial application and:

(a)   the fact that IFRS 9 is not applied to items that have already been derecognised as of the date of initial application;

(b)   the initial business model determination; and

(c)   the elections for the fair value option and the fair value through other comprehensive income presentation alternative at the date of initial application.

BC7.34F   In providing views on their preferred transition approach for the project to replace IAS 39, investors consistently emphasised a need for comparable period-to-period information—that is, information that enabled them to understand the effect of the transition from IAS 39 to IFRS 9. Investors, irrespective of their preferred approach, noted that the mix of transition requirements between phases, and the modifications to retrospective application in the classification and measurement phase, would diminish the usefulness of comparative financial statements. Many also noted that the partial restatement of comparative financial statements could create either confusion or a misleading impression of period-to-period comparability.

BC7.34G   Some investor respondents, despite sharing the views in the preceding paragraph, favoured the presentation of comparative financial statements with full retrospective application of all project phases (ie including hedge accounting) as the preferred way of achieving comparability. Some of the respondents who favoured full retrospective application agreed that the modifications to retrospective application would diminish the usefulness of comparative financial statements but believed that the effect of the modifications would not be significant.

BC7.34H Due to the variation in transition requirements of the phases in the project to replace IAS 39, other investors did not favour the presentation of restated comparative financial statements. Their primary concern was having information that enabled them to understand the effect of the transition from IAS 39 to IFRS 9. They did not believe that restating comparative financial statements on the basis of the transition requirements across the phases of IFRS 9 would necessarily provide that information.

BC7.34I In addition to feedback on their preferred approach to understanding the effect of the transition to IFRS 9, investors also provided information about what they focus on when analysing financial instruments in financial statements. They noted that the statement of profit or loss and other comprehensive income (and restatement of it in comparative periods) is less important to their analysis than the statement of financial position, aside from situations where it allows for a link to the statement of financial position (for example net interest income). Similarly, where restatement means primarily the presentation of historical fair value changes, comparative information is less useful as extrapolation is not possible in the same way as it is for amortised cost information.

BC7.34J Investors also provided feedback on those disclosures that would be useful in understanding the transition from IAS 39 to IFRS 9. They cited examples that they found useful on the transition from other GAAPs to IFRS in Europe in 2005. It was also noted that disclosures similar to those required by IFRS 7 for transfers of financial assets between classification categories would be useful—ie disclosures about reclassifications are also useful when the reclassifications result from applying a new accounting standard.

BC7.34K In the light of this feedback received, the IASB considered whether modified transition disclosures could provide the information necessary for investors to understand the effect of the transition from IAS 39 to IFRS 9, while reducing the burden on preparers that would result from the restatement of comparative financial statements. The IASB also considered whether this approach would address concerns about the diminished usefulness and period-to-period comparability of comparative financial statements due to the different transition requirements of the phases of the project to replace IAS 39. The IASB believes that modified disclosures can achieve these objectives and decided to require modified transition disclosures instead of the restatement of comparative financial statements.

BC7.34L The IASB noted that much of the information requested by investors was already required by IAS 8 and IFRS 7 on transition from IAS 39 to IFRS 9. The IASB also noted that it was not modifying the requirements of IAS 8. The IASB, however, decided that the reclassification disclosures in IFRS 7 (as amended by IFRS 9 (2009)) should be required on transition from IAS 39 to IFRS 9, irrespective of whether they would normally be required due to a change in business model. The IASB also specified that the reclassification disclosures, and other disclosures required when initially applying IFRS 9, should allow reconciliations between the measurement categories in accordance with IAS 39 and IFRS 9 and individual line items in the financial statements or classes of financial instruments. This would provide useful information that would enable users to understand the transition from IAS 39 to IFRS 9.

BC7.34M   The IASB also considered whether the transition disclosures should be required if the entity presents restated comparative financial statements, or only if they are not provided. The IASB noted that the disclosures provide useful information to investors on transition from IAS 39 to IFRS 9, irrespective of whether comparative financial statements are restated. The IASB also believed that the burden of these comparative transition disclosures for preparers would not be unreasonable because it was based largely on existing disclosure requirements and should require disclosure of information available as a result of preparing for transition. Consequently, the IASB decided to require these disclosures even if restated comparative financial statements are provided. However, the IASB did not want to unduly burden those who were in the process of applying IFRS 9 early by requiring disclosures that the entity was not previously required to provide. Consequently, for entities that initially apply the classification and measurement requirements from 1 January 2012 until 31 December 2012, the IASB decided to permit, but not require, the presentation of the additional disclosures. If an entity elects to provide these disclosures when initially applying IFRS 9 between 1 January 2012 and 31 December 2012, it would not be required to restate comparative periods. (Paragraphs BC7.63–BC7.68 describe the IASB's subsequent decisions on disclosures at transition to IFRS 9.)

Transition related to the requirements added to IFRS 9 in November 2013

Presentation of 'own credit' gains and losses on financial liabilities

BC7.35   After requirements were added to IFRS 9 in October 2010 to address the effects of changes in own credit risk for liabilities designated under the fair value option, many interested parties requested that the IASB permit an entity to apply those requirements without also applying the other requirements in IFRS 9. That is because markets continued to be volatile and own credit gains or losses remained significant, which accentuated the concerns about the usefulness of presenting gains in profit or loss when an entity is experiencing deterioration in its own credit quality.

BC7.36   In the 2012 Limited Amendments Exposure Draft, the IASB proposed that six months after the completed version of IFRS 9 is issued, entities would no longer be permitted to newly early apply previous versions of IFRS 9. Consequently, entities wishing to apply the classification and measurement requirements after the completed version of IFRS 9 was issued would have to develop and implement the necessary systems changes for applying the new impairment requirements before they would be able to apply the classification and measurement requirements. In effect, that would have made the availability of the own credit requirements for early application dependent on the implementation of an expected credit loss impairment model.

BC7.37   Consequently, in order to make the own credit requirements in IFRS 9 available more quickly, the 2012 Limited Amendments Exposure Draft proposed that once the completed version of IFRS 9 was issued, an entity would be permitted to early apply the requirements for presenting in other comprehensive income the 'own credit' gains or losses on financial liabilities designated under the fair value option without early applying the other requirements of IFRS 9. However, at the time, the IASB noted that its decision to incorporate the possibility to apply early only the own credit requirements into the final version of IFRS 9 instead of IFRS 9 (2010) and later versions, was based on the expectation that there would not be a significant delay in the completion of IFRS 9. In other words, the IASB believed that the own credit requirements would be available for early application at roughly the same time under both approaches. However, the IASB noted that by exposing the proposals as part of the 2012 Limited Amendments Exposure Draft, it would be possible to change this approach if necessary.

BC7.38 Nearly all respondents to the 2012 Limited Amendments Exposure Draft supported the proposal that an entity would be permitted to early apply only the own credit requirements in IFRS 9 without applying any other requirements of IFRS 9 at the same time. However, most of these respondents also asked the IASB to make these requirements available for early application before the IFRS 9 project is completed and the final Standard is issued. Many of these respondents suggested that this could be accomplished by incorporating the own credit requirements into IAS 39, whereas others suggested incorporating the requirements into IFRS 9 (2010) and later versions.

BC7.39 During the redeliberations the IASB confirmed the proposal in the 2012 Limited Amendments Exposure Draft that the own credit requirements should be made available for early application without early applying the other requirements of IFRS 9. However, in order to respond to the feedback that the own credit requirements should be made available as soon as possible, the IASB decided to incorporate those requirements into IFRS 9 (2010) and later versions. The IASB also confirmed its previous decision not to incorporate the own credit requirements into IAS 39 because that Standard is being replaced by IFRS 9.

BC7.40 Although the topic was not within the scope of the 2012 Limited Amendments Exposure Draft, some respondents asked the IASB to reconsider the requirements in IFRS 9 that prohibit an entity from reclassifying (recycling) own credit gains or losses to profit or loss when the financial liability is derecognised. The IASB noted that it is currently discussing the objective of other comprehensive income, including whether amounts should be recycled to profit or loss (and if so, when), in its project on the *Conceptual Framework* and therefore the IASB noted that it would be inappropriate to reconsider those requirements in IFRS 9 before it completes that work.

Transition related to the hedge accounting requirements

BC7.41 IAS 8 states that retrospective application results in the most useful information to users of the financial statements. IAS 8 also states that retrospective application is the preferred approach to transition, unless such retrospective application is impracticable. In such a scenario the entity adjusts the comparative information from the earliest date practicable. In conformity with these requirements, the classification and measurement chapters of IFRS 9 require retrospective application (with some relief in particular circumstances).

BC7.42   The proposals in the 2010 Hedge Accounting Exposure Draft were a significant change from the requirements in IAS 39. However, in accordance with the proposals, a hedge accounting relationship could be designated only prospectively. Consequently, retrospective application was not applicable. This reflects that retrospective application gives rise to similar concerns about using hindsight as retrospective designation of hedging relationships, which is prohibited.

BC7.43   In developing the transition requirements proposed in the 2010 Hedge Accounting Exposure Draft, the IASB considered two alternative approaches:

(a)   prospective application only for new hedging relationships; or

(b)   prospective application for all hedging relationships.

BC7.44   The IASB rejected the approach using prospective application of hedge accounting only for new hedging relationships. This approach would have required the current hedge accounting model in IAS 39 to be maintained until hedge accounting is discontinued for the hedging relationships established in accordance with IAS 39. Also, the proposed disclosures would be provided only for the hedging relationships accounted for in accordance with the proposed model. This approach entails the complexity of applying the two models simultaneously and also involves a set of disclosures that would be inconsistent and difficult to interpret. Because some hedging relationships are long-term, two hedge accounting models would co-exist for a potentially long period. This would make it difficult for users to compare the financial statements of different entities. Comparability would also be difficult when entities apply the old and the new model in the same financial statements, as well as for information provided over time.

BC7.45   Consequently, the IASB proposed prospective application of the proposed hedge accounting requirements for all hedging relationships, while ensuring that 'qualifying' hedging relationships could be moved from the existing model to the proposed model on the adoption date.

BC7.46   Almost all respondents agreed with prospective application of the new hedge accounting requirements to all hedging relationships because that would avoid the administrative burden of maintaining both the IAS 39 model and the new hedge accounting model and would also mitigate the risk of hindsight arising from retrospective designation of hedging relationships. Respondents also noted that prospective application is consistent with hedge accounting transition requirements that were used for previous amendments to IAS 39.

BC7.47   The IASB also received feedback that suggested a general provision, whereby hedging relationships designated under IAS 39 would be automatically 'grandfathered', ie entities could continue applying the requirements of IAS 39 to these hedging relationships. However, consistent with its proposal in the 2010 Hedge Accounting Exposure Draft (see paragraph BC7.44), the IASB decided not to allow the grandfathering of the application of IAS 39. Instead, the IASB retained its original decision that the new hedge accounting requirements are applied to hedging relationships that qualify for hedge accounting in accordance with IAS 39 and this Standard and that those are treated as continuing hedging relationships.

BC7.48   Some respondents supported varying forms of retrospective application. However, consistent with previous hedge accounting transition requirements in IAS 39 and the 2010 Hedge Accounting Exposure Draft, the IASB decided not to allow retrospective application in situations that would require retrospective designation because that would involve hindsight.

BC7.49   Some responses to the 2010 Hedge Accounting Exposure Draft suggested using retrospective application in two particular situations in which the outcomes under IAS 39 and the new hedge accounting model significantly differ but retrospective designation would not be necessary. The particular situations are when an entity under IAS 39 designated as the hedging instrument only changes in the intrinsic value (but not the time value) of an option or changes in the spot element (but not the forward element) of a forward contract. The IASB noted that in both circumstances applying the new requirements for accounting for the time value of options or the forward element of forward contracts would not involve hindsight from retrospective designation but instead use the designation that was previously made under IAS 39. The IASB also noted that in situations in which mismatches between the terms of the hedging instrument and the hedged item exist there might still be some risk of hindsight related to Level 3 fair value measurements when calculating the 'aligned' time value of an option and the 'aligned' forward element of a forward contract. However, the IASB concluded that such hindsight would be limited because hedge accounting was applied to these hedging relationships under IAS 39, meaning that the changes in the intrinsic value of an option or the changes in the value of the spot element of a forward contract had to have a high degree of offset with the changes in value of the hedged risks. Hence, the valuation inputs used for the calculation of the aligned values could not significantly differ from the valuation inputs for the overall fair value of the hedging instruments, which were known from previously applying IAS 39. The IASB also noted that retrospective application in these cases would significantly improve the usefulness of the information for the reasons that underpinned the IASB's decisions on accounting for the time value of options and the forward element of forward contracts (see paragraphs BC6.386–BC6.426). Consequently, the IASB decided to provide for those two particular situations an exception to prospective application of the hedge accounting requirements of this Standard but only for those hedging relationships that existed at the beginning of the earliest comparative period or were designated thereafter. For the forward element of forward contracts retrospective application is permitted but not required because unlike the new treatment for time value of options the new treatment for the forward element of forward contracts is an election. However, in order to address the risk of using hindsight, the IASB decided that on transition this election is only available on an 'all-or-nothing' basis (ie not a hedge-by-hedge basis). IAS 39 did not allow excluding foreign currency basis spreads from the designation of a financial instrument as the hedging instrument. Consequently, the requirement for the time value of options and the forward element of forward contracts, that an entity excluded the part of the financial instrument that represents costs of hedging from the designation as the hedging instrument under IAS 39, does not apply to foreign currency basis spreads. The restriction that retrospective application is available only on an 'all-or-nothing' basis does not apply to foreign currency basis spreads because of the variety of hedging instruments that involve those spreads.

BC7.50 Some respondents asked the IASB to consider allowing discontinuing at the date of initial application of the new hedge accounting requirements hedging relationships designated under IAS 39 and then designating new hedging relationships in a way that is better aligned with the new hedge accounting requirements.

BC7.51 The IASB noted that an entity could revoke designations of hedging relationships without any restriction until the last day of applying IAS 39 in accordance with the requirements in that Standard. Hence, the IASB considered that any specific transition requirements to address this request were unnecessary. However, in order to address some concerns over potential practical transition issues in the context of prospective application, the IASB decided:

(a) to allow an entity to consider the moment it initially applies the new hedge accounting requirements and the moment it ceases to apply the hedge accounting requirements of IAS 39 as the same point in time. The IASB noted that this would avoid any time lag between starting the use of the new hedge accounting model and discontinuing the old hedge accounting model (because the end of the last business day of the previous reporting period often does not coincide with the beginning of the first business day of the next reporting period), which otherwise might involve significant changes in fair values between those points in time and as a result could cause difficulties in applying hedge accounting under the new hedge accounting model for hedging relationships that would otherwise qualify.

(b) to require that an entity uses the hedge ratio in accordance with IAS 39 as the starting point for rebalancing the hedge ratio of a continuing hedging relationship (if applicable) and to recognise any related gain or loss in profit or loss. The IASB considered that any change to the hedge ratio that might be required on transition so that a hedging relationship designated under IAS 39 continues to qualify for hedge accounting should not result in an entity having to discontinue that hedging relationship on transition and then newly designating it. The IASB decided to require the recognition of any gain or loss on rebalancing in profit or loss in a broadly similar manner for ongoing hedge accounting under the new model to address any concerns that hedge ineffectiveness might otherwise be recognised as a direct adjustment to retained earnings on transition. The accounting is broadly similar to that for ongoing hedge accounting under the new model in that the hedge ineffectiveness in the context of rebalancing is recognised in profit or loss. However, in contrast to ongoing hedge accounting under the new model, rebalancing on transition applies because a different hedge ratio has already been used for risk management purposes (but did not coincide with the designation of the hedging relationship under IAS 39). In other words, rebalancing does not reflect a concurrent adjustment for risk management purposes but results in aligning the hedge ratio for accounting purposes with a hedge ratio that was already in place for risk management purposes.

BC7.52 The IASB decided not to change the requirements of IFRS 1 for hedge accounting. The IASB noted that a first-time adopter would need to look at the entire population of possible hedging relationships and assess which ones would meet the qualifying criteria of the new hedge accounting model. To the extent that an entity wants to apply hedge accounting, those hedging relationships should be documented on or before the transition date. This is consistent with the transition requirements for existing users of IFRS and the existing transition requirements of IFRS 1, which state that an entity shall discontinue hedge accounting if it had designated a hedging relationship but that hedging relationship does not meet the qualifying criteria in IAS 39.

Transition related to the requirements added to IFRS 9 in July 2014

Transition related to the limited amendments to the requirements for classifying and measuring financial assets

Assessment of an asset's contractual cash flow characteristics

BC7.53 In accordance with the existing transition provisions in IFRS 9, when IFRS 9 is initially applied, the assessment of an asset's contractual cash flow characteristics is based on the facts and circumstances that existed at the initial recognition of the financial asset, and the resulting classification is applied retrospectively.

BC7.54 The 2012 Limited Amendments Exposure Draft introduced a notion of a modified economic relationship between principal and the consideration for time value of money and credit risk. In that Exposure Draft, the IASB noted that assessing the contractual cash flow characteristics in accordance with the requirements issued in IFRS 9 (2009) requires judgement, but acknowledged that the proposed clarification introduces a greater degree of judgement and presents a greater risk that hindsight will be necessary to make the assessment. Accordingly, the IASB proposed specific transition requirements for situations in which it is impracticable (for example, because of the risk of using hindsight) to assess a modified economic relationship on the basis of the facts and circumstances that existed at initial recognition of the financial asset.

BC7.55 Specifically, the IASB proposed that in cases in which it is impracticable for an entity to apply the assessment of an asset's contractual cash flow characteristics based on the new requirements, an entity would be required to make that assessment without taking into account the specific requirements related to the modified economic relationship. In other words, the IASB proposed that, in those cases, the entity would apply the assessment of the asset's contractual cash flows characteristics as that assessment was set out in the requirements issued in IFRS 9 (2009); ie without the notion of a modified economic relationship.

BC7.56 During its redeliberations of the 2012 Limited Amendments Exposure Draft, the IASB confirmed the notion of a modified time value of money element in the assessment of an asset's contractual cash flows and therefore also confirmed the transition provision described in paragraph BC7.55. The IASB also noted that a similar transition provision is needed for the exception for particular prepayment features described in paragraph B4.1.12 of IFRS 9. That is because an entity will need to determine whether a prepayable financial asset meets the conditions set out in that paragraph on the basis of the facts and circumstances that existed at the initial recognition of the financial asset, including whether the fair value of the prepayment feature was insignificant. The IASB noted that, in some cases, it may be impracticable for an entity to determine whether the fair value of the prepayment feature was insignificant at the date of initial recognition. For example, this determination might be impracticable if the entity did not account for that embedded prepayment feature separately at fair value through profit or loss as an embedded derivative under IAS 39. Consequently, the IASB decided that in cases in which it is impracticable for an entity to assess whether the fair value of a prepayment feature was insignificant based on the facts and circumstances that existed at the initial recognition of the asset, the entity must assess the contractual cash flow characteristics of the financial asset without taking into account the specific exception for prepayment features.

Fair value option

BC7.57   In accordance with paragraph 7.2.9–7.2.10 of IFRS 9, when an entity initially applies the classification and measurement requirements for financial assets, it is:

(a)   permitted to reconsider its fair value option elections for both financial assets and financial liabilities; that is, to elect to apply the fair value option even if an accounting mismatch already existed before the date of initial application and/or revoke the fair value option even if an accounting mismatch continues to exist; and

(b)   required to revoke its fair value option elections for both financial assets and financial liabilities if an accounting mismatch no longer exists at the date of initial application.

BC7.58   In accordance with paragraph 7.2.27 of IFRS 9, the transition provisions described in paragraph BC7.57 are available only when the entity initially applies the classification and measurement requirements for financial assets; ie an entity applies those provisions only once. The relevant rationale is set out in paragraphs BC7.19 and BC7.27–BC7.28.

BC7.59   In the deliberations that led to the publication of the 2012 Limited Amendments Exposure Draft, the IASB noted that if an entity had already applied an earlier version of IFRS 9 (ie IFRS 9 (2009), IFRS 9 (2010) or IFRS 9 (2013)), it would have already applied the transition provisions described in paragraph BC7.57. However, the application of the proposals in the 2012 Limited Amendments Exposure Draft could cause some financial assets to be measured differently as compared to a previous version of IFRS 9 and, as a result, new accounting mismatches could arise.

BC7.60   Accordingly, the IASB proposed that an entity that has already applied a previous version of IFRS 9 should, when it applies the proposals in the 2012 Limited Amendments Exposure Draft, be:

(a)   permitted to apply the fair value option to new accounting mismatches created by the initial application of the proposed amendments to the classification and measurement requirements; and

(b)   required to revoke previous fair value option elections if an accounting mismatch no longer exists as a result of the initial application of the proposed amendments to the classification and measurement requirements.

BC7.61   In other words, an entity would be permitted or required to reconsider its designations under the fair value option only to the extent that previous accounting mismatches no longer exist, or new accounting mismatches are created, as a result of applying the limited amendments to the classification and measurement requirements for financial assets.

BC7.62   During its redeliberations of the 2012 Limited Amendments Exposure Draft, the IASB confirmed the transition provision described above.

Transition disclosures

BC7.63   The IASB decided to clarify the disclosure requirements in IFRS 7 that are relevant to an entity's transition to IFRS 9. That is, the IASB clarified that on transition to IFRS 9, an entity is required to comply with the quantitative disclosures set out in IFRS 7 instead of applying the general quantitative disclosure requirements in other Standards.

BC7.64   Specifically, the IASB amended paragraph 42Q of IFRS 7 to state that an entity need not disclose the line item amounts that would have been reported:

(a)   in prior reporting periods in accordance with IFRS 9; or

(b)   in the current reporting period in accordance with IAS 39.

BC7.65   The IASB noted that requiring disclosure of the line item amounts that would have been reported in prior reporting periods in accordance with IFRS 9 would contradict paragraph 7.2.15 of IFRS 9, which states that an entity need not restate prior periods.

BC7.66   The IASB considered three primary factors in evaluating whether an entity should be required to disclose line item amounts in the current reporting period in accordance with IAS 39:

(a)   the usefulness of the disclosures;

(b)   the cost of providing such disclosures; and

(c)   whether the existing transition disclosure requirements are sufficient and enable users of financial statements to assess the effect of transition to IFRS 9.

BC7.67   In assessing the usefulness of this disclosure, the IASB considered the interaction at transition to IFRS 9 between the requirements for classification and measurement and hedge accounting. The IASB observed that the concept of hedge accounting does not lend itself to making assumptions about what hedge accounting (under IAS 39) might have been. That is because hedge accounting is an elective accounting treatment that allows the resolution of accounting mismatches. In order to apply hedge accounting, an entity must make that election and then, if the hedging relationship meets the qualifying criteria, the entity prospectively applies hedge accounting. In accordance with IAS 39, an entity can also discontinue hedge accounting at any time and for any reason (or for no reason). This means that any IAS 39-based hedge accounting information 'as if applied in the current period' would be based on highly speculative assumptions. Consequently, the IASB noted that it would be inappropriate to disclose hedge accounting in accordance with IAS 39 in the period during which hedge accounting is first applied in accordance with IFRS 9. Given that conclusion, providing line-item disclosures for classification and measurement in the current period in accordance with IAS 39 would be incomplete, because it would not fully or accurately reflect IFRS 9 relative to IAS 39. The IASB also noted that requiring disclosure of IAS 39 amounts in the current period would require entities to incur the costs of running parallel systems, which could be onerous.

BC7.68   In addition, the IASB noted that IFRS 7 already includes modified transition disclosure requirements that focus on changes in the statement of financial position at the date of initial application of IFRS 9 and also focus on the effect on the key financial statement line items for the current period. The IASB believes that these disclosures will allow users of financial statements to assess the effect of transition to IFRS 9. The IASB noted that users of financial statements expressed support for these disclosures because they provide the necessary information to explain the transition.

Transition for first-time adopters of IFRS

BC7.69   The 2012 Limited Amendments Exposure Draft did not propose amendments to IFRS 1. However it specifically requested feedback on transition to IFRS 9 by first-time adopters of IFRS, including whether there are any unique considerations. The IASB stated that the transition to IFRS 9 by first-time adopters would be considered in the redeliberations of the 2012 Limited Amendments Exposure Draft to ensure that they are given adequate lead time to apply IFRS 9 and are not at a disadvantage in comparison to existing IFRS preparers.

BC7.70   Most respondents who provided feedback on this question stated that they were not aware of any unique considerations for first-time adopters. Some specifically stated that the IASB should provide relief to first-time adopters from presenting comparative information that complies with IFRS 9. Generally, this request was made in order to give first-time adopters adequate lead time to prepare for the transition to IFRS 9 and ensure that they are not at a disadvantage compared to existing IFRS preparers.

BC7.71   Consequently, to ensure that first-time adopters are given adequate lead time to apply IFRS 9 and are not at a disadvantage in comparison to existing IFRS preparers, the IASB decided the following:

(a)   first-time adopters are not required to present comparative information that complies with the completed version of IFRS 9 (issued in 2014) if the beginning of their first IFRS reporting period is earlier than the mandatory effective date of IFRS 9 plus one year (ie 1 January 2019). This ensures that a first-time adopter is not required to start applying IFRS 9 before an existing IFRS preparer.

(b)   if a first-time adopter chooses to present comparative information that does not comply with the completed version of IFRS 9 (issued in 2014), it will be required to provide the same disclosures that were required by IFRS 1 for a first-time adopter that transitioned to IFRS 9 (2009) or IFRS 9 (2010) and that chose not to present comparative information that complied with those new Standards. Those disclosures are set out in paragraph E2 of IFRS 1.

Impairment

BC7.72   The 2013 Impairment Exposure Draft proposed that the expected credit loss requirements should be applied retrospectively on initial application, except when it is not possible to determine, without undue cost and effort, whether the credit risk of a financial instrument has increased significantly since initial recognition. If determining the credit risk on a financial instrument when the instrument was initially recognised would require undue cost or effort, the measurement of the loss allowance should always be determined only on the basis of whether the credit risk is low at the reporting date. However, this requirement did not apply to financial instruments whose past due status is used to assess changes in credit risk, because it is assumed that the information will be available to make the assessment.

BC7.73   In addition, the 2013 Impairment Exposure Draft did not require comparative information to be restated. Entities were, however, permitted to provide restated comparative information if it is possible to do so without the use of hindsight.

BC7.74   IAS 8 provides the principles and framework for changes in accounting policies in the absence of specific transition provisions in a Standard. IAS 8 states that, as a general rule, retrospective application results in the most useful information to users of financial statements, and that it is the preferred approach unless it is impracticable to calculate the period-specific effect or the cumulative effect of the change. The definition of impracticability is relevant to situations in which it is not possible to objectively distinguish the historical information that is relevant for estimating expected credit losses from the information that would not have been available at that earlier date (IAS 8 refers to this situation as 'hindsight').

BC7.75   During development of the proposals in the 2013 Impairment Exposure Draft the IASB identified two main issues about retrospective application for the proposed impairment model:

(a)   availability of initial credit risk data—the model relies on entities assessing whether there has been a significant increase in credit risk since the initial recognition of a financial instrument to decide whether they should establish a loss allowance balance at an amount equal to lifetime expected credit losses. Entities told the IASB that they typically do not currently retain information about initial credit risk, so making this assessment on transition is likely to be difficult.

(b)   risk of hindsight—entities have not previously been required to recognise or disclose expected credit losses for accounting purposes. Accordingly, there was a risk that hindsight would be needed to recognise and measure the amount of expected credit losses in prior periods.

Alternatives previously considered and rejected

BC7.76   During the deliberations that resulted in the publication of the 2013 Impairment Exposure Draft, the IASB considered and rejected the following alternatives:

(a)   grandfathering existing requirements—one approach to transition that would have addressed both of the issues set out in paragraph BC7.75 would have been for the IASB to 'grandfather' the existing impairment requirements for existing financial instruments at the date of initial application. That is, entities would continue to apply the IAS 39 impairment requirements to all financial instruments that exist on transition to the proposed requirements. This would have been a form of prospective application of the proposed requirements. This grandfathering approach would have removed the need to measure expected credit losses for periods prior to the application of the proposed requirements, and would also have eliminated the problem of applying the proposed requirements to financial instruments for which information about the credit risk at initial recognition is not available or would have been very burdensome to obtain on transition to the proposed requirements. It would also have allowed the IASB to specify an earlier mandatory effective date than would otherwise be possible if full retrospective application was required (ie retrospective application that also includes a restatement of comparative periods). Although those who are concerned about the potentially significant effect on equity when making the transition to the new model (which may have regulatory consequences for some) may view this approach positively, it would delay the improvements to accounting for expected credit losses and would reduce comparability. In addition, entities would need to prepare information in accordance with both the IAS 39 impairment model and the new impairment model until they derecognised all grandfathered financial instruments, which would be burdensome, at least for some entities. For these reasons, the IASB rejected the grandfathering approach to transition.

(b)   resetting the credit risk at initial recognition of the financial instrument so that it reflects the credit risk at the date that the proposed model is initially applied—this would have been the least burdensome of the three alternatives to apply, because entities would ignore credit history for all financial instruments. An entity would consider deteriorations or improvements in credit risk from the date of initial application of the proposed model, instead of relative to the credit risk at initial recognition. The IASB rejected this approach because it would have ignored changes in credit risk that had occurred since initial recognition and would not have faithfully represented expected credit losses.

(c) recognising a loss allowance at an amount equal to lifetime expected credit losses on transition until derecognition for financial instruments for which an entity does not use initial credit risk information—this alternative would have been relatively simple to apply because there would have been no requirement for an entity to analyse changes in credit risk either at transition or over the life of the relevant instruments. However, this alternative is inconsistent with the objective of the overall model, which is designed to reflect changes in credit risk. This approach would also have resulted in an entity recognising lifetime expected credit losses for financial instruments whose credit risk is actually better than that on initial recognition.

Availability of initial credit risk data

BC7.77 The 2013 Impairment Exposure Draft proposed that an entity should use available information about credit risk at initial recognition for existing financial instruments when it applies the impairment requirements for the first time, unless obtaining such information requires undue cost or effort. For financial instruments for which an entity has not used information about the initial credit risk on transition, an entity would recognise lifetime expected credit losses, except if the credit risk was low, at each reporting date until the financial instrument was derecognised.

BC7.78 The IASB considered that such an approach should be relatively simple to apply, because it would not require any assessment of changes in credit risk for these financial instruments relative to the initial credit risk. In addition, it corresponds with credit risk management systems that assess credit risk as at the reporting date. However, the IASB decided that this relief would not be appropriate when an entity uses the past due status of payments to apply the model, because in these cases an entity would have the necessary information to decide whether a financial instrument has deteriorated since initial recognition.

BC7.79 The IASB acknowledged that if an entity uses an approach that is based solely on credit risk at the reporting date, then, when the entity is deciding the amount of expected credit losses to recognise, that approach will not allow the entity to consider the increases in credit risk that have occurred since initial recognition. Thus, entities would be required to recognise lifetime expected credit losses for a financial instrument for which the credit risk is not considered low, even if the instrument had been priced to reflect that risk and there has not been a significant increase in credit risk since initial recognition. It would also have a more negative impact for entities whose business model focuses on originating or purchasing financial instruments with credit risk that is not low (for example, their credit risk is not equivalent to investment grade). Requiring an assessment of the credit risk alone might encourage the use of information about the initial credit risk on transition to the proposed requirements, which will enhance comparability and the quality of the information provided. However, under some circumstances, such an approach may discourage the use of information about initial credit risk, particularly if an entity is able to absorb lifetime expected credit losses on those financial instruments on transition to the proposed requirements. While acknowledging the inconsistency with the overall model, the IASB decided that such an approach was the best way to balance the provision of useful information with the associated cost of providing it.

BC7.80   The majority of respondents to the 2013 Impairment Exposure Draft supported the proposed transition requirements. Respondents noted that these proposals achieve a balance between the cost to implement the proposals and presenting relevant information. However, respondents asked the IASB to consider practical ways in which to assess whether, at the date of initial application, there have been significant increases in credit risk since initial recognition. Respondents noted that the proposed requirements could effectively result in the loss allowance for all financial instruments that are not considered to have low credit risk to be measured at lifetime expected credit losses if the entity could not obtain information about the credit risk at initial recognition. They argued that if financial instruments were inappropriately measured at lifetime expected credit losses, it might result in large releases of loss allowance balances when the instruments are derecognised.

BC7.81   The IASB considered that the intention was not to penalise entities that could not obtain information about the initial credit risk without undue cost or effort. It also noted that an entity need not have specific information about the initial credit risk of a financial instrument and clarified this in IFRS 9. For example, the IASB noted that if an entity is able to assess the change in credit risk of a financial instrument on the basis of a portfolio analysis, such an approach could similarly be applied on transition to assess the change in credit risk since initial recognition.

Restatement of comparative periods, including the use of hindsight

BC7.82   At the date of initial application of the requirements in IFRS 9, the transition requirements permit, but do not require, the restatement of comparative periods if the necessary information is available without the use of hindsight (see paragraphs BC7.34A–BC7.34M). This was also proposed in the 2013 Impairment Exposure Draft to address the risk of hindsight being used to decide whether lifetime expected credit losses would be required to be recognised in prior periods and, more generally, in measuring expected credit losses in prior periods. This would prevent entities 'looking back' to make those determinations. Instead, at the beginning of the period in which the proposed model were to be initially applied, an entity would adjust the loss allowance to be in accordance with the proposed model at that date, with an adjustment to an opening component of equity. An entity would still apply the proposed model on a (modified) retrospective basis, because the loss allowance balances would be determined on the basis of information about initial credit risk, subject to the transition relief. As a result, an entity would still assess the changes in credit risk since the initial recognition of financial instruments to decide whether, on transition to the new requirements, it should measure the loss allowance at an amount equal to lifetime or 12-month expected credit losses. A prohibition on restating comparatives would mean that an entity could only reflect the loss allowance balances that result from applying the new model in the financial statements from the beginning of the current period in which the entity applies the proposals for the first time.

BC7.83 The IASB noted that another way to address the risk of hindsight might be to allow a long lead time between issuing the new requirements and the mandatory effective date, so that an entity could calculate expected credit losses contemporaneously for comparative periods to provide restated comparative information. However, in considering a longer lead time, the IASB noted the urgency of this project. Establishing a lead time that would allow an entity to apply the proposed model on a retrospective basis, including the provision of restated comparative information, in a way that addresses the risk of hindsight would result in a significant delay between issuing the final requirements and their mandatory application.

BC7.84 The vast majority of respondents agreed with the transition proposals not to require, but to allow, the restatement of comparative information if the necessary information is available without the use of hindsight. Consequently, the IASB confirmed those proposals during redeliberations.

Transition for first-time adopters of IFRS

BC7.85 The 2013 Impairment Exposure Draft did not propose amendments to IFRS 1. However it specifically requested feedback on transition to IFRS 9 by first-time adopters of IFRS, including whether there are any unique considerations. In the redeliberations on the proposals in the 2013 Impairment Exposure Draft, the IASB confirmed that the same transition relief available on the initial application of the requirements in Section 5.5 of IFRS 9 should be available to first-time adopters of IFRS (see also paragraphs BC7.72–BC7.75).

Analysis of the effects of IFRS 9

Introduction

BCE.1 Before the IASB issues new requirements, or makes amendments to existing Standards, it considers the costs and benefits of the new pronouncements. This includes assessing the effects on the costs for both preparers and users of financial statements. The IASB also considers the comparative advantage that preparers have in developing information that would otherwise cost users of financial statements to develop. One of the main objectives of developing a single set of high quality global accounting Standards is to improve the allocation of capital. The IASB therefore takes into account the benefits of economic decision-making resulting from improved financial reporting. The IASB gains insight on the likely effects of the proposals for new or revised Standards through its formal exposure of proposals and through its analysis and consultations with relevant parties through outreach activities.

BCE.2 The IASB conducted extensive outreach activities with interested parties for each phase of IFRS 9. This included extensive discussions with regulators, users of financial statements, preparers and audit firms worldwide. In addition, as part of the Impairment project, the IASB formed the Expert Advisory Panel (EAP) to address some of the operational challenges of an expected cash flow approach and conducted fieldwork to assess the proposals of the 2013 Exposure Draft

Financial Instruments: Expected Credit Losses (the '2013 Impairment Exposure Draft'). This Effects Analysis is based on the feedback received through this process.

BCE.3　　The evaluation of costs and benefits are necessarily qualitative, instead of quantitative. This is because quantifying costs and, particularly, benefits, is inherently difficult. Although other standard-setters undertake similar types of analyses, there is a lack of sufficiently well-established and reliable techniques for quantifying this analysis. Consequently, the IASB sees this Effects Analysis as being part of an evolving process. In addition, the assessment undertaken is that of the likely effects of the new requirements, because the actual effects will not be known until after the new requirements have been applied. These are subsequently analysed through the Post-implementation Review process.

BCE.4　　The IASB is committed to assessing and sharing knowledge about the likely costs of implementing proposed new requirements and the likely associated ongoing costs and benefits of each new Standard—these costs and benefits are collectively referred to as 'effects'.

BCE.5　　In evaluating the likely effects of the proposals, the IASB has considered how:

(a)　　activities would be reported in the financial statements of those applying IFRS;

(b)　　comparability of financial information would be improved both between different reporting periods for the same entity and between different entities in a particular reporting period;

(c)　　more useful financial reporting would result in better economic decision-making;

(d)　　better economic decision-making as a result of improved financial reporting could be achieved;

(e)　　the compliance costs for preparers would likely be affected; and

(f)　　the costs of analysis for users of financial statements would likely be affected.

BCE.6　　Paragraphs BCE.7–BCE.238 describe the IASB's analysis of the likely effects that will result from IFRS 9. It reflects the three phases of IFRS 9, with the analysis of the classification and measurement requirements described in paragraphs BCE.7–BCE.89, the impairment requirements described in paragraphs BCE.90–BCE.173 and the hedge accounting requirements described in paragraphs BCE.174–BCE.238.

Analysis of the effects: classification and measurement

Overview

BCE.7　　Many users of financial statements and other interested parties have told the IASB that the requirements in IAS 39 are difficult to understand, apply and interpret. They have urged the IASB to develop a new Standard for the financial reporting for financial instruments that is principle-based and less complex. The need to enhance the relevance and understandability of information about financial instruments was also raised by respondents to the Discussion Paper *Reducing Complexity in Reporting Financial Instruments* (published in 2008). That need became more urgent in the light of the global financial crisis, so the IASB decided to replace IAS 39 in its entirety as expeditiously as possible.

BCE.8 IFRS 9 is the IASB's response to the need to improve and simplify the financial reporting for financial instruments. The IASB believes that the new classification and measurement requirements address the issue that IAS 39 has many classification categories for financial assets, each with its own rules for determining which financial asset must, or can be, included and how impairment is identified and measured.

BCE.9 Overall, the IASB's assessment is that the classification and measurement requirements in IFRS 9 will bring significant and sustained improvements to the reporting of financial instruments because they:

(a) introduce a logical and clear rationale for the classification and measurement of financial assets. It is a principle-based approach, in contrast to the complex rules in IAS 39, which often result in financial assets being measured on the basis of free choice.

(b) eliminate the complex requirements for bifurcating hybrid financial assets because financial assets will be classified in their entirety.

(c) require reclassification between measurement categories when, and only when, the entity's business model for managing them changes. This eliminates the complex rules for reclassification in IAS 39 and ensures that users of financial statements are always provided with information that reflects how the cash flows on financial assets are expected to be realised.

(d) accommodate known business models with objectives to hold financial assets to collect contractual cash flows or that result in both collecting contractual cash flows and selling financial assets.

(e) respond to the long-standing concerns about the volatility that occurs in profit or loss due to changes in own credit risk when an entity elects to measure non-derivative financial liabilities at fair value. But otherwise the existing accounting for financial liabilities has been retained because it has worked well in practice.

BCE.10 The classification and measurement requirements included in IFRS 9 change many aspects of IAS 39 and these changes will affect a variety of preparers. However, it is difficult to generalise the likely impact on these entities, because it depends on their individual circumstances. In particular, the overall change in the classification of financial assets will depend on the choices previously made by preparers in applying IAS 39, their business models for managing the financial assets and the contractual cash flow characteristics of their financial assets.

BCE.11 It was not the IASB's objective to increase or decrease the application of fair value measurement, instead the IASB wanted to ensure that financial assets are measured in a way that provides useful information to investors and other users of financial statements to predict likely future cash flows. Whether an entity will have more or fewer financial assets measured at fair value through profit or loss as a result of applying IFRS 9 will depend on the way in which the financial assets are being managed (ie the entity's business model) and the characteristics of the instrument's contractual cash flows. For example, a financial asset with contractual cash flows that are solely payments of principal and interest on the principal amount outstanding will be measured at amortised cost, fair value through other comprehensive income or fair value through profit or loss, depending on the entity's business model (ie amortised cost if the financial assets are held to collect the contractual cash flows or fair value through other comprehensive income if the financial assets are held within a business model whose objective is achieved by collecting contractual cash flows and selling the financial assets and otherwise at fair value through profit or loss).

BCE.12 The requirements for the classification of financial liabilities are largely unchanged from IAS 39. This reflects feedback received that the accounting for financial liabilities has worked well in practice, except for the issue of own credit. However, IFRS 9 addresses the own credit issue by requiring the changes in fair value attributable to changes in the liability's credit risk to be recognised in other comprehensive income for financial liabilities that an entity elects to measure at fair value.

BCE.13 The IASB expects that most costs for preparers will be incurred on transition. The ongoing costs will be mitigated primarily by the fact that:

(a) the business model assessment for the classification of a financial asset is determined on an aggregate basis and is a matter of fact (ie consistent with the entity's actual business model rather being simply an accounting concept);

(b) the contractual cash flow assessment for financial assets need not be analysed in all business models; and

(c) the requirements for the classification of financial liabilities are largely unchanged or should not create incremental costs (such as for the new own credit requirements given that entities are already required to disclose the gains or losses recognised for changes in own credit risk).

The IASB's assessment is that the significant improvements in terms of comparability and transparency will outweigh those costs.

How activities would be reported in the financial statements of those applying IFRS

BCE.14 The following analysis focuses on the key differences between the existing classification model in IAS 39 and the new classification and measurement model in IFRS 9 and how the new model will affect financial reporting.

Objective of the classification and measurement requirements of IFRS 9

BCE.15 The classification and measurement requirements are part of the IASB's response to a long recognised need to improve the accounting for financial instruments.

BCE.16 In view of the criticisms of IAS 39, the IASB introduced a single classification approach for all financial assets in IFRS 9 that is principle-based. Its objective is to faithfully represent, in the financial statements, how the cash flows on financial assets are expected to be realised.

BCE.17 The classification approach is based on the entity's business model and thereby focuses on the matter of fact instead of on management's intention or free choice as is often the case in IAS 39. Most interested parties have agreed that information is improved by a single classification approach as introduced by IFRS 9.

BCE.18 The requirements for the classification and measurement of financial liabilities are largely unchanged from IAS 39, except for the own credit requirements, which was a response to long-standing concerns about the volatility that occurs in profit or loss because of changes in an issuer's own credit risk.

Approach to classifying financial assets

BCE.19 IAS 39 requires financial assets to be classified into one of four categories, each having its own eligibility criteria and different measurement requirements. The eligibility criteria are a combination of the nature of the instrument, its manner of use and management choice.

BCE.20 The IASB believed that the best way to address the complexity arising from the different classification categories in IAS 39 was to replace them with a single classification approach based on a logical structure and clear rationale. IFRS 9 requires entities to classify financial assets on the basis of the entity's business model for managing the financial assets and the characteristics of the financial asset's contractual cash flows.

BCE.21 The business model is relevant to the classification because it determines whether an entity's future cash flows will arise from contractual amounts or by realising the fair value. The nature of the contractual cash flows is relevant to ensure that the cash flows on a financial asset can be properly and adequately reflected by amortised cost measurement, which is a simple technique for allocating interest over the life of a financial instrument. In IFRS 9 such simple cash flows are described as being 'solely payments of principal and interest'.

BCE.22 The requirements issued in IFRS 9 (2009) included only two categories for financial assets—amortised cost and fair value through profit or loss. Financial instruments were classified and measured at amortised cost only if:

(a) they are held in a business model whose objective is to hold financial assets in order to collect contractual cash flows ('held to collect' business model); and

(b) their contractual cash flow terms represented solely payments of principal and interest.

In accordance with the requirements issued in IFRS 9 (2009), all other financial assets were measured at fair value through profit or loss.

BCE.23 The completed version of IFRS 9, issued in 2014, introduces a fair value through other comprehensive income measurement category for debt instruments but retains the classification structure that always existed in IFRS 9. Accordingly, a financial asset shall be measured at fair value through other comprehensive income if:

(a)   it is held in a business model whose objective is achieved by both collecting contractual cash flows and selling financial instruments; and

(b)   its contractual cash flows represent solely payments of principal and interest.[38]

In this measurement category the statement of financial position will reflect the fair value carrying amount while amortised cost information will be presented in profit or loss. The difference between the fair value information and amortised cost information will be recognised in other comprehensive income.

BCE.24   The fair value through other comprehensive income measurement category was added to IFRS 9 in response to feedback requesting accommodation of known business models whose objective results in both collecting contractual cash flows and selling financial assets. This means that both amortised cost (ie information about contractual cash flows) and fair value information are relevant. In addition to providing relevant and useful information for financial assets that are held within a 'hold to collect and sell' business model, the introduction of the fair value through other comprehensive income measurement category also addresses potential accounting mismatches that could arise because of the interaction between the accounting for financial assets and the accounting for insurance contract liabilities.

BCE.25   Although the fair value through other comprehensive income measurement category has been introduced, the existing structure of IFRS 9 has been retained. Thus, IFRS 9 still eliminates the specific rules (which dictate how an asset can or must be classified) and accounting choice in IAS 39. For example, the fair value through other comprehensive income measurement category in IFRS 9 is fundamentally different to the available-for-sale measurement category in IAS 39. That is because financial assets are classified on the basis of their contractual cash flow characteristics and of the business model in which they are held. In contrast, the available-for-sale measurement category in IAS 39 is essentially a residual classification and, in many cases, is a free choice.

Bifurcation of embedded features in financial assets

BCE.26   Another key change is that IFRS 9 eliminates the application of the complex, internally inconsistent and rule-based requirements in IAS 39 for the bifurcation of hybrid financial assets.

BCE.27   In accordance with IFRS 9, a financial asset is accounted for in its entirety on the basis of its contractual cash flow features and the business model within which it is held. Thus, under IFRS 9, a hybrid financial asset is classified as a whole using the same classification approach as all other financial assets. That is in contrast to IAS 39, in which components of a financial asset could have been classified and measured separately—resulting in a component of a financial asset being measured at amortised cost or classified as available-for-sale, while some or all of the embedded features were measured at fair value through profit or

---

38 The fair value through other comprehensive income measurement category is available only for debt instruments. It is different from the presentation election set out in paragraph 5.7.5 of IFRS 9 that permits an entity to present in other comprehensive income subsequent changes in the fair value of particular investments in equity instruments.

loss, even though the financial asset was a single instrument that was settled as a whole on the basis of all of its features.

BCE.28   Consequently, IFRS 9 simplifies the classification of hybrid financial instruments. Consistently with all other financial assets, hybrid contracts with financial asset hosts are classified and measured in their entirety, thereby eliminating the complexity of bifurcation for financial assets.

Effect of classification on impairment

BCE.29   IAS 39 requires different impairment assessments and methods for financial assets depending on their classification. Some of those impairments could not be reversed.

BCE.30   During the global financial crisis some users of financial statements were confused, because the same financial assets were impaired differently simply because they were classified differently for accounting purposes.

BCE.31   As a result of the classification requirements issued in IFRS 9 (2009), only financial assets measured at amortised cost were subject to impairment accounting. IFRS 9 (2014) extends the impairment model to financial assets measured at fair value through other comprehensive income. Consequently, the same impairment model is applied for all financial assets that are not measured at fair value through profit or loss (ie financial assets measured at amortised cost and financial assets measured at fair value through other comprehensive income). This replaces the many different impairment methods that are associated with the numerous classification categories in IAS 39 and thereby addresses the criticism that the impairment models in IAS 39 were not aligned and were therefore confusing. In addition, by using the same impairment model, amortised cost information is provided in profit or loss for financial assets measured at fair value through other comprehensive income.

Reclassification

BCE.32   IAS 39 includes complex rules for the reclassification of financial assets, and different entities could choose to reclassify financial assets in different circumstances. In contrast, IFRS 9 requires the reclassification of financial assets when, and only when, the business model for managing those financial assets changes. IFRS 9 states that changes in a business model are demonstrable events and are expected to be very infrequent. For example, a change in a business model can arise from a business combination or if a reporting entity changes the way it manages its financial assets following the acquisition of a new business. By requiring financial assets to be reclassified when the business model changes, IFRS 9 ensures that relevant information is always provided about the cash flows that an entity expects to realise from managing its financial assets.

The cost exception for unquoted equity investments

BCE.33   IAS 39 has an exception to the measurement requirements for investments in unquoted equity instruments that do not have a quoted market price in an active market (and derivatives on such an instrument) and for which fair value cannot therefore be measured reliably. Such financial instruments are measured at cost. IFRS 9 removes this exception, requiring all equity investments (and derivatives on them) to be measured at fair value. However, IFRS 9 provides guidance on when cost may be an appropriate estimate of fair value.

Gains and losses—equity investments

BCE.34   IFRS 9 provides a presentation option for investments in equity instruments that are not held for trading. Otherwise, equity investments are measured at fair value through profit or loss.

BCE.35   IFRS 9 permits an entity to make an irrevocable election on an instrument-by-instrument basis to present in other comprehensive income changes in the fair value of an investment in an equity instrument that is not held for trading. Dividends received from those investments are presented in profit or loss. Gains and losses presented in other comprehensive income cannot be subsequently transferred to profit or loss (ie there is no recycling). However, the entity may transfer the cumulative gain or loss within equity.

BCE.36   Although the IASB believes that fair value provides the most useful information about investments in equity instruments to users of financial statements, the IASB provided this presentation option because it notes that changes in the value of particular investments in equity instruments may not be indicative of the performance of the entity. This would be the case, for example, if the entity holds those equity instruments primarily for non-contractual benefits. Another reason was because users of financial statements often differentiate between fair value changes arising from equity investments held for purposes other than generating investment returns and equity investments held for trading.

BCE.37   The IASB decided to prohibit recycling of gains and losses into profit or loss when an equity investment is derecognised, even though many respondents said that subsequent transfers of fair value changes to profit or loss should be required. These respondents view the sale of an investment as the realisation of the changes in its fair value. However, such recycling of gains and losses would have made it necessary to introduce an impairment test to ensure that impairments were presented on a consistent basis. Impairment accounting for equity investments has been a significant source of complexity in IAS 39. The IASB thus decided that introducing recycling and associated impairment accounting would create application problems in practice and would not significantly improve or reduce the complexity of the financial reporting for financial assets. Accordingly, the IASB decided to prohibit recycling.

BCE.38   Although IFRS 9 prohibits recycling of gains and losses into profit or loss when an equity investment is derecognised, entities are able to transfer the cumulative gain or loss within equity at any time; for example, to provide information on realisation. The IASB considered specific requirements relating to that transfer, such as requiring the accumulated gain or loss to be transferred to retained earnings upon derecognition of the equity investment, but did not adopt such an approach because of jurisdiction-specific restrictions on components of equity. For example, a transfer to retained earnings may give rise to tax consequences in some jurisdictions. However, additional disclosures are required about investments in equity instruments with fair value changes presented in other comprehensive income to provide useful information to users of financial statements about the effect of that presentation for instruments presented in that manner. For example, paragraph 11B of IFRS 7 requires an entity to disclose the cumulative gain or loss on disposal if the entity derecognised investments in equity instruments with fair value changes presented in other comprehensive income during the reporting period.

Main changes to the approach to classifying and measuring financial liabilities

BCE.39　IFRS 9 carries forward almost all of the requirements in IAS 39 for the classification and measurement of financial liabilities, including the bifurcation of particular embedded derivatives. As a result, most financial liabilities, apart from derivatives or financial liabilities that an entity designates under the fair value option, will continue to be measured at amortised cost.

BCE.40　The main concern that the IASB was asked to address in relation to financial liabilities was the so-called 'own credit' issue, whereby changes in the credit risk of a financial liability give rise to gains or losses in profit or loss. For financial liabilities designated under the fair value option, the requirements issued in IFRS 9 (2010) required an entity to present in other comprehensive income changes in the fair value of a financial liability that are attributable to changes in credit risk.[39]

BCE.41　Users of financial statements continued to support the measurement of financial liabilities on the balance sheet at fair value in accordance with the fair value option noting that this provided a useful source of information on a timely basis about changes in an entity's credit quality. However, the requirement to present these fair value changes in other comprehensive income addressed the concern raised by many, including users of financial statements, that reflecting these fair value changes in profit or loss is counterintuitive and does not result in useful information. In particular, the requirement addresses the concern that a gain is recognised in profit or loss as the credit risk on a financial liability increases (ie its credit quality deteriorates).

BCE.42　The requirements issued in IFRS 9 (2010) enabled entities to apply the change to the presentation of such fair value gains and losses only if all the requirements in that Standard for the classification and measurement of financial assets and liabilities were applied. However, the requirements issued in IFRS 9 (2013) changed this requirement. Consequently, prior to the mandatory effective date of IFRS 9 an entity is permitted to apply the requirements for the presentation of own credit in isolation; ie earlier than the other requirements in IFRS 9.

BCE.43　This allows entities to present the effects of own credit in other comprehensive income, thus improving their financial reporting, without also needing to make other changes to their accounting for financial instruments. It makes the own credit requirements available on a more timely basis, particularly because an entity will be able to make this change before undertaking the changes that would be required in order to implement the expected credit loss impairment model.

39　This applies unless that treatment would create or enlarge an accounting mismatch in profit or loss, in which case all changes in fair value are presented in profit or loss.

Early application

BCE.44　In order to address critical issues during the global financial crisis and to make improvements to financial reporting available more quickly, the IASB decided to replace IAS 39 in phases and to allow entities to early apply only some phases of IFRS 9 (although if a later phase was applied, earlier phases were also required to be applied). Consequently, entities had the option to apply only the requirements for financial assets (IFRS 9 (2009)), the requirements for financial assets and financial liabilities (IFRS 9 (2010)) or the requirements for financial assets, financial liabilities and hedge accounting (IFRS 9 (2013)). In contrast, six months from the issue in 2014 of the completed version of IFRS 9, an entity that newly elects to apply IFRS 9 must either apply the entire Standard (ie all of the classification and measurement, impairment and hedge accounting requirements in the completed version of IFRS 9) or apply only the own credit requirements.[40]

BCE.45　This means that before the mandatory effective date of the completed version of IFRS 9, fewer combinations of the accounting for financial instruments will be available than was previously the case. Having multiple versions of IFRS 9 available for early application (in addition to IAS 39) is complex and would significantly reduce the comparability of information that is provided to users of financial statements.

Comparability of financial information

BCE.46　At a high level, classification and measurement, in accordance with both IAS 39 and IFRS 9, requires consideration of similar aspects of financial instruments–their contractual cash flow characteristics and how they are managed. However, IAS 39 and IFRS 9 approach these aspects of financial instruments in very different ways. IAS 39 is complex and rule-based and the classification of financial assets places emphasis on an entity's intentions in respect of individual financial assets and also considers aspects such as the liquidity of the market for a financial asset. IAS 39 also involves an element of free choice. As discussed in the following paragraphs, IFRS 9 provides a logical structure and a clearer rationale for the classification and measurement of financial assets, with less accounting choice. Consequently, differences in financial reporting between reporting periods for an individual entity, and between different entities in a particular reporting period, will more often reflect the differences in underlying economics instead of resulting from differences in accounting choices. Or, put another way, similar financial assets managed in the same way should be classified in the same way for accounting purposes.

The business model assessment

BCE.47　In contrast to IAS 39, the business model assessment in IFRS 9 is determined by how financial assets are actually managed. This is not a question of intention for an individual instrument but is instead based on an assessment of objective

---

40 However, entities have an accounting policy choice between applying the new hedge accounting requirements of IFRS 9 and retaining the existing requirements in IAS 39.

　　　　　© IFRS Foundation

evidence at a higher level of aggregation. As a result, the assessment is a matter of fact, which results in less accounting choice than is available in IAS 39.

BCE.48   The IASB was made aware of differences in the interpretation of these requirements as they were issued in IFRS 9 (2009) so the completed version of IFRS 9 (issued in 2014) reaffirms and supplements the business model principle. It emphasises that the business model assessment focuses on how the entity actually manages financial assets to generate cash flows. In addition, IFRS 9 (2014) enhances the application guidance for the 'hold to collect' business model, addressing particular application questions raised by interested parties since the issue of IFRS 9 in 2009. It expands the discussion about the activities that are commonly associated with the hold to collect business model, clarifying, for example, that entities do not need to hold all assets until maturity and that sales in themselves do not determine the objective of the business model (although information about sales can be useful in determining an entity's business model). The clarifications are expected to improve comparability by enhancing the consistency in how different entities apply the hold to collect business model and classify their financial assets.

BCE.49   As discussed in paragraph BCE.23, a fair value through other comprehensive income measurement category was introduced to IFRS 9 in 2014. The fair value through other comprehensive income measurement category will allow some business models to be better reflected in the financial statements, improving comparability between entities with economically similar instruments that are managed in a similar way.

Reclassifications

BCE.50   A further improvement to the comparability of financial information is that, compared to the complex rules for reclassification in IAS 39, IFRS 9 makes reclassifications between measurement categories mandatory when, and only when, there has been a change in the entity's business model.

BCE.51   The reclassification requirements will enhance comparability because an entity will generally account for its financial instruments consistently over time. The exception will be in the rare circumstance that an entity's business model changes, in which case the required reclassification strengthens comparability because financial assets will be accounted for consistently with how they are managed.

Usefulness of financial information in assessing the future cash flows of an entity

Financial assets

BCE.52   In the Basis for Conclusions on IFRS 9, the IASB acknowledges that some users of financial statements support a single measurement method—fair value—for all financial assets. However, the IASB continues to believe that both amortised cost and fair value can provide useful information to users of financial statements for particular types of financial assets in particular circumstances. In issuing IFRS 9, the IASB did not seek to increase or reduce the use of fair value measurement. Instead, it sought to ensure that information based on a specific measurement attribute is provided when it is relevant. The IASB decided that if the measurement attribute for financial assets and the assets' effect on profit or loss are aligned with both the business model for managing financial assets and their contractual cash flow characteristics, financial reporting will provide relevant information about the timing, amounts and uncertainty of an entity's future cash flows.

The business model

BCE.53   The business model for managing financial assets determines whether their cash flows are realised through the collection of contractual cash flows, the sale of financial assets or both. Consequently, the business model provides information that is useful in assessing the amounts, timing and uncertainty of the entity's future cash flows.

BCE.54   If the objective of an entity's business model is to collect contractual cash flows then, depending on the characteristics of the contractual cash flows, amortised cost measurement in both the statement of financial position and in profit or loss provides information about future cash flows. However, in contrast, if the objective of the business model is achieved by realising cash flows by selling financial assets, fair value measurement provides more relevant information about future cash flows in both the statement of financial position and in profit or loss.

BCE.55   IFRS 9 (2014) clarifies the application guidance for a hold to collect business model that results in financial assets being measured at amortised cost (depending on their contractual cash flow characteristics). The clarification will improve the quality of the financial information and its usefulness in assessing the amounts, timing and uncertainty of an entity's future cash flows by resulting in amortised cost measurement only for financial assets that are held with the objective of collecting contractual cash flows.

BCE.56   Usefulness of financial information will be further improved by the introduction of the fair value through other comprehensive income measurement category to IFRS 9. The fair value through other comprehensive income measurement category results in a fair value carrying amount in the statement of financial position, while the effect on profit or loss would be the same as if the financial assets were measured at amortised cost. This is considered appropriate for such a business model because, by design, both holding and selling activities are taking place, making both amortised cost and fair value information relevant to users of the financial statements. Due to the addition of the fair value through other comprehensive income measurement category, some question whether the classification and measurement approach will still be an improvement over IAS 39. However, in contrast to the available-for-sale measurement category in IAS 39, there is a clear business model in IFRS 9 that results in measurement at fair value through other comprehensive income. This will allow entities to better reflect the way in which financial assets are managed and improves the usefulness of the information provided for those business models in assessing the timing, amounts and uncertainty of an entity's future cash flows. Also, unlike the available-for-sale category in IAS 39, this measurement category has information content—it provides information about the entity's business model.

Contractual cash flow characteristics

BCE.57   Because the effective interest method is not an appropriate method for allocating 'complex' contractual cash flows, the contractual cash flow test in IFRS 9 ensures that amortised cost information is presented only for assets with simple contractual cash flows.

BCE.58   IFRS 9 (2014) makes a number of enhancements to the application guidance on the contractual cash flow characteristics. For example, it provides additional guidance about the attributes of cash flows that provide returns consistent with principal and interest and clarifies that interest is typically represented by a return for the time value of money and credit risk, but also can include other elements, such as a return for liquidity risk. In addition, it clarifies that a financial asset does not have cash flows that are solely payments of principal and interest if the effect of an interest rate tenor mismatch is significant, compared with the cash flows of an instrument that does not contain such a feature but is otherwise identical. In addition, IFRS 9 (2014) relaxes the original requirements in respect to contingencies. It eliminates the distinction between contingent prepayment and extension features and other types of contingent features, clarifying that all contingent features must be assessed in the same way and irrespective of the nature of the contingent event itself. As a result of these clarifications, the IASB expects that financial instruments considered to pay solely principal and interest will be better aligned with the economic concept of principal and interest.

BCE.59   The IASB was also made aware of regulated interest rates in some jurisdictions that are created with an objective of providing a return that is economically consistent with principal and interest, and that do not introduce volatility that is inconsistent with a basic lending arrangement. However, there is a mismatch between the interest rate set and the duration of the interest rate period. IFRS 9 (2014) provides explicit guidance for such financial instruments so that they are, in specific circumstances, considered to have payments that are solely principal and interest cash flows despite their structure. This will allow financial instruments that are considered 'simple' in the relevant jurisdiction to be measured other than at fair value through profit or loss, depending on an entity's business model. This is expected to provide relevant information for the entities that hold such financial assets.

BCE.60   In addition to these questions of clarity, after the publication of IFRS 9 in 2009 some interested parties suggested that bifurcation for financial assets should be reintroduced, partly because of a concern that some financial assets will be measured at fair value through profit or loss in their entirety, whereas under IAS 39 only the derivative component would have been measured at fair value through profit or loss. The IASB believes that the concern is addressed for some financial assets by the clarifications to the principal and interest criterion outlined above. This is because, despite the presence of embedded features, these financial assets may economically have principal and interest cash flows. This is expected to be the case, for example, for many financial instruments with regulated interest rates and financial instruments with interest rate tenor mismatches. However, for other financial assets, for example, when the contractual cash flows are linked to an underlying that is unrelated to principal or interest, such as a commodity price, IFRS 9 (2014) will not change the requirements issued in IFRS 9 (2009). For the reasons discussed in detail in paragraphs BC4.88–BC4.89 and BC4.196–BC4.204, the IASB believes that classifying financial assets in their entirety instead of bifurcating them will result in financial information that is more useful in assessing the amounts, timing and uncertainty of future cash flows.

BCE.61   In addition to providing information that is more useful in assessing future cash flows, the elimination of bifurcation also simplifies the information about financial assets that is provided to users of financial statements. When a financial asset was bifurcated, the components of that financial asset were measured in different ways, and could also have been presented in different places in the financial statements. Consequently, although the settlement of the financial asset takes into consideration all of its contractual terms, it was difficult to understand that financial asset as a whole until settlement took place.

Financial liabilities

BCE.62   In IFRS 9, the IASB made fewer changes to the classification and measurement of financial liabilities than to financial assets. Views received from users of financial statements, and others, indicated that amortised cost is the most appropriate measurement attribute for many financial liabilities, because it reflects the issuer's legal obligation to pay the contractual amounts in the normal course of business (ie on a going concern basis) and, in many cases, the issuer plans to hold liabilities to maturity and pay the contractual amounts.

BCE.63   However, if a liability has structured features (for example, embedded derivatives), amortised cost is difficult to apply and understand because the cash flows can be highly variable. Consequently, the IASB decided to retain the bifurcation requirements in IAS 39 for financial liabilities. The views received by the IASB indicated that the bifurcation approach in IAS 39 is generally working well for financial liabilities and that a new bifurcation approach would most likely have the same classification and measurement outcomes as the approach in IAS 39. The bifurcation approach also reduces the incidence of fair value changes caused by the issuer's own credit risk.

BCE.64   Views received indicated, and the IASB agreed, that the effects of changes in a liability's credit risk ought not to affect profit or loss unless the liability is held for trading, because an entity will generally not realise the effects of changes in the liability's credit risk unless the liability is held for trading. However, many users of financial statements confirmed that fair value information on the balance sheet does provide useful information because, for example, it can provide early information about an entity's credit problems. The IASB thus decided that entities should continue to have the ability to measure their non-derivative liabilities at fair value (subject to the relevant criteria that are unchanged from IAS 39), but that the portion of the fair value change that is a consequence of changes in the financial instrument's credit risk should be recognised in other comprehensive income. The result of the IASB's decisions, including the own credit requirements for financial liabilities described in paragraphs BC5.35–BC5.64, result in information being reported for financial liabilities that is more useful in assessing the amounts, timing and uncertainty of the entity's future cash flows.

BCE.65   The IASB noted that *prima facie* it would seem preferable to eliminate bifurcation for financial liabilities if it was eliminated for financial assets. However, in discussions with users of financial statements they did not raise concerns regarding this apparent asymmetry in treatment.

Equity instruments

BCE.66   IFRS 9 removes the measurement exception for investments in unquoted equity instruments (and derivatives on them). Measuring those instruments at fair value provides the most relevant information to users of financial statements, because, although cost is a reliable and objective amount, it provides little, if any, information with predictive value about the timing, amount and uncertainty of future cash flows arising from the instrument.

BCE.67   The classification model for financial assets in IFRS 9 results in cost-based information when amortised cost is a relevant measure. Because equity instruments do not have cash flows that represent solely payments of principal and interest, the IASB believes that fair value information is always relevant, irrespective of the business model in which the asset is held. In addition, the IASB believes that changes in the fair value of equity investments usually provide relevant information about an entity's performance and should therefore be included in profit or loss. However, the IASB acknowledges that for some equity investments information about fair value may not be considered relevant to profit or loss, such as when an investment is held for strategic purposes. IFRS 9 therefore allows an entity to elect to present fair value changes on equity investments in other comprehensive income as long as the investment is not held for trading. Because this presentation choice was designed for circumstances in which these fair value changes were not relevant to profit or loss, even though the category is not expressly limited to these circumstances, the IASB decided that gains or losses would not be recycled to profit or loss. This decision was also made so that impairment accounting need not be reintroduced for investments in equity instruments to ensure that this complexity was not introduced in IFRS 9.

BCE.68   Accounting for impairment on equity investments, including assessing whether fair value changes are 'significant or prolonged', has been one of the most difficult application areas of IAS 39. Without an impairment model, recycling could not be allowed because of the risk of asymmetry caused by recognising gains in profit or loss with the risk that losses would be retained in other comprehensive income by avoiding derecognition. This would risk reducing the usefulness and representational faithfulness of the information provided.

BCE.69   Some have expressed concerns that this approach may create a disincentive for entities to invest in equity instruments. However, if an entity is of the view that the users of its financial statements need to see the effects in profit or loss of holding equity investments, they need not elect the other comprehensive income presentation. If the other comprehensive income presentation is elected, entities can choose to present the effects of realising fair value changes by, for example, transferring accumulated gains or losses from other comprehensive income to retained earnings.

Reclassifications

BCE.70   IAS 39 permits reclassifications at the entity's discretion in rare circumstances. Users of financial statements consistently commented that these reclassifications decreased the comparability and usefulness of financial reporting. In contrast, IFRS 9 makes reclassifications mandatory when, and only when, there has been a change in business model. The reclassification requirements will enhance useful and relevant information, because reclassification is based on changes in the entity's business model for managing financial assets. This ensures that financial statements always faithfully represent how those financial assets are managed at the reporting date, reflecting the amounts, timing and uncertainty of future cash flows.

Better economic decision-making as a result of improved financial reporting

BCE.71   The IASB believes that the requirements in IFRS 9 satisfy the fundamental qualitative characteristics of useful financial information as stated in Chapter 3 of the IASB's *Conceptual Framework*. That is, they would:

(a)   provide information that is more useful in assessing the amounts, timing and uncertainty of an entity's future cash flows than the information reported in accordance with IAS 39 and is therefore more relevant and timely; and

(b)   reduce accounting choice and instead require classifications that are consistent with economic substance. Consequently, the financial reporting is a more faithful representation than the financial reporting in accordance with IAS 39. It is also more complete and neutral and is supported by economic substance, which will help it to be free from error and verifiable.

In addition, the IASB notes that IFRS 9 enhances the comparability and understandability of the financial information relative to IAS 39.

BCE.72   In assessing whether IFRS 9 would improve financial reporting, the IASB considered the concerns voiced by some interested parties regarding the changes in accounting for financial assets. Some believe that IFRS 9 will result in more financial assets being reported at fair value compared to the requirements in IAS 39, and this concerns them for one or more of the following reasons:

(a)   while fair value might be relevant during times of relative market stability, they considered that it lacks relevance and reliability during times of market instability.

(b)   fair value reporting leads to procyclicality, meaning that it reflects or even magnifies economic or financial fluctuations. For example, in response to changes in fair value, entities may need, or choose, to sell different amounts of financial assets than they normally would, and the entity may have a different estimate of the present value of the future cash flows than is indicated by the fair value or market price; fair value amounts that are lower than the entity's estimate of future cash flows are of particular concern. (Such as when an entity intends to hold an asset to collect its contractual cash flows.)

(c)   fair value reporting may impact the activities of regulated entities. Regulatory reporting uses some of the amounts reported in general purpose financial statements. Consequently, IFRS reporting may have effects for regulated entities. For example, regulated entities (especially banks) are often required to maintain a minimum level of capital reserves. Decreases in the fair value of some financial assets may impact the level of those capital reserves. As a consequence, some expressed concern that regulated entities may decrease lending during an economic downturn, which can further exacerbate the downturn.

BCE.73   Some are of the view that fair value information is less relevant for all financial instruments in times of relative market instability. Others, including the IASB, agree that fair value is not equally relevant for all financial instruments, but believe that fair value is relevant in all market conditions for some financial instruments. Consequently, the IASB believes that the new approach to classifying and measuring financial instruments will provide relevant information that will lead to better economic decision-making throughout economic cycles.

BCE.74   The IASB did not seek to increase or reduce the number of financial instruments that would be measured at fair value. For financial liabilities, the use of fair value is essentially unchanged in IFRS 9 relative to IAS 39 (and in fact, a portion of the fair value changes will now be recognised in other comprehensive income instead of profit or loss). In addition, financial assets are measured at fair value only when it is relevant because of the contractual cash flow characteristics of the asset and/or the entity's business model. Depending on the entity, its particular financial assets and how it manages them, IFRS 9 may actually result in fewer financial assets being measured at fair value than under IAS 39. For example, because of the rule-based criteria for amortised cost measurement under IAS 39, debt securities that are quoted in active markets are typically measured at fair value in accordance with IAS 39, even if they are held within a business model in which assets are managed to collect contractual cash flows. Such financial assets may be measured at amortised cost in accordance with IFRS 9.

BCE.75   The effect on the classification of an entity's financial assets will depend on the choices it made when applying IAS 39, its business models for managing its financial assets and the contractual cash flow characteristics of those financial assets. It is thus not possible to determine the overall changes in the classification of financial assets that will occur. However, the drivers of possible changes can be considered.

BCE.76   The following examples illustrate how the measurement of the financial assets may or may not change when IFRS 9 is first applied:

Example 1

Entity X invests in a portfolio of bonds that are quoted in an active market. The entity generally holds the investments in order to collect their contractual cash flows but would sell them if the instrument no longer meets the credit criteria specified in the entity's documented investment policy (for example, if a bond's credit risk increases so that it is higher than the credit limit as defined by the investment policy for that class of financial instruments at the reporting date).

Instrument A is a bond that pays principal and interest on the principal amount outstanding. In accordance with IAS 39, the entity classified Instrument A as available-for-sale because of the restrictions and tainting rules associated with the held-to-maturity category. At transition to IFRS 9, the entity reclassifies Instrument A to be measured at amortised cost because:

(a)   the financial assets are held within a business model whose objective is to hold assets in order to collect contractual cash flows;[41] and

(b)   the contractual cash flows are solely payments of principal and interest on the principal amount outstanding. The contractual cash flows reflect a return that is consistent with a basic lending arrangement.

Example 2

In contrast, consider the same fact pattern except that the entity invests in the bonds to achieve the business model's objective by both collecting contractual cash flows and selling bonds. Accordingly, upon transition to IFRS 9 the entity reclassifies Instrument A from available-for-sale to the fair value through other comprehensive income measurement category. This is because:

(a)   the financial assets are managed to achieve the business model's objective by both collecting contractual cash flows and selling financial assets; and

(b)   the contractual cash flows are solely payments of principal and interest on the principal amount outstanding. The contractual cash flows reflect a return that is consistent with a basic lending arrangement.

Example 3

Entity Y invests in bonds that are quoted in an active market. The bonds' contractual cash flows are linked to an equity index. The entity holds the bonds to collect the contractual cash flows. In accordance with IAS 39, Entity Y separated the embedded derivative from the financial asset host and measured the embedded derivative at fair value through profit or loss. The host financial asset was classified as available-for-sale. At transition to IFRS 9, Entity Y applies the classification approach to the hybrid financial instrument as a whole. Consequently, it measures the hybrid financial instrument in its entirety at fair value though profit or loss despite a business model that is a 'hold to collect' model. This is because the contractual cash flows introduce exposure to changes in equity prices that do not give rise to contractual cash flows that are solely

---

41 Sales do not contradict the hold to collect business model if they are in response to the increase in the instrument's credit risk.

payments of principal and interest on the principal amount outstanding. Thus, the contractual cash flows are inconsistent with a basic lending arrangement and the instrument must be measured at fair value through profit or loss.

Example 4

Entity Z invests in senior tranches of securitised bonds that are collateralised by mortgage loans. The underlying mortgage loans have payments that are solely payments of principal and interest. Entity Z invests in these senior tranches in order to collect contractual cash flows. The credit risk of the tranches is lower than that of the overall mortgage pool. In accordance with IAS 39, Entity Z determined that there is not an embedded derivative and classified its investment in these senior tranches as available-for-sale. At transition to IFRS 9, if the contractual terms of the senior tranches give rise to payments that are solely payments of principal and interest on the principal amount outstanding, Entity Z measures its investments at amortised cost. However, if the contractual payments are not solely payments of principal and interest on the principal amount outstanding (that is, they are inconsistent with a basic lending arrangement), the senior tranche must be measured at fair value through profit or loss.

BCE.77   The IASB acknowledges that the fair value through other comprehensive income measurement category may affect some regulated banks, because the Basel III regulatory framework removes the 'regulatory filter' for fair value gains or losses recognised in other comprehensive income.[42] Consequently, if this regulatory change remains in place, for those affected the fair value changes of financial assets that are measured at fair value through other comprehensive income will have a direct effect on regulatory capital. However, the addition of the fair value through other comprehensive income measurement category will only have this potential adverse effect on regulatory capital if those financial assets would otherwise have been measured at amortised cost. The objective of the hold to collect business model in IFRS 9 (as issued in 2009) has not been changed. Some financial assets held in business models that would have been measured at fair value through profit or loss can now be measured at fair value through other comprehensive income. In that case, the value changes in other comprehensive income could still affect regulatory capital but the effect on regulatory capital would be a neutral one relative to the requirements issued in IFRS 9 (2009).

BCE.78   The objective of financial reporting should be to provide transparent information that is useful for economic decision-making. The IASB notes that the objective of providing useful information does not contradict the objective of economic stability. Instead, the IASB believes that transparency is essential to maintain stability in the long term.

---

42 Footnote 10 of Basel III: A global regulatory framework for more resilient banks and banking systems ('Basel III'), published by the Basel Committee on Banking Supervision, states 'that '[t]here is no adjustment applied to remove from Common Equity Tier 1 unrealised gains or losses recognised on the balance sheet [the 'regulatory filter'] … The Committee will continue to review the appropriate treatment of unrealised gains, taking into account the evolution of the accounting framework.' In contrast, Basel II did contain a regulatory filter.

The likely effect on compliance costs for preparers, both on initial application and on an ongoing basis

BCE.79   As with all new requirements, the IASB acknowledges that different areas of the requirements will have different effects and hence different types of costs and benefits will arise when considering both preparers and users of financial statements. Given that the new classification model for financial assets is based on the entity's business model for managing its financial assets and those assets' contractual cash flow characteristics, it is reasonable to conclude that the costs incurred and the benefits obtained in complying with the new requirements will depend on the entity's business model and the contractual cash flow characteristics of its financial assets.

BCE.80   Entities will incur a one-time cost on initial application such as costs for:

(a)   developing new processes, systems and controls;

(b)   undertaking the initial analysis of business models and contractual cash flows on transition;

(c)   creating capabilities for new eligible presentations, if intended to be used (for example, the presentation of the change in the fair value of equity investments in other comprehensive income);

(d)   educating accounting functions and obtaining expert advice for compliance; and

(e)   explaining to users of financial statements the differences between the information produced under IAS 39 and IFRS 9.

BCE.81   The IASB believes that the transition to IFRS 9 and the associated costs (as well as the ongoing costs of applying IFRS 9) will depend on the individual circumstances of the entity, ie the type (and diversity of) business models for its financial assets as well as the contractual cash flow characteristics of the instruments. It is therefore difficult to generalise the likely impact on transition on preparers and on their costs.

BCE.82   However, the IASB does not expect preparers to incur significant incremental costs on an ongoing basis in comparison to applying IAS 39. The IASB notes the following initial and ongoing costs and factors that mitigate the ongoing costs of applying IFRS 9 in comparison to IAS 39:

(a)   the need to assess the business model. The entity's business model is determined on a more aggregated basis than an individual financial instrument level that was the basis for classification under IAS 39. An entity's business model is a matter of fact that can be observed by the way in which an entity is managed and information is provided to its management. The assessment is based on, for example, business plans and internal reporting, which should be available. Thus, the reporting is in a manner consistent with the entity's actual business model and entities need not maintain dual reporting models for internal and external reporting.

(b)   the need to assess the contractual cash flows of a financial asset. However:

(i) the contractual cash flows need not be analysed in all business models. They only need to be analysed to assess cash flows for the held to collect and the held to collect or sell business models.

(ii) financial assets with more complex cash flows are expected to already have an analysis in place to assess the need to bifurcate and to measure the fair value of the asset in its entirety (under the fair value option) or in part in accordance with IAS 39; and

(iii) in other cases an entity is expected to already analyse contractual cash flows in order to determine the fair value for disclosure purposes in accordance with IFRS 7, particularly for assets below Level 1 of the fair value hierarchy.

BCE.83 In addition, the IASB notes that eliminating bifurcation and tainting for financial assets measured at amortised cost, as well as introducing a single impairment method, will simplify compliance with the classification and measurement requirements for financial assets.

BCE.84 Furthermore, for financial liabilities, the classification and measurement model is largely unchanged from IAS 39, except for the own credit requirements for financial liabilities designated as at fair value through profit or loss under the fair value option. Entities are already required to disclose the gains or losses recognised for changes in own credit risk and therefore there should not be any incremental costs to preparers from this change.

BCE.85 Finally, IFRS 9 provides a number of illustrative examples and detailed application guidance that illustrate various aspects of the new Standard. In addition, the IASB has responded to the requests for clarifications and to the application questions raised since the issue of IFRS 9 in 2009. The IASB believes that this will help to reduce the initial and ongoing costs of compliance with the classification and measurement requirements.

BCE.86 For the reasons described in the preceding paragraphs, the IASB believes that the benefits of the improvements to financial reporting will justify the costs to implement and apply the classification and measurement requirements of IFRS 9.

The likely effect on costs of analysis for users of financial statements

BCE.87 The likely benefits of improved reporting are expected to outweigh the costs of analysis for users of financial statements. However, the extent of the benefit will depend on existing practices.

BCE.88 Some of the complexity in IAS 39 is eliminated and it is therefore easier for users of financial statements to understand and use information about financial instruments. In addition, although some users of financial statements favour fair value as a primary measurement attribute for all financial assets, users of financial statements as a group have consistently said that both amortised cost information and fair value information are useful in particular circumstances. The IASB has developed IFRS 9 to provide information that is useful in predicting an entity's future cash flows. In addition, accompanying disclosures provide information that will enable users of financial statements to understand how financial instruments have been classified and measured, and supplementary information from disclosures is available to be used in their financial modelling (for example, the fair value of financial instruments measured at amortised cost).

Conclusion

BCE.89   The requirements result in more relevant and transparent information because they introduce a single classification approach for all financial assets, which always provides users of financial statements with information that reflects how the cash flows on financial assets are expected to be realised given the entity's business model and the nature of the contractual cash flows. In addition, they respond to long standing concerns about the volatility that occurs in profit or loss due to changes in an issuer's own credit risk that was not considered to provide useful information, when an entity elects to measure non-derivative financial liabilities at fair value.

Analysis of the effects: Impairment

Overview

BCE.90   During the global financial crisis, the delayed recognition of credit losses on loans and other financial instruments was identified as a weakness in the existing accounting standards. Specifically, concerns were raised about the timeliness of recognising credit losses because the existing 'incurred loss' model in IAS 39 delays the recognition of credit losses until there is evidence of a credit loss event. The Financial Crisis Advisory Group (FCAG) and others recommended exploring alternatives to the incurred loss model that would use more forward-looking information.

BCE.91   The complexity of having multiple impairment models for financial instruments was also identified as a major concern.

BCE.92   The impairment requirements in IFRS 9 are the IASB's response to the need to improve the accounting for impairment for financial instruments and to remove the complexity of multiple impairment models. The IASB believes that the new impairment requirements address the issue of delayed recognition of credit losses and the complexity of multiple impairment models for financial instruments.

BCE.93   Overall, the IASB's assessment is that the impairment requirements will bring significant and sustained improvements to the reporting of financial instruments because:

(a)   the same impairment model applies to all financial instruments within the scope of IFRS 9 that are subject to impairment accounting. This removes a major source of current complexity.

(b)   entities will be required to recognise a loss allowance at an amount equal to at least 12-month expected credit losses throughout the life of their financial instruments that are subject to impairment accounting. This reduces the systematic overstatement of interest revenue in IAS 39 and acts as a proxy for the recognition of initial expected credit losses over time.

(c)   more timely information will be provided about expected credit losses. The requirements eliminate the threshold for recognising credit losses so that it would no longer be necessary for a credit event to have occurred before credit losses are recognised. Instead, expected credit losses and changes in expected credit losses are always recognised. In particular, IFRS 9 will require:

    (i)   earlier recognition of lifetime expected credit losses for financial instruments relative to IAS 39 (ie instruments with a significant increase in credit risk since initial recognition); and

    (ii)   in addition, 12-month expected credit losses for all other instruments. The amount of expected credit losses will be updated at each reporting date to reflect changes in credit risk since initial recognition. Consequently, the impairment model in IFRS 9 will be more responsive to changes in economic circumstances that affect credit risk.

(d)   the requirements broaden the information that an entity is required to consider when accounting for credit losses. An entity is required to base its measurement of expected credit losses on relevant information about past events, including historical credit loss information for similar financial instruments, current conditions and reasonable and supportable forecasts. Thus, the effects of future credit loss expectations need to be considered. As a result of the broadening of the information that is required to be considered, the impairment model will be more forward looking.

BCE.94   Some interested parties would prefer an impairment model that results in a 'conservative', or prudential, depiction of expected credit losses. Those parties are concerned about higher or lower loss allowances or the 'adequacy' of the loss allowance. They argue that such a depiction would better meet the needs of both the regulators who are responsible for maintaining financial stability and of investors. However, the debate about higher or lower loss allowances or the adequacy of the loss allowance in isolation is primarily a debate for prudential regulators instead of accounting standard-setters. The IASB's objective is not to require higher or lower loss allowances; instead it is to present information to users of financial statements that is neutral and portrays the economic characteristics of the financial instrument at the reporting date. This is consistent with the objectives of financial reporting and the qualitative characteristics in the *Conceptual Framework*. While the IASB does not have an objective to increase allowance balances, loss allowances may quite naturally be higher under IFRS 9 relative to IAS 39. This is because IFRS 9 requires earlier recognition of lifetime expected credit losses as significant increases in credit risk are expected to occur before there is objective evidence of impairment in accordance with IAS 39 and, in addition, 12-month expected credit losses are required to be recognised for all other instruments.[43]

BCE.95 The IASB expects that most costs for preparers will be incurred preparing to transition to the new impairment model. In particular, investments will be required in substantial system changes. The ongoing costs will be mitigated by the fact that several simplifications and clarifications have been put in place that reduce the operational burden of the impairment model in IFRS 9 (see paragraphs BCE.151–BCE.164). The IASB's assessment is that the significant improvements in terms of timeliness of information about expected credit losses and transparency will outweigh those costs.

Objective of the impairment requirements of IFRS 9

BCE.96 The IASB's main objective in developing the impairment model was to provide users of financial statements with more useful information about an entity's expected credit losses on its financial assets and its commitments to extend credit to facilitate their assessment of the amount, timing and uncertainty of future cash flows.

BCE.97 Conceptually, when an entity prices a financial instrument, the credit risk premium in the yield compensates the entity for the initial expected credit losses. For example, at the time of lending, the margin on a financial instrument compensates the lender for the credit risk of the borrower. This means that loss expectations do not give rise to an economic loss at initial recognition. In contrast, subsequent increases in the credit risk of the borrower represent an economic loss. These changes represent an economic loss because they are not priced into the financial instrument. Ideally, to reflect this an entity would include the initial estimate of the expected credit losses in determining the effective interest rate used to recognise interest revenue. Thus, the initial expected credit losses would adjust the interest revenue over the life of the financial asset. The entity would then recognise impairment gains or losses only when changes in the expected credit losses occur. This is what the IASB proposed in the 2009 Impairment Exposure Draft.

BCE.98 In the IASB's view, expected credit losses are most faithfully represented by the proposals in the 2009 Impairment Exposure Draft. Users of financial statements have told the IASB that they support an impairment model that distinguishes between the effect of initial estimates of expected credit losses and subsequent changes in those loss expectations. Many respondents, including the EAP, also supported the concepts in the 2009 Impairment Exposure Draft but said that the proposals would present significant operational challenges.

BCE.99 To overcome the operational challenges of the 2009 Impairment Exposure Draft, the IASB simplified the approach for the recognition of expected credit losses. The impairment model in IFRS 9 seeks to achieve a balance between the benefits

---

43 Purchased credit-impaired assets will not have a 12-month allowance at inception. Instead, the effective interest rate will be adjusted to reflect initial loss expectations and then a loss allowance will be established for all changes in lifetime expected credit losses. Also lifetime expected credit losses are always recognised on trade receivables that do not have a significant financing element and instead of measuring 12-month expected credit losses on assets that have not significantly increased in credit risk, lifetime expected credit losses may be recognised at all times on other trade receivables, lease receivables and contract assets.

of the faithful representation of expected credit losses and the operational cost and complexity. In other words, IFRS 9 seeks to approximate the 2009 Impairment Exposure Draft to the maximum extent possible in a way that is less operationally burdensome and more cost-effective.

BCE.100 IFRS 9 reflects the link between the pricing of financial instruments and the initial recognition of a loss allowance, generally separating the calculation of interest revenue and expected credit losses, by recognising a portion of expected credit losses from initial recognition as a proxy for the yield adjustment and lifetime expected credit losses after there has been a significant increase in the credit risk of a financial instrument. At each reporting date, expected credit losses are measured using updated information.

How activities would be reported in the financial statements of those applying IFRS 9

BCE.101 The analysis in paragraphs BCE.102–BCE.110 focuses on the key differences between the existing impairment model in IAS 39 and the new impairment model in IFRS 9 and how the new impairment model will affect financial reporting.

Single impairment model

BCE.102 IAS 39 requires different impairment assessments and methods for financial assets depending on their classification. Some of those financial asset impairments cannot be reversed. During the global financial crisis, some users of financial statements were confused because the same financial assets were impaired differently simply because they were classified differently for accounting purposes. In contrast, under IFRS 9 the same impairment model is applied to *all* financial instruments subject to impairment accounting. This addresses the criticism that having multiple impairment models in IAS 39 is confusing.

BCE.103 The impairment of debt instruments that are classified as available-for-sale financial assets under IAS 39 was criticised by some users of financial statements, because it is based on fair value fluctuations and is not aligned with the impairment model that is applied to similar financial assets measured at amortised cost. Some questioned the relevance of fair value-based impairment if a financial asset would not be realised through sale.

BCE.104 Similar to financial assets that are measured at amortised cost, in accordance with IFRS 9, the contractual cash flow characteristics of financial assets measured at fair value through other comprehensive income would solely represent payments of principal and interest. In addition, holding financial assets to collect contractual cash flows is an integral feature of the business model. The IASB therefore believes that an impairment model that is based on shortfalls in contractual cash flows and changes in credit risk, instead of changes in fair value, more faithfully reflects the economic reality of expected credit losses that are associated with these financial assets. It is also consistent with both amortised cost and fair value information about these financial assets being provided to the users of financial statements, which was the IASB's objective in introducing the fair value through other comprehensive income measurement category.

BCE.105 Previously, an entity that provided a loan commitment that was not accounted for at fair value through profit or loss and financial guarantee contracts to which IFRS 9 applies but that are not accounted for at fair value through profit or loss, were accounted for in accordance with IAS 37. This was the case even though exposure to credit risk on these instruments is similar to that on loans or other financial instruments and the credit risk is managed in the same way. The IASB therefore concluded that an entity shall apply the same impairment model to those loan commitments and financial guarantee contracts. Aligning the impairment requirements for all credit exposures irrespective of their type reduces operational complexity because, in practice, loan commitments and financial guarantee contracts are often managed using the same credit risk management approach and information systems.

Measurement of expected credit losses

BCE.106 In accordance with IFRS 9, expected credit losses are the present value of expected cash shortfalls over the remaining life of a financial instrument. It requires that the estimates of cash flows are expected values. Consequently, estimates of the amounts and timing of cash flows are the probability-weighted possible outcomes. In the IASB's view, an expected value measurement provides relevant information about the timing, amounts and uncertainty of an entity's future cash flows. It provides information about the risk that the investment might not perform. The amount of expected credit losses will reflect both the risk of a default occurring and the loss amount that would arise if a default were to occur. This is because all financial instruments have a risk of a default occurring. The measurement will therefore reflect that risk of default and not the most likely outcome, as is often the case in practice in accordance with IAS 39.

Timely recognition of expected credit losses

BCE.107 The impairment models in IAS 39 require the recognition of credit losses only once there is objective evidence of impairment or when a credit loss is incurred (thus the impairment model includes a 'recognition threshold'). As a result, the effect of future events, even when expected, cannot be considered. This recognition threshold is perceived to have caused a delay in the recognition of credit losses and was identified during the global financial crisis as a weakness in accounting standards. It also resulted in differences in application because the recognition threshold was applied differently between entities.

BCE.108 IFRS 9 eliminates this threshold. Instead, expected credit losses would always be recognised and updated for changes in credit loss expectations using the best available information at the reporting date. This enables economic credit losses to be better reflected in the financial statements.

BCE.109 Consistent with the recommendations by the G20 Leaders, the FCAG and others, IFRS 9 is more forward-looking and considers a broader range of information than the existing incurred loss model. Such information includes reasonable and supportable forecast information that is available without undue cost or effort.

BCE.110　Consequently, the impairment model in IFRS 9 is expected to be more responsive to changing economic conditions than the existing IAS 39 incurred loss model and requires earlier recognition of expected credit losses.

Comparability of financial information

BCE.111　The IASB acknowledges that the more judgement that is required in the application of an expected credit loss approach, the more subjective the estimates will be, and that this subjectivity will affect the comparability of reported amounts between different entities. Despite the concerns about the application of judgement, in the IASB's view, the new impairment model will improve the comparability of reported amounts. This is because under the incurred loss model in accordance with IAS 39, increases in credit risk are not reported in the absence of a loss event, which limited the comparability of the reported amounts and the effective return on the financial assets. In addition, in practice, the point at which losses were considered to be incurred varied between entities.

BCE.112　In the IASB's view, considering the term structure and initial credit risk when assessing whether lifetime expected credit losses should be recognised will better reflect existing models for measuring credit risk and improve the comparability of the requirements for financial instruments with different maturities and different initial credit risk.

BCE.113　However, any approach that attempts to reflect expected credit losses will be subject to measurement uncertainty and will rely on management's judgement and the quality of the information used. Both qualitative and quantitative disclosures are necessary to assist users of financial statements in understanding and comparing different measures of expected credit losses. Consequently, disclosures are required by IFRS 7 to enable users of the financial statements to identify and understand the inputs, assumptions and techniques applied to identify significant increases in credit risk and measure expected credit losses, the amounts arising from the expected credit losses and the effect of changes in credit risk since initial recognition. The IASB believes that this will lead to greater comparability between different reporting periods of the same entity and assist in enabling comparisons to be made between entities.

Usefulness of financial information in assessing future cash flows of an entity

BCE.114　The IASB noted that the impairment model in IFRS 9 should reflect how an entity approaches credit risk management for different classes of financial instruments and provides information on the effect of the changes in the credit risk of financial instruments since initial recognition.

BCE.115　In assessing the usefulness of the information provided by this approach, the IASB has compared it to the information provided by a general provisioning approach and a fair value approach. In the IASB's view, a general provisioning approach, whereby entities build up reserves to absorb both expected and unexpected credit losses (without any reference to an increase in credit risk) lacks any measurement objective and fails to provide a link between the loss allowance that is recognised and the change in credit risk. Furthermore, a full fair value model does not provide explicit information on expected credit losses. Changes in the fair value of a financial instrument include changes in risks other than credit risk, such as interest rate risk, liquidity risk and market risk. The IASB believes that such an approach does not provide useful information for impairment purposes, because measuring expected credit losses using fair value information is inconsistent with a cost-based measurement that focuses on contractual cash flows.

BCE.116   In the IASB's view, the criterion that determines when lifetime expected credit losses shall be recognised, together with the related disclosure requirements, achieves the best balance between the benefits of distinguishing financial instruments for which there has been a significant increase in credit risk since initial recognition and the costs and complexity of making that assessment.

BCE.117   The IASB is aware that some interested parties favour a lifetime expected credit loss approach, whereby an entity recognises a loss allowance at an amount equal to lifetime expected credit losses from initial recognition, regardless of the credit risk and relative credit pricing of the financial instrument. Under such an approach, the recognition of initial lifetime expected credit losses is triggered by the initial recognition of a financial asset instead of by the increase in credit risk since initial recognition. The IASB believes that this is not appropriate because it would result in financial assets being recognised at a carrying amount that is significantly below fair value on initial recognition and would therefore be inconsistent with the economics of the asset. However, the IASB acknowledges that some users of financial statements find this information useful.

BCE.118   The IASB believes that the impairment requirements in Section 5.5 in IFRS 9 provide useful information by distinguishing between financial instruments for which the credit risk has increased significantly since initial recognition and those financial instruments for which this has not occurred. The feedback to the IASB from the majority of users of financial statements has been that this distinction provides useful information.

Modified financial instruments

BCE.119   As noted in paragraphs BC5.238–BC5.239, the IASB concluded that financial instruments with modified contractual cash flows should be permitted to revert to 12-month expected credit losses in the same way as unmodified financial instruments, if there is no longer a significant increase in credit risk since initial recognition. The IASB believes that such a symmetrical approach faithfully represents the economics of the transaction and that faithful representation should not be sacrificed for anti-abuse purposes.

BCE.120   Some users of financial statements were concerned that such a symmetrical approach would be more permissive than the current IAS 39 requirements. This is because currently in IAS 39 forbearance, as generally used in the regulatory sense, is regarded as an event that indicates objective evidence of impairment. The IASB however notes that because a significant increase in credit risk is determined by reference to the initial credit risk (on the original contractual terms), financial instruments will not necessarily revert to 12-month expected credit losses as a result of a modification of contractual cash flows. IFRS 9 requires an entity to base its assessment of significant increases in credit risk on the credit risk at initial recognition of the original financial instrument (assuming derecognition has not occurred), based on all reasonable and supportable information that is available without undue cost or effort. This includes historical, current and forward-looking information and an assessment of the credit risk over the remaining life of the instrument, which should include the circumstances that led to the modification.

BCE.121 Furthermore, while forbearance may provide objective evidence for the recognition of an incurred loss in accordance with IAS 39, the effect of the modification of contractual cash flows is reflected in the measurement of the impairment loss under that Standard. Consequently, if a modified financial instrument is not considered to have increased significantly in credit risk, it is likely that only a small incurred loss would currently be recognised under IAS 39. As a result, the IASB believes that even if, subsequent to a modification, a loss allowance at an amount equal to 12-month expected credit losses is recognised, it should not result in a smaller loss allowance than would be recognised under IAS 39. The IASB notes that entities are required to disclose the gross carrying amount for modified financial assets for which the loss allowance has reverted back to 12-month expected credit losses during the reporting period.

Better economic decision-making as a result of improved financial reporting

BCE.122 The IASB believes that the new impairment model provides information that is relevant for economic decision-making by depicting changes in the credit risk of financial instruments through the use of a broad range of information, including forward-looking information and the recognition of expected credit losses on a timelier basis. Users of financial statements will also be provided with more information to understand entities' credit risk management processes and the credit risk inherent in their financial instruments. The IASB is of the view that loss allowances should reflect credit loss expectations for financial instruments as at the reporting date.

BCE.123 The IASB acknowledges that the new impairment model would result in an overstatement of expected credit losses for financial assets, and a resulting understatement of the value of the related financial assets, through the recognition of a loss allowance for 12-month expected credit losses. However, the IASB has sought to provide a proxy for the 2009 Impairment Exposure Draft that is less operationally burdensome and more cost-effective. The IASB determined that the impairment requirements in IFRS 9 provides the best balance of the benefits of providing useful information and the costs of providing it. In addition, the overstatement will not be of the same magnitude as if full lifetime expected credit losses were to be recognised on initial recognition. For long-term financial assets and those with a high risk of default occurring as at initial recognition, the difference between a 12-month and lifetime expected credit loss measure can be significant.

BCE.124   Furthermore, relevant information is provided by updating expected credit loss estimates for changes in expectations, by updating the measurement of the loss allowance at each reporting date, and in particular through the recognition of lifetime expected credit losses when there has been a significant increase in credit risk since initial recognition. In addition, information is provided by requiring the calculation of interest revenue on the amortised cost amount (ie net of the loss allowance) of a financial asset when it becomes credit-impaired subsequent to initial recognition.

Regulatory concept of expected credit losses

BCE.125   Some users of financial statements asked the IASB to ensure that the impairment model is both aligned to the prudential capital frameworks and is counter-cyclical, resulting in a loss allowance that is sufficient to absorb all credit losses.

BCE.126   Some prudential regulation and capital adequacy systems, such as the framework developed by the Basel Committee on Banking Supervision, already require financial institutions to calculate 12-month expected credit losses as part of their regulatory capital provisions. However, these estimates only use credit loss experience based on historical events to set out 'provisioning' levels over the entire economic cycle ('through-the-cycle'). Furthermore, through-the-cycle approaches consider a range of possible economic outcomes instead of those that are actually expected at the reporting date. This would result in a loss allowance that is not designed to reflect the economic characteristics of the financial instruments at the reporting date. In addition, the default measures used may be adjusted to reflect a more 'conservative' outlook instead of actual expectations.

BCE.127   The IASB notes that financial reporting, including estimates of expected credit losses, are based on information, circumstances and events at the reporting date. The IASB expects entities to be able to use the systems and processes in place to determine amounts for regulatory purposes as a basis for the application of the impairment requirements in IFRS 9. However, these calculations would have to be adjusted to meet the measurement requirements of IFRS 9.

BCE.128   The IASB acknowledges that any transition adjustments arising on the initial application of IFRS 9 will affect retained earnings, which potentially could have a negative impact on regulatory capital. However, the IASB believes that the objective of financial reporting should be to provide transparent information that is useful to a broad range of users of financial statements and that prudential regulators are best placed to consider how to address the interaction between IFRS and the regulatory requirements. The IASB has discussed the new impairment model and shared information with the Basel Committee on Banking Supervision—through its Accounting Experts Group—throughout the course of the project in order to enable the interaction of the new impairment model with relevant regulatory requirements to be considered. The actual effect on regulatory capital will depend on the decisions made by relevant regulators about the interaction between the IFRS impairment requirements and the prudential requirements.

BCE.129   Some are of the view that loss allowance balances should be used to provide a counter-cyclical effect by building up loss allowances in the good times, to be used in the bad times. This would, however, mask the effect of changes in credit loss expectations. The impairment model in IFRS 9 is based on reasonable and supportable information that is available without undue cost or effort at the reporting date and is designed to reflect economic reality, instead of adjusting the assumptions and inputs applied to achieve a counter-cyclical effect. When credit risk changes, the impairment model will faithfully represent that change. This is consistent with the objective of general purpose financial statements.

BCE.130   Also, because the objective of the new impairment model is to faithfully represent changes in credit risk since initial recognition, the IASB does not believe it would be consistent to also have an objective of ensuring that the recognition of a loss allowance will be sufficient to cover unexpected credit losses. Some users of financial statements would however prefer a representation of credit losses with a conservative or prudential bias, arguing that such a representation would better meet both the needs of regulators who are responsible for maintaining financial stability and those of investors. The majority of users of financial statements that the IASB discussed the impairment requirements with, however supported an impairment model that focuses on expected credit losses and the changes in credit risk since initial recognition.

Fieldwork

BCE.131   The IASB undertook detailed fieldwork during the comment period for the 2013 Impairment Exposure Draft. A key objective of the fieldwork was to understand how responsive the proposed impairment model was expected to be to changes in credit risk expectations over time. It was also designed to provide an understanding of the operational impact of the implementation of the proposals and to provide some directional information about the magnitude of the allowance balance on transition from IAS 39.

BCE.132   In order to understand the responsiveness of the proposed impairment model, the IASB asked participants to use real portfolio information and simulate changes in the credit risk of those portfolios based on a time series of macroeconomic information. To undertake this analysis properly was a very intensive exercise, because it required not only an understanding of existing data but also that entities analyse how they would expect the macroeconomic changes described to affect credit risk over time for their chosen portfolios.[44] Given the intensiveness of the exercise, the sample size was necessarily limited and only 15 participants took part in the fieldwork. However, in order to make the exercise as representative as possible, participants included both financial and non-financial (lessor) entities, multinational and regional (or country)-based businesses, Basel-regulated and non-Basel-regulated entities and entities with various levels of sophistication in credit risk management systems. There was

---

44   The man-hours invested during fieldwork were between 200–250 for smaller businesses, 400–450 for larger businesses and 500–550 for a few participants. The IASB staff invested approximately 400 man-hours, which involved the development of the fieldwork, meetings with participants and portfolio analysis.

also a mixture of the type of portfolios that participants selected, which in aggregate had a total carrying amount in excess of US$500 billion and included:[45]

(a) retail mortgages, including:

  (i) amortising loans;

  (ii) interest only loans; and

  (iii) equity-line loans.

(b) corporate (wholesale) loans;

(c) revolving credit products (for example, credit cards);

(d) lease receivables (for example, vehicle finance); and

(e) other unsecured lending, for example, personal loans/payday loans.

BCE.133 To meet the objective of the fieldwork, participants were asked to measure the loss allowance over a period of five years and apply different impairment requirements for their respective portfolios, including the requirements in IAS 39, the proposals in the 2013 Impairment Exposure Draft and full lifetime expected credit losses for all financial instruments.

BCE.134 While participants were generally able to operationalise the proposals of the 2013 Impairment Exposure Draft, it was not without obstacles. One of the reasons was that there was only a very limited time frame for the fieldwork to be completed in. In addition, by necessity participants could only use information provided as part of the fieldwork or that existed in their credit risk management systems. This meant that the approaches taken could not fully represent those which may ultimately be undertaken. So for retail portfolios, participants were often only able to identify significant increases in credit risk based on past due information plus some adjustments (for example, including restructurings). They found it difficult to incorporate more forward-looking data (for example, macroeconomic data) at a level that enabled them to identify specific financial assets for which there have been significant increases in credit risk since initial recognition.

BCE.135 As a result of this feedback, additional work was undertaken with participants to consider how to ensure that lifetime expected credit losses are recognised for *all* financial instruments for which there have been significant increases in credit risk, even if the significant increase in credit risk is not yet evident on an individual financial instrument level. This has led the IASB to emphasise the need for a portfolio perspective when significant increases in credit risk cannot be identified on an individual financial instrument level to ensure that IFRS 9 is applied on an appropriately forward-looking basis. The work with participants showed that statistical methods and techniques could be used to analyse subportfolios to capture significant increases in credit risk even when that is not evident based on customer-specific information at the level of individual financial instruments.

---

45 The portfolios excluded derivatives and financial guarantee contracts to make the calculations easier and to help participants meet the short deadline of the fieldwork.

BCE.136　Nevertheless, participants in the fieldwork found that the impairment model proposed in the 2013 Impairment Exposure Draft was more responsive to changing economic circumstances in both downturn and upturn macroeconomic environments compared to the IAS 39 model.[46] During a downturn, the loss allowances increased quickly and reached their peak around a year before the lowest point in the economy (reflecting that the data provided was used as forecast data for a 12-month period). During an upturn, the loss allowances recovered faster than those under IAS 39, which often still had a lagging effect from the downturn in the economic cycle. Participants noted that the better an entity is able to incorporate forward-looking and macroeconomic data into its credit risk management models, the more responsive the loss allowance would be to changes in credit risk.

BCE.137　In addition, almost all the participants observed a noticeable increase in the loss allowance on the hypothetical transition date and throughout the economic cycle as compared to IAS 39. For example, on transition, the loss allowance for portfolios other than mortgage portfolios was between 25 per cent and 60 per cent higher compared to the IAS 39 balance and the loss allowance for mortgage portfolios was between 30 per cent and 250 per cent higher compared to the IAS 39 balance. In addition, at the point in the economic cycle when the economic forecast was worst (ie when loss allowances were the highest), the loss allowance measured in accordance with the 2013 Impairment Exposure Draft was between 50 per cent and 150 per cent higher compared to the IAS 39 balance for portfolios other than mortgage portfolios and between 80 per cent and 400 per cent higher compared to the IAS 39 balance for mortgage portfolios.[47, 48]

BCE.138　In performing these calculations, participants that had higher 'incurred but not reported' allowances in accordance with IAS 39 because of longer emergence periods tended to see less of an impact when applying the 2013 Impairment Exposure Draft. In addition, participants that identified and recognised impairment losses on an individual level in a timelier manner under IAS 39 also saw a smaller impact. Finally, participants noted jurisdictional differences because of different macroeconomic factors that affect expected credit losses and therefore the loss allowance.

BCE.139　The IASB notes that it cannot quantify the magnitude of the impact of moving to the new impairment model on an entity's financial reporting. The magnitude of the impact from the requirements in IFRS 9 depends on the financial instruments that an entity holds, when the financial instruments were

---

46　Participants were provided a series of economic information so their proxy forecasting was more accurate than it would be in reality. Although this assessment has imperfections, it nevertheless provided an estimate of the responsiveness of the impairment model.

47　The difference in percentages reflect the extreme effects of differences in expected lives between jurisdictions.

48　This is reflective of the results of the majority of participants in the fieldwork. Excluded from the results, were the responses from participants based on:
(a) qualitative feedback due to timing requirements of the fieldwork; or
(b) the simplified approach (ie measured lifetime expected credit losses on all financial assets) or an absolute approach (for example, when lifetime expected credit losses were recognised on all financial assets of higher credit risk irrespective of whether the credit risk had increased significantly since initial recognition).

originally recognised, how the entity has applied the IAS 39 requirements, the sophistication of the entity's credit risk management systems and the availability of information about, for example, the probabilities of a default occurring, past due statuses and estimates of lifetime expected credit losses for all financial instruments (for example, products, geographical areas and vintages). While all entities will be required to meet the objective of the impairment requirements in Section 5.5 of IFRS 9, in practice, the loss allowance will depend in part on how entities operationalise IFRS 9. The IASB is aware that entities across different jurisdictions have applied the existing impairment requirements in IAS 39 differently, in part as a result of the interaction with local or jurisdictional regulatory definitions and requirements.

BCE.140 Finally, the magnitude of the impact will also depend on the prevalent economic conditions at the time of transitioning to the new requirements. The loss allowance always reflects expectations at the reporting date, so economic conditions at the date of initial application (including forecasts of economic conditions) will affect the loss allowance. The effect on transition will also depend on the information that an entity has available on transition. For example, if an entity is unable to determine the change in credit risk of a financial instrument since initial recognition and will not use past due information to apply the model to that instrument, if it is a low credit risk financial asset, it will have an allowance balance equal to 12-month expected credit losses; otherwise it will have a loss allowance equal to lifetime expected credit losses.

The likely effect on compliance costs for preparers, both at initial application and on an ongoing basis

BCE.141 IFRS 9 seeks to address the cost of identifying deteriorated financial instruments by using significant increases in credit risk as a basis for the distinction. This is intended to ensure that only meaningful changes in credit risk are captured that should align with changes that would be monitored for credit risk management.

BCE.142 The IASB acknowledges that the implementation and ongoing application of an impairment model based on expected credit losses is complex and costly. The costs resulting from the impairment model in IFRS 9 include:

(a) monitoring changes in credit risk of financial instruments since initial recognition and implementing processes to make that assessment; and

(b) calculating expected credit losses including lifetime expected credit losses.

Cost of initial application

BCE.143 The IASB acknowledges that the impairment model in IFRS 9 is different from a credit risk management perspective, because an entity needs to assess the change in credit risk since initial recognition, whereas credit risk managers assess credit risk at a particular date. For example, entities have raised concerns that two loans to the same entity could have different loss allowances when they are originated at different times. Although such a difference in perspective is likely to add cost and complexity to the impairment model, the IASB believes that it is justified because of the underlying concept that a loss only arises when the credit loss expectations on a financial instrument exceed those that are considered when pricing the instrument. Thus, this approach provides information that is useful for users of financial statements.

BCE.144 The implementation of the impairment model will require system changes that may be substantial, and time and resource commitments, resulting in significant costs for most entities with substantial amounts of financial instruments subject to impairment accounting including financial institutions that are already calculating expected credit losses for regulatory purposes. Entities will need to develop new systems and controls to integrate information produced for credit risk management purposes, or elsewhere in their business, into their accounting process. In addition, entities will incur one-time implementation costs to educate personnel in accounting functions to enable them to assess whether the information prepared for credit risk management would suffice to comply with the new impairment requirements. Finally, entities will need to explain to users of financial statements the new impairment model and how it differs from IAS 39 and from the information produced for credit risk management and regulatory purposes. However, these costs are mitigated because the impairment model is based upon changes in credit risk that should be monitored for credit risk management purposes and enables a variety of approaches to be taken to identify such changes, enabling entities to use credit risk information as a basis for implementation.

BCE.145 Participants in outreach activities, preparers responding to the 2013 Impairment Exposure Draft and participants in the fieldwork noted that the cost of implementing the proposed impairment model would depend on how entities segment their portfolios. An entity may, for example, in cases in which the credit risk at origination is similar for particular portfolios, segment its portfolios by credit risk at origination and assess increases in credit risk by comparing the credit risk at the reporting date with the initial credit risk for the relevant portfolio. Thus, the costs of applying the criteria to determine whether lifetime expected credit losses must be recognised would vary depending on the diversity of initial credit risk and the sophistication of credit risk management systems.

BCE.146 The IASB also clarified that a specific or mechanistic assessment is not required. This means that entities need not have explicit probability of default information to assess changes in credit risk, which will enhance the operability of the model and reduce the implementation and ongoing costs.

BCE.147 In addition, the IASB clarified that on initial application of the impairment requirements, entities are permitted to use reasonable and supportable information that is available without undue cost or effort to approximate the credit risk at initial recognition of a financial instrument. Participants in outreach activities and in the fieldwork noted that they would often not have the original credit risk information at transition, which could result in financial instruments being measured inappropriately at lifetime expected credit losses (ie when there have not been in fact a significant increase in credit risk). The IASB clarified the transition requirements because its intention is not to penalise those entities that could not obtain information about the initial credit risk without undue cost or effort. This clarification will enhance the operability of the impairment model and reduce preparers' costs on transition.

BCE.148 For the calculation of expected credit losses (and in particular for the calculation of lifetime expected credit losses), systems need to be updated or newly developed. Field participants used different methods to calculate expected credit losses and noted, for example, that current systems do not discount cash flows used to determine expected credit losses or may discount only to the date of expected default. As a result, systems would need to be modified to discount expected cash flows to the reporting date and to capture the expected timing of credit losses better.

BCE.149 The new disclosure requirements will result in the need to capture more data than under the current disclosure requirements in IFRS 7. Those costs arise on transition to establish the capability to provide those disclosures but will also include ongoing costs. However, if entities embed this in their systems that they use for preparing their financial statements, the ongoing costs can be reduced.

BCE.150 The IASB notes that significant implementation costs are not limited to the impairment model in IFRS 9 and that, regardless of which expected credit loss approach an entity implements, the cost and effort of implementation will be significant. The IASB believes that IFRS 9 appropriately balances the complex requirements of an impairment model based on expected credit losses, with simplifications designed to make the approach more operational, thereby reducing the cost of implementation.

Cost of ongoing application

Interest revenue recognition

BCE.151 The requirement to change the recognition of interest revenue from a gross basis to a net basis at a different level of increase in credit risk compared to when lifetime expected credit losses are recognised (ie when credit losses are incurred) adds a further level of complexity. However, the financial assets that are credit-impaired will be a subset of the financial assets for which lifetime expected credit losses are recognised in accordance with IFRS 9. In addition, because the criteria listed for an instrument to be credit-impaired are the same as the existing incurred loss criteria in IAS 39 (except for the exclusion of 'incurred but not reported'), the IASB believes that the application of these concepts should result in minimal change in practice and will therefore have no significant cost implications for existing IFRS preparers.[49]

Allowance for 12-month expected credit losses

BCE.152 The measurement of a loss allowance at an amount equal to 12-month expected credit losses adds costs and complexity to the impairment model. These costs will be less for financial institutions that are already required to calculate 12-month expected credit losses for prudential purposes; however, that measure would have to be adjusted to meet the measurement requirements of IFRS 9. In

---

49 Almost all participants in the fieldwork considered the proposal to measure interest revenue on the net basis for financial assets that are credit-impaired operable, because it is consistent with the current requirements in IAS 39.

some cases, entities can use information such as loss rates to calculate 12-month expected credit losses, thus building on information that they already use for risk management purposes. However, the cost of measuring a loss allowance at an amount equal to 12-month expected credit losses will be higher for non-Basel II financial institutions and entities that are not financial institutions, because 12-month expected credit losses are a unique calculation that would not normally be required for other purposes. Participants in the fieldwork considered the 12-month allowance to be operational, because information on the 12-month risk of a default occurring is often readily available and already often used (albeit sometimes requiring adjustments) for internal credit risk or regulatory purposes. When information was not readily available internally, participants indicated that information is obtainable in the market to enable this to be determined. However, because of the uniqueness of the calculation, IFRS 9 also provides some relief; for example, the calculation of 12-month expected credit losses is not required for trade receivables, contract assets or lease receivables. In addition, as a result of the 12-month calculation, the lifetime expected credit losses are required to be recognised on fewer financial instruments. As this can be a complex exercise, (see further below in paragraph BCE.155) in effect the 12-month measure also is a source of cost mitigation.

Assessment of significant increases in credit risk

BCE.153 Respondents to the 2009 Impairment Exposure Draft highlighted that the proposals would have required entities to track the initial estimate of lifetime expected credit losses through the credit-adjusted effective interest rate and recognise subsequent changes in the lifetime expected credit losses. This would have led to significant operational challenges and substantial costs, because the effective interest rate information is not contained in the same systems as the credit risk information. To address this, IFRS 9 requires an assessment of the changes in credit risk that have occurred since initial recognition separately from the determination of the effective interest rate. It only requires the effective interest rate to be adjusted for a limited population of financial assets—those that are purchased or originated credit impaired. This reduces the cost of implementation and, in addition, this does not result in an incremental cost for IFRS preparers as this population is unchanged from IAS 39.

BCE.154 Some preparers, particularly credit risk managers, indicated that the tracking of credit risk, in most circumstances, is simpler and more closely aligned to credit risk management practices than the tracking of expected credit losses. To enable the model to be implemented more easily based on existing credit risk management systems, IFRS 9 therefore requires entities to measure and track the initial credit risk instead of changes in expected credit losses to determine whether there has been a significant increase in credit risk since initial recognition.

BCE.155 Some interested parties are concerned that the distinction between financial instruments whose credit risk has increased significantly since initial recognition and financial instruments for which this has not occurred will be operationally challenging. They would prefer lifetime expected credit losses to be measured for all financial instruments (ie also for those financial instruments that have a loss allowance measured at an amount equal to 12-month expected credit losses in accordance with IFRS 9). However, any impairment model that is based on expected credit losses will require monitoring of changes in credit risk to update the expected credit loss amounts. Consequently, differentiating significant changes in credit risk from those that are not, is only an incremental cost to any other impairment model based on expected credit losses. Participants in the fieldwork and respondents to the 2013 Impairment Exposure Draft supported the operability of the impairment proposals for a model in which the measurement of the loss allowance changes when there is a significant increase in credit risk since initial recognition. They stated that this is similar to their credit risk management actions. In addition, it is also expected to be less costly compared to measuring lifetime expected credit losses for all financial instruments. This is because lifetime expected credit losses are most difficult to calculate for long-dated financial assets that are fully performing (ie the 'good' loans, which are measured at 12-month expected credit losses in accordance with IFRS 9), as noted by fieldwork participants. In addition, they observed that lifetime expected credit losses were more sensitive to the underlying assumptions. Their results from the fieldwork showed that updated macroeconomic forecasts led to more volatility in an impairment model based on lifetime expected credit losses for all financial instruments because of the extrapolation effects. They also observed that if lifetime expected credit losses were recognised for all financial instruments the allowance balances increased by at least 100 per cent compared to the 2013 Impairment Exposure Draft for both their mortgages and other portfolios. Finally, they stated that recognising lifetime expected credit losses for financial instruments that have not increased significantly in credit risk is not reflective of the economics of their business.

BCE.156 Some respondents to the 2013 Impairment Exposure Draft were concerned that the assessment of significant increases in credit risk as drafted in that Exposure Draft would require the explicit calculation and storage of the lifetime probability of default curve for a financial instrument to compare the expected remaining lifetime probability of default at inception with the remaining lifetime probability of default at the reporting date. However, the IASB had no intention to prescribe a specific or mechanistic approach to assess whether there has been a significant increase in credit risk. In fact, prescribing a specific method would be contrary to the approach taken by the IASB throughout the development of the new impairment requirements in IFRS 9, whereby the IASB took into account different levels of sophistication of entities and different data availability. Consequently, the IASB has clarified in IFRS 9 that an entity may apply different approaches when assessing whether the credit risk of a financial instrument has increased significantly since initial recognition for different financial instruments. This addresses different levels of sophistication and reduces the operational burden to assess whether a financial instrument shall be measured at lifetime expected credit losses.

BCE.157 In order to further reduce the operational burden of tracking the risk of a default occurring for all financial instruments since initial recognition, IFRS 9 does not require an entity to recognise lifetime expected credit losses on financial instruments with low credit risk at a reporting date, irrespective of the change in credit risk since initial recognition. Consequently, if an entity applies this simplification, it will not need to assess the change in credit risk from initial recognition for financial instruments that have low credit risk on a reporting date (for example, financial instruments whose credit risk is equivalent to investment grade).

BCE.158 The IASB acknowledges that not all entities have advanced credit risk management systems that will enable them to track the changes in credit risk over time. To further reduce the operational burden on such entities, IFRS 9 allows entities to use past due information to determine whether credit risk has increased significantly if information (either on an individual or a portfolio level) that is more forward-looking is not available without undue cost or effort, instead of requiring the implementation of more sophisticated credit risk management systems.

BCE.159 Some preparers were concerned that lifetime expected credit losses would need to be determined for each individual financial instrument, which would add to the operational burden of tracking. However, the IASB clarified that IFRS 9 does not require individual financial instruments to be identifiable as having significantly increased in credit risk in order to recognise lifetime expected credit losses. Financial instruments that share common risk characteristics can be assessed on a collective basis. In particular, IFRS 9 clarifies that the assessment of significant increases in credit risk could be implemented by establishing the maximum credit risk accepted for a particular portfolio on initial recognition (by product type and/or region; the 'origination' credit risk), and then comparing the credit risk of financial instruments in that portfolio at the reporting date with that origination credit risk.[50] In addition, it clarifies that in some cases the assessment of significant increases in credit risk can be implemented through a counterparty assessment instead of an assessment of each individual facility provided to the counterparty as long as such an assessment achieves the objectives of the impairment model and the outcome would not be different to what it would have been if financial instruments had been individually assessed.[51] Both of these clarifications are expected to reduce the operational burden of tracking.

Loan commitments and financial guarantee contracts

BCE.160 IFRS 9 requires the application of the impairment requirements to loan commitments and financial guarantee contracts that are not measured at fair value through profit or loss. While respondents to the 2013 Impairment Exposure Draft widely supported the proposal to recognise a loss allowance for expected credit losses that result from these loan commitments and financial guarantee contracts when there is a present contractual obligation to extend credit, the majority of those respondents noted that expected credit losses on

---

50 Some of the participants in the fieldwork confirmed that this is a more practical way to implement the assessment of significant increases in credit risk for financial instruments, thus making the impairment model more operational.

51 During the fieldwork, some participants were initially concerned that the assessment of significant increases in credit risk is not based on changes in the counterparty's credit risk. However, over the course of the fieldwork, a number of those participants found ways to deal with the difference between the change in the counterparty credit risk and the change in the credit risk of the instrument since origination and stated this to be no longer an area of concern.

some loan commitments should not be estimated over the contractual commitment period. This is because it would be contrary to credit risk management and regulatory reporting, which could result in loss allowances that do not represent the credit losses expected on the off-balance sheet exposures resulting in outcomes for which no actual loss experience exists on which to base the estimates. Participants in the fieldwork who applied the proposed impairment model to credit cards also raised these concerns and suggested that the expected credit loss on these types of loan commitments should be estimated over the behavioural life instead of the contractual life of the instrument. IFRS 9 addresses these concerns and requires expected credit losses for revolving credit facilities, such as credit cards and overdraft facilities, to be measured over the period that the entity expects to be exposed to credit risk and not over the contractual commitment period. This change should enable the measurement of expected credit losses to be more closely aligned to credit risk management systems and enable the loss allowance to more faithfully represent expected credit losses on those exposures.

Simplified approach for trade receivables, contract assets and lease receivables

BCE.161   IFRS 9 addresses the costs and complexities for non-financial institutions and other entities through the simplified approach that removes the need to calculate 12-month expected credit losses and track the increase in credit risk for trade receivables, contract assets and lease receivables.[52]

The effect on entities with less sophisticated credit risk management systems

BCE.162   While a few interested parties have expressed concern that it would be costlier to implement the proposals in some jurisdictions, and for entities that have less sophisticated credit risk management systems, it is the IASB's view that systems and processes that would be required to apply IFRS 9 generally also would be required to manage the entity's business effectively.

BCE.163   However, in order to reduce the operational burden and cost of application for entities, IFRS 9:

   (a)   does not require lifetime expected credit losses to be determined for all financial instruments;

   (b)   has a 'low credit risk' simplification (see paragraph 5.5.10 of IFRS 9);

   (c)   allows entities to use past due information to implement the model (in conjunction with more forward-looking information that is reasonably available without undue cost or effort);

---

52 The non-financial institutions that participated in the fieldwork supported the accounting policy election for lease receivables. They applied the simplified approach because:
   (a) the assets in the portfolio were short term in nature; and
   (b) the simplified approach fitted better into their current credit risk systems, which were not sophisticated systems.
   The majority of the respondents to the 2013 Impairment Exposure Draft also supported the accounting policy election for lease and trade receivables.

(d) does not require a specific approach for assessing whether there has been a significant increase in credit risk, thus enabling entities to build upon their credit risk management information;

(e) clarifies that significant increases in credit risk can be assessed on an individual instrument or a portfolio basis; and

(f) allows entities to use practical expedients when measuring expected credit losses (such as a provision matrix for trade receivables) if doing so is consistent with the principles of IFRS 9.

BCE.164 In addition, IFRS 9 emphasises that an exhaustive search for information is not required. For example, when assessing significant increases in credit risk, entities shall consider all internal and external information that is reasonably available without undue cost or effort. This may mean that entities with little historical information would draw their estimates from internal reports and statistics (which may, for example, have been generated when deciding whether to launch a new product), information that they have about similar products or from peer group experience for comparable financial instruments.

Disclosures

BCE.165 Disclosures are a major contributor to the overall benefits of the model. As mentioned in paragraph BCE.172, the IASB decided to include requirements that provide users of financial statements with information about how an entity manages its credit risk and estimates and measures expected credit losses. The IASB received feedback that a number of the disclosure requirements in the 2013 Impairment Exposure Draft were operationally challenging. With this in mind, the IASB decided on a number of changes and clarifications to reduce the burden of compliance while still providing the information needed by the users of the financial statements.

BCE.166 The IASB considers the requirement in the 2013 Impairment Exposure Draft to provide a reconciliation between the opening balance and the closing balance of the loss allowance and the gross carrying amount of financial assets as a core disclosure. Respondents to the 2013 Impairment Exposure Draft were concerned that this disclosure would be operationally too challenging. Given the feedback raised on operational concerns, the IASB made the disclosure less prescriptive and more principle-based by clarifying that its objective is to provide information about the significant changes in the gross carrying amount that contributed to changes in the loss allowance during the period. In particular, the disclosures are intended to enable users of the financial statements to differentiate between the effects of changes in the amount of exposure (for example, those due to increased lending) and the effect of changes in credit risk. The IASB considers that the requirement, as clarified, is less operationally burdensome but still provides useful information to users of financial statements.

BCE.167 Another important disclosure is the disclosure about modified financial assets. The requirement in the 2013 Impairment Exposure Draft to disclose the gross carrying amount of financial assets that have been modified resulted from a request from users of financial statements to understand the amount of assets that have been modified and subsequently improved in credit risk. The IASB addressed preparers' concerns that the disclosure of the gross carrying amount of modified financial assets for which the measurement objective has changed from lifetime to 12-month expected credit losses during the entire remaining lifetime of the asset (ie until derecognition) would be too onerous, because it would require the tracking of individual assets even after they have returned to a performing status and are no longer closely monitored for credit risk management purposes. Instead, entities shall now only disclose financial assets modified during the reporting period. This still provides an important source of information about the amount of restructuring activity being undertaken while being less burdensome.

The likely effect on costs of analysis for users of financial statements

BCE.168   The IASB believes that users of financial statements will benefit from the timelier information provided about credit risk and the changes in credit risk. The impairment model in IFRS 9 is in strong contrast to the incurred loss model in IAS 39, in which credit losses were only recognised once there was objective evidence that a loss event had occurred. In accordance with IFRS 9, a loss allowance at an amount equal to 12-month expected credit losses will be recognised for all financial instruments unless there has been a significant increase in credit risk since initial recognition, in which case a loss allowance at an amount equal to lifetime expected credit losses should be recognised. Lifetime expected credit losses are therefore recognised earlier than under the incurred loss model in IAS 39, because the credit risk will generally increase significantly before one or more credit loss events occur, particularly given the use of forward-looking information.

BCE.169   The IASB acknowledges that some users of financial statements might have preferred lifetime expected credit losses to be recognised for high credit risk financial instruments that are not purchased or originated credit impaired at initial recognition, whereas only 12-month expected credit losses will be recognised until there has been a significant increase in the credit risk since initial recognition. However, the IASB did not want to create an 'artificial' disincentive for entities to lend to customers with higher credit risk. Furthermore, the IASB believes that full lifetime expected credit losses should not be recognised on initial recognition irrespective of the initial credit risk because financial instruments are priced reflecting initial credit risk expectations. In particular, the IASB was concerned about the effect on the balance sheet carrying amount at initial recognition that would result if lifetime expected credit losses were recognised from inception.

BCE.170   The IASB noted that by reducing the effect on initial recognition by limiting the loss allowance to 12-month expected credit losses the risk of unintended consequences (such as reducing lending to higher risk customers even when correctly priced or reducing lending as the economic environment weakens in order to enable loss allowances to run down creating a gain in profit or loss) would be reduced.

BCE.171   The IASB acknowledges that it would be preferable for users of financial statements if the accounting for expected credit losses was aligned between IFRS and US GAAP. At the time of completing IFRS 9 it appeared likely that accounting for impairment would not be converged despite the efforts of the IASB and the FASB. However, the IASB noted that it was important to improve impairment accounting in accordance with IFRS.

BCE.172   The IASB acknowledges that the assessment of changes in credit risk since initial recognition inherently involves a significant amount of subjectivity and therefore reduces the verifiability and comparability of reported amounts. This inevitably results in costs of analysis to users of financial statements. However, decisions about when credit losses are incurred and the measurement of impairment losses currently in accordance with IAS 39 also involve subjectivity and there is a lack of comparability because of the differences in the application of the incurred loss criteria. IFRS 9 mitigates these issues to some extent by expanding the disclosure requirements to provide users of financial statements with information about the inputs, assumptions and techniques that entities use when assessing the criteria for the recognition of lifetime expected credit losses and the measurement of expected credit losses. For example, a reconciliation is required between the opening balance and the closing balance of the loss allowance and the gross carrying amount of financial assets, which the IASB considers provides useful information about the development and evolution of expected credit losses. Disclosure is also required of information about financial assets with a loss allowance at an amount equal to lifetime expected credit losses that have been modified, including the gross carrying amount of the financial assets and the gain or loss resulting from the modification. Information on modifications is responsive to requests for enhanced information in this area from users of financial statements, because this information was found to be inadequate during the global financial crisis.

Conclusion

BCE.173   The IASB expects that the requirements will provide timelier and more representationally faithful information about an entity's current estimates of expected credit losses and the changes in those estimates over time for all financial instruments subject to impairment accounting. In addition, the requirements include a comprehensive package of disclosures that will help investors to understand the judgements, assumptions and information used by an entity in developing its estimates of expected credit losses. As a result, more relevant and transparent information will be provided to users of financial statements.

Analysis of the effects: Hedge Accounting

Introduction

BCE.174   Throughout the Hedge Accounting project, the IASB performed outreach and consulted with interested parties, with the largest outreach meeting being attended by over 200 participants. The IASB also had extensive discussions with regulators and audit firms worldwide. The analysis in paragraphs BCE.175–BCE.238 is based on the feedback received through this process. Overall, the IASB held over 145 outreach meetings in all the major jurisdictions and also evaluated 247 comment letters received in response to the Exposure Draft *Hedge Accounting*, which was published in 2010 ('2010 Hedge Accounting

Exposure Draft'). The IASB also considered comments received on the draft Standard posted on its website in September 2012.

Overview

BCE.175 Financial reporting should provide transparent information to enable better economic decision-making. Hedge accounting relates to the reporting of risk management activities that entities enter into, to manage their exposures to the risks identified as relevant, from a business perspective.

BCE.176 Over the last decades, the extent and complexity of hedging activities have increased substantially. This has been caused not only by entities' increasing willingness and ability to manage their exposures, but also by the increased availability of financial instruments to manage those exposures.

BCE.177 The hedge accounting requirements in IAS 39 *Financial Instruments: Recognition and Measurement* were complex and rule-based. They involved trying to fit transactions that were originated for risk management purposes into an accounting framework that was largely divorced from the purpose of the transactions. This was pointed out by respondents to the Discussion Paper *Reducing Complexity in Reporting Financial Instruments* (published in 2008) and the sentiment has been confirmed in the outreach and feedback received by the IASB while developing the new hedge accounting requirements.

BCE.178 This also caused difficulties for users of financial statements when trying to understand the information reported in financial statements. Some users of financial statements regarded hedge accounting as being incomprehensible and often removed its effects from their various analyses. Users frequently argued that they had to request additional information (often on a non-GAAP basis) to be able to perform their analyses (for example, making forecasts), because the way in which the hedging activities were accounted for and the disclosures that were provided were often considered not to portray risk management in a useful way. The disclosures under IAS 39 were perceived as too accounting-centric and lacking transparency. This led to entities presenting non-GAAP information in various ways, with various levels of detail across different documents that range from the Management Discussion and Analysis to investor presentations.

BCE.179 The complexity of the hedge accounting model in IAS 39 and the resulting increased importance of non-GAAP information led preparers and users of financial statements to ask the IASB to develop a model that, instead of reporting the results of an accounting-centric exercise, would report the performance of an entity's hedging activities in the financial statements on a basis that was consistent with that entity's risk management activities.

BCE.180 The IASB believes that the new hedge accounting requirements address this issue. Under the new model, it is possible for the financial statements of an entity to reflect its risk management activities instead of simply complying with a rule-based approach, such as the approach in IAS 39.

BCE.181 Overall, the IASB's assessment is that these new requirements will bring significant and sustained improvements to the reporting of hedging activities. In addition, entities will be able to use information that they have prepared for the purpose of undertaking their hedging activities as the basis for demonstrating compliance with the hedge accounting requirements.

BCE.182   The hedge accounting requirements included in IFRS 9 reflect a substantial change from many aspects of hedge accounting in IAS 39. These amendments to hedge accounting will affect a variety of entities, including both financial and non-financial institutions.   The new model will benefit from a more principle-based approach, including the revised eligibility criteria both for hedged items and hedging instruments, and a new objective-based hedge effectiveness assessment. In addition a targeted solution has been introduced for hedges of credit risk using credit derivatives. Entities dealing with hedging of non-financial items are likely to have significant benefits, albeit with some costs to be incurred when implementing the new model. Banks and other financial institutions will also benefit from the general hedge accounting model.

BCE.183   Areas in which it is expected that the new requirements will produce the greatest impact include: hedge effectiveness testing; eligibility of risk components of non-financial instruments; disclosures; accounting for the costs of hedging; aggregated exposures; groups and net positions; the rebalancing and discontinuation of hedging relationships; and hedges of credit risk using credit derivatives.

BCE.184   The IASB expects that most costs for preparers will be incurred at the transition date and will relate to the links that need to be created between the accounting and the risk management functions.   Under the current model for hedge accounting such links have generally been weak or non-existent, reflecting the accounting-centric character of that model. Additional costs will be incurred in explaining to the users of financial statements the impact of the hedging activities. This cost will, however, be mitigated by the fact that, given the greater alignment with risk management, some of the information, although not used for accounting purposes, is already being produced for risk management purposes or is being produced for the reporting of alternative performance measures (the latter often being presented on a non-GAAP basis). In particular, the costs for the hedge effectiveness test for many hedging relationships, especially simple ones, should be reduced on an ongoing basis. The IASB's assessment is that the significant improvements in terms of comparability and transparency will outweigh those costs.

How activities would be reported in the financial statements of those applying IFRS 9

BCE.185   The analysis in paragraphs BCE.186–BCE.238 focuses on the key differences between the existing model in IAS 39 and the new hedge accounting model in this Standard and how the new model will impact financial reporting. In particular, an analysis of some of the key changes introduced by the IFRS 9 hedge accounting model that will change entities' ability to apply hedge accounting is included in paragraphs BCE.190–BCE.205.

Objective of the Standard

BCE.186   During its outreach activities the IASB learnt that both preparers and users of financial statements were frustrated about the lack of connection between actual risk management and the hedge accounting requirements. In particular, preparers found it difficult to reflect their risk management and users of financial statements found it difficult to understand the reflection of risk management on the basis of the hedge accounting requirements in IAS 39. In view of the criticisms received, the IASB, instead of merely considering improvements to the existing model, decided to rethink the entire paradigm of hedge accounting.

BCE.187   The IASB decided that the "objective of hedge accounting is to represent, in the financial statements, the effect of an entity's risk management activities that use financial instruments".[53] This is a principle-based instead of a rule-based approach that focuses on an entity's risk management. Almost all respondents to the 2010 Hedge Accounting Exposure Draft as well as participants in the IASB's outreach activities supported the objective of improving information about risk management through hedge accounting as proposed by the IASB.

BCE.188   Consequently, subject to qualifying criteria, the model developed by the IASB uses the risk management activities of an entity as the foundation for deciding what qualifies (or what does not qualify) for hedge accounting. The aim of the model is to faithfully represent, in the financial statements, the impact of the risk management activities of an entity.

Qualifying hedging instruments

BCE.189   IAS 39 imposed restrictions on what could and what could not be considered as hedging instruments. Respondents to the 2010 Hedge Accounting Exposure Draft questioned the logic behind the arbitrary disallowance of certain types of financial instruments as hedging instruments in IAS 39 even when such financial instruments provided an effective offset for risks managed under common risk management strategies. The key restriction in IAS 39 was the disallowance of designating non-derivative instruments as hedging instruments for hedges of risks other than foreign currency risk.

BCE.190   The IASB decided to expand the types of eligible financial instruments under the new hedge accounting model, to allow non-derivative financial assets and liabilities at fair value through profit or loss to be designated as hedging instruments, ie to acknowledge their effect also for accounting purposes.

BCE.191   The other key change brought in by the new hedge accounting model is the removal of the distinction between combinations of stand-alone written and purchased options and those combined in one contract. The IASB decided that the eligibility of an option contract to be designated as a hedging instrument should depend on its economic substance and risk management objectives instead of its legal form alone. Consequently, the IASB decided that a stand-alone written option would be eligible for designation as a hedging instrument if it is jointly designated with other hedging instruments so that, in combination, they do not result in a net written option.

---

53 See paragraph 6.1.1 of IFRS 9.

© IFRS Foundation

Qualifying hedged items

BCE.192 A key change brought about by the Standard is the ability to hedge a risk component of a non-financial item. The IASB decided to align the treatment of financial and non-financial items to also allow the hedging of risk components in non-financial items, when they are separately identifiable and reliably measurable. This, as noted by many respondents, represents a key aspect of the new hedge accounting model as it allows the accounting to reflect the commercial reality in hedges of non-financial items because, in practice, components of non-financial items are often hedged because hedging the entire item is commercially not viable (because of, for example, a lack of availability of cost effective hedging instruments) or not desired (because, for example, the entity regards accepting the risk as more economical than transferring it to others using hedges). This change will enable such hedges to be reflected in the designation used for hedge accounting, thereby enabling preparers to better reflect, and users of financial statements to better understand, the actual risk management activity and the effectiveness of hedging strategies.

BCE.193 Under IAS 39 hedged items that together constitute an overall net position of assets and liabilities could only be designated in a hedging relationship with the gross position (a group) being the hedged item if certain restrictive criteria were met. These restrictions made achieving hedge accounting for items managed as part of a net position under IAS 39 difficult in practice and made it necessary to designate gross positions instead of the net position that is being economically hedged. This created a disconnect between the accounting and the actual risk management activity.

BCE.194 Consequently, the IASB decided that groups of items (including net positions) would be eligible for hedge accounting. In the case of foreign currency exposures this would mean that all of the actual cash flows included within the group of cash flows being hedged could be designated in line with actual risk management. However, the IASB also decided that for cash flow hedges such net position hedging would not be available for risks other than foreign currency exposures. However, the IASB noted that this did not prevent entities from getting hedge accounting through gross designations that are determined by the net exposure that is monitored for risk management purposes.

BCE.195 In the area of 'risk components', respondents believed that it should be possible to designate a risk component that assumes cash flows that would exceed the actual cash flows of the hedged item, as it reflects risk management in situations in which the hedged item has a negative spread to the benchmark rate. For example, being able to designate a full LIBOR component in a financial instrument that yields LIBOR less a spread (colloquially referred to as 'sub-LIBOR'). Such respondents believed that it should be possible to hedge the LIBOR risk as a benchmark component and treat the spread as a negative residual component, as they hedged their exposure to the variability of cash flows attributable to LIBOR (or a correlated index) using LIBOR swaps.

BCE.196 In its deliberations, the focus was primarily on the sub-LIBOR scenario although the issue is not unique to that situation (see paragraphs BC6.217–BC6.229). In that context, the IASB noted that, for risk management purposes, an entity normally does not try to hedge the entire interest rate of a financial instrument but instead the change in the variability of the cash flows attributable to LIBOR. Such a strategy protects an entity's exposure to benchmark interest rate risk and, importantly, the profit margin of the hedged items (ie the spread relative to the benchmark) is protected against LIBOR changes. This is, of course, only feasible if LIBOR does not fall below the absolute value of the negative spread. However, if LIBOR does fall below the absolute value of that negative spread it would result in 'negative' interest, or interest that is inconsistent with the movement of market interest rates. Consequently, in contrast to exposures with full LIBOR variability, hedging sub-LIBOR exposures means that the entity remains exposed to cash variability in some situations. The IASB noted that allowing a designation that ignores this fact would not faithfully represent the economic phenomenon.

BCE.197   Consequently, in the Standard the IASB retained the restriction in IAS 39 for the designation of risk components when the designated risk component exceeds the total cash flows of the hedged item. However, hedge accounting would still be available in such situations if all the cash flows hedged for a particular risk are designated as the hedged item.

Qualifying criteria for hedge accounting

BCE.198   As with the other aspects of the current hedge accounting model in IAS 39, the IASB received information during outreach and comments from respondents to the 2010 Hedge Accounting Exposure Draft about the hedge effectiveness requirements in IAS 39. The feedback received clearly showed that participants believed that the hedge effectiveness assessment in IAS 39 was formulaic, onerous and difficult to apply. As a consequence, there was often little or no link between the analysis undertaken by risk managers who hedge the risk and the analysis required to apply hedge accounting, and as a result between the hedge accounting and risk management operations. This was reflected, for example, in the fact that hedge accounting could be required to be discontinued in situations in which the hedging relationship was regarded as satisfactory and could be continued from a risk management perspective and for which the entity could achieve hedge accounting again—but only as a new hedging relationship. Also, given the specified bright lines for effectiveness and the accounting consequences of deviating from the same, it made hedge accounting difficult to understand and apply.

BCE.199   To address these concerns, the IASB decided to require an objective-based model for testing hedge effectiveness instead of the bright line test (80–125 per cent) in IAS 39. Instead of setting quantitative thresholds or bright lines, this approach focuses on the achievement of economic offset, a concept used by risk managers when designing and implementing hedging strategies. It also has the benefit of removing the burden of working out hedge effectiveness purely for accounting purposes and instead leverages the assessment done by risk management to ensure compliance with the hedge effectiveness requirements in the Standard. The principles and the concepts behind this change received widespread support.

BCE.200   In addition, IAS 39 did not allow adjustments in the hedging relationship subsequent to designation, except for rollover strategies documented at contract inception, to be treated as adjustments to a continuing hedging relationship.

Consequently, IAS 39 treated such adjustments to an existing hedging relationship as a discontinuation of the original hedging relationship and the start of a new one. The IASB, in its deliberations, noted that this was inconsistent with risk management practices and did not represent the economic phenomenon in practice. There are instances when, although the risk management objective remains the same, adjustments to an existing hedging relationship are made because of changes in circumstances related to the hedging relationship's underlyings or risk variables. The IASB concluded that, in situations in which the original risk management objective remained unaltered, the adjustment to the hedging relationship should be treated as the continuation of the hedging relationship. This will have the effect of enabling changes in risk management to be properly portrayed in hedge accounting.

BCE.201   Under IAS 39 an entity had to discontinue hedge accounting when the hedging relationship ceased to meet the qualifying criteria. Also, the entity had a free choice to discontinue hedge accounting by simply revoking the designation of the hedging relationship, irrespective of the reason behind it. The IASB noted that entities often voluntarily discontinued hedge accounting because of how the effectiveness assessment in IAS 39 worked. The IASB noted that, in some situations, the hedging relationship was discontinued and then restarted even though the risk management objective of the entity had not changed. In the IASB's view, this created a disconnect between the hedge accounting model in IAS 39 and hedging from a risk management perspective. In the light of this, the IASB decided that the ability of an entity to voluntarily revoke a hedge designation, even when all qualifying criteria are met, would no longer be available. However, if the risk management objective for the hedging relationship changes then hedge accounting needs to be discontinued. This will improve the link with risk management by ensuring that once hedge accounting commences it will continue as long as the hedge still qualifies for hedge accounting.

Mechanics of hedge accounting

BCE.202   The IASB considered the fact that the mechanics for hedge accounting in IAS 39 were well established and understood by most interested parties, and therefore decided to retain those hedge accounting mechanics in the new model. The IASB did, however, note that many users of financial statements were confused by the accounting distinction made between cash flow hedges and fair value hedges and how that distinction related to risk and the strategies for managing such risks. Consequently, the IASB decided to include new disclosure requirements in IFRS 7, whereby all disclosures for hedge accounting are presented in a single section in the financial statements with the objective of alleviating this confusion.

BCE.203   Under IAS 39 entities typically designated option-type derivatives as hedging instruments on the basis of their intrinsic value. This meant that the time value that was not designated was required to be presented similarly to financial instruments held for trading. This created a disconnect between the accounting treatment and the risk management view, whereby entities typically consider the time value of an option at contract inception (the premium paid) as a cost of hedging akin to a cost of buying protection (like insurance).

BCE.204 The IASB agreed that the time value of an option could be viewed as a premium paid for protection against risk and, consequently, decided to align the accounting for the time value with the risk management perspective. The IASB took the view that, like the distinction between the different types of costs related to insuring risk, the time value of options should be similarly distinguished. For transaction related hedged items the cumulative change in the fair value of the option's time value should be accumulated in other comprehensive income and should be reclassified in a similar way to that for cash flow hedges. In contrast, for time-period related hedged items the nature of the time value of the option used as the hedging instrument is that of a cost for obtaining protection against a risk over a particular period of time. Hence, the IASB considered that the cost of obtaining the protection should be allocated as an expense over the relevant period on a systematic and rational basis.

BCE.205 The effect of this change is that the time value paid is treated like a cost of hedging instead of as held for trading with the resulting volatility recognised in profit or loss. This enables the costs of such a hedging strategy to be presented in a manner that reflects the inter-relation with the hedging relationship in which the option's intrinsic value is designated, and is consistent with risk management. It also removes a potential disincentive against the use of options as hedging instruments and improves transparency of the costs of hedging.

BCE.206 The IASB made similar changes to the accounting for the forward element of forward contracts and the foreign currency basis spread of hedging instruments.

Accounting for macro hedging

BCE.207 In practice, risk management often considers exposures on an aggregated basis over time. Over time, exposures are either added or removed from the hedged portfolio resulting in what are generally called hedges of 'open positions'. Hedges of open positions introduce significant complexity in the accounting model as the continuous changes in the hedged item need to be monitored and tracked for accounting purposes. The continuous changes in the hedged item also mean there is no direct one-to-one relationship with particular hedges.

BCE.208 The IASB decided not to specifically address open portfolios or the accounting for 'macro hedging' as part of the new hedge accounting model. The IASB noted that under IAS 39 entities often already account for 'macro' activities by applying the general hedge accounting model. The IASB received feedback from financial institutions, as well as from entities outside the financial sector, that addressing situations in which entities use a dynamic risk management strategy was important. Given the nature and complexity of the topic, the IASB has decided to separately deliberate the accounting for macro hedging with the objective of issuing a Discussion Paper.

BCE.209 IFRS 9 (like IAS 39) does not allow cash flow hedges of interest rate risk to be designated on a net position basis but instead on the basis of gross designations. However, so called 'proxy hedging' (when, for example, the designation for hedge accounting purposes is on a gross position basis even though actual risk management typically manages on a net position basis) is still an eligible way to designate a hedged item as long as the designation reflects risk management in that it is related to the same type of risk that is being managed and the financial instruments used for that purpose. Thus, while the separate project continues to explore a more comprehensive model to address the accounting for macro hedging activities, the ability to apply hedge accounting is not expected to change as a result of applying IFRS 9.

BCE.210　In addition, entities can elect to continue to apply the IAS 39 hedge accounting requirements until completion of the project on accounting for macro hedging.

Hedges of credit risk

BCE.211　Financial institutions use credit derivatives to manage their credit risk exposures arising from their lending activities and also, on occasion, to reduce their regulatory capital requirements. However, the credit risk of a financial item is not a risk component that meets the eligibility criteria for hedged items. This is currently a significant issue, particularly for financial institutions because, by using derivatives to manage credit risk, an activity designed to reduce risk, volatility in profit or loss is increased, thereby creating the perception of increased risk.

BCE.212　Many respondents were of the view that the IASB should address the accounting for hedges of credit risk using credit derivatives. Most of them also believed that this is an important issue in practice that the IASB should address.

BCE.213　The IASB decided to use a targeted fair value option to reflect the management of credit risk. The IASB decided to allow the designation of financial instruments, both recognised and unrecognised, to be at fair value through profit or loss if the credit risk of those financial instruments is managed using a credit derivative that is also measured at fair value through profit or loss. This eliminates the accounting mismatch that would otherwise arise from measuring credit derivatives at fair value and hedged items (such as loans) at amortised cost. It also enables entities to appropriately reflect this risk management activity in their financial statements. By allowing entities to make this election also for a proportion of a financial instrument and after its initial recognition, and to subsequently discontinue the fair value measurement for the hedged credit exposure, this approach enables entities to reflect their risk management activity more effectively than using the fair value option (which is available only on initial recognition for the financial instrument in its entirety, and is irrevocable). This becomes important because entities often do not hedge items for their entire life. This targeted fair value option is also available for credit exposures that are outside the scope of this Standard, such as most loan commitments.

Comparability of financial information

BCE.214　The IASB decided that by its very essence, hedge accounting should continue to be voluntary. As a result, there will never be full comparability because, for example, despite identical risk management activity one entity may choose to apply hedge accounting whereas the other may not. However, by improving the link to risk management, which in itself makes hedge accounting less burdensome to apply and facilitates a more useful reflection of risk management activities, increased use of hedge accounting should occur thus improving comparability.

BCE.215   With this in mind the IASB discussed whether it should retain an entity's choice to revoke the designation of a hedging relationship. The IASB decided not to allow the discontinuation of hedge accounting when an entity's risk management objective is unchanged. This will assist in improving comparability.

BCE.216   One of the key contributors to comparability is disclosure. The IASB decided to retain the scope of the hedge accounting disclosures because it provides, to users of financial statements, information on exposures that an entity hedges and for which hedge accounting is applied. For this population of hedging relationships, disclosure is required that will enable users of financial statements to better understand risk management (its effects on cash flows) and the effect of hedge accounting on financial statements. In addition, the IASB decided that all hedge accounting disclosures (ie irrespective of the type of hedge and the type of information required) should be presented in one location within an entity's financial statements. Hedge accounting has been difficult for users of financial statements to understand, which in turn has made risk management difficult to understand. These enhanced disclosures will assist in improving the ability of users of financial statements to compare entities' risk management activities.

Better economic decision making as a result of improved financial reporting

BCE.217   One of the fundamental changes introduced by the Standard is that the entire paradigm of hedge accounting has been changed to align more closely with the risk management activities of an entity. The IASB is of the view that this fundamental shift in focus—whereby the accounting and risk management objectives are brought in congruence—will result in better economic decision making through improved financial reporting. One such example is the accounting for options.

BCE.218   In the IASB's outreach some entities said that the accounting consequences of using options (non-linear instruments) were a consideration in their risk management activities. This was because the undesignated time value of the option was accounted for as at fair value through profit or loss, thereby resulting in significant profit or loss volatility. The IASB has addressed this issue and has better aligned the reported results with the risk management perspective. Time value is now considered to be a cost of hedging instead of a trading position. Similarly, the IASB addressed the accounting for the forward element of forward contracts and the foreign currency basis spread in instruments that hedge foreign currency risk and decided on a treatment similar to that of the time value of options. The latter issue was, for example, of particular concern to entities that raised funds in a currency other than their functional currency.

BCE.219   The IASB expects that these amendments will significantly reduce the accounting considerations affecting risk management decisions and also provide users of financial statements with more useful information about hedging activities, including the cost of such activities, resulting in better economic decision making.

BCE.220   As discussed previously (see paragraphs BCE.189–BCE.190) the IASB decided to expand the types of eligible financial instruments under the new hedge accounting model to allow non-derivative financial assets and liabilities at fair value through profit or loss as eligible hedging instruments. The IASB noted the comments received from respondents that such a treatment enables an entity to better capture its risk management activities in its financial statements. In the IASB's view this will significantly contribute to better economic decision making by capturing established risk management strategies in reported results through hedge accounting. It is particularly relevant for jurisdictions in which the use of derivatives is restricted.

BCE.221   Aligning the treatment of risk components for financial and non-financial items represents a fundamental change in the hedge accounting model, as this will allow entities to better represent their hedging and risk management activities for non-financial items in their financial statements. Entities will be able to more readily designate hedges in a manner that is consistent with risk management and to recognise hedge effectiveness on this basis. The IASB believes that this will significantly improve the usefulness of reported information for entities hedging non-financial items, which will enable preparers to better reflect their performance and result in better economic decision making.

BCE.222   The removal of the bright-line hedge effectiveness requirements will avoid discontinuation of hedging relationships in the financial statements under circumstances in which the hedge is still economically effective. Instead of a percentage-based test that does not meaningfully capture the characteristics of a hedging relationship in all situations, the effectiveness of hedging relationships will be evaluated on the basis of the features that drive their economic success. The new model will ensure that when the economics of a transaction demand that a hedge be rebalanced, such rebalancing does not lead to the hedging relationship being portrayed as discontinued. The IASB believes that such amendments will enable the economic success of an entity's hedging programme to be reflected in the financial statements, thereby leading to better decision making by both management and users of financial statements, because they will be in a better position to make informed judgements about an entity's hedging operations.

BCE.223   The IASB's decision to require the continuation of hedge accounting when a derivative is novated to effect clearing with a central clearing party also improves the usefulness of information for users of financial statements. This is achieved by preventing the discontinuation of hedge accounting and the ineffectiveness that would arise from a new hedging relationship being designated as a replacement.

BCE.224   Risk management also takes into consideration the risk positions that have been created by aggregating exposures that include derivative financial instruments. IAS 39 only allowed derivatives to be designated as hedging instruments, but not to be part of hedged items. Consequently, positions that are a combination of an exposure and a derivative (aggregated exposures) failed to qualify as hedged items. Under the new model an aggregated exposure (comprising a derivative and non-derivative) is an eligible hedged item. Similarly, by modifying the requirements for hedges of groups of items, the accounting for such hedges can now be better represented in the financial statements. Again, the IASB believes that, aligning the accounting model with risk management will result in better information for economic decision making.

BCE.225   This Standard also makes changes to aspects of the accounting for financial instruments outside hedge accounting that allow risk management to be more faithfully represented in the financial statements. One area is the accounting for contracts to buy or sell non-financial items, so called 'own use contracts'. Currently, those contracts are not treated as derivatives in particular circumstances (they are executory contracts that are off the statement of financial position). This can create an artificial perspective when they are measured as part of a portfolio that includes other items that are recognised in the statement of financial position and measured at fair value through profit or loss. By allowing entities to elect to measure own use contracts at fair value through profit or loss, entities are better able to provide information about their risk management activities in the financial statements. The IASB believes that these changes, along with those concerning the management of credit risk, will provide better information for economic decision making.

Compliance costs for preparers

BCE.226   As with all new requirements, the IASB acknowledges that different areas of the requirements will have different effects and hence different types of costs and benefits will arise when considering both preparers and users of financial statements. Given that the new model is based on an entity's risk management practices, it is reasonable to conclude that one of the key drivers of the costs incurred and the benefits obtained, in complying with the new requirements, will be the level of development and the sophistication of the entities' risk management functions.

BCE.227   Entities will incur a one-time cost on initial application to address:

     (a)   development of new processes, systems and controls to integrate information produced for risk management purposes into their accounting processes;

     (b)   creating accounting capabilities for some new eligible accounting treatments (if they are intended to be used—for example, the new accounting for costs of hedging);

     (c)   updating of the documentation for existing hedging relationships on transition to the new requirements;

     (d)   education of accounting functions to enable them to assess whether the information prepared for risk management purposes would suffice to comply with the new hedge accounting requirements; and

     (e)   the need to explain to users of financial statements the difference between the information produced for risk management purposes and the hedge accounting disclosures.

BCE.228   The IASB believes that the costs of the transition, as well as the ongoing costs of applying the new hedge accounting requirements, will very much depend on the individual circumstances of each entity—for example, what type of hedging instruments and hedged items it has, what types of hedges it uses, and how it has implemented hedge accounting in terms of processes and systems. It is therefore difficult to generalise the likely impact of costs on preparers. Broadly, the IASB expects:

(a) entities with more sophisticated risk management functions, that produce reliable information for the entity's own management, will have costs of initial application in establishing better links between those functions and their accounting function, but the ongoing costs of application should then be lower because of the new hedge effectiveness test.

(b) entities that have embedded hedge accounting in their accounting systems may have to adjust their systems, depending on the particular implementation of IAS 39 and what additional new accounting treatments the entity wants to use. Entities using bespoke or self-developed solutions are affected differently from those using standard software. In all cases, the costs are one-off transition costs.

(c) entities that use a master documentation approach, whereby the documentation of individual hedging relationships includes references to master documents that set out risk management strategies or effectiveness testing methods, will have lower costs of making the transition than entities that include that information in full in the documentation of each individual hedging relationship. Those costs are also one-off transition costs.

(d) the new disclosure requirements will result in the need to capture more data than under the current hedge accounting disclosures in IAS 39. Costs arise on transition when the capability to provide those disclosures is created but will also include ongoing costs. However, if entities embed this in their systems that they use for preparing their financial statements the ongoing costs can be significantly reduced.

BCE.229 Overall, given the fact that the new model developed by the IASB is more aligned with the day-to-day risk management activities of an entity, the IASB believes that the following benefits will outweigh the costs of initial implementation and on-going application:

(a) better consistency between accounting and risk management;

(b) better operational efficiency;

(c) less need for non-GAAP information to explain to users of financial statements the impact of hedging for which hedge accounting was not achieved;

(d) reduction in the costs of workarounds to deal with the restrictions in IAS 39; and

(e) standardised and more transparent information, resulting in a better understanding of the company's hedging performance.

BCE.230   In addition to those costs set out in paragraph BCE.228, the IASB notes that one of the key costs of compliance with the hedge accounting requirements of IAS 39 is the infrastructure and resources required to maintain the hedge documentation and effectiveness testing. Under the new model, linking the hedge documentation requirements with that of risk management systems will, in the IASB's view, bring in efficiencies and cost savings as entities integrate such systems. In addition, the new model includes an objective-based effectiveness assessment, which is linked to the way that the hedging relationship is designed and monitored for risk management purposes. This will substantially reduce the costs of ongoing compliance compared with IAS 39.

BCE.231   This will be further reinforced by the fact that the IASB, after due consideration, decided to keep the mechanics of hedge accounting for fair value, cash flow and net investment hedges the same. This will avoid any major costs involved with changing accounting systems both on initial application and on an ongoing basis.

BCE.232   One of the costs involved with the application of any new Standard is the cost of developing ways to implement it. One of the main requests that respondents made to the IASB was to provide examples that would illustrate the various aspects of the new proposals. In response, the IASB has provided detailed guidance whenever possible (for example, detail about the accounting mechanics for aggregated exposures). The IASB believes that this will help in reducing both the initial and ongoing cost of compliance.

BCE.233   The IASB always intended to retain the 'macro fair value hedge accounting model' in IAS 39 pending completion of the project on the accounting for macro hedging. In addition, as noted in paragraphs BCE.208–BCE.209, the IASB is of the view that those using the general requirements in IAS 39 to achieve hedge accounting for their macro hedging activities should be able to continue to do so under the IFRS 9 model. Thus, the ability to apply hedge accounting to macro hedging activities should not be adversely affected by the introduction of IFRS 9. However, the IASB acknowledged that some entities may want to migrate from accounting for their macro hedging activities using IAS 39 directly to any new model for accounting for macro hedging. Consequently, the IASB decided to provide an option to preparers to continue to apply hedge accounting under IAS 39 without requiring them to move to the new hedge accounting model in IFRS 9. This means that those who do not want to change their accounting for macro hedging need not do so until completion of the project on the accounting for macro hedging. This will, however, mean that all of their hedge accounting will continue to be in accordance with IAS 39 (ie the election is made for hedge accounting as a whole).

BCE.234   However, the IASB is of the view that the migration from the accounting for macro hedging using the cash flow hedge accounting requirements in IAS 39 to the accounting using IFRS 9 will not be unduly burdensome for preparers. This is because the new hedge accounting model does not change how risk components of financial items can be designated as hedged items. In addition, while there are changes to the hedge effectiveness requirements, these have introduced simplifications compared with IAS 39. Entities would need to update their documentation of their hedging relationships to reflect the new effectiveness assessment. However, if hedge accounting was applied under IAS 39, the sources of ineffectiveness should be known, and it should be possible to update documentation efficiently by using a master document approach for similar hedges. This can be achieved by one central document being included by a cross reference in the documentation of specific hedging relationships that includes the identification of the specific hedging instruments and hedged items.

Costs of analysis for users of financial statements

BCE.235 Given that the mechanics for hedge accounting were well established and understood by most interested parties, the IASB decided to retain the mechanics of hedge accounting that were in IAS 39 for fair value, cash flow and net investment hedges. Consequently, from the perspective of users of financial statements, the costs in educating themselves about these proposals will be reduced.

BCE.236 The IASB also decided that it would require comprehensive information to be disclosed so that users of financial statements could understand the effects of hedge accounting on the financial statements and so that all hedge accounting disclosures are presented in a single note in the financial statements. This will enable users to access a set of information that is more relevant to their needs and will therefore reduce the need to rely on information prepared on a non-GAAP basis. In addition, they will also benefit from more meaningful information that is more closely linked to the decision making for risk management purposes.

BCE.237 Finally, the IASB expects that users of financial statements will obtain a higher level of transparency from the financial statements of entities applying hedge accounting. This will allow them to better form their own view of the entity's risk management and its effect on reported results. The opportunity for more extensive analyses would, of course, entail costs of performing those analyses, as with any use of financial reporting information.

Conclusion

BCE.238 The IASB expects that preparers will be able to better reflect their risk management activities using hedge accounting under the new model. This should facilitate an increased use of hedge accounting by preparers. In addition, because risk management can be better reflected, and as a result of enhanced disclosures, more relevant and transparent information will be provided to users of financial statements.

General

Summary of main changes from the Exposure Draft
Financial Instruments: Classification and Measurement

BCG.1 The main changes made by IFRS 9 issued in 2009 from the 2009 Exposure Draft *Financial Instruments: Classification and Measurement* (the '2009 Classification and Measurement Exposure Draft') were:

(a) IFRS 9 dealt with the classification and measurement of financial assets only, instead of financial assets and financial liabilities as proposed in the 2009 Classification and Measurement Exposure Draft.

(b) IFRS 9 requires entities to classify financial assets on the basis of the objective of the entity's business model for managing the financial assets and the characteristics of the contractual cash flows. It points out that the entity's business model should be considered first, and that the contractual cash flow characteristics should be considered only for financial assets that are eligible to be measured at amortised cost because of the business model. It states that both classification conditions are essential to ensure that amortised cost provides useful information.

(c) Additional application guidance was added on how to apply the conditions necessary for amortised cost measurement.

(d) IFRS 9 requires a 'look through' approach for investments in contractually linked instruments that effect concentrations of credit risk. The 2009 Classification and Measurement Exposure Draft had proposed that only the most senior tranche could have cash flows that represented payments of principal and interest on the principal amount outstanding.

(e) IFRS 9 requires (unless the fair value option is elected) financial assets purchased in the secondary market to be recognised at amortised cost if the instruments are managed within a business model that has an objective of collecting contractual cash flows and the financial asset has only contractual cash flows representing principal and interest on the principal amount outstanding even if such assets were acquired at a discount that reflects incurred credit losses.

(f) IFRS 9 requires that when an entity elects to present gains and losses on equity instruments measured at fair value in other comprehensive income, dividends are to be recognised in profit or loss. The 2009 Classification and Measurement Exposure Draft had proposed that those dividends would be recognised in other comprehensive income.

(g) IFRS 9 requires reclassifications between amortised cost and fair value classifications when the entity's business model changes. The 2009 Classification and Measurement Exposure Draft had proposed prohibiting reclassification.

(h) For entities that adopt IFRS 9 for reporting periods before 1 January 2012, IFRS 9 provides transition relief from restating comparative information.

(i) IFRS 9 requires additional disclosures for all entities when they first apply the Standard.

Summary of main changes from the Exposure Draft *Fair Value Option for Financial Liabilities*

BCG.2 The main changes from the 2010 Exposure Draft *Fair Value Option for Financial Liabilities* (the '2010 Own Credit Risk Exposure Draft') are:

(a) For liabilities designated under the fair value option, IFRS 9 requires an entity to present the effects of changes in the liability's credit risk in other comprehensive income unless that treatment would create or enlarge an accounting mismatch in profit or loss. If that treatment would create or enlarge an accounting mismatch in profit or loss, the entire fair value change is presented in profit or loss. That was the alternative approach set out in the 2010 Own Credit Risk Exposure Draft. The proposed approach in the 2010 Own Credit Risk Exposure Draft had treated all liabilities designated under the fair value option in the same way and had not addressed cases in which the proposed treatment would create or enlarge an accounting mismatch in profit or loss.

(b) IFRS 9 requires a 'one-step' approach for presenting the effects of changes in a liability's credit risk in the performance statement. That approach requires the effects of changes in a liability's credit risk to be presented directly in other comprehensive income, with the remaining amount of fair value change presented in profit or loss. The 2010 Own Credit Risk Exposure Draft had proposed a 'two-step' approach, which would have required the total fair value change to be presented in profit or loss. The effects of changes in a liability's credit risk would have been backed out and presented in other comprehensive income.

Dissenting opinions

Dissent of James J Leisenring from IFRS 9 *Financial Instruments* (issued 2009)

DO1 Mr Leisenring supports efforts to reduce the complexity of accounting for financial instruments. In that regard, he supports requiring all financial instruments to be measured at fair value, with that measurement being recognised in profit or loss. He finds no compelling reason related to improving financial reporting to reject that approach. It is an approach that maximises comparability and minimises complexity.

DO2 It maximises comparability because all financial instruments would be measured at one attribute within an entity and across entities. No measurement or presentation would change to reflect either arbitrary distinctions or management behaviour or intentions. IFRS 9 emphasises management intentions and behaviour, which substantially undermines comparability.

DO3 Complexity of accounting would be drastically reduced if all financial instruments were measured at fair value. The approach favoured by Mr Leisenring provides at least the following simplifications:

(a) no impairment model is necessary.

(b) criteria for when a given instrument must or can be measured with a given attribute are unnecessary.

(c) there is no need to bifurcate embedded derivatives or to identify financial derivatives.

(d) it eliminates the need for fair value hedge accounting for financial instruments.

(e) it eliminates the disparity in the measurement of derivatives within and outside the scope of IAS 39.

(f) it minimises the incentives for structuring transactions to achieve a particular accounting outcome.

(g) no fair value option would be needed to eliminate accounting mismatches.

(h) it provides a superior foundation for developing a comprehensive standard for the derecognition of financial instruments that is not present in a mixed attribute model.

DO4 Mr Leisenring accepts that measuring more instruments at fair value increases measurement complexity, but this increase is minimal compared with the reductions in complexity that would be otherwise achieved. There is no disagreement that derivatives must be measured at fair value. Those instruments raise the most difficult measurement issues, as cash instruments have many fewer problems. Indeed, some suggestions for an impairment model would measure at fair value the credit loss component of cash instruments. If that were to be the conclusion on impairment (an expected loss approach), it would minimise the incremental fair value measurement complexity of recording at fair value instruments now at amortised cost.

DO5   Mr Leisenring recognises that measuring all instruments at fair value through profit or loss raises presentation issues about disaggregation of fair value changes. However, he does not believe that these issues are insurmountable.

DO6   Investors have often told both the IASB and the FASB that fair value of financial instruments recognised in profit or loss provides the most useful information for their purposes. There is a worldwide demand for an improved and common solution to the accounting for financial instruments. Investors are disappointed that the Board will not take this opportunity to make, with other standard-setters, truly substantive changes rather than these minimal changes that perpetuate all the legitimate concerns that have been expressed about the mixed attribute model.

DO7   IFRS 9 does to some extent reduce complexity but that reduction is minimal. Certain measurement classifications are eliminated but others have been added. Mr Leisenring does not think that, on balance, this is an improvement over IAS 39.

DO8   Fundamental to IFRS 9 is the distinction between financial instruments measured at amortised cost and those at fair value. Mr Leisenring is concerned that neither of the two conditions necessary for that determination is operational. Paragraph BC4.86 criticises IAS 39 because the embedded derivative requirement of that Standard is based on a list of examples. However, the basic classification model of IFRS 9 is based on lists of examples in paragraphs B4.1.4, B4.1.13 and B4.1.14. The examples are helpful but are far from exhaustive of the issues that will be problematic in applying the two criteria for classification at amortised cost.

DO9   Mr Leisenring also thinks that the two criteria are inconsistently applied. When the objective of the entity's business model is to hold the assets to collect the contracted cash flows of an instrument there is no requirement that the entity must actually do so. The cash flow characteristics of the instrument are also ignored when the guidance is applied to investments in contractually linked instruments (tranches). In those circumstances the contractual cash flows of the instrument are ignored and one is required to look through to the composition of assets and liabilities of the issuing entity. This 'look through' requirement is also potentially complex and in Mr Leisenring's opinion is likely to be not very operational. Mr Leisenring also objects to eliminating the requirement to bifurcate derivatives embedded in cash instruments. This objection is primarily because of concern that the two criteria to qualify for amortised cost will not be operational. The pressure on those two conditions will be enormous because there will be an incentive to embed derivatives in a cash instrument in anticipation that the instrument might qualify for amortised cost. Derivatives should be at fair value whether embedded or standing alone and a bifurcation requirement would achieve that accounting. If Mr Leisenring were confident that the criteria for amortised cost could be applied as intended he would not be as concerned because instruments with embedded derivatives would be at fair value in their entirety.

DO10 Mr Leisenring is concerned that, in the current crisis, instruments that have provided some of the most significant losses when measured at fair value would be eligible for amortised cost. That conclusion is not responsive to the present environment. The approach also allows actively traded debt instruments, including treasury securities, to be at amortised cost. These results are unacceptable and reduce the usefulness of reported information for investors.

DO11 The Board is required by its *Framework*[54] to be neutral in its decision-making and to strive to produce neutral information to maximise the usefulness of financial information. IFRS 9 fails in that regard because it produces information based on free choice, management intention and management behaviour. Reporting that will result from this approach will not produce neutral information and diminishes the usefulness of financial reporting.

DO12 The Board is insistent in paragraph BC4.20 that accounting based on a business model is not free choice but never explains why selection of a business model is not a management choice. The existence of a trading account, a fair value option and the objective of a business model are all free choices.

DO13 The classification of selected equity instruments at fair value with the result of the remeasurement reported outside profit or loss is also a free choice. The Board concludes that reporting fair value changes in profit or loss may not reflect the operating performance of an entity. Mr Leisenring could accept accounting for changes in fair value of some instruments outside profit or loss in other comprehensive income. That accounting, however, should not be a free choice and why that presentation is superior in defined circumstances should be developed. In addition, when these securities are sold any realised gains and losses are not 'recycled' to profit or loss. That conclusion is inconsistent with the Board's conclusion that dividends received on these instruments should be reported in profit or loss. Such dividends would represent a return on investment or a form of 'recycling' of changes in the value of the instruments.

DO14 Mr Leisenring believes that a business model is rarely relevant in writing accounting standards. Identical transactions, rights and obligations should be accounted for in the same way if comparability of financial information is to be achieved. The result of applying IFRS 9 ignores any concern for comparability of financial information.

DO15 The credit crisis has provided confirmation that a drastic change in accounting for financial instruments is desirable. However, many have said that while they agree that the approach suggested by Mr Leisenring would be superior, and a significant improvement, the world is not ready to embrace such change. It is unclear to Mr Leisenring what factors need to be present for the optimal solution to be acceptable. He has concluded that it is hard to envisage circumstances that would make the case any more compelling for fundamental change and improvement than the present circumstances. Therefore, IFRS 9 will inevitably preserve a mixed attribute model and the resulting complexity for a significant period of time.

---

54 The reference to the *Framework* is to IASC's *Framework for the Preparation and Presentation of Financial Statements*, adopted by the IASB in 2001. In September 2010 the IASB replaced the *Framework* with the *Conceptual Framework for Financial Reporting*.

DO16 An objective of replacing IAS 39 was to provide a basis for convergence with accounting standards issued by the FASB. Mr Leisenring is concerned that IFRS 9 does not provide such a basis. As a consequence, allowing early adoption of the IFRS is undesirable. For convergence to be achieved significant changes in the IFRS are inevitable. Early adoption of the IFRS will therefore necessitate another costly accounting change when convergence is achieved. Permitting early adoption of this IFRS is also undesirable as it permits a lack of comparability in accounting for many years due to the deferred required effective date.

DO17 Mr Leisenring would accept that if, for reasons other than the desire to provide useful information to investors, his approach is politically unattainable, an alternative could be developed that would be operational. That approach would require all financial assets and financial liabilities to be recorded at fair value through profit or loss except originated loans retained by the originator, trade receivables and accounts payable. If certain derivatives were embedded in an instrument to be accounted for at amortised cost the derivative would be either bifurcated and accounted for at fair value or the entire instrument would be measured at fair value. Either approach would be acceptable.

Dissent of Patricia McConnell from IFRS 9 *Financial Instruments* (2009)

DO1 Ms McConnell believes that fair value is the most relevant and useful measurement attribute for financial assets. However, she acknowledges that many investors prefer not to measure all financial assets at fair value. Those investors believe that both amortised cost and fair value can provide useful information for particular kinds of financial assets in particular circumstances. Therefore, in order to meet the objective of developing high quality, global accounting standards that serve the interests of all investors, Ms McConnell believes that no single measurement attribute should have primacy over another. Thus any new IFRS setting classification and measurement principles for financial assets should require disclosure of sufficient information in the primary financial statements to permit determination of profit or loss and financial position using both amortised cost and fair value. For example, when a measurement attribute other than fair value is used for financial assets, information about fair value should be displayed prominently in the statement of financial position. The Board did not adopt such disclosure in IFRS 9, as discussed in paragraphs BC4.9–BC4.11 of the Board's Basis for Conclusions.

DO2 As stated in paragraph BC4.1, an objective of the Board in developing IFRS 9 was to reduce the number of classification categories for financial instruments. However, Ms McConnell believes that IFRS 9 has not accomplished that objective. IFRS 9 would permit or require the following categories: (1) amortised cost, (2) a fair value option through profit or loss for financial assets that qualify for amortised cost but for which amortised cost would create an accounting mismatch, (3) fair value through profit or loss for debt instruments that fail to qualify for amortised cost, (4) fair value though profit or loss for trading securities, (5) fair value through profit or loss for equity securities not held for trading and (6) fair value through other comprehensive income for equity investments not held for trading. Ms McConnell does not view those six categories as a significant improvement over the six categories in IAS 39; like the categories in IAS 39, they will hinder investors' understanding of an already complex area of financial reporting.

DO3   IFRS 9 sets out two criteria for measuring financial assets at amortised cost: (1) the way the entity manages its financial assets ('business model') and (2) the contractual cash flow characteristics of its financial assets. On the surface, this appears to be an improvement over IAS 39's criterion that was based on management's intention to trade, hold available for sale, hold to maturity, or hold for the foreseeable future. However, Ms McConnell finds it difficult to see how IFRS 9's criterion based on the objective of the entity's business model differs significantly from management's intention. In her opinion selection of a business model is a management choice, as is the decision to have a trading account, use the fair value option for debt instruments or the fair value option for equity instruments with gains and losses reported in other comprehensive income. In paragraphs BC4.20 and BC4.21 the Board argues that selection of a measurement method based on an entity's business model is not a free choice. Ms McConnell does not find the arguments persuasive.

DO4   IFRS 9 permits an entity to make an irrevocable election to present in other comprehensive income changes in the value of any investment in equity instruments that is not held for trading. Ms McConnell could accept accounting for changes in fair value of some instruments outside profit or loss in other comprehensive income. However, that treatment should not be a free choice; criteria for that presentation should be developed. In addition, the Board decided that when those securities are sold any realised gains and losses are not 'reclassified' to profit or loss. That conclusion is inconsistent with the Board's decision to report dividends received on these investments in profit or loss. Such dividends represent a return on investment or a form of 'reclassifying' changes in the value of the instruments.

DO5   In addition, Ms McConnell believes the 'look through' guidance for contractually linked investments (tranches) is an exception to one of the criteria necessary for applying amortised cost, namely the contractual cash flow characteristics of the instrument. In those circumstances the contractual cash flows of the instrument are ignored. Instead an entity is required to 'look through' to the underlying pool of instruments and assess their cash flow characteristics and credit risk relative to a direct investment in the underlying instruments. Ms McConnell believes that this provision adds complexity to the IFRS and reduces the usefulness of the reporting for financial assets. Moreover, since an entity is required to 'look through' only upon initial recognition of the financial asset, subsequent changes in the relative exposure to credit risk over the life of a structured investment vehicle would be ignored. Consequently, Ms McConnell believes it is possible that highly volatile investments, such as those owning sub-prime residential mortgage loans, would be reported at amortised cost.

Dissent of Patricia McConnell from *Mandatory Effective Date of IFRS 9 and Transition Disclosures* (Amendments to IFRS 9 (2009), IFRS 9 (2010) and IFRS 7)

DO1   Ms McConnell concurs with the Board's decision to defer the mandatory effective date of IFRS 9 (2009) and IFRS 9 (2010), but not with its decision to set a mandatory effective date of 1 January 2015. She agrees with the Board that there are compelling reasons for all project phases to be implemented at the same time and, therefore, that the mandatory application of all phases of the project to replace IAS 39 should occur concurrently. However, Ms McConnell does not believe that a mandatory effective date for IFRS 9 (2009) and IFRS 9 (2010) should be established until there is more clarity on the requirements and completion dates of the remaining phases of the project to replace IAS 39, including possible improvements to existing IFRS 9.

DO2   Ms McConnell commends the Board for requiring modified transition disclosures and acknowledges that the modified disclosures will provide useful information that will enable users of financial statements to better understand the transition from IAS 39 to IFRS 9, just as they would provide useful information when financial assets are reclassified in accordance with IFRS 9.

DO3   Although Ms McConnell believes that the modified disclosures are useful, she does not believe that they are an adequate substitute for restated comparative financial statements. Ms McConnell believes that comparative statements are vitally important to users of financial statements. To the extent that the accounting policies applied in comparative financial statements are comparable period-to-period, comparative financial statements enable users to more fully understand the effect of the accounting change on a company's statements of comprehensive income, financial position and cash flows.

DO4   Ms McConnell agrees with the Board that the date of initial application should be defined as a fixed date. In the absence of a fixed date, entities would have to go back to the initial recognition of each individual instrument for classification and measurement. This would be very burdensome, if not impossible. Moreover, particularly because reclassifications in accordance with IFRS 9 only occur (and are required) upon a change in business model for the related group of instruments, reclassifications should be very rare. Consequently, the expected benefit of not naming a fixed date of initial application would not exceed the costs.

DO5   However, Ms McConnell disagrees with defining the date of initial application as the date that an entity first applies this IFRS. She believes that the date of initial application should be defined as the beginning of the earliest period presented in accordance with IFRS 9. This date of initial application would enable entities to compile information in accordance with IFRS 9 while still preparing their external financial reports in accordance with IAS 39. Ms McConnell does not consider that there is a significant risk that entities would use hindsight when applying IFRS 9 to comparative periods prior to those financial statements being reported publicly in accordance with IFRS 9. She also notes that, although it would be costly for entities to prepare financial reporting information in accordance with an extra set of requirements during the comparative period (or periods), this would address concerns on the part of preparers that it is overly burdensome for them to compile information in accordance with IFRS 9 before the date of initial application has passed.

DO6   Ms McConnell acknowledges that defining the date of initial application as the beginning of the earliest date presented would delay the release of financial statements prepared in accordance with IFRS 9 for at least one year, or longer, if the date of initial application were set as she believes it should be. Delays would also result if the mandatory effective date of IFRS 9 was set so that entities could prepare more than one comparative period under IFRS 9 on the basis of requirements in many jurisdictions. Ms McConnell has also considered that it is costly for entities to prepare financial reporting information in accordance with an extra set of requirements during the comparative period (or periods). However, Ms McConnell believes that the benefits to users of financial statements of restated comparative financial statements justify the costs.

Dissent of Patrick Finnegan from the issue in November 2013 of IFRS 9 *Financial Instruments* ('IFRS 9 (2013)')

DO1   Mr Finnegan dissents from the issue of the amendments to IFRS 9 (2013) due to the addition of the requirements related to hedge accounting (Chapter 6 of IFRS 9).

DO2   Mr Finnegan dissents because he disagrees with the decision to provide entities with an accounting policy choice between applying the new hedge accounting requirements of IFRS 9 and retaining the existing hedge accounting requirements in IAS 39 until the completion of the project on the accounting for macro hedging. He believes that such an accounting policy choice combined with the existing approach of replacing IAS 39 in phases creates an unacceptable level of complexity and cost for both preparers and users of financial statements when accounting for financial instruments.

DO3   Mr Finnegan believes that a principal reason for the Board creating an option was to address the concerns of entities who believe that 'proxy hedging' (the use of designations of hedging relationships that do not exactly represent an entity's risk management) would be prohibited under IFRS 9. The Board has made it clear that this is not the case and, therefore, an option to continue to apply the hedge accounting requirements of IAS 39 creates the potential for the misunderstanding and misapplication of the new requirements in IFRS 9.

DO4   Mr Finnegan is concerned that the duration of the option to apply the new hedge accounting requirements is open-ended because it depends on the Board's ability to complete its project on the accounting for macro hedging. Consequently, the length of time that preparers and users of financial statements would be dealing with a variety of complex alternatives related to the accounting for financial instruments is also open-ended. Mr Finnegan believes that this outcome conflicts with the Board's stated goal of making timely improvements to simplify such accounting.

DO5   Mr Finnegan believes that the original goal of the Board to replace IAS 39 in phases was sound, given the initial expectation that a new comprehensive Standard would be completed expeditiously. However, the process of completing the three phases dealing with classification and measurement, impairment, and hedge accounting has proved to be thorny because of many complex and interrelated issues as well as its interaction with the project to create a new Standard for insurance contracts. In the light of that experience, Mr Finnegan believes that preparers and users of financial statements are better served by adopting a new IFRS dealing with all three phases simultaneously because it would involve substantially less cost and complexity and provide more useful information for users of financial statements.

DO6   Mr Finnegan believes that a principal reason for undertaking a fresh examination of the accounting for financial instruments was to achieve converged accounting with US GAAP. The IASB and the FASB are still examining ways of achieving convergence of the accounting for classification and measurement as well as impairment. Mr Finnegan believes that when a classification and measurement model is completed, a reporting entity may need to modify its application of the new requirements for hedge accounting, which would create unnecessary costs for such entities and additional complexity for users of financial statements in their analysis and use of financial statements.

Dissent of Stephen Cooper and Jan Engström from the issue in July 2014 of IFRS 9 *Financial Instruments* ('IFRS 9 (2014)')

DO1   Messrs Cooper and Engström dissent from the issue of IFRS 9 (2014) because of the limited amendments to the classification and measurement requirements for financial assets. They disagree with the introduction of the fair value through other comprehensive income measurement category. They believe that:

(a)   this additional measurement category unnecessarily increases the complexity for the reporting of financial instruments;

(b)   the distinction between the supposed different business models that justify measurement at fair value through other comprehensive income versus measurement at fair value through profit or loss is unclear and does not justify a difference in accounting treatment; and

(c)   faithful representation of insurance contracts in the financial statements does not need the fair value through other comprehensive income measurement category for (some) assets that back insurance liabilities.

DO2   Messrs Cooper and Engström believe that the requirements in IFRS 9 (issued in 2009), which classified financial assets at either amortised cost or fair value through profit or loss, are preferable and should have been retained. However, they support the clarifications to the hold to collect business model and the amendments to the contractual cash flow assessment in IFRS 9 (2014).

Increased complexity that is undesirable and unnecessary

DO3   One of IASB's main objectives for replacing IAS 39 with IFRS 9 is to reduce the complexity of accounting for financial instruments. An important component of that is to reduce the number of categories of financial instruments and the even larger number of different measurement and presentation methods in IAS 39. Interested parties widely supported this objective and Messrs Cooper and Engström believe that it had been achieved in the classification and measurement requirements that were issued in IFRS 9 in 2009. They consider that the introduction of a fair value through other comprehensive income measurement category reverses a significant part of this improvement in reporting.

DO4   Messrs Cooper and Engström believe that, when amortised cost is judged to be the most appropriate basis for reporting, this measurement attribute should be applied consistently throughout the financial statements. Likewise, if fair value provides more relevant information, it should be applied consistently. In their view the fair value through other comprehensive income measurement category provides a confusing mixture of amortised cost and fair value information that will make financial statements more complex and harder to understand. While they accept that in many cases fair value is an important additional piece of information for assets that are appropriately measured and reported at amortised cost, they believe that this fair value information should be provided as supplementary information in the notes, albeit with prominent and clear disclosure.

'A business model whose objective is achieved by both collecting contractual cash flows and selling financial assets' is not a distinct business model

DO5   The amendments are based on the assertion that there are distinct business models that justify accounting for qualifying debt instruments at either fair value through other comprehensive income or fair value through profit or loss. Messrs Cooper and Engström believe that, while the reasons for holding debt instruments outside a hold to collect business model can vary significantly, it is not possible to identify distinct business models or that these reasons justify different accounting. For example, managing assets with the objective of maximising the return on the portfolio through collecting contractual cash flows and opportunistic selling and reinvestment is given as an illustration of a business model whose objective is achieved by both collecting contractual cash flows and selling financial assets (see Example 5 in paragraph B4.1.4C of IFRS 9). However, measurement at fair value through profit or loss is required when assets are managed, and their performance is evaluated, on a 'fair value basis' with collection of contractual cash flows being incidental (see paragraph B4.1.6 of IFRS 9). Messrs Cooper and Engström believe that managing to maximise the return on the portfolio and managing on a fair value basis is a distinction without a difference and is not a valid justification for a very different accounting treatment.

DO6   Messrs Cooper and Engström believe that if fair value is indeed the most appropriate measurement basis then the full fair value change is relevant in assessing overall performance and should be presented within profit or loss. If a portfolio of debt instruments is, for example, managed with the objective of maximising return, then showing in profit or loss only amortised cost-based interest revenue, expected credit losses and realised value changes fails to provide a faithful representation of this economic activity. Furthermore, the use of fair value through other comprehensive income provides an entity with significant freedom to manage profit or loss simply through the selective sale of assets. While Messrs Cooper and Engström believe that all fair value changes should be reported in profit or loss if assets are measured at fair value, they observe that an entity is able to disaggregate fair value gains and losses to highlight particular components (such as the interest yield) if this helps to provide relevant information about performance.

The fair value through other comprehensive income measurement category does not achieve improvements to insurance contracts accounting

DO7   The IASB's decision to introduce the fair value through other comprehensive income measurement category is related to its tentative decision in the Insurance Contracts project that some changes in insurance contract liabilities (ie those arising from changes in the discount rate) would be recognised in other comprehensive income. Messrs Cooper and Engström believe that the use of other comprehensive income for insurance contracts combined with measurement at fair value through other comprehensive income for (some) financial assets that back insurance contract liabilities would lead to unnecessary complexity, a lack of transparency in insurance accounting, and would create opportunities for earnings management through selective realisation of gains or losses on the sale of financial assets and would not faithfully represent the performance of entities engaged in this activity. Accordingly, they believe that the introduction of the fair value through other comprehensive income measurement category in IFRS 9, combined with the use of other comprehensive income for some changes in insurance contract liabilities, will undermine the potential improvements in the quality of financial reporting by entities engaged in issuing insurance contracts that would otherwise result from the introduction of a new insurance contracts Standard.

Appendix A
Previous dissenting opinions

In 2003 and later some IASB members dissented from the issue of IAS 39 and subsequent amendments, and portions of their dissenting opinions relate to requirements that have been carried forward to IFRS 9. Those dissenting opinions are set out below.

Cross references that relate to the requirements that have been carried forward to IFRS 9 have been updated.

Dissent of Anthony T Cope, James J Leisenring and Warren J McGregor from the issue of IAS 39 in December 2003

DO1   Messrs Cope, Leisenring and McGregor dissent from the issue of this Standard.

DO2   Mr Leisenring dissents because he disagrees with the conclusions concerning derecognition, impairment of certain assets and the adoption of basis adjustment hedge accounting in certain circumstances.

DO3   The Standard requires in paragraphs 30 and 31 (now paragraphs 3.2.16 and 3.2.17 of IFRS 9) that to the extent of an entity's continuing involvement in an asset, a liability should be recognised for the consideration received. Mr Leisenring believes that the result of that accounting is to recognise assets that fail to meet the definition of assets and to record liabilities that fail to meet the definition of liabilities. Furthermore, the Standard fails to recognise forward contracts, puts or call options and guarantees that are created, but instead records a fictitious 'borrowing' as a result of rights and obligations created by those contracts. There are other consequences of the continuing involvement approach that has been adopted. For transferors, it results in very different accounting by two entities when they have identical contractual rights and obligations only because one entity once owned the transferred financial asset. Furthermore, the 'borrowing' that is recognised is not accounted for like other loans, so no interest expense may be recorded. Indeed, implementing the proposed approach requires the specific override of measurement and presentation standards applicable to other similar financial instruments that do not arise from derecognition transactions. For example, derivatives created by derecognition transactions are not accounted for at fair value. For transferees, the approach also requires the override of the recognition and measurement requirements applicable to other similar financial instruments. If an instrument is acquired in a transfer transaction that fails the derecognition criteria, the transferee recognises and measures it differently from an instrument that is acquired from the same counterparty separately.

DO4   Mr Leisenring also disagrees with the requirement in paragraph 64 to include an asset that has been individually judged not to be impaired in a portfolio of similar assets for an additional portfolio assessment of impairment. Once an asset is judged not to be impaired, it is irrelevant whether the entity owns one or more similar assets as those assets have no implications for whether the asset that was individually considered for impairment is or is not impaired. The result of this accounting is that two entities could each own 50 per cent of a single loan. Both entities could conclude the loan is not impaired. However, if one of the two entities happens to have other loans that are similar, it would be allowed to recognise an impairment with respect to the loan where the other entity is not. Accounting for identical exposures differently is unacceptable. Mr Leisenring believes that the arguments in paragraph BC115 are compelling.

DO5   Mr Leisenring also dissents from paragraph 98 which allows but does not require basis adjustment for hedges of forecast transactions that result in the recognition of non-financial assets or liabilities. This accounting results in always adjusting the recorded asset or liability at the date of initial recognition away from its fair value. It also records an asset, if the basis adjustment alternative is selected, at an amount other than its cost as defined in IAS 16 *Property, Plant and Equipment* and further described in paragraph 16 of that Standard. If a derivative were to be considered a part of the cost of acquiring an asset, hedge accounting in these circumstances should not be elective to be consistent with IAS 16. Mr Leisenring also objects to creating this alternative as a result of an improvement project that ostensibly had as an objective the reduction of alternatives. The non-comparability that results from this alternative is both undesirable and unnecessary.

DO6   Mr Leisenring also dissents from the application guidance in paragraph AG71[55] and in particular the conclusion contained in paragraph BC98. He does not believe that an entity that originates a contract in one market should measure the fair value of the contract by reference to a different market in which the transaction did not take place. If prices change in the transacting market, that price change should be recognised when subsequently measuring the fair value of the contract. However, there are many implications of switching between markets when measuring fair value that the Board has not yet addressed. Mr Leisenring believes a gain or loss should not be recognised based on the fact a transaction could occur in a different market.

DO7   Mr Cope dissents from paragraph 64 and agrees with Mr Leisenring's analysis and conclusions on loan impairment as set out above in paragraph DO4. He finds it counter-intuitive that a loan that has been determined not to be impaired following careful analysis should be subsequently accounted for as if it were impaired when included in a portfolio.

DO8   Mr Cope also dissents from paragraph 98, and, in particular, the Board's decision to allow a free choice over whether basis adjustment is used when accounting for hedges of forecast transactions that result in the recognition of non-financial assets or non-financial liabilities. In his view, of the three courses of action open to the Board—retaining IAS 39's requirement to use basis adjustment, prohibiting basis adjustment as proposed in the June 2002 Exposure Draft,[56] or providing a choice—the Board has selected the worst course. Mr Cope believes that the best approach would have been to prohibit basis adjustment, as proposed in the Exposure Draft, because, in his opinion, basis adjustments result in the recognition of assets and liabilities at inappropriate amounts.

---

55 IFRS 13 *Fair Value Measurement*, issued in May 2011, now contains the requirements for measuring fair value.

56 Exposure Draft *Proposed Amendments to IAS 32, Financial Instruments: Disclosure and Presentation, and IAS 39, Financial Instruments: Recognition and Measurement*.

DO9   Mr Cope believes that increasing the number of choices in international standards is bad policy. The Board's decision potentially creates major differences between entities choosing one option and those choosing the other. This lack of comparability will adversely affect users' ability to make sound economic decisions.

DO10   In addition, Mr Cope notes that entities that are US registrants may choose not to adopt basis adjustment in order to avoid a large reconciling difference to US GAAP. Mr Cope believes that increasing differences between IFRS-compliant entities that are US registrants and those that are not is undesirable.

DO11   Mr McGregor dissents from paragraph 98 and agrees with Mr Cope's and Mr Leisenring's analyses and conclusions as set out above in paragraphs DO5 and DO8–DO10.

DO12   Mr McGregor also dissents from this Standard because he disagrees with the conclusions about impairment of certain assets.

DO13   Mr McGregor disagrees with paragraphs 67 and 69, which deal with the impairment of equity investments classified as available for sale. These paragraphs require impairment losses on such assets to be recognised in profit or loss when there is objective evidence that the asset is impaired. Previously recognised impairment losses are not to be reversed through profit and loss when the assets' fair value increases. Mr McGregor notes that the Board's reasoning for prohibiting reversals through profit or loss of previously impaired available-for-sale equity investments, set out in paragraph BC130 of the Basis for Conclusions, is that it '... could not find an acceptable way to distinguish reversals of impairment losses from other increases in fair value'. He agrees with this reasoning but believes that it applies equally to the recognition of impairment losses in the first place. Mr McGregor believes that the significant subjectivity involved in assessing whether a reduction in fair value represents an impairment (and thus should be recognised in profit or loss) or another decrease in value (and should be recognised directly in equity) will at best lead to a lack of comparability within an entity over time and between entities, and at worst provide an opportunity for entities to manage reported profit or loss.

DO14   Mr McGregor believes that all changes in the fair value of assets classified as available for sale should be recognised in profit or loss. However, such a major change to the Standard would need to be subject to the Board's full due process. At this time, to overcome the concerns expressed in paragraph DO13, he believes that for equity investments classified as available for sale, the Standard should require all changes in fair value below cost to be recognised in profit or loss as impairments and reversals of impairments and all changes in value above cost to be recognised in equity. This approach treats all changes in value the same way, no matter what their cause. The problem of how to distinguish an impairment loss from another decline in value (and of deciding whether there is an impairment in the first place) is eliminated because there is no longer any subjectivity involved. In addition, the approach is consistent with IAS 16 *Property, Plant and Equipment* and IAS 38 *Intangible Assets*.

DO15   Mr McGregor disagrees with paragraph 106 of the Standard and with the consequential amendments to paragraph 27[57] of IFRS 1 *First-time Adoption of International Financial Reporting Standards*. Paragraph 106 requires entities to apply the derecognition provisions prospectively to financial assets. Paragraph 27 of IFRS 1 requires first-time adopters to apply the derecognition provisions of IAS 39 (as revised in 2003) prospectively to non-derivative financial assets and financial liabilities. Mr McGregor believes that existing IAS 39 appliers should apply the derecognition provisions retrospectively to financial assets, and that first-time adopters should apply the derecognition provisions of IAS 39 retrospectively to all financial assets and financial liabilities. He is concerned that financial assets may have been derecognised under the original IAS 39 by entities that were subject to it, which might not have been derecognised under the revised IAS 39. He is also concerned that non-derivative financial assets and financial liabilities may have been derecognised by first-time adopters under previous GAAP that would not have been derecognised under the revised IAS 39. These amounts may be significant in many cases. Not requiring recognition of such amounts will result in the loss of relevant information and will impair the ability of users of financial statements to make sound economic decisions.

Dissent of Mary E Barth, Robert P Garnett and Geoffrey Whittington from the issue in June 2005 of *The Fair Value Option* (Amendment to IAS 39)

DO1   Professor Barth, Mr Garnett and Professor Whittington dissent from the amendment to IAS 39 *Financial Instruments: Recognition and Measurement—The Fair Value Option*. Their dissenting opinions are set out below.

DO2   These Board members note that the Board considered the concerns expressed by the prudential supervisors on the fair value option as set out in the December 2003 version of IAS 39 when it finalised IAS 39. At that time the Board concluded that these concerns were outweighed by the benefits, in terms of simplifying the practical application of IAS 39 and providing relevant information to users of financial statements, that result from allowing the fair value option to be used for any financial asset or financial liability. In the view of these Board members, no substantive new arguments have been raised that would cause them to revisit this conclusion. Furthermore, the majority of constituents have clearly expressed a preference for the fair value option as set out in the December 2003 version of IAS 39 over the fair value option as contained in the amendment.

DO3   Those Board members note that the amendment introduces a series of complex rules, including those governing transition which would be entirely unnecessary in the absence of the amendment. There will be consequential costs to preparers of financial statements, in order to obtain, in many circumstances, substantially the same result as the much simpler and more easily understood fair value option that was included in the December 2003 version of IAS 39. They believe that the complex rules will also inevitably lead to differing interpretations of the eligibility criteria for the fair value option contained in the amendment.

---

57   As a result of the revision of IFRS 1 in November 2008, paragraph 27 became paragraph B2.

DO4   These Board members also note that, for paragraph 9(b)(i) (now paragraphs 4.1.5 and 4.2.2(a) of IFRS 9), application of the amendment may not mitigate, on an ongoing basis, the anomaly of volatility in profit or loss that results from the different measurement attributes in IAS 39 any more than would the option in the December 2003 version of IAS 39. This is because the fair value designation is required to be continued even if one of the offsetting instruments is derecognised. Furthermore, for paragraphs 9(b)(i), 9(b)(ii) and 11A (now paragraphs 4.1.5, 4.2.2 and 4.3.5 of IFRS 9), the fair value designation continues to apply in subsequent periods, irrespective of whether the initial conditions that permitted the use of the option still hold. Therefore, these Board members question the purpose of and need for requiring the criteria to be met at initial designation.

Appendix B
Amendments to the Basis for Conclusions on other Standards

The amendments in this appendix to the Basis for Conclusions on other Standards are necessary in order to ensure consistency with IFRS 9 and the related amendments to other Standards.

* * * * *

The amendments contained in this appendix when IFRS 9 was issued in 2014 have been incorporated into the Basis for Conclusions on the relevant Standards included in this volume.

IASB documents published to accompany

IFRS 10

Consolidated Financial Statements

The text of the unaccompanied standard, IFRS 10, is contained in Part A of this edition. Its effective date when issued was 1 January 2013. The text of the Accompanying Guidance on IFRS 10 is contained in Part B of this edition. This part presents the following documents:

BASIS FOR CONCLUSIONS

APPENDICES TO THE BASIS FOR CONCLUSIONS
Previous Board approvals and dissenting opinions
Amendments to the Basis for Conclusions on other IFRSs

CONTENTS

Basis for Conclusions on
IFRS 10 *Consolidated Financial Statements*

This Basis for Conclusions accompanies, but is not part of, IFRS 10.

Introduction

BC1   This Basis for Conclusions summarises the International Accounting Standards Board's considerations in developing IFRS 10 *Consolidated Financial Statements*. Individual Board members gave greater weight to some factors than to others. Unless otherwise stated, any reference below to IAS 27 is to IAS 27 *Consolidated and Separate Financial Statements*, and to IAS 28 is to IAS 28 *Investments in Associates*.

BC2   The Board added a project on consolidation to its agenda to deal with divergence in practice in applying IAS 27 and SIC-12 *Consolidation—Special Purpose Entities*. For example, entities varied in their application of the control concept:

(a)   in circumstances in which an investor controls an investee but the investor has less than a majority of the voting rights of the investee (and voting rights are clearly the basis for control).

(b)   in circumstances involving special purpose entities (to which the notion of 'economic substance' in SIC-12 applied).

(c)   in circumstances involving agency relationships.

(d)   in circumstances involving protective rights.

BC3   IAS 27 required the consolidation of entities that are controlled by a reporting entity, and it defined control as the power to govern the financial and operating policies of an entity so as to obtain benefits from its activities. SIC-12, which interpreted the requirements of IAS 27 in the context of special purpose entities,[1] placed greater emphasis on risks and rewards. This perceived conflict of emphasis had led to inconsistent application of the concept of control. This was aggravated by a lack of clear guidance on which investees were within the scope of IAS 27 and which were within the scope of SIC-12. As a result, assessing control sometimes resulted in a quantitative assessment of whether the investor had a majority of the risks. Such tests based on sharp 'bright line' distinctions created structuring opportunities to achieve particular accounting outcomes.

BC4   The global financial crisis that started in 2007 highlighted a lack of transparency about the risks to which investors were exposed from their involvement with 'off balance sheet vehicles' (such as securitisation vehicles), including those that they had set up or sponsored. As a result, the G20 leaders, the Financial Stability

---

1   To maintain consistency with the terminology used in the original documents this Basis for Conclusions refers to 'special purpose entities (SPEs)' when discussing SIC-12 and 'structured entities' when discussing the exposure draft ED 10 *Consolidated Financial Statements* and the related deliberations and redeliberations. SIC-12 described an SPE as an entity that may be created to accomplish a narrow and well-defined objective, often created with legal arrangements that impose strict and sometimes permanent limits on the decision-making powers of its governing board, trustee or management over the SPE's operations. ED 10 defined a structured entity as an entity whose activities are restricted to the extent that those activities are, in essence, not directed by voting or similar rights.

Board and others asked the Board to review the accounting and disclosure requirements for such 'off balance sheet vehicles'.

BC5 In developing IFRS 10, the Board considered the responses to ED 10 *Consolidated Financial Statements*, published in December 2008. Respondents to ED 10 pointed out that the Board and the US Financial Accounting Standards Board (FASB), in their Memorandum of Understanding, had agreed to work towards developing common standards on consolidation by 2011. Therefore, they asked the boards to discuss the consolidation project jointly to ensure that the ensuing standards contained identical, not only similar, requirements. As a result, the Board's deliberations in developing IFRS 10 were conducted jointly with the FASB from October 2009.

BC6 The FASB decided in January 2011 that it would not change the consolidation requirements in US generally accepted accounting principles (GAAP) at this time with one exception. The FASB tentatively decided that it would propose changes to the consolidation requirements relating to both variable interest entities and voting interest entities in the context of assessing whether a decision maker is a principal or an agent. Those proposals would be similar to the requirements developed jointly by the IASB and the FASB regarding the principal/agent assessment, which are included in IFRS 10.

BC7 ED 10 proposed disclosure requirements for consolidated and unconsolidated investees. In its deliberation of the responses to those proposals, the Board decided to combine the disclosure requirements for interests in subsidiaries, joint arrangements, associates and unconsolidated structured entities within a single comprehensive standard, IFRS 12 *Disclosure of Interests in Other Entities*. The Basis for Conclusions accompanying IFRS 12 summarises the Board's considerations in developing that IFRS, including its consideration of responses to the disclosure proposals in ED 10. Accordingly, IFRS 10 does not include disclosure requirements and this Basis for Conclusions does not describe the Board's consideration of responses to the proposed disclosure requirements in ED 10.

The structure of IFRS 10 and the Board's decisions

BC8 IFRS 10 replaces the requirements and guidance in IAS 27 relating to consolidated financial statements. It also replaces SIC-12. As part of its consolidation project, the Board is examining how an investment entity accounts for its interests in subsidiaries, joint ventures and associates and what, if any, additional disclosures might be made about those interests. The Board expects to publish an exposure draft on investment entities later in 2011.[2]

BC9 In developing IFRS 10, the Board did not reconsider all the requirements that are included in the IFRS. The scope in paragraph 4 and the accounting requirements for consolidated financial statements in paragraphs 19–25 and

---

2 *Investment Entities* (Amendments to IFRS 10, IFRS 12 and IAS 27), issued in October 2012, introduced an exception to the principle that all subsidiaries shall be consolidated. The amendments define an investment entity and require a parent that is an investment entity to measure its investments in particular subsidiaries at fair value through profit or loss instead of consolidating those subsidiaries. These amendments are discussed in paragraphs BC215–BC317.

B86–B99 were carried forward from IAS 27 or SIC-12 to IFRS 10 without being reconsidered by the Board because their reconsideration was not part of the Board's consolidation project.

BC10 When revised in 2003, IAS 27 was accompanied by a Basis for Conclusions summarising the considerations of the Board, as constituted at the time, in reaching some of its conclusions in that Standard. That Basis for Conclusions was subsequently updated to reflect amendments to the Standard. The Board has incorporated into this Basis for Conclusions material from the Basis for Conclusions on IAS 27 that discusses matters that the Board has not reconsidered. That material is contained in paragraphs denoted by numbers with the prefix BCZ. In those paragraphs cross-references to the IFRS have been updated accordingly and minor necessary editorial changes have been made.

BC11 In order to portray the historical background of IFRS 10, the documents recording the Board's approval of the revision of IAS 27 in 2003 and the subsequent amendments are set out after this Basis for Conclusions. In addition, in 2003 and later, some Board members dissented from the revision of IAS 27 and subsequent amendments, and portions of their dissenting opinions relate to requirements that have been carried forward to IFRS 10. Those dissenting opinions are set out after the Basis for Conclusions.

Presentation of consolidated financial statements (2003 revision)

Exemption from preparing consolidated financial statements

BCZ12 Paragraph 7 of IAS 27 (as revised in 2000) required consolidated financial statements to be presented. However, paragraph 8 permitted a parent that was a wholly-owned or virtually wholly-owned subsidiary not to prepare consolidated financial statements. In 2003 the Board considered whether to withdraw or amend this exemption from the general requirement.

BCZ13 The Board decided to retain an exemption, so that entities in a group that are required by law to produce financial statements available for public use in accordance with International Financial Reporting Standards, in addition to consolidated financial statements, would not be unduly burdened.

BCZ14 The Board noted that in some circumstances users can find sufficient information for their purposes about a subsidiary from either its separate financial statements or the consolidated financial statements. In addition, the users of financial statements of a subsidiary often have, or can get access to, more information.

BCZ15 Having concluded that it should retain an exemption, the Board decided to modify the circumstances in which an entity would be exempt and considered the following criteria.

Unanimous agreement of the owners of the minority interests[3]

BCZ16   The 2002 exposure draft proposed to extend the exemption to a parent that is not wholly-owned if the owners of the minority interests, including those not otherwise entitled to vote, unanimously agree.

BCZ17   Some respondents disagreed with this proposal, largely because of the practical difficulties in obtaining responses from all the minority shareholders. Acknowledging this argument, the Board decided that the exemption should be available to a parent that is not wholly-owned when the owners of the minority interests have been informed about, and do not object to, consolidated financial statements not being presented.

Exemption available only to non-public entities

BCZ18   The Board believed that the information needs of users of financial statements of entities whose debt or equity instruments are traded in a public market were best served when investments in subsidiaries, jointly controlled entities and associates were accounted for in accordance with IAS 27, IAS 28 and IAS 31 *Interests in Joint Ventures*.[4] It therefore decided that the exemption from preparing consolidated financial statements should not be available to such entities or to entities in the process of issuing instruments in a public market.

Scope of consolidated financial statements (2003 revision)

Scope exclusions

BCZ19   Paragraph 13 of IAS 27 (as revised in 2000) required a subsidiary to be excluded from consolidation when control is intended to be temporary or when the subsidiary operates under severe long-term restrictions.

Temporary control

BCZ20   In 2003 the Board considered whether to remove this scope exclusion and thereby converge with other standard-setters that had recently eliminated a similar exclusion.   It decided to consider this question as part of a comprehensive standard dealing with asset disposals. It decided to retain an exemption from consolidating a subsidiary when there is evidence that the subsidiary is acquired with the intention of disposing of it within twelve months and that management is actively seeking a buyer. The Board's exposure draft ED 4 *Disposal of Non-current Assets and Presentation of Discontinued Operations* proposed to measure and present assets held for sale in a consistent manner irrespective of whether they are held by an investor or in a subsidiary. Therefore, ED 4 proposed to eliminate the exemption from consolidation when control is intended to be temporary and it contained a draft consequential amendment to IAS 27 to achieve this.[5]

---

3   IAS 27 (as amended in 2008) changed the term 'minority interest' to 'non-controlling interest'.
4   IAS 31 was superseded by IFRS 11 *Joint Arrangements* issued in May 2011.
5   In March 2004 the Board issued IFRS 5 *Non-current Assets Held for Sale and Discontinued Operations*. IFRS 5 removed this scope exclusion and eliminated the exemption from consolidation when control is intended to be temporary. For further discussion see the Basis for Conclusions on IFRS 5.

Severe long-term restrictions impairing ability to transfer funds to the parent

BCZ21   The Board decided to remove the exclusion of a subsidiary from consolidation when there are severe long-term restrictions that impair a subsidiary's ability to transfer funds to the parent. It did so because such circumstances may not preclude control. The Board decided that a parent, when assessing its ability to control a subsidiary, should consider restrictions on the transfer of funds from the subsidiary to the parent. In themselves, such restrictions do not preclude control.

BCZ22–   [Deleted]
BCZ28

Exemption from preparing consolidated financial statements for an intermediate parent of an investment entity

BC28A   In December 2014, the Board amended IFRS 10 to confirm that the exemption from preparing consolidated financial statements set out in paragraph 4(a) of IFRS 10 is available to a parent entity that is a subsidiary of an investment entity. This question came about because an investment entity may measure all of its subsidiaries at fair value through profit or loss in accordance with paragraph 31 of IFRS 10. This decision was consistent with the proposal in the Exposure Draft *Investment Entities: Applying the Consolidation Exception* (Proposed amendments to IFRS 10 and IAS 28), which was published in June 2014.

BC28B   Paragraph 4(a)(iv) of IFRS 10, which is one of the criteria for the exemption from preparing consolidated financial statements, previously specified the requirement that the entity's ultimate or any intermediate parent 'produces consolidated financial statements that are available for public use and comply with IFRSs.' The IFRS Interpretations Committee was asked whether the exemption set out in paragraph 4(a) was available to a parent entity that is a subsidiary of an ultimate, or any intermediate, investment entity parent, if the conditions set out in paragraph 4(a)(i)–(iii) are met, but the investment entity parent does not consolidate any of its subsidiaries. Instead, the investment entity parent prepares financial statements in which all of its subsidiaries are measured at fair value through profit or loss in accordance with paragraph 31 of IFRS 10.

BC28C   The Board observed that the exemption for intermediate parent entities was provided because the cost of requiring each intermediate parent entity within a group to prepare consolidated financial statements would outweigh the benefits in cases in which the conditions in paragraph 4(a) of IFRS 10 are met. The Board had previously decided that the conditions in paragraph 4(a) provide safeguards for the users of the intermediate parent's financial statements. In addition, the Board noted that the combination of information available in the consolidated financial statements of the higher level parent and the separate financial statements of the intermediate parent entity provide useful information to users.

BC28D   The Board additionally observed that, when an investment entity measures its interest in a subsidiary at fair value, the disclosures required by IFRS 12 are supplemented by those required in IFRS 7 *Financial Instruments: Disclosures* and

IFRS 13 *Fair Value Measurement*. Accordingly, the Board decided that this combination of information is sufficient to support the decision to retain the existing exemption from presenting consolidated financial statements for a subsidiary of an investment entity that is itself a parent entity. The Board noted that requiring an intermediate parent that is a subsidiary of an investment entity to prepare consolidated financial statements could result in significant additional costs, without commensurate benefit. The Board noted that this would be contrary to its intention in requiring investment entities to measure investments at fair value, which was to provide more relevant information at a reduced cost, as described in paragraphs BC309 and BC314 of IFRS 10.

BC28E   The Board also decided to amend paragraph 17 of IAS 28 *Investments in Associates and Joint Ventures* for the same reasons. Paragraph 17 of IAS 28 uses the same criteria as paragraph 4(a) of IFRS 10 to provide an exemption from applying the equity method for entities that are subsidiaries and that hold interests in associates and joint ventures.

BC28F   Furthermore, the Board decided to amend paragraph 6(b) of IFRS 12 to clarify that the relevant disclosure requirements in IFRS 12 apply to an investment entity. Paragraph 6 of IFRS 12 previously stated that IFRS 12 did not apply to an entity's separate financial statements without stating the applicability of IFRS 12 to investment entities. The Board decided to clarify that this scope exclusion does not apply to the financial statements of a parent that is an investment entity and has measured all of its subsidiaries at fair value through profit or loss in accordance with paragraph 31 of IFRS 10. In such cases, the investment entity shall present the disclosures relating to investment entities required by IFRS 12.

Control as the basis for consolidation

BC29   The Board's objective in issuing IFRS 10 is to improve the usefulness of consolidated financial statements by developing a single basis for consolidation and robust guidance for applying that basis to situations where it has proved difficult to assess control in practice and divergence has evolved (see paragraphs BC2–BC4). The basis for consolidation is control and it is applied irrespective of the nature of the investee.

BC30   Almost all respondents to ED 10 supported control as the basis for consolidation. However, some noted that it can be difficult to identify an investor that has power over investees that do not require substantive continuous decision-making. They suggested that exposure to risks and rewards should be used as a proxy for control when power is not evident. Some respondents were also concerned that applying the proposed control definition to all investees could lead to more structuring opportunities than was the case when applying the requirements in IAS 27 and SIC-12. Others did not think that ED 10 expressed with sufficient clarity the importance of risks and rewards when assessing control.

BC31   The Board confirmed its view that control should be the only basis for consolidation—an investor should consolidate an investee and present in its consolidated financial statements the investee's assets, liabilities, equity, income, expenses and cash flows, if the investor has the current ability to direct those activities of the investee that significantly affect the investee's returns and can benefit by using that ability. An investor that is exposed, or has rights, to variable returns from its involvement with an investee but does not have power over the investee so as to affect the amount of the investor's return from its involvement does not control the investee.

BC32   Control as the basis for consolidation does not mean that the consideration of risks and rewards is unimportant when assessing control of an investee. The more an investor is exposed to risks and rewards from its involvement with an investee, the greater the incentive for the investor to obtain decision-making rights that give it power. However, risks and rewards and power are not necessarily perfectly correlated. Therefore, the Board confirmed that exposure to risks and rewards (referred to in IFRS 10 as variable returns) is an *indicator of control* and an important factor to consider when assessing control, but an investor's exposure to risks and rewards alone does not determine that the investor has control over an investee.

BC33   The Board observed that to conclude that exposure to risks and rewards is anything more than an indicator of control would be inconsistent with a control model that contains both a power element and a returns element.

BC34   The Board confirmed that an investor must have exposure to risks and rewards in order to control an investee—without any exposure to risks and rewards (ie variable returns) an investor is unable to benefit from any power that it might have and therefore cannot control an investee.

BC35   In reaching its conclusions regarding control as the basis for consolidation, the Board also noted the following:

(a)   One of the main objectives of the consolidation project is to develop a consistent basis for determining when an investor should consolidate an investee, irrespective of the nature of the investee. Some respondents to ED 10 suggested including a particular level of exposure to risks and rewards as a presumption of, or proxy for, control, in the context of investees that are not directed through voting or similar rights. The Board concluded that introducing such a presumption for a particular set of investees would contradict the objective of developing a single consistent basis for consolidation that applies to all investees.

(b)   Having a different consolidation model for some investees necessitates defining precisely those investees to which that model applies. There have been difficulties, in practice, in identifying which investees are special purpose entities to which SIC-12 applied. A number of respondents to ED 10 noted that any attempt to split the continuum of investee types into distinct populations and to subject the different populations of entities to different consolidation models would lead to divergence in practice for investees that are not clearly in the specified population sets. For that reason, the Board decided not to carry forward the distinction proposed in ED 10 between different types of investees when assessing control (see paragraphs BC71–BC75).

(c) Including exposure to risks and rewards as a presumption of, or proxy for, control in particular situations puts more pressure on the measurement of that exposure. The Board was particularly concerned that the need to measure risks and rewards might result in the adoption of a consolidation model based on quantitative criteria (for example, a model focused on the majority of risks and rewards). Any quantitative analysis of risks and rewards would inevitably be complex and, as a consequence, difficult to understand, apply and audit. The Board noted that, depending on the specific facts and circumstances, a quantitative model might identify a controlling party that is different from the party that a qualitative analysis of the power over, and returns from, an investee would identify as the controlling party. The Board's analysis is consistent with concerns raised by the FASB's constituents on the quantitative consolidation model in Interpretation 46 (Revised) *Consolidation of Variable Interest Entities*. The FASB has since issued Statement of Financial Accounting Standard No. 167 *Amendments to FIN 46 (Revised)* to amend Interpretation 46 to require a qualitative analysis focusing on the power over and returns from an investee to determine control.[6]

(d) The Board believes that having a control model that applies to all investees is likely to reduce the opportunities for achieving a particular accounting outcome that is inconsistent with the economics of an investor's relationship with an investee—ie it will reduce structuring opportunities.

BC36 The Board does not regard control and risks and rewards as competing models. The exposure to risks and rewards, or variable returns as it is expressed in IFRS 10, is an essential element of control. In the great majority of cases the approaches would lead to the same accounting conclusions. However, a control-based model forces an investor to consider all its rights in relation to the investee rather than relying on arbitrary bright lines that are associated with risks and rewards approaches, such as paragraph 10(c) and (d) of SIC-12, which referred to control if the investor has rights to obtain the majority of the benefits of the investee or if the investor retains the majority of the risks related to the investee. The Board believes that an investor will, generally, want to control an investee when it has significant economic exposure. This should reduce the likelihood of structuring simply to achieve a particular accounting outcome.

Reputational risk

BC37 During the financial crisis, some financial institutions provided funding or other support to securitisation or investment vehicles because they established or promoted those vehicles. Rather than allowing them to fail and facing a loss of reputation, the financial institutions stepped in, and in some cases took control of the vehicles. ED 10 did not make any explicit reference to reputational risk in relation to control because the Board decided that having

---

6 SFAS 167 was subsequently nullified by Accounting Standards Update No. 2009-17. The requirements of SFAS 167 have been included in Accounting Standards Update No. 2009-17.

reputational risk in isolation is not an appropriate basis for consolidation. The term 'reputational risk' relates to the risk that failure of an investee would damage an investee's reputation and, therefore, that of an investor or sponsor, compelling the investor or sponsor to provide support to an investee in order to protect its reputation, even though the investor or sponsor has no legal or contractual requirement to do so.

BC38   Respondents to ED 10 agreed with the Board, almost unanimously, that reputational risk is not an appropriate basis for consolidation. Some, however, were of the view that reputational risk is part of an investor's exposure to risks and rewards and should be considered when determining control of an investee.

BC39   The Board believes that reputational risk is part of an investor's exposure to risks and rewards, albeit a risk that arises from non-contractual sources. For that reason, the Board concluded that when assessing control, reputational risk is a factor to consider along with other facts and circumstances. It is not an indicator of power in its own right, but may increase an investor's incentive to secure rights that give the investor power over an investee.

Definition of control

BC40   IFRS 10 states that an investor controls an investee when the investor is exposed, or has rights, to variable returns from its involvement with the investee and has the current ability to affect those returns through its power over the investee.

BC41   The definition of control includes three elements, namely an investor's:

(a)   power over the investee;

(b)   exposure, or rights, to variable returns from its involvement with the investee; and

(c)   ability to use its power over the investee to affect the amount of the investor's returns.

Power

BC42   ED 10 proposed that in order to control an investee, an investor must have the power to direct the activities of that investee. IAS 27 defines control as the power to govern the financial and operating policies of an entity. The Board decided to change the definition of control because even though power is often obtained by governing the strategic operating and financing policies of an investee, that is only one of the ways in which power to direct the activities of an investee can be achieved. An investor can have the power to direct the activities of an investee through decision-making rights that relate to particular activities of an investee. Indeed, referring to the power to govern the financial and operating policies of an investee would not necessarily apply to investees that are not directed through voting or similar rights.

BC43   Respondents to ED 10 did not object to changing the definition of control to power to direct the activities of an investee. Many were confused, however, about what the Board meant by 'power to direct' and which 'activities' the Board had in mind. They asked for a clear articulation of the principle behind the term 'power to direct'. They also expressed the view that power should relate to significant activities of an investee, and not those activities that have little effect on the investee's returns.

BC44 ED 10 described various characteristics of power—power need not be absolute; power need not have been exercised; power precludes others from controlling an investee. ED 10 also implied that power could arise from rights that appeared to be exercisable only at some point in the future when particular circumstances arise or events happen. Respondents to ED 10 were confused about whether power referred to the legal or contractual power to direct, or to the ability to direct, which does not necessarily require the investor to have the legal or contractual right to direct the activities. Some respondents to ED 10 also commented that the statement that power precludes others from controlling an investee was confusing because it implied that an investor with less than a majority of the voting rights in an investee could never have power.

BC45 In response to the comments from respondents, the Board considered whether power should refer to having the *legal* or *contractual right* to direct the activities, or the *ability* to direct the activities.

BC46 According to a legal or contractual right approach, some would suggest that an investor has power only when it has an unassailable legal or contractual right to direct. This means having the right to make decisions about the activities of an investee that could potentially be contrary to the wishes of others in every possible scenario, within the boundaries of protective rights. Therefore, for example, an investor with less than half the voting rights of an investee could not have power unless it had additional legal or contractual rights (see paragraph BC101). Also, potential voting rights would not affect the assessment of control until exercised or converted because in and of themselves they do not give the holder the contractual right to direct. A consistent application of this view to 'kick-out' (removal) or similar rights would suggest that a decision maker could never have power when such rights are held by others because those rights could be exercised to remove the decision maker.

BC47 Supporters of the legal or contractual right approach point out that this approach requires less judgement than other approaches and, accordingly, is likely to result in more consistent application of the control definition. They are also concerned that other approaches might result in an investor frequently changing its assessment of control because of changes in circumstances. These changes could be outside the control of the investor (for example, changes in the shareholdings of others or market changes that affect the terms and conditions of potential voting rights).

BC48 The Board acknowledged that defining power as the legal or contractual right to direct the activities of an investee would require less judgement than some other approaches. Nonetheless, the Board rejected that approach because it would create opportunities for an investor to ignore those circumstances in which the Board believes that an investor controls an investee without having the unassailable legal or contractual right to direct the activities of the investee.

BC49 In addition, the Board concluded that preparers and others should be able to apply the judgement required by an 'ability' approach, as long as the principles underlying that approach were articulated clearly and the IFRS included application guidance, illustrating how control should be assessed.

BC50 Consequently, the Board concluded that power should refer to having the *current ability* to direct the activities of an investee. The Board observed that the current ability to direct the activities of an investee would, in all cases, arise from rights (such as voting rights, potential voting rights, rights within other arrangements, or a combination of these).

BC51 In addition, an investor would have the current ability to direct the relevant activities if that investor were able to make decisions at the time that those decisions need to be taken.

BC52 The Board also noted that an investor can have the current ability to direct the activities of an investee even if it does not actively direct the activities of the investee. Conversely, an investor is not assumed to have the current ability to direct simply because it is actively directing the activities of an investee. For example, an investor that holds a 70 per cent voting interest in an investee (when no other relevant factors are present) has the current ability to direct the activities of the investee even if it has not exercised its right to vote. Even if the remaining 30 per cent of voting rights were held by a single party actively exercising its voting rights, that minority shareholder would not have power.

BC53 The Board also noted that having the current ability to direct the activities of an investee is not limited to being able to act today. There may be steps to be taken in order to act—for example, an investor may need to initiate a meeting before it can exercise its voting or other rights that give it power. However, such a delay would not prevent the investor from having power, assuming that there are no other barriers that would prevent the investor from exercising its rights when it chooses to do so.

BC54 In addition, the Board observed that for some investees, particularly those with most of their operating and financing decisions predetermined, decisions that significantly affect the returns of the investee are not made continuously. Such decisions may be made only if particular events occur or circumstances arise. For such investees, having the ability to make those decisions if and when they arise is a source of a current ability to direct the relevant activities.

BC55 When discussing the principles underlying power, the Board rejected the assertion that an 'ability' approach could result in an investee moving *frequently* in and out of consolidation because of changes that are outside the control of the investor (see paragraph BC47). Changes as to which party controls an investee could occur according to any control model, including a 'contractual rights' model, when relevant facts and circumstances change. For a discussion of concerns in respect to changes in market conditions and the assessment of potential voting rights see paragraphs BC124 and BC152.

Relevant activities

BC56 ED 10 did not propose explicit guidance explaining the activities of an investee to which the definition of control referred. In response to comments received from respondents, the Board decided to clarify that in order to control an investee an investor must have the current ability to direct the activities of the investee that *significantly affect the investee's returns* (ie the relevant activities).

BC57   The comments on ED 10 suggested that such a clarification would be particularly helpful when assessing control of investees that are not directed through voting or similar rights and for which there may be multiple parties with decision-making rights over different activities.

BC58   If an investor controls such an investee, its power should relate to the activities of the investee that significantly affect the investee's returns, rather than administrative activities that have little or no effect on the investee's returns. For an investee that is not directed through voting or similar rights it can be difficult to determine which investor, if any, meets the power element of the control definition. There is also a risk that, without adding the modifier 'significant', an investor with very little ability to affect the returns could be considered to have power over that investee (for example, if the investor has the ability to direct the most significant of a number of insignificant activities that have little effect on the investee's returns).

BC59   Although the guidance included in IFRS 10 in this respect would be particularly helpful in the context of investees that are not directed through voting or similar rights, the Board concluded that the amended wording would work well for all investees. For an investee that is directed through voting or similar rights, it is generally the case that a range of operating and financing activities are those that significantly affect the investee's returns—for example, selling goods or services, purchasing inventory, making capital expenditures or obtaining finance. In that case, an investor that is able to determine the strategic operating and financing policies of the investee would usually have power.

Returns

BC60   The definition of control in IFRS 10 uses the concept of returns in two ways.

BC61   In order to have power over an investee an investor must have the current ability to direct the relevant activities, ie the activities that significantly affect the investee's returns. The link to returns was included in the first element of control in order to clarify that having the current ability to direct inconsequential activities is not relevant to the assessment of power and control (see paragraph BC58).

BC62   The second element of control requires the investor's involvement with the investee to provide the investor with rights, or exposure, to variable returns. This retains the concept that control conveys the rights to returns from an investee. To have control an investor must have power over the investee, exposure or rights to returns from its involvement with the investee and the ability to use its power to affect its own returns. Control is not a synonym of power, because equating power and control would result in incorrect conclusions in situations when an agent acts on behalf of others. ED 10 used the term 'returns' rather than 'benefits' because 'benefits' are often interpreted as implying only positive returns.

BC63   The Board confirmed its intention to have a broad definition of 'returns' that would include synergistic returns as well as more direct returns, for example, dividends or changes in the value of an investment. In practice, an investor can benefit from controlling an investee in a variety of ways. The Board concluded that to narrow the definition of returns would artificially restrict those ways of benefiting.

BC64   Although some respondents to ED 10 commented that 'returns' could be interpreted narrowly to refer only to financial returns such as dividends, the Board believed that the broad description of returns included in the IFRS should ensure that the Board's intention to have a broad definition is clear. The Board also confirmed that an investor's returns could have the potential to be wholly positive, wholly negative or both positive and negative.

BC65   When assessing control of an investee, an investor determines whether it is exposed, or has rights, to variable returns from its involvement with the investee. The Board considered whether this criterion should refer to involvement through instruments that must absorb variability, in the sense that those instruments reduce the exposure of the investee to risks that cause variability.

BC66   Some instruments are designed to transfer risk from a reporting entity to another entity. During its deliberations, the Board concluded that such instruments create variability of returns for the other entity but do not typically expose the reporting entity to variability of returns from the performance of the other entity. For example, assume an entity (entity A) is established to provide investment opportunities for investors who wish to have exposure to entity Z's credit risk (entity Z is unrelated to any other party involved in the arrangement). Entity A obtains funding by issuing to those investors notes that are linked to entity Z's credit risk (credit-linked notes) and uses the proceeds to invest in a portfolio of risk-free financial assets. Entity A obtains exposure to entity Z's credit risk by entering into a credit default swap (CDS) with a swap counterparty. The CDS passes entity Z's credit risk to entity A, in return for a fee paid by the swap counterparty. The investors in entity A receive a higher return that reflects both entity A's return from its asset portfolio and the CDS fee. The swap counterparty does not have involvement with entity A that exposes it to variability of returns from the performance of entity A because the CDS transfers variability to entity A, rather than absorbing variability of returns of entity A.

BC67   Consequently, the Board decided that it was not necessary to refer specifically to instruments that absorb variability, although it expects that an investor will typically have rights, or be exposed, to variability of returns through such instruments.

Link between power and returns

BC68   To have control, an investor must have power and exposure or rights to variable returns and be able to use that power to affect its own returns from its involvement with the investee. Thus, power and the returns to which an investor is exposed, or has rights to, must be linked. The link between power and returns does not mean that the proportion of returns accruing to an investor needs to be perfectly correlated with the amount of power that the investor has. The Board noted that many parties can have the right to receive variable returns from an investee (eg shareholders, debt providers and agents), but only one party can control an investee.

Control is not shared

BC69   ED 10 proposed that only one party, if any, can control an investee. The Board confirmed this in deliberating IFRS 10. (See further comments regarding joint arrangements in paragraph BC83.)

BC70   ED 10 proposed that an investor need not have absolute power to control an investee. Other parties can have protective rights relating to the activities of an investee. For example, limits on power are often imposed by law or regulations. Similarly, other parties—such as non-controlling interests—may hold protective rights that limit the power of the investor. During its redeliberations the Board confirmed that an investor can control an investee even if other entities have protective rights relating to the activities of the investee. Paragraphs BC93–BC124 discuss rights that give an investor power over an investee.

Assessing control

BC71   In developing IFRS 10 the Board, while acknowledging that the factors to be considered in assessing control will vary, had the objective of developing a control model that applies the same concept of control as the basis for consolidation to all investees, irrespective of their nature.

BC72   In ED 10, the Board set out specific factors to consider when assessing control of a structured entity. ED 10 defined a structured entity as an entity whose activities are restricted to the extent that those activities are, in essence, not directed by voting or similar rights.

BC73   The Board's intention when including the subsection specifically for structured entities was as a convenience for those assessing control of traditional operating entities that are typically controlled through voting rights—the Board did not want to force those assessing control of traditional operating entities to read, and assess whether to apply, all the guidance relating to structured entities if that guidance was not relevant.

BC74   However, the vast majority of respondents to ED 10 were opposed to creating a subset of investees for which different guidance would apply when assessing control. In their view, such an approach would perpetuate problems faced in applying the guidance in IAS 27 and SIC-12—two control models leading to inconsistent application and, therefore, potential arbitrage by varying investee-specific characteristics. Respondents also noted that the guidance provided for structured entities should apply generally to all investees. Therefore, they suggested that there should be a single section that combines guidance on assessing control of all investees.

BC75   The Board was persuaded by this reasoning and decided to combine the guidance for assessing control of an investee within a single section, noting that its intention is to have a single basis for consolidation that could be applied to all investees and that that basis is control. However, the Board acknowledged that the way in which control would need to be assessed would vary depending on the nature of investees.

Understanding the purpose and design of an investee

BC76   Some respondents to ED 10 expressed the view that involvement in the design of an investee (with restricted activities) is a strong indicator of control and, indeed, in some situations, they would conclude that involvement in the design alone is sufficient to meet the power element of the control definition. SIC-12 included this notion as one of its indicators of control and the accompanying Basis for Conclusions explained that:

> SPEs [special purpose entities] frequently operate in a predetermined way so that no entity has explicit decision-making authority over the SPE's ongoing activities after its formation (ie they operate on 'autopilot'). Virtually all rights, obligations, and aspects of activities that could be controlled are predefined and limited by contractual provisions specified or scheduled at inception. In these circumstances, control may exist for the sponsoring party or others with a beneficial interest, even though it may be particularly difficult to assess, because virtually all activities are predetermined. However, the predetermination of the activities of the SPE through an 'autopilot' mechanism often provides evidence that the ability to control has been exercised by the party making the predetermination for its own benefit at the formation of the SPE and is being perpetuated.

BC77   When developing IFRS 10 the Board confirmed the position in ED 10 that being involved in setting up an investee was not, in and of itself, sufficient to conclude that an investor has control. Being involved in the design does not necessarily mean that an investor has decision-making rights to direct the relevant activities. Often several parties are involved in the design of an investee and the final structure of the investee includes whatever is agreed to by all those parties (including investors, the sponsor of the investee, the transferor(s) of the assets held by the investee and other parties involved in the transaction).

BC78   Although the success of, for example, a securitisation will depend on the assets that are transferred to the securitisation vehicle, the transferor might not have any further involvement with the vehicle and thereby may not have any decision-making rights to direct the relevant activities. The benefits from being involved in setting up a vehicle could cease as soon as the vehicle is established. The Board concluded that, in isolation, being involved in setting up an investee would not be an appropriate basis for consolidation.

BC79   The Board confirmed, however, that considering the purpose and design of an investee is important when assessing control. Understanding the purpose and design of an investee is the means by which an investor identifies the relevant activities, the rights from which power arises and who holds those rights. It can also assist in identifying investors that may have sought to secure control and whose position should be understood and analysed when assessing control.

BC80   The Board noted that understanding the purpose and design of an investee also involves consideration of all activities and returns that are closely related to the investee, even though they might occur outside the legal boundaries of the investee. For example, assume that the purpose of a securitisation vehicle is to allocate risks (mainly credit risk) and benefits (cash flows received) of a portfolio of receivables to the parties involved with the vehicle. The vehicle is designed in such a way that the only activity that can be directed, and can significantly affect the returns from the transaction, is managing those receivables when they default. An investor might have the current ability to direct those activities that significantly affect the returns of the transaction by, for example, writing a put option on the receivables that is triggered when the receivables default. The design of the vehicle ensures that the investor has decision-making authority over the relevant activities at the only time that such decision-making authority is required. In this situation, the terms of the put agreement are integral to the overall transaction and the establishment of the investee. Therefore, the terms of the put agreement would be considered together with the founding documents of the investee to conclude whether the investor has the current ability to direct the activities of the securitisation vehicle that significantly affect the returns of the transaction (even before the default of the receivables).

Different activities significantly affect the returns

BC81   IAS 27, SIC-12 and ED 10 did not specifically address situations in which multiple parties have decision-making authority over the activities of an investee. Some respondents to ED 10 questioned how the control model would be applied in such situations. Respondents were concerned that the absence of specific guidance would create structuring opportunities to avoid the consolidation of structured entities—they asserted that, without any guidance, power could easily be disguised and divided among different parties so that it could be argued that no one would have power over the investee.

BC82   The Board identified the following situations in which multiple parties may have decision-making authority over the activities of an investee:

(a)   joint control

(b)   shared decision-making that is not joint control

(c)   multiple parties that each have unilateral decision-making rights to direct different activities of an investee that significantly affect the investee's returns.

Joint control

BC83   IFRS 11 *Joint Arrangements* defines joint control as the contractually agreed sharing of control of an arrangement. Joint control exists only when decisions about the relevant activities require the unanimous consent of the parties sharing control. When two or more parties have joint control of an investee, no single party controls that investee and, accordingly, the investee is not consolidated. IFRS 11 is applicable to all investees for which two or more parties have joint control. The Board confirmed that IFRS 10 does not change or amend the arrangements that are now within the scope of IFRS 11.

Shared decision-making that is not joint control

BC84   The power to direct the relevant activities can be shared by multiple parties but those rights may not meet the definition of joint control. For example, five parties each own 20 per cent of entity Z, and each has one seat on entity Z's board of directors. All strategic operating and financing decisions (ie decisions in respect of the activities that significantly affect the returns of entity Z) require the consent of any four of the five directors. The five parties do not jointly control entity Z because unanimous consent is not required for decisions relating to the activities of entity Z that significantly affect its returns. Nevertheless, it is clear that the power to direct the activities of entity Z is shared and no single party controls entity Z. Again, the Board confirmed that the requirements of IFRS 10 do not change or amend the application of IFRSs to such situations.

Multiple parties with decision-making rights

BC85   When discussing the sharing of power, the Board noted that for most investees it will be clear that one party or body has decision-making authority to direct the activities of an investee that significantly affect the investee's returns. For example, for an investee that is directed by voting or similar rights, the governing body or board of directors would typically be responsible for strategic decision-making. Thus, the current ability to direct that body would be the basis for power.

BC86   Nonetheless, it is possible that more than one party has decision-making authority over different activities of an investee and that each such activity may significantly affect the investee's returns—respondents to ED 10 noted the following as examples: multi-seller conduits, multi-seller securitisations, and investees for which the assets are managed by one party and the funding is managed by another. The Board was persuaded by the comments from respondents that IFRS 10 should specifically address situations for which multiple parties each have unilateral decision-making rights to direct different activities of the investee.

BC87   The Board considered whether, for such investees, none of the parties controls the investee because the ability to direct the activities is shared. If those different activities, in fact, significantly affect the returns of the investee, some would reason that it would be artificial to force the parties involved to conclude that one activity is more important than the others. An investor might be required to consolidate an investee when the investor would not have the power to direct *all* the activities of the investee that significantly affect the investee's returns.

BC88   Nonetheless, the Board decided that when two or more unrelated investors each have unilateral decision-making rights over different activities of an investee that significantly affect the investee's returns, the investor that has the current ability to direct the activities of the investee that *most* significantly affect the investee's returns meets the power element of the control definition. The expectation is that one investor will have that ability to direct the activities that *most* significantly affect the investee's returns and consequently would be deemed to have power. In effect, power is attributed to the party that looks most like the party that controls the investee. However, the Board decided not to prescribe a specific mechanism for assessing which activities of an investee *most* significantly affect the investee's returns.

BC89 The Board was concerned about creating the potential to avoid consolidation if an investor were to conclude that it has power only when it has the current ability to direct *all* the relevant activities. Such a requirement would be open to abuse because an investor could avoid consolidation by involving other parties in an investee's decision-making.

BC90 The Board's conclusions result in greater potential for an investee to be consolidated because one party would be deemed to have power when multiple parties have unilateral decision-making authority over different activities of an investee.

BC91 In reaching its conclusions, the Board noted that the situation in which two or more investors (individually or as a group) have decision-making rights over different activities of an investee that significantly affect the investee's returns is not expected to arise frequently. This is because one party or body usually has overall decision-making responsibility for an investee (see paragraph BC85). The Board believes that its conclusions in this respect will ensure that it does not create an incentive to structure investees to achieve an accounting outcome by involving multiple parties in decision-making when there is no business rationale to do so.

BC92 The Board noted that in situations where two or more parties have the current ability to direct the activities that most significantly affect the investee's returns and if unanimous consent is required for those decisions IFRS 11 applies.

Rights that give an investor power

BC93 IAS 27 and SIC-12 do not include guidance on rights that give an investor power, other than voting rights and potential voting rights. In addition, neither discusses the effect that such rights held by other parties have on the rights of an investor.

BC94 The Board addressed this issue to some extent in ED 10 by including guidance on protective rights. However, comments from respondents to ED 10 suggested that the guidance was not sufficient.

BC95 The Board decided to address the insufficiency by providing additional guidance about the activities that an investor must be able to direct in order to have power (ie those activities that significantly affect the investee's returns) and by providing guidance on when those rights are substantive. The Board believes that including such guidance should help an investor to determine whether it controls an investee, or whether the rights held by other parties are sufficient to prevent an investor from controlling an investee.

Voting rights

BC96 As with IAS 27 and ED 10, the Board decided to include guidance in IFRS 10 that addresses the assessment of control of investees that are controlled by voting rights.

Majority of voting rights

BC97 The Board carried forward the concept from IAS 27, with a modification to the words, that an investor that holds more than half the voting rights of an investee has power over the investee when those voting rights give the investor the current ability to direct the relevant activities (either directly or by appointing the members of the governing body). The Board concluded that such an investor's voting rights are sufficient to give it power over the investee regardless of whether it has exercised its voting power, unless those rights are not substantive or there are separate arrangements providing another entity with power over the investee (such as through a contractual arrangement over decision-making or substantive potential voting rights).

Less than a majority of voting rights

BC98   In October 2005[7] the Board stated that IAS 27 contemplates that there are circumstances in which an investor can control an investee without owning more than half the voting rights of that investee. The Board accepted that at that time IAS 27 did not provide clear guidance about the particular circumstances in which this will occur and that, as a consequence, there was likely to be diversity in practice.

BC99   The Board decided that in ED 10 it would explain clearly that an investor can control an investee even if the investor does not have more than half the voting rights, as long as the investor's voting rights are sufficient to give the investor the current ability to direct the relevant activities. ED 10 included an example of when a dominant shareholder holds voting rights and all other shareholdings are widely dispersed, and those other shareholders do not actively co-operate when they exercise their votes, so as to have more voting power than the dominant shareholder.

BC100   Respondents to ED 10 expressed mixed views about whether an investor could ever control an investee with less than half the voting rights and without other contractual rights relating to the activities of the investee.

BC101   Some who supported a 'contractual rights' control model believe that an investor with less than half the voting rights of an investee (and without other contractual rights) cannot control that investee. They reasoned that this is because the investor contractually does not have the unassailable right to direct the activities of the other investee in every possible scenario and cannot necessarily block the actions of others.

BC102   Supporters of the 'contractual rights' model believe that power should not be defined in a way that relies on the inactivity of other shareholders, as would be the case in an 'ability' model. In addition, they believe that if an investor wishes to control an investee, that investor would need to have a majority of the voting rights, or further contractual rights (in addition to its voting rights if necessary) that guarantee its power over the investee.

BC103   Other respondents supported the 'ability' model proposed in ED 10. They agreed with the Board that there are situations in which an investor with less than half the voting rights of an investee can control that investee, even when the investor does not have other contractual rights relating to the activities of the investee.

---

7   The October 2005 edition of *IASB Update* included a statement from the Board outlining its views on control with less than a majority of voting rights.

However, they asked the Board to clarify when that would be the case. In particular, they questioned the following:

(a)   The proposals in the exposure draft implied that an investor might have to consolidate an investee simply because the remaining shareholdings are widely dispersed or attendance at shareholder meetings is low, even though the investor might hold only a low percentage of voting rights in that investee (eg 10 per cent or 15 per cent).

(b)   The proposals implied that an investor might be forced to obtain information about the shareholder structure, the degree of organisation and the other shareholders' future intentions. This would be particularly difficult to obtain if the investor owned a low percentage of the voting rights of an investee.

BC104   The Board noted the concerns raised by respondents but concluded that it would be inappropriate to limit power to situations in which an investor would have the contractual right to direct the activities of an investee, for the reasons noted in paragraphs BC45–BC50. Specifically in the context of voting rights, the Board believes that there are situations in which an investor can control an investee even though it does not own more than half the voting rights of an investee and does not have other contractual rights relating to the activities of the investee.

BC105   In reaching that conclusion, the Board noted that jurisdictions have differing legal and regulatory requirements relating to the protection of shareholders and investors. Those requirements often determine or influence the rights held by shareholders and consequently have an influence on the ability of an investor to have power over an investee with less than half the voting rights. For that reason, the Board concluded that drawing a line at 50 per cent in terms of voting power could lead to inappropriate consolidation conclusions in some jurisdictions.

BC106   The Board also concluded that an 'ability' model would result in more appropriate consolidation conclusions not only when applied in different jurisdictions, but also when applied to all investees. This is because the 'ability' model would be applied consistently to all investees by considering the rights held by the investor, as well as the rights held by other parties, when assessing control. For example, in the context of voting rights, an investor would assess whether its voting and any other contractual rights would be sufficient to give it the current ability to direct the relevant activities, or whether the voting and other rights held by other shareholders could prevent it from directing the relevant activities if those shareholders chose to act. The model would be applied in a similar way when other parties hold potential voting rights, kick-out rights or similar rights.

BC107   In response to the concerns raised by respondents to ED 10, the Board clarified that its intentions were neither to require the consolidation of all investees, nor to require an investor that owns a low percentage of voting rights of an investee (such as 10 per cent or 15 per cent) to consolidate that investee. An investor should always assess whether its rights, including any voting rights that it owns, are sufficient to give it the current ability to direct the relevant activities. That assessment requires judgement, considering all available evidence.

BC108   The Board decided to add application requirements setting out some of the factors to consider when applying that judgement to situations in which no single party holds more than half the voting rights of an investee. In particular, the Board decided to clarify that it expects that:

(a)   the more voting rights an investor holds (ie the larger its absolute holding), the more likely it will have power over an investee;

(b)   the more voting rights an investor holds relative to other vote holders (ie the larger its relative holding), the more likely the investor will have power over an investee; and

(c)   the more parties that would need to act together to outvote the investor, the more likely the investor will have power over an investee.

BC109   The Board also noted that, in some cases, considering the voting rights and potential voting rights that an investor and others hold, together with contractual rights, will be sufficient to determine whether the investor has power. However, in other cases these factors may not be sufficient to enable a determination to be made and additional evidence would need to be considered for an investor to determine whether it has power. IFRS 10 sets out additional factors to be considered in these circumstances. In particular, the Board noted that the fewer voting rights an investor holds and the fewer parties that would need to act together to outvote the investor, the more reliance would need to be placed on additional evidence to determine whether the investor has power.

BC110   The Board also decided to clarify that if, after all available evidence has been considered, the evidence is not sufficient to conclude that the investor has power, the investor should not consolidate the investee. If an investor controls an investee, that conclusion is reached on the basis of evidence that is sufficient to conclude that the investor's rights give it the current ability to direct the relevant activities. The Board's intention was not to create a presumption that in the absence of evidence to the contrary the shareholder with the largest proportion of voting rights controls an investee.

BC111   It might be the case that when an investor initially acquires voting rights in an investee and assesses control solely by considering the size of that holding and the voting rights held by others, sufficient evidence is not available to conclude that the investor has power. If that is the case, the investor would not consolidate the investee. However, the assessment should be reconsidered as additional evidence becomes available. For example, the voting rights held by an investor and others may be unchanged but over time the investor may have been able to appoint a majority of the investee's board of directors and may have entered into significant transactions with the investee, thereby enabling the overall assessment to be made that the investor now has control and should consolidate the investee.

Potential voting rights

BC112   An investor might own options, convertible instruments or other instruments that, if exercised, would give the investor voting rights.

BC113   IAS 27 referred to those instruments as potential voting rights. According to that standard, the existence and effect of potential voting rights that are currently exercisable or convertible were considered when assessing control. If the options or convertible instruments that give an investor potential voting rights are currently exercisable, IAS 27 required the investor to treat those potential voting rights as if they were current voting rights. According to IAS 27, the investor had to consider all facts and circumstances except the intentions of management and the financial ability to exercise or convert such rights.

BC114　Because of the revised definition of control, the Board reconsidered potential voting rights in developing the guidance in IFRS 10.

BC115　The questions that the Board considered with respect to potential voting rights were:

　　(a)　Can potential voting rights give the holder the current ability to direct the relevant activities of an investee to which those potential voting rights relate?

　　(b)　If so, in what situations do potential voting rights give the holder the current ability to direct the relevant activities of that investee?

BC116　The Board proposed in ED 10 that an investor should assess whether its power from holding potential voting rights, considered together with other facts and circumstances, gives it power over the investee. Such an investor would have power if the governing body acts in accordance with the wishes of the investor, the counterparty to the instrument acts as an agent for the investor or the investor has particular contractual rights that give it power.

BC117　Most respondents to ED 10 agreed that unexercised potential voting rights, taken in conjunction with other facts and circumstances, could give an investor power. However, many were confused by the application guidance—how would one know whether the decisions of the governing body were in accordance with the wishes of the investor? The respondents suggested that the other situations described in the discussion of power through potential voting rights could lead to power for reasons other than the potential voting rights instrument.

BC118　The Board concluded that the guidance in IFRS 10 that addresses control should apply to potential voting rights, ie when assessing control, an investor should consider all rights that it and other parties hold, including potential voting rights, to determine whether its rights are sufficient to give it control.

BC119　The Board observed that concluding that such instruments always or never give the holder control would cause inappropriate consolidation decisions in some cases.

BC120　Accordingly, the Board concluded that potential voting rights can give the holder the current ability to direct the relevant activities. This will be the case if those rights are substantive and on exercise or conversion (when considered together with any other existing rights the holder has) they give the holder the current ability to direct the relevant activities. The holder of such potential voting rights has the contractual right to 'step in', obtain voting rights and subsequently exercise its voting power to direct the relevant activities—thus the holder has the current ability to direct the activities of an investee at the time that decisions need to be taken if those rights are substantive.

BC121   The Board noted that the holder of such potential voting rights is, in effect, in the same position as a passive majority shareholder or the holder of substantive kick-out rights. The control model would provide that, in the absence of other factors, a majority shareholder controls an investee even though it can take time for the shareholder to organise a meeting and exercise its voting rights. In a similar manner, it can take time for a principal to remove or 'kick out' an agent. The holder of potential voting rights must also take steps to obtain its voting rights. In each case, the question is whether those steps are so significant that they prevent the investor from having the current ability to direct the relevant activities of an investee.

BC122   The Board observed that if power was characterised as requiring either the contractual right to direct the activities or active direction of the activities, the holder of unexercised potential voting rights would never have power without other contractual rights. However, power is the current ability to direct the activities of an investee. As such, the Board concluded that there are situations in which substantive potential voting rights can give the holder power before exercise or conversion to obtain those rights.

BC123   In response to comments from respondents to add clarity about when the holder of potential voting rights has power and to ensure that the control model is applied consistently, the Board added guidance and application examples to help assess when potential voting rights are substantive. Although that assessment requires judgement, the Board believes that an investor should be able to apply the judgement required. This is because potential voting rights exist for a reason—the terms and conditions of the instruments reflect that reason. Therefore, an assessment of the terms and conditions of the instrument (ie the purpose and design of the instrument) should provide information about whether the instrument was designed to give the holder power before exercise or conversion.

BC124   Some constituents were concerned about whether the proposed model would lead to frequent changes in the control assessment solely because of changes in market conditions—would an investor consolidate and deconsolidate an investee if potential voting rights moved in and out of the money? In response to those comments, the Board noted that determining whether a potential voting right is substantive is not based solely on a comparison of the strike or conversion price of the instrument and the then current market price of its underlying share. Although the strike or conversion price is one factor to consider, determining whether potential voting rights are substantive requires a holistic approach, considering a variety of factors. This includes assessing the purpose and design of the instrument, considering whether the investor can benefit for other reasons such as by realising synergies between the investor and the investee, and determining whether there are any barriers (financial or otherwise) that would prevent the holder of potential voting rights from exercising or converting those rights. Accordingly, the Board believes that a change in market conditions (ie the market price of the underlying shares) alone would not typically result in a change in the consolidation conclusion.

Delegated power (agency relationships)

BC125   IAS 27 and SIC-12 did not contain requirements or guidance to assess whether a decision maker is an agent or principal. The absence of guidance has allowed divergence to develop in practice. The Board decided to introduce principles that address agency relationships to reduce this divergence.

BC126   ED 10 proposed criteria to identify an agency relationship on the basis of the following assumptions:

(a)   Both the principal and the agent seek to maximise their own benefits. Therefore, the principal is likely to introduce additional measures that are intended to ensure that the agent does not act against the interest of the principal. For example, the principal may have rights to remove the agent with or without cause.

(b)   A principal has no incentive to remunerate an agent more than what is commensurate with the services provided. Accordingly, remuneration that is not commensurate with the services provided is an indicator that a decision maker is not an agent.

BC127   ED 10 included guidance on dual roles and addressed situations in which an investor holds voting rights, both directly and on behalf of other parties as an agent. The exposure draft proposed that when assessing whether an investor acts as an agent or a principal, the investor would exclude the voting rights that it holds as an agent only if it could demonstrate that it is obliged to act in the best interests of other parties or has implemented policies and procedures that ensure the independence of the decision maker in its role as an agent from that as a holder of voting rights directly.

BC128   Most respondents to ED 10 agreed with the Board that the consolidation standard should provide application guidance to identify an agency relationship. However, some respondents believed that the exposure draft was not clear on whether the Board intended the proposed application guidance to be limited to legal or contractual agency relationships. Most respondents agreed that the form of remuneration can be an indicator of an agency relationship. However, many found the application guidance, in this respect, confusing. They did not agree with the dual role guidance that required an investor to assess in aggregate its rights as an agent and a principal. Nor did they believe that such an investor should automatically exclude its rights as an agent from the control assessment.

BC129   In response to those comments, the Board decided to base its principal/agent guidance on the thinking developed in agency theory. Jensen and Meckling (1976) define an agency relationship as 'a contractual relationship in which one or more persons (the principal) engage another person (the agent) to perform some service on their behalf which involves delegating some decision-making authority to the agent.'[8]

BC130   The Board clarified that, as defined, an agent is obliged to act in the best interests of the parties that delegated the power (ie the principal or principals)

---

8   M C Jensen and W H Meckling, *Theory of the Firm: Managerial Behavior Agency Costs and Ownership Structure*, Journal of Financial Economics 1976, pp. 305–360.

and not other parties by way of a wider fiduciary responsibility. The Board did not think it would be appropriate to conclude that every party that is obliged, by law or contract, to act in the best interests of other parties is an agent for the purposes of assessing control. This conclusion, in effect, assumes that a decision maker that is legally or contractually obliged to act in the best interests of other parties will always do so, even if that decision maker receives the vast majority of the returns that are influenced by its decision-making. Although this assumption might be appropriate for some decision makers, the Board observed that it would not be appropriate for all, in particular many investees that are not directed through voting or similar rights. Almost every investment or asset manager could contend that it is contractually obliged to act in the best interests of others. This conclusion could result in virtually every investee that is not directed through voting or similar rights being unconsolidated.

BC131   The Board observed that the difficulty in developing guidance that addresses agency relationships is that the link between power and returns is often missing. To have control, an investor must have power and be able to use that power for its own benefit.

BC132   If a decision maker receives a return that is relatively insignificant or varies insignificantly, most would be comfortable concluding that the decision maker uses any decision-making authority delegated to it to affect the returns received by others—this is because the decision maker would not have power for its own benefit. Similarly, if the decision maker held a substantial investment in the investee (say, a 95 per cent investment), most would conclude that the decision maker uses any decision-making authority delegated to it primarily to affect the returns it receives—the decision maker would have power for its own benefit. But at what point, between insignificant and very significant, does the decision maker change from using any decision-making authority primarily for others to using its authority primarily for itself?

BC133   The Board concluded that the guidance in IFRS 10 that addresses control should apply to agency relationships, ie when assessing control, a decision maker should consider whether it has the current ability to direct the relevant activities of an investee that it manages to affect the returns it receives, or whether it uses the decision-making authority delegated to it primarily for the benefit of other parties.

BC134   The Board observed that a decision maker always acts as an agent of another party when that other party holds a unilateral substantive right to remove the decision maker. Therefore, a substantive removal right that is held by a single party is a conclusive indicator of an agency relationship.

BC135   At the FASB's round-table meeting on consolidation in November 2010, participants asked whether a board of directors (or other governing body) can be evaluated as one party when considering whether a single party holds substantive removal rights. The IASB observed that the function of such governing bodies is to act as a fiduciary for the investors and therefore any rights given to an investee's board of directors (or other governing body) is a pass-through mechanism for the exercise of the investors' rights. Thus, the governing body itself cannot be considered to have or restrict decision-making authority over the investee. Rather it is the rights given to such a governing body by the investors and their effect on the decision-making authority that should be considered. Consequently, a governing body is not generally viewed as a single party.

BC136　In the absence of a substantive removal right that is held by a single party, judgement must be applied when assessing whether a decision maker acts as a principal or an agent. That assessment includes considering the overall relationship between the decision maker, the entity being managed and the other interest holders, taking into account all available evidence.

BC137　With the exception of substantive removal rights that are held by one party, no single factor would provide conclusive evidence of an agency relationship. The Board observed that, depending on the facts and circumstances, a particular factor may be a strong indicator of an agency relationship and would receive a greater weighting than other factors when assessing control. However, the weighting would depend on the relevant facts and circumstances in each case and it would be inappropriate to specify that any factor would always be more important than the others.

Scope of decision-making authority

BC138　One of the factors to consider when assessing whether a decision maker is an agent or principal is the scope of its decision-making authority. The Board considered whether a decision maker would always be considered an agent if the breadth of its decision-making authority were restricted by contractual arrangements. The Board rejected such a conclusion for two reasons. First, it noted that it is rare for a parent to have unrestricted power over a subsidiary because debt providers or non-controlling interests often have protective rights that restrict the decision-making powers of a parent to some extent. Consequently, it would be difficult to set a particular threshold of restriction on decision-making that would automatically lead to a conclusion that the decision maker is an agent. The second reason was that it would inappropriately lead to many investees, such as securitisation vehicles, not being classified as a controlled entity by a decision maker even though it might have significant economic interests in the investee as well as discretion in making decisions about the relevant activities of the investee. The Board observed that a decision maker can have power over an investee if it has discretion in directing the relevant activities, even if those activities are restricted when the investee is established.

Rights held by other parties

BC139　When considering rights held by other parties in the context of a principal/agent analysis, the Board noted that an entity would assess whether those rights are substantive in the same way as any other rights held by other parties, such as voting rights. An entity would assess whether those rights give their holders the practical ability to prevent the decision maker from directing the activities of the investee if the holders choose to exercise those rights.

BC140　Some constituents said that it would be beneficial to address liquidation rights held by other parties. The Board observed that removal rights are defined as 'rights to deprive the decision maker of its decision-making authority' and that some other rights (such as some liquidation rights) may have the same effect on the decision-making authority as removal rights. If those other rights meet the definition of removal rights, they should be treated as such regardless of their label. Therefore, the Board concluded that there was no need to add further guidance in this respect in the IFRS.

Exposure to variability of returns

BC141 The Board considered whether to specify that in the absence of other parties having substantive removal rights, a decision maker that receives a particular level of returns or exposure to variability of returns would be deemed to control an investee (for example, exposure to more than half of the variability of returns of an investee). However, the Board rejected developing a model that would specify a particular level of returns that would result in the determination of an agency relationship. Rather, the Board concluded that the more a decision maker is exposed to the variability of returns from its involvement with an investee, the more likely it is that the decision maker is a principal.

BC142 Although prescribing a quantitative approach for assessing returns, and specifying a particular level of returns, might lead to more consistent application of the requirements by removing some of the judgement required, the Board observed that such an approach was likely to lead to inappropriate consolidation conclusions in some situations. It would create a bright line that might encourage structuring to achieve a particular accounting outcome. The Board also noted that when assessing agency relationships, a decision maker's exposure to variability of returns is not necessarily correlated with the amount of power that it has, unlike the general assumption when investees are controlled by voting rights. Therefore, a decision maker does not necessarily have any more power over an investee when it is exposed, for example, to more than half of the variability of an investee's returns than when it is not.

Relationship with other parties

BC143 The Board decided that an investor should, when assessing control, consider the nature of its relationships with other parties. An investor may conclude that the nature of its relationship with other parties is such that those other parties are acting on the investor's behalf (they are 'de facto agents'). Such a relationship need not involve a contractual arrangement, thereby creating a non-contractual agency relationship. The Board concluded that a party is a de facto agent when the investor has, or those that direct the activities of the investor have, the ability to direct that party to act on the investor's behalf.

BC144 ED 10 included a list of examples of parties that often act for the investor. The Board's intention was that an investor would look closely at its relationships with such parties and assess whether the party is acting on behalf of the investor.

BC145 Some respondents said that the list of examples of parties that often act on behalf of an investor was not helpful because they could think of circumstances in which it would be appropriate to regard each of the parties as agents of the investor and other circumstances when it would not. Respondents were unclear about the consequences of concluding that a party acts for an investor.

BC146   The Board clarified its intentions by stating that, when assessing control, an investor would consider its de facto agent's decision-making rights and exposure (or rights) to variable returns together with its own as if the rights were held by the investor directly. In reaching this decision, the Board noted that it would be inappropriate to assume that all other parties listed in paragraph B75 would *always* or *never* act for the investor. It acknowledged that the assessment of whether the nature of the relationship between the investor and the other party is such that the other party is a de facto agent requires judgement, including consideration of the nature of the relationship and the way that the parties interact with each other.

Control of specified assets

BC147   ED 10 introduced the term 'silo'—an investee within a legal structure—without defining it, noting that an investee can comprise more than one entity. This would be the case when the legal and contractual arrangements relating to an investee give one party control of a particular set of assets and liabilities, whereas another party might have control over another set of assets and liabilities within the investee. Respondents to ED 10 requested more guidance in order to apply the concept in practice.

BC148   In response to those requests, IFRS 10 includes application requirements regarding interests in specified assets. This guidance is consistent with the current guidance in US GAAP in that it sets out when a portion of an investee is treated as a separate entity for the purposes of consolidation. The Board noted that this situation arises most often in the context of investees that are not directed through voting or similar rights. However, the Board decided that to restrict the application requirements to investees that are not directed through voting or similar rights would be contrary to the objective of developing a control model that is applied consistently to all investees. In addition, the Board was not aware of any reason for such a restriction. Therefore, the guidance regarding interests in specified assets is applicable to all investees. This is in contrast with US GAAP, which applies this guidance only to portions of variable interest entities.

Continuous assessment

BC149   ED 10 proposed that an investor should assess control continuously. This is because the Board believes that the assessment of control requires consideration of all facts and circumstances and it would be impossible to develop reconsideration criteria that would apply to every situation in which an investor obtains or loses control of an investee. Therefore, the reassessment of control only when particular reconsideration criteria are met would lead to inappropriate consolidation decisions in some cases.

BC150   Most respondents to ED 10 did not comment on the requirement to assess control continuously. Some questioned whether the continuous assessment of control could be interpreted as requiring preparers to reassess control at the end of each reporting period.

BC151　The Board confirmed the proposal in ED 10 to require an investor to assess control continuously, and clarified that this would mean reassessing control when there is a change in relevant facts and circumstances that suggest that there is a change to one or more of the three elements of control. Such reassessment would not be restricted to each reporting date, nor would the requirement necessarily demand the reassessment of all control or potential control relationships at each reporting date.

BC152　Participants in the FASB's round-table meeting on consolidation held in November 2010 expressed concern about the reassessment of control (including a decision maker's status as principal or agent) when there are changes in market conditions, in particular the reassessment of control in the context of potential voting rights. In response to those concerns, the IASB decided to add guidance to address the reassessment of control (including a decision maker's status as principal or agent) when there are changes in market conditions (for the reassessment of control in the context of potential voting rights see paragraph BC124). The Board observed that a change in market conditions alone would not generally affect the consolidation conclusion, or the status as a principal or an agent, for two reasons. The first is that power arises from substantive rights, and assessing whether those rights are substantive includes the consideration of many factors, not only those that are affected by a change in market conditions. The second is that an investor is not required to have a particular specified level of exposure to variable returns in order to control an investee. If that were the case, fluctuations in an investor's expected returns might result in changes in the consolidation conclusion.

BC153　Nonetheless, the Board confirmed that control should be reassessed when relevant facts and circumstances change to such an extent that there is a change in one or more of the three elements of control or in the overall relationship between a principal and an agent.

Accounting requirements

Consolidation procedures

BC154　The application requirements in IFRS 10 explain how potential voting rights should be accounted for in the consolidated financial statements. Paragraphs B89–B91 replace the guidance previously included in the implementation guidance accompanying IAS 27, but are not intended to change consolidation procedures.

Non-controlling interests (2003 revision and 2008 amendments)

BCZ155　The 2008 amendments to IAS 27 changed the term 'minority interest' to 'non-controlling interest'. The change in terminology reflects the fact that the owner of a minority interest in an entity might control that entity and, conversely, that the owners of a majority interest in an entity might not control the entity. 'Non-controlling interest' is a more accurate description than 'minority interest' of the interest of those owners who do not have a controlling interest in an entity.

BCZ156　Non-controlling interest was defined in IAS 27 as the equity in a subsidiary not attributable, directly or indirectly, to a parent (this definition is now in IFRS 10). Paragraph 26 of IAS 27 (as revised in 2000) required minority (non-controlling) interests to be presented in the consolidated balance sheet (statement of financial position) separately from liabilities and the equity of the shareholders of the parent.

BCZ157　As part of its revision of IAS 27 in 2003, the Board amended this requirement to require minority (non-controlling) interests to be presented in the consolidated statement of financial position within equity, separately from the equity of the shareholders of the parent. The Board concluded that a minority (non-controlling) interest is not a liability because it did not meet the definition of a liability in the *Framework for the Preparation and Presentation of Financial Statements* (replaced in 2010 by the *Conceptual Framework for Financial Reporting*).

BCZ158　Paragraph 49(b) of the *Framework* (now paragraph 4.4(b) of the *Conceptual Framework*) stated that a liability is a present obligation of the entity arising from past events, the settlement of which is expected to result in an outflow from the entity of resources embodying economic benefits. Paragraph 60 of the *Framework* (now paragraph 4.15 of the *Conceptual Framework*) explained that an essential characteristic of a liability is that the entity has a present obligation and that an obligation is a duty or responsibility to act or perform in a particular way. The Board noted that the existence of a minority (non-controlling) interest in the net assets of a subsidiary does not give rise to a present obligation, the settlement of which is expected to result in an outflow of economic benefits from the group.

BCZ159　Instead, the Board noted that minority (non-controlling) interests represent the residual interest in the net assets of those subsidiaries held by some of the shareholders of the subsidiaries within the group, and therefore met the *Framework*'s definition of equity. Paragraph 49(c) of the *Framework* (now paragraph 4.4(c) of the *Conceptual Framework*) stated that equity is the residual interest in the assets of the entity after deducting all its liabilities.

Attribution of losses (2008 amendments)

BCZ160　IAS 27 (as revised in 2003) stated that when losses attributed to the minority (non-controlling) interests exceed the minority's interests in the subsidiary's equity, the excess, and any further losses applicable to the minority, is allocated against the majority interest except to the extent that the minority has a binding obligation and is able to make an additional investment to cover the losses.

BCZ161　In 2005 the Board decided that this treatment was inconsistent with its conclusion that non-controlling interests are part of the equity of the group, and proposed that an entity should attribute total comprehensive income applicable to non-controlling interests to those interests, even if this results in the non-controlling interests having a deficit balance.

BCZ162　If the parent enters into an arrangement that places it under an obligation to the subsidiary or to the non-controlling interests, the Board believes that the entity should account for that arrangement separately and the arrangement should not affect how the entity attributes comprehensive income to the controlling and non-controlling interests.

BCZ163　Some respondents to the 2005 exposure draft agreed with the proposal, noting that non-controlling interests share proportionately in the risks and rewards of the subsidiary and that the proposal was consistent with the classification of non-controlling interests as equity.

BCZ164　Other respondents disagreed, often on the grounds that controlling and non-controlling interests have different characteristics and should not be treated the same way. They argued that there was no need to change the guidance in IAS 27 (as revised in 2003) (ie that an entity should allocate excess losses to the controlling interest unless the non-controlling interests have a binding obligation and are able to make an additional investment to cover the losses). The reasons given by those respondents were:

(a)　The non-controlling interests are not compelled to cover the deficit (unless they have specifically agreed to do so) and it is reasonable to assume that, if the subsidiary requires additional capital in order to continue operations, the non-controlling interests would abandon their investments. In contrast, respondents asserted that in practice the controlling interest often has an implicit obligation to maintain the subsidiary as a going concern.

(b)　Often guarantees or other support arrangements by the parent protect the non-controlling interests from losses of the subsidiary in excess of equity and do not affect the way losses are attributed to the controlling and non-controlling interests. Respondents argued that allocating those losses to the parent and non-controlling interests and recognising separately a guarantee would not reflect the underlying economics, which are that only the parent absorbs the losses of the subsidiary. In their view, it would be misleading for financial statements to imply that the non-controlling interests have an obligation to make additional investments.

(c)　Recognising guarantees separately is contrary to the principle of the non-recognition of transactions between owners.

(d)　Loss allocation should take into account legal, regulatory or contractual constraints, some of which may prevent entities from recognising negative non-controlling interests, especially for regulated businesses (eg banks and insurers).

BCZ165　The Board considered these reasons but observed that, although it is true that non-controlling interests have no further obligation to contribute assets to the subsidiary, neither does the parent. Non-controlling interests participate proportionally in the risks and rewards of an investment in the subsidiary.

BCZ166　Some respondents asked the Board to provide guidance on the accounting for guarantees and similar arrangements between the parent and the subsidiary or the non-controlling interests. They also suggested that the Board should require additional disclosures about inter-company guarantees and the extent of deficits, if any, of non-controlling interests.

BCZ167　The Board considered these requests but observed that this was an issue wider than negative non-controlling interests. For example, the parent is not necessarily responsible for the liabilities of a subsidiary, and often there are factors that restrict the ability of a parent to move assets in a group, which means that the assets of the group are not necessarily freely available to the parent. The Board decided that it would be more appropriate to address comprehensively disclosures about non-controlling interests (disclosures about non-controlling interests are included in IFRS 12).

Changes in ownership interests in subsidiaries (2008 amendments)

BCZ168   The Board decided that after control of an entity is obtained, changes in a parent's ownership interest that do not result in a loss of control are accounted for as equity transactions (ie transactions with owners in their capacity as owners). This means that no gain or loss from these changes should be recognised in profit or loss. It also means that no change in the carrying amounts of the subsidiary's assets (including goodwill) or liabilities should be recognised as a result of such transactions.

BCZ169   The Board reached this conclusion because it believed that the approach adopted in the amendments was consistent with its previous decision that non-controlling interests are a separate component of equity (see paragraphs BCZ156–BCZ159).

BCZ170   Some respondents agreed that non-controlling interests are equity but said that they should be treated as a special class of equity. Others disagreed with the requirement because in their view recognising transactions with non-controlling interests as equity transactions would mean that the Board had adopted an entity approach whereas they preferred a proprietary approach. The Board disagreed with this characterisation of the accounting treatment, noting that the accounting proposed was a consequence of classifying non-controlling interests as equity. The Board did not consider comprehensively the entity and proprietary approaches as part of the amendments to IAS 27 in 2008.

BCZ171   Many respondents to the 2005 exposure draft suggested alternative approaches for the accounting for changes in controlling ownership interests. The most commonly suggested alternative would result in increases in controlling ownership interests giving rise to the recognition of additional goodwill, measured as the excess of the purchase consideration over the carrying amount of the separately identified assets in the subsidiary attributable to the additional interest acquired.

BCZ172   Some respondents suggested that when an entity reduces its ownership interest in a subsidiary, without losing control, it should recognise a gain or loss attributable to the controlling interest. They would measure that gain or loss as the difference between the consideration received and the proportion of the carrying amount of the subsidiary's assets (including recognised goodwill) attributable to the ownership interest being disposed of. Respondents supporting this alternative said that it would provide relevant information about the gains and losses attributable to the controlling interest arising on the partial disposal of ownership interests in subsidiaries.

BCZ173   The Board rejected this alternative. Recognising a change in any of the assets of the business, including goodwill, was inconsistent with the Board's decision in IFRS 3 *Business Combinations* (as revised in 2008) that obtaining control in a business combination is a significant economic event. That event causes the initial recognition and measurement of all the assets acquired and liabilities assumed in the business combination. Subsequent transactions with owners should not affect the measurement of those assets and liabilities.

BCZ174 The parent already controls the assets of the business, although it must share the income from those assets with the non-controlling interests. By acquiring the non-controlling interests the parent is obtaining the rights to some, or all, of the income to which the non-controlling interests previously had rights. Generally, the wealth-generating ability of those assets is unaffected by the acquisition of the non-controlling interests. That is to say, the parent is not investing in more or new assets. It is acquiring more rights to the income from the assets it already controls.

BCZ175 By acquiring some, or all, of the non-controlling interests the parent will be allocated a greater proportion of the profits or losses of the subsidiary in periods after the additional interests are acquired. The adjustment to the controlling interest will be equal to the unrecognised share of the value changes that the parent will be allocated when those value changes are recognised by the subsidiary. Failure to make that adjustment will cause the controlling interest to be overstated.

BCZ176 The Board noted that accounting for changes in controlling ownership interests as equity transactions, as well as ensuring that the income of the group and the reported controlling interests are faithfully represented, is less complex than the other alternatives considered.

BCZ177 Some respondents disagreed with the proposal because they were concerned about the effect on reported equity of the subsequent acquisition of non-controlling interests by the parent. They seemed to be particularly concerned about the effect on the reported leverage of an entity that acquires non-controlling interests and whether this might, for example, cause those entities to have to renegotiate loan agreements.

BCZ178 The Board observed that all acquisitions of an entity's equity reduce the entity's equity, regardless of whether it is an acquisition of the parent's ordinary or preference shares or non-controlling interests. Hence, the treatment of a subsequent acquisition of non-controlling interests is consistent with the general accounting for the acquisition by an entity of instruments classified as equity.

BCZ179 The Board understands the importance of providing owners of the parent with information about the total changes in their reported equity. Therefore, the Board decided to require entities to present in a separate schedule the effects of any changes in a parent's ownership interest in a subsidiary that do not result in a loss of control on the equity attributable to owners of the parent (this disclosure requirement is now in IFRS 12).

Loss of control (2008 amendments)

BCZ180 A parent loses control of a subsidiary when it loses the power to govern the financial and operating policies of an investee so as to obtain benefit from its activities. Loss of control can result from the sale of an ownership interest or by other means, such as when a subsidiary issues new ownership interests to third parties. Loss of control can also occur in the absence of a transaction. It may, for example, occur on the expiry of an agreement that previously allowed an entity to control a subsidiary.

BCZ181   On loss of control, the parent-subsidiary relationship ceases to exist. The parent no longer controls the subsidiary's individual assets and liabilities. Therefore, the parent derecognises the individual assets, liabilities and equity related to that subsidiary.   Equity includes any non-controlling interests as well as amounts previously recognised in other comprehensive income in relation to, for example, foreign currency translation.

BCZ182   The Board decided that any investment the parent has in the former subsidiary after control is lost should be measured at fair value at the date that control is lost and that any resulting gain or loss should be recognised in profit or loss. Some respondents disagreed with that decision.   They asserted that the principles for revenue and gain recognition in the *Framework* would not be satisfied for the retained interest. The Board disagreed with those respondents. Measuring the investment at fair value reflected the Board's view that the loss of control of a subsidiary is a significant economic event.   The parent-subsidiary relationship ceases to exist and an investor-investee relationship begins that differs significantly from the former parent-subsidiary relationship. Therefore, the new investor-investee relationship is recognised and measured initially at the date when control is lost.

BCZ183   The Board decided that the loss of control of a subsidiary is, from the group's perspective, the loss of control over some of the group's individual assets and liabilities. Accordingly, the general requirements in IFRSs should be applied in accounting for the derecognition from the group's financial statements of the subsidiary's assets and liabilities. If a gain or loss previously recognised in other comprehensive income would be reclassified to profit or loss on the separate disposal of those assets and liabilities, the parent reclassifies the gain or loss from equity to profit or loss on the indirect disposal of those assets and liabilities through loss of control of a subsidiary.

BCZ184   The Board also discussed the accounting when an entity transfers its shares in a subsidiary to its own shareholders with the result that the entity loses control of the subsidiary (commonly referred to as a spin-off). The International Financial Reporting Interpretations Committee had previously discussed this matter, but decided not to add the matter to its agenda while the business combinations project was in progress. The Board observed that the issue was outside the scope of the business combinations project.   Therefore, the Board decided not to address the measurement basis of distributions to owners in the amendments to IAS 27.

Multiple arrangements

BCZ185   The Board considered whether its decision that a gain or loss on the disposal of a subsidiary should be recognised only when that disposal results in a loss of control could give rise to opportunities to structure transactions to achieve a particular accounting outcome. For example, would an entity be motivated to structure a transaction or arrangement as multiple steps to maximise gains or minimise losses if an entity were planning to dispose of its controlling interest in a subsidiary? Consider the following example. Entity P controls 70 per cent of entity S. Entity P intends to sell all of its 70 per cent controlling interest in entity S. Entity P could initially sell 19 per cent of its ownership interest in entity S without loss of control and then, soon afterwards, sell the remaining 51 per cent and lose control. Alternatively, entity P could sell all of its 70 per cent interest in entity S in one transaction. In the first case, any difference between the amount by which the non-controlling interests are adjusted and the fair value of the consideration received on the sale of the 19 per cent interest would be recognised directly in equity, whereas the gain or loss from the sale of the remaining 51 per cent interest would be recognised in profit or loss. In the second case, a gain or loss on the sale of the whole 70 per cent interest would be recognised in profit or loss.

BCZ186   The Board noted that the opportunity to conceal losses through structuring would be reduced by the requirements of IAS 36 *Impairment of Assets* and IFRS 5 *Non-current Assets Held for Sale and Discontinued Operations*. Paragraph 12 of IAS 36 includes significant changes to how an entity uses or expects to use an asset as one of the indicators that the asset might be impaired.

BCZ187   Once an asset meets the criteria to be classified as held for sale (or is included in a disposal group that is classified as held for sale), it is excluded from the scope of IAS 36 and is accounted for in accordance with IFRS 5. In accordance with paragraph 20 of IFRS 5 'an entity shall recognise an impairment loss for any initial or subsequent write-down of the asset (or disposal group) to fair value less costs to sell...'. Therefore, if appropriate, an impairment loss would be recognised for the goodwill and non-current assets of a subsidiary that will be sold or otherwise disposed of before control of the subsidiary is lost. Accordingly, the Board concluded that the principal risk is the minimising of gains, which entities are unlikely to strive to do.

BCZ188   The Board decided that the possibility of such structuring could be overcome by requiring entities to consider whether multiple arrangements should be accounted for as a single transaction to ensure that the principle of faithful representation is adhered to. The Board believes that all the terms and conditions of the arrangements and their economic effects should be considered in determining whether multiple arrangements should be accounted for as a single arrangement. Accordingly, the Board included indicators in paragraph 33 of IAS 27 (as revised in 2008) to assist in identifying when multiple arrangements that result in the loss of control of a subsidiary should be treated as a single arrangement (those indicators are now in paragraph B97 of IFRS 10).

BCZ189   Some respondents disagreed with the indicators that were provided in the exposure draft. They said that the need for guidance on when multiple arrangements should be accounted for as a single arrangement indicates a conceptual weakness in the accounting model developed in the exposure draft. Moreover, such guidance would be unnecessary under other alternatives for accounting for decreases in ownership interests. The Board acknowledges that guidance on multiple arrangements would be unnecessary under some other accounting alternatives. However, the Board does not accept that this means that those models are conceptually superior.

BCZ190   Some respondents suggested that IAS 27 should include examples rather than indicators for when multiple transactions should be treated as a single transaction or arrangement, but that those examples should not be regarded as a complete list. The Board considered that suggestion, but decided to confirm the indicators that were proposed in the exposure draft. The Board believed that the indicators could be applied to a variety of situations and were preferable to providing what could be an endless list of examples to try to capture every possible arrangement.

BC190A–   *[These paragraphs refer to amendments that are not yet effective, and are therefore not*
BC190O   *included in this edition.]*

Effective date and transition

Effective date

BC191   The Board decided to align the effective date for the IFRS with the effective date for IFRS 11, IFRS 12, IAS 27 *Separate Financial Statements* and IAS 28. When making this decision, the Board noted that the five IFRSs all deal with the assessment of, and related accounting and disclosure requirements about, a reporting entity's special relationships with other entities (ie when the reporting entity has control or joint control of, or significant influence over, another entity). As a result, the Board concluded that applying IFRS 10 without also applying the other four IFRSs could cause unwarranted confusion.

BC192   The Board usually sets an effective date of between twelve and eighteen months after issuing an IFRS. When deciding the effective date for those IFRSs, the Board considered the following factors:

   (a)   the time that many countries require for translation and for introducing the mandatory requirements into law.

   (b)   the consolidation project was related to the global financial crisis that started in 2007 and was accelerated by the Board in response to urgent requests from the leaders of the G20, the Financial Stability Board, users of financial statements, regulators and others to improve the accounting and disclosure of an entity's 'off balance sheet' activities.

   (c)   the comments received from respondents to the Request for Views *Effective Date and Transition Methods* that was published in October 2010 regarding implementation costs, effective date and transition requirements of the IFRSs to be issued in 2011. Most respondents did not identify the consolidation and joint arrangements IFRSs as having a high impact in terms of the time and resources that their implementation would require. In addition, only a few respondents commented that the effective dates of those IFRSs should be aligned with those of the other IFRSs to be issued in 2011.

BC193   With these factors in mind, the Board decided to require entities to apply the five IFRSs for annual periods beginning on or after 1 January 2013.

BC194   The majority of the respondents to the Request for Views supported early application of the IFRSs to be issued in 2011. Respondents stressed that early application was especially important for first-time adopters in 2011 and 2012.

The Board was persuaded by these arguments and decided to permit early application of IFRS 10 but only if an entity applies it in conjunction with the other IFRSs (ie IFRS 11, IFRS 12, IAS 27 (as amended in 2011) and IAS 28 (as amended in 2011)) to avoid a lack of comparability among financial statements, and for the reasons noted in paragraph BC191 that triggered the Board's decision to set the same effective date for all five IFRSs. Even though an entity should apply the five IFRSs at the same time, the Board noted that an entity should not be prevented from applying any of the disclosure requirements of IFRS 12 early if by doing so users gained a better understanding of the entity's relationships with other entities.

Transition

BC195   IAS 8 *Accounting Policies, Changes in Accounting Estimates and Errors* states that retrospective application results in the most useful information to users because the information presented for all periods is comparable.

BC196   In reaching its conclusions, the Board observed that IFRS 10 might result in an investor consolidating investees that were not previously consolidated or not consolidating investees that were previously consolidated. If an investor is required to consolidate a previously unconsolidated investee and has been accounting for its investment in that investee using proportionate consolidation or the equity method, the Board noted that the investor would often have the information available to consolidate the investee retrospectively as if IFRS 10 had always been in place. This is also likely to be the case if an investor no longer consolidates an investee that it previously consolidated but would now have to account for its investment in the investee using the equity method.

BC196A   IFRS 3 *Business Combinations* was initially issued in 2004 and was then substantially revised in 2008. Those revisions apply prospectively. The Board noted that, when developing the transition guidance in paragraphs C4–C4A, it had not specified which version of IFRS 3 should be used when an investor concludes that it shall consolidate an investee that was not previously consolidated and over which control was obtained before the effective date of IFRS 3 (revised in 2008). Applying the current version of IFRS 3 in such cases may provide more comparable information.

BC196B   However, as noted in BC196, if an investor has been accounting for its investment in such an investee using proportionate consolidation or the equity method, it will have already identified the fair values, goodwill and other amounts required to apply IFRS 3 (issued in 2004). Allowing investors to use existing information in such cases reduces the risk of using hindsight and may provide a more reliable basis for consolidation. Consequently, if control was obtained before the effective date of IFRS 3 (2008), the Board decided to allow entities to use either IFRS 3 (2008) or IFRS 3 (2004) in applying the transition requirements.

BC196C   Similarly, IAS 27 *Consolidated and Separate Financial Statements*, as issued in 2003, was substantially revised in 2008. Those revisions apply prospectively. The requirements of IAS 27 (revised in 2008) have been carried forward into IFRS 10. For the same reasons as those described in BC196A–BC196B relating to IFRS 3, if control was obtained before the effective date of IAS 27 (2008), the Board also decided to allow entities to use either IAS 27 (2008) or IAS 27 (2003) in applying the transition requirements.

BC197 In addition, the Board acknowledged that retrospective application of IFRS 10 may not be practicable in some circumstances. If an investor on initial application of IFRS 10 consolidates an investee it previously did not consolidate and it is impracticable to apply the provisions of IFRS 10 retrospectively, the reporting entity would apply the acquisition method in IFRS 3 with the acquisition date being the beginning of the earliest period for which application of those requirements is practicable (goodwill would not be recognised for an investee that is not a business).

BC198 If an investor on initial application of IFRS 10 ceases to consolidate an investee that was previously consolidated, the investor measures its retained interest in the investee on the date of initial application, at the amount at which the interest would have been measured if the requirements of IFRS 10 had been effective when the investor first became involved with (but did not obtain control in accordance with this IFRS), or lost control of, the investee. If, in accordance with IFRS 10, the investor never obtained control, then it would eliminate the previous consolidation from the date that it first became involved with the investee and account for that interest in accordance with other IFRSs as applicable. Alternatively, the investor may have obtained control in accordance with both IAS 27 and IFRS 10, but then later lost control in accordance with IFRS 10 but not IAS 27. In this case, the investor would cease to consolidate from the date control was lost as defined by IFRS 10. If measurement of the retained interest at the date the investor first became involved with (but did not obtain control in accordance with this IFRS), or lost control of, the investee is impracticable, the investor would apply the requirements in IFRS 10 for accounting for a loss of control at the beginning of the earliest period for which application of those requirements is practicable. The earliest period may be the current period.

BC199 As stated in paragraph BC192, respondents to the Request for Views also commented on the transition requirements of the IFRSs to be issued in 2011. In relation to the transition requirements relating to consolidation, the Board noted that the majority of the respondents to the Request for Views had agreed with limited retrospective application for IFRS 10.

BC199A The Board identified a need to clarify the transition guidance that was intended to achieve limited retrospective application of IFRS 10. The Board noted that the main intention when issuing IFRS 10 was to ensure consistent accounting for transactions when IFRS 10 was applied for the first time (ie 1 January 2013 for a calendar-year entity, assuming no early application). In other words, the intention was to use the date of initial application as the point at which to determine the interests that should be accounted for in accordance with IFRS 10. The Board also noted that the intention was to provide transition relief if the consolidation conclusion would be the same whether applying IAS 27/SIC-12 or IFRS 10 at the date that IFRS 10 was applied for the first time. The Board concluded that, in those situations, the incremental benefit to users of applying IFRS 10 retrospectively would not outweigh the costs.

BC199B   Consequently, the Board confirmed that the 'date of initial application' means the beginning of the annual reporting period for which IFRS 10 is applied for the first time. The Board amended the transition guidance to confirm that an entity is not required to make adjustments to the previous accounting for its involvement with entities if the consolidation conclusion reached at the date of initial application is the same whether applying IAS 27/SIC-12 or IFRS 10. In making this clarification, the Board confirmed that the transition relief in paragraph C3(b) would also apply to interests in investees that were disposed of before the date of initial application of IFRS 10, (ie 1 January 2013 for a calendar-year entity, assuming no early application).

BC199C   In clarifying how an entity should retrospectively adjust its comparative information on initial application of IFRS 10, the Board acknowledged that presenting all adjusted comparatives would be burdensome for preparers in jurisdictions where several years of comparatives are required. Without changing the requirement to apply the recognition and measurement requirements of IFRS 10 retrospectively, the Board decided to limit the requirement to present adjusted comparatives to the annual period immediately preceding the date of initial application. This is consistent with the minimum comparative disclosure requirements contained in IAS 1 *Presentation of Financial Statements* as amended by *Annual Improvements to IFRSs 2009–2011 Cycle* (issued May 2012). Those amendments confirmed that when an entity applies a changed accounting policy retrospectively, it shall present, as a minimum, three statements of financial position (ie 1 January 2012, 31 December 2012 and 31 December 2013 for a calendar-year entity, assuming no early application of this IFRS) and two of each of the other statements (IAS 1 paragraphs 40A–40B). Notwithstanding this requirement, the Board confirmed that an entity is not prohibited from presenting adjusted comparative information for earlier periods. The Board noted that if all comparative periods are not adjusted then entities should be required to state that fact, clearly identify the information that has not been adjusted, and explain the basis on which it has been prepared.

BC199D   The Board also considered the disclosure requirements of IAS 8 *Accounting Policies, Changes in Accounting Estimates and Errors*. On the initial application of an IFRS, paragraph 28(f) of IAS 8 requires an entity to disclose, for the current period and for each prior period presented, the amount of any adjustment for each financial statement line item affected. Changes in the consolidation conclusion on transition to IFRS 10 are likely to affect many line items throughout the financial statements. The Board agreed that this requirement would be burdensome for preparers and so agreed to limit the disclosure of the quantitative impact of any changes in the consolidation conclusion to only the annual period immediately preceding the date of initial application. An entity may also present this information for the current period or for earlier comparative periods, but is not required to do so.

BC199E   The Board considered whether IFRS 1 *First-time Adoption of Financial Reporting Standards* should be amended to allow first-time adopters to use the transition guidance of IFRS 10. It was noted that some respondents to the exposure draft had commented that, particularly when an investee is disposed of or control is lost during the comparative period, the cost of providing temporary consolidation information is not justified. The Board noted that this raised broader issues with the application of IFRS 1 and, rather than address this issue in the context of clarifying IFRS 10 transition relief, it would be more appropriately addressed in the context of IFRS 1 itself.

Transitional provisions (2008 amendments)

BCZ200   To improve the comparability of financial information across entities, amendments to IFRSs are usually applied retrospectively. Therefore, the Board proposed in its 2005 exposure draft to require retrospective application of the amendments to IAS 27, on the basis that the benefits of retrospective application outweigh the costs. However, in that exposure draft the Board identified two circumstances in which it concluded that retrospective application would be impracticable:

(a)   accounting for increases in a parent's ownership interest in a subsidiary that occurred before the effective date of the amendments. Therefore, the accounting for any previous increase in a parent's ownership interest in a subsidiary before the effective date of the amendments should not be adjusted.

(b)   accounting for a parent's investment in a former subsidiary for which control was lost before the effective date of the amendments. Therefore, the carrying amount of any investment in a former subsidiary should not be adjusted to its fair value on the date when control was lost. In addition, an entity should not recalculate any gain or loss on loss of control of a subsidiary if the loss of control occurred before the effective date of the amendments.

BCZ201   The Board concluded that the implementation difficulties and costs associated with applying the amendments retrospectively in these circumstances outweigh the benefits of improved comparability of financial information. Therefore, the Board decided to require prospective application. In addition, the Board concluded that identifying those provisions for which retrospective application of the amendments would be impracticable, and thus prospective application would be required, would reduce implementation costs and result in greater comparability between entities.

BCZ202   Some respondents were concerned that the transitional provisions were different for increases and decreases in ownership interests. They argued that accounting for decreases in non-controlling interests retrospectively imposes compliance costs that are not justifiable, mainly because the requirement to account for increases prospectively reduces comparability anyway. The Board accepted those arguments and decided that prospective application would be required for all changes in ownership interests (those transitional provisions are now in Appendix C of IFRS 10). The revised transitional provisions will lead to increases and decreases in ownership interests being treated symmetrically and the recasting of financial statements being limited to disclosure and presentation. The recognition and measurement of previous transactions will not be changed upon transition.

BCZ203   In response to practical concerns raised by respondents, the Board also decided to require prospective application of the requirement to allocate losses in excess of the non-controlling interests in the equity of a subsidiary to the non-controlling interests, even if that would result in the non-controlling interests being reported as a deficit balance (this transitional provision is now in Appendix C of IFRS 10).

Withdrawal of IAS 27 (2008) and SIC-12

BC204 IFRS 10 identifies the principle of control and determines how to identify whether an investor controls an investee and therefore should consolidate the investee. IFRS 10 also identifies the principles for preparation of consolidated financial statements. IFRS 10 supersedes the requirements related to consolidated financial statements in IAS 27 (as amended in 2008) and SIC-12.

BC205 IFRS 10 does not address the accounting for investments in subsidiaries, jointly controlled entities and associates in separate financial statements as specified in IAS 27. The parts of IAS 27 that relate to separate financial statements have been included in the amended IAS 27.

Summary of main changes from ED 10

BC206 The main changes made by IFRS 10 from the exposure draft ED 10 published in 2008 are:

    (a)   IFRS 10 includes application guidance on all the following topics:

        (i)   the meaning of 'power', 'activities' and 'returns' within the definition of control.

        (ii)   when assessing control of an investee:

- understanding the purpose and design of an investee.

- different activities of an investee that significantly affect the investee's returns.

- a discussion of rights that give an investor power and protective rights.

- power to direct the activities of an investee without a majority of the voting rights, including potential voting rights.

- contractual and non-contractual agency relationships.

    (b)   IFRS 10 requires retrospective application of its requirements subject to the practicability exemption in IAS 8. The exposure draft had proposed prospective application using the requirements of IFRS 3 or the requirements relating to the loss of control on the date of first applying the IFRS.[9]

---

9   *Investment Entities* (Amendments to IFRS 10, IFRS 12 and IAS 27), issued in October 2012, introduced an exception to the principle that all subsidiaries shall be consolidated. The amendments define an investment entity and require a parent that is an investment entity to measure its investments in particular subsidiaries at fair value through profit or loss instead of consolidating those subsidiaries. These amendments are discussed in paragraphs BC215–BC317.

Cost-benefit considerations

BC207   The objective of general purpose financial reporting is to provide information about the financial position, performance and changes in financial position of a reporting entity that is useful to a wide range of users in making economic decisions. To attain this objective, the Board seeks to ensure that an IFRS will meet a significant need and that the overall benefits of the resulting information justify the costs of providing it. Although the costs of implementing a new IFRS might not be borne evenly, users of financial statements benefit from improvements in financial reporting, thereby facilitating the functioning of markets for capital and credit and the efficient allocation of resources in the economy.

BC208   The evaluation of costs and benefits is necessarily subjective. In making its judgement, the Board considered the following:

(a)   the costs incurred by preparers of financial statements;

(b)   the costs incurred by users of financial statements when information is not available;

(c)   the comparative advantage that preparers have in developing information, compared with the costs that users would incur to develop surrogate information;

(d)   the benefit of better economic decision-making as a result of improved financial reporting; and

(e)   the costs of transition for users, preparers and others.

BC209   The Board observed that IFRS 10 will improve the usefulness of consolidated financial statements by developing a single basis for consolidation (control) and robust guidance for applying that basis to situations in which it has proved difficult to assess control in practice and divergence has evolved. IFRS 10 introduces a definition of control of an investee that is applied consistently when assessing whether an investor should consolidate an investee, irrespective of the nature of the investee. IFRS 10 also requires retrospective application of the requirements subject to the practicability exemptions in IAS 8 that will result in comparable information for all periods presented.

BC210   Users prefer information that is comparable from reporting period to reporting period for an individual entity and between different entities in a particular reporting period. The Board concluded that IFRS 10 provides much clearer principles that underlie the definition of control of an investee and provides more application guidance when assessing control than the requirements it replaces. As a consequence, users should have more comparable and verifiable information about the activities controlled by the reporting entity.

BC211   If the requirements in an IFRS are not clear, or there is no guidance, the preparer will often have to seek independent advice and engage with its auditors to resolve uncertainty about how to account for a particular type of transaction. These costs should decrease if the requirements in the revised IFRS are clearer. Accordingly, because IFRS 10 addresses the concerns conveyed to the Board about the absence of guidance in IAS 27 and SIC-12, the Board concluded that preparers will benefit from the new requirements. The Board accepts that any new IFRS will cause preparers to incur one–off costs associated with learning the new requirements and reassessing their accounting. However, the Board's assessment is that the benefits from providing clearer principles and more application guidance outweigh those costs.

BC212   The changes to the definition of control will inevitably lead to some reporting entities consolidating some entities that were previously not consolidated and ceasing consolidation of some entities, or both. The Board does not think it is appropriate to consider whether there will be 'more or less consolidation' by applying the new proposals. However, the clarifications in relation to less than a majority of the voting rights will lead to more consolidation. In the case of what SIC-12 referred to as special purpose entities, the Board believes that the new requirements will result in more appropriate consolidation.

BC213   Given the benefits for users and preparers noted in paragraphs BC209–BC211 the Board believes that the benefits of IFRS 10 outweigh the costs.

BC214   This project also considered disclosure requirements in relation to consolidation. Those requirements, and the related costs and benefits, are assessed in the Basis for Conclusions on IFRS 12.

Exception to consolidation for investment entities (2012 amendments)

Background

BC215   In October 2012, the Board issued *Investment Entities* (Amendments to IFRS 10, IFRS 12 and IAS 27), which provides an exception to consolidation for a class of entities that are defined as 'investment entities'. The Board added the Investment Entities project to its agenda in the course of its deliberations on IFRS 10 as a response to the comments received on ED 10.

BC216   The Board had considered this issue previously. In 2002, the respondents to the Exposure Draft of IAS 27 asked the Board to provide an exception to consolidation for the subsidiaries of venture capital organisations, private equity entities and similar organisations. At that time, the Board decided not to introduce such an exception because it did not think that it should differentiate between the types of entity, or the types of investment, when applying a control model of consolidation. It also did not agree that management's reasons for holding an investment should determine whether or not that investment is consolidated. The Board concluded that for investments under the control of venture capital organisations, private equity entities and similar organisations, users' information needs are best served by financial statements in which those investments are consolidated, thus revealing the extent of the operations of the entities they control.

BC217   The scope of the proposals in ED 10 was the same as the scope of the proposals in IAS 27. IAS 27 required reporting entities to consolidate all controlled entities, regardless of the nature of the reporting entity. Respondents to ED 10 questioned the usefulness of financial statements of investment entities that consolidate investees that the investment entity controls. They pointed out that some national accounting requirements, including United States Generally Accepted Accounting Principles (US GAAP), have historically provided industry-specific guidance that requires investment entities to measure all of their investments, including those that they control, at fair value. The respondents argued that an investment entity holds investments for the sole purpose of capital appreciation, investment income (such as dividends or interest), or both. Users of the financial statements of these investment entities told the Board that the fair value of the investments and an understanding of how the investment entity measures the fair value of its investments is the most useful information.

BC218   Furthermore, respondents to ED 10 argued that consolidated financial statements of an investment entity may hinder users' ability to assess an investment entity's financial position and results, because it emphasises the financial position, operations and cash flows of the investee, rather than those of the investment entity. Often, an investment entity holds non-controlling interests in some entities that are reported at fair value, as well as controlling interests in other entities that are consolidated in accordance with current principles in IFRSs. Reporting investments on more than one basis hinders comparability within the financial statements, because all investments are held by an investment entity for a similar purpose—returns from capital appreciation, investment income, or both. In addition, some of the items consolidated may be measured at historical cost, which distorts the performance assessment of the investment entity and does not reflect the way in which the business of the entity is managed.

BC219   Respondents to ED 10 also argued that when an investment entity consolidates entities that it controls, it is not required to provide the disclosures related to fair value measurements that would be required if the subsidiaries were measured at fair value. For example, IFRS 7 relates only to recognised financial assets and liabilities. There is no requirement to provide disclosures related to fair value for investments in consolidated subsidiaries. Information about fair value and the methodology and inputs used for determining fair value is vital for users to make investment decisions about investment entities. Investors in an investment entity are interested in the fair value of their interest in that entity and often transact with it on a fair value basis (ie their investment in the investment entity is based on a share of the net assets of that entity). Reporting the fair value of substantially all of the net assets of an investment entity allows the investors in that entity to more easily identify the value of their share of those net assets.

BC220   In response to this feedback, the Board published an Exposure Draft *Investment Entities* (*Investment Entities* ED) in August 2011. The *Investment Entities* ED proposed that investment entities would be required to measure their investments in subsidiaries (except those subsidiaries that provide investment–related services) at fair value through profit or loss in accordance with IFRS 9 *Financial Instruments* (or IAS 39,[10] if IFRS 9 has not yet been adopted).[11] The majority of respondents to

10 IFRS 9 *Financial Instruments* replaced IAS 39. IFRS 9 applies to all items that were previously within the scope of IAS 39.

the *Investment Entities* ED broadly supported the proposed exception to consolidation for the reasons outlined in paragraphs BC217–BC219.

BC221 The Board conducted its deliberations leading to the publication of the *Investment Entities* ED and the final investment entities requirements jointly with the FASB. The similarities and differences between the investment entities guidance in IFRS and US GAAP are discussed further in paragraphs BC289–BC291.

Scope of the project

BC222 The *Investment Entities* ED proposed a limited-scope exception to consolidation for investment entities. A number of respondents to the *Investment Entities* ED asked the Board to expand the scope of its proposals.

BC223 Some respondents asked the Board to expand the scope of the project to require an investment entity to measure all of its investments at fair value. However, the Board noted that, in most cases, existing IFRSs require or permit investments held by an investment entity to be measured at fair value. For example an entity:

(a) may elect the fair value option in IAS 40 *Investment Property*; and

(b) would be required to measure its financial assets at fair value through profit or loss in accordance with IFRS 9 (or IAS 39[12]) when those assets are managed on a fair value basis.

Consequently, the Board decided to limit the scope of the project to only providing an exception to consolidation for investment entities.

BC224 Other respondents requested an extension of the proposed exception to consolidation. In particular, respondents from the insurance industry requested an exception to consolidating their interests in insurance investment funds. They argued that presenting the fair value of their interests in insurance investment funds as a single line item, along with a single line item for the current value of their liability to policyholders who receive the returns from those investment funds, would provide more useful information to users than consolidation. The Board noted that providing an exception to consolidation for insurers' interests in insurance investment funds is outside the scope of the Investment Entities project, which was meant to provide an exception to consolidation for investment entities. In addition, any additional exceptions to consolidation would require the Board to do further work to define the entities that could apply those exceptions. The Board noted that this additional exception to consolidation was not contemplated in the scope of the project nor was it exposed for comment. Consequently, the Board decided not to extend the proposed exception to consolidation.

---

11 In December 2014, the Board issued *Investment Entities: Applying the Consolidation Exception* (Amendments to IFRS 10, IFRS 12 and IAS 28). These amendments clarified which subsidiaries of an investment entity are consolidated in accordance with paragraph 32 of IFRS 10, instead of being measured at fair value through profit or loss (see paragraphs BC240A–BC240I).

12 IFRS 9 *Financial Instruments* replaced IAS 39. IFRS 9 applies to all items that were previously within the scope of IAS 39.

BC225   Other respondents asked the Board to provide guidance permitting an investor in an investment entity to use the reported net asset value (NAV) per share of that investment entity as a practical expedient for measuring the fair value of its investment in that investment entity. Similar guidance exists in US GAAP. The Board considered providing such a practical expedient in their deliberations on IFRS 13 but decided against it because, at the time, there was no specific accounting guidance for investment entities in IFRS and because there are different practices for calculating NAVs in jurisdictions around the world. The Board decided that it is outside the scope of the Investment Entities project to provide fair value measurement guidance for investments in investment entities. The Board developed the definition of an investment entity to identify which entities should qualify for an exception to consolidation. The definition was not designed to decide which entities should qualify for a fair value measurement practical expedient. Moreover, the Board still has concerns that NAV could be calculated differently in different jurisdictions. Consequently, the Board decided not to provide an NAV practical expedient for fair value measurement as part of the Investment Entities project.

BC226   The Board has decided to adopt an entity-based approach to the exception to consolidation. That is, the exception to consolidation is based on the type of entity that owns the subsidiary. The Board considered providing an asset-based approach to the exception to consolidation. Under an asset-based approach, an entity would consider its relationship with, and the characteristics of, each of its subsidiaries (that is, each individual asset) to decide whether fair value measurement is more appropriate than consolidation. However, the Board decided to retain the entity-based exception to consolidation that was proposed in the *Investment Entities* ED. The Board was concerned that an asset-based approach would significantly broaden the exception to consolidation by making the exception available to any entity holding relevant assets. This would represent a significant conceptual change to the consolidation model that the Board has developed in this IFRS. In addition, the Board believes that investment entities have a unique business model that makes reporting subsidiaries at fair value more appropriate than consolidation. An entity-based approach captures the unique business model of investment entities.

BC227   The Board also considered providing an option to allow investment entities to either consolidate subsidiaries or measure them at fair value through profit or loss. However, the Board believes that providing this option would be inconsistent with their view that fair value information is the most relevant information for all investment entities. Moreover, providing an option would reduce comparability between different investment entities. Consequently, the Board decided that an investment entity should be required to measure its subsidiaries at fair value through profit or loss.

Approach to assessing investment entity status

BC228   In the *Investment Entities* ED, the Board proposed six criteria that must be met in order for an entity to qualify as an investment entity. These criteria were based on guidance in US GAAP (Topic 946 *Financial Services—Investment Companies* in the *FASB Accounting Standards Codification*®).

BC229   Many respondents expressed concern that requiring an entity to meet all six criteria proposed in the *Investment Entities* ED would be too prescriptive. They thought that the proposed criteria inappropriately focused on the structure of an investment entity rather than on its business model and did not allow for the use of judgement in determining whether an entity is an investment entity. These respondents stated that a less prescriptive approach to assessing the criteria would result in more consistent reporting by entities with similar business models.

BC230   In addition, many respondents argued that the six proposed criteria in the *Investment Entities* ED did not provide a general description of an investment entity and an explanation of why fair value measurement is more relevant for the subsidiaries of an investment entity. Because the concept of an investment entity is new to IFRS, those respondents argued that the guidance should include a more general definition of an investment entity (rather than merely criteria to be an investment entity) and a justification for the exception to consolidation.

BC231   In response to the comments from respondents, the Board decided to provide a definition of an investment entity based on some of the criteria originally proposed in the *Investment Entities* ED. An entity that meets the definition of an investment entity would not consolidate its controlled subsidiaries (other than those subsidiaries that provide investment-related services or activities).[13]

BC232   The Board agreed with respondents who stated that some of the proposed criteria were too strict and would inappropriately exclude some structures from qualifying as investment entities. The Board believes that there are structures in practice in which an entity does not meet one or more of the criteria that were described in the *Investment Entities* ED, but should still qualify as an investment entity. For example, the *Investment Entities* ED required an investment entity to have more than one investor; the Board thinks that some pension funds, sovereign wealth funds, and other investment funds with a single investor should qualify as investment entities. Moreover, respondents commented that the application guidance in the *Investment Entities* ED provided too many exceptions to the strict criteria.

BC233   Consequently, the Board decided that an entity would not be required to satisfy the remaining criteria to meet the definition of an investment entity and qualify for the exception to consolidation. However, the Board noted that the remaining criteria represent typical characteristics of an investment entity and decided to include these typical characteristics in the investment entities guidance to help entities determine whether they qualify as an investment entity. If an entity does not display one or more of the typical characteristics, it indicates that additional judgement is required in determining whether the entity meets the definition of an investment entity. Consequently, the Board

---

13   In December 2014, the Board issued *Investment Entities: Applying the Consolidation Exception* (Amendments to IFRS 10, IFRS 12 and IAS 28). These amendments clarified which subsidiaries of an investment entity are consolidated in accordance with paragraph 32 of IFRS 10, instead of being measured at fair value through profit or loss (see paragraphs BC240A–BC240I).

also decided that an investment entity that does not have one or more of the typical characteristics would be required to disclose how it still meets the definition of an investment entity.

BC234   The Board thinks that it is very unlikely that an entity that displays none of the typical characteristics of an investment entity would meet the definition of one. However, it may be possible in rare circumstances. For example, a pension fund that has a single investor and does not issue equity ownership interests could qualify as an investment entity even if it only holds a single investment temporarily (eg at commencement or wind-down of the entity).

BC235   The Board believes that defining an investment entity and describing its typical characteristics achieves a balance between clearly defining those entities that qualify for the exception to consolidation and avoiding the use of bright lines. In addition, this approach allows the definition to stand on its own, with application guidance providing clarification rather than exceptions.

Definition of an investment entity

BC236   The definition of an investment entity has three essential elements that differentiate investment entities from other types of entities.

Investment management services

BC237   The Board noted that one of the essential activities of an investment entity is that it obtains funds from investors in order to provide those investors with investment management services. The Board believes that this provision of investment management services differentiates investment entities from other entities. Consequently, the Board decided that the definition of an investment entity should state that an investment entity obtains funds from an investor or investors and provides the investor(s) with investment management services.

Business purpose

BC238   The Board believes that an entity's activities and business purpose are critical to determining whether it is an investment entity. An investment entity collects funds from investors and invests those funds to obtain returns solely from capital appreciation, investment income, or both. Consequently, the Board decided that the definition of an investment entity should state that an investment entity commits to its investor(s) that its business purpose is to provide investment management services and invest funds solely for returns from capital appreciation, investment income, or both.

BC239   The *Investment Entities* ED did not allow an entity to qualify as an investment entity if it provided substantive investment-related services to third parties. While some respondents agreed with this, others argued that an investment entity should be allowed to provide such services to third parties. They argued that the provision of these investment-related services to third parties is simply an extension of the investment entity's investing activities and should not prohibit an entity from qualifying as an investment entity. The Board agreed with these arguments, concluding that the provision of such services is within the business model of an investment entity. Although such an entity may earn fee income from the provision of investment-related services, its sole business purpose is still investing for capital appreciation, investment income, or both (whether that is for itself, for its investors or for external parties).

BC240   The Board noted that an investment entity may sometimes hold an interest in a subsidiary that provides investment-related services for its investment activities. The Board did not think that the existence of such a subsidiary should prohibit an entity from qualifying as an investment entity, even if those services were substantial or were provided to third parties in addition to the entity. The Board views such services as an extension of the operations of the investment entity and therefore concluded that subsidiaries that provide those services should be consolidated.

BC240A   In December 2014, the Board issued *Investment Entities: Applying the Consolidation Exception* (Amendments to IFRS 10, IFRS 12 and IAS 28). This amended paragraphs 32, BC85C and B85E of IFRS 10 to clarify which subsidiaries of an investment entity should be consolidated instead of being measured at fair value. The amendments were made in response to a request for the Board to clarify how to apply paragraph 32 when the subsidiary of an investment entity itself meets the definition of an investment entity and provides services that relate to the parent's investment activities.

BC240B   The Board decided to clarify that an investment entity shall measure at fair value through profit or loss all of its subsidiaries that are themselves investment entities. This is consistent with its decision not to distinguish between investment entity subsidiaries established for different purposes (see paragraph BC272). This was supported by the majority of respondents to both the *Investment Entities* ED and the Exposure Draft *Investment Entities: Applying the Consolidation Exception* (Proposed amendments to IFRS 10 and IAS 28), published in June 2014 (the 'Consolidation Exception ED').

BC240C   Some respondents to the *Consolidation Exception* ED suggested that requiring an investment entity to measure each investment entity subsidiary at fair value as a single item results in a loss of information about each subsidiary's underlying investments and the activities of that subsidiary. They suggested that an investment entity parent should be able to apply a 'dual-model' of consolidation, which would allow an investment entity parent to show its directly and indirectly held investments at fair value while consolidating other activities. This is similar to the asset-based approach previously rejected by the Board (see paragraph BC226).

BC240D   The Board acknowledged some of the potential benefits of an asset-based approach. In particular, this approach may better avoid some structuring issues, particularly in multi-layer groups in which different types of subsidiaries are held at different levels within the group. However, the Board decided that developing a broader principle-based approach, together with guidance to enable consistent application, would be too difficult to achieve within the limited scope of the consolidation exception clarification project. In addition, the Board decided that such an approach and related guidance could not be developed within the short time frame that was needed to provide the necessary clarification before the end of 2014. These decisions were, in part, based on the variety of suggestions provided by respondents to the *Consolidation Exception* ED about which activities should be consolidated and which should be measured at fair value.

BC240E   The Board noted that the requirement in paragraph 32 of IFRS 10 to consolidate particular subsidiaries of an investment entity was intended to be a limited exception, capturing only operating subsidiaries that support the investment entity parent's investing activities as an extension of the operations of the investment entity parent. It was not intended to capture subsidiaries that are themselves investment entities. The definition of an investment entity requires that the investment entity's business purpose and, therefore, its core activity is providing investment management services to its investors and investing the funds obtained from its investors solely for returns from capital appreciation, investment income, or both. When the Board decided that providing investment-related services to third parties would not prevent an entity from qualifying as an investment entity, it recognised that investment entities could benefit from synergies between the core investing activities and the provision of investment-related services to third parties.

BC240F   The Board noted that, therefore, when an entity assesses whether it qualifies as an investment entity, it considers whether providing services to third parties is ancillary to its core investing activities. However, the definition of an investment entity requires that the purpose of the entity is to invest solely for capital appreciation, investment income (such as dividends, interest and rental income) or both (see paragraph B85B of IFRS 10). Consequently, an entity whose main purpose is to provide investment-related services in exchange for consideration from third parties has a business purpose that is different from the business purpose of an investment entity. This is because the entity's main activity is earning fee income in exchange for its services. In contrast, for an entity that qualifies as an investment entity, such fee income, which could be substantial in amount, will be derived from its core investment activities, which are designed for earning capital appreciation, investment income or both.

BC240G   The Board decided that requiring an investment entity to measure all of its subsidiaries that are themselves investment entities at fair value through profit or loss is consistent with the entity-based approach and decided to confirm its proposal in the *Consolidation Exception* ED. Consequently, when an investment entity parent assesses whether a subsidiary should be measured at fair value in accordance with paragraph 31 of IFRS 10 or, instead, should be consolidated in accordance with paragraph 32 of IFRS 10, the parent assesses whether the subsidiary meets the definition of an investment entity. If so, the investment entity parent measures its investment entity subsidiary at fair value through profit or loss in accordance with paragraph 31.

BC240H   If the subsidiary is not an investment entity, the investment entity parent assesses whether the main activities undertaken by the subsidiary support the core investment activities of the parent. If so, the subsidiary's activities are considered to be an extension of the parent's core investing activities and the subsidiary would be consolidated in accordance with paragraph 32 of IFRS 10. The Board noted that a subsidiary of an investment entity that provides support services to its parent and other members of the group, such as administration, treasury, payroll and accounting services, is considered to be providing those services as an extension of the operations of the parent. Such a non-investment entity subsidiary would be consolidated in accordance with paragraph 32 of IFRS 10.

BC240I   The Board concluded that these outcomes are consistent with its basic decision that measuring all investments of investment entities at fair value through profit or loss provides the most relevant information, except for operating subsidiaries that act as an extension of the investment entity parent.

BC241   The Board considered prohibiting investment entities from engaging in some activities, such as providing financial support to its investees or actively managing its investees. However, the Board understands that an investment entity may engage in these activities in order to maximise the overall value of the investee (ie to maximise capital appreciation), rather than to obtain other benefits. Consequently, the Board believes that these activities can be consistent with the overall activities of an investment entity and should not be prohibited as long as they do not represent a separate substantial business activity or source of income other than capital appreciation.

BC242   The Board was concerned that an entity that meets the definition of an investment entity could be inserted into a larger corporate structure to achieve a particular accounting outcome. For example, a parent entity could use an 'internal' investment entity subsidiary to invest in subsidiaries that may be making losses (eg research and development activities on behalf of the overall group) and would record its investments at fair value, rather than reflecting the underlying activities of the investee. To address these concerns and to emphasise the business purpose of an investment entity, the Board decided to include a requirement that an investment entity, or other members of the group containing the entity, should not obtain benefits from its investees that would be unavailable to other parties that are not related to the investee. In the Board's view, this is one of the factors that differentiate an investment entity from a non-investment entity holding company. If an entity or another member of the group containing the entity obtains benefits from its investees that are unavailable to other investors, then the investment will benefit that entity or the group in some operating or strategic capacity and the entity will therefore not qualify as an investment entity.

BC243   However, the Board also clarified that an investment entity may have more than one investment in the same industry, market or geographical area in order to benefit from synergies that increase the capital appreciation of those investments. It noted that such a fact pattern may be common in the private equity industry. Some Board members expressed concern that allowing transactions or synergies between investments may artificially increase the fair value of each investment and, consequently, inappropriately increase the assets reported by the investment entity. However, the Board decided that trading transactions or synergies that arise between the investments of an investment entity should not be prohibited because their existence does not necessarily mean that the investment entity is receiving any returns beyond solely capital appreciation, investment income, or both.

Exit strategy

BC244 The Board believes that a parent with operating subsidiaries often plans to own and operate its subsidiaries indefinitely to realise returns from those operations. However, the Board does not think that an entity that holds its investments indefinitely, especially its subsidiaries, should qualify as an investment entity. Accordingly, the Board considered requiring an exit strategy for substantially all investments held by an investment entity, including debt investments.

BC245 However, respondents to the *Investment Entities* ED noted that some investment funds that would otherwise qualify as investment entities may hold a significant amount of debt investments to maturity and therefore would not have an exit strategy for those debt investments. For example, the Board understands that, in some cases, private equity funds may make both debt and equity investments in their investees. The debt investments may have shorter maturities than the anticipated term of the fund's equity investment and may be held to maturity. Moreover, an investment entity may hold debt instruments to maturity to manage liquidity risk or to mitigate the risk from holding other types of more volatile investments. Although the entity does not have an exit strategy for these debt investments, it does not plan to hold them indefinitely—even if the entity does not plan to sell these investments before maturity, the vast majority of debt investments have a limited life.

BC246 The Board decided that such an entity should not be prohibited from qualifying as an investment entity, provided that substantially all of its investments (including debt investments) are measured at fair value. The Board noted that debt investments may be measured at fair value in accordance with IFRS 9 or IAS 39[14] even in the absence of an exit strategy.

BC247 However, the Board decided that an investment entity must have an exit strategy for substantially all of its investments that can be held indefinitely (typically equity investments and non-financial assets). The Board does not think it is appropriate for an entity to qualify for an exception to consolidation if that entity is holding equity investments indefinitely and is not planning to realise capital appreciation from those investments. Although the exit strategy may vary depending on circumstances, potential exit strategies that include a substantive time frame for exiting from the investment should still be identified and documented for equity and non-financial investments in order to meet the definition of an investment entity.

BC248 The Board noted that an entity may fail to meet this component of the definition of an investment entity if it is formed in connection with an investment entity investee for legal, regulatory, tax or similar business reasons (eg a 'blocker' entity or a 'master-feeder' structure), and that that investee holds investments on behalf of the entity. The Board decided that the entity should not be prohibited from qualifying as an investment entity merely because it does not have an exit strategy for the investee, if that investee qualifies as an investment entity and has appropriate exit strategies for its own investments.

---

14 IFRS 9 *Financial Instruments* replaced IAS 39. IFRS 9 applies to all items that were previously within the scope of IAS 39.

Fair value measurement

BC249   In the development of IFRS 10 and the *Investment Entities* ED, the Board heard that fair value information is the primary driver of the decision-making processes both of the management of, and the investors in, investment entities. Many respondents stated that both management and investors evaluate the performance of an investment entity by reference to the fair value of its investments. The Board heard that some investors in investment entities disregard the consolidated financial statements of investment entities and instead rely on non-GAAP fair value reports.

BC250   The basis for the exception to consolidation that is provided to investment entities is that fair value information is the most relevant for an investment entity's investments, including its investments in subsidiaries. The Board therefore decided that an essential feature of the definition of an investment entity is that the entity would use existing IFRS requirements or accounting policy options to measure substantially all of its investments at fair value. The Board does not think that an entity that fails to elect the fair value measurement options available in IAS 28 *Investments in Associates and Joint Ventures* or IAS 40, or that accounts for more than an insignificant amount of its financial assets at amortised cost under IFRS 9 or IAS 39,[15] should qualify as an investment entity.

BC251   The Board noted that some investments may be measured at fair value in the statement of financial position, with fair value changes recognised in other comprehensive income rather than through profit or loss, and agreed that this would satisfy the fair value measurement element of the definition of an investment entity.

BC252   The Board considers that a significant distinguishing characteristic of an investment entity is that investors in an investment entity are primarily interested in fair value and make their investing decisions based on the fair value of the investment entity's underlying investments. The Board notes that this is partly because, in many cases, investors in an investment entity transact with it on a fair value basis (for example, on the basis of a net asset value per share, which is calculated using the fair value of the entity's underlying investments). Similarly, the Board believes that fair value should also be used by an investment entity's key management personnel to assess the entity's performance and to make investing decisions. Consequently, the Board decided that, in order to meet the definition of an investment entity, an entity should demonstrate that fair value is the primary measurement attribute used to evaluate the performance of its investments, both internally and externally.

Regulatory requirements

BC253   The Board considered whether to include a reference to regulatory requirements in the definition of an investment entity. The Board noted that the FASB proposed, in their own Exposure Draft, that any entity that was regulated as an investment company under the US Securities and Exchange Commission's Investment Company Act of 1940 would automatically be considered to be an

---

15 IFRS 9 *Financial Instruments* replaced IAS 39. IFRS 9 applies to all items that were previously within the scope of IAS 39.

investment company for US GAAP financial reporting purposes. Some respondents to the Board's *Investment Entities* ED also asked the Board to include a reference to regulatory requirements in the definition of an investment entity, which would allow any entity regulated as an investment entity to fall within the scope of the investment entity requirements.

BC254 However, the Board was concerned that:

(a) the regulatory requirements in different jurisdictions may result in similar entities qualifying as an investment entity in one jurisdiction but not in another;

(b) regulatory requirements may change over time, resulting in an ever-changing population of entities that would be eligible for an exception to consolidation; and

(c) it would have no control over which entities would qualify for the exception to consolidation.

Consequently, the Board decided not to reference regulatory requirements in the definition of an investment entity.

Typical characteristics of investment entities

BC255 The Board identified several 'typical characteristics' of an investment entity. The Board decided that these typical characteristics could be used to help an entity decide if it meets the definition of an investment entity. The absence of any of these typical characteristics may indicate that an entity does not meet the definition of an investment entity. However, an entity that does not display all of these typical characteristics could, nevertheless, meet the definition of an investment entity.

BC256 The Board identified the following typical characteristics of an investment entity:

(a) more than one investment (paragraphs BC257–BC258);

(b) more than one investor (paragraphs BC259–BC260);

(c) unrelated investors (paragraphs BC261–BC262); and

(d) ownership interests (paragraphs BC263–BC267).

More than one investment

BC257 The *Investment Entities* ED proposed that an investment entity should hold more than one investment. However, respondents provided examples of entities that they believed should qualify as investment entities, but that only hold a single investment. These included single investment funds set up because the required minimum investment is too high for individual investors, or investment funds that hold a single investment temporarily.

BC258 The Board agreed with these arguments and therefore decided that an investment entity would not be required to hold more than one investment. However, the Board understands that investment entities typically invest in more than one investment as a means of diversifying their portfolio and maximising their returns. Consequently, investing in more than one investment is described as a typical characteristic of an investment entity in this IFRS.

More than one investor

BC259 The presence of more than one investor was originally proposed as a requirement in the *Investment Entities* ED. However, respondents provided many examples of investment funds with a single investor. These included funds that temporarily have a single investor, government-owned investment funds, funds wholly-owned by pension plans and endowments, and funds set up by an investment manager for an unrelated single investor with a unique investment strategy.

BC260 The Board does not think that there is a conceptual reason why an investment fund with a single investor should be disqualified from being an investment entity. However, the Board thinks that having more than one investor would make it less likely that the entity, or other members of the group that contains the entity, would obtain benefits other than capital appreciation or investment income from its investment. Consequently, the Board decided to include the presence of more than one investor as a typical characteristic of an investment entity rather than as part of the definition of an investment entity.

Unrelated investors

BC261 The *Investment Entities* ED proposed that an investment entity be required to have investors that are unrelated to the entity or its parent (if any), partly to prevent entities from structuring around the requirement to have more than one investor. However, respondents provided examples of entities with related investors that they believed should qualify as investment entities. For example, a separate 'parallel' entity may be formed to allow the employees of an investment entity to invest in a fund that mirrors the investments in the main fund. The Board agreed with the respondents' arguments and decided that an investment entity would not be required to have investors that are unrelated to the investment entity or to other members of the group that contains the investment entity.

BC262 However, the Board understands that investment entities typically have unrelated investors. Again, having unrelated investors is one way to help ensure that the entity, or another member of the group that contains the entity, does not receive returns from investments that are other than capital appreciation or investment income. Having investors that are unrelated to the entity or its parent (if any), is therefore described as a typical characteristic of an investment entity in this IFRS.

Ownership interests

BC263 An investment entity would typically have ownership interests in the form of equity or similar (eg partnership) interests that entitle investors to a proportionate share of the net assets of the investment entity. This characteristic explains in part why fair value is more relevant to investment entity investors: each unit of ownership in the investment entity entitles an investor to a proportionate share of the net assets of that investment entity. The value of each ownership interest is linked directly to the fair value of the investment entity's investments.

BC264   However, the Board believes that this form of ownership interests in an entity should not be the deciding factor as to whether it is an investment entity. Respondents provided examples of entities that do not have units of ownership in the form of equity or similar interests but provide investors with a proportionate share of their net assets. For example, a pension fund or sovereign wealth fund with a single direct investor may have beneficiaries that are entitled to the net assets of the investment fund, but do not have ownership units. In addition, respondents noted that funds with different share classes or funds in which investors have discretion to invest in individual assets would be disqualified from investment entity status because they did not provide each investor with a proportionate share of net assets.

BC265   The Board does not believe that an entity that provides its investors only a return of their investment plus interest should qualify as an investment entity. Fair value information is more relevant to investors that are entitled to a specifically identifiable portion of the investment entity's net assets and are, therefore, exposed to the upside and downside of the investment entity's performance.

BC266   However, the Board agreed that the requirement proposed in the *Investment Entities* ED (that an investment entity's ownership interests entitle investors to a proportionate share of its net assets) would have inappropriately excluded certain structures from investment entity status. As an alternative, the Board considered requiring that an investment entity's ownership interests be in the form of equity or similar interests. However, the Board was concerned that this would put too much emphasis on the debt/equity classification in IAS 32 *Financial Instruments: Presentation* and would inappropriately exclude some structures whose ownership interests were classified as debt. Moreover, the Board was also concerned that including the 'ownership interest' concept as part of the definition of an investment entity would put too much emphasis on the form of the entity, rather than emphasising its business model.

BC267   Consequently, the Board decided not to include ownership interests as part of the definition of an investment entity but that it should instead be regarded as a typical characteristic of an investment entity.

Reassessment and change of status

BC268   The Board included guidance in the *Investment Entities* ED on reassessing investment entity status. A few respondents asked the Board to clarify this guidance.

BC269   In the *Investment Entities* ED, the Board proposed that an entity would reassess its investment entity status whenever facts or circumstances changed. The Board decided to retain this requirement unchanged because it is consistent with the requirements for reassessment elsewhere in IFRS, including the general reassessment requirements in IFRS 10. The Board noted that they do not believe that the reassessment of facts and circumstances in other situations is considered unduly onerous for preparers or their auditors.

BC270   The Board decided that, when an entity loses investment entity status, it should account for that change as a 'deemed acquisition'. That is, the investment entity would use the fair value of the investment at the date of the change of status as the 'deemed' consideration transferred to obtain control of the investee. This recognises the change in status in the same way as a business combination achieved in stages, as described in IFRS 3. This would result in the recognition of goodwill or a gain on a bargain purchase.

BC271   The Board also decided that, when an entity becomes an investment entity, the entity should account for the change in status as a 'deemed disposal' or 'loss of control' of its subsidiaries. The fair value of the investment at the date of the change of status should be used as the consideration received when applying the guidance in IFRS 10. The Board considered how to account for the gain or loss on the 'deemed disposal' and decided to recognise it as a gain or loss in profit or loss. This treats the change in the business purpose of the investor as a significant economic event and is consistent with the rationale for gains and losses being recognised in profit or loss in IFRS 10 when control is lost.

Parent of an investment entity

Investment entity parent of an investment entity subsidiary

BC272   The *Investment Entities* ED proposed that an investment entity would measure all of its subsidiaries at fair value (except for those subsidiaries providing investment-related services), even those investees who were themselves investment entities. Some respondents questioned this proposal and suggested that at least some investment entity subsidiaries should be consolidated (for example, wholly-owned investment entity subsidiaries that are created for legal, tax or regulatory purposes). However, the Board thinks that fair value measurement of all an investment entity's subsidiaries (except for those subsidiaries providing investment-related services or activities) would provide the most useful information and therefore decided to retain this proposal. The Board considered requiring an investment entity to consolidate only those investment entity subsidiaries that are formed for legal, tax or regulatory purposes, but decided against this because there is no conceptual basis for distinguishing between different investment entity subsidiaries. Moreover, the Board thinks that it would be very difficult to distinguish between an investment entity subsidiary formed for a specific legal, tax or regulatory purpose and those that are set up only for other business reasons.

BC273   The Board considered whether it should require certain investment entity parents to attach the financial statements of their investment entity subsidiaries to the parent's financial statements. Some respondents argued that it would be essential for users of the financial statements of an investment entity parent to have information about the underlying investments of its investment entity subsidiary, particularly when the investment entity parent has only one investment entity subsidiary (eg 'master-feeder funds').

BC274   However, the Board decided against requiring financial statements of an investment entity subsidiary to be attached to the financial statements of an investment entity parent. The Board believed that it would be difficult to define which types of structures should be covered by such a requirement. Moreover, the Board thought that such a requirement would be inconsistent with the proposal that fair value information is always the most relevant information for investment entities.

Non-investment entity parent of an investment entity subsidiary

BC275   The Board also considered whether to retain investment entity accounting in the financial statements of a non-investment entity parent. In the *Investment Entities* ED, the Board proposed that a non-investment entity parent of an investment entity subsidiary would be required to consolidate all of its subsidiaries; that is, the exception to consolidation available to an investment entity would not be available to its non-investment entity parent.

BC276   The Board noted that the majority of respondents disagreed with the proposal, arguing that if fair value information is more relevant than consolidation at an investment entity subsidiary level, it is also more relevant information at the non-investment entity parent level.

BC277   The Board acknowledged the comments received but decided to retain the proposal to require all non-investment entity parents to consolidate all of their subsidiaries.

BC278   The Board has decided to provide an exception to consolidation because of the unique business model of investment entities. Non-investment entities do not have this unique business model; they have other substantial activities besides investing, or do not manage substantially all of their assets on a fair value basis. Consequently, the argument for a fair value measurement requirement is weakened at a non-investment entity level.

BC279   The Board also noted that the decision to define an investment entity and describe its typical characteristics rather than requiring an investment entity to meet a number of criteria has increased the population of entities that could qualify as investment entities, and has also increased the amount of judgement needed to determine whether an entity is an investment entity. For example, an entity with a single investor, or an entity that provides day-to-day management services or strategic advice to its subsidiary, can qualify as an investment entity under this IFRS, when such entities would have been excluded under the *Investment Entities* ED.

BC280   The Board was concerned that some of these changes would increase the likelihood that a non-investment entity parent could achieve different accounting outcomes by holding subsidiaries directly or indirectly through an investment entity. The Board noted that, for example, a non-investment entity parent may elect to hold subsidiaries through an investment entity subsidiary in order to hide leverage or loss-making activities.

BC281   In addition, the Board considered the practical difficulties in retaining the exception to consolidation when a non-investment entity parent and an investment entity subsidiary invest in the same investment or when an investment entity subsidiary holds a subsidiary that invests in the equity of a non-investment entity parent.

BC282   The Board noted that the retention of the specialised accounting used by an investment company subsidiary at a non-investment company level is a long-standing requirement in US GAAP. However, US GAAP has industry-specific guidance for a number of industries, and the application of that industry-specific guidance by a subsidiary is retained by a parent entity, regardless of whether the parent entity is part of that industry. IFRSs generally do not contain such industry-specific guidance.

BC283   Some respondents to the *Investment Entities* ED noted that not retaining the fair value accounting of an investment entity subsidiary in its non-investment entity parent's financial statements seems inconsistent with IAS 28 *Investments in Associates and Joint Ventures*. IAS 28 allows a parent that indirectly holds an investment in an associate through a venture capital organisation, mutual fund, unit trust or similar entity to measure that portion of the investment at fair value through profit or loss in accordance with IFRS 9 or IAS 39.[16] The Board acknowledged the inconsistency but thought it was important to keep the retention of fair value accounting that is currently allowed for venture capital organisations, mutual funds, unit trusts and similar entities. The Board also noted that the difference between using the equity method and fair value measurement for investments in associates and joint ventures is smaller than that between consolidation and fair value measurement for investments in subsidiaries.

Transition

BC284   The Board proposed in the *Investment Entities* ED that the exception to consolidation should be applied prospectively. Some respondents disagreed with the proposal, arguing that retrospective application would result in more useful information. In addition, they noted that retrospective application should not be onerous because investment entities would be expected to have information about the fair value of their investments. Those respondents also argued that retrospective application would be consistent with the other transition requirements in IFRS 10.

BC285   The Board agreed with these arguments and decided to require retrospective application of the exception to consolidation, subject to specific transition reliefs, such as:

(a)   a relief for when it is impracticable to identify the fair value of investments;

(b)   a relief for when an investment entity disposes of investments prior to the date of initial application; and

(c)   a relief from providing comparative information for more than one period preceding the date of initial application.

BC286   The Board also noted that entities that adopt these amendments early may not have adopted IFRS 13, which has an effective date of 1 January 2013. Consequently, the Board decided that when an investment entity has not yet adopted IFRS 13, it may use the fair value amounts previously reported to investors or to management, as long as those amounts represent the amount for

---

16   IFRS 9 *Financial Instruments* replaced IAS 39. IFRS 9 applies to all items that were previously within the scope of IAS 39.

which the investment could have been exchanged between knowledgeable, willing parties in an arm's length transaction at the date of the valuation. The Board noted that if previously used fair value measurements are not available, it may be impracticable to measure fair value without using hindsight. In such cases, transition relief is available.

BC287 The Board also decided to require first-time adopters to apply the requirements retrospectively, subject to specific transition reliefs.[17]

BC287A The Board decided that no specific transition guidance was needed and, therefore, an entity should apply *Investment Entities: Applying the Consolidation Exception* (Amendments to IFRS 10, IFRS 12 and IAS 28) retrospectively in accordance with IAS 8. However, the Board decided that an entity need only present the quantitative information required by paragraph 28(f) of IAS 8 for the annual period immediately preceding the date of initial application of this IFRS (the 'immediately preceding period') when the amendments are first applied.

Effective date and early application

BC288 The Board decided on a 1 January 2014 effective date for the requirements for investment entities. The Board noted that because these requirements provide an exception to consolidation, they should have the same effective date as the revised consolidation requirements in IFRS 10 (annual periods beginning on or after 1 January 2013). However, given that the investment entities requirements were published in October 2012, the Board did not believe that a 1 January 2013 effective date would give adequate time for implementation between the publication and effective dates. However, the Board decided to permit early application of the investment entity requirements. The Board noted that it expects many entities to apply the requirements early. Some investments in subsidiaries may not have been consolidated in accordance with IAS 27 and SIC-12 but, without the exception to consolidation, would need to be consolidated in accordance with IFRS 10. The Board noted that it would be potentially confusing to users of financial statements and time-consuming for the investment entity to consolidate a subsidiary in one accounting period and then carry the same investee at fair value in the following period. In addition, investment entities should already have the fair value information needed for implementation. Finally, the exception to consolidation has been a long-standing request from the investment entity industry. Consequently, the Board believes that many investment entities will want to adopt the requirements early.

Joint deliberations with the FASB

BC289 The Board deliberated this project jointly with the FASB. US GAAP has had comprehensive accounting guidance for investment companies for many years (contained in Topic 946 *Investment Companies*). By deliberating this project jointly,

---

17 *Annual Improvements to IFRS Standards 2014–2016 Cycle*, issued in December 2016, amended IFRS 1 *First-time Adoption of International Financial Reporting Standards* by deleting the short-term exemption for first-time adopters (see paragraph BC99 of IFRS 1), because it was no longer applicable.

the boards hoped to achieve as similar guidance as possible. To that end, they came up with similar definitions of investment entities and guidance on how to assess investment entity status.

BC290 However, the scope of the project was different for the IASB and the FASB. The IASB's Investment Entities project started during the deliberations on the Consolidations project and was only intended to provide an exception to consolidation for investment entities. The FASB was seeking to improve and converge the definition of an investment company with that of the IASB because it already has comprehensive accounting and reporting guidance for investment companies.

BC291 While the boards reached many common decisions, as a result of this scope difference, and other jurisdictional differences, the IASB and the FASB came to different decisions in a number of areas. These include:

(a) whether there should be a requirement that an investment entity measure and evaluate substantially all of its investments on a fair value basis rather than identifying such an activity as a typical characteristic of an investment entity;

(b) whether there should be a reference to existing regulatory requirements in the definition of an investment entity;

(c) whether an investment entity is permitted to provide investment-related services to third parties other than its own investors;

(d) the accounting by an investment entity parent for an investment entity subsidiary; and

(e) the accounting by a non-investment entity parent for an investment entity subsidiary.

Effects analysis for investment entities

BC292 The Board is committed to assessing and sharing knowledge about the likely costs of implementing proposed new requirements and the likely ongoing costs and benefits of each new IFRS—the costs and benefits are collectively referred to as 'effects'. The Board gains insight on the likely effects of the proposals for new or revised IFRSs through its formal exposure of proposals, analysis and consultations with relevant parties.

BC293 In evaluating the likely effects of introducing an exception to consolidation for investment entities to IFRS 10, the Board has considered the following factors:

(a) how the changes to IFRS 10 affect the financial statements of an investment entity;

(b) how those changes improve the comparability of financial information between different reporting periods for an investment entity and between different investment entities in a particular reporting period;

(c) how the changes will improve the quality of the financial information available to investors and its usefulness in assessing the future cash flows of an investment entity;

(d) how users will benefit from better economic decision-making as a result of improved financial reporting;

(e) the likely effect on compliance costs for preparers, both on initial application and on an ongoing basis; and

(f) whether the likely costs of analysis for users are affected.

Financial statements of investment entities

BC294 Before the exception to consolidation for investment entities was issued, IFRS 10 (and its predecessor, IAS 27) required reporting entities to consolidate all controlled entities, regardless of the nature of the reporting entity. Consequently, the assets, liabilities and non-controlling interests of each subsidiary were aggregated with those of the parent to represent the group of entities as a single reporting entity.

BC295 Respondents to ED 10 argued that an investment entity often holds non-controlling investments in some entities that are reported at fair value, as well as subsidiaries that are consolidated in accordance with current principles in IFRS. Reporting investments on more than one basis hinders comparability within the financial statements, because all investments are held by an investment entity for a similar purpose—capital appreciation, investment income, or both. In addition, some of the items consolidated would be measured at historical cost, which distorts the performance assessment of the investment entity and does not reflect the way in which the business of the entity is managed.

BC296 The exception to consolidation will change the way in which an investment entity parent reports its interest in an entity that it controls. Rather than consolidating its subsidiaries, an investment entity is now required to recognise a subsidiary as a single-line investment measured at fair value through profit or loss in accordance with IFRS 9 (or IAS 39,[18] if IFRS 9 has not yet been adopted).

BC297 Accordingly, the exception to consolidation will affect investment entities that hold, as investments, controlling interests in other entities. However, although the changes are important to those entities affected, the changes are only expected to affect a narrow range of entities. Only those entities that meet the definition of an investment entity and hold controlling interests in other entities will be affected by these changes.

BC298 The entities most likely to be affected are:

(a) private equity or venture capital funds; these have business models in which it is more likely that it would be beneficial to take a larger interest in a company, or control investees through debt and equity investment.

(b) master-feeder or fund-of-funds structures where an investment entity parent has controlling interests in investment entity subsidiaries.

---

18 IFRS 9 *Financial Instruments* replaced IAS 39. IFRS 9 applies to all items that were previously within the scope of IAS 39.

BC299   Some pension funds and sovereign wealth funds may also be affected; these may meet the definition of an investment entity and may also hold controlling investments in other entities.

BC300   Other types of entities may meet the definition of an investment entity, such as mutual funds and other regulated investment funds, but are less likely to hold controlling investments in other entities. Instead, they tend to hold lower levels of investments in a wider range of entities. Consequently, the exception to consolidation is less likely to affect these entities.

Comparability

BC301   An investment entity's control of an investee may change from one reporting period to the next. Without the exception to consolidation, an investment entity could be required to consolidate an investment in one period and present it as an investment measured at fair value through profit or loss in the following period (or vice versa). This would reduce comparability between reporting periods. With the introduction of the exception to consolidation, an investment entity can report all investments at fair value, regardless of whether those investments are controlled. This will improve the comparability between reporting periods.

BC302   Many respondents to ED 10 and the *Investment Entities* ED pointed out that some national accounting requirements, including US GAAP, have historically had industry-specific guidance that requires investment entities to measure investments that they control at fair value. Some of these respondents argued that investment entities were actively choosing to adopt those national accounting requirements rather than IFRS so that they could measure all of their investments at fair value. Respondents also pointed out that some investment entities that followed IFRS provided non-GAAP information about the fair value of all of their investments. Consequently, comparability of the financial statements of different investment entities was hindered. The Board expects the introduction of the exception to consolidation to encourage adoption of IFRS among investment entities and to eliminate the need to provide non-GAAP information about fair value. This should improve the comparability of financial statements of different investment entities.

Usefulness of financial statements in assessing the future cash flows of an entity

BC303   Consolidated financial statements of an investment entity emphasise the financial position, operations and cash flows of the investee, rather than merely those of the investment entity. The exception to consolidation will reduce the information about the cash flows of those subsidiaries. However, the main business purpose of an investment entity is to invest funds solely for capital appreciation, investment income, or both. The relevant cash flows relating to these activities are those of the investment entity itself. Consolidating the cash flows of a subsidiary may hinder users' ability to predict the cash flows that may be passed on to investors. The Board therefore believes that these amendments will improve the quality of the financial information reported by an investment entity and will make that information more useful in assessing the future cash flows of the investment entity.

Better economic decision-making

BC304   One of the essential features of an investment entity is that, in order to make better investment decisions, it measures and evaluates substantially all of its investments on a fair value basis. Presenting consolidated financial statements does not reflect this method of management. Requiring an investment entity to account for its investments in subsidiaries at fair value provides a better insight into the information that management uses to evaluate the performance of its investments.

BC305   In addition, investors in an investment entity are typically entitled to a proportionate share of the net assets of the entity when they withdraw their investment. Reporting the fair value of substantially all of the net assets of the investment entity allows the investors to more easily identify the value of their share of those net assets. As a result, the Board expect significant benefits for most users of investment entity financial statements arising from the provision of more fair value information.

BC306   However, some respondents in some jurisdictions objected to the exception to consolidation because it undermines the control-based approach to consolidation used in IFRS 10. These respondents noted that an exception to consolidation would deprive financial statement users of information about the activities of subsidiaries and the economic effects of the relationships between an investment entity and its subsidiaries. In addition, some respondents expressed concern that an exception to consolidation may encourage structuring to avoid consolidation, which would result in a loss of such information to users.

BC307   The Board acknowledges these arguments, but notes that the exception to consolidation has been introduced in response to comments from users that the most useful information for an investment entity is the fair value of its investments. Users also commented that consolidated financial statements of an investment entity may hinder users' ability to assess an investment entity's financial position and results, because it emphasises the financial position, operations and cash flows of the investee, rather than those of the investment entity.

BC308   In developing these amendments, the Board deliberately restricted the population of entities that would qualify for the exception to consolidation. In particular, the Board prohibited the use of the exception to consolidation by non-investment entity parents of investment entities, in order to address respondents' concerns about structuring and to restrict the use of the exception to situations where fair value information would be more relevant than information arising from the consolidation of subsidiaries.

Effect on compliance costs for preparers

BC309   The Board expects that the introduction of the exception to consolidation will result in significant compliance cost savings for preparers, particularly on an ongoing basis. This expectation is based on the feedback the Board has received from respondents to the *Investment Entities* ED and conversations with entities that are expected to qualify as investment entities.

BC310   On initial application, there may be some costs involved in identifying and documenting some of the additional disclosures introduced. In particular, investment entities will need to collect information to comply with the general disclosure requirements of IFRS 7, IFRS 13 and the amended requirements of IFRS 12. However, the Board has been told that the majority of investment entities will already have much of the fair value information that they need in order to comply with the new requirements, because they already measure substantially all of their investments on a fair value basis and many elect to provide this information to their investors already. The Board expects this to mitigate the initial and ongoing costs of applying the exception to consolidation.

BC311   In arriving at its decisions, the Board has considered those costs and believes that the benefits of the information produced as a result of its decisions would outweigh the costs of providing that information. In addition, the initial application costs will be more than offset by the cost savings resulting from the removal of the need to gather information from subsidiaries in order to consolidate details of their financial performance, position and cash flows on a line-by-line basis.

BC312   As described in paragraphs BC275–BC283, the Board decided not to expand the scope of the project to allow a non-investment entity parent to retain the fair value accounting of its investment entity subsidiary. Consequently, the compliance cost savings described above will not be available to non-investment entity parents. Because these entities are not within the scope of these amendments, they may incur ongoing costs because they will have two different bases of accounting within the group. At the investment entity subsidiary level, subsidiaries held by the investment entity will be measured at fair value, but at the non-investment entity parent level, those subsidiaries will be consolidated.

How the costs of analysis for users are affected

BC313   The likely effect of these amendments on the costs of analysis for users of financial statements is expected to be outweighed by the benefits of improved reporting, given that these amendments have been developed on request from users. However, the extent of the benefit will depend on existing practice.

BC314   In general, these amendments will provide improved information about the fair values of investments and the way in which the fair value is measured. Such information could reduce the cost of analysis by providing information more directly to users of financial statements. However, in many cases, investment entities already provide investors with fair value information, although this is often done in an alternative report rather than in the financial statements. This serves to emphasise that the main benefit of the changes is a reduction in costs to preparers because it eliminates what they see as a cumbersome reporting requirement that has little value.

BC315   For analysts or potential investors that use financial statements to analyse investment entities from different countries, the existing problems of diversity in accounting models creates costs that would be reduced by standardised accounting requirements.

BC316   In addition, the Board expects that the requirement to apply the exception to consolidation retrospectively will mitigate some of the transition costs for users. However, some of the transition reliefs will mean that users may receive less information on transition. In particular, the fact that investment entities will be required to provide only one period of comparative information may affect users who might otherwise receive more than one period of comparative information. However, again, the Board expects the benefits to outweigh the costs incurred as a result of the implementation of these amendments.

Summary

BC317   In summary, the cost savings resulting from implementing these amendments are expected to be significant for investment entities and the users of their financial statements. Additionally, the implementation of the investment entities amendments should result in the benefits of increased comparability between entities and across jurisdictions, and more relevant reporting of information used by investors in making economic decisions.

Appendix
Previous Board approvals and dissenting opinions

Approval by the Board of IAS 27 issued in December 2003

International Accounting Standard 27 *Consolidated and Separate Financial Statements* (as revised in 2003) was approved for issue by thirteen of the fourteen members of the International Accounting Standards Board. Mr Yamada dissented. His dissenting opinion is set out after the previous Board approvals.

Sir David Tweedie	Chairman
Thomas E Jones	Vice-Chairman
Mary E Barth	
Hans-Georg Bruns	
Anthony T Cope	
Robert P Garnett	
Gilbert Gélard	
James J Leisenring	
Warren J McGregor	
Patricia L O'Malley	
Harry K Schmid	
John T Smith	
Geoffrey Whittington	
Tatsumi Yamada	

Approval by the Board of amendments to IAS 27 issued in January 2008

The amendments to International Accounting Standard 27 *Consolidated and Separate Financial Statements* in 2008 were approved for issue by nine of the fourteen members of the International Accounting Standards Board. Messrs Danjou, Engström, Garnett, Gélard and Yamada dissented. Their dissenting opinions are set out after the previous Board approvals.

Sir David Tweedie	Chairman
Thomas E Jones	Vice-Chairman
Mary E Barth	
Hans-Georg Bruns	
Anthony T Cope	
Philippe Danjou	
Jan Engström	
Robert P Garnett	
Gilbert Gélard	
James J Leisenring	
Warren J McGregor	
Patricia L O'Malley	
John T Smith	
Tatsumi Yamada	

Dissenting opinions

Dissent of Tatsumi Yamada from IAS 27 (as revised in 2003)

Cross-references have been updated.

DO1   Mr Yamada dissents from this Standard because he believes that the change in classification of minority interests in the consolidated balance sheet, that is to say, the requirement that it be shown as equity, should not be made as part of the Improvements project. He agrees that minority interests do not meet the definition of a liability under the *Framework for the Preparation and Presentation of Financial Statements*,[19] as stated in paragraph BCZ158 of the Basis for Conclusions, and that the current requirement, for minority interests to be presented separately from liabilities and the parent shareholders' equity, is not desirable. However, he does not believe that this requirement should be altered at this stage. He believes that before making the change in classification, which will have a wide variety of impacts on current consolidation practices, various issues related to this change need to be considered comprehensively by the Board. These include consideration of the objectives of consolidated financial statements and the accounting procedures that should flow from those objectives. Even though the Board concluded as noted in paragraph BC27, he believes that the decision related to the classification of minority interests should not be made until such a comprehensive consideration of recognition and measurement is completed.[20]

DO2   Traditionally, there are two views of the objectives of consolidated financial statements; they are implicit in the parent company view and the economic entity view. Mr Yamada believes that the objectives, that is to say, what information should be provided and to whom, should be considered by the Board before it makes its decision on the classification of minority interests in IAS 27. He is of the view that the Board is taking the economic entity view without giving enough consideration to this fundamental issue.

DO3   Step acquisitions are being discussed in the second phase of the Business Combinations project, which is not yet finalised at the time of finalising IAS 27 under the Improvements project. When the ownership interest of the parent increases, the Board has tentatively decided that the difference between the consideration paid by the parent to minority interests and the carrying value of the ownership interests acquired by the parent is recognised as part of equity, which is different from the current practice of recognising a change in the amount of goodwill. If the parent retains control of a subsidiary but its ownership interest decreases, the difference between the consideration received

---

19   IASC's *Framework for the Preparation and Presentation of Financial Statements* was adopted by the IASB in 2001. In September 2010 the IASB replaced the *Framework* with the *Conceptual Framework for Financial Reporting*.

20   Paragraph BC27 of the Basis for Conclusions on IAS 27 (as revised in 2003) was deleted as part of the amendments to IAS 27 in 2008. The paragraph stated: The Board acknowledged that this decision gives rise to questions about the recognition and measurement of minority interests but it concluded that the proposed presentation is consistent with current standards and the *Framework* and would provide better comparability than presentation in the consolidated balance sheet with either liabilities or parent shareholders' equity. It decided that the recognition and measurement questions should be addressed as part of its project on business combinations.

       © IFRS Foundation

by the parent and the carrying value of the ownership interests transferred is also recognised as part of equity, which is different from the current practice of recognising a gain or a loss. Mr Yamada believes that the results of this discussion are predetermined by the decision related to the classification of minority interests as equity. The changes in accounting treatments are fundamental and he believes that the decision on which of the two views should govern the consolidated financial statements should be taken only after careful consideration of the ramifications. He believes that the amendment of IAS 27 relating to the classification of minority interests should not be made before completion of the second phase of the Business Combinations project.

Dissent of Philippe Danjou, Jan Engström, Robert P Garnett, Gilbert Gélard and Tatsumi Yamada from the amendments to IAS 27 issued in January 2008 on the accounting for non-controlling interests and the loss of control of a subsidiary

Cross-references have been updated.

DO1   Messrs Danjou, Engström, Garnett, Gélard and Yamada dissent from the 2008 amendments to IAS 27.

Accounting for changes in ownership interests in a subsidiary

DO2   Messrs Danjou, Engström, Gélard and Yamada do not agree that acquisitions of non-controlling interests in a subsidiary by the parent should be accounted for in full as equity transactions.

DO3   Those Board members observe that the consideration paid for an additional interest in a subsidiary will reflect the additional interest's share in:

(a)   the carrying amount of the subsidiary's net assets at that date;

(b)   additionally acquired goodwill; and

(c)   unrecognised increases in the fair value of the subsidiary's net assets (including goodwill) since the date when control was obtained.

DO4   Paragraphs 23 and B96 of IFRS 10 require such a transaction to be accounted for as an equity transaction, by adjusting the relative interests of the parent and the non-controlling interests. As a consequence, the additionally acquired goodwill and any unrecognised increases in the fair value of the subsidiary's net assets would be deducted from equity. Those Board members disagree that such accounting faithfully represents the economics of such a transaction.

DO5   Those Board members believe that an increase in ownership interests in a subsidiary is likely to provide additional benefits to the parent. Although control has already been obtained, a higher ownership interest might increase synergies accruing to the parent, for example, by meeting legal thresholds provided in company law, which would give the parent an additional level of discretion over the subsidiary. If the additional ownership interest has been acquired in an arm's length exchange transaction in which knowledgeable, willing parties exchange equal values, these additional benefits are reflected in the purchase price of the additional ownership interest. Those Board members believe that the acquisition of non-controlling interests by the parent should give rise to the recognition of goodwill, measured as the excess of the consideration transferred over the carrying amount of the subsidiary's net assets attributable to the additional interest acquired. Those Board members acknowledge that this amount also includes unrecognised increases in the fair value of the subsidiary's net assets since the date when control was obtained. However, on the basis of cost-benefit considerations, they believe that it is a reasonable approximation of the additionally acquired goodwill.

DO6   Messrs Danjou, Gélard and Yamada agree that, in conformity with the *Framework for the Preparation and Presentation of Financial Statements*,[21] non-controlling interests should be presented within the group's equity, because they are not liabilities. However, they believe that until the debates over the objectives of consolidated financial statements (ie what information should be provided and to whom) and the definition of the reporting entity have been settled at the conceptual level, transactions between the parent and non-controlling interests should not be accounted for in the same manner as transactions in which the parent entity acquires its own shares and reduces its equity. In their view, non-controlling interests cannot be considered equivalent to the ordinary ownership interests of the owners of the parent. The owners of the parent and the holders of non-controlling interests in a subsidiary do not share the same risks and rewards in relation to the group's operations and net assets because ownership interests in a subsidiary share only the risks and rewards associated with that subsidiary.

DO7   In addition, Messrs Danjou and Gélard observe that IFRS 3 *Business Combinations* (as revised in 2008) provides an option to measure non-controlling interests in a business combination as their proportionate share of the acquiree's net identifiable assets rather than at their fair value. However, paragraph BC207 of the Basis for Conclusions on IFRS 3 (as revised in 2008) states that accounting for the non-controlling interests at fair value is conceptually superior to this alternative measurement. This view implies that the subsidiary's portion of goodwill attributable to the non-controlling interests at the date when control was obtained is an asset at that date and there is no conceptual reason for it no longer to be an asset at the time of any subsequent acquisitions of non-controlling interests.

DO8   Mr Garnett disagrees with the treatment of changes in controlling interests in subsidiaries after control is established (paragraphs BCZ168–BCZ179 of the Basis for Conclusions). He believes that it is important that the consequences of such changes for the owners of the parent entity are reported clearly in the financial statements.

DO9   Mr Garnett believes that the amendments to IAS 27 adopt the economic entity approach that treats all equity interests in the group as being homogeneous. Transactions between controlling and non-controlling interests are regarded as mere transfers within the total equity interest and no gain or loss is recognised on such transactions. Mr Garnett observes that the non-controlling interests represent equity claims that are restricted to particular subsidiaries, whereas the controlling interests are affected by the performance of the entire group. The consolidated financial statements should therefore report performance from the perspective of the controlling interest (a parent entity perspective) in addition to the wider perspective provided by the economic entity approach. This implies the recognition of additional goodwill on purchases, and gains or losses on disposals of the parent entity's interest in a subsidiary.

DO10   If, as Mr Garnett would prefer, the full goodwill method were not used (see paragraphs DO7–DO10 of the dissenting views on IFRS 3), the acquisition of an

---

21 IASC's *Framework for the Preparation and Presentation of Financial Statements* was adopted by the IASB in 2001. In September 2010 the IASB replaced the *Framework* with the *Conceptual Framework for Financial Reporting*.

additional interest in a subsidiary would give rise to the recognition of additional purchased goodwill, measured as the excess of the consideration transferred over the carrying amount of the subsidiary's net assets attributable to the additional interest acquired.

DO11   Mr Garnett does not agree with the requirement in paragraph B96 of this IFRS that, in respect of a partial disposal of the parent's ownership interest in a subsidiary that does not result in a loss of control, the carrying amount of the non-controlling interests should be adjusted to reflect the change in the parent's interest in the subsidiary's net assets. On the contrary, he believes that the carrying amount of the non-controlling interests should be adjusted by the fair value of the consideration paid by the non-controlling interests to acquire that additional interest.

DO12   Mr Garnett also believes that it is important to provide the owners of the parent entity with information about the effects of a partial disposal of holdings in subsidiaries, including the difference between the fair value of the consideration received and the proportion of the carrying amount of the subsidiary's assets (including purchased goodwill) attributable to the disposal.

Loss of control

DO13   Mr Garnett disagrees with the requirement in paragraph B98 of this IFRS that if a parent loses control of a subsidiary, it measures any retained investment in the former subsidiary at fair value and any difference between the carrying amount of the retained investment and its fair value is recognised in profit or loss, because the retained investment was not part of the exchange. The loss of control of a subsidiary is a significant economic event that warrants deconsolidation. However, the retained investment has not been sold. Under current IFRSs, gains and losses on cost method, available-for-sale and equity method investments are recognised in profit or loss only when the investment is sold (other than impairment). Mr Garnett would have recognised the effect of measuring the retained investment at fair value as a separate component of other comprehensive income instead of profit or loss.

Accounting for losses attributable to non-controlling interests

DO14   Mr Danjou disagrees with paragraph B94 of this IFRS according to which losses can be attributed without limitation to the non-controlling interests even if this results in the non-controlling interests having a deficit balance.

DO15   In many circumstances, in the absence of any commitment or binding obligation of the non-controlling interests to make an additional investment to cover the excess losses of the subsidiary, the continuation of the operations of a subsidiary will be funded through the contribution of additional capital by the parent and with the non-controlling interests being diluted. In those circumstances, the deficit balance attributable to the non-controlling interests that would result from the amendment in paragraph B94 does not present faithfully the equity of the consolidating entity.

DO16 Mr Danjou believes that the Standard should therefore not preclude the allocation against the parent equity of losses that exceed the non-controlling interests in a consolidated subsidiary when the facts and circumstances are as outlined in paragraph DO15.

Appendix
Amendments to the Basis for Conclusions on other IFRSs

This appendix contains amendments to the Basis for Conclusions on other IFRSs that are necessary in order to ensure consistency with IFRS 10 and the related amendments to other IFRSs. Amended footnotes are shown with new text underlined and deleted text struck through.

* * * * *

The amendments contained in this appendix when IFRS 10 was issued in 2011 have been incorporated into the Basis for Conclusions on the relevant IFRSs published in this volume.

IASB documents published to accompany

IFRS 11

Joint Arrangements

The text of the unaccompanied standard, IFRS 11, is contained in Part A of this edition. Its effective date when issued was 1 January 2013. The text of the Accompanying Guidance on IFRS 11 is contained in Part B of this edition. This part presents the following documents:

BASIS FOR CONCLUSIONS

APPENDIX TO THE BASIS FOR CONCLUSIONS
Amendments to the Basis for Conclusions on other IFRSs

Contents

Basis for Conclusions on IFRS 11 *Joint Arrangements*

This Basis for Conclusions accompanies, but is not part of, IFRS 11.

Introduction

BC1   This Basis for Conclusions summarises the International Accounting Standards Board's considerations in reaching the conclusions in IFRS 11 *Joint Arrangements*. Individual Board members gave greater weight to some factors than to others.

BC2   The Board added the joint ventures project to its agenda as part of the project to reduce differences between International Financial Reporting Standards (IFRSs) and US generally accepted accounting principles (GAAP). The requirements of IFRS 11 were not deliberated by the US Financial Accounting Standards Board (FASB).

BC3   The Board focused its deliberations on enhancing the faithful representation of joint arrangements that an entity provides in its financial statements, by establishing a principle-based approach to accounting for joint arrangements, and by requiring enhanced disclosures. Even though the Board focused its efforts on improving the reporting of joint arrangements, the result is that the requirements of the IFRS achieve closer convergence with US GAAP than did IAS 31 *Interests in Joint Ventures*, which IFRS 11 supersedes.

Objective

BC4   IFRS 11 sets out requirements for the recognition and measurement of an entity's interest in joint arrangements. The requirements for the disclosure of an entity's interest in joint arrangements have been included in IFRS 12 *Disclosure of Interests in Other Entities* (see paragraphs BC52–BC55). IFRS 11 is concerned principally with addressing two aspects of IAS 31 that the Board regarded as impediments to high quality reporting of joint arrangements: first, that the structure of the arrangement was the only determinant of the accounting, and second, that an entity had a choice of accounting treatment for interests in jointly controlled entities.

BC5   The Board did not reconsider all the requirements in IAS 31. For example, the Board did not reconsider the equity method. Accordingly, this Basis for Conclusions does not discuss requirements of IAS 31 that the Board did not reconsider.

BC6   The Board published its proposals in an exposure draft, ED 9 *Joint Arrangements*, in September 2007 with a comment deadline of 11 January 2008. The Board received over 110 comment letters on the exposure draft.

The problems with IAS 31

BC7   IAS 31 established different accounting requirements depending on whether the arrangements were structured through an entity. Jointly controlled operations and jointly controlled assets were arrangements that did not require the establishment of an entity or financial structure that is separate from the parties. IAS 31 required parties to these arrangements to recognise assets, liabilities, revenues and expenses arising from the arrangements. When arrangements were structured through an entity, IAS 31 classified them as jointly controlled entities. Parties with interests in jointly controlled entities accounted for them using proportionate consolidation or, as an alternative, the equity method.

BC8 The problem with basing different accounting requirements solely on the existence of an entity, combined with the choice of accounting treatment for jointly controlled entities, was that some arrangements that gave the parties similar rights and obligations were accounted for differently and, conversely, arrangements that gave the parties different rights and obligations were accounted for similarly. The Board's policy is to exclude options in accounting treatment from accounting standards whenever possible. Such options can lead to similar transactions being accounted for in different ways and, therefore, can impair comparability.

Improving IAS 31 with the principles of IFRS 11

BC9 In the Board's view, the accounting for joint arrangements should reflect the rights and obligations that the parties have as a result of their interests in the arrangements, regardless of those arrangements' structure or legal form. This is the principle that IFRS 11 establishes for parties to a joint arrangement when accounting for their interests in the arrangements. However, the Board acknowledges that sometimes the structure or the legal form of the joint arrangements is decisive in determining the parties' rights and obligations arising from the arrangements and, consequently, in determining the classification of the joint arrangements (see paragraphs BC26 and BC31).

BC10 Entities applying IAS 31 were required to choose the same accounting treatment (ie proportionate consolidation or equity method) when accounting for all of their interests in jointly controlled entities. Applying the same accounting treatment to all the interests that an entity has in different jointly controlled entities might not always lead to the faithful representation of each of those interests. For example, an entity whose policy was to account for all of its interests in jointly controlled entities using proportionate consolidation might have recognised assets and liabilities proportionately even though this did not faithfully represent the entity's rights and obligations in the assets and liabilities of particular joint arrangements. Conversely, an entity might have accounted for all of its interests in jointly controlled entities using the equity method, when the recognition of the entity's rights and obligations in particular joint arrangements would instead have led to the recognition of assets and liabilities.

BC11 The accounting for joint arrangements required by the IFRS is not a function of an entity's accounting policy choice but is, instead, determined by an entity applying the principles of the IFRS to each of its joint arrangements and recognising, as a result, the rights and obligations arising from each of them. The Board concluded that proportionate consolidation is not an appropriate method to account for interests in joint arrangements when the parties have neither rights to the assets, nor obligations for the liabilities, relating to the arrangement. The Board also concluded that the equity method is not an appropriate method to account for interests in joint arrangements when parties have rights to the assets, and obligations for the liabilities, relating to the arrangement. The Board believes that it is misleading for users of financial statements if an entity recognises assets and liabilities for which it does not have rights or obligations, or does not recognise assets and liabilities for which it does have rights and obligations.

BC12　The Board also reconsidered the disclosure requirements in IAS 31 for interests in joint arrangements. The Board believes that the disclosure requirements in IFRS 12 will enable users to gain a better understanding of the nature and extent of an entity's operations undertaken through joint arrangements.

Scope

BC13　The IFRS should be applied by all entities that are a party to a joint arrangement. The IFRS does not change the two essential characteristics that IAS 31 required arrangements to have in order to be deemed 'joint ventures', ie that a contractual arrangement that binds the parties to the arrangement exists, and that the contractual arrangement establishes that two or more of those parties have joint control of the arrangement.

BC14　The Board believes that the new definition of control and the application requirements to assess control in IFRS 10 *Consolidated Financial Statements* will assist entities in determining whether an arrangement is controlled or jointly controlled, and in that respect it might cause entities to reconsider their previous assessment of their relationship with the investee. Despite the changes that these reassessments might cause, the Board believes that arrangements that were within the scope of IAS 31 would generally also be within the scope of IFRS 11.

Scope exception

BC15　The Board reconsidered the scope exception of IAS 31 that had also been proposed in ED 9. The Board concluded that the scope exception in ED 9 for interests in joint ventures held by venture capital organisations, or mutual funds, unit trusts and similar entities, including investment-linked insurance funds, that are measured at fair value through profit or loss in accordance with IFRS 9 *Financial Instruments*, is more appropriately characterised as a measurement exemption, not as a scope exception.

BC16　The Board observed that when venture capital organisations, or mutual funds, unit trusts and similar entities, including investment-linked insurance funds, conclude that they have an interest in a joint arrangement, this is because the arrangement has the characteristics of a joint arrangement as specified in IFRS 11 (ie a contractual arrangement exists that establishes that two or more parties have joint control of the arrangement).

BC17　The Board also observed that the scope exception in ED 9 did not relate to the fact that these arrangements do not have the characteristics of joint arrangements, but to the fact that for investments held by venture capital organisations, or mutual funds, unit trusts and similar entities, including investment-linked insurance funds, fair value measurement provides more useful information for users of the financial statements than would application of the equity method.

BC18   Accordingly, the Board decided to maintain the option that permits such entities to measure their interests in joint ventures at fair value through profit or loss in accordance with IFRS 9, but clarified that this is an exemption from the requirement to measure interests in joint ventures using the equity method, rather than an exception to the scope of IFRS 11 for joint ventures in which these entities have interests.

Joint arrangements

BC19   The Board decided to use the term 'joint arrangement', rather than 'joint venture', to describe arrangements that are subject to the requirements of the IFRS. As noted in paragraph BC13, the IFRS does not change the two essential characteristics that IAS 31 required for arrangements to be 'joint ventures': a contractual arrangement that binds the parties to the arrangement exists, and the contractual arrangement establishes that two or more of those parties have joint control of the arrangement.

Joint control

BC20   In ED 9, the proposed definition of 'joint arrangement' required 'shared decision-making' by all the parties to the arrangement. Some respondents questioned how 'shared decision-making' was intended to operate and how it differed from 'joint control'. The Board introduced the term 'shared decision-making' in the exposure draft instead of 'joint control' because control was defined in IAS 27 *Consolidated and Separate Financial Statements* in the context of having power over the financial and operating policies of an entity.[1] During its redeliberation of ED 9, the Board concluded that in joint arrangements, it is the activity undertaken by the parties that is the matter over which the parties share control or share decision-making, regardless of whether the activity is conducted in a separate entity. Consequently, the Board concluded that 'joint control' is a term that expresses better than 'shared decision-making' that the control of the activity that is the subject matter of the arrangement is shared among the parties with joint control of the arrangement.

BC21   The Board did not reconsider the concept of 'joint control' as defined in IAS 31 or in ED 9 (ie the requirement of unanimous consent for the decisions that give the parties control of an arrangement). However, the definition of 'joint control' in the IFRS is different from those in IAS 31 and ED 9. The reason for the change is to align the definition of 'joint control' with the definition of 'control' in IFRS 10. IFRS 11 directs parties to an arrangement to assess first whether all the parties, or a group of the parties, control the arrangement collectively, on the basis of the definition of control and corresponding guidance in IFRS 10. Once an entity has concluded that the arrangement is collectively controlled by all the parties, or by a group of the parties, joint control exists only when decisions

---

1   The consolidation requirements in IAS 27 were replaced by IFRS 10 *Consolidated Financial Statements* issued in 2011 and the definition of control was revised.

about the activities that significantly affect the returns of the arrangement (ie the relevant activities) require the unanimous consent of those parties.

BC22 In response to concerns expressed by some respondents who pointed out that, unlike IAS 31, ED 9 did not include the term 'investors in a joint arrangement', the Board clarified during its redeliberation of ED 9 that not all the parties to a joint arrangement need to have joint control for the arrangement to be a joint arrangement. Indeed, some of the parties to a joint arrangement can have joint control whereas others, although able to participate, do not have joint control of the arrangement. The Board decided to use the terms 'joint operators' to designate parties with joint control of a 'joint operation' and 'joint venturers' to designate parties with joint control of a 'joint venture' (see paragraph BC24).

BC23 The Board observed that the parties to a joint arrangement might agree to change or modify the governance and decision-making process of the arrangement at any time. As a result of such a change, a party might gain or lose joint control of the arrangement. Consequently, the Board concluded that if facts and circumstances change, the parties to a joint arrangement should reassess whether they are parties with joint control of the arrangement.

Types of joint arrangement

BC24 The IFRS classifies joint arrangements into two types—'joint operations' and 'joint ventures'. Parties with joint control of a joint operation have rights to the assets, and obligations for the liabilities, relating to the arrangement ('joint operators'), whereas parties with joint control of a joint venture ('joint venturers') have rights to the net assets of the arrangement.

BC25 The classification of joint arrangements into two types was considered by the Board in its redeliberation of the exposure draft. ED 9 proposed to classify joint arrangements into three types—'joint operations', 'joint assets' and 'joint ventures'. The Board observed that in some instances it might be difficult to assess whether an arrangement is a 'joint operation' or a 'joint asset'. This is because elements from both types of joint arrangement are sometimes present (in many arrangements joint assets are also jointly operated, and therefore such arrangements could be viewed as a 'joint asset' or as a 'joint operation'). Additionally, both types of joint arrangement result in the same accounting outcome (ie recognition of assets and liabilities and corresponding revenues and expenses). For these reasons, the Board decided to merge 'joint operations' and 'joint assets' into a single type of joint arrangement called 'joint operation'. This decision simplifies the IFRS by aligning the two types of joint arrangement presented by the IFRS (ie 'joint operations' and 'joint ventures') with the two possible accounting outcomes (ie recognition of assets, liabilities, revenues and expenses, or recognition of an investment accounted for using the equity method).

BC26 The Board observed that when the parties do not structure their joint arrangement through a separate vehicle (ie arrangements that were formerly 'jointly controlled operations' and 'jointly controlled assets' in IAS 31), the parties determine in the contractual arrangements their rights to the assets, and their obligations for the liabilities, relating to the arrangement. Such arrangements are joint operations.

BC27　In reaching this conclusion, the Board acknowledged the possibility that parties to a joint arrangement that is not structured through a separate vehicle might establish terms in the contractual arrangement under which the parties have rights only to the net assets of the arrangement. The Board thought that this possibility was likely to be rare and that the benefits of introducing an additional assessment in the classification of joint arrangements when these are not structured through separate vehicles would not outweigh the costs of increasing the complexity of the IFRS. This is because in the vast majority of cases, accounting for joint arrangements that are not structured through separate vehicles on a gross basis leads to a faithful representation of the parties' rights and obligations arising from those arrangements.

BC28　The Board acknowledged that classifying jointly controlled entities in IAS 31 into joint operations or joint ventures in the IFRS requires an entity to assess its rights and obligations arising from these arrangements, which will require the entity to exercise judgement.

BC29　The Board considered whether the definition of a 'business', as defined in IFRS 3 *Business Combinations*, would be helpful in distinguishing between a joint venture and a joint operation. Because a 'business' can be found in all types of joint arrangement, the Board decided not to pursue this approach.

BC30　The Board also concluded that there should not be a rebuttable presumption that the arrangement is a joint venture when it has been structured through a separate vehicle. The Board decided that parties to a joint arrangement that is structured through a separate vehicle should assess the classification of the arrangement by taking into consideration all facts and circumstances. The Board noted that an entity should take into consideration the legal form of the separate vehicle, the terms agreed in the contractual arrangement and, when relevant, any other facts and circumstances.

BC31　In taking this approach, the Board observed that the legal form of the separate vehicle in which the joint arrangement is structured provides an initial indicator of the parties' rights to the assets, and obligations for the liabilities, relating to the arrangement. The exception is when the legal form of the separate vehicle does not confer separation between the parties and the vehicle. In such a case, the Board concluded that the assessment of the rights and obligations conferred upon the parties by the legal form of that separate vehicle would be sufficient to conclude that the arrangement is a joint operation.

BC32　The Board believes that the selection of a particular legal form is in many cases driven by the intended economic substance that the particular legal form delivers. However, the Board observed that in some cases the choice of a particular legal form responds to tax, regulatory requirements or other reasons that can alter the intended economic substance initially sought by the parties to the arrangement. In those instances, the parties might use their contractual arrangements to modify the effects that the legal form of the arrangement would otherwise have on their rights and obligations.

BC33   The Board noted that other facts and circumstances might also affect the rights and obligations of the parties to a joint arrangement and, ultimately, affect the classification of the arrangement. Therefore, the parties should recognise the assets and liabilities relating to an arrangement if the parties designed the arrangement so that its activities primarily aimed to provide the parties with an output (ie the parties are entitled to substantially all the economic benefits of the assets relating to the arrangement) and they are, as a result of the design of the arrangement, obliged to settle the liabilities relating to the arrangement.

BC34   The IFRS defines 'joint ventures' as arrangements whereby the parties that have joint control of the arrangement (ie the joint venturers) have rights to the net assets of the arrangement. The Board observed that the term 'net assets' in the definition of joint ventures aimed to portray that the joint venturers have rights to an investment in the arrangement. However, such a definition (ie 'rights to the net assets of the arrangement') would not prevent a joint venturer from having a net liability position arising from its involvement in the joint venture. This could happen, for example, if the joint venture had incurred losses that had reduced the joint venturer's investment to zero, and as a result of the joint venturer having provided a guarantee to cover any losses that the joint venture might incur, the joint venturer has an obligation for those losses. The Board observed that neither the provision of the guarantee by the joint venturer, nor the liability assumed by the joint venturer as a result of the joint venture incurring losses, determines that the arrangement is a joint operation.

BC35   Many respondents to ED 9 were concerned that joint ventures could be merely 'residuals'. This is because these respondents interpreted joint ventures to mean that after parties had identified rights to individual assets or obligations for expenses or financing, joint ventures would be merely any remaining assets and liabilities of the arrangement. As a result of these concerns, the Board clarified that the unit of account of a joint arrangement is the activity that two or more parties have agreed to control jointly, and that a party should assess its rights to the assets, and obligations for the liabilities, relating to that activity. Consequently, the term 'joint venture' refers to a jointly controlled activity in which the parties have an investment.

BC36   During its redeliberation of ED 9, the Board made it clear that different joint arrangements or different types of joint arrangement can be established beneath the umbrella of a single arrangement or framework agreement to deal with, for example, different activities that are interrelated. The Board also observed the possibility that within the same separate vehicle the parties may undertake different activities in which they have different rights to the assets, and obligations for the liabilities, relating to these different activities resulting in different types of joint arrangement conducted within the same separate vehicle. However, the Board acknowledged that even though this situation is conceptually possible, it would be rare in practice.

BC37   The Board observed that the rights and obligations of parties to joint arrangements might change over time. This might happen, for example, as a result of a change in the purpose of the arrangement that might trigger a reconsideration of the terms of the contractual arrangements. Consequently, the Board concluded that the assessment of the type of joint arrangement needs to be a continuous process, to the extent that facts and circumstances change.

Financial statements of parties to a joint arrangement

Joint operation

BC38   In relation to the accounting for a party's interest in a joint operation, some respondents to ED 9 enquired how proportionate consolidation differed from the recognition of (or recognition of shares of) assets, liabilities, revenues and expenses arising from a joint operation. The Board noted that there are two main differences between recognising assets, liabilities, revenues and expenses relating to the activity of the joint operation and proportionate consolidation. The first difference relates to the fact that the rights and obligations, as specified in the contractual arrangement, that an entity has with respect to the assets, liabilities, revenues and expenses relating to a joint operation might differ from its ownership interest in the joint operation. The IFRS requires an entity with an interest in a joint operation to recognise assets, liabilities, revenues and expenses according to the entity's shares in the assets, liabilities, revenues and expenses of the joint operation as determined and specified in the contractual arrangement, rather than basing the recognition of assets, liabilities, revenues and expenses on the ownership interest that the entity has in the joint operation. The second difference from proportionate consolidation is that the parties' interests in a joint operation are recognised in their separate financial statements. Consequently, there is no difference in what is recognised in the parties' separate financial statements and the parties' consolidated financial statements or the parties' financial statements in which investments are accounted for using the equity method.

BC39   Respondents also suggested that the IFRS should provide more clarity in stating the requirements for the accounting for shares of assets in joint operations. Many respondents to ED 9 were not clear whether parties to a joint operation that had rights to the assets should recognise a 'right to use' or a 'right to a share' or whether they should instead directly recognise 'their share of the joint assets, classified according to the nature of the asset'. The concern raised by this uncertainty was the different accounting implications of these interpretations—ie accounting for rights or accounting for shares of assets. The Board concluded that a party to a joint operation should recognise its assets or its share of any assets in accordance with the IFRSs applicable to the particular assets.

BC40   An additional concern raised by some respondents to ED 9 was how the unit of account relating to the share of assets and liabilities to be accounted for by the parties to a joint operation should be delineated. The Board observed that ED 9 had not been intended to change this aspect of IAS 31, where the 'share' is determined in accordance with the contractual arrangement. The Board concluded that the contractual arrangement generally delineates the 'share' or 'part' not only of the assets or liabilities of the parties to joint operations, but also of their 'share' of any revenues and expenses arising from the joint operation.

Joint venture

BC41 In relation to the accounting for interests in joint ventures, the Board decided that entities should recognise their interests using the equity method in accordance with IAS 28 *Investments in Associates and Joint Ventures*, unless the entity is exempted from applying the equity method as stated in that standard. In reaching that conclusion, the Board considered the views of some respondents to ED 9 who pointed out that joint control and significant influence are different. Proponents of this view argue that it is not appropriate to account for an associate and a joint venture in the same way using the equity method. Although the Board acknowledged that significant influence and joint control are different, the Board concluded that, except for specific circumstances that are addressed in IAS 28 (as amended in 2011), the equity method is the most appropriate method to account for joint ventures because it is a method that accounts for an entity's interest in the net assets of an investee. Reconsideration of the equity method was outside the scope of the joint ventures project.

BC42 Other respondents expressed concerns about the elimination of proportionate consolidation. Those respondents believe that proportionate consolidation more faithfully represents the economic substance of the arrangements, and better meets the information needs of users of financial statements. The Board acknowledged these concerns, but observed that the approach in the IFRS is consistent with its view of what constitutes the economic substance of an entity's interests in joint arrangements, a view that it concedes may differ from that of those respondents. This seems inevitable given that, the evidence suggests that in accounting for interests in jointly controlled entities approximately half of the entities applying IFRSs use proportionate consolidation and half use the equity method. The variation in practice, which is facilitated by the option in IAS 31, is a prime motivation for developing IFRS 11 (see paragraphs BC7 and BC8). That variation will, inevitably, be a source of disagreement.

BC43 The Board believes that the accounting for joint arrangements should faithfully reflect the rights and obligations that the parties have in respect of the assets and liabilities relating to the arrangement. In that respect, the Board observes that the activities that are the subject of different joint arrangements might be operationally very similar, but that the contractual terms agreed by the parties to these joint arrangements might confer on the parties very different rights to the assets, and obligations for the liabilities, relating to such activities. Consequently, the Board believes that the economic substance of the arrangements does not depend exclusively on whether the activities undertaken through joint arrangements are closely related to the activities undertaken by the parties on their own, or on whether the parties are closely involved in the operations of the arrangements. Instead, the economic substance of the arrangements depends on the rights and obligations assumed by the parties when carrying out such activities. It is those rights and obligations that the accounting for joint arrangements should reflect.

BC44 The Board observes that the IFRS requires parties to account for assets and liabilities when the contractual arrangement specifies that they have rights to the assets and obligations for the liabilities. The Board believes that accounting for joint arrangements that is based on the principles of the IFRS will contribute not only to improving the faithful representation of an entity's interests in joint arrangements, but also to enhancing comparability. This is because arrangements in which the parties have rights to the assets and obligations for the liabilities will require the same accounting treatment. In the same way, arrangements in which the parties have rights to the net assets of the arrangement will also require the same accounting treatment.

BC45 The Board does not believe that the elimination of proportionate consolidation will cause a loss of information for users of financial statements. This is because the disclosure requirements in IFRS 12, when compared with IAS 31, will improve the quality of the information provided to users relating to an entity's interest in joint ventures. The disclosure requirements in IFRS 12 will provide users with information about individual joint ventures when those joint ventures are material to the reporting entity. In addition, the Board notes that the summarised financial information required in IFRS 12 results in a higher degree of detail than did IAS 31, which gives users a better basis for assessing the effect on the reporting entity of the activities carried out through joint ventures.

Accounting for acquisitions of interests in joint operations

BC45A The IFRS Interpretations Committee (the Interpretations Committee) reported to the IASB that practice differed in accounting for the acquisition of interests in jointly controlled operations or jointly controlled assets, as specified in IAS 31.[2] In particular, the Interpretations Committee noted diversity in practice if the activity of the jointly controlled operations or jointly controlled assets constitutes a business, as defined in IFRS 3.

BC45B The principal approaches observed in practice were:

(a) **IFRS 3 approach:** some preparers of IFRS financial statements, when accounting for the acquisition of interests in jointly controlled operations or jointly controlled assets in which the activity constitutes a business, applied IFRS 3 and the guidance on business combinations in other IFRSs. Identifiable assets and liabilities were measured, subject to the exceptions in IFRS 3, at fair value and the residual was recognised as goodwill. Furthermore, transaction costs were not capitalised and deferred taxes were recognised on initial recognition of assets and liabilities. Only guidance on business combinations in IFRS 3 and other IFRSs that was not appropriate for the acquisition of an interest in jointly controlled operations or jointly controlled assets was not applied, for example, the guidance on non-controlling interests.

(b) **cost approach:** others allocated the total cost of acquiring the interest in the joint operation to the individual identifiable assets on the basis of their relative fair values. Accordingly, any premium paid was allocated to the identifiable assets rather than being recognised as goodwill. Transaction costs were capitalised and deferred taxes were not

---

2 IFRS 11 *Joint Arrangements* shall be applied for annual periods beginning on or after 1 January 2013. It replaces IAS 31 *Interests in Joint Ventures*.

recognised, because of the initial recognition exceptions in paragraphs 15 and 24 of IAS 12 *Income Taxes*.

(c) **hybrid approach:** a third group of preparers of IFRS financial statements only applied the principles on business combinations accounting in IFRS 3 and other IFRSs to issues that were not addressed elsewhere in IFRS. Identifiable assets and liabilities were measured at fair value, with exceptions, and the residual was recognised as a separate asset, ie goodwill. Transaction costs, however, were capitalised and contingent liabilities and deferred taxes were not recognised because these issues were considered as being addressed elsewhere in IFRS. Deferred taxes were not recognised, because of the initial recognition exceptions in paragraphs 15 and 24 of IAS 12.

BC45C The different approaches have led to different accounting outcomes, in particular:

(a) in accounting for premiums paid in excess of the value of the identifiable net assets;

(b) in capitalising or expensing acquisition-related costs; and

(c) in accounting for deferred tax assets and deferred tax liabilities that arise from the initial recognition of assets and liabilities.

BC45D The IASB noted that the diversity in practice resulted from the fact that IAS 31 did not give specific guidance on the accounting for acquisitions of interests in jointly controlled operations or jointly controlled assets, the activity of which constitutes a business, as defined in IFRS 3. The IASB was concerned that this diversity in practice may continue in the accounting for acquisitions of interests in joint operations, as defined in IFRS 11, when the activities of those joint operations constitute businesses. Arrangements that were formerly 'jointly controlled operations' and 'jointly controlled assets' in IAS 31 are joint operations in IFRS 11 (see paragraph BC26). As was the case in IAS 31, a joint operator recognises its (share in the) assets, liabilities, revenue and expenses relating to such arrangements.

BC45E The IASB considered the guidance in current IFRS on the acquisition of an interest in a business. The IASB recognised that the acquisition of an interest in a joint operation does not meet the definition of a business combination in IFRS 3. Nonetheless, the IASB concluded that the most appropriate approach to account for an acquisition of an interest in a joint operation in which the activity of the joint operation constitutes a business, as defined in IFRS 3, is to apply all of the principles on business combinations accounting in IFRS 3 and other IFRSs that do not conflict with the guidance in this IFRS.

BC45F The IASB reached this conclusion because:

(a) it considers that separate recognition of goodwill, when present, is preferable to allocating premiums to identifiable assets acquired on the basis of relative fair values;

(b) it thinks that an approach that limits the application of business combinations accounting only to issues that are not addressed elsewhere in IFRS lacks a strong conceptual basis; and

(c)   the guidance in IFRS 3 and other IFRSs on business combinations give a comprehensive and consistent set of accounting principles for the different components of such complex transactions as acquisitions of interests in businesses.

BC45G   The IASB also concluded that an entity that is acquiring an interest in a joint operation in which the activity of the joint operation constitutes a business, as defined in IFRS 3, shall disclose the relevant information that is specified in IFRS 3 and other IFRSs on business combinations. This is because these requirements are an integral part of the financial reporting about the acquisition of interests in businesses.

BC45H   Consequently, the IASB amended IFRS 11 to address the accounting for both the acquisition of an interest in a joint operation in which the activity of the joint operation constitutes a business, as defined in IFRS 3, and the related disclosure requirements, as a means to resolve the diversity in practice.

BC45I   The IASB noted that the fact patterns raised with the Interpretations Committee were limited to circumstances involving a business, as defined in IFRS 3. The IASB noted that IFRS already provides guidance for the acquisition of an interest in an asset or a group of assets that is not a business, as defined in IFRS 3. Consequently, the amendments apply only when an entity acquires an interest in a joint operation in which the activity constitutes a business, as defined in IFRS 3, either on formation of that joint operation or when acquiring an interest in an existing joint operation.

BC45J   The Exposure Draft *Acquisition of an Interest in a Joint Operation* (Proposed amendment to IFRS 11), which was published in December 2012, used the term 'relevant principles on business combinations accounting in IFRS 3 and other IFRSs' to describe the principles that have to be applied in accounting for the acquisition of an interest in a joint operation in which the activity constitutes a business. In analysing the comment letters on the Exposure Draft, the IASB noted divergent understanding of what the 'relevant principles on business combinations accounting in IFRS 3 and other IFRSs' are, within the context of the proposed amendment.

BC45K   In order to avoid diversity in practice from the application of the term 'relevant principles on business combinations accounting in IFRS 3 and other IFRSs', the IASB decided to replace this term with 'all of the principles on business combinations accounting in IFRS 3 and other IFRSs that do not conflict with the guidance in this IFRS'. In addition, to aid understanding the application guidance includes a non-exhaustive list of five principles related to business combinations accounting in IFRS 3 and other IFRSs that do not conflict with the principles in this IFRS. Four of them relate to the areas in which the Interpretations Committee observed different accounting outcomes from the application of different approaches to the accounting for acquisitions of interests in jointly controlled operations or jointly controlled assets in which the activity constitutes a business (see paragraphs BC45B–BC45C).

BC45L   The IASB also noted that the reference to 'all of the principles on business combinations accounting in IFRS 3 and other IFRSs' is ambiguous for acquisitions of additional interests in joint operations that result in the joint operator retaining joint control of the joint operation. It might be understood as a reference to either:

(a) paragraph 42 of IFRS 3 with the result of remeasuring a previously held interest in a joint operation on the acquisition of an additional interest while retaining joint control; or

(b) paragraph 23 of IFRS 10 with the result of not remeasuring a previously held interest in a joint operation on the acquisition of an additional interest while retaining joint control.

BC45M   In order to resolve this ambiguity, the IASB decided to clarify that previously held interests in a joint operation are not remeasured if the joint operator retains joint control. Paragraph 23 of IFRS 10 addresses the accounting for the acquisition of an additional interest in a business that is already controlled by the acquirer. This is the analogous transaction to the acquisition of an interest in a business that is already jointly controlled by the acquirer and will continue to be jointly controlled by it. Paragraph 42 of IFRS 3 instead addresses the acquisition of an interest that results in the acquirer obtaining control over the business. This is the analogous transaction to the acquisition of an interest in a business that results in the acquirer obtaining joint control of the business.

BC45N   The IASB decided to add a scope exclusion for joint operations under common control to the amendments to IFRS 11. The IASB concluded that the amendments to IFRS 11 should not require the application of all of the principles on business combinations accounting for transactions that would be outside the scope of IFRS 3 if control, rather than joint control, would be obtained or retained by the acquirer.

Transactions between an entity and a joint operation in which that entity is a joint operator and incorporation of SIC-13 into the IFRS

BC46   In its redeliberation of ED 9, the Board noted that the exposure draft was silent on the accounting for transactions between an entity and a joint operation in which that entity is a joint operator. The Board observed that the IFRS did not aim to change the accounting procedures that entities applied when accounting for such transactions in accordance with IAS 31, but it did acknowledge that the IFRS should state what those requirements were.

BC47   The Board also decided to include the requirements for the accounting for transactions entered into between a joint venturer and a joint venture, including the consensus of SIC-13 *Jointly Controlled Entities—Non-Monetary Contributions by Venturers*, in IAS 28 (as amended in 2011).

Reporting interests in joint arrangements in the financial statements of parties that participate in, but do not have joint control of, a joint arrangement

BC48   The Board decided to clarify in the IFRS that an arrangement can be a joint arrangement even though not all of its parties have joint control of the arrangement. This was consistent with IAS 31, which defined an 'investor in a joint venture' as a party to a joint venture that does not have joint control of that joint venture. The Board noted, however, that relating the term 'investor' exclusively to parties with no joint control of the arrangement can be confusing because the parties with joint control of the arrangement are also investors in those arrangements. Accordingly, the Board modified the language in the IFRS to avoid that confusion. However, even though in its redeliberation of ED 9 the Board highlighted that the IFRS establishes recognition and measurement requirements for the parties with joint control of a joint arrangement, the Board decided to address the accounting requirements for parties that participate in, but do not have joint control of, a joint arrangement, to reduce divergence in practice.

BC49　In relation to parties that participate in, but do not have joint control of, a joint arrangement that is a joint operation, the Board focused its discussions on those parties for which the contractual arrangements specify that they have rights to the assets, and obligations for the liabilities, relating to the joint operation. The Board concluded that, even though those parties are not joint operators, they do have rights and obligations for the assets, liabilities, revenues and expenses relating to the joint operation, which they should recognise in accordance with the terms of the contractual arrangement.

BC50　The Board considered that the requirements in IAS 31 for parties that participate in, but do not have joint control of, joint ventures were appropriate and therefore decided to carry them forward to the IFRS. Consequently, such a party should account for its investment in accordance with IFRS 9 or, if that party has significant influence over the joint venture, in accordance with IAS 28 (as amended in 2011).

Joint operation held for sale

BC51　ED 9 was silent on how an entity should account for an interest in a joint operation that is classified as held for sale. The Board decided that a joint operator should account for an interest in a joint operation that is classified as held for sale in accordance with IFRS 5 *Non-current Assets Held for Sale and Discontinued Operations*. The Board also confirmed that the guidance in IFRS 5 for the classification of a disposal group as held for sale would apply to interests in joint operations held for sale.

Disclosure

BC52　As part of its redeliberation of ED 9 and ED 10 *Consolidated Financial Statements*, the Board identified an opportunity to integrate and make consistent the disclosure requirements for subsidiaries, joint arrangements, associates and unconsolidated structured entities, and to present those requirements in a single IFRS.

BC53　The Board observed that IAS 27 (as revised in 2003), IAS 28 (as revised in 2003) and IAS 31 contained many similar disclosure requirements. ED 9 had already proposed amendments to the disclosure requirements for joint ventures and associates to align the disclosure requirements for those two types of investments more closely. The Board noted that the majority of respondents agreed with the proposals in ED 9 to align the disclosures for joint ventures with the disclosures in IAS 28 for associates.

BC54   As a result, the Board combined the disclosure requirements for interest with subsidiaries, joint arrangements, associates and unconsolidated structured entities within a single comprehensive standard, IFRS 12.

BC55   The Basis for Conclusions accompanying IFRS 12 summarises the Board's considerations in developing that IFRS, including its review of responses to the disclosure proposals in ED 9. Accordingly, IFRS 11 does not include disclosure requirements and this Basis for Conclusions does not incorporate the Board's considerations of responses to the proposed disclosure requirements in ED 9.

Effective date

BC56   The Board decided to align the effective date for the IFRS with the effective date for IFRS 10, IFRS 12, IAS 27 *Separate Financial Statements* and IAS 28 (as amended in 2011). When making this decision, the Board noted that the five IFRSs all deal with the assessment of, and related accounting and disclosure requirements about, a reporting entity's special relationships with other entities (ie when the reporting entity has control or joint control of, or significant influence over, another entity). As a result, the Board concluded that applying IFRS 11 without also applying the other four IFRSs could cause unwarranted confusion.

BC57   The Board usually sets an effective date of between twelve and eighteen months after issuing an IFRS. When deciding the effective date for those IFRSs, the Board considered the following factors:

(a)   the time that many countries require for translation and for introducing the mandatory requirements into law.

(b)   the consolidation project was related to the global financial crisis that started in 2007 and was accelerated by the Board in response to urgent requests from the leaders of the G20, the Financial Stability Board, users of financial statements, regulators and others to improve the accounting and disclosure of an entity's 'off balance sheet' activities.

(c)   the comments received from respondents to the Request for Views *Effective Date and Transition Methods* that was published in October 2010 regarding implementation costs, effective date and transition requirements of the IFRSs to be issued in 2011. Most respondents did not identify the consolidation and joint arrangements IFRSs as having a high impact in terms of the time and resources that their implementation would require. In addition, only a few respondents commented that the effective dates of those IFRSs should be aligned with those of the other IFRSs to be issued in 2011.

BC58   With those factors in mind, the Board decided to require entities to apply the five IFRSs for annual periods beginning on or after 1 January 2013.

BC59   Most respondents to the Request for Views supported early application of the IFRSs to be issued in 2011. Respondents stressed that early application was especially important for first-time adopters in 2011 and 2012. The Board was persuaded by these arguments and decided to permit early application of IFRS 11 but only if an entity applies it in conjunction with the other IFRSs (ie IFRS 10, IFRS 12, IAS 27 (as amended in 2011) and IAS 28 (as amended in

2011)) to avoid a lack of comparability among financial statements, and for the reasons noted in paragraph BC56 that triggered the Board's decision to set the same effective date for all five IFRSs. Even though an entity should apply the five IFRSs at the same time, the Board noted that an entity should not be prevented from providing any information required by IFRS 12 early if by doing so users gained a better understanding of the entity's relationships with other entities.

Transition

BC60   The exposure draft proposed retrospective application of the requirements. In its redeliberation of ED 9, the Board observed that entities affected by the changes introduced by the IFRS would have enough time to prepare to apply the new requirements retrospectively. The Board was informed of a few cases in which entities, on the basis of their analysis of the proposals in ED 9, had already changed their accounting for interests in joint arrangements retrospectively, taking advantage of the accounting option that IAS 31 offered to jointly controlled entities.

BC61   However, in its discussions, the Board considered the views of some respondents to ED 9 who had expressed their concern about applying the requirements retrospectively, because of undue cost and effort. In response to these concerns, the Board decided that in the case of changing from proportionate consolidation to the equity method, an entity should not adjust retrospectively any differences between the accounting methods of proportionate consolidation and equity method, but should instead aggregate the carrying amounts of the assets and liabilities, including any goodwill arising from acquisition, that the entity had previously proportionately consolidated into a single line investment as at the beginning of the earliest period presented.

BC62   The Board also decided that the opening balance of the investment should be tested for impairment in accordance with paragraphs 40–43 of IAS 28 (as amended in 2011), with any resulting impairment loss being adjusted against retained earnings at the beginning of the earliest period presented.

BC63   The Board also considered the case when an arrangement that was previously proportionately consolidated has a negative net asset position on transition. In such a case, an entity should assess whether it has legal or constructive obligations in relation to those negative net assets. The Board concluded that if the entity does not have legal or constructive obligations in relation to the negative net assets, it should not recognise the corresponding liability but it should adjust retained earnings at the beginning of the earliest period presented. The entity should also be required to disclose this fact along with its cumulative unrecognised share of losses of the joint venture as at the beginning of the earliest period presented and at the date at which the IFRS is first applied.

BC64   The Board also considered requiring disclosures to help users of financial statements to understand the consequences of the accounting change for those joint arrangements that would be changing from proportionate consolidation to the equity method. To address this need, the Board decided that an entity should disclose a breakdown of the assets and liabilities that have been aggregated into the single line investment as at the beginning of the earliest period presented.

BC65   The Board redeliberated the transition requirements for entities changing from the equity method to accounting for assets and liabilities in respect of their interest in a joint operation. The Board decided to require an entity to recognise each of the assets, including any goodwill arising from acquisition, and the liabilities relating to its interest in the joint operation at its carrying amount on the basis of the information used by the entity in applying the equity method, instead of requiring the entity to remeasure its share of each of those assets and liabilities at the date of transition. The Board did not believe that the costs of requiring entities to remeasure the assets and liabilities relating to the joint operation as a result of the accounting change would outweigh the benefits.

BC66   The Board observed that changing from the equity method to accounting for assets and liabilities in respect of an entity's interest in a joint operation could result in the net amount of the assets and liabilities recognised being either higher or lower than the investment (and any other items that formed part of the entity's net investment in the arrangement) derecognised. In the first case, the Board noted that assets and liabilities recognised could be higher than the investment derecognised when the entity had previously impaired the carrying amount of the investment. The Board observed that, in accordance with IAS 28 (as amended in 2011), such an impairment loss would not have been allocated to any asset, including goodwill, that formed part of the carrying amount of the investment and that as a result, the net amount of the underlying assets and liabilities could be higher than the carrying amount of the investment. To address this, the Board concluded that in such a case, an entity should first adjust the difference against any goodwill related to the investment, with any remaining difference adjusted against retained earnings at the beginning of the earliest period presented. In the second case, the Board noted that the net amount of the assets and liabilities recognised could be lower than the investment derecognised when, for example, an entity applied the same percentage interest to all the underlying assets and liabilities of its investee when determining the carrying amount of its investment using the equity method. However, for some of those underlying assets the entity could have a lower interest when accounting for it as a joint operation. The Board concluded that in such a case, an entity should adjust any difference between the net amount of the assets and liabilities recognised and the investment (and any other items that formed part of the entity's net investment in the arrangement) derecognised against retained earnings at the beginning of the earliest period presented.

BC67   The Board also redeliberated the transition requirements for entities accounting for an interest in a joint operation in its separate financial statements when the entity had previously accounted for this interest at cost or in accordance with IFRS 9. As stated in paragraph BC38, the Board observed that the parties' interests in a joint operation are recognised in their separate financial statements, resulting in no difference between what is recognised in the parties' separate financial statements and in the parties' consolidated financial statements. The Board decided that an entity should adjust any difference between the investment derecognised and the assets and liabilities recognised in respect of the entity's interest in a joint operation against retained earnings at the beginning of the earliest period presented.

BC68   The Board also considered requiring disclosures to help users of financial statements to understand the consequences of the accounting change from the equity method to accounting for assets and liabilities, and when accounting for an interest in a joint operation in the separate financial statements of an entity when the entity had previously accounted for this interest at cost or in accordance with IFRS 9. The Board decided that in both cases, an entity should provide a reconciliation between the investment derecognised and the breakdown of the assets and liabilities recognised, together with any remaining difference adjusted against retained earnings, at the beginning of the earliest period presented.

BC69   As stated in paragraph BC57, respondents to the Request for Views also commented on the transition requirements of the IFRSs to be issued in 2011. In relation to the transition requirements relating to the consolidation and joint arrangements IFRSs, the Board noted that the majority of the respondents to the Request for Views had agreed with the tentative decisions that the Board had previously made at the time of the consultation on the transition requirements for those IFRSs.

BC69A   In June 2012, the Board amended the transition guidance in Appendix C to IFRS 10 *Consolidated Financial Statements*. When making those amendments, the Board decided to limit the requirement to present adjusted comparatives to the annual period immediately preceding the date of initial application of IFRS 10. This is consistent with the minimum comparative disclosure requirements contained in IAS 1 *Presentation of Financial Statements* as amended by *Annual Improvements to IFRSs 2009–2011 Cycle* (issued May 2012). Those amendments confirmed that when an entity applies a changed accounting policy retrospectively, it shall present, as a minimum, three statements of financial position (ie 1 January 2012, 31 December 2012 and 31 December 2013 for a calendar-year entity, assuming no early application of this IFRS) and two of each of the other statements (IAS 1 paragraphs 40A–40B). Notwithstanding this requirement, the Board confirmed that an entity is not prohibited from presenting adjusted comparative information for earlier periods. The Board also decided to make similar amendments to the transition guidance in Appendix C to this IFRS and Appendix C to IFRS 12 *Disclosure of Interests in Other Entities* to be consistent with this decision. The Board noted that if all comparative periods are not adjusted then entities should be required to state that fact, clearly identify the information that has not been adjusted, and explain the basis on which it has been prepared.

BC69B   The Board also considered the disclosure requirements of IAS 8 *Accounting Policies, Changes in Accounting Estimates and Errors*. On the initial application of an IFRS, paragraph 28(f) of IAS 8 requires an entity to disclose, for the current period and for each prior period presented, the amount of any adjustment for each financial statement line item affected. Changes in the accounting for a joint arrangement on transition to IFRS 11 are likely to affect many line items throughout the financial statements. The Board agreed that this requirement would be burdensome for preparers and so agreed to limit the disclosure of the quantitative impact of any changes in the accounting for a joint arrangement to only the annual period immediately preceding the first annual period for which IFRS 11 is applied. An entity may also present this information for the current period or for earlier comparative periods, but is not required to do so.

Accounting for acquisitions of interests in joint operations

BC69C   The IASB considered the transition provisions and effective date of the amendments to IFRS 11. The IASB noted that applying all of the principles of business combinations accounting in IFRS 3 and other IFRSs that do not conflict with the guidance in this IFRS to transactions that have previously been accounted for by applying one of the divergent approaches presented in paragraph BC45B might involve the use of hindsight in determining the acquisition-date fair values of the identifiable assets and liabilities that are to be recognised as part of the transaction and in performing the impairment test for goodwill. Consequently, the IASB decided that an entity would apply the amendments to IFRS 11 prospectively for transactions occurring in annual periods beginning on or after 1 January 2016 with early application permitted.

Summary of main changes from ED 9

BC70   The main changes from the exposure draft ED 9 are:

(a)   IFRS 11 applies to all entities that have an interest in a joint arrangement. The scope exception in the exposure draft for venture capital organisations, or mutual funds, unit trusts and similar entities, including investment-linked insurance funds, has been removed and has been recharacterised as an exemption from the requirement to measure investments in joint ventures in accordance with the equity method.

(b)   IFRS 11 replaces the term 'shared decisions' introduced by ED 9 with the term 'joint control'. As in IAS 31, 'joint control' is one of the features that, along with the existence of a contractual arrangement, defines 'joint arrangements'.

(c)   IFRS 11 classifies joint arrangements into two types—'joint operations' and 'joint ventures'. Each type of joint arrangement is aligned with a specific accounting requirement. ED 9 had classified joint arrangements into three types—'joint operations', 'joint assets' and 'joint ventures'.

(d)   IFRS 11 provides application requirements to assist entities in the classification of their joint arrangements. The IFRS requires an entity to determine the type of joint arrangement in which it is involved by considering its rights and obligations. In particular, the IFRS requires an entity to give consideration to the structure and legal form of the arrangement, to the terms agreed by the parties in the contractual arrangement and, when relevant, it should also consider other facts and circumstances.

(e)   IFRS 11 clarifies that not all the parties to a joint arrangement need to have joint control for the arrangement to be a joint arrangement. As a result, some of the parties to a joint arrangement might participate in the joint arrangement, but might not have joint control of it.

(f)   The consensus of SIC-13 has been incorporated into IAS 28 (as amended in 2011), and SIC-13 is accordingly withdrawn. ED 9 had proposed to incorporate the consensus of SIC-13 into the standard on joint arrangements.

(g)   The disclosure requirements have been placed in IFRS 12. ED 9 had proposed to incorporate the disclosure requirements for joint arrangements into the standard on joint arrangements.

(h)   IFRS 11 does not require an entity to adjust the differences between the proportionate consolidation method and the equity method retrospectively when an entity changes from proportionate consolidation to the equity method when accounting for its joint ventures. Instead, it requires an entity to recognise its investment in a joint venture as at the beginning of the earliest period presented, by measuring it as the aggregate of the carrying amounts of the assets and liabilities that the entity had previously proportionately consolidated, including any goodwill arising from acquisition. ED 9 had proposed retrospective application of the requirements.

Cost-benefit considerations

BC71   The objective of general purpose financial reporting is to provide financial information about the reporting entity that is useful to existing and potential investors, lenders and other creditors in making decisions about providing resources to the entity. To attain this objective, the Board seeks to ensure that an IFRS will meet a significant need and that the overall benefits of the resulting information justify the costs of providing it. Although the costs to implement a new IFRS might not be borne evenly, users of financial statements benefit from improvements in financial reporting, thereby facilitating the functioning of markets for capital and credit and the efficient allocation of resources in the economy.

BC72   The evaluation of costs and benefits is necessarily subjective. In making its judgement, the Board considered the following:

(a)   the costs incurred by preparers of financial statements;

(b)   the costs incurred by users of financial statements when information is not available;

(c)   the comparative advantage that preparers have in developing information, compared with the costs that users would incur to develop surrogate information;

(d)   the benefit of better economic decision-making as result of improved financial reporting; and

(e)   the costs of transition for users, preparers and others.

BC73   The Board concluded that the IFRS benefits preparers and users of financial statements. This is because the accounting for joint arrangements in the IFRS follows a principle-based approach. This approach has allowed the Board to remove the accounting option in IAS 31 so that each type of joint arrangement (ie 'joint operations' and 'joint ventures') is accounted for on a consistent basis. This contributes to enhancing the verifiability, comparability and understandability of these arrangements in entities' financial statements.

BC74   In the IFRS, the accounting for joint arrangements depends on the rights and obligations arising from the arrangement (not exclusively on whether the parties have chosen a particular structure or legal form to carry out their arrangements, or on the consistent application of an accounting policy—proportionate consolidation or equity method). Thus, the IFRS promotes greater comparability by applying the same approach to different joint arrangements.

BC75   The Board believes that basing the accounting on the principles in the IFRS results in enhanced verifiability, comparability and understandability, to the benefit of both preparers and users. First, verifiability and understandability are enhanced because the accounting reflects more faithfully the economic phenomena that it purports to represent (ie an entity's rights and obligations arising from its arrangements), which allows them to be better understood. Second, requiring the same accounting for each type of arrangement will enable entities to account for joint arrangements consistently: arrangements that confer on the parties rights to the assets and obligations for the liabilities are joint operations and arrangements that confer on the parties rights to the net assets are joint ventures. Consistency in the accounting for joint arrangements will help to achieve comparability among financial statements, which will enable users to identify and understand similarities in, and differences between, different arrangements.

BC76   The Board noted that the costs that preparers will have to bear when applying the IFRS to their arrangements are concentrated in the assessment of the type of joint arrangement rather than in the accounting for the arrangements. This is because entities accounting for joint arrangements in accordance with IAS 31 were not required to classify their arrangements on the basis of their rights and obligations arising from the arrangement, but instead on whether the arrangement was structured in an entity. The IFRS will require entities to assess the type of joint arrangement in which they are involved when those arrangements have been structured through a separate vehicle. Even though the classification of the joint arrangements represents an additional assessment that was not required in IAS 31, the application requirements in the IFRS that should assist preparers in the classification of their arrangements are not unduly complex. The Board does not think that the additional assessment that the IFRS will require for the classification of arrangements will result in an undue cost to preparers.

BC77   The Board noted that the IFRS, by comparison with the exposure draft, simplifies the proposals by aligning the types of joint arrangement with the accounting methods. The Board concluded that once an entity has determined the classification of the arrangement, the accounting for the arrangement will follow accounting procedures that have not been modified by the IFRS (ie entities will either account for assets and liabilities or they will account for an investment using the equity method). However, the Board acknowledged that the requirement for joint operations to be accounted for in the same way in the entity's consolidated financial statements as in the entity's separate financial statements might lead to additional costs to entities in jurisdictions in which separate financial statements are required to be reported in accordance with IFRSs. This is because those requirements might cause entities to perform additional manual procedures such as reconciliations between the statutory accounts and the tax returns, and might require an entity to provide additional explanations of the impact of the changes to, for example, its creditors. Except for these costs and any other costs required on transition, the costs of accounting for joint arrangements once the entities have determined their classification will remain unchanged as a result of the IFRS.

BC78　　The Board concluded that enhanced verifiability, comparability and understandability result in a more faithful representation of joint arrangements in the financial statements of the entities that are involved in such arrangements, and that those benefits outweigh the costs that preparers might incur when implementing the IFRS.

Appendix
Amendments to the Basis for Conclusions on other IFRSs

This appendix contains amendments to the Basis for Conclusions on other IFRSs that are necessary in order to ensure consistency with IFRS 11 and the related amendments to other IFRSs. Amended paragraphs are shown with new text underlined and deleted text struck through.

* * * * *

The amendments contained in this appendix when IFRS 11 was issued in 2011 have been incorporated into the Basis for Conclusions on the relevant IFRSs published in this volume.

IASB documents published to accompany

IFRS 12

Disclosure of Interests in Other Entities

The text of the unaccompanied standard, IFRS 12, is contained in Part A of this edition. Its effective date when issued was 1 January 2013. This part presents the following documents:

BASIS FOR CONCLUSIONS

CONTENTS

Basis for Conclusions on
IFRS 12 *Disclosure of Interests in Other Entities*

This Basis for Conclusions accompanies, but is not part of, IFRS 12.

Introduction

BC1　This Basis for Conclusions summarises the International Accounting Standards Board's considerations in developing IFRS 12 *Disclosure of Interests in Other Entities*. Individual Board members gave greater weight to some factors than to others.

BC2　Users of financial statements have consistently requested improvements to the disclosure of a reporting entity's interests in other entities to help identify the profit or loss and cash flows available to the reporting entity and determine the value of a current or future investment in the reporting entity.

BC3　They highlighted the need for better information about the subsidiaries that are consolidated, as well as an entity's interests in joint arrangements and associates that are not consolidated but with which the entity has a special relationship.

BC4　The global financial crisis that started in 2007 also highlighted a lack of transparency about the risks to which a reporting entity was exposed from its involvement with structured entities, including those that it had sponsored.

BC5　IFRS 12 addresses the disclosure of a reporting entity's interests in other entities when the reporting entity has a special relationship with those other entities, ie it controls another entity, has joint control of or significant influence over another entity or has an interest in an unconsolidated structured entity.

BC6　In developing IFRS 12, the Board considered the responses to its exposure drafts, ED 9 *Joint Arrangements* and ED 10 *Consolidated Financial Statements*. ED 9 proposed amendments to the disclosure requirements for joint ventures and associates to align more closely the disclosure requirements for those two types of investments. ED 10 proposed amendments to the disclosure requirements for subsidiaries and new disclosure requirements for unconsolidated structured entities.

BC7　During its consideration of the responses to ED 9 and ED 10, the Board identified an opportunity to integrate and make consistent the disclosure requirements for subsidiaries, joint arrangements, associates and unconsolidated structured entities and present those requirements in a single IFRS. The Board observed that the disclosure requirements of IAS 27 *Consolidated and Separate Financial Statements*, IAS 28 *Investments in Associates* and IAS 31 *Interests in Joint Ventures* overlapped in many areas. In addition, many respondents to ED 10 commented that the disclosure requirements for interests in unconsolidated structured entities should not be located in a consolidation standard. Therefore, the Board concluded that a combined disclosure standard for interests in other entities would make it easier to understand and apply the disclosure requirements for subsidiaries, joint ventures, associates and unconsolidated structured entities.

BC8　The Board decided to extend the scope of IFRS 12 to interests in joint operations. A joint operation is a joint arrangement that is not necessarily structured through an entity that is separate from the parties to the joint arrangement.

Therefore, an interest in a joint operation does not necessarily represent an interest in another entity. The Board decided to include disclosure requirements for joint operations in IFRS 12 because it believes that the benefits of having all disclosure requirements for joint arrangements in one place outweighs the disadvantages of including disclosure requirements about interests in joint operations in a standard that otherwise deals with an entity's interests in other entities.

Clarification of the scope of the Standard (amendments issued in December 2016)

BC8A   The Board was asked to clarify the scope of IFRS 12 with respect to interests in entities within the scope of IFRS 5 *Non-current Assets Held for Sale and Discontinued Operations*. Paragraph B17 states that an entity is not required to disclose summarised financial information in accordance with paragraphs B10–B16 for interests classified as held for sale. However, the requirements in paragraph 5B of IFRS 5 made it unclear whether all other requirements in IFRS 12 apply to interests in entities classified as held for sale or discontinued operations in accordance with IFRS 5.

BC8B   The Board noted that it had not intended to exempt an entity from all of the disclosure requirements in IFRS 12 with respect to interests in entities classified as held for sale or discontinued operations. The objective of IFRS 12 (ie to disclose information that enables users of financial statements to evaluate the nature of, and risks associated with, interests in other entities, and the effects of those interests on financial statements) is relevant to interests in other entities, regardless of whether they are within the scope of IFRS 5.

BC8C   Accordingly, in *Annual Improvements to IFRS Standards 2014–2016 Cycle*, the Board added paragraph 5A to clarify that, except as described in paragraph B17, the requirements in IFRS 12 apply to interests in entities within the scope of IFRS 5—ie interests that are classified (or included in a disposal group that is classified) as held for sale, held for distribution to owners in their capacity as owners, or discontinued operations. Paragraph 5A refers only to interests that are classified as held for sale or discontinued operations because the clarification was needed only for interests referred to in paragraph 5B of IFRS 5.

BC8D   A few respondents to the Board's proposals suggested that the Board consider which requirements in IFRS 12 are particularly relevant for interests in entities within the scope of IFRS 5, and specify that an entity applies only those relevant requirements.

BC8E   The Board decided not to change the proposals in this respect. Although acknowledging that some requirements in IFRS 12 might be more relevant to interests within the scope of IFRS 5 than others, the Board noted that this is also true for interests not within the scope of IFRS 5. This is because the relevance of each disclosure requirement for particular interests depends on the specific facts and circumstances relating to such interests. This is implicit in the requirements in paragraph 4, which require an entity to apply judgement in determining the amount of information to disclose about its interests in other entities to satisfy the disclosure objective.

BC8F   In response to the Board's proposal to apply the amendments retrospectively, a few respondents asked the Board to consider whether to provide transition relief for interests in entities disposed of before or during the first year of application.

BC8G   The Board decided not to provide such transition relief because: (a) the incremental costs of collecting data and preparing information are not expected to be significant—this is because such information is needed for disclosure before the interests are classified as held for sale or discontinued operations; and (b) it would be inconsistent with IFRS 12, which requires disclosure even when an entity no longer has any contractual involvement with another entity.

BC8H   The Board decided on an effective date of 1 January 2017 for the amendments. Because the requirements in IFRS 12 generally apply only to annual financial statements, an effective date of 1 January 2017 would typically mean that the earliest an entity would be required to apply the amendments would be within financial statements for the year ended 31 December 2017. Accordingly, an effective date of 1 January 2017 provides an entity with more than a year to prepare to implement the amendments. In addition, the Board noted that the amendments are clarifying in nature.

BC8I   The Board decided that an option to apply the amendments early is not necessary. This is because an entity is not prohibited from disclosing additional information.

The structure of IFRS 12 and the Board's deliberations

BC9   IFRS 12 replaces the disclosure requirements in IAS 27, IAS 28 and IAS 31, except for the disclosure requirements that apply only when preparing separate financial statements, which are included in IAS 27 *Separate Financial Statements*.

BC10   Unless otherwise stated, any references in this Basis for Conclusions to:

(a)   IAS 27 are to IAS 27 *Consolidated and Separate Financial Statements*.

(b)   IAS 28 are to IAS 28 *Investments in Associates*.

(c)   IAS 31 are to IAS 31 *Interests in Joint Ventures*.

BC11   In developing IFRS 12, the Board did not reconsider all the requirements that are included in the IFRS. The requirements in paragraphs 11, 18 and 19 relate to disclosures about some of the accounting requirements in IFRS 10 *Consolidated Financial Statements*, which were carried forward from IAS 27 to IFRS 10 without being reconsidered by the Board. Consequently, the Board did not reconsider the requirements in those paragraphs. In addition, the requirements in paragraph 22 relate to disclosures about the application of the equity method and restrictions on the ability of joint ventures and associates to transfer funds to the reporting entity. The Board did not reconsider the equity method as part of its joint ventures project. Consequently, and with the exception of its decision to align the requirements for joint ventures and associates as stated in paragraph BC6, the requirements in paragraph 22 were carried forward from IAS 28 without being reconsidered by the Board. Accordingly, when the Board approved IFRS 12 for issue, it brought forward from IAS 27 and IAS 28 without reconsideration the requirements now in paragraphs 11, 18, 19 and 22 of IFRS 12.

BC12 When revised in 2003, IAS 27 was accompanied by a Basis for Conclusions summarising the considerations of the Board, as constituted at the time, in reaching some of its conclusions in that standard. The Basis for Conclusions was subsequently updated to reflect amendments to the standard. For convenience, the Board has incorporated into its Basis for Conclusions on IFRS 12 material from the Basis for Conclusions on IAS 27 that discusses the requirements in paragraphs 18 and 19 that the Board has not reconsidered. That material is contained in paragraphs BC37–BC41. In those paragraphs cross-references to the IFRS have been updated accordingly and minor necessary editorial changes have been made.

BC13 As part of its consolidation project, the Board is examining how an investment entity accounts for its interests in subsidiaries, joint ventures and associates and what, if any, additional disclosures might be made about those interests. The Board expects to publish later in 2011 an exposure draft on investment entities.[1]

Significant judgements and assumptions

BC14 The assessment of whether an entity controls another entity sometimes requires judgement. Paragraph 122 of IAS 1 *Presentation of Financial Statements* requires an entity to disclose the judgements that management has made in the process of applying the entity's accounting policies and that have the most significant effect on the amounts recognised in the financial statements.

BC15 IAS 27 and IAS 28 supplemented the general disclosure requirement in IAS 1 with more specific requirements relating to an entity's decision about whether it controls or has significant influence over another entity. Those standards required disclosure of information when an entity's control or significant influence assessment was different from the presumptions of control or significant influence in IAS 27 and IAS 28 (ie more than 50 per cent voting power for control and 20 per cent or more voting power for significant influence).

BC16 The Board decided to replace the specific disclosure requirements in IAS 27 and IAS 28 with a principle that an entity must disclose all significant judgements and assumptions made in determining the nature of its interest in another entity or arrangement, and in determining the type of joint arrangement in which it has an interest. Moreover, the requirement for such disclosures should not be limited to particular scenarios. Instead, disclosure should be required for all situations in which an entity applies significant judgement in assessing the nature of its interest in another entity. The disclosure requirements formerly in IAS 27 and IAS 28 in this respect were included as examples of situations for which significant judgement might need to be applied.

---

1 *Investment Entities* (Amendments to IFRS 10, IFRS 12 and IAS 27), issued in October 2012, introduced an exception to the principle that all subsidiaries shall be consolidated. The amendments define an investment entity and require a parent that is an investment entity to measure its investments in particular subsidiaries at fair value through profit or loss instead of consolidating those subsidiaries. In addition, the amendments introduce new disclosure requirements related to investment entities in IFRS 12 *Disclosure of Interests in Other Entities* and IAS 27 *Separate Financial Statements*. The amendments are discussed in paragraphs BC215–BC317 of IFRS 10 *Consolidated Financial Statements*, and the disclosure requirements are discussed in paragraphs BC61A–BC61H of this IFRS.

BC17   ED 10 proposed that, for two particular scenarios for which the control assessment was different, an entity should provide information, in aggregate, that would help users evaluate the accounting consequences of the decision to consolidate another entity.

BC18   Most users supported the proposal. However, other respondents to ED 10 expressed the view that disclosing such quantitative information about the accounting consequences was a step too far. They were concerned that such a disclosure would encourage 'second-guessing' by users of financial statements and, therefore, replace the judgement made by management with that made by users of financial statements.

BC19   The Board acknowledged those concerns, but observed that consideration of different scenarios is common practice when analysing financial statements and does not necessarily mean that the judgement of management is replaced with that of other parties. However, the Board noted that IFRS 3 *Business Combinations* requires an entity to disclose information that enables users of financial statements to evaluate the nature and financial effect of a business combination—ie when an entity obtains control of another business or businesses. Furthermore, if an entity's assessment that it does not control another entity requires significant judgement, the entity will often conclude that it has either joint control of or significant influence over that other entity. The Board observed that IFRS 12 will require an entity to disclose quantitative information about its interests in joint ventures and associates, and information about its exposure to risk from its interests in unconsolidated structured entities. Therefore, the Board concluded that there was no need for a separate requirement to disclose quantitative information to help assess the accounting consequences of an entity's decision to consolidate (or not to consolidate) another entity.

Interests in subsidiaries

BC20   IFRS 12 requires an entity to disclose information that enables users of financial statements

(a)   to understand:

(i)   the composition of the group; and

(ii)   the interest that non-controlling interests have in the group's activities and cash flows; and

(b)   to evaluate:

(i)   the nature and the effect of significant restrictions on its ability to access and use assets of the group, and settle liabilities of the group;

(ii)   the nature of, and changes in, the risks associated with its interests in consolidated structured entities;

(iii)   the consequences of changes in the parent's ownership interest in a subsidiary that do not result in a loss of control; and

(iv)   the consequences of losing control of a subsidiary during the reporting period.

Composition of the group and non-controlling interests

BC21   Consolidated financial statements present the financial position, comprehensive income and cash flows of the group as a single entity. They ignore the legal boundaries of the parent and its subsidiaries. However, those legal boundaries could affect the parent's access to and use of assets and other resources of its subsidiaries and, therefore, affect the cash flows that can be distributed to the shareholders of the parent.

BC22   When the Board was developing IFRS 12, users informed the Board that, as part of their analysis of financial statements, they need to identify profit or loss and cash flows attributable to the shareholders of the parent and those attributable to non-controlling interests.

BC23   IAS 1 provides some of the information necessary to perform the valuations by requiring an entity to present:

(a)   in the statement of financial position, the non-controlling interest within equity;

(b)   in the statement of comprehensive income, profit or loss and total comprehensive income for the period attributable to the non-controlling interest; and

(c)   in the statement of changes in equity, a reconciliation between the non-controlling interest at the beginning of the period and the end of the period.

BC24   Although confirming that the presentation requirements in IAS 1 provide important information, users of financial statements requested additional information to enable them to make better estimates of future profit or loss and cash flows attributable to the shareholders of the parent. The Board was advised that, in particular, an analyst requires information about the non-controlling interests' share of the profit or loss, cash flows and net assets of subsidiaries with material non-controlling interests.

BC25   Those users of financial statements also requested specific disclosure requirements in this respect, rather than simply a disclosure objective as was proposed in ED 10. In their view, only specific disclosure requirements would enhance their ability to estimate the profit or loss and cash flows attributable to the ordinary shareholders of the parent and provide comparable information for different entities. Users specifically requested additional financial information about consolidated entities.

BC26   The Board was convinced by those comments and decided to require an entity to provide the following information for each subsidiary that has non-controlling interests that are material to the group:

(a)   *the name of the subsidiary*, because naming subsidiaries that have non-controlling interests that are material to the group helps users search for other information that might be useful for their analysis of the subsidiary.

(b) *the principal place of business (and country of incorporation, if different)*, because this helps users understand the political, economic and currency risks associated with those subsidiaries and the laws with which those subsidiaries must comply.

(c) *the proportion of ownership interests held by non-controlling interests; if different, the proportion of voting rights held by non-controlling interests; profit or loss allocated to non-controlling interests and accumulated non-controlling interests at the end of the reporting period*, because this information helps users understand the profit or loss and cash flows attributable to the shareholders of the parent and the amount attributable to non-controlling interests.

(d) *summarised financial information for the subsidiary*, because this information helps users understand the profit or loss and cash flows attributable to the shareholders of the parent and the amount attributable to non-controlling interests.

BC27 The Board believes that the disclosures required will help users when estimating future profit or loss and cash flows by identifying, for example:

(a) the assets and liabilities that are held by subsidiaries;

(b) risk exposures of particular group entities (eg by identifying which subsidiaries hold debt); and

(c) those subsidiaries that generate significant cash flows.

BC28 In reaching its decision, the Board noted that users have consistently requested additional financial information about consolidated entities for many years. Although users have requested financial information about all subsidiaries that are material to the group, the Board decided to require financial information only for those subsidiaries with material non-controlling interests. A requirement to disclose information about subsidiaries with immaterial or no non-controlling interests might prove to be onerous to prepare without any significant benefit for users, who are expected to benefit most from having financial information about subsidiaries with material non-controlling interests. Summarised financial information about subsidiaries with material non-controlling interests helps users predict how future cash flows will be distributed among those with claims against the entity including the non-controlling interests.

BC29 In addition, the Board does not think that this requirement to provide information about subsidiaries with material non-controlling interests will be particularly onerous to prepare. This is because an entity should have the information available in preparing its consolidated financial statements.

Restrictions on assets and liabilities

BC30 IAS 27 required disclosures about the nature and extent of significant restrictions on the ability of subsidiaries to transfer funds to the parent. Users of financial statements noted that, in addition to legal requirements, the existence of non-controlling interests in a subsidiary might restrict the subsidiary's ability to transfer funds to the parent or any of its other subsidiaries. However, the disclosure requirement in IAS 27 regarding significant restrictions did not refer explicitly to non-controlling interests.

BC31 Accordingly, the Board decided to amend the requirement in IAS 27 to disclose restrictions in order to clarify that the information disclosed should include the nature and extent to which protective rights of non-controlling interests can restrict the entity's ability to access and use the assets and settle the liabilities of a subsidiary.

BC32 In response to concerns raised by respondents to ED 10 about the extent of the disclosure requirement, the Board decided to limit the disclosures to information about the nature and effect of *significant* restrictions on an entity's ability to access and use assets or settle liabilities of the group. In reaching that decision, the Board confirmed that the proposal was never intended to require an entity to disclose, for example, a list of all the protective rights held by non-controlling interests that are embedded in law and regulation.

BC33 The Board also confirmed that the restrictions required to be disclosed by IFRS 12 are those that exist because of the legal boundaries within the group, such as restrictions on transferring cash between group entities. The requirement in IFRS 12 is not intended to replicate those in other IFRSs relating to restrictions, such as those in IAS 16 *Property, Plant and Equipment* or IAS 40 *Investment Property*.

Risks associated with an entity's interests in consolidated structured entities

BC34 An entity can be exposed to risks from both consolidated and unconsolidated structured entities. The Board concluded that it would help users of financial statements in understanding an entity's exposure to risks if the entity disclosed the terms of contractual arrangements that could require it to provide financial support to a consolidated structured entity, including events or circumstances that could expose the entity to a loss.

BC35 The Board concluded for the same reason that an entity should disclose its risk exposure from non-contractual obligations to provide support to both consolidated and unconsolidated structured entities (see paragraphs BC102–BC106).

BC36 The Board noted that US generally accepted accounting principles (GAAP) require similar disclosures, which have been well received by users of financial statements in the US.

Changes in ownership interests in subsidiaries

BC37 In its deliberations in the second phase of the business combinations project, the US Financial Accounting Standards Board (FASB) decided to require entities with one or more partially-owned subsidiaries to disclose in the notes to the consolidated financial statements a schedule showing the effects on the controlling interest's equity of changes in a parent's ownership interest in a subsidiary that do not result in a loss of control.

BC38   In the exposure draft proposing amendments to IAS 27 published in 2005, the Board did not propose to require this disclosure. The Board noted that IFRSs require this information to be provided in the statement of changes in equity or in the notes to the financial statements. This is because IAS 1 requires an entity to present, within the statement of changes in equity, a reconciliation between the carrying amount of each component of equity at the beginning and end of the period, disclosing separately each change.

BC39   Many respondents to the 2005 exposure draft requested more prominent disclosure of the effects of transactions with non-controlling interests on the equity of the owners of the parent. Therefore, the Board decided to converge with the FASB's disclosure requirement and to require that if a parent has equity transactions with non-controlling interests, it should disclose in a separate schedule the effects of those transactions on the equity of the owners of the parent.

BC40   The Board understands that some users will be interested in information pertaining only to the owners of the parent. The Board expected that the presentation and disclosure requirements of IAS 27, as amended in 2008, would meet their information needs. (These presentation and disclosure requirements are now included in IFRS 12.)

Loss of control

BC41   The Board decided that the amount of any gain or loss arising on the loss of control of a subsidiary, including the portion of the gain or loss attributable to recognising any investment retained in the former subsidiary at its fair value at the date when control is lost, and the line item in the statement of comprehensive income in which the gains or losses are recognised should be disclosed. This disclosure requirement, which took effect from 1 July 2009, provides information about the effect of the loss of control of a subsidiary on the financial position at the end of, and performance for, the reporting period.

Interests in joint arrangements and associates

BC42   The Board proposed in ED 9 to align the disclosure requirements for joint ventures and associates by proposing consequential amendments to IAS 28 and by extending the application of some disclosure requirements in IAS 28 to investments in joint ventures.

BC43   During its consideration of responses to ED 9, the Board questioned whether it was possible to achieve further alignment between the disclosure requirements for joint ventures and associates, to the extent that the nature of the particular type of interest does not justify different disclosure requirements. Although joint control is different from significant influence, the Board concluded that the disclosure requirements for joint arrangements and associates could share a common disclosure objective—to disclose information that enables users of financial statements to evaluate the nature, extent and financial effects of an entity's interests in joint arrangements and associates, and the nature of the risks associated with those interests.

Nature, extent and financial effects of interests in joint arrangements and associates

BC44 In response to requests from users of financial statements, the Board proposed in ED 9 that an entity should disclose a list and description of investments in significant joint ventures and associates. Respondents to ED 9 generally welcomed the proposal. The Board decided to carry the proposals forward into IFRS 12 with some modifications as described in paragraphs BC45 and BC46.

BC45 The Board decided to require the information for joint arrangements and associates that are material to the reporting entity rather than for significant joint arrangements and associates. The *Conceptual Framework for Financial Reporting* defines materiality whereas the term 'significant' is undefined and can be interpreted differently. Consequently, the Board decided to replace 'significant' with 'material', which is also used in IFRS 3. The Board noted that materiality should be assessed in relation to an entity's consolidated financial statements or other primary financial statements in which joint ventures and associates are accounted for using the equity method.

BC46 In addition, the Board noted that ED 9 unintentionally changed the application of the requirement in IAS 31 to provide a description of interests in all joint arrangements to interests in joint ventures only. As such, the Board modified the requirement so that it would continue to be required for all joint arrangements that are material to an entity.

Summarised financial information

BC47 IAS 28 and IAS 31 required disclosure of aggregated summarised financial information relating to joint ventures and associates. In response to requests from users of financial statements, ED 9 proposed to expand the requirements so that summarised financial information would be provided for each joint venture that is material to an entity.

BC48 Respondents to ED 9 generally agreed that summarised financial information should be provided. Some had concerns about confidentiality when providing summarised financial information on an individual basis for some joint ventures that were established to implement a single project. Others, including users of financial statements, were concerned that the elimination of proportionate consolidation would result in a loss of information. They therefore requested more detailed disclosures so that the effect of joint ventures on the activities of an entity could be better understood. They stated that there was a need for a detailed breakdown of current assets and current and non-current liabilities (in particular, cash and financial liabilities excluding trade payables and provisions), which would help users understand the net debt position of joint ventures. These users also highlighted the need for a more detailed breakdown of amounts presented in the statement of comprehensive income (such as depreciation and amortisation) that would help when valuing an entity's investment in a joint venture.

BC49 ED 9 proposed that an entity should present summarised financial information for each material joint venture on the basis of its proportionate interest in the joint venture. The Board reconsidered the proposal, noting that it would be confusing to present the entity's share of the assets, liabilities and revenue of a joint venture or associate when the entity has neither rights to, nor obligations for, the assets and liabilities of the joint venture or associate. Rather, the entity has an interest in the net assets of the joint ventures or associates. Consequently, the Board concluded that an entity should present the summarised financial information for each material joint venture on a '100 per cent' basis, and reconcile that to the carrying amount of its investment in the joint venture or associate.

BC50 The Board observed that the requirement to present the amounts on a '100 per cent' basis would be appropriate only when the information is disclosed for individual joint ventures and associates. This is because presenting the financial information on a '100 per cent' basis when aggregating that information for all joint ventures or associates would not result in useful information when the entity holds different percentage ownership interests in its joint ventures or associates. In addition, some users and respondents to ED 9 recommended that the disclosures for associates should be aligned with those for joint ventures because investments in associates can be material and are often strategic to an investor with significant influence. Accordingly, the Board decided that summarised financial information should also be provided for each material associate.

BC51 Nonetheless, the minimum line item disclosures required for each material associate would be less than those required for each material joint venture. The Board noted that an entity is generally more involved with joint ventures than with associates because joint control means that the entity has a right of veto over decisions relating to the relevant activities of the joint venture. Accordingly, the different nature of the relationship between a joint venturer and its joint ventures from that between an investor and its associates warrants a different level of detail in the disclosures of summarised financial information.

BC52 The Board also considered the views of some users who suggested that summarised financial information should be required for joint operations. Assets and liabilities arising from joint operations are an entity's assets and liabilities and consequently are recognised in the entity's financial statements. Those assets and liabilities would be accounted for in accordance with the requirements of applicable IFRSs, and would be subject to the relevant disclosure requirements of those IFRSs. Therefore the Board concluded that entities should not be required to provide summarised financial information separately for joint operations.

Commitments

BC53 ED 9 proposed that an entity should disclose any capital commitments that it has relating to its interests in joint arrangements. IAS 31 had similar requirements.

BC54 When discussing responses to ED 9, the Board examined two aspects of the proposals. The first was whether an entity should separately disclose commitments relating to all types of joint arrangements. The second was the need to maintain the adjective 'capital' when referring to commitments.

BC55 In response to concerns raised by respondents to ED 9, the Board reconsidered the proposals to disclose commitments for all types of joint arrangements.

Respondents said that disclosure of commitments relating to joint operations would be of limited value because such commitments would be included within the disclosures of the entity itself. The Board was convinced by those reasons and decided not to require separate disclosure of commitments relating to an entity's interests in joint operations.

BC56 Regarding the nature of the commitments to be disclosed, the Board noted that 'capital commitment' is not a defined term in IFRSs. Consequently, 'capital' could potentially be interpreted to restrict the disclosures only to those commitments that would result in the capitalisation of assets. Instead, the Board concluded that the objective of the disclosure requirement was to provide information about all unrecognised commitments that could result in future operating, investing or financing cash outflows, or in any other type of outflow of resources from the entity in relation to its interests in joint ventures. Consequently, the Board decided to remove 'capital' from the requirement to disclose commitments.

Contingent liabilities

BC57 ED 9 carried forward the requirement in IAS 31 regarding contingent liabilities and proposed that an entity should separately disclose contingent liabilities relating to its interests in joint arrangements. The Board reconsidered that proposal in response to concerns raised by respondents to ED 9 who stated that separate disclosure of contingent liabilities relating to joint operations would be of limited value for the reasons noted in paragraph BC55.

BC58 The Board was again convinced by those reasons and, accordingly, decided not to require separate disclosure of contingent liabilities relating to an entity's interests in joint operations.

Disclosure requirements for venture capital organisations, mutual funds, unit trusts or similar entities that have an interest in a joint venture or associate

BC59 IAS 28 and IAS 31 established specific disclosure requirements for an entity that had investments in joint ventures or associates when the entity is a venture capital organisation, mutual fund, unit trust or similar entity, including investment-linked insurance funds. The Board discussed whether IFRS 12 should retain the specific disclosure requirements for those types of entities, or whether the disclosure requirements should be the same for all types of entities with interests in joint ventures or associates.

BC60 With the exception of those disclosures that are required only when using the equity method, the Board concluded that the disclosure requirements for interests in joint ventures and associates should be the same for all entities, regardless of whether those entities are venture capital organisations, mutual funds, unit trusts or similar entities. This decision is consistent with the Board's decision to remove the scope exclusion in IAS 28 and IAS 31 for those entities. The Board decided that such entities that hold interests in joint ventures and associates should not be excluded from the relevant standards. Rather, they are simply permitted to use a different measurement basis (ie fair value) for their investments.

Fair value of investments in joint ventures for which there are published price quotations

BC61   IAS 28 required an entity to disclose the fair value of investments in associates for which published price quotations were available. Such quotations might also be available for joint ventures. Consequently, the Board decided to align this disclosure requirement by requiring an entity to disclose the fair value of investments in joint ventures for which there are published price quotations.

Investment entities

BC61A   *Investment Entities* (Amendments to IFRS 10, IFRS 12 and IAS 27) introduced a requirement for investment entities to measure their investments in particular subsidiaries at fair value through profit or loss instead of consolidating them. The Board also decided on specific disclosure requirements for investment entities.

BC61B   In deciding on the appropriate disclosure requirements for investment entities, the Board noted that investment entities would be required to make the disclosures already contained in other Standards. In particular, the disclosure requirements in IFRS 7 *Financial Instruments: Disclosures*, IFRS 13 *Fair Value Measurement* and IAS 24 *Related Party Disclosures* are likely to be relevant for users of investment entity financial statements.

BC61C   Users told the Board that disclosures relating to the valuation methodology used for measuring fair value and the underlying inputs are essential to their analyses. This information is already required by IFRS 7 and by IFRS 13 when reporting investments at fair value through profit or loss or other comprehensive income in accordance with IFRS 9 *Financial Instruments* or IAS 39 *Financial Instruments: Recognition and Measurement*.[2] Accordingly, the Board decided that it was not necessary to propose any additional disclosure requirements relating to the fair value measurements made by investment entities.

BC61D   In the Exposure Draft *Investment Entities* (the *Investment Entities* ED), the Board proposed that an investment entity would be required to meet a disclosure objective that addressed all of an investment entity's investing activities. The *Investment Entities* ED also gave a number of examples of ways in which an investment entity could meet that disclosure objective. Respondents generally supported the disclosure guidance. However, the Board noted that it was outside the scope of the Investment Entities project to require all investment entities to provide disclosures about their investing activities. Consequently, the Board decided to remove the disclosure objective and the examples on how to meet the objective from the final requirements. Because the Investment Entities project focuses on providing an exception to consolidation, the Board decided to limit additional disclosures to information about unconsolidated subsidiaries.

---

2   IFRS 9 *Financial Instruments* replaced IAS 39. IFRS 9 applies to all items that were previously within the scope of IAS 39.

BC61E   The Board also decided to require an investment entity to disclose the fact that it has applied the exception to consolidation, noting that such a disclosure would represent useful information. Moreover, the Board decided to require an investment entity to disclose when it does not display one or more of the typical characteristics of an investment entity, along with a justification of why it still meets the definition of an investment entity.

BC61F   The Board considered whether all of the disclosures in this IFRS should apply to the investments in unconsolidated subsidiaries, associates and joint ventures of investment entities. The Board decided that some (eg summarised financial information and information about non-controlling interests) are not applicable to investment entities and are inconsistent with the assertion that fair value information is the most relevant information for investment entities. Consequently, the Board decided to specify the IFRS 12 requirements applicable to the unconsolidated subsidiaries, associates and joint ventures held by investment entities.

BC61G   Consistently with the principles in this IFRS, the Board decided to require an investment entity to disclose when any explicit or implicit financial support has been provided to entities that it controls. The Board concluded that it would help users of financial statements to understand an investment entity's exposure to risk.

BC61H   The Board decided that an investment entity should disclose the nature and extent of any significant restrictions (eg resulting from borrowing arrangements or regulatory requirements) on the ability of investees to transfer funds to the investment entity in the form of cash dividends, or repayment of loans or advances. The Board considered this requirement to be useful for investors because such restrictions could potentially affect distributions to investors of the investment entity's returns from investments.

BC61I   In December 2014, the Board issued *Investment Entities: Applying the Consolidation Exception* (Amendments to IFRS 10, IFRS 12 and IAS 28). This amended paragraph 6(b) of IFRS 12 to clarify the applicability of IFRS 12 to the financial statements of an investment entity. In June 2014, the Board published the Exposure Draft *Investment Entities: Applying the Consolidation Exception* (Proposed amendments to IFRS 10 and IAS 28) (the 'Consolidation Exception ED'). The comments received in response to the *Consolidation Exception* ED highlighted a lack of clarity about the applicability of IFRS 12 to the financial statements of an investment entity. In particular, the respondents to the *Consolidation Exception* ED pointed out that paragraph 6 of IFRS 12 stated that the Standard did not apply to an entity's separate financial statements without stating the applicability of IFRS 12 to an investment entity. The Board noted that, in contrast, paragraph 16A of IAS 27 *Separate Financial Statements* requires that an investment entity shall present the disclosures relating to investment entities required by IFRS 12. Accordingly, in response to the feedback received, the Board decided to clarify that the scope exclusion in paragraph 6(b) does not apply to the financial statements of a parent that is an investment entity and has measured all of its subsidiaries at fair value through profit or loss in accordance with paragraph 31 of IFRS 10. In such a case, the investment entity shall present the disclosures relating to investment entities required by IFRS 12. The Board also noted that if an investment entity has a subsidiary that it consolidates in accordance with paragraph 32 of IFRS 10, the disclosure requirements in IFRS 12 apply to the financial statements in which the investment entity consolidates that subsidiary.

Interests in unconsolidated structured entities

The need for the disclosure requirements

BC62   IAS 27 did not require disclosures relating to interests in unconsolidated entities. The Board was asked by users of financial statements, regulators and others (such as the G20 leaders and the Financial Stability Board) to improve the disclosure requirements for what are often described as 'off balance sheet' activities. Unconsolidated structured entities, particularly securitisation vehicles and asset-backed financings, were identified as forming part of such activities.

BC63   The Board concluded that when an entity has an interest in an unconsolidated structured entity, users of financial statements would benefit from information about the risks to which the entity is exposed from that interest. Such information is relevant in assessing the amount, timing and uncertainty of the entity's future cash flows.

BC64   As proposed in ED 10, IFRS 12 requires an entity to disclose information that enables users of financial statements to evaluate the nature of, and risks associated with, the entity's interest in unconsolidated structured entities.

BC65   Virtually all respondents to ED 10 agreed that there is a need for improved disclosures about an entity's exposure to risk from 'off balance sheet' activities. However, respondents expressed differing views on the nature and amount of information that should be disclosed. Some, including users of financial statements, supported the approach proposed in ED 10 to require disclosure of risks arising from interests in unconsolidated structured entities.

BC66   Other respondents pointed out that an entity can be exposed to the same risks from having interests in all types of entities. Therefore, they questioned why an entity should be required to provide particular information about its exposure to risk from its interests in unconsolidated structured entities, but not with other unconsolidated entities.

BC67   Some respondents were also concerned that the proposals would duplicate the risk disclosures in IFRS 7 *Financial Instruments: Disclosures*. IFRS 7 requires an entity to disclose qualitative and quantitative information about risks arising from financial instruments that the entity holds. Those respondents expressed the view that ED 10 proposed disclosures about the counterparties of financial instruments to which the disclosure requirements in IFRS 7 already apply.

BC68   In addition, some respondents disagreed with the proposals because they suspected that the Board had included the proposed disclosures as a 'safety net' because it was concerned that some structured entities might fail the consolidation criteria in ED 10, even though, in their view, consolidation would be appropriate.

BC69   When deliberating the responses to ED 10, the Board agreed with those respondents who emphasised that disclosures about unconsolidated structured entities cannot replace robust consolidation requirements. The disclosures proposed were never intended to compensate for weaknesses in the control definition. IFRS 10 documents the Board's determination to develop appropriate and robust consolidation criteria. Rather, the disclosure proposals were intended to complement the consolidation criteria, focusing on an entity's exposure to risk from interests in structured entities that the entity rightly does not consolidate because it does not control them.

BC70   The Board acknowledged that the same types of risks that the disclosure proposals in ED 10 were intended to capture can arise from an entity's interests in other types of entities and that it may be appropriate to develop risk disclosures that apply to an entity's interests in all types of unconsolidated entities. However, the Board noted that when it proposed the disclosure requirements in ED 10, it intended to provide a timely response to particular information needs identified during the global financial crisis that started in 2007. More specifically, users and regulators had expressed concerns about the lack of disclosure relating to investment and securitisation activities that an entity conducts through structured entities. They asked the Board to introduce specific risk disclosures for an entity's interests in unconsolidated structured entities because those particular interests had exposed entities to significant risks in the past. The proposed disclosure requirements in ED 10 were intended to meet those requests. To go beyond structured entities would delay addressing the concerns raised, which would not be beneficial to users.

BC71   The Board also noted that addressing disclosures for interests in unconsolidated structured entities would be an opportunity to align the disclosure requirements in IFRSs and US GAAP in this respect.

BC72   Regarding IFRS 7, the Board agreed with respondents that both requirements will often result in disclosure of the same underlying risks. What is different is how the disclosure requirements describe an entity's risk exposure. IFRS 7 requires qualitative and quantitative disclosures about the credit, liquidity, market and other risks associated with financial instruments. IFRS 12 adopts a different perspective and requires an entity to disclose its exposure to risk from its interest in a structured entity.

BC73   The Board believes that information from both perspectives assists users of financial statements in their analysis of an entity's exposure to risk—the disclosures in IFRS 7 by identifying those financial instruments that create risk, and the disclosures in IFRS 12 by providing, when relevant, information about:

(a)   the extent of an entity's transactions with structured entities;

(b)   concentrations of risk that arise from the nature of the entities with which the entity has transactions; and

(c)   particular transactions that expose the entity to risk.

BC74   Accordingly, the Board concluded that although the disclosures in IFRS 7 and IFRS 12 regarding unconsolidated structured entities might overlap to some extent, they complement each other.

BC75   The Board was also persuaded by information received from users of financial statements in the US, who had been using the disclosures required by US GAAP for variable interest entities in their analysis. Those users confirmed that the new disclosures provided them with information that was not previously available to them, but which they regarded as important for a thorough understanding of an entity's exposure to risk.

BC76   Many of those users referred also to the global financial crisis and emphasised that a better understanding of an entity's interests in unconsolidated structured entities might have helped to identify earlier the extent of risks to which entities were exposed. Accordingly, those users stated that the new disclosures had significantly improved the quality of financial reporting and strongly encouraged the Board to require similar disclosures for IFRS preparers.

BC77   The Board considered whether an entity should be required to disclose the information for interests in unconsolidated structured entities as well as for interests in joint ventures or associates if a joint venture or an associate meets the definition of a structured entity. The Board concluded that an entity should provide information that meets both sets of disclosure requirements if it has interests in joint ventures or associates that are structured entities. In reaching this conclusion, the Board noted that an entity should capture most, and in some cases all, of the disclosures required for interests in unconsolidated structured entities by providing the disclosures for interests in joint ventures and associates. Accordingly, the Board does not think that this conclusion should significantly increase the amount of information that an entity would be required to provide.

The scope of the risk disclosures

Interests in unconsolidated structured entities

BC78   In response to concerns raised by respondents to ED 10 about the scope of the risk disclosures, the Board considered whether it should try to define 'interests in' more narrowly, for example, by stating that an entity would be required to disclose information only about interests that give rise to exposure to loss beyond amounts recognised in its financial statements. However, the Board concluded that any such attempt to narrow the definition of 'interests in' would complicate the guidance and would probably exclude disclosure of information that users would find useful.

BC79   The Board also considered whether to require disclosure of significant interests in structured entities—some respondents to ED 10 had suggested clarifying that an entity would not be required to disclose information about insignificant interests with structured entities. The Board decided against adding 'significant' for a number of reasons. First, the Board noted that because the concept of materiality underpins the disclosure requirements in IFRS 12 as it does in all other IFRSs, an entity would be required to disclose only information that is material as defined and described in the *Conceptual Framework*. The Board also noted that the term 'significant' is not defined in IFRSs. Comments received on other projects suggest that 'significant' is interpreted in different ways. The Board concluded that, without defining the term, adding 'significant' would be of no benefit to those using IFRS 12 to prepare or audit financial statements.

BC80   The Board decided to retain the wider definition of 'interest in' (ie an entity's involvement with another entity, whether contractual or non-contractual, that exposes the entity to variability of returns from the performance of the other entity). The Board was convinced by comments received from US preparers, auditors and users about their experience with the US GAAP requirements to disclose information about involvement with variable interest entities. Involvement is not defined by US GAAP but is interpreted in a way similar to how 'interest in' is defined in IFRS 12. US preparers and users generally agreed with the scope of the disclosure requirements—US users of financial statements thought that the revised disclosure requirements provided them with an appropriate degree of detail; US preparers and accountants thought that the disclosure requirements allow entities to focus on presenting information that is considered relevant for users of financial statements. US preparers and accountants also noted that both the aggregation guidance and the requirement that an entity should determine, in the light of facts and circumstances, how much detail it must give to satisfy the disclosure requirements provide sufficient flexibility for preparers.

BC81   Consequently, the Board decided to include in IFRS 12 the requirement to consider the level of detail necessary to meet the disclosure objectives and to include aggregation principles and guidance to assist preparers when determining what level of detail is appropriate.

The definition of a structured entity

BC82   IFRS 12 introduces the term 'structured entity'. The type of entity the Board envisages being characterised as a structured entity is unlikely to differ significantly from an entity that SIC-12 *Consolidation—Special Purpose Entities* described as a special purpose entity (SPE). SIC-12 described an SPE as an entity created to accomplish a narrow and well–defined objective, listing as examples entities established to effect a lease, research and development activities or a securitisation of financial assets.

BC83   The Board considered whether to define a structured entity in a way similar to a variable interest entity (VIE) in US GAAP. US GAAP defines a VIE, in essence, as an entity whose activities are not directed through voting or similar rights. In addition, the total equity at risk in a VIE is not sufficient to permit the entity to finance its activities without additional subordinated financial support. US GAAP contains extensive application guidance to help determine the sufficiency of the equity, including a 10 per cent equity threshold that is generally used to determine whether an entity's equity is sufficient. The Board decided against this approach because it would introduce complicated guidance solely for disclosure purposes that was not previously in IFRSs.

BC84   The Board therefore decided to define a structured entity as an entity that has been designed so that voting rights are not the dominant factor in deciding who controls the entity. The Board also decided to include guidance similar to that included in SIC-12 to reflect the Board's intention that the term 'structured entity' should capture a set of entities similar to SPEs in SIC-12. The Board also decided to incorporate some of the attributes of a VIE included in US GAAP. In particular, a structured entity is an entity whose equity is often not sufficient to permit the entity to finance its activities without additional subordinated financial support. The Board reasoned that users had requested risk disclosures relating to structured entities because being involved with such entities inherently exposes an entity to more risk than being involved with traditional operating entities. The increased risk exposure arises because, for example, the entity has restricted activities, is created to pass risks and returns arising from specified assets to investors, or there is insufficient equity to fund losses on the assets, if they arise.

BC85 The definition does not state that if an entity has insufficient equity at risk, it would always be deemed to be a structured entity. There are two reasons for this. The first is that such a definition would require extensive application guidance to help determine the sufficiency of the equity, similar to US GAAP, to which the Board was opposed for the reasons noted in paragraph BC83. The second is that the Board feared that some traditional operating entities might be caught by such a definition when it had no intention of doing so. For example, a traditional operating entity whose financing had been restructured following a downturn in activities might be deemed to be a structured entity, which was not what the Board intended.

Nature of interest

BC86 IFRS 12 requires an entity to disclose information that enables users of financial statements to understand the nature of, and changes in, the risks associated with its interests in structured entities (see paragraphs BC92–BC114). As a consequence, an entity would be required to provide disclosures about its exposure to risk when it has sponsored an unconsolidated structured entity and has retained an interest in the structured entity, for example by holding debt or equity instruments of the structured entity.

BC87 However, that decision would not require an entity to provide disclosures if the entity does not retain any interest in the structured entity through explicit or implicit involvement. The Board received views from many constituents who reasoned that sponsoring a structured entity can create risks for an entity, even though the entity might not retain any interest in the structured entity. If the structured entity encounters difficulties, it is possible that the sponsor could be challenged on its advice or actions, or might choose to act to protect its reputation.

BC88 IFRS 12 also requires disclosure regarding the provision of financial and other support to a structured entity when there is no contractual obligation to do so and about any current intentions to provide financial support or other assistance in the future (see paragraphs BC102–BC106). Although helpful, the disclosure provides an incomplete picture of an entity's exposure to risk from its sponsoring activities because:

(a) the disclosure requirement applies only when the entity has provided, or intends to provide, financial support to a structured entity.

(b) an entity's exposure to risk from its sponsoring activities is broader than the risk to provide implicit support to the structured entity. For example, an entity that does not intend to provide any implicit support might be exposed to litigation risk from sponsoring a failed structured entity.

(c) there is currently no other disclosure requirement that would inform users of financial statements about an entity's risk exposure from its sponsoring activities. For example, the disclosure requirements in IFRS 7 do not result in such information because there is usually no financial instrument associated with the sponsorship that would trigger the disclosures. The disclosure requirements relating to transfers of financial assets apply only if an entity has transferred its own financial assets to the structured entities that it sponsors. In addition, an unconsolidated structured entity is unlikely to meet the definition of a related party in IAS 24 *Related Party Disclosures*.

BC89   Users said that it would be useful to have information about the scale of an entity's operations that is derived from transactions with unconsolidated structured entities, ie to have more information about an entity's business model and the risks associated with that business model. This would be particularly useful to help understand the likely effect on the performance of an entity attributable to either a loss of income or a restriction on the entity's ability to carry out its usual business activities if there were a significant decrease in the use of structured entities for investing or financing purposes. They noted that during the global financial crisis that started in 2007 investors became concerned about the extent to which entities had been involved with structured investment vehicles. However, few entities disclosed information about the extent of their involvement in establishing such vehicles. It was, therefore, difficult to assess the potential exposure an entity might have. Those users also confirmed that their request for such information precedes the global financial crisis, and is not simply a reaction to it.

BC90   In response to requests from users and others, the Board decided to require an entity to disclose income derived from, and asset information about, structured entities that the entity has sponsored. The Board noted that the requirements are not intended to help assess the actual risk of failure or recourse to an entity. Rather, they would give a sense of the scale of the operations an entity had managed with these types of transactions and the extent of the entity's reliance on such entities to facilitate its business. For this reason, the Board concluded that the asset information disclosed should refer not only to assets transferred by the sponsor but to all assets transferred to the structured entity during the reporting period. The information provided would be a signpost that would enable users to identify when to ask for further information.

BC91   Because an entity is required to disclose information about its exposure to risk when it retains an interest in an unconsolidated structured entity, the Board decided that the requirement to disclose income and asset information when acting as a sponsor should be required only when an entity has not provided disclosures about the nature of its risks from that interest in the unconsolidated structured entity.

Nature of risks

BC92   ED 10 proposed that an entity should disclose information to help users of financial statements evaluate the nature and extent of the entity's risk from its interests in unconsolidated structured entities. To support that objective, the exposure draft proposed that an entity should disclose the carrying amounts of its assets and liabilities relating to its interests in structured entities, its maximum exposure to loss and the reported amount of assets of structured entities. ED 10 also listed other information (such as information about the assets and funding of structured entities) that might be useful to an assessment of the risks to which an entity is exposed.

BC93   Users generally supported the disclosures proposed. However, other respondents to ED 10, although agreeing that risk disclosures were required, thought that the proposed disclosure requirements were too prescriptive. In their view, an entity should be allowed to disclose its risk exposure on the basis of the information generated by its internal risk reporting system rather than on the basis of the information proposed in ED 10.

BC94   Although agreeing with respondents that an entity should generally be allowed to tailor its disclosures to meet the specific information needs of its users, the Board decided that the disclosure requirements should contain a minimum set of requirements that should be applied by all entities. The Board was convinced by comments from users who pointed out that without any specific disclosure requirements, comparability would be impaired and an entity might not disclose information that users find important.

BC95   Users of financial statements confirmed that information about an entity's exposure to loss from its interests in unconsolidated structured entities and supplementary information about the financial position of both the entity and the structured entity is relevant to their analysis of financial statements.

The assets of structured entities

BC96   The Board was persuaded by the views of respondents who argued that disclosure of assets held by structured entities without information about the funding of the assets is of limited use, and could be difficult to interpret. Therefore, the Board decided to require an entity to disclose information about the nature, purpose, size and activities of a structured entity and how the structured entity is financed. The Board concluded that this requirement should provide users with sufficient information about the assets held by structured entities and the funding of those assets, without requiring specific disclosure of the assets of unconsolidated structured entities in which the entity has an interest in all circumstances. If relevant to an assessment of its exposure to risk, an entity would be required to provide additional information about the assets and funding of structured entities.

Exposure to loss

BC97   The Board acknowledged that, sometimes, information about an entity's expected losses might be more relevant than information about its maximum exposure to loss and that the disclosure of either amount would require the application of judgement. However, if IFRS 12 required the disclosure of expected losses only, the Board was concerned that an entity might often identify a positive expected value of returns from its interests in unconsolidated structured entities and, as a consequence, would not disclose any loss exposure. Accordingly, the Board retained the requirement to disclose an entity's maximum exposure to loss from interests in unconsolidated structured entities.

BC98   The Board decided not to provide a definition of what represents a loss but to leave it to an entity to identify what constitutes a loss in the particular context of that reporting entity. The entity should then disclose how it has determined its maximum loss exposure.

BC99   The Board acknowledged that it may not always be possible to calculate the maximum exposure to loss, such as when a financial instrument exposes an entity to theoretically unlimited losses. The Board decided that when this is the case an entity should disclose the reasons why it is not possible to calculate its maximum exposure to loss.

BC100   Lastly, the Board decided to require an entity to disclose a comparison of the carrying amounts of the assets and liabilities in its statement of financial position and its maximum exposure to loss. This is because the information will provide users with a better understanding of the differences between the maximum loss exposure and the expectation of whether it is likely that an entity will bear all or only some of those losses. In the past, maximum exposure to loss information (when it was provided) was often accompanied by a statement that the information did not in any way represent the losses to be incurred. The Board reasoned that this disclosure requirement should help an entity explain why the maximum exposure to loss is unrepresentative of its actual exposure if that is the case.

BC101   The Board also noted that the disclosures required regarding an entity's exposure to loss mirror those required by US GAAP, which have been well received by users of financial statements in the US.

Providing financial support without having an obligation to do so

BC102   ED 10 proposed requiring the disclosure of support that an entity has provided to unconsolidated structured entities without having a contractual obligation to do so.

BC103   Most respondents to ED 10 agreed with the proposed disclosures, noting that an entity's past actions may be an important factor in considering the substance of its relationship with structured entities. Some, however, questioned the proposal to disclose any current intentions to provide support to a structured entity and questioned how to interpret 'support'.

BC104   The Board agreed with those respondents who thought that it would be unreasonable to expect an entity to include forward-looking disclosures about a decision that might be made in the future. However, the Board concluded that IFRS 12 should retain the requirement to disclose any current intentions to provide non-contractual financial or other support because if an entity has decided that it will provide support (ie it has current intentions to do so), this should be disclosed.

BC105   The Board decided not to define 'support' because a definition of support would either be so broad that it would be an ineffective definition or invite structuring so as to avoid the disclosure. The Board believes that financial support is widely understood as a provision of resources to another entity, either directly or indirectly. In the case of implicit arrangements, the support is provided without having the contractual obligation to do so. Nonetheless, the Board decided to include some examples of financial support in IFRS 12. In order to address respondents' concerns about distinguishing this provision of financial support from any other commercial transaction, the Board clarified that the disclosure is required when an entity has provided non-contractual support to an unconsolidated structured entity in which it previously had or currently has an interest.

BC106   The Board also decided to extend the requirement to support provided to both consolidated and unconsolidated structured entities. US GAAP includes this requirement and users confirmed that they find the disclosure of such information useful.

Risks arising from previous involvement with unconsolidated structured entities

BC107   The actions of some entities during the global financial crisis that started in 2007 demonstrated that an entity can have exposure to risk from involvement with a structured entity, even though it may not control or have any contractual involvement with that entity at the reporting date. For example, failure of a structured entity might damage an entity's reputation, compelling the entity to provide support to the structured entity in order to protect its reputation, even though the entity has no legal or contractual requirement to do so.

BC108   The Board considered how best to address requests to improve the disclosure requirements in this area. The difficulty faced by the Board was to determine which disclosures might help assess an entity's exposure to reputational risk in advance of a financial crisis happening.

BC109   The Board considered asking for five-year historical information about the assets transferred to unconsolidated structured entities that the reporting entity had sponsored. However, the Board concluded that historical information beyond that required by paragraph 27 of the IFRS would not necessarily provide any useful information about the risks to which a sponsor is currently exposed. Information at the reporting date about total assets of unconsolidated structured entities that an entity had sponsored might be useful. However, this information would be difficult, if not impossible, for entities to provide because the entity does not control, or have an interest in, the structured entity at the reporting date. The Board also considered whether to ask for additional information when a particular triggering event occurred (for example, when a structured entity holds troubled assets). However, again, the Board rejected such an approach. Requiring additional disclosures only when the triggering event happens would probably yield information that was too late to be useful.

BC110   The Board decided that the objective in this respect is that an entity should provide information about its exposure to risk associated with its interests in structured entities, regardless of whether that risk arises from having an existing interest in the entity or from being involved with the entity in previous periods. Therefore the Board decided to define 'an interest in an entity' as contractual or non-contractual involvement that exposes the entity to variability of returns. In addition, the Board decided to state explicitly that the disclosures about an entity's exposure to risk should include risk that arises from previous involvement with a structured entity even if an entity no longer has any contractual involvement with the structured entity at the end of the reporting period.

Additional information that might be relevant to an assessment of risk

BC111　When the Board included a list of other information that might be relevant to an assessment of risk in ED 10, it did not intend each item in the list of proposed supplemental disclosures to apply in all circumstances, ie no item was intended to be mandatory. Rather, the Board thought that all the proposed disclosures had the potential to provide important information. Depending on a particular set of facts and circumstances, some of the proposed disclosures would be very relevant whereas others would not. Therefore, an entity might be expected to provide some, but not all, of the disclosures included in the list.

BC112　The difficulty facing the Board was that preparers and users generally have differing views about the level of prescriptive detail to include in disclosure requirements. Preparers generally propose having clear disclosure principles but with a limited number of prescriptive disclosure requirements. They believe that each reporting entity should be able to determine what information meets the disclosure principles on the basis of the particular facts and circumstances surrounding the entity. Users, on the other hand, prefer to have prescriptive disclosure requirements so that the information provided by preparers is comparable.

BC113　The Board's intentions regarding the disclosure of exposure to risk is for an entity to disclose information that is important when assessing that exposure, but not to cloud the information with unnecessary detail that would be considered irrelevant. If an entity has a large exposure to risk because of transactions with a particular unconsolidated structured entity, then the Board would expect extensive disclosure about that exposure. In contrast, if the entity has very limited exposure to risk, little disclosure would be required.

BC114　The Board decided to retain a list of examples of disclosures that might be relevant to emphasise the level of detail that would be required when an entity has a large exposure to risk from its interests in unconsolidated structured entities. However, the Board decided to make clear that the list of additional information that, depending on the circumstances, might be relevant is a list of examples of information that might be relevant and not a list of requirements that should be applied regardless of the circumstances.

Effective date and transition

BC115　The Board decided to align the effective date for the IFRS with the effective date for IFRS 10, IFRS 11 *Joint Arrangements*, IAS 27 *Separate Financial Statements* and IAS 28 *Investments in Associates and Joint Ventures*. When making this decision, the Board noted that the five IFRSs all deal with the assessment of, and related accounting and disclosure requirements about, a reporting entity's special relationships with other entities (ie when the reporting entity has control or joint control of, or significant influence over, another entity). As a result, the

Board concluded that applying IFRS 12 without also applying the other four IFRSs could cause unwarranted confusion.

BC116　The Board usually sets an effective date of between twelve and eighteen months after issuing an IFRS. When deciding the effective date for those IFRSs, the Board considered the following factors:

(a)　the time that many countries require for translation and for introducing the mandatory requirements into law.

(b)　the consolidation project was related to the global financial crisis that started in 2007 and was accelerated by the Board in response to urgent requests from the leaders of the G20, the Financial Stability Board, users of financial statements, regulators and others to improve the accounting and disclosure of an entity's 'off balance sheet' activities.

(c)　the comments received from respondents to the Request for Views *Effective Date and Transition Methods* that was published in October 2010 regarding implementation costs, effective date and transition requirements of the IFRSs to be issued in 2011. Most respondents did not identify the consolidation and joint arrangements IFRSs as having a high impact in terms of the time and resources that their implementation would require. In addition, only a few respondents commented that the effective dates of those IFRSs should be aligned with those of the other IFRSs to be issued in 2011.

BC117　With those factors in mind, the Board decided to require entities to apply the five IFRSs for annual periods beginning on or after 1 January 2013.

BC118　Most respondents to the Request for Views supported early application of the IFRSs to be issued in 2011. Respondents stressed that early application was especially important for first-time adopters in 2011 and 2012. The Board was persuaded by these arguments and decided to permit early application of the five IFRSs (ie IFRS 10, IFRS 11, IFRS 12, IAS 27 (as amended in 2011) and IAS 28 (as amended in 2011)) but only if an entity applies all those IFRSs.

BC119　Notwithstanding that decision, the Board noted that an entity should not be prevented from providing any information required by IFRS 12 early if by doing so users gained a better understanding of the entity's relationships with other entities. In reaching that decision, the Board observed that if an entity chooses to apply some, but not all, of the requirements of IFRS 12 early, the entity would be required to continue to apply the disclosure requirements of IAS 27, IAS 28 and IAS 31 until such time that it applies all the requirements of IFRS 12.

BC119A　In June 2012, the Board amended the transition guidance in Appendix C to IFRS 10 *Consolidated Financial Statements*. When making those amendments, the Board decided to limit the requirement to present adjusted comparatives to the annual period immediately preceding the date of initial application of IFRS 10. This is consistent with the minimum comparative disclosure requirements contained in IAS 1 *Presentation of Financial Statements* as amended by *Annual Improvements to IFRSs 2009–2011 Cycle* (issued May 2012). Those amendments confirmed that when an entity applies a changed accounting policy retrospectively, it shall present, as a minimum, three statements of financial position (ie 1 January 2012, 31 December 2012 and 31 December 2013 for a calendar-year entity, assuming no early application of this IFRS) and two of each of the other statements (IAS 1 paragraphs 40A–40B). The Board also decided to make similar amendments to the transition guidance in Appendix C to IFRS 11 *Joint Arrangements* and Appendix C to this IFRS to be consistent with this decision.

BC119B   IFRS 12 introduces new disclosures relating to unconsolidated structured entities. Feedback from interested parties informed the Board that the changes to their accounting and reporting systems that are needed to capture this information were more onerous than originally envisaged, particularly in respect of comparative periods prior to the effective date of IFRS 12. Consequently, the Board decided to provide additional transition relief by eliminating the requirement to present comparatives for this information for periods beginning before the first year that IFRS 12 is applied.

BC119C   The Board decided that no specific transition guidance was needed and, therefore, an entity should apply *Investment Entities: Applying the Consolidation Exception* (Amendments to IFRS 10, IFRS 12 and IAS 28) retrospectively in accordance with IAS 8 *Accounting Policies, Changes in Accounting Estimates and Errors*.

Summary of main changes from ED 9 and ED 10

BC120   The main changes from the exposure drafts ED 9 and ED 10 are:

(a)   The disclosure requirements for subsidiaries, joint arrangements, associates and unconsolidated structured entities are included in IFRS 12, separately from the accounting requirements relating to an entity's interests in those entities. ED 9 and ED 10 had proposed that the disclosure requirements would be located with the accounting requirements in IAS 28, IFRS 10 and IFRS 11. (paragraphs BC7 and BC8)

(b)   IFRS 12 includes application guidance dealing with the aggregation of information disclosed in accordance with the requirements of the IFRS.

(c)   IFRS 12 requires the disclosure of significant judgements and assumptions made in determining whether an entity has a special relationship (ie control, joint control or significant influence) with another entity. ED 10 had proposed disclosure of the basis of an entity's assessment of whether it controls another entity in particular scenarios. (paragraphs BC14–BC19)

(d)   IFRS 12 requires the disclosure of summarised financial information for subsidiaries that have non-controlling interests that are material to the entity. ED 9 had proposed disclosing a list of significant subsidiaries. (paragraphs BC21–BC29)

(e)   IFRS 12 requires disclosure of the nature of, and risks associated with, an entity's interests in consolidated structured entities. (paragraphs BC34–BC36)

(f)   IFRS 12 requires the disclosure of summarised financial information for each material joint venture and associate, and requires more detailed information for joint ventures than for associates. ED 9 had proposed less detailed summarised financial information for each material joint venture and summarised financial information in aggregate for associates. (paragraphs BC47–BC52)

(g)   IFRS 12 requires entities that are venture capital organisations, mutual funds, unit trusts and similar entities to provide all the disclosures relating to interests in joint ventures and associates. ED 9 proposed that such entities would be required to provide only some of the disclosures relating to interests in joint ventures and associates. (paragraphs BC59 and BC60)

(h)   IFRS 12 does not require the disclosure of the reported amount of assets held by structured entities in which an entity has an interest. ED 10 had proposed disclosing such information. (paragraph BC96)

Convergence with US GAAP

BC121   Most of the disclosure requirements for consolidated and unconsolidated structured entities are similar to those for variable interest entities in Subtopic 810-10 in the *FASB Accounting Standards Codification*®. The Board developed many of those disclosure requirements in conjunction with the FASB, following the Financial Stability Board's recommendation to work with other accounting standard-setters to achieve international convergence in this area. However, IFRS 12 goes further than the disclosure requirements in Subtopic 810-10 because it requires an entity to disclose information about:

(a)   the interest that non-controlling interests have in the activities of a consolidated structured entity; and

(b)   the risks from sponsoring an unconsolidated structured entity for which the entity does not provide other risk disclosures.

BC122   IFRS 12 also includes more detailed disclosure requirements than US GAAP for subsidiaries, joint arrangements and associates (eg summarised financial information for subsidiaries with material non-controlling interests, and material joint ventures and associates).

Cost-benefit considerations

BC123   The objective of financial statements is to provide information about the financial position, performance and changes in financial position of an entity that is useful to a wide range of users in making economic decisions. To attain this objective, the Board seeks to ensure that an IFRS will meet a significant need and that the overall benefits of the resulting information justify the costs of providing it. Although the costs to implement a new IFRS might not be borne evenly, users of financial statements benefit from improvements in financial reporting, thereby facilitating the functioning of markets for capital and credit and the efficient allocation of resources in the economy.

BC124   The evaluation of costs and benefits is necessarily subjective. In making its judgement, the Board considers the following:

(a)   the costs incurred by preparers of financial statements;

(b)   the costs incurred by users of financial statements when information is not available;

(c)   the comparative advantage that preparers have in developing information, compared with the costs that users would incur to develop surrogate information;

(d)   the benefit of better economic decision-making as a result of improved financial reporting; and

(e)   the costs of transition for users, preparers and others.

BC125   The Board observed that IFRS 12 will improve the ability of users to understand consolidated financial statements by requiring disclosure of information about the interests that non-controlling interests have in the group's activities. IFRS 12 will also improve users' understanding of the special relationships that a reporting entity has with entities that are not consolidated (ie the relationships with joint arrangements, associates and unconsolidated structured entities).

BC126   In particular, an entity was not previously required to provide information specifically about its exposure to risk from interests in structured entities. The requirements in IFRS 12 relating to interests in unconsolidated structured entities respond to the conclusions of the G20 leaders and the recommendations of international bodies such as the Financial Stability Board following the global financial crisis that started in 2007. The G20 leaders and the Financial Stability Board recommended that the IASB should accelerate its work on enhancing disclosure requirements for 'off balance sheet' vehicles (such as structured investment vehicles), in particular to ensure that entities are required to disclose their exposure to risk and potential losses associated with their involvement with such vehicles.

BC127   During the development of IFRS 12, the Board consulted users of financial statements, who confirmed the benefit of having more information about:

(a)   an entity's exposure to risk from interests in structured entities;

(b)   non-controlling interests within the group; and

(c)   joint arrangements and associates.

BC128   There are costs involved in the adoption and ongoing application of IFRS 12. Those costs will depend on the nature and complexity of the relationships that a reporting entity has with other entities. However, given the benefits for users noted in paragraphs BC125–BC127, the Board believes that the benefits of IFRS 12 outweigh the costs.

IASB documents published to accompany

IFRS 13

Fair Value Measurement

The text of the unaccompanied standard, IFRS 13, is contained in Part A of this edition. Its effective date when issued was 1 January 2013. The text of the Accompanying Guidance on IFRS 13 is contained in Part B of this edition.

BASIS FOR CONCLUSIONS

APPENDIX TO THE BASIS FOR CONCLUSIONS
Amendments to the Basis for Conclusions on other IFRSs

CONTENTS

SUMMARY OF MAIN CHANGES FROM THE EXPOSURE DRAFT BC244
APPENDIX
Amendments to the Basis for Conclusions on other IFRSs

Basis for Conclusions on
IFRS 13 *Fair Value Measurement*

This Basis for Conclusions accompanies, but is not part of, IFRS 13.

Introduction

BC1   This Basis for Conclusions summarises the considerations of the International Accounting Standards Board (IASB) in reaching the conclusions in IFRS 13 *Fair Value Measurement*. It includes the reasons for accepting particular views and rejecting others. Individual IASB members gave greater weight to some factors than to others.

BC2   IFRS 13 is the result of the IASB's discussions about measuring fair value and disclosing information about fair value measurements in accordance with International Financial Reporting Standards (IFRSs), including those held with the US national standard-setter, the Financial Accounting Standards Board (FASB), in their joint project on fair value measurement.

BC3   As a result of those discussions, the FASB amended particular aspects of Topic 820 *Fair Value Measurement* in the *FASB Accounting Standards Codification®* (which codified FASB Statement of Financial Accounting Standards No. 157 *Fair Value Measurements* (SFAS 157)). The FASB separately developed a Basis for Conclusions summarising its considerations in reaching the conclusions resulting in those amendments.

Overview

BC4   Some IFRSs require or permit entities to measure or disclose the fair value of assets, liabilities or their own equity instruments. Because those IFRSs were developed over many years, the requirements for measuring fair value and for disclosing information about fair value measurements were dispersed and in many cases did not articulate a clear measurement or disclosure objective.

BC5   As a result, some of those IFRSs contained limited guidance about how to measure fair value, whereas others contained extensive guidance and that guidance was not always consistent across those IFRSs that refer to fair value. Inconsistencies in the requirements for measuring fair value and for disclosing information about fair value measurements have contributed to diversity in practice and have reduced the comparability of information reported in financial statements.

BC6   To remedy that situation, the IASB added a project to its agenda with the following objectives:

(a)   to establish a single set of requirements for all fair value measurements required or permitted by IFRSs to reduce complexity and improve consistency in their application, thereby enhancing the comparability of information reported in financial statements;

(b)   to clarify the definition of fair value and related guidance to communicate the measurement objective more clearly;

(c)   to enhance disclosures about fair value measurements that will help users of financial statements assess the valuation techniques and inputs used to develop fair value measurements; and

(d)   to increase the convergence of IFRSs and US generally accepted accounting principles (GAAP).

BC7   IFRS 13 is the result of that project. IFRS 13 is a single source of fair value measurement guidance that clarifies the definition of fair value, provides a clear framework for measuring fair value and enhances the disclosures about fair value measurements. It is also the result of the efforts of the IASB and the FASB to ensure that fair value has the same meaning in IFRSs and in US GAAP and that their respective fair value measurement and disclosure requirements are the same (except for minor differences in wording and style; see paragraphs BC237 and BC238 for the differences between IFRS 13 and Topic 820).

BC8   IFRS 13 applies to IFRSs that require or permit fair value measurements or disclosures. It does not introduce new fair value measurements, nor does it eliminate practicability exceptions to fair value measurements (eg the exception in IAS 41 *Agriculture* when an entity is unable to measure reliably the fair value of a biological asset on initial recognition). In other words, IFRS 13 specifies *how* an entity should measure fair value and disclose information about fair value measurements. It does not specify *when* an entity should measure an asset, a liability or its own equity instrument at fair value.

Background

BC9   The IASB and the FASB began developing their fair value measurement standards separately.

BC10   The FASB began working on its fair value measurement project in June 2003. In September 2005, during the FASB's redeliberations on the project, the IASB added to its agenda a project to clarify the meaning of fair value and to provide guidance for its application in IFRSs.

BC11   In September 2006 the FASB issued SFAS 157 (now in Topic 820). Topic 820 defines fair value, establishes a framework for measuring fair value and requires disclosures about fair value measurements.

BC12   In November 2006 as a first step in developing a fair value measurement standard, the IASB published a discussion paper *Fair Value Measurements*. In that discussion paper, the IASB used SFAS 157 as a basis for its preliminary views because of the consistency of SFAS 157 with the existing fair value measurement guidance in IFRSs and the need for increased convergence of IFRSs and US GAAP. The IASB received 136 comment letters in response to that discussion paper. In November 2007 the IASB began its deliberations for the development of the exposure draft *Fair Value Measurement*.

BC13   In May 2009 the IASB published that exposure draft, which proposed a definition of fair value, a framework for measuring fair value and disclosures about fair value measurements. Because the proposals in the exposure draft were developed using the requirements of SFAS 157, there were many similarities between them. However, some of those proposals were different from the requirements of SFAS 157 and many of them used wording that was similar, but not identical, to the wording in SFAS 157. The IASB received 160 comment letters in response to the proposals in the exposure draft. One of the most prevalent comments received was a request for the IASB and the FASB to work together to develop common fair value measurement and disclosure requirements in IFRSs and US GAAP.

BC14 In response to that request, the IASB and the FASB agreed at their joint meeting in October 2009 to work together to develop common requirements. The boards concluded that having common requirements for fair value measurement and disclosure would improve the comparability of financial statements prepared in accordance with IFRSs and US GAAP. In addition, they concluded that having common requirements would reduce diversity in the application of fair value measurement requirements and would simplify financial reporting. To achieve those goals, the boards needed to ensure that fair value had the same meaning in IFRSs and US GAAP and that IFRSs and US GAAP had the same fair value measurement and disclosure requirements (except for minor differences in wording and style). Consequently, the FASB agreed to consider the comments received on the IASB's exposure draft and to propose amendments to US GAAP if necessary.

BC15 The boards began their joint discussions in January 2010. They discussed nearly all the issues together so that each board would benefit from hearing the rationale for the other board's decisions on each issue. They initially focused on the following:

(a) differences between the requirements in Topic 820 and the proposals in the IASB's exposure draft;

(b) comments received on the IASB's exposure draft (including comments received from participants at the IASB's round-table meetings held in November and December 2009); and

(c) feedback received on the implementation of Topic 820 (eg issues discussed by the FASB's Valuation Resource Group).

BC16 In March 2010 the boards completed their initial discussions. As a result of those discussions, in June 2010 the FASB issued a proposed Accounting Standards Update (ASU) *Fair Value Measurements and Disclosures (Topic 820): Amendments for Common Fair Value Measurement and Disclosure Requirements in U.S GAAP and IFRSs* and the IASB re-exposed a proposed disclosure of the unobservable inputs used in a fair value measurement (*Measurement Uncertainty Analysis Disclosure for Fair Value Measurements*). The IASB concluded that it was necessary to re-expose that proposal because in their discussions the boards agreed to require a measurement uncertainty analysis disclosure that included the effect of any interrelationships between unobservable inputs (a requirement that was not proposed in the May 2009 exposure draft and was not already required by IFRSs). The IASB received 92 comment letters on the re-exposure document.

BC17 In September 2010, after the end of the comment periods on the IASB's re-exposure document and the FASB's proposed ASU, the boards jointly considered the comments received on those exposure drafts. The boards completed their discussions in March 2011.

BC18   Throughout the process, the IASB considered information from the IFRS Advisory Council, the Analysts' Representative Group and the IASB's Fair Value Expert Advisory Panel (see paragraph BC177) and from other interested parties.

Scope

BC19   The boards separately discussed the scope of their respective fair value measurement standards because of the differences between IFRSs and US GAAP in the measurement bases specified in other standards for both initial recognition and subsequent measurement.

BC20   IFRS 13 applies when another IFRS requires or permits fair value measurements or disclosures about fair value measurements (and measurements, such as fair value less costs to sell, based on fair value or disclosures about those measurements), except in the following circumstances:

(a)   The measurement and disclosure requirements of IFRS 13 do not apply to the following:

(i)   share-based payment transactions within the scope of IFRS 2 *Share-based Payment*;

(ii)   leasing transactions within the scope of IAS 17 *Leases*; and

(iii)   measurements that have some similarities to fair value but are not fair value, such as net realisable value in accordance with IAS 2 *Inventories* and value in use in accordance with IAS 36 *Impairment of Assets*

(b)   The disclosures required by IFRS 13 are not required for the following:

(i)   plan assets measured at fair value in accordance with IAS 19 *Employee Benefits*;

(ii)   retirement benefit plan investments measured at fair value in accordance with IAS 26 *Accounting and Reporting by Retirement Benefit Plans*; and

(iii)   assets for which recoverable amount is fair value less costs of disposal in accordance with IAS 36

BC21   The exposure draft proposed introducing a new measurement basis for IFRS 2, a market-based value. The definition of *market-based value* would have been similar to the exit price definition of fair value except that it would specify that the measurement does not take into account market participant assumptions for vesting conditions and reload features. Respondents pointed out that some items measured at fair value in IFRS 2 were consistent with the proposed definition of fair value, not with the proposed definition of market-based value, and were concerned that there could be unintended consequences of moving forward with a market-based value measurement basis in IFRS 2. The IASB agreed with those comments and concluded that amending IFRS 2 to distinguish between measures that are fair value and those based on fair value would require new measurement guidance for measures based on fair value. The IASB concluded that such guidance might result in unintended changes in practice with regard to measuring share-based payment transactions and decided to exclude IFRS 2 from the scope of IFRS 13.

BC22 The IASB concluded that applying the requirements in IFRS 13 might significantly change the classification of leases and the timing of recognising gains or losses for sale and leaseback transactions. Because there is a project under way to replace IAS 17, the IASB concluded that requiring entities to make potentially significant changes to their accounting systems for the IFRS on fair value measurement and then for the IFRS on lease accounting could be burdensome.

BC23 The exposure draft proposed that the disclosures about fair value measurements would be required for the fair value of plan assets in IAS 19 and the fair value of retirement benefit plan investments in IAS 26. In its project to amend IAS 19 the IASB decided to require an entity to disaggregate the fair value of the plan assets into classes that distinguish the risk and liquidity characteristics of those assets, subdividing each class of debt and equity instruments into those that have a quoted market price in an active market and those that do not. As a result, the IASB decided that an entity does not need to provide the disclosures required by IFRS 13 for the fair value of plan assets or retirement benefit plan investments.

BC24 The exposure draft was not explicit about whether the measurement and disclosure requirements in the exposure draft applied to measurements based on fair value, such as fair value less costs to sell in IFRS 5 *Non-current Assets Held for Sale and Discontinued Operations* or IAS 41. In the boards' discussions, they concluded that the measurement and disclosure requirements should apply to all measurements for which fair value is the underlying measurement basis (except that the disclosure requirements would not apply to assets with a recoverable amount that is fair value less costs of disposal in IAS 36; see paragraphs BC218–BC221). Consequently, the boards decided to clarify that the measurement and disclosure requirements apply to both fair value measurements and measurements based on fair value. The boards also decided to clarify that the measurement and disclosure requirements do not apply to measurements that have similarities to fair value but are not fair value, such as net realisable value in accordance with IAS 2 or value in use in accordance with IAS 36.

BC25 The boards decided to clarify that the measurement requirements apply when measuring the fair value of an asset or a liability that is not measured at fair value in the statement of financial position but for which the fair value is disclosed (eg for financial instruments subsequently measured at amortised cost in accordance with IFRS 9 *Financial Instruments* or IAS 39 *Financial Instruments: Recognition and Measurement*[1] and for investment property subsequently measured using the cost model in accordance with IAS 40 *Investment Property*).

BC26 The IASB decided that two of the proposals about scope in the exposure draft were not necessary:

---

1   IFRS 9 *Financial Instruments* replaced IAS 39. IFRS 9 applies to all items that were previously within the scope of IAS 39.

(a)   The exposure draft proposed excluding financial liabilities with a demand feature in IAS 39[2] from the scope of an IFRS on fair value measurement. In the light of the comments received, the IASB confirmed its decision when developing IAS 39 that the fair value of financial liabilities with a demand feature cannot be less than the present value of the demand amount (see paragraphs BC101–BC103) and decided to retain the term *fair value* for such financial liabilities.

(b)   The exposure draft proposed replacing the term *fair value* with another term that reflects the measurement objective for reacquired rights in a business combination in IFRS 3 *Business Combinations*. In the redeliberations, the IASB concluded that because IFRS 3 already describes the measurement of reacquired rights as an exception to fair value, it was not necessary to change that wording.

Measurement

Definition of fair value

Clarifying the measurement objective

BC27   IFRS 13 defines fair value as:

> The price that would be received to sell an asset or paid to transfer a liability in an orderly transaction between market participants at the measurement date.

BC28   IFRS 13 also provides a framework that is based on an objective to estimate the price at which an orderly transaction to sell the asset or to transfer the liability would take place between market participants at the measurement date under current market conditions (ie an exit price from the perspective of a market participant that holds the asset or owes the liability at the measurement date).

BC29   That definition of fair value retains the exchange notion contained in the previous definition of fair value in IFRSs:

> The amount for which an asset could be exchanged, or a liability settled, between knowledgeable, willing parties in an arm's length transaction.

BC30   Like the previous definition of fair value, the revised definition assumes a hypothetical and orderly exchange transaction (ie it is not an actual sale or a forced transaction or distress sale). However, the previous definition of fair value:

(a)   did not specify whether an entity is buying or selling the asset;

(b)   was unclear about what is meant by settling a liability because it did not refer to the creditor, but to knowledgeable, willing parties; and

(c)   did not state explicitly whether the exchange or settlement takes place at the measurement date or at some other date.

BC31   The IASB concluded that the revised definition of fair value remedies those deficiencies. It also conveys more clearly that fair value is a market-based

---

2   IFRS 9 *Financial Instruments* replaced IAS 39. IFRS 9 applies to all items that were previously within the scope of IAS 39.

measurement, and not an entity-specific measurement, and that fair value reflects current market conditions (which reflect market participants', not the entity's, current expectations about future market conditions).

BC32   In determining how to define fair value in IFRSs, the IASB considered work done in its project to revise IFRS 3. In that project, the IASB considered whether differences between the definitions of fair value in US GAAP (an explicit exit price) and IFRSs (an exchange amount, which might be interpreted in some situations as an entry price) would result in different measurements of assets acquired and liabilities assumed in a business combination. That was a particularly important issue because in many business combinations the assets and liabilities are non-financial.

BC33   The IASB asked valuation experts to take part in a case study involving the valuation of the identifiable assets acquired and liabilities assumed in a sample business combination. The IASB learned that differences between an exit price and an exchange amount (which might be interpreted as an entry price in a business combination) were unlikely to arise, mainly because transaction costs are not a component of fair value in either definition. The IASB observed that although the definitions used different words, they articulated essentially the same concepts.

BC34   However, the valuation experts identified potential differences in particular areas. The valuation experts told the IASB that an exit price for an asset acquired or a liability assumed in a business combination might differ from an exchange amount if:

   (a)   an entity's intended use for an acquired asset is different from its highest and best use by market participants (ie when the acquired asset provides defensive value); or

   (b)   a liability is measured on the basis of settling it with the creditor rather than transferring it to a third party and the entity determines that there is a difference between those measurements. Paragraphs BC80–BC82 discuss perceived differences between the settlement and transfer notions.

BC35   With respect to highest and best use, the IASB understood that the ways of measuring assets on the basis of their defensive value (ie the value associated with improving the prospects of the entity's other assets by preventing the acquired asset from being used by competitors) in accordance with US GAAP at the time IFRS 3 was issued were still developing. As a consequence, the IASB thought it was too early to assess the significance of any differences that might result. With respect to liabilities, it was also not clear at that time whether entities would use different valuation techniques to measure the fair value of liabilities assumed in a business combination. In the development of IFRS 13, the IASB observed the discussions of the FASB's Valuation Resource Group to learn from the implementation of SFAS 157 and Topic 820 in US GAAP.

Fair value as a current exit price

BC36   The definition of fair value in IFRS 13 is a current exit price. That definition in and of itself is not a controversial issue. Many respondents thought the proposal to define fair value as a current, market-based exit price was appropriate because that definition retains the notion of an exchange between unrelated, knowledgeable and willing parties in the previous definition of fair value in IFRSs, but provides a clearer measurement objective. Other respondents thought an entry price would be more appropriate in some situations (eg at initial recognition, such as in a business combination).

BC37   However, the issue of *when* fair value should be used as a measurement basis in IFRSs is controversial. There is disagreement about the following:

(a)   which assets and liabilities should be measured at fair value (eg whether fair value should be restricted to assets and liabilities with quoted prices in active markets that the entity intends to sell or transfer in the near term);

(b)   when those assets and liabilities should be measured at fair value (eg whether the measurement basis should change when markets have become less active); and

(c)   where any changes in fair value should be recognised.

BC38   Although IFRS 13 does not address when fair value should be used as a measurement basis for a particular asset or liability or revisit when fair value has been used in IFRSs, the IASB did consider whether each use of the term *fair value* in IFRSs was consistent with an exit price definition (see paragraphs BC41–BC45). Furthermore, IFRS 13 will inform the IASB in the future as it considers whether to require fair value as a measurement basis for a particular type of asset or liability.

BC39   The IASB concluded that an exit price of an asset or a liability embodies expectations about the future cash inflows and outflows associated with the asset or liability from the perspective of a market participant that holds the asset or owes the liability at the measurement date. An entity generates cash inflows from an asset by using the asset or by selling it. Even if an entity intends to generate cash inflows from an asset by using it rather than by selling it, an exit price embodies expectations of cash flows arising from the use of the asset by selling it to a market participant that would use it in the same way. That is because a market participant buyer will pay only for the benefits it expects to generate from the use (or sale) of the asset. Thus, the IASB concluded that an exit price is always a relevant definition of fair value for assets, regardless of whether an entity intends to use an asset or sell it.

BC40   Similarly, a liability gives rise to outflows of cash (or other economic resources) as an entity fulfils the obligation over time or when it transfers the obligation to another party. Even if an entity intends to fulfil the obligation over time, an exit price embodies expectations of related cash outflows because a market participant transferee would ultimately be required to fulfil the obligation. Thus, the IASB concluded that an exit price is always a relevant definition of fair value for liabilities, regardless of whether an entity intends to fulfil the liability or transfer it to another party that will fulfil it.

BC41   In developing the revised definition of fair value, the IASB completed a standard-by-standard review of fair value measurements required or permitted in IFRSs to assess whether the IASB or its predecessor intended each use of fair value to be a current exit price measurement basis. If it became evident that a current exit price was not the intention in a particular situation, the IASB would use another measurement basis to describe the objective. The other likely measurement basis candidate was a current entry price. For the standard-by-standard review, the IASB defined current entry price as follows:

> The price that would be paid to buy an asset or received to incur a liability in an orderly transaction between market participants (including the amount imposed on an entity for incurring a liability) at the measurement date.

BC42　That definition of current entry price, like fair value, assumes a hypothetical orderly transaction between market participants at the measurement date. It is not necessarily the same as the price an entity paid to acquire an asset or received to incur a liability, eg if that transaction was not at arm's length. In discussions with interested parties, the IASB found that most people who assert that an asset or a liability should be measured using an entry price measurement basis, rather than an exit price measurement basis, would actually prefer to use the entity's actual transaction price (or cost), not the market-based current entry price defined above. The IASB observed that in some cases there is not an actual transaction price (eg when a group of assets is acquired but the unit of account is an individual asset, or when a biological asset regenerates) and, as a result, an assumed, or hypothetical, price must be used.

BC43　During the standard-by-standard review, the IASB asked various parties to provide information on whether, in practice, they interpreted fair value in a particular context in IFRSs as a current entry price or a current exit price. The IASB used that information in determining whether to define fair value as a current exit price, or to remove the term *fair value* and use the terms current *exit price* and *current entry price* depending on the measurement objective in each IFRS that used the term *fair value*.

BC44　As a result of the standard-by-standard review, the IASB concluded that a current entry price and a current exit price will be equal when they relate to the same asset or liability on the same date in the same form in the same market. Therefore, the IASB considered it unnecessary to make a distinction between a current entry price and a current exit price in IFRSs with a market-based measurement objective (ie fair value), and the IASB decided to retain the term fair value and define it as a current exit price.

BC45　The IASB concluded that some fair value measurement requirements in IFRSs were inconsistent with a current exit price or the requirements for measuring fair value. For those fair value measurements, IFRS 13 excludes the measurement from its scope (see paragraphs BC19–BC26).

The asset or liability

BC46　IFRS 13 states that a fair value measurement takes into account the characteristics of the asset or liability, eg the condition and location of the asset and restrictions, if any, on its sale or use. Restrictions on the sale or use of an asset affect its fair value if market participants would take the restrictions into account when pricing the asset at the measurement date. That is consistent with the fair value measurement guidance already in IFRSs. For example:

(a)   IAS 40 stated that an entity should identify any differences between the property being measured at fair value and similar properties for which observable market prices are available and make the appropriate adjustments; and

(b)   IAS 41 referred to measuring the fair value of a biological asset or agricultural produce in its present location and condition.

BC47   The IASB concluded that IFRS 13 should describe how to measure fair value, not what is being measured at fair value. Other IFRSs specify whether a fair value measurement considers an individual asset or liability or a group of assets or liabilities (ie the unit of account). For example:

(a)   IAS 36 states that an entity should measure the fair value less costs of disposal for a cash-generating unit when assessing its recoverable amount.

(b)   In IAS 39[3] and IFRS 9 the unit of account is generally an individual financial instrument.

The transaction

BC48   The exposure draft proposed that the transaction to sell an asset or transfer a liability takes place in the most advantageous market to which the entity has access. That was different from the approach in Topic 820, which refers to the principal market for the asset or liability or, in the absence of a principal market, the most advantageous market for the asset or liability. The IASB concluded that in most cases the principal market for an asset or a liability will be the most advantageous market and that an entity need not continuously monitor different markets in order to determine which market is most advantageous at the measurement date. That proposal contained a presumption that the market in which the entity normally enters into transactions for the asset or liability is the most advantageous market and that an entity may assume that the principal market for the asset or liability is the most advantageous market.

BC49   Many respondents agreed with the most advantageous market notion because most entities enter into transactions that maximise the price received to sell an asset or minimise the price paid to transfer a liability. Furthermore, they thought that a most advantageous market notion works best for all assets and liabilities, regardless of the level of activity in a market or whether the market for an asset or a liability is observable.

BC50   However, some respondents were concerned about the difficulty with identifying and selecting the most advantageous market when an asset or a liability is exchanged in multiple markets throughout the world. Other respondents found the guidance confusing because it was not clear whether the most advantageous market must be used or how the market in which the entity normally enters into transactions relates to the principal market or to the most advantageous market. In general, respondents preferred the approach in Topic 820.

---

3   IFRS 9 *Financial Instruments* replaced IAS 39. IFRS 9 applies to all items that were previously within the scope of IAS 39.

BC51　Although the boards think that in most cases the principal market and the most advantageous market would be the same, they concluded that the focus should be on the principal market for the asset or liability and decided to clarify the definition of the principal market.

BC52　Some respondents to the exposure draft stated that the language in US GAAP was unclear about whether the principal market should be determined on the basis of the volume or level of activity *for the asset or liability* or on the volume or level of activity *of the reporting entity's transactions in a particular market*. Consequently, the boards decided to clarify that the principal market is the market for the asset or liability that has the greatest volume or level of activity *for the asset or liability*. Because the principal market is the most liquid market for the asset or liability, that market will provide the most representative input for a fair value measurement. As a result, the boards also decided to specify that a transaction to sell an asset or to transfer a liability takes place in the principal (or most advantageous) market, provided that the entity can access that market on the measurement date.

BC53　In addition, the boards concluded that an entity normally enters into transactions in the principal market for the asset or liability (ie the most liquid market, assuming that the entity can access that market). As a result, the boards decided to specify that an entity can use the price in the market in which it normally enters into transactions, unless there is evidence that the principal market and that market are not the same. Consequently, an entity does not need to perform an exhaustive search for markets that might have more activity for the asset or liability than the market in which that entity normally enters into transactions. Thus, IFRS 13 addresses practical concerns about the costs of searching for the market with the greatest volume or level of activity for the asset or liability.

BC54　The boards also concluded that the determination of the most advantageous market (which is used in the absence of a principal market) for an asset or a liability takes into account both transaction costs and transport costs. However, regardless of whether an entity measures fair value on the basis of the price in the principal market or in the most advantageous market, the fair value measurement takes into account transport costs, but not transaction costs (see paragraphs BC60–BC62 for a discussion on transport and transaction costs). That is consistent with the proposal in the exposure draft.

Market participants

BC55　IFRS 13 states that a fair value measurement is a market-based measurement, not an entity-specific measurement. Therefore, a fair value measurement uses the assumptions that market participants would use when pricing the asset or liability.

BC56　The previous definition of fair value in IFRSs referred to 'knowledgeable, willing parties in an arm's length transaction'. The IASB concluded that the previous definition expressed the same notion as the definition of fair value in IFRS 13, but that the previous definition was less clear. Thus, IFRS 13 defines market participants as buyers and sellers in the principal (or most advantageous) market for the asset or liability who are independent of each other (ie they are not related parties), knowledgeable about the asset or liability, and able and willing to enter into a transaction for the asset or liability.

Independence

BC57 IFRS 13 states that market participants are independent of each other (ie they are not related parties). That is consistent with the proposal in the exposure draft. Given that proposal, some respondents noted that in some jurisdictions entities often have common ownership (eg state-owned enterprises or entities with cross ownership) and questioned whether transactions observed in those jurisdictions would be permitted as an input into a fair value measurement. The boards decided to clarify that the price in a related party transaction may be used as an input into a fair value measurement if the entity has evidence that the transaction was entered into at market terms. The boards concluded that this is consistent with IAS 24 *Related Party Disclosures*.

Knowledge

BC58 The exposure draft stated that market participants were presumed to be as knowledgeable as the entity about the asset or liability. Some respondents questioned that conclusion because they thought the entity might have access to information that is not available to other market participants (information asymmetry).

BC59 In the IASB's view, if a market participant is willing to enter into a transaction for an asset or a liability, it would undertake efforts, including usual and customary due diligence efforts, necessary to become knowledgeable about the asset or liability and would factor any related risk into the measurement.

The price

BC60 IFRS 13 states that the price used to measure fair value should not be reduced (for an asset) or increased (for a liability) by the costs an entity would incur when selling the asset or transferring the liability (ie transaction costs).

BC61 Some respondents stated that transaction costs are unavoidable when entering into a transaction for an asset or a liability. However, the IASB noted that the costs may differ depending on how a particular entity enters into a transaction. Therefore, the IASB concluded that transaction costs are not a characteristic of an asset or a liability, but a characteristic of the transaction. That decision is consistent with the requirements for measuring fair value already in IFRSs. An entity accounts for those costs in accordance with relevant IFRSs.

BC62 Transaction costs are different from transport costs, which are the costs that would be incurred to transport the asset from its current location to its principal (or most advantageous) market. Unlike transaction costs, which arise from a transaction and do not change the characteristics of the asset or liability, transport costs arise from an event (transport) that does change a characteristic of an asset (its location). IFRS 13 states that if location is a characteristic of an asset, the price in the principal (or most advantageous) market should be adjusted for the costs that would be incurred to transport the asset from its current location to that market. That is consistent with the fair value measurement guidance already in IFRSs. For example, IAS 41 required an entity to deduct transport costs when measuring the fair value of a biological asset or agricultural produce.

Application to non-financial assets

Distinguishing between financial assets, non-financial assets and liabilities

BC63   The exposure draft stated that the concepts of highest and best use and valuation premise would not apply to financial assets or to liabilities.

The IASB reached that conclusion for the following reasons:

(a)   Financial assets do not have alternative uses because a financial asset has specific contractual terms and can have a different use only if the characteristics of the financial asset (ie the contractual terms) are changed. However, a change in characteristics causes that particular asset to become a different asset. The objective of a fair value measurement is to measure the asset that exists at the measurement date.

(b)   Even though an entity may be able to change the cash flows associated with a liability by relieving itself of the obligation in different ways, the different ways of doing so are not alternative uses. Moreover, although an entity might have entity-specific advantages or disadvantages that enable it to fulfil a liability more or less efficiently than other market participants, those entity-specific factors do not affect fair value.

(c)   Those concepts were originally developed within the valuation profession to value non-financial assets, such as land.

BC64   Before the amendments to Topic 820, US GAAP specified that the concepts of highest and best use and valuation premise applied when measuring the fair value of assets, but it did not distinguish between financial assets and non-financial assets.

BC65   The FASB agreed with the IASB that the concepts of highest and best use and valuation premise are relevant when measuring the fair value of non-financial assets, and are not relevant when measuring the fair value of financial assets or the fair value of liabilities. The boards also concluded that those concepts do not apply to an entity's own equity instruments because those arrangements, similar to financial instruments, typically have specific contractual terms. Paragraphs BC108–BC131 describe the boards' rationale in developing the requirements for measuring the fair value of financial assets and financial liabilities with offsetting positions in market risks and counterparty credit risk.

BC66   Some respondents to the FASB's proposed ASU were concerned that limiting the highest and best use concept to non-financial assets removed the concept of value maximisation by market participants, which they considered fundamental to a fair value measurement for financial assets and financial liabilities.

BC67   The boards decided to clarify that although there are no excess returns available from holding financial assets and financial liabilities within a portfolio (because in an efficient market, the price reflects the benefits that market participants would derive from holding the asset or liability in a diversified portfolio), a fair value measurement assumes that market participants seek to maximise the fair value of a financial or non-financial asset or to minimise the fair value of a financial or non-financial liability by acting in their economic best interest in a transaction to sell the asset or to transfer the liability in the principal (or most advantageous) market for the asset or liability. Such a transaction might involve grouping assets and liabilities in a way in which market participants would enter into a transaction, if the unit of account in other IFRSs does not prohibit that grouping.

Highest and best use

BC68   Highest and best use is a valuation concept used to value many non-financial assets (eg real estate). The highest and best use of a non-financial asset must be physically possible, legally permissible and financially feasible. In developing the proposals in the exposure draft, the IASB concluded that it was necessary to describe those three criteria, noting that US GAAP at the time did not.

BC69   Some respondents asked for further guidance about whether a use that is legally permissible must be legal at the measurement date, or if, for example, future changes in legislation can be taken into account. The IASB concluded that a use of an asset does not need to be legal at the measurement date, but must not be legally prohibited in the jurisdiction (eg if the government of a particular country has prohibited building or development in a protected area, the highest and best use of the land in that area could not be to develop it for industrial use). The illustrative examples that accompany IFRS 13 show how an asset can be zoned for a particular use at the measurement date, but how a fair value measurement can assume a different zoning if market participants would do so (incorporating the cost to convert the asset and obtain that different zoning permission, including the risk that such permission would not be granted).

BC70   IFRS 13 states that fair value takes into account the highest and best use of an asset from the perspective of market participants. That is the case even if an entity acquires an asset but, to protect its competitive position or for other reasons, the entity does not intend to use it actively or does not intend to use the asset in the same way as other market participants (eg if an intangible asset provides defensive value because the acquirer holds the asset to keep it from being used by competitors). When revising IFRS 3 in 2008, the IASB decided that an entity must recognise such an asset at fair value because the intention of IFRS 3 was that assets, both tangible and intangible, should be measured at their fair values regardless of how or whether the acquirer intends to use them (see paragraph BC262 of IFRS 3). IFRS 13 sets out requirements for measuring the fair value of those assets.

BC71   IFRS 13 does not require an entity to perform an exhaustive search for other potential uses of a non-financial asset if there is no evidence to suggest that the current use of an asset is not its highest and best use. The IASB concluded that an entity that seeks to maximise the value of its assets would use those assets at their highest and best use and that it would be necessary for an entity to consider alternative uses of those assets only if there was evidence that the current use of the assets is not their highest and best use (ie an alternative use would maximise their fair value). Furthermore, after discussions with valuation professionals, the IASB concluded that in many cases it would be unlikely for an asset's current use not to be its highest and best use after taking into account the costs to convert the asset to the alternative use.

BC72 When the IASB was developing the proposals in the exposure draft, users of financial statements asked the IASB to consider how to account for assets when their highest and best use within a group of assets is different from their current use by the entity (ie when there is evidence that the current use of the assets is not their highest and best use, and an alternative use would maximise their fair value). For example, the fair value of a factory is linked to the value of the land on which it is situated. The fair value of the factory would be nil if the land has an alternative use that assumes the factory is demolished. The IASB concluded when developing the exposure draft that measuring the factory at nil would not provide useful information when an entity is using that factory in its operations. In particular, users would want to see depreciation on that factory so that they could assess the economic resources consumed in generating cash flows from its operation. Therefore, the exposure draft proposed requiring an entity to separate the fair value of the asset group into its current use and fair value components.

BC73 Respondents found that proposal confusing and thought that calculating two values for a non-financial asset would be costly. As a result, the boards decided that when an entity uses a non-financial asset in a way that differs from its highest and best use (and that asset is measured at fair value), the entity must simply disclose that fact and why the asset is being used in a manner that differs from its highest and best use (see paragraphs BC213 and BC214).

Valuation premise

Terminology

BC74 As an application of the highest and best use concept, the exposure draft identified two valuation premises that may be relevant when measuring the fair value of an asset:

(a) The *in-use valuation premise*, which applies when the highest and best use of an asset is to use it with other assets or with other assets and liabilities as a group. The in-use valuation premise assumes that the exit price would be the price for a sale to a market participant that has, or can obtain, the other assets and liabilities needed to generate cash inflows by using the asset (complementary assets and the associated liabilities).

(b) The *in-exchange valuation premise*, which applies when the highest and best use of an asset is to use it on a stand-alone basis. It assumes that the sale would be to a market participant that uses the asset on a stand-alone basis.

BC75 Many respondents found the terms *in use* and *in exchange* confusing because they thought that the terminology did not accurately reflect the objective of the valuation premise (ie in both cases the asset is being exchanged, and both cases involve an assessment of how the asset will be used by market participants). In addition, some respondents stated that the in-use valuation premise could be confused with the term *value in use*, as defined in IAS 36.

BC76   In response, the boards decided to remove the terms *in use* and *in exchange* and instead describe the objective of the valuation premise: the valuation premise assumes that an asset would be used either (a) in combination with other assets or with other assets and liabilities (formerly referred to as *in use*) or (b) on a stand-alone basis (formerly referred to as *in exchange*). Respondents to the FASB's proposed ASU generally supported that proposal. The boards concluded that the change improves the understandability of the valuation premise concept.

Valuation premise for a single non-financial asset

BC77   IFRS 13 states that the valuation premise assumes that the non-financial asset being measured at fair value is sold on its own (at the unit of account level) and should be measured accordingly, even if transactions in the asset are typically the result of sales of the asset as part of a group of assets or a business. Even when an asset is used in combination with other assets, the exit price for the asset is a price for that asset individually because a fair value measurement assumes that a market participant (buyer) of the asset already holds the complementary assets and the associated liabilities. Because the buyer is assumed to hold the other assets (and liabilities) necessary for the asset to function, that buyer would not be willing to pay more for the asset solely because it was sold as part of a group. That conclusion is consistent with the conclusion reached in IFRS 3 for measuring the fair value of the identifiable assets acquired in a business combination.

Valuation premise for specialised non-financial assets

BC78   Some respondents to the exposure draft expressed concerns about using an exit price notion for specialised non-financial assets that have a significant value when used together with other non-financial assets, for example in a production process, but have little value if sold for scrap to another market participant that does not have the complementary assets. They were concerned that an exit price would be based on that scrap value (particularly given the requirement to maximise the use of observable inputs, such as market prices) and would not reflect the value that an entity expects to generate by using the asset in its operations. However, IFRS 13 clarifies that this is not the case. In such situations, the scrap value for an individual asset would be irrelevant because the valuation premise assumes that the asset would be used in combination with other assets or with other assets and liabilities. Therefore, an exit price reflects the sale of the asset to a market participant that has, or can obtain, the complementary assets and the associated liabilities needed to use the specialised asset in its own operations. In effect, the market participant buyer steps into the shoes of the entity that holds that specialised asset.

BC79   It is unlikely in such a situation that a market price, if available, would capture the value that the specialised asset contributes to the business because the market price would be for an unmodified asset. When a market price does not capture the characteristics of the asset (eg if that price represents the use of the asset on a stand-alone basis, not installed or otherwise configured for use, rather than in combination with other assets, installed and configured for use), that price will not represent fair value. In such a situation, an entity will need to measure fair value using another valuation technique (such as an income approach) or the cost to replace or recreate the asset (such as a cost approach) depending on the circumstances and the information available.

Application to liabilities

General principles

BC80   The exposure draft proposed that a fair value measurement assumes that a liability is transferred to a market participant at the measurement date because the liability that is the subject of the fair value measurement remains outstanding (ie it is owed by the entity and is not settled with the counterparty or otherwise extinguished at the measurement date). Because the liability is assumed to be transferred to a market participant, the liability remains outstanding and the market participant transferee, like the entity, would be required to fulfil it. The same concept applies to an entity's own equity instrument, as discussed in paragraphs BC104–BC107.

BC81   In many cases, an entity might not intend (or be able) to transfer its liability to a third party. For example, an entity might have advantages relative to the market that would make it more beneficial for the entity to fulfil the liability using its own internal resources or the counterparty might not permit the liability to be transferred to another party. However, the IASB concluded that a fair value measurement provides a market benchmark to use as a basis for assessing an entity's advantages or disadvantages in performance or settlement relative to the market (for both assets and liabilities). Therefore, when a liability is measured at fair value, the relative efficiency of an entity in settling the liability using its own internal resources appears in profit or loss over the course of its settlement, and not before.

BC82   Furthermore, even if an entity is unable to transfer its liability to a third party, the IASB concluded that the transfer notion was necessary in a fair value measurement because that notion captures market participants' expectations about the liquidity, uncertainty and other factors associated with the liability, whereas a settlement notion may not because it may incorporate entity-specific factors. In the IASB's view, the fair value of a liability from the perspective of a market participant that owes the liability is the same regardless of whether it is settled or transferred. That is because:

(a)   both a settlement and a transfer of a liability reflect all costs that would be incurred to fulfil the obligation, including the market-based profit an entity and a market participant transferee desire to earn on all their activities.

(b)   an entity faces the same risks when fulfilling an obligation that a market participant transferee faces when fulfilling that obligation. Neither the entity nor the market participant transferee has perfect knowledge about the timing and amount of the cash outflows, even for financial liabilities.

(c)   a settlement in a fair value measurement does not assume a settlement with the counterparty over time (eg as principal and interest payments become due), but a settlement at the measurement date. Accordingly, the settlement amount in a fair value measurement reflects the present value of the economic benefits (eg payments) the counterparty would have received over time.

As a result, the IASB concluded that similar thought processes are needed to estimate both the amount to settle a liability and the amount to transfer that liability.

BC83   The exposure draft proposed that an entity could estimate the amount at which a liability could be transferred in a transaction between market participants by using the same methodology that would be used to measure the fair value of the liability held by another entity as an asset (ie the fair value of the corresponding asset). If the liability was traded as an asset, the observed price would also represent the fair value of the issuer's liability. If there was no corresponding asset (eg as would be the case with a decommissioning liability), the fair value of the liability could be measured using a valuation technique, such as the present value of the future cash outflows that market participants would expect to incur in fulfilling the obligation.

BC84   That proposal was consistent with the approach in Topic 820 in US GAAP (in August 2009, after the IASB's exposure draft was published, the FASB amended Topic 820 to provide additional guidance about measuring the fair value of liabilities). However, Topic 820 provided more guidance than the IASB's exposure draft, including additional examples for applying that guidance. Because the guidance in Topic 820 was consistent with but not identical to the proposals in the IASB's exposure draft, the boards worked together to develop a combination of the two.

BC85   The boards concluded that the objective of a fair value measurement of a liability when using a valuation technique (ie when there is not an observable market to provide pricing information about the transfer of the liability) is to estimate the price that would be paid to transfer the liability in an orderly transaction between market participants at the measurement date under current market conditions.

BC86   Therefore, the boards decided to describe how an entity should measure the fair value of a liability when there is no observable market to provide pricing information about the transfer of a liability. For example, IFRS 13 states that an entity may measure the fair value of a liability by using a quoted price for an identical or a similar liability held by another party as an asset or by using another valuation technique (such as an income approach).

BC87   The boards clarified that regardless of the approach used, when there is no observable market price for the transfer of a liability and the identical liability is held by another party as an asset, an entity measures the fair value of the liability from the perspective of a market participant that holds the identical liability as an asset at the measurement date. That approach is consistent with the exposure draft and US GAAP.

BC88   Thus, in the boards' view, the fair value of a liability equals the fair value of a properly defined corresponding asset (ie an asset whose features mirror those of the liability), assuming an exit from both positions in the same market. In reaching their decision, the boards considered whether the effects of illiquidity could create a difference between those values. The boards noted that the effects of illiquidity are difficult to differentiate from credit-related effects. The boards concluded that there was no conceptual reason why the liability value would diverge from the corresponding asset value in the same market because the contractual terms are the same, unless the unit of account for the liability is different from the unit of account for the asset or the quoted price for the asset relates to a similar (but not identical) liability held as an asset.

BC89   Furthermore, the boards concluded that in an efficient market, the price of a liability held by another party as an asset must equal the price for the corresponding asset. If those prices differed, the market participant transferee (ie the party taking on the obligation) would be able to earn a profit by financing the purchase of the asset with the proceeds received by taking on the liability. In such cases the price for the liability and the price for the asset would adjust until the arbitrage opportunity was eliminated.

BC90   The exposure draft stated that when using a present value technique to measure the fair value of a liability that is not held by another party as an asset, an entity should include the compensation that a market participant would require for taking on the obligation. Topic 820 contained such a requirement. Respondents asked for clarification on the meaning of compensation that a market participant would require for taking on the obligation. Therefore, the boards decided to provide additional guidance about the compensation that market participants would require, such as the compensation for taking on the responsibility of fulfilling an obligation and for assuming the risk associated with an uncertain obligation (ie the risk that the actual cash outflows might differ from the expected cash outflows). The boards concluded that including this description will improve the application of the requirements for measuring the fair value of liabilities that are not held as assets.

BC91   Some respondents to the FASB's proposed ASU requested clarification about applying risk premiums when measuring the fair value of a liability that is not held by another party as an asset (eg a decommissioning liability assumed in a business combination) when using a present value technique. They noted that the description of present value techniques described adjustments for risk as *additions* to the discount rate, which they agreed was consistent with asset valuation, but not necessarily consistent with liability valuation in the absence of a corresponding asset. The boards reasoned that from a market participant's perspective, compensation for the uncertainty related to a liability results in an increase to the amount that the market participant would expect to receive for assuming the obligation. If that compensation was accounted for in the discount rate, rather than in the cash flows, it would result in a reduction of the discount rate used in the fair value measurement of the liability. Therefore, the boards concluded that, all else being equal, the risk associated with an asset decreases the fair value of that asset, whereas the risk associated with a liability increases the fair value of that liability. However, the boards decided not to prescribe how an entity would adjust for the risk inherent in an asset or a liability, but to state that the objective is to ensure that the fair value measurement takes that risk into account. That can be done by adjusting the cash flows or the discount rate or by adding a risk adjustment to the present value of the expected cash flows (which is another way of adjusting the cash flows).

Non-performance risk

BC92   IFRS 13 states that a fair value measurement assumes that the fair value of a liability reflects the effect of non-performance risk, which is the risk that an entity will not fulfil an obligation. Non-performance risk includes, but is not limited to, an entity's own credit risk (credit standing). That is consistent with the fair value measurement guidance already in IFRSs. For example, IAS 39[4] and IFRS 9 referred to making adjustments for credit risk if market participants would reflect that risk when pricing a financial instrument. However, there was inconsistent application of that principle because:

(a)   IAS 39 and IFRS 9 refer to credit risk generally and do not specifically refer to the reporting entity's *own* credit risk; and

(b)   there were different interpretations about how an entity's own credit risk should be reflected in the fair value of a liability using the settlement notion in the previous definition of fair value because it is unlikely that the counterparty would accept a different amount as settlement of the obligation if the entity's credit standing changed.

BC93   As a result, some entities took into account changes in their own credit risk when measuring the fair value of their liabilities, whereas other entities did not. Consequently, the IASB decided to clarify in IFRS 13 that the fair value of a liability includes an entity's own credit risk.

BC94   In a fair value measurement, the non-performance risk related to a liability is the same before and after its transfer. Although the IASB acknowledges that such an assumption is unlikely to be realistic for an actual transaction (because in most cases the reporting entity transferor and the market participant transferee are unlikely to have the same credit standing), the IASB concluded that such an assumption was necessary when measuring fair value for the following reasons:

(a)   A market participant taking on the obligation would not enter into a transaction that changes the non-performance risk associated with the liability without reflecting that change in the price (eg a creditor would not generally permit a debtor to transfer its obligation to another party of lower credit standing, nor would a transferee of higher credit standing be willing to assume the obligation using the same terms negotiated by the transferor if those terms reflect the transferor's lower credit standing).

---

4   IFRS 9 *Financial Instruments* replaced IAS 39. IFRS 9 applies to all items that were previously within the scope of IAS 39.

(b) Without specifying the credit standing of the entity taking on the obligation, there could be fundamentally different fair values for a liability depending on an entity's assumptions about the characteristics of the market participant transferee.

(c) Those who might hold the entity's obligations as assets would consider the effect of the entity's credit risk and other risk factors when pricing those assets (see paragraphs BC83–BC89).

The FASB reached the same conclusions when developing SFAS 157 and ASU No. 2009-05 *Fair Value Measurements and Disclosures (Topic 820): Measuring Liabilities at Fair Value.*

BC95 Few respondents questioned the usefulness of reflecting non-performance risk in the fair value measurement of a liability at initial recognition. However, many questioned the usefulness of doing so after initial recognition, because they reasoned that it would lead to counter-intuitive and potentially confusing reporting (ie gains for credit deterioration and losses for credit improvements). The IASB understands that these concerns are strongly held, but concluded that addressing them was beyond the scope of the fair value measurement project. The purpose of that project was to define fair value, not to determine when to use fair value or how to present changes in fair value. A measurement that does not consider the effect of an entity's non-performance risk is not a fair value measurement. The IASB addressed those concerns in developing IFRS 9 (issued in October 2010).

Liabilities issued with third-party credit enhancements

BC96 IFRS 13 includes requirements for measuring the fair value of a liability issued with an inseparable third-party credit enhancement from the issuer's perspective. Those requirements are consistent with Topic 820.

BC97 A credit enhancement (also referred to as a guarantee) may be purchased by an issuer that combines it with a liability, such as debt, and then issues the combined security to an investor. For example, debt may be issued with a financial guarantee from a third party that guarantees the issuer's payment obligations. Generally, if the issuer of the liability fails to meet its payment obligations to the investor, the guarantor has an obligation to make the payments on the issuer's behalf and the issuer has an obligation to the guarantor. By issuing debt combined with a credit enhancement, the issuer is able to market its debt more easily and can either reduce the interest rate paid to the investor or receive higher proceeds when the debt is issued.

BC98 The boards concluded that the measurement of a liability should follow the unit of account of the liability for financial reporting purposes. When the unit of account for such liabilities is the obligation without the credit enhancement, the fair value of the liability from the issuer's perspective will not equal its fair value as a guaranteed liability held by another party as an asset. Therefore, the fair value of the guaranteed liability held by another party as an asset would need to be adjusted because any payments made by the guarantor in accordance with the guarantee result in a transfer of the issuer's debt obligation from the investor to the guarantor. The issuer's resulting debt obligation to the guarantor has not been guaranteed. Consequently, the boards decided that if the third-party credit enhancement is accounted for separately from the liability, the fair value of that obligation takes into account the credit standing of the issuer and not the credit standing of the guarantor.

Restrictions preventing transfer

BC99   A restriction on an entity's ability to transfer its liability to another party is a function of the requirement to fulfil the obligation and the effect of such a restriction normally is already reflected in the price. As a result, IFRS 13 states that the fair value of a liability should not be adjusted further for the effect of a restriction on its transfer if that restriction is already included in the other inputs to the fair value measurement. However, if an entity is aware that a restriction on transfer is not already reflected in the price (or in the other inputs used in the measurement), the entity would adjust those inputs to reflect the existence of the restriction.

BC100   The boards concluded that there are two fundamental differences between the fair value measurement of an asset and the fair value measurement of a liability that justify different treatments for asset restrictions and liability restrictions. First, restrictions on the transfer of a liability relate to the performance of the obligation (ie the entity is legally obliged to satisfy the obligation and needs to do something to be relieved of the obligation), whereas restrictions on the transfer of an asset relate to the marketability of the asset. Second, nearly all liabilities include a restriction preventing the transfer of the liability, whereas most assets do not include a similar restriction. As a result, the effect of a restriction preventing the transfer of a liability, theoretically, would be consistent for all liabilities and, therefore, would require no additional adjustment beyond the factors considered in determining the original transaction price. The inclusion of a restriction preventing the sale of an asset typically results in a lower fair value for the restricted asset than for the non-restricted asset, all other factors being equal.

Measurement of financial liabilities with a demand feature[5]

BC101   In developing IFRS 13, the IASB confirmed its decision in developing IAS 39 that the fair value of a financial liability with a demand feature cannot be less than the amount payable on demand, discounted from the first date that the amount could be required to be repaid.

BCZ102 Some comments received on the exposure draft published in 2002 preceding IAS 39 requested clarification of how to measure the fair value of financial liabilities with a demand feature (eg demand deposits) when the fair value measurement option is applied or the liability is otherwise measured at fair value. In other words, could the fair value be less than the amount payable on demand, discounted from the first date that an amount could be required to be paid (the demand amount), such as the amount of the deposit discounted for the period that the entity expects the deposit to be outstanding? Some commentators believed that the fair value of financial liabilities with a demand

---

5   IFRS 9 *Financial Instruments* replaced IAS 39. IFRS 9 applies to all items that were previously within the scope of IAS 39.

feature is less than the demand amount, for reasons that include the consistency of such measurement with how those financial liabilities are treated for risk management purposes.

BCZ103   In developing IAS 39 the IASB agreed that this issue should be clarified. It confirmed that the fair value of a financial liability with a demand feature is not less than the amount payable on demand, discounted from the first date that the amount could be required to be paid (this is now in paragraph 47 of IFRS 13). That conclusion is the same as in the original IAS 32 *Financial Instruments: Disclosure and Presentation* (issued by the IASB's predecessor body, IASC, in 1995), which is now IAS 32 *Financial Instruments: Presentation*. The IASB noted that in many cases, the market price observed for such financial liabilities is the price at which they are originated between the customer and the deposit-taker—ie the demand amount. It also noted that recognising a financial liability with a demand feature at less than the demand amount would give rise to an immediate gain on the origination of such a deposit, which the IASB believes is inappropriate.

Application to an entity's own equity instruments[6]

BC104   The exposure draft and Topic 820 stated that although the definition of fair value refers to assets and liabilities, it also should be applied to an instrument measured at fair value that is classified in an entity's own shareholders' equity. Respondents to the discussion paper asked for explicit guidance for measuring the fair value of such instruments because Topic 820 did not contain explicit guidance. Consequently, the boards decided to describe how an entity should measure the fair value of its own equity instruments (eg when an acquirer issues equity in consideration for an acquiree in a business combination).

BC105   The exposure draft proposed requiring an entity to measure the fair value of its own equity instruments from the perspective of a market participant that holds the instrument as an asset. That was because the issuer of an equity instrument can exit from that instrument only if the instrument ceases to exist or if the entity repurchases the instrument from the holder. The FASB agreed with that conclusion.

BC106   The boards also noted that some instruments may be classified as liabilities or equity, depending on the characteristics of the transaction and the characteristics of the instrument. Examples of such instruments include contingent consideration issued in a business combination in accordance with IFRS 3 and equity warrants issued by an entity in accordance with IAS 39[7] or IFRS 9. The boards concluded that the requirements for measuring the fair value of an entity's own equity instruments should be consistent with the requirements for measuring the fair value of liabilities. Consequently, the boards decided to clarify that the accounting classification of an instrument should not affect that instrument's fair value measurement.

---

6   IFRS 9 *Financial Instruments* replaced IAS 39. IFRS 9 applies to all items that were previously within the scope of IAS 39.

7   IFRS 9 *Financial Instruments* replaced IAS 39. IFRS 9 applies to all items that were previously within the scope of IAS 39.

BC107　The boards decided to clarify that the objective of a fair value measurement for liabilities and an entity's own equity instruments should be an exit price from the perspective of a market participant that holds the instrument as an asset at the measurement date if there is a corresponding asset, regardless of whether there is an observable market for the instrument as an asset. That decision is consistent with the boards' decisions about the requirements for measuring the fair value of a liability.

Application to financial assets and financial liabilities with offsetting positions in market risks or counterparty credit risk[8]

BC108　An entity that holds a group of financial assets and financial liabilities is exposed to market risks (ie interest rate risk, currency risk or other price risk) and to the credit risk of each of the counterparties. Financial institutions and similar entities that hold financial assets and financial liabilities often manage those instruments on the basis of the entity's net exposure to a particular market risk (or risks) or to the credit risk of a particular counterparty.

BC109　The previous requirements in IFRSs and US GAAP for measuring the fair value of financial assets and financial liabilities that are managed in this way were expressed differently. Therefore, the boards concluded that it is important that IFRSs and US GAAP express the requirements for measuring the fair value of those financial instruments in the same way.

BC110　When applying IFRSs, entities applied IFRS 9 or IAS 39, which permitted an entity to take into account the effects of offsetting positions in the same market risk (or risks) when measuring the fair value of a financial asset or financial liability. Many entities were using the same approach for offsetting positions in the credit risk of a particular counterparty by analogy.

BC111　When applying US GAAP, many entities applied the in-use valuation premise when measuring the fair value of such financial assets and financial liabilities. In other words, an entity would take into account how the fair value of each financial asset or financial liability might be affected by the combination of that asset or liability with other financial assets or financial liabilities held by the entity. Other entities applied the in-exchange valuation premise to the entity's net risk exposure and assumed that the transaction took place for the net position, not for the individual assets and liabilities making up that position. Those differing applications of the valuation premise arose because Topic 820 did not specify the valuation premise for financial assets.

BC112　In developing the exposure draft, the IASB concluded that the fair value of a financial asset reflects any benefits that market participants would derive from holding that asset within a diversified portfolio. An entity derives no incremental value from holding a financial asset within a portfolio. Furthermore, the IASB noted that the valuation premise related only to assets, not to liabilities, and as such could not be applied to portfolios of financial instruments that include financial liabilities. Therefore, the exposure draft

---

8　IFRS 9 *Financial Instruments* replaced IAS 39. IFRS 9 applies to all items that were previously within the scope of IAS 39.

proposed that the in-exchange valuation premise must be used to measure the fair value of a financial asset. The IASB also proposed an amendment to IAS 39 making it explicit that the unit of account for financial instruments is the individual financial instrument at all levels of the fair value hierarchy (Level 1, 2 or 3).

BC113 The boards understand that although the approaches used to measure the fair value of financial assets and financial liabilities were expressed differently in IFRSs and US GAAP, they resulted in similar fair value measurement conclusions in many cases. However, the FASB was aware that before the amendments Topic 820 was sometimes interpreted more broadly than the FASB intended, such as when an entity used the in-use valuation premise to measure the fair value of a group of financial assets when the entity did not have offsetting positions in a particular market risk (or risks) or counterparty credit risk. That interpretation led the IASB to propose requiring the in-exchange valuation premise for financial assets in its exposure draft.

BC114 The IASB's proposal to require the fair value of a financial asset to be measured using the in-exchange valuation premise was one of the more controversial proposals in the exposure draft. That proposal, combined with a proposed amendment to IAS 39 about the unit of account for financial instruments, led respondents to believe that the fair value of financial assets cannot reflect the fact that those assets are held within a portfolio, even when an entity manages its financial instruments on the basis of the entity's net exposure, rather than its gross exposure, to market risks and credit risk.

BC115 Respondents were concerned that the proposal in the exposure draft would separate the valuation of financial instruments for financial reporting from the entity's internal risk management practices. In addition, they were concerned about the systems changes that would be necessary to effect a change in practice. To preserve the relationship between financial reporting and risk management, some respondents asked whether they would be able to apply the bid-ask spread guidance to each of the individual instruments so that the sum of the fair values of the individual instruments equals the value of the net position.

BC116 Other respondents suggested that the IASB should continue to allow the practice that has developed using paragraph AG72 of IAS 39, which stated:

> When an entity has assets and liabilities with offsetting market risks, it may use mid-market prices as a basis for establishing fair values for the offsetting risk positions and apply the bid or asking price to the net open position as appropriate.

BC117 The previous requirements in IFRSs and US GAAP did not clearly specify the relationship between the fair value measurement of financial instruments and how an entity manages its net risk exposure. For example, Topic 820, IAS 39 and IFRS 9 did not explicitly address how the following meet the objective of a fair value measurement for financial instruments:

(a) Entities typically do not manage their exposure to market risks and credit risk by *selling* a financial asset or transferring a financial liability (eg by unwinding a transaction). Instead, they manage their risk exposure by entering into a transaction for another financial instrument (or instruments) that would result in an offsetting position in the same risk. The resulting measurement represents the fair value of the net risk exposure, not the fair value of an individual financial instrument. The sum of the fair values of the individual instruments is not equal to the fair value of the net risk exposure.

(b)   An entity's net risk exposure is a function of the other financial instruments held by the entity and of the entity's risk preferences (both of which are entity-specific decisions and, thus, do not form part of a fair value measurement). Market participants may hold different groups of financial instruments or may have different risk preferences, and it is those factors that are taken into account when measuring fair value. However, the boards understand that market participants holding that particular group of financial instruments and with those particular risk preferences would be likely to price those financial instruments similarly (ie using similar valuation techniques and similar market data). As a result, the market participants' measurement of those financial instruments within that particular group is a market-based measurement, and a measurement using an entity's risk preferences would not be a fair value measurement, but an entity-specific measurement.

BC118   Consequently, the boards decided to permit an exception to the requirements in IFRS 13 and Topic 820 for measuring fair value when an entity manages its financial assets and financial liabilities on the basis of the entity's net exposure to market risks or to the credit risk of a particular counterparty. Respondents to the FASB's proposed ASU generally supported that proposal and stated that it was consistent with current practice for measuring the fair value of such financial assets and financial liabilities.

BC119   That exception permits an entity to measure the fair value of a group of financial assets and financial liabilities on the basis of the price that would be received to sell a net long position (ie asset) for a particular risk exposure or to transfer a net short position (ie liability) for a particular risk exposure in an orderly transaction between market participants at the measurement date under current market conditions, subject to specific requirements.

Scope of paragraph 52

BC119A   After issuing IFRS 13, the IASB was made aware that it was not clear whether the scope of the exception for measuring the fair value of a group of financial assets and financial liabilities on a net basis (the 'portfolio exception') includes all contracts that are within the scope of IAS 39 or IFRS 9. The exception is set out in paragraph 48 and the scope of the exception is set out in paragraph 52. In particular, the IASB was asked whether the scope of the portfolio exception included contracts that are accounted for as if they were financial instruments, but that do not meet the definitions of financial assets or financial liabilities in IAS 32. Examples of such a situation would be some contracts to buy or sell a non-financial item that can be settled net in cash by another financial instrument or by exchanging financial instruments as if the contracts were financial instruments within the scope of, and accounted for in accordance with, IAS 39 or IFRS 9.

BC119B   The IASB did not intend to exclude from the scope of the portfolio exception any contracts that are within the scope of IAS 39 or IFRS 9. Consequently, the IASB amended paragraph 52 of this Standard to clarify that the portfolio exception applies to all contracts within the scope of, and accounted for in accordance with, IAS 39 or IFRS 9, regardless of whether they meet the definitions of financial assets or financial liabilities as defined in IAS 32.

Evidence of managing financial instruments on the basis of the net risk exposure

BC120   IFRS 13 states that to use the exception, an entity must provide evidence that it consistently manages its financial instruments on the basis of its net exposure to market risks or credit risk. In addition, the entity must be required (or must have elected, for example, in accordance with the fair value option) to measure the financial instruments at fair value on a recurring basis. The boards concluded that if an entity does not manage its risk exposure on a net basis and does not manage its financial instruments on a fair value basis, the entity should not be permitted to measure the fair value of its financial instruments on the basis of the entity's net risk exposure.

BC121   The boards decided to require an entity to provide evidence that it manages its net risk exposure consistently from period to period. The boards decided this because an entity that can provide evidence that it manages its financial instruments on the basis of its net risk exposure would do so consistently for a particular portfolio from period to period, and not on a net basis for that portfolio in some periods and on a gross basis in other periods. Some respondents to the FASB's proposed ASU found that requirement limiting because they noted that the composition of a portfolio changes continually as the entity rebalances the portfolio and changes its risk exposure preferences over time. Although the entity does not need to maintain a static portfolio, the boards decided to clarify that the entity must make an accounting policy decision (in accordance with IAS 8 *Accounting Policies, Changes in Accounting Estimates and Errors*) to use the exception described in paragraphs BC118 and BC119. The boards also decided that the accounting policy decision could be changed if the entity's risk exposure preferences change. In that case the entity can decide not to use the exception but instead to measure the fair value of its financial instruments on an individual instrument basis. However, if the entity continues to value a portfolio using the exception, it must do so consistently from period to period.

Exposure to market risks

BC122   The boards decided that an entity could apply the bid-ask spread guidance to the entity's net position in a particular market risk (rather than to each individual financial instrument included in that position) only if the market risks that are being offset are substantially the same. Some respondents to the FASB's proposed ASU asked for additional guidance on what is meant by *substantially the same* given the different instruments and types of instruments that might make up a portfolio. In addition, they were concerned that the proposed requirement that the market risks be substantially the same meant that there could be no basis risk in the portfolio or, conversely, that the basis risk would not be reflected in the fair value measurement.

BC123 Consequently, the boards decided to include additional guidance for determining whether market risks are substantially the same. The boards held discussions with several financial institutions that manage their financial assets and financial liabilities on the basis of their net exposure to market risks. From those discussions, the boards concluded that when measuring fair value on the basis of an entity's net exposure to market risks, the entity should not combine a financial asset that exposes it to a particular market risk with a financial liability that exposes it to a different market risk that does not mitigate either of the market risk exposures that the entity faces. The boards also concluded that it is not necessary that the grouping of particular financial assets and financial liabilities results in an entity having no basis risk because the fair value measurement would take into account any basis risk. Furthermore, on the basis of their discussions with financial institutions, the boards concluded that an entity should not combine a financial asset that exposes it to a particular market risk over a particular duration with a financial liability that exposes it to substantially the same market risk over a different duration without taking into account the fact that the entity is fully exposed to that market risk over the time period for which the market risks are not offset. If there is a time period in which a market risk is not offset, the entity may measure its net exposure to that market risk over the time period in which the market risk is offset and must measure its gross exposure to that market risk for the remaining time period (ie the time period in which the market risk is not offset).

Exposure to the credit risk of a particular counterparty

BC124 Because the bid-ask spread (which is the basis for making adjustments for an entity's exposure to market risk to arrive at the fair value of the net position) does not include adjustments for counterparty credit risk (see paragraph BC164), the boards decided to specify that an entity may take into account its net exposure to the credit risk of a particular counterparty when applying the exception.

BC125 The boards decided that when measuring fair value, an entity may consider its net exposure to credit risk when it has entered into an arrangement with a counterparty that mitigates its credit risk exposure in the event of default (eg a master netting agreement). On the basis of their discussions with financial institutions the boards concluded that a fair value measurement reflects market participants' expectations about the likelihood that such an arrangement would be legally enforceable.

BC126 Some respondents to the FASB's proposed ASU asked whether the existence of a master netting agreement was necessary or whether other credit mitigating arrangements could be taken into account in the fair value measurement. The boards decided to clarify that in a fair value measurement, an entity must take into account other arrangements that mitigate credit risk, such as an agreement that requires the exchange of collateral on the basis of each party's net exposure to the credit risk of the other party, if market participants would expect such arrangements to be legally enforceable in the event of default.

BC127   The boards acknowledged that the group of financial assets and financial liabilities for which an entity manages its net exposure to a particular market risk (or risks) could differ from the group of financial assets and financial liabilities for which an entity manages its net exposure to the credit risk of a particular counterparty because it is unlikely that all contracts would be with the same counterparty.

Relationship between measurement and presentation

BC128   In some cases the basis for the presentation of financial instruments in the statement of financial position differs from the basis for the measurement of those financial instruments. For example, that would be the case if an IFRS does not require or permit financial instruments to be presented on a net basis. The FASB's proposed ASU stated that the exception would not apply to financial statement presentation (ie an entity must comply with the financial statement presentation requirements specified in other standards).

BC129   The boards discussed the different approaches to measurement and presentation, particularly in the light of their currently differing requirements for offsetting financial assets and financial liabilities. In IAS 32 an entity may not use net presentation unless specific criteria are met, whereas in US GAAP many entities are able to use net presentation in their financial statements. However, the criteria for net presentation in US GAAP relate to credit risk, not to market risks. As a result, the presentation and measurement bases are different when an entity applies bid-ask adjustments on a net basis but is required to present fair value information on a gross basis (although generally the financial instruments with bid-ask adjustments would qualify for net presentation in US GAAP because of the existence of master netting agreements and other credit risk mitigating arrangements).

BC130   The boards concluded that a relationship between presentation and measurement is not necessary and that adjustments for market risks or credit risk (ie portfolio-level adjustments) are a matter of measurement rather than presentation. They reasoned that fair value measurements are meant to reflect (a) the risk exposure faced by the entity and (b) how that risk exposure would be priced by market participants (which is one reason the boards decided to permit the exception; see paragraph BC117). When pricing financial instruments, a market participant would take into account the other instruments it holds to the extent that those instruments reduce or enhance its overall risk exposure. That is a consequence of requiring or permitting financial instruments to be measured at fair value. The boards' considerations for requiring net or gross presentation of financial instruments are different from those for requiring net or gross measurement.

BC131   Some respondents asked for additional guidance for allocating the bid-ask and credit adjustments to the individual assets and liabilities that make up the group of financial assets and financial liabilities. Although any allocation method is inherently subjective, the boards concluded that a quantitative allocation would be appropriate if it was reasonable and consistently applied. Therefore, the boards decided not to require a particular method of allocation.

Fair value at initial recognition[9]

BC132   The exposure draft proposed guidance for measuring fair value at initial recognition, using both observable and unobservable inputs (as appropriate). The exposure draft also proposed a list of indicators specifying when the transaction price might not be the best evidence of the fair value of an asset or a liability at initial recognition.

BC133   Respondents generally agreed with the list of indicators, but thought that the wording used implied that those were the only indicators, rather than examples of indicators. They suggested that the IFRS on fair value measurement should use the wording in US GAAP. The boards agreed with respondents that the list of indicators was not exhaustive and decided to use the wording in Topic 820.

BC134   Some respondents suggested that market inactivity should be included in the list of indicators. The boards concluded that market inactivity is not an indicator that the transaction price may not represent fair value, but an indicator that the entity should do further work to determine whether the transaction price represents fair value.

BC135   The exposure draft did not address the recognition of a day 1 gain or loss but stated that an entity would recognise such gains or losses unless another IFRS specifies otherwise. For example, IAS 39 and IFRS 9 state that an entity cannot recognise a day 1 gain or loss for a financial instrument unless its fair value is evidenced by a quoted price in an active market for an identical asset or liability or based on a valuation technique that uses only data from observable markets. In contrast, IFRS 3 and IAS 41 require the recognition of day 1 gains or losses even when fair value is measured using unobservable inputs.

BC136   The IASB concluded that fair value should be measured at initial recognition without regard to whether it would result in a gain or loss at initial recognition of the asset or liability. Respondents' views ranged from the view that the transaction price is the best evidence of fair value at initial recognition unless the fair value is measured using only observable inputs (the approach in IAS 39 and IFRS 9) to the view that the transaction price might sometimes, but not always, represent fair value at initial recognition, and that the degree of observability of inputs is not always the best indicator of whether this is the case (the approach in US GAAP).

BC137   Many respondents suggested that IFRSs and US GAAP should have the same requirements for recognising gains or losses at initial recognition. The boards concluded that determining whether to recognise a day 1 gain or loss was beyond the scope of the fair value measurement project. The boards noted that the measurement basis at initial recognition of financial instruments in IFRSs and US GAAP is not always the same, and so the boards could not address comparability at this time. As a result, the boards decided that an entity would refer to relevant IFRSs for the asset or liability when determining whether to

---

9   IFRS 9 *Financial Instruments* replaced IAS 39. IFRS 9 applies to all items that were previously within the scope of IAS 39.

recognise those amounts. The boards concluded that if the relevant IFRS does not specify whether and, if so, where to recognise those amounts, the entity should recognise them in profit or loss.

BC138 Although the IASB did not change the recognition threshold, it amended IAS 39[10] and IFRS 9 to clarify that the fair value of financial instruments at initial recognition should be measured in accordance with IFRS 13 and that any deferred amounts arising from the application of the recognition threshold in IAS 39 and IFRS 9 are separate from the fair value measurement. In other words, the recognition threshold in IAS 39 and IFRS 9 is not a constraint when measuring fair value. Rather, it determines whether (and when) the resulting difference (if any) between fair value at initial recognition and the transaction price is recognised.

Short-term receivables and payables

BC138A After issuing IFRS 13, the IASB was made aware that an amendment to IFRS 9 and IAS 39, which resulted in the deletion of paragraphs B5.4.12 and AG79 respectively, might be perceived as removing the ability to measure short-term receivables and payables with no stated interest rate at invoice amounts without discounting, when the effect of not discounting is immaterial. The IASB did not intend to change the measurement requirements for those short-term receivables and payables, noting that paragraph 8 of IAS 8 already permits entities not to apply accounting policies set out in accordance with IFRSs when the effect of applying them is immaterial.

Valuation techniques

BC139 When measuring fair value, the objective of using a valuation technique is to estimate the price at which an orderly transaction would take place between market participants at the measurement date under current market conditions.

BC140 To meet that objective, the exposure draft proposed that valuation techniques used to measure fair value should be consistent with the market approach, income approach or cost approach. Such valuation techniques are consistent with those already described in IFRSs and with valuation practice.

BC141 Respondents generally agreed with the descriptions of the three valuation techniques. Some respondents questioned whether a cost approach is consistent with an exit price definition of fair value because they think that the cost to replace an asset is more consistent with an entry price than an exit price. The IASB noted that an entity's cost to replace an asset would equal the amount that a market participant buyer of that asset (that would use it similarly) would pay to acquire it (ie the entry price and the exit price would be equal in the same market). Thus, the IASB concluded that the cost approach is consistent with an exit price definition of fair value.

---

10 IFRS 9 *Financial Instruments* replaced IAS 39. IFRS 9 applies to all items that were previously within the scope of IAS 39.

Single versus multiple valuation techniques

BC142 IFRS 13 does not contain a hierarchy of valuation techniques because particular valuation techniques might be more appropriate in some circumstances than in others. The IASB concluded that determining the appropriateness of valuation techniques in the circumstances requires judgement and noted that Topic 820 and the fair value measurement guidance already in IFRSs do not contain a hierarchy of valuation techniques. For example, IAS 41 acknowledged that in some cases the various approaches used by an entity might suggest different fair value conclusions for a biological asset or agricultural produce, but that the entity should consider the reasons for the differences to arrive at a fair value within a reasonable range.

Valuation adjustments

BC143 Some respondents asked for more explicit requirements about applying valuation adjustments (including risk adjustments related to the uncertainty inherent in the inputs used in a fair value measurement; see paragraphs BC149 and BC150). They found the descriptions of valuation adjustments in the IASB's Fair Value Expert Advisory Panel's October 2008 report *Measuring and disclosing the fair value of financial instruments in markets that are no longer active* helpful (see paragraph BC177). In addition, regulators asked the IASB to address measurement uncertainty to ensure that fair value measurements are not overstated or understated in the statement of financial position, thus improving the quality of information available to users of financial statements.

BC144 Although the exposure draft was not explicit with respect to valuation adjustments, it stated that an entity must use the assumptions that market participants would use in pricing the asset or liability, including assumptions about the risk inherent in a particular valuation technique or in the inputs to the valuation technique. That implicitly included measurement uncertainty.

BC145 The boards noted that entities found the IASB's Fair Value Expert Advisory Panel's report helpful when measuring the fair value of financial instruments during a period of market inactivity. As a result, the boards decided to describe the valuation adjustments that entities might need to make when using a valuation technique because market participants would make those adjustments when pricing a financial asset or financial liability under the market conditions at the measurement date, including adjustments for measurement uncertainty. Those valuation adjustments include the following:

(a) an adjustment to a valuation technique to take into account a characteristic of an asset or a liability that is not captured by the valuation technique (the need for such an adjustment is typically identified during calibration of the value calculated using the valuation technique with observable market information).

(b) applying the point within the bid-ask spread that is most representative of fair value in the circumstances.

(c) an adjustment to take into account non-performance risk (eg an entity's own credit risk or the credit risk of the counterparty to a transaction).

(d)   an adjustment to take into account measurement uncertainty (eg when there has been a significant decrease in the volume or level of activity when compared with normal market activity for the asset or liability, or similar assets or liabilities, and the entity has determined that the transaction price or quoted price does not represent fair value).

BC146   The boards decided that it would be appropriate to apply such valuation adjustments if those adjustments are consistent with the objective of a fair value measurement. Valuation adjustments may help avoid an understatement or overstatement of a fair value measurement and should be applied when a valuation technique or the inputs to a valuation technique do not capture factors that market participants would take into account when pricing an asset or a liability at the measurement date, including assumptions about risk.

Consistency constraint

BC147   IFRS 13 emphasises the need for consistency in the valuation technique or techniques used to measure fair value. It does not preclude a change in valuation technique, provided that the change results in a measurement that is equally or more representative of fair value in the circumstances. The exposure draft proposed requiring an entity to disclose the effect of a change in valuation technique on a fair value measurement (similar to the disclosures required by IAS 8 for a change in valuation technique). Respondents did not support that proposal because they thought it would be difficult to determine whether a change in fair value was attributable to a change in the valuation technique used or attributable to changes in other factors (such as changes in the observability of the inputs used in the measurement).

BC148   The IASB agreed with those respondents and decided that in the absence of an error (eg in the selection or application of a particular valuation technique), revisions resulting from a change in the valuation technique or its application should be accounted for as a change in accounting estimate in accordance with IAS 8. The IASB concluded that disclosing the effect of a change in valuation technique on the fair value measurement or requiring the disclosures in IAS 8 for a change in accounting estimate would not be cost-beneficial.

Inputs to valuation techniques

Assumptions about risk

BC149   In IFRS 13 inputs refer broadly to the assumptions that market participants would use when pricing the asset or liability, including assumptions about risk. The IASB decided that a necessary input to a valuation technique is an adjustment for risk because market participants would make such an adjustment when pricing an asset or a liability. Therefore, including an adjustment for risk ensures that the measurement reflects an exit price for the asset or liability, ie the price that would be received in an orderly transaction to sell an asset or paid in an orderly transaction to transfer the liability at the measurement date under current market conditions.

BC150   The IASB accepted that it might be difficult for an entity to quantify a risk adjustment in some cases, but concluded that this difficulty does not justify the exclusion of this input if market participants would take it into account. The exposure draft focused on the need to adjust for the risk inherent in a particular valuation technique used to measure fair value, such as a pricing model (model risk) and the risk inherent in the inputs to the valuation technique (input risk). That proposal was consistent with US GAAP.

Observable and unobservable inputs

BC151   IFRS 13 distinguishes between observable inputs and unobservable inputs, and requires an entity to maximise the use of relevant observable inputs and minimise the use of unobservable inputs (consistently with the fair value measurement guidance that was already in IFRSs). Respondents to the exposure draft expressed concerns about being required to use observable inputs during the global financial crisis that started in 2007 when the available observable inputs were not representative of the asset or liability being measured at fair value. Given that feedback, the IASB wanted to ensure that observability was not the only criterion applied when selecting the inputs to a valuation technique. Consequently, IFRS 13 focuses on *relevant* observable inputs because the IASB noted that in some cases the available observable inputs will require an entity to make significant adjustments to them given the characteristics of the asset or liability and the circumstances at the measurement date (eg market conditions).

Application of premiums and discounts in a fair value measurement

BC152   The exposure draft proposed an amendment to IAS 39[11] making it explicit that the unit of account for a financial instrument is the individual financial instrument at all levels of the fair value hierarchy. That proposal in effect would have prohibited the application of premiums and discounts related to the size of an entity's holding in a fair value measurement categorised within any level of the fair value hierarchy for financial instruments within the scope of IAS 39. The IASB proposed that amendment for the following reasons:

(a)   The unit of account for a financial instrument should not depend on an instrument's categorisation within the fair value hierarchy.

(b)   Market participants will enter into a transaction to sell a financial instrument that maximises the fair value of an asset or minimises the fair value of a liability. An entity's decision to sell at a less advantageous price because it sells an entire holding rather than each instrument individually is a factor specific to that reporting entity.

BC153   Before the amendments to Topic 820, US GAAP generally prohibited any adjustment to a quoted price in an active market for an identical asset or liability for a fair value measurement categorised within Level 1 of the fair value hierarchy (including either a blockage factor, which was described as an adjustment to a quoted price for an asset or a liability when the normal daily trading volume for the asset or liability is not sufficient to absorb the quantity held and therefore placing orders to sell the asset or liability in a single transaction might affect the quoted price, or any other premium or discount).

---

11   IFRS 9 *Financial Instruments* replaced IAS 39. IFRS 9 applies to all items that were previously within the scope of IAS 39.

However, Topic 820 did not specify whether a blockage factor (or another premium or discount, such as a control premium or a non-controlling interest discount) should be applied in a fair value measurement categorised within Level 2 or Level 3 of the fair value hierarchy if market participants would take it into account when pricing the asset or liability.

BC154 Respondents interpreted the proposal in the exposure draft as being consistent with Topic 820 for fair value measurements categorised within Level 1 of the fair value hierarchy, but they thought it was inconsistent with Topic 820 for fair value measurements categorised within Level 2 and Level 3. For example, some respondents thought that the IASB intended to prohibit the application of any premiums or discounts (such as a control premium) for fair value measurements categorised within Level 2 and Level 3 of the fair value hierarchy even when market participants would take into account a premium or discount when pricing the asset or liability for a particular unit of account.

BC155 Some respondents supported the proposal for fair value measurements categorised within Level 1 of the fair value hierarchy even though, in their view, entities do not typically exit a position on an individual instrument basis (eg by entering into a transaction to sell a single share of equity). Those respondents understood the boards' concerns about verifiability within Level 1. Other respondents stated that the fair value measurement should reflect the fair value of the entity's *holding*, not of each individual instrument within that holding (ie they did not agree that the unit of account for a financial instrument should be a single instrument). Those respondents maintained that the principle should be that the unit of account reflects how market participants would enter into a transaction for the asset or liability. They asserted that market participants would not (and often cannot) sell individual items. The FASB received similar comments when developing SFAS 157. The boards concluded that such concerns were outside the scope of the fair value measurement project because the project addressed *how* to measure fair value and not *what* is measured at fair value.

BC156 In addition, the comments received on the exposure draft indicated that respondents had different interpretations of the term *blockage factor*. Many respondents interpreted a blockage factor as any adjustment made because of the size of an asset or a liability. In the boards' view, there is a difference between size being a characteristic of the asset or liability and size being a characteristic of the entity's holding. Accordingly, the boards clarified that a blockage factor encompasses the latter and is not relevant in a fair value measurement because a fair value measurement reflects the value of the asset or liability to a market participant for a particular unit of account and is not necessarily representative of the value of the entity's entire holding.

BC157 Given the description of a blockage factor, the boards concluded that an entity's decision to realise a blockage factor is specific to that entity, not to the asset or liability. In many cases the unit of account for a financial instrument for financial reporting is the individual financial instrument. In such cases the size of an entity's holding is not relevant in a fair value measurement. An entity would realise a blockage factor when that entity decides to enter into a transaction to sell a block consisting of a large number of identical assets or liabilities. Therefore, blockage factors are conceptually similar to transaction costs in that they will differ depending on how an entity enters into a transaction for an asset or a liability. The boards concluded that if an entity decides to enter into a transaction to sell a block, the consequences of that decision should be recognised when the decision is carried out regardless of the level of the fair value hierarchy in which the fair value measurement is categorised.

BC158 Therefore, the boards decided to clarify that the application of premiums and discounts in a fair value measurement is related to the characteristics of the asset or liability being measured at fair value and its unit of account. IFRS 13 specifies that when a Level 1 input is not available, a fair value measurement should incorporate premiums or discounts if market participants would take them into account in a transaction for the asset or liability. Paragraph BC168 describes the IASB's rationale for requiring an entity to use Level 1 inputs without adjustment whenever available. However, the boards decided to clarify that the application of premiums or discounts must be consistent with the unit of account in the IFRS that requires or permits the fair value measurement.

BC159 The boards decided not to provide detailed descriptions of premiums and discounts or to provide detailed guidance about their application in a fair value measurement. They reasoned that such descriptions and guidance would be too prescriptive because the application of premiums and discounts in a fair value measurement depends on the facts and circumstances at the measurement date. In the boards' view, different facts and circumstances might lead to particular premiums or discounts being relevant for some assets and liabilities but not for others (eg in different jurisdictions). Furthermore, the boards did not intend to preclude the use of particular premiums or discounts, except for blockage factors.

Inputs based on bid and ask prices

BC160 In some situations, inputs might be determined on the basis of bid and ask prices, eg an input from a dealer market, in which the bid price represents the price the dealer is willing to pay and the ask price represents the price at which the dealer is willing to sell. IAS 39 required the use of bid prices for asset positions and ask prices for liability positions. IAS 36 and IAS 38 *Intangible Assets* had similar requirements.

BC161 The exposure draft proposed that a fair value measurement should use the price within the bid-ask spread that is most representative of fair value in the circumstances. Furthermore, the exposure draft stated that the bid-ask spread guidance applied at all levels of the fair value hierarchy, when bid and ask prices are relevant (see paragraph BC165), and did not preclude the use of mid-market pricing or other pricing conventions that are used by market participants as a practical expedient.

BC162 Many respondents supported the proposal because in their experience different market participants enter into transactions at different prices within a bid-ask spread. Some respondents preferred a single bid-ask spread pricing method, as described in IAS 39, because it would maximise the consistency and comparability of fair value measurements using bid and ask prices.

BC163   The IASB observed that, in many situations, bid and ask prices establish the boundaries within which market participants would negotiate the price in the exchange for the asset or liability. Having clarified the fair value measurement objective, the IASB concluded that an entity should use judgement in meeting that objective. Accordingly, IFRS 13 states that a fair value measurement should use the price within the bid-ask spread that is most representative of fair value in the circumstances, and that the use of bid prices for asset positions and ask prices for liability positions is permitted but is not required.

BC164   IAS 39 stated that the *bid-ask spread* includes only transaction costs. In IAS 39 other adjustments to arrive at fair value (eg for counterparty credit risk) were not included in the term *bid-ask spread*. Some respondents asked whether the proposed bid-ask guidance reflected that view. Although the boards decided not to specify what, if anything, is in a bid-ask spread besides transaction costs, in the boards' view the bid-ask spread does not include adjustments for counterparty credit risk (see paragraphs BC124–BC127 for a discussion on adjustments for counterparty credit risk when measuring fair value). Therefore, an entity will need to make an assessment of what is in the bid-ask spread for an asset or a liability when determining the point within the bid-ask spread that is most representative of fair value in the circumstances.

BC165   Some respondents noted that there could be a difference between entry prices and exit prices when entities enter into transactions at different points within the bid-ask spread. For example, an entity might buy an asset at the ask price (entry price) and measure fair value using the bid price (exit price). The boards concluded that bid-ask spreads are only relevant for financial instruments and in markets in which an intermediary (eg a broker) is necessary to bring together a buyer and a seller to engage in a transaction (ie when the buyer and seller need an intermediary to find one another). When measuring the fair value of a non-financial asset or non-financial liability, the notion of a bid-ask spread will not be relevant because the buyers and sellers in the principal (or most advantageous) market have already found one another and are assumed to have negotiated the transaction price (ie fair value).

Fair value hierarchy

BC166   IFRS 13 uses a three-level fair value hierarchy, as follows:

     (a)   Level 1 comprises unadjusted quoted prices in active markets for identical assets and liabilities.

     (b)   Level 2 comprises other observable inputs not included within Level 1 of the fair value hierarchy.

     (c)   Level 3 comprises unobservable inputs (including the entity's own data, which are adjusted if necessary to reflect the assumptions market participants would use in the circumstances).

BC167   The IASB noted that many IFRSs already contained an implicit fair value hierarchy by referring to observable market transactions or measuring fair value using a valuation technique. For example, the following three-level measurement hierarchy was implicit in IAS 39 and IFRS 9:

     (a)   financial instruments quoted in an active market;

(b)   financial instruments whose fair value is evidenced by comparison with other observable current market transactions in the same instrument (ie without modification or repackaging) or based on a valuation technique whose variables include only data from observable markets; and

(c)   financial instruments whose fair value is determined in whole or in part using a valuation technique based on assumptions that are not supported by prices from observable current market transactions in the same instrument (ie without modification or repackaging) and not based on available observable market data.

Level 1 inputs

BC168   Level 1 inputs are unadjusted quoted prices in active markets for identical assets and liabilities. The IASB concluded that those prices generally provide the most reliable evidence of fair value and should be used to measure fair value whenever available.

BC169   IFRS 13 defines an active market as a market in which transactions for the asset or liability take place with sufficient frequency and volume to provide pricing information on an ongoing basis. The IASB concluded that although different words are used, that definition is consistent with the definitions of an active market already in IFRSs:

(a)   IASs 36, 38 and 41 stated that an active market is one in which '(i) the items traded in the market are homogeneous; (ii) willing buyers and sellers can normally be found at any time; and (iii) prices are available to the public.'

(b)   IAS 39 and IFRS 9 stated that an active market is one in which 'quoted prices are readily and regularly available from an exchange, dealer, broker, industry group, pricing service or regulatory agency, and those prices represent actual and regularly occurring market transactions on an arm's length basis.'

BC170   IFRS 13 states that when an entity holds a large number of similar assets and liabilities that are required to be measured at fair value and a quoted price in an active market is not readily accessible for each of those assets and liabilities, the entity can use an alternative pricing method that does not rely exclusively on quoted prices as a practical expedient (although the resulting fair value measurement is a lower level measurement). For example, an entity might hold a large number of similar debt instruments (such as sovereign debt securities) and use matrix pricing, which does not rely exclusively on quoted prices, to measure the fair value of those instruments. In such a situation, although a Level 1 input is used to measure fair value, the fair value measurement would not be categorised within Level 1 of the fair value hierarchy. That is a departure from the principle that a fair value measurement should maximise the use of relevant observable inputs. However, the IASB regards this particular practical expedient as justified on cost-benefit grounds.

Level 2 inputs

BC171   Level 2 inputs are all inputs other than quoted prices included in Level 1 that are observable (either directly or indirectly) for the asset or liability. The IASB concluded that it is appropriate to include in Level 2 market-corroborated inputs that might not be directly observable, but are based on or supported by observable market data, because such inputs are less subjective than unobservable inputs classified within Level 3.

Level 3 inputs

BC172   Level 3 inputs are unobservable inputs for the asset or liability.

BC173   Some respondents stated that it would be misleading to describe a measurement using significant unobservable inputs as a fair value measurement. They also expressed concerns that unobservable inputs may include entity-specific factors that market participants would not consider. Therefore, they suggested that the IASB should use a different label for measurements that use significant unobservable inputs. However, the IASB concluded that it would be more helpful to users of financial statements to use the label *fair value* for all three levels of the hierarchy described in the exposure draft, for the following reasons:

(a)   The proposed definition of fair value identifies a clear objective for valuation techniques and the inputs to them: consider all factors that market participants would consider and exclude all factors that market participants would exclude. An alternative label for Level 3 measurements would be unlikely to identify such a clear objective.

(b)   The distinction between Levels 2 and 3 is inevitably subjective. It is undesirable to adopt different measurement objectives on either side of such a subjective boundary.

Rather than requiring a different label for measurements derived using significant unobservable inputs, the IASB concluded that concerns about the subjectivity of those measurements are best addressed by requiring enhanced disclosure for those measurements (see paragraphs BC187–BC210).

BC174   The IASB accepts that the starting point for Level 3 inputs might be estimates developed by the entity. However, the entity must adjust those inputs if reasonably available information indicates that other market participants would use different data when pricing the asset or liability or there is something particular to the entity that is not available to other market participants (eg an entity-specific synergy).

BC175   Some respondents expressed concerns that an entity would be compelled by its auditors or regulators to undertake exhaustive efforts to obtain information about the assumptions that market participants would use when pricing the asset or liability. Furthermore, they were concerned that their judgement would be questioned when asserting the absence of contrary data. IFRS 13 states that such exhaustive efforts would not be necessary. However, when information about market participant assumptions is reasonably available, an entity cannot ignore it.

Measuring fair value when the volume or level of activity for an asset or a liability has significantly decreased

BC176 The global financial crisis that started in 2007 emphasised the importance of having common fair value measurement requirements in IFRSs and US GAAP, particularly for measuring fair value when the market activity for an asset or a liability declines. As a result, and consistently with the recommendations of the Group of Twenty (G20) Leaders, the Financial Stability Board and the IASB's and FASB's Financial Crisis Advisory Group, the IASB and the FASB worked together to develop common requirements for measuring the fair value of assets and liabilities when markets are no longer active.

BC177 In May 2008 the IASB set up a Fair Value Expert Advisory Panel in response to recommendations made by the Financial Stability Forum (now the Financial Stability Board) to address the measurement and disclosure of financial instruments when markets are no longer active. The Panel's discussions were observed by FASB staff. In October 2008 the IASB staff published a staff report on the Panel's discussions.

BC178 Also in response to the global financial crisis, in April 2009 the FASB issued FASB Staff Position (FSP) No. FAS 157-4 *Determining Fair Value When the Volume and Level of Activity for the Asset or Liability Have Significantly Decreased and Identifying Transactions That Are Not Orderly*. That FSP was codified in Topic 820 and provides guidance for:

(a) measuring fair value when the volume or level of activity for the asset or liability has significantly decreased; and

(b) identifying circumstances that indicate a transaction is not orderly.

BC179 IASB published a Request for Views that asked respondents whether they believed that the guidance in that FSP was consistent with the Panel's report. The IASB also asked members of the Fair Value Expert Advisory Panel the same question. The IASB received 69 responses to the Request for Views. The respondents to the Request for Views and the members of the Fair Value Expert Advisory Panel indicated that the FSP was consistent with the Panel's report. As a result, the IASB included the guidance from FSP FAS 157-4 in the exposure draft.

BC180 Respondents to the exposure draft generally agreed with the proposed guidance and found it consistent with the concepts in the IASB's Fair Value Expert Advisory Panel's report and in US GAAP. However, some respondents noted that the words used in the exposure draft were different from those used in US GAAP and wondered whether the requirements were meant to be different. The boards acknowledged those concerns and decided to align the wording. In addition, the boards decided to clarify that the requirements pertain to when there has been a significant decline in the volume or level of activity for the asset or liability, not to assets and liabilities for which there is typically no observable market.

BC181 Furthermore, the boards concluded that when applying IFRS 13 and Topic 820 an entity should focus on whether an observed transaction price is the result of an orderly transaction, not only on the level of activity in a market, because even in a market with little activity, transactions can be orderly. Accordingly, the boards concluded that an entity should consider observable transaction prices unless there is evidence that the transaction is not orderly. If an entity does not have sufficient information to determine whether a transaction is orderly, it performs further analysis to measure fair value.

BC182   Also as a result of the global financial crisis, there was a particularly urgent need to improve transparency of fair value measurements for financial instruments. To address that need, the IASB amended IFRS 7 *Financial Instruments: Disclosures* in March 2009. The amended disclosures about fair value measurements have been relocated to IFRS 13.

Disclosure

BC183   The disclosures about fair value measurements in IFRSs vary, although many require, at a minimum, information about the methods and significant assumptions used in the measurement, and whether fair value was measured using observable prices from recent market transactions for the same or a similar asset or liability.

BC184   The IASB decided that having established a framework for measuring fair value, it should also enhance and harmonise the disclosures about fair value measurements. The IASB decided to limit the disclosures to fair values measured in the statement of financial position after initial recognition, whether those measurements are made on a recurring or non-recurring basis, because other IFRSs address the disclosure of fair values at initial recognition (eg IFRS 3 requires disclosure of the measurement of assets acquired and liabilities assumed in a business combination).

BC185   The objective of the disclosures in IFRS 13 is to provide users of financial statements with information about the valuation techniques and inputs used to develop fair value measurements and how fair value measurements using significant unobservable inputs affected profit or loss or other comprehensive income for the period. To meet those objectives, the disclosure framework (a) combines the disclosures currently required by IFRSs and US GAAP and (b) provides additional disclosures that users of financial statements suggested would be helpful in their analyses. In developing the disclosures, the IASB used information received from users and preparers of financial statements and the IASB's Fair Value Expert Advisory Panel.

Distinguishing between recurring and non-recurring fair value measurements

BC186   The disclosures in US GAAP differentiate fair value measurements that are recurring from those that are non-recurring. The exposure draft did not propose differentiating recurring from non-recurring fair value measurements and required the same information about all fair value measurements. However, users of financial statements asked the IASB to include the same principles for disclosing information about fair value measurements in IFRSs that are in US GAAP. As a result, the boards decided to differentiate the two types of fair value measurements and to describe their differences.

Information about fair value measurements categorised within Level 3 of the fair value hierarchy

BC187   The boards received requests from users of financial statements for more information about fair value measurements categorised within Level 3 of the fair value hierarchy. The following sections describe the boards' response to those requests.

Quantitative information

BC188   The exposure draft proposed requiring an entity to disclose the methods and inputs used in a fair value measurement, including the information used to develop those inputs. That proposal was developed using feedback from users of financial statements and the IASB's Fair Value Expert Advisory Panel. Although the proposal was not explicit, the IASB intended that the information about the inputs used in the measurement would be quantitative.

BC189   Before the amendments to Topic 820, US GAAP required an entity to provide a description of the inputs used when measuring the fair value of an asset or a liability that is categorised within Level 2 or Level 3 of the fair value hierarchy. Topic 820 was not explicit about whether that description needed to include quantitative information.

BC190   Users of financial statements asked the boards to clarify that entities must provide quantitative information about the inputs used in a fair value measurement, particularly information about unobservable inputs used in a measurement categorised within Level 3 of the fair value hierarchy. When limited or no information is publicly available, disclosures about such information help users to understand the measurement uncertainty inherent in the fair value measurement.

BC191   Therefore, the boards decided to clarify that an entity should disclose *quantitative* information about the significant unobservable inputs used in a fair value measurement categorised within Level 3 of the fair value hierarchy.

BC192   Some respondents to the FASB's proposed ASU questioned the usefulness of quantitative information about the unobservable inputs used in a fair value measurement because of the level of aggregation required in those disclosures. The boards noted that the objective of the disclosure is not to enable users of financial statements to replicate the entity's pricing models, but to provide enough information for users to assess whether the entity's views about individual inputs differed from their own and, if so, to decide how to incorporate the entity's fair value measurement in their decisions. The boards concluded that the information required by the disclosure will facilitate comparison of the inputs used over time, providing users with information about changes in management's views about particular unobservable inputs and about changes in the market for the assets and liabilities within a particular class. In addition, that disclosure might facilitate comparison between entities with similar assets and liabilities categorised within Level 3 of the fair value hierarchy.

BC193   IFRS 13 and Topic 820 state that an entity should determine appropriate classes of assets and liabilities on the basis of the nature, characteristics and risks of the assets and liabilities, noting that further disaggregation might be required for fair value measurements categorised within Level 3 of the fair value hierarchy. Consequently, the boards concluded that the meaningfulness of the disclosure of quantitative information used in Level 3 fair value measurements will depend on an entity's determination of its asset and liability classes.

BC194 Some respondents to the IASB's re-exposure document and the FASB's proposed ASU suggested requiring quantitative information about the unobservable inputs used in fair value measurements categorised within Level 2 of the fair value hierarchy because determining whether to categorise fair value measurements within Level 2 or Level 3 can be subjective. The boards concluded that for a fair value measurement to be categorised within Level 2 of the fair value hierarchy, the unobservable inputs used, if any, must not be significant to the measurement in its entirety. As a result, the boards decided that quantitative information about unobservable inputs would be of limited use for those measurements.

BC195 In addition, the boards understand that fair value is sometimes measured on the basis of prices in prior transactions (eg adjustments to the last round of financing for a venture capital investment) or third-party pricing information (eg broker quotes). Such measurements might be categorised within Level 3 of the fair value hierarchy. In such cases, the boards concluded that an entity should be required to disclose how it has measured the fair value of the asset or liability, but that it should not need to create quantitative information (eg an implied market multiple or future cash flows) to comply with the disclosure requirement if quantitative information other than the prior transaction price or third-party pricing information is not used when measuring fair value. However, the boards concluded that when using a prior transaction price or third-party pricing information, an entity cannot ignore other quantitative information that is reasonably available. If there was an adjustment to the price in a prior transaction or third-party pricing information that is significant to the fair value measurement in its entirety, that adjustment would be an unobservable input about which the entity would disclose quantitative information even if the entity does not disclose the unobservable information used when pricing the prior transaction or developing the third-party pricing information.

Level 3 reconciliation for recurring fair value measurements

BC196 The exposure draft proposed requiring an entity to provide a reconciliation from the opening balances to the closing balances of fair value measurements categorised within Level 3 of the fair value hierarchy. IFRS 7 required such a disclosure for financial instruments after it was amended in March 2009 to introduce a three-level fair value hierarchy, and to require more detailed information about fair value measurements categorised within Level 3 of the fair value hierarchy. In addition, many IFRSs already required a similar reconciliation for all fair value measurements, not only for those that are categorised within Level 3 of the fair value hierarchy.

BC197 Some respondents agreed with the proposed reconciliation disclosure because they thought it would help meet the objective to provide meaningful information to users of financial statements about the relative subjectivity of fair value measurements. Other respondents thought that the disclosure requirement would be onerous and did not believe that the benefits would outweigh the costs, particularly for non-financial assets and liabilities. The IASB received similar feedback on the proposed amendments to IFRS 7. However, users of financial statements told the IASB that the disclosures made in accordance with US GAAP and IFRS 7 were helpful, particularly in the light of the global financial crisis that started in 2007. They indicated that the disclosures allowed them to make more informed judgements and to segregate the effects of fair value measurements that are inherently subjective, thereby enhancing their ability to assess the quality of an entity's reported earnings. Consequently, the IASB decided to require an entity to provide such a reconciliation.

BC198   The exposure draft and IFRS 7 did not distinguish between *realised* and *unrealised* gains or losses. That was because those documents referred to *gains or losses attributable to assets and liabilities held at the end of the reporting period*, which the IASB meant to be equivalent to unrealised gains or losses (ie realised gains or losses result from the sale, disposal or settlement of an asset or a liability, and therefore the asset or liability is no longer held by the entity at the reporting date, whereas unrealised gains or losses relate to changes in the fair value of an asset or a liability that is held by the entity at the reporting date). Respondents to the exposure draft wondered whether the different terminology used in the exposure draft and in Topic 820 meant that the disclosure proposed for IFRSs would be different from the disclosure required by US GAAP. To ensure that there would be no differences in interpretation of the requirements in IFRSs and US GAAP, the IASB decided to use the terms *realised* and *unrealised* in the reconciliation disclosure.

BC199   The IASB concluded that the disclosure should focus on recurring fair value measurements because it would be difficult to reconcile the opening balances to the closing balances for non-recurring fair value measurements when the carrying amount of an asset or a liability is not determined on the basis of fair value at each reporting period. For example, it would be difficult to reconcile changes in fair value when an asset held for sale is recognised at its carrying amount in accordance with IFRS 5 in one period and at fair value less costs to sell in the next period. The information gained from requiring a reconciliation of changes in fair value from one period to the next is not available when requiring changes resulting from the use of different measurement bases from one period to the next.

Valuation processes

BC200   The boards decided to require an entity to disclose the valuation processes used for fair value measurements categorised within Level 3 of the fair value hierarchy (including, for example, how an entity decides its valuation policies and procedures and analyses changes in fair value measurements from period to period). They made that decision because users of financial statements told the boards that information about an entity's valuation processes helps them assess the relative subjectivity of the entity's fair value measurements, particularly for those categorised within Level 3 of the fair value hierarchy.

BC201   In addition, the requirements in IFRS 13 are consistent with the conclusions of the IASB's Fair Value Expert Advisory Panel as described in its report in October 2008.

Sensitivity to changes in unobservable inputs

BC202   The exposure draft proposed requiring a quantitative sensitivity analysis for fair value measurements categorised within Level 3 of the fair value hierarchy. That proposal was taken from the requirement in IFRS 7 to disclose a sensitivity analysis if changing any of the unobservable inputs used in the measurement to reasonably possible alternative assumptions would change the fair value significantly. Although in IFRS 7 that disclosure was required for financial assets and financial liabilities measured at fair value, under the proposal it would have been required for all assets and liabilities measured at fair value.

BC203   In August 2009 the FASB proposed a similar disclosure requirement in its proposed ASU *Fair Value Measurements and Disclosures (Topic 820): Improving Disclosures about Fair Value Measurements*, although that proposal would have required an entity to take into account the effect of interrelationships between inputs. Very few respondents to that proposed ASU supported the proposed disclosure, stating that it would not provide useful information and would be costly and operationally challenging. However, users were supportive of the proposed disclosure. The FASB decided to defer the consideration of a sensitivity analysis disclosure requirement to the joint fair value measurement project.

BC204   In the boards' discussions about that sensitivity analysis disclosure, they considered whether the IASB's proposed disclosure and that in IFRS 7 would be improved if the boards required an entity to include the effect of interrelationships between unobservable inputs, thereby showing a range of fair values (exit prices) that reasonably could have been measured in the circumstances as of the measurement date. Because that refinement of the disclosure was not included in the IASB's May 2009 exposure draft and was not required by IFRS 7, the IASB needed to expose the proposal to require the sensitivity analysis including the effect of interrelationships between unobservable inputs. That disclosure was referred to in the IASB's re-exposure document and the FASB's proposed ASU in June 2010 as a *measurement uncertainty analysis disclosure*.

BC205   Respondents to the FASB's proposed ASU and the IASB's re-exposure document were concerned about whether the proposal would be operational (those comments were consistent with those received on the FASB's proposed ASU in August 2009). Although that proposal was in response to requests from users of financial statements to require additional information about the measurement uncertainty inherent in fair value measurements (particularly those categorised within Level 3 of the fair value hierarchy), the responses from preparers of financial statements indicated that the costs associated with preparing such a disclosure would outweigh the benefits to users once the information had been aggregated by class of asset or liability. As an alternative to the proposal, those respondents suggested that the boards should require a qualitative assessment of the subjectivity of fair value measurements categorised within Level 3 of the fair value hierarchy, as well as an alternative quantitative approach that would be less costly to prepare (see paragraphs BC188–BC195).

BC206　Therefore, the boards decided to require an entity to provide a narrative description, by class of asset or liability, of the sensitivity of a recurring fair value measurement categorised within Level 3 of the fair value hierarchy to changes in the unobservable inputs used in the measurement if a change in those inputs to a different amount would result in a significantly higher or lower fair value measurement. If there are interrelationships between those inputs and other unobservable inputs, the boards decided to require an entity to provide a description of those interrelationships and of how they might magnify or mitigate the effect of changes in the unobservable inputs on the fair value measurement. The boards concluded that such information would provide users of financial statements with information about how the selection of unobservable inputs affects the valuation of a particular class of assets or liabilities. The boards expect that the narrative description will focus on the unobservable inputs for which quantitative information is disclosed because those are the unobservable inputs that the entity has determined are most significant to the fair value measurement. They will continue to assess whether a quantitative measurement uncertainty analysis disclosure would be practical after issuing IFRS 13, with the aim of reaching a conclusion about whether to require such a disclosure at a later date.

BC207　The boards concluded that a narrative description about sensitivity provides users of financial statements with information about the directional effect of a change in a significant unobservable input on a fair value measurement. That disclosure, coupled with quantitative information about the inputs used in fair value measurements categorised within Level 3 of the fair value hierarchy, provides information for users to assess whether the entity's views about individual inputs differed from their own and, if so, to decide how to incorporate the entity's fair value measurement in their decisions. In addition, that disclosure provides information about the pricing model for those users who are not familiar with the valuation of a particular class of assets or liabilities (eg complex financial instruments).

BC208　In addition to the narrative sensitivity analysis disclosure, IFRS 13 requires a quantitative sensitivity analysis for financial instruments that are measured at fair value and categorised within Level 3 of the fair value hierarchy (ie the disclosure that was previously in IFRS 7). The IASB decided to move that requirement from IFRS 7 to IFRS 13 so that all the fair value measurement disclosure requirements in IFRSs are in a single location. When developing IFRS 7, the IASB concluded that information about the sensitivities of fair value measurements to the main valuation assumptions would provide users of financial statements with a sense of the potential variability of the measurement. In forming that conclusion, the IASB considered the view that disclosure of sensitivities could be difficult, particularly when there are many assumptions to which the disclosure would apply and those assumptions are interdependent. However, the IASB noted that a detailed quantitative disclosure of sensitivity to all assumptions is not required (only those that could result in a significantly different estimate of fair value are required) and that the disclosure does not require the entity to reflect interdependencies between assumptions when making the disclosure.

BC209   The boards concluded that the objective of the narrative and quantitative sensitivity analysis disclosures about fair value are different from the objectives of other disclosures that an entity may be required to make in IFRSs and US GAAP, such as the market risk sensitivity analysis disclosure required by IFRS 7 (see paragraph 40 of IFRS 7). The IASB concluded that even though there is some overlap in those disclosures, the objective of each disclosure is different: the market risk sensitivity analysis disclosure in IFRS 7 provides information about an entity's exposure to future changes in market risks (ie currency risk, interest rate risk and other price risk), whereas the fair value measurement disclosures provide information about the sensitivity of the fair value measurement at the measurement date to changes in unobservable inputs for those fair value measurements with the greatest level of subjectivity (ie fair value measurements categorised within Level 3 of the fair value hierarchy). In addition, the market risk sensitivity analysis disclosure in IFRS 7 relates only to financial instruments (as does the quantitative sensitivity analysis disclosure in IFRS 13), whereas the narrative sensitivity analysis disclosure in IFRS 13 relates to all assets and liabilities measured at fair value.

BC210   The IASB identified the following differences between the market risk and fair value sensitivity analysis disclosures:

(a)   The market risk disclosure is not specific to financial instruments measured at fair value, but also relates to financial instruments measured at amortised cost.

(b)   The market risk disclosure focuses on the effect on profit or loss and equity, not specifically on the change in value.

(c)   The market risk disclosure focuses only on the entity's exposure to market risks (ie interest rate risk, currency risk or other price risk), whereas the fair value disclosures take into account the effect on a fair value measurement of changes in significant unobservable inputs.

(d)   The market risk disclosure does not distinguish between observable and unobservable inputs (or level in the fair value hierarchy, ie Level 1, 2 or 3), whereas the fair value disclosures relate only to the unobservable inputs used in fair value measurements categorised within Level 3 of the fair value hierarchy.

Transfers between Levels 1 and 2 of the fair value hierarchy

BC211   The exposure draft proposed requiring an entity to disclose the amounts of *significant* transfers into or out of Level 1 and Level 2 of the fair value hierarchy and the reasons for those transfers. That disclosure was also required in Topic 820. In their discussions, the boards decided instead to require a disclosure of *any* transfers into or out of Levels 1 and 2. Respondents to the FASB's proposed ASU generally did not support that proposal because it would require an entity to monitor all transfers on a daily basis, regardless of whether those transfers were significant. In addition, respondents were concerned about the accuracy of information about all transfers because there can be an unclear distinction between less active Level 1 fair value measurements and more active Level 2 fair value measurements.

BC212   The boards concluded that the objective of the disclosure is to provide information that will help users of financial statements assess changes in market and trading activity (the entity's or others') so that users can (a) incorporate into their analyses the entity's future liquidity risk and (b) analyse the entity's exposure to the relative subjectivity of its fair value measurements. In the boards' view, the only way to provide that information, and to reduce the subjectivity involved in preparing the information, is to require information about *all* transfers between Level 1 and Level 2 of the fair value hierarchy.

When an entity uses a non-financial asset in a way that differs from its highest and best use

BC213   The boards decided to require an entity to disclose information about when it uses a non-financial asset in a way that differs from its highest and best use (when that asset is measured at fair value in the statement of financial position or when its fair value is disclosed). The boards concluded that such a disclosure provides useful information for users of financial statements that rely on fair value information when forecasting future cash flows, whether that fair value information is presented in the statement of financial position or is disclosed in the notes. Users told the boards that they would need to know how non-financial assets are being used and how that use fits with an entity's strategic and operating plans.

BC214   The boards considered whether to limit the disclosure to some non-financial assets and not others. The boards concluded that because the measurement and disclosure requirements are principle-based, those requirements should not need to be amended in the future if the boards should decide to use fair value as the measurement basis for particular assets or liabilities. Therefore, the disclosure is required for any non-financial asset measured at fair value that an entity uses in a way that differs from its highest and best use.

The categorisation within the level of the fair value hierarchy for items that are not measured at fair value in the statement of financial position

BC215   IFRS 7 requires an entity to disclose the fair value of financial instruments even if they are not measured at fair value in the statement of financial position. An example is a financial instrument that is measured at amortised cost in the statement of financial position.

BC216   The boards decided to require an entity to disclose the level of the fair value hierarchy in which an asset or a liability (financial or non-financial) would be categorised if that asset or liability had been measured at fair value in the statement of financial position. The boards concluded that such a disclosure would provide meaningful information about the relative subjectivity of that fair value measurement.

BC217   Respondents to the IASB's exposure draft and the FASB's proposed ASU were concerned about the cost associated with preparing that disclosure because it is not always clear in which level a fair value measurement would be categorised. The boards concluded that even if determining the level in which to categorise a fair value measurement requires judgement, the benefits of doing so outweigh the costs. Therefore, the boards decided to require an entity to disclose the level of the fair value hierarchy in which an asset or a liability would be categorised if that asset or liability had been measured at fair value in the statement of financial position.

Assets with a recoverable amount that is fair value less costs of disposal

BC218 Because IAS 36 requires disclosures that are specific to impaired assets, the exposure draft did not propose requiring the disclosures about fair value measurements for assets with a recoverable amount that is fair value less costs of disposal in IAS 36. Some respondents (mainly users of financial statements) noted that the disclosures about impaired assets are different in IFRSs and in US GAAP (which requires assets to be tested for impairment by comparing their carrying amounts with their fair values) and asked the IASB to minimise those differences to ensure that users have access to similar information for their analyses of impaired assets.

BC219 The IASB noted that the disclosure requirements in IAS 36 were developed specifically to ensure consistency in the disclosure of information about impaired assets so that the same type of information is provided whether the recoverable amount was determined on the basis of value in use or fair value less costs of disposal. Consequently, the IASB did not think it would be appropriate to require an entity to provide information when the recoverable amount is determined on the basis of fair value less costs of disposal (ie as required by IFRS 13) that is significantly different from what the entity would provide when the recoverable amount is determined on the basis of value in use.

BC220 Although IFRSs and US GAAP have different impairment models, the IASB concluded that requiring the following information (in addition to what IAS 36 currently requires) about impaired assets measured at fair value less costs of disposal would improve comparability between entities applying IFRSs and those applying US GAAP as well as increase the convergence of IFRSs and US GAAP:

(a) the fair value less costs of disposal;

(b) the level of the fair value hierarchy within which the fair value less costs of disposal is categorised in its entirety (Level 1, 2 or 3);

(c) if applicable, changes to valuation techniques and reasons for those changes; and

(d) quantitative information about significant inputs used when measuring fair value less costs of disposal (along with a conforming amendment to the disclosures about value in use).

BC221 In addition, those disclosures are consistent with the disclosures required for non-recurring fair value measurements in IFRS 13 and in US GAAP.

Interim financial reporting

BC222 For financial instruments, the exposure draft proposed that particular fair value disclosures required in annual financial statements would also be required for interim financial reports. That differed from the approach proposed for non-financial assets and non-financial liabilities, for which there is no specific fair value disclosure requirement beyond the existing requirements in IAS 34 *Interim Financial Reporting*.

BC223 Respondents generally thought that the principle underlying IAS 34 addresses when disclosures should be updated in interim financial reports. Some respondents thought the costs of providing updated information outweighed the benefits to users of financial statements of having that information.

BC224 The IASB decided to include in IAS 34 an explicit requirement to provide updated disclosures because it concluded that the benefit of having incremental disclosures for financial instruments outweighed the associated costs given the increased interest in those instruments during the global financial crisis that started in 2007.

Effective date and transition

BC225 When deciding the effective date for IFRS 13, the IASB considered the comments received on the Request for Views *Effective Date and Transition Methods*. Many respondents said that the effective date should allow enough time for them to put the necessary systems in place to ensure that their accounting policies and models meet the requirements of IFRS 13. Some of those respondents, particularly those with many assets and liabilities measured at fair value, requested a later effective date. Other respondents requested an earlier effective date, mainly for comparability reasons and because in their view many entities might have inadvertently already started applying the revised concepts.

BC226 The IASB concluded that although IFRS 13 is a major new standard, it does not require any new fair value measurements and it does not fundamentally change many of the requirements for measuring fair value or for disclosing information about those measurements. The IASB concluded that in many respects, IFRS 13 uses different words to articulate the concepts already present in IFRSs. However, the IASB also considered the time that a particular country might require for translation and for introducing the mandatory requirements into law.

BC227 Consequently, the IASB decided that IFRS 13 should be effective for annual periods beginning on or after 1 January 2013. Because IFRS 13 applies when other IFRSs require or permit fair value measurements (and does not introduce any new fair value measurements), the IASB believes that the extended transition period for IFRS 13 provides enough time for entities, their auditors and users of financial statements to prepare for implementation of its requirements.

BC228 The IASB decided to permit early application of IFRS 13 because that would allow entities to apply the measurement and disclosure requirements as soon as practicable, thereby improving comparability in measurement and transparency in disclosures. That would also improve comparability with entities applying US GAAP.

BC229 The exposure draft proposed prospective application because the IASB concluded that a change in the methods used to measure fair value would be inseparable from a change in the fair value measurements (ie as new events occur or as new information is obtained, eg through better insight or improved judgement). Respondents to the exposure draft and the Request for Views supported that proposal. Therefore, the IASB concluded that IFRS 13 should be applied prospectively (in the same way as a change in accounting estimate).

BC230 To achieve comparability in future periods, the IASB decided to require the disclosures in IFRS 13 for the first interim period in which the IFRS is initially applied. However, those disclosures need not be presented in periods before initial application of the IFRS because it would be difficult to apply some of the requirements in IFRS 13 without the use of hindsight in selecting the inputs that would have been appropriate in prior periods.

BC230A *Annual Improvements Cycle 2011–2013* issued in December 2013 amended paragraph 52 and added paragraph C4 to clarify the scope of the portfolio exception. It considered the transition provisions and effective date of the amendments to IFRS 13. It decided that an entity should apply that amendment for annual periods beginning on or after 1 July 2014. In order to be consistent with the prospective initial application of IFRS 13, the IASB decided that an entity would apply the amendment to IFRS 13 prospectively from the beginning of the annual period in which IFRS 13 was initially applied.

Application in emerging and transition economies

BC231 During the development of IFRS 13, the IASB received information from entities in emerging and transition economies that had concerns about applying the fair value measurement principles in IFRS 13 in their jurisdictions. Common concerns included the following:

(a) The fair value measurement guidance is not detailed enough to allow them to measure fair value on a consistent basis.

(b) There is limited availability of practitioners in their jurisdictions who have the skills to apply the guidance (and as a result entities might be unfamiliar with applying the necessary judgements).

(c) There is limited access to market data to develop fair value measurements because there are few deep and liquid markets, there are often few willing buyers and sellers and prices often fluctuate considerably within short periods of time.

(d) Models, inputs and assumptions may be new and may not be comparable across entities because of rapidly developing socio-economic changes.

(e) Measuring fair value (and preparing the resulting disclosures) could be expensive.

BC232 The IASB noted that because fair value is used in many IFRSs, knowledge about its application is necessary for applying IFRSs generally and noted that the concerns raised are not specific to entities in emerging and transition economies. Entities in developed economies faced similar challenges during the global financial crisis that started in 2007 and asked the IASB for guidance for measuring the fair value of equity instruments without active markets given the requirement to recognise them at fair value in IFRS 9. Furthermore, the IASB concluded that there should not be a different threshold for measuring fair value depending on jurisdiction. Only by performing fair value measurements will entities applying IFRSs learn how to do those measurements appropriately and robustly.

BC233 Therefore, the IASB concluded that entities applying IFRSs would benefit from educational material to accompany IFRS 13. The IFRS Foundation sometimes publishes educational material that is leveraged from the standard-setting process to reinforce the goal of promoting the adoption and consistent application of a single set of high quality international accounting standards. The IASB asked the staff to develop educational material on fair value measurement that describes at a high level the thought process for measuring assets, liabilities and an entity's own equity instruments at fair value consistent with the objective of a fair value measurement.

BC234 The IASB concluded that any educational material developed must benefit all entities equally. Thus, the educational material cannot benefit entities in emerging and transition economies without being made available to entities in developed economies.

BC235 The IASB staff and the FASB staff will liaise during the development of the educational material.

Convergence with US GAAP

BC236 As noted above, the fair value measurement project was a joint project with the FASB. The boards worked together to ensure that fair value has the same meaning in IFRSs and in US GAAP and that their respective fair value measurement and disclosure requirements are the same (except for minor differences in wording and style).

BC237 The boards worked together to ensure that, to the extent possible, IFRS 13 and Topic 820 are identical. The following style differences remain:

(a) There are differences in references to other IFRSs and US GAAP—For example, regarding related party transactions, IFRS 13 refers to IAS 24 *Related Party Disclosures* and Topic 820 refers to Topic 850 *Related Party Disclosures*.

(b) There are differences in style—For example, IFRS 13 refers to *an entity* and Topic 820 refers to *a reporting entity*.

(c) There are differences in spelling—For example, IFRS 13 refers to *labour costs* and Topic 820 refers to *labor costs*.

(d) There are differences in whether references are to a particular jurisdiction or are generic—For example, IFRS 13 refers to *risk-free government securities* and Topic 820 refers to *US Treasury securities*.

The boards concluded that those differences will not result in inconsistent interpretations in practice by entities applying IFRSs or US GAAP.

BC238   In addition, IFRS 13 and Topic 820 have the following differences:

(a)   There are different accounting requirements in IFRSs and US GAAP for measuring the fair value of investments in investment companies. Topic 946 *Financial Services—Investment Companies* in US GAAP requires an investment company to recognise its underlying investments at fair value at each reporting period. Topic 820 provides a practical expedient that permits an entity with an investment in an investment company to use as a measure of fair value in specific circumstances the reported net asset value without adjustment. IFRS 10 *Consolidated Financial Statements* requires an investment company to consolidate its controlled underlying investments. Because IFRSs do not have accounting requirements that are specific to investment companies, the IASB decided that it would be difficult to identify when such a practical expedient could be applied given the different practices for calculating net asset values in jurisdictions around the world. For example, investment companies may report in accordance with national GAAP, which may have recognition and measurement requirements that differ from those in IFRSs (ie the underlying investments might not be measured at fair value, or they might be measured at fair value in accordance with national GAAP, not IFRSs). The boards are reviewing the accounting for investment companies as part of a separate project.[12]

(b)   There are different requirements for measuring the fair value of a financial liability with a demand feature. In US GAAP, Topic 825 *Financial Instruments* and Topic 942 *Financial Services—Depository and Lending* describe the fair value measurement of a deposit liability as the amount payable on demand at the reporting date. In IFRSs, IFRS 13 states that the fair value measurement of a financial liability with a demand feature (eg demand deposits) cannot be less than the present value of the amount payable on demand. That requirement in IFRS 13 was relocated unchanged from IAS 39 and IFRS 9 as a consequence of the IASB's fair value measurement project.

(c)   There are different disclosure requirements in IFRSs and US GAAP. For example:

(i)   Because IFRSs generally do not allow net presentation for derivatives, the amounts disclosed for fair value measurements categorised within Level 3 of the fair value hierarchy might differ. The boards are reviewing the presentation requirements for offsetting financial assets and financial liabilities in their joint project on the accounting for financial instruments.

---

12 In October 2012 the Board issued *Investment Entities* (Amendments to IFRS 10, IFRS 12 and IAS 27), which required investment entities, as defined in IFRS 10 *Consolidated Financial Statements*, to measure their investments in subsidiaries, other than those providing investment-related services or activities, at fair value through profit or loss. In their redeliberations on the Investment Entities project, the Board considered providing a net asset value practical expedient. However, the Board decided against this because there are different calculation methods in different jurisdictions and it is outside the scope of the Investment Entities project to provide fair value measurement guidance for investments in investment entities.

    (ii)   IFRSs require a quantitative sensitivity analysis for financial instruments that are measured at fair value and categorised within Level 3 of the fair value hierarchy (that disclosure was previously in IFRS 7). The boards will analyse the feasibility of incorporating information about interrelationships between unobservable inputs into a quantitative measurement uncertainty analysis disclosure. After completing that analysis, the boards will decide whether to require such a disclosure.

    (iii)   Topic 820 has different disclosure requirements for non-public entities. The FASB concluded that some of the disclosures should not be required for non-public entities because of the characteristics of the users of the financial statements of those entities. The FASB considered the ability of those users to access information about the financial position of the entity and the relevance to those users of the information that would be provided by the requirements in the disclosure amendments. In contrast, the IASB recently completed a project on the accounting for small and medium-sized entities. As a result, the *IFRS for Small and Medium-Sized Entities* addresses the accounting for entities that do not have public accountability, and the disclosures about their fair value measurements.

Cost-benefit considerations

BC239   The objective of general purpose financial reporting is to provide financial information about the reporting entity that is useful to existing and potential investors, lenders and other creditors in making decisions about providing resources to the entity. To meet that objective, the IASB seeks to ensure that an IFRS will meet a significant need and that the overall benefits of the resulting information justify the costs of providing it. Although the costs to implement a new standard might not be borne evenly, users of financial statements benefit from improvements in financial reporting, thereby facilitating the functioning of markets for capital and credit and the efficient allocation of resources in the economy.

BC240   The evaluation of costs and benefits is necessarily subjective. In making its judgement, the IASB considers the following:

    (a)   the costs incurred by preparers of financial statements;

    (b)   the costs incurred by users of financial statements when information is not available;

    (c)   the comparative advantage that preparers have in developing information, compared with the costs that users would incur to develop surrogate information; and

    (d)   the benefit of better economic decision-making as a result of improved financial reporting.

BC241   IFRS 13 defines fair value, provides a framework for measuring fair value and requires disclosures about fair value measurements. A clear definition of fair value, together with a framework for measuring fair value that eliminates inconsistencies across IFRSs that have contributed to diversity in practice, should improve consistency in application, thereby enhancing the comparability of information reported in financial statements.

BC242   The disclosures about fair value measurements would increase transparency and improve the quality of information provided to users of financial statements. In developing the disclosure requirements in IFRS 13, the IASB obtained input from users and preparers of financial statements and other interested parties to enable the IASB to assess whether the disclosures could be provided within reasonable cost-benefit constraints.

BC243   Although the framework for measuring fair value builds on current practice and requirements, some methods in IFRS 13 may result in a change to practice for some entities. Furthermore, some entities will need to make systems and operational changes, thereby incurring incremental costs. Other entities also might incur incremental costs in applying the measurement and disclosure requirements. However, the IASB concluded that the benefits resulting from increased consistency in application of fair value measurement requirements and enhanced comparability of fair value information and improved communication of that information to users of financial statements will continue. On balance, the IASB concluded that improvements in financial reporting resulting from the application of the requirements in IFRS 13 will exceed the increased costs of applying the requirements.

Summary of main changes from the exposure draft

BC244   The main changes from the proposals in the exposure draft published in May 2009 are as follows:

(a)   IFRS 13 excludes from its scope share-based payment transactions in IFRS 2 and leasing transactions in IAS 17. The exposure draft proposed the following:

(i)   replacing the term *fair value* with another term that reflects the measurement objective for share-based payment transactions in IFRS 2 and for reacquired rights in a business combination in IFRS 3.

(ii)   excluding financial liabilities with a demand feature in IAS 39[13] from the scope of an IFRS on fair value measurement.

The exposure draft did not propose excluding leasing transactions from the scope of an IFRS on fair value measurement.

(b)   IFRS 13 requires fair value to be measured using the price in the principal market for the asset or liability, or in the absence of a principal market, the most advantageous market for the asset or liability. The exposure draft proposed that fair value should be measured using the price in the most advantageous market.

---

13   IFRS 9 *Financial Instruments* replaced IAS 39. IFRS 9 applies to all items that were previously within the scope of IAS 39.

(c) IFRS 13 states that market participants have a reasonable understanding about the asset or liability and the transaction using all available information, including information that might be obtained through due diligence efforts that are usual and customary. The exposure draft stated that market participants are presumed to be as knowledgeable as the entity about the asset or liability (ie there was no information asymmetry between market participants and the entity).

(d) IFRS 13 contains detailed guidance for measuring the fair value of liabilities, including the compensation market participants would require to assume the liability and how a third-party credit enhancement affects the fair value of a liability. The exposure draft provided high level guidance.

(e) IFRS 13 contains detailed guidance for measuring the fair value of an entity's own equity instruments. That guidance is consistent with the guidance for measuring the fair value of a liability. The exposure draft proposed requiring an entity to measure the fair value of its own equity instruments by reference to the fair value of the instrument held by a market participant as an asset (ie the corresponding asset) without providing information about when the fair value of the equity instrument might differ from the fair value of the corresponding asset.

(f) IFRS 13 provides guidance for measuring the fair value of financial assets and financial liabilities with offsetting positions in market risks or counterparty credit risk. The exposure draft proposed requiring financial assets to be measured using an in-exchange valuation premise.

(g) IFRS 13 states that classes of asset or liability for disclosure purposes should be determined on the basis of the nature, characteristics and risks of the asset or liability and the level of the fair value hierarchy within which the fair value measurement is categorised. The exposure draft did not provide guidance for determining the appropriate class of asset or liability for disclosures about fair value measurements.

(h) IFRS 13 provides examples of policies for when to recognise transfers between levels of the fair value hierarchy, such as the date of the transfer, the beginning of the reporting period or the end of the reporting period. IFRS 13 also states that the policy about the timing of recognising transfers must be the same for transfers into a level as that for transfers out of a level. The exposure draft did not provide guidance for determining when transfers are deemed to have occurred or propose to require an entity to disclose its policy for determining when transfers between levels are recognised.

(i) IFRS 13 requires a narrative discussion of the sensitivity of a fair value measurement categorised within Level 3 of the fair value hierarchy to changes in significant unobservable inputs and any interrelationships between those inputs that might magnify or mitigate the effect on the measurement. It also requires a quantitative sensitivity analysis for financial instruments categorised within Level 3 of the fair value hierarchy (that disclosure was relocated from IFRS 7). The exposure draft proposed a quantitative sensitivity analysis for assets and liabilities categorised within Level 3 of the fair value hierarchy. The IASB re-exposed that proposal, including a requirement to take into account the interrelationships between unobservable inputs in the analysis (referred to as a measurement uncertainty analysis disclosure). Respondents were concerned about whether the proposal would be operational. The boards will continue to assess whether a quantitative measurement uncertainty analysis disclosure would be practical after the IFRS is issued, with the aim of reaching a conclusion about whether to require such a disclosure at a later date.

(j)   IFRS 13 requires an entity to disclose information about its valuation processes (eg valuation policies and procedures) for fair value measurements categorised within Level 3 of the fair value hierarchy. The disclosure is similar to the description of valuation processes in the IASB's Fair Value Expert Advisory Panel's October 2008 report.

(k)   If the highest and best use of a non-financial asset differs from its current use, IFRS 13 requires an entity to disclose that fact and why the asset is being used in a manner that differs from its highest and best use. The exposure draft proposed requiring an entity to disclose the value of the asset assuming its current use, the amount by which the fair value of the asset differs from its fair value in its current use (ie the incremental value of the asset group) and the reasons the asset is being used in a manner that differs from its highest and best use.

Appendix
Amendments to the Basis for Conclusions on other IFRSs

This appendix contains amendments to the Basis for Conclusions on other IFRSs that are necessary in order to ensure consistency with IFRS 13 and the related amendments to other IFRSs. Amended paragraphs are shown with new text underlined and deleted text struck through.

* * * * *

The amendments contained in this appendix when IFRS 13 was issued in 2011 have been incorporated into the Basis for Conclusions on the relevant IFRSs published in this volume.

IASB documents published to accompany

IFRS 14

Regulatory Deferral Accounts

The text of the unaccompanied standard, IFRS 14, is contained in Part A of this edition. Its effective date when issued was 1 January 2016. The text of the Accompanying Guidance on IFRS 14 is contained in Part B of this edition. This part presents the following documents:

BASIS FOR CONCLUSIONS

DISSENTING OPINIONS

Contents

© IFRS Foundation

Basis for Conclusions on
IFRS 14 *Regulatory Deferral Accounts*

This Basis for Conclusions accompanies, but is not part of, IFRS 14.

Introduction

BC1   This Basis for Conclusions summarises the considerations of the International Accounting Standards Board (IASB) in reaching the conclusions in IFRS 14 *Regulatory Deferral Accounts*. Individual IASB members gave greater weight to some factors than to others.

BC2   The IASB and the IFRS Interpretations Committee (the 'Interpretations Committee') received several requests for guidance on whether rate-regulated entities can or should recognise, in their IFRS financial statements, a regulatory deferral or variance account debit or credit balance as a result of price or rate regulation by regulatory bodies or governments. Some national accounting standard-setting bodies permit or require such balances to be recognised as assets and liabilities under some circumstances, depending on the type of rate regulation in force. In such cases, these regulatory deferral account balances are often referred to as 'regulatory assets' and 'regulatory liabilities'. However, as explained in this Basis for Conclusions (see paragraphs BC11–BC12 and BC21), the term 'regulatory deferral account balances' has been chosen as a neutral descriptor for these items for the purpose of this Standard.

BC3   US generally accepted accounting principles (US GAAP) have recognised the economic effect of certain types of rate regulation since at least 1962. In 1982, the US national standard-setter, the Financial Accounting Standards Board (FASB) issued SFAS 71 *Accounting for the Effects of Certain Types of Regulation*.[1] SFAS 71 formalised many of those principles. In the absence of specific national guidance, practice in many other jurisdictions followed SFAS 71. In the financial statements of rate-regulated entities that apply such guidance, regulatory deferral account balances are often incorporated into the carrying amount of items such as property, plant and equipment and intangible assets, or are recognised as separate items in the financial statements.

BC4   In June 2005, the Interpretations Committee received a request about SFAS 71. The request asked whether an entity could apply SFAS 71 in accordance with the hierarchy in paragraphs 10–12 of IAS 8 *Accounting Policies, Changes in Accounting Estimates and Errors* when selecting an accounting policy in the absence of specific guidance in IFRS.

BC5   The Interpretations Committee previously discussed the possible recognition of regulatory deferral account debit balances as part of its project on service concessions. As a result of its consideration at that time, the Interpretations Committee concluded that "entities applying IFRS should recognise only assets that qualified for recognition in accordance with the IASB's *Framework for the*

---

1   The guidance in SFAS 71, together with subsequent amendments and related guidance, has now been incorporated into Topic 980 *Regulated Operations* in the FASB *Accounting Standards Codification*®.

Preparation and Presentation of Financial Statements[2] ... and relevant accounting standards, such as IAS 11 *Construction Contracts*, IAS 18 *Revenue*, IAS 16 *Property, Plant and Equipment* and IAS 38 *Intangible Assets*." In other words, the Interpretations Committee thought that an entity should recognise 'regulatory assets' only to the extent that they meet the criteria to be recognised as assets in accordance with existing IFRS.

BC6   The Interpretations Committee concluded that the recognition criteria in SFAS 71 were not fully consistent with the recognition criteria in IFRS. Applying the guidance in SFAS 71 would result in the recognition of regulatory deferral account balances under certain circumstances that would not meet the recognition criteria of relevant Standards. Consequently, the requirements of SFAS 71 were not indicative of the requirements of IFRS. The Interpretations Committee decided not to add a project on regulatory assets to its agenda.

BC7   In January 2008, the Interpretations Committee received a second request to consider whether rate-regulated entities could or should recognise a regulatory liability (or a regulatory asset) as a result of rate regulation by regulatory bodies or governments. The Interpretations Committee again decided not to add the issue to its agenda for several reasons. Importantly, it concluded that divergence did not seem to be significant in practice for entities that were applying IFRS. The established practice of almost all entities is to eliminate regulatory deferral account balances when IFRS is adopted and not to recognise such balances in IFRS financial statements. However, the Interpretations Committee also noted that rate regulation is widespread and significantly affects the economic environment of many entities.

BC8   The IASB noted the ongoing requests for guidance on this issue. It also considered the comments that had been received on the Interpretations Committee's tentative agenda decisions. Those comments pointed out that although divergence in IFRS practice did not exist, several jurisdictions whose local accounting principles permitted or required the recognition of regulatory deferral account balances would be adopting IFRS in the near future. This would increase pressure for definitive guidance on the recognition of regulatory deferral account balances as assets or liabilities.

BC9   Consequently, in December 2008, the IASB added a project on rate-regulated activities to its agenda and subsequently, in July 2009, published an Exposure Draft Rate-regulated Activities (the '2009 ED'). The responses to the 2009 ED raised complex and fundamental issues at a conceptual level. In September 2010, the IASB decided that the complex technical issues could not be resolved quickly, and suspended the project until it had considered whether to include rate-regulated activities in its future agenda. The 2011 Agenda Consultation asked stakeholders to provide their views as to which projects the IASB should give priority.[3] The responses to this consultation, received through comment

---

2   In September 2010, the IASB replaced the *Framework for the Preparation and Presentation of Financial Statements* with the *Conceptual Framework for Financial Reporting*. The definitions of assets and liabilities and the criteria for recognising them in the statement of financial position were unchanged.

3   In July 2011, the IASB published a formal Request for Views document to provide a channel for formal public input on the broad aspects of our agenda-setting process.

letters and other outreach activities, persuaded the IASB to prioritise addressing the unresolved issues related to rate-regulated activities.

BC10 As a result of its agenda-setting process, in September 2012 the IASB decided to add to its agenda a comprehensive project on rate-regulated activities to investigate these complex issues. In addition, the *Conceptual Framework for Financial Reporting* (the *'Conceptual Framework'*) is currently being reviewed and updated. The outcome of the Rate-regulated Activities project will be influenced by the outcome of the *Conceptual Framework* project. The initial objective is to develop a Discussion Paper for each of these projects, which the IASB hopes will provide a basis for developing guidance in the long term.[4] It also decided, in December 2012, to develop an interim Standard on the accounting for regulatory deferral accounts that would apply until the completion of the comprehensive project. This Standard is the result of that decision.

Reasons for issuing this Standard

BC11 Many rate-regulated entities think that recognising regulatory deferral account balances as assets and liabilities would provide more relevant information and would provide a more faithful representation of their rate-regulated activities than the established practice in IFRS currently. They suggest that rate regulation creates special conditions that support the recognition of regulatory deferral account balances, even when those balances consist of deferred costs that other Standards require to be recognised as an expense in the period in which they are incurred. The 2009 ED, which proposed that regulatory deferral account balances should be recognised when arising from activities that are subject to a specific type of rate regulation (referred to in the 2009 ED as "cost-of-service rate regulation"), raised expectations that the IASB had agreed that there was merit to the arguments used to support recognition of such balances as assets and liabilities.

BC12 Consequently, some respondents have noted that, although the case has not been made conclusively for amending IFRS to permit or require the recognition of regulatory deferral account balances as assets and liabilities, neither has it been made conclusively for an approach that eliminates such balances and changes existing accounting policies. These policies are being widely applied in accordance with some national GAAPs, and are familiar to many users of financial statements in jurisdictions that currently permit or require the recognition of rate-regulated items.

BC13 The IASB recognises that discontinuing the recognition of regulatory deferral account balances in advance of the conclusion of the comprehensive Rate-regulated Activities project could be a significant barrier to the adoption of IFRS for entities for which regulatory deferral account balances represent a significant proportion of net assets. This has led to an industry-specific 'carve-out' from the application of IFRS in at least one jurisdiction that has otherwise adopted IFRS, to allow rate-regulated entities to continue to use local GAAP (or, in some cases, US GAAP). In addition, there are examples of 'carve-ins'

---

4   The IASB published, in July 2013, the Discussion Paper *A Review of the Conceptual Framework for Financial Reporting*. The deadline for comments was 14 January 2014.

being created that introduce specific guidance for rate-regulated activities that overlies IFRS requirements as issued by the IASB. However, the interaction of such guidance when it is in conflict with the requirements of IFRS can create diversity of application in practice.

BC14 During outreach, some respondents told the IASB that, in many jurisdictions, the accounting policies developed for regulatory deferral account balances are based on US GAAP or local GAAP that provides similar guidance. This is understood to provide a reasonable level of comparability for regulatory deferral account balances across jurisdictions. However, different approaches to accommodating existing practice for such balances have reduced comparability for users of financial statements in these jurisdictions, because the rest of the items in the financial statements are now accounted for using different accounting frameworks (for example, IFRS, US GAAP or local GAAP), depending on which approach has been adopted. In some cases, the development of these carve-in or carve-out options has been in direct response to the publication of the 2009 ED.

BC15 The IASB acknowledges the difficult practice problems related to this issue. The IASB has, therefore, decided to issue this Standard, which allows entities that currently recognise regulatory deferral account balances in accordance with their previous GAAP to continue to do so when making the transition to IFRS. In accordance with paragraph 5, an entity is only eligible to apply this Standard if it:

(a) is subject to oversight and/or approval from an authorised body (the rate regulator);

(b) recognised regulatory deferral account balances in its financial statements in accordance with its previous GAAP; and

(c) elected to apply the requirements of this Standard in its first IFRS financial statements.

BC16 Consequently, an entity that does not recognise regulatory deferral account balances in accordance with its previous GAAP in the period immediately preceding its first IFRS financial statements is not eligible to apply this Standard in order to start recognising such balances. An entity would not, therefore, be eligible if, for example:

(a) the entity did not have any relevant rate-regulated activities in the period before it made the transition to IFRS but then acquires or commences rate-regulated activities after the date that it adopts IFRS; or

(b) the entity is a newly formed business and adopts IFRS in its first IFRS financial statements.

BC17 The IASB thinks that this restriction balances the needs of preparers and users in jurisdictions that currently recognise regulatory deferral account balances in accordance with previous GAAP, and those that already prepare IFRS financial statements and do not recognise such balances.

BC18 A Standard that permits first-time adopters of IFRS to continue to apply their existing policies for the recognition, measurement, impairment and derecognition of regulatory deferral account balances will help those entities avoid having to make a major change to their accounting policies for regulatory deferral account balances until the comprehensive Rate-regulated Activities project is completed. The related presentation and disclosure requirements should help to reduce the disruption to information available for trend analyses for these entities on transition to IFRS, until the IASB can consider these issues in its comprehensive project. This would enable rate-regulated entities to overcome the barrier noted in paragraph BC13 and, consequently, to make the transition to IFRS.

BC19 Although comparability will be improved overall by having more entities applying IFRS, the IASB acknowledges that permitting only a limited population of entities to recognise regulatory deferral account balances will introduce some inconsistency and diversity into IFRS practice for the treatment of regulatory deferral account balances, when it does not currently exist. In order to improve comparability between IFRS preparers that are subject to rate regulation but that do not recognise regulatory deferral account balances and entities that are permitted to recognise such balances in accordance with this Standard, the IASB decided to require segregated presentation of these balances. The IASB thinks that the resulting presentation and disclosure requirements in this Standard will help to minimise the impact of introducing this inconsistency, and that the benefits to users and preparers of financial statements outweigh the costs.

BC20 The IASB thinks that the following benefits of this Standard justify introducing this diversity:

(a) it is likely to remove a major barrier to the adoption of IFRS for entities for which regulatory deferral account balances represent a significant proportion of net assets;

(b) it should reduce the risk of entities adopting locally developed carve-ins or carve-outs that would otherwise create greater diversity of accounting treatment and greater confusion for users of financial statements. Having more entities applying IFRS would ensure that their other activities are reported in accordance with IFRS, thereby increasing comparability for those other assets and liabilities; and

(c) it is likely to improve transparency and consistency in the way that regulatory deferral account balances and movements in those balances are presented, thereby highlighting the impact of recognising such items and improving comparability between those entities that recognise such balances in accordance with the Standard.

BC21 However, the IASB noted that, by issuing this Standard, it is not anticipating the outcome of the comprehensive Rate-regulated Activities project referred to in paragraph BC10. Consequently, regulatory deferral account balances are not described as regulatory assets or regulatory liabilities in this Standard because the IASB has yet to decide whether they meet the definitions of assets or liabilities in the *Conceptual Framework*. The separation of these balances from the amounts that are recognised as assets and liabilities in accordance with other Standards is designed to maintain the integrity of the application of existing Standards.

Scope

BC22   This Standard does not allow entities to recognise regulatory deferral account balances if those entities have a dominant position in a market and decide to self-regulate to avoid the potential government intervention that might occur if it were perceived to be abusing its dominant position. Instead, it requires there to be a formal rate regulator involved to ensure that the rate-regulatory mechanism in place is supported by statute or regulation and that the regulatory mechanism binds the entity.

BC23   However, the IASB does not intend to exclude entities that are regulated by their own governing body in cases in which:

(a)   the governing body sets prices both in the interests of the customers and to ensure the financial viability of the entity within a specified framework; and

(b)   the framework is subject to oversight and/or approval by an authorised body that is empowered by statute or regulation.

BC24   This situation could arise, for example, when the entity conducts previously state-run activities and the government delegates regulatory powers to an entity (that may be state-controlled) within a statutory framework that is overseen by an authorised body of the government. Another example is a co-operative that may be subject to some form of regulatory oversight in order to obtain preferential loans, tax relief or other incentives to maintain the supply of goods or services that the government consider to be essential or near essential.

BC25   This Standard does not address an entity's accounting for reporting to rate regulators (regulatory accounting). Rate regulators may require a regulated entity to maintain its accounts in a form that permits the rate regulator to obtain the information that is needed for regulatory purposes. Rate regulators' actions are based on many considerations. This Standard neither limits nor endorses a rate regulator's actions.

BC26   Although rate regulators can affect the timing of the recovery of the costs or the reversal of over-recoveries through future increases and decreases in rates, they cannot change the characteristics of assets and liabilities that exist and that are accounted for in accordance with IFRS. The IASB has not, therefore, introduced any changes to the accounting for assets or liabilities that are already addressed in other Standards. Those items should be accounted for in accordance with those Standards, irrespective of whether the entity is subject to rate regulation or not.

BC27   Consequently, the IASB decided that the scope of the Standard should be limited to specifying how an entity reports the differences that arise between the regulatory accounting requirements of rate regulators and the accounting that would otherwise be required in financial statements that are prepared in accordance with IFRS, in the absence of this Standard.

Recognition, measurement, impairment and derecognition

Temporary exemption from paragraph 11 of IAS 8

BC28   As noted in paragraph BC7, the established practice in IFRS has been that rate-regulated entities do not recognise regulatory deferral accounts in IFRS financial statements. Some IASB members are concerned that entities that will recognise regulatory deferral account balances in accordance with this Standard could give the appearance of being compliant with IFRS while being inconsistent with the stated objectives of the IASB, ie to provide users of financial statements with financial information that is transparent, comparable and of high quality. The IASB did not consider the exemption from parts of IAS 8 lightly, but introduced this interim step to lower a significant barrier to adopting IFRS for some jurisdictions, pending the completion of the comprehensive Rate-regulated Activities project. This step is also intended to minimise disruption, both for users (for example, a lack of continuity of information available for trend analyses) and preparers (for example, extensive system changes) when entities in these jurisdictions make the transition to IFRS.

BC29   The IASB has been told that the majority of the national standard-setting bodies that permit or require the recognition of regulatory deferral account balances in accordance with local GAAP do so using the requirements of US GAAP (Topic 980 *Regulated Operations* in the FASB *Accounting Standards Codification*®) or local requirements that are based on US GAAP. Consequently, the IASB does not expect there to be significant diversity in the accounting for regulatory deferral account balances in jurisdictions that currently apply regulatory accounting in financial statements.

BC30   Paragraph 12 of IAS 8 could permit Topic 980 or similar local GAAP requirements to be applied in IFRS financial statements, but only to the extent that those national GAAPs do not conflict with the sources of guidance listed in paragraph 11 of IAS 8 (ie other Standards and the *Conceptual Framework*). As noted in paragraph BC6, the Interpretations Committee concluded that the recognition criteria in SFAS 71 (now incorporated into Topic 980) were not fully consistent with the recognition criteria in IFRS. This is because some regulatory deferral account balances are specifically prohibited from being recognised as assets and liabilities by other Standards. It is this conflict with the sources listed in paragraph 11 of IAS 8 that has prevented almost all existing IFRS preparers from recognising regulatory deferral account balances. Consequently, the IASB has decided that entities within the scope of this Standard should be granted a temporary exemption from paragraph 11 of IAS 8 in order to overcome the restriction on the use of the sources of accounting guidance referred to in paragraph 12 of IAS 8.

BC31   When developing IFRS 4 *Insurance Contracts* and IFRS 6 *Exploration for and Evaluation of Mineral Resources*, the IASB considered whether they should require an entity to follow its national accounting requirements (ie national GAAP) when accounting for insurance contracts or the exploration for and evaluation of mineral resources respectively to prevent the selection of accounting policies that do not form a comprehensive basis of accounting. Consistent with its conclusions in those Standards, the IASB concluded that defining national GAAP would have posed problems. Further definitional problems could have arisen because some entities do not apply the national GAAP of their own country. For example, some non-US entities with rate-regulated activities apply US GAAP (Topic 980). Moreover, it is unusual and, arguably, beyond the IASB's mandate to impose requirements set by another body.

BC32 Consequently, the IASB decided that an entity could continue to follow the accounting policies that it was using when it first applied the IFRS requirements, provided that they satisfy the requirements of paragraphs 10 and 12 of IAS 8. This should help to ensure that those policies are generally accepted in the local jurisdiction, either because the local GAAP allows the use of another standard-setter's pronouncement or because of accepted industry practice. The IASB decided to adopt the same approach in this Standard that it adopted with IFRSs 4 and 6, for the same reasons.

Changes in accounting policies

BC33 IAS 8 prohibits a change in accounting policies that is not required by a Standard, unless the change will result in information that is reliable and more relevant. Paragraph 15 of IAS 8 explains that this is because users of financial statements need to be able to compare the financial statements of an entity over time to identify trends in financial position, financial performance and cash flows. Consistent with its conclusions in IFRSs 4 and 6, the IASB decided to permit changes in accounting policies for regulatory deferral account balances if they make the financial statements more relevant and no less reliable, or more reliable and no less relevant, judged in accordance with the criteria in IAS 8.

BC34 As previously noted, the IASB has started the research phase of a comprehensive project to investigate how IFRS financial statements might reflect the effects of rate regulation (see paragraph BC10). Until that project is completed, the IASB wishes to minimise disruption to information used for trend analyses of IFRS financial statements and thus the limitation on changes in accounting policy is intended to be restrictive. The established practice in IFRS has been that almost all rate-regulated entities do not recognise regulatory deferral account balances in IFRS financial statements. Consequently, the IASB thinks that changing an accounting policy to start to recognise such balances, or to recognise a wider range of such balances by modifying a previous GAAP policy, when that changed policy might need to change again following the completion of the Rate-regulated Activities project, would not make the financial statements more reliable. The scope of this Standard and the restriction on changes in accounting policies in paragraphs 13–15, therefore, prohibit entities that currently do not recognise regulatory deferral account balances from starting to do so.

BC35 The IASB wished to avoid imposing unnecessary changes of accounting policy as a result of applying this Standard. However, it did not want to prevent entities that currently recognise regulatory deferral account balances from ceasing to recognise them when adopting IFRS because this would be consistent with the established IFRS practice. The IASB thinks that this would result in an entity presenting more comparable information with existing IFRS preparers, which would bring the financial statements closer to the criteria in IAS 8. The IASB has, therefore, decided that the continued recognition of regulatory deferral account balances in accordance with this Standard should be optional. An entity that is eligible to apply this Standard but that elects not to apply it and, consequently, ceases to recognise its regulatory deferral account balances, is not required to apply any of the disclosure requirements of this Standard. However, such entities, and other entities that are not eligible to apply this Standard, are not prohibited from providing supplementary disclosures, such as those set out in paragraphs 30–36.

BC36 In addition, this Standard contains some specific accounting requirements for presentation that may require entities to change the presentation of regulatory deferral account balances that they recognise in accordance with their previous GAAP accounting policies. The IASB thinks that these changes, together with the specific disclosure requirements set out in this Standard, will improve comparability and understandability, and provide relevant information to users.

Interaction with other Standards

BC37 Any specific exception, exemption or additional requirements related to the interaction of this Standard with other Standards is contained within this Standard. The IASB thinks that, except for IFRS 1, other Standards should not be subject to consequential amendments relating only to this Standard because its application is restricted to a limited population of entities. In addition, it is intended to be applicable only as a short-term interim solution until the comprehensive Rate-regulated Activities project is completed.

BC38 As previously noted, in order to apply this Standard an eligible entity must elect to apply it in the entity's first IFRS financial statements. Consequently, a first-time adopter will initially apply this Standard at the same time as it applies IFRS 1. Paragraph D8B of IFRS 1 provides an exemption to allow first-time adopters to use, as the deemed cost at the date of transition to IFRS, the previous GAAP carrying amount of items of property, plant and equipment or intangible assets that are used, or were previously used, in operations subject to rate regulation. For the purposes of that exemption, paragraph D8B defined operations that are subject to rate regulation in the context of a cost-plus or cost-of-service type of rate regulation. The IASB has decided to make a consequential amendment to paragraph D8B of IFRS 1 to make the definition of rate regulation used in that paragraph consistent with the definition used in this Standard. This will ensure that a first-time adopter that applies this Standard is not prohibited from using the exemptions available to other first-time adopters in IFRS 1.

Recoverability

BC39 Although the approval by the rate regulator may not guarantee that a regulatory deferral account balance will be recovered (or reversed) through future sales, it does provide a high degree of assurance that the anticipated economic benefits will flow to or from the entity. In some cases, an entity may incur costs several months or even years before the rate regulator formally approves them. The IASB concluded that, in such cases, judgement is required to determine whether the costs can be considered recoverable. Consequently, the IASB decided not to develop specific recognition or impairment requirements for these circumstances, but instead decided that an entity should continue to apply its previous GAAP accounting policies for the recognition and measurement of such amounts.

Presentation

Cost of self-constructed or internally generated assets

BC40 The IASB noted that in some cases, a rate regulator requires, for rate-setting purposes, an entity to include, as part of the cost of property, plant and equipment or other assets, amounts that would not be included by non-rate-regulated entities. For example, a rate regulator might specify how to calculate the carrying value of an item of property, plant and equipment for rate-setting purposes (the rate-base or regulatory value), which might differ from the method required by IAS 16.

BC41 The IASB acknowledges that at least two alternatives exist for accounting for these amounts: present them separately or include them within the amounts presented for property, plant and equipment or other assets. Proponents of the first alternative think that regulatory deferral account balances that would be recognised as a result of this Standard do not have the same characteristics as assets and liabilities that would be recognised in accordance with other Standards. Consequently, proponents of this alternative think that all amounts that qualify for recognition as regulatory deferral account balances should be presented separately from the assets and liabilities that are recognised in accordance with other Standards, instead of being included within the carrying amount of the item of property, plant and equipment or other asset.

BC42 Proponents of the second alternative think that some regulatory deferral account balances that would be recognised as a result of this Standard are so closely related to other assets of the entity that accounting for them separately does not provide additional information to users. Proponents of this alternative think that when regulatory assets are complementary to other assets and have similar useful lives, there is no need to incur the costs of separate accounting. Instead, they think that the other assets should be measured at the amount allowed for rate-regulatory purposes. In accordance with this alternative, an entity includes the regulatory deferral account balances in the cost of the asset that is recognised in accordance with other Standards as a single asset. This approach is consistent with that applied in US GAAP (Topic 980).

BC43 The IASB will consider this issue as part of the comprehensive Rate-regulated Activities project. For the purpose of this Standard, the IASB has decided to require the first alternative. This decision does not change the relief available to first-time adopters using the deemed cost exemption provided by paragraph D8B of IFRS 1 (see paragraph BC38). This is consistent with the IASB's decision not to introduce any changes to the accounting for assets and liabilities that are already addressed in other Standards (see paragraph BC26). Some IASB members think that this separate presentation is essential until the consideration of the more fundamental issues about accounting for rate-regulated activities is completed through the comprehensive project.

Separate presentation in the primary financial statements

BC44   Many of the items included in regulatory deferral account balances would not otherwise be capitalised as assets (or liabilities) in the absence of the temporary exemption from paragraph 11 of IAS 8 that is contained in this Standard (see paragraph BC30). Consequently, and consistent with the IASB's decision discussed in paragraph BC43, the Standard requires the total of all regulatory deferral account debit balances and the total of all regulatory deferral account credit balances to be presented as separate line items in the statement of financial position. Similarly, the net movement between the opening and closing balances is presented separately within the statement(s) of profit or loss and other comprehensive income, split between amounts related to other comprehensive income and amounts related to profit or loss. Any movements not related to profit or loss or other comprehensive income, such as amounts acquired or disposed of, are disclosed in the reconciliation of opening and closing balances required by paragraph 33.

BC45   In addition, the IASB concluded that presenting the regulatory impact separately would provide more useful information about the regulatory environment and would be consistent with the enhancing qualitative characteristic of comparability in paragraphs QC20–QC25 of the *Conceptual Framework*. In particular, it would enable users to more directly compare the property, plant and equipment or intangible assets of comparable rate-regulated entities (in addition to comparing them to those of non-rate-regulated entities), regardless of whether they recognise regulatory deferral account balances in their financial statements. This would also result in more consistent application of IFRS for all other transactions or activities, irrespective of whether an entity has rate-regulated activities and the type of rate-regulatory environment that the entity is subject to.

BC46   The IASB concluded that the separate presentation of regulatory deferral account balances, especially those amounts that are often permitted by national GAAP practices to be included within the carrying amounts of property, plant and equipment and other assets, is an important improvement because it contributes to increased transparency in financial reporting. The IASB noted that a first-time adopter of IFRS may apply the deemed cost exemption in paragraph D8B of IFRS 1, which allows adopters to use their previous GAAP carrying amounts at the date of transition to IFRS. This exemption provides relief for first-time adopters that would otherwise be required to separate out the regulatory component of the carrying amount of sometimes very large and old items of property, plant and equipment or intangible assets at the date of transition to IFRS, which may be impracticable. The IASB has made a consequential amendment to the scope of the IFRS 1 exemption to make it consistent with the scope of this Standard. Consequently, entities that apply this Standard will only need to isolate the regulatory deferral account amounts for those items on a prospective basis from the date of transition to IFRS. The IASB also noted that the information required for separate presentation on an ongoing basis is normally available in any case, due to the information requirements of rate regulators.

Current/non-current allocation and offset

BC47   Regulatory deferral account balances arise from specific individual costs (income) that the rate regulator requires or permits to be deferred to future periods. The rates charged for goods or services in the current period may be intended to recover a combination of past costs, current costs and, in some cases, anticipated future costs. Although the rate regulator may specify the period over which the recovery of the regulatory deferral account balances is intended, judgement may be needed to identify the costs that the revenue billed in a period recovers. This means that detailed scheduling of the timing of recovery or reversal of each regulatory deferral account debit or credit balance may be needed for the purpose of identifying which amounts should be classed as current or for determining which amounts would be recovered or reversed in the same period for the purposes of offsetting. Consequently, the IASB has decided that regulatory deferral account balances should not be presented as current or non-current and that debit and credit balances should not be offset in the statement of financial position. Instead, this Standard requires information about the period(s) over which regulatory deferral account balances are expected to be recovered or reversed to be disclosed. An entity is not, however, prohibited from identifying current and non-current amounts within the information disclosed if the relevant information is available.

Disclosure

BC48   In December 2012, the IASB launched a survey on disclosures, which was directed at preparers, users and others interested in or affected by disclosure requirements. The results were discussed in a public discussion forum on *Disclosures in Financial Reporting* in January 2013. The survey and the discussion forum were aimed at assisting the IASB to gain a clearer picture on the perceived "disclosure problem" (ie identifying disclosure requirements that create a burden for preparers but do not provide users with sufficient relevant information). The views of most financial statement preparers that took part in these events identified the primary problem as the disclosure requirements being too extensive, with not enough being done to exclude immaterial information, which has been referred to as "disclosure overload". Similarly, many users of financial statements felt that preparers could do more to improve the communication of relevant information within the financial statements, rather than leaving users to sift through large amounts of data.

BC49   With this in mind, this Standard sets out a general objective for disclosure as well as a list of detailed items that might be useful in achieving that objective. The IASB has previously concluded that it is unnecessary, in general, to state explicitly that specified disclosures relate only to material items because all Standards are governed by the concept of materiality as described in IAS 1 *Presentation of Financial Statements* and in IAS 8. The IASB has decided, consistent with its previous conclusions, not to specifically refer to materiality in this Standard. However, this Standard contains other explicit guidance to clarify that preparers should use their judgement to decide which of the detailed items are necessary to achieve the objective and what level of detail to provide.

BC50   The IASB thinks that an understanding of an entity's different types of rate-regulated activities is important for understanding the entity as a whole. In addition, an understanding of each class of regulatory deferral account is considered important because that can provide information about the nature of the rate regulation and the potential timing of related cash flows. Consequently, this Standard requires the disclosure of qualitative and quantitative information for each type of an entity's rate-regulated activities and each class of regulatory deferral account balance, because this will provide information that is more useful in assessing the impact of different rate-regulatory environments.

BC51   The IASB thinks that most entities that already recognise regulatory deferral account balances in accordance with US GAAP, or similar requirements or practices in other jurisdictions, currently provide most of the information required to be disclosed by paragraph 33 of this Standard. However, the IASB observed that the information is often disclosed in various places throughout the financial statements in a way that can make it difficult for a user to appreciate the overall effect that rate regulation has had on the amounts recognised in the financial statements. Consequently, this Standard requires that entities meet the disclosure requirements by providing a table, containing aggregated information, and showing a reconciliation of the movements in the carrying amounts in the statement of financial position of the various categories of regulatory items. This table will be required unless another format is more appropriate. The IASB noted that such a table, presenting information in a structured manner, would assist financial statement users in understanding how the entity's reported financial position and comprehensive income have been affected by rate regulation.

Location of qualitative disclosures

BC52   The IASB observed that many entities provide, often in the management commentary reports that accompany the financial statements, a qualitative description of the nature and extent of the effect of rate regulation on its activities. The IASB acknowledges that the nature and extent of rate regulation can have a significant impact on the amount and timing of revenue and cash flows of a rate-regulated entity. Hence, the IASB concluded that such disclosures should be part of the financial statements and they could be given either in the financial statements or incorporated by cross-reference from the financial statements to some other statement that is available to users of the financial statements on the same terms as the financial statements and at the same time. This approach is intended to reduce duplication of information and is consistent with some types of risk disclosure required by IFRS 7 *Financial Instruments: Disclosures*.

Effective date and transition

BC53   This Standard will only be available to first-time adopters of IFRS and will need to be applied retrospectively at the date of transition to IFRS. The IASB usually intends to allow a minimum of one year between the date when wholly new Standards or major amendments to Standards are issued and the date when implementation is required. Consequently, the IASB has set 1 January 2016 as the effective date for this Standard. Earlier application is permitted to make the benefits outlined in paragraph BC20 available at the earliest opportunity.

BC54　The IASB concluded that no explicit relief from full retrospective application of the Standard is needed because existing recognition, measurement, impairment and derecognition policies are continued when this Standard is applied. First-time adopters of IFRS can use the deemed cost exemption for property, plant and equipment and intangible assets that is already available in IFRS 1 that allows first-time adopters to use their previous GAAP carrying amounts at the date of transition to IFRS. Consequently, they will only need to change their presentation policies for these items to isolate the regulatory deferral account amounts on a prospective basis from the date of transition to IFRS.

Summary of main changes from the Exposure Draft *Regulatory Deferral Accounts*

BC55　The proposed definition of the rate regulator included the term "or contract" when establishing the authority of the rate regulator. Some respondents to the Exposure Draft *Regulatory Deferral Accounts*, which was published in April 2013 (the '2013 ED'), were concerned that this term resulted in the definition being too broad. Those respondents assumed that the intention of including the entity's own governing body was to (appropriately) capture those cases in which an entity conducts previously state-run monopolistic activities and is consequently delegated regulatory powers by the government. However, the respondents were concerned that the scope could be applied, by analogy, to other commercial entities having monopolistic features. This concern was raised within the context of entities that, in the absence of an external regulator, self-regulate (for example, by formally agreeing this with investors through the articles of association or other contractual arrangement). Entities may do this to avoid potential government intervention if they might otherwise be perceived to be abusing their strong market position.

BC56　Consequently, the IASB decided to refine the definition of the rate regulator to exclude self-regulation and instead require the rate regulator to be supported by statute or other formal regulations.

BC57　In addition, the definitions of rate regulation and the rate regulator were further refined to clarify that the regulation can permit some flexibility in the prices to be charged, within a range of prices established or approved by the rate regulator.

BC58　The scope criterion in paragraph 7(b) of the 2013 ED, which proposed that the price established by regulation (the rate) should be designed to recover the entity's allowable costs of providing the regulated goods or services, has been removed. The IASB was persuaded by arguments from some respondents that this criterion was inconsistent with the underlying objective of the IASB to reduce barriers to the adoption of IFRS. In addition, retaining this criterion may be perceived as prejudging the outcome of the comprehensive project.

BC59　The other main changes from the proposals in the 2013 ED are as follows:

(a)　application guidance has been added to:

(i)   clarify some group accounting issues. Paragraph 19 of IFRS 10 *Consolidated Financial Statements* requires that a "parent shall prepare consolidated financial statements using uniform accounting policies for like transactions and other events in similar circumstances". Consequently, if a parent recognises regulatory deferral account balances in accordance with this Standard, it shall apply the same accounting policies for the recognition, measurement, impairment and derecognition of regulatory deferral account balances arising from the rate-regulated activities of all of its subsidiaries, even if some of those subsidiaries do not recognise such balances in their own financial statements. A similar requirement applies to an investor applying the equity method to investments in associates and joint ventures.

(ii)   introduce a limited exception to IFRS 3 *Business Combinations* to require the continuation of the acquirer's previous GAAP accounting policies for the recognition and measurement of regulatory deferral account balances acquired or assumed in a business combination. The IASB noted that, if an acquirer does not recognise regulatory deferral account balances in accordance with this Standard, but subsequently acquires a subsidiary that does recognise such balances, the acquirer is not eligible to apply this Standard. Consequently, the acquirer is not eligible to recognise the acquiree's regulatory deferral account balances within the consolidated financial statements.

(iii)   clarify that an entity is not prohibited from recognising new regulatory deferral account balances for timing differences that are created as a consequence of a change in an accounting policy for other items required by IFRS. The IASB noted that the recognition of timing differences between its applied accounting policies and rate-regulatory requirements is a key element of what regulatory deferral account balances represent. When an entity adopts IFRS, the accounting policies that it uses in its opening IFRS statement of financial position may differ from those that it used at the same date when it used its previous GAAP. Such changes in accounting policies may create new timing differences that will be recorded by the entity in regulatory deferral accounts. For example, the rate regulator might allow pension costs to be reflected in rates when benefits or other costs are paid. The previous GAAP accounting policy for pension costs may have been consistent with this 'as paid' policy and thus no regulatory deferral account balance would have existed for those costs. However, IAS 19 *Employee Benefits* requires pension costs to be attributed to periods of service in accordance with the plan's benefit formula, or in some cases on a straight-line basis. For defined benefit pension costs, this would create a new timing difference for which a regulatory deferral account balance would be created. Some respondents were concerned that the prohibition to change accounting policies would prevent such newly created regulatory deferral account balances from being recognised. However, this was not the IASB's intention, because the recognition of such timing differences would be consistent with the recognition of other timing differences already recognised as regulatory deferral account balances.

(b) the requirement to continue previous GAAP accounting policies for the recognition, measurement and impairment of regulatory deferral account balances has been extended to include derecognition.

(c) the requirement to present the net movement in regulatory deferral account balances in the statement of profit or loss and other comprehensive income has been modified to require the net movement to be split between amounts related to items reported in profit or loss and those reported in other comprehensive income. The IASB was persuaded by those respondents that stated that the proposal to recognise all net movements in regulatory deferral account balances in a single line item in the profit or loss section of the statement of profit or loss and other comprehensive income could be confusing or misleading when a material portion of the movement related to items that are recognised in other comprehensive income.

(d) the references to materiality as a factor to consider in deciding the level of detail to disclose has been deleted. The IASB noted that the consideration of materiality is already dealt with in IAS 1 and IAS 8. The IASB is currently assessing the adequacy of the guidance contained in those Standards as part of its Disclosure Initiative project.

BC60 A few respondents to the 2013 ED asked for additional guidance for the application of IAS 34 *Interim Financial Reporting*. In particular, they requested that it should be made clear that separate line items for regulatory deferral account balances and movements therein should also be included in a condensed set of financial statements. However, the IASB did not agree that additional guidance is necessary. Paragraph 10 of IAS 34 requires that condensed financial statements "shall include, at a minimum, each of the headings and subtotals that were included in its most recent annual financial statements and the selected explanatory notes as required by this Standard." In addition, paragraphs 15–15A of IAS 34 require that an entity shall include an explanation of events and transactions that are significant to an understanding of the changes in the financial position and performance of the entity.

BC61 The IASB concluded that the existing requirements, together with the detailed year-end information required in this Standard, are sufficient to provide users with the relevant information to understand the regulatory deferral account balances that are recognised.

BC62 The Illustrative examples and the Basis for Conclusions on the 2013 ED contained some educational background information about rate regulation, which was not related specifically to the contents of the proposed requirements. This background information has been deleted from this Standard.

Effects analysis

BC63   The IASB is committed to assessing and sharing knowledge about the likely costs of implementing new requirements and the likely ongoing costs and benefits of each new Standard. The costs and benefits are collectively referred to as 'effects'. The IASB gains insight on the likely effects of the proposals for new or revised Standards through its formal exposure of proposals, analysis and consultations with relevant parties.

BC64   In evaluating the likely effects of permitting rate-regulated entities that are first-time adopters of IFRS to continue to recognise regulatory deferral account balances, the IASB has considered the following factors:

(a)   how the changes to the presentation of regulatory deferral account balances affect the financial statements of a rate-regulated entity;

(b)   whether the changes improve the comparability of financial information between different reporting periods for a rate-regulated entity and between different rate-regulated entities in a particular reporting period;

(c)   whether the changes improve the quality of financial information that is available to investors and its usefulness in assessing the future cash flows of a rate-regulated entity;

(d)   whether users will benefit from better economic decision-making as a result of improved financial reporting;

(e)   the likely effect on compliance costs for preparers, both on initial application and on an ongoing basis; and

(f)   whether the likely costs of analysis for users are affected.

Financial statements of rate-regulated entities

BC65   The scope of this Standard is limited to first-time adopters of IFRS that already recognise regulatory deferral account balances in their financial statements in accordance with their previous GAAP. Consequently, the financial statements of rate-regulated entities that already apply IFRS, or that do not otherwise recognise such balances, will not be affected by this Standard.

BC66   This Standard permits rate-regulated entities within its scope to continue to apply their existing recognition, measurement, impairment and derecognition policies for regulatory deferral account balances. Consequently, the application of this Standard should have little or no impact on the net assets or the net profit reported in the financial statements.

BC67   However, the presentation of some regulatory deferral account balances will be changed to isolate the impact of their recognition and present this impact as separate line items within the statement of financial position and the statement of profit or loss and other comprehensive income. In particular, some regulatory deferral account balances that would be presented within the carrying amount of items of property, plant and equipment, intangible assets and inventories in accordance with previous GAAP will, in future, be presented separately from those classes of asset in accordance with this Standard.

Comparability

BC68   The IASB acknowledges that the requirements of this Standard will reduce comparability in some ways, but thinks that this reduction will be outweighed by other improvements in comparability that will result from applying the requirements in this Standard.

BC69   As noted in paragraph BC19, permitting only a limited population of entities to recognise regulatory deferral account balances will introduce some inconsistency and diversity into IFRS practice, when it does not currently exist. However, this is mitigated by the requirements to isolate the regulatory deferral account balances, and the movements in those balances, into separate line items in the financial statements.

BC70   The IASB is aware that many rate-regulated entities view the inability to recognise regulatory deferral account balances in IFRS financial statements as a major barrier to the adoption of IFRS. Although many of these entities are understood to use similar policies for the recognition and measurement of these balances, they use different frameworks of accounting for the preparation and presentation of the financial statements as a whole. The IASB thinks that reducing the barriers for these entities to adopt IFRS will improve the comparability of the financial statements of rate-regulated entities across jurisdictions.

BC71   In addition, the IASB thinks that the requirements to isolate the regulatory deferral account balances, and the movements in those balances, from other items in the financial statements will increase the transparency of these items. This will provide greater comparability across those entities within the scope of this Standard. This will, as a result, assist users of financial statements to understand more clearly the impact of recognising regulatory deferral account balances, and will allow direct comparisons not only against those entities that will be permitted to recognise these balances, but also against entities that do not recognise them.

Usefulness in assessing the future cash flows of an entity

BC72   Rate regulation imposes a framework for establishing prices that can be charged to customers for goods or services. Consequently, a rate-regulated entity is usually unable to react quickly in order to change its selling price in response to changes in its operating or other costs. Many of those who support the recognition of regulatory deferral account balances in financial statements argue that these balances provide some indication of the impact of these time delays on the cash flows that will be generated through future sales that will be made at a higher or lower price. The disclosures required by this Standard should provide more information about the amount and expected timing of the recovery or reversal of the regulatory deferral account balances recognised.

Better economic decision-making

BC73   The IASB has been told by many users in jurisdictions that currently permit or require regulatory deferral account balances to be recognised in financial statements that the information about those balances is useful in making

© IFRS Foundation

economic decisions. At the same time, many other users of IFRS financial statements have noted that the inclusion of such balances could be confusing because it is not clear whether they meet the definitions of assets and liabilities. As a result, these users think that it is unclear what these balances represent.

BC74   The IASB thinks that this Standard will allow entities within its scope to continue to provide information that some users find useful, but that the presentation requirements will provide clarity to avoid confusion for those who are not familiar with the recognition of regulatory deferral account balances.

BC75   In particular, the IASB thinks that the improvements in comparability noted in paragraphs BC69–BC71 will provide users of financial statements with more information to help them better understand the impact of rate regulation on those rate-regulated entities that will be able to continue to recognise regulatory deferral account balances in accordance with this Standard.

Effect on compliance costs for preparers

BC76   This Standard will not change the recognition or measurement policies of entities within its scope, and thus will not result in any cost change in this respect. However, the IASB acknowledges that the separate presentation of regulatory deferral account balances is likely to result in changes to most existing presentation policies. Existing policies of entities within the scope of this Standard usually require or permit certain regulatory deferral account balances to be included within the carrying amount of items of property, plant and equipment and other assets. The separate presentation required by this Standard may add some cost on an ongoing basis, because preparers would need to track some of the differences between the regulatory amounts and those reported in the financial statements in more detail than is currently required.

BC77   However, the cost on the initial application of this Standard would largely be mitigated by the exemption that is already contained in paragraph D8B of IFRS 1. This exemption applies to first-time adopters of IFRS that hold items of property, plant and equipment or intangible assets that are, or were previously, used in operations subject to rate regulation. It allows those first-time adopters to use the previous GAAP carrying amount of such an item at the date of transition to IFRS as deemed cost. Consequently, the additional administrative burden of tracking changes need only apply on a prospective basis for differences arising after the date of transition.

BC78   In addition, the IASB understands that in many regulatory regimes, the regulatory accounting requirements require that regulatory deferral account balances are recorded in separate accounts within the entity's financial record-keeping system, at least until such time that the regulator issues a formal rate decision. Consequently, the IASB thinks that the incremental costs of retaining this separation beyond the time normally required by the regulator should not be significant.

How the costs of analysis for users are affected

BC79   The likely effect of these requirements on the costs of analysis for users of financial statements is expected to be outweighed by the benefits of improved reporting. Some users have commented that information related to the impact that rate regulation has on the amount, timing and certainty of returns and cash flows is important. The IASB think that the segregated presentation and related disclosures required by this Standard will highlight more clearly this impact. As noted in paragraph BC66, the requirements should have little or no impact on the net assets or the net profit reported in the financial statements of those entities within the scope of this Standard. Consequently, there is expected to be little disruption to the information available for trend analyses. Although the changes to the presentation of the amounts may cause some initial costs to be incurred, the IASB thinks that the added transparency introduced by this Standard will provide users with clearer and more comparable information.

Dissenting opinions

Dissent of Messrs Edelmann, Gomes and Zhang

DO1   Messrs Edelmann, Gomes and Zhang voted against the publication of IFRS 14.

Reduced comparability and inconsistency with existing IFRS practice

DO2   The established practice in IFRS has been that rate-regulated entities do not recognise regulatory deferral account balances in IFRS financial statements. Consequently, almost all rate-regulated entities around the world that previously recognised regulatory deferral account balances in their financial statements in accordance with their previous GAAP did not continue to recognise such balances but instead, derecognised them when they first adopted IFRS. In the view of Messrs Edelmann, Gomes and Zhang, to now permit an unknown population of rate-regulated entities to recognise these balances when adopting IFRS will introduce inconsistent accounting treatment into IFRS reporting and will reduce existing comparability.

DO3   In addition, Messrs Edelmann, Gomes and Zhang disagree with permitting first-time adopters of IFRS to continue to measure the regulatory deferral account balances that are recognised in the statement of financial position using their previous GAAP accounting policies. They believe that further inconsistency might be introduced by entities continuing to apply existing practices that might not be comparable with other entities that have different existing practices. In their view, isolating the impact of recognising regulatory deferral account balances by presenting them separately is not sufficient to eliminate the effect of this inconsistency. Messrs Edelmann, Gomes and Zhang are also concerned that entities might encounter operational difficulties in applying other general Standards to regulatory deferral account balances because there is uncertainty as to whether these balances are assets and liabilities, and there is no single clear and consistent recognition and measurement policy for them. This in turn might create additional diversity and further reduce comparability in practice.

Creating uncertainty for potential future adopters of IFRS

DO4   Messrs Edelmann, Gomes and Zhang acknowledge that this Standard is intended to be a practical and short-term interim solution to address a significant barrier to the adoption of IFRS in some jurisdictions. They note that a major argument for this Standard is to avoid rate-regulated entities having to make a major change to their accounting policies when making the transition to IFRS (ie derecognise their regulatory deferral account balances in accordance with the current established practice in IFRS of almost all rate-regulated entities) until guidance can be developed through the comprehensive project on rate-regulated activities (see paragraph BC18). However, they also note that this argument is not new, and nor is it specific to this particular subject. Despite this argument, when developing major projects, the IASB does not usually introduce interim Standards to be applied only by first-time adopters of IFRS. In particular, the IASB did not decide to introduce an interim Standard when it worked on the Exposure Draft *Rate-regulated Activities*, published in July 2009 (the '2009 ED'), which, at that time, would have equally avoided the issue for many entities in jurisdictions that have since adopted IFRS.

DO5   In addition, Messrs Edelmann, Gomes and Zhang note that the majority of IFRS Advisory Council members, at their meeting in October 2012, did not support the development of an interim Standard that would permit the continuation of existing previous GAAP policies. Many of those members warned against setting a precedent of implementing a policy of adopting an interim solution whenever a major standard-setting project is activated. Messrs Edelmann, Gomes and Zhang are concerned that developing an interim solution in this situation might create uncertainty as to what the IASB's approach might be when major projects are being researched in the future.

Recognition is contrary to the *Conceptual Framework for Financial Reporting*

DO6   Messrs Gomes and Zhang also disagree with permitting regulatory deferral account balances to be recognised in the statement of financial position because they do not think that all such balances meet the definitions of assets and liabilities in the IASB's *Conceptual Framework*. This is one of the issues that the comprehensive Rate-regulated Activities project is looking to resolve. Consequently, the IASB has stated that IFRS 14 does not anticipate the outcome of the comprehensive project, and uses the neutral term 'regulatory deferral account balances' instead of 'regulatory assets' and 'regulatory liabilities' (see paragraph BC21). However, Messrs Gomes and Zhang believe that permitting them to be included in the statement of financial position is equivalent to recognising them as assets and liabilities, which, in their view, is contrary to the current accounting principles in the *Conceptual Framework* and the application of existing Standards.

DO7   In addition, Messrs Gomes and Zhang are concerned that allowing regulatory deferral account balances to be recognised in the financial statements is contrary to the IASB's objectives of requiring high-quality, transparent and comparable information in financial statements by requiring similar transactions and events to be accounted for and reported in a similar way. The IASB acknowledges that rate regulators have different objectives for regulatory reporting than the IASB has for financial reporting. In the view of Messrs Gomes and Zhang, allowing regulatory deferral account balances to be recognised will effectively allow the objectives of the rate regulator(s) to take precedence over the objectives of general purpose financial reporting, as expressed in the *Conceptual Framework*. In particular, they believe that allowing regulatory deferral account balances to be recognised effectively allows the objectives of the rate regulator(s) for setting rates and smoothing out the volatility, which results from real economic events, to be reflected in the financial statements. Messrs Gomes and Zhang think that this is inconsistent with paragraph OB17 of the *Conceptual Framework*, which notes the importance of depicting the effects of transactions and other events and circumstances on a reporting entity's economic resources and claims in the periods in which those effects occur, even if the resulting cash receipts and payments occur in a different period.

IASB documents published to accompany

IFRS 15

Revenue from Contracts with Customers

The text of the unaccompanied standard, IFRS 15, is contained in Part A of this edition. Its effective date when issued was 1 January 2017. In September 2015 the Board issued *Effective Date of IFRS 15* which deferred the effective date to 1 January 2018. The text of the Accompanying Guidance on IFRS 15 is contained in Part B of this edition. This part presents the following documents:

BASIS FOR CONCLUSIONS

DISSENTING OPINION

APPENDICES TO THE BASIS FOR CONCLUSIONS
A Comparison of IFRS 15 and Topic 606
B Amendments to the Basis for Conclusions on other Standards

CONTENTS

Basis for Conclusions on IFRS 15 *Revenue from Contracts with Customers*

This Basis for Conclusions accompanies, but is not part of, IFRS 15.

Introduction

BC1   This Basis for Conclusions summarises the joint considerations of the International Accounting Standards Board (IASB) and the US national standard-setter, the Financial Accounting Standards Board (FASB), in reaching the conclusions in their standards, IFRS 15 *Revenue from Contracts with Customers* and Topic 606, which is introduced into the FASB *Accounting Standards Codification®* by the Accounting Standards Update 2014-09 *Revenue from Contracts with Customers*. It includes the reasons for accepting particular views and rejecting others. Individual Board members gave greater weight to some factors than to others.

BC1A   In April 2016, the IASB issued *Clarifications to IFRS 15* Revenue from Contracts with Customers. The objective of these amendments is to clarify the IASB's intentions when developing the requirements in IFRS 15 but not to change the underlying principles of IFRS 15. Further details are contained in paragraphs BC27A–BC27H. In some cases, the boards made the same amendments to IFRS 15 and Topic 606. In other cases, the boards did not make the same amendments to the standards. The FASB also amended Topic 606 for issues for which the IASB concluded that it was not necessary to amend IFRS 15. The IASB added a further practical expedient to the transition requirements, which the FASB decided not to provide. Accordingly, Appendix A *Comparison of IFRS 15 and Topic 606* to this Basis for Conclusions has been updated to reflect the differences between the amendments to IFRS 15 and the amendments to Topic 606.

Overview

BC2   IFRS 15 and Topic 606 are the result of the IASB's and the FASB's joint project to improve the financial reporting of revenue under International Financial Reporting Standards (IFRS) and US Generally Accepted Accounting Principles (US GAAP). The boards undertook this project because their requirements for revenue needed improvement for the following reasons:

(a)   US GAAP comprised broad revenue recognition concepts and detailed guidance for particular industries or transactions, which often resulted in different accounting for economically similar transactions.

(b)   the previous revenue Standards in IFRS had different principles and were sometimes difficult to understand and apply to transactions other than simple ones. In addition, IFRS had limited guidance on important topics such as revenue recognition for multiple-element arrangements. Consequently, some entities that were applying IFRS referred to parts of US GAAP to develop an appropriate revenue recognition accounting policy.

(c)   the disclosures required under both IFRS and US GAAP were inadequate and often did not provide users of financial statements with information to sufficiently understand revenue arising from contracts with customers.

BC3   IFRS 15 and Topic 606[1] eliminate those inconsistencies and weaknesses by providing a comprehensive revenue recognition model that applies to a wide range of transactions and industries. The comprehensive model also improves previous IFRS and US GAAP by:

(a)   providing a more robust framework for addressing revenue recognition issues;

(b)   improving comparability of revenue recognition practices across entities, industries, jurisdictions and capital markets;

(c)   simplifying the preparation of financial statements by reducing the amount of guidance to which entities must refer; and

(d)   requiring enhanced disclosures to help users of financial statements better understand the nature, amount, timing and uncertainty of revenue that is recognised.

Background

BC4   In December 2008, the boards published for public comment the Discussion Paper *Preliminary Views on Revenue Recognition in Contracts with Customers* and received more than 200 comment letters in response. In the Discussion Paper, the boards proposed the general principles of a contract-based revenue recognition model with a measurement approach that was based on an allocation of the transaction price. That revenue recognition model was developed after extensive discussions by the boards on alternative models for recognising and measuring revenue (see paragraphs BC16–BC27).

BC5   Respondents to the Discussion Paper generally supported the objective of developing a comprehensive revenue recognition model for both IFRS and US GAAP. Most respondents also generally supported the recognition and measurement principles proposed in the Discussion Paper, which are the basic building blocks of the revenue recognition model. In particular, the Discussion Paper introduced the concepts that a contract contains performance obligations for the entity to transfer goods or services to a customer and that revenue is recognised when the entity satisfies its performance obligations as a result of the customer obtaining control of those goods or services.

BC6   Respondents to the Discussion Paper were mainly concerned about the following proposals:

---

1   Unless indicated otherwise, all references to IFRS 15 in this Basis for Conclusions can be read as also referring to Topic 606.

(a)   identifying performance obligations only on the basis of the timing of the transfer of the good or service to the customer. Respondents commented that this would be impractical, especially when many goods or services are transferred over time to the customer (for example, in construction contracts).

(b)   using the concept of control to determine when a good or service is transferred. Respondents asked the boards to clarify the application of the concept of control to avoid the implication that the proposals would require completed contract accounting for all construction contracts (ie revenue is recognised only when the customer obtains legal title or physical possession of the completed asset).

BC7   The boards considered those comments when developing the Exposure Draft *Revenue from Contracts with Customers* (the FASB's Exposure Draft was a proposed Accounting Standards Update), which was published in June 2010 (the '2010 Exposure Draft'). Nearly 1,000 comment letters were received from respondents representing a wide range of industries, including construction, manufacturing, telecommunications, technology, pharmaceutical, biotechnology, financial services, consulting, media and entertainment, energy and utilities, freight and logistics, and industries with significant franchising operations, such as hospitality and quick-service restaurant chains. The boards and their staffs also consulted extensively on the proposals in the 2010 Exposure Draft by participating in round-table discussions, conferences, working group sessions, discussion forums and one-to-one discussions that were held across all major geographical regions.

BC8   The boards also received a substantial number of comment letters in response to a question asked by the FASB on whether the proposals should apply to non-public entities. Almost all of those comment letters were from respondents associated with sections of the US construction industry (for example, private construction contractors, accounting firms that serve those contractors and surety providers who use the financial statements of construction contractors when deciding whether to guarantee that those contractors will meet their obligations under a contract). Those respondents also raised concerns about the application of the proposed model to non-public entities. Those issues were considered and discussed separately by the FASB.

BC9   With the exception of many of the responses from non-public entities in the construction industry, most of the feedback from the comment letters and from the consultation activities generally supported the boards' proposal for a comprehensive revenue recognition model for both IFRS and US GAAP. Moreover, most respondents supported the core principle of that model, which was that an entity should recognise revenue to depict the transfer of goods or services to a customer in an amount that reflects the amount of consideration that the entity expects to receive for those goods or services.

BC10   Almost all respondents to the 2010 Exposure Draft indicated that the boards should clarify further the operation of the core principle. In particular, respondents were concerned about the application of the following:

(a) the concept of control and, in particular, the application of the indicators of the transfer of control to service contracts and to contracts for the transfer of an asset over time to a customer as it is being constructed (for example, a work-in-progress asset).

(b) the principle of distinct goods or services for identifying performance obligations in a contract. Many respondents were concerned that the proposed principle would lead to inappropriate disaggregation of the contract.

BC11 The boards addressed those concerns during the redeliberations of the proposals in the 2010 Exposure Draft. As the redeliberations of those proposals drew to a close, the boards decided to issue a revised Exposure Draft for public comment to provide interested parties with an opportunity to comment on the revisions that the boards had made since the 2010 Exposure Draft was published. The boards decided unanimously that it was appropriate to go beyond their established due process and re-expose their revised revenue proposals, because of the importance of revenue to all entities and to avoid unintended consequences in the recognition of revenue for specific contracts or industries. The revised Exposure Draft *Revenue from Contracts with Customers* was published in November 2011 (the '2011 Exposure Draft') and approximately 350 comment letters were received from respondents representing a wide range of industries. As in the case of the 2010 Exposure Draft, the boards and their staffs consulted extensively on the proposals in the 2011 Exposure Draft. This consultation also included all major geographical regions and occurred in a number of formats. Many of the discussions focused on detailed analyses related to the application of the revenue recognition model and the principles in the 2011 Exposure Draft.

BC12 Almost all respondents continued to support the core principle of the revenue recognition model, which is that an entity should recognise revenue to depict the transfer of promised goods or services to customers in an amount that reflects the consideration to which the entity expects to be entitled in exchange for those goods or services. Moreover, most of the feedback from the comment letters and from the consultation activities generally supported the revisions to the boards' proposed revenue recognition model in the 2011 Exposure Draft. However, respondents raised issues or questions on some of the proposals in the 2011 Exposure Draft. That feedback could be broadly divided into three categories:

(a) requests for clarifications and further refinements—such as on the criteria for identifying performance obligations, determining when a performance obligation is satisfied over time and constraining estimates of variable consideration;

(b) difficulties in the practical application of the requirements—such as on the time value of money (referred to as a significant financing component in IFRS 15) and the retrospective application of the proposed Standard; and

(c) disagreement with some of the proposed requirements for the following topics:

(i) identifying onerous performance obligations;

© IFRS Foundation

      (ii)   disclosing information about revenue;

      (iii)   applying the requirements for licences; and

      (iv)   applying the allocation principles to contracts that are prevalent in the telecommunications industry.

BC13   The boards addressed those concerns during the redeliberations of the proposals in the 2011 Exposure Draft. The boards' discussion of those concerns and their conclusions are included in the relevant sections of this Basis for Conclusions.

Why make the change?

BC14   Throughout the project, some respondents questioned the need to replace the requirements for revenue recognition, particularly because those requirements seemed to work reasonably well in practice and provided useful information about the different types of contracts for which they were intended.

      (a)   For US GAAP, some questioned whether a new revenue recognition model was necessary, because Accounting Standards Update No. 2009-13 *Revenue Recognition (Topic 605): Multiple-Deliverable Revenue Arrangements* resolved some of the issues that the Revenue Recognition project had originally intended to resolve. Furthermore, the *FASB Accounting Standards Codification®* (the Codification) had simplified the process of accessing and researching previous requirements for revenue.

      (b)   For IFRS, some indicated that the IASB could have improved, rather than replace, its previous revenue Standards by developing additional requirements for critical issues (for example, multiple-element arrangements).

BC15   The boards acknowledged that it would have been possible to improve many of the previous revenue recognition requirements without replacing them. However, even after the changes to US GAAP mentioned in paragraph BC14(a), the requirements in US GAAP would have continued to result in inconsistent accounting for revenue and, consequently, would not have provided a robust framework for addressing revenue recognition issues in the future. Furthermore, amending the requirements would have failed to achieve one of the goals of the Revenue Recognition project, which was to develop a common revenue standard for IFRS and US GAAP that entities could apply consistently across industries, jurisdictions and capital markets. Because revenue is a crucial number to users of financial statements, the boards decided that a common standard on revenue for IFRS and US GAAP is an important step toward achieving the goal of a single set of high-quality global accounting standards. To be consistent with that goal, the boards noted that previous revenue recognition requirements in IFRS and US GAAP should not be used to supplement the principles in IFRS 15.

Alternative revenue recognition models

BC16   During the early stages of their Revenue Recognition project, the boards considered various alternative revenue recognition models, including the following:

(a)   the basis for recognising revenue—specifically, whether an entity should recognise revenue only when it transfers a promised good or service to a customer (a contract-based revenue recognition principle) or when (or as) the entity undertakes a productive activity (which could be an activity that is undertaken regardless of whether a contract exists); and

(b)   the basis for measuring revenue—specifically, whether revenue should be measured at an allocated customer consideration amount (ie the transaction price) or at a current exit price.

Basis for recognising revenue

BC17   In the Discussion Paper, the boards proposed a principle to recognise revenue on the basis of the accounting for the asset or the liability arising from a contract with a customer. The boards had two reasons for developing a standard on revenue that applies only to contracts with customers. First, contracts to provide goods or services to customers are important economic phenomena and are crucial to most entities. Second, most previous revenue recognition requirements in IFRS and US GAAP focused on contracts with customers. The boards decided that focusing on the recognition and measurement of the asset or liability arising from a contract with a customer and the changes in that asset or liability over the life of the contract would bring discipline to the earnings process approach. Consequently, it would result in entities recognising revenue more consistently than they did under previous revenue recognition requirements.

BC18   Upon entering into a contract with a customer, an entity obtains rights to receive consideration from the customer and assumes obligations to transfer goods or services to the customer (performance obligations). The combination of those rights and performance obligations gives rise to a (net) asset or a (net) liability depending on the relationship between the remaining rights and the performance obligations. The contract is an asset (a contract asset) if the measure of the remaining rights exceeds the measure of the remaining performance obligations. Conversely, the contract is a liability (a contract liability) if the measure of the remaining performance obligations exceeds the measure of the remaining rights.

BC19   By definition, revenue from a contract with a customer cannot be recognised until a contract exists. Conceptually, revenue recognition could occur at the point at which an entity enters into a contract with a customer. For an entity to recognise revenue at contract inception (before either party has performed), the measure of the entity's rights must exceed the measure of the entity's performance obligations. This could occur if the rights and obligations were measured at current exit prices and would lead to revenue recognition because of an increase in a contract asset. However, as described in paragraph BC25, the boards proposed in the Discussion Paper that performance obligations should be measured at the same amount as the rights in the contract at contract inception, thereby precluding the recognition of a contract asset and revenue at contract inception.

BC20   Therefore, the boards decided that revenue should be recognised only when an entity transfers a promised good or service to a customer, thereby satisfying a performance obligation in the contract. That transfer results in revenue recognition, because upon satisfying a performance obligation an entity no longer has that obligation to provide the good or service. Consequently, its position in the contract increases—either its contract asset increases or its contract liability decreases—and that increase leads to revenue recognition.

BC21 Although, conceptually, revenue arises from an increase in a contract asset or a decrease in a contract liability, the boards articulated the requirements in terms of the recognition and measurement of revenue rather than the recognition and measurement of the contract. The boards noted that focusing on the timing and amount of revenue from a contract with a customer would simplify the requirements. Feedback from respondents to the Discussion Paper and the 2010 and 2011 Exposure Drafts confirmed that view.

BC22 Nearly all respondents to the Discussion Paper agreed with the boards' view that an entity generally should not recognise revenue if there is no contract with a customer. However, some respondents requested that the boards instead develop an activities model in which revenue would be recognised as the entity undertakes activities in producing or providing goods or services, regardless of whether those activities result in the transfer of goods or services to the customer. Those respondents reasoned that recognising revenue over time, for example, throughout long-term construction or other service contracts, regardless of whether goods or services are transferred to the customer, would provide users of financial statements with more useful information.

BC23 However, the boards noted the following concerns about an activities model:

(a) revenue recognition would not have been based on accounting for the contract. In an activities model, revenue arises from increases in the entity's assets, such as inventory or work-in-progress, rather than only from rights under a contract. Consequently, conceptually, an activities model does not require a contract with a customer for revenue recognition, although revenue recognition could be precluded until a contract exists. However, that would have resulted in revenue being recognised at contract inception for any activities completed to that point.

(b) it would have been counterintuitive to many users of financial statements. An entity would have recognised consideration as revenue when the customer had not received any promised goods or services in exchange.

(c) there would have been potential for abuse. An entity could have accelerated revenue recognition by increasing its activities (for example, production of inventory) at the end of a reporting period.

(d) it would have resulted in a significant change to previous revenue recognition requirements and practices. In many of those requirements, revenue was recognised only when goods or services were transferred to the customer. For example, previous requirements in IFRS required revenue from the sale of a good to be recognised when the entity transferred ownership of the good to the customer. The boards also observed that the basis for percentage-of-completion accounting in previous revenue recognition requirements could be viewed as similar to the core principle in IFRS 15.

BC24   Accordingly, the boards did not develop an activities model and they maintained their view that a contract-based revenue recognition principle is the most appropriate principle for a general revenue recognition standard for contracts with customers.

Basis for measuring revenue

BC25   The boards decided that an allocated transaction price approach should be applied to measure performance obligations. Using that approach, an entity would allocate the transaction price to each performance obligation in the contract (see paragraphs BC181 and BC266). In the Discussion Paper, the boards considered an alternative approach to measure performance obligations directly at current exit prices. However, the boards rejected that approach for the following reasons:

(a)   an entity would have recognised revenue before transferring goods or services to the customer at contract inception if the measure of rights to consideration exceeded the measure of the remaining performance obligations. That would have been a typical occurrence at contract inception, because the transaction price often includes amounts that enable an entity to recover its costs to obtain a contract.

(b)   any errors in identifying or measuring performance obligations could have affected revenue recognised at contract inception.

(c)   a current exit price (ie the price that would be received to sell an asset or paid to transfer a liability) for the remaining performance obligations is typically not observable and an estimated current exit price could be complex and costly to prepare and difficult to verify.

BC26   Almost all respondents supported the boards' proposal to measure performance obligations using an allocated transaction price approach.

BC27   In the Discussion Paper, the boards also considered whether it would be appropriate to require an alternative measurement approach for some types of performance obligations (for example, performance obligations with highly variable outcomes, for which an allocated transaction price approach may not result in useful information). However, the boards decided that the benefits of accounting for all performance obligations within the scope of the requirements using the same measurement approach outweighed any concerns about using that approach for some types of performance obligations. The boards also noted that a common type of contract with customers that has highly variable outcomes would be an insurance contract, which is excluded from the scope of IFRS 15.

Clarifications to IFRS 15 (amendments issued in April 2016)

BC27A   After issuing IFRS 15 and Topic 606 in May 2014, the boards formed the Transition Resource Group (TRG) for Revenue Recognition to support implementation of these standards. One of the objectives of the TRG is to inform the boards about implementation issues to help the boards determine what, if any, action should be undertaken to address those issues. The substantial majority of the submissions from stakeholders regarding the implementation of IFRS 15, as discussed by the TRG, were determined to be sufficiently addressed by the requirements in IFRS 15. However, the TRG's discussions on five topics indicated potential differences of views on how to implement the requirements and, therefore, were considered by the boards. Those topics were:

(a)   identifying performance obligations;

(b)   principal versus agent considerations;

(c)   licensing;

(d)   collectability; and

(e)   measuring non-cash consideration.

BC27B   The boards also received requests from some stakeholders for practical expedients in respect of the following:

(a)   accounting for contract modifications that occurred before transition to IFRS 15;

(b)   for entities electing to use the full retrospective transition method, accounting for a contract completed under previous revenue Standards before transition to IFRS 15; and

(c)   assessing whether a sales tax (or a similar tax) is collected on behalf of a third party.

BC27C   The boards discussed the five topics and the possible practical expedients, and each board decided to make amendments to clarify the requirements in IFRS 15 and Topic 606 respectively. As a result, the IASB issued *Clarifications to IFRS 15* in April 2016 making targeted amendments to IFRS 15 with respect to three of the five topics considered—identifying performance obligations, principal versus agent considerations and licensing. The IASB concluded that it was not necessary to amend IFRS 15 with respect to the other two topics—collectability and measuring non-cash consideration. In respect of the practical expedients, the IASB provided transition relief for modified contracts and completed contracts.

BC27D   In reaching its conclusions to make clarifying amendments and provide transition relief to IFRS 15, the IASB considered the need to balance being responsive to issues raised to help entities implement IFRS 15 but, at the same time, not creating a level of uncertainty about IFRS 15 to the extent that the IASB's actions might be disruptive to the implementation process. The IASB noted that, when new Standards are issued, there are always initial questions that arise. Those questions are generally resolved as entities, auditors and others work through them over time, and gain a better understanding of the new requirements. The IASB also considered the effect of any differences between its decisions and those made by the FASB.

BC27E   With these wider considerations in mind, the IASB decided to apply a high hurdle when considering whether to amend IFRS 15 and, thus, to minimise changes to the extent possible. On this basis, the IASB made clarifying amendments to IFRS 15 only when (a) it considered those amendments to be essential to clarifying the IASB's intentions when developing the requirements in IFRS 15; or (b) it viewed the benefits of retaining converged requirements as greater than any potential costs of amending the requirements.

BC27F The FASB decided to make more extensive amendments to Topic 606, as explained in paragraph BC27G. The FASB issued amendments to the application guidance in Topic 606 on principal versus agent considerations, Accounting Standards Update (ASU) *2016-08, Revenue from Contracts with Customers (Topic 606): Principal versus Agent Considerations (Reporting Revenue Gross versus Net)*, in March 2016. The FASB is expected to issue two further ASUs:

(a) one ASU for its amendments to the requirements with respect to identifying performance obligations and the application guidance on licensing; and

(b) another ASU for its amendments to the requirements in Topic 606 with respect to the other topics and the practical expedients.

BC27G The FASB's amendments to Topic 606 are the same as the IASB's amendments to IFRS 15 with respect to (a) the requirements on identifying performance obligations relating to the determination of whether an entity's promise to transfer a good or service to a customer is distinct within the context of the contract; and (b) the application guidance on principal versus agent considerations. The FASB made further amendments regarding some other requirements on identifying performance obligations. In relation to licensing, the boards made the same clarifying amendments for sales-based and usage-based royalties. The boards decided to make different amendments to the application guidance relating to identifying the nature of an entity's promise in granting a licence. The FASB also decided to amend Topic 606 for other issues relating to licensing for which the IASB decided not to make any amendments to IFRS 15. The FASB has also decided (a) to amend Topic 606 with respect to collectability and measuring non-cash consideration and (b) to provide an accounting policy election to present all sales taxes on a net basis. The FASB decided to provide similar transition relief to that provided in IFRS 15 for contract modifications. However, with respect to completed contracts, the FASB decided to (a) amend the definition of a completed contract; and (b) provide transition relief, similar to the relief provided by the IASB, only for entities that apply Topic 606 in accordance with paragraph 606-10-65-1(d)(2) (equivalent to paragraph C3(b) of IFRS 15).

BC27H Because of the different decisions of the boards, Appendix A *Comparison of IFRS 15 and Topic 606* to this Basis for Conclusions has been updated. The IASB's considerations together with an overview of the FASB's considerations (based on both the amendments to Topic 606 issued and decisions made by the FASB until March 2016) in reaching their respective decisions are explained in the following paragraphs.

Topics for which both the IASB and FASB decided to amend IFRS 15 and Topic 606

Topic	Reference
Identifying performance obligations	paragraphs BC116A–BC116U
Principal versus agent considerations	paragraphs BC385A–BC385Z
Licensing	paragraphs BC414A–BC414Y paragraphs BC421A–BC421J
Practical expedients on transition	paragraphs BC445A–BC445B paragraphs BC445J–BC445R

Topics for which the IASB decided not to amend IFRS 15 but the FASB decided to amend Topic 606

Topic	Reference
Collectability	paragraphs BC46A–BC46H
Presentation of sales taxes (determining the transaction price)	paragraphs BC188A–BC188D
Non-cash consideration	paragraphs BC254A–BC254H
Definition of a completed contract	paragraphs BC445C–BC445I

Scope

BC28   The boards decided that IFRS 15 should apply only to a subset of revenue as defined in each of the boards' conceptual frameworks (ie revenue from contracts with customers). Revenue from transactions or events that does not arise from a contract with a customer is not within the scope of IFRS 15 and, therefore, those transactions or events will continue to be recognised in accordance with other Standards, for example:

(a)   dividends received (although these requirements existed in previous revenue Standards in IFRS, the IASB has moved them unchanged, and without changing their effect, into IFRS 9 *Financial Instruments*);

(b)   non-exchange transactions (for example, donations or contributions received);

(c)   for IFRS, changes in the value of biological assets, investment properties and the inventory of commodity broker-traders; and

(d)   for US GAAP, changes in regulatory assets and liabilities arising from alternative revenue programmes for rate-regulated entities in the scope of Topic 980 on regulated operations. (The FASB decided that the revenue arising from those assets or liabilities should be presented separately from revenue arising from contracts with customers. Therefore, the FASB made amendments to Subtopic 980-605 *Regulated Operations—Revenue Recognition*.)

BC29　The boards decided not to amend the existing definitions of revenue in each of their conceptual frameworks. The boards decided that they will consider the definition of revenue when they revise their respective conceptual frameworks. However, the IASB decided to carry forward into IFRS 15 the description of revenue from the IASB's *Conceptual Framework for Financial Reporting* rather than the definition of revenue from a previous revenue Standard. The IASB noted that the definition in a previous revenue Standard referred to 'gross inflow of economic benefits' and it had concerns that some might have misread that reference as implying that an entity should recognise as revenue a prepayment from a customer for goods or services. As described in paragraphs BC17–BC24, the principle is that revenue is recognised in accordance with IFRS 15 as a result of an entity satisfying a performance obligation in a contract with a customer. In addition, the FASB decided to carry forward a definition of revenue that is based on the definition in FASB Concepts Statement No. 6 *Elements of Financial Statements*.

BC30　The converged definitions of a contract and a customer establish the scope of IFRS 15.

Definition of a contract (Appendix A)

BC31　The boards' definition of contract is based on common legal definitions of a contract in the United States and is similar to the definition of a contract used in IAS 32 *Financial Instruments: Presentation*. The IASB decided not to adopt a single definition of a contract for both IAS 32 and IFRS 15, because the IAS 32 definition implies that contracts can include agreements that are not enforceable by law. Including such agreements would have been inconsistent with the boards' decision that a contract with a customer must be enforceable by law for an entity to recognise the rights and obligations arising from that contract. The IASB also noted that amending the IAS 32 definition would have posed the risk of unintended consequences in accounting for financial instruments.

BC32　The definition of a contract emphasises that a contract exists when an agreement between two or more parties creates enforceable rights and obligations between those parties. The boards noted that the agreement does not need to be in writing to be a contract. Whether the agreed-upon terms are written, oral or evidenced otherwise (for example, by electronic assent), a contract exists if the agreement creates rights and obligations that are enforceable against the parties. Determining whether a contractual right or obligation is enforceable is a question to be considered within the context of the relevant legal framework (or equivalent framework) that exists to ensure that the parties' rights and obligations are upheld. The boards observed that the factors that determine enforceability may differ between jurisdictions. Although there must be enforceable rights and obligations between parties for a contract to exist, the boards decided that the performance obligations within the contract could include promises that result in the customer having a valid expectation that the entity will transfer goods or services to the customer even though those promises are not enforceable (see paragraph BC87).

BC33 The boards decided to complement the definition of a contract by specifying criteria that must be met before an entity can apply the revenue recognition model to that contract (see paragraph 9 of IFRS 15). Those criteria are derived mainly from previous revenue recognition requirements and other existing standards. The boards decided that when some or all of those criteria are not met, it is questionable whether the contract establishes enforceable rights and obligations. The boards' rationale for including those criteria is discussed in paragraphs BC35–BC46.

BC34 The boards also decided that those criteria would be assessed at contract inception and would not be reassessed unless there is an indication that there has been a significant change in facts and circumstances (see paragraph 13 of IFRS 15). The boards decided that it was important to reassess the criteria in those cases, because that change might clearly indicate that the remaining contractual rights and obligations are no longer enforceable. The word 'remaining' in paragraph 13 of IFRS 15 indicates that the criteria would be applied only to those rights and obligations that have not yet transferred. That is, an entity would not include in the reassessment (and therefore would not reverse) any receivables, revenue or contract assets already recognised.

The parties have approved the contract and are committed to perform their respective obligations (paragraph 9(a))

BC35 The boards decided to include this criterion because if the parties to a contract have not approved the contract, it is questionable whether that contract is enforceable. Some respondents questioned whether oral and implied contracts could meet this criterion, especially if it is difficult to verify an entity's approval of that contract. The boards noted that the form of the contract does not, in and of itself, determine whether the parties have approved the contract. Instead, an entity should consider all relevant facts and circumstances in assessing whether the parties intend to be bound by the terms and conditions of the contract. Consequently, in some cases, the parties to an oral or an implied contract (in accordance with customary business practices) may have agreed to fulfil their respective obligations. In other cases, a written contract may be required to determine that the parties to the contract have approved it.

BC36 In addition, the boards decided that the parties should be committed to performing their respective obligations under the contract. However, the boards decided that an entity and a customer would not always need to be committed to fulfilling all of their respective rights and obligations for a contract to meet the requirements in paragraph 9(a) of IFRS 15. For example, a contract might include a requirement for the customer to purchase a minimum quantity of goods from the entity each month, but the customer's past practice indicates that the customer is not committed to always purchasing the minimum quantity each month and the entity does not enforce the requirement to purchase the minimum quantity. In that example, the criterion in paragraph 9(a) of IFRS 15 could still be satisfied if there is evidence that demonstrates that the customer and the entity are substantially committed to the contract. The boards noted that requiring all of the rights and obligations to be fulfilled would have inappropriately resulted in no recognition of revenue for some contracts in which the parties are substantially committed to the contract.

The entity can identify each party's rights regarding the goods or services to be transferred (paragraph 9(b))

BC37   The boards decided to include this criterion because an entity would not be able to assess the transfer of goods or services if it could not identify each party's rights regarding those goods or services.

The entity can identify the payment terms for the goods or services to be transferred (paragraph 9(c))

BC38   The boards decided to include this criterion because an entity would not be able to determine the transaction price if it could not identify the payment terms in exchange for the promised goods or services.

BC39   Respondents from the construction industry questioned whether an entity can identify the payment terms for orders for which the scope of work may already have been defined even though the specific amount of consideration for that work has not yet been determined and may not be finally determined for a period of time (sometimes referred to as unpriced change orders or claims). The boards clarified that their intention is not to preclude revenue recognition for unpriced change orders if the scope of the work has been approved and the entity expects that the price will be approved. The boards noted that, in those cases, the entity would consider the requirements for contract modifications (see paragraphs BC76–BC83).

The contract has commercial substance (paragraph 9(d))

BC40   The boards decided to include 'commercial substance' as a criterion when they discussed whether revenue should be recognised in contracts with customers that include non-monetary exchanges. Without that requirement, entities might transfer goods or services back and forth to each other (often for little or no cash consideration) to artificially inflate their revenue. Consequently, the boards decided that an entity should not recognise revenue from a non-monetary exchange if the exchange has no commercial substance.

BC41   The boards decided to describe commercial substance in paragraph 9(d) of IFRS 15 in a manner that is consistent with its existing meaning in other financial reporting contexts, such as existing requirements for non-monetary exchange transactions. The boards also observed that this criterion is important in all contracts (not only non-monetary exchanges) because without commercial substance it is questionable whether an entity has entered into a transaction that has economic consequences. Consequently, the boards decided that all contracts should have commercial substance before an entity can apply the other requirements in the revenue recognition model.

It is probable that the entity will collect the consideration to which it will be entitled (paragraph 9(e))

BC42   The boards included the criterion in paragraph 9(e) of IFRS 15 (which acts like a collectability threshold) because they concluded that the assessment of a customer's credit risk was an important part of determining whether a contract is valid. Furthermore, the boards decided to include this criterion as a consequence of their decision that customer credit risk should not affect the measurement or presentation of revenue (see paragraphs BC259–BC265).

BC43 The boards decided that a collectability threshold is an extension of the other requirements in paragraph 9 of IFRS 15 on identifying the contract. In essence, the other criteria in paragraph 9 require an entity to assess whether the contract is valid and represents a genuine transaction. The collectability threshold is related to that assessment because a key part of assessing whether a transaction is valid is determining the extent to which the customer has the ability and the intention to pay the promised consideration. In addition, entities generally only enter into contracts in which it is probable that the entity will collect the amount to which it will be entitled.

BC44 The boards noted that the term 'probable' has different meanings under US GAAP and IFRS. Under US GAAP, the term was initially defined in Topic 450 *Contingencies* as 'likely to occur' whereas under IFRS, probable is defined as 'more likely than not'. The boards noted that using the same term which has different meanings in US GAAP and IFRS could result in accounting that is not converged when determining whether the criterion in paragraph 9(e) of IFRS 15 is met. However, the boards noted that the term 'probable' was used in some of the collectability thresholds in their previous revenue recognition requirements and both boards wanted to maintain consistency with those requirements. (The term 'reasonably assured' was also used in collectability thresholds in some parts of US GAAP. However, in this context, the FASB understood that in practice, probable and reasonably assured had similar meanings.) In addition, the boards observed that in most transactions, an entity would not enter into a contract with a customer in which there was significant credit risk associated with that customer without also having adequate economic protection to ensure that it would collect the consideration. Consequently, the boards decided that there would not be a significant practical effect of the different meaning of the same term because the population of transactions that would fail to meet the criterion in paragraph 9(e) of IFRS 15 would be small.

BC45 In determining whether it is probable that an entity will collect the amount of consideration to which the entity will be entitled, an entity might first need to determine the amount of consideration to which the entity will be entitled. This is because, in some circumstances, the amount of consideration to which an entity will be entitled may be less than the price stated in the contract. This could be because the entity might offer the customer a price concession (see paragraph 52 of IFRS 15) or because the amount of consideration to which an entity will be entitled varies for other reasons, such as the promise of a bonus. In either of those circumstances, an entity considers whether it is probable that the entity will collect the amount of consideration to which it will be entitled when the uncertainty relating to that consideration is resolved. The entity assesses whether it is probable of collecting that amount by considering both of the following:

(a) the ability (ie the financial capacity) of the customer to pay the amount of consideration to which the entity will be entitled in exchange for the goods or services transferred.

(b)   the customer's intention to pay that amount. The boards observed that an assessment of the customer's intention would require an entity to consider all of the facts and circumstances, including the past practice of that customer or customer class. The boards noted that this assessment should be made on the assumption that the amount will be due (ie the corresponding performance obligation will be satisfied and the consideration is not subject to further variability that might affect the entity's entitlement to that consideration).

BC46   In addition, the boards specified in paragraph 9(e) of IFRS 15 that an entity should assess only the consideration to which it will be entitled in exchange for the goods or services that will be transferred to a customer. Therefore, if the customer were to fail to perform as promised and consequently the entity would respond to the customer's actions by not transferring any further goods or services to the customer, the entity would not consider the likelihood of payment for those goods or services that would not be transferred.

Clarifications to IFRS 15 (amendments issued in April 2016)—topics for which the IASB decided not to amend IFRS 15

BC46A   The TRG discussed an implementation question raised by stakeholders about how to apply the collectability criterion in paragraph 9(e) of IFRS 15 in instances in which the entity has received non-refundable consideration from a customer assessed as having poor credit quality. The discussion informed the boards that there are potentially different interpretations of:

(a)   how to apply the collectability criterion in paragraph 9(e) when it is not probable that the total consideration promised in the contract is collectable; and

(b)   when to recognise the non-refundable consideration received from the customer as revenue in accordance with paragraph 15 of IFRS 15 when the contract does not meet the criteria in paragraph 9 of IFRS 15.

Assessing collectability

BC46B   Paragraph 9(e) requires an entity to assess whether it is probable that it will collect the consideration to which it will be entitled in exchange for the goods or services that will be transferred to the customer. This assessment forms part of Step 1 of IFRS 15 *Identify the contract(s) with a customer*. The TRG's discussions informed the boards that some stakeholders interpreted this requirement to mean that an entity should assess the probability of collecting all of the consideration promised in the contract. Under this interpretation, some contracts with customers that are assessed as having poor credit quality would not meet the criteria in paragraph 9(e), even though they are otherwise valid contracts. Other stakeholders asserted that those contracts would be valid if the entity has the ability to protect itself from credit risk.

BC46C   The boards noted that the assessment in paragraph 9(e) requires an entity to consider how the entity's contractual rights to the consideration relate to its performance obligations. That assessment considers the entity's exposure to the customer's credit risk and the business practices available to the entity to manage its exposure to credit risk throughout the contract. For example, an entity may be able to stop providing goods or services to the customer or require advance payments. This is consistent with the explanation of the boards' considerations as described in paragraph BC46.

BC46D The FASB decided to amend the implementation guidance and illustrations in Topic 606 to clarify that an entity should assess the collectability of the consideration promised in a contract for the goods or services that will be transferred to the customer rather than assessing the collectability of the consideration promised in the contract for all of the promised goods or services.

BC46E Having considered the wider implications of amending IFRS 15 before its effective date, the IASB concluded that the existing requirements in IFRS 15 and the explanations in paragraphs BC42–BC46 are sufficient. The IASB noted that it expects practice to develop consistently with the boards' intentions in developing the collectability criterion in paragraph 9(e). The IASB does not expect the FASB's anticipated clarifications to the paragraph equivalent to paragraph 9(e) in Topic 606 to result in any additional differences in outcomes. In reaching its decision, the IASB observed that an entity will generally not enter into a contract with a customer if the entity does not consider it to be probable that the entity will collect the consideration to which it will be entitled in exchange for the goods or services that will be transferred to the customer. This is consistent with the boards' reasoning in paragraph BC43. It was not the boards' intention that many contracts should fail the condition in paragraph 9(e). On this basis, the IASB thinks that the population of contracts to which any clarification to paragraph 9(e) might apply is small.

Contract termination

BC46F Paragraph 15 specifies when an entity should recognise any consideration received from a customer as revenue when the contract does not meet Step 1 of the revenue recognition model. Paragraph 15(b) states that an entity should recognise revenue when the contract has been terminated and the consideration received from the customer is non-refundable. The TRG's discussions informed the boards about potential diversity in stakeholders' understanding of when a contract is terminated. The assessment of when a contract is terminated affects when an entity recognises revenue in a contract that does not meet Step 1 of the revenue recognition model. Some stakeholders asserted that a contract is terminated when an entity stops transferring promised goods or services to the customer. Other stakeholders asserted that a contract is terminated only when the entity stops pursuing collection from the customer. Stakeholders noted that those two events often occur at different points in time. For example, entities sometimes pursue collection for a significant period of time after they have stopped transferring promised goods or services to the customer. As a result, non-refundable consideration received from the customer might be recognised as a liability for a significant period of time during which an entity pursues collection, even though the entity may have stopped transferring promised goods or services to the customer and has no further obligations to transfer goods or services to the customer.

BC46G The FASB decided to amend paragraph 606-10-25-7 of Topic 606 (equivalent to paragraph 15 of IFRS 15) to add an additional event in which an entity should recognise any consideration received as revenue. This amendment is expected to allow an entity to recognise any consideration received as revenue when (a) the entity has transferred control of the goods or services to which the consideration received relates; (b) the entity has stopped transferring additional goods or services and has no obligation to transfer additional goods or services; and (c) the consideration received from the customer is non-refundable.

BC46H   The IASB noted that contracts often specify that an entity has the right to terminate the contract in the event of non-payment by the customer and that this would not generally affect the entity's rights to recover any amounts owed by the customer. The IASB also noted that an entity's decision to stop pursuing collection would not typically affect the entity's rights and the customer's obligations under the contract with respect to the consideration owed by the customer. On this basis, the IASB concluded that the existing requirements in IFRS 15 are sufficient for an entity to conclude, without any additional clarification, that a contract is terminated when it stops providing goods or services to the customer. Some IASB members also expressed concerns about the potential for unintended consequences relating to other areas of IFRS if contract termination were to be defined in IFRS 15. Consequently, the IASB decided not to amend paragraph 15.

Accounting for contracts that do not meet the criteria in paragraph 9

BC47   The boards decided to include the requirements in paragraphs 14–16 of IFRS 15 in response to questions from some respondents about how an entity should account for its rights and obligations when a contract does not meet the criteria in paragraph 9 of IFRS 15. Those respondents were concerned that if a contract did not meet the criteria in paragraph 9 of IFRS 15, in the absence of specific requirements, an entity would seek alternative guidance and potentially apply the revenue recognition model by analogy, which might not result in appropriate accounting. Consequently, the boards specified that in cases in which the contract does not meet the criteria in paragraph 9 of IFRS 15, an entity should recognise the consideration received as revenue only when one of the events in paragraph 15 of IFRS 15 has occurred or the entity reassesses the criteria in paragraph 9 of IFRS 15 and the contract subsequently meets those criteria.

BC48   The requirements in paragraph 15 are consistent with the boards' rationale for paragraph 9 of IFRS 15, which is to filter out contracts that may not be valid and that do not represent genuine transactions, and therefore recognising revenue for those contracts would not provide a faithful representation of such transactions. The requirements therefore preclude an entity from recognising any revenue until the contract is either complete or cancelled or until a subsequent reassessment indicates that the contract meets all of the criteria in paragraph 9 of IFRS 15. The boards noted that this approach is similar to the 'deposit method' that was previously included in US GAAP and that was applied when there was no consummation of a sale.

BC49   The boards considered whether to include asset derecognition requirements (and therefore cost recognition requirements) for assets related to a contract that does not meet the criteria in paragraph 9 of IFRS 15. However, the boards decided not to include requirements for asset derecognition for these types of transactions, because including those requirements would be outside the scope of this project. (However, the FASB added some asset derecognition guidance to other Standards for transactions outside the scope of the requirements—that is, for the transfer of non-financial assets. See paragraphs BC494–BC503.) The boards noted that entities should apply existing IFRS and US GAAP to assets related to contracts that do not meet the criteria in paragraph 9 of IFRS 15.

Wholly unperformed contracts

BC50   The boards decided that IFRS 15 should not apply to wholly unperformed contracts if each party to the contract has the unilateral enforceable right to terminate the contract without penalty. Those contracts would not affect an entity's financial position or performance until either party performs. In contrast, there could be an effect on an entity's financial position and performance if only one party could terminate a wholly unperformed contract without penalty. For instance, if only the customer could terminate the wholly unperformed contract without penalty, the entity is obliged to stand ready to perform at the discretion of the customer. Similarly, if only the entity could terminate the wholly unperformed contract without penalty, it has an enforceable right to payment from the customer if it chooses to perform.

BC51   In accordance with IFRS 15, an entity's rights and obligations in wholly unperformed non-cancellable contracts are measured at the same amount and, therefore, would offset each other at inception. However, by including those contracts within the scope of IFRS 15, an entity would provide additional information about a change in its financial position that resulted from entering into those contracts, that is, disclosing the amount of transaction price allocated to the remaining performance obligations in that wholly unperformed contract (see paragraph 120 of IFRS 15).

Definition of a customer (paragraph 6 and Appendix A)

BC52   The boards decided to define the term 'customer' to enable an entity to distinguish contracts that should be accounted for under IFRS 15 (ie contracts with customers) from contracts that should be accounted for under other requirements.

BC53   The definition of a customer in IFRS 15 refers to an entity's ordinary activities. Some respondents asked the boards to clarify the meaning of ordinary activities; however, the boards decided not to provide additional requirements, because the notion of ordinary activities is derived from the definitions of revenue in the boards' respective conceptual frameworks. In particular, the IASB's *Conceptual Framework* description of revenue refers specifically to the 'ordinary activities of an entity' and the definition of revenue in FASB Concepts Statement No. 6 refers to the notion of an entity's 'ongoing major or central operations'. As noted in paragraph BC29, the boards did not reconsider those definitions as part of the Revenue Recognition project.

BC54   Some respondents asked the boards to clarify whether the parties to some common types of contracts (for example, contracts with collaborators or partners) would meet the definition of a customer. However, the boards decided that it would not be feasible to develop application guidance that would apply uniformly to various industries because the nature of the relationship (ie supplier-customer versus collaboration or partnership) would depend on specific terms and conditions in those contracts. The boards observed that in many arrangements highlighted by respondents, an entity would need to consider all relevant facts and circumstances, such as the purpose of the activities undertaken by the counterparty, to determine whether the counterparty is a customer. Examples of arrangements in which an entity would need to make that assessment are as follows:

(a) collaborative research and development efforts between biotechnology and pharmaceutical entities or similar arrangements in the aerospace and defence, technology and healthcare industries or in higher education;

(b) arrangements in the oil and gas industry in which partners in an offshore oil and gas field may make payments to each other to settle any differences between their proportionate entitlements to production volumes from the field during a reporting period; and

(c) arrangements in the not-for-profit industry in which an entity receives grants and sponsorship for research activity and the grantor or sponsor may specify how any output from the research activity will be used.

BC55 The boards noted that a contract with a collaborator or a partner (for example, a joint arrangement as defined in IFRS 11 *Joint Arrangements* or a collaborative arrangement within the scope of Topic 808 *Collaborative Arrangements*) could also be within the scope of IFRS 15 if that collaborator or partner meets the definition of a customer for some or all of the terms of the arrangement.

BC56 The boards also noted that in some cases it might be appropriate for an entity to apply the principles of IFRS 15 to some transactions with collaborators or partners. For example, an entity might consider applying IFRS 15 to a collaborative arrangement or partnership, provided such application is appropriate in accordance with IAS 8 *Accounting Policies, Changes in Accounting Estimates and Errors* or, for an entity applying US GAAP, provided there are not more relevant authoritative requirements in US GAAP.

BC57 Notwithstanding the boards' decision that only contracts with customers should be accounted for under IFRS 15, the boards also decided that some of the requirements in IFRS 15 should apply to the transfer of non-financial assets that are not an output of an entity's ordinary activities (see paragraphs BC494–BC503).

Exchanges of products to facilitate a sale to another party (paragraph 5(d))

BC58 In industries with homogeneous products, it is common for entities in the same line of business to exchange products to facilitate sales to customers or potential customers other than the parties to the exchange. For example, an oil supplier may swap inventory with another oil supplier to reduce transport costs, meet immediate inventory needs, or otherwise facilitate the sale of oil to the end customer. The boards noted that the party exchanging inventory with the entity meets the definition of a customer, because it has contracted with the entity to obtain an output of the entity's ordinary activities. Consequently, in the absence of specific requirements, an entity might recognise revenue once for the exchange of inventory and then again for the sale of the inventory to the end customer. The boards decided that this outcome would be inappropriate for the following reasons:

(a)   it would have grossed up revenues and expenses and made it difficult for users of financial statements to assess the entity's performance and gross margins during the reporting period; and

(b)   some view the counterparty in those arrangements as also acting as a supplier and not as a customer.

BC59   The boards considered modifying the definition of a customer. However, they rejected that alternative because of concerns about unintended consequences. Consequently, the boards decided to exclude from the scope of IFRS 15 transactions involving non-monetary exchanges between entities in the same line of business to facilitate sales to customers or to potential customers. The FASB noted such exchanges should remain within the scope of Topic 845 on non-monetary transactions.

Contracts with customers outside the scope of the requirements (paragraph 5)

BC60   The boards also excluded from the scope of IFRS 15 three types of contracts with customers that they are addressing in other Standards:

(a)   leases;

(b)   insurance contracts; and

(c)   financial instruments and other contractual rights or obligations within the scope of the boards' other Standards.

BC61   Some respondents asked the FASB to clarify what is meant by 'contractual rights or obligations' in paragraph 5 of the requirements, because those respondents stated that it is unclear whether financial instrument arrangements that are addressed elsewhere in the Codification, such as letters of credit and loan commitments (addressed in Topic 440 *Commitments*), would be included within the scope of Topic 606. The FASB noted that its intention is that if specific requirements in other Topics of the Codification deal with a transaction, the more detailed requirements from those other Topics should be applied rather than the requirements in Topic 606. For example, the FASB decided to exclude from the scope of Topic 606 guarantees (other than product warranties) that are within the scope of Topic 460 *Guarantees*, because the focus of the existing accounting requirements for those guarantee arrangements relates primarily to recognising and measuring a guarantee liability.

BC62   Some respondents reasoned that excluding some contracts with customers from the scope of IFRS 15 (such as those identified in paragraph BC60) could perpetuate the development of industry-specific or transaction-specific revenue recognition guidance, which would be inconsistent with the Revenue Recognition project's stated objective. The boards disagreed with that view. In the boards' view, IFRS 15 provides them with a framework for considering revenue issues in other standard-setting projects. The boards decided that, within the context of those other projects, a different basis of accounting for those contracts with customers might provide users of financial statements with more relevant information.

BC63 Other respondents identified what they perceived to be a contradiction within the scope requirements in IFRS 15 and IFRS 9. Those respondents stated that some of the requirements for accounting for contract assets (which would meet the definition of a financial asset) are inconsistent with the requirements in financial instruments Standards for accounting for financial assets. For example, in some cases a contract asset is not required to be adjusted for the time value of money (see paragraph BC236), and in other cases the contract asset might initially be measured at an amount that excludes some of the expected cash flows if the transaction price includes variable consideration (see paragraphs BC189–BC223). However, the IASB disagreed with those respondents. The IASB noted that the requirements in paragraph 5 of IFRS 15 (together with paragraph 2(k) of IAS 39 *Financial Instruments: Recognition and Measurement*, which is a consequential amendment to IAS 39 added by IFRS 15) are clear that when a contract asset is within the scope of IFRS 15, it is not within the scope of IFRS 9.

Contracts partially within the scope of other Standards (paragraph 7)

BC64 Some contracts with customers are partially within the scope of IFRS 15 and partially within the scope of other Standards (for example, a lease with a service contract). The boards decided that it would be inappropriate in those cases for an entity to account for the entire contract in accordance with one standard or another. This is because it could result in different accounting outcomes depending on whether the goods or services were sold on a stand-alone basis or together with other goods or services.

BC65 The boards considered whether the requirements in IFRS 15 should be the default approach for separating a contract and allocating consideration to each part. However, specific issues could arise in separating contracts that are not within the scope of IFRS 15. For example, a financial instrument or an insurance contract might require an entity to provide services that are best accounted for in accordance with IFRS 9, Subtopic 942-605 *Financial Services—Depository and Lending—Revenue Recognition*, IFRS 4 *Insurance Contracts*, or Subtopic 944-605 *Financial Services—Insurance—Revenue Recognition*.

BC66 Consequently, the boards decided that if other Standards specify how to separate and/or initially measure parts of a contract, an entity should first apply those Standards. In other words, the more specific Standard would take precedence in accounting for a part of a contract and any residual consideration should be allocated to the part(s) of the contract within the scope of IFRS 15. This rationale is consistent with the principle in IFRS 15 related to scope, which is that another Standard should be applied to a portion of the contract or arrangement if that Standard provides specific requirements for that portion of the contract or arrangement. The boards' decision is also consistent with the requirements for multiple-element arrangements in US GAAP that were replaced by Topic 606.

The boards noted that this decision results in any discount in the overall arrangement being allocated to the portion of the arrangement within the scope of IFRS 15.

Identifying the contract (paragraphs 9–16)

BC67   The boards decided that the revenue recognition model would apply to a contract with a customer only when the criteria in paragraph 9 of IFRS 15 are met. The rationale for those criteria is described in paragraphs BC33–BC46.

BC68   IFRS 15 applies to a single contract with a customer. In many cases, the contract that is accounted for separately will be the individual contract negotiated with the customer. However, the structure and scope of a contract can vary depending on how the parties to the contract decide to record their agreement. For instance, there may be legal or commercial reasons for the parties to use more than one contract to document the sale of related goods or services or to use a single contract to document the sale of unrelated goods or services. One of the boards' objectives in developing IFRS 15 is that the accounting for a contract should depend on an entity's present rights and obligations rather than on how the entity structures the contract.

Applying IFRS 15 at a portfolio level

BC69   IFRS 15 specifies the accounting required for an individual contract. Many entities have a large number of contracts and as a result some respondents noted practical challenges in applying the model on a contract-by-contract basis. These respondents questioned whether it would always be necessary to apply IFRS 15 on a contract-by-contract basis. The boards observed that the way in which an entity applies the model to its contracts is not a matter for which the boards should specify requirements. Nonetheless, in the light of the feedback, the boards decided to include a practical expedient in paragraph 4 of IFRS 15 to acknowledge that a practical way to apply IFRS 15 to some contracts may be to use a 'portfolio approach'. The boards acknowledged that an entity would need to apply judgement in selecting the size and composition of the portfolio in such a way that the entity reasonably expects that application of the revenue recognition model to the portfolio would not differ materially from the application of the revenue recognition model to the individual contracts or performance obligations in that portfolio. In their discussions, the boards indicated that they did not intend for an entity to quantitatively evaluate each outcome and, instead, the entity should be able to take a reasonable approach to determine the portfolios that would be appropriate for its types of contracts.

BC70   The boards observed that because it is a practical way to apply IFRS 15, the portfolio approach may be particularly useful in some industries in which an entity has a large number of similar contracts and applying the model separately for each contract may be impractical. For example, entities in the telecommunications industry explained that implementing accounting systems to determine the stand-alone selling price for the promised goods or services in each contract and, in turn, allocating the transaction price to the performance obligations identified in that contract would be complex and costly (see paragraphs BC287–BC293).

Combination of contracts (paragraph 17)

BC71   The boards decided to include requirements in paragraph 17 of IFRS 15 for when an entity should combine two or more contracts and account for them as a single contract. This is because, in some cases, the amount and timing of revenue might differ depending on whether an entity accounts for two or more contracts separately or accounts for them as one contract.

BC72   The boards decided that entering into contracts at or near the same time is a necessary condition for the contracts to be combined. That decision is consistent with the objective of identifying the contract that is to be accounted for as the unit of account because that assessment is also performed at contract inception.

BC73   The boards decided that in addition to entering into contracts at or near the same time, the contracts should satisfy one or more of the criteria in paragraph 17 of IFRS 15 for the contracts to be combined. The boards observed that when either criterion (a) or (b) in paragraph 17 of IFRS 15 is met, the relationship between the consideration in the contracts (ie the price interdependence) is such that if those contracts were not combined, the amount of consideration allocated to the performance obligations in each contract might not faithfully depict the value of the goods or services transferred to the customer. The boards decided to include the criterion in paragraph 17(c) of IFRS 15 to avoid the possibility that an entity could effectively bypass the requirements for identifying performance obligations depending on how the entity structures its contracts.

BC74   The boards clarified that for two or more contracts to be combined, they should be with the same customer. However, the boards acknowledged that in some situations, contracts with related parties (as defined in IAS 24 *Related Party Disclosures* and Topic 850 *Related Party Disclosures*) should be combined if there are interdependencies between the separate contracts with those related parties. Thus, in those situations, combining the contracts with related parties results in a more appropriate depiction of the amount and timing of revenue recognition.

BC75   The boards also considered whether to specify that all contracts should be combined if they were negotiated as a package to achieve a single commercial objective, regardless of whether those contracts were entered into at or near the same time with the same customer. However, the boards decided not to do this, primarily because they were concerned that doing so could have had the unintended consequence of an entity combining too many contracts and not faithfully depicting the entity's performance. Furthermore, the boards decided that an entity should apply judgement to determine whether a contract is entered into 'at or near the same time'. However, the boards noted that the longer the period between the commitments of the parties to the contracts, the more likely it is that the economic circumstances affecting the negotiations have changed.

Contract modifications (paragraphs 18–21)

BC76   The boards observed that previous revenue recognition requirements did not include a general framework for accounting for contract modifications. Therefore, the boards decided to include requirements regarding contract modifications in IFRS 15 to improve consistency in the accounting for contract modifications. As the revenue recognition model developed, the boards proposed different approaches to account for contract modifications. However, each approach was developed with the overall objective of faithfully depicting an entity's rights and obligations in the modified contract. The boards concluded that to faithfully depict the rights and obligations arising from a modified contract, an entity should account for some modifications prospectively and for other modifications on a cumulative catch-up basis.

BC77 The boards decided that a contract modification should be accounted for prospectively if the additional promised goods or services are distinct and the pricing for those goods or services reflects their stand-alone selling price (see paragraph 20 of IFRS 15). The boards decided that when those criteria are met, there is no economic difference between an entity entering into a separate contract for the additional goods or services and an entity modifying an existing contract.

BC78 The boards also decided that a contract modification should be accounted for prospectively when the goods or services to be provided after the modification are distinct from the goods or services already provided (see paragraph 21(a) of IFRS 15). The boards decided that this should be the case regardless of whether the pricing of the additional promised goods or services reflected their stand-alone selling prices. This is because accounting for those types of modifications on a cumulative catch-up basis could be complex and may not necessarily faithfully depict the economics of the modification, because the modification is negotiated after the original contract and is based on new facts and circumstances. Therefore, this approach avoids opening up the accounting for previously satisfied performance obligations and, thus, avoids any adjustments to revenue for satisfied performance obligations.

BC79 Some respondents were concerned that an entity would also be required to use a cumulative catch-up basis to account for modifications to a contract with a single performance obligation that is made up of a series of distinct goods or services. Those contracts typically include repetitive services, such as energy contracts or mobile phone airtime services. The boards considered those concerns and clarified in paragraph 21(a) of IFRS 15 that the determination of whether a modification is accounted for prospectively depends on whether the remaining promises in the contract are for distinct goods or services. This is the case even if an entity determines that it has a single performance obligation, provided that the performance obligation represents a series of distinct goods or services (see paragraphs BC113–BC116).

BC80 The boards decided that if the remaining goods or services are not distinct and are part of a single performance obligation that is partially satisfied (ie a performance obligation satisfied over time), an entity should recognise the effect of the modification on a cumulative catch-up basis. This requires an entity to update the transaction price and the measure of progress towards complete satisfaction of a performance obligation, both of which may change as a result of the contract modification. That approach is particularly relevant to, and generally accepted in, the construction industry because a modification to those types of contracts would typically not result in the transfer of additional goods or services that are distinct from those promised in the existing contract.

BC81 Respondents also asked how the requirements for contract modifications would apply to unpriced change orders (see paragraph BC39) and contract claims (ie specific modifications in which the changes in scope and price are unapproved or in dispute). IFRS and US GAAP previously included specific guidance for unpriced change orders and contract claims within construction-type and production-type contracts. The boards decided that it was unnecessary to provide specific requirements for the accounting for these types of modifications because IFRS 15 includes the relevant requirements, specifically:

(a) paragraphs 18 and 19 of IFRS 15 require an entity to determine whether the rights and obligations of the parties to the contract that are created or changed by the unpriced change order or contract claim are enforceable;

(b) paragraph 19 of IFRS 15 requires an entity to estimate the change to the transaction price for the unpriced change order or contract claim; and

(c) paragraph 21 of IFRS 15 requires an entity to determine whether the unpriced change order or contract claim should be accounted for on a prospective basis or a cumulative catch-up basis.

Interaction between changes in the transaction price and contract modifications

BC82 The 2011 Exposure Draft proposed that an entity would account for contract modifications that result only in a change in the contract price on a cumulative catch-up basis because this would be consistent with the requirements for changes in the transaction price (as a result of changes in the estimate of variable consideration). In their redeliberations, the boards noted that the proposal would result in very different accounting outcomes depending on whether a distinct good or service was included in the modification. This is because modifications that change only the price would be accounted for on a cumulative catch-up basis, whereas modifications in which a distinct good or service (no matter how small) is added to the contract at the same time as a price change would be accounted for on a prospective basis. Furthermore, the boards noted that changes in the transaction price arising from a contract modification and changes in the expectations of variable consideration are the result of different economic events—a change in the expectation of variable consideration arises from a change in a variable that was identified and agreed upon at contract inception, whereas a change in price arising from a contract modification arises from a separate and subsequent negotiation between the parties to the contract. Consequently, the boards decided that a contract modification resulting only in a change in the contract price should be accounted for in a manner that is consistent with other contract modifications.

BC83 Some respondents requested that the boards clarify how an entity should allocate a change in the transaction price that occurs after a modification of the contract (that is accounted for in accordance with paragraph 21(a) of IFRS 15) but the change in the transaction price is attributable to an amount of variable consideration promised before the modification. This may occur because the estimate of the amount of variable consideration in the initial contract has changed or is no longer constrained. Specifically, those respondents asked whether, in those circumstances, an entity should allocate the corresponding change in the transaction price to the performance obligations in the modified contract, or to the performance obligations identified in the contract before the modification (ie the initial contract), including to performance obligations that were satisfied before the modification. In response to that feedback, the boards clarified in paragraph 90 of IFRS 15 that the allocation of the change in transaction price in those circumstances depends on whether, and the extent to which, the change in the transaction price is attributable to an amount of variable consideration promised before the modification. In providing that clarification, the boards noted that it would be appropriate in those circumstances to allocate a change in the transaction price to the performance obligations identified in the initial contract, if the promised variable consideration and the resolution of the uncertainty associated with that amount of variable consideration are not affected by the contract modification.

Identifying performance obligations

Definition of a performance obligation (Appendix A)

BC84   IFRS 15 distinguishes between obligations to provide goods or services to a customer and other obligations by defining those obligations to provide goods or services as performance obligations. The notion of a performance obligation is similar to the notions of deliverables, components or elements of a contract in previous revenue Standards. Although the notion of a performance obligation is implicit in previous revenue Standards, the term 'performance obligation' has not been defined previously.

BC85   The boards' objective in developing the definition of a performance obligation was to ensure that entities appropriately identify the unit of account for the goods and services promised in a contract with a customer. The boards decided that because the revenue recognition model is an allocated transaction price model, identifying a meaningful unit of account that depicts the goods and services in the contract is fundamental for the purpose of recognising revenue on a basis that faithfully depicts the entity's performance in transferring the promised goods or services to the customer.

BC86   The boards decided that a performance obligation could be either of the following:

(a)   a good or service (or a bundle of goods or services) that is distinct (see paragraphs BC94–BC112); or

(b)   a series of distinct goods or services that are substantially the same and have the same pattern of transfer (see paragraphs BC113–BC116).

Identifying the promised goods or services (paragraphs 24–25)

BC87   Before an entity can identify its performance obligations in a contract with a customer, the entity would first need to identify all of the promised goods or services in that contract. The boards noted that in many cases, all of the promised goods or services in a contract might be identified explicitly in that contract. However, in other cases, promises to provide goods or services might be implied by the entity's customary business practices. The boards decided that such implied promises should be considered when determining the entity's performance obligations, if those practices create a valid expectation of the customer that the entity will transfer a good or service (for example, some when-and-if-available software upgrades). The boards also noted that the implied promises in the contract do not need to be enforceable by law. If the customer has a valid expectation, then the customer would view those promises as part of the negotiated exchange (ie goods or services that the customer expects to receive and for which it has paid). The boards noted that in the absence of these requirements developed by the boards, an entity might recognise all of the consideration in a contract as revenue even though the entity continues to have remaining (implicit) promises related to the contract with the customer.

BC88 Some respondents suggested that some promised goods or services should be excluded from the scope of IFRS 15 and accounted for as marketing expenses or incidental obligations, even though those promises would meet the definition of a performance obligation. Examples of such promised goods or services may include 'free' handsets provided by telecommunication entities, 'free' maintenance provided by automotive manufacturers and customer loyalty points awarded by supermarkets, airlines and hotels. Those respondents stated that revenue should be recognised only for the main goods or services for which the customer has contracted and not for what they consider to be marketing incentives and other incidental obligations.

BC89 The boards observed that when a customer contracts with an entity for a bundle of goods or services, it can be difficult and subjective for the entity to identify the main goods or services for which the customer has contracted. In addition, the outcome of that assessment could vary significantly depending on whether the entity performs the assessment from the perspective of its business model or from the perspective of the customer. Consequently, the boards decided that all goods or services promised to a customer as a result of a contract give rise to performance obligations because those promises were made as part of the negotiated exchange between the entity and its customer. Although the entity might consider those goods or services to be marketing incentives or incidental goods or services, they are goods or services for which the customer pays and to which the entity should allocate consideration for purposes of revenue recognition. However, the boards observed that in some cases, an entity might provide incentives to a customer that would not represent a performance obligation if those incentives are provided independently of the contract that they are designed to secure. (See paragraphs BC386–BC395 for additional discussion on marketing incentives and the accounting for customer options to acquire additional goods or services.)

BC90 For similar reasons, the boards decided not to exempt an entity from accounting for performance obligations that the entity might regard as being perfunctory or inconsequential.[2] Instead, an entity should assess whether those performance obligations are immaterial to its financial statements as described in IAS 8 and FASB Concepts Statement No. 8 *Conceptual Framework for Financial Reporting*.

BC91　To help an entity identify the promised goods or services, IFRS 15 provides examples of the types of promises that can represent goods or services to the customer. In response to feedback received, the boards clarified that the following can also represent promised goods or services:

(a)　providing a service of standing ready or making goods or services available (see paragraph BC160); and

(b)　granting rights to goods or services to be provided in the future (see paragraph BC92).

BC92　The boards observed that it was important to clarify that granting a right to goods or services to be provided in the future, such as when an entity makes a promise to provide goods or services to its customer's customer, would give rise to performance obligations for the entity. Those types of promises exist in distribution networks in various industries but are particularly common in the automotive industry. For example, when a manufacturer sells a motor vehicle to its customer (a dealer), the manufacturer may also promise to provide additional goods or services (such as maintenance) to the dealer's customer. IFRS 15 requires an entity to identify all of the promises—both explicit and implicit—that are made to the customer as part of the contract with that customer. Consequently, a promise of a good or service (such as maintenance) that the customer can pass on to its customer would be a performance obligation if the promise could be identified (explicitly or implicitly) in the contract with the customer. However, the boards noted that some promised goods or services might not represent performance obligations if those promises did not exist (explicitly or implicitly) at the time that the parties agreed to the contract.

BC93　The boards also clarified that an entity should not account for activities it may perform that do not transfer goods or services to the customer. This may occur in many contracts in which an entity undertakes separate activities that do not directly transfer goods or services to the customer (for example, service contracts that require significant setup costs), even though those activities are required to successfully transfer the goods or services for which the customer has contracted. The boards decided that including those activities as performance obligations would have been inconsistent with the core revenue recognition principle because those activities do not result in a transfer of goods or services to the customer.

2　The FASB subsequently decided to amend Topic 606 to state that an entity is not required to assess whether promised goods or services are performance obligations if they are immaterial within the context of the contract with the customer. The IASB's considerations for deciding not to make similar amendments to IFRS 15 are explained in paragraphs BC116A–BC116E.

Identifying when promises represent performance obligations (paragraphs 22–30)

BC94   Contracts with customers can include many promises to transfer goods or services. In the Discussion Paper, the boards proposed that an entity should review the timing of the transfer of the promised goods or services to identify the performance obligations that it should account for separately. Respondents to the Discussion Paper were concerned that this proposal would have required an entity to account separately for every promised good or service in a contract that is transferred at a different time, which would not be practical for many contracts, especially for long-term service and construction contracts. Consequently, the boards decided to provide clearer requirements that result in an entity identifying performance obligations in a way that is practical and results in a pattern of revenue recognition that faithfully depicts the transfer of goods or services to the customer.

BC95   In developing those requirements, the boards observed that in many contracts, identifying the promised goods or services that an entity should account for separately is straightforward. Consequently, the boards developed a principle for identifying performance obligations that separates promised goods or services in a relevant way when applied across the various industries and transactions within the scope of IFRS 15. That principle is the notion of a distinct good or service. The term 'distinct', in an ordinary sense, suggests something that is different, separate or dissimilar. A majority of respondents agreed with using the principle of distinct goods or services to identify the performance obligations in a contract. However, many asked the boards to refine and further clarify the requirements for determining when a good or service is distinct.

BC96   Consequently, the boards decided that for a good or service to be distinct, the criteria in paragraph 27 of IFRS 15 must be met. The boards' deliberations of those criteria are discussed in the following sections.

Capable of being distinct

BC97   The boards decided that a good or service must possess some specified minimum characteristics to be accounted for separately. Specifically, the good or service must be capable of being distinct—that is, the good or service is capable of providing a benefit to the customer either on its own or together with other resources that are readily available to the customer. The boards were concerned that requiring an entity to account separately (and estimate a stand-alone selling price) for a good or service that is not capable of providing a benefit to the customer might result in information that would not be relevant to users of financial statements. For example, if an entity transferred a machine to the customer, but the machine is only capable of providing a benefit to the customer after an installation process that only the entity can provide, the machine would not be distinct.

BC98   The 2010 Exposure Draft addressed this notion of a minimum characteristic by proposing that a good or service should have a distinct function—that is, the good or service should have utility either on its own or together with other goods or services that the customer has acquired from the entity or that are sold separately by the entity or another entity. Respondents requested additional guidance on the meaning of 'distinct function' because they considered that almost any element of a contract could have utility in combination with other goods or services.

BC99 Consequently, the boards refined the notion of distinct function and developed the criterion in paragraph 27(a) of IFRS 15. In addition, the boards included the requirements in paragraph 28 of IFRS 15 (which were derived from the Basis for Conclusions on the 2011 Exposure Draft) to help an entity apply that criterion and assess whether a customer can benefit from the good or service on its own or together with other resources. Those requirements focus on the notion of economic benefits, which many respondents explained was helpful in assessing whether the customer can benefit from the good or service on its own or together with other resources. The boards noted that, conceptually, any good or service that is regularly sold separately should be able to be used on its own or with other resources. Otherwise, there would be no market for an entity to provide that good or service on a stand-alone basis.

BC100 The boards observed that the assessment of whether the 'customer can benefit from the goods or services on its own' should be based on the characteristics of the goods or services themselves instead of the way in which the customer may use the goods or services. Consequently, an entity would disregard any contractual limitations that might preclude the customer from obtaining readily available resources from a source other than the entity.

BC101 The attributes of a distinct good or service are comparable to previous revenue recognition requirements for identifying separate deliverables in a multiple-element arrangement, which specified that a delivered item must have 'value to the customer on a stand-alone basis' for an entity to account for that item separately. However, the boards decided against using that terminology to avoid the implication that an entity must assess the customer's intended use for the promised goods or services in identifying the performance obligations in a contract. The boards observed that it would be difficult, if not impossible, for an entity to know the customer's intentions in a given contract.

Distinct within the context of the contract[3]

BC102 In some cases, even though the individual goods or services promised as a bundle of goods or services might be capable of being distinct, those goods or services should not be accounted for separately because it would not result in a faithful depiction of the entity's performance in that contract. As an example, many construction-type and production-type contracts involve transferring to the customer many goods and services that are capable of being distinct (such as various building materials, labour and project management services). However,

---

3 *Clarifications to IFRS 15* issued in April 2016 amended paragraphs 27 and 29 of IFRS 15 to clarify that the objective of assessing whether an entity's promises to transfer goods or services to the customer are separately identifiable is to determine whether the entity's promise is to transfer (a) each of those goods or services; or (b) a combined item or items to which the promised goods or services are inputs. Amendments were also made to the factors in paragraph 29 to more clearly align them with the revised 'separately identifiable' principle. Paragraphs BC102–BC112 should therefore be read together with paragraphs BC116F–BC116Q, which explain the boards' considerations in making these amendments.

identifying all of those individual goods and services as separate performance obligations would be impractical and, more importantly, it would neither faithfully represent the nature of the entity's promise to the customer nor result in a useful depiction of the entity's performance. This is because it would result in an entity recognising and measuring revenue when the materials and other inputs to the construction or production process are provided, instead of recognising and measuring revenue when the entity performs (and uses those inputs) in the construction or production of the item (or items) for which the customer has contracted. Consequently, the boards decided that, when identifying whether goods or services are distinct, an entity should not only consider the characteristics of an individual good or service (see paragraph 27(a) of IFRS 15) but should also consider whether the promise to transfer the good or service is separately identifiable (ie distinct within the context of the contract, see paragraph 27(b) of IFRS 15).

BC103 During the development of IFRS 15, the existence of 'separable risks' was identified as a basis for assessing whether a good or service is distinct within the context of the contract. In that assessment, the individual goods or services in a bundle would not be distinct if the risk that an entity assumes to fulfil its obligation to transfer one of those promised goods or services to the customer is a risk that is inseparable from the risk relating to the transfer of the other promised goods or services in that bundle. The boards considered whether to specify 'separable risks' as a necessary attribute of a distinct good or service. However, the boards decided that the concept of 'separable risks' may not be a practical criterion for determining whether a good or service is distinct.

BC104 To make the notion of separable risks more operable, the boards considered other approaches for articulating the notion. However, the boards rejected those approaches for the following reasons:

(a) distinct profit margin—in some cases, entities may decide to assign the same margin to various goods or services, even though those goods or services use different resources and are subject to different risks. In addition, for some goods or services, especially software and other types of intellectual property, cost is not a significant factor in determining price and, therefore, margins could be highly variable because they may be determined by the customer's ability to pay or to obtain substitute goods or services from another entity.

(b) criteria based on the notions of goods or services that are significantly modified or customised, and highly interrelated goods or services that require an entity to provide a significant service of integrating those goods or services—respondents explained that while these are relevant factors to consider to determine whether a good or service is distinct, expressing those factors as criteria could be too restrictive because they could force bundling or unbundling that did not reflect the economics of the arrangement.

BC105 Consequently, the boards decided to specify in paragraph 27(b) of IFRS 15 that the objective in identifying whether a promised good or service is distinct within the context of the contract is to determine whether an entity's promise to transfer that good or service is separately identifiable from other promises in the contract. The notion of 'separately identifiable' is based on the notion of separable risks in paragraph BC103 (ie whether the risk that an entity assumes to fulfil its obligation to transfer one of those promised goods or services to the customer is a risk that is inseparable from the risk relating to the transfer of the other promised goods or services). The boards observed that determining whether the entity's promise to transfer a good or service is separately identifiable requires judgement, taking into account all of the facts and circumstances. The boards decided to assist entities in making that judgement by including the factors in paragraph 29 of IFRS 15.

BC106   The boards observed that the factors in paragraph 29 of IFRS 15 are not mutually exclusive. On the contrary, because the factors are based on the same underlying principle of inseparable risks, the boards noted that in many cases more than one of the factors might apply to a contract with a customer. However, each factor was developed because it may be more applicable for particular contracts or industries. The rationale for each factor is discussed in paragraphs BC107–BC112.

Significant integration service (paragraph 29(a))

BC107   In circumstances in which an entity provides an integration service, the risk of transferring individual goods or services is inseparable, because a substantial part of the entity's promise to a customer is to ensure the individual goods or services are incorporated into the combined output. Thus, the individual goods or services are inputs to produce a single output. The boards observed that this factor may be relevant in many construction contracts in which the contractor provides an integration (or contract management) service to manage and co-ordinate the various construction tasks and to assume the risks associated with the integration of those tasks. Moreover, the integration service will require a contractor to co-ordinate the tasks performed by any subcontractors and ensure that those tasks are performed in accordance with the contract specifications, thus ensuring the individual goods or services are appropriately incorporated into the combined item for which the customer has contracted.

BC108   The boards observed that this factor could apply to industries other than the construction industry. For example, some software development contracts with significant integration services will similarly have promised goods and services that meet the criterion in paragraph 27(b) of IFRS 15. However, the boards did not intend for this factor to be applied too broadly to software integration services for which the risk that the entity assumes in integrating the promised goods or services is negligible (for example, a simple installation of software that does not require significant modification). Therefore, to provide some additional clarification for many software-type contracts, the boards included the factor in paragraph 29(b) of IFRS 15.

Significant modification or customisation (paragraph 29(b))

BC109   In some industries, such as the software industry, the notion of inseparable risks is more clearly illustrated by assessing whether one good or service significantly modifies or customises another good or service. This is because if a good or service modifies or customises another good or service in the contract, each good or service is being assembled together (ie as inputs) to produce a combined output for which the customer has contracted.

BC110 For example, an entity may promise to provide a customer with existing software and also promise to customise that software so that it will function with the customer's existing infrastructure such that the entity is providing the customer with a fully integrated system. In this case, if the customisation service requires the entity to significantly modify the existing software in such a way that the risks of providing the software and the customisation service are inseparable, the entity may conclude that the promises to transfer the software and the customisation service would not be separately identifiable and, therefore, those goods or services would not be distinct within the context of the contract.

Highly dependent or highly interrelated (paragraph 29(c))

BC111 The boards decided to include the factor in paragraph 29(c) of IFRS 15 because, in some cases, it might be unclear whether the entity is providing an integration service (see paragraph 29(a)) or whether the goods or services are significantly modified or customised (see paragraph 29(b)). However, the individual goods and services in the contract may still not be separately identifiable from the other goods or services promised in the contract. This may be because the goods or services are highly dependent on, or highly interrelated with, other promised goods or services in the contract in such a way that the customer could not choose to purchase one good or service without significantly affecting the other promised goods or services in the contract.

BC112 Consider the following example—an entity agrees to design an experimental new product for a customer and to manufacture 10 prototype units of that product. The specifications for the product include functionality that has yet to be proved. Consequently, the entity will be required to continue to revise the design of the product during the construction and testing of the prototypes and make any necessary modifications to in-progress or completed prototypes. The entity expects that most or all of the units to be produced may require some rework because of design changes made during the production process. In that case, the customer may not be able to choose whether to purchase only the design service or the manufacturing service without significantly affecting one or the other. This is because the risk of providing the design service is inseparable from the manufacturing service. Thus, although each promise may have benefit on its own, within the context of the contract, they are not separately identifiable. This is because the entity determines that each promise is highly dependent on, and highly interrelated with, the other promises in the contract.

A series of distinct goods or services that are substantially the same and have the same pattern of transfer (paragraph 22(b))

BC113 The boards decided to specify that a promise to transfer a series of distinct goods or services that are substantially the same and that have the same pattern of transfer to the customer would be a single performance obligation if two criteria are met. The boards decided to include this notion as part of the definition of a performance obligation to simplify the application of the model and to promote consistency in the identification of performance obligations in circumstances in which the entity provides the same good or service consecutively over a period of time (for example, a repetitive service arrangement). To be accounted for as a single performance obligation, each of those promised goods or services must be performance obligations satisfied over time in accordance with paragraph 35 of IFRS 15.

BC114 The boards observed that without this part of the definition, applying the model might present some operational challenges when an entity provides a series of distinct goods or services that are substantially the same. Otherwise, the entity would be required to identify multiple distinct goods or services, allocate the transaction price to each of the resulting performance obligations on a stand-alone selling price basis and then recognise revenue when those performance obligations are satisfied. For example, in a repetitive service contract such as a cleaning contract, transaction processing or a contract to deliver electricity, an entity would be required to allocate the overall consideration to each increment of service (for example, each hour of cleaning) to be provided in the contract. The boards decided that it would not be cost-effective to apply the model in this manner and determined that including paragraph 22(b) of IFRS 15 as part of the definition of a performance obligation would alleviate costs. This is because when paragraph 22(b) of IFRS 15 applies (ie the contract includes a promise to transfer a series of distinct goods or services that are substantially the same and have the same pattern of transfer to the customer), an entity will identify a single performance obligation and allocate the transaction price to the performance obligation. The entity will then recognise revenue by applying a single measure of progress to that performance obligation.

BC115 The boards noted that if an entity determines it has a performance obligation that meets the criterion in paragraph 22(b) of IFRS 15, an entity should consider the distinct goods or services in the contract, rather than the performance obligation, for the purposes of contract modifications and the allocation of variable consideration.

BC116 In their redeliberations, the boards observed that paragraph 22(b) of IFRS 15 applies to goods or services that are delivered consecutively, rather than concurrently. The boards noted that IFRS 15 would not need to specify the accounting for concurrently delivered distinct goods or services that have the same pattern of transfer. This is because, in those cases, an entity is not precluded from accounting for the goods or services as if they were a single performance obligation, if the outcome is the same as accounting for the goods and services as individual performance obligations.

Clarifications to IFRS 15 (amendments issued in April 2016)

Promised goods or services that are immaterial within the context of the contract

BC116A The TRG discussed an implementation question about whether an entity should identify items or activities as promised goods or services that were not identified as deliverables or components under previous revenue Standards. A specific concern was raised about the boards' decision (see paragraph BC90) not to exempt an entity from accounting for performance obligations that the entity might regard as being perfunctory or inconsequential. Some stakeholders held the view that IFRS 15 might require an entity to identify significantly more performance obligations than would have been the case under previous revenue Standards.

BC116B   In response to stakeholders' concerns, the FASB decided to amend Topic 606 to state that an entity is not required to assess whether promised goods or services are performance obligations if they are immaterial within the context of the contract with the customer. The FASB decided to specify that an entity is required to consider whether a promised good or service is material only at the contract level because it would be unduly burdensome to require an entity to aggregate and determine the effect on its financial statements of those items or activities determined to be immaterial at the contract level. In addition, the FASB decided to specify that an entity is required to accrue the costs, if any, to transfer immaterial goods or services to the customer in instances in which the costs will be incurred after the satisfaction of the performance obligation (and recognition of revenue) to which those immaterial goods or services relate.

BC116C   Having considered the wider implications of amending IFRS 15, the IASB decided that it was not necessary to incorporate similar wording into IFRS 15. The TRG's discussion highlighted that the concerns raised primarily related to potential changes to practice under US GAAP. Previous revenue Standards under IFRS did not contain similar language to the guidance issued by the staff of the US Securities and Exchange Commission on inconsequential or perfunctory performance obligations. The TRG's discussion also indicated that IFRS stakeholders can understand and apply the requirements of IFRS 15 in this area.

BC116D   In its deliberations, the IASB expressed the view that the concerns raised relate to the application of materiality concepts rather than the application of the requirements in IFRS 15. As described in paragraph BC84, the boards intended the notion of a performance obligation to be similar to the notions of deliverables, components or elements of a contract in previous revenue Standards. The IASB noted that IFRS 15 requires an entity to identify performance obligations rather than promised goods or services. Accordingly, although an entity makes an assessment of the goods or services promised in a contract in order to identify material performance obligations, the boards did not intend to require an entity to individually identify every possible promised good or service.

BC116E   In reaching its decision, the IASB also observed that the explanation in paragraph BC90 should be read within the context of the boards' explanation of the development of IFRS 15 rather than as implying that an entity is required to identify perfunctory or inconsequential goods or services promised in a contract. One of the reasons that the IASB decided not to introduce an exemption for perfunctory or inconsequential performance obligations is that it was not considered necessary, both because of how the concept of 'distinct' is applied and also because of the application of materiality. In assessing promised goods or services and identifying performance obligations, entities should consider not only materiality considerations but also the overall objective of IFRS 15. The IASB further noted that materiality is an overarching concept that applies throughout IFRS and not just when it is mentioned explicitly.

Identifying performance obligations (paragraphs 27–30)

BC116F   The TRG discussed issues relating to the principle in paragraph 27(b) regarding when a promised good or service is separately identifiable (ie distinct within the context of a contract) and the supporting factors in paragraph 29. The discussion informed the boards about potential diversity in stakeholders' understanding and indicated that there was a risk of paragraph 29(c) being applied more broadly than intended, resulting in promised goods or services being inappropriately combined and accounted for as a single performance obligation. Stakeholders asked about the application of this factor to scenarios in which one of the promised goods or services is dependent on the transfer of the other, such as a contract for equipment and related consumables that are required for the equipment to function. Some stakeholders suggested that, although the promised goods or services may be capable of being distinct, if one of the goods or services was dependent on the other, the promised goods or services would not be distinct within the context of the contract.

BC116G   In the light of the TRG discussions, the IASB was initially of the view that the discussions highlighted educational needs and that, given the nature of the issues raised, amendments to IFRS 15 were not required and that the examples accompanying IFRS 15 could be clarified to illustrate the application of the requirements. Consequently, in its Exposure Draft *Clarifications to IFRS 15*, the IASB proposed to add some new examples, and to amend some of the existing examples that accompany IFRS 15. The FASB decided to propose amendments to Topic 606 to clarify the guidance relating to the identification of performance obligations. In particular, their proposed amendments included expanding the articulation of the 'separately identifiable' principle and reframing the existing factors in paragraph 606-10-25-21 (paragraph 29 of IFRS 15) to align them with the amended principle.

BC116H   Some respondents to the IASB's Exposure Draft asked for the amendments proposed by the FASB to be incorporated into paragraph 29 of IFRS 15. They expressed concerns about differences in wording between IFRS and US GAAP and also indicated that the FASB's proposed amendments would improve the understanding of the separately identifiable principle and the operability of the requirements. Step 2 is a fundamental part of IFRS 15 that affects accounting in subsequent steps of the revenue recognition model. Consequently, in its redeliberations of the amendments the IASB concluded that the benefits of retaining converged requirements on this topic outweigh the potential costs of amending the requirements. Accordingly, the IASB decided to amend IFRS 15 to clarify the principle and the factors that indicate when two or more promises to transfer goods or services are not separately identifiable. Those amendments are the same as the FASB's related amendments to Topic 606.

BC116I   Although the wording describing the separately identifiable principle in paragraph 29 has been amended, the amendments clarify the boards' intentions and are not a change to the underlying principle. The boards observed that applying the principle in paragraph 27(b) requires judgement, taking into account facts and circumstances (see paragraph BC105). Even after amending the factors in paragraph 29 of IFRS 15, the boards recognise that judgement will be needed to determine whether promised goods or services are distinct within the context of the contract.

BC116J The amendments are intended to convey that an entity should evaluate whether its promise, within the context of the contract, is to transfer each good or service individually or a combined item (or items) that comprises the individual goods or services promised in the contract. Therefore, entities should evaluate whether the promised goods or services in the contract are outputs or, instead, are inputs to a combined item (or items). In many cases, the inputs to a combined item concept might be further explained as a situation in which an entity's promise to transfer goods or services results in a combined item that is more than (or substantively different from) the sum of those individual promised goods and services. For example, in a contract to build a wall, the promise to provide bricks and the promise to provide labour are not separately identifiable from each other within the context of the contract because those promises together comprise the promise to the customer to build the wall.

BC116K The boards previously considered the concept of 'separable risks' (see paragraph BC103) as an alternative basis for assessing whether an entity's promise to transfer a good or service is separately identifiable from other promises in the contract. Although the boards decided not to use this terminology in IFRS 15, the notion of separable risks continues to influence the separately identifiable principle. The evaluation of whether an entity's promise is separately identifiable considers the relationship between the various goods or services within the contract in the context of the process of fulfilling the contract. Therefore, an entity should consider the level of integration, interrelation or interdependence among the promises to transfer goods or services. The boards observed that rather than considering whether one item, by its nature, depends on the other (ie whether two items have a functional relationship), an entity evaluates whether there is a transformative relationship between the two items in the process of fulfilling the contract.

BC116L The boards decided to reframe the factors in paragraph 29 of IFRS 15 to more clearly align them with the revised wording of the separately identifiable principle. This clarification emphasises that the separately identifiable principle is applied within the context of the bundle of promised goods or services in the contract rather than within the context of each individual promised good or service. The separately identifiable principle is intended to identify when an entity's performance in transferring a bundle of goods or services in a contract is fulfilling a single promise to a customer. Accordingly, the boards revised the wording to emphasise that an entity should evaluate whether two or more promised goods or services each significantly affect the other (and, therefore, are highly interdependent or highly interrelated) in the contract. Furthermore, the boards concluded that it may be clearer to structure those factors to identify when the promises in a bundle of promised goods or services are *not* separately identifiable and, therefore, constitute a single performance obligation.

BC116M   In addition to reframing the factors in the context of a bundle of goods or services, the boards amended the factor relating to a significant integration service in paragraph 29(a) of IFRS 15 to clarify two related issues—that application of this factor is not limited to circumstances that result in a single output, and that a combined output may include more than one phase, element or unit. This concept is illustrated by the example in paragraph BC112, in which an entity agrees to design an experimental product for a customer and to manufacture 10 prototype units of that product. In the example, the design and production of the units is an iterative process and the significant integration service provided by the entity relates to all 10 prototype units.

BC116N   The TRG's discussions also highlighted that some stakeholders may have been interpreting the factors supporting paragraph 27(b) as a series of criteria. Paragraph 29, where the factors are set out, provides a non-exhaustive list of factors to consider; not all of those factors need to exist (or not exist) to conclude that the entity's promises to transfer goods or services are not (are) separately identifiable. Similarly, the boards also noted that the factors are not intended to be criteria that are evaluated independently of the separately identifiable principle. Given the wide variety of revenue arrangements that are within the scope of IFRS 15, the boards expect that there will be some instances for which the factors will be less relevant to the evaluation of the separately identifiable principle. Consequently, entities should consider the objective of the principle, not just the factors provided in paragraph 29 of IFRS 15.

BC116O   Stakeholders also asked about the effect of contractual restrictions on the identification of performance obligations. Accordingly, one of the examples added (Case D of Example 11) illustrates the boards' observation in paragraph BC100 of IFRS 15 that an entity should focus on the characteristics of the promised goods or services themselves instead of on the way in which the customer might be required to use the goods or services.

BC116P   The IASB decided that it was not necessary to add some of the examples that the FASB included in its amendments to Topic 606. In particular, the IASB concluded that an example relating to whether an anti-virus software licence is distinct from when-and-if-available updates to the software during the licence period (Example 10, Case C in Topic 606) was unnecessary. The IASB thought that this additional example was not required because Example 55 that accompanies IFRS 15 illustrates the application of the requirements on identifying performance obligations to a similar fact pattern.

BC116Q   Respondents to the Exposure Draft expressed concern that the proposed Example 10, Case B may imply that any contract manufacturing or similar arrangement would be a single performance obligation comprising goods that are not distinct. There are some similarities between the fact pattern in the example and other contracts with customers that involve project management, the production of customised goods or the manufacture of a series of identical goods. However, an entity should evaluate the nature of its promise(s) to a customer within the context of the contract. Example 10, Case B illustrates a scenario in which the entity is contractually required to undertake a significant effort to establish a customised production process specifically in order to produce the highly complex, specialised devices for which the customer has contracted. As a result, the entity's promise is to establish and provide a service of producing the contracted devices based on the customer's specifications. In contrast, other manufacturing scenarios may involve the development of a production process that can be used to produce goods for multiple contracts with the same or additional customers. In that case, the contract may not include a promise to establish a customised production process.

Shipping and handling activities

BC116R   Some stakeholders in the United States expressed differing views about when shipping and handling activities that occur after the transfer of control to the customer should be accounted for as a promised service or as a fulfilment activity. Under previous revenue Standards, entities often did not account for shipping provided in conjunction with the sale of their goods as an additional service. As a result, some stakeholders raised cost-benefit concerns and asked whether relief should be provided in respect of shipping and handling activities from the general requirement to assess the goods or services promised in a contract with a customer in order to identify performance obligations.

BC116S   When the boards discussed these concerns, board members noted that shipping and handling activities that occur before the customer obtains control of the related good are fulfilment activities. However, if control of a good has been transferred to a customer, shipping and handling services are provided in relation to the customer's good, which may indicate that the entity is providing a service to the customer.

BC116T   In response to the cost-benefit concerns raised by stakeholders, the FASB decided to amend Topic 606 to:

(a)   permit an entity, as an accounting policy election, to account for shipping and handling activities that occur after the customer has obtained control of a good as fulfilment activities; and

(b)   explicitly state that shipping and handling activities that occur before the customer obtains control of the related good are fulfilment activities.

BC116U   Having considered the wider implications of amending IFRS 15, the IASB decided not to make a similar amendment, for the following reasons:

(a)   An accounting policy choice for shipping and handling activities after control of goods has been transferred to the customer would create an exception to the revenue recognition model and potentially reduce comparability between entities. Paragraph 22 of IFRS 15 requires an entity to assess the goods or services promised in a contract with a customer in order to identify performance obligations. The introduction of a policy choice would override this requirement.

(b)   In addition, a policy choice is applicable to all entities. Consequently, it is possible that entities with significant shipping operations would make different policy elections. This would make it more difficult for users of financial statements to understand and compare the revenue reported by different entities, including those within the same industry.

The IASB acknowledged that, because the policy choice is not available in IFRS 15, this gives rise to a difference between IFRS 15 and Topic 606.

Satisfaction of performance obligations (paragraphs 31–45)

BC117 Revenue is recognised when (or as) goods or services are transferred to a customer. This is because an entity satisfies its performance obligation by transferring control of the promised good or service underlying that performance obligation to the customer. Consequently, assessing when control of a good or service is transferred is a critical step in applying IFRS 15.

Control

BC118 Most previous revenue Standards required an entity to assess the transfer of a good or service by considering the transfer of risks and rewards of ownership. However, the boards decided that an entity should assess the transfer of a good or service by considering when the customer obtains control of that good or service, for the following reasons:

(a) Both goods and services are assets that a customer acquires (even if many services are not recognised as an asset because those services are simultaneously received and consumed by the customer), and the boards' existing definitions of an asset use control to determine when an asset is recognised or derecognised.

(b) Assessing the transfer of goods or services using control should result in more consistent decisions about when goods or services are transferred, because it can be difficult for an entity to judge whether an appropriate level of the risks and rewards of ownership of a good or service has been transferred to the customer if the entity retains some risks and rewards.

(c) A risks-and-rewards approach could conflict with identifying performance obligations. For example, if an entity transfers a product to a customer but retains some risks associated with that product, an assessment based on risks and rewards might result in the entity identifying a single performance obligation that could be satisfied (and therefore revenue would be recognised) only after all the risks are eliminated. However, an assessment based on control might appropriately identify two performance obligations—one for the product and another for a remaining service, such as a fixed price maintenance agreement. Those performance obligations would be satisfied at different times.

BC119 Many respondents to both the 2010 and the 2011 Exposure Drafts agreed with using control to determine when a good or service is transferred to a customer. However, some respondents indicated that the transfer of the risks and rewards of ownership is sometimes a helpful indicator that control has transferred (see paragraph BC154).

Developing the notion of control

BC120 The boards' description of control is based on the meaning of control in the definitions of an asset in the boards' respective conceptual frameworks. Thus, the boards determined that control of a promised good or service (ie an asset) is the customer's ability to direct the use of, and obtain substantially all of the remaining benefits from, the asset. The components that make up the description of control are explained as follows:

(a)   ability—a customer must have the present right to direct the use of, and obtain substantially all of the remaining benefits from, an asset for an entity to recognise revenue. For example, in a contract that requires a manufacturer to produce an asset for a particular customer, it might be clear that the customer will ultimately have the right to direct the use of, and obtain substantially all of the remaining benefits from, the asset. However, the entity should not recognise revenue until the customer has actually obtained that right (which, depending on the contract, might occur during production or afterwards).

(b)   direct the use of—a customer's ability to direct the use of an asset refers to the customer's right to deploy that asset in its activities, to allow another entity to deploy that asset in its activities, or to restrict another entity from deploying that asset.

(c)   obtain the benefits from—the customer must have the ability to obtain substantially all of the remaining benefits from an asset for the customer to obtain control of it. Conceptually, the benefits from a good or service are potential cash flows (either an increase in cash inflows or a decrease in cash outflows). A customer can obtain the benefits directly or indirectly in many ways, such as by using, consuming, disposing of, selling, exchanging, pledging or holding an asset.

BC121   The boards observed that the assessment of when control has transferred could be applied from the perspective of either the entity selling the good or service or the customer purchasing the good or service. Consequently, revenue could be recognised when the seller surrenders control of a good or service or when the customer obtains control of that good or service. Although in many cases both perspectives lead to the same result, the boards decided that control should be assessed primarily from the perspective of the customer. That perspective minimises the risk of an entity recognising revenue from undertaking activities that do not coincide with the transfer of goods or services to the customer.

Applying the notion of control

BC122   As described in paragraph BC119, many respondents agreed with using control as the basis for assessing when the transfer of a promised good or service (ie an asset) occurs. However, most respondents to the 2010 Exposure Draft explained that the definition was most helpful when applied to performance obligations for the transfer of goods. They commented that applying the concept of control is straightforward in those cases because, typically, it is clear that an asset has transferred from the entity to its customer. They noted, however, that the requirements were more difficult to apply to performance obligations for services and construction-type contracts, because it could be difficult to determine when a customer obtains control of a service. This is because in many service contracts the service asset is simultaneously created and consumed and, therefore, is never recognised as an asset by the customer. Even in the case of a construction contract in which there is a recognisable asset, it can be difficult to assess whether a customer has the ability to direct the use of, and obtain substantially all of the remaining benefits from, a partially completed asset that the seller is creating. Consequently, many respondents in the construction industry were concerned that they would be required to change their revenue recognition policy from using a percentage-of-completion method to a completed contract method (ie on the basis that the transfer of assets occurs only upon transfer of legal title or physical possession of the finished asset, which typically occurs upon contract completion). Those respondents explained that the outcome of applying the completed contract method to their contracts with customers would not be a faithful depiction of the economics of those contracts.

BC123 As a result, some respondents suggested that the boards provide guidance for the transfer of control of services separately from the guidance for goods. However, the boards observed that it would be difficult to clearly define a service and not all contracts that are commonly regarded as services result in a transfer of resources to customers over time. Furthermore, the boards decided that the notion of control should apply equally to both goods and services. Consequently, to address respondents' concerns, the boards decided to specify requirements that focus on the attribute of the timing of when a performance obligation is satisfied (ie when a good or service is transferred to a customer). Accordingly, IFRS 15 includes criteria for determining whether a performance obligation is satisfied over time. Those criteria are explained in the following paragraphs.

Performance obligations satisfied over time (paragraphs 35–37)

BC124 The boards developed the criteria in paragraph 35 of IFRS 15 to provide an objective basis for assessing when control transfers over time and, thus, when a performance obligation is satisfied over time.

Customer simultaneously receives and consumes benefits as entity performs (paragraph 35(a))

BC125 In many typical service contracts, the entity's performance creates an asset only momentarily, because that asset is simultaneously received and consumed by the customer. In those cases, the simultaneous receipt and consumption of the asset that has been created means that the customer obtains control of the entity's output as the entity performs and, thus, the entity's performance obligation is satisfied over time. For example, consider an entity that promises to process transactions on behalf of a customer. The customer simultaneously receives and consumes a benefit as each transaction is processed.

BC126 The boards observed that there may be service-type contracts in which it is unclear whether the customer receives and consumes the benefit of the entity's performance over time. This is because the notion of 'benefit' can be subjective. Consider, for example, a freight logistics contract in which the entity has agreed to transport goods from Vancouver to New York City. Many respondents suggested that the customer receives no benefit from the entity's performance until the goods are delivered to New York City. However, the boards observed that the customer does benefit from the entity's performance as it occurs because if the goods were delivered only part way (for example, to Chicago), another entity would not need to substantially re-perform the entity's performance to date—that is, another entity would not need to take the goods back to Vancouver to deliver them to New York City. The boards observed that, in those cases, the assessment of whether another entity would need to substantially re-perform the performance completed to date can be used as an objective basis for determining whether the customer receives benefit from the entity's performance as it is provided.

BC127   The boards decided that an entity should disregard any contractual or practical limitations when it assesses the 'simultaneously receives and consumes' criterion and whether another entity would need to substantially re-perform the performance completed to date. This is because the objective of this criterion is to determine whether control of the goods or services has already been transferred to the customer. This is done by using a hypothetical assessment of what another entity would need to do if it were to take over the remaining performance. Thus, actual practical or contractual limitations on the remaining performance would have no bearing on the assessment of whether the entity has transferred control of the goods or services provided to date.

BC128   The boards also observed that this criterion is not intended to apply to contracts in which the entity's performance is not immediately consumed by the customer, which would be typical in cases in which the entity's performance results in an asset (such as work-in-progress). Consequently, an entity that applies IFRS 15 to contracts in which the entity's performance results in an asset (which could be intangible) being created or enhanced should consider the criteria in paragraph 35(b) and (c) of IFRS 15.

Performance creates or enhances an asset that the customer controls as it is created (paragraph 35(b))

BC129   The boards included this criterion to address situations in which an entity's performance creates or enhances an asset that a customer clearly controls as the asset is created or enhanced. In those cases, because the customer controls any work in progress, the customer is obtaining the benefits of the goods or services that the entity is providing and, thus, the performance obligation is satisfied over time. For example, in the case of a construction contract in which the entity is building on the customer's land, the customer generally controls any work in progress arising from the entity's performance.

BC130   The boards observed that the basis for this criterion is consistent with the rationale for using the 'percentage-of-completion' revenue recognition approach in previous revenue guidance in US GAAP. That guidance acknowledged that in many construction contracts the entity has, in effect, agreed to sell its rights to the asset (ie work-in-progress) as the entity performs. Accordingly, the parties have agreed, in effect, to a continuous sale (ie the customer controls the work-in-progress) that occurs as the work progresses.

BC131   Many respondents explained that this criterion would be straightforward and helpful in cases in which the customer clearly controls the asset that is being constructed or enhanced. However, the boards observed that for some performance obligations, it may be unclear whether the asset that is created or enhanced is controlled by the customer. Consequently, it may be more challenging to determine when control transfers in those cases and, therefore, the boards developed a third criterion in paragraph 35(c) of IFRS 15.

Performance does not create an asset with an alternative use to the entity and the entity has an enforceable right to payment for performance completed to date (paragraph 35(c))

BC132   The boards observed that, in some cases, applying the criteria in paragraph 35(a) and (b) of IFRS 15 could be challenging. Consequently, the boards developed a third criterion to help with the assessment of control. The boards observed that this criterion may be necessary for services that may be specific to a customer (for example, consulting services that ultimately result in a professional opinion for the customer) but also for the creation of tangible (or intangible) goods.

BC133   The notions of 'alternative use' and 'right to payment' are described in the following paragraphs.

Performance does not create an asset with an alternative use

BC134   The boards developed the notion of alternative use to exclude the circumstances in which the entity's performance would not result in the transfer of control of goods or services to the customer over time. This is because when the entity's performance creates an asset with an alternative use to the entity, the entity could readily direct the asset to another customer and, therefore, the customer would not control the asset as it is being created. This may occur in the creation of many standard inventory-type items for which the entity has the discretion to substitute across different contracts with customers. In those cases, the customer cannot control the asset because the customer does not have the ability to restrict the entity from directing that asset to another customer.

BC135   Conversely, when an entity creates an asset that is highly customised for a particular customer, the asset would be less likely to have an alternative use. This is because the entity would incur significant costs to reconfigure the asset for sale to another customer (or would need to sell the asset for a significantly reduced price). In that case, the customer could be regarded as receiving the benefit of that performance and, consequently, as having control of the goods or services (ie the asset being created) as the performance occurs. (However, an entity would also need to consider whether a right to payment exists to conclude that control transfers over time, see paragraphs BC142–BC148.)

BC136   In assessing whether the asset has an alternative use, the entity would need to consider practical limitations and contractual restrictions on directing the asset for another use. In determining whether the entity is limited practically from directing the asset for another use, the boards decided that an entity should consider the characteristics of the asset that will ultimately be transferred to the customer. This is because, for some assets, it is not the period of time for which the asset has no alternative use that is the critical factor in making the assessment but, instead, whether the asset that is ultimately transferred could be redirected without a significant cost of rework. This may occur in some manufacturing contracts in which the basic design of the asset is the same across all contracts, but the customisation is substantial. Consequently, redirecting the asset in its completed state to another customer would require significant rework.

BC137   Although the level of customisation might be a helpful factor to consider when assessing whether an asset has an alternative use, the boards decided that it should not be a determinative factor. This is because in some cases (for example, some real estate contracts), an asset may be standardised but may still not have an alternative use to an entity, as a result of substantive contractual restrictions that preclude the entity from readily directing the asset to another customer. If a contract precludes an entity from transferring an asset to another customer and that restriction is substantive, the entity does not have an alternative use for that asset because it is legally obliged to direct the asset to the customer. Consequently, this indicates that the customer controls the asset as it is created, because the customer has the present ability to restrict the entity from directing that asset to another customer (an entity would also need to consider whether a right to payment exists to conclude that control of the asset transfers over time as it is created, see paragraphs BC142–BC148). The boards observed that contractual restrictions are often relevant in real estate contracts, but might also be relevant in other types of contracts.

BC138   The boards also noted that contractual restrictions that provide a protective right to the customer would not be sufficient to establish that an asset has no alternative use to the entity. The boards observed that a protective right typically results in the entity having the practical ability to physically substitute or redirect the asset without the customer being aware of or objecting to the change. For example, a contract might state that an entity cannot transfer a good because a customer has legal title to the goods in the contract. However, the customer's legal title to the goods is intended to protect the customer in the event of the entity's liquidation and the entity can physically substitute and redirect the goods to another customer for little cost. In this example, the contractual restriction is merely a protective right and does not indicate that control of the goods have transferred to the customer.

BC139   Some respondents observed that requiring an entity to consider contractual and practical restrictions in paragraph 35(c) of IFRS 15 seems to contradict the requirements in paragraph B4 of IFRS 15 to ignore contractual and practical limitations when applying the criterion in paragraph 35(a) of IFRS 15. The boards noted that this difference is appropriate. Although the objective of both criteria is to assess when control transfers over time, each criterion provides a different method for assessing when that control transfers, because the criteria were designed to apply to different scenarios.

BC140   The boards decided that the assessment of alternative use should be completed only at contract inception and should not be updated. Otherwise, an entity would need to continually reassess whether the asset has an alternative use, which could lead to a pattern of performance (and, therefore, revenue recognition) that is not useful.

BC141   The boards also decided that while the notion of alternative use is a necessary part of the criterion in paragraph 35(c), it is not enough to conclude that a customer controls an asset. Consequently, the boards decided that to

© IFRS Foundation

demonstrate that a customer controls an asset that has no alternative use as it is being created, an entity must also have an enforceable right to payment for performance completed to date.

The entity has an enforceable right to payment for performance completed to date

BC142   The boards decided that there is a link between the assessment of control and the factors of no alternative use and a 'right to payment'. This is because if an asset that an entity is creating has no alternative use to the entity, the entity is effectively constructing an asset at the direction of the customer. Consequently, the entity will want to be economically protected from the risk of the customer terminating the contract and leaving the entity with no asset or an asset that has little value to the entity. That protection will be established by requiring that if the contract is terminated, the customer must pay for the entity's performance completed to date. This is consistent with other exchange contracts in which a customer would typically be obliged to pay only if it has received control of goods or services in the exchange. Consequently, the fact that the customer is obliged to pay for the entity's performance (or, in other words, is unable to avoid paying for that performance) suggests that the customer has obtained the benefits from the entity's performance.

BC143   The boards intended the term 'right to payment' to refer to a payment that compensates an entity for its performance completed to date rather than, for example, a payment of a deposit or a payment to compensate the entity for inconvenience or loss of profit. This is because the underlying objective of the criterion is to determine whether the entity is transferring control of goods or services to the customer as an asset is being created for that customer. Consequently, assuming there is rational behaviour and that there are no broader perceived economic benefits that might exist outside the scope of the contract with the customer, the entity would only agree to transfer control of the goods or services to the customer if the entity is compensated for the costs associated with fulfilling the contract and it receives a profit margin that includes a return on those costs.

BC144   The boards noted that the compensation to which the entity would be entitled upon termination by the customer might not always be the contract margin, because the value transferred to a customer in a prematurely terminated contract may not be proportional to the value if the contract was completed. However, the boards decided that to demonstrate compensation for performance completed to date, the compensation should be based on a reasonable proportion of the entity's expected profit margin or be a reasonable return on the entity's cost of capital. Furthermore, the boards noted that the focus should be on the amount to which the entity would be entitled upon termination rather than the amount to which the entity might ultimately be willing to settle for in a negotiation. Consequently, the boards clarified their intention about what a 'reasonable profit margin' is intended to represent in paragraph B9 of IFRS 15.

BC145   In addition, the boards clarified that an entity need not have a present unconditional right to payment but, instead, it must have an enforceable right to demand and/or retain payment for performance completed to date if the customer were to terminate the contract without cause before completion. For example, consider a consulting contract in which the consulting entity agrees to provide a report at the end of the contract for a fixed amount that is conditional on providing that report. If the entity were performing under that contract, it would have a right to payment for performance completed to date if the terms of the contract (or other law) require the customer to compensate the entity for its work completed to date if the customer terminates the contract without cause before completion. The boards clarified this notion because the contractual payment terms in the contract might not always align with the entity's enforceable rights to payment for performance completed to date.

BC146 A few respondents asked whether a 100 per cent non-refundable upfront payment would meet the 'right to payment for performance completed to date' criterion (ie because a 100 per cent payment would at least compensate the entity for work completed to date throughout the contract). The boards decided that that type of payment would meet that criterion if the entity's right to retain (and not refund) that payment would be enforceable if the customer terminated the contract. Furthermore, the boards noted that the right to payment should be enforceable; otherwise, it is questionable whether the entity actually has a right to payment. Consequently, the boards included the factors in paragraph B12 of IFRS 15 to help an entity determine whether the right to payment would be enforceable.

BC147 The boards also decided to clarify that an entity could have an enforceable right to payment in some cases in which a customer might not have a right to terminate the contract or might have a right to terminate the contract only at specified times. This would be the case if the contract or other laws in the jurisdiction require the entity and the customer to complete their respective obligations (often referred to as specific performance).

Right to payment as a separate revenue recognition criterion

BC148 The boards considered but rejected specifying a right to payment as a more overarching criterion in determining when revenue is recognised, for the following reasons:

(a) an entity must have a contract to recognise revenue in accordance with IFRS 15 and a component of a contract is a right to payment.

(b) the core revenue recognition principle is about determining whether goods or services have been transferred to a customer, not whether the entity has a right to payment (although it is an important part of determining whether a contract exists—see paragraphs BC31–BC46). Including a right to payment as an overarching criterion for determining when a performance obligation is satisfied could have potentially overridden that revenue recognition principle.

(c) a right to payment does not necessarily indicate a transfer of goods or services (for example, in some contracts, customers are required to make non-refundable upfront payments and do not receive any goods or services in exchange). In cases in which the customer clearly receives benefits as the entity performs, as in many service contracts, the possibility that the entity will ultimately not retain the payment for its performance is addressed in the measurement of revenue. For example, in some service contracts in which the customer simultaneously receives and consumes benefits as the entity performs, the customer may be able to terminate the contract and receive a full refund of any consideration paid. The boards decided that in those cases, because the entity is transferring services to the customer, it should recognise revenue subject to an assessment of whether it should constrain the amount of the transaction price to which it is entitled (see paragraphs BC203–BC223).

Agreements for the construction of real estate

BC149 In developing the requirements for assessing when goods or services transfer to the customer, the boards considered the diversity in practice from applying previous revenue recognition requirements in IFRS that were specific to the construction of real estate. That diversity in practice resulted from the difficulty in determining when control of real estate transferred to the customer over time by applying the previous IFRS revenue recognition criteria to complex contracts with different facts and circumstances.

BC150 The boards envisage that the diversity in practice should be reduced by the requirements in paragraphs 35–37 of IFRS 15, which provide specific requirements for determining when goods or services transfer over time. However, the boards observe that the pattern of transfer may be different for different real estate contracts because it will depend on the relevant facts and circumstances of each contract. For example, some real estate contracts may result in an asset that cannot (under the terms of the contract) be readily directed to another customer (ie the entity's performance does not create an asset with an alternative use to the entity), and the contracts require the customer to pay for performance completed to date (thus meeting the criterion in paragraph 35(c) of IFRS 15). However, other real estate contracts that create an asset with no alternative use to the entity may not require the customer to pay for performance completed to date. Therefore, an entity would reach a different conclusion on the pattern of transfer for those contracts.

BC151 Some respondents applying IFRS in the residential real estate industry supported the addition of the criteria for determining whether a performance obligation is satisfied over time, because they reasoned it would assist them in assessing whether revenue could be recognised over time as construction of residential units in a multi-unit real estate development occurs. Other respondents in this industry explained that although they were able to conclude that their performance does not create an asset with an alternative use, they were unable to meet the 'right to payment for performance completed to date' criterion. This would mean that they would be able to recognise revenue only at the point in time when each unit transfers to the customer (often only after construction is complete and the customer has physical possession), which they stated would be an inappropriate depiction of their performance.

BC152 However, the boards concluded that if either of the criteria in paragraph 35(c) of IFRS 15 is not met, recognising revenue over time would not faithfully depict the entity's performance and the entity's and the customer's respective rights and obligations in the contract. Furthermore, the boards decided that clarifying the 'no alternative use and right to payment for performance completed to date' criterion would ensure greater certainty and consistency in recognising revenue for multi-unit residential real estate developments.

Performance obligations satisfied at a point in time (paragraph 38)

BC153   The boards decided that all performance obligations that do not meet the criteria for being satisfied over time should be accounted for as performance obligations satisfied at a point in time. For performance obligations satisfied at a point in time, the performance obligation is satisfied at the point in time when control of the goods or services transfers to the customer. The boards included indicators of the transfer of control in paragraph 38 of IFRS 15.

BC154   Many respondents commented that the indicators were useful for contracts for the sales of goods to assist an entity in determining when it has transferred control of an asset (whether tangible or intangible). The boards included the indicator 'the customer has the significant risks and rewards of ownership of the asset' because of comments from respondents who disagreed with the boards' initial proposal to eliminate considerations of the 'risks and rewards of ownership' from the recognition of revenue. Respondents observed that risks and rewards can be a helpful factor to consider when determining the transfer of control, as highlighted by the IASB in IFRS 10 *Consolidated Financial Statements*, and can often be a consequence of controlling an asset. The boards decided that adding risks and rewards as an indicator provides additional guidance, but does not change the principle of determining the transfer of goods or services on the basis of the transfer of control.

BC155   Some respondents questioned whether all of the indicators would need to be present for an entity to conclude that it had transferred control of a good or service. Some respondents also questioned what an entity should do if some but not all of the indicators were present. In their redeliberations, the boards emphasised that the indicators in paragraph 38 of IFRS 15 are not a list of conditions that must be met before an entity can conclude that control of a good or service has transferred to a customer. Instead, the indicators are a list of factors that are often present if a customer has control of an asset and that list is provided to assist entities in applying the principle of control in paragraph 31 of IFRS 15.

BC156   The boards considered including an indicator that the 'design or function of the good or service is customer-specific'. However, the boards decided not to include this indicator in IFRS 15, because it would apply mainly to service contracts (for example, construction-type contracts) and it would be unnecessary in the light of the requirements for determining when performance obligations are satisfied over time. As described in paragraphs BC134–BC141, the notion of customer-specific design or function has been developed into the criterion of 'an asset with no alternative use to the entity'.

BC157   Respondents also suggested additional indicators such as the entity's lack of continuing involvement in the good or service (for example, a call option on a delivered good). The boards included application guidance to help an entity assess the transfer of control in circumstances in which put or call options exist in a contract with a customer (see paragraphs BC422–BC433).

Measuring progress towards complete satisfaction of a performance obligation (paragraphs 39–45 and B14–B19)

BC158   The boards decided that when an entity determines that a performance obligation is satisfied over time, it should determine how much revenue to recognise in each reporting period by measuring its progress towards complete satisfaction of the performance obligation.

BC159   There are various methods that an entity might use to measure its progress towards complete satisfaction of a performance obligation. Because of the breadth of the scope of IFRS 15, the boards decided that it would not be feasible to consider all possible methods and prescribe when an entity should use each method. Accordingly, an entity should use judgement when selecting an appropriate method of measuring progress towards complete satisfaction of a performance obligation. That does not mean that an entity has a 'free choice'. The requirements state that an entity should select a method of measuring progress that is consistent with the clearly stated objective of depicting the entity's performance—that is, the satisfaction of an entity's performance obligation—in transferring control of goods or services to the customer.

BC160   To meet that objective of depicting the entity's performance, an entity would need to consider the nature of the promised goods or services and the nature of the entity's performance. For example, in a typical health club contract, the entity's promise is to stand ready for a period of time (ie by making the health club available), rather than providing a service only when the customer requires it. In this case, the customer benefits from the entity's service of making the health club available. This is evidenced by the fact that the extent to which the customer uses the health club does not, in itself, affect the amount of the remaining goods or services to which the customer is entitled. In addition, the customer is obliged to pay the consideration regardless of whether it uses the health club. Consequently, in those cases, the entity would need to select a measure of progress based on its service of making goods or services available, instead of when the customer uses the goods or services made available to them.

BC161   The boards decided that an entity should apply the selected method for measuring progress consistently for a particular performance obligation and also across contracts that have performance obligations with similar characteristics. An entity should not use different methods to measure its performance in satisfying the same or similar performance obligations, otherwise that entity's revenue would not be comparable in different reporting periods. The boards also noted that if an entity were permitted to apply more than one method to measure its performance in fulfilling a performance obligation, it would effectively bypass the requirements for identifying performance obligations.

BC162   Although the boards did not consider all possible methods and prescribe when an entity should use each method, they observed that there are broadly two methods that the entity might consider when determining the method of measuring progress towards complete satisfaction of the performance obligation—that is, output and input methods. Requirements for the application of those methods are included in the application guidance (see paragraphs B14–B19 of IFRS 15).

Output methods

BC163 Output methods recognise revenue on the basis of direct measurements of the value to the customer of the goods or services transferred to date (for example, surveys of performance completed to date, appraisals of results achieved, milestones reached, time elapsed and units delivered or units produced). When applying an output method, 'value to the customer' refers to an objective measure of the entity's performance in the contract. However, value to the customer is not intended to be assessed by reference to the market prices or stand-alone selling prices of the individual goods or services promised in the contract, nor is it intended to refer to the value that the customer perceives to be embodied in the goods or services.

BC164 The boards decided that, conceptually, an output measure is the most faithful depiction of an entity's performance because it directly measures the value of the goods or services transferred to the customer. However, the boards observed that it would be appropriate for an entity to use an input method if that method would be less costly and would provide a reasonable proxy for measuring progress.

BC165 In the redeliberations, some respondents, particularly those in the contract manufacturing industry, requested the boards to provide more guidance on when units-of-delivery or units-of-production methods would be appropriate. Those respondents observed that such methods appear to be output methods and, therefore, questioned whether they would always provide the most appropriate depiction of an entity's performance. The boards observed that such methods may be appropriate in some cases; however, they may not always result in the best depiction of an entity's performance if the performance obligation is satisfied over time. This is because a units-of-delivery or a units-of-production method ignores the work in progress that belongs to the customer. When that work in progress is material to either the contract or the financial statements as a whole, the boards observed that using a units-of-delivery or a units-of-production method would distort the entity's performance because it would not recognise revenue for the assets that are created before delivery or before production is complete but are controlled by the customer.

BC166 The boards also observed that a units-of-delivery or a units-of-production method may not be appropriate if the contract provides both design and production services because, in this case, each item produced or delivered may not transfer an equal amount of value to the customer. However, a units-of-delivery method may be an appropriate method for measuring progress for a long-term manufacturing contract of standard items that individually transfer an equal amount of value to the customer on delivery. Thus, the boards clarified that in selecting an output method for measuring progress and determining whether a units-of-delivery or a units-of-production method is appropriate, an entity should consider its facts and circumstances and select the method that depicts the entity's performance and the transfer of control of the goods or services to the customer.

BC167 The boards also decided that, in some circumstances, as a practical expedient, another appropriate output method is to recognise revenue at the amount of consideration to which an entity has a right to invoice. This method is appropriate if the amount of consideration that the entity has a right to invoice corresponds directly with the value to the customer of each incremental good or service that the entity transfers to the customer (ie the entity's performance completed to date). This may occur, for example, in a services contract in which an entity invoices a fixed amount for each hour of service provided.

Input methods

BC168 Input methods recognise revenue on the basis of an entity's efforts or inputs towards satisfying a performance obligation (for example, resources consumed, labour hours expended, costs incurred, time elapsed or machine hours used) relative to the total expected inputs to satisfy the performance obligation.

BC169 In some contracts, an entity promises to transfer both goods and services to a customer, but the customer takes control of the goods, which represent a significant part of the performance obligation, at a different time from that of the services (for example, the customer obtains control of the goods before they are installed). If those goods and services are not distinct, then the entity would have a single performance obligation. Because there is diversity in practice about how to apply an input method to measure progress in such situations, the boards decided to provide additional guidance related to uninstalled materials.

Uninstalled materials

BC170 The boards decided to clarify that the adjustment to the input method for uninstalled materials is intended to ensure that the input method meets the objective of measuring progress towards complete satisfaction of a performance obligation, as described in paragraph 39 of IFRS 15—that is, to depict an entity's performance.

BC171 The boards observed that if a customer obtains control of the goods before they are installed by an entity, then it would be inappropriate for the entity to continue to recognise the goods as inventory. Instead, the entity should recognise revenue for the transferred goods in accordance with the core principle of IFRS 15. The boards also observed that if the entity applies a cost-to-cost method of measuring progress (ie costs incurred compared with total expected costs), the entity might (in the absence of clear requirements) include the cost of the goods in the cost-to-cost calculation and, therefore, recognise a contract-wide profit margin for the transfer of the goods. The boards noted that recognising a contract-wide profit margin before the goods are installed could overstate the measure of the entity's performance and, therefore, revenue would be overstated. Alternatively, requiring an entity to estimate a profit margin that is different from the contract-wide profit margin could be complex and could effectively create a performance obligation for goods that are not distinct (thus bypassing the requirements for identifying performance obligations). Therefore, the boards decided that, in specified circumstances, an entity should recognise revenue for the transfer of the goods but only in an amount equal to the cost of those goods. In those circumstances, an entity should also exclude the costs of the goods from the cost-to-cost calculation to be consistent with the cost-to-cost methodology.

BC172   The boards noted that the adjustment to the cost-to-cost measure of progress for uninstalled materials is generally intended to apply to a subset of goods in a construction-type contract—that is, only to those goods that have a significant cost relative to the contract and only if the entity is essentially providing a simple procurement service to the customer. For goods that meet the conditions in paragraph B19(b) of IFRS 15, recognising revenue to the extent of the costs of those goods ensures that the depiction of the entity's profit (or margin) in the contract is similar to the profit (or margin) that the entity would recognise if the customer had supplied those goods themselves for the entity to install or use in the construction activity.

BC173   Some respondents disagreed with the requirements that an entity recognise a profit margin of zero on the transfer of the uninstalled materials to the customer. In their view, recognising different profit margins for different parts of a single performance obligation is inconsistent with the principle of identifying performance obligations. Other respondents disagreed with recognising revenue for uninstalled materials at a zero profit margin because it might not properly depict an entity's rights under the contract (for example, if the entity was entitled on termination of the contract to a payment at an amount that reflects the contract-wide margin for all work performed, including the transfer of uninstalled materials to the customer).

BC174   The boards considered those arguments but decided that the adjustment to the input method specified in paragraph B19(b) of IFRS 15 will ensure that the input method meets the objective of measuring progress to depict an entity's performance. The boards disagreed with the concern raised by some respondents that paragraph B19(b) of IFRS 15 is inconsistent with the principle of identifying performance obligations. Although the outcome of applying paragraph B19(b) of IFRS 15 is that some goods or services that are part of a single performance obligation attract a margin, while any uninstalled materials attract only a zero margin, that difference arises only as a consequence of the need to adjust the cost-to-cost calculation so that the input method faithfully depicts the entity's performance in the contract.

BC175   To be consistent with their decision on uninstalled materials, the boards also clarified that if an entity selects an input method such as cost-to-cost to measure its progress, the entity should adjust the measure of progress if including some of those costs incurred (for example, inefficiencies and wasted materials) would distort the entity's performance in the contract.

Inefficiencies and wasted materials

BC176   Paragraph B19 of IFRS 15 acknowledges that a shortcoming of input methods is that there may not be a direct relationship between an entity's inputs and the transfer of control of goods or services to a customer. This would be the case if the cost-to-cost method includes costs attributable to wasted materials or other inefficiencies that do not contribute to the satisfaction of a performance obligation. Consequently, an entity should exclude the effects of any inputs that do not depict the transfer of control of goods or services to the customer (for example, the costs of wasted materials, labour or other resources to fulfil the contract that were not reflected in the price of the contract). In that regard, the requirements in paragraph B19 of IFRS 15 can be viewed as a reminder that a mechanical application of the cost-to-cost method might not always provide a faithful depiction of the entity's performance.

BC177   As part of their redeliberations, the boards considered whether more guidance should be provided on the notions of inefficiency and wasted materials. For instance, some respondents asked if the assessment should focus on entity-specific inefficiencies or market-driven inefficiencies, and some requested a clear distinction between the accounting for normal expected wasted materials and the accounting for abnormal wasted materials.

BC178   The boards acknowledged the concerns but decided that it would not be feasible to develop additional guidance that would clearly and consistently identify the costs of inefficiencies and wasted materials that should be excluded from a cost-to-cost measure of progress. Instead, the boards decided to emphasise that the objective of measuring progress towards complete satisfaction of the performance obligation is to depict an entity's performance in the contract and therefore a cost-to-cost calculation may require adjustment if some of the costs incurred do not contribute to the progress in the contract.

Reasonable measures of progress

BC179   The boards clarified that when selecting a method to measure progress and, thus, determining when to recognise revenue, an entity should recognise revenue for its performance only if it can reasonably measure its progress towards complete satisfaction of the performance obligation. Some asked whether an entity's inability to measure progress would mean that costs would also be deferred. However, the boards observed that unless the entity can recognise an asset from the costs to fulfil a contract in accordance with paragraph 95 of IFRS 15, those costs would not represent an asset of the entity and, therefore, should be recognised as expenses as they are incurred.

BC180   The boards also concluded that in cases in which an entity cannot reasonably measure its progress towards complete satisfaction of a performance obligation, but nevertheless expects eventually to recover the costs incurred in satisfying the performance obligation, the entity should recognise at least some amount of revenue to reflect the fact that it is making progress in satisfying the performance obligation. Consequently, the boards decided that in those cases, an entity should recognise revenue for the satisfaction of the performance obligation only to the extent of the costs incurred. (That method is consistent with previous revenue recognition requirements in both IFRS and US GAAP for measuring progress.) However, the boards also decided that an entity should stop using that method when it can reasonably measure its progress towards complete satisfaction of the performance obligation.

Measurement of revenue (paragraphs 46–90)

BC181   The boards decided that an entity should measure revenue based on an allocated transaction price approach. Using that approach, an entity allocates the transaction price to each performance obligation at an amount that depicts the amount of consideration to which the entity expects to be entitled in exchange for satisfying each performance obligation. That allocation determines the amount of revenue that an entity recognises when (or as) it satisfies each performance obligation. Most respondents supported the allocated transaction price approach.

BC182 The boards considered, but rejected, an alternative measurement approach, which would have been to measure the remaining performance obligations directly at the end of each reporting period. The boards observed that this alternative would have made accounting for the contract more complex. In addition, the boards expected that in many cases it would have provided users of financial statements with little additional information, either because the values of goods or services promised are not inherently volatile or because the effect of any volatility that might exist is limited when an entity transfers the goods or services to the customer over a relatively short time. Paragraphs BC25–BC27 include additional discussion on rejected measurement approaches.

BC183 The allocated transaction price approach generally requires an entity to follow three main steps to determine the amount of revenue that can be recognised for satisfied performance obligations. Those steps are as follows:

(a) determine the transaction price for the contract;

(b) allocate the transaction price to performance obligations; and

(c) recognise revenue at the amount allocated to the satisfied performance obligation.

Determining the transaction price (paragraphs 47–72)

BC184 Determining the transaction price is an important step in the revenue recognition model because the transaction price is the amount that an entity allocates to the performance obligations in a contract and ultimately recognises as revenue.

BC185 The boards decided to define the transaction price as the amount of consideration to which an entity expects to be entitled in exchange for transferring goods or services. Consequently, the objective in determining the transaction price at the end of each reporting period is to predict the total amount of consideration to which the entity will be entitled from the contract. In developing IFRS 15, the boards decided that the transaction price should not be adjusted for the effects of the customer's credit risk (see paragraphs BC259–BC265) unless the contract includes a significant financing component (see paragraphs BC229–BC247).

BC186 The boards clarified that the transaction price should include only amounts (including variable amounts) to which the entity has rights under the present contract. For example, the transaction price does not include estimates of consideration from the future exercise of options for additional goods or services or from future change orders. Until the customer exercises the option or agrees to the change order, the entity does not have a right to consideration.

BC187 The boards also clarified that the amounts to which the entity has rights under the present contract can be paid by any party (ie not only by the customer). For example, in the healthcare industry, an entity may determine the transaction price based on amounts to which it will be entitled to payment from the patient, insurance companies and/or governmental organisations. This may also occur in other industries in which an entity receives a payment from a manufacturer as a result of the manufacturer issuing coupons or rebates directly to the entity's customer. However, it would not include amounts collected on behalf of another party such as some sales taxes and value added taxes in some jurisdictions.

BC188 Determining the transaction price when a customer promises to pay a fixed amount of cash consideration (ie an amount that will not vary) will be simple. However, determining the transaction price may be more difficult in the following cases:

(a) the promised amount of consideration is variable (see paragraphs BC189–BC202), which will also require an entity to consider whether it should constrain the estimated amount of consideration to be included in the transaction price (see paragraphs BC203–BC223);

(b) the contract has a significant financing component (see paragraphs BC229–BC247);

(c) the promised amount of consideration is in a form other than cash (see paragraphs BC248–BC254); and

(d) there is consideration payable to the customer by the entity (see paragraphs BC255–BC258).

Clarifications to IFRS 15 (amendments issued in April 2016)—topics for which the IASB decided not to amend IFRS 15 (presentation of sales taxes)

BC188A Paragraph 47 of IFRS 15 specifies that amounts collected on behalf of third parties, such as some sales taxes, are excluded from the determination of the transaction price. Entities are therefore required to identify and assess sales taxes to determine whether to include or exclude those taxes from the transaction price.

BC188B After the issuance of Topic 606 and IFRS 15, some US stakeholders expressed concerns about the cost and complexity of assessing tax laws in each jurisdiction, because many entities operate in numerous jurisdictions, and the laws in some jurisdictions are unclear about which party to the transaction is primarily obligated for payment of the taxes. These stakeholders also stated that the variety of, and changes in, tax laws among jurisdictions contributes to that complexity. Consequently, some preparers and auditors asked the boards to amend the Standard to add a practical expedient to reduce the complexity and practical difficulties in assessing whether a sales tax is collected on behalf of a third party. An accounting policy choice to either include or exclude all sales taxes in or from revenue was available in the previous revenue standards under US GAAP.

BC188C The FASB decided to amend Topic 606 to provide an accounting policy election that permits an entity to exclude from the measurement of the transaction price all taxes assessed by a governmental authority that are both imposed on, and concurrent with, a specific revenue-producing transaction and collected from customers (for example, sales taxes, use taxes, value added taxes, and some excise taxes). Taxes assessed on an entity's total gross receipts or imposed during the inventory procurement process are excluded from the scope of the election.

BC188D   The IASB decided not to provide a similar accounting policy choice, for the following reasons:

(a)   It would reduce the comparability of revenue between entities operating under different tax regimes in different jurisdictions, as well as between entities operating in the same jurisdictions to the extent that they choose different approaches.

(b)   The previous revenue Standards under IFRS contained requirements applicable to sales tax similar to those in IFRS 15. Consequently, assessing whether sales taxes are collected on behalf of a third party is not a new requirement for IFRS preparers.

(c)   It would create an exception to the revenue recognition model that does not reflect the economics of the arrangement in cases for which a sales (or similar) tax is a tax on the entity rather than a tax collected by the entity from the customer on behalf of a tax authority.

The IASB acknowledged that, because the policy choice is not available in IFRS 15, this gives rise to a difference between IFRS 15 and Topic 606.

Variable consideration (paragraphs 50–59)

BC189   The boards noted that in contracts with customers in which the promised consideration is variable, an entity needs to estimate the amount of consideration to which the entity expects to be entitled. Consequently, the boards decided to provide requirements that address:

(a)   identifying when variable consideration is present in a contract with a customer (see paragraphs BC190–BC194);

(b)   the methods for estimating variable consideration (see paragraphs BC195–BC202);

(c)   when those estimates of variable consideration should be constrained and, thus, not included in the transaction price (see paragraphs BC203–BC223); and

(d)   how to account for subsequent changes in the transaction price (see paragraphs BC224–BC228).

Identifying variable consideration

BC190   The boards noted that variable consideration can arise in any circumstance in which the consideration to which the entity will be entitled under the contract may vary. The examples in paragraph 51 of IFRS 15 include common types of variable consideration that may occur in a contract with a customer.

BC191   The boards observed that consideration can be variable even in cases in which the stated price in the contract is fixed. This is because the entity may be entitled to the consideration only upon the occurrence or non-occurrence of a future event. Consider, for example, a fixed-price service contract in which the customer pays upfront and the terms of the contract provide the customer with a full refund of the amount paid if the customer is dissatisfied with the service at any time. In those cases, the consideration is variable because the entity might be entitled to all of the consideration or none of the consideration if the customer exercises its right to a refund.

BC192 The contract will often specify the terms that result in the consideration being classified as variable. However, in some cases the promised consideration may be variable because the facts and circumstances indicate that the entity may accept a lower price than that stated in the contract (ie the contract contains an implicit price concession). The boards observed that an entity's customary business practices, published policies or specific statements may provide evidence that the entity is willing to accept a lower price in exchange for the promised goods and services. For example, an entity might grant a price concession to a customer for goods that were previously sold to that customer to enable the customer to discount the goods and, therefore, more easily sell them to a third party. The boards noted that in many cases, price concessions are likely to be granted to enhance a customer relationship to encourage future sales to that customer.

BC193 The boards decided that an entity should also consider all facts and circumstances to determine whether the entity will accept a lower amount of consideration than the price stated in the contract. For example, an entity might enter into a contract with a new customer with a strategy to develop the customer relationship. In that case, although there may not be past evidence that the entity will provide a price concession, there may be other factors present that result in the entity concluding that it will accept a lower price than that stated in the contract.

BC194 The boards observed that in some cases it may be difficult to determine whether the entity has implicitly offered a price concession or whether the entity has chosen to accept the risk of default by the customer of the contractually agreed-upon consideration (ie customer credit risk). The boards noted that an entity should use judgement and consider all relevant facts and circumstances in making that determination. The boards observed that this judgement was being applied under previous revenue recognition requirements. Consequently, the boards decided not to develop detailed requirements for differentiating between a price concession and impairment losses.

The method for estimating the variable consideration

BC195 The boards decided to specify that an entity should estimate variable consideration using either the expected value or the most likely amount, depending on which method the entity expects will better predict the amount of consideration to which the entity will be entitled (see paragraph 53 of IFRS 15). The boards noted that this is not intended to be a 'free choice'; an entity needs to consider which method it expects to better predict the amount of consideration to which it will be entitled and apply that method consistently for similar types of contracts.

BC196 The boards concluded on the methods to estimate the transaction price in response to the feedback on the 2010 Exposure Draft. That exposure draft proposed that when the consideration in a contract is variable, an entity should measure the transaction price (at its expected value) using only a probability-weighted method. A probability-weighted method reflects the full range of possible consideration amounts, weighted by their respective probabilities. Many respondents to the 2010 Exposure Draft disagreed with measuring the transaction price using a probability-weighted method because they reasoned it would:

(a)   add complexity and be costly to apply; and

(b)   impede the reporting of meaningful results in all circumstances because, for example, it could result in an entity determining the transaction price at an amount of consideration that the entity could never obtain under the contract.

BC197   Some respondents suggested that the boards not specify a measurement model and, instead, require that the transaction price be determined using management's best estimate. Many noted that this would provide management with the flexibility to estimate on the basis of its experience and available information, without the documentation that would be required when a measurement model is specified.

BC198   In their redeliberations, the boards reaffirmed their decision to specify an objective and an appropriate measurement method for estimating the transaction price. This is because specifying an objective and an appropriate measurement method would provide the necessary framework to ensure rigour in the process of estimation. Furthermore, without such a framework, the measurement of revenue might not be understandable to users of financial statements and might lack comparability between entities.

BC199   However, in their redeliberations, the boards reconsidered what the appropriate measurement method(s) should be. They noted that a probability-weighted method reflects all of the uncertainties existing in the transaction price at the end of the reporting period. Therefore, it best reflects the conditions that are present at the end of each reporting period. For instance, it reflects the possibility of receiving a greater amount of consideration as well as the risk of receiving a lesser amount. However, the boards observed that users of financial statements are most interested in knowing the total amount of consideration that will ultimately be realised from the contract. Consequently, the boards decided that for the estimate of the transaction price to be meaningful at the end of each reporting period, it should be an amount that the entity expects to better predict the amount of consideration to which it will be entitled (the boards decided to address the issue of credit risk separately—see paragraphs BC259–BC265).

BC200   The boards observed that in some cases, a probability-weighted estimate (ie an expected value) predicts the amount of consideration to which an entity will be entitled. For example, that is likely to be the case if the entity has a large number of contracts with similar characteristics. However, the boards agreed with respondents that an expected value may not always faithfully predict the consideration to which an entity will be entitled. For example, if the entity is certain to receive one of only two possible consideration amounts in a single contract, the expected value would not be a possible outcome in accordance with the contract and, therefore, might not be relevant in predicting the amount of consideration to which the entity will be entitled. The boards decided that in those cases, another method—the most likely amount method—is necessary to estimate the transaction price. This is because the most likely amount method identifies the individual amount of consideration in the range of possible consideration amounts that is more likely to occur than any other individual outcome.

BC201   Theoretically, although an entity using the most likely amount method must consider all possible outcomes to identify the most likely one, in practice, there is no need to quantify the less probable outcomes. Similarly, in practice, estimating the expected value using a probability-weighted method does not require an entity to consider all possible outcomes using complex models and techniques, even if an entity has extensive data and can identify many outcomes. In many cases, a limited number of discrete outcomes and probabilities can often provide a reasonable estimate of the distribution of possible outcomes. Therefore, the boards decided that neither of the two approaches should be too costly or complex to apply.

BC202   The boards also decided that, to provide better information to users, an entity should apply one method consistently throughout the contract when estimating the effect of an uncertainty on the amount of variable consideration to which the entity expects to be entitled. However, the boards observed that this would not mean an entity would need to use one method to measure each uncertainty in a single contract. Instead, an entity may use different methods for different uncertainties.

Constraining estimates of variable consideration

BC203   The boards decided that to provide useful information to users of financial statements, some estimates of variable consideration should not be included in the transaction price. This would be the case if the estimate of variable consideration (and consequently the amount of revenue recognised) is too uncertain and, therefore, may not faithfully depict the consideration to which the entity will be entitled in exchange for the goods or services transferred to the customer. In that case, the boards decided that an entity should constrain the estimate of variable consideration to be included in the transaction price.

BC204   Many respondents agreed that it was necessary to include some form of constraint on the recognition of revenue that results from variable consideration because a significant portion of errors in financial statements under previous revenue recognition requirements have related to the overstatement or premature recognition of revenue. However, the boards noted that their intention was not to eliminate the use of estimates, which are commonplace and necessary in financial reporting, but instead to ensure that those estimates are robust and result in useful information. This is because revenue is an important metric and users of financial statements explained that it is critical that those estimates of variable consideration be included in revenue only when there is a high degree of confidence that revenue will not be reversed in a subsequent reporting period.

BC205   In developing the requirements for constraining estimates of variable consideration, the boards considered the following:

(a)   the objective of constraining estimates of variable consideration and specifying a level of confidence (see paragraphs BC206–BC213);

(b)   application of the requirements for constraining estimates of variable consideration and sales-based and usage-based royalties on licences of intellectual property (see paragraphs BC214–BC219); and

(c)   whether the requirements for constraining estimates of variable consideration should be included in the determination of the transaction price (Step 3 of the revenue recognition model) or the determination of the cumulative amount of revenue recognised when a performance obligation is satisfied (Step 5 of the revenue recognition model) (see paragraphs BC220–BC223).

The objective of constraining estimates of variable consideration and specifying a level of confidence

BC206   In their redeliberations, the boards decided that it would be helpful to clarify the objective for constraining estimates of variable consideration. In making their decision, the boards considered the feedback received from users of financial statements. The majority of users of financial statements that were consulted indicated that the most relevant measure for revenue in a reporting period would be one that will not result in a significant reversal in a subsequent period. This is because an amount that would not reverse in the future would help users of financial statements better predict future revenues of an entity. Therefore, the boards decided that the focus for constraining revenue should be on possible downward adjustments (ie revenue reversals), rather than on all revenue adjustments (ie both downward and upward adjustments). Specifically, the boards decided that an entity should include some or all of an estimate of variable consideration in the transaction price only to the extent it is highly probable that a significant revenue reversal will not occur.

BC207   The boards acknowledge that the requirement to constrain estimates of variable consideration and the objective they have defined creates a tension with the notion of neutrality in the boards' respective conceptual frameworks. This is because the boards' decision introduces a downward bias into estimates that will be included in the transaction price. However, the boards decided that this bias was reasonable because users of financial statements indicated that revenue is more relevant if it is not expected to be subject to significant future reversals.

BC208   In the redeliberations, preparers and auditors indicated that meeting the objective of constraining estimates of variable consideration would be difficult if no level of confidence was specified, for instance, if the boards merely specified that an entity should include variable consideration to the extent that it expects that doing so would not result in a significant revenue reversal. Many also observed that omitting a level of confidence from the objective could result in diversity in practice if entities interpreted the implicit confidence level in different ways (for example, some might interpret the implicit confidence level as virtually certain while others might presume it to mean more likely than not).

BC209   Consequently, the boards decided that specifying a level of confidence would provide clarity and thus ensure more consistent application of the requirements to constrain estimates of variable consideration. In determining the appropriate level of confidence, the boards considered whether they could use the proposal in the 2011 Exposure Draft that constrained revenue to the amount to which an entity would be reasonably assured to be entitled. However, many respondents to the 2011 Exposure Draft were unsure about what the boards intended by using the term 'reasonably assured'. Those respondents observed that the term is used elsewhere in IFRS, US GAAP and auditing requirements and further noted that its meaning is often interpreted differently in those contexts.

BC210   The boards also considered using terminology that has not previously been used in IFRS and US GAAP. However, the boards decided that any new term that was used might result in diversity in practice, because entities might interpret the new term in different ways. Consequently, the boards decided that the most appropriate level of confidence would be 'highly probable' for IFRS and 'probable' for US GAAP as a result of the usage of those terms in existing requirements.

BC211   The boards observed that the term 'probable' is widely used and understood in practice in the United States and is defined in US GAAP as 'the future event or events are likely to occur' (Topic 450). In contrast, the term 'probable' is defined in IFRS as 'more likely than not' (IFRS 5 *Non-current Assets Held for Sale and Discontinued Operations* and IAS 37 *Provisions, Contingent Liabilities and Contingent Assets*). Therefore, to achieve the same meaning in IFRS as US GAAP, the boards decided to use the term 'highly probable' for IFRS purposes and 'probable' for US GAAP purposes. The boards noted that this is consistent with the approach that the IASB adopted in developing IFRS 5, for which the IASB used the term 'highly probable' to achieve the same meaning as 'probable' in US GAAP (see paragraph BC81 of IFRS 5).

BC212   The boards observed that the analysis an entity would undertake to determine if its estimate met the required level of confidence would still be largely qualitative. Specifically, that analysis would require the entity to use judgement and consider the factors in paragraph 57 of IFRS 15 to assess whether it was highly probable that a significant revenue reversal would not occur. In other words, the boards did not expect that an entity would need to prepare a quantitative analysis each time it assessed the likelihood of whether a significant revenue reversal could occur. Therefore, the boards concluded that including a confidence level would not result in application of the requirements that is too costly or complex.

BC213   The factors in paragraph 57 of IFRS 15 were derived in part from previous requirements in US GAAP on estimating sales returns. Those indicators were also proposed in the 2010 and the 2011 Exposure Drafts and respondents generally agreed that the indicators were relevant and helpful. In their redeliberations, the boards also decided to add an indicator in paragraph 57(d) of IFRS 15 to address the circumstances in which there is no explicit requirement to adjust the price stated in the contract, but the entity has a past practice of offering a broad range of price concessions (or similar types of price adjustments). This is because the boards observed that a practice of offering a broad range of price concessions would increase the probability that a significant revenue reversal would occur if the entity included the contractual amount of consideration in the transaction price.

Application of the requirements to constrain estimates of variable consideration

BC214 The requirements for constraining estimates of variable consideration first require an entity to estimate the consideration to which the entity will be entitled (see paragraph 53 of IFRS 15). The entity then assesses whether the objective of the requirements for constraining estimates of variable consideration can be met—that is by determining whether it is highly probable that a significant revenue reversal will not occur when the uncertainty associated with the variable consideration is subsequently resolved. If the entity determines that it is highly probable that the inclusion of its estimate will not result in a significant revenue reversal, that amount is included in the transaction price.

BC215 Although some respondents explained that they reasoned that these requirements would inappropriately require a two-step process, the boards observed that an entity would not be required to strictly follow those two steps if the entity's process for estimating variable consideration already incorporates the principles on which the requirements for constraining estimates of variable consideration are based. For example, an entity might estimate revenue from sales of goods with a right of return. In that case, the entity might not practically need to estimate the expected revenue and then apply the constraint requirements to that estimate, if the entity's calculation of the estimated revenue incorporates the entity's expectations of returns at a level at which it is highly probable that the cumulative amount of revenue recognised would not result in a significant revenue reversal.

BC216 The requirements for constraining estimates of variable consideration require an entity to assess whether a significant revenue reversal would not occur for the amount of cumulative revenue recognised for a satisfied (or partially satisfied) performance obligation. This is because the boards did not intend for an entity to inappropriately recognise revenue by offsetting the risk of a future revenue reversal for a satisfied (or partially satisfied) performance obligation against expected revenue from future performance.

BC217 The requirements for constraining estimates of variable consideration also require an entity to assess the magnitude of a significant revenue reversal for both variable consideration and fixed consideration. For example, if the consideration for a single performance obligation included a fixed amount and a variable amount, the entity would assess the magnitude of a possible revenue reversal of the variable amount relative to the total consideration (ie variable and fixed consideration). This is because the objective of constraining estimates of variable consideration is focused on a possible revenue reversal of the amount of cumulative revenue recognised for a performance obligation, rather than on a reversal of only the variable consideration allocated to that performance obligation.

BC218   The boards noted that in some cases, when an entity applies the requirements for constraining estimates of variable consideration, the entity might determine that it should not include the entire estimate of the variable consideration in the transaction price when it is not highly probable that doing so would not result in a significant revenue reversal. However, the entity might determine that it is highly probable that including some of the estimate of the variable consideration in the transaction price would not result in a significant revenue reversal. The boards decided that, in such cases, the entity should include that amount in the estimate of the transaction price. Respondents to both the 2010 and the 2011 Exposure Drafts supported including some of the variable consideration in the transaction price (and therefore recognising that portion as revenue when the entity satisfies the related performance obligation) if including that amount would meet the objective of the requirements for constraining estimates of variable consideration.

BC219   However, the boards decided that for a licence of intellectual property for which the consideration is based on the customer's subsequent sales or usage, an entity should not recognise any revenue for the uncertain amounts until the uncertainty is resolved (ie when the customer's subsequent sales or usage occurs). The boards included these requirements because both users and preparers of financial statements generally indicated that if an entity recognised a minimum amount of revenue for those contracts it would not provide relevant information (see paragraphs BC419–BC421).

Constraining the estimate of the transaction price (Step 3) or constraining the cumulative amount of revenue that is recognised (Step 5)

BC220   During the development of the requirements for constraining estimates of variable consideration, the boards considered where in the revenue recognition model it would be most appropriate to apply those requirements.

BC221   Some respondents suggested that if the objective is to constrain the measurement of revenue, it might be more appropriate to constrain the transaction price (ie include a constraint at Step 3). In contrast, if the objective is to limit the amount of revenue recognised, it might be more appropriate to constrain the cumulative amount of revenue recognised (ie include a constraint at Step 5). However, the boards observed that those are not truly independent objectives because the measurement of revenue determines the amount of revenue recognised. In other words, the requirements for constraining estimates of variable consideration restrict revenue recognition and use measurement uncertainty as the basis for determining if (or how much) revenue should be recognised. The boards noted that applying the requirements for constraining estimates of variable consideration to the transaction price or to the cumulative amount of revenue recognised should have an equal effect on the amount of revenue recognised in a contract.

BC222   Consequently, the boards decided that the requirements for constraining estimates of variable consideration should be incorporated into the determination of the transaction price because feedback from respondents indicated that this would be consistent with the way in which management often considers variable consideration.

BC223 Respondents in the asset management and hotel management industries questioned whether constraining the transaction price would result in a pattern of revenue recognition that would faithfully depict their performance under the contract. In many of the contracts in those industries, when a portion of the variable consideration becomes fixed, it relates only to the performance for the period. The boards observed that the requirements for allocating variable consideration (see paragraphs BC284–BC293) would ensure that the revenue recognised would faithfully depict the performance in such a contract.

Subsequent changes in the transaction price

BC224 After contract inception, an entity will revise its expectations about the amount of consideration to which it expects to be entitled as uncertainties are resolved or as new information about remaining uncertainties becomes available. To depict conditions that exist at the end of each reporting period (and changes in conditions during the reporting period), the boards decided that an entity should update its estimate of the transaction price throughout the contract. The boards concluded that reflecting current assessments of the amount of consideration to which the entity expects to be entitled will provide more useful information to users of financial statements than retaining the initial estimates, especially for long-term contracts that are subject to significant changes in conditions during the life of the contract.

BC225 The boards considered whether an entity should do either of the following if the transaction price changes during a contract:

 (a) recognise those changes in profit or loss when the changes occur; or

 (b) allocate those changes to performance obligations.

BC226 The boards rejected the alternative of recognising the entire amount of a change in the estimate of the transaction price in profit or loss when that change occurs. In the boards' view, that alternative could have resulted in a pattern of revenue recognition that would not faithfully depict the pattern of the transfer of goods or services. Moreover, recognising revenue immediately (and entirely) for a change in the estimate of the transaction price would have been prone to abuse in practice. The boards considered whether changes in the estimate of the transaction price could be presented as a gain or loss separately from revenue, thus preserving the pattern of revenue recognition. However, the boards rejected that alternative because the total amount of revenue recognised for the contract would not have equalled the amount of consideration to which the entity was entitled under the contract.

BC227 Instead, the boards decided that an entity should allocate a change in the transaction price to all the performance obligations in the contract, subject to the conditions in paragraphs 87–90 of IFRS 15 (see paragraph BC286). This is because the cumulative revenue recognised will then depict the revenue that the entity would have recognised at the end of the subsequent reporting period, if the entity had the information at contract inception. Consequently, the transaction price that is allocated to performance obligations that have already been satisfied should be recognised as revenue (or as a reduction of revenue) immediately.

BC228   The boards noted that in some cases, an entity might make an estimate of the amount of variable consideration to include in the transaction price at the end of a reporting period. However, information relating to the variable consideration might arise between the end of the reporting period and the date when the financial statements are authorised for issue. The boards decided not to provide guidance on the accounting in these situations because they noted that the accounting for subsequent events is already addressed in IAS 10 *Events after the Reporting Period* and Topic 855 *Subsequent Events*.

The existence of a significant financing component in the contract (paragraphs 60–65)

BC229   Some contracts with customers include a financing component. The financing component may be explicitly identified in the contract or be implied by the contractual payment terms of the contract. A contract that has a financing component includes, conceptually, two transactions—one for the sale and one for the financing. The boards decided to require an entity to adjust the promised amount of consideration for the effects of financing components if those financing components are significant, for the following reasons:

(a)   not recognising a financing component could misrepresent the revenue of a contract. For example, if a customer pays in arrears, ignoring the financing component of the contract would result in full revenue recognition on the transfer of the good or service, despite the fact that the entity is providing a service of financing to the customer.

(b)   in some contracts, entities (or customers) consider the timing of the cash flows in a contract. Consequently, identifying a significant financing component acknowledges an important economic feature of the contract, which is that the contract includes a financing arrangement as well as the transfer of goods or services. A contract in which the customer pays for a good or service when that good or service is transferred to the customer may be significantly different from a contract in which the customer pays before or after the good or service is transferred in order to provide or receive a financing benefit.

BC230   The objective of adjusting the promised amount of consideration for the effects of a significant financing component is to reflect, in the amount of revenue recognised, the 'cash selling price' of the underlying good or service at the time that the good or service is transferred. The boards observed that adjusting the promised consideration to obtain the cash selling price may only be required when the timing of payments specified in the contract provides the customer or the entity with a significant benefit of financing the transfer of goods or services to the customer. This is because, in other cases, the timing of payments may be for a purpose other than financing, such as protection for non-performance. This is described further in the following paragraphs.

Determining whether a contract includes a significant financing component

BC231   The boards considered whether the requirements for identifying a financing component should be based only on whether payment is due either significantly before, or significantly after, the transfer of goods or services to the customer.

However, a number of respondents explained that this might have required an entity to adjust for the time value of money when the parties did not contemplate a financing arrangement as part of the negotiated terms of the contract. Those respondents explained that, in some cases, although there is a significant period of time between the transfer of the goods or services and the payment, the reason for that timing difference is not related to a financing arrangement between the entity and the customer. The boards agreed with those respondents and clarified their intention by specifying in paragraph 60 of IFRS 15 that an entity should adjust for financing only if the timing of payments specified in the contract provides the customer or the entity with a significant benefit of financing.

BC232   The boards also decided to remove the term 'time value of money' from the discussion about adjustments for financing components, to reflect their decision that the focus is on whether the payment terms provide the customer or the entity with a significant benefit of financing. This is because the term 'time value of money' is a broader economic term that may suggest that it is necessary to adjust the promised amount of consideration in circumstances other than when the cash sales price may differ from the contractual payments. In addition, the boards decided to refine the factors in paragraph 61 of IFRS 15 that an entity should consider when deciding whether a contract includes a significant financing component. Those factors require evaluation of:

(a)   the difference, if any, between the amount of promised consideration and the cash selling price of the promised goods or services. If the entity (or another entity) sells the same good or service for a different amount of consideration depending on the timing of the payment terms, this generally provides observable data that the parties are aware that there is a financing component in the contract. This factor is presented as an indicator because in some cases the difference between the cash selling price and the consideration promised by the customer is due to factors other than financing (see paragraph BC233).

(b)   the combined effect of (1) the expected length of time between when the entity transfers the promised goods or services to the customer and when the customer pays for those goods or services and (2) the prevailing interest rates in the relevant market. Although the boards decided that the difference in timing between the transfer of goods and services and payment for those goods and services is not determinative, the combined effect of timing and the prevailing interest rates may provide a strong indication that a significant benefit of financing is being provided.

BC233   In addition, the boards included criteria in paragraph 62 of IFRS 15 to clarify the circumstances in which a contract does *not* provide the customer or the entity with a significant benefit of financing:

(a)   the customer has paid for the goods or services in advance and, the timing of the transfer of those goods or services is at the discretion of the customer. The boards noted that for some types of goods or services, such as prepaid phone cards and customer loyalty points, the customer will pay for those goods or services in advance and the transfer of those goods or services to the customer is at the customer's discretion. The boards expected that, in those cases, the purpose of the payment terms is not related to a financing arrangement between the parties. In addition, the boards decided that the costs of requiring an entity to account for the time value of money in these cases would outweigh any perceived benefit because the entity would need to continually estimate when the goods or services will transfer to the customer.

(b) a substantial amount of the consideration promised by the customer is variable and that consideration varies on the basis of factors that are outside the control of the customer or the entity. The boards observed that for some arrangements, the primary purpose of the specified timing or amount of the payment terms might not be to provide the customer or the entity with a significant benefit of financing but, instead, to resolve uncertainties that relate to the consideration for the goods or services. For example, in a royalty arrangement, the entity and the customer might not be willing to fix the price and timing of payment because there are significant uncertainties about the goods or services. The primary purpose of those payment terms may be to provide the parties with assurance of the value of the goods or services rather than to provide significant financing to the customer.

(c) the difference between the promised consideration and the cash selling price of the good or service arises for reasons other than the provision of financing to either the customer or the entity. In some circumstances, a payment in advance or in arrears in accordance with the typical payment terms of an industry or jurisdiction may have a primary purpose other than financing. For example, a customer may retain or withhold some consideration that is payable only on successful completion of the contract or on achievement of a specified milestone. Alternatively, the customer might be required to pay some consideration upfront to secure a future supply of limited goods or services. The primary purpose of those payment terms may be to provide the customer with assurance that the entity will complete its obligations satisfactorily under the contract, rather than to provide financing to the customer or the entity respectively.

BC234 The boards also observed that for many contracts, an entity will not need to adjust the promised amount of customer consideration because the effects of the financing component will not materially change the amount of revenue that should be recognised in relation to a contract with a customer. In other words, for those contracts, the financing component will not be significant. During their redeliberations, the boards clarified that an entity should consider only the *significance* of a financing component at a contract level rather than consider whether the financing is *material* at a portfolio level. The boards decided that it would have been unduly burdensome to require an entity to account for a financing component if the effects of the financing component were not material to the individual contract, but the combined effects for a portfolio of similar contracts were material to the entity as a whole.

Practical reliefs from the significant financing component requirements

BC235　　Some previous requirements required an entity to recognise the effects of a significant financing component with a customer only if the time period exceeded a specified period, often one year. For example, Subtopic 835-30 *Interest—Imputation of Interest*, excluded 'transactions with customers or suppliers in the normal course of business that are due in customary trade terms not exceeding approximately one year'. The boards decided to include similar relief in IFRS 15 from the requirements to account for a significant financing component in circumstances in which the period between when the entity transfers the promised goods or services to the customer, and when the customer pays for those goods or services, is one year or less (see paragraph 63 of IFRS 15). The boards observed that, as with the other practical expedients in IFRS 15, an entity should apply the practical expedient consistently to similar contracts in similar circumstances.

BC236　　The boards acknowledged that the relief could produce arbitrary outcomes in some cases because the financing component could be material for short-term contracts with high implicit interest rates and, conversely, could be immaterial for long-term contracts with low implicit interest rates. However, the boards decided to exempt an entity from accounting for the effects of any significant financing component on contracts with an expected duration of one year or less for the following reasons:

　　(a)　　application of IFRS 15 would be simplified. This is because an entity would not be required to:

　　　　(i)　　conclude whether those contracts contain the attributes of a financing component that are significant to those contracts (see paragraph BC232); and

　　　　(ii)　　determine the interest rate that is implicit within those contracts.

　　(b)　　the effect on the pattern of profit recognition should be limited because the exemption would apply only to financing arrangements that are expected to expire within 12 months (ie when either the customer pays or the entity performs).

BC237　　Some respondents also suggested that the boards should exempt an entity from reflecting in the measurement of the transaction price the effect of a significant financing component associated with advance payments from customers. Those respondents commented that accounting for any effects of a significant financing component arising from advance payments would result in the following:

　　(a)　　change previous practices in which entities typically did not recognise the effects of the financing implicit in advance payments;

(b)   revenue that is higher than the cash received (for example, if the discount rate implicit in the contract resulted in the accretion of interest of CU21[4] over two years, revenue would be recognised in the amount of the CU121 rather than the CU100 in cash that was paid in advance); and

(c)   not reflect the economics of the arrangement when the customer pays in advance for reasons other than financing (for example, the customer has significant credit risk or is compensating the entity for incurring upfront contract costs).

BC238   The boards decided not to exempt an entity from accounting for the effects of a significant financing component for advance payments. This is because ignoring the effects of advance payments could substantially skew the amount and pattern of profit recognition if the advance payment is significant and the primary purpose of that payment is to provide financing to the entity. Consider the example in which an entity requires a customer to pay in advance for a long-term construction contract, because the entity requires financing to obtain materials for the contract. If the entity did not require the customer to pay in advance, the entity would need to obtain the financing from a third party and, consequently, would charge the customer a relatively higher amount to cover the finance costs incurred. However, in either scenario the goods or services transferred to the customer are the same; it is only the party providing the financing to the entity that changes. Consequently, the entity's revenue should be consistent regardless of whether it receives the significant financing benefit from the customer or from a third party.

Discount rate

BC239   The boards considered whether the discount rate used to adjust the promised amount of consideration for the effects of a significant financing component should be a risk-free rate or a risk-adjusted rate. A risk-free rate would have been observable and simple to apply in many jurisdictions and it would have avoided the costs of determining a rate specific to each contract. However, the boards decided that using a risk-free rate would not result in useful information, because the resulting interest rate would not have reflected the characteristics of the parties to the contract. In addition, the boards noted that it would not necessarily have been appropriate to use any rate explicitly specified in the contract because the entity might offer 'cheap' financing as a marketing incentive and, therefore, using that rate would not have resulted in an appropriate recognition of profit over the life of the contract. Consequently, the boards decided that an entity should apply the rate used in a financing transaction between the entity and its customer that does not involve the provision of goods or services because that rate reflects the characteristics of the party receiving financing in the contract. That rate also reflects the customer's creditworthiness, among other risks.

BC240   Some respondents mentioned that determining the discount rate that would be used in a separate financing transaction between an entity and a customer would be difficult and costly because most entities within the scope of IFRS 15 do not enter into separate financing transactions with their customers. In

---

4   Monetary items in the Basis for Conclusions are denominated as 'currency units' (CU).

addition, it would have been impractical for entities with large volumes of customer contracts to determine a discount rate specifically for each individual customer.

BC241 The boards addressed many of those concerns by providing both the exemption for contracts with a term of up to one year from being considered to have a significant financing component and the factors in paragraph 62 of IFRS 15, which describe when there is no significant financing component that needs to be accounted for. The boards expect that in those remaining contracts in which an entity is required to account separately for the financing component, the entity and its customer will typically negotiate the contractual payment terms separately after considering factors such as inflation rates and the customer's credit risk. Therefore, an entity should have access to sufficient information to determine the discount rate that would be used in a separate financing between the entity and the customer.

Re-evaluating the discount rate used for a significant financing component

BC242 Some respondents asked whether an entity would be required to revise the discount rate used in determining the amount of a significant financing component if there was a change in circumstances.

BC243 The boards clarified that an entity should not update the discount rate for a change in circumstances because an entity should reflect in the measurement of the transaction price only the discount rate that is determined at contract inception. They also observed that it would be impractical for an entity to update the transaction price for changes in the assessment of the discount rate.

Presentation of the effect of a significant financing component

BC244 As a result of the boards' decision on the existence of a significant financing component (see paragraphs BC229–BC243), a contract with a customer that has a significant financing component would be separated into a revenue component (for the notional cash sales price) and a loan component (for the effect of the deferred or advance payment terms). Consequently, the accounting for a trade receivable arising from a contract that has a significant financing component should be comparable to the accounting for a loan with the same features. Consider the following example: Customer A purchases a good on credit and promises to pay CU1,000 in three years. The present value of this trade receivable is CU751. Now consider Customer B who borrows CU751 from a bank with a promise to pay CU1,000 in three years. Customer B uses the loan to purchase the same good as Customer A. Economically, those transactions are the same, but, in the absence of the requirements in IFRS 15 to account for a significant financing component, the form of the transaction would determine whether an entity would recognise revenue of CU751 or CU1,000 (ie on a discounted or an undiscounted basis). For this reason, paragraphs 60–65 of IFRS 15 require a contract with a financing component that is significant to the contract to be separated, which results in the same revenue recognition for both transactions.

BC245　The boards observed that the presentation, in the statement of comprehensive income, of any impairment losses from long-term trade receivables (ie receivables arising from the financing components of contracts with customers) would be consistent with the presentation of impairment losses for other types of financial assets within the scope of the boards' respective financial instruments Standards. The boards decided that impairment losses on short-term trade receivables (ie receivables arising from contracts with customers that do not have separately identified financing components) should be presented in the statement of comprehensive income in a consistent manner with impairment losses on long-term trade receivables (see paragraphs BC259–BC265).

BC246　The boards decided that an entity should present the effect of the financing (ie the unwinding of the discount) separately from revenue from contracts with customers, as interest revenue or interest expense, rather than as a change to the measurement of revenue. This is because contracts with financing components that are significant have distinct economic characteristics—one relating to the transfer of goods or services to the customer and one relating to a financing arrangement—and those characteristics should be accounted for and presented separately.

BC247　The boards noted that some entities (for example, banks and other entities with similar types of operations) regularly enter into financing transactions and, therefore, interest represents income arising from ordinary activities for those entities. The boards noted that the requirements in paragraph 65 of IFRS 15 do not preclude an entity from presenting interest as a type of revenue in circumstances in which the interest represents income from the entity's ordinary activities.

Non-cash consideration (paragraphs 66–69)

BC248　When an entity receives cash from a customer in exchange for a good or service, the transaction price and, therefore, the amount of revenue, should be the amount of cash received (ie the value of the inbound asset). To be consistent with that approach, the boards decided that an entity should measure non-cash consideration at fair value. The non-cash consideration could be in the form of goods or services, but it may also be in the form of a financial instrument or property, plant and equipment. For example, an entity might receive an electrical substation in exchange for connecting houses in a new residential development to the electricity network.

BC249　The boards decided that if an entity cannot reasonably estimate the fair value of the non-cash consideration, it should measure the promised consideration indirectly by reference to the stand-alone selling price of the goods or services promised in exchange for the consideration. That approach is consistent both with requirements in previous revenue Standards in IFRS and with requirements for other situations in which the fair value of the assets surrendered in exchange for assets received may be estimated more reliably. (For instance, IFRS 2 *Share-based Payment* and Subtopic 505-50 *Equity-Based Payments to Non-Employees* state that if the fair value of the goods or services received cannot be estimated reliably, then the entity measures them indirectly by reference to the fair value of the granted equity instrument.)

BC250   Some respondents observed that estimates of fair value of non-cash consideration may vary like other types of variable consideration that the entity will receive in cash. For example, an entity's entitlement to a bonus that will be received in non-cash consideration may also depend on the occurrence or non-occurrence of a future event. Consequently, those respondents asked the boards to clarify whether the requirements for constraining estimates of variable consideration (see paragraphs 56–58 of IFRS 15) should be applied to estimates of the fair value of non-cash consideration.

BC251   The boards observed that while the fair value of the non-cash consideration could change because of the occurrence or non-occurrence of a future event, it could also vary because of the form of the consideration. That is, the fair value could vary because of changes in the price or value of the non-cash consideration, such as a change in the price per share.

BC252   The boards decided that it would be most appropriate to apply the requirements for constraining estimates of variable consideration to the same types of variability regardless of whether the amount that will be received will be in the form of cash or non-cash consideration. Consequently, the boards decided to constrain variability in the estimate of the fair value of the non-cash consideration if that variability relates to changes in the fair value for reasons other than the form of the consideration (ie for reasons other than changes in the price of the non-cash consideration). For example, if an entity is entitled to a performance bonus that is payable in the form of non-cash consideration, the entity would apply the requirements for constraining estimates of variable consideration to the uncertainty of whether the entity will receive the bonus, because that uncertainty is related to something other than the form of the consideration (ie the entity's performance). The boards observed that this principle is not that different from previous revenue recognition requirements under US GAAP for changes in the fair value of equity instruments that are granted as consideration in exchange for goods or services, although those requirements differentiated between the variability on the basis of performance conditions and market conditions (which were defined terms in those requirements).

BC253   The boards also observed that once recognised, any asset arising from the non-cash consideration would be measured and accounted for in accordance with other relevant requirements (for example, IFRS 9 or Topic 320 *Investments—Debt and Equity Securities* or Topic 323 *Equity Method And Joint Ventures*).

BC254   The FASB noted that the requirements in Topic 606 will result in the removal of previous requirements for the accounting for share-based payments received by an entity in exchange for goods or services. Those previous requirements provided detailed guidance for the measurement and recognition of revenue when the consideration was in the form of shares or share options. However, the FASB decided to remove those requirements because equity instruments are merely another form of non-cash consideration. Therefore, equity instruments received as promised consideration in a contract with a customer would be accounted for consistently with other forms of non-cash consideration.

Clarifications to IFRS 15 (amendments issued in April 2016)—topics for which the IASB decided not to amend IFRS 15

BC254A   The TRG discussed the following implementation questions raised by stakeholders in connection with applying IFRS 15 to contracts that involve non-cash consideration:

(a)   At which date should the fair value of non-cash consideration be measured in determining the transaction price?

(b)   How should the constraint on variable consideration be applied to transactions for which the fair value of non-cash consideration might vary due to both the form of the consideration and for other reasons?

Date of measurement of non-cash consideration

BC254B   Paragraph 66 of IFRS 15 requires non-cash consideration to be measured at fair value (or by reference to the stand-alone selling price of the goods or services promised to the customer if an entity cannot reasonably estimate fair value of the non-cash consideration). The TRG's discussion informed the boards that the measurement date for non-cash consideration is unclear and could be interpreted as one of several dates: (a) at contract inception; (b) when the non-cash consideration is received; or (c) at the earlier of when the non-cash consideration is received and when the related performance obligation is satisfied.

BC254C   In its discussions, the IASB observed that this issue has important interactions with other Standards (including IFRS 2 *Share-based Payment* and IAS 21 *The Effects of Changes in Foreign Exchange Rates*) and, thus, any decisions made would create a risk of potential unintended consequences. Accordingly, the IASB decided that, if needed, issues relating to the measurement of non-cash consideration should be considered more comprehensively in a separate project.

BC254D   The FASB decided to amend the guidance in Topic 606 to require non-cash consideration to be measured at its fair value at contract inception. In the FASB's view, measuring non-cash consideration at contract inception is most consistent with the requirements in Topic 606 on determining the transaction price and on allocating the transaction price to performance obligations. The FASB also expects this approach to be typically less costly and less complex to apply in practice than other alternatives.

BC254E   The IASB acknowledged that, because it has concluded that a change equivalent to that decided by the FASB is not needed, the use of a measurement date other than contract inception would not be precluded under IFRS. Consequently, it is possible that diversity between IFRS and US GAAP entities could arise in practice. The IASB observed that, unlike US GAAP, existing IFRS does not contain any specific requirements about the measurement date for non-cash consideration for revenue transactions. In addition, discussions with some stakeholders highlighted that any practical effect of different measurement dates would arise in only limited circumstances. The IASB also noted that paragraph 126 of IFRS 15 requires an entity to disclose information about the methods, inputs and assumptions used for measuring non-cash consideration.

Application of the variable consideration constraint to changes in fair value of non-cash consideration

BC254F   The TRG discussed the concerns raised by some stakeholders that it is not clear whether the variable consideration requirements in paragraphs 56–58 of IFRS 15 apply in circumstances in which the fair value of non-cash consideration varies due to both the form of the consideration and for other reasons. In particular, some stakeholders are concerned that bifurcating the effects of variability might be challenging in some circumstances.

BC254G   The FASB decided to amend Topic 606 to specify that the constraint on variable consideration applies only to variability that arises for reasons other than the form of the consideration. Paragraph 68 of IFRS 15 indicates that the requirements for constraining estimates of variable consideration are applied if the fair value of the non-cash consideration promised by a customer varies for reasons other than only the form of the consideration (for example, a change in the exercise price of a share option because of the entity's performance). The FASB observed that applying the variable consideration requirements to both types of variability might not provide users of financial statements with useful information, because the timing of revenue recognition might differ for similar transactions settled in different forms of consideration (for example, cash and shares). Additionally, the inclusion of a minor performance condition could significantly affect the amount of non-cash consideration that would be subject to the constraint on variable consideration.

BC254H   The IASB noted that paragraph BC252 explains that the boards decided to constrain variability in the estimate of the fair value of the non-cash consideration if that variability relates to changes in the fair value for reasons other than the form of the consideration (ie for reasons other than changes in the price of the non-cash consideration). The IASB also noted the view of some TRG members that in practice it might be difficult to distinguish between variability in the fair value due to the form of the consideration and other reasons, in which case applying the variable consideration constraint to the whole of the estimate of the non-cash consideration might be more practical. However, for reasons similar to those discussed in paragraph BC254E, the IASB decided not to amend IFRS 15 for this issue. Consequently, the IASB acknowledged that differences may arise between an entity reporting under IFRS and an entity reporting under US GAAP.

Consideration payable to a customer (paragraphs 70–72)

BC255   In some cases, an entity pays consideration to one of its customers or to its customer's customer (for example, an entity may sell a product to a dealer or distributor and subsequently pay a customer of that dealer or distributor). That consideration might be in the form of a payment in exchange for goods or services received from the customer, a discount or refund for goods or services provided to the customer, or a combination of both.

BC256   To help an entity distinguish between those types of payments, the boards decided that the only circumstance in which an entity should account for any good or service received in the same way as for other purchases from suppliers is if the good or service is distinct. Previous requirements in US GAAP on the consideration that a vendor gives to a customer used the term 'identifiable benefit', which was described as a good or service that is 'sufficiently separable from the recipient's purchase of the vendor's products such that the vendor could have entered into an exchange transaction with a party other than a purchaser of its products or services in order to receive that benefit'. The boards concluded that the principle in IFRS 15 for assessing whether a good or service is distinct is similar to the previous requirements in US GAAP.

BC257   The amount of consideration received from a customer for goods or services, and the amount of any consideration paid to that customer for goods or services, could be linked even if they are separate events. For instance, a customer may pay more for goods or services from an entity than it would otherwise have paid if it was not receiving a payment from the entity. Consequently, the boards decided that to depict revenue faithfully in those cases, any amount accounted for as a payment to the customer for goods or services received should be limited to the fair value of those goods or services, with any amount in excess of the fair value being recognised as a reduction of the transaction price.

BC258   If the payment of consideration is accounted for as a reduction of the transaction price, an entity would recognise less revenue when it satisfies the related performance obligation(s). However, in some cases, an entity promises to pay consideration to a customer only after it has satisfied its performance obligations and, therefore, after it has recognised revenue. When this is the case, a reduction in revenue should be recognised immediately. Accordingly, the boards clarified that the reduction of revenue is recognised at the later of when the entity transfers the goods or services to the customer and when the entity promises to pay the consideration. By using the phrase 'promises to pay', the boards clarified that an entity should reflect in the transaction price payments to customers that are conditional on future events (for example, a promise to pay a customer that is conditional on the customer making a specified number of purchases would be reflected in the transaction price when the entity makes the promise).

Customer credit risk

BC259   The 2010 Exposure Draft proposed that an entity would recognise revenue at the amount that the entity expects to *receive* from the customer. In other words, the customer's credit risk would be reflected in the measurement of the transaction price allocated to the performance obligations in the contract.

BC260   Many respondents to the 2010 Exposure Draft commented specifically about the proposed requirements for customer credit risk. Although some respondents agreed with the proposal that the transaction price should reflect the customer's credit risk, nearly all respondents (including preparers, users of financial statements and securities regulators) expressed concerns about applying that concept in practice. In particular, many users of financial statements commented that they would prefer revenue to be measured at the 'gross' amount so that revenue growth and receivables management (or bad debts) could be analysed separately. Those users of financial statements indicated that they were interested in assessing the performance of an entity's sales function and receivables collection function separately because those functions are often managed separately. However, that information would not be available if an entity's assessment of sales and collectability were reflected only on a 'net' basis in the revenue line.

BC261 After considering that feedback, the boards decided not to adopt that proposal. Instead, in the 2011 Exposure Draft, the boards proposed that revenue should be recognised at the amount to which the entity expects to be entitled, which would not reflect any adjustments for amounts that the entity might not be able to collect from the customer. However, to provide transparency to all users of financial statements for the portion of the entity's gross revenue that is expected to be uncollectable, the boards proposed to link the presentation of the revenue line and the impairment loss line. Consequently, the 2011 Exposure Draft proposed that initial and subsequent impairment losses (and reversals) on transactions that did not include a significant financing component should be presented as a separate line item adjacent to the revenue line item.

BC262 In redeliberating the 2011 Exposure Draft, the boards considered the following challenges arising from the proposed linked presentation of revenue and impairment losses:

(a) different interpretations might have emerged about whether the reported revenue amount of the entity is the gross revenue before the impairment losses that are presented adjacent to revenue or the net revenue after those impairment losses.

(b) the impairment losses that would have been presented as a separate line item adjacent to the revenue line item might have related to uncollectable consideration that had been recognised as revenue in previous reporting periods. Consequently, there would not necessarily be a connection between the revenue recognised in a particular reporting period and the impairment losses that would have been presented adjacent to the revenue line item in that period.

(c) the impairment losses on short-term trade receivables (ie receivables arising from contracts with customers that do not have separately identified financing components) would have been presented differently from all other financial assets that are subject to impairment. This is because the impairment losses for short-term trade receivables would have been presented adjacent to revenue, whereas for all other financial assets, impairment losses would have been presented together with other expense items in the statement of comprehensive income. For the reasons described in paragraphs BC244–BC247, those other financial assets would have included receivables arising from contracts with customers that include a financing component that is significant to the contract.

BC263 The boards considered addressing some of those challenges by requiring that initial impairment losses be presented adjacent to the revenue line item and subsequent impairment losses be presented as a separate expense. The boards observed that this approach would have provided a clearer link between revenue and the impairment losses related to the revenue recognised in that period. However, many respondents noted that it would have been challenging to distinguish between initial and subsequent impairment losses without incurring significant costs to obtain the information.

BC264   Consequently, the boards decided to modify the presentation requirements for impairment losses and to require disclosure of impairment losses on short-term trade receivables arising from a contract with a customer separate from other impairment losses (if not otherwise presented and subject to the usual materiality considerations). The boards decided that this approach is the most appropriate because it addresses the challenges identified in the 2011 Exposure Draft and still provides users of financial statements with the information that they had said would be most useful, which is gross revenue to provide revenue trend information and the impairment loss to provide information on receivables management (or bad debts). Furthermore, the boards noted that this would provide greater consistency with the accounting for impairment losses on contracts with customers that include a significant financing component.

BC265   However, the boards were concerned that for some transactions in which there is significant credit risk at contract inception, an entity might recognise revenue for the transfer of goods or services and, at the same time, recognise a significant bad debt expense. The boards decided that in those cases, 'grossing up' revenue and recognising a significant impairment loss would not faithfully represent the transaction and would not provide useful information. Consequently, the boards included the criterion in paragraph 9(e) of IFRS 15 (see paragraphs BC42–BC46).

Allocating the transaction price to performance obligations (paragraphs 73–86)

BC266   The boards decided that an entity should generally allocate the transaction price to all performance obligations in proportion to the stand-alone selling prices of the goods or services underlying each of those performance obligations at contract inception (ie on a relative stand-alone selling price basis). They decided that in most cases an allocation based on stand-alone selling prices faithfully depicts the different margins that may apply to promised goods or services.

BC267   Most respondents agreed with the requirement to allocate the transaction price on a relative stand-alone selling price basis. Some of those respondents observed that the requirements were broadly consistent with previous changes to US GAAP for multiple-element arrangements. However, respondents expressed concerns about the following topics:

(a)   estimating the stand-alone selling price; and

(b)   allocating discounts and contingent consideration.

Estimating stand-alone selling prices (paragraphs 76–80)

BC268   IFRS 15 specifies that if an entity does not have an observable price from selling a good or service separately, the entity should instead estimate the stand-alone selling price. Paragraph 79 of IFRS 15 includes examples of suitable estimation methods for estimating the stand-alone selling price. However, the boards decided not to preclude or prescribe any particular method for estimating a stand-alone selling price so long as the estimate is a faithful representation of the price at which the entity would sell the distinct good or service if it were sold separately to the customer. The boards clarified that the method used by the entity to estimate a stand-alone selling price should maximise the use of observable inputs and should be applied consistently to estimate the stand-alone selling price of other goods or services with similar characteristics.

BC269　The boards observed that many entities may already have robust processes for determining stand-alone selling prices on the basis of reasonably available data points and the effects of market considerations and entity-specific factors. However, other entities may need to develop processes for estimating selling prices of goods or services that are typically not sold separately. The boards decided that when developing those processes, an entity should consider all reasonably available information on the basis of the specific facts and circumstances. That information might include the following:

(a)　reasonably available data points (for example, a stand-alone selling price of the good or service, the costs incurred to manufacture or provide the good or service, related profit margins, published price listings, third-party or industry pricing and the pricing of other goods or services in the same contract);

(b)　market conditions (for example, supply and demand for the good or service in the market, competition, restrictions and trends);

(c)　entity-specific factors (for example, business pricing strategies and practices); and

(d)　information about the customer or class of customer (for example, type of customer, geographical region and distribution channel).

Residual approach

BC270　In response to questions from respondents, the boards decided to specify that a residual approach might be a suitable technique for estimating the stand-alone selling price of a good or service. Using a residual approach, an entity would estimate a stand-alone selling price of a good or service on the basis of the difference between the total transaction price and the (observable) stand-alone selling prices of other goods or services in the contract.

BC271　The boards also decided to specify how and when an entity can use the residual approach as an estimation method in paragraph 79(c) of IFRS 15. Specifically, in situations in which one or more promised goods or services have a stand-alone selling price that is highly variable or uncertain. In specifying those circumstances, the boards were particularly mindful of the challenges in determining stand-alone selling prices in contracts for intellectual property and other intangible products. In those arrangements, the pricing can be highly variable because there is little or no incremental cost to the entity in providing those goods or services to a customer. In those circumstances, the most reliable way of determining the stand-alone selling price in the contract will often be to use a residual approach. For the same reason, the boards noted that the residual approach might be appropriate in situations in which an entity has not yet established the selling price for a good or service that previously has not been sold on a stand-alone basis.

BC272 Most respondents agreed with the boards' proposals on the residual approach. However, some respondents, particularly those in the software industry, asked the boards to clarify whether they could use a residual approach if there is more than one good or service in the contract with highly variable or uncertain stand-alone selling prices. Those respondents observed that this may occur in contracts that include three or more performance obligations, in which at least one of the performance obligations has an observable stand-alone selling price. The boards decided that even if a contract includes more than one good or service with a highly variable or uncertain stand-alone selling price, an entity should not be prevented from applying the residual approach because it may still be a reliable method for determining the stand-alone selling price. However, the boards observed that using the residual approach when there are two or more goods or services with highly variable or uncertain stand-alone selling prices may require an entity to use a combination of techniques to estimate the stand-alone selling prices as follows:

(a) apply the residual approach to estimate the aggregate of the stand-alone selling prices for all the promised goods or services with highly variable or uncertain stand-alone selling prices; and

(b) then use another technique to estimate the stand-alone selling prices of each of those promised goods or services with highly variable or uncertain stand-alone selling prices.

BC273 In determining whether the estimate is reasonable, the boards observed that it was important to understand that the residual approach for estimating the stand-alone selling price of a promised good or service is different from the residual method permitted under previous revenue Standards. This is because in IFRS 15 the residual approach is used to determine the stand-alone selling price of a distinct good or service. By definition, the outcome of this approach cannot realistically result in a stand-alone selling price of zero if the good or service is in fact distinct because to be distinct that good or service must have value on a stand-alone basis. In contrast, the residual method in previous revenue Standards could have resulted in an outcome of zero because the residual method was an allocation method. Thus, under previous revenue recognition requirements, zero could be the only amount of consideration that remained to be allocated to a performance obligation. Consequently, the boards noted that if the residual approach in paragraph 79(c) of IFRS 15 results in no, or very little, consideration being allocated to a good or service or a bundle of goods or services, the entity should consider whether that estimate is appropriate in those circumstances.

Specifying a hierarchy of evidence

BC274 The boards decided not to specify a hierarchy of evidence to determine the stand-alone selling price of a good or service. Instead, they decided to emphasise that an entity should maximise the use of observable inputs when developing estimates of stand-alone selling prices.

BC275 Most respondents agreed with the boards' decision not to prescribe a hierarchy of evidence for estimating a stand-alone selling price. However, some respondents recommended that the boards should specify a hierarchy of evidence, because specifying a hierarchy of evidence for determining stand-alone selling prices (and requiring disclosures using that hierarchy) would enhance the quality and reliability of an entity's reported revenues. The hierarchy suggested by those respondents was similar to that in previous revenue Standards:

(a) if vendor-specific objective evidence of a selling price is available, an entity would use this price to determine the selling price of a promised good or service;

(b) if vendor-specific objective evidence is not available, an entity would determine the selling price using third-party evidence, if available; and

(c) if third-party evidence is not available, an entity would use its best estimate of the selling price.

BC276   The boards observed that IFRS 15 requires an entity to use observable prices when a good or service is sold separately by the entity (which is similar to a vendor-specific objective evidence notion). It is only when a good or service is not sold separately that an entity is required to estimate the stand-alone selling price. In that estimation process, an entity is still required to maximise the use of observable inputs. The boards noted that in the hierarchy in paragraph BC275 there is little distinction between third-party evidence and a best estimate of a selling price. For instance, third-party evidence of a selling price might require adjustments to reflect differences in either (a) the good or service (because the third-party price could be for a similar, rather than an identical, good or service) or (b) pricing strategies between the third party and the entity. Therefore, the boards affirmed their decision not to specify a hierarchy in IFRS 15. Instead, the boards decided that it was important to emphasise that an entity should maximise the use of observable inputs when developing estimates of stand-alone selling prices.

Allocating discounts and variable consideration (paragraphs 81–86)

BC277   A consequence of allocating the transaction price on a relative stand-alone selling price basis is that any discount in the contract is allocated proportionately to each of the performance obligations in the contract. Some respondents noted that this would not always faithfully depict the amount of consideration to which an entity is entitled for satisfying a particular performance obligation. For example, those respondents noted that the allocation of the discount could result in a loss on one part of the contract although the contract as a whole may be profitable (for example, the contract contains both a high-margin item and a low-margin item). They suggested that the boards should permit an entity to allocate the discount in a contract using one of the following alternatives:

(a) a management approach, in which an entity would assess which promised good or service is priced at a discount to its stand-alone selling price.

(b) a residual approach, in which any discount in the contract would be allocated entirely to the satisfied performance obligations.

(c)   a profit margin approach, in which an entity would allocate the discount in a contract in proportion to the individual profit margin on each performance obligation. The individual profit margin for each performance obligation is the difference between the stand-alone selling price and the direct costs of the good or service underlying each performance obligation.

BC278   Another consequence of allocating the transaction price on a relative stand-alone selling price basis is that any amount of consideration that is variable will be allocated to each of the performance obligations in the contract. Some respondents noted that this allocation will not always faithfully depict the amount of consideration to which an entity is entitled upon satisfying a particular performance obligation, if the variable consideration does not relate to all of the performance obligations in the contract. Many suggested that any adjustment in the transaction price as a result of variable amounts should be allocated only to the performance obligation(s) to which the variable amounts relate.

BC279   The boards noted that the objective of the revenue recognition model is for an entity to recognise revenue in the amount of consideration to which it expects to be entitled from the customer in exchange for transferring goods or services. The relative stand-alone selling price basis allocation is simply a method to achieve that objective rather than being the allocation principle.

BC280   However, the boards also noted that allocating the transaction price on a relative stand-alone selling price basis brings rigour and discipline to the process of allocating the transaction price and, therefore, enhances comparability both within an entity and across entities. Consequently, the boards decided that it should be the default method for allocating the transaction price. However, they agreed with respondents that it might not always result in a faithful depiction of the amount of consideration to which the entity expects to be entitled from the customer. Accordingly, in paragraphs 81–86 of IFRS 15, the boards specified the circumstances in which other methods should be used.

Allocating discounts (paragraphs 81–83)

BC281   IFRS 15 requires an entity to allocate a discount entirely to one or more, but not all, performance obligations in the contract if the entity has observable selling prices for each performance obligation in the contract and those observable stand-alone selling prices provide evidence that the entire discount in the contract is specifically attributable to one or more of those performance obligations. Those requirements are largely based on the 'contract segmentation' principle that was included in the 2010 Exposure Draft, which only allowed a discount to be allocated entirely to one or more performance obligations on the basis of goods or services that are priced independently.

BC282   Some respondents questioned whether the requirements in paragraph 82 of IFRS 15 for allocating a discount are too restrictive and, therefore, might yield outcomes that are inconsistent with the economics of some transactions. However, the boards noted that the requirements are included to maintain the rigour and discipline of a stand-alone selling price allocation and, thus, appropriately restrict the situations in which a discount should not be allocated pro rata to all performance obligations in the contract.

BC283 The boards also noted that paragraph 82 of IFRS 15 would typically apply to contracts for which there are at least three performance obligations. This is because an entity could demonstrate that a discount relates to two or more performance obligations when it has observable information supporting the stand-alone selling price of a group of those promised goods or services when they are sold together. The boards noted that it may be possible for an entity to have sufficient evidence to be able to allocate a discount to only one performance obligation in accordance with the criteria in paragraph 82, but the boards expected that this could only occur in rare cases.

Allocating variable consideration (paragraphs 84–86)

BC284 The boards agreed with respondents that it would not always be appropriate for an entity to allocate the variable consideration in a transaction price to all of the performance obligations in a contract. For example, an entity may contract to provide two products at different times with a bonus that is contingent on the timely delivery of only the second product. In that example, it might be inappropriate to attribute variable consideration included in the transaction price to both products. Similarly, an entity may contract to provide two products at different times with a fixed amount for the first product that represents that product's stand-alone selling price, and a variable amount that is contingent on the delivery of the second product. That variable amount might be excluded from the estimate of the transaction price (ie because of the requirements for constraining estimates of the transaction price). In that case, it might be inappropriate to attribute the fixed consideration included in the transaction price to both products. Consequently, the boards specified the criteria in paragraphs 84–86 of IFRS 15 to identify the circumstances in which an entity should allocate the variable consideration entirely to a performance obligation or to a distinct good or service (that forms part of a single performance obligation) rather than to the contract as a whole. The boards decided that those criteria are necessary to ensure an appropriate allocation of the transaction price when there is variable consideration in the transaction price.

BC285 The boards clarified in paragraph 84(b) of IFRS 15 that variable consideration can be allocated to distinct goods or services even if those goods or services form a single performance obligation. The boards made this clarification to ensure that an entity can, in some cases, attribute the reassessment of variable consideration to only the satisfied portion of a performance obligation when that performance obligation meets the criterion in paragraph 22(b) of IFRS 15. Consider the example of a contract to provide hotel management services for one year (ie a single performance obligation in accordance with paragraph 22(b) of IFRS 15) in which the consideration is variable and determined based on two per cent of occupancy rates. The entity provides a daily service of management that is distinct and the uncertainty related to the consideration is also resolved on a daily basis when the occupancy occurs. In those circumstances, the boards did not intend for an entity to allocate the variable consideration determined on a daily basis to the entire performance obligation (ie the promise to provide management services over a one-year period). Instead, the variable consideration should be allocated to the distinct service to which the variable consideration relates, which is the daily management service.

Changes in transaction price

BC286 The boards also decided to specify that any subsequent changes in the transaction price should be allocated in a manner that is consistent with the allocation methodology at contract inception. This ensures that changes in the estimate of the variable consideration that are included in (or excluded from) the transaction price are allocated to the performance obligation(s) to which the variable consideration relates. Consequently, the boards specified in paragraph 89 of IFRS 15 that an entity should allocate a change in the transaction price entirely to one or more distinct goods or services if the criteria in paragraph 85 of IFRS 15 are met.

Contingent revenue cap and the portfolio approach to allocation

BC287 Some respondents disagreed with the boards' proposal that the transaction price should be allocated on a relative stand-alone selling price basis. Those respondents (primarily from the telecommunications and cable television industries) disagreed because allocating the transaction price using relative stand-alone selling prices on a contract-by-contract basis could be complex and costly for their industries. This is because entities in those industries:

(a) have a high volume of contracts with various potential configurations;

(b) provide multiple goods and services in those contracts;

(c) include a discount in the contracts; and

(d) provide the goods or services at different times.

BC288 Those respondents also disagreed with allocating the transaction price on the basis of relative stand-alone selling prices because it would provide a revenue recognition pattern that they considered would not be useful to users of their financial statements.

BC289 Those respondents requested that the boards should carry forward previous revenue recognition requirements in US GAAP (previously referred to as 'the contingent revenue cap'). Those requirements were previously used by many telecommunications entities applying US GAAP and IFRS. In the respondents' view, carrying forward those requirements would have simplified the application of the revenue recognition model by limiting the amount of consideration that a telecommunications entity could allocate to a handset that is bundled with network services to the amount that is not contingent on the delivery of network services in the future. Consequently, revenue would have been recognised at the amount that the customer paid for the handset at contract inception when the handset was transferred to the customer. The remaining contractual payments would have been recognised subsequently as revenue as the entity provided network services to the customer. Many users of financial statements of entities in the telecommunications industry agreed that this revenue recognition pattern would have been useful because it closely relates to the timing of cash received.

BC290 Respondents from the telecommunications industry commented that without a contingent revenue cap, not only will the application of the revenue recognition model be complex, but revenue will also be recognised for delivering a handset in an amount that exceeds the amount of consideration paid for the handset. In their view, this is inappropriate because it will not be useful to users of their financial statements and, in a separate objection, because they will be entitled to collect the excess only when they provide the network services. Consequently, they reasoned that the contract asset that will result from recognising revenue for delivery of the handset will not meet the definition of an asset. In addition, they suggested that without a contingent revenue cap, the model will be complex and costly to apply because of the high volume of contracts that they will have to manage and the various potential configurations of handsets and network service plans.

BC291 However, the boards decided not to carry forward the contingent revenue cap for the following reasons:

(a) limiting the amount of consideration that can be allocated to a satisfied performance obligation is tantamount to cash-basis accounting and does not meet the core principle of IFRS 15. This is because revenue recognised would not depict the amount of consideration to which an entity expects to be entitled for the delivered good or service. Consequently, the contingent revenue cap could result in economically similar contracts being accounted for differently.

(b) the contingent revenue cap can result in the recognition of losses if the contract is profitable. That would occur if the amount allocated to a satisfied performance obligation is limited to an amount (potentially to zero) that is less than the expenses recognised for the costs of providing the good or service (unless those costs are deferred). However, costs relating to a good or service already transferred to a customer would not give rise to an asset.

(c) recognising a contract asset in the situation described in paragraph BC290 is appropriate because the entity has a valuable contractual right as a result of satisfying a performance obligation and that right meets the definition of an asset. That right exists even if the entity does not have the unconditional right to collect consideration from the customer. This is because if the entity were to transfer the remaining rights and performance obligations in the contract to a third party after it had delivered a handset, it would expect to be compensated for that past performance.

(d) applying the contingent cap more broadly than it was applied in previous revenue Standards could have had far-reaching consequences. For example, in many service contracts (including construction contracts), it is appropriate to recognise revenue when services are provided even though the amount of consideration is contingent on the entity's future performance. Otherwise, the entity would not recognise any revenue until reaching a contract milestone or potentially until completion of the contract (which would not depict the transfer of goods or services to the customer).

(e) although the consequences for construction and other service contracts could have been reduced by limiting the amount allocated to satisfied performance obligations (rather than limiting the amount allocated to a satisfied portion of a single performance obligation), the boards decided that this would have created an arbitrary distinction and would have put additional pressure on the criteria for identifying performance obligations.

(f) for many contracts that were previously accounted for under the contingent revenue cap, the amount of consideration allocated to delivered items was not contingent because, even if the customer cancelled the contract, the customer would have been obliged to pay for the delivered item(s). For example, in some contracts for the sale of a handset and network services, either the contract was not cancellable or, if it was, the customer was obliged to pay a termination fee that corresponded with the value of the handset that was delivered upfront (even if the entity might choose not to enforce payment of that fee).

BC292 In addition, the boards decided not to introduce an exception to the revenue recognition model for telecommunications and similar contracts because they do not view those contracts as being different from other contracts in which an entity transfers a bundle of goods or services. Furthermore, the boards decided that IFRS 15 provides a more consistent basis for recognising revenue and produces results in accounting that more closely match the underlying economics of transactions.

BC293 The boards also observed that entities in the telecommunications industry may be able to simplify the application of the model by using portfolio techniques (as envisioned by the practical expedient specified in paragraph 4 of IFRS 15) to allocate the transaction price for a group of similar contracts (see paragraphs BC69–BC70). The boards considered whether they should provide more specific guidance as to when an entity could use a portfolio approach for allocating the transaction price. However, the boards decided not to do so because they were concerned that any further guidance (for example, by including criteria that an entity would need to meet to apply a portfolio approach) might make the practical expedient less useful across entities or jurisdictions.

Onerous performance obligations

BC294 In the 2010 and the 2011 Exposure Drafts, the boards proposed including requirements for identifying and measuring onerous performance obligations in contracts with customers (ie an 'onerous test'). In those proposals, the boards concluded that an onerous test was needed because the initial measurements of performance obligations are not routinely updated. In addition, the boards noted that including an onerous test would achieve greater convergence of IFRS and US GAAP.

BC295 However, many respondents to the 2010 and the 2011 Exposure Drafts disagreed with the onerous test and highlighted a number of practical application difficulties. Furthermore, many explained that strict application of the onerous test would have resulted in recognition of liabilities in cases in which the outcome of fulfilling a single performance obligation was onerous but the outcome of fulfilling the entire contract would be profitable. A number of respondents suggested removing the onerous test from the revenue proposals because, in addition to being complex and difficult to apply, the requirements for recognition of onerous losses are already sufficiently addressed in other Standards. Those respondents commented that:

(a) for IFRS, the onerous test in IAS 37 and the requirements in IAS 2 *Inventories* already provide sufficient guidance for determining when to recognise losses arising from contracts with customers.

(b) for US GAAP, existing requirements for recognition of losses from contracts are adequate and if a change to those requirements is necessary, that change could instead be handled in a separate project that addresses liabilities in Topic 450.

BC296 The boards agreed that existing requirements in both IFRS and US GAAP could adequately identify onerous contracts. Furthermore, the boards noted that although their existing requirements for onerous contracts are not identical, they are not aware of any pressing practice issues resulting from the application of those existing requirements. Consequently, the boards decided that IFRS 15 should not include an onerous test. Instead, entities applying IFRS or US GAAP will use their respective existing requirements for the identification and measurement of onerous contracts.

Contract costs (paragraphs 91–104)

Incremental costs of obtaining a contract (paragraphs 91–94)

BC297 The boards decided that an entity should recognise as an asset the incremental costs of obtaining a contract with a customer if the entity expects to recover those costs. The boards defined the incremental costs of obtaining a contract as the costs that an entity incurs in its efforts to obtain a contract that would not have been incurred if the contract had not been obtained. The boards acknowledged that, in some cases, an entity's efforts to recognise an asset from incremental acquisition costs might exceed the financial reporting benefits. Consequently, as a practical expedient, the boards decided to allow an entity to recognise those costs as expenses when incurred for contracts in which the amortisation period for the asset that the entity otherwise would have recognised is one year or less.

BC298 The boards considered requiring an entity to recognise all of the costs of obtaining a contract as expenses when those costs are incurred. The boards observed that, conceptually, an entity may obtain a contract asset as a result of its efforts to obtain a contract (because the measure of the remaining rights might exceed the measure of the remaining obligations). However, because the principle in IFRS 15 requires an entity to recognise a contract asset and revenue only as a result of satisfying a performance obligation in the contract, the boards observed that on the basis of that reasoning, the contract asset would be measured at zero at contract inception and any costs of obtaining a contract would therefore be recognised as expenses when incurred.

BC299 Many respondents disagreed with recognising all costs to obtain a contract as expenses when incurred because those costs meet the definition of an asset in some cases. In addition, they noted the following:

(a) other Standards require some of the costs of obtaining a contract to be included in the carrying amount of an asset on initial recognition; and

(b) the recognition of the costs of obtaining a contract as expenses would be inconsistent with the tentative decisions in the boards' projects on leases and insurance contracts.

BC300 During the redeliberations, the boards decided that, in some cases, it might be misleading for an entity to recognise all the costs of obtaining a contract as expenses, when incurred. For example, the boards observed that recognising the full amount of a sales commission as an expense at inception of a long-term service contract (when that sales commission is reflected in the pricing of that contract and is expected to be recovered) would fail to acknowledge the existence of an asset.

BC301 Consequently, the boards decided that an entity would recognise an asset from the costs of obtaining a contract and would present the asset separately from the contract asset or the contract liability. To limit the acquisition costs to those that can be clearly identified as relating specifically to a contract, the boards decided that only the incremental costs of obtaining a contract should be included in the measurement of the asset, if the entity expects to recover those costs. The boards decided that determining whether other costs relate to a contract is too subjective.

BC302 The boards noted that it might be difficult for some entities to determine whether a commission payment is incremental to obtaining a new contract (for example, payment of a commission might depend on the entity successfully acquiring several contracts). The boards considered whether to allow an accounting policy election for contract costs, under which an entity would have been able to choose to recognise an asset from the acquisition costs or recognise those costs as an expense (with disclosure of the accounting policy election). The boards noted that this would have been consistent with previous revenue recognition requirements in US GAAP for public entities. However, the boards noted that introducing accounting policy elections into IFRS 15 would have reduced comparability and therefore would not have met one of the key objectives of the Revenue Recognition project to improve comparability in accounting among entities and industries. Consequently, the boards decided not to allow entities an accounting policy election with respect to contract acquisition costs.

BC303 The FASB noted that depending on the specific facts and circumstances of the arrangement between an asset manager and the other parties in the relationship, the application of the requirements for incremental costs of obtaining a contract might have resulted in different accounting for sales commissions paid to third-party brokers (ie in some cases the commission would have been recognised as an asset while in others it would have been recognised as an expense). The FASB observed that it had not intended the application of the cost requirements to result in an outcome for these specific types of sales commissions that would be different from applying existing US GAAP. Consequently, the FASB decided to retain the specific cost requirements for investment companies in paragraph 946-605-25-8 of the Codification which has been moved to Subtopic 946-720 *Financial Services—Investment Companies—Other Expenses*.

Costs to fulfil a contract (paragraphs 95–98)

BC304   The boards developed requirements for accounting for some costs to fulfil a contract. Those requirements were developed in response to concerns that the proposals in the Discussion Paper focused on how an entity should recognise revenue in a contract without considering how the entity should account for the costs to fulfil a contract. Some respondents, particularly those from the construction industry, said that requirements for profit margin recognition are as important as requirements for revenue recognition. Other respondents, mainly preparers who apply US GAAP, were concerned about the withdrawal of requirements for costs that were developed specifically for their own industries.

BC305   The cost requirements in IFRS 15 are intended to achieve the following:

(a)   fill the gap arising from the withdrawal of previous revenue Standards—IFRS 15 will result in the withdrawal of some requirements for contract costs, in particular, the previous requirements for accounting for construction contracts.

(b)   improve current practice—the cost requirements provide clearer requirements for accounting for some costs to fulfil a contract (for example, setup costs for services) and result in an entity no longer having to rely on, or analogise to, requirements that were not developed specifically for contracts with customers. For instance, in accounting for setup costs, an entity applying US GAAP may previously have needed to analogise to the guidance on the deferral of direct loan origination costs in paragraph 310-20-25-2 of the Codification. An entity applying IFRS may have evaluated those costs in accordance with IAS 38 *Intangible Assets*. Specifying clear requirements will also result in greater consistency in practice.

(c)   promote convergence in accounting for contract costs—more costs will be accounted for similarly under IFRS and US GAAP (although total consistency in accounting for costs to fulfil a contract will not be achieved unless the boards align their respective Standards on inventories; property, plant and equipment; intangible assets and impairment of assets).

BC306   Most respondents supported the boards' inclusion of requirements that address some of the costs to fulfil a contract. Some respondents recommended that the boards address cost requirements comprehensively in a separate project. However, because cost requirements are included in many Standards (such as the ones described in paragraph BC305(c)), the boards noted that this would require reconsideration of those Standards and, therefore, decided against broadening the scope of the cost requirements.

BC307 Because the boards decided not to reconsider all cost requirements comprehensively, paragraphs 91–98 of IFRS 15 specify the accounting for contract costs that are not within the scope of other Standards. Consequently, if the other Standards preclude the recognition of any asset arising from a particular cost, an asset cannot then be recognised under IFRS 15 (for example, in IFRS, initial operating losses, such as those incurred while demand for an item builds, will continue to be accounted for in accordance with paragraph 20(b) of IAS 16 and, in US GAAP, pre-production costs under long-term supply arrangements will continue to be accounted for in accordance with paragraphs 340-10-25-5 through 25-8 of the Codification).

BC308 IFRS 15 clarifies that only costs that give rise to resources that will be used in satisfying performance obligations in the future and that are expected to be recovered are eligible for recognition as assets. Those requirements ensure that only costs that meet the definition of an asset are recognised as such and that an entity is precluded from deferring costs merely to normalise profit margins throughout a contract by allocating revenue and costs evenly over the life of the contract. To provide a clear objective for recognising and measuring an asset arising from the costs to fulfil a contract, the boards decided that only costs that relate directly to a contract should be included in the cost of the asset.

Amortisation and impairment (paragraphs 99–104)

BC309 The boards decided that an entity should amortise the asset recognised from the costs of obtaining and fulfilling a contract in accordance with the pattern of transfer of goods or services to which the asset relates. Respondents broadly agreed; however, some asked the boards to clarify whether those goods or services could relate to future contracts. Consequently, the boards clarified that in amortising the asset in accordance with the transfer of goods or services to which the asset relates, those goods or services could be provided under a specifically anticipated (ie future) contract. That conclusion is consistent with the notion of amortising an asset over its useful life and with other Standards. However, amortising the asset over a longer period than the initial contract would not be appropriate in situations in which an entity pays a commission on a contract renewal that is commensurate with the commission paid on the initial contract. In that case, the acquisition costs from the initial contract do not relate to the subsequent contract.

BC310 The boards considered testing a recognised asset arising from fulfilment costs for impairment using one of the existing impairment tests in their respective requirements (for example, IAS 2 and IAS 36 *Impairment of Assets* or Topic 330 *Inventory*, Topic 360 *Property, Plant and Equipment* and Subtopic 985-20 *Software—Costs of Software to Be Sold, Leased, or Marketed*). However, the boards decided that an entity should consider only the economic benefits in the contract with the customer and, consequently, the impairment test should be based on comparing the carrying amount of the asset with the remaining amount of promised consideration in exchange for the goods or services to which the asset relates, less the remaining costs of providing those goods or services. The boards decided that for purposes of impairment testing, the entity should consider future cash flows that may be too uncertain to include in the recognition of revenue (see paragraphs BC203–BC223). The boards decided this because their objective for measuring and recognising impairments of contract acquisition and fulfilment costs is different from the measurement objective for revenue. The impairment objective is to determine whether the carrying amount of the contract acquisition and fulfilment costs asset is recoverable. Consequently, the measurement objective is consistent with other impairment methods in IFRS and US GAAP that include an assessment of customer credit risk and expectations of whether amounts of variable consideration will be received.

BC311   The FASB decided that an entity should not reverse an impairment charge when the reasons for the impairment no longer exist. Conversely, the IASB decided that the impairment charge should be reversed in those circumstances under IFRS. The boards acknowledged that this would result in entities accounting differently for those contract costs using IFRS and US GAAP. However, the boards decided that it is important for the requirements to be consistent with their respective impairment models for other types of assets and those impairment models differ in their accounting for reversals of impairments.

Learning curve

BC312   A 'learning curve' is the effect of efficiencies realised over time when an entity's costs of performing a task (or producing a unit) decline in relation to how many times the entity performs that task (or produces that unit). The phenomenon of a learning curve can exist independently of a contract with a customer. For example, a typical manufacturer that produces units of inventory would become more efficient in its production process over time. Some respondents asked how to apply the proposals to account for the effects of learning costs in a contract with a customer.

BC313   The boards noted that IFRS 15 addresses the accounting for the effects of learning costs if both of the following conditions are satisfied:

(a)   an entity has a single performance obligation to deliver a specified number of units; and

(b)   the performance obligation is satisfied over time.

BC314   In that situation, an entity recognises revenue by selecting a method of measuring progress that depicts the transfer over time of the good or service to the customer. An entity would probably select a method (for example, cost-to-cost) that results in the entity recognising more revenue and expense for the early units produced relative to the later units. That effect is appropriate because of the greater value of the entity's performance in the early part of the contract because, if an entity were to sell only one unit, it would charge the customer a higher price for that unit than the average unit price the customer pays when the customer purchases more than one unit.

BC315   In other situations, an entity may promise to deliver a specified number of units in a contract, but that promise does not give rise to a single performance obligation that is satisfied over time. The boards decided that, in those situations, an entity should apply the requirements of other Standards (for example, IAS 2) for the following reasons:

(a)   if an entity incurs costs to fulfil a contract without also satisfying a performance obligation over time, the entity probably would be creating an asset included within the scope of other Standards (for example, the costs of producing tangible units would accumulate as inventory, and the entity would select an appropriate method of measuring that inventory). In those cases, the boards decided that an entity should not account for the learning curve differently depending on whether or not a contract exists.

(b)   the type of contract described in this paragraph is not the type of contract typically entered into by respondents who asked how the requirements of IFRS 15 would apply to learning curve effects (in most cases, those respondents enter into contracts that would be accounted for as a performance obligation satisfied over time).

BC316   The boards, however, acknowledged the diversity in practice when accounting (in accordance with other Standards) for the costs of products produced under long-term production programmes, but agreed that they could not address these matters as part of the Revenue Recognition project.

Presentation (paragraphs 105–109)

BC317   The boards decided that the remaining rights and performance obligations in a contract should be accounted for and presented on a net basis, as either a contract asset or a contract liability. The boards noted that the rights and obligations in a contract with a customer are interdependent—the right to receive consideration from a customer depends on the entity's performance and, similarly, the entity performs only as long as the customer continues to pay. The boards decided that those interdependencies are best reflected by accounting and presenting on a net basis the remaining rights and obligations in the statement of financial position.

BC318   The boards considered whether the rights and performance obligations in contracts that are subject to the legal remedy of specific performance should be presented on a gross basis, that is, as separate assets and liabilities. The boards observed that in the event of a breach of contract, some contracts require the entity and the customer to perform as specified in the contract. Consequently, unlike most contracts that can be settled net, specific performance contracts generally result in a two-way flow of resources between the customer and the entity. Specific performance contracts are akin to financial contracts that are settled by physical delivery rather than by a net cash payment and for which the units of account are the individual assets and liabilities arising from the contractual rights and obligations.

BC319   However, the boards decided against making an exception for specific performance contracts. This is because the remedy of specific performance is relatively rare and is not available in all jurisdictions. In addition, it is only one of a number of possible remedies that could be awarded by a court if legal action were taken for breach of contract.

BC320   The boards decided that IFRS 15 should not specify whether an entity is required to present its contract assets and contract liabilities as separate line items in the statement of financial position. Instead, an entity should apply the general principles for the presentation of financial statements to determine whether to present contract assets and contract liabilities separately in the statement of financial position. For example, IAS 1 *Presentation of Financial Statements* requires an entity to present separately each class of similar items and items of a dissimilar nature or function unless they are immaterial.

BC321 The boards also observed that some industries have historically used different labels to describe contract assets and contract liabilities or may recognise them in more than one line item either in the financial statements or in the notes. Because that additional detail is often useful to users of those financial statements, the boards decided that an entity could use different descriptions of contract assets, contract liabilities and receivables, and could use additional line items to present those assets and liabilities if the entity also provides sufficient information for users of financial statements to be able to distinguish them.

Relationship between contract assets and receivables

BC322 When an entity performs first by satisfying a performance obligation before a customer performs by paying the consideration, the entity has a contract asset—a right to consideration from the customer in exchange for goods or services transferred to the customer.

BC323 In many cases, that contract asset is an unconditional right to consideration—a receivable—because only the passage of time is required before payment of that consideration is due. However, in other cases, an entity satisfies a performance obligation but does not have an unconditional right to consideration, for example, because it first needs to satisfy another performance obligation in the contract. The boards decided that when an entity satisfies a performance obligation but does not have an unconditional right to consideration, an entity should recognise a contract asset in accordance with IFRS 15. The boards noted that making the distinction between a contract asset and a receivable is important because doing so provides users of financial statements with relevant information about the risks associated with the entity's rights in a contract. That is because although both would be subject to credit risk, a contract asset is also subject to other risks, for example, performance risk.

BC324 Once an entity has an unconditional right to consideration, it should present that right as a receivable separately from the contract asset and account for it in accordance with other requirements (for example, IFRS 9 or Topic 310). The boards decided that IFRS 15 need not address the accounting for receivables in addition to revenue recognition. Issues such as the measurement (or impairment) of receivables and disclosures relating to those assets are already addressed in IFRS and US GAAP.

BC325 In many cases, an unconditional right to consideration arises when the entity satisfies the performance obligation and invoices the customer. For example, a payment for goods or services is typically due and an invoice is issued when the entity has transferred the goods or services to the customer. However, the act of invoicing the customer for payment does not indicate whether the entity has an unconditional right to consideration. For instance, the entity may have an unconditional right to consideration before it invoices (unbilled receivable) if only the passage of time is required before payment of that consideration is due. In other cases, an entity can have an unconditional right to consideration before it has satisfied a performance obligation. For example, an entity may enter into a non-cancellable contract that requires the customer to pay the consideration a month before the entity provides goods or services. In those cases, on the date when payment is due, the entity has an unconditional right to consideration. (However, in those cases, the entity should recognise revenue only after it transfers the goods or services.)

BC326   The boards observed that in some cases, an entity will have an unconditional right to consideration, even though the entity may be required to refund some or all of that consideration in the future. In those cases, the possible obligation to refund consideration in the future will not affect the entity's present right to be entitled to the gross amount of consideration. In those cases, the boards observed that an entity may recognise a receivable and a refund liability (for example, when a right of return exists).

Disclosure (paragraphs 110–129)

BC327   Some of the main criticisms from regulators and users of financial statements about prior revenue Standards in IFRS and US GAAP related to the disclosure requirements. Broadly, regulators and users of financial statements found the disclosure requirements to be inadequate and lacking cohesion with the disclosure of other items in the financial statements. This lack of cohesion made it difficult to understand an entity's revenues, as well as the judgements and estimates made by the entity in recognising those revenues. For example, many users of financial statements observed that entities presented revenue in isolation, with the result that users of financial statements could not relate revenue to the entity's financial position. Consequently, one of the boards' goals in undertaking the Revenue Recognition project was to provide users of financial statements with more useful information through improved disclosure requirements. Many respondents broadly supported that goal. However, respondents' views about the proposed disclosure requirements in the 2011 Exposure Draft were polarised—users of financial statements supported the proposed disclosure requirements because those requirements would have been a significant improvement over previous requirements. In contrast, other respondents (primarily preparers) noted that, when viewed as a whole, the proposed disclosure requirements would have resulted in voluminous disclosures and they questioned whether the proposed disclosures were justifiable on a cost-benefit basis.

BC328   Because of those polarised views, the boards held workshops with users of financial statements and preparers between September and December 2012 in London (United Kingdom), Tokyo (Japan), and Norwalk and New York City (United States). The objective of those workshops was to discuss issues on disclosure and transition and to identify potential solutions to address both users' needs for useful information and preparers' concerns about the costs of providing that information. As a result of the feedback provided through workshops, other outreach efforts and the comment letters, the boards refined the disclosure requirements proposed in the 2011 Exposure Draft. Those refinements and the reasons for the boards' decisions are explained in paragraphs BC330–BC361.

BC329 The boards noted that the disclosure requirements in paragraphs 110–129 of IFRS 15 are comprehensive and represent a significant improvement from previous requirements. Some may observe that the overall volume of disclosure has increased compared with previous revenue disclosure requirements. However, the boards observed that, to some extent, concerns about the increased volume were the inevitable consequence of addressing the shortcoming in the previous disclosure requirements. In addition, the boards noted that many entities provide voluntary revenue disclosures outside the financial statements and the boards concluded that the increase in disclosure is necessary to improve previous disclosure practices and the usefulness of financial reporting.

Disclosure objective and materiality (paragraphs 110–112)

BC330 The boards decided that, consistently with other recent Standards, IFRS 15 should specify an objective for the revenue disclosures. In the boards' view, a clear objective improves the interpretation and implementation of the disclosure requirements. This is because a preparer can assess whether the overall quality and informational value of its revenue disclosures are sufficient to meet the stated objectives. The boards also observed that specifying an overall disclosure objective avoids the need for detailed and prescriptive disclosure requirements to accommodate the many and varied types of contracts with customers that are within the scope of IFRS 15.

BC331 The boards also decided to include disclosure requirements to help an entity meet the disclosure objective. However, those disclosures should not be viewed as a checklist of minimum disclosures, because some disclosures may be relevant for some entities or industries but may be irrelevant for others. The boards also observed that it is important for an entity to consider the disclosures together with the disclosure objective and materiality. Consequently, paragraph 111 of IFRS 15 clarifies that an entity need not disclose information that is immaterial.

Contracts with customers

BC332 To provide context for the disclosures, the boards decided to require an entity to disclose the amount of revenue recognised from contracts with customers. The FASB noted that in the absence of a general financial statement presentation standard, it would require an entity to present or disclose the amount of revenue recognised from contracts with customers. However, the IASB noted that the general principles of IAS 1 would apply and, therefore, an entity would need to disclose the amount of revenue recognised from contracts with customers in the notes to the financial statements only if it was not otherwise presented.

BC333 In addition to the amount of revenue recognised, the boards also decided to require an entity to disclose impairment losses from contracts with customers (if not presented in the statement of comprehensive income). The boards made this decision as a consequence of their previous decisions not to reflect customer credit risk in the measurement of the transaction price and, therefore, the amount of revenue recognised for transactions that do not include a significant financing component (see paragraphs BC259–BC265). This is reflected in the core principle of IFRS 15 that specifies that an entity recognise revenue at an amount that reflects the consideration to which the entity expects to be entitled.

BC334   In the light of those decisions, the boards decided that separately disclosing (or presenting) the impairment losses on contracts with customers provides the most relevant information to users of financial statements.

Disaggregation of revenue (paragraphs 114–115)

BC335   Revenue recognised in the statement of comprehensive income is a composite amount arising from many contracts with customers. This is because revenue can arise from the transfer of different goods or services and from contracts that involve different types of customers or markets. Users of financial statements explained that understanding those differences was critical to their analyses. Consequently, the boards decided to require an entity to provide disaggregated revenue information to help users of financial statements understand the composition of the revenue from contracts with customers recognised in the current period.

BC336   In developing the requirements for disclosing disaggregated revenue, the boards observed that some previous revenue recognition requirements required revenue to be disaggregated into its significant categories, including revenue arising from goods or services. However, because the most useful disaggregation of revenue depends on various entity-specific or industry-specific factors, the boards decided that IFRS 15 should not prescribe any specific factor to be used as the basis for disaggregating revenue from contracts with customers. Instead, the boards decided to specify in paragraph 114 of IFRS 15 an objective for providing disaggregated information. The boards noted that specifying an objective will result in the most useful information for users of financial statements, because it enables an entity to disaggregate revenue into categories that are meaningful for its business. In addition, specifying an objective should result in disaggregation that is neither too aggregated nor too detailed.

BC337   The boards also decided to provide application guidance because of requests for additional guidance about how to implement the objective and, in particular, how to determine the appropriate categories that an entity may use to disaggregate revenue from contracts with customers. The application guidance explains that the most appropriate categories depend on facts and circumstances; however, an entity should consider how revenue is disaggregated in other communications or for the purposes of evaluating financial performance. This is because entities often already disaggregate revenue in those communications and the categories used may be those that are most useful for users of financial statements and that meet the objective in paragraph 114 of IFRS 15. The application guidance also includes a list of examples of categories (for example, geographical region or product type) by which an entity might disaggregate its revenue. The boards noted that the list of categories was compiled as examples that could be applied to many different entities, industries and contracts. As a result, the list should not be viewed either as a checklist or as an exhaustive list. However, the boards observed that an entity may need to disaggregate by more than one category to meet the objective.

BC338 The boards also decided to require that an entity explain the relationship between the disaggregated revenue information required by paragraph 114 of IFRS 15 and the segment information required by IFRS 8 *Operating Segments* and Topic 280 *Segment Reporting*. The boards decided this because users of financial statements explained that it is critical to their analyses to understand not only the composition of revenue, but also how that revenue relates to other information provided in segment disclosures such as costs of goods sold, expenses and assets used.

BC339 In developing the requirements, the boards also considered whether the current segment reporting requirements in IFRS 8 and Topic 280 provided adequate information for users of financial statements in understanding the composition of revenue. Those requirements require an entity to disaggregate and disclose revenue for each operating segment (reconciled to total revenue). In addition, those requirements also require an entity to disaggregate total revenue by products or services (or by groups of similar products or services) and geographical areas—if the entity's operating segments are not based on those factors.

BC340 However, despite some similarity to segment reporting, the boards decided to require disaggregated revenue information for revenue from contracts with customers in IFRS 15 because some entities are exempt from providing segment disclosures (for example, entities that are not listed on a public stock exchange). Furthermore, the boards observed that segment information might be based on non-GAAP information (ie the revenue that is reported to the chief operating decision maker may be recognised and measured on a basis that is not in accordance with IFRS 15). The boards also observed that the objective of providing segment information in accordance with IFRS 8 or Topic 280 is different from the objective for the disaggregation disclosure in IFRS 15 and, therefore, segment revenue disclosures may not always provide users of financial statements with enough information to help them understand the composition of revenue recognised in the period. Nonetheless, the boards clarified in paragraph 112 of IFRS 15 that an entity does not need to provide disaggregated revenue disclosures if the information about revenue provided in accordance with IFRS 8 or Topic 280 meets the requirements specified in paragraph 114 of IFRS 15 and those revenue disclosures are based on the recognition and measurement requirements in IFRS 15.

Contract balances (paragraphs 116–118)

BC341 Users of financial statements explained that they need to understand the relationship between the revenue recognised in a reporting period and the changes in the balances of the entity's contract assets and contract liabilities (ie contract balances) to assess the nature, amount, timing and uncertainty of revenue and cash flows arising from an entity's contracts with customers. Those users of financial statements noted that even though many entities currently recognise working capital balances such as unbilled receivables and deferred revenue, previous revenue recognition requirements did not require adequate disclosure about the relationship between those balances and the amount of revenue recognised. Consequently, the 2010 and the 2011 Exposure Drafts proposed that an entity disclose a reconciliation of the contract asset and the contract liability balances in a tabular format.

BC342 However, many preparers strongly opposed any requirements to reconcile the contract asset and the contract liability balances in a tabular format. Those preparers noted that it would be costly to compile and present the information because it was not tracked. Preparers also questioned the usefulness of this reconciliation to users of financial statements, because the information was not used by management. In contrast, users of financial statements reiterated that some of the information in the reconciliation would be useful, including the information about contract liabilities, which would provide greater transparency about future revenues, which is critical to their analyses. However, users of financial statements also acknowledged that the rigid format of the proposed reconciliation had limitations that would have reduced its usefulness. This is because, for example, changes in contract assets and contract liabilities would have been disclosed on an aggregate basis (ie changes in contract assets would have been offset by changes in contract liabilities) and, therefore, the extent of the changes in contract balances (and the reasons for those changes) would have been obscured.

BC343 In the discussion at the disclosure and transition workshops in 2012 (see paragraph BC328), preparers agreed that they could provide further information about contract balances that would be useful to users of financial statements. However, to limit the costs of providing that information, those preparers explained that they need greater flexibility in the format of this disclosure. Users of financial statements emphasised that it was critical to them to have information on the movements in the contract balances presented separately because it would help them understand information about the following:

(a) the amount of the opening balance of the contract liability balance that will be recognised as revenue during the period; and

(b) the amount of the opening balance of the contract asset that will be transferred to accounts receivable or collected in cash during the period.

BC344 Before addressing concerns about format, the boards considered whether they could address the cost concerns of preparers by limiting the scope of the reconciliation requirements to only contract balances for specific types of contracts (for example, long-term contracts). They did this because many users of financial statements observed that information about contract balances would be particularly important for entities that enter into long-term contracts with customers or that carry significant contract liability balances for other reasons (for example, prepaid service contracts). However, the boards rejected this alternative for the following reasons:

(a) it would have been difficult to clearly identify the types of contracts or industries for which a reconciliation would (or would not) provide useful information.

(b)   limiting the scope of the reconciliation would have added complexity. This is because limiting the scope could have resulted in excluding some of an entity's contract assets and contract liabilities from the reconciliation and, therefore, additional information would have been required to relate the reconciled amounts of contract assets or contract liabilities to those recognised in the statement of financial position.

(c)   information on contract balances is useful for other contracts, in addition to long-term contracts, because, for example, there may be a number of contracts or businesses that have significant timing differences between payment and performance.

BC345   In the light of their decision not to limit the scope of the disclosure, the boards considered whether they could instead modify the format of the disclosure to address the concerns of preparers and users of financial statements. The boards observed that neither users of financial statements nor preparers supported the format proposed in the 2010 and the 2011 Exposure Drafts because users of financial statements were concerned that the information about the movements in the contract balances was too aggregated to be useful and because preparers were concerned about the cost of compliance with such a rigid format. The boards acknowledged that a previously rejected alternative format of a gross reconciliation of contract balances (ie to show the remaining contractual rights and performance obligations in separate columns) would have been inappropriate because it would not respond to preparers' concerns about costs. This is because the cost of preparing and auditing the gross reconciliation would have been high, and possibly higher than the 'net' reconciliation proposed in the 2011 Exposure Draft, because an entity would have been required to measure all unperformed contracts which would have required a high level of judgement.

BC346   Consequently, the boards decided that, instead of requiring a tabular reconciliation of the aggregate contract balances, they would require an entity to disclose qualitative and quantitative information about the entity's contract balances (see paragraphs 116–118 of IFRS 15). This approach balances the needs of users of financial statements with preparers' concerns because the qualitative and quantitative disclosures provide users of financial statements with the information they requested (ie information on when contract assets are typically transferred to accounts receivable or collected as cash and when contract liabilities are recognised as revenue). In addition, the boards decided that those disclosures would be more cost-effective than a reconciliation. The boards also observed that this approach would not result in a significant change for many entities that are already disclosing similar information. For example, the boards observed that some long-term construction entities already disclosed information relating to balances similar to contract assets and contract liabilities—often referred to as 'due from customers' or 'unbilled accounts receivable' and 'due to customers' or 'deferred revenue'.

BC347   The boards also decided to require that an entity disclose the amount of revenue recognised in the period that relates to amounts allocated to performance obligations that were satisfied (or partially satisfied) in previous periods (for example, as a result of a change in transaction price or estimates related to the constraint on revenue recognised). Disclosing those amounts provides relevant information about the timing of revenue recognition that was not a result of performance in the current period and thus provides useful information about the current period operating results and on predicting future revenues. In addition, the boards noted that this information is not provided elsewhere in the financial statements. Finally, the boards noted that, consistent with general materiality requirements, they did not expect this disclosure to be provided if the amounts are immaterial.

Disclosure of the transaction price allocated to the remaining performance obligations (paragraphs 120–122)

BC348   Many users of financial statements explained that information about the amount and timing of revenue that the entity expects to recognise from its existing contracts would be useful in their analyses of revenue. They also explained that the information would be most useful for long-term contracts, because those contracts typically have the most significant amounts of unrecognised revenue.

BC349   The boards observed that a number of entities often voluntarily disclose information about their long-term contracts, which is commonly referred to as 'backlog' information. (Some entities are also required to produce this information outside the financial statements in regulatory filings.) However, this information is typically presented outside the financial statements and may not be comparable across entities because there is not a common definition of backlog.

BC350   In the light of those factors, the boards decided to specify disclosure requirements to capture information about the amount and timing of revenue that an entity expects to recognise from the remaining performance obligations in the entity's existing contracts. The boards observed that by disclosing that information, an entity would provide users of the entity's financial statements with additional information about the following:

(a)   the amount and expected timing of revenue to be recognised from the remaining performance obligations in existing contracts;

(b)   trends relating to the amount and expected timing of revenue to be recognised from the remaining performance obligations in existing contracts;

(c)   risks associated with expected future revenue (for example, some observe that revenue is more uncertain if an entity does not expect to satisfy a performance obligation until a much later date); and

(d)   the effect of changes in judgements or circumstances on an entity's revenue.

BC351   Many respondents (including most preparers) disagreed with the boards' decision to require such information to be disclosed in the financial statements. Those respondents highlighted different reasons for their disagreement, as follows:

(a) the disclosure would be difficult and costly to prepare and audit because existing accounting systems are not designed to track and capture the required information, including the information on scheduling the timing of the satisfaction of those remaining performance obligations.

(b) the information provided by the disclosure could be misinterpreted because, depending on the nature of the entity's business(es), the disclosure may give prominence to only a relatively small subset of the entity's potential future revenues. In addition, the disclosure may include less information than the entity previously included in its backlog disclosure because future and cancellable executory contracts are excluded from the scope of the disclosure.

(c) the information appeared to be forward-looking in nature and thus should not be presented in the notes to the financial statements.

BC352 In redeliberating the disclosure requirements, taking into consideration the feedback received at the disclosure workshops, the boards observed that the requirement to disclose information about remaining performance obligations should not impose significant incremental costs on an entity because the entity is already required by the revenue recognition requirements to determine and allocate the transaction price to the remaining performance obligations. Nonetheless, the boards decided to address preparers' concerns about costs of preparation as follows:

(a) providing practical expedients to limit the scope of the disclosure (see paragraph 121 of IFRS 15). The boards decided that including the practical expedient in paragraph 121(a) of IFRS 15 would ease the burden for the preparation of the disclosure and yet would not significantly decrease the usefulness of the information for users of financial statements. This is because users indicated that information for remaining performance obligations is most critical to their analyses when the contracts are long-term. In addition, including the practical expedient in paragraph 121(b) of IFRS 15 would maintain the relief provided to an entity in paragraph B16 of IFRS 15 on measuring progress for those performance obligations (ie performance obligations for which the entity has a right to consideration that corresponds directly with its performance completed to date). The boards provided practical expedients rather than specifically limiting the scope because some preparers commented that it would be easier for them to comply with the requirement from an accounting systems and processes perspective if they could choose to include all of their remaining performance obligations in the disclosure.

(b) eliminating the prescriptive approach to disclosing when the entity expects to satisfy its remaining performance obligations (see paragraph 120 of IFRS 15). Initially, the boards proposed that an entity should follow a prescriptive approach in determining when the entity expects to satisfy its remaining performance obligations (ie by requiring a quantitative disclosure of the remaining performance obligations, scheduled into one-year time bands). However, many respondents disagreed with that proposal on the basis that the rigid nature of the prescribed time bands would imply a degree of precision in the timing of revenue recognition that may not exist and, furthermore, would increase the costs of preparation. In response to that feedback, the boards decided to permit an entity to estimate and present such information either on a quantitative basis, with time bands that are most appropriate for the duration of the remaining performance obligations (ie not necessarily one-year time bands) or by using qualitative information (or both).

BC353   Some users of financial statements also asked for more information to be provided about the relationship between the amounts disclosed as an entity's remaining performance obligations and the entity's contract liabilities. (A contract liability arises if an entity receives consideration from a customer before the entity satisfies its performance obligations to the customer.) This is because the amount of the remaining performance obligations for which cash has been received is useful information. However, the boards noted that contract liabilities are a subset of the amounts disclosed as the transaction price allocated to the remaining performance obligations and paragraph 116(a) of IFRS 15 already requires the contract liability balance to be disclosed. Consequently, the boards decided that no further disclosures should be required.

Performance obligations (paragraph 119)

BC354   Previous requirements in IFRS and US GAAP require entities to disclose their accounting policies for recognising revenue (see paragraph 10(e) of IAS 1 and the requirements in Topic 235 *Notes to Financial Statements*). However, users of financial statements suggested that in many cases, an entity provides a 'boilerplate' description of the accounting policy adopted without explaining how the accounting policy relates to the contracts that the entity enters into with customers. To address this criticism, paragraph 119 of IFRS 15 requires that an entity disclose information about its performance obligations in contracts with customers. This disclosure complements the accounting policy disclosure requirements in existing Standards by requiring an entity to provide more descriptive information about its performance obligations.

Significant judgements (paragraphs 123–126)

BC355   IFRS and US GAAP have general requirements for disclosing significant accounting estimates and judgements made by an entity. Because of the importance placed on revenue by users of financial statements, the boards decided to require specific disclosures about the estimates used and the judgements made in determining the amount and timing of revenue recognition.

Assets recognised from the costs to obtain or fulfil a contract with a customer (paragraphs 127–128)

BC356   The boards decided to require that an entity disclose information about assets that it recognises from the costs to obtain or fulfil a contract, because information about those assets is useful to users. That information will help users of financial statements understand the types of costs that the entity has recognised as assets and how those assets are subsequently amortised or impaired. The boards also decided that this disclosure was necessary to replace some of the previous disclosure requirements that were superseded by IFRS 15.

BC357   The boards decided not to require that information to be provided as a reconciliation because the cost of providing such a rigid disclosure would outweigh the benefit to users. In addition, most users agreed that the disclosure about the assets recognised from the costs to obtain or fulfil a contract did not need to be provided as a reconciliation to provide relevant information. Consequently, the boards decided to require disclosure of only the most critical information about assets recognised from the costs to obtain or fulfil a contract.

Disclosures required for interim financial reports

BC358   The boards observed that in the absence of more specific disclosure requirements for interim financial reports, an entity should apply IAS 34 *Interim Financial Reporting* or Topic 270 *Interim Reporting* to determine the information about revenue from contracts with customers that the entity should disclose in its interim financial reports. Those requirements require, as a general principle, an entity to disclose information about significant changes in its financial position and performance since the end of the last annual reporting period. The boards considered whether to amend IAS 34 and Topic 270 to specify that the entity provide the same quantitative disclosures about revenue in its interim financial reports as those in its annual financial statements.

BC359   Many preparers and other respondents broadly disagreed with the boards' proposals to make amendments to IAS 34 and Topic 270. They explained that requiring all of the quantitative disclosures in interim financial reports would be too burdensome and difficult to achieve in the short time frames required for interim reporting. In contrast, users of financial statements had mixed views. Some users (including nearly all US-based users) suggested that IAS 34 and Topic 270 should be amended to require the quantitative disclosures because of the importance of revenue and the need to have timely disclosures provided regularly in the interim financial reports. However, other users of financial statements explained that only the information about the disaggregation of revenue was critical to their interim analyses. Those users of financial statements also explained that timeliness in interim reporting was critical and that a requirement to provide other interim disclosures might unnecessarily delay the issuance of interim financial reports.

BC360   The IASB and the FASB reached different decisions on the amendments to IAS 34 and Topic 270. The IASB decided to amend IAS 34 to only add specific requirements that an entity should disclose disaggregated revenue information in interim financial reports. For all other disclosures related to revenue from contracts with customers, the IASB decided that the general principles of IAS 34 should apply. The IASB decided to add to IAS 34 a requirement to disclose disaggregated revenue information because users of financial statements explained that disaggregation was critical to their analyses and because the information is typically already provided in interim financial statements; therefore, the requirement should not result in an entity incurring significant incremental costs. Furthermore, the general principle of IAS 34 to disclose information about an entity's significant changes in financial position and

© IFRS Foundation

performance should provide users of financial statements with the other information they need about revenue at an interim reporting period. The IASB decided not to make further changes to IAS 34 without a more comprehensive review of the role of disclosure in interim financial reporting.

BC361 The FASB decided to amend Topic 270 to require the same quantitative disclosures about revenue in its interim financial reports as those in its annual financial statements (excluding the cost disclosures). The FASB noted that it is helpful to provide entities with certainty about the information that should be provided in interim financial reports. In addition, the FASB observed that an entity would be compiling most of the information required for the disclosures on an interim basis for the purposes of revenue recognition, and therefore disclosing that information might not result in a significant amount of incremental costs. The FASB also observed that this information is useful to users of financial statements in assessing an entity's current and future financial performance.

Application guidance (paragraphs B2–B89)

BC362 The boards decided to include application guidance to clarify how the principles in IFRS 15 should be applied, including how those principles should be applied to features found in a number of typical contracts with customers. Some of that application guidance has been included based on previous requirements in IFRS or US GAAP that arose as a result of entities requesting clarification in more complex areas of revenue recognition. However, to be consistent with the objective of developing a single revenue recognition model, the boards did not provide requirements that would have applied only to specific industries (see paragraphs BC2–BC3).

Sale with a right of return (paragraphs B20–B27)

BC363 In some contracts, an entity transfers a good to a customer and also grants the customer the right to return it. The boards decided that, conceptually, a contract with a right of return includes at least two performance obligations—a performance obligation to provide the good to the customer and a performance obligation for the return right service, which is a stand-ready obligation to accept the goods returned by the customer during the return period.

BC364 In relation to performance obligations to provide customers with goods, the boards decided that, in effect, an entity has made an uncertain number of sales. This is because it is only after the return right expires that the entity will know with certainty how many sales it has made (ie how many sales did not fail). Consequently, the boards decided that an entity should not recognise revenue for the sales that are expected to fail as a result of customers exercising their return rights. Instead, the entity should recognise a liability for its obligation to refund amounts to customers.

BC365 The boards decided that in determining the amount of revenue to recognise (ie the amount of the refund obligation), an entity should use the principles for recognising and measuring variable consideration. Using those principles, an entity would recognise revenue only to the extent that it is highly probable that a significant reversal in the amount of cumulative revenue recognised will not occur when the uncertainty associated with the right of return is subsequently resolved. When the entity determines that it cannot recognise all of the consideration received as revenue for the sale of goods with a right of return, the entity would recognise some of the consideration received as a refund liability.

BC366　The boards considered whether to account for the return right service as a performance obligation, in addition to any refund liability that is recognised. If an entity does not recognise a performance obligation for the return right service, it should recognise all of the revenue and margin in the contract once the customer obtains control of the good. That outcome might not faithfully depict the entity's performance under the contract. However, the boards noted that accounting for the return right service as a performance obligation, in addition to the refund liability, would typically require the entity to estimate the stand-alone selling price of that service. Because, in many cases, the number of returns is expected to be only a small percentage of the total sales and the return period is often short (such as 30 days), the boards decided that the incremental information provided to users of financial statements by accounting for the return right service as a performance obligation would not have justified the complexities and costs of doing so. Consequently, the boards decided that the return right service should not be accounted for as a performance obligation.

BC367　A return right gives an entity a contractual right to recover the good from a customer if the customer exercises its option to return the good and obtain a refund. The boards decided that the right to recover the good should be recognised as an asset rather than offset against the refund liability. The boards observed that recognising the asset separately from the refund liability provides greater transparency and ensures that the asset is considered for impairment testing.

Warranties (paragraphs B28–B33)

BC368　When an entity sells a product (whether that product is a good or service) to a customer, the entity may also provide the customer with a warranty on that product. The warranty might be described as, for example, a manufacturer's warranty, a standard warranty or an extended warranty. The boards decided to provide specific requirements for applying the revenue recognition model to warranties, because many contracts with customers for the sale of products include a warranty and the nature of that warranty may vary across products, entities and jurisdictions.

BC369　In the Discussion Paper, the boards proposed accounting for all warranties consistently because a unifying feature of all warranties is that an entity promises to stand ready to replace or repair the product in accordance with the terms and conditions of the warranty. The Discussion Paper proposed that a promise to stand ready would provide a customer with a service of warranty coverage, which would have been a performance obligation to which revenue would be attributed. However, most respondents to the Discussion Paper stated that the accounting for warranties should reflect the fact that some product warranties are different from others. Some warranties protect the customer from defects that exist when the product is transferred to the customer and other warranties protect the customer from faults that arise after the product has been transferred to the customer. Those respondents commented that the customer does not receive a separate service if the warranty only protects the customer from the product defects that were present at the time of sale. Consequently, any subsequent repairs or replacements to remedy those defects are additional costs of providing the product and, therefore, relate to an entity's past performance.

BC370　In the light of that feedback, the boards decided to account for some warranties differently from others. The boards considered distinguishing warranties on the basis of when the fault in the products arises; however, respondents explained that such a distinction was not operational. Therefore, the boards decided to distinguish warranties on the basis of whether the warranty provides the customer with a service in addition to the assurance that the related product complies with the agreed-upon specifications. Specifically, the boards decided that when the warranty provides a service (ie a service-type warranty), the warranty should be accounted for as a performance obligation.

Warranties that are performance obligations (service-type warranties)

BC371　For some types of warranties, an entity either sells separately or negotiates separately with a customer so that the customer can choose whether to purchase the warranty coverage. That fact provides objective evidence that the promised warranty provides a service to the customer in addition to the promised product. Consequently, the boards decided that this type of promised warranty is a performance obligation in accordance with paragraphs 22–30 of IFRS 15.

BC372　The boards decided that warranties that are not sold separately by the entity, or negotiated separately with the customer, should also be identified as performance obligations if the facts and circumstances suggest that the warranty (or a part of the warranty) provides a service to the customer, in addition to the assurance that the entity's past performance was as specified in the contract. The boards noted the following about this decision:

(a)　it provides a clear principle that allows an entity to account for economically similar warranties in a similar manner, regardless of whether the warranties are separately priced or negotiated;

(b)　it is consistent with the general principles for identifying performance obligations; and

(c)　it removes the bright line in previous US GAAP that distinguishes between different types of warranties based solely on whether the warranty is separately priced.

BC373　A warranty that meets the requirements in paragraphs B28–B33 of IFRS 15 to be accounted for as a performance obligation might also meet the criteria for classification as an insurance contract. However, only warranties issued directly by a third party would be accounted for as insurance contracts according to the proposals in the boards' respective projects on the accounting for insurance contracts.

Warranties that are not performance obligations (assurance-type warranties)

BC374   The boards considered whether an assurance-type warranty should be accounted for as either of the following:

(a)   a separate liability to replace or repair a defective product; or

(b)   an unsatisfied performance obligation, because the entity has not provided the customer with a product that is free from defects at the time of sale.

BC375   The proposals in the 2010 Exposure Draft would have required an entity that provides an assurance-type warranty to a customer to assess whether it had satisfied its performance obligation to transfer the product specified in the contract. The entity would have been required to determine the likelihood of the existence of defective products that it had sold to customers and their quantity and, as a consequence, not recognise revenue to the extent that those performance obligations were not satisfied. An advantage of that proposal would have been that an entity would not have recognised the entire transaction price as revenue when the product transferred to the customer, because a portion of the transaction price would not have been recognised as revenue until the entity had repaired or replaced the products that were expected to be defective. However, the boards decided not to retain that proposal, mainly for the following practical reasons:

(a)   there would have been complexities associated with the requirements for an entity to continue to recognise as 'inventory' products that had been delivered to customers and that were expected to be defective; and

(b)   any margin attributable to the repair or replacement of a product in an assurance-type warranty would have been unlikely to significantly distort the pattern of recognition of the overall contract margin.

BC376   Accordingly, the boards decided that an entity should recognise an assurance-type warranty as a separate liability to replace or repair a defective product. Consequently, an entity should recognise a warranty liability and corresponding expense when it transfers the product to the customer and the liability should be measured in accordance with IAS 37 or Topic 460 *Guarantees*. In contrast to the accounting for service-type warranties, an entity should not attribute any of the transaction price (and therefore revenue) to an assurance-type warranty. Some warranties may include both assurance features and service features. The boards decided that if an entity cannot reasonably account for those assurance features of the warranty separately from the service features, the entity should be allowed to account for the warranties together as a single performance obligation. That accounting ensures that the entity does not overstate the recognition of revenue at the time that the product transfers to the customer and also relieves the entity from identifying and accounting separately for the two components of the warranty coverage.

Statutory warranties

BC377   In some jurisdictions, the law requires an entity to provide warranties with the sale of its products. The law might state that an entity is required to repair or

© IFRS Foundation

replace products that develop faults within a specified period from the time of sale. Consequently, those statutory warranties may appear to be service-type warranties because they cover faults arising after the time of sale, not merely defects existing at the time of sale. However, the boards decided that the law can be viewed as simply operationalising an assurance-type warranty. In other words, the objective of those statutory warranties is to protect the customer against the risk of purchasing a defective product. But rather than requiring the entity to determine whether the product was defective at the time of sale, the law presumes that if a fault arises within a specified period (which can vary depending on the nature of the product), the product was defective at the time of sale. Consequently, these statutory warranties should be accounted for as assurance-type warranties.

Product liability laws

BC378   The boards clarified that product liability laws do not give rise to performance obligations. Those laws typically require an entity to pay compensation if one of its products causes harm or damage. The boards noted that an entity should not recognise a performance obligation arising from those laws because the performance obligation in a contract is to transfer the product to the customer. To the extent that an entity expects the product(s) to be defective, the entity should recognise a liability for the expected costs to repair or replace the product (see paragraph B33 of IFRS 15). Any obligation of the entity to pay compensation for the damage or harm that its product causes is separate from the performance obligation. The boards noted that an entity should account for this obligation separately from the contract with the customer and in accordance with the requirements for loss contingencies in IAS 37 or Topic 450.

Principal versus agent considerations (paragraphs B34–B38)[5]

BC379   Previous revenue Standards required an entity to assess whether it was acting as a principal or an agent when goods or services were transferred to a customer. That assessment was necessary to determine whether an entity should recognise revenue for the gross amount of customer consideration (if the entity was determined to be a principal) or for a net amount after the supplier was compensated for its goods or services (if the entity was determined to be an agent).

BC380   IFRS 15 also requires an entity to determine whether it is a principal or an agent. This is because the performance obligations of principals and agents are different. A principal controls the goods or services before they are transferred to a customer. Consequently, the principal's performance obligation is to transfer those goods or services to the customer. Therefore, recognising revenue

---

5   *Clarifications to IFRS 15* issued in April 2016 amended the application guidance in paragraphs B34–B38 and, as a consequence, amended paragraph BC383. The objective of amending the application guidance in paragraphs B34–B38 is to (a) provide a better framework to be applied when assessing whether an entity is a principal or an agent; (b) clarify the application of the control principle to intangible goods and services; and (c) clarify the role of the indicators in paragraph B37 when applying the control principle. Paragraphs BC379–BC385 should therefore be read together with paragraphs BC385A–BC385Z, which explain the boards' considerations for amending the application guidance.

at the gross amount of the customer consideration faithfully depicts the consideration to which the entity is entitled for the transfer of the goods and services. In contrast, an agent does not control the goods or services before they are transferred to a customer. The agent merely facilitates the sale of goods or services between a principal and the customer. Consequently, an agent's performance obligation is to arrange for another party to provide the goods or services to the customer. Therefore, the transaction price attributable to an agent's performance obligation is the fee or commission that the agent receives for providing those services.

BC381   The boards observed that identifying an entity's promise (ie the performance obligation) in a contract is fundamental to the determination of whether the entity is acting as a principal or an agent. This is because identifying the nature of the entity's performance obligation is necessary for the entity to determine whether it controls the goods or services that have been promised before they are transferred to a customer. For example, a travel agent could be the principal in some contracts with customers if the travel agent determines that its promise is to provide a right to a flight (ie a ticket), instead of a promise to provide the flight. However, to conclude whether they are a principal or an agent, the travel agent would need to also consider whether it controlled that right before transferring it to the customer, which may occur when the travel agent purchases the tickets in advance for sales to future customers.

BC382   The nature of the entity's promise may not always be readily apparent. For that reason, the boards included indicators in paragraph B37 of IFRS 15 to help an entity determine whether the entity controls the goods or services before transferring them and thus whether the entity is a principal or an agent. Those indicators are based on indicators that were included in previous revenue recognition requirements in IFRS and US GAAP. However, as noted in paragraph BC380, the indicators in IFRS 15 have a different purpose than previous revenue recognition requirements in that they are based on the concepts of identifying performance obligations and the transfer of control of goods or services.

BC383   After an entity identifies its promise and determines whether it is the principal or the agent, the entity would recognise revenue when it satisfies its performance obligation. This would, for an entity that is a principal, occur when control of the promised goods or services transfers to the customer. The boards observed that in some contracts in which the entity is the agent, control of the goods or services promised to the customer might transfer before the customer receives the goods or services from the principal. For example, an entity that issues loyalty points to its customers when they purchase goods or services from the entity might satisfy its performance obligation with respect to the loyalty points on issuing those points to the customers if:

(a)   the points entitle the customers to future discounted purchases with another party (ie the points represent a material right to a future discount); and

(b)   the entity determines that it is an agent (ie its promise is to arrange for the customers to be provided with points) and the entity does not control those points before they are transferred to the customer.

BC384   In contrast, the boards observed that if the points entitle the customers to future goods or services to be provided by the entity, the entity may conclude it is not an agent. This is because the entity's promise is to provide those future goods or services and thus the entity controls both the points and the future goods or services before they are transferred to the customer. In these cases, the entity's performance obligation may only be satisfied when the future goods or services are provided.

BC385   In other cases, the points may entitle customers to choose between future goods or services provided by either the entity or another party. The boards observed that in those cases, to determine when the performance obligation is satisfied, the entity would need to consider the nature of its performance obligation. This is because until the customer has chosen the goods or services to be provided (and thus whether the entity or the third party will provide those goods or services), the entity is obliged to stand ready to deliver goods or services. Thus, the entity may not satisfy its performance obligation until such time as it either delivers the goods or services or is no longer obliged to stand ready. The boards also observed that if the customer subsequently chooses the goods or services from another party, the entity would need to consider whether it was acting as an agent and thus should recognise revenue for only a fee or commission that the entity received from providing the services to the customer and the third party. The boards noted that this is consistent with previous revenue recognition requirements in IFRS for customer loyalty programmes.

Clarifications to IFRS 15 (amendments issued in April 2016)

BC385A   The TRG discussed a number of issues in relation to paragraphs B34–B38 of IFRS 15. Some stakeholders asked whether control is always the basis for determining whether an entity is a principal or an agent, and how the control principle and the indicators in paragraph B37 work together. Other stakeholders asked how to apply the control principle to contracts involving intangible goods or services. In the light of those discussions and the feedback received, the boards discussed, and decided to clarify, the principal versus agent guidance by making the same targeted amendments to the application guidance and the related Illustrative Examples in IFRS 15 and Topic 606.

BC385B   When another party is involved in providing goods or services to a customer, the amendments to the application guidance clarify how an entity determines whether it is a principal or an agent. These amendments focus on (a) the need for appropriately identifying the good or service that is transferred to the customer (the 'specified good or service'); and (b) determining whether the entity has promised to provide the specified good or service itself (ie the entity is a principal) or to arrange for the specified good or service to be provided to the customer by the other party (ie the entity is an agent). The entity determines the nature of its promise on the basis of whether the entity controls the specified good or service before that good or service is transferred to the customer. Throughout the guidance on principal versus agent considerations, the boards decided to refer to the *specified good or service* transferred to the customer (as in paragraph B34), rather than the *performance obligation*. This is because use of the term 'performance obligation' would have been confusing if the entity is an agent. An agent's performance obligation is to arrange for the other party to provide its goods or services to the customer; it does not promise to provide the goods or services itself to the end customer. Accordingly, the specified good or service to be provided to the end customer is not the performance obligation of the agent.

Principle for determining whether an entity is a principal or an agent

BC385C Paragraph B34 requires an entity to determine whether it is a principal or an agent on the basis of whether the nature of the entity's promise is a performance obligation to provide the specified goods or services itself (ie the entity is a principal) or to arrange for those goods or services to be provided by another party (ie the entity is an agent). Assessing whether the entity controls the specified good or service before it is transferred to the customer is the basis for determining the nature of the entity's promise.

BC385D The boards observed that in order for an entity to conclude that it is providing the specified good or service to the customer, it must first control that good or service (as defined in paragraph 33). The entity cannot provide the specified good or service to a customer if the entity does not first control the good or service to be provided. If an entity controls the specified good or service before that good or service is transferred to the customer, the entity is the principal in the transaction with the customer. If the entity does not control the specified good or service before that good or service is transferred to a customer, the entity is not a principal in the transaction with the customer. The boards noted that their considerations in this respect are explained in paragraph BC380.

BC385E In addition, the boards noted that an entity that itself manufactures a good or performs a service is always a principal if the entity transfers control of that good or service to another party. Such an entity does not need to evaluate whether it is a principal or an agent using the guidance in paragraphs B34–B38 because the entity transfers the good or provides the service directly to its customer, without the involvement of another party. If the entity transfers a good or provides a service to an intermediary that is a principal in providing that good or service to an end customer (whether individually or as part of a distinct bundle of goods or services), the entity's customer is the intermediary.

BC385F Because of the concerns highlighted in the TRG's discussions, the boards decided to clarify the following aspects of the application guidance on principal versus agent considerations:

(a) the relationship between the control principle and the indicators in paragraph B37; and

(b) the application of the control principle to intangible goods and services.

The relationship between control and the indicators in paragraph B37

BC385G The boards observed that the questions about the relationship between the assessment of control and the indicators of control in paragraph B37 arose, at least in part, because the indicators in that paragraph were carried forward from IAS 18 *Revenue* and Topic 605 *Revenue Recognition*. IAS 18 had a principle for this assessment (based on risks and rewards) that was different from the control principle in IFRS 15 and, although Topic 605 did not explicitly include a principle, the indicators in Topic 605 were understood to be indicators of risks and rewards. In addition, the structure of the analysis in Examples 45–48 accompanying IFRS 15 added to the confusion.

BC385H The boards' considerations (explained in paragraph BC382) highlight that the indicators in paragraph B37 were included to support an entity's assessment of whether it controls a specified good or service before transfer in scenarios for which that assessment might be difficult. The indicators (a) do not override the assessment of control; (b) should not be viewed in isolation; (c) do not constitute a separate or additional evaluation; and (d) should not be considered a checklist of criteria to be met, or factors to be considered, in all scenarios. Considering one or more of the indicators will often be helpful and, depending on the facts and circumstances, individual indicators will be more or less relevant or persuasive to the assessment of control.

BC385I The boards acknowledged that the indicators are similar to those in IAS 18 and Topic 605, but also noted their considerations in this respect, explained in paragraph BC382. Paragraph BC382 explains that the boards decided to carry over some of the indicators in previous revenue recognition Standards even though those indicators have a different purpose in IFRS 15. In IFRS 15, the indicators support the concepts of identifying performance obligations and the transfer of control of goods or services. Accordingly, the boards had expected that the conclusions about principal versus agent under IFRS 15 could be different in some scenarios from those reached under the previous revenue recognition Standards. Furthermore, the boards observed that, although exposure to risks and rewards alone does not give an entity control, exposure to risks and rewards can be a helpful factor to consider in determining whether an entity has obtained control (see paragraph 38).

BC385J The boards decided to amend the indicators in paragraph B37 to more clearly establish a link between the control principle and the indicators by:

(a) reframing the indicators as indicators of when an entity controls a specified good or service before transfer, rather than as indicators that an entity does not control the specified good or service before transfer.

(b) adding guidance to explain how each indicator supports the assessment of control as defined in paragraph 33 of IFRS 15. This should help entities apply indicators that are similar to those in the previous revenue recognition Standards but within the context of the control principle in IFRS 15.

(c) removing the indicator relating to the form of the consideration. Although that indicator might sometimes be helpful in assessing whether an entity is an agent, the boards concluded that it would not be helpful in assessing whether an entity is a principal.

(d) removing the indicator relating to exposure to credit risk. The feedback on the Exposure Draft *Clarifications to IFRS 15* highlighted that exposure to credit risk is generally not a helpful indicator when assessing whether an entity controls the specified good or service. Stakeholders observed that the credit risk indicator in the previous revenue guidance has been problematic from the perspective of entities trying to use exposure to credit risk to override stronger evidence of agency. The boards concluded that removing the credit risk indicator should reduce some of the complexity in the principal versus agent evaluation because the credit risk indicator will typically be less relevant, or not relevant, to the evaluation for contracts within the scope of IFRS 15.

(e) clarifying that the indicators are not an exhaustive list and merely support the assessment of control—they do not replace or override that assessment. The boards decided to explicitly state that one or more of the indicators might provide more persuasive evidence to support the assessment of control in different scenarios.

BC385K In the light of the IASB's decision to generally apply a high hurdle when considering whether to amend IFRS 15, the IASB initially thought that it would not be necessary to add explanatory text to each indicator in paragraph B37 to establish a link to the concept of control. In the IASB's view, clarity about the interaction between the control principle and the indicators could have been achieved by amending only the Illustrative Examples. The IASB noted concerns about adding explanatory text to the indicators in paragraph B37 because of (a) the risk of new questions arising with respect to those additional explanations; and (b) the risk that some of those additional explanations might be used inappropriately to reach a conclusion that an entity is a principal when the entity is an agent. Nonetheless, despite those concerns, the IASB decided to amend the indicators in paragraph B37 of IFRS 15 in order to align the wording of the amendments with the wording of those made by the FASB. The IASB concluded that the benefits of retaining converged requirements on this topic outweigh the potential costs of amending the requirements.

The use of the indicators in paragraph B37 rather than the indicators in paragraph 38

BC385L Some stakeholders asked why the indicators in paragraph B37 are different from the indicators on the satisfaction of performance obligations (paragraph 38), noting that both sets of indicators relate to control. The boards observed that the indicators in paragraph 38 are indicators of the point in time at which the customer obtains control of the promised good or service. Accordingly, the indicators in paragraph 38 serve a different purpose than the indicators in paragraph B37. The indicators in paragraph 38 are not intended to indicate whether the customer obtains control of a promised asset—within the context of IFRS 15 as a whole, it is assumed that the customer will obtain control of the promised asset at some point—instead, they are intended to indicate when the customer has obtained control. In contrast, the indicators in paragraph B37 are intended to indicate whether the entity controls a specified good or service before that good or service is transferred to the customer.

Application of the control principle to intangible goods and services

BC385M The boards observed that at least some of the difficulty that stakeholders had in applying the control principle, in particular to intangible goods and services, was linked to challenges in identifying the specified good or service to be provided to the customer. The boards observed that this also had frequently been a challenge for entities under previous revenue recognition Standards.

BC385N   The principal versus agent considerations relate to the application of Step 2 of the revenue recognition model. Appropriately identifying the good or service to be provided is a critical step in appropriately identifying whether the nature of an entity's promise is to act as a principal or an agent. When the appropriate specified good or service is identified, the assessment of control is often relatively straightforward, even when the specified good or service is an intangible good or a service. For example, the specified good or service to be provided to the customer could be:

(a)   a right to goods or services (see paragraph 26). For example, the airline ticket (a right to fly) in Example 47 and the meal voucher (a right to a meal) in Example 48 accompanying IFRS 15; or

(b)   a bundle of goods or services that are not distinct from each other (for example, the specialised equipment in Example 46 accompanying IFRS 15).

BC385O   The boards observed that when the specified good or service to be provided to the customer is a right to goods or services to be provided in the future by another party, the entity would determine whether its performance obligation is a promise to provide a right to goods or services or whether it is arranging for the other party to provide that right. The fact that the entity will not provide the goods or services itself is not determinative. Instead, the entity evaluates whether it controls the right to goods or services before that right is transferred to the customer. In doing so, it is often relevant to assess whether the right is created only when it is obtained by the customer, or whether the right to goods or services exists before the customer obtains the right. If the right does not exist before the customer obtains it, an entity would be unable to control that right before it is transferred to the customer.

BC385P   Some respondents to the Exposure Draft stated that it could be difficult in some cases to determine whether the specified good or service is the right to a good or service to be provided by another party or the underlying good or service itself (for example, in the case of Example 47, whether the specified good or service is the right to the flight (the ticket) or the flight itself). The boards observed that a careful consideration of the facts and circumstances, and exercise of judgement may be required in identifying the specified good or service (just as identifying an entity's performance obligations outside the context of a principal versus agent evaluation will often require judgement). The boards also observed that assessing whether an entity controls a right to a good or service to be provided by another party is important to the principal versus agent evaluation. The boards noted that the Illustrative Examples accompanying IFRS 15 on principal versus agent considerations have been designed to address and explain scenarios in which the specified good or service is a right to a good or service to be provided by another party (as in Example 47 accompanying IFRS 15) and scenarios in which the specified good or service is the underlying service itself (as in Example 46A accompanying IFRS 15).

BC385Q   The boards also observed that the specified good or service to which the control principle is applied should be a distinct good or service, or a distinct bundle of goods or services. If individual goods or services are not distinct from each other, then they may be, for example, merely inputs to a combined item and are each only part of a single promise to the customer. Accordingly, an entity should evaluate the nature of its promise (ie to act as a principal or an agent) within the context of the promise to the customer, rather than for part of that promise. Consequently, for contracts in which goods or services provided by another party are inputs to a combined item (or items) for which the customer has contracted, the entity assesses whether it controls the combined item before that item is transferred to the customer.

BC385R When a specified good or service is a distinct bundle of goods or services, the principal versus agent analysis may, in some cases, be straightforward. The boards concluded (in paragraph B35A(c)) that when an entity provides a significant service of integrating two or more goods or services into the combined output that is the specified good or service for which the customer contracted, it controls that specified good or service before it is transferred to the customer. When the entity provides a significant integration service it controls the inputs to the combined item that is the specified good or service (including goods or services provided by another party that are inputs to the specified good or service). The entity controls the inputs by directing their use to create the combined item. In that case, the inputs provided by the other party would be a fulfilment cost to the entity. In contrast, if a third party provides the significant integration service, then the entity's customer for its goods or services (which would be inputs to the specified good or service) is likely to be the other party.

BC385S Consequently, the boards decided to clarify the thought process to be applied when assessing whether an entity is a principal or an agent by specifically requiring an entity to identify the specified good or service before applying the control principle to each specified good or service. The amended paragraph B34 and the additional paragraph B34A should:

(a) provide a better framework for assessing whether an entity is a principal or an agent.

(b) emphasise the importance of appropriately identifying the specified good or service (which could be a right to a good or service to be provided by another party) that will be transferred to the customer.

(c) clarify that the specified good or service (ie the unit of account for the principal versus agent evaluation) is each distinct good or service (or distinct bundle of goods or services). Accordingly, those paragraphs also clarify that, because a contract with a customer could include more than one specified good or service, an entity could be a principal for one or more specified goods or services in a contract and an agent for others.

(d) emphasise that control (as defined in paragraph 33 of IFRS 15) is the determining factor when assessing whether an entity is a principal or an agent.

BC385T The IASB noted that, in many respects, paragraph B34A simply points to other relevant parts of the requirements in IFRS 15. Accordingly, the IASB did not view the inclusion of that additional paragraph as essential to clarifying the requirements in IFRS 15. In its view, clarity about the thought process to be applied could have been achieved by amending only the Illustrative Examples.

Nonetheless, given the concerns raised by stakeholders, the IASB concluded that including paragraph B34A would be helpful to the principal versus agent evaluation, and would align the wording of the amendments with the wording of those made by the FASB. Therefore, the IASB concluded that the benefits of adding the paragraph outweigh the potential costs of amending the requirements.

Assessment of control of a service

BC385U   The TRG's discussions highlighted concerns about the application of the control principle to services to be provided to a customer. Questions discussed included how an entity (other than the service provider) could control a service before that service is transferred to the customer, because a service comes into existence only at the moment that it is delivered. The boards observed that an entity can control a service to be provided by another party when it controls the right to the specified service from the other party that will be provided to the customer. The entity then either transfers the right to the service to the customer (for example, the airline ticket in Example 47) or uses its right to direct the other party to provide the service to the customer on the entity's behalf (ie to satisfy the entity's performance obligation in the contract with the customer), such as in Example 46A. Determining whether the entity controls a right to a specified service requires consideration of the facts and circumstances. The boards noted that contracts involving services provided by another party in which the entity is a principal can be broadly categorised as follows:

(a)   Contracts in which an entity provides the customer with a right to a future service to be provided by another party, such as the right to a specified flight (in the form of a ticket) to be provided by an airline (as discussed in paragraph BC385O).

(b)   Contracts in which the service provided by the other party is not distinct from other goods or services promised to the customer, and the entity directs the use of that service to create the combined item that is the specified good or service for which the customer has contracted (as discussed in paragraphs BC385Q–BC385R). Paragraph B35A(c) states that this scenario would exist whenever the entity provides a significant service of integrating the service provided by another party into the specified good or service for which the customer has contracted. Example 46 accompanying IFRS 15 illustrates this scenario.

(c)   Contracts in which an entity directs another party to provide the service to the customer on the entity's behalf in satisfying the entity's performance obligation. Example 46A accompanying IFRS 15 illustrates this scenario.

BC385V   The boards observed that determining whether an entity is a principal or an agent may be more difficult in the third category of contracts listed above in which the entity has entered into a contract with a customer and has engaged another party (a subcontractor) to satisfy a performance obligation within that contract on its behalf. In these contracts, the entity assesses whether it controls a right to the specified services. An entity could control the right to the specified services by entering into a contract with the subcontractor and defining the services to be performed by the subcontractor on the entity's behalf. In that scenario, which is illustrated in Example 46A, the entity obtains the right to the services of the subcontractor and then directs the subcontractor to provide the services to the customer on the entity's behalf. This scenario is equivalent to the entity fulfilling the contract using its own resources rather than engaging another party to do so. The entity would remain responsible for the satisfactory provision of services in accordance with the contract with the customer. In other scenarios in which the specified services provided to the customer are provided by another party and the entity did not have the ability to direct those services, the entity would typically be an agent. In those scenarios, the entity is likely to be facilitating (and arranging for) the provision of services by the other party rather than controlling the rights to the services that the entity then directs to the customer.

BC385W   The boards noted that paragraph B35 explains that an entity that is a principal in a contract may satisfy a performance obligation by itself or it may engage another party to satisfy some or all of a performance obligation on its behalf. The boards decided to add further explanation (paragraph B35A) to clarify the assessment of control of a service by explaining the scenarios in which a principal can control a service to be provided by another party. The boards also decided to add Example 46A to the Illustrative Examples accompanying IFRS 15 to illustrate the application of control to services.

Estimating revenue as a principal

BC385X   Some TRG participants asked how an entity that is a principal would estimate the amount of revenue to recognise if it were not aware of the amounts being charged to end customers by an intermediary that is an agent. The IASB observed that this question is largely unrelated to the application guidance on principal versus agent considerations in paragraph B34–B38 of IFRS 15, but rather relates to applying the requirements in paragraphs 46–90 on determining the consideration to which an entity is entitled. The IASB noted that the situations in which an entity that is a principal may be unaware of the amount charged to end customers by an intermediary that is an agent are generally limited to situations in which the intermediary (a) has some flexibility in setting prices; or (b) is procuring the good or service on behalf of the end customer. The IASB concluded that the issue does not require any clarifications or additional guidance because the issue is expected to affect a limited number of entities and contracts.

BC385Y   The FASB has also decided not to amend Topic 606 to address this issue. This is mainly because the FASB had observed that the situations in which an entity that is a principal is (and expects to remain) unaware of the amount charged by an intermediary that is an agent to the end customer are not pervasive and the issue affects only a limited number of entities and contracts. For those limited situations, the FASB is of the view that the determination of whether revenue may be estimated is based on an assessment of the requirements for determining the transaction price and estimating variable consideration.

BC385Z   The IASB did not specifically consider how the transaction price requirements would be applied in those situations but concluded that an entity that is a principal would generally be expected to be able to apply judgement and determine the consideration to which it is entitled using all relevant facts and circumstances available to it.

Customer options for additional goods or services (paragraphs B39–B43)

BC386   In some contracts, customers are given an option to purchase additional goods or services. The boards considered when those options should be accounted for as a performance obligation. During those discussions, the boards observed that it can be difficult to distinguish between the following:

(a)   an option that the customer pays for (often implicitly) as part of an existing contract, which would be a performance obligation to which part of the transaction price is allocated; and

(b)   a marketing or promotional offer that the customer did not pay for and, although made at the time of entering into a contract, is not part of the contract and that would not be a performance obligation in that contract.

BC387   Similar difficulties in distinguishing between an option and an offer have arisen in US GAAP for the software industry. Previous US GAAP revenue recognition requirements for the software industry specified that an offer of a discount on future purchases of goods or services was presumed to be a separate option in the contract, if that discount was significant and also incremental both to the range of discounts reflected in the pricing of other elements in that contract and to the range of discounts typically given in comparable transactions. Those notions of 'significant' and 'incremental' form the basis for the principle of a material right that is used to differentiate between an option and a marketing or promotional offer. However, the boards observed that even if the offered discount is not incremental to other discounts in the contract, it nonetheless could, in some cases, give rise to a material right to the customer. Consequently, the boards decided not to carry forward that part of the previous revenue recognition requirements from US GAAP into IFRS 15.

BC388   Some respondents asked the boards to clarify whether specific options, such as customer loyalty points, should be accounted for as a performance obligation when the arrangement involves more than two parties. This often occurs in a credit card arrangement in which an entity provides the credit card holder with points based on the amount of purchases made at other entities (often referred to as 'merchants'). The boards determined that the assessment of whether any loyalty points represent a performance obligation requires an analysis of the facts and circumstances in each arrangement. The boards decided not to provide any further guidance because the issue was specific to the credit card industry and the boards observed that these arrangements are often complex and can vary significantly. Furthermore, the boards noted that IFRS 15 includes all the requirements to enable entities to account for the various arrangements.

Allocating the transaction price

BC389   In accordance with IFRS 15, an entity is required to determine the stand-alone selling price of the option so that it can allocate part of the transaction price to that performance obligation. In some cases, the stand-alone selling price of the option may be directly observable. In many cases though, the stand-alone selling price of the option will need to be estimated.

BC390   Option pricing models can be used to estimate the stand-alone selling price of an option. The price of an option includes the intrinsic value of the option (ie the value of the option if it were exercised today) and its time value (ie the value of the option that depends on the time until the expiry and the volatility of the price of the underlying goods or services). The boards decided that the benefits to users of financial statements of allocating some of the transaction price to the price and availability guarantees inherent in the time value component of the option price would not have justified the costs and difficulties to do so. However, the boards decided that an entity should be able to readily obtain the inputs necessary to measure the intrinsic value of the option in accordance with paragraph B42 of IFRS 15 and that those calculations should be relatively straightforward and intuitive. This measurement approach is consistent with the application guidance that was provided for measuring customer loyalty points in previous revenue recognition requirements in IFRS.

Renewal options

BC391   A renewal option gives a customer the right to acquire additional goods or services of the same type as those supplied under an existing contract. This type of option could be described as a renewal option within a relatively short contract (for example, a one-year contract with an option to renew that contract for a further year at the end of the first and second years) or a cancellation option within a longer contract (for example, a three-year contract that allows the customer to discontinue the contract at the end of each year). A renewal option could be viewed similarly to other options to provide additional goods or services. In other words, the renewal option could be a performance obligation in the contract if it provides the customer with a material right that it otherwise could not obtain without entering into that contract.

BC392   However, there are typically a series of options in cases in which a renewal option provides a customer with a material right. In other words, to exercise any option in the contract, the customer must have exercised all the previous options in the contract. The boards decided that determining the stand-alone selling price of a series of options would have been complex because doing so would have required an entity to identify various inputs, such as the stand-alone selling prices for the goods or services for each renewal period and the likelihood that the customers will renew for the subsequent period. In other words, the entity would have had to consider the entire potential term of the contract to determine the amount of the transaction price from the initial period that should be deferred until later periods.

BC393   For that reason, the boards decided to provide an entity with a practical alternative to estimating the stand-alone selling price of the option. The practical alternative requires an entity to include the optional goods or services that it expects to provide (and corresponding expected customer consideration) in the initial measurement of the transaction price. In the boards' view, it is simpler for an entity to view a contract with renewal options as a contract for its expected term (ie including the expected renewal periods) rather than as a contract with a series of options.

BC394 The boards developed two criteria to distinguish renewal options from other options to acquire additional goods or services. The first criterion specifies that the additional goods or services underlying the renewal options must be similar to those provided under the initial contract—that is, an entity continues to provide what it was already providing. Consequently, it is more intuitive to view the goods or services underlying such options as part of the initial contract. In contrast, customer loyalty points and many discount vouchers should be considered to be separate deliverables in the contract, because the underlying goods or services may be of a different nature.

BC395 The second criterion specifies that the additional goods or services in the subsequent contracts must be provided in accordance with the terms of the original contract. Consequently, the entity's position is restricted because it cannot change those terms and conditions and, in particular, it cannot change the pricing of the additional goods or services beyond the parameters specified in the original contract. That too is different from examples such as customer loyalty points and discount vouchers. For example, if an airline offers flights to customers in exchange for points from its frequent flyer programme, the airline is not restricted, because it can subsequently determine the number of points that are required to be redeemed for any particular flight. Similarly, when an entity grants discount vouchers, it has typically not restricted itself with respect to the price of the subsequent goods or services against which the discount vouchers will be redeemed.

Customers' unexercised rights (breakage) (paragraphs B44–B47)

BC396 Some respondents asked the boards to provide guidance on how to account for a customer's non-refundable prepayment for the right to receive goods or services in the future. Common examples include the purchase of gift cards and non-refundable tickets.

BC397 The boards noted that the requirements for the allocation of the transaction price to customer options implicitly explains how to account for situations in which the customer does not exercise all of its contractual rights to those goods or services (ie breakage). However, the boards decided to clarify how to account for breakage in situations in which there is only one performance obligation in the contract (ie how to account for breakage in customer options when there is no need to allocate the transaction price and, therefore, no need to determine a stand-alone selling price).

BC398 Consequently, the boards included application guidance on the accounting for breakage. Those requirements require the same pattern of revenue recognition as the requirements for customer options. Thus, an entity should recognise revenue from breakage as it performs under the contract on the basis of the transfer of the goods or services promised in the contract. This effectively increases the transaction price allocated to the individual goods or services transferred to the customer to include the revenue from the entity's estimate of unexercised rights. The boards decided that this approach represents the most appropriate pattern of revenue recognition for breakage, because if an entity expected that customers would exercise all of their rights (ie if the entity did not expect any breakage), it might increase the price of its goods or services. For example, an airline that sells non-refundable tickets would presumably charge a higher price per ticket if there was no expectation of breakage.

BC399   The boards also decided that an entity should recognise revenue for breakage only if it is highly probable that doing so would not result in a subsequent significant revenue reversal (see paragraphs 56–58 of IFRS 15). Otherwise, the entity's performance obligation to stand ready to provide future goods or services could be understated.

BC400   The boards considered but rejected an approach that would have required an entity to recognise estimated breakage as revenue immediately on the receipt of prepayment from a customer. The boards decided that because the entity has not performed under the contract, recognising revenue would not have been a faithful depiction of the entity's performance and could also have understated its obligation to stand ready to provide future goods or services.

BC401   Some respondents questioned whether the accounting for breakage is consistent with that for customer options in IFRS 15. Those respondents explained that for customer options, breakage is taken into account when determining the stand-alone selling price of the option as required by paragraph B42 of IFRS 15. Therefore, those respondents were concerned that when the consideration is allocated between the option and another performance obligation, some of the breakage on the option would be recognised when the other performance obligation is satisfied, which could occur before any rights under the options are exercised by the customer. However, the boards observed that when there are two (or more) performance obligations, IFRS 15 requires an entity to allocate the overall consideration between the performance obligations based on their relative stand-alone selling prices and, therefore, any discount on the combined bundle of goods or services is allocated on that basis (unless the entity meets the requirements in paragraph 82 or 85 of IFRS 15 to allocate on another basis). In other words, any difference between the sum of the stand-alone selling prices of the option and the other promised goods or services compared with the overall consideration would be recognised when (or as) the entity transfers the goods or services promised in the contract, which is consistent with the pattern of revenue recognition for breakage when there is only one performance obligation.

Licensing (paragraphs B52–B63B)[6]

BC402   In the 2011 Exposure Draft, the boards proposed that a licence grants a customer a right to use, but not own, intellectual property of the entity. Consequently, the 2011 Exposure Draft viewed the nature of the promised asset in a licence as a right to use an intangible asset that is transferred at a point in time. This is

---

6   *Clarifications to IFRS 15* issued in April 2016 deleted paragraph B57 and added paragraph B59A of IFRS 15 to clarify the application guidance on determining the nature of the entity's promise in granting a licence of intellectual property. Paragraphs BC402–BC414 should therefore be read together with paragraphs BC414A–BC414Y, which explain the IASB's considerations in amending the application guidance.

because the boards' view at that time was that there is a point at which the customer obtains the ability to direct the use of, and obtain substantially all of the benefits from, the right to use the intellectual property. However, the 2011 Exposure Draft also explained that revenue may be recognised over time for some contracts that include a licence if that licence is not distinct from other promises in the contract that may transfer to the customer over time.

BC403   In the light of the feedback received on the 2011 Exposure Draft, the boards reconsidered whether the nature of the promised asset in a licence is always a right that transfers at a point in time. In the examples they considered, the boards observed that licences vary significantly and include a wide array of different features and economic characteristics, which lead to significant differences in the rights provided by a licence. In some of the examples, the boards observed that the customer might be viewed as not obtaining control of the licence at a point in time. This is because the intellectual property to which the customer has obtained rights is dynamic and will change as a result of the entity's continuing involvement in its intellectual property, including activities that affect that intellectual property. In those cases, the customer may not be able to direct the use of, and obtain substantially all of the remaining benefits from, the licence at the time of transfer. In other words, what the licence provides to the customer is access to the intellectual property in the form in which it exists at any given moment. (Those notions were supported by some respondents who opposed the proposal in the 2011 Exposure Draft that all distinct licences represent the transfer of a right to use an intangible asset.)

BC404   Consequently, the boards decided to specify criteria for determining whether the nature of the entity's promise in granting a licence is to provide a customer with a right to access the entity's intellectual property as it exists throughout the licence period, or a right to use the entity's intellectual property as it exists at a point in time when the licence is granted. The boards noted that these criteria were necessary to distinguish between the two types of licences, rather than strictly relying on the control requirements, because it is difficult to assess when the customer obtains control of assets in a licence without first identifying the nature of the entity's performance obligation.

BC405   However, the boards observed that before applying the criteria, an entity should assess the goods or services promised in the contract and identify, as performance obligations, the promises that transfer the goods or services to the customer.

Identifying the performance obligations

BC406   The boards observed that, as is the case with other contracts, contracts that include a licence require an assessment of the promises in the contract and the criteria for identifying performance obligations (see paragraphs 27–30 of IFRS 15). This would include an assessment of whether the customer can benefit from the licence on its own or together with other resources that are readily available (see paragraph 27(a) of IFRS 15) and whether the licence is separately identifiable from other goods or services in the contract (see paragraph 27(b) of IFRS 15). The boards observed that this assessment may sometimes be challenging because the customer can often obtain benefit from the licence on its own (ie the licence is capable of being distinct). However, in many cases, the customer can benefit from the licence only with another good or service that is also promised (explicitly or implicitly) in the contract; therefore, the licence is not separately identifiable from other goods or services in the contract. This may occur when:

(a) a licence forms a component of a tangible good and is integral to the good's functionality—software (ie a licence) is often included in tangible goods (for example, a car) and in most cases, significantly affects how that good functions. In those cases, the customer cannot benefit from the licence on its own (see paragraph 27(a) of IFRS 15) because the licence is integrated into the good (see paragraph 29(a) of IFRS 15); that is, the licence is an input to produce that good, which is an output.

(b) a licence that the customer can benefit from only in conjunction with a related service—this may occur when an entity provides a service, such as in some hosting or storage services, that enables the customer to use a licence, such as software, only by accessing the entity's infrastructure. In those cases, the customer does not take control of the licence and, therefore, cannot benefit from (or use) the licence on its own (see paragraph 27(a) of IFRS 15) without the hosting service. In addition, the use of the licence is highly dependent on, or highly interrelated with, the hosting service (see paragraph 29(c) of IFRS 15).

BC407 If the customer cannot benefit from the licence on its own, and/or the licence cannot be separated from other promises in the contract, the licence would not be distinct and thus would be combined with those other promises (see paragraph 30 of IFRS 15). The entity would then determine when the single performance obligation is satisfied on the basis of when the good or service (ie the output) is transferred to the customer. The boards noted that in some cases the combined good or service transferred to the customer may have a licence as its primary or dominant component. When the output that is transferred is a licence or when the licence is distinct, the entity would apply the criteria in paragraph B58 of IFRS 15 to determine whether the promised licence provides the customer with access to the entity's intellectual property or a right to use the entity's intellectual property.

Developing the criteria for licences that provide a right to access

BC408 As noted in paragraph BC404, the boards decided to specify criteria in paragraph B58 of IFRS 15 for determining if the intellectual property will change and, thus, if a licence provides a customer with a right to access the entity's intellectual property. If those criteria are not met, the licence provides the customer with a right to use an entity's intellectual property as that intellectual property exists (in the form and with the functionality) at the point in time when the licence transfers to the customer. To ensure that all licences are accounted for as either a right of access or a right to use, the boards decided to specify criteria for only one type of licence. In determining for which type of licence they should develop criteria, the boards observed that it was easier to determine when the intellectual property to which the customer has rights was changing (ie was dynamic), rather than when it was static.

BC409   In developing the criteria, the boards observed that the main factor that results in the intellectual property changing is when the contract requires, or the customer reasonably expects, that the entity undertakes activities that do not directly transfer goods or services to a customer (ie they do not meet the definition of a performance obligation). The activities may be part of an entity's ongoing and ordinary activities and customary business practices. However, the boards noted that it was not enough that the entity undertook activities, but also that those activities affected the intellectual property to which the customer has rights and, thus, exposes the customer to positive or negative effects. In those cases, the customer will essentially be using the most recent form of the intellectual property throughout the licence period. The boards observed that when the activities do not affect the customer, the entity is merely changing its own asset, which, although it may affect the entity's ability to provide future licences, would not affect the determination of what the licence provides or what the customer controls.

BC410   The boards noted that the assessment of the criteria would not be affected by other promises in the contract to transfer goods or services (ie performance obligations) that are separate from the licence. This is because the nature and pattern of transfer of each (separate) performance obligation in a contract would not affect the timing of other promised goods or services in the contract and, thus, would not affect the identification of the rights provided by the licence. This is because, by definition, a performance obligation is separate from the other promises in the contract. Consider a contract to provide a car and ongoing maintenance services—that is, two distinct goods or services (and thus two separate performance obligations). In this case, it seems counterintuitive to include the promise to provide a (separate) maintenance service when determining the nature and timing of the entity's performance related to the transfer of the car. A similar example can be drawn from a contract that includes a software licence and a promise to provide a service of updating the customer's software (sometimes included in a contract as post-contract support), in which the post-contract support is identified as a distinct good or service. This is because the entity would not consider the post-contract support when determining when control of the software transfers to the customer. In other words, a promise to transfer separate updates to the licence would not be considered in the assessment of the criteria in paragraph B58 of IFRS 15 and, furthermore, would be specifically excluded by criterion (c) in that paragraph.

BC411   The boards also noted that an entity would exclude the factors specified in paragraph B62 of IFRS 15 for the following reasons:

(a)   restrictions of time, geographical region or use that define the attributes of the asset conveyed in a licence—an entity would not consider restrictions of time, geographical region or use, because they define attributes of the rights transferred rather than the nature of the underlying intellectual property and the rights provided by the licence. Consider, for example, a term licence that permits the customer to show a movie in its theatre six times over the next two years. The restrictions in that example determine the nature of the asset that the entity has obtained (ie six showings of the movie), rather than the nature of the underlying intellectual property (ie the underlying movie).

(b) guarantees provided by the entity that it has a valid patent to intellectual property and that it will defend and maintain that patent—guarantees that the entity has a valid patent would not be included in the assessment of the criteria for determining the rights provided in a licence, because those promises are part of the entity's representation that the intellectual property is legal and valid (this notion was previously included in the 2011 Exposure Draft).

BC412 In developing the criteria, the boards considered, but rejected, differentiating licences based on the following factors:

(a) term of the licence—the length of a licence term is a restriction that represents an attribute of the asset transferred and does not provide information on the nature of the underlying intellectual property or on the nature of the entity's promise. For those reasons, the licence term does not depict when a customer obtains control of the promised licence.

(b) exclusivity—the 2010 Exposure Draft proposed to distinguish between licences (ie whether they were a performance obligation satisfied over time or at a point in time) on the basis of whether the licence was exclusive. Many respondents to the 2010 Exposure Draft explained that a distinction based on exclusivity was inconsistent with the control principle, because exclusivity does not affect the determination of the entity's performance. In addition, respondents stated that a distinction based on exclusivity would not be operational, because it would require the boards to provide more clarity on how the term 'exclusive' would be interpreted. The boards observed that exclusivity is another restriction that represents an attribute of the asset transferred, rather than the nature of the underlying intellectual property or the entity's promise in granting a licence.

(c) consumption of the underlying intellectual property—the boards also considered but rejected an approach that would differentiate between licences on the basis of the amount of the underlying intellectual property that was used up, or consumed by, a licence. This is because the intellectual property can be divided in many ways such as by time, geographical region or other restriction on use, and the rights can be provided to more than one customer at the same time through different licences. Consequently, it would be difficult for an entity to determine how much of the intellectual property was consumed by a particular licence.

(d) payment terms—the boards decided not to use payment terms to differentiate between licences. This is because payment terms are not indicative of whether the licence provides the customer with a right to access or right to use the intellectual property of the entity and thus when the performance obligation is satisfied. Instead, payment terms will be agreed by the customer and the entity and will reflect other economic factors such as credit risk and potential cash flows of the asset.

BC413 The boards also considered whether to include a criterion that differentiated the nature of an entity's promise when the promised consideration is dependent on the customer's sales from, or usage of, the licence (often referred to as a sales-based or a usage-based royalty). As a criterion for differentiating licences, this would have resulted in *all* of the promised consideration being recognised over time for such licences, including any fixed amount. The boards decided not to include royalties as a criterion for differentiating licences, because the existence of a sales-based or a usage-based royalty does not solely define performance over time. However, the boards observed that, in some cases, the existence of a sales-based or a usage-based royalty can indicate a 'shared economic interest' between the entity and the customer in the intellectual property being licensed and therefore the customer could reasonably expect that the entity will undertake activities that affect the intellectual property to which the licence relates. The boards also decided, however, to include an exception for the revenue recognition pattern of sales-based or usage-based royalties (see paragraphs BC415–BC421).

When is the performance obligation satisfied?

BC414 The boards observed that when the licence provides the customer with a right to access the entity's intellectual property, the promised licence represents a performance obligation satisfied over time because the customer will simultaneously receive and benefit from the entity's performance as the performance occurs—that is, the criterion in paragraph 35(a) of IFRS 15 will be met. However, when the licence provides the customer with a right to use the entity's intellectual property, the boards decided that the performance obligation will be satisfied at a point in time. In those cases, an entity would need to assess the point in time at which the performance obligation is satisfied (ie when the customer obtains control of the licence) by applying paragraph 38 of IFRS 15. The boards also decided to specify that control of a licence could not transfer before the beginning of the period during which the customer can use and benefit from the licenced property. If the customer cannot use and benefit from the licenced property then, by definition, it does not control the licence. The boards noted that when viewed from the entity's perspective, performance may appear to be complete when a licence has been provided to the customer, even if the customer cannot yet use that licence. However, the boards observed that the definition of control in paragraph 33 of IFRS 15 focuses on the customer's perspective, as explained in paragraph BC121.

Clarifications to IFRS 15 (amendments issued in April 2016)

BC414A The TRG discussed issues relating to the application of the licensing guidance in IFRS 15. The main issues discussed related to:

(a) determining the nature of the entity's promise in granting a licence of intellectual property;

(b) the scope and applicability of the sales-based and usage-based royalties exception;

(c) the effect of contractual restrictions in a licence on identifying the performance obligations in the contract; and

(d) when the guidance on determining the nature of the entity's promise in granting a licence applies.

BC414B In the light of those discussions and the feedback received, the IASB decided to clarify the application guidance on licensing and the accompanying Illustrative Examples to improve its operability and understandability. In some cases, the IASB concluded that a clarification is not necessary because there is adequate guidance in IFRS 15 with sufficient explanation of the boards' considerations in the Basis for Conclusions. Except for the scope and applicability of the sales-based and usage-based royalties exception, the FASB reached different conclusions about whether and how to address stakeholder concerns.

Determining the nature of the entity's promise in granting a licence of intellectual property

BC414C IFRS 15 specifies criteria in paragraph B58 for determining whether the nature of the entity's promise in granting a licence is to provide a customer with a right to access the entity's intellectual property as it exists throughout the licence period, or a right to use the entity's intellectual property as it exists at a point in time when the licence is granted. In developing IFRS 15, the boards noted that these criteria were necessary because it is difficult to assess when the customer obtains control of assets in a licence without first identifying the nature of the entity's performance obligation.

BC414D Paragraph B57 of IFRS 15 (now deleted, see paragraph BC414J) explained that the determination of whether an entity's promise to grant a licence provides a customer with a right to access or a right to use an entity's intellectual property is based on whether the customer can direct the use of, and obtain substantially all of the remaining benefits from, a licence at the point in time at which the licence is granted. A customer can direct the use of, and obtain substantially all the benefits from, the intellectual property, if the intellectual property to which the customer has rights is not significantly affected by activities of the entity. In contrast, a customer cannot direct the use of, and obtain substantially all of the remaining benefits from, a licence at the point in time at which the licence is granted if the intellectual property to which the customer has rights changes throughout the licence period. The intellectual property will change when the entity continues to be involved with its intellectual property and undertakes activities that significantly affect the intellectual property to which the customer has rights. Paragraph B58 provides criteria to help an entity assess whether its activities 'change' the intellectual property to which the customer has rights, including whether the expected activities of the entity significantly affect the intellectual property to which the customer has rights.

BC414E Stakeholders agree that activities that change the form or functionality of the intellectual property would represent activities that affect the intellectual property to which the customer has rights. However, stakeholders have indicated that it was unclear whether the reference in IFRS 15 to changes in the intellectual property solely refers to changes in the form or functionality of the intellectual property, or also includes changes in the value of the intellectual property. This had resulted in different interpretations about how to apply the criteria in paragraph B58(a). Some stakeholders held the view that, for activities to significantly affect the intellectual property to which the customer has rights, those activities must be expected to change the form or functionality of that intellectual property. They thought that changes that solely affect the value of the intellectual property do not significantly affect the intellectual property to which the customer has rights. Others thought that activities that significantly affect the value of the intellectual property are sufficient to conclude that the licence provides a right to access the intellectual property.

BC414F   The IASB decided to clarify the requirements of paragraph B58(a) by providing additional application guidance on when activities change the intellectual property to which the customer has rights in such a way that the ability of the customer to obtain benefit from the intellectual property is significantly affected. The IASB noted that the reference to form or functionality in paragraph B61 (and the Illustrative Examples and the Basis for Conclusions) was not intended to suggest that the nature of a licence is a right to access intellectual property only if the entity's activities significantly affect the form or functionality of the intellectual property to which the customer has rights. Determining the nature of a licence is defined by the criteria in paragraph B58, which do not refer to form or functionality.

BC414G   Paragraph B59A clarifies that the assessment of whether the entity's activities significantly change the intellectual property to which the customer has rights is based on whether those activities affect the intellectual property's ability to provide benefit to the customer. In some cases, the ability of the intellectual property to provide benefit to the customer is derived from the form or functionality of the intellectual property to which the customer has rights and, in other cases, from the value of that intellectual property. If the activities are expected to significantly change the form or functionality of the intellectual property, those activities are considered to significantly affect the customer's ability to obtain benefit from the intellectual property. If the activities do not significantly change the form or functionality, but the ability of the customer to obtain benefit from the intellectual property is substantially derived from, or dependent upon, the entity's activities after the licence is granted, then the activities are also considered to significantly affect the intellectual property (as long as those activities do not result in the transfer of a good or service to the customer). In these cases, it is not necessary for those activities to change the form or functionality of the intellectual property to significantly affect the ability of the customer to obtain benefit from the intellectual property. For example, in some circumstances (eg many licences of brands), the benefit of the intellectual property is derived from its value and the entity's activities to support or maintain that value.

BC414H   The IASB observed that intellectual property that has significant stand-alone functionality derives a substantial portion of its benefit from that functionality. Consequently, if the entity's activities do not significantly change the form or functionality of such intellectual property, then the entity's activities will not significantly affect the customer's ability to derive benefit from that intellectual property. Therefore, the IASB clarified that in these cases the criterion in paragraph B58(a) would not be met and the licence would be a right to use the intellectual property as it existed at the time that it was transferred.

BC414I   The IASB has not defined the term 'significant stand-alone functionality' but has made clarifications to the Illustrative Examples to illustrate when the intellectual property to which the customer has rights might have significant stand-alone functionality. In many cases, it will be clear when intellectual property has significant stand-alone functionality. If there is no significant stand-alone functionality, the benefit to the customer might be derived substantially from the value of the intellectual property and the entity's activities to support or maintain that value. The IASB noted, however, that an entity may need to apply judgement to determine whether the intellectual property to which the customer has rights has significant stand-alone functionality.

BC414J   The IASB has deleted paragraph B57. This is in response to stakeholder concerns that paragraph B57 has contributed to the confusion about whether the reference to change solely refers to changes in the form or functionality of intellectual property or also includes changes in the value of intellectual property. The IASB is of the view that the addition of paragraph B59A provides clarity about the intended meaning of change in intellectual property, which makes the discussion in paragraph B57 redundant within the context of the application guidance. The discussion in paragraph B57 explained the IASB's logic for the requirements for determining whether an entity's promise to grant a licence provides a customer with either a right to access or a right to use an entity's intellectual property. Accordingly, the IASB has incorporated the content of paragraph B57 into this Basis for Conclusions.

BC414K   Having considered the wider implications of amending IFRS 15 before its effective date, the IASB decided to clarify the approach to determining the nature of an entity's promise in providing a licence, rather than change that approach. The IASB is of the view that stakeholder concerns have been addressed adequately by providing greater clarity about how to apply the requirements within the Standard. The IASB acknowledge that, in some cases, the outcome of using its clarified approach may differ from the outcome achieved using the alternative approach contained in the amendments issued by the FASB (see paragraphs BC414L–BC414N).

Alternative approach developed by the FASB

BC414L   The FASB developed an alternative approach to determine whether a licence constitutes a right to access or a right to use, based on the nature of the intellectual property. The FASB explained that the basis for this approach is whether an entity's promise to a customer includes supporting or maintaining the intellectual property to which the customer has rights, which in turn largely depends on whether the intellectual property has significant stand-alone functionality.

BC414M   The FASB decided that intellectual property is either:

(a)   functional intellectual property, which is intellectual property that has significant stand-alone functionality and derives a substantial portion of its utility (ie its ability to provide benefit or value) from its significant stand-alone functionality. In this case, a customer generally obtains a licence for the right to use intellectual property unless the functionality of the intellectual property is expected to substantively change during the licence period as a result of activities of the entity that do not transfer a good or service to the customer and the customer is contractually or practically required to use the updated intellectual property; or

(b) symbolic intellectual property, which is intellectual property that does not have significant stand-alone functionality. Substantially all of the utility of symbolic intellectual property is derived from its association with the entity's past or ongoing activities, including its ordinary business activities. In this case, a customer obtains a licence for the right to access intellectual property.

BC414N The FASB's approach looks to the nature of the intellectual property to determine whether the entity's activities significantly affect the intellectual property to which the customer has rights. The FASB's approach has the potential to result in some licences of symbolic intellectual property being classified as a right to access intellectual property, even though there is no expectation that the entity will undertake activities after making the intellectual property available to the customer. For example, the entity may own a brand that it does not support or maintain, but still grants licences to customers to use the brand in television or movie productions that are set in a time period during which the brand was active. Nonetheless, the FASB decided to adopt this alternative approach on the basis of feedback that the approach would be more operable than the approach contained in Topic 606 when it was issued in May 2014, particularly for entities with a significant number of licensing arrangements and those with diversified operations.

Contractual restrictions in a licence and the identification of performance obligations

BC414O Some stakeholders suggested that it was unclear whether particular types of contractual restrictions would affect the identification of the promised goods or services in the contract. For example, an arrangement might grant a customer a licence of a well-known television programme or movie for a period of time (for example, three years), but the customer might be restricted to showing that licensed content only once per year during each of those three years. Those stakeholders acknowledged that paragraph B62 is clear that restrictions of time, geographical region or use do not affect the licensor's determination about whether the licence is satisfied over time or at a point in time. However, in their view, it was unclear whether contractual restrictions affect the entity's identification of its promises in the contract (ie whether the airing restrictions affect whether the entity has granted one licence or three licences). Subsequent to the publication, in July 2015, of the Exposure Draft *Clarifications to IFRS 15*, the TRG discussed some further examples considering whether particular contractual restrictions create separate promises or, instead, merely define attributes of a promise. The TRG also discussed time attributes within the context of applying paragraph B61 of IFRS 15 to renewals of, or extensions to, existing licences (see paragraphs BC414S–BC414U).

BC414P Having considered the wider implications of amending IFRS 15 before its effective date, the IASB decided that no clarification on the identification of performance obligations in a contract containing one or more licences was necessary. This is because, in its view, the clarifications made to IFRS 15 by the amendments issued in April 2016 will assist all entities in applying the requirements for identifying performance obligations contained in paragraphs 22–30 of IFRS 15. Paragraphs BC405–BC406 of IFRS 15 explain that, as is the case with other contracts, contracts that include a promise to grant a licence to a customer require an assessment of the promises in the contract using the criteria for identifying performance obligations (see paragraphs 27–30 of IFRS 15). This assessment is done before applying the criteria to determine the nature of an entity's promise in granting a licence. Consequently, the entity considers all of the contractual terms to determine whether the promised rights result in the transfer to the customer of one or more licences. In making this determination, judgement is needed to distinguish contractual provisions that create promises to transfer rights to use the entity's intellectual property from contractual provisions that establish when, where and how those rights may be used.

BC414Q   The IASB considered Example 59 in the Illustrative Examples accompanying IFRS 15. The entity concludes that its only performance obligation is to grant the customer a right to use the music recording. When, where and how the right can be used is defined by the attributes of time (two years), geographical scope (Country A) and permitted use (in commercials). If, instead, the entity had granted the customer rights to use the recording for two different time periods in two geographical locations, for example, years X1–X3 in Country A and years X2–X4 in Country B, the entity would need to use the criteria for identifying performance obligations in paragraphs 27–30 of IFRS 15 to determine whether the contract included one licence covering both countries or separate licences for each country.

BC414R   The FASB decided to amend Topic 606 to confirm that the requirements about contractual restrictions of the nature described in paragraph B62 do not replace the requirement for the entity to identify the number of licences promised in the contract. Similarly to the IASB, the FASB also observed that judgement is often required in distinguishing a contract that contains a single licence with multiple attributes from a contract that contains multiple licences to the customer that represent separate performance obligations.

Renewals of licences of intellectual property

BC414S   As noted in paragraph BC414O, the TRG discussed the application of paragraph B61 of IFRS 15 within the context of licence renewals. Paragraph B61 states that '... revenue cannot be recognised for a licence that provides a right to use the entity's intellectual property before the beginning of the period during which the customer is able to use and benefit from the licence'. Some stakeholders asked whether paragraph B61 applies to the renewal of an existing licence or whether the entity could recognise revenue for the renewal when the parties agree to the renewal.

BC414T   The discussion at the TRG indicated that this is an area in which judgement is needed. This is because when the entity and the customer enter into a contract to renew (or extend the period of) an existing licence, the entity will evaluate whether the renewal or extension should be treated as a new licence or, alternatively, as a modification of the existing contract. A modification would be accounted for in accordance with the contract modifications requirements in paragraphs 18–21 of IFRS 15. The IASB noted that, although some diversity may arise, IFRS 15 provides a more extensive framework for applying judgement than its predecessor, IAS 18. Again, having considered the wider implications of amending IFRS 15 before its effective date, the IASB decided that a clarification about the application of the contract modification requirements specifically for renewals of licensing arrangements was not necessary.

BC414U The FASB decided to amend Topic 606 and provide an additional example to specify that the entity would generally not recognise revenue relating to the renewal until the beginning of the licence renewal period. Consequently, in some cases, this may result in the recognition of revenue with respect to the renewal or extension at a later date using Topic 606 than using IFRS 15.

When to consider the nature of the entity's promise in granting a licence

BC414V Paragraph B55 requires an entity to apply the general revenue recognition model (paragraphs 31–38) to determine whether a performance obligation that contains a licence that is not distinct (in accordance with paragraph 27) is satisfied at a point in time or over time. Since IFRS 15 was issued, some stakeholders have asked when the licensing guidance on determining the nature of an entity's promise applies to a performance obligation that contains a licence and other goods or services. Some held the view that paragraph B55 suggests that an entity would consider the nature of its promise in granting a licence only when the licence is distinct. Others noted that an entity would have to consider the nature of its promise in granting a licence, even when the licence is not distinct, to (a) determine whether a single performance obligation that includes a licence of intellectual property is satisfied over time or at a point in time; and (b) measure progress towards complete satisfaction of that single performance obligation if it is satisfied over time.

BC414W Again, having considered the wider implications of amending IFRS 15 before its effective date, the IASB decided that a clarification in this respect is not necessary. IFRS 15 and the explanatory material in the Basis for Conclusions provide adequate guidance to account for a licence that is combined with another good or service in a single performance obligation. An entity will, however, need to apply judgement to determine the nature of the performance obligation, and to select a method of measuring progress that is consistent with the objective of depicting the entity's performance.

BC414X In making this judgement, the IASB noted that it did not intend for an entity to disregard the guidance on determining the nature of its promise in granting a licence when applying the general revenue recognition model. In some cases, it might be necessary for an entity to consider the nature of its promise in granting a licence even when the licence is not distinct. The IASB discussed an example in which an entity grants a 10-year licence that is not distinct from a one-year service arrangement. The IASB noted that a distinct licence that provides access to an entity's intellectual property over a 10-year period could not be considered completely satisfied before the end of the access period. The IASB observed that it would, therefore, be inappropriate to conclude that a single performance obligation that includes that licence is satisfied over the one-year period of the service arrangement. Paragraph BC407 further highlights that an entity considers the nature of its promise in granting the licence if the licence is the primary or dominant component (ie the predominant item) of a single performance obligation.

BC414Y The FASB decided to make amendments that explicitly state that an entity considers the nature of its promise in granting a licence when applying the general revenue recognition model to a single performance obligation that includes a licence and other goods or services (ie when applying the requirements in Topic 606 equivalent to those set out in paragraphs 31–45 of IFRS 15). Consequently, when the licence is not the predominant item of a single performance obligation, this may result in an entity that applies Topic 606 considering the nature of its promise in granting a licence in a greater number of circumstances than an entity applying IFRS 15.

Consideration in the form of sales-based or usage-based royalties[7]

BC415 The boards decided that for a licence of intellectual property for which the consideration is based on the customer's subsequent sales or usage, an entity should not recognise any revenue for the variable amounts until the uncertainty is resolved (ie when a customer's subsequent sales or usage occurs). The boards had proposed a similar requirement in the 2011 Exposure Draft because both users and preparers of financial statements indicated that it would not be useful for an entity to recognise a minimum amount of revenue for those contracts. This is because that approach would inevitably have required the entity to report, throughout the life of the contract, significant adjustments to the amount of revenue recognised at inception of the contract as a result of changes in circumstances, even though those changes in circumstances are not related to the entity's performance. The boards observed that this would not result in relevant information, particularly in contracts in which the sales-based or usage-based royalty is paid over a long period of time.

BC416 In redeliberating the 2011 Exposure Draft, the boards observed that because the restriction for a sales-based or usage-based royalty on a licence of intellectual property was structured to apply to only a particular type of transaction, other economically similar types of transactions might be accounted for differently. For example, the restriction would not apply to tangible goods that include a significant amount of intellectual property and, instead, any variable consideration to which the entity is entitled in exchange for those tangible goods would be considered under the general requirements for constraining estimates of variable consideration. Some respondents questioned the conceptual rationale for including a restriction that could in some cases result in an outcome that was not consistent with the requirement to recognise some or all of an estimate of variable consideration. Others asked whether they could apply the restriction by analogy if the promised good or service had characteristics similar to a licence of intellectual property and the consideration

---

7 *Clarifications to IFRS 15* issued in April 2016 added paragraphs B63A–B63B of IFRS 15 to clarify when an entity should recognise revenue for a sales-based or usage-based royalty using the requirement in paragraph B63 of IFRS 15. Paragraphs BC415–BC421 should therefore be read together with paragraphs BC421A–BC421J, which explain the boards' considerations in amending the application guidance.

depended on the customer's future actions. Consequently, the boards considered whether they should do either of the following:

(a) expand the scope of paragraph B63 of IFRS 15 to constrain all estimates of variable consideration when that consideration depends on the customer's future actions; or

(b) develop a general principle that could be applied to all contracts that would achieve broadly the same outcomes.

Expand the scope

BC417 The boards considered whether to expand the restriction for a sales-based or usage-based royalty on a licence of intellectual property, whereby revenue recognition would be constrained to zero for any performance obligation when the amount that an entity is entitled to is based on a customer's future actions. However, the boards decided not to introduce this principle into IFRS 15. This is because it would have prevented an entity from recognising any revenue when the goods and services were transferred in cases in which the entity could estimate the variable consideration and meet the objective of constraining estimates of variable consideration.

BC418 The boards also observed that expanding the scope to constrain revenue when consideration is based on the customer's future actions would also have increased complexity. It would have required the boards to create another exception to maintain the requirements for accounting for customer rights of return, which also results in consideration that is dependent on the customer's future actions.

Develop a general principle

BC419 The boards also considered whether the restriction for a sales-based or usage-based royalty on a licence of intellectual property could be incorporated into a general principle. The boards considered various ways of articulating this principle, including doing so on the basis of the timing of satisfaction of a performance obligation—that is, whether the performance obligation is satisfied over time or at a point in time. Specifically, if the performance obligation to which the variable consideration related was satisfied at a point in time, an entity would include an estimate of variable consideration in the transaction price only to the extent that it is highly probable that a significant reversal in the amount of cumulative revenue recognised will not occur when the uncertainty associated with the variable consideration is subsequently resolved. Conversely, if the performance obligation to which the variable consideration related was satisfied over time, an entity could include any estimate in the transaction price (even a minimum amount) provided that the objective of constraining estimates of variable consideration could be met.

BC420 This approach was based on the rationale that, for a performance obligation satisfied at a point in time, recognition of revenue that could be adjusted up or down would not be a meaningful depiction of the consideration for the related goods or services and, furthermore, any future adjustments to the transaction price (and therefore revenue) would have little correlation with the entity's performance in that period. Conversely, when a performance obligation is satisfied over time, the initial recognition of some but not all of the estimate of variable consideration would be affected by the entity's future performance, so future adjustments to the transaction price would provide useful information because they explain whether the entity's subsequent performance was beneficial (ie the minimum amount is increased) or detrimental (ie the minimum amount is subject to an unexpected reversal). However, the boards rejected this approach because it would have added complexity to the model that would outweigh the benefit.

BC421   Consequently, the boards decided against applying the restriction for sales-based or usage-based royalties on intellectual property more broadly. Although the boards acknowledge that the requirements in paragraph B63 of IFRS 15 constitute an exception that might not be consistent with the principle of recognising some or all of the estimate of variable consideration, they decided that this disadvantage was outweighed by the simplicity of these requirements, as well as by the relevance of the resulting information for this type of transaction. The boards also noted that because this is a specific requirement intended for only limited circumstances, entities should not apply it by analogy to other types of promised goods or services or other types of variable consideration.

Clarifications to IFRS 15 (amendments issued in April 2016)

BC421A   Paragraph B63 requires an entity to recognise revenue for a sales-based or usage-based royalty promised in exchange for a licence of intellectual property when the later of the following events occurs: (a) the customer's subsequent sales or usage; and (b) the performance obligation to which some or all of the sales-based or usage-based royalty has been allocated has been satisfied (or partially satisfied). This guidance in paragraph B63 is referred to as the 'royalties constraint'.

BC421B   Stakeholders had indicated that it was unclear when a sales-based or usage-based royalty is 'promised in exchange for a licence'. Some stakeholders held the view that the royalties constraint applies whenever the royalty relates to a licence of intellectual property, regardless of whether the royalty is also consideration for other goods or services in the contract. Other stakeholders had suggested that the royalties constraint applies only when the royalty relates solely to a licence that is distinct in accordance with paragraph 27 of IFRS 15 or only when the licence is the predominant item to which the royalty relates. Stakeholders had also indicated that it was unclear whether a single sales-based or usage-based royalty should be split into a portion to which the royalties constraint would apply and a portion to which it would not, for example, when the royalty relates to a licence and another good or service that is not a licence.

BC421C   In response to stakeholder concerns, the boards decided to clarify the application of the royalties constraint as follows:

(a)   the royalties constraint applies whenever a licence of intellectual property is the sole or predominant item to which the royalty relates; and

(b)   an entity should not split a single royalty into a portion subject to the royalties constraint and a portion that is subject to the general constraint on variable consideration contained in paragraphs 50–59 of IFRS 15.

Applying the royalties constraint

BC421D   The boards decided to clarify in paragraph B63A that the royalties constraint applies to those arrangements for which the licence is the predominant item to which the royalty relates. This is because users of financial statements are likely to view those arrangements as licensing arrangements. The boards had previously observed in paragraph BC415 that it would not be useful for an entity to recognise a minimum amount of revenue for licences of intellectual property for which the consideration is based on the customer's sales or usage. Applying the royalties constraint only when the royalty relates solely to a licence that is distinct in accordance with paragraph 27 of IFRS 15 might unduly restrict its application.

BC421E   The boards observed that judgement is required to determine when a licence is the predominant item to which a sales-based or usage-based royalty relates. However, the judgement needed for that determination is likely to be less than the judgement needed to apply the general requirements on variable consideration to those arrangements that would fall outside the scope of the royalties constraint if that scope were to be more restrictive.

BC421F   The boards decided against changing the scope of the royalties constraint, including expanding it beyond those situations for which a licence is the predominant item to which a royalty relates. This is because doing so would capture arrangements for which the boards previously concluded that the royalties constraint should not apply (for example, sales of intellectual property or sales of tangible goods that include intellectual property). As noted in paragraphs BC416 and BC421, the royalties constraint is intended to apply only to limited circumstances involving licences of intellectual property and, therefore, entities cannot apply it by analogy to other types of transactions.

BC421G   The boards observed that an entity might conclude that a licence is the predominant item to which a sales-based or usage-based royalty relates when there is more than one performance obligation. This conclusion might be reached regardless of whether the entity concludes that the royalty can be allocated entirely to one performance obligation in accordance with the requirements for allocating variable consideration in paragraphs 84–85 of IFRS 15. The boards also observed that the royalties constraint would also apply when the royalty predominantly relates to two or more licences promised in a contract, rather than a single licence.

BC421H   The boards made consistent clarifying amendments to the Illustrative Examples to more clearly support the conclusions reached about when a sales-based royalty would be recognised. However, the boards decided not to amend paragraph B63 or provide further Illustrative Examples for more complex fact patterns.

BC421I   In reaching this decision, the IASB considered a similar example to Example 60 accompanying IFRS 15 and concluded that when a time-based measure of progress appropriately depicts an entity's performance under the licence, recognising the sales-based royalty as and when the customer's sales occur would generally be appropriate. This is because, as noted in paragraph BC219, the objective of the royalties constraint is to prevent an entity from recognising revenue for uncertain amounts until the uncertainty is resolved (ie when the customer's subsequent sales or usage occurs). In effect, the requirement in paragraph B63 constrains the amount of revenue that can be recognised when or as a performance obligation is satisfied, rather than constraining the total amount of the transaction price to be allocated. Paragraph B63(b) reflects one of the key principles of IFRS 15, which is to recognise revenue only when (or as) an entity satisfies a performance obligation. If the entity has satisfied (or partially satisfied) the performance obligation to which the royalty relates, paragraph B63(a) further constrains the recognition of revenue until the uncertainty about the amount of revenue is resolved. Consequently, an entity recognises revenue from a sales-based or usage-based royalty when (or as) the customer's subsequent sales or usage occur, unless recognition in that manner would accelerate the recognition of revenue for the performance obligation to which the royalty solely or partially relates ahead of the entity's performance towards complete satisfaction of the performance obligation based on an appropriate measure of progress.

Splitting a royalty

BC421J   Paragraph B63B of IFRS 15 clarifies that an entity should recognise revenue from a sales-based or usage-based royalty wholly in accordance with either the requirement in paragraph B63 (if paragraph B63 applies) or the requirements on variable consideration contained in paragraphs 50–59 of IFRS 15 (if paragraph B63 does not apply). The boards made this clarification in paragraph B63B because the boards concluded that (a) it would be more complex to account for part of a royalty under the royalties constraint and another part under the general requirements for variable consideration; and (b) doing so would not provide any additional useful information to users of financial statements. This is because splitting a royalty would result in an entity recognising an amount at contract inception that would reflect neither the amount to which the entity expects to be entitled based on its performance, nor the amount to which the entity has become legally entitled during the period.

Repurchase agreements (paragraphs B64–B76)

BC422   When developing the requirements for control, the boards considered how an entity should apply the requirements to contracts in which the entity sells an asset and also enters into a repurchase agreement (either in the same contract or in another contract).

BC423   The boards observed that repurchase agreements generally come in three forms—forwards, call options and put options. However, the boards decided that an arrangement in which an entity subsequently decides to repurchase a good after transferring control of that good to a customer would not constitute a repurchase agreement as described in paragraph B64 of IFRS 15. This is because the entity's subsequent decision to repurchase a good without reference to any pre-existing contractual right does not affect the customer's ability to direct the use of, and obtain substantially all of the remaining benefits from, the good upon initial transfer. In other words, the customer is not obliged to resell that good to the entity as a result of the initial contract. The boards observed that in those cases, the entity should, however, consider whether the customer obtained control of the good initially and may need to consider the requirements for principal versus agent in paragraphs B34–B38 of IFRS 15.

A forward or a call option

BC424   If an entity has an obligation or a right to repurchase an asset (ie a forward or a call option, respectively), the boards decided that the customer does not obtain control of the asset and, therefore, no revenue should be recognised. This is because the customer is constrained in its ability to direct the use of, and obtain substantially all of the remaining benefits from, the asset. Because the customer is obliged to return, or to stand ready to return, the asset to the entity, the customer cannot use up or consume the entire asset. Moreover, the customer cannot sell the asset to another party (unless that sale is subject to a repurchase agreement, in which case the customer's benefit from the sale is constrained).

BC425   Theoretically, a customer is not constrained in its ability to direct the use of, and obtain substantially all the benefits from, the asset if an entity agrees to repurchase, at the prevailing market price, an asset from the customer that is substantially the same and is readily available in the marketplace. However, the boards noted that an entity would be unlikely to enter into such a transaction.

BC426   The boards decided that an entity would account for a forward or a call option as a lease or a financing arrangement, depending on the relationship between the repurchase amount and the original selling price. The FASB also decided to specify that when the forward or call option accounted for as a lease is part of a sale-leaseback transaction, the contract should be accounted for as a financing transaction. Otherwise, the FASB observed that an entity would have been required to account for the transaction as a lease and then as a leaseback, which would not have been appropriate.

BC427   The boards noted that an entity would not need to consider the likelihood that a call option can be exercised, because the existence of the call option effectively limits the customer's ability to control the asset. However, the boards observed that if the call option is non-substantive, that option should be ignored in assessing whether and when the customer obtains control of a good or service (to be consistent with the general requirement for any non-substantive term in a contract).

A put option

BC428   The boards decided that if the sale and repurchase agreement resulted in an entity's obligation to repurchase the asset at a customer's request (ie a put option), the customer would obtain control of the asset because the customer is neither obliged to return the asset nor obliged to stand ready to do so. Consequently, the customer has the ability to direct the use of, and obtain substantially all of the remaining benefits from, the asset (ie the customer can sell, use up or consume the entire asset and choose not to exercise the put option). The boards decided that the entity should account for its obligation to stand ready to repurchase the asset, to be consistent with the accounting for the sale of a product with a right of return (see paragraphs BC363–BC367). That results in the entity recognising the following:

(a) a liability for its obligation to repurchase the asset, measured at the amount of the consideration expected to be paid to the customer;

(b) an asset for the entity's right to receive that asset upon settling that liability, measured at an amount that may or may not equal the entity's previous carrying value of the asset; and

(c) revenue on transfer of the asset for the difference between the sales price of the asset and the liability recognised for the obligation to repurchase the asset.

BC429 Some respondents questioned whether that accounting would be appropriate in all cases in which a customer has a put option. For instance, some noted that the contract appears to be economically similar to a lease with a purchase option rather than to a right of return. That might be the case if the entity is required to repurchase the asset at a price that is lower than the original sales price and the surrounding facts and circumstances indicate that the customer will exercise its put option. In those cases, the difference between the original sales price and the repurchase price can be viewed as the amount that the customer pays for a right to use the asset, thereby compensating the entity for the decline in the value of the asset. Some respondents noted that, in other cases, the contract is, in effect, a financing arrangement.

BC430 The boards agreed with those respondents and decided that if a customer has a right to require an entity to repurchase the asset at a price that is lower than the original sales price and the customer has a significant economic incentive to exercise that right, then the customer does not obtain control of the asset. Although the customer is not obliged to exercise its put option, the fact that it has a significant economic incentive to exercise that right means that it would probably incur a loss if it did not do so. (For example, the repurchase price may be set significantly above the expected market value of the asset at the date of the repurchase. However, the boards observed that an entity should consider factors other than the price when determining that it has a significant economic incentive to exercise its right.) The boards decided that in those cases, the existence of the option effectively restricts the customer's ability to direct the use of, and obtain substantially all of the remaining benefits from, the asset. For similar reasons, the boards decided that if the customer has the unconditional right to require the entity to repurchase the asset at a price that is greater than the original sales price, and higher than the expected market value of the asset, the customer does not obtain control of the asset.

BC431 The boards also considered whether other arrangements should be accounted for as a lease, such as when an entity provides its customer with a guaranteed amount to be paid on resale (ie a guaranteed minimum resale value). Accounting for those transactions as leases would be consistent with previous US GAAP, and a number of respondents, primarily from the automotive industry, explained that they viewed the transactions to be economically similar. However, the boards observed that while the cash flows may be similar, the customer's ability to control the asset in each case is different. If the customer has a put option that it has significant economic incentive to exercise, the customer is restricted in its ability to consume, modify or sell the asset. However, when the entity guarantees that the customer will receive a minimum amount of sales proceeds, the customer is not constrained in its ability to direct the use of, and obtain substantially all of the benefits from, the asset. Thus, the boards decided that it was not necessary to expand the requirements for repurchase agreements to consider guaranteed amounts of resale.

Accounting for repurchase agreements in which the customer does not obtain control of the asset

BC432   If an entity enters into a contract with a repurchase agreement and the customer does not obtain control of the asset, the boards decided the following:

(a)   the contract should be accounted for as a lease in accordance with IAS 17 *Leases* or Topic 840 *Leases* if the customer is paying for a right to use the asset; and

(b)   the contract is a financing arrangement if the net consideration that the entity receives is equal to or less than zero (ie the entity is paying interest).

BC433   To ensure consistent accounting in IFRS and US GAAP for a financing arrangement that arises from a contract with a customer, the boards decided to provide guidance consistent with Subtopic 470-40 *Debt—Product Financing Arrangements*. Consequently, the FASB decided to amend the guidance in Subtopic 470-40 that discusses arrangements in which an entity sells a product to another entity and, in a related transaction, agrees to repurchase the product. However, the FASB decided not to amend Subtopic 470-40 for transactions in which an entity arranges for another party to purchase products on its behalf and agrees to purchase those products from the other party. In those cases, the entity is required to recognise the products as an asset and to recognise a related liability when the other party purchases the product. The FASB noted that although IFRS 15 results in similar accounting when the other party acts as an agent of the entity (ie the other party does not obtain control of the products), Subtopic 470-40 provides explicit requirements for transactions in which no sale has occurred.

Transition, effective date and early application (paragraphs C1–C9)

Transition (paragraphs C2–C8A)

BC434   The boards decided that an entity should apply IFRS 15 using either of the following methods:

(a)   retrospectively to each prior reporting period presented in accordance with IAS 8 or Topic 250 *Accounting Changes and Error Corrections*, subject to some optional practical expedients (see paragraphs BC435–BC438); or

(b)   retrospectively with the cumulative effect of initially applying IFRS 15 recognised as an adjustment to the opening balance of retained earnings at the date of initial application (see paragraphs BC439–BC444).

Retrospective application

BC435   The 2010 and 2011 Exposure Drafts proposed that an entity should apply the requirements retrospectively in accordance with IAS 8 or Topic 250. Retrospective application ensures that all contracts with customers are recognised and measured consistently both in the current period and in the comparative periods presented, regardless of whether those contracts were entered into before or after the requirements became effective. Furthermore, retrospective application provides users of financial statements with useful trend information across the current period and comparative periods. Feedback received from users of financial statements confirmed that retrospective application would be the most useful transition approach for them to be able to understand trends in revenue.

BC436   In contrast to the feedback received from users of financial statements, many respondents commented that applying the requirements retrospectively would be burdensome, especially for entities with long-term contracts or large and complex multiple-element arrangements. The main concerns raised by those respondents were as follows:

(a)   it may not be possible to obtain historical information for contracts that were completed under previous revenue Standards in IFRS or US GAAP because the relevant information is no longer retained by the entity.

(b)   applying IFRS 15 retrospectively (particularly to completed contracts) may not result in a materially different pattern of revenue recognition, and the significant costs incurred to confirm this fact would not provide much benefit to users of financial statements. For example, for contracts that were considered to be completed (as assessed under previous revenue Standards) several years before the date of initial application, an entity would, theoretically, need to obtain the relevant information to ensure that there was no effect on the pattern of revenue recognition in the financial statements in the year of initial application.

(c)   presenting the effect of IFRS 15 in the comparative years would incur significant preparation and audit costs, because a change in revenue could affect many other line items in the financial statements (such as deferred tax, receivables, interest and foreign currency gains/losses) as well as items that reference an entity's revenue in the financial statements (such as taxes, statutory reporting and financing arrangements).

(d)   the historical information needed to estimate stand-alone selling prices of goods or services in a contract with many performance obligations may not exist.

(e)   entities make assumptions and estimates throughout a contract's life, and it may not be possible to recreate the circumstances that apply historically without the use of hindsight.

Retrospective application with practical expedients (paragraphs C4–C6)

BC437 The boards decided that although retrospective application would generally impose increased preparation costs, those costs would be outweighed by the increased benefits to users of financial statements. Consequently, the boards considered how the burden of retrospective application could be eased while, at the same time, retaining the benefits of comparability and consistency that retrospective application would provide. To ease the burden of transition without sacrificing comparability, the boards decided to allow an entity to elect to use one or more of the following practical expedients when applying IFRS 15 retrospectively.

Practical expedient	Rationale
Reducing the number of contracts that require restatement[a]	
For contracts completed before the date of initial application of IFRS 15, an entity need not restate contracts that begin and end within the same annual reporting period.	In considering whether an entity should be required to review and restate all contracts completed before the date of initial application, the boards decided that trend information should be preserved for completed contracts that span annual reporting periods. Consequently, the boards decided to limit the relief to only those contracts that begin and end within the same annual reporting period, because the amount and timing of revenue recognition relating to those contracts would not change between annual reporting periods. The boards noted that this relief would significantly reduce the transition burden on entities that have a large number of short-term contracts.

A consequence of this relief is that revenue reported in interim periods before and after the effective date would not necessarily be accounted for on a comparable basis. The boards expect that an entity would not elect to use this relief if it operates in an industry in which comparability across interim reporting periods is particularly important to users of financial statements. |

continued...

...*continued*

Practical expedient	Rationale
Simplifying how an entity restates contracts with customers[b]	
For contracts completed before the date of initial application of IFRS 15 and that have variable consideration, an entity may use the transaction price at the date that the contract was completed rather than estimating variable consideration amounts in the comparative reporting periods.	Full retrospective application of IFRS 15 in accordance with IAS 8 or Topic 250 would require an entity to determine the estimates that it would have made at each of the reporting dates in the comparative periods. The boards considered that making those estimates in the comparative years would increase the complexity and costs of retrospective application. By allowing an entity to use hindsight in estimating variable consideration, the boards decided that transition would be simplified for the following reasons: (a) it would reduce the amount of information that an entity would need to collect throughout the transition period; and (b) the entity would not need to determine the transaction price at the end of each period.

continued...

© IFRS Foundation

...*continued*

Practical expedient	Rationale
Simplifying retrospective application of other aspects of the requirements	
For all reporting periods presented before the date of initial application of IFRS 15, an entity need not disclose the amount of the transaction price allocated to the remaining performance obligations and an explanation of when the entity expects to recognise that amount as revenue (as specified in paragraph 120 of IFRS 15).	The boards decided that the disclosure of the amount of the transaction price allocated to the remaining performance obligations (as would be required by paragraph 120 of IFRS 15) should not be required for periods presented before the date of initial application of IFRS 15 for the following reasons: (a) the disclosure would be most useful for the current period; and (b) the disclosure could be burdensome to prepare for comparative years, especially when trying to avoid the use of hindsight to estimate the transaction price and the expected timing of satisfaction of those performance obligations.

(a) *Clarifications to IFRS 15* issued in April 2016 amended paragraph C5 of IFRS 15 to add a further practical expedient to permit an entity not to restate contracts that are completed contracts at the beginning of the earliest period presented. This practical expedient, if applied, would further reduce the number of contracts that require restatement. The IASB's considerations in adding the practical expedient are explained in paragraphs BC445M–BC445N.

(b) *Clarifications to IFRS 15* issued in April 2016 amended paragraph C5 and added paragraph C7A to add a further practical expedient to simplify how an entity restates contracts with customers that are modified before transition to IFRS 15. The boards' considerations in adding the practical expedient are explained in paragraphs BC445O–BC445R.

BC438   As a result of the practical expedients providing some relief from applying IFRS 15 retrospectively, the boards also decided to supplement the transitional disclosure requirements of IAS 8 or Topic 250 to require an entity to provide additional disclosure if it elects to use one or more of the practical expedients. Accordingly, paragraph C6 of IFRS 15 requires an entity to provide an explanation to users of financial statements about which practical expedients were used and, to the extent reasonably possible, a qualitative assessment of the estimated effect of applying those practical expedients.

Retrospective application with the cumulative effect recognised in the current period (paragraphs C7–C8)

BC439   The boards decided to develop an alternative transition method to ease the burden of retrospectively applying IFRS 15 because feedback from preparers and auditors indicated that, although helpful, the practical expedients (see paragraph BC437) would not mitigate much of the implementation challenge of a retrospective transition approach. In contrast, users of financial statements generally supported the requirements for retrospective application with practical expedients because it would provide them with useful information on transition and assist their financial statement analyses.

BC440　As a result of those differing views, transition was one of the topics discussed at four disclosure and transition workshops that were held in late 2012 with both users and preparers of financial statements (see paragraph BC328). During those workshops, users of financial statements acknowledged that another transition method might be appropriate to ease the burden of transition; however, they emphasised their need for trend information, regardless of which method is used.

BC441　After considering this feedback, the boards decided that as an alternative to retrospective application with practical expedients, an entity could apply IFRS 15 (including the requirements for costs) retrospectively, with the cumulative effect of initially applying IFRS 15 recognised in the current year (referred to as the 'cumulative catch-up' transition method). Specifically, the cumulative effect would be an adjustment to the appropriate opening balance of equity in the year of initial application (ie comparative years would not be restated) for contracts that are not completed at the date of initial application.[8] (The boards clarified that a completed contract is a contract in which the entity has fully performed in accordance with revenue recognition requirements in effect before the date of initial application. Thus, a completed contract would include a contract for which the entity's performance was complete but there was a change in the transaction price after the date of initial application.)[9] The boards observed that the cumulative catch-up transition method responds to feedback from auditors and preparers by eliminating the need to restate prior periods and thus reducing costs.

BC442　The boards noted that applying the cumulative catch-up transition method results in consistent presentation of contracts under previous IFRS or US GAAP during the comparative years and in consistent presentation of any contracts not yet completed at the date of initial application under IFRS 15 in the current year. However, because the comparative information will not be restated under the cumulative catch-up transition method, the boards decided to require additional disclosures to help users of financial statements understand the effect on trend information. Consequently, when an entity uses the cumulative catch-up transition method, it is required to disclose the following information for reporting periods that include the date of initial application:

8　*Clarifications to IFRS 15* issued in April 2016 amended paragraph C7 of IFRS 15 to permit an entity using the transition method described in paragraph C3(b) to apply IFRS 15 (a) only to contracts that are not completed contracts at the date of initial application (as originally required in paragraph C7 when IFRS 15 was issued); or (b) to all contracts including completed contracts at the date of initial application. The boards' considerations in amending paragraph C7 are explained in paragraphs BC445J–BC445L.

9　The FASB subsequently decided to amend the definition of a completed contract as a contract for which all or substantially all of the revenue was recognised in accordance with the revenue guidance that was in effect before the date of initial application of Topic 606. The IASB's considerations for deciding not to amend the definition, together with an overview of the FASB's considerations for amending the definition, are explained in paragraphs BC445C–BC445I.

(a)   the amount by which each financial statement line item is affected in the current year as a result of the entity applying IFRS 15 rather than previous revenue Standards in IFRS; and

(b)   an explanation of the reasons for the significant changes in those financial statement line items.

BC443   In other words, to provide the required disclosures, an entity would apply both IFRS 15 and the previous revenue Standards in the year of initial application. Despite requiring an entity to account for revenue transactions in the year of initial application using two different sets of accounting requirements, the boards decided that this method would reduce the overall cost of applying IFRS 15 while still providing information about trends that was requested by users of financial statements.

BC444   The boards also considered other transition methods as alternatives to the cumulative catch-up method to try to ease the burden of retrospective application. For example, the boards considered requiring a prospective approach that would require entities to apply IFRS 15 only to new contracts or those that are materially modified on or after the date of initial application. However, the boards rejected this approach because prospective application would not result in consistent presentation of existing contracts and new contracts and thus would reduce comparability. In addition, this approach would not provide useful trend information for users of financial statements until existing contracts have been fully satisfied after the date of initial application. Furthermore, the boards observed that this approach would require some entities to incur significant costs of maintaining two accounting systems for contracts that are accounted for in accordance with IFRS 15 and previous revenue Standards in IFRS, until all existing contracts have been completed, which could take many years for entities with long-term contracts.

Other relief

BC445   If an entity applies IFRS 15 retrospectively in accordance with paragraph C3(a) of IFRS 15 (ie without electing to use the cumulative catch-up transition method), comparative information *would* be restated. Consequently, the IASB clarified that if an entity applies IFRS 15 retrospectively in accordance with paragraph C3(a), it is not required to provide the current year transition disclosure in paragraph 28(f) of IAS 8.

Clarifications to IFRS 15 (amendments issued in April 2016)

BC445A   The boards discussed requests from some stakeholders for further transition relief in respect of (a) accounting for a completed contract (as defined in paragraph C2(b)) on transition to IFRS 15; and (b) accounting for modifications to a contract that occurred before transition to IFRS 15. The IASB decided (a) to expand the application of the transition method described in paragraph C3(b) by allowing an entity a choice to apply IFRS 15 to all contracts including completed contracts; and (b) to provide transition relief for contract modifications. The FASB decided to make similar amendments to Topic 606. The IASB additionally decided to allow an entity using the transition method described in paragraph C3(a) not to restate completed contracts at the beginning of the earliest period presented. The following paragraphs explain the boards' considerations in providing the additional practical expedients.

Completed contracts

BC445B   The boards considered the following questions about the transition requirements in IFRS 15 with respect to a completed contract:

(a)   definition of and accounting for a completed contract.

(b)   providing an entity applying paragraph C3(b) of IFRS 15 with the choice of applying IFRS 15 to all contracts including completed contracts at the date of initial application.

(c)   permitting an entity applying paragraph C3(a) of IFRS 15 not to restate completed contracts at the beginning of the earliest period presented.

Definition of and accounting for a completed contract

BC445C   Some stakeholders, mainly in the US, highlighted potential difficulties with respect to the definition of a completed contract in paragraph C2(b) and the accounting for a completed contract once IFRS 15 becomes effective. They were unclear whether the boards intended that any previously unrecognised revenue from a completed contract that is not transitioned to IFRS 15 would continue to be accounted for in accordance with the previous revenue Standards. In addition, referring to the words 'transferred all of the goods or services' in the definition of a completed contract, they commented that:

(a)   *transfer* of goods or services is a notion that is introduced in IFRS 15 and does not exist in previous revenue Standards.

(b)   it is unclear how an entity would continue to account for a completed contract in accordance with the previous revenue Standards, which would be withdrawn once IFRS 15 becomes effective.

(c)   the boards' considerations explained in paragraph BC444 for rejecting a prospective transition method do not support the use of the previous revenue Standards once IFRS 15 becomes effective. As explained in paragraph BC444, one of the reasons for rejecting prospective transition methods was the 'significant costs of maintaining two accounting systems...until all existing contracts have been completed, which could take many years for entities with long-term contracts'.

BC445D   The IASB concluded that it was not necessary to change the definition of a completed contract to address the issues raised. In relation to the words 'transferred all of the goods or services' in the definition of a completed contract, the IASB noted that it did not intend that an entity would apply the 'transfer of control' notion in IFRS 15 to goods or services identified in accordance with previous revenue Standards. The IASB noted that paragraph BC441 refers to performance in accordance with previous revenue Standards. Consequently, in many situations the term 'transferred' would mean 'delivered' within the context of contracts for the sale of goods and 'performed' within the context of contracts for rendering services and construction contracts. In some situations, the entity would use judgement when determining whether it has transferred goods or services to the customer. For example, an entity may need to use judgement to determine when it has transferred rights to use its assets (for example, rights granted within a licence agreement), because there is no specific guidance on the transfer or delivery of such rights in IAS 18.

BC445E   The IASB observed that if an entity chooses not to apply IFRS 15 to completed contracts in accordance with paragraph C5(a)(ii) or the amended paragraph C7, only contracts that are not completed contracts are included in the transition to IFRS 15. The entity would continue to account for the completed contracts in accordance with its accounting policies based on the previous revenue Standards. The IASB's decision, when it issued IFRS 15 in May 2014, was not to require such an entity to apply IFRS 15 either prospectively or retrospectively to completed contracts.

BC445F   Furthermore, the IASB also observed that its rationale for rejecting a prospective transition method because of the costs of maintaining two systems is less relevant to completed contracts for two reasons. First, the IASB expects the volume of completed contracts with unrecognised revenue at the date of transition to IFRS 15 to be significantly less than the volume of all ongoing contracts that would be included in the transition to IFRS 15. Second, for many completed contracts, the IASB does not expect the accounting under previous revenue Standards to continue for many years after transition, because the goods or services have been transferred before the transition to IFRS 15.

BC445G   Some stakeholders expressed a view that accounting for completed contracts using the previous revenue Standards after IFRS 15 becomes effective would not provide useful financial information to users of financial statements. When developing the transition method described in paragraph C3(b), the boards considered feedback from users of financial statements and decided to require an entity to provide additional disclosures to help users understand the effect of that transition method on trend information (see paragraphs BC442–BC443). The IASB observed that as part of the disclosures required by paragraph C8 an entity could provide additional information about the amount of revenue recognised using previous revenue Standards, if the entity concludes that such information would be helpful to users. In addition, when selecting a transition method, the IASB expects that an entity would consider whether the selected transition method provides useful information to users of its financial statements. If the entity were to conclude that excluding completed contracts from the transition to IFRS 15 would not provide useful information to users, and if that is an important consideration for the entity, then the entity could decide to include completed contracts in its transition to IFRS 15.

BC445H   The FASB decided to amend Topic 606 to define a completed contract as a contract for which all (or substantially all) of the revenue was recognised in accordance with the previous revenue Standards. The FASB believes that the objective of the transition guidance in Topic 606 should be to ensure that all (or substantially all) of the revenue from contracts with customers that is recognised after transition to Topic 606 should be recognised in accordance with Topic 606. Accordingly, the FASB decided to amend the definition of a completed contract so that an entity would apply Topic 606 to all contracts for which all (or substantially all) of the revenue was not recognised under the previous revenue Standards. The FASB acknowledged that an entity would need to apply judgement in some cases to determine whether a contract is completed.

BC445I   The IASB observed that the boards' different decisions regarding amendments to the definition of a completed contract give rise to a difference between IFRS 15 and Topic 606. However, the IASB noted that an entity could avoid the consequences of the different definitions by choosing to apply IFRS 15 retrospectively to all contracts including completed contracts (see paragraph BC445K).

Providing an entity applying IFRS 15 in accordance with paragraph C3(b) with the choice of applying IFRS 15 to all contracts including completed contracts at the date of initial application

BC445J   The boards decided to amend paragraph C7 to provide an entity with a choice of applying IFRS 15 in accordance with paragraph C3(b) either (a) only to contracts that are not completed contracts at the date of initial application (which was the original requirement in paragraph C7 when IFRS 15 was issued); or (b) to all contracts including completed contracts at the date of initial application. The boards acknowledged that this choice might result in a decrease in comparability between entities. However, the boards observed that applying the transition method described in paragraph C3(b) to all contracts, including completed contracts, at the date of initial application could result in financial information that is more comparable with financial information provided by entities using the transition method described in paragraph C3(a). Furthermore, the IASB observed that any decrease in comparability between entities because of the choice will be transitory.

BC445K   The IASB also observed that:

(a)   an entity that wishes to use the transition method described in paragraph C3(b) and also avoid the consequences of the different definitions of a completed contract in IFRS 15 and Topic 606 could choose to apply IFRS 15 in accordance with paragraph C3(b) to all contracts including contracts that are completed contracts at the date of initial application; and

(b)   some entities will find applying the transition method described in paragraph C3(b) to all contracts less complex operationally than continuing to account for completed contracts under previous revenue Standards and all other contracts under IFRS 15, or using the method described in paragraph C3(a).

BC445L   The FASB observed that allowing the choice may help mitigate some of the unanticipated financial reporting consequences that some entities may experience as a result of its amendments to the definition of a completed contract.

Permitting an entity applying IFRS 15 in accordance with paragraph C3(a) not to restate completed contracts at the beginning of the earliest period presented

BC445M   The IASB decided to provide an additional practical expedient to permit an entity applying IFRS 15 in accordance with paragraph C3(a) not to restate contracts that are completed contracts at the beginning of the earliest period presented. The IASB noted that reducing the population of contracts to which IFRS 15 applies (the consequence of applying this practical expedient) could reduce the effort and cost of initial application of IFRS 15. In addition, the IASB observed that a similar expedient is currently given to first-time adopters in paragraph D35 of IFRS 1 *First-time Adoption of International Financial Reporting Standards*.

BC445N   The FASB decided not to provide a similar expedient to the transition guidance because it concluded that application of such an expedient would not faithfully depict a full retrospective application of Topic 606. The IASB acknowledged that the expedient could affect the comparability of financial information under the full retrospective method, but concluded that this would be outweighed by the benefit provided by the reduced transition costs.

Modified contracts

BC445O   Some stakeholders highlighted that applying the requirements in paragraphs 20–21 of IFRS 15 to past contract modifications could be complex, especially if the entity has long-term contracts that are modified frequently. To simplify how an entity retrospectively applies IFRS 15 to its contracts with customers, the boards decided to provide an additional practical expedient that would permit an entity to use hindsight when evaluating contract modifications when making the transition to IFRS 15. Consequently, when restating contracts on transition to IFRS 15, an entity could either (a) follow the requirements in paragraphs 20–21; or (b) use the new practical expedient in paragraph C5(c) of IFRS 15. The new practical expedient allows the entity to reflect the aggregate effect of all past contract modifications when identifying the performance obligations, and determining and allocating the transaction price, instead of accounting for the effects of each contract modification separately. The boards observed that the practical expedient would provide some cost relief and yet would result in financial information that closely aligns with the financial information that would be available under IFRS 15 without the expedient.

BC445P   The boards' conclusions on the date at which this practical expedient should be applied are not fully aligned. Both boards decided that an entity applying IFRS 15 in accordance with paragraph C3(a) should apply the practical expedient at the beginning of the earliest period presented. For an entity applying Topic 606 in accordance with paragraph 606-10-65-1(d)(2) (equivalent to paragraph C3(b) of IFRS 15), the FASB decided that the entity should apply the practical expedient at the date of initial application. However, the IASB decided that an entity applying IFRS 15 in accordance with paragraph C3(b) may apply the practical expedient either (a) at the beginning of the earliest period presented; or (b) at the date of initial application.

BC445Q   The IASB observed that without the choice of the date at which the practical expedient is applied, entities that apply IFRS 15 in accordance with paragraph C3(b), especially entities with a large number of contracts subject to frequent modifications (for example, some telecommunication companies), might have practical difficulties if they are required to wait until the date of initial application for finalising the cumulative effect of past contract modifications. This is because of the large number of contracts that would have to be evaluated in a relatively short time. Those entities highlighted that the benefit of the practical expedient would be considerably constrained if they cannot finalise the cumulative effect of past contract modifications ahead of the date of initial application of IFRS 15. The IASB observed that this decision creates a difference between IFRS 15 and Topic 606. However, an entity applying IFRS 15 in accordance with paragraph C3(b) could avoid the different reporting outcomes between IFRS 15 and Topic 606 by choosing to apply the practical expedient at the date of initial application.

BC445R The boards considered, but rejected, permitting an entity to account for the unsatisfied performance obligations in a modified contract at transition as if the original contract were terminated and a new contract created as of the transition date. This would be computationally simpler because it eliminates the need to evaluate the effects of modifications before transition to IFRS 15. Under this approach, the amount of consideration allocated to the unsatisfied performance obligations would be the total consideration promised by the customer (including amounts already received) less any amounts already recognised as revenue under previous revenue Standards. Although this might significantly reduce the cost and complexity of applying the transition requirements to contract modifications, the approach was rejected by the boards because it could result in financial information that differed significantly from that under IFRS 15 without the expedient.

Transition to Clarifications to IFRS 15

BC445S The IASB decided to require an entity to apply the amendments to IFRS 15 retrospectively in accordance with IAS 8. In reaching its decision to require retrospective application, the IASB observed that the amendments were intended to clarify the IASB's intentions when developing the requirements in IFRS 15 rather than to change the underlying principles of IFRS 15. The IASB decided not to allow prospective application of the amendments because that would reduce comparability in the limited cases that the amendments may have resulted in significant changes to an entity's application of IFRS 15. This is consistent with feedback received from users of financial statements during the development of IFRS 15 highlighting that retrospective application would be the most useful transition method for them to understand trends in revenue.

BC445T By requiring an entity to apply the amendments as if those amendments had been included in IFRS 15 at the date of initial application, the IASB observed that:

(a) if the entity applies both IFRS 15 and Clarifications to IFRS 15 at the same time, any effect of applying the amendments would be reflected in the effects of initially applying IFRS 15.

(b) if the entity applies Clarifications to IFRS 15 after the date of initial application of IFRS 15, the effects of initially applying IFRS 15 would be restated for the effects, if any, of initially applying the amendments.

BC445U The outcome of retrospective application of Clarifications to IFRS 15 will depend on which transition method an entity chooses when it first applies IFRS 15. The choice of the transition method will determine, for example, whether periods before the date of initial application of IFRS 15 are restated as well as the amount and date of the adjustment to retained earnings. Retrospective application of *Clarifications to IFRS 15* will affect only those reporting periods and those contracts to which IFRS 15 is applied. For example, consider an entity that applies IFRS 15 in accordance with paragraph C3(b) on 1 January 2017 and *Clarifications to IFRS 15* on 1 January 2018. Retrospective application of *Clarifications to IFRS 15* would not require the restatement of financial information before 1 January 2017 for the effects of the amendments. Any effect of applying the amendments would be included in a restated cumulative effect adjustment as of 1 January 2017.

Effective date and early application (paragraphs C1–C1B)

Effective date[10]

BC446   In the 2011 Exposure Draft, the boards indicated that the effective date of IFRS 15 would be set to ensure that the start of the earliest comparative period for an entity that is required to present two comparative annual periods (in addition to the current annual period) would be after the final requirements are issued. The boards developed this approach in response to feedback obtained from interested parties through a number of activities, including:

(a)   the IASB's Request for Views on *Effective Dates and Transition Methods* and the FASB's Discussion Paper *Effective Dates and Transition Methods* (October 2010);

(b)   the boards' joint investor outreach questionnaire (April 2011); and

(c)   consultation with systems providers and preparers in 2010 and 2011.

BC447   On the basis of that proposed formula for setting an effective date and of the estimated issue date of IFRS 15 at the time of their decision, the boards would have set the effective date as 1 January 2016. However, many respondents, including respondents in industries for which there could be significant process and system changes required to comply with IFRS 15 (for example, in the telecommunications and software industries), indicated that the proposed formula would not provide them with adequate time. Specifically, those respondents explained that providing only a short time before the earliest comparative period would not be sufficient to ensure that processes and systems were in place to capture the information that would be required to apply IFRS 15 retrospectively. Some respondents further explained that because of the large volume of contracts in their businesses, it would be far more cost-effective to process the information on a real-time basis to ensure that the adjustments to the financial statements were being calculated during the transition period, rather than attempting to retrospectively calculate the adjustments at the date of initial application.

BC448   The boards considered whether their decision to permit an alternative transition method (see paragraphs BC439–BC444) would provide sufficient relief that an effective date of 1 January 2016, would be appropriate. However, the boards noted that if a contract is not completed at the date of initial application, the

---

10   The boards subsequently deferred the effective date of IFRS 15 and Topic 606 by one year. See paragraphs BC453A–BC453H.

entity would need to apply IFRS 15 to that entire contract to calculate any cumulative effect that would be recognised in the opening retained earnings in the year of initial application. The boards noted that the industries that would be most affected generally have contracts with durations that would result in those industries still having only a few months to prepare their processes and systems to capture the required information on a real-time basis.

BC449 Consequently, the FASB decided to require that a public entity apply Topic 606 for annual reporting periods beginning after 15 December 2016, and the IASB decided to require that an entity apply IFRS 15 for annual reporting periods beginning on or after 1 January 2017. Although the effective dates are not identical, the boards noted that this difference has resulted from precedents in IFRS and US GAAP. Furthermore, the difference is not significant and the boards did not expect that it would result in a difference in the way that an entity considers the effective date.

BC450 The boards acknowledged that the period of time from which IFRS 15 is issued until its effective date is longer than usual. However, in this case, the boards decided that a delayed effective date is appropriate because of the unique attributes of IFRS 15, including the wide range of entities that will be affected and the potentially significant effect that a change in revenue recognition has on other financial statement line items.

BC451 To ensure consistency with the IASB's requirements in IAS 34, the FASB clarified that the first set of interim financial reports in which Topic 606 will apply is the first set of interim financial reports after the effective date (ie 31 March 2017 for a calendar year-end entity). The FASB also decided that this is appropriate because of the relatively long lead time that has been provided to entities.

Early application

BC452 The FASB decided not to allow entities to apply Topic 606 early, because doing so would have reduced the comparability of financial reporting in the period up to the date of initial application.[11] Although the IASB agreed that allowing early application would reduce the comparability of financial reporting in the period up to the date of initial application, the IASB noted that IFRS 15 improves accounting for revenue in areas in which there was little guidance under previous revenue Standards in IFRS and, thus, entities should not be precluded from applying IFRS 15 before its effective date. Furthermore, the IASB noted that IFRS 15 should resolve some pressing issues in practice arising from previous revenue recognition requirements. For example, the requirements for determining whether a performance obligation is satisfied over time should address the current diversity in practice associated with the application of the interpretation of IFRS on the construction of real estate.

BC453 The boards observed that the IASB-only decision to permit early application should not result in differences after the date of initial application in the

---

11 The FASB subsequently amended Topic 606 to allow all entities to apply the Standard early for annual periods beginning after 15 December 2016. See paragraph BC453H.

accounting for revenue between entities applying US GAAP and those applying IFRS that apply IFRS 15 early, even for contracts that straddle the date of initial application.

Deferral of effective date (amendment issued in September 2015)

BC453A   After issuing IFRS 15 and Topic 606, the IASB and the FASB formed a joint Transition Resource Group (TRG) for Revenue Recognition to support the implementation of the Standard. The TRG discussed submissions from stakeholders and its discussions on five topics indicated potential differences of views on how to implement the requirements in IFRS 15. Consequently, those topics were discussed by the boards and each board decided to propose targeted amendments to IFRS 15 and Topic 606. The IASB published an Exposure Draft *Clarifications to IFRS 15* in July 2015. In the light of those proposed amendments, the IASB and the FASB each discussed whether to defer the effective date of the Standard.

BC453B   The IASB observed that changing the effective date of a Standard shortly after its issuance creates uncertainty for stakeholders and has the potential to set a bad precedent. The effective date is set after consideration of information obtained in the exposure process about the time needed to implement the requirements. Accordingly, the IASB would consider changing the effective date only in exceptional circumstances. The IASB noted that it had already provided a considerable amount of time between issuing IFRS 15 and the effective date, anticipating that some entities would be required to change information technology systems and processes when applying the Standard. The IASB has also provided substantive relief on transition to IFRS 15 by giving entities a choice of transition methods, one of which does not involve the restatement of comparative financial information. In addition, the IASB observed that the proposed amendments noted in paragraph BC453A are expected to clarify, rather than change, the requirements of the Standard.

BC453C   Nonetheless, the IASB decided to propose a deferral of the effective date of IFRS 15 by one year to 1 January 2018 because of the combination of the following factors that result in the circumstances surrounding the implementation of IFRS 15 being exceptional:

(a)   The IASB acknowledged that, although intended to provide clarity, the proposed amendments to IFRS 15 noted in paragraph BC453A may affect some entities that would wish to apply any amendments at the same time as they first apply IFRS 15. Those entities are likely to wish to avoid reporting changes to revenue when first implementing the Standard and then, within a year or two, potentially reporting further changes to revenue as a result of applying any amendments to the Standard. For those entities, a deferral of the effective date by one year would provide additional time to implement any amendments to the Standard.

(b)   IFRS 15 was issued later than had been anticipated when the IASB set the effective date of the Standard, which absorbed some of the implementation time that entities were expecting to have.

  (c) IFRS 15 is a converged Standard with Topic 606—although this was not the only consideration, the IASB observed that there are benefits for a broad range of stakeholders of retaining an effective date that is aligned with the effective date of Topic 606.

BC453D Accordingly, the IASB published the Exposure Draft *Effective Date of IFRS 15* in May 2015 proposing to defer the effective date of IFRS 15 by one year.

BC453E The IASB concluded that a one-year deferral would be sufficient in terms of providing additional time to implement IFRS 15. IASB members observed that the issuance of IFRS 15 in May 2014 had been later than anticipated by some months, not years. Accordingly, a deferral of the effective date of IFRS 15 for anything longer than one year would unnecessarily delay transition by many entities to a new Standard that the IASB views as a substantial improvement to financial reporting.

BC453F Almost all respondents to the Exposure Draft agreed with the proposal to defer the effective date of IFRS 15 for one or more of the reasons noted by the IASB, some noting the exceptional nature of the circumstances surrounding the implementation of IFRS 15. Most also agreed that a one-year deferral should be sufficient and would improve the quality of implementation.

BC453G In the light of the feedback received, the IASB confirmed its decision to defer the effective date of the Standard. The IASB did not change its previous decision to permit early application of IFRS 15.

BC453H For factors similar to those considered by the IASB, the FASB issued an Accounting Standards Update 2015-14 *Revenue from Contracts with Customers (Topic 606): Deferral of the Effective Date* in August 2015 also deferring the effective date of Topic 606 for all entities by one year. Consequently, a public entity would be required to apply Topic 606 to annual reporting periods beginning after 15 December 2017. The FASB decided to permit early application of Topic 606 by all entities, but not before the original effective date of Topic 606 for a public entity (ie annual reporting periods beginning after 15 December 2016).

Clarifications to IFRS 15 (amendments issued in April 2016)

BC453I As explained in paragraph BC453C, one of the considerations of the IASB in deferring the effective date of IFRS 15 from 1 January 2017 to 1 January 2018 was that the deferral would provide additional time to entities that wish to implement *Clarifications to IFRS 15* along with IFRS 15. Consequently, the IASB set an effective date for *Clarifications to IFRS 15* that aligns with the revised effective date of IFRS 15.

BC453J Furthermore, the IASB decided that an entity should be permitted to apply *Clarifications to IFRS 15* earlier than its effective date. This would allow an entity the choice of either:

  (a) applying *Clarifications to IFRS 15* on the same date as it first applies IFRS 15; or

  (b) applying *Clarifications to IFRS 15* at a date later than when it early applies IFRS 15.

In other words, an entity that has decided to early apply IFRS 15 would have the flexibility to apply *Clarifications to IFRS 15* either together with the Standard or at a subsequent date.

Analysis of the effects of IFRS 15

BC454 The objective of financial statements is to provide information about the financial position, financial performance and cash flows of an entity that is useful to a wide range of users of financial statements in making economic decisions. To attain that objective, the boards try to ensure that new requirements meet a significant need and that the overall benefits to economic decision-making that would result from improved financial reporting justify the costs of providing such information. For example, the boards consider the comparative advantage that preparers have in developing information, compared with the costs that users of financial statements would incur to develop surrogate information. In this evaluation, the boards recognise that the costs of implementing a new standard might not be borne evenly by participants in the financial reporting system. However, both the users of financial statements and the entities that prepare those financial statements benefit from improvements in financial reporting that facilitate the functioning of markets for capital, including credit and the efficient allocation of resources in the economy.

BC455 The IASB is committed to assessing and sharing knowledge about the likely costs of implementing new requirements and the likely, associated ongoing costs and benefits of each new Standard—these costs and benefits are collectively referred to as 'effects'. The evaluation of these effects is necessarily subjective and qualitative. This is because quantifying costs and, particularly, benefits, is inherently difficult. Although other standard-setters undertake similar types of analyses, there is a lack of sufficiently well-established and reliable techniques for quantifying this analysis. Consequently, the IASB sees this analysis of the effects as being part of an evolving process. In addition, the assessment undertaken is that of the likely effects of the new requirements because the actual effects would not be known until after the new requirements had been applied. These are subsequently analysed through the Post-implementation Review process.

Overview

BC456 As explained in paragraphs BC2–BC3, the boards developed IFRS 15 to eliminate the inconsistencies and weaknesses in previous revenue recognition requirements and to improve disclosure requirements related to revenue. However, throughout the project, many preparers and some users of financial statements explained that they did not perceive significant weaknesses in previous revenue recognition requirements. Therefore, those preparers and users questioned whether the benefits of applying a new revenue standard would justify the costs of implementing that standard.

BC457 To gain insight on the likely effects of IFRS 15, the boards conducted extensive consultation with interested parties through the formal exposure of the proposals and outreach activities. This consultation included three formal exposure documents—a Discussion Paper and two Exposure Drafts—in response to which the boards received and assessed more than 1,500 comment letters. Over the course of the project, the boards and staff also held more than 650 meetings with users of financial statements, preparers, auditors, regulators and other interested parties in a wide range of industries and a number of jurisdictions. Those meetings included general educational sessions about the proposals and in-depth discussions in relation to particular topics. Some meetings also focused on gaining an understanding of the effects of the proposals in specific industries or on particular transactions. In some cases, the boards undertook additional outreach in those specific industries or on those particular topics for which there were significant operational or other concerns about the effects of the boards' proposals. For example, because of the disparate views of preparers and users of financial statements on the topic of disclosure requirements, the boards sought further feedback in four workshops that brought user and preparer groups together to discuss how to balance the requirements to be more useful for users of financial statements and less burdensome for preparers (see paragraph BC328). In addition, because of the effect of the principles for allocating the transaction price on a typical mobile phone contract, the boards also held a number of meetings with representatives from the telecommunications industry to better understand their concerns and so that those concerns could be considered during redeliberations. The boards' consideration of the feedback received from this industry and their conclusions is included in paragraphs BC287–BC293 and BC473–BC476.

BC458   The boards considered in their redeliberations all of the feedback received and, as a result, decided to modify or clarify many aspects of the revenue recognition model to reduce the burden of implementing and applying the proposed requirements. Discussion of this feedback and the resulting changes in different aspects of the model are included throughout the Basis for Conclusions and are summarised in this analysis of the effects.

BC459   Overall, the boards concluded that the improvements to financial reporting would justify the costs of implementing IFRS 15. In making this assessment, the boards considered:

(a)   how revenue from contracts with customers would be reported in the financial statements;

(b)   how the comparability of financial information would be improved and the benefit of better economic decision-making as a result of improved financial reporting;

(c)   the likely compliance costs for preparers of financial statements; and

(d)   the likely costs of analysis for users of financial statements.

Reporting revenue from contracts with customers in the financial statements

BC460   IFRS 15 replaces the previous limited revenue recognition requirements in IFRS and the broad revenue recognition concepts and industry-specific requirements in US GAAP with a robust and comprehensive framework that is applied to all revenue contracts with customers (except for lease, insurance and financial instruments contracts which fall within the scope of other Standards). This framework provides a basis that should be more easily applied to complex transactions and that provides timely guidance for evolving revenue transactions.

BC461 The framework in IFRS 15 also fills a gap by providing requirements for revenue transactions that had not previously been addressed comprehensively, such as transactions for revenue for the provision of services and for revenue resulting from licences of intellectual property. In addition, IFRS 15 provides requirements for issues such as contract modifications that were previously addressed only for a particular industry. IFRS 15 also provides improved requirements for some transactions such as multiple-element arrangements (see paragraphs BC470–BC472).

BC462 By providing a comprehensive framework, one of the most significant effects of IFRS 15 in reporting revenue from contracts with customers is greater consistency in the accounting for economically similar transactions. This is because the diversity in practice that developed as a result of weaknesses in previous revenue recognition requirements in IFRS and US GAAP would be eliminated. However, the previous inconsistencies in the accounting and the diversity in practice that existed before the issuance of IFRS 15 may mean that the nature and extent of the changes would likely vary between entities and industries. For example, some industries, such as the telecommunications and software industries, may have significant changes. This is because those industries had narrow and transaction-specific industry revenue recognition requirements in US GAAP (which were often referred to by entities applying IFRS). However, other industries, such as the construction industry, may see minimal changes overall but significant changes for particular entities or jurisdictions that may have interpreted previous requirements differently to apply to their specific transactions. For other contracts, such as straightforward retail transactions, IFRS 15 would have little, if any, effect. The boards were aware of those varying effects when developing IFRS 15 and took them into account in their decision-making. In many cases, the boards observed that the requirements in IFRS 15 may be broadly consistent with previous revenue recognition requirements or practices, thus limiting the effects of IFRS 15 for many entities.

BC463 In making their assessment of the nature of the changes in the reporting of revenue from contracts with customers (ie the recognition and measurement of revenue), the boards observed that the following parts of the revenue recognition model are expected to result in the most significant changes for some entities:

(a) transfer of control: basis for the timing of revenue recognition;

(b) identification of performance obligations in a contract;

(c) allocating the transaction price to performance obligations based on relative stand-alone selling prices; and

(d) measurement of revenue.

Transfer of control: basis for the timing of revenue recognition

BC464 Previous revenue recognition requirements typically determined the timing of revenue recognition depending on whether the asset transferred was a good or a service. Both IFRS and US GAAP required revenue to be recognised for goods when risks and rewards transferred and, for services, as the service was performed. However, both approaches presented challenges in determining when to recognise revenue and often resulted in accounting for economically similar transactions differently. For example, when determining when to recognise revenue for the transfer of a good, it was often difficult for an entity to judge whether a preponderance (or some other balance) of the risks and rewards had been transferred to the customer. In some contracts, there could be significant difficulty in interpreting whether the asset to be transferred was a good or a service, therefore, making it difficult to rationalise why for one asset, revenue should be recognised only when the asset was complete (ie a good), whereas for another asset, revenue should be recognised continuously as that asset is created (ie a service). Some of this difficulty was due to the vague and narrow definition of services in US GAAP and the lack of clear rationale (ie a Basis for Conclusions) in IFRS for why, in some cases, revenue should be recognised for a service over time. In some cases, entities that applied IFRS consulted the rationale in US GAAP for why revenue would be recognised over time for a service. That rationale explained that this was because the entity was transferring a service continuously. However, that rationale did not address many specific application questions in IFRS about determining whether specific items met the definition of a service. In response, the IASB developed an Interpretation to help clarify whether the construction of real estate would be accounted for as a good or a service (ie a performance obligation satisfied at a point in time or over time). However, many observed that the principle in that Interpretation was difficult to understand and apply.

BC465 In the light of the challenges with previous revenue recognition requirements, the boards observed that applying the single framework in IFRS 15 to determine the timing of revenue recognition for both goods *and* services would improve the consistency in accounting for revenue. This is because the framework would be applied to the attributes of the goods and services transferred, together with the terms of the contract, rather than only to the type of contract. In addition, the boards determined that the core principle in IFRS 15, based on the notion of transferring control, would further improve the consistency of reporting because it would provide a more objective assessment for determining the timing of revenue recognition.

BC466 The boards noted that the application of the core principle may not result in changes for all contracts. For example, the boards acknowledge that for construction contracts, the application of the criteria for when a good or service transfers over time (and thus, is a performance obligation satisfied over time) in IFRS 15 would likely broadly result in the same accounting as required by previous revenue recognition requirements for contracts that met the definition of 'services'. However, the boards observed that the application of IFRS 15 could result in changes for those contracts for which, under previous revenue recognition requirements, it may have been difficult to conclude that the contracted activities were services. This may occur in some manufacturing service contracts and contracts for the construction of residential real estate.

Application guidance: licensing

BC467 Previous revenue recognition requirements did not determine the timing of revenue recognition for licences based on an assessment of whether the licence was a good or a service. However, those previous requirements were limited and industry-specific. For example, in US GAAP, revenue recognition for licences differed depending on the industry (for example, franchisors, media and entertainment and software) and often was based on features of the licence (for example, licence period or payment terms). Therefore, the previous revenue recognition requirements did not coalesce into a single principle or rule. In IFRS, previous revenue recognition requirements for licences required revenue to be recognised 'in accordance with the substance of the agreement'. However, because those requirements provided minimal guidance on how an entity should assess the 'substance of the agreement', there was significant diversity in practice for the accounting for licences.

BC468 The boards included in IFRS 15 application guidance on how an entity should assess and account for its licence arrangements. That guidance is anchored in applying key steps of the revenue recognition model—specifically, identifying the performance obligations in a contract and assessing the transfer of control, which the boards operationalised by differentiating between two types of licences. The boards also decided to include in the application guidance the rationale for the guidance and additional illustrative examples to explain the intention, objective and application of those steps and the differentiation between licences.

BC469 The detailed application guidance for licences in IFRS 15 is intended to help entities determine when a licence is transferred to a customer and thus when revenue can be recognised. Because of the previous diversity in practice in revenue recognition for licences, the addition of the application guidance in IFRS 15 may change practice for some entities. However, the boards observed that the diversity and inconsistencies that previously existed meant that some changes in practice would have occurred regardless of how the boards decided to apply the revenue recognition model to licences.

Identification of performance obligations in a contract

BC470 The boards cited deficiencies in previous IFRS and US GAAP in the accounting for arrangements with multiple elements as one of the reasons for adding the Revenue Recognition project to its agenda. Although US GAAP was improved after the Revenue Recognition project began, deficiencies still existed. For example, there was no definition of a 'deliverable' in previous US GAAP, even though the term was used to determine the unit of account for revenue transactions. IFRS had even fewer requirements because it only acknowledged that revenue could be recognised for 'separately identifiable components of a single transaction', without providing guidance on how to determine what constituted a 'separately identifiable component'.

BC471   IFRS 15 addresses those weaknesses by defining promised goods or services that should be accounted for separately as performance obligations. IFRS 15 defines a performance obligation and provides criteria and factors for identifying performance obligations, which are based on the notion of distinct goods or services. These requirements were developed on the basis of extensive consultation and attempts to separate contracts in a meaningful and cost-effective way with intuitive outcomes.

BC472   The boards observed that the requirements in IFRS 15 for identifying performance obligations may not result in significant changes for many entities. This is because many entities have developed practices to separate contracts with customers in a manner that was similar to the requirements in IFRS 15. However, the boards observed that because there were specific requirements in previous US GAAP, there would be a change in the accounting for incidental obligations and marketing incentives (see paragraphs BC87–BC93). This is because the requirements in IFRS 15 would require an entity to identify and recognise revenue for those goods or services, when previously they may have been recognised as an expense or ignored for the purposes of revenue recognition. The boards observed that two industries that would be particularly affected by this change are the automotive industry (which previously recognised as an expense the promise of maintenance with the purchase of an automobile) and the telecommunications industry (which sometimes did not attribute any revenue to the handsets provided as part of a bundled offering).

Allocating the transaction price to performance obligations based on relative stand-alone selling prices

BC473   Previous revenue recognition requirements in IFRS and US GAAP for the allocation of consideration in multiple-element arrangements were different. Before IFRS 15, there were no general requirements in IFRS for allocation of consideration (there were some specific requirements in an Interpretation for one type of transaction—that is, customer loyalty points). This was due in part to the lack of guidance on defining an element or unit of account for revenue. In contrast, US GAAP specified that an allocation of the consideration to multiple-elements should be made on a relative selling price basis for some industries. US GAAP also included explicit requirements for some industries on determining the selling price of an item, which required an entity to use vendor-specific objective evidence, but it also permitted the use of estimation techniques in some cases. However, the allocation requirements in the software industry strictly prohibited allocation to individual elements unless the entity obtained vendor-specific objective evidence for all elements of the contract. Because there was often no vendor-specific objective evidence available for one or more undelivered elements, revenue recognition was delayed until all elements had been delivered.

BC474   Although the principle for allocating the transaction price in IFRS 15 is broadly consistent with previous US GAAP for some industries—that is, allocating the transaction price on a relative stand-alone selling price basis—there may be a change in some outcomes, in particular in the software industry. This is because the boards decided to eliminate the restrictive, industry-specific requirements in US GAAP for allocating consideration in software arrangements (ie the requirement to have vendor-specific objective evidence for all elements in the arrangements before consideration can be allocated). Instead, IFRS 15 requires an entity to estimate the stand-alone selling price of a good or service, if the stand-alone selling price is not directly observable. The boards observed that this change would permit an entity in the software industry to better depict performance by recognising revenue for performance obligations when they are satisfied, instead of when all performance in a contract is complete. In some instances, the boards observed that this may permit entities to eliminate the disclosure of non-GAAP measures that were created because the outcomes from applying previous revenue recognition requirements did not faithfully depict an entity's performance.

BC475 The boards observed that the requirements for allocating the transaction price in IFRS 15, in conjunction with the requirements for identifying performance obligations, may also result in a significant change in the accounting for bundled arrangements in the automotive and telecommunications industries. As explained in paragraph BC457, the boards' consideration of the feedback received from the telecommunications industry and their conclusions are included in paragraphs BC287–BC293.

BC476 The boards observed that even though IFRS 15 may result in significant differences in the allocation of the transaction price to performance obligations (and consequently in the amount and timing of the recognition of revenue) in some industries, the change was necessary to provide greater consistency in the recognition of revenue across industries. In addition, the boards observed that the effects were a consequence of the boards' objectives of eliminating industry-specific requirements and defining a common framework that could be applied to all revenue transactions. Furthermore, the boards observed that the allocation requirements in IFRS 15 would result in accounting for a transaction in a manner that more closely reflects the underlying economics.

Measurement of revenue

BC477 Previous requirements for the measurement of revenue in US GAAP were limited and differed for goods and for services. US GAAP did not provide specific requirements for how to measure revenue for goods, but it nevertheless restricted the amount of revenue that could be recognised for goods to the amount that was fixed or determinable. IFRS required revenue to be recognised for the transfer of goods and services at the fair value of the consideration received/receivable; but, there was no guidance on how to apply that principle because IFRS 13 *Fair Value Measurement* was not effective until 1 January 2013. Consequently, that principle was not consistently applied. In addition, IFRS contained little guidance on how to measure variable consideration. However, both IFRS and US GAAP indicated that the amount of revenue to be recognised for services should be limited to an amount that could be 'estimated reliably'.

BC478 Thus, IFRS 15 appears to be a significant change from previous revenue recognition requirements because it introduces a customer consideration model and measures revenue using the transaction price, which is defined as the amount to which the entity expects to be entitled in exchange for transferring goods or services. However, previous practices were broadly consistent with this approach and many entities determined the amount of revenue on the basis of the amounts the customer promised to pay. Where IFRS 15 differs from previous revenue recognition requirements is in the additional guidance it provides for estimating consideration when it is variable and in constraining those estimates to ensure revenue is not overstated. In addition, IFRS 15 provides requirements related to other aspects of measuring revenue such as accounting for significant financing components, non-cash consideration and consideration payable to a customer.

BC479   The additional guidance includes two methods for estimating variable consideration, which may not substantially change the amount of revenue recognised in many industries in which robust estimation methods have been developed over time. However, it may result in changes in the timing of revenue recognised in other cases, for which estimation of variable consideration was either prohibited or not used in the recognition of revenue. For example, in some distribution channels, entities may not have estimated the price of a good or service when that price depended on the eventual sale to an end customer. In those cases, revenue was not recognised until that final sale occurred. The boards concluded that the additional guidance for estimation methods should ensure that performance is better reflected in the financial statements in those cases and should provide greater consistency in estimating variable consideration. The additional guidance would also provide users of financial statements with more transparency on the estimation process, which was often masked with undefined terms such as 'best estimates'.

BC480   In addition, the requirements for constraining estimates of variable consideration provide entities with a more specific approach for assessing the likelihood of an entity being entitled to variable consideration and, therefore, whether or not to include an estimate of that variable consideration in the amount of revenue recognised. It would also give users of financial statements more confidence in the amount of revenue recognised in the financial statements by requiring a consistent approach to estimating the amount of variable consideration to which an entity is entitled. The boards included the requirements for constraining estimates of variable consideration in part because of feedback from users of financial statements who demanded that estimates should be of high quality, but also because a significant portion of errors in financial statements have related to the overstatement of revenue.

Improved comparability of financial information and better economic decision-making

BC481   Before the issuance of IFRS 15, there were significant differences in accounting for economically similar revenue transactions, both within and across industries for entities applying US GAAP. There was also significant diversity in practice in accounting for revenue transactions for entities applying IFRS. Those differences made it difficult for users of financial statements to understand and compare revenue numbers. As explained in paragraphs BC460–BC480, some of this diversity arose because there were limited revenue recognition requirements in IFRS in general and on particular topics. Furthermore, the requirements that were provided were difficult to apply to complex transactions, in part because there was no rationale for those requirements (ie there was no Basis for Conclusions). Those differences also arose because previous revenue recognition requirements in US GAAP were voluminous and often industry-specific or transaction-specific, which also created difficulty for users of financial statements in interpreting the information about revenue. The boards noted that the diversity in practice and challenges to users were often amplified for entities applying IFRS because some preparers selectively referenced US GAAP.

BC482   Analysis of revenue by users of financial statements was made even more difficult because previous disclosure requirements for revenue were inadequate. Consequently, users of financial statements found it difficult to understand an entity's revenues, as well as the judgements and estimates made by that entity in recognising those revenues. However, many entities acknowledged a need to provide investors with additional information about revenue and therefore provided this information in other reports outside the financial statements (for example, in earnings releases and shareholder reports).

BC483   By providing a robust, comprehensive framework that would be applied by entities applying both IFRS and US GAAP, IFRS 15 would eliminate the previous diversity in practice and create greater comparability across entities, industries and reporting periods. In addition, the boards observed that a common revenue Standard should make the financial reporting of revenue comparable between entities that prepare financial statements in accordance with IFRS or US GAAP, resulting in a significant benefit to users. Furthermore, by providing a rationale for the requirements (ie a Basis for Conclusions), the framework should be more easily applied to a broad range of transactions and contracts.

BC484   In addition, IFRS 15 provides comprehensive disclosure requirements that should greatly improve the information about revenue reported in the financial statements (see paragraphs BC327–BC361). Specifically, the information about revenue would enable users of financial statements to better understand an entity's contracts with customers and revenue from those contracts and to better predict cash flows. This information should also help users of financial statements to make more informed economic decisions. The boards acknowledged that these improvements may increase the costs of the application of IFRS 15 for preparers. However, the boards concluded that these costs were necessary to improve the usefulness of financial reporting in an area that is critical for users of financial statements to the analysis and understanding of an entity's performance and prospects.

BC485   During outreach, the boards learned that the disclosures required by IFRS 15 may help some entities to eliminate various alternative reporting measures that were created because previous revenue recognition requirements did not adequately depict their performance. Conversely, the boards noted that other industries in which changes may be more significant may be required to create alternative performance measures to help users understand the difference between previous accounting requirements and the requirements under IFRS 15. However, because the requirements adequately depict performance, the boards do not expect that these performance measures would be necessary in the longer term.

Compliance costs for preparers

BC486   As with any new requirements, there will be costs to implement IFRS 15. The breadth of industries and entities that will be required to apply IFRS 15, and the diversity in practice that existed under previous revenue recognition requirements, make it difficult to generalise the costs to preparers. However, because of the breadth of industries and entities that will be affected, most entities will incur at least some costs. Broadly, the boards expect that a majority of preparers may incur the following costs:

(a)   costs to implement changes in or develop new systems, processes and controls used to gather and archive contract data, make required estimates and provide required disclosures, possibly including fees paid to external consultants;

(b)   costs to hire additional employees that may be needed to comply with IFRS 15 and modify processes and internal controls accordingly;

(c)   incremental fees paid to external auditors to audit the financial statements in the period of initial application of IFRS 15;

(d)   costs required to educate management, finance and other personnel about the effects of IFRS 15; and

(e)   costs required to educate users of financial statements about the effects on the financial statements.

BC487   Many of the costs listed in paragraph BC486 will be non-recurring, because they will be incurred only upon initial application of IFRS 15. However, some entities that expect significant changes as a result of applying IFRS 15 expect that the continued application of IFRS 15 will likely cause the following long-term increases in costs:

(a)   increase in audit fees because of the increased volume of disclosures and the difficulty of auditing some of the required estimates (for example, estimates of stand-alone selling price and variable consideration);

(b)   costs to maintain improved systems and make modifications for transactions; and

(c)   higher personnel costs.

BC488   The boards considered those costs in their analysis of the effects for the Standard as a whole and in relation to specific provisions in IFRS 15 when making their decisions. Board members and staff consulted extensively across a wide range of industries and jurisdictions to better understand some of the operational issues arising from the proposals in the Discussion Paper and both Exposure Drafts. The boards took that feedback into consideration in their redeliberations and, as a result, modified or clarified many aspects of the revenue recognition model to reduce the burden of implementing and applying the requirements. Those decisions and their rationale are documented throughout the Basis for Conclusions in relation to specific aspects of the model such as variable consideration and significant financing components. Those clarifications and modifications included:

(a) clarifying the use of portfolios—the boards clarified that many entities would not need to develop systems to account for each contract individually, especially entities that have a large volume of similar contracts with similar classes of customer. In those cases, the boards noted that entities may apply the requirements to a portfolio of similar contracts.

(b) practical expedients—the boards added some practical expedients (for example, in the requirements for adjusting the transaction price for significant financing components) to simplify compliance with the requirements in circumstances in which the boards determined that applying the practical expedient would have a limited effect on the amount or timing of revenue recognition.

(c) disclosure requirements—the boards eliminated the rigidity in the disclosure requirements proposed in the 2011 Exposure Draft that required entities to provide a detailed reconciliation of their contract balances. Instead, the boards decided to require only the opening and closing balances as well as some information on the changes in those balances. The boards also provided similar relief for the reconciliation proposed in the 2011 Exposure Draft for the costs to obtain or fulfil a contract.

(d) transition requirements—the boards expected that the costs of the systems and operational changes would be incurred primarily during the transition from previous revenue recognition requirements to IFRS 15. Therefore, to ease implementation costs and complexities associated with transition to IFRS 15, the boards decided to provide practical expedients that an entity may elect to use when applying the requirements retrospectively. In addition, the boards introduced an alternative transition method (ie the cumulative catch-up transition method) that would alleviate the costs of transition for many entities because it would not require restatement of prior periods.

(e) additional illustrations—the boards responded to requests from respondents to provide examples that would illustrate the various aspects of IFRS 15 by providing educational guidance designed to help with implementation and understandability wherever possible. The boards concluded that this would help to reduce both the initial and ongoing cost of compliance, as well as enhancing the consistency of application and therefore comparability of financial statements.

Costs of analysis for users of financial statements

BC489 The boards note that, as with all new requirements, there will be an educational and adjustment period for users of financial statements, during which they may incur costs. Those costs may include costs to modify their processes and analyses. However, the costs are likely to be non-recurring and are likely to be offset by a longer-term reduction in costs from the additional information that would be provided by the improved disclosure requirements. Users of financial statements may also observe a longer-term reduction in education costs, because of the common framework created by IFRS 15, which applies across jurisdictions, industries and transactions.

BC490   In the boards' view, the significant benefits to users of financial statements from IFRS 15 will justify the costs that the users may incur. Those benefits include:

(a)   greater comparability and consistency of reporting revenue from contracts with customers;

(b)   a better depiction of entities' performance; and

(c)   improved understanding of entities' contracts and revenue-generating activities.

Conclusion

BC491   The boards concluded that the issuance of IFRS 15[12] achieves their objectives as outlined in paragraph BC3. This is because IFRS 15 provides a robust and comprehensive framework that:

(a)   will apply to a broad range of transactions and industries and will improve the comparability of the recognition of revenue across industries and jurisdictions;

(b)   can be applied to complex transactions and evolving transactions, resulting in greater consistency in the recognition of revenue; and

(c)   will require enhanced disclosures that will improve the understandability of revenue, which is a critical part of the analysis of an entity's performance and prospects.

BC492   In the light of these achievements, the boards determined that the issuance of IFRS 15 would result in an overall improvement to financial reporting. The boards also concluded that these benefits would be ongoing and would justify the costs of implementing IFRS 15 (for example, systems and operational changes) that would be incurred primarily during the transition from previous revenue recognition requirements.

BC493   However, because of differences in their previous revenue recognition requirements, the boards noted that their rationale for the conclusion that IFRS 15 results in 'an improvement to financial reporting' was slightly different. The differences in their rationale are as follows:

(a)   Previous revenue recognition requirements in US GAAP were rules-based and provided specific requirements for particular transactions and industries. In addition, there were transactions that were not directly in the scope of specific guidance. Consequently, economically similar transactions were often accounted for differently. Overall, the robust and comprehensive framework in Topic 606 should improve comparability in the accounting for economically similar transactions and should result in accounting that better reflects the economics of those transactions.

---

12   As indicated in footnote 1, unless indicated otherwise, all references to IFRS 15 in this Basis for Conclusions can be read as also referring to Topic 606 in the FASB's Accounting Standards Codification®.

(b) As described in paragraph BC460, the previous revenue recognition requirements in IFRS were limited. In particular, IFRS did not include general requirements related to many key issues in revenue recognition such as multiple-element arrangements and how to allocate consideration to those elements. In addition, the lack of a Basis for Conclusions in those previous revenue recognition requirements in IFRS created challenges in assessing how to apply the principles in those requirements. In combination, these factors contributed to diversity in practice across jurisdictions and industries. By providing a comprehensive framework and a Basis for Conclusions, IFRS 15 should be a significant improvement to the previous revenue recognition requirements. Consequently, IFRS 15 should eliminate that previous diversity in practice and thus improve financial reporting.

Consequential amendments

Sales of assets that are not an output of an entity's ordinary activities

BC494 For the transfer of non-financial assets that are not an output of an entity's ordinary activities, the boards decided to amend their respective Standards to require that an entity apply the requirements from IFRS 15 for the following topics:

(a) control—to determine when to derecognise the asset.

(b) measurement—to determine the amount of the gain or loss to recognise when the asset is derecognised (including any constraints on the transaction price because it is variable).

BC495 The FASB also decided to apply the requirements from Topic 606 for the existence of a contract to transfer a non-financial asset. Those requirements require an entity to determine whether the parties are committed to perform under the contract, which can be difficult in sales of real estate in which the seller has provided significant financing to the purchaser.

BC496 Those amendments will result in changes to IAS 16 *Property, Plant and Equipment*, IAS 38 and IAS 40 *Investment Property* and to Topic 360 and Topic 350 *Intangibles—Goodwill and Other*. The changes to those Standards will result in the same accounting requirements under IFRS and US GAAP for the transfer of non-financial assets that are not an output of an entity's ordinary activities. However, because the requirements in those Standards were previously different under IFRS and US GAAP, the boards have different reasons for making those changes.

Consequential amendments to US GAAP

BC497 A contract for the sale of real estate that is an output of an entity's ordinary activities meets the definition of a contract with a customer and, therefore, is within the scope of Topic 606. Because Subtopic 360-20 *Real Estate Sales* provided requirements for recognising profit on *all* real estate sales, regardless of whether real estate is an output of an entity's ordinary activities, the FASB considered the implications of retaining the requirements in Subtopic 360-20 for contracts that are not within the scope of Topic 606. The FASB noted that retaining those requirements could result in an entity recognising the profit or loss on a real estate sale differently, depending on whether the transaction is a contract with a customer. However, there is economically little difference between the sale of real estate that is an output of the entity's ordinary activities and the sale of real estate that is not. Consequently, the difference in accounting should relate only to the presentation of the profit or loss in the statement of comprehensive income—revenue and expense or gain or loss.

BC498 Consequently, the FASB decided to amend Topic 360 and create Subtopic 610-20 *Gains and Losses from the Derecognition of Nonfinancial Assets* to require that an entity apply the requirements in Topic 606 for the existence of a contract, for control, and for measurement of a contract for the transfer of real estate (including in-substance real estate) that is not an output of the entity's ordinary activities. If the real estate is a business (and not an in-substance non-financial asset), the requirements in Subtopic 810-10 for consolidation apply.

BC499 The FASB also decided to specify that an entity apply the requirements in Topic 606 for the existence of a contract, for control and for measurement to contracts for the transfer of all non-financial assets in non-revenue transactions, such as tangible assets within the scope of Topic 360 and intangible assets within the scope of Topic 350. The primary reason for that decision was the lack of clear requirements in US GAAP for accounting for the transfer of non-financial assets when those assets are not an output of an entity's ordinary activities and do not constitute a business or non-profit activity. In addition, the FASB decided, due to the lack of guidance in Topics 350 and 360, to add guidance for how to account for a contract that fails to meet the criteria in paragraph 606-10-25-1.

Consequential amendments to IFRS

BC500 In IFRS, an entity selling an asset within the scope of IAS 16, IAS 38 or IAS 40 would have applied the recognition principles of the previous revenue Standards in IFRS to determine when to derecognise the asset and, in determining the gain or loss on the transfer, would have measured the consideration at fair value. However, the IASB noted that there is diversity in practice in the recognition of the gain or loss when the transfer of those assets involves variable consideration, because the previous revenue Standard in IFRS did not provide specific requirements for variable consideration. The IASB decided that requiring application of the requirements in IFRS 15 for control and for measurement (including constraining the amount of variable consideration used in determining the gain or loss) would eliminate the diversity in practice because the requirements in IFRS 15 provide a clear principle for accounting for variable consideration.

BC501 The IASB considered whether it should retain fair value as the measurement basis for transfers of non-financial assets within the scope of IAS 16, IAS 38 and IAS 40. However, the IASB rejected this proposal and, as explained in paragraph BC500, decided to require that an entity apply the measurement requirements in IFRS 15 to transfers of non-financial assets that are not an output of the entity's ordinary activities, for the following reasons:

(a) measuring the gain on the transfers of non-financial assets that are not an output of the entity's ordinary activities by using the same requirements as for measuring revenue provides users of financial statements with useful information. The IASB decided that it would provide useful information if entities apply the requirements for constraining estimates of variable consideration to any gain that will be recognised on the transfer of the non-financial asset. The IASB acknowledged that in some cases this may result in a loss on the transfer when the transferred asset has a cost basis that is greater than the constrained consideration, which may occur when the asset has a cost basis that is determined using fair value. However, the IASB noted that this outcome is appropriate and useful to users, because of the significant uncertainty about the variable consideration. The IASB also noted that this outcome is consistent with the outcome in a transaction with a customer in which the variable consideration is constrained, but the entity has transferred control of the good or service to the customer.

(b) it is not necessary to measure the gains on the transfers of non-financial assets to be consistent with other asset disposals, such as disposals of an entity, that are accounted for at fair value in accordance with other Standards (for example, IFRS 10). This is because transfers of non-financial assets that are not an output of an entity's ordinary activities are more like transfers of assets to customers, rather than other asset disposals.

(c) applying the measurement requirements in IFRS 15 achieves consistency with US GAAP.

A separate project

BC502 The boards also considered whether they should consider the changes to the guidance on transfers of non-financial assets in a separate project. The boards noted that undertaking a separate project would mean that changes to existing Standards would not be made until that project had been completed and became effective. Because of the boards' other standard-setting priorities, and the time required to complete all relevant due process steps for issuing a standard, it might be several years before the existing requirements were replaced. The boards observed that the implications of not proceeding with the proposed consequential amendments would have been as follows:

(a) for IFRS reporters, the IASB would have needed to amend IAS 16, IAS 38 and IAS 40 to include the revenue recognition criteria from previous revenue Standards in IFRS. This would have resulted in different recognition and measurement requirements for transfers of non-financial assets as compared to contracts with customers.

(b) for US GAAP reporters, there would have been two sets of recognition and measurement requirements for real estate sales, depending on whether the transfer was with a customer. In addition, no specific requirements would have been provided in US GAAP for transfers of non-financial assets (other than real estate) within the scope of Subtopic 360-10 (for example, equipment) or Topic 350 (for example, intangible assets).

BC503   Consequently, the boards reaffirmed their decision in the 2011 Exposure Draft that consequential amendments should be made, because this results in consistency in the accounting for the transfers of non-financial assets between IFRS and US GAAP, addresses the lack of requirements for the accounting for transfers of non-financial assets in US GAAP and eliminates possible complexities that might result from retaining separate recognition criteria for transfers of non-financial assets in IFRS.

Transition for first-time adopters of IFRS

BC504   During redeliberations of the transition requirements, the IASB considered whether to amend IFRS 1 *First-time Adoption of International Financial Reporting Standards* to allow a first-time adopter of IFRS to use the same transition methods for adopting IFRS 15 as specified in paragraph C3 of IFRS 15 as follows:

(a)   retrospectively to each prior period presented in accordance with IAS 8, subject to the practical expedients in paragraph C5 of IFRS 15; and

(b)   retrospectively with the cumulative effect of initially applying IFRS 15 recognised at the date of initial application (for a first-time adopter of IFRS, this would be the entity's first IFRS reporting period) in accordance with paragraphs C7–C8 of IFRS 15.

BC505   The IASB decided that the practical expedients in paragraph C5 of IFRS 15 should also apply to a first-time adopter, because both first-time adopters and entities that already apply IFRS would face similar challenges. The IASB observed that IFRS 1 requires that the accounting policies effective at the end of the first IFRS reporting period are applied to all reporting periods from the date of transition to IFRS onwards. This is identical to retrospective application for entities already applying IFRS. Some IASB members also noted that in many jurisdictions that have not yet adopted IFRS, revenue standards are similar to current IFRS. In those jurisdictions, the starting point for transition for a first-time adopter will be similar to entities already applying IFRS.

BC506   The IASB also clarified that, for any of the practical expedients in paragraph C5 of IFRS 15 that the entity uses, the entity should apply that expedient consistently to all reporting periods presented and disclose which expedients have been used, together with the estimated effect of applying those expedients (see paragraph C6 of IFRS 15).

BC507   Paragraphs BC439–BC444 explain the boards' rationale for including an additional transition method in IFRS 15. That method requires an entity (that is not a first-time adopter of IFRS) to apply IFRS 15 retrospectively with the cumulative effect of initially applying IFRS 15 recognised in the current year (referred to as the 'cumulative catch-up' transition method). Using the cumulative catch-up transition method, an entity would apply the requirements retrospectively only to contracts that are not completed at the beginning of the date of initial application (which, if applied to a first-time adopter would be the entity's first IFRS reporting period).

BC508 However, the IASB decided not to amend IFRS 1 to permit first-time adopters of IFRS to use the cumulative catch-up transition method because it is not consistent with the principles of IFRS 1. This is because it would eliminate comparability within a first-time adopter's first IFRS financial statements by providing relief from restating comparative years. The IASB also observed that the cumulative catch-up transition method may not reduce the burden of retrospective application because it would potentially require two separate reconciliations of equity—one for the transition to IFRS, which would be recognised in the earliest comparative period, and one for the transition to IFRS 15, which would be recognised at the beginning of the entity's first IFRS reporting period. This would not only be challenging for preparers, but might also be confusing for users of financial statements.

BC509 Despite deciding not to amend IFRS 1 to allow first-time adopters to use the cumulative catch-up transition method, the IASB decided to amend IFRS 1 to provide an optional exemption for first-time adopters from the requirements of IFRS 15 in accounting for contracts completed before the earliest period presented. Under this exemption, a first-time adopter would not be required to restate all of its contracts for which it has recognised all of its revenue in accordance with its previous GAAP before the earliest period presented.

Summary of main changes from the 2011 Exposure Draft

BC510 The main changes from the proposals in the 2011 Exposure Draft are as follows:

(a) IFRS 15 includes additional requirements related to identifying a contract with a customer. Specifically, IFRS 15 includes an additional criterion that must be met before an entity can apply the requirements in IFRS 15 to a contract. This criterion in paragraph 9(e) of IFRS 15 requires an entity to conclude that it is probable that a customer will pay the consideration to which the entity will be entitled by assessing the customer's ability and intention to pay. In addition, IFRS 15 provides guidance for accounting for contracts that do not meet the specified criteria and thus cannot apply IFRS 15.

(b) IFRS 15 clarifies the objective of the requirements for constraining estimates of variable consideration and provides a level of confidence of 'highly probable' for determining when to include those estimates in the transaction price. This represents a change from the 2011 Exposure Draft, which specified that an entity could only recognise revenue for estimates of variable consideration when an entity was 'reasonably assured' that it would be entitled to that amount.

(c) IFRS 15 provides additional guidance on the allocation of the transaction price to performance obligations:

(i)   the residual approach may be used for two or more goods or services with highly variable or uncertain stand-alone selling prices if at least one good or service has a stand-alone selling price that is not highly variable or uncertain; and

(ii)   allocation of a discount among performance obligations should be done before using the residual approach to estimate the stand-alone selling price for a good or service with a highly variable or uncertain stand-alone selling price.

(d)   IFRS 15 carries forward from the 2011 Exposure Draft the principles related to identifying performance obligations in a contract and determining whether a performance obligation is satisfied over time. However, IFRS 15 clarifies those principles and provides additional guidance for entities in applying those principles.

(e)   IFRS 15 provides additional guidance for determining when a customer obtains control of a licence, by distinguishing between licences that provide a right to access the entity's intellectual property as it exists throughout the licence period and licences that provide a right to use the entity's intellectual property as it exists at the point in time at which the licence is granted. This determination will affect whether the entity satisfies its performance obligation to transfer a licence at a point in time or over time. This represents a change from the 2011 Exposure Draft, which specified that all licences were transferred to the customer at the point in time at which the customer obtained control of the rights. IFRS 15 also clarifies that before determining when the licence transfers to the customer, an entity considers the promises in the contract and applies the requirements for identifying performance obligations.

(f)   IFRS 15 does not include the requirements proposed in the 2011 Exposure Draft to test a performance obligation to determine whether it is onerous.

(g)   IFRS 15 clarifies the disclosures required for revenue from contracts with customers. Specifically, it requires an entity to provide a combination of qualitative and quantitative information about contract balances. The 2011 Exposure Draft required this disclosure to be provided as a reconciliation of contract balances.

(h)   IFRS 15 provides entities with an additional transition method that does not require a restatement of prior periods. The 2011 Exposure Draft proposed only one transition method (ie a retrospective transition method with practical expedients) that requires a restatement of all previous periods presented.

Dissenting Opinion

Dissenting Opinion from *Clarifications to IFRS 15* Revenue from Contracts with Customers as issued in April 2016

DO1   Mr Ochi voted against the publication of *Clarifications to IFRS 15* Revenue from Contracts with Customers. He agrees with all of the clarifying amendments to IFRS 15 and the additional transition reliefs. However, he disagrees with the IASB's decision to require entities to apply *Clarifications to IFRS 15* retrospectively as if those amendments had been included in IFRS 15 at the date of initial application.

DO2   Referring to the IASB's considerations explained in paragraph BC445T, he thinks that requiring an entity that has applied IFRS 15 before applying these amendments to restate the effects of initially applying IFRS 15 for the effects, if any, of initially applying the amendments is inconsistent with allowing early application of IFRS 15. That entity might be required to restate some contracts twice, first on initially applying IFRS 15 and again on initial application of these amendments. Furthermore, that entity is deprived of the benefit of the new practical expedients added by the IASB.

DO3   Mr Ochi does not disagree with issuing clarifications, if absolutely necessary, to a Standard before its effective date. However, the IASB's actions in issuing any such clarifying amendments should not be perceived as penalising those entities that begin their implementation process early and rewarding those that delay. Such perceptions could discourage entities from starting the implementation of any new Standard on a timely basis.

DO4   Mr Ochi noted that the effective date of the new leases Standard has been set so as to provide a long initial implementation period. In that regard, he believes that allowing early application of a Standard supports the smooth application of new Standards.

DO5   To encourage early application of Standards, he thinks that the IASB should, when deciding the transition requirements for amendments such as *Clarifications to IFRS 15*, give due consideration to those entities that have already early applied the Standard or are in advanced stages of preparing to do so. When deciding the transition requirements, he thinks it is not just a question of considering the extent or potential effect of any clarifications to a Standard; rather it is a matter of principle.

Appendix A
Comparison of IFRS 15 and Topic 606[13]

A1   IFRS 15, together with the FASB's Topic 606, issued in May 2014 completes a joint effort by the IASB and the FASB to improve financial reporting by creating a common revenue standard for IFRS and US GAAP that can be applied consistently across various transactions, industries and capital markets. In IFRS 15 and Topic 606, the boards achieved their goal of reaching the same conclusions on all requirements for the accounting for revenue from contracts with customers. However, there are some minor differences in the standards as issued in May 2014, which are as follows:

     (a)   **Collectability threshold**—the boards included an explicit collectability threshold as one of the criteria that a contract must meet before an entity can recognise revenue. For a contract to meet that criterion, an entity must conclude that it is probable that it will collect the consideration to which it will be entitled in exchange for the goods or services that will be transferred to the customer. In setting the threshold, the boards acknowledged that the term 'probable' has different meanings in IFRS and in US GAAP. However, the boards decided to set the threshold at a level that is consistent with previous revenue recognition practices and requirements in IFRS and in US GAAP. (See paragraphs BC42–BC46.)

     (b)   **Interim disclosure requirements**—the boards noted that the general principles in their respective interim reporting requirements (IAS 34 *Interim Financial Reporting* and Topic 270 *Interim Reporting*) would apply to revenue from contracts with customers. However, the IASB decided to also amend IAS 34 to specifically require the disclosure of disaggregated information of revenue from contracts with customers in interim financial reports. The FASB similarly decided to amend Topic 270, to require a public entity to disclose disaggregated revenue information in interim financial reports, but also made amendments to require information about both contract balances and remaining performance obligations to be disclosed on an interim basis. (See paragraphs BC358–BC361.)

     (c)   **Early application and effective date**—paragraph C1 of IFRS 15 allows entities to apply the requirements early, whereas Topic 606 prohibits a public entity from applying the requirements earlier than the effective date.[14] In addition, the effective date for IFRS 15 is for annual reporting periods beginning on or after 1 January 2017, whereas Topic 606 has an

---

13 This Appendix reflects the differences between IFRS 15 and Topic 606 when those standards were issued in May 2014 updated to reflect the issue of *Clarifications to IFRS 15* in April 2016.

14 The FASB subsequently amended Topic 606 in August 2015 to allow all entities to apply the standard early for annual periods beginning after 15 December 2016. See paragraph BC453H.

effective date for public entities for annual reporting periods beginning after 15 December 2016.[15] (See paragraphs BC452–BC453.)

(d) **Impairment loss reversal**—paragraph 104 of IFRS 15 requires an entity to reverse impairment losses, which is consistent with the requirements for the impairment of assets within the scope of IAS 36 *Impairment of Assets*. In contrast, consistent with other areas of US GAAP, Topic 606 does not allow an entity to reverse an impairment loss on an asset that is recognised in accordance with the guidance on costs to obtain or fulfil a contract. (See paragraphs BC309–BC311.)

(e) **Non-public entity requirements**—there are no specific requirements included in IFRS 15 for non-public entities. Entities that do not have public accountability may apply *IFRS for Small and Medium-sized Entities*. Topic 606 applies to non-public entities, although some specific reliefs relating to disclosure, transition and effective date have been included in Topic 606 for non-public entities.

A1A   As explained in paragraph BC1A, the IASB issued *Clarifications to IFRS 15* in April 2016, which differed in some respects from the amendments to Topic 606 issued by the FASB, and those expected to be issued by the FASB based on its decisions, until March 2016. The differences are as follows:

(a) **Collectability criterion**—The FASB decided to amend paragraph 606-10-25-1(e) of Topic 606 (equivalent to paragraph 9(e) of IFRS 15), and add implementation guidance and illustrations to clarify that an entity should assess the collectability of the consideration promised in a contract for the goods or services that will be transferred to the customer rather than assessing the collectability of the consideration promised in the contract for all of the promised goods or services. The IASB did not make similar amendments to IFRS 15. (See paragraphs BC46B–BC46E.)

(b) **Revenue recognition for contracts with customers that do not meet the Step 1 criteria**—The FASB decided to amend paragraph 606-10-25-7 of Topic 606 (equivalent to paragraph 15 of IFRS 15) to add an event in which an entity recognises any consideration received as revenue when (a) the entity has transferred control of the goods or services to which the consideration received relates; (b) the entity has stopped transferring additional goods or services and has no obligation to transfer additional goods or services; and (c) the consideration received from the customer is non-refundable. The IASB did not make similar amendments to IFRS 15. (See paragraphs BC46F–BC46H.)

(c) **Promised goods or services that are immaterial within the context of the contract**—The FASB decided to amend Topic 606 to state that an entity is not required to assess whether promised goods or services are performance obligations if they are immaterial within the context of the contract with the customer. The IASB did not make similar amendments to IFRS 15. (See paragraphs BC116A–BC116E.)

---

15 The IASB issued *Effective Date of IFRS 15* in September 2015 deferring the effective date of IFRS 15 by one year. Similarly, the FASB amended Topic 606 in August 2015 deferring the effective date of Topic 606 by one year. See paragraphs BC453A–BC453H.

(d) **Shipping and handling activities**—The FASB decided to amend Topic 606 to permit an entity, as an accounting policy election, to account for shipping and handling activities that occur after the customer has obtained control of a good as fulfilment activities. The IASB decided not to make a similar amendment to IFRS 15. (See paragraphs BC116R–BC116U.)

(e) **Presentation of sales taxes**—The FASB decided to amend Topic 606 to provide an accounting policy election that permits an entity to exclude from the measurement of the transaction price all taxes assessed by a governmental authority that are both imposed on and concurrent with a specific revenue-producing transaction and collected from customers (for example, sales taxes, use taxes, value added taxes and some excise taxes). The IASB decided not to provide a similar accounting policy choice in IFRS 15. (See paragraphs BC188A–BC188D.)

(f) **Non-cash consideration**—The FASB decided to amend Topic 606 to require non-cash consideration to be measured at its fair value at contract inception. The FASB also decided to specify that the constraint on variable consideration applies only to variability in the fair value of the non-cash consideration that arises for reasons other than the form of the consideration. The IASB did not make similar amendments to IFRS 15. (See paragraphs BC254A–BC254H.)

(g) **Licensing**

(i) **Determining the nature of the entity's promise in granting a licence of intellectual property**—IFRS 15 and Topic 606 require entities to determine whether the nature of an entity's promise in granting a licence is a right to use or a right to access the entity's intellectual property. The IASB did not amend the criteria in IFRS 15 to determine the nature of the licence but clarified that the assessment of whether the entity's activities significantly change the intellectual property to which the customer has rights is based on whether those activities affect the intellectual property's ability to provide benefit to the customer. The FASB decided to amend the criteria to determine the nature of the licence by requiring an entity to classify the intellectual property underlying the licence as functional or symbolic based on whether the intellectual property has significant stand-alone functionality. A licence to functional intellectual property is considered a right to use, while a licence to symbolic intellectual property is considered a right to access the underlying intellectual property. (See paragraphs BC414C–BC414N.)

(ii) **Contractual restrictions in a licence and the identification of performance obligations**—The FASB decided to amend Topic 606 to clarify that the requirements about contractual restrictions of the nature described in paragraph B62 do not replace the requirement for the entity to identify the number of licences promised in the contract. The IASB did not make similar amendments to IFRS 15. (See paragraphs BC414O–BC414R.)

      (iii)   **Renewals of licences of intellectual property**—The FASB decided to amend Topic 606 and provide an additional example to specify that the entity would generally not recognise revenue from the transfer of the renewal licence until the beginning of the licence renewal period. The IASB did not make similar amendments. (See paragraphs BC414S–BC414U.)

      (iv)   **When to consider the nature of an entity's promise in granting a licence**—The FASB decided to make amendments that explicitly state that an entity considers the nature of its promise in granting a licence when applying the general revenue recognition model to a single performance obligation that includes a licence and other goods or services. The IASB did not make similar amendments to IFRS 15. (See paragraphs BC414V–BC414Y.)

  (h)   **Completed contracts**—The FASB decided to amend the definition of a completed contract to be a contract for which all (or substantially all) of the revenue was recognised in accordance with the previous revenue Standards. The IASB did not make a similar amendment to IFRS 15. (See paragraphs BC445C–BC445I.) Furthermore, the IASB added a practical expedient to allow an entity applying IFRS 15 in accordance with paragraph C3(a) not to restate contracts that are completed contracts at the beginning of the earliest period presented. The FASB decided not to provide the practical expedient. (See paragraphs BC445M–BC445N.)

  (i)   **Date of application of the contract modifications practical expedient**—For an entity applying Topic 606 in accordance with paragraph 606-10-65-1(d)(2) (equivalent to paragraph C3(b) of IFRS 15), the FASB decided that the entity should apply the practical expedient at the date of initial application. However, the IASB decided that an entity applying IFRS 15 in accordance with paragraph C3(b) may apply the practical expedient either (a) at the beginning of the earliest period presented; or (b) at the date of initial application. (See paragraphs BC445O–BC445R.)

A2   IFRS 15 and Topic 606 have been structured to be consistent with the style of other Standards in IFRS and US GAAP (respectively). As a result, the paragraph numbers of IFRS 15 and Topic 606 are not the same. The wording in most of the paragraphs is consistent because IFRS 15 and Topic 606 were issued in May 2014 as a common revenue standard for IFRS and US GAAP. However, the wording in some paragraphs differs because of the different amendments to IFRS 15 and Topic 606 (see paragraph A1A). The following table illustrates how the paragraphs of IFRS 15 and Topic 606, and the related illustrative examples, correspond. Paragraphs in which the wording differs are marked with '*'. The table reflects amendments issued by the FASB, and those expected to be issued by the FASB based on its decisions, until March 2016.

IASB	FASB
MAIN FEATURES	**OVERVIEW AND BACKGROUND**
N/A	606-10-05-1
IN7	606-10-05-2
IN8	606-10-05-3
	606-10-05-4
IN9	606-10-05-5
N/A	606-10-05-6

OBJECTIVE	
1	606-10-10-1
Meeting the Objective	
2	606-10-10-2
3	606-10-10-3
4	606-10-10-4

SCOPE	
Entities	
N/A	606-10-15-1
Transactions	
5	606-10-15-2
6	606-10-15-3
7	606-10-15-4
8	606-10-15-5

RECOGNITION	
Identifying the Contract	
9	606-10-25-1*
10	606-10-25-2
11	606-10-25-3*
12	606-10-25-4
13	606-10-25-5
14	606-10-25-6
15	606-10-25-7*
16	606-10-25-8
Combination of Contracts	
17	606-10-25-9
Contract Modifications	
18	606-10-25-10
19	606-10-25-11
20	606-10-25-12
21	606-10-25-13
Identifying Performance Obligations	
22	606-10-25-14
23	606-10-25-15
Promises in Contracts with Customers	
24	606-10-25-16*
N/A	606-10-25-16A through 25-16B*
25	606-10-25-17*
Distinct Goods or Services	
26	606-10-25-18
N/A	606-10-25-18A through 25-18B*
27	606-10-25-19
28	606-10-25-20
29	606-10-25-21
30	606-10-25-22

continued...

...continued

RECOGNITION	
Satisfaction of Performance Obligations	
31	606-10-25-23
32	606-10-25-24
33	606-10-25-25
34	606-10-25-26
Performance Obligations Satisfied Over Time	
35	606-10-25-27
36	606-10-25-28
37	606-10-25-29
Performance Obligations Satisfied at a Point in Time	
38	606-10-25-30
Measuring Progress towards Complete Satisfaction of a Performance Obligation	
39	606-10-25-31
40	606-10-25-32
Methods for Measuring Progress	
41	606-10-25-33
42	606-10-25-34
43	606-10-25-35
Reasonable Measures of Progress	
44	606-10-25-36
45	606-10-25-37

MEASUREMENT	
46	606-10-32-1
Determining the Transaction Price	
47	606-10-32-2
N/A	606-10-32-2A*
48	606-10-32-3
49	606-10-32-4

continued...

...continued

MEASUREMENT	
Variable Consideration	
50	606-10-32-5
51	606-10-32-6
52	606-10-32-7
53	606-10-32-8
54	606-10-32-9
Refund Liabilities	
55	606-10-32-10
Constraining Estimates of Variable Consideration	
56	606-10-32-11
57	606-10-32-12
58	606-10-32-13
Reassessment of Variable Consideration	
59	606-10-32-14
The Existence of a Significant Financing Component in the Contract	
60	606-10-32-15
61	606-10-32-16
62	606-10-32-17
63	606-10-32-18
64	606-10-32-19
65	606-10-32-20
Non-cash Consideration	
66	606-10-32-21*
67	606-10-32-22
68	606-10-32-23*
69	606-10-32-24
Consideration Payable to a Customer	
70	606-10-32-25
71	606-10-32-26
72	606-10-32-27

continued...

...continued

MEASUREMENT	
Allocating the Transaction Price to Performance Obligations	
73	606-10-32-28
74	606-10-32-29
75	606-10-32-30
Allocation Based on Stand-alone Selling Prices	
76	606-10-32-31
77	606-10-32-32
78	606-10-32-33
79	606-10-32-34
80	606-10-32-35
Allocation of a Discount	
81	606-10-32-36
82	606-10-32-37
83	606-10-32-38
Allocation of Variable Consideration	
84	606-10-32-39
85	606-10-32-40
86	606-10-32-41
Changes in the Transaction Price	
87	606-10-32-42
88	606-10-32-43
89	606-10-32-44
90	606-10-32-45

CONTRACT COSTS	
Overview and Background	
N/A	340-40-05-1
N/A	340-40-05-2

continued...

...*continued*

CONTRACT COSTS	
Scope and Scope Exceptions	
N/A	340-40-15-1
N/A	340-40-15-2
N/A	340-40-15-3
Incremental Costs of Obtaining a Contract	
91	340-40-25-1
92	340-40-25-2
93	340-40-25-3
94	340-40-25-4
Costs to Fulfil a Contract	
95	340-40-25-5
96	340-40-25-6
97	340-40-25-7
98	340-40-25-8
Amortisation and Impairment	
99	340-40-35-1
100	340-40-35-2
101	340-40-35-3
102	340-40-35-4
103	340-40-35-5
104	340-40-35-6

PRESENTATION	
105	606-10-45-1
106	606-10-45-2
107	606-10-45-3
108	606-10-45-4
109	606-10-45-5

DISCLOSURE	
110	606-10-50-1
111	606-10-50-2
112	606-10-50-3
Contracts with Customers	
113	606-10-50-4
Disaggregation of Revenue	
114	606-10-50-5
115	606-10-50-6
N/A	606-10-50-7
Contract Balances	
116	606-10-50-8
117	606-10-50-9
118	606-10-50-10
N/A	606-10-50-11
Performance Obligations	
119	606-10-50-12
Transaction Price Allocated to the Remaining Performance Obligations	
120	606-10-50-13
121	606-10-50-14
122	606-10-50-15
N/A	606-10-50-16
Significant Judgements in the Application of this Standard	
123	606-10-50-17
Determining the Timing of Satisfaction of Performance Obligations	
124	606-10-50-18
125	606-10-50-19
Determining the Transaction Price and the Amounts Allocated to Performance Obligations	
126	606-10-50-20
N/A	606-10-50-21

continued...

...continued

DISCLOSURE	
Assets Recognised from the Costs to Obtain or Fulfil a Contract with a Customer	
N/A	340-40-50-1
127	340-40-50-2
128	340-40-50-3
N/A	340-40-50-4
129	340-40-50-5
N/A	340-40-50-6
Practical Expedients	
129	606-10-50-22
N/A	606-10-50-23

TRANSITION AND EFFECTIVE DATE	
Appendix C	606-10-65-1*

APPLICATION GUIDANCE	
B1	606-10-55-3*
Assessing Collectability	
N/A	606-10-55-3A through 55-3C*
Performance Obligations Satisfied Over Time	
B2	606-10-55-4
Simultaneous Receipt and Consumption of the Benefits of the Entity's Performance	
B3	606-10-55-5
B4	606-10-55-6
Customer Controls the Asset as it is Created or Enhanced	
B5	606-10-55-7
Entity's Performance Does Not Create an Asset with an Alternative Use	
B6	606-10-55-8
B7	606-10-55-9
B8	606-10-55-10

continued...

...*continued*

APPLICATION GUIDANCE	
Right to Payment for Performance Completed to Date	
B9	606-10-55-11
B10	606-10-55-12
B11	606-10-55-13
B12	606-10-55-14
B13	606-10-55-15
Methods for Measuring Progress Towards Complete Satisfaction of a Performance Obligation	
B14	606-10-55-16
Output Methods	
B15	606-10-55-17
B16	606-10-55-18
B17	606-10-55-19
Input Methods	
B18	606-10-55-20
B19	606-10-55-21
Sale with a Right of Return	
B20	606-10-55-22
B21	606-10-55-23
B22	606-10-55-24
B23	606-10-55-25
B24	606-10-55-26
B25	606-10-55-27
B26	606-10-55-28
B27	606-10-55-29

continued...

...*continued*

APPLICATION GUIDANCE	
Warranties	
B28	606-10-55-30
B29	606-10-55-31
B30	606-10-55-32
B31	606-10-55-33
B32	606-10-55-34
B33	606-10-55-35
Principal Versus Agent Considerations	
B34	606-10-55-36
B34A	606-10-55-36A
B35	606-10-55-37
B35A	606-10-55-37A
B35B	606-10-55-37B
B36	606-10-55-38
B37	606-10-55-39
B37A	606-10-55-39A
B38	606-10-55-40
Customer Options for Additional Goods or Services	
B39	606-10-55-41
B40	606-10-55-42
B41	606-10-55-43
B42	606-10-55-44
B43	606-10-55-45
Customers' Unexercised Rights	
B44	606-10-55-46
B45	606-10-55-47
B46	606-10-55-48
B47	606-10-55-49

continued...

...*continued*

APPLICATION GUIDANCE	
Non-refundable Upfront Fees (and Some Related Costs)	
B48	606-10-55-50
B49	606-10-55-51
B50	606-10-55-52
B51	606-10-55-53
Licensing	
B52	606-10-55-54*
B53	606-10-55-55
B54	606-10-55-56
B55	606-10-55-57*
B56	606-10-55-58*
Determining the Nature of the Entity's Promise	
B57 [Deleted]	N/A*
N/A	606-10-55-59*
B58 and B59A	606-10-55-60, 55-62 through 55-63A*
B59	606-10-55-61 [Superseded]*
B60	606-10-55-58A*
B61	606-10-55-58B through 55-58C*
B62	606-10-55-64 through 55-64A*
Sales-Based or Usage-Based Royalties	
B63	606-10-55-65
B63A–B63B	606-10-55-65A through 55-65B
Repurchase Agreements	
B64	606-10-55-66
B65	606-10-55-67
A Forward or a Call Option	
B66	606-10-55-68
B67	606-10-55-69
B68	606-10-55-70
B69	606-10-55-71

continued...

...continued

APPLICATION GUIDANCE	
A Put Option	
B70	606-10-55-72
B71	606-10-55-73
B72	606-10-55-74
B73	606-10-55-75
B74	606-10-55-76
B75	606-10-55-77
B76	606-10-55-78
Consignment Arrangements	
B77	606-10-55-79
B78	606-10-55-80
Bill-and-Hold Arrangements	
B79	606-10-55-81
B80	606-10-55-82
B81	606-10-55-83
B82	606-10-55-84
Customer Acceptance	
B83	606-10-55-85
B84	606-10-55-86
B85	606-10-55-87
B86	606-10-55-88
Disclosure of Disaggregated Revenue	
B87	606-10-55-89
B88	606-10-55-90
B89	606-10-55-91

ILLUSTRATIONS	
IE1	606-10-55-92
N/A	606-10-55-93

IDENTIFYING THE CONTRACT	
IE2	606-10-55-94*
Example 1—Collectability of the Consideration	
IE3	606-10-55-95
IE4	606-10-55-96*
IE5	606-10-55-97*
IE6	606-10-55-98*
N/A	606-10-55-98A through 55-98L*
Example 2—Consideration Is Not the Stated Price—Implicit Price Concession	
IE7	606-10-55-99
IE8	606-10-55-100
IE9	606-10-55-101
Example 3—Implicit Price Concession	
IE10	606-10-55-102
IE11	606-10-55-103
IE12	606-10-55-104
IE13	606-10-55-105
Example 4—Reassessing the Criteria for Identifying a Contract	
IE14	606-10-55-106
IE15	606-10-55-107
IE16	606-10-55-108
IE17	606-10-55-109

CONTRACT MODIFICATIONS	
IE18	606-10-55-110
Example 5—Modification of a Contract for Goods	
IE19	606-10-55-111
IE20	606-10-55-112
IE21	606-10-55-113
IE22	606-10-55-114
IE23	606-10-55-115
IE24	606-10-55-116
Example 6—Change in the Transaction Price after a Contract Modification	
IE25	606-10-55-117
IE26	606-10-55-118
IE27	606-10-55-119
IE28	606-10-55-120
IE29	606-10-55-121
IE30	606-10-55-122
IE31	606-10-55-123
IE32	606-10-55-124
Example 7—Modification of a Services Contract	
IE33	606-10-55-125
IE34	606-10-55-126
IE35	606-10-55-127
IE36	606-10-55-128
Example 8—Modification Resulting in a Cumulative Catch-Up Adjustment to Revenue	
IE37	606-10-55-129
IE38	606-10-55-130
IE39	606-10-55-131
IE40	606-10-55-132
IE41	606-10-55-133

continued...

...*continued*

CONTRACT MODIFICATIONS	
Example 9—Unapproved Change in Scope and Price	
IE42	606-10-55-134
IE43	606-10-55-135

IDENTIFYING PERFORMANCE OBLIGATIONS	
IE44	606-10-55-136*
Example 10—Goods and Services Not Distinct	
IE45	606-10-55-137
IE46	606-10-55-138
IE47	606-10-55-139
IE48	606-10-55-140
IE48A–IE48C	606-10-55-140A through 55-140C
N/A	606-10-55-140D through 55-140F*
Example 11—Determining Whether Goods or Services Are Distinct	
IE49	606-10-55-141
IE50	606-10-55-142
IE51	606-10-55-143*
IE52	606-10-55-144
IE53	606-10-55-145
IE54	606-10-55-146
IE55	606-10-55-147
IE56	606-10-55-148
IE57	606-10-55-149
IE58	606-10-55-150*
IE58A–IE58K	606-10-55-150A through 55-150K

continued...

...*continued*

IDENTIFYING PERFORMANCE OBLIGATIONS	
Example 12—Explicit and Implicit Promises in a Contract	
IE59	606-10-55-151
IE60	606-10-55-152
IE61	606-10-55-153
IE61A	606-10-55-153A
IE62	606-10-55-154
IE63	606-10-55-155*
IE64	606-10-55-156
IE65	606-10-55-157
IE65A	606-10-55-157A
Example 12A—Series of Distinct Goods or Services	
N/A	606-10-55-157B through 55-157E*

PERFORMANCE OBLIGATIONS SATISFIED OVER TIME	
IE66	606-10-55-158
Example 13—Customer Simultaneously Receives and Consumes the Benefits	
IE67	606-10-55-159
IE68	606-10-55-160
Example 14—Assessing Alternative Use and Right to Payment	
IE69	606-10-55-161
IE70	606-10-55-162
IE71	606-10-55-163
IE72	606-10-55-164
Example 15—Asset Has No Alternative Use to the Entity	
IE73	606-10-55-165
IE74	606-10-55-166
IE75	606-10-55-167
IE76	606-10-55-168

continued...

...continued

PERFORMANCE OBLIGATIONS SATISFIED OVER TIME	
Example 16—Enforceable Right to Payment for Performance Completed to Date	
IE77	606-10-55-169
IE78	606-10-55-170
IE79	606-10-55-171
IE80	606-10-55-172
Example 17—Assessing Whether a Performance Obligation Is Satisfied at a Point in Time or Over Time	
IE81	606-10-55-173
IE82	606-10-55-174
IE83	606-10-55-175
IE84	606-10-55-176
IE85	606-10-55-177
IE86	606-10-55-178
IE87	606-10-55-179
IE88	606-10-55-180
IE89	606-10-55-181
IE90	606-10-55-182

MEASURING PROGRESS TOWARDS COMPLETE SATISFACTION OF A PERFORMANCE OBLIGATION	
IE91	606-10-55-183
Example 18—Measuring Progress When Making Goods or Services Available	
IE92	606-10-55-184
IE93	606-10-55-185
IE94	606-10-55-186

continued...

...continued

MEASURING PROGRESS TOWARDS COMPLETE SATISFACTION OF A PERFORMANCE OBLIGATION	
Example 19—Uninstalled Materials	
IE95	606-10-55-187
IE96	606-10-55-188
IE97	606-10-55-189
IE98	606-10-55-190
IE99	606-10-55-191
IE100	606-10-55-192

VARIABLE CONSIDERATION	
IE101	606-10-55-193
Example 20—Penalty Gives Rise to Variable Consideration	
IE102	606-10-55-194
IE103	606-10-55-195
IE104	606-10-55-196
Example 21—Estimating Variable Consideration	
IE105	606-10-55-197
IE106	606-10-55-198
IE107	606-10-55-199
IE108	606-10-55-200

CONSTRAINING ESTIMATES OF VARIABLE CONSIDERATION	
IE109	606-10-55-201
Example 22—Right of Return	
IE110	606-10-55-202
IE111	606-10-55-203
IE112	606-10-55-204
IE113	606-10-55-205
IE114	606-10-55-206
IE115	606-10-55-207

continued...

...continued

CONSTRAINING ESTIMATES OF VARIABLE CONSIDERATION	
Example 23—Price Concessions	
IE116	606-10-55-208
IE117	606-10-55-209
IE118	606-10-55-210
IE119	606-10-55-211
IE120	606-10-55-212
IE121	606-10-55-213
IE122	606-10-55-214
IE123	606-10-55-215
Example 24—Volume Discount Incentive	
IE124	606-10-55-216
IE125	606-10-55-217
IE126	606-10-55-218
IE127	606-10-55-219
IE128	606-10-55-220
Example 25—Management Fees Subject to the Constraint	
IE129	606-10-55-221
IE130	606-10-55-222
IE131	606-10-55-223
IE132	606-10-55-224
IE133	606-10-55-225

THE EXISTENCE OF A SIGNIFICANT FINANCING COMPONENT IN THE CONTRACT	
IE134	606-10-55-226
Example 26—Significant Financing Component and Right of Return	
IE135	606-10-55-227
IE136	606-10-55-228
IE137	606-10-55-229
IE138	606-10-55-230
IE139	606-10-55-231
IE140	606-10-55-232
Example 27—Withheld Payments on a Long-Term Contract	
IE141	606-10-55-233
IE142	606-10-55-234
Example 28—Determining the Discount Rate	
IE143	606-10-55-235
IE144	606-10-55-236
IE145	606-10-55-237
IE146	606-10-55-238
IE147	606-10-55-239
Example 29—Advance Payment and Assessment of the Discount Rate	
IE148	606-10-55-240
IE149	606-10-55-241
IE150	606-10-55-242
IE151	606-10-55-243
Example 30—Advance Payment	
IE152	606-10-55-244
IE153	606-10-55-245
IE154	606-10-55-246

continued...

...continued

ALLOCATING THE TRANSACTION PRICE TO PERFORMANCE OBLIGATIONS	
Example 34—Allocating a Discount	
IE167	606-10-55-259
IE168	606-10-55-260
IE169	606-10-55-261
IE170	606-10-55-262
IE171	606-10-55-263
IE172	606-10-55-264
IE173	606-10-55-265
IE174	606-10-55-266
IE175	606-10-55-267
IE176	606-10-55-268
IE177	606-10-55-269
Example 35—Allocation of Variable Consideration	
IE178	606-10-55-270
IE179	606-10-55-271
IE180	606-10-55-272
IE181	606-10-55-273
IE182	606-10-55-274
IE183	606-10-55-275
IE184	606-10-55-276
IE185	606-10-55-277
IE186	606-10-55-278
IE187	606-10-55-279

CONTRACT COSTS	
IE188	340-40-55-1
Example 36—Incremental Costs of Obtaining a Contract	
IE189	340-40-55-2
IE190	340-40-55-3
IE191	340-40-55-4
Example 37—Costs That Give Rise to an Asset	
IE192	340-40-55-5
IE193	340-40-55-6
IE194	340-40-55-7
IE195	340-40-55-8
IE196	340-40-55-9

PRESENTATION	
IE197	606-10-55-283
Example 38—Contract Liability and Receivable	
IE198	606-10-55-284
IE199	606-10-55-285
IE200	606-10-55-286
Example 39—Contract Asset Recognised for the Entity's Performance	
IE201	606-10-55-287
IE202	606-10-55-288
IE203	606-10-55-289
IE204	606-10-55-290
Example 40—Receivable Recognised for the Entity's Performance	
IE205	606-10-55-291
IE206	606-10-55-292
IE207	606-10-55-293
IE208	606-10-55-294

DISCLOSURE	
IE209	606-10-55-295
Example 41—Disaggregation of Revenue—Quantitative Disclosure	
IE210	606-10-55-296
IE211	606-10-55-297
Example 42—Disclosure of the Transaction Price Allocated to the Remaining Performance Obligations	
IE212	606-10-55-298
IE213	606-10-55-299
IE214	606-10-55-300
IE215	606-10-55-301
IE216	606-10-55-302
IE217	606-10-55-303
IE218	606-10-55-304
IE219	606-10-55-305
Example 43—Disclosure of the Transaction Price Allocated to the Remaining Performance Obligations—Qualitative Disclosure	
IE220	606-10-55-306
IE221	606-10-55-307

WARRANTIES	
IE222	606-10-55-308
Example 44—Warranties	
IE223	606-10-55-309*
IE224	606-10-55-310
IE225	606-10-55-311
IE226	606-10-55-312
IE227	606-10-55-313
IE228	606-10-55-314
IE229	606-10-55-315

PRINCIPAL VERSUS AGENT CONSIDERATIONS	
IE230	606-10-55-316

Example 45—Arranging for the Provision of Goods or Services (Entity is an Agent)

IE231	606-10-55-317
IE232	606-10-55-318
IE232A–IE232C	606-10-55-318A through 55-318C
IE233	606-10-55-319

Example 46—Promise to Provide Goods or Services (Entity is a Principal)

IE234	606-10-55-320
IE235	606-10-55-321
IE236	606-10-55-322
IE237	606-10-55-323
IE237A–IE237B	606-10-55-323A through 55-323B
IE238	606-10-55-324

Example 46A—Promise to Provide Goods or Services (Entity Is a Principal)

IE238A–IE238G	606-10-55-324A through 55-324G

Example 47—Promise to Provide Goods or Services (Entity is a Principal)

IE239	606-10-55-325
IE240	606-10-55-326
IE241	606-10-55-327
IE242	606-10-55-328
IE242A–IE242C	606-10-55-328A through 55-328C
IE243	606-10-55-329

continued...

...*continued*

PRINCIPAL VERSUS AGENT CONSIDERATIONS	
Example 48—Arranging for the Provision of Goods or Services (Entity is an Agent)	
IE244	606-10-55-330
IE245	606-10-55-331
IE246	606-10-55-332
IE247	606-10-55-333
IE247A–IE247B	606-10-55-333A through 55-333B
IE248	606-10-55-334
Example 48A—Entity Is a Principal and an Agent in the Same Contract	
IE248A–IE248F	606-10-55-334A through 55-334F

CUSTOMER OPTIONS FOR ADDITIONAL GOODS OR SERVICES	
IE249	606-10-55-335
Example 49—Option That Provides the Customer with a Material Right (Discount Voucher)	
IE250	606-10-55-336
IE251	606-10-55-337
IE252	606-10-55-338
IE253	606-10-55-339
Example 50—Option That Does Not Provide the Customer with a Material Right (Additional Goods or Services)	
IE254	606-10-55-340
IE255	606-10-55-341
IE256	606-10-55-342

continued...

...*continued*

CUSTOMER OPTIONS FOR ADDITIONAL GOODS OR SERVICES	
Example 51—Option That Provides the Customer with a Material Right (Renewal Option)	
IE257	606-10-55-343
IE258	606-10-55-344
IE259	606-10-55-345
IE260	606-10-55-346
IE261	606-10-55-347
IE262	606-10-55-348
IE263	606-10-55-349
IE264	606-10-55-350
IE265	606-10-55-351
IE266	606-10-55-352
Example 52—Customer Loyalty Programme	
IE267	606-10-55-353
IE268	606-10-55-354
IE269	606-10-55-355
IE270	606-10-55-356

NON-REFUNDABLE UPFRONT FEES	
IE271	606-10-55-357
Example 53—Non-refundable Upfront Fee	
IE272	606-10-55-358
IE273	606-10-55-359
IE274	606-10-55-360

LICENSING	
IE275	606-10-55-361*
Example 54—Right to Use Intellectual Property	
IE276	606-10-55-362
IE277	606-10-55-363 through 55-363B*

continued...

...continued

LICENSING	
Example 55—Licence of Intellectual Property	
IE278	606-10-55-364
IE279	606-10-55-365
IE279A	606-10-55-365A
IE280	606-10-55-366*
Example 56—Identifying a Distinct Licence	
IE281	606-10-55-367*
IE282	606-10-55-368*
IE283	606-10-55-369
IE284	606-10-55-370*
IE285	606-10-55-371
IE286	606-10-55-372
IE286A	606-10-55-372A
IE287	606-10-55-373*
IE288	606-10-55-374*
Example 57—Franchise Rights	
IE289	606-10-55-375*
IE290	606-10-55-376*
IE291	606-10-55-377
IE292	606-10-55-378*
IE293	606-10-55-379*
IE294	606-10-55-380*
IE295	606-10-55-381*
IE296	606-10-55-382*

continued...

...*continued*

LICENSING	
Example 58—Access to Intellectual Property	
IE297	606-10-55-383*
IE298	606-10-55-384
IE299	606-10-55-385*
IE300	606-10-55-386*
IE301	606-10-55-387*
IE302	606-10-55-388*
Example 59—Right to Use Intellectual Property	
IE303	606-10-55-389
IE304	606-10-55-390
IE305	606-10-55-391*
IE306	606-10-55-392*
N/A	606-10-55-392A through 55-392D*
Example 60—Sales-based royalty for a licence of intellectual property	
IE307	606-10-55-393
IE308	606-10-55-394
Example 61—Access to Intellectual Property	
IE309	606-10-55-395
IE310	606-10-55-396*
IE311	606-10-55-397*
IE312	606-10-55-398*
IE313	606-10-55-399*
Example 61A—Right to Use Intellectual Property	
N/A	606-10-55-399A through 55-399J*
Example 61B—Distinguishing Multiple Licences from Attributes of a Single Licence	
N/A	606-10-55-399K through 55-399O*

REPURCHASE AGREEMENTS	
IE314	606-10-55-400
Example 62—Repurchase Agreements	
IE315	606-10-55-401
IE316	606-10-55-402
IE317	606-10-55-403
IE318	606-10-55-404
IE319	606-10-55-405
IE320	606-10-55-406
IE321	606-10-55-407

BILL-AND-HOLD ARRANGEMENTS	
IE322	606-10-55-408
Example 63—Bill-and-Hold Arrangement	
IE323	606-10-55-409
IE324	606-10-55-410
IE325	606-10-55-411
IE326	606-10-55-412
IE327	606-10-55-413

Appendix B
Amendments to the Basis for Conclusions on other Standards

The amendments in this appendix to the Basis for Conclusions on other Standards are necessary in order to ensure consistency with IFRS 15 and the related amendments to other Standards.

* * * * *

The amendments contained in this appendix when IFRS 15 was issued in 2014 have been incorporated into the Basis for Conclusions on the relevant Standards included in this volume.

IASB documents published to accompany

IAS 1

Presentation of Financial Statements

The text of the unaccompanied standard, IAS 1, is contained in Part A of this edition. Its effective date when issued was 1 January 2009. The text of the Accompanying Guidance on IAS 1 is contained in Part B of this edition. This part presents the following documents:

BASIS FOR CONCLUSIONS

APPENDIX TO THE BASIS FOR CONCLUSIONS
Amendments to the Basis for Conclusions on other IFRSs

DISSENTING OPINIONS

CONTENTS

Basis for Conclusions on
IAS 1 *Presentation of Financial Statements*

This Basis for Conclusions accompanies, but is not part of, IAS 1.

The International Accounting Standards Board revised IAS 1 Presentation of Financial Statements in 2007 as part of its project on financial statement presentation. It was not the Board's intention to reconsider as part of that project all the requirements in IAS 1.

For convenience, the Board has incorporated into this Basis for Conclusions relevant material from the Basis for Conclusions on the revision of IAS 1 in 2003 and its amendment in 2005. Paragraphs have been renumbered and reorganised as necessary to reflect the new structure of the Standard.

Introduction

BC1   The International Accounting Standards Committee (IASC) issued the first version of IAS 1 *Disclosure of Accounting Policies* in 1975. It was reformatted in 1994 and superseded in 1997 by IAS 1 *Presentation of Financial Statements*.[1] In 2003 the International Accounting Standards Board revised IAS 1 as part of the Improvements project and in 2005 the Board amended it as a consequence of issuing IFRS 7 *Financial Instruments: Disclosures*. In 2007 the Board revised IAS 1 again as part of its project on financial statement presentation. This Basis for Conclusions summarises the Board's considerations in reaching its conclusions on revising IAS 1 in 2003, on amending it in 2005 and revising it in 2007. It includes reasons for accepting some approaches and rejecting others. Individual Board members gave greater weight to some factors than to others.

The Improvements project—revision of IAS 1 (2003)

BC2   In July 2001 the Board announced that, as part of its initial agenda of technical projects, it would undertake a project to improve a number of standards, including IAS 1. The project was undertaken in the light of queries and criticisms raised in relation to the standards by securities regulators, professional accountants and other interested parties. The objectives of the Improvements project were to reduce or eliminate alternatives, redundancies and conflicts within standards, to deal with some convergence issues and to make other improvements. The Board's intention was not to reconsider the fundamental approach to the presentation of financial statements established by IAS 1 in 1997.

BC3   In May 2002 the Board published an exposure draft of proposed *Improvements to International Accounting Standards*, which contained proposals to revise IAS 1. The Board received more than 160 comment letters. After considering the responses the Board issued in 2003 a revised version of IAS 1. In its revision the Board's main objectives were:

   (a)   to provide a framework within which an entity assesses how to present fairly the effects of transactions and other events, and assesses whether the result of complying with a requirement in an IFRS would be so misleading that it would not give a fair presentation;

---

1   IASC did not publish a Basis for Conclusions.

(b) to base the criteria for classifying liabilities as current or non-current solely on the conditions existing at the balance sheet date;

(c) to prohibit the presentation of items of income and expense as 'extraordinary items';

(d) to specify disclosures about the judgements that management has made in the process of applying the entity's accounting policies, apart from those involving estimations, and that have the most significant effect on the amounts recognised in the financial statements; and

(e) to specify disclosures about sources of estimation uncertainty at the balance sheet date that have a significant risk of causing a material adjustment to the carrying amounts of assets and liabilities within the next financial year.

BC4   The following sections summarise the Board's considerations in reaching its conclusions as part of its Improvements project in 2003:

(a) departures from IFRSs (paragraphs BC23–BC30)

(b) criterion for exemption from requirements (paragraphs BC34–BC36)

(c) effect of events after the reporting period on the classification of liabilities (paragraphs BC39–BC48)

(d) results of operating activities (paragraphs BC55 and BC56)

(e) minority interest (paragraph BC59)[2]

(f) extraordinary items (paragraphs BC60–BC64)

(g) disclosure of the judgements management has made in the process of applying the entity's accounting policies (paragraphs BC77 and BC78)

(h) disclosure of major sources of estimation uncertainty (paragraphs BC79–BC84).

Amendment to IAS 1—*Capital Disclosures* (2005)

BC5   In August 2005 the Board issued an Amendment to IAS 1–*Capital Disclosures*. The amendment added to IAS 1 requirements for disclosure of:

(a) the entity's objectives, policies and processes for managing capital.

(b) quantitative data about what the entity regards as capital.

(c) whether the entity has complied with any capital requirements; and if it has not complied, the consequences of such non-compliance.

BC6   The following sections summarise the Board's considerations in reaching its conclusions as part of its amendment to IAS 1 in 2005:

(a) disclosures about capital (paragraphs BC85–BC89)

---

2   In January 2008 the IASB issued an amended IAS 27 *Consolidated and Separate Financial Statements*, which amended 'minority interest' to 'non-controlling interests'. The consolidation requirements in IAS 27 were superseded by IFRS 10 *Consolidated Financial Statements* issued in May 2011. The term 'non-controlling interests' and the requirements for non-controlling interests were not changed.

(b)   objectives, policies and processes for managing capital (paragraphs BC90 and BC91)

(c)   externally imposed capital requirements (paragraphs BC92–BC97)

(d)   internal capital targets (paragraphs BC98–BC100).

Amendments to IAS 32 and IAS 1—*Puttable Financial Instruments and Obligations Arising on Liquidation* (2008)

BC6A   In July 2006 the Board published an exposure draft of proposed amendments to IAS 32 and IAS 1 relating to the classification of puttable instruments and instruments with obligations arising only on liquidation. The Board subsequently confirmed the proposals and in February 2008 issued an amendment that now forms part of IAS 1.

Presentation of Items of Other Comprehensive Income (Amendments to IAS 1)

BC6B   In May 2010 the Board published an exposure draft of proposed amendments to IAS 1 relating to the presentation of items of other comprehensive income (OCI). The Board subsequently modified and confirmed the proposals and in June 2011 issued *Presentation of Items of Other Comprehensive Income* (Amendments to IAS 1). The amendments were developed in a joint project with the US national standard-setter, the Financial Accounting Standards Board (FASB), with the aim of aligning the presentation of OCI so that information in financial statements prepared by entities using IFRSs and entities using US generally accepted accounting principles (GAAP) can be more easily compared.

Financial statement presentation—Joint project

BC7   In September 2001 the Board added to its agenda the performance reporting project (in March 2006 renamed the 'financial statement presentation project'). The objective of the project was to enhance the usefulness of information presented in the income statement. The Board developed a possible new model for reporting income and expenses and conducted preliminary testing. Similarly, in the United States, the Financial Accounting Standards Board (FASB) added a project on performance reporting to its agenda in October 2001, developed its model and conducted preliminary testing. Constituents raised concerns about both models and about the fact that they were different.

BC8   In April 2004 the Board and the FASB decided to work on financial statement presentation as a joint project. They agreed that the project should address presentation and display not only in the income statement, but also in the other statements that, together with the income statement, would constitute a complete set of financial statements—the balance sheet, the statement of changes in equity, and the cash flow statement. The Board decided to approach the project in two phases. Phase A would address the statements that constitute a complete set of financial statements and the periods for which they are required to be presented. Phase B would be undertaken jointly with the FASB and would address more fundamental issues relating to presentation and display of information in the financial statements, including:

(a) consistent principles for aggregating information in each financial statement.

(b) the totals and subtotals that should be reported in each financial statement.

(c) whether components of other comprehensive income should be reclassified to profit or loss and, if so, the characteristics of the transactions and events that should be reclassified and when reclassification should be made.

(d) whether the direct or the indirect method of presenting operating cash flows provides more useful information.

BC9 In March 2006, as a result of its work in phase A, the Board published an exposure draft of proposed amendments to IAS 1—*A Revised Presentation*. The Board received more than 130 comment letters. The exposure draft proposed amendments that affected the presentation of owner changes in equity and the presentation of comprehensive income, but did not propose to change the recognition, measurement or disclosure of specific transactions and other events required by other IFRSs. It also proposed to bring IAS 1 largely into line with the US standard—SFAS 130 *Reporting Comprehensive Income*. After considering the responses to the exposure draft the Board issued a revised version of IAS 1. The FASB decided to consider phases A and B issues together, and therefore did not publish an exposure draft on phase A.

BC10 The following sections summarise the Board's considerations in reaching its conclusions as part of its revision in 2007:

(a) general purpose financial statements (paragraphs BC11–BC13)

(b) titles of financial statements (paragraphs BC14–BC21)

(c) equal prominence (paragraph BC22)

(d) a statement of financial position as at the beginning of the earliest comparative period (paragraphs BC31 and BC32)

(e) IAS 34 *Interim Financial Reporting* (paragraph BC33)

(f) reporting owner and non-owner changes in equity (paragraphs BC37 and BC38)

(g) reporting comprehensive income (paragraphs BC49–BC54)

(h) subtotal for profit or loss (paragraphs BC57 and BC58)

(i) other comprehensive income-related tax effects (paragraphs BC65–BC68)

(j) reclassification adjustments (paragraphs BC69–BC73)

(k) effects of retrospective application or retrospective restatement (paragraph BC74)

(l) presentation of dividends (paragraph BC75)

(m) IAS 7 *Cash Flow Statements* (paragraph BC76)

(n) presentation of measures per share (paragraphs BC101–BC104)

(o) effective date and transition (paragraph BC105)

(p)   differences from SFAS 130 (paragraph BC106).

Definitions

General purpose financial statements (paragraph 7)

BC11   The exposure draft of 2006 proposed a change to the explanatory paragraph of what 'general purpose financial statements' include, in order to produce a more generic definition of a set of financial statements. Paragraph 7 of the exposure draft stated:

> General purpose financial statements include those that are presented separately or within other *public* documents such as a *regulatory filing* or report to shareholders. [emphasis added]

BC12   Respondents expressed concern about the proposed change. They argued that it could be understood as defining as general purpose financial statements any financial statement or set of financial statements filed with a regulator and could capture documents other than annual reports and prospectuses. They saw this change as expanding the scope of IAS 1 to documents that previously would not have contained all of the disclosures required by IAS 1. Respondents pointed out that the change would particularly affect some entities (such as small private companies and subsidiaries of public companies with no external users of financial reports) that are required by law to place their financial statements on a public file.

BC13   The Board acknowledged that in some countries the law requires entities, whether public or private, to report to regulatory authorities and include information in those reports that could be beyond the scope of IAS 1. Because the Board did not intend to extend the definition of general purpose financial statements, it decided to eliminate the explanatory paragraph of what 'general purpose financial statements' include, while retaining the definition of 'general purpose financial statements'.

Financial statements

Complete set of financial statements

Titles of financial statements (paragraph 10)

BC14   The exposure draft of 2006 proposed changes to the titles of some of the financial statements—from 'balance sheet' to 'statement of financial position', from 'income statement' to 'statement of profit or loss' and from 'cash flow statement' to 'statement of cash flows'. In addition, the exposure draft proposed a 'statement of recognised income and expense' and that all owner changes in equity should be included in a 'statement of changes in equity'. The Board did not propose to make any of these changes of nomenclature mandatory.

BC15   Many respondents opposed the proposed changes, pointing out that the existing titles had a long tradition and were well understood. However, the Board reaffirmed its view that the proposed new titles better reflect the function of each financial statement, and pointed out that an entity could choose to use other titles in its financial report.

BC16   The Board reaffirmed its conclusion that the title 'statement of financial position' not only better reflects the function of the statement but is consistent with the *Framework for the Preparation and Presentation of Financial Statements*, which contains several references to 'financial position'. Paragraph 12 of the *Framework*[3] states that the objective of financial statements is to provide information about the financial position, performance and changes in financial position of an entity; paragraph 19 of the *Framework* states that information about financial position is primarily provided in a balance sheet. In the Board's view, the title 'balance sheet' simply reflects that double entry bookkeeping requires debits to equal credits. It does not identify the content or purpose of the statement. The Board also noted that 'financial position' is a well-known and accepted term, as it has been used in auditors' opinions internationally for more than 20 years to describe what the 'balance sheet' presents. The Board decided that aligning the statement's title with its content and the opinion rendered by the auditor would help the users of financial statements.

BC17   As to the other statements, respondents suggested that renaming the balance sheet the 'statement of financial position' implied that the 'cash flow statement' and the 'statement of recognised income and expense' do not also reflect an entity's financial position. The Board observed that although the latter statements reflect changes in an entity's financial position, neither can be called a 'statement of changes in financial position', as this would not depict their true function and objective (ie to present cash flows and performance, respectively). The Board acknowledged that the titles 'income statement' and 'statement of profit or loss' are similar in meaning and could be used interchangeably, and decided to retain the title 'income statement' as this is more commonly used.

BC18   The title of the proposed new statement, the 'statement of recognised income and expense', reflects a broader content than the former 'income statement'. The statement encompasses both income and expenses recognised in profit or loss and income and expenses recognised outside profit or loss.

BC19   Many respondents opposed the title 'statement of recognised income and expense', objecting particularly to the use of the term 'recognised'. The Board acknowledged that the term 'recognised' could also be used to describe the content of other primary statements as 'recognition', explained in paragraph 82 of the *Framework*, is 'the process of incorporating in the balance sheet or income statement an item that meets the definition of an element and satisfies the criteria for recognition set out in paragraph 83.' Many respondents suggested the term 'statement of comprehensive income' instead.

BC20   In response to respondents' concerns and to converge with SFAS 130, the Board decided to rename the new statement a 'statement of comprehensive income'. The term 'comprehensive income' is not defined in the *Framework* but is used in IAS 1 to describe the change in equity of an entity during a period from transactions, events and circumstances other than those resulting from transactions with owners in their capacity as owners. Although the term 'comprehensive income' is used to describe the aggregate of all components of

---

3   References to the *Framework* are to IASC's *Framework for the Preparation and Presentation of Financial Statements*, adopted by the IASB in 2001. In September 2010 the IASB replaced the *Framework* with the *Conceptual Framework for Financial Reporting*.

comprehensive income, including profit or loss, the term 'other comprehensive income' refers to income and expenses that under IFRSs are included in comprehensive income but excluded from profit or loss.

BC20A   In May 2010 the Board published the exposure draft *Presentation of Items of Other Comprehensive Income* (proposed amendments to IAS 1) relating to the presentation of items of other comprehensive income (OCI). One of the proposals in the exposure draft related to the title of the statement containing profit or loss and other comprehensive income. The Board proposed this change so that it would be clear that the statement had two components: profit or loss and other comprehensive income. A majority of the respondents to the exposure draft supported the change and therefore the Board confirmed the proposal in June 2011. IAS 1 allows preparers to use other titles for the statement that reflect the nature of their activities.

BC20B   Several other IFRSs refer to the 'statement of comprehensive income'. The Board considered whether it should change all such references to 'statement of profit or loss and other comprehensive income'. The Board noted that the terminology used in IAS 1 is not mandatory and that 'statement of comprehensive income' is one of the examples used in the standard. The Board decided that there was little benefit in replacing the title 'statement of comprehensive income' in other IFRSs or 'income statement' with the 'statement of profit or loss'. However, the Board did change the terminology when an IFRS made reference to the two-statement option.

BC21   In finalising its revision, the Board confirmed that the titles of financial statements used in this Standard would not be mandatory. The titles will be used in future IFRSs but are not required to be used by entities in their financial statements. Some respondents to the exposure draft expressed concern that non-mandatory titles will result in confusion. However, the Board believes that making use of the titles non-mandatory will allow time for entities to implement changes gradually as the new titles become more familiar.

Equal prominence (paragraphs 11 and 12)

BC22   The Board noted that the financial performance of an entity is not assessed by reference to a single financial statement or a single measure within a financial statement. The Board believes that the financial performance of an entity can be assessed only after all aspects of the financial statements are taken into account and understood in their entirety. Accordingly, the Board decided that in order to help users of the financial statements to understand the financial performance of an entity comprehensively, all financial statements within the complete set of financial statements should be presented with equal prominence.

Departures from IFRSs (paragraphs 19–24)

BC23   IAS 1 (as issued in 1997) permitted an entity to depart from a requirement in a Standard 'in the extremely rare circumstances when management concludes that compliance with a requirement in a Standard would be misleading, and therefore that departure from a requirement is necessary to achieve a fair presentation' (paragraph 17, now paragraph 19). When such a departure occurred, paragraph 18 (now paragraph 20) required extensive disclosure of the facts and circumstances surrounding the departure and the treatment adopted.

BC24   The Board decided to clarify in paragraph 15 of the Standard that for financial statements to present fairly the financial position, financial performance and cash flows of an entity, they must represent faithfully the effects of transactions and other events in accordance with the definitions and recognition criteria for assets, liabilities, income and expenses set out in the *Framework*.

BC25   The Board decided to limit the occasions on which an entity should depart from a requirement in an IFRS to the extremely rare circumstances in which management concludes that compliance with the requirement would be so misleading that it would conflict with the objective of financial statements set out in the *Framework*. Guidance on this criterion states that an item of information would conflict with the objective of financial statements when it does not represent faithfully the transactions, other events or conditions that it either purports to represent or could reasonably be expected to represent and, consequently, it would be likely to influence economic decisions made by users of financial statements.

BC26   These amendments provide a framework within which an entity assesses how to present fairly the effects of transactions, other events and conditions, and whether the result of complying with a requirement in an IFRS would be so misleading that it would not give a fair presentation.

BC27   The Board considered whether IAS 1 should be silent on departures from IFRSs. The Board decided against making that change, because it would remove the Board's capability to specify the criteria under which departures from IFRSs should occur.

BC28   Departing from a requirement in an IFRS when considered necessary to achieve a fair presentation would conflict with the regulatory framework in some jurisdictions. The revised IAS 1 takes into account the existence of different regulatory requirements. It requires that when an entity's circumstances satisfy the criterion described in paragraph BC25 for departure from a requirement in an IFRS, the entity should proceed as follows:

(a)   When the relevant regulatory framework requires—or otherwise does not prohibit—a departure from the requirement, the entity should make that departure and the disclosures set out in paragraph 20.

(b)   When the relevant regulatory framework prohibits departure from the requirement, the entity should, to the maximum extent possible, reduce the perceived misleading aspects of compliance by making the disclosures set out in paragraph 23.

This amendment enables entities to comply with the requirements of IAS 1 when the relevant regulatory framework prohibits departures from accounting standards, while retaining the principle that entities should, to the maximum extent possible, ensure that financial statements provide a fair presentation.

BC29   After considering the comments received on the exposure draft of 2002, the Board added to IAS 1 a requirement in paragraph 21 to disclose the effect of a departure from a requirement of an IFRS in a prior period on the current period's financial statements. Without this disclosure, users of the entity's financial statements could be unaware of the continuing effects of prior period departures.

BC30 In view of the strict criteria for departure from a requirement in an IFRS, IAS 1 includes a rebuttable presumption that if other entities in similar circumstances comply with the requirement, the entity's compliance with the requirement would not be so misleading that it would conflict with the objective of financial statements set out in the *Framework*.

Materiality and aggregation (paragraphs 29–31)

BC30A The Board was informed at the Discussion Forum *Financial Reporting Disclosure* in January 2013, in its related survey and by other sources, that there are difficulties applying the concept of materiality in practice. Some are of the view that these difficulties contribute to a disclosure problem, namely, that there is both too much irrelevant information and not enough relevant information in financial statements. A number of factors have been identified for why materiality may not be applied well in practice. One of these is that the guidance on materiality in IFRS is not clear.

BC30B Some think that the statement in IAS 1 that an entity need not provide a specific disclosure if the information is not material means that an entity does not need to present an item in the statement(s) of profit or loss and other comprehensive income, the statement of financial position, the statement of cash flows and the statement of changes in equity, but must instead disclose it in the notes. However, the Board noted that the concept of materiality is applicable to financial statements, which include the notes, and not only to those statements.

BC30C Some are of the view that when IFRS states that a specific disclosure is required, the concept of materiality does not apply to those disclosure requirements, ie disclosures specifically identified in IFRS are required irrespective of whether they result in material information. In addition, some people think that when a line item is presented, or a material item is otherwise recognised, in the statement(s) of profit or loss and other comprehensive income and the statement of financial position, all the disclosures in IFRS specified for that item must be disclosed. The Board observed that paragraph 31 of IAS 1 is clear that the concept of materiality applies to specific disclosures required by an IFRS and therefore an entity does not have to disclose information required by an IFRS if that information would not be material.

BC30D The Board understands that these misconceptions may have arisen because of the wording that is used when specifying presentation or disclosure requirements in IFRS; for example, the use of the words 'as a minimum'. For this reason, the Board removed the phrase 'as a minimum' in paragraph 54 of IAS 1, which lists line items for presentation in the statement of financial position. This also makes the requirement broadly consistent with the corresponding requirement in paragraph 82 of IAS 1 for the profit or loss section of the statement of comprehensive income or the statement of profit or loss.

BC30E On the basis of its observations and conclusions set out in paragraphs BC30A–BC30D, the Board added a new paragraph, paragraph 30A, and amended paragraph 31 of IAS 1.

BC30F   Paragraph 30A was added to IAS 1 to highlight that when an entity decides how it aggregates information in the financial statements, it should take into consideration all relevant facts and circumstances. Paragraph 30A emphasises that an entity should not reduce the understandability of its financial statements by providing immaterial information that obscures the material information in financial statements or by aggregating material items that have different natures or functions. Obscuring material information with immaterial information in financial statements makes the material information less visible and therefore makes the financial statements less understandable. The amendments do not actually prohibit entities from disclosing immaterial information, because the Board thinks that such a requirement would not be operational; however, the amendments emphasise that disclosure should not result in material information being obscured.

BC30G   The Exposure Draft *Disclosure Initiative* (Proposed amendments to IAS 1) (the 'March 2014 Exposure Draft'), which was published in March 2014, also proposed that an entity should not 'disaggregate' information in a manner that obscures useful information. Disaggregation is often used to describe the process of expanding totals, subtotals and line items into further items that themselves may reflect the aggregated results of transactions or other events. Because the process of expanding totals, subtotals and line items is more likely to increase the transparency of information rather than obscuring it, the Board decided not to include the term disaggregation in paragraph 30A of IAS 1. In addition, the Board was of the view that items resulting from the process of disaggregation that themselves reflect the aggregated results of transactions would be covered by paragraphs 29–31 of IAS 1.

BC30H   The Board amended paragraph 31 of IAS 1 to highlight that materiality also applies to disclosures specifically required by IFRS. In addition, to highlight that materiality not only involves decisions about excluding information from the financial statements, the Board amended paragraph 31 to reiterate the notion already stated in paragraph 17(c) of IAS 1 that materiality also involves decisions about whether to include additional information in the financial statements. Consequently, an entity should make additional disclosures when compliance with the specific requirements in IFRS is insufficient to enable users of financial statements to understand the impact of particular transactions, other events and conditions on the entity's financial position and financial performance.

BC30I   The Board noted that the definition of 'material' in paragraph 7 of IAS 1 discusses omissions or misstatements of items being material if they could individually or collectively influence economic decisions. The Board considered making amendments to paragraph 31 of IAS 1 to say that an entity need not provide a specific disclosure if the information provided by that disclosure is not material, either individually or collectively. However, the Board decided not to make that change since the definition of material already incorporates the notions of individual and collective assessment and, therefore, reference to the term material in paragraph 31 is sufficient to incorporate this concept.

BC30J   In the March 2014 Exposure Draft the Board proposed to use the term 'present' to refer to line items, subtotals and totals on the statement(s) of profit or loss and other comprehensive income, the statement of financial position, the statement of cash flows and the statement of changes in equity, and the term 'disclose' to mean information in the notes. However, respondents to the March 2014 Exposure Draft did not support the distinction between present and disclose because they considered that the terminology has not been used consistently throughout IAS 1 and that any changes in how these terms are used should be done as part of a comprehensive review of IAS 1. Because of this, and because making such comprehensive changes to IAS 1 would be outside the scope of these amendments, the Board did not finalise the proposed changes regarding use of the terms present and disclose.

Comparative information

A statement of financial position as at the beginning of the earliest comparative period (paragraph 39)

BC31   The exposure draft of 2006 proposed that a statement of financial position as at the beginning of the earliest comparative period should be presented as part of a complete set of financial statements. This statement would provide a basis for investors and creditors to evaluate information about the entity's performance during the period. However, many respondents expressed concern that the requirement would unnecessarily increase disclosures in financial statements, or would be impracticable, excessive and costly.

BC32   By adding a statement of financial position as at the beginning of the earliest comparative period, the exposure draft proposed that an entity should present three statements of financial position and two of each of the other statements. Considering that financial statements from prior years are readily available for financial analysis, the Board decided to require only two statements of financial position, except when the financial statements have been affected by retrospective application or retrospective restatement, as defined in IAS 8 *Accounting Policies, Changes in Accounting Estimates and Errors*, or when a reclassification has been made. In those circumstances three statements of financial position are required.

Clarification of requirements for comparative information

BC32A   In *Annual Improvements 2009–2011 Cycle* (issued in May 2012) the Board addressed a request to clarify the requirements for providing comparative information for:

(a)   the comparative requirements for the opening statement of financial position when an entity changes accounting policies, or makes retrospective restatements or reclassifications, in accordance with IAS 8 *Accounting Policies, Changes in Accounting Estimates and Errors*; and

(b)   the requirements for providing comparative information when an entity provides financial statements beyond the minimum comparative information requirements.

Opening statement of financial position

BC32B   In *Annual Improvements 2009–2011 Cycle* (issued in May 2012) the Board addressed a request to clarify the appropriate date for the opening statement of financial position. The Board decided to amend the current requirements in IAS 1 that relate to the presentation of a statement of financial position for the beginning of the earliest comparative period presented in cases of changes in accounting policies, retrospective restatements or reclassifications to clarify that the appropriate date for the opening statement of financial position is the beginning of the preceding period.

BC32C   The Board also decided to change the previous requirements so that related notes to this opening statement of financial position are no longer required to be presented. The Board's decision to give this relief was based on the fact that circumstances in which an entity changes an accounting policy, or makes a retrospective restatement or a reclassification in accordance with IAS 8, are considered narrow, specific and limited. However, the circumstances in which an entity chooses to provide additional financial statements (ie on a voluntary basis) can be viewed as more generic and may arise for different reasons. Accordingly, this relief is not available when additional financial statements are provided on a voluntary basis.

BC32D   The Board added the guidance in paragraph 40A(a) to clarify when an opening statement of financial position provides useful information and, should therefore be required. Paragraph 40A(b) is a reminder that the concept of materiality should be considered in applying the guidance in paragraph 40A(a). The Board noted that the entity would still be required to disclose the information required by IAS 8 for changes in accounting policies and retrospective restatements.

Comparative information beyond minimum requirements

BC32E   In *Annual Improvements 2009–2011 Cycle* (issued in May 2012) the Board addressed a request to clarify the requirements for providing comparative information. Specifically, the Board was asked to consider whether an entity should be required to present a complete set of financial statements when it provides financial statements beyond the minimum comparative information requirements (ie additional comparative information). In response to this request, the Board decided to clarify that additional financial statement information need not be presented in the form of a complete set of financial statements for periods beyond the minimum requirements. The Board also noted that additional comparative information might include:

(a)   information that is presented voluntarily, beyond the information that is included within a complete set of financial statements; or

(b)   comparative information that is required by law or other regulations but that is not required by IFRSs.

BC32F   The Board also decided to amend paragraphs 38–41 of IAS 1 to clarify that, when additional comparative information (that is not required by IFRSs) is provided by an entity, this information should be presented in accordance with IFRSs and the entity should present comparative information in the related notes for that additional information. The Board determined that requiring full notes for additional information in accordance with paragraph 38C is necessary to ensure that the additional information that the entity provides is balanced and results in financial statements that achieve a fair presentation.

BC32G   In the light of the concerns raised by interested parties, the Board decided that the amendments should be introduced through the Annual Improvements process instead of through the Financial Statement Presentation project, so that the changes could be made more quickly.

IAS 34 *Interim Financial Reporting*

BC33   The Board decided not to reflect in paragraph 8 of IAS 34 (ie the minimum components of an interim financial report) its decision to require the inclusion of a statement of financial position as at the beginning of the earliest comparative period in a complete set of financial statements. IAS 34 has a year-to-date approach to interim reporting and does not replicate the requirements of IAS 1 in terms of comparative information.

Criterion for exemption from requirements (paragraphs 41–44)

BC34   IAS 1 as issued in 1997 specified that when the presentation or classification of items in the financial statements is amended, comparative amounts should be reclassified unless it is impracticable to do so. Applying a requirement is impracticable when the entity cannot apply it after making every reasonable effort to do so.

BC35   The exposure draft of 2002 proposed a different criterion for exemption from particular requirements. For the reclassification of comparative amounts, and its proposed new requirement to disclose key assumptions and other sources of estimation uncertainty at the end of the reporting period (discussed in paragraphs BC79–BC84), the exposure draft proposed that the criterion for exemption should be that applying the requirements would require undue cost or effort.

BC36   In the light of respondents' comments on the exposure draft, the Board decided that an exemption based on management's assessment of undue cost or effort was too subjective to be applied consistently by different entities. Moreover, balancing costs and benefits was a task for the Board when it sets accounting requirements rather than for entities when they apply them. Therefore, the Board retained the 'impracticability' criterion for exemption. This affects the exemptions now set out in paragraphs 41–43 and 131 of IAS 1. Impracticability is the only basis on which IFRSs allow specific exemptions from applying particular requirements when the effect of applying them is material.[4]

Reporting owner and non-owner changes in equity

BC37   The exposure draft of 2006 proposed to separate changes in equity of an entity during a period arising from transactions with owners in their capacity as owners (ie all owner changes in equity) from other changes in equity (ie non-owner changes in equity). All owner changes in equity would be presented in the statement of changes in equity, separately from non-owner changes in equity.

---

4   In 2006 the IASB issued IFRS 8 *Operating Segments*. As explained in paragraphs BC46 and BC47 of the Basis for Conclusions on IFRS 8, that IFRS includes an exemption from some requirements if the necessary information is not available and the cost to develop it would be excessive.

BC38　Most respondents welcomed this proposal and saw this change as an improvement of financial reporting, by increasing the transparency of those items recognised in equity that are not reported as part of profit or loss. However, some respondents pointed out that the terms 'owner' and 'non-owner' were not defined in the exposure draft, the *Framework* or elsewhere in IFRSs, although they are extensively used in national accounting standards. They also noted that the terms 'owner' and 'equity holder' were used interchangeably in the exposure draft. The Board decided to adopt the term 'owner' and use it throughout IAS 1 to converge with SFAS 130, which uses the term in the definition of 'comprehensive income'.

Statement of financial position

Information to be presented in the statement of financial position (paragraphs 54–55A)

BC38A　Paragraph 54 of IAS 1 lists line items that are required to be presented in the statement of financial position. The Board has been informed that some have interpreted that list as prescriptive and that those line items cannot be disaggregated. There is also a perception by some that IFRS prevents them from presenting subtotals in addition to those specifically required by IFRS.

BC38B　Paragraph 55 of IAS 1 requires an entity to present additional line items, headings and subtotals when their presentation is relevant to an understanding of the entity's financial position. This highlights that the line items listed for presentation in paragraph 54 of IAS 1 should be disaggregated and that subtotals should be presented, when relevant. Paragraphs 78 and 98 of IAS 1 give examples of potential disaggregations of line items in the statement of financial position and the statement(s) of profit or loss and other comprehensive income.

BC38C　Consequently, the Board:

(a)　removed the wording 'as a minimum' from paragraph 54 of IAS 1 (see paragraph BC30D) to address the possible misconception that this wording prevents entities from aggregating the line items specified in paragraph 54 if those specified line items are immaterial; and

(b)　clarified that the presentation requirements in paragraphs 54–55 may be fulfilled by disaggregating a specified line item.

BC38D　The Board noted that there are similar presentation requirements in paragraph 85 of IAS 1 for the statement(s) of profit or loss and other comprehensive income. The Board therefore amended those requirements to make them consistent.

BC38E　Some respondents to the proposals suggested that the Board should make clear that the line items listed in paragraph 54 of IAS 1 are required 'when material'. The Board decided not to state that the line items are only required when material, because materiality is generally not referenced specifically in disclosure requirements in IFRS and so including a specific reference in this case could make it less clear that materiality applies to other disclosure requirements.

BC38F   The Board understands that some are concerned about the presentation of subtotals, in addition to those specified in IFRS, in the statement of financial position and the statement(s) of profit or loss and other comprehensive income. Those with this concern think that some subtotals can be misleading, for example, because they are given undue prominence. The Board noted that paragraphs 55 and 85 of IAS 1 require the presentation of subtotals when such presentation is relevant to an understanding of the entity's financial position or financial performance.

BC38G   The Board therefore included additional requirements in IAS 1 to help entities apply paragraphs 55 and 85. These additional requirements supplement the existing guidance on fair presentation in paragraphs 15 and 17 of IAS 1. They are designed to clarify the factors that should be considered when fairly presenting subtotals in the statement of financial position and the statement(s) of profit or loss and other comprehensive income. Specifically, the subtotal should:

(a)   be comprised of line items made up of amounts recognised and measured in accordance with IFRS.

(b)   be understandable. It should be clear what line items are included in the subtotal by the way that the subtotal is presented and labelled. For example, if an entity presents a commonly reported subtotal, but excludes items that would normally be considered as part of that subtotal, the label should reflect what has been excluded.

(c)   be consistent from period to period. The subtotal should be consistently presented and calculated from period to period (in accordance with paragraph 45 of IAS 1), subject to possible changes in accounting policy or estimates assessed in accordance with IAS 8.

(d)   not be displayed with more prominence than those subtotals and totals required in IFRS for either the statement(s) of profit or loss and other comprehensive income or the statement of financial position.

Current assets and current liabilities (paragraphs 68 and 71)

BC38H   As part of its improvements project in 2007, the Board identified inconsistent guidance regarding the current/non-current classification of derivatives. Some might read the guidance included in paragraph 71 as implying that financial liabilities classified as held for trading in accordance with IAS 39 *Financial Instruments: Recognition and Measurement*[5] are always required to be presented as current.

BC38I   The Board expects the criteria set out in paragraph 69 to be used to assess whether a financial liability should be presented as current or non-current. The

---

5   IFRS 9 *Financial Instruments* replaced IAS 39. IFRS 9 applies to all items that were previously within the scope of IAS 39. This paragraph refers to matters relevant when IAS 1 was issued.

'held for trading' category in paragraph 9 of IAS 39[6] is for measurement purposes and includes financial assets and liabilities that may not be held primarily for trading purposes.

BC38J The Board reaffirmed that if a financial liability is held primarily for trading purposes it should be presented as current regardless of its maturity date. However, a financial liability that is not held for trading purposes, such as a derivative that is not a financial guarantee contract or a designated hedging instrument, should be presented as current or non-current on the basis of its settlement date. For example, derivatives that have a maturity of more than twelve months and are expected to be held for more than twelve months after the reporting period should be presented as non-current assets or liabilities.

BC38K Therefore, the Board decided to remove the identified inconsistency by amending the examples of current liabilities in paragraph 71. The Board also amended paragraph 68 in respect of current assets to remove a similar inconsistency.

Classification of the liability component of a convertible instrument (paragraph 69)

BC38L As part of its improvements project in 2007, the Board considered the classification of the liability component of a convertible instrument as current or non-current. Paragraph 69(d) of IAS 1 states that when an entity does not have an unconditional right to defer settlement of a liability for at least twelve months after the reporting period, the liability should be classified as current. According to the *Framework*, conversion of a liability into equity is a form of settlement.

BC38M The application of these requirements means that if the conversion option can be exercised by the holder at any time, the liability component would be classified as current. This classification would be required even if the entity would not be required to settle unconverted instruments with cash or other assets for more than twelve months after the reporting period.

BC38N IAS 1 and the *Framework* state that information about the liquidity and solvency positions of an entity is useful to users. The terms 'liquidity' and 'solvency' are associated with the availability of cash to an entity. Issuing equity does not result in an outflow of cash or other assets of the entity.

BC38O The Board concluded that classifying the liability on the basis of the requirements to transfer cash or other assets rather than on settlement better reflects the liquidity and solvency position of an entity, and therefore it decided to amend IAS 1 accordingly.

BC38P The Board discussed the comments received in response to its exposure draft of proposed *Improvements to IFRSs* published in 2007 and noted that some respondents were concerned that the proposal in the exposure draft would apply to all liabilities, not just those that are components of convertible instruments as originally contemplated in the exposure draft. Consequently, in

---

6 IFRS 9 *Financial Instruments* replaced IAS 39. IFRS 9 applies to all items that were previously within the scope of IAS 39. This paragraph refers to matters relevant when IAS 1 was issued.

Improvements to IFRSs issued in April 2009, the Board amended the proposed wording to clarify that the amendment applies only to the classification of a liability that can, at the option of the counterparty, be settled by the issue of the entity's equity instruments.

Effect of events after the reporting period on the classification of liabilities (paragraphs 69–76)

BC39   Paragraph 63 of IAS 1 (as issued in 1997) included the following:

> An enterprise should continue to classify its long-term interest-bearing liabilities as non-current, even when they are due to be settled within twelve months of the balance sheet date if:
>
> (a)   the original term was for a period of more than twelve months;
>
> (b)   the enterprise intends to refinance the obligation on a long-term basis; and
>
> (c)   that intention is supported by an agreement to refinance, or to reschedule payments, which is completed before the financial statements are authorised for issue.

BC40   Paragraph 65 stated:

> Some borrowing agreements incorporate undertakings by the borrower (covenants) which have the effect that the liability becomes payable on demand if certain conditions related to the borrower's financial position are breached. In these circumstances, the liability is classified as non-current only when:
>
> (a)   the lender has agreed, prior to the authorisation of the financial statements for issue, not to demand payment as a consequence of the breach; and
>
> (b)   it is not probable that further breaches will occur within twelve months of the balance sheet date.

BC41   The Board considered these requirements and concluded that refinancing, or the receipt of a waiver of the lender's right to demand payment, that occurs after the reporting period should not be taken into account in the classification of a liability.

BC42   Therefore, the exposure draft of 2002 proposed:

(a)   to amend paragraph 63 to specify that a long-term financial liability due to be settled within twelve months of the balance sheet date should not be classified as a non-current liability because an agreement to refinance, or to reschedule payments, on a long-term basis is completed after the balance sheet date and before the financial statements are authorised for issue. This amendment would not affect the classification of a liability as non-current when the entity has, under the terms of an existing loan facility, the discretion to refinance or roll over its obligations for at least twelve months after the balance sheet date.

(b)   to amend paragraph 65 to specify that a long-term financial liability that is payable on demand because the entity breached a condition of its loan agreement should be classified as current at the balance sheet date even if the lender has agreed after the balance sheet date, and before the financial statements are authorised for issue, not to demand payment as a consequence of the breach. However, if the lender has agreed by the balance sheet date to provide a period of grace within which the entity can rectify the breach and during which the lender cannot demand immediate repayment, the liability is classified as non-current if it is due for settlement, without that breach of the loan agreement, at least twelve months after the balance sheet date and:

(i)   the entity rectifies the breach within the period of grace; or

(ii)   when the financial statements are authorised for issue, the period of grace is incomplete and it is probable that the breach will be rectified.

BC43   Some respondents disagreed with these proposals. They advocated classifying a liability as current or non-current according to whether it is expected to use current assets of the entity, rather than strictly on the basis of its date of maturity and whether it is callable at the end of the reporting period. In their view, this would provide more relevant information about the liability's future effect on the timing of the entity's resource flows.

BC44   However, the Board decided that the following arguments for changing paragraphs 63 and 65 were more persuasive:

(a)   refinancing a liability after the balance sheet date does not affect the entity's liquidity and solvency *at the balance sheet date*, the reporting of which should reflect contractual arrangements in force on that date. Therefore, it is a non-adjusting event in accordance with IAS 10 *Events after the Balance Sheet Date* and should not affect the presentation of the entity's balance sheet.

(b)   it is illogical to adopt a criterion that 'non-current' classification of short-term obligations expected to be rolled over for at least twelve months after the balance sheet date depends on whether the roll-over is at the discretion of the entity, and then to provide an exception based on refinancing occurring after the balance sheet date.

(c)   in the circumstances set out in paragraph 65, unless the lender has waived its right to demand immediate repayment or granted a period of grace within which the entity may rectify the breach of the loan agreement, the financial condition of the entity at the balance sheet date was that the entity did not hold an absolute right to defer repayment, based on the terms of the loan agreement. The granting of a waiver or a period of grace changes the terms of the loan agreement. Therefore, an entity's receipt from the lender, after the balance sheet date, of a waiver or a period of grace of at least twelve months does not change the nature of the liability to non-current until it occurs.

BC45   IAS 1 now includes the amendments proposed in 2002, with one change. The change relates to the classification of a long-term loan when, at the end of the reporting period, the lender has provided a period of grace within which a breach of the loan agreement can be rectified, and during which period the lender cannot demand immediate repayment of the loan.

BC46   The exposure draft proposed that such a loan should be classified as non-current if it is due for settlement, without the breach, at least twelve months after the balance sheet date and:

(a)   the entity rectifies the breach within the period of grace; or

(b)   when the financial statements are authorised for issue, the period of grace is incomplete and it is probable that the breach will be rectified.

BC47   After considering respondents' comments, the Board decided that the occurrence or probability of a rectification of a breach after the reporting period is irrelevant to the conditions existing at the end of the reporting period. The revised IAS 1 requires that, for the loan to be classified as non-current, the period of grace must end at least twelve months after the reporting period (see paragraph 75). Therefore, the conditions (a) and (b) in paragraph BC46 are redundant.

BC48   The Board considered arguments that if a period of grace to remedy a breach of a long-term loan agreement is provided before the end of the reporting period, the loan should be classified as non-current regardless of the length of the period of grace. These arguments are based on the view that, at the end of the reporting period, the lender does not have an unconditional legal right to demand repayment before the original maturity date (ie if the entity remedies the breach during the period of grace, it is entitled to repay the loan on the original maturity date). However, the Board concluded that an entity should classify a loan as non-current only if it has an unconditional right to defer settlement of the loan for at least twelve months after the reporting period. This criterion focuses on the legal rights of the entity, rather than those of the lender.

Statement of comprehensive income

Reporting comprehensive income (paragraph 81)

BC49   The exposure draft of 2006 proposed that all non-owner changes in equity should be presented in a single statement or in two statements. In a single-statement presentation, all items of income and expense are presented together. In a two-statement presentation, the first statement ('income statement') presents income and expenses recognised in profit or loss and the second statement ('statement of comprehensive income') begins with profit or loss and presents, in addition, items of income and expense that IFRSs require or permit to be recognised outside profit or loss. Such items include, for example, translation differences related to foreign operations and gains or losses on available-for-sale financial assets.[7] The statement of comprehensive income does not include transactions with owners in their capacity as owners. Such transactions are presented in the statement of changes in equity.

BC50   Respondents to the exposure draft had mixed views about whether the Board should permit a choice of displaying non-owner changes in equity in one statement or two statements. Many respondents agreed with the Board's proposal to maintain the two-statement approach and the single-statement

---

7   IFRS 9 Financial Instruments eliminated the category of available-for-sale financial assets. This paragraph refers to matters relevant when IAS 1 was issued.

approach as alternatives and a few urged the Board to mandate one of them. However, most respondents preferred the two-statement approach because it distinguishes profit or loss and total comprehensive income; they believe that with the two-statement approach, the 'income statement' remains a primary financial statement. Respondents supported the presentation of two separate statements as a transition measure until the Board develops principles to determine the criteria for inclusion of items in profit or loss or in other comprehensive income.

BC51 The exposure draft of 2006 expressed the Board's preference for a single statement of all non-owner changes in equity. The Board provided several reasons for this preference. All items of non-owner changes in equity meet the definitions of income and expenses in the *Framework*. The *Framework* does not define profit or loss, nor does it provide criteria for distinguishing the characteristics of items that should be included in profit or loss from those items that should be excluded from profit or loss. Therefore, the Board decided that it was conceptually correct for an entity to present all non-owner changes in equity (ie all income and expenses recognised in a period) in a single statement because there are no clear principles or common characteristics that can be used to separate income and expenses into two statements.

BC52 However, in the Board's discussions with interested parties, it was clear that many were strongly opposed to the concept of a single statement. They argued that there would be undue focus on the bottom line of the single statement. In addition, many argued that it was premature for the Board to conclude that presentation of income and expense in a single statement was an improvement in financial reporting without also addressing the other aspects of presentation and display, namely deciding what categories and line items should be presented in a statement of recognised income and expense.

BC53 In the light of these views, although it preferred a single statement, the Board decided that an entity should have the choice of presenting all income and expenses recognised in a period in one statement or in two statements. An entity is prohibited from presenting components of income and expense (ie non-owner changes in equity) in the statement of changes in equity.

BC54 Many respondents disagreed with the Board's preference and thought that a decision at this stage would be premature. In their view the decision about a single-statement or two-statement approach should be subject to further consideration. They urged the Board to address other aspects of presentation and display, namely deciding which categories and line items should be presented in a 'statement of comprehensive income'. The Board reaffirmed its reasons for preferring a single-statement approach and agreed to address other aspects of display and presentation in the next stage of the project.

BC54A In *Presentation of Items of Other Comprehensive Income* published in May 2010 the Board proposed to eliminate the option to present all items of income and expense recognised in a period in two statements, thereby requiring presentation in a continuous statement displaying two sections: *profit or loss* and *other comprehensive income*. The Board also proposed to require items of OCI to be classified into items that might be reclassified (recycled) to profit or loss in subsequent periods and items that would not be reclassified subsequently.

BC54B   In its deliberations on financial instruments and pensions the Board discussed the increasing importance of consistent presentation of items of OCI. Both projects will increase the number of items presented in OCI, particularly items that will not be reclassified subsequently to profit or loss. Therefore the Board thought it important that all income and expenses that are components of the total non-owner changes in equity should be presented transparently.

BC54C   The Board has no plans to eliminate profit or loss as a measure of performance. Profit or loss will be presented separately and will remain the required starting point for the calculation of earnings per share.

BC54D   The Board had previously received responses to similar proposals for a single statement of comprehensive income. In October 2008 the Board and the FASB jointly published a discussion paper, *Preliminary Views on Financial Statement Presentation*. In that paper, the boards proposed eliminating the alternative presentation formats for comprehensive income and to require an entity to present comprehensive income and its components in a single statement. The boards asked for views on that proposal. The responses were split on whether an entity should present comprehensive income and its components in a single statement or in two separate statements. In general, respondents supporting a single statement of comprehensive income said that it would lead to greater transparency, consistency and comparability. Furthermore, the process of calculating financial ratios would be made easier.

BC54E   Respondents disagreeing with the proposal for a single statement of comprehensive income urged the boards to defer any changes to the guidance on the statement of comprehensive income until the boards had completed a project to revise the guidance on what items should be presented in OCI. Those respondents also said that a single statement would undermine the importance of profit or loss by making it a subtotal and that presenting total comprehensive income as the last number in the statement would confuse users. They also feared that requiring all items of income and expense to be presented in a single statement was the first step by the boards towards eliminating the notion of profit or loss. In addition, they argued that the items that are presented in OCI are different from items presented in profit or loss. Therefore they preferred either to keep the presentation of profit or loss separate from the presentation of OCI or to allow management to choose to present them either in a single statement or in two statements.

BC54F   In the responses to the exposure draft of May 2010 many of the respondents objected to the proposals to remove the option to present all items of income and expense in two statements. The arguments used by those objecting were much the same as those received on the discussion paper. However, many respondents, regardless of their views on the proposed amendments, said that the Board should establish a conceptual basis for what should be presented in OCI. Those opposed to a continuous statement cited OCI's lack of a conceptual definition and therefore believed that OCI should not be presented in close proximity to profit or loss because this would confuse users. However, users generally said that the lack of a conceptual framework made it difficult to distinguish the underlying economics of items reported in profit or loss (net income) from items reported in other comprehensive income. Although users also asked for a conceptual framework for OCI, most supported the notion of a single statement of comprehensive income.

BC54G   Another issue on which many respondents commented was the reclassification (recycling) of OCI items. Those respondents said that in addition to addressing the conceptual basis for the split between profit or loss and OCI the Board should set principles for which OCI items should be reclassified (recycled) to profit or loss and when they should be reclassified. The Board acknowledges that it has not set out a conceptual basis for how it determines whether an item should be presented in OCI or in profit or loss. It also agrees that it has not set out principles to determine whether items should be reclassified to profit or loss. Those matters were not within the scope of this project, which focused on presentation, and therefore the Board has not addressed them at this time. However, the Board is consulting on its future agenda, which could lead to those matters becoming part of the work programme.

BC54H   In the light of the response the Board confirmed in June 2011 the requirement for items of OCI to be classified into items that will not be reclassified (recycled) to profit or loss in subsequent periods and items that might be reclassified.

BC54I   The Board also decided not to mandate the presentation of profit or loss in a continuous statement of profit or loss and other comprehensive income but to maintain an option to present two statements. The Board did this in the light of the negative response to its proposal for a continuous statement and the resistance to this change signified by a majority of respondents.

BC54J   The FASB also proposed in its exposure draft to mandate a continuous statement of comprehensive income but decided in the light of the responses not to go as far as mandating a single statement and instead to allow the two-statement option. Nevertheless, the changes made by the FASB are a significant improvement for US GAAP, which previously allowed an option to present OCI items in stockholders' equity or in the notes to the financial statements.

BC54K   In 2013 the IFRS Interpretations Committee reported to the Board that there was uncertainty about the requirements in paragraph 82A of IAS 1 for presenting an entity's share of items of other comprehensive income of associates and joint ventures accounted for using the equity method. The Board agreed that paragraph 82A allowed for diverse interpretations, and therefore decided to amend IAS 1 as follows:

(a)   to clarify that paragraph 82A requires entities to present the share of other comprehensive income of associates and joint ventures accounted for using the equity method, separated into the share of items that:

(i)   will not be reclassified subsequently to profit or loss; and

(ii)   will be reclassified subsequently to profit or loss when specific conditions are met.

(b)   to amend the Guidance on Implementing IAS 1 to reflect the clarification of paragraph 82A.

The Board noted that whether an amount is reclassified to profit or loss is determined by the nature of the underlying item. It also noted that the timing of reclassification is usually determined by the actions of the investee. It may however also be triggered by the investor, which would be the case on the disposal of the investee by the investor.

BC54L The feedback received on the March 2014 Exposure Draft included requests for the Board to clarify whether the investor's share of the other comprehensive income of its associate or joint venture should be presented net or gross of tax and the applicability of the guidance in paragraphs 90–91 of IAS 1 in this regard. The Board noted that an investor's share of other comprehensive income of associates or joint ventures is after tax and non-controlling interests of the associate or joint venture, as illustrated in the Guidance on Implementing IAS 1. It also noted that the disclosure requirements in paragraphs 90–91 do not apply to the tax of the associate or joint venture that is already reflected in the investor's share of other comprehensive income of the associate or joint venture. However, the Board noted that if the investor itself is liable for tax in respect of its share of other comprehensive income of the associate or joint venture, then paragraphs 90–91 would apply to this tax. Therefore, the Board decided not to add additional guidance to IAS 1 on this topic.

Results of operating activities

BC55 IAS 1 omits the requirement in the 1997 version to disclose the results of operating activities as a line item in the income statement. 'Operating activities' are not defined in IAS 1, and the Board decided not to require disclosure of an undefined item.

BC56 The Board recognises that an entity may elect to disclose the results of operating activities, or a similar line item, even though this term is not defined. In such cases, the Board notes that the entity should ensure that the amount disclosed is representative of activities that would normally be regarded as 'operating'. In the Board's view, it would be misleading and would impair the comparability of financial statements if items of an operating nature were excluded from the results of operating activities, even if that had been industry practice. For example, it would be inappropriate to exclude items clearly related to operations (such as inventory write-downs and restructuring and relocation expenses) because they occur irregularly or infrequently or are unusual in amount. Similarly, it would be inappropriate to exclude items on the grounds that they do not involve cash flows, such as depreciation and amortisation expenses.

Subtotal for profit or loss (paragraph 82)

BC57 As revised, IAS 1 requires a subtotal for profit or loss in the statement of comprehensive income. If an entity chooses to present comprehensive income by using two statements, it should begin the second statement with profit or loss—the bottom line of the first statement (the 'income statement')—and display the components of other comprehensive income immediately after that. The Board concluded that this is the best way to achieve the objective of equal prominence (see paragraph BC22) for the presentation of income and expenses. An entity that chooses to display comprehensive income in one statement should include profit or loss as a subtotal within that statement.

BC58　The Board acknowledged that the items included in profit or loss do not possess any unique characteristics that allow them to be distinguished from items that are included in other comprehensive income. However, the Board and its predecessor have required some items to be recognised outside profit or loss. The Board will deliberate in the next stage of the project how items of income and expense should be presented in the statement of comprehensive income.

Information to be presented in the profit or loss section or the statement of profit or loss (paragraphs 85–85B)

BC58A　In December 2014 the Board issued *Disclosure Initiative* (Amendments to IAS 1). Those amendments included amendments to paragraph 85 of IAS 1 and the addition of paragraph 85A. These amendments are consistent with similar amendments to the requirements for the statement of financial position and therefore the Basis for Conclusions for these amendments has been included in the section dealing with that statement (see paragraphs BC38A–BC38G).

BC58B　In addition to those amendments, the Board decided to require entities to present line items in the statement(s) of profit or loss and other comprehensive income that reconcile any subtotals presented in accordance with paragraphs 85–85A of IAS 1 with those that are required in IFRS for the statement(s) of profit or loss and other comprehensive income. Consequently, it added paragraph 85B to IAS 1. The purpose of this requirement is to help users of financial statements understand the relationship between the subtotals presented in accordance with paragraph 85 and the specific totals and subtotals required in IFRS to address concerns that that relationship would not be clear. The Board noted that such a requirement is already implicit in existing IFRS requirements. IFRS requires entities to present aggregated information as line items when such presentation provides material information. Consequently, because all recognised items of income and expense must be included in the statement(s) of profit or loss and other comprehensive income totals, any intervening line items and subtotals necessarily reconcile. However, the Board decided to make the requirement more explicit for the statement(s) of profit or loss and other comprehensive income to help users of financial statements understand the relationship between subtotals and totals presented in the statement(s) of profit or loss and other comprehensive income.

Minority interest (paragraph 83)[8]

BC59　IAS 1 requires the 'profit or loss attributable to minority interest' and 'profit or loss attributable to owners of the parent' each to be presented in the income statement in accordance with paragraph 83. These amounts are to be presented as allocations of profit or loss, not as items of income or expense. A similar requirement has been added for the statement of changes in equity, in paragraph 106(a). These changes are consistent with IAS 27 *Consolidated and Separate Financial Statements*, which requires that in a consolidated balance sheet

---

8　In January 2008 the IASB issued an amended IAS 27 *Consolidated and Separate Financial Statements*, which amended 'minority interest' to 'non-controlling interests'. The consolidation requirements in IAS 27 were superseded by IFRS 10 *Consolidated Financial Statements* issued in May 2011. The term 'non-controlling interests' and the requirements for non-controlling interests were not changed.

(now called 'statement of financial position'), minority interest is presented within equity because it does not meet the definition of a liability in the *Framework*.

Extraordinary items (paragraph 87)

BC60   IAS 8 *Net Profit or Loss for the Period, Fundamental Errors and Changes in Accounting Policies* (issued in 1993) required extraordinary items to be disclosed in the income statement separately from the profit or loss from ordinary activities. That standard defined 'extraordinary items' as 'income or expenses that arise from events or transactions that are clearly distinct from the ordinary activities of the enterprise and therefore are not expected to recur frequently or regularly'.

BC61   In 2002, the Board decided to eliminate the concept of extraordinary items from IAS 8 and to prohibit the presentation of items of income and expense as 'extraordinary items' in the income statement and the notes. Therefore, in accordance with IAS 1, no items of income and expense are to be presented as arising from outside the entity's ordinary activities.

BC62   Some respondents to the exposure draft of 2002 argued that extraordinary items should be presented in a separate component of the income statement because they are clearly distinct from all of the other items of income and expense, and because such presentation highlights to users of financial statements the items of income and expense to which the least attention should be given when predicting an entity's future performance.

BC63   The Board decided that items treated as extraordinary result from the normal business risks faced by an entity and do not warrant presentation in a separate component of the income statement. The nature or function of a transaction or other event, rather than its frequency, should determine its presentation within the income statement. Items currently classified as 'extraordinary' are only a subset of the items of income and expense that may warrant disclosure to assist users in predicting an entity's future performance.

BC64   Eliminating the category of extraordinary items eliminates the need for arbitrary segregation of the effects of related external events—some recurring and others not—on the profit or loss of an entity for a period. For example, arbitrary allocations would have been necessary to estimate the financial effect of an earthquake on an entity's profit or loss if it occurs during a major cyclical downturn in economic activity. In addition, paragraph 97 of IAS 1 requires disclosure of the nature and amount of material items of income and expense.

Other comprehensive income—related tax effects (paragraphs 90 and 91)

BC65   The exposure draft of 2006 proposed to allow components of 'other recognised income and expense' (now 'other comprehensive income') to be presented before tax effects ('gross presentation') or after their related tax effects ('net presentation'). The 'gross presentation' facilitated the traceability of other comprehensive income items to profit or loss, because items of profit or loss are generally displayed before tax. The 'net presentation' facilitated the identification of other comprehensive income items in the equity section of the statement of financial position. A majority of respondents supported allowing both approaches. The Board reaffirmed its conclusion that components of other comprehensive income could be displayed either (a) net of related tax effects or (b) before related tax effects.

BC66 Regardless of whether a pre-tax or post-tax display was used, the exposure draft proposed to require disclosure of the amount of income tax expense or benefit allocated separately to individual components of other comprehensive income, in line with SFAS 130. Many respondents agreed in principle with this disclosure, because they agreed that it helped to improve the clarity and transparency of such information, particularly when components of other comprehensive income are taxed at rates different from those applied to profit or loss.

BC67 However, most respondents expressed concern about having to trace the tax effect for each one of the components of other comprehensive income. Several observed that the tax allocation process is arbitrary (eg it may involve the application of subjectively determined tax rates) and some pointed out that this information is not readily available for some industries (eg the insurance sector), where components of other comprehensive income are multiple and tax allocation involves a high degree of subjectivity. Others commented that they did not understand why tax should be attributed to components of comprehensive income line by line, when this is not a requirement for items in profit or loss.

BC68 The Board decided to maintain the disclosure of income tax expense or benefit allocated to each component of other comprehensive income. Users of financial statements often requested further information on tax amounts relating to components of other comprehensive income, because tax rates often differed from those applied to profit or loss. The Board also observed that an entity should have such tax information available and that a disclosure requirement would therefore not involve additional cost for preparers of financial statements.

BC68A In its exposure draft *Presentation of Items of Other Comprehensive Income* published in May 2010 the Board proposed requiring that income tax on items presented in OCI should be allocated between items that will not be subsequently reclassified to profit or loss and those that might be reclassified, if the items in OCI are presented before tax. Most respondents agreed with this proposal as this would be in line with the existing options in IAS 1 regarding presentation of income tax on OCI items. Therefore the Board confirmed the proposal in June 2011.

Reclassification adjustments (paragraphs 92–96)

BC69 In the exposure draft of 2006, the Board proposed that an entity should separately present reclassification adjustments. These adjustments are the amounts reclassified to profit or loss in the current period that were previously recognised in other comprehensive income. The Board decided that adjustments necessary to avoid double-counting items in total comprehensive income when those items are reclassified to profit or loss in accordance with IFRSs. The Board's view was that separate presentation of reclassification adjustments is essential to inform users of those amounts that are included as income and expenses in different periods—as income or expenses in other comprehensive income in previous periods and as income or expenses in profit or loss in the current period. Without such information, users may find it difficult to assess the effect of reclassifications on profit or loss and to calculate the overall gain or loss associated with available-for-sale financial assets,[9] cash flow hedges and on translation or disposal of foreign operations.

BC70 Most respondents agreed with the Board's decision and believe that the disclosure of reclassification adjustments is important to understanding how components recognised in profit or loss are related to other items recognised in equity in two different periods. However, some respondents suggested that the Board should use the term 'recycling', rather than 'reclassification' as the former term is more common. The Board concluded that both terms are similar in meaning, but decided to use the term 'reclassification adjustment' to converge with the terminology used in SFAS 130.

BC71 The exposure draft proposed to allow the presentation of reclassification adjustments in the statement of recognised income and expense (now 'statement of comprehensive income') or in the notes. Most respondents supported this approach.

BC72 Some respondents noted some inconsistencies in the definition of 'reclassification adjustments' in the exposure draft (now paragraphs 7 and 93 of IAS 1). Respondents suggested that the Board should expand the definition in paragraph 7 to include gains and losses recognised in current periods in addition to those recognised in earlier periods, to make the definition consistent with paragraph 93. They commented that, without clarification, there could be differences between interim and annual reporting, for reclassifications of items that arise in one interim period and reverse out in a different interim period within the same annual period.

BC73 The Board decided to align the definition of reclassification adjustments with SFAS 130 and include an additional reference to 'current periods' in paragraph 7.

Statement of changes in equity

Effects of retrospective application or retrospective restatement (paragraph 106(b))

BC74 Some respondents to the exposure draft of 2006 asked the Board to clarify whether the effects of retrospective application or retrospective restatement, as defined in IAS 8, should be regarded as non-owner changes in equity. The Board noted that IAS 1 specifies that these effects are included in the statement of changes in equity. However, the Board decided to clarify that the effects of retrospective application or retrospective restatement are not changes in equity in the period, but provide a reconciliation between the previous period's closing balance and the opening balance in the statement of changes in equity.

---

9 IFRS 9 *Financial Instruments* eliminated the category of available-for-sale financial assets. This paragraph refers to matters relevant when IAS 1 was issued.

Reconciliation for each component of other comprehensive income (paragraphs 106(d)(ii) and 106A)

BC74A   Paragraph 106(d) requires an entity to provide a reconciliation of changes in each component of equity. In *Improvements to IFRSs* issued in May 2010, the Board clarified that entities may present the required reconciliations for each component of other comprehensive income either in the statement of changes in equity or in the notes to the financial statements.

Presentation of dividends (paragraph 107)

BC75   The Board reaffirmed its conclusion to require the presentation of dividends in the statement of changes in equity or in the notes, because dividends are distributions to owners in their capacity as owners and the statement of changes in equity presents all owner changes in equity. The Board concluded that an entity should not present dividends in the statement of comprehensive income because that statement presents non-owner changes in equity.

Statement of cash flows

IAS 7 *Cash Flow Statements* (paragraph 111)

BC76   The Board considered whether the operating section of an indirect method statement of cash flows should begin with total comprehensive income instead of profit or loss as is required by IAS 7 *Cash Flow Statements*. When components of other comprehensive income are non-cash items, they would become reconciling items in arriving at cash flows from operating activities and would add items to the statement of cash flows without adding information content. The Board concluded that an amendment to IAS 7 is not required; however, as mentioned in paragraph BC14 the Board decided to relabel this financial statement as 'statement of cash flows'.

Notes

Structure (paragraphs 112–116)

BC76A   The Board is aware that some had interpreted paragraph 114 of IAS 1 as requiring a specific order for the notes. Paragraph 114 stated that 'an entity normally presents notes in the [following] order' and then listed a particular order for the notes. Some think that the use of 'normally' makes it difficult for an entity to vary the order of the notes from the one that is listed in paragraph 114; for example, by disclosing the notes in order of importance or disclosing related information together in sections.

BC76B   Investors' feedback indicates that some investors prefer an entity to vary the order of the notes from the one that is listed in paragraph 114 of IAS 1. Other investors would prefer entities to use that order because they think it will increase comparability between periods and across entities.

BC76C   The Board considered the use of the word normally in paragraph 114 of IAS 1 and concluded that it was not intended that entities be required to disclose their notes in that order. Instead, it thinks that the order listed was intended to provide an example of how an entity could order the notes and that the term normal was not meant to imply that alternative ordering of the notes is 'abnormal'. The Board therefore amended IAS 1 to clarify that the order listed in paragraph 114 is an example of how an entity could order or group its notes in a systematic manner. The Board also made amendments to clarify that significant accounting policies do not need to be disclosed in one note, but instead can be included with related information in other notes.

BC76D   The Board also noted the requirement in paragraph 113 of IAS 1 for entities to, as far as practicable, present the notes in a systematic manner. In the Board's view, this means that there must be a system or reason behind the ordering and grouping of the notes. For example, notes could be ordered by importance to the entity, in the order line items are presented in the financial statements or a combination of both. The Board amended paragraph 113 to clarify that an entity should consider the effect on the understandability and comparability of its financial statements when determining the order of the notes. The Board acknowledged that there is a trade-off between understandability and comparability; for example, ordering notes to increase understandability could mean that comparability, including consistency, between entities and periods is reduced. In particular, the Board acknowledged that consistency in the order of the notes for a specific entity from period to period is important. The Board noted that it would generally be helpful for users of financial statements if the ordering of notes by an entity is consistent and noted that it does not expect the order of an entity's notes to change frequently. A change in the order of the notes previously determined to be an optimal mix of understandability and comparability should generally result from a specific event or transaction, such as a change in business. The Board also noted that the existing requirements in paragraph 45 of IAS 1 for consistency of presentation still apply.

BC76E   The Board also observed that electronic versions of financial statements can make it easier to search for, locate and compare information within the financial statements, between periods and between entities.

Disclosure of accounting policies (paragraphs 117–121)

BC76F   Paragraph 117 of IAS 1 requires significant accounting policies to be disclosed and gives guidance, along with paragraphs 118–124 of IAS 1, about what a significant accounting policy could be. That guidance includes, as examples of significant accounting policies, the income taxes accounting policy and the foreign currency accounting policy.

BC76G   Some suggested that it is not helpful to provide the income taxes accounting policy as an example of a policy that users of financial statements would expect to be disclosed. Being liable to income taxes is typical for many entities and it was not clear, from the example, what aspect of the entity's operations would make a user of financial statements expect an accounting policy on income taxes to be disclosed. Consequently, the example does not illustrate why an accounting policy on income taxes is significant. The Board also thought that the foreign currency accounting policy example in paragraph 120 of IAS 1 was unhelpful for the same reasons and therefore deleted the income taxes and foreign currency examples.

Disclosure of the judgements that management has made in the process of applying the entity's accounting policies (paragraphs 122–124)

BC77 The revised IAS 1 requires disclosure of the judgements, apart from those involving estimations, that management has made in the process of applying the entity's accounting policies and that have the most significant effect on the amounts recognised in the financial statements (see paragraph 122). An example of these judgements is how management determines whether financial assets are held-to-maturity investments.[10] The Board decided that disclosure of the most important of these judgements would enable users of financial statements to understand better how the accounting policies are applied and to make comparisons between entities regarding the basis on which managements make these judgements.

BC78 Comments received on the exposure draft of 2002 indicated that the purpose of the proposed disclosure was unclear. Accordingly, the Board amended the disclosure explicitly to exclude judgements involving estimations (which are the subject of the disclosure in paragraph 125) and added another four examples of the types of judgements disclosed (see paragraphs 123 and 124).

Disclosure of major sources of estimation uncertainty (paragraphs 125–133)

BC79 IAS 1 requires disclosure of the assumptions concerning the future, and other major sources of estimation uncertainty at the end of the reporting period, that have a significant risk of causing a material adjustment to the carrying amounts of assets and liabilities within the next financial year. For those assets and liabilities, the proposed disclosures include details of:

(a) their nature; and

(b) their carrying amount as at the end of the reporting period (see paragraph 125).

BC80 Determining the carrying amounts of some assets and liabilities requires estimation of the effects of uncertain future events on those assets and liabilities at the end of the reporting period. For example, in the absence of recently observed market prices used to measure the following assets and liabilities, future-oriented estimates are necessary to measure the recoverable amount of classes of property, plant and equipment, the effect of technological obsolescence of inventories, provisions subject to the future outcome of litigation in progress, and long-term employee benefit liabilities such as pension obligations. These estimates involve assumptions about items such as the risk adjustment to cash flows or discount rates used, future changes in salaries and future changes in prices affecting other costs. No matter how diligently an entity estimates the carrying amounts of assets and liabilities subject to significant estimation uncertainty at the end of the reporting period, the reporting of point estimates in the statement of financial position cannot

---

10 IFRS 9 *Financial Instruments* eliminated the category of held-to-maturity financial assets. This paragraph refers to matters relevant when IAS 1 was issued.

provide information about the estimation uncertainties involved in measuring those assets and liabilities and the implications of those uncertainties for the period's profit or loss.

BC81　The *Framework* states that 'The economic decisions that are made by users of financial statements require an evaluation of the ability of an entity to generate cash and cash equivalents and of the timing and certainty of their generation.' The Board decided that disclosure of information about assumptions and other major sources of estimation uncertainty at the end of the reporting period enhances the relevance, reliability and understandability of the information reported in financial statements. These assumptions and other sources of estimation uncertainty relate to estimates that require management's most difficult, subjective or complex judgements. Therefore, disclosure in accordance with paragraph 125 of the revised IAS 1 would be made in respect of relatively few assets or liabilities (or classes of them).

BC82　The exposure draft of 2002 proposed the disclosure of some 'sources of measurement uncertainty'. In the light of comments received that the purpose of this disclosure was unclear, the Board decided:

(a)　to amend the subject of that disclosure to 'sources of estimation uncertainty at the end of the reporting period'; and

(b)　to clarify in the revised Standard that the disclosure does not apply to assets and liabilities measured at fair value based on recently observed market prices (see paragraph 128 of IAS 1).

BC83　When assets and liabilities are measured at fair value on the basis of recently observed market prices, future changes in carrying amounts would not result from using estimates to measure the assets and liabilities at the end of the reporting period. Using observed market prices to measure assets or liabilities obviates the need for estimates at the end of the reporting period. The market prices properly reflect the fair values at the end of the reporting period, even though future market prices could be different. The objective of fair value measurement is to reflect fair value at the measurement date, not to predict a future value.[11]

BC84　IAS 1 does not prescribe the particular form or detail of the disclosures. Circumstances differ from entity to entity, and the nature of estimation uncertainty at the end of the reporting period has many facets. IAS 1 limits the scope of the disclosures to items that have a significant risk of causing a material adjustment to the carrying amounts of assets and liabilities within the next financial year. The longer the future period to which the disclosures relate, the greater the range of items that would qualify for disclosure, and the less specific are the disclosures that could be made about particular assets or liabilities. A period longer than the next financial year might obscure the most relevant information with other disclosures.

11　IFRS 13 *Fair Value Measurement*, issued in May 2011, defines fair value and contains the requirements for measuring fair value.

Disclosures about capital (paragraphs 134 and 135)

BC85 In July 2004 the Board published an exposure draft—ED 7 *Financial Instruments: Disclosures*. As part of that project, the Board considered whether it should require disclosures about capital.

BC86 The level of an entity's capital and how it manages capital are important factors for users to consider in assessing the risk profile of an entity and its ability to withstand unexpected adverse events. The level of capital might also affect the entity's ability to pay dividends. Consequently, ED 7 proposed disclosures about capital.

BC87 In ED 7 the Board decided that it should not limit the requirements for disclosures about capital to entities that are subject to external capital requirements (eg regulatory capital requirements established by legislation or other regulation). The Board believes that information about capital is useful for all entities, as is evidenced by the fact that some entities set internal capital requirements and norms have been established for some industries. The Board noted that the capital disclosures are not intended to replace disclosures required by regulators. The Board also noted that the financial statements should not be regarded as a substitute for disclosures to regulators (which may not be available to all users) because the function of disclosures made to regulators may differ from the function of those to other users. Therefore, the Board decided that information about capital should be required of all entities because it is useful to users of general purpose financial statements. Accordingly, the Board did not distinguish between the requirements for regulated and non-regulated entities.

BC88 Some respondents to ED 7 questioned the relevance of the capital disclosures in an IFRS dealing with disclosures relating to financial instruments. The Board noted that an entity's capital does not relate solely to financial instruments and, thus, capital disclosures have more general relevance. Accordingly, the Board included these disclosures in IAS 1, rather than IFRS 7 *Financial Instruments: Disclosures*, the IFRS resulting from ED 7.

BC89 The Board also decided that an entity's decision to adopt the amendments to IAS 1 should be independent of the entity's decision to adopt IFRS 7. The Board noted that issuing a separate amendment facilitates separate adoption decisions.

Objectives, policies and processes for managing capital (paragraph 136)

BC90 The Board decided that disclosure about capital should be placed in the context of a discussion of the entity's objectives, policies and processes for managing capital. This is because the Board believes that such a discussion both communicates important information about the entity's capital strategy and provides the context for other disclosures.

BC91 The Board considered whether an entity can have a view of capital that differs from what IFRSs define as equity. The Board noted that, although for the purposes of this disclosure capital would often equate with equity as defined in IFRSs, it might also include or exclude some components. The Board also noted that this disclosure is intended to give entities the opportunity to describe how they view the components of capital they manage, if this is different from what IFRSs define as equity.

Externally imposed capital requirements (paragraph 136)

BC92 The Board considered whether it should require disclosure of any externally imposed capital requirements. Such a capital requirement could be:

(a) an industry-wide requirement with which all entities in the industry must comply; or

(b) an entity-specific requirement imposed on a particular entity by its prudential supervisor or other regulator.

BC93 The Board noted that some industries and countries have industry-wide capital requirements, and others do not. Thus, the Board concluded that it should not require disclosure of industry-wide requirements, or compliance with such requirements, because such disclosure would not lead to comparability between different entities or between similar entities in different countries.

BC94 The Board concluded that disclosure of the existence and level of entity-specific capital requirements is important information for users, because it informs them about the risk assessment of the regulator. Such disclosure improves transparency and market discipline.

BC95 However, the Board noted the following arguments against requiring disclosure of externally imposed entity-specific capital requirements.

(a) Users of financial statements might rely primarily on the regulator's assessment of solvency risk without making their own risk assessment.

(b) The focus of a regulator's risk assessment is for those whose interests the regulations are intended to protect (eg depositors or policyholders). This emphasis is different from that of a shareholder. Thus, it could be misleading to suggest that the regulator's risk assessment could, or should, be a substitute for independent analysis by investors.

(c) The disclosure of entity-specific capital requirements imposed by a regulator might undermine that regulator's ability to impose such requirements. For example, the information could cause depositors to withdraw funds, a prospect that might discourage regulators from imposing requirements. Furthermore, an entity's regulatory dialogue would become public, which might not be appropriate in all circumstances.

(d) Because different regulators have different tools available, for example formal requirements and moral suasion, a requirement to disclose entity-specific capital requirements could not be framed in a way that would lead to the provision of information that is comparable across entities.

(e) Disclosure of capital requirements (and hence, regulatory judgements) could hamper clear communication to the entity of the regulator's assessment by creating incentives to use moral suasion and other informal mechanisms.

(f)   Disclosure requirements should not focus on entity-specific capital requirements in isolation, but should focus on how entity-specific capital requirements affect how an entity manages and determines the adequacy of its capital resources.

(g)   A requirement to disclose entity-specific capital requirements imposed by a regulator is not part of Pillar 3 of the Basel II Framework developed by the Basel Committee on Banking Supervision.

BC96   Taking into account all of the above arguments, the Board decided not to require quantitative disclosure of externally imposed capital requirements. Rather, it decided to require disclosures about whether the entity complied with any externally imposed capital requirements during the period and, if not, the consequences of non-compliance. This retains confidentiality between regulators and the entity, but alerts users to breaches of capital requirements and their consequences.

BC97   Some respondents to ED 7 did not agree that breaches of externally imposed capital requirements should be disclosed. They argued that disclosure about breaches of externally imposed capital requirements and the associated regulatory measures subsequently imposed could be disproportionately damaging to entities. The Board was not persuaded by these arguments because it believes that such concerns indicate that information about breaches of externally imposed capital requirements may often be material by its nature. The *Framework* states that 'Information is material if its omission or misstatement could influence the economic decisions of users taken on the basis of the financial statements.' Similarly, the Board decided not to provide an exemption for temporary non-compliance with regulatory requirements during the year. Information that an entity is sufficiently close to its limits to breach them, even on a temporary basis, is useful for users.

Internal capital targets

BC98   The Board proposed in ED 7 that the requirement to disclose information about breaches of capital requirements should apply equally to breaches of internally imposed requirements, because it believed the information is also useful to a user of the financial statements.

BC99   However, this proposal was criticised by respondents to ED 7 for the following reasons:

(a)   The information is subjective and, thus, not comparable between entities. In particular, different entities will set internal targets for different reasons, so a breach of a requirement might signify different things for different entities. In contrast, a breach of an external requirement has similar implications for all entities required to comply with similar requirements.

(b)   Capital targets are not more important than other internally set financial targets, and to require disclosure only of capital targets would provide users with incomplete, and perhaps misleading, information.

(c)   Internal targets are estimates that are subject to change by the entity. It is not appropriate to require the entity's performance against this benchmark to be disclosed.

(d)   An internally set capital target can be manipulated by management. The disclosure requirement could cause management to set the target so that it would always be achieved, providing little useful information to users and potentially reducing the effectiveness of the entity's capital management.

BC100   As a result, the Board decided not to require disclosure of the capital targets set by management, whether the entity has complied with those targets, or the consequences of any non-compliance. However, the Board confirmed its view that when an entity has policies and processes for managing capital, qualitative disclosures about these policies and processes are useful. The Board also concluded that these disclosures, together with disclosure of the components of equity and their changes during the year (required by paragraphs 106–110), would give sufficient information about entities that are not regulated or subject to externally imposed capital requirements.

Puttable financial instruments and obligations arising on liquidation

BC100A The Board decided to require disclosure of information about puttable instruments and instruments that impose on the entity an obligation to deliver to another party a pro rata share of the net assets of the entity only on liquidation that are reclassified in accordance with paragraphs 16E and 16F of IAS 32. This is because the Board concluded that this disclosure allows users of financial statements to understand the effects of any reclassifications.

BC100B The Board also concluded that entities with puttable financial instruments classified as equity should be required to disclose additional information to allow users to assess any effect on the entity's liquidity arising from the ability of the holder to put the instruments to the issuer. Financial instruments classified as equity usually do not include any obligation for the entity to deliver a financial asset to another party. Therefore, the Board concluded that additional disclosures are needed in these circumstances. In particular, the Board concluded that entities should disclose the expected cash outflow on redemption or repurchase of those financial instruments that are classified as equity and information about how that amount was determined. That information allows liquidity risk associated with the put obligation and future cash flows to be evaluated.

Presentation of measures per share

BC101   The exposure draft of 2006 did not propose to change the requirements of IAS 33 *Earnings per Share* on the presentation of basic and diluted earnings per share. A majority of respondents agreed with this decision. In their opinion, earnings per share should be the only measure per share permitted or required in the statement of comprehensive income and changing those requirements was beyond the scope of this stage of the financial statement presentation project.

BC102   However, some respondents would like to see alternative measures per share whenever earnings per share is not viewed as the most relevant measure for financial analysts (ie credit rating agencies that focus on other measures). A few respondents proposed that an entity should also display an amount per share for total comprehensive income, because this was considered a useful measure. The Board did not support including alternative measures per share in the financial statements, until totals and subtotals, and principles for aggregating and disaggregating items, are addressed and discussed as part of the next stage of the financial statement presentation project.

BC103   Some respondents also interpreted the current provisions in IAS 33 as allowing de facto a display of alternative measures in the income statement. In its deliberations, the Board was clear that paragraph 73 of IAS 33 did not leave room for confusion. However, it decided that the wording in paragraph 73 could be improved to clarify that alternative measures should be shown 'only in the notes'. This will be done when IAS 33 is revisited or as part of the annual improvements process.

BC104   One respondent commented that the use of the word 'earnings' was inappropriate in the light of changes proposed in the exposure draft and that the measure should be denominated 'profit or loss per share', instead. The Board considered that this particular change in terminology was beyond the scope of IAS 1.

Transition and effective date

BC105   The Board is committed to maintaining a 'stable platform' of substantially unchanged standards for annual periods beginning between 1 January 2006 and 31 December 2008. In addition, some preparers will need time to make the system changes necessary to comply with the revisions to IAS 1. Therefore, the Board decided that the effective date of IAS 1 should be annual periods beginning on or after 1 January 2009, with earlier application permitted.

BC105A   The exposure draft *Presentation of Items of Other Comprehensive Income* published in May 2010 proposed changes to presentation of items of OCI. The Board finalised these changes in June 2011 and decided that the effective dates for these changes should be for annual periods beginning on or after 1 July 2012, with earlier application permitted. The Board did not think that a long transition period was needed as the changes to presentation are small and the presentation required by the amendments is already allowed under IAS 1.

BC105B   The Board had consulted on the effective date and transition requirements for this amendment in its *Request for Views on Effective Dates and Transition Requirements* in October 2010 and the responses to that document did not give the Board any reason to reconsider the effective date and the transition requirements.

Disclosure Initiative (Amendments to IAS 1)

BC105C   The Board decided that *Disclosure Initiative* (Amendments to IAS 1) should be applied for annual periods beginning on or after 1 January 2016 with early application permitted.

BC105D   The Board noted that these amendments clarify existing requirements in IAS 1. They provide additional guidance to assist entities to apply judgement when meeting the presentation and disclosure requirements in IFRS. These amendments do not affect recognition and measurement. They should not result in the reassessment of the judgements about presentation and disclosure made in periods prior to the application of these amendments.

BC105E   Paragraph 38 of IAS 1 requires an entity to present comparative information for all amounts reported in the current period financial statements and for narrative or descriptive information 'if it is relevant to understanding the current period's financial statements'. If an entity alters the order of the notes or the information presented or disclosed compared to the previous year, it also adjusts the comparative information to align with the current period presentation and disclosure. For that reason, IAS 1 already provides relief from having to disclose comparative information that is not considered relevant in the current period and requires comparative information for new amounts presented or disclosed in the current period.

BC105F   The March 2014 Exposure Draft proposed that if an entity applies these amendments early that it should disclose that fact. However, the Board removed this requirement and stated in the transition provisions that an entity need not disclose the fact that it has applied these amendments (regardless of whether the amendments have been applied for annual periods beginning on or after 1 January 2016 or if they have been applied early). This is because the Board considers that these amendments are clarifying amendments that do not directly affect an entity's accounting policies or accounting estimates. Similarly, an entity does not need to disclose the information required by paragraphs 28–30 of IAS 8 in relation to these amendments. The Board noted that if an entity decides to change its accounting policies as a result of applying these amendments then it would be required to follow the existing requirements in IAS 8 in relation to those accounting policy changes.

Differences from SFAS 130

BC106   In developing IAS 1, the Board identified the following differences from SFAS 130:

(a)   **Reporting and display of comprehensive income** Paragraph 22 of SFAS 130 permits a choice of displaying comprehensive income and its components, in one or two statements of financial performance or in a statement of changes in equity. IAS 1 (as revised in 2007) does not permit display in a statement of changes in equity.

(b)   **Reporting other comprehensive income in the equity section of a statement of financial position** Paragraph 26 of SFAS 130 specifically states that the *total of other comprehensive income* is reported separately from retained earnings and additional paid-in capital in a statement of financial position at the end of the period. A descriptive title such as *accumulated other comprehensive income* is used for that component of equity. An entity discloses accumulated balances for each classification in that separate component of equity in a statement of financial position, in a statement of changes in equity, or in notes to the financial statements. IAS 1 (as revised in 2007) does not specifically require the display of a total of accumulated other comprehensive income in the statement of financial position.

(c) **Display of the share of other comprehensive income items of associates and joint ventures accounted for using the equity method** Paragraph 82 of IAS 1 (as revised in 2007) requires the display in the statement of comprehensive income of the investor's share of the investee's other comprehensive income. Paragraph 122 of SFAS 130 does not specify how that information should be displayed. An investor is permitted to combine its proportionate share of other comprehensive income amounts with its own other comprehensive income items and display the aggregate of those amounts in an income statement type format or in a statement of changes in equity.

Appendix
Amendments to the Basis for Conclusions on other IFRSs

This appendix contains amendments to the Basis for Conclusions on other IFRSs that are necessary in order to ensure consistency with the revised IAS 1. Amended paragraphs are shown with the new text underlined and deleted text struck through.

* * * * *

The amendments contained in this appendix when this Standard was revised in 2007 have been incorporated into the relevant IFRSs published in this volume.

Dissenting opinions

Dissent of Mary E Barth, Anthony T Cope, Robert P Garnett and James J Leisenring from IAS 1 (as revised in September 2007)

DO1   Professor Barth and Messrs Cope, Garnett and Leisenring voted against the issue of IAS 1 *Presentation of Financial Statements* in 2007. The reasons for their dissent are set out below.

DO2   Those Board members agree with the requirement to report all items of income and expense separately from changes in net assets that arise from transactions with owners in their capacity as owners. Making that distinction clearly is a significant improvement in financial reporting.

DO3   However, they believe that the decision to permit entities to divide the statement of comprehensive income into two separate statements is both conceptually unsound and unwise.

DO4   As noted in paragraph BC51, the *Framework*[12] does not define profit or loss, or net income. It also does not indicate what criteria should be used to distinguish between those items of recognised income and expense that should be included in profit or loss and those items that should not. In some cases, it is even possible for identical transactions to be reported inside or outside profit or loss. Indeed, in that same paragraph, the Board acknowledges these facts, and indicates that it had a preference for reporting all items of income and expense in a single statement, believing that a single statement is the conceptually correct approach. Those Board members believe that some items of income and expense that will potentially bypass the statement of profit and loss can be as significant to the assessment of an entity's performance as items that will be included. Until a conceptual distinction can be developed to determine whether any items should be reported in profit or loss or elsewhere, financial statements will lack neutrality and comparability unless all items are reported in a single statement. In such a statement, profit or loss can be shown as a subtotal, reflecting current conventions.

DO5   In the light of those considerations, it is puzzling that most respondents to the exposure draft that proposed these amendments favoured permitting a two-statement approach, reasoning that it 'distinguishes between profit and loss and total comprehensive income' (paragraph BC50). Distinguishing between those items reported in profit or loss and those reported elsewhere is accomplished by the requirement for relevant subtotals to be included in a statement of comprehensive income. Respondents also stated that a two-statement approach gives primacy to the 'income statement'; that conflicts with the Board's requirement in paragraph 11 of IAS 1 to give equal prominence to all financial statements within a set of financial statements.

DO6   Those Board members also believe that the amendments are flawed by offering entities a choice of presentation methods. The Board has expressed a desire to

---

12 The reference to the *Framework* is to IASC's *Framework for the Preparation and Presentation of Financial Statements*, adopted by the IASB in 2001. In September 2010 the IASB replaced the *Framework* with the *Conceptual Framework for Financial Reporting*.

reduce alternatives in IFRSs. The *Preface to International Financial Reporting Standards*, in paragraph 13,[13] states: 'the IASB intends not to permit choices in accounting treatment ... and will continue to reconsider ... those transactions and events for which IASs permit a choice of accounting treatment, with the objective of reducing the number of those choices.' The *Preface* extends this objective to both accounting and reporting. The same paragraph states: 'The IASB's objective is to require like transactions and events to be accounted for *and reported* in a like way and unlike transactions and events to be accounted for *and reported* differently' (emphasis added). By permitting a choice in this instance, the IASB has abandoned that principle.

DO7 Finally, the four Board members believe that allowing a choice of presentation at this time will ingrain practice, and make achievement of the conceptually correct presentation more difficult as the long-term project on financial statement presentation proceeds.

---

13 Paragraph 13, slightly amended, is now paragraph 12 of the *Preface*, as amended at September 2010.

Dissent of Paul Pacter from *Presentation of Items of Other Comprehensive Income* (Amendments to IAS 1)

DO1　Mr Pacter voted against issuing the amendments to IAS 1 *Presentation of Financial Statements* set out in *Presentation of Items of Other Comprehensive Income* in June 2011. Mr Pacter believes that the Board has missed a golden opportunity to align the performance statement with the Board's *Conceptual Framework* and, thereby, improve information for users of IFRS financial statements.

DO2　Mr Pacter believes that ideally this project should have provided guidance, to the Board and to those who use IFRSs, on which items of income and expense (if any) should be presented as items of other comprehensive income (OCI) and which of those (if any) should subsequently be recycled through profit or loss. Mr Pacter acknowledges and accepts that this project has a more short-term goal – 'to improve the consistency and clarity of the presentation of items of OCI'. He believes that this project fails to deliver on that objective, for the following reasons:

(a)　Consistency is not achieved because the standard allows choice between presenting performance in a single performance statement or two performance statements. Users of financial statements—and the Board itself—have often said that accounting options are not helpful for understandability and comparability of financial statements.

(b)　Clarity is not achieved because allowing two performance statements is inconsistent with the *Conceptual Framework*. The *Conceptual Framework* defines two types of items that measure an entity's performance—income and expenses. Mr Pacter believes that all items of income and expense should be presented in a single performance statement with appropriate subtotals (including profit or loss, if that can be defined) and supporting disclosures. This is consistent with reporting all assets and liabilities in a single statement of financial position, rather than multiple statements. Unfortunately, neither IAS 1 nor any other IFRS addresses criteria for which items are presented in OCI. And the recent history of which items are presented in OCI suggests that the decisions are based more on expediency than conceptual merit. In Mr Pacter's judgement, that is all the more reason to have all items of income and expense reported in a single performance statement.

DO3　Mr Pacter believes that the Board should breathe new life into its former project on performance reporting as a matter of urgency.

IASB documents published to accompany

IAS 2

Inventories

The text of the unaccompanied standard, IAS 2, is contained in Part A of this edition. Its effective date when issued was 1 January 2005. This part presents the following documents:

BASIS FOR CONCLUSIONS

Basis for Conclusions on
IAS 2 *Inventories*

This Basis for Conclusions accompanies, but is not part of, IAS 2.

Introduction

BC1   This Basis for Conclusions summarises the International Accounting Standards Board's considerations in reaching its conclusions on revising IAS 2 *Inventories* in 2003. Individual Board members gave greater weight to some factors than to others.

BC2   In July 2001 the Board announced that, as part of its initial agenda of technical projects, it would undertake a project to improve a number of Standards, including IAS 2. The project was undertaken in the light of queries and criticisms raised in relation to the Standards by securities regulators, professional accountants and other interested parties. The objectives of the Improvements project were to reduce or eliminate alternatives, redundancies and conflicts within Standards, to deal with some convergence issues and to make other improvements. In May 2002 the Board published its proposals in an Exposure Draft of *Improvements to International Accounting Standards*, with a comment deadline of 16 September 2002. The Board received over 160 comment letters on the Exposure Draft.

BC3   Because the Board's intention was not to reconsider the fundamental approach to the accounting for inventories established by IAS 2, this Basis for Conclusions does not discuss requirements in IAS 2 that the Board has not reconsidered.

Scope

Reference to historical cost system

BC4   Both the objective and the scope of the previous version of IAS 2 referred to 'the accounting treatment for inventories under the historical cost system.' Some had interpreted those words as meaning that the Standard applied only under a historical cost system and permitted entities the choice of applying other measurement bases, for example fair value.

BC5   The Board agreed that those words could be seen as permitting a choice, resulting in inconsistent application of the Standard. Accordingly, it deleted the words 'in the context of the historical cost system in accounting for inventories' to clarify that the Standard applies to all inventories that are not specifically exempted from its scope.

Inventories of broker-traders

BC6   The Exposure Draft proposed excluding from the scope of the Standard inventories of non-producers of agricultural and forest products and mineral ores to the extent that these inventories are measured at net realisable value in accordance with well-established industry practices. However, some respondents disagreed with this scope exemption for the following reasons:

(a) the scope exemption should apply to all types of inventories of broker-traders;

(b) established practice is for broker-traders to follow a mark-to-market approach rather than to value these inventories at net realisable value;

(c) the guidance on net realisable value in IAS 2 is not appropriate for the valuation of inventories of broker-traders.

BC7 The Board found these comments persuasive. Therefore it decided that the Standard should not apply to the measurement of inventories of:

(a) producers of agricultural and forest products, agricultural produce after harvest, and minerals and mineral products, to the extent that they are measured at net realisable value (as in the previous version of IAS 2), or

(b) commodity broker-traders when their inventories are measured at fair value less costs to sell.

BC8 The Board further decided that the measurement of the effect of inventories on profit or loss for the period needed to be consistent with the measurement attribute of inventories for which such exemption is allowed. Accordingly, to qualify under (a) or (b), the Standard requires changes in the recognised amount of inventories to be included in profit or loss for the period. The Board believes this is particularly appropriate in the case of commodity broker-traders because they seek to profit from fluctuations in prices and trade margins.

Cost formulas

BC9 The combination of the previous version of IAS 2 and SIC-1 *Consistency—Different Cost Formulas for Inventories* allowed some choice between first-in, first-out (FIFO) or weighted average cost formulas (benchmark treatment) and the last-in, first-out (LIFO) method (allowed alternative treatment). The Board decided to eliminate the allowed alternative of using the LIFO method.

BC10 The LIFO method treats the newest items of inventory as being sold first, and consequently the items remaining in inventory are recognised as if they were the oldest. This is generally not a reliable representation of actual inventory flows.

BC11 The LIFO method is an attempt to meet a perceived deficiency of the conventional accounting model (the measurement of cost of goods sold expense by reference to outdated prices for the inventories sold, whereas sales revenue is measured at current prices). It does so by imposing an unrealistic cost flow assumption.

BC12 The use of LIFO in financial reporting is often tax-driven, because it results in cost of goods sold expense calculated using the most recent prices being deducted from revenue in the determination of the gross margin. The LIFO method reduces (increases) profits in a manner that tends to reflect the effect that increased (decreased) prices would have on the cost of replacing inventories sold. However, this effect depends on the relationship between the prices of the most recent inventory acquisitions and the replacement cost at the end of the period. Thus, it is not a truly systematic method for determining the effect of changing prices on profits.

BC13 The use of LIFO results in inventories being recognised in the balance sheet at amounts that bear little relationship to recent cost levels of inventories. However, LIFO can distort profit or loss, especially when 'preserved' older 'layers' of inventory are presumed to have been used when inventories are substantially reduced. It is more likely in these circumstances that relatively new inventories will have been used to meet the increased demands on inventory.

BC14 Some respondents argued that the use of LIFO has merit in certain circumstances because it partially adjusts profit or loss for the effects of price changes. The Board concluded that it is not appropriate to allow an approach that results in a measurement of profit or loss for the period that is inconsistent with the measurement of inventories for balance sheet purposes.

BC15 Other respondents argued that in some industries, such as the oil and gas industry, inventory levels are driven by security considerations and often represent a minimum of 90 days of sales. They argue that, in these industries, the use of LIFO better reflects an entity's performance because inventories held as security stocks are closer to long-term assets than to working capital.

BC16 The Board was not convinced by these arguments because these security stocks do not match historical layers under a LIFO computation.

BC17 Other respondents argued that in some cases, for example, when measuring coal dumps, piles of iron or metal scraps (when stock bins are replenished by 'topping up'), the LIFO method reflects the actual physical flow of inventories.

BC18 The Board concluded that valuation of these inventories follows a direct costing approach where actual physical flows are matched with direct costs, which is a method different from LIFO.

BC19 The Board decided to eliminate the LIFO method because of its lack of representational faithfulness of inventory flows. This decision does not rule out specific cost methods that reflect inventory flows that are similar to LIFO.

BC20 The Board recognised that, in some jurisdictions, use of the LIFO method for tax purposes is possible only if that method is also used for accounting purposes. It concluded, however, that tax considerations do not provide an adequate conceptual basis for selecting an appropriate accounting treatment and that it is not acceptable to allow an inferior accounting treatment purely because of tax regulations and advantages in particular jurisdictions. This may be an issue for local taxation authorities.

BC21 IAS 2 continues to allow the use of both the FIFO and the weighted average methods for interchangeable inventories.

Cost of inventories recognised as an expense in the period

BC22   The Exposure Draft proposed deleting paragraphs in the previous version of IAS 2 that required disclosure of the cost of inventories recognised as an expense in the period, because this disclosure is required in IAS 1 *Presentation of Financial Statements*.

BC23   Some respondents observed that IAS 1 does not specifically require disclosure of the cost of inventories recognised as an expense in the period when presenting an analysis of expenses using a classification based on their function. They argued that this information is important to understand the financial statements. Therefore the Board decided to require this disclosure specifically in IAS 2.

IASB documents published to accompany

IAS 7

Statement of Cash Flows

The text of the unaccompanied standard, IAS 7, is contained in Part A of this edition. Its effective date when issued was 1 January 1994. The text of the Accompanying Guidance on IAS 7 is contained in Part B of this edition. This part presents the following documents:

BASIS FOR CONCLUSIONS

DISSENTING OPINION

Basis for Conclusions on
IAS 7 *Statement of Cash Flows*

This Basis for Conclusions accompanies, but is not part of, IAS 7.

BC1   This Basis for Conclusions summarises the considerations of the International Accounting Standards Board in reaching its conclusions on amending IAS 7 *Statement of Cash Flows* as part of *Improvements to IFRSs* issued in April 2009. Individual Board members gave greater weight to some factors than to others.

BC2   IAS 7 was developed by the International Accounting Standards Committee in 1992 and was not accompanied by a Basis for Conclusions. This Basis refers to clarification of guidance on classification of cash flows from investing activities.

Classification of expenditures on unrecognised assets

BC3   In 2008 the International Financial Reporting Interpretations Committee (IFRIC) reported to the Board that practice differed for the classification of cash flows for expenditures incurred with the objective of generating future cash flows when those expenditures are not recognised as assets in accordance with IFRSs. Some entities classified such expenditures as cash flows from operating activities and others classified them as investing activities. Examples of such expenditures are those for exploration and evaluation activities, which IFRS 6 *Exploration for and Evaluation of Mineral Resources* permits to be recognised as either an asset or an expense depending on the entity's previous accounting policies for those expenditures. Expenditures on advertising and promotional activities, staff training, and research and development could also raise the same issue.

BC4   The IFRIC decided not to add this issue to its agenda but recommended that the Board should amend IAS 7 to state explicitly that only an expenditure that results in a recognised asset can be classified as a cash flow from investing activity.

BC5   In 2008, as part of its annual improvements project, the Board considered the principles in IAS 7, specifically guidance on the treatment of such expenditures in the statement of cash flows. The Board noted that even though paragraphs 14 and 16 of IAS 7 appear to be clear that only expenditure that results in the recognition of an asset should be classified as cash flows from investing activities, the wording is not definitive in this respect. Some might have misinterpreted the reference in paragraph 11 of IAS 7 for an entity to assess classification by activity that is most appropriate to its business to imply that the assessment is an accounting policy choice.

BC6   Consequently, in *Improvements to IFRSs* issued in April 2009, the Board removed the potential misinterpretation by amending paragraph 16 of IAS 7 to state explicitly that only an expenditure that results in a recognised asset can be classified as a cash flow from investing activities.

BC7   The Board concluded that this amendment better aligns the classification of cash flows from investing activities in the statement of cash flows and the presentation of recognised assets in the statement of financial position, reduces divergence in practice and, therefore, results in financial statements that are easier for users to understand.

BC8   The Board also amended the Basis for Conclusions on IFRS 6 to clarify the Board's view that the exemption in IFRS 6 applies only to recognition and measurement of exploration and evaluation assets, not to the classification of related expenditures in the statement of cash flows, for the same reasons set out in paragraph BC7.

Changes in liabilities arising from financing activities (paragraphs 44A–44E)

Background to the January 2016 Amendments

BC9   In January 2016 the Board amended IAS 7 to require entities to provide disclosures that enable users of financial statements to evaluate changes in liabilities arising from financing activities. The amendments were in response to requests from users, including those received at the Board's *Financial Reporting Disclosure Discussion Forum* in January 2013 and reflected in the resulting Feedback Statement ('the Feedback Statement'), which was issued in May 2013. Users highlighted that understanding an entity's cash flows is critical to their analysis and that there is a need for improved disclosures about an entity's debt, including changes in debt during the reporting period. The Feedback Statement noted that users had been consistently asking for the Board to introduce a requirement for entities to disclose and explain a net debt reconciliation.

BC10   In early 2014, to understand the reasons for their requests for more disclosure about net debt, the Board undertook a survey of investors. The survey sought information about why investors seek to understand the changes in debt between the beginning and the end of a reporting period. The survey also sought input on disclosures about cash and cash equivalents. On the basis of the survey, the Board identified that investors use a net debt reconciliation in their analysis of the entity:

(a)   to check their understanding of the entity's cash flows, because it provides a reconciliation between the statement of financial position and the statement of cash flows;

(b)   to improve their confidence in forecasting the entity's future cash flows when they can use a reconciliation to check their understanding of the entity's cash flows;

(c)   to provide information about the entity's sources of finance and how those sources have been used over time; and

(d)   to help them understand the entity's exposure to risks associated with financing.

BC11   The survey helped the Board to understand why investors were calling for improved disclosures about changes in debt during the reporting period. The Board noted that one challenge in responding to this need was that debt is not defined or required to be disclosed in current IFRS Standards. The Board noted that finding a commonly agreed definition of debt would be difficult. However, the Board decided that it could use the definition of financing activities in IAS 7. It therefore decided to propose a requirement to disclose a reconciliation between the amounts in the opening and the amounts in the closing statements of financial position for liabilities for which cash flows were, or future cash flows will be, classified as financing activities in the statement of cash flows.

BC12   IAS 7 defines financing activities as activities that result in changes in the size and composition of the contributed equity and borrowings of the entity. The Board proposed that a reconciliation of liabilities arising from financing activities would provide the information about debt that users of financial statements were requesting.

BC13   In December 2014 the Board published an Exposure Draft *Disclosure Initiative* (Proposed amendments to IAS 7) ('the 2014 Exposure Draft') seeking views on the proposals for a reconciliation of liabilities arising from financing activities.

Feedback on the proposals set out in the Exposure Draft

BC14   The feedback received on the 2014 Exposure Draft provided evidence that the disclosure would provide users of financial statements with the information they were seeking in order to analyse an entity's cash flows. The Board decided to finalise the amendments to IAS 7 ('the 2016 Amendments'); paragraphs BC15–BC24 set out how the Board responded to the feedback received on the 2014 Exposure Draft.

The objective of the disclosure

BC15   Feedback on the 2014 Exposure Draft noted that the proposal did not set out a disclosure objective, and consequently it was not sufficiently clear how entities would determine the most appropriate way to provide the required disclosure. The Board agreed with this feedback and included an objective within the requirement set out in paragraph 44A of the 2016 Amendments.

BC16   In setting the disclosure objective the Board decided the objective should reflect the needs of the users of financial statements, including those summarised in paragraph BC10.

Application of the 2016 Amendments to financial institutions

BC17   Some respondents to the 2014 Exposure Draft from financial institutions stated that the proposals would provide little or no relevant information to users of their financial statements because:

(a)   only some of the sources of finance for a financial institution are classified as 'financing activities' (for example, deposits from customers provide finance but in practice the resulting cash flows are typically classified as operating cash flows). A reconciliation may therefore provide an incomplete picture of the changes in the financing structure of a financial institution; and

(b)   other disclosure requirements (for example, comprehensive regulatory disclosure requirements) may already result in sufficient disclosure about an entity's financing structure.

© IFRS Foundation

BC18   After taking into consideration the feedback from respondents from financial institutions, the Board decided that the disclosure requirement could be satisfied in various ways, and not only by providing a reconciliation. The Board noted that when an entity is considering whether it has fulfilled the disclosure requirement, it should take into consideration:

（a）   the extent to which information about changes in liabilities arising from financing activities provides relevant information to its users, considering the needs of users summarised in paragraph BC10; and

（b）   whether the entity is satisfying the disclosure requirement through other disclosures included in the financial statements.

BC19   The Board therefore decided that a reconciliation between the opening and closing balances in the statement of financial position for liabilities arising from financing activities is one way to fulfil the disclosure requirement but should not be a mandatory format.

Information that supplements the disclosures

BC20   Some respondents to the 2014 Exposure Draft expressed a concern that the proposals in the Exposure Draft were too restrictive because, in their view:

（a）   the proposed disclosure would not include liabilities that an entity considers to be sources of finance although the entity does not classify them as financing activities (for example, pension liabilities); and

（b）   entities that already provided a net debt reconciliation (a reconciliation of movements in a net balance comprising debt less cash and cash equivalents) would be prevented from providing such a reconciliation, even if users would find it useful.

BC21   The Board did not intend to prevent entities from providing information required by paragraph 44A in a format that combines it with information about changes in other assets and liabilities. For example, an entity could provide that information as part of a net debt reconciliation, as described in paragraph BC20(b). To ensure users can identify the information required by paragraph 44A, the format selected needs to distinguish that information from information about changes in other assets and liabilities. In finalising the 2016 Amendments, the Board clarified these points in paragraph 44E.

Financial assets

BC22   Some respondents to the 2014 Exposure Draft asked the Board to clarify whether changes in financial assets held to hedge financial liabilities could also be included in the disclosure required by the 2016 Amendments. The Board noted that paragraph G.2 of the Guidance on implementing IFRS 9 *Financial Instruments* states that cash flows arising from a hedging instrument are classified as operating, investing or financing activities, on the basis of the classification of the cash flows arising from the hedged item. Consequently, the Board clarified in paragraph 44C that changes in financial assets held to hedge financial liabilities are included in the disclosure required by paragraph 44A.

Cost-benefit considerations

BC23   The Board considered the feedback received on perceived costs and benefits in finalising the 2016 Amendments. The Board noted that there will be initial costs for preparers to update information technology systems to enable changes in liabilities arising from financing activities to be tracked and collated. The Board also acknowledged that disclosing additional information could result in costs relating to extending the existing internal controls and audit processes of the entity. However, the Board noted that much of the information is already available to preparers. It also noted that the 2016 Amendments do not change the recognition or measurement for liabilities arising from financing activities; instead, they track changes in those items. Consequently, the Board concluded that it does not foresee any significant ongoing cost related to providing this information, and that the informational benefits to users of financial statements would outweigh the costs.

Illustrative example

BC24   Some respondents to the 2014 Exposure Draft stated that the example proposed within the Exposure Draft was too simplistic and might not help preparers in disclosing relevant information, because in practice the reconciliation would be more detailed. To address this feedback, the Board inserted a further example in the illustrative examples accompanying IAS 7.

Other disclosures

BC25   To supplement the current disclosure requirements in paragraph 48 of IAS 7 the 2014 Exposure Draft proposed additional disclosure requirements about an entity's liquidity such as restrictions that affect an entity's decision to use cash and cash equivalent balances. However, in the light of the responses, the Board decided that further work is needed before it can determine whether and how to finalise requirements arising from that proposal. The Board decided to continue that work without delaying the improvements to financial reporting that it expects will result from adding paragraphs 44A–44E to IAS 7. The Board may also, in due course, consider adding to its technical work programme a project that would look at liquidity disclosures more broadly.

Transition and effective date

Amendments to IAS 7

BC26   The Board concluded that timely application of the 2016 Amendments would respond to a long-standing request from users of financial statements. Thus, the Board decided that the 2016 Amendments should be applied for annual reporting periods beginning on or after 1 January 2017, with early application permitted.

BC27   Because the 2016 Amendments were issued in January 2016, which is less than one year before the beginning of the period when some entities could be required to apply them, the Board exempted entities from providing comparative information when they first apply the amendments.

Dissenting opinion

Dissent of Mr Takatsugu Ochi from *Disclosure Initiative* (Amendments to IAS 7)

DO1   Mr Ochi voted against the publication of *Disclosure Initiative* (Amendments to IAS 7) (the 2016 Amendments). The reasons for his dissent are set out below.

DO2   Mr Ochi believes that financial statements that reflect the 2016 Amendments may provide incomplete information about an entity's management of liquidity. The objective of the 2016 Amendments is to require disclosures that enable users to evaluate changes in liabilities arising from financing activities, including both changes arising from cash flows and non-cash changes. However, Mr Ochi thinks that users of financial statements are seeking clearer information about entities' management of liquidity risk. Consequently, he thinks that the information provided by the 2016 Amendments will not meet users' needs. Mr Ochi thinks that the Board has issued these amendments without setting a clear vision of overall improvements to the disclosure about an entity's liquidity risk management. He thinks that this could confuse and mislead users of financial statements.

DO3   The objective mentioned in paragraph DO2 refers to liabilities arising from financing activities. Paragraph 44C specifies that those liabilities are liabilities for which cash flows were, or future cash flows will be, classified in the statement of cash flows as cash flows from financing activities. However, Mr Ochi thinks that specifying the scope of the disclosure requirement in this way does not capture the information that users need. This is because changes in liabilities arising from financing activities are different from the information used to assess liquidity risk management. Because IAS 7 permits an entity to classify some cash flows (such as interest payments) as either operating or financing, the understanding of what constitutes changes in liabilities arising from financing activities may vary among preparers. In Mr Ochi's view, preparers may have a more precise understanding about what constitutes information on liquidity risk than simply understanding changes in liabilities arising from financing activities.

DO4   Mr Ochi also thinks that if an entity provides the disclosures required by paragraph 44A in combination with disclosure of changes in the amount of cash and cash equivalents and does not disclose information about the location and availability of the cash and cash equivalents, the disclosure is sometimes irrelevant to how an entity manages liquidity. If users expect to obtain a full picture of an entity's liquidity risk management as a result of the 2016 Amendments, they may be confused and misled.

DO5   Mr Ochi thinks that providing the disclosure may require excessive work and hence may be inefficient from a preparer's point of view. He notes that the Board may conduct research regarding the effectiveness of IAS 7. Because he regards IAS 7 as having some significant shortcomings, he believes that issuing amendments based on the existing statement of cash flows is not a worthwhile endeavour. He also thinks that it could reduce the clarity of the statement of cash flows.

DO6   Mr Ochi also has a significant concern regarding the costs required to prepare the disclosure. Although the 2016 Amendments are disclosure-only amendments, all reporting entities will need to consider providing this disclosure. For this disclosure, an entity may be required to adjust items already presented as operating and financing activities in a statement of cash flows (for example, interest payments that are classified as operating activities), which may require system changes. Concurrently, an entity may also have to initiate system changes to prepare for applying IFRS 9 *Financial Instruments* and IFRS 15 *Revenue from Contracts with Customers* (both effective on 1 January 2018) as well as IFRS 16 *Leases* (effective on 1 January 2019). Mr Ochi believes that the costs that will be incurred by entities as a consequence of those other changes will be considerable and he thinks that this fact is not reflected in the conclusion the Board had reached as a consequence of its assessment of costs pertaining to this disclosure. Taking these matters into consideration, Mr Ochi believes that the costs of the 2016 Amendments will outweigh the benefits.

IASB documents published to accompany

IAS 8

Accounting Policies, Changes in Accounting Estimates and Errors

The text of the unaccompanied standard, IAS 8, is contained in Part A of this edition. Its effective date when issued was 1 January 2005. The text of the Accompanying Guidance on IAS 8 is contained in Part B of this edition. This part presents the following documents:

BASIS FOR CONCLUSIONS

Basis for Conclusions on
IAS 8 *Accounting Policies, Changes in Accounting Estimates and Errors*

This Basis for Conclusions accompanies, but is not part of, IAS 8.

Introduction

BC1   This Basis for Conclusions summarises the International Accounting Standards Board's considerations in reaching its conclusions on revising IAS 8 *Net Profit or Loss for the Period, Fundamental Errors and Changes in Accounting Policies* in 2003. Individual Board members gave greater weight to some factors than to others.

BC2   In July 2001 the Board announced that, as part of its initial agenda of technical projects, it would undertake a project to improve a number of Standards, including IAS 8. The project was undertaken in the light of queries and criticisms raised in relation to the Standards by securities regulators, professional accountants and other interested parties. The objectives of the Improvements project were to reduce or eliminate alternatives, redundancies and conflicts within Standards, to deal with some convergence issues and to make other improvements. In May 2002 the Board published its proposals in an Exposure Draft of *Improvements to International Accounting Standards*, with a comment deadline of 16 September 2002. The Board received over 160 comment letters on the Exposure Draft.

BC3   The Standard includes extensive changes to the previous version of IAS 8. The Board's intention was not to reconsider all of the previous Standard's requirements for selecting and applying accounting policies, and accounting for changes in accounting policies, changes in accounting estimates and corrections of errors. Accordingly, this Basis for Conclusions does not discuss requirements in IAS 8 that the Board did not reconsider.

Removing allowed alternative treatments

BC4   The previous version of IAS 8 included allowed alternative treatments of voluntary changes in accounting policies (paragraphs 54–57) and corrections of fundamental errors (paragraphs 38–40). Under those allowed alternatives:

(a)   the adjustment resulting from retrospective application of a change in an accounting policy was included in profit or loss for the current period; and

(b)   the amount of the correction of a fundamental error was included in profit or loss for the current period.

BC5   In both circumstances, comparative information was presented as it was presented in the financial statements of prior periods.

BC6   The Board identified the removal of optional treatments for changes in accounting policies and corrections of errors as an important improvement to the previous version of IAS 8. The Standard removes the allowed alternative treatments and requires changes in accounting policies and corrections of prior period errors to be accounted for retrospectively.

BC7 The Board concluded that retrospective application made by amending the comparative information presented for prior periods is preferable to the previously allowed alternative treatments because, under the now required method of retrospective application:

(a) profit or loss for the period of the change does not include the effects of changes in accounting policies or errors relating to prior periods.

(b) information presented about prior periods is prepared on the same basis as information about the current period, and is therefore comparable. This information possesses a qualitative characteristic identified in the *Framework for the Preparation and Presentation of Financial Statements*,[1] and provides the most useful information for trend analysis of income and expenses.

(c) prior period errors are not repeated in comparative information presented for prior periods.

BC8 Some respondents to the Exposure Draft argued that the previously allowed alternative treatments are preferable because:

(a) correcting prior period errors by restating prior period information involves an unjustifiable use of hindsight;

(b) recognising the effects of changes in accounting policies and corrections of errors in current period profit or loss makes them more prominent to users of financial statements; and

(c) each amount credited or debited to retained earnings as a result of an entity's activities has been recognised in profit or loss in some period.

BC9 The Board concluded that restating prior period information to correct a prior period error does not involve an unjustifiable use of hindsight because prior period errors are defined in terms of a failure to use, or misuse of, reliable information that was available when the prior period financial statements were authorised for issue and could reasonably be expected to have been obtained and taken into account in the preparation and presentation of those financial statements.

BC10 The Board also concluded that the disclosures about changes in accounting policies and corrections of prior period errors in paragraphs 28, 29 and 49 of the Standard should ensure that their effects are sufficiently prominent to users of financial statements.

BC11 The Board further concluded that it is less important for each amount credited or debited to retained earnings as a result of an entity's activities to be recognised in profit or loss in some period than for the profit or loss for each period presented to represent faithfully the effects of transactions and other events occurring in that period.

---

1 IASC's *Framework for the Preparation and Presentation of Financial Statements* was adopted by the IASB in 2001. In September 2010 the IASB replaced the *Framework* with the *Conceptual Framework for Financial Reporting*.

Eliminating the distinction between fundamental errors and other material prior period errors

BC12　The Standard eliminates the distinction between fundamental errors and other material prior period errors. As a result, all material prior period errors are accounted for in the same way as a fundamental error was accounted for under the retrospective treatment in the previous version of IAS 8. The Board concluded that the definition of 'fundamental errors' in the previous version was difficult to interpret consistently because the main feature of the definition—that the error causes the financial statements of one or more prior periods no longer to be considered to have been reliable—was also a feature of all material prior period errors.

Applying a Standard or an Interpretation that specifically applies to an item

BC13　The Exposure Draft proposed that when a Standard or an Interpretation applies to an item in the financial statements, the accounting policy (or policies) applied to that item is (are) determined by considering the following in descending order:

(a)　the Standard (including any Appendices that form part of the Standard);

(b)　the Interpretation;

(c)　Appendices to the Standard that do not form a part of the Standard; and

(d)　Implementation Guidance issued in respect of the Standard.

BC14　The Board decided not to set out a hierarchy of requirements for these circumstances. The Standard requires only applicable IFRSs to be applied. In addition, it does not mention Appendices.

BC15　The Board decided not to rank Standards above Interpretations because the definition of International Financial Reporting Standards (IFRSs) includes Interpretations, which are equal in status to Standards. The rubric to each Standard clarifies what material constitutes the requirements of an IFRS and what is Implementation Guidance.[2] The term 'Appendix' is retained only for material that is part of an IFRS.

Pronouncements of other standard-setting bodies

BC16　The Exposure Draft proposed that in the absence of a Standard or an Interpretation specifically applying to an item, management should develop and apply an accounting policy by considering, among other guidance, pronouncements of other standard-setting bodies that use a similar conceptual framework to develop accounting standards. Respondents to the Exposure Draft commented that this could *require* entities to consider the pronouncements of

---

2　In 2007 the Board was advised that paragraphs 7 and 9 may appear to conflict, and may be misinterpreted to require mandatory consideration of Implementation Guidance. The Board amended paragraphs 7, 9 and 11 by *Improvements to IFRSs* issued in May 2008 to state that only guidance that is identified as an integral part of IFRSs is mandatory.

various other standard-setting bodies when IASB guidance does not exist. Some commentators argued that, for example, it could require consideration of all components of US GAAP on some topics. After considering these comments, the Board decided that the Standard should indicate that considering such pronouncements is voluntary (see paragraph 12 of the Standard).

BC17 As proposed in the Exposure Draft, the Standard states that pronouncements of other standard-setting bodies are used only if they do not conflict with:

(a) the requirements and guidance in IFRSs dealing with similar and related issues; and

(b) the definitions, recognition criteria and measurement concepts for assets, liabilities, income and expenses in the *Framework*.[3]

BC18 The Standard refers to the most recent pronouncements of other standard-setting bodies because if pronouncements are withdrawn or superseded, the relevant standard-setting body no longer thinks they include the best accounting policies to apply.

BC19 Comments received indicated that it was unclear from the Exposure Draft whether a change in accounting policy following a change in a pronouncement of another standard-setting body should be accounted for under the transitional provisions in that pronouncement. As noted above, the Standard does not mandate using pronouncements of other standard-setting bodies in any circumstances. Accordingly, the Board decided to clarify that such a change in accounting policy is accounted for and disclosed as a voluntary change in accounting policy (see paragraph 21 of the Standard). Thus, an entity is precluded from applying transitional provisions specified by the other standard-setting body if they are inconsistent with the treatment of voluntary changes in accounting policies specified by the Standard.

Materiality

BC20 The Standard states that accounting policies specified by IFRSs need not be applied when the effect of applying them is immaterial. It also states that financial statements do not comply with IFRSs if they contain material errors, and that material prior period errors are to be corrected in the first set of financial statements authorised for issue after their discovery. The Standard includes a definition of material omissions or misstatements, which is based on the description of materiality in IAS 1 *Presentation of Financial Statements* (as issued in 1997) and in the *Framework*.

BC21 The former *Preface to Statements of International Accounting Standards* stated that International Accounting Standards were not intended to apply to immaterial items. There is no equivalent statement in the *Preface to International Financial Reporting Standards*. The Board received comments that the absence of such a statement from the *Preface* could be interpreted as requiring an entity to apply accounting policies (including measurement requirements) specified by IFRSs to

---

3 In September 2010 the IASB replaced the *Framework* with the *Conceptual Framework for Financial Reporting*.

immaterial items. However, the Board decided that the application of the concept of materiality should be in Standards rather than in the *Preface*.

BC22 The application of the concept of materiality is set out in two Standards. IAS 1 (as revised in 2007) continues to specify its application to disclosures. IAS 8 specifies the application of materiality in applying accounting policies and correcting errors (including errors in measuring items).

Criterion for exemption from requirements

BC23 The previous version of IAS 8 included an impracticability criterion for exemption from retrospective application of voluntary changes in accounting policies and retrospective restatement for fundamental errors, and from making related disclosures, when the allowed alternative treatment of those items was not applied. The Exposure Draft proposed instead an exemption from retrospective application and retrospective restatement when it gives rise to undue cost or effort.

BC24 In the light of comments received on the Exposure Draft, the Board decided that an exemption based on management's assessment of undue cost or effort is too subjective to be applied consistently by different entities. Moreover, the Board decided that balancing costs and benefits is a task for the Board when it sets accounting requirements rather than for entities when they apply those requirements. Therefore, the Board decided to retain the impracticability criterion for exemption in the previous version of IAS 8. This affects the exemptions in paragraphs 23–25, 39 and 43–45 of the Standard. Impracticability is the only basis on which specific exemptions are provided in IFRSs from applying particular requirements when the effect of applying them is material.[4]

Definition of 'impracticable'

BC25 The Board decided to clarify the meaning of 'impracticable' in relation to retrospective application of a change in accounting policy and retrospective restatement to correct a prior period error.

BC26 Some commentators suggested that retrospective application of a change in accounting policy and retrospective restatement to correct a prior period error are impracticable for a particular prior period whenever significant estimates are required as of a date in that period. However, the Board decided to specify a narrower definition of impracticable because the fact that significant estimates are frequently required when amending comparative information presented for prior periods does not prevent reliable adjustment or correction of the comparative information. Thus, the Board decided that an inability to distinguish objectively information that both provides evidence of circumstances that existed on the date(s) as at which those amounts are to be recognised, measured or disclosed and would have been available when the financial statements for that prior period were authorised for issue from other

---

4   In 2006 the IASB issued IFRS 8 *Operating Segments*. As explained in paragraphs BC46 and BC47 of the Basis for Conclusions on IFRS 8, that IFRS includes an exemption from some requirements if the necessary information is not available and the cost to develop it would be excessive.

information is the factor that prevents reliable adjustment or correction of comparative information for prior periods (see part (c) of the definition of 'impracticable' and paragraphs 51 and 52 of the Standard).

BC27 The Standard specifies that hindsight should not be used when applying a new accounting policy to, or correcting amounts for, a prior period, either in making assumptions about what management's intentions would have been in a prior period or estimating the amounts in a prior period. This is because management's intentions in a prior period cannot be objectively established in a later period, and using information that would have been unavailable when the financial statements for the prior period(s) affected were authorised for issue is inconsistent with the definitions of retrospective application and retrospective restatement.

Applying the impracticability exemption

BC28 The Standard specifies that when it is impracticable to determine the cumulative effect of applying a new accounting policy to all prior periods, or the cumulative effect of an error on all prior periods, the entity changes the comparative information as if the new accounting policy had been applied, or the error had been corrected, prospectively from the earliest date practicable (see paragraphs 25 and 45 of the Standard). This is similar to paragraph 52 of the previous version of IAS 8, but it is no longer restricted to changes in accounting policies. The Board decided to include such provisions in the Standard because it agrees with comments received that it is preferable to require prospective application from the start of the earliest period practicable than to permit a change in accounting policy only when the entity can determine the cumulative effect of the change for all prior periods at the beginning of the current period.

BC29 Consistently with the Exposure Draft's proposals, the Standard provides an impracticability exemption from retrospective application of changes in accounting policies, including retrospective application of changes made in accordance with the transitional provisions in an IFRS. The previous version of IAS 8 specified the impracticability exemption for retrospective application of only *voluntary* changes in accounting policies. Thus, the applicability of the exemption to changes made in accordance with the transitional provisions in an IFRS depended on the text of that IFRS. The Board extended the applicability of the exemption because it decided that the need for the exemption applies equally to all changes in accounting policies applied retrospectively.

Disclosures about impending application of newly issued IFRSs

BC30 The Standard requires an entity to provide disclosures when it has not yet applied a new IFRS that has been issued but is not yet effective. The entity is required to disclose that it has not yet applied the IFRS, and known or reasonably estimable information relevant to assessing the possible impact that initial application of the new IFRS will have on the entity's financial statements in the period of initial application (paragraph 30). The Standard also includes guidance on specific disclosures the entity should consider when applying this requirement (paragraph 31).

BC31   Paragraphs 30 and 31 of the Standard differ from the proposals in the Exposure
        Draft in the following respects:

    (a)   they specify that an entity needs to disclose information only if it is
            known or reasonably estimable. This clarification responds to comments
            on the Exposure Draft that the proposed disclosures would sometimes be
            impracticable.

    (b)   whereas the Exposure Draft proposed to mandate the disclosures now in
            paragraph 31, the Standard sets out these disclosures as items an entity
            should consider disclosing to meet the general requirement in
            paragraph 30. This amendment focuses the requirement on the
            objective of the disclosure, and, in response to comments on the
            Exposure Draft that the proposed disclosures were more onerous than
            the disclosures in US GAAP, clarifies that the Board's intention was to
            converge with US requirements, rather than to be more onerous.

Recognising the effects of changes in accounting estimates

BC32   The Exposure Draft proposed to retain without exception the requirement in the
        previous version of IAS 8 that the effect of a change in accounting estimate is
        recognised in profit or loss in:

    (a)   the period of the change, if the change affects that period only; or

    (b)   the period of the change and future periods, if the change affects both.

BC33   Some respondents to the Exposure Draft disagreed with requiring the effects of
        all changes in accounting estimates to be recognised in profit or loss.
        They argued that this is inappropriate to the extent that a change in an
        accounting estimate gives rise to changes in assets and liabilities, because the
        entity's equity does not change as a result. These commentators also argued that
        it is inappropriate to preclude recognising the effects of changes in accounting
        estimates directly in equity when that is required or permitted by a Standard or
        an Interpretation. The Board concurs, and decided to provide an exception to
        the requirement described in paragraph BC32 for these circumstances.

IASB documents published to accompany

IAS 10

Events after the Reporting Period

The text of the unaccompanied standard, IAS 10, is contained in Part A of this edition. Its effective date when issued was 1 January 2005. This part presents the following documents:

BASIS FOR CONCLUSIONS

Basis for Conclusions on
IAS 10 *Events after the Reporting Period*[1]

This Basis for Conclusions accompanies, but is not part of, IAS 10.

Introduction

BC1   This Basis for Conclusions summarises the International Accounting Standards Board's considerations in reaching its conclusions on revising IAS 10 *Events After the Balance Sheet Date* in 2003. Individual Board members gave greater weight to some factors than to others.

BC2   In July 2001 the Board announced that, as part of its initial agenda of technical projects, it would undertake a project to improve a number of Standards, including IAS 10. The project was undertaken in the light of queries and criticisms raised in relation to the Standards by securities regulators, professional accountants and other interested parties. The objectives of the Improvements project were to reduce or eliminate alternatives, redundancies and conflicts within Standards, to deal with some convergence issues and to make other improvements. In May 2002 the Board published its proposals in an Exposure Draft of *Improvements to International Accounting Standards*, with a comment deadline of 16 September 2002. The Board received over 160 comment letters on the Exposure Draft.

BC3   Because the Board's intention was not to reconsider the fundamental approach to the accounting for events after the balance sheet date established by IAS 10, this Basis for Conclusions does not discuss requirements in IAS 10 that the Board has not reconsidered.

Limited clarification

BC4   For this limited clarification of IAS 10 the main change made is in paragraphs 12 and 13 (paragraphs 11 and 12 of the previous version of IAS 10). As revised, those paragraphs state that if dividends are declared after the balance sheet date,[2] an entity shall not recognise those dividends as a liability at the balance sheet date. This is because undeclared dividends do not meet the criteria of a present obligation in IAS 37 *Provisions, Contingent Liabilities and Contingent Assets*. The Board discussed whether or not an entity's past practice of paying dividends could be considered a constructive obligation. The Board concluded that such practices do not give rise to a liability to pay dividends.[3]

---

1   In September 2007 the IASB amended the title of IAS 10 from *Events after the Balance Sheet Date* to *Events after the Reporting Period* as a consequence of the amendments in IAS 1 *Presentation of Financial Statements* (as revised in 2007).

2   IAS 1 *Presentation of Financial Statements* (as revised in 2007) replaced the term 'balance sheet date' with 'end of the reporting period'.

3   In 2007 the Board was advised that paragraph 13, taken in isolation, could be read to imply that a liability should be recognised in some circumstances on the basis that a constructive obligation exists, such as when there is an established pattern of paying a dividend. Therefore, the Board amended paragraph 13 by *Improvements to IFRSs* issued in May 2008 to state that no such obligation exists.

IASB documents published to accompany

IAS 12

Income Taxes

The text of the unaccompanied standard, IAS 12, is contained in Part A of this edition. Its effective date when issued was 1 January 1998. The text of the Accompanying Guidance on IAS 12 is contained in Part B of this edition. This part presents the following documents:

BASIS FOR CONCLUSIONS

Basis for Conclusions on IAS 12 *Income Taxes*

This Basis for Conclusions accompanies, but is not part of, IAS 12.

Introduction

BC1   When IAS 12 *Income Taxes* was issued by the International Accounting Standards Committee in 1996 to replace the previous IAS 12 *Accounting for Taxes on Income* (issued in July 1979), the Standard was not accompanied by a Basis for Conclusions. This Basis for Conclusions is not comprehensive. It summarises only the International Accounting Standards Board's considerations in making the amendments to IAS 12 contained in *Deferred Tax: Recovery of Underlying Assets* issued in December 2010. Individual Board members gave greater weight to some factors than to others.

BC1A   In August 2014 the Board published an Exposure Draft of proposed amendments to IAS 12 to clarify the requirements on recognition of deferred tax assets for unrealised losses on debt instruments measured at fair value. The Board subsequently modified and confirmed the proposals and in January 2016 issued *Recognition of Deferred Tax Assets for Unrealised Losses* (Amendments to IAS 12). The Board's considerations and reasons for its conclusions are discussed in paragraphs BC37–BC62.

BC2   The Board amended IAS 12 to address an issue that arises when entities apply the measurement principle in IAS 12 to temporary differences relating to investment properties that are measured using the fair value model in IAS 40 *Investment Property*.

BC3   In March 2009 the Board published an exposure draft, *Income Tax* (the 2009 exposure draft), proposing a new IFRS to replace IAS 12. In the 2009 exposure draft, the Board addressed this issue as part of a broad proposal relating to the determination of tax basis. In October 2009 the Board decided not to proceed with the proposals in the 2009 exposure draft and announced that, together with the US Financial Accounting Standards Board, it aimed to conduct a fundamental review of the accounting for income tax in the future. In the meantime, the Board would address specific significant current practice issues.

BC4   In September 2010 the Board published proposals for addressing one of those practice issues in an exposure draft *Deferred Tax: Recovery of Underlying Assets* with a 60-day comment period. Although that is shorter than the Board's normal 120-day comment period, the Board concluded that this was justified because the amendments were straightforward and the exposure draft was short. In addition, the amendments were addressing a problem that existed in practice and needed to be solved as soon as possible. The Board considered the comments it received on the exposure draft and in December 2010 issued the amendments to IAS 12. The Board intends to address other practice issues arising from IAS 12 in due course, when other priorities on its agenda permit this.

Recovery of revalued non-depreciable assets

BC5   In December 2010, the Board incorporated in paragraph 51B of IAS 12 the consensus previously contained in SIC Interpretation 21 *Income Taxes—Recovery of Revalued Non-Depreciable Assets*. However, because paragraph 51C addresses investment property carried at fair value, the Board excluded such assets from the scope of paragraph 51B. Paragraphs BC6 and BC7 set out the basis that the Standing Interpretations Committee (SIC) gave for the conclusions it reached in developing the consensus expressed in SIC-21.

BC6   The SIC noted that the *Framework for the Preparation and Presentation of Financial Statements*[1] stated that an entity recognises an asset if it is probable that the future economic benefits associated with the asset will flow to the entity. Generally, those future economic benefits will be derived (and therefore the carrying amount of an asset will be recovered) through sale, through use, or through use and subsequent sale. Recognition of depreciation implies that the carrying amount of a depreciable asset is expected to be recovered through use to the extent of its depreciable amount, and through sale at its residual value. Consistently with this, the carrying amount of a non-depreciable asset, such as land having an unlimited life, will be recovered only through sale. In other words, because the asset is not depreciated, no part of its carrying amount is expected to be recovered (ie consumed) through use. Deferred taxes associated with the non-depreciable asset reflect the tax consequences of selling the asset.

BC7   The SIC noted that the expected manner of recovery is not predicated on the basis of measuring the carrying amount of the asset. For example, if the carrying amount of a non-depreciable asset is measured at its value in use, the basis of measurement does not imply that the carrying amount of the asset is expected to be recovered through use, but through its residual value upon ultimate disposal.

Recovery of investment properties

Reason for the exception

BC8   IAS 12 applies the principle that the measurement of deferred tax liabilities and deferred tax assets should reflect the tax consequences that would follow from the manner in which the entity expects to recover or settle the carrying amount of its assets and liabilities. In many cases, however, an entity expects to rent out investment property to earn rental income and then sell it to gain from capital appreciation at some point in the future. Without specific plans for disposal of the investment property, it is difficult and subjective to estimate how much of the carrying amount of the investment property will be recovered through cash flows from rental income and how much of it will be recovered through cash flows from selling the asset.

BC9   It is particularly difficult and subjective to determine the entity's expected manner of recovery for investment property that is measured using the fair

---

1   IASC's *Framework for the Preparation and Presentation of Financial Statements* was adopted by the IASB in 2001. In September 2010 the IASB replaced the *Framework* with the *Conceptual Framework for Financial Reporting*.

value model in IAS 40. In contrast, for investment property that is measured using the cost model in IAS 40, the Board believes that the estimates required for depreciation establish the expected manner of recovery because there is a general presumption that an asset's carrying amount is recovered through use to the extent of the amount subject to depreciation and through sale to the extent of the residual value.

BC10 To address this issue, the Board introduced an exception to the principle in IAS 12 that applies when an entity adopts an accounting policy of remeasuring investment property at fair value. The purpose of the exception is to reflect the entity's expectation of recovery of the investment property in a practical manner that involves little subjectivity.

BC11 Many respondents to the exposure draft of September 2010 commented that the Board should develop application guidance rather than creating an exception. The Board could have achieved a similar result in some cases by providing application guidance on how to apply the underlying principle to investment property. However, the Board chose an exception because it is simple, straightforward and can avoid unintended consequences by a strict definition of its scope. In fact, this exception is very similar to application guidance. However, it is technically an exception because, in some cases, the asset's carrying amount is assumed to be recovered entirely through sale even though an entity expects it to be recovered partly through sale and partly through use.

BC12 The Board also noted that application guidance would not resolve a practice issue that arises when the future income generated from an asset is expected to exceed the carrying amount of that asset and that future income will be subject to two or more different tax regimes. In those situations, IAS 12 provides no basis for determining which tax rate and tax base apply to the recovery of the carrying amount. The Board concluded that the practical way to resolve this issue was to create an exception that determines the manner of recovery of an asset within the scope of that exception.

Scope of the exception

BC13 The Board understands that the concerns raised in practice relate primarily to investment property measured using the fair value model in IAS 40. The Board proposed in the exposure draft that the exception should also apply to property, plant and equipment or intangible assets measured using the revaluation model in IAS 16 *Property, Plant and Equipment* or IAS 38 *Intangible Assets*. That was because in assessing the difficulty and subjectivity involved in determining the expected manner of recovering the carrying amount of the underlying asset, there is no underlying difference between regularly fair valuing assets through a revaluation accounting policy and applying a fair value measurement model.

BC14 Many respondents disagreed with the proposal to include property, plant and equipment or intangible assets measured using the revaluation model in IAS 16 or IAS 38 in the scope of the exception. They stated that many items of property, plant and equipment are recovered through use rather than through sale, and that this is consistent with the definition of property, plant and equipment in IAS 16. In addition, many respondents disagreed with the presumption of recovery through sale when the underlying assets are intangible assets for similar reasons. They also warned of unintended consequences that could arise because of the varying nature of intangible assets. Many respondents suggested limiting the scope of the exception to investment properties measured using the fair value model in IAS 40. Having considered those comments, the Board adopted that suggestion.

BC15 Some respondents supported inclusion of property, plant and equipment in the scope of the exception, including property, plant and equipment measured on a cost basis, because of their concerns about the lack of discounting deferred tax assets and deferred tax liabilities and about a possible double-counting of tax effects (see paragraph BC19). However, the Board concluded that considering concerns about the lack of discounting and about the possible double-counting was outside the limited scope of the amendments.

BC16 The Board made it clear that the exception also applies on initial measurement of investment property acquired in a business combination if the investment property will subsequently be measured using the fair value model in IAS 40. If the exception did not apply in these circumstances, deferred taxes might reflect the tax consequences of use at the acquisition date, but at a later date reflect the tax consequences of sale. The Board believes that measurement of deferred taxes at the acquisition date should be consistent with the subsequent measurement of the same deferred taxes. For the same reason, the Board concluded that the exception should not apply to investment property initially measured at fair value in a business combination if the entity subsequently uses the cost model.

BC17 Having considered the responses to the exposure draft, the Board decided not to extend the exception to other underlying assets and liabilities that are measured at fair value, including financial instruments or biological assets. This is because the Board understands that the most significant current practice issues relate to investment property. In addition, the Board wished to avoid unintended consequences of expanding the scope to other assets and liabilities that are measured on a fair value basis.

BC18 The Board concluded that the amendments should apply to all temporary differences that arise relating to underlying assets within the scope of the exception, not just those separate temporary differences created by the remeasurement of the underlying asset. This is because the unit of account applied in determining the manner of recovery in the Standard is the underlying asset as a whole, not the individual temporary differences.

Measurement basis

BC19 The Board decided that when the exception applies, there should be a presumption that deferred taxes should be measured to reflect the tax consequences of recovering the carrying amount of the investment property entirely through sale. In making that decision, the Board considered various views expressed by interested parties, which included, but were not limited to the following:

(a) the tax effect would be double-counted in some situations if deferred taxes are measured on the basis of the tax consequences of use, because the investment property is measured at fair value, which reflects some of these tax consequences; and

(b)   presuming sale is consistent with a fair value measurement basis that reflects the price that would be received if the investment property is sold.

BC20   Many respondents to the exposure draft said that choosing a measurement basis of fair value is an accounting policy choice that does not imply or predict recovery of the investment property through sale. Many also said that the proposed exception would solve the double-counting problem partially but not completely. The Board noted that the aim of the exception was neither to link the accounting policy with measurement of deferred taxes (see paragraph BC7), nor to remove completely the double-counting of tax effects (see paragraph BC15). The aim of this exception is to provide a practical approach when determination of the expected manner of recovery is difficult and subjective.

BC21   In many cases when an entity chooses the fair value model for investment property, investment properties are recovered through sale. Even if an investment property earns income through rental use in a given period, the value of the future earnings capacity of the investment property will often not decrease and that value will ultimately be realised through sale. Therefore, the Board retained its proposal to introduce a presumption of recovery through sale.

BC22   The Board made that presumption rebuttable because the Board believes that it is not always appropriate to assume the recovery of investment property through sale. The Board initially proposed in the exposure draft that the presumption of recovery through sale is not appropriate when the entity has clear evidence that it will consume the asset's economic benefits throughout its economic life. The Board set a criterion that refers to consumption of the asset's economic benefits, rather than to the recovery of the carrying amount, because the Board understands that there is diverse practice regarding the meaning of the recovery of the carrying amount through use or through sale.

BC23   After considering the responses to the exposure draft, the Board reworded the rebuttable presumption so that clear evidence would not be required to rebut it. Instead, the presumption is rebutted if an asset is held within a business model whose objective is to consume substantially all of the economic benefits embodied in the investment property over time, rather than through sale. Many respondents were concerned that, because clear evidence is an ambiguous term, the requirement to gather clear evidence would have been onerous for entities that have no problem applying the existing principle in IAS 12, and could have led to abuse by entities that choose whether to gather clear evidence to achieve a favourable result. The Board chose to use the term 'business model' because it is already used in IFRS 9 *Financial Instruments* and would not depend on management's intentions for an individual asset. Many respondents were concerned that the presumption would lead to inappropriate results in some cases because it would not be rebutted if a minor scrap value would be recovered through sale. The Board also reworded the rebuttable presumption in order to respond to those concerns. The Board also made it clear that the presumption of recovery through sale cannot be rebutted if the asset is non-depreciable because that fact implies that no part of the carrying amount of the asset would be consumed through use (see paragraph BC6).

BC24   The Board also considered other approaches to the measurement of deferred tax liabilities and deferred tax assets when the exception applies, specifically whether deferred taxes should be measured on the basis of the lower of the tax consequences of recovery through use and through sale. However, the Board rejected such an approach, noting that it would have created:

(a)   conceptual and practical concerns about whether deferred tax assets should be measured to reflect the lower of, or higher of, the tax consequences of use and of sale;

(b)   a measurement basis that some believe would be arbitrary; and

(c)   concerns that entities might be required to measure deferred taxes on a basis that is inconsistent with their expectations of recovery of the carrying amount of the underlying asset.

BC25   Some respondents to the exposure draft drew the mistaken conclusion that the exposure draft required presumption of *immediate* sale at the end of the reporting period when assessing the presumption of recovery through sale. The Board observed that paragraph 47 of IAS 12 requires deferred tax assets and liabilities to be measured at the tax rates that are expected to apply to the period when the asset is realised or the liability is settled on the basis of tax rates (and tax laws) that have been enacted or substantively enacted by the end of the reporting period. This requirement applies even when the presumption of recovery through sale is used. For clarification, the Board adjusted the illustrative example following paragraph 51C to reflect the requirement in paragraph 47.

BC26   In the exposure draft, the Board proposed to withdraw SIC-21. However, many respondents commented that SIC-21 should be retained in order to avoid unintended consequences. Having considered the responses to the exposure draft, the Board decided to incorporate SIC-21 into IAS 12 in its entirety after excluding from the scope of SIC-21 the investment property subject to the requirement in paragraph 51C.

Assessment of deferred tax assets

BC27   The Board inserted paragraph 51E to confirm that the requirements in paragraphs 24–33 (deductible temporary differences) and paragraphs 34–36 (unused tax losses and unused tax credits) relating to assessment of deferred tax assets continue to apply even when the presumption of recovery through sale arises. The Board did not think that additional guidance would be necessary.

Disclosure requirement

BC28   The Board proposed in the exposure draft disclosure of the fact of, and reasons for, the rebuttal of the presumption of recovery through sale if the entity has rebutted the presumption. However, many respondents said that this disclosure would add little or no value to the financial statements. IAS 1 *Presentation of Financial Statements* already requires disclosures regarding material judgements. Thus, there is no need to disclose a particular judgement on specific types of assets. The Board was convinced by those arguments and did not proceed with the proposed disclosure requirement.

The costs and benefits of the amendments to IAS 12

BC29   Computation of the tax consequences of selling assets is complex in some tax jurisdictions and there are concerns that the amendments to IAS 12 will increase the administrative burden for some entities in those tax jurisdictions.

BC30   However, the Board believes that the benefit of providing the exception outweighs this potential increase in administrative burden for some entities. This is because the purpose of the exception is to enable preparers to measure deferred taxes in these circumstances in the least subjective manner and in so doing enhance the comparability of financial information about deferred taxes for the benefit of users of financial statements. It is also expected to result in an overall reduction of the administrative burden for entities that have previously had to consider the tax consequence of both use and sale of an investment property when measuring deferred taxes.

BC31   Many respondents to the exposure draft said that entities would not benefit from the amendments in jurisdictions in which this practice issue did not exist but would suffer from an increased administrative burden as a result of the amendments. Their criticism mainly focused on the rebuttable presumption, as discussed in paragraphs BC22 and BC23. They also said that the disclosure requirement proposed in the exposure draft would be onerous.

BC32   After considering the responses to the exposure draft, the Board narrowed the scope of the exception to apply only to investment property carried at fair value. It reworded the rebuttable presumption so that clear evidence would no longer be required to rebut the presumption. The Board also did not pursue the proposed disclosure requirement regarding the fact of, and reason for, the rebuttal. After those changes, the Board believes that the amendments will not be onerous for entities that have previously been able to establish without difficulty how they expect to recover investment property carried at fair value.

Transition and effective date

BC33   IAS 8 *Accounting Policies, Changes in Accounting Estimates and Errors* requires an entity to apply retrospectively a change in accounting policy resulting from the initial application of an IFRS that does not have a transition provision. The Board did not include any transition provision in the amendments because, in the Board's view, it would not be unduly burdensome for entities to apply the changes to IAS 12 retrospectively.

BC34   The Board acknowledges that the amendments may add some administrative burden if they apply to investment property acquired in a business combination that occurred in a previous reporting period. For example, it could be difficult to restate goodwill and recalculate previous impairment reassessments if some information is not available and an entity is unable to separate the effects of hindsight. However, the Board reasoned that the amendments apply only to specific circumstances. Moreover, IAS 8 provides sufficient guidance to deal with cases when it might be impracticable to reassess impairment of goodwill or recoverability of deferred tax assets.

BC35   Consequently, the Board concluded that the cost of requiring retrospective application is outweighed by the benefit of consistent application of the amendments by entities to all periods presented in the financial statements. Accordingly, the Board decided that entities should apply the amendments to IAS 12 retrospectively in accordance with IAS 8.

First-time adoption of IFRSs

BC36   The Board identified no reason to adjust the exception for application by a first-time adopter at its date of transition to IFRSs.

Recognition of Deferred Tax Assets for Unrealised Losses (2016 amendments)

BC37   The IFRS Interpretations Committee (the 'Interpretations Committee') was asked to provide guidance on how an entity determines, in accordance with IAS 12, whether to recognise a deferred tax asset when:

(a)   the entity has a debt instrument that is classified as an available-for-sale financial asset in accordance with IAS 39 *Financial Instruments: Recognition and Measurement*.[2] Changes in the market interest rate result in a decrease in the fair value of the debt instrument to below its cost (ie it has an 'unrealised loss');

(b)   it is probable that the issuer of the debt instrument will make all the contractual payments;

(c)   the tax base of the debt instrument is cost;

(d)   tax law does not allow a loss to be deducted on a debt instrument until the loss is realised for tax purposes;

(e)   the entity has the ability and intention to hold the debt instrument until the unrealised loss reverses (which may be at its maturity);

(f)   tax law distinguishes between capital gains and losses and ordinary income and losses. While capital losses can only be offset against capital gains, ordinary losses can be offset against both capital gains and ordinary income; and

(g)   the entity has insufficient taxable temporary differences and no other probable taxable profits against which the entity can utilise deductible temporary differences.

BC38   The Interpretations Committee reported to the Board that practice differed because of divergent views on the following questions:

(a)   Do decreases in the carrying amount of a fixed-rate debt instrument for which the principal is paid on maturity always give rise to a deductible temporary difference if this debt instrument is measured at fair value and if its tax base remains at cost? In particular, do they give rise to a deductible temporary difference if the debt instrument's holder expects

---

2   IFRS 9 *Financial Instruments* replaced IAS 39. IFRS 9 applies to all items that were previously within the scope of IAS 39. Under IFRS 9, the same question arises for debt instruments measured at fair value.

to recover the carrying amount of the asset by use, ie continuing to hold it, and if it is probable that the issuer will pay all the contractual cash flows? (see paragraphs BC39–BC45)

(b)　Does an entity assume that it will recover an asset for more than its carrying amount when estimating probable future taxable profit against which deductible temporary differences are assessed for utilisation if such recovery is probable? This question is relevant when taxable profit from other sources is insufficient for the utilisation of the deductible temporary differences related to debt instruments measured at fair value. In this case, an entity may only be able to recognise deferred tax assets for its deductible temporary differences if it is probable that it will collect the entire cash flows from the debt instrument and therefore recover it for more than its carrying amount. (see paragraphs BC46–BC54)

(c)　When an entity assesses whether it can utilise deductible temporary differences against probable future taxable profit, does that probable future taxable profit include the effects of reversing deductible temporary differences? (see paragraphs BC55–BC56)

(d)　Does an entity assess whether a deferred tax asset is recognised for each deductible temporary difference separately or in combination with other deductible temporary differences? This question is relevant, for example, when tax law distinguishes capital gains and losses from other taxable gains and losses and capital losses can only be offset against capital gains. (see paragraphs BC57–BC59)

Existence of a deductible temporary difference

BC39　In the case of many debt instruments, the collection of the principal on maturity does not increase or decrease taxable profit that is reported for tax purposes. This is the case in the example illustrating paragraph 26(d) of IAS 12. Interest is paid at the contractual rate each year, and on maturity of the debt instrument the issuer pays the principal of CU1,000. In this example, if the investor continues to hold the debt instrument, the investor only pays taxes on the interest income. The collection of the principal does not trigger any tax payments.

BC40　Because the collection of the principal does not increase or decrease the taxable profit that is reported for tax purposes, some thought that the collection of the principal is a non-taxable event. Sometimes, tax law does not explicitly address whether the collection of the principal has tax consequences. Consequently, proponents of this view thought that a difference between the carrying amount of the debt instrument in the statement of financial position and its higher tax base does not give rise to a deductible temporary difference, if this difference results from a loss that they expect will not be realised for tax purposes.

BC41　Those who held this view thought that the loss would not be realised for tax purposes if the entity has the ability and intention to hold the debt instrument over the period until the loss reverses, which might be until maturity, and it is probable that the entity will receive all the contractual cash flows. In this case, differences between the carrying amount of the debt instrument in the statement of financial position and its tax base reverse over the period to maturity, as a result of continuing to hold the debt instrument.

BC42   The Board considered the guidance in IAS 12 on the identification of temporary differences and rejected the reasoning presented in paragraphs BC40 and BC41. Paragraphs 20 and 26(d) of IAS 12 specify that a difference between the carrying amount of an asset measured at fair value and its higher tax base gives rise to a deductible temporary difference. This is because the calculation of a temporary difference in IAS 12 is based on the premise that the entity will recover the carrying amount of an asset, and hence economic benefits will flow to the entity in future periods to the extent of the asset's carrying amount at the end of the reporting period. In contrast, the view presented in paragraphs BC40 and BC41 is based on the assessment of the economic benefits that are expected at maturity. The Board noted that the existence of a deductible temporary difference depends solely on a comparison of the carrying amount of an asset and its tax base at the end of the reporting period, and is not affected by possible future changes in the carrying amount.

BC43   Consequently, the Board concluded that decreases below cost in the carrying amount of a fixed-rate debt instrument measured at fair value for which the tax base remains at cost give rise to a deductible temporary difference. This applies irrespective of whether the debt instrument's holder expects to recover the carrying amount of the debt instrument by sale or by use, ie continuing to hold it, or whether it is probable that the issuer will pay all the contractual cash flows. Normally, the collection of the entire principal does not increase or decrease taxable profit that is reported for tax purposes, because the tax base equals the inflow of taxable economic benefits when the principal is paid. Typically, the tax base of the debt instrument is deducted either on sale or on maturity.

BC44   The economic benefit embodied in the related deferred tax asset arises from the ability of the holder of the debt instrument to achieve future taxable gains in the amount of the deductible temporary difference without paying taxes on those gains. In contrast, an entity that acquires the debt instrument described in the example illustrating paragraph 26(d) of IAS 12 for its fair value at the end of Year 2 (in the example, CU918) and continues to hold it, has to pay taxes on a gain of CU82, whereas the entity in that example will not pay any taxes on the collection of the CU1,000 of principal. The Board concluded that it was appropriate for the different tax consequences for these two holders of the same instrument to be reflected in the deferred tax accounting for the debt instrument.

BC45   The Board has added an example after paragraph 26 of IAS 12 to illustrate the identification of a deductible temporary difference in the case of a fixed-rate debt instrument measured at fair value for which the principal is paid on maturity.

Recovering an asset for more than its carrying amount

BC46   The Board noted that paragraph 29 of IAS 12 identifies taxable profit in future periods as one source of taxable profits against which an entity can utilise deductible temporary differences. Future taxable profit has to be probable to justify the recognition of deferred tax assets.

BC47   The guidance in paragraph 29 of IAS 12 does not refer to the carrying amount of assets within the context of estimating probable future taxable profit. Some thought, however, that the carrying amount of an asset to which a temporary difference is related limits the estimate of future taxable profit. They argued that accounting for deferred taxes should be based on consistent assumptions, which implies that an entity cannot assume that, for one and the same asset, the entity will recover it:

(a)   for its carrying amount when determining deductible temporary differences and taxable temporary differences; as well as

(b)   for more than its carrying amount when estimating probable future taxable profit against which deductible temporary differences are assessed for utilisation.

BC48   Consequently, proponents of this view thought that an entity cannot assume that it will collect the entire principal of CU1,000 in the example illustrating paragraph 26(d) of IAS 12 when determining probable future taxable profit. Instead, they thought that an entity must assume that it will collect only the carrying amount of the asset.

BC49   The Board noted however that determining temporary differences and estimating probable future taxable profit against which deductible temporary differences are assessed for utilisation are two separate steps and the carrying amount of an asset is relevant only to determining temporary differences. The carrying amount of an asset does not limit the estimation of probable future taxable profit. In its estimate of probable future taxable profit, an entity includes the probable inflow of taxable economic benefits that results from recovering an asset. This probable inflow of taxable economic benefits may exceed the carrying amount of the asset.

BC50   Moreover, a limitation on the estimate of probable future taxable profit by the carrying amount of assets can lead to inappropriate results in other scenarios. For example, a significant part of the assets of a profitable manufacturing entity is property, plant and equipment and inventories. Property, plant and equipment may be measured using the cost model (paragraph 30 of IAS 16 *Property, Plant and Equipment)* and inventories are measured at the lower of cost and net realisable value (paragraph 9 of IAS 2 *Inventories*). If such an entity expects to generate future taxable profit, it may be inconsistent to assume that it will only recover these assets for their carrying amount. This is because a significant part of the manufacturing entity's probable future taxable profit results from using those assets to generate taxable profit in excess of their carrying amount.

BC51   If a limitation such as the one described in paragraph BC50 was made, then, for the purpose of consistency, the entity would need to assume that it will not recover any of its assets for more than their carrying amount. The Board decided that it would not be appropriate to limit the estimate of probable future taxable profit to the carrying amount of related assets only for assets to which temporary differences are related, because there is no basis for a different assessment that would depend on whether a deductible temporary difference is related to an asset or not.

BC52   Some respondents to the Exposure Draft expressed concern that the guidance might be applied more broadly, and in their view, inappropriately, to other assets, and not merely to debt instruments measured at fair value. Some other respondents were concerned that any guidance would give the false impression that future taxable profit should be estimated on an individual asset basis. The Board noted that the principle that the estimate of probable future taxable profit includes an expected recovery of assets for more than their carrying amounts is not limited to any specific type or class of assets.

BC53   However, the Board also noted that there are cases in which it may not be probable that an asset will be recovered for more than its carrying amount. An entity should not inappropriately assume that an asset will be recovered for more than its carrying amount. The Board thought that this is particularly important when the asset is measured at fair value. In response to that concern, the Board noted that entities will need to have sufficient evidence on which to base their estimate of probable future taxable profit, including when that estimate involves the recovery of an asset for more than its carrying amount. For example, in the case of a fixed-rate debt instrument measured at fair value, the entity may judge that the contractual nature of future cash flows, as well as the assessment of the likelihood that those contractual cash flows will be received, adequately supports the conclusion that it is probable that it will recover the fixed-rate debt instrument for more than its carrying amount, if the expected cash flows exceed the debt instrument's carrying amount. The Board thought that such an example could enhance understanding and reduce the risk of arbitrary estimates of future taxable profit.

BC54   The Board has added paragraph 29A to IAS 12 to clarify to what extent an entity's estimate of future taxable profit (paragraph 29) includes amounts from recovering assets for more than their carrying amounts.

Probable future taxable profit against which deductible temporary differences are assessed for utilisation

BC55   The Interpretations Committee observed that there is uncertainty about how to determine probable future taxable profit against which deductible temporary differences are assessed for utilisation when this profit is being assessed to determine the recognition of all deferred tax assets. The uncertainty relates to whether the probable future taxable profit should include or exclude deductions that will arise when those deductible temporary differences reverse.

BC56   The Board noted that deductible temporary differences are utilised by deduction against taxable profit, excluding deductions arising from reversal of those deductible temporary differences. Consequently, taxable profit used for assessing the utilisation of deductible temporary differences is different from taxable profit on which income taxes are payable, as defined in paragraph 5 of IAS 12. If those deductions were not excluded, then they would be counted twice. The Board has amended paragraph 29(a) to clarify this.

Combined versus separate assessment

BC57   The Board considered the guidance in IAS 12 on the recognition of deferred tax assets. Paragraph 24 of IAS 12 requires deferred tax assets to be recognised only to the extent of probable future taxable profit against which the deductible temporary differences can be utilised. Paragraph 27 explains that:

(a)   the deductible temporary differences are utilised when their reversal results in deductions that are offset against taxable profits of future periods; and

(b)   economic benefits in the form of reductions in tax payments will flow to the entity only if it earns sufficient taxable profits against which the deductions can be offset.

BC58   The Board noted that:

(a)   tax law determines which deductions are offset against taxable income in determining taxable profits. The Board also noted that paragraph 5 of IAS 12 defines taxable profit as the profit of a period, determined in accordance with the rules established by the taxation authorities, upon which income taxes are payable.

(b)   no deferred tax asset is recognised if the reversal of the deductible temporary difference will not lead to tax deductions.

BC59   Consequently, if tax law offsets a deduction against taxable income on an entity basis, without segregating deductions from different sources, an entity carries out a combined assessment of all its deductible temporary differences relating to the same taxation authority and the same taxable entity. However, if tax law offsets specific types of losses only against a particular type, or types, of income (for example, if tax law limits the offset of capital losses to capital gains), an entity assesses a deductible temporary difference in combination with other deductible temporary differences of that type(s), but separately from other deductible temporary differences. Segregating deductible temporary differences in accordance with tax law and assessing them on such a basis is necessary to determine whether taxable profits are sufficient to utilise deductible temporary differences. The Board has added paragraph 27A to IAS 12 to clarify this.

Transition

BC60   The Board decided to require the adjustment of comparative information for any earlier periods presented. However, this amendment allows the change in opening equity of the earliest comparative period presented that arises upon the first application of the amendment to be recognised in opening retained earnings (or in another component of equity, as appropriate), without the need to allocate the change between opening retained earnings and other components of equity. This is to avoid undue cost and effort.

BC61   The Board noted that, with the exception of the amounts that would have to be adjusted within equity, the accounting required by these amendments is based on amounts and estimates at the end of the reporting periods. The changes to the accounting are mechanical in nature and so the Board expects that the cost of adjusting comparatives should not exceed the benefits of greater comparability.

BC62 The Board has not added additional transition relief for first-time adopters. This is consistent with the fact that IFRS 1 *First-time Adoption of International Financial Reporting Standards* does not include an exception to, or exemption from, the retrospective application of the requirements in IAS 12.

IASB documents published to accompany

IAS 16

Property, Plant and Equipment

The text of the unaccompanied standard, IAS 16, is contained in Part A of this edition. Its effective date when issued was 1 January 2005. This part presents the following documents:

BASIS FOR CONCLUSIONS

DISSENTING OPINION

Contents

© IFRS Foundation

Basis for Conclusions on
IAS 16 *Property, Plant and Equipment*

This Basis for Conclusions accompanies, but is not part of, IAS 16.

Introduction

BC1   This Basis for Conclusions summarises the International Accounting Standards Board's considerations in reaching its conclusions on revising IAS 16 *Property, Plant and Equipment* in 2003. Individual Board members gave greater weight to some factors than to others.

BC2   In July 2001 the Board announced that, as part of its initial agenda of technical projects, it would undertake a project to improve a number of Standards, including IAS 16. The project was undertaken in the light of queries and criticisms raised in relation to the Standards by securities regulators, professional accountants and other interested parties. The objectives of the Improvements project were to reduce or eliminate alternatives, redundancies and conflicts within Standards, to deal with some convergence issues and to make other improvements. In May 2002 the Board published its proposals in an Exposure Draft of *Improvements to International Accounting Standards*, with a comment deadline of 16 September 2002. The Board received over 160 comment letters on the Exposure Draft.

BC2A   *Agriculture: Bearer Plants* (Amendments to IAS 16 and IAS 41), issued in June 2014, amended the scope of IAS 16 to include bearer plants. IAS 41 *Agriculture* applies to the produce growing on those bearer plants. The amendments define a bearer plant and require bearer plants to be accounted for as property, plant and equipment in accordance with IAS 16. These amendments are discussed in paragraphs BC38–BC117.

BC3   Because the Board's intention was not to reconsider the fundamental approach to the accounting for property, plant and equipment that was established by IAS 16, this Basis for Conclusions does not discuss requirements in IAS 16 that the Board has not reconsidered.

Scope

BC4   The Board clarified that the requirements of IAS 16 apply to items of property, plant and equipment that an entity uses to develop or maintain (a) biological assets and (b) mineral rights and mineral reserves such as oil, natural gas and similar non-regenerative resources. The Board noted that items of property, plant and equipment that an entity uses for these purposes possess the same characteristics as other items of property, plant and equipment.

Recognition

BC5   In considering potential improvements to the previous version of IAS 16, the Board reviewed its subsequent expenditure recognition principle for two reasons. First, the existing subsequent expenditure recognition principle did not align with the asset recognition principle in the *Framework*.[1] Second, the Board noted difficulties in practice in making the distinction it required between expenditures that maintain, and those that enhance, an item of property, plant and equipment. Some expenditures seem to do both.

BC6   The Board ultimately decided that the separate recognition principle for subsequent expenditure was not needed. As a result, an entity will evaluate all its property, plant and equipment costs under IAS 16's general recognition principle. Also, if the cost of a replacement for part of an item of property, plant and equipment is recognised in the carrying amount of an asset, then an entity will derecognise the carrying amount of what was replaced to avoid carrying both the replacement and the replaced portion as assets. This derecognition occurs whether or not what is replaced is a part of an item that the entity depreciates separately.

BC7   The Board's decision on how to handle the recognition principles was not reached easily. In the Exposure Draft (ED), the Board proposed to include within IAS 16's general recognition principle only the recognition of subsequent expenditures that are replacements of a part of an item of property, plant and equipment. Also in the ED, the Board proposed to modify the subsequent expenditure recognition principle to distinguish more clearly the expenditures to which it would continue to apply.

BC8   Respondents to the ED agreed that it was appropriate for subsequent expenditures that were replacements of a part of an item of property, plant and equipment that an entity depreciated separately to be covered by the general recognition principle. However, the respondents argued, and the Board agreed, that the modified second principle was not clearer because it would result in an entity recognising in the carrying amount of an asset and then depreciating subsequent expenditures that were for the day-to-day servicing of items of property, plant and equipment, those that might commonly be regarded as for 'repairs and maintenance'. That result was not the Board's intention.

BC9   In its redeliberation of the ED, the Board concluded it could not retain the proposed modified subsequent expenditure recognition principle. It also concluded that it could not revert to the subsequent expenditure principle in the previous version of IAS 16 because, if it did, nothing was improved; the *Framework* conflict was not resolved and the practice issues were not addressed.

BC10   The Board concluded that it was best for all subsequent expenditures to be covered by IAS 16's general recognition principle. This solution had the following advantages:

(a)   use of IAS 16's general recognition principle fits the *Framework*.

(b)   use of a single recognition principle is a straightforward approach.

---

1   References to the *Framework* are to IASC's *Framework for the Preparation and Presentation of Financial Statements*, adopted by the IASB in 2001. In September 2010 the IASB replaced the *Framework* with the *Conceptual Framework for Financial Reporting*.

(c)   retaining IAS 16's general recognition principle and combining it with the derecognition principle will result in financial statements that reflect what is occurring, ie both the flow of property, plant and equipment through an entity and the economics of the acquisition and disposal process.

(d)   use of one recognition principle fosters consistency. With two principles, consistency is not achieved unless it is clear when each should apply. Because IAS 16 does not address what constitutes an 'item' of property, plant and equipment, this clarity was not assured because some might characterise a particular cost as the initial cost of a new item of property, plant and equipment and others might regard it as a subsequent cost of an existing item of property, plant and equipment.

BC11   As a consequence of placing all subsequent expenditures under IAS 16's general recognition principle, the Board also included those expenditures under IAS 16's derecognition principle. In the ED, the Board proposed the derecognition of the carrying amount of a part of an item that was depreciated separately and was replaced by a subsequent expenditure that an entity recognised in the carrying amount of the asset under the general recognition principle. With this change, replacements of a part of an item that are not depreciated separately are subject to the same approach.

BC12   The Board noted that some subsequent expenditures on property, plant and equipment, although arguably incurred in the pursuit of future economic benefits, are not sufficiently certain to be recognised in the carrying amount of an asset under the general recognition principle. Thus, the Board decided to state in the Standard that an entity recognises in profit or loss as incurred the costs of the day-to-day servicing of property, plant and equipment.

Classification of servicing equipment

BC12A   In *Annual Improvements 2009–2011 Cycle* (issued in May 2012) the Board responded to a request to address a perceived inconsistency in the classification requirements for servicing equipment. Paragraph 8 of IAS 16 was unclear on the classification of servicing equipment as inventory or property, plant and equipment and led some to think that servicing equipment used during more than one period would be classified as part of inventory. The Board decided to clarify that items such as spare parts, stand-by equipment and servicing equipment shall be recognised as property, plant and equipment when they meet the definition of property, plant and equipment. If they do not meet this definition they are classified as inventory. In the light of respondents' comments to the June 2011 exposure draft, the Board did not make explicit reference to the classification of particular types of equipment, because the definition of property, plant and equipment already provides sufficient guidance. The Board also deleted from paragraph 8 the requirement to account for spare parts and servicing equipment as property, plant and equipment only if they were used in connection with an item of property, plant and equipment because this requirement was too restrictive when compared with the definition of property, plant and equipment.

Measurement at recognition

Asset dismantlement, removal and restoration costs

BC13 The previous version of IAS 16 provided that in initially measuring an item of property, plant and equipment at its cost, an entity would include the cost of dismantling and removing that item and restoring the site on which it is located to the extent it had recognised an obligation for that cost. As part of its deliberations, the Board evaluated whether it could improve this guidance by addressing associated issues that have arisen in practice.

BC14 The Board concluded that the relatively limited scope of the Improvements project warranted addressing only one matter. That matter was whether the cost of an item of property, plant and equipment should include the initial estimate of the cost of dismantlement, removal and restoration that an entity incurs as a consequence of using the item (instead of as a consequence of acquiring it). Therefore, the Board did not address how an entity should account for (a) changes in the amount of the initial estimate of a recognised obligation, (b) the effects of accretion of, or changes in interest rates on, a recognised obligation or (c) the cost of obligations an entity did not face when it acquired the item, such as an obligation triggered by a law change enacted after the asset was acquired.

BC15 The Board observed that whether the obligation is incurred upon acquisition of the item or while it is being used, its underlying nature and its association with the asset are the same. Therefore, the Board decided that the cost of an item should include the costs of dismantlement, removal or restoration, the obligation for which an entity has incurred as a consequence of having used the item during a particular period other than to produce inventories during that period. An entity applies IAS 2 *Inventories* to the costs of these obligations that are incurred as a consequence of having used the item during a particular period to produce inventories during that period. The Board observed that accounting for these costs initially in accordance with IAS 2 acknowledges their nature. Furthermore, doing so achieves the same result as including these costs as an element of the cost of an item of property, plant and equipment, depreciating them over the production period just completed and identifying the depreciation charge as a cost to produce another asset (inventory), in which case the depreciation charge constitutes part of the cost of that other asset.

BC16 The Board noted that because IAS 16's initial measurement provisions are not affected by an entity's subsequent decision to carry an item under the cost model or the revaluation model, the Board's decision applies to assets that an entity carries under either treatment.

Asset exchange transactions

BC17 Paragraph 22 of the previous version of IAS 16 indicated that if (a) an item of property, plant and equipment is acquired in exchange for a similar asset that has a similar use in the same line of business and has a similar fair value or (b) an item of property, plant and equipment is sold in exchange for an equity interest in a similar asset, then no gain or loss is recognised on the transaction.

The cost of the new asset is the carrying amount of the asset given up (rather than the fair value of the purchase consideration given for the new asset).

BC18   This requirement in the previous version of IAS 16 was consistent with views that:

(a)   gains should not be recognised on exchanges of assets unless the exchanges represent the culmination of an earning process;

(b)   exchanges of assets of a similar nature and value are not a substantive event warranting the recognition of gains; and

(c)   requiring or permitting the recognition of gains from such exchanges enables entities to 'manufacture' gains by attributing inflated values to the assets exchanged, if the assets do not have observable market prices in active markets.

BC19   The approach described above raised issues about how to identify whether assets exchanged are similar in nature and value. The Board reviewed this topic, and noted views that:

(a)   under the *Framework*, the recognition of income from an exchange of assets does not depend on whether the assets exchanged are dissimilar;

(b)   income is not necessarily earned only at the culmination of an earning process, and in some cases it is arbitrary to determine when an earning process culminates;

(c)   generally, under both measurement bases after recognition that are permitted under IAS 16, gain recognition is not deferred beyond the date at which assets are exchanged; and

(d)   removing 'existing carrying amount' measurement of property, plant and equipment acquired in exchange for similar assets would increase the consistency of measurement of acquisitions of assets.

BC20   The Board decided to require in IAS 16 that all items of property, plant and equipment acquired in exchange for non-monetary assets or a combination of monetary and non-monetary assets should be measured at fair value, except that, if the exchange transaction lacks commercial substance or the fair value of neither of the assets exchanged can be determined reliably, then the cost of the asset acquired in the exchange should be measured at the carrying amount of the asset given up.

BC21   The Board added the 'commercial substance' test in response to a concern raised in the comments it received on the ED. This concern was that, under the Board's proposal, an entity would measure at fair value an asset acquired in a transaction that did not have commercial substance, ie the transaction did not have a discernible effect on an entity's economics. The Board agreed that requiring an evaluation of commercial substance would help to give users of the financial statements assurance that the substance of a transaction in which the acquired asset is measured at fair value (and often, consequentially, a gain on the disposal of the transferred asset is recognised in income) is the same as its legal form.

BC22   The Board concluded that in evaluating whether a transaction has commercial substance, an entity should calculate the present value of the post-tax cash flows that it can reasonably expect to derive from the portion of its operations affected by the transaction. The discount rate should reflect the entity's current assessment of the time value of money and the risks specific to those operations rather than those that marketplace participants would make.

BC23   The Board included the 'reliable measurement' test for using fair value to measure these exchanges to minimise the risk that entities could 'manufacture' gains by attributing inflated values to the assets exchanged. Taking into consideration its project for the convergence of IFRSs and US GAAP, the Board discussed whether to change the manner in which its 'reliable measurement' test is described. The Board observed this was unnecessary because it believes that its guidance and that contained in US GAAP are intended to have the same meaning.

BC24   The Board decided to retain, in IAS 18 *Revenue*,[2] its prohibition on recognising revenue from exchanges or swaps of goods or services of a similar nature and value. The Board has on its agenda a project on revenue recognition and does not propose to make any significant amendments to IAS 18 until that project is completed.

Measurement after recognition

Revaluation model

BC25   The Board is taking part in research activities with national standard-setters on revaluations of property, plant and equipment. This research is intended to promote international convergence of standards. One of the most important issues is identifying the preferred measurement attribute for revaluations. This research could lead to proposals to amend IAS 16.

Revaluation method–proportionate restatement of accumulated depreciation when an item of property, plant and equipment is revalued

BC25A   The IFRS Interpretations Committee reported to the Board that practice differed in calculating the accumulated depreciation for an item of property, plant and equipment that is measured using the revaluation method in cases in which the residual value, the useful life or the depreciation method has been re-estimated before a revaluation.

BC25B   Paragraph 35(a) required that, in instances in which the gross carrying amount is revalued, the revalued accumulated depreciation is restated proportionately with the change in the gross carrying amount.

BC25C   The submission noted that applying the same proportionate factor to restate the accumulated depreciation as for the change in the gross carrying amount has caused problems in practice if the residual value, the useful life or the

---

2   IFRS 15 *Revenue from Contracts with Customers*, issued in May 2014, replaced IAS 18 *Revenue*. IFRS 15 also excludes from its scope non-monetary exchanges between entities in the same line of business to facilitate sales to customers, or to potential customers, other than the parties to the exchange.

depreciation method has been re-estimated before the revaluation. The submission used an example in which both the gross carrying amount and the carrying amount were revalued.

BC25D   In such cases, divergent views existed as to how to calculate the accumulated depreciation when the item of property, plant and equipment is revalued:

(a)   some think that the restatement of the accumulated depreciation is not always proportionate to the change in the gross carrying amount and that paragraph 35(a) should be amended accordingly.

(b)   others are of the opinion that the accumulated depreciation and the gross carrying amount should always be restated proportionately when applying paragraph 35(a). The difference between the amount required for a proportionate restatement of the depreciation and the actual restatement of the depreciation required for the gross carrying amount to result in a carrying amount equal to the revalued amount being treated as an accounting error in accordance with IAS 8 *Accounting Policies, Changes in Accounting Estimates and Errors*.

BC25E   The definition of 'carrying amount' in paragraph 6 is "the amount at which an asset is recognised after deducting any accumulated depreciation and accumulated impairment loss". The Board noted that, when revaluing an item of property, plant and equipment, the definition implies that the accumulated depreciation is calculated as the difference between the gross carrying amount and the carrying amount, after taking into account accumulated impairment losses.

BC25F   The Board agrees with the proponents of the view presented in paragraph BC25D(a) that the restatement of the accumulated depreciation is not always proportionate to the change in the gross carrying amount. The Board noted that the accumulated depreciation would not be able to be restated proportionately to the gross carrying amount in situations in which both the gross carrying amount and the carrying amount are revalued non-proportionately to each other. It was noted that this was the case regardless of whether there had been a re-estimation of residual value, the useful life or the depreciation method in a prior period.

BC25G   For example, when the revalued amounts for the gross carrying amount and the carrying amount both reflect non-proportionate observable data, it is demonstrated that accumulated depreciation cannot be proportionately restated to the gross carrying amount in order for the carrying amount to equal the gross carrying amount less any accumulated depreciation and accumulated impairment losses. In that respect, the Board thinks that the requirements in paragraph 35(a) may be perceived as being inconsistent with the definition of carrying amount.

BC25H   In addition, the Board noted that the second sentence in paragraph 35(a) reinforced that inconsistency because it states that proportionate restatement is often used when an asset is revalued by means of applying an index to determine its replacement cost. It reinforced the inconsistency because the determination of the accumulated depreciation does not depend on the selection of the valuation technique used for the revaluation under the revaluation model for property, plant and equipment.

BC25I   Consequently, the Board decided to:

(a)   amend paragraph 35(a) to state that the gross carrying amount is adjusted in a manner that is consistent with the revaluation of the carrying amount;

(b)   amend paragraph 35(a) to state that the accumulated depreciation is calculated as the difference between the gross carrying amount and the carrying amount after taking into account accumulated impairment losses; and

(c)   delete the references to valuation methods in paragraph 35(a)–(b).

The Board also decided to amend paragraph 35(b) to be consistent with the wording used in those amendments.

BC25J   The Board decided to include wording in paragraph 35(a) to require an entity to take into account accumulated impairment losses when adjusting the depreciation on revaluation. This was to ensure that when future revaluation increases occur, the correct split, in accordance with paragraph 39 of IAS 16 and paragraph 119 of IAS 36 *Impairment of Assets*, is made between profit or loss and other comprehensive income when reversing prior accumulated impairment losses.

Depreciation: unit of measure

BC26   The Board's discussions about the potential improvements to the depreciation principle in the previous version of IAS 16 included consideration of the unit of measure an entity uses to depreciate its items of property, plant and equipment. Of particular concern to the Board were situations in which the unit of measure is the 'item as a whole' even though that item may be composed of significant parts with individually varying useful lives or consumption patterns. The Board did not believe that, in these situations, an entity's use of approximation techniques, such as a weighted average useful life for the item as a whole, resulted in depreciation that faithfully represents an entity's varying expectations for the significant parts.

BC27   The Board sought to improve the previous version of IAS 16 by proposing in the ED revisions to existing guidance on separating an item into its parts and then further clarifying in the Standard the need for an entity to depreciate separately any significant parts of an item of property, plant and equipment. By doing so an entity will also separately depreciate the item's remainder.

Depreciation: depreciable amount

BC28   During its discussion of depreciation principles, the Board noted the concern that, under the cost model, the previous version of IAS 16 does not state clearly why an entity deducts an asset's residual value from its cost to determine the asset's depreciable amount. Some argue that the objective is one of precision, ie reducing the amount of depreciation so that it reflects the item's net cost. Others argue that the objective is one of economics, ie stopping depreciation if, because of inflation or otherwise, an entity expects that during its useful life an asset will increase in value by an amount greater than it will diminish.

BC29 The Board decided to improve the previous version of IAS 16 by making clear the objective of deducting a residual value in determining an asset's depreciable amount. In doing so, the Board did not adopt completely either the 'net cost' or the 'economics' objective. Given the concept of depreciation as a cost allocation technique, the Board concluded that an entity's expectation of increases in an asset's value, because of inflation or otherwise, does not override the need to depreciate it. Thus, the Board changed the definition of residual value to the amount an entity could receive for the asset currently (at the financial reporting date) if the asset were already as old and worn as it will be when the entity expects to dispose of it. Thus, an increase in the expected residual value of an asset because of past events will affect the depreciable amount; expectations of future changes in residual value other than the effects of expected wear and tear will not.

Depreciation: depreciation period

BC30 The Board decided that the useful life of an asset should encompass the entire time it is available for use, regardless of whether during that time it is in use or is idle. Idle periods most commonly occur just after an asset is acquired and just before it is disposed of, the latter while the asset is held either for sale or for another form of disposal.

BC31 The Board concluded that, whether idle or not, it is appropriate to depreciate an asset with a limited useful life so that the financial statements reflect the consumption of the asset's service potential that occurs while the asset is held. The Board also discussed but decided not to address the measurement of assets held for sale. The Board concluded that whether to apply a different measurement model to assets held for sale—which may or may not be idle—was a different question and was beyond the scope of the Improvements project.

BC32 In July 2003 the Board published ED 4 *Disposal of Non-current Assets and Presentation of Discontinued Operations*. ED 4 was published as part of the Board's short-term convergence project, the scope of which was broader than that of the Improvements project. In ED 4, the Board proposed that an entity should classify some of its assets as 'assets held for sale' if specified criteria are met. Among other things, the Board proposed that an entity should cease depreciating an asset classified in this manner, irrespective of whether the asset is idle. The basis for this proposal was that the carrying amount of an asset held for sale will be recovered principally through sale rather than future operations, and therefore accounting for the asset should be a process of valuation rather than allocation. The Board will amend IAS 16 accordingly when ED 4 is finalised.

Depreciation: depreciation method

BC33 The Board considered how an entity should account for a change in a depreciation method. The Board concluded that a change in a depreciation method is a change in the technique used to apply the entity's accounting policy to recognise depreciation as an asset's future economic benefits are consumed. Therefore, it is a change in an accounting estimate.

BC33A   The IASB decided to amend IAS 16 to address the concerns regarding the use of a revenue-based method for depreciating an asset. The IASB's decision was in response to a request to clarify the meaning of the term 'consumption of the expected future economic benefits embodied in the asset' when determining the appropriate amortisation method for intangible assets of service concession arrangements (SCA) that are within the scope of IFRIC 12 *Service Concession Arrangements*. The issue raised is related to the application of paragraphs 97–98 of IAS 38 *Intangible Assets* although the IASB decided to address the issue broadly, rather than limit it only to intangible assets arising in an SCA.

BC33B   The IASB observed that a revenue-based depreciation method is one that allocates an asset's depreciable amount based on revenues generated in an accounting period as a proportion of the total revenues expected to be generated over the asset's useful economic life. The total revenue amount is affected by the interaction between units (ie quantity) and price and takes into account any expected changes in price.

BC33C   The IASB observed that paragraph 60 of IAS 16 states that the depreciation method used shall reflect the pattern in which the asset's future economic benefits are expected to be consumed by the entity. The IASB noted that even though revenue could sometimes be considered to be a measurement of the output generated by the asset, revenue does not, as a matter of principle, reflect the way in which an item of property, plant and equipment is used or consumed. The IASB observed that the price component of revenue may be affected by inflation and noted that inflation has no bearing upon the way in which an asset is consumed.

BC33D   On the basis of the guidance in IAS 16, the IASB proposed to clarify in the Exposure Draft *Clarification of Acceptable Methods of Depreciation and Amortisation* (Proposed amendments to IAS 16 and IAS 38) (the 'ED') that a method of depreciation that is based on revenue generated from an activity that includes the use of an asset is not appropriate, because it reflects a pattern of economic benefits being generated from operating the business (of which the asset is part) rather than the economic benefits being consumed through the use of the asset.

BC33E   During its redeliberations of the ED the IASB decided to reaffirm its conclusion that the use of a revenue-based method is not appropriate, because the principle in paragraph 60 of IAS 16 is that the "depreciation method shall reflect the pattern in which the asset's future economic benefits are expected to be consumed by the entity". A method that is based on revenue generated from an activity that includes the use of an asset would be, in contrast, a method based on the generation of future economic benefits from the use of the asset. As a result of the feedback received on the ED, the IASB also decided not to retain the comments that it had included in the Basis for Conclusions on the ED on the limited circumstances in which a revenue-based method gives the same result as a units of production method. Many respondents to the ED found these comments contradictory to the guidance proposed in the Standard.

BC33F   In the ED the IASB proposed to provide guidance to clarify the role of obsolescence in the application of the diminishing balance method. In response to the comments received about the proposed guidance the IASB decided to change the focus of this guidance. The IASB decided to explain that expected future reductions in the selling price of an item could indicate the expectation of technical or commercial obsolescence of the asset, which, in turn, might reflect a reduction of the future economic benefits embodied in the asset. The IASB noted that the expectation of technical or commercial obsolescence is relevant for estimating both the pattern of consumption of future economic benefits and the useful life of an asset. The IASB noted that the diminishing balance method is an accepted depreciation methodology in paragraph 62 of IAS 16, which is capable of reflecting an accelerated consumption of the future economic benefits embodied in the asset.

BC33G   Some respondents to the ED suggested that the IASB should define the notion of 'consumption of economic benefits' and provide guidance in this respect. During its redeliberations the IASB decided against doing so, noting that explaining the notion of consumption of economic benefits would require a broader project.

BC33H   *[This paragraph refers to amendments that are not yet effective, and is therefore not included in this edition.]*

Derecognition

Derecognition date

BC34   The Board decided that an entity should apply the revenue recognition principle in IAS 18[3] for sales of goods to its gains from the sales of items of property, plant and equipment. The requirements in that principle ensure the representational faithfulness of an entity's recognised revenue. Representational faithfulness is also the appropriate objective for an entity's recognised gains. However, in IAS 16, the revenue recognition principle's criteria drive derecognition of the asset disposed of rather than recognition of the proceeds received. Applying the principle instead to the recognition of the proceeds might lead to the conclusion that an entity will recognise a deferred gain. Deferred gains do not meet the definition of a liability under the *Framework*. Thus, the Board decided that an entity does not derecognise an item of property, plant and equipment until the requirements in IAS 18 to recognise revenue on the sale of goods are met.

Gain classification

BC35   Although the Board concluded that an entity should apply the recognition principle for revenue from sales of goods to its recognition of gains on disposals of items of property, plant and equipment, the Board concluded that the respective approaches to income statement display should differ. The Board concluded that users of financial statements would consider these gains and the proceeds from an entity's sale of goods in the course of its ordinary activities

---

3   IFRS 15 *Revenue from Contracts with Customers*, issued in May 2014, replaced IAS 18 *Revenue* and amended paragraph 69 of IAS 16 for consistency with the requirements in IFRS 15.

differently in their evaluation of an entity's past results and their projections of future cash flows. This is because revenue from the sale of goods is typically more likely to recur in comparable amounts than are gains from sales of items of property, plant and equipment. Accordingly, the Board concluded that an entity should not classify as revenue gains on disposals of items of property, plant and equipment.

Assets held for rental to others[4]

BC35A   The Board identified that, in some industries, entities are in the business of renting and subsequently selling the same assets.

BC35B   The Board noted that the Standard prohibits classification as revenue of gains arising from derecognition of items of property, plant and equipment. The Board also noted that paragraph BC35 states the reason for this is 'users of financial statements would consider these gains and the proceeds from an entity's sale of goods in the course of its ordinary activities differently in their evaluation of an entity's past results and their projections of future cash flows.'

BC35C   Consistently with that reason, the Board concluded that entities whose ordinary activities include renting and subsequently selling the same assets should recognise revenue from both renting and selling the assets. In the Board's view, the presentation of gross selling revenue, rather than a net gain or loss on the sale of the assets, would better reflect the ordinary activities of such entities.

BC35D   The Board concluded that the disclosure requirements of IAS 16, IAS 2 and IAS 18[5] would lead an entity to disclose relevant information for users.

BC35E   The Board also concluded that paragraph 14 of IAS 7 *Statement of Cash Flows* should be amended to present within operating activities cash payments to manufacture or acquire such assets and cash receipts from rents and sales of such assets.

BC35F   The Board discussed the comments received in response to its exposure draft of proposed *Improvements to International Financial Reporting Standards* published in 2007 and noted that a few respondents would prefer the issue to be included in one of the Board's major projects such as the revenue recognition project or the financial statement presentation project. However, the Board noted that the proposed amendment would improve financial statement presentation before those projects could be completed and decided to add paragraph 68A as previously exposed. A few respondents raised the concern that the term 'held for sale' in the amendment could be confused with the notion of held for sale in accordance with IFRS 5 *Non-current Assets Held for Sale and Discontinued Operations*. Consequently, the Board clarified in the amendment that IFRS 5 should not be applied in those circumstances.

---

4   Paragraphs BC35A–BC35F were added as a consequence of amendments to IAS 16 by *Improvements to IFRSs* issued in May 2008. At the same time, the Board also amended paragraph 6 by replacing the term 'net selling price' in the definition of 'recoverable amount' with 'fair value less costs to sell' for consistency with the wording used in IFRS 5 *Non-current Assets Held for Sale and Discontinued Operations* and IAS 36.

5   IFRS 15 *Revenue from Contracts with Customers*, issued in May 2014, replaced IAS 18 *Revenue*.

Transitional provisions

BC36   The Board concluded that it would be impracticable for an entity to determine retrospectively whether a previous transaction involving an exchange of non-monetary assets had commercial substance. This is because it would not be possible for management to avoid using hindsight in making the necessary estimates as of earlier dates. Accordingly, the Board decided that in accordance with the provisions of IAS 8 an entity should consider commercial substance only in evaluating the initial measurement of future transactions involving an exchange of non-monetary assets.

BC36A   *Annual Improvements to IFRSs 2010–2012 Cycle*, issued in December 2013, amended paragraph 35. The Board also decided that the amendment should be required to be applied to all revaluations occurring in annual periods beginning on or after the date of initial application of the amendments and in the immediately preceding annual period. The Board was concerned that the costs of full retrospective application might outweigh the benefits.

Summary of changes from the Exposure Draft

BC37   The main changes from the ED proposals to the revised Standard are as follows:

   (a)   The ED contained two recognition principles, one applying to subsequent expenditures on existing items of property, plant and equipment. The Standard contains a single recognition principle that applies to costs incurred initially to acquire an item and costs incurred subsequently to add to, replace part of or service an item. An entity applies the recognition principle to the latter costs at the time it incurs them.

   (b)   Under the approach proposed in the ED, an entity measured an item of property, plant and equipment acquired in exchange for a non-monetary asset at fair value irrespective of whether the exchange transaction in which it was acquired had commercial substance. Under the Standard, a lack of commercial substance is cause for an entity to measure the acquired asset at the carrying amount of the asset given up.

   (c)   Compared with the Standard, the ED did not as clearly set out the principle that an entity separately depreciates at least the parts of an item of property, plant and equipment that are of significant cost.

   (d)   Under the approach proposed in the ED, an entity derecognised the carrying amount of a replaced part of an item of property, plant and equipment if it recognised in the carrying amount of the asset the cost of the replacement under the general recognition principle. In the Standard, an entity also applies this approach to a replacement of a part of an item that is not depreciated separately.

   (e)   In finalising the Standard, the Board identified further necessary consequential amendments to IFRS 1, IAS 14, IAS 34, IAS 36, IAS 37, IAS 38, IAS 40, SIC-13, SIC-21, SIC-22 and SIC-32.

Accounting for bearer plants (2014 amendments)

Overview

BC38 The Board observed that there is a class of biological assets, bearer plants, that are held by an entity solely to grow produce over their productive life. The Board's principal decision underlying the 2014 amendments is that bearer plants should be treated as property, plant and equipment, for which the accounting is prescribed in IAS 16. IAS 16 permits the use of either a cost model or a revaluation model.

Background

BC39 Prior to the 2014 amendments, IAS 41 required all biological assets related to agricultural activity to be measured at fair value less costs to sell based on the principle that their biological transformation is best reflected by fair value measurement. IAS 41 defines 'biological transformation' as follows:

> Biological transformation comprises the processes of growth, degeneration, production, and procreation that cause qualitative or quantitative changes in a biological asset.

BC40 IAS 41 has a single accounting treatment for all bearer and consumable biological assets within its scope. IAS 41 only distinguishes between bearer and consumable biological assets for disclosure purposes (see paragraphs 43–44 of IAS 41).

BC41 Stakeholders told the Board that they think that fair value measurement is not appropriate for mature bearer biological assets such as oil palms and rubber trees because they are no longer undergoing significant biological transformation. The use of mature bearer biological assets such as these is seen by many as similar to that of manufacturing. Consequently, they said that a cost model should be permitted for those bearer biological assets, because it is permitted for property, plant and equipment. They also said that they had concerns about the cost, complexity and practical difficulties of fair value measurements of bearer biological assets in the absence of markets for those assets, and about the volatility from recognising changes in the fair value less costs to sell in profit or loss. Furthermore, they asserted that investors, analysts and other users of financial statements adjust the reported profit or loss to eliminate the effects of changes in the fair values of these bearer biological assets.

BC42 Most respondents who cited agriculture in their responses to the Board's 2011 Agenda Consultation raised concerns in relation to fair value measurement of plantations, for example oil palm and rubber trees plantations, and favoured a limited-scope project for these bearer biological assets to address the concerns in paragraph BC41. Only a small number of respondents favoured a broader consideration of IAS 41 or a Post-implementation Review, or said that there is no need to amend IAS 41.

BC43 Before the limited-scope project for bearer biological assets was added to its work programme, the Board was monitoring the work undertaken by the Asian-Oceanian Standard-Setters Group (AOSSG), primarily by the Malaysian

Accounting Standards Board (MASB), on a proposal to remove some bearer biological assets from the scope of IAS 41 and account for them in accordance with IAS 16. Those proposals were discussed several times by national standard-setters, the Board's Emerging Economies Group (EEG) and the IFRS Advisory Council. Feedback from these meetings indicated strong support for the AOSSG/MASB proposals and for the Board to start a limited-scope project for bearer biological assets.

BC44　In September 2012 the Board decided to add to its agenda a limited-scope project for bearer biological assets, with the aim of considering whether to account for some or all of them as property, plant and equipment, thereby permitting use of a cost model. The limited-scope project was supported by the following reasons:

(a)　it addressed the accounting treatment for those biological assets for which respondents to the 2011 Agenda Consultation had concerns. It also had significant support among national standard-setters and other interested parties. Furthermore, on the basis of feedback from the 2011 Agenda Consultation and other outreach, the expected changes under the project would be likely to reduce compliance costs for preparers and would not adversely affect users of financial statements.

(b)　it had the advantage of timeliness compared to a more comprehensive project. The Board was able to use the research performed by the MASB and address the main issues relatively quickly. A more comprehensive project would have had to wait for space on the Board's agenda and, once started, might have taken several years.

BC45　The Board decided that it had received sufficient information to develop an Exposure Draft (ED) from work performed by the MASB, meetings of national standard-setters, feedback from preparers on the 2011 Agenda Consultation and user outreach performed by staff. Furthermore, the project was expected to result in limited changes that were sought by both users and preparers of financial statements, as explained in more detail in the analysis of the likely effects of the amendments in paragraphs BC99–BC117. Consequently, the Board decided that the project could proceed without a Discussion Paper and developed an ED that was issued in June 2013.

Changes to the proposals in the ED

BC46　The Board received 72 comment letters on the ED. The vast majority of respondents supported the proposal in the ED to account for bearer plants in accordance with IAS 16. Three additional issues raised by respondents were:

(a)　extend the scope of the amendments to other biological assets (see paragraphs BC54–BC58);

(b)　do not require fair value measurement of growing produce (see paragraphs BC75–BC78); and

(c)　provide guidance on when a bearer plant is in the 'location and condition necessary for it to be capable of operating in the manner intended by management' in accordance with paragraph 16(b) of IAS 16—ie when it reaches maturity (see paragraph BC82).

BC47   As a result of the Board's redeliberations of the issues raised on the ED, three changes were made to the proposed amendments in the ED, other than drafting changes. Those three changes were:

(a)   modifying criterion (c) of the definition of a bearer plant (see paragraph BC62);

(b)   clarifying the transition provisions (see paragraph BC96); and

(c)   exempting entities from the disclosure requirements in paragraph 28(f) of IAS 8 for the current period in both the amendments to IAS 16 and the amendments to IAS 41 (see paragraph BC97).

Paragraphs BC48–BC117 summarise the Board's considerations in developing the amendments and its reasons for only making limited changes to the amendments proposed in the ED.

Scope of the amendments

BC48   The Board decided that, before it could consider whether some or all bearer biological assets should be accounted for in accordance with IAS 16 instead of IAS 41, it first needed to define bearer biological assets for the purposes of the amendments. The Board initially discussed four options when deciding on the scope:

(a)   Option 1: no-alternative-use model. Limit the scope of the amendments to IAS 41 to biological assets that are solely used in the production or supply of agricultural produce (ie only used as bearer biological assets) and that are expected to be used for more than one period.

(b)   Option 2: predominant-use model. Limit the scope of the amendments to IAS 41 to biological assets that are used predominantly in the production or supply of agricultural produce (ie used primarily as bearer biological assets) and that are expected to be used for more than one period.

(c)   Option 3: no-alternative-use model—plants only. This is the same as Option 1 except that it would only include plants, not livestock.

(d)   Option 4: predominant-use model—plants only. This is the same as Option 2 except that it would only include plants, not livestock.

BC49   The Board's first consideration when setting the scope of the amendments to IAS 41 was whether to follow a 'no-alternative-use' model or a 'predominant-use' model. The Board observed that many types of livestock that are used as bearer biological assets by an entity also have a common alternative use as a consumable biological asset. For example, an entity may choose to rear a sheep for its wool (bearer attribute) and/or for its meat (consumable attribute). It was also observed that some trees are cultivated both for their lumber, for example, for furniture production (consumable attribute) and for their fruit (bearer attribute).

BC50   The Board observed that a predominant-use model would be more difficult to apply than a no-alternative-use model because it would require additional judgement to be applied in order to determine the predominant use, and would need to address the consequences of reclassifications between IAS 16 and IAS 41 if the predominant use changes. In contrast, if the scope is restricted to biological assets that are solely used as bearer biological assets, the need to apply judgement and make reclassifications would be expected to be rare.

BC51   The Board further noted that, if an entity intends to sell a biological asset as agricultural produce after it has been used as a bearer biological asset for a period of time, fair value measurement would provide useful information about the future economic benefits from the future sale of the asset. Furthermore, if a biological asset is commonly sold as agricultural produce, there will often be an active market for sale of that biological asset separately from land, meaning that fair value information is likely to be readily available and easier to apply than cost measurement. The Board also noted that the concerns raised by respondents to the 2011 Agenda Consultation generally relate to plants that do not have an alternative use to the entity and that do not have a market value separate from the land component. Consequently, any sales transactions that take place in the market are likely to be of bearer plants plus land, and possibly whole plantations. For these reasons, the Board decided to limit the scope to biological assets that are solely used as bearer biological assets.

BC52   The Board's second consideration when setting the scope was whether livestock should be included within the amendments to IAS 41. The Board observed that including livestock would make the use of a cost model more complex. Unlike plants, livestock is not attached to land and there is usually an active market for it, meaning that fair value information is likely to be readily available and easier to apply than cost measurement. As noted in paragraph BC51, concerns raised by respondents to the 2011 Agenda Consultation mainly relate to plants, not livestock. Consequently, the Board decided to restrict the scope to plants.

BC53   On the basis of the considerations in paragraphs BC49–BC52, the Board decided on Option 3.

BC54   Many respondents to the ED said that the concerns outlined by interested parties in paragraph BC41 about fair value measurement and the Board's reasoning in the ED for accounting for bearer plants in accordance with IAS 16 (repeated in paragraphs BC63–BC68) apply equally to other biological assets, such as bearer livestock and plants predominantly used to produce agricultural produce. These respondents said that there was no conceptual basis for singling out bearer plants and that all biological assets used in the production or supply of agricultural produce should be accounted for in the same way.

BC55   During redeliberations of the proposals in the ED, the Board noted that the limited-scope project was added to the Board's agenda to respond to concerns raised by respondents to the 2011 Agenda Consultation, which were raised primarily about plants used solely to bear agricultural produce, for example, oil palm and rubber tree plantations. When the limited-scope project was added to the Board's agenda, the Board had noted that it did not have the resources at that time to perform a comprehensive review of IAS 41. However, the Board had observed that a limited-scope project could be addressed quickly.

BC56   Most respondents to the ED who suggested expanding the scope to livestock did not acknowledge that a key reason the Board limited the scope to bearer plants was the complexities of measuring the initial cost of bearer livestock. A few respondents disagreed with the Board's observation in paragraph BC52 that a cost model would be complex to implement for bearer livestock and noted that cost-based models are used for livestock in some jurisdictions. However, they did not provide any further information on how a cost model like the one in IAS 16 can be applied to livestock.

BC57 The Board observed that before and during development of the amendments it had received significant information from interested parties about the consequences of including bearer plants in IAS 16. However, the Board noted that it had only received limited information about these issues within the context of other biological assets. The Board agreed that the scope of the project should not be expanded without understanding whether IAS 16 is appropriate and can be applied consistently to those biological assets. The Board observed that obtaining this understanding would take time and delay completion of the ED. The Board also noted that such requests for an expanded scope would increase the complexity of the project and raise conceptual issues that did not belong in a limited-scope project but instead in a comprehensive review of IAS 41.

BC58 The Board agreed that the amendments address an immediate need for plantation businesses and are generally perceived by respondents to result in a significant improvement in financial reporting. Consequently, the Board decided not to expand the limited scope of the amendments with the aim of finalising the amendments quickly.

BC59 The ED defined a bearer plant as a plant that is:

(a) used in the production or supply of agricultural produce;

(b) expected to bear produce for more than one period; and

(c) not intended to be sold as a living plant or harvested as agricultural produce, except for incidental scrap sales.

BC60 The Board noted that some crops are perennial plants because their roots remain in the ground to sprout for the next period's crop. An example would be sugarcane if its roots are retained for a second harvest. The Board agreed that if an entity retains the roots to bear produce for more than one period and the roots are not later sold, the roots would meet the definition of a bearer plant. The Board decided that this did not need to be clarified in the amendments and most respondents to the ED agreed.

BC61 Some respondents to the ED asked for guidance on applying the definition of a bearer plant to a range of plants. Because of the diversity of bearer plants, the Board decided not to add guidance on specific types of plants.

BC62 The Board decided to amend criterion (c) of the definition to state 'has a remote likelihood of being sold as agricultural produce, except for incidental scrap sales' to ensure that the amendment captures only those plants used solely in the production or supply of agricultural produce. The Board also clarified in the definition that a bearer plant is a living plant. No other changes were made to the proposed definition.

Basis for accounting for bearer plants in IAS 16

BC63   The Board considered whether the current requirements in IAS 16 for property, plant and equipment are appropriate for bearer plants and also considered the concerns raised by interested parties in paragraph BC41. The Board concluded that applying IAS 16 to bearer plants is appropriate. Paragraphs BC64–BC68 explain the reasons supporting the Board's conclusion.

Support for the use of IAS 16

BC64   Prior to the 2014 amendments, IAS 41 required all biological assets related to agricultural activity to be measured at fair value less costs to sell, based on the principle that their biological transformation is best reflected by fair value measurement. However, mature bearer plants are fully grown and so, apart from bearing produce, biological transformation is no longer significant in generating future economic benefits. Bearer plants are used solely to grow produce over several periods. After this time they are usually scrapped. Consequently, the only significant future economic benefits from bearer plants arise from selling the agricultural produce that they create.

BC65   The Board noted that while fair value measurement may provide an indication of the quality and productive capacity of the bearer plants at a point in time, it is less important to users of financial statements than it is for biological assets whose value may be realised through sale as agricultural produce.

BC66   Bearer plants meet the definition of property, plant and equipment. The use of mature bearer plants to produce agricultural produce is similar to the use of machinery to manufacture goods. The manner in which an entity derives economic benefits from bearer plants and a production plant is similar and that manner differs from biological assets that are harvested for sale. The progressive decline in the future earning potential of a bearer plant over its life is also similar to other depreciable assets, for example, plant and machinery.

BC67   There is an assumption inherent in the *Conceptual Framework* that accounting for similar assets in similar ways enhances the decision-usefulness of the reported information. The land upon which bearer plants are growing, the structures used to support their growth and the agricultural machinery are measured in accordance with IAS 16. Although bearer plants are dissimilar in form to plant and machinery, similarities in how they are used supports accounting for them in the same way.

Cost-benefit considerations

BC68   The Board noted that, on the basis of the responses to the 2011 Agenda Consultation and the outreach performed by the staff, the costs of measuring bearer plants at fair value are perceived by many preparers to exceed the benefits to users of financial statements. The Board also observed that nearly all investors and analysts consulted during the outreach performed by the staff said that the IAS 41 fair value information about bearer plants has limited use to them. The main reasons given by the investors and analysts were:

(a) information about operating performance and cash flows is more relevant to their forecasting and analysis. Consequently, they eliminate changes in the fair value less costs to sell of bearer plants from the figures used for their analysis.

(b) there are concerns about relying on the fair value measurements because valuations involve significant management judgement, have the potential for manipulation, and assumptions vary significantly between companies.

(c) fair value information about bearer plants is not very useful without fair value information about the related land, land improvements, agricultural machinery, etc.

Biological transformation

BC69 The IAS 41 fair value model is based on the principle that biological transformation is best reflected by fair value measurement. Once bearer plants mature, they are held by an entity solely to grow produce and so, apart from bearing produce, their biological transformation is no longer significant in generating future economic benefits. Consequently, the Board decided bearer plants should be accounted for under IAS 16 instead of IAS 41 (see paragraphs BC63–BC68). However, the Board noted that the same argument is not true for bearer plants before they reach maturity and bear produce. Until they reach maturity, bearer plants are in a growth phase and so undergo significant biological transformation. Furthermore, the Board noted that the produce growing on the bearer plants is undergoing biological transformation until it is harvested (for example, grapes growing on a grape vine). Paragraphs BC70–BC79 explain the reasons supporting the Board's conclusions regarding bearer plants before they reach maturity and the produce growing on the bearer plants.

Accounting for bearer plants before they mature

BC70 The Board considered whether a fair value approach or a cost accumulation approach should be applied to bearer plants before they reach maturity.

BC71 The Board noted that, before they mature, bearer plants undergo biological transformation and this distinguishes them from self-constructed property, plant and equipment. Such biological transformation would not be reflected by a cost accumulation approach. The Board further noted that a fair value approach would be consistent with the principle in IAS 41 that biological transformation is best reflected by fair value measurement.

BC72 However, the Board noted that IAS 16 does not incorporate internal profit in the measurement of a self-constructed item of machinery. By analogy, biological transformation should not be included either. The Board further noted that most of the investors and analysts consulted during the outreach performed by the staff said that the IAS 41 fair value information about bearer plants is of limited use to them and that the measurement of the fair values of bearer plants is particularly subjective during the early years of the life cycle of those bearer plants. For these reasons the Board decided that bearer plants should be measured at accumulated cost before they reach maturity. The Board also observed that it would be simpler to keep bearer plants in IAS 16 throughout their life. Virtually all respondents to the ED supported measuring bearer plants using a cost accumulation approach before they mature.

Accounting for produce growing on a bearer plant

BC73   The Board considered whether produce should be recognised at fair value less costs to sell only at the point of harvest or from the date that it starts to grow.

BC74   The Board observed that the produce is a consumable biological asset growing on the bearer plant and the growth of the produce directly increases the expected revenue from the sale of the produce. Consequently, fair value measurement of the growing produce provides useful information to users of financial statements about future cash flows that an entity will actually realise. In contrast the bearer plants themselves are not sold and the changes in the fair value of the bearer plants do not directly influence the entity's future cash flows. The Board also observed that produce will ultimately be detached from the bearer plants and is normally sold separately, meaning it has a market value on its own. This is in contrast to many bearer plants that are unlikely to have an observable market value on their own because they can only be sold while attached to the land.

BC75   Many respondents to the ED acknowledged the conceptual reasons for accounting for produce at fair value less costs to sell, but expressed concern with the likely practical challenges. Some respondents suggested only requiring fair value less costs to sell to be measured at the point of harvest, or providing additional relief from fair value measurement on the basis of cost-benefit considerations. Other respondents suggested accounting for produce using a cost model before harvest, similarly to inventories or work in progress. Several respondents said further guidance should be provided on how to measure the produce at fair value.

BC76   The Board acknowledged that measuring produce growing on bearer plants at fair value less costs to sell might sometimes be difficult to apply in practice. However, it was noted that similar difficulties are encountered when measuring the fair value less costs to sell of produce growing in the ground. Consequently, the Board decided that it would be inconsistent to provide additional relief from fair value measurement for produce growing on a bearer plant and not also for other biological assets within the scope of IAS 41.

BC77   The Board observed that if preparers encounter significant practical difficulties on initial measurement of produce, they should consider whether they meet the requirements of the exemptions in paragraphs 10(c) and 30 of IAS 41. Paragraph 10(c) of IAS 41 states that an entity shall recognise a biological asset only when the fair value or cost of the asset can be measured reliably. Paragraph 30 of IAS 41 requires a biological asset to be measured using a cost model if fair value measurement is determined to be clearly unreliable. The Board noted that this limited-scope project was not intended to address the fair value model in IAS 41. Consequently, the Board agreed not to further discuss the exemptions in IAS 41 as part of this project.

BC78   On the basis of the considerations above, the Board decided to reaffirm that produce is a biological asset within the scope of IAS 41 and consequently should be measured at fair value less costs to sell with changes recognised in profit and loss as the produce grows. This would maintain the consistency of accounting for produce growing in the ground and produce growing on a bearer plant. Consequently, the Board decided to keep the produce within the scope of IAS 41.

BC79   The Board noted that most of the areas for which respondents to the ED asked for additional guidance were specific to a particular type of bearer plant or produce. The Board decided that because of the specialised nature and diversity of bearer plants and produce it would be too difficult for the Board to develop additional guidance on measuring the fair value of produce.

Application of the IAS 16 requirements to bearer plants

Unit of measure

BC80   Agricultural activity is often a continuous process, meaning that older plants are continuously removed from service and replaced. The Board noted that, if bearer plants are accounted for using a cost model, this continuous process needs to be made discrete. Consequently, the question arises as to what the unit of measure is—for example, is it the individual plant or some larger aggregation, such as a field or a planting cycle?

BC81   The Board noted that IAS 16 does not prescribe the unit of measure, or the extent to which items can be aggregated and treated as a single item of property, plant and equipment. Consequently, applying the recognition criteria in IAS 16 to bearer plants will require judgement. This would give an entity flexibility, depending on its circumstances, to decide how to aggregate individual plants for the purpose of determining a measurable unit of bearer plants. The Board noted that accounting for an aggregation of plants would be similar to accounting for a large quantity of equipment that is acquired or constructed in batches. For example a company may construct a large number of moulds for use within its business. Some aggregation of the moulds would usually be necessary for determining an item of property, plant and equipment. Consequently, the Board decided that the requirements for the unit of measure in IAS 16 would provide sufficient guidance for bearer plants without modification.

Point of maturity

BC82   Most respondents to the ED requested additional guidance on when a bearer plant is in the 'location and condition necessary for it to be capable of operating in the manner intended by management' in accordance with paragraph 16(b) of IAS 16—ie when it is deemed to have reached maturity. For example, an oil palm may start to grow produce after two years, but only reach its maximum yield after seven years. Respondents suggested either defining the date of maturity to be 'the date of the first harvest of commercial value' or 'the date commercial quantities of produce are produced'. The Board noted that without further clarification these terms would not assist entities in applying judgement in this area and would be likely to lead to interpretation requests in the future. The Board also noted that a similar scenario arises for a factory or retail outlet that is not yet capable of operating at full capacity and did not think that this was a major issue in practice. Consequently, the Board decided not to add guidance in this area.

Other recognition and measurement requirements of the cost model

BC83   The Board considered whether the other recognition and measurement requirements of the cost model in IAS 16 were sufficient to address the unique costs of growing bearer plants both before and after they reach maturity. The following were the main requests for guidance raised by respondents to the ED:

(a)   how to assess what is an abnormal amount of wastage/mortality during the growth phase of the bearer plants. The Board noted that there is a similar issue when an entity constructs a large number of fragile items of machinery for use within the business.

(b)   the nature of costs that can be capitalised before maturity. The Board noted that although the examples in IAS 16 are about non-living items, paragraph 17(a)–(b) and (e) of IAS 16 adequately covers the types of costs incurred to cultivate and grow bearer plants.

(c)   allocation of costs after maturity between the growing fruit and the bearer plant. The Board noted that an entity may recognise all costs as an expense after maturity unless they meet the criteria for capitalisation as part of bearer plants in accordance with paragraph 7 of IAS 16. Consequently, such guidance would not be necessary.

(d)   transfers between IAS 16 and IAS 41 if the entity changes its intention for a bearer plant or if scrap sales are no longer considered incidental. The Board noted that it would be rare for transfers to take place between IAS 16 and IAS 41 for bearer plants, particularly in the light of the Board's decision to change criterion (c) of the definition of a bearer plant to 'has a remote likelihood of being sold as agricultural produce, except for incidental scrap sales' (see paragraph BC62).

BC84   The Board decided that the current principles in IAS 16 are sufficient to cater for bearer plants without modification or supplement.

BC85   Some respondents to the ED requested guidance on the application of other Standards to bearer plants, for example, IAS 17 *Leases*, IAS 20 *Accounting for Government Grants and Disclosure of Government Assistance*, IAS 23 *Borrowing Costs* and IAS 36 *Impairment of Assets*. However, when commenting on those Standards, respondents did not highlight issues unique to bearer plants. The Board noted that bearer plants meet the definition of property, plant and equipment in IAS 16 and are accounted for as property, plant and equipment. Consequently, bearer plants are items of property, plant and equipment when applying other Standards.

Disclosure requirements of the cost model

BC86 The Board considered the disclosure requirements in IAS 16 and decided that they could be applied to bearer plants without modification. The Board also considered whether any additional disclosures should be required for bearer plants.

BC87 Some Board members were concerned that if entities move from a fair value model to a cost model for bearer plants, decision-useful information about the fair values of bearer plants and the assumptions used to determine those fair value measurements would be lost. However, the Board noted that most of the investors and analysts consulted during the user outreach performed by the staff said that fair value information about bearer plants has limited use to them without fair value information about the related land, agricultural machinery, etc. Furthermore, virtually all respondents to the ED said that disclosure of fair value information about bearer plants and/or information about the significant inputs used in valuation techniques should not be required.

BC88 The Board noted that there is no clear basis for requiring fair value disclosures for bearer plants when such disclosures are not required for the rest of the property, plant and machinery involved in the process of growing the produce. It also noted that there is also no clear basis for requiring entities with bearer plants to provide fair value disclosures for their land when these disclosures are not required for land used for other purposes. The Board further acknowledged that the limited-scope project was not intended to address fair value disclosure requirements for other assets in IAS 16. Consequently, the Board decided not to require additional fair value disclosures for entities with bearer plants.

BC89 During user outreach, many investors and analysts told the staff that instead of using fair value information they use other information, for example, about yield, acreage and age of bearer plants. This information is usually obtained via the presentations made to analysts, the front of annual reports (for example, in the Management Commentary) or is otherwise received directly from companies. Many respondents to the ED acknowledged that disclosures about productivity and future cash flows are useful to users of financial statements, but most said that such disclosures should not be mandatory and belonged outside the financial statements.

BC90 Some respondents to the ED noted that disclosure of non-financial measures of physical quantities of biological assets and output of agricultural produce is currently required for all biological assets in paragraph 46 of IAS 41. They said that including bearer plants in IAS 16 would mean that this disclosure requirement would no longer apply to them. The Board observed that this is likely to have a limited effect in practice because the disclosures in paragraph 46 of IAS 41 will continue to apply to the produce in IAS 41 as follows:

(a) paragraph 46(a) and (b)(ii) of IAS 41—the Board noted that the disclosures made by entities in accordance with paragraphs 46(a) and (b)(ii) would be the same regardless of whether those paragraphs refer to the entire plant or only the produce.

(b)   paragraph 46(b)(i) of IAS 41—the Board noted that paragraph 46(b)(i) now applies to physical quantities of produce instead of physical quantities of entire plants. The Board noted that paragraph 46(b)(i) does not stipulate the type of non-financial measures or estimates that an entity needs to provide. The Board also noted that plantation companies generally provide more information about productivity of bearer plants outside the financial statements than is required by paragraph 46 of IAS 41 and would be likely to continue to disclose their chosen non-financial measures of bearer plants even if this paragraph only refers to produce.

Consequently, the Board decided not to add the disclosures in paragraph 46 of IAS 41 to IAS 16.

BC91   The Board observed that agricultural activity is diverse and it would be difficult to identify specific productivity disclosures that would provide useful information for users of financial statements and cover all types of bearer plants. The Board also observed that if additional productivity disclosures were included in IAS 16 for bearer plants (other than those in paragraph 46 of IAS 41), it would be difficult to justify requiring them in IAS 16 for bearer plants and not in IAS 41 for other biological assets. The Board noted that reconsidering the disclosure requirements of IAS 41 was outside the scope of this project. Consequently, the Board decided not to add any additional disclosures in IAS 16 for bearer plants.

Revaluation model

BC92   IAS 16 permits entities to choose either the cost model or the revaluation model for each class of property, plant and equipment. The Board decided that the same accounting policy options should be permitted for bearer plants. Consequently, the Board decided that the revaluation model in IAS 16 should be permitted for bearer plants.

BC93   Most respondents to the ED supported allowing entities an option to use the revaluation model. However, some respondents asked for guidance on applying the revaluation model to bearer plants. The Board decided that the requirements of the revaluation model are clear without additional guidance and it noted its expectation that the vast majority of entities with bearer plants will use the cost model for the reasons set out in paragraph BC103. Consequently, the Board confirmed that the revaluation model would be permitted for bearer plants and decided not to add additional guidance.

Positioning of requirements

BC94   The Board observed that there was some benefit to keeping all of the requirements for agricultural activity together. However, the Board noted that the requirements in IAS 16 would be applied to bearer plants with virtually no modification. Furthermore, bearer plants meet the definition of property, plant and equipment and are used like property, plant and equipment within the business. Virtually all respondents to the ED supported including bearer plants within the scope of IAS 16. The Board thus confirmed that it would include bearer plants within the scope of IAS 16.

Transition requirements

Current IFRS preparers

BC95   The Board noted that if an entity currently measures its bearer plants at fair value less costs to sell and has not previously collected cost information, collecting this information to measure the cost of those bearer plants may be costly. If bearer plants have long life cycles, entities could be required to look back several decades in order to obtain the necessary information. Consequently, for cost-benefit reasons, the Board decided that the amendments to IAS 16 should permit the use of fair value as deemed cost for items of bearer plants at the beginning of the earliest comparative period presented in the financial statements. The Board also noted that the amendments address an immediate need for entities with bearer plants. Consequently, the Board decided that the amendments should be available for early application.

BC96   Virtually all respondents to the ED supported the transition requirements without change. However, some respondents said that the Board should clarify how to account for differences between fair value and the carrying value determined in accordance with IAS 41 (fair value less costs to sell) at the transition date. The Board agreed.

BC97   The Board noted that on the initial application of the amendments, paragraph 28(f) of IAS 8 would require an entity to disclose, for the current period and for each prior period presented, the amount of any adjustment for each financial statement line item affected. The Board observed that requiring this disclosure requirement for the current year would be burdensome because it would require an entity to maintain dual systems in the year of initial application. The Board noted that not requiring this disclosure for the current year would be consistent with its other decisions during the project. Consequently for both the amendments to IAS 16 and the amendments to IAS 41, the Board decided to exempt entities from providing the disclosure required by paragraph 28(f) for the current period. Entities would still be required to provide those disclosures for each prior period presented in the financial statements.

First-time adoption of IFRS

BC98   Consistent with the reasoning for accounting for bearer plants as property, plant and equipment (see paragraphs BC63–BC68), the Board decided that the same deemed cost exemptions provided for property, plant and equipment in IFRS 1 *First-time Adoption of International Financial Reporting Standards* should be available for bearer plants. Virtually all respondents to the ED supported this requirement for first-time adopters of IFRSs. The Board thus confirmed the proposals for first-time adopters. The Board noted that no consequential amendments to IFRS 1 were required because bearer plants are accounted for as items of property, plant and equipment. Consequently, exemptions already provided in IFRS 1 would address first-time application issues related to bearer plants.

Analysis of the likely effects of the amendments

BC99   The following paragraphs describe the Board's analysis of the likely effects that will result from the amendments to the requirements for the accounting for bearer plants.

BC100   The Board is committed to assessing and sharing knowledge about the likely costs of implementing new requirements, and the likely ongoing application costs and benefits of each new or revised Standard—the costs and benefits are collectively referred to as 'effects'.

BC101   The Board gains insight on the likely effects of the proposals for new or revised Standards through its formal exposure of proposals and through its fieldwork, analysis and consultations with relevant parties through outreach activities. The likely effects are assessed:

      (a)   in the light of the Board's objective of financial reporting transparency; and

      (b)   in comparison to the existing financial reporting requirements.

BC102   In evaluating the likely effects of the amendments, the Board has considered the following issues (see paragraphs BC106–BC117):

      (a)   how the changes are likely to affect how bearer plants are reported in the financial statements of those applying IFRS;

      (b)   whether those changes improve the comparability of financial statements between different reporting periods for an individual entity and between different entities in a particular reporting period;

      (c)   whether the changes will improve the ability of users of financial statements to assess the future cash flows of an entity;

      (d)   whether the improvements to financial reporting will result in better economic decision-making;

      (e)   the likely effect on compliance costs for preparers, both on initial application and on an ongoing basis; and

      (f)   whether the likely costs of analysis for users of financial statements, including the costs of extracting data, identifying how it has been measured and adjusting it for the purposes of including that data in, for example, a valuation model, are affected.

BC103   The amendments will permit entities to apply either the cost model or the revaluation model, in accordance with IAS 16, for bearer plants. The Board expects that most entities will choose the cost model instead of the revaluation model, because:

      (a)   the revaluation model would not eliminate the main concerns raised by preparers, in particular the cost and complexity of regularly measuring the fair value of bearer plants.

(b)   most entities apply a cost model to agricultural land and machinery and the Board expects that those entities would favour using a consistent approach for all assets used in the production of income, including bearer plants.

(c)   IAS 16 only permits the revaluation model to be used if the fair value of bearer plants can be measured reliably. Many entities with bearer plants told the Board that fair value estimations are often complex and subjective. If fair value cannot be measured reliably, use of the revaluation model would be precluded.

BC104   Consequently, the analysis of the likely effects in paragraphs BC106–BC117 only considers the likely effects of applying the IAS 16 cost model in comparison to the IAS 41 fair value model.

BC105   If entities choose to account for bearer plants using the revaluation model in IAS 16, the most significant effect would be to require changes in the revalued amount, which approximates fair value, to be recognised in other comprehensive income. Currently, changes in fair value less costs to sell are recognised in profit or loss under IAS 41.

How the amendments are likely to affect how activities are reported

BC106   The amendments will only affect specific types of agricultural activity, namely those entities with bearer plants.

BC107   Assuming that current IFRS adopters choose to apply the cost model in IAS 16 to bearer plants the main changes will be as follows:

Effect	Fair value model in IAS 41	Cost model in IAS 16	Effect
Financial position	Measured at fair value less costs to sell (together with the produce).	Measured at cost less any accumulated depreciation and any accumulated impairment losses. (Produce measured separately at fair value less costs to sell.)	Net asset amounts are likely to be lower for the cost model than the fair value model during the earlier part of the productive life of a bearer plant. This is because the future cash flows that can be generated by the bearer plant, and reflected in a fair value measurement, will likely be higher than the cost on initial recognition. Over time, the carrying amounts measured in accordance with the two models are expected to converge as the asset approaches the end of its productive life.

continued...

...continued

Effect	Fair value model in IAS 41	Cost model in IAS 16	Effect
Profit or loss	Changes in fair value less costs to sell are recognised in profit or loss. Costs may be recognised as an expense immediately or capitalised. If they are capitalised there is an equal reduction in the change in the fair value less costs to sell.	The depreciation charge for each period, and any impairment loss, will be recognised in profit or loss.	Over the life of the bearer plants the net amount recognised in profit or loss will likely be the same whether applying the fair value model or the cost model. However, if an entity applies the fair value model the effect on profit or loss will be variable (changes in fair value). If an entity applies the cost model the effect on profit or loss is likely to be more systematic (depreciation, with possible impairment).

How the amendments affect the comparability of financial statements

Comparability between entities

BC108   The Board does not expect the amendments to significantly reduce the comparability between entities because:

(a)   IAS 41 requires biological assets to be accounted for using the fair value model. The Board does not expect the choice of accounting policy in IAS 16 to reduce comparability between entities with bearer plants because most entities are expected to choose the cost model for the reasons explained in paragraph BC103.

(b)   The primary benefits of using fair value for biological assets are that fair value captures biological development (ie the growth of the produce) and is closely aligned with how the entity expects to convert the asset to cash (ie through sale). The Board has retained fair value for the produce of a bearer plant (for which these primary benefits are applicable) while aligning the accounting for the bearer plant with the accounting for property, plant and equipment. The Board considers that this change will improve comparability by distinguishing between types of biological asset.

(c)   The Board observed that some entities may elect to measure bearer plants at fair value on initial application of the amendments and use that fair value as its deemed cost at that date, while others may elect to apply the amendments retrospectively (eg if they currently use a cost model in accordance with IAS 16 for management purposes). However, the Board noted that if there is any lack of comparability between entities on initial application, it is just as likely to arise from the aggregation of costs incurred at different dates as from the use of fair value as deemed cost by some but not all entities. Furthermore, the use of fair value as the deemed cost for bearer plants means that an entity will report the same cost data as if it had acquired bearer plants with the same remaining service potential at the date of transition to IFRS, eg if it had purchased an area of plantation on that date.

Comparability between reporting periods for an individual entity

BC109 The Board does not expect the amendments to significantly reduce the comparability between reporting periods for an individual entity choosing the cost model. This is because under IAS 41 the change in the fair value less costs to sell of bearer plants can fluctuate significantly between reporting periods as a result of small changes in assumptions. Furthermore, most investors and analysts consulted during the user outreach performed by staff said that they eliminate the change in the fair value less costs to sell of bearer plants when comparing an entity's operating performance between reporting periods.

BC110 Currently, bearer plants are accounted for in a different way from the land, land improvements and agricultural machinery used in the production process. In most cases entities account for these assets at cost under IAS 16. Consequently, accounting for the bearer plants under IAS 16 will improve comparability between the producing assets of the entity by accounting for similar assets in similar ways.

How the amendments will improve a user's ability to assess future cash flows

BC111 IAS 41 currently requires bearer plants to be measured at fair value less costs to sell. Consequently, the requirement to measure fair value applies to both the bearer plant and the produce growing on the bearer plant. As a result of the amendments, only the produce growing on bearer plants will be measured at fair value less costs to sell.

BC112 The produce of bearer plants is usually grown for sale. Consequently, fair value changes in the produce have a direct relationship to the expectations of future cash flows that the entity will receive on sale. In contrast, bearer plants are normally held by an entity for the whole of their useful life and then scrapped, so changes in fair value are not directly recognised as cash flows on sale of the bearer plants. Consequently, the Board thinks that providing separate fair value information for the produce is likely to improve the ability of users of the financial statements to assess future cash flows.

BC113 During the project the staff sought the views of investors and analysts that use the financial statements of companies with bearer plants. Many of these investors and analysts told the staff that they focus on cash flows that an entity is expected to realise. These investors and analysts said that the fair value of bearer plants is not considered in their analysis because the bearer plants themselves are not sold and the changes in the fair value of the bearer plants do not directly influence the entity's future cash flows. Furthermore, some of these investors and analysts said that they would prefer a cost model for bearer plants because it provides a better basis to forecast future capital expenditure than a fair value model.

How the amendments will affect economic decision-making and the costs of analysis for users of financial statements

BC114   There is an assumption inherent in the *Conceptual Framework* that accounting for similar assets in similar ways enhances the usefulness of the reported information. Although bearer plants are dissimilar in form to plant and machinery, similarities in how they are used provides support for accounting for them in the same way.

BC115   As a result of the amendments, users of financial statements will generally receive cost information about bearer plants instead of fair value information. This is not expected to result in less relevant information for users of financial statements because nearly all investors and analysts consulted during the user outreach performed by staff said that the IAS 41 fair value information about bearer plants is of limited use to them for the reasons set out in paragraph BC68.

Effect on the compliance costs for preparers

BC116   Preparers of financial statements have expressed concern that, in the absence of active markets for bearer plants, fair value measurements are complex, time-consuming and costly, especially for entities that hold large plantations with varying maturities, yield profiles and locations. The amendments respond to this concern and are expected to significantly reduce costs for preparers of financial statements by permitting a cost model for bearer plants. However, entities will still be required to perform the following fair value measurements:

(a)   the produce growing on the bearer plants will still be measured at fair value less costs to sell. The Board's reasoning for requiring the produce to be measured at fair value less costs to sell is set out in paragraphs BC73–BC79.

(b)   as is the case for all items of property, plant and equipment, bearer plants will be subject to an impairment test under IAS 36. Consequently, if there is an indication that bearer plants are impaired at the reporting date, the entity would be required to estimate the recoverable amount of the asset (or its cash-generating unit). The recoverable amount of an asset or a cash-generating unit is the higher of its fair value less costs of disposal and its value in use.

BC117   Nevertheless, the amendments will reduce compliance costs for the majority of entities because:

(a)   the Board thinks that measuring the produce at fair value less costs to sell would be less complex than measuring the bearer plants and produce together at fair value less costs to sell. This is because the produce is growing on the bearer plants only for a short period and so the valuation of produce will not involve forecasting over long time periods. Furthermore, there is usually an active market for the harvested produce, whereas there is rarely an active market for bearer plants and observable market prices generally exist only for many bearer plants together with the land.

(b) IAS 41 currently requires entities to determine the fair value less costs to sell of bearer plants at each reporting date. As a result of the amendments, an entity applying the cost model in accordance with IAS 16 would be required to estimate the recoverable amount of an item of bearer plants (or the relevant cash-generating unit) only if there are indicators of impairment at the reporting date. In general, bearer plants do not generate cash flows independently of the land. Consequently, the impairment test would take place at the cash-generating unit level. If the fair value of the land is greater than the carrying amount of the cash-generating unit containing the land and bearer plants, the cash-generating unit would not be impaired. Consequently, as a result of the amendments, fair value measurements are expected to be less frequent.

Dissenting opinions

Dissent of Mary Tokar from *Clarification of Acceptable Methods of Depreciation and Amortisation* (Amendments to IAS 16 and IAS 38) as issued in May 2014

DO1   Ms Tokar is dissenting from the publication of this amendment. She does not object to the IASB's objective of clarifying acceptable methods of depreciation and amortisation, nor to its conclusions to preclude revenue-based depreciation and nor to the introduction of a rebuttable presumption that revenue cannot be used as a basis for amortisation of intangibles. She also agrees that expectations of obsolescence should be considered when determining the useful life of an asset and selecting an amortisation or depreciation method that reflects the pattern of consumption of the asset. However, she is concerned that the amendments will not fully resolve the practice issue that was originally raised with the IFRS Interpretations Committee. She believes that the amendments are not sufficiently clear regarding what evidence is required to overcome the presumption and instead support the use of revenue as the basis for amortisation of an intangible asset. She believes that further guidance should be included to explain when the pattern of consumption of economic benefits is the same as the pattern in which revenue is generated.

Dissent of Patrick Finnegan and Patricia McConnell from *Agriculture: Bearer Plants* (Amendments to IAS 16 and IAS 41) June 2014

DO1   Mr Finnegan and Ms McConnell voted against the publication of *Agriculture: Bearer Plants* (Amendments to IAS 16 and IAS 41) issued in June 2014 (the 'June 2014 Amendment') because they believe that including bearer plants within the scope of IAS 16 *Property, Plant and Equipment* instead of IAS 41 *Agriculture* will eliminate information about the fair value changes in bearer plants and the underlying assumptions used to estimate those changes. Information about the fair values of all biological assets including bearer plants is critical both to managing agricultural activities and to investing in entities that engage in those activities. Without such information, investors are unable to assess changes in expectations of future net cash inflows for an entity engaged in agricultural activity. The fact that published price quotations have developed throughout the world for orchards and plantations that include bearer plants demonstrates the importance of fair value information to those who invest in agricultural activities.

DO2   IAS 41 prescribes the accounting for agricultural activity, that is, the management by an entity of the biological transformation of living animals or plants (biological assets) for sale, into agricultural produce or into additional biological assets. The underlying principle of IAS 41 is that fair value measurement best reflects the biological transformation of biological assets. It requires measurement at fair value less costs to sell (referred to hereafter as fair value) from initial recognition of biological assets up to and including the point of harvest, other than when fair value cannot be measured reliably on initial recognition.

DO3   The June 2014 Amendment changes the measurement for one subset of biological assets, bearer plants, from fair value to a cost-based measure. Bearer plants are plants that are used only in the production or supply of agricultural produce and are expected to bear produce for more than one period. The June 2014 Amendment includes bearer plants within the scope of IAS 16. Consequently, entities would be permitted to choose either the cost model or the revaluation model for bearer plants. All other biological assets related to agricultural activity will remain under the fair value model in IAS 41, including bearer animals.

The importance of fair value information for biological assets

DO4   Fundamentally, IAS 41 is a Standard on accounting for biological transformation. Biological transformation of bearer assets occurs both prior to maturity and after maturity. A cost model ignores biological transformation when it occurs. That is why IAS 41 requires fair value measurement. The Basis for Conclusions of IAS 41 states:

> "Those who support fair value measurement argue that the effects of changes brought about by biological transformation are best reflected by reference to the fair value changes in biological assets. They believe that fair value changes in biological assets have a direct relationship to changes in expectations of future economic benefits to the entity."

Mr Finnegan and Ms McConnell see no reason to abandon that principle with respect to bearer plants. Consequently, they do not agree that prior to maturity, bearer plants should be measured at accumulated cost. They do not believe that accounting for bearer plants in the same way as for self-constructed items of property, plant and equipment will provide users of financial statements with information that is useful to an understanding of the agricultural entity's performance for the period or of its productive capacity at a point in time.

DO5   While maturing, bearer plants are undergoing biological transformation. Mr Finnegan and Ms McConnell continue to believe that fair value measurement for the biological transformation process provides the best information about bearer assets' quality and quantitative changes during their growth period. They also believe that the fair value of bearer plants at maturity provides the best measure of an entity's resources being placed into the production of produce at maturity. Investors need that information to assess management's stewardship of the resources invested in the production process and the performance of the entity using those resources. Consequently, they believe that bearer plants must be measured at fair value while maturing because fair value provides users of financial statements with the best information about an important aspect of an agricultural entity's performance and management stewardship.

DO6   They also reject the view that biological transformation of bearer assets is no longer a key element for understanding the future net cash flows to an entity once such assets reach maturity. By definition, biological transformation is not limited to merely the growth process to maturity, but also includes the cycles of production and degeneration, which are critical phases in the life cycle of bearer assets. Fair value measurements of bearer assets throughout their lives provide information about the effectiveness and efficiency of the production process, and about the capability of such assets to generate net cash inflows into the future. In contrast, depreciation of the cost of a mature bearer asset only approximates the biological transformation of a bearer asset throughout its productive life and has only an indirect relationship, at best, to changes in future net cash inflows.

Effects of the use of fair value measurement

DO7   Mr Finnegan and Ms McConnell acknowledge that measuring bearer plants at fair value may sometimes be difficult. In particular, the Board has been told that the fair value of bearer plants is particularly subjective during the early years of their life cycle. However, Mr Finnegan and Ms McConnell note that IAS 41 contains an exception from fair value for biological assets for which quoted market prices are not available and for which alternative fair value measurements are determined to be clearly unreliable on initial recognition. They believe that this exception is sufficient to deal with the concerns about the reliability of fair value measures of bearer plants during the early years of their life cycle. They also note that entities throughout the world have been applying IAS 41 in a wide variety of agricultural activities since 2003. In fact, some national accounting standards required or recommended measurement of bearer assets at fair values even before IAS 41 was issued. They do not believe that measuring fair value of bearer plants, in general, is any more difficult than measuring fair value for other biological assets such as bearer animals. Furthermore, they believe that applying a cost measure to bearer plants may be equally as difficult in some situations. Fair value measurements are required in assessing bearer plants for impairment, and surely those who are urging a reversion to a cost model for bearer assets would not suggest that impairment should be ignored because fair value measurement may sometimes be difficult. Moreover, the June 2014 Amendment would permit fair value measurements as a pure accounting policy choice. Mr Finnegan and Ms McConnell believe that accounting should reflect underlying economic circumstances and should not merely be left to choice. The existing fair value exception in IAS 41 is based on circumstances (measurement reliability), and is not an accounting policy choice.

DO8   In addition to concerns about the reliability of fair value measures, entities with bearer assets expressed concern about the volatility that arises from recognising changes in the fair value of the bearer plants in profit or loss and said that users of financial statements adjust reported profit or loss to eliminate the effects of changes in fair values of bearer biological assets. Mr Finnegan and Ms McConnell accept the view that the use of fair value for bearer assets makes the analysis of profit or loss and financial position more difficult. At the same time, they note that price volatility is an indicator of risk, and risk assessment is part of an analyst's job. Mr Finnegan and Ms McConnell note that sound financial statement analysis will always adjust reported profit or loss and financial position for the effects of unusual or non-recurring changes in reported information. However, if critical information about changes in the economic benefits arising in an agricultural operation is not reported, such analysis is impaired or not possible at all.

DO9   Mr Finnegan and Ms McConnell believe that instead of ignoring the fair value volatility, which a cost model does, volatility should be addressed as a matter of financial statement presentation—such as by putting the fair value changes in other comprehensive income. They note that under the June 2014 Amendment, the bearer assets will be within the scope of IAS 16 and revaluation will be permitted. If an entity were to choose revaluation, the change in the revaluation amount (which approximates fair value) would be reported in other comprehensive income. Consequently, they believe that requiring fair value measurement during the entirety of the bearer plant's life cycle with the fair value changes reported in other comprehensive income would be consistent with permitting revaluation of the bearer asset. Furthermore, Mr Finnegan and Ms McConnell believe that such a change would preserve relevant information for investors through prominent display in the primary financial statements, while addressing the concerns of those who believe that fair value changes distort profit or loss.

Current proposals are not improvements to IFRS

DO10   Mr Finnegan and Ms McConnell believe that if bearer assets are measured at accumulated cost, then at a minimum, the fair value of the bearer plants should be a required disclosure, including information about the valuation techniques and key inputs/assumptions used. However, the 2014 Amendment is not requiring disclosure of fair value. Consequently, critical information is being eliminated from the financial statements of entities engaged in agricultural activities using bearer assets. Mr Finnegan and Ms McConnell do not believe that this is an improvement to financial reporting. In January 2013, the Trustees of the IFRS Foundation approved a new *Due Process Handbook* that specifies, among other things, the criteria for new Standards or major improvements. The main criteria (in addition to pervasiveness of the issue) are (a) whether there is a deficiency in the way particular types of transactions or activities are reported in financial reports, and (b) the importance of the matter to those who use financial reports. Mr Finnegan and Ms McConnell believe that, from a user perspective, there is no deficiency in the accounting for, and disclosures about, bearer assets in IAS 41 and that fair value information is important (indeed essential) to those who use the financial reports of entities engaged in agricultural activity.

DO11   In the user outreach performed by the staff, most investors and analysts said that fair value information about bearer plants is of either limited or no use to them *without* fair value information about the related land, agricultural machinery, etc. Instead of meeting the needs of users by providing this additional fair value information to make the fair value of bearer plants more useful, the Board has chosen to withdraw the requirement to provide the fair value of bearer plants. In the view of Mr Finnegan and Ms McConnell this solution does not adequately address the needs of users of financial statements.

DO12   A better solution would have been for the Board to require the fair value of bearer plants in combination with the fair value of the land to which such plants are attached. One of the weaknesses in IAS 41 is that it does not require the use of fair value to measure land to which bearer plants are attached. This is a weakness because the value of bearer plants is inextricably tied to the value of the land. By understanding the value of the bearer plants and the land, investors know the true potential of an entity's future net cash inflows. A historical cost model for either or both is incapable of providing such information.

DO13   As just discussed, Mr Finnegan and Ms McConnell do not believe the June 2014 Amendment represents an improvement to IFRS and, in fact, represents a step towards lowering the quality of the information available in the financial statements of entities engaged in agricultural activities. The June 2014 Amendment therefore fails to meet the Board's own criteria for a new or amended Standard.

IASB documents published to accompany

IAS 17

Leases

The text of the unaccompanied standard, IAS 17, is contained in Part A of this edition. Its effective date when issued was 1 January 2005. The text of the Accompanying Guidance on IAS 17 is contained in Part B of this edition. This part presents the following documents:

BASIS FOR CONCLUSIONS

DISSENTING OPINION

Basis for Conclusions on IAS 17 *Leases*

This Basis for Conclusions accompanies, but is not part of, IAS 17.

Introduction

BC1　This Basis for Conclusions summarises the International Accounting Standards Board's considerations in reaching its conclusions on revising IAS 17 *Leases* in 2003. Individual Board members gave greater weight to some factors than to others.

BC2　In July 2001 the Board announced that, as part of its initial agenda of technical projects, it would undertake a project to improve a number of Standards, including IAS 17. The project was undertaken in the light of queries and criticisms raised in relation to the Standards by securities regulators, professional accountants and other interested parties. The objectives of the Improvements project were to reduce or eliminate alternatives, redundancies and conflicts within existing Standards, to deal with some convergence issues and to make other improvements. In May 2002 the Board published its proposals in an Exposure Draft of *Improvements to International Accounting Standards*, with a comment deadline of 16 September 2002. The Board received over 160 comment letters on the Exposure Draft.

BC3　Because the Board's intention was not to reconsider the fundamental approach to the accounting for leases established by IAS 17, this Basis for Conclusions does not discuss requirements in IAS 17 that the Board has not reconsidered.

Classification of leases—leases of land and buildings (2003 amendment)

BC4　Paragraph 14 of the Standard requires a lease of land with an indefinite economic life to be normally classified as an operating lease, unless title is expected to pass to the lessee by the end of the lease term. The previous version of IAS 17 (as amended in 2000) was not explicit about how to classify a lease of land and buildings.

BC5　This is a matter of concern in countries where property rights are obtained under long-term leases and the substance of those leases differs little from buying a property. Therefore, the Board decided to deal with this matter in its Improvements project in 2001 and not to defer its resolution until the more fundamental project on leases was completed.

BC6　The Board noted that two approaches are applied in practice. The first is to treat such a lease as a single unit and to classify it as an operating lease in its entirety. The second is to split the lease into two elements—a lease of land and a lease of buildings. The Board decided that the first approach does not adequately reflect the assets controlled by the entity or their usage and financing. It is also inconsistent with the classification and the measurement of other leases. Therefore, the Board rejected the first approach of classifying a lease of land and buildings as an operating lease in its entirety.

© IFRS Foundation

BC7   The Board agreed on the second approach of splitting the lease into two elements—a lease of land and a lease of buildings. The land element would normally be classified as an operating lease in accordance with paragraph 14 of the revised Standard and the buildings element classified as an operating or finance lease by applying the conditions in paragraphs 7–13. The Board noted that generally accepted accounting principles in Australia, Canada and the United States all explicitly require a lease of land and buildings to be split into two elements.

BC8   The Board also discussed a third approach, namely whether to delete the requirement (in paragraph 14 of the Standard) normally to classify a lease of land as an operating lease when title does not pass at the end of the lease and to require such a lease to be classified as a finance lease when all other conditions for finance lease classification in the Standard are met. The Board noted that such an accounting treatment would conflict with the criteria for lease classification in the Standard, which are based on the extent to which the risks and rewards incidental to ownership of a leased asset lie with the lessor or the lessee. Indeed, land normally has an indefinite economic life and hence there are significant risks and rewards associated with the land at the end of the lease term, which do not pass to the lessee. Therefore, the Board rejected this approach when issuing the amendments to IAS 17 in December 2003.

Land element in long-term leases (2009 amendment)[1]

BC8A   As part of its annual improvements project in 2007, the Board reconsidered the decisions it made in 2003, specifically the perceived inconsistency between the general lease classification guidance in paragraphs 7–13 and the specific lease classification guidance in paragraphs 14 and 15 related to long-term leases of land and buildings. The Board concluded that the guidance in paragraphs 14 and 15 might lead to a conclusion on the classification of land leases that does not reflect the substance of the transaction.

BC8B   For example, consider a 999-year lease of land and buildings. In this situation, significant risks and rewards associated with the land during the lease term would have been transferred to the lessee despite there being no transfer of title.

BC8C   The Board noted that the lessee in leases of this type will typically be in a position economically similar to an entity that purchased the land and buildings. The present value of the residual value of the property in a lease with a term of several decades would be negligible. The Board concluded that the accounting for the land element as a finance lease in such circumstances would be consistent with the economic position of the lessee.

BC8D   The Board noted that this amendment reversed the decision it made in amending IAS 17 in December 2003. The Board also noted that the amendment differed from the International Financial Reporting Interpretations Committee's agenda decision in March 2006 based on the IAS 17 guidance that such long-term leases of land would be classified as an operating lease unless title or significant risks and rewards of ownership passed to the lessee, irrespective of

---

1   Paragraphs BC8A–BC8F were added as a consequence of amendments to IAS 17 made by *Improvements to IFRSs* issued in April 2009.

the term of the lease. However, the Board believed that this change improves the accounting for leases by removing a rule and an exception to the general principles applicable to the classification of leases.

BC8E   Some respondents to the exposure draft proposing this amendment agreed with the direction of this proposal but suggested that it should be incorporated into the Board's project on leases. The Board acknowledged that the project on leases is expected to produce a standard in 2011. However, the Board decided to issue the amendment now because of the improvement in accounting for leases that would result and the significance of this issue in countries in which property rights are obtained under long-term leases. Therefore, the Board decided to remove this potential inconsistency by deleting the guidance in paragraphs 14 and 15.

BC8F   Some respondents raised concerns about the proposed requirement to apply the amendment retrospectively. The land and buildings elements of a long-term finance lease may have different amortisation bases. Accordingly, entities must obtain relative fair values even when both elements are classified as finance leases. The Board noted that this information should already be available because entities would have had to obtain it to adopt the 2003 amendment to IAS 17 that required the split between land and buildings elements for the purposes of lease classification. However, the Board acknowledged that the fair values at the inception of the leases might not be available in some situations. The Board noted that determining the fair value of the land element at the inception of long-term leases in these instances would require the use of hindsight and might not achieve comparability. Accordingly, the Board decided not to require retrospective application when the necessary information is not available. The Board also rejected prospective application of the amendment because the land element in existing long-term leases would be accounted for inconsistently. Therefore, the Board decided to adopt the modified retrospective transition requirement in paragraph 68A of IAS 17.

Allocation of minimum lease payments between land and buildings

BC9   The Exposure Draft proposed that the allocation of the minimum lease payments between land and buildings should be made in proportion to their relative fair values at the inception of the lease. Respondents to the Exposure Draft questioned whether the allocation basis referred to the land and buildings components of the fair value of the property or the fair value of those components to the extent they were the subject of the lease.

BC10   The Board noted that an allocation of the minimum lease payments by reference to the relative fair values of the land and buildings would not reflect the fact that land often has an indefinite economic life, and therefore would be expected to maintain its value beyond the lease term. In contrast, the future economic benefits of a building are likely to be used up, at the least to some extent, over the lease term. Therefore, it would be reasonable to expect that the lease payments relating to the building would be set at a level that enabled the lessor not only to make a return on initial investment, but also to recoup the value of the building used up over the term of the lease. In the case of land, the lessor would not normally need compensation for using up the land.

BC11 Therefore, the Board decided to clarify in the Standard that the allocation of the minimum lease payments is weighted to reflect their role in compensating the lessor, and not by reference to the relative fair values of the land and buildings. In other words, the weighting should reflect the lessee's leasehold interest in the land and the buildings. In the extreme case that a building is fully depreciated over the lease term, the minimum lease payments would need to be weighted to provide a return plus the full depreciation of the building's value at the inception of the lease. The leasehold interest in the land would, assuming a residual value that equals its value at the inception of the lease, have a weighting that reflects only a return on the initial investment.

Impracticability of split between land and buildings

BC12 A question that arises is how to treat leases for which it is not possible to measure the two elements reliably (eg because similar land and buildings are not sold or leased separately). One possibility would be to classify the entire lease as a finance lease. This would prevent a lessee from avoiding finance lease treatment for the buildings by asserting that it cannot separately measure the two elements. However, it may be apparent from the circumstances that classifying the entire lease as a finance lease is not representationally faithful. In view of this, the Board decided that when it is not possible to measure the two elements reliably, the entire lease should be classified as a finance lease unless it is clear that both elements should be classified as an operating lease.

Exception to the requirement to separate the land and buildings elements

BC13 The Board discussed whether to allow or require an exception from the requirement to separate the land and buildings elements in cases in which the present value of the land element at the inception of the lease is small in relation to the value of the entire lease. In such cases the benefits of separating the lease into two elements and accounting for each separately may not outweigh the costs. The Board noted that generally accepted accounting principles in Australia, Canada and the United States allow or require such leases to be classified and accounted for as a single unit, with finance lease treatment being used when the relevant criteria are met. The Board decided to allow land and buildings to be treated as a single unit when the land element is immaterial.

BC14 Some respondents to the Exposure Draft requested guidance on how small the relative value of the land element needs to be in relation to the total value of the lease. The Board decided not to introduce a bright line such as a specific percentage threshold. The Board decided that the normal provisions on materiality should apply.

Transitional provisions

BC15 The Board decided that the requirement to separate the land and buildings elements in a lease of land and buildings should be applied retrospectively. It noted that there will be cases when it will be impracticable to reassess the treatment of these leases retrospectively, because doing so requires estimating what the fair value of the two elements was at the inception of the lease, which may have been many years before. The Board also noted that IAS 8 *Accounting Policies, Changes in Accounting Estimates and Errors* contains guidance on when it is impracticable to apply retrospectively a change in accounting policy and therefore decided not to provide specific transitional provisions for the implementation of this revision to IAS 17.

Inception of the lease and commencement of the lease term

BC16   The previous version of IAS 17 did not define the commencement of the lease term. It implicitly assumed that commencement (when the lease begins) and inception (when the agreement is entered into) are simultaneous. Some respondents questioned what should happen if there is a time lag between the two dates, particularly if the amounts change—for example, because the asset is under construction and the final cost is not known at inception. The Standard now specifies that recognition takes place at commencement, based on values measured at inception. However, if the lease is adjusted for changes in the lessor's costs between the inception of the lease and the commencement of the lease term, the effect of any such changes is deemed to have taken place at inception. These revisions are consistent with generally accepted accounting principles in Australia, Canada and the United States, and are consistent with the present accounting treatment of most ordinary purchases and sales.

BC17   In agreeing on this treatment, the Board noted that measurement at commencement would have been more satisfactory in principle. However, this cannot be done properly within the framework of IAS 17 because the Standard generally requires a finance lease receivable or payable to be recognised at an amount based on the fair value of the asset, which is inappropriate at any date after inception.

Leases in the financial statements of lessors other than manufacturers and dealers

BC18   Lessors may incur direct costs in negotiating a lease, such as commissions, brokers' fees and legal fees. The previous version of IAS 17 contained a choice on how to account for such costs—they might be either charged as an expense as incurred or allocated over the lease term. The choice of treatment applied to operating and finance leases. In the case of a finance lease, paragraph 33 of the previous version of IAS 17 stated that allocation over the lease term might be achieved by recognising the cost as an expense and, in the same period, recognising an equal amount of unearned finance income.

BC19   The Board decided that this treatment was not in accordance with the *Framework for the Preparation and Presentation of Financial Statements*.[2] Its effect was to recognise some future finance income as income and an asset at the commencement of the lease term. However, at that date, the *Framework*'s definitions of income and assets are not met. Therefore, the Board decided that if direct costs incurred by

---

2   IASC's *Framework for the Preparation and Presentation of Financial Statements* was adopted by the IASB in 2001. In September 2010 the IASB replaced the *Framework* with the *Conceptual Framework for Financial Reporting*.

lessors are to be allocated over the lease term, this should be achieved by including them in the carrying amount of the lease asset.

BC20   The Board noted that standard-setters in Australia, Canada, France, Japan, the United Kingdom and the United States either permit or require initial direct costs to be allocated over the lease term. The Board also noted that other Standards permit or require the recognition of a range of similar costs in the carrying amount of assets, generally subject to those costs being directly attributable to the acquisition of the asset in question. Hence, for reasons of convergence and comparability with other Standards, the Board decided to require initial direct costs to be included in the carrying amount of the lease asset.

BC21   For consistency with other Standards, in particular IAS 39 *Financial Instruments: Recognition and Measurement*,[3] the Board decided that recognition in the carrying amount of assets should be restricted to costs that are incremental and directly attributable to negotiating and arranging a lease.

---

3   IFRS 9 *Financial Instruments* replaced IAS 39. IFRS 9 applies to all items that were previously within the scope of IAS 39. This paragraph refers to matters relevant when IAS 17 was issued.

Dissenting opinion

Dissent of James J Leisenring from the amendment issued in April 2009

DO1   Mr Leisenring dissents from the amendment to IAS 17 *Leases* made by *Improvements to IFRSs* issued in April 2009.

DO2   Mr Leisenring believes that the amendment inappropriately permits an accounting that does not reflect the economic position of the lessee. In his view, land normally has an indefinite economic life, unlike other properties with finite useful lives. Therefore, it is not the lessee's land at the end of the lease even if the lease term is 999 years. He does not believe that a lessee is in a position economically similar to the purchaser of the land. Any appreciation in the land value does not accrue to the lessee at the termination of the lease. Furthermore, it is unclear how long the lease term must be for the Board to conclude that a lessee and a purchaser are in the same economic position.

DO3   This amendment also reverses the decision the Board made in amending IAS 17 in December 2003 and creates a divergence from US generally accepted accounting principles. Mr Leisenring agrees with some respondents that it is best to incorporate this amendment into the Board's broader project on lease accounting.

IASB documents published to accompany

IAS 19

Employee Benefits

The text of the unaccompanied standard, IAS 19, is contained in Part A of this edition. Its effective date when issued was 1 January 1999. The text of the Accompanying Guidance on IAS 19 is contained in Part B of this edition. This part presents the following documents:

BASIS FOR CONCLUSIONS

APPENDIX TO THE BASIS FOR CONCLUSIONS

Amendments to the Basis for Conclusions on other IFRSs

DISSENTING OPINIONS

Contents

COST-BENEFIT CONSIDERATIONS: AMENDMENTS ISSUED IN 2011   BC280

APPENDIX
Amendments to the Basis for Conclusions on other IFRSs

DISSENTING OPINIONS

Basis for Conclusions on
IAS 19 *Employee Benefits*

Introduction

BC1   This Basis for Conclusions summarises the International Accounting Standards Board's considerations in reaching its conclusions on IAS 19 *Employee Benefits*. Individual Board members gave greater weight to some factors than to others.

BC2   The Board's predecessor, the International Accounting Standards Committee (IASC), approved IAS 19 *Employee Benefits* in 1998, replacing a previous version of the standard. IASC developed the revision of IAS 19 in 1998 following its consideration of the responses to its exposure draft E54 *Employee Benefits* published in 1996. Since that date, IASC and the Board have made the following amendments that are still relevant:

(a)   In October 2000 IASC extended the definition of plan assets (see paragraphs BC178–BC190) and introduced recognition and measurement requirements for reimbursements (see paragraphs BC195–BC199).

(b)   In December 2004 the Board amended the accounting for multi-employer plans and group plans (see paragraphs BC35–BC38 and BC40–BC50).

(c)   In June 2011 the Board eliminated previous options for deferred recognition of changes in the net defined benefit liability (asset), amended where those changes should be recognised, amended the disclosure requirements for defined benefit plans and multi-employer plans, and made a number of other amendments (see paragraphs BC3–BC13).

Amendments made in 2011

BC3   Accounting for post-employment benefit promises is an important financial reporting issue. Anecdotal evidence and academic research suggested that many users of financial statements did not fully understand the information that entities provided about post-employment benefits under the requirements of IAS 19 before the amendments made in 2011. Both users and preparers of financial statements criticised those accounting requirements for failing to provide high quality, transparent information about post-employment benefits. For example, delays in the recognition of gains and losses give rise to misleading amounts in the statement of financial position and the existence of various options for recognising gains and losses and a lack of clarity in the definitions lead to poor comparability.

BC4   In July 2006 the Board added to its agenda a project on the accounting for post-employment benefit promises in response to calls for a comprehensive review of the accounting for post-employment benefit promises to improve the quality and transparency of financial statements. However, a comprehensive project to address all areas of post-employment benefit accounting could take many years to complete. Nevertheless, the Board recognised a short-term need to provide users of financial statements with better information about post-employment benefit promises.

BC5 Accordingly, the Board undertook a limited scope project, and in March 2008 the Board published a discussion paper *Preliminary Views on Amendments to IAS 19 Employee Benefits* that included the Board's preliminary views on the following areas of IAS 19:

(a) the deferred recognition of some gains and losses arising from defined benefit plans.

(b) presentation of the changes in the net defined benefit liability or asset.

(c) accounting for employee benefits that are based on contributions and a promised return and employee benefits with a 'higher of' option (contribution-based promises).

BC6 The discussion paper also asked respondents to identify:

(a) any additional issues that should be addressed in this project given that its objective was to address specific issues in a limited time frame.

(b) what disclosures the Board should consider as part of its review of disclosures.

BC7 The IASB received 150 comment letters in response to that discussion paper. In the light of those responses, the Board deferred its review of contribution-based promises to a possible future project. The Board considered the additional issues raised in those responses and extended the scope of the project to include:

(a) a review of the disclosures for defined benefit plans and multi-employer plans; and

(b) additional issues raised in the responses to the discussion paper and matters that had been submitted to the International Financial Reporting Interpretations Committee (IFRIC) for interpretation that the Board considered could be addressed expeditiously, would not require a fundamental review of defined benefit obligation measurement and would lead to an improvement in the reporting of defined benefit plans.

BC8 In April 2010 the Board published an exposure draft *Defined Benefit Plans* (the 2010 ED). The Board received 227 comment letters in response. In addition to the formal consultation provided by the 2010 ED, the Board undertook an extensive programme of outreach activities during the exposure period with a wide range of users and preparers of financial statements, regulators and others interested in the financial reporting of employee benefits from a wide variety of geographical areas.

BC9 Some respondents to the 2010 ED and the discussion paper requested a comprehensive review of the accounting for employee benefits, preferably as a joint project with the US national standard-setter, the Financial Accounting Standards Board (FASB), and questioned why the Board was addressing employee benefits in a limited scope project, expressing concern that successive changes could be disruptive. The Board reiterated its previous concern that a comprehensive review of the accounting for employee benefits would take many years to complete and that there was an urgent need to improve the financial reporting of employee benefits in the short term, so that users of financial statements receive more useful and understandable information.

BC10　In June 2011 the Board issued amendments to IAS 19 that targeted improvements in the following areas:

(a)　recognition of changes in the net defined benefit liability (asset) (see paragraphs BC65–BC100), including:

(i)　immediate recognition of defined benefit cost (see paragraphs BC70–BC72).

(ii)　disaggregation of defined benefit cost into components (see paragraphs BC73–BC87).

(iii)　recognition of remeasurements in other comprehensive income (see paragraphs BC88–BC100).

(b)　plan amendments, curtailments and settlements (see paragraphs BC152–BC173).

(c)　disclosures about defined benefit plans (see paragraphs BC203–BC252).

(d)　accounting for termination benefits (see paragraphs BC11 and BC254–BC268).

(e)　miscellaneous issues, including:

(i)　the classification of employee benefits (see paragraphs BC16–BC24).

(ii)　current estimates of mortality rates (see paragraph BC142).

(iii)　tax and administration costs (see paragraphs BC121–BC128).

(iv)　risk-sharing and conditional indexation features (see paragraphs BC143–BC150).

(f)　some matters that had been submitted to the IFRIC for interpretation, including:

(i)　IFRIC rejection March 2007—Special wage tax (see paragraphs BC121–BC124).

(ii)　IFRIC rejection November 2007—Treatment of employee contributions (see paragraphs BC143–BC150).

(iii)　IFRIC rejection January 2008—Pension promises based on performance hurdles (see paragraphs BC143–BC150).

(iv)　IFRIC rejection May 2008—Settlements (see paragraph BC163).

BC11　The Board issued the amendments resulting from the 2010 ED together with amendments relating to termination benefits resulting from the exposure draft *Proposed Amendments to IAS 37* Provisions, Contingent Liabilities and Contingent Assets *and IAS 19* Employee Benefits (the 2005 ED), published in June 2005. The Board concluded that it would be better to issue both sets of amendments

© IFRS Foundation

together rather than delay the completion of the amendments for termination benefits until it completed its work on IAS 37 *Provisions, Contingent Liabilities and Contingent Assets*.

Matters not addressed as part of the limited scope project

BC12 Respondents to the 2010 ED and the discussion paper raised matters that were outside the scope of this project (such as measurement of the defined benefit obligation). The Board did not consider these matters in detail. Any project addressing issues beyond the scope of the targeted improvements would be subject to the Board's agenda-setting process.

BC13 In selecting issues to address, the Board discussed the following issues, but took no action in the amendments made in 2011.

(a) *Contribution-based promises*—The discussion paper included proposals on contribution-based promises. The Board will consider whether to develop those proposals further if it undertakes a comprehensive review of employee benefit accounting.

(b) *Discount rate for employee benefits*—The Board did not proceed with the proposals in its exposure draft *Discount Rate for Employee Benefits*, published in August 2009. The Board decided it would address issues relating to the discount rate only in the context of a fundamental review (see paragraphs BC138 and BC139).

(c) *The effect of expected future salary increases on the attribution of benefits*—The 2010 ED proposed that expected future salary increases should be included in determining whether a benefit formula expressed in terms of current salary allocates a materially higher level of benefit to later years. The Board did not proceed with that proposal because it is closely related to a fundamental review of the accounting for contribution-based promises (see paragraphs BC117–BC120).

(d) *Exemption for entities participating in multi-employer defined benefit plans*—The Board rejected a proposal to permit all entities participating in a multi-employer defined benefit plan to account for these plans as defined contribution plans. The Board concluded that extending that exemption would be contrary to its general approach of limiting exceptions. The Board also believes that such an exemption would not be appropriate for all multi-employer plans, such as when an entity becomes a dominant participant in a multi-employer plan, perhaps because other participants leave the plan (see paragraph BC39).

(e) *IFRIC-related matters*—The Board did not incorporate into IAS 19 the requirements of IFRIC 14 *IAS 19—The Limit on a Defined Benefit Asset, Minimum Funding Requirements and their Interaction*. Incorporating IFRIC 14 would require changes to the drafting, which could have unintended consequences. The Board also considered other questions received by the IFRIC but concluded that it would not amend IAS 19 at this time.

Employee Benefits Working Group

BC14 The Board established an Employee Benefits Working Group in 2007 to help by providing a variety of expert perspectives, including those of auditors, preparers and users of financial statements, actuaries and regulators. The group consisted of senior professionals with extensive practical experience in the operation, management, valuation, financial reporting, auditing or regulation of a variety of post-employment benefit arrangements.

BC15 Members of the group assisted the Board by reviewing early drafts of the amendments made in 2011, and the preceding discussion paper and exposure draft. The Board greatly appreciates the time and energy that group members have devoted to this process and the quality of their contributions.

Classification of benefits

Short-term employee benefits: amendments issued in 2011

BC16 The amendments made in 2011 clarify that the classification of benefits as short-term employee benefits depends on the period between the end of the annual reporting period in which the employee renders the service that gives rise to the benefit and the date when the benefit is expected to be settled.

BC17 The Board's objective in defining the scope of the short-term employee benefits classification was to identify the set of employee benefits for which a simplified measurement approach would not result in measuring those benefits at an amount different from the general measurement requirements of IAS 19.

BC18 The Board concluded that the classification of a short-term employee benefit on the basis of the timing of expected settlement would best meet this objective and would be most consistent with the measurement basis in IAS 19.

BC19 Other alternatives that the Board considered for the basis for classification of short-term employee benefits included:

(a) *The earliest possible settlement date (ie entitlement)*—The Board rejected this alternative because it would have the result that a benefit classified as a short-term employee benefit could be measured at an amount materially different from its present value. For example, this could occur if an employee is entitled to a benefit within twelve months, but the benefit is not expected to be settled until many years later.

(b) *The latest possible settlement date*—The Board rejected this alternative because, although the latest possible settlement date would be consistent with the Board's objective of minimising differences between the measurement of short-term employee benefits and the measurement of the same benefits using the model for post-employment benefits, this would result in the smallest set of benefits that would meet the definition.

BC20 However, classifying short-term employee benefits on the basis of expected settlement raises the following additional concerns:

(a) *Unit of account*—the expected settlement date is determined on the basis of a combination of the characteristics of the benefits and the characteristics of the employees, and would reflect the actuarial assumptions for a particular year rather than the characteristics of the benefits promised. The Board concluded that the classification of the benefits should reflect the characteristics of the benefits, rather than the demographic or financial assumptions at a point in time.

(b) *Splitting benefits into components*—some benefits are expected to be settled over a period of time. The Board concluded that an entity should classify a benefit as a short-term employee benefit if the whole of the benefit is expected to be settled before twelve months after the end of the annual reporting period in which the related service was provided. This will ensure that the benefit is measured on the same basis throughout its life and is consistent with the measurement requirements of paragraph 69.

(c) *Reclassification*—if the expected settlement date of a benefit classified initially as a short-term employee benefit changes subsequently to a date more than twelve months after the end of the reporting period, then the undiscounted amount of that benefit could differ materially from its present value. The Board concluded that the classification of a short-term employee benefit should be revisited if it no longer meets the definition. This maintains the objective that the benefits should not be measured at an amount that would differ materially from their present value. However, the Board concluded that a temporary change in expectation should not trigger reclassification because such a change would not be indicative of a change in the underlying characteristics of the benefit. The Board noted that reclassification of a benefit from other long-term employee benefits to short-term employee benefits is less of a concern because in that case measuring the benefit at its undiscounted amount should not differ materially from measuring the benefit at its present value.

BC21 Other approaches that the Board considered for addressing the concerns above included:

(a) *Unit of account*—by requiring an entity to classify benefits on an employee-by-employee basis. The Board concluded that this would not be practical and would not meet the objectives of the classification.

(b) *Reclassification*—prohibiting the entity from revising the classification of a short-term employee benefit after initial classification. This approach would maintain continuity of measurement throughout the life of the benefit, but the Board rejected it because measuring the benefit at the undiscounted amount could result in an amount that differs from its present value if the entity no longer expects to settle the benefit before twelve months after the end of the annual reporting period.

Long-term employee benefits: exposure draft published in 2010

BC22 The Board considered combining post-employment benefits and other long-term employee benefits into a single category. The main differences between accounting for other long-term benefits and accounting for post-employment benefits were:

(a) the previous option to defer recognition of actuarial gains and losses ('the corridor'); and

(b) the previous requirement to recognise unvested past service cost over the vesting period.

BC23 As proposed in the 2010 ED, the Board removed these differences in 2011. In the light of that proposal, the 2010 ED also proposed the removal of the distinction between post-employment benefits and other long-term employee benefits. However, many respondents to the 2010 ED did not support this removal of that distinction. They did not think that the recognition and disclosure requirements for post-employment benefits were appropriate for other long-term employee benefits, because in their view:

(a) the costs of applying the recognition and disclosure requirements for post-employment benefits to other long-term employee benefits outweigh the benefits.

(b) accounting for other long-term employee benefits was not originally within the scope of the project. Accounting for other long-term employee benefits was not an area they viewed as requiring improvement.

BC24 After reviewing the responses to the 2010 ED, the Board decided not to combine post-employment and other long-term employee benefits into a single category for the reasons expressed by respondents.

Short-term employee benefits

Paid absences

BC25 Some argue that an employee's entitlement to future paid absences does not create an obligation if that entitlement is conditional on future events other than future service. However, IASC concluded in 1998 that an obligation arises as an employee renders service that increases the employee's entitlement (conditional or unconditional) to future paid absences; for example, accumulating paid sick leave creates an obligation because any unused entitlement increases the employee's entitlement to sick leave in future periods. The probability that the employee will be sick in those future periods affects the measurement of that obligation, but does not determine whether that obligation exists.

BC26 IASC considered three alternative approaches to measuring the obligation that results from unused entitlement to accumulating paid absences:

(a) recognise the entire unused entitlement as a liability, on the basis that any future payments are made first out of unused entitlement and only subsequently out of entitlement that will accumulate in future periods (a FIFO approach);

(b) recognise a liability to the extent that future payments for the employee group as a whole are expected to exceed the future payments that would have been expected in the absence of the accumulation feature (a group LIFO approach); or

(c) recognise a liability to the extent that future payments for individual employees are expected to exceed the future payments that would have been expected in the absence of the accumulation feature (an individual LIFO approach).

These methods are illustrated by the following example.

BC Example 1

An entity has 100 employees, who are each entitled to five working days of paid sick leave for each year. Unused sick leave may be carried forward for one year. Such leave is taken first out of the current year's entitlement and then out of any balance brought forward from the previous year (a LIFO basis).

At 31 December 20X1 the average unused entitlement is two days per employee. The entity expects, on the basis of past experience that is expected to continue, that 92 employees will take no more than four days of paid sick leave in 20X2 and that the remaining 8 employees will take an average of six and a half days each.

Method (a):   *The entity recognises a liability equal to the undiscounted amount of 200 days of sick pay (two days each, for 100 employees). It is assumed that the first 200 days of paid sick leave result from the unused entitlement.*

Method (b):   *The entity recognises no liability because paid sick leave for the employee group as a whole is not expected to exceed the entitlement of five days each in 20X2.*

Method (c):   *The entity recognises a liability equal to the undiscounted amount of 12 days of sick pay (one and a half days each, for 8 employees).*

BC27 IASC selected method (c), the individual LIFO approach, because that method measures the obligation at the present value of the additional future payments that are expected to arise solely from the accumulation feature. IAS 19 notes that, in many cases, the resulting liability will not be material.

Post-employment benefits

Distinction between defined contribution plans and defined benefit plans

Defined contribution plans

BC28   IAS 19 before its revision in 1998 defined:

(a)   **defined contribution plans** as retirement benefit plans under which amounts to be paid as retirement benefits are determined by reference to contributions to a fund together with investment earnings thereon; and

(b)   **defined benefit plans** as retirement benefit plans under which amounts to be paid as retirement benefits are determined by reference to a formula usually based on employees' remuneration and/or years of service.

BC29   IASC considered these definitions unsatisfactory because they focused on the benefit receivable by the employee, rather than on the cost to the entity. The definitions introduced in 1998 focused on the downside risk that the cost to the entity may increase. The definition of defined contribution plans does not exclude the upside potential that the cost to the entity may be less than expected.

Defined benefit plans: amendments issued in 2011

BC30   The amendments made in 2011 clarify that the existence of a benefit formula does not, by itself, create a defined benefit plan, but rather that there needs to be a link between the benefit formula and contributions that creates a legal or constructive obligation to contribute further amounts to meet the benefits specified by the benefit formula. This amendment to paragraph 29 addressed a concern that can arise when a plan has a benefit formula determining the benefits to be paid if there are sufficient plan assets, but not requiring the employer to pay additional contributions if there are insufficient plan assets to pay those benefits. In effect, the benefit payments are based on the lower of the benefit formula and the plan assets available. The amendments clarify that such a plan is a defined contribution plan.

Multi-employer plans and state plans

BC31   An entity may not always be able to obtain sufficient information from multi-employer plans to use defined benefit accounting. IASC considered three approaches to this problem:

(a)   use defined contribution accounting for some and defined benefit accounting for others;

(b)   use defined contribution accounting for all multi-employer plans, with additional disclosure where the multi-employer plan is a defined benefit plan; or

(c)   use defined benefit accounting for those multi-employer plans that are defined benefit plans. However, where sufficient information is not available to use defined benefit accounting, an entity should disclose that fact and use defined contribution accounting.

BC32   IASC believed that there was no conceptually sound, workable and objective way to draw a distinction so that an entity could use defined contribution accounting for some multi-employer defined benefit plans and defined benefit accounting for others. In addition, IASC believed that it was misleading to use defined contribution accounting for multi-employer plans that are defined benefit plans. This is illustrated by the case of French banks that used defined contribution accounting for defined benefit pension plans operated under industry-wide collective agreements on a pay-as-you-go basis. Demographic trends made these plans unsustainable and a major reform in 1993 replaced them by defined contribution arrangements for future service. At that point, the banks were compelled to quantify their obligations. Those obligations had previously existed, but had not been recognised as liabilities.

BC33   IASC concluded that an entity should use defined benefit accounting for those multi-employer plans that are defined benefit plans. However, where sufficient information is not available to use defined benefit accounting, an entity should disclose that fact and use defined contribution accounting. IASC applied the same principle to state plans, observing that most state plans are defined contribution plans.

BC34   In response to comments on E54, IASC considered a proposal to exempt wholly-owned subsidiaries (and their parents) participating in group defined benefit plans from the recognition and measurement requirements in their individual non-consolidated financial statements, on cost-benefit grounds. IASC concluded that such an exemption would not be appropriate.

Multi-employer plans: amendments issued in 2004

BC35   In April 2004 the IFRIC published a draft Interpretation, D6 *Multi-employer Plans*, which proposed the following guidance on how multi-employer plans should apply defined benefit accounting, if possible:

(a)   The plan should be measured in accordance with IAS 19 using assumptions appropriate for the plan as a whole.

(b)   The plan should be allocated to plan participants so that they recognise an asset or liability that reflects the impact of the surplus or deficit on the future contributions from the participant.

BC36   The concerns raised by respondents to D6 about the availability of the information about the plan as a whole, the difficulties in making an allocation as proposed and the resulting lack of usefulness of the information provided by defined benefit accounting were such that the IFRIC decided not to proceed with the proposals.

BC37   When discussing group plans (see paragraphs BC40–BC50) in 2004 the Board noted that, if there were a contractual agreement between a multi-employer plan and its participants on how a surplus would be distributed or a deficit funded, the same principle that applied to group plans should apply to multi-employer plans, ie the participants should recognise an asset or liability. In relation to the funding of a deficit, the Board regarded this principle as consistent with the recognition of a provision in accordance with IAS 37.

BC38 The Board therefore clarified that a participant in a multi-employer defined benefit plan must recognise the asset or liability arising from that contractual agreement if the participant:

(a) accounts for that participation on a defined contribution basis in accordance with paragraph 34 because it has insufficient information to apply defined benefit accounting, but

(b) has a contractual agreement that determines how a surplus would be distributed or a deficit funded.

Multi-employer plans: exposure draft published in 2010

BC39 The Board considered and rejected a proposal to permit all entities participating in multi-employer defined benefit plans to account for those plans as defined contribution plans. The Board concluded that extending that exemption would be contrary to its general approach of limiting exceptions. In the Board's view such an exemption would not be appropriate for all multi-employer plans, such as when an entity becomes a dominant participant in a multi-employer plan, perhaps because other participants leave the plan.

Group plans: amendments issued in 2004

BC40 Some constituents asked the Board to consider whether entities participating in a group defined benefit plan should, in their separate or individual financial statements, either have an unqualified exemption from defined benefit accounting or be able to treat the plan as a multi-employer plan.

BC41 In developing the exposure draft *Actuarial Gains and Losses, Group Plans and Disclosures* published in April 2004 (the 2004 ED), the Board did not agree that an unqualified exemption from defined benefit accounting for group defined benefit plans in the separate or individual financial statements of group entities was appropriate. In principle, the requirements of International Financial Reporting Standards (IFRSs) should apply to separate or individual financial statements in the same way as they apply to any other financial statements. Following that principle would mean amending IAS 19 to allow group entities that participate in a plan that meets the definition of a multi-employer plan, except that the participants are under common control, to be treated as participants in a multi-employer plan in their separate or individual financial statements.

BC42 However, in the 2004 ED the Board concluded that entities within a group should always be presumed to be able to obtain the necessary information about the plan as a whole. This implies that, in accordance with the requirements for multi-employer plans, defined benefit accounting should be applied if there is a consistent and reliable basis for allocating the assets and obligations of the plan.

BC43 In the 2004 ED the Board acknowledged that entities within a group might not be able to identify a consistent and reliable basis for allocating the plan that results in the entity recognising an asset or liability that reflects the extent to which a surplus or deficit in the plan would affect its future contributions. This is because there may be uncertainty in the terms of the plan about how surpluses will be used or deficits funded across the consolidated group. However, the Board concluded that entities within a group should always be able to make at least a consistent and *reasonable* allocation, for example on the basis of a percentage of pensionable pay.

BC44 The Board then considered whether, for some group entities, the benefits of defined benefit accounting using a consistent and reasonable basis of allocation were worth the costs involved in obtaining the information. The Board decided that this was not the case for entities that meet criteria similar to those in IAS 27 *Consolidated and Separate Financial Statements*[1] for the exemption from preparing consolidated financial statements.

BC45 The 2004 ED therefore proposed the following for entities that participate in a plan that would meet the definition of a multi-employer plan except that the participants are under common control:

(a) If the entities meet the criteria as proposed in the 2004 ED, they should be treated as if they were participants in a multi-employer plan. This means that if there is no consistent and reliable basis for allocating the assets and liabilities of the plan, the entity should use defined contribution accounting and provide additional disclosures.

(b) In all other cases, the entities should be required to apply defined benefit accounting by making a consistent and reasonable allocation of the assets and liabilities of the plan.

BC46 Respondents to the 2004 ED generally supported the proposal to extend the requirements on multi-employer plans to group entities. However, many disagreed with the criteria proposed in the 2004 ED, for the following reasons:

(a) The proposed amendments and the interaction with D6 (see paragraphs BC35–BC38) were unclear.

(b) The provisions for multi-employer accounting should be extended to a listed parent company.

(c) The provisions for multi-employer accounting should be extended to group entities with listed debt.

(d) The provisions for multi-employer plan accounting should be extended to all group entities, including partly-owned subsidiaries.

(e) There should be a blanket exemption from defined benefit accounting for all group entities.

BC47 The Board agreed that the proposed requirements for group plans were unnecessarily complex. The Board also concluded that it would be better to treat group plans separately from multi-employer plans because of the difference in information available to the participants: in a group plan, information about the plan as a whole should generally be available. The Board

---

1 The consolidation requirements in IAS 27 were superseded by IFRS 10 *Consolidated Financial Statements* issued in May 2011. The criteria for the exemption from preparing consolidated financial statements were not changed.

further noted that, if the parent wishes to comply with IFRSs in its separate financial statements or wishes its subsidiaries to comply with IFRSs in their individual financial statements, then it must obtain and provide the necessary information at least for the purposes of disclosure.

BC48   The Board noted that, if there were a contractual agreement or stated policy on charging the net defined benefit cost to group entities, that agreement or policy would determine the cost for each entity. If there is no such contractual agreement or stated policy, the entity that is the sponsoring employer bears the risk relating to the plan by default. The Board therefore concluded that a group plan should be allocated to the individual entities within a group in accordance with any contractual agreement or stated policy. If there is no such agreement or policy, the net defined benefit cost is allocated to the sponsoring employer. The other group entities recognise a cost equal to any contribution collected by the sponsoring employer.

BC49   This approach has the advantages of (a) all group entities recognising the cost they have to bear for the defined benefit promise and (b) being simple to apply.

BC50   The Board also noted that participation in a group plan is a related party transaction. As such, disclosures are required to comply with IAS 24 *Related Party Disclosures*. IAS 24 requires an entity to disclose the nature of the related party relationship as well as information about the transactions and outstanding balances necessary for an understanding of the potential effect of the relationship on the financial statements. The Board noted that information about each of (a) the policy on charging the defined benefit cost, (b) the policy on charging current contributions and (c) the status of the plan as a whole was required to give an understanding of the potential effect of the participation in the group plan on the entity's separate or individual financial statements.

State plan and group plan disclosures: amendments issued in 2011

BC51   The amendments made in 2011 updated, without reconsideration, the disclosure requirements for entities that participate in state plans or defined benefit plans that share risks between various entities under common control, to be consistent with the disclosure requirements for multi-employer plans and defined benefit plans. However, those amendments permit an entity to include those disclosures by cross-reference to the required disclosures in another group entity's financial statements, if specified conditions are met.

Defined benefit plans: recognition and measurement

BC52   Although IAS 19 before its revision in 1998 did not deal explicitly with the recognition of retirement benefit obligations as a liability, it is likely that most entities recognised a liability for retirement benefit obligations at the same time under the requirements in IAS 19 before and after its revision in 1998. However, the requirements in IAS 19 before and after its revision in 1998 differed in the measurement of the resulting liability.

BC53   Paragraph 63 of IAS 19 is based on the definition of, and recognition criteria for, a liability in IASC's *Framework for the Preparation and Presentation of Financial*

Statements.[2] The *Framework* defined a liability as 'a present obligation of the entity arising from past events, the settlement of which is expected to result in an outflow from the entity of resources embodying economic benefits'. The *Framework* stated that an item which meets the definition of a liability should be recognised if:

(a) it is probable that any future economic benefit associated with the item will flow from the entity; and

(b) the item has a cost or value that can be measured with reliability.

BC54 IASC believed that:

(a) an entity has an obligation under a defined benefit plan when an employee has rendered service in return for the benefits promised under the plan. Paragraphs 70–74 deal with the attribution of benefit to individual periods of service in order to determine whether an obligation exists.

(b) an entity should use actuarial assumptions to determine whether the entity will pay those benefits in future reporting periods (see paragraphs 75–98).

(c) actuarial techniques allow an entity to measure the obligation with sufficient reliability to justify recognition of a liability.

BC55 IASC believed that an obligation exists even if a benefit is not vested, in other words if the employee's right to receive the benefit is conditional on future employment. For example, consider an entity that provides a benefit of CU100[3] to employees who remain in service for two years. At the end of the first year, the employee and the entity are not in the same position as at the beginning of the first year, because the employee will need to work for only one more year, instead of two, before becoming entitled to the benefit. Although there is a possibility that the benefit may not vest, that difference is an obligation and, in IASC's view, should result in the recognition of a liability at the end of the first year. The measurement of that obligation at its present value reflects the entity's best estimate of the probability that the benefit may not vest.

Measurement date

BC56 Some national standards permit entities to measure the present value of defined benefit obligations at a date up to three months before the end of the reporting period. However, IASC decided that entities should measure the present value of defined benefit obligations, and the fair value of any plan assets, at the end of the reporting period. Consequently, if an entity carries out a detailed valuation of the obligation at an earlier date, the results of that valuation should be updated to take account of any significant transactions and other significant changes in circumstances up to the balance sheet date (end of the reporting period).

---

2 In September 2010 the Board replaced the *Framework* with the *Conceptual Framework for Financial Reporting.*

3 In this Basis for Conclusions monetary amounts are denominated in 'currency units (CU)'.

BC57   In response to comments on E54, IASC clarified that full actuarial valuation was not required at the end of the reporting period, provided that an entity determined the present value of defined benefit obligations and the fair value of any plan assets with sufficient regularity that the amounts recognised in the financial statements did not differ materially from the amounts that would be determined at the balance sheet date.

Interim reporting: effects of the amendments issued in 2011

BC58   The 2010 ED did not propose any substantial amendments to the requirements in IAS 34 *Interim Financial Reporting*. Respondents to the 2010 ED were concerned that the requirements for the immediate recognition of changes in the net defined benefit liability (asset) would imply that entities should remeasure the net defined benefit liability (asset) at each interim reporting date.

BC59   The Board noted that an entity is not always required to remeasure a net defined benefit liability (asset) for interim reporting purposes under IAS 19 and IAS 34. Both indicate that the entity needs to exercise judgement in determining whether it needs to remeasure the net defined benefit liability (asset) at the end of the (interim or annual) reporting period.

BC60   The amendments made in 2011 require an entity to recognise remeasurements in the period in which they arise. Thus, remeasurements are now more likely to have a material effect on the amount recognised in the financial statements than would have been the case before those amendments if an entity elected to defer recognition of actuarial gains and losses. It follows that entities previously deferring recognition of some gains and losses are now more likely to judge that remeasurement is required for interim reporting.

BC61   The Board considered setting out explicitly whether an entity should remeasure a net defined benefit liability (asset) at interim dates. However, in the Board's view, such a change would be an exemption from the general requirements of IAS 34 and consequently it decided against such an amendment. The Board is not aware of concerns with the application of these interim reporting requirements for entities that applied the immediate recognition option under the previous version of IAS 19.

BC62   Some respondents to the 2010 ED asked the Board to clarify whether the assumptions used to determine defined benefit cost for subsequent interim periods should reflect the assumptions used at the end of the prior financial year or for the most recent measurement of the defined benefit obligation (for example, in an earlier interim period or in determining the effect of a plan amendment or settlement).

BC63   The Board noted that if assumptions for each interim reporting period were updated to the most recent interim date, the measurement of the entity's annual amounts would be affected by how frequently the entity reports, ie whether the entity reports quarterly, half-yearly or with no interim period. In the Board's view this would not be consistent with the requirements of paragraphs 28 and 29 of IAS 34.

BC64   Similarly, in the Board's view, there is no reason to distinguish between the periods before and after a plan amendment, curtailment or settlement in determining current service cost and net interest, ie determining how much service the employee has rendered to date and the effect of the time value of money to date. The remeasurement of the defined benefit obligation in the event of a plan amendment, curtailment or settlement is required in order to determine past service cost and the gain or loss on settlement. In accordance with paragraph B9 of IAS 34 the assumptions underlying the calculation of current service cost and net interest are based on the assumptions at the end of the prior financial year.

Recognition: amendments issued in 2011

BC65   The amendments made in 2011 require entities to recognise all changes in the net defined benefit liability (asset) in the period in which those changes occur, and to disaggregate and recognise defined benefit cost as follows:

(a)   service cost, relating to the cost of the services received, in profit or loss.

(b)   net interest on the net defined benefit liability (asset), representing the financing effect of paying for the benefits in advance or in arrears, in profit or loss.

(c)   remeasurements, representing the period-to-period fluctuations in the amounts of defined benefit obligations and plan assets, in other comprehensive income.

BC66   Before those amendments, IAS 19 permitted three options for the recognition of actuarial gains and losses:

(a)   leaving actuarial gains and losses unrecognised if they were within a 'corridor' and deferred recognition of actuarial gains and losses outside the corridor in profit or loss;

(b)   immediate recognition in profit or loss; or

(c)   immediate recognition in other comprehensive income. Actuarial gains and losses recognised in other comprehensive income are transferred directly to retained earnings.

BC67   The amendments in 2011 made the following changes to the recognition requirements:

(a)   immediate recognition—elimination of the corridor (paragraphs BC70–BC72).

(b)   redefining the components of defined benefit cost (paragraphs BC73–BC87).

(c)   recognition of the remeasurements component in other comprehensive income (paragraphs BC88–BC100).

BC68   Many respondents to the 2010 ED agreed that the Board should address within the project the disaggregation of defined benefit cost and where the components of defined benefit cost should be recognised. However, some respondents said that the determination of an appropriate disaggregation method was intrinsically linked to the accounting model and should not be considered until there is a fundamental review of IAS 19. The Board considered the components of defined benefit cost in the context of the accounting model of IAS 19. In the Board's view, the disaggregation requirements are consistent with that model and provide useful information.

BC69 Others said that the Board should not address those matters until it completes its project on financial statement presentation, including the conceptual basis for deciding whether items should ultimately be reclassified to profit or loss from other comprehensive income. However, the Board concluded that improving the understandability and comparability of the changes in the net defined benefit liability or asset would be necessary if changes are to be recognised immediately, and that improving the understandability of those changes should not be delayed until it completes its project on financial statement presentation.

Immediate recognition: elimination of the corridor

BC70 In the Board's view, immediate recognition provides information that is more relevant to users of financial statements than the information provided by deferred recognition. It also provides a more faithful representation of the financial effect of defined benefit plans on the entity and is easier for users to understand. In contrast, deferred recognition can produce misleading information: for example,

(a) an asset may be recognised in the statement of financial position, even when a plan is in deficit; or

(b) the statement of comprehensive income may include gains and losses that arise from economic events that occurred in past periods.

BC71 In addition, eliminating accounting options makes it easier for users to compare entities.

BC72 Most respondents supported the proposal to recognise all changes in the present value of the defined benefit obligation and in the fair value of plan assets when they occur. However, some respondents expressed concerns about immediate recognition:

(a) *Measurement model requires further work*—some respondents expressed the view that the measurement model needs a comprehensive review and that it would be disruptive to move to immediate recognition of changes arising from the measurement model in IAS 19. However, in the Board's view, deferred recognition makes accounting for defined benefit plans obscure and difficult for users to understand. Consequently, the Board decided not to delay the introduction of the requirement for immediate recognition.

(b) *Relevance of information*—some respondents expressed the view that some changes to the net defined benefit liability (asset) occurring in a period are not relevant to the measurement of a long-term liability. This is because past gains or losses may be offset by future losses or gains. However, in the Board's view it is not inevitable that future gains or losses will occur and offset past losses or gains.

(c) *Volatility*—many respondents were concerned that volatility might result if an entity reported all changes in the net defined benefit liability (asset) in each period and that this volatility would impede year-on-year comparability, and would obscure the profitability of the entity's core business. However, the Board believes that a measure should be volatile if it faithfully represents transactions and other events that are themselves volatile, and that financial statements should not omit such information. In the Board's view, that information should be presented in a way that is most useful to users of financial statements. Therefore, the Board introduced a presentation that allows users of financial statements to isolate remeasurements of the entity's net defined benefit liability (asset) (see paragraphs BC88–BC100).

(d) *Behavioural and social consequences*—some respondents expressed concerns that immediate recognition might have adverse behavioural and social consequences. For example, they were concerned that entities might try to eliminate short-term volatility by making long-term economically inefficient decisions about the allocation of plan assets, or by making socially undesirable amendments to plan terms. However, in the Board's view, it is not the responsibility of accounting standard-setters to encourage or discourage particular behaviour. Their responsibility is to set standards that result in the provision of relevant information that faithfully represents an entity's financial position, financial performance and cash flows so that users of that information can make well-informed decisions.

(e) *Potential effect on debt covenants*—some respondents were concerned that immediate recognition could lead to difficulties with debt covenants based on earnings or net assets, and impair entities' ability to pay dividends because of legal restrictions based on amounts in financial statements. In the Board's view, it is up to the entity and the holder of a covenant to determine whether to insulate a debt covenant from the effects of a new or amended accounting standard or to determine how they might renegotiate any existing covenant.

Components of defined benefit cost: service cost

BC73 The service cost component includes current service cost, past service cost and any gain or loss on settlement, but excludes changes in the defined benefit obligation that result from changes in demographic assumptions that are included in the remeasurements component together with other actuarial gains and losses. In the Board's view, including the effect of changes in demographic assumptions in the service cost component would combine amounts with different predictive values and, consequently, the service cost component is more relevant for assessing an entity's continuous operational costs if it does not include changes in past estimates of service cost. Most respondents agreed with the proposals in the 2010 ED that service cost should exclude changes in demographic assumptions.

Components of defined benefit cost: net interest

BC74   The amendments made in 2011 require an entity to calculate net interest on the net defined benefit liability (asset) using the same discount rate used to measure the defined benefit obligation (the net interest approach).

BC75   The amendments are consistent with the view that a net defined benefit liability is equivalent to a financing amount owed by the entity to the plan or to the employees. The economic cost of that financing is interest cost, calculated using the rate specified in paragraph 83. Similarly, a net defined benefit asset is an amount owed by the plan or by the employees to the entity. The entity accounts for the present value of economic benefits that it expects to receive from the plan or from the employees in the form of reductions in future contributions or as refunds. The entity discounts those economic benefits using the rate specified in paragraph 83.

BC76   In the Board's view, a net interest approach provides more understandable information than would be the case if finance income and expenses were to be determined separately on the plan assets and defined benefit obligation that combine to make a net defined benefit liability (asset). The net interest approach results in an entity recognising interest income when the plan has a surplus, and interest cost when the plan has a deficit.

BC77   The Board concluded that, in principle, the change in value of any asset can be divided into an amount that arises from the passage of time and amounts that arise from other changes. The interest cost on the defined benefit obligation arises from the passage of time. Consequently, the 2010 ED proposed that the net interest component of defined benefit cost should include not only the interest cost on the defined benefit obligation, but also the part of the return on plan assets that arises from the passage of time. In addition, the Board concluded that, to be consistent with the principle of separating components of defined benefit cost with different predictive implications, the net interest component should not include the part of the return on plan assets that does not arise from the passage of time.

BC78   The Board found it difficult to identify a practical method for identifying the change in the fair value of plan assets that arises from the passage of time, particularly for assets that do not bear explicit interest. The Board rejected approximations to this amount using:

(a)   the expected return on plan assets (as required by IAS 19 before the amendments made in 2011) because it could not be determined in an objective way, and because it might include a return that is not simply attributable to the passage of time; and

(b)   dividends (but not capital gains) received on equity plan assets and interest earned on debt plan assets. In the Board's view, dividends are not a faithful representation of the time value of money.

BC79   Consequently, the 2010 ED proposed that entities should calculate interest income on plan assets using the rate used to discount the defined benefit obligation. This approach produces interest income that is equivalent to determining a net interest on the net defined benefit liability (asset). The difference between the actual return on assets and the interest income on plan assets is included in the remeasurements component (see paragraph BC86).

BC80   Respondents generally agreed with the principle that the net interest component should include changes both in the defined benefit obligation and in plan assets that arise from the passage of time. However, some supported the approach proposed in the 2010 ED and others supported the expected return approach used in IAS 19 before the amendments made in 2011 (ie based on the expected return on plan assets).

BC81   The Board agreed with the views of respondents who reasoned that the net interest approach is a simple and pragmatic solution that is consistent with the presentation in the statement of financial position and, by reflecting the underlying economics of the net defined benefit liability (asset), provides more relevant and understandable information than the expected return approach. The net interest approach represents the economics of the entity's decision on how to finance the plan by reporting net interest income when the plan is in surplus and net interest expense when the plan is in deficit.

BC82   Respondents to the 2010 ED expressed concerns that:

(a)   plan assets may be made up of many different types of investments. The return on high quality corporate bonds would be arbitrary and would not be a faithful representation of the return that investors require or expect from each type of asset. However, in the Board's view, using the same rate as the rate used to discount the liability is a practical approach that:

(i)   would not require an entity to make a subjective judgement on how to divide the return on plan assets into an interest component and a remeasurement.

(ii)   results in amounts recognised in profit or loss that reflect the effect of the time value of money on both the defined benefit obligation and on plan assets. Consequently, the amounts recognised in profit or loss reflect the differences between funded and unfunded plans.

(b)   the requirements in paragraph 83 for determining the discount rate can result in economically similar defined benefit obligations being reported at different amounts, depending on whether there is a deep market in high quality corporate bonds. As noted in paragraph BC13, the Board considered improving the discount rate requirements of IAS 19, but decided to defer consideration of the discount rate until it decides whether to review measurement of the defined benefit obligation as a whole.

BC83   The Board considered the expected return approach, but noted that:

(a)   although the expected return approach is consistent with the discount rate used in the measurement of the plan assets at fair value, the net interest approach better represents the economics of the net defined benefit liability (asset) and consequently provides more comparable information on the changes in that net amount presented in the statement of financial position.

(b)   although the expected return approach is not theoretically more subjective than the net interest approach, in practice it is more likely that observable information will not be available to determine the expected return than is the case for the discount rate used for the net interest approach.

(c)   the expected return approach results in the reporting of the expected performance of the plan assets, regardless of their actual performance during the period. For a high risk investment, this has the effect of recognising the anticipated higher return in profit or loss, and the effect of higher risk in other comprehensive income. In contrast, the net interest approach recognises in other comprehensive income both the higher return and the effects of higher risk.

BC84   Supporters of both the net interest approach and the expected return approach reasoned that their favoured approach produces more relevant, comparable and understandable information. These contrasting views may reflect how different respondents consider the net defined benefit liability (asset) recognised in the statement of financial position as either comprising two components (the plan assets and the defined benefit obligation), which are measured separately but presented together (the gross view), or representing a single amount owed to, or from, the plan (the net view). These differences in views may also reflect differences in plan design, such as the degree of an entity's control over the plan assets. The expected return approach is more consistent with the gross view and the net interest approach is more consistent with the net view. The Board concluded that the net view is more consistent with the presentation of the net defined benefit liability (asset) in the statement of financial position, and therefore the disaggregation of the defined benefit cost in the statement of comprehensive income should also be based on the net view.

BC85   Supporters of both the net interest approach and the expected return approach reasoned that their approach does not provide an uneconomic incentive to invest assets in a particular way. In coming to its conclusion, the Board did not aim to encourage or discourage any particular behaviour, but considered which approach would provide the most relevant information that faithfully represents the changes in the plan assets and defined benefit obligation.

Components of defined benefit cost: remeasurements

BC86   As a result of the Board's decisions on the service cost and net interest components, the amendments made in 2011 define the remeasurement component as comprising:

(a)   actuarial gains and losses on the defined benefit obligation;

(b)   the return on plan assets, excluding amounts included in net interest on the net defined benefit liability (asset); and

(c)   any changes in the effect of the asset ceiling, excluding the amount included in net interest on the net defined benefit liability (asset).

BC87   The definition of remeasurements differs from the definition of actuarial gains and losses in IAS 19 before the amendments made in 2011 because the introduction of the net interest approach changed the disaggregation of the return on plan assets and the effect of the asset ceiling.

Components of defined benefit cost: recognition of the remeasurements component

BC88   As described in paragraphs BC70–BC72, the amendments made in 2011 eliminated deferred recognition. To distinguish the remeasurement component from service cost and net interest in an informative way, the 2010 ED proposed that entities should recognise the remeasurements component as an item of other comprehensive income, thus removing the previous option to recognise in profit or loss all changes in the net defined benefit liability (asset). The Board noted that although changes included in the remeasurements component may provide more information about the uncertainty and risk of future cash flows, they provide less information about the likely amount and timing of those cash flows.

BC89   Most respondents agreed with the proposal in the 2010 ED to recognise remeasurements in other comprehensive income. But some respondents expressed the following concerns:

    (a)   *Remeasurements in profit or loss*—some respondents did not support the proposal in the 2010 ED because, in their view:

        (i)   there is no conceptual basis for recognising amounts in other comprehensive income, thus recognition in profit or loss would be more appropriate.

        (ii)   the fact that the remeasurements component's predictive value is different from that of other components should not lead to the conclusion that this component should be recognised in other comprehensive income, but instead should indicate that there is a need to present this component as a separate line item in profit or loss.

        (iii)   if changes in assumptions are not recognised in profit or loss in the same way as service costs, this might encourage mis-estimation of service costs to achieve an accounting result.

    (b)   *Remeasurements option*—some respondents expressed the view that the Board should maintain the option to recognise remeasurements in profit or loss:

        (i)   because the Board should not eliminate this option until it develops a principle for determining which items should be recognised in profit or loss and which items should be recognised in other comprehensive income;

        (ii)   because recognising remeasurements in profit or loss is the conceptually best method;

        (iii)   to keep the accounting simple for entities with small plans; and

(iv) because recognising remeasurements in other comprehensive income may lead to an accounting mismatch (eg for an unfunded plan, if the entity holds assets to fund the obligation, and gains and losses on the assets are recognised in profit or loss).

(c) *Reclassification to profit or loss*—some respondents were concerned that amounts recognised in other comprehensive income are not reclassified to profit or loss in subsequent periods because:

(i) the amounts in other comprehensive income would never be recognised in profit or loss.

(ii) this change diverges from US generally accepted accounting principles (GAAP), because amounts in other comprehensive income under US GAAP are subsequently reclassified to profit or loss.

BC90 In finalising the amendments made in 2011, the Board confirmed the proposal made in the 2010 ED that an entity should recognise remeasurements in other comprehensive income. The Board acknowledged that the *Conceptual Framework* and IAS 1 do not describe a principle that would identify the items an entity should recognise in other comprehensive income rather than in profit or loss. However, the Board concluded that the most informative way to disaggregate the components of defined benefit cost with different predictive values is to recognise the remeasurements component in other comprehensive income.

BC91 The Board considered and rejected alternative approaches that would address some of the concerns expressed in paragraph BC89(a) and (b) for the reasons discussed in paragraphs BC92–BC98. Subsequent reclassification of amounts recognised in other comprehensive income to profit or loss is discussed in paragraph BC99.

Components of defined benefit cost: other approaches to recognising remeasurements

BC92 The Board considered the following alternatives for recognising the remeasurements component:

(a) previous options in IAS 19 for immediate recognition (paragraph BC93).

(b) recognition of all components in profit or loss (paragraphs BC94–BC96).

(c) a hybrid approach requiring recognition of the remeasurements component in other comprehensive income or profit or loss in different circumstances (paragraphs BC97 and BC98).

BC93 Before its amendment in 2011, IAS 19 permitted two methods for recognising actuarial gains and losses immediately: in profit or loss or in other comprehensive income. Many respondents to the 2010 ED suggested that the Board should permit an entity to recognise remeasurements either in profit or loss or in other comprehensive income. Retaining those options would have allowed entities with small plans to keep the accounting simple and would have allowed entities to eliminate the accounting mismatches noted in paragraph BC89(b). However, the Board concluded that eliminating options would improve financial reporting.

BC94 Some respondents to the 2010 ED expressed the view that entities should recognise all components of defined benefit cost within profit or loss, rather than using other comprehensive income for some items. They offered the following reasons for their position:

(a) Some indicated that the *Framework* and IAS 1 do not describe a principle that would identify the items an entity should recognise in other comprehensive income rather than in profit or loss.

(b) Some believe that an entity should show amounts relating to defined benefit plans in aggregate, as a single net amount arising from personnel or employment expense, in conformity with the presentation of a single net amount in the statement of financial position.

BC95 However, most respondents to the 2010 ED expressed the view that it would be inappropriate to recognise in profit or loss short-term fluctuations in an item that is long-term in nature. The Board concluded that in the light of the improved presentation of items of other comprehensive income in its amendment to IAS 1 issued in June 2011, the most informative way to disaggregate the components of defined benefit cost with different predictive values is to recognise the remeasurement component in other comprehensive income.

BC96 Many respondents urged the Board to carry out a project to identify what items of income and expense an entity should recognise in other comprehensive income, and whether an entity should subsequently reclassify items recognised in other comprehensive income to profit or loss. If the Board carries out such a project, the Board may need in due course to revisit its decisions on the recognition of the remeasurements component.

BC97 The Board noted that an accounting mismatch could arise for entities that hold assets to fund the obligation that do not qualify as plan assets because an entity would recognise changes in the defined benefit obligation in other comprehensive income, but changes in the carrying amount of those assets in profit or loss. The Board considered whether to permit (or perhaps require) entities to recognise the remeasurement component in profit or loss if that would reduce or eliminate an accounting mismatch from profit or loss.

BC98 However, the Board did not pursue such a hybrid approach because doing so would have required the Board to add significant complexity to the requirements in IAS 19 to address matters such as the following:

(a) introducing criteria to identify an accounting mismatch.

(b) determining whether to make such an election irrevocable, and whether an entity could revisit its election if there are changes in facts (such as in the case of a plan amendment, merger or plans switching between funded and unfunded status).

Components of defined benefit cost: reclassification to profit or loss

BC99 Both before and after the amendments made in 2011, IAS 19 prohibits subsequent reclassification of remeasurements from other comprehensive income to profit or loss. The Board prohibited such reclassification because:

(a) there is no consistent policy on reclassification to profit or loss in IFRSs, and it would have been premature to address this matter in the context of the amendments made to IAS 19 in 2011.

(b) it is difficult to identify a suitable basis to determine the timing and amount of such reclassifications.

Components of defined benefit cost: cumulative remeasurements

BC100 The 2010 ED proposed to carry forward the requirement that an entity should transfer amounts recognised in other comprehensive income directly to retained earnings. However, IFRSs do not define the phrase 'retained earnings' and the Board has not discussed what it should mean. Moreover, there exist jurisdiction-specific restrictions on components of equity. The amendments made in 2011 permit an entity to transfer the cumulative remeasurements within equity, and do not impose specific requirements on that transfer.

The asset ceiling

BC101 In some cases, paragraph 63 of IAS 19 requires an entity to recognise an asset. E54 proposed that the amount of the asset recognised should not exceed the aggregate of the present values of:

(a) any refunds expected from the plan; and

(b) any expected reduction in future contributions arising from the surplus.

In approving E54, IASC took the view that an entity should not recognise an asset at an amount that exceeds the present value of the future benefits that are expected to flow to the entity from that asset. This view was consistent with IASC's proposal in its exposure draft E55 *Impairment of Assets* that assets should not be carried at more than their recoverable amount. IAS 19 before its revision in 1998 contained no such restriction.

BC102 Some commentators argued that the limit in E54 was not operable because it would require an entity to make extremely subjective forecasts of expected refunds or reductions in contributions. In response to those comments, IASC agreed that the limit should reflect the available refunds or reductions in contributions.

An additional minimum liability

BC103 IASC considered whether it should require an entity to recognise an additional minimum liability where:

(a) an entity's immediate obligation if it discontinued a plan at the balance sheet date would be greater than the present value of the liability that would otherwise be recognised on the statement of financial position.

(b) vested post-employment benefits are payable at the date when an employee leaves the entity. Consequently, because of the effect of discounting, the present value of the vested benefit would be greater if an employee left immediately after the balance sheet date than if the employee completed the expected period of service.

(c) the present value of vested benefits exceeds the amount of the liability that would otherwise be recognised in the balance sheet. Before the amendments made to IAS 19 in 2011 this could have occurred where a large proportion of the benefits were fully vested and an entity had not recognised actuarial losses or past service cost.

BC104 One example of a requirement for an entity to recognise an additional minimum liability was in the US standard SFAS 87 *Employers' Accounting for Pensions*: the minimum liability was based on current salaries and excluded the effect of deferring some past service cost and actuarial gains and losses. If the minimum liability exceeded the obligation measured on the normal projected salary basis (with deferred recognition of some types of income and expense), the excess was recognised as an intangible asset (not exceeding the amount of any unamortised past service cost, with any further excess deducted directly from equity) and as an additional minimum liability.

BC105 IASC believed that such additional measures of the liability were potentially confusing and did not provide relevant information. They would also conflict with the *Framework*'s assumption that the entity is a going concern and with its definition of a liability. IAS 19 does not require the recognition of an additional minimum liability. Some of the circumstances discussed in the preceding two paragraphs might have given rise to contingent liabilities requiring disclosure under IAS 37.

Recognition of defined benefit cost as part of an asset: amendments issued in 2011

BC106 IAS 19 requires an entity to recognise defined benefit costs as income or expense unless another IFRS requires or permits their inclusion in the cost of an asset. Some respondents to the 2010 ED asked the Board to clarify whether remeasurements recognised in other comprehensive income result in income or expense that is eligible for inclusion in the cost of an asset. Some respondents said that recognising remeasurements as part of an asset and then recognising that asset as an expense in profit or loss would be inconsistent with the Board's conclusion that reclassification from other comprehensive income to profit or loss should be prohibited.

BC107 In relation to determining the cost of an asset, IFRSs include no principle distinguishing between income and expense presented in profit or loss and income and expense recognised in other comprehensive income. In the Board's view, whether an item is included in the cost of an asset depends on its nature and whether it meets the definition of cost in the relevant IFRS for that asset. Furthermore, in the Board's view this would be consistent with its conclusions on the reclassification of amounts recognised in other comprehensive income because amounts recognised as part of an asset would not be recognised in other comprehensive income first. Accordingly, the Board added no further guidance on this matter.

Actuarial valuation method

BC108 IAS 19 before its revision in 1998 permitted both accrued benefit valuation methods (benchmark treatment) and projected benefit valuation methods (allowed alternative treatment). The two groups of methods were based on fundamentally different, and incompatible, views of the objectives of accounting for employee benefits:

(a) **accrued benefit methods** (sometimes known as 'benefit', 'unit credit' or 'single premium' methods) determine the present value of employee benefits attributable to service to date; but

(b) **projected benefit methods** (sometimes described as 'cost', 'level contribution' or 'level premium' methods) project the estimated total obligation at retirement and then calculate a level funding cost, taking into account investment earnings, that will provide the total benefit at retirement.

BC109 The two methods may have similar effects on the income statement, but only by chance or if the number and age distribution of participating employees remain relatively stable over time. There can be significant differences in the measurement of liabilities under the two groups of methods. For these reasons, IASC believed that a requirement to use a single group of methods would significantly enhance comparability.

BC110 IASC considered whether it should continue to permit projected benefit methods as an allowed alternative treatment while introducing a new requirement to disclose information equivalent to the use of an accrued benefit method. However, IASC believed that disclosure cannot rectify inappropriate accounting in the balance sheet and income statement. IASC concluded that projected benefit methods were not appropriate, and should be eliminated, because such methods:

(a) focus on future events (future service) as well as past events, whereas accrued benefit methods focus only on past events;

(b) generate a liability that does not represent a measure of any real amount and can be described only as the result of cost allocations; and

(c) do not attempt to measure fair value and cannot, therefore, be used in a business combination, as required by IAS 22 *Business Combinations*.[4] If an entity used an accrued benefit method in a business combination, it would not be feasible for the entity to use a projected benefit method to account for the same obligation in subsequent periods.

BC111 IAS 19 before its revision in 1998 did not specify which forms of accrued benefit valuation method should be permitted under the benchmark treatment. IAS 19 as revised in 1998 required a single accrued benefit method: the most widely used accrued benefit method, which is known as the projected unit credit method (sometimes known as the 'accrued benefit method pro-rated on service' or as the 'benefit/years of service method').

BC112 IASC acknowledged that the elimination of projected benefit methods, and of accrued benefit methods other than the projected unit credit method, had cost implications. However, with modern computing power, it would be only

---

4 IAS 22 was withdrawn in 2004 and replaced by IFRS 3 *Business Combinations*.

marginally more expensive to run a valuation on two different bases and the advantages of improved comparability would outweigh the additional cost.

BC113 An actuary may sometimes recommend, for example in the case of a closed fund, a method other than the projected unit credit method for funding purposes. Nevertheless, IASC agreed to require the use of the projected unit credit method in all cases because that method was more consistent with the accounting objectives laid down in IAS 19 as revised in 1998.

Attributing benefit to periods of service

BC114 As explained in paragraph BC54, IASC believed that an entity has an obligation under a defined benefit plan when an employee has rendered service in return for the benefits promised under the plan. IASC considered three alternative methods of accounting for a defined benefit plan that attributes different amounts of benefit to different periods:

(a) apportion the entire benefit on a straight-line basis over the entire period to the date when further service by the employee will lead to no material amount of further benefits under the plan, other than from further salary increases.

(b) apportion benefit under the plan's benefit formula. However, a straight-line basis should be used if the plan's benefit formula attributes a materially higher benefit to later years.

(c) apportion the benefit that vests at each interim date on a straight-line basis over the period between that date and the previous interim vesting date.

The three methods are illustrated by the following two examples.

BC Example 2

A plan provides a benefit of CU400 if an employee retires after more than ten and less than twenty years of service and a further benefit of CU100 (CU500 in total) if an employee retires after twenty or more years of service.

The amounts attributed to each year are as follows:

	Years 1–10	Years 11–20
Method (a)	25	25
Method (b)	40	10
Method (c)	40	10

BC Example 3

A plan provides a benefit of CU100 if an employee retires after more than ten and less than twenty years of service and a further benefit of CU400 (CU500 in total) if an employee retires after twenty or more years of service.

The amounts attributed to each year are as follows:

	Years 1–10	Years 11–20
Method (a)	25	25
Method (b)	25	25
Method (c)	10	40

Note: this plan attributes a higher benefit to later years, whereas the plan in BC Example 2 attributes a higher benefit to earlier years.

BC115   In approving E54, IASC adopted method (a) on the grounds that this method was the most straightforward and that there were no compelling reasons to attribute different amounts of benefit to different years, as would occur under either of the other methods.

BC116   A significant minority of commentators on E54 favoured following the benefit formula (or alternatively, if the standard were to retain straight-line attribution, the recognition of a minimum liability based on the benefit formula). IASC agreed with these comments and decided to require the method described in paragraph BC114(b).

Attributing benefit to periods of service: exposure draft published in 2010

BC117   Paragraph 70 requires an entity to attribute benefits on a straight-line basis if an employee's service in later years will lead to a materially higher level of benefit than in earlier years. If a benefit formula is expressed as a constant proportion of current salary, some believe that expected future salary increases are not included in determining whether the benefit formula allocates a higher level of benefit in later years.

BC118   However, if that view is taken, the attribution for career average salary benefits (benefits described as a percentage of the average salary multiplied by the number of years of service) would differ from the attribution for current salary benefits (benefits described as a percentage of current salary), even though such benefits could be the same economically. In the Board's view, benefits that are economically the same should be measured similarly regardless of how the benefit formula describes them. Consequently, the 2010 ED proposed that expected future salary increases should be included in determining whether a benefit formula expressed in terms of current salary allocates a materially higher level of benefit in later years.

BC119   Some respondents to the 2010 ED disagreed with that proposal for the reason that:

(a)   service in previous or subsequent periods does not change the benefit increment earned in a particular year; and

(b)   the fact that the entity remunerates later periods of service at higher levels is an intrinsic part of the plans and there is no reason for smoothing costs over all periods of service—they are not intended to remunerate for overall services on a straight-line basis.

BC120   The Board concluded that it should not address this issue at this stage because the issue is closely related to a fundamental review of the accounting for contribution-based promises that the Board decided was beyond the scope of the project (see paragraph BC13).

Actuarial assumptions—tax payable by the plan: amendments issued in 2011

BC121   The amendments made in 2011 clarify that:

(a)   the estimate of the defined benefit obligation includes the present value of taxes payable by the plan if they relate to service before the reporting date or are imposed on benefits resulting from that service, and

(b)   other taxes should be included as a reduction to the return on plan assets.

BC122   The Board noted that IAS 19 requires an entity to estimate the ultimate cost of providing long-term employee benefits. Thus, if the plan is required to pay taxes when it ultimately provides benefits, the taxes payable will be part of the ultimate cost. Similarly, the ultimate cost would include any taxes payable by the plan when the contribution relates to service before the period (such as in the case of contributions to reduce a deficit).

BC123   Some respondents to the 2010 ED asked the Board to address:

(a)   country-specific tax regimes;

(b)   taxes paid by the employer; and

(c)   taxes on the return on plan assets.

BC124   However, the Board noted that a wide variety of taxes on pension costs exists worldwide and it is a matter of judgement whether they are income taxes within the scope of IAS 12 *Income Taxes*, costs of liabilities within the scope of IAS 37, or costs of employee benefits within the scope of IAS 19. Given the variety of tax arrangements, the Board decided that it could not address issues beyond those relating to taxes payable by the plan itself in a reasonable period of time and therefore did not address them in the amendment made in 2011.

Actuarial assumptions—administration costs: amendments issued in 2011

BC125   The amendments made in 2011 require administration costs to be recognised when the administration services are provided, with costs relating to the management of plan assets deducted from the return on plan assets. Before those amendments, IAS 19 required that costs of administering the plan, other than those included in the actuarial assumptions used to measure the defined benefit obligation, should be deducted from the return on plan assets. But IAS 19 did not specify which costs should be included in those actuarial assumptions.

BC126   In the Board's view, the treatment of plan administration costs should depend on the nature of those costs. Therefore, the 2010 ED proposed that:

(a)   costs of managing plan assets should be the only administration costs that are deducted in determining the return on plan assets (that is part of the remeasurements component). Other administration costs, eg the cost of administering benefit payments, are unrelated to the plan assets.

(b)   the present value of the defined benefit obligation should include the present value of costs relating to the administration of benefits attributable to current or past service. This is consistent with the measurement objective that the defined benefit obligation should be determined on the basis of the ultimate cost of the benefits.

BC127   Respondents to the 2010 ED raised practical concerns, including how entities should identify and estimate costs of managing plan assets and other administration services, and how the other administration services costs should be allocated to current, past and future service. In response to those concerns, the Board decided that an entity should recognise administration costs when the administration services are provided. This practical expedient avoids the need to attribute costs between current and past service and future service.

BC128   In some cases, a total fee is charged for both managing plan assets and other administration services, but in the Board's view the cost of managing plan assets would not be excessively costly or difficult to estimate under these circumstances. An entity could estimate such costs by estimating the administration costs if there were no plan assets, or by observing the prices for such services in the market.

Actuarial assumptions—discount rate

BC129   One of the most important issues in measuring defined benefit obligations is the selection of the criteria used to determine the discount rate. According to IAS 19 before its revision in 1998, the discount rate that was assumed in determining the actuarial present value of promised retirement benefits reflected the long-term rates, or an approximation thereto, at which such obligations were expected to be settled. IASC rejected the use of such a rate because it was not relevant for an entity that does not contemplate settlement and it was an artificial construct, because there may be no market for settlement of such obligations.

BC130 Some believe that, for funded benefits, the discount rate should be the expected rate of return on the plan assets actually held by a plan, because the return on plan assets represents faithfully the expected ultimate cash outflow (ie future contributions). IASC rejected this approach because the fact that a fund has chosen to invest in particular kinds of asset does not affect the nature or amount of the obligation. In particular, assets with a higher expected return carry more risk and an entity should not recognise a smaller liability merely because the plan has chosen to invest in riskier assets with a higher expected return. Consequently, the measurement of the obligation should be independent of the measurement of any plan assets actually held by a plan.

BC131 The most significant decision was whether the discount rate should be a risk-adjusted rate (one that attempts to capture the risks associated with the obligation). Some expressed the view that the most appropriate risk-adjusted rate is given by the expected return on an appropriate portfolio of plan assets that would, over the long term, provide an effective hedge against such an obligation. An appropriate portfolio might include:

(a) fixed interest securities for obligations to former employees to the extent that the obligations are not linked, in form or in substance, to inflation;

(b) index-linked securities for index-linked obligations to former employees; and

(c) equity securities for benefit obligations towards current employees that are linked to final pay. This is based on the view that the long-term performance of equity securities is correlated with general salary progression in the economy as a whole and hence with the final-pay element of a benefit obligation.

It is important to note that the portfolio actually held need not necessarily be an appropriate portfolio in this sense. Indeed, in some countries, regulatory constraints may prevent plans from holding an appropriate portfolio. For example, in some countries, plans are required to hold a specified proportion of their assets in the form of fixed interest securities. Furthermore, if an appropriate portfolio is a valid reference point, it is equally valid for both funded and unfunded plans.

BC132 Those who support using the interest rate on an appropriate portfolio as a risk-adjusted discount rate argue that:

(a) portfolio theory suggests that the expected return on an asset (or the interest rate inherent in a liability) is related to the undiversifiable risk associated with that asset (or liability). Undiversifiable risk reflects not the variability of the returns (payments) in absolute terms but the correlation of the returns (or payments) with the returns on other assets. If cash inflows from a portfolio of assets react to changing economic conditions over the long term in the same way as the cash outflows of a defined benefit obligation, the undiversifiable risk of the obligation (and hence the appropriate discount rate) must be the same as that of the portfolio of assets.

(b)   an important aspect of the economic reality underlying final salary plans is the correlation between final salary and equity returns that arises because they both reflect the same long-term economic forces. Although the correlation is not perfect, it is sufficiently strong that ignoring it will lead to systematic overstatement of the liability. In addition, ignoring this correlation will result in misleading volatility due to short-term fluctuations between the rate used to discount the obligation and the discount rate that is implicit in the fair value of the plan assets. These factors will deter entities from operating defined benefit plans and lead to switches from equities to fixed-interest investments. Where defined benefit plans are largely funded by equities, this could have a serious impact on share prices. This switch will also increase the cost of pensions. There will be pressure on companies to remove the apparent (but non-existent) shortfall.

(c)   if an entity settled its obligation by purchasing an annuity, the insurance company would determine the annuity rates by looking to a portfolio of assets that provides cash inflows that substantially offset all the cash flows from the benefit obligation as those cash flows fall due. Consequently, the expected return on an appropriate portfolio measures the obligation at an amount that is close to its market value. In practice, it is not possible to settle a final pay obligation by buying annuities because no insurance company would insure a final pay decision that remained at the discretion of the person insured. However, evidence can be derived from the purchase or sale of businesses that include a final salary pension scheme. In this situation the vendor and purchaser would negotiate a price for the pension obligation by reference to its present value, discounted at the rate of return on an appropriate portfolio.

(d)   although investment risk is present even in a well-diversified portfolio of equity securities, any general decline in securities would, in the long term, be reflected in declining salaries. Because employees accepted that risk by agreeing to a final salary plan, the exclusion of that risk from the measurement of the obligation would introduce a systematic bias into the measurement.

(e)   time-honoured funding practices in some countries use the expected return on an appropriate portfolio as the discount rate. Although funding considerations are distinct from accounting issues, the long history of this approach calls for careful scrutiny of any other proposed approach.

BC133   Those who oppose a risk-adjusted rate argue that:

(a)   it is incorrect to look at returns on assets in determining the discount rate for liabilities.

(b) if a sufficiently strong correlation between asset returns and final pay actually existed, a market for final salary obligations would develop, yet this has not happened. Furthermore, where any such apparent correlation does exist, it is not clear whether the correlation results from shared characteristics of the portfolio and the obligations or from changes in the contractual pension promise.

(c) the return on equity securities does not correlate with other risks associated with defined benefit plans, such as variability in mortality, timing of retirement, disability and adverse selection.

(d) in order to evaluate a liability with uncertain cash flows, an entity would normally use a discount rate lower than the risk-free rate, but the expected return on an appropriate portfolio is higher than the risk-free rate.

(e) the assertion that final salary is strongly correlated with asset returns implies that final salary will tend to decrease if asset prices fall, yet experience shows that salaries tend not to decline.

(f) the notion that equities are not risky in the long term, and the associated notion of long-term value, are based on the fallacious view that the market always bounces back after a crash. Shareholders do not get credit in the market for any additional long-term value if they sell their shares today. Even if some correlation exists over long periods, benefits must be paid as they become due. An entity that funds its obligations with equity securities runs the risk that equity prices may be down when benefits must be paid. In addition, the hypothesis that the real return on equities is uncorrelated with inflation does not mean that equities offer a risk-free return, even in the long term.

(g) the expected long-term rate of return on an appropriate portfolio cannot be determined sufficiently objectively in practice to provide an adequate basis for an accounting standard. The practical difficulties include specifying the characteristics of the appropriate portfolio, selecting the time horizon for estimating returns on the portfolio and estimating those returns.

BC134 IASC had not identified clear evidence that the expected return on an appropriate portfolio of assets provides a relevant and reliable indication of the risks associated with a defined benefit obligation, or that such a rate can be determined with reasonable objectivity. Consequently, IASC decided that the discount rate should reflect the time value of money, but should not attempt to capture those risks. Furthermore, the discount rate should not reflect the entity's own credit rating, because otherwise an entity with a lower credit rating would recognise a smaller liability. IASC decided that the rate that best achieves these objectives is the yield on high quality corporate bonds. In countries where there is no deep market in such bonds, the yield on government bonds should be used.

BC135 Another issue was whether the discount rate should be the long-term average rate, based on past experience over a number of years, or the current market yield at the balance sheet date for an obligation of the appropriate term. Those who supported a long-term average rate expressed the view that:

(a) a long-term approach is consistent with the transaction-based historical cost approach that was either required or permitted by other International Accounting Standards.

(b) point in time estimates aim at a level of precision that is not attainable in practice and lead to volatility in reported profit that may not be a faithful representation of changes in the obligation, but may simply reflect an unavoidable inability to predict accurately the future events that are anticipated in making period-to-period measurements.

(c) for an obligation based on final salary, neither market annuity prices nor simulation by discounting expected future cash flows can determine an unambiguous annuity price.

(d) over the long term, a suitable portfolio of plan assets may provide a reasonably effective hedge against an employee benefit obligation that increases in line with salary growth. However, there is much less assurance that, at a given measurement date, market interest rates will match the salary growth built into the obligation.

BC136 IASC decided that the discount rate should be determined by reference to market yields at the balance sheet date, because:

(a) there is no rational basis for expecting efficient market prices to drift towards any assumed long-term average, because prices in a market of sufficient liquidity and depth incorporate all publicly available information and are more relevant and reliable than an estimate of long-term trends by any individual market participant.

(b) the cost of benefits attributed to service during the current period should reflect prices of that period.

(c) if expected future benefits are defined in terms of projected future salaries that reflect current estimates of future inflation rates, the discount rate should be based on current market interest rates (in nominal terms), because these also reflect current market expectations of inflation rates.

(d) if plan assets are measured at a current value (ie fair value), the related obligation should be discounted at a current discount rate in order to avoid introducing irrelevant volatility through a difference in the measurement basis.

BC137 The reference to market yields at the balance sheet date did not mean that short-term discount rates should be used to discount long-term obligations. IAS 19 requires that the discount rate should reflect market yields (at the balance sheet date) on bonds with an expected term that is consistent with the expected term of the obligations.

Actuarial assumptions—discount rate: exposure draft published in 2009

BC138   The discount rate requirements in IAS 19 may result in an entity reporting a significantly higher defined benefit obligation in a jurisdiction that does not have a deep market in high quality corporate bonds than it would in a similar jurisdiction that does have a deep market in such bonds, even when the underlying obligations are very similar.

BC139   To address this issue, in August 2009 the Board published an exposure draft *Discount Rate for Employee Benefits*, that proposed eliminating the requirement to use a government bond rate if there is no deep market in high quality corporate bonds. However, responses to that exposure draft indicated that the proposed amendment raised more complex issues than had been expected. After considering those responses, the Board decided not to proceed with the proposals but to address issues relating to the discount rate only in the context of a fundamental review (see paragraph BC13(b)).

Actuarial assumptions—salaries, benefits and medical costs

BC140   Some argue that estimates of future increases in salaries, benefits and medical costs should not affect the measurement of assets and liabilities until they are granted, on the grounds that:

(a)   future increases are future events; and

(b)   such estimates are too subjective.

BC141   IASC believed that the assumptions were used not to determine whether an obligation exists, but to measure an existing obligation on a basis that provides the most relevant measure of the estimated outflow of resources. If no increase was assumed, this was an implicit assumption that no change will occur and it would be misleading to assume no change if an entity did expect a change. IAS 19 maintains the requirement in IAS 19 before its revision in 1998 that measurement should take account of estimated future salary increases. IASC also believed that increases in future medical costs can be estimated with sufficient reliability to justify incorporation of those estimated increases in the measurement of the obligation.

Actuarial assumptions—mortality: amendments issued in 2011

BC142   The amendments made in 2011 make explicit that the mortality assumptions used to determine the defined benefit obligation are current estimates of the expected mortality rates of plan members, both during and after employment. In the Board's view, current mortality tables might need to be adjusted for expected changes in mortality (such as expected mortality improvement) to provide the best estimate of the amount that reflects the ultimate cost of settling the defined benefit obligation.

Actuarial assumptions—risk-sharing: amendments issued in 2011

BC143   The amendments made in 2011 clarify that:

(a)   the effect of employee and third-party contributions should be considered in determining the defined benefit cost, the present value of the defined benefit obligation and the measurement of any reimbursement rights.

(b)   the benefit to be attributed to periods of service in accordance with paragraph 70 of IAS 19 is net of the effect of any employee contributions in respect of service.[5]

(c)   any conditional indexation should be reflected in the measurement of the defined benefit obligation, whether the indexation or changes in benefits are automatic or are subject to a decision by the employer, the employee or a third party, such as trustees or administrators of the plan.

(d)   if any limits exist on the legal and constructive obligation to pay additional contributions, the present value of the defined benefit obligation should reflect those limits.

BC144   Some defined benefit plans include features that share the benefits of a surplus or the cost of a deficit between the employer and the plan participants. Similarly, some defined benefit plans provide benefits that are conditional to some extent on whether there are sufficient assets in the plan to fund them. Such features share risk between the entity and the plan participants and affect the ultimate cost of the benefits. Hence, the 2010 ED proposed to clarify that the present value of the defined benefit obligation should reflect the best estimate of the effect of risk-sharing and conditional indexation features. Many respondents agreed with that proposal.

BC145   However, some respondents expressed doubts about whether the proposals could adequately address risk-sharing features because of the existing defined benefit and defined contribution distinction and because of the existing measurement model for defined benefit plans. They suggested that the Board should not address risk-sharing features until it conducted a fundamental review of classification and measurement in order to address the whole spectrum of plans from defined contribution to defined benefit (including contribution-based promises). However, the Board observed that the current model is based on the ultimate cost of the benefit, and thus should be able to take into account risk-sharing features that reduce the ultimate cost of the benefit to the entity.

BC146   Many respondents requested further clarification on:

(a)   conditional indexation (paragraphs BC147–BC149); and

(b)   other points (paragraph BC150).

---

5   *Defined Benefit Plans: Employee Contributions*, issued in November 2013, clarified the requirements that relate to how contributions from employees or third parties that are linked to service should be attributed to periods of service. In addition, it permits a practical expedient if the amount of the contributions is independent of the number of years of service. See paragraphs BC150G–BC150Q.

Conditional indexation

BC147   Some defined benefit plans provide conditional indexation (such as additional benefits contingent on returns on plan assets). In general, according to paragraph 88, the measurement of the benefit obligation must reflect the best estimate of any future effect of such conditional indexation. However, some respondents noted that the strict separation of the measurement of plan assets and liabilities under IAS 19 results in a mismatch: the conditional indexation is included in the present value of the defined benefit obligation, but not in the measurement of the plan assets. Some argue that the effect of conditional indexation should not be included in the measurement of the liability until the underlying returns are included in the measurement of the plan assets.

BC148   In the Board's view, projecting the benefit on the basis of current assumptions of future investment performance (or other criteria to which the benefits are indexed) is consistent with estimating the ultimate cost of the benefit, which is the objective of the measurement of the defined benefit obligation, as stated in paragraph 76. The Board also considered other changes to the measurement approach, such as using option pricing techniques to capture the effect of the conditional indexation in a manner consistent with the fair value of the plan assets. However, the Board rejected those alternatives because they would require changing the fundamental measurement of the defined benefit obligation. The Board noted that concerns regarding measurement of benefits with conditional indexation are similar to concerns regarding the measurement of contribution-based promises discussed in its 2008 discussion paper. Addressing these concerns was beyond the scope of the amendments made in 2011.

BC149   Some respondents interpreted the 2010 ED as proposing that in determining the effect of conditional indexation, an entity would be required to project the future funding position (on the basis used to set contribution rates) and then establish the effect that the funding level might have on future benefits and contribution requirements. These respondents believe that projecting the funding position would involve a significant amount of additional work and that in most regions it would be very difficult to establish a suitable adjustment to the liabilities to reflect the effect of conditional indexation based on the funding position. In the Board's view, an entity should estimate the likely conditional indexation of benefits based on the current funding status of the plan, consistently with how financial assumptions are determined in accordance with paragraph 80. Paragraph 80 requires financial assumptions to be based on market expectations at the end of the reporting period for the period over which the obligations are to be settled.

Other clarifications

BC150   The Board clarified the following points in the light of responses to the 2010 ED:

(a)   Contributions from employees in respect of service should be attributed to periods of service in accordance with paragraph 70 using the benefit formula, or on a straight-line basis (ie the back-end loading test and attribution in paragraph 70 should be based on the net benefit).[6] This reflects the Board's view that contributions from employees can be viewed as a negative benefit. In addition, the Board noted that a portion of future employee contributions may be connected with salary increases included in the defined benefit obligation. Applying the same method of attribution to that portion of the contribution and the salary increases avoids an inconsistency.

(b)   An entity would apply judgement in determining whether a change in an input is a change in the terms of the benefit (resulting in past service cost) or a change in an assumption (resulting in an actuarial gain or loss). This clarification is consistent with guidance that existed in IAS 19 before 2011, describing how to address employee contributions for medical costs.

(c)   The best estimate of the ultimate cost of the benefits reflects the best estimate of the effect of terms of the plan that require or allow a change to the level of benefit, or that provide other benefit options, regardless of whether the benefits are adjustable by the entity, by the managers of the plan, or by the employees.

(d)   The measurement of the defined benefit obligation takes account of the effect of any limit on contributions by the employer (see paragraph 91). In the Board's view, this is consistent with the objective of determining the ultimate cost of the benefits. The Board concluded that the effect of such a limit should be determined over the shorter of the expected life of the plan and the expected life of the entity. Determining the limit over a period longer than the current period is necessary to identify whether the effect of the limit is temporary or permanent. For example, the service cost may be higher than the maximum contribution amount in the current period, but if in subsequent years the service cost is lower than the contribution amount, then the effect of the limit is more of a deferral of current period contributions than a limit on the total contributions required.

(e)   The amendments relating to risk-sharing are not intended to be limited to particular relationships. Some respondents noted that some plans' risks are shared not only with employees, but also with other parties (such as the government). In the Board's view, an entity should consider such arrangements in determining the defined benefit obligation. Nevertheless, entities need to consider whether those contributions are reimbursements as described in paragraphs 116–119 (and therefore must be recognised as reimbursement rights) or reductions in the defined benefit obligation.

---

6   *Defined Benefit Plans: Employee Contributions*, issued in November 2013, clarified the requirements that relate to how contributions from employees or third parties that are linked to service should be attributed to periods of service. In addition, it permits a practical expedient if the amount of the contributions is independent of the number of years of service. See paragraphs BC150G–BC150Q.

Actuarial assumptions—discount rate: regional market issue

BC150A The Board was asked to clarify the requirements of IAS 19 to determine the discount rate in a regional market sharing the same currency (for example, the Eurozone). The issue arose because some think that the basket of high quality corporate bonds should be determined at a country level, and not at a currency level, because paragraph 83 of IAS 19 states that in countries in which there is no deep market in such bonds, the market yields at the end of the reporting period on government bonds shall be used.

BC150B The Board noted that paragraph 83 of IAS 19 states that the currency and term of the corporate bonds or government bonds shall be consistent with the currency and estimated term of the post-employment benefit obligations.

BC150C The Board decided to amend paragraph 83 of IAS 19 in order to clarify that the depth of the market for high quality corporate bonds should be assessed at a currency level.

BC150D Some respondents to the Exposure Draft *Annual Improvements to IFRSs 2012–2014 Cycle* (the '2013 Annual Improvements Exposure Draft'), published in December 2013, suggested to the Board that it should clarify the objectives and the rationale underlying the selection and use of the discount rate for post-employment benefit obligations. The Board noted that the IFRS Interpretations Committee (the 'Interpretations Committee') had already discussed a potential broader amendment relating to the discount rate and, after several meetings, recommended that the determination of the discount rate for post-employment benefit obligations should be addressed in the Board's research project on discount rates.

BC150E Some respondents to the 2013 Annual Improvements Exposure Draft suggested to the Board that it should clarify whether the proposed amendment prohibits an entity that operates in a country/regional market in which there is a deep market for high quality corporate bonds from using only the high quality corporate bonds issued in its own country/regional market. The Board noted that the amendment only clarifies that the depth of the market for high quality corporate bonds should be assessed at a currency level and not a country/regional market level. It does not require that the basket of high quality corporate bonds used to determine the discount rate for post-employment obligations must include all the high quality corporate bonds issued in a currency.

BC150F Some respondents to the 2013 Annual Improvements Exposure Draft expressed concerns about the potential effects of the amendment on countries that have adopted a currency as their official or legal currency without being members of a regional market or part of one with a common currency. They think that the proposed amendment could result in anomalous outcomes in these countries, because a discount rate determined from high quality corporate bonds denominated in a stronger currency could be inconsistent with the inflation rate (and the other assumptions) used in these countries to determine the cost of providing post-employment benefits. The Board noted that this anomaly is not unique to the fact pattern raised. Instead, inflation rates in one location may be different to those in another, even if they are in the same country, state or regional market with a shared currency. In the Board's view, an analysis of the potential effect of the amendment would not provide useful additional information. The Board concluded that the amendment is an improvement that should not be delayed for a narrow range of situations that the Board had already considered in proposing the amendment.

Contributions from employees or third parties: amendments issued in 2013

BC150G   In 2012, the Interpretations Committee received two submissions that requested clarification of the accounting requirements set out in paragraph 93 of IAS 19 for contributions from employees or third parties.

BC150H   The Interpretations Committee considered whether some types of contributions from employees or third parties to a defined benefit plan should reduce the cost of short-term employee benefits instead of reducing the cost of post-employment benefits.   The Interpretations Committee observed that the wording in paragraph 93 of IAS 19 appeared to suggest that all employee contributions that are linked to service should be attributed to periods of service as a reduction of service cost (ie as a negative benefit). However, employee contributions that are linked solely to the employee's service rendered in the same period in which those contributions are payable (for example, contributions that are a fixed percentage of salary throughout the period of the employment) might also be considered to be a reduction of the cost of short-term employee benefits (ie a reduction in salary).   Consequently, the Interpretations Committee recommended to the IASB that it should amend IAS 19 regarding the accounting for such contributions.

BC150I   In the IASB's view, contributions from employees or third parties that are required by the terms of a defined benefit plan should form part of the post-employment benefit rather than the short-term employee benefit. Consequently, such contributions should be attributed to periods of service as a reduction of service cost (ie as a negative benefit). However, the IASB acknowledged the general concern about the complexity of the required calculations that could result from the requirement to attribute the net benefit to periods of service. The IASB thus concluded that the costs of applying the attribution requirements to some simple types of contributory plans outweighed the benefits and so the IASB decided to add a practical expedient to paragraph 93.

BC150J   Consequently, in March 2013, the IASB published the Exposure Draft ED/2013/4 Defined Benefit Plans: Employee Contributions ('ED/2013/4'), which proposed amendments to paragraph 93 of IAS 19. In ED/2013/4 the IASB proposed that some contributions from employees or third parties may be excluded from being attributed to periods of service as a negative benefit.   Instead, those contributions could be recognised as a reduction in the service cost in the period in which they are payable if, and only if, they are linked solely to the employee's service rendered in that period. An example of such a situation would be contributions based on an employee's salary at a fixed percentage that does not depend on the number of years of service by the employee to the employer. On the other hand, if an employee is required to contribute a higher percentage of salary in later years of service, then the contributions are not linked solely to the employee's service that is rendered in the period in which the contributions are payable.

BC150K   When developing ED/2013/4, the IASB observed that paragraph 93 first states that contributions from employees or third parties in respect of service are attributed to periods of service as a negative benefit in accordance with paragraph 70, and then states that the net benefit is attributed in accordance with paragraph 70. The references to both the negative benefit and net benefit might cause confusion as to whether the back-end loading test in paragraph 70 is required to be performed on the net benefit, or on the gross benefit and the negative benefit separately. The IASB observed that performing the test on the net benefit would add complexity and that the outcome of that test would differ from the outcome of performing the test on the gross benefit and the negative benefit separately. Consequently, the IASB proposed to specify in paragraph 93 that the contributions from employees or third parties that are not solely linked to current-year service should be attributed to periods of service using the same method of attribution as the gross benefit in accordance with paragraph 70.

BC150L   A total of 63 respondents commented on ED/2013/4. The majority of respondents supported the proposed amendments, but about half of them requested either further clarification of the scope of the practical expedient or the addition of application guidance or examples.

BC150M   Some respondents requested clarification of whether they could apply the proposed practical expedient if the amount of the contributions depended on the employee's age instead of the number of years of service (age-based contributions). The IASB observed that examples illustrating the proposed practical expedient in ED/2013/4 implied two criteria—one is whether contributions are a fixed percentage of salary and the other is whether the contributions are independent of the number of years of service.

BC150N   The IASB considered whether contributions should have to meet either or both of the criteria to qualify for the practical expedient. In some circumstances, age-based contributions could approximate contributions that depend on the number of years of service, because both of the contribution formulas depend on time. However, age-based contributions are independent of the number of years of service. For example, the terms of a plan require employee contributions of four per cent of salary for the first ten years and then six per cent thereafter. The increase to six per cent is not only related to the service in the current year, but is also related to the first ten years of service, which is a prerequisite for the change in the contribution percentage. If the terms of the plan required employee contributions of four per cent of salary if the employee was 30 years old or younger and six per cent if the employee was more than 30 years old, then an employee would be required to contribute either four per cent or six per cent regardless of the length of their service. In other words, the contributions paid for each year are not dependent on prior service.

BC150O   Consequently, the IASB decided that the practical expedient should be permitted if the amount of the contributions is independent of the number of years of service. This principle would also help to clarify whether the practical expedient would apply to other types of contribution arrangements, including contributions that are a fixed amount (as opposed to a fixed percentage) regardless of the number of years of service.

BC150P   One respondent to ED/2013/4 was concerned that some might interpret the requirements to attribute contributions from employees or third parties to periods of service to mean that the accumulated value of contributions should be deducted from both the defined benefit obligation and the plan assets. The IASB noted that the plan assets and the defined benefit obligation would increase by the amount of the contributions paid. This is because the contributions that are paid increase the employer's obligation to the employees even if those contributions are attributed to other periods of service to reflect the net cost to the employer.

BC150Q   When developing the amendments, the IASB observed that paragraph 94 sets out requirements for the accounting for changes in employee or third-party contributions. The IASB noted that the requirements in that paragraph apply to contributions that are attributed to periods of service using the same attribution method that is required by paragraph 70 for the gross benefit. Consequently, the IASB decided to amend paragraph 94 to clarify the scope of the requirements in that paragraph.

Curtailments and settlements

BC151   Under IAS 19 before its revision in 1998, curtailment and settlement gains were recognised when the curtailment or settlement occurred, but losses were recognised when it was probable that the curtailment or settlement would occur. IASC concluded that management's intention to curtail or settle a defined benefit plan was not a sufficient basis to recognise a loss. IAS 19 revised in 1998 required that curtailment and settlement losses, as well as gains, should be recognised when the curtailment or settlement occurs. The guidance on the recognition of curtailments and settlements conformed to the proposals in E59 *Provisions, Contingent Liabilities and Contingent Assets.*

Plan amendments, curtailments and settlements: amendments issued in 2011

BC152   The amendments made in 2011:

(a)   require immediate recognition of all past service cost (paragraphs BC154–BC159); and

(b)   amend the definitions of past service cost, curtailments and settlements (paragraphs BC160–BC163).

BC153   The Board also considered other approaches to account for plan amendments and settlements (paragraphs BC164–BC173).

Immediate recognition—past service cost

BC154   The amendments made in 2011 require an entity to recognise both vested and unvested past service cost in the period of the plan amendment that gives rise to the past service cost. Before that amendment, IAS 19 required immediate recognition for *vested* past service cost and recognition over the vesting period for *unvested* past service cost.

BC155   Many respondents to the 2010 ED supported the proposal for immediate recognition of unvested past service cost. Other respondents objected to the proposal for the reasons set out below:

(a)   Most plan amendments are initiated with the intention of benefiting the entity in future periods. Moreover, the principle in IAS 19 is that employee benefit expense is recognised in the period when the employee must provide the service needed to qualify for the benefit. It would be more consistent with that principle to require recognition of unvested past service cost over the remaining service periods until vesting.

(b)   Recognising unvested past service cost over the vesting period would be consistent with what the Board thought were the best conceptual answers that it adopted in IFRS 2 *Share-based Payment*.

(c)   The proposal may provide potential for arbitrage. If unvested past service cost were recognised immediately, an entity could change how much of the total expense is recognised by changing the past service period without changing the amount and timing of benefits.

BC156   For the following reasons, the Board confirmed the requirement to recognise both vested and unvested past service cost immediately:

(a)   IAS 19 requires an entity to attribute benefits to periods of service in accordance with the benefit formula, even if the benefits are conditional on future employment. Therefore, recognising unvested past service cost immediately is consistent with the recognition of unvested current service cost that IAS 19 treats as an obligation in paragraph 72. The Board noted that recognising unvested past service cost immediately would not be consistent with IFRS 2. However, in the Board's view, internal consistency within IAS 19 is more desirable than consistency with IFRS 2.

(b)   The Board acknowledged that recognising unvested past service cost immediately may introduce an opportunity for accounting arbitrage by selection of the benefit formula, but recognising unvested past service cost over the vesting period may also be open to accounting arbitrage. If an entity recognised unvested past service cost over the vesting period, an entity could change how much of the total expense is recognised by changing the amount subject to vesting conditions and the vesting period. Any approach to attributing unvested benefits to periods of service is arbitrary. However, recognising unvested past service cost immediately is more consistent with paragraph 72 and the recognition of unvested current service cost.

BC157   Before the amendments made in 2011, an entity recognised curtailments resulting from a significant reduction in the number of employees covered by the plan when the entity was demonstrably committed to making the reduction. The amendments made in 2011 require an entity to recognise a plan amendment and a curtailment when they occur.

BC158   Some respondents to the 2010 ED asked the Board to clarify whether, in the context of a plan amendment or curtailment, 'occurs' means when the change is announced, when it is executed or when the change is effective. If a plan amendment or curtailment occurs in isolation (ie it is not triggered by a settlement, termination benefit or restructuring), determining when the plan amendment occurs requires the exercise of judgement. The timing of recognition would depend on the individual facts and circumstances and how they interact with the constructive obligation requirements in paragraphs 61 and 62. The Board concluded that providing further guidance on when a plan amendment 'occurs' is beyond the scope of the amendments made in 2011.

BC159   The amendments made in 2011 also:

(a)   remove the 'demonstrably committed' recognition criterion for termination benefits (paragraphs BC258–BC260); and

(b)   align the recognition of related plan amendments, curtailments, termination benefits and restructuring costs (paragraphs BC262–BC268).

Definitions of past service cost, curtailments and settlements

BC160   The Board noted that recognising unvested past service cost immediately results in the same accounting for past service cost and curtailments. As a result, the amendments made in 2011 revised the definitions of plan amendments and curtailments. Before those amendments, IAS 19 defined the curtailment of a plan as follows:

> A curtailment occurs when an entity either:
>
> (a)   is demonstrably committed to make a significant reduction in the number of employees covered by a plan; or
>
> (b)   amends the terms of a defined benefit plan so that a significant element of future service by current employees will no longer qualify for benefits, or will qualify only for reduced benefits.

BC161   The distinction between past service cost and curtailments was necessary in IAS 19 before the amendments made in 2011 because curtailments were recognised immediately, but unvested past service cost was recognised over the vesting period. However, because the amendments made in 2011 require immediate recognition of unvested past service costs, there is no longer any reason for the distinction between past service cost and the second part of the definition of curtailments. Accordingly, the Board removed the second part of that definition. Consequently, past service cost will include amounts attributed to past service resulting from any plan amendment and would be recognised immediately.

BC162   The Board retained the first part of the definition of curtailments. This distinguishes the closure of a plan to a significant number of employees (which is closer to a plan amendment) and an increase in estimated employee turnover (which is closer to a change in actuarial assumption). Thus, if a reduction in the number of employees is judged significant, then an entity accounts for it in the same way as for a plan amendment, and if not significant an entity will have to determine whether it is a change in actuarial assumption or a plan amendment. Because IAS 19 now treats plan amendments and curtailments in the same way, it now treats gains or losses on a curtailment as one form of past service cost.

BC163　The amendment made in 2011 clarifies that a settlement is a payment of benefits that is not set out in the terms of the plan. The payment of benefits that are set out in the terms of the plan, including terms that provide members with options on the nature of benefit payment such as an option to take a lump sum instead of an annuity, would be included in the actuarial assumptions. Therefore, any difference between an estimated benefit payment and the actual benefit payment is an actuarial gain or loss.

Other alternatives considered for accounting for plan amendments and settlements

BC164　The Board considered two other alternatives:

(a) *Confirming the proposals in the 2010 ED*—the 2010 ED proposed that past service cost and a gain or loss on curtailment should be included in the service cost component and a gain or loss on settlement should be included in the remeasurements component (see paragraphs BC165–BC170).

(b) *Remeasurements approach*—requiring past service cost and a gain or loss on curtailment or settlement to be included in the remeasurements component (see paragraphs BC171–BC173).

Other alternatives considered: confirming the proposals in the 2010 ED

BC165　The Board's view in developing the 2010 ED was that gains and losses arise on settlements because of a difference between the defined benefit obligation, as remeasured at the transaction date, and the settlement amount. Therefore, the 2010 ED proposed that:

(a) gains and losses on settlements should be treated in the same way as actuarial gains and losses, by being included in the remeasurements component; and

(b) the effect of plan amendments and curtailments should be included in the service cost component.

BC166　Many respondents to the 2010 ED supported the proposals for the recognition of past service cost and gains and losses on curtailments in profit or loss and the recognition of gains and losses on routine settlements in other comprehensive income. But many respondents disagreed with the proposal to recognise the effects of settlements in other comprehensive income, for the following reasons:

(a) There is overlap between the definitions of settlements, curtailments and plan amendments and the transactions usually happen at the same time, so it can be difficult to allocate the gains and losses between them. Requiring different accounting treatments for settlements, curtailments and plan amendments would introduce practical difficulties, diversity in practice and structuring opportunities.

(b) Settlements with third parties typically involve additional cost (such as a profit margin for the third party) and the effect of management's decision to incur this additional cost should be reflected in profit or loss when that transaction occurs.

(c) Recognising a gain or loss on derecognition of a liability in other comprehensive income seems inconsistent with other IFRSs that require a gain or loss on derecognition of a liability to be recognised in profit or loss.

(d) If settlements are the result of an event accounted for separately in profit or loss, then the gain or loss on settlement should be recognised in the same place as that event.

(e) A settlement can be interpreted as an 'action' of the plan sponsor, so the argument that past service cost should be recognised in profit or loss 'because [the plan amendment] occurs [when] an entity takes an action that reduces the benefits provided by the plan to employees' (Basis for Conclusions on 2010 ED, paragraph BC48) is applicable for the treatment of settlements as well.

BC167 Some interpret the definition of settlements as overlapping with the definitions of plan amendments, curtailments and changes in actuarial assumptions. If a transaction closes a plan and eliminates all further legal or constructive obligations, the transaction may have elements of plan amendments, curtailments and changes in actuarial assumptions because the definitions are not mutually exclusive. For example, if an entity negotiates a lump sum to be paid in connection with the closure of a defined benefit plan, one view is that the entire change in the defined benefit obligation is a settlement, because the lump sum eliminates all further legal and constructive obligations. The other view is that the effect of eliminating future pay growth, earlier payment than expected and the conversion of the benefits to a lump sum is a plan amendment and curtailment, with the settlement occurring when the payment is made.

BC168 In the Board's view, it is not clear whether the definitions overlap (because the definitions are not mutually exclusive) or whether it is merely difficult to distinguish the effects of a plan amendment, curtailment and settlement when they occur together. However, entities would need to distinguish these items if entities were required to include the amount relating to each in a different component of defined benefit cost.

BC169 The Board decided to treat past service cost and gains and losses arising from settlements (defined as non-routine settlements in the 2010 ED) as part of the service cost component. This does not require entities to make a distinction between those items if they occur at the same time. It is also consistent with the requirements in IAS 19 before the amendments made in 2011, and with the recognition in profit or loss of amounts from other related transactions, such as termination benefits and restructuring costs.

BC170 Such an approach requires a distinction between routine benefit payments and settlements (ie routine and non-routine settlements as defined in the 2010 ED), because a gain or loss on a settlement is included in the service cost component, and a gain or loss on a routine benefit payment is included in remeasurements. However, respondents appeared less concerned about making this distinction than about making one between plan amendments and settlements.

Other alternatives considered: remeasurements approach

BC171 Some respondents suggested that the effect of past service cost and gains or losses on settlement should be included in the remeasurements component. Such an approach would not require a distinction between past service cost, gains and losses on settlements and actuarial gains and losses. The gains and losses arising from all of these transactions would be included in the remeasurements component.

BC172 These respondents justified including the effects of plan amendments in the remeasurements component on the basis that past service cost provides less information about the amount and timing of future cash flows than does current service cost. Respondents noted that this would have the effect of limiting the service cost component to current service cost, and would maintain the Board's conclusion that amounts with different predictive value should be presented separately. Furthermore, such an approach would eliminate the requirement to distinguish between past service cost, the effects of settlements, and actuarial gains and losses for the purpose of presentation.

BC173 However, the Board concluded that past service cost and gains and losses on settlements arise as a result of a new transaction, as opposed to the remeasurement of a prior period transaction, and therefore should be differentiated from remeasurements of the defined benefit obligation. In addition, a plan amendment or settlement might occur as part of a related restructuring or termination benefit, for which the resulting gain or loss is recognised in profit or loss.

Plan assets

BC174 IAS 19 requires explicitly that the defined benefit liability or asset should be recognised as the defined benefit obligation after deducting plan assets (if any) out of which the obligations are to be settled directly (see paragraph 8). IASC noted that this was already widespread, and probably universal, practice. IASC believed that plan assets reduce (but do not extinguish) an entity's own obligation and result in a single, net liability. Although the presentation of that net liability as a single amount in the balance sheet differs conceptually from the offsetting of separate assets and liabilities, IASC decided that the definition of plan assets should be consistent with the offsetting criteria in IAS 32 *Financial Instruments: Disclosure and Presentation*.[7] IAS 32 states that a financial asset and a financial liability should be offset and the net amount reported in the balance sheet when an entity:

(a) has a legally enforceable right to set off the recognised amounts; and

(b) intends either to settle on a net basis, or to realise the asset and settle the liability simultaneously.

BC175 IAS 19 as revised in 1998 defined plan assets as assets (other than non-transferable financial instruments issued by the reporting entity) held by an entity (a fund) that satisfies all of the following conditions:

(a) The entity is legally separate from the reporting entity.

---

7 In 2005 the IASB amended IAS 32 as *Financial Instruments: Presentation*.

(b)   The assets of the fund are to be used only to settle the employee benefit obligations, are not available to the entity's own creditors and cannot be returned to the entity (or can be returned to the entity only if the remaining assets of the fund are sufficient to meet the plan's obligations).

(c)   To the extent that sufficient assets are in the fund, the entity will have no legal or constructive obligation to pay the related employee benefits directly.

BC176   In issuing IAS 19 in 1998, IASC considered whether the definition of plan assets should include a fourth condition: that the entity does not control the fund. IASC concluded that control is not relevant in determining whether the assets in a fund reduce an entity's own obligation.

BC177   In response to comments on E54, IASC modified the definition of plan assets to exclude non-transferable financial instruments issued by the reporting entity. If this had not been done, an entity could reduce its liabilities, and increase its equity, by issuing non-transferable equity instruments to a defined benefit plan.

Plan assets: amendments issued in 2000

BC178   In 1999 IASC began a limited scope project to consider the accounting for assets held by a fund that satisfies parts (a) and (b) of the definition set out in paragraph BC175, but does not satisfy condition (c) because the entity retains a legal or constructive obligation to pay the benefits directly. IAS 19 before the amendments made in 2000 did not address assets held by such funds.

BC179   IASC considered two main approaches to such funds:

(a)   a **net** approach—the entity recognises its entire obligation as a liability after deducting the fair value of the assets held by the fund; and

(b)   a **gross** approach—the entity recognises its entire obligation as a liability and recognises its rights to a refund from the fund as a separate asset.

BC180   Supporters of a net approach made one or more of the following arguments:

(a)   A gross presentation would be misleading, because:

(i)   where conditions (a) and (b) of the definition in paragraph BC175 are met, the entity does not control the assets held by the fund; and

(ii)   even if the entity retains a legal obligation to pay the entire amount of the benefits directly, this legal obligation is a matter of form rather than substance.

(b)   A gross presentation would be an unnecessary change from current practice, which generally permits a net presentation. It would introduce excessive complexity into the standard, for limited benefit to users, given that paragraph 140(a) already requires disclosure of the gross amounts.

(c)   A gross approach may lead to measurement difficulties because of the interaction with the 10 per cent corridor that existed for the obligation before the amendments made to IAS 19 in 2011.

(d)   A net approach might be viewed as analogous to the treatment of joint and several liabilities under paragraph 29 of IAS 37. An entity recognises a provision for the part of the obligation for which an outflow of resources embodying economic benefits is probable. The part of the obligation that is expected to be met by other parties is treated as a contingent liability.

BC181   Supporters of a gross approach advocated that approach for one or more of the following reasons:

(a)   Paragraph BC174 gives a justification for presenting defined benefit obligations net of plan assets. The explanation focuses on whether offsetting is appropriate. Part (c) of the 1998 definition focuses on offsetting. This suggests that assets that satisfy parts (a) and (b) of the definition, but fail part (c), should be treated in the same way as plan assets for recognition and measurement purposes, but should be shown gross in the balance sheet without offsetting.

(b)   If offsetting is allowed when condition (c) is not met, this would seem to be equivalent to permitting a net presentation for 'in-substance defeasance' and other analogous cases where IAS 32 indicates explicitly that offsetting is inappropriate. IASC rejected 'in-substance defeasance' for financial instruments (see IAS 39 *Financial Instruments: Recognition and Measurement*[8] paragraph AG59) and there was no obvious reason to permit it in accounting for defined benefit plans. In these cases the entity retains an obligation that should be recognised as a liability and the entity's right to reimbursement from the plan is a source of economic benefits that should be recognised as an asset. Offsetting would be permitted if the conditions in paragraph 42 of IAS 32 are satisfied.

(c)   IASC decided in IAS 37 to require a gross presentation for reimbursements related to provisions, even though this was not previously general practice. There is no conceptual reason to require a different treatment for employee benefits.

(d)   Although some consider that a gross approach requires an entity to recognise assets that it does not control, others believe that this view is incorrect. A gross approach requires the entity to recognise an asset representing its right to receive reimbursement from the fund that holds those assets. It does not require the entity to recognise the underlying assets of the fund.

(e)   In a plan with plan assets that meet the definition adopted in 1998, the employees' first claim is against the fund—they have no claim against the entity if sufficient assets are in the fund. In the view of some, the fact that employees must first claim against the fund is more than just a difference in form—it changes the substance of the obligation.

---

8   IFRS 9 *Financial Instruments* replaced IAS 39. IFRS 9 applies to all items that were previously within the scope of IAS 39. The requirements in paragraph AG59 of IAS 39 were relocated to paragraph B3.3.3 of IFRS 9.

(f)   Defined benefit plans might be regarded under SIC-12 *Consolidation—Special Purpose Entities*[9] as special purpose entities that the entity controls—and that it should consolidate. Because the offsetting criterion in IAS 19 was consistent with offsetting criteria in other International Accounting Standards, it was relatively unimportant whether the pension plan is consolidated in cases where the obligation and the plan assets qualify for offset. If the assets are presented as a deduction from the related benefit obligations in cases where condition (c) is not met, it could become important to assess whether the entity should consolidate the plan.

BC182   Some argued that a net approach should be permitted when an entity retains an obligation to pay the entire amount of the benefits directly, but the obligation was considered unlikely to have any substantive effect in practice. IASC concluded that it would not be practicable to establish guidance of this kind that could be applied in a consistent manner.

BC183   IASC also considered the possibility of adopting a 'linked presentation' that UK Financial Reporting Standard FRS 5 *Reporting the Substance of Transactions* required for non-recourse finance. Under FRS 5, the balance sheet presents both the gross amount of the asset and, as a direct deduction, the related non-recourse debt. Supporters of this approach argued that it portrays the close link between related assets and liabilities without compromising general offsetting requirements. Opponents of the linked presentation argued that it creates a form of balance sheet presentation that IASC had not previously used and might cause confusion. IASC decided not to adopt the linked presentation.

BC184   IASC concluded that a net presentation is justified where there are restrictions (including restrictions that apply on bankruptcy of the reporting entity) on the use of the assets so that the assets can be used only to pay or fund employee benefits. Accordingly, it modified the definition of plan assets set out in paragraph BC175 by:

(a)   emphasising that the creditors of the entity should not have access to the assets held by the fund, even on bankruptcy of the reporting entity; and

(b)   deleting condition (c), so that the existence of a legal or constructive obligation to pay the employee benefits directly does not preclude a net presentation, and modifying condition (b) to explicitly permit the fund to reimburse the entity for paying the long-term employee benefits.

BC185   When an entity retains a direct obligation to the employees, IASC acknowledged that the net presentation was inconsistent with the derecognition requirements for financial instruments in IAS 39[10] and with the offsetting requirements in IAS 32. However, in IASC's view, the restrictions on the use of the assets created a sufficiently strong link with the employee benefit obligations that a net

---

9   SIC-12 *Consolidation—Special Purpose Entities* was withdrawn and superseded by IFRS 10 *Consolidated Financial Statements* issued in May 2011. There is no longer specific accounting guidance for special purpose entities because IFRS 10 applies to all types of entities.

10   IFRS 9 *Financial Instruments* replaced IAS 39. IFRS 9 applies to all items that were previously within the scope of IAS 39. This paragraph refers to matters relevant when IAS 19 was issued.

presentation was more relevant than a gross presentation, even if the entity retained a direct obligation to the employees.

BC186   IASC believed that such restrictions were unique to employee benefit plans and did not intend to permit this net presentation for other liabilities if the conditions then in IAS 32 and IAS 39 were not met. Accordingly, condition (a) in the new definition refers to the reason for the existence of the fund. IASC believed that an arbitrary restriction of this kind was the only practical way to permit a pragmatic exception to IASC's general offsetting criteria without permitting an unacceptable extension of this exception to other cases.

BC187   In some plans in some countries, an entity is entitled to receive a reimbursement of employee benefits from a separate fund, but the entity has discretion to delay receipt of the reimbursement or to claim less than the full reimbursement. Some argue that this element of discretion weakens the link between the benefits and the reimbursement so much that a net presentation is not justifiable. They believe that the definition of plan assets should exclude assets held by such funds and that a gross approach should be used in such cases. IASC concluded that the link between the benefits and the reimbursement was strong enough in such cases that a net approach was still appropriate.

BC188   IASC's proposal for extending the definition of plan assets was set out in exposure draft E67 *Pension Plan Assets*, published in July 2000. The vast majority of the 39 respondents to E67 supported the proposal.

BC189   A number of respondents to E67 proposed a further extension of the definition to include particular insurance policies that have similar economic effects to funds whose assets qualify as plan assets under the revised definition proposed in E67. Accordingly, IASC extended the definition of plan assets to include some insurance policies (described in IAS 19 as qualifying insurance policies) that satisfy the same conditions as other plan assets. These decisions were implemented in amendments to IAS 19 approved by IASC in October 2000.

BC190   A qualifying insurance policy is not necessarily an insurance contract as defined in IFRS 4 *Insurance Contracts*.

Plan assets—measurement

BC191   IAS 19 before its revision in 1998 stated that plan assets are valued at fair value, but did not define fair value. However, other International Accounting Standards defined fair value as 'the amount for which an asset could be exchanged or a liability settled between knowledgeable, willing parties in an arm's length transaction'.[11] This might be taken to imply that no deduction is made for the estimated costs that would be necessary to sell the asset (in other words, it is a mid-market value, with no adjustment for transaction costs). However, some argue that a plan will eventually have to dispose of its assets in order to pay benefits. Consequently, IASC concluded in E54 that plan assets

---

11   IFRS 13 *Fair Value Measurement*, issued in May 2011, defines fair value, describes the effect transaction costs have on a fair value measurement and addresses the application of bid and ask prices when measuring fair value.

should be measured at market value. Market value was defined, as in IAS 25 *Accounting for Investments*,[12] as the amount obtainable from the sale of an asset, in an active market.

BC192 Some commentators on E54 felt that the proposal to measure plan assets at market value would not be consistent with IAS 22 *Business Combinations*[13] and with the measurement of financial assets as proposed in the discussion paper *Accounting for Financial Assets and Financial Liabilities* published by IASC's Financial Instruments Steering Committee in March 1997. Consequently, IASC decided that plan assets should be measured at fair value.

BC193 Some argue that concerns about volatility in reported profit should be countered by permitting or requiring entities to measure plan assets at a market-related value that reflects changes in fair value over an arbitrary period, such as five years. IASC believed that the use of market-related values would add excessive and unnecessary complexity and that the combination of the 'corridor' approach to actuarial gains and losses with deferred recognition outside the 'corridor' was sufficient to deal with concerns about volatility.[14]

BC194 IASC decided that there should not be a different basis for measuring investments that have a fixed redemption value and those that match the obligations of the plan, or specific parts thereof. IAS 26 *Accounting and Reporting by Retirement Benefit Plans* permits such investments to be measured on an amortised cost basis.

Reimbursements: amendments issued in 2000

BC195 Paragraph 48 states that an entity recognises its rights under an insurance policy as an asset if the policy is held by the entity itself. IAS 19 before the amendments made in 2000 did not address the measurement of these insurance policies. The entity's rights under the insurance policy might be regarded as a financial asset. However, rights and obligations arising under insurance contracts are excluded from the scope of IAS 39.[15] In addition, IAS 39 does not apply to 'employers' rights and obligations under employee benefit plans, to which IAS 19 *Employee Benefits* applies'. Paragraphs 46–49 discuss insured benefits in distinguishing defined contribution plans and defined benefit plans, but this discussion does not deal with measurement.

BC196 In reviewing the definition of plan assets (see paragraphs BC178–BC190), IASC reviewed the treatment of insurance policies that an entity holds in order to fund employee benefits. Even under the revised definition adopted in 2000, the entity's rights under an insurance policy that is not a qualifying insurance policy (as defined in the 2000 revision of IAS 19) are not plan assets.

---

12 IAS 25 was superseded by IAS 39 *Financial Instruments: Recognition and Measurement* and IAS 40 *Investment Property*. IFRS 9 *Financial Instruments* replaced IAS 39. IFRS 9 applies to all items that were previously within the scope of IAS 39. This paragraph refers to matters relevant when IAS 19 was issued.

13 IAS 22 was withdrawn in 2004 and replaced by IFRS 3 *Business Combinations*.

14 The amendments made in 2011 eliminated the 10 per cent corridor from IAS 19.

15 IFRS 9 *Financial Instruments* replaced IAS 39. IFRS 9 applies to all items that were previously within the scope of IAS 39. This paragraph refers to matters relevant when IAS 19 was issued.

BC197   In 2000 IASC introduced recognition and measurement requirements for reimbursements under such insurance policies (see paragraphs 116–119). IASC based those requirements on the treatment of reimbursements under paragraphs 53–58 of IAS 37. In particular, IAS 19 requires an entity to recognise a right to reimbursement of post-employment benefits as a separate asset, rather than as a deduction from the related obligations. In all other respects (for example, the treatment of actuarial gains and losses), the standard requires an entity to treat such reimbursement rights in the same way as plan assets. This requirement reflects the close link between the reimbursement right and the related obligation.

BC198   Paragraph 115 states that where plan assets include insurance policies that exactly match the amount and timing of some or all of the benefits payable under the plan, the plan's rights under those insurance policies are measured at the same amount as the related obligations. Paragraph 119 extends that conclusion to insurance policies that are assets of the entity itself.

BC199   IAS 37 states that the amount recognised for the reimbursement should not exceed the amount of the provision. Paragraph 116 contains no similar restriction, because the limit in paragraph 64 already applies to prevent the recognition of a net defined benefit asset that exceeds the asset ceiling.

Defined benefit plans—presentation of assets and liabilities

BC200   IASC decided not to specify whether an entity should distinguish current and non-current portions of assets and liabilities arising from post-employment benefits, because such a distinction may sometimes be arbitrary.

Defined benefit plans—presentation of defined benefit cost: amendments issued in 2011

BC201   The amendments made in 2011 do not specify how an entity should present the service cost and net interest components in profit or loss. Instead, an entity is required to present them in accordance with the requirements of IAS 1 *Presentation of Financial Statements*, consistently with IAS 19 before the amendments made in 2011.

BC202   The Board also considered:

    (a)   requiring the net interest component to be included in the finance cost line item of IAS 1, as proposed in the 2010 ED. However, if the Board had adopted this approach, it would have needed to consider whether the requirement would apply when the net interest component represents income because IAS 1 requires only finance cost and not finance income to be presented separately. The Board would also have needed to consider in due course whether it should apply similar treatment to amounts related to the passage of time in other projects, such as revenue recognition, insurance contracts and leases. The Board concluded that this would be beyond the scope of the project and that it should consider this aspect of presentation in the statement of profit or loss and other comprehensive income more broadly as part of the financial statement presentation project.

(b)   amending IAS 1 to require a separate line item for the net interest component or to require presentation of a line item that would combine service cost and net interest. The Board concluded that although these amounts would be material to many entities, there is no reason to single out post-employment benefits for special treatment in the statement of profit or loss and other comprehensive income. If an entity thinks that information about pensions is sufficiently important to the users of its financial statements, IAS 1 already permits that entity to provide disaggregated information in the performance statements. The Board would also have had to consider the implications of adding mandatory line items to IAS 1 if the entity presented its expenses by function. The Board concluded that this was beyond the scope of the project.

Defined benefit plans—disclosures: amendments issued in 2011

BC203   The amendments made in 2011 updated the disclosure requirements, because of concerns:

(a)   that the disclosures required by the previous version of IAS 19 did not enable users of financial statements to understand the financial effect of liabilities and assets arising from defined benefit plans on the financial statements as a whole.

(b)   that the volume of disclosures about defined benefit plans in many financial statements risked reducing understandability and usefulness by obscuring important information. This concern was particularly pronounced for multinational entities that have many varied plans in many jurisdictions.

BC204   The disclosure amendments made in 2011 related to:

(a)   disclosure objectives (paragraphs BC212–BC214).

(b)   the characteristics of the defined benefit plan and amounts in the financial statements (paragraphs BC215–BC228).

(c)   the amount, timing and uncertainty of the entity's future cash flows (paragraphs BC229–BC243).

(d)   multi-employer defined benefit plans (paragraphs BC245–BC252).

BC205   Paragraph BC244 discusses disclosures considered but rejected by the Board.

BC206   In reviewing the disclosure requirements, the Board considered:

(a)   the comment letters on the discussion paper and the 2010 ED.

(b)   publications from other bodies interested in financial reporting, including the Pro-active Accounting Activities in Europe (PAAinE) discussion paper *The Financial Reporting of Pensions*; the UK Accounting Standards Board (ASB) Reporting Statement *Retirement Benefits – Disclosures*; and FASB Staff Position No.132(R) *Employers' Disclosures about Postretirement Benefit Plan Assets* (FSP FAS 132(R)–1).

(c)   proposals from the Investors Technical Advisory Committee (ITAC) of the FASB for a 'principle-based' disclosure framework, and a draft discussion paper on the disclosure of information in financial statements, prepared by the staff of the Canadian Accounting Standards Board (AcSB).

(d)   advice received from the Global Preparers' Forum and the Board's Analyst Representative Group and Employee Benefits Working Group.

(e)   the need to update the disclosure requirements in IAS 19 to reflect developments in IFRSs on disclosures, in particular IFRS 7 *Financial Instruments: Disclosures* and IFRS 13 *Fair Value Measurement*.

The Board's approach to disclosures about defined benefit plans

BC207   The Board sought an approach that:

(a)   provides sufficient disclosures about defined benefit plans when those plans are material to the entity's operations.

(b)   provides users of financial statements with relevant information that is not obscured by excessive detail.

BC208   Accordingly, the amendments made in 2011 introduced explicit objectives for disclosures about defined benefit plans.

BC209   In developing the proposals in the 2010 ED, the Board noted that entities must comply with the general materiality requirements in paragraphs 17(c) and 31 of IAS 1, including the requirement to disclose additional information if necessary, and that the financial statements need not contain disclosures that are not material.

BC210   However, some respondents were concerned that entities might have difficulty in exercising judgement when assessing the materiality of disclosures because:

(a)   there is no universal quantitative criterion for defined benefit plans for separating material disclosure items from immaterial ones; and

(b)   the notion of materiality seems best suited to a binary decision (whether to provide or omit a particular disclosure) and is not well suited to determining the extent of disclosure required to meet a disclosure requirement or to determining the overall balance with other disclosure requirements.

BC211   Although many respondents supported the inclusion of disclosure objectives, they believed that supplementing the objectives with an extensive list of disclosure requirements would not achieve the result that the Board intended. Many supported a principle-based approach to disclosure that would put more emphasis on meeting the disclosure objectives. Some suggested that it would be better if the Board supported the disclosure objectives through the use of 'encouraged but not required' disclosures or by including examples illustrating the application of the disclosure objectives in different circumstances. In response to these concerns the Board included a requirement that an entity should consider the level of disclosure necessary to satisfy the disclosure objectives and how much emphasis to place on each requirement.

Selecting disclosure objectives

BC212 The Board considered whether it should require the same disclosure objectives for defined benefit plans as for long-term financial instruments and insurance contracts. All three expose the entity to similar risks, including risks that the ultimate cost of settling the liability may vary from the amount estimated and risks arising from the complexity of measuring the liability. Many respondents stated that the disclosures in IAS 19 do not provide users of financial statements with the information about risk that is provided for other assets and liabilities. However, the Board concluded that much of the information required by IFRS 7 and IFRS 4 *Insurance Contracts* for assets would be unnecessary in depicting an entity's involvement with a defined benefit plan because:

(a) the entity may not manage plan assets directly and may not have an unrestricted ability to access the economic benefits from those assets. Thus, plan assets differ from assets held directly by the entity. Consequently, disclosures about market risk and credit risk of plan assets are less relevant than for assets an entity holds directly. Moreover, an entity may have limited information about them.

(b) liquidity risk arises from the timing and amount of contributions that the entity is required to make to the plan and not from the need to meet directly the payments required by the defined benefit obligation.

BC213 Accordingly, the Board focused the disclosure objectives in IAS 19 on the matters most relevant to users of the employer's financial statements, ie information that:

(a) explains the characteristics of the defined benefit plans.

(b) identifies and explains the amounts in the financial statements arising from the defined benefit plans.

(c) describes how involvement in defined benefit plans affects the amount, timing and uncertainty of the entity's future cash flows.

BC214 In response to suggestions by respondents, the Board included a requirement for entities to disclose additional information if required to meet the disclosure objectives.

Characteristics of the defined benefit plan and amounts in the financial statements

BC215 The disclosures about the characteristics of defined benefit plans and the amounts in the financial statements arising from defined benefit plans are based on those in IAS 19 before the amendments made in 2011 with the following changes:

(a) additional information about exposure to risk (paragraphs BC216–BC218);

(b) distinguishing between actuarial gains and losses arising from demographic and financial assumptions (paragraph BC219);

(c) not requiring an entity to distinguish between plan amendments, curtailments and settlements if they occur together (paragraph BC220);

(d)   stating a principle for the disaggregation of plan assets rather than listing the categories required (paragraphs BC221–BC226); and

(e)   stating a principle for the disclosure of significant actuarial assumptions rather than listing the assumptions required to be disclosed (paragraphs BC227 and BC228).

Exposure to risk

BC216   The amendments in 2011 require entities to provide a narrative description of exposure to risk arising from their involvement with the plan. The 2010 ED proposal for additional disclosure regarding risk was in response to requests from users.

BC217   Some respondents to the 2010 ED suggested limiting the narrative disclosure about risk to any risks that are specific to the entity, or that are unusual, so that it does not result in boilerplate disclosure regarding generic risks to which all entities with defined benefit plans are exposed.

BC218   The Board agreed with respondents that requiring disclosure of all material risks would result in extensive generic disclosures that would not be particularly useful. However, in the Board's view it would not be practical to limit the disclosure to risks that are specific or unusual without providing a clear definition of those terms. Instead, the amendments in 2011 require an entity to focus the disclosure on risks that the entity judges to be significant or unusual.

Actuarial gains and losses arising from demographic and financial assumptions

BC219   The amendments made to IAS 19 in 2011 require entities to disclose the effect of changes in demographic assumptions separately from the effect of changes in financial assumptions. Some respondents to the 2010 ED stated that this separation would be arbitrary because of the interrelationships between some actuarial assumptions, particularly between financial assumptions. For example, discount rates may be correlated with inflation rates. However, the Board observed that, in general, financial assumptions are less intertwined with demographic assumptions than with other financial assumptions. Thus, the Board concluded that it would not be unduly difficult to distinguish the effects of changes in financial assumptions from the effects of changes in demographic assumptions.

Plan amendments, curtailments and settlements

BC220   The amendments made in 2011 retain similar disclosure for plan amendments, curtailments and settlements. However, the Board agreed with the views of respondents to the 2010 ED that when plan amendments, curtailments and settlements occur together, requiring entities to distinguish them for disclosure would be excessive. Therefore, the amendments do not require an entity to distinguish them when they occur together.

Plan assets

BC221 The amendments made in 2011 replace the minimum list of categories for the disaggregation of plan assets with a requirement to disaggregate the fair value of the plan assets:

(a) into assets that have a quoted price in an active market and assets that do not; and

(b) into classes that distinguish the risk and liquidity characteristics of those assets.

BC222 In addition to stating the principle for the disaggregation, the 2010 ED proposals would have required an entity to distinguish, at a minimum, debt instruments and equity instruments that have a quoted market price in an active market from those that do not. The proposals also specified a list of minimum categories into which an entity should disaggregate plan assets (based on the categories in IAS 19 at that time).

BC223 Respondents to the 2010 ED agreed with the principle of the disaggregation, but noted that the proposed minimum categories may not always meet that principle. The Board agreed with respondents that entities should focus on the principle of the disclosure: to disaggregate plan assets into classes that distinguish the risk and liquidity characteristics of those assets. In support of that principle, the amendments provide a list of example categories that would allow entities to adapt their disclosures to the nature and risks of the assets in their plans.

BC224 Some respondents also had concerns about the requirement to distinguish assets that have a quoted market price from those that do not. They indicated that disaggregating debt and equity instruments into those that have a quoted market price and those that do not would result in extensive disclosures that would be unlikely to add much to the understandability of the financial statements. However, users have requested information about the level of measurement uncertainty in items measured at fair value, such as the fair value hierarchy in IFRS 13. Therefore, the Board retained the proposal to disaggregate debt and equity instruments into those that have a quoted market price and those that do not.

BC225 In coming to this conclusion, the Board noted that this disaggregation requirement would be less onerous than the requirement in IFRS 13 to disaggregate on the basis of a three-level hierarchy.

BC226 Some hold the view that entities should disclose disaggregated information about how they invest plan assets. However, the Board concluded that extensive disaggregated information about plan assets is not necessary for users of the employer entity's financial statements because the entity does not hold those assets directly. Similarly, the Board concluded that for plan assets the disclosures about fair value required by IFRS 13 would not be relevant.

Actuarial assumptions

BC227 The amendments made in 2011 replace the previous mandatory list of actuarial assumptions with a requirement to disclose the significant actuarial assumptions used to determine the present value of the defined benefit obligation.

BC228 The Board did not specify particular assumptions for which disclosure is required, because particular disclosures may not be needed in every case to meet the disclosure objectives. Indeed, such disclosures may obscure important information with excessive detail. Accordingly, the 2010 ED proposed an approach in which entities would use judgement to determine which actuarial assumptions require disclosure. Respondents to the 2010 ED generally supported this proposal.

Amount, timing and uncertainty of future cash flows

BC229 The amendments made in 2011 improve the required disclosures about the amount, timing and uncertainty of future cash flows in the following respects:

(a) information about asset-liability matching strategies (paragraphs BC230–BC234);

(b) sensitivity analysis (paragraphs BC235–BC239); and

(c) information about the funding and duration of the liability (paragraphs BC240–BC243).

Asset-liability matching strategies

BC230 The amendments made in 2011 require an entity to disclose information about its asset-liability matching strategy.

BC231 In developing the proposals in the 2010 ED, the Board considered requiring entities to discuss their strategies for mitigating risks arising from defined benefit plans. However, the Board concluded that such a requirement would result in generic disclosure that would not provide enough specific information to be useful to users of financial statements. Nonetheless, in the Board's view, information about an entity's use of asset-liability matching strategies, or about the use of techniques such as annuities or longevity swaps to manage longevity risk, would provide additional information on how the entity manages the risk inherent in its defined benefit plan. Accordingly, the 2010 ED proposed a requirement to disclose information about these items.

BC232 Respondents' views on the proposals regarding asset-liability matching strategies were mixed. Some respondents to the 2010 ED supported the disclosure, whereas others expressed the view that it should be part of a broader disclosure regarding risk management and investment strategy or that it should be removed altogether. Those who believed that it should be part of a broader discussion about risks suggested linking the disclosure with the requirement to describe the nature of risks to which the plan exposes the entity, by requiring the entity to describe how it manages those risks. Respondents also noted that the disclosure could be better integrated with the disclosures on plan assets. Respondents that did not support the asset-liability matching disclosure were concerned that:

(a)   any disclosure of strategy would be generic and boilerplate;

(b)   a user would be able to perform a better assessment using the disclosures on plan assets and on defined benefit obligations (ie the results of such a strategy are more relevant than a narrative discussion); and

(c)   the requirement might be interpreted as implying that all entities should be performing asset-liability matching.

BC233   In the Board's view, disclosure about the asset-liability matching strategy may be more useful than disclosure about the general investment strategy because an asset-liability matching strategy aims to match the amount and timing of cash inflow from plan assets with those of cash outflow from the defined benefit obligation.

BC234   The amendments require the entity to disclose details of asset-liability matching strategies used by the plan or the entity, if any, and do not intend to imply that all plans or entities should be performing asset-liability matching.

Sensitivity analysis

BC235   The amendments made in 2011 require an entity to disclose how the effect of reasonably possible changes to significant actuarial assumptions affect the defined benefit obligation.

BC236   Users of financial statements have consistently emphasised the fundamental importance of sensitivity analyses to their understanding of the risks underlying the amounts recognised in the financial statements.

BC237   In the Board's view, a sensitivity analysis on the net defined benefit liability (asset) would be more useful than a sensitivity analysis on the defined benefit obligation only. However, the Board concluded that a sensitivity analysis on the net defined benefit liability (asset) should not be required because, for example, showing how the fair value of equities would respond to changes in the assumptions used to measure the present value of the defined benefit obligation would be complex and difficult to perform.

BC238   The Board proposed in the 2010 ED a sensitivity analysis for service cost showing how the service cost would have varied in response to changes in assumptions that were reasonably possible at the beginning of the period. Many respondents did not see the relevance of disclosing how the effect of a change to an assumption at the beginning of the reporting period would have affected current service cost. The Board agreed with this view and consequently withdrew that proposal.

BC239   Respondents expressed the following concerns about the sensitivity analysis on the defined benefit obligation:

(a)   The sensitivity disclosure would not take into account the correlations between various actuarial assumptions. Some respondents suggested that a scenario analysis would be more useful. The Board concluded that, although a scenario analysis could provide more useful information, the complexity and cost of producing the information would outweigh the benefits.

(b) Some respondents were concerned that carrying out a series of sensitivity analyses on several actuarial assumptions would be onerous. Some requested that the sensitivity analysis should be limited to the assumptions that have a significant effect on the financial statements, such as the discount rate. The Board agreed with these respondents that in many cases the discount rate would be one of the most significant assumptions. However, depending on the plan and other facts and circumstances, other assumptions might be significant. The 2010 ED proposed that the sensitivity analysis should apply only to 'significant actuarial assumptions'. Consequently, the Board confirmed that proposal.

(c) Some respondents raised a concern that a 'reasonably possible' change is open to subjectivity and suggested that IAS 19 should specify a quantitative range. However, although setting the range to a particular percentage might improve comparability, the Board was concerned that a quantitative range might not reflect the reasonably possible ranges in different circumstances. The Board noted that requiring sensitivity on the basis of changes in the relevant actuarial assumption that were 'reasonably possible' at that date is consistent with the sensitivity disclosure requirements of other standards, such as IFRS 7.

Information about the funding and duration of the liability

BC240 The amendments made in 2011 require an entity to disclose:

(a) a narrative description of any funding arrangement and funding policy;

(b) the amount of expected contribution in the next year (carried forward from the previous version of IAS 19); and

(c) information about the maturity profile of the obligation, including the weighted average duration.

BC241 To provide users with information about the effect of a defined benefit plan on an entity's future cash flow, the 2010 ED proposed that an entity should discuss the factors that may cause contributions to differ from service cost. However, many respondents suggested that a disclosure about the effect of a defined benefit plan on an entity's future cash flows should instead focus on:

(a) the funding arrangement and funding policy; and

(b) the amount and timing of expected contributions and benefit payments.

BC242 In the Board's view, the disclosures suggested by respondents will be more relevant to users in assessing the risk related to changes in contribution and forecasting how much cash outflow will be incurred to cover the employee benefits than the proposal in the 2010 ED, discussed further in paragraph BC244(d).

BC243 Accordingly, the Board concluded that disclosing when, on average, the liabilities of a defined benefit plan mature would help users to understand the profile of cash flows required to meet the obligation. The Board considered requiring entities to disclose a maturity analysis of the obligation but, because the cost of such a disclosure might be onerous, the Board concluded that an entity should be required to disclose only the weighted average duration of the obligation. However, the amendments include a maturity analysis as an example of additional disclosures that could meet the disclosure objectives. The disclosure of the average duration provides information similar to the maturity analysis and will enhance the usefulness of other disclosures, such as the disclosure of actuarial assumptions dependent on the duration.

Other disclosures considered but rejected by the Board

BC244 The Board also considered, but rejected, requiring disclosure of:

(a) *actuarial assumptions and the process used to determine them*—the 2010 ED proposed that if the disclosure of demographic assumptions (such as mortality) would be difficult to interpret without additional demographic information, the entity should explain how it made those actuarial assumptions. Few respondents supported that proposal. Respondents commented that the disclosure would lead to boilerplate descriptions that would not be particularly helpful and that users rely on the entity, its actuaries and auditors to ensure that the demographic assumptions are reasonable. The Board agreed with these views and withdrew the proposal.

(b) *an alternative measure of the long-term employee benefit liability*—the 2010 ED proposed that entities should disclose the defined benefit obligation, excluding projected growth in salaries (sometimes referred to as the accumulated benefit obligation). Many respondents said that the relevance of such a disclosure would vary by country and by plan and that it would be inappropriate to require a disclosure simply because it would be relevant to some users in limited circumstances. The Board agreed with those respondents and withdrew the proposal.

(c) *disaggregation of the defined benefit obligation*—some respondents suggested that instead of the proposed disclosure as described in paragraph BC244(b), a more relevant disclosure would be a disaggregation of the defined benefit obligation showing, for example, vested benefits, accrued but unvested benefits, future salary increases, other constructive obligations and amounts owing to active members, deferred members and pensioners. The Board concluded that disaggregating the defined benefit obligation to distinguish components with different risk characteristics, as suggested by some respondents, would better meet the disclosure objectives, but requiring any particular disaggregation would be costly for preparers. However, disaggregation of the defined benefit obligation is included as an example of additional information that an entity may provide in order to meet the disclosure objectives.

(d) *factors that may cause contributions to differ from service cost*—in the Board's view, information about the effect of a surplus or deficit on the timing and amount of an entity's contributions is useful. Consequently, the 2010 ED proposed disclosure of factors that could cause contributions over the next five years to differ from current service cost. Many respondents did not support that proposal, observing that an entity's cash flows would be determined by funding requirements and not by the service cost as determined in accordance with IAS 19. Consequently, a discussion of those factors would not be relevant to a user's understanding of the entity's cash flows. The Board agreed with those respondents and withdrew the proposal.

(e) *historical information*—the amendments made in 2011 deleted the previous requirement to disclose historical information over five years about amounts in the statement of financial position and experience adjustments. The Board concluded that this requirement provided information about the defined benefit plan that was already available in previous financial statements and therefore was redundant.

Multi-employer plans

BC245   The amendments made in 2011 require disclosures for multi-employer defined benefit plans based on those in the previous version of IAS 19 with the following additional disclosure:

(a)   qualitative information about any agreed deficit or surplus allocation on wind-up of the plan, or the amount that is required to be paid on withdrawal of the entity from the plan (paragraphs BC247–BC249).

(b)   the expected contribution for the next annual period (paragraph BC250).

(c)   the level of participation in a multi-employer plan (paragraphs BC251 and BC252).

BC246   In the Board's view, entities participating in a defined benefit multi-employer plan face greater risks than other entities: for example, risks that result from actions by other participants in the plan. Respondents to the discussion paper expressed the view that the disclosures in IAS 19 were insufficient to inform users about the potential effect on the amount, timing and uncertainty of future cash flows associated with an entity's participation in multi-employer defined benefit plans. Accordingly, the 2010 ED proposed additional disclosures about participation in a multi-employer plan and respondents generally welcomed those proposals.

Withdrawal obligations

BC247   IAS 37 requires an entity to disclose information about contingent liabilities and IAS 19 notes that contingent liabilities may arise from an entity's participation in a multi-employer plan. The Board identified two cases in which such information may be relevant, namely withdrawal from the plan and the wind-up of a plan. In the Board's view, disclosure of the withdrawal liability should be limited to qualitative information, for the following reasons:

(a)   If an entity is not committed to withdrawing from the plan, the plan is not committed to being wound up or a withdrawal liability has not been agreed between the entity and the plan, determining the withdrawal liability would be difficult. Furthermore, additional measurement requirements would have to be developed as well as further disclosure about the assumptions used.

(b) Withdrawal is not always an option for an entity. However, the Board decided that an entity should disclose whether it is unable to withdraw from a plan because that would be useful information for a user of the financial statements.

(c) The cost of obtaining the information would make the disclosure onerous if it were required for all entities in all circumstances. Moreover, an entity may be unable to obtain the information.

BC248 Some respondents stated that disclosure of a withdrawal liability should not be required because different plans or jurisdictions use different assumptions to determine the withdrawal amount, and therefore the amounts are not comparable. The Board did not agree with that view. The amount required to withdraw from a plan faithfully represents the obligation, whether that amount is determined on the same basis as for another plan or on a different basis. If the amounts are determined on the basis of different underlying requirements, the actual amounts required to withdraw will differ.

BC249 The Board noted that if it is probable that the entity will withdraw from the plan, any additional liability should be recognised and measured under IAS 37. This requirement was implicit in IAS 19, but the Board made it explicit in the amendments made in 2011. Requiring entities to recognise an additional liability when it is probable that the entity will withdraw from the plan also converges with similar requirements in US GAAP.

Future contributions

BC250 The Board agreed with respondents' views that the proposal in the 2010 ED for an entity to disclose the contributions for the next five years would require estimates that may be difficult to determine and very subjective. Thus the Board aligned this disclosure with the general requirement for defined benefit plans, which requires an entity to disclose the expected contribution for a defined benefit plan for the next annual period. The Board confirmed the proposal in the ED for a narrative description of any funding arrangement and funding policy. That requirement is consistent with the requirement for single employer defined benefit plans.

Level of participation

BC251 The amendments made in 2011 require an entity that accounts for its participation in a multi-employer defined benefit plan as a defined contribution plan to disclose an indication of the level of its participation in the plan compared with other plan participants. Together with information about the whole plan, that disclosure provides information about the effect of any surplus or deficit on the amount, timing and uncertainty of an entity's future cash flows.

BC252 The Board provided examples of measures that might indicate the entity's level of participation, but did not specify a particular measure because a single measure may not be relevant in all cases.

Other long-term employee benefits

Death-in-service benefits

BC253   E54 proposed guidance on cases where death-in-service benefits are not insured externally and are not provided through a post-employment benefit plan. IASC concluded that such cases will be rare. Accordingly, IASC deleted the guidance on death-in-service benefits.

Termination benefits: amendments issued in 2011

BC254   The proposals in the 2005 ED proposed to align the accounting for termination benefits with the requirements in FASB Accounting Standards Codification (ASC) Topic 420 *Exit or Disposal Cost Obligations* (FASB ASC Topic 420), relating to 'one-time termination benefits' and FASB ASC Topic 712 *Compensation—Nonretirement Postemployment Benefits*, relating to 'special termination benefits'. The Board acknowledged that differences with US GAAP would remain following the introduction of these amendments. Nonetheless, the Board believed that the proposed amendments would converge with some US GAAP requirements and would improve the accounting for termination benefits. The proposals for termination benefits complemented proposed amendments to the requirements on restructurings in IAS 37 in the 2005 ED. The Board received 123 comment letters in response to the proposals in the 2005 ED.

BC255   The Board considered the following:

(a)   benefits payable in exchange for future service (see paragraphs BC256 and BC257);

(b)   recognition of termination benefits (see paragraphs BC258–BC260);

(c)   measurement of termination benefits (see paragraph BC261); and

(d)   interaction with restructuring costs, plan amendments, curtailments and settlements (see paragraphs BC262–BC268).

Benefits payable in exchange for services

BC256   IAS 19 requires an entity to account for termination benefits separately from other employee benefits, because the event that gives rise to a present obligation is the termination of employment rather than employee service. In contrast, FASB ASC Topic 420 regards some involuntary termination benefits as being provided in exchange for employees' future services (or, expressed another way, a 'stay bonus'). In such cases under US GAAP, an entity recognises the cost of those benefits over the period of the employees' service, consistently with the accounting for other employee benefits.

BC257   In the 2005 ED, the Board proposed that IAS 19 should specify recognition requirements for an entity providing termination benefits in exchange for future service, consistent with Topic 420. However, when finalising the amendments made in 2011, the Board noted the potential for confusion caused by accounting for some benefits provided in exchange for future service as termination benefits. The Board concluded that treating benefits provided in exchange for future service as short-term or other long-term employee benefits or post-employment benefits would result in the same recognition as is required under Topic 420 (ie the cost of those benefits would be recognised over the period of service), and would maintain the existing distinction between benefits provided in exchange for termination of employment and benefits provided in exchange for services.

Recognition

BC258　IAS 19 before the amendments made in 2011 specified that an entity should recognise termination benefits when the entity was demonstrably committed to providing those benefits. In revisiting that conclusion, the Board considered the following circumstances:

(a)　an offer of termination benefits that an entity can withdraw at its own discretion before acceptance by the employee.

(b)　an offer of termination benefits that an entity cannot withdraw, including benefits provided as a result of an entity's decision to terminate an employee's employment (ie if the employee has no choice but to accept what is given).

BC259　The Board decided that the factor determining the timing of recognition is the entity's inability to withdraw the offer of termination benefits. In the circumstances in (a) this would be when the employee accepts the offer and in the circumstances in (b) this would be when the entity communicates a termination plan to the affected employees. The Board concluded that until these events occur the employer has discretion to avoid paying termination benefits and, therefore, a liability does not exist.

BC260　The criteria in Topic 420 relating to the termination plan are similar to the criteria in IAS 19 before the amendments made in 2011 for establishing whether an entity is demonstrably committed to a termination plan and, therefore, should recognise termination benefits. However, there was no requirement in that version of IAS 19 to communicate the plan of termination to employees. The Board added a requirement specifying that an entity does not have a present obligation to provide termination benefits until it has communicated its plan of termination to each of the affected employees. The Board also replaced the criteria in IAS 19 relating to the plan of termination with those in Topic 420. Although those criteria were very similar, the Board concluded that it would be better if they were identical.

Measurement

BC261　IAS 19 before the amendments made in 2011 required termination benefits that become due more than twelve months after the reporting date to be discounted, but provided no further measurement guidance. The Board amended the standard to state explicitly that the measurement of termination benefits should be consistent with the measurement requirements for the nature of the underlying benefits.

Interaction between plan amendments, curtailments, settlements, termination benefits and restructuring costs

BC262   In finalising the amendments made in 2011, the Board decided that an entity should:

(a)   recognise a plan amendment or curtailment when it occurs (paragraphs BC154–BC159); and

(b)   recognise termination benefits when the entity can no longer withdraw the offer of those benefits (paragraphs BC258–BC260).

BC263   Respondents to the 2010 ED were concerned about the accounting interactions between plan amendments, curtailments, settlements, termination benefits and restructurings because they often occur together, and it could be difficult to distinguish the gain or loss that arises from each transaction if they have different recognition requirements or are included in different components of defined benefit cost. Some respondents to the 2010 ED suggested aligning the timing of recognition of amounts resulting from plan amendments, curtailments, settlements, termination benefits and restructuring if they are related.

BC264   The requirements of IAS 19 before the amendments made in 2011 aligned the timing of recognition for a curtailment with the timing of recognition of a related restructuring, and suggested that when an entity recognises termination benefits the entity may also have to account for a curtailment. The objective of these requirements was to ensure that any gain or loss on curtailment is recognised at the same time as an expense resulting from a related termination benefit, from a restructuring provision or from both. In IAS 19 before the amendments made in 2011 and IAS 37, the recognition criteria for termination benefits and restructuring provisions were very similar and would have resulted in related termination benefits and restructuring being recognised together because both required recognition when an entity was demonstrably committed to the transaction.

BC265   The 2005 ED proposed to amend the timing of recognition of curtailments from being aligned with a related restructuring to being aligned with a related termination benefit. The 2010 ED did not include this amendment because the Board was in the process of finalising the amendments for termination benefits at the time.

BC266   To avoid an inconsistency in the timing of recognition for related transactions, the Board decided that:

(a)   past service cost should be recognised at the earlier of:

(i)   when the plan amendment occurs; and

(ii)   when any related restructuring costs or termination benefits are recognised.

(b)   termination benefits should be recognised at the earlier of:

(i)   when the entity can no longer withdraw the offer of those benefits; and

(ii)   when any related restructuring costs are recognised.

BC267   The Board also considered other approaches, including the proposal in the 2010 ED to align the timing of recognition for a plan amendment or curtailment with a related termination benefit but not with a related restructuring. In the Board's view the amendments made in 2011 have the following benefits over other approaches:

(a)   They align the timing of recognition for related transactions for all combinations of curtailments, termination benefits and restructurings (which is consistent with the current requirements).

(b)   They include the stand-alone recognition criteria developed for plan amendments and curtailments (ie that the plan amendment will be recognised when it occurs).

BC268   The 2005 ED proposed that the specific recognition criterion for restructuring costs should be withdrawn from IAS 37. If the Board confirms this proposal as part of its future discussion, then the references to the timing of recognition for restructuring costs will become redundant and the timing of recognition for plan amendments and curtailments will be aligned only with the timing of recognition for termination benefits. The Board will review the timing of recognition for restructuring costs when it finalises the amendments to IAS 37 resulting from the 2005 ED.

Transition

BC269   The amendments made in 2011 are to be applied retrospectively in accordance with the general requirements of IAS 8 *Accounting Policies, Changes in Accounting Estimates and Errors*, with two exceptions:

(a)   The carrying amount of assets outside the scope of IAS 19 need not be adjusted for changes in employee benefit costs that were included in the carrying amount before the beginning of the financial year in which the amendments are first applied. Thus entities may recognise previously unrecognised actuarial gains and losses and past service cost by adjusting equity, instead of by allocating part of those adjustments against the carrying amount of assets such as inventories. In the Board's view, such an allocation could have been costly and would have provided little or no benefit to users.

(b)   In financial statements for periods beginning before 1 January 2014, an entity need not provide comparatives for the disclosures about the sensitivity of the defined benefit obligation. The Board provided this exemption to provide sufficient lead time for entities to implement the necessary systems.

First-time adopters

BC270   For entities adopting IFRSs for the first time, the amendments made in 2011 are to be applied retrospectively as required by IFRS 1 *First-time Adoption of International Financial Reporting Standards*. The Board included a temporary exemption for entities adopting IFRSs to use paragraph 173(b) for the same reasons as given in paragraph BC269(b).[16]

Early application

BC271　The amendments made in 2011 will improve the accounting and, in particular, the disclosures provided by a reporting entity in relation to its participation in defined benefit plans. In addition, some of the amendments address existing problems in applying IAS 19 in practice. The Board noted that the majority of the amendments made in 2011 are permitted by the previous version of IAS 19. Consequently, the Board permitted early application of all the amendments made in 2011.

Transition provisions for *Defined Benefit Plans: Employee Contributions*

BC271A　In ED/2013/4, the IASB proposed retrospective application and to permit earlier application of the amendments. The majority of the respondents supported those proposals. Some respondents questioned whether retrospective application was practicable because some calculations might require information that is not readily available. The IASB observed that in current practice, contributions from employees or third parties are generally reduced from service cost without being attributed to periods of service. The proposed amendments are intended to provide relief so that entities can deduct contributions from service cost in the period in which the service is rendered, which was common practice prior to the 2011 amendments to IAS 19. The impact of retrospective application would therefore be minimal in those cases. Consequently, the IASB decided to retain the requirement for retrospective application.

BC271B　The amendments to IAS 19 published in 2011 are effective for annual periods beginning on or after 1 January 2013. In the IASB's view, the objective of the amendments published in 2013 is to provide relief in the accounting for contributions from employees or third parties and, therefore, the effective date should be set as early as possible, while allowing jurisdictions to have sufficient time to prepare for the new requirements. Consequently, the IASB decided that the effective date of the amendments should be 1 July 2014, with earlier application permitted.

Annual Improvements to IFRSs 2012–2014 Cycle

BC271C　*Annual Improvements to IFRSs 2012–2014 Cycle*, issued in September 2014, amended paragraph 83. The Board noted that for some entities a full retrospective application of the amendment could be burdensome. Consequently, the Board decided that the amendment should be applied from the beginning of the earliest comparative period presented in the first financial statements in which an entity applies the amendment. Any initial adjustment arising from the application of the amendment should be recognised in opening retained earnings of the earliest comparative period presented.

16　*Annual Improvements to IFRS Standards 2014–2016 Cycle*, issued in December 2016, amended IFRS 1 *First-time Adoption of International Financial Reporting Standards* by deleting the short-term exemption for first-time adopters (see paragraph BC99 of IFRS 1), because it was no longer applicable.

Summary of changes from the 2010 ED and 2005 ED: amendments issued in 2011

BC272 The main changes from the 2010 ED are:

(a) The amendments do not specify where in profit or loss an entity should present the net interest component. The 2010 ED proposed that an entity should include the net interest component as part of finance cost in profit or loss.

(b) The amendments require gains and losses on settlement to be included in service cost. The 2010 ED proposed that gains and losses on settlement should be included in remeasurements.

(c) The amendments do not require the following disclosures proposed in the 2010 ED:

(i) the defined benefit obligation, excluding projected growth in salaries;

(ii) sensitivity of current service cost to changes in actuarial assumptions; and

(iii) a description of the process used to determine the demographic actuarial assumptions.

(d) The amendments align the timing of recognition for plan amendments, termination benefits and restructuring costs. The 2010 ED proposed aligning the timing of recognition for plan amendments and termination benefits only.

(e) The amendments do not:

(i) combine the post-employment and other long-term employee benefit categories, as had been proposed in the 2010 ED.

(ii) state whether expected future salary increases should be included in determining whether a benefit formula allocates a materially higher level of benefit to later years, as had been proposed in the 2010 ED.

(iii) incorporate IFRIC 14 *IAS 19—The Limit on a Defined Benefit Asset, Minimum Funding Requirements and their Interaction* as had been proposed in the 2010 ED.

BC273 The main changes from the 2005 ED are:

(a) The amendment requires entities to recognise termination benefits when the entity can no longer withdraw an offer of those benefits. The 2005 ED proposed that voluntary termination benefits should be recognised when accepted by the employee, and that involuntary termination benefits should be recognised when the entity has a plan that meets specified criteria.

(b) The amendment clarifies the measurement requirements for termination benefits.

Convergence with US GAAP: amendments issued in 2011

Multi-employer plan disclosures

BC274 In March 2010 the FASB announced a new project to review disclosures about an employer's participation in a multi-employer plan and to develop disclosure requirements that would give better information about the risks that an entity faces by participating in a multi-employer plan. The FASB published a proposed Accounting Standards Update in the second quarter of 2010 with disclosure requirements similar to those relating to multi-employer defined benefit plans. The FASB expects to issue a final Accounting Standards Update in 2011.

Recognition of defined benefit cost

BC275 The amendments made in 2011 result in the measurement of an entity's surplus or deficit in a defined benefit plan in the statement of financial position, consistently with the requirements in US GAAP. Although both US GAAP and IAS 19 require the immediate recognition of changes in the net defined benefit liability (asset), there are differences in where those changes are recognised.

BC276 US GAAP defines net periodic pension cost[17] as comprising current service cost, interest cost on the defined benefit obligation, expected return on plan assets, amortisation of unrecognised prior service cost (if any), gains or losses recognised and amortised after exceeding a specified corridor (if any), amortisation of unrecognised initial net obligation and/or initial net asset. The IAS 19 requirements for the disaggregation of defined benefit cost and recognition of the components of defined benefit cost differ from the requirements in US GAAP as follows:

(a) *Disaggregation of the return on plan assets*—US GAAP distinguishes the expected return on plan assets and the difference between the expected and actual returns. The net interest approach in IAS 19 distinguishes an implied interest income on plan assets and the difference between the implied interest income and actual returns.

(b) *Past service cost*—US GAAP recognises past service cost in other comprehensive income initially, and then reclassifies past service cost from other comprehensive income to profit or loss in subsequent periods. IAS 19 requires past service cost to be included together with current service cost in profit or loss.

(c) *Reclassification*—US GAAP requires the reclassification of amounts recognised in other comprehensive income to profit or loss in subsequent periods. IAS 19 prohibits subsequent reclassification.

Termination benefits

BC277 FASB ASC Topic 420 specifies the accounting for a class of termination benefits known as 'one-time termination benefits'. Topic 420 requires an entity to recognise a 'stay bonus' over the period of the employees' service and to recognise other termination benefits when the entity has a plan of termination

---

17 FASB ASC Section 715-30-20 *Defined Benefit Plans—Pension Glossary*

that meets specified criteria. The amendments made in 2011 distinguish benefits provided in exchange for service and benefits provided in exchange for the termination of employment. A 'stay bonus' would not be classified as a termination benefit under IAS 19 because it is provided in exchange for service and, therefore, would be attributed to periods of service in accordance with paragraph 70 of IAS 19.

BC278 FASB ASC Topic 712 specifies the accounting for a class of termination benefits known as 'special termination benefits'. Topic 712 requires an entity to recognise these special termination benefits when the employees accept the employer's offer of termination benefits. The amendments made to IAS 19 in 2011 are consistent with those requirements. Topic 712 also specifies the accounting for a class of termination benefits known as 'contractual termination benefits'. Topic 712 requires an entity to recognise contractual termination benefits when it is probable that employees will be entitled to benefits and the amount can be reasonably estimated. The amendments made in 2011 do not converge with those requirements; instead, IAS 19 requires those benefits to be recognised when an entity can no longer withdraw an offer of those benefits.

BC279 FASB ASC Topic 420 specifies that an entity should measure 'one-time' termination benefits at fair value (or at an amount based on fair value for benefits provided in exchange for future service). The Board did not align the measurement requirements of IAS 19 for termination benefits with those of Topic 420. When an entity provides termination benefits through a post-employment defined benefit plan (for example, by enhancing retirement benefits) the Board concluded that it would be unduly complex to specify that an entity should measure the benefits at fair value. To do so would require the effect of the changes to the plan arising from the termination of employment to be isolated, on a continuous basis, from the remainder of the plan.

Cost-benefit considerations: amendments issued in 2011

BC280 The objective of financial statements is to provide information about the financial position, performance and changes in financial position of an entity that is useful to a wide range of users in making economic decisions. To attain this objective, the Board seeks to ensure that an IFRS will meet a significant need and that the overall benefits of the resulting information justify the costs of providing it. Although the costs to implement changes to existing requirements might not be borne evenly, users of financial statements benefit from improvements in financial reporting, thereby facilitating the functioning of markets for capital and credit and the efficient allocation of resources in the economy.

BC281 The evaluation of costs and benefits is necessarily subjective. In making its judgement, the Board considered the following:

(a)   the costs incurred by preparers of financial statements.

(b)   the costs incurred by users of financial statements when information is not available.

(c) the comparative advantage that preparers have in developing information, compared with the costs that users would incur to develop surrogate information.

(d) the benefit of better economic decision-making as a result of improved financial reporting.

(e) the costs of transition for users, preparers and others.

BC282 The objective of the amendments made in 2011 is to improve the usefulness of information available to users for their assessment of the amounts, timing and uncertainty of future cash flows arising from defined benefit plans of the entity. However, the Board also considered the cost of implementing the proposed amendments and applying them on a continuous basis. In evaluating the relative costs and benefits of the proposed amendments, the Board was assisted by the information received in meetings with its Employee Benefits Working Group.

BC283 The amendments should improve the ability of users to understand the financial reporting for post-employment benefits by:

(a) reporting changes in the carrying amounts of defined benefit obligations and changes in the fair value of plan assets in a more understandable way;

(b) eliminating some recognition options that were allowed by IAS 19, thus improving comparability;

(c) clarifying requirements that have resulted in diverse practices; and

(d) improving information about the risks arising from an entity's involvement in defined benefit plans.

BC284 Costs will be involved in the adoption and continuing application of the amendments. Those costs will depend on the complexity of an entity's defined benefit arrangements and the options in IAS 19 that the entity currently elects to apply. However, those costs should be minimal because in order to apply the previous version of IAS 19 entities need to obtain much of the information that the amendments require. Consequently, the Board believes that the benefits of the amendments outweigh the costs.

Appendix
Amendments to the Basis for Conclusions on other IFRSs

This appendix contains amendments to the Basis for Conclusions (and related appendices) on other IFRSs that are necessary in order to ensure consistency with IAS 19 and the related amendments to other IFRSs. Amended paragraphs are shown with new text underlined and deleted text struck through.

* * * * *

The amendments contained in this appendix when IAS 19, as amended in 2011, was issued have been incorporated into the Basis for Conclusions on the relevant IFRSs published in this volume.

© IFRS Foundation

Dissenting opinions

Dissent of James J Leisenring and Tatsumi Yamada from the issue in December 2004 of *Actuarial Gains and Losses, Group Plans and Disclosures* (Amendment to IAS 19)[18]

Mr Leisenring

DO1 Mr Leisenring dissents from the issue of the Amendment to IAS 19 Employee Benefits—*Actuarial Gains and Losses, Group Plans and Disclosures*.

DO2 Mr Leisenring dissents because he disagrees with the deletion of the last sentence in paragraph 40 and the addition of paragraphs 41 and 42. He believes that group entities that give a defined benefit promise to their employees should account for that defined benefit promise in their separate or individual financial statements. He further believes that separate or individual financial statements that purport to be prepared in accordance with IFRSs should comply with the same requirements as other financial statements that are prepared in accordance with IFRSs. He therefore disagrees with the removal of the requirement for group entities to treat defined benefit plans that share risks between entities under common control as defined benefit plans and the introduction instead of the requirements of paragraph 41.

DO3 Mr Leisenring notes that group entities are required to give disclosures about the plan as a whole but does not believe that disclosures are an adequate substitute for recognition and measurement in accordance with the requirements of IAS 19.

Mr Yamada

DO4 Mr Yamada dissents from the issue of the Amendment to IAS 19 Employee Benefits—*Actuarial Gains and Losses, Group Plans and Disclosures*.

DO5 Mr Yamada agrees that an option should be added to IAS 19 that allows entities that recognise actuarial gains and losses in full in the period in which they occur to recognise them outside profit or loss in a statement of recognised income and expense, even though under the previous IAS 19 they can be recognised in profit or loss in full in the period in which they occur. He agrees that the option provides more transparent information than the deferred recognition options commonly chosen under IAS 19. However, he also believes that all items of income and expense should be recognised in profit or loss in some period. Until they have been so recognised, they should be included in a component of equity separate from retained earnings. They should be transferred from that separate component of equity into retained earnings when they are recognised in profit or loss. Mr Yamada does not, therefore, agree with the requirements of paragraph 93D.[19]

---

18 Cross-references have been updated.
19 The amendments to IAS 19 made in 2011 deleted paragraph 93D.

DO6   Mr Yamada acknowledges the difficulty in finding a rational basis for recognising actuarial gains and losses in profit or loss in periods after their initial recognition in a statement of recognised income and expense when the plan is ongoing. He also acknowledges that, under IFRSs, some gains and losses are recognised directly in a separate component of equity and are not subsequently recognised in profit or loss. However, Mr Yamada does not believe that this justifies expanding this treatment to actuarial gains and losses.

DO7   The cumulative actuarial gains and losses could be recognised in profit or loss when a plan is wound up or transferred outside the entity. The cumulative amount recognised in a separate component of equity would be transferred to retained earnings at the same time. This would be consistent with the treatment of exchange gains and losses on subsidiaries that have a measurement currency different from the presentation currency of the group.

DO8   Therefore, Mr Yamada believes that the requirements of paragraph 93D mean that the option is not an improvement to financial reporting because it allows gains and losses to be excluded permanently from profit or loss and yet be recognised immediately in retained earnings.

Dissent of Jan Engström and Tatsumi Yamada from the issue in June 2011 of IAS 19 as amended

Mr Engström

DO1   Mr Engström voted against the amendments made to IAS 19 in 2011. The project was a limited scope project focused on bringing the full post-employment benefit onto the statement of financial position and on eliminating the corridor approach.

DO2   In Mr Engström's view, during the project it has become increasingly clear that a review of the measurement principles is much needed— something not included in the limited scope of the project. During the recent financial crisis the defined benefit obligation could be as much as 50 per cent higher in one company compared with an identical defined benefit obligation in another company operating in an adjacent country, with basically equal macroeconomic parameters, due to the imperfections in measurement requirements of IAS 19.

DO3   In Mr Engström's view, the amendments to IAS 19 made in 2011 introduce some radical changes from a principle point of view by not requiring some income and expenses truly related to a company's activities ever to be presented in profit or loss, indeed actually prohibiting such presentation. The adjustments of the defined benefit obligation, and of the plan assets, have for many companies been a very significant amount and by presenting income and expenses resulting from these adjustments only in other comprehensive income this project continues the gradual erosion of the concept of profit or loss.

DO4   Mr Engström sees no reason why the remeasurements component could not be subsequently reclassified to profit or loss on a reasonable basis consistently with the assumptions used to measure the defined benefit obligation.

DO5   Mr Engström would favour a comprehensive review of IAS 19, including a review of measurement, and he would prefer presentation to be decided only after the IASB has taken a stance on what profit or loss is, what other comprehensive income is and what should be subsequently reclassified into profit or loss.

DO6   As a consequence of these amendments made to IAS 19, and of the option introduced in IFRS 9 *Financial Instruments*, some material amounts may never be presented in profit or loss. IFRS 9 introduced an option to present some gains and losses on equity instruments not held for trading in other comprehensive income, without subsequent reclassification to profit or loss. In Mr Engström's view, these recent ad hoc decisions push financial reporting de facto towards a single income statement as some matters truly related to a company's activities are never to be presented in profit or loss.

Mr Yamada

DO7   Mr Yamada voted against the amendments made to IAS 19 in 2011.

DO8   Mr Yamada agrees with the Board's view in paragraph BC70 that immediate recognition of all changes in the fair values of plan assets and in the defined benefit obligation in the period in which those changes occur provides information that is more relevant to users of financial statements than the information provided by deferred recognition. Mr Yamada also agrees that immediate recognition provides a more faithful representation of defined benefit plans and is easier for a user to understand.

DO9   However, Mr Yamada does not agree with:

(a)   the disaggregation of defined benefit cost (see paragraph DO10);

(b)   the definition of net interest and remeasurements of the net defined benefit liability (asset) (see paragraphs DO11–DO14); and

(c)   the presentation of remeasurements of the net defined benefit liability (asset) in other comprehensive income (see paragraphs DO15–DO17).

Disaggregation of defined benefit cost

DO10   In Mr Yamada's view the disaggregation of defined benefit cost into components (ie service cost, net interest and remeasurements) in profit or loss and other comprehensive income in paragraph 120 is not consistent with the presentation of plan assets and the defined benefit obligation in the statement of financial position. In his view, to be consistent with the presentation of a single net defined benefit liability (asset) in the statement of financial position, the presentation of changes in the net defined benefit liability (asset) should be a single net amount presented in profit or loss. Therefore, he does not agree with paragraph 134 not to specify how to present service cost and net interest on the net defined benefit liability (asset). He understands the usefulness of disaggregated information, but believes that an appropriate way of providing information on the components of defined benefit cost is to show them in the notes to the financial statements.

Definition of net interest and remeasurements on the net defined benefit liability (asset)

DO11   Mr Yamada sees no principle behind the disaggregation described in paragraph 120 (ie service cost, net interest and remeasurements). In particular, in his view the approach for calculating net interest on the net defined benefit liability (asset) is not an improvement in financial reporting.

DO12   In Mr Yamada's view there is no reason for requiring the component of the return on plan assets presented in profit or loss to be determined using the rate used to discount the defined benefit obligation as is in paragraph 125. He agrees with the respondents' concerns summarised in paragraph BC82 that plan assets may be made up of many different types of investments, and that 'the return on high quality corporate bonds would be arbitrary and would not be a faithful representation of the return that investors require or expect from each type of asset.' Therefore, in his view, it does not provide more useful information to use the rate used to discount the defined benefit obligation in place of the previous requirement to use expected return on plan assets.

DO13   Mr Yamada does not agree that the Board should require 'using the same rate [for plan assets] as the rate used to discount the liability [as] a practical approach that ... would not require an entity to make a subjective judgement on how to divide the return on plan assets into an interest component and a remeasurement' (paragraph BC82). He agrees that determining the 'expected return on plan assets' that is used by the previous version of IAS 19 requires judgement by management, but this does not mean that the 'expected return on plan assets' is unreliable. In his view, estimating the 'expected return on plan assets' requires the same degree of judgement as do other accounting estimates.

DO14   In Mr Yamada's view, there is no clear explanation about the nature of the remeasurements component, nor why disaggregation of this amount is appropriate. In the previous version of IAS 19, actuarial gains and losses on plan assets were defined as experience adjustments, ie the effects of differences between the previous actuarial assumptions (the expected return on assets) and what actually occurred. However, paragraph BC86 explains the nature of the remeasurements component as being a residual after determining the service cost and net interest components, and simply restates the definition of remeasurements in paragraph 7.

Presentation of remeasurements in other comprehensive income

DO15   Paragraph BC88 sets out the Board's reasoning that the remeasurement component should be presented in other comprehensive income because 'although changes included in the remeasurements component may provide more information about the uncertainty and risk of future cash flows, they provide less information about the likely amount and timing of those cash flows'. Mr Yamada does not agree with that reasoning because, in his view, the actual return on plan assets provides information about the performance of plan assets during the period, but the disaggregation of the actual return into interest income and a remeasurements component does not provide information about the likely timing and amount of future cash flows. Therefore, in his view, it does not represent faithfully the performance of plan assets if the actual returns on plan assets in excess of the interest income on plan assets are presented in other comprehensive income and not presented in profit or loss when they occur. Instead, all the components should be presented in profit or loss when they occur. Therefore, he does not agree with paragraph 120(c). In his view the amount representing remeasurements does not have a clearly defined characteristic that justifies its presentation in other comprehensive income.

DO16   Mr Yamada notes that the definition of net interest on the net defined benefit liability (asset) results in the difference between the rate used to discount the defined benefit obligation applied to plan assets and the actual return on plan assets being presented in other comprehensive income. To do so eliminates from profit or loss the effects of differences between the actual return on plan assets and the rate applied to the defined benefit obligation. In his view the elimination of these differences introduces a type of smoothing mechanism. Thus, in his view the proposal is not an improvement on the previous version of IAS 19.

DO17   Given that the Board decided to present part of the defined benefit cost (ie remeasurements) in other comprehensive income, he is of the view that the Board should have retained the notion of actuarial gains and losses in the previous version of IAS 19 (paragraphs 93A–93D) rather than introduce a similar but not clearly better new notion of 'remeasurements'. This would mean that the expected return on plan assets is recognised in profit or loss and the difference between the expected return on plan assets and the actual return on plan assets is recognised in other comprehensive income. As stated in paragraph DO15, in Mr Yamada's view, this difference gives better information than the revised remeasurement component.

IASB document published to accompany

IAS 20

Accounting for Government Grants and Disclosure of Government Assistance

The text of the unaccompanied standard, IAS 20, is contained in Part A of this edition. Its effective date when issued was 1 January 1984. This part presents the following documents:

BASIS FOR CONCLUSIONS

Basis for Conclusions on IAS 20 *Accounting for Government Grants and Disclosure of Government Assistance*

This Basis for Conclusions accompanies, but is not part of, IAS 20.

BC1   This Basis for Conclusions summarises the International Accounting Standards Board's considerations in amending IAS 20 *Accounting for Government Grants and Disclosure of Government Assistance* as part of *Improvements to IFRSs* issued in May 2008.

BC2   IAS 20 was developed by the International Accounting Standards Committee in 1983 and did not include a Basis for Conclusions. This Basis refers to the insertion of paragraphs 10A and 43 and the deletion of paragraph 37. Those changes require government loans with below-market rates of interest to be recognised and measured in accordance with IAS 39 *Financial Instruments: Recognition and Measurement*[1] and the benefit of the reduced interest to be accounted for using IAS 20.

Accounting for loans from government with a below-market rate of interest

BC3   The Board identified an apparent inconsistency between the guidance in IAS 20 and IAS 39.[2] It related to the accounting for loans with a below-market rate of interest received from a government. IAS 20 stated that no interest should be imputed for such a loan, whereas IAS 39 required all loans to be recognised at fair value, thus requiring interest to be imputed to loans with a below-market rate of interest.

BC4   The Board decided to remove this inconsistency. It believed that the imputation of interest provides more relevant information to a user of the financial statements. Accordingly the Board amended IAS 20 to require that loans received from a government that have a below-market rate of interest should be recognised and measured in accordance with IAS 39. The benefit of the government loan is measured at the inception of the loan as the difference between the cash received and the amount at which the loan is initially recognised in the statement of financial position. This benefit is accounted for in accordance with IAS 20.

BC5   Noting that applying IAS 39 to loans retrospectively may require entities to measure the fair value of loans at a past date, the Board decided that the amendment should be applied prospectively to new loans.

---

1   IFRS 9 *Financial Instruments* replaced IAS 39. IFRS 9 applies to all items that were previously within the scope of IAS 39. This paragraph refers to matters relevant when IAS 20 was amended in 2008.
2   IFRS 9 *Financial Instruments* replaced IAS 39. IFRS 9 applies to all items that were previously within the scope of IAS 39. This paragraph refers to matters relevant when IAS 20 was amended in 2008.

IASB documents published to accompany

IAS 21

The Effects of Changes in Foreign Exchange Rates

The text of the unaccompanied standard, IAS 21, is contained in Part A of this edition. Its effective date when issued was 1 January 2005. This part presents the following documents:

BASIS FOR CONCLUSIONS

Basis for Conclusions on
IAS 21 *The Effects of Changes in Foreign Exchange Rates*

This Basis for Conclusions accompanies, but is not part of, IAS 21.

Paragraph BC1 was amended and paragraphs BC25A–BC25F were added in relation to the amendment to IAS 21 issued in December 2005.

In this Basis for Conclusions the terminology has not been amended to reflect the changes made by IAS 1 Presentation of Financial Statements *(as revised in 2007).*

Introduction

BC1   This Basis for Conclusions summarises the International Accounting Standards Board's considerations in reaching its conclusions on revising IAS 21 *The Effects of Changes in Foreign Exchange Rates* in 2003, and on the amendment to IAS 21 *Net Investment in a Foreign Operation* in December 2005. Individual Board members gave greater weight to some factors than to others.

BC2   In July 2001 the Board announced that, as part of its initial agenda of technical projects, it would undertake a project to improve a number of Standards, including IAS 21. The project was undertaken in the light of queries and criticisms raised in relation to the Standards by securities regulators, professional accountants and other interested parties. The objectives of the Improvements project were to reduce or eliminate alternatives, redundancies and conflicts within Standards, to deal with some convergence issues and to make other improvements. In May 2002 the Board published its proposals in an Exposure Draft of *Improvements to International Accounting Standards*, with a comment deadline of 16 September 2002. The Board received over 160 comment letters on the Exposure Draft.

BC3   Because the Board's intention was not to reconsider the fundamental approach to accounting for the effects of changes in foreign exchange rates established by IAS 21, this Basis for Conclusions does not discuss requirements in IAS 21 that the Board has not reconsidered.

Functional currency

BC4   The term 'reporting currency' was previously defined as 'the currency used in presenting the financial statements'. This definition comprises two separate notions (which were identified in SIC-19 *Reporting Currency—Measurement and Presentation of Financial Statements under IAS 21 and IAS 29*):

- the measurement currency (the currency in which the entity measures the items in the financial statements); and

- the presentation currency (the currency in which the entity presents its financial statements).

The Board decided to revise the previous version of IAS 21 to incorporate the SIC-19 approach of separating these two notions. The Board also noted that the term 'functional currency' is more commonly used than 'measurement currency' and decided to adopt the more common term.

BC5   The Board noted a concern that the guidance in SIC-19 on determining a measurement currency could permit entities to choose one of several currencies, or to select an inappropriate currency. In particular, some believed that SIC-19 placed too much emphasis on the currency in which transactions are denominated and too little emphasis on the underlying economy that determines the pricing of those transactions. To meet these concerns, the Board defined functional currency as 'the currency of the primary economic environment in which the entity operates'. The Board also provided guidance on how to determine the functional currency (see paragraphs 9–14 of the Standard). This guidance draws heavily on SIC-19 and equivalent guidance in US and other national standards, but also reflects the Board's decision that some factors merit greater emphasis than others.

BC6   The Board also discussed whether a foreign operation that is integral to the reporting entity (as described in the previous version of IAS 21) could have a functional currency that is different from that of its 'parent'.[1] The Board decided that the functional currencies will always be the same, because it would be contradictory for an integral foreign operation that 'carries on business as if it were an extension of the reporting enterprise's operations'[2] to operate in a primary economic environment different from its parent.

BC7   It follows that it is not necessary to translate the results and financial position of an integral foreign operation when incorporating them into the financial statements of the parent—they will already be measured in the parent's functional currency. Furthermore, it is not necessary to distinguish between an integral foreign operation and a foreign entity. When a foreign operation's functional currency is different from that of its parent, it is a foreign entity, and the translation method in paragraphs 38–49 of the Standard applies.

BC8   The Board also decided that the principles in the previous version of IAS 21 for distinguishing an integral foreign operation from a foreign entity are relevant in determining an operation's functional currency. Hence it incorporated these principles into the Standard in that context.

BC9   The Board agreed that the indicators in paragraph 9 are the primary indicators for determining the functional currency and that paragraphs 10 and 11 are secondary. This is because the indicators in paragraphs 10 and 11 are not linked to the primary economic environment in which the entity operates but provide additional supporting evidence to determine an entity's functional currency.

Presentation currency

BC10   A further issue is whether an entity should be permitted to present its financial statements in a currency (or currencies) other than its functional currency. Some believe it should not. They believe that the functional currency, being the currency of the primary economic environment in which the entity operates, most usefully portrays the economic effect of transactions and events on the entity. For a group that comprises operations with a number of functional

---

1   The term 'parent' is used broadly in this context to mean an entity that has a branch, associate or joint venture, as well as one with a subsidiary.

2   IAS 21 (revised 1993), paragraph 24

currencies, they believe that the consolidated financial statements should be presented in the functional currency that management uses when controlling and monitoring the performance and financial position of the group. They also believe that allowing an entity to present its financial statements in more than one currency may confuse, rather than help, users of those financial statements. Supporters of this view believe that any presentation in a currency other than that described above should be regarded as a 'convenience translation' that is outside the scope of IFRSs.

BC11   Others believe that the choice of presentation currency should be limited, for example, to the functional currency of one of the substantive entities within a group. However, such a restriction might be easily overcome—an entity that wished to present its financial statements in a different currency might establish a substantive, but relatively small operation with that functional currency.

BC12   Still others believe that, given the rising trend towards globalisation, entities should be permitted to present their financial statements in any currency. They note that most large groups do not have a single functional currency, but rather comprise operations with a number of functional currencies. For such entities, they believe it is not clear which currency should be the presentation currency, or why one currency is preferable to another. They also point out that management may not use a single currency when controlling and monitoring the performance and financial position of such a group. In addition, they note that in some jurisdictions, entities are required to present their financial statements in the local currency, even when this is not the functional currency.[3] Hence, if IFRSs required the financial statements to be presented in the functional currency, some entities would have to present two sets of financial statements: financial statements that comply with IFRSs presented in the functional currency and financial statements that comply with local regulations presented in a different currency.

BC13   The Board was persuaded by the arguments in the previous paragraph. Accordingly, it decided that entities should be permitted to present their financial statements in any currency (or currencies).

BC14   The Board also clarified that the Standard does not prohibit the entity from providing, as supplementary information, a 'convenience translation'. Such a 'convenience translation' may display financial statements (or selected portions of financial statements) in a currency other than the presentation currency, as a convenience to some users. The 'convenience translation' may be prepared using a translation method other than that required by the Standard. These types of 'convenience translations' should be clearly identified as supplementary information to distinguish them from information required by IFRSs and translated in accordance with the Standard.

---

3   This includes entities operating in another country and, for example, publishing financial statements to comply with a listing requirement of that country.

© IFRS Foundation

Translation method

BC15   The Board debated which method should be used to translate financial statements from an entity's functional currency into a different presentation currency.

BC16   The Board agreed that the translation method should not have the effect of substituting another currency for the functional currency. Put another way, presenting the financial statements in a different currency should not change the way in which the underlying items are measured. Rather, the translation method should merely express the underlying amounts, as measured in the functional currency, in a different currency.

BC17   Given this, the Board considered two possible translation methods. The first is to translate all amounts (including comparatives) at the most recent closing rate. This method has several advantages: it is simple to apply; it does not generate any new gains and losses; and it does not change ratios such as return on assets. This method is supported by those who believe that the process of merely expressing amounts in a different currency should preserve the relationships among amounts as measured in the functional currency and, as such, should not lead to any new gains or losses.

BC18   The second method considered by the Board is the one that the previous version of IAS 21 required for translating the financial statements of a foreign operation.[4] This method results in the same amounts in the presentation currency regardless of whether the financial statements of a foreign operation are:

(a)   first translated into the functional currency of another group entity (eg the parent) and then into the presentation currency, or

(b)   translated directly into the presentation currency.

BC19   This method avoids the need to decide the currency in which to express the financial statements of a multinational group before they are translated into the presentation currency. As noted above, many large groups do not have a single functional currency, but comprise operations with a number of functional currencies. For such entities it is not clear which functional currency should be chosen in which to express amounts before they are translated into the presentation currency, or why one currency is preferable to another. In addition, this method produces the same amounts in the presentation currency for a stand-alone entity as for an identical subsidiary of a parent whose functional currency is the presentation currency.

BC20   The Board decided to require the second method, ie that the financial statements of any entity (whether a stand-alone entity, a parent or an operation within a group) whose functional currency differs from the presentation currency used by the reporting entity are translated using the method set out in paragraphs 38–49 of the Standard.

---

4   This is to translate balance sheet items at the closing rate and income and expense items at actual (or average) rates, except for an entity whose functional currency is that of a hyperinflationary economy.

BC21   With respect to translation of comparative amounts, the Board adopted the approach required by SIC-30 for:

(a)   an entity whose functional currency is not the currency of the hyperinflationary economy (assets and liabilities in the comparative balance sheet are translated at the closing rate at the date of that balance sheet and income and expenses in the comparative income statement are translated at exchange rates at the dates of the transactions); and

(b)   an entity whose functional currency is the currency of a hyperinflationary economy, and for which the comparative amounts are being translated into the currency of a hyperinflationary economy (both balance sheet and income statement items are translated at the closing rate of the most recent balance sheet presented).

BC22   However, the Board decided not to adopt the SIC-30 approach for the translation of comparatives for an entity whose functional currency is the currency of a hyperinflationary economy, and for which the comparative amounts are being translated into a presentation currency of a non-hyperinflationary economy. The Board noted that in such a case, the SIC-30 approach requires restating the comparative amounts from those shown in last year's financial statements for both the effects of inflation and for changes in exchange rates. If exchange rates fully reflect differing price levels between the two economies to which they relate, the SIC-30 approach will result in the same amounts for the comparatives as were reported as current year amounts in the prior year financial statements. Furthermore, the Board noted that in the prior year, the relevant amounts had been already expressed in the non-hyperinflationary presentation currency, and there was no reason to change them. For these reasons the Board decided to require that all comparative amounts are those presented in the prior year financial statements (ie there is no adjustment for either subsequent changes in the price level or subsequent changes in exchange rates).

BC23   The Board decided to incorporate into the Standard most of the disclosure requirements of SIC-30 *Reporting Currency—Translation from Measurement Currency to Presentation Currency* that apply when a different translation method is used or other supplementary information, such as an extract from the full financial statements, is displayed in a currency other than the functional currency (see paragraph 57 of the Standard). These disclosures enable users to distinguish information prepared in accordance with IFRSs from information that may be useful to users but is not the subject of IFRSs, and also tell users how the latter information has been prepared.

Capitalisation of exchange differences

BC24   The previous version of IAS 21 allowed a limited choice of accounting for exchange differences that arise 'from a severe devaluation or depreciation of a currency against which there is no practical means of hedging and that affects liabilities which cannot be settled and which arise directly on the recent acquisition of an asset'.[5] The benchmark treatment was to recognise such exchange differences in profit or loss. The allowed alternative was to recognise them as an asset.

BC25   The Board noted that the allowed alternative (of recognition as an asset) was not in accordance with the *Framework for the Preparation and Presentation of Financial Statements*[6] because exchange losses do not meet the definition of an asset. Moreover, recognition of exchange losses as an asset is neither allowed nor required by any liaison standard-setter, so its deletion would improve convergence. Finally, in many cases when the conditions for recognition as an asset are met, the asset would be restated in accordance with IAS 29 *Financial Reporting in Hyperinflationary Economies*. Thus, to the extent that an exchange loss reflects hyperinflation, this effect is taken into account by IAS 29. For all of these reasons, the Board removed the allowed alternative treatment and the related SIC Interpretation is superseded.

Net investment in a foreign operation

BC25A The principle in paragraph 32 is that exchange differences arising on a monetary item that is, in substance, part of the reporting entity's net investment in a foreign operation are initially recognised in a separate component of equity[7] in the consolidated financial statements of the reporting entity. Among the revisions to IAS 21 made in 2003 was the provision of guidance on this principle that required the monetary item to be denominated in the functional currency of either the reporting entity or the foreign operation. The previous version of IAS 21 did not include such guidance.

BC25B The requirements can be illustrated by the following example. Parent P owns 100 per cent of Subsidiary S. Parent P has a functional currency of UK sterling. Subsidiary S has a functional currency of Mexican pesos. Parent P grants a loan of 100 US dollars to Subsidiary S, for which settlement is neither planned nor likely to occur in the foreseeable future. IAS 21 (as revised in 2003) requires the exchange differences arising on the loan to be recognised in profit or loss in the consolidated financial statements of Parent P, whereas those differences would be recognised initially in equity in the consolidated financial statements of Parent P, if the loan were to be denominated in sterling or Mexican pesos.

BC25C After the revised IAS 21 was issued in 2003, constituents raised the following concerns:

   (a)   It is common practice for a monetary item that forms part of an entity's investment in a foreign operation to be denominated in a currency that is not the functional currency of either the reporting entity or the foreign operation. An example is a monetary item denominated in a currency that is more readily convertible than the local domestic currency of the foreign operation.

---

5   IAS 21 (revised 1993), paragraph 21.
6   In September 2010 the IASB replaced the *Framework* with the *Conceptual Framework for Financial Reporting*.
7   As a consequence of the revision of IAS 1 *Presentation of Financial Statements* in 2007 such differences are recognised in other comprehensive income.

(b)   An investment in a foreign operation denominated in a currency that is not the functional currency of the reporting entity or the foreign operation does not expose the group to a greater foreign currency exchange difference than arises when the investment is denominated in the functional currency of the reporting entity or the foreign operation. It simply results in exchange differences arising in the foreign operation's individual financial statements and the reporting entity's separate financial statements.

(c)   It is not clear whether the term 'reporting entity' in paragraph 32 should be interpreted as the single entity or the group comprising a parent and all its subsidiaries. As a result, constituents questioned whether the monetary item must be transacted between the foreign operation and the reporting entity, or whether it could be transacted between the foreign operation and any member of the consolidated group, ie the reporting entity or any of its subsidiaries.

BC25D   The Board noted that the nature of the monetary item referred to in paragraph 15 is similar to an equity investment in a foreign operation, ie settlement of the monetary item is neither planned nor likely to occur in the foreseeable future. Therefore, the principle in paragraph 32 to recognise exchange differences arising on a monetary item initially in a separate component of equity effectively results in the monetary item being accounted for in the same way as an equity investment in the foreign operation when consolidated financial statements are prepared. The Board concluded that the accounting treatment in the consolidated financial statements should not be dependent on the currency in which the monetary item is denominated, nor on which entity within the group conducts the transaction with the foreign operation.

BC25E   Accordingly, in 2005 the Board decided to amend IAS 21. The amendment requires exchange differences arising on a monetary item that forms part of a reporting entity's net investment in a foreign operation to be recognised initially in a separate component of equity in the consolidated financial statements. This requirement applies irrespective of the currency of the monetary item and of whether the monetary item results from a transaction with the reporting entity or any of its subsidiaries.

BC25F   The Board also proposed amending IAS 21 to clarify that an investment in a foreign operation made by an associate of the reporting entity is not part of the reporting entity's net investment in that foreign operation. Respondents to the exposure draft disagreed with this proposal. Many respondents said that the proposed amendment added a detailed rule that was not required because the principle in paragraph 15 was clear. In redeliberations, the Board agreed with those comments and decided not to proceed with that proposed amendment.

Goodwill and fair value adjustments

BC26   The previous version of IAS 21 allowed a choice of translating goodwill and fair value adjustments to assets and liabilities that arise on the acquisition of a foreign entity at (a) the closing rate or (b) the historical transaction rate.

BC27   The Board agreed that, conceptually, the correct treatment depends on whether goodwill and fair value adjustments are part of:

(a)   the assets and liabilities of the acquired entity (which would imply translating them at the closing rate); or

(b)   the assets and liabilities of the parent (which would imply translating them at the historical rate).

BC28   The Board agreed that fair value adjustments clearly relate to the identifiable assets and liabilities of the acquired entity and should therefore be translated at the closing rate.

BC29   Goodwill is more complex, partly because it is measured as a residual. In addition, the Board noted that difficult issues can arise when the acquired entity comprises businesses that have different functional currencies (eg if the acquired entity is a multinational group). The Board discussed how to assess any resulting goodwill for impairment and, in particular, whether the goodwill would need to be 'pushed down' to the level of each different functional currency or could be accounted for and assessed at a higher level.

BC30   One view is that when the parent acquires a multinational operation comprising businesses with many different functional currencies, any goodwill may be treated as an asset of the parent/acquirer and tested for impairment at a consolidated level. Those who support this view believe that, in economic terms, the goodwill is an asset of the parent because it is part of the acquisition price paid by the parent. Thus, they believe, it would be incorrect to allocate the goodwill to the many acquired businesses and translate it into their various functional currencies. Rather, the goodwill, being treated as an asset of the parent, is not exposed to foreign currency risks, and translation differences associated with it should not be recognised. In addition, they believe that such goodwill should be tested for impairment at a consolidated level. Under this view, allocating or 'pushing down' the goodwill to a lower level, such as each different functional currency within the acquired foreign operation, would not serve any purpose.

BC31   Others take a different view. They believe that the goodwill is part of the parent's net investment in the acquired entity. In their view, goodwill should be treated no differently from other assets of the acquired entity, in particular intangible assets, because a significant part of the goodwill is likely to comprise intangible assets that do not qualify for separate recognition. They also note that goodwill arises only because of the investment in the foreign entity and has no existence apart from that entity. Lastly, they point out that when the acquired entity comprises a number of businesses with different functional currencies, the cash flows that support the continued recognition of goodwill are generated in those different functional currencies.

BC32   The Board was persuaded by the reasons set out in the preceding paragraph and decided that goodwill is treated as an asset of the foreign operation and translated at the closing rate. Consequently, goodwill should be allocated to the level of each functional currency of the acquired foreign operation. This means that the level to which goodwill is allocated for foreign currency translation purposes may be different from the level at which the goodwill is tested for impairment. Entities follow the requirements in IAS 36 *Impairment of Assets* to determine the level at which goodwill is tested for impairment.

Disposal or partial disposal of a foreign operation[8]

BC33   In the second phase of the business combinations project the Board decided that the loss of control, significant influence or joint control of an entity is accounted for as a disposal for the purposes of IAS 21. Accordingly, a former parent accounts for the loss of control over a subsidiary as a disposal of the subsidiary, even if the former subsidiary becomes an associate or jointly controlled entity[9] of the former parent. Similarly an investor accounts for the loss of significant influence over an associate or the loss of joint control over a jointly controlled entity as a disposal. The Board decided that the change in the nature of the investment is a significant economic event.

BC34   The Board also decided in the second phase of the business combinations project that:

(a)   changes in the parent's ownership interest in a subsidiary that do not result in a loss of control are accounted for as equity transactions (ie transactions with owners in their capacity as owners);

(b)   if a parent loses control of a subsidiary, the parent reclassifies from equity to profit or loss (as a reclassification adjustment) the parent's share of the exchange differences recognised in other comprehensive income relating to a foreign operation in that subsidiary; and

(c)   if an investor loses significant influence over an associate or loses joint control over a jointly controlled entity, the investor reclassifies from equity to profit or loss (as a reclassification adjustment) the exchange differences recognised in other comprehensive income relating to a foreign operation in that associate or jointly controlled entity.

The amendments in paragraphs 48A–49 of the Standard reflect those decisions for the disposal or partial disposal of a foreign operation.

BC35   As part of *Cost of an Investment in a Subsidiary, Jointly Controlled Entity or Associate* (Amendments to IFRS 1 *First-time Adoption of International Financial Reporting Standards* and IAS 27 *Consolidated and Separate Financial Statements*), issued in May 2008, the Board amended IAS 27 to remove the definition of the 'cost method'. The cost method required an entity to recognise distributions as income only if they came from post-acquisition retained earnings. Distributions received in excess of such profits were regarded as a recovery of the investment and were recognised as a reduction of its cost. Consequently, the Board amended paragraph 49 to remove the reference to pre-acquisition profits and to clarify

---

8   This heading and paragraphs BC33 and BC34 were added as a consequence of amendments to IAS 27 *Consolidated and Separate Financial Statements* made as part of the second phase of the business combinations project in 2008. The consolidation requirements in IAS 27 were superseded by IFRS 10 *Consolidated Financial Statements* issued in May 2011. The accounting requirements did not change.

9   'Jointly controlled entities' were defined in IAS 31 *Interests in Joint Ventures*. IFRS 11 *Joint Arrangements*, issued in May 2011, replaced IAS 31 and changed the terminology.

that a dividend accounted for in accordance with paragraph 38A of IAS 27 cannot be a disposal or partial disposal of a net investment in IAS 21.[10]

Disposal or partial disposal of a foreign operation (amendment 2011)

BC36   During its redeliberation of the exposure draft ED 9 *Joint Arrangements*, the Board reconsidered whether its decision in the second phase of the business combinations project to characterise loss of joint control or loss of significant influence as a significant economic event (ie in the same way that loss of control is characterised as a significant economic event) was appropriate. If it were, the Board thought that the entity should be required to recalibrate the accounting as required by IFRS 10 *Consolidated Financial Statements*. However, the Board concluded that, although significant, the events are fundamentally different. In the case of loss of control, the cessation of the parent-subsidiary relationship results in the derecognition of assets and liabilities because the composition of the group changes. If joint control or significant influence is lost the composition of the group is unaffected.

BC37   The Board also noted that retaining the characterisation of significant economic event in the case of loss of joint control or significant influence when the retained interest is a financial asset is unnecessary. IFRS 9 already requires that in such cases the retained interest (ie a financial asset) must be measured at fair value.

BC38   In the case of loss of joint control when significant influence is maintained, the Board acknowledged that the investor-investee relationship changes and, consequently, so does the nature of the investment. However, in this instance, both investments (ie the joint venture and the associate) continue to be measured using the equity method. Considering that there is neither a change in the group boundaries nor a change in the measurement requirements, the Board concluded that losing joint control and retaining significant influence is not an event that warrants remeasurement of the retained interest at fair value.

BC39   Consequently, the Board removed all descriptions that characterise loss of joint control or significant influence as a significant economic event as introduced in the second phase of the Board's project on business combinations.

BC40   The Board also decided to align the conclusions reached on the loss of joint control when significant influence is maintained with the requirements in IAS 21 so that the change from joint control to significant influence is treated as a 'partial' disposal rather than deemed to be an 'entire' disposal. As a consequence, the Board concluded that when an entity loses joint control of a joint arrangement that includes a foreign operation but retains significant influence, an entity reclassifies to profit or loss only the proportionate share of the cumulative amount of the exchange differences recognised in other comprehensive income relating to a foreign operation in that joint arrangement.

---

10 The consolidation guidance was removed from IAS 27 and the Standard was renamed *Separate Financial Statements* by IFRS 10 *Consolidated Financial Statements* issued in May 2011. The accounting requirements for dividends were not changed.

IASB documents published to accompany

IAS 23

Borrowing Costs

The text of the unaccompanied standard, IFRS 10, is contained in Part A of this edition. Its effective date when issued was 1 January 2009. The text of the Accompanying Guidance on IAS 23 is contained in Part B of this edition. This part presents the following documents:

BASIS FOR CONCLUSIONS

APPENDIX TO THE BASIS FOR CONCLUSIONS
Amendments to Basis for Conclusions on other pronouncements

DISSENTING OPINIONS

Basis for Conclusions on
IAS 23 *Borrowing Costs*

This Basis for Conclusions accompanies, but is not part of, IAS 23.

Introduction

BC1   This Basis for Conclusions summarises the International Accounting Standards Board's considerations in reaching its conclusions on revising IAS 23 *Borrowing Costs* in 2007. Individual Board members gave greater weight to some factors than to others.

BC2   The revisions to IAS 23 result from the Board's Short-term Convergence project. The project is being conducted jointly with the United States standard-setter, the Financial Accounting Standards Board (FASB). The objective of the project is to reduce differences between IFRSs and US generally accepted accounting principles (GAAP) that are capable of resolution in a relatively short time and can be addressed outside major projects. The revisions to IAS 23 are principally concerned with the elimination of one of the two treatments that exist for borrowing costs directly attributable to the acquisition, construction or production of a qualifying asset. The application of only one method will enhance comparability. For the reasons set out below, the Board decided to eliminate the option of immediate recognition of such borrowing costs as an expense. It believes this will result in an improvement in financial reporting as well as achieving convergence in principle with US GAAP.

BC3   The Board considered whether to seek convergence on the detailed requirements for the capitalisation of borrowing costs directly attributable to the acquisition, construction or production of a qualifying asset. However, the Board noted statements by the US Securities and Exchange Commission (SEC) and the European Commission that the IASB and FASB should focus their short-term convergence effort on eliminating major differences of principle between IFRSs and US GAAP. For their purposes, convergence on the detailed aspects of accounting treatments is not necessary. The Board further noted that both IAS 23 and SFAS 34 *Capitalization of Interest Cost* were developed some years ago. Consequently, neither set of specific provisions may be regarded as being of a clearly higher quality than the other. Therefore, the Board concluded that it should not spend time and resources considering aspects of IAS 23 beyond the choice between capitalisation and immediate recognition as an expense. This Basis for Conclusions does not, therefore, discuss aspects of IAS 23 that the Board did not reconsider. Paragraphs BC19–BC26 analyse the differences between IAS 23 and SFAS 34.

Amendments to the scope

Assets measured at fair value

BC4   The exposure draft of proposed amendments to IAS 23 proposed excluding from the scope of IAS 23 assets measured at fair value. Some respondents objected to the proposal, interpreting the scope exclusion as limiting capitalisation of borrowing costs to qualifying assets measured at cost. The Board confirmed its decision not to require capitalisation of borrowing costs relating to assets that are measured at fair value. The measurement of such assets will not be affected by the amount of borrowing costs incurred during their construction or production period. Therefore, requirements on how to account for borrowing costs are unnecessary, as paragraphs B61 and B62 of the Basis for Conclusions on IAS 41 *Agriculture* explain. But the Board noted that the exclusion of assets measured at fair value from the requirements of IAS 23 does not prohibit an entity from presenting items in profit or loss as if borrowing costs had been capitalised on such assets before measuring them at fair value.

Inventories that are manufactured, or otherwise produced, in large quantities on a repetitive basis

BC5 The US standard, SFAS 34, requires an entity to recognise as an expense interest costs for inventories that are routinely manufactured or otherwise produced in large quantities on a repetitive basis because, in the FASB's view, the informational benefit from capitalising interest costs does not justify the cost. The exposure draft did not make an exception for borrowing costs relating to such inventories. The exposure draft, therefore, proposed to require an entity to capitalise borrowing costs relating to inventories that are manufactured in large quantities on a repetitive basis and take a substantial period of time to get ready for sale. Respondents argued that capitalising those borrowing costs would create a significant administrative burden, would not be informative to users and would create a reconciling item between IFRSs and US GAAP.

BC6 The Board decided to exclude from the scope of IAS 23 inventories that are manufactured, or otherwise produced, in large quantities on a repetitive basis, even if they take a substantial period of time to get ready for sale. The Board acknowledges the difficulty in both allocating borrowing costs to inventories that are manufactured in large quantities on a repetitive basis and monitoring those borrowing costs until the inventory is sold. It concluded that it should not require an entity to capitalise borrowing costs on such inventories because the costs of capitalisation are likely to exceed the potential benefits.

Elimination of the option of immediate recognition as an expense of borrowing costs directly attributable to the acquisition, construction or production of a qualifying asset

BC7 The previous version of IAS 23 permitted two treatments for accounting for borrowing costs that are directly attributable to the acquisition, construction or production of a qualifying asset. They could be capitalised or, alternatively, recognised immediately as an expense. SFAS 34 requires the capitalisation of such borrowing costs.

BC8 The Board proposed in the exposure draft to eliminate the option of immediate recognition as an expense. Many respondents disagreed with the Board's proposal in the exposure draft, arguing that:

(a) borrowing costs should not be the subject of a short-term convergence project.

(b) the Board had not explored in sufficient detail the merits of both accounting options.

(c) the proposal did not result in benefits for users of financial statements because:

(i) it addressed only one of the differences between IAS 23 and SFAS 34.

(ii) comparability would not be enhanced because the capital structure of an entity could affect the cost of an asset.

(iii) credit analysts reverse capitalised borrowing costs when calculating coverage ratios.

(d) the costs of implementing the capitalisation model in IAS 23 would be burdensome.

(e) the proposal was not consistent with the Board's approach on other projects (in particular, the second phase of the Business Combinations project).

BC9 The Board concluded that borrowing costs that are directly attributable to the acquisition, construction or production of a qualifying asset are part of the cost of that asset. During the period when an asset is under development, the expenditures for the resources used must be financed. Financing has a cost. The cost of the asset should include all costs necessarily incurred to get the asset ready for its intended use or sale, including the cost incurred in financing the expenditures as a part of the asset's acquisition cost. The Board reasoned that recognising immediately as an expense borrowing costs relating to qualifying assets does not give a faithful representation of the cost of the asset.

BC10 The Board confirmed that the objective of the project is not to achieve full convergence on all aspects of accounting for borrowing costs. Rather, it is to reduce differences between IFRSs and US GAAP that are capable of resolution in a relatively short time. The removal of a choice of accounting treatment and convergence in principle with US GAAP will enhance comparability. The Board acknowledges that capitalising borrowing costs does not achieve comparability between assets that are financed with borrowings and those financed with equity. However, it achieves comparability among all non-equity financed assets, which is an improvement.

BC11 A requirement to recognise immediately as an expense borrowing costs relating to qualifying assets would not enhance comparability. Rather, comparability between assets that are internally developed and those acquired from third parties would be impaired. The purchase price of a completed asset purchased from a third party would include financing costs incurred by the third party during the development phase.

BC12 Respondents to the exposure draft argued that requiring the capitalisation of borrowing costs is not consistent with the Board's proposal in the second phase of the Business Combinations project to require an entity to treat as an expense acquisition costs relating to a business combination. The Board disagrees with those respondents. Acquisition costs as defined in the context of a business combination are different from borrowing costs incurred in constructing or producing a qualifying asset. Borrowing costs are part of the cost necessarily incurred to get the asset ready for its intended use or sale. Acquisition costs relating to a business combination are costs incurred for services performed to help with the acquisition, such as due diligence and professional fees. They are not costs of assets acquired in a business combination.

BC13 The Board concluded that the additional benefits in terms of higher comparability, improvements in financial reporting and achieving convergence in principle with US GAAP exceed any additional costs of implementation. Achieving convergence in principle with US GAAP on this topic is a milestone in the Memorandum of Understanding published by the FASB and IASB in February 2006, which is a step towards removal of the requirement imposed on foreign registrants with the SEC to reconcile their financial statements to US GAAP.

BC14 The Board observes that there is an unavoidable cost of complying with any new financial reporting standard. Accordingly, the Board carefully considers the costs and benefits of any new pronouncement. In this case, the Board has not been told that preparers who elected to capitalise borrowing costs under the previous version of IAS 23 found doing so unnecessarily burdensome. In the Board's judgement, any additional costs of capitalising an item of cost of an asset are offset by the advantage of having all entities account for that item in the same way.

Effective date and transition

BC15 Development of a qualifying asset may take a long time. Additionally, some assets currently in use may have undergone and completed their production or construction process many years ago. If the entity has been following the accounting policy of immediately recognising borrowing costs as an expense, the costs of gathering the information required to capitalise them retrospectively and to adjust the carrying amount of the asset may exceed the potential benefits. Hence, the Board decided to require prospective application, which was supported by respondents to the exposure draft.

BC16 The Board noted that the revisions would result in information that is more comparable between entities. On that basis, if an entity wished to apply the revised Standard from any date before the effective date, users of the entity's financial statements would receive more useful and comparable information than previously.

BC17 Therefore, an entity is permitted to apply the revised Standard from any designated date before the effective date. However, if an entity applies the Standard from such an earlier date, it should apply the Standard to all qualifying assets for which the commencement date for capitalisation is on or after that designated date.

BC18 The Board recognises that the Standard may require an entity that reconciles its IFRS financial statements to US GAAP to maintain two sets of capitalisation information—one set that complies with the requirements of IAS 23 and one that complies with the requirements of SFAS 34. The Board wishes to avoid imposing on such entities the need to maintain two sets of capitalisation information. Therefore, before the effective date, the Board will consider what actions it might take to avoid this outcome.

Differences between IAS 23 and SFAS 34

BC19　The following paragraphs summarise the main differences between IAS 23 and SFAS 34.

Definition of borrowing costs

BC20　IAS 23 uses the term 'borrowing costs' whereas SFAS 34 uses the term 'interest costs'. 'Borrowing costs' reflects the broader definition in IAS 23, which encompasses interest and other costs, such as:

(a)　exchange differences arising from foreign currency borrowings to the extent that they are regarded as an adjustment to interest costs;.[1]and

(b)　~~amortisation of ancillary costs incurred in connection with the arrangement of borrowings.~~

BC21　EITF Issue No. 99–9 concludes that derivative gains and losses (arising from the effective portion of a derivative instrument that qualifies as a fair value hedge) are part of the capitalised interest cost. IAS 23 does not address such derivative gains and losses.

Definition of a qualifying asset

BC22　The main differences are as follows:

(a)　IAS 23 defines a qualifying asset as one that takes a substantial period of time to get ready for its intended use or sale. The SFAS 34 definition does not include the term *substantial*.

(b)　IAS 23 excludes from its scope qualifying assets that are measured at fair value. SFAS 34 does not address assets measured at fair value.

(c)　SFAS 34 includes as qualifying assets investments in investees accounted for using the equity method, in some circumstances.[2] Such investments are not qualifying assets according to IAS 23.

(d)　SFAS 34 does not permit the capitalisation of interest costs on assets acquired with gifts or grants that are restricted by the donor or grantor in some situations. IAS 23 does not address such assets.

1　In 2007 the Board was advised that some of the components of borrowing costs in paragraph 6 are broadly equivalent to the components of interest expense calculated using the effective interest method in accordance with IAS 39 *Financial Instruments: Recognition and Measurement*. Consequently, the Board amended paragraph 6 to refer to the relevant guidance in IAS 39 when describing the components of borrowing costs. Subsequently, IFRS 9 *Financial Instruments* replaced IAS 39. IFRS 9 applies to all items that were previously within the scope of IAS 39.

2　While the investee has activities in progress necessary to commence its planned principal operations provided that the investee's activities include the use of funds to acquire qualifying assets for its operations.

Measurement

BC23   When an entity borrows funds specifically for the purpose of obtaining a qualifying asset:

(a)   IAS 23 requires an entity to capitalise the actual borrowing costs incurred on that borrowing. SFAS 34 states that an entity may use the rate of that borrowing.

(b)   IAS 23 requires an entity to deduct any income earned on the temporary investment of actual borrowings from the amount of borrowing costs to be capitalised. SFAS 34 does not generally permit this deduction, unless particular tax-exempt borrowings are involved.

BC24   SFAS 34 requires an entity to use judgement in determining the capitalisation rate to apply to the expenditures on the asset—an entity selects the borrowings that it considers appropriate to meet the objective of capitalising the interest costs incurred that otherwise could have been avoided. When an entity borrows funds generally and uses them to obtain a qualifying asset, IAS 23 permits some flexibility in determining the capitalisation rate, but requires an entity to use all outstanding borrowings other than those made specifically to obtain a qualifying asset.

Disclosure requirements

BC25   IAS 23 requires disclosure of the capitalisation rate used to determine the amount of borrowing costs eligible for capitalisation. SFAS 34 does not require this disclosure.

BC26   SFAS 34 requires disclosure of the total amount of interest cost incurred during the period, including the amount capitalised and the amount recognised as an expense. IAS 23 requires disclosure only of the amount of borrowing costs capitalised during the period. IAS 1 *Presentation of Financial Statements* requires the disclosure of finance costs for the period.

BC27   [Deleted]

Appendix
Amendments to Basis for Conclusions on other pronouncements

This appendix contains amendments to the Basis for Conclusions on other pronouncements that are necessary in order to ensure consistency with the revised IAS 23.

* * * * *

The amendments contained in this appendix when IAS 23 was issued in 2007 have been incorporated into the text of the Basis for Conclusions on IFRS 1 and IFRICs 1 and 12.

© IFRS Foundation

Dissenting opinions

Dissent of Anthony T Cope, Philippe Danjou and Robert P Garnett

DO1 The Board's decision to require the capitalisation of borrowing costs relating to qualifying assets will cause a significant change in accounting for the many preparers that currently apply the benchmark treatment of recognising borrowing costs as an expense. Messrs Cope, Danjou and Garnett believe that such a change will require the establishment of cumbersome measurement processes and monitoring of capitalised costs over a long period. This is likely to involve considerable accounting work and incremental auditing costs.

DO2 Users of financial statements responding to the exposure draft did not support the change because they saw no informational benefit in a model that capitalises costs, other than the capitalisation of the actual economic cost of capital of the investment. In addition, Messrs Cope, Danjou and Garnett believe that a standard requiring the capitalisation of borrowing costs should discuss more extensively which assets qualify for the purpose of capitalising which borrowing costs.

DO3 As a consequence, Messrs Cope, Danjou and Garnett dissent because, in their view, the costs of this particular change will far outweigh the benefits to users.

DO4 In addition, this requirement to capitalise borrowing costs will achieve only limited convergence with US GAAP—differences will remain that could lead to materially different capitalised amounts. Furthermore, entities that are required to reconcile net income and shareholders' equity to US GAAP already have the option to capitalise borrowing costs and, thus, may recognise amounts that are more comparable to, albeit still potentially materially different from, those recognised in accordance with US GAAP.

DO5 The Memorandum of Understanding published by the FASB and the IASB states that trying to eliminate differences between standards that are both in need of significant improvement is not the best use of resources. Messrs Cope, Danjou and Garnett support the convergence work programme, but only if it results in higher quality standards and improved financial reporting. They are of the opinion that IAS 23 and SFAS 34 are both in need of significant improvement and should not have been addressed as part of short-term convergence.

IASB documents published to accompany

IAS 24

Related Party Disclosures

The text of the unaccompanied standard, IAS 24, is contained in Part A of this edition. Its effective date when issued was 1 January 2011. The text of the Accompanying Guidance on IAS 24 is contained in Part B of this edition. This part presents the following documents:

BASIS FOR CONCLUSIONS

APPENDIX TO THE BASIS FOR CONCLUSIONS
Amendment to the Basis for Conclusions on IAS 19 *Employee Benefits*

DISSENTING OPINION

Basis for Conclusions on IAS 24 *Related Party Disclosures*

This Basis for Conclusions accompanies, but is not part of, IAS 24.

Introduction

BC1 This Basis for Conclusions summarises the International Accounting Standards Board's considerations in reaching its conclusions on revising IAS 24 *Related Party Disclosures* in 2003 and 2009. Individual Board members gave greater weight to some factors than to others.

BC2 In July 2001 the Board announced that, as part of its initial agenda of technical projects, it would undertake a project to improve a number of standards, including IAS 24. The project was undertaken in the light of queries and criticisms raised in relation to the standards by securities regulators, professional accountants and other interested parties. The objectives of the Improvements project were to reduce or eliminate alternatives, redundancies and conflicts within existing standards, to deal with some convergence issues and to make other improvements. In May 2002 the Board published its proposals in an exposure draft of *Improvements to International Accounting Standards* (the 2002 ED), with a comment deadline of 16 September 2002. The Board received over 160 comment letters on the exposure draft. After reviewing the responses, the Board issued a revised version of IAS 24 in December 2003.

BC3 In February 2007 the Board published an exposure draft *State-controlled Entities and the Definition of a Related Party* (the 2007 ED), proposing:

(a) an exemption from the disclosure requirements in IAS 24 for transactions between entities that are controlled, jointly controlled or significantly influenced by a state ('state-controlled entities'[1]); and

(b) amendments to the definition of a related party.

BC4 The Board received 72 comment letters on the 2007 ED. After considering those comments, in December 2008 the Board published revised proposals in an exposure draft *Relationships with the State* (the 2008 ED). The 2008 ED:

(a) presented revised proposals for state-controlled entities; and

(b) proposed one further amendment to the definition of a related party.

BC5 The Board received 75 comment letters on the 2008 ED. After reviewing the responses, the Board issued a revised version of IAS 24 in November 2009.

BC6 Because the Board's intention was not to reconsider the fundamental approach to related party disclosures established by IAS 24, this Basis for Conclusions discusses only the following requirements in IAS 24:

(a) management compensation (paragraphs BC7–BC10);

---

1 In finalising the revised version of IAS 24 in 2009, the Board replaced the term 'state' with 'government'.

(b)   related party disclosures in separate financial statements (paragraphs BC11–BC17);

(c)   definition of a related party (paragraphs BC18–BC32);

(d)   government-related entities (paragraphs BC33–BC48); and

(e)   other minor changes made in 2009 (paragraph BC49).

Management compensation

BC7   The version of IAS 24 issued by the Board's predecessor in 1984 had no exemption for the disclosure of key management personnel compensation. In developing the 2002 ED, the Board proposed that the disclosure of management compensation, expense allowances and similar items paid in the ordinary course of business should not be required because:

(a)   the approval processes for key management personnel compensation in some jurisdictions remove the rationale for related party disclosures;

(b)   privacy issues arise in some jurisdictions where accountability mechanisms other than disclosure in financial statements exist; and

(c)   requiring these disclosures placed weight on the determination of 'key management personnel' and 'compensation', which was likely to prove contentious. In addition, comparability of these disclosures would be unlikely until measurement requirements are developed for all forms of compensation.

BC8   However, some respondents to the 2002 ED objected to the proposed exemption because they were concerned that information relating to management compensation is relevant to users' information needs and that an exemption based on 'items paid in the ordinary course of business' could lead to abuse. Establishing a disclosure exemption on such a criterion without a definition of the terms could lead to exempting other transactions with management from being disclosed, because they could all be structured as 'compensation paid in the ordinary course of an entity's operations'. Respondents argued that such an exemption could lead to abuse because it could potentially apply to any transactions with management.

BC9   The Board was persuaded by the respondents' views on the 2002 ED and decided that the Standard should require disclosure of key management personnel compensation because:

(a)   the principle underpinning the requirements in IAS 24 is that transactions with related parties should be disclosed, and key management personnel are related parties of an entity.

(b)   key management personnel compensation is relevant to decisions made by users of financial statements when it represents a material amount. The structure and amount of compensation are major drivers in the implementation of the business strategy.

(c)   the benefit of this information to users of financial statements largely outweighs the potential lack of comparability arising from the absence of recognition and measurement requirements for all forms of compensation.

BC10   The Board believes that although some jurisdictions have processes for approving compensation for key management personnel in an attempt to ensure an arm's length result, it is clear that some jurisdictions do not. Furthermore, although approval processes for management compensation may involve other parties such as shareholders or investors, key management personnel may still have a significant input. In addition, the Board noted that disclosing key management personnel compensation would improve transparency and comparability, thereby enabling users of financial statements to make a better assessment of the impact of such compensation on the entity's financial position and profit or loss. The Board also noted that the definition of key management personnel and the guidance on compensation in IAS 19 *Employee Benefits* are sufficient to enable entities to disclose the relevant information.

Related party disclosures in separate financial statements

BC11   The version of IAS 24 issued by the Board's predecessor in 1984 exempted disclosures about related party transactions in:

(a)   parents' financial statements when they are made available or published with the consolidated statements; and

(b)   financial statements of a wholly-owned subsidiary if its parent is incorporated in the same country and provides consolidated financial statements in that country.

BC12   In the 2002 ED the Board proposed to continue exempting separate financial statements of parents and financial statements of wholly-owned subsidiaries from disclosures about any related parties in specified circumstances. It proposed that disclosure of related party transactions and outstanding balances in the separate financial statements of a parent or the financial statements of a wholly-owned subsidiary would not be required, but only if those statements were made available or published with consolidated financial statements for the group.

BC13   The Board proposed to retain this exemption so that entities that are required by law to produce financial statements available for public use in accordance with International Financial Reporting Standards (IFRSs) in addition to the group's consolidated financial statements would not be unduly burdened. The Board noted that in some circumstances, users can find sufficient information for their purposes regarding a subsidiary from either its financial statements or the group's consolidated financial statements. In addition, the users of financial statements of a subsidiary often have, or can obtain access to, more information. The Board also noted that users should be aware that amounts recognised in the financial statements of a wholly-owned subsidiary can be affected significantly by the subsidiary's relationship with its parent.

BC14   However, respondents to the 2002 ED objected to this exemption, on the grounds that disclosure of related party transactions and outstanding balances is essential information for external users, who need to be aware of the level of support provided by related parties. The respondents also argued that financial statements prepared in accordance with IFRSs could be presented on a stand-alone basis. Therefore, financial statements prepared on the basis of this proposed exemption would not achieve a fair presentation without related party disclosures.

BC15   The Board was persuaded by those arguments and decided to require the disclosure of related party transactions and outstanding balances in separate financial statements of a parent, investor or venturer in addition to the disclosure requirements in IAS 27 *Consolidated and Separate Financial Statements*,[2] IAS 28 *Investments in Associates*[3] and IAS 31 *Interests in Joint Ventures*.[4]

BC16   The Board noted that the financial statements of an entity that is part of a consolidated group may include the effects of extensive intragroup transactions. Indeed, potentially all of the revenues and expenses for such an entity may derive from related party transactions. The Board concluded that the disclosures required by IAS 24 are essential to understanding the financial position and financial performance of such an entity and therefore should be required for separate financial statements presented in accordance with IAS 27.

BC17   The Board also believed that disclosure of such transactions is essential because the external users need to be aware of the interrelationships between related parties, including the level of support provided by related parties, to assist external users in their economic decisions.

Definition of a related party

BC18   The definition of a related party in IAS 24 was widely considered to be too complex and difficult to apply in practice. The Board noted that the existing definition of a related party had weaknesses: it was cumbersome and included several cross-references that made it difficult to read (and to translate). Therefore, the 2007 and 2008 EDs proposed revised definitions.

BC19   In revising the definition, the Board adopted the following approach:

      (a)   When an entity assesses whether two parties are related, it would treat significant influence as equivalent to the relationship that exists between an entity and a member of its key management personnel. However, those relationships are not as close as a relationship of control or joint control.

      (b)   If two entities are both subject to control (or joint control) by the same entity or person, the two entities are related to each other.

---

2   The consolidation guidance was removed from IAS 27 and the Standard was renamed *Separate Financial Statements* by IFRS 10 *Consolidated Financial Statements* issued in May 2011. The accounting requirements for separate financial statements were not changed.

3   In May 2011, the Board amended IAS 28 and changed its title to *Investments in Associates and Joint Ventures*.

4   IFRS 11 *Joint Arrangements*, issued in May 2011, replaced IAS 31.

(c)   If one entity (or person) controls (or jointly controls) a second entity and the first entity (or person) has significant influence over a third entity, the second and third entities are related to each other.

(d)   Conversely, if two entities are both subject to significant influence by the same entity (or person), the two entities are not related to each other.

(e)   If the revised definition treats one party as related to a second party, the definition should also treat the second party as related to the first party, by symmetry.

BC20   The new definition was not intended to change the meaning of a related party except in the three respects detailed in paragraphs BC21–BC26. The 2008 ED proposed other amendments to the definition for one additional case that had been inadvertently omitted from the 2007 ED and the elimination of further inconsistencies (paragraphs BC27–BC29). In finalising the amendments in 2009, the Board also removed the term 'significant voting power' from the definition of a related party (paragraphs BC30 and BC31).

An associate of a subsidiary's controlling investor

BC21   First, the Board considered the relationship between an associate and a subsidiary of an investor that has significant influence over the associate. The Board observed that when an associate prepares individual or separate financial statements, its investor is a related party. If the investor has a subsidiary, that subsidiary is also related to the associate, because the subsidiary is part of the group that has significant influence over the associate. Although the definition in the 2003 version of IAS 24 incorporated such relationships, the Board concluded that the revised definition should state this more clearly.

BC22   In contrast, when a subsidiary prepares individual or separate financial statements, an associate of the subsidiary's controlling investor was not a related party as defined in the 2003 version of IAS 24. The subsidiary does not have significant influence over the associate, nor is it significantly influenced by the associate.

BC23   However, the Board decided that, for the same reasons that the parties described in paragraph BC21 are related, the parties described in paragraph BC22 are also related. Thus, the Board amended the definition of a related party to include the relationship discussed in paragraph BC22.

BC24   Furthermore, the Board decided that in the situations described in paragraphs BC21 and BC22, if the investor is a person who has significant influence over one entity and control or joint control over another entity, sufficient influence exists to warrant concluding that the two entities are related.

Two associates of a person

BC25   Secondly, the Board considered the relationship between associates of the investor. IAS 24 does not define associates as related to each other if the investor is an entity. This is because there is insufficient influence through the common investment in two associates. However, the Board noted a discrepancy in that if a person significantly influences one entity and a close member of that person's family significantly influences another entity, those entities were treated as related parties of each other. The Board amended the definition to exclude the entities described in the latter scenario, thereby ensuring a consistent treatment of associates.

Investments of members of key management personnel

BC26   Thirdly, IAS 24 treats some investees of the key management personnel of a reporting entity as related to that entity. However, the definition in the 2003 version of IAS 24 did not include the reciprocal of this—ie for the financial statements of the investee, the other entity managed by the key management personnel was not a related party. To eliminate this inconsistency, the Board amended the definition so that for both sets of financial statements the entities are related parties.

Joint control

BC27   Respondents to the 2007 ED pointed out that one case had been excluded from the restructured definition without being explicitly stated as a change to IAS 24. When a person has joint control over a reporting entity and a close member of that person's family has joint control or significant influence over the other entity, the 2003 version of IAS 24 defined the other entity as related to the reporting entity.

BC28   The Board noted that joint control is generally regarded as influence that is stronger than significant influence. Therefore, the Board concluded that the relationship described in paragraph BC27 should continue to be treated as a related party relationship.

BC29   The definition in the 2003 version of IAS 24 did not include the reciprocal of the case described in paragraph BC27, nor did it deal with cases when a person or a third entity has joint control or significant influence over the two entities. The definition proposed in the 2007 ED would not have rectified these omissions. The Board decided to include these cases in the definition, to treat similar relationships in a consistent manner. In summary, whenever a person or entity has both joint control over a second entity and joint control or significant influence over a third entity, the amendments described in this paragraph and paragraph BC27 treat the second and third entities as related to each other.

Removal of 'significant voting power'

BC30   Respondents to the 2007 and 2008 EDs raised concerns about the term 'significant voting power' in the definition of a related party. They identified anomalies in its use such as when significant voting power created a related party relationship only when that power is held by individuals, not when that power is held by an entity. A further anomaly arose because two entities were classified as related to each other when a third person was a member of the key management personnel of one and had significant voting power in the other; however, they were not treated as related when a third person had significant voting power in both entities.

BC31   In response to these comments, the Board deleted the reference to 'significant voting power' because it was undefined, used inconsistently and created unnecessary complexity. The Board concluded that if the effect of 'significant voting power' was considered to be the same as 'significant influence', its deletion would have no effect because 'significant influence' is in the definition. On the other hand, if the effect of 'significant voting power' was considered to be different from that of 'significant influence', IAS 24 did not explain what that difference was.

Other minor changes to the definition of a related party

BC32　The revisions to IAS 24 in 2009 included the following other minor changes:

(a)　The definition of a **related party** is amended:

(i)　to replace references to 'individual' with 'person';

(ii)　to clarify that an associate includes subsidiaries of an associate and a joint venture includes subsidiaries of the joint venture; and

(iii)　to clarify that two entities are not related parties simply because a member of key management personnel of one entity has significant influence over the other entity.

(b)　The definition of a **close member of the family** is amended:

(i)　to replace references to 'individual' with 'person'; and

(ii)　to delete 'may' from the list of examples to state that close members of a person's family include (rather than 'may include') that person's spouse or domestic partner and children.

Government-related entities

Exemption (paragraph 25)

BC33　The version of IAS 24 that preceded its revision in 2003 did not require 'state-controlled' entities to disclose transactions with other such entities. The revised version of IAS 24 issued in 2003 omitted this exemption because at the time the Board concluded that the disclosure requirements would not be a burden for those entities.

BC34　Subsequently concerns were raised that in environments where government control is pervasive, compliance with IAS 24 was problematic. To address those concerns, the 2007 ED proposed an exemption from the disclosure requirements now in paragraph 18 of IAS 24 for government-related entities. In developing that proposal, the Board noted the following:

(a)　It can be difficult to identify other government-related entities, particularly in jurisdictions with a large number of such entities. Such entities might not even be aware that an entity with which they have transactions is a related party.

(b)　For these transactions, the cost of meeting the requirements in IAS 24 was not always offset by the benefit of increased information for users of financial statements. More specifically:

(i)　extensive disclosures were required for transactions that are unaffected by the relationship;

(ii) if some entities are not aware that their transactions are with other government-related entities, the disclosures provided would be incomplete; and

(iii) transactions that are affected by the relationship might well be obscured by excessive disclosures about unaffected transactions.

(c) Some governments establish subsidiaries, joint ventures and associates to compete with each other. In this case, transactions between such entities are likely to be conducted as if they are unrelated parties.

BC35 Respondents to the 2007 ED generally supported an exemption for government-related entities. However, they expressed concerns about the complexity of the specific proposal and asked the Board to clarify various aspects of it. After considering all comments received, the Board proposed a revised exemption for those entities in the 2008 ED.

BC36 Respondents to the 2008 ED generally supported the revised proposal, but some argued that the exemption should not apply to transactions:

(a) between members of a group that is controlled by a government (paragraph BC37); and

(b) between government-related entities that are related for a reason in addition to their relationship with the same government (paragraph BC38).

BC37 Some respondents reasoned that the exemption should not apply to transactions between members of a group that is controlled by a government, for example between a government-related entity and its parent or its fellow subsidiaries. Those respondents noted that the relationship within such a group might sometimes be closer and more influential than between government-related entities in an environment where government control is pervasive. However, for the following reasons the Board concluded that the exemption should also apply within such groups:

(a) Sometimes, requiring disclosure in such cases would negate the purpose of the exemption and could lead to significant differences in the level of disclosure when the substance of the relationships and transactions could be very similar. For example, suppose one government controls all entities directly but another government has similar entities and controls them all through a single holding company. The entities controlled by the first government would all qualify for the exemption but those controlled by the second government would not.

(b) Requiring disclosure in such cases would place considerable pressure on the definition of the boundary between government and entities controlled by the government. For example, suppose a government controls entities through an intermediate institution. It would be necessary to determine whether that institution is an entity controlled by the government (in which case the exemption would not apply) or part of the government (in which case the exemption would apply). This may be answered easily if the institution is a company incorporated under normal company law that simply happens to have the government as a controlling shareholder. It may be less clear if the institution is, for example, a government agency or department.

BC38 The Board identified only one case when government-related entities might be related to each other for reasons other than their relationships with the same government: a government might control both a post-employment benefit plan and the sponsoring employer. However, the main transactions between such a plan and the sponsoring employer are (a) employer contributions and (b) investments by the plan in the employer or in assets used by the employer. IAS 19 already requires a sponsoring employer to disclose most, if not all, of the information that IAS 24 would require if the exemption did not apply. Thus the Board concluded that no significant loss of disclosure would arise from applying the exemption in these cases.

BC39 Paragraph BC34 explains why the Board provided an exemption from the disclosure requirements in paragraph 18 of IAS 24 for government-related entities. It was beyond the scope of the project to consider whether similar exemptions would be appropriate in other circumstances.

BC40 Some respondents to the 2008 ED noted that many financial institutions had recently become government-related entities when governments took significant and sometimes controlling equity interests in them during the global financial crisis. They queried whether the exemption was appropriate in such cases. In finalising the amendments in 2009, the Board identified no reason to treat such entities differently from other government-related entities. The Board noted that in addition to the disclosure requirements in IAS 24, IAS 20 *Accounting for Government Grants and Disclosure of Government Assistance* requires the reporting entity to disclose information about the receipt of government grants or assistance.

BC41 Respondents to the 2008 ED noted that the proposed definition of 'state' was similar to the definition of 'government' in IAS 20. To avoid confusion and provide consistency, the Board adopted the latter definition when finalising the amendments to IAS 24 in 2009. The Board decided that it need not provide a more comprehensive definition or additional guidance on how to determine what is meant by 'government'. In the Board's view, a more detailed definition could not capture every conceivable government structure across every jurisdiction. In addition, judgement is required by the reporting entity when applying the definition because every jurisdiction has its own way of organising government-related activities.

Disclosure requirements when the exemption applies (paragraph 26)

BC42 The Board considered whether the disclosure requirements in paragraph 26:

(a)   met the objective of IAS 24 (paragraphs BC43–BC46); and

(b)   were operational (paragraphs BC47 and BC48).

BC43 The objective of IAS 24 is to provide 'disclosures necessary to draw attention to the possibility that [the entity's] financial position and profit or loss may have been affected by the existence of related parties and by transactions and outstanding balances, including commitments, with such parties.' To meet that objective, paragraph 26 requires some disclosure when the exemption applies. Those disclosures are intended to put users on notice that related party transactions have occurred and to give an indication of their extent. The Board did not intend to require the reporting entity to identify **every** government-related entity, or to quantify in detail **every** transaction with such entities, because such a requirement would negate the exemption.

BC44 Some respondents to the 2008 ED were concerned that qualitative disclosure of individually significant related party transactions alone would not meet the objective of IAS 24 and that combining individually significant transactions with collectively significant transactions would not provide sufficient transparency. The Board concluded that it should require an entity to disclose:

(a) the nature and amount of each individually significant transaction; and

(b) quantitative or qualitative information about other types of transactions that are collectively, but not individually, significant.

BC45 The Board noted that this requirement should not be too onerous for the reporting entity because:

(a) individually significant transactions should be a small subset, by number, of total related party transactions;

(b) the reporting entity should know what those transactions are; and

(c) reporting such items on an exceptional basis takes into account cost-benefit considerations.

BC46 The Board also noted that more disclosure of individually significant transactions would better meet the objective of IAS 24 because this approach focuses on transactions that, through their nature or size, are of more interest to users and are more likely to be affected by the related party relationship.

BC47 Some respondents raised concerns about whether the reporting entity would be able to identify whether the counterparty to individually significant or collectively significant transactions is a related party because it is controlled, jointly controlled or significantly influenced by the same government. The problem of identifying all such counterparties was one of the primary reasons for the exemption.

BC48 However, as discussed in paragraph BC43, it was not the Board's intention to require the reporting entity to identify every government-related entity, or to quantify every transaction with such entities. Moreover, individually significant transactions are likely to attract more scrutiny by management. The Board concluded that management will know, or will apply more effort in establishing, who the counterparty to an individually significant transaction is and will have, or be able to obtain, background information on the counterparty.

Other minor changes made in 2009

BC49   The revisions to IAS 24 in 2009 included the following other changes:

     (a)   The list of examples of **related party transactions** is amended to include in paragraph 21(i) commitments to do something if a particular event occurs or does not occur in the future, including executory contracts. The Board concluded that commitments were one type of transaction, but to avoid doubt decided to make explicit reference to them.

     (b)   Paragraph 3 relating to the **scope** of IAS 24 is amended to clarify that the Standard applies to individual, as well as separate and consolidated, financial statements because individual financial statements relate to something different from the defined term in IAS 27.[5]

     (c)   Paragraph 34 of IFRS 8 *Operating Segments* is amended. The Board recognised that in applying the requirements in IFRS 8 it may not be practicable or meaningful to regard all government-related entities as a single customer, especially for environments in which government control is pervasive.

     (d)   A consequential amendment to the Basis for Conclusions on IAS 19 draws attention to the new definition of a related party. The definition of a qualifying insurance policy in IAS 19 refers to this definition.

Key management personnel

BC50   The Board was asked to address the identification and disclosure of related party transactions that arise when a management entity provides key management personnel services to a reporting entity. The Board understood that divergence existed because some reporting entities do not identify this as a related party transaction. Of those who do identify this as a related party transaction, some reporting entities would disclose the compensation paid by the management entity to those employees or directors of the management entity that act as key management personnel of the reporting entity. Other reporting entities would disclose the service fee that is paid or payable to the management entity, which is incurred by the reporting entity.

BC51   The Board noted that IAS 24 is unclear as to what information to disclose for key management personnel when those persons are not employees of the reporting entity. To address the diversity in disclosures that has arisen from IAS 24 being unclear, the Board decided to amend the definition of 'related party'. The amendment clarified that a management entity that provides key management services to a reporting entity is deemed to be a related party of the reporting entity. In discussing these proposals, the Board acknowledged that the relationship between the management entity and the reporting entity is not symmetrical. The reporting entity is not a related party of the management

---

5   The consolidation guidance was removed from IAS 27 and the Standard was renamed *Separate Financial Statements* by IFRS 10 *Consolidated Financial Statements* issued in May 2011. The definition of separate financial statements was not changed.

entity solely as a consequence of being a customer of the management entity. The reporting entity cannot affect the management entity's activities, financial position or profit except through some other relationship. Consequently, the reporting entity is required to disclose the amount incurred for the service fee paid or payable to the management entity that employs, or has as directors, the persons that provide the key management personnel services. As a result of identifying the management entity as a related party of the reporting entity, the Board noted that the reporting entity is also required to disclose other transactions with the management entity, for example, loans, under the existing disclosure requirements of IAS 24 with respect to related parties.

BC52　The Board was informed of concerns that it is impracticable to access the detailed information that is required in paragraph 17 when compensation is paid to a separate management entity as fees. The Board therefore decided to provide relief so that the reporting entity is not required to disclose the components of compensation to key management personnel that is paid through another entity. Instead, amounts incurred in respect of key management personnel compensation or key management personnel services, paid or payable to another entity, shall be disclosed in accordance with paragraph 18A.

Appendix
Amendment to the Basis for Conclusions on IAS 19 *Employee Benefits*

This Appendix contains an amendment to the Basis for Conclusions on IAS 19 that is necessary in order to ensure consistency with IAS 24.

* * * * *

The amendment contained in this appendix when IAS 24 (as revised) was issued in 2009 has been incorporated into the Basis for Conclusions on IAS 19 published in this volume.

Dissenting opinion

Dissent of Robert P Garnett

DO1   Mr Garnett disagrees with the Board's decision to exempt only government-related entities from the requirements of paragraph 18 to disclose information about all transactions with related parties. He also disagrees with the decision not to require all entities to provide information about each individually significant transaction with a related party as set out in paragraph 26(b)(i).

DO2   The Basis for Conclusions sets out clearly the need to remove the unnecessary burden of collecting data for all transactions, entered into and priced on normal business terms, because the counterparty was identified as a related party. It also explains the need to inform investors of individually significant transactions with related parties. Mr Garnett agrees with the explanations in paragraphs BC33–BC48.

DO3   Paragraph 25, however, restricts these changes to entities that are controlled, jointly controlled or significantly influenced by the same government. Mr Garnett sees no reason to make such a distinction, other than to provide limited relief to certain entities.

IASB documents published to accompany

IAS 27

Separate Financial Statements

The text of the unaccompanied standard, IAS 27, is contained in Part A of this edition. Its effective date when issued was 1 January 2013. The text of the Accompanying Guidance on IAS 27 is contained in Part B of this edition. This part presents the following documents:

BASIS FOR CONCLUSIONS

DISSENTING OPINION

Basis for Conclusions on
IAS 27 *Separate Financial Statements*

This Basis for Conclusions accompanies, but is not part of, IAS 27.

Introduction

BC1   This Basis for Conclusions summarises the International Accounting Standards Board's considerations in reaching its conclusions on issuing IAS 27 *Consolidated and Separate Financial Statements* in 2003, and amending IAS 27 in 2008 and again in 2011. Individual Board members gave greater weight to some factors than to others. Unless otherwise noted, references below to IAS 27 are to previous versions of the Standard.

BC2   The amendment of IAS 27 in 2011 resulted from the Board's project on consolidation. A new IFRS, IFRS 10 *Consolidated Financial Statements*, addresses the principle of control and requirements relating to the preparation of consolidated financial statements. As a result, IAS 27 now contains requirements relating only to separate financial statements. This change is reflected in the Standard's amended title, *Separate Financial Statements*.

BC3   In approving the publication of IFRS 10 in 2011, the Board also approved consequential amendments to IAS 27 that removed from the Standard all requirements relating to consolidated financial statements.

BC4   At the same time, the Board relocated to IAS 27 requirements from IAS 28 *Investments in Associates* and IAS 31 *Interests in Joint Ventures* regarding separate financial statements. Those requirements are in paragraphs 6–8 of the Standard. Given the extent of the material that has been removed or relocated, the Board decided, for clarity, to renumber the paragraphs in the amended IAS 27. The definitions and wording in the Standard were also updated to be consistent with the requirements in IFRS 10, IFRS 11 *Joint Arrangements*, IFRS 12 *Disclosure of Interests in Other Entities*, and IAS 28 *Investments in Associates and Joint Ventures*.

BC5   When issued in 2003, IAS 27 was accompanied by a Basis for Conclusions summarising the considerations of the Board, as constituted at the time, in reaching its conclusions. The Basis for Conclusions was subsequently updated to reflect amendments to the Standard.

BC6   This Basis for Conclusions now includes only the Board's considerations on separate financial statements. Cross-references have been updated accordingly and minor necessary editorial changes have been made. The paragraphs discussing consolidated financial statements have been relocated to the Basis for Conclusions on IFRS 10 as appropriate.

Consolidation exemption available for non-public entities

BC7   The Board decided that a parent that meets the criteria in paragraph 4(a) of IFRS 10 for exemption from the requirement to prepare consolidated financial statements should, in its separate financial statements, account for those subsidiaries in the same way as other parents, joint venturers with interests in joint ventures or investors in associates account for investments in their separate financial statements. The Board draws a distinction between accounting for such investments as equity investments and accounting for the economic entity that the parent controls. In relation to the former, the Board decided that each category of investment should be accounted for consistently.

BC8 The Board decided that the same approach to accounting for investments in separate financial statements should apply irrespective of the circumstances for which they are prepared. Thus, a parent that presents consolidated financial statements, and a parent that does not because it is exempted, should present the same form of separate financial statements.

Investment entities

BC8A *Investment Entities* (Amendments to IFRS 10, IFRS 12 and IAS 27), issued in October 2012, introduced an exception to the principle in IFRS 10 that all subsidiaries shall be consolidated. The amendments define an investment entity and require a parent that is an investment entity to measure its investments in particular subsidiaries at fair value through profit or loss in accordance with IFRS 9 *Financial Instruments* (or IAS 39 *Financial Instruments: Recognition and Measurement*,[1] if IFRS 9 has not yet been adopted) instead of consolidating those subsidiaries. Consequently, the Board decided to amend IAS 27 to require an investment entity to also measure its investments in subsidiaries at fair value through profit or loss in its separate financial statements. The Board also made corresponding amendments to the disclosure requirements for an investment entity's separate financial statements, noting that if an investment entity prepares separate financial statements as its only financial statements, it is still appropriate for the investment entity to make the disclosures otherwise required in IFRS 12 about its interests in subsidiaries.

Measurement of investments in subsidiaries, joint ventures and associates in separate financial statements

2003 revision

BC9 IAS 27 (as revised by the Board's predecessor body in 2000) permitted entities to measure investments in subsidiaries in any one of three ways in the parent's separate financial statements. These were at cost, using the equity method, or as available-for-sale[2] financial assets in accordance with IAS 39 *Financial Instruments: Recognition and Measurement*.[3] IAS 28 *Investments in Associates* permitted the same choices for investments in associates in separate financial statements, and IAS 31 *Interests in Joint Ventures* stated that IAS 31 did not indicate a preference for any particular treatment for accounting for interests in joint ventures in a joint venturer's separate financial statements. However, in 2003 the Board decided to

---

1 IFRS 9 *Financial Instruments* replaced IAS 39. IFRS 9 applies to all items that were previously within the scope of IAS 39.
2 IFRS 9 *Financial Instruments* eliminated the category of available-for-sale financial assets.
3 IFRS 9 *Financial Instruments* replaced IAS 39. IFRS 9 applies to all items that were previously within the scope of IAS 39.

require the use of cost or IAS 39 for all investments included in separate financial statements and to remove the equity method as one of the measurement options.

BC10   Although the equity method would provide users with some profit or loss information similar to that obtained from consolidation, the Board noted that such information is reflected in the investor's consolidated or individual financial statements and does not need to be provided to the users of its separate financial statements. For separate financial statements, the focus is upon the performance of the assets as investments. The Board concluded that separate financial statements prepared using either the fair value method in accordance with IAS 39[4] or the cost method would be relevant. Using the fair value method in accordance with IAS 39 would provide a measure of the economic value of the investments. Using the cost method can result in relevant information, depending on the purpose of preparing the separate financial statements. For example, they may be needed only by particular parties to determine the dividend income from subsidiaries.

Equity method in separate financial statements (amendments issued in 2014)

BC10A   In their responses to the Board's 2011 Agenda Consultation, some respondents said that:

(a)   the laws of some countries require listed companies to present separate financial statements prepared in accordance with local regulations, and those local regulations require the use of the equity method to account for investments in subsidiaries, joint ventures and associates; and

(b)   in most cases, the use of the equity method would be the only difference between the separate financial statements prepared in accordance with IFRS and those prepared in accordance with local regulations.

BC10B   Those respondents strongly supported the inclusion of the equity method as one of the options for measuring investments in subsidiaries, joint ventures and associates in the separate financial statements of an entity. In May 2012, the Board decided to consider restoring the option to use the equity method in separate financial statements through a narrow-scope project. Consequently, the Board issued an Exposure Draft in December 2013, the proposals in which would facilitate convergence of local GAAP in those jurisdictions with IFRS for separate financial statements, and that would help to reduce compliance costs for some entities without the loss of information.

Definition of separate financial statements

BC10C   Some respondents to the Exposure Draft commented that the proposed amendments to paragraphs 4 and 6 of IAS 27 create an inconsistency in the definition of 'separate financial statements', especially for an investor that has investments in associates or joint ventures and no investments in subsidiaries. The financial statements of such an investor in which the investments in joint

---

4   In May 2011 the Board issued IFRS 13 *Fair Value Measurement*, which contains requirements for measuring fair value.

ventures and associates are accounted for using the equity method would be the investor's primary financial statements as well as its separate financial statements. Consequently, they assert that there could be confusion about the applicability of the disclosure requirements in IAS 27 and IFRS 12. IFRS 12 does not apply to an entity's separate financial statements.

BC10D   The Board noted that the financial statements of an investor that has no investments in subsidiaries, and has investments in associates or joint ventures that are required by IAS 28 to be accounted for using the equity method, are not separate financial statements. Consequently, in those financial statements, such an investor is required to comply with the disclosure requirements in IFRS 12. As a logical consequence, such an investor is less likely to prepare separate financial statements in which investments in associates or joint ventures are accounted for using the equity method. If such an investor presents separate financial statements, the Board expects that the investor is likely to account for its investments in associates or joint ventures either at cost or in accordance with IFRS 9.

BC10E   The Board also noted that an investor that is exempted in accordance with paragraph 17 of IAS 28 from applying the equity method to its investments in joint ventures and associates may elect to present separate financial statements in which the investor elects to account for those investments using the equity method. In those separate financial statements, the investor is not required to present the information required by IFRS 12 for its investments in joint ventures and associates (see paragraph 6(b) of IFRS 12).

Application of the equity method

BC10F   IAS 28 contains guidance on the application of the equity method. IAS 28 notes that many of the procedures that are appropriate for the application of the equity method are similar to the consolidation procedures described in IFRS 10 (see paragraph 26 of IAS 28).

BC10G   In general, the application of the equity method to investments in subsidiaries, joint ventures and associates in the separate financial statements of an entity is expected to result in the same net assets and profit or loss attributable to the owners as in the entity's consolidated financial statements. However, there could be situations in which applying the equity method in separate financial statements to investments in subsidiaries would give a different result compared to the consolidated financial statements. Some of those situations are:

(a)   *impairment testing requirements in IAS 28.* For an investment in a subsidiary accounted for in separate financial statements using the equity method, goodwill that forms part of the carrying amount of the investment in the subsidiary is not tested for impairment separately. Instead, the entire carrying amount of the investment in the subsidiary is tested for impairment in accordance with IAS 36 *Impairment of Assets* as a single asset. However, in the consolidated financial statements of the entity, because goodwill is recognised separately, it is tested for impairment by applying the requirements in IAS 36 for testing goodwill for impairment.

(b)   *subsidiary that has a net liability position.* IAS 28 requires an investor to discontinue recognising its share of further losses when its cumulative share of losses of the investee equals or exceeds its interest in the investee, unless the investor has incurred legal or constructive obligations or made payments on behalf of the investee, in which case a liability is recognised, whereas there is no such requirement in relation to the consolidated financial statements.

(c)   *capitalisation of borrowing costs incurred by a parent in relation to the assets of a subsidiary.* IAS 23 *Borrowing Costs* notes that, in some circumstances, it may be appropriate to include all borrowings of the parent and its subsidiaries when computing a weighted average of the borrowing costs. When a parent borrows funds and its subsidiary uses them for the purpose of obtaining a qualifying asset, in the consolidated financial statements of the parent the borrowing costs incurred by the parent are considered to be directly attributable to the acquisition of the subsidiary's qualifying asset. However, this would not be appropriate in the separate financial statements of the parent if the parent's investment in the subsidiary is a financial asset, which is not a qualifying asset.

Some respondents to the Exposure Draft asked the Board to consider providing additional guidance to align the carrying amount of a subsidiary in the parent's separate financial statements with the net assets of the subsidiary that are attributable to the parent in the parent's consolidated financial statements. The Board concluded that creating any additional guidance within IAS 28 to eliminate such differences was outside the scope of this project. The Board was concerned that the development of such guidance would not be possible without adequate research and analysis, which would delay the amendments. Consequently, the Board decided not to consider these requests.

BC10H   Some respondents to the Exposure Draft commented that IAS 28 should be amended to provide guidance on the application of the equity method to a subsidiary in the separate financial statements of the parent. The Board concluded that amending IAS 28 to provide such guidance was outside the scope of the project, and a parent that has elected to apply the equity method to account for its subsidiaries in its separate financial statements should follow the methodology in IAS 28 as applicable to an associate or a joint venture.

2008 amendments

BC11   As part of its annual improvements project begun in 2007, the Board identified an apparent inconsistency with IFRS 5 *Non-current Assets Held For Sale and Discontinued Operations.* The inconsistency related to the accounting by a parent in its separate financial statements when investments it accounts for in accordance with IAS 39 are classified as held for sale in accordance with IFRS 5. Paragraph 10 requires an entity that prepares separate financial statements to account for such investments that are classified as held for sale (or included in a disposal group that is classified as held for sale) in accordance with IFRS 5 if they are measured at cost. However, financial assets that an entity accounts for in accordance with IAS 39 are excluded from IFRS 5's measurement requirements.

BC12   Paragraph BC13 of the Basis for Conclusions on IFRS 5 explains that the Board decided that non-current assets should be excluded from the measurement scope of IFRS 5 only 'if (i) they are already carried at fair value with changes in fair value recognised in profit or loss or (ii) there would be difficulties in determining their fair value less costs to sell.'[5] The Board acknowledged in the Basis for Conclusions on IFRS 5 that not all financial assets within the scope of IAS 39 are recognised at fair value with changes in fair value recognised in profit or loss, but it did not want to make any further changes to the accounting for financial assets at that time.

BC13   Therefore, the Board amended paragraph 10 by *Improvements to IFRSs* issued in May 2008 to align the accounting in separate financial statements for those investments that are accounted for in accordance with IAS 39 with the measurement exclusion that IFRS 5 provides for other assets that are accounted for in accordance with IAS 39 before classification as held for sale. Thus, an entity should continue to account for such investments in accordance with IAS 39 when they meet the held for sale criteria in IFRS 5.

Dividend received from a subsidiary, a joint venture or an associate

BC14   Before *Cost of an Investment in a Subsidiary, Jointly Controlled Entity or Associate* was issued in May 2008, IAS 27 described a 'cost method'. This required an entity to recognise distributions as income only if they came from post-acquisition retained earnings. Distributions received in excess of such retained earnings were regarded as a recovery of investment and were recognised as a reduction in the cost of the investment. To apply that method retrospectively upon first-time adoption of IFRSs in its separate financial statements, an investor would need to know the subsidiary's pre-acquisition retained earnings in accordance with IFRSs.

BC15   Restating pre-acquisition retained earnings would be a task tantamount to restating the business combination (for which IFRS 1 *First-time Adoption of International Financial Reporting Standards* provides an exemption in Appendix C). It might involve subjective use of hindsight, which would diminish the relevance and reliability of the information. In some cases, the restatement would be time-consuming and difficult. In other cases, it would be impossible (because it would involve making judgements about the fair values of the assets and liabilities of a subsidiary at the acquisition date).

BC16   Therefore, in *Cost of an Investment in a Subsidiary*, an exposure draft of proposed amendments to IFRS 1 (published in January 2007), the Board proposed to give first-time adopters an exemption from restating the retained earnings of the subsidiary at the date of acquisition for the purpose of applying the cost method.

BC17   In considering the responses to that exposure draft, the Board observed that the principle underpinning the cost method is that a return of an investment should be deducted from the carrying amount of the investment. However, the wording in the previous version of IAS 27 created a problem in some

---

5   In May 2011 the Board issued IFRS 13 *Fair Value Measurement*, which contains requirements for measuring fair value.

jurisdictions because it made specific reference to retained earnings as the means of making that assessment. The Board decided that the best way to resolve this issue was to delete the definition of the cost method.

BC18 In removing the definition of the cost method, the Board concluded that an investor should recognise a dividend from a subsidiary, a joint venture or an associate as income in its separate financial statements. Consequently, the requirement to separate the retained earnings of an entity into pre-acquisition and post-acquisition components as a method for assessing whether a dividend is a recovery of its associated investment has been removed from IFRSs.

BC19 To reduce the risk that removing the definition of the cost method would lead to investments in subsidiaries, joint ventures and associates being overstated in the separate financial statements of the investor, the Board proposed that the related investment should be tested for impairment in accordance with IAS 36.

BC20 The Board published its revised proposals in *Cost of an Investment in a Subsidiary, Jointly Controlled Entity or Associate*, an exposure draft of proposed amendments to IFRS 1 and IAS 27, in December 2007. Respondents generally supported the proposed amendments to IAS 27, except for the proposal to require impairment testing of the related investment when an investor recognises a dividend. In the light of the comments received, the Board revised its proposal and identified specific indicators of impairment. This was done to narrow the circumstances in which impairment testing of the related investment would be required when an investor recognises a dividend (see paragraph 12(h) of IAS 36). The Board included the amendments in *Cost of an Investment in a Subsidiary, Jointly Controlled Entity or Associate* issued in May 2008.

Measurement of cost in the separate financial statements of a new parent

BC21 In 2007 the Board received enquiries about the application of paragraph 10(a) when a parent reorganises the structure of its group by establishing a new entity as its parent. The new parent obtains control of the original parent by issuing equity instruments in exchange for existing equity instruments of the original parent.

BC22 In this type of reorganisation, the assets and liabilities of the new group and the original group are the same immediately before and after the reorganisation. In addition, the owners of the original parent have the same relative and absolute interests in the net assets of the new group immediately after the reorganisation as they had in the net assets of the original group before the reorganisation. Finally, this type of reorganisation involves an existing entity and its shareholders agreeing to create a new parent between them. In contrast, many transactions or events that result in a parent-subsidiary relationship are initiated by a parent over an entity that will be positioned below it in the structure of the group.

BC23 Therefore, the Board decided that in applying paragraph 10(a) *in the limited circumstances in which a parent establishes a new parent in this particular manner*, the new parent should measure the cost of its investment in the original parent at the carrying amount of its share of the equity items shown in the separate financial statements of the original parent at the date of the reorganisation. In

December 2007 the Board published an exposure draft proposing to amend IAS 27 to add a paragraph with that requirement.

BC24 In response to comments received from respondents to that exposure draft, the Board modified the drafting of the amendment (paragraphs 13 and 14) to clarify that it applies to the following types of reorganisations when they satisfy the criteria specified in the amendment:

(a) reorganisations in which the new parent does not acquire all the equity instruments of the original parent. For example, a new parent might issue equity instruments in exchange for ordinary shares of the original parent, but not acquire the preference shares of the original parent. In addition, a new parent might obtain control of the original parent, but not acquire all the ordinary shares of the original parent.

(b) the establishment of an intermediate parent within a group, as well as the establishment of a new ultimate parent of a group.

(c) reorganisations in which an entity that is not a parent establishes a new entity as its parent.

BC25 In addition, the Board clarified that the amendment focuses on the measurement of one asset—the new parent's investment in the original parent in the new parent's separate financial statements. The amendment does not apply to the measurement of any other assets or liabilities in the separate financial statements of either the original parent or the new parent or in the consolidated financial statements.

BC26 The Board included the amendment in *Cost of an Investment in a Subsidiary, Jointly Controlled Entity or Associate* issued in May 2008.

BC27 The Board did not consider the accounting for other types of reorganisations or for common control transactions more broadly. Accordingly, paragraphs 13 and 14 apply only when the criteria in those paragraphs are satisfied. Therefore, the Board expects that entities would continue to account for transactions that do not satisfy the criteria in paragraphs 13 and 14 in accordance with their accounting policies for such transactions. The Board plans to consider the definition of common control and the accounting for business combinations under common control in a future project on common control transactions.

Disclosure (2011 amendments)

BC28 When IAS 27 was amended in 2011, the Board clarified the disclosures required by an entity preparing separate financial statements so that the entity would be required to disclose the principal place of business (and country of incorporation, if different) of significant investments in subsidiaries, joint ventures and associates and, if applicable, of the parent that prepares consolidated financial statements that comply with IFRSs. IAS 27 (as amended in 2008) had previously required the disclosure of the country of incorporation or residence of such entities. The clarification of the disclosure requirement is more consistent with those requirements in other IFRSs (eg IFRS 12 and IAS 1 *Presentation of Financial Statements*) that also require disclosure of the principal place of business and country of incorporation.

Effective date (2011 amendments)

BC29　The Board decided to align the effective date for the Standard with the effective date for IFRS 10, IFRS 11, IFRS 12 and IAS 28 (as amended in 2011). When making this decision, the Board noted that the five IFRSs all deal with the assessment of, and related accounting and disclosure requirements about, a reporting entity's special relationships with other entities (ie when the reporting entity has control or joint control of, or significant influence over, another entity). As a result, the Board concluded that applying IAS 27 without also applying the other four IFRSs could cause unwarranted confusion.

BC30　The Board usually sets an effective date of between twelve and eighteen months after issuing an IFRS. When deciding the effective date for the five IFRSs, the Board considered the following factors:

(a)　the time that many countries require for translation and for introducing the mandatory requirements into law.

(b)　the consolidation project was related to the global financial crisis that started in 2007 and was accelerated by the Board in response to urgent requests from the leaders of the G20, the Financial Stability Board, users of financial statements, regulators and others to improve the accounting and disclosure of an entity's 'off balance sheet' activities.

(c)　the comments received from respondents to the Request for Views *Effective Date and Transition Methods* that was published in October 2010 regarding implementation costs, effective date and transition requirements of the IFRSs to be issued in 2011. Most respondents did not identify the consolidation and joint arrangements IFRSs as having a high impact in terms of the time and resources that their implementation would require. In addition, only a few respondents commented that the effective dates of those IFRSs should be aligned with those of the other IFRSs to be issued in 2011.

BC31　With these factors in mind, the Board decided to require entities to apply the five IFRSs for annual periods beginning on or after 1 January 2013.

BC32　Most respondents to the Request for Views supported early application of the IFRSs to be issued in 2011. Respondents stressed that early application was especially important for first-time adopters in 2011 and 2012. The Board was persuaded by these arguments and decided to permit early application of IAS 27 but only if an entity applies it in conjunction with the other IFRSs (ie IFRS 10, IFRS 11, IFRS 12 and IAS 28 (as amended in 2011)) to avoid a lack of comparability among financial statements, and for the reasons noted in paragraph BC29 that triggered the Board's decision to set the same effective date for all five IFRSs. Even though an entity should apply the five IFRSs at the same time, the Board noted that an entity should not be prevented from providing any information required by IFRS 12 early if by doing so users gained a better understanding of the entity's relationships with other entities.

Transition requirements (2014 amendments)

BC33   Some respondents to the Exposure Draft suggested that the Board should consider providing some form of relief to make the transition to accounting for investments in subsidiaries, joint ventures and associates using the equity method easier. However, the Board noted that an entity should be able to use the information that is used for consolidation of the subsidiary in its consolidated financial statements for applying the equity method to the investment in the subsidiary in its separate financial statements. Investments in associates and joint ventures (after applying the transition provisions of IFRS 11) are accounted for using the equity method in the consolidated financial statements, which means that an entity need not perform any additional procedures and can use the same information in its separate financial statements. The Board also noted that many entities would be able to draw on the information in the financial statements of its ultimate, or any intermediate, parent in order to calculate the carrying amount of its investment in a subsidiary, joint venture and associate on the initial application of these amendments. Furthermore, the application of the equity method in separate financial statements is optional and not mandatory. Consequently, the Board concluded that additional transition relief was not needed and that an entity that elects to use the equity method should be required to apply the amendments retrospectively in accordance with IAS 8.

Dissenting Opinion

Dissent of Mary E Barth and Philippe Danjou from *Cost of an Investment in a Subsidiary, Jointly Controlled Entity or Associate* (Amendments to IFRS 1 and IAS 27) issued in May 2008

Cross-references have been updated.

DO1   Professor Barth and Mr Danjou voted against the publication of *Cost of an Investment in a Subsidiary, Jointly Controlled Entity or Associate* (Amendments to IFRS 1 *First-time Adoption of International Financial Reporting Standards* and IAS 27 *Consolidated and Separate Financial Statements*). The reasons for their dissent are set out below.

DO2   These Board members disagree with the **requirement** in paragraphs 13 and 14 of IAS 27 that when a reorganisation satisfies the criteria specified in those paragraphs and the resulting new parent accounts for its investment in the original parent at cost in accordance with paragraph 10(a) of IAS 27, the new parent must measure the cost at the carrying amount of its share of the equity items shown in the separate financial statements of the original parent at the date of the reorganisation.

DO3   These Board members acknowledge that a new parent could choose to apply paragraph 10(b) of IAS 27 and account for its investment in the original parent in accordance with IAS 39 *Financial Instruments: Recognition and Measurement*.[6] However, the new parent then would be required to account for the investment in accordance with IAS 39 in subsequent periods and to account for all other investments in the same category in accordance with IAS 39.

DO4   These Board members also acknowledge, as outlined in paragraph BC23 of the Basis for Conclusions on IAS 27, that this type of reorganisation is different from other types of reorganisations in that the assets and liabilities of the new group and the original group are the same immediately before and after the reorganisation, as are the interests of the owners of the original parent in the net assets of those groups. Therefore, using the previous carrying amount to measure the cost of the new parent's investment in the original parent might be appropriate on the basis that the separate financial statements of the new parent would reflect its position as part of a pre-existing group.

DO5   However, these Board members believe that it is inappropriate to preclude a new parent from measuring the cost of its investment in the original parent at the fair value of the shares that it issues as part of the reorganisation. Separate financial statements are prepared to reflect the parent as a separate legal entity (ie not considering that the entity might be part of a group). Although such a reorganisation does not change the assets and liabilities of the group and therefore should have no accounting effect at the consolidated level, from the perspective of the new parent as a separate legal entity, its position has

---

6   IFRS 9 *Financial Instruments* replaced IAS 39. IFRS 9 applies to all items that previously were within the scope of IAS 39.

changed—it has issued shares and acquired an investment that it did not have previously. Also, in many jurisdictions, commercial law or corporate governance regulations require entities to measure new shares that they issue at the fair value of the consideration received for the shares.

DO6 These Board members believe that the appropriate measurement basis for the new parent's cost of its investment in the original parent depends on the Board's view of separate financial statements. The Board is or will be discussing related issues in the reporting entity phase of its *Conceptual Framework* project and in its project on common control transactions. Accordingly, these Board members believe that the Board should have permitted a new parent to measure the cost of its investment in the original parent either at the carrying amount of its share of the equity items shown in the separate financial statements of the original parent or at the fair value of the equity instruments that it issues until the Board discusses the related issues in its projects on reporting entity and common control transactions.

IASB documents published to accompany

IAS 28

Investments in Associates and Joint Ventures

The text of the unaccompanied standard, IAS 28, is contained in Part A of this edition. Its effective date when issued was 1 January 2013. The text of the Accompanying Guidance on IAS 28 is contained in Part B of this edition. This part presents the following documents:

BASIS FOR CONCLUSIONS

DISSENTING OPINIONS

CONTENTS

**BASIS FOR CONCLUSIONS ON
IAS 28 *INVESTMENTS IN ASSOCIATES AND JOINT
VENTURES***

Basis for Conclusions on
IAS 28 *Investments in Associates and Joint Ventures*

This Basis for Conclusions accompanies, but is not part of, IAS 28.

Introduction

BC1   This Basis for Conclusions summarises the International Accounting Standards Board's considerations in reaching its conclusions on amending IAS 28 *Investments in Associates* in 2011. Individual Board members gave greater weight to some factors than to others.

BC2   The amendment of IAS 28 resulted from the Board's project on joint ventures. When discussing that project, the Board decided to incorporate the accounting for joint ventures into IAS 28 because the equity method is applicable to both joint ventures and associates.

BC3   As a result, the title of IAS 28 was changed to *Investments in Associates and Joint Ventures*. Because the Board's intention was not to reconsider the fundamental approach to the accounting for investments in associates established by IAS 28, the Board has incorporated into its Basis for Conclusions on IAS 28 material from the Basis for Conclusions on IAS 28 (as revised in 2003) that the Board has not reconsidered.

The structure of IAS 28 and the Board's deliberations

BC4   IAS 28 as amended in 2011 superseded IAS 28 (as revised in 2003 and amended in 2010). As stated in paragraph BC3, in amending IAS 28, the Board did not reconsider all the Standard's requirements. The requirements in paragraphs 5–11, 15, 22–23, 25–28 and 32–43 relate to the assessment of significant influence and to the equity method and its application, and paragraphs 12–14 relate to the accounting for potential voting rights. With the exception of the Board's decision to incorporate the accounting for joint ventures into IAS 28, those paragraphs were carried forward from IAS 28 and from the Guidance on Implementing IAS 27 *Consolidated and Separate Financial Statements*, IAS 28 *Investments in Associates* and IAS 31 *Interests in Joint Ventures* that was withdrawn when IFRS 10 *Consolidated Financial Statements*, IFRS 11 *Joint Arrangements* and IAS 28 (as amended in 2011) were issued. As a result, those paragraphs were not reconsidered by the Board.

BC5   When revised in 2003 IAS 28 was accompanied by a Basis for Conclusions summarising the considerations of the Board, as constituted at the time, in reaching its conclusions. That Basis for Conclusions was subsequently updated to reflect amendments to the Standard.

BC6   The Board has incorporated into its Basis for Conclusions on IAS 28 (as amended in 2011) material from the previous Basis for Conclusions because it discusses matters that the Board has not reconsidered. That material is contained in paragraphs denoted by numbers with the prefix BCZ. In those paragraphs cross-references have been updated accordingly and minor necessary editorial changes have been made.

BC7   One Board member dissented from an amendment to IAS 28 issued in May 2008, which has been carried forward to IAS 28 (as amended in 2011). His dissenting opinion is also set out after this Basis for Conclusions.

BC8   The requirements in paragraphs 2, 16–21, 24 and 29–31 relate to matters addressed within the joint ventures project that led to amendments to IAS 28. Paragraphs describing the Board's considerations in reaching its conclusions on IAS 28 are numbered with the prefix BC.

BC9   As part of its project on consolidation, the Board is examining how an investment entity accounts for its interests in subsidiaries, joint ventures and associates. The outcome might affect how organisations such as venture capital organisations, or mutual funds, unit trusts and similar entities account for their interests in joint ventures and associates. The Board expects to publish later in 2011 an exposure draft on investment entities.[1,2]

Scope

BC10   During its redeliberation of the exposure draft ED 9 *Joint Arrangements*, the Board reconsidered the scope exception of IAS 31 that had also been proposed in ED 9. The Board concluded that the scope exception in ED 9 for interests in joint ventures held by venture capital organisations, or mutual funds, unit trusts and similar entities, including investment-linked insurance funds, that are measured at fair value through profit or loss in accordance with IFRS 9 *Financial Instruments* is more appropriately characterised as a measurement exemption, and not as a scope exception.

BC11   The Board observed that IAS 28 had a similar scope exception for investments in associates held by venture capital organisations, or mutual funds, unit trusts and similar entities, including investment-linked insurance funds, that are measured at fair value through profit or loss in accordance with IFRS 9.

BC12   The Board observed that the scope exception in ED 9 and IAS 28 related not to the fact that these arrangements do not have the characteristics of joint arrangements or those investments are not associates, but to the fact that for investments held by venture capital organisations, or mutual funds, unit trusts and similar entities including investment-linked insurance funds, fair value measurement provides more useful information for users of the financial statements than would application of the equity method.

BC13   Accordingly, the Board decided to maintain the option that permits venture capital organisations, or mutual funds, unit trusts and similar entities including investment-linked insurance funds to measure their interests in joint ventures

---

1   In October 2012 the Board issued *Investment Entities* (Amendments to IFRS 10, IFRS 12 and IAS 27), which required investment entities, as defined in IFRS 10 *Consolidated Financial Statements*, to measure their investments in subsidiaries, other than those providing investment-related services or activities, at fair value through profit or loss. The amendments did not introduce any new accounting requirements for investments in associates or joint ventures.

2   In December 2014, the IASB issued *Investment Entities: Applying the Consolidation Exception* (Amendments to IFRS 10, IFRS 12 and IAS 28). The amendments introduced relief to permit a non-investment entity investor in an associate or joint venture that is an investment entity to retain the fair value through profit or loss measurement applied by the associate or joint venture to its subsidiaries (see paragraphs BC46A–BC46G).

and associates at fair value through profit or loss in accordance with IFRS 9, but clarified that this is an exemption from the requirement to measure interests in joint ventures and associates using the equity method, rather than an exception to the scope of IAS 28 for the accounting for joint ventures and associates held by those entities.

BC14   As a result of that decision and of the decision to incorporate the accounting for joint ventures into IAS 28, the Board decided that IAS 28 should be applied to the accounting for investments held by all entities that have joint control of, or significant influence over, an investee.

Significant influence

Potential voting rights

BC15   In its deliberation of the amendments to IAS 28, the Board considered whether the requirements now in paragraphs 7–9 of IAS 28 regarding potential voting rights when assessing significant influence should be changed to be consistent with the requirements developed in the consolidation project.

BC16   The Board observed that the definition of significant influence in IAS 28 (ie 'the power to participate in the financial and operating policy decisions of the investee but is not control or joint control of those policies') was related to the definition of control as it was defined in IAS 27. The Board had not considered the definition of significant influence when it amended IAS 28 and concluded that it would not be appropriate to change one element of significant influence in isolation. Any such consideration should be done as part of a wider review of the accounting for associates.

BC16A–
BC16L   *[These paragraphs refer to an amendment that is not yet effective, and are therefore not included in this edition.]*

Application of the equity method

Temporary joint control and significant influence (2003 revision)

BCZ17   In IFRS 5 *Non-current Assets Held for Sale and Discontinued Operations* the Board decided not to exempt an entity from applying the equity method for accounting for its investments in joint ventures and associates when joint control of, or significant influence over, an investee is intended to be temporary.

Severe long-term restrictions impairing ability to transfer funds to the investor (2003 revision)

BCZ18   The Board decided not to exempt an entity from applying the equity method for accounting for its investments in joint ventures or associates when severe long-term restrictions impaired a joint venture or an associate's ability to transfer funds to the investor. It did so because such circumstances may not preclude the entity's joint control of, or significant influence over, the joint venture or the associate. The Board decided that an entity should, when assessing its ability to exercise joint control of, or significant influence over, an investee, consider restrictions on the transfer of funds from the joint venture or from the associate to the entity. In themselves, such restrictions do not preclude the existence of joint control or significant influence.

Non-coterminous year-ends (2003 revision)

BCZ19   The exposure draft that preceded the revision of IAS 28 in 2003 proposed to limit to three months any difference between the reporting dates of an entity and its associate or its joint venture when applying the equity method. Some respondents to that exposure draft believed that it could be impracticable for the entity to prepare financial statements as of the same date when the date of the entity's financial statements and those of the associate or joint venture differ by more than three months. The Board noted that a three-month limit operates in several jurisdictions and it was concerned that a longer period, such as six months, would lead to the recognition of stale information. Therefore, it decided to retain the three-month limit.

Exemption from applying the equity method: subsidiary of an investment entity

BC19A   In December 2014, the Board amended IFRS 10 to confirm that the exemption from preparing consolidated financial statements set out in paragraph 4(a) of IFRS 10 is available to a parent entity that is a subsidiary of an investment entity. The Board also decided to amend paragraph 17 of IAS 28 for the same reasons. Paragraph 17 of IAS 28 uses the same criteria as paragraph 4(a) of IFRS 10 to provide an exemption from applying the equity method for entities that are subsidiaries and that hold interests in associates and joint ventures.

Exemption from applying the equity method: measuring an associate or joint venture at fair value (amendments issued in December 2016)

BC19B   When an investment in an associate or joint venture is held by, or is held indirectly through, a venture capital organisation, or a mutual fund, unit trust and similar entities including investment-linked insurance funds, the entity may elect, in accordance with paragraph 18 of IAS 28, to measure that investment at fair value through profit or loss. The Board received a request to clarify whether the entity is able to choose between applying the equity method or measuring the investment at fair value for each investment, or whether instead the entity applies the same accounting to all of its investments in associates and joint ventures.

BC19C   The Board noted that, before it was revised in 2011, IAS 28 *Investments in Associates* permitted a venture capital organisation, or a mutual fund, unit trust and similar entities to elect to measure investments in an associate at fair value through profit or loss separately for each associate. However, after the revision, it had become less clear whether such an election was still available to those entities. The Board noted that it did not consider changing these requirements when revising IAS 28 in 2011, and any lack of clarity that arose as a consequence of the amendments in 2011 was unintentional.

BC19D   Accordingly, in *Annual Improvements to IFRS Standards 2014–2016 Cycle*, the Board amended paragraph 18 of IAS 28 to clarify that a venture capital organisation, or a mutual fund, unit trust and similar entities may elect, at initial recognition, to measure investments in an associate or joint venture at fair value through profit or loss separately for each associate or joint venture.

BC19E   In addition, paragraph 36A of IAS 28 permits an entity that is not an investment entity to retain the fair value measurement applied by its associates and joint ventures (that are investment entities) when applying the equity method. The Board also decided to amend that paragraph to clarify that this choice is available, at initial recognition, for each investment entity associate or joint venture.

BC19F   Some respondents to the Board's proposals said that it was not clear whether, in its separate financial statements, a venture capital organisation or a mutual fund, unit trust and similar entities:

(a)   could choose to measure investments in an associate or joint venture at fair value through profit or loss for each associate or joint venture; or

(b)   would be required to measure all such investments at fair value through profit or loss, on the grounds that paragraph 10 of IAS 27 *Separate Financial Statements* requires the same accounting for each category of investments and paragraph 11 of IAS 27 requires investments measured at fair value in accordance with IAS 28 to be measured at fair value in separate financial statements. If this were to be the case, those respondents note that such an outcome would appear to be inconsistent with the objective of the amendments to IAS 28.

BC19G   The Board noted that 'category' is not defined in IFRS Standards, but is used in a number of Standards. For example, IFRS 7 *Financial Instruments: Disclosures* uses 'category' to refer to groupings of financial assets and financial liabilities that are measured in different ways—for example, financial assets measured at fair value through profit or loss is one category of financial asset and financial assets measured at amortised cost is another category of financial asset. The Board observed that paragraph 10 of IAS 27 should not be read to mean that, in all circumstances, all investments in associates are one 'category' of investment and all investments in joint ventures are one 'category' of investment. The issue raised by respondents arises only if the requirement in paragraph 10 of IAS 27 were to be interpreted in that way. An entity that elects to measure some associates or joint ventures at fair value through profit or loss in accordance with paragraph 18 of IAS 28 would retain that measurement basis for those associates and joint ventures in its separate financial statements, as required by paragraph 11 of IAS 27. The entity could then choose to measure its remaining associates and joint ventures either at cost, in accordance with IFRS 9 or using the equity method in accordance with paragraph 10 of IAS 27.

BC19H   In response to the Board's proposal to apply the amendments retrospectively, some respondents questioned whether the information needed would be available without the use of hindsight. Others suggested providing transition relief for entities that previously interpreted IAS 28 as requiring the same accounting for all investments in associates and joint ventures. They suggested that, when first applying the amendments, such entities should be allowed to elect to measure each existing investment either at fair value through profit or loss or using the equity method.

BC19I The Board decided to retain retrospective application of the amendments because the amendments are expected to affect only a narrow population of entities, and such entities (being venture capital organisations, or mutual funds, unit trusts and similar entities) would typically be expected to have fair value information for their investments for management purposes. In addition, if the costs of applying the amendments retrospectively are considered excessive, an entity can choose not to change any of its previous decisions regarding measurement. This is because retrospective application of a choice of measurement for each associate or joint venture, in effect, means that an entity is not required to reassess its previous decisions. The Board also noted that retrospective application in accordance with IAS 8 *Accounting Policies, Changes in Accounting Estimates and Errors* means that an entity will not use hindsight when first applying the amendments—paragraph 53 of IAS 8 states that hindsight should not be used when applying a new accounting policy to a prior period, either in making assumptions about what management's intentions would have been in a prior period or in estimating the amounts recognised, measured and disclosed in a prior period.

Exemptions from applying the equity method: partial use of fair value measurement of associates

BC20 The Board received a request to clarify whether different measurement bases can be applied to portions of an investment in an associate when part of the investment is not accounted for using the equity method in accordance with paragraph 18 of IAS 28, but it is instead measured at fair value through profit or loss in accordance with IFRS 9. The Board initially deliberated this amendment to IAS 28 as part of the *Improvements to IFRSs* issued in April 2010; however, at its meeting in February 2010 the Board decided to address this issue within the joint ventures project.

BC21 The Board noted that two views exist with respect to measurement. The first view identifies all direct and indirect interests held in the associate either by the parent or through any of its subsidiaries, and then applies IAS 28 to the entire investment in the associate. In accordance with this view, there is only one investment in the associate and it should be accounted for as a single unit. The second view identifies all direct and indirect interests held in an associate, but then allows the use of the measurement exemption to portions of an investment in an associate if the portion is held by a venture capital organisation, or a mutual fund, unit trust and similar entities including investment-linked insurance funds, regardless of whether those entities have significant influence over their portion of the investment in the associate. The Board agreed with the second view and therefore amended IAS 28. The Board decided that equivalent guidance on the partial use of fair value for the measurement of investments in joint ventures should not be provided because the Board thought that such events would be unlikely in practice.

BC22 The Board also discussed whether the partial use of fair value should be allowed only in the case of venture capital organisations, or mutual funds, unit trusts and similar entities including investment-linked insurance funds, that have designated their portion of the investment in the associate at fair value through profit or loss in their own financial statements. The Board noted that several situations might arise in which those entities do not measure their portion of the investment in the associate at fair value through profit or loss. In those situations, however, from the group's perspective, the appropriate determination of the business purpose would lead to the measurement of this portion of the investment in the associate at fair value through profit or loss in the consolidated financial statements. Consequently, the Board decided that an entity should be able to measure a portion of an investment in an associate held by a venture capital organisation, or a mutual fund, unit trust and similar entities including investment-linked insurance funds, at fair value through profit or loss regardless of whether this portion of the investment is measured at fair value through profit or loss in those entities' financial statements.

Classification as held for sale

BC23   ED 9 proposed that an entity should account for an interest in a joint venture that is classified as held for sale in accordance with IFRS 5.

BC24   During its redeliberation of ED 9 the Board noted that the exposure draft *Improvements to IFRSs* published in August 2009 had proposed to amend IFRS 5 so as to require an entity to classify as held for sale its interest in an associate, or in a jointly controlled entity, when it is committed to a sale plan involving loss of significant influence or loss of joint control. Those proposals aimed to clarify that all the interest ('the whole interest') an entity had in an associate or a joint venture had to be classified as held for sale if the entity was committed to a sale plan involving loss of, significant influence over, or joint control of that interest.

BC25   The Board observed that those proposals were not aligned with the decisions made during the Board's redeliberation of ED 9 to remove all descriptions that associated the loss of joint control and the loss of significant influence with the term 'significant economic event' as introduced in the second phase of the Board's project on business combinations (see paragraphs BC28–BC31).

BC26   The Board decided that classifying an interest as held for sale should be on the basis of whether the intended disposal meets the criteria for classification as held for sale in accordance with IFRS 5, rather than on whether the entity had lost joint control of, or significant influence over, that interest. As a result, the Board concluded that when the disposal of an interest, or a portion of an interest, in a joint venture or an associate fulfilled the criteria for classification as held for sale in accordance with IFRS 5, an entity should classify the whole interest, or a portion of the interest, as held for sale.

BC27   The Board decided that, in the case of a partial disposal, an entity should maintain the use of the equity method for the retained interest in the joint venture or associate until the portion classified as held for sale is finally disposed of. The Board reasoned that even if the entity has the intention of selling a portion of an interest in an associate or a joint venture, until it does so it still has significant influence over, or joint control of, that investee. After the disposal, an entity should measure the retained interest in the joint venture or associate in accordance with IFRS 9 or in accordance with IAS 28 if the entity still has significant influence over, or joint control of, the retained interest.

Discontinuing the use of the equity method

BC28   During its redeliberation of ED 9, the Board reconsidered whether its decision in the second phase of the business combinations project to characterise loss of joint control or loss of significant influence as a significant economic event (ie in the same way that loss of control is characterised as a significant economic event) was appropriate. If it were, the Board thought that the entity should be required to recalibrate the accounting as required by IFRS 10. However, the Board concluded that, although significant, the events are fundamentally different. In the case of loss of control, the cessation of the parent-subsidiary relationship results in the derecognition of assets and liabilities because the composition of the group changes. If joint control or significant influence is lost the composition of the group is unaffected.

BC29   The Board also noted that retaining the characterisation of significant economic event in the case of loss of joint control or significant influence when the retained interest is a financial asset is unnecessary. IFRS 9 already requires that in such cases the retained interest (ie a financial asset) must be measured at fair value.

BC30   In the case of loss of joint control when significant influence is maintained, the Board acknowledged that the investor-investee relationship changes and, consequently, so does the nature of the investment. However, in this instance, both investments (ie the joint venture and the associate) continue to be measured using the equity method. Considering that there is neither a change in the group boundaries nor a change in the measurement requirements, the Board concluded that losing joint control and retaining significant influence is not an event that warrants remeasurement of the retained interest at fair value.

BC31   Consequently, the Board removed all descriptions that characterise loss of joint control or significant influence as a significant economic event as introduced in the second phase of the Board's project on business combinations.

Incorporation of SIC-13

BC32   In the joint ventures project, the Board decided to extend the requirements and guidance in IAS 28 for the accounting for 'downstream' and 'upstream' transactions between an entity and its associate to the accounting for transactions between an entity and its joint venture.

BC33   In ED 9, the Board proposed to incorporate into the standard on joint arrangements the consensus of SIC-13 *Jointly Controlled Entities—Non-Monetary Contributions by Venturers*. Because the Board relocated all the requirements for the accounting for joint ventures into IAS 28, the Board incorporated the consensus of SIC-13 into IAS 28 and extended it to associates.

BC34   The Board noted that the consensus of SIC-13 regarding non-monetary contributions made by a venturer[3] to a joint venture is consistent with IAS 28, except for the following aspect. SIC-13 established three exceptions for the recognition of gains or losses attributable to the equity interests of the other

---

3   IFRS 11 *Joint Arrangements*, issued in May 2011, uses the term 'joint venturers' to designate parties that have joint control of a joint venture.

© IFRS Foundation

parties. In response to comments raised by some respondents to ED 9, the Board redeliberated the need to incorporate into IAS 28 the exceptions included in SIC-13 for the recognition by an entity of the portion of a gain or loss attributable to the interests of other unrelated investors in the investee.

BC35   The Board concluded that only when the transaction lacks commercial substance should there be an exception for the recognition of gains or losses to be carried forward from the consensus of SIC-13 into IAS 28, because the other two exceptions in SIC-13 (ie 'the significant risks and rewards of ownership of the contributed non-monetary asset(s) have not been transferred to the jointly controlled entity' and 'the gain or loss on the non-monetary contribution cannot be measured reliably') either relate to requirements that are not aligned with the principles and requirements of IFRS 11 or relate to a criterion for the recognition of gain or losses (ie 'reliability of measurement') that is already included in the *Conceptual Framework for Financial Reporting*.

BCZ36   To the extent that the entity also receives monetary or non-monetary assets dissimilar to the assets contributed in addition to equity interests in the investee, the realisation of which is not dependent on the future cash flows of the investee, the earnings process is complete. Accordingly, an entity should recognise in full in profit or loss the portion of the gain or loss on the non-monetary contribution relating to the monetary or non-monetary assets received.

BC37   Additionally, the Board considered whether the requirements in IAS 31 for recognition of losses when downstream or upstream transactions provide evidence of a reduction in the net realisable value or impairment loss of the assets transacted or contributed were still relevant and decided to bring them forward to IAS 28.

BC37A–   *[These paragraphs refer to amendments that are not yet effective, and are therefore not*
BC37J   *included in this edition.]*

Recognition of losses (2003 revision)

BCZ38   The 2000 version of IAS 28 and SIC-20 *Equity Accounting Method—Recognition of Losses* restricted application of the equity method when, in accounting for the entity's share of losses, the carrying amount of the investment is reduced to zero.

BCZ39   The Board decided that the base to be reduced to zero should be broader than residual equity interests and should also include other non-equity interests that are in substance part of the net investment in the associate or joint venture, such as long-term receivables. Therefore, the Board decided to withdraw SIC-20.

BCZ40   The Board also noted that if non-equity investments are not included in the base to be reduced to zero, an entity could restructure its investment to fund the majority in non-equity investments to avoid recognising the losses of the associate or joint venture under the equity method.

BCZ41   In widening the base against which losses are to be recognised, the Board also clarified the application of the impairment provisions of IAS 39 *Financial Instruments: Recognition and Measurement*[4] to the financial assets that form part of the net investment.

Impairment losses (2008 amendment)

BCZ42   In 2008 the Board identified unclear guidance in IAS 28 regarding the extent to which an impairment reversal should be recognised as an adjustment to the carrying amount of an investment in an associate or in a joint venture.

BCZ43   The Board noted that applying the equity method involves adjusting the entity's share of the impairment loss recognised by the associate or joint venture on assets such as goodwill or property, plant and equipment to take account of the acquisition date fair values of those assets. The Board proposed in the exposure draft *Improvements to International Financial Reporting Standards* published in October 2007 that an additional impairment recognised by the entity, after applying the equity method, should not be allocated to any asset, including goodwill, that forms part of the carrying amount of the investment. Therefore, such an impairment should be reversed in a subsequent period to the extent that the recoverable amount of the investment increases.

BCZ44   Some respondents to the exposure draft expressed the view that the proposed amendment was not consistent with IAS 39 (regarding reversal of an impairment loss on an available-for-sale equity instrument[5]), or with IAS 36 *Impairment of Assets* (regarding the allocation of an impairment loss to goodwill and any reversal of an impairment loss relating to goodwill).

BCZ45   In its redeliberations, the Board affirmed its previous decisions but, in response to the comments made, decided to clarify the reasons for the amendments. The Board decided that an entity should not allocate an impairment loss to any asset that forms part of the carrying amount of the investment in the associate or joint venture because the investment is the only asset that the entity controls and recognises.

BCZ46   The Board also decided that any reversal of this impairment loss should be recognised as an adjustment to the investment in the associate or joint venture to the extent that the recoverable amount of the investment increases. This requirement is consistent with IAS 36, which permits the reversal of impairment losses for assets other than goodwill. The Board did not propose to align the requirements for the reversal of an impairment loss with those in IAS 39[6] relating to equity instruments, because an entity recognises an impairment loss on an investment in an associate or joint venture in accordance with IAS 36, rather than in accordance with IAS 39.

---

4   IFRS 9 *Financial Instruments* replaced IAS 39. IFRS 9 applies to all items that previously were within the scope of IAS 39.
5   IFRS 9 *Financial Instruments* eliminated the category of available-for-sale financial assets.
6   IFRS 9 *Financial Instruments* replaced IAS 39. IFRS 9 applies to all items that previously were within the scope of IAS 39.

Retaining the fair value measurement applied by an associate or joint venture that is an investment entity

BC46A   In October 2012, the Board issued *Investment Entities* (Amendments to IFRS 10, IFRS 12 and IAS 27), which required investment entities, as defined in IFRS 10, to measure most investments in subsidiaries at fair value through profit or loss. The amendments did not introduce any new accounting requirements for investments in associates or joint ventures. This is because paragraphs 18–19 of IAS 28 already allowed an investment entity to measure its investments in associates and joint ventures at fair value through profit or loss in accordance with IFRS 9. A wider range of entities, including venture capital organisations, or mutual funds, unit trusts and similar entities including investment-linked insurance funds, may also elect to measure their investments in associates and joint ventures in the same way.

BC46B   Paragraph 33 of IFRS 10 requires a non-investment entity parent of an investment entity to consolidate all entities that it controls, including those controlled through an investment entity subsidiary. This is consistent with the proposal contained in the Exposure Draft *Investment Entities* (the 'Investment Entities ED'), which was published in August 2011. Some respondents to the *Investment Entities* ED noted that this seemed inconsistent with paragraphs 18–19 of IAS 28, which allow a wider group of entities than only investment entities to measure their investments in associates and joint ventures at fair value through profit or loss. The Board acknowledged this inconsistency, and explained its reasons for not amending IAS 28 in line with IFRS 10, in paragraph BC283 of IFRS 10.

BC46C   Subsequently, the IFRS Interpretations Committee (the 'Interpretations Committee') received a request to clarify whether an entity that is not an investment entity should, when applying the equity method of accounting for its investment in an associate or joint venture that is an investment entity, retain the fair value measurement that is applied by that associate or joint venture to its subsidiaries or, instead, 'unwind' that treatment and apply consolidation procedures. Members of the Interpretations Committee had mixed views on the matter and, because of the need to provide clarity before the end of 2014, the matter was passed to the Board.

BC46D   The Board noted that the scope of the amendment in the *Investment Entities* ED was restricted to providing an exception to the consolidation requirements for investment entity parents. This exception reflects the unique business model of an investment entity, for which fair value information is more relevant than consolidation. This unique business model is not applicable to a non-investment entity parent. Consequently, paragraph 33 of IFRS 10 requires a non-investment entity parent of an investment entity to consolidate all entities that it controls, both directly and indirectly through an investment entity. This requires the non-investment entity parent to unwind the fair value through profit or loss measurement used by its investment entity subsidiaries for indirectly held subsidiaries.

BC46E   The Board also noted that paragraphs 35–36 of IAS 28, which require the use of uniform accounting policies, would apply for a non-investment entity investor and its investment entity associates or joint ventures. This would mean that the subsidiaries of those investment entity associates and joint ventures should be consolidated into the financial statements of those associates and joint ventures prior to the equity method being applied. The Board noted that this is conceptually consistent with the requirement in IFRS 10 for a non-investment entity parent to consolidate subsidiaries held through an investment entity subsidiary.

BC46F   However, some Board members raised concerns about the potentially significant practical difficulties or additional costs that may arise for an entity in unwinding the fair value through profit or loss measurement applied by an investment entity associate or joint venture for their interests in subsidiaries. Some Board members noted that the degree of practical difficulty is different depending on whether the investee is an associate or joint venture. In addition, some Board members noted the structuring risks highlighted in paragraph BC280 of IFRS 10 and noted that an investor's ability to achieve different accounting outcomes by holding investments through an investment entity investee is different depending on whether the investee is an associate or a joint venture. Consequently, in the Exposure Draft *Investment Entities: Applying the Consolidation Exception* (Proposed amendments to IFRS 10 and IAS 28) (the '*Consolidation Exception* ED'), which was published in June 2014, the Board proposed to provide relief to non-investment entity investors for their interests in investment entity associates, but not for their interests in investment entity joint ventures.

BC46G   The practicality and cost concerns were noted by the majority of respondents to the *Consolidation Exception* ED. However, the majority of respondents disagreed with the proposal to limit the relief to interests in investment entity associates, noting that the practicality and cost issues also applied to interests in joint ventures. In addition, some respondents disagreed with the concerns about the risk of structuring, noting that the difference between significant influence and joint control is much smaller than the difference between control and joint control. Consequently, the Board decided to provide relief to non-investment entity investors in both investment entity associates and joint ventures and to retain the consistency in treatment in applying the equity method to both associates and joint ventures. This relief permits, but does not require, a non-investment entity investor to retain the fair value through profit or loss measurement applied by an investment entity associate or joint venture for their subsidiaries when applying the equity method.

Effective date and transition

BC47   The Board decided to align the effective date for the Standard with the effective date for IFRS 10, IFRS 11, IFRS 12 *Disclosure of Interests in Other Entities* and IAS 27 *Separate Financial Statements*. When making this decision, the Board noted that the five IFRSs all deal with the assessment of, and related accounting and disclosure requirements about, a reporting entity's special relationships with other entities (ie when the reporting entity has control or joint control of, or significant influence over, another entity). As a result, the Board concluded that applying IAS 28 without also applying the other four IFRSs could cause unwarranted confusion.

BC48   The Board usually sets an effective date of between twelve and eighteen months after issuing an IFRS. When deciding the effective date for those IFRSs, the Board considered the following factors:

(a)   the time that many countries require for translation and for introducing the mandatory requirements into law.

(b)   the consolidation project was related to the global financial crisis that started in 2007 and was accelerated by the Board in response to urgent requests from the leaders of the G20, the Financial Stability Board, users of financial statements, regulators and others to improve the accounting and disclosure of an entity's 'off balance sheet' activities.

(c)   the comments received from respondents to the Request for Views *Effective Date and Transition Methods* that was published in October 2010 regarding implementation costs, effective date and transition requirements of the IFRSs to be issued in 2011. Most respondents did not identify the consolidation and joint arrangements IFRSs as having a high impact in terms of the time and resources that their implementation would require. In addition, only a few respondents commented that the effective dates of those IFRSs should be aligned with those of the other IFRSs to be issued in 2011.

BC49   With those factors in mind, the Board decided to require entities to apply the five IFRSs for annual periods beginning on or after 1 January 2013.

BC50   Most respondents to the Request for Views supported early application of the IFRSs to be issued in 2011. Respondents stressed that early application was especially important for first-time adopters in 2011 and 2012. The Board was persuaded by these arguments and decided to permit early application of IAS 28 but only if an entity applies it in conjunction with the other IFRSs (ie IFRS 10, IFRS 11, IFRS 12 and IAS 27 (as amended in 2011)) to avoid a lack of comparability among financial statements, and for the reasons noted in paragraph BC47 that triggered the Board's decision to set the same effective date for all five IFRSs. Even though an entity should apply the five IFRSs at the same time, the Board noted that an entity should not be prevented from providing any information required by IFRS 12 early if by doing so users gained a better understanding of the entity's relationships with other entities.

BC50A   The Board decided that no specific transition guidance was needed and, therefore, an entity should apply *Investment Entities: Applying the Consolidation Exception* (Amendments to IFRS 10, IFRS 12 and IAS 28) retrospectively in accordance with IAS 8 *Accounting Policies, Changes in Accounting Estimates and Errors*.

General

Withdrawal of IAS 28 (2003 revision)

BC51   IAS 28 *Investments in Associates and Joint Ventures* replaces IAS 28 *Investments in Associates* (as revised in 2003 and amended in 2010). IAS 28 (as amended in 2011) incorporates the accounting for joint ventures and includes some amendments discussed by the Board during its redeliberation of the exposure draft ED 9.

Disclosure

BC52　IAS 28 does not address the disclosure requirements for entities with joint control of, or significant influence over, an investee. As part of its redeliberation of ED 9 and ED 10 *Consolidated Financial Statements*, the Board identified an opportunity to integrate and make consistent the disclosure requirements for subsidiaries, joint arrangements, associates and unconsolidated structured entities, and to present those requirements in a single IFRS.

BC53　The Board observed that IAS 27, IAS 28 and IAS 31 contained many similar disclosure requirements. ED 9 had already proposed amendments to the disclosure requirements for joint ventures and associates to align the disclosure requirements for those two types of investments more closely. The Board noted that the majority of respondents agreed with the proposals in ED 9 to align the disclosures for joint ventures with the disclosures in IAS 28 for associates.

BC54　As a result, the Board combined the disclosure requirements for interest with subsidiaries, joint arrangements, associates and unconsolidated structured entities within a single comprehensive standard, IFRS 12.

BC55　The Basis for Conclusions accompanying IFRS 12 summarises the Board's considerations in developing that IFRS, including its review of responses to the disclosure proposals in ED 9. Accordingly, IAS 28 does not include disclosure requirements and this Basis for Conclusions does not incorporate the Board's considerations of responses to the proposed disclosure requirements in ED 9.

Summary of main changes from IAS 28 (2003 revision)

BC56　The main changes from the previous version of IAS 28 are as follows:

(a)　The accounting for joint ventures has been incorporated into the Standard.

(b)　The scope exception for venture capital organisations, or mutual funds, unit trusts and similar entities, including investment-linked insurance funds has been eliminated and has been characterised as a measurement exemption from the requirement to measure investments in associates and joint ventures in using the equity method.

(c)　IAS 28 now permits an entity that has an investment in an associate, a portion of which is held indirectly through venture capital organisations, or mutual funds, unit trusts and similar entities including investment-linked insurance funds, to elect to measure that portion of the investment in the associate at fair value through profit or loss in accordance with IFRS 9 regardless of whether these entities have significant influence over that portion of the investment.

(d)　IAS 28 requires a portion of an investment in an associate or a joint venture to be classified as held for sale if the disposal of that portion of the interest would fulfil the criteria to be classified as held for sale in accordance with IFRS 5.

(e)　The consensus of SIC-13 has been incorporated into IAS 28. As a result, gains and losses resulting from a contribution of a non-monetary asset to an associate or a joint venture in exchange for an equity interest in an associate or a joint venture are recognised only to the extent of unrelated investors' interests in the associate or joint venture, except when the contribution lacks commercial substance, as that term is described in IAS 16 *Property, Plant and Equipment*.

(f) The disclosure requirements have been placed in IFRS 12.

Dissenting opinion on amendment issued in May 2008

Dissent of Tatsumi Yamada

DO1   Mr Yamada voted against one of the amendments to IAS 28 *Investments in Associates* issued in *Improvements to IFRSs* in May 2008.

DO2   Mr Yamada believes it is inappropriate not to allocate any additional impairment losses to the goodwill and other assets that form part of the carrying amount of the investment in the associate. In his view, because he believes that an investor can identify attributable goodwill when it makes an investment, all impairment losses recognised with respect to the investor's investment in an associate should be allocated to the goodwill and other assets that form part of the carrying amount of the investment.

DO3   Mr Yamada also believes that all impairment losses allocated to goodwill should not be subsequently reversed. In his view the non-allocation of impairment losses to goodwill as required by the amendment and the subsequent reversal of such impairment losses in substance leads to the recognition of internally generated goodwill. He believes that the amendment to IAS 28 is not consistent with paragraphs 124 and 125 of IAS 36 *Impairment of Assets*, which prohibit the reversal of impairment losses related to goodwill.

IASB document published to accompany

IAS 29

Financial Reporting in Hyperinflationary Economies

The text of the unaccompanied standard, IAS 29, is contained in Part A of this edition. Its effective date when issued was 1 January 1990. This part presents the following documents:

BASIS FOR CONCLUSIONS

Basis for Conclusions on
IAS 29 *Financial Reporting in Hyperinflationary Economies*

This Basis for Conclusions accompanies, but is not part of, IAS 29.

BC1   This Basis for Conclusions summarises the International Accounting Standards Board's considerations in reaching its conclusions on amending IAS 29 *Financial Reporting in Hyperinflationary Economies* in 2008. Individual Board members gave greater weight to some factors than to others.

BC2   Paragraph 6 of the previous version of the Standard did not reflect the fact that a number of assets and liabilities may or must be measured on the basis of a current value rather than a historical value. Therefore, the Board included examples rather than a definitive list of such items by *Improvements to IFRSs* issued in May 2008.

IASB documents published to accompany

IAS 32

Financial Instruments: Presentation

The text of the unaccompanied standard, IAS 32, is contained in Part A of this edition. Its effective date when issued was 1 January 2005. The text of the Accompanying Guidance on IAS 32 is contained in Part B of this edition. This part presents the following documents:

BASIS FOR CONCLUSIONS

DISSENTING OPINIONS

CONTENTS

Basis for Conclusions on
IAS 32 *Financial Instruments: Presentation*

This Basis for Conclusions accompanies, but is not part of, IAS 32.

BC1 This Basis for Conclusions summarises the International Accounting Standards Board's considerations in reaching its conclusions on revising IAS 32 *Financial Instruments: Disclosure and Presentation*[1] in 2003. Individual Board members gave greater weight to some factors than to others.

BC2 In July 2001 the Board announced that, as part of its initial agenda of technical projects, it would undertake a project to improve a number of Standards, including IAS 32 and IAS 39 *Financial Instruments: Recognition and Measurement*.[2] The objectives of the Improvements project were to reduce the complexity in the Standards by clarifying and adding guidance, eliminating internal inconsistencies, and incorporating into the Standards elements of Standing Interpretations Committee (SIC) Interpretations and IAS 39 implementation guidance. In June 2002 the Board published its proposals in an Exposure Draft of proposed amendments to IAS 32 *Financial Instruments: Disclosure and Presentation* and IAS 39 *Financial Instruments: Recognition and Measurement*, with a comment deadline of 14 October 2002. The Board received over 170 comment letters on the Exposure Draft.

BC3 Because the Board did not reconsider the fundamental approach to the accounting for financial instruments established by IAS 32 and IAS 39, this Basis for Conclusions does not discuss requirements in IAS 32 that the Board has not reconsidered.

BC3A In July 2006 the Board published an exposure draft of proposed amendments to IAS 32 relating to the classification of puttable instruments and instruments with obligations arising on liquidation. The Board subsequently confirmed the proposals and in 2008 issued an amendment that now forms part of IAS 32. A summary of the Board's considerations and reasons for its conclusions is in paragraphs BC50–BC74.

Scope

BC3B In November 2013 the Board amended the scope of IAS 32 so that it conformed to the scope of IAS 39 as amended in November 2013 regarding the accounting for some executory contracts (which was changed as a result of replacing the hedge accounting requirements in IAS 39).

BC3C IFRS 9 replaced IAS 39 and consequentially in July 2014 the scope of IAS 39 was relocated to IFRS 9.

---

1 In August 2005, the IASB relocated all disclosures relating to financial instruments to IFRS 7 *Financial Instruments: Disclosures*. The paragraphs relating to disclosures that were originally published in this Basis for Conclusions were relocated, if still relevant, to the Basis for Conclusions on IFRS 7.

2 IFRS 9 *Financial Instruments* replaced IAS 39. IFRS 9 applies to all items that were previously within the scope of IAS 39.

Definitions (paragraphs 11–14 and AG3–AG24)

Financial asset, financial liability and equity instrument (paragraphs 11 and AG3–AG14)

BC4　The revised IAS 32 addresses the classification as financial assets, financial liabilities or equity instruments of financial instruments that are indexed to, or settled in, an entity's own equity instruments. As discussed further in paragraphs BC6–BC15, the Board decided to preclude equity classification for such contracts when they (a) involve an obligation to deliver cash or another financial asset or to exchange financial assets or financial liabilities under conditions that are potentially unfavourable to the entity, (b) in the case of a non-derivative, are not for the receipt or delivery of a fixed number of shares or (c) in the case of a derivative, are not for the exchange of a fixed number of shares for a fixed amount of cash or another financial asset. The Board also decided to preclude equity classification for contracts that are derivatives on derivatives on an entity's own equity. Consistently with this decision, the Board also decided to amend the definitions of financial asset, financial liability and equity instrument in IAS 32 to make them consistent with the guidance about contracts on an entity's own equity instruments. The Board did not reconsider other aspects of the definitions as part of this project to revise IAS 32, for example the other changes to the definitions proposed by the Joint Working Group in its Draft Standard *Financial Instruments and Similar Items* published by the Board's predecessor body, IASC, in 2000.

Foreign currency denominated pro rata rights issues

BC4A　In 2005 the International Financial Reporting Interpretations Committee (IFRIC) was asked whether the equity conversion option embedded in a convertible bond denominated in a foreign currency met IAS 32's requirements to be classified as an equity instrument. IAS 32 states that a derivative instrument relating to the purchase or issue of an entity's own equity instruments is classified as equity only if it results in the exchange of a fixed number of equity instruments for a fixed amount of cash or other assets. At that time, the IFRIC concluded that if the conversion option was denominated in a currency other than the issuing entity's functional currency, the amount of cash to be received in the functional currency would be variable. Consequently, the instrument was a derivative liability that should be measured at its fair value with changes in fair value included in profit or loss.

BC4B　However, the IFRIC also concluded that this outcome was not consistent with the Board's approach when it introduced the 'fixed for fixed' notion in IAS 32. Therefore, the IFRIC decided to recommend that the Board amend IAS 32 to permit a conversion or stand-alone option to be classified as equity if the exercise price was fixed in any currency. In September 2005 the Board decided not to proceed with the proposed amendment.

BC4C　In 2009 the Board was asked by the IFRIC to consider a similar issue. This issue was whether a right entitling the holder to receive a fixed number of the issuing entity's own equity instruments for a fixed amount of a currency other than the issuing entity's functional currency (foreign currency) should be accounted for as a derivative liability.

BC4D　These rights are commonly described as 'rights issues' and include rights, options and warrants. Laws or regulations in many jurisdictions throughout the world require the use of rights issues when raising capital. The entity issues one or more rights to acquire a fixed number of additional shares pro rata to all existing shareholders of a class of non-derivative equity instruments. The exercise price is normally below the current market price of the shares. Consequently, a shareholder must exercise its rights if it does not wish its proportionate interest in the entity to be diluted. Issues with those characteristics are discussed in IFRS 2 *Share-based Payment* and IAS 33 *Earnings per Share*.

BC4E　The Board was advised that rights with the characteristics discussed above were being issued frequently in the current economic environment. The Board was also advised that many issuing entities fixed the exercise price of the rights in currencies other than their functional currency because the entities were listed in more than one jurisdiction and might be required to do so by law or regulation. Therefore, the accounting conclusions affected a significant number of entities in many jurisdictions. In addition, because these are usually relatively large transactions, they can have a substantial effect on entities' financial statement amounts.

BC4F　The Board agreed with the IFRIC's 2005 conclusion that a contract with an exercise price denominated in a foreign currency would not result in the entity receiving a fixed amount of cash. However, the Board also agreed with the IFRIC that classifying rights as derivative liabilities was not consistent with the substance of the transaction. Rights issues are issued only to existing shareholders on the basis of the number of shares they already own. In this respect they partially resemble dividends paid in shares.

BC4G　The Board decided that a financial instrument that gives the holder the right to acquire a fixed number of the entity's own equity instruments for a fixed amount of any currency is an equity instrument if, and only if, the entity offers the financial instrument pro rata to all of its existing owners of the same class of its own non-derivative equity instruments.

BC4H　In excluding grants of rights with these features from the scope of IFRS 2, the Board explicitly recognised that the holder of the right receives it as a holder of equity instruments, ie as an owner. The Board noted that IAS 1 *Presentation of Financial Statements* requires transactions with owners in their capacity as owners to be recognised in the statement of changes in equity rather than in the statement of comprehensive income.

BC4I　Consistently with its conclusion in IFRS 2, the Board decided that a pro rata issue of rights to all existing shareholders to acquire additional shares is a transaction with an entity's owners in their capacity as owners. Consequently, those transactions should be recognised in equity, not comprehensive income. Because the Board concluded that the rights were equity instruments, it decided to amend the definition of a financial liability to exclude them.

BC4J   Some respondents to the exposure draft expressed concerns that the wording of the amendment was too open-ended and could lead to structuring risks. The Board rejected this argument because of the extremely narrow amendment that requires the entity to treat all of its existing owners of the same class of its own non-derivative equity instruments equally. The Board also noted that a change in the capital structure of an entity to create a new class of non-derivative equity instruments would be transparent because of the presentation and disclosure requirements in IFRSs.

BC4K   The Board decided not to extend this conclusion to other instruments that grant the holder the right to purchase the entity's own equity instruments such as the conversion feature in convertible bonds. The Board also noted that long-dated foreign currency rights issues are not primarily transactions with owners in their capacity as owners. The equal treatment of all owners of the same class of equity instruments was also the basis on which, in IFRIC 17 *Distributions of Non-cash Assets to Owners*, the IFRIC distinguished non-reciprocal distributions to owners from exchange transactions. The fact that the rights are distributed pro rata to existing shareholders is critical to the Board's conclusion to provide an exception to the 'fixed for fixed' concept in IAS 32 as this is a narrow targeted transaction with owners in their capacity as owners.

Presentation (paragraphs 15–50 and AG25–AG39)

Liabilities and equity (paragraphs 15–27 and AG25–AG29)

BC5   The revised IAS 32 addresses whether derivative and non-derivative contracts indexed to, or settled in, an entity's own equity instruments are financial assets, financial liabilities or equity instruments. The original IAS 32 dealt with aspects of this issue piecemeal and it was not clear how various transactions (eg net share settled contracts and contracts with settlement options) should be treated under the Standard. The Board concluded that it needed to clarify the accounting treatment for such transactions.

BC6   The approach agreed by the Board can be summarised as follows:

A contract on an entity's own equity is an equity instrument if, and only if:

(a)   it contains no contractual obligation to transfer cash or another financial asset, or to exchange financial assets or financial liabilities with another entity under conditions that are potentially unfavourable to the entity; and

(b)   if the instrument will or may be settled in the entity's own equity instruments, it is either (i) a non-derivative that includes no contractual obligation for the entity to deliver a variable number of its own equity instruments, or (ii) a derivative that will be settled by the entity exchanging a fixed amount of cash or another financial asset for a fixed number of its own equity instruments.

No contractual obligation to deliver cash or another financial asset (paragraphs 17–20, AG25 and AG26)

Puttable instruments (paragraph 18(b))

BC7　The Board decided that a financial instrument that gives the holder the right to put the instrument back to the entity for cash or another financial asset is a financial liability of the entity. Such financial instruments are commonly issued by mutual funds, unit trusts, co-operative and similar entities, often with the redemption amount being equal to a proportionate share in the net assets of the entity. Although the legal form of such financial instruments often includes a right to the residual interest in the assets of an entity available to holders of such instruments, the inclusion of an option for the holder to put the instrument back to the entity for cash or another financial asset means that the instrument meets the definition of a financial liability. The classification as a financial liability is independent of considerations such as when the right is exercisable, how the amount payable or receivable upon exercise of the right is determined, and whether the puttable instrument has a fixed maturity.

BC7A　The Board reconsidered its conclusions with regards to some puttable instruments and amended IAS 32 in February 2008 (see paragraphs BC50–BC74).

BC8　The Board noted that the classification of a puttable instrument as a financial liability does not preclude the use of descriptors such as 'net assets attributable to unitholders' and 'change in net assets attributable to unitholders' on the face of the financial statements of an entity that has no equity (such as some mutual funds and unit trusts) or whose share capital is a financial liability under IAS 32 (such as some co-operatives). The Board also agreed that it should provide examples of how such entities might present their income statement[3] and balance sheet[4] (see Illustrative Examples 7 and 8).

Implicit obligations (paragraph 20)

BC9　The Board did not debate whether an obligation can be established implicitly rather than explicitly because this is not within the scope of an improvements project. This question will be considered by the Board in its project on revenue, liabilities and equity. Consequently, the Board retained the existing notion that an instrument may establish an obligation indirectly through its terms and conditions (see paragraph 20). However, it decided that the example of a preference share with a contractually accelerating dividend which, within the foreseeable future, is scheduled to yield a dividend so high that the entity will be economically compelled to redeem the instrument, was insufficiently clear. The example was therefore removed and replaced with others that are clearer and deal with situations that have proved problematic in practice.

3　IAS 1 *Presentation of Financial Statements* (as revised in 2007) requires an entity to present all income and expense items in one statement of comprehensive income or in two statements (a separate income statement and a statement of comprehensive income).

4　IAS 1 (revised 2007) replaced the term 'balance sheet' with 'statement of financial position'.

Settlement in the entity's own equity instruments (paragraphs 21–24 and AG27)

BC10   The approach taken in the revised IAS 32 includes two main conclusions:

(a)   When an entity has an obligation to purchase its own shares for cash (such as under a forward contract to purchase its own shares), there is a financial liability for the amount of cash that the entity has an obligation to pay.

(b)   When an entity uses its own equity instruments 'as currency' in a contract to receive or deliver a variable number of shares whose value equals a fixed amount or an amount based on changes in an underlying variable (eg a commodity price), the contract is not an equity instrument, but is a financial asset or a financial liability. In other words, when a contract is settled in a variable number of the entity's own equity instruments, or by the entity exchanging a fixed number of its own equity instruments for a variable amount of cash or another financial asset, the contract is not an equity instrument but is a financial asset or a financial liability.

When an entity has an obligation to purchase its own shares for cash, there is a financial liability for the amount of cash that the entity has an obligation to pay.

BC11   An entity's obligation to purchase its own shares establishes a maturity date for the shares that are subject to the contract. Therefore, to the extent of the obligation, those shares cease to be equity instruments when the entity assumes the obligation. This treatment under IAS 32 is consistent with the treatment of shares that provide for mandatory redemption by the entity. Without a requirement to recognise a financial liability for the present value of the share redemption amount, entities with identical obligations to deliver cash in exchange for their own equity instruments could report different information in their financial statements depending on whether the redemption clause is embedded in the equity instrument or is a free-standing derivative contract.

BC12   Some respondents to the Exposure Draft suggested that when an entity writes an option that, if exercised, will result in the entity paying cash in return for receiving its own shares, it is incorrect to treat the full amount of the exercise price as a financial liability because the obligation is conditional upon the option being exercised. The Board rejected this argument because the entity has an obligation to pay the full redemption amount and cannot avoid settlement in cash or another financial asset for the full redemption amount unless the counterparty decides not to exercise its redemption right or specified future events or circumstances beyond the control of the entity occur or do not occur. The Board also noted that a change would require a reconsideration of other provisions in IAS 32 that require liability treatment for obligations that are conditional on events or choices that are beyond the entity's control. These include, for example, (a) the treatment of financial instruments with contingent settlement provisions as financial liabilities for the full amount of the conditional obligation, (b) the treatment of preference shares that are redeemable at the option of the holder as financial liabilities for the full amount of the conditional obligation, and (c) the treatment of financial instruments (puttable instruments) that give the holder the right to put the instrument back to the issuer for cash or another financial asset, the amount of which is determined by reference to an index, and which therefore has the potential to increase and decrease, as financial liabilities for the full amount of the conditional obligation.

When an entity uses its own equity instruments as currency in a contract to receive or deliver a variable number of shares, the contract is not an equity instrument, but is a financial asset or a financial liability.

BC13   The Board agreed that it would be inappropriate to account for a contract as an equity instrument when an entity's own equity instruments are used as currency in a contract to receive or deliver a variable number of shares whose value equals a fixed amount or an amount based on changes in an underlying variable (eg a net share-settled derivative contract on gold or an obligation to deliver as many shares as are equal in value to CU10,000). Such a contract represents a right or obligation of a specified amount rather than a specified equity interest. A contract to pay or receive a specified amount (rather than a specified equity interest) is not an equity instrument. For such a contract, the entity does not know, before the transaction is settled, how many of its own shares (or how much cash) it will receive or deliver and the entity may not even know whether it will receive or deliver its own shares.

BC14   In addition, the Board noted that precluding equity treatment for such a contract limits incentives for structuring potentially favourable or unfavourable transactions to obtain equity treatment. For example, the Board believes that an entity should not be able to obtain equity treatment for a transaction simply by including a share settlement clause when the contract is for a specified value, rather than a specified equity interest.

BC15   The Board rejected the argument that a contract that is settled in the entity's own shares must be an equity instrument because no change in assets or liabilities, and thus no gain or loss, arises on settlement of the contract. The Board noted that any gain or loss arises before settlement of the transaction, not when it is settled.

Contingent settlement provisions (paragraphs 25 and AG28)

BC16   The revised Standard incorporates the conclusion previously in SIC-5 *Classification of Financial Instruments—Contingent Settlement Provisions* that a financial instrument for which the manner of settlement depends on the occurrence or non-occurrence of uncertain future events, or on the outcome of uncertain circumstances that are beyond the control of both the issuer and the holder (ie a 'contingent settlement provision'), is a financial liability.

BC17   The amendments do not include the exception previously provided in paragraph 6 of SIC-5 for circumstances in which the possibility of the entity being required to settle in cash or another financial asset is remote at the time the financial instrument is issued. The Board concluded that it is not consistent with the definitions of financial liabilities and equity instruments to classify an obligation to deliver cash or another financial asset as a financial liability only when settlement in cash is probable. There is a contractual obligation to transfer economic benefits as a result of past events because the entity is unable to avoid a settlement in cash or another financial asset unless an event occurs or does not occur in the future.

BC18　　However, the Board also concluded that contingent settlement provisions that would apply only in the event of liquidation of an entity should not influence the classification of the instrument because to do so would be inconsistent with a going concern assumption. A contingent settlement provision that provides for payment in cash or another financial asset only on the liquidation of the entity is similar to an equity instrument that has priority in liquidation and therefore should be ignored in classifying the instrument.

BC19　　Additionally, the Board decided that if the part of a contingent settlement provision that could require settlement in cash or a variable number of own shares is not genuine, it should be ignored for the purposes of classifying the instrument. The Board also agreed to provide guidance on the meaning of 'genuine' in this context (see paragraph AG28).

Settlement options (paragraphs 26 and 27)

BC20　　The revised Standard requires that if one of the parties to a contract has one or more options as to how it is settled (eg net in cash or by exchanging shares for cash), the contract is a financial asset or a financial liability unless all of the settlement alternatives would result in equity classification. The Board concluded that entities should not be able to circumvent the accounting requirements for financial assets and financial liabilities simply by including an option to settle a contract through the exchange of a fixed number of shares for a fixed amount. The Board had proposed in the Exposure Draft that past practice and management intentions should be considered in determining the classification of such instruments. However, respondents to the Exposure Draft noted that such requirements can be difficult to apply because some entities do not have any history of similar transactions and the assessment of whether an established practice exists and of what is management's intention can be subjective. The Board agreed with these comments and accordingly concluded that past practice and management intentions should not be determining factors.

Alternative approaches considered

BC21　　In finalising the revisions to IAS 32 the Board considered, but rejected, a number of alternative approaches:

(a)　　To classify as an equity instrument any contract that will be settled in the entity's own shares. The Board rejected this approach because it does not deal adequately with transactions in which an entity is using its own shares as currency, eg when an entity has an obligation to pay a fixed or determinable amount that is settled in a variable number of its own shares.

(b)   To classify a contract as an equity instrument only if (i) the contract will be settled in the entity's own shares, and (ii) the changes in the fair value of the contract move in the same direction as the changes in the fair value of the shares from the perspective of the counterparty. Under this approach, contracts that will be settled in the entity's own shares would be financial assets or financial liabilities if, from the perspective of the counterparty, their value moves inversely with the price of the entity's own shares. An example is an entity's obligation to buy back its own shares. The Board rejected this approach because its adoption would represent a fundamental shift in the concept of equity. The Board also noted that it would result in a change to the classification of some transactions, compared with the existing Framework[5] and IAS 32, that had not been exposed for comment.

(c)   To classify as an equity instrument a contract that will be settled in the entity's own shares unless its value changes in response to something other than the price of the entity's own shares. The Board rejected this approach to avoid an exception to the principle that non-derivative contracts that are settled in a variable number of an entity's own shares should be treated as financial assets or financial liabilities.

(d)   To limit classification as equity instruments to outstanding ordinary shares, and classify as financial assets or financial liabilities all contracts that involve future receipt or delivery of the entity's own shares. The Board rejected this approach because its adoption would represent a fundamental shift in the concept of equity. The Board also noted that it would result in a change to the classification of some transactions compared with the existing IAS 32 that had not been exposed for comment.

Compound financial instruments (paragraphs 28–32 and AG30–AG35)

BC22   The Standard requires the separate presentation in an entity's balance sheet[6] of liability and equity components of a single financial instrument. It is more a matter of form than a matter of substance that both liabilities and equity interests are created by a single financial instrument rather than two or more separate instruments. The Board believes that an entity's financial position is more faithfully represented by separate presentation of liability and equity components contained in a single instrument.

---

5   References to the Framework are to IASC's Framework for the Preparation and Presentation of Financial Statements, adopted by the IASB in 2001. In September 2010 the IASB replaced the Framework with the Conceptual Framework for Financial Reporting.

6   IAS 1 (as revised in 2007) replaced the term 'balance sheet' with 'statement of financial position'.

Allocation of the initial carrying amount to the liability and equity components (paragraphs 31, 32 and AG36–AG38 and Illustrative Examples 9–12)

BC23   The previous version of IAS 32 did not prescribe a particular method for assigning the initial carrying amount of a compound financial instrument to its separated liability and equity components. Rather, it suggested approaches that might be considered, such as:

(a)   assigning to the less easily measurable component (often the equity component) the residual amount after deducting from the instrument as a whole the amount separately determined for the component that is more easily determinable (a 'with-and-without' method); and

(b)   measuring the liability and equity components separately and, to the extent necessary, adjusting these amounts pro rata so that the sum of the components equals the amount of the instrument as a whole (a 'relative fair value' method).

BC24   This choice was originally justified on the grounds that IAS 32 did not deal with the measurement of financial assets, financial liabilities and equity instruments.

BC25   However, since the issue of IAS 39,[7] IFRSs contain requirements for the measurement of financial assets and financial liabilities. Therefore, the view that IAS 32 should not prescribe a particular method for separating compound financial instruments because of the absence of measurement requirements for financial instruments is no longer valid. IAS 39, paragraph 43, requires a financial liability to be measured on initial recognition at its fair value. Therefore, a relative fair value method could result in an initial measurement of the liability component that is not in compliance with IAS 39.

BC26   After initial recognition, a financial liability that is classified as at fair value through profit or loss is measured at fair value under IAS 39,[8] and other financial liabilities are measured at amortised cost. If the liability component of a compound financial instrument is classified as at fair value through profit or loss, an entity could recognise an immediate gain or loss after initial recognition if it applies a relative fair value method. This is contrary to IAS 32, paragraph 31, which states that no gain or loss arises from recognising the components of the instrument separately.

BC27   Under the *Framework*, and IASs 32 and 39, an equity instrument is defined as any contract that evidences a residual interest in the assets of an entity after deducting all of its liabilities. Paragraph 67 of the *Framework*[9] further states that the amount at which equity is recognised in the balance sheet is dependent on the measurement of assets and liabilities.

BC28   The Board concluded that the alternatives in IAS 32 to measure on initial recognition the liability component of a compound financial instrument as a

---

7   IFRS 9 *Financial Instruments* replaced IAS 39. The requirements of paragraph 43 of IAS 39 relating to the initial measurement of financial assets were relocated to paragraph 5.1.1 of IFRS 9.

8   IFRS 9 *Financial Instruments* replaced IAS 39. IFRS 9 applies to all items that were previously within the scope of IAS 39.

9   now paragraph 4.22 of the *Conceptual Framework*

residual amount after separating the equity component or on the basis of a relative fair value method should be eliminated. Instead the liability component should be measured first (including the value of any embedded non-equity derivative features, such as an embedded call feature), and the residual amount assigned to the equity component.

BC29   The objective of this amendment is to make the requirements about the entity's separation of the liability and equity components of a single compound financial instrument consistent with the requirements about the initial measurement of a financial liability in IAS 39 and the definitions in IAS 32 and the *Framework* of an equity instrument as a residual interest.

BC30   This approach removes the need to estimate inputs to, and apply, complex option pricing models to measure the equity component of some compound financial instruments. The Board also noted that the absence of a prescribed approach led to a lack of comparability among entities applying IAS 32 and that it therefore was desirable to specify a single approach.

BC31   The Board noted that a requirement to use the with-and-without method, under which the liability component is determined first, is consistent with the proposals of the Joint Working Group of Standard Setters in its Draft Standard and Basis for Conclusions in *Financial Instruments and Similar Items*, published by IASC in December 2000 (see Draft Standard, paragraphs 74 and 75 and Application Supplement, paragraph 318).

Treasury shares (paragraphs 33, 34 and AG36)

BC32   The revised Standard incorporates the guidance in SIC-16 *Share Capital—Reacquired Own Equity Instruments (Treasury Shares)*. The acquisition and subsequent resale by an entity of its own equity instruments represents a transfer between those holders of equity instruments who have given up their equity interest and those who continue to hold an equity instrument, rather than a gain or loss to the entity.

BC32A   [This paragraph refers to amendments that are not yet effective, and is therefore not included in this edition.]

Interest, dividends, losses and gains (paragraphs 35–41 and AG37)

Costs of an equity transaction (paragraphs 35 and 37–39)

BC33   The revised Standard incorporates the guidance in SIC-17 *Equity—Costs of an Equity Transaction*. Transaction costs incurred as a necessary part of completing an equity transaction are accounted for as part of the transaction to which they relate. Linking the equity transaction and costs of the transaction reflects in equity the total cost of the transaction.

Income tax consequences of distributions to holders of an equity instrument and of transaction costs of an equity transaction

BC33A   In *Annual Improvements 2009–2011 Cycle* (issued in May 2012) the Board addressed perceived inconsistencies between IAS 12 *Income Taxes* and IAS 32 *Financial*

Instruments: Presentation with regards to recognising the consequences of income tax relating to distributions to holders of an equity instrument and to transaction costs of an equity transaction. Paragraph 52B of IAS 12 requires the recognition of the income tax consequences of dividends in profit or loss except when the circumstances described in paragraph 58(a) and (b) of IAS 12 arise. However, paragraph 35 of IAS 32 required the recognition of income tax relating to distributions to holders of an equity instrument in equity (prior to the amendment).

BC33B   The Board noted that the intention of IAS 32 was to follow the requirements in IAS 12 for accounting for income tax relating to distributions to holders of an equity instrument and to transaction costs of an equity transaction. Consequently, the Board decided to add paragraph 35A to IAS 32 to clarify this intention.

BC33C   The Board noted that this amendment is not intended to address the distinction between income tax consequences of dividends in accordance with paragraph 52B, and withholding tax for dividends in accordance with paragraph 65A, of IAS 12. In this respect, the Board observed that the income tax consequences of distributions to holders of an equity instrument are recognised in profit or loss in accordance with paragraph 52B of IAS 12. Consequently, to the extent that the distribution relates to income arising from a transaction that was originally recognised in profit or loss, the income tax on the distribution should be recognised in profit or loss. However, if the distribution relates to income or to a transaction that was originally recognised in other comprehensive income or equity, the entity should apply the exception in paragraph 58(a) of IAS 12, and recognise the income tax consequences of the distribution outside of profit or loss. The Board also observed that, in accordance with paragraph 65A, when an entity pays dividends to its shareholders the portion of the dividends paid or payable to taxation authorities as withholding tax is charged to equity as part of the dividends.

BC34–
BC48   [Deleted]

Summary of changes from the Exposure Draft

BC49   The main changes from the Exposure Draft's proposals are as follows:

(a)   The Exposure Draft proposed to define a financial liability as a contractual obligation to deliver cash or another financial asset to another entity or to exchange financial instruments with another entity under conditions that are potentially unfavourable. The definition in the Standard has been expanded to include some contracts that will or may be settled in the entity's own equity instruments. The Standard's definition of a financial asset has been similarly expanded.

(b)   The Exposure Draft proposed that a financial instrument that gives the holder the right to put it back to the entity for cash or another financial asset is a financial liability. The Standard retains this conclusion, but provides additional guidance and illustrative examples to assist entities that, as a result of this requirement, either have no equity as defined in IAS 32 or whose share capital is not equity as defined in IAS 32.

(c) The Standard retains and clarifies the proposal in the Exposure Draft that terms and conditions of a financial instrument may indirectly create an obligation.

(d) The Exposure Draft proposed to incorporate in IAS 32 the conclusion previously in SIC-5. This is that a financial instrument for which the manner of settlement depends on the occurrence or non-occurrence of uncertain future events or on the outcome of uncertain circumstances that are beyond the control of both the issuer and the holder is a financial liability. The Standard clarifies this conclusion by requiring contingent settlement provisions that apply only in the event of liquidation of an entity or are not genuine to be ignored.

(e) The Exposure Draft proposed that a derivative contract that contains an option as to how it is settled meets the definition of an equity instrument if the entity had all of the following: (i) an unconditional right and ability to settle the contract gross; (ii) an established practice of such settlement; and (iii) the intention to settle the contract gross. These conditions have not been carried forward into the Standard. Rather, a derivative with settlement options is classified as a financial asset or a financial liability unless all the settlement alternatives would result in equity classification.

(f) The Standard provides explicit guidance on accounting for the repurchase of a convertible instrument.

(g) The Standard provides explicit guidance on accounting for the amendment of the terms of a convertible instrument to induce early conversion.

(h) The Exposure Draft proposed that a financial instrument that is an equity instrument of a subsidiary should be eliminated on consolidation when held by the parent, or presented in the consolidated balance sheet within equity when not held by the parent (as a minority interest[10] separate from the equity of the parent). The Standard requires all terms and conditions agreed between members of the group and the holders of the instrument to be considered when determining if the group as a whole has an obligation that would give rise to a financial liability. To the extent there is such an obligation, the instrument (or component of the instrument that is subject to the obligation) is a financial liability in consolidated financial statements.

(i)–(j) [deleted]

(k) In August 2005, the IASB issued IFRS 7 *Financial Instruments: Disclosures*. As a result, disclosures relating to financial instruments, if still relevant, were relocated to IFRS 7.

---

10 In January 2008 the IASB issued an amended IAS 27 *Consolidated and Separate Financial Statements*, which amended 'minority interest' to 'non-controlling interests'. The consolidation requirements in IAS 27 were superseded by IFRS 10 *Consolidated Financial Statements* issued in May 2011. The term 'non-controlling interests' and the requirements for non-controlling interests were not changed.

Amendments for some puttable instruments and some instruments that impose on the entity an obligation to deliver to another party a pro rata share of the net assets of the entity only on liquidation

Amendment for puttable instruments

BC50   As discussed in paragraphs BC7 and BC8, puttable instruments meet the definition of a financial liability and the Board concluded that all such instruments should be classified as liabilities. However, constituents raised the following concerns about classifying such instruments as financial liabilities if they represent the residual claim to the net assets of the entity:

(a)   On an ongoing basis, the liability is recognised at not less than the amount payable on demand. This can result in the entire market capitalisation of the entity being recognised as a liability depending on the basis for which the redemption value of the financial instrument is calculated.

(b)   Changes in the carrying value of the liability are recognised in profit or loss. This results in counter-intuitive accounting (if the redemption value is linked to the performance of the entity) because:

(i)   when an entity performs well, the present value of the settlement amount of the liabilities increases, and a loss is recognised.

(ii)   when the entity performs poorly, the present value of the settlement amount of the liability decreases, and a gain is recognised.

(c)   It is possible, again depending on the basis for which the redemption value is calculated, that the entity will report negative net assets because of unrecognised intangible assets and goodwill, and because the measurement of recognised assets and liabilities may not be at fair value.

(d)   The issuing entity's statement of financial position portrays the entity as wholly, or mostly, debt funded.

(e)   Distributions of profits to shareholders are recognised as expenses. Hence, it may appear that profit or loss is a function of the distribution policy, not performance.

Furthermore, constituents contended that additional disclosures and adapting the format of the statement of comprehensive income and statement of financial position did not resolve these concerns.

BC51   The Board agreed with constituents that many puttable instruments, despite meeting the definition of a financial liability, represent a residual interest in the net assets of the entity. The Board also agreed with constituents that additional disclosures and adapting the format of the entity's financial statements did not resolve the problem of the lack of relevance and understandability of that current accounting treatment. Therefore, the Board decided to amend IAS 32 to improve the financial reporting of these instruments.

BC52   The Board considered the following ways to improve the financial reporting of instruments that represent a residual interest in the net assets of the entity:

(a)   to continue to classify these instruments as financial liabilities, but amend their measurement so that changes in their fair value would not be recognised;

(b)   to amend IAS 32 to require separation of all puttable instruments into a put option and a host instrument; or

(c)   to amend IAS 32 to provide a limited scope exception so that financial instruments puttable at fair value would be classified as equity, if specified conditions were met.

Amend the measurement of some puttable financial instruments so that changes in their fair value would not be recognised

BC53   The Board decided against this approach because:

(a)   it is inconsistent with the principle in IAS 32 and IAS 39[11] that only equity instruments are not remeasured after their initial recognition;

(b)   it retains the disadvantage that entities whose instruments are all puttable would have no equity instruments; and

(c)   it introduces a new category of financial liabilities to IAS 39, and thus increases complexity.

Separate all puttable instruments into a put option and a host instrument

BC54   The Board concluded that conducting further research into an approach that splits a puttable share into an equity component and a written put option component (financial liability) would duplicate efforts of the Board's longer-term project on liabilities and equity. Consequently, the Board decided not to proceed with a project at this stage to determine whether a puttable share should be split into an equity component and a written put option component.

Classify as equity instruments puttable instruments that represent a residual interest in the entity

BC55   The Board decided to proceed with proposals to amend IAS 32 to require puttable financial instruments that represent a residual interest in the net assets of the entity to be classified as equity provided that specified conditions are met. The proposals represented a limited scope exception to the definition of a financial liability and a short-term solution, pending the outcome of the longer-term project on liabilities and equity. In June 2006 the Board published an exposure draft proposing that financial instruments puttable at fair value that meet specific criteria should be classified as equity.

BC56   In response to comments received from respondents to that exposure draft, the Board amended the criteria for identifying puttable instruments that represent

---

11   IFRS 9 *Financial Instruments* replaced IAS 39. IFRS 9 applies to all items that were previously within the scope of IAS 39.

a residual interest in the entity, to those included in paragraphs 16A and 16B. The Board decided on those conditions for the following reasons:

(a)   to ensure that the puttable instruments, as a class, represent the residual interest in the net assets of the entity;

(b)   to ensure that the proposed amendments are consistent with a limited scope exception to the definition of a financial liability; and

(c)   to reduce structuring opportunities that might arise as a result of the amendments.

BC57   The Board decided that the instrument must entitle the holder to a pro rata share of the net assets on liquidation because the net assets on liquidation represent the ultimate residual interest of the entity.

BC58   The Board decided that the instrument must be in the class of instruments that is subordinate to all other classes of instruments on liquidation in order to represent the residual interest in the entity.

BC59   The Board decided that all instruments in the class that is subordinate to all other classes of instruments must have identical contractual terms and conditions. In order to ensure that the class of instruments as a whole is the residual class, the Board decided that no instrument holder in that class can have preferential terms or conditions in its position as an owner of the entity.

BC60   The Board decided that the puttable instruments should contain no contractual obligation to deliver a financial asset to another entity other than the put. That is because the amendments represent a limited scope exception to the definition of a financial liability and extending that exception to instruments that also contain other contractual obligations is not appropriate. Moreover, the Board concluded that if the puttable instrument contains another contractual obligation, that instrument may not represent the residual interest because the holder of the puttable instrument may have a claim to some of the net assets of the entity in preference to other instruments.

BC61   As well as requiring a direct link between the puttable instrument and the performance of the entity, the Board also decided that there should be no financial instrument or contract with a return that is more residual. The Board decided to require that there must be no other financial instrument or contract that has total cash flows based substantially on the performance of the entity and has the effect of significantly restricting or fixing the return to the puttable instrument holders. This criterion was included to ensure that the holders of the puttable instruments represent the residual interest in the net assets of the entity.

BC62   An instrument holder may enter into transactions with the issuing entity in a role other than that of an owner. The Board concluded that it is inappropriate to consider cash flows and contractual features related to the instrument holder in a non-owner role when evaluating whether a financial instrument has the features set out in paragraph 16A or paragraph 16C. That is because those cash flows and contractual features are separate and distinct from the cash flows and contractual features of the puttable financial instrument.

BC63   The Board also decided that contracts (such as warrants and other derivatives) to be settled by the issue of puttable financial instruments should be precluded from equity classification. That is because the Board noted that the amendments represent a limited scope exception to the definition of a financial liability and extending that exception to such contracts is not appropriate.

Amendment for obligations to deliver to another party a pro rata share of the net assets of the entity only on liquidation

BC64   Issues similar to those raised by constituents relating to classification of puttable financial instruments apply to some financial instruments that create an obligation only on liquidation of the entity.

BC65   In the exposure draft published in June 2006, the Board proposed to exclude from the definition of a financial liability a contractual obligation that entitles the holder to a pro rata share of the net assets of the entity only on liquidation of the entity. The liquidation of the entity may be:

(a)   certain to occur and outside the control of the entity (limited life entities); or

(b)   uncertain to occur but at the option of the holder (for example, some partnership interests).

BC66   Respondents to that exposure draft were generally supportive of the proposed amendment.

BC67   The Board decided that an exception to the definition of a financial liability should be made for instruments that entitle the holder to a pro rata share of the net assets of an entity only on liquidation if particular requirements are met. Many of those requirements, and the reasons for them, are similar to those for puttable financial instruments. The differences between the requirements are as follows:

(a)   there is no requirement that there be no other contractual obligations;

(b)   there is no requirement to consider the expected total cash flows throughout the life of the instrument;

(c)   the only feature that must be identical among the instruments in the class is the obligation for the issuing entity to deliver to the holder a pro rata share of its net assets on liquidation.

The reason for the differences is the timing of settlement of the obligation. The life of the financial instrument is the same as the life of the issuing entity; the extinguishment of the obligation can occur only at liquidation. Therefore, the Board concluded that it was appropriate to focus only on the obligations that exist at liquidation. The instrument must be subordinate to all other classes of instruments and represent the residual interests only at that point in time. However, if the instrument contains other contractual obligations, those obligations may need to be accounted for separately in accordance with the requirements of IAS 32.

Non-controlling interests

BC68 The Board decided that puttable financial instruments or instruments that impose on the entity an obligation to deliver to another party a pro rata share of the net assets of the entity only on liquidation should be classified as equity in the separate financial statements of the issuer if they represent the residual class of instruments (and all the relevant requirements are met). The Board decided that such instruments were not the residual interest in the consolidated financial statements and therefore that non-controlling interests that contain an obligation to transfer a financial asset to another entity should be classified as a financial liability in the consolidated financial statements.

Analysis of costs and benefits

BC69 The Board acknowledged that the amendments made in February 2008 are not consistent with the definition of a liability in the *Framework*, or with the underlying principle of IAS 32, which is based on that definition. Consequently, those amendments added complexity to IAS 32 and introduced the need for detailed rules. However, the Board also noted that IAS 32 contains other exceptions to its principle (and the definition of a liability in the *Framework*) that require instruments to be classified as liabilities that otherwise would be treated as equity. Those exceptions highlight the need for a comprehensive reconsideration of the distinctions between liabilities and equity, which the Board is undertaking in its long-term project.

BC70 In the interim, the Board concluded that classifying as equity the instruments that have all the features and meet the conditions in paragraphs 16A and 16B or paragraphs 16C and 16D would improve the comparability of information provided to the users of financial statements. That is because financial instruments that are largely equivalent to ordinary shares would be consistently classified across different entity structures (eg some partnerships, limited life entities and co-operatives). The specified instruments differ from ordinary shares in one respect; that difference is the obligation to deliver cash (or another financial asset). However, the Board concluded that the other characteristics of the specified instruments are sufficiently similar to ordinary shares for the instruments to be classified as equity. Consequently, the Board concluded that the amendments will result in financial reporting that is more understandable and relevant to the users of financial statements.

BC71 Furthermore, in developing the amendments, the Board considered the costs to entities of obtaining information necessary to determine the required classification. The Board believes that the costs of obtaining any new information would be slight because all of the necessary information should be readily available.

BC72 The Board also acknowledged that one of the costs and risks of introducing exceptions to the definition of a financial liability is the structuring opportunities that may result. The Board concluded that financial structuring opportunities are minimised by the detailed criteria required for equity classification and the related disclosures.

BC73 Consequently, the Board believed that the benefits of the amendments outweigh the costs.

BC74   The Board took the view that, in most cases, entities should be able to apply the amendments retrospectively. The Board noted that IAS 8 *Accounting Policies, Changes in Accounting Estimates and Errors* provides relief when it is impracticable to apply a change in accounting policy retrospectively as a result of a new requirement. Furthermore, the Board took the view that the costs outweighed the benefits of separating a compound financial instrument with an obligation to deliver a pro rata share of the net assets of the entity only on liquidation when the liability component is no longer outstanding on the date of initial application. Hence, there is no requirement on transition to separate such compound instruments.

Amendments to the application guidance for offsetting financial assets and financial liabilities

Background

BC75   Following requests from users of financial statements and recommendations from the Financial Stability Board, in June 2010 the IASB and the US national standard-setter, the Financial Accounting Standards Board (FASB), added a project to their respective agendas to improve, and potentially achieve convergence of, the requirements for offsetting financial assets and financial liabilities. The boards made this decision because the differences in their requirements for offsetting financial assets and financial liabilities cause significant differences between amounts presented in statements of financial position prepared in accordance with IFRSs and amounts presented in statements of financial position prepared in accordance with US GAAP. This is particularly so for entities that have large amounts of derivative activities.

BC76   Consequently, in January 2011 the Board published the exposure draft *Offsetting Financial Assets and Financial Liabilities*. The proposals in the exposure draft would have established a common approach with the FASB. The exposure draft also proposed disclosures about financial assets and financial liabilities that are subject to set-off rights and related arrangements (such as collateral agreements), and the effect of those rights and arrangements on an entity's financial position.

BC77   As a result of the feedback received on the exposure draft, the IASB and the FASB decided to maintain their current offsetting models. However, the boards noted that requiring common disclosures of gross and net information would be helpful for users of financial statements. Accordingly, the boards agreed on common disclosure requirements by amending and finalising the disclosures that were initially proposed in the exposure draft. The amendments *Disclosures—Offsetting Financial Assets and Financial Liabilities* (Amendments to IFRS 7) were issued in December 2011.

BC78   In addition, the IASB decided to add application guidance to IAS 32 to address inconsistencies identified in applying some of the offsetting criteria. This included clarifying the meaning of 'currently has a legally enforceable right of set-off' and that some gross settlement systems may be considered equivalent to net settlement.

Requirements for offsetting financial assets and financial liabilities

Criterion that an entity 'currently has a legally enforceable right to set off the recognised amounts' (paragraph 42(a))

BC79　To meet the criterion in paragraph 42(a) of IAS 32, an entity must currently have a legally enforceable right to set off the recognised amounts. However, IAS 32 did not previously provide guidance on what was meant by 'currently has a legally enforceable right to set off'. Feedback from the exposure draft revealed inconsistencies in the application of this criterion by IFRS preparers. Consequently, the Board decided to include application guidance in IAS 32 (paragraphs AG38A–AG38D) to clarify the meaning of this criterion.

BC80　The Board believes that the net amounts of financial assets and financial liabilities presented in the statement of financial position should represent an entity's exposure in the normal course of business and its exposure if one of the parties will not or cannot perform under the terms of the contract. The Board therefore clarified in paragraph AG38B that to meet the criterion in paragraph 42(a) of IAS 32 a right of set-off is required to be legally enforceable in the normal course of business, the event of default and the event of insolvency or bankruptcy of the entity and all of the counterparties. The right must exist for all counterparties so that if an event occurs for one of the counterparties, including the entity, the other counterparty or parties will be able to enforce the right of set-off against the party that has defaulted or gone insolvent or bankrupt.

BC81　If a right of set-off cannot be enforced in the event of default and in the event of insolvency or bankruptcy, then offsetting would not reflect the economic substance of the entity's rights and obligations and would therefore not meet the objective of offsetting in paragraph 43 of IAS 32. The Board uses the term 'in the event of default and in the event of insolvency or bankruptcy' to describe scenarios where an entity will not or cannot perform under the contract.

BC82　The use of the word 'currently' in paragraph 42(a) of IAS 32 means that the right of set-off cannot be contingent on a future event. If a right of set-off were contingent or conditional on a future event an entity would not currently have a (legally enforceable) right of set-off. The right of set-off would not exist until the contingency occurred, if at all.

BC83　In addition, the Board believes that the passage of time or uncertainties in amounts to be paid do not preclude an entity from currently having a (legally enforceable) right of set-off. The fact that the payments subject to a right of set-off will only arise at a future date is not in itself a condition or a form of contingency that prevents offsetting in accordance with paragraph 42(a) of IAS 32.

BC84　However, if the right of set-off is not exercisable during a period when amounts are due and payable, then the entity does not meet the offsetting criterion as it has no right to set off those payments. Similarly, a right of set-off that could disappear or that would no longer be enforceable after a future event that could take place in the normal course of business or in the event of default, or in the event of insolvency or bankruptcy, such as a ratings downgrade, would not meet the currently (legally enforceable) criterion in paragraph 42(a) of IAS 32.

BC85 The application of the word 'currently' in paragraph 42(a) of IAS 32 was not a source of inconsistency in practice but rather a question that arose as a result of the wording in the exposure draft. Consequently, the Board decided that further application guidance was only required for the legal enforceability part of the criterion.

BC86 In developing the proposals in the exposure draft, the Board concluded that the net amount represents the entity's right or obligation if (a) the entity has the ability to insist on net settlement or to enforce net settlement in all situations (ie the exercise of that right is not contingent on a future event), (b) that ability is assured, and (c) the entity intends to receive or pay a single net amount, or to realise the asset and settle the liability simultaneously.

BC87 Some respondents were concerned that the terms 'in all situations' and 'the ability is assured' as referred to in paragraph BC86 create a higher hurdle than IAS 32 today. The Board however believes that the conclusions in the exposure draft are consistent with the offsetting criteria and principle in IAS 32, specifically paragraphs 42, 43, 46 and 47. In addition, the application guidance in paragraph AG38B of IAS 32 addresses respondents' concerns by clarifying the circumstances in which an entity should be able to net (ie what 'in all situations' means), and by requiring legal enforceability in such circumstances, a term commonly used in applying IAS 32 today.

Applicability to all counterparties

BC88 The proposals in the exposure draft required that the right of set-off be legally enforceable in the event of default and in the event of insolvency or bankruptcy of 'one of the counterparties' (including the entity itself). There were differing views as to whether the requirement that the right of set-off must be enforceable in the event of the entity's default and/or insolvency or bankruptcy changed the criteria in IAS 32 today.

BC89 Some respondents disagreed that the right of set-off must be enforceable in the events of default and insolvency or bankruptcy of the entity. Although consideration is given to enforceability today to achieve offsetting in accordance with IAS 32, some have only focused on the effects of the insolvency or bankruptcy of the counterparty. These respondents questioned whether legal opinions as to enforceability in the event of their own insolvency or bankruptcy could be obtained and considered this to be a change in practice from IAS 32 that could increase costs and the burden for preparers. They also believed that such a requirement would be inconsistent with the going concern basis of preparation for financial statements.

BC90 Other respondents, however, agreed that, to represent the entity's net exposure at all times, the right of set-off must be enforceable in the insolvency or bankruptcy of all of the counterparties to the contract.

BC91   The Board believes that limiting the enforcement of the right of set-off to the event of default and the event of insolvency or bankruptcy of the counterparty (and not the entity itself) is not consistent with the principle and objective of offsetting in IAS 32.

BC92   If a right of set-off cannot also be enforced in the event of default and in the event of insolvency or bankruptcy of the entity, then offsetting would not reflect the economic substance of the entity's rights and obligations or the financial position of the entity (ie offsetting would not reflect an entity's expected future cash flows from settling two or more separate financial instruments in accordance with paragraph 43 of IAS 32) and would therefore not meet the objective of offsetting in IAS 32.

BC93   Consequently, the Board decided to clarify that, to meet the offsetting criterion in paragraph 42(a) of IAS 32, a right of set-off must be enforceable in the event of default and in the event of insolvency or bankruptcy of both the entity and its counterparties (paragraphs AG38A and AG38B of IAS 32).

Criterion that an entity 'intends either to settle on a net basis, or to realise the asset and settle the liability simultaneously' (paragraph 42(b))

BC94   In the exposure draft the boards noted that offsetting financial assets and financial liabilities is appropriate and reflects the financial position of an entity only if the entity has, in effect, a right to, or an obligation for, only the net amount (ie the entity has, in effect, a single net financial asset or net financial liability). The amount resulting from offsetting must also reflect the entity's expected future cash flows from settling two or more separate financial instruments. This is consistent with the principle in paragraph 43 of IAS 32.

BC95   When developing that principle the boards understood that entities may currently have a legally enforceable right and desire to settle net, but may not have the operational capabilities to effect net settlement. The gross positions would be settled at the same moment such that the outcome would not be distinguishable from net settlement. As a result the boards included simultaneous settlement as a practical exception to net settlement. Simultaneous settlement was intended to capture payments that are essentially equivalent to actual net settlement. The proposals in the exposure draft also defined simultaneous settlement as settlement 'at the same moment'.

BC96   Simultaneous settlement as 'at the same moment' is already a concept in paragraph 48 of IAS 32 that enables an entity to meet the criterion in paragraph 42(b) of IAS 32. However, feedback received during outreach indicated that there was diversity in practice related to the interpretation of 'simultaneous settlement' in IAS 32. Many preparers and accounting firms have interpreted paragraph 48 of IAS 32 to mean that settlement through a clearing house always meets the simultaneous settlement criterion even if not occurring at the same moment.

BC97   Respondents also noted that settlement of two positions by exchange of gross cash flows at exactly the same moment (simultaneously) rarely occurs in practice today. They argued that 'simultaneous' is not operational and ignores settlement systems that are established to achieve what is economically considered to be net exposure.

BC98 Some preparers also indicated that settlement through some gross settlement mechanisms, though not simultaneous, effectively results in the same exposure as in net settlement or settlement at the same moment and are currently considered to meet the requirements in IAS 32, without actually taking place 'at the same moment'. For particular settlement mechanisms, once the settlement process commences, the entity is not exposed to credit or liquidity risk over and above the net amount and therefore the process is equivalent to net settlement.

BC99 Paragraph 48 of IAS 32 states that simultaneous settlement results in 'no exposure to credit or liquidity risk'. In its redeliberations the Board considered gross settlement mechanisms with features that both (i) eliminate credit and liquidity risk; and (ii) process receivables and payables in a single settlement process. The Board agreed that gross settlement systems with such features are effectively equivalent to net settlement.

BC100 To clarify the application of the IAS 32 offsetting criteria and to reduce diversity in practice, the Board therefore clarified the principle behind net settlement and included an example of a gross settlement system with characteristics that would satisfy the IAS 32 criterion for net settlement in paragraph AG38F of IAS 32.

BC101 However, the Board decided not to refer specifically to clearing houses or central counterparties when describing systems that may be treated as equivalent to net settlement for the purposes of the set-off criterion. Systems that meet the principle in paragraph AG38F of IAS 32 may be referred to by different names in different jurisdictions. Referring to specific types of settlement systems may exclude other systems that are also considered equivalent to net settlement. In addition, the Board did not want to imply that settlement through specific systems would always meet the net settlement criterion. Entities must determine whether a system meets the principle in paragraph AG38F of IAS 32 by determining whether or not the system eliminates or results in insignificant credit and liquidity risk and processes receivables and payables in the same settlement process or cycle.

Offsetting collateral amounts

BC102 The proposals in the exposure draft specifically prohibited offsetting assets pledged as collateral (or the right to reclaim the collateral pledged) or the obligation to return collateral sold with the associated financial assets and financial liabilities. A number of respondents disagreed with the proposed treatment of collateral and noted that the proposed prohibition was more restrictive than the offsetting criteria in paragraph 42 of IAS 32.

BC103 The offsetting criteria in IAS 32 do not give special consideration to items referred to as 'collateral'. The Board confirmed that a recognised financial instrument referred to as collateral should be set off against the related financial asset or financial liability in the statement of financial position if, and only if, it meets the offsetting criteria in paragraph 42 of IAS 32. The Board also noted that if an entity can be required to return or receive back collateral, the entity would not currently have a legally enforceable right of set-off in all of the following circumstances: in the normal course of business, the event of default and the event of insolvency or bankruptcy of one of the counterparties.

BC104   Because no particular practice concerns or inconsistencies were brought to the Board's attention related to the treatment of collateral in accordance with the offsetting criteria in IAS 32, and as the concerns that arose originated from the proposals in the exposure draft, the Board did not consider it necessary to add application guidance for the treatment of collateral.

Unit of account

BC105   Neither IAS 32 nor the exposure draft specifies the unit of account to which the offsetting requirements should be applied. During the outreach performed on the exposure draft, it became apparent that there was diversity in practice regarding the unit of account that was used for offsetting in accordance with IAS 32.

BC106   Entities in some industries (for example, energy producers and traders) apply the offsetting criteria to identifiable cash flows. Other entities apply the offsetting criteria to entire financial assets and financial liabilities. For those entities (for example, financial institutions), applying the offsetting criteria to individual identifiable cash flows (portions of financial assets and financial liabilities) within contracts would be impractical and burdensome, even though requiring application of the offsetting criteria to entire financial instruments results in less offsetting in the statement of financial position.

BC107   The Board acknowledged that the focus of the offsetting model is the entity's net exposure and expected future cash flows from settling the related financial instruments.

BC108   The Board also noted that some of the entities for whom the offsetting requirements are most relevant are those that would have the most significant operational challenges with applying the model to individual cash flows (such as financial institutions with large derivative activities). This is important to consider because IAS 32 requires offsetting if the offsetting criteria are met.

BC109   On the other hand, if the application of the offsetting criteria to individual cash flows was prohibited, entities in some industries (for example, energy producers and traders) that apply the criteria in IAS 32 to individual cash flows of financial instruments, and achieve set-off on that basis today, would no longer be permitted to do so.

BC110   The Board considered clarifying the application guidance in IAS 32 to indicate that offsetting should apply to individual cash flows of financial instruments. However, if it made such clarification, the Board felt that it would be necessary to consider an exemption from this requirement on the basis of operational complexity. This would result in the offsetting requirements still being applied differently between entities.

BC111   Although different interpretations of the unit of account are applied today, the Board concluded that this does not result in inappropriate application of the offsetting criteria. The benefits of amending IAS 32 would not outweigh the costs for preparers and therefore the Board decided not to amend the application guidance to IAS 32 on this subject.

Cost-benefit considerations

BC112 Before issuing an IFRS or an amendment to an IFRS, the Board seeks to ensure that it will meet a significant need and that the overall benefits of the resulting information will justify the costs of providing it. The Board issued *Offsetting Financial Assets and Financial Liabilities* (Amendments to IAS 32) to eliminate inconsistencies in the application of the offsetting criteria in paragraph 42 of IAS 32 by clarifying the meaning of 'currently has a legally enforceable right of set-off' and that some gross settlement systems may be considered equivalent to net settlement.

BC113 Some respondents were concerned that requiring a right of set-off to be enforceable in the event of default and in the event of insolvency or bankruptcy of the entity would increase the cost of applying the offsetting criteria in IAS 32, if, for example, they needed to obtain additional legal opinions on enforceability. However, the Board noted that without this clarification the offsetting criteria would continue to be applied inconsistently, and the resulting offsetting would be inconsistent with the offsetting objective in IAS 32. This would also reduce comparability for users of financial statements. Consequently, the Board concluded that the benefit of clarifying this criterion outweighed the cost to preparers of applying these amendments.

BC114 During redeliberations the Board also considered feedback received on the proposals in the exposure draft related to the treatment of collateral and unit of account. However, as described in greater detail in other sections of this Basis for Conclusions, the Board did not consider it necessary to add application guidance for the treatment of these items.

BC115 The amendments to the IAS 32 application guidance (paragraphs AG38A–AG38F of IAS 32) are intended to clarify the Board's objective for the offsetting criteria and therefore eliminate inconsistencies noted in applying paragraph 42 of IAS 32.

BC116 Based on the considerations described in the Basis for Conclusions of these amendments, and summarised in paragraphs BC112–BC115, the Board concluded that the benefits of *Offsetting Financial Assets and Financial Liabilities* (Amendments to IAS 32) outweigh the costs to preparers of applying those amendments.

Transition and effective date

BC117 During redeliberations, the Board originally decided to require retrospective application of the application guidance in paragraphs AG38A–AG38F of IAS 32 for annual periods beginning on or after 1 January 2013. The Board did not expect significant changes in practice as a result of the clarifications made to the application guidance and hence aligned the effective date and transition of these amendments with that of *Disclosures—Offsetting Financial Assets and Financial Liabilities* (Amendments to IFRS 7), issued in December 2011.

BC118   However, the Board received additional feedback from some preparers that the clarifications to the application guidance could change their practice. These preparers indicated that they needed more time to evaluate the effects of the amendments. They indicated that it would be difficult for them to make this assessment in time to allow application of the amendments to the application guidance for the first comparative reporting period.

BC119   Preparers therefore requested that the Board consider aligning the effective date of the amendments with the then revised effective date of IFRS 9 *Financial Instruments* (1 January 2015),[12] with earlier application permitted. This would give them sufficient time to determine if there would be any changes to their financial statements.

BC120   The Board believed that the amendments to the IAS 32 application guidance should be effective as soon as possible to ensure comparability of financial statements prepared in accordance with IFRSs. In addition, the Board did not consider that the effective date needed to be aligned with that of IFRS 9. However, the Board also understood the concerns of preparers. The Board therefore decided to require the amendments to the IAS 32 application guidance to be effective for periods beginning 1 January 2014 with earlier application permitted. This would provide a balance between the time needed to implement the amendments with the need for consistent application of the IAS 32 offsetting requirements.

---

12   In the completed version of IFRS 9, issued in July 2014, the Board specified that entities must adopt the completed version of IFRS 9 for annual periods beginning on or after 1 January 2018.

Dissenting opinions

Dissent of James J Leisenring from the issue of IAS 32 in December 2003

DO1   Mr Leisenring dissents from IAS 32 because, in his view, the conclusions about the accounting for forward purchase contracts and written put options on an issuer's equity instruments that require physical settlement in exchange for cash are inappropriate. IAS 32 requires a forward purchase contract to be recognised as though the future transaction had already occurred. Similarly it requires a written put option to be accounted for as though the option had already been exercised. Both of these contracts result in combining the separate forward contract and the written put option with outstanding shares to create a synthetic liability.

DO2   Recording a liability for the present value of the fixed forward price as a result of a forward contract is inconsistent with the accounting for other forward contracts. Recording a liability for the present value of the strike price of an option results in recording a liability that is inconsistent with the *Framework*[13] as there is no present obligation for the strike price. In both instances the shares considered to be subject to the contracts are outstanding, have the same rights as any other shares and should be accounted for as outstanding. The forward and option contracts meet the definition of a derivative and should be accounted for as derivatives rather than create an exception to the accounting required by IAS 39.[14] Similarly, if the redemption feature is embedded in the equity instrument (for example, a redeemable preference share) rather than being a free-standing derivative contract, the redemption feature should be accounted for as a derivative.

DO3   Mr Leisenring also objects to the conclusion that a purchased put or call option on a fixed number of an issuer's equity instruments is not an asset. The rights created by these contracts meet the definition of an asset and should be accounted for as assets and not as a reduction in equity. These contracts also meet the definition of derivatives that should be accounted for as such consistently with IAS 39.

---

13 The reference to the *Framework* is to IASC's *Framework for the Preparation and Presentation of Financial Statements*, adopted by the IASB in 2001. In September 2010 the IASB replaced the *Framework* with the *Conceptual Framework for Financial Reporting*.

14 IFRS 9 *Financial Instruments* replaced IAS 39. IFRS 9 applies to all items that were previously within the scope of IAS 39.

Dissent of Mary E Barth and Robert P Garnett from the issue of *Puttable Financial Instruments and Obligations Arising on Liquidation* (Amendments to IAS 32 and IAS 1) in February 2008

DO1   Professor Barth and Mr Garnett voted against the publication of *Puttable Financial Instruments and Obligations Arising on Liquidation* (Amendments to IAS 32 and IAS 1 *Presentation of Financial Statements*). The reasons for their dissent are set out below.

DO2   These Board members believe that the decision to permit entities to classify as equity some puttable financial instruments and some financial instruments that entitle the holder to a pro rata share of the net assets of the entity only on liquidation is inconsistent with the *Framework*.[15] The contractual provisions attached to those instruments give the holders the right to put the instruments to the entity and demand cash. The *Framework*'s definition of a liability is that it is a present obligation of the entity arising from a past event, the settlement of which is expected to result in an outflow of resources of the entity. Thus, financial instruments within the scope of the amendments clearly meet the definition of a liability in the *Framework*.

DO3   These Board members do not agree with the Board that an exception to the *Framework* is justified in this situation. First, the Board has an active project on the *Framework*, which will revisit the definition of a liability. Although these Board members agree that standards projects can precede decisions in the *Framework* project, the discussions to date in the *Framework* project do not make it clear that the Board will modify the existing elements definitions in such a way that these instruments would be equity. Second, the amendments would require disclosure of the expected cash outflow on redemption or repurchase of puttable instruments classified as equity. These disclosures are similar to those for financial liabilities; existing standards do not require similar disclosure for equity instruments. The Board's decision to require these disclosures reveals its implicit view these instruments are, in fact, liabilities. Yet, the *Framework* is clear that disclosure is not a substitute for recognition. Third, these Board members see no cost-benefit or practical reasons for making this exception. The amendments require the same or similar information to be obtained and disclosed as would be the case if these obligations were classified as liabilities. Existing standards offer presentation alternatives for entities that have no equity under the *Framework*'s definitions.

DO4   These Board members also do not agree with the Board that there are benefits to issuing these amendments. First, paragraph BC70 in the Basis for Conclusions states that the amendments will result in more relevant and understandable financial reporting. However, as noted above, these Board members do not believe that presenting as equity items that meet the *Framework*'s definition of a liability results in relevant information. Also as noted above, existing standards offer presentation alternatives that result in understandable financial reporting.

---

15   References to the *Framework* are to IASC's *Framework for the Preparation and Presentation of Financial Statements*, adopted by the IASB in 2001. In September 2010 the IASB replaced the *Framework* with the *Conceptual Framework for Financial Reporting*.

DO5   Second, paragraph BC70 states that the amendments would increase comparability by requiring more consistent classification of financial instruments that are largely equivalent to ordinary shares. These Board members believe that the amendments decrease comparability. These instruments are not comparable to ordinary shares because these instruments oblige the entity to transfer its economic resources; ordinary shares do not. Also, puttable instruments and instruments that entitle the holder to a pro rata share of the net assets of the entity only on liquidation will be classified as equity by some entities and as liabilities by other entities, depending on whether the other criteria specified in the amendments are met. Thus, these amendments account similarly for economically different instruments, which decreases comparability.

DO6   Finally, these Board members do not believe that the amendments are based on a clear principle. Rather, they comprise several paragraphs of detailed rules crafted to achieve a desired accounting result. Although the Board attempted to craft these rules to minimise structuring opportunities, the lack of a clear principle leaves open the possibility that economically similar situations will be accounted for differently and economically different situations will be accounted for similarly. Both of these outcomes also result in lack of comparability.

Dissent of James J Leisenring and John T Smith from the issue of *Classification of Rights Issues* in October 2009

DO1 Messrs Leisenring and Smith dissent from the amendment *Classification of Rights Issues* for the reasons set out below.

DO2 Mr Smith agrees with the concept of accounting for a rights issue as equity in specified circumstances and supports both the IFRIC recommendation and staff recommendation in July 2009 that the Board make 'an extremely narrow amendment' to IAS 32 to deal with this issue. However, he dissents because he believes the change is not extremely narrow and will provide a means for an entity to use its equity instruments as a way to engage in speculative foreign currency transactions and structure them as equity transactions, a concern identified by the Board in the Basis for Conclusions on IAS 32.

DO3 In their comment letters on the exposure draft, some respondents expressed concerns that the wording of the amendment was too open-ended and could lead to structuring risks. Mr Smith believes that these concerns are well-founded because there is no limitation on what qualifies as a class of equity. Without some limitation, an entity could, for example, establish a foreign currency trading subsidiary, issue shares to a non-controlling interest and deem the shares to be a class of equity in the consolidated group.

DO4 The staff acknowledged the concerns expressed in comment letters that a new class of equity could be created for the purpose of obtaining a desired accounting treatment. However, the Board decided not to attempt to limit such structuring opportunities. The Board was concerned that a requirement that a pro rata offer of rights must be made to all existing owners (rather than only all existing owners of a particular class) of equity instruments would mean that the amendment would not be applicable to most of the transactions to which the Board intended the amendment to apply.

DO5 Instead of trying to narrow the amendment, the Board simply acknowledged that under the amendment, 'You could set up a new class of shares today and one minute later issue shares to that class and ... speculate in foreign currency without it going through the income statement.' Mr Smith believes the Board should have explored other alternatives. Mr Smith believes that the Board should have sought solutions that could in fact provide a means of narrowing the amendment to limit structuring while accommodating appropriate transactions.

DO6 Mr Smith believes that structuring opportunities could be curtailed significantly if some limitations were placed on the type of class of equity instruments that qualify for the exemption. There are a number of factors or indicators that could have been incorporated into the amendment that would limit the exception. For example, the amendment could have specified that non-controlling interests do not constitute a class. The amendment could have further required that qualification for the exemption is limited to those classes of equity instruments in which (a) ownership in the class is diverse or (b) the class is registered on an exchange and shares are exchanged in the marketplace or (c) shares in that class when issued were offered to the public at large and sold in more than one jurisdiction and there was no agreement to subsequently offer rights to shares of the entity; and the amount of capital provided by the class is substantial relative to the other classes of equity. Clearly, some combination of these and other alternatives could have been used to limit structuring opportunities. Mr Smith believes that a better solution could have been found and without introducing some limits around the type of class of equity instruments that qualify, the Board did not produce an extremely narrow amendment.

DO7   Mr Leisenring agrees that when an entity issues rights to acquire its own equity instruments those rights should be classified as equity. However, he does not accept that the issue must be pro rata to all existing shareholders of a class of non-derivative equity instruments. He does not accept that whether or not the offer is pro rata is relevant to determining if the transaction meets the definition of a liability.

DO8   Paragraph BC4J suggests that the Board limited its conclusion to those transactions issued on a pro rata basis because of concerns about structuring risks. If that is of concern the suggestions contained in Mr Smith's dissent would be much more effective and desirable than introducing a precedent that transactions such as this rights offering must simply be pro rata to be considered a transaction with owners as owners.

DO9   Mr Leisenring would have preferred to conclude that a right granted for a fixed amount of a currency was a 'fixed for fixed' exchange rather than create additional conditions to the determination of a liability.

IASB documents published to accompany

IAS 33

Earnings per Share

The text of the unaccompanied standard, IAS 33, is contained in Part A of this edition. Its effective date when issued was 1 January 2005. The text of the Accompanying Guidance on IAS 33 is contained in Part B of this edition. This part presents the following documents:

BASIS FOR CONCLUSIONS

Basis for Conclusions on
IAS 33 *Earnings per Share*

This Basis for Conclusions accompanies, but is not part of, IAS 33.

Introduction

BC1　This Basis for Conclusions summarises the International Accounting Standards Board's considerations in reaching its conclusions on revising IAS 33 *Earnings Per Share* in 2003. Individual Board members gave greater weight to some factors than to others.

BC2　In July 2001 the Board announced that, as part of its initial agenda of technical projects, it would undertake a project to improve a number of Standards, including IAS 33. The project was undertaken in the light of queries and criticisms raised in relation to the Standards by securities regulators, professional accountants and other interested parties. The objectives of the Improvements project were to reduce or eliminate alternatives, redundancies and conflicts within Standards, to deal with some convergence issues and to make other improvements. In May 2002 the Board published its proposals in an Exposure Draft of *Improvements to International Accounting Standards*, with a comment deadline of 16 September 2002. The Board received over 160 comment letters on the Exposure Draft.

BC3　Because the Board's intention was not to reconsider the fundamental approach to the determination and presentation of earnings per share established by IAS 33, this Basis for Conclusions does not discuss requirements in IAS 33 that the Board has not reconsidered.

Presentation of parent's separate earnings per share

BC4　The Exposure Draft published in May 2002 proposed deleting paragraphs 2 and 3 of the previous version of IAS 33, which stated that when the parent's separate financial statements and consolidated financial statements are presented, earnings per share need be presented only on the basis of consolidated information.

BC5　Some respondents expressed concern that the presentation of two earnings per share figures (one for the parent's separate financial statements and one for the consolidated financial statements) might be misleading.

BC6　The Board noted that disclosing the parent's separate earnings per share amount is useful in limited situations, and therefore decided to retain the option. However, the Board decided that the Standard should prohibit presentation of the parent's separate earnings per share amounts in the consolidated financial statements (either on the face of the financial statements or in the notes).

Contracts that may be settled in ordinary shares or cash

BC7　The Exposure Draft proposed that an entity should include in the calculation of the number of potential ordinary shares in the diluted earnings per share calculation contracts that may be settled in ordinary shares or cash, at the issuer's option, based on a rebuttable presumption that the contracts will be settled in shares. This proposed presumption could be rebutted if the issuer had acted through an established pattern of past practice, published policies, or by having made a sufficiently specific current statement indicating to other parties the manner in which it expected to settle, and, as a result, the issuer had created a valid expectation on the part of those other parties that it would settle in a manner other than by issuing shares.

BC8   The majority of the respondents on the Exposure Draft agreed with the proposed treatment of contracts that may be settled in ordinary shares or cash at the issuer's option. However, the Board decided to withdraw the notion of a rebuttable presumption and to incorporate into the Standard the requirements of SIC-24 *Earnings Per Share—Financial Instruments and Other Contracts that May Be Settled in Shares*. SIC-24 requires financial instruments or other contracts that may result in the issue of ordinary shares of the entity to be considered potential ordinary shares of the entity.

BC9   Although the proposed treatment would have converged with that required by several liaison standard-setters, for example, in US SFAS 128 *Earnings per Share*, the Board concluded that the notion of a rebuttable presumption is inconsistent with the stated objective of diluted earnings per share. The US Financial Accounting Standards Board has agreed to consider this difference as part of the joint short-term convergence project with the IASB.

Calculation of year-to-date diluted earnings per share

BC10   The Exposure Draft proposed the following approach to the year-to-date calculation of diluted earnings per share:

     (a)   The number of potential ordinary shares is a year-to-date weighted average of the number of potential ordinary shares included in each interim diluted earnings per share calculation, rather than a year-to-date weighted average of the number of potential ordinary shares weighted for the period they were outstanding (ie without regard for the diluted earnings per share information reported during the interim periods).

     (b)   The number of potential ordinary shares is computed using the average market price during the interim periods, rather than using the average market price during the year-to-date period.

     (c)   Contingently issuable shares are weighted for the interim periods in which they were included in the computation of diluted earnings per share, rather than being included in the computation of diluted earnings per share (if the conditions are satisfied) from the beginning of the year-to-date reporting period (or from the date of the contingent share agreement, if later).

BC11   The majority of the respondents on the Exposure Draft disagreed with the proposed approach to the year-to-date calculation of diluted earnings per share. The most significant argument against the proposed approach was that the proposed calculation of diluted earnings per share could result in an amount for year-to-date diluted earnings per share that was different for entities that report more frequently, for example, on a quarterly or half-yearly basis, and for entities that report only annually. It was also noted that this problem would be exacerbated for entities with seasonal businesses.

BC12 The Board considered whether to accept that differences in the frequency of interim reporting would result in different earnings per share amounts being reported. However, IAS 34 *Interim Financial Reporting* states 'the frequency of an entity's reporting (annual, half-yearly, or quarterly) should not affect the measurement of its annual results. To achieve that objective, measurements for interim reporting purposes should be made on a year-to-date basis.'

BC13 The Board also considered whether it could mandate the frequency of interim reporting to ensure consistency between all entities preparing financial statements in accordance with IFRSs, ie those that are brought within the scope of IAS 33 by virtue of issuing publicly traded instruments or because they elect to present earnings per share. However, IAS 34 states that, 'This Standard does not mandate which entities should be required to publish interim financial reports, how frequently, or how soon after the end of an interim period.' The frequency of interim reporting is mandated by securities regulators, stock exchanges, governments, and accountancy bodies, and varies by jurisdiction.

BC14 Although the proposed approach for the calculation of year-to-date diluted earnings per share would have converged with US SFAS 128, the Board concluded that the approach was inconsistent with IAS 34 and that it could not mandate the frequency of interim reporting. The US Financial Accounting Standards Board has agreed to consider this difference as part of the joint short-term convergence project with the IASB as well as the issue noted in paragraph BC9.

Other changes

BC15 Implementation questions have arisen since the previous version of IAS 33 was issued, typically concerning the application of the Standard to complex capital structures and arrangements. In response, the Board decided to provide additional application guidance in the Appendix as well as illustrative examples on more complex matters that were not addressed in the previous version of IAS 33. These matters include the effects of contingently issuable shares, potential ordinary shares of subsidiaries, joint ventures or associates, participating equity instruments, written put options, and purchased put and call options.

IASB documents published to accompany

IAS 34

Interim Financial Reporting

The text of the unaccompanied standard, IAS 34, is contained in Part A of this edition. Its effective date when issued was 1 January 1999. The text of the Accompanying Guidance on IAS 34 is contained in Part B of this edition. This part presents the following documents:

BASIS FOR CONCLUSIONS

Basis for Conclusions on
IAS 34 *Interim Financial Reporting*

This Basis for Conclusions accompanies, but is not part of, IAS 34.

BC1 This Basis for Conclusions summarises the International Accounting Standards Board's considerations in amending paragraphs 15–18 of IAS 34 *Interim Financial Reporting* as part of *Improvements to IFRSs* issued in May 2010. Those changes aim to emphasise the disclosures principles in IAS 34 and to add further guidance to illustrate how to apply these principles.

BC2 IAS 34 was developed by the International Accounting Standards Committee (IASC) in 1998 and did not include a Basis for Conclusions.

Significant events and transactions

BC3 In *Improvements to IFRSs* issued in May 2010, the Board addressed requests for clarification of the disclosures required by IAS 34 when considered against changes in the disclosure requirements of other IFRSs. IAS 34 was issued by the Board's predecessor body, IASC, in 1998. In the light of recent improvements to disclosure requirements, many users of financial statements asked the Board to consider whether particular disclosures required by IFRS 7 *Financial Instruments: Disclosures* for annual financial statements should also be required in interim financial statements. IAS 34 sets out disclosure principles to determine what information should be disclosed in an interim financial report. The Board concluded that amending IAS 34 to place greater emphasis on those principles and the inclusion of additional examples relating to more recent disclosure requirements, ie fair value measurements, would improve interim financial reporting.

BC4 As part of *Improvements to IFRSs* issued in May 2010, the Board deleted paragraph 18 of IAS 34 because it repeats paragraph 10 of IAS 34 and because the Board's intention is to emphasise those disclosures that are required rather than those that are not required.

Content of an interim financial report

BC5 As part of *Annual Improvements 2009–2011 Cycle* (issued in May 2012) the Board amended paragraph 5 to achieve consistency with paragraphs 10(ea) and 10(f) of IAS 1 *Presentation of Financial Statements*.

Selected explanatory notes

BC6 In *Annual Improvements 2009–2011 Cycle* (issued in May 2012) the Board decided to clarify the requirements on segment information for total assets and liabilities for each reportable segment to enhance consistency with the requirements in paragraph 23 of IFRS 8 *Operating Segments*. The amendment clarifies that the total assets and liabilities for a particular reportable segment are required to be disclosed if, and only if:

(a)   a measure of total assets or of total liabilities (or both) is regularly provided to the chief operating decision maker; and

(b)   there has been a material change from those measures disclosed in the last annual financial statements for that reportable segment.

Other disclosures incorporated by cross-reference to information outside the interim financial statements

BC7   The Board received a request to clarify the meaning of disclosure of information 'elsewhere in the interim financial report' as used in IAS 34. The submitter noted that the definition of 'interim financial report' in paragraph 4 of IAS 34 was not sufficiently clear with respect to whether the interim financial report covers only the information reported under IFRS (meaning the IFRS interim financial statements) or whether it also includes management reports or other elements in addition to IFRS interim financial statements.

BC8   The Board observed that presenting information 'elsewhere in the interim financial report' in accordance with paragraph 16A of IAS 34 is unclear. In the Exposure Draft *Annual Improvements to IFRSs 2012–2014 Cycle* (the '2013 Annual Improvements Exposure Draft'), published in December 2013, the Board proposed to clarify that an entity discloses information elsewhere in the interim financial report when it incorporates disclosures by cross-reference to information in another statement. This information should be available to users of the interim financial statements on the same terms as the interim financial statements and at the same time.

BC9   Some respondents to the 2013 Annual Improvements Exposure Draft observed that the proposed amendment seemed to suggest that the interim financial report was not a single report and that, instead, it included multiple documents. In response to these comments, the Board observed that in accordance with paragraphs 4 and 8 of IAS 34, an interim financial report is a single report that includes a set of condensed financial statements and selected explanatory notes. The Board further clarified that the amendment is not extending the scope of the interim financial report, because the disclosures required in paragraph 16A(a)–(k) of IAS 34 are part of the selected explanatory notes (and therefore part of the interim financial report), even if they are presented in another statement, such as a management commentary or risk report. If they are not presented, the interim financial report would be incomplete.

BC10   In response to the comments received on the 2013 Annual Improvements Exposure Draft the Board decided to clarify what was meant by the requirement that disclosures incorporated by cross-reference should be made available 'on the same terms' as the financial statements. This means that users of the financial statements should have access to the referenced material on the same basis as they have for accessing the financial statements from where the reference is made.

IASB documents published to accompany

IAS 36

Impairment of Assets

The text of the unaccompanied IAS 36 is contained in Part A of this edition. Its effective date when issued was 31 March 2004. The text of the Basis for Conclusions on IAS 36 is contained in Part B of this edition. This part presents the following accompanying document:

BASIS FOR CONCLUSIONS

DISSENTING OPINIONS

CONTENTS

Basis for Conclusions on
IAS 36 *Impairment of Assets*

The International Accounting Standards Board revised IAS 36 as part of its project on business combinations. It was not the Board's intention to reconsider as part of that project all of the requirements in IAS 36.

The previous version of IAS 36 was accompanied by a Basis for Conclusions summarising the former International Accounting Standards Committee's considerations in reaching some of its conclusions in that Standard. For convenience the Board has incorporated into its own Basis for Conclusions material from the previous Basis for Conclusions that discusses (a) matters the Board did not reconsider and (b) the history of the development of a standard on impairment of assets. That material is contained in paragraphs denoted by numbers with the prefix BCZ. Paragraphs describing the Board's considerations in reaching its own conclusions are numbered with the prefix BC.

In this Basis for Conclusions the terminology has not been amended to reflect the changes made by IAS 1 Presentation of Financial Statements *(as revised in 2007).*

In developing IFRS 13 Fair Value Measurement, *issued in May 2011, the Board changed the definition of fair value less costs to sell. As a consequence all references to 'fair value less costs to sell' in IAS 36 were replaced with 'fair value less costs of disposal'. This Basis for Conclusions has not been amended to reflect that change.*

Introduction

BC1   This Basis for Conclusions summarises the International Accounting Standards Board's considerations in reaching the conclusions in IAS 36 *Impairment of Assets*. Individual Board members gave greater weight to some factors than to others.

BC2   The International Accounting Standards Committee (IASC) issued the previous version of IAS 36 in 1998. It has been revised by the Board as part of its project on business combinations. That project had two phases. The first resulted in the Board issuing simultaneously in 2004 IFRS 3 *Business Combinations* and revised versions of IAS 36 and IAS 38 *Intangible Assets*. The Board's intention in revising IAS 36 as part of the first phase of the project was not to reconsider all of the requirements in IAS 36. The changes to IAS 36 were primarily concerned with the impairment tests for intangible assets with indefinite useful lives (hereafter referred to as 'indefinite-lived intangibles') and goodwill. The second phase of the project on business combinations resulted in the Board issuing simultaneously in 2008 a revised IFRS 3 and an amended version of IAS 27 *Consolidated and Separate Financial Statements*.[1] The Board amended IAS 36 to reflect its decisions on the measurement of a non-controlling interest in an acquiree (see paragraph BC170A). The Board has not deliberated the other requirements in IAS 36. Those other requirements will be considered by the Board as part of a future project on impairment of assets.

---

1   The consolidation requirements in IAS 27 were superseded by IFRS 10 *Consolidated Financial Statements* issued in May 2011.

BC3　　The previous version of IAS 36 was accompanied by a Basis for Conclusions summarising IASC's considerations in reaching some of its conclusions in that Standard. For convenience, the Board has incorporated into this Basis for Conclusions material from the previous Basis for Conclusions that discusses matters the Board did not consider. That material is contained in paragraphs denoted by numbers with the prefix BCZ. The views expressed in paragraphs denoted by numbers with the prefix BCZ are those of IASC.

Scope (paragraph 2)

BCZ4　　IAS 2 *Inventories* requires an enterprise to measure the recoverable amount of inventory at its net realisable value. IASC believed that there was no need to revise this requirement because it was well accepted as an appropriate test for recoverability of inventories. No major difference exists between IAS 2 and the requirements included in IAS 36 (see paragraphs BCZ37–BCZ39).

BCZ5　　IAS 11 *Construction Contracts*[2] and IAS 12 *Income Taxes* already deal with the impairment of assets arising from construction contracts and deferred tax assets respectively. Under both IAS 11 and IAS 12, recoverable amount is, in effect, determined on an undiscounted basis. IASC acknowledged that this was inconsistent with the requirements of IAS 36. However, IASC believed that it was not possible to eliminate that inconsistency without fundamental changes to IAS 11 and IAS 12. IASC had no plans to revise IAS 11 or IAS 12.

BCZ6　　IAS 19 *Employee Benefits* contains an upper limit on the amount at which an enterprise should recognise an asset arising from employee benefits. Therefore, IAS 36 does not deal with such assets. The limit in IAS 19 is determined on a discounted basis that is broadly compatible with the requirements of IAS 36.[3]

BCZ7　　IAS 39 *Financial Instruments: Recognition and Measurement*[4] sets out the requirements for impairment of financial assets.

BCZ8　　IAS 36 is applicable to all assets, unless specifically excluded, regardless of their classification as current or non-current. Before IAS 36 was issued, there was no International Accounting Standard on accounting for the impairment of current assets other than inventories.

Measuring recoverable amount (paragraphs 18–57)

BCZ9　　In determining the principles that should govern the measurement of recoverable amount, IASC considered, as a first step, what an enterprise will do if it discovers that an asset is impaired. IASC concluded that, in such cases, an enterprise will either keep the asset or dispose of it. For example, if an enterprise discovers that the service potential of an asset has decreased:

2　IFRS 15 *Revenue from Contracts with Customers*, issued in May 2014, replaced IAS 11 *Construction Contracts*. IFRS 15 includes requirements for the impairment of some assets arising from contracts with customers and amended paragraph 2 of IAS 36 for consistency with the requirements of IFRS 15.

3　sentence deleted when IAS 19 *Employee Benefits* was amended in 2011.

4　IFRS 9 *Financial Instruments* replaced IAS 39. IFRS 9 applies to all items that were previously within the scope of IAS 39.

    (a)   the enterprise may decide to sell the asset if the net proceeds from the sale would provide a higher return on investment than continuing use in operations; or

    (b)   the enterprise may decide to keep the asset and use it, even if its service potential is lower than originally expected. Some reasons may be that:

        (i)   the asset cannot be sold or disposed of immediately;

        (ii)   the asset can be sold only at a low price;

        (iii)   the asset's service potential can still be recovered but only with additional efforts or expenditure; or

        (iv)   the asset could still be profitable although not to the same extent as expected originally.

IASC concluded that the resulting decision from a rational enterprise is, in substance, an investment decision based on estimated net future cash flows expected from the asset.

BCZ10   IASC then considered which of the following four alternatives for determining the recoverable amount of an asset would best reflect this conclusion:

    (a)   recoverable amount should be the sum of undiscounted future cash flows.

    (b)   recoverable amount should be the asset's fair value: more specifically, recoverable amount should be derived primarily from the asset's market value. If market value cannot be determined, then recoverable amount should be based on the asset's value in use as a proxy for market value.[5]

    (c)   recoverable amount should be the asset's value in use.

    (d)   recoverable amount should be the higher of the asset's net selling price and value in use.[6]

Each of these alternatives is discussed below.

BCZ11   It should be noted that fair value, net selling price and value in use all reflect a present value calculation (implicit or explicit) of estimated net future cash flows expected from an asset:

    (a)   fair value[7] reflects the market's expectation of the present value of the future cash flows to be derived from the asset;

    (b)   net selling price reflects the market's expectation of the present value of the future cash flows to be derived from the asset, less the direct incremental costs to dispose of the asset; and

    (c)   value in use is the enterprise's estimate of the present value of the future cash flows to be derived from continuing use and disposal of the asset.

---

5   IFRS 13 *Fair Value Measurement*, issued in May 2011, defines fair value and contains the requirements for measuring fair value. As a result the term 'market value' has been changed to 'fair value'.

6   In IFRS 5 *Non-current Assets Held for Sale and Discontinued Operations*, issued by the IASB in 2004, the term 'net selling price' was replaced in IAS 36 by 'fair value less costs to sell'.

7   IFRS 13, issued in May 2011, defines fair value and contains the requirements for measuring fair value.

These bases all consider the time value of money and the risks that the amount and timing of the actual cash flows to be received from an asset might differ from estimates. Fair value and net selling price may differ from value in use because the market may not use the same assumptions as an individual enterprise.

Recoverable amount based on the sum of undiscounted cash flows

BCZ12   Some argue that recoverable amount should be measured as the sum of undiscounted future cash flows from an asset. They argue that:

(a)   historical cost accounting is not concerned with measuring the economic value of assets. Therefore, the time value of money should not be considered in estimating the amount that will be recovered from an asset.

(b)   it is premature to use discounting techniques without further research and debates on:

(i)   the role of discounting in the financial statements; and

(ii)   how assets should be measured generally.

If financial statements include assets that are carried on a variety of different bases (historical cost, discounted amounts or other bases), this will be confusing for users.

(c)   identifying an appropriate discount rate will often be difficult and subjective.

(d)   discounting will increase the number of impairment losses recognised. This, coupled with the requirement for reversals of impairment losses, introduces a volatile element into the income statement. It will make it harder for users to understand the performance of an enterprise.

A minority of commentators on E55 *Impairment of Assets* supported this view.

BCZ13   IASC rejected measurement of recoverable amount based on the sum of undiscounted cash flows because:

(a)   the objective of the measurement of recoverable amount is to reflect an investment decision. Money has a time value, even when prices are stable. If future cash flows were not discounted, two assets giving rise to cash flows of the same amount but with different timings would show the same recoverable amount. However, their current market values would be different because all rational economic transactions take account of the time value of money.

(b)   measurements that take into consideration the time value of money are more relevant to investors, other external users of financial statements and management for resource allocation decisions, regardless of the general measurement basis adopted in the financial statements.

(c)   many enterprises were already familiar with the use of discounting techniques, particularly for supporting investment decisions.

(d) discounting was already required for other areas of financial statements that are based on expectations of future cash flows, such as long-term provisions and employee benefit obligations.

(e) users are better served if they are aware on a timely basis of assets that will not generate sufficient returns to cover, at least, the time value of money.

Recoverable amount based on fair value

BCZ14 IAS 32 *Financial Instruments: Disclosure and Presentation*[8] and a number of other International Accounting Standards define fair value[9] as:

> '… the amount for which an asset could be exchanged, or a liability settled, between knowledgeable, willing parties in an arm's length transaction …'

BCZ15 International Accounting Standards include the following requirements or guidance for measuring fair value:[10]

(a) for the purpose of revaluation of an item of property, plant or equipment to its fair value, IAS 16 *Property, Plant and Equipment* indicates that fair value is usually an asset's market value, normally determined by appraisal undertaken by professionally qualified valuers and, if no market exists, fair value is based on the asset's depreciated replacement cost.

(b) for the purpose of revaluation of an intangible asset to its fair value, IASC proposed in E60 *Intangible Assets* that fair value be determined by reference to market values obtained from an active market. E60 proposed a definition of an active market.[11]

(c) IASC proposed revisions to IAS 22 (see E61 *Business Combinations*) so that fair value would be determined without consideration of the acquirer's intentions for the future use of an asset.[12]

(d) IAS 39[13] indicates that if an active market exists, the fair value of a financial instrument is based on a quoted market price. If there is no active market, fair value is determined by using estimation techniques such as market values of similar types of financial instruments, discounted cash flow analysis and option pricing models.

BCZ16 Some argue that the only appropriate measurement for the recoverable amount of an asset is fair value (based on observable market prices or, if no observable

---

8 In 2005 the IASB amended IAS 32 as *Financial Instruments: Presentation*.
9 IFRS 13, issued in May 2011, defines fair value as an exit price.
10 IFRS 13, issued in May 2011, defines fair value and contains the requirements for measuring fair value. As a consequence the relevant requirements in IAS 16 and IAS 39 have been deleted from those Standards.
11 IASC approved an International Accounting Standard on intangible assets in 1998.
12 IASC approved revisions to IAS 22 *Business Combinations* in 1998.
13 The Board's project to revise IAS 32 and IAS 39 in 2003 resulted in the relocation of the requirements on fair value measurement from IAS 32 to IAS 39. Subsequently to that, IFRS 9 *Financial Instruments* replaced IAS 39. IFRS 9 applies to all items that were previously within the scope of IAS 39. In 2011 the Board's project on fair value measurement resulted in the relocation of the requirements for measuring fair value to IFRS 13.

market prices exist, estimated considering prices for similar assets and the results of discounted future cash flow calculations).[14] Proponents of fair value argue that:

(a) the purpose of measuring recoverable amount is to estimate a market value, not an enterprise-specific value. An enterprise's estimate of the present value of future cash flows is subjective and in some cases may be abused. Observable market prices that reflect the judgement of the marketplace are a more reliable measurement of the amounts that will be recovered from an asset. They reduce the use of management's judgement.

(b) if an asset is expected to generate greater net cash inflows for the enterprise than for other participants, the superior returns are almost always generated by internally generated goodwill stemming from the synergy of the business and its management team. For consistency with IASC's proposals in E60 that internally generated goodwill should not be recognised as an asset, these above-market cash flows should be excluded from assessments of an asset's recoverable amount.

(c) determining recoverable amount as the higher of net selling price and value in use is tantamount to determining two diverging measures whilst there should be only one measure to estimate recoverable amount.

A minority of commentators on E55 supported measuring recoverable amount at fair value (based on observable market prices or, if no observable market prices exist, estimated considering prices for similar assets and the results of discounted future cash flow calculations).

BCZ17 IASC rejected the proposal that an asset's recoverable amount should be determined by reference to its fair value (based on observable market prices or, if no observable market prices exist, estimated considering prices for similar assets and the results of discounted future cash flow calculations). The reasons are the following:

(a) IASC believed that no preference should be given to the market's expectation of the recoverable amount of an asset (basis for fair value when market values are available and for net selling price) over a reasonable estimate performed by the individual enterprise that owns the asset (basis for fair value when market values are not available and for value in use). For example, an enterprise may have information about future cash flows that is superior to the information available in the marketplace. Also, an enterprise may plan to use an asset in a manner different from the market's view of the best use.

(b) market values are a way to estimate fair value but only if they reflect the fact that both parties, the acquirer and the seller, are willing to enter a transaction. If an enterprise can generate greater cash flows by using an asset than by selling it, it would be misleading to base recoverable

---

14 IFRS 13, issued in May 2011, describes valuation techniques for measuring the fair value of an asset that is being used (and would not be sold) by an entity, eg a current replacement cost valuation technique.

amount on the market price of the asset because a rational enterprise would not be willing to sell the asset. Therefore, recoverable amount should not refer only to a transaction between two parties (which is unlikely to happen) but should also consider an asset's service potential from its use by the enterprise.

(c) IASC believed that in assessing the recoverable amount of an asset, it is the amount that an enterprise can expect to recover from that asset, including the effect of synergy with other assets, that is relevant.

The following two examples illustrate the proposal (rejected by IASC) that an enterprise should measure an asset's recoverable amount at its fair value (primarily based on observable market values if these values are available).

Example 1

10 years ago, an enterprise bought its headquarters building for 2,000. Since then, the real estate market has collapsed and the building's market value at balance sheet date is estimated to be 1,000. Disposal costs of the building would be negligible. The building's carrying amount at the balance sheet date is 1,500 and its remaining useful life is 30 years. The building meets all the enterprise's expectations and it is likely that these expectations will be met for the foreseeable future. As a consequence, the enterprise has no plans to move from its current headquarters. The value in use of the building cannot be determined because the building does not generate independent cash inflows. Therefore, the enterprise assesses the recoverable amount of the building's cash-generating unit, that is, the enterprise as a whole. That calculation shows that the building's cash-generating unit is not impaired.

Proponents of fair value (primarily based on observable market values if these values are available) would measure the recoverable amount of the building at its market value (1,000) and, hence, would recognise an impairment loss of 500 (1,500 less 1,000), even though calculations show that the building's cash-generating unit is not impaired.

IASC did not support this approach and believed that the building was not impaired. IASC believed that, in the situation described, the enterprise would not be willing to sell the building for 1,000 and that the assumption of a sale was not relevant.

Example 2

At the end of 20X0, an enterprise purchased a computer for 100 for general use in its operations. The computer is depreciated over 4 years on a straight-line basis. Residual value is estimated to be nil. At the end of 20X2, the carrying amount of the computer is 50. There is an active market for second-hand computers of this type. The market value of the computer is 30. The enterprise does not intend to replace the computer before the end of its useful life. The computer's cash-generating unit is not impaired.

Proponents of fair value (primarily based on observable market values if these values are available) would measure the recoverable amount of the computer at its market value (30) and, therefore, would recognise an impairment loss of 20 (50 less 30) even though the computer's cash-generating unit is not impaired.

IASC did not support this approach and believed that the computer was not impaired as long as:

(a)   *the enterprise was not committed to dispose of the computer before the end of its expected useful life; and*

(b)   *the computer's cash-generating unit was not impaired.*

BCZ18   If no deep and liquid market exists for an asset, IASC considered that value in use would be a reasonable estimate of fair value. This is likely to happen for many assets within the scope of IAS 36: observable market prices are unlikely to exist for goodwill, most intangible assets and many items of property, plant and equipment. Therefore, it is likely that the recoverable amount of these assets, determined in accordance with IAS 36, will be similar to the recoverable amount based on the fair value of these assets.

BCZ19   For some assets within the scope of IAS 36, observable market prices exist or consideration of prices for similar assets is possible. In such cases, the asset's net selling price will differ from the asset's fair value only by the direct incremental costs of disposal. IASC acknowledged that recoverable amount as the higher of net selling price and value in use would sometimes differ from fair value primarily based on market prices (even if the disposal costs are negligible). This is because, as explained in paragraph BCZ17(a), the market may not use the same assumptions about future cash flows as an individual enterprise.[15]

BCZ20   IASC believed that IAS 36 included sufficient requirements to prevent an enterprise from using assumptions different from the marketplace that are unjustified. For example, an enterprise is required to determine value in use using:

(a)   cash flow projections based on reasonable and supportable assumptions and giving greater weight to external evidence; and

(b)   a discount rate that reflects current market assessments of the time value of money and the risks specific to the asset.

---

15   IFRS 13, issued in May 2011, describes the objective of a fair value measurement and the use of market participant assumptions.

Recoverable amount based on value in use

BCZ21 Some argue that value in use is the only appropriate measurement for the recoverable amount of an asset because:

(a) financial statements are prepared under a going concern assumption. Therefore, no consideration should be given to an alternative measurement that reflects a disposal, unless this reflects the enterprise's intentions.

(b) assets should not be carried at amounts higher than their service potential from use by the enterprise. Unlike value in use, a market value does not necessarily reflect the service potential of an asset.

Few commentators on E55 supported this view.

BCZ22 IASC rejected this proposal because:

(a) if an asset's net selling price is higher than its value in use, a rational enterprise will dispose of the asset. In this situation, it is logical to base recoverable amount on the asset's net selling price to avoid recognising an impairment loss that is unrelated to economic reality.

(b) if an asset's net selling price is greater than its value in use, but management decides to keep the asset, the extra loss (the difference between net selling price and value in use) properly falls in later periods because it results from management's decision in these later periods to keep the asset.

Recoverable amount based on the higher of net selling price and value in use[16]

BCZ23 The requirement that recoverable amount should be the higher of net selling price and value in use stems from the decision that measurement of the recoverable amount of an asset should reflect the likely behaviour of a rational management. Furthermore, no preference should be given to the market's expectation of the recoverable amount of an asset (basis for net selling price) over a reasonable estimate performed by the individual enterprise which owns the asset (basis for value in use) or vice versa (see paragraphs BCZ17–BCZ20 and BCZ22). It is uncertain whether the assumptions of the market or the enterprise are more likely to be true. Currently, perfect markets do not exist for many of the assets within the scope of IAS 36 and it is unlikely that predictions of the future will be entirely accurate, regardless of who makes them.

BCZ24 IASC acknowledged that an enterprise would use judgement in determining whether an impairment loss needed to be recognised. For this reason, IAS 36 included some safeguards to limit the risk that an enterprise may make an over-optimistic (pessimistic) estimate of recoverable amount:

(a) IAS 36 requires a formal estimate of recoverable amount whenever there is an indication that:

(i) an asset may be impaired; or

---

16 In IFRS 5 *Non-current Assets Held for Sale and Discontinued Operations*, issued by the IASB in 2004, the term 'net selling price' was replaced in IAS 36 by 'fair value less costs to sell'.

© IFRS Foundation

(ii) an impairment loss may no longer exist or may have decreased.

For this purpose, IAS 36 includes a relatively detailed (although not exhaustive) list of indicators that an asset may be impaired (see paragraphs 12 and 111 of IAS 36).

(b) IAS 36 provides guidelines for the basis of management's projections of future cash flows to be used to estimate value in use (see paragraph 33 of IAS 36).

BCZ25 IASC considered the cost of requiring an enterprise to determine both net selling price and value in use, if the amount determined first is below an asset's carrying amount. IASC concluded that the benefits of such a requirement outweigh the costs.

BCZ26 The majority of the commentators on E55 supported IASC's view that recoverable amount should be measured at the higher of net selling price and value in use.

Assets held for disposal

BCZ27 IASC considered whether the recoverable amount of an asset held for disposal should be measured only at the asset's net selling price. When an enterprise expects to dispose of an asset within the near future, the net selling price of the asset is normally close to its value in use. Indeed, the value in use usually consists mostly of the net proceeds to be received for the asset, since future cash flows from continuing use are usually close to nil. Therefore, IASC believed that the definition of recoverable amount as included in IAS 36 is appropriate for assets held for disposal without a need for further requirements or guidance.

Other refinements to the measurement of recoverable amount

Replacement cost as a ceiling

BCZ28 Some argue that the replacement cost of an asset should be adopted as a ceiling for its recoverable amount. They argue that the value of an asset to the business would not exceed the amount that the enterprise would be willing to pay for the asset at the balance sheet date.

BCZ29 IASC believed that replacement cost techniques are not appropriate to measuring the recoverable amount of an asset. This is because replacement cost measures the cost of an asset and not the future economic benefits recoverable from its use and/or disposal.

Appraisal values

BCZ30 In some cases, an enterprise might seek external appraisal of recoverable amount. External appraisal is not a separate technique in its own right. IASC believed that if appraisal values are used, an enterprise should verify that the external appraisal follows the requirements of IAS 36.

Net selling price (paragraphs 25–29)[17]

BCZ31   IAS 36 defines net selling price as the amount obtainable from the sale of an asset in an arm's length transaction between knowledgeable, willing parties, less the incremental costs directly attributable to the disposal of the asset.

BCZ32   In other words, net selling price reflects the market's expectations of the future cash flows for an asset after the market's consideration of the time value of money and the risks inherent in receiving those cash flows, less the disposal costs.

BCZ33   Some argue that direct incremental costs of disposal should not be deducted from the amount obtainable from the sale of an asset because, unless management has decided to dispose of the asset, the going concern assumption should apply.

BCZ34   IASC believed that it is appropriate to deduct direct incremental costs of disposal in determining net selling price because the purpose of the exercise is to determine the net amount that an enterprise could recover from the sale of an asset at the date of the measurement and to compare it with the alternative of keeping the asset and using it.

BCZ35   IAS 36 indicates that termination benefits (as defined in IAS 19 *Employee Benefits*) and costs associated with reducing or reorganising a business following the disposal of an asset are not direct incremental costs to dispose of the asset. IASC considered these costs as incidental to (rather than a direct consequence of) the disposal of an asset. In addition, this guidance is consistent with the direction of the project on provisions.[18]

BCZ36   Although the definition of 'net selling price' would be similar to a definition of 'net fair value', IASC decided to use the term 'net selling price' instead of 'net fair value'. IASC believed that the term 'net selling price' better describes the amount that an enterprise should determine and that will be compared with an asset's value in use.

Net realisable value

BCZ37   IAS 2 *Inventories* defines net realisable value as:

'... the estimated selling price in the ordinary course of business ... less the estimated costs necessary to make the sale ...'

BCZ38   For the purpose of determining recoverable amount, IASC decided not to use the term 'net realisable value' as defined in IAS 2 because:

(a)   IAS 2's definition of net realisable value does not refer explicitly to transactions carried out on an arm's length basis.

---

17   In IFRS 5 *Non-current Assets Held for Sale and Discontinued Operations*, issued by the IASB in 2004, the term 'net selling price' was replaced in IAS 36 by 'fair value less costs to sell'.

18   IASC approved an International Accounting Standard on provisions, contingent liabilities and contingent assets in 1998.

(b)   net realisable value refers to an estimated selling price in the ordinary course of business. In certain cases, net selling price will reflect a forced sale, if management is compelled to sell immediately.

(c)   it is important that net selling price uses, as a starting point, a selling price agreed between knowledgeable, willing buyers and sellers. This is not explicitly mentioned in the definition of net realisable value.

BCZ39   In most cases, net selling price and net realisable value will be similar. However, IASC did not believe that it was necessary to change the definition of net realisable value used in IAS 2 because, for inventories, the definition of net realisable value is well understood and seems to work satisfactorily.

Value in use (paragraphs 30–57 and Appendix A)

BCZ40   IAS 36 defines value in use as the present value of the future cash flows expected to be derived from an asset.

Expected value approach

BCZ41   Some argue that, to better reflect uncertainties in timing and amounts inherent in estimated future cash flows, expected future cash flows should be used in determining value in use. An expected value approach considers all expectations about possible future cash flows instead of the single, most likely, future cash flows.

Example
An enterprise estimates that there are two scenarios for future cash flows: a first possibility of future cash flows amounts to 120 with a 40 per cent probability and a second possibility amounts to 80 with a 60 per cent probability. *The most likely future cash flows would be 80 and the expected future cash flows would be 96 (80 × 60% + 120 × 40%).*

BCZ42   In most cases, it is likely that budgets/forecasts that are the basis for cash flow projections will reflect a single estimate of future cash flows only. For this reason, IASC decided that an expected value approach should be permitted but not required.

Future cash flows from internally generated goodwill and synergy with other assets

BCZ43   IASC rejected a proposal that estimates of future cash inflows should reflect only future cash inflows relating to the asset that was initially recognised (or the remaining portion of that asset if part of it has already been consumed or sold). The purpose of such a requirement would be to avoid including in an asset's value in use future cash inflows from internally generated goodwill or from synergy with other assets. This would be consistent with IASC's proposal in E60 *Intangible Assets* to prohibit the recognition of internally generated goodwill as an asset.[19]

BCZ44   In many cases, it will not be possible in practice to distinguish future cash inflows from the asset initially recognised from the future cash inflows from internally generated goodwill or a modification of the asset. This is particularly true when businesses are merged or once an asset has been enhanced by subsequent expenditure. IASC concluded that it is more important to focus on whether the carrying amount of an asset will be recovered rather than on whether the recovery stems partly from internally generated goodwill.

BCZ45   The proposal—that future cash inflows should reflect only future cash inflows relating to the asset that was initially recognised—would also conflict with the requirement under IAS 36 that cash flow projections should reflect reasonable and supportable assumptions that represent management's best estimate of the set of economic conditions that will exist over the remaining useful life of the asset (see paragraph 33 of IAS 36). Therefore, the Standard requires that future cash inflows should be estimated for an asset in its current condition, whether or not these future cash inflows are from the asset that was initially recognised or from its subsequent enhancement or modification.

Example

Several years ago, an enterprise purchased a customer list with 10,000 addresses that it recognised as an intangible asset. The enterprise uses this list for direct marketing of its products. Since initial recognition, about 2,000 customer addresses have been deleted from the list and 3,000 new customer addresses added to it. The enterprise is determining the value in use of the customer list.

Under the proposal (rejected by IASC) that an enterprise should reflect only future cash inflows relating to the asset that was initially recognised, the enterprise would consider only those future cash inflows generated by the remaining 8,000 (10,000 less 2,000) customers from the list acquired.

Under IAS 36, an enterprise considers the future cash inflows generated by the customer list in its current condition, ie by all 11,000 customers (8,000 plus 3,000).

Value in use estimated in a foreign currency (paragraph 54)

BCZ46   In response to comments from field test participants, paragraph 54 of IAS 36 includes guidance on calculating the value in use of an asset that generates future cash flows in a foreign currency. IAS 36 indicates that value in use in a foreign currency is translated into the reporting currency[20] using the spot exchange rate at the balance sheet date.

---

19   IASC approved an International Accounting Standard on intangible assets in 1998.
20   In IAS 21 *The Effects of Changes in Foreign Exchange Rates*, as revised by the IASB in 2003, the term 'reporting currency' was replaced by 'functional currency'.

BCZ47   If a currency is freely convertible and traded in an active market, the spot rate reflects the market's best estimate of future events that will affect that currency. Therefore, the only available unbiased estimate of a future exchange rate is the current spot rate, adjusted by the difference in expected future rates of general inflation in the two countries to which the currencies belong.

BCZ48   A value in use calculation already deals with the effect of general inflation since it is calculated either by:

(a)   estimating future cash flows in nominal terms (ie including the effect of general inflation and specific price changes) and discounting them at a rate that includes the effects of general inflation; or

(b)   estimating future cash flows in real terms (ie excluding the effect of general inflation but including the effect of specific price changes) and discounting them at a rate that excludes the effect of general inflation.

BCZ49   To use a forward rate to translate value in use expressed in a foreign currency would be inappropriate. This is because a forward rate reflects the market's adjustment for the differential in interest rates. Using such a rate would result in double-counting the time value of money (first in the discount rate and then in the forward rate).

BCZ50   Even if a currency is not freely convertible or is not traded in an active market—with the consequence that it can no longer be assumed that the spot exchange rate reflects the market's best estimate of future events that will affect that currency—IAS 36 indicates that an enterprise uses the spot exchange rate at the balance sheet date to translate value in use estimated in a foreign currency. This is because IASC believed that it is unlikely that an enterprise can make a more reliable estimate of future exchange rates than the current spot exchange rate.

BCZ51   An alternative to estimating the future cash flows in the currency in which they are generated would be to estimate them in another currency as a proxy and discount them at a rate appropriate for this other currency. This solution may be simpler, particularly where cash flows are generated in the currency of a hyperinflationary economy (in such cases, some would prefer using a hard currency as a proxy) or in a currency other than the reporting currency. However, this solution may be misleading if the exchange rate varies for reasons other than changes in the differential between the general inflation rates in the two countries to which the currencies belong. In addition, this solution is inconsistent with the approach under IAS 29 *Financial Reporting in Hyperinflationary Economies*, which does not allow, if the reporting currency[21] is the currency of a hyperinflationary economy, translation into a hard currency as a proxy for restatement in terms of the measuring unit current at the balance sheet date.

---

21 In IAS 21 *The Effects of Changes in Foreign Exchange Rates*, as revised by the IASB in 2003, the term 'reporting currency' was replaced by 'functional currency'.

Discount rate (paragraphs 55–57 and A15–A21)

BCZ52 The purpose of discounting future cash flows is to reflect the time value of money and the uncertainties attached to those cash flows:

(a) assets that generate cash flows soon are worth more than those generating the same cash flows later. All rational economic transactions will take account of the time value of money. The cost of not receiving a cash inflow until some date in the future is an opportunity cost that can be measured by considering what income has been lost by not investing that money for the period. The time value of money, before consideration of risk, is given by the rate of return on a risk-free investment, such as government bonds of the same duration.

(b) the value of the future cash flows is affected by the variability (ie the risks) associated with the cash flows. Therefore, all rational economic transactions will take risk into account.

BCZ53 As a consequence IASC decided:

(a) to reject a discount rate based on a historical rate—ie the effective rate implicit when an asset was acquired. A subsequent estimate of recoverable amount has to be based on prevailing interest rates because management's decisions about whether to keep the asset are based on prevailing economic conditions. Historical rates do not reflect prevailing economic conditions.

(b) to reject a discount rate based on a risk-free rate, unless the future cash flows have been adjusted for all the risks specific to the asset.

(c) to require that the discount rate should be a rate that reflects current market assessments of the time value of money and the risks specific to the asset. This rate is the return that investors would require if they were to choose an investment that would generate cash flows of amounts, timing and risk profile equivalent to those that the enterprise expects to derive from the asset.

BCZ54 In principle, value in use should be an enterprise-specific measure determined in accordance with the enterprise's own view of the best use of that asset. Logically, the discount rate should be based on the enterprise's own assessment both of the time value of money and of the risks specific to the future cash flows from the asset. However, IASC believed that such a rate could not be verified objectively. Therefore, IAS 36 requires that the enterprise should make its own estimate of future cash flows but that the discount rate should reflect, as far as possible, the market's assessment of the time value of money. Similarly, the discount rate should reflect the premium that the market would require from uncertain future cash flows based on the distribution estimated by the enterprise.

BCZ55 IASC acknowledged that a current asset-specific market-determined rate would rarely exist for the assets covered by IAS 36. Therefore, an enterprise uses current market-determined rates for other assets (as similar as possible to the asset under review) as a starting point and adjusts these rates to reflect the risks specific to the asset for which the cash flow projections have not been adjusted.

Additional guidance included in the Standard in 2004

Elements reflected in value in use (paragraphs 30–32)

BC56 The Exposure Draft of Proposed Amendments to IAS 36 proposed, and the revised Standard includes, additional guidance to clarify:

(a) the elements that are reflected in an asset's value in use; and

(b) that some of those elements (ie expectations about possible variations in the amount or timing of future cash flows, the price for bearing the uncertainty inherent in the asset, and other factors that market participants would reflect in pricing the future cash flows the entity expects to derive from the asset) can be reflected either as adjustments to the future cash flows or as adjustments to the discount rate.

The Board decided to include this additional guidance in the Exposure Draft in response to a number of requests from its constituents for clarification of the requirements in the previous version of IAS 36 on measuring value in use.

BC57 Respondents to the Exposure Draft generally agreed with the proposals. Those that disagreed varied widely in their views, arguing that:

(a) IAS 36 should be amended to permit entities to measure value in use using methods other than discounting of future cash flows.

(b) when measuring the value in use of an intangible asset, entities should be required to reflect the price for bearing the uncertainty inherent in the asset as adjustments to the future cash flows.

(c) it is inconsistent with the definition of value in use to reflect in that measure the other factors that market participants would reflect in pricing the future cash flows the entity expects to derive from the asset—this element refers to market pricing of an asset rather than to the value to the entity of the asset. Other factors should be reflected in value in use only to the extent that they affect the cash flows the entity can achieve from the asset.

BC58 In considering (a) above, the Board observed that the measure of recoverable amount in IAS 36 (ie higher of value in use and fair value less costs to sell) stems from IASC's decision that an asset's recoverable amount should reflect the likely behaviour of a rational management, with no preference given to the market's expectation of the recoverable amount of an asset (ie fair value less costs to sell) over a reasonable estimate performed by the entity that controls the asset (ie value in use) or vice versa (see paragraph BCZ23). In developing the Exposure Draft and revising IAS 36, the Board concluded that it would be inappropriate to modify the measurement basis adopted in the previous version of IAS 36 for determining recoverable amount until the Board considers and resolves the broader question of the appropriate measurement objective(s) in accounting. Moreover, IAS 36 does not preclude the use of other valuation techniques in estimating fair value less costs to sell. For example, paragraph 27 of the Standard states that 'If there is no binding sale agreement or active market for an asset, fair value less costs to sell is based on the best information available to reflect the amount that an entity could obtain, at the balance sheet date, from the disposal of the asset in an arm's length transaction between knowledgeable, willing parties, after deducting the costs of disposal.'[22]

BC59 In considering (b) above, the Board observed that the previous version of IAS 36 permitted risk adjustments to be reflected either in the cash flows or in the discount rate, without indicating a preference. The Board could see no justification for amending this approach to require risk adjustments for uncertainty to be factored into the cash flows, particularly given the Board's inclination to avoid modifying the requirements in the previous version of IAS 36 for determining recoverable amount until it considers and resolves the broader question of measurement in accounting. Additionally, the Board as part of its consultative process conducted field visits and round-table discussions during the comment period for the Exposure Draft.[23] Many field visit participants indicated a preference for reflecting such risk adjustments in the discount rate.

BC60 In considering (c) above, the Board observed that the measure of value in use adopted in IAS 36 is not a pure 'entity-specific' measure. Although the cash flows used as the starting point in the calculation represent entity-specific cash flows (ie they are derived from the most recent financial budgets/forecasts approved by management and represent management's best estimate of the set of economic conditions that will exist over the remaining useful life of the asset), their present value is required to be determined using a discount rate that reflects current market assessments of the time value of money and the risks specific to the asset. Paragraph 56 of the Standard (paragraph 49 of the previous version of IAS 36) clarifies that 'A rate that reflects current market assessments of the time value of money and the risks specific to the asset is the return that investors would require if they were to choose an investment that would generate cash flows of amounts, timing and risk profile equivalent to those that the entity expects to derive from the asset.' In other words, an asset's value in use reflects how the market would price the cash flows that management expects to derive from that asset.

BC61 Therefore, the Board concluded that:

(a) it is consistent with the measure of value in use adopted in IAS 36 to include in the list of elements the other factors that market participants would reflect in pricing the future cash flows the entity expects to derive from the asset.

(b) all of the elements proposed in the Exposure Draft (and listed in paragraph 30 of the revised Standard) should be reflected in the calculation of an asset's value in use.

---

22 IFRS 13, issued in May 2011, contains the requirements for measuring fair value. As a consequence paragraph 27 of IAS 36 has been deleted.

23 The field visits were conducted from early December 2002 to early April 2003, and involved IASB members and staff in meetings with 41 companies in Australia, France, Germany, Japan, South Africa, Switzerland and the United Kingdom. IASB members and staff also took part in a series of round-table discussions with auditors, preparers, accounting standard-setters and regulators in Canada and the United States on implementation issues encountered by North American companies during first-time application of US Statements of Financial Accounting Standards 141 *Business Combinations* and 142 *Goodwill and Other Intangible Assets*, and the equivalent Canadian Handbook Sections, which were issued in June 2001.

to be the arm's length price the entity paid to acquire the unit, adjusted for disposal costs and for any changes in economic circumstances between the transaction date and the date at which the estimate is made.

(c)   if the unit's fair value less costs to sell were to be otherwise estimated, it would also reflect the market's assessment of the expected net benefits any acquirer would be able to derive from restructuring the unit or from future capital expenditure on the unit.

BC70   Therefore, all else being equal, the unit's recoverable amount would be its fair value less costs to sell, rather than its value in use. As such, the net benefits of the restructuring would be reflected in the unit's recoverable amount, meaning that an impairment loss would arise only to the extent of any material disposal costs.

BC71   The Board acknowledged that treating the newly acquired unit's fair value less costs to sell as its recoverable amount seems inconsistent with the reason underpinning a 'higher of fair value less costs to sell and value in use' recoverable amount measurement objective. Measuring recoverable amount as the higher of fair value less costs to sell and value in use is intended to reflect the economic decisions that are made when an asset becomes impaired: is it better to sell or keep using the asset?

BC72   Nevertheless, the Board concluded that:

(a)   amending IAS 36 to include in value in use calculations the costs and benefits of future restructurings to which the entity is not yet committed would be a significant change to the concept of value in use adopted in the previous version of IAS 36. That concept is 'value in use for the asset in its current condition'.

(b)   the concept of value in use in IAS 36 should not be modified as part of the Business Combinations project, but should be reconsidered only once the Board considers and resolves the broader question of the appropriate measurement objectives in accounting.

BC73   The second issue the Board considered related to what some respondents suggested was a conflict between the requirements in paragraphs 27(b) and 37 of the previous version of IAS 36 (now paragraphs 33(b) and 44). Paragraph 27(b) required value in use to be based on the most recent forecasts approved by management—which would be likely to reflect management's intentions in relation to future restructurings and future capital expenditure—whereas paragraph 37 required value in use to exclude the effects of a future restructuring to which the enterprise is not yet committed and future capital expenditure that will improve or enhance the asset in excess of its originally assessed standard of performance.[27]

---

27   The requirement to exclude future capital expenditure that will improve or enhance the asset in excess of its originally assessed standard of performance was amended in 2003 as a consequential amendment arising from the revision of IAS 16 *Property, Plant and Equipment*. Paragraph 44 of IAS 36 now requires estimates of future cash flows to exclude future cash inflows or outflows that are expected to arise from improving or enhancing the asset's performance.

BC74   The Board concluded that it is clear from the Basis for Conclusions on the previous version of IAS 36 that IASC's intention was that value in use should be calculated using estimates of future cash inflows for an asset in its current, condition. The Board nevertheless agreed with respondents that the requirement for value in use to be based on the most recent forecasts approved by management could be viewed as inconsistent with paragraph 37 of the previous version of IAS 36 when those forecasts include either future restructurings to which the entity is not yet committed or future cash flows associated with improving or enhancing the asset's performance.

BC75   Therefore, the Board decided to clarify, in what is now paragraph 33(b) of the revised Standard, that cash flow projections should be based on the most recent financial budgets/forecasts that have been approved by management, but should exclude any estimated future cash inflows or outflows expected to arise from future restructurings or from improving or enhancing the asset's performance. The Board also decided to clarify that when a cash-generating unit contains assets with different estimated useful lives (or, similarly, when an asset comprises components with different estimated useful lives), the replacement of assets (components) with shorter lives is considered to be part of the day-to-day servicing of the unit (asset) when estimating the future cash flows associated with the unit (asset).

Using present value techniques to measure value in use (paragraphs A1–A14)

BC76   The Exposure Draft proposed additional application guidance on using present value techniques in measuring value in use. The Board decided to include this additional guidance in the Exposure Draft in response to requests for clarification of the requirements in the previous version of IAS 36 on measuring value in use.

BC77   Respondents to the Exposure Draft were generally supportive of the additional guidance. Those that were not varied in their views, suggesting that:

(a)   limiting the guidance to a brief appendix to IAS 36 is insufficient.

(b)   although the guidance is useful, it detracts from the main purpose of IAS 36, which is to establish accounting principles for impairment testing assets. Therefore, the guidance should be omitted from the Standard.

(c)   entities should be required to use an expected cash flow approach to measure value in use.

(d)   an expected cash flow approach is not consistent with how transactions are priced by management and should be prohibited.

BC78   In considering (a) and (b) above, the Board noted that the respondents that commented on the additional guidance generally agreed that it is useful and sufficient.

BC79   In considering (c) and (d) above, the Board observed that the previous version of IAS 36 did not require value in use to be calculated using an expected cash flow approach, nor did it prohibit such an approach. The Board could see no justification for requiring or prohibiting the use of an expected cash flow approach, particularly given the Board's inclination to avoid modifying the requirements in the previous version of IAS 36 for determining recoverable amount until it considers and resolves the broader measurement issues in accounting. Additionally, in relation to (d), some field visit participants said that they routinely undertake sensitivity and statistical analysis as the basis for using an expected value approach to budgeting/forecasting and strategic decision-making.

BC80 Therefore, the Board decided to include in the revised Standard the application guidance on using present value techniques that was proposed in the Exposure Draft.

Income taxes

Consideration of future tax cash flows

BCZ81 Future income tax cash flows may affect recoverable amount. It is convenient to analyse future tax cash flows into two components:

(a) the future tax cash flows that would result from any difference between the tax base of an asset (the amount attributed to it for tax purposes) and its carrying amount, after recognition of any impairment loss. Such differences are described in IAS 12 *Income Taxes* as 'temporary differences'.

(b) the future tax cash flows that would result if the tax base of the asset were equal to its recoverable amount.

BCZ82 For most assets, an enterprise recognises the tax consequences of temporary differences as a deferred tax liability or deferred tax asset in accordance with IAS 12. Therefore, to avoid double-counting, the future tax consequences of those temporary differences—the first component referred to in paragraph BCZ81—are not considered in determining recoverable amount (see further discussion in paragraphs BCZ86–BCZ89).

BCZ83 The tax base of an asset on initial recognition is normally equal to its cost. Therefore, net selling price[28] implicitly reflects market participants' assessment of the future tax cash flows that would result if the tax base of the asset were equal to its recoverable amount. Therefore, no adjustment is required to net selling price to reflect the second component referred to in paragraph BCZ81.

BCZ84 In principle, value in use should include the present value of the future tax cash flows that would result if the tax base of the asset were equal to its value in use—the second component referred to in paragraph BCZ81. Nevertheless it may be burdensome to estimate the effect of that component. This is because:

(a) to avoid double-counting, it is necessary to exclude the effect of temporary differences; and

---

28 In IFRS 5 *Non-current Assets Held for Sale and Discontinued Operations*, issued by the IASB in 2004, the term 'net selling price' was replaced in IAS 36 by 'fair value less costs to sell'.

(b) value in use would need to be determined by an iterative and possibly complex computation so that value in use itself reflects a tax base equal to that value in use.

For these reasons, IASC decided to require an enterprise to determine value in use by using pre-tax future cash flows and, hence, a pre-tax discount rate.

Determining a pre-tax discount rate

BCZ85 In theory, discounting post-tax cash flows at a post-tax discount rate and discounting pre-tax cash flows at a pre-tax discount rate should give the same result, as long as the pre-tax discount rate is the post-tax discount rate adjusted to reflect the specific amount and timing of the future tax cash flows. The pre-tax discount rate is not always the post-tax discount rate grossed up by a standard rate of tax.

Example

This example illustrates that a post-tax discount rate grossed-up by a standard rate of tax is not always an appropriate pre-tax discount rate.

At the end of 20X0, the carrying amount of an asset is 1,757 and its remaining useful life is 5 years. The tax base in 20X0 is the cost of the asset. The cost is fully deductible at the end of 20X1. The tax rate is 20%. The discount rate for the asset can be determined only on a post-tax basis and is estimated to be 10%. At the end of 20X0, cash flow projections determined on a pre-tax basis are as follows:

		20X1	20X2	20X3	20X4	20X5
(1)	Pre-tax cash flows (CF)	800	600	500	200	100

Value in use determined using post-tax cash flows and a post-tax discount rate

End of 20X0		20X1	20X2	20X3	20X4	20X5
(2)	Deduction of the cost of					
	the asset	(1,757)	–	–	–	–
(3)	Tax CF [((1) – (2)) × 20%]	(191)	120	100	40	20
(4)	Post-tax CF [(1) – (3)]	991	480	400	160	80
(5)	Post-tax CF discounted at					
	10%	901	396	301	109	50
Value in use [Σ (5)] =						1,757

continued...

...continued

Example

Value in use determined using pre-tax cash flows and a pre-tax discount rate (determined by grossing-up the post-tax discount rate)

Pre-tax discount rate (grossed-up) [10%/(100% − 20%)] 12.5%

End of 20X0		20X1	20X2	20X3	20X4	20X5
(6)	Pre-tax CF discounted at					
	12.5%	711	475	351	125	55
Value in use [Σ(6)] =						1,717

Determination of the 'real' pre-tax discount rate

A pre-tax discount rate can be determined by an iterative computation so that value in use determined using pre-tax cash flows and a pre-tax discount rate equals value in use determined using post-tax cash flows and a post-tax discount rate. In the example, the pre-tax discount rate would be 11.2%.

End of 20X0		20X1	20X2	20X3	20X4	20X5
(7)	Pre-tax CF discounted at					
	11.2%	718	485	364	131	59
Value in use [Σ(7)] =						1,757

The 'real' pre-tax discount rate differs from the post-tax discount rate grossed-up by the standard rate of tax depending on the tax rate, the post-tax discount rate, the timing of the future tax cash flows and the useful life of the asset. Note that the tax base of the asset in this example has been set equal to its cost at the end of 20X0. Therefore, there is no deferred tax to consider in the balance sheet.

Interaction with IAS 12

BCZ86   IAS 36 requires that recoverable amount should be based on present value calculations, whereas under IAS 12 an enterprise determines deferred tax assets and liabilities by comparing the carrying amount of an asset (a present value if the carrying amount is based on recoverable amount) with its tax base (an undiscounted amount).

BCZ87   One way to eliminate this inconsistency would be to measure deferred tax assets and liabilities on a discounted basis. In developing the revised version of IAS 12 (approved in 1996), there was not enough support to require that deferred tax assets and liabilities should be measured on a discounted basis. IASC believed there was still not consensus to support such a change in existing practice. Therefore, IAS 36 requires an enterprise to measure the tax effects of temporary differences using the principles set out in IAS 12.

BCZ88   IAS 12 does not permit an enterprise to recognise certain deferred tax liabilities and assets. In such cases, some believe that the value in use of an asset, or a cash-generating unit, should be adjusted to reflect the tax consequences of recovering its pre-tax value in use. For example, if the tax rate is 25 per cent, an enterprise must receive pre-tax cash flows with a present value of 400 in order to recover a carrying amount of 300.

BCZ89　IASC acknowledged the conceptual merit of such adjustments but concluded that they would add unnecessary complexity. Therefore, IAS 36 neither requires nor permits such adjustments.

Comments by field visit participants and respondents to the December 2002 Exposure Draft

BC90　In revising IAS 36, the Board considered the requirement in the previous version of IAS 36 for:

(a)　income tax receipts and payments to be excluded from the estimates of future cash flows used to measure value in use; and

(b)　the discount rate used to measure value in use to be a pre-tax rate that reflects current market assessments of the time value of money and the risks specific to the asset for which the future cash flow estimates have not been adjusted.

BC91　The Board had not considered these requirements when developing the Exposure Draft. However, some field visit participants and respondents to the Exposure Draft stated that using pre-tax cash flows and pre-tax discount rates would be a significant implementation issue for entities. This is because typically an entity's accounting and strategic decision-making systems are fully integrated and use post-tax cash flows and post-tax discount rates to arrive at present value measures.

BC92　In considering this issue, the Board observed that the definition of value in use in the previous version of IAS 36 and the associated requirements on measuring value in use were not sufficiently precise to give a definitive answer to the question of what tax attribute an entity should reflect in value in use. For example, although IAS 36 specified discounting pre-tax cash flows at a pre-tax discount rate—with the pre-tax discount rate being the post-tax discount rate adjusted to reflect the specific amount and timing of the future tax cash flows—it did not specify *which* tax effects the pre-tax rate should include. Arguments could be mounted for various approaches.

BC93　The Board decided that any decision to amend the requirement in the previous version of IAS 36 for pre-tax cash flows to be discounted at a pre-tax discount rate should be made only after the Board has resolved the issue of what tax attribute should be reflected in value in use. The Board decided that it should not try to resolve this latter issue as part of the Business Combinations project—decisions on the treatment of tax in value in use calculations should be made only as part of its conceptual project on measurement. Therefore, the Board concluded it should not amend as part of the current revision of IAS 36 the requirement to use pre-tax cash flows and pre-tax discount rates when measuring value in use.

BC94　However, the Board observed that, conceptually, discounting post-tax cash flows at a post-tax discount rate and discounting pre-tax cash flows at a pre-tax discount rate should give the same result, as long as the pre-tax discount rate is the post-tax discount rate adjusted to reflect the specific amount and timing of the future tax cash flows. The pre-tax discount rate is generally not the post-tax discount rate grossed up by a standard rate of tax.

Recognition of an impairment loss (paragraphs 58–64)

BCZ95   IAS 36 requires that an impairment loss should be recognised whenever the recoverable amount of an asset is below its carrying amount. IASC considered various criteria for recognising an impairment loss in the financial statements:

(a)   recognition if it is considered that the impairment loss is permanent ('permanent criterion');

(b)   recognition if it is considered probable that an asset is impaired, ie if it is probable that an enterprise will not recover the carrying amount of the asset ('probability criterion'); and

(c)   immediate recognition whenever recoverable amount is below the carrying amount ('economic criterion').

Recognition based on a 'permanent' criterion

BCZ96   Supporters of the 'permanent' criterion argue that:

(a)   this criterion avoids the recognition of temporary decreases in the recoverable amount of an asset.

(b)   the recognition of an impairment loss refers to future operations; it is contrary to the historical cost system to account for future events. Also, depreciation (amortisation) will reflect these future losses over the expected remaining useful life of the asset.

This view was supported by only a few commentators on E55 *Impairment of Assets*.

BCZ97   IASC decided to reject the 'permanent' criterion because:

(a)   it is difficult to identify whether an impairment loss is permanent. There is a risk that, by using this criterion, recognition of an impairment loss may be delayed.

(b)   this criterion is at odds with the basic concept that an asset is a resource that will generate future economic benefits. Cost-based accrual accounting cannot reflect events without reference to future expectations. If the events that led to a decrease in recoverable amount have already taken place, the carrying amount should be reduced accordingly.

Recognition based on a 'probability' criterion

BCZ98   Some argue that an impairment loss should be recognised only if it is considered probable that the carrying amount of an asset cannot be fully recovered. Proponents of a 'probability' criterion are divided between:

(a)   those who support the use of a recognition trigger based on the sum of the future cash flows (undiscounted and without allocation of interest costs) as a practical approach to implementing the 'probability' criterion; and

(b)   those who support reflecting the requirements in IAS 10 (reformatted 1994) *Contingencies and Events Occurring After the Balance Sheet Date*.[29]

Sum of undiscounted future cash flows (without interest costs)

BCZ99   Some national standard-setters use the 'probability' criterion as a basis for recognition of an impairment loss and require, as a practical approach to implementing that criterion, that an impairment loss should be recognised only if the sum of the future cash flows from an asset (undiscounted and without allocation of interest costs) is less than the carrying amount of the asset. An impairment loss, when recognised, is measured as the difference between the carrying amount of the asset and its recoverable amount measured at fair value (based on quoted market prices or, if no quoted market prices exist, estimated considering prices for similar assets and the results of valuation techniques, such as the sum of cash flows discounted to their present value, option-pricing models, matrix pricing, option-adjusted spread models and fundamental analysis).[30]

BCZ100   One of the characteristics of this approach is that the bases for recognition and measurement of an impairment loss are different. For example, even if the fair value of an asset is lower than its carrying amount, no impairment loss will be recognised if the sum of undiscounted cash flows (without allocation of interest costs) is greater than the asset's carrying amount. This might occur, especially if an asset has a long useful life.

BCZ101   Those who support using the sum of undiscounted future cash flows (without allocation of interest costs) as a recognition trigger argue that:

(a)   using a recognition trigger based on undiscounted amounts is consistent with the historical cost framework.

(b)   it avoids recognising temporary impairment losses and creating potentially volatile earnings that may mislead users of financial statements.

(c)   net selling price[31] and value in use are difficult to substantiate—a price for the disposal of an asset or an appropriate discount rate is difficult to estimate.

(d)   it is a higher threshold for recognising impairment losses. It should be relatively easy to conclude that the sum of undiscounted future cash flows will equal or exceed the carrying amount of an asset without incurring the cost of allocating projected cash flows to specific future periods.

This view was supported by a minority of commentators on E55 *Impairment of Assets*.

---

29   The requirements relating to contingencies in the 1994 version of IAS 10 were replaced in 1998 with the requirements in IAS 37 *Provisions, Contingent Liabilities and Contingent Assets*.

30   IFRS 13, issued in May 2011, contains the requirements for measuring fair value.

31   In IFRS 5 *Non-current Assets Held for Sale and Discontinued Operations*, issued by the IASB in 2004, the term 'net selling price' was replaced in IAS 36 by 'fair value less costs to sell'.

BCZ102   IASC considered the arguments listed above but rejected this approach because:

   (a)   when it identifies that an asset may be impaired, a rational enterprise will make an investment decision. Therefore, it is relevant to consider the time value of money and the risks specific to an asset in determining whether an asset is impaired. This is particularly true if an asset has a long useful life.

   (b)   IAS 36 does not require an enterprise to estimate the recoverable amount of each [depreciable] asset every year but only if there is an indication that an asset may be materially impaired. An asset that is depreciated (amortised) in an appropriate manner is unlikely to become materially impaired unless events or changes in circumstances cause a sudden reduction in the estimate of recoverable amount.

   (c)   probability factors are already encompassed in the determination of value in use, in projecting future cash flows and in requiring that recoverable amount should be the higher of net selling price and value in use.

   (d)   if there is an unfavourable change in the assumptions used to determine recoverable amount, users are better served if they are informed about this change in assumptions on a timely basis.

Probability criterion based on IAS 10 (reformatted 1994)

BCZ103   IAS 10 required the amount of a contingent loss to be recognised as an expense and a liability if:

   (a)   it was probable that future events will confirm that, after taking into account any related probable recovery, an asset had been impaired or a liability incurred at the balance sheet date; and

   (b)   a reasonable estimate of the amount of the resulting loss could be made.

BCZ104   IASC rejected the view that an impairment loss should be recognised based on the requirements in IAS 10 because:

   (a)   the requirements in IAS 10 were not sufficiently detailed and would have made a 'probability' criterion difficult to apply.

   (b)   those requirements would have introduced another unnecessary layer of probability. Indeed, as mentioned above, probability factors are already encompassed in estimates of value in use and in requiring that recoverable amount should be the higher of net selling price and value in use.

Recognition based on an 'economic' criterion

BCZ105   IAS 36 relies on an 'economic' criterion for the recognition of an impairment loss—an impairment loss is recognised whenever the recoverable amount of an asset is below its carrying amount. This criterion was already used in many International Accounting Standards before IAS 36, such as IAS 9 *Research and Development Costs*, IAS 22 *Business Combinations*, and IAS 16 *Property, Plant and Equipment*.

BCZ106 IASC considered that an 'economic' criterion is the best criterion to give information which is useful to users in assessing future cash flows to be generated by the enterprise as a whole. In estimating the time value of money and the risks specific to an asset in determining whether the asset is impaired, factors, such as the probability or permanence of the impairment loss, are subsumed in the measurement.

BCZ107 The majority of commentators on E55 supported IASC's view that an impairment loss should be recognised based on an 'economic' criterion.

Revalued assets: recognition in the income statement versus directly in equity

BCZ108 IAS 36 requires that an impairment loss on a revalued asset should be recognised as an expense in the income statement[32] immediately, except that it should be recognised directly in equity[33] to the extent that it reverses a previous revaluation on the same asset.

BCZ109 Some argue that, when there is a clear reduction in the service potential (for example, physical damage) of a revalued asset, the impairment loss should be recognised in the income statement.

BCZ110 Others argue that an impairment loss should always be recognised as an expense in the income statement. The logic of this argument is that an impairment loss arises only where there is a reduction in the estimated future cash flows that form part of the business's operating activities. Indeed, according to IAS 16, whether or not an asset is revalued, the depreciation charge is always recognised in the income statement. Supporters of this view question why the treatment of an impairment loss on a revalued asset should be different to depreciation.

BCZ111 IASC believed that it would be difficult to identify whether an impairment loss is a downward revaluation or a reduction in service potential. Therefore, IASC decided to retain the treatment used in IAS 16 and to treat an impairment loss of a revalued asset as a revaluation decrease (and similarly, a reversal of an impairment loss as a subsequent revaluation increase).

BCZ112 For a revalued asset, the distinction between an 'impairment loss' ('reversal of an impairment loss') and another 'revaluation decrease' ('revaluation increase') is important for disclosure purposes. If an impairment loss that is material to the enterprise as a whole has been recognised or reversed, more information on how this impairment loss is measured is required by IAS 36 than for the recognition of a revaluation in accordance with IAS 16.

Cash-generating units (paragraphs 66–73)

BCZ113 Some support the principle of determining recoverable amount on an individual asset basis only. This view was expressed by a few commentators on E55. They argued that:

---

32 IAS 1 *Presentation of Financial Statements* (as revised in 2007) requires an entity to present all income and expense items in one statement of comprehensive income or in two statements (a separate income statement and a statement of comprehensive income).

33 As a consequence of the revision of IAS 1 (revised 2007) an impairment loss is recognised in other comprehensive income.

(a)   it would be difficult to identify cash-generating units at a level other than the business as a whole and, therefore, impairment losses would never be recognised for individual assets; and

(b)   it should be possible to recognise an impairment loss, regardless of whether an asset generates cash inflows that are independent from those of other assets or groups of assets. Commentators quoted examples of assets that have become under-utilised or obsolete but that are still in use.

BCZ114   IASC acknowledged that identifying the lowest level of independent cash inflows for a group of assets would involve judgement. However, IASC believed that the concept of cash-generating units is a matter of fact: assets work together to generate cash flows.

BCZ115   In response to requests from commentators on E55, IAS 36 includes additional guidance and examples for identifying cash-generating units and for determining the carrying amount of cash-generating units. IAS 36 emphasises that cash-generating units should be identified for the lowest level of aggregation of assets possible.

Internal transfer pricing (paragraph 70)

BC116   The previous version of IAS 36 required that if an active market exists for the output produced by an asset or a group of assets:

(a)   that asset or group of assets should be identified as a cash-generating unit, even if some or all of the output is used internally; and

(b)   management's best estimate of the future market prices for the output should be used in estimating:

(i)   the future cash inflows that relate to the internal use of the output when determining the value in use of this cash-generating unit; and

(ii)   the future cash outflows that relate to the internal use of the output when determining the value in use of the entity's other cash-generating units.

BC117   The requirement in (a) above has been carried forward in the revised Standard. However, some respondents to the Exposure Draft asked for additional guidance to clarify the role of internal transfer pricing versus prices in an arm's length transaction when developing cash flow forecasts. The Board decided to address this issue by amending the requirement in (b) above to deal more broadly with cash-generating units whose cash flows are affected by internal transfer pricing, rather than just cash-generating units whose internally consumed output could be sold on an active market.

BC118   Therefore, the Standard clarifies that if the cash inflows generated by *any* asset or cash-generating unit are affected by internal transfer pricing, an entity should use management's best estimate of future prices that could be achieved in arm's length transactions in estimating:

(a)   the future cash inflows used to determine the asset's or cash-generating unit's value in use; and

(b)   the future cash outflows used to determine the value in use of other assets or cash-generating units affected by the internal transfer pricing.

Testing indefinite-lived intangibles for impairment

BC119   As part of the first phase of its Business Combinations project, the Board concluded that:

(a)   an intangible asset should be regarded as having an indefinite useful life when, based on an analysis of all relevant factors (eg legal, regulatory, contractual, competitive and economic), there is no foreseeable limit on the period over which the asset is expected to generate net cash inflows for the entity; and

(b)   an indefinite-lived intangible should not be amortised, but should be tested regularly for impairment.

An outline of the Board's deliberations on each of these issues is provided in the Basis for Conclusions on IAS 38 *Intangible Assets*.

BC120   Having reached these conclusions, the Board then considered the form that the impairment test for indefinite-lived intangibles should take. The Board concluded that:

(a)   an indefinite-lived intangible should be tested for impairment annually, or more frequently if there is any indication that it may be impaired; and

(b)   the recoverable amounts of such assets should be measured, and impairment losses (and reversals of impairment losses) in respect of those assets should be accounted for, in accordance with the requirements in IAS 36 for assets other than goodwill.

Paragraphs BC121–BC126 outline the Board's deliberations in reaching its conclusion about the frequency and timing of impairment testing indefinite-lived intangibles. Paragraphs BC129 and BC130 outline the Board's deliberations in reaching its conclusions about measuring the recoverable amount of such assets and accounting for impairment losses and reversals of impairment losses.

Frequency and timing of impairment testing (paragraphs 9 and 10(a))

BC121   In developing the Exposure Draft, the Board observed that requiring assets to be remeasured when they are impaired is a valuation concept rather than one of cost allocation. This concept, which some have termed 'the recoverable cost concept', focuses on the benefits to be derived from the asset in the future, rather than on the process by which the cost or other carrying amount of the asset should be allocated to particular accounting periods. Therefore, the purpose of an impairment test is to assess whether the carrying amount of an asset will be recovered through use or sale of the asset. Nevertheless, allocating the depreciable amount of an asset with a limited useful life on a systematic basis over that life provides some assurance against the asset's carrying amount exceeding its recoverable amount. The Board acknowledged that non-amortisation of an intangible asset increases the reliance that must be placed on impairment reviews of that asset to ensure that its carrying amount does not exceed its recoverable amount.

BC122   Accordingly, the Exposure Draft proposed that indefinite-lived intangibles should be tested for impairment at the end of each annual reporting period. The Board concluded, however, that testing such assets annually for impairment is not a substitute for management being aware of events occurring or circumstances changing between annual tests that indicate a possible impairment. Therefore, the Exposure Draft also proposed that an entity should be required to test such assets for impairment whenever there is an indication of possible impairment, and not wait until the next annual test.

BC123   The respondents to the Exposure Draft generally supported the proposal to test indefinite-lived intangibles for impairment annually and whenever there is an indication of possible impairment. Those that disagreed argued that requiring an annual impairment test would be excessively burdensome, and recommended requiring an impairment test only when there is an indication that an indefinite-lived intangible might be impaired. After considering these comments the Board:

(a)   reaffirmed its view that non-amortisation of an intangible asset increases the reliance that must be placed on impairment reviews of that asset to ensure that its carrying amount does not exceed its recoverable amount.

(b)   concluded that IAS 36 should require indefinite-lived intangibles to be tested for impairment annually and whenever there is an indication of possible impairment.

BC124   However, as noted in paragraph BC122, the Exposure Draft proposed that the annual impairment tests for indefinite-lived intangibles should be performed at the end of each annual period. Many respondents to the Exposure Draft disagreed that IAS 36 should mandate the timing of the annual impairment tests. They argued that:

(a)   it would be inconsistent with the proposal (now a requirement) that the annual impairment test for a cash-generating unit to which goodwill has been allocated may be performed at any time during an annual period, provided the test is performed at the same time every year. There is no justification for providing less flexibility in the timing of the annual impairment test for indefinite-lived intangibles.

(b)   if the impairment test for an indefinite-lived intangible is linked to the impairment test for goodwill (ie if the indefinite-lived intangible is assessed for impairment at the same cash-generating unit level as goodwill, rather than individually or as part of a smaller cash-generating unit), the requirement to measure its recoverable amount at the end of the annual period could result in the cash-generating unit to which it (and the goodwill) belongs being tested for impairment at least twice each annual period, which is too burdensome. For example, assume a cash-generating unit contains goodwill and an indefinite-lived intangible, and that the indefinite-lived intangible is assessed for impairment at the same cash-generating unit level as goodwill. Assume also that the entity reports quarterly, has a December year-end, and decides to test goodwill for impairment at the end of the third quarter to coincide with the completion of its annual strategic planning/budgeting process. The proposal that the annual impairment test for an indefinite-lived intangible should be performed at the end of each annual period would mean that the entity would be required:

(i) to calculate at the end of each September the recoverable amount of the cash-generating unit, compare it with its carrying amount, and, if the carrying amount exceeds the recoverable amount, recognise an impairment loss for the unit by reducing the carrying amount of goodwill and allocating any remaining impairment loss to the other assets in the unit, including the indefinite-lived intangible.

(ii) to perform the same steps again each December to test the indefinite-lived intangible for impairment.

(iii) to perform the same steps again at any other time throughout the annual period if there is an indication that the cash-generating unit, the goodwill or the indefinite-lived intangible may be impaired.

BC125 In considering these comments, the Board indicated a preference for requiring entities to perform the recoverable amount calculations for both goodwill and indefinite-lived intangibles at the end of the annual period. However, the Board acknowledged that, as outlined in paragraph BC124(b), impairment tests for indefinite-lived intangibles will sometimes be linked to impairment tests for goodwill, and that many entities would find it difficult to perform all those tests at the end of the annual period.

BC126 Therefore, consistently with the annual impairment test for goodwill, the Standard permits the annual impairment test for an indefinite-lived intangible to be performed at any time during an annual period, provided it is performed at the same time every year.

Carrying forward a recoverable amount calculation (paragraph 24)

BC127 The Standard permits the most recent detailed calculation of the recoverable amount of an indefinite-lived intangible to be carried forward from a preceding period for use in the current period's impairment test, provided all of the criteria in paragraph 24 of the Standard are met.

BC128 Integral to the Board's decision that indefinite-lived intangibles should be tested for impairment annually was the view that many entities should be able to conclude that the recoverable amount of such an asset is greater than its carrying amount without actually recomputing recoverable amount. However, the Board concluded that this would be the case only if the last recoverable amount determination exceeded the carrying amount by a substantial margin, and nothing had happened since then to make the likelihood of an impairment loss other than remote. The Board concluded that, in such circumstances, permitting a detailed calculation of the recoverable amount of an indefinite-lived intangible to be carried forward from the preceding period for use in the current period's impairment test would significantly reduce the costs of applying the impairment test, without compromising its integrity.

Measuring recoverable amount and accounting for impairment losses and reversals of impairment losses

BC129   The Board could see no compelling reason why the measurement basis adopted for determining recoverable amount and the treatment of impairment losses and reversals of impairment losses for one group of identifiable assets should differ from those applying to other identifiable assets. Adopting different methods would impair the usefulness of the information provided to users about an entity's identifiable assets, because both comparability and reliability, which rest on the notion that similar transactions are accounted for in the same way, would be diminished. Therefore, the Board concluded that the recoverable amounts of indefinite-lived intangibles should be measured, and impairment losses and reversals of impairment losses in respect of those assets should be accounted for, consistently with other identifiable assets covered by the Standard.

BC130   The Board expressed some concern over the measurement basis adopted in the previous version of IAS 36 for determining recoverable amount (ie higher of value in use and net selling price) and its treatment of impairment losses and reversals of impairment losses for assets other than goodwill. However, the Board's intention in revising IAS 36 was *not* to reconsider the general approach to impairment testing. Accordingly, the Board decided that it should address concerns over that general approach as part of its future re-examination of IAS 36 in its entirety, rather than as part of its Business Combinations project.

Testing goodwill for impairment (paragraphs 80–99)

BC131   [Deleted]

BC131A   The Board concluded that goodwill should not be amortised and instead should be tested for impairment annually, or more frequently if events or changes in circumstances indicate that it might be impaired. IAS 22 *Business Combinations* required acquired goodwill to be amortised on a systematic basis over the best estimate of its useful life. There was a rebuttable presumption that its useful life did not exceed twenty years from initial recognition. If that presumption was rebutted, acquired goodwill was required to be tested for impairment in accordance with the previous version of IAS 36 at least at each financial year-end, even if there was no indication that it was impaired.

BC131B   In considering the appropriate accounting for acquired goodwill after its initial recognition, the Board examined the following three approaches:

(a)   straight-line amortisation but with an impairment test whenever there is an indication that the goodwill might be impaired;

(b)   non-amortisation but with an impairment test annually or more frequently if events or changes in circumstances indicate that the goodwill might be impaired; and

(c)   permitting entities a choice between approaches (a) and (b).

BC131C   The Board concluded, and the respondents to ED 3 *Business Combinations* that expressed a clear view on this issue generally agreed, that entities should not be allowed a choice between approaches (a) and (b). Permitting such choices impairs the usefulness of the information provided to users of financial statements because both comparability and reliability are diminished.

BC131D   The respondents to ED 3 who expressed a clear view on this issue generally supported approach (a). They put forward the following arguments in support of that approach:

(a)   acquired goodwill is an asset that is consumed and replaced by internally generated goodwill. Therefore, amortisation ensures that the acquired goodwill is recognised in profit or loss and no internally generated goodwill is recognised as an asset in its place, consistently with the general prohibition in IAS 38 on the recognition of internally generated goodwill.

(b)   conceptually, amortisation is a method of allocating the cost of acquired goodwill over the periods it is consumed, and is consistent with the approach taken to other intangible and tangible fixed assets that do not have indefinite useful lives. Indeed, entities are required to determine the useful lives of items of property, plant and equipment, and allocate their depreciable amounts on a systematic basis over those useful lives. There is no conceptual reason for treating acquired goodwill differently.

(c)   the useful life of acquired goodwill cannot be predicted with a satisfactory level of reliability, nor can the pattern in which that goodwill diminishes be known. However, systematic amortisation over an albeit arbitrary period provides an appropriate balance between conceptual soundness and operationality at an acceptable cost: it is the only practical solution to an intractable problem.

BC131E   In considering these comments, the Board agreed that achieving an acceptable level of reliability in the form of representational faithfulness while striking some balance with what is practicable was the primary challenge it faced in deliberating the subsequent accounting for goodwill. The Board observed that the useful life of acquired goodwill and the pattern in which it diminishes generally are not possible to predict, yet its amortisation depends on such predictions. As a result, the amount amortised in any given period can be described as at best an arbitrary estimate of the consumption of acquired goodwill during that period. The Board acknowledged that if goodwill is an asset, in some sense it must be true that goodwill acquired in a business combination is being consumed and replaced by internally generated goodwill, provided that an entity is able to maintain the overall value of goodwill (by, for example, expending resources on advertising and customer service). However, consistently with the view it reached in developing ED 3, the Board remained doubtful about the usefulness of an amortisation charge that reflects the consumption of acquired goodwill, when the internally generated goodwill replacing it is not recognised. Therefore, the Board reaffirmed the conclusion it reached in developing ED 3 that straight-line amortisation of goodwill over an arbitrary period fails to provide useful information. The Board noted that both anecdotal and research evidence supports this view.

BC131F   In considering respondents' comments summarised in paragraph BC131D(b), the Board noted that although the useful lives of both goodwill and tangible fixed assets are directly related to the period over which they are expected to generate net cash inflows for the entity, the expected physical utility to the entity of a tangible fixed asset places an upper limit on the asset's useful life. In other words, unlike goodwill, the useful life of a tangible fixed asset could never extend beyond the asset's expected physical utility to the entity.

BC131G   The Board reaffirmed the view it reached in developing ED 3 that if a rigorous and operational impairment test could be devised, more useful information would be provided to users of an entity's financial statements under an approach in which goodwill is not amortised, but instead tested for impairment annually or more frequently if events or changes in circumstances indicate that the goodwill might be impaired. After considering respondents' comments to the exposure draft of proposed amendments to IAS 36 on the form that such an impairment test should take, the Board concluded that a sufficiently rigorous and operational impairment test could be devised.

BC132   Paragraphs BC133–BC177 outline the Board's deliberations on the form that the impairment test for goodwill should take:

(a)   paragraphs BC137–BC159 discuss the requirements relating to the allocation of goodwill to cash-generating units and the level at which goodwill is tested for impairment.

(b)   paragraphs BC160–BC170 discuss the requirements relating to the recognition and measurement of impairment losses for goodwill, including the frequency of impairment testing.

(c)   paragraphs BC171–BC177 discuss the requirements relating to the timing of goodwill impairment tests.

BC133   As a first step in its deliberations, the Board considered the objective of the goodwill impairment test and the measure of recoverable amount that should be adopted for such a test. The Board observed that recent North American standards use fair value as the basis for impairment testing goodwill, whereas the previous version of IAS 36 and the United Kingdom standard are based on an approach under which recoverable amount is measured as the higher of value in use and net selling price.

BC134   The Board also observed that goodwill acquired in a business combination represents a payment made by an acquirer in anticipation of future economic benefits from assets that are not capable of being individually identified and separately recognised. Goodwill does not generate cash flows independently of other assets or groups of assets and therefore cannot be measured directly. Instead, it is measured as a residual amount, being the excess of the cost of a business combination over the acquirer's interest in the net fair value of the acquiree's identifiable assets, liabilities and contingent liabilities. Moreover, goodwill acquired in a business combination and goodwill generated after that business combination cannot be separately identified, because they contribute jointly to the same cash flows.[34]

BC135　The Board concluded that because it is not possible to measure separately goodwill generated internally after a business combination and to factor that measure into the impairment test for acquired goodwill, the carrying amount of goodwill will always be shielded from impairment by that internally generated goodwill. Therefore, the Board took the view that the objective of the goodwill impairment test could at best be to ensure that the carrying amount of goodwill is recoverable from future cash flows expected to be generated by both acquired goodwill and goodwill generated internally after the business combination.

BC136　The Board noted that because goodwill is measured as a residual amount, the starting point in any goodwill impairment test would have to be the recoverable amount of the operation or unit to which the goodwill relates, regardless of the measurement basis adopted for determining recoverable amount. The Board decided that until it considers and resolves the broader question of the appropriate measurement objective(s) in accounting, identifying the appropriate measure of recoverable amount for that unit would be problematic. Therefore, although the Board expressed concern over the measurement basis adopted in IAS 36 for determining recoverable amount, it decided that it should not depart from that basis when measuring the recoverable amount of a unit whose carrying amount includes acquired goodwill. The Board noted that this would have the added advantage of allowing the impairment test for goodwill to be integrated with the impairment test in IAS 36 for other assets and cash-generating units that include goodwill.

Allocating goodwill to cash-generating units (paragraphs 80–87)

BC137　The previous version of IAS 36 required goodwill to be tested for impairment as part of impairment testing the cash-generating units to which it relates. It employed a 'bottom-up/top-down' approach under which the goodwill was in effect tested for impairment by allocating its carrying amount to each of the smallest cash-generating units to which a portion of that carrying amount could be allocated on a reasonable and consistent basis.

BC138　Consistently with the previous version of IAS 36, the Exposure Draft proposed that:

(a)　goodwill should be tested for impairment as part of impairment testing the cash-generating units to which it relates; and

(b)　the carrying amount of goodwill should be allocated to each of the smallest cash-generating units to which a portion of that carrying amount can be allocated on a reasonable and consistent basis.

However, the Exposure Draft proposed additional guidance clarifying that a portion of the carrying amount of goodwill should be regarded as capable of being allocated to a cash-generating unit on a reasonable and consistent basis

---

34　In the second phase of its business combinations project, the Board revised the definition and measurement of goodwill in IFRS 3. See paragraph 32 and Appendix A of IFRS 3 (as revised in 2008).

only when that unit represents the lowest level at which management monitors the return on investment in assets that include the goodwill. That cash-generating unit could not, however, be larger than a segment based on the entity's primary reporting format determined in accordance with IAS 14 *Segment Reporting*.

BC139 In developing this proposal, the Board noted that because acquired goodwill does not generate cash flows independently of other assets or groups of assets, it can be tested for impairment only as part of impairment testing the cash-generating units to which it relates. However, the Board was concerned that in the absence of any guidance on the precise meaning of 'allocated on a reasonable and consistent basis', some might conclude that when a business combination enhances the value of all of the acquirer's pre-existing cash-generating units, any goodwill acquired in that business combination should be tested for impairment only at the level of the entity itself. The Board concluded that this should not be the case. Rather, there should be a link between the level at which goodwill is tested for impairment and the level of internal reporting that reflects the way an entity manages its operations and with which the goodwill naturally would be associated. Therefore, it was important to the Board that goodwill should be tested for impairment at a level at which information about the operations of an entity and the assets that support them is provided for internal reporting purposes.

BC140 In redeliberating this issue, the Board noted that respondents' and field visit participants' comments indicated that the Board's intention relating to the allocation of goodwill had been widely misunderstood, with many concluding that goodwill would need to be allocated to a much lower level than that intended by the Board. For example, some respondents and field visit participants were concerned that the proposal to allocate goodwill to such a low level would force entities to allocate goodwill arbitrarily to cash-generating units, and therefore to develop new or additional reporting systems to perform the test. The Board confirmed that its intention was that there should be a link between the level at which goodwill is tested for impairment and the level of internal reporting that reflects the way an entity manages its operations. Therefore, except for entities that do not monitor goodwill at or below the segment level, the proposals relating to the level of the goodwill impairment test should *not* cause entities to allocate goodwill arbitrarily to cash-generating units. Nor should they create the need for entities to develop new or additional reporting systems.

BC141 The Board observed from its discussions with field visit participants that much of the confusion stemmed from the definition of a 'cash-generating unit', when coupled with the proposal in paragraph 73 of the Exposure Draft for goodwill to be allocated to each 'smallest cash-generating unit to which a portion of the carrying amount of the goodwill can be allocated on a reasonable and consistent basis'. Additionally, field visit participants and respondents were unclear about the reference in paragraph 74 of the Exposure Draft to 'the lowest level at which management monitors the return on investments in assets that include goodwill', the most frequent question being 'what level of management?' (eg board of directors, chief executive officer, or segment management).

BC142   The Board noted that once its intention on this issue was clarified for field visit participants, they all, with the exception of one company that believes goodwill should be tested for impairment at the entity level, supported the level at which the Board believes goodwill should be tested for impairment.

BC143   The Board also noted the comment from a number of respondents and field visit participants that for some organisations, particularly those managed on a matrix basis, the proposal for cash-generating units to which the goodwill is allocated to be no larger than a segment based on the entity's *primary* reporting format could result in an outcome that is inconsistent with the Board's intention, ie that there should be a link between the level at which goodwill is tested for impairment and the level of internal reporting that reflects the way an entity manages its operations. The following example illustrates this point:

> A company managed on a matrix basis is organised primarily on a geographical basis, with product groups providing the secondary basis of segmentation. Goodwill is acquired as part of an acquisition of a product group that is present in several geographical regions, and is then monitored on an ongoing basis for internal reporting purposes as part of the product group/secondary segment. It is feasible that the secondary segment might, depending on the definition of 'larger', be 'larger' than a primary segment.

BC144   Therefore, the Board decided:

    (a)   that the Standard should require each unit or group of units to which goodwill is allocated to represent the lowest level within the entity at which the goodwill is monitored for internal management purposes.

    (b)   to clarify in the Standard that acquired goodwill should, from the acquisition date, be allocated to each of the acquirer's cash-generating units, or groups of cash-generating units, that are expected to benefit from the combination, irrespective of whether other assets or liabilities of the acquiree are assigned to those units or groups of units.

    (c)   to replace the proposal for cash-generating units or groups of units to which goodwill is allocated to be no larger than a segment based on the entity's *primary* reporting format, with the requirement that they be no larger than a segment based on either the entity's primary or the entity's secondary reporting format. The Board concluded that this amendment is necessary to ensure that entities managed on a matrix basis are able to test goodwill for impairment at the level of internal reporting that reflects the way they manage their operations.[35]

BC145   Some respondents to the Exposure Draft raised the following additional concerns on the allocation of goodwill for impairment testing purposes:

    (a)   mandating that goodwill should be allocated to at least the segment level is inappropriate—it will often result in arbitrary allocations, and entities would need to develop new or additional reporting systems.

---

35 In 2006 IAS 14 was replaced by IFRS 8 *Operating Segments*. IFRS 8 does not require disclosure of primary and secondary segment information. See paragraph BC150A.

                                  © IFRS Foundation

(b)　for convergence reasons, the level of the goodwill impairment test should be the same as the level in US Financial Accounting Standards Board Statement of Financial Accounting Standards No. 142 *Goodwill and Other Intangible Assets* (SFAS 142) (ie the reporting unit level).

(c)　cash-generating units that constitute businesses with similar characteristics should, as is required by SFAS 142, be aggregated and treated as single units, notwithstanding that they may be monitored independently for internal purposes.

BC146　In relation to (a), the Board reaffirmed the conclusion it reached when developing the Exposure Draft that requiring goodwill to be allocated to at least the segment level is necessary to avoid entities erroneously concluding that, when a business combination enhances the value of all of the acquirer's pre-existing cash-generating units, any goodwill acquired in that combination could be tested for impairment only at the level of the entity itself.

BC147　In relation to (b), the Board noted that SFAS 142 requires goodwill to be tested for impairment at a level of reporting referred to as a 'reporting unit'. A reporting unit is an operating segment (as defined in SFAS 131 *Disclosures about Segments of an Enterprise and Related Information*[36]) or one level below an operating segment (referred to as a component). A component of an operating segment is a reporting unit if the component constitutes a business for which discrete financial information is available and segment management regularly reviews the operating results of that component. However, two or more components of an operating segment must be aggregated and deemed a single reporting unit if the components have similar economic characteristics. An operating segment is deemed to be a reporting unit if all of its components are similar, if none of its components is a reporting unit, or if it comprises only a single component.

BC148　Therefore, unlike IAS 36, SFAS 142 places a limit on how far goodwill can be 'pushed down' for impairment testing (ie one level below an operating segment).

BC149　In deciding not to converge with SFAS 142 on the level of the goodwill impairment test, the Board noted the following findings from the field visits and North American round-table discussions:

(a)　most of the US registrant field visit participants stated that the Board's proposals on the level of the goodwill impairment test would result, in practice, in goodwill being tested for impairment at the same level at which it is tested in accordance with SFAS 142. However, several stated that under the Board's proposals, goodwill would be tested for impairment at a lower level than under SFAS 142. Nevertheless, they believe that the Board's approach provides users and management with more useful information.

36　The basis for identifying 'operating segments' under SFAS 131 differs from the basis for identifying segments based on the entity's primary reporting format under IAS 14. SFAS 131 defines an operating segment as a component of an enterprise (a) that engages in business activities from which it may earn revenues and incur expenses, including revenues and expenses relating to transactions with other components of the enterprise; (b) whose operating results are regularly reviewed by the enterprise's chief operating decision maker to make decisions about resources to be allocated to the segment and assess its performance; and (c) for which discrete financial information is available. IAS 14 was replaced by IFRS 8 in 2006. See paragraph BC150A.

(b) several round-table participants stated that they (or, in the case of audit firm participants, their clients) manage and have available information about their investments in goodwill at a lower level than the level of the SFAS 142 impairment test. They expressed a high level of dissatisfaction at being prevented by SFAS 142 from recognising goodwill impairments that they knew existed at these lower levels, but which 'disappeared' once the lower level units were aggregated with other units containing sufficient 'cushions' to offset the impairment loss.

BC150   In considering suggestion (c) in paragraph BC145, the Board observed that aggregating units that constitute businesses with similar characteristics could result in the disappearance of an impairment loss that management *knows* exists in a cash-generating unit because the units with which it is aggregated contain sufficient cushions to offset the impairment loss. In the Board's view, if, because of the way an entity is managed, information about goodwill impairment losses is available to management at a particular level, that information should also be available to the users of the entity's financial statements.

BC150A In 2006 IFRS 8 replaced IAS 14 and changed the basis for identifying segments. Under IAS 14, two sets of segments were identified—one based on related products and services, and the other on geographical areas. Under IFRS 8, operating segments are identified on the basis of internal reports that are regularly reviewed by the entity's chief operating decision maker in order to allocate resources to the segment and assess its performance. The objective of the change was to improve the disclosure of segment information, not to change the requirements of IAS 36 relating to the allocation of goodwill for impairment testing. The previous wording of the requirement in IAS 36 that each unit or group of units to which goodwill is allocated shall 'not be larger than a segment based on either the entity's primary or the entity's secondary reporting format determined in accordance with IAS 14' has been amended by IFRS 8 to 'not be larger than an operating segment determined in accordance with IFRS 8'. The arguments set out above in support of the original requirement based on segments determined in accordance with IAS 14 support the revised requirements based on segments determined in accordance with the requirements in IFRS 8.

BC150B Entities adopting IFRS 8 must reconsider the allocation of goodwill to cash-generating units because of the definition of operating segment introduced by IFRS 8. That definition affects the determination of the largest unit permitted by paragraph 80 of IAS 36 for testing goodwill for impairment. In 2008 the Board was made aware that divergent views had developed regarding the largest unit permitted by IAS 36 for impairment testing of goodwill. One view was that the unit is the operating segment level as defined in paragraph 5 of IFRS 8 *before* the aggregation permitted by paragraph 12 of IFRS 8. The other view was that the unit is the operating segment level as defined in paragraph 5 of IFRS 8 *after* the aggregation permitted by paragraph 12 of IFRS 8. The Board noted that the lowest level of the entity at which management monitors goodwill as required in paragraph 80(a) is the same as the lowest level of operating segments at which the chief operating decision maker regularly reviews operating results as defined in IFRS 8. The Board also noted that the linkage of the entity's goodwill monitoring level with the entity's internal reporting level is intentional, as described in paragraph BC140. The Board noted that aggregating operating segments for goodwill impairment testing into a unit larger than the level at which goodwill is monitored contradicts the rationale underlying IAS 36, as set out in paragraphs BC145–BC150. In addition, meeting the aggregation criteria of similar economic characteristics permitted in IFRS 8 does not automatically result in groups of cash-generating units that are expected to benefit from the synergies of allocated goodwill. Similarly, the aggregated segments do not necessarily represent business operations that are economically interdependent or work in concert to recover the goodwill being assessed for impairment. Therefore, in *Improvements to IFRSs* issued in April 2009, the Board amended paragraph 80(b) to state that the required unit for goodwill impairment in IAS 36 is not larger than the operating segment level as defined in paragraph 5 of IFRS 8 before the permitted aggregation.

Completing the initial allocation of goodwill (paragraphs 84 and 85)

BC151 If the initial allocation of goodwill acquired in a business combination cannot be completed before the end of the annual period in which the business combination is effected, the Exposure Draft proposed, and the revised Standard requires, that the initial allocation should be completed before the end of the first annual period beginning after the acquisition date. In contrast, ED 3 proposed, and IFRS 3 requires, that if the initial accounting for a business combination can be determined only provisionally by the end of the period in which the combination is effected, the acquirer should:

(a) account for the combination using those provisional values; and

(b) recognise any adjustments to those provisional values as a result of completing the initial accounting within twelve months of the acquisition date.[37]

BC152 Some respondents to the Exposure Draft questioned why the period to complete the initial allocation of goodwill should differ from the period to complete the initial accounting for a business combination. The Board's view is that acquirers should be allowed a longer period to complete the goodwill allocation, because that allocation often might not be able to be performed until after the initial accounting for the combination is complete. This is because the cost of the combination or the fair values at the acquisition date of the acquiree's identifiable assets, liabilities or contingent liabilities, and therefore the amount of goodwill acquired in the combination, would not be finalised until the initial accounting for the combination in accordance with IFRS 3 is complete.

---

37 In the second phase of its business combinations project, the Board clarified that adjustments to provisional values should be made only to reflect new information obtained about facts and circumstances that existed as of the acquisition date that, if known, would have affected the measurement of the amounts recognised as of that date. Such adjustments should be made within the measurement period, which shall not exceed one year from the acquisition date.

Disposal of a portion of a cash-generating unit containing goodwill (paragraph 86)

BC153   The Exposure Draft proposed that when an entity disposes of an operation within a cash-generating unit to which goodwill has been allocated, the goodwill associated with that operation should be:

(a)   included in the carrying amount of the operation when determining the gain or loss on disposal; and

(b)   measured on the basis of the relative values of the operation disposed of and the portion of the cash-generating unit retained.

BC154   This proposal has been carried forward in the Standard with one modification. The Standard requires the goodwill associated with the operation disposed of to be measured on the basis of the relative values of the operation disposed of and the portion of the cash-generating unit retained, unless the entity can demonstrate that some other method better reflects the goodwill associated with the operation disposed of.

BC155   In developing the Exposure Draft, the Board concluded that the proposed level of the impairment test would mean that goodwill could not be identified or associated with an asset group at a level lower than the cash-generating unit to which the goodwill is allocated, except arbitrarily. However, the Board also concluded that when an operation within that cash-generating unit is being disposed of, it is appropriate to presume that some amount of goodwill is associated with that operation. Thus, an allocation of the goodwill should be required when the part of the cash-generating unit being disposed of constitutes an operation.

BC156   Some respondents to the Exposure Draft suggested that although in most circumstances goodwill could not be identified or associated with an asset group at a level lower than the cash-generating unit or group of cash-generating units to which it is allocated for impairment testing, there may be some instances when this is not so. For example, assume an acquiree is integrated with one of the acquirer's pre-existing cash-generating units that did not include any goodwill in its carrying amount. Assume also that almost immediately after the business combination the acquirer disposes of a loss-making operation within the cash-generating unit. The Board agreed with respondents that in such circumstances, it might reasonably be concluded that no part of the carrying amount of goodwill has been disposed of, and therefore no part of its carrying amount should be derecognised by being included in the determination of the gain or loss on disposal.

Reorganisation of reporting structure (paragraph 87)

BC157   The Exposure Draft proposed that when an entity reorganises its reporting structure in a way that changes the composition of cash-generating units to which goodwill has been allocated, the goodwill should be reallocated to the units affected using a relative value approach similar to that used when an entity disposes of an operation within a cash-generating unit.

BC158   In developing the Exposure Draft, the Board concluded that a reorganisation that changes the composition of a cash-generating unit to which goodwill has been allocated gives rise to the same allocation problem as disposing of an operation within that unit. Therefore, the same allocation methodology should be used in both cases.

BC159   As a result, and consistently with the Board's decision to modify its proposal on allocating goodwill when an entity disposes of an operation, the revised Standard requires an entity that reorganises its reporting structure in a way that changes the composition of one or more cash-generating units to which goodwill has been allocated:

(a)   to reallocate the goodwill to the units affected; and

(b)   to perform this reallocation using a relative value approach similar to that used when an entity disposes of an operation within a cash-generating unit (group of cash-generating units), unless the entity can demonstrate that some other method better reflects the goodwill associated with the reorganised units (groups of units).

Recognition and measurement of impairment losses (paragraphs 88–99 and 104)

Background to the proposals in the Exposure Draft

BC160   The Exposure Draft proposed a two-step approach for impairment testing goodwill. The first step involved using a screening mechanism for identifying potential goodwill impairments, whereby goodwill allocated to a cash-generating unit would be identified as potentially impaired only when the carrying amount of the unit exceeded its recoverable amount. If an entity identified the goodwill allocated to a cash-generating unit as potentially impaired, an entity would then determine whether the goodwill allocated to the unit was impaired by comparing its recoverable amount, measured as the 'implied value' of the goodwill, with its carrying amount. The implied value of goodwill would be measured as a residual, being the excess of:

(a)   the recoverable amount of the cash-generating unit to which the goodwill has been allocated, over

(b)   the net fair value of the identifiable assets, liabilities and contingent liabilities the entity would recognise if it acquired the cash-generating unit in a business combination on the date of the impairment test (excluding any identifiable asset that was acquired in a business combination but not recognised separately from goodwill at the acquisition date).

BC161   In developing the Exposure Draft, the Board's discussion focused first on how the recoverable amount of goodwill allocated to a cash-generating unit could be separated from the recoverable amount of the unit as a whole, given that goodwill generated internally after a business combination could not be measured separately. The Board concluded that a method similar to the method an acquirer uses to allocate the cost of a business combination to the net assets acquired could be used to measure the recoverable amount of goodwill after its initial recognition. Thus, the Board decided that some measure of the net assets of a cash-generating unit to which goodwill has been allocated should be subtracted from the recoverable amount of that unit to determine a current implied value for the goodwill. The Board concluded that the measure of the net assets of a cash-generating unit described in paragraph BC160(b) would result in the best estimate of the current implied value of the goodwill, given that goodwill generated internally after a business combination could not be measured separately.

BC162 Having decided on the most appropriate measure of the recoverable amount of goodwill, the Board then considered how often an entity should be required to test goodwill for impairment. Consistently with its conclusions about indefinite-lived intangibles, the Board concluded that non-amortisation of goodwill increases the reliance that must be placed on impairment tests to ensure that the carrying amount of goodwill does not exceed its recoverable amount. Accordingly, the Board decided that goodwill should be tested for impairment annually. However, the Board also concluded that the annual test is not a substitute for management being aware of events occurring or circumstances changing between annual tests indicating a possible impairment of goodwill. Therefore, the Board decided that an entity should also be required to test goodwill for impairment whenever there is an indication of possible impairment.

BC163 After the Board decided on the frequency of impairment testing, it expressed some concern that the proposed test would not be cost-effective. This concern related primarily to the requirement to determine the fair value of each identifiable asset, liability and contingent liability within a cash-generating unit that would be recognised by the entity if it had acquired the cash-generating unit in a business combination on the date of the impairment test (to estimate the implied value of goodwill).

BC164 Therefore, the Board decided to propose as a first step in the impairment test for goodwill a screening mechanism similar to that in SFAS 142. Under SFAS 142, goodwill is tested for impairment by first comparing the fair value of the reporting unit to which the goodwill has been allocated for impairment testing purposes with the carrying amount of that unit. If the fair value of the unit exceeds its carrying amount, the goodwill is regarded as not impaired. An entity need estimate the implied fair value of goodwill (using an approach consistent with that described in paragraph BC160) only if the fair value of the unit is less than its carrying amount.

The Board's redeliberations

BC165 Many respondents disagreed with the proposal to adopt a two-step approach to impairment testing goodwill. In particular, the second step of the proposed impairment test and the method for measuring any impairment loss for the goodwill caused considerable concern. Respondents provided the following conceptual arguments against the proposed approach:

(a) by drawing on only some aspects of the SFAS 142 two-step approach, the result is a hybrid between fair values and value in use. More particularly, not measuring goodwill's implied value as the difference between the unit's fair value and the net fair value of the identifiable net assets in the unit, but instead measuring it as the difference between the unit's recoverable amount (ie higher of value in use and fair value less costs to sell) and the net fair value of the identifiable net assets in the unit, results in a measure of goodwill that conceptually is neither fair value nor recoverable amount. This raises questions about the conceptual validity of measuring goodwill impairment losses as the difference between goodwill's implied value and carrying amount.

(b) it seems inconsistent to consider goodwill separately for impairment testing when other assets within a unit are not considered separately but are instead considered as part of the unit as a whole, particularly given that goodwill, unlike many other assets, cannot generate cash inflows independently of other assets. The previous version of IAS 36 is premised on the notion that if a series of independent cash flows can be generated only by a group of assets operating together, impairment losses should be considered only for that group of assets as a whole—individual assets within the group should not be considered separately.

(c) concluding that the recoverable amount of goodwill—which cannot generate cash inflows independently of other assets—should be measured separately for measuring impairment losses makes it difficult to understand how the Board could in the future reasonably conclude that such an approach to measuring impairment losses is also not appropriate for other assets. In other words, if it adopts the proposed two-step approach for goodwill, the Board could in effect be committing itself to an 'individual asset/fair value' approach for measuring impairments of all other assets. A decision on this issue should be made only as part of a broad reconsideration of the appropriate measurement objective for impairment testing generally.

(d) if goodwill is considered separately for impairment testing using an implied value calculation when other assets within a unit are considered only as part of the unit as a whole, there will be asymmetry: unrecognised goodwill will shield the carrying value of other assets from impairment, but the unrecognised value of other assets will not shield the carrying amount of goodwill from impairment. This seems unreasonable given that the unrecognised value of those other assets cannot then be recognised. Additionally, the carrying amount of a unit will be less than its recoverable amount whenever an impairment loss for goodwill exceeds the unrecognised value of the other assets in the unit.

BC166 Additionally, respondents, field visit participants and North American round-table participants raised the following concerns about the practicability and costs of applying the proposed two-step approach:

(a) many companies would be required regularly to perform the second step of the impairment test, and therefore would need to determine the fair values of each identifiable asset, liability and contingent liability within the impaired unit(s) that the entity would recognise if it acquired the unit(s) in a business combination on the date of the impairment test. Although determining these fair values would not, for some companies, pose significant practical challenges (because, for example, fair value information for their significant assets is readily available), most would need to engage, on a fairly wide scale and at significant cost, independent valuers for some or all of the unit's assets. This is particularly the case for identifying and measuring the fair values of unrecognised internally generated intangible assets.

(b)   determining the fair values of each identifiable asset, liability and contingent liability within an impaired unit is likely to be impracticable for multi-segmented manufacturers that operate multi-product facilities servicing more than one cash-generating unit. For example, assume an entity's primary basis of segmentation is geographical (eg Europe, North America, South America, Asia, Oceania and Africa) and that its secondary basis of segmentation is based on product groups (vaccinations, over-the-counter medicines, prescription medicines and vitamins/dietary supplements).[38] Assume also that:

(i)   the lowest level within the entity at which the goodwill is monitored for internal management purposes is one level below primary segment (eg the vitamins business in North America), and that goodwill is therefore tested for impairment at this level;

(ii)   the plants and distribution facilities in each geographical region manufacture and distribute for all product groups; and

(iii)   to determine the carrying amount of each cash-generating unit containing goodwill, the carrying amount of each plant and distribution facility has been allocated between each product group it services.

If, for example, the recoverable amount of the North American vitamins unit were less than its carrying amount, measuring the implied value of goodwill in that unit would require a valuation exercise to be undertaken for *all* North American assets so that a portion of each asset's fair value can then be allocated to the North American vitamins unit. These valuations are likely to be extremely costly and virtually impossible to complete within a reasonable time period (field visit participants' estimates ranged from six to twelve months). The degree of impracticability will be even greater for those entities that monitor, and therefore test, goodwill at the segment level.

BC167   In considering the above comments, the Board noted that:

(a)   all of the US registrant field visit participants and North American round-table participants that have had to perform the second step of the SFAS 142 impairment test were compelled to engage, at significant cost, independent valuers.

(b)   the impairment model proposed in the Exposure Draft, although based on the two-step approach in SFAS 142, differed from the SFAS 142 test and would be unlikely to result in convergence for the following reasons:

---

38   In 2006 IAS 14 was replaced by IFRS 8 *Operating Segments* which does not require disclosure of primary and secondary segment information. See paragraph BC150A.

© IFRS Foundation

(i)   the recoverable amount of a unit to which goodwill is allocated in accordance with IAS 36 would be the higher of the unit's value in use and fair value less costs to sell, rather than fair value. Many of the US registrant field visit participants stated that the measure of recoverable amount they would use under IAS 36 would differ from the fair value measure they would be required to use under SFAS 142.

(ii)   the level at which goodwill is tested for impairment in accordance with SFAS 142 will often be higher than the level at which it would be tested under IAS 36. Many of the US registrant field visit participants stated that goodwill would be tested for impairment in accordance with IAS 36 at a lower level than under SFAS 142 because of either: (1) the limit SFAS 142 places on how far goodwill can be 'pushed down' for impairment testing (ie one level below an operating segment); or (2) the requirement in SFAS 142 to aggregate components with similar economic characteristics. Nevertheless, these participants unanimously agreed that the IAS 36 approach provides users and management with more useful information. The Board also noted that many of the North American round-table participants stated that they (or, in the case of audit firm participants, their clients) manage and have available information about their investments in goodwill at a level lower than a reporting unit as defined in SFAS 142. Many of these participants expressed a high level of dissatisfaction at being prevented by SFAS 142 from recognising goodwill impairments that they knew existed at these lower levels, but 'disappeared' once the lower level units were aggregated with other units containing sufficient 'cushions' to offset the impairment loss.

BC168   The Board also noted that, unlike SFAS 142, it had as its starting point an impairment model in IAS 36 that integrates the impairment testing of *all* assets within a cash-generating unit, including goodwill. Unlike US generally accepted accounting principles (GAAP), which use an undiscounted cash flow screening mechanism for impairment testing long-lived assets other than goodwill, IAS 36 requires the recoverable amount of an asset or cash-generating unit to be measured whenever there is an indication of possible impairment. Therefore, if at the time of impairment testing a 'larger' unit to which goodwill has been allocated there is an indication of a possible impairment in an asset or 'smaller' cash-generating unit included in that larger unit, an entity is required to test that asset or smaller unit for impairment first. Consequently, the Board concluded that it would be reasonable in an IAS 36 context to presume that an impairment loss for the larger unit would, after all other assets and smaller units are assessed for impairment, be likely to relate to the goodwill in the unit. Such a presumption would not be reasonable if an entity were following US GAAP.

BC169   The Board considered converging fully with the SFAS 142 approach. However, although supporting convergence, the Board was concerned that the SFAS 142 approach would not provide better information than an approach under which goodwill is tested for impairment at a lower level (thereby removing many of the 'cushions' protecting the goodwill from impairment) but with the amount of any impairment loss for goodwill measured in accordance with the one-step approach in the previous version of IAS 36.

BC170 The Board concluded that the complexity and costs of applying the two-step approach proposed in the Exposure Draft would outweigh the benefits of that approach. Therefore, the Board decided to retain the approach to measuring impairments of goodwill included in the previous version of IAS 36. Thus, the Standard requires any excess of the carrying amount of a cash-generating unit (group of units) to which goodwill has been allocated over its recoverable amount to be recognised first as an impairment loss for goodwill. Any excess remaining after the carrying amount of goodwill has been reduced to zero is then recognised by being allocated to the other assets of the unit pro rata with their carrying amounts.

Changes as a result of 2008 revisions to IFRS 3 (Appendix C)

BC170A As a result of the changes to IFRS 3 (as revised in 2008), the requirements in Appendix C of the Standard and the related illustrative examples have been amended to reflect the two ways of measuring non-controlling interests: at fair value and as a proportion of the identifiable net assets of the acquiree. Appendix C has also been modified to clarify the requirements of the Standard.

Timing of impairment tests (paragraphs 96–99)

BC171 To reduce the costs of applying the test, and consistently with the proposals in the Exposure Draft, the Standard permits the annual impairment test for a cash-generating unit (group of units) to which goodwill has been allocated to be performed at any time during an annual period, provided the test is performed at the same time every year. Different cash-generating units (groups of units) may be tested for impairment at different times. However, if some or all of the goodwill allocated to a unit (group of units) was acquired in a business combination during the current annual period, that unit (group of units) must be tested for impairment before the end of the current annual period.

BC172 The Board observed that acquirers can sometimes 'overpay' for an acquiree, resulting in the amount initially recognised for the business combination and the resulting goodwill exceeding the recoverable amount of the investment. The Board concluded that the users of an entity's financial statements are provided with representationally faithful, and therefore useful, information about a business combination if such an impairment loss is recognised by the acquirer in the annual period in which the business combination occurs.

BC173 The Board was concerned that it might be possible for entities to delay recognising such an impairment loss until the annual period after the business combination if the Standard included only a requirement to impairment test cash-generating units (groups of units) to which goodwill has been allocated on an annual basis at any time during a period. Therefore, the Board decided to include in the Standard the added requirement that if some or all of the goodwill allocated to a unit (group of units) was acquired in a business combination during the current annual period, the unit (group of units) should be tested for impairment before the end of that period.

Sequence of impairment tests (paragraph 97)

BC174   The Standard requires that if the assets (cash-generating units) constituting the cash-generating unit (group of units) to which goodwill has been allocated are tested for impairment at the same time as the unit (group of units) containing the goodwill, those other assets (units) should be tested for impairment before the unit (group of units) containing the goodwill.

BC175   The Board observed that assets or cash-generating units making up a unit or group of units to which goodwill has been allocated might need to be tested for impairment at the same time as the unit or group of units containing the goodwill when there is an indication of a possible impairment of the asset or smaller unit. The Board concluded that to assess whether the unit or group of units containing the goodwill, and therefore whether the goodwill, is impaired, the carrying amount of the unit or group of units containing the goodwill would need first to be adjusted by recognising any impairment losses relating to the assets or smaller units within that unit or group of units.

Carrying forward a recoverable amount calculation (paragraph 99)

BC176   Consistently with the impairment test for indefinite-lived intangibles, the Standard permits the most recent detailed calculation of the recoverable amount of a cash-generating unit (group of units) to which goodwill has been allocated to be carried forward from a preceding period for use in the current period's impairment test, provided all of the criteria in paragraph 99 are met.

BC177   Integral to the Board's decision that goodwill should be tested for impairment annually was the view that many entities should be able to conclude that the recoverable amount of a cash-generating unit (group of units) to which goodwill has been allocated is greater than its carrying amount without actually recomputing recoverable amount. However, again consistently with its conclusions about indefinite-lived intangibles, the Board concluded that this would be the case only if the last recoverable amount determination exceeded the carrying amount of the unit (group of units) by a substantial margin, and nothing had happened since that last determination to make the likelihood of an impairment loss other than remote. The Board concluded that in such circumstances, permitting a detailed calculation of the recoverable amount of a cash-generating unit (group of units) to which goodwill has been allocated to be carried forward from the preceding period for use in the current period's impairment test would significantly reduce the costs of applying the impairment test, without compromising its integrity.

Allocating an impairment loss between the assets of a cash-generating unit (paragraphs 104–107)

BCZ178   IAS 36 includes requirements for the allocation of an impairment loss for a cash-generating unit that differ from the proposals in E55. In particular, E55 proposed that an impairment loss should be allocated:

(a)   first, to goodwill;

(b)   secondly, to intangible assets for which no active market exists;

(c)   thirdly, to assets whose net selling price[39] is less than their carrying amount; and

(d)   then, to the other assets of the unit on a pro-rata basis based on the carrying amount of each asset in the unit.

BCZ179   The underlying reasons for making this proposal were that:

(a)   an impairment loss for a cash-generating unit should be allocated, in priority, to assets with the most subjective values. Goodwill and intangible assets for which there is no active market were considered to be in that category. Intangible assets for which there is no active market were considered to be similar to goodwill (IASC was thinking of brand names, publishing titles etc).

(b)   if the net selling price of an asset is less than its carrying amount, this was considered a reasonable basis for allocating part of the impairment loss to that asset rather than to other assets.

BCZ180   Many commentators on E55 objected to the proposal on the grounds that:

(a)   not all intangible assets for which no active market exists are similar to goodwill (for example, licences and franchise rights). They disagreed that the value of intangible assets is always more subjective than the value of tangible assets (for example, specialised plant and equipment).

(b)   the concept of cash-generating units implies a global approach for the assets of the units and not an asset-by-asset approach.

In response to these comments, IASC decided to withdraw E55's proposal for the allocation of an impairment loss to intangible assets and assets whose net selling price is less than their carrying amount.

BCZ181   IASC rejected a proposal that an impairment loss for a cash-generating unit should be allocated first to any obviously impaired asset. IASC believed that if the recoverable amount of an obviously impaired asset can be determined for the individual asset, there is no need to estimate the recoverable amount of the asset's cash-generating unit. If the recoverable amount of an individual asset cannot be determined, it cannot be said that the asset is obviously impaired because an impairment loss for a cash-generating unit relates to all of the assets of that unit.

Reversing impairment losses for assets other than goodwill (paragraphs 110–123)

BCZ182   IAS 36 requires that an impairment loss for an asset other than goodwill should be reversed if, and only if, there has been a change in the estimates used to determine an asset's recoverable amount since the last impairment loss was recognised.

---

39   In IFRS 5 *Non-current Assets Held for Sale and Discontinued Operations*, issued by the IASB in 2004, the term 'net selling price' was replaced in IAS 36 by 'fair value less costs to sell'.

BCZ183   Opponents of reversals of impairment losses argue that:

(a)   reversals of impairment losses are contrary to the historical cost accounting system. When the carrying amount is reduced, recoverable amount becomes the new cost basis for an asset. Consequently, reversing an impairment loss is no different from revaluing an asset upward. Indeed, in many cases, recoverable amount is similar to the measurement basis used for the revaluation of an asset. Hence, reversals of impairment losses should be either prohibited or recognised directly in equity as a revaluation.

(b)   reversals of impairment losses introduce volatility in reported earnings. Periodic, short-term income measurements should not be affected by unrealised changes in the measurement of a long-lived asset.

(c)   the result of reversals of impairment losses would not be useful to users of financial statements since the amount of a reversal under IAS 36 is limited to an amount that does not increase the carrying amount of an asset above its depreciated historical cost. Neither the amount reversed nor the revised carrying amount have any information content.

(d)   in many cases, reversals of impairment losses will result in the implicit recognition of internally generated goodwill.

(e)   reversals of impairment losses open the door to abuse and income 'smoothing' in practice.

(f)   follow-up to verify whether an impairment loss needs to be reversed is costly.

BCZ184   IASC's reasons for requiring reversals of impairment losses were the following:

(a)   it is consistent with the *Framework*[40] and the view that future economic benefits that were not previously expected to flow from an asset have been reassessed as probable.

(b)   a reversal of an impairment loss is not a revaluation and is consistent with the historical cost accounting system as long as the reversal does not result in the carrying amount of an asset exceeding its original cost less amortisation/depreciation, had the impairment loss not been recognised. Accordingly, the reversal of an impairment loss should be recognised in the income statement and any amount in excess of the depreciated historical cost should be accounted for as a revaluation.

(c)   impairment losses are recognised and measured based on estimates. Any change in the measurement of an impairment loss is similar to a change in estimate. IAS 8 *Net Profit or Loss for the Period, Fundamental Errors and Changes in Accounting Policies*[41] requires that a change in accounting estimate should be included in the determination of the net profit or loss

---

40   The reference to the *Framework* is to IASC's *Framework for the Preparation and Presentation of Financial Statements*, adopted by the IASB in 2001. In September 2010 the IASB replaced the *Framework* with the *Conceptual Framework for Financial Reporting*.

41   IAS 8 *Net Profit or Loss for the Period, Fundamental Errors and Changes in Accounting Policies* was superseded in 2003 by IAS 8 *Accounting Policies, Changes in Accounting Estimates and Errors*.

in (a) the period of the change, if the change affects the period only, or (b) the period of the change and future periods, if the change affects both.

(d)   reversals of impairment losses provide users with a more useful indication of the potential for future benefits of an asset or group of assets.

(e)   results of operations will be more fairly stated in the current period and in future periods because depreciation or amortisation will not reflect a previous impairment loss that is no longer relevant. Prohibition of reversals of impairment losses may lead to abuses such as recording a significant loss one year with the resulting lower amortisation/depreciation charge and higher profits in subsequent years.

BCZ185   The majority of commentators on E55 supported IASC's proposals for reversals of impairment losses.

BCZ186   IAS 36 does not permit an enterprise to recognise a reversal of an impairment loss just because of the unwinding of the discount. IASC supported this requirement for practical reasons only. Otherwise, if an impairment loss is recognised and recoverable amount is based on value in use, a reversal of the impairment loss would be recognised in each subsequent year for the unwinding of the discount. This is because, in most cases, the pattern of depreciation of an asset is different from the pattern of value in use. IASC believed that, when there is no change in the assumptions used to estimate recoverable amount, the benefits from recognising the unwinding of the discount each year after an impairment loss has been recognised do not justify the costs involved. However, if a reversal is recognised because assumptions have changed, the discount unwinding effect is included in the amount of the reversal recognised.

Reversing goodwill impairment losses (paragraph 124)

BC187   Consistently with the proposal in the Exposure Draft, the Standard prohibits the recognition of reversals of impairment losses for goodwill. The previous version of IAS 36 required an impairment loss for goodwill recognised in a previous period to be reversed when the impairment loss was caused by a specific external event of an exceptional nature that was not expected to recur, and subsequent external events had occurred that reversed the effect of that event.

BC188   Most respondents to the Exposure Draft agreed that reversals of impairment losses for goodwill should be prohibited. Those that disagreed argued that reversals of impairment losses for goodwill should be treated in the same way as reversals of impairment losses for other assets, but limited to circumstances in which the impairment loss was caused by specific events beyond the entity's control.

BC189   In revising IAS 36, the Board noted that IAS 38 *Intangible Assets* prohibits the recognition of internally generated goodwill. Therefore, if reversals of impairment losses for goodwill were permitted, an entity would need to establish the extent to which a subsequent increase in the recoverable amount of goodwill is attributable to the recovery of the acquired goodwill within a cash-generating unit, rather than an increase in the internally generated goodwill within the unit. The Board concluded that this will seldom, if ever, be possible. Because the acquired goodwill and internally generated goodwill contribute jointly to the same cash flows, any subsequent increase in the recoverable amount of the acquired goodwill is indistinguishable from an increase in the internally generated goodwill. Even if the specific external event that caused the recognition of the impairment loss is reversed, it will seldom, if ever, be possible to determine that the effect of that reversal is a corresponding increase in the recoverable amount of the acquired goodwill. Therefore, the Board concluded that reversals of impairment losses for goodwill should be prohibited.

BC190 The Board expressed some concern that prohibiting the recognition of reversals of impairment losses for goodwill so as to avoid recognising internally generated goodwill might be viewed by some as inconsistent with the impairment test for goodwill. This is because the impairment test results in the carrying amount of goodwill being shielded from impairment by internally generated goodwill. This has been described by some as 'backdoor' capitalisation of internally generated goodwill.

BC191 However, the Board was not as concerned about goodwill being shielded from the recognition of impairment losses by internally generated goodwill as it was about the direct recognition of internally generated goodwill that might occur if reversals of impairment losses for goodwill were permitted. As discussed in paragraph BC135, the Board is of the view that it is not possible to devise an impairment test for acquired goodwill that removes the cushion against the recognition of impairment losses provided by goodwill generated internally after a business combination.

Disclosures for cash-generating units containing goodwill or indefinite-lived intangibles (paragraphs 134 and 135)

Background to the proposals in the Exposure Draft

BC192 The Exposure Draft proposed requiring an entity to disclose a range of information about cash-generating units whose carrying amounts included goodwill or indefinite-lived intangibles. That information included:

(a) the carrying amount of goodwill and the carrying amount of indefinite-lived intangibles.

(b) the basis on which the unit's recoverable amount had been determined (ie value in use or net selling price).

(c) the amount by which the unit's recoverable amount exceeded its carrying amount.

(d) the key assumptions and estimates used to measure the unit's recoverable amount and information about the sensitivity of that recoverable amount to changes in the key assumptions and estimates.

BC193 If an entity reports segment information in accordance with IAS 14 *Segment Reporting*, the Exposure Draft proposed that this information should be disclosed in aggregate for each segment based on the entity's primary reporting format. However, the Exposure Draft also proposed that the information would be disclosed separately for a cash-generating unit when:

(a) the carrying amount of the goodwill or indefinite-lived intangibles allocated to the unit was significant in relation to the total carrying amount of goodwill or indefinite-lived intangibles; or

(b) the basis for determining the unit's recoverable amount differed from the basis used for the other units within the segment whose carrying amounts include goodwill or indefinite-lived intangibles; or

(c) the nature of, or value assigned to the key assumptions or growth rate on which management based its determination of the unit's recoverable amount differed significantly from that used for the other units within the segment whose carrying amounts include goodwill or indefinite-lived intangibles.

BC194 In deciding to propose these disclosure requirements in the Exposure Draft, the Board observed that non-amortisation of goodwill and indefinite-lived intangibles increases the reliance that must be placed on impairment tests of those assets to ensure that their carrying amounts do not exceed their recoverable amounts. However, the nature of impairment tests means that the carrying amounts of such assets and the related assertion that those carrying amounts are recoverable will normally be supported only by management's projections. Therefore, the Board decided to examine ways in which the reliability of the impairment tests for goodwill and indefinite-lived intangibles could be improved. As a first step, the Board considered including a subsequent cash flow test in the revised Standard, similar to that included in UK Financial Reporting Standard 11 *Impairment of Fixed Assets and Goodwill* (FRS 11).

Subsequent cash flow test

BC195 FRS 11 requires an entity to perform a subsequent cash flow test to confirm, ex post, the cash flow projections used to measure a unit's value in use when testing goodwill for impairment. Under FRS 11, for five years following each impairment test for goodwill in which recoverable amount has been based on value in use, the actual cash flows achieved must be compared with those forecast. If the actual cash flows are so much less than those forecast that use of the actual cash flows in the value in use calculation could have required recognition of an impairment in previous periods, the original impairment calculations must be re-performed using the actual cash flows, but without revising any other cash flows or assumptions (except those that change as a direct consequence of the occurrence of the actual cash flows, for example where a major cash inflow has been delayed for a year). Any impairment identified must then be recognised in the current period, unless the impairment has reversed and the reversal of the loss satisfies the criteria in FRS 11 regarding reversals of impairment losses for goodwill.

BC196 The Board noted the following arguments in support of including a similar test in the revised Standard:

(a) it would enhance the reliability of the goodwill impairment test by preventing the possibility of entities avoiding the recognition of impairment losses by using over-optimistic cash flow projections in the value in use calculations.

(b) it would provide useful information to users of an entity's financial statements because a record of actual cash flows continually less than forecast cash flows tends to cast doubt on the reliability of current estimates.

BC197 However, the subsequent cash flow test is designed only to prevent entities from avoiding goodwill write-downs. The Board observed that, given current trends in 'big bath' restructuring charges, the greater risk to the quality of financial reporting might be from entities trying to write off goodwill without adequate justification in an attempt to 'manage' the balance sheet. The Board also observed that:

(a) the focus of the test on cash flows ignores other elements in the measurement of value in use. As a result, it does not produce representationally faithful results in a present value measurement system. The Board considered incorporating into the recalculation performed under the test corrections of estimates of other elements in the measurement of value in use. However, the Board concluded that specifying which elements to include would be problematic. Moreover, adding corrections of estimates of those other elements to the test would, in effect, transform the test into a requirement to perform a comprehensive recalculation of value in use for each of the five annual reporting periods following an impairment test.

(b) the amount recognised as an impairment loss under the test is the amount of the impairment that would have been recognised, provided changes in estimates of remaining cash flows and changes in discount and growth rates are ignored. Therefore, it is a hypothetical amount that does not provide decision-useful information—it is neither an estimate of a current amount nor a prediction of ultimate cash flows.

(c) the requirement to perform the test for each of the five annual reporting periods following an impairment test could result in an entity having to maintain as many as five sets of 5-year computations for each cash-generating unit to which goodwill has been allocated. Therefore, the test is likely to be extremely burdensome, particularly if an entity has a large number of such units, without producing understandable or decision-useful information.

BC198 Therefore, the Board decided not to propose a subsequent cash flow test in the Exposure Draft. However, the Board remained committed to finding some way of improving the reliability of the impairment tests for goodwill and indefinite-lived intangibles, and decided to explore improving that reliability through disclosure requirements.

Including disclosure requirements in the revised Standard

BC199   In developing the Exposure Draft, the Board observed that the *Framework*[42] identifies reliability as one of the key qualitative characteristics that information must possess to be useful to users in making economic decisions. To be reliable, information must be free from material error and bias and be able to be depended upon to represent faithfully that which it purports to represent. The *Framework* identifies relevance as another key qualitative characteristic that information must possess to be useful to users in making economic decisions. To be relevant, information must help users to evaluate past, present or future events, or confirm or correct their past evaluations.

BC200   The Board observed that information that assists users in evaluating the reliability of other information included in the financial statements is itself relevant, increasing in relevance as the reliability of that other information decreases.   For example, information that assists users in evaluating the reliability of the amount recognised for a provision is relevant because it helps users to evaluate the effect of both a past event (ie the economic consequences of the past event giving rise to the present obligation) and a future event (ie the amount of the expected future outflow of economic benefits required to settle the obligation). Accordingly, IAS 37 *Provisions, Contingent Liabilities and Contingent Assets* requires an entity to disclose, for each class of provision, information about the uncertainties surrounding the amount and timing of expected outflows of economic benefits, and the major assumptions concerning future events that may affect the amount required to settle the obligation and have been reflected in the amount of the provision.

BC201   The Board concluded that because information that assists users in evaluating the reliability of other information is itself relevant, an entity should disclose information that assists users in evaluating the reliability of the estimates used by management to support the carrying amounts of goodwill and indefinite-lived intangibles.

BC202   The Board also concluded that such disclosures would provide users with more useful information for evaluating the reliability of the impairment tests for goodwill and indefinite-lived intangibles than the information that would be provided by a subsequent cash flow test.

BC203   The Board then considered how some balance might be achieved between the objective of providing users with useful information for evaluating the reliability of the estimates used by management to support the carrying amounts of goodwill and indefinite-lived intangibles, and the potential magnitude of those disclosures.

BC204   The Board decided that a reasonable balance might be achieved between the objective of the disclosures and their potential magnitude by requiring:

---

42   The references to the *Framework* are to IASC's *Framework for the Preparation and Presentation of Financial Statements*, adopted by the IASB in 2001. In September 2010 the IASB replaced the *Framework* with the *Conceptual Framework for Financial Reporting*.

(a) information to be disclosed on an aggregate basis for each segment based on the entity's primary reporting format that includes in its carrying amount goodwill or indefinite-lived intangibles; but

(b) information for a particular cash-generating unit within that segment to be excluded from the aggregate information and disclosed separately when either:

(i) the basis (ie net selling price or value in use), methodology or key assumptions used to measure its recoverable amount differ from those used to measure the recoverable amounts of the other units in the segment; or

(ii) the carrying amount of the goodwill or indefinite-lived intangibles in the unit is significant in relation to the total carrying amount of goodwill or indefinite-lived intangibles.

The Board's redeliberations

BC205 After considering respondents' and field visit participants' comments, the Board confirmed its previous conclusion that information that assists users in evaluating the reliability of other information is itself relevant, increasing in relevance as the reliability of that other information decreases. Therefore, entities should be required to disclose information that assists users in evaluating the reliability of the estimates used by management to support the carrying amounts of goodwill and indefinite-lived intangibles. The Board noted that almost all field visit participants and many respondents expressed explicit support of its conclusion that, because non-amortisation of goodwill and indefinite-lived intangibles increases the reliance that must be placed on impairment tests of those assets, some additional disclosure is necessary to provide users with information for evaluating the reliability of those impairment tests.

BC206 However, it was clear from field visit participants' responses that the proposed disclosures could not be meaningfully aggregated at the segment level to the extent the Board had hoped might be the case. As a result, the proposal to require the information to be disclosed on an aggregate basis for each segment, but with disaggregated disclosures for cash-generating units in the circumstances set out in paragraph BC193 would not result in a reasonable balance between the objective of the disclosures and their potential magnitude.

BC207 The Board was also sympathetic to field visit participants' and respondents' concerns that the proposed disclosures went beyond their intended objective of providing users with relevant information for evaluating the reliability of the impairment tests for goodwill and indefinite-lived intangibles. For example, field visit participants and respondents argued that:

(a) it would be extremely difficult to distil the recoverable amount calculations into concise but meaningful disclosures because those calculations typically are complex and do not normally result in a single point estimate of recoverable amount—a single value for recoverable amount would normally be determined only when the bottom-end of the recoverable amount range is less than a cash-generating unit's carrying amount. These difficulties make it doubtful that the information, particularly the sensitivity analyses, could be produced on a timely basis.

(b)   disclosing the proposed information, particularly the values assigned to, and the sensitivity of, each key assumption on which recoverable amount calculations are based, could cause significant commercial harm to an entity. Users of financial statements might, for example, use the quantitative disclosures as the basis for initiating litigation against the entity, its board of directors or management in the highly likely event that those assumptions prove less than accurate. The increased litigation risk would either encourage management to use super-conservative assumptions, thereby resulting in improper asset write-downs, or compel management to engage independent experts to develop all key assumptions and perform the recoverable amount calculations. Additionally, many of the field visit participants expressed concern over the possible impact that disclosing such information might have on their ability to defend themselves in various legal proceedings.

BC208   Therefore, the Board considered the following two interrelated issues:

(a)   if the proposed disclosures went beyond their intended objective, what information *should* be disclosed so that users have sufficient information for evaluating the reliability of impairment tests for goodwill and indefinite-lived intangibles?

(b)   how should this information be presented so that there is an appropriate balance between providing users with information for evaluating the reliability of the impairment tests, and the potential magnitude of those disclosures?

BC209   As a result of its redeliberations, the Board decided:

(a)   not to proceed with the proposal to require information for evaluating the reliability of the impairment tests for goodwill and indefinite-lived intangibles to be disclosed in aggregate for each segment and separately for cash-generating units within a segment in specified circumstances. Instead, the Standard requires this information to be disclosed only for each cash-generating unit (group of units) for which the carrying amount of goodwill or indefinite-lived intangibles allocated to that unit (group of units) is significant in comparison with the entity's total carrying amount of goodwill or indefinite-lived intangibles.

(b)   not to proceed with the proposal to require an entity to disclose the amount by which the recoverable amount of a cash-generating unit exceeds its carrying amount. Instead, the Standard requires an entity to disclose this information only if a reasonably possible change in a key assumption on which management has based its determination of the unit's (group of units') recoverable amount would cause the unit's (group of units') carrying amount to exceed its recoverable amount.

(c)   not to proceed with the proposal to require an entity to disclose the value assigned to each key assumption on which management based its recoverable amount determination, and the amount by which that value must change, after incorporating any consequential effects of that change on the other variables used to measure recoverable amount, in order for the unit's recoverable amount to be equal to its carrying amount. Instead, the Standard requires an entity to disclose a description of each key assumption on which management has based its recoverable amount determination, management's approach to determining the value(s) assigned to each key assumption, whether those value(s) reflect past experience or, if appropriate, are consistent with external sources of information, and, if not, how and why they differ from past experience or external sources of information. However, if a reasonably possible change in a key assumption would cause the unit's (group of units') carrying amount to exceed its recoverable amount, the entity is also required to disclose the value assigned to the key assumption, and the amount by which that value must change, after incorporating any consequential effects of that change on the other variables used to measure recoverable amount, in order for the unit's (group of units') recoverable amount to be equal to its carrying amount.

(d)   to require information about key assumptions to be disclosed also for any key assumption that is relevant to the recoverable amount determination of multiple cash-generating units (groups of units) that individually contain insignificant amounts of goodwill or indefinite-lived intangibles, but contain, in aggregate, significant amounts of goodwill or indefinite-lived intangibles.

Changes as a result of *Improvements to IFRSs* (2008)[43]

BC209A   The Board noted that the disclosures that IAS 36 requires when value in use is used to determine recoverable amount differ from those required when fair value less costs to sell is used. These differing requirements appear inconsistent when a similar valuation methodology (discounted cash flows) has been used. Therefore, as part of *Improvements to IFRSs* issued in May 2008, the Board decided to require the same disclosures for fair value less costs to sell and value in use when discounted cash flows are used to estimate recoverable amount.

Changes as a result of IFRS 13 *Fair Value Measurement*

BC209B   In developing IFRS 13, issued in May 2011, the Board was asked by users of financial statements to minimise the differences between the disclosures made about impaired assets in IFRSs and in US GAAP (which requires assets to be tested for impairment by comparing their carrying amount with their fair value). The Board noted that the disclosure requirements in IAS 36 were developed specifically to ensure consistency in the disclosure of information about impaired assets so that the same type of information is provided whether the recoverable amount was determined on the basis of value in use or fair value less costs of disposal. Consequently, the Board did not think it would be appropriate to require an entity to provide information when the recoverable amount is determined on the basis of fair value less costs of disposal (ie those

---

43   This heading and paragraph BC209A were added by *Improvements to IFRSs* issued in May 2008.

supporting it. Consequently, the IASB decided to incorporate that proposal into Exposure Draft ED/2013/1, but did not request comments in response to this topic.

BC209K   A total of 74 respondents commented on Exposure Draft ED/2013/1. Even though the vast majority of the respondents supported the proposed amendments, a few respondents believed that, when impairment losses were calculated by reference to the recoverable amount determined on the basis of fair value less costs of disposal, the amendments would result in the disclosure requirements being broader than the disclosures that would be required if the same impairment losses were calculated by reference to the recoverable amount determined on the basis of value in use. The IASB noted that it had already taken the decision to require this incremental disclosure when it first amended IAS 36 as a result of issuing IFRS 13. As mentioned in paragraph BC209G, that decision had been taken on the grounds that those amendments would improve comparability between the disclosures presented in the financial statements of entities applying IFRS and the disclosures presented in the financial statements of those applying US GAAP.

BC209L   During the development of IFRS 13, the IASB also noted that not all of the additional disclosure requirements for the recoverable amount determined on the basis of fair value less costs of disposal would be applicable for the recoverable amount determined on the basis of value in use. The requirement of disclosing the level of the fair value hierarchy within which the fair value measurement of the impaired asset is categorised would, for example, not be applicable to a measurement based on value in use. In addition, the IASB noted that the amendments to paragraph 130(f) would help to align the disclosure requirements for fair value less costs of disposal for impaired assets with the disclosure requirements in paragraph 134(e) for fair value less costs of disposal for each cash-generating unit for which the carrying amount of goodwill or intangible assets with indefinite useful lives allocated to that unit is significant in comparison with an entity's total carrying amount of goodwill or intangible assets with indefinite useful lives.

BC209M   Exposure Draft ED/2013/1 also proposed to remove the term 'material' from paragraph 130. When developing these proposals, the IASB concluded that it was unnecessary to state explicitly that the disclosure requirements in paragraph 130 relate to assets (including goodwill) or cash-generating units, for which a material impairment loss has been recognised or reversed during the period, because all IFRSs are governed by the concept of materiality as described in IAS 1 *Presentation of Financial Statements* (see paragraph 31 of IAS 1) and IAS 8 *Accounting Policies, Changes in Accounting Estimates and Errors*. Some respondents to Exposure Draft ED/2013/1 were opposed to removing this term because they thought that, by removing it, it would become unclear whether the disclosure requirements in paragraph 130 apply only when a material impairment loss has been recognised or reversed during the period. They were also concerned that the elimination of the term 'material' in paragraph 130 could impact the understanding of the requirements in paragraph 131 that deal with the disclosure of immaterial items on an aggregate basis.

BC209N   The IASB had not intended to change the scope of the disclosure requirements in paragraph 130. In addition, the IASB concluded that the removal of the term 'material' in paragraph 130 should not impact the disclosure requirements in paragraph 131. Consequently, the IASB concluded that the rationale for removing the term 'material', as presented in Exposure Draft ED/2013/1, was still valid and, as a result, the IASB confirmed the removal of that term in the final amendments.

BC209O   The IASB decided not to retain in the final amendments the last sentence of paragraph 130(f), as proposed in Exposure Draft ED/2013/1. That sentence stated that an "... entity is not required to provide the disclosures required by IFRS 13". The IASB noted that IFRS 13 already excludes from the scope of its disclosure requirements assets for which the recoverable amount is fair value less costs of disposal in accordance with IAS 36. As a result, the IASB concluded that that sentence in paragraph 130(f) was redundant and could cause confusion and therefore decided to remove it from the final amendments.

BC209P   Exposure Draft ED/2013/1 proposed to include an illustrative example of the requirements in paragraph 130(b) and the proposed requirements in paragraph 130(f)(ii). Some respondents questioned the usefulness of that illustrative example, which did not illustrate all of the disclosures that are required for the recoverable amount of impaired assets based on fair value less costs of disposal. In their view, such an illustrative example could be misleading rather than helpful, because it might suggest that no other disclosures are required. On the basis of these comments, and because the IASB noted that Illustrative Example 15 to IFRS 13 includes similar disclosures to the ones included in the proposed illustrative example, it decided not to incorporate the proposed example in the final amendments.

BC209Q   On the basis of the respondents' comments, the IASB decided to proceed with the final amendments subject to only minor drafting modifications.

Transitional provisions (paragraphs 138–140)

BC210   If an entity elects to apply IFRS 3 from any date before the effective dates outlined in IFRS 3, it is also required to apply IAS 36 from that same date. Paragraphs BC181–BC184 of the Basis for Conclusions on IFRS 3 outline the Board's deliberations on this issue.[44]

BC211   Otherwise, IAS 36 is applied:

(a)   to goodwill and intangible assets acquired in business combinations for which the agreement date is on or after 31 March 2004; and

(b)   to all other assets prospectively from the beginning of the first annual period beginning on or after 31 March 2004.

BC212   In developing the requirements set out in paragraph BC211, the Board considered whether entities should be required:

(a)   to apply retrospectively the revised impairment test for goodwill; and

---

44   The Board issued a revised IFRS 3 in 2008. This paragraph relates to IFRS 3 as issued in 2004.

(b)   to apply retrospectively the requirement prohibiting reversals of impairment losses for goodwill and therefore eliminate any reversals recognised before the date the revised Standard was issued.

BC213   The Board concluded that retrospective application of the revised impairment test for goodwill would be problematic for the following reasons:

(a)   it was likely to be impossible in many cases because the information needed may not exist or may no longer be obtainable.

(b)   it would require the determination of estimates that would have been made at a prior date, and therefore would raise the problem of how the effect of hindsight could be separated from the factors existing at the date of the impairment test.

BC214   The Board also noted that the requirement for goodwill to be tested for impairment annually, irrespective of whether there is any indication that it may be impaired, will ensure that by the end of the first period in which the Standard is effective, all recognised goodwill acquired before its effective date would be tested for impairment.

BC215   In the case of reversals of impairment losses for goodwill, the Board acknowledged that requiring the elimination of reversals recognised before the revised Standard's effective date might seem appropriate, particularly given the Board's reasons for prohibiting reversals of impairment losses for goodwill (see paragraphs BC187–BC191). The Board concluded, however, that the previous amortisation of that goodwill, combined with the requirement for goodwill to be tested for impairment at least annually, ensures that the carrying amount of the goodwill does not exceed its recoverable amount at the end of the reporting period in which the Standard is effective. Therefore, the Board concluded that the Standard should apply on a prospective basis.

Transitional impairment test for goodwill

BC216   Given that one of the objectives of the first phase of the Business Combinations project was to seek international convergence on the accounting for goodwill, the Board considered whether IAS 36 should include a transitional goodwill impairment test similar to that included in SFAS 142. SFAS 142 requires goodwill to be tested for impairment annually, and between annual tests if an event occurs or circumstances change and would be more likely than not to reduce the fair value of a reporting unit below its carrying amount. The transitional provisions in SFAS 142 require the impairment test for goodwill to be applied prospectively. However, a transitional goodwill impairment test must be performed as of the *beginning* of the fiscal year in which SFAS 142 is applied in its entirety. An impairment loss recognised as a result of a transitional test is recognised as the effect of a change in accounting principle, rather than as an impairment loss. In addition to the transitional test, SFAS 142 requires an entity to perform the required annual goodwill impairment test in the year that SFAS 142 is initially applied in its entirety. In other words, the transitional goodwill impairment test may not be regarded as the initial year's annual test unless an entity designates the beginning of its fiscal year as the date for its annual goodwill impairment test.

BC217 The FASB concluded that goodwill that was not regarded as impaired under US GAAP before SFAS 142 was issued could be determined to be impaired if the SFAS 142 impairment test was applied to that goodwill at the date an entity initially applied SFAS 142. This is because, under previous US GAAP, entities typically tested goodwill for impairment using undiscounted estimates of future cash flows. The FASB further concluded that:

(a) the preponderance of any transitional impairment losses was likely to result from the change in methods and treating those losses as stemming from changes in accounting principles would therefore be more representationally faithful.

(b) given that a transitional impairment loss should be reported as a change in accounting principle, the transitional goodwill impairment test should ideally apply as of the date SFAS 142 is initially applied.

BC218 The Board observed that under the previous version of IAS 36, goodwill that was amortised over a period exceeding 20 years was required to be tested for impairment at least at each financial year-end. Goodwill that was amortised over a period not exceeding 20 years was required to be tested for impairment at the balance sheet date if there was an indication that it might be impaired. The revised Standard requires goodwill to be tested for impairment annually or more frequently if there is an indication the goodwill might be impaired. It also carries forward from the previous version of IAS 36 (a) the indicators of impairment, (b) the measure of recoverable amount (ie higher of value in use and fair value less costs to sell), and (c) the requirement for an impairment loss for a cash-generating unit to be allocated first to reduce the carrying amount of any goodwill allocated to the unit.

BC219 Therefore, goodwill tested for impairment in accordance with the previous version of the revised Standard immediately before the beginning of the reporting period in which the revised Standard becomes effective (because it was being amortised over a period exceeding 20 years or because there was an indicator of impairment) could not be identified as impaired under IAS 36 at the beginning of the period in which it becomes effective. This is because application of the Standard results in a goodwill impairment loss being identified only if the carrying amount of the cash-generating unit (group of units) to which the goodwill has been allocated exceeds its recoverable amount, and the impairment test in the previous version of IAS 36 ensures that this will not be the case.

BC220 The Board concluded that there would be only one possible situation in which a transitional impairment test might give rise to the recognition of an impairment loss for goodwill. This would be when goodwill being amortised over a period not exceeding 20 years was, immediately before the beginning of the period in which the revised Standard becomes effective, impaired in the absence of any indicator of impairment that ought reasonably to have been considered by the entity. The Board concluded that this is likely to be a rare occurrence.

BC221 The Board observed that any such impairment loss would nonetheless be recognised as a consequence of applying the requirement in IAS 36 to test goodwill for impairment at least annually. Therefore, the only benefit of applying a transitional impairment test would be, in those rare cases, to separate the impairment loss arising before the period in which the revised Standard is effective from any impairment loss arising after the beginning of that period.

BC222 The Board concluded that given the rare circumstances in which this issue would arise, the benefit of applying a transitional goodwill impairment test would be outweighed by the added costs of the test. Therefore, the Board decided that the revised Standard should not require a transitional goodwill impairment test.

Transitional impairment test for indefinite-lived intangibles

BC223 SFAS 142 also requires a transitional impairment test to be applied, as of the beginning of the fiscal year in which that Standard is initially applied, to intangible assets recognised before the effective date of SFAS 142 that are reassessed as having indefinite useful lives. An impairment loss arising from that transitional impairment test is recognised as the effect of a change in accounting principle rather than as an impairment loss. As with goodwill:

(a) intangible assets that cease being amortised upon initial application of SFAS 142 are tested for impairment in accordance with SFAS 142 using a different method from what had previously applied to those assets. Therefore, it is possible that such an intangible asset not previously regarded as impaired might be determined to be impaired under SFAS 142.

(b) the FASB concluded that the preponderance of any transitional impairment losses would be likely to result from the change in impairment testing methods. Treating those losses as stemming from changes in accounting principles is therefore more representationally faithful.

BC224 The Board considered whether IAS 36 should include a transitional impairment test for indefinite-lived intangibles similar to that in SFAS 142.

BC225 The Board observed that the previous version of IAS 38 *Intangible Assets* required an intangible asset being amortised over a period exceeding 20 years to be tested for impairment at least at each financial year-end in accordance with the previous version of IAS 36. An intangible asset being amortised over a period not exceeding 20 years was required, under the previous version of IAS 36, to be tested for impairment at the balance sheet date only if there was an indication the asset might be impaired. The revised Standard requires an indefinite-lived intangible to be tested for impairment at least annually. However, it also requires that the recoverable amount of such an asset should continue to be measured as the higher of the asset's value in use and fair value less costs to sell.

BC226 As with goodwill, the Board concluded that the revised Standard should not require a transitional impairment test for indefinite-lived intangibles because:

(a)   the only circumstance in which a transitional impairment test might give rise to the recognition of an impairment loss would be when an indefinite-lived intangible previously being amortised over a period not exceeding 20 years was, immediately before the beginning of the period in which the revised Standard is effective, impaired in the absence of any indicator of impairment that ought reasonably to have been considered by the entity.

(b)   any such impairment loss would nonetheless be recognised as a consequence of applying the requirement in the Standard to test such assets for impairment at least annually. Therefore, the only benefit of such a test would be to separate the impairment loss arising before the period in which the revised Standard is effective from any impairment loss arising after the beginning of that period.

(c)   given the extremely rare circumstances in which this issue is likely to arise, the benefit of applying a transitional impairment test is outweighed by the added costs of the test.

Early application (paragraph 140)

BC227   The Board noted that the issue of any Standard demonstrates its opinion that application of the Standard will result in more useful information being provided to users about an entity's financial position, performance or cash flows. On that basis, a case exists for permitting, and indeed encouraging, entities to apply IAS 36 before its effective date. However, the Board also considered that permitting a revised Standard to be applied before its effective date potentially diminishes comparability between entities in the period(s) leading up to that effective date, and has the effect of providing entities with an option.

BC228   The Board concluded that the benefit of providing users with more useful information about an entity's financial position, performance and cash flows by permitting early application of IAS 36 outweighs the disadvantages of potentially diminished comparability. Therefore, entities are encouraged to apply the requirements of IAS 36 before its effective date. However, given that the revision of IAS 36 is part of an integrated package, IAS 36 requires IFRS 3 and IAS 38 (as revised in 2004) to be applied at the same time.

Transitional provision for *Improvements to IFRSs* (2009)

BC228A   The Board considered the transition provisions and effective date of the amendment to paragraph 80(b). The Board noted that the assessment of goodwill impairment might involve the use of hindsight in determining the fair values of the cash-generating units at the end of a past reporting period. Considering practicability, the Board decided that the effective date should be for annual periods beginning on or after 1 January 2010 although the Board noted that the effective date of IFRS 8 is 1 January 2009. Therefore, the Board decided that an entity should apply the amendment to paragraph 80(b) made by *Improvements to IFRSs* issued in April 2009 prospectively for annual periods beginning on or after 1 January 2010.

Transition provisions for *Recoverable Amount Disclosures for Non-Financial Assets*

BC228B   In Exposure Draft ED/2013/1, the IASB proposed retrospective application and to permit earlier application of the amendments. The vast majority of the respondents supported those proposals.

BC228C   The IASB decided to retain in the final amendments the transition requirements proposed in Exposure Draft ED/2013/1 that meant that entities should not provide comparative information for the prior period if they are not also applying IFRS 13 in that period. The objective of such transition requirements is to make these amendments have the same effect as if they had been issued when the IASB issued IFRS 13.

Summary of main changes from the Exposure Draft

BC229   The following are the main changes from the Exposure Draft:

(a)   the Exposure Draft proposed that an intangible asset with an indefinite useful life should be tested for impairment at the end of each annual period by comparing its carrying amount with its recoverable amount. The Standard requires such an intangible asset to be tested for impairment annually by comparing its carrying amount with its recoverable amount. The impairment test may be performed at any time during an annual period, provided it is performed at the same time every year, and different intangible assets may be tested for impairment at different times. However, if such an intangible asset was initially recognised during the current annual period, the Standard requires that intangible asset to be tested for impairment before the end of the current annual period.

(b)   the Exposure Draft proposed that the cash flow projections used to measure value in use should be based on reasonable and supportable assumptions that take into account both past actual cash flows and management's past ability to forecast cash flows accurately. This proposal has not been included in the Standard. Instead, the Standard includes guidance clarifying that management:

(i)   should assess the reasonableness of the assumptions on which its current cash flow projections are based by examining the causes of differences between past cash flow projections and actual cash flows; and

(ii)   should ensure that the assumptions on which its current cash flow projections are based are consistent with past actual outcomes, provided the effects of subsequent events or circumstances that did not exist when those actual cash flows were generated make this appropriate.

(c)   the Exposure Draft proposed that if an active market exists for the output produced by an asset or a group of assets, that asset or group of assets should be identified as a cash-generating unit, even if some or all of the output is used internally. In such circumstances, management's best estimate of future market prices for the output should be used in estimating the future cash flows used to determine the unit's value in use. The Exposure Draft also proposed that when estimating future cash flows to determine the value in use of cash-generating units using the output, management's best estimate of future market prices for the output should be used. The Standard similarly requires that if an active market exists for the output produced by an asset or a group of assets, that asset or group of assets should be identified as a cash-generating unit, even if some or all of the output is used internally. However, the Standard clarifies that if the cash inflows generated by *any* asset or cash-generating unit are affected by internal transfer pricing, an entity should use management's best estimate of future price(s) that could be achieved in arm's length transactions in estimating:

(i)　the future cash inflows used to determine the asset's or cash-generating unit's value in use; and

(ii)　the future cash outflows used to determine the value in use of other assets or cash-generating units affected by the internal transfer pricing.

(d)　the Exposure Draft proposed that goodwill acquired in a business combination should be allocated to one or more cash-generating units, with each of those units representing the smallest cash-generating unit to which a portion of the carrying amount of the goodwill could be allocated on a reasonable and consistent basis. The Exposure Draft also proposed that:

(i)　a portion of the carrying amount of goodwill should be regarded as capable of being allocated to a cash-generating unit on a reasonable and consistent basis only when that unit represents the lowest level at which management monitors the return on investment in assets that include the goodwill.

(ii)　each cash-generating unit should not be larger than a segment based on the entity's primary reporting format determined in accordance with IAS 14 *Segment Reporting*.

The Standard requires goodwill acquired in a business combination to be allocated to each of the acquirer's cash-generating units, or groups of cash-generating units, that are expected to benefit from the synergies of the combination, irrespective of whether other assets or liabilities of the acquiree are assigned to those units or groups of units. The Standard also requires each unit or group of units to which the goodwill is so allocated: (1) to represent the lowest level within the entity at which the goodwill is monitored for internal management purposes; and (2) to be not larger than a segment based on either the entity's primary or the entity's secondary reporting format determined in accordance with IAS 14.

(e)　the Exposure Draft proposed that when an entity disposes of an operation within a cash-generating unit to which goodwill has been allocated, the goodwill associated with that operation should be:

(i)   included in the carrying amount of the operation when determining the gain or loss on disposal; and

(ii)   measured on the basis of the relative values of the operation disposed of and the portion of the cash-generating unit retained.

This proposal has been included in the Standard with one modification. The Standard requires the goodwill associated with the operation disposed of to be measured on the basis of the relative values of the operation disposed of and the portion of the cash-generating unit retained, unless the entity can demonstrate that some other method better reflects the goodwill associated with the operation disposed of.

(f)   the Exposure Draft proposed that when an entity reorganises its reporting structure in a way that changes the composition of cash-generating units to which goodwill has been allocated, the goodwill should be reallocated to the units affected using a relative value approach similar to that used when an entity disposes of an operation within a cash-generating unit. The Standard similarly requires an entity that reorganises its reporting structure in a way that changes the composition of one or more cash-generating units to which goodwill has been allocated to reallocate the goodwill to the units (groups of units) affected. However, the Standard requires this reallocation to be performed using a relative value approach similar to that used when an entity disposes of an operation within a cash-generating unit, unless the entity can demonstrate that some other method better reflects the goodwill associated with the reorganised units (groups of units).

(g)   the Exposure Draft proposed a two-step approach for impairment testing goodwill. The first step involved using a screening mechanism for identifying potential goodwill impairments, whereby goodwill allocated to a cash-generating unit would be identified as potentially impaired only when the carrying amount of the unit exceeded its recoverable amount.   If an entity identified the goodwill allocated to a cash-generating unit as potentially impaired, an entity would then determine whether the goodwill allocated to the unit was impaired by comparing its recoverable amount, measured as the implied value of the goodwill, with its carrying amount. The implied value of goodwill would be measured as a residual, being the excess of the recoverable amount of the cash-generating unit to which the goodwill has been allocated, over the net fair value of the identifiable assets, liabilities and contingent liabilities the entity would recognise if it acquired the cash-generating unit in a business combination on the date of the impairment test. The Standard requires any excess of the carrying amount of a cash-generating unit (group of units) to which goodwill has been allocated over its recoverable amount to be recognised first as an impairment loss for goodwill. Any excess remaining after the carrying amount of goodwill has been reduced to zero is then recognised by being allocated to the other assets of the unit pro rata with their carrying amounts.

(h) the Exposure Draft proposed requiring an entity to disclose information about cash-generating units whose carrying amounts included goodwill or indefinite-lived intangibles. That information included the carrying amount of goodwill and the carrying amount of indefinite-lived intangibles, the basis on which the unit's recoverable amount had been determined (ie value in use or net selling price), the amount by which the unit's recoverable amount exceeded its carrying amount, the key assumptions and estimates used to measure the unit's recoverable amount and information about the sensitivity of that recoverable amount to changes in the key assumptions and estimates. If an entity reports segment information in accordance with IAS 14, the Exposure Draft proposed that this information should be disclosed in aggregate for each segment based on the entity's primary reporting format. However, the Exposure Draft also proposed that the information would be disclosed separately for a cash-generating unit if specified criteria were met. The Standard:

    (i) does not require information for evaluating the reliability of the impairment tests for goodwill and indefinite-lived intangibles to be disclosed in aggregate for each segment and separately for cash-generating units within a segment when specified criteria are met. Instead, the Standard requires this information to be disclosed for each cash-generating unit (group of units) for which the carrying amount of goodwill or indefinite-lived intangibles allocated to that unit (group of units) is significant in comparison with the entity's total carrying amount of goodwill or indefinite-lived intangibles.

    (ii) does not require an entity to disclose the amount by which the recoverable amount of a cash-generating unit exceeds its carrying amount. Instead, the Standard requires an entity to disclose this information only if a reasonably possible change in a key assumption on which management has based its determination of the unit's (group of units') recoverable amount would cause the unit's (group of units') carrying amount to exceed its recoverable amount.

    (iii) does not require an entity to disclose the value assigned to each key assumption on which management has based its recoverable amount determination, and the amount by which that value must change, after incorporating any consequential effects of that change on the other variables used to measure recoverable amount, in order for the unit's recoverable amount to be equal to its carrying amount. Instead, the Standard requires an entity to disclose a description of each key assumption on which management has based its recoverable amount determination, management's approach to determining the value(s) assigned to each key assumption, whether those value(s) reflect past experience or, if appropriate, are consistent with external sources of information, and, if not, how and why they differ from past experience or external sources of information. However, if a reasonably possible change in a key assumption would cause the unit's (group of units') carrying amount to exceed its recoverable amount, the entity is also required to disclose the value assigned to the key assumption, and the amount by which that value must change, after incorporating any consequential effects of that change on the other variables used to measure recoverable amount, in order for the unit's (group of units') recoverable amount to be equal to its carrying amount.

(iv) requires information about key assumptions to be disclosed for any key assumption that is relevant to the recoverable amount determination of multiple cash-generating units (groups of units) that individually contain insignificant amounts of goodwill or indefinite-lived intangibles, but which contain, in aggregate, significant amounts of goodwill or indefinite-lived intangibles.

History of the development of a standard on impairment of assets

BCZ230   In June 1996, IASC decided to prepare an International Accounting Standard on Impairment of Assets. The reasons for developing a Standard on impairment of assets were:

(a) to combine the requirements for identifying, measuring, recognising and reversing an impairment loss in one Standard to ensure that those requirements are consistent;

(b) the previous requirements and guidance in International Accounting Standards were not detailed enough to ensure that enterprises identified, recognised and measured impairment losses in a similar way, eg there was a need to eliminate certain alternatives for measuring an impairment loss, such as the former option not to use discounting; and

(c) IASC decided in March 1996 to explore whether the amortisation period of intangible assets and goodwill could, in certain rare circumstances, exceed 20 years if those assets were subject to detailed and reliable annual impairment tests.

BCZ231   In April 1997, IASC approved Exposure Draft E55 *Impairment of Assets*. IASC received more than 90 comment letters from over 20 countries. IASC also performed a field test of E55's proposals. More than 20 companies from various business sectors and from 10 different countries participated in the field test. About half of the field test participants prepared their financial statements using International Accounting Standards and the other half reported using other Standards. Field test participants completed a detailed questionnaire and most of them were visited by IASC staff to discuss the results of the application of E55's proposals to some of their assets. A brief summary of the comment letters received on E55 and the results of the field test was published in IASC *Insight* in December 1997.

BCZ232   In October 1997, IASC, together with the Accounting Standards Boards in Australia, Canada, New Zealand, the United Kingdom and the United States, published a discussion paper entitled *International Review of Accounting Standards*

Specifying a Recoverable Amount Test for Long-Lived Assets (Jim Paul, from the staff of the Australian Accounting Research Foundation, was the principal author). This discussion paper resulted from the discussions of a 'working group' consisting of some Board members and senior staff members from the standard-setting bodies listed above and IASC. The paper:

(a)   noted the key features of the working group members' existing or proposed accounting standards that require an impairment test, and compared those standards; and

(b)   proposed the views of the working group on the major issues.

BCZ233   In April 1998, after considering the comments received on E55 and the results of the field test, IASC approved IAS 36 *Impairment of Assets*.

Dissenting opinions

Dissent of Anthony T Cope, James J Leisenring and Geoffrey Whittington

DO1   Messrs Cope and Leisenring and Professor Whittington dissent from the issue of IAS 36.

DO2   Messrs Cope and Leisenring and Professor Whittington dissent because they object to the impairment test that the Standard requires for goodwill.

DO3   Messrs Cope and Leisenring agree with the prohibition, in paragraph 54 of IFRS 3 *Business Combinations*, of amortisation of goodwill.[45] Research and experience have demonstrated that the amortisation of goodwill produces data that is meaningless, and perhaps even misleading. However, if goodwill is not amortised, its special nature mandates that it should be accounted for with caution. The Basis for Conclusions on IAS 36 (paragraph BC131) states that 'if a rigorous and operational impairment test [for goodwill] could be devised, more useful information would be provided to users of an entity's financial statements under an approach in which goodwill is not amortised, but instead tested for impairment annually or more frequently if events or changes in circumstances indicate that the goodwill might be impaired.' Messrs Cope and Leisenring agree with that statement. However, they believe that the impairment test to which a majority of the Board has agreed lacks the rigour to satisfy that condition.

DO4   Messrs Cope and Leisenring share the reservations of some Board members, as noted in paragraph BC130 of the Basis for Conclusions on IAS 36, about an impairment test based on measuring the recoverable amount of an asset, and particularly an asset with an indefinite life, as the higher of fair value less costs to sell or value in use. Messrs Cope and Leisenring are content, however, for the time being to defer consideration of that general measurement issue, pending more research and debate on measurement principles. (They note that the use of fair value would achieve significant convergence with US GAAP.) But a much more rigorous effort must be made to determine the recoverable amount of goodwill, however measured, than the Board's revised impairment test. The 'two-step' method originally proposed by the Board in the Exposure Draft of Proposed Amendments to IAS 36 and IAS 38 was a more useful approach to determining the 'implied value' of goodwill. That test should have been retained.

DO5   Messrs Cope and Leisenring recognise that some constituents raised objections to the complexity and potential cost of the requirements proposed in the Exposure Draft. However, they believe that many commentators misunderstood the level at which the Board intended impairment testing to be undertaken. This was demonstrated during the field-testing of the Exposure Draft. Furthermore, the provisions of paragraph 99 of IAS 36, specifying when impairment testing need not be undertaken, provide generous relief from the

---

45 The Board issued a revised IFRS 3 in 2008. The amortisation of goodwill is prohibited, but the paragraph reference no longer exists in IFRS 3 (as revised in 2008).

necessity of making frequent calculations. They would have preferred to meet those objections by specifying that the goodwill impairment test should be at the level set out in US Financial Accounting Standards Board's Statement of Financial Accounting Standards No. 142 *Goodwill and Other Intangible Assets*.

DO6   Professor Whittington believes that there are two aspects of the proposed impairment test that are particularly unsatisfactory. First, the failure to eliminate the shield from impairment provided by the internally generated goodwill of the acquiring entity at acquisition. This is discussed in paragraph DO7. Second, the lack of a subsequent cash flow test. This is discussed in paragraphs DO8–DO10. The inability to eliminate the shield from impairment provided by internally generated goodwill accruing after the acquisition date is also a problem. However, there is no obvious practical way of dealing with this problem within the framework of conventional impairment tests.

DO7   When an acquired business is merged with an acquirer's existing operations, the impairment test in IAS 36 does not take account of the acquirer's pre-existing internally generated goodwill. Thus, the pre-existing internally generated goodwill of the acquirer provides a shield against impairment additional to that provided by subsequent internally generated goodwill. Professor Whittington believes that the impairment test would be more rigorous if it included a requirement similar to that in UK Financial Reporting Standard 11 *Impairment of Fixed Assets and Goodwill*, which recognises, for purposes of impairment testing, the implied value of the acquirer's goodwill existing at the time of acquisition.

DO8   The subsequent cash flow test is discussed in paragraphs BC195–BC198 of the Basis for Conclusions on IAS 36. A subsequent cash flow test substitutes in past impairment tests the cash flows that actually occurred for those that were estimated at the time of the impairment tests, and requires a write-down if the revised estimates would have created an impairment loss for goodwill. It is thus a correction of an estimate. Such a test is incorporated in FRS 11.

DO9   The Board's reasons for rejecting the subsequent cash flow test are given in paragraph BC197(a)–(c). The preamble to paragraph BC197 claims that the subsequent cash flow test is misdirected because excessive write-downs of goodwill may be a problem that should be prevented. However, the subsequent cash flow test requires only realistic write-downs (based on actual outcomes), not excessive ones. If the statement in paragraph BC197 is correct, this may point to another deficiency in the impairment testing process that requires a different remedy.

DO10   Paragraph BC197(a) asserts that 'it does not produce representationally faithful results' because it ignores other elements in the measurement of value in use. As explained above, it merely substitutes the outcome cash flow for the estimate, which should have a clear meaning and provides a safeguard against over-optimism in the estimation of cash flows. If corrections of estimates of other elements, such as variations that have occurred in interest rates, were considered important in this context, they could be incorporated in the calculation. Paragraph BC197(b) seems to raise the same point as paragraph BC197(a), as to the meaning of the impairment loss under the test. Paragraph BC197(c) complains about the excessive burden that a subsequent cash flow test might impose. Professor Whittington notes that the extent of the burden depends, of course, upon the frequency with which the test is applied. He also notes that the extensive disclosure requirements currently associated with the impairment test might be reduced if the subsequent cash flow test were in place.

IASB documents published to accompany

IAS 38

Intangible Assets

The text of the unaccompanied standard, IAS 38, is contained in Part A of this edition. Its effective date when issued was 31 March 2004. The text of the Accompanying Guidance on IAS 38 is contained in Part B of this edition. This part presents the following documents:

BASIS FOR CONCLUSIONS
DISSENTING OPINIONS

Contents

Basis for Conclusions on
IAS 38 *Intangible Assets*

The International Accounting Standards Board revised IAS 38 as part of its project on business combinations. It was not the Board's intention to reconsider as part of that project all of the requirements in IAS 38.

The previous version of IAS 38 was accompanied by a Basis for Conclusions summarising the former International Accounting Standards Committee's considerations in reaching some of its conclusions in that Standard. For convenience the Board has incorporated into its own Basis for Conclusions material from the previous Basis for Conclusions that discusses (a) matters the Board did not reconsider and (b) the history of the development of a standard on intangible assets. That material is contained in paragraphs denoted by numbers with the prefix BCZ. Paragraphs describing the Board's considerations in reaching its own conclusions are numbered with the prefix BC.

Introduction

BC1   This Basis for Conclusions summarises the International Accounting Standards Board's considerations in reaching the conclusions in IAS 38 *Intangible Assets*. Individual Board members gave greater weight to some factors than to others.

BC2   The International Accounting Standards Committee (IASC) issued the previous version of IAS 38 in 1998. It has been revised by the Board as part of its project on business combinations. That project has two phases. The first has resulted in the Board issuing simultaneously IFRS 3 *Business Combinations* and revised versions of IAS 38 and IAS 36 *Impairment of Assets*. Therefore, the Board's intention in revising IAS 38 as part of the first phase of the project was not to reconsider all of the requirements in IAS 38. The changes to IAS 38 are primarily concerned with:

(a)   the notion of 'identifiability' as it relates to intangible assets;

(b)   the useful life and amortisation of intangible assets; and

(c)   the accounting for in-process research and development projects acquired in business combinations.

BC3   With the exception of research and development projects acquired in business combinations, the Board did not reconsider the requirements in the previous version of IAS 38 on the recognition of internally generated intangible assets. The previous version of IAS 38 was accompanied by a Basis for Conclusions summarising IASC's considerations in reaching some of its conclusions in that Standard. For convenience, the Board has incorporated into this Basis for Conclusions material from the previous Basis for Conclusions that discusses the recognition of internally generated intangible assets (see paragraphs BCZ29–BCZ46) and the history of the development of a standard on intangible assets (see paragraphs BCZ104–BCZ110). The views expressed in paragraphs BCZ29–BCZ46 and BCZ104–BCZ110 are those of IASC.

Definition of an intangible asset (paragraph 8)

BC4   An intangible asset was defined in the previous version of IAS 38 as 'an identifiable non-monetary asset without physical substance held for use in the production or supply of goods or services, for rental to others, or for administrative services'. The definition in the revised Standard eliminates the requirement for the asset to be held for use in the production or supply of goods or services, for rental to others, or for administrative services.

BC5   The Board observed that the essential characteristics of intangible assets are that they:

(a)   are resources controlled by the entity from which future economic benefits are expected to flow to the entity;

(b)   lack physical substance; and

(c)   are identifiable.

The Board concluded that the purpose for which an entity holds an item with these characteristics is not relevant to its classification as an intangible asset, and that all such items should be within the scope of the Standard.

Identifiability (paragraph 12)

BC6   Under the Standard, as under the previous version of IAS 38, a non-monetary asset without physical substance must be identifiable to meet the definition of an intangible asset. The previous version of IAS 38 did not define 'identifiability', but stated that an intangible asset could be distinguished from goodwill if the asset was separable, but that separability was not a necessary condition for identifiability. The revised Standard requires an asset to be treated as meeting the identifiability criterion in the definition of an intangible asset when it is separable, or when it arises from contractual or other legal rights, regardless of whether those rights are transferable or separable from the entity or from other rights and obligations.

Background to the Board's deliberations

BC7   The Board was prompted to consider the issue of 'identifiability' as part of the first phase of its Business Combinations project as a result of changes during 2001 to the requirements in Canadian and United States standards on the separate recognition of intangible assets acquired in business combinations. The Board observed that intangible assets comprise an increasing proportion of the assets of many entities, and that intangible assets acquired in a business combination are often included in the amount recognised as goodwill, despite the requirements in IAS 22 *Business Combinations* and IAS 38 for them to be recognised separately from goodwill. The Board agreed with the conclusion reached by the Canadian and US standard-setters that the usefulness of financial statements would be enhanced if intangible assets acquired in a business combination were distinguished from goodwill. Therefore, the Board concluded that the IFRS arising from the first phase of the Business Combinations project should provide a definitive basis for identifying and recognising intangible assets acquired in a business combination separately from goodwill.

© IFRS Foundation

BC8   In revising IAS 38 and developing IFRS 3, the Board affirmed the view in the previous version of IAS 38 that identifiability is the characteristic that conceptually distinguishes other intangible assets from goodwill. The Board concluded that to provide a definitive basis for identifying and recognising intangible assets separately from goodwill, the concept of identifiability needed to be articulated more clearly.

Clarifying identifiability (paragraph 12)

BC9   Consistently with the guidance in the previous version of IAS 38, the Board concluded that an intangible asset can be distinguished from goodwill if it is separable, ie capable of being separated or divided from the entity and sold, transferred, licensed, rented or exchanged. Therefore, in the context of intangible assets, separability signifies identifiability, and intangible assets with that characteristic that are acquired in a business combination should be recognised as assets separately from goodwill.

BC10   However, again consistently with the guidance in the previous version of IAS 38, the Board concluded that separability is not the only indication of identifiability. The Board observed that, in contrast to goodwill, the values of many intangible assets arise from rights conveyed legally by contract or statute. In the case of acquired goodwill, its value arises from the collection of assembled assets that make up an acquired entity or the value created by assembling a collection of assets through a business combination, such as the synergies that are expected to result from combining entities or businesses. The Board also observed that, although many intangible assets are both separable and arise from contractual-legal rights, some contractual-legal rights establish property interests that are not readily separable from the entity as a whole. For example, under the laws of some jurisdictions some licences granted to an entity are not transferable except by sale of the entity as a whole. The Board concluded that the fact that an intangible asset arises from contractual or other legal rights is a characteristic that distinguishes it from goodwill. Therefore, intangible assets with that characteristic that are acquired in a business combination should be recognised as assets separately from goodwill.

Non-contractual customer relationships (paragraph 16)

BC11   The previous version of IAS 38 and the Exposure Draft of Proposed Amendments to IAS 38 stated that 'An entity controls an asset if the entity has the power to obtain the future economic benefits flowing from the underlying resource and also can restrict the access of others to those benefits'. The documents then expanded on this by stating that 'in the absence of legal rights to protect, or other ways to control, the relationships with customers or the loyalty of the customers to the entity, the entity usually has insufficient control over the economic benefits from customer relationships and loyalty to consider that such items meet the definition of intangible assets'.

BC12   However, the Draft Illustrative Examples accompanying ED 3 *Business Combinations* stated that 'If a customer relationship acquired in a business combination does not arise from a contract, the relationship is recognised as an intangible asset separately from goodwill if it meets the separability criterion. Exchange transactions for the same asset or a similar asset provide evidence of separability of a non-contractual customer relationship and might also provide information about exchange prices that should be considered when estimating fair value.' Whilst respondents to the Exposure Draft generally agreed with the Board's conclusions on the definition of identifiability, some were uncertain about the relationship between the separability criterion for establishing whether a non-contractual customer relationship is identifiable, and the control concept for establishing whether the relationship meets the definition of an asset. Additionally, some respondents suggested that non-contractual customer relationships would, under the proposal in the Exposure Draft, be separately recognised if acquired in a business combination, but not if acquired in a separate transaction.

BC13   The Board observed that exchange transactions for the same or similar non-contractual customer relationships provide evidence not only that the item is separable, but also that the entity is able to control the expected future economic benefits flowing from that relationship. Similarly, if an entity separately acquires a non-contractual customer relationship, the existence of an exchange transaction for that relationship provides evidence both that the item is separable, and that the entity is able to control the expected future economic benefits flowing from the relationship. Therefore, the relationship would meet the intangible asset definition and be recognised as such. However, in the absence of exchange transactions for the same or similar non-contractual customer relationships, such relationships acquired in a business combination would not normally meet the definition of an 'intangible asset'—they would not be separable, nor would the entity be able to demonstrate that it controls the expected future economic benefits flowing from that relationship.

BC14   Therefore, the Board decided to clarify in paragraph 16 of IAS 38 that in the absence of legal rights to protect customer relationships, exchange transactions for the same or similar non-contractual customer relationships (other than as part of a business combination) provide evidence that the entity is nonetheless able to control the future economic benefits flowing from the customer relationships. Because such exchange transactions also provide evidence that the customer relationships are separable, those customer relationships meet the definition of an intangible asset.

Criteria for initial recognition

BC15   In accordance with the Standard, as with the previous version of IAS 38, an intangible asset is recognised if, and only if:

(a)   it is probable that the expected future economic benefits that are attributable to the asset will flow to the entity; and

(b)   the cost of the asset can be measured reliably.

In revising IAS 38 the Board considered the application of these recognition criteria to intangible assets acquired in business combinations. The Board's deliberations on this issue are set out in paragraphs BC16–BC25.

Acquisition as part of a business combination (paragraphs 33–38)

BC16   [Deleted]

BC16A   The Board observed that in a business combination both criteria, the probability criterion and the reliability of measurement criterion, will always be met.

Probability recognition criterion

BC17   In revising IAS 38, the Board observed that the fair value of an intangible asset reflects market expectations about the probability that the future economic benefits associated with the intangible asset will flow to the acquirer. In other words, the effect of probability is reflected in the fair value measurement of an intangible asset.[1] Therefore, the probability recognition criterion is always considered to be satisfied for intangible assets acquired in business combinations.

BC18   The Board observed that this highlights a general inconsistency between the recognition criteria for assets and liabilities in the *Framework*[2] (which states that an item meeting the definition of an element should be recognised only if it is probable that any future economic benefits associated with the item will flow to or from the entity, and the item can be measured reliably) and the fair value measurements required in, for example, a business combination. However, the Board concluded that the role of probability as a criterion for recognition in the *Framework* should be considered more generally as part of a forthcoming Concepts project.

Reliability of measurement recognition criterion

BC19   [Deleted]

BC19A   In developing IFRS 3, the IASB noted that the fair values of identifiable intangible assets acquired in a business combination are normally measurable with sufficient reliability to be recognised separately from goodwill. The effects of uncertainty because of a range of possible outcomes with different probabilities are reflected in measuring the asset's fair value;[3] the existence of such a range does not demonstrate an inability to measure fair value reliably. IAS 38 (as revised in 2004) included a rebuttable presumption that the fair value of an intangible asset with a finite useful life acquired in a business combination can be measured reliably. The Board had concluded that it might not always be possible to measure reliably the fair value of an asset that has an underlying contractual or legal basis. However, IAS 38 (revised 2004) provided that the only circumstances in which it might not be possible to measure reliably the fair value of an intangible asset acquired in a business combination that arises from legal or other contractual rights were if it either:

        (a)   is not separable; or

---

1   IFRS 13 *Fair Value Measurement*, issued in May 2011, defines fair value and contains the requirements for measuring fair value.

2   References to the *Framework* are to IASC's *Framework for the Preparation and Presentation of Financial Statements*, adopted by the IASB in 2001. In September 2010 the IASB replaced the *Framework* with the *Conceptual Framework for Financial Reporting*.

3   IFRS 13, issued in May 2011, contains the requirements for measuring fair value.

(b)   is separable, but there is no history or evidence of exchange transactions for the same or similar assets, and otherwise estimating fair value would depend on immeasurable variables.

BC19B   In developing the 2005 Business Combinations exposure draft, the Board concluded that separate recognition of intangible assets, on the basis of an estimate of fair value, rather than subsuming them in goodwill, provides better information to the users of financial statements even if a significant degree of judgement is required to estimate fair value. For this reason, the Board decided to propose consequential amendments to IAS 38 to remove the reliability of measurement criterion for intangible assets acquired in a business combination. In redeliberating the proposals in the 2005 Business Combinations exposure draft, the Board affirmed those amendments to IAS 38.

BC19C   When the Board developed IFRS 3 (as revised in 2008), it decided that if an intangible asset acquired in a business combination is separable or arises from contractual or other legal rights, sufficient information exists to measure the fair value of the asset reliably. The Board made related amendments to IAS 38 to reflect that decision. However, the Board identified additional amendments that were needed to reflect clearly its decisions on the accounting for intangible assets acquired in a business combination. Consequently, in *Improvements to IFRSs* issued in April 2009, the Board amended paragraphs 36 and 37 of IAS 38 to clarify the Board's intentions.

BC19D   Additionally, in *Improvements to IFRSs* issued in April 2009, the Board amended paragraphs 40 and 41 of IAS 38 to clarify the description of valuation techniques commonly used to measure intangible assets at fair value[4] when assets are not traded in an active market. The Board also decided that the amendments should be applied prospectively because retrospective application might require some entities to remeasure fair values associated with previous transactions. The Board does not think this is appropriate because the remeasurement might involve the use of hindsight in those circumstances.

BC20–
BC25   [Deleted]

Separate acquisition (paragraphs 25 and 26)

BC26   Having decided to include paragraphs 33–38 in IAS 38, the Board also decided that it needed to consider the role of the probability and reliability of measurement recognition criteria for separately acquired intangible assets.

BC27   Consistently with its conclusion about the role of probability in the recognition of intangible assets acquired in business combinations, the Board concluded that the probability recognition criterion is always considered to be satisfied for separately acquired intangible assets. This is because the price an entity pays to acquire separately an intangible asset normally reflects expectations about the probability that the expected future economic benefits associated with the intangible asset will flow to the entity. In other words, the effect of probability is reflected in the cost of the intangible asset.

---

4   IFRS 13, issued in May 2011, contains the requirements for measuring fair value. As a consequence paragraphs 40 and 41 of IAS 38 have been deleted.

BC28   The Board also concluded that when an intangible asset is separately acquired in exchange for cash or other monetary assets, sufficient information should exist to measure the cost of that asset reliably. However, this might not be the case when the purchase consideration comprises non-monetary assets. Therefore, the Board decided to carry forward from the previous version of IAS 38 guidance clarifying that the cost of a separately acquired intangible asset can usually be measured reliably, particularly when the purchase consideration is cash or other monetary assets.

Internally generated intangible assets (paragraphs 51–67)

BCZ29   The controversy relating to internally generated intangible assets surrounds whether there should be:

(a)   a requirement to recognise internally generated intangible assets in the balance sheet whenever certain criteria are met;

(b)   a requirement to recognise expenditure on all internally generated intangible assets as an expense;

(c)   a requirement to recognise expenditure on all internally generated intangible assets as an expense, with certain specified exceptions; or

(d)   an option to choose between the treatments described in (a) and (b) above.

Background on the requirements for internally generated intangible assets

BCZ30   Before IAS 38 was issued in 1998, some internally generated intangible assets (those that arose from development expenditure) were dealt with under IAS 9 *Research and Development Costs*. The development of, and revisions to, IAS 9 had always been controversial.

BCZ31   Proposed and approved requirements for the recognition of an asset arising from development expenditure and other internally generated intangible assets had been the following:

(a)   in 1978, IASC approved IAS 9 *Accounting for Research and Development Activities*. It required expenditure on research and development to be recognised as an expense when incurred, except that an enterprise had the option to recognise an asset arising from development expenditure whenever certain criteria were met.

(b)   in 1989, Exposure Draft E32 *Comparability of Financial Statements* proposed retaining IAS 9's option to recognise an asset arising from development expenditure if certain criteria were met and identifying:

(i)   as a preferred treatment, recognising all expenditure on research and development as an expense when incurred; and

(ii)   as an allowed alternative treatment, recognising an asset arising from development expenditure whenever certain criteria were met.

The majority of commentators on E32 did not support maintaining an option or the proposed preferred treatment.

(c) in 1991, Exposure Draft E37 *Research and Development Costs* proposed requiring the recognition of an asset arising from development expenditure whenever certain criteria were met. In 1993, IASC approved IAS 9 *Research and Development Costs* based on E37.

(d) in 1995, consistently with IAS 9, Exposure Draft E50 *Intangible Assets* proposed requiring internally generated intangible assets—other than those arising from development expenditure, which would still have been covered by IAS 9—to be recognised as assets whenever certain criteria were met.

(e) in 1997, Exposure Draft E60 *Intangible Assets* proposed:

   (i) retaining E50's proposals for the recognition of internally generated intangible assets; but

   (ii) extending the scope of the Standard on intangible assets to deal with all internally generated intangible assets—including those arising from development expenditure.

(f) in 1998, IASC approved:

   (i) IAS 38 *Intangible Assets* based on E60, with a few minor changes; and

   (ii) the withdrawal of IAS 9.

BCZ32 From 1989, the majority view at IASC and from commentators was that there should be only one treatment that would require an internally generated intangible asset—whether arising from development expenditure or other expenditure—to be recognised as an asset whenever certain recognition criteria are met. Several minority views were strongly opposed to this treatment but there was no clear consensus on any other single treatment.

Combination of IAS 9 with the Standard on intangible assets

BCZ33 The reasons for not retaining IAS 9 as a separate Standard were that:

(a) IASC believed that an identifiable asset that results from research and development activities is an intangible asset because knowledge is the primary outcome of these activities. Therefore, IASC supported treating expenditure on research and development activities similarly to expenditure on activities intended to create any other internally generated intangible assets.

(b) some commentators on E50, which proposed to exclude research and development expenditures from its scope,

   (i) argued that it was sometimes difficult to identify whether IAS 9 or the proposed Standard on intangible assets should apply, and

   (ii) perceived differences in accounting treatments between IAS 9 and E50's proposals, whereas this was not IASC's intent.

BCZ34 A large majority of commentators on E60 supported including certain aspects of IAS 9 with the proposed Standard on intangible assets and the withdrawal of IAS 9. A minority of commentators on E60 supported maintaining two separate

Standards. This minority supported the view that internally generated intangible assets should be dealt with on a case-by-case basis with separate requirements for different types of internally generated intangible assets. These commentators argued that E60's proposed recognition criteria were too general to be effective in practice for all internally generated intangible assets.

BCZ35   IASC rejected a proposal to develop separate standards (or detailed requirements within one standard) for specific types of internally generated intangible assets because, as explained above, IASC believed that the same recognition criteria should apply to all types of internally generated intangible assets.

Consequences of combining IAS 9 with IAS 38

BCZ36   The requirements in IAS 38 and IAS 9 differ in the following main respects:

(a)   IAS 9 limited the amount of expenditure that could initially be recognised for an asset arising from development expenditure (ie the amount that formed the cost of such an asset) to the amount that was probable of being recovered from the asset. Instead, IAS 38 requires that:

(i)   all expenditure incurred from when the recognition criteria are met until the asset is available for use should be accumulated to form the cost of the asset; and

(ii)   an enterprise should test for impairment, at least annually, an intangible asset that is not yet available for use. If the cost recognised for the asset exceeds its recoverable amount, an enterprise recognises an impairment loss accordingly. This impairment loss should be reversed if the conditions for reversals of impairment losses under IAS 36 *Impairment of Assets* are met.

(b)   IAS 38 permits an intangible asset to be measured after recognition at a revalued amount less subsequent amortisation and subsequent impairment losses. IAS 9 did not permit this treatment. However, it is highly unlikely that an active market (the condition required to revalue intangible assets) will exist for an asset that arises from development expenditure.

(c)   IAS 38 requires consideration of residual values in determining the depreciable amount of an intangible asset. IAS 9 prohibited the consideration of residual values. However, IAS 38 sets criteria that make it highly unlikely that an asset that arises from development expenditure would have a residual value above zero.

BCZ37   IASC believed that, in practice, it would be unlikely that the application of IAS 38 would result in differences from the application of IAS 9.

Recognition of expenditure on all internally generated intangible assets as an expense

BCZ38   Those who favour the recognition of expenditure on all internally generated intangible assets (including development expenditure) as an expense argue that:

(a)   internally generated intangible assets do not meet the *Framework*'s requirements for recognition as an asset because:

(i) the future economic benefits that arise from internally generated intangible assets cannot be distinguished from future economic benefits that arise from internally generated goodwill; and/or

(ii) it is impossible to distinguish reliably the expenditure associated with internally generated intangible assets from the expenditure associated with enhancing internally generated goodwill.

(b) comparability of financial statements will not be achieved. This is because the judgement involved in determining whether it is probable that future economic benefits will flow from internally generated intangible assets is too subjective to result in similar accounting under similar circumstances.

(c) it is not possible to assess reliably the amount that can be recovered from an internally generated intangible asset, unless its fair value can be determined by reference to an active market.[5] Therefore, recognising an internally generated intangible asset for which no active market exists at an amount other than zero may mislead investors.

(d) a requirement to recognise internally generated intangible assets at cost if certain criteria are met results in little, if any, decision-useful or predictive information because:

(i) demonstration of technological feasibility or commercial success in order to meet the recognition criteria will generally not be achieved until substantial expenditure has been recognised as an expense. Therefore, the cost recognised for an internally generated intangible asset will not reflect the total expenditure on that asset.

(ii) the cost of an internally generated intangible asset may not have any relationship to the value of the asset.

(e) in some countries, users are suspicious about an enterprise that recognises internally generated intangible assets.

(f) the added costs of maintaining the records necessary to justify and support the recognition of internally generated intangible assets do not justify the benefits.

Recognition of internally generated intangible assets

BCZ39 Those who support the mandatory recognition of internally generated intangible assets (including those resulting from development expenditure) whenever certain criteria are met argue that:

(a) recognition of an internally generated intangible asset if it meets the definition of an asset and the recognition criteria is consistent with the *Framework*. An enterprise can, in some instances:

(i) determine the probability of receiving future economic benefits from an internally generated intangible asset; and

---

5 IFRS 13, issued in May 2011, defines an active market.

      (ii)   distinguish the expenditure on this asset from expenditure on internally generated goodwill.

(b)   there has been massive investment in intangible assets in the last two decades. There have been complaints that:

    (i)   the non-recognition of investments in intangible assets in the financial statements distorts the measurement of an enterprise's performance and does not allow an accurate assessment of returns on investment in intangible assets; and

    (ii)   if enterprises do not track the returns on investment in intangible assets better, there is a risk of over- or under-investing in important assets. An accounting system that encourages such behaviour will become an increasingly inadequate signal, both for internal control purposes and for external purposes.

(c)   certain research studies, particularly in the United States, have established a cost-value association for research and development expenditures. The studies establish that capitalisation of research and development expenditure yields value-relevant information to investors.

(d)   the fact that some uncertainties exist about the value of an asset does not justify a requirement that no cost should be recognised for the asset.

(e)   it should not matter for recognition purposes whether an asset is purchased externally or developed internally. Particularly, there should be no opportunity for accounting arbitrage depending on whether an enterprise decides to outsource the development of an intangible asset or develop it internally.

IASC's view in approving IAS 38

BCZ40   IASC's view—consistently reflected in previous proposals for intangible assets—was that there should be no difference between the requirements for:

(a)   intangible assets that are acquired externally; and

(b)   internally generated intangible assets, whether they arise from development activities or other types of activities.

Therefore, an internally generated intangible asset should be recognised whenever the definition of, and recognition criteria for, an intangible asset are met. This view was also supported by a majority of commentators on E60.

BCZ41   IASC rejected a proposal for an allowed alternative to recognise expenditure on internally generated intangible assets (including development expenditure) as an expense immediately, even if the expenditure results in an asset that meets the recognition criteria. IASC believed that a free choice would undermine the comparability of financial statements and the efforts of IASC to reduce the number of alternative treatments in International Accounting Standards.

Differences in recognition criteria for internally generated intangible assets and purchased intangible assets

BCZ42   IAS 38 includes specific recognition criteria for internally generated intangible assets that expand on the general recognition criteria for intangible assets. It is assumed that these criteria are met implicitly whenever an enterprise acquires an intangible asset. Therefore, IAS 38 requires an enterprise to demonstrate that these criteria are met for internally generated intangible assets only.

Initial recognition at cost

BCZ43   Some commentators on E50 and E60 argued that the proposed recognition criteria in E50 and E60 were too restrictive and that they would prevent the recognition of many intangible assets, particularly internally generated intangible assets. Specifically, they disagreed with the proposals (retained in IAS 38) that:

(a)   an intangible asset should not be recognised at an amount other than its cost, even if its fair value can be determined reliably; and

(b)   expenditure on an intangible asset that has been recognised as an expense in prior periods should not be reinstated.

They argued that these principles contradict the *Framework* and quoted paragraph 83 of the *Framework*,[6] which specifies that an item that meets the definition of an asset should be recognised if, among other things, its '*cost or value* can be measured with reliability'. These commentators supported recognising an intangible asset—an internally generated intangible asset—at its fair value, if, among other things, its fair value can be measured reliably.

BCZ44   IASC rejected a proposal to allow the initial recognition of an intangible asset at fair value (except if the asset is acquired in a business combination, in exchange for a dissimilar asset[7] or by way of a government grant) because:

(a)   this is consistent with IAS 16 *Property, Plant and Equipment*. IAS 16 prohibits the initial recognition of an item of property, plant or equipment at fair value (except in the specific limited cases as those in IAS 38).

(b)   it is difficult to determine the fair value of an intangible asset reliably if no active market exists for the asset.[8] Since active markets with the characteristics set out in IAS 38 are highly unlikely to exist for internally generated intangible assets, IASC did not believe that it was necessary to make an exception to the principles generally applied for the initial recognition and measurement of non-financial assets.

(c)   the large majority of commentators on E50 supported the initial recognition of intangible assets at cost and the prohibition of the reinstatement of expenditure on an intangible item that was initially recognised as an expense.

---

6   now paragraph 4.38 of the *Conceptual Framework*

7   IAS 16 *Property, Plant and Equipment* (as revised in 2003) requires an entity to measure an item of property, plant and equipment acquired in exchange for a non-monetary asset or assets, or a combination of monetary and non-monetary assets, at fair value unless the exchange transaction lacks commercial substance. Previously, an entity measured such an acquired asset at fair value unless the exchanged assets were similar. The IASB concluded that the same measurement criteria should apply to intangible assets acquired in exchange for a non-monetary asset or assets, or a combination of monetary and non-monetary assets.

8   IFRS 13, issued in May 2011, defines an active market.

Application of the recognition criteria for internally generated intangible assets

BCZ45   IAS 38 specifically prohibits the recognition as intangible assets of brands, mastheads, publishing titles, customer lists and items similar in substance that are internally generated. IASC believed that internally generated intangible items of this kind would rarely, and perhaps never, meet the recognition criteria in IAS 38. However, to avoid any misunderstanding, IASC decided to set out this conclusion in the form of an explicit prohibition.

BCZ46   IAS 38 also clarifies that expenditure on research, training, advertising and start-up activities will not result in the creation of an intangible asset that can be recognised in the financial statements. Whilst some view these requirements and guidance as being too restrictive and arbitrary, they are based on IASC's interpretation of the application of the recognition criteria in IAS 38. They also reflect the fact that it is sometimes difficult to determine whether there is an internally generated intangible asset distinguishable from internally generated goodwill.

2008 Amendments[9]

BC46A   Paragraph 68 states that expenditure on an internally developed intangible item shall be recognised as an expense when it is incurred. The Board noted that it was unclear to some constituents how this should be interpreted. For example, some believed that an entity should recognise expenditure on advertising and promotional activities as an expense when it received the goods or services that it would use to develop or communicate the advertisement or promotion. Others believed that an entity should recognise an expense when the advertisement or promotion was delivered to its customers or potential customers. Therefore, the Board decided to amend paragraph 69 to clarify the meaning of 'incurred'.

BC46B   The Board noted that advertising and promotional activities enhance or create brands or customer relationships, which in turn generate revenues. Goods or services that are acquired to be used to undertake advertising or promotional activities have no other purpose than to undertake those activities. In other words, the only benefit of those goods or services is to develop or create brands or customer relationships, which in turn generate revenues. Internally generated brands or customer relationships are not recognised as intangible assets.

BC46C   The Board concluded that it would be inconsistent for an entity to recognise an asset in respect of an advertisement that it had not yet published if the economic benefits that might flow to the entity as a result of publishing the advertisement are the same as those that might flow to the entity as a result of the brand or customer relationship that it would enhance or create. Therefore, the Board concluded that an entity should not recognise as an asset goods or services that it had received in respect of its future advertising or promotional activities.

BC46D   In reaching this conclusion the Board noted that, if an entity pays for advertising goods or services in advance and the other party has not yet provided

---

9   This heading and paragraphs BC46A–BC46I were added by *Improvements to IFRSs* issued in May 2008.

those goods or services, the entity has a different asset. That asset is the right to receive those goods and services. Therefore, the Board decided to retain paragraph 70, which allows an entity to recognise as an asset the right to receive those goods or services. However, the Board did not believe that this paragraph should be used as a justification for recognising an asset beyond the point at which the entity gained a right to access the related goods or received the related services. Therefore, the Board decided to amend the paragraph to make clear that a prepayment may be recognised by an entity only until that entity has gained a right to access to the related goods or has received the related services.

BC46E   The Board noted that when the entity has received the related goods or services, it ceases to have the right to receive them. Because the entity no longer has an asset that it can recognise, it recognises an expense. However, the Board was concerned that the timing of delivery of goods should not be the determinant of when an expense should be recognised. The date on which physical delivery is obtained could be altered without affecting the commercial substance of the arrangement with the supplier. Therefore, the Board decided that an entity should recognise an expense for goods when they have been completed by the supplier in accordance with a contract to supply them and the entity could ask for delivery in return for payment—in other words, when the entity had gained a right to access the related goods.

BC46F   A number of commentators on the exposure draft of proposed *Improvements to International Financial Reporting Standards* published in 2007 thought that it was unclear when the Board intended an expense to be recognised. In response to those comments, the Board added paragraph 69A to clarify when entities would gain a right to access goods or receive services.

BC46G   The Board also received a number of comments arguing that mail order catalogues are not a form of advertising and promotion but instead give rise to a distribution network. The Board rejected these arguments, believing that the primary objective of mail order catalogues is to advertise goods to customers. To avoid confusion, the Board decided to include mail order catalogues in the Standard as an example of advertising activities.

BC46H   Some respondents who argued that the cost of mail order catalogues should be capitalised suggested that making an analogy to web site costs in SIC-32 *Intangible Assets—Web Site Costs* would be appropriate. The Board agreed and concluded that its proposed amendments would result in accounting that is almost identical to that resulting from the application of SIC-32. In particular, SIC-32 requires the cost of content (to the extent that it is developed to advertise and promote products and services) to be recognised as an expense as it is incurred. The Board concluded that in the case of a mail order catalogue, the majority of the content is intended to advertise and promote products and services. Therefore, permitting the cost of catalogues to be capitalised while at the same time requiring the cost of developing and uploading web site content used to advertise and promote an entity's products to be recognised as an expense would base the accounting on the nature of the media (paper or electronic) used to deliver the content rather than the nature of the expenditure.

BC46I   The Board also noted that SIC-32 permits expenditure on an internally developed web site to be capitalised only in the 'application and infrastructure development stage'. It requires costs associated with developing the functionality and infrastructure that make a web site operate to be capitalised. In the Board's view, the electronic infrastructure capitalised in accordance with SIC-32 is analogous to the property, plant and equipment infrastructure—for example, a sign—that permits advertising to be displayed to the public not the content that is displayed on that sign.

Subsequent accounting for intangible assets

BC47   The Board initially decided that the scope of the first phase of its Business Combinations project should include a consideration of the subsequent accounting for intangible assets acquired in business combinations. To that end, the Board initially focused its attention on the following three issues:

    (a)   whether an intangible asset with a finite useful life and acquired in a business combination should continue to be accounted for after initial recognition in accordance with IAS 38.

    (b)   whether, and under what circumstances, an intangible asset acquired in a business combination could be regarded as having an indefinite useful life.

    (c)   how an intangible asset with an indefinite useful life (assuming such an asset exists) acquired in a business combination should be accounted for after initial recognition.

BC48   However, during its deliberations of the issues in (b) and (c) of paragraph BC47, the Board decided that any conclusions it reached on those issues would equally apply to recognised intangible assets obtained other than in a business combination. The Board observed that amending the requirements in the previous version of IAS 38 only for intangible assets acquired in business combinations would create inconsistencies in the accounting for intangible assets depending on how they are obtained. Thus, similar items would be accounted for in dissimilar ways. The Board concluded that creating such inconsistencies would impair the usefulness of the information provided to users about an entity's intangible assets, because both comparability and reliability (which rests on the notion of representational faithfulness, ie that similar transactions are accounted for in the same way) would be diminished. Therefore, the Board decided that any amendments to the requirements in the previous version of IAS 38 to address the issues in (b) and (c) of paragraph BC47 should apply to all recognised intangible assets, whether generated internally or acquired separately or as part of a business combination.

BC49   Before beginning its deliberations of the issues identified in paragraph BC47, the Board noted the concern expressed by some that, because of the subjectivity involved in distinguishing goodwill from other intangible assets as at the acquisition date, differences between the subsequent treatment of goodwill and other intangible assets increases the potential for intangible assets to be misclassified at the acquisition date. The Board concluded, however, that adopting the separability and contractual or other legal rights criteria provides a reasonably definitive basis for separately identifying and recognising intangible assets acquired in a business combination. Therefore, the Board decided that its analysis of the accounting for intangible assets after initial recognition should have regard only to the nature of those assets and not to the subsequent treatment of goodwill.

Accounting for intangible assets with finite useful lives acquired in business combinations

BC50   The Board observed that the previous version of IAS 38 required an intangible asset to be measured after initial recognition:

(a)   at cost less any accumulated amortisation and any accumulated impairment losses; or

(b)   at a revalued amount, being the asset's fair value, determined by reference to an active market,[10] at the date of revaluation less any subsequent accumulated amortisation and any subsequent accumulated impairment losses. Under this approach, revaluations must be made with such regularity that at the balance sheet date the carrying amount of the asset does not differ materially from its fair value.

Whichever of the above methods was used, the previous version of IAS 38 required the depreciable amount of the asset to be amortised on a systematic basis over the best estimate of its useful life.

BC51   The Board observed that underpinning the requirement for all intangible assets to be amortised is the notion that they all have determinable and finite useful lives. Setting aside the question of whether, and under what circumstances, an intangible asset could be regarded as having an indefinite useful life, an important issue for the Board to consider was whether a departure from the above requirements would be warranted for intangible assets acquired in a business combination that have finite useful lives.

BC52   The Board observed that any departure from the above requirements for intangible assets with finite lives acquired in business combinations would create inconsistencies between the accounting for recognised intangible assets based wholly on the means by which they are obtained. In other words, similar items would be accounted for in dissimilar ways. The Board concluded that creating such inconsistencies would impair the usefulness of the information provided to users about an entity's intangible assets, because both comparability and reliability would be diminished.

BC53   Therefore, the Board decided that intangible assets with finite useful lives acquired in business combinations should continue to be accounted for in accordance with the above requirements after initial recognition.

---

10   IFRS 13, issued in May 2011, defines an active market.

Impairment testing intangible assets with finite useful lives (paragraph 111)

BC54 The previous version of IAS 38 required the recoverable amount of an intangible asset with a finite useful life that is being amortised over a period of more than 20 years, whether or not acquired in a business combination, to be measured at least at each financial year-end.

BC55 The Board observed that the recoverable amount of a long-lived tangible asset needs to be measured only when, in accordance with IAS 36 *Impairment of Assets*, there is an indication that the asset may be impaired. The Board could see no conceptual reason for requiring the recoverable amounts of some identifiable assets being amortised over very long periods to be determined more regularly than for other identifiable assets being amortised or depreciated over similar periods. Therefore, the Board concluded that the recoverable amount of an intangible asset with a finite useful life that is amortised over a period of more than 20 years should be determined only when, in accordance with IAS 36, there is an indication that the asset may be impaired. Consequently, the Board decided to remove the requirement in the previous version of IAS 38 for the recoverable amount of such an intangible asset to be measured at least at each financial year-end.

BC56 The Board also decided that all of the requirements relating to impairment testing intangible assets should be included in IAS 36 rather than in IAS 38. Therefore, the Board relocated to IAS 36 the requirement in the previous version of IAS 38 that an entity should estimate at the end of each annual reporting period the recoverable amount of an intangible asset not yet available for use, irrespective of whether there is any indication that it may be impaired.

Residual value of an intangible asset with a finite useful life (paragraph 100)

BC57 In revising IAS 38, the Board considered whether to retain for intangible assets with finite useful lives the requirement in the previous version of IAS 38 for the residual value of an intangible asset to be assumed to be zero unless:

(a) there is a commitment by a third party to purchase the asset at the end of its useful life; or

(b) there is an active market[11] for the asset and:

(i) the asset's residual value can be determined by reference to that market; and

(ii) it is probable that such a market will exist at the end of the asset's useful life.

BC58 The Board observed that the definition in the previous version of IAS 38 (as amended by IAS 16 when revised in 2003) of residual value required it to be estimated as if the asset were already of the age and in the condition expected at the end of the asset's useful life. Therefore, if the useful life of an intangible asset was shorter than its economic life because the entity expected to sell the

---

11 IFRS 13, issued in May 2011, defines an active market.

asset before the end of that economic life, the asset's residual value would not be zero, irrespective of whether the conditions in paragraph BC57(a) or (b) are met.

BC59 Nevertheless, the Board observed that the requirement for the residual value of an intangible asset to be assumed to be zero unless the specified criteria are met was included in the previous version of IAS 38 as a means of preventing entities from circumventing the requirement in that Standard to amortise all intangible assets. Excluding this requirement from the revised Standard for finite-lived intangible assets would similarly provide a means of circumventing the requirement to amortise such intangible assets—by claiming that the residual value of such an asset was equal to or greater than its carrying amount, an entity could avoid amortising the asset, even though its useful life is finite. The Board concluded that it should not, as part of the Business Combinations project, modify the criteria for permitting a finite-lived intangible asset's residual value to be other than zero. However, the Board decided that this issue should be addressed as part of a forthcoming project on intangible assets.

Useful lives of intangible assets (paragraphs 88–96)

BC60 Consistently with the proposals in the Exposure Draft of Proposed Amendments to IAS 38, the Standard requires an intangible asset to be regarded by an entity as having an indefinite useful life when, based on an analysis of all of the relevant factors, there is no foreseeable limit to the period over which the asset is expected to generate net cash inflows for the entity.

BC61 In developing the Exposure Draft and the revised Standard, the Board observed that the useful life of an intangible asset is related to the expected cash inflows that are associated with that asset. The Board observed that, to be representationally faithful, the amortisation period for an intangible asset generally should reflect that useful life and, by extension, the cash flow streams associated with the asset. The Board concluded that it is possible for management to have the intention and the ability to maintain an intangible asset in such a way that there is no foreseeable limit on the period over which that particular asset is expected to generate net cash inflows for the entity. In other words, it is conceivable that an analysis of all the relevant factors (ie legal, regulatory, contractual, competitive, economic and other) could lead to a conclusion that there is no foreseeable limit to the period over which a particular intangible asset is expected to generate net cash inflows for the entity.

BC62 For example, the Board observed that some intangible assets are based on legal rights that are conveyed in perpetuity rather than for finite terms. As such, those assets may have cash flows associated with them that may be expected to continue for many years or even indefinitely. The Board concluded that if the cash flows are expected to continue for a finite period, the useful life of the asset is limited to that finite period. However, if the cash flows are expected to continue indefinitely, the useful life is indefinite.

BC63 The previous version of IAS 38 prescribed a presumptive maximum useful life for intangible assets of 20 years. In developing the Exposure Draft and the revised Standard, the Board concluded that such a presumption is inconsistent with the view that the amortisation period for an intangible asset should, to be representationally faithful, reflect its useful life and, by extension, the cash flow streams associated with the asset. Therefore, the Board decided not to include in the revised Standard a presumptive maximum useful life for intangible assets, even if they have finite useful lives.

BC64 Respondents to the Exposure Draft generally supported the Board's proposal to remove from IAS 38 the presumptive maximum useful life and instead to require useful life to be regarded as indefinite when, based on an analysis of all of the relevant factors, there is no foreseeable limit to the period of time over which the intangible asset is expected to generate net cash inflows for the entity. However, some respondents suggested that an inability to determine clearly the useful life of an asset applies equally to many items of property, plant and equipment. Nonetheless, entities are required to determine the useful lives of those items of property, plant and equipment, and allocate their depreciable amounts on a systematic basis over those useful lives. Those respondents suggested that there is no conceptual reason for treating intangible assets differently.

BC65 In considering these comments, the Board noted the following:

(a) an intangible asset's useful life would be regarded as indefinite in accordance with IAS 38 only when, based on an analysis of all of the relevant factors, there is no foreseeable limit to the period of time over which the asset is expected to generate net cash inflows for the entity. Difficulties in accurately determining an intangible asset's useful life do not provide a basis for regarding that useful life as indefinite.

(b) although the useful lives of both intangible and tangible assets are directly related to the period during which they are expected to generate net cash inflows for the entity, the expected physical utility to the entity of a tangible asset places an upper limit on the asset's useful life. In other words, the useful life of a tangible asset could never extend beyond the asset's expected physical utility to the entity.

The Board concluded that tangible assets (other than land) could not be regarded as having indefinite useful lives because there is always a foreseeable limit to the expected physical utility of the asset to the entity.

Useful life constrained by contractual or other legal rights (paragraphs 94–96)

BC66 The Board noted that the useful life of an intangible asset that arises from contractual or other legal rights is constrained by the duration of those rights. The useful life of such an asset cannot extend beyond the duration of those rights, and may be shorter. Accordingly, the Board concluded that in determining the useful life of an intangible asset, consideration should be given to the period that the entity expects to use the intangible asset, which is subject to the expiration of the contractual or other legal rights.

BC67 However, the Board also observed that such rights are often conveyed for limited terms that may be renewed. It therefore considered whether renewals should be assumed in determining the useful life of such an intangible asset. The Board noted that some types of licences are initially issued for finite periods but renewals are routinely granted at little cost, provided that licensees have complied with the applicable rules and regulations. Such licences are traded at prices that reflect more than the remaining term, thereby indicating that renewal at minimal cost is the general expectation. However, renewals are not assured for other types of licences and, even if they are renewed, substantial costs may be incurred to secure their renewal.

BC68 The Board concluded that because the useful lives of some intangible assets depend, in economic terms, on renewal and on the associated costs of renewal, the useful lives assigned to those assets should reflect renewal when there is evidence to support renewal without significant cost.

BC69 Respondents to the Exposure Draft generally supported this conclusion. Those that disagreed suggested that:

(a) when the renewal period depends on the decision of a third party and not merely on the fulfilment of specified conditions by the entity, it gives rise to a contingent asset because the third-party decision affects not only the cost of renewal but also the probability of obtaining it. Therefore, useful life should reflect renewal only when renewal is not subject to third-party approval.

(b) such a requirement would be inconsistent with the basis used to measure intangible assets at the date of a business combination, particularly contractual customer relationships. For example, it is not clear whether the fair value of a contractual customer relationship includes an amount that reflects the probability that the contract will be renewed. The possibility of renewal would have a fair value regardless of the costs required to renew. This means the useful life of a contractual customer relationship could be inconsistent with the basis used to determine the fair value of the relationship.[12]

BC70 In relation to (a) above, the Board observed that if renewal by the entity is subject to third-party (eg government) approval, the requirement that there be evidence to support the entity's ability to renew would compel the entity to make an assessment of the likely effect of the third-party approval process on the entity's ability to renew. The Board could see no conceptual basis for narrowing the requirement to situations in which the contractual or legal rights are not subject to the approval of third parties.

BC71 In relation to (b) above, the Board observed the following:

(a) the requirements relating to renewal periods address circumstances in which *the entity* is able to renew the contractual or other legal rights, notwithstanding that such renewal may, for example, be conditional on the entity satisfying specified conditions, or subject to third-party approval. Paragraph 94 of the Standard states that '... the useful life of the intangible asset shall include the renewal period(s) only if there is evidence to support renewal *by the entity* [emphasis added] without significant cost.' The ability to renew a customer contract normally rests with the customer and not with the entity.

---

12 IFRS 13, issued in May 2011, contains the requirements for measuring fair value.

(b)   the respondents seem to regard as a single intangible asset what is, in substance, two intangible assets—one being the customer contract and the other being the related customer relationship. Expected renewals by the customer would affect the fair value of the customer relationship intangible asset, rather than the fair value of the customer contract. Therefore, the useful life of the customer contract would not, under the Standard, extend beyond the term of the contract, nor would the fair value of that customer contract reflect expectations of renewal by the customer. In other words, the useful life of the customer contract would not be inconsistent with the basis used to determine its fair value.

BC72   However, in response to respondents' suggestions, the Board included paragraph 96 in the Standard to provide additional guidance on the circumstances in which an entity should be regarded as being able to renew the contractual or other legal rights without significant cost.

Intangible assets with finite useful lives (paragraph 98)[13]

BC72A   The last sentence of paragraph 98 previously stated, 'There is rarely, if ever, persuasive evidence to support an amortisation method for intangible assets with finite useful lives that results in a lower amount of accumulated amortisation than under the straight-line method.' In practice, this wording was perceived as preventing an entity from using the units of production method to amortise assets if it resulted in a lower amount of accumulated amortisation than the straight-line method. However, using the straight-line method could be inconsistent with the general requirement of paragraph 38 that the amortisation method should reflect the expected pattern of consumption of the expected future economic benefits embodied in an intangible asset. Consequently, the Board decided to delete the last sentence of paragraph 98.

Amortisation method (paragraphs 97–98C)

BC72B   The IASB decided to amend IAS 38 to address concerns regarding the use of a revenue-based method for amortising an intangible asset. The IASB's decision was in response to a request to clarify the meaning of the term 'consumption of the expected future economic benefits embodied in the asset' when determining the appropriate amortisation method for intangible assets of service concession arrangements (SCA) that are within the scope of IFRIC 12 *Service Concession Arrangements*. The issue raised is related to the application of paragraphs 97–98 of IAS 38, although the IASB decided to address the issue broadly, rather than limit it only to intangible assets arising in an SCA.

BC72C   A revenue-based amortisation method is one that allocates an asset's amortisable amount based on revenues generated in an accounting period as a proportion of the total revenues expected to be generated over the asset's useful economic life. The total revenue amount is affected by the interaction between units (ie quantity) and price and takes into account any expected changes in price. The IASB observed that the price component of revenue may be affected by inflation and noted that inflation has no bearing upon the way in which the asset is consumed.

---

13 This heading and paragraph BC72A were added by *Improvements to IFRSs* issued in May 2008.

BC72D   The IASB observed that paragraph 97 of IAS 38 states that the amortisation method used shall reflect the pattern in which the intangible asset's future economic benefits are expected to be consumed by the entity.

BC72E   On the basis of the guidance in IAS 38 the IASB proposed to clarify in the Exposure Draft *Clarification of Acceptable Methods of Depreciation and Amortisation* (Proposed amendments to IAS 16 and IAS 38) (the 'ED') that a method of amortisation that is based on revenue generated from an activity that includes the use of an asset is not appropriate, because it reflects a pattern of economic benefits being generated from operating the business (of which the asset is part) rather than the economic benefits being consumed through the use of the asset.

BC72F   During its redeliberations of the ED the IASB decided to include a rebuttable presumption that revenue is generally presumed to be an inappropriate basis for measuring the consumption of the economic benefits embodied in the intangible asset. The IASB also considered the question of whether there could be circumstances in which revenue could be used to reflect the pattern in which the future economic benefits of the intangible asset are expected to be consumed.

BC72G   In finalising the proposed amendments to IAS 38, the IASB decided to make clear in the Standard that the presumption precluding the use of revenue as a basis for amortisation could be overcome in two circumstances. One of those circumstances is when it can be demonstrated that revenue is highly correlated with the consumption of the economic benefits embodied in an intangible asset. The IASB also noted that another circumstance in which revenue could be used is when the right embodied by an intangible asset is expressed as a total amount of revenue to be generated (rather than time, for example), in such a way that the generation of revenue is the measurement used to determine when the right expires. The IASB noted that, in this case, the pattern of consumption of future economic benefits that is embodied in the intangible asset is defined by reference to the total revenue earned as a proportion of the contractual maximum and, consequently, the amount of revenue generated contractually reflects the consumption of the benefits that are embodied in the asset.

BC72H   The IASB also analysed situations in which an intangible asset is used in multiple activities to provide multiple revenue streams. Some respondents commented that the application of a units of production method did not seem practicable, because the units of production were not homogeneous. For example, the producer of a motion picture will typically use the intellectual property embodied in the film to generate cash flows through exhibiting the film in theatres, licensing the rights to characters to manufacturers of toys and other goods, selling DVDs or digital copies of the film and licensing broadcast rights to television broadcasters. Some respondents thought that the best way to amortise the cost of the intellectual property embodied in the film was to use a revenue-based method, because revenue was considered a common denominator to reflect a suitable proxy of the pattern of consumption of all the benefits received from the multiple activities in which the intellectual property could be used.

BC72I   The IASB acknowledged that determining an appropriate amortisation method for situations in which an intangible asset is used in multiple activities, and generates multiple cash flow streams in different markets, requires judgement. The IASB considered suggestions that an intangible asset should be componentised for amortisation purposes in circumstances in which the asset is used to generate multiple cash flow streams. It observed that separating an asset into different components is not a new practice in business or in IFRS—it is routinely done for property, plant and equipment and IAS 16 provides guidance in this respect—but refrained from developing guidance in this respect for intangible assets.

BC72J   The IASB also decided to provide guidance on how an entity could identify an amortisation method in response to some respondents who observed that further guidance was required in the application of paragraph 98 of IAS 38, which is limited to providing a description of the amortisation methods most commonly used. During its deliberations the IASB determined that, when choosing an amortisation method, an entity could determine the predominant limiting factor for the use of the intangible asset. For example, a contract could be limited by a number of years (ie time), a number of units produced or an amount of revenue to be generated. The IASB clarified that identifying such a predominant limiting factor is only a starting point for the identification of the amortisation method and an entity may apply another basis if the entity determines that it more closely reflects the expected pattern of consumption of economic benefits.

BC72K   In the ED the IASB proposed to provide guidance to clarify the role of obsolescence in the application of the diminishing balance method. In response to the comments received about the proposed guidance, the IASB decided to change the focus of this guidance to explain that expected future reductions in the selling price of an item that was produced using an intangible asset could indicate the expectation of technological or commercial obsolescence of the asset, which, in turn, might reflect a reduction of the future economic benefits embodied in the asset. The IASB noted that the expectation of technical or commercial obsolescence is relevant for estimating both the pattern of consumption of future economic benefits and the useful life of an asset. The IASB noted that the diminishing balance method is an accepted amortisation methodology in paragraph 98 of IAS 38, which is capable of reflecting an accelerated consumption of the future economic benefits embodied in the asset.

BC72L   Some respondents to the ED suggested that the IASB should define the notion of 'consumption of economic benefits' and provide guidance in this respect. During its redeliberations the IASB decided against doing so, noting that explaining the notion of consumption of economic benefits would require a broader project.

Consistency in the use of the phrase 'units of production'

BC72M   The IASB decided to make consistent the phrase 'units of production method' and has therefore amended the instances of the phrase 'unit of production method'.

Accounting for intangible assets with indefinite useful lives (paragraphs 107–110)

BC73 Consistently with the proposals in the Exposure Draft, the Standard prohibits the amortisation of intangible assets with indefinite useful lives. Therefore, such assets are measured after initial recognition at:

(a) cost less any accumulated impairment losses; or

(b) a revalued amount, being fair value determined by reference to an active market[14] less any accumulated impairment losses.

Non-amortisation

BC74 In developing the Exposure Draft and the revised Standard, the Board observed that many assets yield benefits to an entity over several periods. Amortisation is the systematic allocation of the cost (or revalued amount) of an asset, less any residual value, to reflect the consumption over time of the future economic benefits embodied in that asset. Thus, if there is no foreseeable limit on the period during which an entity expects to consume the future economic benefits embodied in an asset, amortisation of that asset over, for example, an arbitrarily determined maximum period would not be representationally faithful. Respondents to the Exposure Draft generally supported this conclusion.

BC75 Consequently, the Board decided that intangible assets with indefinite useful lives should not be amortised, but should be subject to regular impairment testing. The Board's deliberations on the form of the impairment test, including the frequency of impairment testing, are included in the Basis for Conclusions on IAS 36. The Board further decided that regular re-examinations should be required of the useful life of an intangible asset that is not being amortised to determine whether circumstances continue to support the assessment that the useful life is indefinite.

Revaluations

BC76 Having decided that intangible assets with indefinite useful lives should not be amortised, the Board considered whether an entity should be permitted to carry such assets at revalued amounts. The Board could see no conceptual justification for precluding some intangible assets from being carried at revalued amounts solely on the basis that there is no foreseeable limit to the period over which an entity expects to consume the future economic benefits embodied in those assets.

BC77 As a result, the Board decided that the Standard should permit intangible assets with indefinite useful lives to be carried at revalued amounts.

Revaluation method—proportionate restatement of accumulated amortisation when an intangible asset is revalued

BC77A The IFRS Interpretations Committee reported to the Board that practice differed in calculating the accumulated depreciation for an item of property, plant and

---

14 IFRS 13, issued in May 2011, defines an active market.

equipment that is measured using the revaluation method in cases in which the residual value, the useful life or the depreciation method has been re-estimated before a revaluation.

BC77B The reasons for making the change are further explained in paragraphs BC25A–BC25G of IAS 16.

BC77C The Board noted that the issue in paragraphs BC25A–BC25G of IAS 16 regarding accumulated depreciation upon revaluation could also occur when revaluing an intangible asset under IAS 38, because both IAS 16 and IAS 38 have the same requirements for accumulated depreciation/amortisation when revaluing items of property, plant and equipment/intangible assets. Differences in the revaluation models for items of property, plant and equipment and intangible assets do not result in different models for restating accumulated depreciation/amortisation. For example, IAS 38 requires that the fair value of an intangible asset is measured by reference to an active market. Otherwise, the revaluation model cannot be applied. However, IAS 38 requires fair value measurement by reference to an active market only for the carrying amount of an intangible asset in contrast to its gross carrying amount.

BC77D Consequently, the Board decided to amend paragraph 80(a) to state that:

(a) the gross carrying amount is adjusted in a manner that is consistent with the revaluation of the carrying amount; and

(b) the accumulated amortisation is calculated as the difference between the gross carrying amount and the carrying amount after taking into account accumulated impairment losses.

The Board also decided to amend paragraph 80(b) to be consistent with the wording used in those amendments.

BC77E The Board decided to include wording in paragraph 80(a) to require an entity to take into account accumulated impairment losses when adjusting the amortisation on revaluation. This was to ensure that when future revaluation increases occur, the correct split according to paragraph 85 of IAS 38 and paragraph 119 of IAS 36 is made between profit or loss and other comprehensive income when reversing prior accumulated impairment losses.

Research and development projects acquired in business combinations

BC78 The Board considered the following issues in relation to in-process research and development (IPR&D) projects acquired in a business combination:

(a) whether the proposed criteria for recognising intangible assets acquired in a business combination separately from goodwill should also be applied to IPR&D projects;

(b) the subsequent accounting for IPR&D projects recognised as assets separately from goodwill; and

(c) the treatment of subsequent expenditure on IPR&D projects recognised as assets separately from goodwill.

The Board's deliberations on issue (a), although included in the Basis for Conclusions on IFRS 3, are also, for the sake of completeness, outlined below.

BC79 The Board did not reconsider as part of the first phase of its Business Combinations project the requirements in the previous version of IAS 38 for internally generated intangibles and expenditure on the research or development phase of an internal project. The Board decided that a reconsideration of those requirements is outside the scope of this project.

Initial recognition separately from goodwill

BC80 The Board observed that the criteria in IAS 22 *Business Combinations* and the previous version of IAS 38 for recognising an intangible asset acquired in a business combination separately from goodwill applied to all intangible assets, including IPR&D projects. Therefore, in accordance with those Standards, any intangible item acquired in a business combination was recognised as an asset separately from goodwill when it was identifiable and could be measured reliably, and it was probable that any associated future economic benefits would flow to the acquirer. If these criteria were not satisfied, the expenditure on the cost or value of that item, which was included in the cost of the combination, was part of the amount attributed to goodwill.

BC81 The Board could see no conceptual justification for changing the approach in IAS 22 and the previous version of IAS 38 of using the same criteria for all intangible assets acquired in a business combination when assessing whether those assets should be recognised separately from goodwill. The Board concluded that adopting different criteria would impair the usefulness of the information provided to users about the assets acquired in a combination because both comparability and reliability would be diminished. Therefore, IAS 38 and IFRS 3 require an acquirer to recognise as an asset separately from goodwill any of the acquiree's IPR&D projects that meet the definition of an intangible asset. This will be the case when the IPR&D project meets the definition of an asset and is identifiable, ie is separable or arises from contractual or other legal rights.

BC82 Some respondents to the Exposure Draft of Proposed Amendments to IAS 38 expressed concern that applying the same criteria to all intangible assets acquired in a business combination to assess whether they should be recognised separately from goodwill results in treating some IPR&D projects acquired in business combinations differently from similar projects started internally. The Board acknowledged this point, but concluded that this does not provide a basis for subsuming those acquired intangible assets within goodwill. Rather, it highlights a need to reconsider the conclusion in the Standard that an intangible asset can never exist in respect of an in-process research project and can exist in respect of an in-process development project only once all of the Standard's criteria for deferral have been satisfied. The Board decided that such a reconsideration is outside the scope of its Business Combinations project.

Subsequent accounting for IPR&D projects acquired in a business combination and recognised as intangible assets

BC83   The Board observed that the previous version of IAS 38 required all recognised intangible assets to be accounted for after initial recognition at:

(a)   cost less any accumulated amortisation and any accumulated impairment losses; or

(b)   revalued amount, being the asset's fair value, determined by reference to an active market,[15] at the date of revaluation less any subsequent accumulated amortisation and any subsequent accumulated impairment losses.

Such assets included: IPR&D projects acquired in a business combination that satisfied the criteria for recognition separately from goodwill; separately acquired IPR&D projects that satisfied the criteria for recognition as an intangible asset; and recognised internally developed intangible assets arising from development or the development phase of an internal project.

BC84   The Board could see no conceptual justification for changing the approach in the previous version of IAS 38 of applying the same requirements to the subsequent accounting for all recognised intangible assets. Therefore, the Board decided that IPR&D projects acquired in a business combination that satisfy the criteria for recognition as an asset separately from goodwill should be accounted for after initial recognition in accordance with the requirements applying to the subsequent accounting for other recognised intangible assets.

Subsequent expenditure on IPR&D projects acquired in a business combination and recognised as intangible assets (paragraphs 42 and 43)

BC85   The Standard requires subsequent expenditure on an IPR&D project acquired separately or in a business combination and recognised as an intangible asset to be:

(a)   recognised as an expense when incurred if it is research expenditure;

(b)   recognised as an expense when incurred if it is development expenditure that does not satisfy the criteria for recognition as an intangible asset in paragraph 57; and

(c)   added to the carrying amount of the acquired IPR&D project if it is development expenditure that satisfies the recognition criteria in paragraph 57.

BC86   In developing this requirement the Board observed that the treatment required under the previous version of IAS 38 of subsequent expenditure on an IPR&D project acquired in a business combination and recognised as an asset separately from goodwill was unclear. Some suggested that the requirements in the previous version of IAS 38 relating to expenditure on research, development, or the research or development phase of an internal project should be applied.

---

15   IFRS 13, issued in May 2011, defines an active market.

However, others argued that those requirements were ostensibly concerned with the initial recognition and measurement of internally generated intangible assets. Instead, the requirements in the previous version of IAS 38 dealing with subsequent expenditure should be applied. Under those requirements, subsequent expenditure on an intangible asset after its purchase or completion would have been recognised as an expense when incurred unless:

(a) it was probable that the expenditure would enable the asset to generate future economic benefits in excess of its originally assessed standard of performance; and

(b) the expenditure could be measured and attributed to the asset reliably.

If these conditions were satisfied, the subsequent expenditure would be added to the carrying amount of the intangible asset.

BC87 The Board observed that this uncertainty also existed for separately acquired IPR&D projects that satisfied the criteria in the previous version of IAS 38 for recognition as intangible assets.

BC88 The Board noted that applying the requirements in the Standard for expenditure on research, development, or the research or development phase of an internal project to subsequent expenditure on IPR&D projects acquired in a business combination and recognised as assets separately from goodwill would result in such subsequent expenditure being treated inconsistently with subsequent expenditure on other recognised intangible assets. However, applying the subsequent expenditure requirements in the previous version of IAS 38 to subsequent expenditure on IPR&D projects acquired in a business combination and recognised as assets separately from goodwill would result in research and development expenditure being accounted for differently depending on whether a project is acquired or started internally.

BC89 The Board concluded that until it has had the opportunity to review the requirements in IAS 38 for expenditure on research, development, or the research or development phase of an internal project, more useful information will be provided to users of an entity's financial statements if all such expenditure is accounted for consistently. This includes subsequent expenditure on a separately acquired IPR&D project that satisfies the Standard's criteria for recognition as an intangible asset.

Transitional provisions (paragraphs 129–132)

BC90 If an entity elects to apply IFRS 3 from any date before the effective dates outlined in IFRS 3, it is also required to apply IAS 38 prospectively from that same date. Otherwise, IAS 38 applies to the accounting for intangible assets acquired in business combinations for which the agreement date is on or after 31 March 2004, and to the accounting for all other intangible assets prospectively from the beginning of the first annual reporting period beginning on or after 31 March 2004. IAS 38 also requires an entity, on initial application, to reassess the useful lives of intangible assets. If, as a result of that reassessment, the entity changes its useful life assessment for an asset, that change is accounted for as a change in an accounting estimate in accordance with IAS 8 *Accounting Policies, Changes in Accounting Estimates and Errors*.

BC91 The Board's deliberations on the transitional issues relating to the initial recognition of intangible assets acquired in business combinations and the impairment testing of intangible assets are addressed in the Basis for Conclusions on IFRS 3 and the Basis for Conclusions on IAS 36, respectively.

BC92 In developing the requirements outlined in paragraph BC90, the Board considered the following three questions:

(a) should the useful lives of, and the accounting for, intangible assets already recognised at the effective date of the Standard continue to be determined in accordance with the requirements in the previous version of IAS 38 (ie by amortising over a presumptive maximum period of twenty years), or in accordance with the requirements in the revised Standard?

(b) if the revised Standard is applied to intangible assets already recognised at its effective date, should the effect of a reassessment of an intangible asset's useful life as a result of the initial application of the Standard be recognised retrospectively or prospectively?

(c) should entities be required to apply the requirements in the Standard for subsequent expenditure on an acquired IPR&D project recognised as an intangible asset retrospectively to expenditure incurred before the effective date of the revised Standard?

BC93 In relation to the first question above, the Board noted its previous conclusion that the most representationally faithful method of accounting for intangible assets is to amortise those with finite useful lives over their useful lives with no limit on the amortisation period, and not to amortise those with indefinite useful lives. Thus, the Board concluded that the reliability and comparability of financial statements would be diminished if the Standard was not applied to intangible assets recognised before its effective date.

BC94 On the second question, the Board observed that a reassessment of an asset's useful life is regarded throughout IFRSs as a change in an accounting estimate, rather than a change in an accounting policy. For example, in accordance with the Standard, as with the previous version of IAS 38, if a new estimate of the expected useful life of an intangible asset is significantly different from previous estimates, the change must be accounted for as a change in accounting estimate in accordance with IAS 8. IAS 8 requires a change in an accounting estimate to be accounted for prospectively by including the effect of the change in profit or loss in:

(a) the period of the change, if the change in estimate affects that period only; or

(b) the period of the change and future periods, if the change in estimate affects both.

BC95 Similarly, in accordance with IAS 16 *Property, Plant and Equipment*, if a new estimate of the expected useful life of an item of property, plant and equipment is significantly different from previous estimates, the change must be accounted for prospectively by adjusting the depreciation expense for the current and future periods.

BC96 Therefore, the Board decided that a reassessment of useful life resulting from the initial application of IAS 38, including a reassessment from a finite to an indefinite useful life, should be accounted for as a change in an accounting estimate. Consequently, the effect of such a change should be recognised prospectively.

BC97 The Board considered the view that because the previous version of IAS 38 required intangible assets to be treated as having a finite useful life, a change to an assessment of indefinite useful life for an intangible asset represents a change in an accounting policy, rather than a change in an accounting estimate. The Board concluded that, even if this were the case, the useful life reassessment should nonetheless be accounted for prospectively. This is because retrospective application would require an entity to determine whether, at the end of each reporting period before the effective date of the Standard, the useful life of an intangible asset was indefinite. Such an assessment requires an entity to make estimates that would have been made at a prior date, and therefore raises problems in relation to the role of hindsight, in particular, whether the benefit of hindsight should be included or excluded from those estimates and, if excluded, how the effect of hindsight can be separated from the other factors existing at the date for which the estimates are required.

BC98 On the third question, and as noted in paragraph BC86, it was not clear whether the previous version of IAS 38 required subsequent expenditure on acquired IPR&D projects recognised as intangible assets to be accounted for:

(a) in accordance with its requirements for expenditure on research, development, or the research or development phase of an internal project; or

(b) in accordance with its requirements for subsequent expenditure on an intangible asset after its purchase or completion.

The Board concluded that subsequent expenditure on an acquired IPR&D project that was capitalised under (b) above before the effective date of the Standard might not have been capitalised had the Standard applied when the subsequent expenditure was incurred. This is because the Standard requires such expenditure to be capitalised as an intangible asset only when it is development expenditure and all of the criteria for deferral are satisfied. In the Board's view, those criteria represent a higher recognition threshold than (b) above.

BC99 Thus, retrospective application of the revised Standard to subsequent expenditure on acquired IPR&D projects incurred before its effective date could result in previously capitalised expenditure being reversed. Such reversal would be required if the expenditure was research expenditure, or it was development expenditure and one or more of the criteria for deferral were not satisfied at the time the expenditure was incurred. The Board concluded that determining whether, at the time the subsequent expenditure was incurred, the criteria for deferral were satisfied raises the same hindsight issues discussed in paragraph BC97: it would require assessments to be made as of a prior date, and therefore raises problems in relation to how the effect of hindsight can be separated from factors existing at the date of the assessment. In addition, such assessments could, in many cases, be impossible: the information needed may not exist or no longer be obtainable.

BC100   Therefore, the Board decided that the Standard's requirements for subsequent expenditure on acquired IPR&D projects recognised as intangible assets should not be applied retrospectively to expenditure incurred before the revised Standard's effective date. The Board noted that any amounts previously included in the carrying amount of such an asset would, in any event, be subject to the requirements for impairment testing in IAS 36.

Revaluation method—proportionate restatement of accumulated amortisation when an intangible asset is revalued

BC100A   *Annual Improvements to IFRSs 2010–2012 Cycle*, issued in December 2013, amended paragraph 80. The Board also decided that the amendment should be required to be applied to all revaluations occurring in annual periods beginning on or after the date of initial application of the amendment and in the immediately preceding annual period. The Board was concerned that the costs of full retrospective application might outweigh the benefits.

Early application (paragraph 132)

BC101   The Board noted that the issue of any Standard reflects its opinion that application of the Standard will result in more useful information being provided to users about an entity's financial position, performance or cash flows. On that basis, a case exists for permitting, and indeed encouraging, entities to apply the revised Standard before its effective date. However, the Board also considered the assertion that permitting a revised Standard to be applied before its effective date potentially diminishes comparability between entities in the period(s) leading up to that effective date, and has the effect of providing entities with an option.

BC102   The Board concluded that the benefit of providing users with more useful information about an entity's financial position and performance by permitting early application of the Standard outweighs the disadvantages of potentially diminished comparability. Therefore, entities are encouraged to apply the requirements of the revised Standard before its effective date, provided they also apply IFRS 3 and IAS 36 (as revised in 2004) at the same time.

Summary of main changes from the Exposure Draft

BC103   The following are the main changes from the Exposure Draft of Proposed Amendments to IAS 38:

(a)   The Standard includes additional guidance clarifying the relationship between the separability criterion for establishing whether a non-contractual customer relationship is identifiable, and the control concept for establishing whether the relationship meets the definition of an asset. In particular, the Standard clarifies that in the absence of legal rights to protect customer relationships, exchange transactions for the same or similar non-contractual customer relationships (other than as part of a business combination) provide evidence that the entity is nonetheless able to control the future economic benefits flowing from the customer relationships. Because such exchange transactions also provide evidence that the customer relationships are separable, those customer relationships meet the definition of an intangible asset (see paragraphs BC11–BC14).

(b) The Exposure Draft proposed that, except for an assembled workforce, an intangible asset acquired in a business combination should always be recognised separately from goodwill; there was a presumption that sufficient information would always exist to measure reliably its fair value. The Standard states that the fair value of an intangible asset acquired in a business combination can *normally* be measured with sufficient reliability to qualify for recognition separately from goodwill. If an intangible asset acquired in a business combination has a finite useful life, there is a rebuttable presumption that its fair value can be measured reliably (see paragraphs BC16–BC25).

(c) The Exposure Draft proposed, and the Standard requires, that the useful life of an intangible asset arising from contractual or other legal rights should not exceed the period of those rights. However, if the rights are conveyed for a limited term that can be renewed, the useful life should include the renewal period(s) only if there is evidence to support renewal by the entity without significant cost. Additional guidance has been included in the Standard to clarify the circumstances in which an entity should be regarded as being able to renew the contractual or other legal rights without significant cost (see paragraphs BC66–BC72).

History of the development of a standard on intangible assets

BCZ104 IASC published a Draft Statement of Principles on Intangible Assets in January 1994 and an Exposure Draft E50 *Intangible Assets* in June 1995. Principles in both documents were consistent as far as possible with those in IAS 16 *Property, Plant and Equipment*. The principles were also greatly influenced by the decisions reached in 1993 during the revisions to the treatment of research and development costs and goodwill.

BCZ105 IASC received about 100 comment letters on E50 from over 20 countries. Comment letters on E50 showed that the proposal for the amortisation period for intangible assets—a 20-year ceiling for almost all intangible assets, as required for goodwill in IAS 22 (revised 1993)—raised significant controversy and created serious concerns about the overall acceptability of the proposed standard on intangible assets. IASC considered alternative solutions and concluded in March 1996 that, if an impairment test that is sufficiently robust and reliable could be developed, IASC would propose deleting the 20-year ceiling on the amortisation period for both intangible assets and goodwill.

BCZ106 In August 1997, IASC published proposals for revised treatments for intangible assets and goodwill in Exposure Drafts E60 *Intangible Assets* and E61 *Business*

© IFRS Foundation

Combinations. This followed the publication of Exposure Draft E55 *Impairment of Assets* in May 1997, which set out detailed proposals for impairment testing.

BCZ107 E60 proposed two major changes to the proposals in E50:

(a) as explained above, revised proposals for the amortisation of intangible assets; and

(b) combining the requirements relating to all internally generated intangible assets in one standard. This meant including certain aspects of IAS 9 *Research and Development Costs* in the proposed standard on intangible assets and withdrawing IAS 9.

BCZ108 Among other proposed changes, E61 proposed revisions to IAS 22 to make the requirements for the amortisation of goodwill consistent with those proposed for intangible assets.

BCZ109 IASC received about 100 comment letters on E60 and E61 from over 20 countries. The majority of the commentators supported most of the proposals in E60 and E61, although some proposals still raised significant controversy. The proposals for impairment tests were also supported by most commentators on E55.

BCZ110 After considering the comments received on E55, E60 and E61, IASC approved:

(a) IAS 36 *Impairment of Assets* (April 1998);

(b) IAS 38 *Intangible Assets* (July 1998);

(c) a revised IAS 22 *Business Combinations* (July 1998); and

(d) withdrawal of IAS 9 *Research and Development Costs* (July 1998).

Dissenting opinions

Dissent of Geoffrey Whittington from IAS 38 issued in March 2004

DO1   Professor Whittington dissents from the issue of this Standard because it does not explicitly require the probability recognition criterion in paragraph 21(a) to be applied to intangible assets acquired in a business combination, notwithstanding that it applies to all other intangible assets.

DO2   The reason given for this (paragraphs 33 and BC17) is that fair value is the required measurement on acquisition of an intangible asset as part of a business combination, and fair value incorporates probability assessments. Professor Whittington does not believe that the *Framework*[16] precludes having a prior recognition test based on probability, even when subsequent recognition is at fair value. Moreover, the application of probability may be different for recognition purposes: for example, it may be the 'more likely than not' criterion used in IAS 37 *Provisions, Contingent Liabilities and Contingent Assets*, rather than the 'expected value' approach used in the measurement of fair value.

DO3   This inconsistency between the recognition criteria in the *Framework* and fair values is acknowledged in paragraph BC18. In Professor Whittington's view, the inconsistency should be resolved before changing the recognition criteria for intangible assets acquired in a business combination.

---

16   The references to the *Framework* are to IASC's *Framework for the Preparation and Presentation of Financial Statements*, adopted by the IASB in 2001. In September 2010 the IASB replaced the *Framework* with the *Conceptual Framework for Financial Reporting*.

Dissent of James J Leisenring from amendments issued in May 2008

DO1   Mr Leisenring dissents from the amendments to IAS 38 *Intangible Assets* made by *Improvements to IFRSs* issued in May 2008.

DO2   Mr Leisenring believes that the Board's amendments introduce a logical flaw into IAS 38. Paragraph 68 states that 'expenditure on an intangible item shall be recognised as an expense when it is incurred unless' specific conditions apply. The amendments to paragraph 69 include guidance on the accounting for expenditure on a tangible rather than an intangible item and therefore the amendment to paragraph 69 is inconsistent with paragraph 68.

DO3   Extending the application of IAS 38 to tangible assets used for advertising also raises application concerns. Are signs constructed by a restaurant chain at their location an advertising expense in the period of construction? Would the costs of putting an entity's name on trucks, airplanes and buildings be an advertising expense in the year incurred? The logic of this amendment would suggest an affirmative answer to these questions even though the result of the expenditure benefits several periods.

DO4   Mr Leisenring believes that if an entity acquires goods, including items such as catalogues, film strips or other materials, the entity should determine whether those goods meet the definition of an asset. In his view, IAS 38 is not relevant for determining whether goods acquired by an entity and which may be used for advertising should be recognised as an asset.

DO5   Mr Leisenring agrees that the potential benefit that might result from having advertised should not be recognised as an intangible asset in accordance with IAS 38.

Dissent of Mary Tokar from *Clarification of Acceptable Methods of Depreciation and Amortisation* (Amendments to IAS 16 and IAS 38) as issued in May 2014

DO1   Ms Tokar is dissenting from the publication of this amendment. She does not object to the IASB's objective of clarifying acceptable methods of depreciation and amortisation, nor to its conclusions to preclude revenue-based depreciation and nor to the introduction of a rebuttable presumption that revenue cannot be used as a basis for amortisation of intangibles. She also agrees that expectations of obsolescence should be considered when determining the useful life of an asset and selecting an amortisation or depreciation method that reflects the pattern of consumption of the asset. However, she is concerned that the amendments will not fully resolve the practice issue that was originally raised with the IFRS Interpretations Committee. She believes that the amendments are not sufficiently clear regarding what evidence is required to overcome the presumption and instead support the use of revenue as the basis for amortisation of an intangible asset. She believes that further guidance should be included to explain when the pattern of consumption of economic benefits is the same as the pattern in which revenue is generated.

IASB documents published to accompany

IAS 39

Financial Instruments: Recognition and Measurement

The text of the unaccompanied standard, IAS 39, is contained in Part A of this edition. Its effective date when issued was 1 January 2005. The text of the Accompanying Guidance on IAS 39 is contained in Part B of this edition. This part presents the following documents:

BASIS FOR CONCLUSIONS

DISSENTING OPINIONS

CONTENTS

Basis for Conclusions on
IAS 39 *Financial Instruments: Recognition and Measurement*

This Basis for Conclusions accompanies, but is not part of, IAS 39.

In this Basis for Conclusions the terminology has not been amended to reflect the changes made by IAS 1 Presentation of Financial Statements *(as revised in 2007).*

References to the Framework *are to IASC's* Framework for the Preparation and Presentation of Financial Statements, *adopted by the IASB in 2001. In September 2010 the IASB replaced the* Framework *with the* Conceptual Framework for Financial Reporting.

IFRS 9 Financial Instruments *replaced IAS 39. However, the Board did not reconsider most of the requirements of IAS 39 relating to scope, classification and measurement of financial liabilities or derecognition of financial assets and financial liabilities. Accordingly the following were relocated to IFRS 9: paragraphs BC11C, BC15–BC24Y, BC30–BC79A and BC85–BC104.*

BC1 This Basis for Conclusions summarises the International Accounting Standards Board's considerations in reaching the conclusions on revising IAS 39 *Financial Instruments: Recognition and Measurement* in 2003. Individual Board members gave greater weight to some factors than to others.

BC2– [Deleted]
BC130

Hedging

BC131 The Exposure Draft proposed few changes to the hedge accounting guidance in the original IAS 39. The comments on the Exposure Draft raised several issues in the area of hedge accounting suggesting that the Board should consider these issues in the revised IAS 39. The Board's decisions with regard to these issues are presented in the following paragraphs.

Consideration of the shortcut method in SFAS 133

BC132 SFAS 133 *Accounting for Derivative Instruments and Hedging Activities* issued by the FASB allows an entity to assume no ineffectiveness in a hedge of interest rate risk using an interest rate swap as the hedging instrument, provided specified criteria are met (the 'shortcut method').

BC133 The original IAS 39 and the Exposure Draft precluded the use of the shortcut method. Many comments received on the Exposure Draft argued that IAS 39 should permit use of the shortcut method. The Board considered the issue in developing the Exposure Draft, and discussed it in the round-table discussions that were held in the process of finalising IAS 39.

BC134 The Board noted that, if the shortcut method were permitted, an exception would have to be made to the principle in IAS 39 that ineffectiveness in a hedging relationship is measured and recognised in profit or loss. The Board agreed that no exception to this principle should be made, and therefore concluded that IAS 39 should not permit the shortcut method.

BC135 Additionally, IAS 39 permits the hedging of portions of financial assets and financial liabilities in cases when US GAAP does not. The Board noted that under IAS 39 an entity may hedge a portion of a financial instrument (eg interest rate risk or credit risk), and that if the critical terms of the hedging instrument and the hedged item are the same, the entity would, in many cases, recognise no ineffectiveness.

Hedges of portions of financial assets and financial liabilities (paragraphs 81, 81A, AG99A and AG99B)

BC135A   IAS 39 permits a hedged item to be designated as a portion of the cash flows or fair value of a financial asset or financial liability. In finalising the Exposure Draft *Fair Value Hedge Accounting for a Portfolio Hedge of Interest Rate Risk*, the Board received comments that demonstrated that the meaning of a 'portion' was unclear in this context. Accordingly, the Board decided to amend IAS 39 to provide further guidance on what may be designated as a hedged portion, including confirmation that it is not possible to designate a portion that is greater than the total cash flows of the asset or liability.

Expected effectiveness (paragraphs AG105–AG113)

BC136   Qualification for hedge accounting is based on expectations of future effectiveness (prospective) and evaluation of actual effectiveness (retrospective). In the original IAS 39, the prospective test was expressed as 'almost fully offset', whereas the retrospective test was 'within a range of 80–125 per cent'. The Board considered whether to amend IAS 39 to permit the prospective effectiveness to be within the range of 80–125 per cent rather than 'almost fully offset'. The Board noted that an undesirable consequence of such an amendment could be that entities would deliberately underhedge a hedged item in a cash flow hedge so as to reduce recognised ineffectiveness. Therefore, the Board initially decided to retain the guidance in the original IAS 39.

BC136A   However, when subsequently finalising the requirements for portfolio hedges of interest rate risk, the Board received representations from constituents that some hedges would fail the 'almost fully offset' test in IAS 39, including some hedges that would qualify for the shortcut method in US GAAP and thus be assumed to be 100 per cent effective. The Board was persuaded that the concern described in the previous paragraph that an entity might deliberately underhedge would be met by an explicit statement that an entity could not deliberately hedge less than 100 per cent of the exposure on an item and designate the hedge as a hedge of 100 per cent of the exposure. Therefore, the Board decided to amend IAS 39:

(a)   to remove the words 'almost fully offset' from the prospective effectiveness test, and replace them by a requirement that the hedge is expected to be 'highly effective'. (This amendment is consistent with the wording in US GAAP.)

(b)   to include a statement in the Application Guidance in IAS 39 that if an entity hedges less than 100 per cent of the exposure on an item, such as 85 per cent, it shall designate the hedged item as being 85 per cent of the exposure and shall measure ineffectiveness on the basis of the change in the whole of that designated 85 per cent exposure.

BC136B Additionally, comments made in response to the Exposure Draft *Fair Value Hedge Accounting for a Portfolio Hedge of Interest Rate Risk* demonstrated that it was unclear how the prospective effectiveness test was to be applied. The Board noted that the objective of the test was to ensure there was firm evidence to support an expectation of high effectiveness. Therefore, the Board decided to amend the Standard to clarify that an expectation of high effectiveness may be demonstrated in various ways, including a comparison of past changes in the fair value or cash flows of the hedged item that are attributable to the hedged risk with past changes in the fair value or cash flows of the hedging instrument, or by demonstrating a high statistical correlation between the fair value of cash flows of the hedged item and those of the hedging instrument. The Board noted that the entity may choose a hedge ratio of other than one to one in order to improve the effectiveness of the hedge as described in paragraph AG100.

Hedges of portions of non-financial assets and non-financial liabilities for risk other than foreign currency risk (paragraph 82)

BC137 The Board considered comments on the Exposure Draft that suggested that IAS 39 should permit designating as the hedged risk a risk portion of a non-financial item other than foreign currency risk.

BC138 The Board concluded that IAS 39 should not be amended to permit such designation. It noted that in many cases, changes in the cash flows or fair value of a portion of a non-financial hedged item are difficult to isolate and measure. Moreover, the Board noted that permitting portions of non-financial assets and non-financial liabilities to be designated as the hedged item for risk other than foreign currency risk would compromise the principles of identification of the hedged item and effectiveness testing that the Board has confirmed because the portion could be designated so that no ineffectiveness would ever arise.

BC139 The Board confirmed that non-financial items may be hedged in their entirety when the item the entity is hedging is not the standard item underlying contracts traded in the market. In this context, the Board decided to clarify that a hedge ratio of other than one-to-one may maximise expected effectiveness, and to include guidance on how the hedge ratio that maximises expected effectiveness can be determined.

Loan servicing rights

BC140 The Board also considered whether IAS 39 should permit the interest rate risk portion of loan servicing rights to be designated as the hedged item.

BC141 The Board considered the argument that interest rate risk can be separately identified and measured in loan servicing rights, and that changes in market interest rates have a predictable and separately measurable effect on the value of loan servicing rights. The Board also considered the possibility of treating loan servicing rights as financial assets (rather than non-financial assets).

BC142 However, the Board concluded that no exceptions should be permitted for this matter. The Board noted that (a) the interest rate risk and prepayment risk in loan servicing rights are interdependent, and thus inseparable, (b) the fair values of loan servicing rights do not change in a linear fashion as interest rates increase or decrease, and (c) concerns exist about how to isolate and measure the interest rate risk portion of a loan servicing right. Moreover, the Board expressed concern that in jurisdictions in which loan servicing right markets are not developed, the interest rate risk portion may not be measurable.

BC143　The Board also considered whether IAS 39 should be amended to allow, on an elective basis, the inclusion of loan servicing rights in its scope provided that they are measured at fair value with changes in fair value recognised immediately in profit or loss. The Board noted that this would create two exceptions to the general principles in IAS 39. First, it would create a scope exception because IAS 39 applies only to financial assets and financial liabilities; loan servicing rights are non-financial assets. Second, *requiring* an entity to measure loan servicing rights at fair value through profit or loss would create a further exception, because this treatment is optional (except for items that are held for trading). The Board therefore decided not to amend the scope of IAS 39 for loan servicing rights.

Whether to permit hedge accounting using cash instruments

BC144　In finalising the amendments to IAS 39, the Board discussed whether an entity should be permitted to designate a financial asset or financial liability other than a derivative (ie a 'cash instrument') as a hedging instrument in hedges of risks other than foreign currency risk. The original IAS 39 precluded such designation because of the different bases for measuring derivatives and cash instruments. The Exposure Draft did not propose a change to this limitation. However, some commentators suggested a change, noting that entities do not distinguish between derivative and non-derivative financial instruments in their hedging and other risk management activities and that entities may have to use a non-derivative financial instrument to hedge risk if no suitable derivative financial instrument exists.

BC145　The Board acknowledged that some entities use non-derivatives to manage risk. However, it decided to retain the restriction against designating non-derivatives as hedging instruments in hedges of risks other than foreign currency risk. It noted the following arguments in support of this conclusion:

(a)　The need for hedge accounting arises in part because derivatives are measured at fair value, whereas the items they hedge may be measured at cost or not recognised at all. Without hedge accounting, an entity might recognise volatility in profit or loss for matched positions. For non-derivative items that are not measured at fair value or for which changes in fair value are not recognised in profit or loss, there is generally no need to adjust the accounting of the hedging instrument or the hedged item to achieve matched recognition of gains and losses in profit or loss.

(b)　To allow designation of cash instruments as hedging instruments would diverge from US GAAP: SFAS 133 precludes the designation of non-derivative instruments as hedging instruments except for some foreign currency hedges.

(c)   To allow designation of cash instruments as hedging instruments would add complexity to the Standard. More financial instruments would be measured at an amount that represents neither amortised cost nor fair value. Hedge accounting is, and should be, an exception to the normal measurement requirements.

(d)   If cash instruments were permitted to be designated as hedging instruments, there would be much less discipline in the accounting model because, in the absence of hedge accounting, a non-derivative may not be selectively measured at fair value. If the entity subsequently decides that it would rather not apply fair value measurement to a cash instrument that had been designated as a hedging instrument, it can breach one of the hedge accounting requirements, conclude that the non-derivative no longer qualifies as a hedging instrument and selectively avoid recognising the changes in fair value of the non-derivative instrument in equity (for a cash flow hedge) or profit or loss (for a fair value hedge).

(e)   The most significant use of cash instruments as hedging instruments is to hedge foreign currency exposures, which is permitted under IAS 39.

Whether to treat hedges of forecast transactions as fair value hedges

BC146   The Board considered a suggestion made in some of the comment letters received on the Exposure Draft that a hedge of a forecast transaction should be treated as a fair value hedge, rather than as a cash flow hedge. Some argued that the hedge accounting provisions should be simplified by having only one type of hedge accounting. Some also raised concern about an entity's ability, in some cases, to choose between two hedge accounting methods for the same hedging strategy (ie the choice between designating a forward contract to sell an existing asset as a fair value hedge of the asset or a cash flow hedge of a forecast sale of the asset).

BC147   The Board acknowledged that the hedge accounting provisions would be simplified, and their application more consistent in some situations, if the Standard permitted only one type of hedge accounting. However, the Board concluded that IAS 39 should continue to distinguish between fair value hedge accounting and cash flow hedge accounting. It noted that removing either type of hedge accounting would narrow the range of hedging strategies that could qualify for hedge accounting.

BC148   The Board also noted that treating a hedge of a forecast transaction as a fair value hedge is not appropriate for the following reasons: (a) it would result in the recognition of an asset or liability before the entity has become a party to the contract; (b) amounts would be recognised in the balance sheet that do not meet the definitions of assets and liabilities in the *Framework*; and (c) transactions in which there is no fair value exposure would be treated as if there were a fair value exposure.

Hedges of firm commitments (paragraphs 93 and 94)

BC149   The previous version of IAS 39 required a hedge of a firm commitment to be accounted for as a cash flow hedge. In other words, hedging gains and losses, to the extent that the hedge is effective, were initially recognised in equity and were subsequently 'recycled' to profit or loss in the same period(s) that the hedged firm commitment affected profit or loss (although, when basis adjustment was used, they adjusted the initial carrying amount of an asset or liability recognised in the meantime). Some believe this is appropriate because cash flow hedge accounting for hedges of firm commitments avoids partial recognition of the firm commitment that would otherwise not be recognised. Moreover, some believe it is conceptually incorrect to recognise the hedged fair value exposure of a firm commitment as an asset or liability merely because it has been hedged.

BC150   The Board considered whether hedges of firm commitments should be treated as cash flow hedges or fair value hedges. The Board concluded that hedges of firm commitments should be accounted for as fair value hedges.

BC151   The Board noted that, in concept, a hedge of a firm commitment is a fair value hedge. This is because the fair value of the item being hedged (the firm commitment) changes with changes in the hedged risk.

BC152   The Board was not persuaded by the argument that it is conceptually incorrect to recognise an asset or liability for a firm commitment merely because it has been hedged. It noted that for all fair value hedges, applying hedge accounting has the effect that amounts are recognised as assets or liabilities that would otherwise not be recognised. For example, assume an entity hedges a fixed rate loan asset with a pay-fixed, receive-variable interest rate swap. If there is a loss on the swap, applying fair value hedge accounting requires the offsetting gain on the loan to be recognised, ie the carrying amount of the loan is increased. Thus, applying hedge accounting has the effect of recognising a part of an asset (the increase in the loan's value attributable to interest rate movements) that would otherwise not have been recognised. The only difference in the case of a firm commitment is that, without hedge accounting, none of the commitment is recognised, ie the carrying amount is zero. However, this difference merely reflects that the historical cost of a firm commitment is usually zero. It is not a fundamental difference in concept.

BC153   Furthermore, the Board's decision converges with SFAS 133, and thus eliminates practical problems and eases implementation for entities that report under both standards.

BC154   However, the Board clarified that a hedge of the foreign currency risk of a firm commitment may be treated as either a fair value hedge or a cash flow hedge because foreign currency risk affects both the cash flows and the fair value of the hedged item. Accordingly a foreign currency cash flow hedge of a forecast transaction need not be re-designated as a fair value hedge when the forecast transaction becomes a firm commitment.

Basis adjustments (paragraphs 97–99)

BC155   The question of basis adjustment arises when an entity hedges the future purchase of an asset or the future issue of a liability. One example is that of a US entity that expects to make a future purchase of a German machine that it will pay for in euro. The entity enters into a derivative to hedge against possible future changes in the US dollar/euro exchange rate. Such a hedge is classified as a cash flow hedge under IAS 39, with the effect that gains and losses on the hedging instrument (to the extent that the hedge is effective) are initially recognised in equity.[1] The question the Board considered is what the accounting should be once the future transaction takes place. In its deliberations on this issue, the Board discussed the following approaches:

    (a)   to remove the hedging gain or loss from equity and recognise it as part of the initial carrying amount of the asset or liability (in the example above, the machine). In future periods, the hedging gain or loss is automatically recognised in profit or loss by being included in amounts such as depreciation expense (for a fixed asset), interest income or expense (for a financial asset or financial liability), or cost of sales (for inventories). This treatment is commonly referred to as 'basis adjustment'.

    (b)   to leave the hedging gain or loss in equity. In future periods, the gain or loss on the hedging instrument is 'recycled' to profit or loss in the same period(s) as the acquired asset or liability affects profit or loss. This recycling requires a separate adjustment and is not automatic.

BC156   It should be noted that both approaches have the same effect on profit or loss and net assets for all periods affected, so long as the hedge is accounted for as a cash flow hedge. The difference relates to balance sheet presentation and, possibly, the line item in the income statement.

BC157   In the Exposure Draft, the Board proposed that the 'basis adjustment' approach for forecast transactions (approach (a)) should be eliminated and replaced by approach (b) above. It further noted that eliminating the basis adjustment approach would enable IAS 39 to converge with SFAS 133.

BC158   Many of the comments received from constituents disagreed with the proposal in the Exposure Draft. Those responses argued that it would unnecessarily complicate the accounting to leave the hedging gain or loss in equity when the hedged forecast transaction occurs. They particularly noted that tracking the effects of cash flow hedges after the asset or liability is acquired would be complicated and would require systems changes. They also pointed out that treating hedges of firm commitments as fair value hedges has the same effect as a basis adjustment when the firm commitment results in the recognition of an asset or liability. For example, for a perfectly effective hedge of the foreign currency risk of a firm commitment to buy a machine, the effect is to recognise the machine initially at its foreign currency price translated at the forward rate in effect at the inception of the hedge rather than the spot rate. Therefore, they

---

1   As a consequence of the revision of IAS 1 *Presentation of Financial Statements* in 2007 such gains and losses are recognised in other comprehensive income.

questioned whether it is consistent to treat a hedge of a firm commitment as a fair value hedge while precluding basis adjustments for hedges of forecast transactions.

BC159 Others believe that a basis adjustment is difficult to justify in principle for forecast transactions, and also argue that such basis adjustments impair comparability of financial information. In other words, two identical assets that are purchased at the same time and in the same way, except for the fact that one was hedged, should not be recognised at different amounts.

BC160 The Board concluded that IAS 39 should distinguish between hedges of forecast transactions that will result in the recognition of a *financial* asset or a *financial* liability and those that will result in the recognition of a *non-financial* asset or a *non-financial* liability.

Basis adjustments for hedges of forecast transactions that will result in the recognition of a financial asset or a financial liability

BC161 For hedges of forecast transactions that will result in the recognition of a financial asset or a financial liability, the Board concluded that basis adjustments are not appropriate. Its reason was that basis adjustments cause the initial carrying amount of acquired assets (or assumed liabilities) arising from forecast transactions to move away from fair value and hence would override the requirement in IAS 39 to measure a financial instrument initially at its fair value.

BC161A If a hedged forecast transaction results in the recognition of a financial asset or a financial liability, paragraph 97 of IAS 39 required the associated gains or losses on hedging instruments to be reclassified from equity to profit or loss as a reclassification adjustment in the same period or periods during which the hedged item affects profit or loss (such as in the periods that interest income or interest expense is recognised).

BC161B The Board was informed that there was uncertainty about how paragraph 97 should be applied when the designated cash flow exposure being hedged differs from the financial instrument arising from the hedged forecast cash flows.

BC161C   The example below illustrates the issue:

> An entity applies the guidance in the answer to Question F.6.2 of the guidance on implementing IAS 39.[a] On 1 January 20X0 the entity designates forecast cash flows for the risk of variability arising from changes in interest rates. Those forecast cash flows arise from the repricing of existing financial instruments and are scheduled for 1 April 20X0. The entity is exposed to variability in cash flows for the three-month period beginning on 1 April 20X0 attributable to changes in interest rate risk that occur from 1 January 20X0 to 31 March 20X0.
>
> The occurrence of the forecast cash flows is deemed to be highly probable and all the other relevant hedge accounting criteria are met.
>
> The financial instrument that results from the hedged forecast cash flows is a five-year interest-bearing instrument.
>
> (a) IFRS 9 *Financial Instruments* deletes the guidance in IAS 39.

BC161D   Paragraph 97 required the gains or losses on the hedging instrument to be reclassified from equity to profit or loss as a reclassification adjustment in the same period or periods during which the asset acquired or liability assumed affected profit or loss. The financial instrument that was recognised is a five-year instrument that will affect profit or loss for five years. The wording in paragraph 97 suggested that the gains or losses should be reclassified over five years, even though the cash flows designated as the hedged item were hedged for the effects of interest rate changes over only a three-month period.

BC161E   The Board believes that the wording of paragraph 97 did not reflect the underlying rationale in hedge accounting, ie that the gains or losses on the hedging instrument should offset the gains or losses on the hedged item, and the offset should be reflected in profit or loss by way of reclassification adjustments.

BC161F   The Board believes that in the example set out above the gains or losses should be reclassified over a period of three months beginning on 1 April 20X0, and not over a period of five years beginning on 1 April 20X0.

BC161G   Consequently, in *Improvements to IFRSs* issued in April 2009, the Board amended paragraph 97 of IAS 39 to clarify that the gains or losses on the hedged instrument should be reclassified from equity to profit or loss during the period that the hedged forecast cash flows affect profit or loss. The Board also decided that to avoid similar confusion paragraph 100 of IAS 39 should be amended to be consistent with paragraph 97.

Basis adjustments for hedges of forecast transactions that will result in the recognition of a non-financial asset or a non-financial liability

BC162   For hedges of forecast transactions that will result in the recognition of a non-financial asset or a non-financial liability, the Board decided to permit entities a choice of whether to apply basis adjustment.

BC163   The Board considered the argument that changes in the fair value of the hedging instrument are appropriately included in the initial carrying amount of the recognised asset or liability because such changes represent a part of the 'cost' of that asset or liability. Although the Board has not yet considered the broader issue of what costs may be capitalised at initial recognition, the Board believes that its decision to provide an option for basis adjustments in the case of non-financial items will not pre-empt that future discussion. The Board also recognised that financial items and non-financial items are not necessarily measured at the same amount on initial recognition, because financial items are measured at fair value and non-financial items are measured at cost.

BC164   The Board concluded that, on balance, providing entities with a choice in this case was appropriate. The Board took the view that allowing basis adjustments addresses the concern that precluding basis adjustments complicates the accounting for hedges of forecast transactions. In addition, the number of balance sheet line items that could be affected is quite small, generally being only property, plant and equipment, inventory and the cash flow hedge line item in equity. The Board also noted that US GAAP precludes basis adjustments and that applying a basis adjustment is inconsistent with the accounting for hedges of forecast transactions that will result in the recognition of a financial asset or a financial liability. The Board acknowledged the merits of these arguments, and recognised that by permitting a choice in IAS 39, entities could apply the accounting treatment required by US GAAP.

Hedging using internal contracts

BC165   IAS 39 does not preclude entities from using internal contracts as a risk management tool, or as a tracking device in applying hedge accounting for external contracts that hedge external positions. Furthermore, IAS 39 permits hedge accounting to be applied to transactions between entities in the same group in the *separate reporting* of those entities. However, IAS 39 does not permit hedge accounting for transactions between entities in the same group in consolidated financial statements. The reason is the fundamental requirement of consolidation that the accounting effects of internal contracts should be eliminated in consolidated financial statements, including any internally generated gains or losses. Designating internal contracts as hedging instruments could result in non-elimination of internal gains and losses and have other accounting effects. The Exposure Draft did not propose any change in this area.

BC166   To illustrate, assume the banking book division of Bank A enters into an internal interest rate swap with the trading book division of the same bank. The purpose is to hedge the net interest rate risk exposure in the banking book of a group of similar fixed rate loan assets funded by floating rate liabilities. Under the swap, the banking book pays fixed interest payments to the trading book and receives variable interest rate payments in return. The bank wants to designate the internal interest rate swap in the banking book as a hedging instrument in its consolidated financial statements.

BC167   If the internal swap in the banking book is designated as a hedging instrument in a cash flow hedge of the liabilities, and the internal swap in the trading book is classified as held for trading, internal gains and losses on that internal swap would not be eliminated. This is because the gains and losses on the internal swap in the banking book would be recognised in equity[2] to the extent the hedge is effective and the gains and losses on the internal swap in the trading book would be recognised in profit or loss.

BC168 If the internal swap in the banking book is designated as a hedging instrument in a fair value hedge of the loan assets and the internal swap in the trading book is classified as held for trading, the changes in the fair value of the internal swap would offset both in total net assets in the balance sheet and profit or loss. However, without elimination of the internal swap, there would be an adjustment to the carrying amount of the hedged loan asset in the banking book to reflect the change in the fair value attributable to the risk hedged by the internal contract. Moreover, to reflect the effect of the internal swap the bank would in effect recognise the fixed rate loan at a floating interest rate and recognise an offsetting trading gain or loss in the income statement. Hence the internal swap would have accounting effects.

BC169 Some respondents to the Exposure Draft and some participants in the round-tables objected to not being able to obtain hedge accounting in the consolidated financial statements for internal contracts between subsidiaries or between a subsidiary and the parent (as illustrated above). Among other things, they emphasised that the use of internal contracts is a key risk management tool and that the accounting should reflect the way in which risk is managed. Some suggested that IAS 39 should be changed to make it consistent with US GAAP, which allows the designation of internal derivative contracts as hedging instruments in cash flow hedges of forecast foreign currency transactions in specified, limited circumstances.

BC170 In considering these comments, the Board noted that the following principles apply to consolidated financial statements:

(a) financial statements provide financial information about an entity or group as a whole (as that of a single entity). Financial statements do not provide financial information about an entity as if it were two separate entities.

(b) a fundamental principle of consolidation is that intragroup balances and intragroup transactions are eliminated in full. Permitting the designation of internal contracts as hedging instruments would require a change to the consolidation principles.

(c) it is conceptually wrong to permit an entity to recognise internally generated gains and losses or make other accounting adjustments because of internal transactions. No external event has occurred.

(d) an ability to recognise internally generated gains and losses could result in abuse in the absence of requirements about how entities should manage and control the associated risks. It is not the purpose of accounting standards to prescribe how entities should manage and control risks.

---

2   As a consequence of the revision of IAS 1 *Presentation of Financial Statements* in 2007 such gains and losses are recognised in other comprehensive income.

(e)   permitting the designation of internal contracts as hedging instruments violates the following requirements in IAS 39:

    (i)   the prohibition against designating as a hedging instrument a non-derivative financial asset or non-derivative financial liability for other than foreign currency risk. To illustrate, if an entity has two offsetting internal contracts and one is the designated hedging instrument in a fair value hedge of a non-derivative asset and the other is the designated hedging instrument in a fair value hedge of a non-derivative liability, from the entity's perspective the effect is to designate a hedging relationship between the asset and the liability (ie a non-derivative asset or non-derivative liability is used as the hedging instrument).

    (ii)   the prohibition on designating a net position of assets and liabilities as the hedged item. To illustrate, an entity has two internal contracts. One is designated in a fair value hedge of an asset and the other in a fair value hedge of a liability. The two internal contracts do not fully offset, so the entity lays off the net risk exposure by entering into a net external derivative. In that case, the effect from the entity's perspective is to designate a hedging relationship between the net external derivative and a net position of an asset and a liability.

    (iii)   the option to fair value assets and liabilities does not extend to portions of assets and liabilities.

(f)   the Board is considering separately whether to make an amendment to IAS 39 to facilitate fair value hedge accounting for portfolio hedges of interest rate risk. The Board believes that that is a better way to address the concerns raised about symmetry with risk management systems than permitting the designation of internal contracts as hedging instruments.

(g)   the Board decided to permit an option to measure any financial asset or financial liability at fair value with changes in fair value recognised in profit or loss. This enables an entity to measure matching asset/liability positions at fair value without a need for hedge accounting.

BC171   The Board reaffirmed that it is a fundamental principle of consolidation that any accounting effect of internal contracts is eliminated on consolidation. The Board decided that no exception to this principle should be made in IAS 39. Consistently with this decision, the Board also decided not to explore an amendment to permit internal derivative contracts to be designated as hedging instruments in hedges of some forecast foreign currency transactions, as is permitted by SFAS 138 *Accounting for Certain Derivative Instruments and Certain Hedging Activities*.

BC172   The Board also decided to clarify that IAS 39 does not preclude hedge accounting for transactions between entities in the same group in individual or separate financial statements of those entities because they are not internal to the entity (ie the individual entity).

BC172A   Previously, paragraphs 73 and 80 referred to the need for hedging instruments to involve a party external to the reporting entity. In doing so, they used a segment as an example of a reporting entity. However, IFRS 8 *Operating Segments* requires disclosure of information that is reported to the chief operating decision maker even if this is on a non-IFRS basis. Therefore, the two IFRSs appeared to conflict. In *Improvements to IFRSs* issued in May 2008 and April 2009, the Board removed from paragraphs 73 and 80 references to the designation of hedging instruments at the segment level.

Eligible hedged items in particular situations (paragraphs AG99BA, AG99E, AG99F, AG110A and AG110B)

BC172B   The Board amended IAS 39 in July 2008 to clarify the application of the principles that determine whether a hedged risk or portion of cash flows is eligible for designation in particular situations. This followed a request by the IFRIC for guidance.

BC172C   The responses to the exposure draft *Exposures Qualifying for Hedge Accounting* demonstrated that diversity in practice existed, or was likely to occur, in two situations:

(a)   the designation of a one-sided risk in a hedged item

(b)   the designation of inflation as a hedged risk or portion in particular situations.

Designation of a one-sided risk in a hedged item

BC172D   The IFRIC received requests for guidance on whether an entity can designate a purchased option in its entirety as the hedging instrument in a cash flow hedge of a highly probable forecast transaction in such a way that all changes in the fair value of the purchased option, including changes in the time value, are regarded as effective and would be recognised in other comprehensive income. The exposure draft proposed to amend IAS 39 to clarify that such a designation was not allowed.

BC172E   After considering the responses to the exposure draft, the Board confirmed that the designation set out in paragraph BC172D is not permitted.

BC172F   The Board reached that decision by considering the variability of future cash flow outcomes resulting from a price increase of a forecast commodity purchase (a one-sided risk). The Board noted that the forecast transaction contained no separately identifiable risk that affects profit or loss that is equivalent to the time value of a purchased option hedging instrument (with the same principal terms as the designated risk). The Board concluded that the intrinsic value of a purchased option, but not its time value, reflects a one-sided risk in a hedged item. The Board then considered a purchased option designated in its entirety as the hedging instrument. The Board noted that hedge accounting is based on a principle of offsetting changes in fair value or cash flows between the hedging instrument and the hedged item. Because a designated one-sided risk does not contain the time value of a purchased option hedging instrument, the Board noted that there will be no offset between the cash flows relating to the time value of the option premium paid and the designated hedged risk. Therefore, the Board concluded that a purchased option designated in its entirety as the hedging instrument of a one-sided risk will not be perfectly effective.

Designation of inflation in particular situations

BC172G   The IFRIC received a request for guidance on whether, for a hedge of a fixed rate financial instrument, an entity can designate inflation as the hedged item. The exposure draft proposed to amend IAS 39 to clarify that such a designation was not allowed.

BC172H   After considering the responses to the exposure draft, the Board acknowledged that expectations of future inflation rates can be viewed as an economic component of nominal interest. However, the Board also noted that hedge accounting is an exception to normal accounting principles for the hedged item (fair value hedges) or hedging instrument (cash flow hedges). To ensure a disciplined use of hedge accounting the Board noted that restrictions regarding eligible hedged items are necessary, especially if something other than the entire fair value or cash flow variability of a hedged item is designated.

BC172I   The Board noted that paragraph 81 permits an entity to designate as the hedged item something other than the entire fair value change or cash flow variability of a financial instrument. For example, an entity may designate some (but not all) risks of a financial instrument, or some (but not all) cash flows of a financial instrument (a 'portion').

BC172J   The Board noted that, to be eligible for hedge accounting, the designated risks and portions must be separately identifiable components of the financial instrument, and changes in the fair value or cash flows of the entire financial instrument arising from changes in the designated risks and portions must be reliably measurable. The Board noted that these principles were important in order for the effectiveness requirements set out in paragraph 88 to be applied in a meaningful way. The Board also noted that deciding whether designated risks and portions are separately identifiable and reliably measurable requires judgement. However, the Board confirmed that unless the inflation portion is a contractually specified portion of cash flows and other cash flows of the financial instrument are not affected by the inflation portion, inflation is not separately identifiable and reliably measurable and is not eligible for designation as a hedged risk or portion of a financial instrument.

Fair value hedge accounting for a portfolio hedge of interest rate risk

Background

BC173   The Exposure Draft of proposed improvements to IAS 39 published in June 2002 did not propose any substantial changes to the requirements for hedge accounting as they applied to a portfolio hedge of interest rate risk. However, some of the comment letters on the Exposure Draft and participants in the round-table discussions raised this issue. In particular, some were concerned that portfolio hedging strategies they regarded as effective hedges would not have qualified for fair value hedge accounting in accordance with previous versions of IAS 39. Rather, they would have either:

(a)   not qualified for hedge accounting at all, with the result that reported profit or loss would be volatile; or

(b)   qualified only for cash flow hedge accounting, with the result that reported equity would be volatile.

BC174   In the light of these concerns, the Board decided to explore whether and how IAS 39 could be amended to enable fair value hedge accounting to be used more readily for portfolio hedges of interest rate risk. As a result, in August 2003 the Board published a second Exposure Draft, *Fair Value Hedge Accounting for a Portfolio Hedge of Interest Rate Risk*, with a comment deadline of 14 November 2003. More than 120 comment letters were received. The amendments proposed in this second Exposure Draft were finalised in March 2004. Paragraphs BC135A–BC136B and BC175–BC220 summarise the Board's considerations in reaching conclusions on the issues raised.

Scope

BC175   The Board decided to limit any amendments to IAS 39 to applying fair value hedge accounting to a hedge of interest rate risk on a portfolio of items. In making this decision it noted that:

(a)   implementation guidance on IAS 39[3] explains how to apply cash flow hedge accounting to a hedge of the interest rate risk on a portfolio of items.

(b)   the issues that arise for a portfolio hedge of interest rate risk are different from those that arise for hedges of individual items and for hedges of other risks. In particular, the three issues discussed in paragraph BC176 do not arise in combination for such other hedging arrangements.

The issue: why fair value hedge accounting was difficult to achieve in accordance with previous versions of IAS 39

BC176   The Board identified the following three main reasons why a portfolio hedge of interest rate risk might not have qualified for fair value hedge accounting in accordance with previous versions of IAS 39.

(a)   Typically, many of the assets that are included in a portfolio hedge are prepayable, ie the counterparty has a right to repay the item before its contractual repricing date. Such assets contain a prepayment option whose fair value changes as interest rates change. However, the derivative that is used as the hedging instrument typically is not prepayable, ie it does not contain a prepayment option. When interest rates change, the resulting change in the fair value of the hedged item (which is prepayable) differs from the change in fair value of the hedging derivative (which is not prepayable), with the result that the hedge may not meet IAS 39's effectiveness tests.[4] Furthermore, prepayment risk may have the effect that the items included in a portfolio hedge fail the requirement[5] that a group of hedged assets or liabilities must be 'similar' and the related requirement[6] that 'the change in fair value attributable

---

3   IFRS 9 *Financial Instruments* deleted the guidance on implementing IAS 39.
4   see IAS 39, paragraph AG105
5   see IAS 39, paragraph 78
6   see IAS 39, paragraph 83

to the hedged risk for each individual item in the group shall be expected to be approximately proportional to the overall change in fair value attributable to the hedged risk of the group of items'.

(b) IAS 39[7] prohibits the designation of an overall net position (eg the net of fixed rate assets and fixed rate liabilities) as the hedged item. Rather, it requires individual assets (or liabilities), or groups of similar assets (or similar liabilities), that share the risk exposure equal in amount to the net position to be designated as the hedged item. For example, if an entity has a portfolio of CU100 of assets and CU80 of liabilities, IAS 39 requires that individual assets or a group of similar assets of CU20 are designated as the hedged item. However, for risk management purposes, entities often seek to hedge the net position. This net position changes each period as items are repriced or derecognised and as new items are originated. Hence, the individual items designated as the hedged item also need to be changed each period. This requires de- and redesignation of the individual items that constitute the hedged item, which gives rise to significant systems needs.

(c) Fair value hedge accounting requires the carrying amount of the hedged item to be adjusted for the effect of changes in the hedged risk.[8] Applied to a portfolio hedge, this could involve changing the carrying amounts of many thousands of individual items. Also, for any items subsequently de-designated from being hedged, the revised carrying amount must be amortised over the item's remaining life.[9] This, too, gives rise to significant systems needs.

BC177 The Board decided that any change to IAS 39 must be consistent with the principles that underlie IAS 39's requirements on derivatives and hedge accounting. The three principles that are most relevant to a portfolio hedge of interest rate risk are:

(a) derivatives should be measured at fair value;

(b) hedge ineffectiveness should be identified and recognised in profit or loss;[10] and

(c) only items that are assets and liabilities should be recognised as such in the balance sheet. Deferred losses are not assets and deferred gains are not liabilities. However, if an asset or liability is hedged, any change in its fair value that is attributable to the hedged risk should be recognised in the balance sheet.

Prepayment risk

BC178 In considering the issue described in paragraph BC176(a), the Board noted that a prepayable item can be viewed as a combination of a non-prepayable item and a prepayment option. It follows that the fair value of a fixed rate prepayable item changes for two reasons when interest rates move:

---

7   see IAS 39, paragraph AG101
8   see IAS 39, paragraph 89(b)
9   see IAS 39, paragraph 92
10 Subject to the same materiality considerations that apply in this context as throughout IFRSs.

　　　　　　　© IFRS Foundation

(a) the fair value of the contracted cash flows to the contractual repricing date changes (because the rate used to discount them changes); and

(b) the fair value of the prepayment option changes (reflecting, among other things, that the likelihood of prepayment is affected by interest rates).

BC179 The Board also noted that, for risk management purposes, many entities do not consider these two effects separately. Instead they incorporate the effect of prepayments by grouping the hedged portfolio into repricing time periods based on *expected* repayment dates (rather than contractual repayment dates). For example, an entity with a portfolio of 25-year mortgages of CU100 may expect 5 per cent of that portfolio to repay in one year's time, in which case it schedules an amount of CU5 into a 12-month time period. The entity schedules all other items contained in its portfolio in a similar way (ie on the basis of expected repayment dates) and hedges all or part of the resulting overall net position in each repricing time period.

BC180 The Board decided to permit the scheduling that is used for risk management purposes, ie on the basis of expected repayment dates, to be used as a basis for the designation necessary for hedge accounting. As a result, an entity would not be required to compute the effect that a change in interest rates has on the fair value of the prepayment option embedded in a prepayable item. Instead, it could incorporate the effect of a change in interest rates on prepayments by grouping the hedged portfolio into repricing time periods based on expected repayment dates. The Board noted that this approach has significant practical advantages for preparers of financial statements, because it allows them to use the data they use for risk management. The Board also noted that the approach is consistent with paragraph 81 of IAS 39, which permits hedge accounting for a portion of a financial asset or financial liability. However, as discussed further in paragraphs BC193–BC206, the Board also concluded that if the entity changes its estimates of the time periods in which items are expected to repay (eg in the light of recent prepayment experience), ineffectiveness will arise, regardless of whether the revision in estimates results in more or less being scheduled in a particular time period.

BC181 The Board also noted that if the items in the hedged portfolio are subject to different amounts of prepayment risk, they may fail the test in paragraph 78 of being similar and the related requirement in paragraph 83 that the change in fair value attributable to the hedged risk for each individual item in the group is expected to be approximately proportional to the overall change in fair value attributable to the hedged risk of the group of items. The Board decided that, in the context of a portfolio hedge of interest rate risk, these requirements could be inconsistent with the Board's decision, set out in the previous paragraph, on how to incorporate the effects of prepayment risk. Accordingly, the Board decided that they should not apply. Instead, the financial assets or financial liabilities included in a portfolio hedge of interest rate risk need only share the risk being hedged.

Designation of the hedged item and liabilities with a demand feature

BC182 The Board considered two main ways to overcome the issue noted in paragraph BC176(b). These were:

(a) to designate the hedged item as the overall net position that results from a portfolio containing assets and liabilities. For example, if a repricing time period contains CU100 of fixed rate assets and CU90 of fixed rate liabilities, the net position of CU10 would be designated as the hedged item.

(b) to designate the hedged item as a portion of the assets (ie assets of CU10 in the above example), but not to require individual assets to be designated.

BC183 Some of those who commented on the Exposure Draft favoured designation of the overall net position in a portfolio that contains assets and liabilities. In their view, existing asset-liability management (ALM) systems treat the identified assets and liabilities as a natural hedge. Management's decisions about additional hedging focus on the entity's remaining net exposure. They observe that designation based on a portion of either the assets or the liabilities is not consistent with existing ALM systems and would entail additional systems costs.

BC184 In considering questions of designation, the Board was also concerned about questions of measurement. In particular, the Board observed that fair value hedge accounting requires measurement of the change in fair value of the hedged item attributable to the risk being hedged. Designation based on the net position would require the assets and the liabilities in a portfolio each to be measured at fair value (for the risk being hedged) in order to compute the fair value of the net position. Although statistical and other techniques can be used to estimate these fair values, the Board concluded that it is not appropriate to assume that the change in fair value of the hedging instrument is equal to the change in fair value of the net position.

BC185 The Board noted that under the first approach in paragraph BC182 (designating an overall net position), an issue arises if the entity has liabilities that are repayable on demand or after a notice period (referred to below as 'demandable liabilities'). This includes items such as demand deposits and some types of time deposits. The Board was informed that, when managing interest rate risk, many entities that have demandable liabilities include them in a portfolio hedge by scheduling them to the date when they *expect* the total amount of demandable liabilities in the portfolio to be due because of net withdrawals from the accounts in the portfolio. This expected repayment date is typically a period covering several years into the future (eg 0–10 years hence). The Board was also informed that some entities wish to apply fair value hedge accounting based on this scheduling, ie they wish to include demandable liabilities in a fair value portfolio hedge by scheduling them on the basis of their expected repayment dates. The arguments for this view are:

(a) it is consistent with how demandable liabilities are scheduled for risk management purposes. Interest rate risk management involves hedging the interest rate margin resulting from assets and liabilities and not the fair value of all or part of the assets and liabilities included in the hedged portfolio. The interest rate margin of a specific period is subject to variability as soon as the amount of fixed rate assets in that period differs from the amount of fixed rate liabilities in that period.

(b) it is consistent with the treatment of prepayable assets to include demandable liabilities in a portfolio hedge based on expected repayment dates.

(c) as with prepayable assets, expected maturities for demandable liabilities are based on the historical behaviour of customers.

(d) applying the fair value hedge accounting framework to a portfolio that includes demandable liabilities would not entail an immediate gain on origination of such liabilities because all assets and liabilities enter the hedged portfolio at their carrying amounts. Furthermore, IAS 39 requires the carrying amount of a financial liability on its initial recognition to be its fair value, which normally equates to the transaction price (ie the amount deposited).[11]

(e) historical analysis shows that a base level of a portfolio of demandable liabilities, such as chequing accounts, is very stable. Whilst a portion of the demandable liabilities varies with interest rates, the remaining portion—the base level—does not. Hence, entities regard this base level as a long-term fixed rate item and include it as such in the scheduling that is used for risk management purposes.

(f) the distinction between 'old' and 'new' money makes little sense at a portfolio level. The portfolio behaves like a long-term item even if individual liabilities do not.

BC186 The Board noted that this issue is related to that of how to measure the fair value of a demandable liability. In particular, it interrelates with the requirement in IAS 39 that the fair value of a liability with a demand feature is not less than the amount payable on demand, discounted from the first date that the amount could be required to be paid.[12] This requirement applies to all liabilities with a demand feature, not only to those included in a portfolio hedge.

BC187 The Board also noted that:

(a) although entities, when managing risk, may schedule demandable liabilities based on the expected repayment date of the total balance of a portfolio of accounts, the deposit liabilities included in that balance are unlikely to be outstanding for an extended period (eg several years). Rather, these deposits are usually expected to be withdrawn within a short time (eg a few months or less), although they may be replaced by new deposits. Put another way, the balance of the portfolio is relatively stable only because withdrawals on some accounts (which usually occur relatively quickly) are offset by new deposits into others. Thus, the liability being hedged is actually the forecast replacement of existing deposits by the receipt of new deposits. IAS 39 does not permit a hedge

---

11 IFRS 9 *Financial Instruments* replaced IAS 39.
12 IFRS 9 *Financial Instruments* replaced IAS 39.

of such a forecast transaction to qualify for fair value hedge accounting. Rather, fair value hedge accounting can be applied only to the liability (or asset) or firm commitment that exists today.

(b) a portfolio of demandable liabilities is similar to a portfolio of trade payables. Both comprise individual balances that usually are expected to be paid within a short time (eg a few months or less) and replaced by new balances. Also, for both, there is an amount—the base level—that is expected to be stable and present indefinitely. Hence, if the Board were to permit demandable liabilities to be included in a fair value hedge on the basis of a stable base level created by expected replacements, it should similarly allow a hedge of a portfolio of trade payables to qualify for fair value hedge accounting on this basis.

(c) a portfolio of similar core deposits is not different from an individual deposit, other than that, in the light of the 'law of large numbers', the behaviour of the portfolio is more predictable. There are no diversification effects from aggregating many similar items.

(d) it would be inconsistent with the requirement in IAS 39 that the fair value of a liability with a demand feature is not less than the amount payable on demand, discounted from the first date that the amount could be required to be paid, to schedule such liabilities for hedging purposes using a different date. For example, consider a deposit of CU100 that can be withdrawn on demand without penalty. IAS 39 states that the fair value of such a deposit is CU100. That fair value is unaffected by interest rates and does not change when interest rates move. Accordingly, the demand deposit cannot be included in a fair value hedge of interest rate risk—there is no fair value exposure to hedge.

BC188 For these reasons, the Board concluded that demandable liabilities should not be included in a portfolio hedge on the basis of the expected repayment date of the *total balance of a portfolio* of demandable liabilities, ie including expected rollovers or replacements of existing deposits by new ones. However, as part of its consideration of comments received on the Exposure Draft, the Board also considered whether a demandable liability, such as a demand deposit, could be included in a portfolio hedge based on the expected repayment date of the *existing balance of individual deposits*, ie ignoring any rollovers or replacements of existing deposits by new deposits. The Board noted the following.

(a) For many demandable liabilities, this approach would imply a much earlier expected repayment date than is generally assumed for risk management purposes. In particular, for chequing accounts it would probably imply an expected maturity of a few months or less. However, for other demandable liabilities, such as fixed term deposits that can be withdrawn only by the depositor incurring a significant penalty, it might imply an expected repayment date that is closer to that assumed for risk management.

(b) This approach implies that the *fair value* of the demandable liability should also reflect the expected repayment date of the existing balance, ie that the fair value of a demandable deposit liability is the present value of the amount of the deposit discounted from the expected repayment date. The Board noted that it would be inconsistent to permit fair value hedge accounting to be based on the expected repayment date, but to measure the fair value of the liability on initial recognition on a different basis. The Board also noted that this approach would give rise to a difference on initial recognition between the amount deposited and the fair value recognised in the balance sheet. This, in turn, gives rise to the issue of what the difference represents. Possibilities the Board considered include (i) the value of the depositor's option to withdraw its money before the expected maturity, (ii) prepaid servicing costs or (iii) a gain. The Board did not reach a conclusion on what the difference represents, but agreed that if it were to require such differences to be recognised, this would apply to all demandable liabilities, not only to those included in a portfolio hedge. Such a requirement would represent a significant change from present practice.

(c) If the fair value of a demandable deposit liability at the date of initial recognition is deemed to equal the amount deposited, a fair value portfolio hedge based on an expected repayment date is unlikely to be effective. This is because such deposits typically pay interest at a rate that is significantly lower than that being hedged (eg the deposits may pay interest at zero or at very low rates, whereas the interest rate being hedged may be LIBOR or a similar benchmark rate). Hence, the fair value of the deposit will be significantly less sensitive to interest rate changes than that of the hedging instrument.

(d) The question of how to fair value a demandable liability is closely related to issues being debated by the Board in other projects, including Insurance (phase II), Revenue Recognition, Leases and Measurement. The Board's discussions in these other projects are continuing and it would be premature to reach a conclusion in the context of portfolio hedging without considering the implications for these other projects.

BC189 As a result, the Board decided:

(a) to confirm the requirement in IAS 39 that 'the fair value of a financial liability with a demand feature (eg a demand deposit) is not less than the amount payable on demand, discounted from the first date that the amount could be required to be paid',[13] and

(b) consequently, that a demandable liability cannot qualify for fair value hedge accounting for any time period beyond the shortest period in which the counterparty can demand payment.

The Board noted that, depending on the outcome of its discussions in other projects (principally Insurance (phase II), Revenue Recognition, Leases and Measurement), it might reconsider these decisions at some time in the future.

BC190 The Board also noted that what is designated as the hedged item in a portfolio hedge affects the relevance of this issue, at least to some extent. In particular, if the hedged item is designated as a portion *of the assets* in a portfolio, this issue is irrelevant. To illustrate, assume that in a particular repricing time period an

---

13 IFRS 9 *Financial Instruments* replaced IAS 39.

entity has CU100 of fixed rate assets and CU80 of what it regards as fixed rate liabilities and the entity wishes to hedge its net exposure of CU20. Also assume that all of the liabilities are demandable liabilities and the time period is later than that containing the earliest date on which the items can be repaid. If the hedged item is designated as CU20 of *assets*, then the demandable *liabilities* are not included in the hedged item, but rather are used only to determine how much of the assets the entity wishes to designate as being hedged. In such a case, whether the demandable liabilities can be designated as a hedged item in a fair value hedge is irrelevant. However, if the overall net position were to be designated as the hedged item, because the net position comprises CU100 of assets and CU80 of demandable liabilities, whether the demandable liabilities can be designated as a hedged item in a fair value hedge becomes critical.

BC191   Given the above points, the Board decided that a portion of assets or liabilities (rather than an overall net position) may be designated as the hedged item, to overcome part of the demandable liabilities issue. It also noted that this approach is consistent with IAS 39,[14] whereas designating an overall net position is not. IAS 39[15] prohibits an overall net position from being designated as the hedged item, but permits a similar effect to be achieved by designating an amount of assets (or liabilities) equal to the net position.

BC192   However, the Board also recognised that this method of designation would not fully resolve the demandable liabilities issue. In particular, the issue is still relevant if, in a particular repricing time period, the entity has so many demandable liabilities whose earliest repayment date is before that time period that (a) they comprise nearly all of what the entity regards as its fixed rate liabilities and (b) its fixed rate liabilities (including the demandable liabilities) exceed its fixed rate assets in this repricing time period. In this case, the entity is in a net liability position. Thus, it needs to designate an amount of the *liabilities* as the hedged item. But unless it has sufficient fixed rate liabilities other than those that can be demanded before that time period, this implies designating the demandable liabilities as the hedged item. Consistently with the Board's decision discussed above, such a hedge does not qualify for fair value hedge accounting. (If the liabilities are non-interest bearing, they cannot be designated as the hedged item in a cash flow hedge because their cash flows do not vary with changes in interest rates, ie there is no cash flow exposure to interest rates. However, the hedging relationship may qualify for cash flow hedge accounting if designated as a hedge of associated assets.)

What portion of assets should be designated and the impact on ineffectiveness

BC193   Having decided that a portion of assets (or liabilities) could be designated as the hedged item, the Board considered how to overcome the systems problems noted in paragraph BC176(b) and (c). The Board noted that these problems arise from designating individual assets (or liabilities) as the hedged item. Accordingly, the Board decided that the hedged item could be expressed as an *amount* (of assets or liabilities) rather than as individual assets or liabilities.

---

14   see IAS 39, paragraph 84
15   see IAS 39, paragraph AG101

BC194   The Board noted that this decision—that the hedged item may be designated as an amount of assets or liabilities rather than as specified items—gives rise to the issue of how the amount designated should be specified. The Board considered comments received on the Exposure Draft that it should not specify any method for designating the hedged item and hence measuring effectiveness. However, the Board concluded that if it provided no guidance, entities might designate in different ways, resulting in little comparability between them. The Board also noted that its objective, when permitting an amount to be designated, was to overcome the systems problems associated with designating individual items whilst achieving a very similar accounting result. Accordingly, it concluded that it should require a method of designation that closely approximates the accounting result that would be achieved by designating individual items.

BC195   Additionally, the Board noted that designation determines how much, if any, ineffectiveness arises if actual repricing dates in a particular repricing time period vary from those estimated or if the estimated repricing dates are revised. Taking the above example of a repricing time period in which there are CU100 of fixed rate assets and the entity designates as the hedged item an amount of CU20 of assets, the Board considered two approaches (a layer approach and a percentage approach) that are summarised below.

Layer approach

BC196   The first of these approaches, illustrated in figure 1, designates the hedged item as a 'layer' (eg (a) the bottom layer, (b) the top layer or (c) a portion of the top layer) of the assets (or liabilities) in a repricing time period. In this approach, the portfolio of CU100 in the above example is considered to comprise a hedged layer of CU20 and an unhedged layer of CU80.

Figure 1: Illustrating the designation of an amount of assets as a layer

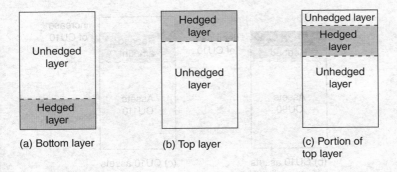

(a) Bottom layer   (b) Top layer   (c) Portion of top layer

BC197   The Board noted that the layer approach does not result in the recognition of ineffectiveness in all cases when the estimated amount of assets (or liabilities) changes. For example, in a bottom layer approach (see figure 2), if some assets prepay earlier than expected so that the entity revises downward its estimate of the amount of assets in the repricing time period (eg from CU100 to CU90), these reductions are assumed to come first from the unhedged top layer (figure 2(b)). Whether any ineffectiveness arises depends on whether the downward revision reaches the hedged layer of CU20. Thus, if the bottom layer is designated as the hedged item, it is unlikely that the hedged (bottom) layer will be reached and that any ineffectiveness will arise. Conversely, if the top layer is designated (see figure 3), any downward revision to the estimated amount in a repricing time period will reduce the hedged (top) layer and ineffectiveness will arise (figure 3(b)).

Figure 2: Illustrating the effect on changes in prepayments in a bottom layer approach

(a) Original expectation

(b) CU10 assets prepay earlier than expected

(c) CU10 assets prepay later than expected

Figure 3: Illustrating the effect on changes in prepayments in a top layer approach

(a) Original expectation

(b) CU10 assets prepay earlier than expected

(c) CU10 assets prepay later than expected

BC198   Finally, if some assets prepay *later* than expected so that the entity revises *upwards* its estimate of the amount of assets in this repricing time period (eg from CU100 to CU110, see figures 2(c) and 3(c)), no ineffectiveness arises no matter how the layer is designated, on the grounds that the hedged layer of CU20 is still there and that was all that was being hedged.

Percentage approach

BC199　The percentage approach, illustrated in figure 4, designates the hedged item as a percentage of the assets (or liabilities) in a repricing time period. In this approach, in the portfolio in the above example, 20 per cent of the assets of CU100 in this repricing time period is designated as the hedged item (figure 4(a)). As a result, if some assets prepay *earlier* than expected so that the entity revises *downwards* its estimate of the amount of assets in this repricing time period (eg from CU100 to CU90, figure 4(b)), ineffectiveness arises on 20 per cent of the decrease (in this case ineffectiveness arises on CU2). Similarly, if some assets prepay *later* than expected so that the entity revises *upwards* its estimate of the amount of assets in this repricing time period (eg from CU100 to CU110, figure 4(c)), ineffectiveness arises on 20 per cent of the increase (in this case ineffectiveness arises on CU2).

Figure 4: Illustrating the designation of an amount of assets as a percentage

Arguments for and against the layer approach

BC200　The arguments for the layer approach are as follows:

(a)　Designating a bottom layer would be consistent with the answers to Questions F.6.1 and F.6.2 of the Guidance on Implementing IAS 39, which allow, for a cash flow hedge, the 'bottom' portion of reinvestments of collections from assets to be designated as the hedged item.[16]

(b)　The entity is hedging interest rate risk rather than prepayment risk. Any changes to the portfolio because of changes in prepayments do not affect how effective the hedge was in mitigating interest rate risk.

16　IFRS 9 *Financial Instruments* deleted the guidance on implementing IAS 39.

(c) The approach captures all ineffectiveness on the hedged portion. It merely allows the hedged portion to be defined in such a way that, at least in a bottom layer approach, the first of any potential ineffectiveness relates to the unhedged portion.

(d) It is correct that no ineffectiveness arises if changes in prepayment estimates cause more assets to be scheduled into that repricing time period. So long as assets equal to the hedged layer remain, there is no ineffectiveness and upward revisions of the amount in a repricing time period do not affect the hedged layer.

(e) A prepayable item can be viewed as a combination of a non-prepayable item and a prepayment option. The designation of a bottom layer can be viewed as hedging a part of the life of the non-prepayable item, but none of the prepayment option. For example, a 25-year prepayable mortgage can be viewed as a combination of (i) a non-prepayable, fixed term, 25-year mortgage and (ii) a written prepayment option that allows the borrower to repay the mortgage early. If the entity hedges this asset with a 5-year derivative, this is equivalent to hedging the first five years of component (i). If the position is viewed in this way, no ineffectiveness arises when interest rate changes cause the value of the prepayment option to change (unless the option is exercised and the asset prepaid) because the prepayment option was not hedged.

BC201 The arguments against the layer approach are as follows:

(a) The considerations that apply to a fair value hedge are different from those that apply to a cash flow hedge. In a cash flow hedge, it is the cash flows associated with the reinvestment of probable future collections that are hedged. In a fair value hedge it is the fair value of the assets that currently exist.

(b) The fact that no ineffectiveness is recognised if the amount in a repricing time period is re-estimated upwards (with the effect that the entity becomes underhedged) is not in accordance with IAS 39. For a fair value hedge, IAS 39 requires that ineffectiveness is recognised both when the entity becomes overhedged (ie the derivative exceeds the hedged item) and when it becomes underhedged (ie the derivative is smaller than the hedged item).

(c) As noted in paragraph BC200(e), a prepayable item can be viewed as a combination of a non-prepayable item and a prepayment option. When interest rates change, the fair value of both of these components changes.

(d) The objective of applying fair value hedge accounting to a hedged item designated in terms of an amount (rather than as individual assets or liabilities) is to obtain results that closely approximate those that would have been obtained if individual assets or liabilities had been designated as the hedged item. If individual prepayable assets had been designated as the hedged item, the change in both the components noted in (c) above (to the extent they are attributable to the hedged risk) would be recognised in profit or loss, both when interest rates increase and when they decrease. Accordingly, the change in the fair value of the hedged asset would differ from the change in the fair value of the hedging derivative (unless that derivative includes an equivalent prepayment option) and ineffectiveness would be recognised for the difference. It follows that in the simplified approach of designating the hedged item as an amount, ineffectiveness should similarly arise.

(e) *All* prepayable assets in a repricing time period, and not just a layer of them, contain a prepayment option whose fair value changes with changes in interest rates. Accordingly, when interest rates change, the fair value of the hedged assets (which include a prepayment option whose fair value has changed) will change by an amount different from that of the hedging derivative (which typically does not contain a prepayment option), and ineffectiveness will arise. This effect occurs regardless of whether interest rates increase or decrease—ie regardless of whether re-estimates of prepayments result in the amount in a time period being more or less.

(f) Interest rate risk and prepayment risk are so closely interrelated that it is not appropriate to separate the two components referred to in paragraph BC200(e) and designate only one of them (or a part of one of them) as the hedged item. Often the biggest single cause of changes in prepayment rates is changes in interest rates. This close relationship is the reason why IAS 39 prohibits a held-to-maturity asset[17] from being a hedged item with respect to either interest rate risk or prepayment risk. Furthermore, most entities do not separate the two components for risk management purposes. Rather, they incorporate the prepayment option by scheduling amounts based on expected maturities. When entities choose to use risk management practices—based on not separating prepayment and interest rate risk—as the basis for designation for hedge accounting purposes, it is not appropriate to separate the two components referred to in paragraph BC200(e) and designate only one of them (or a part of one of them) as the hedged item.

(g) If interest rates change, the effect on the fair value of a portfolio of prepayable items will be different from the effect on the fair value of a portfolio of otherwise identical but non-prepayable items. However, using a layer approach, this difference would not be recognised—if both portfolios were hedged to the same extent, both would be recognised in the balance sheet at the same amount.

BC202 The Board was persuaded by the arguments in paragraph BC201 and rejected layer approaches. In particular, the Board concluded that the hedged item should be designated in such a way that if the entity changes its estimates of the repricing time periods in which items are expected to repay or mature (eg in the light of recent prepayment experience), ineffectiveness arises. It also concluded that ineffectiveness should arise both when estimated prepayments decrease, resulting in more assets in a particular repricing time period, and when they increase, resulting in fewer.

---

17 IFRS 9 eliminated the category of held-to-maturity.

Arguments for a third approach—measuring directly the change in fair value of the entire hedged item

BC203   The Board also considered comments on the Exposure Draft that:

(a)   some entities hedge prepayment risk and interest rate risk separately, by hedging to the expected prepayment date using interest rate swaps, and hedging possible variations in these expected prepayment dates using swaptions.

(b)   the embedded derivatives provisions of IAS 39 require some prepayable assets to be separated into a prepayment option and a non-prepayable host contract (unless the entity is unable to measure separately the prepayment option, in which case it treats the entire asset as held for trading). This seems to conflict with the view in the Exposure Draft that the two risks are too difficult to separate for the purposes of a portfolio hedge.[18]

BC204   In considering these arguments, the Board noted that the percentage approach described in paragraph AG126(b) is a proxy for measuring the change in the fair value of the *entire* asset (or liability)—including any embedded prepayment option—that is attributable to changes in interest rates. The Board had developed this proxy in the Exposure Draft because it had been informed that most entities (a) do not separate interest rate risk and prepayment risk for risk management purposes and hence (b) were unable to value the change in the value of the entire asset (including any embedded prepayment option) that is attributable to changes in the hedged interest rates. However, the comments described in paragraph BC203 indicated that in some cases, entities may be able to measure this change in value directly. The Board noted that such a direct method of measurement is conceptually preferable to the proxy described in paragraph AG126(b) and, accordingly, decided to recognise it explicitly. Thus, for example, if an entity that hedges prepayable assets using a combination of interest rate swaps and swaptions is able to measure directly the change in fair value of the entire asset, it could measure effectiveness by comparing the change in the value of the swaps and swaptions with the change in the fair value of the entire asset (including the change in the value of the prepayment option embedded in them) that is attributable to changes in the hedged interest rate. However, the Board also decided to permit the proxy proposed in the Exposure Draft for those entities that are unable to measure directly the change in the fair value of the entire asset.

Consideration of systems requirements

BC205   Finally, the Board was informed that, to be practicable in terms of systems needs, any approach should not require tracking of the amount in a repricing time period for multiple periods. Therefore it decided that ineffectiveness should be calculated by determining the change in the estimated amount in a repricing time period between one date on which effectiveness is measured and the next, as described more fully in paragraphs AG126 and AG127. This requires the entity to track how much of the change in each repricing time period

---

18   IFRS 9 replaced IAS 39.

between these two dates is attributable to revisions in estimates and how much is attributable to the origination of new assets (or liabilities). However, once ineffectiveness has been determined as set out above, the entity in essence starts again, ie it establishes the new amount in each repricing time period (including new items that have been originated since it last tested effectiveness), designates a new hedged item, and repeats the procedures to determine ineffectiveness at the next date it tests effectiveness. Thus the tracking is limited to movements between one date when effectiveness is measured and the next. It is not necessary to track for multiple periods. However, the entity will need to keep records relating to each repricing time period (a) to reconcile the amounts for each repricing time period with the total amounts in the two separate line items in the balance sheet (see paragraph AG114(f)), and (b) to ensure that amounts in the two separate line items are derecognised no later than when the repricing time period to which they relate expires.

BC206　　The Board also noted that the amount of tracking required by the percentage approach is no more than what would be required by any of the layer approaches. Thus, the Board concluded that none of the approaches was clearly preferable from the standpoint of systems needs.

The carrying amount of the hedged item

BC207　　The last issue noted in paragraph BC176 is how to present in the balance sheet the change in fair value of the hedged item. The Board noted the concern of respondents that the hedged item may contain many—even thousands of—individual assets (or liabilities) and that to change the carrying amounts of each of these individual items would be impracticable. The Board considered dealing with this concern by permitting the change in value to be presented in a single line item in the balance sheet. However, the Board noted that this could result in a decrease in the fair value of a financial asset (financial liability) being recognised as a financial liability (financial asset). Furthermore, for some repricing time periods the hedged item may be an asset, whereas for others it may be a liability. The Board concluded that it would be incorrect to present together the changes in fair value for such repricing time periods, because to do so would combine changes in the fair value of assets with changes in the fair value of liabilities.

BC208　　Accordingly, the Board decided that two line items should be presented, as follows:

(a)　　for those repricing time periods for which the hedged item is an asset, the change in its fair value is presented in a single separate line item within assets; and

(b)　　for those repricing time periods for which the hedged item is a liability, the change in its fair value is presented in a single separate line item within liabilities.

BC209　　The Board noted that these line items represent changes in the fair value of the hedged item. For this reason, the Board decided that they should be presented next to financial assets or financial liabilities.

Derecognition of amounts included in the separate line items

Derecognition of an asset (or liability) in the hedged portfolio

BC210   The Board discussed how and when amounts recognised in the separate balance sheet line items should be removed from the balance sheet. The Board noted that the objective is to remove such amounts from the balance sheet in the same periods as they would have been removed had individual assets or liabilities (rather than an amount) been designated as the hedged item.

BC211   The Board noted that this objective could be fully met only if the entity schedules individual assets or liabilities into repricing time periods and tracks both for how long the scheduled individual items have been hedged and how much of each item was hedged in each time period. In the absence of such scheduling and tracking, some assumptions would need to be made about these matters and, hence, about how much should be removed from the separate balance sheet line items when an asset (or liability) in the hedged portfolio is derecognised. In addition, some safeguards would be needed to ensure that amounts included in the separate balance sheet line items are removed from the balance sheet over a reasonable period and do not remain in the balance sheet indefinitely. With these points in mind, the Board decided to require that:

(a)   whenever an asset (or liability) in the hedged portfolio is derecognised—whether through earlier than expected prepayment, sale or write-off from impairment—any amount included in the separate balance sheet line item relating to that derecognised asset (or liability) should be removed from the balance sheet and included in the gain or loss on derecognition.

(b)   if an entity cannot determine into which time period(s) a derecognised asset (or liability) was scheduled:

(i)   it should assume that higher than expected prepayments occur on assets scheduled into the first available time period; and

(ii)   it should allocate sales and impairments to assets scheduled into all time periods containing the derecognised item on a systematic and rational basis.

(c)   the entity should track how much of the total amount included in the separate line items relates to each repricing time period, and should remove the amount that relates to a particular time period from the balance sheet no later than when that time period expires.

Amortisation

BC212   The Board also noted that if the designated hedged amount for a repricing time period is reduced, IAS 39[19] requires that the separate balance sheet line item described in paragraph 89A relating to that reduction is amortised on the basis of a recalculated effective interest rate. The Board noted that for a portfolio hedge of interest rate risk, amortisation based on a recalculated effective interest rate could be complex to determine and could demand significant additional

---

19   see paragraph 92

systems requirements. Consequently, the Board decided that in the case of a portfolio hedge of interest rate risk (and only in such a hedge), the line item balance may be amortised using a straight-line method when a method based on a recalculated effective interest rate is not practicable.

The hedging instrument

BC213   The Board was asked by commentators to clarify whether the hedging instrument may be a portfolio of derivatives containing offsetting risk positions. Commentators noted that previous versions of IAS 39 were unclear on this point.

BC214   The issue arises because the assets and liabilities in each repricing time period change over time as prepayment expectations change, as items are derecognised and as new items are originated. Thus the net position, and the amount the entity wishes to designate as the hedged item, also changes over time. If the hedged item decreases, the hedging instrument needs to be reduced. However, entities do not normally reduce the hedging instrument by disposing of some of the derivatives contained in it. Instead, entities adjust the hedging instrument by entering into new derivatives with an offsetting risk profile.

BC215   The Board decided to permit the hedging instrument to be a portfolio of derivatives containing offsetting risk positions for both individual and portfolio hedges. It noted that all of the derivatives concerned are measured at fair value. It also noted that the two ways of adjusting the hedging instrument described in the previous paragraph can achieve substantially the same effect. Therefore the Board clarified paragraph 77 to this effect.

Hedge effectiveness for a portfolio hedge of interest rate risk

BC216   Some respondents to the Exposure Draft questioned whether IAS 39's effectiveness tests[20] should apply to a portfolio hedge of interest rate risk. The Board noted that its objective in amending IAS 39 for a portfolio hedge of interest rate risk is to permit fair value hedge accounting to be used more easily, whilst continuing to meet the principles of hedge accounting. One of these principles is that the hedge is highly effective. Thus, the Board concluded that the effectiveness requirements in IAS 39 apply equally to a portfolio hedge of interest rate risk.

BC217   Some respondents to the Exposure Draft sought guidance on how the effectiveness tests are to be applied to a portfolio hedge. In particular, they asked how the prospective effectiveness test is to be applied when an entity periodically 'rebalances' a hedge (ie adjusts the amount of the hedging instrument to reflect changes in the hedged item). The Board decided that if the entity's risk management strategy is to change the amount of the hedging instrument periodically to reflect changes in the hedged position, that strategy affects the determination of the term of the hedge. Thus, the entity needs to demonstrate that the hedge is expected to be highly effective only for the period until the amount of the hedging instrument is next adjusted. The Board noted that this decision does not conflict with the requirement in paragraph 75 that 'a hedging relationship may not be designated for only a portion of the time

---

20   see paragraph AG105

period during which a hedging instrument remains outstanding'. This is because the entire hedging instrument is designated (and not only some of its cash flows, for example, those to the time when the hedge is next adjusted). However, expected effectiveness is assessed by considering the change in the fair value of the entire hedging instrument only for the period until it is next adjusted.

BC218   A third issue raised in the comment letters was whether, for a portfolio hedge, the retrospective effectiveness test should be assessed for all time buckets in aggregate or individually for each time bucket. The Board decided that entities could use any method to assess retrospective effectiveness, but noted that the chosen method would form part of the documentation of the hedging relationship made at the inception of the hedge in accordance with paragraph 88(a) and hence could not be decided at the time the retrospective effectiveness test is performed.

Transition to fair value hedge accounting for portfolios of interest rate risk

BC219   In finalising the amendments to IAS 39, the Board considered whether to provide additional guidance for entities wishing to apply fair value hedge accounting to a portfolio hedge that had previously been accounted for using cash flow hedge accounting. The Board noted that such entities could apply paragraph 101(d) to revoke the designation of a cash flow hedge and re-designate a new fair value hedge using the same hedged item and hedging instrument, and decided to clarify this in the Application Guidance. Additionally, the Board concluded that clarification was not required for first-time adopters because IFRS 1 already contained sufficient guidance.

BC220   The Board also considered whether to permit retrospective designation of a portfolio hedge. The Board noted that this would conflict with the principle in paragraph 88(a) that 'at the inception of the hedge there is formal designation and documentation of the hedging relationship' and accordingly, decided not to permit retrospective designation.

Novation of derivatives and continuation of hedge accounting

BC220A   The IASB received an urgent request to clarify whether an entity is required to discontinue hedge accounting for hedging relationships in which a derivative has been designated as a hedging instrument in accordance with IAS 39 when that derivative is novated to a central counterparty (CCP) due to the introduction of a new law or regulation.[21]

BC220B   The IASB considered the derecognition requirements of IAS 39 to determine whether the novation in such a circumstance leads to the derecognition of an existing derivative that has been designated as a hedging instrument. The IASB

---

21 In this context, the term 'novation' indicates that the parties to a derivative agree that one or more clearing counterparties replace their original counterparty to become the new counterparty to each of the parties. For this purpose, a clearing counterparty is a central counterparty or an entity or entities, for example, a clearing member of a clearing organisation or a client of a clearing member of a clearing organisation, that are acting as counterparty in order to effect clearing by a central counterparty.

noted that a derivative should be derecognised only when it meets both the derecognition criteria for a financial asset and the derecognition criteria for a financial liability in circumstances in which the derivative involves two-way payments between parties (ie the payments are or could be from and to each of the parties).

BC220C   The IASB observed that paragraph 17(a) of IAS 39 requires that a financial asset is derecognised when the contractual rights to the cash flows from the financial asset expire. The IASB noted that through novation to a CCP, a party (Party A) to the original derivative has new contractual rights to cash flows from a (new) derivative with the CCP, and this new contract replaces the original contract with a counterparty (Party B). Thus the original derivative with Party B has expired and as a consequence the original derivative through which Party A has engaged with Party B shall meet the derecognition criteria for a financial asset.[22]

BC220D   The IASB also observed that paragraph AG57(b) of IAS 39 states that a financial liability is extinguished when the debtor is legally released from primary responsibility for the liability. The IASB noted that the novation to the CCP would release Party A from the responsibility to make payments to Party B and also would oblige Party A to make payments to the CCP. Consequently, the original derivative through which Party A has transacted with Party B also meets the derecognition criteria for a financial liability.[23]

BC220E   Consequently, the IASB concluded that the novation of a derivative to a CCP would be accounted for as the derecognition of the original derivative and the recognition of the (new) novated derivative.

BC220F   Taking into account the conclusion of the assessment on the derecognition requirements, the IASB considered paragraphs 91(a) and 101(a) of IAS 39, which require an entity to discontinue hedge accounting prospectively if the hedging instrument expires or is sold, terminated or exercised. The IASB noted that novation to a CCP would require the entity to discontinue hedge accounting because the derivative that was designated as a hedging instrument has been derecognised and consequently the hedging instrument in the existing hedging relationship no longer exists.

BC220G   The IASB, however, was concerned about the financial reporting effects that would arise from novations that result from new laws or regulations. The IASB noted that the requirement to discontinue hedge accounting meant that although an entity could designate the new derivative as the hedging instrument in a new hedging relationship, this could result in more hedge ineffectiveness, especially for cash flow hedges, compared to a continuing hedging relationship. This is because the derivative that would be newly designated as the hedging instrument would be on terms that would be different from a new derivative, ie it was unlikely to be 'at-market' (for example, a non-option derivative such as a swap or forward might have a significant fair value) at the time of the novation. The IASB also noted that there would be an increased risk that the hedging relationship would fail to fall within the 80–125 per cent hedge effectiveness range required by IAS 39.

---

22 IFRS 9 replaced IAS 39.
23 IFRS 9 replaced IAS 39.

BC220H   The IASB, taking note of these financial reporting effects, was convinced that accounting for the hedging relationship that existed before the novation as a continuing hedging relationship, in this specific situation, would provide more useful information to users of financial statements. The IASB also considered the feedback from outreach that involved the members of the International Forum of Accounting Standard Setters (IFASS) and securities regulators and noted that this issue is not limited to a specific jurisdiction because many jurisdictions have introduced, or are expected to mandate, laws or regulations that encourage or require the novation of derivatives to a CCP.

BC220I   The IASB noted that the widespread legislative changes across jurisdictions were prompted by a G20 commitment to improve transparency and regulatory oversight of over-the-counter (OTC) derivatives in an internationally consistent and non-discriminatory way. Specifically, the G20 agreed to improve OTC derivatives markets so that all standardised OTC derivatives contracts are cleared through a CCP.

BC220J   The IASB also considered the draft requirements of the forthcoming hedge accounting chapter of IFRS 9. The IASB noted that those draft requirements also would require hedge accounting to be discontinued if the novation to a CCP occurs.

BC220K   Consequently, the IASB decided to publish, in January 2013, the Exposure Draft *Novation of Derivatives and Continuation of Hedge Accounting* ('ED/2013/2'), which proposed amendments to IAS 39 and IFRS 9. In ED/2013/2, the IASB proposed to amend paragraphs 91(a) and 101(a) of IAS 39 to provide relief from discontinuing hedge accounting when the novation to a CCP is required by new laws or regulations and meets certain criteria. The IASB decided to set the comment period for those proposals to 30 days. The IASB noted that the reduced comment period was necessary because the amendments should be completed urgently because the new laws or regulations to effect CCP clearing of OTC derivatives would come into force within a short period; the contents of the proposed amendments were short; and there was likely to be a broad consensus on the topic.

BC220L   When developing ED/2013/2, the IASB tentatively decided that the terms of the novated derivative should be unchanged other than the change in counterparty, however, the IASB noted that, in practice, other changes may arise as a direct consequence of the novation. For example, in order to enter into a derivative with a CCP it may be necessary to make adjustments to the collateral arrangements. Such narrow changes that are a direct consequence of or are incidental to the novation were acknowledged in the proposed amendments. However, this would not include changes to, for example, the maturity of the derivatives, the payment dates, or the contractual cash flows or the basis of their calculation, except for charges that may arise as a consequence of transacting with a CCP.

BC220M   When developing ED/2013/2, the IASB also discussed whether to require an entity to disclose that it has been able to continue hedge accounting by applying the relief provided by these proposed amendments to IAS 39 and IFRS 9. The IASB tentatively decided that it was not appropriate to mandate specific disclosure in this situation because, from the perspective of a user of financial statements, the hedge accounting would be continuing.

BC220N   A total of 78 respondents commented on ED/2013/2. The vast majority of respondents agreed that the proposed amendments are necessary. However, a few respondents expressed disagreement with the proposal on the basis that they disagreed with the IASB's conclusion that hedge accounting would be required to be discontinued as a result of such novations. In expressing such disagreement some noted that IAS 39 expressly acknowledges that certain replacements or rollovers of hedging instruments are not expirations or terminations for the purposes of discontinuing hedge accounting. The IASB noted that this exception applies if '[a] replacement or rollover is part of the entity's documented hedging strategy' (IAS 39.91(a) and IAS 39.101(a)). The IASB questioned whether replacement of a contract as a result of unforeseen legislative changes (even if documented) fits the definition of a replacement that is part of a 'documented hedging strategy'.

BC220O   Even though the vast majority of respondents agreed with the proposal, a considerable majority of respondents disagreed with the scope of the proposed amendments. They believed that the proposed scope of 'novation required by laws or regulations' is too restrictive and that the scope therefore should be expanded by removing this criterion. In particular, they argued that voluntary novation to a CCP should be provided with the same relief as novation required by laws or regulations. A few respondents further requested that the scope should not be limited to novation to a central counterparty and that novation in other circumstances should also be considered.

BC220P   In considering respondents' comments, the IASB noted that voluntary novation to a CCP could be prevalent in some circumstances such as novation in anticipation of regulatory changes, novation due to operational ease, and novation induced but not actually mandated by laws or regulations as a result of the imposition of charges or penalties. The IASB also noted that many jurisdictions would not require the existing stock of outstanding historical derivatives to be moved to CCPs, although this was encouraged by the G20 commitment.

BC220Q   The IASB observed, however, that for hedge accounting to continue voluntary novation to a CCP should be associated with laws or regulations that are relevant to central clearing of derivatives. The IASB noted that while a novation need not be required by laws or regulations for hedge accounting to be allowed to continue, allowing all novations to CCPs to be accommodated was broader than the IASB had intended. In addition, the IASB agreed that hedge accounting should continue when novations are performed as a consequence of laws or regulations or the introduction of laws of regulations but noted that the mere possibility of laws or regulations being introduced was not a sufficient basis for the continuation of hedge accounting.

BC220R   Some respondents were concerned that restricting the relief to novation directly to a CCP was too narrow. In considering respondents' comments, the IASB noted that in some cases a CCP has a contractual relationship only with its 'clearing members', and therefore an entity must have a contractual relationship with a clearing member in order to transact with a CCP; a clearing member of a CCP provides a clearing service to its client who cannot access a CCP directly. The IASB also noted that some jurisdictions are introducing a so-called 'indirect clearing' arrangement in their laws or regulations to effect clearing with a CCP, by which a client of a clearing member of a CCP provides a (indirect) clearing service to its client in the same way as a clearing member of a CCP provides a clearing service to its client. In addition, the IASB observed that an intragroup novation also can occur in order to access a CCP; for example, if only particular group entities can transact directly with a CCP.

BC220S   On the basis of respondents' comments, the IASB decided to expand the scope of the amendments by providing relief for novations to entities other than a CCP if such novation is undertaken with the objective of effecting clearing with a CCP rather than limiting relief to situations in which novation is directly to a CCP. The IASB decided that in these circumstances the novation had occurred in order to effect clearing through a CCP, albeit indirectly. The IASB thus decided also to include such novations in the scope of the amendments because they are consistent with the objective of the proposed amendments—they enable hedge accounting to continue when novations occur as a consequence of laws or regulations or the introduction of laws or regulations that increase the use of CCPs. However, the IASB noted that when parties to a hedging instrument enter into novations with different counterparties (for example, with different clearing members), these amendments only apply if each of those parties ultimately effects clearing with the same central counterparty.

BC220T   Respondents raised a concern about the phrase 'if and only if' that was used in ED/2013/2 when describing that the relief is provided 'if and only if' the criteria are met. In considering respondents' comments, the IASB noted that ED/2013/2 was intended to address a narrow issue—novation to CCPs—and therefore changing the phrase 'if and only if' to 'if' would target the amendment on the fact patterns that the IASB sought to address. The IASB noted that this would have the effect of requiring an analysis of whether the general conditions for continuation of hedge accounting are satisfied in other cases (for example, as was raised by some respondents, in determining the effect of intragroup novations in consolidated financial statements).

BC220U   The IASB decided to make equivalent amendments to the forthcoming chapter on hedge accounting that will be incorporated into IFRS 9, as proposed in ED/2013/2; no respondents opposed this proposal.

BC220V   ED/2013/2 did not propose any additional disclosures. The vast majority of respondents agreed with this. The IASB confirmed that additional disclosures are not required. However, the IASB noted that an entity may consider disclosures in accordance with IFRS 7 *Financial Instruments: Disclosures*, which requires qualitative and quantitative disclosures about credit risk.

BC220W   The IASB also decided to retain in the final amendments the transition requirements proposed in ED/2013/2 so that the amendments should apply retrospectively and early application should be permitted. The IASB noted that even with retrospective application, if an entity had previously discontinued hedge accounting, as a result of a novation, that (pre-novation) hedge accounting relationship could not be reinstated because doing so would be inconsistent with the requirements for hedge accounting (ie hedge accounting cannot be applied retrospectively).

BC221– [Deleted]
BC222

Dissenting opinions

Dissent of John T Smith from the issue in March 2004 of *Fair Value Hedge Accounting for a Portfolio Hedge of Interest Rate Risk* (Amendments to IAS 39)

DO1   Mr Smith dissents from these Amendments to IAS 39 Financial Instruments: Recognition and Measurement—*Fair Value Hedge Accounting for a Portfolio Hedge of Interest Rate Risk*. He agrees with the objective of finding a macro hedging solution that would reduce systems demands without undermining the fundamental accounting principles related to derivative instruments and hedging activities. However, Mr Smith believes that some respondents' support for these Amendments and their willingness to accept IAS 39 is based more on the extent to which the Amendments reduce recognition of ineffectiveness, volatility of profit or loss, and volatility of equity than on whether the Amendments reduce systems demands without undermining the fundamental accounting principles.

DO2   Mr Smith believes some decisions made during the Board's deliberations result in an approach to hedge accounting for a portfolio hedge that does not capture what was originally intended, namely a result that is substantially equivalent to designating an individual asset or liability as the hedged item. He understands some respondents will not accept IAS 39 unless the Board provides still another alternative that will further reduce reported volatility. Mr Smith believes that the Amendments already go beyond their intended objective. In particular, he believes that features of these Amendments can be applied to smooth out ineffectiveness and achieve results substantially equivalent to the other methods of measuring ineffectiveness that the Board considered when developing the Exposure Draft. The Board rejected those methods because they did not require the immediate recognition of all ineffectiveness. He also believes those features could be used to manage earnings.

IASB documents published to accompany

IAS 40

Investment Property

The text of the unaccompanied standard, IAS 40, is contained in Part A of this edition. Its effective date when issued was 1 January 2005. The text of the Accompanying Guidance on IAS 40 is contained in Part B of this edition. This part presents the following documents:

IASB BASIS FOR CONCLUSIONS ON IAS 40 (AS REVISED IN 2003)

IASC BASIS FOR CONCLUSIONS ON IAS 40 (2000)

Basis for Conclusions on IAS 40 *Investment Property*

This Basis for Conclusions accompanies, but is not part of, IAS 40.

Introduction

BC1   This Basis for Conclusions summarises the International Accounting Standards Board's considerations in reaching its conclusions on revising IAS 40 *Investment Property* in 2003. Individual Board members gave greater weight to some factors than to others.

BC2   In July 2001 the Board announced that, as part of its initial agenda of technical projects, it would undertake a project to improve a number of Standards, including IAS 40. The project was undertaken in the light of queries and criticisms raised in relation to the Standards by securities regulators, professional accountants and other interested parties. The objectives of the Improvements project were to reduce or eliminate alternatives, redundancies and conflicts within Standards, to deal with some convergence issues and to make other improvements. In May 2002 the Board published its proposals in an Exposure Draft of *Improvements to International Accounting Standards*, with a comment deadline of 16 September 2002. The Board received over 160 comment letters on the Exposure Draft.

BC3   Because the Board's intention was not to reconsider the fundamental approach to the accounting for investment property established by IAS 40, this Basis for Conclusions does not discuss requirements in IAS 40 that the Board has not reconsidered. The IASC Basis for Conclusions on IAS 40 (2000) follows this Basis.

Scope

Property interests held under an operating lease

BC4   Paragraph 14 of IAS 17 *Leases* requires a lease of land with an indefinite economic life to be classified as an operating lease, unless title is expected to pass to the lessee by the end of the lease term. Without the provisions of IAS 40 as amended, this operating lease classification would prevent a lessee from classifying its interest in the leased asset as an investment property in accordance with IAS 40. As a result, the lessee could not remeasure its interest in the leased asset to fair value and recognise any change in fair value in profit or loss. However, in some countries, interests in property (including land) are commonly—or exclusively—held under long-term operating leases. The effect of some of these leases differs little from buying a property outright. As a result, some contended that such leases should be accounted for as finance leases or investment property, or as both.

BC5   The Board discussed possible solutions to this issue. In particular, it considered deleting paragraph 14 of IAS 17, so that a long-term lease of land would be classified as a finance lease (and hence could qualify as an investment property) when the conditions for finance lease classification in paragraphs 4–13 of IAS 17 are met. However, the Board noted that this would not resolve all cases encountered in practice. Some leasehold interests held for investment would remain classified as operating leases (eg leases with significant contingent rents), and hence could not be investment property in accordance with IAS 40.

BC6   In the light of this, the Board decided to state separately in paragraph 6 (rather than amend IAS 40's definition of investment property) that a lessee's interest in property that arises under an operating lease could qualify as investment property. The Board decided to limit this amendment to entities that use the fair value model in IAS 40, because the objective of the amendment is to permit use of the fair value model for similar property interests held under finance and operating leases. Put another way, a lessee that uses the cost model for a property would not be permitted to recognise operating leases as assets. The Board also decided to make the change optional, ie a lessee that has an interest in property under an operating lease is allowed, but not required, to classify that property interest as investment property (provided the rest of the definition of investment property is met). The Board confirmed that this classification alternative is available on a property-by-property basis.

BC7   When a lessee's interest in property held under an operating lease is accounted for as an investment property, the Board decided that the initial carrying amounts of that interest and the related liability are to be accounted for as if the lease were a finance lease. This decision places such leases in the same position as investment properties held under finance leases in accordance with the previous version of IAS 40.

BC8   In doing so, the Board acknowledged that this results in different measurement bases for the lease asset and the lease liability. This is also true for owned investment properties and debt that finances them. However, in accordance with IAS 39 *Financial Instruments: Recognition and Measurement*,[1] as revised in 2003, an entity can elect to measure such debt at fair value, but lease liabilities cannot be remeasured in accordance with IAS 17.

BC9   The Board considered changing the scope of IAS 39, but concluded that this would lead to a fundamental review of lease accounting, especially in relation to contingent rentals. The Board decided that this was beyond the limited revisions to IAS 40 to facilitate application of the fair value model to some operating leases classified as investment properties. The Board did, however, indicate that it wished to revisit this issue in a later project on lease accounting. The Board also noted that this was the view of the Board of the former IASC as expressed in its Basis for Conclusions, in paragraphs B25 and B26.[2]

BC10   Finally, the Board noted that the methodology described in paragraphs 40 and 50(d) of IAS 40, whereby a fair valuation of the property that takes all lease obligations into account is adjusted by adding back any liability that is

---

1   IFRS 9 *Financial Instruments* replaced IAS 39. IFRS 9 applies to all items that were previously within the scope of IAS 39. This paragraph refers to matters relevant when IAS 40 was issued.

2   These paragraphs in the IASC Basis are no longer relevant and have been deleted.

recognised for these obligations, would, in practice, enable entities to ensure that net assets in respect of the leased interest are not affected by the use of different measurement bases.[3]

BC10A   [This paragraph refers to amendments that are not yet effective, and is therefore not included in this edition.]

The choice between the cost model and the fair value model

BC11   The Board also discussed whether to remove the choice in IAS 40 of accounting for investment property using a fair value model or a cost model.

BC12   The Board noted that IASC had included a choice for two main reasons. The first was to give preparers and users time to gain experience with using a fair value model. The second was to allow time for countries with less-developed property markets and valuation professions to mature. The Board decided that more time is needed for these events to take place (IAS 40 became mandatory only for periods beginning on or after 1 January 2001). The Board also noted that requiring the fair value model would not converge with the treatment required by most of its liaison standard-setters. For these reasons, the Board decided not to eliminate the choice as part of the Improvements project, but rather to keep the matter under review with a view to reconsidering the option to use the cost model at a later date.

BC13   The Board did not reconsider IAS 40 in relation to the accounting by lessors. The definition of investment property requires that such a property is held by the owner or a lessee under a finance lease. As indicated above, the Board agreed to allow a lessee under an operating lease, in specified circumstances, also to be a 'holder'. However, a lessor that has provided a property to a lessee under a finance lease cannot be a 'holder'. Such a lessor has a lease receivable, not an investment property.

BC14   The Board did not change the requirements for a lessor that leases property under an operating lease that is classified and accounted for by the lessee as investment property. The Board acknowledged that this would mean that two parties could both account as if they 'hold' interests in the property. This could occur at various levels of lessees who become lessors in a manner consistent with the definition of an investment property and the election provided for operating leases. Lessees who use the property in the production or supply of goods or services or for administrative purposes would not be able to classify that property as an investment property.

Scope

Investment property under construction

BC15   In response to requests for guidance, the Board revisited the exclusion of investment property under construction from the scope of IAS 40. The Board

---

3   Subsequently, the Board concluded that the drafting of paragraph 50(d) was misleading because it implied that the fair value of an investment property asset held under a lease was equal to the net fair value plus the carrying amount of any recognised lease liability. Therefore, in Improvements to IFRSs issued in May 2008 the Board amended paragraph 50(d) to clarify the intended meaning.

noted that investment property being redeveloped remained in the scope of the Standard and that the exclusion of investment property under construction gave rise to a perceived inconsistency. In addition, the Board concluded that with increasing experience with the use of fair value measures since the Standard was issued, entities were more able to measure reliably the fair value of investment property under construction. Therefore, in the exposure draft of proposed *Improvements to International Financial Reporting Standards* published in 2007 the Board proposed amending the scope of the Standard to include investment property under construction.

BC16 Many respondents supported the Board's proposal. However, many expressed concern that including in IAS 40 investment property under construction might result in fewer entities measuring investment property at fair value. This was because the fair value model in the Standard requires an entity to establish whether fair value can be determined reliably when a property first becomes an investment property. If not, the property is accounted for using the cost model until it is disposed of. In some situations, the fair value of investment property under construction cannot be measured reliably but the fair value of the completed investment property can. In these cases, including in the Standard investment property under construction would have required the properties to be accounted for using the cost model even after construction had been completed.

BC17 Therefore, the Board concluded that, in addition to including investment property under construction within the scope of the Standard, it would also amend the Standard to allow investment property under construction to be measured at cost if fair value cannot be measured reliably until such time as the fair value becomes reliably measurable or construction is completed (whichever comes earlier).

Classification of property as investment property or owner-occupied property

Acquisition of investment property: interrelationship with IFRS 3

BC18 The IFRS Interpretations Committee (the 'Interpretations Committee') reported to the Board that practice differed in delineating the scope of IFRS 3 *Business Combinations* and IAS 40:

(a) some considered both Standards as mutually exclusive if investment property with associated insignificant ancillary services, as specified in paragraph 11 of IAS 40, is acquired. They view property, together with any associated insignificant ancillary services, as being a single 'unit of account' and they consider this unit of account to be one asset called 'investment property'.

(b) others did not view IFRS 3 and IAS 40 as being mutually exclusive if investment property with associated insignificant ancillary services, as specified in paragraph 11 of IAS 40, is acquired; nor did they view the definitions of a business as defined in Appendix A of IFRS 3 and investment property as defined in paragraph 5 of IAS 40 as being interrelated. They think that an entity that acquires investment property has to determine whether it meets both definitions.

BC19   The Board noted that paragraphs 7–14 of IAS 40 have been developed to differentiate investment property from owner-occupied property and to define the scope of IAS 40 to distinguish it from the scope of IAS 16 *Property, Plant and Equipment*. In addition, neither IFRS 3 nor IAS 40 contains a limitation in its scope that restricts its application when the other Standard applies, ie there is nothing within the scope of each Standard to suggest that they are mutually exclusive. The Board also noted that the wording of IAS 40 is not sufficiently clear about the interrelationship between the two Standards.

BC20   The Board agreed with the proponents of the view presented in paragraph BC18(b) that IFRS 3 and IAS 40 are not mutually exclusive. It amended IAS 40 to state explicitly that judgement is also needed to determine whether the transaction is the acquisition of an asset or a group of assets or is a business combination within the scope of IFRS 3. That judgement is not based on paragraphs 7–14 of IAS 40 but is instead based on the guidance in IFRS 3. Only the judgement needed to distinguish investment property from owner-occupied property is based on those paragraphs.

BC21   Consequently, the Board clarified the interrelationship between the two Standards by adding paragraph 14A and a heading before paragraph 6 to IAS 40.

Effective date and transition

BC22   *Annual Improvements Cycle 2011–2013* issued in December 2013 added headings before paragraph 6 and after paragraph 84 and added paragraphs 14A, 84A and 85D to clarify the interrelationship between IFRS 3 and IAS 40. It considered the provisions for transition and the effective date of the amendment to IAS 40. The Board noted that applying IFRS 3 to transactions that have previously been accounted for as the acquisition of an asset or a group of assets might involve the use of hindsight when determining the fair values, at acquisition date, of the identifiable assets acquired and of the liabilities assumed as part of the business combination transaction. However, it also noted that the amendment is only a clarification of the interrelationship between IFRS 3 and IAS 40. Consequently, it decided that an entity would apply the amendments to IAS 40 prospectively for annual periods beginning on or after 1 July 2014, but an entity may choose to apply the amendment to individual transactions that occurred prior to the beginning of the first annual period occurring on or after the effective date only if the information needed is available to the entity.

Transfers of investment property

BC23   The Board received a question regarding the application of paragraph 57, which specifies requirements on transfers to, or from, investment property. The question asked whether an entity transfers property under construction or development previously classified as inventory to investment property when there is evidence of a change in use, even if that evidence is not specifically listed in paragraph 57(a)–(d).

BC24   Paragraph 57 requires transfers to, or from, investment property when, and only when, there is a change in use of property supported by evidence. The Board noted that the words 'when, and only when' in this paragraph are important to ensure that a transfer is limited to situations in which a change in use has occurred. The Board observed that the list of circumstances that provide evidence of a change in use specified in paragraph 57(a)–(d) of IAS 40 was drafted such that it was exhaustive (as shown by the references to 'when and only when' and 'evidenced by' in that paragraph).

BC25   The Board decided, however, to amend paragraph 57 so that it reflects the principle that a change in use would involve (a) an assessment of whether a property meets, or has ceased to meet, the definition of investment property; and (b) supporting evidence that a change in use has occurred. Applying this principle, an entity transfers property under construction or development to, or from, investment property when, and only when, there is a change in the use of such property, supported by evidence.

BC26   The Board also re-characterised the list of circumstances in paragraph 57(a)–(d) as a non-exhaustive list of examples to be consistent with the principle described in paragraph BC25.

BC27   Respondents to the Board's proposals asked whether management's intended use of a property would provide sufficient evidence of a change in use of a property under construction or development. The Board decided to confirm in paragraph 57 that, in isolation, a change in management's intentions would not be enough to support a transfer of property. This is because management's intentions, alone, do not provide evidence of a change in use—an entity must have taken observable actions to support such a change.

BC28   Some other respondents asked the Board to explain what provides substantive evidence of a change in use. The Board decided that such explanation is not needed. An entity assesses the specific facts and circumstances when applying paragraph 57, and paragraph 14 notes that judgement is needed to determine whether a property qualifies as investment property.

BC29   Respondents agreed with the Board's decision to re-characterise the list of circumstances in paragraph 57(a)–(d). However, some respondents were concerned that this list appeared to apply only to completed properties and, thus, they suggested that the Board add examples for a change in use of properties under construction or development. In response, the Board decided to amend paragraph 57(a) (ie to include 'commencement of development with a view to owner-occupation') and paragraph 57(d) (ie to refer to 'inception' of an operating lease, because at this point the construction of the related property might not be complete).

Transition

BC30   The Board proposed that an entity apply the amendments retrospectively. However, some respondents disagreed. They said that retrospective application might be impossible for some entities without the use of hindsight, or could be complex and burdensome in some situations—for example, in determining the exact point at which there was evidence of a change in use in prior periods, or in obtaining fair values at transfer dates in the past. Those respondents suggested either prospective application or, alternatively, retrospective application with some practical expedients.

BC31   In considering the comments, the Board observed the following:

(a)   the amounts recognised on the date of initial application would be unaffected by the transition approach for some previous changes in use, for example, transfers between investment property and owner-occupied property for entities that use the cost model.

(b)   applying the amendments retrospectively could be complex or may require the use of hindsight for some previous changes in use, for example, transfers from investment property measured using the fair value model to owner-occupied property that occurred some considerable time ago.

(c)   a prospective approach would require entities to apply the amendments only to changes in use that occur on or after the date of initial application. Such an approach might prevent an entity from reclassifying some property to reflect the conditions that exist on the date of initial application.

BC32   To address the concerns raised, the Board developed the transition method in paragraph 84C to ease the burden of applying the amendments retrospectively and to ensure that, on transition, an entity classifies property consistently with the amended Standard. If an entity uses this transition method, the Board decided to require specific disclosure of any reclassification of property at the date of initial application as part of the reconciliation of the carrying amount of investment property that is already required to be provided. This disclosure informs users of financial statements about changes to the carrying amount of investment property at the date of transition that do not reflect an underlying change in use of the property at that date.

BC33   The Board also noted that, depending on the properties held and previous changes in use that occurred, an entity may be able to apply the amendments retrospectively without the use of hindsight. If that is the case, the Board decided that the entity should not be prevented from doing so.

Contents

Basis for Conclusions on
IAS 40 (2000) *Investment Property*

This Basis for Conclusions accompanies, but is not part of, IAS 40. It was issued by the Board of the former International Accounting Standards Committee (IASC) in 2000. Apart from the deletion of paragraphs B10–B20, B25 and B26, this Basis has not been revised by the IASB—those paragraphs are no longer relevant and have been deleted to avoid the risk that they might be read out of context. However, cross-references to paragraphs in IAS 40 as issued in 2000 have been marked to show the corresponding paragraphs in IAS 40 as revised by the IASB in 2003 (superseded references are struck through and new references are underlined). Paragraphs are treated as corresponding if they broadly address the same matter even though the guidance may differ. In addition, the text has been annotated where references to material in other standards are no longer valid, following the revision of those standards. Reference should be made to the IASB's Basis for Conclusions on the amendments made in 2003.

Background

B1   The IASC Board (the "Board") approved IAS 25 *Accounting for Investments* in 1986. In 1994, the Board approved a reformatted version of IAS 25 presented in the revised format adopted for International Accounting Standards from 1991. Certain terminology was also changed at that time to bring it into line with then current IASC practice. No substantive changes were made to the original approved text.

B2   IAS 25 was one of the standards that the Board identified for possible revision in E32 *Comparability of Financial Statements*. Following comments on the proposals in E32, the Board decided to defer consideration of IAS 25, pending further work on Financial Instruments. In 1998, the Board approved IAS 38 *Intangible Assets* and IAS 39 *Financial Instruments: Recognition and Measurement*,[4] leaving IAS 25 to cover investments in real estate, commodities and tangible assets such as vintage cars and other collectors' items.

B3   In July 1999, the Board approved E64 *Investment Property*, with a comment deadline of 31 October 1999. The Board received 121 comment letters on E64. Comment letters came from various international organisations, as well as from 28 individual countries. The Board approved IAS 40 *Investment Property* in March 2000. Paragraph B67 below summarises the changes that the Board made to E64 in finalising IAS 40.

B4   IAS 40 permits entities to choose between a fair value model and a cost model. As explained in paragraphs B47–B48 below, the Board believes that it is impracticable, at this stage, to require a fair value model for all investment property. At the same time, the Board believes that it is desirable to permit a fair value model. This evolutionary step forward will allow preparers and users to gain greater experience working with a fair value model and will allow time for certain property markets to achieve greater maturity.

---

4   IFRS 9 *Financial Instruments* replaced IAS 39. IFRS 9 applies to all items that were previously within the scope of IAS 39. This paragraph refers to matters relevant when IAS 40 was issued.

Need for a Separate Standard

B5   Some commentators argued that investment property should fall within the scope of IAS 16 *Property, Plant and Equipment*, and that there is no reason to have a separate standard on investment property. They believe that:

(a)   it is not possible to distinguish investment property rigorously from owner-occupied property covered by IAS 16 and without reference to management intent. Thus, a distinction between investment property and owner-occupied property will lead to a free choice of different accounting treatments in some cases; and

(b)   the fair value accounting model proposed in E64 is not appropriate, on the grounds that fair value is not relevant and, in some cases, not reliable in the case of investment property. The accounting treatments in IAS 16 are appropriate not only for owner-occupied property, but also for investment property.

B6   Having reviewed the comment letters, the Board still believes that the characteristics of investment property differ sufficiently from the characteristics of owner-occupied property that there is a need for a separate Standard on investment property. In particular, the Board believes that information about the fair value of investment property, and about changes in its fair value, is highly relevant to users of financial statements. The Board believes that it is important to permit a fair value model for investment property, so that entities can report fair value information prominently. The Board tried to maintain consistency with IAS 16, except for differences dictated by the choice of a different accounting model.

Scope

Investment Property Entities

B7   Some commentators argued that the Standard should cover only investment property held by entities that specialise in owning such property (and, perhaps, also other investments) and not cover investment property held by other entities. The Board rejected this view because the Board could find no conceptual and practical way to distinguish rigorously any class of entities for which the fair value model would be less or more appropriate.

Investment Property Reportable Segments

B8   Some commentators suggested that the Board should limit the scope of the Standard to entities that have a reportable segment whose main activity is investment property. These commentators argued that an approach linked to reportable segments would require an entity to adopt the fair value model when the entity considers investment property activities to be an important element of its financial performance and would allow an entity to adopt IAS 16 in other cases.

B9   An approach linked to reportable segments would lead to lack of comparability between investment property held in investment property segments and investment property held in other segments. For this reason, the Board rejected such an approach.

B10–
B20   [Deleted]

Property Occupied by Another Entity in the Same Group

B21   In some cases, an entity owns property that is leased to, and occupied by, another entity in the same group. The property does not qualify as investment property in consolidated financial statements that include both entities, because the property is owner-occupied from the perspective of the group as a whole. However, from the perspective of the individual entity that owns it, the property is investment property if it meets the definition set out in the Standard.

B22   Some commentators believe that the definition of investment property should exclude properties that are occupied by another entity in the same group. Alternatively, they suggest that the Standard should not require investment property accounting in individual financial statements for properties that do not qualify as investment property in consolidated financial statements. They believe that:

(a)   it could be argued (at least in some such cases) that the property does not meet the definition of investment property from the perspective of a subsidiary whose property is occupied by another entity in the same group—the subsidiary's motive for holding the property is to comply with a directive from its parent and not necessarily to earn rentals or to benefit from capital appreciation. Indeed, the intragroup lease may not be priced on an arm's length basis;

(b)   this requirement would lead to additional valuation costs that would not be justified by the limited benefits to users. For groups with subsidiaries that are required to prepare individual financial statements, the cost could be extensive as entities may create a separate subsidiary to hold each property;

(c)   some users may be confused if the same property is classified as investment property in the individual financial statements of a subsidiary and as owner-occupied property in the consolidated financial statements of the parent; and

(d)   there is a precedent for a similar exemption (relating to disclosure, rather than measurement) in paragraph 4(c) of IAS 24 *Related Party Disclosures*, which does not require disclosures in a wholly-owned subsidiary's financial statements if its parent is incorporated in the same country and provides consolidated financial statements in that country.[5]

B23   Some commentators believe that the definition of investment property should exclude property occupied by any related party. They argue that related parties often do not pay rent on an arm's length basis, that it is often difficult to establish whether the rent is consistent with pricing on an arm's length basis and that rental rates may be subject to arbitrary change. They suggest that fair values are less relevant where property is subject to leases that are not priced on an arm's length basis.

---

5   IAS 24 *Related Party Disclosures* as revised by the IASB in 2003 no longer provides the exemption mentioned in paragraph B22(d).

B24 The Board could find no justification for treating property leased to another entity in the same group (or to another related party) differently from property leased to other parties. Therefore, the Board decided that an entity should use the same accounting treatment, regardless of the identity of the lessee.

B25–
B26 [Deleted]

Government Grants

B27 IAS 20 *Accounting for Government Grants and Disclosure of Government Assistance* permits two methods of presenting grants relating to assets—either setting up a grant as deferred income and amortising the income over the useful life of the asset or deducting the grant in arriving at the carrying amount of the asset. Some believe that both of those methods reflect a historical cost model and are inconsistent with the fair value model set out in this Standard. Indeed, Exposure Draft E65 *Agriculture*, which proposes a fair value model for biological assets, addresses certain aspects of government grants, as these are a significant factor in accounting for agriculture in some countries.

B28 Some commentators urged IASC to change the accounting treatment of government grants related to investment property. However, most commentators agreed that IASC should not deal with this aspect of government grants now. The Board decided not to revise this aspect of IAS 20 in the project on Investment Property.

B29 Some commentators suggested that IASC should begin a wider review of IAS 20 as a matter of urgency. In early 2000, the G4+1 group of standard setters published a Discussion Paper *Accounting by Recipients for Non-Reciprocal Transfers, Excluding Contributions by Owners: Their Definition, Recognition and Measurement*. The Board's work plan does not currently include a project on the accounting for government grants or other forms of non-reciprocal transfer.

Definition of Investment Property

B30 The definition of investment property excludes:

(a) owner-occupied property—covered by IAS 16 *Property, Plant and Equipment*. Under IAS 16, such property is carried at either depreciated cost or revalued amount less subsequent depreciation. In addition, such property is subject to an impairment test; and

(b) property held for sale in the ordinary course of business—covered by IAS 2 *Inventories*. IAS 2 requires an entity to carry such property at the lower of cost and net realisable value.

B31 These exclusions are consistent with the existing definitions of property, plant and equipment in IAS 16 and inventories in IAS 2. This ensures that all property is covered by one, and only one, of the three Standards.

B32 Some commentators suggested that property held for sale in the ordinary course of business should be treated as investment property rather than as inventories (covered by IAS 2). They argued that:

(a) it is difficult to distinguish property held for sale in the ordinary course of business from property held for capital appreciation; and

      (b)   it is illogical to require a fair value model for land and buildings held for long-term capital appreciation (investment property) when a cost model is still used for land and buildings held for short-term sale in the ordinary course of business (inventories).

B33   The Board rejected this suggestion because:

      (a)   if fair value accounting is used for property held for sale in the ordinary course of business, this would raise wider questions about inventory accounting that go beyond the scope of this project; and

      (b)   it is arguably more important to use fair value accounting for property that may have been acquired over a long period and held for several years (investment property) than for property that was acquired over a shorter period and held for a relatively short time (inventories). With the passage of time, cost-based measurements become increasingly irrelevant. Also, an aggregation of costs incurred over a long period is of questionable relevance.

B34   Some commentators suggested requiring (or at least permitting) entities, particularly financial institutions such as insurance companies, to use the fair value model for their owner-occupied property. They argued that some financial institutions regard their owner-occupied property as an integral part of their investment portfolio and treat it for management purposes in the same way as property leased to others. In the case of insurance companies, the property may be held to back policyholder liabilities. The Board believes that property used for similar purposes should be subject to the same accounting treatment. Accordingly, the Board concluded that no class of entities should use the fair value model for their owner-occupied property.

B35   Some commentators suggested that the definition of investment property should exclude property held for rentals, but not for capital appreciation. In their view, a fair value model may be appropriate for dealing activities, but is inappropriate where an entity has historically held rental property for many years and has no intention of selling it in the foreseeable future. They consider that holding property for long-term rental is a service activity and the assets used in that activity should be treated in the same way as assets used to support other service activities. In their view, holding an investment in property in such cases is similar to holding "held-to-maturity investments", which are measured at amortised cost under IAS 39.[6]

B36   In the Board's view, the fair value model provides useful information about property held for rental, even if there is no immediate intention to sell the property. The economic performance of a property can be regarded as being made up of both rental income earned during the period (net of expenses) and changes in the value of future net rental income. The fair value of an investment property can be regarded as a market-based representation of the value of the future net rental income, regardless of whether the entity is likely to sell the property in the near future. Also, the Standard notes that fair value is

---

6   IFRS 9 *Financial Instruments* eliminated the held-to-maturity category. This paragraph discusses matters relevant when IAS 40 was issued.

                     © IFRS Foundation

determined without deducting costs of disposal—in other words, the use of the fair value model is not intended as a representation that a sale could, or should, be made in the near future.[7]

B37   The classification of hotels and similar property was controversial throughout the project and commentators on E64 had mixed views on this subject. Some see hotels essentially as investments, while others see them essentially as operating properties. Some requested a detailed rule to specify whether hotels (and, perhaps, other categories of property, such as restaurants, bars and nursing homes) should be classified as investment property or as owner-occupied property.

B38   The Board concluded that it is preferable to distinguish investment property from owner-occupied property on the basis of general principles, rather than have arbitrary rules for specific classes of property. Also, it would inevitably be difficult to establish rigorous definitions of specific classes of property to be covered by such rules. Paragraphs 9–11 11–13 of the Standard discuss cases such as hotels in the context of the general principles that apply when an entity provides ancillary services.

B39   Some commentators requested quantitative guidance (such as a percentage) to clarify whether an "insignificant portion" is owner-occupied (paragraph 8 10) and whether ancillary services are "significant" (paragraphs 9–11 11–13 of the Standard). As for similar cases in other Standards, the Board concluded that quantitative guidance would create arbitrary distinctions.

Subsequent Expenditure

B40   Some believe that there is no need to capitalise subsequent expenditure in a fair value model and that all subsequent expenditure should be recognised as an expense. However, others believe—and the Board agreed—that the failure to capitalise subsequent expenditure would lead to a distortion of the reported components of financial performance. Therefore, the Standard requires that an entity should determine whether subsequent expenditure should be capitalised using a test similar to the test used for owner-occupied property in IAS 16.

B41   Some commentators suggested that the test for capitalising subsequent expenditure should not refer to the originally assessed standard of performance. They felt that it is impractical and irrelevant to judge against the originally assessed standard of performance, which may relate to many years in the past. Instead, they suggested that subsequent expenditure should be capitalised if it enhances the previously assessed standard of performance—for example, if it increases the current market value of the property or is intended to maintain its competitiveness in the market. The Board saw some merit in this suggestion.

B42   Nevertheless, the Board believes that a reference to the previously assessed standard of performance would require substantial additional guidance, might not change the way the Standard is applied in practice and might cause

---

7   IFRS 13 *Fair Value Measurement*, issued in May 2011, defines fair value and contains the requirements for measuring fair value.

confusion. The Board also concluded that it was important to retain the existing reference to the originally assessed standard of performance[8] to be consistent with IAS 16 and IAS 38.

Subsequent Measurement

Accounting Model

B43 Under IAS 25, an entity was permitted to choose from among a variety of accounting treatments for investment property (depreciated cost under the benchmark treatment in IAS 16 *Property, Plant and Equipment*, revaluation with depreciation under the allowed alternative treatment in IAS 16, cost less impairment under IAS 25 or revaluation under IAS 25).[9]

B44 E64 proposed that all investment property should be measured at fair value. Supporters of the fair value model believe that fair values give users of financial statements more useful information than other measures, such as depreciated cost. In their view, rental income and changes in fair value are inextricably linked as integral components of the financial performance of an investment property and measurement at fair value is necessary if that financial performance is to be reported in a meaningful way.

B45 Supporters of the fair value model also note that an investment property generates cash flows largely independently of the other assets held by an entity. In their view, the generation of independent cash flows through rental or capital appreciation distinguishes investment property from owner-occupied property. The production or supply of goods or services (or the use of property for administrative purposes) generates cash flows that are attributable not merely to property, but also to other assets used in the production or supply process. Proponents of the fair value model for investment property argue that this distinction makes a fair value model more appropriate for investment property than for owner-occupied property.

B46 Those who oppose measurement of investment property at fair value argue that:

(a) there is often no active market for investment property (unlike for many financial instruments). Real estate transactions are not frequent and not homogeneous. Each investment property is unique and each sale is subject to significant negotiations. As a result, fair value measurement will not enhance comparability because fair values are not determinable on a reliable basis, especially in countries where the valuation profession is less well established. A depreciated cost measurement provides a more consistent, less volatile, and less subjective measurement;

---

8   IAS 16 *Property, Plant and Equipment* as revised by the IASB in 2003 requires all subsequent costs to be covered by its general recognition principle and eliminated the requirement to reference the originally assessed standard of performance. IAS 40 was amended as a consequence of the change to IAS 16.

9   IAS 16 *Property, Plant and Equipment* as revised by the IASB in 2003 eliminated all references to 'benchmark' treatment and 'allowed alternative' treatments. They are replaced with cost model and revaluation model.

(b)   IAS 39[10] does not require fair value measurement for all financial assets, even some that are realised more easily than investment property. It would be premature to consider extending the fair value model until the Joint Working Group on financial instruments has completed its work;

(c)   a cost basis is used for "shorter term" assets (such as inventories) for which fair value is, arguably, more relevant than for "held for investment" assets; and

(d)   measurement at fair value is too costly in relation to the benefits to users.

B47   This is the first time that the Board has proposed requiring a fair value accounting model for non-financial assets. The comment letters on E64 showed that although many support this step, many others still have significant conceptual and practical reservations about extending a fair value model to non-financial assets, particularly (but not exclusively) for entities whose main activity is not to hold property for capital appreciation. Also, some entities feel that certain property markets are not yet sufficiently mature for a fair value model to work satisfactorily. Furthermore, some believe that it is impossible to create a rigorous definition of investment property and that this makes it impracticable to require a fair value model at present.

B48   For those reasons, the Board believes that it is impracticable, at this stage, to require a fair value model for investment property. At the same time, the Board believes that it is desirable to permit a fair value model. This evolutionary step forward will allow preparers and users to gain greater experience working with a fair value model and will allow time for certain property markets to achieve greater maturity.

B49   IAS 40 permits entities to choose between a fair value model and a cost model. An entity should apply the model chosen to all its investment property. [This choice is not available to a lessee accounting for an investment property under an operating lease as if it were a finance lease—refer to the IASB's Basis for Conclusions on the amendments made in 2003.] The fair value model is the model proposed in E64: investment property should be measured at fair value and changes in fair value should be recognised in the income statement. The cost model is the benchmark treatment[11] in IAS 16 *Property, Plant and Equipment*: investment property should be measured at depreciated cost (less any accumulated impairment losses). An entity that chooses the cost model should disclose the fair value of its investment property.

B50   Under IAS 8 *Net Profit or Loss for the Period, Fundamental Errors and Changes in Accounting Policies*,[12] a change in accounting policies from one model to the other model should be made only if the change will result in a more appropriate presentation of events or transactions.[13] The Board concluded that this is highly

---

10 IFRS 9 *Financial Instruments* replaced IAS 39. IFRS 9 applies to all items that were previously within the scope of IAS 39. This paragraph refers to matters relevant when IAS 40 was issued.

11 IAS 16 *Property, Plant and Equipment* as revised by the IASB in 2003 eliminated all references to 'benchmark' treatment and 'allowed alternative' treatments.

12 revised by the IASB in 2003 as IAS 8 *Accounting Policies, Changes in Accounting Estimates and Errors*

13 The IASB conformed the terminology used in paragraph 31 to the terminology used in IAS 8 by *Improvements to IFRSs* issued in May 2008.

unlikely to be the case for a change from the fair value model to the cost model and paragraph 25 31 of the Standard reflects this conclusion.

B51　　The Board believes that it is undesirable to permit three different accounting treatments for investment property. Accordingly, if an entity does not adopt the fair value model, the Standard requires the entity to use the benchmark treatment in IAS 16 and does not permit the use of the allowed alternative treatment. However, an entity may still use the allowed alternative for other properties covered by IAS 16.[14]

Guidance on Fair Value[15]

B52　　The valuation profession will have an important role in implementing the Standard. Accordingly, in developing its guidance on the fair value of investment property, the Board considered not only similar guidance in other IASC literature, but also International Valuation Standards (IVS) issued by the International Valuation Standards Committee (IVSC). The Board understands that IVSC intends to review, and perhaps revise, its Standards in the near future.

B53　　The Board believes that IASC's concept of fair value is similar to the IVSC concept of market value. IVSC defines market value as "the estimated amount for which an asset should exchange on the date of valuation between a willing buyer and a willing seller in an arm's length transaction after proper marketing wherein the parties had each acted knowledgeably, prudently and without compulsion". The Board believes that the guidance in paragraphs 29–30 36, 37 and 32–38 39–44 of the Standard is, in substance (and largely in wording as well), identical with guidance in IVS 1.[16]

B54　　Paragraphs 31 38 and 39–46 45–52 have no direct counterpart in the IVSC literature. The Board developed much of this material in response to commentators on E64, who asked for more detailed guidance on determining the fair value of investment property. In developing this material, the Board considered guidance on fair value in other IASC Standards and Exposure Drafts, particularly those on financial instruments (IAS 32 and IAS 39[17]), intangible assets (IAS 38) and agriculture (E65).[18]

Independent Valuation

B55　　Some commentators believe that fair values should be determined on the basis of an independent valuation, to enhance the reliability of the fair values reported. Others believe, on cost-benefit grounds, that IASC should not require (and perhaps not even encourage) an independent valuation. They believe that it is for preparers to decide, in consultation with auditors, whether an entity has

---

14　IAS 16 *Property, Plant and Equipment* as revised by the IASB in 2003 eliminated all references to 'benchmark' treatment and 'allowed alternative' treatments.

15　IFRS 13, issued in May 2011, contains the requirements for measuring fair value.

16　The requirements for measuring fair value in IFRS 13, issued in May 2011, differ in some respects from the guidance for measuring market value in accordance with IVS 1. IFRS 13 deleted paragraphs 36, 37 and 42–44 of IAS 40.

17　IFRS 9 *Financial Instruments* replaced IAS 39. IFRS 9 applies to all items that were previously within the scope of IAS 39. This paragraph refers to matters relevant when IAS 40 was issued.

18　IFRS 13, issued in May 2011, defines fair value and contains the requirements for measuring fair value. As a consequence paragraphs 38, 45–47, 49 and 51 of IAS 40 have been deleted.

sufficient internal resources to determine reliable fair values. Some also believe that independent valuers with appropriate expertise are not available in some markets.

B56   The Board concluded that an independent valuation is not always necessary. Therefore, as proposed in E64, the Standard encourages, but does not require, an entity to determine the fair value of all investment property on the basis of a valuation by an independent valuer who holds a recognised and relevant professional qualification and who has recent experience in the location and category of the investment property being valued. This approach is consistent with the approach to actuarial valuations in IAS 19 *Employee Benefits* (see IAS 19, paragraph 57).[19]

Inability to Measure Fair Value Reliably

B57   E64 included a rebuttable presumption that an entity will be able to determine reliably the fair value of property held to earn rentals or for capital appreciation. E64 also proposed a reliability exception: IAS 16 should be applied if evidence indicates clearly, when an entity acquires or constructs a property, that fair value will not be determinable reliably on a continuing basis.

B58   Some commentators opposed various aspects of this proposal, on one or more of the following grounds:

(a)   the rebuttable presumption underestimates the difficulties of determining fair value reliably. This will often be impossible, particularly where markets are thin or where there is not a well-established valuation profession;

(b)   the accounting model under IAS 16 includes an impairment test under IAS 36. However, it is illogical to rely on an impairment test when fair value cannot be determined using cash flow projections, because an impairment test under IAS 36 is also difficult in such cases;

(c)   where fair value cannot be determined reliably, this fact does not justify charging depreciation. Instead, the property in question should be measured at cost less impairment losses; and

(d)   to avoid the danger of manipulation, all efforts should be made to determine fair values, even in a relatively inactive market. Even without an active market, a range of projected cash flows is available. If there are problems in determining fair value, an entity should measure the property at the best estimate of fair value and disclose limitations on the reliability of the estimate. If it is completely impossible to determine fair value, fair value should be deemed to be zero.

B59   The Board concluded that the rebuttable presumption and the reliability exception should be retained, but decided to implement them in a different way. In E64, they were implemented by excluding a property from the definition of investment property if the rebuttable presumption was overcome. Some commentators felt that it was confusing to include such a reliability exception

---

19   Paragraph 57 was renumbered as paragraph 59 when IAS 19 was amended in 2011.

in a definition. Accordingly, the Board moved the reliability exception from the definition to the section on subsequent measurement (paragraphs 47–49 53–55).

B60 Under E64, an entity should not stop using the fair value model if comparable market transactions become less frequent or market prices become less readily available. Some commentators disagreed with this proposal. They argued that there may be cases when reliable estimates are no longer available and that it would be misleading to continue fair value accounting in such cases. The Board decided that it is important to keep the E64 approach, because otherwise entities might use a reliability exception as an excuse to discontinue fair value accounting in a falling market.[20]

B61 In cases where the reliability exception applies, E64 proposed that an entity should continue to apply IAS 16 until disposal of the property. Some commentators proposed that an entity should start applying the fair value model once the fair value becomes measurable reliably. The Board rejected this proposal because it would inevitably be a subjective decision to determine when fair value has become measurable reliably and this subjectivity could lead to inconsistent application.

B62 E64 proposed no specific disclosure where the reliability exception applies. Some commentators felt that disclosure would be important in such cases. The Board agreed and decided to include disclosures consistent with paragraph 170(b) of IAS 39[21] (see paragraphs 68 and 69(e) 78 and 79(e) of IAS 40). Paragraph 170(b) of IAS 39 requires disclosures for financial assets whose fair value cannot be reliably measured.

Gains and Losses on Remeasurement to Fair Value

B63 Some commentators argued that there should be either a requirement or an option to recognise changes in the fair value of investment property in equity, on the grounds that:

(a) the market for property is not liquid enough and market values are uncertain and variable. Investment property is not as liquid as financial instruments and IAS 39 allows an option for available-for-sale investments;[22]

(b) until performance reporting issues are resolved more generally, it is premature to require recognition of fair value changes in the income statement;

(c) recognition of unrealised gains and losses in the income statement increases volatility and does not enhance transparency, because revaluation changes will blur the assessment of an entity's operating performance. It may also cause a presumption that the unrealised gains are available for distribution as dividends;

---

20 IFRS 13, issued in May 2011, discusses the measurement of fair value when the volume or level of activity for an asset has significantly decreased.

21 In August 2005, the IASB relocated all disclosures relating to financial instruments to IFRS 7 *Financial Instruments: Disclosures*.

22 IFRS 9 *Financial Instruments* eliminated the category of available-for-sale financial assets.

(d) recognition in equity is more consistent with the historical cost and modified historical cost conventions that are a basis for much of today's accounting. For example, it is consistent with IASC's treatment of revaluations of property, plant and equipment under IAS 16 and with the option available for certain financial instruments under IAS 39;[23]

(e) for properties financed by debt, changes in the fair value of the properties resulting from interest rate changes should not be recognised in the income statement, since the corresponding changes in the fair value of the debt are not recognised under IAS 39;

(f) under paragraphs 92 and 93 of the *Framework*,[24] income should be recognised only when it can be measured with sufficient certainty. For example, IAS 11 *Construction Contracts*[25] requires certain conditions before an entity can use the percentage-of-completion method. These conditions are not normally met for investment property; and

(g) results from operations should be distinguished from changes in values. For example, under IAS 21, unrealised exchange differences on a foreign entity[26] are recognised in equity.

B64 Some commentators suggested that increases should be recognised in equity and decreases should be recognised in profit or loss. This is similar to the revaluation model that forms the allowed alternative treatment[27] in IAS 16 (except for the lack of depreciation).

B65 As proposed in E64, the Board concluded that, in a fair value model, changes in the fair value of investment property should be recognised in the income statement as part of profit or loss for the period. The arguments for this approach include the following:

(a) the conceptual case for the fair value model is built largely on the view that this provides the most relevant and transparent view of the financial performance of investment property. Given this, it would be inconsistent to permit or require recognition in equity;

(b) recognition of fair value changes in equity would create a mismatch because net rental income would be recognised in the income statement, whereas the related consumption of the service potential (recognised as depreciation under IAS 16) would be recognised in equity. Similarly, maintenance expenditure would be recognised as an expense while related increases in fair value would be recognised in equity;

---

23 IFRS 9 *Financial Instruments* replaced IAS 39. IFRS 9 applies to all items that were previously within the scope of IAS 39. This paragraph refers to matters relevant when IAS 40 was issued.

24 The reference to the *Framework* is to IASC's *Framework for the Preparation and Presentation of Financial Statements*, adopted by the IASB in 2001. In September 2010 the IASB replaced the *Framework* with the *Conceptual Framework for Financial Reporting*. Paragraphs 92 and 93 are now paragraphs 4.47 and 4.48 of the *Conceptual Framework*.

25 IFRS 15 *Revenue from Contracts with Customers*, issued in May 2014, replaced IAS 11 *Construction Contracts*.

26 In IAS 21 *The Effects of Changes in Foreign Exchange Rates*, as revised by the IASB in 2003, the term 'foreign entity' was replaced by 'foreign operation'.

27 IAS 16 *Property, Plant and Equipment* as revised by the IASB in 2003 eliminated all references to 'benchmark' treatment and 'allowed alternative' treatments.

(c) using this approach, there is no need to resolve some difficult and controversial issues that would arise if changes in the fair value of investment property were recognised in equity. These issues include the following:

 (i) should fair value changes previously recognised in equity be transferred ("recycled") to profit or loss on disposal of investment property; and

 (ii) should fair value changes previously recognised in equity be transferred ("recycled") to profit or loss when investment property is impaired? If so, how should such impairment be identified and measured; and

(d) given the difficulty in defining investment property rigorously, entities will sometimes have the option of applying the investment property standard or either of the two treatments in IAS 16. It would be undesirable to include two choices in the investment property standard, as this would give entities a choice (at least occasionally) between four different treatments.

Transfers

B66 When an owner-occupied property carried under the benchmark treatment under IAS 16 becomes an investment property, the measurement basis for the property changes from depreciated cost to fair value. The Board concluded that the effect of this change in measurement basis should be treated as a revaluation under IAS 16 at the date of change in use. The result is that:

(a) the income statement excludes cumulative net increases in fair value that arose before the property became investment property. The portion of this change that arose before the beginning of the current period does not represent financial performance of the current period; and

(b) this treatment creates comparability between entities that had previously revalued the property under the allowed alternative treatment in IAS 16 and those entities that had previously used the IAS 16 benchmark treatment.[28]

Summary of Changes to E64

B67 The most important change between E64 and the final Standard was the introduction of the cost model as an alternative to the fair value model. The other main changes are listed below.

(a) The guidance on determining fair value was expanded, to clarify the following:[29]

---

28 IAS 16 *Property, Plant and Equipment* as revised by the IASB in 2003 eliminated all references to 'benchmark' treatment and 'allowed alternative' treatments.

29 IFRS 13, issued in May 2011, contains the requirements for measuring fair value and for disclosing information about fair value measurements. As a consequence paragraphs 37, 38, 45–47, 49, 51 and 75(d) of IAS 40 have been deleted.

(i) the fair value of investment property is not reduced by transaction costs that may be incurred on sale or other disposal (paragraph 30 37 of the Standard). This is consistent with the measurement of financial assets under paragraph 69 of IAS 39.[30] E64 was silent on the treatment of such costs;

(ii) measurement is based on valuation at the balance sheet date (paragraph 31 38);

(iii) the best evidence of fair value is normally given by current prices on an active market for similar property in the same location and condition and subject to similar lease and other contracts (paragraph 39 45). In the absence of such evidence, fair value reflects information from a variety of sources and an entity needs to investigate reasons for any differences between the information from different sources (paragraphs 40–41 46 and 47);

(iv) market value differs from value in use as defined in IAS 36 *Impairment of Assets* (paragraph 43 49);

(v) there is a need to avoid double counting of investment property and separately recognised assets and liabilities. Integral equipment (such as elevators or air-conditioning) is generally included in the investment property, rather than recognised separately (paragraph 44 50);

(vi) the fair value of investment property does not reflect future capital expenditure that will improve or enhance the asset and does not reflect the related future benefits from this future expenditure (paragraph 45 51);

(vii) an entity uses IAS 37 to account for any provisions associated with investment property (paragraph 46 52); and

(viii) in the exceptional cases when fair value cannot be determined reliably, measurement is under the IAS 16 benchmark treatment[31] only (in such cases, revaluation under IAS 16 would also not be reliable) and residual value is assumed to be zero (given that fair value cannot be determined reliably) (paragraphs 47–48 53 and 54).

(b) In relation to the scope of the Standard and the definition of investment property:

(i) paragraph 3 4 now clarifies that the Standard does not apply to forests and similar regenerative natural resources and to mineral rights, the exploration for and extraction of minerals, oil, natural gas and similar non-regenerative resources. This wording is consistent with a similar scope exclusion in IAS 16 *Property, Plant and Equipment*. The Board did not wish to prejudge its decision on

---

30 Paragraph 69 was replaced by paragraph 46 when the Board revised IAS 39 in 2003. IFRS 9 *Financial Instruments* deleted paragraph 46 of IAS 39.

31 IAS 16 *Property, Plant and Equipment* as revised by the IASB in 2003 eliminated all references to 'benchmark' treatment and 'allowed alternative' treatments.

the treatment of such items in the current projects on Agriculture and the Extractive Industries;

(ii) land held for a currently undetermined future use is a further example of investment property (paragraph 6(b) 8(b)), on the grounds that a subsequent decision to use such land as inventory or for development as owner-occupied property would be an investment decision;

(iii) new examples of items that are not investment property are: property held for future use as owner-occupied property, property held for future development and subsequent use as owner-occupied property, property occupied by employees (whether or not the employees pay rent at market rates) and owner-occupied property awaiting disposal (paragraph 7(c) 9(c));

(iv) property that is being constructed or developed for future use as investment property is now covered by IAS 16 and measured at cost, less impairment losses, if any (paragraph 7(d) 9(d)). E64 proposed that investment property under construction should be measured at fair value; and

(v) the reference to reliable measurement of fair value (and the related requirements in paragraphs 14–15 of E64) was moved from the definition of investment property into the section on subsequent measurement (paragraphs 47–49 53–55).

(c) New paragraph 20 23 deals with start up costs, initial operating losses and abnormal wastage (based on paragraphs 17 and 18 of IAS 16[32]). The Board considered adding guidance on the treatment of incidental revenue earned during the construction of investment property. However, the Board concluded that this raised an issue in the context of IAS 16 and decided that it was beyond the scope of this project to deal with this.

(d) There is an explicit requirement on determining gains or losses on disposal (paragraph 62 69). This is consistent with IAS 16, paragraph 56.[33] There are also new cross-references to:

(i) IAS 17 Leases and IAS 18 Revenue,[34] as guidance for determining the date of disposal (paragraph 61 67); and

(ii) IAS 37 Provisions, Contingent Liabilities and Contingent Assets, for liabilities retained after disposal (paragraph 64 71).

(e) The Standard states explicitly that an entity should transfer an investment property to inventories when the entity begins to develop the property for subsequent sale in the ordinary course of business (paragraphs 51(b) and 52 57(b) and 58). E64 proposed that all transfers

---

32 In IAS 16 Property, Plant and Equipment as revised by the IASB in 2003, paragraphs 17 and 18 were replaced by paragraphs 19–22.

33 In IAS 16 Property, Plant and Equipment as revised by the IASB in 2003, paragraph 56 was replaced by paragraphs 68 and 71.

34 IFRS 15 Revenue from Contracts with Customers, issued in May 2014, replaced IAS 18 Revenue and amended paragraph 67 of IAS 40 for consistency with the requirements in IFRS 15.

from investment properties to inventories should be prohibited. The Standard also deals more explicitly than E64 with certain other aspects of transfers.

(f) New disclosure requirements include:[35]

(i) extension of the required disclosure on methods and significant assumptions, which are now to include disclosure of whether fair value was supported by market evidence, or whether the estimate is based on other data (which the entity should disclose) because of the nature of the property and the lack of comparable market data (paragraph ~~66(b)~~ 75(d));

(ii) disclosures of rental income and direct operating expenses (paragraph ~~66(d)~~ 75(f)); and

(iii) disclosures in the exceptional cases when fair value is not reliably determinable (paragraphs ~~68 and 69(e)~~ 78 and 79(e)).

(g) E64 proposed a requirement to disclose the carrying amount of unlet or vacant investment property. Some commentators argued that this disclosure was impracticable, particularly for property that is partly vacant. Some also felt that this is a matter for disclosure in a financial review by management, rather than in the financial statements. The Board deleted this disclosure requirement. It should be noted that some indication of vacancy levels may be available from the required disclosure of rental income and from the IAS 17 requirement to disclose cash flows from non-cancellable operating leases (split into less than one year, one to five years and more than five years).

(h) E64 included no specific transitional provisions, which means that IAS 8 would apply. There is a risk that restatement of prior periods might allow entities to manipulate their reported profit or loss for the period by selective use of hindsight in determining fair values in prior periods. Accordingly, the Board decided to prohibit restatement in the fair value model, except where an entity has already publicly disclosed fair values for prior periods (paragraph ~~70~~ 80).

---

35 IFRS 13, issued in May 2011, contains the requirements for measuring fair value and for disclosing information about fair value measurements. As a consequence paragraphs 37, 38, 45–47, 49, 51 and 75(d) of IAS 40 have been deleted.

IASB documents published to accompany

IAS 41

Agriculture

The text of the unaccompanied standard, IAS 41, is contained in Part A of this edition. Its effective date when issued was 1 January 2003. The text of the Accompanying Guidance on IAS 41 is contained in Part B of this edition. This part presents the following documents:

BASIS FOR CONCLUSIONS

BASIS FOR IASC'S CONCLUSIONS ON IAS 41

DISSENTING OPINIONS

Basis for Conclusions on IAS 41 *Agriculture*

This Basis for Conclusions accompanies, but is not part of, IAS 41.

Introduction

BC1   This Basis for Conclusions summarises the International Accounting Standards Board's considerations in reaching its conclusions on amending IAS 41 *Agriculture* by *Improvements to IFRSs* in May 2008 and by *Agriculture: Bearer Plants* (Amendments to IAS 16 and IAS 41)[1] in June 2014. Individual Board members gave greater weight to some factors than to others.

BC2   Because the Board's intention was not to reconsider the fundamental approach to the accounting for agriculture established by IAS 41, this Basis for Conclusions does not discuss requirements in IAS 41 that the Board has not reconsidered. The IASC Basis for Conclusions on IAS 41 follows this Basis.

Scope (2008 and 2014 amendments)

Costs to sell (paragraph 5) – 2008 amendments

BC3   Before the *Improvements to IFRSs* issued in May 2008, IAS 41 used the term 'point-of-sale costs'. This term was not used elsewhere in IFRSs. The term 'costs to sell' is used in IFRS 5 *Non-current Assets Held for Sale and Discontinued Operations* and IAS 36 *Impairment of Assets*. The Board decided that 'point-of-sale costs' and 'costs to sell' meant the same thing in the context of IAS 41. The word 'incremental' in the definition of 'costs to sell' excludes costs that are included in the fair value measurement of a biological asset, such as transport costs. It includes costs that are necessary for a sale to occur but that would not otherwise arise, such as commissions to brokers and dealers, levies by regulatory agencies and commodity exchanges, and transfer taxes and duties. Both terms relate to transaction costs arising at the point of sale.

BC4   Therefore, the Board decided to replace the terms 'point-of-sale costs' and 'estimated point-of-sale costs' with 'costs to sell' to make IAS 41 consistent with IFRS 5 and IAS 36.

Produce growing on bearer plants – 2014 amendments

BC4A   Before *Agriculture: Bearer Plants* (Amendments to IAS 16 and IAS 41) was issued in June 2014, IAS 41 required all biological assets related to agricultural activity to be measured at fair value less costs to sell. However, the Board observed that there is a class of biological assets, bearer plants, that are held by an entity solely to grow produce over their productive life. The Board's principal decision

---

1   *Agriculture: Bearer Plants* (Amendments to IAS 16 and IAS 41), issued in June 2014, introduced a definition of a bearer plant. The amendments require biological assets meeting the definition of a bearer plant to be accounted for as property, plant and equipment in accordance with IAS 16 *Property, Plant and Equipment* and as such the amendments are more comprehensively discussed in paragraphs BC38–BC117 of IAS 16. The produce growing on the bearer plants is within the scope of IAS 41. A summary of the specific changes to IAS 41 are discussed in paragraphs BC4A–BC4E of this Standard.

underlying the 2014 amendments is that bearer plants should be treated as property, plant and equipment. Accordingly, the Board decided to account for bearer plants as property, plant and equipment in accordance with the requirements in IAS 16 *Property, Plant and Equipment*.

BC4B Nevertheless the Board noted that the same argument is not true for the produce growing on the bearer plants that is undergoing biological transformation until it is harvested (for example, grapes growing on a grape vine). The Board observed that the produce is a consumable biological asset growing on the bearer plant and the growth of the produce directly increases the expected revenue from the sale of the produce. Consequently, fair value measurement of the growing produce provides useful information to users of financial statements about future cash flows that an entity is expected to realise. In contrast the bearer plants themselves are not sold and the changes in the fair value of the bearer plants do not directly influence the entity's future cash flows. The Board also observed that produce will ultimately be detached from the bearer plants and is normally sold separately, meaning it has a market value on its own. This is in contrast to many bearer plants that are unlikely to have an observable market value on their own because they can only be sold while attached to the land.

BC4C The Board acknowledged that measuring produce growing on bearer plants at fair value less costs to sell sometimes might be difficult to apply in practice. However, it was noted that similar difficulties are encountered when measuring the fair value less costs to sell of the produce growing in the ground. Consequently, the Board decided that it would be inconsistent to provide additional relief from fair value measurement for produce growing on a bearer plant and not also for other biological assets within the scope of IAS 41. The Board observed that if preparers encounter significant practical difficulties on initial measurement of produce, they should consider whether they meet the requirements of the exemptions in paragraphs 10(c) and 30 of IAS 41.

BC4D Consequently, the Board decided to reaffirm that produce is a biological asset within the scope of IAS 41 and should be measured at fair value less costs to sell with changes recognised in profit and loss as the produce grows. This would maintain consistency of accounting for produce growing in the ground and produce growing on a bearer plant. Consequently, the Board decided to keep the produce within the scope of IAS 41.

BC4E The Board noted that most of the areas for which respondents asked for additional guidance were specific to a particular type of bearer plant or produce. The Board decided that because of the specialised nature and diversity of bearer plants and produce it would be too difficult for the Board to develop additional guidance on measuring the fair value of produce.

Recognition and measurement – 2008 amendments

Discount rate (paragraph 20)

BC5 As part of the annual improvements project begun in 2007, the Board reconsidered whether it is appropriate to require a pre-tax discount rate in paragraph 20 when measuring fair value.[2] The Board noted that a fair value measurement should take into account the attributes, including tax attributes, that a market participant would consider when pricing an asset or liability.

BC6 The Board noted that a willing buyer would factor into the amount that it would be willing to pay the seller to acquire an asset (or would receive to assume a liability) all incremental cash flows that would benefit that buyer. Those incremental cash flows would be reduced by expected income tax payments using appropriate tax rates (ie the tax rate of a market participant buyer). Accordingly, fair value takes into account future income taxes that a market participant purchasing the asset (or assuming the liability) would be expected to pay (or to receive), without regard to an entity's specific tax situation.[3]

BC7 Therefore, the Board decided to keep the requirement to use a current market-based discount rate but in *Improvements to IFRSs* issued in May 2008 removed the reference to a pre-tax discount rate in paragraph 20.

Additional biological transformation (paragraph 21)

BC8 Sometimes the fair value of an asset in its current location and condition is estimated using discounted cash flows. Paragraph 21 could be read to exclude from such calculations increases in cash flows arising from 'additional biological transformation'. Diversity in practice had developed from different interpretations of this requirement. The Board decided that not including these cash flows resulted in a carrying amount that is not representative of the asset's fair value. The Board noted that an entity should consider the risks associated with cash flows from 'additional biological transformation' in determining the expected cash flows, the discount rate, or some combination of the two. Therefore, the Board decided to amend IAS 41 to remove the prohibition on an entity taking into account the cash flows resulting from 'additional biological transformation' when estimating the fair value of a biological asset.[4]

BC9 In its exposure draft of proposed *Improvements to International Financial Reporting Standards* published in 2007, the Board proposed changing the definition of biological transformation to include harvest. This was because the Board wished to make clear that harvest altered the condition of a biological asset. Some commentators objected to this change on the basis that harvest is a human activity rather than a biological transformation. The Board agreed with this argument and decided not to include the harvest in the definition of biological transformation. Instead, the Board amended the Standard to refer to biological transformation or harvest when applicable to make clear that harvest changes the condition of an asset.

---

2   IFRS 13 *Fair Value Measurement*, issued in May 2011, defines fair value and contains the requirements for measuring fair value.

3   IFRS 13, issued in May 2011, defines fair value and contains the requirements for measuring fair value.

4   IFRS 13, issued in May 2011, contains the requirements for measuring fair value. As a consequence, paragraph 21 of IAS 41 has been deleted.

BC10   Because applying the changes discussed in paragraphs BC8 and BC9 retrospectively might require some entities to remeasure the fair value of biological assets at a past date, the Board decided that these amendments should be applied prospectively.

CONTENTS

Basis for IASC's Conclusions on
IAS 41 *Agriculture*

This Basis for Conclusions accompanies, but is not part of, IAS 41. It was prepared by the IASC Staff in 2000 but was not approved by the IASC Board. It summarises the Board's reasons for:

(a)   initiating and proposing an International Accounting Standard on agriculture; and

(b)   accepting or rejecting certain alternative views.

Individual Board members gave greater weight to some factors than to others.

This Basis has not been revised by the IASB and the terminology has not been amended to reflect the changes made by Improvements to IFRSs *issued in May 2008.*

Background

B1   In 1994, the IASC Board (the 'Board') decided to develop an International Accounting Standard on agriculture and appointed a Steering Committee to help define the issues and develop possible solutions. In 1996, the Steering Committee published a Draft Statement of Principles ('DSOP') setting out the issues, alternatives, and the Steering Committee's proposals for resolving the issues and inviting public comment. In response, 42 comment letters were received. The Steering Committee reviewed the comments, revised certain of its recommendations, and submitted them to the Board.

B2   In July 1999, the Board approved Exposure Draft E65 *Agriculture* with a comment deadline of 31 January 2000. The Board received 62 comment letters on E65. They came from various international organisations, as well as from 28 individual countries. In April 2000, the IASC Staff sent a questionnaire to entities that undertake agricultural activity in an attempt to determine the reliability of the fair value measurement proposed in E65 and received 20 responses from 11 countries. In December 2000, after considering the comments on E65 and responses to the questionnaire, the Board approved IAS 41 *Agriculture* (the Standard). Paragraph B82 below summarises the changes that the Board made to E65 in finalising the Standard.

The need for an International Accounting Standard on agriculture

B3   A main objective of the IASC is to develop International Accounting Standards that are relevant in the general purpose financial statements of all businesses. While most International Accounting Standards apply to entities in all activities, some International Accounting Standards, for example IAS 30 *Disclosures in the Financial Statements of Banks and Similar Financial Institutions*[5] and IAS 40 *Investment Property*, deal with issues that arise in particular activities. IASC has also undertaken industry-specific projects on insurance and extractive industries.

---

5   In August 2005, IFRS 7 *Financial Instruments: Disclosures* superseded IAS 30.

B4   Diversity in accounting for agricultural activity has occurred because:

(a)   prior to the development of the Standard, assets related to agricultural activity and changes in those assets were excluded from the scope of International Accounting Standards:

(i)   IAS 2 *Inventories* excluded 'producers' inventories of livestock, agricultural and forest products ... to the extent that they are measured at net realisable value in accordance with well established practices in certain industries';

(ii)   IAS 16 *Property, Plant and Equipment* did not apply to 'forests and similar regenerative natural resources';

(iii)   IAS 18 *Revenue*[6] did not deal with revenue arising from 'natural increases in herds, and agricultural and forest products'; and

(iv)   IAS 40 *Investment Property* did not apply to 'forests and similar regenerative natural resources';

(b)   accounting guidelines for agricultural activity developed by national standard setters have, in general, been piecemeal, developed to resolve a specific issue related to a form of agricultural activity of significance to that country; and

(c)   the nature of agricultural activity creates uncertainty or conflicts when applying traditional accounting models, particularly because the critical events associated with biological transformation (growth, degeneration, production, and procreation) that alter the substance of biological assets are difficult to deal with in an accounting model based on historical cost and realisation.

B5   Most business organisations involved in agricultural activity are small, independent, cash and tax focused, family-operated business units, often perceived as not being required to produce general purpose financial statements. Some believe that because of this an International Accounting Standard on agriculture would not have widespread application. However, even small agricultural entities seek outside capital and subsidies, particularly from banks or government agencies, and these capital providers increasingly request financial statements. Moreover, an international trend towards deregulation, an increasing number of cross-border listings and more investment have resulted in increasing scale, scope, and commercialism of agricultural activity. This has created a greater need for financial statements based on sound and generally accepted accounting principles. For the above reasons, in 1994 the Board added to its agenda a project on agriculture.

B6   The DSOP specifically asked for views on the feasibility of developing a comprehensive International Accounting Standard on agriculture. Some commentators felt that the diversity of agricultural activity prevents the development of a single International Accounting Standard on accounting for all agricultural activities. Others said that different principles should attach to

---

6   IFRS 15 *Revenue from Contracts with Customers*, issued in May 2014, replaced IAS 18 *Revenue*. IFRS 15 also does not address revenue arising from 'natural increases in herds, and agricultural and forest products'.

agricultural activity with short and long production cycles. Some cited the need to develop International Accounting Standards that are simple to apply and broad in application. Commentators on the DSOP also noted that agriculture is a significant industry in many countries, particularly in developing and newly industrialised countries. In many such countries it is the most important industry.

B7 After considering the comments on the DSOP, the Board reaffirmed its conclusion that an International Accounting Standard is needed. The Board believes that the principles set forth in the Standard have wide application and provide a clear set of principles.

Scope

B8 The Standard prescribes, among other things, the accounting treatment for biological assets and for the initial measurement of agricultural produce harvested from an entity's biological assets at the point of harvest. However, the Standard does not deal with the processing of agricultural produce after harvest, since the Board did not consider it appropriate to undertake a partial revision of IAS 2 *Inventories* which deals with the accounting treatment for inventories under the historical cost system.[7] The processing after harvest is accounted for under IAS 2 or another applicable International Accounting Standard (for example, if an entity harvests logs[8] and decides to use them for constructing its own building, IAS 16 *Property, Plant and Equipment* is applied in accounting for the logs).

B9 Some may think of such processing as agricultural activity, particularly if it is done by the same entity that developed the agricultural produce (for example, the processing of grapes into wine by a vintner who has grown the grapes). While such processing may be a logical and natural extension of agricultural activity, and the events taking place may bear some similarity to biological transformation, such processing is not included within the definition of agricultural activity in the Standard.

B10 In particular, the Board considered whether to include circumstances where there is a long ageing or maturation process after harvest (for example, for wine production from grapes and cheese production from milk) in the scope of the Standard. Those who believe that the Standard should cover such processing argue that:

(a) such a long ageing or maturation process is similar to biological transformation and fundamental to assessing the performance of an entity; and

(b) many agricultural entities are vertically integrated and involved in, for example, producing both grapes and wine.

---

7 The term 'historical cost system' is no longer applicable owing to revisions made to IAS 2 in December 2003.

8 As the result of an amendment by the IASB, contained in *Improvements to IFRSs* issued in May 2008, 'logs' is an example of produce that has been processed rather than an example of unprocessed produce.

B11 The Board decided not to include such circumstances in the scope of the Standard because of concerns about difficulties in differentiating them from other manufacturing processes (such as conversion of raw materials into marketable inventories as defined in IAS 2). The Board concluded that the requirements in IAS 2 or another applicable International Accounting Standard would be suited to accounting for such processes.

B12 The Board also considered whether to deal with contracts for the sale of a biological asset or agricultural produce and government grants related to agricultural activity in the Standard. These issues are discussed below (see paragraphs B47–54 and B63–73).

Measurement

Biological assets

Fair value versus cost

B13 The Standard requires an entity to use a fair value approach in measuring its biological assets related to agricultural activity as proposed in the DSOP and E65, except for cases where the fair value cannot be measured reliably on initial recognition.

B14 Those who support fair value measurement argue that the effects of changes brought about by biological transformation are best reflected by reference to the fair value changes in biological assets. They believe that fair value changes in biological assets have a direct relationship to changes in expectations of future economic benefits to the entity.

B15 Those who support fair value measurement also note that the transactions entered into to effect biological transformation often have only a weak relationship with the biological transformation itself and, thus, a more distant relationship to expected future economic benefits. For example, patterns of growth in a plantation forest directly affect expectations of future economic benefits but differ markedly, in timing, from patterns of cost incurrence. No income might be reported until first harvest and sale (perhaps 30 years) in a plantation forestry entity using a transaction-based, historical cost accounting model. On the other hand, income is measured and reported throughout the period until initial harvest if an accounting model is used that recognises and measures biological growth using current fair values.

B16 Further, those who support fair value measurement cite reasons for concluding that fair value has greater relevance, reliability, comparability, and understandability as a measurement of future economic benefits expected from biological assets than historical cost, including:

(a) many biological assets are traded in active markets with observable market prices. Active markets for these assets provide a reliable measure of market expectations of future economic benefits. The presence of such markets significantly increases the reliability of market value as an indicator of fair value;

(b)   measures of the cost of biological assets are sometimes less reliable than measures of fair value because joint products and joint costs can create situations in which the relationship between inputs and outputs is ill-defined, leading to complex and arbitrary allocations of cost between the different outcomes of biological transformation. Such allocations become even more arbitrary if biological assets generate additional biological assets (offspring) and the additional biological assets are also used in the entity's own agricultural activity;

(c)   relatively long and continuous production cycles, with volatility in both the production and market environment, mean that the accounting period often does not depict a full cycle. Therefore, period-end measurement (as opposed to time of transaction) assumes greater significance in deriving a measure of current period financial performance or position. The less significant current year harvest is in relation to total biological transformation, the greater the significance of period-end measures of asset change (growth and degeneration). In relatively high turnover, short production cycle, highly controlled agricultural systems (for example, broiler chicken or mushroom production) in which the majority of biological transformation and harvesting occurs within a year, the relationship between cost and future economic benefits appears more stable. This apparent stability does not alter the relationship between current market value and future economic benefits, but it makes the difference in measurement method less significant; and

(d)   different sources of replacement animals and plants (home-grown or purchased) give rise to different costs in a historical cost approach. Similar assets should give rise to similar expectations with regard to future benefits. Considerably enhanced comparability and understandability result when similar assets are measured and reported using the same basis.

B17   Those who oppose measuring biological assets at fair value believe there is superior reliability in cost measurement because historical cost is the result of arm's length transactions, and therefore provides evidence of an open-market value at that point in time, and is independently verifiable. More importantly, they believe fair value is sometimes not reliably measurable and that users of financial statements may be misled by presentation of numbers that are indicated as being fair value but are based on subjective and unverifiable assumptions. Information regarding fair value can be provided other than in a single number in the financial statements. They believe the scope of the Standard is too broad. They also argue that:

(a)   market prices are often volatile and cyclical and not appropriate as a basis of measurement;

(b)   it may be onerous to require fair valuation at each balance sheet date, especially if interim reports are required;

(c) the historical cost convention is well established and commonly used. The use of any other basis should be accompanied by a change in the IASC *Framework for the Preparation and Presentation of Financial Statements*[9] (the '*Framework*'). For consistency with other International Accounting Standards and other activities, biological assets should be measured at their cost;

(d) cost measurement provides more objective and consistent measurement;

(e) active markets may not exist for some biological assets in some countries. In such cases, fair value cannot be measured reliably, especially during the period of growth in the case of a biological asset that has a long growth period (for example, trees in a plantation forest);

(f) fair value measurement results in recognition of unrealised gains and losses and contradicts principles in International Accounting Standards on recognition of revenue; and

(g) market prices at a balance sheet date may not bear a close relationship to the prices at which assets will be sold, and many biological assets are not held for sale.

B18 The *Framework* is neutral with respect to the choice of measurement basis, identifying that a number of different bases are employed to different degrees and in varying combinations, though noting that historical cost is most commonly adopted. The alternatives specifically identified are historical cost, current cost, realisable value, and present value. Precedents for fair value measurement exist in other International Accounting Standards.

B19 The Board concluded that the Standard should require a fair value model for biological assets related to agricultural activity because of the unique nature and characteristics of agricultural activity. However, the Board also concluded that, in some cases, fair value cannot be measured reliably. Some respondents to the questionnaire, as well as some commentators on E65, expressed significant concern about the reliability of fair value measurement for some biological assets, arguing that:

(a) active markets do not exist for some biological assets, in particular for those with a long growth period;

(b) present value of expected net cash flows is often an unreliable measure of fair value due to the need for, and use of, subjective assumptions (for example, about weather); and

(c) fair value cannot be measured reliably prior to harvest.

Some commentators on E65 suggested that the Standard should include a reliability exception for cases where no active market exists.

B20 The Board decided there was a need to include a reliability exception for cases where market-determined prices or values are not available and alternative estimates of fair value are determined to be clearly unreliable. In those cases,

---

9 References to the *Framework* are to IASC's *Framework for the Preparation and Presentation of Financial Statements*, which was adopted by the IASB in 2001. In September 2010 the IASB replaced the *Framework* with the *Conceptual Framework for Financial Reporting*.

biological assets should be measured at their cost less any accumulated depreciation and any accumulated impairment losses. In determining cost, accumulated depreciation and accumulated impairment losses, an entity considers IAS 2 *Inventories*, IAS 16 *Property, Plant and Equipment* and IAS 36 *Impairment of Assets*.

B21   The Board rejected a benchmark treatment of fair value and an allowed alternative treatment of historical cost because of the greater comparability and understandability achieved by a mandatory fair value approach in the presence of active markets. The Board is also uncomfortable with options in International Accounting Standards.

Treatment of point-of-sale costs

B22   The Standard requires that a biological asset should be measured at its fair value less estimated point-of-sale costs. Point-of-sale costs include commissions to brokers and dealers, levies by regulatory agencies and commodity exchanges, and transfer taxes and duties. Point-of-sale costs exclude transport and other costs necessary to get assets to a market. Such transport and other costs are deducted in determining fair value (that is, fair value is a market price less transport and other costs necessary to get an asset to a market).[10]

B23   E65 proposed that pre-sale disposal costs that will be incurred to place an asset on the market (such as transport costs) should be deducted in determining fair value, if a biological asset will be sold in an active market in another location. However, E65 did not specify the treatment of point-of-sale costs. Some commentators suggested that the Standard should clarify the treatment of point-of-sale costs, as well as pre-sale disposal costs.

B24   Some argue that point-of-sale costs should not be deducted in a fair value model. They argue that fair value less estimated point-of-sale costs would be a biased estimate of markets' estimate of future cash flows, because point-of-sale costs would in effect be recognised as an expense twice if the acquirer pays point-of-sale costs on acquisition; once related to the initial acquisition of biological assets and once related to the immediate measurement at fair value less estimated point-of-sale costs. This would occur even when point-of-sale costs would not be incurred until a future period or would not be paid at all for a bearer biological asset that will not be sold.

B25   On the other hand, some believe that point-of-sale costs should be deducted in a fair value model. They believe that the carrying amount of an asset should represent the economic benefits that are expected to flow from the asset. They argue that fair value less estimated point-of-sale costs would represent the markets' estimate of the economic benefits that are expected to flow to the entity from that asset at the balance sheet date. They also argue that failure to deduct estimated point-of-sale costs could result in a loss being deferred until a sale occurs.

---

10   IFRS 13, issued in May 2011, describes how transport costs are factored into a fair value measurement.

B26 The Board concluded that fair value less estimated point-of-sale costs is a more relevant measurement of biological assets, acknowledging that, in particular, failure to deduct estimated point-of-sale costs could result in a loss being deferred.

Hierarchy in fair value measurement[11]

B27 The Standard requires that, if an active market exists for a biological asset, the quoted price in that market is the appropriate basis for determining the fair value of that asset. If an active market does not exist, an entity uses market-determined prices or values (such as the most recent market transaction price) when available. However, in some circumstances, market-determined prices or values may not be available for a biological asset in its present condition. In these circumstances, the Standard indicates that an entity uses the present value of expected net cash flows[12] from the asset.

B28 E65 proposed that, if an active market exists for a biological asset, an entity should use the market price in the active market. If an active market does not exist, E65 proposed that an entity should consider other measurement bases such as the price of the most recent transaction for the same type of asset, sector benchmarks, and present value of expected net cash flows. E65 did not set a hierarchy in cases where no active market exists; that is, E65 did not indicate which basis is preferable to the other bases.

B29 The Board considered setting an explicit hierarchy in cases where no active market exists. Some believe that using market-determined prices or values; for example, the most recent market transaction price, would always be preferable to present value of expected net cash flows. On the other hand, some believe that market-determined prices or values would not necessarily be preferable to present value of expected net cash flows, especially when an entity uses market prices for similar assets with adjustment to reflect differences.

B30 The Board concluded that a detailed hierarchy would not provide sufficient flexibility to appropriately deal with all the circumstances that may arise and decided not to set a detailed hierarchy in cases where no active market exists. However, the Board decided to indicate that an entity uses all available market-determined prices or values since otherwise there is a possibility that entities may opt to use present value of expected net cash flows from the asset even when useful market-determined prices or values are available. Of the 20 companies that responded to the questionnaire, six companies used present value of expected net cash flows as a basis of fair value measurement and, in addition, two companies indicated that it was impossible to measure their biological assets reliably since the present value of expected net cash flows would not be reliable (as they would need to use present value as a basis).

---

11 IFRS 13, issued in May 2011, defines an active market and contains a three-level fair value hierarchy for the inputs used in the valuation techniques used to measure fair value.

12 Paragraph 20 of the previous version of IAS 41 required entities to use a pre-tax discount rate when measuring fair value. The IASB decided to maintain the requirement to use a current market-based discount rate but removed the reference to a pre-tax discount rate by *Improvements to IFRSs* issued in May 2008.

B31 When an entity has access to different markets, the Standard indicates that the entity uses the most relevant one. For example, if an entity has access to two active markets, it uses the price existing in the market expected to be used. Some believe that the most advantageous price in the accessible markets should be used. The Standard reflects the view that the most relevant measurement results from using the market expected to be used.

Frequency of fair value measurement

B32 Some argue that less frequent measurement of fair value should be permitted because of concerns about burdens on entities. The Board rejected this approach because of the:

(a) continuous nature of biological transformation;

(b) lack of direct relationships between financial transactions and the outcomes of biological transformation; and

(c) general availability of reliable measures of fair value at reasonable cost.

Independent valuation

B33 A significant number of commentators on the DSOP indicated that, if present value of expected net cash flows is used to determine fair value, an external independent valuation should be required. The Board rejected this proposal since it believes that external independent valuations are not commonly used for certain agricultural activity and it would be burdensome to require an external independent valuation. The Board believes that it is for entities to decide how to determine fair value reliably, including the extent to which independent valuers need to be involved.

Inability to measure fair value reliably

B34 As noted previously, the Board decided to include a reliability exception in the Standard for cases where fair value cannot be measured reliably on initial recognition. The Standard indicates a presumption that fair value can be measured reliably for a biological asset. However, that presumption can be rebutted only on initial recognition for a biological asset for which market-determined prices or values are not available and for which alternative estimates of fair value are determined to be clearly unreliable. In such a case, that biological asset should be measured at its cost less any accumulated depreciation and any accumulated impairment losses. Once the fair value of such a biological asset becomes reliably measurable, the Standard requires that an entity should start measuring the biological asset at its fair value less estimated point-of-sale costs.

B35 Some believe that, if an entity was previously using the reliability exception, the entity should not be allowed to start fair value measurement (that is, an entity should continue to use a cost basis). They argue that it could be a subjective decision to determine when fair value has become reliably measurable and that this subjectivity could lead to inconsistent application and, potentially, abuse. The Board noted, however, that in agricultural activity, it is likely that fair value becomes measurable more reliably as biological transformation occurs and that fair value measurement is preferable to cost in those cases. Thus, the Board decided to require fair value measurement once fair value becomes reliably measurable.

B36   If an entity has previously measured a biological asset at its fair value less estimated point-of-sale costs, the Standard requires that the entity should continue to measure the biological asset at its fair value less estimated point-of-sale costs until disposal. Some argue that reliable estimates may cease to be available. The Board believed that this would rarely, if ever, occur. Accordingly, the Board decided to prohibit entities from changing their measurement basis from fair value to cost, because otherwise an entity might use a reliability exception as an excuse to discontinue fair value accounting in a falling market.

B37   If an entity uses the reliability exception, the Standard requires additional disclosures. The additional disclosures include information on biological assets held at the end of the period such as a description of the assets and an explanation of why fair value cannot be measured reliably. The additional disclosures also include the gain or loss recognised for the period on disposal of biological assets measured at cost less any accumulated depreciation and any accumulated impairment losses, even though those biological assets are not held at the end of the period.

Gains and losses

B38   The Standard requires that a gain or loss arising on initial recognition of a biological asset and from a change in fair value less estimated point-of-sale costs of a biological asset should be included in net profit or loss[13] for the period in which it arises. Those who support this treatment argue that biological transformation is a significant event that should be included in net profit or loss because:

(a)   the event is fundamental to understanding an entity's performance; and

(b)   this is consistent with the accrual basis of accounting.

B39   Some commentators on the DSOP and E65 argued that fair value changes should be included directly in equity, through the statement of changes in equity, until realised, arguing that:

(a)   the effects of biological transformation cannot be measured reliably and, therefore, should not be reported as income;

(b)   fair value changes should only be included in net profit or loss when the earnings process is complete;

(c)   recognition of unrealised gains and losses in net profit or loss increases volatility of earnings;

(d)   the results of biological transformation may never be realised, particularly given the risks to which biological assets are exposed; and

---

13   IAS 1 *Presentation of Financial Statements* (revised in 2003) replaced the term 'net profit or loss' with 'profit or loss'.

(e)   it is premature to require recognition of fair value changes in net profit or loss, until performance reporting issues are resolved.

B40   The Board rejected requiring changes in fair value to be included directly in equity since it is difficult to find any conceptual basis for reporting any portion of the changes in fair value of biological assets related to agricultural activity directly in equity. No distinction is made in the *Framework* between recognition in the balance sheet and recognition in the income statement.

Agricultural produce

B41   The Standard requires that agricultural produce harvested from an entity's biological assets should be measured at its fair value less estimated point-of-sale costs at the point of harvest. Such measurement is the cost at that date when applying IAS 2 *Inventories* or another applicable International Accounting Standard.

B42   The Board noted that the same basis of measurement should generally be applied to agricultural produce on initial recognition and to the biological asset from which it is harvested. Because the fair value of a biological asset takes into account the condition of the agricultural produce that will be harvested from the biological asset, it would be illogical to measure the agricultural produce at cost when the biological asset is measured at fair value. For example, the fair value of a sheep with half fleece will differ from the fair value of a similar sheep with full fleece. It would be inconsistent and distort reporting of current period performance if, upon shearing, the shorn fleece is measured at its cost when the fair value of the sheep is reduced by the fair value of the fleece.

B43   As noted previously, certain biological assets are measured at their cost less any accumulated depreciation and any accumulated impairment losses, if the reliability exception is applied. Some argue that a reliability exception should exist for measurement of agricultural produce. The Board rejected this view because many of the arguments for a reliability exception do not apply to agricultural produce. For example, markets more often exist for agricultural produce than for biological assets. The Board also noted that it is generally not practicable to reliably determine the cost of agricultural produce harvested from biological assets.

B44   With regard to measurement after harvest, some argue that agricultural produce should be measured at its fair value both at the point of harvest and at each balance sheet date until sold, consumed, or otherwise disposed of. They argue that this approach would ensure that all agricultural produce of a similar type is measured similarly irrespective of date of harvest, thus enhancing comparability and consistency.

B45   The Board concluded that fair value less estimated point-of-sale costs at the point of harvest should be the cost when applying IAS 2 or another applicable International Accounting Standard, since this is consistent with the historical cost accounting model applied to manufacturing processes in general and other types of inventory.

B46   In reaching the above conclusion, the Board noted that entities undertaking agricultural activity sometimes purchase agricultural produce for resale, and other entities often engage in processing purchased agricultural produce into consumable products. If agricultural produce would be measured at its fair value after harvest, a desire for consistency would suggest revaluing purchased inventories as well, and such a treatment would be inconsistent with IAS 2. The Board did not consider it appropriate to undertake a partial revision of IAS 2.

Sales contracts

B47 Entities often enter into contracts to sell at a future date their biological assets or agricultural produce. The Standard indicates that contract prices are not necessarily relevant in determining fair value and that the fair value of a biological asset or agricultural produce is not adjusted because of the existence of a contract.

B48 E65 did not propose how to account for a contract for the sale of a biological asset or agricultural produce. Some commentators suggested prescribing the treatment of sales contracts since such sales contracts are common in certain agricultural activity. Some commentators also pointed out that certain sales contracts are not within the scope of IAS 39 *Financial Instruments: Recognition and Measurement*[14] and that no other International Accounting Standards deal with those contracts.

B49 Some argue that contract prices should be used in measuring the related biological assets when an entity expects to settle the contract by delivery and believe this would result in the most relevant carrying amount for the biological asset. Others argue that contract prices are not necessarily relevant in measuring the biological assets at fair value since fair value reflects the current market in which a willing buyer and seller would enter into a transaction.[15]

B50 The Board concluded that contract prices should not be used in measuring related biological assets, because contract prices do not necessarily reflect the current market in which a willing buyer and seller would enter into a transaction and therefore do not necessarily represent the fair value of assets. The Board wished to maintain a consistent approach to the measurement of assets. The Board instead considered whether it might require that sales contracts be measured at fair value. It is logical to measure a sales contract at fair value to the extent that a related biological asset is also measured at fair value.

B51 However, the Board noted that to achieve symmetry between the measurement of a biological asset and a related sales contract the Standard would have to carefully restrict the sales contracts to be measured at fair value. An entity may enter into a contract to sell agricultural produce to be harvested from the entity's biological assets. The Board concluded that it would not be appropriate to require fair value measurement for a contract to sell agricultural produce that does not yet exist (for example, milk to be harvested from a cow), since no related asset has yet been recognised or measured at fair value and to do so would be beyond the scope of the project on agriculture.

---

14 IFRS 9 *Financial Instruments* replaced IAS 39. IFRS 9 applies to all items that were previously within the scope of IAS 39.

15 IFRS 13, issued in May 2011, contains the requirements for measuring fair value.

B52 Thus, the Board considered restricting the sales contracts to be measured at fair value to those for the sale of an entity's existing biological assets and agricultural produce. However, the Board noted that it is difficult to differentiate existing agricultural produce from agricultural produce that does not exist. For example:

(a) if an entity enters into a contract to sell fully-grown wheat at a future date and has half-grown wheat at a balance sheet date, it seems clear that the wheat to be delivered under the contract does not yet exist at the balance sheet date; but

(b) on the other hand, if an entity enters into a contract to sell mature cattle at a future date and has mature cattle at a balance sheet date, it could be argued that the cattle exist in the form in which they will be sold at the balance sheet date. However, it could also be argued that the cattle do not yet exist in the form in which they will be sold at the balance sheet date since further biological transformation will occur between the balance sheet date and the date of delivery.

B53 The Board also noted that the Standard would have to require an entity to stop fair value measurement for sales contracts once agricultural produce to be sold under the contract is harvested from an entity's biological assets, since accounting for agricultural produce is not dealt with in the Standard except for initial measurement and IAS 2 *Inventories* or another applicable International Accounting Standard applies after harvest. It would be illogical to continue fair value measurement when the agricultural produce is measured at historical cost. The Board noted that it would be anomalous to require an entity to start measuring a contract at fair value once the related asset exists and to stop doing that at a later date.

B54 The Board concluded that no solution is practicable without a complete review of the accounting for commodity contracts that are not within the scope of IAS 39.[16] Because of the above difficulties, the Board concluded that the Standard should not deal with the measurement of sales contracts that are not within the scope of IAS 39. Instead, the Board decided to include an observation that those sales contracts may be onerous contracts under IAS 37 *Provisions, Contingent Liabilities and Contingent Assets*.

Land related to agricultural activity

B55 The Standard does not establish any new principles for land related to agricultural activity. Rather, an entity follows IAS 16 *Property, Plant and Equipment* or IAS 40 *Investment Property* depending on which standard is appropriate in the circumstances. IAS 16 requires land to be measured either at its cost less any accumulated impairment losses, or at a revalued amount. IAS 40 requires land that is investment property to be measured at its fair value, or cost less any accumulated impairment losses.

B56 Some argue that land attached to biological assets related to agricultural activity should also be measured at its fair value. They argue that fair value

---

16 IFRS 9 *Financial Instruments* replaced IAS 39. IFRS 9 applies to all items that were previously within the scope of IAS 39.

measurement of land results in consistency of measurement with the fair value measurement of biological assets. They also argue that it is sometimes difficult to measure the fair value of such biological assets separately from the land since an active market often exists for the combined assets (that is, land and biological assets; for example, trees in a plantation forest).

B57 The Board rejected this approach, primarily because requiring the fair value measurement of land related to agricultural activity would be inconsistent with IAS 16.

Intangible assets

B58 The Standard does not establish any new principles for intangible assets related to agricultural activity. Rather, an entity follows IAS 38 *Intangible Assets*. IAS 38 requires an intangible asset, after initial recognition, to be measured at its cost less any accumulated amortisation and impairment losses, or at a revalued amount.

B59 E65 proposed that an entity should be encouraged to follow the revaluation alternative in IAS 38 for intangible assets related to agricultural activity, to enhance consistency of measurement with the fair value measurement of biological assets. Some commentators on E65 disagreed with having the encouragement. They argued that a unique treatment for intangible assets related to agricultural activity is not warranted.

B60 The Board did not include the encouragement in E65 in the Standard. The Board concluded that IAS 38 should be applied to intangible assets related to agricultural activity, as it is to intangible assets related to other activities.

Subsequent expenditure

B61 The Standard does not explicitly prescribe how to account for subsequent expenditure related to biological assets. E65 proposed that costs of producing and harvesting biological assets should be charged to expense when incurred and that costs that increase the number of units of biological assets owned or controlled by the entity should be added to the carrying amount of the asset.

B62 Some believe that there is no need to capitalise subsequent expenditure in a fair value model and that all subsequent expenditure should be recognised as an expense. Some also argue that it would sometimes be difficult to prescribe which costs should be recognised as expenses and which costs should be capitalised; for example, in the case of vet fees paid for delivering a calf. The Board decided not to explicitly prescribe the accounting for subsequent expenditure related to biological assets in the Standard, because it believes to do so is unnecessary with a fair value measurement approach.

Government grants

B63 The Standard requires that an unconditional government grant related to a biological asset measured at its fair value less estimated point-of-sale costs should be recognised as income when, and only when, the government grant becomes receivable. If a government grant is conditional, including where a government grant requires an entity not to engage in specified agricultural activity, an entity should recognise the government grant as income when, and only when, the conditions attaching to the government grant are met.

B64 The Standard requires a different treatment from IAS 20 *Accounting for Government Grants and Disclosure of Government Assistance* in the circumstances described above. IAS 20 is to be applied only to government grants related to biological assets measured at cost less any accumulated depreciation and any accumulated impairment losses.

B65 IAS 20 requires that government grants should not be recognised until there is reasonable assurance that:

(a) the entity will comply with the conditions attaching to them; and

(b) the grants will be received.

IAS 20 also requires that government grants should be recognised as income over the periods necessary to match them with the related costs that they are intended to compensate, on a systematic basis. In relation to the presentation of government grants related to assets, IAS 20 permits two methods—setting up a government grant as deferred income or deducting the government grant from the carrying amount of the asset.

B66 The latter method of presentation—deducting a government grant from the carrying amount of the related asset—is inconsistent with a fair value model in which an asset is measured and presented at its fair value. Using the deduction from carrying value approach, an entity would first deduct the government grant from the carrying amount of the related asset and then measure that asset at its fair value. In effect, an entity would recognise a government grant as income immediately, even for a conditional government grant. This conflicts with the requirement in IAS 20 that government grants should not be recognised until there is reasonable assurance that the entity will comply with the conditions attaching to them.

B67 Because of the above, the Board concluded that there was a need to deal with government grants related to biological assets measured at their fair value. Some argued that IASC should begin a wider review of IAS 20 rather than provide special rules in individual International Accounting Standards. The Board acknowledged that this might be a more appropriate approach, but concluded that such a review would be beyond the scope of the project on agriculture. Instead, the Board decided to deal with government grants in the Standard, since the Board noted that government grants related to agricultural activity are common in some countries.

B68 E65 proposed that, if an entity receives a government grant in respect of a biological asset that is measured at its fair value and the grant is unconditional, the entity should recognise the grant as income when the government grant becomes receivable. E65 also proposed that, if a government grant is conditional, the entity should recognise it as income when there is reasonable assurance that the conditions are met.

B69 The Board noted that, if a government grant is conditional, an entity is likely to have costs and ongoing obligations associated with satisfying the conditions attaching to the government grant. It may be possible that the inflow of economic benefits is much less than the amount of the government grant. Given that possibility, the Board acknowledged that the criterion for recognising income from a conditional government grant in E65, when there is reasonable assurance that the conditions are met, may give rise to income recognition that is inconsistent with the *Framework*. The *Framework* indicates that income is recognised in the income statement when an increase in future economic benefits related to an increase in an asset or a decrease in a liability has arisen that can be measured reliably. The Board also noted that it would inevitably be a subjective decision as to when there is reasonable assurance that the conditions are met and that this subjectivity could lead to inconsistent income recognition.

B70   The Board considered two alternative approaches:

(a)   an entity should recognise a conditional government grant as income when it is probable that the entity will meet the conditions attaching to the government grant; and

(b)   an entity should recognise a conditional government grant as income when the entity meets the conditions attaching to the government grant.

B71   Proponents of approach (a) argue that this approach is generally consistent with the revenue recognition requirements in IAS 18 *Revenue*.[17] IAS 18 requires that revenue should be recognised, among other things, when it is probable that the economic benefits associated with the transaction will flow to the entity.

B72   Proponents of approach (b) believe that, until the conditions attaching to the government grant are met, a liability should be recognised under the *Framework* rather than income since an entity has a present obligation to satisfy the conditions arising from past events. They also argue that income recognition under approach (a) would still be subjective and inconsistent with the recognition criteria indicated in the *Framework*.

B73   The Board concluded that approach (b) is more appropriate. The Board also decided that a government grant that requires an entity not to engage in specified agricultural activity should also be accounted for in the same way as a conditional government grant related to a biological asset measured at its fair value less estimated point-of-sale costs.

Disclosure

Separate disclosure of physical and price changes

B74   The Standard encourages, but does not require, separate disclosure of the effects of the factors resulting in changes to the carrying amount of biological assets, physical change and price change, when there is a production cycle of more than one year. Physical change is attributable to changes in the assets themselves while price change is attributable to changes in unit fair values.

B75   Some argue that the separate disclosure should be required since it is useful in appraising current period performance and future prospects in relation to

---

17   IFRS 15 *Revenue from Contracts with Customers*, issued in May 2014, replaced IAS 18 *Revenue*.

production from, and maintenance and renewal of, biological assets. Others argue that it may be impracticable to separate these elements and the two components cannot be separated reliably.

B76 The Board concluded that the separate disclosure should not be required because of practicability concerns. However, the Board decided to encourage the separate disclosure, given that such disclosure may be useful and practically determinable in some circumstances. The separate disclosure is not encouraged when the production cycle is less than one year (for example, when raising broiler chickens or growing cereal crops) since that information is less useful in that circumstance.

B77 Some argue that physical changes should be included in net profit or loss and that price changes should be included directly in equity, through the statement of changes in equity. The Board rejected this approach because both components are indicative of management's performance.

Disaggregation of the gain or loss

B78 The Standard requires that an entity should disclose the aggregate gain or loss arising during the current period on initial recognition of biological assets and agricultural produce and from the change in fair value less estimated point-of-sale costs of biological assets. The Standard does not require or encourage disaggregating the gain or loss, except that the Standard encourages separate disclosure of physical changes and price changes as discussed above.

B79 The Board considered requiring, or encouraging, disclosure of the gain or loss on a disaggregated basis; for example, requiring separate disclosure of the gain or loss related to biological assets and the gain or loss related to agricultural produce. Those who supported disaggregating the gain or loss believe that such information is useful in appraising current period performance in relation to biological transformation. Others argued that disaggregation would be impracticable and require a subjective procedure.

Other disclosures

B80 E65 proposed disclosing the:

(a) extent to which the carrying amount of biological assets reflects a valuation by an external independent valuer, or if there has been no valuation by an external independent valuer, that fact;

(b) activities that are unsustainable with an estimated date of cessation of the activities;

(c) aggregate carrying amount of an entity's agricultural land and the basis (cost or revalued amount) on which the carrying amount was determined under IAS 16 *Property, Plant and Equipment*; and

(d) carrying amount of agricultural produce either on the face of the balance sheet or in the notes.

B81 The Board did not include the above disclosures in the Standard. The Board noted that requiring item (a) above would not be appropriate since external independent valuations are not commonly used for assets related to agricultural activity, unlike for certain other assets such as investment property. The Board also noted that item (b) is not required in other International Accounting Standards and a unique disclosure requirement is not warranted for agricultural activity. Items (c) and (d) would be outside the scope of the Standard and covered by other International Accounting Standards (IAS 16 or IAS 2 *Inventories*).

Summary of changes to E65

B82   The Standard made the following principal changes to the proposals in E65:

(a)   The Standard includes a reliability exception for biological assets on initial recognition. If the exception is applied, the biological asset should be measured at its cost less any accumulated depreciation and any accumulated impairment losses (paragraph 30 of the Standard). As a consequence, the Standard includes disclosure requirements consistent with paragraph 170(b) of IAS 39 *Financial Instruments: Recognition and Measurement*[18] and paragraph 68 of IAS 40 *Investment Property*[19] (paragraphs 54(a)–(c) and 55 of the Standard), and consistent with paragraphs 60(b)–(d) and 60(e)(v)–(vii) of IAS 16 *Property, Plant and Equipment*[20] (paragraphs 54(d)–(f) and 55).

(b)   If the reliability exception is applied but fair value subsequently becomes reliably measurable and, therefore, an entity has started measuring the biological assets at their fair value less estimated point-of-sale costs, the Standard requires the entity to disclose a description of the biological assets, an explanation of why fair value has become reliably measurable, and the effect of the change (paragraph 56).

(c)   E65 did not specify how to account for point-of-sale costs (such as commissions to brokers). The Standard requires that biological assets and agricultural produce should be measured at their fair value less estimated point-of-sale costs (paragraphs 12–13).

(d)   E65 included net realisable value as one of the measurement bases in cases where no active market exists. Net realisable value was deleted from the bases since it is not a market-determined value.

(e)   The Standard indicates that market-determined prices or values are used when available. The Standard also indicates that, in some circumstances, market-determined prices or values may not be available for an asset in its present condition. In these circumstances, an entity uses the present value of expected net cash flows (paragraphs 18–20).

(f)   Guidance on the performance of present value calculations was added (paragraphs 21–23).

---

18 Paragraph 170(b) of IAS 39 was replaced by paragraph 90 of IAS 32 *Financial Instruments: Disclosure and Presentation* when the IASB revised those standards in 2003. In 2005, the IASB relocated all disclosures relating to financial instruments to IFRS 7 *Financial Instruments: Disclosures.*

19 Paragraph 68 of IAS 40 was replaced by paragraph 78 when the IASB revised IAS 40 in 2003.

20 Paragraph 60 of IAS 16 was replaced by paragraph 73 when IAS 16 was revised in 2003.

(g) E65 did not specify how to account for contracts for the sale of a biological asset or agricultural produce. The Standard indicates that the fair value of a biological asset or agricultural produce is not adjusted because of the existence of a sales contract (paragraph 16).

(h) E65 did not explicitly indicate that a gain or loss may arise on initial recognition of agricultural produce. The Standard clarifies that a gain or loss may arise on initial recognition of agricultural produce; for example, as a result of harvesting and that such a gain or loss should be included in net profit or loss[21] for the period in which it arises (paragraphs 28–29).

(i) E65 proposed that costs of producing and harvesting biological assets should be charged to expense when incurred, and that costs that increase the number of units of biological assets owned or controlled by the entity should be added to the carrying amount of the asset. The Standard does not explicitly prescribe how to account for subsequent expenditure related to biological assets.

(j) E65 proposed that an entity should recognise a conditional government grant as income when there is reasonable assurance that the conditions are met. The Standard requires that a conditional government grant related to a biological asset measured at its fair value less estimated point-of-sale costs, including where a government grant requires an entity not to engage in specified agricultural activity, should be recognised as income when, and only when, the conditions attaching to the government grant are met. The Standard also indicates that IAS 20 *Accounting for Government Grants and Disclosure of Government Assistance* is applied to a government grant related to a biological asset measured at its cost less any accumulated depreciation and any accumulated impairment losses (paragraphs 34–35 and 37).

(k) E65 provided the following encouragements specific to agricultural activity with regard to alternative treatments allowed in other International Accounting Standards, to achieve consistency with the accounting treatment of activities covered by E65:

(i) analysing expenses by nature, as set out in IAS 1 *Presentation of Financial Statements*; and

(ii) revaluing certain intangible assets used in agricultural activity if an active market exists, as set out in IAS 38 *Intangible Assets*.

The Board did not include these encouragements in the Standard. The Board noted that IAS 1 and IAS 38 apply to entities that undertake agricultural activity, as well as to those in other activities.

---

21 IAS 1 *Presentation of Financial Statements* (revised in 2003) replaced the term 'net profit or loss' with 'profit or loss'.

(l)   New disclosure requirements include disclosing the:

    (i)   basis for making distinctions between consumable and bearer biological assets or between mature and immature biological assets, when an entity provides a quantified description of each group of biological assets (paragraph 43);

    (ii)   methods and significant assumptions applied in determining the fair value of each group of agricultural produce at the point of harvest (paragraph 47);

    (iii)   fair value less estimated point-of-sale costs of agricultural produce harvested during the period, determined at the point of harvest (paragraph 48);

    (iv)   increases resulting from business combinations in the reconciliation of the carrying amount of biological assets (paragraph 50(e)); and

    (v)   significant decreases expected in the level of government grants related to agricultural activity covered by the Standard (paragraph 57(c)).

(m)   E65 proposed disclosing the:

    (i)   extent to which the carrying amount of biological assets reflects a valuation by an external independent valuer or, if there has been no valuation by an external independent valuer, that fact;

    (ii)   activities that are unsustainable with an estimated date of cessation of the activities;

    (iii)   aggregate carrying amount of an entity's agricultural land and the basis (cost or revalued amount) on which the carrying amount was determined under IAS 16; and

    (iv)   carrying amount of agricultural produce either on the face of the balance sheet or in the notes.

The Standard does not include the above disclosures.

(n)   The amendment to IAS 17 *Leases* now clarifies that IAS 17 should not be applied to the measurement by:

    (i)   lessees of biological assets held under finance leases; and

    (ii)   lessors of biological assets leased out under operating leases.

Biological assets held under finance leases and those leased out under operating leases are measured under the Standard rather than IAS 17. A lease of a biological asset is classified as a finance lease or operating lease under IAS 17. If a lease is classified as a finance lease, the lessee recognises the leased biological asset under IAS 17 and thereafter measures and presents it under the Standard. In that case, the lessee makes disclosures both under the Standard and IAS 17. A lessor of a biological asset under an operating lease measures and presents the biological asset under the Standard, and makes disclosures both under the Standard and IAS 17.

Dissenting Opinions

Dissent of Patrick Finnegan and Patricia McConnell

DO1   Mr Finnegan and Ms McConnell voted against the publication of *Agriculture: Bearer Plants* (Amendments to IAS 16 and IAS 41) issued in June 2014 (the 'June 2014 Amendment') because they believe that including bearer plants within the scope of IAS 16 *Property, Plant and Equipment* instead of IAS 41 *Agriculture* will eliminate information about the fair value changes in bearer plants and the underlying assumptions used to estimate those changes. Information about the fair values of all biological assets including bearer plants is critical both to managing agricultural activities and to investing in entities that engage in those activities. Without such information, investors are unable to assess changes in expectations of future net cash inflows for an entity engaged in agricultural activity. The fact that published price quotations have developed throughout the world for orchards and plantations that include bearer plants demonstrates the importance of fair value information to those who invest in agricultural activities.

DO2   IAS 41 prescribes the accounting for agricultural activity, that is, the management by an entity of the biological transformation of living animals or plants (biological assets) for sale, into agricultural produce or into additional biological assets. The underlying principle of IAS 41 is that fair value measurement best reflects the biological transformation of biological assets. It requires measurement at fair value less costs to sell (referred to hereafter as fair value) from initial recognition of biological assets up to and including the point of harvest, other than when fair value cannot be measured reliably on initial recognition.

DO3   The June 2014 Amendment changes the measurement for one subset of biological assets, bearer plants, from fair value to a cost-based measure. Bearer plants are plants that are used only in the production or supply of agricultural produce and are expected to bear produce for more than one period. The June 2014 Amendment includes bearer plants within the scope of IAS 16. Consequently, entities would be permitted to choose either the cost model or the revaluation model for bearer plants. All other biological assets related to agricultural activity will remain under the fair value model in IAS 41, including bearer animals.

The importance of fair value information for biological assets

DO4   Fundamentally, IAS 41 is a Standard on accounting for biological transformation. Biological transformation of bearer assets occurs both prior to maturity and after maturity. A cost model ignores biological transformation when it occurs. That is why IAS 41 requires fair value measurement. The Basis for Conclusions of IAS 41 states:

> "Those who support fair value measurement argue that the effects of changes brought about by biological transformation are best reflected by reference to the fair value changes in biological assets. They believe that fair value changes in biological assets have a direct relationship to changes in expectations of future economic benefits to the entity."

Mr Finnegan and Ms McConnell see no reason to abandon that principle with respect to bearer plants. Consequently, they do not agree that prior to maturity, bearer plants should be measured at accumulated cost. They do not believe that accounting for bearer plants in the same way as for self-constructed items of property, plant and equipment will provide users of financial statements with information that is useful to an understanding of the agricultural entity's performance for the period or of its productive capacity at a point in time.

DO5   While maturing, bearer plants are undergoing biological transformation. Mr Finnegan and Ms McConnell continue to believe that fair value measurement for the biological transformation process provides the best information about bearer assets' quality and quantitative changes during their growth period. They also believe that the fair value of bearer plants at maturity provides the best measure of an entity's resources being placed into the production of produce at maturity. Investors need that information to assess management's stewardship of the resources invested in the production process and the performance of the entity using those resources. Consequently, they believe that bearer plants must be measured at fair value while maturing because fair value provides users of financial statements with the best information about an important aspect of an agricultural entity's performance and management stewardship.

DO6   They also reject the view that biological transformation of bearer assets is no longer a key element for understanding the future net cash flows to an entity once such assets reach maturity. By definition, biological transformation is not limited to merely the growth process to maturity, but also includes the cycles of production and degeneration, which are critical phases in the life cycle of bearer assets. Fair value measurements of bearer assets throughout their lives provide information about the effectiveness and efficiency of the production process, and about the capability of such assets to generate net cash inflows into the future. In contrast, depreciation of the cost of a mature bearer asset only approximates the biological transformation of a bearer asset throughout its productive life and has only an indirect relationship, at best, to changes in future net cash inflows.

Effects of the use of fair value measurement

DO7   Mr Finnegan and Ms McConnell acknowledge that measuring bearer plants at fair value may sometimes be difficult. In particular, the Board has been told that the fair value of bearer plants is particularly subjective during the early years of their life cycle. However, Mr Finnegan and Ms McConnell note that IAS 41 contains an exception from fair value for biological assets for which quoted market prices are not available and for which alternative fair value measurements are determined to be clearly unreliable on initial recognition. They believe that this exception is sufficient to deal with the concerns about the reliability of fair value measures of bearer plants during the early years of their life cycle. They also note that entities throughout the world have been applying IAS 41 in a wide variety of agricultural activities since 2003. In fact, some national accounting standards required or recommended measurement of bearer assets at fair values even before IAS 41 was issued. They do not believe that measuring fair value of bearer plants, in general, is any more difficult than measuring fair value for other biological assets such as bearer animals. Furthermore, they believe that applying a cost measure to bearer plants may be equally as difficult in some situations. Fair value measurements are required in assessing bearer plants for impairment, and surely those who are urging a reversion to a cost model for bearer assets would not suggest that impairment should be ignored because fair value measurement may sometimes be difficult. Moreover, the June 2014 Amendment would permit fair value measurements as a pure accounting policy choice. Mr Finnegan and Ms McConnell believe that accounting should reflect underlying economic circumstances and should not merely be left to choice. The existing fair value exception in IAS 41 is based on circumstances (measurement reliability), and is not an accounting policy choice.

DO8   In addition to concerns about the reliability of fair value measures, entities with bearer assets expressed concern about the volatility that arises from recognising changes in the fair value of the bearer plants in profit or loss and said that users of financial statements adjust reported profit or loss to eliminate the effects of changes in fair values of bearer biological assets. Mr Finnegan and Ms McConnell accept the view that the use of fair value for bearer assets makes the analysis of profit or loss and financial position more difficult. At the same time, they note that price volatility is an indicator of risk, and risk assessment is part of an analyst's job. Mr Finnegan and Ms McConnell note that sound financial statement analysis will always adjust reported profit or loss and financial position for the effects of unusual or non-recurring changes in reported information. However, if critical information about changes in the economic benefits arising in an agricultural operation is not reported, such analysis is impaired or not possible at all.

DO9   Mr Finnegan and Ms McConnell believe that instead of ignoring the fair value volatility, which a cost model does, volatility should be addressed as a matter of financial statement presentation—such as by putting the fair value changes in other comprehensive income. They note that under the June 2014 Amendment, the bearer assets will be within the scope of IAS 16 and revaluation will be permitted. If an entity were to choose revaluation, the change in the revaluation amount (which approximates fair value) would be reported in other comprehensive income. Consequently, they believe that requiring fair value measurement during the entirety of the bearer plant's life cycle with the fair value changes reported in other comprehensive income would be consistent with permitting revaluation of the bearer asset. Furthermore, Mr Finnegan and Ms McConnell believe that such a change would preserve relevant information for investors through prominent display in the primary financial statements, while addressing the concerns of those who believe that fair value changes distort profit or loss.

Current proposals are not improvements to IFRS

DO10   Mr Finnegan and Ms McConnell believe that if bearer assets are measured at accumulated cost, then at a minimum, the fair value of the bearer plants should be a required disclosure, including information about the valuation techniques and key inputs/assumptions used. However, the 2014 Amendment is not requiring disclosure of fair value. Consequently, critical information is being eliminated from the financial statements of entities engaged in agricultural activities using bearer assets. Mr Finnegan and Ms McConnell do not believe that this is an improvement to financial reporting. In January 2013, the Trustees of the IFRS Foundation approved a new *Due Process Handbook* that specifies, among other things, the criteria for new Standards or major improvements. The main criteria (in addition to pervasiveness of the issue) are (a) whether there is a deficiency in the way particular types of transactions or activities are reported in financial reports, and (b) the importance of the matter to those who use financial reports. Mr Finnegan and Ms McConnell believe that, from a user perspective, there is no deficiency in the accounting for, and disclosures about, bearer assets in IAS 41 and that fair value information is important (indeed essential) to those who use the financial reports of entities engaged in agricultural activity.

DO11   In the user outreach performed by the staff, most investors and analysts said that fair value information about bearer plants is of either limited or no use to them *without* fair value information about the related land, agricultural machinery, etc. Instead of meeting the needs of users by providing this additional fair value information to make the fair value of bearer plants more useful, the Board has chosen to withdraw the requirement to provide the fair value of bearer plants. In the view of Mr Finnegan and Ms McConnell this solution does not adequately address the needs of users of financial statements.

DO12   A better solution would have been for the Board to require the fair value of bearer plants in combination with the fair value of the land to which such plants are attached. One of the weaknesses in IAS 41 is that it does not require the use of fair value to measure land to which bearer plants are attached. This is a weakness because the value of bearer plants is inextricably tied to the value of the land. By understanding the value of the bearer plants and the land, investors know the true potential of an entity's future net cash inflows. A historical cost model for either or both is incapable of providing such information.

DO13   As just discussed, Mr Finnegan and Ms McConnell do not believe the June 2014 Amendment represents an improvement to IFRS and, in fact, represents a step towards lowering the quality of the information available in the financial statements of entities engaged in agricultural activities. The June 2014 Amendment therefore fails to meet the Board's own criteria for a new or amended Standard.

Documents published to accompany

IFRIC 1

Changes in Existing Decommissioning, Restoration and Similar Liabilities

The text of the unaccompanied Interpretation, IFRIC 1, is contained in Part A of this edition. Its effective date when issued was 1 September 2004. The text of the Accompanying Guidance on IFRIC 1 is contained in Part B of this edition. This part presents the following documents:

BASIS FOR CONCLUSIONS

BC2   IAS 16 Property, Plant and Equipment requires the cost of an item of property, plant and equipment to include the initial estimate of the costs of dismantling and removing an asset and restoring the site on which it is located, the obligation for which an entity incurs either when the item is acquired or as a consequence of having used the item during a particular period for purposes other than to produce inventories during that period.

BC3   IAS 37 Provisions, Contingent Liabilities and Contingent Assets requires that the measurement of the liability, both initially and subsequently, should be the estimated expenditure required to settle the present obligation at the balance sheet date, end of the reporting period and should reflect a current market-based discount rate. It requires provisions to be reviewed at each balance sheet date the end of each reporting period and adjusted to reflect the current best estimate. Hence, when the effect of a change in estimated outflows of resources embodying economic benefits and/or the discount rate is material, that change should be recognised.

BC4   The IFRIC was asked to address how to account for changes in decommissioning, restoration and similar liabilities. The issue is whether changes in the liability should be recognised in current period profit or loss, or added to (or deducted from) the cost of the related asset. IAS 16 contains requirements for the initial capitalisation of decommissioning costs and IAS 37 contains requirements for measuring the resulting liability; neither specifically addresses accounting for the effect of changes in the liability. The IFRIC was informed that different views exist, resulting in a risk of divergent practices developing.

BC5   Accordingly, the IFRIC decided to develop guidance on accounting for the changes. In so doing, the IFRIC recognised that the measurement of the liability is inherently subjective, and its settlement may be very far in the future, and estimating the timing and amount of the outflow of resources embodying economic benefits required to settle the obligation and/or the discount rate often involves the exercise of considerable judgement. Hence, it is likely that revisions to the initial estimate will be made.

Basis for Conclusions on
IFRIC Interpretation 1 *Changes in Existing Decommissioning, Restoration and Similar Liabilities*

This Basis for Conclusions accompanies, but is not part of, IFRIC 1.

The original text has been marked up to reflect the revision of IAS 1 Presentation of Financial Statements *in 2007: new text is underlined and deleted text is struck through.*

Introduction

BC1   This Basis for Conclusions summarises the IFRIC's considerations in reaching its consensus. Individual IFRIC members gave greater weight to some factors than to others.

Background

BC2   IAS 16 *Property, Plant and Equipment* requires the cost of an item of property, plant and equipment to include the initial estimate of the costs of dismantling and removing an asset and restoring the site on which it is located, the obligation for which an entity incurs either when the item is acquired or as a consequence of having used the item during a particular period for purposes other than to produce inventories during that period.

BC3   IAS 37 *Provisions, Contingent Liabilities and Contingent Assets* requires that the measurement of the liability, both initially and subsequently, should be the estimated expenditure required to settle the present obligation at the ~~balance sheet date~~ end of the reporting period and should reflect a current market-based discount rate. It requires provisions to be reviewed at ~~each balance sheet date~~ the end of each reporting period and adjusted to reflect the current best estimate. Hence, when the effect of a change in estimated outflows of resources embodying economic benefits and/or the discount rate is material, that change should be recognised.

BC4   The IFRIC was asked to address how to account for changes in decommissioning, restoration and similar liabilities. The issue is whether changes in the liability should be recognised in current period profit or loss, or added to (or deducted from) the cost of the related asset. IAS 16 contains requirements for the initial capitalisation of decommissioning costs and IAS 37 contains requirements for measuring the resulting liability; neither specifically addresses accounting for the effect of changes in the liability. The IFRIC was informed that differing views exist, resulting in a risk of divergent practices developing.

BC5   Accordingly, the IFRIC decided to develop guidance on accounting for the changes. In so doing, the IFRIC recognised that the estimation of the liability is inherently subjective, since its settlement may be very far in the future and estimating (a) the timing and amount of the outflow of resources embodying economic benefits (eg cash flows) required to settle the obligation and (b) the discount rate often involves the exercise of considerable judgement. Hence, it is likely that revisions to the initial estimate will be made.

Scope

BC6　The scope of the Interpretation addresses the accounting for changes in estimates of existing liabilities to dismantle, remove and restore items of property, plant and equipment that fall within the scope of IAS 16 and are recognised as a provision under IAS 37. The Interpretation does not apply to changes in estimated liabilities in respect of costs that fall within the scope of other IFRSs, for example, inventory or production costs that fall within the scope of IAS 2 *Inventories*. The IFRIC noted that decommissioning obligations associated with the extraction of minerals are a cost either of the property, plant and equipment used to extract them, in which case they are within the scope of IAS 16 and the Interpretation, or of the inventory produced, which should be accounted for under IAS 2.

Basis for Consensus

BC7　The IFRIC reached a consensus that changes in an existing decommissioning, restoration or similar liability that result from changes in the estimated timing or amount of the outflow of resources embodying economic benefits required to settle the obligation, or a change in the discount rate, should be added to or deducted from the cost of the related asset and depreciated prospectively over its useful life.

BC8　In developing its consensus, the IFRIC also considered the following three alternative approaches for accounting for changes in the outflow of resources embodying economic benefits and changes in the discount rate:

(a)　capitalising only the effect of a change in the outflow of resources embodying economic benefits that relate to future periods, and recognising in current period profit or loss all of the effect of a change in the discount rate.

(b)　recognising in current period profit or loss the effect of all changes in both the outflow of resources embodying economic benefits and the discount rate.

(c)　treating changes in an estimated decommissioning, restoration and similar liability as revisions to the initial liability and the cost of the asset. Under this approach, amounts relating to the depreciation of the asset that would have been recognised to date would be reflected in current period profit or loss and amounts relating to future depreciation would be capitalised.

BC9　The IFRIC rejected alternative (a), because this approach does not treat changes in the outflow of resources embodying economic benefits and in the discount rate in the same way, which the IFRIC agreed is important, given that matters such as inflation can affect both the outflow of economic benefits and the discount rate.

BC10　In considering alternative (b), the IFRIC observed that recognising all of the change in the discount rate in current period profit or loss correctly treats a change in the discount rate as an event of the present period. However, the

IFRIC decided against alternative (b) because recognising changes in the estimated outflow of resources embodying economic benefits in current period profit or loss would be inconsistent with the initial capitalisation of decommissioning costs under IAS 16.

BC11   Alternative (c) was the approach proposed in draft Interpretation D2 *Changes in Decommissioning, Restoration and Similar Liabilities*, published on 4 September 2003. In making that proposal, the IFRIC regarded the asset, from the time the liability for decommissioning is first incurred until the end of the asset's useful life, as the unit of account to which decommissioning costs relate. It therefore took the view that revisions to the estimates of those costs, whether through revisions to estimated outflows of resources embodying economic benefits or revisions to the discount rate, ought to be accounted for in the same manner as the initial estimated cost. The IFRIC still sees merit in this proposal, but concluded on balance that, under current standards, full prospective capitalisation should be required for the reasons set out in paragraphs BC12–BC18.

IAS 8 and a change in accounting estimate

BC12   IAS 8 *Accounting Policies, Changes in Accounting Estimates and Errors* requires an entity to recognise a change in an accounting estimate prospectively by including it in profit or loss in the period of the change, if the change affects that period only, or the period of the change and future periods, if the change affects both. To the extent that a change in an accounting estimate gives rise to changes in assets or liabilities, or relates to an item of equity, it is required to be recognised by adjusting the asset, liability or equity item in the period of change.

BC13   Although the IFRIC took the view that the partly retrospective treatment proposed in D2 is consistent with these requirements of IAS 8, most responses to the draft Interpretation suggested that IAS 8 would usually be interpreted as requiring a fully prospective treatment. The IFRIC agreed that IAS 8 would support a fully prospective treatment also, and this is what the Interpretation requires.

IAS 16 and changes in accounting estimates for property, plant and equipment

BC14   Many responses to the draft Interpretation argued that the proposal in D2 was inconsistent with IAS 16, which requires other kinds of change in estimate for property, plant and equipment to be dealt with prospectively. For example, as IAS 8 also acknowledges, a change in the estimated useful life of, or the expected pattern of consumption of the future economic benefits embodied in, a depreciable asset affects depreciation expense for the current period and for each future period during the asset's remaining useful life. In both cases, the effect of the change relating to the current period is recognised in profit or loss in the current period. The effect, if any, on future periods is recognised in profit or loss in those future periods.

BC15   Some responses to the draft Interpretation noted that a change in the estimate of a residual value is accounted for prospectively and does not require a catch-up adjustment. They observed that liabilities relating to decommissioning costs can be regarded as negative residual values, and suggested that the Interpretation should not introduce inconsistent treatment for similar events. Anomalies could result if two aspects of the same change are dealt with differently—for example, if the useful life of an asset was extended and the present value of the decommissioning liability reduced as a result.

BC16   The IFRIC agreed that it had not made a sufficient case for treating changes in estimates of decommissioning and similar liabilities differently from other changes in estimates for property, plant and equipment. The IFRIC understood that there was no likelihood of the treatment of other changes in estimate for such assets being revisited in the near future.

BC17   The IFRIC also noted that the anomalies that could result from its original proposal, if other changes in estimate were dealt with prospectively, were more serious than it had understood previously, and that a fully prospective treatment would be easier to apply consistently.

BC18   The IFRIC had been concerned that a fully prospective treatment could result in either unrealistically large assets or negative assets, particularly if there are large changes in estimates toward the end of an asset's life. The IFRIC noted that the first concern could be dealt with if the assets were reviewed for impairment in accordance with IAS 36 *Impairment of Assets*, and that a zero asset floor could be applied to ensure that an asset did not become negative if cost estimates reduced significantly towards the end of its life. The credit would first be applied to write the carrying amount of the asset down to nil and then any residual credit adjustment would be recognised in profit or loss. These safeguards are included in the final consensus.

Comparison with US GAAP

BC19   In reaching its consensus, the IFRIC considered the US GAAP approach in Statement of Financial Accounting Standards No. 143, *Accounting for Asset Retirement Obligations* (SFAS 143). Under that standard, changes in estimated cash flows are capitalised as part of the cost of the asset and depreciated prospectively, but the decommissioning obligation is not required to be revised to reflect the effect of a change in the current market-assessed discount rate.

BC20   The treatment of changes in estimated cash flows required by this Interpretation is consistent with US GAAP, which the proposal in D2 was not. However, the IFRIC agreed that because IAS 37 requires a decommissioning obligation to reflect the effect of a change in the current market-based discount rate (see paragraph BC3), it was not possible to disregard changes in the discount rate. Furthermore, SFAS 143 did not treat changes in cash flows and discount rates in the same way, which the IFRIC had agreed was important.

The interaction of the Interpretation and initial recognition under IAS 16

BC21   In developing the Interpretation, the IFRIC considered the improvements that have been made to IAS 16 by the Board and agreed that it would explain the interaction of the two.

BC22   IAS 16 (as revised in 2003) clarifies that the initial measurement of the cost of an item of property, plant and equipment should include the cost of dismantling and removing the item and restoring the site on which it is located, if this obligation is incurred either when the item is acquired or as a consequence of having used the item during a particular period for purposes other than to produce inventories during that period. This is because the Board concluded that whether the obligation is incurred upon acquisition of the item or as a consequence of using it, the underlying nature of the cost and its association with the asset are the same.

BC23   However, in considering the improvements to IAS 16, the Board did not address how an entity would account for (a) changes in the amount of the initial estimate of a recognised obligation, (b) the effects of accretion of, or changes in interest rates on, a recognised obligation or (c) the cost of obligations that did not exist when the entity acquired the item, such as an obligation triggered by a change in a law enacted after the asset is acquired. The Interpretation addresses issues (a) and (b).

The interaction of the Interpretation and the choice of measurement model under IAS 16

BC24   IAS 16 allows an entity to choose either the cost model or the revaluation model for measuring its property, plant and equipment, on a class-by-class basis. The IFRIC's view is that the measurement model that an entity chooses under IAS 16 would not be affected by the Interpretation.

BC25   Several responses to the draft Interpretation sought clarification of how it should be applied to revalued assets. The IFRIC noted that:

(a)   if the entity chooses the revaluation model, IAS 16 requires the valuation to be kept sufficiently up to date that the carrying amount does not differ materially from that which would be determined using fair value at the balance sheet date.[1] This Interpretation requires a change in a recognised decommissioning, restoration or similar liability generally to be added to or deducted from the cost of the asset. However, a change in the liability does not, of itself, affect the *valuation* of the asset for financial reporting purposes, because (to ensure that it is not counted twice) the separately recognised liability is excluded from its valuation.

(b)   rather than changing the valuation of the asset, a change in the liability affects the difference between what would have been reported for the asset under the cost model, under this Interpretation, and its valuation. In other words, it changes the revaluation surplus or deficit that has previously been recognised for the asset. For example, if the liability increases by CU20, which under the cost model would have been added to the cost of the asset, the revaluation surplus reduces (or the revaluation deficit increases) by CU20. Under the revaluation model set out in IAS 16, cumulative revaluation surpluses for an asset are

---

1   IAS 1 *Presentation of Financial Statements* (revised 2007) replaced the term 'balance sheet date' with 'end of the reporting period'.

accounted for in equity,[2] and cumulative revaluation deficits are accounted for in profit or loss. The IFRIC decided that changes in the liability relating to a revalued asset should be accounted for in the same way as other changes in revaluation surpluses and deficits under IAS 16.

(c) although a change in the liability does not directly affect the value of the asset for financial reporting purposes, many events that change the value of the liability may also affect the value of the asset, by either a greater or lesser amount. The IFRIC therefore decided that, for revalued assets, a change in a decommissioning liability indicates that a revaluation may be required. Any such revaluation should be taken into account in determining the amount taken to profit or loss under (b) above. If a revaluation is done, IAS 16 requires all assets of the same class to be revalued.

(d) the depreciated cost of an asset (less any impairment) should not be negative, regardless of the valuation model, and the revaluation surplus on an asset should not exceed its value. The IFRIC therefore decided that, if the reduction in a liability exceeds the carrying amount that would have been recognised had the asset been carried under the cost model, the excess reduction should always be taken to profit or loss. For example, if the depreciated cost of an unimpaired asset is CU25, and its revalued amount is CU100, there is a revaluation surplus of CU75. If the decommissioning liability associated with the asset is reduced by CU30, the depreciated cost of the asset should be reduced to nil, the revaluation surplus should be increased to CU100 (which equals the value of the asset), and the remaining CU5 of the reduction in the liability should be taken to profit or loss.

The unwinding of the discount

BC26 The IFRIC considered whether the unwinding of the discount is a borrowing cost for the purposes of IAS 23 *Borrowing Costs*. This question arises because if the unwinding of the discount rate were deemed a borrowing cost for the purposes of IAS 23, in certain circumstances this amount might be capitalised under the allowed alternative treatment of capitalisation.[3] The IFRIC noted that IAS 23 addresses funds borrowed specifically for the purpose of obtaining a particular asset. It agreed that a decommissioning liability does not fall within this description since it does not reflect funds (ie cash) borrowed. Hence, the IFRIC concluded that the unwinding of the discount is not a borrowing cost as defined in IAS 23.

BC27 The IFRIC agreed that the unwinding of the discount as referred to in paragraph 60 of IAS 37 should be reported in profit or loss in the period it occurs.

---

2 As a consequence of the revision of IAS 1 *Presentation of Financial Statements* in 2007 the increase is recognised in other comprehensive income and accumulated in equity under the heading of revaluation surplus.

3 In March 2007, IAS 23 was revised to require the previously allowed alternative treatment of capitalisation. Capitalisation of borrowing costs for a qualifying asset becomes the only accounting treatment. That revision does not affect the reasoning set out in this Basis for Conclusions.

Disclosures

BC28   The IFRIC considered whether the Interpretation should include disclosure guidance and agreed that it was largely unnecessary because IAS 16 and IAS 37 contain relevant guidance, for example:

(a)   IAS 16 explains that IAS 8 requires the disclosure of the nature and effect of changes in accounting estimates that have an effect in the current period or are expected to have a material effect in subsequent periods, and that such disclosure may arise from changes in the estimated costs of dismantling, removing or restoring items of property, plant and equipment.

(b)   IAS 37 requires the disclosure of:

(i)   a reconciliation of the movements in the carrying amount of the provision for the period.

(ii)   the increase during the period in the discounted amount arising from the passage of time and the effect of any change in the discount rate.

(iii)   a brief description of the nature of the obligation and the expected timing of any resulting outflows of economic benefits.

(iv)   an indication of the uncertainties about the amount or timing of those outflows, and where necessary the disclosure of the major assumptions made concerning future events (eg future interest rates, future changes in salaries, and future changes in prices).

BC29   However, in respect of assets measured using the revaluation model, the IFRIC noted that changes in the liability would often be taken to the revaluation surplus. These changes reflect an event of significance to users, and the IFRIC agreed that they should be given prominence by being separately disclosed and described as such in the statement of changes in equity.[4]

Transition

BC30   The IFRIC agreed that preparers that already apply IFRSs should apply the Interpretation in the manner required by IAS 8, which is usually retrospectively. The IFRIC could not justify another application method, especially when IAS 37 requires retrospective application.

BC31   The IFRIC noted that, in order to apply the Interpretation retrospectively, it is necessary to determine both the timing and amount of any changes that would have been required by the Interpretation. However, IAS 8 specifies that:

(a)   if retrospective application is not practicable for all periods presented, the new accounting policy shall be applied retrospectively from the earliest practicable date; and

---

4   As a consequence of the revision of IAS 1 *Presentation of Financial Statements* in 2007 such changes are presented in the statement of comprehensive income.

(b)   if it is impracticable to determine the cumulative effect of applying the new accounting policy at the start of the current period, the policy shall be applied prospectively from the earliest date practicable.

BC32   The IFRIC noted that IAS 8 defines a requirement as impracticable when an entity cannot apply it after making every reasonable effort to do so, and gives guidance on when this is so.

BC33   However, the provisions of IAS 8 on practicability do not apply to IFRS 1 *First-time Adoption of International Financial Reporting Standards*. Retrospective application of this Interpretation at the date of transition to IFRSs, which is the treatment required by IFRS 1 in the absence of any exemptions, would require first-time adopters to construct a historical record of all such adjustments that would have been made in the past. In many cases this will not be practicable. The IFRIC agreed that, as an alternative to retrospective application, an entity should be permitted to include in the depreciated cost of the asset at the date of transition an amount calculated by discounting the liability at that date back to, and depreciating it from, when it was first incurred. This Interpretation amends IFRS 1 accordingly.

Document published to accompany
IFRIC 2

Members' Shares in Co-operative Entities and Similar Instruments

The text of the unaccompanied Interpretation, IFRIC 2, is contained in Part A of this edition. Its effective date when issued was 1 September 2004. This part presents the following documents:

BASIS FOR CONCLUSIONS

Basis for Conclusions on
IFRIC Interpretation 2 *Members' Shares in Co-operative Entities and Similar Instruments*

This Basis for Conclusions accompanies, but is not part of, IFRIC 2.

Introduction

BC1   This Basis for Conclusions summarises the IFRIC's considerations in reaching its consensus. Individual IFRIC members gave greater weight to some factors than to others.

Background

BC2   In September 2001, the Standing Interpretations Committee instituted by the former International Accounting Standards Committee (IASC) published Draft Interpretation SIC D-34 *Financial Instruments – Instruments or Rights Redeemable by the Holder*. The Draft Interpretation stated: 'The issuer of a Puttable Instrument should classify the entire instrument as a liability.'

BC3   In 2001 the International Accounting Standards Board (IASB) began operations in succession to IASC. The IASB's initial agenda included a project to make limited amendments to the financial instruments standards issued by IASC. The IASB decided to incorporate the consensus from Draft Interpretation D-34 as part of those amendments. In June 2002 the IASB published an exposure draft of amendments to IAS 32 *Financial Instruments: Disclosure and Presentation* that incorporated the proposed consensus from Draft Interpretation D-34.

BC4   In their responses to the Exposure Draft and in their participation in public round-table discussions held in March 2003, representatives of co-operative banks raised questions about the application of the principles in IAS 32 to members' shares. This was followed by a series of meetings between IASB members and staff and representatives of the European Association of Co-operative Banks. After considering questions raised by the bank group, the IASB concluded that the principles articulated in IAS 32 should not be modified, but that there were questions about the application of those principles to co-operative entities that should be considered by the IFRIC.

BC5   In considering the application of IAS 32 to co-operative entities, the IFRIC recognised that a variety of entities operate as co-operatives and these entities have a variety of capital structures. The IFRIC decided that its proposed Interpretation should address some features that exist in a number of co-operatives. However, the IFRIC noted that its conclusions and the examples in the Interpretation are not limited to the specific characteristics of members' shares in European co-operative banks.

Basis for consensus

BC6   Paragraph 15 of IAS 32 states:

> The issuer of a financial instrument shall classify the instrument, or its component parts, on initial recognition as a financial liability, a financial asset or an equity instrument in accordance with the *substance of the contractual arrangement* and the definitions of a financial liability, a financial asset and an equity instrument. [Emphasis added]

BC7   In many jurisdictions, local law or regulations state that members' shares are equity of the entity. However, paragraph 17 of IAS 32 states:

> With the exception of the circumstances described in paragraphs 16A and 16B or paragraphs 16C and 16D, a critical feature in differentiating a financial liability from an equity instrument is *the existence of a contractual obligation of one party to the financial instrument (the issuer) either to deliver cash or another financial asset to the other party (the holder)* or to exchange financial assets or financial liabilities with the holder under conditions that are potentially unfavourable to the issuer. Although the holder of an equity instrument may be entitled to receive a pro rata share of any dividends or other distributions of equity, the issuer does not have a contractual obligation to make such distributions because it cannot be required to deliver cash or another financial asset to another party. [Emphasis added]

BC8   Paragraphs cited in the examples in the Appendix and in the paragraphs above show that, under IAS 32, the terms of the contractual agreement govern the classification of a financial instrument as a financial liability or equity. If the terms of an instrument create an unconditional obligation to transfer cash or another financial asset, circumstances that might restrict an entity's ability to make the transfer when due do not alter the classification as a financial liability. If the terms of the instrument give the entity an unconditional right to avoid delivering cash or another financial asset, the instrument is classified as equity. This is true even if other factors make it likely that the entity will continue to distribute dividends or make or other payments. In view of those principles, the IFRIC decided to focus on circumstances that would indicate that the entity has the unconditional right to avoid making payments to a member who has requested that his or her shares be redeemed.

BC9   The IFRIC identified two situations in which a co-operative entity has an unconditional right to avoid the transfer of cash or another financial asset. The IFRIC acknowledges that there may be other situations that may raise questions about the application of IAS 32 to members' shares. However, it understands that the two situations are often present in the contractual and other conditions surrounding members' shares and that interpretation of those two situations would eliminate many of the questions that may arise in practice.

BC10   The IFRIC also noted that an entity assesses whether it has an unconditional right to avoid the transfer of cash or another financial asset on the basis of local laws, regulations and its governing charter in effect at the date of classification. This is because it is local laws, regulations and the governing charter in effect at the classification date, together with the terms contained in the instrument's documentation that constitute the terms and conditions of the instrument at that date. Accordingly, an entity does not take into account expected future amendments to local law, regulation or its governing charter.

The right to refuse redemption (paragraph 7)

BC11 An entity may have the unconditional right to refuse redemption of a member's shares. If such a right exists, the entity does not have the obligation to transfer cash or another financial asset that IAS 32 identifies as a critical characteristic of a financial liability.

BC12 The IFRIC considered whether the entity's history of making redemptions should be considered in deciding whether the entity's right to refuse requests is, in fact, unconditional. The IFRIC observed that a history of making redemptions may create a reasonable expectation that all future requests will be honoured. However, holders of many equity instruments have a reasonable expectation that an entity will continue a past practice of making payments. For example, an entity may have made dividend payments on preference shares for decades. Failure to make those payments would expose the entity to significant economic costs, including damage to the value of its ordinary shares. Nevertheless, as outlined in IAS 32 paragraph AG26 (cited in paragraph A3), a holder's expectations about dividends do not cause a preferred share to be classified as a financial liability.

Prohibitions against redemption (paragraphs 8 and 9)

BC13 An entity may be prohibited by law or its governing charter from redeeming members' shares if doing so would cause the number of members' shares, or the amount of paid-in capital from members' shares, to fall below a specified level. While each individual share might be puttable, a portion of the total shares outstanding is not.

BC14 The IFRIC concluded that conditions limiting an entity's ability to redeem members' shares must be evaluated sequentially. Unconditional prohibitions like those noted in paragraph 8 of the consensus prevent the entity from *incurring a liability* for redemption of all or some of the members' shares, regardless of whether it would otherwise be able to satisfy that financial liability. This contrasts with conditional prohibitions that prevent payments being made only if specified conditions—such as liquidity constraints—are met. Unconditional prohibitions prevent a liability from coming into existence, whereas the conditional prohibitions may only defer the payment of a liability already incurred. Following this analysis, an unconditional prohibition affects classification when an instrument subject to the prohibition is issued or when the prohibition is enacted or added to the entity's governing charter. In contrast, conditional restrictions such as those described in paragraphs 19 and AG25 of IAS 32 do not result in equity classification.

BC15 The IFRIC discussed whether the requirements in IAS 32 can be applied to the classification of members' shares as a whole subject to a partial redemption prohibition. IAS 32 refers to 'a financial instrument', 'a financial liability' and 'an equity instrument'. It does not refer to groups or portfolios of instruments. In view of this the IFRIC considered whether it could apply the requirements in IAS 32 to the classification of members' shares subject to partial redemption prohibitions. The application of IAS 32 to a prohibition against redeeming some portion of members' shares (eg 500,000 shares of an entity with 1,000,000 shares outstanding) is unclear.

BC16   The IFRIC noted that classifying a group of members' shares using the individual instrument approach could lead to misapplication of the principle of 'substance of the contract' in IAS 32. The IFRIC also noted that paragraph 23 of IAS 32 requires an entity that has entered into an agreement to purchase its own equity instruments to recognise a financial liability for the present value of the redemption amount (eg for the present value of the forward repurchase price, option exercise price or other redemption amount) even though the shares subject to the repurchase agreement are not individually identified. Accordingly, the IFRIC decided that for purposes of classification there are instances when IAS 32 does not require the individual instrument approach.

BC17   In many situations, looking at either individual instruments or all of the instruments governed by a particular contract would result in the same classification as financial liability or equity under IAS 32. Thus, if an entity is prohibited from redeeming any of its members' shares, the shares are not puttable and are equity. On the other hand, if there is no prohibition on redemption and no other conditions apply, members' shares are puttable and the shares are financial liabilities. However, in the case of partial prohibitions against redemption, the classification of members' shares governed by the same charter will differ, depending on whether such a classification is based on individual members' shares or the group of members' shares as a whole. For example, consider an entity with a partial prohibition that prevents it from redeeming 99 per cent of the highest number of members' shares ever outstanding. The classification based on individual shares considers each share to be potentially puttable and therefore a financial liability. This is different from the classification based on all of the members' shares. While each member's share may be redeemable individually, 99 per cent of the highest number of shares ever outstanding is not redeemable in any circumstances other than liquidation of the entity and therefore is equity.

Measurement on initial recognition (paragraph 10)

BC18   The IFRIC noted that when the financial liability for the redemption of members' shares that are redeemable on demand is initially recognised, the financial liability is measured at fair value in accordance with paragraph 49 of IAS 39 *Financial Instruments: Recognition and Measurement*.[1] Paragraph 49 states: 'The fair value of a financial liability with a demand feature (eg a demand deposit) is not less than the amount payable on demand, discounted from the first date that the amount could be required to be paid'. Accordingly, the IFRIC decided that the fair value of the financial liability for redemption of members' shares redeemable on demand is the maximum amount payable under the redemption provisions of its governing charter or applicable law. The IFRIC also considered situations in which the number of members' shares or the amount of paid-in capital subject to prohibition against redemption may change. The IFRIC

---

1   IFRS 9 *Financial Instruments* replaced IAS 39. Paragraph 49 of IAS 39 was ultimately relocated to paragraph 47 of IFRS 13 *Fair Value Measurement*. Paragraph BC18 refers to matters relevant when IFRIC 2 was issued.

concluded that a change in the level of a prohibition against redemption should lead to a transfer between financial liabilities and equity.

Subsequent measurement

BC19   Some respondents requested additional guidance on subsequent measurement of the liability for redemption of members' shares. The IFRIC noted that the focus of this Interpretation was on clarifying the classification of financial instruments rather than their subsequent measurement. Also, the IASB has on its agenda a project to address the accounting for financial instruments (including members' shares) that are redeemable at a pro rata share of the fair value of the residual interest in the entity issuing the financial instrument. The IASB will consider certain measurement issues in this project. The IFRIC was also informed that the majority of members' shares in co-operative entities are not redeemable at a pro rata share of the fair value of the residual interest in the co-operative entity thereby obviating the more complex measurement issues. In view of the above, the IFRIC decided not to provide additional guidance on measurement in the Interpretation.

Presentation

BC20   The IFRIC noted that entities whose members' shares are not equity could use the presentation formats included in paragraphs IE32 and IE33 of the Illustrative Examples with IAS 32.

Alternatives considered

BC21   The IFRIC considered suggestions that:

(a)   members' shares should be classified as equity until a member has requested redemption. That member's share would then be classified as a financial liability and this treatment would be consistent with local laws. Some commentators believe this is a more straightforward approach to classification.

(b)   the classification of members' shares should incorporate the probability that members will request redemption. Those who suggest this view observe that experience shows this probability to be small, usually within 1–5 per cent, for some types of co-operative. They see no basis for classifying 100 per cent of the members' shares as liabilities on the basis of the behaviour of 1 per cent.

BC22   The IFRIC did not accept those views. Under IAS 32, the classification of an instrument as financial liability or equity is based on the 'substance of the contractual arrangement and the definitions of a financial liability, a financial asset and an equity instrument.' In paragraph BC7 of the Basis for Conclusions on IAS 32, the IASB observed:

> Although the legal form of such financial instruments often includes a right to the residual interest in the assets of an entity available to holders of such instruments, the inclusion of an option for the holder to put the instrument back to the entity for cash or another financial asset means that the instrument meets the definition of a financial liability. The classification as a financial liability is independent of

considerations such as when the right is exercisable, how the amount payable or receivable upon exercise of the right is determined, and whether the puttable instrument has a fixed maturity.

BC23　The IFRIC also observed that an approach similar to that in paragraph BC21(a) is advocated in the Dissenting Opinion of one Board member on IAS 32. As the IASB did not adopt that approach its adoption here would require an amendment to IAS 32.

Transition and effective date (paragraph 14)

BC24　The IFRIC considered whether its Interpretation should have the same transition and effective date as IAS 32, or whether a later effective date should apply with an exemption from IAS 32 for members' shares in the interim. Some co-operatives may wish to amend their governing charter in order to continue their existing practice under national accounting requirements of classifying members' shares as equity. Such amendments usually require a general meeting of members and holding a meeting may not be possible before the effective date of IAS 32.

BC25　After considering a number of alternatives, the IFRIC decided against any exemption from the transition requirements and effective date in IAS 32. In reaching this conclusion, the IFRIC noted that it was requested to provide guidance on the application of IAS 32 when it is first adopted by co-operative entities, ie from 1 January 2005. Also, the vast majority of those who commented on the draft Interpretation did not object to the proposed effective date of 1 January 2005. Finally, the IFRIC observed that classifying members' shares as financial liabilities before the date that the terms of these shares are amended will affect only 2005 financial statements, as first-time adopters are not required to apply IAS 32 to earlier periods. As a result, any effect of the Interpretation on first-time adopters is expected to be limited. Furthermore, the IFRIC noted that regulators are familiar with the accounting issues involved. A co-operative entity may be required to present members' shares as a liability until the governing charter is amended. The IFRIC understands that such amendments, if adopted, could be in place by mid-2005. Accordingly, the IFRIC decided that the effective date for the Interpretation would be annual periods beginning on or after 1 January 2005.

Document published to accompany

IFRIC 4

Determining whether an Arrangement contains a Lease

The text of the unaccompanied Interpretation, IFRIC 4, is contained in Part A of this edition. Its effective date when issued was 1 January 2006. The text of the Accompanying Guidance on IFRIC 4 is contained in Part B of this edition. This part presents the following documents:

BASIS FOR CONCLUSIONS

Basis for Conclusions on
IFRIC Interpretation 4 *Determining whether an Arrangement contains a Lease*

This Basis for Conclusions accompanies, but is not part of, IFRIC 4.

Introduction

BC1   This Basis for Conclusions summarises the IFRIC's considerations in reaching its consensus. Individual IFRIC members gave greater weight to some factors than to others.

Background (paragraphs 1–3)

BC2   The IFRIC noted that arrangements have developed in recent years that do not take the legal form of a lease but convey rights to use items for agreed periods of time in return for a payment or series of payments. Examples of such arrangements are set out in paragraph 1 of the Interpretation. The IFRIC observed that these arrangements share many features of a lease because a lease is defined in paragraph 4 of IAS 17 *Leases* as 'an agreement whereby the lessor conveys to the lessee in return for a payment or series of payments *the right to use an asset* for an agreed period of time' (emphasis added). The IFRIC noted that all arrangements meeting the definition of a lease should be accounted for in accordance with IAS 17 (subject to the scope of that Standard) regardless of whether they take the legal form of a lease. In other words, just as the Standing Interpretations Committee concluded in SIC-27 *Evaluating the Substance of Transactions Involving the Legal Form of a Lease* that an arrangement that is described as a lease is not necessarily accounted for as a lease, the IFRIC concluded that an arrangement can be within the scope of IAS 17 even if it is not described as a lease. The IFRIC therefore decided that it should issue guidance to assist in determining whether an arrangement is, or contains, a lease.

BC3   The IFRIC published Draft Interpretation D3 *Determining whether an Arrangement contains a Lease* for public comment in January 2004 and received 51 comment letters in response to its proposals. In addition, in order to understand better the practical issues that would have arisen on implementing the proposed Interpretation, IASB staff met a number of preparer constituents.

BC4   There was broad support for the IFRIC issuing an Interpretation on this topic (even among those respondents who disagreed with the criteria in D3 for determining whether a lease exists). However, some respondents to D3 questioned whether the proposals were a legitimate *interpretation* of IAS 17. In particular, some suggested that the proposals anticipated the Board's current research project on leasing.

BC5   In considering these comments, the IFRIC concluded that they primarily arose from its observation in the Basis for Conclusions on D3 that 'the lease asset under IAS 17 is the right to use [and] that this asset should not be confused with the underlying item [in the arrangement]' (eg an item of property, plant or equipment). As a result, the IFRIC understood that some respondents were concerned that D3 was requiring (or permitting) purchasers (lessees) to recognise an intangible asset for the right of use, even for leases classified as operating leases.

BC6 During redeliberation, the IFRIC affirmed its view that conceptually IAS 17 regards the asset as the right of use (although it acknowledged that in a finance lease, a lessee recognises an asset and accounts for that asset as if it were within the scope of IAS 16 *Property, Plant and Equipment* or IAS 38 *Intangible Assets*). However, the IFRIC decided to emphasise that the objective of the Interpretation is only to identify whether an arrangement contains a lease, not to change the requirements of IAS 17. Accordingly, having identified a lease, an entity accounts for that lease in accordance with IAS 17. This includes following the requirements of paragraphs 7–19 of IAS 17 to determine whether the lease should be classified as an operating lease or as a finance lease. This means, for example, that if a purchaser satisfies the criteria in the Interpretation, it (a) recognises an asset only if substantially all the risks and rewards incidental to ownership are transferred and (b) treats the recognised asset as a leased item, rather than an intangible asset for the right to use that item.

BC7 The IFRIC reconsidered its use of the term 'item' in D3 (as in right to use an item). The IFRIC noted that it had used 'item' rather than 'asset' to refer to the underlying asset in the arrangement (eg an item of property, plant or equipment) in order to emphasise that the asset that is the subject of the Interpretation is the right of use and not the underlying item or asset. However, given that many found the use of the term confusing, the IFRIC decided in finalising the Interpretation to revert to the phrase in IAS 17 'right to use an asset'.

Multiple-element arrangements

BC8 The IFRIC observed that many of the arrangements that fall within the scope of the Interpretation are likely to involve services as well as a right to use an asset. In other words, the arrangement is what is sometimes referred to as a multiple-element arrangement. The IFRIC concluded that IAS 17 allows for separate recognition of a lease that is embedded or contained within a multiple-element arrangement because IAS 17 states (paragraph 3) that it applies to 'agreements that transfer the right to use assets even though substantial services by the lessor may be called for in connection with the operation or maintenance of such assets.' In addition, the definition of minimum lease payments in paragraph 4 of IAS 17 clarifies that such payments exclude costs for services. The Interpretation therefore addresses whether a multiple-element arrangement contains a lease and not just whether an *entire* arrangement is a lease.

Portions of an asset (paragraph 3)

BC9 The Interpretation (like D3) does not address what constitutes the underlying asset in the arrangement. In other words, it does not address when a portion of a larger asset can be the subject of a lease.

BC10 Some respondents to D3 suggested that this omission pointed to a flaw in the proposals. They were troubled by the potential inconsistency between the accounting for a take-or-pay arrangement for substantially all of the output from a specific asset (which could have contained a lease) and one for a smaller portion of the output (which would not have been required to be treated as containing a lease). Other respondents argued that D3 would have allowed undue flexibility and that the IFRIC should either explicitly rule out portions or provide additional guidance to clarify which portions should be recognised (for example, those that are physically distinguishable).

BC11   From an early stage in this project, the IFRIC decided that it should not address the issue of portions and should focus on the main question, ie what constitutes a lease. The IFRIC noted that the subject of portions was important in itself and had much wider applicability than the Interpretation. The IFRIC affirmed this view during its redeliberations and therefore rejected the suggestion that it also should address portions in the Interpretation. The IFRIC also concluded that it would be inappropriate to specify that the Interpretation should not be applied to an arrangement that contains a right to use a portion of an asset (whether that portion be a physically distinguishable portion of an asset, or defined by reference to the output of the asset or the time the asset is made available) because this would conflict with IAS 17. The IFRIC agreed that the phrase 'right to use an asset' does not preclude the asset being a portion of a larger asset.

BC12   However, in the light of comments from respondents, the IFRIC decided to clarify that the Interpretation should be applied to arrangements in which the underlying asset would represent the unit of account in either IAS 16 or IAS 38.

Scope (paragraph 4)

BC13   The objective of the Interpretation is to determine whether an arrangement contains a lease that falls within the scope of IAS 17. The lease is then accounted for in accordance with that Standard. Because the Interpretation should not be read as overriding any of the requirements of IAS 17, the IFRIC decided that it should clarify that if an arrangement is found to be, or contains, a lease or licensing agreement that is excluded from the scope of IAS 17, an entity need not apply IAS 17 to that lease or licensing agreement.

BC14   The IFRIC considered whether the scope of the Interpretation might overlap with IAS 39 *Financial Instruments: Recognition and Measurement*.[1] In particular it noted the view that an arrangement for output might meet the definition of a derivative under IAS 39 but also be determined to contain a lease under this Interpretation. The IFRIC concluded that there should not be an overlap because an arrangement for output that is a derivative would not meet the criteria in paragraphs 6–9 of the Interpretation. In particular, the IFRIC noted that such an arrangement would be for a product with a quoted market price available in an active market and would therefore be unlikely to depend upon the use of a specifically identified asset.

BC14A   The IFRIC considered whether the scope of the Interpretation might overlap with IFRIC 12, which was developed from draft Interpretations D12–D14. In

---

1   IFRS 9 *Financial Instruments* replaced IAS 39. IFRS 9 applies to all items that were previously within the scope of IAS 39.

particular it noted the views expressed by some respondents to the proposals that the contractual terms of some public-to-private service concession arrangements would be regarded as leases under IFRIC 4 and would also be regarded as meeting the scope criterion of D12–D14. The IFRIC did not regard the choice between accounting treatments as appropriate because it could lead to different accounting treatments for contracts that have similar economic effects. The IFRIC therefore amended IFRIC 4 to specify that if a public-to-private service concession arrangement met the scope requirements of IFRIC 12 it would not be within the scope of IFRIC 4.

Consensus (paragraphs 6–15)

Criteria for determining whether an arrangement contains a lease (paragraphs 6–9)

BC15 In D3 the IFRIC proposed that three criteria would all need to be satisfied for an arrangement to be, or contain, a lease:

(a) The arrangement depends upon a specific item or items (the item). The item need not be explicitly identified by the contractual provisions of the arrangement. Rather it may be implicitly identified because it is not economically feasible or practical for the supplier to fulfil the arrangement by providing use of alternative items.

(b) The arrangement conveys a right to use the item for a specific period of time such that the purchaser is able to exclude others from using the item.

(c) Payments under the arrangement are made for the time that the item is made available for use rather than for actual use of the item.

BC16 D3 also proposed that arrangements in which there is only a remote possibility that parties other than the purchaser will take more than an insignificant amount of the output produced by an item would meet the second of the criteria above.

BC17 In its Basis for Conclusions on D3, the IFRIC drew attention to the similarities between its Interpretation and Issue No. 01-8 *Determining Whether an Arrangement Contains a Lease* published by the US Emerging Issues Task Force (EITF) in May 2003. The IFRIC concluded that '[a]lthough the wording of Issue 01-8 and the draft Interpretation differ, ... a similar assessment of whether an arrangement contains a lease is likely under both interpretations.'

BC18 Some respondents disagreed with the IFRIC's conclusion and suggested that the differences between the two interpretations were, in fact, significant. The IFRIC, however, maintained its original conclusion. In particular, it noted that both it and the EITF had concluded that a right of use can be conveyed in arrangements in which purchasers have rights to acquire the output that will be produced by an asset, regardless of any right or ability physically to operate or control access to that asset. Accordingly, many take-or-pay (and similar contracts) would have been similarly assessed under the two interpretations.

BC19 Nonetheless, the IFRIC agreed that some arrangements would be regarded as leases under Issue 01-8 but not under D3. The IFRIC concluded that there were two main reasons for this. First, the effect of the third criterion in D3 ('payments under the arrangement are made for the time that the item is made available for use rather than for actual use of the item') was that a purchaser would always be required to assume some pricing risk in an arrangement for there to be a lease. This is not the case under Issue 01-8. Secondly, the second criterion in D3 ('the arrangement conveys a right to use the item ... such that the purchaser is able to exclude others from using the item') suggested that a right of use is conveyed in an arrangement for the output from an asset only when the purchaser is taking *substantially all* of the output from a specific asset. Under Issue 01-8, a right of use is also conveyed if the purchaser controls or operates the underlying specific asset while taking more than a *minor amount* of the output from an asset.

BC20   The IFRIC noted that the definition of a lease in IAS 17 is similar to its definition in the US standard SFAS 13 *Accounting for Leases*. Given this, the IFRIC concluded that there was no compelling reason for different assessments of whether an arrangement contains a lease under IFRSs and US GAAP. Furthermore, the IFRIC was sympathetic to the practical difficulties highlighted by some respondents that would arise in cases when an agreement would need to be assessed against two similar, but different, sets of criteria. Therefore, the IFRIC decided that it should seek to eliminate the differences between the approach in D3 and Issue 01-8 for determining whether an arrangement contains a lease. The IFRIC concluded that the most effective way of achieving this objective would be to modify its criteria to conform them more fully to the approach in Issue 01-8.

BC21   The IFRIC decided that as far as possible it should adopt the actual words from Issue 01-8, subject to differences between IAS 17 and SFAS 13. It concluded that differences in wording would not promote convergence and would be likely to cause confusion. Therefore, paragraphs 7–9 are virtually identical to Issue 01-8, except that:

    (a)   the Interpretation uses the term 'asset' rather than 'property, plant or equipment' as in Issue 01-8. The IFRIC noted that IAS 17 covers a broader range of leases than SFAS 13 and that there was no reason for restricting this Interpretation only to items of property, plant or equipment.

    (b)   the phrase 'more than a minor amount of the output' in Issue 01-8 has been expressed as 'more than an insignificant amount of the output'. This is because the latter is the more customary form of words under IFRSs and is therefore consistent with other Standards. In this context, however, the IFRIC intends 'minor' and 'insignificant' to have the same meaning.

BC22   Apart from small modifications to the wording of the first criterion in D3, the effect of converging fully with the criteria in Issue 01-8 for determining whether an arrangement contains a lease is that the second and third criteria in D3 are replaced by one criterion, requiring the arrangement to convey to the purchaser the right to control the use of the underlying asset.

BC23   Although the requirements for determining whether an arrangement contains a lease are the same under IFRSs and US GAAP, the IFRIC emphasises that any lease identified by the Interpretation may be accounted for differently under IFRSs and US GAAP because of differences between their respective leasing standards.

Fulfilment of the arrangement is dependent on the use of a specific asset (paragraphs 7 and 8)

BC24   The IFRIC agreed that a specific asset needs to be identified in the arrangement for there to be a lease. The IFRIC concluded that this follows from the definition of a lease, which refers to a 'right to use *an* asset' (emphasis added). The IFRIC also observed that dependence on a specifically identified asset is a feature that distinguishes a lease from other arrangements that also convey rights to use assets but are not leases (eg some service arrangements).

BC25   However, the IFRIC concluded that the identification of the asset in the arrangement need not be explicit. Rather, the facts and circumstances could implicitly identify an asset because it would not be economically feasible or practical for the supplier to perform its obligation by providing the use of alternative assets. Examples of when an asset may be implicitly identified are when the supplier owns only one suitable asset; the asset used to fulfil the contract needs to be at a particular location or specialised to the purchaser's needs; and the supplier is a special purpose entity formed for a limited purpose.[2]

BC26   Some respondents to D3 noted that the effect of this first criterion is that the *purchaser's* accounting could depend on how the *supplier* chooses to fulfil the arrangement. They noted that the purchaser might have no control over this because (in form) the purchaser has contracted for output. Some respondents were also troubled by the lack of comparability, because similar arrangements for the output of an asset could be accounted for differently according to whether they depend on the use of a specific asset.

BC27   In response to the first of these comments, the IFRIC noted that how an entity chooses to obtain a product normally determines the accounting treatment; for example, an entity requiring power may choose to lease a power plant or connect to the grid and the two options would result in different accounting. Although in the respondents' example the choice is the supplier's (rather than the purchaser's), the IFRIC concluded that the critical matter is the end position of the entity (ie is there a lease?) not how it got to that position (ie whether it chose that outcome or it was imposed).

BC28   In response to the second comment, the IFRIC observed that it is important to consider the combined effect of the criteria in the Interpretation rather than considering the criteria individually. On reconsidering the proposals in D3 and the requirements of Issue 01-8, the IFRIC concluded that in the context of current IFRSs, in which executory contracts are generally not accounted for, the Interpretation identifies contracts (or an element therein) that for a purchaser warrant recognition (if the definition of a finance lease is satisfied). The IFRIC concluded that identifying and accounting for the lease element would represent an improvement to existing accounting practice.

---

2   SIC-12 *Consolidation—Special Purpose Entities* was withdrawn and superseded by IFRS 10 *Consolidated Financial Statements* issued in May 2011. There is no longer specific accounting guidance for special purpose entities because IFRS 10 applies to all types of entities.

Arrangement conveys a right to use the asset (paragraph 9)

BC29   Following Issue 01-8, the Interpretation specifies that a right of use can be conveyed if any of three criteria is satisfied.

BC30   The first two criteria consider the purchaser's ability to control physically the use of the underlying asset, either through operations or access, while obtaining or controlling more than an insignificant amount of the output of the asset. For example, a purchaser's ability to operate the asset may be evidenced by its ability to hire, fire or replace the operator of the asset or its ability to specify significant operating policies and procedures in the arrangement (as opposed to a right to monitor the supplier's activities) with the supplier having no ability to change such policies and procedures.

BC31   In D3 the IFRIC explained that it did not regard the ability of a purchaser to operate physically the underlying asset as determinative of whether a right of use has been conveyed. The IFRIC noted that asset managers 'operate' assets, but this does not necessarily convey a right of use. However, the IFRIC noted that under Issue 01-8, in addition to the ability to operate the asset, the purchaser has to be taking more than a minor amount of the output. The IFRIC agreed that in such cases the arrangement would convey a right of use.

BC32   The IFRIC agreed with the EITF that a right of use has been conveyed in arrangements in which the purchaser has the ability to control physically the use of the underlying asset through access (while obtaining or controlling more than a minor amount of the output of the asset). The IFRIC noted that in such arrangements the purchaser would have the ability to restrict the access of others to economic benefits of the underlying asset.

BC33   The third criterion for determining whether a right of use has been conveyed considers whether the purchaser is taking all or substantially all of the output or other utility of the underlying asset.

BC34   As noted above, D3 similarly specified that a right of use could be conveyed in arrangements in which there is only a remote possibility that other parties could take more than an insignificant amount of the output of an asset. Among the respondents who disagreed with the proposals in D3, it was this criterion that was considered most troublesome. They disagreed that, in certain specified circumstances, a purchaser's right to acquire the output from an asset could be equated with a right of use that asset. Among the arguments put to the IFRIC were:

    (a)   A right of use requires the purchaser to have the ability to control the way in which the underlying asset is used during the term of the arrangement: for example, the right for the purchaser's employees to assist or supervise the operation of the asset.

    (b)   In addition to the right to the output, the purchaser needs to have control over the delivery profile of the output; in other words it also needs the ability to determine when the output flows, otherwise it is simply consuming the output of the underlying asset rather than using the asset in its business.

(c)   In most supply arrangements, the purchaser would not have access to the plant in the event of default by the supplier but would receive damages. The absence of this right points to there not being a lease. If the arrangement did contain a lease, the purchaser would have the ability to receive the output from the plant in the arrangement by replacing the original supplier with another service provider.

(d)   D3 dismisses 'risks and rewards incidental to ownership' of the asset in determining whether an arrangement contains a lease. Therefore, arrangements in which the supplier retains significantly all of the risks and rewards of operation and ownership of the asset could be deemed to contain leases. However, in such arrangements the supplier's cash flows may have significantly more potential for variability than a 'true' lessor and the supplier may demand a return significantly above the market rate for a lessor.

BC35   In its redeliberations, the IFRIC reaffirmed its view that a purchaser that is taking substantially all of the output from an asset has the ability to restrict the access of others to the output from that asset. The purchaser therefore has a right of use because it controls access to the economic benefits to be derived from the asset. The IFRIC therefore did not agree that the absence of the ability to control physically the way in which the underlying asset is used precludes the existence of a right of use (although, as noted above, such an ability may indicate that a right of use has been conveyed).

BC36   With respect to the other points, the IFRIC noted the following:

(a)   A purchaser that is taking substantially all of the output from an asset in cases when it is remote that others will be taking more than an insignificant amount of the output does in effect determine when the output flows.

(b)   In most straightforward leases, any lessee that terminates the lease because of default by the lessor would no longer have access to the asset. Furthermore, in many leases that contain both a right of use and a service element, the related service contract does not operate independently (eg the lessee cannot terminate the service element alone). Indeed, the IFRIC noted that the purchaser's entitlement to damages in the event of default by the supplier indicates that a right of use was originally conveyed, and that the supplier is compensating the purchaser for withdrawing that right.

(c)   Risks and rewards are in general relevant for determining lease classification rather than whether an arrangement is a lease. The IFRIC noted that in many straightforward short-term operating leases, substantially all the risks and rewards are retained by the lessor. Even if it were desirable to specify that a certain level of risks and rewards needed to be transferred for there to be a lease, the IFRIC was doubtful that such a criterion could be made operable. Nonetheless, an arrangement that conveys the right to use an asset will also convey certain risks and rewards incidental to ownership. Therefore, the transfer of risks and rewards of ownership may indicate that the arrangement conveys the right to use an asset. For example, if an arrangement's pricing provides for a fixed capacity charge designed to recover the supplier's capital investment in the underlying asset, the pricing may be persuasive evidence that it is remote that parties other than the purchaser will take more than an insignificant amount of the output or other utility that will be produced or generated by the asset, and the criterion in paragraph 9(c) is satisfied.

BC37　In adopting the approach from Issue 01-8, the IFRIC has specified that an arrangement for all or substantially all of the output from a specific asset does not convey the right to use the asset if the price that the purchaser will pay is contractually fixed per unit of output or equal to the current market price per unit of output as of the time of delivery of the output. This is because in such cases the purchaser is paying for a product or service rather than paying for the right to use the asset. In D3, the IFRIC proposed making a similar distinction by the combination of the second and third criteria (see paragraph BC15(b) and (c) above).

BC38　The IFRIC noted that its Interpretation could result in take-or-pay arrangements, in which purchasers are committed to purchase substantially all of the output from specific assets, being determined to contain leases. This is because in such arrangements the purchaser makes payments for the time that the underlying asset is made available for use rather than on the basis of actual use or output (resulting in the arrangement's pricing being neither fixed per unit of output nor equal to the current market price per unit of output). In many take-or-pay arrangements, the purchaser is contractually committed to pay the supplier regardless of whether the purchaser uses the underlying asset or obtains the output from that asset. Payments are therefore made for the right to use that asset. The IFRIC agreed that the overall effect of such a take-or-pay arrangement is similar to that of a lease plus contracts for related services and supplies (such as contracts for the operation of the asset and the purchase of inputs).

BC39　The IFRIC observed that if an arrangement contains a lease, and the lease is an operating lease, applying the Interpretation is likely to result in the same assets, liabilities and expenses being recognised as if no lease had been identified. However, the IFRIC noted that IAS 17 requires lessors and lessees to recognise operating lease payments on a straight-line basis over the lease term (unless another systematic basis is more representative of the time pattern of the benefit derived from the leased asset), and thus adjustments to the recognition profile of the payments for the lease element might be required in some instances. Also, the IFRIC noted that the Interpretation would often result in additional disclosure, because IAS 17 requires the lessor and lessee to disclose the future minimum lease payments. The IFRIC observed that, for a purchaser, the arrangements discussed in the Interpretation typically represent significant future commitments, and yet these commitments are not specifically required to be disclosed in the financial statements by Standards other than IAS 17. The IFRIC concluded that bringing such arrangements within the scope of IAS 17 would provide users of financial statements with relevant information that is useful for assessing the purchaser's solvency, liquidity and adaptability. The IFRIC acknowledged that the disclosed information might relate only to the lease element of the arrangement; however, it agreed that it would be beyond the scope of this Interpretation to address disclosure of executory contracts more generally.

Assessing or reassessing whether an arrangement contains a lease (paragraphs 10 and 11)

BC40   In D3 the IFRIC proposed that the assessment of whether an arrangement contains a lease should be made at the inception of the arrangement on the basis of the facts and circumstances existing at that time and that, consistently with IAS 17, an arrangement should be reassessed only if there was a change in the terms of the arrangement. Hence, under D3, a supplier that subsequently obtained additional assets with which it could fulfil the arrangement, would not have reassessed the arrangement.

BC41   Some respondents disagreed with this conclusion and argued that the analogy with the requirements for reclassifying a lease in IAS 17 was not relevant because the objective of the Interpretation is to determine whether an arrangement is within the scope of IAS 17. They noted that since this depends on factors such as whether the arrangement depends on a specific asset, it was logical that reassessment should be required if those factors change.

BC42   The IFRIC was persuaded by this argument and concluded that it outweighed the concerns that it had expressed in D3 about it being unduly burdensome to require purchasers to reassess arrangements. The IFRIC also noted that its proposal in D3 was different from Issue 01-8. Given that it had modified its approach to determining whether a lease exists to converge with Issue 01-8, the IFRIC decided that it should also specify the same treatment as Issue 01-8 for reassessments.

BC43   The IFRIC noted that the requirements in paragraphs 10 and 11 relate only to determining when the arrangement should be reassessed and that they do not alter the requirements of IAS 17. Hence if an arrangement that contains a lease is required to be reassessed and found still to contain a lease, the lease is reclassified as a finance lease or operating lease only if so required by paragraph 13 of IAS 17.

Separating payments for the lease from other payments (paragraphs 12–15)

BC44   D3 proposed, and the Interpretation requires, payments in an arrangement containing both a lease and other elements (eg services) to be separated into those for the lease and those for other elements on the basis of their relative fair values. The IFRIC concluded that fair value is the most relevant and faithful representation of the underlying economics of the transaction.

BC45   The IFRIC noted that this requirement could be more onerous for purchasers than for suppliers, particularly when a purchaser has no access to the supplier's pricing information. The IFRIC therefore agreed that it should provide some guidance to assist purchasers in separating the lease from other elements in the arrangement. Nonetheless, the IFRIC acknowledged that in rare cases it might be impracticable for the purchaser to separate the payments reliably. The IFRIC noted that if this was the case and the lease was a finance lease, then the requirements of IAS 17 would ensure that the purchaser would not capitalise an amount greater than the fair value of the asset (since paragraph 20 of IAS 17 requires a lessee to recognise a finance lease asset at the fair value of the leased property or, if lower, the present value of the minimum lease payments). Accordingly, the IFRIC decided to specify that in such cases the purchaser should recognise the fair value of the underlying asset as the leased asset. If the lease is an operating lease and it is impracticable to separate the payments reliably, the IFRIC agreed, as a practical accommodation, that the purchaser should disclose all the payments under the arrangement when disclosing the minimum lease payments, and state that these also include payment for other elements in the arrangement.

BC46   Some respondents to D3 noted that if a purchaser with an operating lease does not separate the payments, the usefulness of the disclosures required by IAS 17 would be reduced. The IFRIC agreed that the minimum lease payments are often used by users of financial statements to estimate the value of assets held under operating leases and therefore concluded that lease payments that also include payments for other elements should be disclosed separately.

Transition (paragraph 17)

BC47   D3 proposed, and the Interpretation requires, retrospective application. Some respondents proposed that the Interpretation should be applied only to new arrangements starting after its effective date. Two main arguments were put forward in support of this view:

(a)   convergence with Issue 01-8 (which applies to arrangements starting or modified after the beginning of an entity's next reporting period beginning after 28 May 2003); and

(b)   to ease transition, particularly in the case of longer arrangements that started some years ago and where it might be difficult to make the assessments required by D3 retrospectively.

BC48   The IFRIC noted that EITF Abstracts are usually applied prospectively. In contrast, IFRSs (including Interpretations) are applied retrospectively following the principle articulated in IAS 8 *Accounting Policies, Changes in Accounting Estimates and Errors*. The IFRIC could see no compelling argument for departing from this principle. The IFRIC also noted that unless it were to specify exactly the same effective date as Issue 01-8 (which was before D3 was published), reconciling items with US GAAP would still arise.

BC49   In addition, the IFRIC decided that the continuation of some arrangements for many years emphasised the need for retrospective application. Without retrospective application, an entity could be accounting for similar arrangements differently for many years with a consequent loss of comparability.

BC50   However, the IFRIC was sympathetic to the practical difficulties raised by full retrospective application, in particular the difficulty of going back potentially many years and determining whether the criteria would have been satisfied at that time. Although IAS 8 provides relief from fully retrospective application in cases where such treatment would be impracticable, the IFRIC decided that it should provide transitional relief for existing preparers of IFRSs in the Interpretation itself. The IFRIC emphasises that this relief does not alter the transition requirements of IAS 17 and therefore if an arrangement is determined to contain a lease an entity applies IAS 17 from the inception of the arrangement.

Document published to accompany

IFRIC 5

Rights to Interests arising from Decommissioning, Restoration and Environmental Rehabilitation Funds

The text of the unaccompanied Interpretation, IFRIC 5, is contained in Part A of this edition. Its effective date when issued was 1 January 2006. This part presents the following documents:

BASIS FOR CONCLUSIONS

Basis for Conclusions on IFRIC Interpretation 5 *Rights to Interests arising from Decommissioning, Restoration and Environmental Rehabilitation Funds*

This Basis for Conclusions accompanies, but is not part of, IFRIC 5.

The original text has been marked up to reflect the revision of IAS 1 Presentation of Financial Statements *in 2007: new text is underlined and deleted text is struck through.*

Introduction

BC1   This Basis for Conclusions summarises the IFRIC's considerations in reaching its consensus. Individual IFRIC members gave greater weight to some factors than to others.

Background (paragraphs 1–3)

BC2   The IFRIC was informed that an increasing number of entities with decommissioning obligations are contributing to a separate fund established to help fund those obligations. The IFRIC was also informed that questions have arisen in practice over the accounting treatment of interests in such funds and that there is a risk that divergent practices may develop. The IFRIC therefore concluded that it should provide guidance to assist in answering the questions in paragraph 6, in particular on the accounting for the asset of the right to receive reimbursement from a fund. On the issue of whether the fund should be consolidated or equity accounted, the IFRIC concluded that the normal requirements of IAS 27 *Consolidated and Separate Financial Statements*, SIC-12 *Consolidation—Special Purpose Entities*, IAS 28 *Investments in Associates*[1] or IAS 31 *Interests in Joint Ventures*[2] apply and that there is no need for interpretative guidance.[3] The IFRIC published its proposed Interpretation on 15 January 2004 as D4 *Decommissioning, Restoration and Environmental Rehabilitation Funds*.

BC3   Paragraphs 1–3 describe ways in which entities might arrange to fund their decommissioning obligations. Those that are within the scope of the Interpretation are specified in paragraphs 4–6.

Scope (paragraphs 4 and 5)

BC4   D4 did not precisely define the scope because the IFRIC believed that the large variety of schemes in operation would make any definition inappropriate. However, some respondents to D4 disagreed and commented that the absence of any definition made it unclear when the Interpretation should be applied. As a result, the IFRIC has specified the scope by identifying the features that

---

1   In May 2011, the Board amended IAS 28 and changed its title to *Investments in Associates and Joint Ventures*.

2   IFRS 11 *Joint Arrangements*, issued in May 2011, replaced IAS 31.

3   The consolidation requirements in IAS 27 and SIC-12 were superseded by IFRS 10 *Consolidated Financial Statements* issued in May 2011.

make an arrangement a decommissioning fund. It has also described the different types of fund and the features that may (or may not) be present.

BC5   The IFRIC considered whether it should issue a wider Interpretation that addresses similar forms of reimbursement, or whether it should prohibit the application of the Interpretation to other situations by analogy. The IFRIC rejected any widening of the scope, deciding instead to concentrate on the matter referred to it. The IFRIC also decided that there was no reason to prohibit the application of the Interpretation to other situations by analogy and thus the hierarchy of criteria in paragraphs 7–12 of IAS 8 *Accounting Policies, Changes in Accounting Estimates and Errors* would apply, resulting in similar accounting for reimbursements under arrangements that are not decommissioning funds, but have similar features.

BC6   The IFRIC considered comments from respondents that a contributor may have an interest in the fund that extends beyond its right to reimbursement. In response, the IFRIC added clarification that a residual interest in a fund, such as a contractual right to distributions once all the decommissioning has been completed or on winding up the fund, may be an equity instrument within the scope of IAS 39 *Financial Instruments: Recognition and Measurement*.[4]

Basis for consensus

Accounting for an interest in a fund (paragraphs 7–9)

BC7   The IFRIC concluded that the contributor should recognise a liability unless the contributor is not liable to pay decommissioning costs even if the fund fails to pay. This is because the contributor remains liable for the decommissioning costs. Additionally, IAS 37 *Provisions, Contingent Liabilities and Contingent Assets* provides that:

(a)   when an entity remains liable for expenditure, a provision should be recognised even where reimbursement is available; and

(b)   if the reimbursement is virtually certain to be received when the obligation is settled, then it should be treated as a separate asset.

BC8   In concluding that the contributor should recognise separately its liability to pay decommissioning costs and its interest in the fund, the IFRIC also noted the following:

(a)   There is no legally enforceable right to set off the rights under the decommissioning fund against the decommissioning liabilities. Also, given that the main objective is reimbursement, it is likely that settlement will not be net or simultaneous. Accordingly, treating these rights and liabilities as analogous to financial assets and financial liabilities would not result in offset because the offset criteria in IAS 32 *Financial Instruments: Disclosure and Presentation*[5] are not met.

4   IFRS 9 *Financial Instruments* replaced IAS 39. IFRS 9 applies to all items that were previously within the scope of IAS 39.

5   In August 2005, IAS 32 was amended as IAS 32 *Financial Instruments: Presentation*.

(b)   Treating the decommissioning obligation as analogous to a financial liability would not result in derecognition through extinguishment. If the fund does not assume the obligation for decommissioning, the criteria in IAS 39[6] for derecognition of financial liabilities through extinguishment are not met. At best, the fund acts like an in-substance defeasance that does not qualify for derecognition of the liability.

(c)   It would not be appropriate to treat decommissioning funds as analogous to pension funds, which are presented net of the related liability. This is because, in allowing a net presentation for pension plans in IAS 19 *Employee Benefits*, the International Accounting Standards Board's predecessor organisation, IASC, stated that it believed the situation is 'unique to employee benefit plans and [it did] not intend to permit this net presentation for other liabilities if the conditions in IAS 32 and IAS 39[7] are not met' (IAS 19, Basis for Conclusions paragraph BC68I).[8]

BC9   As to the accounting for the contributor's interest in the fund, the IFRIC noted that some interests in funds would be within the scope of IAS 27, IAS 28, IAS 31[9] or SIC-12. As noted in paragraph BC2, the IFRIC concluded that, in such cases, the normal requirements of those Standards would apply and there is no need for interpretative guidance.

BC10   Otherwise, the IFRIC concluded that the contributor has an asset for its right to receive amounts from the fund.

The right to receive reimbursement from a fund and amendment to the scope of IAS 39[10]

BC11   The IFRIC noted that under existing IFRSs, there are two forms of rights to reimbursement that would be accounted for differently:

(a)   A contractual right to receive reimbursement in the form of cash. This meets the definition of a financial asset and is within the scope of IAS 39. Such a financial asset would be classified as an available-for-sale financial asset[11] (unless accounted for using the fair value option) because it does not meet the definitions of a financial asset held for trading, a held-to-maturity investment or a loan or receivable.

(b)   A right to reimbursement other than a contractual right to receive cash. This does not meet the definition of a financial asset and is within the scope of IAS 37.

BC12   The IFRIC concluded that both these forms of reimbursement have economically identical effects. Therefore accounting for both forms in the same way would

---

6   IFRS 9 *Financial Instruments* replaced IAS 39. IFRS 9 applies to all items that were previously within the scope of IAS 39.

7   IFRS 9 *Financial Instruments* replaced IAS 39. IFRS 9 applies to all items that were previously within the scope of IAS 39.

8   Paragraph BC68I was renumbered as paragraph BC186 when IAS 19 was amended in 2011.

9   IFRS 11 *Joint Arrangements*, issued in May 2011, replaced IAS 31.

10   IFRS 9 *Financial Instruments* replaced IAS 39. IFRS 9 applies to all items that were previously within the scope of IAS 39.

11   IFRS 9 *Financial Instruments* eliminated the categories of available-for-sale and held-to-maturity financial assets.

provide relevant and reliable information to a user of the financial statements. However, the IFRIC noted that this did not appear possible under existing IFRSs because some such rights are within the scope of IAS 39, and others are not. Therefore, it asked the Board to amend the scope of IAS 39 to exclude rights to reimbursement for expenditure required to settle:

(a)   a provision that has been recognised in accordance with IAS 37; and

(b)   obligations that had been originally recognised as provisions in accordance with IAS 37, but are no longer provisions because their timing or amount is no longer uncertain. An example of such a liability is one that was originally recognised as a provision because of uncertainty about the timing of the cash outflow, but subsequently becomes another type of liability because the timing is now certain.

BC13   This amendment was approved by the Board and is set out in the Appendix of IFRIC 5.[12] As a result, all such rights to reimbursement are within the scope of IAS 37.

BC14   The IFRIC noted that paragraph 53 of IAS 37 specifies the accounting for rights to receive reimbursement. It requires this right to reimbursement to be separately recognised when it is virtually certain that reimbursement will be received if the contributor settles the obligation. The IFRIC also noted that this paragraph prohibits the recognition of an asset in excess of the recognised liability. For example, rights to receive reimbursement to meet decommissioning liabilities that have yet to be recognised as a provision are not recognised. Accordingly, the IFRIC concluded that when the right to reimbursement is virtually certain to be received if the contributor settles its decommissioning obligation, it should be measured at the lower of the amount of the decommissioning obligation recognised and the reimbursement right.

BC15   The IFRIC discussed whether the reimbursement right should be measured at:

(a)   the contributor's share of the fair value of the net assets of the fund attributable to contributors, taking into account any inability to access any surplus of the assets of the fund over eligible decommissioning costs (with any obligation to make good potential defaults of other contributors being treated separately as a contingent liability); or

(b)   the fair value of the reimbursement right (which would normally be lower than (a) because of the risks involved, such as the possibility that the contributor may be required to make good defaults of other contributors).

BC16   The IFRIC noted that the right to reimbursement relates to a decommissioning obligation for which a provision would be recognised and measured in accordance with IAS 37. Paragraph 36 of IAS 37 requires such provisions to be measured at 'the best estimate of the expenditure required to settle the present obligation at the ~~balance sheet date~~ end of the reporting period'. The IFRIC noted that the amount in paragraph BC15(a)—ie the contributor's share of the fair value of the net assets of the fund attributable to contributors, taking into account any inability to access any surplus of the assets of the fund over eligible

---

12   The amendment has been incorporated into the text of IAS 39 as published in this volume.

decommissioning costs—is the best estimate of the amount available to the contributor to reimburse it for expenditure it had incurred to pay for decommissioning. Thus, the amount of the asset recognised would be consistent with the amount of the liability recognised.

BC17   In contrast, the IFRIC noted that the amount in paragraph BC15(b)—ie the fair value of the reimbursement right—would take into account the factors such as liquidity that the IFRIC believed to be difficult to measure reliably. Furthermore, this amount would be lower than that in paragraph BC15(a) because it reflects the possibility that the contributor may be required to make potential additional contributions in the event of default by other contributors. The IFRIC noted that its decision that the obligation to make potential additional contributions should be treated as a contingent liability in accordance with IAS 37 (see paragraphs BC22–BC25) would result in double-counting of the risk of the additional contribution being required if the measure in paragraph BC15(b) were to be used.

BC18   Consequently, the IFRIC concluded that the approach in paragraph BC15(a) would provide the most useful information to users.

The asset cap

BC19   Many respondents to D4 expressed concern about the 'asset cap' that is imposed by the requirement in paragraph 9. This asset cap limits the amount recognised as a reimbursement asset to the amount of the decommissioning obligation recognised. These respondents argued that rights to benefit in excess of this amount give rise to an additional asset, separate from the reimbursement asset. Such an additional asset may arise in a number of ways, for example:

(a)   the contributor has the right to benefit from a repayment of any surplus in the fund that exists once all the decommissioning has been completed or on winding up the fund.

(b)   the contributor has the right to benefit from reduced contributions to the fund or increased benefits from the fund (eg by adding new sites to the fund for no additional contributions) in the future.

(c)   the contributor expects to obtain benefit from past contributions in the future, based on the current and planned level of activity. However, because contributions are made before the decommissioning obligation is incurred, IAS 37 prevents recognition of an asset in excess of the obligation.

BC20   The IFRIC concluded that a right to benefit from a repayment of any surplus in the fund that exists once all the decommissioning has been completed or on winding up the fund may be an equity instrument within the scope of IAS 39,[13] in which case IAS 39 would apply. However, the IFRIC agreed that an asset should not be recognised for other rights to receive reimbursement from the fund. Although the IFRIC had sympathy with the concerns expressed by constituents that there may be circumstances in which it would seem appropriate to recognise an asset in excess of the reimbursement right, it

---

13   IFRS 9 *Financial Instruments* replaced IAS 39. IFRS 9 applies to all items that were previously within the scope of IAS 39.

© IFRS Foundation

concluded that it would be inconsistent with paragraph 53 of IAS 37 (which requires that 'the amount recognised for the reimbursement should not exceed the amount of the provision') to recognise this asset. The IFRIC also noted that the circumstances in which this additional asset exists are likely to be limited, and apply only when a contributor has restricted access to a surplus of fund assets that does not give it control, joint control or significant influence over a fund. The IFRIC expects that most such assets would not meet the recognition criteria in the *Framework*[14] because they are highly uncertain and cannot be measured reliably.

BC21　The IFRIC also considered arguments that there should not be a difference between the treatment of a surplus when a fund is accounted for as a subsidiary, joint venture or associate, and when it is not. However, the IFRIC noted that, under IFRSs, restrictions on assets in subsidiaries, joint ventures or associates do not affect recognition of those assets. Hence it concluded that the difference in treatment between funds accounted for as subsidiaries, joint ventures or associates and those accounted for as a reimbursement right is inherent in IFRSs. The IFRIC also concluded that this is appropriate because, in the former case, the contributor exercises a degree of control not present in the latter case.

Obligations to make additional contributions (paragraph 10)

BC22　In some cases, a contributor has an obligation to make potential additional contributions, for example, in the event of the bankruptcy of another contributor.

BC23　The IFRIC noted that by 'joining' the fund, a contributor may assume the position of guarantor of the contributions of the other contributors, and hence become jointly and severally liable for the obligations of other contributors. Such an obligation is a present obligation of the contributor, but the outflow of resources associated with it may not be probable. The IFRIC noted a parallel with the example in paragraph 29 of IAS 37, which states that 'where an entity is jointly and severally liable for an obligation, the part of the obligation that is expected to be met by other parties is treated as a contingent liability.' Accordingly, the IFRIC concluded that a liability would be recognised by the contributor only if it is probable that it will make additional contributions. The IFRIC noted that such a contingent liability may arise both when the contributor's interest in the fund is accounted for as a reimbursement right and when it is accounted for in accordance with IAS 27, IAS 28, IAS 31[15] or SIC-12.

BC24　The IFRIC considered the argument that an obligation to make good potential shortfalls of other contributors is a financial instrument (ie a financial guarantee) as defined in IAS 32 and hence should be accounted for in accordance with IAS 39.[16] The grounds for this point of view are that the contributor has an

---

14　The reference to the *Framework* is to IASC's *Framework for the Preparation and Presentation of Financial Statements*, adopted by the IASB in 2001. In September 2010 the IASB replaced the *Framework* with the *Conceptual Framework for Financial Reporting*.

15　IFRS 11 *Joint Arrangements*, issued in May 2011, replaced IAS 31.

16　IFRS 9 *Financial Instruments* replaced IAS 39. IFRS 9 applies to all items that were previously within the scope of IAS 39.

obligation to deliver cash to the fund, and the fund has a right to receive cash from the contributor if a shortfall in contributions arises. However, the IFRIC noted that:

(a)   a contractual obligation to make good shortfalls of other contributors is a financial guarantee. Financial guarantee contracts that provide for payments to be made if the debtor fails to make payment when due are excluded from the scope of IAS 39.

(b)   when the obligation is not contractual, but rather arises as a result of regulation, it is not a financial liability as defined in IAS 32 nor is it within the scope of IAS 39.

BC25   Therefore, the IFRIC concluded that an obligation to make additional contributions in the event of specified circumstances should be treated as a contingent liability in accordance with IAS 37.

Disclosure (paragraphs 11–13)

BC26   The IFRIC noted that the contributor may not be able to access the assets of the fund (including cash or cash equivalents) for many years (eg until it undertakes the decommissioning), if ever. Therefore, the IFRIC concluded that the nature of the contributor's interest and the restriction on access should be disclosed. The IFRIC also concluded that this disclosure is equally relevant when a contributor's interest in a fund is accounted for by consolidation, proportional consolidation[17] or using the equity method because the contributor's ability to access the underlying assets may be similarly restricted.

Effective date and transition (paragraphs 14 and 15)

BC27   D4 proposed that the Interpretation should be effective for annual periods beginning on a date set at three months after the Interpretation was finalised. The IFRIC considered the view of some respondents that the Interpretation should apply from 1 January 2005 (an earlier date) on the grounds that this is the date from which many entities will adopt IFRSs, and hence adopting the Interpretation at that time would promote comparability between periods. However, the IFRIC noted its general practice is to allow at least three months between finalising an Interpretation and its application, to enable entities to obtain the Interpretation and implement any necessary systems changes. In addition, the IFRIC considered the Board's concern that the amendment to IAS 39[18] issued as part of the Interpretation would change the 'stable platform' of Standards that are in force for entities that will apply IFRSs for the first time in 2005. Therefore, the IFRIC decided to require that the Interpretation should be applied for annual periods beginning on or after 1 January 2006, with earlier application encouraged.

---

17   IFRS 11 *Joint Arrangements*, issued in May 2011, replaced IAS 31. IFRS 11 does not permit an entity to use 'proportional consolidation' for accounting for interests in joint ventures.

18   IFRS 9 *Financial Instruments* replaced IAS 39. IFRS 9 applies to all items that were previously within the scope of IAS 39.

BC28   The IFRIC observed that the implementation of the Interpretation is not expected to be problematic. Therefore, the IFRIC concluded that IAS 8 should apply. Respondents to D4 did not disagree with this conclusion.

Document published to accompany

IFRIC 6

Liabilities arising from Participating in a Specific Market—Waste Electrical and Electronic Equipment

The text of the unaccompanied Interpretation, IFRIC 6, is contained in Part A of this edition. Its effective date when issued was 1 December 2005. This part presents the following documents:

BASIS FOR CONCLUSIONS

Basis for Conclusions on
IFRIC Interpretation 6 *Liabilities arising from Participating in a Specific Market—Waste Electrical and Electronic Equipment*

This Basis for Conclusions accompanies, but is not part of, IFRIC 6.

BC1 This Basis for Conclusions summarises the IFRIC's considerations in reaching its consensus. Individual IFRIC members gave greater weight to some factors than to others.

BC2 The IFRIC was informed that the European Union's Directive on Waste Electrical and Electronic Equipment (WE&EE) had given rise to questions about when a liability for the decommissioning of WE&EE for certain goods should be recognised. The IFRIC therefore decided to develop an Interpretation that would provide guidance regarding what constitutes an obligating event in the circumstances created by the Directive.

BC3 The IFRIC's proposals were set out in Draft Interpretation D10 *Liabilities arising from Participating in a Specific Market—Waste Electrical and Electronic Equipment*, which was published in November 2004. The IFRIC received 22 comment letters on the proposals.

BC4 The Directive indicates that it is participation in the market during the measurement period that triggers the obligation to meet the costs of waste management.

BC5 For example, an entity selling electrical equipment in 20X4 has a market share of 4 per cent for that calendar year. It subsequently discontinues operations and is thus no longer in the market when the waste management costs for its products are allocated to those entities with market share in 20X7. With a market share of 0 per cent in 20X7, the entity's obligation is zero. However, if another entity enters the market for electronic products in 20X7 and achieves a market share of 3 per cent in that period, then that entity's obligation for the costs of waste management from earlier periods will be 3 per cent of the total costs of waste management allocated to 20X7, even though the entity was not in the market in those earlier periods and has not produced any of the products for which waste management costs are allocated to 20X7.

BC6 The IFRIC concluded that the effect of the cost attribution model specified in the Directive is that the making of sales during the measurement period is the 'past event' that requires recognition of a provision under IAS 37 *Provisions, Contingent Liabilities and Contingent Assets* over the measurement period. Aggregate sales for the period determine the entity's obligation for a proportion of the costs of waste management allocated to that period. The measurement period is independent of the period when the cost allocation is notified to market participants. The timing of the obligating event may also be independent of the particular period in which the activities to perform the waste management are undertaken and the related costs incurred. Incurring costs in the performance of the waste management activities is a separate matter from incurring the obligation to share in the ultimate cost of those activities.

BC7   Some constituents asked the IFRIC to consider the effect of the following possible national legislation: the waste management costs for which a producer is responsible because of its participation in the market during a specified period (for example 20X6) are not based on the market share of the producer during that period but on the producer's participation in the market during a previous period (for example 20X5). The IFRIC noted that this affects only the measurement of the liability and that the obligating event is still participation in the market during 20X6.

BC8   The IFRIC considered whether its conclusion is undermined by the principle that the entity will continue to operate as a going concern. If the entity will continue to operate in the future, it treats the costs of doing so as future costs. For these future costs, paragraph 18 of IAS 37 emphasises that 'Financial statements deal with the financial position of an entity at the end of its reporting period and not its possible position in the future. Therefore, no provision is recognised for costs that need to be incurred to operate in the future.'

BC9   The IFRIC considered an argument that manufacturing or selling products for use in private households constitutes a past event that gives rise to a constructive obligation. Allocating waste management costs on the basis of market share would then be a matter of measurement rather than recognition. Supporters of this argument emphasise the definition of a constructive obligation in paragraph 10 of IAS 37 and point out that in determining whether past actions of an entity give rise to an obligation it is necessary to consider whether a change in practice is a realistic alternative. These respondents believed that when it would be necessary for an entity to take some unrealistic action in order to avoid the obligation then a constructive obligation exists and should be accounted for.

BC10   The IFRIC rejected this argument, concluding that a stated intention to participate in a market during a future measurement period does not create a constructive obligation for future waste management costs. In accordance with paragraph 19 of IAS 37, a provision can be recognised only in respect of an obligation that arises independently of the entity's future actions. For historical household equipment the obligation is created only by the future actions of the entity. If an entity has no market share in a measurement period, it has no obligation for the waste management costs relating to the products of that type which it had previously manufactured or sold and which otherwise would have created an obligation in that measurement period. This differentiates waste management costs, for example, from warranties (see Example 1 in the guidance on implementing IAS 37), which represent a legal obligation even if the entity exits the market. Consequently, no obligation exists for the future waste management costs until the entity participates in the market during the measurement period.

Document published to accompany

IFRIC 7

Applying the Restatement Approach under IAS 29 Financial Reporting in Hyperinflationary Economies

The text of the unaccompanied Interpretation, IFRIC 7, is contained in Part A of this edition. Its effective date when issued was 1 March 2006. The text of the Accompanying Guidance on IFRIC 7 is contained in Part B of this edition. This part presents the following documents:

BASIS FOR CONCLUSIONS

Basis for Conclusions on
IFRIC Interpretation 7 *Applying the Restatement Approach under IAS 29 Financial Reporting in Hyperinflationary Economies*

This Basis for Conclusions accompanies, but is not part of, IFRIC 7.

In this Basis for Conclusions the terminology has not been amended to reflect the changes made by IAS 1 Presentation of Financial Statements *(as revised in 2007).*

Introduction

BC1   This Basis for Conclusions summarises the IFRIC's considerations in reaching its consensus. Individual IFRIC members gave greater weight to some factors than to others.

Background

BC2   The IFRIC was asked for guidance on how an entity should restate its financial statements when it starts to apply IAS 29 *Financial Reporting in Hyperinflationary Economies.* There was uncertainty whether the opening balance sheet at the beginning of the reporting period should be restated to reflect changes in prices before that date.

BC3   In addition, there was uncertainty about the measurement of comparative deferred tax items in the opening balance sheet. IAS 29 states that at the balance sheet date deferred tax items of the restated financial statements should be measured in accordance with IAS 12 *Income Taxes.* However, it was not clear how an entity should account for the corresponding deferred tax figures.

BC4   In response, the IFRIC developed and published Draft Interpretation D5 *Applying IAS 29* Financial Reporting in Hyperinflationary Economies *for the First Time* for public comment in March 2004. It received 30 letters in response to the proposals.

Basis for consensus

The restatement approach

BC5   In developing D5, the IFRIC observed that the purpose of restating financial statements in hyperinflationary economies in accordance with IAS 29 is to reflect the effect on an entity of changes in general purchasing power. Paragraph 2 of IAS 29 states:

> In a hyperinflationary economy, reporting of operating results and financial position in the local currency without restatement is not useful. Money loses purchasing power at such a rate that comparison of amounts from transactions and other events that have occurred at different times, even within the same accounting period, is misleading.

This purpose applies to the financial statements of the first reporting period in which an entity identifies the existence of hyperinflation in the economy of its functional currency as well as to subsequent reporting periods (if the criteria for a hyperinflationary economy are still met).

BC6 The IFRIC considered the meaning of paragraph 4 of IAS 29, which states:

> ... this Standard applies to the financial statements of any entity from the beginning of the reporting period in which it identifies the existence of hyperinflation in the country in whose currency it reports.

The IFRIC noted that some may interpret this provision as restricting the restatement of an entity's opening balance sheet in the reporting period in which it identifies the existence of hyperinflation. Consequently, the opening balance sheet should be restated to reflect the change in a general price index for the reporting period only and not for changes in a general price index before the beginning of the reporting period, even though some balance sheet items may have been acquired or assumed before that date. However, the IFRIC also noted that paragraph 34 of IAS 29 requires:

> *Corresponding figures for the previous reporting period*, whether they were based on a historical cost approach or a current cost approach, are restated by applying a general price index so that the comparative financial statements are *presented in terms of the measuring unit current at the end of the reporting period*. Information that is disclosed in respect of earlier periods is also expressed in terms of the measuring unit current at the end of the reporting period ... [emphasis added]

BC7 The IFRIC considered a possible inconsistency between the restriction in paragraph 4 of IAS 29 and the requirement in paragraph 34. The IFRIC noted that paragraph 4 is a scope paragraph, which identifies when an entity has to comply with the Standard. The paragraph clarifies that an entity applies the requirements of the Standard to its financial statements from the beginning of the reporting period to the balance sheet date and not only from the date when it identifies the existence of hyperinflation. However, paragraph 4 does not deal with the restatement and presentation of the financial statements (either at the balance sheet date or in relation to the comparative figures). Hence, paragraph 4 of IAS 29 does not exclude from the restatement of an entity's opening balance sheet changes in the general price level before the beginning of the reporting period in which the entity identifies the existence of hyperinflation.

BC8 The IFRIC concluded that, in the context of the purpose of the Standard, the restatement of the financial statements for the reporting period in which an entity identifies the existence of hyperinflation should be consistent with the restatement approach applied in subsequent reporting periods.

BC9 Some respondents to D5 expressed concerns about whether the restatement approach in IAS 29 was always practicable for preparers and whether it provided decision-useful information to users. Though the IFRIC understood those concerns, the IFRIC observed that such concerns reflected broader aspects related to the accounting for hyperinflation in general, rather than how an entity has to apply the current Standard.

BC10   Nevertheless, the IFRIC considered how an entity should apply the Standard if, for example, detailed records of the acquisition dates of items of property, plant and equipment are not available. The IFRIC noted that, in those circumstances, paragraph 16 of IAS 29 states:

> ... In these rare circumstances, it may be necessary, in the first period of application of this Standard, to use an independent professional assessment of the value of the items as the basis for their restatement.

The IFRIC also noted that a similar exemption exists when a general price index may not be available. Paragraph 17 of IAS 29 states:

> ... In these circumstances, it may be necessary to use an estimate based, for example, on the movements in the exchange rate between the functional currency and a relatively stable foreign currency.

BC11   The IFRIC observed that, in developing IFRS 1 *First-time Adoption of International Financial Reporting Standards*, the International Accounting Standards Board discussed whether IFRS 1 should exempt first-time adopters of IFRSs from the effects of restatement in their first IFRS financial statements. Paragraph BC67 of IFRS 1 states:

> Some argued that the cost of restating financial statements for the effects of hyperinflation in periods before the date of transition to IFRSs would exceed the benefits, particularly if the currency is no longer hyperinflationary. However, the Board concluded that such restatement should be required, because hyperinflation can make unadjusted financial statements meaningless or misleading.

BC12   However, the IFRIC also observed that first-time adopters of IFRSs could use, for example, the fair value at transition date as deemed cost for property, plant and equipment, and, in some instances, also for investment property and intangible assets. Hence, if a first-time adopter that would otherwise have to apply IAS 29 at its transition to IFRSs applies the fair value measurement exemption of IFRS 1, it would apply IAS 29 to periods only after the date for which the fair value was determined. Such remeasurements would therefore reduce the need for a first-time adopter to restate its financial statements.

BC13   The IFRIC noted that the exemptions from the general restatement approach for preparers that already apply IFRSs, as stated in paragraph BC10 above, apply only in specific circumstances, whereas a first-time adopter may always elect to use the fair value remeasurement exemption for property, plant and equipment in IFRS 1. Nevertheless, the IFRIC concluded that the application of the exemptions in the Standards is clear and, therefore, extending the exemptions in IAS 29 to permit preparers that already apply IFRSs to elect fair value remeasurement of property, plant and equipment when applying the restatement approach under IAS 29 would require amendments of the Standard itself, rather than an Interpretation.

BC14   Respondents to D5 also argued that the procedures, as proposed to be clarified, are inconsistent with the accounting for a change in functional currency under IAS 21 *The Effect of Changes in Foreign Exchange Rates*, which in their view is comparable to moving into a state of hyperinflation. Moreover, they noted that retrospective application is also inconsistent with the US GAAP approach, which accounts for a change in hyperinflation status prospectively.

BC15 In relation to the reference to a change in functional currency, the IFRIC observed that the existence of hyperinflation may (but not necessarily should) initiate such a change. The IFRIC noted that a change in functional currency is a change in the currency that is normally used to determine the pricing of an entity's transactions. As clarified in paragraph BC5 above, the purpose of restatement for the effects of hyperinflation is to reflect the effect of changes in purchasing power in the economy of an entity's functional currency. Therefore, the IFRIC did not believe that the application of accounting for hyperinflation should be based on the accounting for the change in an entity's functional currency.

BC16 The IFRIC also observed that respondents' reference to prospective application under US GAAP reflects requirements only for investments in foreign entities in hyperinflationary economies. In this case, paragraph 11 of SFAS 52 *Foreign Currency Translation* states:

> The financial statements of a foreign entity in a highly inflationary economy shall *be remeasured as if the functional currency were the reporting currency.* Accordingly, the financial statements of those entities shall be remeasured into the reporting currency according to the requirements of paragraph 10 ... [emphasis added]

Therefore, under US GAAP a foreign entity's financial statements are remeasured into its investor's functional currency. The IFRIC noted that this approach is different from the restate/translate approach under IFRSs. US GAAP provides different guidance for reporting entities operating with a hyperinflationary functional currency. APB Statement No. 3 *Financial Statements Restated for General Price-Level Changes* is also based on a restatement approach, and would require retrospective application, as under IAS 29. The IFRIC observed that for the purpose of presenting comparative amounts in a different presentation currency under IFRSs paragraphs 42(b) and 43 of IAS 21 apply. In such instances, an entity will have relief from the required restatement of comparatives under IAS 29. Paragraph BC22 of IAS 21 explains the reasoning for this specific exemption as follows:

> ... If exchange rates fully reflect differing price levels between the two economies to which they relate, the SIC-30 approach will result in the same amounts for the comparatives as were reported as current year amounts in the prior year financial statements. Furthermore, the Board noted that in the prior year, the relevant amounts had been already expressed in the non-hyperinflationary presentation currency, and there was no reason to change them.

BC17 D5 proposed that applying the restatement approach under IAS 29 should be regarded as a change in circumstances, rather than a change in accounting policy. Some respondents to D5 believed this was inconsistent. This is because IAS 8 *Accounting Policies, Changes in Accounting Estimates and Errors*, paragraph 16, states that a change in circumstances is not a change in accounting policy and an entity would not apply IAS 29 retrospectively. However, the IFRIC observed that IAS 29 contains specific requirements on this point, as noted in paragraphs BC5–BC16 above. The IFRIC concluded that the opening balance sheet for the reporting period in which an entity identifies the existence of hyperinflation ought to be restated as if the entity had always applied the restatement approach under IAS 29. The IFRIC reconfirmed its view that this treatment is similar to the retrospective application of a change in accounting policy described in IAS 8.

Deferred tax items

BC18   The IFRIC was asked for guidance on the accounting for deferred tax items when an entity restates its financial statements according to IAS 29. In particular, the IFRIC was asked for guidance on measuring deferred tax items in the opening balance sheet for the reporting period in which an entity identifies the existence of hyperinflation.

BC19   The IFRIC observed that paragraph 32 of IAS 29 states:

> The restatement of financial statements in accordance with this Standard may give rise to differences between the carrying amount of individual assets and liabilities in the balance sheet and their tax bases. These differences are accounted for in accordance with IAS 12 *Income Taxes*.

Therefore, at the closing balance sheet date of the reporting period an entity remeasures its deferred tax items on the basis of the restated financial statements, rather than by applying the general restatement provisions for monetary items or non-monetary items. However, the IFRIC noted that it was not clear how an entity should account for its comparative deferred tax items.

BC20   In developing D5, the IFRIC considered the following options:

(a)   restatement of deferred tax items as monetary items;

(b)   restatement of deferred tax items as non-monetary items; or

(c)   remeasurement of deferred tax items as if the economy of the entity's functional currency had always been hyperinflationary.

BC21   D5 proposed clarifying that deferred tax items are neither clearly monetary nor non-monetary in nature. This was because deferred tax items are determined by the assets' (and liabilities') relative carrying amounts and tax bases. However, some respondents to D5 objected to that view, for various reasons. Some argued that deferred tax items, by nature, are received or paid in a fixed or determinable number of units of currency, and so should be considered as monetary items in accordance with paragraph 8 of IAS 21. Others noted that general practice is to classify deferred taxes as non-monetary items.

BC22   When considering respondents' comments the IFRIC confirmed that its conclusion in paragraph BC17 above should also apply to deferred tax items. In other words, the deferred tax items in the opening balance sheet for the reporting period in which an entity identifies the existence of hyperinflation should be calculated as if the environment had always been hyperinflationary, ie option (c) in paragraph BC20. Although the IFRIC acknowledged that deferred tax items may meet the definition of monetary items it noted that the purposes of option (c) would not be achieved if opening deferred tax were restated in the same manner as applied generally for monetary items.

BC23   The IFRIC observed that some respondents to D5 suggested that deferred tax items in the opening balance sheet should be remeasured after restating the opening balance sheet with the measurement unit current at the closing balance sheet date of the reporting period. In the IFRIC's view, that proposal would (in case of a deferred tax liability) overstate the deferred tax item recognised in the opening balance sheet and, accordingly, understate the costs recognised in the reporting period. This is because the loss on the tax base caused by the inflation in the reporting period would be recognised directly in opening equity. The IFRIC illustrated this by the following example:

> At the end of Year 1, a non-monetary asset is restated at the measurement unit current at that date. Its restated amount is CU1,000[1] and its tax base is CU500. If the tax rate is 30 per cent, the entity would remeasure a deferred tax liability of CU150. In Year 2 inflation is 100 per cent. Assuming that nothing has changed the entity would, in its restated financial statements, recognise an asset of CU2,000 (both at the closing balance sheet date of the reporting period and in the comparative figures). At the closing balance sheet date, the deferred tax liability is remeasured at CU450 ((CU2,000 − CU500) × 0.3). However, if the comparative deferred tax liability is remeasured after restating the asset by the measuring unit current at the closing balance sheet date of the reporting period, the entity should recognise an opening deferred tax liability of CU450, and there would be no impact on profit or loss (CU450 − CU450). On the other hand, if the comparatives are stated as proposed in D5, the restated opening deferred tax liability would be CU300 ((CU1,000 − CU500) × 0.3) × 100% + CU150). Accordingly, the entity should recognise a loss of CU150 (CU450 − CU300), which is the loss of purchasing power on the tax base in the reporting period.

BC24   The IFRIC observed that paragraph 18 of Appendix A to IAS 12 explains:[2]

> Non-monetary assets are restated in terms of the measuring unit current at the balance sheet date (see IAS 29 *Financial Reporting in Hyperinflationary Economies*) and no equivalent adjustment is made for tax purposes. *(notes: (1) the deferred tax is charged in the income statement;[3] and (2) if, in addition to the restatement, the non-monetary assets are also revalued, the deferred tax relating to the revaluation is charged to equity[4] and the deferred tax relating to the restatement is charged in the income statement.)*

BC25   Consequently, the IFRIC confirmed its conclusion that restatement of comparative deferred tax items would require an entity, first, to remeasure its deferred tax items on the basis of the financial statements of the previous reporting period, which have been restated by applying a general price index reflecting the price level at the end of that period. Secondly, the entity should restate those calculated deferred tax items by the change in the general price level for the reporting period.

---

1   In this example monetary amounts are denominated in 'currency units (CU)'.
2   Paragraph 18 has been amended as a consequence of the changes made by IAS 1 *Presentation of Financial Statements* (as revised in 2007).
3   IAS 1 (revised 2007) requires an entity to present all income and expense items in one statement of comprehensive income or in two statements (a separate income statement and a statement of comprehensive income).
4   Under IAS 1 (revised 2007), such effect is recognised in other comprehensive income.

Documents published to accompany

IFRIC 10

Interim Financial Reporting and Impairment

The text of the unaccompanied Interpretation, IFRIC 10, is contained in Part A of this edition. Its effective date when issued was 1 November 2006. This part presents the following documents:

BASIS FOR CONCLUSIONS

Basis for Conclusions on
IFRIC Interpretation 10 *Interim Financial Reporting and Impairment*

This Basis for Conclusions accompanies, but is not part of, IFRIC 10.

BC1   This Basis for Conclusions summarises the IFRIC's considerations in reaching its consensus. Individual IFRIC members gave greater weight to some factors than to others.

BC2   IAS 34 requires an entity to apply the same accounting policies in its interim financial statements as it applies in its annual financial statements. For annual financial statements, IAS 36 prohibits an entity from reversing an impairment loss on goodwill that it recognised in a prior annual period. Similarly, IAS 39[1] prohibits an entity from reversing in a subsequent annual period an impairment loss on an investment in an equity instrument or in a financial asset carried at cost. These requirements might suggest that an entity should not reverse in a subsequent interim period an impairment loss on goodwill or an investment in an equity instrument or in a financial asset carried at cost that it had recognised in a prior interim period. Such impairment losses would not be reversed even if no loss, or a smaller loss, would have been recognised had the impairment been assessed only at the end of the subsequent interim period.

BC3   However, IAS 34 requires year-to-date measures in interim financial statements. This requirement might suggest that an entity should reverse in a subsequent interim period an impairment loss it recognised in a prior interim period. Such impairment losses would be reversed if no loss, or a smaller loss, would have been recognised had the impairment been assessed only at the end of the subsequent interim period.

BC4   The IFRIC released Draft Interpretation D18 *Interim Financial Reporting and Impairment* for public comment in January 2006. It received more than 50 letters in response.

BC5   The IFRIC noted that many of the respondents believed that in attempting to address contradictions between standards, D18 was beyond the scope of the IFRIC. Some believed that the issue addressed could be better resolved by amending IAS 34. Before finalising its views, the IFRIC asked the International Accounting Standards Board to consider this point. The Board, however, did not wish to amend IAS 34 and asked the IFRIC to continue with its Interpretation.

BC6   Respondents to D18 were divided on whether the proposed Interpretation should prohibit the reversal of impairment losses on goodwill or investments in equity instruments or in financial assets carried at cost that had been recognised in interim periods. The IFRIC considered these responses but maintained its view that such losses should not be reversed in subsequent financial statements. The IFRIC observed that the wide divergence of views evident from respondents' letters underlined the need for additional guidance and it therefore decided to issue the Interpretation with few changes from D18.

---

1   IFRS 9 *Financial Instruments* replaced IAS 39. IFRS 9 applies to all items that were previously within the scope of IAS 39.

BC7　　　The IFRIC considered the example of Entity A and Entity B, which each hold the same equity investment with the same acquisition cost. Entity A prepares quarterly interim financial statements and Entity B prepares half-yearly financial statements. The entities have the same year-end. The IFRIC noted that if there was a significant decline in the fair value of the equity instrument below its cost in the first quarter, Entity A would recognise an impairment loss in its first quarter interim financial statements. However, if the fair value of the equity instrument subsequently recovered, so that by the half-year date there had not been a significant decline in fair value below cost, Entity B would not recognise an impairment loss in its half-yearly financial statements if it tested for impairment only at its half-yearly reporting dates. Therefore, unless Entity A reversed the impairment loss that had been recognised in an earlier interim period, the frequency of reporting would affect the measurement of its annual results when compared with Entity B's approach. The IFRIC also noted that the recognition of an impairment loss could similarly be affected by the timing of the financial year-ends of the two entities.

BC8　　　The IFRIC noted that the illustrative examples accompanying IAS 34 provide examples of applying the general recognition and measurement principles of that standard, and that paragraph B36 states that IAS 34 requires an entity to apply the same impairment testing, recognition, and reversal criteria at an interim date as it would at the end of its financial year.

BC9　　　The IFRIC concluded that the prohibitions on reversals of recognised impairment losses on goodwill in IAS 36 and on investments in equity instruments and in financial assets carried at cost in IAS 39[2] should take precedence over the more general statement in IAS 34 regarding the frequency of an entity's reporting not affecting the measurement of its annual results.

BC10　　Furthermore, the IFRIC concluded that the rationale for the non-reversal of impairment losses relating to goodwill and investments in equity instruments, as set out in paragraph BC189 of IAS 36 and paragraph BC130 of IAS 39, applies at both interim and annual reporting dates.

BC11　　The IFRIC considered a concern that this conclusion could be extended to other areas of potential conflict between IAS 34 and other standards. The IFRIC has not studied those areas and therefore has not identified any general principles that might apply both to the Interpretation and to other areas of potential conflict. The IFRIC therefore added a prohibition against extending the consensus by analogy to other areas of potential conflict between IAS 34 and other standards.

BC12　　D18 proposed fully retrospective application. A number of comment letters stated that this could be read as being more onerous than the first-time adoption requirements of IAS 36. The IFRIC revised the wording of the transition requirements to make clear that the Interpretation should not be applied to periods before an entity's adoption of IAS 36 in the case of goodwill impairments and IAS 39 in the case of impairments of investments in equity instruments or in financial assets carried at cost.

2　　In November 2009 and October 2010 the Board amended some of the requirements of IAS 39 and relocated them to IFRS 9 *Financial Instruments*. IFRS 9 applies to all items within the scope of IAS 39.

Documents published to accompany

IFRIC 12

Service Concession Arrangements

The text of the unaccompanied Interpretation, IFRIC 12, is contained in Part A of this edition. Its effective date when issued was 1 January 2008. The text of the Accompanying Guidance on IFRIC 12 is contained in Part B of this edition. This part presents the following documents:

BASIS FOR CONCLUSIONS

Basis for Conclusions on
IFRIC Interpretation 12 *Service Concession Arrangements*

This Basis for Conclusions accompanies, but is not part of, IFRIC 12.

Introduction

BC1   This Basis for Conclusions summarises the IFRIC's considerations in reaching its consensus. Individual IFRIC members gave greater weight to some factors than to others.

Background (paragraphs 1–3)

BC2   SIC-29 *Service Concession Arrangements: Disclosures* (formerly *Disclosure—Service Concession Arrangements*) contains disclosure requirements in respect of public-to-private service arrangements, but does not specify how they should be accounted for.

BC3   There was widespread concern about the lack of such guidance. In particular, operators wished to know how to account for infrastructure that they either constructed or acquired for the purpose of a public-to-private service concession arrangement, or were given access to for the purpose of providing the public service. They also wanted to know how to account for other rights and obligations arising from these types of arrangements.

BC4   In response to this concern, the International Accounting Standards Board asked a working group comprising representatives of the standard-setters of Australia, France, Spain and the United Kingdom (four of the countries that had expressed such concern) to carry out initial research on the subject. The working group recommended that the IFRIC should seek to clarify how certain aspects of existing accounting standards were to be applied.

BC5   In March 2005 the IFRIC published for public comment three draft Interpretations: D12 *Service Concession Arrangements—Determining the Accounting Model*, D13 *Service Concession Arrangements—The Financial Asset Model* and D14 *Service Concession Arrangements—The Intangible Asset Model*. In response to the proposals 77 comment letters were received. In addition, in order to understand better the practical issues that would have arisen on implementing the proposed Interpretations, IASB staff met various interested parties, including preparers, auditors and regulators.

BC6   Most respondents to D12–D14 supported the IFRIC's proposal to develop an Interpretation. However, nearly all respondents expressed concern with fundamental aspects of the proposals, some urging that the project be passed to the Board to develop a comprehensive standard.

BC7   In its redeliberation of the proposals the IFRIC acknowledged that the project was a large undertaking but concluded that it should continue its work because, given the limited scope of the project, it was by then better placed than the Board to deal with the issues in a timely way.

Terminology

BC8   SIC-29 used the terms 'Concession Provider' and 'Concession Operator' to describe, respectively, the grantor and operator of the service arrangement. Some commentators, and some members of the IFRIC, found these terms confusingly similar. The IFRIC decided to adopt the terms 'grantor' and 'operator', and amended SIC-29 accordingly.

Scope (paragraphs 4–9)

BC9   The IFRIC observed that public-to-private service arrangements take a variety of forms. The continued involvement of both grantor and operator over the term of the arrangement, accompanied by heavy upfront investment, raises questions over what assets and liabilities should be recognised by the operator.

BC10   The working group recommended that the scope of the IFRIC's project should be restricted to public-to-private service concession arrangements.

BC11   In developing the proposals the IFRIC decided to address only arrangements in which the grantor (a) controlled or regulated the services provided by the operator, and (b) controlled any significant residual interest in the infrastructure at the end of the term of the arrangement. It also decided to specify the accounting treatment only for infrastructure that the operator constructed or acquired from a third party, or to which it was given access by the grantor, for the purpose of the arrangement. The IFRIC concluded that these conditions were likely to be met in most of the public-to-private arrangements for which guidance had been sought.

BC12   Commentators on the draft Interpretations argued that the proposals ignored many arrangements that were found in practice, in particular, when the infrastructure was leased to the operator or, conversely, when it was held as the property, plant and equipment of the operator before the start of the service arrangement.

BC13   In considering these comments, the IFRIC decided that the scope of the project should not be expanded because it already included the arrangements most in need of interpretative guidance and expansion would have significantly delayed the Interpretation. The scope of the project was considered at length during the initial stage, as indicated above. The IFRIC confirmed its view that the proposed Interpretation should address the issues set out in paragraph 10. Nonetheless, during its redeliberation the IFRIC considered the range of typical arrangements for private sector participation in the provision of public services, including some that were outside the scope of the proposed Interpretation. The IFRIC decided that the Interpretation could provide references to relevant standards that apply to arrangements outside the scope of the Interpretation without giving guidance on their application. If experience showed that such guidance was needed, a separate project could be undertaken at a later date. Information Note 2 contains a table of references to relevant standards for the types of arrangements considered by the IFRIC.

Private-to-private arrangements

BC14 Some respondents to the draft Interpretations suggested that the scope of the proposed Interpretation should be extended to include private-to-private service arrangements. The IFRIC noted that addressing the accounting for such arrangements was not the primary purpose of the project because the IFRIC had been asked to provide guidance for public-to-private arrangements that meet the requirements set out in paragraph 5 and have the characteristics described in paragraph 3. The IFRIC noted that application by analogy would be appropriate under the hierarchy set out in paragraphs 7–12 of IAS 8 *Accounting Policies, Changes in Accounting Estimates and Errors*.

Grantor accounting

BC15 The Interpretation does not specify the accounting by grantors, because the IFRIC's objective and priority were to establish guidance for operators. Some commentators asked the IFRIC to establish guidance for the accounting by grantors. The IFRIC discussed these comments but reaffirmed its view. It noted that in many cases the grantor is a government body, and that IFRSs are not designed to apply to not-for-profit activities in the private sector, public sector or government, though entities with such activities may find them appropriate (see *Preface to IFRSs* paragraph 9).

Existing assets of the operator

BC16 The Interpretation does not specify the treatment of existing assets of the operator because the IFRIC decided that it was unnecessary to address the derecognition requirements of existing standards.

BC17 Some respondents asked the IFRIC to provide guidance on the accounting for existing assets of the operator, stating that the scope exclusion would create uncertainty about the treatment of these assets.

BC18 In its redeliberations the IFRIC noted that one objective of the Interpretation is to address whether the operator should recognise as its property, plant and equipment the infrastructure it constructs or to which it is given access. The accounting issue to be addressed for existing assets of the operator is one of derecognition, which is already addressed in IFRSs (IAS 16 *Property, Plant and Equipment*). In the light of the comments received from respondents, the IFRIC decided to clarify that certain public-to-private service arrangements may convey to the grantor a right to use existing assets of the operator, in which case the operator would apply the derecognition requirements of IFRSs to determine whether it should derecognise its existing assets.

The significant residual interest criterion

BC19 Paragraph 5(b) of D12 proposed that for a service arrangement to be within its scope the residual interest in the infrastructure handed over to the grantor at the end of the arrangement must be significant. Respondents argued, and the IFRIC agreed, that the significant residual interest criterion would limit the usefulness of the guidance because a service arrangement for the entire physical life of the infrastructure would be excluded from the scope of the guidance. That result was not the IFRIC's intention. In its redeliberation of the proposals, the IFRIC decided that it would not retain the proposal that the residual interest in the infrastructure handed over to the grantor at the end of the arrangement must be significant. As a consequence, 'whole of life' infrastructure (ie where the infrastructure is used in a public-to-private service arrangement for the entirety of its useful life) is within the scope of the Interpretation.

Treatment of the operator's rights over the infrastructure (paragraph 11)

BC20   The IFRIC considered the nature of the rights conveyed to the operator in a service concession arrangement. It first examined whether the infrastructure used to provide public services could be classified as property, plant and equipment of the operator under IAS 16. It started from the principle that infrastructure used to provide public services should be recognised as property, plant and equipment of the party that controls its use. This principle determines which party should recognise the property, plant and equipment as its own. The reference to control stems from the *Framework*:[1]

     (a)   an asset is defined by the *Framework* as 'a resource controlled by the entity as a result of past events and from which future economic benefits are expected to flow to the entity.'

     (b)   the *Framework* notes that many assets are associated with legal rights, including the right of ownership. It goes on to clarify that the right of ownership is not essential.

     (c)   rights are often unbundled. For example, they may be divided proportionately (undivided interests in land) or by specified cash flows (principal and interest on a bond) or over time (a lease).

BC21   The IFRIC concluded that treatment of infrastructure that the operator constructs or acquires or to which the grantor gives the operator access for the purpose of the service arrangement should be determined by whether it is controlled by the grantor in the manner described in paragraph 5. If it is so controlled (as will be the case for all arrangements within the scope of the Interpretation), then, regardless of which party has legal title to it during the arrangement, the infrastructure should not be recognised as property, plant and equipment of the operator because the operator does not control the use of the public service infrastructure.

BC22   In reaching this conclusion the IFRIC observed that it is control of the right to use an asset that determines recognition under IAS 16 and the creation of a lease under IAS 17 *Leases*. IAS 16 defines property, plant and equipment as tangible items that 'are held for use in the production or supply of goods or services, for rental to others or for administrative purposes ...'. It requires items within this definition to be recognised as property, plant and equipment unless another standard requires or permits a different approach. As an example of a different approach, it highlights the requirement in IAS 17 for recognition of leased

---

1   References to the *Framework* are to IASC's *Framework for the Preparation and Presentation of Financial Statements*, adopted by the IASB in 2001. In September 2010 the IASB replaced the *Framework* with the *Conceptual Framework for Financial Reporting*.

property, plant and equipment to be evaluated on the basis of the transfer of risks and rewards. That standard defines a lease as 'an agreement whereby the lessor conveys to the lessee in return for a series of payments the right to use an asset' and it sets out the requirements for classification of leases. IFRIC 4 *Determining whether an Arrangement contains a Lease* interprets the meaning of right to use an asset as 'the arrangement conveys the right to control the use of the underlying asset.'

BC23   Accordingly, it is only if an arrangement conveys the right to control the use of the underlying asset that reference is made to IAS 17 to determine how such a lease should be classified. A lease is classified as a finance lease if it transfers substantially all the risks and rewards incidental to ownership. A lease is classified as an operating lease if it does not transfer substantially all the risks and rewards incidental to ownership.

BC24   The IFRIC considered whether arrangements within the scope of IFRIC 12 convey 'the right to control the use of the underlying asset' (the public service infrastructure) to the operator. The IFRIC decided that, if an arrangement met the conditions in paragraph 5, the operator would not have the right to control the use of the underlying asset and should therefore not recognise the infrastructure as a leased asset.

BC25   In arrangements within the scope of the Interpretation the operator acts as a service provider. The operator constructs or upgrades infrastructure used to provide a public service. Under the terms of the contract the operator has access to operate the infrastructure to provide the public service on the grantor's behalf. The asset recognised by the operator is the consideration it receives in exchange for its services, not the public service infrastructure that it constructs or upgrades.

BC26   Respondents to the draft Interpretations disagreed that recognition should be determined solely on the basis of control of use without any assessment of the extent to which the operator or the grantor bears the risks and rewards of ownership. They questioned how the proposed approach could be reconciled to IAS 17, in which the leased asset is recognised by the party that bears substantially all the risks and rewards incidental to ownership.

BC27   During its redeliberation the IFRIC affirmed its decision that if an arrangement met the control conditions in paragraph 5 of the Interpretation the operator would not have the right to control the use of the underlying asset (public service infrastructure) and should therefore not recognise the infrastructure as its property, plant and equipment under IAS 16 or the creation of a lease under IAS 17. The contractual service arrangement between the grantor and operator would not convey the right to use the infrastructure to the operator. The IFRIC concluded that this treatment is also consistent with IAS 18 *Revenue*[2] because, for arrangements within the scope of the Interpretation, the second condition of paragraph 14 of IAS 18 is not satisfied. The grantor retains continuing managerial involvement to the degree usually associated with ownership and control over the infrastructure as described in paragraph 5.

2   IFRS 15 *Revenue from Contracts with Customers*, issued in May 2014, replaced IAS 18 *Revenue*.

BC28   In service concession arrangements rights are usually conveyed for a limited period, which is similar to a lease. However, for arrangements within the scope of the Interpretation, the operator's right is different from that of a lessee: the grantor retains control over the use to which the infrastructure is put, by controlling or regulating what services the operator must provide, to whom it must provide them, and at what price, as described in paragraph 5(a). The grantor also retains control over any significant residual interest in the infrastructure throughout the period of the arrangement. Unlike a lessee, the operator does not have a right of use of the underlying asset: rather it has access to operate the infrastructure to provide the public service on behalf of the grantor in accordance with the terms specified in the contract.

BC29   The IFRIC considered whether the scope of the Interpretation might overlap with IFRIC 4. In particular, it noted the views expressed by some respondents that the contractual terms of certain service arrangements would be regarded as leases under IFRIC 4 and would also be regarded as meeting the scope criterion set out in paragraph 5 of IFRIC 12. The IFRIC did not regard the choice between accounting treatments as appropriate because it could lead to different accounting treatments for contracts that have similar economic effects. In the light of comments received the IFRIC amended the scope of IFRIC 4 to specify that if a service arrangement met the scope requirements of IFRIC 12 it would not be within the scope of IFRIC 4.

Recognition and measurement of arrangement consideration (paragraphs 12 and 13)

BC30   The accounting requirements for construction and service contracts are addressed in IAS 11 *Construction Contracts*[3] and IAS 18[4]. They require revenue to be recognised by reference to the stage of completion of the contract activity. IAS 18 states the general principle that revenue is measured at the fair value of the consideration received or receivable. However, the IFRIC observed that the fair value of the construction services delivered may in practice be the most appropriate method of establishing the fair value of the consideration received or receivable for the construction services. This will be the case in service concession arrangements, because the consideration attributable to the construction activity often has to be apportioned from a total sum receivable on the contract as a whole and, if it consists of an intangible asset, may also be subject to uncertainty in measurement.

3   IFRS 15 *Revenue from Contracts with Customers*, issued in May 2014, replaced IAS 11 *Construction Contracts* and IAS 18 *Revenue*. IFRS 15 requires revenue to be recognised when (or as) an entity satisfies a performance obligation by transferring a promised good or service to a customer. IFRS 15 measures the revenue by (a) determining the amount of consideration to which an entity expects to be entitled in exchange for transferring promised goods or services to a customer; and (b) allocating that amount to the performance obligations.

4   IFRS 15 *Revenue from Contracts with Customers*, issued in May 2014, replaced IAS 11 *Construction Contracts* and IAS 18 *Revenue*. IFRS 15 requires revenue to be recognised when (or as) an entity satisfies a performance obligation by transferring a promised good or service to a customer. IFRS 15 measures the revenue by (a) determining the amount of consideration to which an entity expects to be entitled in exchange for transferring promised goods or services to a customer; and (b) allocating that amount to the performance obligations.

BC31   The IFRIC noted that IAS 18[5] requires its recognition criteria to be applied separately to identifiable components of a single transaction in order to reflect the substance of the transaction. For example, when the selling price of a product includes an identifiable amount for subsequent servicing, that amount is deferred and is recognised as revenue over the period during which the service is performed. The IFRIC concluded that this requirement was relevant to service arrangements within the scope of the Interpretation. Arrangements within the scope of the Interpretation involve an operator providing more than one service, ie construction or upgrade services, and operation services. Although the contract for each service is generally negotiated as a single contract, its terms call for separate phases or elements because each separate phase or element has its own distinct skills, requirements and risks. The IFRIC noted that, in these circumstances, IAS 18 paragraphs 4 and 13 require the contract to be separated into two separate phases or elements, a construction element within the scope of IAS 11[6] and an operations element within the scope of IAS 18. Thus the operator might report different profit margins on each phase or element. The IFRIC noted that the amount for each service would be identifiable because such services were often provided as a single service. The IFRIC also noted that the combining and segmenting criteria of IAS 11 applied only to the construction element of the arrangement.

BC32   In some circumstances, the grantor makes a non-cash payment for the construction services, ie it gives the operator an intangible asset (a right to charge users of the public service) in exchange for the operator providing construction services. The operator then uses the intangible asset to generate further revenues from users of the public service.

BC33   Paragraph 12 of IAS 18[7] states:

> When goods are sold or services are rendered in exchange for dissimilar goods or services, the exchange is regarded as a transaction which generates revenue. The revenue is measured at the fair value of the goods or services received, adjusted by the amount of any cash or cash equivalents transferred. When the fair value of the goods or services received cannot be measured reliably, the revenue is measured at the fair value of the goods or services given up, adjusted by the amount of any cash or cash equivalents transferred.

---

5   IFRS 15 *Revenue from Contracts with Customers*, issued in May 2014, replaced IAS 11 *Construction Contracts* and IAS 18 *Revenue*. IFRS 15 requires revenue to be recognised when (or as) an entity satisfies a performance obligation by transferring a promised good or service to a customer. IFRS 15 measures the revenue by (a) determining the amount of consideration to which an entity expects to be entitled in exchange for transferring promised goods or services to a customer; and (b) allocating that amount to the performance obligations.

6   IFRS 15 *Revenue from Contracts with Customers*, issued in May 2014, replaced IAS 11 *Construction Contracts* and IAS 18 *Revenue*. IFRS 15 requires revenue to be recognised when (or as) an entity satisfies a performance obligation by transferring a promised good or service to a customer. IFRS 15 measures the revenue by (a) determining the amount of consideration to which an entity expects to be entitled in exchange for transferring promised goods or services to a customer; and (b) allocating that amount to the performance obligations.

7   IFRS 15 *Revenue from Contracts with Customers*, issued in May 2014, replaced IAS 18 *Revenue*. IFRS 15 requires an entity to measure non-cash consideration at fair value, unless the entity cannot reasonably estimate the fair value of the non-cash consideration. In such cases, IFRS 15 requires the entity to measure the consideration indirectly by reference to the stand-alone selling price of the goods or services promised to the customer in exchange for the consideration.

BC34   The IFRIC noted that total revenue does not equal total cash inflows. The reason for this outcome is that, when the operator receives an intangible asset in exchange for its construction services, there are two sets of inflows and outflows rather than one. In the first set, the construction services are exchanged for the intangible asset in a barter transaction with the grantor. In the second set, the intangible asset received from the grantor is used up to generate cash flows from users of the public service. This result is not unique to service arrangements within the scope of the Interpretation. Any situation in which an entity provides goods or services in exchange for another dissimilar asset that is subsequently used to generate cash revenues would lead to a similar result.

BC35   Some IFRIC members were uncomfortable with such a result, and would have preferred a method of accounting under which total revenues were limited to the cash inflows. However, they accepted that it is consistent with the treatment accorded to a barter transaction, ie an exchange of dissimilar goods or services.

Consideration given by the grantor to the operator (paragraphs 14–19)

BC36   The IFRIC observed that the contractual rights that the operator receives in exchange for providing construction services can take a variety of forms. They are not necessarily rights to receive cash or other financial assets.

BC37   The draft Interpretations proposed that the nature of the operator's asset depended on who had the primary responsibility to pay the operator for the services. The operator should recognise a financial asset when the grantor had the primary responsibility to pay the operator for the services. The operator should recognise an intangible asset in all other cases.

BC38   Respondents to the draft Interpretations argued that determining which accounting model to apply by looking at who has the primary responsibility to pay the operator for the services, irrespective of who bears demand risk (ie ability and willingness of users to pay for the service), would result in an accounting treatment that did not reflect the economic substance of the arrangement. Respondents were concerned that the proposal would require operators with essentially identical cash flow streams to adopt different accounting models. This would impair users' understanding of entities involved in providing public-to-private service concession arrangements. Several gave the example of a shadow toll road and a toll road, where the economics (demand risk) of the arrangements would be similar, pointing out that under the proposals the two arrangements would be accounted for differently. In the light of comments received on the proposals, the IFRIC decided to clarify (see paragraphs 15–19) the extent to which an operator should recognise a financial asset and an intangible asset.

BC39   Responses to the draft Interpretations provided only limited information about the impact of the proposals. To obtain additional information, IASB staff arranged for discussions with preparers, auditors and regulators. The consensus of those consulted was that the identity of the payer has no effect on the risks to the operator's cash flow stream. The operator typically relies on the terms of the service arrangement contract to determine the risks to its cash flow stream. The operator's cash flows may be guaranteed by the grantor, in which case the grantor bears demand risk, or the operator's cash flows may be conditional on usage levels, in which case the operator bears demand risk.

BC40 The IFRIC noted that the operator's cash flows are guaranteed when (a) the grantor agrees to pay the operator specified or determinable amounts whether or not the public service is used (sometimes known as take-or-pay arrangements) or (b) the grantor grants a right to the operator to charge users of the public service and the grantor guarantees the operator's cash flows by way of a shortfall guarantee described in paragraph 16. The operator's cash flows are conditional on usage when it has no such guarantee but must obtain its revenue either directly from users of the public service or from the grantor in proportion to public usage of the service (road tolls or shadow tolls for example).

A financial asset (operator's cash flows are guaranteed by the grantor)

BC41 Paragraph 11 of IAS 32 *Financial Instruments: Presentation* defines a financial asset to include 'a contractual right to receive cash or another financial asset from another entity'. Paragraph 13 of that standard clarifies that 'contractual' refers to 'an agreement between two or more parties that has clear economic consequences that the parties have little, if any, discretion to avoid, usually because the agreement is enforceable by law.'

BC42 The IFRIC decided that a financial asset should be recognised to the extent that the operator has an unconditional present right to receive cash from or at the direction of the grantor for the construction services; and the grantor has little, if any, discretion to avoid payment, usually because the agreement is enforceable by law. The operator has a contractual right to receive cash for the construction services if the grantor contractually guarantees the operator's cash flows, in the manner described in paragraph 16. The IFRIC noted that the operator has an unconditional right to receive cash to the extent that the grantor bears the risk (demand risk) that the cash flows generated by the users of the public service will not be sufficient to recover the operator's investment.

BC43 The IFRIC noted that:

(a) an agreement to pay for the shortfall, if any, between amounts received from users of the service and specified or determinable amounts does not meet the definition of a financial guarantee in paragraph 9 of IAS 39 *Financial Instruments: Recognition and Measurement*[8] because the operator has an unconditional contractual right to receive cash from the grantor. Furthermore, the amendments made to IAS 39 in August 2005 by *Financial Guarantee Contracts* do not address the treatment of financial guarantee contracts by the holder. The objective of the amendments was to ensure that issuers of financial guarantee contracts recognise a liability for the obligations the guarantor has undertaken in issuing that guarantee.

---

8 IFRS 9 *Financial Instruments* replaced IAS 39. IFRS 9 applies to all items that were previously within the scope of IAS 39.

(b)   users or the grantor may pay the contractual amount receivable directly to the operator. The method of payment is a matter of form only. In both cases the operator has a present, unconditional, contractual right to receive the specified or determinable cash flows from or at the direction of the grantor. The nature of the operator's asset is not altered solely because the contractual amount receivable may be paid directly by users of the public service. The IFRIC observed that accounting for these contractual cash flows in accordance with IASs 32 and 39 faithfully reflects the economics of the arrangements, which is to provide finance to the operator for the construction of the infrastructure.

Operator's cash flows are contingent on the operator meeting specified quality or efficiency requirements

BC44   The IFRIC concluded that the definition of a financial asset is met even if the contractual right to receive cash is contingent on the operator meeting specified quality or efficiency requirements or targets. Before the grantor is required to pay the operator for its construction services, the operator may have to ensure that the infrastructure is capable of generating the public services specified by the grantor or that the infrastructure is up to or exceeds operating standards or efficiency targets specified by the grantor to ensure a specified level of service and capacity can be delivered. In this respect the operator's position is the same as that of any other entity in which payment for goods or services is contingent on subsequent performance of the goods or service sold.

BC45   Therefore IFRIC 12 treats the consideration given by the grantor to the operator as giving rise to a financial asset irrespective of whether the contractual amounts receivable are contingent on the operator meeting levels of performance or efficiency targets.[9]

An intangible asset (operator's cash flows are conditional on usage)

BC46   IAS 38 *Intangible Assets* defines an intangible asset as 'an identifiable non-monetary asset without physical substance'. It mentions licences as examples of intangible assets. It describes an asset as being identifiable when it arises from contractual rights.

BC47   The IFRIC concluded that the right of an operator to charge users of the public service meets the definition of an intangible asset, and therefore should be accounted for in accordance with IAS 38. In these circumstances the operator's revenue is conditional on usage and it bears the risk (demand risk) that the cash flows generated by users of the public service will not be sufficient to recover its investment.

BC48   In the absence of contractual arrangements designed to ensure that the operator receives a minimum amount (see paragraphs BC53 and BC54), the operator has no contractual right to receive cash even if receipt of the cash is highly probable.

---

9   IFRS 15 *Revenue from Contracts with Customers*, issued in May 2014, replaced IAS 18 *Revenue*. IFRS 15 requires an entity to recognise a financial asset to the extent that it has an unconditional contractual right to receive cash or another financial asset. This is also discussed in paragraph 16 of IFRIC 12.

Rather, the operator has an opportunity to charge those who use the public service in the future. The operator bears the demand risk and hence its commercial return is contingent on users using the public service. The operator's asset is a licence, which would be classified as an intangible asset within the scope of IAS 38. And, as clarified in paragraph AG10 of the application guidance in IAS 32:

> Physical assets (such as inventories, property, plant and equipment), leased assets and intangible assets (such as patents and trademarks) are not financial assets. Control of such physical and intangible assets creates an opportunity to generate an inflow of cash or another financial asset, but it does not give rise to a present right to receive cash or another financial asset.

BC49   The IFRIC considered whether a right to charge users unsupported by any shortfall guarantee from the grantor could be regarded as an indirect right to receive cash arising from the contract with the grantor. It concluded that although the operator's asset might have characteristics that are similar to those of a financial asset, it would not meet the definition of a financial asset in IAS 32: the operator would not at the balance sheet date have a contractual right to receive cash from another entity. That other entity (ie the user) would still have the ability to avoid any obligation. The grantor would be passing to the operator an opportunity to charge users in future, not a present right to receive cash.

Contractual arrangements that eliminate substantially all variability in the operator's return

BC50   The IFRIC considered whether agreements incorporating contractual arrangements designed to eliminate substantially all variability in the operator's return would meet the definition of a financial asset, for example:

(a)   the price charged by the operator would be varied by regulation designed to ensure that the operator received a substantially fixed return; or

(b)   the operator would be permitted to collect revenues from users or the grantor until it achieved a specified return on its investment, at which point the arrangement would come to an end.

BC51   The IFRIC noted that, as a result of such contractual arrangements, the operator's return would be low risk. Only if usage were extremely low would the contractual mechanisms fail to give the operator the specified return. The likelihood of usage being that low could be remote. Commercially, the operator's return would be regarded as fixed, giving its asset many of the characteristics of a financial asset.

BC52   However, the IFRIC concluded that the fact that the operator's asset was low risk did not influence its classification. IAS 32 does not define financial assets by reference to the amount of risk in the return—it defines them solely by reference to the existence or absence of an unconditional contractual right to receive cash. There are other examples of licences that offer the holders of the rights predictable, low risk returns, but such licences are not regarded as giving the holder a contractual right to cash. And there are other industries in which price regulation is designed to provide the operators with substantially fixed returns—but the rights of operators in these other industries are not classified as financial assets as a result. The operator's asset is a variable term licence, which would be classified as an intangible asset within the scope of IAS 38.

A financial asset and an intangible asset

BC53　The IFRIC concluded that if the operator is paid for its construction services partly by a financial asset and partly by an intangible asset it is necessary to account separately for each component of the operator's consideration. The IFRIC included the requirement to account separately for each component (sometimes known as a bifurcated arrangement) of the operator's consideration in response to a concern raised on the draft Interpretations. The concern was that, in some arrangements, both parties to the contract share the risk (demand risk) that the cash flows generated by users of the public service will not be sufficient to recover the operator's investment. In order to achieve the desired sharing of risk, the parties often agree to arrangements under which the grantor pays the operator for its services partly by a financial asset and partly by granting a right to charge users of the public service (an intangible asset). The IFRIC concluded that in these circumstances it would be necessary to divide the operator's consideration into a financial asset component for any guaranteed amount of cash or other financial asset and an intangible asset for the remainder.

BC54　The IFRIC concluded that the nature of consideration given by the grantor to the operator is determined by reference to the contract terms and when it exists, relevant contract law. The IFRIC noted public-to-private service agreements are rarely if ever the same; technical requirements vary by sector and country. Furthermore, the terms of the contractual agreement may also depend on the specific features of the overall legal framework of the particular country. Public-to-private service contract laws, where they exist, may contain terms that do not have to be repeated in individual contracts.

Contractual obligations to restore the infrastructure to a specified level of serviceability (paragraph 21)

BC55　The IFRIC noted that IAS 37 *Provisions, Contingent Liabilities and Contingent Assets* prohibits an entity from providing for the replacement of parts of its own property, plant and equipment. IAS 16 requires such costs to be recognised in the carrying amount of an item of property, plant and equipment if the recognition criteria in paragraph 7 are met. Each part of an item of property, plant and equipment with a cost that is significant in relation to the total cost of the item is depreciated separately. The IFRIC concluded that this prohibition would not apply to arrangements within the scope of the Interpretation because the operator does not recognise the infrastructure as its own property, plant and equipment. The operator has an unavoidable obligation that it owes to a third party, the grantor, in respect of the infrastructure. The operator should recognise its obligations in accordance with IAS 37.

BC56　The IFRIC considered whether the Interpretation should contain guidance on the timing of recognition of the obligations. It noted that the precise terms and circumstances of the obligations would vary from contract to contract. It concluded that the requirements and guidance in IAS 37 were sufficiently clear to enable an operator to identify the period(s) in which different obligations should be recognised.

Borrowing costs (paragraph 22)

BC57   IAS 23 *Borrowing Costs* permits borrowing costs to be capitalised as part of the cost of a qualifying asset to the extent that they are directly attributable to its acquisition, construction or production until the asset is ready for its intended use or sale. That Standard defines a qualifying asset as 'an asset that necessarily takes a substantial period of time to get ready for its intended use or sale'.

BC58   For arrangements within the scope of the Interpretation, the IFRIC decided that an intangible asset (ie the grantor gives the operator a right to charge users of the public service in return for construction services) meets the definition of a qualifying asset of the operator because generally the licence would not be ready for use until the infrastructure was constructed or upgraded. A financial asset (ie the grantor gives the operator a contractual right to receive cash or other financial asset in return for construction services) does not meet the definition of a qualifying asset of the operator. The IFRIC observed that interest is generally accreted on the carrying value of financial assets.

BC59   The IFRIC noted that financing arrangements may result in an operator obtaining borrowed funds and incurring associated borrowing costs before some or all of the funds are used for expenditure relating to construction or operation services. In such circumstances the funds are often temporarily invested. Any investment income earned on such funds is recognised in accordance with IAS 39,[10] unless the operator adopts the allowed alternative treatment, in which case investment income earned during the construction phase of the arrangement is accounted for in accordance with paragraph 16 of IAS 23.[11]

Financial asset (paragraphs 23–25)[12]

BC60   Paragraph 9 of IAS 39 identifies and defines four categories of financial asset: (i) those held at fair value through profit or loss; (ii) held-to-maturity investments; (iii) loans and receivables; and (iv) available-for-sale financial assets.

BC61   Paragraph 24 of IFRIC 12 assumes that public-to-private service arrangement financial assets will not be categorised as held-to-maturity investments. Paragraph 9 of IAS 39 states that a financial asset may not be classified as a held-to-maturity investment if it meets the definition of a loan or receivable. An asset that meets the definition of a held-to-maturity investment will meet the definition of a loan or receivable unless:

10 IFRS 9 *Financial Instruments* replaced IAS 39. IFRS 9 applies to all items that were previously within the scope of IAS 39.

11 In March 2007, IAS 23 was revised to require the previously allowed alternative treatment of capitalisation. Therefore, an entity is required to capitalise borrowing costs as part of the cost of a qualifying asset to the extent that they are directly attributable to its acquisition, construction or production until the asset is ready for its intended use or sale. That revision does not affect the reasoning set out in this Basis for Conclusions.

12 IFRS 9 *Financial Instruments* replaced IAS 39. IFRS 9 applies to all items that were previously within the scope of IAS 39.

(a)   it is quoted in an active market; or

(b)   the holder may not recover substantially all of its initial investment, other than because of credit deterioration.

It is not envisaged that a public-to-private service arrangement financial asset will be quoted in an active market. Hence the circumstances of (a) will not arise. In the circumstances of (b), the asset must be classified as available for sale (if not designated upon initial recognition as at fair value through profit or loss).

BC62   The IFRIC considered whether the contract would include an embedded derivative if the amount to be received by the operator could vary with the quality of subsequent services to be provided by the operator or performance or efficiency targets to be achieved by the operator. The IFRIC concluded that it would not, because the definition of a derivative in IAS 39 requires, among other things, that the variable is not specific to a party to the contract. The consequence is that the contract's provision for variations in payments does not meet the definition of a derivative and, accordingly, the requirements of IAS 39 in relation to embedded derivatives do not apply. The IFRIC observed that if the amount to be received by the operator is conditional on the infrastructure meeting quality or performance or efficiency targets as described in paragraph BC44, this would not prevent the amount from being classified as a financial asset. The IFRIC also concluded that during the construction phase of the arrangement the operator's asset (representing its accumulating right to be paid for providing construction services) should be classified as a financial asset when it represents cash or another financial asset due from or at the direction of the grantor.

Intangible asset (paragraph 26)

BC63   The Interpretation requires the operator to account for its intangible asset in accordance with IAS 38. Among other requirements, IAS 38 requires an intangible asset with a finite useful economic life to be amortised over that life. Paragraph 97 states that 'the amortisation method used shall reflect the pattern in which the asset's future economic benefits are expected to be consumed by the entity.'

BC64   The IFRIC considered whether it would be appropriate for intangible assets under paragraph 26 to be amortised using an 'interest' method of amortisation, ie one that takes account of the time value of money in addition to the consumption of the intangible asset, treating the asset more like a monetary than a non-monetary asset. However, the IFRIC concluded that there was nothing unique about these intangible assets that would justify use of a method of depreciation different from that used for other intangible assets. The IFRIC noted that paragraph 98 of IAS 38 provides for a number of amortisation methods for intangible assets with finite useful lives. These methods include the straight-line method, the diminishing balance method and the units of production method. The method used is selected on the basis of the expected pattern of consumption of the expected future economic benefits embodied in the asset and is applied consistently from period to period, unless there is a change in the expected pattern of consumption of those future economic benefits.

BC65   The IFRIC noted that interest methods of amortisation are not permitted under IAS 38. Therefore, IFRIC 12 does not provide exceptions to permit use of interest methods of amortisation.

BC66   The IFRIC considered when the operator should first recognise the intangible asset. The IFRIC concluded that the intangible asset (the licence) received in exchange for construction services should be recognised in accordance with general principles applicable to contracts for the exchange of assets or services.

BC67   The IFRIC noted that it is current practice not to recognise executory contracts to the extent that they are unperformed by both parties (unless the contract is onerous). IAS 37 describes executory contracts as 'contracts under which neither party has performed any of its obligations or both parties have partially performed their obligations to an equal extent'. Paragraph 91 of the *Framework*[13] states:

> In practice, obligations under contracts that are equally proportionately unperformed (for example, liabilities for inventory ordered but not yet received) are generally not recognised as liabilities in the financial statements.

BC68   Therefore, the IFRIC concluded that contracts within the scope of the Interpretation should not be recognised to the extent that they are executory. The IFRIC noted that service concession arrangements within the scope of the Interpretation are generally executory when the contracts are signed. The IFRIC also concluded that during the construction phase of the arrangement the operator's asset (representing its accumulating right to be paid for providing construction services) should be classified as an intangible asset to the extent that it represents a right to receive a right (licence) to charge users of the public service (an intangible asset).

Items provided to the operator by the grantor (paragraph 27)

BC69   For service arrangements within the scope of the Interpretation, pre-existing infrastructure items made available to the operator by the grantor for the purpose of the service arrangement are not recognised as property, plant and equipment of the operator.

BC70   However, different considerations apply to other assets provided to the operator by the grantor if the operator can keep or deal with the assets as it wishes. Such assets become assets of the operator and so should be accounted for in accordance with general recognition and measurement principles, as should the obligations undertaken in exchange for them.

BC71   The IFRIC considered whether such assets would represent government grants, as defined in paragraph 3 of IAS 20 *Accounting for Government Grants and Disclosure of Government Assistance*:

---

13   now paragraph 4.46 of the *Conceptual Framework*

> Government grants are assistance by government in the form of transfers of resources to an entity in return for past or future compliance with certain conditions relating to the operating activities of the entity. They exclude those forms of government assistance which cannot reasonably have a value placed upon them and transactions with government which cannot be distinguished from the normal trading transactions of the entity.

The IFRIC concluded that if such assets were part of the overall consideration payable by the grantor on an arms' length basis for the operator's services, they would not constitute 'assistance'. Therefore, they would not meet the definition of government grants in IAS 20 and that standard would not apply.

Transition (paragraphs 29 and 30)

BC72   IAS 8 *Accounting Policies, Changes in Accounting Estimates and Errors* states that an entity shall account for a change in accounting policy resulting from initial application of an Interpretation in accordance with any specific transitional provisions in that Interpretation. In the absence of any specific transitional provisions, the general requirements of IAS 8 apply. The general requirement in IAS 8 is that the changes should be accounted for retrospectively, except to the extent that retrospective application would be impracticable.

BC73   The IFRIC noted that there are two aspects to retrospective determination: reclassification and remeasurement. The IFRIC took the view that it will usually be practicable to determine retrospectively the appropriate classification of all amounts previously included in an operator's balance sheet, but that retrospective remeasurement of service arrangement assets might not always be practicable.

BC74   The IFRIC noted that, when retrospective restatement is not practicable, IAS 8 requires prospective application from the earliest practicable date, which could be the start of the current period. Under prospective application, the operator could be applying different accounting models to similar transactions, which the IFRIC decided would be inappropriate. The IFRIC regarded it as important that the correct accounting model should be consistently applied.

BC75   The Interpretation reflects these conclusions.

Amendments to IFRS 1

BC76   The amendments to IFRS 1 *First-time Adoption of International Financial Reporting Standards* are necessary to ensure that the transitional arrangements are available to both existing users and first-time adopters of IFRSs. The IFRIC believes that the requirements will ensure that the balance sheet will exclude any items that would not qualify for recognition as assets and liabilities under IFRSs.

Summary of changes from the draft Interpretations

BC77   The main changes from the IFRIC's proposals are as follows:

(a)   The proposals were published in three separate draft Interpretations, D12 *Service Concession Arrangements—Determining the Accounting Model*, D13 *Service Concession Arrangements—The Financial Asset Model* and D14 *Service Concession Arrangements—The Intangible Asset Model*. In finalising IFRIC 12, the IFRIC combined the three draft Interpretations.

(b)   By contrast with IFRIC 12 the draft Interpretations did not explain the reasons for the scope limitations and the reasons for the control approach adopted by the IFRIC in paragraph 5. The IFRIC added Information Note 2 to IFRIC 12 to provide references to standards that apply to arrangements outside the scope of the Interpretation.

(c)   The scope of the proposals did not include 'whole of life infrastructure' (ie infrastructure used in a public-to-private service arrangement for its entire useful life). IFRIC 12 includes 'whole of life infrastructure' within its scope.

(d)   Under the approach proposed, an entity determined the appropriate accounting model by reference to whether the grantor or the user had primary responsibility to pay the operator for the services provided. IFRIC 12 requires an entity to recognise a financial asset to the extent that the operator has an unconditional contractual right to receive cash from or at the direction of the grantor. The operator should recognise an intangible asset to the extent that it receives a right to charge users of the public service.

(e)   By contrast with IFRIC 12, the draft Interpretations implied that the nature of asset recognised (a financial asset or an intangible asset) by the operator as consideration for providing construction services determined the accounting for the operation phase of the arrangement.

(f)   Under the approach proposed in the draft Interpretations, an entity could capitalise borrowing costs under the allowed alternative treatment in IAS 23. IFRIC 12 requires borrowing costs to be recognised as an expense in the period in which they are incurred unless the operator has a contractual right to receive an intangible asset (a right to charge users of the public service), in which case borrowing costs attributable to the arrangement may be capitalised in accordance with the allowed alternative treatment under IAS 23.[14]

(g)   In finalising IFRIC 12, the IFRIC decided to amend IFRIC 4.

---

14 In March 2007, IAS 23 was revised to require the previously allowed alternative treatment of capitalisation. Therefore, an entity is required to capitalise borrowing costs as part of the cost of a qualifying asset to the extent that they are directly attributable to its acquisition, construction or production until the asset is ready for its intended use or sale. That revision does not affect the reasoning set out in this Basis for Conclusions.

Documents published to accompany

IFRIC 14

IAS 19—The Limit on a Defined Benefit Asset, Minimum Funding Requirements and their Interaction

The text of the unaccompanied Interpretation, IFRIC 14, is contained in Part A of this edition. Its effective date when issued was 1 January 2008. The text of the Accompanying Guidance on IFRIC 14 is contained in Part B of this edition. This part presents the following documents:

BASIS FOR CONCLUSIONS

Basis for Conclusions on
IFRIC Interpretation 14 *IAS 19—The Limit on a Defined Benefit Asset, Minimum Funding Requirements and their Interaction*

This Basis for Conclusions accompanies, but is not part of, IFRIC 14.

The original text has been marked up to reflect the revision of IAS 1 Presentation of Financial Statements *in 2007: new text is underlined and deleted text is struck through.*

BC1   This Basis for Conclusions summarises the IFRIC's considerations in reaching its consensus. Individual IFRIC members gave greater weight to some factors than to others.

BC2   The IFRIC noted that practice varies significantly with regard to the treatment of the effect of a minimum funding requirement on the limit placed by paragraph 64 of IAS 19 *Employee Benefits* on the amount of a defined benefit asset. The IFRIC therefore decided to include this issue on its agenda. In considering the issue, the IFRIC also became aware of the need for general guidance on determining the limit on the measurement of the defined benefit asset, and for guidance on when that limit makes a minimum funding requirement onerous.

BC3   The IFRIC published D19 *IAS 19—The Asset Ceiling: Availability of Economic Benefits and Minimum Funding Requirements* in August 2006. In response, the IFRIC received 48 comment letters.

BC3A   In November 2009 the International Accounting Standards Board amended IFRIC 14 to remove an unintended consequence arising from the treatment of prepayments in some circumstances when there is a minimum funding requirement (see paragraphs BC30A–BC30D).

Definition of a minimum funding requirement

BC4   D19 referred to statutory or contractual minimum funding requirements. Respondents to D19 asked for further guidance on what constituted a minimum funding requirement. The IFRIC decided to clarify that for the purpose of the Interpretation a minimum funding requirement is any requirement for the entity to make contributions to *fund* a post-employment or other long-term defined benefit plan.

Interaction between IAS 19 and minimum funding requirements

BC5   Funding requirements would not normally affect the accounting for a plan under IAS 19. However, paragraph 64 of IAS 19 limits the amount of the net defined benefit asset to the available economic benefit. The interaction of a minimum funding requirement and this limit has two possible effects:

   (a)   the minimum funding requirement may restrict the economic benefits available as a reduction in future contributions, and

(b)   the limit may make the minimum funding requirement onerous because contributions payable under the requirement in respect of services already received may not be available once they have been paid, either as a refund or as a reduction in future contributions.

BC6   These effects raised general questions about the availability of economic benefits in the form of a refund or a reduction in future contributions.

Availability of the economic benefit

BC7   One view of 'available' would limit the economic benefit to the amount that is realisable immediately at the end of the reporting period ~~balance sheet date~~.

BC8   The IFRIC disagreed with this view. The *Framework*[1] defines an asset as a resource 'from which future economic benefits are expected to flow to the entity'. Therefore, it is not necessary for the economic benefit to be realisable immediately. Indeed, a reduction in future contributions cannot be realisable immediately.

BC9   The IFRIC concluded that a refund or reduction in future contributions is available if it could be realisable at some point during the life of the plan or when the plan liability is settled. Respondents to D19 were largely supportive of this conclusion.

BC10   In the responses to D19, some argued that an entity may expect to use the surplus to give improved benefits. Others noted that future actuarial losses might reduce or eliminate the surplus. In either case there would be no refund or reduction in future contributions. The IFRIC noted that the existence of an asset at the end of the reporting period ~~balance sheet date~~ depends on whether the entity has the right to obtain a refund or reduction in future contributions. The existence of the asset at that date is not affected by possible future changes to the amount of the surplus. If future events occur that change the amount of the surplus, their effects are recognised when they occur. Accordingly, if the entity decides to improve benefits, or future losses in the plan reduce the surplus, the consequences are recognised when the decision is made or the losses occur. The IFRIC noted that such events of future periods do not affect the existence or measurement of the asset at the end of the reporting period ~~balance sheet date~~.

The asset available as a refund of a surplus

BC11   The IFRIC noted that a refund of a surplus could potentially be obtained in three ways:

(a)   during the life of the plan, without assuming that the plan liabilities have to be settled in order to get the refund (eg in some jurisdictions, the entity may have a right to a refund during the life of the plan, irrespective of whether the plan liabilities are settled); or

---

1   The reference to the *Framework* is to IASC's *Framework for the Preparation and Presentation of Financial Statements*, adopted by the IASB in 2001. In September 2010 the IASB replaced the *Framework* with the *Conceptual Framework for Financial Reporting*.

(b)   assuming the gradual settlement of the plan liabilities over time until all members have left the plan; or

(c)   assuming the full settlement of the plan liabilities in a single event (ie as a plan wind-up).

BC12   The IFRIC concluded that all three ways should be considered in determining whether an economic benefit was available to the entity. Some respondents to D19 raised the question of when an entity controls an asset that arises from the availability of a refund, in particular if a refund would be available only if a third party (for example the plan trustees) gave its approval. The IFRIC concluded that an entity controlled the asset only if the entity has an unconditional right to the refund. If that right depends on actions by a third party, the entity does not have an unconditional right.

BC13   If the plan liability is settled by an immediate wind-up, the costs associated with the wind-up may be significant. One reason for this may be that the cost of annuities available on the market is expected to be significantly higher than that implied by the IAS 19 basis. Other costs include the legal and other professional fees expected to be incurred during the winding-up process. Accordingly, a plan with an apparent surplus may not be able to recover any of that surplus on wind-up.

BC14   The IFRIC noted that the available surplus should be measured at the amount that the entity could receive from the plan. The IFRIC decided that in determining the amount of the refund available on wind-up of the plan, the amount of the costs associated with the settlement and refund should be deducted if paid by the plan.

BC15   The IFRIC noted that the costs of settling the plan liability would be dependent on the facts and circumstances of the plan and it decided not to issue any specific guidance in this respect.

BC16   The IFRIC also noted that the present value of the defined benefit obligation and the fair value of assets are both measured on a present value basis[2] and therefore take into account the timing of the future cash flows. The IFRIC concluded that no further adjustment for the time value of money needs to be made when measuring the amount of a refund determined as the full amount or a proportion of the surplus that is realisable at a future date.

The asset available in the form of a future contribution reduction

BC17   The IFRIC decided that the amount of the contribution reduction available to the entity should be measured with reference to the amount that the entity would have been required to pay had there been no surplus. The IFRIC concluded that is represented by the cost to the entity of accruing benefits in the plan, in other words by the future IAS 19 service cost. Respondents to D19 broadly supported this conclusion.

---

2   IFRS 13 *Fair Value Measurement*, issued in May 2011, defines fair value and contains the requirements for measuring fair value. IFRS 13 does not specify a particular valuation technique for measuring the fair value of plan assets.

              © IFRS Foundation

BC18   When the issue of the availability of reductions in future contributions was first raised with the IFRIC, some expressed the view that an entity should recognise an asset only to the extent that there was a formal agreement between the trustees and the entity specifying contributions payable lower than the IAS 19 service cost. The IFRIC disagreed, concluding instead that an entity is entitled to assume that, in general, it will not be required to make contributions to a plan in order to maintain a surplus and hence that it will be able to reduce contributions if the plan has a surplus. (The effects of a minimum funding requirement on this assumption are discussed below.)

BC19   The IFRIC considered the assumptions that underlie the calculation of the future service cost. In respect of the discount rate, IAS 19 requires the measurement of the present value of the future contribution reduction to be based on the same discount rate as that used to determine the present value of the defined benefit obligation.

BC20   The IFRIC considered whether the term over which the contribution reduction should be calculated should be restricted to the expected future working lifetime of the active membership. The IFRIC disagreed with that view. The IFRIC noted that the entity could derive economic benefit from a reduction in contributions beyond that period. The IFRIC also noted that increasing the term of the calculation has a decreasing effect on the incremental changes to the asset because the reductions in contributions are discounted to a present value. Thus, for plans with a large surplus and no possibility of receiving a refund, the available asset will be limited even if the term of the calculation extends beyond the expected future working lifetime of the active membership to the expected life of the plan. This is consistent with paragraph BC77 of the Basis for Conclusions on IAS 19,[3] which states that 'the limit [on the measurement of the defined benefit asset] is likely to come into play *only* where ... the plan is very mature and has a very large surplus that is more than large enough to eliminate *all* future contributions and cannot be returned to the entity' (emphasis added). If the contribution reduction were determined by considering only the term of the expected future working lifetime of the active membership, the limit on the measurement of the defined benefit asset would come into play much more frequently.

BC21   Most respondents to D19 were supportive of this view. However, some argued that the term should be the shorter of the expected life of the plan and the expected life of the entity. The IFRIC agreed that the entity could not derive economic benefits from a reduction in contributions beyond its own expected life and has amended the Interpretation accordingly.

BC22   Next, the IFRIC considered what assumptions should be made about a future workforce. D19 proposed that the assumptions for the demographic profile of the future workforce should be consistent with the assumptions underlying the calculation of the present value of the defined benefit obligation at the end of the reporting period balance sheet date. Some respondents noted that the calculation of service costs for future periods requires assumptions that are not required for the calculation of the defined benefit obligation. In particular, the

---

3   As a result of the amendments to IAS 19 in June 2011, paragraph BC77 was deleted.

assumptions underlying the present value of the defined benefit obligation calculation do not include an explicit assumption for new entrants.

BC23   The IFRIC agreed that this is the case. The IFRIC noted that assumptions are needed in respect of the size of the future workforce and future benefits provided by the plan. The IFRIC decided that the future service cost should be based on the situation that exists at the end of the reporting period ~~balance sheet date~~ determined in accordance with IAS 19. Therefore, increases in the size of the workforce or the benefits provided by the plan should not be anticipated. Decreases in the size of the workforce or the benefits should be included in the assumptions for the future service cost at the same time as they are treated as curtailments in accordance with IAS 19.

The effect of a minimum funding requirement on the economic benefit available as a refund

BC24   The IFRIC considered whether a minimum funding requirement to make contributions to a plan in force at the end of the reporting period ~~balance sheet date~~ would restrict the extent to which a refund of surplus is available. The IFRIC noted that there is an implicit assumption in IAS 19 that the specified assumptions represent the best estimate of the eventual outcome of the plan in economic terms, while a requirement to make additional contributions is often a prudent approach designed to build in a risk margin for adverse circumstances. Moreover, when there are no members left in the plan, the minimum funding requirement would have no effect. This would leave the IAS 19 surplus available. To the extent that the entity has a right to this eventual surplus, the IAS 19 surplus would be available to the entity, regardless of the minimum funding restrictions in force at the end of the reporting period ~~balance sheet date~~. The IFRIC therefore concluded that the existence of a minimum funding requirement may affect the timing of a refund but does not affect whether it is ultimately available to the entity.

The effect of a minimum funding requirement on the economic benefit available as a reduction in future contributions

BC25   The entity's minimum funding requirements at a given date can be analysed into the contributions that are required to cover (a) an existing shortfall for past service on the minimum funding basis and (b) future service.

BC26   Contributions required to cover an existing shortfall may give rise to a liability, as discussed in paragraphs BC31–BC37 below. But they do not affect the availability of a reduction in future contributions for future service.

BC27   In contrast, future contribution requirements in respect of future service do not generate an additional liability at the end of the reporting period ~~balance sheet date~~ because they do not relate to past services received by the entity. However, they may reduce the extent to which the entity can benefit from a reduction in future contributions. Therefore, the IFRIC decided that the available asset from a contribution reduction should be calculated as the present value of the IAS 19 future service cost less the minimum funding contribution requirement in respect of future service in each year.

BC28   If the minimum funding contribution requirement is consistently greater than the IAS 19 future service cost, that calculation may be thought to imply that a liability exists. However, as noted above, an entity has no liability at the <u>end of the reporting period</u> <s>balance sheet date</s> in respect of minimum funding requirements that relate to future service. The economic benefit available from a reduction in future contributions can be nil, but it can never be a negative amount.

BC29   The respondents to D19 were largely supportive of these conclusions.

BC30   The IFRIC noted that future changes to regulations on minimum funding requirements might affect the available surplus. However, the IFRIC decided that, just as the future service cost was determined on the basis of the situation existing at the <u>end of the reporting period</u> <s>balance sheet date</s>, so should the effect of a minimum funding requirement. The IFRIC concluded that when determining the amount of an asset that might be available as a reduction in future contributions, an entity should not consider whether the minimum funding requirement might change in the future. The respondents to D19 were largely supportive of these conclusions.

Prepayments of a minimum funding requirement

BC30A   If an entity has prepaid future minimum funding requirement contributions and that prepayment will reduce future contributions, the prepayment generates economic benefits for the entity. However, to the extent that the future minimum funding requirement contributions exceeded future service costs, the original version of IFRIC 14 did not permit entities to consider those economic benefits in measuring a defined benefit asset. After issuing IFRIC 14, the Board reviewed the treatment of such prepayments. The Board concluded that such a prepayment provides an economic benefit to the entity by relieving the entity of an obligation to pay future minimum funding requirement contributions that exceed future service cost. Therefore, considering those economic benefits in measuring a defined benefit asset would convey more useful information to users of financial statements. In May 2009 the Board published that conclusion in an exposure draft *Prepayments of a Minimum Funding Requirement*. After considering the responses to that exposure draft, the Board amended IFRIC 14 by issuing *Prepayments of a Minimum Funding Requirement* in November 2009.

BC30B   Some respondents noted that the amendments increase the effect of funding considerations on the measurement of a defined benefit asset and liability and questioned whether funding considerations should ever affect the measurement. However, the Board noted that the sole purpose of the amendments was to eliminate an unintended consequence in IFRIC 14. Thus, the Board did not re-debate the fundamental conclusion of IFRIC 14 that funding is relevant to the measurement when an entity cannot recover the additional cost of a minimum funding requirement in excess of the IAS 19 service cost.

BC30C   Many respondents noted that the proposals made the assessment of the economic benefit available from a prepayment different from the assessment for a surplus arising from actuarial gains. Most agreed that a prepayment created an asset, but questioned why the Board did not extend the underlying principle to other surpluses that could be used to reduce future payments of minimum funding requirement contributions.

BC30D   The Board did not extend the scope of the amendments to surpluses arising from actuarial gains because such an approach would need further thought and the Board did not want to delay the amendments for prepayments. However, the Board may consider the matter further in a future comprehensive review of pension cost accounting.

Onerous minimum funding requirements

BC31   Minimum funding requirements for contributions to cover an existing minimum funding shortfall create an obligation for the entity at the end of the reporting period balance sheet date because they relate to past service. Nonetheless, usually minimum funding requirements do not affect the measurement of the defined benefit asset or liability under IAS 19. This is because the contributions, once paid, become plan assets and the additional net liability for the funding requirement is nil. However, the IFRIC noted that the limit on the measurement of the defined benefit asset in paragraph 64 of IAS 19 may make the funding obligation onerous, as follows.

BC32   If an entity is obliged to make contributions and some or all of those contributions will not subsequently be available as an economic benefit, it follows that when the contributions are made the entity will not be able to recognise an asset to that extent. However, the resulting loss to the entity does not arise on the payment of the contributions but earlier, at the point at which the obligation to pay arises.

BC33   Therefore, the IFRIC concluded that when an entity has an obligation under a minimum funding requirement to make additional contributions to a plan in respect of services already received, the entity should reduce the balance sheet asset or increase the liability recognised in the statement of financial position to the extent that the minimum funding contributions payable to the plan will not be available to the entity either as a refund or a reduction in future contributions.

BC34   Respondents to D19 broadly supported this conclusion. But some questioned whether the draft Interpretation extended the application of paragraph 64 of IAS 19 too far. They argued that it should apply only when an entity has a defined benefit asset. In particular, it should not be used to classify a funding requirement as onerous, thereby creating an additional liability to be recognised beyond that arising from the other requirements of IAS 19. Others agreed that such a liability existed, but questioned whether it fell within the scope of IAS 19 rather than IAS 37 *Provisions, Contingent Liabilities and Contingent Assets*.

BC35   The IFRIC did not agree that the Interpretation extends the application of paragraph 64 of IAS 19. Rather, it applies the principles in IAS 37 relating to onerous contracts in the context of the requirements of IAS 19, including paragraph 64. On the question whether the liability falls within the scope of IAS 19 or IAS 37, the IFRIC noted that employee benefits are excluded from the scope of IAS 37. The IFRIC therefore confirmed that the interaction of a minimum funding requirement and the limit on the measurement of the defined benefit asset could result in a decrease in a defined benefit asset or an increase in a defined benefit liability.

BC36–
BC37   [Deleted]

Transitional provisions

BC38   In D19, the IFRIC proposed that the draft Interpretation should be applied retrospectively. The draft Interpretation required immediate recognition of all adjustments relating to the minimum funding requirements. The IFRIC therefore argued that retrospective application would be straightforward.

BC39   Respondents to D19 noted that paragraph 58A[4] of IAS 19 causes the limit on the defined benefit asset to affect the deferred recognition of actuarial gains and losses. Retrospective application of the Interpretation could change the amount of that limit for previous periods, thereby also changing the deferred recognition of actuarial gains and losses. Calculating these revised amounts retrospectively over the life of the plan would be costly and of little benefit to users of financial statements.

BC40   The IFRIC agreed with this view. The IFRIC therefore amended the transitional provisions so that IFRIC 14 is to be applied only from the beginning of the first period presented in the financial statements for annual periods beginning on or after the effective date.

Summary of changes from D19

BC41   The Interpretation has been altered in the following significant respects since it was exposed for comment as D19:

(a)   The issue of when an entity controls an asset arising from the availability of a refund has been clarified (paragraphs BC10 and BC12).

(b)   Requirements relating to the assumptions underlying the measurement of a reduction in future contributions have been clarified (paragraphs BC22 and BC23).

(c)   The transitional requirements have been changed from retrospective application to application from the beginning of the first period presented in the first financial statements to which the Interpretation applies (paragraphs BC38–BC40).

(d)   In November 2009 the Board amended IFRIC 14 to require entities to recognise as an economic benefit any prepayment of minimum funding requirement contributions. At the same time, the Board removed references to 'present value' from paragraphs 16, 17, 20 and 22 and 'the surplus in the plan' from paragraph 16 because these references

---

4   IAS 19 (as amended in June 2011) eliminated deferred recognition of actuarial gains and losses and deleted paragraph 58A.

duplicated references in paragraph 64 of IAS 19. The Board also amended the term 'future accrual of benefits' to 'future service' for consistency with the rest of IAS 19.

(e) In June 2011 the Board issued an amended IAS 19 that eliminated the deferred recognition of actuarial gains and losses. As a consequence of that amendment, the Board deleted paragraphs 25 and 26, amended paragraphs 1, 6, 17, 24 and amended Examples 1–4 in the illustrative examples accompanying IFRIC 14. As a result of those changes paragraphs BC36 and BC37 of this Basis for Conclusions were deleted and paragraph BC5 was amended. Lastly, cross-references to IAS 19 were updated.

© IFRS Foundation

Document published to accompany

IFRIC 16

Hedges of a Net Investment in a Foreign Operation

The text of the unaccompanied Interpretation, IFRIC 16, is contained in Part A of this edition. Its effective date when issued was 1 October 2008. The text of the Accompanying Guidance on IFRIC 16 is contained in Part B of this edition. This part presents the following documents:

BASIS FOR CONCLUSIONS

Basis for Conclusions on IFRIC Interpretation 16 *Hedges of a Net Investment in a Foreign Operation*

This Basis for Conclusions accompanies, but is not part of, IFRIC 16.

Introduction

BC1   This Basis for Conclusions summarises the IFRIC's considerations in reaching its consensus. Individual IFRIC members gave greater weight to some factors than to others.

Background

BC2   The IFRIC was asked for guidance on accounting for the hedge of a net investment in a foreign operation in the consolidated financial statements. Interested parties had different views of the risks eligible for hedge accounting purposes. One issue is whether the risk arises from the foreign currency exposure to the functional currencies of the foreign operation and the parent entity, or whether it arises from the foreign currency exposure to the functional currency of the foreign operation and the presentation currency of the parent entity's consolidated financial statements.

BC3   Concern was also raised about which entity within a group could hold a hedging instrument in a hedge of a net investment in a foreign operation and in particular whether the parent entity holding the net investment in a foreign operation must also hold the hedging instrument.

BC4   Accordingly, the IFRIC decided to develop guidance on the accounting for a hedge of the foreign currency risk arising from a net investment in a foreign operation.

BC5   The IFRIC published draft Interpretation D22 *Hedges of a Net Investment in a Foreign Operation* for public comment in July 2007 and received 45 comment letters in response to its proposals.

Consensus

Hedged risk and hedged item

Functional currency versus presentation currency (paragraph 10)

BC6   The IFRIC received a submission suggesting that the method of consolidation can affect the determination of the hedged risk in a hedge of a net investment in a foreign operation. The submission noted that consolidation can be completed by either the direct method or the step-by-step method. In the direct method of consolidation, each entity within a group is consolidated directly into the ultimate parent entity's presentation currency when preparing the consolidated financial statements. In the step-by-step method, each intermediate parent entity prepares consolidated financial statements, which are then consolidated into its parent entity until the ultimate parent entity has prepared consolidated financial statements.

BC7 The submission stated that if the direct method was required, the risk that qualifies for hedge accounting in a hedge of a net investment in a foreign operation would arise only from exposure between the functional currency of the foreign operation and the presentation currency of the group. This is because each foreign operation is translated only once into the presentation currency. In contrast, the submission stated that if the step-by-step method was required, the hedged risk that qualifies for hedge accounting is the risk between the functional currencies of the foreign operation and the immediate parent entity into which the entity was consolidated. This is because each foreign operation is consolidated directly into its immediate parent entity.

BC8 In response to this, the IFRIC noted that IAS 21 *The Effects of Changes in Foreign Exchange Rates* does not specify a method of consolidation for foreign operations. Furthermore, paragraph BC18 of the Basis for Conclusions on IAS 21 states that the method of translating financial statements will result in the same amounts in the presentation currency regardless of whether the direct method or the step-by-step method is used. The IFRIC therefore concluded that the consolidation mechanism should not determine what risk qualifies for hedge accounting in the hedge of a net investment in a foreign operation.

BC9 However, the IFRIC noted that its conclusion would not resolve the divergence of views on the foreign currency risk that may be designated as a hedge relationship in the hedge of a net investment in a foreign operation. The IFRIC therefore decided that an Interpretation was needed.

BC10 The IFRIC considered whether the risk that qualifies for hedge accounting in a hedge of a net investment in a foreign operation arises from the exposure to the functional currency of the foreign operation in relation to the presentation currency of the group or the functional currency of the parent entity, or both.

BC11 The answer to this question is important when the presentation currency of the group is different from an intermediate or ultimate parent entity's functional currency. If the presentation currency of the group and the functional currency of the parent entity are the same, the exchange rate being hedged would be identified as that between the parent entity's functional currency and the foreign operation's functional currency. No further translation adjustment would be required to prepare the consolidated financial statements. However, when the functional currency of the parent entity is different from the presentation currency of the group, a translation adjustment will be included in other comprehensive income to present the consolidated financial statements in a different presentation currency. The issue, therefore, is how to determine which foreign currency risk may be designated as the hedged risk in accordance with IAS 39 *Financial Instruments: Recognition and Measurement*[1] in the hedge of a net investment in a foreign operation.

---

1   IFRS 9 *Financial Instruments* replaced the hedge accounting requirements in IAS 39. However, the requirements regarding hedges of a net investment in a foreign operation were retained from IAS 39 and relocated to IFRS 9.

BC12　　The IFRIC noted the following arguments for permitting hedge accounting for a hedge of the presentation currency:

　　(a)　If the presentation currency of the group is different from the ultimate parent entity's functional currency, a difference arises on translation that is recognised in other comprehensive income. It is argued that a reason for allowing hedge accounting for a net investment in a foreign operation is to remove from the financial statements the fluctuations resulting from the translation to a presentation currency. If an entity is not allowed to use hedge accounting for the exposure to the presentation currency of the group when it is different from the functional currency of the parent entity, there is likely to be an amount included in other comprehensive income that cannot be offset by hedge accounting.

　　(b)　IAS 21 requires an entity to reclassify from equity to profit or loss as a reclassification adjustment any foreign currency translation gains and losses included in other comprehensive income on disposal of a foreign operation. An amount in other comprehensive income arising from a different presentation currency is therefore included in the amount reclassified to profit or loss on disposal. The entity should be able to include the amount in a hedging relationship if at some stage it is recognised along with other reclassified translation amounts.

BC13　　The IFRIC noted the following arguments for allowing an entity to designate hedging relationships solely on the basis of differences between functional currencies:

　　(a)　The functional currency of an entity is determined on the basis of the primary economic environment in which that entity operates (ie the environment in which it generates and expends cash). However, the presentation currency is an elective currency that can be changed at any time. To present amounts in a presentation currency is merely a numerical convention necessary for the preparation of financial statements that include a foreign operation. The presentation currency will have no economic effect on the parent entity. Indeed, a parent entity may choose to present financial statements in more than one presentation currency, but can have only one functional currency.

　　(b)　IAS 39 requires a hedging relationship to be effective in offsetting changes in fair values or cash flows attributable to the hedged risk. A net investment in a foreign operation gives rise to an exposure to changes in exchange rate risk for a parent entity. An economic exchange rate risk arises only from an exposure between two or more functional currencies, not from a presentation currency.

BC14　　When comparing the arguments in paragraphs BC12 and BC13, the IFRIC concluded that the presentation currency does not create an exposure to which an entity may apply hedge accounting. The functional currency is determined on the basis of the primary economic environment in which the entity operates. Accordingly, functional currencies create an economic exposure to changes in cash flows or fair values; a presentation currency never will. No commentators on the draft Interpretation disagreed with the IFRIC's conclusion.

Eligible risk (paragraph 12)

BC15   The IFRIC considered which entity's (or entities') functional currency may be used as a reference point for the hedged risk in a net investment hedge. Does the risk arise from the functional currency of:

(a)   the immediate parent entity that holds directly the foreign operation;

(b)   the ultimate parent entity that is preparing its financial statements; or

(c)   the immediate, an intermediate or the ultimate parent entity, depending on what risk that entity decides to hedge, as designated at the inception of the hedge?

BC16   The IFRIC concluded that the risk from the exposure to a different functional currency arises for any parent entity whose functional currency is different from that of the identified foreign operation. The immediate parent entity is exposed to changes in the exchange rate of its directly held foreign operation's functional currency. However, indirectly every entity up the chain of entities to the ultimate parent entity is also exposed to changes in the exchange rate of the foreign operation's functional currency.

BC17   Permitting only the ultimate parent entity to hedge its net investments would ignore the exposures arising on net investments in other parts of the entity. Conversely, permitting only the immediate parent entity to undertake a net investment hedge would imply that an indirect investment does not create a foreign currency exposure for that indirect parent entity.

BC18   The IFRIC concluded that a group must identify which risk (ie the functional currency of which parent entity and of which net investment in a foreign operation) is being hedged. The specified parent entity, the hedged risk and hedging instrument should all be designated and documented at the inception of the hedge relationship. As a result of comments received on the draft Interpretation, the IFRIC decided to emphasise that this documentation should also include the entity's strategy in undertaking the hedge as required by IAS 39.

Amount of hedged item that may be hedged (paragraphs 11 and 13)

BC19   In the draft Interpretation the IFRIC noted that, in financial statements that include a foreign operation, an entity cannot hedge the same risk more than once. This comment was intended to remind entities that IAS 39 does not permit multiple hedges of the same risk. Some respondents asked the IFRIC to clarify the situations in which the IFRIC considered that the same risk was being hedged more than once. In particular, the IFRIC was asked whether the same risk could be hedged by different entities within a group as long as the amount of risk being hedged was not duplicated.

BC20   In its redeliberations, the IFRIC decided to clarify that the carrying amount of the net assets of a foreign operation that may be hedged in the consolidated financial statements of a parent depends on whether any lower level parent of the foreign operation has hedged all or part of the net assets of that foreign operation and that accounting has been maintained in the parent's consolidated financial statements. An intermediate parent entity can hedge some or all of the risk of its net investment in a foreign operation in its own consolidated financial statements. However, such hedges will not qualify for hedge accounting at the ultimate parent entity level if the ultimate parent entity has also hedged the same risk. Alternatively, if the risk has not been hedged by the ultimate parent entity or another intermediate parent entity, the hedge relationship that qualified in the immediate parent entity's consolidated financial statements will also qualify in the ultimate parent entity's consolidated financial statements.

BC21   In its redeliberations, the IFRIC also decided to add guidance to the Interpretation to illustrate the importance of careful designation of the amount of the risk being hedged by each entity in the group.

Hedging instrument

Location of the hedging instrument (paragraph 14) and assessment of hedge effectiveness (paragraph 15)

BC22   The IFRIC discussed where in a group structure a hedging instrument may be held in a hedge of a net investment in a foreign operation. Guidance on the hedge of a net investment in a foreign operation was originally included in IAS 21. This guidance was moved to IAS 39 to ensure that the hedge accounting guidance included in paragraph 88 of IAS 39 would also apply to the hedges of net investments in foreign operations.

BC23   The IFRIC concluded that any entity within the group, other than the foreign operation being hedged, may hold the hedging instrument, as long as the hedging instrument is effective in offsetting the risk arising from the exposure to the functional currency of the foreign operation and the functional currency of the specified parent entity. The functional currency of the entity holding the instrument is irrelevant in determining effectiveness.

BC24   ~~The IFRIC concluded that the foreign operation being hedged could not hold the hedging instrument because that instrument would be part of, and denominated in the same currency as, the net investment it was intended to hedge. In this circumstance, hedge accounting is unnecessary. The foreign exchange differences between the parent's functional currency and both the hedging instrument and the functional currency of the net investment will automatically be included in the group's foreign currency translation reserve as part of the consolidation process. The balance of the discussion in this Basis for Conclusions does not repeat this restriction.~~[2]

BC24A   Paragraph 14 of IFRIC 16 originally stated that the hedging instrument could not be held by the foreign operation whose net investment was being hedged. The restriction was included in draft Interpretation D22 (from which IFRIC 16 was developed) and attracted little comment from respondents. As originally explained in paragraph BC24, the IFRIC concluded, as part of its redeliberations, that the restriction was appropriate because the foreign exchange differences between the parent's functional currency and both the hedging instrument and

---

2   Paragraph BC24 was deleted and paragraphs BC24A–BC24D and paragraph BC40A added as a consequence of *Improvements to IFRSs* issued in April 2009.

the functional currency of the net investment would automatically be included in the group's foreign currency translation reserve as part of the consolidation process.

BC24B   After IFRIC 16 was issued, it was brought to the attention of the International Accounting Standards Board that this conclusion was not correct. Without hedge accounting, part of the foreign exchange difference arising from the hedging instrument would be included in consolidated profit or loss. Therefore, in *Improvements to IFRSs* issued in April 2009, the Board amended paragraph 14 of IFRIC 16 to remove the restriction on the entity that can hold hedging instruments and deleted paragraph BC24.

BC24C   Some respondents to the exposure draft *Post-implementation Revisions to IFRIC Interpretations* (ED/2009/1) agreed that a parent entity should be able to use a derivative held by the foreign operation being hedged as a hedge of the net investment in that foreign operation. However, those respondents recommended that the amendment should apply only to derivative instruments held by the foreign operation being hedged. They asserted that a non-derivative financial instrument would be an effective hedge of the net investment only if it were issued by the foreign operation in its own functional currency and this would have no foreign currency impact on the profit or loss of the consolidated group. Consequently, they thought that the rationale described in paragraph BC24B to support the amendment did not apply to non-derivative instruments.

BC24D   In its redeliberations, the Board confirmed its previous decision that the amendment should not be restricted to derivative instruments. The Board noted that paragraphs AG13–AG15 of IFRIC 16 illustrate that a non-derivative instrument held by the foreign operation does not need to be considered to be part of the parent's net investment. As a result, even if it is denominated in the foreign operation's functional currency a non-derivative instrument could still affect the profit or loss of the consolidated group. Consequently, although it could be argued that the amendment was not required to permit non-derivative instruments to be designated as hedges, the Board decided that the proposal should not be changed.

BC25   The IFRIC also concluded that to apply the conclusion in paragraph BC23 when determining the effectiveness of a hedging instrument in the hedge of a net investment, an entity computes the gain or loss on the hedging instrument by reference to the functional currency of the parent entity against whose functional currency the hedged risk is measured, in accordance with the hedge documentation. This is the same regardless of the type of hedging instrument used. This ensures that the effectiveness of the instrument is determined on the basis of changes in fair value or cash flows of the hedging instrument, compared with the changes in the net investment as documented. Thus, any effectiveness test is not dependent on the functional currency of the entity holding the instrument. In other words, the fact that some of the change in the hedging instrument is recognised in profit or loss by one entity within the group and some is recognised in other comprehensive income by another does not affect the assessment of hedge effectiveness.

BC26　　In the draft Interpretation the IFRIC noted Question F.2.14 in the guidance on implementing IAS 39, on the location of the hedging instrument, and considered whether that guidance could be applied by analogy to a net investment hedge. The answer to Question F.2.14 concludes:

> IAS 39 does not require that the operating unit that is exposed to the risk being hedged be a party to the hedging instrument.

This was the only basis for the IFRIC's conclusion regarding which entity could hold the hedging instrument provided in the draft Interpretation. Some respondents argued that the Interpretation should not refer to implementation guidance as the sole basis for an important conclusion.[3]

BC27　　In its redeliberations, the IFRIC considered both the International Accounting Standards Board's amendment to IAS 21 in 2005 and the objective of hedging a net investment described in IAS 39 in addition to the guidance on implementing IAS 39.

BC28　　In 2005 the Board was asked to clarify which entity is the reporting entity in IAS 21 and therefore what instruments could be considered part of a reporting entity's net investment in a foreign operation. In particular, constituents questioned whether a monetary item must be transacted between the foreign operation and the reporting entity to be considered part of the net investment in accordance with IAS 21 paragraph 15, or whether it could be transacted between the foreign operation and any member of the consolidated group.

BC29　　In response the Board added IAS 21 paragraph 15A to clarify that 'The entity that has a monetary item receivable from or payable to a foreign operation described in paragraph 15 may be any subsidiary of the group.' The Board explained its reasons for the amendment in paragraph BC25D of the Basis for Conclusions:

> The Board concluded that the accounting treatment in the consolidated financial statements should not be dependent on the currency in which the monetary item is denominated, nor on which entity within the group conducts the transaction with the foreign operation.

In other words, the Board concluded that the relevant reporting entity is the group rather than the individual entity and that the net investment must be viewed from the perspective of the group. It follows, therefore, that the group's net investment in any foreign operation, and its foreign currency exposure, can be determined only at the relevant parent entity level. The IFRIC similarly concluded that the fact that the net investment is held through an intermediate entity does not affect the economic risk.

BC30　　Consistently with the Board's conclusion with respect to monetary items that are part of *the net investment*, the IFRIC concluded that monetary items (or derivatives) that are *hedging instruments* in a hedge of a net investment may be held by any entity within the group and the functional currency of the entity holding the monetary items can be different from those of either the parent or the foreign operation. The IFRIC, like the Board, agreed with constituents who noted that a hedging item denominated in a currency that is not the functional

---

3　　IFRS 9 replaced IAS 39.

currency of the entity holding it does not expose the group to a greater foreign currency exchange difference than arises when the instrument is denominated in that functional currency.

BC31   The IFRIC noted that its conclusions that the hedging instrument can be held by any entity in the group and that the foreign currency is determined at the relevant parent entity level have implications for the designation of hedged risks. As illustrated in paragraph AG5 of the application guidance, these conclusions make it possible for an entity to designate a hedged risk that is not apparent in the currencies of the hedged item or the foreign operation. This possibility is unique to hedges of net investments. Consequently, the IFRIC specified that the conclusions in the Interpretation should not be applied by analogy to other types of hedge accounting.

BC32   The IFRIC also noted that the objective of hedge accounting as set out in IAS 39 is to achieve offsetting changes in the values of the *hedging instrument* and of the *net investment* attributable to the hedged risk. Changes in foreign currency rates affect the value of the entire *net investment* in a foreign operation, not only the portion IAS 21 requires to be recognised in profit or loss in the absence of hedge accounting but also the portion recognised in other comprehensive income in the parent's consolidated financial statements. As noted in paragraph BC25, it is the total change in the hedging instrument as result of a change in the foreign currency rate with respect to the parent entity against whose functional currency the hedged risk is measured that is relevant, not the component of comprehensive income in which it is recognised.

Reclassification from other comprehensive income to profit or loss (paragraphs 16 and 17)

BC33   In response to requests from some respondents for clarification, the IFRIC discussed what amounts from the parent entity's foreign currency translation reserve in respect of both the hedging instrument and the foreign operation should be recognised in profit or loss in the parent entity's consolidated financial statements when the parent disposes of a foreign operation that was hedged. The IFRIC noted that the amounts to be reclassified from equity to profit or loss as reclassification adjustments on the disposition are:

(a)   the cumulative amount of gain or loss on a hedging instrument determined to be an effective hedge that has been reflected in other comprehensive income (IAS 39 paragraph 102), and

(b)   the cumulative amount reflected in the foreign currency translation reserve in respect of that foreign operation (IAS 21 paragraph 48).

BC34   The IFRIC noted that when an entity hedges a net investment in a foreign operation, IAS 39 requires it to identify the cumulative amount included in the group's foreign currency translation reserve as a result of applying hedge accounting, ie the amount determined to be an effective hedge. Therefore, the IFRIC concluded that when a foreign operation that was hedged is disposed of, the amount reclassified to profit or loss from the foreign currency translation reserve in respect of the hedging instrument in the consolidated financial statements of the parent should be the amount that IAS 39 requires to be identified.

Effect of consolidation method

BC35　Some respondents to the draft Interpretation argued that the method of consolidation creates a difference in the amounts included in the ultimate parent entity's foreign currency translation reserve for individual foreign operations that are held through intermediate parents. These respondents noted that this difference may become evident only when the ultimate parent entity disposes of a second tier subsidiary (ie an indirect subsidiary).

BC36　The difference becomes apparent in the determination of the amount of the foreign currency translation reserve that is subsequently reclassified to profit or loss. An ultimate parent entity using the direct method of consolidation would reclassify the cumulative foreign currency translation reserve that arose between its functional currency and that of the foreign operation. An ultimate parent entity using the step-by-step method of consolidation might reclassify the cumulative foreign currency translation reserve reflected in the financial statements of the intermediate parent, ie the amount that arose between the functional currency of the foreign operation and that of the intermediate parent, translated into the functional currency of the ultimate parent.

BC37　In its redeliberations, the IFRIC noted that the use of the step-by-step method of consolidation does create such a difference for an *individual* foreign operation although the aggregate net amount of foreign currency translation reserve for all the foreign operations is the same under either method of consolidation. At the same time, the IFRIC noted that the method of consolidation *should not* create such a difference for an individual foreign operation, on the basis of its conclusion that the economic risk is determined in relation to the ultimate parent's functional currency.

BC38　The IFRIC noted that the amount of foreign currency translation reserve for an individual foreign operation determined by the direct method of consolidation reflects the economic risk between the functional currency of the foreign operation and that of the ultimate parent (if the parent's functional and presentation currencies are the same). However, the IFRIC noted that IAS 21 does not require an entity to use this method or to make adjustments to produce the same result. The IFRIC also noted that a parent entity is not precluded from determining the amount of the foreign currency translation reserve in respect of a foreign operation it has disposed of as if the direct method of consolidation had been used in order to reclassify the appropriate amount to profit or loss. However, it also noted that making such an adjustment on the disposal of a foreign operation is an accounting policy choice and should be followed consistently for the disposal of all net investments.

BC39　The IFRIC noted that this issue arises when the net investment disposed of was not hedged and therefore is not strictly within the scope of the Interpretation. However, because it was a topic of considerable confusion and debate, the IFRIC decided to include a brief example illustrating its conclusions.

Transition (paragraph 19)

BC40　In response to respondents' comments, the IFRIC clarified the Interpretation's transitional requirements. The IFRIC decided that entities should apply the conclusions in this Interpretation to existing hedging relationships on adoption and cease hedge accounting for those that no longer qualify. However, previous hedge accounting is not affected. This is similar to the transition requirements in IFRS 1 *First-time Adoption of International Financial Reporting Standards* paragraph 30,[4] for relationships accounted for as hedges under previous GAAP.

Effective date of amended paragraph 14

BC40A   The Board amended paragraph 14 in April 2009. In ED/2009/01 the Board proposed that the amendment should be effective for annual periods beginning on or after 1 October 2008, at the same time as IFRIC 16. Respondents to the exposure draft were concerned that permitting application before the amendment was issued might imply that an entity could designate hedge relationships retrospectively, contrary to the requirements of IAS 39. Consequently, the Board decided that an entity should apply the amendment to paragraph 14 made in April 2009 for annual periods beginning on or after 1 July 2009. The Board also decided to permit early application but noted that early application is possible only if the designation, documentation and effectiveness requirements of paragraph 88 of IAS 39 and of IFRIC 16 are satisfied at the application date.

Summary of main changes from the draft Interpretation

BC41   The main changes from the IFRIC's proposals are as follows:

(a)   Paragraph 11 clarifies that the carrying amount of the net assets of a foreign operation that may be hedged in the consolidated financial statements of a parent depends on whether any lower level parent of the foreign operation has hedged all or part of the net assets of that foreign operation and that accounting has been maintained in the parent's consolidated financial statements.

(b)   Paragraph 15 clarifies that the assessment of effectiveness is not affected by whether the hedging instrument is a derivative or a non-derivative instrument or by the method of consolidation.

(c)   Paragraphs 16 and 17 and the illustrative example clarify what amounts should be reclassified from equity to profit or loss as reclassification adjustments on disposal of the foreign operation.

(d)   Paragraph 19 clarifies transitional requirements.

(e)   The appendix of application guidance was added to the Interpretation. Illustrative examples accompanying the draft Interpretation were removed.

(f)   The Basis for Conclusions was changed to set out more clearly the reasons for the IFRIC's conclusions.

---

4   Paragraph B6 in the revised version of IFRS 1 issued in November 2008.

Document published to accompany

IFRIC 17

Distributions of Non-cash Assets to Owners

The text of the unaccompanied Interpretation, IFRIC 17, is contained in Part A of this edition. Its effective date when issued was 1 July 2009. The text of the Accompanying Guidance on IFRIC 17 is contained in Part B of this edition. This part presents the following documents:

BASIS FOR CONCLUSIONS

Basis for Conclusions on
IFRIC Interpretation 17 *Distributions of Non-cash Assets to Owners*

This Basis for Conclusions accompanies, but is not part of, IFRIC 17.

Introduction

BC1　This Basis for Conclusions summarises the IFRIC's considerations in reaching its consensus. Individual IFRIC members gave greater weight to some factors than to others.

BC2　At present, International Financial Reporting Standards (IFRSs) do not address how an entity should measure distributions to owners acting in their capacity as owners (commonly referred to as dividends). The IFRIC was told that there was significant diversity in practice in how entities measured distributions of non-cash assets.

BC3　The IFRIC published draft Interpretation D23 *Distributions of Non-cash Assets to Owners* for public comment in January 2008 and received 56 comment letters in response to its proposals.

Scope (paragraphs 3–8)

Should the Interpretation address all transactions between an entity and its owners?

BC4　The IFRIC noted that an asset distribution by an entity to its owners is an example of a transaction between an entity and its owners. Transactions between an entity and its owners can generally be categorised into the following three types:

(a)　exchange transactions between an entity and its owners.

(b)　non-reciprocal transfers of assets by owners of an entity to the entity. Such transfers are commonly referred to as contributions from owners.

(c)　non-reciprocal transfers of assets by an entity to its owners. Such transfers are commonly referred to as distributions to owners.

BC5　The IFRIC concluded that the Interpretation should not address exchange transactions between an entity and its owners because that would probably result in addressing all related party transactions. In the IFRIC's view, such a scope was too broad for an Interpretation. Instead, the IFRIC concluded that the Interpretation should focus on distributions of assets by an entity to its owners acting in their capacity as owners.

BC6　In addition, the IFRIC decided that the Interpretation should not address distributions in which owners of the same class of equity instrument are not all treated equally. This is because, in the IFRIC's view, such distributions might imply that at least some of the owners receiving the distributions indeed gave up something to the entity and/or other owners. In other words, such distributions might be more in the nature of exchange transactions.

Should the Interpretation address all types of asset distributions?

BC7　The IFRIC was told that there was significant diversity in the measurement of the following types of non-reciprocal distributions of assets by an entity to its owners acting in their capacity as owners:

(a)　distributions of non-cash assets (eg items of property, plant and equipment, businesses as defined in IFRS 3, ownership interests in another entity or disposal groups as defined in IFRS 5 *Non-current Assets Held for Sale and Discontinued Operations*) to its owners; and

(b)　distributions that give owners a choice of receiving either non-cash assets or a cash alternative.

BC8　The IFRIC noted that all distributions have the same purpose, ie to distribute assets to an entity's owners. It therefore concluded that the Interpretation should address the measurement of all types of asset distributions with one exception set out in paragraph 5 of the Interpretation.

A scope exclusion: a distribution of an asset that is ultimately controlled by the same party or parties before and after the distribution

BC9　In the Interpretation, the IFRIC considered whether it should address how an entity should measure a distribution of an asset (eg an ownership interest in a subsidiary) that is ultimately controlled by the same party or parties before and after the distribution. In many instances, such a distribution is for the purpose of group restructuring (eg separating two different businesses into two different subgroups). After the distribution, the asset is still controlled by the same party or parties.

BC10　In addition, the IFRIC noted that dealing with the accounting for a distribution of an asset within a group would require consideration of how a transfer of any asset within a group should be accounted for in the separate or individual financial statements of group entities.

BC11　For the reasons described in paragraphs BC9 and BC10, the IFRIC concluded that the Interpretation should not deal with a distribution of an asset that is ultimately controlled by the same party or parties before and after the distribution.

BC12　In response to comments received on the draft Interpretation, the IFRIC redeliberated whether the scope of the Interpretation should be expanded to include a distribution of an asset that is ultimately controlled by the same party or parties before and after the distribution. The IFRIC decided not to expand the scope of the Interpretation in the light of the Board's decision to add a project to its agenda to address common control transactions.

BC13　The IFRIC noted that many commentators believed that most distributions of assets to an entity's owners would be excluded from the scope of the Interpretation by paragraph 5. The IFRIC did not agree with this conclusion. It noted that in paragraph B2 of IFRS 3 *Business Combinations* (as revised in 2008), the Board concluded that a group of individuals would be regarded as controlling an entity only when, as a result of contractual arrangements, they collectively have the power to govern its financial and operating policies so as to obtain benefits from its activities. In addition, in *Cost of an Investment in a Subsidiary, Jointly Controlled Entity or Associate* in May 2008, the Board clarified in the amendments to IAS 27 *Consolidated and Separate Financial Statements* that the distribution of equity interests in a new parent to shareholders in exchange for their interests in the existing parent was not a common control transaction.[1]

BC14 Consequently, the IFRIC decided that the Interpretation should clarify that unless there is a contractual arrangement among shareholders to control the entity making the distribution, transactions in which the shares or the businesses of group entities are distributed to shareholders outside the group (commonly referred to as a spin-off, split-off or demerger) are not transactions between entities or businesses under common control. Therefore they are within the scope of the Interpretation.

BC15 Some commentators on D23 were concerned about situations in which an entity distributes some but not all of its ownership interests in a subsidiary and retains control. They believed that the proposed accounting for the distribution of ownership interests representing a non-controlling interest in accordance with D23 was inconsistent with the requirements of IAS 27 (as amended in 2008). That IFRS requires changes in a parent's ownership interest in a subsidiary that do not result in a loss of control to be accounted for as equity transactions. The IFRIC had not intended the Interpretation to apply to such transactions so did not believe it conflicted with the requirements of IAS 27. As a result of the concerns expressed, the IFRIC amended the Interpretation to make this clear.

BC16 Some commentators on D23 were also concerned about situations in which a subsidiary with a non-controlling interest distributes assets to both the parent and the non-controlling interests. They questioned why only the distribution to the controlling entity is excluded from the scope of the Interpretation. The IFRIC noted that when the parent controls the subsidiary before and after the transaction, the entire transaction (including the distribution to the non-controlling interest) is not within the scope of the Interpretation and is accounted for in accordance with IAS 27.

BC17 Distributions to owners may involve significant portions of an entity's operations. In such circumstances, sometimes referred to as split-off, some commentators on D23 were concerned that it would be difficult to determine which of the surviving entities had made the distribution. They thought that it might be possible for each surviving entity to recognise the distribution of the other. The IFRIC agreed with commentators that identifying the distributing entity might require judgement in some circumstances. However, the IFRIC concluded that the distribution could be recognised in only one entity's financial statements.

---

1 The consolidation guidance was removed from IAS 27 and the Standard was renamed *Separate Financial Statements* by IFRS 10 *Consolidated Financial Statements* issued in May 2011. The accounting requirements for transactions between owners did not change.

When to recognise a dividend payable (paragraph 10) and amendment to IAS 10

BC18   D23 did not address when an entity should recognise a liability for a dividend payable and some respondents asked the IFRIC to clarify this issue. The IFRIC noted that in IAS 10 *Events after the Reporting Period* paragraph 13 states that 'If dividends are declared (ie the dividends are appropriately authorised and no longer at the discretion of the entity) after the reporting period but before the financial statements are authorised for issue, the dividends are not recognised as a liability at the end of the reporting period because no obligation exists at that time.'

BC19   Some commentators stated that in many jurisdictions a commonly held view is that the entity has discretion until the shareholders approve the dividend. Therefore, constituents holding this view believe a conflict exists between 'declared' and the explanatory phrase in the brackets in IAS 10 paragraph 13. This is especially true when the sentence is interpreted as 'declared by *management but before the shareholders' approval*'. The IFRIC concluded that the point at which a dividend is appropriately authorised and no longer at the discretion of the entity will vary by jurisdiction.

BC20   Therefore, as a consequence of this Interpretation the IFRIC decided to recommend that the Board amend IAS 10 to remove the perceived conflict in paragraph 13. The IFRIC also noted that the principle on when to recognise a dividend was in the wrong place within the IASB's authoritative documents. The Board agreed with the IFRIC's conclusions and amended IAS 10 as part of its approval of the Interpretation. The Board confirmed that this Interpretation had not changed the principle on when to recognise a dividend payable; however, the principle was moved from IAS 10 into the Interpretation and clarified but without changing the principle.

How should an entity measure a dividend payable? (paragraphs 11–13)

BC21   IFRSs do not provide guidance on how an entity should measure distributions to owners. However, the IFRIC noted that a number of IFRSs address how a liability should be measured. Although IFRSs do not specifically address how an entity should measure a dividend payable, the IFRIC decided that it could identify potentially relevant IFRSs and apply their principles to determine the appropriate measurement basis.

Which IFRSs are relevant to the measurement of a dividend payable?

BC22   The IFRIC considered all IFRSs that prescribe the accounting for a liability. Of those, the IFRIC concluded that IAS 37 *Provisions, Contingent Assets and Contingent Liabilities* and IAS 39 *Financial Instruments: Recognition and Measurement*[2] were the most likely to be relevant. The IFRIC concluded that other IFRSs were not

---

2   IFRS 9 *Financial Instruments* replaced IAS 39. IFRS 9 applies to all items that were previously within the scope of IAS 39.

applicable because most of them addressed only liabilities arising from exchange transactions and some of them were clearly not relevant (eg IAS 12 *Income Taxes*). As mentioned above, the Interpretation addresses only non-reciprocal distributions of assets by an entity to its owners.

BC23   Given that all types of distributions have the purpose of distributing assets to owners, the IFRIC decided that all dividends payable should be measured the same way, regardless of the types of assets to be distributed. This also ensures that all dividends payable are measured consistently.

BC24   Some believed that IAS 39 was the appropriate IFRS to be used to measure dividends payable. They believed that, once an entity declared a distribution to its owners, it had a contractual obligation to distribute the assets to its owners. However, IAS 39 would not cover dividends payable if they were considered to be non-contractual obligations. In addition, IAS 39 covers some but not all obligations that require an entity to deliver non-cash assets to another entity. It does not cover a liability to distribute non-financial assets to owners. The IFRIC therefore concluded that it was not appropriate to conclude that all dividends payable should be within the scope of IAS 39.

BC25   The IFRIC then considered IAS 37, which is generally applied in practice to determine the accounting for liabilities other than those arising from executory contracts and those addressed by other IFRSs. IAS 37 requires an entity to measure a liability on the basis of the best estimate of the expenditure required to settle the present obligation at the end of the reporting period. Consequently, in D23 the IFRIC decided that it was appropriate to apply the principles in IAS 37 to all dividends payable (regardless of the types of assets to be distributed). The IFRIC decided that to apply IAS 37 to measure a liability for an obligation to distribute non-cash assets to owners, an entity should consider the fair value of the assets to be distributed. The fair value of the assets to be distributed is clearly relevant no matter which approach in IAS 37 is taken to determine the best estimate of the expenditure required to settle the liability.

BC26   However, in response to comments received on D23, the IFRIC reconsidered whether the Interpretation should specify that all dividends payable should be measured in accordance with IAS 37. The IFRIC noted that many respondents were concerned that D23 might imply that the measurement attribute in IAS 37 should always be interpreted to be fair value. This was not the intention of D23 as that question is part of the Board's project to amend IAS 37. In addition, many respondents were not certain whether measuring the dividend payable 'by reference to' the fair value of the assets to be distributed required measurement at their fair value or at some other amount.

BC27   Therefore, the IFRIC decided to modify the proposal in D23 to require the dividend payable to be measured at the fair value of the assets to be distributed, without linking to any individual standard its conclusion that fair value is the most relevant measurement attribute. The IFRIC also noted that if the assets being distributed constituted a business, its fair value could be different from the simple sum of the fair value of the component assets and liabilities (ie it includes the value of goodwill or the identified intangible assets).

Should any exception be made to the principle of measuring a dividend payable at the fair value of the assets to be distributed?

BC28   Some are concerned that the fair value of the assets to be distributed might not be reliably measurable in all cases. They believe that exceptions should be made in the following circumstances:

(a)   An entity distributes an ownership interest of another entity that is not traded in an active market and the fair value of the ownership interest cannot be measured reliably. The IFRIC noted that IAS 39[3] does not permit investments in equity instruments that do not have a quoted market price in an active market[4] and whose fair value cannot be measured reliably to be measured at fair value.

(b)   An entity distributes an intangible asset that is not traded in an active market and therefore would not be permitted to be carried at a revalued amount in accordance with IAS 38 *Intangible Assets*.

BC29   The IFRIC noted that in accordance with IAS 39 paragraphs AG80 and AG81,[5] the fair value of equity instruments that do not have a quoted price in an active market[6] is reliably measurable if:

(a)   the variability in the range of reasonable fair value estimates is not significant for that instrument, or

(b)   the probabilities of the various estimates within the range can be reasonably assessed and used in estimating fair value.

BC30   The IFRIC noted that, when the management of an entity recommends a distribution of a non-cash asset to its owners, one or both of the conditions for determining a reliable measure of the fair value of equity instruments that do not have a quoted price in an active market is likely to be satisfied. Management would be expected to know the fair value of the asset because management has to ensure that all owners of the entity are informed of the value of the distribution. For this reason, it would be difficult to argue that the fair value of the assets to be distributed cannot be determined reliably.

---

3   IFRS 9 *Financial Instruments* requires all investments in equity instruments to be measured at fair value.

4   IFRS 13 *Fair Value Measurement*, issued in May 2011, defines fair value and contains the requirements for measuring fair value. IFRS 13 defines a Level 1 input as a quoted price in an active market for an identical asset or liability. Level 2 inputs include quoted prices for identical assets or liabilities in markets that are not active. As a result IFRS 9 refers to such equity instruments as 'an equity instrument that does not have a quoted price in an active market for an identical instrument (ie a Level 1 input)'.

5   IFRS 9 *Financial Instruments* deleted paragraphs AG80 and AG81 of IAS 39. IFRS 13 *Fair Value Measurement*, issued in May 2011, defines fair value and contains requirements for measuring fair value. IFRS 13 defines a Level 1 input as a quoted price in an active market for an identical asset or liability. Level 2 inputs include quoted prices for identical assets or liabilities in markets that are not active. As a result IFRS 9 refers to such equity instruments as 'an equity instrument that does not have a quoted price in an active market for an identical instrument (ie a Level 1 input)'.

6   IFRS 13 *Fair Value Measurement*, issued in May 2011, defines fair value and contains requirements for measuring fair value. IFRS 13 defines a Level 1 input as a quoted price in an active market for an identical asset or liability. Level 2 inputs include quoted prices for identical assets or liabilities in markets that are not active. As a result IFRS 9 refers to such equity instruments as 'an equity instrument that does not have a quoted price in an active market for an identical instrument (ie a Level 1 input)'.

BC31   In addition, the IFRIC recognised that in some cases the fair value of an asset must be estimated. As mentioned in paragraph 86 of the *Framework for the Preparation and Presentation of Financial Statements*,[7] the use of reasonable estimates is an essential part of the preparation of financial statements and does not undermine their reliability.

BC32   The IFRIC noted that a reason why IAS 38 and IAS 39[8] require some assets to be measured using a historical cost basis is cost-benefit considerations. The cost of determining the fair value of an asset not traded in an active market at the end of each reporting period could outweigh the benefits. However, because an entity would be required to determine the fair value of the assets to be distributed only once at the time of distribution, the IFRIC concluded that the benefit (ie informing users of the financial statements of the value of the assets distributed) outweighs the cost of determining the fair value of the assets.

BC33   Furthermore, the IFRIC noted that dividend income, regardless of whether it is in the form of cash or non-cash assets, is within the scope of IAS 18 *Revenue*[9] and is required to be measured at the fair value of the consideration received. Although the Interpretation does not address the accounting by the recipient of the non-cash distribution, the IFRIC concluded that the Interpretation did not impose a more onerous requirement on the entity that makes the distribution than IFRSs have already imposed on the recipient of the distribution.

BC34   For the reasons described in paragraphs BC28–BC33, the IFRIC concluded that no exceptions should be made to the requirement that the fair value of the asset to be distributed should be used in measuring a dividend payable.

Whether an entity should remeasure the dividend payable (paragraph 13)

BC35   The IFRIC noted that paragraph 59 of IAS 37 requires an entity to review the carrying amount of a liability at the end of each reporting period and to adjust the carrying amount to reflect the current best estimate of the liability. Other IFRSs such as IAS 19 *Employee Benefits* similarly require liabilities that are based on estimates to be adjusted each reporting period. The IFRIC therefore decided that the entity should review and adjust the carrying amount of the dividend payable to reflect its current best estimate of the fair value of the assets to be distributed at the end of each reporting period and at the date of settlement.

BC36   The IFRIC concluded that, because any adjustments to the best estimate of the dividend payable reflect changes in the estimated value of the distribution, they should be recognised as adjustments to the amount of the distribution. In accordance with IAS 1 *Presentation of Financial Statements* (as revised in 2007), distributions to owners are required to be recognised directly in the statement of

---

7   now paragraph 4.41 of the *Conceptual Framework*. References to the *Framework* are to IASC's *Framework for the Preparation and Presentation of Financial Statements*, adopted by the IASB in 2001. In September 2010 the IASB replaced the *Framework* with the *Conceptual Framework for Financial Reporting*.

8   IFRS 9 *Financial Instruments* eliminated the requirement in IAS 39 for some assets to be measured using a historical cost basis.

9   IFRS 15 *Revenue from Contracts with Customers*, issued in May 2014, replaced IAS 18 *Revenue*. IFRS 15 does not address dividends. Dividends should be accounted for in accordance with IFRS 9, or IAS 39 if applicable.

changes in equity. Similarly, adjustments to the amount of the distribution are also recognised directly in the statement of changes in equity.

BC37   Some commentators argued that the changes in the estimated value of the distribution should be recognised in profit or loss because changes in liabilities meet the definition of income or expenses in the *Framework*. However, the IFRIC decided that the gain or loss on the assets to be distributed should be recognised in profit or loss when the dividend payable is settled. This is consistent with other IFRSs (IAS 16, IAS 38, IAS 39[10]) that require an entity to recognise in profit or loss any gain or loss arising from derecognition of an asset. The IFRIC concluded that the changes in the dividend payable before settlement related to changes in the estimate of the distribution and should be accounted for in equity (ie adjustments to the amount of the distribution) until settlement of the dividend payable.

When the entity settles the dividend payable, how should it account for any difference between the carrying amount of the assets distributed and the carrying amount of the dividend payable? (paragraph 14)

BC38   When an entity distributes the assets to its owners, it derecognises both the assets distributed and the dividend payable.

BC39   The IFRIC noted that, at the time of settlement, the carrying amount of the assets distributed would not normally be greater than the carrying amount of the dividend payable because of the recognition of impairment losses required by other applicable standards. For example, paragraph 59 of IAS 36 *Impairment of Assets* requires an entity to recognise an impairment loss in profit or loss when the recoverable amount of an asset is less than its carrying amount. The recoverable amount of an asset is the higher of its fair value less costs to sell and its value in use in accordance with paragraph 6 of IAS 36. When an entity has an obligation to distribute the asset to its owners in the near future, it would not seem appropriate to measure an impairment loss using the asset's value in use. Furthermore, IFRS 5 requires an entity to measure an asset held for sale at the lower of its carrying amount and its fair value less costs to sell. Consequently, the IFRIC concluded that when an entity derecognises the dividend payable and the asset distributed, any difference will always be a credit balance (referred to below as the credit balance).

BC40   In determining how the credit balance should be accounted for, the IFRIC first considered whether it should be recognised as an owner change in equity.

BC41   The IFRIC acknowledged that an asset distribution was a transaction between an entity and its owners. The IFRIC also observed that distributions to owners are recognised as owner changes in equity in accordance with IAS 1 (as revised in 2007). However, the IFRIC noted that the credit balance did not arise from the distribution transaction. Rather, it represented the cumulative unrecognised

---

10   IFRS 9 *Financial Instruments* replaced IAS 39. IFRS 9 applies to all items that were previously within the scope of IAS 39.

gain associated with the asset. It reflects the performance of the entity during the period the asset was held until it was distributed.

BC42   Some might argue that, since an asset distribution does not result in the owners of an entity losing the future economic benefits of the asset, the credit balance should be recognised directly in equity. This view would be based upon the proprietary perspective in which the reporting entity does not have substance of its own separate from that of its owners. However, the IFRIC noted that the *Framework* requires an entity to consider the effect of a transaction from the perspective of the entity for which the financial statements are prepared. Under the entity perspective, the reporting entity has substance of its own, separate from that of its owners. In addition, when there is more than one class of equity instruments, the argument that all owners of an entity have effectively the same interest in the asset would not be valid.

BC43   For the reasons described in paragraphs BC41 and BC42, the IFRIC concluded that the credit balance should not be recognised as an owner change in equity.

BC44   The IFRIC noted that, as explained in the Basis for Conclusions on IAS 1, the Board explicitly prohibited any income or expenses (ie non-owner changes in equity) from being recognised directly in the statement of changes in equity. Any such income or expenses must be recognised as items of comprehensive income first.

BC45   The statement of comprehensive income in accordance with IAS 1 includes two components: items of profit or loss, and items of other comprehensive income. The IFRIC therefore discussed whether the credit balance should be recognised in profit or loss or in other comprehensive income.

BC46   IAS 1 does not provide criteria for when an item should be recognised in profit or loss. However, paragraph 88 of IAS 1 states: 'An entity shall recognise all items of income and expense in a period in profit or loss unless an IFRS requires or permits otherwise.'

BC47   The IFRIC considered the circumstances in which IFRSs require items of income and expense to be recognised as items of other comprehensive income, mainly as follows:

(a)   some actuarial gains or losses arising from remeasuring defined benefit liabilities provided that specific criteria set out in IAS 19 are met.

(b)   a revaluation surplus arising from revaluation of an item of property, plant and equipment in accordance with IAS 16 or revaluation of an intangible asset in accordance with IAS 38.

(c)   an exchange difference arising from the translation of the results and financial positions of an entity from its functional currency into a presentation currency in accordance with IAS 21 *The Effects of Changes in Foreign Exchange Rates.*

(d)   an exchange difference arising from the translation of the results and financial position of a foreign operation into a presentation currency of a reporting entity for consolidation purposes in accordance with IAS 21.

(e)   a change in the fair value of an available-for-sale[11] investment in accordance with IAS 39.

(f)   a change in the fair value of a hedging instrument qualifying for cash flow hedge accounting in accordance with IAS 39.[12]

BC48   The IFRIC concluded that the requirement in IAS 1 prevents any of these ite7ms from being applied by analogy to the credit balance. In addition, the IFRIC noted that, with the exception of the items described in paragraph BC47(a)–(c), the applicable IFRSs require the items of income and expenses listed in paragraph BC47 to be reclassified to profit or loss when the related assets or liabilities are derecognised. Those items of income and expenses are recognised as items of other comprehensive income when incurred, deferred in equity until the related assets are disposed of (or the related liabilities are settled), and reclassified to profit or loss at that time.

BC49   The IFRIC noted that, when the dividend payable is settled, the asset distributed is also derecognised. Therefore, given the existing requirements in IFRSs, even if the credit balance were recognised as an item of other comprehensive income, it would have to be reclassified to profit or loss immediately. As a result, the credit balance would appear three times in the statement of comprehensive income—once recognised as an item of other comprehensive income, once reclassified out of other comprehensive income to profit or loss and once recognised as an item of profit or loss as a result of the reclassification. The IFRIC concluded that such a presentation does not faithfully reflect what has occurred. In addition, users of financial statements were likely to be confused by such a presentation.

BC50   Moreover, when an entity distributes its assets to its owners, it loses the future economic benefit associated with the assets distributed and derecognises those assets. Such a consequence is, in general, similar to that of a disposal of an asset. IFRSs (eg IAS 16, IAS 38, IAS 39[13] and IFRS 5) require an entity to recognise in profit or loss any gain or loss arising from the derecognition of an asset. IFRSs also require such a gain or loss to be recognised when the asset is derecognised. As mentioned in paragraph BC42, the *Framework* requires an entity to consider the effect of a transaction from the perspective of an entity for which the financial statements are prepared. For these reasons, the IFRIC concluded that the credit balance and gains or losses on derecognition of an asset should be accounted for in the same way.

BC51   Furthermore, paragraph 92 of the *Framework*[14] states: 'Income is recognised in the income statement when an increase in future economic benefits related to an increase in an asset or *a decrease of a liability* has arisen that can be measured reliably' (emphasis added). At the time of the settlement of a dividend payable, there is clearly a decrease in a liability. Therefore, the credit balance should be recognised in profit or loss in accordance with paragraph 92 of the *Framework*. Some might argue that the entity does not receive any additional economic

---

11   IFRS 9 *Financial Instruments* eliminated the category of available-for-sale financial assets.
12   IFRS 9 *Financial Instruments* replaced the hedge accounting requirements in IAS 39.
13   IFRS 9 *Financial Instruments* replaced IAS 39. IFRS 9 applies to all items that were previously within the scope of IAS 39.
14   now paragraph 4.47 of the *Conceptual Framework*

benefits when it distributes the assets to its owners. As mentioned in paragraph BC41, the credit balance does not represent any additional economic benefits to the entity. Instead, it represents the unrecognised economic benefits that the entity obtained while it held the assets.

BC52 The IFRIC also noted that paragraph 55 of the *Framework*[15] states: 'The future economic benefits embodied in an asset may flow to the entity in a number of ways. For example, an asset may be: (a) used singly or in combination with other assets in the production of goods or services to be sold by the entity; (b) exchanged for other assets; (c) used to settle a liability; or (d) *distributed to the owners of the entity* [emphasis added].'

BC53 In the light of these requirements, in D23 the IFRIC concluded that the credit balance should be recognised in profit or loss. This treatment would give rise to the same accounting results regardless of whether an entity distributes non-cash assets to its owners, or sells the non-cash assets first and distributes the cash received to its owners. Most commentators on D23 supported the IFRIC's conclusion and its basis.

BC54 Some IFRIC members believed that it would be more appropriate to treat the distribution as a single transaction with owners and therefore recognise the credit balance directly in equity. This alternative view was included in D23 and comments were specifically invited. However, this view was not supported by commentators. To be recognised directly in equity, the credit balance must be considered an owner change in equity in accordance with IAS 1. The IFRIC decided that the credit balance does not arise from the distribution transaction. Rather, it represents the increase in value of the assets. The increase in the value of the asset does not meet the definition of an owner change in equity in accordance with IAS 1. Rather, it meets the definition of income and should be recognised in profit and loss.

BC55 The IFRIC recognised respondents' concerns about the potential 'accounting mismatch' in equity resulting from measuring the assets to be distributed at carrying amount and measuring the dividend payable at fair value. Consequently, the IFRIC considered whether it should recommend that the Board amend IFRS 5 to require the assets to be distributed to be measured at fair value.

BC56 In general, IFRSs permit remeasurement of assets only as the result of a transaction or an impairment. The exceptions are situations in which the IFRSs prescribe current measures on an ongoing basis as in IASs 39 and 41 *Agriculture*, or permit them as accounting policy choices as in IASs 16, 38 and 40 *Investment Property*. As a result of its redeliberations, the IFRIC concluded that there was no support in IFRSs for requiring a remeasurement of the assets because of a decision to distribute them. The IFRIC noted that the mismatch concerned arises only with respect to assets that are not carried at fair value already. The IFRIC also noted that the accounting mismatch is the inevitable consequence of IFRSs using different measurement attributes at different times with different triggers for the remeasurement of different assets and liabilities.

---

15 now paragraph 4.10 of the *Conceptual Framework*

BC57 If a business is to be distributed, the fair value means the fair value of the business to be distributed. Therefore, it includes goodwill and intangible assets. However, internally generated goodwill is not permitted to be recognised as an asset (paragraph 48 of IAS 38). Internally generated brands, mastheads, publishing titles, customer lists and items similar in substance are not permitted to be recognised as intangible assets (paragraph 63 of IAS 38). In accordance with IAS 38, the carrying amounts of internally generated intangible assets are generally restricted to the sum of expenditure incurred by an entity. Consequently, a requirement to remeasure an asset that is a business would contradict the relevant requirements in IAS 38.

BC58 Furthermore, in addition to the lack of consistency with other IFRSs, changing IFRS 5 this way (ie to require an asset held for distribution to owners to be remeasured at fair value) would create internal inconsistency within IFRS 5. There would be no reasonable rationale to explain why IFRS 5 could require assets that are to be sold to be carried at the lower of fair value less costs to sell and carrying value but assets to be distributed to owners to be carried at fair value. The IFRIC also noted that this 'mismatch' would arise only in the normally short period between when the dividend payable is recognised and when it is settled. The length of this period would often be within the control of management. Therefore, the IFRIC decided not to recommend that the Board amend IFRS 5 to require assets that are to be distributed to be measured at fair value.

Amendment to IFRS 5

BC59 IFRS 5 requires an entity to classify a non-current asset (or disposal group) as held for sale if its carrying amount will be recovered principally through a sale transaction rather than through continuing use. IFRS 5 also sets out presentation and disclosure requirements for a discontinued operation.

BC60 When an entity has an obligation to distribute assets to its owners, the carrying amount of the assets will no longer be recovered principally through continuing use. The IFRIC decided that the information required by IFRS 5 is important to users of financial statements regardless of the form of a transaction. Therefore, the IFRIC concluded that the requirements in IFRS 5 applicable to non-current assets (or disposal groups) classified as held for sale and to discontinued operations should also be applied to assets (or disposal groups) held for distribution to owners.

BC61 However, the IFRIC concluded that requiring an entity to apply IFRS 5 to non-current assets (disposal groups) held for distribution to owners would require amendments to IFRS 5. This is because, in the IFRIC's view, IFRS 5 at present applies only to non-current assets (disposal groups) held for sale.

BC62 The Board discussed the IFRIC's proposal at its meeting in December 2007. The Board agreed with the IFRIC's conclusion that IFRS 5 should be amended to apply to non-current assets held for distribution to owners as well as to assets held for sale. However, the Board noted that IFRS 5 requires an entity to classify a non-current asset as held for sale when the sale is highly probable and the entity is *committed* to a plan to sell (emphasis added). Consequently, the Board directed the IFRIC to invite comments on the following questions:

(a) Should an entity apply IFRS 5 when it is committed to make a distribution or when it has an obligation to distribute the assets concerned?

(b) Is there a difference between those dates?

(c) If respondents believe that there is a difference between the dates and that an entity should apply IFRS 5 at the commitment date, what is the difference? What indicators should be included in IFRS 5 to help an entity to determine that date?

BC63 On the basis of the comments received, the IFRIC noted that, in many jurisdictions, shareholders' approval is required to make a distribution. Therefore, in such jurisdictions there could be a difference between the commitment date (ie the date when management is committed to the dividend) and the obligation date (ie the date when the dividend is approved by the shareholders). On the other hand, some commentators think that, when a distribution requires shareholders' approval, the entity cannot be committed until that approval is obtained: in that case, there would be no difference between two dates.

BC64 The IFRIC concluded that IFRS 5 should be applied at the commitment date at which time the assets must be available for immediate distribution in their present condition and the distribution must be *highly probable*. For the distribution to be highly probable, it should meet essentially the same conditions required for assets held for sale. Further, the IFRIC concluded that the probability of shareholders' approval (if required in the jurisdiction) should be considered as part of the assessment of whether the distribution is highly probable. The IFRIC noted that shareholder approval is also required for the sale of assets in some jurisdictions and concluded that similar consideration of the probability of such approval should be required for assets held for sale.

BC65 The Board agreed with the IFRIC's conclusions and amended IFRS 5 as part of its approval of the Interpretation.

Summary of main changes from the draft Interpretation

BC66 The main changes from the IFRIC's proposals in D23 are as follows:

(a) Paragraphs 3–8 were modified to clarify the scope of the Interpretation.

(b) Paragraph 10 clarifies when to recognise a dividend payable.

(c) Paragraphs 11–13 were modified to require the dividend payable to be measured at the fair value of the assets to be distributed without linking the IFRIC's conclusion that fair value is the most relevant measurement attribute to any individual standard.

(d) Illustrative examples were expanded to set out clearly the scope of the Interpretation.

(e) The Interpretation includes the amendments to IFRS 5 and IAS 10.

(f) The Basis for Conclusions was changed to set out more clearly the reasons for the IFRIC's conclusions.

Document published to accompany

IFRIC 19

Extinguishing Financial Liabilities with Equity Instruments

The text of the unaccompanied Interpretation, IFRIC 19, is contained in Part A of this edition. Its effective date when issued was 1 July 2010. This part presents the following documents:

BASIS FOR CONCLUSIONS

Basis for Conclusions on IFRIC Interpretation 19 *Extinguishing Financial Liabilities with Equity Instruments*

This Basis for Conclusions accompanies, but is not part of, IFRIC 19.

Introduction

BC1   This Basis for Conclusions summarises the IFRIC's considerations in reaching its consensus. Individual IFRIC members gave greater weight to some factors than to others.

BC2   The IFRIC received a request for guidance on the application of IAS 39 *Financial Instruments: Recognition and Measurement*[1] and IAS 32 *Financial Instruments: Presentation* when an entity issues its own equity instruments to extinguish all or part of a financial liability. The question is how the entity should recognise the equity instruments issued.

BC3   The IFRIC noted that lenders manage loans to entities in financial difficulty in a variety of ways including one or more of the following:

(a)   selling the loans in the market to other investors/lenders;

(b)   renegotiating the terms of the loan (eg extension of the maturity date or lower interest payments); or

(c)   accepting the creditor's equity instruments in full or partial settlement of the liability (sometimes referred to as a 'debt for equity swap').

BC4   The IFRIC was informed that there was diversity in practice in how entities measure the equity instruments issued in full or partial settlement of a financial liability following renegotiation of the terms of the liability. Some recognise the equity instruments at the carrying amount of the financial liability and do not recognise any gain or loss in profit or loss. Others recognise the equity instruments at the fair value of either the liability extinguished or the equity instruments issued and recognise a difference between that amount and the carrying amount of the financial liability in profit or loss.

BC5   In August 2009 the IFRIC published draft Interpretation D25 *Extinguishing Financial Liabilities with Equity Instruments* for public comment. It received 33 comment letters in response to the proposals.

Scope

BC6   The IFRIC concluded that its Interpretation should address only the accounting by an entity when the terms of a financial liability are renegotiated and result in the entity issuing equity instruments to a creditor of the entity to extinguish part or all of the liability. It does not address the accounting by the creditor because other IFRSs already set out the relevant requirements.

---

1   IFRS 9 *Financial Instruments* replaced IAS 39. IFRS 9 applies to all items that were previously within the scope of IAS 39.

BC7   The IFRIC considered whether to provide guidance on transactions in which the creditor is also a direct or indirect shareholder and is acting in its capacity as an existing direct or indirect shareholder. The IFRIC concluded that the Interpretation should not address such transactions. It noted that determining whether the issue of equity instruments to extinguish a financial liability in such situations is considered a transaction with an owner in its capacity as an owner would be a matter of judgement depending on the facts and circumstances.

BC8   In its redeliberations, the IFRIC clarified that transactions when the creditor and the entity are controlled by the same party or parties before and after the transaction are outside the scope of the Interpretation when the substance of the transaction includes an equity distribution by, or contribution to, the entity. The IFRIC acknowledged that the allocation of consideration between the extinguishment of all or part of a financial liability and the equity distribution or contribution components may not always be reliably measured.

BC9   Some respondents questioned whether the Interpretation should be applied to transactions when the extinguishment of the financial liability by issuing equity shares is in accordance with the original terms of the liability. In its redeliberations the IFRIC decided that these transactions should be excluded from the scope of the Interpretation, noting that IAS 32 includes specific guidance on those financial instruments.

Are an entity's equity instruments 'consideration paid'?

BC10   The IFRIC noted that IFRSs do not contain specific guidance on the measurement of an entity's equity instruments issued to extinguish all or part of a financial liability. Paragraph 41 of IAS 39[2] requires an entity to recognise in profit or loss the difference between the carrying amount of the financial liability extinguished and the consideration paid. That paragraph describes 'consideration paid' as including non-cash assets transferred, or liabilities assumed, and does not specifically mention equity instruments issued. Consequently, some are of the view that equity instruments are not 'consideration paid'.

BC11   Holders of this view believe that, because IFRSs are generally silent on how to measure equity instruments on initial recognition (see paragraph BC15), a variety of practices has developed. One such practice is to recognise the equity instruments issued at the carrying amount of the financial liability extinguished.

BC12   However, the IFRIC observed that both IFRS 2 *Share-based Payment* and IFRS 3 *Business Combinations* make it clear that equity instruments are used as consideration to acquire goods and services as well as to obtain control of businesses.

BC13   The IFRIC also observed that the issue of equity instruments to extinguish a financial liability could be analysed as consisting of two transactions—first, the

---

2   IFRS 9 *Financial Instruments* replaced IAS 39. IFRS 9 applies to all items that were previously within the scope of IAS 39.

issue of new equity instruments to the creditor for cash and second, the creditor accepting payment of that amount of cash to extinguish the financial liability.

BC14　As a result of its analysis, the IFRIC concluded that the equity instruments issued to extinguish a financial liability are 'consideration paid' in accordance with paragraph 41 of IAS 39.

How should the equity instruments be measured?

BC15　The IFRIC observed that although IFRSs do not contain a general principle for the initial recognition and measurement of equity instruments, guidance on specific transactions exists, including:

(a)　*initial recognition of compound instruments* (IAS 32). The amount allocated to the equity component is the residual after deducting the fair value of the financial liability component from the fair value of the entire compound instrument.

(b)　*cost of equity transactions and own equity instruments ('treasury shares') acquired and reissued or cancelled* (IAS 32). No gain or loss is recognised in profit or loss on the purchase, sale, issue or cancellation of an entity's own equity instruments. These are transactions with an entity's owners in their capacity as owners.

(c)　*equity instruments issued in share-based payment transactions* (IFRS 2). For equity-settled share-based payment transactions, the entity measures the goods or services received, and the corresponding increase in equity, directly, at the fair value of the goods or services received, unless that fair value cannot be estimated reliably. If the entity cannot estimate reliably the fair value of the goods or services received (eg transactions with employees), the entity measures their value, and the corresponding increase in equity, indirectly, by reference to the fair value of the equity instruments granted.

(d)　*consideration transferred in business combinations* (IFRS 3). The total consideration transferred in a business combination is measured at fair value. It includes the acquisition-date fair values of any equity interests issued by the acquirer.

BC16　The IFRIC noted that the general principle of IFRSs is that equity is a residual and should be measured initially by reference to changes in assets and liabilities (the *Framework*[3] and IFRS 2). IFRS 2 is clear that when goods or services are received in return for the issue of equity instruments, the increase in equity is measured directly at the fair value of the goods or services received.

BC17　The IFRIC decided that the same principles should apply when equity instruments are issued to extinguish financial liabilities. However, the IFRIC was concerned that entities might encounter practical difficulties in measuring the fair value of both the equity instruments issued and the financial liability, particularly when the entity is in financial difficulty. Therefore, the IFRIC

3　References to the *Framework* are to IASC's *Framework for the Preparation and Presentation of Financial Statements*, adopted by the IASB in 2001. In September 2010 the IASB replaced the *Framework* with the *Conceptual Framework for Financial Reporting*.

decided in D25 that equity instruments issued to extinguish a financial liability should be measured initially at the fair value of the equity instruments issued or the fair value of the liability extinguished, whichever is more reliably determinable.

BC18 However, in response to comments received on D25, the IFRIC reconsidered whether the entity should initially measure equity instruments issued to a creditor to extinguish all or part of a financial liability at the fair value of the equity instruments issued or the fair value of the liability extinguished. The IFRIC noted that many respondents proposed that a preferred measurement basis should be determined to avoid an 'accounting choice' developing in practice, acknowledging that both measurement approaches would need to be used to identify which was more reliably determinable.

BC19 Therefore the IFRIC decided to modify the proposal in D25 and identify a preferred measurement basis. In identifying this preferred measurement basis, the IFRIC noted that many respondents considered that the principles in IFRS 2 and the *Framework* referred to in paragraph BC16 support a measurement based on the fair value of the liability extinguished.

BC20 However, some respondents argued that the fair value of the equity issued should be the proposed measurement basis. They pointed out that this approach would be consistent with the consensus that the issue of an entity's equity instruments is consideration paid in accordance with paragraph 41 of IAS 39.[4] They also argued that the fair value of the equity issued best reflects the total amount of consideration paid in the transaction, which may include a premium that the creditor requires to renegotiate the terms of the financial liability.

BC21 The IFRIC considered that the fair value of the equity issued should be the proposed measurement basis for the reasons described in paragraph BC20. Consequently the IFRIC concluded that an entity should initially measure equity instruments issued to a creditor to extinguish all or part of a financial liability at the fair value of the equity instruments issued, unless that fair value cannot be reliably measured. If the fair value of the equity instruments issued cannot be reliably measured then these equity instruments should initially be measured to reflect the fair value of the liability extinguished.

BC22 In redeliberations, the IFRIC noted that these transactions often take place in situations when the terms of the financial liability are breached and the liability becomes repayable on demand. The IFRIC agreed with comments received that paragraph 49 of IAS 39 is not applied in measuring the fair value of all or part of a financial liability extinguished in these situations.[5] This is because the extinguishment transaction suggests that the demand feature is no longer substantive.

---

4   IFRS 9 *Financial Instruments* replaced IAS 39. IFRS 9 applies to all items that were previously within the scope of IAS 39.

5   IFRS 9 *Financial Instruments* replaced IAS 39. Paragraph 49 of IAS 39 was ultimately relocated to paragraph 47 of IFRS 13 *Fair Value Measurement*. Paragraph BC22 refers to matters relevant when IFRIC 19 was issued.

BC23   In response to comments, the IFRIC also clarified that the equity instruments issued should be recognised initially and measured at the date the financial liability (or part of that liability) is extinguished. This is consistent with paragraphs BC341 and BC342 of the Basis for Conclusions on IFRS 3, which discuss the views on whether equity instruments issued as consideration in a business combination should be measured at fair value at the agreement date or acquisition date, concluding that measurement should be at the acquisition date.

How should a difference between the carrying amount of the financial liability and the consideration paid be accounted for?

BC24   In accordance with paragraph 41 of IAS 39,[6] the entity should recognise a gain or loss in profit or loss for any difference between the carrying amount of the financial liability extinguished and the consideration paid. This requirement is consistent with the *Framework's* discussion of income:

(a)   Income is increases in economic benefits during the accounting period in the form of inflows or enhancements of assets or *decreases of liabilities that result in increases in equity*, other than those relating to contributions from equity participants. (paragraph 70(a))[7] (emphasis added)

(b)   Gains represent other items that meet the definition of income and may, or may not, arise in the course of the ordinary activities of an entity. Gains represent increases in economic benefits ... (paragraph 75)[8]

(c)   Income may also result from the settlement of liabilities. For example, an entity may provide goods and services to a lender in settlement of an obligation to repay an outstanding loan. (paragraph 77)[9]

Full extinguishment

BC25   The IFRIC noted that, as discussed in paragraph BC13, a transaction in which an entity issues equity instruments to extinguish a liability can be analysed as first, the issue of new equity instruments to the creditor for cash and second, the creditor accepting payment of that amount of cash to extinguish the financial liability. Consistently with paragraph BC24, when the creditor accepts cash to extinguish the liability, the entity should recognise a gain or loss in profit or loss.

BC26   Similarly, the IFRIC noted that, in accordance with IAS 32, when an entity amends the terms of a convertible instrument to induce early conversion, the entity recognises in profit or loss the fair value of any additional consideration paid to the holder. Thus, the IFRIC concluded that when an entity settles an instrument by issuing its own equity instruments and that settlement is not in accordance with the original terms of the financial liability, the entity should recognise a gain or loss in profit or loss.

---

6   IFRS 9 *Financial Instruments* replaced IAS 39. IFRS 9 applies to all items that were previously within the scope of IAS 39.

7   now paragraph 4.25(a) of the *Conceptual Framework*

8   now paragraph 4.30 of the *Conceptual Framework*

9   now paragraph 4.32 of the *Conceptual Framework*

BC27　　As a result of its conclusions, the IFRIC decided that the entity should recognise a gain or loss in profit or loss. This gain or loss is equal to the difference between the carrying amount of the financial liability and the fair value of the equity instruments issued, or fair value of the liability extinguished if the fair value of the equity instruments issued cannot be reliably measured.

Partial extinguishment

BC28　　The IFRIC also observed that the restructuring of a financial liability can involve both the partial settlement of the liability by the issue of equity instruments to the creditor and the modification of the terms of the liability that remains outstanding. Therefore, the IFRIC decided that the Interpretation should also apply to partial extinguishments. In the case of a partial extinguishment, the discussion in paragraphs BC25–BC27 applies to the part of the liability extinguished.

BC29　　Many respondents requested clarification of the guidance on partial extinguishment included in D25. During its redeliberations, the IFRIC acknowledged that the issue of an entity's equity shares may reflect consideration paid for both the extinguishment of part of a financial liability and the modification of the terms of the part of the liability that remains outstanding.

BC30　　The IFRIC decided that to reflect this, an entity should allocate the consideration paid between the part of the liability extinguished and the part of the liability that remains outstanding. The entity would consider this allocation in determining the profit or loss to be recognised on the part of the liability extinguished and in its assessment of whether the terms of the remaining liability have been substantially modified.

BC31　　The IFRIC concluded that providing additional guidance on determining whether the terms of the part of the financial liability that remains outstanding has been substantially modified in accordance with paragraph 40 of IAS 39[10] was outside the scope of the Interpretation.

Presentation

BC32　　The IFRIC decided that an entity should disclose the gain or loss on the extinguishment of the financial liability by the issue of equity instruments as a separate line item in profit or loss or in the notes. This requirement is consistent with the *Framework* and the requirements in other IFRSs, for example:

(a)　　When gains are recognised in the income statement, they are usually displayed separately because knowledge of them is useful for the purpose of making economic decisions. (paragraph 76 of the *Framework*)[11]

(b)　　An entity shall present additional line items, headings and subtotals in the statement of comprehensive income and the separate income statement (if presented), when such presentation is relevant to an

---

10　IFRS 9 *Financial Instruments* replaced IAS 39. IFRS 9 applies to all items that were previously within the scope of IAS 39.

11　now paragraph 4.31 of the *Conceptual Framework*

understanding of the entity's financial performance. (paragraph 85 of IAS 1 *Presentation of Financial Statements*)

(c) An entity shall disclose net gains or net losses on financial liabilities either in the statement of comprehensive income or in the notes. (paragraph 20 of IFRS 7 *Financial Instruments: Disclosures*)

Transition

BC33   The IFRIC decided that the Interpretation should be applied retrospectively even though it acknowledged that determining fair values retrospectively may be problematic. The IFRIC noted that IAS 8 *Accounting Policies, Changes in Accounting Estimates and Errors* provides guidance on circumstances in which retrospective application might be impracticable. The IFRIC concluded that it was preferable to require entities that could apply the Interpretation retrospectively to do so, rather than requiring all entities to apply it prospectively to future transactions. However, to simplify transition, the IFRIC also concluded that it should require retrospective application only from the beginning of the earliest comparative period presented because application to earlier periods would result only in a reclassification of amounts within equity.

Summary of main changes from the draft Interpretation

BC34   The main changes from the IFRIC's proposals in D25 are as follows:

(a)   Paragraph 3 was added because the IFRIC identified specific transactions that are outside of the scope of the Interpretation.

(b)   Paragraph 6 was modified to state that measurement should be based on the fair value of the equity instruments issued, unless that fair value cannot be reliably measured.

(c)   Paragraph 7 was added to reflect the modification to paragraph 6. It also clarifies the intention of the IFRIC that in measuring the fair value of a financial liability extinguished that includes a demand feature (eg a demand deposit), paragraph 49 of IAS 39[12] is not applied.

(d)   Paragraph 8 was added, and paragraph 10 was modified, to clarify how the Interpretation should be applied when only part of the financial liability is extinguished by the issue of equity instruments.

(e)   Paragraph 9 was modified to state when the equity instruments issued should be initially measured.

---

12   IFRS 9 *Financial Instruments* replaced IAS 39. Paragraph 49 of IAS 39 was ultimately relocated to paragraph 47 of IFRS 13 *Fair Value Measurement*. Paragraph BC22 refers to matters relevant when IFRIC 19 was issued.

Document published to accompany

IFRIC 20

Stripping Costs in the Production Phase of a Surface Mine

The text of the unaccompanied Interpretation, IFRIC 20, is contained in Part A of this edition. Its effective date when issued was 1 January 2013. The text of the Accompanying Guidance on IFRIC 20 is contained in Part B of this edition. This part presents the following documents:

BASIS FOR CONCLUSIONS

Basis for Conclusions on
IFRIC Interpretation 20 *Stripping Costs in the Production Phase of a Surface Mine*

This Basis for Conclusions accompanies, but is not part of, IFRIC 20.

Introduction

BC1   This Basis for Conclusions summarises the IFRS Interpretations Committee's considerations in reaching its consensus. Individual Committee members gave greater weight to some factors than to others.

Background

BC2   The Committee received a request to issue guidance on the accounting for waste removal ('stripping') costs incurred in the production phase of a surface mine ('production stripping costs'). Accounting for production stripping costs is challenging, because the costs that are incurred may benefit both future and current period production, and there is no specific guidance in IFRSs that addresses this issue.

BC3   Consequently, there is diversity in practice in accounting for production stripping costs—some entities recognise production stripping costs as an expense (a cost of production), some entities capitalise some or all production stripping costs on the basis of a 'life-of-mine ratio' calculation or some similar basis, and some capitalise the costs associated with specific betterments. The Committee decided to develop an Interpretation in response to this diversity in practice.

Scope

BC4   This Interpretation gives guidance on the accounting for stripping costs incurred in the production phase of a surface mine. In developing the Interpretation, the Committee decided to focus only on surface mining activities and not on underground mining activities. This Interpretation applies to the activity of surface mining and therefore to all types of natural resources that are extracted using this process. Where this Interpretation refers to 'extraction of mineral ore', it applies equally to surface mining activities used to extract other natural resources that may not be embedded in an ore deposit but are nevertheless extracted using a surface mining activity, for example coal. However, the Committee decided not to address oil and natural gas extraction, including the question of whether oil sands extraction was a surface mining activity, when it determined the scope of this Interpretation.

BC5   The Committee decided not to include stripping costs incurred during the development phase of a surface mine because there is no significant diversity in practice in accounting for such costs. During the development phase of a surface mine (before production begins), stripping costs are usually capitalised as part of the depreciable cost of building, developing and constructing the mine if it is probable that these costs will be recovered through future mining activity.

These capitalised costs are depreciated or amortised on a systematic basis, usually by using the units of production method, once production begins.

Consensus

Recognition of production stripping costs as an asset

BC6 The Committee decided that an entity may create two benefits by undertaking stripping activity (and incurring stripping costs). These benefits are the extraction of the ore in the current period and improved access to the ore body for a future period. The result of this is that the activity creates an inventory asset and a non-current asset.

BC7 The asset recognition criteria included in paragraph 9 of this Interpretation are those referred to in paragraph 4.44 of the *Conceptual Framework for Financial Reporting*. An additional criterion is, however, also included in this Interpretation for recognising the stripping activity asset—that the entity can specifically identify the 'component' of the ore body for which access is being improved. All three criteria must be met for the costs to qualify for recognition as an asset. If the criteria are not met, a stripping activity asset will not be recognised.

BC8 'Component' refers to the specific volume of the ore body that is made more accessible by the stripping activity. The identified component of the ore body would typically be a subset of the total ore body of the mine. A mine may have several components, which are identified during the mine planning stage. As well as providing a basis for measuring the costs reliably at recognition stage, identification of components of the ore body is necessary for the subsequent depreciation or amortisation of the stripping activity asset, which will take place as that identified component of the ore body is mined.

BC9 Identifying components of the ore body requires judgement. The Committee understands that an entity's mine plan will provide the information required to allow these judgements to be made with reasonable consistency.

BC10 This Interpretation also states that the stripping cost asset should be recognised as 'part' of an existing asset. 'Part' refers to the addition to, or enhancement of, the existing asset that relates to the stripping activity asset. The Committee took the view that the stripping activity asset was more akin to being a part of an existing asset, rather than being an asset in its own right. The stripping activity asset might add to or improve a variety of existing assets, for example the mine property (land), the mineral deposit itself, an intangible right to extract the ore or an asset that originated in the mine development phase.

BC11 The Committee decided that it is not necessary for the Interpretation to define whether the benefit created by the stripping activity is tangible or intangible in nature—this will be determined from the nature of the related underlying existing asset.

Initial measurement of the stripping activity asset

BC12 IAS 16 paragraph 16(b) states that the cost of an item of property, plant and equipment includes 'any costs directly attributable to bringing the asset to the location and condition necessary ...'. Examples of the types of costs that the Committee would expect to be included as directly attributable overhead costs (paragraph 12 of the Interpretation) would include an allocation of salary costs of the mine supervisor overseeing that component of the mine, and an allocation of rental costs of any equipment that was hired specifically to perform the stripping activity.

BC13 The Committee thought that it was important to be guided by the principle contained in paragraph 21 of IAS 16 when addressing incidental operations in the Interpretation. The Committee is aware that a number of activities are carried out simultaneously in a mine operation, and it thought that it was important for the entity to be aware of what constitutes production stripping activity, and what does not, when considering the measurement of the stripping activity asset. An example of such an incidental operation would be building an access road in the area in which the stripping campaign is taking place.

BC14 The Committee noted that, when inventory is produced at the same time as the stripping activity asset is created, it may be difficult in practice to measure the separate cost of each benefit directly. The Committee agreed that an allocation basis would be needed in order to differentiate between the cost of the inventory produced and the cost of the stripping activity asset.

BC15 In its discussions of the most appropriate allocation basis, the Committee rejected any basis that was based on sales values. The Committee considered that such a basis in the context of stripping costs would be inappropriate because it was not closely linked to the activity taking place. Furthermore, if the current sales price of the relevant mineral was used in determining the allocation basis, the same current sales price would be applied to the volume of the mineral in both the extracted ore and the identified component. Hence the relevant variable would be the volume of mineral in both the extracted ore and the identified component, ie the current sales price would not change the allocation basis. The Committee understood that applying a future sales price basis would involve practical difficulties and that it would be costly in comparison to the benefit that it would provide. From the outreach performed by the staff, the Committee understood that identifying a future sales price for ore that will be mined in the future can be difficult, given the volatility of market prices for many minerals. Further complexities may arise when more than one mineral is present (whether by-products or joint products) when the ore is extracted.

BC16 The Committee decided to require an allocation approach that was based on a relevant production measure, because a production measure was considered to be a good indicator of the nature of the benefits that are generated for the activity taking place in the mine. The production measure basis requires an entity to identify when a level of activity has taken place beyond what would otherwise be expected for the inventory production in the period, and that may have given rise to a future access benefit.

Subsequent measurement of the stripping activity asset

BC17 The Committee decided that the cost of the stripping activity asset should be depreciated or amortised over the expected useful life of the identified component of the ore body that is made more accessible by the activity, on a basis that best reflects the consumption of economic benefits. The units of production method is commonly used, and would be focused only on the identified component of the ore body, the access to which has been improved by the stripping activity. Because the life of the identified component is expected to be only a part of the entire life of the mine, the stripping activity asset will be depreciated or amortised over a shorter period than the life of the mine, unless the stripping activity provides improved access to the whole of the remaining ore body, for example, towards the end of a mine's useful life when the identified component represents the final part of the ore body to be extracted.

BC18　The Committee decided that the principles of this Interpretation would also be applicable to an entity that subsequently accounts for its mine assets at revaluation, although the Committee noted that this method was seldom used. The Committee decided that the subsequent measurement basis of the stripping activity asset should follow that of the existing asset of which it is a part, that is, if the existing asset is measured using a cost basis, then the stripping activity asset would also be measured using a cost basis. The Committee also decided that there was no need for specific impairment guidance to be given and expects that the principles in IAS 36 *Impairment of Assets* would be applied to the existing asset of which the stripping activity asset is a part, and not at the level of the stripping activity asset itself.

Transition

BC19　Because of the complex and lengthy nature of many mining operations, and the past diversity of practice in respect of this issue, the Committee concluded that the cost of applying the change in accounting policy retrospectively would exceed the benefit that would be gained from doing so. The Committee therefore decided that this Interpretation shall require prospective application to production stripping costs incurred on or after the beginning of the earliest period presented.

BC20　The Committee decided to follow the principles in IAS 8 *Accounting Policies, Changes in Accounting Estimates and Errors* on transition. It decided to require recognition of any predecessor stripping asset balances (see paragraph A3) as at the beginning of the earliest period presented, in opening retained earnings at that date, if such balances could not be identified with a remaining component of the ore body that was made more accessible by the stripping activity.

BC21　The Committee noted that any liability balances resulting from prior production stripping activity that existed at the transition date would not be recognised under the principles described in the Interpretation. The Committee understood from the comments received on the draft Interpretation that such balances were uncommon, and therefore did not think that it needed to provide any guidance on recognition of liability balances, because constituents may find it confusing.

Document published to accompany

IFRIC 21

Levies

The text of the unaccompanied Interpretation, IFRIC 21, is contained in Part A of this edition. Its effective date when issued was 1 January 2014. The text of the Accompanying Guidance on IFRIC 21 is contained in Part B of this edition. This part presents the following documents:

BASIS FOR CONCLUSIONS

Basis for Conclusions on IFRIC Interpretation 21 *Levies*

This Basis for Conclusions accompanies, but is not part of, IFRIC 21.

Introduction

BC1   This Basis for Conclusions summarises the considerations of the IFRS Interpretations Committee (the Interpretations Committee) in reaching its consensus. The Interpretations Committee received a request to clarify whether, under certain circumstances, IFRIC 6 *Liabilities arising from Participating in a Specific Market—Waste Electrical and Electronic Equipment* should be applied by analogy to identify the obligating event that gives rise to the recognition of a liability for other levies imposed by governments on entities. The question relates to when to recognise a liability to pay a levy that is accounted for in accordance with IAS 37 *Provisions, Contingent Liabilities and Contingent Assets*.

BC2   In particular, the request was for the Interpretations Committee to clarify how an entity should account for levies when the calculation for the levies is based on financial data that relates to a period before the period that contains the activity that triggers the payment of the levy. This is the case if, for example, the activity that triggers the payment of the levy, as identified by the legislation, occurs in 20X1 and the calculation of the levy is based on financial data for 20X0 (see Illustrative Example 2).

BC3   The Interpretations Committee was informed that there was diversity in practice in how entities account for the obligation to pay such a levy.

Scope

BC4   One of the questions that was submitted was how to account for levies whose calculation basis uses data such as the gross amount of revenue, assets or liabilities. The Interpretations Committee noted that those levies do not meet the definition of income taxes provided in IAS 12 *Income Taxes* because they are not based on taxable profit. In two Agenda Decisions (published in March 2006 and May 2009), the Interpretations Committee (then called the IFRIC) noted that the term 'taxable profit' implies a notion of a net rather than a gross amount. In those Agenda Decisions, the Interpretations Committee also observed that any taxes that are not within the scope of other Standards (such as IAS 12) are within the scope of IAS 37. The Interpretations Committee further observed that IAS 37 contains a definition of a liability and that a provision is defined in IAS 37 as a liability of uncertain timing or amount. The Interpretations Committee noted that the same recognition requirements should apply to provisions to pay a levy and to liabilities to pay a levy whose timing and amount is certain. Consequently, this Interpretation also addresses the accounting for a liability to pay a levy whose timing and amount is certain.

BC5   The Interpretations Committee noted that IAS 37 does not apply to executory contracts unless they are onerous, so the Interpretations Committee decided that this Interpretation should therefore not apply to executory contracts unless they are onerous.

BC6   The Interpretations Committee decided that, for the purposes of this Interpretation, a levy is an outflow of resources embodying economic benefits that is imposed by governments on entities in accordance with legislation (ie laws and/or regulations), other than those outflows of resources that are within the scope of other Standards (such as income taxes that are within the scope of IAS 12). Amounts that are collected by entities on behalf of governments (such as value added taxes) and remitted to governments are not outflows of resources embodying economic benefits for the entities that collect and remit those amounts. The Interpretations Committee decided to use the definition of the term 'government' provided in IAS 20 *Accounting for Government Grants and Disclosure of Government Assistance* and IAS 24 *Related Party Disclosures*.

BC7   The Interpretations Committee noted that a payment made by an entity for the acquisition of an asset, or for the rendering of services under a contractual agreement with a government, does not meet the definition of a levy. For the purposes of this Interpretation, levies are imposed by governments and therefore do not arise from contractual agreements. Similarly, the Interpretations Committee noted that this Interpretation does not apply to the accounting for trade discounts and volume rebates agreed between a seller and a purchaser under a contractual agreement.

BC8   The Interpretations Committee decided that this Interpretation should not address the accounting for fines and other penalties. Fines and penalties are paid as a consequence of the breach of laws and/or regulations, whereas levies are paid as a consequence of complying with laws and/or regulations.

BC9   The Interpretations Committee decided that an entity should not be required to apply this Interpretation to liabilities that arise from emissions trading schemes. The IASB decided in 2011 to add a project on this topic to its research agenda. The Interpretations Committee thinks that it would be better to address the accounting for liabilities that arise from emissions trading schemes in a comprehensive project on all recognition and measurement issues related to emissions trading schemes.

BC10   The Interpretations Committee decided not to withdraw IFRIC 6 because it provides useful information on the accounting for liabilities within its scope. The Interpretations Committee noted that the consensus in IFRIC 6 is consistent with the consensus in this Interpretation, and concluded that a scope exclusion for liabilities for waste management within the scope of IFRIC 6 is not necessary.

BC11   The Interpretations Committee decided that this Interpretation should provide guidance on applying IAS 37 to a liability to pay a levy and should not address the accounting for the costs arising from recognising the liability to pay a levy. The Interpretations Committee observed that other Standards would determine whether the recognition of a liability to pay a levy gives rise to an asset or an expense.

What is the obligating event that gives rise to the recognition of a liability to pay a levy?

BC12   According to the definition in paragraph 10 of IAS 37, an obligating event is an event that creates a legal or constructive obligation that results in an entity having no realistic alternative to settling the obligation. According to paragraph 14(a) of IAS 37, a provision should be recognised only when an entity has a present obligation as a result of a past event. The Interpretations Committee noted that the main consequence of these requirements is that there can be only one single obligating event. The Interpretations Committee acknowledged that, in some circumstances, an obligating event can occur only if other events have occurred previously. For example, for some levies, the entity paying the levy must have undertaken an activity both in the previous and in the current periods in order to be obliged to pay the levy. The Interpretations Committee noted that the activity undertaken in the previous period is necessary, but not sufficient, to create a present obligation.

BC13 Consequently, the Interpretations Committee concluded that the obligating event that gives rise to a liability to pay a levy is the activity that triggers the payment of the levy, as identified by the legislation. In other words, the liability to pay a levy is recognised when the activity that triggers the payment of the levy occurs, as identified by the legislation. For example, if the activity that triggers the payment of the levy is the generation of revenue in 20X1 and the calculation of that levy is based on the revenue generated in 20X0, the obligating event for that levy is the generation of revenue in 20X1 (see Illustrative Example 2). The date on which the levy is paid does not affect the timing of recognition of the liability to pay a levy, because the obligating event is the activity that triggers the payment of the levy (and not the payment of the levy itself).

BC14 The Interpretations Committee noted that some respondents to the draft Interpretation think that the result of the proposed accounting does not provide a fair representation of the economic effects of recurring levies when the liability is recognised at a point in time and gives rise to an expense, although these respondents acknowledged that the proposed accounting in the draft Interpretation is a technically correct interpretation of the requirements in IAS 37. Those respondents think that the substance of a recurring levy is that it is an expense associated with a specific period (and not an expense triggered on a specific date). The Interpretations Committee concluded that this Interpretation is needed to address the diversity in practice and that it provides consistent information about an entity's obligations to pay levies. The Interpretations Committee also observed that this Interpretation does not address the accounting for the costs arising from recognising a liability to pay a levy and that other Standards would determine whether the recognition of the liability to pay a levy gives rise to an asset or an expense. Some respondents to the draft Interpretation asked the Interpretations Committee to consider the effect of economic compulsion to continue to operate in a future period and of going concern assumption on the accounting for levies. The Interpretations Committee's conclusions are set out below.

Does economic compulsion to continue to operate in a future period create a constructive obligation to pay a levy that will be triggered by operating in that future period?

BC15 The Interpretations Committee considered an argument that, if it would be necessary for an entity to take unrealistic action in order to avoid an obligation to pay a levy that would otherwise be triggered by operating in the future, then a constructive obligation to pay the levy exists and a liability should be recognised. For example, if the activity that triggers the payment of the levy occurs in 20X1 and the calculation of the levy is based on financial data for 20X0 (as in Illustrative Example 2), some argue that a liability should be recognised in 20X0. Supporters of this argument point to the definition of a constructive obligation in paragraph 10 of IAS 37 and conclude that an entity might have no realistic alternative other than to continue to operate in the next period (ie 20X1). For example, they note that an entity may operate in a regulated market and may not be able to stop operating without a long period of run-off.

BC16 The Interpretations Committee rejected this argument, noting that if this rationale were applied, many types of future expenditure within the scope of IAS 37 would be recognised as liabilities. Indeed, in many cases, entities have no realistic alternative but to pay expenditures to be incurred in the future. The Interpretations Committee noted that, in accordance with paragraphs 18–19 of IAS 37:

(a) no provision is recognised for costs that need to be incurred to operate in the future; and

(b) it is only those obligations arising from past events existing independently of an entity's future conduct of its business that are recognised as provisions.

BC17 As a result, the Interpretations Committee concluded that, when an entity is economically compelled to incur operating costs that relate to the future conduct of the business, that compulsion does not create a constructive obligation and thus does not lead to the entity recognising a liability. This point is illustrated in the examples accompanying IAS 37.

BC18 The Interpretations Committee noted that a levy is triggered as a result of undertaking an activity in a specified period, as identified by the legislation. As a result, the Interpretations Committee concluded that there is no constructive obligation to pay a levy that relates to the future conduct of the business, even if:

(a) it is economically unrealistic for the entity to avoid the levy if it has the intention of continuing in business;

(b) there is a legal requirement to incur the levy if the entity does continue in business;

(c) it would be necessary for an entity to take unrealistic action to avoid paying the levy, such as to sell, or stop operating, property, plant and equipment;

(d) the entity made a statement of intent (and has the ability) to operate in the future period(s); or

(e) the entity has a legal, regulatory or contractual requirement to operate in the future period(s).

BC19 Consequently, the Interpretations Committee concluded that an entity does not have a constructive obligation at a reporting date to pay a levy that will be triggered by operating in a future period as a result of the entity being economically compelled to continue to operate in that future period.

Does the going concern assumption imply that an entity has a present obligation to pay a levy that will be triggered by operating in a future period?

BC20   The Interpretations Committee noted that this issue is related to the basis of preparation of financial statements. Some question whether the going concern assumption affects the timing of the recognition of the liability to pay a levy.

BC21   The Interpretations Committee observed that IAS 1 *Presentation of Financial Statements* sets out general features for the financial statements, including the accrual basis of accounting and the going concern assumption. The Interpretations Committee noted that, when an entity prepares financial statements on a going concern basis, it shall also comply with all the recognition and measurement requirements of IFRS. Consequently, the Interpretations Committee concluded that the going concern assumption cannot lead to the recognition of a liability that does not meet the definitions and recognition criteria set out in IAS 37.

BC22   Specifically, the Interpretations Committee concluded that the preparation of financial statements under the going concern assumption does not imply that an entity has a present obligation to pay a levy that will be triggered by operating in a future period. Paragraphs 18–19 of IAS 37 specify that no provision is recognised in that case.

Does the recognition of a liability to pay a levy arise at a point in time or does it, in some circumstances, arise progressively over time?

BC23   The Interpretations Committee observed that most of the liabilities in IAS 37 and in the Illustrative Examples accompanying IAS 37 are recognised at a point in time, that is, when the obligating event occurs. Nevertheless, they noted that, in one example accompanying IAS 37, the liability is recognised progressively over time.

BC24   In Illustrative Example 3 accompanying IAS 37, an entity operates an offshore oilfield and is required to restore the seabed because of damage caused by the extraction of oil. According to this example, the restoration costs that arise through the extraction of oil are recognised as a liability when the oil is extracted. The Interpretations Committee noted that in this example, the damage is directly caused by the extraction of oil, and that more damage occurs when more oil is extracted. Thus, the outcome is that the liability for damage caused over time is recognised progressively over time as the entity extracts oil and causes damage to the environment.

BC25   The Interpretations Committee discussed whether this outcome is linked to a recognition issue or to a measurement issue and concluded that this is a recognition issue, because the obligating event (ie the damage caused by the extraction of oil) occurs progressively over a period of time. In accordance with paragraph 19 of IAS 37, the Interpretations Committee noted that a present obligation exists only to the extent of the damage caused to date to the environment, because the entity has no present obligation to rectify the damage that will result from the extraction of oil in the future (ie the future conduct of its business).

BC26   Consequently, the Interpretations Committee concluded that the liability to pay a levy is recognised progressively if the obligating event (ie the activity that triggers the payment of the levy, as identified by the legislation) occurs over a period of time. For example, if the obligating event is the generation of revenue over a period of time, the corresponding liability is recognised as the entity generates that revenue (see Illustrative Example 1).

What is the obligating event that gives rise to the recognition of a liability to pay a levy that is triggered if a minimum threshold is reached?

BC27   The draft Interpretation did not address the accounting for levies that are triggered if a minimum revenue threshold is reached. However, many respondents to the draft Interpretation emphasised the importance of providing guidance on this issue. The Interpretations Committee agreed with the respondents' comments and concluded that this Interpretation should provide guidance on the accounting for levies with minimum thresholds. The Interpretations Committee decided that the accounting for the liability to pay such levies should be consistent with the principles established in paragraphs 8 and 11 of this Interpretation.

BC28   For example, if a levy is triggered when a minimum activity threshold is reached (such as a minimum amount of revenue or sales generated or outputs produced), the obligating event is the reaching of that activity threshold. If a levy is triggered as the entity undertakes an activity above a minimum level of activity (such as revenue or sales generated or outputs produced in excess of the minimum amount specified in the legislation), the obligating event is the activity that is undertaken after the threshold is reached (see Illustrative Example 4). If a levy is triggered if an entity operates on a specified date, as identified by the legislation, provided that a minimum threshold is reached in a previous period (such as a minimum amount of revenue, a minimum number of employees, or a minimum amount of assets and liabilities), the obligating event is the entity operating on the specified date as identified by the legislation after having reached the threshold in the previous period. In that case, the reaching of the threshold in the previous period is necessary, but not sufficient, to create a present obligation.

Are the principles for recognising a liability to pay a levy in the annual financial statements and in the interim financial report the same?

BC29   IAS 34 *Interim Financial Reporting* (paragraph 29) states that the same recognition principles should be applied in the annual financial statements and in the interim financial report. By applying the requirements of IAS 34 (paragraphs 31–32 and 39, as illustrated by paragraphs B2, B4 and B11 of the Illustrative Examples accompanying IAS 34), no liability would be recognised at the end of an interim reporting period if the obligating event has not yet occurred. For example, an entity does not have an obligation at the end of an interim reporting period if the present obligation arises only at the end of the annual reporting period. Similarly, if a present obligation to pay a levy exists at the end of an interim reporting period, the liability should be recognised.

BC30   The Interpretations Committee observed that paragraph 16A of IAS 34 requires the disclosure of explanatory comments about the nature and amount of items affecting liabilities that are unusual because of their nature, size or incidence and about the events after the interim period that have not been reflected in the financial statements for the interim period. If necessary, an entity would therefore provide disclosures about levies that are recognised in the interim financial report or that will be recognised in future interim financial reports.

© IFRS Foundation

Document published to accompany

IFRIC 22

Foreign Currency Transactions and Advance Consideration

The text of the unaccompanied Interpretation, IFRIC 22, is contained in Part A of this edition. Its effective date when issued was 1 January 2018. The text of the Accompanying Guidance on IFRIC 22 is contained in Part B of this edition. This part presents the following documents:

BASIS FOR CONCLUSIONS

Basis for Conclusions on IFRIC 22
Foreign Currency Transactions and Advance Consideration

This Basis for Conclusions accompanies, but is not part of, IFRIC 22.

Introduction

BC1   This Basis for Conclusions summarises the considerations of the IFRS Interpretations Committee (the Interpretations Committee) in reaching its consensus.

Background

BC2   The Interpretations Committee received a question asking how to determine the exchange rate to use in applying IAS 21 *The Effects of Changes in Foreign Exchange Rates* when recognising revenue. The question addressed a circumstance in which an entity receives advance consideration in a foreign currency. IAS 21 does not specifically address such a circumstance.

BC3   The Interpretations Committee noted that the feedback from its outreach on the question indicated that:

   (a)   the issue affects a number of jurisdictions, and particularly affects the construction industry.

   (b)   diverse reporting methods are applied. Some entities recognise revenue using the spot exchange rate between the functional currency and the foreign currency at the date of the receipt of the advance consideration and others use the exchange rate at the date that revenue is recognised.

BC4   To address the issue, in October 2015 the Interpretations Committee published a draft Interpretation *Foreign Currency Transactions and Advance Consideration* for public comment. It received 45 comment letters. The Interpretations Committee considered the comments received in developing this Interpretation.

Scope

Foreign currency transactions other than revenue transactions

BC5   The question received related specifically to revenue transactions. However, in discussing the issue, the Interpretations Committee noted that a similar question arises for other transactions when consideration is denominated in a foreign currency and is paid or received in advance. For example:

   (a)   purchases and sales of property, plant and equipment;

   (b)   purchases and sales of intangible assets;

   (c)   purchases and sales of investment property;

   (d)   purchases of inventory;

   (e)   purchases of services;

   (f)   entering into lease contracts; and

(g)   receipt of some government grants.

BC6   In addition, the Interpretations Committee noted that IAS 21 applies to all foreign currency transactions, not only to revenue transactions in a foreign currency. Consequently, the Interpretations Committee decided that the Interpretation applies to a foreign currency transaction (or part of it) when an entity recognises a non-monetary asset or non-monetary liability arising from the payment or receipt of advance consideration. Respondents to the draft Interpretation generally supported the scope proposed by the Interpretations Committee.

Income taxes and insurance contracts

BC7   The Interpretations Committee decided that an entity is not required to apply the Interpretation to income taxes, or to insurance contracts (including reinsurance contracts) that it issues or reinsurance contracts that it holds.

BC8   The Interpretations Committee concluded that it is important to avoid unintended consequences for income taxes because of the complexities that arise from the interplay with deferred tax. Similarly, the Interpretations Committee concluded that it is important to avoid unintended consequences for insurance contracts. The International Accounting Standards Board's project on Insurance Contracts is at an advanced stage and it would be inappropriate to require a change in accounting before the application of the forthcoming insurance contracts Standard.

Non-cash consideration

BC9   Advance consideration may be denominated in a foreign currency, but in a form other than cash. For example, an entity may receive equity instruments, or an item of inventory that has a fair value determined in a foreign currency, in exchange for the provision of services.

BC10   IAS 21 applies to both cash and non-cash foreign currency transactions. Accordingly, the Interpretations Committee determined that the Interpretation applies to both cash and non-cash transactions when an entity recognises a non-monetary asset or non-monetary liability arising from advance consideration in a foreign currency.

Transactions measured at fair value on initial recognition

BC11   Paragraph 23(c) of IAS 21 requires an entity to translate non-monetary items measured at fair value in a foreign currency using the exchange rate at the date when the fair value was measured. Consequently, the Interpretations Committee decided that the Interpretation does not apply to foreign currency transactions for which the related asset, expense or income is initially measured at fair value.

BC12   The Interpretations Committee also decided the Interpretation does not apply to foreign currency transactions for which the related asset, expense or income is initially measured at the fair value of the consideration paid or received at a date other than the date of the transaction specified in this Interpretation. This is because the date of measurement of the fair value used to measure the asset, expense or income on initial recognition would determine the date of the transaction.

Monetary and non-monetary items

BC13   The payment or receipt of advance consideration generally gives rise to the recognition of a non-monetary asset or non-monetary liability. However, an advance payment or receipt could give rise to a monetary asset or liability instead of a non-monetary asset or liability.

BC14   When the asset or liability is a monetary item, paragraphs 28–29 of IAS 21 require an entity to recognise an exchange difference in profit or loss for any change in the exchange rate between the transaction date and the date of settlement of that asset or liability. Consequently, the question about which exchange rate to use on initial recognition of the related asset, expense or income arises only when the advance consideration gives rise to the recognition of a non-monetary asset or non-monetary liability. Accordingly, the Interpretations Committee decided that this Interpretation applies only in circumstances in which an entity recognises a non-monetary asset or non-monetary liability arising from advance consideration.

BC15   Some respondents to the draft Interpretation requested guidance in determining whether the payment or receipt of advance consideration gives rise to a monetary or non-monetary asset or liability. These respondents said that, for some transactions, this assessment can be difficult.

BC16   In considering the request, the Interpretations Committee noted that the Interpretation is not adding a new requirement to determine whether an item is monetary or non-monetary—this requirement already exists in IAS 21. The Interpretation simply clarifies which exchange rate to use for particular transactions. The Interpretations Committee decided that it was outside the scope of this Interpretation to provide application guidance on the definition of monetary and non-monetary items.

BC17   Nonetheless, the Interpretations Committee acknowledged that an entity may need to apply judgement in determining whether an item is monetary or non-monetary. It also noted references in Standards and *The Conceptual Framework for Financial Reporting* (the *Conceptual Framework*) that may be helpful in determining whether an item is monetary or non-monetary. These references include:

(a)   paragraph 16 of IAS 21;

(b)   paragraph AG11 of IAS 32 *Financial Instruments: Presentation*; and

(c)   paragraph 4.17 of *The Conceptual Framework*.

Consensus

The date of the transaction

BC18   Paragraph 22 of IAS 21 defines the date of the transaction for the purpose of determining the exchange rate to use on initial recognition of a foreign currency transaction as 'the date on which the transaction first qualifies for recognition in accordance with IFRSs'.

BC19   The Interpretations Committee observed that there could be two ways of identifying 'the transaction' for the purpose of determining the exchange rate to use on initial recognition:

    (a)   the 'one-transaction' approach—the receipt or payment of consideration and the transfer of the goods or services are all considered to be part of the same transaction. Thus, the date of the transaction is determined by the date on which the first element of the transaction qualifies for recognition applying the relevant Standards.

    (b)   the 'multi-transaction' approach—the receipt or payment of consideration and the transfer of the goods or services are considered to be separate transactions, each of which has its own 'date of the transaction' when it first qualifies for recognition applying the relevant Standards.

BC20   The one-transaction approach is consistent with the notion that purchases and sales represent exchange transactions, and the payment and transfer of goods or services are inherently interdependent. Accordingly, if the first element of the transaction to be recognised is a non-monetary asset or non-monetary liability, that would determine the date of the transaction for the purpose of recognising the related asset, expense or income (or part of it).

BC21   The multi-transaction approach treats the transfer of goods or services and the receipt or payment of consideration as two separate transactions. This approach would result in a date of the transaction that is the same as the date of recognition of the related asset, expense or income (or part of it), regardless of the timing of the payment or receipt of consideration.

BC22   The Interpretations Committee decided that the one-transaction approach is a more appropriate interpretation of IAS 21 when the payment or receipt of advance consideration gives rise to a non-monetary asset or non-monetary liability. This is because:

    (a)   it reflects that an entity is typically no longer exposed to foreign exchange risk in respect of the transaction to the extent that it has received or paid advance consideration. After receipt of advance consideration in a foreign currency, the entity can decide whether to hold the foreign currency consideration and be exposed to foreign exchange risk. After payment of advance consideration in a foreign currency, the entity is no longer exposed to foreign exchange risk in respect of that amount.

(b)   the obligation to perform (reflected in the recognition of a non-monetary liability) and the subsequent fulfilment of that obligation (which gives rise to income) are interdependent and are part of the same transaction.

(c)   the right to receive assets, goods or services (reflected in the recognition of a non-monetary asset) and the receipt of those assets, goods or services are inherently interdependent.

(d)   it is consistent with the treatment of non-monetary assets and non-monetary liabilities applying paragraph 23(b) of IAS 21, because an entity does not subsequently update the translated amounts of such items.

BC23   In addition, considering paragraph 22 of IAS 21, the Interpretations Committee concluded that, for a transaction to qualify for recognition in accordance with the Standards, an entity must record the transaction in its financial statements with a value. The Interpretations Committee observed that paragraph 4.46 of the *Conceptual Framework* notes that 'in practice, obligations under contracts that are equally proportionately unperformed (for example, liabilities for inventory ordered but not yet received) are generally not recognised as liabilities in the financial statements'. Consequently, the Interpretations Committee concluded the date on which an entity first recognises the transaction in its financial statements with a value determines the date of the transaction. If an entity recognises a non-monetary asset or non-monetary liability arising from advance consideration, the date of initial recognition of that asset or liability is the date of the transaction. The date of initial recognition of the non-monetary asset or non-monetary liability is generally the date on which the entity pays or receives the advance consideration.

Multiple payments

BC24   If only part of the consideration is received or paid in advance, then an entity has initially recognised only part of the transaction as a non-monetary asset or non-monetary liability. In that case, applying this Interpretation, an entity determines the date of the transaction for only that part of the related asset, expense or income for which consideration has been received or paid in advance. If there are subsequent advance payments or receipts, the date(s) of the transaction for the remaining part(s) of the related asset, expense or income will be the date(s) on which the entity recognises those subsequent advance receipts or payments. Correspondingly, if part of the consideration is paid in arrears, the date(s) of the transaction for the remaining part(s) of the related asset, expense or income will be the date(s) on which the entity initially recognises that (those) part(s) of the asset, expense or income in its financial statements applying applicable Standards.

BC25   The Interpretations Committee observed that this treatment reflects that an entity typically has no foreign exchange risk in respect of foreign currency amounts already paid or received, but is still exposed to foreign exchange risk in respect of any unpaid consideration.

Embedded derivatives

BC26   The Interpretations Committee was asked to clarify how the Interpretation applies to an embedded derivative that requires separation at contract inception. The Interpretations Committee decided it was not necessary to clarify this matter in the Interpretation. The Interpretation Committee noted that paragraph 24 of IAS 21 requires an entity to determine the carrying amount of an item in conjunction with other relevant Standards. Consequently, an entity first evaluates transactions for embedded derivatives that require separation at contract inception before applying the requirements in IAS 21 or this Interpretation.

BC27   The Interpretations Committee further noted that, if an entity separately accounts for an embedded derivative, the requirements of the Interpretation apply to a remaining host contract denominated in a foreign currency when consideration has been paid or received in advance as they do to other such foreign currency transactions.

Illustrative examples

BC28   Some respondents to the draft Interpretation suggested including an example to illustrate how the Interpretation applies to transactions with a significant financing component. The Interpretations Committee decided not to include an example because it concluded that any such example would interpret other Standards.

Interaction with the presentation of exchange differences arising on monetary items

BC29   The Interpretations Committee considered the interaction of the Interpretation with the presentation of exchange differences on the settlement or retranslation of monetary items that, applying paragraphs 28–29 of IAS 21, an entity recognises in profit or loss in the period in which they arise.

BC30   The Interpretations Committee decided that presentation of exchange differences in profit or loss is outside the scope of the issue being addressed in the Interpretation. This is because the Interpretation addresses only how to determine the 'date of the transaction' for the purpose of determining the exchange rate to use on initial recognition of the related asset, expense or income on the derecognition of a non-monetary asset or non-monetary liability arising from advance consideration in a foreign currency.

Transition

BC31   The Interpretations Committee observed that retrospective application of the Interpretation may be burdensome, in particular for foreign currency transactions involving purchases of assets. Consequently, the Interpretations Committee decided that, on initial application, entities should have the option not to retrospectively adjust assets, expenses and income (or parts of them) that had been recognised before the beginning of the reporting period in which the

Interpretation is first applied or the beginning of a prior reporting period presented as comparative information in the period in which the Interpretation is first applied.

BC32 If an entity uses this option and applies the Interpretation prospectively as permitted in paragraph A2(b), the entity does not restate amounts recognised before either the beginning of the reporting period in which the entity first applies the Interpretation (if paragraph A2b(i) is applied) or the beginning of a prior reporting period presented as comparative information in the period in which the entity first applies the Interpretation (if paragraph A2b(ii) is applied).

First-time adopters

BC33 The Interpretations Committee received feedback that first-time adopters of IFRS Standards may also find retrospective application burdensome. Consequently, the Interpretations Committee decided that first-time adopters should not be required to apply the Interpretation to assets, expenses and income initially recognised before the date of transition to IFRS Standards. Accordingly, this Interpretation amends IFRS 1 *First-time Adoption of International Financial Reporting Standards*.

Material published to accompany

SIC-7

Introduction of the Euro

The text of the unaccompanied Interpretation, SIC 7, is contained in Part A of this edition. Its effective date when issued was 1 June 1998. This part presents the following documents:

BASIS FOR CONCLUSIONS

Basis for Conclusions on
SIC Interpretation 7 *Introduction of the Euro*

This Basis for Conclusions accompanies, but is not part of, SIC-7.

[The original text has been marked up to reflect the revision of IAS 21 in 2003 and IAS 1 in 2007 and the amendment of IAS 27 in 2008:[1] new text is underlined and deleted text is struck through.]

5   IAS 21.23~~11~~(a) requires that foreign currency monetary items (as defined by IAS 21.8~~07~~) be reported using the closing rate at ~~each balance sheet date~~ the end of each reporting period. According to IAS 21.28~~15~~, exchange differences arising from the translation of monetary items generally should be recognised as income or as expenses in the period in which they arise. The effective start of the EMU after the reporting period ~~balance sheet date~~ does not change the application of these requirements at the end of the reporting period ~~balance sheet date~~; in accordance with IAS 10.10~~28~~[2] it is not relevant whether or not the closing rate can fluctuate after the ~~balance sheet date~~ reporting period.

6   IAS 21.5~~14~~ states that the Standard does not apply to ~~deal with~~ hedge accounting~~, except in restricted circumstances~~. Therefore, this Interpretation does not address how foreign currency hedges should be accounted for. IAS 8.~~42~~ would allow such a change in accounting policy only if the change would result in a more appropriate presentation of events or transactions.[3] The effective start of EMU, of itself, does not justify a change to an entity's established accounting policy related to ~~anticipatory~~ hedges of forecast transactions because the changeover does not affect the economic rationale of such hedges. Therefore, the changeover should not alter the accounting policy where gains and losses on financial instruments used as ~~anticipatory~~ hedges of forecast transactions are ~~currently deferred~~ initially recognised in ~~equity~~ other comprehensive income and matched with the related income or expense in a future period.

7   IAS 21.48~~37~~ requires the cumulative amount of exchange differences relating to the translation of the financial statements of a foreign operation ~~entity which~~ that have been ~~deferred in equity~~ recognised in other comprehensive income and accumulated in a separate component of equity in accordance with IAS 21.~~17,~~ ~~19 or 30~~32 or 39(c) to be ~~recognised as income or expenses~~ reclassified from equity to profit or loss in the same period in which the gain or loss on disposal or partial disposal of the foreign operation ~~entity~~ is recognised. The fact that the cumulative amount of exchange differences will be fixed under EMU does not justify immediate recognition as income or expenses ~~since~~ because the wording and the rationale of IAS 21.48~~37~~ clearly preclude such a treatment.

~~8   Under the Allowed Alternative Treatment of IAS 21.21, exchange differences resulting from severe devaluations of currencies are included in the carrying~~

---

1 The consolidation requirements in IAS 27 were superseded, and IAS 27 was renamed *Separate Financial Statements*, by IFRS 10 *Consolidated Financial Statements* issued in May 2011.

2 ~~IAS 10 (revised in 1999), paragraph 20, contains similar requirements.~~

3 As SIC-7 was issued before IAS 39, the previous version of this Interpretation could refer only to the entity's own accounting policies on the matter. The accounting for hedges was subsequently covered under IAS 39 *Financial Instruments: Recognition and Measurement*. In November 2013 the Board replaced the hedge accounting requirements in IAS 39 and relocated them to IFRS 9 *Financial Instruments*.

~~amount of the related assets in certain limited circumstances. Those circumstances do not apply to the currencies participating in the changeover since the event of severe devaluation is incompatible with the required stability of participating currencies.~~

Material published to accompany

SIC-10

Government Assistance—No Specific Relation to Operating Activities

The text of the unaccompanied Intrepretation, SIC 10, is contained in Part A of this edition. Its effective date when issued was 1 August 1998. This part presents the following documents:

BASIS FOR CONCLUSIONS

Basis for Conclusions on
SIC Interpretation 10 *Government Assistance—No Specific Relation to Operating Activities*

This Basis for Conclusions accompanies, but is not part of, SIC-10.

4   IAS 20.03 defines government grants as assistance by the government in the form of transfers of resources to an entity in return for past or future compliance with certain conditions relating to the operating activities of the entity. The general requirement to operate in certain regions or industry sectors in order to qualify for the government assistance constitutes such a condition in accordance with IAS 20.03. Therefore, such assistance falls within the definition of government grants and the requirements of IAS 20 apply, in particular paragraphs 12 and 20, which deal with the timing of recognition as income.

Material published to accompany

SIC-15

Operating Leases—Incentives

The text of the unaccompanied Interpretation, SIC-15, is contained in Part A of this edition. Its effective date when issued was 1 January 1999. The text of the Basis for Conclusions on SIC-15 is contained in Part B of this edition. The text of the Accompanying Guidance on SIC-15 is contained in Part B of this edition. This part presents the following documents:

BASIS FOR CONCLUSIONS

Basis for Conclusions on
SIC Interpretation 15 *Operating Leases—Incentives*

This Basis for Conclusions accompanies, but is not part of, SIC-15.

[The original text has been marked up to reflect the revision of IASs 8 and 17 in 2003 and of IAS 1 in 2007: new text is underlined and deleted text is struck through.]

7   Paragraph 35 of the *Framework*[1] explains that if information is to represent faithfully the transactions and events that it purports to represent, it is necessary that transactions and events are accounted for and presented in accordance with their substance and economic reality and not merely their legal form. IAS 1.20(b)(ii) 8.10(b)(ii) also requires the application of accounting policies which reflect economic substance.

8   Paragraph 22 of the *Framework*[2] and IAS 1.2527 require the preparation of financial statements under the accrual basis of accounting. IAS 17.3325 and IAS 17.5042 specify the basis on which lessees and lessors respectively should recognise amounts payable or receivable under operating leases.

9   The underlying substance of operating lease arrangements is that the lessor and lessee exchange the use of an asset for a specified period for the consideration of a net amount of money. The accounting periods in which this net amount is recognised by either the lessor or the lessee is not affected by the form of the agreement or the timing of payments. Payments made by a lessor to or on behalf of a lessee, or allowances in rental cost made by a lessor, as incentives for the agreement of a new or renewed lease are an inseparable part of the net amount receivable or payable under the operating lease.

10   Costs incurred by the lessor as incentives for the agreement of new or renewed operating leases are not considered to be part of those initial costs which may be recognised as an expense in the income statements in the period in which they are incurred are added to the carrying amount of the leased asset and recognised as an expense over the lease term on the same basis as the lease income in accordance with under IAS 17.5244. Initial costs, such as direct costs for administration, advertising and consulting or legal fees, are incurred by a lessor to arrange a contract, whereas incentives in an operating lease are, in substance, related to the consideration for the use of the leased asset.

11   Costs incurred by the lessee on its own behalf are accounted for using the applicable recognition requirements. For example, relocation costs are recognised as an expense in profit or loss the income statement in the period in which they are incurred. The accounting for such costs does not depend on whether or not they are effectively reimbursed through an incentive arrangement as they are not related to the consideration for the use of the leased asset.

---

1   Paragraph 35 was superseded by Chapter 3 of the *Conceptual Framework*. References to the *Framework* are to IASC's *Framework for the Preparation and Presentation of Financial Statements*, adopted by the IASB in 2001. In September 2010 the IASB replaced the *Framework* with the *Conceptual Framework for Financial Reporting*.

2   Paragraph 22 was not carried forward into the *Conceptual Framework*.

Material published to accompany

SIC-25

Income Taxes—Changes in the Tax Status of an Entity or its Shareholders

The text of the unaccompanied Interpretation, SIC 25, is contained in Part A of this edition. Its effective date when issued was 15 July 2000. This part presents the following documents:

BASIS FOR CONCLUSIONS

Basis for Conclusions on
SIC Interpretation 25 *Income Taxes—Changes in the Tax Status of an Entity or its Shareholders*

This Basis for Conclusions accompanies, but is not part of, SIC-25.

[The original text has been marked up to reflect the amendment to IAS 12 in 2003, and the revision of IAS 38 Intangible Assets *in 2004 and IAS 1* Presentation of Financial Statements *in 2007: new text is underlined and deleted text is struck through.]*

5	IAS 12.58 requires current and deferred tax to be included in ~~the net~~ profit or loss for the period, except to the extent the tax arises from a transaction or event that is recognised <u>outside profit or loss either in other comprehensive income or</u> directly in equity, in the same or a different period, (or arises from a business combination ~~that is an acquisition~~). IAS 12.61<u>A</u> requires ~~that~~ current and deferred tax <u>to</u> be <u>recognised outside profit or loss</u> ~~charged or credited directly to equity~~ if the tax relates to items that are <u>recognised</u> ~~credited or charged~~, in the same or a different period, <u>outside profit or loss</u> ~~directly to equity~~.
5A	<u>IAS 12.62 identifies examples of circumstances in which a transaction or event is recognised in other comprehensive income as permitted or required by another IFRS. All of these circumstances result in changes in the recognised amount of equity through recognition in other comprehensive income.</u>
6	IAS 12.62<u>A</u> identifies examples of circumstances in which a transaction or event is recognised directly in equity as ~~is~~ permitted or required by another <u>IFRS</u> ~~International Financial Reporting Standard~~. All of these circumstances result in changes in the recognised amount of equity through recognition of a credit or charge directly to equity.
7	IAS 12.65 explains that where the tax base of a revalued asset changes, any tax consequence is recognised <u>in other comprehensive income</u> ~~directly in equity~~ only to the extent <u>that</u> a related accounting revaluation was or is expected to be recognised <u>in other comprehensive income</u> ~~directly in equity~~ (revaluation surplus).
8	Because tax consequences recognised <u>outside profit or loss, whether in other comprehensive income or</u> directly in equity, must relate to a transaction or event recognised <u>outside profit or loss</u> ~~directly in equity~~ in the same or a different period, the cumulative amount of tax ~~charged or credited directly to equity~~ <u>recognised outside profit or loss</u> can be expected to be the same amount that would have been <u>recognised outside profit or loss</u> ~~charged or credited directly to equity~~ if the new tax status had applied previously. IAS 12.63(b) acknowledges that determining the tax consequences of a change in the tax rate or other tax rules that affects a deferred tax asset or liability and relates to an item previously <u>recognised outside profit or loss</u> ~~charged or credited to equity~~ may prove to be difficult. Because of this, IAS 12.63 suggests that an allocation may be necessary.

Material published to accompany

SIC-27

Evaluating the Substance of Transactions Involving the Legal Form of a Lease

The text of the unaccompanied Interpretation, SIC-27, is contained in Part A of this edition. Its effective date when issued was 31 December 2001. The text of the Accompanying Guidance on SIC-27 is contained in Part B of this edition. This part presents the following documents:

BASIS FOR CONCULSIONS

Basis for Conclusions on
SIC Interpretation 27 *Evaluating the Substance of Transactions Involving the Legal Form of a Lease*

This Basis for Conclusions accompanies, but is not part of, SIC-27.

[The requirements of IAS 39 relating to classification and measurement of items within the scope of IAS 39 were relocated to IFRS 9 Financial Instruments. *To avoid confusion with earlier amendments marked up on the original text to reflect the revision of IAS 39 in 2003 and the subsequent issue of IFRS 4, paragraphs 14 and 15 have been amended for consistency with IFRS 9. References to the* Framework *are to IASC's* Framework for the Preparation and Presentation of Financial Statements, *adopted by the IASB in 2001. In September 2010 the IASB replaced the* Framework *with the* Conceptual Framework for Financial Reporting.*]

12   Paragraph 9 of IAS 11 *Construction Contracts*[1] requires a group of contracts to be treated as a single contract when the group of contracts is negotiated as a single package, the contracts are so closely interrelated that they are, in effect, part of a single project with an overall profit margin, and the contracts are performed concurrently or in a continuous sequence. In such a situation, a series of transactions that involve the legal form of a lease are linked and accounted for as one transaction, because the overall economic effect cannot be understood without reference to the series of transactions as a whole.

13   An agreement is accounted for as a lease in accordance with IAS 17 when it conveys to the lessee in return for a payment or series of payments the right to use an asset for an agreed period of time. For information to represent faithfully the transactions it purports to represent, paragraph 35 of the *Framework*[2] indicates that it is necessary that transactions are accounted for and presented in accordance with their substance and economic reality, not merely their legal form.

14   When an Entity does not control the assets that will be used to satisfy the lease payment obligations, and is not obligated to pay the lease payments, it does not recognise the assets and lease payment obligations, because the definitions of an asset and a liability have not been met. This is different from the circumstance when an Entity controls the assets, is obligated to pay the lease payments, and then later transfers assets to a third party (including a trust). In that circumstance, the transfer of assets (sometimes called an 'in-substance' defeasance) does not by itself relieve the Entity of its primary obligation, in the absence of legal release. A financial asset and a financial liability, or a portion of either, are derecognised only when the requirements of paragraphs 3.2.1–3.2.23, 3.3.1–3.3.4, B3.2.1–B3.2.17 and B3.3.1–B3.3.7 of IFRS 9 are met.

15   IFRS 4 provides guidance for recognising and measuring financial guarantees and similar instruments that provide for payments to be made if the debtor fails to make payments when due, if that contract transfers significant insurance risk

---

1   IFRS 15 *Revenue from Contracts with Customers*, issued in May 2014, replaced IAS 11 *Construction Contracts*. IFRS 15 requires contracts to be combined if they meet specified criteria.

2   superseded by Chapter 3 of the *Conceptual Framework*. References to the *Framework* are to IASC's *Framework for the Preparation and Presentation of Financial Statements*, adopted by the IASB in 2001. In September 2010 the IASB replaced the *Framework* with the *Conceptual Framework for Financial Reporting*.

to the issuer. Financial guarantee contracts that provide for payments to be made in response to changes in relation to a variable (sometimes referred to as an 'underlying') are subject to IAS 39.[3]

16   IAS 18[4] addresses the accounting treatment of revenue. Paragraph 75 of the *Framework*[5] indicates that gains are no different in nature from revenue. Therefore, the requirements of IAS 18 apply by analogy or otherwise. Example 14(c) in the illustrative examples accompanying IAS 18 states that a fee earned on the execution of a significant act, which is much more significant than any other act, is recognised as income when the significant act has been completed. The example also indicates that it is necessary to distinguish between fees earned on completion of a significant act and fees related to future performance or risks retained.

---

3   IFRS 9 *Financial Instruments* replaced IAS 39. IFRS 9 applies to all items that were previously within the scope of IAS 39.

4   IFRS 15 *Revenue from Contracts with Customers*, issued in May 2014, replaced IAS 18 *Revenue*. IFRS 15 eliminated the guidance on recognising revenue on the execution of a significant act.

5   now paragraph 4.30 of the *Conceptual Framework*

Material published to accompany

SIC-29

Service Concession Arrangements: Disclosures

The text of the unaccompanied Interpretation, SIC 29, is contained in Part A of this edition. Its effective date when issued was 31 December 2001. This part presents the following documents:

BASIS FOR CONCLUSIONS

Basis for Conclusions on
SIC Interpretation 29 *Service Concession Arrangements: Disclosures*

This Basis for Conclusions accompanies, but is not part of, SIC-29.

[The original text of paragraphs 8 and 9 has been marked up to reflect the revision of IAS 1 in 2003 and 2007 and the issue of IFRIC 12 in 2006: new text is underlined and deleted text is struck through.]

8   Paragraph 15 of the *Framework*[1] states that the economic decisions taken by users of financial statements require an evaluation of the ability of the entity to generate cash and cash equivalents and of the timing and certainty of their generation. Paragraph 21 of the *Framework*[1] states that financial statements also contain notes and supplementary schedules and other information. For example, they may contain additional information that is relevant to the needs of users about the items in the statement of financial position balance sheet and statement of comprehensive income statement. They may also include disclosures about the risks and uncertainties affecting the entity and any resources and obligations not recognised in the statement of financial position balance sheet.

9   A service concession arrangement often has provisions or significant features that warrant disclosure of information necessary to assist in assessing the amount, timing and certainty of future cash flows, and the nature and extent of the various rights and obligations involved. The rights and obligations associated with the services to be provided usually involve a high level of public involvement (eg to provide electricity to a city). Other obligations could include significant acts such as building an infrastructure asset (eg power plant) and delivering that asset to the Concession Provider grantor at the end of the concession period.

      The text of paragraph 10 has been marked up to reflect the revision of IAS 1 in 2007. Previous amendments to the paragraph, reflecting the revision of IAS 1 in 2003, have been incorporated into the text to avoid confusion with the new amendments in 2007.

10   IAS 1.112(c)103(c) requires an entity's notes to provide additional information that is not presented elsewhere in the financial statements on the face of the balance sheet, income statement, statement of changes in equity or cash flow statement, but is relevant to an understanding of any of them. The definition of notes in IAS 1.7 11 indicates that notes provide narrative descriptions or disaggregations of items disclosed in the statement of financial position balance sheet, statement of comprehensive income, separate income statement (if presented), statement of changes in equity and statement of cash flows statement, as well as information about items that do not qualify for recognition in those statements.

---

1   superseded by Chapter 1 of the *Conceptual Framework*. References to the *Framework* are to IASC's *Framework for the Preparation and Presentation of Financial Statements*, adopted by the IASB in 2001. In September 2010 the IASB replaced the *Framework* with the *Conceptual Framework for Financial Reporting*.

Material published to accompany

SIC-32

Intangible Assets—Web Site Costs

The text of the unaccompanied Interpretation, SIC-32, is contained in Part A of this edition. Its effective date when issued was 25 March 2002. The text of the Accompanying Guidance on SIC-32 is contained in Part B of this edition. This part presents the following documents:

BASIS FOR CONCLUSIONS

Basis for Conclusions on
SIC Interpretation 32 *Intangible Assets—Web Site Costs*

This Basis for Conclusions accompanies, but is not part of, SIC-32.

[The original text has been marked up to reflect the revision of IAS 16 in 2003 and the subsequent issue of IFRS 3: new text is underlined and deleted text is struck through.]

11 An intangible asset is defined in IAS 38.87 as an identifiable non-monetary asset without physical substance held for use in the production or supply of goods or services, for rental to others, or for administrative purposes. IAS 38.98 provides computer software as a common example of an intangible asset. By analogy, a web site is another example of an intangible asset.

12 IAS 38.6856 requires expenditure on an intangible item to be recognised as an expense when incurred unless it forms part of the cost of an intangible asset that meets the recognition criteria in IAS 38.18–.6755. IAS 38.6957 requires expenditure on start-up activities to be recognised as an expense when incurred. An entity developing its own web site for internal or external access is not undertaking a start-up activity to the extent that an internally generated intangible asset is created. The requirements and guidance in IAS 38.52–.6740.55, in addition to the general requirements described in IAS 38.2119 for recognition and initial measurement of an intangible asset, apply to expenditure incurred on the development of an entity's own web site. As described in IAS 38.65–.6753–.55, the cost of a web site recognised as an internally generated intangible asset comprises all expenditure that can be directly attributed, or allocated on a reasonable and consistent basis, and is necessary to creating, producing and preparing the asset for it to be capable of operating in the manner intended by management its intended use.

13 IAS 38.5442 requires expenditure on research (or on the research phase of an internal project) to be recognised as an expense when incurred. The examples provided in IAS 38.5644 are similar to the activities undertaken in the Planning stage of a web site's development. Consequently, expenditure incurred in the Planning stage of a web site's development is recognised as an expense when incurred.

14 IAS 38.5745 requires an intangible asset arising from the development phase of an internal project to be recognised only if an entity can demonstrate fulfilment of the six criteria specified. One of the criteria is to demonstrate how a web site will generate probable future economic benefits (IAS 38.5745(d)). IAS 38.6048 indicates that this criterion is met by assessing the economic benefits to be received from the web site and using the principles in IAS 36 *Impairment of Assets*, which considers the present value of estimated future cash flows from continuing use of the web site. Future economic benefits flowing from an intangible asset, as stated in IAS 38.17, may include revenue from the sale of products or services, cost savings, or other benefits resulting from the use of the asset by the entity. Therefore, future economic benefits from a web site may be assessed when the web site is capable of generating revenues. A web site developed solely or primarily for advertising and promoting an entity's own products and services is not recognised as an intangible asset, because the entity

cannot demonstrate the future economic benefits that will flow. Consequently, all expenditure on developing a web site solely or primarily for promoting and advertising an entity's own products and services is recognised as an expense when incurred.

15 Under IAS 38.21~~19~~, an intangible asset is recognised if, and only if, it meets specified criteria. IAS 38.65~~53~~ indicates that the cost of an internally generated intangible asset is the sum of expenditure incurred from the date when the intangible asset first meets the specified recognition criteria. When an entity acquires or creates content for purposes other than to advertise and promote an entity's own products and services, it may be possible to identify an intangible asset (eg a licence or a copyright) separate from a web site. However, a separate asset is not recognised when expenditure is directly attributed, ~~or allocated on a reasonable and consistent basis,~~ to creating, producing, and preparing the web site for it to be capable of operating in the manner intended by management ~~its intended use~~ — the expenditure is included in the cost of developing the web site.

16 IAS 38.69~~57~~(c) requires expenditure on advertising and promotional activities to be recognised as an expense when incurred. Expenditure incurred on developing content that advertises and promotes an entity's own products and services (eg digital photographs of products) is an advertising and promotional activity, and consequently recognised as an expense when incurred ~~in accordance with IAS 38.57(c).~~

17 ~~Once development of a web site is complete, an enterprise begins the activities described in the Operating stage. Subsequent expenditure to enhance or maintain an enterprise's own web site is recognised as an expense when incurred unless it meets the recognition criteria in IAS 38.60. IAS 38.61 explains that if the expenditure is required to maintain the asset at its originally assessed standard of performance, then the expenditure is recognised as an expense when incurred.[1]__ Once development of a web site is complete, an entity begins the activities described in the Operating stage. Subsequent expenditure to enhance or maintain an entity's own web site is recognised as an expense when incurred unless it meets the recognition criteria in IAS 38.18. IAS 38.20 explains that most subsequent expenditures are likely to maintain the future economic benefits embodied in an existing intangible asset rather than meet the definition of an intangible asset and the recognition criteria set out in IAS 38. In addition, it is often difficult to attribute subsequent expenditure directly to a particular intangible asset rather than to the business as a whole. Therefore, only rarely will subsequent expenditure—expenditure incurred after the initial recognition of a purchased intangible asset or after completion of an internally generated intangible asset—be recognised in the carrying amount of an asset.[2]

---

1 ~~IAS 16 *Property, Plant and Equipment* as revised by the IASB in 2003 requires all subsequent costs to be covered by its general recognition principle and eliminated the requirement to reference the originally assessed standard of performance. IAS 38 was amended as a consequence of the change to IAS 16 and the paragraphs specifically referred to were eliminated. This paragraph has been struck through to avoid any confusion.~~

2 The new text was added by IFRS 3 *Business Combinations* in 2004.

18   An intangible asset is measured after initial recognition by applying the requirements of IAS 38.72–.8763–.78. The <u>revaluation model</u> <s>Allowed Alternative Treatment</s> in IAS 38.7564 is applied only when the fair value of an intangible asset can be determined by reference to an active market.[3] However, as an active market is unlikely to exist for web sites, the <u>cost model</u> <s>Benchmark Treatment</s> applies. Additionally, <s>since IAS 38.84 states that an intangible asset always has a finite useful life, a web site that is recognised as an asset is amortised over the best estimate of its useful life under IAS 38.79. As</s> <u>as</u> indicated in IAS 38.9281, many intangible assets are susceptible to technological obsolescence, and given the history of rapid changes in technology, the useful life of web sites will be short.

---

3   <u>IFRS 13 *Fair Value Measurement*, issued in May 2011, defines fair value and contains the requirements for measuring fair value. IFRS 13 defines an active market.</u>

               © IFRS Foundation

IASB document published to accompany

IFRS Practice Statement 1

Management Commentary
A framework for presentation

IFRS Practice Statement 1 *Management Commentary* was issued in December 2010 for application from 8 December 2010. The text of Practice Statement 1 is contained in Part B of this edition. This part presents the following accompanying document:

BASIS FOR CONCLUSIONS

Basis for Conclusions

This Basis for Conclusions accompanies, but is not part of, the Practice Statement.

Introduction

BC1   This Basis for Conclusions summarises the International Accounting Standard Board's considerations in developing the IFRS Practice Statement *Management Commentary*. Individual Board members gave greater weight to some factors than to others.

BC2   The Practice Statement was approved by the Board for issue as non-binding guidance, after considering the responses to its public consultation on the discussion paper *Management Commentary* and the exposure draft *Management Commentary*.

BC3   The purpose of financial statements is to provide information about the financial position, financial performance and cash flows of an entity that is useful to a wide range of users in making economic decisions (paragraph 9 of IAS 1 *Presentation of Financial Statements*). Financial statements prepared for that purpose meet the common needs of most users. However, financial statements do not provide all the information that users need to make economic decisions because the financial statements largely portray the financial effects of past events and do not provide non-financial measures of performance or a discussion of future prospects and plans.

BC4   Management commentary supplements and complements the financial statements. The Board's objective in issuing the Practice Statement is to improve the usefulness of the information provided in an entity's management commentary so that, when it is provided in conjunction with the financial statements, users are better able to make decisions about providing resources to the entity.

BC5   Governments, securities regulators, stock exchanges and professional accountancy bodies often require entities whose debt or equity securities are publicly traded to publish management commentary. Management commentary encompasses reporting that jurisdictions may describe as management's discussion and analysis (MD&A), operating and financial review (OFR), business review or management's report.

BC6   This Basis for Conclusions discusses the following matters:

      (a)   background (paragraphs BC7–BC11);

      (b)   objective (paragraphs BC12–BC14);

      (c)   scope (paragraphs BC15–BC17);

      (d)   identification of management commentary (paragraphs BC18–BC21);

      (e)   users of management commentary (paragraphs BC22–BC25);

      (f)   purpose of management commentary (paragraphs BC26–BC28);

      (g)   principles for the presentation of management commentary (paragraphs BC29–BC44);

(h)   presentation (paragraphs BC45 and BC46);

(i)   elements of management commentary (paragraphs BC47–BC49); and

(j)   placement of disclosure within the financial reports (paragraphs BC50–BC53).

Background

BC7   In late 2002 the Board set up a project team comprising representatives from the national standard-setters in Germany, New Zealand and the United Kingdom and from the Canadian Institute of Chartered Accountants. The project team examined the potential for issuing a standard or guidance on management commentary. In October 2005 the Board published the results of the project team's research in a discussion paper *Management Commentary*.

BC8   In the discussion paper, the project team presented its views on the users, objective and qualitative characteristics of management commentary. The project team also described essential elements (described as 'content elements' in the discussion paper) of management commentary and a possible framework for use by standard-setters in distinguishing between information that would appear in management commentary and information that would appear in the notes to the financial statements.

BC9   In 2009 the Board published an exposure draft *Management Commentary*. The exposure draft took into account the proposals contained in the discussion paper and respondents' comments on those proposals. It also reflected developments in narrative reporting at the regulatory level in a variety of jurisdictions and the Board's recent work on the *Conceptual Framework for Financial Reporting*, specifically the work on the exposure draft *An improved Conceptual Framework for Financial Reporting: Chapter 1: The Objective of Financial Reporting* and *Chapter 2: Qualitative Characteristics and Constraints of Decision-useful Financial Reporting Information* (May 2008). Importantly, the exposure draft *Management Commentary* included a proposal to publish the proposals in the exposure draft as non-binding guidance, not as an International Financial Reporting Standard (IFRS).

BC10   Most respondents supported the Board's proposal in the exposure draft to issue guidance. In developing the Practice Statement, the Board considered responses to this proposal and on other issues such as applying the qualitative characteristics to information in management commentary, including application guidance and illustrative examples in the Practice Statement and whether forecasts must be included in management commentary as forward-looking information.

BC11   The Board observed that management commentary meets the definition of 'other financial reporting' described in paragraph 7 of the *Preface to International Financial Reporting Standards*. Thus the Board decided that management commentary is within the boundaries of financial reporting and within the scope of the *Conceptual Framework*. Consequently, management commentary is also within the scope and authority of the Board.

Objective

BC12   The Practice Statement sets out a non-binding framework to guide the presentation of management commentary. The Board's intention in issuing the Practice Statement is to foster good practice in management commentary reporting by permitting an entity's management to exercise discretion in tailoring its commentary to the entity's particular circumstances.

BC13   Although the Practice Statement is not an IFRS and is not binding, the Board believes the Statement will promote comparability across all entities that present management commentary to accompany their IFRS financial statements, thereby improving the usefulness of the financial reports to users.

BC14   The Board considered the view that a non-binding practice statement would not result in improvements in financial reporting. However, the Board decided that a practice statement would provide useful guidance for entities, and its flexible application would benefit entities in jurisdictions that have local requirements or regulations. Furthermore, the Board believes that a practice statement might encourage entities that are not accustomed to presenting management commentary to provide it for users. The existence of a practice statement might also encourage jurisdictions to adopt it as their own.

Scope

BC15   The Board believes that the Practice Statement may prove useful to entities that are not accustomed to presenting management commentary. It may also be useful for entities that are already accustomed to presenting reports setting out commentary by management because of local requirements or regulations imposed by the public exchanges on which their securities are listed, provided the Practice Statement does not contradict those requirements or regulations. Thus, the Board decided that the Practice Statement could be applied by entities that present management commentary that relates to financial statements that have been prepared in accordance with IFRSs.

BC16   The Board decided to provide guidance on the content of management commentary in the form of a non-binding practice statement, rather than an IFRS, because it believes it is up to individual jurisdictions to make their own judgements on:

    (a)   whether entities should be required to include management commentary in addition to their IFRS financial statements and whether inclusion is necessary to assert compliance with IFRSs;

    (b)   the level of assurance to which management commentary should be subjected;

    (c)   the necessity of 'safe harbour' provisions in relation to the inclusion of forward-looking information;[1] and

    (d)   the type of entity that should present management commentary.

---

1   A safe harbour is a provision of a statute or a regulation that reduces or eliminates a party's liability under the law, on the condition that the party performed its actions in good faith.

BC17   The Board's decision to issue a practice statement and not an IFRS means that entities applying IFRSs are not required to comply with the Practice Statement, unless specifically required by their jurisdiction. Furthermore, non-compliance with the Practice Statement does not prevent the entity's financial statements from complying with IFRSs, if they otherwise do so. Additionally, the entity's financial statements may comply with IFRSs if an entity has not provided management commentary during a particular financial year.

Identification of management commentary

BC18   The positioning of management commentary relative to the financial statements varies among jurisdictions that require management commentary. In some jurisdictions, management commentary accompanies the annual financial statements in a printed report to shareholders. In others, management commentary is contained within separate annual regulatory filings.

BC19   The Board considered whether it would be desirable to incorporate management commentary within the financial statements, perhaps by adding textual material and other information within the notes to the financial statements. The Board rejected this idea on the ground that management commentary should supplement and complement the financial statements. Consequently, the Board concluded that management commentary should not be placed within the financial statements themselves.

BC20   The Board also decided to link management commentary to the financial statements because, as noted in paragraph BC33, management commentary is designed to supplement and complement information provided in a related set of financial statements. The Board observed that providing management commentary without (at minimum) identifying the related financial statements might be misleading for users. Consequently, the Board decided that when an entity presents management commentary that relates to IFRS financial statements, it should either make the financial statements available with the commentary or identify the financial statements to which the commentary relates. The Board noted that because the Practice Statement does not require entities to prepare management commentary, IFRS financial statements can be made available for use without a corresponding management commentary.

BC21   In the Board's view, it is important for users of the financial reports to be able to distinguish information contained in the reports using the Practice Statement from information that is prepared using IFRSs and from information that may be useful to users but is neither the subject of the Practice Statement nor the requirements in IFRSs. While the Board concluded that preparers should not be required to include a formal confirmation that they have complied with the Practice Statement, because the Statement is not binding, it did agree that it would be helpful if preparers included in management commentary an explanation of the extent to which the Practice Statement has been followed. The Board also concluded that it would be misleading if preparers were to assert compliance with the Practice Statement if they did not comply with the Practice Statement in its entirety.

Users of management commentary

BC22   In September 2010 the Board published two chapters of the *Conceptual Framework*: Chapter 1: *The objective of general purpose financial reporting* and Chapter 3: *Qualitative characteristics of useful financial information*. In the Board's view, management commentary is within the scope of the *Conceptual Framework*. The two aspects of the Practice Statement most affected by the *Conceptual Framework* are the definition of users and the qualitative characteristics (see paragraphs BC41–BC43) of management commentary.

BC23   In most jurisdictions, the requirements or guidance on management commentary specify that the information should be directed to meeting the needs of investors, or a narrower group such as existing shareholders. In some jurisdictions there has been debate about which users should be the focus of management commentary—with many constituents taking the view that management commentary should meet the needs of all stakeholders.

BC24   The Board reasoned that given that management commentary forms a part of financial reporting and is within the scope of the *Conceptual Framework*, it follows that information provided by management commentary should focus on the same users as do general purpose financial reports.

BC25   Therefore, the Board concluded that the primary users of management commentary are those identified in paragraph OB2 of Chapter 1 of the *Conceptual Framework*: 'existing and potential investors, lenders and other creditors'.

Purpose of management commentary

BC26   The Board agreed that the purpose of management commentary is to provide, from management's perspective, context for the financial statements. This is consistent with the objectives stated in regulations and guidance in many jurisdictions. For example, guidance issued by the US Securities and Exchange Commission (SEC) in December 2003 states that the purpose of Management's Discussion and Analysis (MD&A) is 'not complicated'. It is to provide users with information 'necessary to an understanding of [a company's] financial condition, changes in financial condition and results of operations' (SEC, Regulation S–K, Item 303).

BC27   The content of management commentary is not necessarily bound to the reporting period described by the financial statements to which it relates. Some information within management commentary looks to the future. The Board concluded that the inclusion of forward-looking information within management commentary helps users of the financial reports assess whether past performance is indicative of future performance and whether the progress of the entity is in line with management's stated objectives.

BC28   The Board defined the term 'progress' in the Appendix on the basis of the usage of the term 'development' in the European Union's requirement for 'at least a fair review of the development of the company's business and of its position' (Article 46 of the Fourth Council Directive on the annual accounts of certain types of companies (78/660/EEC)). The Board did not use the term 'development' in the Practice Statement, because it is already defined in IFRSs.

Principles for the presentation of management commentary

Management's view

BC29   The principle in paragraph 12(a) raises the issue of what is meant by 'management'. The term 'key management personnel' is defined in IAS 24 *Related Party Disclosures* to mean 'those persons having authority and responsibility for planning, directing and controlling the activities of the entity, directly or indirectly, including any director (whether executive or otherwise) of that entity' (paragraph 9 of IAS 24).

BC30   The Board noted that determining who presents and approves management commentary may not be limited to 'key management personnel' and is likely to depend on jurisdictional requirements. For example, in the United Kingdom the Companies Act 2006 requires a business review as part of the directors' report. For quoted companies, the requirements are reflected in the UK Accounting Standards Board's (ASB's) OFR Reporting Statement, which recommends that an OFR should be the analysis by the directors. Furthermore, it is the directors who are responsible for approving the business review or OFR. There are similar requirements in Canada, France and Germany. Therefore, the Board determined that referring to 'management' would enable entities to apply the principle in paragraph 12(a) given their jurisdictional requirements.

BC31   The Board observed that the principle that management commentary should describe management's view of the financial statements has its roots in regulation. For example, the first of the SEC objectives requires that MD&A:

> ... provide a narrative explanation of a company's financial statements that enables investors to see the company through the eyes of management. [SEC, Regulation S-K, Item 303]

That requirement has also been enshrined in securities regulation in Canada and in the UK ASB's OFR Reporting Statement.

BC32   The Board noted a study that suggests that, with few exceptions, the information important to management in managing the business is the same information that is important to capital providers in assessing performance and prospects. Consequently, the Board decided that management commentary should derive from the same information that is important to management.

Supplement and complement the financial statements

BC33   Paragraph BC11 points out that the Board observed that management commentary meets the definition of 'other financial reporting' in the Preface. In addition, the Board noted that the principle of providing information to supplement and complement the financial statements in effect formalises the statement in paragraph 7 of the *Preface* that:

> Other financial reporting comprises information provided outside financial statements that assists in the interpretation of a complete set of financial statements or improves users' ability to make efficient economic decisions.

BC34   To provide context for the principle of supplementing and complementing the financial statements is the example of commentary for a defined benefit pension plan that has a deficit. In this example, management could supplement and complement the disclosure in the financial statements by providing a narrative explanation of the nature of the deficit and the conditions and events that led to the deficit (eg poor returns on plan assets or the demographics of those covered by the plan). Furthermore, management could provide helpful information related to the plan that is not otherwise disclosed in the financial statements, but is important to the management of the plan (eg changing investment managers or focusing on specific investment opportunities).

Forward-looking information

BC35   The Board observed that in many jurisdictions, requirements relating to management commentary focus on information that helps users of the financial reports to assess the entity's prospects. These requirements have their roots in regulation, specifically in the MD&A requirements of the SEC. The third of the SEC objectives for MD&A reporting is:

> ... to provide information about the quality of, and potential variability of, a company's earnings and cash flow, so that investors can ascertain the likelihood that past performance is indicative of future performance. [SEC, Regulation S-K, Item 303]

BC36   This US regulatory requirement for the inclusion of information that helps investors assess prospects is found in both Canadian securities regulations and the European Modernisation Directive. The Directive has in turn been transposed into legislation in EU Member States.

BC37   The Board agreed with the inclusion of forward-looking information in management commentary for the reasons specified in the SEC MD&A requirements.

BC38   Many respondents to the exposure draft were concerned about the focus on forward-looking information. However, the Board decided that forward-looking information is important. Explanations of management's perspective of the entity's direction, targets and prospects, in addition to explanations of past events, can help users of the financial reports to develop expectations about the entity from its past performance and current state. Furthermore, the Board observed that the Practice Statement allows flexibility for management in determining to what extent management commentary includes forward-looking information. In particular, the Board observed that the Practice Statement clearly indicates that the extent of forward-looking information will be influenced by the regulatory and legal environment within which the entity operates. Moreover, although disclosure of forward-looking information is encouraged in many jurisdictions, this does not necessarily mean providing forecasts or projections. The Board notes that in some jurisdictions there are safe harbour provisions to restrict liability claims or regulatory provisions, or both, for forward-looking information. However, those safe harbour provisions require cautionary statements to be included with the forward-looking information.

BC39　The Board considered the view that forward-looking information might present an over-optimistic picture of the entity. However, the Board observes that forward-looking information must possess the qualitative characteristics, including faithful representation, and thus must be neutral. Furthermore, management must disclose its assumptions used in providing the forward-looking information, thus enabling users to evaluate the reasonableness of the assumptions.

BC40　An example of what the Board envisages as forward-looking information that does not include forecasts or projections is again the commentary that could be provided for a defined benefit pension plan that has a deficit (described in paragraph BC34). In that example, management could provide forward-looking information by explaining management's objectives and strategies for remedying the plan deficit. These strategies might include a planned future increase in contributions, changes in investment strategy or changes to the plan. Management could also provide an explanation of how general market trends or other risks might affect the deficit and the strategies of management for remedying the deficit. This disclosure could include some quantitative information, but it is not necessarily a forecast or a projection.

BC41　In developing the exposure draft, the Board considered the view that detailed application guidance or illustrative examples are necessary to put into operation the guidance around forward-looking information included in the Practice Statement. However, the Board decided not to include such detailed guidance because there is a risk that undue emphasis could be placed on the application guidance or illustrative examples. Furthermore, the Board observed that such guidance or examples could be misinterpreted and thus reduce the flexibility in applying the framework. Many respondents to the exposure draft supported the Board's decision not to include detailed application guidance or illustrative examples.

Qualitative characteristics

BC42　As a result of the Board concluding that management commentary is within the scope of the *Conceptual Framework*, the Practice Statement specifies that the appropriate qualitative characteristics are those identified in Chapter 3 of the *Conceptual Framework* (see paragraph BC22). The qualitative characteristics in Chapter 3 will therefore be applied to both financial statements and management commentary.

BC43　In discussing the application of the qualitative characteristics to management commentary, the Board considered how the concept of balance (ie the inclusion of both bad news and good news) relates to the qualitative characteristics in general and the application of the qualitative characteristic of verifiability in particular. The Board decided that balance is equivalent to neutrality, in the context described in Chapter 3 of the *Conceptual Framework*. Consequently, the Board reasoned that because neutrality is a characteristic of faithful representation, balance is subsumed within faithful representation.

BC44　Furthermore, the Board decided that information in management commentary, including forward-looking information, can possess the qualitative characteristic of verifiability as it is described in Chapter 3. Paragraph QC26 of

Chapter 3 indicates that 'verifiability means that different knowledgeable and independent observers could reach consensus'. Expressed differently, the information presented is capable of being tested, either by observation or experiment. The Board observed that for forward-looking information, the test to ensure verifiability may be one of reasonableness: do the assumptions that support the forward-looking information in financial reports make sense?

Presentation

BC45   The Board agreed that it should be management's responsibility to decide both the content of its management commentary and the best way to present that content (ie the form). The Board observed that providing flexibility in both the content and form of management commentary reduces the risk that management will adopt a boilerplate approach to the presentation of management commentary.

BC46   Because management commentary supplements and complements the financial statements, the Board decided that management commentary should be consistent with the financial statements, particularly in terms of its presentation of segment information. The Board noted that, if the financial statements include segment information, the information presented in the management commentary should reflect that segmentation. The Board observed that this information is relevant for understanding the entity as a whole.

Elements of management commentary

BC47   The Board noted that specifying disclosures for management commentary may be more difficult than specifying information to be disclosed in the notes to the financial statements. The types of activities that are critical to an entity are specific to that entity. As a consequence, regulators have tended to identify the elements that reflect the type of content that they expect to see in management commentary rather than defining the elements themselves. The Board decided that following a similar approach would generate more meaningful disclosures, because entities can discuss those matters most relevant to their individual circumstances. Some Board members requested that the Practice Statement should include a detailed list of items (eg critical accounting estimates), even though they recognise that the elements and the framework would lead to discussion of those items. However, the Board wishes to avoid a checklist-compliance mentality, which might result from specifying a detailed list.

User needs

BC48   The Board decided to include the five elements described in paragraphs 24–40 of the Practice Statement as based upon the needs of existing and potential investors, lenders and other creditors as the primary users of management commentary information. The table below relates the five elements to the Board's assessment of the needs of the primary users of management commentary.

Elements	User needs
Nature of the business	The knowledge of the business in which an entity is engaged and the external environment in which it operates.
Objectives and strategies	To assess the strategies adopted by the entity and the likelihood that those strategies will be successful in meeting management's stated objectives.
Resources, risks and relationships	A basis for determining the resources available to the entity as well as obligations to transfer resources to others; the ability of the entity to generate long-term, sustainable net inflows of resources; and the risks to which those resource-generating activities are exposed, both in the near term and in the long term.
Results and prospects	The ability to understand whether an entity has delivered results in line with expectations and, implicitly, how well management has understood the entity's market, executed its strategy and managed the entity's resources, risks and relationships.
Performance measures and indicators	The ability to focus on the critical performance measures and indicators that management uses to assess and manage the entity's performance against stated objectives and strategies.

BC49   The Board observed that information in management commentary will be of interest to users other than the primary users described in paragraph 8 of the Practice Statement. As a result, the Board noted that management may need to consider the extent to which commenting on issues relevant to a wider user group may be appropriate given the degree of those issues' influence on the performance of the entity and its value. The Board also noted that management commentary should not, however, be seen as a replacement for other forms of reporting addressed to a wider stakeholder group.

Placement of disclosure within the financial reports

BC50   The Board noted that neither IFRSs nor the *Conceptual Framework* include principles to guide the Board's approach for establishing disclosure requirements. Thus, it is not always clear whether information belongs in the notes to the financial statements or in management commentary.

BC51   In December 2007 the Board decided to defer its work on a framework for disclosure and instead wait for the phase *Boundaries of financial reporting, and presentation and disclosure* (phase E) of the conceptual framework project. The Board noted that phase E includes the development of disclosure principles.

Consequently, the Board views phase E of the conceptual framework as the appropriate project to resolve questions about the placement of disclosures in the financial reports.

BC52 The Board acknowledges that until phase E is completed, overlap will exist between the type of information that is disclosed in the notes to the financial statements and the type of information that is disclosed in management commentary. In the light of this overlap, the Board decided that it was important to establish management commentary as a disclosure tool, before resolving questions of placement.

BC53 The Board acknowledges that some entities already present management commentary and it has addressed this overlap in one area, which is the risk disclosures required by IFRS 7 *Financial Instruments: Disclosures*. IFRS 7 permits management to provide required risk disclosures either in the financial statements or in management commentary, if the disclosure in management commentary is cross-referenced in the financial statements and management commentary is provided at the same time and under the same terms as the financial statements. However, IFRS 7 and the Practice Statement do not address auditing matters related to the location of those disclosures.

IASB document published to accompany

IFRS Practice Statement 2

Making Materiality Judgements

IFRS Practice Statement 2 *Making Materiality Judgements* was issued in September 2017 for application from 14 September 2017. The text of Practice Statement 2 is contained in Part B of this edition. This part presents the following accompanying document:

BASIS FOR CONCLUSIONS

Basis for Conclusions on the IFRS Practice Statement 2 *Making Materiality Judgements*

This Basis for Conclusions accompanies, but is not part of, the IFRS Practice Statement 2 Making Materiality Judgements *(Practice Statement). It summarises the considerations of the International Accounting Standards Board (Board) when developing the Practice Statement. Individual Board members gave greater weight to some factors than to others.*

Background

BC1   The Board was informed at the Discussion Forum on Financial Reporting Disclosure in January 2013, through feedback on the 2014 Exposure Draft of proposed amendments to IAS 1 *Presentation of Financial Statements* and from other sources, that entities experience difficulties making materiality judgements when preparing financial statements. Some entities are unsure how to make materiality judgements and tend to use disclosure requirements in IFRS Standards as if they were items on a checklist, rather than using judgement when deciding what information to provide in financial statements. Some stakeholders stated that these difficulties and practices contribute to a disclosure problem—namely, entities provide too much irrelevant information and not enough relevant information in their financial statements.

BC2   Some stakeholders suggested that one of the factors contributing to these difficulties was the lack of guidance on materiality in IFRS Standards, particularly on how entities should make materiality judgements about information disclosed in the notes to the financial statements. In the light of this feedback, the Board decided to provide further guidance. The aim of the Board is to promote a behavioural change in the way entities prepare their financial statements, encouraging a greater exercise of judgement when determining what information to include or not to include in those statements.

BC3   In October 2015, the Board published the Exposure Draft IFRS Practice Statement *Application of Materiality to Financial Statements* (Practice Statement ED). The Board developed the Practice Statement ED after considering the input obtained from outreach and consultations with the IFRS Advisory Council; the Accounting Standards Advisory Forum (ASAF); the World Standard-Setters; the Global Preparers Forum (GPF); the Capital Markets Advisory Committee (CMAC); representatives of the International Auditing and Assurance Standards Board and the International Organization of Securities Commissions; and a number of other accounting professionals, academics and representatives of other regulatory bodies.[1]

BC4   The Board received 95 comment letters in response to the Practice Statement ED. The Board also conducted outreach on the proposals in the Practice Statement ED, including consultation with the ASAF, the CMAC and the GPF. Responses to the Practice Statement ED indicated widespread support for the Board to issue

---

1   The IFRS Advisory Council, the Accounting Standards Advisory Forum (ASAF), the Global Preparers Forum (GPF) and the Capital Markets Advisory Committee (CMAC) are the Board's advisory bodies. The World Standard-Setters is a meeting of accounting standard-setters organised by the Board.

practical guidance on making materiality judgements in the preparation of financial statements. The Board considered the input it received on the Practice Statement ED when developing this Practice Statement.

Form of the guidance

BC5   The Practice Statement sets out non-mandatory guidance with the aim of assisting entities in making materiality judgements when preparing general purpose financial statements. Entities applying IFRS Standards are not required to comply with the Practice Statement to state compliance with those Standards. Nevertheless, the Board expects the Practice Statement to help promote a greater understanding of the role of materiality in applying IFRS Standards and of how judgement should be exercised to assess materiality in preparing financial statements. The Board expects that better understanding of the role of materiality will ultimately make financial statements more useful and easier to understand.

BC6   The Board decided to provide guidance on how to make materiality judgements in the form of a non-mandatory Practice Statement because:

(a)   issuing mandatory requirements in a Standard could risk appearing prescriptive, which could undermine the emphasis on entities applying their judgement in the assessment of materiality; and

(b)   issuing guidance as a separate non-mandatory document, rather than as non-mandatory implementation guidance supporting a specific Standard, such as IAS 1, would help to emphasise that the concept of materiality is pervasive throughout IFRS Standards.

BC7   Moreover, the Board was told that adding mandatory requirements in a Standard could risk creating conflicts with local legal or regulatory frameworks. Nevertheless, the Board observed that even though some jurisdictions might have legal or regulatory requirements that interact with IFRS materiality requirements, this should not result in a conflict with the guidance in the Practice Statement, provided that those local requirements do not prevent an entity from applying the requirements in IFRS Standards. No respondents to the Practice Statement ED and no participants in the outreach organised by the Board reported such a circumstance.

BC8   Furthermore, this Practice Statement does not change any requirements in IFRS Standards or introduce any new requirements. The Board decided that non-mandatory status was more appropriate.

BC9   Finally, the Board issued a Practice Statement rather than asking the IFRS Foundation staff to develop educational material because a Practice Statement is subject to full due process, including public consultation, and is more accessible than educational material.

BC10   Responses to the Practice Statement ED indicated widespread agreement with the considerations that led the Board to include its guidance in a non-mandatory Practice Statement.

Scope

BC11 The objective of this Practice Statement is to provide entities with guidance on making materiality judgements when preparing general purpose financial statements in accordance with IFRS Standards. The Board discussed whether to broaden the audience of the Practice Statement by also addressing it to other parties involved in financial reporting, but concluded that the Practice Statement should only be addressed to those involved in the preparation of the financial statements. The Board noted, however, that the Practice Statement is also likely to help other parties, such as auditors, users of financial statements, regulators and enforcers, understand the approach an entity follows in making materiality judgements when preparing its financial statements.

BC12 The Board discussed whether the Practice Statement should also be addressed to entities applying the *IFRS for SMEs*® Standard. However, the *IFRS for SMEs* Standard is a separate and stand-alone accounting framework based on full IFRS Standards with modifications to reflect cost-benefit considerations specific to small and medium sized entities and the need of users of the financial statements of such entities. The *IFRS for SMEs* Standard does not refer to the concept of primary users as included in the *Conceptual Framework for Financial Reporting (Conceptual Framework)* and does not include recent changes to full IFRS Standards (eg that an entity shall not reduce the understandability of its financial statements by obscuring material information with immaterial information). Therefore, the Board decided that the Practice Statement is not intended for entities applying the *IFRS for SMEs* Standard. The *IFRS for SMEs* Standard permits, but does not require, entities to refer to guidance available in full IFRS Standards. Those entities may therefore refer to the guidance in the Practice Statement in the same way they consider the requirements and guidance in full IFRS Standards dealing with similar and related issues in developing and applying accounting policies when the *IFRS for SMEs* Standard does not specifically address a transaction, other event or condition.

BC13 Materiality is a general concept widely used for financial reporting and other purposes. For example, auditors usually assess materiality when making judgements about the nature, timing and extent of the work to be done to express an opinion as to whether the financial statements are prepared, in all material respects, in accordance with an applicable financial reporting framework. Some respondents to the Practice Statement ED noted that preparers and auditors of financial statements assess materiality using a comparable approach—they both focus on information that could reasonably be expected to influence decisions of the users of an entity's financial statements. The Board discussed whether to include in the Practice Statement a reference to the assessment of materiality for auditing or other purposes, but decided to focus its guidance on the preparation of financial statements only. Assessing materiality for purposes other than the preparation of financial statements is beyond the scope of this Practice Statement. Moreover, referring to different applications of the concept of materiality might cause confusion.

General characteristics of materiality

Definition of material

BC14   The Board has discussed the definition of 'material' and whether to change or clarify that definition in its Principles of Disclosure project. In September 2017, on the basis of those discussions, the Board published the Exposure Draft *Definition of Material (Proposed amendments to IAS 1 and IAS 8)* (Definition of Material ED). The Definition of Material ED proposes refining the definition of material by incorporating the existing description of material information in paragraph 7 of IAS 1[2] and emphasising the need to ensure material information is not obscured, as described in paragraph 30A of IAS 1. IFRS Standards already include both concepts; consequently, the Practice Statement includes these notions. The Board considered whether to postpone issuing this Practice Statement until the completion of the Definition of Material project. However, the Board concluded that providing guidance on making materiality judgements as quickly as possible would be useful and responded to requests for guidance.

BC15   Moreover, the Board observed that, since the proposed amendments in the Definition of Material ED do not constitute substantive changes to the existing requirements in IFRS Standards, they are unlikely to result in a change in practice for most entities or to significantly affect entities' financial statements. Therefore, the guidance in this Practice Statement would not be affected by the proposed amendments, other than by the possible need to update the definition of material quoted in the document.

Materiality judgements are pervasive

BC16   The Board discussed whether to focus the guidance in the Practice Statement on IFRS presentation and disclosure requirements only, but concluded that the need for materiality judgements is pervasive in the preparation of financial statements, also encompassing recognition and measurement requirements. Consequently, the Board provided, throughout the Practice Statement, guidance on how to make materiality judgements in the context of recognition and measurement as well as of presentation and disclosure.

Primary users and their information needs

BC17   The Practice Statement explains that, when making its materiality assessments, an entity should consider the primary users of its financial statements—its primary users—as defined by the *Conceptual Framework*, that is, existing and potential investors, lenders and other creditors. The Board discussed whether it would be appropriate to emphasise the existence, among those primary users, of different subsets of users whose information needs might differ. However, the Board concluded that requiring an entity to identify different subsets of primary users, or focusing on any special information needs and expectations those users might have, could create a tension with the definition of general purpose financial statements, which focuses on the common information needs of a wide

---

2   '... the assessment needs to take into account how users [...] could *reasonably* be expected to be influenced in making economic decisions' [emphasis added].

range of users. Consequently, the Practice Statement refers to the three categories of primary users identified in the *Conceptual Framework*—existing and potential investors, lenders and other creditors.

BC18   Furthermore, the Board decided to emphasise in the Practice Statement that the primary users of an entity's financial statements include potential investors, lenders and other creditors, as well as existing ones. The Board concluded this would address concerns some stakeholders expressed about an inappropriate focus on specific existing users; the Board decided to make clear that an entity cannot narrow the information provided in its financial statements by focusing only on its existing users' information needs.

BC19   An entity considers decisions its primary users make on the basis of the financial statements when deciding what information to include in those statements. Consequently, the Board decided the Practice Statement should describe primary users' decisions and related information needs as set out in the *Conceptual Framework*. Primary users' decisions depend on the returns they expect from the resources they provide to an entity. Expectations about returns, in turn, depend on primary users' assessment of the amount, timing and uncertainty of the future cash inflows to the entity, as well as on the assessment of management's stewardship of the entity's resources.

BC20   The Board further considered the *Conceptual Framework* when developing its guidance on the information needs of primary users an entity should consider when making materiality judgements. Providing all the information existing and potential investors, lenders and other creditors need is not the objective of general purpose financial statements. The Board clarified that an entity is not required to address information needs that respond to unique or individual information requests. An entity should aim to meet primary users' common information needs. In developing its guidance, the Board clarified that, to avoid losing information relevant to one category of primary users (among the three identified in the *Conceptual Framework*), the common information needs are not limited to the information needs simultaneously shared across all categories of primary users. An entity separately identifies the common information needs for each of the three categories, and meets the total of these needs.

Interaction with local laws and regulations

BC21   The Board discussed the interaction of materiality requirements in IFRS Standards with local laws and regulations in the light of stakeholders' comments relating to potential conflicts between the guidance in the Practice Statement ED and local legal or regulatory requirements. The Board noted that the Practice Statement provides guidance on making materiality judgements when preparing financial statements in accordance with IFRS Standards; it does not provide guidance on how to apply local legal or regulatory requirements.

BC22   Nevertheless, the Board acknowledged that local requirements might affect information provided in the financial statements. In these circumstances, an entity must comply with the materiality requirements in IFRS Standards, but the Standards do not prohibit the disclosure of additional information required by local laws or regulations, even if that information is not material according to

IFRS Standards. A conflict would only occur if local laws or regulations prohibit the inclusion of information that is material for the purpose of IFRS Standards. No respondents to the Practice Statement ED and no participants in the outreach organised by the Board reported such a circumstance.

BC23   When information in addition to that required by IFRS Standards is provided in the financial statements, paragraph 30A of IAS 1 requires an entity to ensure that material information required by the Standards is not obscured. The Board observed that the appropriate organisation of information in the financial statements would allow an entity to meet that requirement.

Making materiality judgements

BC24   Respondents commenting on the Practice Statement ED welcomed the fact it gathered guidance on materiality from multiple IFRS Standards. However, some respondents suggested it would be useful to also describe the practical steps an entity follows when making materiality judgements in the preparation of its financial statements. The Board developed a four-step process (materiality process) in consultation with the ASAF, the CMAC and the GPF. The description of the materiality process illustrates the role materiality plays in the preparation of financial statements and clarifies how a materiality judgement is made. The materiality process also identifies the factors an entity should consider when making materiality judgements.

BC25   Consistent with the non-mandatory status of the Practice Statement, the Board developed the materiality process as an example of the approach an entity may follow in making materiality judgements, but clarified that the materiality process includes the materiality requirements an entity must apply to state compliance with IFRS Standards.

BC26   The Board considered whether to focus its guidance on the application of judgement or to illustrate the overall process of which materiality judgements are a part. However, as some respondents to the Practice Statement ED noted, describing the overall process helps an entity understand how materiality judgements can influence the preparation of its financial statements, as well as how the various materiality decisions are connected with each other.

BC27   The Board included Step 1 (identify) to provide an entity with a clear starting point for its assessments. Stakeholders largely agreed that an entity should use the requirements in IFRS Standards to identify information that primary users might need to make decisions about providing resources to the entity. When using the requirements in IFRS Standards, an entity benefits from the assessment the Board makes when developing IFRS Standards—when developing a Standard the Board identifies information it expects will meet the needs of a broad range of primary users. The Board also considered that some information not specified in IFRS Standards might be necessary to enable primary users to understand the impact of an entity's transactions, other events and conditions on the entity's financial position, financial performance and cash flows. Therefore, the Board decided that the entity's knowledge about its primary users' common information needs should be an additional input to Step 1. On the basis of that knowledge, an entity should consider whether to include additional information not specified by IFRS Standards in its financial statements.

BC28   Step 2 (assess) describes factors an entity should consider in identifying whether an item of information is material. The Board concluded that the application of judgement in assessing whether information is material involves both quantitative and qualitative considerations. Respondents to the Practice Statement ED also agreed that, in making materiality judgements, an entity should consider both quantitative and qualitative factors. The Practice Statement includes some examples of materiality factors. However, the Board decided to describe a limited number of factors rather than provide an exhaustive list of considerations to be taken into account.

BC29   The Board decided to include some guidance in the materiality process on the way an entity should reflect its materiality judgements. Step 3 (organise) deals with the output of an entity's materiality judgements and provides guidance the entity might want to consider to make its financial statements easier to understand. The Board recommends that an entity considers the different roles of the primary financial statements and the notes in deciding whether to present an item of information separately in the primary financial statements, to aggregate it with other information and/or to disclose the information in the notes. However, the Board decided not to provide further guidance on those topics in the Practice Statement. A discussion of the roles of the different components of the financial statements, as well as of the implications of those roles, has been included in the *Principles of Disclosure* Discussion Paper, which the Board published in March 2017.

BC30   Step 4 (review) gives an entity the opportunity to 'step back', once it has prepared its draft financial statements, and consider the information from an aggregated perspective. The Board discussed whether this step duplicates the assessment performed in Step 2 and clarified that an entity makes its materiality judgements in Step 2, but then reviews these judgements once a draft of the financial statements is available. In Step 2, an entity based its assessment on the expected financial statements as a whole, while it was still preparing its draft. In Step 4, an entity checks its assessment against the actual draft financial statements—this review may lead the entity to revisit the assessment performed in Step 2, provide additional information in the financial statements, remove immaterial information or reorganise existing information.

Specific topics

Prior-period information

BC31   When discussing materiality judgements about prior-period information included in financial statements, the Board acknowledged some legal or regulatory requirements might set out the amount of prior-period information to include in the financial statements. However, the Board decided that providing guidance on making materiality judgements about prior-period information in the Practice Statement would be necessary to promote behavioural change consistently across all parts of the financial statements and to encourage entities to exercise greater judgement when determining what information to include or not to include in financial statements.

BC32   The Board developed the guidance in the Practice Statement in the light of the minimum comparative information required by IAS 1. However, the Board acknowledged that an entity needs to consider any legal or regulatory requirements when making materiality judgements about prior-period information. Consequently, the Board decided to explain that, in its current-period financial statements, an entity may summarise prior-period information, compared to the way it was included in prior-period financial statements, except when local laws or regulations demand otherwise. The Board also clarified that an entity that wishes to state compliance with IFRS Standards cannot provide less information than the information required by the Standards, even if local laws and regulations permit otherwise.

BC33   The Board also emphasised that, when providing prior-period information in addition to the minimum comparative information required by IFRS Standards, information has to be provided in accordance with those Standards and should not obscure material information. Some stakeholders asked whether providing prior-period information at the same level of detail as current-period information could be seen as obscuring material information in the current-period financial statements. The Board does not expect that such prior-period information would obscure current-period material information.

Errors

BC34   The Board discussed whether to include in the Practice Statement guidance to help entities determine whether an error is material. The Board noted that the assessment of whether an error could reasonably be expected to influence primary users' decisions is an integral part of the preparation of the financial statements, and therefore concluded that the Practice Statement should address this topic. The Board noted that the materiality factors an entity would apply to conclude whether an error is material are the same as those described in the materiality process. Consequently, there is no need to provide any specific additional guidance. In the 'Errors' section, the Practice Statement suggests that an entity refer to the considerations described in the materiality process.

BC35   Respondents to the Practice Statement ED asked the Board to also address the situation in which an entity faces errors generated by the accumulation over several periods of errors that were immaterial both in individual prior periods and cumulatively over all prior periods (sometimes called 'cumulative errors'). The Board concluded it would be helpful to clarify that, in such circumstances:

(a)   materiality judgements about cumulative errors that an entity made at the time the prior-period financial statements were authorised for issue need not be revisited in the current period, provided those judgements were reasonable at the time they were made and the entity considered information that was available, or was reasonably expected to be available, at that time; however

(b)   an entity needs to assess whether cumulative errors have become material to the current-period financial statements.

BC36   The Board decided to include a statement in the Practice Statement to remind an entity that a cumulative error must be corrected if it becomes material to the current-period financial statements. The Board discussed whether to provide further guidance on how to correct such an error, but concluded that the Practice Statement should focus on how to make materiality judgements, instead of dealing with the consequences of these judgements. IAS 8 contains the requirements on the correction of errors.

BC37   The Practice Statement ED included some wording implying that if an entity intentionally misstates or omits information to achieve a particular presentation or result, such an error is always material. Respondents to the Practice Statement ED commented that the wording appears inconsistent with paragraph 41 of IAS 8 *Accounting Policies, Changes in Accounting Estimates and Errors*. Paragraph 41 of IAS 8 does not characterise such errors as material, however, it requires the correction of all errors made intentionally to achieve a particular presentation of an entity's financial position, financial performance or cash flows. The Board decided to align the wording in the Practice Statement with the wording of paragraph 41 of IAS 8.

Information about covenants

BC38   When discussing whether the existence of a covenant, or similar contractual terms, could influence materiality judgements, the Board identified two concerns:

(a)   do any specific considerations apply in making materiality judgements on information about the existence and terms of a covenant, or a covenant breach?

(b)   does the existence of a covenant influence materiality judgements about information other than about the existence of the covenant, or a covenant breach, included in the financial statements?

BC39   In respect of the first concern, the Board concluded that, in addition to the materiality factors described in the materiality process, materiality judgements are specifically influenced by the consequences of a breach occurring and the likelihood of that breach occurring. In particular, the Board clarified that, regardless of the significance of the consequences of a breach occurring, information about the covenant is not material if the likelihood of the breach occurring is remote. In providing this clarification, the Board applied the disclosure threshold set in paragraph 28 of IAS 37 *Provisions, Contingent Liabilities and Contingent Assets* regarding the disclosure of contingent liabilities.

BC40   In respect of the second concern, the Board discussed including in the Practice Statement guidance stating that the existence of a covenant should not influence an entity's assessment of the materiality of other information in the financial statements. In other words, an entity is not required to reperform its materiality assessments the closer it gets to breaching a covenant. However, some stakeholders observed that such guidance would conflict with existing guidance developed by other parties on the assessment of the materiality of errors. To avoid creating any confusion among preparers and others involved in financial reporting, the Board decided not to include in the Practice Statement guidance on the impact of covenants on materiality assessments.

Materiality judgements for interim reporting

BC41   The Board discussed whether to provide guidance on how to make materiality judgements when preparing an interim financial report. The Board concluded that, when preparing an interim financial report, an entity should consider the same materiality factors it considers in preparing its annual financial statements. However, the Board also noted that it would be helpful to explain any additional considerations relevant to making a materiality judgement in the preparation of an interim financial report. In particular, the Board noted that it would be helpful to explain how the different time period and purposes of an interim financial report, compared to the annual financial statements, affect materiality judgements, as well as to address some practical concerns raised by respondents to the Practice Statement ED.

Likely effects of this Practice Statement

BC42   The Board is committed to assessing and sharing knowledge about the likely costs of implementing proposed new requirements and guidance—the costs and benefits are collectively referred to as 'effects'. The Practice Statement is designed to provide guidance on how to make materiality judgements in the preparation of financial statements. The Practice Statement does not change any requirements in IFRS Standards or introduce any new requirements. With no changes in existing requirements and given that the application of the Practice Statement is not required to state compliance with IFRS Standards, the Board concluded that a separate effects analysis was not necessary.

BC43   The expected effects of the Practice Statement have been considered as part of the Board's discussions. The Board expects the Practice Statement will:

(a)   enhance awareness of the role of materiality in helping to promote positive changes in behaviour (such as to discourage rigid adherence to checklists by an entity preparing financial statements);

(b)   encourage an entity to exercise judgement to a greater extent when preparing financial statements, which should lead to a reduction in boilerplate disclosures and redundant information and provide a framework for assessing the need in the financial statements for information that is additional to disclosure requirements specified by IFRS Standards; and

(c)   provide a useful reference point for discussions between an entity, its auditors and regulators on the assessment of materiality, which could help facilitate agreement.

BC44   The Board does not expect any significant costs associated with the application of the Practice Statement because it introduces no new requirements nor is the application of the Practice Statement mandatory. However, some implementation costs might be faced by an entity that has previously relied on a checklist approach when preparing its financial statements. The Board expects such an entity would apply more judgement when deciding what information to include in the financial statements, if it follows the guidance in the Practice Statement. The Board concluded that the benefits of higher-quality disclosures and easier access to information for primary users of financial statements exceed the implementation costs required when entities apply judgement in preparing financial statements, rather than following a checklist. Conversely, an entity already applying appropriate judgement in the preparation of its financial statements would incur no additional implementation costs and could benefit from the issue of the Practice Statement in its interaction with auditors and other stakeholders.

BC45 The effects the Board expects from the Practice Statement were assessed against the comments received on the Practice Statement ED. Overall, respondents confirmed the Board's expectations and welcomed the proposal to issue the Practice Statement.

Interaction with the Board's other projects

BC46 The Board decided to issue this Practice Statement before the finalisation of the Principle of Disclosures project, for which a Discussion Paper was published in March 2017; the Definition of Material project, for which an Exposure Draft was published in September 2017; or the *Conceptual Framework* project—the revised *Conceptual Framework* is expected to be issued in 2018. The Board considered whether to postpone issuing this Practice Statement until the completion of one or more of those projects; however, it concluded that it would be useful to provide guidance on making materiality judgements as quickly as possible, to respond to requests for guidance. Moreover, the Board concluded that the finalisation of these projects would be unlikely to affect the guidance in the Practice Statement.

Approvals by the Board of Annual Improvements to IFRS Standards

Approval by the Board of *Improvements to IFRSs* issued in May 2008

In May 2008 the International Accounting Standards Board issued *Improvements to IFRSs*. The document contained miscellaneous amendments to International Financial Reporting Standards (IFRSs) and the related Bases for Conclusions and guidance made in the Board's first annual improvements project.

The annual improvements project provides a vehicle for making non-urgent but necessary amendments to IFRSs. The amendments have been incorporated into the text of the IFRSs set out in this edition.

Improvements to IFRSs was approved for issue by the thirteen members of the International Accounting Standards Board, except that:

- Mr Yamada dissented from one of the amendments to IAS 28 *Investments in Associates*.

- Mr Leisenring dissented from one of the amendments to IAS 38 *Intangible Assets*.

The dissenting opinions of those Board members are set out after the Basis for Conclusions on the IFRSs affected.

Sir David Tweedie	Chairman
Thomas E Jones	Vice-Chairman
Mary E Barth	
Stephen Cooper	
Philippe Danjou	
Jan Engström	
Robert P Garnett	
Gilbert Gélard	
James J Leisenring	
Warren J McGregor	
John T Smith	
Tatsumi Yamada	
Wei-Guo Zhang	

Approval by the Board of *Improvements to IFRSs* issued in April 2009

In April 2009 the International Accounting Standards Board issued *Improvements to IFRSs*. The document contained miscellaneous amendments to International Financial Reporting Standards (IFRSs) and the related Bases for Conclusions and guidance made in the Board's second annual improvements project.

The annual improvements project provides a vehicle for making non-urgent but necessary amendments to IFRSs. The amendments have been incorporated into the text of the IFRSs set out in this edition.

Improvements to IFRSs was approved for issue by the fourteen members of the International Accounting Standards Board, except that:

- Mr Cooper dissented from the amendment to IFRS 8 *Operating Segments*.

- Mr Leisenring dissented from the amendment to IAS 17 *Leases*.

The dissenting opinions of those Board members are set out after the Basis for Conclusions on the IFRSs affected.

Sir David Tweedie	Chairman
Thomas E Jones	Vice-Chairman
Mary E Barth	
Stephen Cooper	
Philippe Danjou	
Jan Engström	
Robert P Garnett	
Gilbert Gélard	
Prabhakar Kalavacherla	
James J Leisenring	
Warren J McGregor	
John T Smith	
Tatsumi Yamada	
Wei-Guo Zhang	

Approval by the Board of *Improvements to IFRSs* issued in May 2010

In May 2010 the International Accounting Standards Board issued *Improvements to IFRSs*. The document contained miscellaneous amendments to International Financial Reporting Standards (IFRSs) and the related Bases for Conclusions and guidance made in the Board's third annual improvements project.

The annual improvements project provides a vehicle for making non-urgent but necessary amendments to IFRSs. The amendments have been incorporated into the text of the IFRSs set out in this edition.

Improvements to IFRSs was approved for issue by the fifteen members of the International Accounting Standards Board.

Sir David Tweedie   Chairman

Stephen Cooper

Philippe Danjou

Jan Engström

Patrick Finnegan

Robert P Garnett

Gilbert Gélard

Amaro Luiz de Oliveira Gomes

Prabhakar Kalavacherla

James J Leisenring

Patricia McConnell

Warren J McGregor

John T Smith

Tatsumi Yamada

Wei-Guo Zhang

© IFRS Foundation

Approval by the Board of *Annual Improvements 2009–2011 Cycle* published in May 2012

Annual Improvements 2009–2011 Cycle was approved for publication by the fourteen members of the International Accounting Standards Board.

Hans Hoogervorst	Chairman
Ian Mackintosh	Vice-Chairman
Stephen Cooper	
Philippe Danjou	
Jan Engström	
Patrick Finnegan	
Amaro Luiz de Oliveira Gomes	
Prabhakar Kalavacherla	
Patricia McConnell	
Takatsugu Ochi	
Paul Pacter	
Darrel Scott	
John T Smith	
Wei-Guo Zhang	

Approval by the Board of *Annual Improvements to IFRSs 2010–2012 Cycle* published in December 2013

Annual Improvements to IFRSs 2010–2012 Cycle was approved for publication by the sixteen members of the International Accounting Standards Board.

Hans Hoogervorst	Chairman
Ian Mackintosh	Vice-Chairman
Stephen Cooper	
Philippe Danjou	
Martin Edelmann	
Jan Engström	
Patrick Finnegan	
Amaro Luiz de Oliveira Gomes	
Gary Kabureck	
Prabhakar Kalavacherla	
Patricia McConnell	
Takatsugu Ochi	
Darrel Scott	
Chungwoo Suh	
Mary Tokar	
Wei-Guo Zhang	

Approval by the Board of *Annual Improvements to IFRSs 2011–2013 Cycle* published in December 2013

Annual Improvements to IFRSs 2011–2013 Cycle was approved for publication by the sixteen members of the International Accounting Standards Board.

Hans Hoogervorst	Chairman
Ian Mackintosh	Vice-Chairman
Stephen Cooper	
Philippe Danjou	
Martin Edelmann	
Jan Engström	
Patrick Finnegan	
Amaro Luiz de Oliveira Gomes	
Gary Kabureck	
Prabhakar Kalavacherla	
Patricia McConnell	
Takatsugu Ochi	
Darrel Scott	
Chungwoo Suh	
Mary Tokar	
Wei-Guo Zhang	

Approval by the Board of *Annual Improvements to IFRSs 2012–2014 Cycle* issued in September 2014

Annual Improvements to IFRSs 2012–2014 Cycle was approved for issue by the fourteen members of the International Accounting Standards Board.

Hans Hoogervorst	Chairman
Ian Mackintosh	Vice-Chairman
Stephen Cooper	
Philippe Danjou	
Amaro Luiz de Oliveira Gomes	
Martin Edelmann	
Patrick Finnegan	
Gary Kabureck	
Suzanne Lloyd	
Takatsugu Ochi	
Darrel Scott	
Chungwoo Suh	
Mary Tokar	
Wei-Guo Zhang	

Approval by the Board of *Annual Improvements to IFRS Standards 2014–2016 Cycle* issued in December 2016

Annual Improvements to IFRS Standards 2014–2016 Cycle was approved for issue by the 11 members of the International Accounting Standards Board.

Hans Hoogervorst	Chairman
Suzanne Lloyd	Vice-Chair
Stephen Cooper	
Martin Edelmann	
Amaro Gomes	
Gary Kabureck	
Takatsugu Ochi	
Darrel Scott	
Chungwoo Suh	
Mary Tokar	
Wei-Guo Zhang	

NOTES

NOTES

NOTES

NOTES

NOTES

NOTES

NOTES

NOTES

NOTES

NOTES

NOTES

NOTES

NOTES

NOTES